SUPPLEMENT XVIII

Charles Frederick Briggs to Robert Wrigley

American Writers
A Collection of Literary Biographies

JAY PARINI

Editor in Chief

SUPPLEMENT XVIII
Charles Frederick Briggs to Robert Wrigley

CHARLES SCRIBNER'S SONS

A part of Gale, Cengage Learning

Detroit • New York • San Francisco • New Haven, Conn • Waterville, Maine • London

American Writers Supplement XVIII

Editor in Chief: Jay Parini

Project Editor: Joseph Palmisano

Contributing Project Editor: Michelle Kazensky

Permissions: Margaret Abendroth, Vernon English, Sara Teller

Composition and Electronic Capture: Gary Leach

Manufacturing: Rhonda A. Dover

Publisher: Jim Draper

Product Manager: Janet Witalec

LIBRARY OF CONGRESS CATALOGING-IN-PUBLICATION DATA

American writers: a collection of literary biographies / Leonard Unger, editor in chief.
p. cm.
The 4-vol. main set consists of 97 of the pamphlets originally published as the University of Minnesota pamphlets on American writers; some have been rev. and updated. The supplements cover writers not included in the original series.
Supplement 2, has editor in chief, A. Walton Litz; Retrospective suppl. 1, c1998, was edited by A. Walton Litz & Molly Weigel; Suppl. 5–7 have as editor-in-chief, Jay Parini.
Includes bibliographies and index.
Contents: v. 1. Henry Adams to T.S. Eliot — v. 2. Ralph Waldo Emerson to Carson McCullers — v. 3. Archibald MacLeish to George Santayana — v. 4. Isaac Bashevis Singer to Richard Wright — Supplement[s]: 1, pt. 1. Jane Addams to Sidney Lanier. 1, pt. 2. Vachel Lindsay to Elinor Wylie. 2, pt. 1. W.H. Auden to O. Henry. 2, pt. 2. Robinson Jeffers to Yvor Winters. — 4, pt. 1. Maya Angelou to Linda Hogan. 4, pt. 2. Susan Howe to Gore Vidal — Suppl. 5. Russell Banks to Charles Wright — Suppl. 6. Don DeLillo to W. D. Snodgrass — Suppl. 7. Julia Alvarez to Tobias Wolff — Suppl. 8. T.C. Boyle to August Wilson. — Suppl. 11 Toni Cade Bambara to Richard Yates.
ISBN 0-684-19785-5 (set) — ISBN 0-684-13662-7
1. American literature—History and criticism. 2. American literature—Bio-bibliography. 3. Authors, American—Biography. I. Unger, Leonard. II. Litz, A. Walton. III. Weigel, Molly. IV. Parini, Jay. V. University of Minnesota pamphlets on American writers.

PS129 .A55
810'.9
[B] 73-001759

Gale
27500 Drake Rd.
Farmington Hills, MI, 48331-3535

ISBN-13: ISBN-13: 978-0-684-31552-2
ISBN-10: ISBN-10: 0-684-31552-1

Printed in the United States of America
1 2 3 4 5 6 7 12 11 10 09 08

Acknowledgments

Acknowledgment is gratefully made to those publishers and individuals who permitted the use of the following material in copyright. Every effort has been made to secure permission to reprint copyrighted material.

BOB DYLAN Dylan, Bob. From "Blowin' in the Wind," in *Lyrics 1962–2001.* Simon and Schuster, 2004. Copyright © 1962 by Warner Bros., Inc. Copyright © renewed 1990 Special Rider Music. All rights reserved. International copyright secured. Reprinted by permission./ Dylan, Bob. From "A Hard Rain's A-Gonna Fall," in *Lyrics 1962–2001.* Simon and Schuster, 2004. Copyright © 1963 by Warner Bros., Inc. Copyright © renewed 1991 Special Rider Music. All rights reserved. International copyright secured. Reprinted by permission./ Dylan, Bob. From "It's All Over Now, Baby Blue," in *Lyrics 1962–2001.* Simon and Schuster, 2004. Copyright © 1965 by Warner Bros., Inc. Copyright © renewed 1993 Special Rider Music. All rights reserved. International copyright secured. Reprinted by permission./ Dylan, Bob. From "The Times They Are A-Changin'," in *Lyrics 1962–2001.* Simon and Schuster, 2004. Copyright © 1963, 1964 by Warner Bros., Inc. Copyright © renewed 1991 Special Rider Music. All rights reserved. International copyright secured. Reprinted by permission./ Dylan, Bob. From "When the Ship Comes In," in *Lyrics 1962–2001.* Simon and Schuster, 2004. Copyright © 1963 by Warner Bros., Inc. Copyright © renewed 1991 Special Rider Music. All rights reserved. International copyright secured. Reprinted by permission./ Dylan, Bob. From "It's Alright, Ma (I'm Only Bleeding)," in *Lyrics 1962–2001.* Simon and Schuster, 2004. Copyright © 1965 by Warner Bros., Inc. Copyright © renewed 1993 Special Rider Music. All rights reserved. International copyright secured. Reprinted by permission./ Dylan, Bob. From "Idiot Wind," in *Lyrics 1962–2001.* Simon and Schuster, 2004. Copyright © 1974 by Ram's Horn Music. All rights reserved. International copyright secured. Reprinted by permission./ Dylan, Bob. From "Ballad of a Thin Man," in *Lyrics 1962–2001.* Simon and Schuster, 2004. Copyright © 1965 by Warner Bros., Inc. Copyright © renewed 1993 Special Rider Music. All rights reserved. International copyright secured. Reprinted by permission./ Dylan, Bob. From "Summer Days," in *Lyrics 1962–2001.* Simon and Schuster, 2004. Copyright © 2001 Special Rider Music. All rights reserved. International copyright secured. Reprinted by permission./ Dylan, Bob. From "Love Minus Zero/No Limit," in *Lyrics 1962–2001.* Simon and Schuster, 2004. Copyright © 1965 by Warner Bros., Inc. Copyright © renewed 1993 Special Rider Music. All rights reserved. International copyright secured. Reprinted by permission.

MARGARET EDSON Edson, Margaret. From *Wit.* Faber and Faber, Inc., 1999. Copyright © 1993, 1999 by Margaret Edson. All rights reserved. Reprinted by permission of Faber & Faber, Inc., an affiliate of Farrar, Straus and Giroux, LLC./ *The Washington Post,* February 27, 2000, for "A Teacher's Wit and Wisdom: Margaret Edson, Finding Lessons in Her Sole Play," by Nelson Pressley. Copyright © 2000 The Washington Post. Reprinted by permission of the author.

JON KRAKAUER Krakauer, Jon. From *Eiger Dreams.* The Lyons Press, 1990. Copyright © 1990 by Jon Krakauer. Reproduced by permission.

MARILYN NELSON Waniek, Marilyn Nelson. From *For the Body.* Louisiana State University Press, 1978. Copyright © 1978 by Marilyn Nelson Waniek. All rights reserved. Reproduced by permission./ Rasmussen, Halfdan. From *Hundreds of Hens and Other Poems for Children.* Translated by Marilyn Nelson and Pamela Espeland. Black Willow Press, 1982. Text copyright © Marilyn Nelson Waniek and Pamela Espeland. All rights reserved. Reproduced by permission./ Espeland, Pamela and Nelson, Marilyn. From *The Cat Walked Through the Casserole.* Carolrhoda, 1984. Text copyright © 1984 by Pamela Espeland and Marilyn Nelson Waniek. All rights reserved. Reproduced by Carolrhoda, a division of Lerner Publishing Group./ Waniek, Marilyn Nelson. From *Mama's Promises.* Louisiana State University Press, 1985. Copyright © 1985 by Marilyn Nelson Waniek. All rights reserved. Reproduced by permission./ Waniek, Marilyn Nelson. From *The Homeplace.* Louisiana State University Press, 1990. Copyright © 1989, 1990 by Marilyn Nelson Waniek. All rights reserved. Reproduced by permission./ Waniek, Marilyn Nelson. From *Partial Truth.* Kutenai Press, 1992. Copyright © 1992 by Marilyn Nelson Waniek. Copyright © 1992 by Eric Spencer. Reproduced by permission./ Waniek, Marilyn Nelson. From *Magnificat.* Louisiana State University Press, 1994. Copyright © 1994 by Marilyn Nelson Waniek. All rights reserved. Reproduced by permission./ Nelson, Marilyn. From *The Fields of Praise.* Louisiana State University Press, 1997. Copyright © 1994, 1995, 1996, 1997 by Marilyn Nelson. All rights reserved. Reproduced by permission./ Nelson, Marilyn. From *She-Devil Circus.* Aralia, 2001. Copyright © 2001 by Marilyn Nelson. Reproduced by permission./ Nelson, Marilyn. From *A Wreath for Emmett Till.* Houghton Mifflin, 2005. Text copyright © 2005 by Marilyn Nelson. All rights reserved. Reprinted by permission of Houghton Mifflin Harcourt Publishing Company./ Nelson, Marilyn. From *The Cachoeira Tales and Other Poems.* Louisiana State University Press, 2005. Copyright © 2005 by Marilyn Nelson. All rights reserved. Reproduced by permission./ Nelson, Marilyn. From *Triolets for*

Triolet. Curbstone Press, Ltd, 2001. Copyright © 2001 by Marilyn Nelson. All rights reserved. Reproduced by permission./ Pederson, Inge. From *The Thirteenth Month.* Translated by Marilyn Nelson. Oberlin College Press, 2005. Introduction and translations copyright © 2005 by Marilyn Nelson. Reproduced by permission.

JANISSE RAY Ray, Janisse. From *Naming the Unseen.* University of Montana, 1996. Copyright © 1996 by Janisse Ray. Reproduced by permission.

CONRAD RICHTER Richter, Conrad. From *A Country of Strangers.* Alfred Knopf, 1966. Copyright © 1966 by Conrad Richter. Reproduced by permission of Alfred Knopf, a division of Random House, Inc.

ROBERT WRIGLEY Wrigley, Robert. From *The Sinking of Clay City.* Copper Canyon Press, 1979. Copyright © 1979 Robert Wrigley. Used by permission of Penguin, a division of Penguin Group (USA) Inc. and the author./ Wrigley, Robert. From *Moon in a Mason Jar; and, What My Father Believed: Two Volumes of Poetry.* University of Illinois Press, 1986. Copyright © 1986, 1991, 1998 by Robert Wrigley. Used with permission of the poet and the University of Illinois Press./ Wrigley, Robert. From *What My Father Believed.* University of Illinois Press, 1991. Copyright © 1991 by Robert Wrigley. Used with permission of the author./ Wrigley, Robert. From *In the Bank of Beautiful Sins.* Penguin Group, 1995. Copyright © 1995 Robert Wrigley. Used by permission of Penguin, a division of Penguin Group (USA) Inc. and the author./ Wrigley, Robert. From *Reign of Snakes.* Penguin Group, 1999. Copyright © 1999 by Robert Wrigley. Used by permission of Penguin, a division of Penguin Group (USA) Inc. and the author./ Wrigley, Robert. From *Lives of the Animals* Penguin Group, 2003. Copyright © 2003 Robert Wrigley. In the U.S. used by permission of Penguin Group (USA) Inc. In the U.K. reproduced by permission of the author./ *The Hudson Review,* v. LIX, winter, 2007. Copyright © 2007 by Robert Wrigley. Reprinted by permission from *The Hudson Review.*

List of Subjects

Introduction ix

List of Contributors xi

CHARLES FREDERICK BRIGGS 1
Bette S. Weidman

BOB DYLAN 19
Ian Bickford

MARGARET EDSON 35
Angela Garcia

PERCIVAL EVERETT 53
Tracie Church Guzzio

WILLIAM HOFFMAN 69
William L. Frank

HA JIN 89
Deborah Kay Ferrell

JON KRAKAUER 105
Susan Butterworth

NELLA LARSEN 119
Whitney Womack Smith

JONATHAN LETHEM 135
Bert Almon

ALICE McDERMOTT 155
Paul Johnston

MARILYN NELSON 171
Kim Bridgford

JANISSE RAY 189
Joan Wylie Hall

CONRAD RICHTER 207
David R. Johnson

PAUL WILLIAM RYAN 223
Joseph G. Ramsey

BUDD SCHULBERG 241
Tom Cerasulo

SUSAN WARNER 257
Laurie Ousley

DOROTHY WEST 277
Whitney Womack Smith

ROBERT WRIGLEY 293
Richard Wakefield

Cumulative Index 309

Authors List 569

Introduction

"Literature is as old as speech," said John Steinbeck, in his Nobel Prize acceptance speech in 1962. "It grew out of human need for it, and it has not changed except to become more needed." The fact is we need books of poetry, novels, plays, and memoirs. We need the solace they provide, their inspiration, their guiding light. The great authors of the world are spiritual mentors, and they teach us ways to grow and think. They offer directions for living. They amuse us, they console us. The books they write are speech, human language, in a refined and heightened state of activity. We have always needed good writing, and—as Steinbeck suggests—we need this writing even more now, when the threat from the larger culture is overwhelming, and books must contend with MTV, cable television, movies, radio, and countless new media.

In this eighteenth supplement of *American Writers,* we offer eighteen articles on writers of fiction, drama (including film), and poetry (including song lyrics, in the case of Bob Dylan). Each of the writers discussed is accomplished, having made a major contribution to one or more of the genres of literature, and none of them has yet been featured in this series. These articles are meant to provide an introductory guide to these writers, although many of them rise to a level of criticism that will interest even those with considerable expertise in the subject. Certainly each of the subjects discussed may be considered a primary example of "human speech" in the terms that Steinbeck proposed.

This series had its origin in a series of biographical monographs that appeared between 1959 and 1972. *The Minnesota Pamphlets on American Writers* were incisively written and informative, treating ninety-seven American writers in a way that attracted a devoted following of readers. The series proved invaluable to a generation of students and teachers, who could depend on these reliable and interesting critiques of major figures. The idea of reprinting these essays occurred to Charles Scribner, Jr. (1921–1995). The series appeared in four volumes entitled *American Writers: A Collection of Literary Biographies* (1974). Since then, eighteen supplements have appeared, treating well over two hundred American writers: poets, novelists, playwrights, essayists, and autobiographers. We have discussed not only "literary" writers but popular ones as well, sometimes taking the measure of those in the field of genre fiction, for example. Yet the idea has been consistent with the original series: to provide clear, informative essays aimed at the general reader and intelligent student. These essays often rise to a remarkably high level of craft and vision, but they are meant to introduce an author of some importance in American literature, and to provide a sense of the scope and nature of the career under review. A certain amount of biographical and historical context is also provided, giving a context for the work itself—on the assumption that no work of literature arises from nowhere. Every poem or novel, play or memoir, roots in its time and place.

The writers of these articles are teachers and scholars. Most have published books and articles in their field, and several are well-known writers of poetry or fiction as well as critics. As anyone glancing through this collection will see, they have all been held to a high standard of good writing and sound scholarship, and a great deal of attention has been paid to revealing the career of each writer as it unfolds in time, with some focus on the critical reception of individual works. Each of the essays

concludes with a bibliography of works by the author, followed by a select bibliography of critical works about the author; these latter references are intended to direct the reading of those who wish to pursue the subject further.

In this eighteenth supplement, we treat a wide range of authors from the past and present. Among them are three interesting writers from the nineteenth and early to mid-twentieth centuries, including Susan Warner, Charles Frederick Briggs, Conrad Richter, Nella Larsen, Dorothy West, Budd Schulberg, and Paul William Ryan. They were each popular in their time (Schulberg is still alive, in his nineties), and they continue to attract a discerning readership. The main focus of this supplement, however, is contemporary literature. We examine the work of Bob Dylan, the great song writer and singer—this is something of a departure for this series, but we firmly believe that Dylan writes songs of genuine literary value, and he has also published important books. Among the recent authors discussed are Margaret Edson, Percival Everett, William Hoffman, Ha Jin, Jon Krakauer, Jonathan Lethem, Alice McDermott, Marilyn Nelson, Janisse Ray, and Robert Wrigley. Each of these has attracted a following, won awards, and gotten a good deal of critical attention in newspapers and journals; but few of them have yet to receive the kind of sustained critical focus that we offer here.

As Steinbeck said, literature is human speech, and the writing examined in these pages is quite remarkable for its brilliance and enduring value. My belief is that this supplement performs a useful service in this regard, providing substantial introductions to American writers from the past and present who have managed to change the lives of their readers (or, in Dylan's case, his listeners). These articles will assist readers in the difficult but rewarding work of close reading.

—*JAY PARINI*

Contributors

Bert Almon. Poet, critic, and biographer, Bert Almon teaches English at the University of Alberta. He is the author of *William Humphrey: Destroyer of Myths* (North Texas State University Press, 1998), *This Stubborn Self: Texas Autobiographies* (TCU Press, 2001), and eight collections of poetry. He has published articles on American, English, Canadian, and Australian writers. JONATHAN LETHEM

Ian Bickford. Ian Bickford is a visiting assistant professor of English at Bard College at Simon's Rock and a student in the Ph.D. program in English at the City University of New York Graduate Center, where he is writing a dissertation titled "The Thief of Paradise: John Milton and Seventh-day Adventism." His poetry and other writings have appeared in *Agni, LIT, Post Road, Beloit Poetry Review, Colorado Review, Sleeping Fish, Smartish Pace, Asheville Poetry Review, Oxford Encyclopedia of American Literature,* and elsewhere. He has been the recipient of a Mayers fellowship at the Huntington Library. He lives in Pownal, Vermont. BOB DYLAN

Kim Bridgford. Kim Bridgford is a professor of English at Fairfield University and editor of *Dogwood* and *Mezzo Cammin.* Her books include *Undone,* nominated for the Pulitzer Prize; *Instead of Maps,* nominated for the Poets' Prize; and *In the Extreme: Sonnets about World Records,* winner of the Donald Justice Prize. In addition, she has written on such poets as Sharon Olds, Dana Gioia, Mark Jarman, Brigit Pegeen Kelly, Mark Doty, and Micheal O'Siadhail. She is currently working on a three-book poetry/photography project with visual artist Jo Yarrington, focusing on journey and sacred space in Iceland, Venezuela, and Bhutan. MARILYN NELSON

Susan Butterworth. Susan Butterworth is a professor of English at Salem State College, where she teaches courses in literature, research, and writing. She has written reference articles for such volumes as the *Oxford Encyclopedia of American Literature, American Writers, British Writers, Magill's Survey of World Literature, Musicians and Composers of the Twentieth Century, Critical Survey of Mystery and Detective Fiction,* among many others. She also writes and publishes creative nonfiction, travel and memoir writing, and literary biography. JON KRAKAUER

Tom Cerasulo. Tom Cerasulo holds the Shaughness Family Chair for the Study of the Humanities at Elms College. He has published on film adaptations and on the cultural history of American authorship. His recent work appears in *Arizona Quarterly, MELUS, The Litchfield Review,* and *Studies in American Culture.* He is currently writing a book that reconsiders Hollywood's effect on American literary authors. BUDD SCHULBERG

Deborah Kay Ferrell. Deborah Kay Ferrell earned a doctorate in creative writing and American literature from Florida State University. She has been the recipient of a Florida Arts Council grant for her fiction. Currently, she is an associate professor of English at SUNY–Finger Lakes Community College, where she teaches courses in writing, cinema, and American literature. She recently completed a novel on her experiences with the Cuban-American community in Miami. HA JIN

William L. Frank. William L. Frank is a professor emeritus and former dean of the College of Arts and Sciences at Longwood College. Before teaching at Longwood, he served for four years in the U.S. Air Force and taught at the University of Southern Mississippi, Northwestern University, Delta State University, and

the University of Southeast Missouri. He has published books and articles on Sherwood Bonner, William Hoffman, Robert Penn Warren, and Allen Wier. He resides in Rice, Virginia, with his wife. They have three children and eight grandchildren. WILLIAM HOFFMAN

Angela Garcia. Angela Garcia earned a master's degree in English from the University of California, Davis. She has taught in El Salvador, as well as California schools. Having recently moved to Corvallis, Oregon, she is employed as a freelance online writer, as well as a professional scorer for Pearson and the Educational Testing Service. MARGARET EDSON

Tracie Church Guzzio. Tracie Church Guzzio is an associate professor of English at the State University of New York at Plattsburgh, where she teaches courses in African American literature, literary theory, and human rights literature. She has published criticism on various African American writers and was co-editor of *The Encyclopedia of African-American Literature.* She recently completed a manuscript on the work of John Edgar Wideman, and she is currently working on a study of post-traumatic narratives and African American literature. PERCIVAL EVERETT

Joan Wylie Hall. Joan Wylie Hall teaches Southern literature and other American literary genres at the University of Mississippi. Author of *Shirley Jackson: A Study of the Short Fiction* and editor of the interview collection *Conversations with Audre Lorde,* she has published essays on Willa Cather, William Faulkner, Josephine Humphreys, Anna Deavere Smith, Ruth McEnery Stuart, Eudora Welty, Tennessee Williams, among others. She contributed the Ann Patchett essay to *American Writers Supplement XII.* JANISSE RAY

David R. Johnson. David R. Johnson is a professor of English at Lafayette College. He is the author of *Conrad Richter: A Writer's Life* and has written on Ernest Hemingway, John Steinbeck, Harold Frederic, and on aspects of American literature and culture. CONRAD RICHTER

Paul Johnston. Paul Johnston is an associate professor of English at the State University of New York at Plattsburgh, where he teaches courses in colonial and nineteenth-century American literature, as well as nature writing courses. He has published articles on Nathaniel Hawthorne, Henry Wadsworth Longfellow and the Fireside Poets, Susan and James Fenimore Cooper, Jonathan Edwards, Thomas Merton, and Barry Lopez. He is currently writing a study of Catholicism in nineteenth-century American literature. ALICE MCDERMOTT

Laurie Ousley. Laurie Ousley is a faculty member at the Nichols School. She has published a collection of essays about children's literature titled *To See the Wizard: Politics and the Literature of Childhood,* which includes her essay "'Well-read people are less likely to be evil': Intellectual Development and Justice in Lemony Snicket's *A Series of Unfortunate Events.*" She has also published in *Legacy* and has an essay forthcoming in *Mother Knows Best: Talking Back to the "Experts".* She is currently working on a study of political intentions within young readers' literature from the nineteenth century to the present-day. SUSAN WARNER

Joseph G. Ramsey. Joseph G. Ramsey is an assistant professor of English at Fisher College and a recent graduate of Tufts University's Ph.D. program in English. His current research focuses on U.S. proletarian literature and the intersections between left-wing movements and twentieth-century U.S. mass culture. Along with Graham Barnfield and Victor Cohen, Ramsey co-edited a special issue of the e-journal *Reconstruction* focusing on the theme of "class, culture, and public intellectuals." Work from his dissertation "Red Pulp: Radicalism and Repression in Mid-20th Century U.S. 'Genre' Fiction" is forthcoming in *Mediations* and *Reconstruction 8.4,* while his film criticism has appeared in such journals as *Cultural Logic, Socialism and Democracy,* and *Counterpunch.* PAUL WILLIAM RYAN

Whitney Womack Smith. Whitney Womack Smith is an associate professor of English and

an affiliate in women's studies and black world studies at Miami University Hamilton. Her research focuses on the transatlantic relationships and dialogues among nineteenth-century British and American women writers. She has published articles and biographical entries on Harriet Beecher Stowe, Rebecca Harding Davis, Elizabeth Gaskell, Elizabeth Siddal, and Margaret Sackville. NELLA LARSEN, DOROTHY WEST

Richard Wakefield. Richard Wakefield has taught composition and American literature at Tacoma Community and the University of Washington for over twenty-five years. He has also been a literary critic for the *Seattle Times* for over twenty years. His collection of poetry, *East of Early Winters,* was published by the University of Evansville Press and received the Richard Wilbur Award. ROBERT WRIGLEY

Bette S. Weidman. Bette S. Weidman is an associate professor of English at Queens College of the City University of New York, where she has been teaching American literature since 1968. She also serves as director of American studies at Queens College and held a Fulbright fellowship in India in 1997. She has written on Charles Frederick Briggs, Henry David Thoreau, Herman Melville, Margaret Fuller and other antebellum authors, as well as on Native American literature and historic photographs. CHARLES FREDERICK BRIGGS

SUPPLEMENT XVIII

Charles Frederick Briggs to Robert Wrigley

CHARLES FREDERICK BRIGGS

(1804—1877)

Bette S. Weidman

CHARLES FREDERICK BRIGGS played an influential role in the development of American literature in the antebellum period through his work as a novelist, as a writer of sketches and short fiction for periodicals, and as the founding editor of two important magazines. He was also the author of hundreds of unsigned book reviews and columns of cultural commentary circulating in the press of the young country. His four novels, rich in social satire, give a view of pre–Civil War urban scenes and the shipboard experience of crews aboard American vessels, accompanied by acute analysis of the influence of economics and social class; this work made popularly available forms and themes that later writers like Herman Melville (1819–1891) and Theodore Dreiser (1871–1945) would absorb and develop. Briggs also made an original contribution to American literary satire in his witty fictional letters published in newspapers in the 1840s and again in the 1870s, making him a forerunner of the humorists Artemus Ward, Josh Billings, Petroleum Nasby, and Mark Twain.

Charles Briggs's forty years of largely anonymous literary labor, dating from his emergence in 1839 as the hitherto unknown author of a popular success, *The Adventures of Harry Franco,* to his death in 1877, on the day he composed the last of his "Brewsterville" letters for the weekly *Independent,* were rooted in New York City, where he was a passionately engaged citizen. His contemporaries acknowledged his interest in the architecture and social life of the city by appointing him to civic organizations, among them the American Art-Union, the Copyright Club, and the committee that planned Central Park. From 1853 through 1877, Briggs wrote the unsigned introductions to *Trow's New York City Directory,* showing that his fictional metropolitan portraits had a basis in street-by-street familiarity with the growing city. Most of all, he identified his point of view, in the perilous 1840s and 1850s, with "the meridian of Broadway," which he imagined, hopefully, as a harmonizing alternative to the approaching conflict of North and South.

LIFE

Charles Frederick Briggs was born in the town of Siasconset at the eastern edge of the island of Nantucket, Massachusetts, on December 30, 1804. He was the fourth child of six born to Sally Coffin and Jonathan Briggs, a merchant engaged in the China trade. Their families had long been settled in this seacoast town thirty miles off the coast of the New England mainland but not at all peripheral to the trade routes vital to the early Republic. Nantucket, and particularly his birthplace, known as 'Sconset, made a lasting impression on Briggs, who always reached back to it for his definition of true moral values.

When he was establishing his literary reputation in the pages of the *Knickerbocker, or New-York Monthly Magazine,* in 1840, he wrote a short history and appreciation of Nantucket, noting its founding by Thomas Macy, who had been forced to flee colonial Massachusetts for harboring Quakers. The sublime beauty of the ocean, the vigor and challenge of the fishing and whaling industries, the modesty and hospitality of the inhabitants, gave Briggs his earliest real education. In a later autobiographical article, he wrote:

> When a very small boy, I used to climb to the top of high hills for the pleasure of reveling in the fresh breeze as it flew by; and my first dream of freedom was the open sea, where there was nothing between me and the winds. Many a time have I wished

> myself one of the dwarf cedars that fringed the bleak hill at the back of my father's house,—the winds seem to take such a delight in rustling through them. Many a winter's night in my boyhood have I heard the nor'westers carousing in the forest, roaring and screeching among their dry branches, and wished myself among them.
>
> ("The Winds," pp. 52–53)

But economic woes abbreviated this happy childhood as President Thomas Jefferson's Embargo Acts of 1807 and 1808 severely limited New England shipping. The War of 1812 put an end to Jonathan Briggs's prosperity; his ships were seized by the British and he was jailed for bankruptcy. Thirty-three years later, in a letter to his friend James Russell Lowell (1819–1891), Charles Briggs recalled a sharp memory of being taken to a "strange-looking building with a high fence around it," where his uncle lifted him up to the bars to see his father. His later work shows that he never forgot the sudden experience of poverty and the sting of unjust laws.

Jonathan Briggs's sons went to sea to redeem the family's fortunes, the oldest, William, becoming captain of the ship *Phoebe,* and Charles, the third son, making at least two voyages as a merchant sailor, one to Liverpool and the other to South America. We know he was at sea by the age of twenty, as he records in a letter to Lowell that he dashed from Liverpool to a London bookshop in 1824 to purchase an early copy of the last canto of Lord Byron's *Don Juan.* The source of his literary interests is unknown, as he wrote later to a Nantucket friend that he had grown up "without a soul caring if [he] knew [his] letters." Remarkably well self-educated, he favored Jonathan Swift, Henry Fielding, and the witty satire of Restoration comedy. His omnivorous reading in early manhood prepared him well for his later work reviewing a great variety of new books for magazines and newspapers.

Glimpsing the attractions of the growing city of New York from the harbor, Briggs took up land-based mercantile pursuits, eventually becoming a full partner in the wholesale grocers' firm of Ransom E. Wood, Charles F. Briggs, and William H. Mather, located at 47 Water Street. Although Briggs lived and worked in New York for the rest of his life, he marked his commitment to Nantucket values by marrying his cousin Deborah Rawson, on May 16, 1836. The publication of Briggs's novel *The Adventures of Harry Franco* in 1839 made his reputation as a satiric humorist and launched his literary career.

Although he worked at multiple jobs for much of his life, his literary ambitions and his commitment to the development of a national literature never wavered. In the absence of international copyright law, periodicals that paid authors were shaping American literary production; Briggs's work can be found, unsigned and under the pseudonym of Harry Franco, in all sorts of periodicals, from the *Knickerbocker* to the *Union Magazine of Literature and Art*; *American Magazine: A Whig Journal of Politics, Literature and Art*; *U.S. Magazine and Democratic Review*; *Boston Miscellany of Literature and Fashion*; *Liberator*; *National Anti-Slavery Standard*; *Graham's Gentlemen's and Ladies' Magazine*; *Hartford Courant*; and many others. Briggs wrote two more novels in 1843 and 1844: *The Haunted Merchant,* a Dickensian tragicomedy, and *Working a Passage; or, Life on a Liner,* a novelized critique of living and working conditions on American merchant vessels.

During the early years of his life as a merchant-turned-writer, Briggs developed two important friendships. He met the portrait painter William Page (1811–1885) as a result of art criticism he wrote for Park Benjamin's newspaper, *New World.* Briggs was an early and ardent supporter of American painting and became a shareholder in the Apollo Association, formed for the support of native artists in 1839. A few years later Briggs was on the Committee of Management of the group, which became the American Art-Union. He was influential in selecting paintings to be purchased and exhibited and prepared the organization's 1843 and 1844 annual reports. He praised Page's realism, defended his portrayal of nudity, and extended the hand of friendship to Page, whose domestic life was in turmoil. In turn, Page introduced him to the young poet James Russell Lowell. One cannot overstate the importance of Briggs's friendships with Page and Lowell. Their substantial preserved correspondence provides valuable detail about the lives of

all three men, who encouraged and supported each other for twenty years. In 1847, Lowell included a literary portrait of Briggs in his famous "A Fable for Critics" and also made him a New Year's gift of the manuscript and all the proceeds of its publication.

In the early 1840s, Charles and Deborah Briggs moved to a rural retreat on Staten Island, which was developing as a spacious suburb for the growing city. Briggs called his first cottage "Willowbrook," possibly after the north-shore waterway near the present-day campus of the College of Staten Island. Soon he moved to larger home he jokingly called "Bishop's Terrace," in honor of his wife's bishop, or bustle, hanging out on a clothesline. Staten Island historians think that this house was located in the region known as Dutch Farms, where Ralph Waldo Emerson's brother, Judge William Emerson, lived, as well as Henry James, Sr. Lowell came to Staten Island to visit an eye specialist, Dr. Samuel Mackenzie Elliott, who lived in the neighborhood today called New Brighton. Briggs's friends Sydney Howard Gay and George William Curtis also lived in this vicinity, home to the island's abolitionist community.

Briggs realized the dream of creating a magazine of his own in January 1845, when he founded the weekly *Broadway Journal,* promising to print only original material and undertaking an ambitious role in reviewing new books. Politically, the *Broadway Journal* hoped to establish a third voice to balance those of Boston and South Carolina. Briggs deplored the rapidly polarizing discourse of New England abolitionists and the Southern apologists for slavery; he hoped his *Journal* would be a means of communication and a rational alternative in American politics. The *Broadway Journal* was antislavery but not abolitionist; it made an effort to print Southern writers. But as Briggs's chief supporters were his New England friends, he made a tactical error in accepting Edgar Allan Poe as coeditor; Poe emphasized the magazine's alliance with the South and undermined its subscription list. Briggs gave up his hopes by the second number and, before the end of 1846, Poe ran the enterprise into the ground. The *Broadway Journal* is remembered today for its serious format, anticipating the *New York Review of Books*; its negative reception of Margaret Fuller's *Woman in the Nineteenth Century* (1845); and its first publication of many of Poe's stories and poems.

In 1847, Charles and Deborah Briggs moved to Brooklyn to await the birth of their daughter, Charlotte. From this time to the end of his life, Briggs's name can be found in Brooklyn street directories at various addresses, sometimes also identified by the profession of editor or clerk. His belated fatherhood, coming after eleven years of marriage and the loss, in 1844, of an infant son, was a great pleasure to him. He confessed to Lowell that the world turned more smoothly for him after Charlotte's birth. Briggs went to work for the *New York Mirror,* a daily with a weekly edition, publishing a series of letters from a fictional foreign correspondent parodying the letters of Nathaniel Parker Willis and Margaret Fuller then appearing in New York newspapers. He used these "Pinto letters" to promote his antislavery views by satiric indirection. He then wrote a final novel, *The Trippings of Tom Pepper,* a string of satiric vignettes (first serialized in the *Mirror* from 1847 to 1850) in which he mocked the American dogma that virtuous behavior will bring worldly success. *The Trippings of Tom Pepper* (published in two volumes, in 1847 and 1850) culminates in a withering portrait of the New York literati.

Among the jobs of literary work that Briggs took on in 1847–1848, the most notable are the notes he wrote to the architectural drawings of William H. Ranlett. Ranlett made sketches of homes of varying pretensions and costs, and Briggs developed short essays that explored the relationships of men to their homes. The drawings and essays were published as *The Architect* in 1849, and they follow up on an interest in architecture that Briggs had been elaborating since his early days as a writer for the *Knickerbocker.*

During the 1850s, Briggs continued to write for a variety of magazine and newspapers, but in 1853, he succeeded in collaborating with George William Curtis to interest the publisher George Palmer Putnam in sponsoring a new magazine.

The *Broadway Journal* was reborn on a more ambitious scale as *Putnam's Monthly Magazine,* which Briggs served as editor from 1853 to 1855. Among the distinctions of this landmark in American literary history, *Putnam's* under Briggs published Melville's short stories "Bartleby the Scrivener," "The Encantadas," the installments of *Israel Potter,* and "The Lightning Rod Man" as well as Henry David Thoreau's "An Excursion to Canada." James Fenimore Cooper, Henry Wadsworth Longfellow, James Russell Lowell, and Edmund Quincy contributed prose serials that testified to the editor's support of local color and realism. Briggs's interest in engravings gave space to a valuable series called "New York Daguerreotyped."

Although its political orientation was liberal and antislavery, rather than abolitionist, Briggs had secured enough allies to prevent *Putnam's* from meeting the fate of the *Broadway Journal.* In 1856, Putnam himself took over the editorship and the magazine gradually stopped publishing. In the five years before and during the Civil War Briggs turned to newspaper journalism, helping Henry J. Raymond edit the daily *New York Times.*

In his 1884 reminiscence *Fifty Years Among Authors, Editors, and Publishers,* J. C. Derby remembered Briggs as one of the "brightest and most popular humorous men of the day." Along with Artemus Ward, Josh Billings, T. B. Aldrich and others, Briggs frequented George W. Carleton's bookstore and lunched at "Pfaff's celebrated German restaurant, in a Broadway basement, near Bleecker Street, the rendezvous at that day of the so-called Bohemians" (p. 239). The thirty-six-year-old freelance journalist Walt Whitman, who was about to publish the first edition of *Leaves of Grass* (1855), also frequented Pfaff's; whether or not the two ever met, Briggs would have despised Whitman's politics, because as a regular Democrat, Whitman had campaigned for U.S. presidents Martin Van Buren and James Polk and supported Polk's imperialist war with Mexico (1846–1848).

In 1855, Briggs contributed to an anthology honoring Lewis Gaylord Clark, of the *Knickerbocker,* his own first editor. He collaborated with Augustus Maverick on *The Story of the Telegraph* (1858), based on their *Times* dispatches. Still writing hundreds of reviews, he finally noticed the third edition of *Leaves of Grass,* characterizing its author, in the *Times,* as "uncultured, rude, defiant and arrogant ... a rough diamond" (May 19, 1860, Books Supplement, p. 1). In 1862 he reviewed the display of Matthew Brady's daguerreotypes of Antietam.

In the uneasy years of the war, Briggs edited the short-lived *Irving Magazine* and wrote the articles on William Page and Henry Fielding for the *New American Cyclopedia* (1864). He provided an introductory essay for the new series of *Putnam's* in 1868 and undoubtedly wrote reviews until December 1870, when the magazine merged into *Scribner's Monthly.* His life was shaped by the tremendous amount of literary labor, much of it anonymous, that he put into the establishment of an American literary culture.

Settled in Brooklyn Heights for the twenty years since Charlotte's birth, in his last years Briggs attended the Congregational Church of the Pilgrims, where the pastor was a scholar, Richard Storrs, also president of the Long Island Historical Society. He pointedly did not choose the nearby church of the flamboyant Henry Ward Beecher.

In 1870, a neighbor on Livingston Street, Theodore Tilton, editor of the daily *Brooklyn Union* and the weekly *Independent,* engaged Briggs to assist him by reporting on financial news. Soon, however, a sorry affair disrupted Tilton's life. Fifteen years earlier, Tilton had reported on Henry Ward Beecher's oratory; he became the preacher's friend and follower and married a Sunday school teacher from Beecher's church, Elizabeth Richards. In 1870, Tilton learned that his wife and Beecher had committed adultery. After a Machiavellian intervention by Henry Bowen, who owned the *Union* and the *Independent* and who had also been cuckolded by Beecher, Tilton lost his journalistic positions. He also lost his social position as a result of the ignominy brought on him by his radical supporter, the prophetess of free love Victoria Woodhull. Benjamin Tracy, a Brooklyn lawyer, bought the *Union* and made Briggs editor in chief.

Although he benefited by Tilton's tragedy, Briggs took no pleasure in it; he scrupulously kept his family and himself out of the affair, although his home was only a few doors from the one occupied by the unhappy Tiltons. While the daily *Union* was a journalistic success, Briggs preferred to work at the weekly *Independent.* In 1874, he provided the annual Christmas story for the *Independent* and inaugurated a new series of fictional correspondence, this time masquerading as Elder Brewster of Brewsterville. Elder Brewster commented freely, sharply, and satirically on the presidential election of Rutherford B. Hayes versus Samuel Tilden and on the mores of the citizens of Brewsterville. The Brewsterville letters appeared eight times, until the black-bordered June 20, 1877, issue of the *Independent* announced the author's sudden death at age seventy-three, of a heart attack, following a pleasant evening entertaining friends.

Deborah Briggs outlived her husband by twenty-two years, staying on in Brooklyn until she was ninety-five years old, accompanied by Charlotte, who remained unmarried. Both women were devoted to Briggs's memory; Charlotte reported, in a letter to Charles Eliot Norton, how much pleasure reading his biography of James Russell Lowell gave to her aged mother. Living on until 1928, Charlotte Briggs cared for her father's literary remains, lending his letters to biographers of Lowell and Poe but always pleading for their return. No one has yet located her father's manuscripts, although she gave his correspondence with Lowell to the Houghton Library at Harvard University. The Briggs family is buried in the Moravian Cemetery, New Dorp, Staten Island.

HARRY FRANCO

During the undocumented years of his life in the early 1830s, when Briggs was transforming himself from a wandering sailor to a rooted New Yorker, he must have tried several employments, experiencing firsthand some of the troubles that later beset his first hero, Harry Franco. Like his creator, a boy from the provinces, Harry is repeatedly cheated of his money and his ideals in a comic episodic plot influenced by the works of Tobias Smollett and Henry Fielding but directed at particularly American social contradictions. The novel's subtitle, *A Tale of the Great Panic,* places its criticism of social life in the context of the volatility of economic conditions. Even at the end of the book, when Franco has experienced sincere religious conversion, he is still not free of the uncertainties imposed by forces stronger than his will or virtue.

Franco, whose name carries the echo of Benjamin Franklin, one of Briggs's favorite autobiographers, must make his own way in New York City. His father, like his author's, has been bankrupted by Jefferson's Embargo and, moreover, disinherited. Unlike Briggs, however, Harry Franco has been nurtured on expectations of an inheritance; his dreams fail to prepare him for the ruthlessness of the city, where his innocence of the game of manners lays bare the sectional hostilities, drunkenness and debauchery, and threat of violence so close to the surface of American life.

If Briggs experimented with writing prior to the publication of *The Adventures of Harry Franco* in 1839, his efforts are well concealed by the practice of journalistic anonymity. He later wrote that he hid his literary efforts under a bushel. We know he gave some of his own experience as a merchant sailor in South America to Harry Franco. But unlike Briggs himself, Franco does not work his way up to partnership in a wholesale grocer's firm; instead, his autobiography is a fiction intended to reveal Franco's foolish investments in pseudo-gentility and pride, as he pursues the beautiful Georgiana DeLancey.

As Franco makes his way in the city, he is cheated by a dandified dry-goods salesman, J. Lummucks; sold worthless real estate by a con man named Doitt; victimized by a lawyer, Mr. Slobber; and cursed by a Southern orator, Colonel Sylvanus Spliteer. In each of these comic episodes, Briggs is interested in the social failure, not the characters themselves. At the start of his literary career, he shows that his treatment of slavery is not going to be directly critical but shaped to make the slaveholder visible as corrupt and morally discredited. Colonel Spliteer curses

Harry as the "son of a northern abolitionist" (Vol. 1, p. 40), because at the boardinghouse table Harry innocently drinks from what he takes to be a common bottle of wine. The terms of the curse lead Spliteer's henchmen to assault Franco, presuming he is enticing away Spliteer's black servant. Lucky to escape a lynching, the boy is hauled before a judge, the napkins he used to mop up spilled wine alleged to be abolitionist handbills. Finally revealed as having committed only a breach of manners, Franco is forgiven and invited to drink with the colonel and the judge, who behave so grossly that their titles lose their sanctity for the boy. The incident is still not closed, for a newspaperman, irked at his exclusion from the courtroom, picks up the outlines of the story and represents Franco as a bold insurgent; he derides Harry's appearance and demands that he be tarred, feathered, and ridden out of town. Horrified at this impending fate, Harry appeals to Spliteer for protection and is reassured by that benevolent gentleman: "nobody cares anything about a newspaper, for although there is nothing which men read more eagerly, there is nothing which they heed so little, not even their Bibles" (Vol. 1, p. 64).

Franco describes his encounters with men of the city with great candor and feeling; the reader, seeing beyond the innocence of the boy, understands the irony of the author in revealing slavery as the national paranoia and greed as the urban pastime. But in addition to his satiric purpose, Briggs also weights the city scenes with a ballast of realistic description. One of his favorite sites is the Battery:

> The sky was bright and blue and a thousand penons and signals, and the flags of many nations, gracefully floated upon the breeze. The magnificent proportions of the ships, with their beautiful figureheads, and rich gilding and bright waists, and tall taper masts and outstretched spars, filled me with amazement; and the countless multitudes of smaller vessels, their curious and varying shapes and the regular confusion of ropes and spars, gave me no less astonishment.
>
> (Vol. 1, p. 152)

If the Battery gives evidence of New York's prosperity and natural beauty, the Five Points slum area is proof of the squalor that also exists in the city. Franco, wandering into the crowded, littered slum streets, is driven to thoughts of suicide when he sees how human beings starve amid the wealth of the city. The reader will have to wait ten years for Herman Melville's *Redburn* before encountering another such immersion of innocence in the city.

Briggs's own childhood poverty established unfailing sensitivity to the cruelty of deprivation, a theme to which he recurs in all of his novels. Franco's realistic descriptions of the great disparity between rich and poor do not cause him to omit portraits of those, neither wealthy nor destitute, who lead a marginal existence: the apple woman, the Negro girl hawking hot corn, the cartmen reading their penny papers, the old secondhand book dealer:

> "Close by was a negro opening hard-shelled clams, with a red flannel shirt on his back, and a bell crowned beaver hat on his head. Not far from him was a young girl in a black silk dress and a tattered leghorn hat, selling ice cream."
>
> (Vol. 2, p. 2)

There is a Whitmanesque touch to these details, recorded for their own sake. The closely observed city scenes in *Harry Franco* are forerunners of similar sketches of New York and Liverpool in the later novels; they indicate Briggs's continuing fascination with the spectacle of everyday life in early-nineteenth-century New York, with its oyster cellars, firehouses, and counting houses. This aspect of his work links Briggs with the later writers William Dean Howells, Hamlin Garland, and most of all, Dreiser.

After a substantial experience of failure in the city, his efforts bringing him no closer to the distant Georgiana, Franco enlists as a sailor aboard a merchant vessel bound for South America. He strikes up his first genuine friendship with a handsome, popular sailor, Jerry Bowhorn, a literary ancestor of Melville's Jack Chase, with whom he jumps ship in Buenos Aires. They travel across the pampas, noting that polite manners conceal brutality among gauchos and outlaws. Somewhat inconsistently, perhaps as a sign of Briggs's nationalism, Franco has no trouble recognizing the corruption of Buenos Aires, though he is blind to it at home.

The Adventures of Harry Franco, highly praised by the *Knickerbocker* editor Lewis Gaylord Clark, made such a stir in literary circles in 1839 that one would not be surprised to learn that it had eventually caught the eye of another young aspiring sailor-turned-writer, who a few years later also jumped ship with a congenial companion in an even more exotic locale. Herman Melville may even have remembered the most striking episode in *The Adventures of Harry Franco,* when the boy sails home from Argentina on an American sloop of war. Resisting the tyranny of a lieutenant who orders him flogged, Franco climbs to the topmost spar and falls into the sea. The punishment is ordered because Harry will not betray his fellow crewmembers, who smuggled liquor onto the vessel. In springing into the rigging to escape the brutal command, Franco refuses to bend his spirit to an official tyranny. In describing his ascent and fall from the main topmast, Briggs wrote some of his most vivid prose. In Melville's *White-Jacket,* published in 1850, the hero's fall from that same topmost yard results in his freeing himself from the strangling garment that had set him apart from his fellows. In Briggs's book the experience also represents the mysterious confrontation with death that brings about a deeper identification with other human beings. Harry experiences a sense of solidarity with the sailors, symbolized by their generous subscription, which was missing in the world of the city. The interlude at sea is written in a different tone from the rest of Franco's adventures. Burlesque is almost absent, and Franco is given a chance, finally, to show that he is made of better stuff than the common run of sentimental heroes.

In this book, however, it is an essential part of the satire that the hero's growth in understanding does not significantly affect his fate. Though Harry returns to the city a more confident and somewhat more developed character, he cannot change his condition by his own merit. He travels to New Orleans to deal in the cotton market, but fails; in desperation, seeking a gambling den, he wanders by mistake into a religious congregation. Guided by an old slave, he takes a seat and the words of the sermon "fall upon [his] heart" (Vol. 2, p. 220). A reversal of his fortunes comes about through a lucky speculation by his father; this finally makes him a worthy suitor for Georgiana, as her guardian has lost his fortune in the same economic turmoil. The country village of Harry's childhood has been renamed Francoville, and a pretentious mansion erected in place of his old home. Seeking Georgiana, Harry is caught in a shipwreck, after a storm that adds natural disaster to the symbolic weight of economic disorder. Eventually he conveniently floats ashore on the North Carolina beach where Georgiana is waiting.

Just as the English heroes of Fielding and Smollett traditionally rediscover their aristocratic parentage, Franco also comes to wealth and position. However, this is not as a result of his lengthy strenuous exertion but, instead, of his father's attainment of wealth by chance. In *Harry Franco,* Briggs burlesques an American compromise with the system of an established elite. Like Harriet Martineau, Charles Dickens, and other English observers of nineteenth-century American society, Briggs saw that Americans, despite their vaunted ideals of democracy, set up social patterns that approximate those of the British aristocracy that they profess to despise. Although Franco achieves his fortune and his beloved, he is only temporarily secure, for the shape of the novel's plot emphasizes the fragility of any security in a tumultuous world.

While the plot is full of variety and witty complication, the narrative style is also of interest. *The Adventures of Harry Franco* begins as a retrospective first-person narrative, the speaker an older and wiser Harry than the boy who is being described. This distance contributes to the ironic detachment Briggs seeks. As the narrative proceeds, the gap between narrator and actor narrows to emphasize dramatic action; Harry loses his opening sophistication but regains it at the novel's end, where he ties up the loose ends of the story and meditates on the difference between fiction and history.

The Adventures of Harry Franco introduced Briggs to the reading public as a comic satirist interested in urban social interactions and economic inequalities. Of course his readers

preferred to laugh at the comic situations rather than heed the serious social criticism. As a sign of the uncritical merging of author and character, Briggs was known in the literary world as Harry Franco; his work can still be found more easily under this pseudonym than under his real name. When James Russell Lowell paid Briggs the compliment of a portrait in his "A Fable for Critics," he remembered him as Harry Franco.

BRIGGS AT THE KNICKERBOCKER

Briggs's literary career was launched by the favorable review given *The Adventures of Harry Franco* in the pages of the New York *Knickerbocker,* a conservative monthly periodical addressed to the tastes of prosperous merchants and lawyers. Edited by Lewis Gaylord Clark, who purchased it in 1834 and kept it going until 1861, the *Knickerbocker* had published such notable writers as Washington Irving, James Fenimore Cooper, William Cullen Bryant, Fitz-Greene Halleck, Henry Wadsworth Longfellow, and John Greenleaf Whittier by 1839, the year in which Clark enlisted Briggs as a regular contributor. Devoted to celebrating the vitality of New York City, the *Knickerbocker* disavowed New England transcendentalism and abolitionism and defended high protective tariffs, Whig candidates, and orthodox Christianity.

The *Knickerbocker*'s politics did not entirely coincide with that of its new contributor, but the connection was useful to a writer making his reputation and evidently profitable to Clark, eagerly enlisting new voices to promote circulation. In August 1839, Briggs began a series of articles called "Gimcrackery," which he promised would be lighthearted. Yet the second installment, "The Story of Poppy Van Buster," while it begins as a comic portrait of an old man devoted to the preservation of his house in a sea of urban change, ends as tragedy. In spite of the persistence of old Van Buster, he is the victim of modern times. His wooden mansion of 1779 is razed by the mayor and the city council, while Poppy wanders about the changed town in search of his cousin, with whom he wants to share a treasure of prerevolutionary currency. The story sharply criticizes the demolition of old New York in the name of profit and new fashions. A reverse Rip Van Winkle, instead of leaving its old man contentedly surviving into the new political dispensation, Briggs's story ends with the old Dutchman hanging himself from the single remaining beam of his house, a victim of political and economic forces he cannot fight.

The third "Gimcrack" offers the first two chapters of a narrative that later became Briggs's second novel, *The Haunted Merchant* (1843). The story of an orphan boy adopted by a lonely rich merchant, this work was projected as the first of a series to be called *Bankrupt Stories.* Intended as a kind of Decameron, in which ten bankrupt merchants would retrieve their wealth by telling their stories, the series never materialized beyond the first volume. The novel's theme springs from Briggs's childhood experience and its literary influence is Dickens, a favorite with American readers in this period. But Briggs's Dickensian hero falls victim to jealousy and corruption. Briggs targets the distortions of lives devoted to the accumulation of wealth, false values resulting in imitative art and architecture. The hero, John Tremlett, eventually commits suicide, but not before Briggs has used his experiences to satirize transcendental schoolteaching (through a character modeled on Bronson Alcott), to explore the complexities of Southern slaveholding, to reveal the corruption of a political ward meeting, and to praise Quaker honesty and wholesome values. Not all of these episodes appeared in the *Knickerbocker,* where they would have been offensive to Clark's readers.

Instead, Briggs suspended "The Haunted Merchant" in favor of a fourth "Gimcrack" in which he imagines a future world, in which all contemporary social evils are corrected: "Women enjoy the same privileges as men; servants are unknown, and all government is at an end" (November 1939, p. 425). He retrieves a newspaper of that day, *The Minors' Mirror,* which is edited by a society of infants still contending for their rights. Some of the comedy is heavy-handed, some of it topical, but one can still tease

out the humorous criticism of contemporary journalism.

The two best "Gimcracks" in the series are the fifth, "A Ride in an Omnibus" (December 1839) and the sixth, "Siasconset: How It Arose and What It Is" (March 1840).

The omnibus ride takes the reader on a trip down New York City's Broadway in a "long white carriage, drawn by four horses of as many different colors, and with a figure of Minerva painted upon its central panel" (p. 542), bound for Bowling Green. The daring young driver takes up a challenge from a driver from the opposition line, and the two vehicles hurtle down the great street, passing by the city's landmarks and interfered with by old market women, pigs, charcoal wagons, butcher's carts, and overloaded drays, arriving at a Swiftian climax before the race is over. All of Briggs's relish for city scenes and his rich local knowledge are displayed in this vigorous essay. Quite in contrast, his sixth "Gimcrack" memorializes his tranquil birthplace, reviewing its history of political resistance to tyranny and persecution and its capable brave whaling fleet, ending in a tribute to its matchless codfish and a recipe for New England chowder that roused a controversy among the *Knickerbocker*'s readers (explored by Perry Miller in his 1956 volume *The Raven and the Whale*).

In addition to the "Gimcracks," Briggs made numerous other contributions to the *Knickerbocker,* under the pseudonym of "Harry Franco." These include a humorous sketch of sea travel with vigorous views of ocean phenomena and stirring descriptions of danger at sea, concluding with literary criticism aimed at James Fenimore Cooper that anticipates that of Mark Twain. "The Day-Dream of a Grocer" (November 1841) is another example of Briggs's rendering of metropolitan scenes with a critique of unequal distribution of wealth and the injustice served by courts of law. Modern readers have an easy opportunity to read "Harry Franco" in the pages of the *Knickerbocker* and the other magazines to which he contributed, thanks to digitizing technology that makes much of his work retrievable online simply by typing in his famous pseudonym.

WORKING A PASSAGE

Briggs's third novel, *Working a Passage; or, Life on a Liner,* first published in 1844, is narrated in the first person by a young man of good family who leaves New York for Europe during a cholera epidemic, hoping both to avoid the pestilence and to enhance his education with visits to London, Paris, Florence, and Rome. Unluckily, when he reaches Paris to collect his bill of credit, he discovers that his father has died insolvent. To avoid further debt, he determines to work his passage home on a shabby American merchant vessel that is poorly run and provisioned. The narrative offers a realistic description of the life and work of sailors, as the narrator adjusts to losing his status as a "soft hand" in favor of becoming a "hard hand." Incompetence and bad weather abort the journey, and after a short stay in Liverpool, where the narrator observes the lives of the poor and socially marginalized, he takes ship on a New York liner, and the clash of democratic ideals and military methods becomes the theme of the book.

Like many of his countrymen, Briggs had been alarmed by an event that took place in the U.S. Navy on November 26, 1842, when on board the brig *Somers,* Captain Slidell MacKenzie had three sailors hanged for plotting mutiny, without giving them the benefit of civil trials. In his novel, Briggs writes, "The authority of a shipmaster, like that of a slave-owner, is too great not to be abused" (p. 57). He framed *Working a Passage* as an argument against the abuse and exploitation of sailors, thus providing a model for the younger writer Herman Melville to follow, five years later, when he composed *White-Jacket* (1849).

In *Working a Passage,* Briggs treats rough sailors with compassion. At the mercy of ignorant, quirky commanders, inadequately fed and sheltered, they are understandably demoralized; their condition illustrates the "inequalities of civilized life, where one portion of the people are privileged to live without work, and the other portion are doomed to work without living" (p. 57). Briggs took sharp note of those conditions that, in the eighteenth and nineteenth centuries,

caused some sailors to see the political ramifications of their situations and find effective means of resistance. Scholars since the late twentieth century have identified this racial and political consciousness with the term "the Black Atlantic."

Briggs's directness and the clarity of his descriptions make the short volume memorable for the quality of its prose. This realistic writing, thick with detail, may have caught the ear of young Melville, trying in these years to write his first novels. Briggs's description of Liverpool reminds the reader of Melville's later Ishmael, who set out in the *Pequod* to escape the "damp drizzly November in [his] soul" (*Moby-Dick,* 1851). It was evidently a state of mind and weather familiar to both writers:

> It was the last day of November, a cold, dreary, drizzling day; a dirty yellowish vapor hung over the city, so impervious to the sun's rays. ... A suffocating stench of coal smoke pervaded the atmosphere, and everything dripped, dripped, dripped dismally with rain; the gutters poured out never failing streams of muddy water, too thick and slow to make a bubble; most of the shops had gas lights burning, and the fish women with their baskets of herrings upon their heads, as they waded their miserable rounds, seemed too disheartened to cry their scaly commodities.
>
> (pp. 14–15)

Throughout the novel, food is used to distinguish "soft hands" from "hard hands." While the captain and his guests eat a breakfast of mutton chops, fried ham, hot rolls, buckwheat cakes, omelets, and coffee, the sailors survive on scrapings from mahogany-like salt beef. The continuing use of food is brought to a skillful climax at the book's end. In the next-to-last chapter, the sailors' spokesman, Jack Plasket, is revolted by the mishandling of the sailors' poor supper. He opposes the captain by tossing the filthy meat overboard; Plasket prefers hunger to being "fed like dogs" (p. 76). The sailors grumble briefly at the loss of their supper, but they bear their privation with dignity in the manner of those accustomed to it. The book's final chapter describes a parallel incident, a loss sustained by the privileged class, borne with far less aplomb.

Officers aboard the liner, a few days before their arrival in port, decide to kill the green turtle they have been fattening and banquet on turtle and champagne. Briggs indicates their anticipation and excitement; he describes the odors emanating from the galley, the jovial attitude of usually grim passengers, and the exaggerated politeness of the group as they walk into dinner. As the cook carries the precious tureen across the deck, the fascinated sailor at the wheel, our narrator, forgets his job. The ship lurches, the tureen slips, and the soup is lost, to the unbearable chagrin of the self-indulged privileged class. In *Working a Passage,* Briggs's democrat may go hungry, but he wins a moral victory over the plutocrats of American society.

THE BROADWAY JOURNAL

After more than five years of struggling to publish in magazines that failed to satisfy his standards of independence and intelligence, Briggs arranged to put forth a journal of his own. Combining his resources with those of a printer and a publisher, he issued a prospectus for his new magazine. It would respect the ideal of international copyright, even in the absence of such a law, by permitting only original matter into its pages: "Essays, Criticisms in Art and Literature, Domestic and Foreign Correspondence, and Literary and Scientific Intelligence." It would present original illustrations and demonstrate interest in the design of public buildings. The weekly journal would "espouse the cause of no political party, but would hold itself free to condemn or approve any men or measures that a patriotic regard for the welfare of the country might dictate" (p. 1).

The first number of the *Broadway Journal* appeared on January 4, 1845, with a full "Introductory" explaining its name and character:

> Broadway is confessedly the finest street in the first city of the New World. It is the great artery through which flows the best blood of our system. All the elegance of our continent permeates through it. If there is a handsome equipage set up, its first appearance is in Broadway. The most elegant shops in the city line its sides; the finest buildings are found there, and all the fashions exhibit their first gloss upon its sidewalks. Although it has a character of

> its own, the traveler often forgets himself walking through it, and imagines himself in London or Paris. Wall Street pours its wealth into its broad channel and all the dealers in intellectual works are here centered; every exhibition of art is found here, and the largest caravan series in the world border upon it. Its pavement has been trod by every distinguished man that has visited our continent; those who travel through it are refreshed by the most magnificent fountains in the world. It has a sunny side, too, where we have opened our office of delivery. It terminates at one end in the finest square in the city, doubtless in the Union, and at the other, in the Battery, unrivalled for its entire beauty by any marine parade in the world. So travelers say. For ourselves, we have seen many in the old world and the new, but none that equal it. As Paris is France, and London, England, so is Broadway, New York; and New York is fast becoming, if she be not already, America, in spite of South Carolina and Boston.
>
> (p. 1)

Moved to rare exuberance by the spectacle of the city and his hope for the new magazine, Briggs put aside his critical eye and offered a tribute to American material progress. The challenge of his last statement, that New York could find a middle ground between the North and the South, remained to be tested. Briggs planned to gain a national readership, keeping a line of Northern influence to the South. His *Journal* was to be antislavery, not as an isolated political program but as a natural outgrowth of its hatred of all forms of social injustice.

One of the most important features of the new magazine was a series called "American Prose Writers." To support native writing Briggs also undertook a substantial section of book and magazine reviewing. The *Broadway Journal* often included portraits of urban conditions, revealing the little immigrant children, barefooted in winter, sweeping the street corners for pennies, while fat, prosperous lawyers hurry by in their high boots. Briggs used the magazine to continue his crusade against corruption in the U.S. Navy. He introduced a series of satirical engravings, the most striking of which appeared on March 29, 1845, after annexation of Texas. Under the title "Portrait of an Annexationist," the artist has sketched the figure of Satan, crowned with iron horns, receiving the news from Texas with the greatest glee, anticipating "visions of fields of carnage ... of broken-hearted widows; of weeping orphans, of national debts ... and innumerable other delights which he feels sure will follow on the heels of annexation" (p. 200).

The most pointedly personal of the engravings was a satiric portrait of Briggs's fellow journalist Margaret Fuller, for whom his acrimony was unabated through the 1840s. Her book *Woman in the Nineteenth Century* had aroused Briggs's disagreement. His reviewer, Lydia Maria Child, wrote the first mild notice of the book in February 1845, but on March 8, 1845, along with the engraving, Briggs published a second discussion of the book that took issue with Fuller's feminism, contending that the woman who is sexually unfulfilled "sees things through a false medium ... her nature is distorted and unnatural" (p. 145). Opposing female suffrage, he brought down upon the *Journal* the wrath of his liberal readership.

Soon after, seeking allies, he added the name of Edgar Allan Poe to the masthead of the *Journal.* Poe cultivated his Southern connections and completed the alienation of Briggs's New England readership. Despite the excellence of its articles on New York architecture, its interesting fiction by Briggs and by Poe, its articles by William Page on the use of color in painting, Briggs found himself losing control of the *Journal,* as Poe monopolized much of its space to carry on his vendetta against Henry Wadsworth Longfellow, whom he accused of plagiarism. When Poe escalated the issue into the "little Longfellow war," it was clear that Briggs had miscalculated Poe's value to the magazine. Briggs's moderation on abolitionism had alienated Lowell and the New Englanders, who officially withdrew their support of the *Broadway Journal* in the Boston *Liberator* for 28 March 1845. Then Poe, seeking an outlet for his work, negotiated with the *Journal*'s publisher, John Bisco, to buy out Briggs's share in the magazine. The end of Briggs's dream of an independent literary journal was so abrupt that the story he was in the process of serializing, "Adventures of a Gentleman in Search of a Dinner," was left forever unfinished. His long-anticipated dinner repeatedly postponed

by comic circumstances, the gentleman remained hungry, much like the editor, who had to wait eight years, until *Putnam's* offered him the chance to satisfy his editorial ambitions.

THE LETTERS OF PINTO: 1846–1847

After the loss of the *Broadway Journal,* Briggs resumed publishing in a variety of magazines, offering a notable series of sketches on urban life, "City Articles," to his old editor, Clark, at the *Knickerbocker,* but his steadiest employer in 1846 was the new editor of the *New York Mirror,* Hiram Fuller. Fuller's pro-war pro-Polk political stance was repugnant to Briggs, but Fuller allowed him a good measure of freedom in return for as many book reviews and sketches as Briggs could produce.

On July 4, 1846, an outspoken American named Ferdinand Mendes Pinto made his first appearance on the foreign correspondence pages of the *Mirror.* Briggs used as a pseudonym the name of an adventurer that William Congreve, in his 1695 play *Love for Love,* had made the proverbial epithet for a liar. He conceived the idea of a fictional foreign correspondent partly as a witty response to the letters of Margaret Fuller, then appearing in Horace Greeley's *Tribune,* and partly as a satire on the recently published edition *Pencillings by the Way* (1841), the collected European letters of Nathaniel Parker Willis. In Pinto, Briggs created a self-assured Yankee whose personality was modeled on the genteel, pretentious Willis and on the self-centered, oblivious Margaret Fuller.

Briggs's fictional letters fitted into the *Mirror* seamlessly, as daily newspapers in the 1840s were composed of political discussions, observations on social life, and reports of local events, many of them in the form of letters. In addition, Briggs had many literary models to inspire him, from Jonathan Swift and Oliver Goldsmith to Benjamin Franklin and Washington Irving. His friend Lowell was planning fictional letters on abolition purporting to be written by "Hosea Biglow." When he took up his pen to satirize Fuller and Willis, Briggs could expect his audience to recognize and appreciate the genre.

Willis venerated European aristocracy, a sycophancy Briggs despised; Margaret Fuller, at the start of her European tour, sought to meet literary celebrities and to impress them with her own erudition. Pinto shares these tastes, but Briggs takes a step away from his models by also making Pinto into a patriot and a defender of his country's "peculiar institution." So while he eagerly accepts an invitation to a shooting party at the estate of the British prime minister, he takes offense at being seated at breakfast beside the African Alexander Dumas. Traveling on to the estate of the Duke of Argyle, he is mortified to meet up with Margaret Fuller, who is pontificating to the famous critic Christopher North, but he is forced to leave Inverary when he is introduced to "the notorious runaway slave," Frederick Douglass:

> My blood was at boiling heat, in a moment, and drawing myself up at my full length, I said with a proud air to his Grace, before all his noble guess; "Sir, as the representative of a free and enlightened country—as a republican—I resent this insult. I find that the days of exclusiveness and gentility are gone, and in their place those of reformers and abolitionists and amalgamations have come. The glory of Europe has departed. I will return to my own country." This cut them to the quick, and to disguise their feelings, they set up a loud laugh. But I was determined to mortify them still more, and immediately walked grandly out of the castle, with the intention of going directly to the inn. I took nothing with me but my hat, and stalked proudly across the lawn to the road which leads into the village. The night was dark and cold, and soon a thick fog set in and I lost my way. But I scorned to cry for assistance and walked straight on, and presently found myself nearly up to my middle in a bog.
>
> ("Pinto Letter 8" in *Studies in the American Renaissance,* p. 114)

The bog, of course, is an apt metaphor for the dead end Briggs saw in the defense of slavery. Unlike the abolitionists, however, he prefers pointing out absurdity to moralizing.

Pinto meets Miss Fuller again at the wedding of Robert Browning and Elizabeth Barrett, an affair he disparages for its asceticism. When a toast is offered to the "American ambassador," intended for the historian George Bancroft, Fuller rises to accept it! Anticipating the "ugly Ameri-

can," she attempts to buy Shakespeare's house and move it to America. The Pinto letters not only mock the overreaching of this American but also satirize the moral imperviousness and sentimentality of the British aristocracy, as in the description of Mayfair's grief at the departure of Tom Thumb and the death of Paul Dombey. But the Pinto letters are strongest on Pinto's struggles with his "patriotism," when he repeatedly encounters Frederick Douglass in the homes of British aristocracy. Briggs's genius is to complicate the satire by mocking Margaret Fuller directly while also mocking her critic Pinto, by making him ridiculous in his objections to Dumas and Douglass. Lowell thought the antislavery satire in the Pinto letters too good to be lost. In all, Briggs wrote eighteen Pinto letters, which belong to the tradition of American satire that culminated in the work of Mark Twain (1835–1910).

THE TRIPPINGS OF TOM PEPPER

Always alert to absurdity and pretension, Briggs must have noted the publication of Fanny Forrester's *Trippings in Authorland* (1846). He borrowed part of the title and the concept for his fourth and last novel, *The Trippings of Tom Pepper* (published in two volumes, 1847 and 1850), a savage satire of the New York literary society he knew so well. His *Trippings* was first serialized in the *Mirror* in columns adjoining Dickens's *Dombey and Son,* juxtaposing a homegrown work to the popular British reprint.

Illegitimate and orphaned, Tom Pepper spends his childhood on his native Cape Cod. Stowing away on a New York–bound packet, he falls under the influence of a kind merchant who sees him as unspoiled and who offers to help him to find his father, in return for Tom's promise to live a life of truth-telling as he makes his way in the city. His vow to live by the truth enmeshes Tom in a series of misadventures with money-lenders, lawyers, and, ultimately, literati, observed by Tom at a soiree hosted by "Lizzy Gil," the note-shaver's daughter. Briggs based this character on the figures of Anne Charlotte Lynch and Elizabeth Frieze Ellet, two contemporaries involved in a scandal with Poe.

Briggs could expect his sophisticated readers to recognize Myrtle Pipps, "the American G. P. R. James," as a portrait of the proslavery Southern novelist and historian William Gilmore Simms. Fitch Greenwood and his wife, translators from the Swedish, represent William and Mary Howitt, the British writers of a volume called *The Homes and Haunts of the Most Eminent British Poets,* reviewed negatively by Briggs on June 24, 1847, in the *National Anti-Slavery Standard.* Infuriated by Howitt's treatment of Jonathan Swift, Briggs had written, "The gossiping, book-peddling writer of literary catchpennies could no more comprehend the qualities of such a mind as that which conceived the Tale of a Tub, than a mud-paddling duck could understand the movements of an eagle" (p. 15). As he worked, Briggs saw the inclusive possibilities of his "soiree," to which he also invites satiric representations of Cornelius Mathews and Evert Duyckinck, prominent members of the "Young America" literary movement, and finally, "Austin Wicks," his stand-in for Edgar Allan Poe. Assembling all of those who had angered or wronged him since the *Broadway Journal* years, Briggs dramatizes a fracas caused by Poe that undermines the credibility and moral decency of the whole group.

More than the overflow of revengeful feelings, Briggs's satire fulfills a genuine moral purpose in castigating the politics and personalities of the New York literati, reminding them to cleanse themselves of posturing, jealousy, and imitativeness. Among the figures with which Briggs fills his two-volume novel are portraits of Margaret Fuller, as "Sophia Ruby"; William Page, as the bohemian artist "Ardent"; and Hiram Fuller, the editor of the *Mirror,* as "Mr. Wilton." The only literary figure of significance missing from Briggs's narrative is introduced in the dedication to "Matthew Trueman," as the reader for whom the book was written. "Matthew Trueman" was the pseudonym used by Lowell when he wrote a prose piece for the *Broadway Journal* condemning slavery and annexation in terms too strong for the practical editor. The "great moral lesson" that Briggs tells Matthew Trueman he has illustrated in his book is not the surface les-

son that truth-telling is the only path to happiness but, rather, the underlying fact that ideals must be accommodated to social realities.

Briggs ends Tom Pepper's *Trippings* with his discovery of a wealthy British father who makes it possible for him to marry a poor, humble girl like his abandoned mother and retire to a rural location. Of course, no such retirement was possible for his creator, who was finishing his double-decker novel and beginning his editorship of *Holden's Dollar Magazine* at the same time. Intended to correspond to the penny papers, *Holden's* was to achieve a circulation of thirty thousand, bringing to the working class a serious magazine filled with book reviews and articles on notable figures and issues.

PUTNAM'S MONTHLY

After a stint as clerk in the debenture room at the New York Custom House, a modest plum of political patronage that fell to him through Hiram Fuller, the editor of the *Mirror*, Briggs interested his friend George William Curtis in the development of a new literary magazine as ambitious as the *Broadway Journal* but more securely established. Together, the friends put their plan to the publisher George Palmer Putnam as a counterweight to the popular *Harper's Magazine*, which was filled with British reprints. *Putnam's Monthly* was to print only original material, as its publisher was an earnest advocate of international copyright law.

Putnam's under Briggs is remembered today for its publication of Melville's now-famous short stories, Thoreau's prose, and distinguished work by Cooper, Lowell, Longfellow, Quincy, and others, all of whom were published anonymously in the style of the day. *Putnam's* was openly antislavery in its political orientation and included serious reviews, notably Briggs's reviews of Henry David Thoreau's *Walden* (1854) and of Harriet Beecher Stowe's *Uncle Tom's Cabin* (1852). In addition, copyright legislation is a recurring theme in the magazine, with Briggs responding to Whig criticism regarding the topic.

Putnam's included commentary on art and architecture as well as on women and the women's movement, a topic on which Briggs remained conservative. When moved to passion, he resorted to an old option: the invention of a fictional character. Because of the practice of journalistic anonymity, it is difficult to identify all of Briggs's contributions to the magazine, but it is likely that he invented the Quaker character Bildad Hardhed to express his opposition to the war hawks of the mid-1850s. Described within the February 1855 "Editorial Notes," Hardhed appeared in the editorial offices of *Putnam's* to confront General Delablueblazes, whose central belief was "in time of peace, prepare for war." Bildad opposes the military man's espousal of war as a solution to political problems: "Shall the fair young wife, who now laughs to her crowing baby, in the coming years see the child brought home a mutilated man?" (p. 205).

One can still browse through the sturdy bound volumes of *Putnam's* with pleasure and profit, reading frank evaluations of race relations; an analysis of the culture of Wall Street; detailed discussions, accompanied by engravings, of New York City theaters and concert rooms; letters on international copyright; and amusing fictional sketches and serials. In early 1853, Briggs published a lengthy piece on "The Polar Seas and Sir John Franklin," still a topic of great interest, a thorough discussion of "Woman and the Woman's Movement," and a thoughtful review article on Harriet Beecher Stowe, "Uncle Tomitudes." Antebellum intellectuals must have found *Putnam's* indispensable.

Briggs looked upon the editorship of *Putnam's* as the zenith of his career, the best effort he could summon on behalf of a national literature. As an obituary notice written by Charles Richardson on July 5, 1877, in the *Independent* would later point out, *Putnam's "was* Mr. Briggs in his prime" (p. 3). In one of the last numbers of *Putnam's* that appeared under his editorship, Briggs enumerated his duties. He calculated that he had to wade through thirty thousand pages of manuscripts each year, avoid the appearance of hard-heartedness in rejecting contributions, "do" the books, overcome literary pirates, succeed in being the exponent of national thought and the supporter of what is right and

true, and—at the same time—please public taste! After eighteen months of editing *Putnam's,* Briggs was optimistic about the future of the literature he was trying to shape. He concluded his tenure as editor by remarking in the April 1855 "Editorial Notes" that his magazine had already succeeded in publishing superb American writers; that *Putnam's* "leaved and flowered so soon and so luxuriantly," he asserted, "shows unusual pith and vigor" in the young American literature. He went on to write, in the prophetic style of Whitman:

> Who knows how many, in every village in the country, and in the solitary houses, too—as from Henry Thoreau's seven dollar palace in the woods—have already written to publishers; or have by them, in secret nooks, piles of scratched paper, their tickets for immortality—or at the very least are meditating, *alta sub mente repostum,* what the coming years shall make known?
>
> (p. 442)

ELDER BREWSTER OF BREWSTERVILLE

Briggs undertook his last creative work for the literary weekly the *Independent* in 1875. In 1910, George Cary Eggleston wrote:

> The *Independent* exercised an influence upon the thought and life of the American people such as no periodical publication of its class exercises in this later time. ... Its circulation of more than three hundred thousand exceeded that of all the other publications of its class combined, and more important still, it was spread all over the country, from Maine to California.
>
> (*Recollections of a Varied Life,* p. 107)

In his affiliation with the *Independent,* then, Briggs demonstrated that, even as a septuagenarian, he had not lost touch with important periodicals and the group of young writers through whose work American literature would enter the twentieth century. Briggs was these young writers' link with previous generations; as one of them, Charles Richardson, later wrote in the *Independent,* "To share his editorial room was an education in the history of the nineteenth century; and in gentle courtesy and a singular uniformity of manner as well" (p. 3).

For the *Independent,* Briggs wrote the column "Personalities," filled with thumbnail obituaries and witty characterizations. On the last day of 1874, he contributed a retrospective called "The Good Old Times: New York Fifty Years Ago," and in 1876 he contributed the *Independent*'s traditional Christmas story, "The Widow's Wish," vintage Briggs in its satire on venality in the church and the marketplace. But the most important of his contributions are the eight fictional letters from "Brewsterville."

On January 4, 1877, the *Independent* promised a new feature to its growing readership; along with a new serial by Petroleum Nasby, it would run a series of "rich, racy, and truthful communications from Elder Brewster, Jr. of Brewsterville, Mass, on men and things, religion and politics, and every 'top topic,' as it comes up."

> The Elder is a descendent of the old Puritan stock, and he has spent a lifetime in thinking, rather than writing; so our readers will have "an old man for counsel" all through the year. The Elder's notions may be a little old-fashioned and peculiar but they will not err on the side of shoddyism, cowardice or fashionable infidelity.
>
> (p. 4)

Briggs's new set of fictional letters was launched on January 11, 1877. They established the voice of a prominent elder in a small New England town writing to the readers of the *Independent* with political and social commentary. Elder Brewster supports Rutherford B. Hayes in preference to the Democrat, Samuel Tilden, and he is full of righteous indignation at the jockeying for political patronage shown by the Democrats. Of course, he has his own candidate, his brother, for the plum of the postmastership of Brewsterville. He gets seriously exercised about the issue of invoking prayers for Congress as they count electoral votes, but his hotheaded son, Amzi, prefers to raise a military company to assist at the inauguration of their candidate. Amzi is the family realist: "Father, I tell you how it is. It is no use praying for Congress while it has a Democratic majority of seventy. Wait until the next Congress, when the majority will not be more than five or six, and then I will join in, and we may hope to do some good" (p. 4).

As usual in Briggs's satire, the central figure is not only the maker of satiric jabs but the object of them also. In the second letter, published on February 8, 1877, "A Brewsterville Croesus," the elder engages the local rich man in a dialogue about his "worthless dross," but betrays his willingness to accept a gift. Elder Brewster visits the town Croesus again in "The Great Sleigh-Ride of Brewsterville," trying unsuccessfully to raise funds for a winter festival. The old Scrooge refuses even to lend his sleigh bells, but the townspeople take up the challenge, construct a great ark into which seventy-two people climb, and set out for the neighboring town, where they participate in a communal celebration, complete with music and dancing. This letter, with its jolly journey through a winter landscape, is a rural match for Briggs's earlier "A Ride in an Omnibus." Its scene is a contribution to New England regionalism and Elder Brewster's Puritan scruples are acknowledged, even as his son, Amzi, leads the wild youth:

> For my own part, I did not look on at the dancing; and, feeling quite certain that it would be no use to expostulate, I sat down with Brother Scudder, from West Hopkins, who had come with his parishioners, and had a very satisfactory talk with him upon the subject of evolution, which has been very much discussed in these parts of late.
>
> (p. 1)

Later letters engage the millionaire neighbor in a discussion of the uses of wealth and its redistribution, describe Brewster's attempt to defuse a riot after the election of Hayes, and become quite complex in analyzing Brewsterville's response to Hayes's appointment of Frederick Douglass as marshall of the District of Columbia. The elder remembers a lecture by Douglass in Brewsterville before the war, when the orator had to spend the time following his lecture in the town cemetery, since no one would invite him home. Brewster devotes a letter to Mrs. Hayes and her preference for plain attire and includes his distaste for the Mormons, eventually bringing his commentary home to Boss Tweed, imprisoned for graft. There is a grafter in Brewsterville, as well, Deacon Upton, who exposes his motives to the elder and asks, unsuccessfully, for his protection.

The last letter from Brewsterville, published alongside its author's obituary, on June 28, 1877, returns to the figure of Frederick Douglass, who is reported in the press as urging emancipated slaves to acquire money and property. The elder, however, reads in the same newspaper a report of the sorry treatment of a wealthy Jewish banker of New York, who was not welcome at the Grand Union Hotel of Saratoga. He assures the *Independent*'s readers that Seligman would be welcome in Brewsterville's top hotel, where there are so many empty rooms that even a repentant rebel officer, "if it were Jeff Davis himself," would be welcome. As usual, Briggs's satire comes home to sting: "As to Jews, I should be glad to see some of them here, and I can promise them the best seats for hearing in our *church.* Nobody here will be offended by any display they make of diamonds, rubies, or pearls." Elder Brewster cuts the ground from beneath his best attempt at a truly liberal attitude by his display of submerged bigotry.

Finding new subjects in the postwar social scene susceptible to his style of satire, Briggs was developing a paradigm for the North in Brewsterville. In the late 1870s, he saw American society in the grip of the same contradictions that had plagued it in the expanding 1840s, and he asked, in his last letter, a troubling question: "Are we so well persuaded that anything has happened down south since Abraham Lincoln was elected for the first time?"

BRIGGS FOR TODAY'S READERS

Briggs is most interesting to today's readers for his mature satire in the fictional Pinto letters and the letters from Brewsterville. We see him working in an American vernacular form to address his contemporaries on social issues such as economic inequality and racial injustice, which continue to resonate in American culture. In spite of his conservatism on women's issues and his initial resistance to embracing abolition, he grasped the significance of the figures of Margaret Fuller and Frederick Douglass, the two figures of his day who best represented radical change. As a man of the city, with a deep appreciation of the

built environment, he provides modern readers with a rare experience of nineteenth-century New York City. A 2001 issue of *PMLA* reprinted Briggs's story, "Elegant Tom Dillar," with commentary from Stephanie P. Browner on its sophisticated treatment of economic volatility and the minstrel show, suggesting that buried in the prolific anonymous literary production of this period there may be other gems of his acute social analysis.

In the past, scholars have turned to Briggs's substantial private correspondence with his friends and colleagues to gather information for biographies of James Russell Lowell, William Page, and Edgar Allan Poe, or, like Perry Miller, they have used the letters to compose a pioneering portrait of his literary world. Cultural theorists in the early twenty-first century have shown renewed interest in Briggs's life and work as they explore his central role in the transatlantic circulation of literary texts, described by Meredith McGill as "the culture of reprinting."

Selected Bibliography

WORKS OF CHARLES FREDERICK BRIGGS

NOVELS

The Adventures of Harry Franco: A Tale of the Great Panic. 2 vols. New York: Frederic Saunders, 1839. (This first edition, represented by a copy in the New York Public Library, was reproduced as a photographic reprint by Garrett Press, New York, in 1969, with an introduction by Bette S. Weidman.)

Bankrupt Stories. New York: John Allen, 1843. (*The Haunted Merchant,* the only one of Briggs's *Bankrupt Stories* to be written, can be read online, located under Briggs's name, as part of the Google company's digitization project.)

Working a Passage; or, Life on a Liner (Published for the Benefit of Young Travellers). New York: John Allen, 1844. (A second edition was published by Homans and Ellis of New York, in 1846, with the penultimate chapter. The second edition was reproduced as a photographic reprint by Garrett Press, New York, in 1970, with an introduction by Bette S. Weidman.)

The Trippings of Tom Pepper; or, The Results of Romancing. An Autobiography. 2 vols (volume 1, New York: Burgess, Stringer / W. H. Graham / Long & Brother / J. A. Tuttle / George Dexter, 1847; volume 2, New York: Mirror Office / W. H. Graham / Dewitt & Davenport / Long & Brother / George Dexter, 1850). (This novel was first serialized in the *New York Mirror,* irregularly, in 1847–1850.)

NONFICTION

The Architect. Drawings by William Ranlett. Commentary by Briggs. Vol. 2. New York: William H. Graham, 1849.

Homes of American Authors. Edited by Briggs and G. P. Putnam. New York: Putnam, 1853.

The Story of the Telegraph, and a History of the Great Atlantic Cable: A Complete Record of the Inception, Progress, and Final Success of That Undertaking. With Augustus Maverick. New York: Rudd & Carleton, 1858.

CONTRIBUTIONS TO PUBLISHED BOOKS

"Annual Report." In *Transactions of the Apollo Association, for the Promotion of the Fine Arts in the United States, for the Year 1843.* New York: Printed for the Association by Charles Vinton, 1844. Pp. 3–10.

"Annual Report." In *Transactions of the Apollo Association, for the Promotion of the Fine Arts in the United States, for the Year 1844.* New York: Printed for the Association by John Douglas, 1845. Pp. 3–9.

"The Winds." In *The Missionary Memorial: A Literary and Religious Souvenir.* New York: E. Walker, 1846. Pp. 52–60.

"A Commission of Lunacy" and "Channing." In *Voices of the True-Hearted.* Philadelphia: J. Miller M'Kim, 1846. Pp. 102–104 and 106.

"The Harper"and "A Pair of Sonnets ... Siaconset [and] Coatue." In *Seaweeds from the Shores of Nantucket.* Boston: Crosby, Nichols / New York: C. S. Francis, 1853. Pp. 52-56, 63-64.

Trow's New York City Directory, introduction by Briggs (New York, 1853-1877).

"Benjamin Franklin." In *Homes of American Statesmen.* New York: G. P. Putnam, 1854. P. 65.

"A Literary Martyrdom." In *Knickerbocker Gallery.* New York: S. Hueston, 1855. Pp. 481–491.

PERIODICALS

Knickerbocker (1839–1846).

New World (1840–1844).

Broadway Journal (1845).

United States Democratic Review (1846).

New York Mirror (1846–1850).

Holden's Dollar Magazine (1848–1850).

New York Times (1852–1862).

Putnam's Magazine (1853–1855).

Irving Magazine (1861).

Brooklyn Union (1870–1873).

Independent (1875–1877).

Briggs's work appeared under the pseudonym of "Harry Franco" and unsigned in the above New York periodicals. However, in the absence of copyright legislation, his work was probably widely copied, without attribution.

MANUSCRIPTS AND OTHER PAPERS

The only Briggs literary manuscript located as of 2008 is a short piece, "A Caution to Sea Travellers," held in the Henry E. Huntington Library, San Marino, California. Genealogical and birth records are in the Vital Records of Nantucket, Nantucket Atheneum. Significant collections of letters by and to Briggs are located in the following libraries, listed in order of importance: Lowell Collection, Houghton Library, Harvard University; Archives of American Art, Detroit, Michigan; New York Public Library, Duyckinck, Berg, and Miscellaneous Collections; Boston Public Library; Massachusetts Historical Society; and Columbia University, Special Collections.

CRITICAL AND BIOGRAPHICAL STUDIES

Browner, Stephanie P. "Documenting Cultural Politics: A *Putnam*'s Short Story." *PMLA* 116, no. 2:397–415 (March 2001).

Derby, J. C. *Fifty Years Among Authors, Editors, and Publishers.* New York: C. W. Carleton, 1884.

Duberman, Martin. *James Russell Lowell.* Boston: Houghton Mifflin, 1966.

Eggleston, George Cary. *Recollections of a Varied Life.* New York: H. Holt, 1910.

Greenspan, Ezra. *George Palmer Putnam, Representative American Publisher.* University Park, Pa.: Pennsylvania State University Press, 2000.

McGill, Meredith. *American Literature and the Culture of Reprinting, 1834–1853.* Philadelphia: University of Pennsylvania Press, 2003.

Miller, Perry. *The Raven and the Whale.* New York: Harcourt, Brace, 1956.

Mott, Frank Luther. *A History of American Magazines.* 5 vols. Cambridge, Mass.: Belknap Press of Harvard University Press, 1938–1968.

Norton, Charles Eliot. *The Letters of James Russell Lowell.* 2 vols. New York: Harper and Bros., 1894.

Poe, Edgar Allan. *The Literati.* New York: J. S. Redfield, 1850.

Putnam, George Haven. *Memories of a Publisher, 1865–1915.* New York: G. P. Putnam, 1915.

Shamir, Milette. *Inexpressible Privacy: The Interior Life of Antebellum American Literature.* Philadelphia: University of Pennsylvania Press, 2006.

Taylor, Joshua. *William Page, the American Titian.* Chicago: University of Chicago Press, 1957.

Tilton, Theodore. *Sanctum Sanctorum; or, Proof-sheets from an Editor's Table.* New York: Sheldon, 1870.

Weidman, Bette S. "*The Broadway Journal*: A Casualty of Abolition Politics." *Bulletin of the New York Public Library* 73, no. 2:94–113 (February 1969).

———. *Charles Frederick Briggs: A Critical Biography.* Ph.D. dissertation, Columbia University, 1968.

———. "The Pinto Letters of Charles Frederick Briggs." In *Studies in the American Renaissance.* Edited by Joel Myerson. Boston: Twayne, 1979.

Woodberry, George. *The Life of Edgar Allan Poe.* Boston: Houghton Mifflin, 1909.

BOB DYLAN

(1941—)

Ian Bickford

BOB DYLAN TOURED England in 1965 and again in 1966. Accompanying him on both occasions was filmmaker D. A. Pennebaker, documenting the commotion of Dylan's abrupt and enormous fame in what would become *Dont Look Back* (1967) and *Eat the Document* (1972). Pennebaker's dominant venture in the first of these documentaries was to reveal the contrasts and narrate the tensions between an uptight, aging establishment (largely represented by members of the press) and a hip, enthusiastic, liberated younger generation. In the second film, however, the same youthful crowds discover their own capacity for cantankerousness as they criticize and indeed boo Dylan's new, loud, plugged-in performances. A young man stares defiantly at the camera long enough to speculate that England might very well have something of her own to offer, some variety of cultural icon, entirely commensurate to the brilliance of the American visitor: "Shakespeare," he suggests by way of example, and then, piquantly, "perhaps."

Equally a symptom and an idiosyncrasy of the way in which Bob Dylan entered into, then occupied, the center of popular culture, the placement of Dylan within a literary rather than a musical canon had by this time become routine. Indeed, the palpable skepticism in this particular British youth's comparison of Dylan to Shakespeare derives its irony from a readiness on the part of scores of his peers to acknowledge Dylan as nothing less than a literary giant, someone who *un*-ironically might be compared to and potentially upstage the brightest, the greatest, the reigning representatives of canonical literature, past and present. That Dylan was a writer of songs, moreover that for most of the first decade of his professional career he published *nothing but* songs, with even the printed lyrical verses accompanying his albums described in one instance as "Some Other Kinds Of Songs," only adds to the complexity of the popular resolve that this singer was not only a singer but also a poet, his songs not only songs but also poems, his influence exceeding the scope of anything to be found on record albums. Poetry, from this perspective, was a context of sufficient cultural authority for Dylan's accomplishments to be measured—positively or negatively—within it. To cast his compositions as poetry was essentially to claim for them an unambiguous status.

A secondary effect of the rhetoric enthroning Dylan as a poet, meanwhile, was to disturb the very definition of poetry, to stage an incursion against the limits of what was possible within that genre. From the earliest moments of Dylan's career his contested literary eminence comprised not only a line of questioning about Dylan but also an equivalent questioning and projected repositioning of poetry itself, along with a questioning of what it meant to be a poet, especially an American poet, in the middle of the twentieth century. This is why such a miscellany of major literary figures—including John Ciardi, Allen Ginsberg, Norman Mailer, Frank Kermode, Stephen Spender, John Clellon Holmes, Anthony Burgess, Kenneth Rexroth, John Berryman, Philip Larkin, and Robert Lowell—all found it necessary at one time or another to take up the question of Dylan as a poet. In the 1960s and 1970s the question became a variety of litmus tests for one's position within a fracturing literary world. Writers hastened to define themselves in relationship to an accelerating avant-garde—sometimes oscillating between positions, as in the case of Norman Mailer, who initially declared, with characteristic truculence, "If Dylan's a poet, I'm

a basketball player," yet eventually acknowledged, in a full reversal, "Dylan may prove to be our greatest lyric poet of this period." Even trenchant arguments against Dylan's songs as poetry added to the energy accumulating behind the debate, helping therefore to rank the debate among the most challenging of literary puzzles. Whether Dylan is or is not classifiable as a poet matters less, perhaps, than the extraordinary impact of his music upon literary writers of subsequent but also of prior generations, such as Allen Ginsberg. The unusual quality of Dylan's popularity likewise affected popular tastes in literature: "If Dylan has done nothing else," wrote Henrietta Yurchenco in 1966, "he is responsible for the present widespread interest in poetry."

The songs of Bob Dylan have long occupied a significant place in university curricula. Robert Shelton reports that as early as 1977 "more than one hundred courses had ... been taught on Dylan's poetics alone"; that number has compounded exponentially over the years. Dylan's lyrics appear alongside a more traditional stock of poems in such standard volumes as *The Norton Anthology of Poetry,* and articles on Dylan, or referencing Dylan, or borrowing their obligatory epigraphs from Dylan, regularly appear in mainstream academic journals. The Oxford professor Christopher Ricks, celebrated for his work on Milton, Keats, Tennyson, and T. S. Eliot, lectured and wrote on Bob Dylan for three decades before publishing *Dylan's Visions of Sin* in 2003. The work is a milestone in Dylan scholarship, exploring what Ricks sees as Dylan's superb poetics, especially his facility with rhyme, while never losing track of the experiential peculiarities of listening to a song as opposed to reading a poem.

Dylan's own statements on the appropriateness of discussing his songs in a literary context—of calling him a poet at all—have been as ambivalent as they have been various. When asked in San Francisco on December 3, 1965, whether he considered himself "primarily a singer or a poet," he dodged: "Oh, I think of myself more as a song-and-dance man." Yet, during the same year, at the Beverly Hills press conference, Dylan was more direct:

> *Q: Do you prefer writing poetry or songs?*
>
> B.D.: Poems. I don't have to condense or restrict my thoughts into a song pattern.
>
> (p. 59)

Expressing a preference for writing poetry, Dylan simultaneously distinguishes between endeavors. Poetry and songwriting, he implies, even his own and despite the opinion of most of his fans, are different kinds of writing. Much later, remembering early literary and musical attachments in his autobiographical *Chronicles: Volume One* (2005), Dylan praises the "street ideologies" of such texts as Jack Kerouac's *On the Road* (1957) and Ginsberg's *Howl* (1956) yet complains that nothing comparable could be found among hit singles on the radio: "45 records," he writes, "were incapable of it." On the other hand, "LPs were like the force of gravity. They had covers, back and front, that you could stare at for hours" (p. 35). In full-length records, if not in singles, Dylan saw a possibility for something equivalent to literature, at least in the mystique and authority of covers—covers of books, covers of LPs. Accordingly, Dylan's songs grew in scope throughout the 1960s and into the 1970s, from his 1962 eponymous first album of almost entirely traditional songs, to the instantly iconic, politically challenging material of *The Freewheelin' Bob Dylan* (1963) and *The Times They Are A-Changin'* (1964), to the roiling visions of *Highway 61 Revisited* (1965) and *Blonde on Blonde* (1966), to the literary inflections of *Blood on the Tracks* (1975). Of the single "Like a Rolling Stone," twice the length of most songs receiving radio airplay in 1965 yet reaching number two on the Billboard charts after its release that year, Dylan has said the following: "After writing that [song] I wasn't interested in writing a novel or a play or anything like that. I knew I just had too much. I wanted to write songs" (Scorsese, *No Direction Home*). More than simply a rejection of his literary ambitions, this statement finds Dylan growing into his medium, discovering avenues within it that would not restrict, as he worried at other moments, but instead free, his will to experiment. Now it was not only LPs with impressive front and back covers but also individual songs on the radio that could command full respect, could

express the "street ideologies" *(Chronicles: Volume One)* once available only to books and poems, could have the impact of "a novel or a play or anything like that" (Scorsese, *No Direction Home*).

Abandoning the desire to write a book was no idle sacrifice for Dylan in 1965—nor would he stick to it, exactly. Dylan had signed a contract with the Macmillan Company to produce a volume to which he referred at different moments as a novel, as poetry, and, echoing Hamlet to Polonius, as "a book of words." Later he would confess it was a mistake to promise a book before writing one, but in a September 1965 interview, at that moment still enthusiastic, he mentioned it by its title, *Tarantula,* and announced (optimistically) a December release. Plans for publication were moved to the fall of 1966, whereon, in the tumult of a demanding concert schedule, combined with editing of the second Pennebaker film and constant pressure from trespassing fans, Dylan would suffer a motorcycle accident near his home in Woodstock, New York, and withdraw from all obligations—including his book contract. Review copies of *Tarantula* had already been circulated; pirated editions of these were widely sought. The book's official publication would not occur until 1971, yet in its various iterations *Tarantula* represented a major confirmation of the compass of Dylan's virtuosity. He was, the book proved, a writer whose talents were not constrained to songwriting.

Readers waited more than three decades for a second original book from Bob Dylan. *Chronicles: Volume One* appeared in 2004 to overwhelmingly positive reviews. Between *Tarantula* and *Chronicles*—very different texts, yet thematically linked—several volumes were published of Dylan's lyrics and other miscellaneous writings. Dylan has also cowritten two films: *Renaldo and Clara* (1978) with Sam Shepard and *Masked and Anonymous* (2003) with Larry Charles. His importance as a writer is undoubtedly secure, yet what *kind* of writer and how exactly to position him within an American literary tradition remains uncertain—any resolution confounded in his eclecticism, his unwillingness to rest even momentarily within a genre, within a persona, within a style.

BIOGRAPHY

Robert Allen Zimmerman was born on May 24, 1941, in Duluth, Minnesota, the eldest of two boys. His first performance was on Mother's Day, 1946: the four-year-old Bobby sang "Some Sunday Morning" and "Accentuate the Positive" for delighted, praising relatives. When Bobby was six the family moved to Hibbing, Minnesota, where his father, Abe, whose bout with polio had left him with a pronounced limp, joined Bobby's two uncles in their furniture and appliance business. Bobby's mother, Beatty, remembered her talented son spending significant time alone in his room. "Bob was upstairs quietly becoming a writer for twelve years," she said to Robert Shelton, the journalist who first and famously reviewed Dylan in the *New York Times* and who spent much of his career compiling interviews for a massive biography, *No Direction Home* (1986). While Beatty would prove enormously supportive of Bobby's artistic aspirations and eventually of his success, his earliest activities were, for her, a point of anxiety: "I said to Bobby that you can't go on and on and on and sit and dream and write poems. I was afraid he would end up being a poet! ... In my day, a poet was unemployed and had no ambition." Abe, on the other hand, recalled Bobby's overall aptitude in school, noting only, "History was always a problem for him. ... I used to argue that history only requires you to remember what you had read. He said there was nothing to figure out in history." The comment was perhaps weighted with particular meaning, for Bobby would gain his first notoriety almost immediately upon gaining his first professional recognition when he began, as the transformed Bob Dylan, broadcasting radically revised versions of his personal history—especially those portions of history having to do with his family.

Indeed, if Bobby Zimmerman had no taste for history, Bob Dylan cultivated a remarkable flair for rewriting it. Partly for this reason, the details of his life exist in perpetual tension with

alternative versions, half-truths, revisions and retractions, strategic manipulations. There is perhaps no living person of whom so much has been written whose biography remains so inveterately—and enchantingly—elusive. In *Writing Dylan: The Songs of a Lonesome Traveler,* Larry David Smith argues that "Bob Dylan" is the name for a vast, deliberate, and ultimately coherent artistic vision authored by Robert Zimmerman over the course of nearly a half-century and that, in essence, if Dylan is a poet he is also his own poem. Although somewhat overstated in its thesis—no less than in its style—Smith's book supplies some instruction for examining the circumstances of Dylan's past: before a certain point, an elaborate pattern of biographical misinformation gives way to an equally elaborate confusion; after that point, Dylan seems to have been so purposeful, so precise, and yet so unpredictable in weaving and stitching and patching the fabric of his identity that one struggles to distinguish between the genuine individual and his adopted roles, between, that is, the person and the performance.

This habit—preferring fibs to facts, refusing to tolerate the details of a prosaic upbringing, of ordinary surroundings—began early. Bobby's first band in high school, the Golden Chords, quickly dissolved as Bobby became increasingly fascinated with rock and roll. Classmates remember a riotous performance at the Hibbing High Jacket Jamboree Talent Show, amps turned up loud, Bobby pounding on the piano and screaming the lyrics to "Rock n' Roll Is Here to Stay." The school's principal finally cut the microphones, foreshadowing a probably apocryphal account of the folk patriarch Pete Seeger threatening to cut the cables with an ax at the 1965 Newport Folk Festival, where Dylan yet again surprised an audience with extreme amplification. In 1959, just after graduating from high school, Bobby played piano in the backing band for the regional musician Bobby Vee; he held on to the gig only briefly, performing under the stage name Elston Gunn, but when Vee had a hit later that year with the song "Suzie Baby," Bobby Zimmerman told friends and relatives that *he* was the Bobby Vee they were hearing on their radios. Enrolling at the University of Minnesota in Minneapolis, where he would stay through the end of 1960 but fail almost completely to attend classes, he began using the name Bobby Dillon, then Dylan, changing his name legally to Bob Dylan in 1962. He was feeling his way toward the elasticity of identity for which he would soon be famous, finding that the farther he traveled from home, the farther his identity would stretch.

How he arrived finally at the surname Dylan is one of those disputed affairs which should, as a matter of extensive accumulated evidence, be simple enough to resolve; Dylan, however, has consistently and persistently gone out of his way to agitate the issue, to muddy it as much as possible, to shroud it in the kind of mystery that keeps his biographers searching and his audiences fascinated. The popular theory is that he borrowed his name from Dylan Thomas, yet, if there is truth in this, it must be only fractionally true, given the initial discrepancy of spelling and the likelihood that Dylan was introduced to the Welsh poet's verse only *after* experimenting with homophonic versions of his name. Robert Shelton points to the young Bobby's idolization of the *Gunsmoke* character Matt Dillon, as well as a Hibbing family named Dillion to whom Bobby held some relation. In fact, Dylan petitions Shelton to right the record: "Straighten out in your book that I did not take my name from Dylan Thomas." Much later, interviewed in Martin Scorsese's 2005 documentary of the same title as Shelton's biography (Scorsese and Shelton both derived their title from a line in "Like a Rolling Stone"), Dylan, referring to the sequence of events leading to his new name, said, "It really didn't happen any of the ways I've read about it." Presumably this includes what he read in Shelton's account, an account shaped upon Dylan's own statements and at least informally authorized by him. Hence, *No Direction Home* (the film) corrects and inverts *No Direction Home* (the book), injecting a nearly comic tension between the titles whereby seeking direction leads only to new varieties of misdirection, and "home"—or origin—recedes always further toward indeterminacy. Dylan has frequently used his contact with scholars, biographers, and the

press, including Shelton, with whom he shared a friendship and to whom he owed a considerable debt for effectively introducing his music to the world, as an occasion for renewing control of the details of his life, revising those details wherever necessary, introducing fresh contradictions wherever strategically productive. For example, he insisted to Shelton that he had arrived in New York City at the close of 1960, *not,* as previously believed, at the beginning of 1961, and that he did not go directly to Greenwich Village but spent two months around Times Square, turning tricks. Shelton, attuned to what he calls Dylan's "put-ons," does not assign any particular veracity to the story, and in Scorsese's film Dylan again reverses his rendering, now radically simplifying it: "Got out of the car at George Washington Bridge. Took a subway down to the Village."

Dylan elides these details in *Chronicles: Volume One,* but he does return to the subject of his name, offering yet another version which reinstates Dylan Thomas as central to the narrative. He also writes this: "One of the early presidents of the San Bernardino [Hell's] Angels was Bobby Zimmerman, and he was killed in 1964 on the Bass Lake run. ... That person is gone. That was the end of him." Replacing the former Bobby Zimmerman with a stand-in, a kind of crash-test dummy, Dylan effectively kills himself off, projecting his identity into the death of someone else who happens, conveniently, to bear the same name. He simultaneously conjures his own 1966 motorcycle accident, rumored in its aftermath to have been disfiguring or even fatal. Dylan's identity, by his own design, begins to fracture, to take up residency in new and various bodies, some surviving, some succumbing. Footage included in Scorsese's *No Direction Home* depicts Dylan shortly before his accident, exhausted, frustrated with the intense pressures of his second major English tour, joking, "I think I'm going to get me a new Bob Dylan next week. ... Use the new Bob Dylan, see how long *he* lasts." In concert on Halloween 1964, Dylan famously announced from the stage, "I have my Bob Dylan mask on." His discussion of literary influences in *Chronicles* gives pride of place to a single syntactically intricate line from Arthur Rimbaud: "Je est un autre," or "I is another." The paradox contrived in the rupture of the subject "Je" from its first-person status in the third-person verb form "est" constitutes in its very incoherency a strikingly consistent gesture across Dylan's oeuvre. If Bob Dylan represents nothing but a prosthetic identity for Bobby Zimmerman (who is supposed to have died in one motorcycle accident or another), the prosthesis would logically bear replacement as successive iterations wear out. This network of ideas is central to Todd Haynes's 2007 film *I'm Not There,* in which six different actors of different ages, genders, and ethnicities play a person recognizable as but never called Bob Dylan. The aforementioned line, "Je est un autre," topped Haynes's single-page film proposal to which Dylan granted his rare approval, and one of the film's seven versions of Dylan is actually named Arthur Rimbaud. Haynes clearly understood the importance of Rimbaud to Dylan's overarching aesthetic, and he understood as well that recognition of this importance would be invaluable in gaining Dylan's trust, therefore gaining a green light for the film.

It was in Minneapolis that Dylan was introduced to the songs of Woody Guthrie. Guthrie's impact on Dylan cannot be overstated. Dylan began playing almost exclusively Guthrie compositions in his coffeehouse performances around the folk-oriented "Dinkytown" section of Minneapolis. In the fall of 1960 he read Guthrie's autobiographical *Bound for Glory* (1943), which quickly replaced *On the Road* as his touchstone for American seeking and dreaming. When Dylan learned that Guthrie was hospital-bound in Morris Plains, New Jersey, he decided to pay a visit to his hero. Guthrie suffered from Huntington's chorea, an inherited neurological disorder, deadly as well as profoundly disabling, and Dylan found him languishing in a psychiatric institution, the older singer's mind still sharp but his body given over to uncontrollable tremors and spasms. Visiting him there and, later, at Brooklyn State Hospital, Dylan played guitar and sang for Guthrie, taking requests for Guthrie's own songs. At this point Dylan's repertoire comprised entirely songs written by others. "I wasn't yet the poet musician that I would

become," he writes in *Chronicles.* If Dylan's relationship to Guthrie was derivative, if Dylan copied Guthrie's singing, his style, and even his mannerisms, the stage for such a frank and heartfelt homage was also the platform for an imminent creative leap beyond Guthrie. Dylan's first major foray into songwriting, "Song for Woody," addressed directly to Guthrie and set to one of Guthrie's own melodies, would ambitiously form a connection between Guthrie's declining health in a hospital bed and Dylan's own youthful momentum, thereby describing a transfer of energy if not of identity. When Dylan recorded "Song for Woody" it would be one of only two original compositions on his first album; that album would be the last crafted primarily of borrowed songs until Dylan's return to a traditional songbook in the early 1990s.

In Greenwich Village, 1961, Bob Dylan played as a regular at the Café Wha? and at the legendary Gaslight before his first major performance at Gerde's Folk City, opening for John Lee Hooker. Because Dylan was under the legal age of twenty-one, Gerde's proprietor Mike Porco signed as his guardian for membership in the American Federation of Musicians, local 802, required for wage-earning performers. It was at a later Gerde's appearance with the Greenbriar Boys that Dylan was "discovered" by the *New York Times* critic Robert Shelton. Shelton's September 19, 1961 review was enthusiastic, naming Dylan "one of the most distinctive stylists to play in a Manhattan cabaret in months" and predicting the direction of Dylan's career "to be straight up." Not quite a month later, after having endured rejections for recording contracts from successive folk labels, including, most crushingly, his revered Folkways Records, Dylan met the influential producer and A&R executive John Hammond at Columbia Records during a session with Carolyn Hester, on whose eponymous album Dylan played harmonica. Without requiring an audition—in some versions of the story without ever having heard Dylan sing—Hammond offered Dylan a record deal on the authority of Shelton's review. Dylan signed on the spot.

His first album sold poorly. After its March 1962 release, Dylan was referred to at Columbia as "Hammond's Folly." Dylan expressed personal dissatisfaction with the album and wished almost immediately for an opportunity to supplant it with new material. Meanwhile a romance with Suze Rotolo was proving a watershed for his songwriting, not only in such characteristically arm's-length love songs as "Don't Think Twice, It's All Right" and "Down the Highway" but also in an initially wholehearted embrace of Suze's activism and social consciousness. Dylan had previously shown little interest in politics, but under the tutelage of Suze and her sister Carla, as well as such Village folk personalities as Dave Van Ronk, he began to learn and write about an array of social issues. His second album, *The Freewheelin' Bob Dylan,* released May 1963, includes three songs that would become standards in the 1960s culture of protest. The lyrical yet vague expression of outrage and hope in "Blowin' in the Wind" stands in counterpart to "Masters of War" with its very specific admonition of the American weapons industry, while "Oxford Town" weighed in for civil rights with a powerful if somewhat incredulous response to the episodes of hatred and violence accumulating in the South.

In July 1963 Dylan made his first of several appearances at the Newport Folk Festival, where the singer Joan Baez, only a few months older than Dylan but already a major star in the folk galaxy, extolled him to the audience as a new and crucial voice. During the same month, Peter, Paul and Mary's version of "Blowin' in the Wind" came very close to topping the charts. Dylan joined Martin Luther King Jr. later that summer for the celebrated March on Washington for Jobs and Freedom, performing "Only a Pawn in Their Game" and "Blowin' in the Wind" for an audience numbering in the hundreds of thousands. Only two years after arriving in Greenwich Village an impish midwestern nobody, Bob Dylan found himself endorsed within liberal politics and the folk music establishment as a genius and—in the label he would grow to hate—the voice of a generation. Yet he was already resisting these designations and the public

responsibilities they required. From his first interview with Shelton he had begun developing the system of feints and falsehoods designed to frustrate the media in its efforts to classify him within a particular role or genre, and what began as simple evasion accelerated toward a full-blown mutual antagonism between Dylan and the mainstream press. A cover story in *Newsweek* on November 4, 1963, confirmed Dylan's distrust of the media and left him warier than ever of the consequences of his own fame. The story billed itself as an exposé, airing Dylan's suite of fabrications about his past, specifically about his family, and aggravating an unsubstantiated yet tenacious rumor that "Blowin' in the Wind" had been plagiarized.

It was in the context of this sense of being under attack, of holding a beleaguered position toward a public whose adoration verged on harassment, whose praise resembled a kind of pillorying, that Dylan watched the rest of the year unfold. President John F. Kennedy was shot and killed in his motorcade in Dallas on November 22, and his alleged assassin Lee Harvey Oswald took a deadly bullet two days later. Live television cameras carried the second shooting into the homes of a shocked nation as Oswald collapsed before Jack Ruby's gun. On the 172nd anniversary of the ratification of the Bill of Rights, Friday, December 13, in the ballroom of the Americana Hotel in New York City, Dylan accepted the Thomas Paine Award from the Emergency Civil Liberties Committee for his work contributing to the advancement of equality and rights. He was drunk and nervous, sharing the dais with the novelist and activist James Baldwin, looking out at an audience comprising the Old Left's old guard, and in his speech—after joking that the number of bald heads in the room was an indicator of the event's social irrelevance—he compared himself to Oswald, expressing sympathy with what the president's killer must have felt. The audience booed. Dylan later composed a letter in verse apologizing, not for the substance of his comments but for obstructing the intake of charitable dollars from a suddenly uncharitable crowd. He tried to explain the awkward sense of guilt that he felt about the societal expectations demanded of him, which were both burdensome and not well-defined. It was a mistake, Dylan continued, to lose oneself in a society of blame, to disperse and hence dilute responsibility for such ills as poverty, violence, war, and intolerance across a national community of individuals. Instead the individual must feel these varieties of guilt distilled within himself, must understand himself to share a personal, not a communal, relationship to the violent occurrences of what Dylan, in his letter, calls "the times." These were metaphysical more than political ideas. Dylan expressed them poorly in his speech, only slightly better in his apology. His message, in other words, suffered distortion. From that moment he began to learn to use distortion as a method for enacting, if not always fully communicating, a message. His rapport with audiences would never again be entirely comfortable.

Released in February 1964, *The Times They Are A-Changin'* was even more concertedly political than *The Freewheelin' Bob Dylan,* but this third album quickly gave way to a fourth, the much more personal, lyrical *Another Side of Bob Dylan* (August 1964). By March 1965, with the release of *Bringing It All Back Home,* Dylan had begun what turned out to be the incredibly difficult errand of reclaiming his rock-and-roll roots. Several tracks on *Bringing It All Back Home* include heavy electrical instrumentation, including "Subterranean Homesick Blues," "Maggie's Farm," and "Bob Dylan's 115th Dream," but for the moment Dylan's live performances remained acoustic. After his Newport debut in 1963, Dylan had traveled with Joan Baez for several tour dates during which the two would each play a solo set and Dylan would join Baez onstage for harmonic versions of a number of his songs. Though Baez headed the bill, Dylan earned a slightly higher cut per show. Dylan was Baez's protégé, and she took pleasure in being able to help him at the start of his career. The two singers developed a close friendship and then a romantic liaison that would overtake Dylan's relationship with Suze Rotolo. Baez was leading Dylan into the frenzy of his new life as a celebrity, yet her home in Carmel, California,

where Dylan often stayed, afforded an equivalent refuge from that life. It was understood though unspoken that Dylan would offer Baez the same partnership in the planning of his own future performances; however, when she accompanied him to England in 1965, she found herself relegated to the background. Dylan was now established in his fame and disinclined to share the stage.

An important component of Dylan's break from Baez was his increasing impatience with her faith, shared by folk audiences, that protest, and especially singing as a form of protest, could change the world. Close followers of Dylan could certainly have noticed in the body of his songwriting and in the matter of his public statements a long evolution of his priorities away from politics and protest—after all, as early as 1963 he was distancing himself in interviews from overtly political interpretations of songs like "A Hard Rain's A-Gonna Fall"—yet it took his 1965 performance at Newport to force such a recognition. This was Dylan's third year as one of the festival's headliners, and he used the occasion to dissolve the usual folk formula for performance. Instead of standing onstage alone with his guitar and harmonica, he invited Al Kooper and members of the Paul Butterfield Blues Band to join him; Kooper and Mike Bloomfield had recently performed on the recording of "Like a Rolling Stone," and Dylan told them he wanted to reproduce the feeling and the sound they had achieved in the studio during that session. Mastered bootlegs of the concert capture the band's sharp intensity behind Dylan's strong vocals, yet the audience expressed immediate dissatisfaction at the opening performance of "Maggie's Farm"—a similar rendition to the one they would already have heard, electrified, on *Bringing It All Back Home.* Legend depicts the Newport audience as despairing that Dylan, their idol and exemplar, had sold out to the corporate interests of rock and roll and that his electric guitar and his amplified band were symbolic of his betrayal. It is in this version of the narrative that Pete Seeger, guardian of folk principles, went looking for an ax to cut the cables. Yet if the same audience was capable of accepting, even enjoying, Butterfield's electrified blues earlier in the festival's proceedings, furthermore if plugged-in tracks drew none of the same ire in receptions of *Bringing It All Back Home,* the crowd's recoil must have stemmed at least partly from other causes. Many, including Seeger, report that the engineering of the sound was simply bad, the microphones distorted, the instruments too loud. Dylan played two more songs—one was "Like a Rolling Stone"—then left the stage with the other musicians. He returned alone to play a very short acoustic set, mostly to placate the audience, and bade farewell to the festival with "It's All Over Now, Baby Blue."

This was the first in a long series of shows following the same pattern. Dylan discovered that he could goad an audience into booing simply by strapping on an electric guitar. He began testing this ability, extorting dismay and distaste from concertgoers just as he had already learned to stimulate their adoration. He asked the Hawks—Robbie Robertson, Levon Helm, Garth Hudson, Rick Danko, and Richard Manuel, an alchemical group of musicians who started out together backing the country and rock-and-roll singer Ronnie Hawkins and who would eventually call themselves the Band—to join him for a tour of U.S. cities and Toronto, then Australia, then Great Britain. Helm quickly left the tour, partly, he wrote later in his autobiographical *This Wheel's on Fire: Levon Helm and the Story of the Band* (1993), because he could not endure the continual antagonism emanating from audiences. Much had changed for Dylan in the single year since his first British tour. Pennebaker's camera found wilder hair, unpredictable gestures verging on paroxysmal, and an opaque, amphetamine-charged demeanor. More significantly, the grainy color footage for *Eat the Document* (not released until a 1972 PBS broadcast and even now rarely seen) catches Dylan's energy onstage in counterpoise with disgruntled fans inveighing against the pop sensibilities of "the group" and painting Dylan as a sellout. Dylan began each show with a solo acoustic set, always warmly received, followed by an electric set with the Hawks. During this second half of the show he would trade barbs with hecklers in

the crowd. One shouted, "Judas!"; Dylan replied, "I don't believe you. You're a liar."

The constant battle with his fan base took a toll. Back in the States he faced dozens of additional concert commitments, along with an impending book release and rigorous editing of *Eat the Document,* into which he had injected considerable personal attention and involvement. On July 29, 1966, Dylan suffered his motorcycle accident. Although he has been secretive about the details of this event, his injuries—several fractured vertebrae, by many accounts—seem to have been real but not incapacitating. He allowed exaggerated reports of his accident to circulate as a tactic for escaping the destructive pace of his life. Retreating to what he hoped would be a quiet life in Woodstock, he spent time with his wife, Sara, whom he had married in a private ceremony on November 22, 1965, and their first child, Jesse, born January 6, 1966. Sara had a daughter, Maria, from a prior marriage, and the family continued to grow. Anna Dylan was born on July 11, 1966, Samuel on July 30, 1968, and Jakob on December 9, 1969. Dylan also continued to develop his creative relationship with the Band, writing and recording with them in the basement of their house, Big Pink, in nearby Saugerties. When the results of those sessions finally emerged in 1975 as *The Basement Tapes,* it became apparent that Dylan's most reclusive period was also among his most productive and certainly among his most musically inspired.

The flow of albums continued, albeit at a more leisurely rate than the torrent of his earliest writing. *Highway 61 Revisited* had been released in August 1965 and the double album *Blonde on Blonde* in May 1966. The contemplative *John Wesley Harding* appeared in December 1967, and *Nashville Skyline,* released in April 1969, would prove to be one of Dylan's most popular albums with its country inflections and guest appearance by Johnny Cash on "Girl of the North Country." The early 1970s, however, found Dylan in something of a slump, critically if not creatively. Many considered *Self Portrait* (June 1970) to represent Dylan's worst work, while *New Morning* (October 1970) received an only slightly better response. Late in 1972 Dylan was persuaded by the songwriter and actor Kris Kristofferson to join the director Sam Peckinpah in Durango, Mexico, for the filming of *Pat Garrett and Billy the Kid,* released the following year. Dylan wrote a score for the film and played the minor role of Alias. The film was poorly reviewed, though Dylan's music for it found an appreciative audience.

Dylan was still wary of public appearances. Trespassing fans had continually invaded his privacy in Woodstock, and in an effort to escape what he began to view as their dangerous obsession with him, he moved back to Greenwich Village with his family late in 1969. There the harrying treatment continued: "Dylanologist" A. J. Weberman mined garbage outside Dylan's home on MacDougal Street. Rare concerts included a tribute for the late Woody Guthrie at Carnegie Hall in January 1968; a headlining set at the Isle of Wight Music Festival in late August 1969, concurrent with the Woodstock Music Festival taking place in Dylan's own territory and from which Dylan was conspicuously absent; and participation in George Harrison's Concert for Bangladesh at Madison Square Garden in August 1971. He would not return to full public view until January 1974, when he launched his first large-scale tour since returning from Great Britain eight years earlier. The tour accompanied the release of a new album, *Planet Waves.*

Momentum increased. *Blood on the Tracks,* appearing in January 1975, and *The Basement Tapes,* released in July of the same year, comprised yet another renewal for Bob Dylan, with many critics calling these his best albums to date—no matter that *The Basement Tapes* had been recorded almost a decade prior. Encouraged, Dylan began planning a new variety of tour, inviting old friends such as Joan Baez, Bob Neuwirth, and Ramblin' Jack Elliott, as well as the poets Allen Ginsberg and Peter Orlovsky and musicians T-Bone Burnett, Mick Ronson, David Mansfield, Scarlet Rivera, Rob Stoner, and Howie Wyeth to join him on an improvisational, impressionistic, unstructured circuit of the Northeast, playing concerts both scheduled and unscheduled, everyone traveling together as the Rolling Thunder Revue. Throughout this tour Dylan wore

white makeup on his face and presided over performers who would come and go haphazardly from the stage. Two concerts in support of Rubin "Hurricane" Carter, an African American boxer convicted of murder on questionable evidence and whose trial many felt to have been an example of racial injustice, represented Dylan's return to political demonstration. The Rolling Thunder Revue also doubled as the occasion for Dylan's four-hour film *Renaldo and Clara* (1978), for which Sam Shepard acted as resident screenwriter. Sara Dylan plays Clara, and Bob Dylan, as Renaldo, occupies the film as a sort of fractured, composite identity, at once an outlaw, a pimp, a husband, and a rock star. Ronnie Hawkins, meanwhile, plays a character named Bob Dylan. The film is generally regarded as a failure, but it stands as an enormously ambitious foray for Dylan into a medium with which he could claim only modest experience. In scope it far exceeds—and perhaps was conceived as an amplification of—*Eat the Document,* and Dylan's writing with Shepard, even at its most incomprehensible, is highly imaginative. The best moments in the film are abundantly surprising, even luminous, and, for Dylan, unusually revealing.

Sara and Bob Dylan divorced in June 1977. Many of the songs on the January 1976 album *Desire,* especially the directly confessional "Sara," are occupied with the troubles as well as the felicities of their marriage. The following decade was difficult for Dylan, even by his own account. In 1979, only a few years after pervasive speculation that he had magnified his Jewish heritage into a variety of Zionism, Dylan confused fans by becoming a born-again Christian. The net effect of this decision was to alienate audiences with sermons before concerts and gospel themes dominating three successive albums: *Slow Train Coming* (August 1979), *Saved* (June 1980), and *Shot of Love* (August 1981). Subsequent appearances with Tom Petty and the Heartbreakers and the Grateful Dead were marked, Dylan remembers in *Chronicles,* by a lack of energy and a greater lack of inspiration, although some concert recordings of that period capture Dylan at the top of his vocal capacity. Critics and fans tend to wish the 1980s had never happened for Dylan; certain songs, however, especially from *Infidels* (October 1983) and *Knocked Out Loaded* (July 1986) display a lyrical nuance equal to anything in Dylan's repertoire. Dylan's daughter with backup singer Carolyn Dennis was born on January 31, 1986, and named Desiree Gabrielle Dennis-Dylan. Dylan and Dennis were quietly married in June of that year and quietly divorced in October 1992.

A final album of the 1980s, *Oh Mercy,* recorded in New Orleans with producer Daniel Lanois and released in September 1989, commenced the latest of Dylan's transformations. The album's blues inflections cast forward to Dylan's next project with Lanois, *Time Out of Mind* (September 1997), which brought Dylan three Grammy awards, including one for Best Album. Between *Oh Mercy* and *Time Out of Mind,* Dylan celebrated thirty years in the recording industry with an all-star anniversary concert at Madison Square Garden. He also released two albums of traditional songs and blues: *Good as I Been to You* (November 1992) and *World Gone Wrong* (October 1993). These events found Dylan cycling back to his earliest fascinations as a songwriter. Indeed, his next achievement, *Love and Theft,* released on September 11, 2001, compiles lines and themes from Dylan's lifetime as a reader and listener into taut compositional structures of motif and memory. *Modern Times* (August 2006) explores similar terrain.

Since 1988 Dylan has played over one hundred concerts per year. His film *Masked and Anonymous* premiered at the Sundance Film Festival in January 2003. He published *Chronicles: Volume One* in October of the following year, and May 2006 occasioned the launch of *Theme Time Radio Hour* on XM satellite radio with none other than Bob Dylan as its brusque, mercurial host.

SONGS

Nominees for the 1996 Nobel Prize in Literature included one writer whose only book at that time had been published twenty-five years earlier. He held an honorary doctorate in music from Princeton University although he had never bothered

to attend classes even as an undergraduate at the University of Minnesota. This was clearly an unusual candidate for the world's preeminent literary honor. Still, his nomination meant something, and the writer to whom he found himself a runner-up, the Polish poet Wislawa Szymborska, supplied illuminating remarks in her Nobel Lecture on the uncertainty poets feel toward poetry and toward a society that is in turn uncertain exactly how to deal with—even to recognize—poets. She discussed the wariness with which poets confess to being poets, suggesting that they would rather call themselves almost anything else. She might as well have been talking about Bob Dylan, her fellow nominee, who in 1965 sidestepped the designation of "poet" in favor of "song-and-dance man." Dylan's tongue was only partly in his cheek. He understood that poetry is at once an exclusive and an ill-defined category, and that establishing his work within it would generate expectations and with them limitations. In other words, he wanted to avoid the very debate that tried on one side to boost his writing into an authoritative literary position and on the other to send him back to the lower divisions of the arts, to songwriting as a subclass of writing.

In any case, it was surely not *Tarantula* that earned Dylan his Nobel nomination—though the merits of that book are many—but an intuition of now several generations of audiences that something in Dylan's *other* work, his work in song, was classifiable if not as poetry then at least as literature of some kind. Interviewed shortly before his death for Scorsese's *No Direction Home,* Allen Ginsberg recalled weeping when he heard the song "A Hard Rain's A-Gonna Fall" for the first time and thinking that Dylan had managed to transmit the lessons of a prior generation of writers into a new form, hence a viable future. "Poetry," said Ginsberg, "is words that are empowered, that make your hair stand on end, that you recognize instantly as being some form of subjective truth that has an objective reality to it because somebody's realized it. Then you call it poetry later." The category itself is ex post facto in Ginsberg's understanding, even incidental, applied in the necessity to explain an experience of profound communication. This is simply a different way of approaching Dylan and Szymborska's shared hesitation to endorse the poet's lexicon, which, Ginsberg shows, regards poetry from the wrong end of the process of naming it.

Ginsberg was responding to a quality in Dylan's writing that corresponded to a Beat aesthetic of internal exploration and prophetic language. It is significant that he singled out "A Hard Rain's A-Gonna Fall" from the songs collected on *The Freewheelin' Bob Dylan* insofar as these particular lyrics don't really fit the context of the political ballads and talking blues that typified Dylan's earliest compositions. The "hard rain" of the song was often taken to represent a nuclear rain, but Dylan explicitly resisted this interpretation. In fact, the lyrics build upon an old traditional song, bringing to it the same type of biblical incantation that Ginsberg had pursued in *Howl* and later. This was undoubtedly Dylan's breakthrough composition, and in its context one can see even the much more immediately popular "Blowin' in the Wind"—a favorite of the protest movement—struggling to exceed protest and achieve something more recognizable as prophecy. If first Dylan asks, "How many years can a mountain exist / Before it's washed to the sea?" he soon places himself stumbling "on the side of twelve misty mountains" to "reflect" his message "from the mountain so all souls can see it," and, in a sense, ride the mountainside to its watery grave: "Then I'll stand on the ocean until I start sinkin'". If, moreover, he begins by asking, "How many roads must a man walk down / Before you call him a man?" he answers his own question with a specific number: "I've walked and I've crawled on six crooked highways". Ginsberg was especially impressed with the wisdom of the penultimate line of "A Hard Rain's A-Gonna Fall," its promise to "know my song well before I start singin'". The song ends with a kind of beginning, a statement of readiness, the rehearsal over.

When Dylan sang to his solemn fans at the 1965 Newport Folk Festival that "it's all over now, Baby Blue", he was picking up the same

thread. The "blue-eyed son" of the first line of "A Hard Rain's A-Gonna Fall" emerges again in this new incarnation, but instead of looking into an apocalyptic future, "It's All Over Now, Baby Blue" describes a world already flooded, its "seasick sailors ... rowing home" and "the saints ... comin' through" to mark an end. Unnecessary any longer to "accept it that soon / You'll be drenched to the bone", as Dylan advised in "The Times They Are A-Changin,'" or to anticipate "[t]he hour when the ship comes in" as dreamed of in the song titled for that line, the only course now is to "take what you need ... grab it fast" and "[l]eave your stepping stones behind" to follow willingly when finally "something calls for you." The flood described here is not the drowning of the Pharaoh or the conquering of Goliath as Dylan had once forecast. Instead it is total, threatening to drown the accusers along with the accused. Dylan's audiences at live performances can be counted on to break into a cheer at the following lines from "It's Alright Ma (I'm Only Bleeding)": "Goodness hides behind its gates / But even the president of the United States / Sometimes must have to stand naked." Yet these lines do less to isolate the president as the perpetrator of successive wars and social atrocities than to place each individual in the audience in the same isolated position. To shine a light upon the nakedness of power is to reflect—unsettlingly—that light back upon the individual. Less pronounced and less often noticed are these lines:

> You lose yourself, you reappear
> You suddenly find you got nothing to fear
> Alone you stand with nobody near
> When a trembling distant voice, unclear
> Startles your sleeping ears to hear
> That somebody thinks they really found you.
>
> (*Lyrics: 1962–2001,* p. 157)

That illusion, the illusion of finding someone else in the midst—which is to say the mist—of one's isolation, suddenly makes even the act of plunging from the stepping-stones into the flood in pursuit of a calling voice seem futile, foolish.

Dylan's songs travel farther and farther into this bleak, lonesome environment, eventually finding their rhythm and pulse in what Dylan once described as the "wild mercury sound" of *Bringing It All Back Home, Highway 61 Revisited,* and *Blonde on Blonde.* Even his most commercially successful recording, "Like a Rolling Stone," contributes to the narrative of a fall from precarious confidence into chaos and isolation, and its companion songs on *Highway 61 Revisited* begin to populate the destroyed terrain with an assortment of outlandish characters, as though describing what kind of civilization emerges after the dominant civilization fails. John the Baptist converses with the commander in chief in "Tombstone Blues"; Mister Jones argues with a one-eyed midget in "Ballad of a Thin Man"; God and Abraham negotiate in "Highway 61 Revisited"; Ezra Pound and T. S. Eliot spar in "Desolation Row." A similarly bizarre citizenry inhabits the Basement Tapes, which the critic Greil Marcus imagines as portraying an "Invisible Republic" based on "The Old, Weird America" of traditional music (these phrases are the titles of successive editions of Marcus's seminal book about the Basement Tapes, published in 1997 and 2001).

Christopher Ricks joins Allen Ginsberg in noting Dylan's extraordinary facility with rhyme. Chief among Dylan's rhymes in Ricks's treatment is the opening couplet of the second stanza of "It's All Over Now, Baby Blue": "The highway is for gamblers, better use your sense. / Take what you have gathered from coincidence." Indeed, Ricks writes, "[All] rhymes are a coincidence issuing in a new sense. It is a pure coincidence that *sense* rhymes with *coincidence,* and from this you *gather* something" (p. 34). Ginsberg, for his part, often expressed admiration for a rhymed couplet in "Idiot Wind," among the more vituperative of the songs on *Blood on the Tracks*: "Idiot wind, blowing like a circle around my skull / From the Grand Coulee Dam to the Capitol." Ricks elaborates that the richness in this rhyme extends from the likeness of the Capitol dome to the white expanse of a skull—an eerie image and a critique of statehood and power. One might also notice the inscription (as with compass hands upon a map) of a circle from one national landmark to another, with the individual at its radial center. The singer remains

pivotal to—literally—and yet remote from the span of his republic.

More recently, the songs included on *Love and Theft* reintroduce the thematically persistent flood and its aftermath of wet clothes, washed-out roads, and abandoned street corners. Isolation is yet again a central premise, yet these compositions seem also to confess the thoroughness with which they are connected to a tradition, to history, to the world surrounding them with its "idiot wind." Thirty-five years earlier, in "Ballad of a Thin Man," the mysterious Mister Jones fell under Dylan's fire for the pretensions of being popular with professors, for being "well read" and for having "been through all of F. Scott Fitzgerald's books", whereas now, in "Summer Days," a "worn out star" finds himself reliving nearly word for word a moment from Fitzgerald's *The Great Gatsby* (1925): "She's looking into my eyes, she's holding my hand / She says, [']You can't repeat the past.['] / I say, [']You can't? What do you mean, you can't? Of course you can.[']" Compare these lines to a conversation between Jay Gatsby and Nick Carraway:

> "I wouldn't ask too much of her," I ventured. "You can't repeat the past."
>
> "Can't repeat the past?" he cried incredulously. "Why of course you can!"

In fact, Dylan repeats the past with a nearly obsessive enthusiasm—to such an extent that two later albums, *Love and Theft* and *Modern Times,* have undergone minute critical scrutiny for what some regard as magnificent appropriation of a diversity of cultural texts and what others regard simply as plagiarism. Dylan presumably took the very title *Love and Theft* from a historical text by Eric Lott: *Love and Theft: Blackface Minstrelsy and the American Working Class* (1995). Songs borrow heavily from *Confessions of a Yakuza: A Life in Japan's Underworld* (1991), by Junichi Saga. For *Modern Times,* Dylan turns to a now obscure Civil War–era poet named Henry Timrod for inspiration. If once Dylan stood baffled and remote at the center of his imagined postapocalyptic civilization, he now appears to have cast himself as the historian of that civilization, piecing together its voices, bringing them back to life.

In recognition of his "profound impact on popular music and American culture, marked by lyrical compositions of extraordinary poetic power," Dylan was awarded a Pulitzer Prize Special Citation on April 7, 2008.

TARANTULA

In the introduction to the first official edition of Bob Dylan's *Tarantula*—an introduction titled "Here Lies Tarantula"—the publisher narrates the long process and the series of delays of the book's publication. The manuscript was set aside at Dylan's insistence in 1966 and not revived until 1971. The body of the text is treated as an artifact, promised "the way [Dylan] wrote it when he was twenty-three—just this way." As for its substance, the publisher's introduction admits that in the beginning "We weren't quite sure what to make of the book—except money. We didn't know what Bob was up to." The sense was that a first book by as famous a person as Dylan would be valuable more for its status as a curiosity than for anything it might say. The life of the book in pirated editions and in later published editions certainly confirms this calculation: it is one of those texts widely circulated but infrequently read.

Not unlike Dylan's work in film, *Tarantula* is in fact a serious and ambitious undertaking by an artist possessing remarkable confidence in his distinctive vision and experimental technique—and, problematically, a nearly total disregard for the usual bounds of coherency or linearity. In other words, *Tarantula* fails much as *Renaldo and Clara* fails, its failure of a piece with those elements that make it after all an exciting and rewarding if difficult work of art. One thinks of Dylan's own lines in "Love Minus Zero/No Limit": "[T]here's no success like failure / And ... failure's no success at all." Sam Shepard reports in *The Rolling Thunder Logbook* (1977) that in making *Renaldo and Clara,* Dylan wanted to emulate such great French filmmakers as Marcel Carné and François Truffaut; similarly, the publishers of *Tarantula* remember discussing Rimbaud with Dylan in establishing their mutual hopes for the book. Dylan's taste for the avant-

garde emerges most fully in his work outside music—after all, his music must compete in a popular industry—yet the experimentation of *Tarantula* calls attention to some of the strangeness, the fragmentation and instinct for the absurd to be found in even the most popular of Dylan's songs. Certain characters from *Highway 61 Revisited* and *The Basement Tapes* reappear in *Tarantula,* reminding us that Dylan's images, if ephemeral, are not insubstantial or even fleeting, but they are ephemeral in the manner of ghosts, difficult to catch or fully perceive yet somehow continuous, dependable in their way, haunting a landscape over a long term.

Tarantula alternates stream-of-consciousness prose occasionally likened to (though perhaps not as fully realized as) James Joyce's *Finnegans Wake* with sections of verse that sometimes refer back to and sometimes depart entirely from the prose. The book is divided into chapters, each chapter ending in a lyric epistle signed by an oddly named character: "homer the slut," "Mouse," "Lazy Henry," "truman peyote," "The Law," "louie louie," "your uncle Matilda," "your friend, Friend," et cetera. These names never repeat, though one begins to suspect of them an accumulation of aliases for a small number of consistent voices. Epistles ending certain middle chapters carry no signature, and the last chapter includes no epistle. In general the names of the characters peopling *Tarantula*—in the prose and verse as well as in the epistles—occur in single chapters and not again, though one character, Aretha, appears throughout. Indeed, her name is the first word of the first chapter. Another character, incidental yet hard to ignore, appears late in the book and only long enough to die: It is Dylan himself. When the publisher's introduction plays on this theme with the variation "Here Lies Tarantula," we are to understand the author to be embalmed in his own words. We are also to remember that "lying" happens in three ways: to lie in a grave; to lie open, ready for examination; and to tell a lie, to fib. These paired instances encompass all three meanings. Finally, elsewhere an epistle signed "your benefactor Smokey Horny" recalls Dylan's fascination with floods and with decisions to defect from drowning crowds.

CHRONICLES: VOLUME ONE

Of course, the clearest message of *Tarantula*—and of passages like the one concluding the discussion above—is that nobody will ever "get the message." Its obscurity essentially obviates meaning of any traditional kind. Yet one of Dylan's strengths and one of the reasons his work is so persuasive not only at moments but also in the arc it describes across a career is that within his frequent incoherence he has a remarkable capacity for building larger structures of meaning. One must stand back from them to fully survey their architecture. *Tarantula* marks Dylan's first suicide in text—"here lies bob dylan"—yet we will remember that he also contrives to kill himself off in *Chronicles: Volume One*: "One of the early presidents of the San Bernardino Angels was Bobby Zimmerman, and he was killed in 1964 on the Bass Lake run." If it is a coincidence that Dylan writes his own death into each of his two published books, and if it is furthermore a coincidence that the second death dates to 1964, a year during in which Dylan was hard at work writing the text that would include the first, this must be the kind of coincidence from which we are meant to "*gather* something," as Christopher Ricks suggests. To "stand up & say 'san bernardino' " is a nonsensical act, and to hope for anyone to "get the message" is even more absurd. But if San Bernardino is where Bobby Zimmerman was lost in Dylan's personal mythology, to "go back" there in the chaos of the shipwreck would be an act of recovery, and suddenly the monotone in which the words are to be spoken resembles the "trembling distant voice" from "It's Alright Ma (I'm Only Bleeding)" of "somebody [who] thinks they really found you."

The question "are you a man or a self?" carries some urgency. After all, this is the Bob Dylan who finds it possible to imagine "[getting] ... a new Bob Dylan next week" and who goes out on Halloween with his "Bob Dylan mask on." From such a perspective, *Chronicles* can be read as Dylan's attempt to recover the man within the

self. The book surprised readers upon its publication with its lucidity and directness—radically different from *Tarantula*'s convolutions—yet many critics found Dylan's choice of material to be puzzling. A memoir rather than an autobiography, that is, a book recounting sections of a life, not a life in its entirety, *Chronicles* seems determined to avoid discussing those events most burning to the curiosity of audiences. Three chapters deal with the years in Greenwich Village, yet Dylan brushes aside his motorcycle accident in a single sentence and writes nothing of Newport 1965. Instead readers find lengthy accounts of recording sessions for *New Morning* and *Oh Mercy.* This is partly a reminder that a person exists behind the celebrity whose memory of the things that happened *to* him—moments that stand out as important—may not conform entirely to what his fans remember *of* him. Still, the chapters share a more specific commonality, an idea that Dylan has expressed at intervals that an artist must never remain within a scene, must always seek an exit from any aesthetic room in which he finds himself. In *Chronicles,* Dylan reflects upon those moments when he stood at some variety of brink—the brink of a creative breakthrough, the brink of fame, the brink of depression, the brink of irrelevance. He writes a great deal about the books and authors he turned to at each moment. In the second chapter he mentions Dante's *Inferno*: one possibility for understanding Dylan's self-portrait in *Chronicles* is as a pilgrim lost at successive junctures in a dark wood, probing, in the manner of Dante, for a way out.

Among the most rewarding passages of *Chronicles* are those in which Dylan discusses his influences. We find a diverse and challenging constellation. Suze Rotolo introduced Dylan to the works of the avant-garde artist Red Grooms and playwright Bertolt Brecht. In fact, it was an admiration for Brecht's musical lyrics even more than Guthrie's that spurred Dylan to songwriting. The blues guitarist Robert Johnson emerges as another influence, as well as Elvis Presley, and perhaps most significantly Rimbaud. When Dylan decided to write songs, we learn, he went to the New York Public Library to read archived newspapers in search of an understanding of historical America—this in an era when "topical" songwriters were mining the current dailies for their material. He was especially engaged with the Civil War items in those papers, wherein, as Robert Polito has observed, he may have first discovered the poetry and reporting of Henry Timrod, eventually his source for the album *Modern Times.*

In the Bob Dylan of *Chronicles: Volume One* we discover a careful student of literature, of history, and of people around him, foraging for something he can use, a voice, an exit, a raft in the flood.

Selected Bibliography

WORKS OF BOB DYLAN

Albums

Bob Dylan. 1962.

The Freewheelin' Bob Dylan. 1963.

The Times They Are A-Changin'. 1964.

Another Side of Bob Dylan. 1964.

Bringing It All Back Home. 1965.

Highway 61 Revisited. 1965.

Blonde on Blonde. 1966.

Bob Dylan's Greatest Hits. 1967.

John Wesley Harding. 1967.

Nashville Skyline. 1969.

Self Portrait. 1970.

New Morning. 1970.

Bob Dylan's Greatest Hits. Vol. 2. 1971.

Pat Garrett and Billy the Kid. 1973.

Dylan. 1973.

Planet Waves. 1974.

Before the Flood. 1974.

Blood on the Tracks. 1975.

The Basement Tapes. 1975.

Desire. 1976.

Hard Rain. 1976.

Street Legal. 1978.

Slow Train Coming. 1979.

Saved. 1980.

Shot of Love. 1981.

Infidels. 1983.

Empire Burlesque. 1985.

Biograph. 1985.

Knocked Out Loaded. 1986.

Dylan & the Dead. 1988.

Down in the Groove. 1988.

Oh Mercy. 1989.

Under the Red Sky. 1990.

The Bootleg Series, Vols. 1-3: Rare And Unreleased, 1961-1991. 1991.

Good As I Been to You. 1992.

The 30th Anniversary Concert Celebration. 1993.

World Gone Wrong. 1993.

Bob Dylan's Greatest Hits. Vol. 3. 1994.

MTV Unplugged. 1995.

Time Out Of Mind. 1997.

The Bootleg Series, Vol. 4: Live 1966: The "Royal Albert Hall" Concert. 1998.

Love and Theft. 2001.

The Bootleg Series, Vol. 5: Live 1975: The Rolling Thunder Revue. 2002.

The Bootleg Series, Vol. 6: Live 1964: Concert at Philharmonic Hall. 2004.

The Bootleg Series, Vol. 7: No Direction Home: The Soundtrack. 2005.

Modern Times. 2006.

The Bootleg Series, Vol. 8: Tell Tale Signs: Rare And Unreleased, 1989-2006. 2008.

BOOKS

Tarantula. New York: Macmillan, 1971.

Writings and Drawings. New York: Knopf, 1973.

Chronicles: Volume One. New York: Simon & Schuster, 2004.

Lyrics: 1962–2001. New York: Simon & Schuster, 2004.

FILMS BY AND ABOUT DYLAN

Dont Look Back. Directed by D. A. Pennebaker. Leacock-Pennebaker, 1967.

Eat the Document. Directed by Bob Dylan. 1972.

Renaldo and Clara. Directed by Bob Dylan. Lombard Street Films, 1978.

Masked and Anonymous. Directed by Larry Charles. BBC Films, 2003.

No Direction Home. Directed by Martin Scorsese. Box TV, 2005.

I'm Not There. Directed by Todd Haynes. Killer Films, 2007.

The Other Side of the Mirror: Bob Dylan Live at the Newport Folk Festival, 1963-1965. Directed by Murray Lerner. 2007.

CRITICAL AND BIOGRAPHICAL STUDIES

"Beverly Hills Press Conference." In *The Bob Dylan Companion: Four Decades of Commentary.* Edited by Carl Benson. New York: Schirmer Books, 1998.

Corcoran, Neil, ed. *"Do You, Mr. Jones?": Bob Dylan with the Poets and Professors.* London: Chatto, & Windus, 2002.

Cott, Jonathan, ed. *Bob Dylan, the Essential Interviews.* New York: Wenner Books, 2006.

Gray, Michael. *Song & Dance Man III: The Art of Bob Dylan.* London: Cassell, 2000.

———. *Bob Dylan Encyclopedia.* New York: Continuum, 2006; updated and revised paperback edition, 2008.

Hajdu, David. *Positively 4th Street: The Lives and Times of Joan Baez, Bob Dylan, Mimi Baez Fariña, and Richard Fariña.* New York: Farrar, Straus and Giroux, 2001.

Helm, Levon. *This Wheel's on Fire: Levon Helm and the Story of the Band.* Chicago: A Cappella, 2000.

Heylin, Clinton. *Bob Dylan: Behind the Shades Revisited.* New York: William Morrow, 2001.

Marcus, Greil. *The Old, Weird America: The World of Bob Dylan's Basement Tapes.* New York: Picador, 2001.

———. *Like a Rolling Stone: Bob Dylan at the Crossroads.* New York: Public Affairs, 2005.

Polito, Robert. "Bob Dylan: Henry Timrod Revisited." Poetry Foundation (http://www.poetryfoundation.org/archive/feature.html?id=178703), 2007.

Ricks, Christopher. *Dylan's Visions of Sin.* New York: Ecco, 2003.

Scaduto, Anthony. *Bob Dylan: An Intimate Biography.* New York: Grosset & Dunlap, 1971.

Shelton, Robert. *No Direction Home: The Life and Music of Bob Dylan.* Cambridge, Mass.: Da Capo, 2003.

Shepard, Sam. *The Rolling Thunder Logbook.* New York: Da Capo, 2004.

Smith, Larry David. *Writing Dylan: The Songs of a Lonesome Traveler.* Westport, Conn.: Praeger, 2005.

Sounes, Howard. *Down the Highway.* New York: Grove Press, 2001.

MARGARET EDSON

(1961—)

Angela Garcia

A KINDERGARTEN TEACHER living in Atlanta, Georgia, Margaret Edson has both entertained and discomfited audiences with her biting rendition of a cancer patient's experience in *Wit,* her first play. Edson's work won the Pulitzer Prize for Drama in 1999. The play premiered in Costa Mesa, California, in 1995 before rapidly rising to critical acclaim and box office success in New York City; it reached a wider audience as an Emmy Award–winning Home Box Office cable television movie, directed by Mike Nichols and starring Emma Thompson, in 2001. Other honors include the Drama League of New York Playwright Award (1993) and awards from the Dramatists Guild of America (1998) and the Los Angeles, Connecticut, and New York Drama Critics' Circles, to name just a few.

As a raw look at a professional woman's journeys through cancer and cancer treatment, the contemporary medical system, and end-of-life "care," *Wit* provokes as much as it enlightens. In its characterization of a dying woman, *Wit* is a drama of life at the precipice. The protagonist, the English professor Vivian Bearing, is no truth seeker, in spite of her scholarship—but truth, whether through God's grace or some form of human love or connection, will find her regardless. And so an intellectual decipherer of the *ideas* of life, death, and afterlife discovers herself on the real edge.

While the play strikes a chord with audiences for its timeless examination of the human response to terminal illness, it also offers through Vivian a sharply critical study of current medical practices—in particular, hospital care and doctors' relations with dying patients. At the same time, interspersed with the portrayal of the patient's hospital protocol and treatment, Edson delivers a controversial running commentary on pieces by the seventeenth-century Metaphysical poet John Donne, whose death themes lay both an intellectual and spiritual foundation for *Wit.* At the end the play moves toward a kind of spiritual redemption for Vivian, a dimension that Edson has acknowledged as unrecognized by most critics.

Critics have widely praised the play as a multilayered medical drama, but they often overlook its Christian elements as well as its humor. In an interview with Adrienne Martini for *American Theatre,* Edson asserted, "The play is about redemption, and I'm surprised no one mentions it. ... Grace," she clarifies, "is the opportunity to experience God in spite of yourself, which is what Dr. Bearing ultimately achieves" (p. 22).

Wit's contemporary setting, at the approach of the twenty-first century, renders the idea of God's unconditional saving grace implicitly, and less religiously than Donne's overtly Christian wrestling; nonetheless, the dramatic struggle for meaning and salvation seems to resonate even with secular audiences. After in a sudden diagnosis of stage-four ovarian cancer, the esteemed literature professor Vivian Bearing finds herself, through a course of eight experimental drug treatments at full dose, confined to the hospital bed and at the mercy of pernicious side effects. Through her characterizations, Edson pointedly suggests that, in spite of high-technology treatments and endless clinical research, the contemporary medical system, obsessed with acquiring more and more data, is sadly lacking in a crucial respect: its capability to grant an essential dignity to those making their final transition from life. The author makes plain that in spite of seeming advances in treatment, the system—with a protocol that emphasizes research over humanity—is fundamentally flawed, even inhumane,

and itself intensifies Vivian's emotional suffering at her life's end.

For Vivian, as with all patients, her terminal illness results in a suddenly deepened sense of alienation. Intensifying the psychological and physical isolation and the mounting pain of her battle against cancer is the pervasive spiritual emptiness of the callous hospital environment. This emptiness is echoed throughout the play: from the sterile womb reflected and mocked in the ovarian cancer diagnosis; to the ovaries, Fallopian tubes, and uterus that have been removed; to the glaring lack of friends or family members at the dying woman's bedside.

The well-respected research hospital in *Wit* is largely peopled by doctors, technicians, and clinical fellows (generally male) who may be well-intentioned but seem incapable of empathy. Of the prevailing hierarchy, only the supervising doctor, a researcher, exhibits a modicum of compassion, understanding, respect—or even concern enough to look at a dying patient. In exposing the inhumanity of the hospital environment, the drama (in spite of its more gentle mocking of Vivian's academicism) elevates the protagonist as an underdog and honors her survival struggle. Although its grim focus is relieved by its comic asides, the drama essentially mourns for the neglected but stoic cancer victim in the hospital gown. Only the female nurse, the lowest person in the medical hierarchy, manages to provide exceptional care in her nurturing comforts and attention to Vivian's needs. In the medical arena, *Wit* illuminates the need for quality end-of-life care, scaled down to value individual needs.

In a more spiritual sense, the play suggests the importance of learning to let go. Suffering teaches Vivian to expand her focus and gives her, finally, a willingness to be the student. For most of the play, the scholar exhibits a kind of crossword-puzzle delight in decoding flights of wordplay, showing her mastery of the intellectual side of Donne's poetry (her academic specialization). Yet her critical commentary, while emphasizing the logical and rational, lacks any sense of the passionate faith that fuels Donne's poems. As they dissect the poet's aggressive intelligence, Vivian's lectures and comments ignore any reference to the searches for *truth* that inspire the work. Tellingly, she examines none of Donne's popular erotic or love poems, only the *Holy Sonnets.*

In interviews, Edson seems to deflate the poems, ostensibly reducing them to intellectual exercises—wit for wit's own sake. Yet this general lambasting seems to contradict the inherent power of the poems in the play. On the whole, the language of Donne's poetry interspersed among the academic and clinical jargon serves as an effective means to raise eternal struggles and questions; at the end, the sound and sense of the *Holy Sonnets* honor the sacred in the play in spite of their ostensibly shallow wit.

On the whole, Donne's work stands up to *Wit*'s seeming disembowelment as still being important and meaningful. If the poems were mere puzzles, intended only for highbrow amusement, Sonnets V and VI would not shine so brightly from the dramatic darkness, essentially anchoring and commenting upon the spirituality in the play. And so, even as Edson might reduce or dismiss the poems as unnecessarily complex, or eluding the truth, at *Wit*'s core the play subverts the authorial remarks, in fact showcasing the very poems that Edson professes to be vain intellectual exercises. The overall effect of the drama is one that satirizes not the poems but the scholarship that depends so much on matters of a semicolon versus a comma.

BIOGRAPHY

Born July 4, 1961 in Washington D.C., Margaret Edson was the second child of Peter Edson, a newspaper columnist, and Joyce Winnifred Edson, a medical social worker. She grew up across the street from American University. Julia Louis-Dreyfus, who later was a cast member of popular television series such as *Saturday Night Live* and *Seinfeld,* lived next door; together the two girls would invent dramas with Barbie dolls or act out scenarios of being college girls.

Edson attended public school until fourth grade and then was enrolled in the esteemed

private Sidwell Friends' School during the 1970s, a Quaker institution that boasts Chelsea Clinton among its alumnae. She enjoyed performing in neighborhood plays and also participated in several high school productions, but she never aspired to a career as an actress. Her father died in 1977, when Edson was a teenager; her mother continues her career as a social worker.

Edson went on to study Renaissance history at Smith College in Northampton, Massachusetts (1979–1983), and graduated magna cum laude. Upon graduation she helped a friend move to Indiana, then settled outside Iowa City (where her sister lived) to sell hot dogs by day and work nights in a bar.

Eventually, an interest in monasticism cultivated in college inspired her to spend a year in a French Dominican convent in Rome. Returning from abroad, she took a job as a unit clerk in the cancer and AIDS ward of a research hospital in Manhattan. Her menial job status, she has explained, enabled her to witness and overhear several key incidents that informed her playwriting.

Edson told Nelson Pressley of the *Washington Post* about the summer in which she concentrated her writing of *Wit*:

> In the summer of 1991 [at age 30] Edson quit [a grant-writing] position at St. Francis and got a low-pressure job working in a bike shop near Tenley Circle. In effect, she was taking the summer off so she could write this one little play that had been taking shape in her mind, triggered in part by what she had seen of cancer treatment.
>
> But she would allow herself only the summer to write. She was enrolled at Georgetown University for the fall, ready to pursue a master's in English. She wasn't setting out to become a writer.
>
> "Oh, no," Edson says, horrified by the idea. "That would have been too dangerous for me."
>
> (p. G-1)

Originally intending to complete a Ph.D., Edson enrolled at Georgetown University and, in 1992, finished a master's degree in literature. She wrote her thesis on teaching with poetry. However, as a graduate student, Edson volunteered for her church, St. Margaret's Episcopal, as an English as a Second Language tutor, which awakened her to the possibilities of being a schoolteacher. "I started liking my tutoring more and more," she recalled, "and feeling less and less comfortable in the academy. So at the end of that year, it was clear to me that I wanted to be in the elementary classroom" (p. G-1).

Edson then enrolled in an alternate certification program designed to attract candidates from other professions into public education jobs. Rather than pursue the Ph.D., she began teaching English as a Second Language in the Washington, D.C., public schools. She described to the *Post* her excitement at finding this opportunity that allowed her to begin teaching right away rather than first wade through a one-year, full-time program:

> In inner-city schools, there's about a 40 percent exit rate in the first three years for teachers. Alternative certification programs have a much higher retention rate because people go into it knowing more about it. They're not 21. We were older and sadder and wiser, and had had some kind of experience in the classroom. So I taught ESL for five years, and I never could have done it without this program. It was really the big break of my life.
>
> (p. G-1)

After that teaching spell, the author worked for one school year as a first-grade teacher in 1997. In 1998 Edson moved to Atlanta where her partner, Linda Merrill, an art historian, took a position at the High Museum. Since then, Edson has taught kindergarten in Atlanta. She teaches at John Hope Elementary School and has two sons, Timothy and Peter.

In spite of *Wit*'s spectacular success, Edson does not identify herself as a playwright, telling Pressley in the *Post* interview, "I just wrote this one little play" (p. G-1). Edson was in her fourth year as a teacher by the time her play was produced, and she insists on her commitment to that vocation, which she finds extremely satisfying; she explains that she enjoys handing to five-year-old children what she sees as immense power, the power to read and write. She is adamant that she has no immediate literary or dramatic ambitions (*Wit* may easily be her last play). Taking a matter-of-fact view toward her drama's achievement, Edson has stated that it

was something she "just had to say" at the time, and she has dismissed the idea of writing any more literary works unless she recognizes the same sense of urgency, of needing to say something that can only be said through literature.

The Pulitzer Prize winner's devotion to kindergarten teaching over writing—which Pressley says makes her "arguably the most famous kindergarten teacher in America"—is a drive that has confounded critics. She explained to Pressley:

> The job I have now, 'people person' doesn't even begin to describe it. I'm with my students every minute of the day—lunch, everything. So the isolated languor of the writer is just really not part of my world.
>
> [...] Ms. Rivers in the room next door has made the same choice. Not out of the same number of options. But all my colleagues are doing the same thing I'm doing. People who know me slightly, or who have maybe read about me or heard about me, find it hard to understand. But to people who know me better, it makes perfect sense. They know the ways that I'm ... odd.
>
> (p. G-1)

Although Edson is a graduate of private school, her dedication to public school is pronounced:

> The school where I teach is a Title One, free lunch/ free breakfast school. My students are people who would be ... well-served by good education. I feel very clear about what I'm doing. I'm perfectly sure of the positive impact of what I'm doing. And I'm the only person I know who can say that. Except for the people down the hall, Ms. Rivers next door.
>
> (p. G-1)

WIT: *BACKGROUND AND RECEPTION*

Edson completed the writing of her play during the summer of 1991 as she worked at a bicycle shop. She has offered a small allegory, connecting carpentry to the writing process to describe that process. This choice is probably most fitting, given the play's Christian overtones and its emphasis on humility:

> A friend of ours, in his garden, decided to build a shed. He'd never built anything, and he just got this idea that he was going to build this shed. And so he got all these books and plans, and he poured a foundation. For somebody who'd never built anything to build such a shed was incredible. He worked for the government, came home from work, and worked on this shed. And this was his ... shed. And I was working on my play. We had the same spirit: that whatever else happens, I'm makin' my shed. So now he has his shed. And I have my play.
>
> (p. G-1)

The author has playfully attested that she sent the play to every theater in the country. She cited the reasons her play kept coming back: "cast size, subject, too much talk, too academic, too haughty, too unsure of itself, whether it was funny or sad ... Now people are scratching their heads about it. But it was unanimous" (p. G-1).

Wit received some attention when it won the Drama League's $1,000 prize for an unproduced play in 1993. Edson received a letter of acceptance from South Coast Repertory in Costa Mesa, California, and her work premiered with director Martin Benson in January 1995. The script was cut by an hour, from two acts to one, by Edson together with the dramaturge Jerry Patch and the director Martin Benson. The play later debuted in New Haven, Connecticut, in October 1997, directed by a former classmate of Edson's from Sidwell Friends' School, Derek Anson Jones. "The effect it has now, especially in Derek's production, is of this very fast-swerving drive," she says. "You're brought very quickly over to laughing and then ripped right back into something harrowing—very shocking, in fact. And it happens so quickly and smoothly in his production that it makes me seem like I really know what I'm doing," she explained, laughing.

Before reaching Connecticut, however, *Wit* had already taken the theater world by storm, winning six Los Angeles Drama Critics' Circle Awards in 1996: for best production, performance, writing, directing, lighting, and best world premiere. Edson has reminded her readership of the importance of reading the play aloud—that dramas are meant to be performed. In February 2000, on the heels of winning the Pulitzer, she recalled her delight with finally seeing the finished production—her words and imaginings—enacted onstage:

> It happened exactly like it was in my mind, as though I was whispering to each person what to do. So instead of being astonished by it, it was ... correct. That was the most exciting thing—to have it be exactly as I imagined it, to the tiniest detail, and to have strangers bringing that about. It was so proper, so correct, that it was thrilling. I was delirious. And that hasn't gone away.
>
> (p. G-1)

The Derek Jones production won three Connecticut Drama Critics' Circle Awards in 1998, for best production, performance, and directing. After minor cast changes, Jones guided the play through successful productions at the ninety-nine-seat Manhattan Class Company Theater and subsequently the 499-seat Union Square Theatre in New York City in 1999, where it won New York Drama Critics' Circle, Drama Desk, Drama League, Outer Critics Circle, and Lucille Lortel Awards, among others.

Kathleen Chalfant played Vivian Bearing in the New York production for a year before her brother died of cancer. She has spoken about how the play helped teach her how to help her brother at the end of his life. Jones readied the production for a national tour before he died of AIDS complications in January 2000. Judith Light starred in the national touring company, which opened at the Kennedy Center's Eisenhower Theater.

In a 1999 interview with Jim Lehrer of the PBS television *Newshour,* after winning the Pulitzer, Edson reinforced how her experience with AIDS and cancer patients marked her playwriting: "Since it was such a low-level job, I was able to really see a lot of things first hand. I was sort of unnoticed because I was so insignificant. And so I was able to witness a lot, both the actions of the care-givers and reactions of the patients."

The play has been well-received by the medical community and has been produced in medical schools and hospitals throughout the United States. Doctors have regarded the play as emotionally powerful teaching tools for their medical students, since it advances education on end-of-life care. Medical journal reviews have praised the play, and seen *Wit* as a warning or wake-up call to refocus the education on patient protocol, to reenergize that conversation.

NAMES: CARRYING LIFE'S BURDEN

Like John Donne, who famously played on his name in various puns in his poetry, Vivian's own name plays on at least two identities in the face of death. First, the surname "Bearing" emphasizes Vivian's upright carriage despite the odds, her braggadocio—simultaneously admirable and pathetic. Vivian may come to realize her limits as a human being. Still, for most of the play, she glories in her past triumphs of punctuation in sonnet analysis, and she naturally needs to see herself as powerful when she is at her most powerless—before facing her need to accept, release, and move forward.

Second, the name intimates the cross she bears—the real load she has to carry. For the weight that rests on us all sits most squarely, and painfully, on Vivian's shoulders as her condition worsens. She bears her illness, yes, but also, rather than our vague knowledge of mortality, she carries that knowledge, squared, intensified: she has the *immediate knowledge* of her impending death, her mortality. The professor must also tolerate the cross of isolation; her own predilection toward academic alienation (she has been respected in her profession, not liked) now weighs on her as a terrible aloneness thrust on her by the cancer diagnosis and medical treatment. In *Wit,* however, the weight of the journey is relieved by humor, while the unbearable loneliness of the journey is relieved by the company of the audience, by Vivian's mentor, E.M. Ashford, and by her nurse Susie.

Her first name, by which she is referred in the playwright's directions, Vivian, admits the universal desire to live life, the will to survive: *vivire.* And while Vivian does not exactly rage against the dying of the light, she does not exactly submit either. Instead she performs a kind of song and dance, a comedy routine against the dying of the light. The vaudevillian carryings-on amount in fact to a dodge; as she admits later, she is hiding from the monster that confronts her. But in the meantime she (quite seriously) draws

herself up to her fullest height, summoning the ghosts of publications and lectures past as though again and again to protest her importance against that mortal force.

Most stunningly, in terms of her "aliveness," Vivian is reborn at the end of the play—crucified and resurrected—as she rises up naked to the light. This is how she marks her exit from life and from the drama. Indeed, Edson suggests through this vision that there is truth in the metaphor of the mere comma between life and death and life everlasting. In her final recitation of Holy Sonnet VI, Vivian forgets the originally and correctly punctuated version she has touted throughout *Wit.* As evidenced by her confused state, her treatment may have (falsely) forced the comma back into a semicolon, implying that an insuperable barrier has been posed between those states of life, death and eternal life. She also returns an extra (inaccurate) capital D to Death, as though her enemy has been unnecessarily demonized and dramatized at the end of her life. In effect, Edson suggests that Vivian's medical treatment has made it harder to die and die gracefully. In spite of the treatment efforts to keep her alive at all costs, and even a false Code Blue, Vivian finally rises into her eternal life. Throughout, Vivian thus has remained true to her name and to her nature. Even when her humor veers toward self-parody ("In short, I am a force") or a desire to hide, to escape the pain, overtakes her, the professor's relentless energy manages to light a spark against the awesome power of death.

The clinical fellow Jason, on the other hand, sports the ironic surname Posner (in Scottish, "always prepared"). As one who views his course in bedside manner as a massive waste of time, he remains a callous mechanical figure; when Vivian finally tries to hint at her own fear, Jason stands obtuse. His first name, equally ironically, comes from the Greek and Hebrew: "healer"; "the Lord is salvation." At the end he fails his name as well as his vocation.

COMEDY AND IRONY

As drama, *Wit* dwells in the genre of tragicomedy, or dark comedy. In view of the play's hospital setting and terminal circumstances, its humor—however irreverent, outrageous, or grim—saves. Through Vivian, Edson exhibits a wickedly dry humor that reverberates throughout the work, lightening the bleakness; it ricochets the audience from pathos to laughter and back again.

This comic element works to mitigate the impending tragedy of Vivian's death, (and the reader's own resulting fear of mortality), as consistently humorous dialogue punctures the numbness occasioned by the prognosis. And yes, the humor is, as the title promises, witty, both in Vivian's most satisfying quips and in Donne's logical leaps in his death sonnets. As with Donne, wit is the rapier Vivian favors in her duel with death. By illuminating the difficult march toward death, humor works to defy, defuse, and even transcend death's power.

Comedy is not the only relief in the play. Given the pain inherent in the theme of Edson's work, and its sterile, mercilessly lit interior, other dramatic elements must—for the sake of audience palatability—counter the requisite IV bottles, gowns, and grimly beeping apparatuses. In *Wit*'s patently realistic hospital room, morbidity and hope seem to vie for the soul of the patient. Humor provides the hope. But so does character. Thus Edson's characterization of Vivian as tough rather than sentimental bolsters the play's mood as well. When confronted with pain and mortality, at least in art, the audience seems to crave a character who exhibits a certain measure of bravado. Vivian's asides are full of ironic humor, and her quips also pepper the hospital dialogue, sometimes as cynical response to the doctors' mechanical questions. Edson's unsentimental characterization provides a no-nonsense, typically American slant to the play; when sentiment does enter the picture, through the nurse's empathetic words and actions, it is welcome.

The play as it opens immediately establishes Vivian's sane, sardonic, and acute intelligence, expressed in her talent for irony:

> (VIVIAN BEARING *walks on the empty stage pushing her IV pole. She is fifty, tall and very thin, barefoot, and completely bald. She wears two hospital*

> *gowns—one tied in the front and one tied in the back—a baseball cap, and a hospital ID bracelet. The house lights are at half strength.* VIVIAN *looks out at the audience, sizing them up.*)
>
> VIVIAN: (*In false familiarity, waving and nodding to the audience*) Hi. How are you feeling today? Great. That's just great. (*In her own professorial tone*) This is not my standard greeting, I assure you.
>
> (p. 5)

Immediately (and deceitfully) Vivian establishes herself as master of her situation, just as the medical personnel give a fair imitation of controlling the cancer's growth and spread throughout the play. She also immediately analyzes the audience in a way that mocks the medical establishment's insincere bedside manner. Essentially, her character taps into stereotype, or archetype; Vivian's temperament is as purely formal and academic as an old school lecturer's—albeit one whose coldness is sporadically reprieved by the unexpected grace and warmth of some rollicking one-liners.

Vivian proceeds to establish her self-absorbed, intellectual prowess, even sense of superiority, this time through an ironic and funny explication of the niceties of grammatical analysis:

> There is some debate as to the correct response to this salutation. Should one reply "I feel good," using "feel" as a copulative to link the subject, "I," to its subject complement, "good"; or [...]
>
> I don't know. I am a professor of seventeenth-century poetry, specializing in the Holy Sonnets of John Donne.
>
> (p. 5)

(The comic sexual innuendo of the grammatical term "copulative" is later echoed in the title of her magnum opus, *Ejaculations.*) The vulnerability and confessed ignorance regarding her own condition will echo from this "I don't know" (p. 5) all the way to the whimpered expressions of her fear. But for now Vivian delights in detailing her experience and firing her dry wit:

> I have been asked "How are you feeling today?" while I was throwing up into a plastic washbasin. I have been asked as I was emerging from a four-hour operation with a tube in every orifice, "How are you feeling today?"
>
> I am waiting for the moment when someone asks me this question and I am dead.
>
> I'm a little sorry I'll miss that.
>
> (p. 5)

As if to nudge aside the literary critics, Vivian herself airily intones, as if in passing, the "*ironic significance*" (p. 6) of the hospital gown as viewed in terms of how it makes plain the answer to the seemingly innocuous question she hears again and again from medical staff: "Hi. How are you feeling today?" (p. 6). She goes on to further categorize and critically analyze the literary genre and tone of her own story, one she can recount, even dissect, but not control:

> *Irony* is a literary device that will necessarily be deployed to great effect.
>
> [...] I would prefer that a play about me be cast in the mythic-heroic-pastoral mode, but the facts, most notably stage-four metastatic ovarian cancer, conspire against that.
>
> (p. 6)

In foreseeing her death as an integral part of the plot, Vivian has had to surrender some of the control of the literary elements in her own story, the first of many surrenders. Edson, through Vivian, evokes Shakespeare's famed metaphor of life as a play—a stage—in which we are merely players; one is no longer in control of one's thoughts or actions, even of one's humor, but instead puppeted by a higher Author to whom we will eventually return. Indeed, in yet another level of self-reflexive irony, Vivian is already effectively "onstage" for the medical establishment. The actual stage, set up for the audience too to observe, merely duplicates, even caricatures, this state of clinical observation.

THE MEDICAL AND ACADEMIC AS MIRROR IMAGES

Much of the complexity in Edson's drama derives from undercutting of two highly respected institu-

tions—the medical and academic, the hospital and the university. In fact, it seems that for the playwright, the letters behind the name—Ph.D., M.D.—render the character that much more open to good-natured skewering. Even in the character list Edson includes the letters behind the names, which—in light of the play's deflations—can only be perceived as a questioning, if not mocking, of the significance of credentials (especially at death's door) and of status and ego in both fields.

Edson clearly designs these two rigid disciplines to mirror each other throughout *Wit*; indeed, from the beginning the characters demonstrate that both vocations encourage a signature coldness of demeanor. The play explores the narrowness inherent in both institutions through its portrayal of Vivian's and Jason's tragically circumscribed lives. Despite Vivian's rapid-fire quips and Jason's dosage monitoring, when it comes to a question of life and death, both academic and medical rationales are found wanting. Logic, the playwright suggests, is not nearly enough. The scholar admittedly hides, while the doctor and intern effectively cloak themselves in their assemblage of facts and figures: charts, scans, tests, experiments, dosages. In short, research.

In this, Vivian's and Jason's similarities are riveting. Indeed, Jason's research obsession is only a riff on Vivian's opus, which discusses "every word in extensive detail ... I summarize previous critical interpretations of the text and offer my own analysis. It is exhaustive" (p. 19). Of course she too has concentrated on research to the neglect of any human or social relationship; research-oriented, research-centered, she prides herself on the scholarship and analysis that have composed her career and sighs at the thick-headed students necessary to the teaching component.

Edson paints the medical field in like colors: dense in information and delighting in details of the pathology almost to the point of ecstasy. Vivian's punctuation finds its equivalent in Jason's prized data: measurements and numbers. Her comma equals his dose in milligrams—perversely enjoyed for its own sake. Jason does not even look at his patient during his last two visits before her death, by which time "How are you feeling?" takes on a sinister quality. He has openly stated that the bedside manner is a waste of time.

Yet Vivian does not regret the doubling she witnesses; the recognition of her own self in Jason produces little outward regret. Instead, self-admittedly "uncomfortable with kindness" (p. 34), the career academic initially appears thankful for her intern's awkward formality. The lecture hall, after all, is the atmosphere in which she feels most at home and which she has most enjoyed—where she can display her expertise in logic, problem-solving, and mechanics.

Sometimes this mirroring leads constructively to self-revelation. Jason's coldness spawns in Vivian the memory of her callous, cynical, hurtful response when a student requests an extension to attend her grandmother's funeral. Although she presents the episode cynically and self-consciously, Vivian's regret may be classified as repentance and may, even in Donne's Christian universe, be a step toward her redemption.

While they are parallel in so many ways (Vivian seeks scholarship, not truth—Jason seeks research, not healing), the two characters diverge on an important point. Death forces Vivian's humanity, bringing her to review her life and forcing moments of honest reflection and confessions of human vulnerability. By finally laughing with Susie, who is less educated and knows nothing of poetry, she humbles herself and deepens her human connections. By increments the sardonic wit, the professorial icon, becomes less wooden and, more and more, flesh and blood. Jason, on the other hand, with his love of research, remains seemingly invulnerable until the final scene.

THE "SOLO" IN SOLILOQUY

For the bulk of the play, Vivian's alienation is profound. That the cancer is ovarian serves as a cruel mockery of her sterile womb and seemingly loveless and even friendless life. No mother, spouse, sibling, colleague, student, or child emerges from the woodwork to help Vivian

tell her tale. An archetypal lonely patient, she apparently has no living relatives at all—and despite an illustrious career at a prestigious university, no friends to visit her (although she anticipates a perfunctory, published tribute to her collected Donne criticism). Consequently Vivian offers to the strangers in the room, the audience, the daydreams and thoughts inside her head. As Vivian escapes herself, the audience becomes privy to the most intimate of her thoughts and, occasionally, her revealed emotions. That the audience participates in this way—as a collective listener to Vivian's spirited reflections, privy to the last film reel of this dying woman's mind—establishes a dynamic that counters the rather immobile setting of the sterile hospital room and its potentially sterile dialogue.

It is through her soliloquies and asides that Vivian most intensely illustrates the human desire to transcend illness, even death, through human connection. Like Donne, Vivian refuses to be an island; and so, as the cancer takes its toll, she seeks fellowship, if not outside with the unresponsive medical staff then onward through her own mind to the fourth dimension, the listeners. In a sense she reverts to her childhood self, left alone to read and exult in learning vocabulary—the lonely but fulfilling pursuit that ultimately leads to graduate school, her Ph.D., and her academic career as a successful literature professor.

Like Hamlet, as her alienation deepens, Vivian increasingly expounds to or confides in the audience—although she works to keep her desperation muted. The professor wishes to be perceived as the uncomplaining patient and to be appreciated for her willingness as a research specimen for the medical professionals with whom she insists, and is to some degree granted, equal footing.

CAREER HUBRIS: ACADEMIC AND MEDICAL

As the play opens, Vivian—with her healthy ego—seems blatantly arrogant. Even in her own introduction to the medical establishment when she is first hospitalized, as she is delivered in a wheelchair for an X-ray, Vivian revels in herself and in her status. In another comic turn, her only frame of reference is herself; all paths lead back to the "I".

> TECHNICIAN 1: Name.
>
> VIVIAN: My name? Vivian Bearing.
>
> TECHNICIAN 1: Huh?
>
> VIVIAN: Bearing. B-E-A-R-I-N-G. Vivian. V-I-V-I-A-N.
>
> TECHNICIAN 1: Doctor.
>
> VIVIAN: Yes, I have a Ph.D.
>
> (p. 16)

And a moment later, even as she is pushing her face and head into a metal plate for the X-ray:

> VIVIAN: I have made an immeasurable contribution to the discipline of English literature.
>
> (p. 17)

Given the diagnosis and the setting, this pride already seems irrelevant and even pathetic as the X-ray technician shows no interest in what she is saying—in fact ignores her while he does his job, what he is paid to do, in this case positioning the patient's body for a chest X-ray. This dismissal of the patient's humanity does not bode well for Bearing's future hospitalization. In the same light, her arrogance is rendered poignant and somewhat excusable, under the circumstances of her rapid decline and the inhumane treatment by the medical staff. Whether Vivian's self-absorption—her retreat into the familiar, ego-stroking world of publications and credentials—is a defense mechanism or whether it merely displays her ignorance of what is to follow, she soon finds her power sapped and her physical messages overpowering the mental.

Vivian's pompous assessment of her own career becomes absurdly and increasingly comedic as she boasts that she alphabetized index cards for three years for her professor's "monumental critical edition of Donne's *Devotions upon Emergent Occasions*" (p. 18). The title perhaps reiterates the aching need for some kind of sacredness, ceremony, prayer for when Vivian transitions from life into death and her simulta-

neous emergence into new life. Her own dissertation title, *Ejaculations in Seventeenth-Century Manuscript and Printed Editions of the Holy Sonnets: A Comparison,* further mocks and blasts her self-important scholarship. Although the "ejaculations" presumably refer to Donne's exclamations, the wording conveys a certain prideful masculinity, implying that this successful, renowned professor has positioned herself as a veritable patriarch in her system. An academic Iron Lady, she has needed to be tough to buck the well-documented old-boy tenure system prevalent in her time.

In the male-dominated medical system she has now entered, Vivian herself is the object of analysis. Where the two disciplines so nicely converge is in their perfunctory dissection and analysis. Both fields wield their own terminology of dissection in order to perform their great service to humanity. The intern, in fact, seems—regrettably—in all his visits to the patient's lonely, sterile, and machinated bedside, never to diverge from this jargon.

As a technician (one of a series of three mechanical technicians who "deposit" Vivian into various positions) grudgingly wanders offstage to get her wheelchair, which has disappeared, Vivian continues to enumerate her accomplishments to the audience. This is a prime example of Edson's use of a fluid sort of soliloquy, which slides seamlessly from addressing another character, to—upon that character's (increasingly expected) absence—addressing the always-present audience. Sometimes, in the inherent search for audience, any audience, this shift seems the only dignified response to the scholar's embarrassment and awkwardness at finding herself in such a weak predicament.

Indeed, enmeshed in her false pride, Vivian seems ignorant of her own childlike transparency as she reveals just how important her research is to her overinflated ego. Vivian's own words, as she is bracketed by the obtuse technician on one side and her first exposure to her equally obtuse former student, the intern Jason, on the other side, tell all: "Donne's wit is ... a way to see how good you really are" (p. 20); her great work, *Made Cunningly,* again emphasizes again her mere cleverness over any wisdom.

Yet while she constantly summons her analytical skills to mull over clinical jargon, Vivian usually keeps these reflections to herself (and the audience), as any intellectual protestations are usually ignored by hospital staff. As demonstrated by the supervising physician, Kelekian, and his intern Jason, philosophy and literature count for exactly nothing in a world of the M.D.; just as Vivian may have played the queen bee at her prestigious university department of English, the doctor of medicine is king in his own domain. At best, the doctors address her as "doctor" in return, and Jason does acknowledge her as his former professor, although he reduces it to a mere notch in his belt: "Yeah, I survived Bearing's course. No problem. Heh" (p. 31).

The ego that unites Vivian, Kelekian, and Jason is so focused, driven, obsessed, and self-obsessed that all other considerations fade into obscurity. Dr. Harvey ("battle-worthy soldier," from Old French) Kelekian seems indeed sometimes too eager for battle, and he generally comports himself as a professor with a manner as tough as Vivian's as he leads the interns on their Grand Rounds. King of his castle, Kelekian—perhaps because he is of Vivian's generation—plays a generally warmer role than does his intern. However, he is just as eager to make her cooperate fully in his research experiment and—along with Jason—is equally ruthless in making her comply with his research in spite of the side effects; the full dose of treatment for eight cycles plainly sickens her, especially after the fifth cycle, when she is admitted into isolation with fever and neutropenia.

As a fellow professional, the doctor does view Vivian as an equal of sorts, and he openly commiserates with her exasperation toward students and their lack of thoroughness. And yet he exudes the same factuality and callousness, even obtuseness, of the medical establishment that drums throughout the play. In a scene that sets the mood for her hospital stay, the "alpha" doctor delivers a blunt diagnosis and intones the imperial need for toughness.

Jason takes after his role model with a less humane, busier efficiency. Already nervous during the patient interview, Jason must be continually reminded by Kelekian with the command "clinical" (p. 40) to address the patient and ask her how she is doing—basically to pretend to care. That he proves repeatedly deaf to the falseness of her stock response, "Fine" (p. 54), becomes one of the most pregnant motifs in the play and throws an especially ugly light on Jason's soul.

The terror and agony of illness, combined with the medical world's continued insensitivities, will topple even Vivian's fighting stance, upsetting her trademark relaxed wisecracking. The tough specimen must be shaken into admitting her vulnerability.

No impending death forces, forges, or fires Jason's humanity or spirit. The medical model's obsession with data and its deficit in empathy only become more glaring as the play progresses. From Jason's detailed monologue (and Vivian's witty responses) while his professor lies in stirrups, nothing deters the ruthless objectification of the patient.

Likewise, the group of medical students that enters her hospital room during Grand Rounds in order to observe Vivian's pelvic examination answer Kelekian's quiz questions as if they are game show contestants vying for a prize. They all try to upstage Jason, the star student. This scenario merely deepens the sense of absurdity, grotesqueness, and injustice enabled by the medical protocol in *Wit* and its "up the dose to 2000 milligrams" robotic expediency. Edson clearly means the audience to see this painfully public pelvic exam, with its attendant audience voyeurism and guilt, as an open assault on human dignity.

From the beginning Edson, through Vivian's dry bitter comic reflex, openly critiques Jason's monstrosity, his lack of humanity, in his blatant lack of empathy with the patient. To further illuminate the appalling schism between caregiver and patient, the playwright lets Jason slip with his comment that it is the cancer, not the death, that is awesome to him. This again parallels Vivian's fixation with Donne's cleverness rather than spiritual truth. Too busy establishing herself as a willing candidate for research, however, Vivian, notably, never becomes angry with Jason or medical staff. She is only too able to recognize that she has always been one of them. But the superior facades are doomed to crack. As Vivian nears her death, Jason will fall, his principles as a competent, capable healer called into question. Gradually, throughout the play, Edson builds Jason's behavior—developing his sense of superiority and his unkindness—toward this fall, triggered by a final, blatant disregard toward the patient's expressed will.

By the end of the play, Jason's violation of a Do Not Resuscitate order has sullied the medical profession (as if it needed further sullying in the drama), and he has sabotaged, perhaps destroyed, his medical career through his professional negligence—essentially, through the systematic neglect of the patient's humanity.

FLASHING BACK

Flashbacks—as reminders of the past that bring life into the death-filled scenario peppered with IV bottles—both frame and define *Wit,* and along with the soliloquies, they relieve Vivian's intense isolation. They are necessary in order to gain insight into Vivian's life and career and to establish the real former power of the personage who is being accosted by the body's betrayal. These visions represent Vivian to herself in three of her life's stages.

Edson's use of this technique basically allows the protagonist greater physical movement and emotional range than she can provide in the drama's real time. They also allow the audience to better understand her character—in this case, her loneliness, eagerness, and pride. Flashbacks remind the audience of Vivian's former life, of her power, but they also—ironically, in light of Vivian's peacock display—demonstrate her failings as a scholar and professor.

Vivian works imaginatively to transcend her daily reality through her daydreams—in which she relives her past glories. During these reminiscences, she speaks to us not from madness but

from the need for sanity, for survival. But they effectively pierce the infallible persona Vivian has presented, showing the audience the chinks in the protagonist's armor.

These earlier incarnations are in fact perfectly in keeping with Vivian's present character on stage, not only confirming the traits already visible to the audience but also providing some important psychological background: the precocious child treated too soon as an adult, left to her own devices (the world of reading); the eager graduate student, misguidedly continuing to seek the world in the pages of a book, or in the library, and thereby rejecting life's truths and pleasures; and finally, the overbearing, supercilious professor whose persona, in her lecture hall domain, demands everything and answers to no one.

In the first vision, as a lonely child, Edson establishes Vivian's emotional connection to words and language. A five-year-old Vivian, with her father's cold and distant (indeed professorial) guidance, learns the excitement of deriving meaning from a new word—"soporific." This delight remains with her, and the love of words gives her the emotional solace that she is presumably missing from her parents, throughout her life.

In the second reenactment, as a graduate student, Vivian is gently chided by her wise mentor, E.M. Ashford, for her use of an outdated, incorrectly punctuated copy of Donne's poems. At the time E.M., pointing out the comma in Sonnet X, sees that Vivian cannot recognize the gist of Donne's passionate poem—the triumph of eternal life—but only fastens on the witty implication of the punctuation. The scholar cannot see the forest for the trees: she proves, alas, detail-oriented to a fault. In this flashback, Vivian has matured into a scholar-huntress or predator bent on caging—here, defining—her prey, as she victoriously receives her mentor's wisdom—that the poet's vision of life and death and *eternal life,* "life and life everlasting" (p. 14), are separated by a mere comma.

Her mentor, E.M., shakes her head at the eager young graduate student, addicted to library study to the detriment of her own powers of human experience and observation. "Don't go back to the library. Go out." The truth-seeker must go outside. But typically, and prophetically, Bearing misses this message and goes to the library anyway. From her obsession with punctuation (though deemed important by her mentor, E.M. Ashford, it should not be an end in itself), the reader can only infer that each Bearing work, including her "exhaustive" critical work or compendium, bears information but no truth. Her lack of outside experience surely reduces Vivian's readings of the poems; she neglects Donne's famous love poems, erotic poems, and other sonnets for those focusing on death, perhaps because—she has mentioned neither lover nor spouse—love does not loom large in her experience. Nor does spiritual faith, Donne's prime subject.

Interestingly, Vivian abdicates her critical role when she is hospitalized, but she never questions the treatment or setting. (For reasons unknown, she is never transferred to hospice care, which ostensibly would offer more of the type of nurturing care exemplified by Susie's compassion toward dying patients.) Instead, the prize scholar so eager to please E.M. becomes, somewhat pathetically, a prize patient, eager to participate in the experimental chemotherapy program if her doctors wish this. Her complaints are only expressed as private pain. Some of the play's only references to Christianity are to the pain that "hurts like hell" and Vivian's mantra (which becomes Jason's after her death), "Oh, God" (p. 70). In *Wit* these seem to represent the only overt Christian references America has left: its swearing, sideways glances.

A more considerable chink in Vivian's armor appears with her third and final flashback, one in which she recognizes the power she has misused. When a student begs to miss an examination in order to attend her grandmother's funeral, Vivian flaunts her power without mercy. Her response is negative and cynical. In Vivian's present condition, however, the tables are turned. Vivian is the silently imploring graduate student, seeking kindness, and the intern is the unrelenting professor. Now, as she briefly and cynically moralizes, she can see the flaws in her former callousness and tenacity.

FORMS OF REDEMPTION

Where it exists, redemption comes through the other two female characters in the play: the professor-mentor and the nurse. Susie is a godsend, in more ways than one. She brings out the human response in Vivian, who has fought to keep her loftiness. Vivian laughs with her and actively seeks her motherly care. The nurse, in turn, honestly speaks to Vivian about her diagnosis and explains the details of the Do Not Resuscitate order and so helps her to release the clinging to self and self-importance that have been lifetime impediments to her emotional and spiritual growth. As she gains in mutual understanding with another being, Vivian subtly emerges from her isolation, her hibernation, and wakes into a more enlightened state.

The "uneducated" nurse Susie in fact plays a Mary Magdalene role, offering, along with Bearing's old mentor, E.M., a kind of angelic solace. The dying woman who has turned, in loneliness, mainly to the audience for company and comfort—an expression of sharing limited to soliloquies—is initially repelled by Susie's indulgences of popsicles and pillow-fluffing. And yet Vivian comes to appreciate (and even bait or orchestrate) these ministrations, distasteful as they may have seemed to her at first.

The play's Christian roots, including Donne's Christian passions and reflections, are illuminated in Susie's role. Susie's name refers to the lily, the symbolic flower of death and resurrection that blooms at Easter. But her name is only used in the diminutive, implying that this is a woman seen almost as a child, emphasizing her lesser role in the medical hierarchy. But such humble placement merely reinforces the Christian belief regarding life after death, the Second Coming: "The first shall be last, and the last shall be first." Susie is young and selfless; her Christlike ministrations as a nurse are largely overlooked and ignored by all but Vivian, but they represent more than her doing her job; the nurse, unlike the doctor and the intern in the story, is exalted by her compassion, humanity, and finally her bravery. She is the only one who likes Vivian or who worries about her ("You okay all by yourself?") (p. 33). She is also the only character who advocates, in the face of the drive for more research, for Vivian's comfortable transition into death: "I think you need to talk to Kelekian about lowering the dose for the next cycle. It's too much for her like this," she tells Jason (p. 45).

Susie in fact bears the heaviest truth in her exchange with Vivian about what the patient wishes to do if her heart stops. Does Vivian wish to be resuscitated if she stops breathing (Code Blue)? After initially expressing her wish to be resuscitated, Vivian changes her mind and agrees to the DNR (Do Not Resuscitate) order. Vivian agrees that she must be allowed to die. She exercises her right to the pursuit of happiness, in this case as release from excruciating pain.

While some critics have been uncomfortable with the stereotype of the repressed professor—and what some have seen as the predictability of suffering in order to be granted illumination, or spiritual resuscitation—others have been impressed by one aside that conveys her epiphany:

> [...] Now is not the time for verbal swordplay, for unlikely flights of imagination, and wildly shifting perspectives, for metaphysical conceit, for wit.
>
> And nothing would be worse than a detailed scholarly analysis. Erudition. Interpretation. Complication.
>
> (*Slowly*) Now is a time for simplicity. Now is a time for, dare I say it, kindness.
>
> (*Searchingly*) I thought being extremely smart would take care of it. But I see that I have been found out. Ooohhh.
>
> (pp. 69–70)

After a morphine drip is started, Vivian and Susie share some laughter together over an unknowing remark of Susie's. It is significant that Vivian has dropped her veneer of superiority, her protective shield and armor; she no longer mocks or sneers at another's deficiencies but genuinely learns to laugh *with* another human being, not at their expense. From Jason she has learned not to objectify Susie.

The play's other redeemer, Vivian's mentor, E.M. Ashford ("ash" is rooted in the Norse for "divine" or "God"), represents her only outside visitor, and this eighty-year-old woman acts as a

wise, healing presence, unwittingly witnessing Vivian's transition from life. Like a midwife or doula who is with the mother during a birth, Vivian's mentor essentially guides and delivers her to the afterlife, on the occasion of her death—comforting Vivian and, in reading to her, leaving her with the last words she will hear.

To the ash tree is attributed mystical character, the ash wand or staff being a frequent symbol of healing, enchantment, transformation, and empowerment in matters of destiny, according to Celtic mythology. Norse mythology maintains that the World Tree was a giant ash tree that linked and sheltered all the worlds.

E.M., though a towering scholar and intellect, proves that humane kindness is also possible as a successful woman professor. By now, presumably retired, she also identifies herself as a grandmother: no longer a professor in her professorial status and role, with an academic tome, but a grandmother with a grandmotherly demeanor and a grandmotherly book. And, anathema to Vivian's universe, this turns out to mean no diminishment of character. On the contrary, her grandmotherly, nurturing qualities are just what are needed by Vivian at this moment, just as Susie's maternal comforts are so needed. E.M. echoes the kindliness that Susie has provided, and she brings simple comfort through a sympathetic though necessarily one-sided conversation and via the text she chooses to present to her prodigy, who is crying.

There is no literary interest once the body's deterioration intensifies. Upon E.M.'s "Shall I recite to you? Would you like that? I'll recite something by Donne," the last word of Vivian's life is "Nooooo" (p. 79). At the deathbed, Edson seems to imply, the literary-intellectual song and dance with its attendant status is irrelevant. So, Ashford, who is in town for her grandson's fifth birthday, pulls from her bag Margaret Wise Brown's popular and strange children's tale, *The Runaway Bunny.* In doing so, E.M. achieves a sense of balance with social and human credentials, in spite of her professor emerita glory. (One would never picture Vivian with a children's book.)

This seemingly simple piece of classic children's literature, taken as religious or biblical parable, delivers its own metaphysical wallop within the context of the play: "Once there was a little bunny who wanted to run away. So he said to his mother, 'I am running away.' 'If you run away,' said his mother, 'I will run after you. For you are my little bunny.'" The story furthers the idea that Vivian—like the proud scholar that she is, like the medical establishment, like Edson's complicated Donne—is hiding from death; "Look at that," E.M. points out. "A little allegory of the soul. No matter where it hides, God will find it. See, Vivian?" (p. 80).

The effect is strange, even surreal, but moving nonetheless. It is as though Edson is teaching that this kindergarten redemption, even unacknowledged, is still redemption; the parable could represent the inevitability of God's saving grace. Vivian's "No," taken with the children's book reading, seems also to imply that the simplest tale may say more about the universal issues of life than a poet's complexities. The child's text suggests that when she admits the truth and hits bottom in her weakness and vulnerability, God finds and saves Vivian. Some critics are uncomfortable with the imposition of the children's text, however, and see in this juxtaposition (and in Vivian's earlier analyses) a facile view, or a misreading of Donne's poetry, of which Vivian only gives the reader a glimpse.

Vivian's is a muted and passive-seeming redemption. No explicit generosity of spirit ensues. But there is an acceptance and humility. If anything, she is redeemed in spite of herself, as God scoops her up in the motherly style of the mother bunny; there is little poetic about it. Vivian has been exhausted into surrendering to death, and thus to God's unconditional grace.

The Runaway Bunny, in all its embarrassing implications for Donne and in all its glorious incongruity, is a bedtime story. By reading and lulling her prodigy to sleep, Ashford indeed evokes Donne after all, as the death-sleep analogy is one of Donne's most famous. Donne resorts to dashing logic and, as Edson would have it, clever linguistic subterfuge, in order to ensure that his soul will not be destroyed, and so he

seems to discover anew God's gift of grace, the greatest and wiliest outwitting of the most dangerous force. For Donne, God helps Christians to outmaneuver Death with a capital D, to steal his fire or, like a cartoon character, to do a double take. Donne takes the ultimate villain and leaves him deflated, with empty pockets.

For her part, E.M. keeps up a cheery one-sided conversation to Vivian's occasional moans and bids her farewell with a blessing that is one last literary glance, a nod to Shakespeare's *Hamlet*: "And flights of angels sing thee to thy rest" (p. 80). (Again, the role of literature in *Wit* is elevated; her parting words honor, if not scholarship or criticism, then poetry; they do not dishonor it.) As implicit in their names, Susie and E.M. serve as Vivian's angels. In a seemingly secular story of hellish pain and "infernal tests" (p. 53), these two women bring messages that are not about numbers and measurements, scientific calculations and dosages; they, like Mary's angel or even the three wise men, carry tidings of joy, much-needed solace, and the blessings of connection.

In a 2002 issue of *Christianity and Literature,* Martha Greene Eads addresses the thematic question of redemption in Edson's work, and she sees in the writer a "deep ambivalence about orthodox Christian faith" as well as "related ambivalence about the life of the mind" (p. G-1). Eads believes *Wit* "reflects its author's unusual personal struggle to come to terms with both academia and orthodoxy" but that Edson ultimately "affirms ... a Christian understanding of God's persistent pursuit of His children" (pp. 241–254).

One insistent motif in *Wit* proves to be metamorphosis or, given the play's Christian resonances, incarnation. The drama is stocked with new incarnations (and contradictions). The superstar professor morphs into weak patient, the former student into doctor; the mentor-professor reveals herself as grandmother, and the seemingly not-so-smart nurse as angel or savior. Finally the dead patient is reborn, spiritually, into new life. The hierarchy is upended. Edson recognizes this as a condition of Christianity.

Vivian's final conversion is into one redeemed. If faith or religious belief is not necessary for redemption in the universe of the play, sin may be; but sin is not a problem. It is part of the weak, fallible human condition that allies the reader with Vivian. In Vivian's case, her cardinal sin presents itself as pride—the pride that prohibits her from granting an extension to the student needing to go to a grandmother's funeral, for instance. Vivian's life's pride is evident throughout the play, but, curiously, her callousness toward the student is the only example of Vivian actually actively inflicting hurt on another person.

Possibly Vivian, through witnessing especially Susie's charity as a true angel of mercy, finally recognizes in her humble nurse something of the truth or soul of the poetry she has scrutinized and taught all her life. She learns to see Susie as a person who is as worthy of respect as herself, in contrast to the way she has seen her students in the past. That there is merely a comma between life and death is a facile, glib pronouncement for a scholar bent on advancement; but now this is a lesson she needs to learn firsthand, as Donne himself incarnates Christ in his wasted body during his Final Sermon, and speaks of the soul.

In another moment of Christian symbolism, Vivian rises at the end of the play—crucified and resurrected. After learning to let go of her pride and egotism, and accepting her mortality, she is welcomed into God's grace and love in spite of herself, as Edson has indicated, and she has no choice in the matter. As in Edson's final direction, the stage notes indicate, "*The instant she is naked, and beautiful, reaching for the light—Lights out*" (p. 85).

This exit has been viewed as an excessive focus on physical salvation to the detriment of any larger spiritual message—again, critics have charged, stemming from a misreading of Donne. However, the soul's deliverance may also be inferred from the body's movement into light.

FINAL IMAGES AND UNDERCURRENTS

Indeed, the angel and monster (if not devil), the good and evil in the story, come to a showdown

when Bearing is finally dying. "She's Research!" Jason shouts, finally giving away his true regard for the human patient as a part of his great experiment. "She's NO CODE!" (p. 82). Susie returns in a secular wrestle to fight for the dying Vivian and succeeds in her righteousness to respect the patient's will. And so the audience sees Jason receive his just desserts, and his last words as he ends the play—always ironically—are "Oh, God" (p. 82). It is as though, having just made a terrible, irrevocable mistake in his incipient oncology career, he finally realizes that he is not the god, that there is a higher power. In contrast, the nurse—the lower-class citizen in this hierarchy—proves correct; she is not only correct in her knowledge and information but also right and good. She is bright and victorious, as she is angelic in spirit.

In his means to his research ends, the smug Jason fails, collapses even, weeping at his loss of reputation, which is confirmed by the degrading conversation between medical staff that he can already overhear. At the same time Vivian sheds her gown and bracelet and rises.

Jason cries for his professional failings, not for Vivian's dignity. In the scheme of things, he fails as a human being. His arrogance, even while mirrored by Vivian's, holds the potential for much more tragic consequences than hers because of the nature of his chosen field. The medical power we have handed to institutions is life-or-death, virtually godlike—thus, potentially more self-deceiving.

Edson, then, leaves glaring the lack of thoroughness that Vivian—as well as Dr. Kelekian—have mentioned that they cannot abide in their students. Jason's is not a fatal error—Vivian would eventually die regardless—but it is a transgression against human dignity. It would be an abomination to resuscitate a patient who does not wish to be resuscitated. "The healer" with his Hippocratic Oath is no healer, physically nor emotionally. And the medical establishment has failed its patient through its stubborn focus on the clinical over the individual.

Jason's shouting also speaks to Vivian's career as a decoder of poetry. Vivian is "no code." She is indeed *not* code to be objectified, quantified, and deciphered. She is not a chart, she is not data. She is human, and as such, in God's eyes she is exalted. She is poetry.

Four hundred years after his lifetime (1572–1631), John Donne's words still point the reader to the most essential questions in human experience; they drive us not only to know but also to feel the great forces that shape us. When critics remark upon the multilayered feeling of Margaret Edson's *Wit,* Donne's work is a major factor in the geology. The *Holy Sonnets* work as a Greek chorus in the drama, commenting philosophically and religiously upon the action. As his literary reputation looms, at times as an actual screen lowered sardonically into a hospital scene, Donne's words—particularly Sonnets V and X—lend gravitas to Vivian's own battle. The cancer, its treatment, and the terrifyingly unstoppable progression toward death are themes echoed in these poems; the sonnets reflect the Metaphysical poet's own unabashedly Christian obsessions—spiked as they are with death and crucifixion, resurrection, and rebirth into eternal life.

In his complex images and logic, Donne aims for transcendence. His meter is masterly and evocative—even contemporary, in its often conversational diction; his ragged, intentionally various line rhythms embody their poetic meaning.

From his scandalous elopement to his stately position as English vicar, Donne's life was action-packed. Reflecting this, his work brims not only with wit or intellect but also with sensual appetites and liveliness, deeply felt love and sorrow, and extraordinary, flashing meditations on death. Admittedly, many poems do rely on the semantic, often unsolvable puzzles the professor Vivian loves to examine and try to untangle. And yet, it may be argued, in the best poems, the brilliant wordplay enhances rather than detracts from the sense in the poetry.

That the Metaphysical wordplay dazzles—much like a spectacle or optical illusion—may suggest to some that it has no substance. Yet Donne's logic embraces complexity and contradictions; unlike Vivian, he demonstrates that wit and passion (spiritual or physical)—and espe-

cially *intelligence and compassion*—are not mutually exclusive.

In typical incongruous fashion, *Wit* presents the famous Sonnet VI—"Death Be Not Proud"—with its expression of dominion over death and its magnanimous insistence on eternal life ("one short sleepe past, wee wake eternally"), through Vivian's recitation of it during a pelvic exam. Nonetheless, through Donne's sonnet, the audience is (unthreateningly) presented with this concept, which is enacted full force in the ending scene.

Sonnet V, on the other hand, is presented as a lecture, with Vivian whacking the screen critically. Although it utters her unspoken Christlike plea, "Why should I bee (damned)?" her critical blows (played out in the whacks of her stick) again seem to deflate or diminish the text. However, the same scene undeniably mirrors and bespeaks Vivian's desperate spiritual condition, even as she ridicules the melodrama. In fact, the "overweening *intellect* or overwrought *dramatics*" (p. 50) she perceives in Donne's style are her own. In focusing on Donne's hiding (not actually evident in the sonnet—the speaker pleads for God to forget his sins, not himself), she downplays his despair of his own reason and his plea for mercy. The scholar seems merely puzzled by his plea to God to forget his sins. His "O God, Oh!" she deems unconvincing, but Vivian is to echo these words again and again in her own physical (not spiritual) pain.

In the third flashback, Vivian's students suggest again, to her silent but cynical intellectual encouragement, that in trying to confront death, Donne hides behind his wit. Edson seems to encourage this view. And yet, by letting his words resound in her play, the author suggests that contrary to Vivian's reduction of Donne—through a career of surgically dissecting his language and meaning—Donne's poetry truly *is* a force (the poet, like the play's author, is after all a creator not a critic).

So in his courageous wrestling, spiritual and intellectual, there is evidence in Donne's life and work to suggest that, while Vivian may hide behind her studied application of wit, the poet upon whom she has built her academic career uses his own talents as a means to a larger purpose; in passionately and imaginatively confronting death and God, he voices what is essentially a very human vulnerability and struggle. His art never denies his humanity.

The ghostliness of the author's ending scene vividly embodies an elemental part of Donne's prose and poetry, the resurrection; it stands contrasted with, upon Susie's cancellation of his order, Jason's new anguish and humiliation. Thus the power balance realigns itself, and the two characters are reborn.

Margaret Edson warns us, through *Wit,* that advancement in knowledge may not be advancement in truth. Amid the trappings of secularity, Edson's play reaffirms the need for attention to the soul, and soul's dignity. *Wit* values the individual at her most fragile and vulnerable, and the play helps readers come to terms with their own mortality. It also instructs caregivers in how to help a person die in peace. Many have found that Edson's fantastical ending strangely comforts. No more hospital gowns, no more cap, no more hospital bracelet. Having discarded the institutional uniform and accepted her own humanity and weakness, Vivian, through her dying, enters into the unconditional spiritual grace Donne seeks and affirms—and triumphs.

Selected Bibliography

WORKS OF MARGARET EDSON

Wit. New York: Faber & Faber, 1999.

CRITICAL AND BIOGRAPHICAL STUDIES

Carter, Betty. "John Donne Meets *The Runaway Bunny.*" *Books and Culture,* September–October 1999, pp. 24–26.

Eads, Martha Greene "Margaret Edson." In *Dictionary of Literary Biography. Vol. 266, Twentieth-Century American Dramatists, Fourth Series.* Edited by Christopher J. Wheatley. Detroit: Gale, 2002. Pp. 75–78.

———. "Unwitting Redemption in Margaret Edson's *Wit.*" *Christianity and Literature* 51, no. 2:241–254 (winter 2002).

Lehrer, Jim. "Love and Knowledge." *NewsHour with Jim Lehrer,* April 14, 1999. Transcript available at http://www.pbs.org/newshour/bb/entertainment/jan-june99/edson_4-14.html (Television interview.)

Martini, Adrienne. "The Playwright in Spite of Herself." *American Theatre,* October 1999, pp. 22–25.

Pressley, Nelson. "A Teacher's *Wit* and Wisdom." *Washington Post,* February 27, 2000, p. G-1. (Interview.)

Sykes, John D., Jr. "*Wit,* Pride, and the Resurrection: Margaret Edson's Play and John Donne's Poetry." *Renascence* 55, no. 2:163–174 (winter 2003).

Vanhoutte, Jacqueline. "Cancer and the Common Woman in Margaret Edson's *Wit.*" *Comparative Drama* 36, nos. 3–4:391–410 (fall–winter 2002–2003).

PERCIVAL EVERETT

(1956—)

Tracie Church Guzzio

PERHAPS NO OTHER writer in recent memory has been as difficult to characterize as Percival Everett. His work cannot be easily cataloged or referenced, it cannot be said to reflect any particular theory or trend, and its tone is as variable as the weather—which is perhaps why most reviewers slip into the safe and comfortable term for Everett: experimental. The word might not be completely accurate, but it does capture the spirit if not the substance of Everett's writing. He is a maverick, an uncompromising artist who has managed, despite the oft-required conformity of the publishing world, to follow his own path. Somehow, despite these pressures, he manages to balance an iconoclastic artistic vision and a deep love of mythic storytelling. Like the western environment he adopted as his home, Everett's work is sublime, inspiring, and sometimes unfriendly to visitors. Most critics, while attracted to his novels, have stayed away, not because his work is not worthy of attention, but because it requires a new lens. The critic and reviewer Greil Marcus argues that Everett's career and his position in literary circles is complex because "he has never fit." Unable to categorize him, scholars and critics have largely neglected him.

This barren critical landscape might imply to the casual observer that Everett's work is less significant, intelligent, or artistic than that of other, more celebrated contemporaries, but readers familiar with his canvas know differently. "Absurdist," "esoteric," and "angry" have all been tags used to characterize his fiction. His style, his voracity, his vision, his humor, his critiques—his experimentalism—all evoke names such as Ralph Ellison, Thomas Pynchon, Kurt Vonnegut. However, his writing is also reminiscent of Jonathan Swift, Ishmael Reed, and Horace (yes, he is, after all, very fond of Greek and Latin classics). Just when it seems that he could best be described as a contemporary Aristophanes, he pulls a Euripides out of his bag of tricks. One might accuse him of being a modernist or a postmodernist—or both at the same time. Where does one place a writer whose canon includes revisions of Dionysius, Medea, Tiresias, Icarus, *and* the John Wayne film *The Searchers* and at the same time attempts to write a "history" of African Americans penned by the most notorious political foe of integration in post–World War II America, South Carolina senator Strom Thurmond? Whose work reflects the influences of French poststructuralist theory (especially semiotics), the philosopher Ludwig Wittgenstein, Ralph Ellison, and Laurence Sterne? Who has written a children's book as well as a new introduction to *The Jefferson Bible*? Everett steadfastly refuses to be pinned down. If in our quest to review and analyze our contemporary writers, to place them into anthologies and college classes, we miss that Everett's work captures both the comic and the tragic in the human experience—the sacred and the profane—then we are doing literary studies and ourselves a monumental disservice.

BIOGRAPHY

Everett was born Percival Leonard Everett on December 22, 1956, in Fort Gordon, Georgia (outside of Augusta) to Dorothy Stimson Everett and Percival L. Everett, Sr., then a U.S. Army sergeant, who later became a dentist. The younger Everett's middle-class upbringing in Columbia, South Carolina, was by his own account "average." Unlike many of his literary peers, however, Everett spends little time discussing his personal past, or his personal present. He rarely

gives interviews, and even during some of these he playfully hides from the interviewers' probing questions. He has said that his father instilled in him a love of education. Everett grew up playing blues and jazz guitar, and had a natural affinity for math. While at the University of Miami (AB degree, 1977), he studied biochemistry and philosophy. For a while he was a high school math teacher in Florida, but he soon turned his attention to writing. While completing his A.M. degree in writing at Brown University, Everett began working seriously on his first novel. The novel, *Suder,* was published in 1983. In the years since, Everett has published over twenty books, including novels, short story collections, poetry, and a children's book, *The One That Got Away.* This description of the volume of his work neglects the numerous short stories, reviews, and essays found in *Callaloo.* He has been the fiction editor of this journal of African American and Afro-Caribbean literature and criticism since 1994. This same journal devoted an issue to Everett and his work in 2005. Included in the journal were personal reflections on Everett, poetry celebrating him, an interview, and criticism. Several reproductions of Everett's abstract paintings were also displayed in the opening pages.

His work, despite the relative dearth of published criticism, has nonetheless garnered him several prestigious awards. In 1984 he received the D. H. Lawrence Fellowship at the University of New Mexico. His novel *Zulus* received the New American Writing Award in 1990. By 1994 he had also received the Lila Wallace–Readers Digest Fellowship and the Woodrow Wilson Foundation Award, followed by the PEN/Oakland–Josephine Miles Award for Excellence in Literature based on the collection of short stories *Big Picture* (1996). Everett continued to gain accolades after the publication of *Erasure,* for which he was awarded the Hurston/Wright Legacy Award in 2002. This particular award Everett found ironic given the plot of *Erasure* and its criticism of publishers seeing writers only in terms of race. Other prominent honors have included the American Academy of Arts and Letters Award for Literature in 2003 and a PEN/USA Literary Award (for *Wounded*) in 2006.

His prolific creative writing output remarkably has taken place at the same time that Everett has successfully pursued an academic professional career. He taught at the University of Kentucky and the University of Notre Dame and chaired the American Studies Department at the University of Wyoming in Laramie for one year. In 1992 he began teaching at the University of California at Riverside, where he chaired its creative writing program. In 1998 he joined the faculty of the University of Southern California, where in 2007 he became Distinguished Professor of English. Throughout his tenure at various schools he has taught literary theory, creative writing, film, and American studies. His academic life has not slowed down his production; on the contrary, he has managed to use the institutional framework as material for his novels and as a text itself—critiquing its idiosyncrasies and social constructions.

But his work has not been confined to writing novels, editing *Callaloo,* and teaching college students. In his spare time, Everett works on his ranch in Southern California. He landscaped the area, fosters its gardens, and cares for its animal life (of the mule variety especially). His skill as a carpenter has no doubt helped create and maintain the property, which includes an art studio. And when he cannot be found at USC, on his ranch, or at his second home in Vancouver, British Columbia, Everett can be located in Montana, fly-fishing. Everett's passions, hobbies, jobs, and talents are as varied and as multifaceted as his novels. Clearly, Everett never stops.

EARLY NOVELS

Everett's first novel, *Suder* (1983), was published when he was only twenty-six years old. The work follows the recent trials of Craig Suder, a third baseman for the Seattle Mariners whose career is suffering from a batting slump. His personal life is equally unsuccessful. This is where the reader meets him; thereafter, the novel's course follows him on a series of humorous picaresque adventures after his team puts him on leave. In a story structured as a revisioning of the Icarus myth, all

of Suder's misfortunes are necessary steps as he heads toward a moment of enlightenment and fulfillment.

Unable to find happiness with his talents and depressed by his marriage, Suder, like most picaresque figures, leaves what he knows in order to rediscover himself, to find meaning in his life again. He brings his Charlie Parker album, *Ornithology,* along on the odyssey. The novel's comic tone implies that such a journey can only happen if Suder realizes the absurdity of human existence. Everett designs the novel to suggest there is no direct relationship between the random events of our lives and happiness. The novel's counterpoint sections between the past and the present emphasize this. The flashbacks of Suder's memories of childhood do not provide answers, nor do religion or other institutions, nor does baseball. The blues and jazz at least offer him comfort and a sense of the historical tradition that he shares with other African Americans.

Meaning comes to Suder through his relationships and interconnectedness with others. He soon finds himself caring for an elephant named Renoir and for Jincy, a young white girl, both orphans of a society that sees no value in them. By choosing to create a community with these other rejected beings, Suder embraces his compassion rather than his despair. The eccentricity of this "family" only heightens the absurdity of the novel and of life.

Throughout the novel, bird and flight imagery are associated with Suder and his self-reflective journey. After finding a home for Renoir and Jincy, he soon believes that he can fly: "I decide that flying is a distinct possibility and that being a bird is well worth my while." He decides to be "bird-like" after having given up playing the saxophone which has allowed him to connect to the spirit of Charlie "Bird" Parker. Now that he has found real connection to Renoir and Jincy, he can let the saxophone go, but his desire to feel the power of the music does not leave him. By the end of the novel, Suder is flying. His ability to transcend the pain and futility of his previous life frees him physically from a world that didn't believe in his individuality or his worth. The final scene, and its thematic illustration, is reminiscent of the folktales of "flying Africans" who refused to be defined by the limitations of America. It also echoes the final scene in Toni Morrison's *Song of Solomon,* in which Milkman Dead flies. Though Everett's novel is very different tonally, both the *Song of Solomon* and *Suder* use the image of flight as a trope of African American survival in the face of nihilism.

Everett's second novel, *Walk Me to the Distance,* is as different as from the tone of *Suder* as any novel could be. Published in 1985, the novel follows David Larson, an easterner who has moved to Wyoming. Like other famous heroes of western stories, he seems to be a typical loner. But in comparison with the heroes of dime novels of the past or Hollywood westerns, Larson seems especially adrift. He has not come west to reclaim some romantic ideal of American rugged individualism, to escape the civilization of the East, or to find a stronger connection to the natural world. Instead he has come west because it represents stories he remembers from his youth, although the reader senses that he could easily have wandered anywhere. His apathy is an indication of Larson's own inability to reconcile his feelings about himself and about America after his return from Vietnam.

After a series of relationships with prostitutes, he begins a friendship with a widow called Sixbury. Sixbury owns a sheep ranch and lives an isolated life with her mentally disabled son, Patrick. Like Larson, she lives seemingly with little purpose, hiding her own and her son's disabilities from the world. Larson's sympathy for Sixbury and his own desire to find some meaning in his life encourages him to think: "Maybe I just need someone to protect. And maybe, for once, I want to do the choosing."

Shortly after, Larson finds himself caring for an abandoned Vietnamese seven-year-old girl, whom he calls Butch. For a short time he feels finally like he is protecting someone, until Patrick kidnaps and rapes the child. In a moment of rage and anguish members of the community exact justice on Patrick. And Larson is haunted by his participation in the event made worse by the pain he must see Sixbury endure. Eventually Sixbury, Butch, and Larson find a measure of contentment

together as a family. While Larson does not follow the typical mythic path of the western hero, Everett still imbues him with a sense of honor and duty, qualities commonly found in these literary characters. Because the landscape of America has changed, so must the typical hero. By reconnecting Larson to the community, to a family, Everett also critiques the typical western that celebrates heroic individualism at the expense of human relationships.

Cutting Lisa (1986), Everett's third novel, examines two pivotal moments in the life of John Livesey, an obstetrician. In the prologue we are introduced to Livesey as he is being called in to "aid" in a caesarean section. When John arrives at the hospital he discovers that Gertrude Thompson's husband has performed the surgery himself on his wife. Not because she or the baby were in danger and needed the operation but because, as he tells Livesey, "I wanted to bring my child into the world." Initially disgusted by Thompson's decision, Livesey begins to reflect on the man's motives and is disturbed to discover that he finds the "action somehow beautiful." This early moment in the novel is recalled later as Livesey's own life begins to spin out of control, and he interprets Thompson's act as one of bravery and assertiveness, and even a desire to protect, in a world that no longer makes sense.

Following the death of his wife, Livesey goes to spend time with his son Elgin, a college history professor, and his wife, Lisa. The couple has a daughter, Katy, and they are expecting another baby. During the visit, Livesey becomes closer to his granddaughter and starts a relationship with a beautiful younger woman, Ruth. Livesey soon begins to suspect that his daughter-in-law, Lisa, is having an affair with another man, Greg Yount, and that the child she is carrying belongs to him. He discusses with his friend Oliver whether or not he should tell his son. Oliver suggests to Livesey that the only way to protect his family is to kill the other man. The idea begins to take root in John's mind; he develops a hatred of Yount—seeing the man as an intruding disease or "parasite"—as his own instinct to protect his family grows stronger.

Unable to kill Yount, he develops a new plan that is inspired by Thompson's delivery of his own child. Having finally realized how much he loves his family, he decides to take matters into his own hands. The novel closes with Livesey declaring: "Now I love Lisa" as he prepares to abort the child she is carrying to ensure that his family stays together. Clearly it is a controversial conclusion; nevertheless, Everett's characterization of Livesey argues that the doctor's choice to protect the sanctity of the family redeems his past.

Everett's next novels, *For Her Dark Skin* and *Zulus,* both were released in 1990. *Zulus* won Everett the New American Writing Award the same year. Leaving behind the realistic style of *Walk Me to the Distance* and *Cutting Lisa,* Everett sets this novel in the future and develops his characters in a modernist tone and in fantastical settings. The protagonist is Alice Achitophel, who knows that, unlike most of the women in her society, she is able to bear children. An unlikely outlaw, Alice Achitophel (who is always called by both names) has refused to follow the law that dictates that she be sterilized (nor has she lost the weight that the government has demanded).

In this postapocalyptic dystopia, the government controls everything: what people eat, their bodies, language, history. Everett's metafictional voice in the novel reflects the conflict between control and freedom. Each chapter opens with the author outlining the alphabet: "A is for Achitophel," "B is for blood," and so on. Each letter represents objects as well as historical events and literary characters. As the characters of *Zulus* fight to gain freedom over their own lives, Everett reminds us through the structure of the narrative and his authorial stance that language itself is a tool used for controlling identity and knowledge.

The novel also attempts to deconstruct several "master narratives." It critiques the notions of democracy and freedom, faith and individuality, gender and history. We have seen some of these topics before, but this novel, more than any other of Everett's works to this point, pursues these themes in a writing style that

reflects the poststructuralist attitudes that its subject matter seem to promote.

Once the government discovers that Alice Achitophel is fertile, her life is in danger. Her boss at the Division of Religious Adjustment, Theodore Theodore, aids her in her escape, as do a group of revolutionaries. She soon becomes close to one of them, a man named Kevin Peters. As the novel progresses, Alice Achitophel's self-confidence grows. She finds courage and pride in believing she can have a baby, and her weight (over 300 pounds) makes her feel unique—the characteristics that might have made her a nasty joke in our contemporary world make her a hero in Everett's. The novel seeks to address the conflict between constructed cultural values and real human worth. Eventually the novel reminds us that things are often not what they seem—reality and fiction are difficult to disentangle—and that we too cannot trust too deeply in the narratives that we are presented with.

GOD'S COUNTRY *AND* WATERSHED

In 1994 Everett published two more novels, *The Body of Martin Aquilera* and *God's Country. God's Country* marked Everett's first significant critical success. The work also continued to develop Everett's portrait of the West. The seriocomic work follows the adventures of Curt Marder, whose home has been destroyed and his wife kidnapped by a gang. Everett has admitted that the novel is a parody of the classic John Ford–directed western *The Searchers.* But suffice it to say, Curt Marder is no John Wayne. He does, however, enjoy the same privilege of race. Despite Marder's obvious flaws—including his unethical behavior, ignorance, and greed—he expects that he will prevail and that his "whiteness" guarantees him status and success in the American society of the old West ("white always moves first"). These characteristics are highlighted in his relationship with Bubba, an African American tracker whom Marder hires ostensibly to find his wife (though he seems to care more about his dear, departed dog). Bubba is clearly more intelligent, more honorable, and more capable of making a just civilization out in the "Wild West" than is Marder, but as a black man in America, his second-class status denies him the rewards that being a just man should bring. Everett uses the western landscape of the past to represent "the West" as a culturally dominant image of whiteness and American exceptionalism that transcends the nineteenth-century frontier, thus allowing him to critique current attitudes toward race and the "other." When Marder asks Bubba, "Christ, man, it's 1871, ain't you people ever gonna forget about that slavery stuff?" the contemporary reader catches the grim joke and winces at the same time.

Though the novel's subject is serious, its tone and sometimes its plot, decidedly are not. There is the oft-repeated gag about Marder's despair over his dog (to the neglect of his lost wife), and halfway through the novel most of the characters, including Marder, have forgotten about the kidnapped wife that they are supposedly tracking. Throughout the work there are numerous examples of wordplay and puns. When Bubba and Marder consider the direction of their search, Marder asks Bubba: "Where does the road go? You know?" Bubba answers: "Goes to the town of Cahoots." And Marder's reply: "You think they're in Cahoots?" Everett makes fun of the simple and stereotypical characters and language of the westerns, but the same time, it is clear that he appreciates and even respects the western American heroes and myths (as well as the myths and heroes of western European antiquity).

The figure of Bubba suggests Everett's esteem for these stories. Bubba is an honorable man in an unjust environment. A loner who is quiet, introspective, and mysterious and follows his own brand of ethics and individual responsibility, Bubba recalls the typical western hero, the "last good man." He is also reminiscent of Everett's previous western hero, David Larson, in *Walk Me to the Distance.* This type of hero role should have been occupied by someone like Marder because of his race, position, and situation. Instead, as Leland Krauth points out, Everett creates a character and narrator who "talks too much." His story, like the story of European-American exploration and movement

across the West, takes center stage. Everett reminds us that the history of the West is still primarily a white American one. However, unlike the whites who have power and privilege—including even the pathetic Marder—Bubba defies the barbarism and irrationality of men who "settled" the West. These include characters like the preacher, Simon Phrensie, who continually tries to molest the child Jake (a young girl who has been masquerading as a boy to protect herself).

Everett also portrays historical examples of brutality, such as General George Custer. Custer and his men slaughter peaceful and honorable Native Americans, who elsewhere in the novel prove to be the most conscientious and sensitive community (though they like to play jokes on Marder). It is not the agents of the civilized world that protect the innocent and fight for justice in this version of the western. Instead it is Bubba, himself a victim of corrupt American institutions and ideals, who emerges as the heroic voice. When Jake is threatened, Bubba sends her to stay with Native Americans who will protect her—a reversal of *The Searchers,* where "savages" have raped and killed one young white woman and kidnapped another.

Everett embraces the conventional plot of the western in *God's Country* but overturns it through his characterization of Bubba. Indeed, as Leland Krauth put it in *Callaloo,* "what Everett finally does is recuperate the Western hero." We may never learn his story, but Bubba represents all the lives that were a part of western history but have remained unknown merely because they did not accommodate the images of the American mythic West.

Everett's absurdist characters and situations do not obscure his deeper concerns and criticisms. As this work and other of his novels illustrate, Everett asks his readers to acknowledge the profound ironies in American history, especially in its continued portrait of race and race relations. It is Marder who acts with disregard to others, cheats, lies; it is Phrensie who tries to rape a white woman; it is Custer who is a murderer. Everett's novel asks readers to see beyond the representations of historical truth in America and the racial and ethnic stereotypes still promoted by many of its institutions.

Everett again examines the image of the American West in the novel *Watershed* (1996). This time Everett considers the West of contemporary America but still questions the status of western American mythology and race. The tone of *Watershed* is a little less satiric than that of *God's Country*; nevertheless, Everett still manages to critique American history. He more directly engages historiography and its impact on the lives of non-Europeans in the settling of the West. As the critic William R. Handley points out, it is as "revisionist" of western history as *God's Country* but far less interested in the formulaic western story. *Watershed* is a narrative about many of the issues that still haunt the West: land rights, environmental concerns, and the legacy of the federal government's treatment of Native Americans.

Echoing the arguments by Native American writers such as Leslie Marmon Silko and N. Scott Momaday, *Watershed* directly links ecological problems of the present to the sins of the past. When the book was reprinted in 2003 it included a new introduction by Sherman Alexie, the critically acclaimed author of *Reservation Blues, Smoke Signals,* and *The Lone Ranger and Tonto Fistfight in Heaven.* Alexie argues for Everett's "right" to address Native Americans in his work, despite the fact that he himself once believed "only Native American writers should write about Native Americans." Reading *Watershed* changed his mind. Alexie discovered that Everett highlights the complexity and humanity of his Native American characters as equally as he does that of his African American protagonist, Robert Hawks. Moreover, the novel illustrates the ineluctable connection of blacks, natives, and whites in the history of the West, and makes even Alexie, as he admits, rethink the ways he sees the world. Alexie goes on to suggest that the reason that Everett has been virtually ignored by critics (white and black alike) is because of this ability, which is "threatening" to people's perceptions.

The novel begins with the murder of two FBI agents on the fictional Plata Reservation, an allusion to historical events on the Sioux Pine Ridge

Reservation in the 1970s (the FBI mystery here further alludes to the fictionalized version of these events in the 1992 film *Thunderheart*). Hawks, a scientist, is involved in disputes about land and water rights. His work as a hydrologist foregrounds a larger philosophical and cultural conflict in the novel between the rational world of western discourse and the language of nature embodied by the Native Americans. While Everett is careful not to draw the Native American characters as "noble savages," he reminds the reader that they might know more than scientists about the natural world that Hawks is examining, since they have inhabited it for thousands of years. Interspersed throughout the narrative of the novel are quotations from legal documents and land treaties as well as scientific representations of molecules. Alongside these are Native American chants and poetry. This juxtaposition shows that the authority of language—scientific and legal—belongs to the white Western world, enabling it to strip Native Americans of their land, their culture, and their way of life, ultimately robbing native experience and language of any epistemological agency. The Native American literature and oral history as it is structured in Everett's text should be as relevant as the western discourse and should be considered equally valid. However, readers know that the privileged narratives of American institutions still dominate the landscape. Hawks not only has to decide where he stands politically in this struggle, but also must choose which way he will see and understand the world.

Like the Plata Indians, Hawks has been colonized, but he has internalized it, so that he views himself through the lens of whites. He emerges as a descendant of Ralph Ellison's *Invisible Man.* In later novels, Everett will directly allude to Ellison and his work; in *Watershed,* the reference is more subtle. When the novel opens, Hawks is holed up in a church, reflecting on his name and identity as he begins to share his story with us. The novel's opening is reminiscent of the prologue to *Invisible Man.* When Hawk first arrives on the Plata reservation, he has little direction in his life and initially becomes politically involved out of a kind of listlessness. Like the "invisible man," however, he is enlightened by the novel's end, though unlike Ellison's pre-civil-rights-era character, he transforms into an activist. After discovering the government's involvement in the contamination of the water on the Plata reservation (in a development reminiscent of Silko's *Ceremony*), Hawks knows what he must do. Some aspects of Hawks's stance remain ambivalent by the end of the novel; all he knows with certainty is that his "blood" is his own. However, he has taken a "first step" according to Michael K. Johnson, in understanding "the real effect fiction play(s)" in his life.

Ellison's narrator in *Invisible Man* calls history a "boomerang." Hawks might be comfortable with such a description. In the midst of the conflict between the federal government and the Plata, he recalls his own personal history—one that was scarred by the violence of the civil rights movement in the 1960s. Hawks realizes that both personal and public history is affected by the forces that seek to control or oppress difference in our culture. He also understands that a society's historical memory is no more objective than an individual's interpretation of his or her experiences. His most poignant discovery is the knowledge that past pain will continue to impact the present, no matter how much we attempt to hide from it.

FRENZY, GLYPH, *AND* ERASURE

Frenzy (1997) moves into a completely different landscape and genre from that of *God's Country* and *Watershed.* Everett's retelling of the Dionysius myth is captivating and sensitive at the same time it is comic. Interested in understanding the emotional and passionate life of humans, Everett's Dionysos sends his page, alter ego, and "chronicler" Vlepo out into the world to seek all human experience. A blending of Greek tragedy and fantastic fiction, Everett conjures a tale that illustrates the most ancient and meaningful of stories: the relationship between gods and mortals.

Vlepo travels all over the world and over great expanses of time in his quest to bring Di-

onysos records of human anger, disillusionment, beauty, and love. Along the way, we encounter figures from Greek myth such as Tiresias, Ariadne, Pentheus, and Orpheus and Eurydice. Each story, each character offers a glimpse at human mystery and sublime suffering. Yet Dionysos, whose presence excites and ignites human passion and "frenzy" cannot emotionally comprehend the stories that Vlepo offers him. When Vlepo asks his god and master why Eurydice is crying after Orpheus and she have made love, Dionysos answers: "the sorrow is that I do not know." The most human tragedy in the novel, it appears, belongs to Dionysos, who longs for a mortal existence, for love, and even for death.

Everett had visited Greek myth before in his retelling of Medea in *For Her Dark Skin.* That novel had not found much critical success, but Fiona McCrae, Everett's editor at Graywolf Press, believed that *Frenzy* would build upon the reception of *God's Country* and *Watershed.* When readers and some reviewers questioned an African American writer's choice of Greek myth as his subject matter, *Frenzy* seemed doomed as well. Everett's race played a significant role in the marketing of the book, according to McCrae, and readers stayed away. McCrae suggests that it was publishers' reluctance to sign books written by African Americans on topics not considered "black" and the consequent shelving of *Frenzy* in the "African American Studies" sections of bookstores that directly led to Everett's scathing portrait of the publishing world in his novel *Erasure.* What many failed to see in *Frenzy* was Everett's portrayal of ordinary human events across time and space, shared by men and envied by gods—common tragicomic moments that bind together diverse cultures and peoples.

Everett dedicates *Glyph* (1999) to McCrae. A delightfully nonrealistic tale, *Glyph* may have been written with the intent to present little evidence this time around that could be used by booksellers to place the work in the African American literature section of the local Barnes & Noble. Its initial pages (including "Deconstruction paper") open with words (and even characters) out of Laurence Sterne's *Tristram Shandy.* The narrator begins his story before his birth. The baby, Ralph Townsend, is able to achieve this not by a literary device but because he is a preternatural genius. By the age of ten months he can understand every word that his parents are saying—which is saying a great deal because they are intellectuals: "my father was a poststructuralist and my mother hated his guts." Ralph's father is a failed academic, whose career is so uneventful that by age eighteen his son is overshadowing him.

Before he is two, Ralph is a writer and mathematician, but he has also decided by this point to stop talking. He prefers literature to the spoken word, primarily because he already realizes how inexact language can be. His favorite "bedtime story" is *Tractus Logico Philosophicus* written by the philosopher Ludwig Wittgenstein (but he has also enjoyed "Goldilocks and the Three Bears"). Like any good deconstructionist, he mistrusts language and cultural narratives, but he likes playing with the word "bear" and its homophone "bare." After all, he is still teething, so children's stories amuse him.

He writes letters to Roland Barthes and to Wittgenstein and by the age of four the child genius becomes the object of an attempted kidnapping. Both the government and academia want him (though for different reasons). Little else happens in the novel as far as plot is concerned. Interspersed throughout are puns, attempts at poems, allusions to philosophy texts and titles, and semiotic diagrams.

Not only a satire of academia, jargon, and child-rearing in the late twentieth century, *Glyph* is a whimsically digressive tale that honors Everett's favorite thinkers and writers, not only as intellectual influences, but as larger-than-life characters. A section of the book called "Ralph's Fictive Space" could have easily been called "Percival's Playroom." The reader should not look for meaning, for any profound epiphany. Everett collects his favorite literary toys here and invites the reader on a playdate, complete with footnotes from the babysitter. Everett told the interviewer Kera Bolonik that *Glyph* is the work "closest" to his "heart."

Little Ralph (an allusion to one of Everett's most noted influences, Ralph Ellison) is, by the

way, African American—a detail that both Ralph and Everett want to keep a secret from us as long as possible (remember those pesky booksellers?). In a reflection that seems to be looking forward to Thelonious Ellison in *Erasure,* Ralph tells us that he has kept this hidden from us because the language and the image would have altered our perceptions:

> Have you to this point assumed that I am white? In my reading I discovered that if a character was black, then he at some point was required to comb his Afro hairdo, speak on the street using an obvious, ethnically identifiable idiom, live in a certain part of town, or be called a nigger by someone. White characters, I assumed they were white (often, because of the ways they spoke of other kinds of people) did not seem to need that kind of introduction, or perhaps legitimization, to exist on the page. But you, dear reader, no doubt, whether you share my pigmentation or cultural origins, probably assumed that I was white.
>
> (p. 54)

Ralph Ellison was often accused of not being "black enough" by the generation of African American writers that came after him. He argued against such labels most of his career, once telling critics that his definition of freedom was the power to write any way you wish to. Plagued by some of the same criticism and reaction to his work, Everett connects the two works immediately following the publication of *Frenzy*—which had been reviewed poorly, seemingly on the basis of Everett's skin color and the racial and cultural difference of his topic, Greek mythology—to Ralph Ellison. Any reader looking for "meaning"—especially "authentic" African American meaning—will have a difficult search in *Glyph.* Julian Wolfreys, in his equally playful critical essay, suggests the novel may be a "theoretical exploration of the exhaustion of narrative" and that the only story worth understanding is the one of "endless mutability, the endless difference of narrative." This may be the closest "reading" of the text done by a critic.

Erasure (2001), the novel that grew out of the complaint about Everett's own experiences as an African American in the literary world, ironically became his most critically successful work to date. Like his protagonist, Thelonious Ellison, Everett is a writer and academic whose work has a hard time finding an audience—primarily, according to his editor, because no one knows how to market a book written by an African American author whose subject is not urban gangs and violence but Greek mythology and drama. In *Erasure,* one reviewer of Ellison's latest effort writes: "The novel is finely crafted, with fully developed characters, rich language and subtle play with the plot, but one is lost to understand what this reworking of Aeschylus' *The Persians* has to do with the African American experience." The preceding words could easily be applied, or even have been applied, to Everett's own novels. Disturbed at finding his novels only in the African American Studies section of the bookstore, Ellison falls into professional despair.

This creative and racialized angst is further exacerbated by the appearance and subsequent success of Juanita Mae Jenkins's novel, *We's Lives in da Ghetto.* Jenkins achieves almost instant celebrity, and an Oprah Winfrey–like talk show host invites her to discuss her artistic style and personal experience on television. Jenkins (who it turns out is not from the ghetto after all) fictionalizes a life that conforms to widely held stereotypes of black life. It doesn't matter to the readers ultimately that it isn't a "true" autobiography; it's truer than Jenkins's factual biography because it is what white middle-class America accepts as "true."

Dumbfounded and disgusted by Jenkins's success, Ellison decides to write an "autobiography" of his own. Motivated by financial reasons (he needs to care for his mother), Ellison also wants to pull one over on his audience. As the son of a doctor, and being a well-educated and erudite writer himself, how could anyone believe that his attempt will be accepted as fact? Nevertheless, *My Pafology,* the "true" account of Stagg R. Leigh, becomes a runaway best seller and tops critics' "best of" lists. What Ellison meant as a parody is read as an accurate depiction of black life; "raw and honest," it's "the kind of book they will be reading in high schools thirty years from now." The book goes on to be optioned for a film and considered for a prestigious award. And in a moment of cosmic irony, Ellison is

chosen to be on the selection committee. No one notices the outlandish comic situations in *My Pafology,* nor do they notice the character, Stagg, is an allusion to the infamous Staggerlee or Stackolee of African American urban folktales and toasts.

Of course, we notice these connections, as well as the one heralded by our narrator's names: Thelonious and Ellison. His first name, an allusion to the jazz pianist Thelonious Monk, acts as a reminder that our character, despite all opinions to the contrary, represents African American art; Monk is an icon not only of bebop but also of "cool." As an artist, it may be his isolated manner and his experimental, expressivist, and alienating musical style that Everett wants to signify here. The narrator's work (not to speak of Everett's own) could be described in such terms. But Monk also never compromised his art to fit into commercial tastes.

Ralph Ellison is an even more significant signifier in the protagonist's name. Extending other references to Ellison in his work (including Ralph in *Glyph*), "erasure" implies not only Ralph Ellison's trope of African American invisibility but also denial of any existence whatsoever. History, academia, the media—all the institutions of the novel—try to erase Thelonious Ellison just as publishers have tried to "erase" what Everett writes on the page. At one point, Ellison imagines that he "in fact might become a Rhinehart," referring to the identity-shifting confidence man in the Ralph Ellison novel. Like the narrator in that novel, Thelonious Ellison finds an attraction in someone who has so many identities, so many possibilities, that nothing can pin him down and therefore cannot erase him.

More intimate issues than his acceptance as a writer should be weighing on Thelonious Ellison's mind in the book. His mother's Alzheimer's, his sister's death, his brother's closeted life, and his father's suicide years ago trouble him, but he is unable to express his confusion and pain about them because these are also not "proper subject matter" for African American writers. By denying him the freedom to write what he wants, the world denies his humanity—which is what oppressors must accomplish in order to erase the oppressed. His act of literary minstrelsy may be ultimately empowering, but the conclusion of the novel leaves us with a picture of Thelonious Ellison continuing to "sound" like the urban slang-speaking Stagg. Is the disguise permanent? Or is it another layer of masking and signifying on Ellison's part?

Erasure is possibly the most discussed of all of Everett's works. It has also elicited the most honors, including the Hurston/Wright Award, given to African American writers. Everett considered not accepting the award, given his critique of this type of pigeonholing of writers in the very novel he was winning the award for. Most critics have paid particular attention to the marriage of theory and practice in this work (as in *Glyph*) and to Everett's deconstruction of identity as well as language ("race/erasure"). His editor, McCrae, called him "a genius" and an "original," recalling that Everett only had to think about his own experiences to express the anger found in this book. And the critic Margaret Russert's fine study of the novel emphasizes *Erasure*'s mimetic quality and its semiotic play, particularly Everett's use of the *X* to "signify" both being "x'd" out and the "signing" of the *X* that many illiterate slaves and African Americans used as a "signature." Like *My Pafology,* its novel within a novel, *Erasure* is already appearing in university classes and becoming an important critical standard in African American literary studies.

AMERICAN DESERT *AND* STROM THURMOND

Everett released two more novels in 2004, *American Desert* and *The History of the African-American People (Proposed) by Strom Thurmond,* which he cowrote with his USC colleague James Kincaid. *American Desert* continues Everett's attraction to the western landscape and its mythic narratives, though the novel also satirizes academia and the media. But this western landscape is a broader picture than we have seen in other Everett novels set in this region. Here Everett uses the western desert as a metaphor to describe the barrenness of its civilization, its narratives, and many of its inhabitants.

There are probably more jokes and puns about heads in this novel than in any other work in English (maybe any other language as well). The novel's hero, a college professor at USC who teaches Old English, is depressed about his professional failures (a rejected manuscript and a looming tenure decision, for example) and his personal life. He decides to drown himself in the ocean, only to fail at this plan as well: driving to the beach, he is killed in a car accident where he is beheaded. Miraculously (fantastically) he is still alive, as he proves when he sits up in his coffin—looking like the scarecrow from *The Wizard of Oz*—at his own funeral. He gives new meaning to the intellectual "talking head," as his situation makes national "headlines."

Everett especially lampoons the media in the novel. The news anchors and reporters threaten and manipulate people to get a sensational story. When Ted resists an interview he is accused by the on-camera personality, Barbie Becker, with trying to undermine the "fabric of society" by refusing to concede to the needs of the media. The media's ascendancy as an institution on a level with religion and higher education makes it a target in the novel as yet another citadel of abusive power. By 2004 this was hardly newsworthy, but Everett suggests the media is clearly responsible for many of the present ills in this "American desert."

One of the other narratives responsible for the condition of America is the conservative Christian church. Touted as a "resurrected man," Ted must endure the continual scrutiny of fundamentalists, who quickly decide that his "miracle" is really the work of the devil. Ironically unable to embrace the inscrutable, the leader of the church, Big Daddy, has Ted kidnapped so that he can determine the validity of Ted's life or end it for him. Ted's "resurrection" is viewed as a threat by the faithful—mainly to their power. They do not see miracles anymore. They do not believe in mystery; they believe in the dollar. Little separates them from the government or the media in the way they conduct business or treat people.

Ted, however, is given a new chance at life. He has become a braver individual. And he sees what is truly essential in having a fulfilling life. He had been willing to kill himself rather than deal with the disappointments he faced. After his "death," he is resurrected to a certain degree. He reconnects with his family and with humanity in general, and discovers that while he is no hero he is a "decent man." It is this understanding that transforms him in the novel from a satirical joke to a representative of Everett's themes. As absurdist as this episode has been, Ted emerges as a flawed yet soulful human capable of courage and compassion in the crazy wasteland of modern America.

Everett's other major publication of 2004, *A History of the African American People (Proposed) by Strom Thurmond,* nearly defies description. A satirical epistolary parody, the novel imagines a series of exchanges among Senator Strom Thurmond, publishing executives, and members of Congress and their aides. Everett and Kincaid are metafictional characters who are the ghostwriters of the work. Seen through the letters, Thurmond is a visionary caretaker of the African American way of life, a protector of their history. Besides the obvious targets of the satire, Everett and Kincaid critique the intellectual and artist visionary central to the romantic ideal of American literary heroism. Thurmond fashions himself as one of these men; the audience of the novel knows the truth, but the work should also act as a cautionary tale about passively following the vision of any leader, including those who control even with the best of intentions.

The parody of the publishing world and academic language and life here is far more bitter. Some of the memos between the "ghostwriters" and the editors at Simon & Schuster reflect dissatisfaction with the way publishers "handle" authors and what their "bottom line" is. Much like Everett's criticism of publishers in *Erasure,* in this work editors have little intellectual, critical, or artistic consciousness. And like the journalists in *American Desert* they are most concerned with whatever sensational story they can get their hands on. They are most interested in selling books that feed Americans' vision of themselves, even if it promotes fiction over fact;

Everett and Kincaid have a great deal of fun inverting this characteristic in their portrait of Thurmond.

Their metafictional satire might prove to be the "truest" picture of Thurmond ever produced. It may even be a profound illustration of the limited way America still discusses race relations. It is hard not to see both the humor and an indictment of history of the American mind when the list of things (seriously) that Thurmond can contribute to a historiography of African American life is "what they eat and how" and "their fondness for rape."

WOUNDED *AND* THE WATER CURE

Everett's next two novels took a more serious and unsettling path than did his previous satirical work. They are also less driven by plot. *Wounded* (2005), like many other Everett novels, is set in the contemporary West. Although Everett's West is not without its complexities and disturbing realities, it has offered—at least for a few moments in earlier works—some solace and tranquility from the world's problems. Everett has always questioned the fiction of the West as a psychological retreat as well as a natural one, but some part of Everett or his characters still had some faith in its power. In *Wounded,* however, the image of the West is one that can no longer sustain the American myth.

Violence pervades all western narratives, even Everett's. But the almost clichéd and unrealistic plots of western stories—of cowboys and Indians, outlaws and heroes—gives way here to bloodshed and to villains that exist on the evening news. These are not situations and criminals that can be contained when justice comes to town. The narrator, John Hunt, finds himself mourning the loss of his wife at the same time a young gay man has been murdered by one of his ranch hands. The novel, which takes place in Wyoming, dramatizes a version of the 1998 Matthew Shepard murder in order to investigate the strains of prejudice and fear that remain deeply buried in the western soil.

Hunt himself has been the victim of such fear and loathing, but as he points out, the only "place anyone ever called me nigger to my face was in Cambridge, Mass." Hunt's point, of course, is that racism is an American institution, practiced not exclusively by "rednecks" and "cowpokes" but also by people at Harvard. As the novel unfolds, Hunt's mind slowly changes to reconsider the growing hatred and intolerance as it is practiced in the West. What emerges in his mind is a paradoxical picture of the West as a region celebrated for its beauty and spiritual edification but savagely settled by men who spoke about freedom and democracy but ensured it at the expense of destroying anyone who did not look like or think like them.

As he does in *God's Country,* Everett attempts to recapture the typical hero of the American West—the quiet loner who has come west to escape but also embodies the honor and moral courage of a bygone era. Hunt, like his counterpart Hawks in *Watershed,* moves from indifference to commitment in *Wounded,* ultimately standing up for the weak and the innocent. Hunt also fights for his "vision of the West and his allegiance to (its) unique and beautiful landscape" as Michael K. Johnson argues (p. 9). Hunt has come west to leave behind the institutions and "civilization" of green, ivy-covered New England. He loves the wild desert, the land of the West, and "maybe what the land did to some who lived on it."

The romantic and spiritual associations of the West in Hunt's mind are tested when he considers that the topography is also an attractive site for homophobes, political extremists, and white supremacists. Hunt's battles in the concluding chapters of the book are against racism and prejudice, but they are also about defending his image of America. This same war will be fought by Ishmael Kidder—though under very different circumstances—in Everett's next novel, *The Water Cure.*

Published in 2007, *The Water Cure* is one of Everett's most controversial novels. The title is a reference to torture tactics employed by the U.S. government against terrorism suspects. Far angrier and darker than any other of Everett's

books to date, including *Wounded,* the novel confronts the policies of the George W. Bush administration and the resulting domestic trauma following 9/11 and the U.S. invasion of Iraq. Though the plot revolves around one man's intimate grief, the tone of the novel and its clear allusion to contemporary politics is a very public and direct critique of America. Everett is not his more usual playful self, and the work is a haunting reflection of America's continued loss of moral ground. The relationship explored between private and public trauma in *Wounded* exposes even more rawness here. The book's narrative is even more fractured and difficult to follow than in previous works. It is unclear even to some readers whether or not this is a fantasy of a grieving father or an actualized revenge.

The personal tragedy that illuminates the larger political picture is the emotionally devastating rape and murder of the eleven-year-old daughter of Ishmael Kidder, the novel's protagonist. Kidder's despair leads him to plot revenge against the suspected killer. Kidder's life before the loss of his child had been fairly average and quiet. Divorced from his daughter's mother, Charlotte, he is a loner who writes romance novels. This character biography, including having a retreat in Taos, New Mexico, is very similar to that of Rawley Tucker in Everett's short story "True Romance." Both characters are cynical about love and romance, yet still believe in mythic innocence. For Kidder it is the child who was taken too early, and for Tucker it is the pristine natural beauty of Taos.

Kidder's inability to accept that even the most universally understood image of innocence has been brutalized and destroyed propels him into a philosophical crisis. Despite his generally pessimistic and critical attitude toward people, he expected a certain shared moral and ethical respect and understanding. His response is not only the act of a father in despair, but also the plan of a man at odds with society's growing apathy and disregard for common humanity. Throughout the novel, Kidder writes dialogues, bits of romance plot, and poetry at the same time that he quotes Plato and the Bible. His rage seamlessly merges with these attempts not only to fathom what has happened but also to recover some beauty and some universal meaning.

Considering the caustic bite of some of Everett's previous novels, it might appear that this is a concept that he would satirize or at least question, but in fact there are strains of romantic sentiment in many of his works. Kidder's demand for justice is a desire to restore honor and meaning to his world. The loss of his daughter and this desire to find moral truth again also reflects his attitude toward his country in the years since 9/11. In the midst of a metafictional moment during which Kidder/Everett discusses writing, the reflection on beauty and truth is interrupted by a confession that he is "ashamed" of his country. Its image as the icon of democracy and justice is tainted by its "rape" of the world and its torturing of possibly innocent individuals. As a self-described "jaded" writer, he nevertheless still wants to be "happily naïve" when it comes to believing in honor and heroism. This same faith in American heroism resonates in the character of Bubba in *God's Country.* The seething anger of many of Everett's works exists not because he rejects the American mythic narratives, it is because he resents that America is not fulfilling its promise.

Kidder's plan to achieve justice includes kidnapping, torturing, and perhaps killing the man responsible for his daughter's death. He believes this will restore meaning to his once ordered and sensible life. The reader sees less of this story than glimpses of the past with his daughter and Kidder's wrestling with the inability of language or philosophy to describe and explain his pain. He conducts his torture at the same time he is trying to finish a manuscript for his editor. The more involved he becomes with his violent plan, the less able he is to express himself through the written word. As he begins to turn into a monster, he loses all sense of meaning; his identity, his name, and his past are all unstable constructions. The novel never resolves his conflicts or dilemmas, but its questions are profoundly unsettling in a world experiencing massive violence and loss. Readers are also never certain whether this is in the imagination of Kidder or if he actually carrying out the plot.

Unlike most of Everett's protagonists, Kidder is unable to find connections to people. Those possibilities are lost to him when he realizes he was not there enough for his daughter and when his torture of another human being pushes him irrevocably away from humanity. There is perhaps some limited hope for Kidder: his relationship with his ex-wife is renewed and strengthened by their shared tragedy. But it is unclear whether or not this will have the power to save him.

SHORT FICTION

In addition to the novella *Grand Canyon, Inc.*, Everett has published three collections of short stories: *The Weather and the Women Treat Me Fair* (1987), *Big Picture* (1996), and *Damned If I Do* (2004). Each collection includes stories that appeared elsewhere, including in *Callaloo*. Several of the short stories could be described as antecedents of the novels. A number of the stories are exceptional works on their own, including "The Appropriation of Cultures," "Cerulean," and "Big Picture." Some characters appear in several of the short pieces in *Big Picture,* providing continuity and a developing story cycle. But most of Everett's short fiction is realistic and direct, unlike many of his novels (especially his later ones). Nevertheless, many of the same themes appear, and the requisite satire makes a showing in almost every short tale.

"The Appropriation of Cultures" has gained the most notoriety. Its opening sequence of an African American jazz musician being asked to play "Dixie," the unofficial anthem of the Confederacy, for a group of southern white male college students is thought to be based on some of Everett's own experiences when he played in a band. The moment when the musician, Daniel Barkley, begins to sing the words, "feeling the lyrics, deciding that the lyrics were his, deciding that the song was his," he frees himself and his art from the past. It is a scene often referred to when critics and reviewers discuss Everett—his epiphany as a writer who has the ability to transcend expectations of race and use the material of the past, and all of America, as his canvas.

As varied and unique as Everett's work is, it illustrates some common primary concerns, including the necessity of human connection, the failure of history, the moral obligation to protect the weak and the innocent, a critical respect for myth, a fondness for Western philosophy, and a desire to quietly celebrate the grandeur and beauty of the western landscape. Everett is also engaged in highlighting America's continued inability to look at race and ethnicity without creating damaging stereotypes. And one would have to agree with the critic William Ramsey's observation that "anger in comic guise pervades Everett's fiction." In the years since his first novel appeared, his criticism of such narratives as the American Dream has deepened and has become more personal and poignant. Clearly Everett is losing patience with America's inability or unwillingness to address its social paradoxes and bitter ironies. As an artist and as a cultural critic, Everett continues to try any method to get his "beloved country" to wake up and change its ways. Behind his often resentful mask and numerous artistic disguises lingers a cowpoke optimist looking for the horizon.

Selected Bibliography

WORKS OF PERCIVAL EVERETT

NOVELS

Suder. New York: Viking Press, 1983.

Walk Me to the Distance. New York: Ticknor & Fields, 1985.

Cutting Lisa. New York: Ticknor & Fields, 1986.

For Her Dark Skin. Seattle: Owl Creek Press, 1990.

Zulus. Sag Harbor, N.Y.: Permanent Press, 1990.

The Body of Martin Aquilera. Seattle: Owl Creek Press, 1994.

God's Country. Boston: Faber & Faber, 1994.

Watershed. Saint Paul, Minn.: Graywolf Press, 1996.

Frenzy. Saint Paul, Minn.: Graywolf Press, 1997.

Glyph. Saint Paul, Minn.: Graywolf Press, 1999.

Erasure. New York: Hyperion, 2001.

Grand Canyon, Inc. San Francisco: Versus Press, 2001. (Novella.)

American Desert. New York: Hyperion, 2004.

A History of the African-American People (Proposed) by Strom Thurmond, As Told to Percival Everett and James Kincaid. With James Kincaid. New York: Akashic Books, 2004.

Wounded. Saint Paul, Minn.: Graywolf Press, 2005.

The Water Cure. Saint Paul, Minn.: Graywolf Press, 2007.

COLLECTED SHORT STORIES

The Weather and Women Treat Me Fair: Stories. Little Rock, Ark.: August House, 1987.

Big Picture: Stories. Saint Paul, Minn.: Graywolf Press, 1996.

Damned If I Do: Stories. Saint Paul, Minn.: Graywolf Press, 2004.

OTHER WRITINGS

The One That Got Away. Illustrated by Dirk Zimmer. New York: Houghton Mifflin, 1992. (Children's book.)

Foreword to *Making Callaloo: 25 Years of Black Literature.* Edited by Charles Henry Rowell. New York: St. Martin's Press, 2002. Pp. xv–xvii.

Introduction to *The Jefferson Bible,* by Thomas Jefferson. New York: Akashic Books, 2004.

re:f (gesture). Los Angeles: Black Goat, 2006. (Poetry.)

"Thirty Years of *Callaloo.*" *Callaloo* 30, no. 1:315 (winter 2007).

CRITICAL AND BIOGRAPHICAL STUDIES

Bell, Bernard W. Review of *Erasure. African American Review* 37, nos. 2–3:474–477 (summer–autumn 2003).

Bell, Madison Smartt. "A Note on *God's Country.*" *Callaloo* 28, no. 2:343–344 (spring 2005).

Berben-Masi, Jacqueline. "Percival Everett's Glyph: Prisons of the Body Physical, Political, and Academic." In *In the Grip of the Law: Trials, Prisons, and the Space In Between.* Edited by Monika Fludernik and Greta Olson. Frankfurt, Germany: Peter Lang, 2004. Pp. 223–239.

Handley, William R. "Detecting the Real Fictions of History." *Callaloo* 28, no. 2:305–312 (spring 2005).

Johnson, Michael K. "Looking at the Big Picture: Percival Everett's Western Fiction." *Western American Literature* 42, no. 1:26–53 (spring 2007).

Kincaid, James. "Collaborating with the Sphinx: On Strom." *Callaloo* 28, no. 2:369–371 (spring 2005).

Knight, Michael. "My Friend, Percival." *Callaloo* 28, no. 2:292–296 (spring 2005).

Krauth, Leland. "Undoing and Redoing the Western." *Callaloo* 28, no. 2:313–327 (spring 2005).

Marcus, Greil. "Invisible Scam." *Bookforum,* winter 2002. Available online (http://www.bookforum.com/archive/win_02/marcus.html).

McCrae, Fiona. "Frenzy." *Callaloo* 28, no. 2:328–329 (spring 2005).

Monaghan, Peter. "Satiric Inferno." *Chronicle of Higher Education,* February 11, 2005, p. 30.

Ramsey, William. "Knowing Their Place: Three Black Writers and the Postmodern South." *Southern Literary Journal* 37, no. 2:119–139 (2005).

Russett, Margaret. "Race Under 'Erasure' for Percival Everett, 'A Piece of Fiction.'" *Callaloo* 28, no. 2:358–368 (spring 2005).

Wolfreys, Julian. "'A Self-Referential Density': *Glyph* and the 'Theory' Thing." *Callaloo* 28, no. 2:345–357 (spring 2005).

INTERVIEWS

Bolonik, Kera. "Mules, Men, and Barthes: Percival Everett Talks with *Bookforum.*" *Artforum* 12, no. 3:52–53 (October 2005).

Kincaid, James. "An Interview with Percival Everett." *Callaloo* 28, no. 2:377–381 (spring 2005).

Masiki, Trent. "Irony and Ecstasy: A Profile of Percival Everett." *Poets & Writers* 32:3 (May–June 2004).

WILLIAM HOFFMAN

(1925—)

William L. Frank

HENRY WILLIAM HOFFMAN was born in Charleston, West Virginia, on May 16, 1925. According to Hoffman, the history on his father's side of the family is fairly slender (W. Hoffman, series of personal communications, 2005). He knows that the family originally came from Frankfort, Germany, and one of the early settlers founded the first paper mill in the United States. The family initially settled in what is today Gunpowder Falls, Maryland. During the Civil War Hoffman's great-great-grandfather served in the Army of the Confederacy. Hoffman's own father, Henry William Hoffman Sr., served in World War I, earning a battlefield commission. After the war, although his father offered to send him to college, Henry Hoffman went to work with the Hercules Powder Company in Beckley, West Virginia.

Julia Beckley and Hoffman's father were living in Beckley at the time, where he was working in a coal mine. The two, not quite from opposite sides of the tracks but in the view of Julia's mother close to it, met at a local YMCA dance and were married shortly after. With the unions and coal mine owners in constant conflict Hoffman's father decided the family fortunes might be better in Charleston, West Virginia, where the coal baron and mine owner James Kay, Hoffman's maternal great-grandfather, was both well known and extremely influential. Henry Hoffman went to work immediately at the Consolidated Coal Company, a firm founded by James Kay.

In general, William Hoffman and his sister Janet, three years older, recall the early years in Charleston with fondness and pleasure. At the end of the hilly street they lived on there were numerous caves above the house, and Janet and Bill would spend many afternoons playing and hiding in the caves.

The end—to both the Hoffman happiness and the marriage of Julia and Henry Hoffman—was sudden and swift. Bill Hoffman's recollection, echoed by that of his sister, Janet, is that his father lost his job at the earliest sign of the impending Depression. The family was forced to move into the grand home of the great-grandfather at 1419 Virginia Street in Charleston. They were given the third floor of the home, ruled by their grandmother, Julia's mother, who never could accept Henry Hoffman as a suitable husband for her daughter. Henry Hoffman had by then started a small local trucking company, but he lost it as the Charleston banks began to go under and close. He tried several different lines of work. At one time he sold bonds, and Bill Hoffman recalls feeling a sense of excitement because he thought his father was selling bombs.

Hoffman thinks that his father deserted the family in the early 1930s, about the same year that young Bill started kindergarten in the public school system of Charleston. After that separation, Hoffman recalls, every so often, once or twice a year, as he was walking home from school, a car would pull up beside him, his father would get out, and the two would carry on a short conversation before his father would again drive off, leaving young Bill alone on the sidewalk. During that period Henry Hoffman was living and working in Baltimore, Maryland, not in coal mining per se but with the grading of coal ore.

Deprived for all practical purpose of his father around the age of five, and of his great-grandfather when he was nine, Bill Hoffman appears to have accepted and played well the hand he was dealt. None of the remaining years of the decade of the 1930s is recalled by him with anything except pleasure. Only the references to his mother's health cloud any of his teenage

years. Despite the years of the Great Depression, he recalls that his grandmother always had plenty of money. She always had a new car and a maid seven days a week.

The Depression had little if any effect on the lifestyle of the clan. In general these early years were happy ones. There were, Hoffman remembers, the usual experiences of boyhood, ranging from fights with the neighborhood bullies to strict rules laid down and enforced by his grandmother, such as nothing but church on Sundays, when his friends were permitted to go to the local movie theater in the afternoon. Both Janet and Bill recall summer vacations to beaches in Maryland and to Virginia Beach, and later to beaches in Florida, with the grandmother driving the large family car herself. When the three—or four when Julia was well enough to accompany them—were not at the beach during the summer, Bill would spend the summer vacation period, until he was around fifteen years old, on a farm in Pocahontas County, West Virginia, owned by a Scottish friend of James Kay. It was here that he began his love affair with horses and riding.

The mother that Janet and Bill remember during these years, roughly from 1935 to the summer of 1939, remains to them a shadowy, hazy figure. She was usually either away in Baltimore receiving medical treatment for her depression, or home occasionally confined to bed, but often playing her piano, reading, or greeting frequent visitors to the home. There were visitations to Baltimore, with the children and their grandmother riding the C&O Railroad from Charleston to Baltimore.

One morning in midsummer of 1939 Bill walked downstairs to the grandmother's living room on the first floor and found her in conversation with a colonel from Kentucky Military Institute, Colonel Charles Richmond, the school's owner. Without even introducing Bill to the officer she turned to him and said, "Bill, how would you like to go to Kentucky Military Institute this fall?" So the fall of 1939, the same year of Germany's march into and occupation of Poland, found Bill at KMI, a small, private, prestigious, and expensive school.

Of his first year in military school he recalls it being "awfully tough in many ways, but I loved it! I took a lot of hazing in my freshman year." One of the things he loved was that KMI had a three-month resident semester—from New Year's to Easter—in Venice, Florida. The entire corps of cadets and the faculty traveled by train to their "southern residence" to escape the frigid winter of Lyndon, Kentucky. Although Hoffman had experienced a fairly successful freshman year, passing "most subjects," he underwent an epiphany in his sophomore year. He was promoted to the rank of corporal, and he and other cadets received recognition for academic excellence and achievement in front of the corps of cadets. It was also at KMI where Bill learned to box, took up tennis, and continued to ride horses.

By the time Hoffman graduated from KMI in June 1943 the United States was already fighting a global war on two fronts. Partly because of the military schooling at Kentucky Military Institute and partly because he had flown a plane at the age of fourteen, he tried to enlist in what was then called the Army Air Corps, but he was rejected because of his eyesight and because he did not weigh enough. He then tried to enlist in the U.S. Navy and later the Merchant Marine, but again failed his physicals. The following month he was accepted into the U.S. Army, but his induction was deferred until the end of the summer.

It was not until his arrival at Camp Barkley, Texas, that he was informed he had been assigned to the Medical Corps, an assignment and future duty that would have a profound effect on him for the remainder of his life. Although he weighed only 118 pounds on his five-feet-ten-inch frame, years in military school, swimming, tennis, riding, and boxing had kept him in excellent physical shape.

After Hoffman completed basic training he was sent to El Paso, Texas, for an additional six weeks of advanced training in the army's Tech School. He did so well there that his superiors offered to make him a male nurse, but he declined. At the completion of Tech School—no one called it graduation in those early, hectic days—he received orders to report to Camp

Shanks in Pennsylvania by a future date for further assignment, in all probability bound for England or the European theater of Allied operations.

After a ten-day delay en route, Hoffman took a train north from Fort Lauderdale to Pittsburgh and Camp Shanks, where he reported as ordered. After only a couple of days his outfit was taken by train to Fort Dix, New Jersey, the regular staging area for deployment overseas. As Hoffman tells the story, "One night we were called out and left Fort Dix for New York, there to embark on the *Queen Mary.*" In many ways it was a nightmarish trip: "Everything smelled of vomit, even the food you ate, because vomit was everywhere." (Hoffman was later to use this experience in the third of his World War II novels, *Yancey's War.*) The actual destination of the *Queen Mary* was Edinburgh, Scotland, and from there they went by train to Southampton, England, to await further orders. The unit literally lived on a dock at Southampton for just under a week, June 3 to June 9. It was, of course, on June 6 that one of the largest and most carefully planned invasions in the history of the world began, so Hoffman with his medical unit left for Normandy on what the military refers to as D-Day plus three, or June 9.

Hoffman's unit had by now been assigned to the Ninth Army and consequently saw action in the fall of 1944 in Belgium and Holland. They participated in the famous Battle of the Bulge and continued their advance in crossing the Ruhr, the Rhine, and the Elbe rivers. Although Bill Hoffman had four battle stars by May 1945, he had paid a heavy price for each one. He freely admits he was in "pretty bad shape" at war's end. Like Tyree Shelby in *The Trumpet Unblown,* Hoffman spent several weeks in a military hospital in France and came home on a hospital transport ship. He was next sent to a military hospital in Battle Creek, Michigan. After treatment he was given a thirty-day leave and went home to Charleston, West Virginia. More or less "recovered," he received orders to go to Fort Meade, Maryland, where he received his honorable discharge from the U.S. Army on February 23, 1946. He was still only twenty years old, with a lifetime of war experiences crammed into the previous two years.

THE HAMPDEN-SYDNEY/FARMVILLE/ CHARLOTTE COURT HOUSE YEARS

A scant two days after his honorable discharge Bill Hoffman enrolled in Hampden-Sydney College in southside Virginia, only a few miles south of Farmville off U.S. Highway 15. The college's strong Presbyterian ties, coupled with Hoffman's own strict Presbyterian upbringing, constitute a second major influence on Hoffman and subsequently on his fiction.

Hoffman's reasons for enrolling in Hampden-Sydney, probably the third major influence on his fiction, were threefold. First, his family knew much of the college—two cousins and an uncle had previously attended it—and its strong Presbyterian ties appealed especially to his grandmother. Second, he had initially wanted to attend the University of Virginia at Charlottesville, about sixty miles northwest of Hampden-Sydney and therefore closer to his home in Charleston, but discovered he could not begin at UVA until the following fall. Third, Hampden-Sydney was eager to regain its student population base, which had been more than decimated by the war, and established a special class for World War II veterans that began in February, offering two courses, English I and Algebra-Trig, meeting six days a week for two college credits. As Hoffman later said, "It seemed like the logical place to go." At the time Hoffman attended Hampden-Sydney, students did not select majors or minors. The college offered two degrees, a BA with an emphasis on the humanities and language, and a BS with emphasis on the sciences. Hoffman studied for the BA degree, and in addition to Greek he also studied Latin, French, and German. Taking eighteen hours per semester instead of the usual sixteen, Hoffman graduated in three years instead of the usual four.

Taking a taxing eighteen-hour course load kept him busy, both during the six-day school week and over what was left of a short weekend. Still he found time for a fairly heavy schedule of

intramural sports in volleyball, softball, and tennis. (He played tennis and swam into his seventies.)

Almost before he was ready for it graduation rolled around, and in May 1949 his beloved "Nana" drove to Hampden-Sydney from Charleston to attend his graduation. Hoffman's grades had earned him the right and privilege to receive the first diploma and give the valedictory address, but Hoffman, always diffident, turned down the honor, describing himself at that time as "gun-shy."

Hampden-Sydney College has always enjoyed a reputation for producing doctors, ministers, and lawyers, and Hoffman assumed that after graduation he would attend graduate school and study law. There were no lawyers in the Hoffman-Kay family, although a few older cousins had chosen law as their profession. Because Hoffman had graduated from Hampden-Sydney in three years, he still had a year remaining on his GI Bill, and he decided to enroll in law school at Washington and Lee University in Lexington, Virginia. Along with two close friends, Hoffman arrived at Washington and Lee in the fall of 1949. Upon arrival he discovered that he could defer the law school for a year and take any undergraduate courses he was interested in. He, therefore, elected courses in French, German, philosophy, music, and writing, and as he explains it, "I got hooked on writing." Another member of that same writing class was Tom Wolfe, whose hometown at that time was Richmond, Virginia. Wolfe and Hoffman have remained friends ever since, and when Tom Wolfe gave the commencement address at Longwood College in Farmville in 1987, he told this author that Hoffman's short stories were by far the best written in that class in that year.

Bitten by the writing bug in that one year, 1949–1950, at Washington and Lee, Hoffman has never stopped writing, and in the course of more than fifty years has published fourteen novels, four collections of short stories, and numerous uncollected short stories in top literary quarterlies and magazines. Knowing he needed additional study and training, Hoffman returned to Farmville for the summer of 1950, spending his time reading, writing, and swimming at nearby Goodwin Lake in Prince Edward County. It was almost an idyllic time, and great preparation for his next educational experience, the already well-known Writers Workshop at the University of Iowa, under the direction of Paul Engle. But it was another faculty member at Iowa, Ronald Verlin Cassill, who took Hoffman under his wing, gave him much-needed encouragement, and worked with him on almost a daily basis. But Hoffman did not last out the year. Despite Cassill's encouragement and recognition—he even got a scholarship for him—Hoffman felt lonely and out of place there. He describes it as "cold" and "friendless," even though he met and became lifelong friends with a former member of the Army Air Corps from New York City, Wally Kaminsky. Hoffman left Iowa in April 1951 and returned once more to the comfort and safety of his grandmother's house in Charleston. There he continued to read voraciously and to write, again an important and formative period.

It was during the summer of 1951, following his "escape" from Iowa, that Bill walked out on the porch of his grandmother's home in Charleston to find a body sleeping on his front porch. The body belonged to a former classmate from Iowa, James Weaver of Eugene, Oregon. Weaver was on his way to Washington, D.C., because he had heard of a "Veterans Preference Program" there that guaranteed a job to World War II vets. Weaver convinced Hoffman to join him, and the two set out for Washington. They both did indeed get jobs under that program, at the Department of Defense. Probably because of Hoffman's proficiency in several languages he was hired as a code breaker at a GS-5 level.

The work at the Defense Department was neither challenging nor interesting. Bored again—although on the payroll, on some days he literally did nothing—he resigned that position and decided to go to New York City and look up Wally Kaminsky.

Before looking up Kaminsky, however, Hoffman knew he again had to find employment. He got to New York City in the late afternoon and checked into the Ambassador Hotel. The next day he scanned the want-ad section of the *Times*

and zeroed in on two jobs that appealed to him, one with the New York Public Library and one with the Chase National Bank. Hoffman interviewed for both jobs the same day, first with the library. While the woman who interviewed him was encouraging, she told him she had to consult others. He went immediately to Chase, where he was hired on the spot to work in their foreign department on the night shift.

There is no telling how long such an arrangement might have lasted, and what different turns Hoffman's writing career might have taken, if the academic dean at Hampden-Sydney, Dean Wilson, had not called him one early September morning (1952) and offered him a faculty position teaching English 101 to incoming freshmen. Bill taught at Hampden-Sydney for the next seven years, until 1959.

Initially Hoffman rented a small apartment in Farmville about seven miles from Hampden-Sydney, but when he married Alice Sue Richardson, of Bluefield, West Virginia, on April 17, 1957, they rented a house in Farmville. When Sue became pregnant they realized the growing family would need more space, and they bought a house in the same neighborhood. The Hoffmans had two daughters born to them while residing in Farmville, Ruth Beckley, born on September 23, 1958, and Margaret Kay, born on November 7, 1961.

In 1964 the Hoffmans bought a large historic home in nearby Charlotte Court House in Charlotte County, Virginia. The brick residence, called Wynyard, was built in the 1830s and came with stables, outbuildings, and fifty acres. They were delighted with the beauty and the freedom of the charming home. The acreage afforded them ample room to indulge in what had been for Hoffman a lifelong interest in horses and riding, dating from his childhood summers in Kentucky.

Never wealthy but usually comfortable, Hoffman continued to write, publishing four novels in the next six years. With (by today's standards) modest advances from Doubleday, usually $10,000, the Hoffmans "got by because they'd paid off the farm, raised their own food, drove second-hand cars—and because Bill taught at Hampden-Sydney and also managed to make money in the stock market" (Span, p. 15).

By the mid-1980s the Hoffmans were middle-aged, the children were graduating, and other interests were beckoning. Margaret Kay graduated from Randolph Macon Women's college in the spring of 1984. Sue last participated in "riding to the hounds" in 1986, her decision to retire aided by the falls and broken bones she had endured on several occasions. Bill continued to ride and played tennis and swam into his late seventies. In the early 1980s the Hoffmans were invited by friends to visit on the shore of Chesapeake Bay. Both fell in love with the land, its people, and the scenic beauty. They soon purchased property just out of Mathews, Virginia, in Mathews County on a spit of land with water on three sides. Here they built Wyndor, their vacation home, where they entertained frequently as they had initially done in Charlotte County.

They owned both a powerboat and a sailboat, although Sue was never wholly comfortable with the sailboat, wondering what she would do if Bill took sick or had an accident and she had to sail the boat alone. They also had crab pots "in their front yard," and Hoffman would don his waders and the Hoffmans and their guests would enjoy the fresh seafood.

But with the Hoffmans approaching their mid-seventies the trips to Mathews became fewer and fewer and the upkeep of the Charlotte Court House property more demanding. Knowing it was time to cut back, they sold Wyndor in 1998. As of the summer of 2007 the Hoffmans continue to live on the farm in Charlotte Court House as they have for the past forty-seven years. They attend the local Presbyterian church, where both have served on various governing and service boards and committees. Bill still walks mid-morning to the post office for the *Wall Street Journal,* the *Charlotte Gazette,* and whatever news comes from his agent, his publishers, or his children and grandchildren. He continues correspondence with his many friends and with newfound readers who e-mail with questions and comments. Occasionally he gives readings at the Library of Virginia in Richmond or serves on panels dealing with writing, publishing, or World War II at universi-

ties in the area. They both look forward to occasional trips to Richmond to visit their daughter Ruth Beckley, and they drive to North Carolina to visit their other daughter, Margaret Kay, and her husband, Neil Huffman, and the Hoffmans' three grandchildren.

The marriage between Alice Sue Richardson and Henry William Hoffman has been a strong one. This writer asked Sue if, married to a writer with an unpredictable income, she ever worried about money. Her reply to the question, although brief, speaks volumes: "No, I honestly didn't worry about money. We didn't live high on the hog, and I trusted the Lord."

THE WAR NOVELS: THE TRUMPET UNBLOWN *(1955),* DAYS IN THE YELLOW LEAF *(1958), AND* YANCEY'S WAR *(1966)*

In a long introduction to his article on two of Hoffman's war novels in *The Fictional World of William Hoffman* (2000), the noted poet and critic George Garrett creates a war novel genre and places Hoffman's work squarely in it:

> In the years immediately following the war, and continuing on into the 1960s—thus written and published with first the Korean War and then the War in Vietnam serving at once as background and refresher course—there were a lot of war novels, mainly dealing with World War II, written by Americans and for Americans. ... William Hoffman's two novels dealing directly with World War II unquestionably belong in their company and at the highest rank of the American fiction coming out of World War II.
>
> (p. 89)

Although *The Trumpet Unblown* is actually Hoffman's second novel, it is his first published novel. Early reviews of it mentioned Hemingway as one of the recognizable influences, and Hoffman, himself, has said he read Hemingway, Thomas Hardy, and Stephen Crane. In an early scene in Hemingway's *The Sun Also Rises,* the protagonist, Jake Barnes, picks up a prostitute on his way to meet Lady Brett Ashley for dinner. In the cab on the way to the restaurant, Jake puts his arm around the woman:

> She looked up to be kissed. She touched me with one hand and I put her hand away.
>
> 'Never mind.'
>
> 'What's the matter? You sick?'
>
> 'Yes.'
>
> . . . .
>
> 'You're not a bad type,' she said. 'It's a shame you're sick. We get on well. What's the matter with you, anyway?'
>
> 'I got hurt in the war,' I said.
>
> 'Oh, the dirty war.'
>
> We would probably have gone on and discussed the war and agreed that it was in reality a calamity for civilization and perhaps would have been better avoided. ...
>
> (pp. 15, 17)

The protagonist of Hoffman's novel, Tyree Jefferson Shelby, a blue-blood son of Old Virginia, also discovers that war is indeed dirty. Attached to a medical corps as was Hoffman himself in World War II, Shelby has witnessed unspeakable scenes of horror, mutilation, and death. In one particularly gruesome scene Shelby and his unit discover a locked barn with an overpowering stench. Forcing the doors open, they find ceiling-high layers of rotting bodies. The German SS had rounded up Slavic displaced persons—men, women and children—stacked them, doused them with gasoline, and set them on fire.

Knowing that the German villagers had witnessed the atrocity, Shelby's unit rounds up all the villagers and makes them bury, with their bare hands, each limb and piece of flesh recovered from the barn:

> It took the rest of the day to complete it, and there was much sickness before it was over.
>
> Finally it was finished, and Coger let the Germans go back to their neat little village with its fine old church and religious paintings. The men of the outfit washed as soon as they could to get the smell off, but there was not enough water in the world to wash off that stink. Runcer even forgot to put guards on the alcohol that night.
>
> (p. 200)

But Shelby's very soul is annihilated not only by such horrors, but also by the daily and deadly routine of caring for the sick, the wounded, the dying:

> He fought it as best he could. At first he thought it had something to do with the sleeping capsules and tapered off. That didn't help much. He tried some of the old dreams, but the dreams would no longer come. He talked to himself, saying that what he was doing was as valuable as anything the infantry was doing. He told himself he was saving life and that saving life was better than taking it. But deep down he was ashamed of his part in the war, of its safety and triviality, of its lack of possibility for the colorful act. What did you do in the war? I carried bedpan, gave enemas, dipped catheters into mineral oil and slipped them in.
>
> (p. 132)

By novel's end Shelby has made it home to Richmond and his fiancee, Cotton, but only after a long stay at a rehab center. And he knows he could never live a normal life, marry Cotton, and work in his brother-in-law's brokerage house, have children, go to church—war has stripped him of everything he once thought could be his. Perhaps the influence of Crane's *Red Badge of Courage* and his satiric and ironic peom, "Do Not Weep Maiden, For War Is Kind" could summarize Shelby's plight at novel's end.

As George Garrett put it in his essay, "Clearly with this, his first novel, William Hoffman proved himself once and for all a major writer with the touch and judgment of a master. That it is not better known, that it was not honored in its first brief season, must be attributable to the terrible truths it shows and tells."

Days in the Yellow Leaf was Hoffman's second published novel, but it was the first he wrote. It would have been a wonderful sequel to *The Trumpet Unblown,* for what happens to its protagonist, Tod Young, is precisely what readers would expect to happen to Tyree Shelby. Hoffman even gives the fathers of the two protagonists the same first name, Will. Tod is also a victim of World War II, transformed into a killing machine by his experiences and participation in the war. Thus it is no surprise that he ends up murdering his wife and his best friend when he discovers them in a lovers' tryst.

Tod is exonerated by a jury partially bought off by a combination of his father's influence and position in the community. Although the legal system considered him innocent, Tod knows he is indeed guilty and intends to take his own life in expiation for his sins.

Saved again by his father's intervention, Tod agrees never again to attempt suicide. But Hoffman makes it clear in the novel's conclusion that sin/crime must be paid for. Tod will never again draw a free breath and he will spend the rest of his life in an unforgiving hell.

If Hoffman doesn't insist that some sins consist of the unpardonable sin, he surely suggests it. However, it is the unspeakable effects of war that doom these characters, not any rational acts of their own. Again it is war, the blood-bloated monster, that continues to claim its victims. No wonder that Hoffman has said repeatedly to audiences of his readings and talks that he has never gotten over World War II and its effects on him and on his outlook on life.

Yancey's War, published eighteen years later in 1966, clearly belongs to Hoffman's war novels genre. It is the first of his novels to employ the concept/device of the dual protagonist. The novel seems to belong to Marvin Yancey, an average despicable character who has bribed and brown-nosed his way to the rank of officer in his unit. But it is Charles Elgar who satisfies Robert Penn Warren's definition of a protagonist as one who does something or learns something in the course of the plot/action of a novel.

Yancey, the reader discovers early on, is a volunteer. Why would a highly successful, wealthy, and influential person volunteer to join the Army? One learns that he is trying to atone for his earlier misdeeds and mistakes. Yancey has numerous medals and citations from World War I, but the reader discovers that they are fraudulent—awarded because he was the sole survivor of a battle because he had deserted his unit.

Because Yancey is unable to read a map, he takes a wrong turn and leads his men into a town occupied by the German Army. His unit takes refuge in a house and holds off the Germans for several days. Finally a German flame-throwing tank arrives, and Yancey realizes that his choice

is capture or death. In one heroic moment out of a lifetime of cowardice and fear, Yancey climbs onto the slow-moving tank and drops a hand grenade into its exposed turret. Hoffman seems to say that one heroic act of self-sacrifice can redeem a lifetime of mistakes and misdeeds, a theme he will revisit in *The Land That Drank the Rain.*

THE VIRGINIA/WEST VIRGINIA NOVELS, NOVELS OF PLACE: A PLACE FOR MY HEAD *(1960),* THE DARK MOUNTAINS *(1963),* A WALK TO THE RIVER *(1970), AND* LIES *(2005)*

A Place for My Head was greeted by rave reviews. *The Saturday Review* described it as "A powerful novel of the contemporary South, a town's terrifying hour of decision and a man's desperate struggle for self-discovery and love." The protagonist, Angus McCloud, the last of the McClouds for whom the town was named, still keeps a law office but has few clients and therefore little income except for the small check he receives each month from his father's insurance policy.

Although still a relatively young man Angus is deep into alcoholism and is spiritually dead as well. He cannot function until he drinks and when he drinks he is soon in a drunken stupor. He desperately seeks love but is so hopelessly in love with the aristocratic and married Caroline Gainer that he cannot sustain a relationship with anyone else. He takes his occasional date Laura Lee to a country club dance, but when she fights off his advances on the way home he ends up driving twenty miles to the local house of prostitution and engages the services of his regular whore, Rita, apologizing for paying her with a postdated check because he doesn't even have ten dollars in his bank account.

Angus's chance for a major score comes when he acts on rumors of a large chemical plant coming to town. He and an old family friend form a partnership and build spec houes on the few remaining acres Angus still owns. They borrow heavily from the local bank to finance construction and when the chemical plant announces that the plant will be primarily an automated assembly line operation employing fewer than one hundred people, the majority of whom will be lowly paid, unskilled workers, Angus and his partner are unable to sell a single house. During his affluent and promising months Angus has also been seeing and courting Caroline Gainer, almost estranged from her husband, George, president of the local bank that holds Angus's mortgage. Thus Angus's fall is quicker than his hoped-for ascent: within a few weeks, he loses his spec houses to the bank through foreclosure, and he loses Caroline to George:

> He was able to keep going for a while. His life had a certain momentum which pushed him on whether he cared or not. Then, no matter how bad it became at times, he knew he would not die from it. Even the great loneliness didn't kill. After a while the pain dulled somewhat, and he entered a kind of twilight zone in which there were no emotions.
>
> (p. 400)

In many ways *A Place for My Head* is a modern morality tale echoing three earlier American novels. Faulkner's story of the decline of the Compson family told in his Yoknapatawpha Saga is clearly on Hoffman's mind with the loss of huge family landholdings. Secondly, Angus's dream is similar to that of Jay Gatsby in his pursuit of Daisy and the destruction of that dream equally disastrous. Daisy Buchanan in many of her actions is certainly like Hoffman's Caroline Gainer, and when both characters decide to return to their husbands, the worlds of Jay Gatsby and Angus McCloud cave in. The third similar novel is Dreiser's *Sister Carrie*: both novels end with their protagonists' dreams on hold if not wholly dashed, and both novels end with their protagonists looking out a window and "rocking, rocking, rocking," an action that suggests motion without direction or advancement, much like the imagery in Eliot's "Prufrock" such as the "pair of ragged claws" that drift with the tide.

Hoffman's fourth novel, *The Dark Mountains* (1963), was at the time he wrote and published it his most ambitious novel to date. It was probably necessary for him to write both *The Trumpet Unblown* and *Days* to get over the war that had taken so much from him. But *The Dark Mountains* was in his blood. He had inherited from

both father and grandfather his love and awe of coal and the mountains from which men extracted it. So this novel was for Hoffman a given, a peace offering, a commitment to his family, not because it is biographical, although it is certainly that, but because his particular story had to be told, and there was no other storyteller to tell it. There are twenty-eight chapters in this novel, and probably as many significant characters as there are chapters, but there is only one character larger than life, only one character who carved a town out of the wilderness: the coal baron James MacGlauglin, a characterization based on Hoffman's own grandfather, and this is his story.

It is impossible to suggest in a few pages the range, scope, and depth of Hoffman's study of the coal industry in this novel, or to do justice to some of the finest character studies in modern American literature. As W. L. Frank, Jr. has suggested in an unpublished paper on Hoffman's fiction:

> It is difficult to determine just who the protagonist is in the novel. Is it James MacGlauglin, the owner of the mines worth millions of dollars, who rose from nothing? Is it James St. George, James's grandson who loves his mother's father, James, but despises his own father, a do-nothing alcoholic-transplanted Virginia aristocrat? Or is it Paul Crittendon, the college friend of Jamie's who leaves his once wealthy but now financially troubled family in the comforts of Richmond, Virginia to enter the West Virginia wilderness and work in James' coal mines?

When William Hoffman discusses *The Dark Mountains* he invokes Robert Penn Warren's *All the King's Men,* which Hoffman calls "a most beautifully crafted book." Following one of Warren's techniques in that novel, Hoffman too uses the dual protagonist, as Mary H. Davis argues in her unpublished master's thesis. Also, just as Warren used Huey Long to characterize Willie Stark, Hoffman bases the character of James MacGlauglin on Hoffman's own grandfather, an uneducated Scottish immigrant. Hoffman's fascination with coal mining led him to talk at length with miners as well as to visit operating coal mines as he gathered research for this novel. The end result is a highly realistic novel that traces three generations of the coal mining MacGlauglin family during the years of the development of labor unions. It is James MacGlauglin who accomplishes the American dream. He builds his own town, an industry and a dynasty from the rich coal veins of the mountains of West Virginia, and lives long enough to see the decline and fall of his kingdom, first assaulted and weakened by the miners' union, and finally occupied by U.S. Army troops.

A Walk to the River, Hoffman's sixth novel, is told from the first-person point of view by Jackson LeJohn, another "dead man" of Hoffman's worlds. The novel continues Hoffman's scrutiny of small town characters ruined—brought to their knees—by the town aristocracy or influential citizens who control political power and/or wealth. Only LeJohn is not the pilloried character; he is only the instrument in his position as church elder who drives the preacher from the pulpit as well as from their small town of Black Leaf. The novel opens with LeJohn receiving a visit from a fellow member of the local church's Board of Officers, "Doc" Sutter, who informs him that their preacher, Paul Elgin, has been accused of debauching the wife of Lou Gaines, Black Leaf's most prominent citizen and probably the wealthiest man in town. When the full board meets the members are divided between dismissing Paul immediately and taking more time to investigate the allegations to discover whether it is Lou's wife who is lying or whether the minister's denial is true. It falls to Jackson LeJohn, as Church Board Chairman, to undertake the investigation.

Jackson's search for the truth, which takes him to Richmond and North Carolina, reveals that Caroline Gainer and Paul Elgin had been lovers while living in North Carolina. One of Faulkner's characters says, "The past isn't dead; it's not even past yet," and Jackson discovers enough about Caroline's dark past to cast doubt on her charges against Paul. LeJohn's confrontation of the couple reveals to the board and the reader that Caroline had invited Paul into her home in the belief that her husband would be in Richmond overnight. On his unexpected return, she puts all the blame on Paul.

What then is Hoffman saying in this novel? Pride and social position will always triumph over the truth; money is more important than principle and truth; or, as the poet Gerard Manley Hopkins wrote, "The sots and thralls of this world do thrive, Sir, / More than I that spend life upon thy cause." However, the novel does end on an optimistic note: Jackson has learned that he is not as spiritually dead as he had imagined himself to be at the novel's opening. He will, at least, as Eliot says of his protagonist in *The Waste Land,* begin to put his own house in order:

> I bit down on my sadness. I thought that even pain had goodness. A dead man couldn't suffer. To grieve, a man had to be alive and to care about something.

Although twenty-five years separate *A Walk to the River* (1970) and *Lies* (2005), the latter clearly can be grouped here with Hoffman's other novels that focus on place. *Lies* opens with the protagonist, Wayland Garnett, driving no-longer-familiar roads in search of his past and his roots, remembering scenes from his childhood exploding within him and recalling the years between then and now. Wayland, now sixty-five and married to a trophy wife, Amy, twenty years younger, recalls vividly his mother, "a tall woman worked lean," and his daddy, "even taller than the mama, ... a hunter whose step is so silent he ghosts through woods" (p. 12). And he remembers his daddy talking about his father, who had served under General Joe Johnson with the Army of Tennessee all the way to Atlanta, where he "used his pocket knife to hack free the remains of his own leg tore part off below the knee by grapeshot" (p. 12).

Neither his wife nor their daughter, Jennifer, knows anything about Wayland's roots or his family. He has built his new life with them on a series of lies. It has been forty years since Wayland had left Howell County, Virginia, but as he gets closer to the site of his boyhood home "his stomach felt unsettled, and he realized his palms were moist" (p. 67). A lot has of course happened to Wayland in that interval, the forty years suggesting the symbolic number of Ahab's forty years of whaling, Christ's forty days in the desert, and Moses's forty years of exile.

In what Wayland himself describes as "nothing more than a fruitless journey into an uneasy swamp of nostalgia," he continues both his literal and physical journey as well as his metaphorical one back to his roots, with the question always in his mind as to whether or not he could ever share with his wife and daughter the truth of his past. Thoughts, memories, sights, and smells always return Wayland to other parts of his past life—now to his service during World War II and to the horrors of war, hand-to-hand combat, grenades tearing his buddies apart, and finally to a German counterattack.

With his mind once again very much in present time Wayland finally arrives at his destination, Bellepays, the family home of the Ballards, for whom Wayland worked in those early years, along with his brother, his father until he was injured, then his mother and indeed most of the population, both black and white. When Wayland questions the caretaker he tells him, "The Ballards is gone. ... They gone. All the Ballards is, except them lying in the graveyard" (p. 233).

On the road back to Richmond, Wayland sees a panel truck with the lettering "Meekums Plumbing, Heating & Appliances" painted on the side, and recognizes the driver, his former boyhood chum and best friend, Willie Meekums. Willie echoes the caretaker's words to Wayland: "Nothing's the same, Wayland. It's all changed. Ever'thing has" (p. 246). Perhaps Thomas Wolfe had it right all along: You can't go home again.

Lies is much more than a novel about the past, remembrances, and incidents, people and scenes one wishes one did not remember. It is also a novel of courage, endurance, hope for the future, and ultimately acceptance. Wayland may regret much of his past, most of which was beyond his control, but he is also obviously thankful that the journey has been worthwhile, for in the course of it he has learned that he can at last accept all of his past, the lies but also the truths that he has learned from all of his experiences. Like Tennyson's Ulysses, Wayland has not only learned that he is indeed a part of all that he has met but also like Robert Penn

Warren's Jack Burden in *All the King's Men,* he can now live in peace with himself.

THE PHILOSOPHICAL/SPIRITUAL/ETHICAL NOVELS: A DEATH OF DREAMS *(1973),* THE LAND THAT DRANK THE RAIN *(1982), AND* FURORS DIE *(1989)*

A Death of Dreams (1973), Hoffman's seventh novel, is a story of betrayal, disillusionment, and at least partial recovery if not redemption. Although in an interview with this writer Hoffman has said he has never turned a short story into a novel, *A Death of Dreams* is a fully developed version of the short story entitled "Your Hand, Your Hand," originally published in *Carleton Miscellany* (fall/winter 1971–1972) and republished in Hoffman's first short story collection, *Virginia Reels* (1978).

In a brilliant analysis of the novel published in *The Fictional World of William Hoffman,* Dabney Stuart focuses primarily on the role of the narrative voice in the novel, the novel's imagery, and the role that each of the many minor characters in the novel plays, as well as the psychological development of the novel's protagonist, Guy Dion, and Guy's struggles to find himself and to redefine his relationships with others, especially his long-dead father, his wife, and his two grown children. Stuart is especially praiseworthy of Hoffman's management of time in the novel:

> In *A Death of Dreams* he employs a technique similar to Thomas Mann's in *The Magic Mountain.* He records the days and their patterns exactly for slightly over half the novel, the first seven full days of Guy Dion's sojourn at the hospital, the week of biblical creation, the mystical seven so important to ritual.
>
> (*Fictional World,* p. 100)

Although two months form the novel's principal plot element, Guy Dion (read: "dying") is actually on a spiritual odyssey that will eventually take him beyond the walls of the treatment facility. Guy, although not completely spiritually dead, is slowly dying, reminiscent of many of Graham Greene's characters in such novels as *A Burnt-Out Case* and *The Heart of the Matter.*

What follows, at the novel's conclusion, is its high point, particularly for Hoffman readers who have seen in other works the son's search for his father. Guy flees to the mountains where he had grown up. (For Hoffman, mountains are almost always symbols of power, serenity, strength, endurance, and especially hope.) Guy's destination is Boone, the town of his father's birth and initial prosperity.

Now Boone is a ghost town, inhabited, apparently, by one last, lost soul, whom Guy sees pushing a wheelbarrow:

> 'You don't know how glad I am to see you,' Guy said. Motionless, still holding a board, the old man watched. He wore rubber boots, a long brown overcoat torn at the pockets, and under a black felt hat a white scarf wrapped over his ears and tied under his chin.
>
> (p. 315)

In conversation with the old man of the mountain, Wayne Peters, Guy learns that his father, broke and destitute, lost his house when a flood "brought part of the mountain down." Shortly thereafter Guy's father disappeared: "I told your father there was no place for us old men to go, but he wouldn't stay. He was a dreamer." To which Guy replies, "I wanted to make it right between us." Peters's comment upon the fertility of the land returning—reminiscent of the poet Gerard Manley Hopkins's line, "There lives the dearest freshness deep down things"—brings hope to Guy for the future. "The land's coming back," the old man said. "For a while you couldn't grow anything here because of coal dust, but it's washing off. Fish swim in the streams again. In the woods I cleared a garden plot so rich I don't have to fertilize. I grow spuds and beans and trap me some meat. The animals are coming back too."

In response, Guy surprises even himself as he thinks "I must put my house in order," a verbal echo from part 5 of Eliot's *The Waste Land.* At novel's end Guy is more determined than ever to bring order out of chaos in his own life:

> Wind woke him. The building trembled in gusts. It's finished for me, he thought, and the finality of this knowledge seemed as if it would still his life. Like a child he cried, his fingers over and in his mouth to choke the noise.
>
> At the same time a part of him declined to let go. He wiped his face and eyes. He had never quit,

> though many times there was reason to. As each man has reason to, he thought, yet lifts himself for another crazy, gallant stride into—what? He had a vision of an immense ripening field stretching forever into darkness and a ghostly harvest.
>
> "The grass," the old man mumbled.
>
> I am not without resources, Guy thought, and I decline to quit. In the morning I'll stand from this place to find my father. After we're reconciled, I'll think of ways to put my house in order.
>
> (p. 324)

Hoffman's next novel to be treated in this section, *The Land That Drank the Rain,* has frequently been likened by critics to Henry David Thoreau's *Walden.* The novel is unquestionably the most religious, symbolic, and allegorical of any of Hoffman's fourteen novels. There are many direct and indirect quotations from the Bible. It is a story of sin, perverse sex, expiation, atonement and reconciliation.

The novel opens with its protagonist, Claytor Carson, having driven from California to the Cumberland Mountains of Eastern Kentucky. He sets fire to his yellow Eldorado Cadillac, a symbol of the materialism he has recently renounced. The journey from West to East is a symbolic one, as is the torching of the Caddy, reminiscent of Part III of Eliot's *The Waste Land,* "The Fire Sermon." The flames are symbolic of purgatory and Hell and foreshadow the purification ritual that Claytor is shortly to undergo.

Hoffman suggest in this novel that God does indeed work in mysterious ways, for the means to Claytor's ultimate salvation is Vestil Skank, the illegitimate son of any one of a twenty-eight-member high school football team. Abandoned by his mother and shunned by the townspeople, Vestil, one night, cries out to God to give him a new life elsewhere. Clay overhears the petition and takes it upon himself to free Vestil from his bondage as a male prostitute in the local brothel. The prostitutes are "protected" by a thug named Coon.

When Clay enter the house posing as a client in order to give Vestil the money to flee, he is ushered into room thirty-three. From that moment in the novel, Clay becomes a Christ figure. Successful in giving Vestil the money to escape, Clay is intercepted by Coon, who is ordered by the madam, Miss Lily, to mutilate Clay:

> Coon made a double carving motion. Claytor heard cartilage being sawed and parting, heard it not from outside through his ears, but from inside along his bone, skin, throat, and skull. He closed his eyes. He felt metal more than pain. As blood slid over his cheeks and lips, he tasted the steel of the blade.
>
> (p. 243)

Clay is then allowed to leave the hotel, to bear perpetually the scars of his Calvary. And Hoffman reminds the reader of Christ's ascent as Clay makes his slow, painful journey to his home in the mountains:

> Snow fell faster. ... Claytor swayed past mounds which were again clean. ... A tipple appeared virginal. He left drops of blood in the snow. Wind blew flakes that like wafers settled on cinders. ...
>
> His blood sprinkled snow, the stains sinking like red seeds. ... Slowly he gathered his body to rise. He would climb to the house, clean himself, and meet them standing.
>
> (pp. 244–245)

Clay's ascent, the seasonal setting of the book from late fall through winter to the promise of spring, and the allusions and parallels already cited combine to show Hoffman's thematic intention: Redemption and salvation are always possible, but they can come only after expiation, contrition, and sacrifice.

Furors Die (1989), Hoffman's tenth novel and the last of the Virginia/West Virginia/Kentucky novels set in his beloved mountains, is superbly discussed by Jeanne Nostrandt in her highly original and illuminating essay "Sowing and Reaping in *Furors Die,*" in *The Fictional World of William Hoffman.* Nostrandt suggests that the novel has three parts, much like a three-act play, and credits Hoffman's brief stint as playwright-in-residence at the Barter Theatre in nearby Abingdon, Virginia, in 1967 for the novel's organization and structure. She compares Book 1 to a drama's prologue, which both introduces the novel's Wylie DuVal, born to aristocracy, and Amos "Pinky" Cody, born on the wrong side of the tracks, and reveals their already

emerging characters. Book 2, which Nostrandt terms the "rising action," begins with the summer between graduation from high school and entry into college, and ends with the reader seeing both the initial material success of Wylie and Pinky, and the promise of more, much more to follow. At the beginning of Book 3 both men have taken their places as pillars of their community, and "the stage is set for the falling action with its denouement and resolution." Nostrandt goes on to point out that *Furors Die* is the modern version of the comparison and contrast between the two sides of the typical American character: "the cultivated gentleman and the rough-edged pioneer."

The story is essentially a rich and detailed account of the growing up and coming of age of its two main characters. Wylie has it all, and at an early age: new cars, easy girls, a free-swinging country club lifestyle. Pinky, on the other hand, overly influenced by a frenzied and aggressive mother, a member of a Pentecostal religious sect, outwardly chastises and condemns everything that Wylie represents, yet inwardly and secretly covets and envies Wylie's youthful boozing and sexual liberty. Without contriving incidents or encounters, Hoffman skillfully weaves a plotline that keeps the two lives constantly in focus, so that the reader may discover the gradual weighing and shifting of values on the part of Pinky, and Wylie's attempts to dissociate himself from Pinky.

Because Pinky worked through high school as an office-and-errand boy for Wylie's highly successful father, and especially because on one occasion Pinky talked a frustrated and slightly deranged tenant out of holding Wylie's father as a hostage, Mr. DuVal sends Pinky to Wylie's prep school, White Oak, in Virginia, expecting and demanding that Wylie "look after Pinky." Although Wylie bitterly resents the situation, to retain his father's goodwill and financial support he reluctantly agrees to his father's request, thus bringing the two boys into a relationship that allows the seed of future discord to take deep root.

There are no heroes in this novel, at least not in the modern sense of the term. Neither Wylie nor Pinky can really understand each other, and neither makes any solid attempt to try. And yet Wylie, at least on the surface to those who know him, is not an evil person. In the best tradition of the so-called southern gentleman he is a well-mannered, sociable, highly successful businessman, regular in his attendance at church, a better-than-average tennis player, a generous husband. But like too many in a materialistic yuppie society, Wylie lacks a proper sense of values, of morals. As one of his sexual conquests, Trish, tells him, "We're not moral people. ... It's not your moral code that's hurt, it's your pride." Pride, covetousness, anger, and lust—they are all omnipresent in this novel, with almost every character, major and minor, afflicted with each vice to varying degrees. Ultimately, however, *Furors Die* is not only a parable on the seven deadly sins; it is also, and perhaps primarily, a satire on a greedy, materialistic, mechanistic, and sick society—a society, Hoffman warns, as doomed as the grand schemes and airy monuments built by both the Wylies and the Pinkys of our world.

THE MYSTERY NOVELS AND NOVELS OF DETECTION: GODFIRES *(1985),* TIDEWATER BLOOD *(1998),* BLOOD AND GUILE *(2000), AND* WILD THORN *(2002)*

Godfires, Hoffman's ninth novel, continues the implicit examination of degenerative American society that started with *The Land That Drank the Rain.* In *Godfires,* however, the quest is skillfully hidden with one of the cleverest tales of detective fiction of the twentieth century. The reader is immediately plunged into an entertaining and frequently gripping double whodunit. First, who is the "master" who has imprisoned and shackled the protagonist in a remote cabin deep in the recesses of a swamp and who returns almost daily to teach him about God, sin, expiation, grace, and forgiveness? Second, who is the slayer of Vincent Fallon Farr, an upstanding citizen of the county.

The novel opens with a scene that could have been filmed in one of the endless horror and sci-fi flicks that constituted the "in" movies of the 1980s: the narrator is chained to a cot: "I am

hungry and anxious to be fed." Hoffman then plays with the reader for over two hundred pages, describing "the Master" as an erect military figure who wears a Smith & Wesson .38 police special and sheath knife "used to skin deer"

The most complete and important character in the novel other than the protagonist is Rhea, Vin Farr's widow, a beautiful and complex woman haunted by the ancestral pride that is always present in the massive portrait of her mother that hangs in the living room of the Farr mansion. Rhea tells the protagonist that after the marriage with Vin had begun to sour, "I read a lot, even did a little private drinking, nothing like Vin's. I'd sit in the quietness of the parlor sipping whiskey and looking at my mother's portrait, trying to draw courage from her." Rhea, cursed by the family pride, laments, "I considered leaving him. I went to a Richmond lawyer, yet couldn't go through with divorce because my mother would never have. I was a Dillon woman. We won by lasting."

The murder and its solution are only the background against which Hoffman explores, reveals, and condemns the diseased society of big-town and small-town, urban and rural, late-twentieth-century America. As Hoffman adroitly plants clues along the way for both the protagonist and the reader, he is also simultaneously reminding us of the real problems of a materialistic world. By holding a mirror up to Billy and the others through the commentary of minor characters, Hoffman gives us the power that the poet Robert Burns pleaded for: to see ourselves as others see us. Thus we learn that Vincent Farr, as rich as he already was, still wanted more, and would run over whatever or whoever got in his way.

Godfires, then, continues the scrutiny of a society and a world that Hoffman began to explore in earnest with *The Land That Drank the Rain.* Some of the same themes from that work are carried into *Godfires*—private sin, jaded sex, bonded prostitution—but others, equally damning to the individual and to the larger society, are added: the frenzied twentieth-century pursuit of money and of the power and influence that follow; the dangers of hypocritical and obsessive religion; and prejudice toward fellow humans either of a different lifestyle or of another race, whether consciously or unconsciously ridiculed or ignored.

Hoffman's eleventh novel, *Tidewater Blood,* also a Virginia/West Virginia novel, belongs in the detection category rather than the philosophical/spiritual group primarily because of its setting, plot, and themes. The novel begins with a brief prologue in which we learn that a powerful Tidewater Virginia aristocratic family, while gathered to celebrate its 250-year founding, is blown to pieces while standing on the portico of the family mansion. The attention of the investigating authorities is immediately and solely focused on the black sheep of the family, Charles MacKay LeBlanc. Charley, a Vietnam vet, has brought shame and humiliation to the proud LeBlanc family because he had been court-martialed, sent to Leavenworth, and given a dishonorable discharge. He in turn has repudiated the LeBlanc name, taking the name Jim Moultrie, a name he says he took from a tombstone in Tampa, Florida, but it is nevertheless Charley LeBlanc that the reader follows through the novel.

Tidewater Blood has essentially two main threads running through it. First, it is a story of self-discovery and self-realization on Charley's part; one of Hoffman's major achievements in the course of the novel is the deftness with which he transforms Charles LeBlanc from his initial appearance as a dirty, smelly hermit to a human being with daring, courage, ingenuity, and integrity, an evolution that grows on the reader along with the novel. It is the second most important character in the novel, a woman whom Charley knows only as Blackie and who becomes his companion-in-exile, who is largely responsible for Charley's transformation. Secondly, *Tidewater Blood* is also a novel of revenge. Who could have hated all living descendants of the LeBlanc family passionately enough to arrange for their simultaneous deaths?

Through a process worthy of Poe's detective, C. Auguste Dupin, Charley soon reaches the conclusion that the solution to the crime lies not at the LeBlanc mansion in King County but in the coalfields of West Virginia, the source of the

LeBlanc wealth. Branded as a known felon and fugitive, Charley heads for the hills and mountains of West Virginia, hounded by state police from two states, and narrowly escaping arrest on several occasions. It is Hoffman's insistence that no one can master the present without understanding and accepting the past that clearly places *Tidewater Blood* as one of Hoffman's major thematic achievements.

Blood and Guile (2000), William Hoffman's twelfth novel and his third mystery novel, was initially written as an intended sequel to *Tidewater Blood.* The novel opens with a fatal hunting accident when four of the main characters—Walter Frampton (Charley LeBlanc's attorney from *Tidewater Blood*), Drake Wingo, Cliff Dickens, and Wendell Ripley—arrive at Drake's hunting lodge, which is built on land owned by Wendell, to hunt grouse. On the first morning of the hunt, Wendell is accidently killed. The novel ends with a second fatal hunting accident that involves still another of the four main characters, this time Drake Wingo himself. In between these two scenes the reader accompanies Walter Frampton as he tries to determine why the West Virginia authorities are convinced that there is more to the first accident than would appear to the casual onlooker. Walter, with his background in the law and his firsthand knowledge of police and police procedures, senses immediately that the highly intelligent and well-trained sheriff of Seneca County, Sheriff Bruce Sawyers, is a brilliant and determined investigator who will not rest or sign off on "accident" until he is absolutely certain of the events that took place on that lovely fall day on Blind Sheep Mountain.

Besides the half dozen or so major characters, *Blood and Guile* has an equally satisfying number of minor characters to keep building the action and intrigue. There is the beautiful woman, the gay restaurant owner, the tomboy friend become wealthy stockbroker still admired and desired by Walter. There is even a prince, who has purchased Bellerive, the LeBlanc family ancestral home and gardens that are important in *Tidewater Blood,* That purchase will make Charley Le Blanc a millionaire many times over and will make an important contribution to the novel's major themes.

The novel's setting is similar to that found in *Tidewater Blood.* The locale and action move from Walter's office in Jessup's Wharf in the Tidewater area of Virginia, to and through the city of Richmond, and to the mountains of West Virginia, where both the opening and closing scenes take place except for a brief return to Richmond.

Although *Blood and Guile* is a mystery novel, it nevertheless displays Hoffman's characteristically lyrical language, his evocative imagery, and his highly effective characterizations. As a Shakespeare scholar at Virginia's Longwood University once remarked, when Hoffman writes of Tidewater, one can smell and taste the marsh and salt air, and when he writes of mountain scenery and beauty one can see the soar of the eagle and the flight of the ruffed grouse.

For all of the beauty in the novel, there is also much that is sordid and depressing. When it is obvious to Walter that the local authorities believe they may have a murder on their hands instead of an unfortunate and tragic hunting accident, he attempts to question Drake more closely about the events that led to the shooting. Drake is at best evasive and at worst misleading. When Walter confronts Drake with a plausible scenario that would implicate Drake in the shooting as an accessory to murder, and threatens to share his theory with Sheriff Sawyers, Drake orders Walter to return to the cabin so they can discuss the situation and its implications. Walter refuses and starts back down the mountain to the trail where he had left his car. Drake fires a shotgun charge at Walter, close enough to shatter hemlock boughs, causing them to fall across Walter's shoulders and back. "No farther," Drake said. ... "I mean it, Raff." Walter believes there is nothing to be gained by further conversation with Drake: "I kept moving and waited for the shot, my eyes half-blinded, my throat choked, my body shaking and giving itself to gravity's pull. But Drake didn't shoot."

When Walter returns with Sheriff Sawyers and several deputies to where Walter had last seen Drake, they hear a shot close by. Receiving

no reply to Walter's pleas to Drake to surrender, they soon discover Drake's bloodied body "sprawled among a broken section of rails":

> The Savage lay just beyond the outstretched fingers of Drake's right hand. The shot had smashed his chest, and blood thickly scarlet under the sun's brightness had found and flowed along channels of his hunting jacket. His blue eyes flecked with gold were opened upward, his face splattered with bits of blood and of flesh. Already the green flies had found feast.
>
> (p. 222)

The sordidness has revolved around murder, depression, suicide, homosexuality, cover-ups to protect innocent victims, and unjust accusations of crime. After solving the mysteries involved in the plot, Walter Frampton returns to the peace and serenity of Jessup's Wharf, a haven from the materialistic hedonism of American society.

William Hoffman's thirteenth novel, *Wild Thorn,* is the second of the Charley LeBlanc/ Blackie planned trilogy but is in no way a sequel to *Blood and Guile.* It is, as Henry James would say, a well-made novel with a cast of highly credible and challenging major characters together with Hoffman's wonderful assortment of minor characters, plucked from the Main Streets of small rural towns and settlements scattered throughout Virginia and this novel's principal locale, the mountains of West Virginia.

In addition to the major characters mentioned, others include the mysterious financier, Duncan St. George, his son Angus, and Duncan's striking, beautiful, sexy, and much younger wife, Jeannie Bruce St. George. Rounding out the roll call of major characters is Cousin Ben Henshaw, not a blood relative of Blackie but a close friend of her father, who "still lay buried under the collapsed roof of a drift mine more than a mile back in the mountain that had become his assassin and tombstone." Cousin Ben is one of Hoffman's favorite creations in *Wild Thorn,* an intelligent, private, self-educated, wholly self-reliant man, who "could put a bullet in a bat's eye. And he got himself a bunch of medals over in France" (p. 23). As Faulkner said of Dilsey, Hoffman could say of Ben: "They endured."

When *Wild Thorn* opens, Charley and Blackie are in Montana, living peacefully on rented but extensive land that they someday hope to own, riding their beloved horses and drinking in some of the most breathtaking scenery that God ever created. Instinct, a longing for home, or a mysterious foreboding take Charley and Blackie back to Shawnee County in West Virginia, and back to its only populated town, Cliffside:

> Cliffside had been a twenty-four-hour-a-day roaring blast of new wealth and rowdy miners who as fast as they could take it in hand spent the dollars paid to them by the coal companies. When the rich seams thinned or became depleted, the town bled out, not quickly, but a slow hemorrhaging until it became what it was now, a near corpse.
>
> (p. 8)

Charley and Blackie have come home to West Virginia to see Aunt Jessie Arbuckle, again, no blood kin but a remarkable and self-reliant elderly woman who is the principal caretaker of the mysterious Esmeralda, a semi-wild middle-aged woman who literally lives in the wild with no visible means of support or sustenance except for the loving care and generosity of the Aunt Jessies of Shawnee Valley.

But when Charley and Blackie arrive at Aunt Jessie's cabin, they find yellow plastic police tape cordoning off the cabin and a young deputy sheriff who informs them that Aunt Jessie is dead and her cabin and land are a crime scene. Returning to Cliffside for information from the sheriff's office, Blackie runs into an old nemesis, Sheriff Basil Lester, who'll "kiss any ass that's got the shine of money on it." Lester is not only not helpful, he is downright hostile, but he does let them know that the authorities believe that Aunt Jessie was murdered, and their number-one suspect is poor Esmeralda, who was seen running from Aunt Jessie's cabin carrying a package under her arm.

It is the scene of Esmeralda's flight—recalling Caddy's muddy drawers in Faulkner's *The Sound and the Fury*—that sets in motion the principal events in *Wild Thorn.* Charles, Blackie, and Ben are convinced that Esmeralda could not have killed Aunt Jessie under any set of circumstances. Charley in particular sets out to find the truth so that Esmeralda can be set free from Huntington State Hospital, where she has

been locked up since her apprehension by the state police.

Wild Thorn has all of the ingredients for a superb novel of setting, characterization, theme, and detection. While Charley LeBlanc is not quite an antihero, he certainly is an unsympathetic protagonist. He badgers people unmercifully, suspects the law even when on rare occasions it tries to cooperate with him, ridicules and threatens his brother, Edward, over the financial terms of the settlement of the family inherited fortune, and even betrays Blackie's genuine love for him. Always, however, he wants to protect and provide for Esmeralda, and this perhaps is his saving grace: he wants not for himself but for others. And we are often reminded of his painful past. A dishonorably discharged Vietnam vet who killed a man while doing time in Leavenworth, he has earned the right to be distrustful and suspicious of others and their motives. Perhaps Hoffman best summarizes Charley's plight when, during a visit to a fellow Vietnam vet, Zeke Webb, Charley thinks, "We were both stuck with the absolute knowledge that at any instant everything in the world that had any value to us could be seized and taken away" (p. 173).

Little does Charley realize what a prophet he is. In responding to a note from Jeanne Bruce, Charley arrives at Wild Thorn, the family mansion.. During their meeting he confronts Jeannie with the accusation that it was she who attacked and killed Aunt Jessie. Jeannie admits that she hit Aunt Jessie with her riding whip but denies that the blow led to her death: "Hitting her was a reflex that happened fast without thought. And she didn't fall, cry out or anything. She just sat in her chair and smiled." As Charley attempts to leave the room, "the door from the game room swung fully open, and Duncan stepped through. In his thin, veined hands he held one of his shotguns" (p. 250).

As he is held hostage realizing he may be left in the prison for days, Charley discusses with Duncan the events leading up to Aunt Jessie's death. It gradually becomes clear to Charley who killed Aunt Jessie and why.

Three days later, Pepe, Duncan's house servant, follows instructions to release Charley from his cell. But his release just takes Charley from a physical hell to an emotional and mental one, for, believing that Charley has betrayed her with Jeannie, Blackie has left.

Several days later Blackie does return, but only to pick up her other clothes. When Charley begs her at least to listen to his explanation, her reply is laconic to the extreme: "Nope, I'm gone." After Blackie drives off, Charley visits Esmeralda at the state hospital, and he arranges with the kindly and concerned head doctor to give Esmeralda anything she might need.

Charley then drives off into the night heading south, regretting his affair with Jeannie and losing Blackie, at least temporarily. At the novel's conclusion one knows that somewhere down the road, if not Montana then maybe Florida, Charlie and Blackie will once again be together.

As of January 2008, Hoffman was putting the finishing touches on the third novel of the Charley LeBlanc trilogy. Tentatively and appropriately entitled *Road's End,* the novel focuses on the reunion between Blackie and Charley and suggests the permanence of their relationship after all of the misunderstandings, missed opportunities, and separations.

THE SHORT STORIES

Since the late 1980s Hoffman has received increasing recognition for his short fiction. In 1988 his story "Sweet Armageddon" was chosen by the *Virginia Quarterly Review* as its best story published that year; in 1989 he was awarded, for the second time, the Andrew Nelson Lytle Prize from the *Sewanee Review*; in 1990 he won *Shenandoah*'s Jeanne Charpiot Goodheart Prize for Fiction; in 1993 Longwood College bestowed upon him the John Dos Passos Prize for Excellence in Literature; and in 1995 he was given the Fellowship of Southern Writers Hillsdale Prize for Fiction. In 1996 Hoffman was inducted into the Fellowship of Southern Writers at a ceremony in Chattanooga, Tennessee. In addition, Hoffman holds honorary doctorates from Hampden-Sydney College, Washington and Lee University, and Sewanee.

Hoffman's first short story collection, *Virginia Reels,* was published by the University of Illinois Press in 1978. It contains nine stories, which were earlier published in six periodicals over a period of eleven years, from 1966 through 1977. At the time of the publication of each of these stories Hoffman was living in Farmville and later Charlotte Court House in Virginia, and for many of those years he was teaching at Hampden-Sydney College in Prince Edward County. The nine stories collected here anticipate the setting for the vast majority of Hoffman's stories and novels: Tidewater; Virginia, including the Chesapeake Bay area; Richmond; rural southside Virginia; and the mountains and coal-mining regions of West Virginia where Hoffman grew up.

George Core, editor of the *Sewanee Review,* in which four of these stories first appeared, stated at a seminar on Hoffman in 1988 that the *SR* has published more stories by William Hoffman than by any other writer, living or dead—notes in the remarks on the book's jacket that

> William Hoffman is one of the finest American short-story writers of our time. His stories are beautifully paced and cleanly written: nothing is wasted, everything counts. Here is an author who is a master of the enlivening detail, the casual aside, the necessary idiom. Hoffman's fiction ranges from hilarity to pathos to terror; his humorous response to man's folly is as memorable as his profound vision of man's depravity.

Of the twelve stories that comprise Hoffman's second collection, *By Land, By Sea* (1988), eight take place in rural southside Virginia, Danville, Richmond, and towns and counties adjacent to these; four are set on or near water, and water to Hoffman is the sea—the Atlantic Ocean and the Chesapeake Bay. Regardless of setting, Hoffman's characters and the daily conflicts they confront are, as always, the essence of his fiction.

All eleven of the stories in Hoffman's third collection, *Follow Me Home* (1994) had been previously published: "Dancer," "Abide with Me," "Points," and "Expiation" in the *Sewanee Review*; "Tides" in the *Southern Review*; "Coals," "Boy Up a Tree," and "Business Trip" in *Shenandoah*; "Sweet Armageddon" and "The Secret Garden" in the *Virginia Quarterly Review*; and "Night Sport" in the *Atlantic.* "Night Sport" is one of Hoffman's most chilling works, and the only one of his short stories that could be called a war story, or rather a postwar story, dealing with the effects of war on an individual. It is surprising that in his short fiction Hoffman has written so sparingly about war, since three of his novels are certainly war novels, and Hoffman himself said in a *Farmville Herald* interview (June 6, 1999) that "[i]n most cases I was writing novels and stories simultaneously so they would reflect each other." "Night Sport" is so disturbing that numerous readers of the *Atlantic* wrote in to cancel their subscriptions to protest the story's publication. Its protagonist, Chip, a Vietnam veteran who lost his legs in the war and now lives by himself in a rural area of southside Virginia, has grown increasingly bitter about what the war and society have done to his life. He rejects his family, his former girlfriend, and his mother's well-intentioned but overly sanctimonious minister, and "baits" his house to invite a break-in.

Hoffman's next collection of short fiction, *Doors,* was published in 1999. Once again, all ten stories that appear in it were previously published: "Doors," "Stones," and "Place" in *Shenandoah*; "Roll Call" and "Blood" in the *Virginia Quarterly Review*; and half the stories, "Landings," "Winter Wheat," "Prodigal," "Humility," and "Tenant," in the *Sewanee Review.* In an interview that appeared in the *Farmville Herald* (June 6, 1999) shortly after the book was published, Hoffman, asked why the collection was entitled *Doors,* replied:

> I wanted to start this collection with a story most readers would probably like. I didn't want to scare readers off with a story that might startle too much. Also, in every one of these stories doors occur. So the reader is looking through ten different doors and at the people who live inside that particular structure. ... I wanted readers to see these places as a series of doors and a series of people living beyond the threshold.
>
> (p. 10)

"Doors," then, become the collection's unifying device. In the title story, an aging widow, the story's unnamed first-person narrator, hires the local handyman, Horace Puckett, to rebuild the

ancient furnace in her house. But when Horace knocks at the front door to enter and inspect the furnace, she sends him "around back to the outside basement entrance because I wasn't in the habit of letting laborers come through the front door or the kitchen one either if it could be avoided. I assumed he didn't know better." But by story's end it is Horace who is teaching the once haughty and proud widow about acceptance, dignity, humility, and expiation.

The stories discussed in this chapter reveal much about the short fiction of William Hoffman. They introduce his readers to characters as real and as believable as any in twentieth-century American literature, a number of them as memorable as many of Eudora or William Faulkner's Mississippi characters—characters such as Gormer, the snake-handling minister in "The Spirit in Me," Matthew the avenging farmer in "Winter Wheat," Chip, the psychotic Vietnam vet of "Night Sport," and Dave, the business tycoon approaching seventy who confuses Gail, the young tennis player he has just met, with his deceased wife, Helen, in "Lover." Apart from brilliant and searing characterization, Hoffman gives the reader in his short fiction a strong sense of place. He has done for southside Virginia, the mountains of Virginia and West Virginia, and the Tidewater–Chesapeake Bay area what Faulkner did for the Mississippi delta and the hills of Oxford—we can almost smell the sea breezes of "Sea Tides," "Sea Treader," and "Moorings" and feel the red clay of "A Southern Sojourn" or "Winter Wheat." The themes of Hoffman's stories will remain with his readers: courage, honor, pride, humility, self-sacrifice, loneliness, and love, always love: love of land, love of family, love of father and son, love of country, love for the unloved, love for the forgotten, abused, and ill-used. Fred Chappell's comment in *The Fictional World of William Hoffman* on the author's short fiction offers a refreshing insight:

> His relish for accessible story lines, thematic clarity, informative detail, strong characterization, and satisfying structure is unmistakable. Almost any page shows his enjoyment of these customary elements of fiction composition as well as his quiet proficiency in their application. He rarely writes what we would call an "experimental" story; he probably feels no need, being so expert in the art of straightforward narrative.
>
> (p. 10)

Selected Bibliography

WORKS OF WILLIAM HOFFMAN

Novels

The Trumpet Unblown. Garden City, N.Y.: Doubleday, 1955.

Days in the Yellow Leaf. Garden City, N.Y.: Doubleday, 1958.

A Place for My Head. Garden City, N.Y.: Doubleday, 1960.

The Dark Mountains. Garden City, N.Y.: Doubleday, 1963.

Yancey's War. Garden City, N.Y.: Doubleday, 1966.

A Walk to the River. Garden City, N.Y.: Doubleday, 1970.

A Death of Dreams. Garden City, N.Y.: Doubleday, 1973.

The Land That Drank the Rain. Baton Rouge: Louisiana State University Press, 1982.

Godfires. New York: Viking, 1985.

Furors Die. Baton Rouge: Louisiana State University Press, 1989.

Tidewater Blood. Chapel Hill, N.C.: Algonquin, 1998.

Blood and Guile. New York: HarperCollins, 2000.

Wild Thorn. New York: HarperCollins, 2002.

Lies. Montgomery, Ala.: River City Publishing, 2005.

Short Story Collections

Virginia Reels. Urbana: University of Illinois Press, 1978.

By Land, By Sea. Baton Rouge: Louisiana State University Press, 1988.

Follow Me Home. Baton Rouge: Louisiana State University Press, 1994.

Doors. Columbia: University of Missouri Press, 1999.

Other Works

"The Love Touch." (Unpublished, produced play). Abingdon, Va.: Barter Theatre, August 22–27, 1967.

CRITICAL AND BIOGRAPHICAL STUDIES

Davis, Mary H. "Introduction to the Novels of William Hoffman." Master's thesis, Longwood College (Farmville, Va.), 1980.

Frank, William L., ed. *The Fictional World of William Hoffman.* Columbia: University of Missouri Press, 2000.

Span, Paula. "The Loneliness of the Midlist Author," *Washington Post Magazine,* February 4, 2001, pp. 10–15, 23–29.

WILLIAM HOFFMAN

INTERVIEW

Frank, William. "Hoffman Opens His Door." *Farmville Herald,* June 6, 1999, pp. 1, 10. (An interview with William Hoffman on *Doors.*)

HA JIN

(1956—)

Deborah Kay Ferrell

HA JIN IS perhaps the United States' premier Chinese American poet and fiction writer. Of his dual identity, Jin remarked to Wendy Smith in *Publishers Weekly,* "I don't mind being a Chinese-American writer: my first 29 years were spent in China; it would be insane to erase that."

In 1996 Jin won his first major literary accolade, the Hemingway Foundation/PEN Award, for *Ocean of Words: Army Stories,* a collection that details life in the Chinese Liberation Army. The next year he won the Flannery O'Connor Prize for Short Fiction for *Under the Red Flag,* twelve tales about life in a Chinese village during the Cultural Revolution. *Waiting,* his much-heralded "breakthrough" novel about the conflicts of longing for passionate love and the onus of familial life, received the National Book Award in 1999. In 2000 the novel was the recipient of the PEN/Faulkner Award, which Jin won a second time for *War Trash* in 2005, thereby joining Philip Roth and John Edgar Wideman as one of a handful of writers to have been thus distinguished in the first twenty-five years of the award's history. *War Trash,* the story of Yu Yuan, an officer in the Chinese Army who is taken as a prisoner of war by the Americans in the Korean War, was also a finalist for the Pulitzer Prize that same year.

Jin's success as a writer is all the more remarkable because his formal education was abruptly halted when he was a young boy. He was born Xuefei (shu-Fay) in Liaoning Province in northern China, near the Korean border, on February 21, 1956. Jin is the oldest of five children. His father, Danlin, was a low-ranking military officer and his mother, Yuanfen, was a petty officer. At age seven Jin was sent to military school, which was considered quite an honor at that time, but he remained there for only two years, until 1965. The following year marked the beginning of the Cultural Revolution, and Mao Zedong ordered all of China's schools closed. During this time, Jin was sent home, where he and his entire family suffered from the mass hysteria directed at those who were deemed to be counterrevolutionary. Jin's maternal grandfather had once been a small landowner, and Jin's mother, the writer recalled in an interview with Dwight Garner, suffered especially during those times. "People did terrible things to her," he said. As punishment for who she was and what her father had been, Jin's mother was also intermittently sent away to pick apples for two or three years. Because his parents were away from home frequently, Jin and his siblings were taken care of by an older cousin. Although his father's position in the military afforded his family protection from further persecution, Jin remembers watching the Red Guards burn his father's books in the yard. He also recalls "wrapping a set of secreted encyclopedias with paper and poring over their forbidden pages." For Jin, who wanted to show loyalty to the new regime, to fit in, even to be a hero, the emotional turmoil of his family's adversity and his own yearning for knowledge juxtaposed against the sacrifices that must be made for equality and the Cultural Revolution left an indelible mark. Prominent in his works is the recurrent theme of the moral ambiguities that exist between pursuing individual desire and freedom and doing what is right for the betterment of the whole—family, the military, and society.

For almost a decade, Jin's schooling was interrupted. When he was fourteen years old, fueled by rumors that Russia was going to attack China and determined to prove his devotion to Chairman Mao and his country, Jin lied about his age so that he could enlist in the People's Libera-

tion Army (PLA). In an interview with John Freeman, Jin explained that "[the army] was a better choice, comparatively, than going to work in the countryside." His initial assignment was as an artilleryman, where he was stationed to patrol China's borders with Russia and North Korea. At age sixteen Jin bought his first novel, a Chinese classic, but because of the interruption in his schooling, his reading was stilted and labored. Of his education, Jin has remarked, "I was almost illiterate when I was in the army." Jin began to study the dictionary, and sometimes it took weeks before he could understand enough words to return to the novel and comprehend its meaning. Because he was in such a remote area near the Siberian border, finding anything else to read was nearly impossible until Jin was removed from the front lines and transferred to a base in a city close by. There he finally had greater access to books. While Jin was in the army, his parents sent him two texts of ancient Chinese poems, and he pored over them until committing every line to memory.

Jin was discharged from the military when he was nineteen, and for three years he worked as a telegraph operator for the Harbin Railroad Company on the night shift. Every morning between five and five thirty, Jin began to learn spoken English by tuning in to a radio program that taught catchy phrases such as "Long live Chairman Mao!" Later he listened to English tapes. At age twenty, Jin began to teach himself how to read English with the only title he knew: Friedrich Engels's *The Condition of the Working Class in England.*

The death of Mao Zedong in 1976 also marked the end of the Cultural Revolution, and in 1977 the universities were reopened. Jin, who had always wanted to attend college, sat for the entrance examinations and was admitted to Heilongjiang University in the city of Harbin. Then twenty-one years old, Jin listed five areas he was interested in studying. His first selection was philosophy, but in an interview with Felipe Nieves, the writer recalled, "I was assigned to study English. It was not my choice." Jin spent four years in Harbin, a city that is repeatedly mentioned in his works and from which he took his pen name, Ha Jin ("Ha" being the first Chinese character for "Harbin").

At Heilongjiang University, Jin began to read Faulkner and Hemingway, whose works had been banned during the Cultural Revolution. He found them a welcome addition to John Steinbeck, Jack London, and Langston Hughes, writers who had been deemed suitably proletariat by the former regime. Jin's initial interest in the English language was lackadaisical, and he was only concerned with the opportunities this knowledge could provide him, but when given no other option for study, as he told Andrea Ludlow, "I was always in the slow class, but when your survival is on the line you have no choice." It was the introduction of William Faulkner's writings, in particular, that inspired Jin to major in American literature.

After graduating with a bachelor's degree in English in 1981, Jin continued his studies at Shandong University. While there, he also became enamored with the works of the poet Theodore Roethke and the Nobel laureate Saul Bellow, and he first began to dabble in writing poetry in Chinese. During this time, Jin met Lisha Bian, a mathematics teacher, and they married on July 6, 1982. The following year the couple had their only child, a son, Wen, and in 1984 Jin completed his master's degree.

While at Shandong University, Jin took a graduate class with Beatrice Spade, a history professor who was teaching a course in American literature. She encouraged him to pursue his studies in the United States, and Jin began to apply to colleges that offered doctoral programs in English. In 1985 he traveled to Boston, where he had been accepted at Brandeis University, but he was faced with a heartbreaking decision: while he was allowed to travel on a student visa, the Chinese government insisted that he leave his wife and infant son behind as assurance of his return.

Jin always intended to go back to China, where he planned to find employment as a translator or a teacher. Even the subject of his dissertation on the high modernist poets Ezra Pound, T. S. Eliot, W. H. Auden, and W. B. Yeats was intended for a Chinese job market. In an

interview with Dave Weich on Powells.com, Jin said, "Those four have poems which are related to Chinese texts and poems that reference the culture." At night, Jin began to work a series of odd jobs—busboy, waiter, and house cleaner—to support himself and his family. In 1987 his wife, Lisha, was allowed to leave China and join her husband in Boston, but she left their son, Wen, with her parents. Jin continued to work on his dissertation, and his wife began to learn English, mainly from the television. The show *The Simpsons* and the soap opera *All My Children* were particular favorites.

On April 15, 1989, pro-democracy demonstrators, mainly comprising activists, intellectuals, and students, could no longer contain their frustration at China's government and began to stage protests in Beijing. The couple's anxiety and fear were exacerbated by the fact that they were safe, yet their son remained in China. For two months they watched the horror unfold, and they became increasingly desperate to bring Wen to the United States. Despite China's notoriously cumbersome bureaucracy and layers of paperwork, their son was granted his visa two days before the Tiananmen Square Massacre. Jin has referred to this unexpected expediency as "miraculous."

As tensions mounted, Jin recalled in a 2007 *Newsweek* feature, "I was glued to the TV for three days. ... I was in shock. I had served in the Army to protect the people. Suddenly the whole thing was reversed. I just couldn't reconcile it." For most of the Western world, this incident in history is best symbolized in a photograph taken by Jeff Widener known simply as the "tank picture." A lone young man, dressed in a white shirt and black pants, faces four army tanks that are rolling toward him. At the last minute, the protester was said to be pulled aside by bystanders, but Widener's website states that the young man's fate is unknown. Also disputed is the number of civilians who were killed during the uprisings. Accounts of fatalities vary from the Chinese government's official toll of twenty-three to the Western media's estimate of three thousand. Three political prisoners who were released in 1994 claim that twenty thousand total were slain.

Ha Jin was forever changed by the events that had occurred in his homeland. He and Lisha flew to San Francisco to retrieve their son, who was the last person off the plane. While they watched the rows of passengers walk into the terminal, the eager parents were terrified that something had gone amiss and perhaps Wen had not been able to come. Finally, when they were reunited, the joyous moment was tinged with sadness. The boy, who was five years old, recognized his mother but not his father, whom he had last seen when he was a toddler. Determined to forge a free life for Wen, the young family returned to the Boston area, and among his other jobs, Jin found employment as a night watchman at a plastics factory. It was there that he began fervently to write poems in between performing his hourly security checks. Today Jin laughs when he thinks of that job that he still remembers fondly, despite, as he told Marcia Davis of the *Washington Post,* "There were a lot of chemicals, too. ... Your face would change colors. I couldn't see it but my wife would say 'your face is green.' " Jin only quit the job when the factory moved elsewhere.

BETWEEN SILENCES

With the encouragement of his Brandeis teachers, the poets Allen Grossman and Frank Bidart, Jin published his first book of poetry, *Between Silences: A Voice from China,* in 1990. That same year Jin made the decision to speak and write exclusively in English, a process he has called excruciating and likened to changing his blood. The events of Tiananmen Square had left an indelible mark on the man and the writer, and the collection hints at the themes that would come to characterize much of his work—the absurdities of life under a totalitarian regime, the tragedies of the loss of individual liberty, and the inanities of being subjected to an unwieldy bureaucracy. In his preface Jin writes:

> The People in this book are not merely victims of history. They are also the makers of the history. Without them the history of contemporary China would remain a blank page. ... If what has been said in this book is embarrassing, then truth itself is cold

> and brutal. If not every one of these people, who were never perfect, is worthy of our love, at least their fate deserves our attention and our memory. They should talk and be talked about.
>
> (p. 1)

Prior to the book's publication, Jin had already had success with the collection's opening poem, "The Dead Soldier's Talk," which was accepted by Jonathan Galassi, who was then the poetry editor for the *Paris Review.* Frank Bidart, who was impressed with its remarkable idiom, urged Jin to contact the prestigious literary journal, and Jin did so, reading the poem aloud over the telephone to Galassi. Based on a famous story in China, the poem is narrated in the first person by a soldier who drowned while trying to rescue a statue of Chairman Mao. What is all the more tragic is that the statue was made out of plaster, which easily disintegrates in water. While the young man was lauded in China for his bravery and devotion to the regime, he is restless in his grave, lamenting that no one comes to bring him news of the great leader. The senselessness of heroism juxtaposed against the loss of the individual is all the more heartrending because the poem occurs six years after the soldier's death. Chairman Mao is gravely ill and the Cultural Revolution, and all that the young man died for, is soon to end. Jin's voice is that of an ironic closeness, marked by simplicity of language and starkness of imagery that recalls the tragic life and poetry of Wilfred Owen, the World War I soldier who died on the battlefield, and his most famous ode to the absurdities of war, "Dulce et Decorum Est."

Later poems in the collection focus on the effects of the Cultural Revolution, particularly on children, as their worlds are rent asunder and the traditional bonds of family, friendships, and community are deemed suspicious. One cannot help but recall the image of a young Xuefei who watched as his father's books were burned, the boy who secreted away a set of encyclopedias so that he could attempt his best to read them, and the student who was sent home from boarding school to an uncertain future where joining the army was better than being repatriated to the countryside. Gail Mazur wrote in *Ploughshares* that these poems appear to have been "forged under the most intense pressure to remain silent, in the certainty that to speak freely is to court calamity."

Even after the Tiananmen Square uprisings, Jin had not given up hopes of returning to his homeland; however, the matter was decided for him. When Jin applied for an extension of his student visa to study creative writing at Boston University, the Chinese government turned down his request. It also refused to renew his passport because of Jin's outspokenness against the brutality that he had witnessed from afar. Jin was literally a man without a country, an experience he has described as painfully alienating. What followed were desperate times. He continued to work on his dissertation, but now he faced the uncertainties of finding an academic job in America. Jin decided that the best way to be employable in a highly competitive market was to publish books. His wife, Lisha, was willing to sacrifice with him. More than anything, the couple wanted their son to grow up in a free society.

It was at a poetry reading, when Jin approached Leslie Epstein, the novelist and longtime chair of Boston University's Creative Writing Program, that a friendship was forged and the Chinese émigré's genesis as a fiction writer began. Despite Epstein's concerns about Jin's faltering spoken English, the novelist had enjoyed Jin's poetry, and he agreed to allow Jin to audit a writing workshop. During those days, Jin wrote frantically. In 1993 he completed his dissertation on the high modernist poets and received his Ph.D. from Brandeis. As Jin searched for a job, he recalled to Wendy Smith, "I gradually realized that some of the material I used in my first book of poems would be more effective in short stories; that's how I started to write *Ocean of Words.*" In part due to the success of *Between Silences,* Jin was hired as an assistant professor of creative writing at Emory University in Atlanta. That time period proved to be one of his most prolific. In 1996 he published *Facing Shadows,* his second poetry book, and *Ocean of Words: Army Stories,* based on his first book of poems, the ones that continued to grow.

FACING SHADOWS *AND* OCEAN OF WORDS: ARMY STORIES

Although there is little in *Facing Shadows* that overtly relates to Jin's life in China during the time of the Cultural Revolution, the collection still recalls Jin the soldier. In the poem "War," Jin writes of the duel existence through personal memory of being both in China and the United States. Many of the poems are in the first person, and they reflect Jin's personal devastation over the Tiananmen Square Massacre. In "A Child's Nature," he recounts Wen's arrival in San Francisco and a father's helpless anger that his son's version of what occurred during those tragic two months was so different from what he himself had witnessed on television. The poem reckons with a betrayal that is both political and personal. Not only had the government indoctrinated his son with the belief that the pro-democracy demonstrators deserved their fate but his own family had too.

Other poems reflect guilt, especially over the sacrifices his wife made for their life in the United States and his own failure to take a more definitive stand against the Chinese government, as the political dissidents had. The autobiographical nature of the collection is further revealed as Jin explores his identity as an immigrant. In "Ways of Talking" the permanency and poignancy of exile are clear, yet the ending is hopeful, even optimistic.

In his review of *Facing Shadows,* Jack Granath wrote that "The issues of nationality, tradition, and race that inevitably arise park this work firmly on the couch of contemporary American poetry, with its nervous confessions of identity confusion and unhappiness." And while the following comment might seem dismissive, it, like so many of Jin's poems in this volume, is also hopeful. Granath concluded: "It's just a book that's like a lot of other books. The best poems in it though, show a remarkable talent emerging."

Jin has stated that he worked very hard as a poet at Emory, but while there, he also began to write, edit, and revise stories that would eventually make up his first collection, *Ocean of Words: Army Stories.* These tales are a return to the ideas and themes first explored in *Between the Silences.* Despite the writer's increasing reputation as a gifted poet, he encountered difficulty finding a publisher. By his account, the book was rejected dozens of times before it finally found a home in the now-defunct Zoland Press. According to an article by Amy Yee in the *Asian Wall Street Journal,* one of the letters Jin received stated: "The author deals with the subject in a poetic way but we don't see the market for this work. ... we don't see the point of publishing a Chinese fiction writer." This xenophobia was rationalized by the doubt that an American audience would want to read about stories that take place along the frigid and forbidding borders between Manchuria and Siberia. Further, *Ocean of Words* is confined to stories about the experiences of those who served in the People's Liberation Army. Their world is often claustrophobic and characterized by a general paranoia. Instead of comrades who are mutually supportive, more often than not they watch each other with distrust, ready to report anyone who raises the slightest suspicion to the Regimental Political Department. Tensions are augmented by the political madness in Mainland China and by the ever-present Russian guards on the other side of the border.

In "A Report," the brief opening story, an entire company of paratroopers is out on a routine march, displaying that they are "the flower of our Second Division." However, as they sing a song about soldiers saying good-bye to their mothers, they break into tears. Told from the perspective of the company's political instructor, Chen Jun, he is not only appalled by this embarrassing display of bourgeois emotions but deems the song subversive and counterrevolutionary. He labels it "poisonous" and recommends that the composer's family and political background be investigated. He concludes that: "Our class enemies are still active, and they never got to sleep. ... We must grow another pair of eyes in the backs of our heads so that we can keep them under watch everywhere and at all times."

To emphasize the isolation of the region, and the recurrent theme of the conflicts of Communist Party ideology with the desires of human nature, "Love in the Air" is a story about an awkward

telegraph operator, Kang, who is so desperately lonely that he falls in love with the hand of another operator whose "elegance and fluency" with the dots and dashes he interprets as having "secret meanings." Although Kang's relationship exists only in fantasy, when he learns that the woman, Lili, has been conducting "a love affair in the air" with another operator in his company, he feels betrayed. Devastated by his inability to overcome these bourgeois emotions, Kang feels damned and asks to be reassigned to another unit.

The last story in the collection, the book's title piece, is perhaps the most poignant and autobiographical. "Ocean of Words" resonates with the desire to break free of ideological dogma's constraints on human emotions as the protagonist, a studious soldier, leaves the army to take up the battle with the pen and become a budding writer.

Timothy Wong, writing for *World Literature Today,* asserted that the stories read like translations; for example, Jin refers to a wanton woman as a "broken shoe," and at times he seems to mix cultural metaphors. Rather than "clicking their heels" together, characters are "clapping their heels together." Despite this criticism, Wong also stated:

> With all their surface similarities to so much of "modern" Chinese fiction, these stories are different in a very important way: they challenge Marxist (or Maoist) political ideology not by declaring allegiance to some other ideology but by demonstrating again and again the complexity of human emotion which defies simplistic dogma.
>
> (p. 862)

Despite the trepidations about Jin's stories finding an audience, and problems of translation, both culturally and linguistically, *Ocean of Words* was an undisputed success, proving that a Chinese émigré could write stories about his homeland and garner the prestigious Hemingway Foundation/PEN Award for First Fiction along the way. Amy Yee posited that the reason "an American audience is embracing Mr. Jin's work reflects America's growing desire to understand the history so crucial to shaping the identity of China today."

Of his time at Emory, Ha Jin stated he was driven by fear. In between teaching classes, he would draft his stories and then obsessively revise them. The result was that in the following year, 1997, Jin published *Under the Red Flag,* his second collection of short fiction. Set in the rural town of Dismount Fort, the stories take place during the Cultural Revolution, a time that Jin portrays as plagued by moral breakdown and unimaginable cruelty. The book's characters are ordinary people often caught in social changes that are not of their own making.

The opening story, "In Broad Daylight," is told from the point of view of a young boy who witnesses the public persecution of a prostitute named Mu Ying. Despite the abandonment of past customs where prostitutes were burned alive on a hill named Heaven Lamp, the new way of punishment is simply a variation of an old tradition. Mu Ying must march through the village with a sign around her neck that reads, "I am a Broken Shoe. My Crime Deserves Death." In the riot that ensues, her husband is left dead, and she is abandoned at a bus stop, pleading for someone to help her.

Paul Gray, writing for *Time,* singled out "Winds and Clouds over a Funeral" as the best story in the collection. In it, a Communist official, Ding, is torn between the bourgeois loyalties he feels to his dying mother, whose deathbed desire is to be buried in the tradition of her ancestors, and the dictates of the Party, which decree that all dead must be cremated so as not to waste arable land. Ding realizes that if he follows his mother's wishes, his political enemies will entrap him. Desperate for his own survival, he must recreate the truth and convince himself, in order to justify his actions, that his mother wanted to be cremated. His own son, a recently discharged army soldier, knows of his grandmother's final request, and he is angered by this lapse in filial loyalty, but he must remain silent, for he has learned that in life, as in the military, to speak the truth is to court disaster.

With its Orwellian resonance, perhaps the most horrifying story in the collection is "Resurrection." The story is related in a distant, matter-of-fact manner that only serves to augment the details, so that they have a lasting, haunting effect. "Resurrection" is also probably

the most political of the stories, and it is one that Jin has described as an allegory for his grief over the events that happened in the Tiananmen Square uprisings. Mr. Lu, the protagonist, is caught having sex with his pregnant wife's sister. When officials learn of this liaison, he is forced to write a confession. Mr. Lu's first effort is rejected because of its blandness, and he is instructed to produce no less than one hundred pages of the most intimate details. Unable to do so, when he is confronted by the officials in his own home, Mr. Lu is cornered and ashamed. Desperate, he castrates himself with a pair of scissors. The story's ending is eerily discomfiting. Mr. Lu's self-mutilation has made him a hero for taking such an extreme action to rid himself of his moral corruption, he and his wife are reconciled, and now, "most significant of all, he had a new, normal life."

The ending seems too pat, especially for the devastation that has occurred, yet Jin has done this intentionally to mirror the calamity that resulted in the Tiananmen Square Massacre. Jin waited in vain for a response of any kind—more protests, global sanctions, even lasting acknowledgement of the tragedy. What happened instead were a retreat and a slow return in China to the status quo. Jin has said that in not responding to the bloodshed, we "castrated ourselves."

Under the Red Flag won the prestigious Flannery O'Connor Award for Short Fiction in 1997, and while the book was generally well received, some reviewers, such as Frank Caso of *Booklist,* accused Jin of writing his own propaganda. A reviewer for *Publishers Weekly* was more positive in assessing the stories, asserting that for Jin they are an exploration of "larger themes about human relationships and the effect of government on individual lives."

IN THE POND

Ha Jin's debut novel, *In the Pond,* has the writer returning to familiar territory. In fact, it was originally intended as part of *Under the Red Flag.* However, it expanded in length, causing Jin to separate the two works and transition to longer writing forms. Published in 1998, this slim volume that some have likened to a fable is once again set in the dismal village of Dismount Fort. Although the novel is not necessarily less political than his previous works, Jin has shifted the tone of *In the Pond* to one that is delightfully wry and ironic. Mei Chin, writing for the *New York Times Book Review,* deemed the novel "first and foremost a comedy—naughty, lusty, raucously entertaining." Indeed it is, as the reader becomes enthralled with the protagonist, Shao Bin, a Chinese "everyman," and his unrelenting quest for better housing, a nonproletarian mission if ever there was one. Set just after the death of Chairman Mao, the novel has an old-fashioned quality to it, as if Jin is re-creating the China of his boyhood.

Shao Bin is likable, although a bit of a buffoon. He is a self-taught artist and calligrapher who is unfulfilled by his job in a fertilizer plant. He and his family reside in a commune called the "pond," a stagnant puddle of corruption. Unhappy as he is with his station in life, this would-be intellectual who is familiar with "a lot of ancient stories, even the adventures of Sherlock Holmes," is further dismayed with his living arrangements. When Shao Bin returns from work every evening to his one-room dormitory, where he lives with his wife and young daughter, he covets a place in Worker's Park, the new housing complex.

To assist him in attempting to secure a better apartment, Shao Bin's wife urges him to ingratiate himself with the factory's supervisor, Ma Gong, and party secretary, Liu Shu, even though housing assignments are ostensibly determined by a lottery. When Bin is rejected, he begins his one-man campaign to reveal the corruption of the officials who surround him. As retribution, he stays up at night, drawing and annotating satirical cartoons. When one of his pieces is published in a local newspaper, he is at first terrified, especially when he is publicly denounced by Ma and Liu, who begin to retaliate against Bin by trying to prove that he is insane. What ensues is a series of conflicts countered by more cartoons. Bin vacillates between belittling others and self-aggrandizement as he rationalizes his actions: "Who were Liu Shu and Ma Gong? Two small cadres with glib tongues, uncouth and unlettered.

They were wine vessels and rice bags, their existence only burdening the earth, whereas he had read hundreds of books and was knowledgeable about strategies."

The conflict escalates until Bin is successful at expressing his anger all the way to Beijing. Despite being recognized as an artist and gathering a following of supporters in the capital who have heard his call for reforms, in the end Bin is silenced when Lu and Ma appoint him to the factory's propaganda office. Bin is so thrilled by his perceived victory that he even forgets about the apartment that he once longed for. Phyllis Alesia Perry ended her review of *The Pond* with a statement that is as sad as Bin's bought compliance: "Perhaps Bin's little rebellion solidifies for us what we already suspected: that an individual can ripple the surface of the water for a moment, even if after that moment, the pond again is still."

By this time Ha Jin was regarded as "a Chinese American literary phenomenon," but it was the gentle and beautiful *Waiting* that would earn him mainstream success, with an estimated half-million copies in print. After bouncing from agent to agent, he finally found the literary agent Lane Zachary and a major trade publisher, Pantheon.

WAITING

In an interview with Michael Skube, Jin said that he got the idea for *Waiting* from a story told to him by his wife's parents, both army doctors. When he read a newspaper article about a woman who was trapped in a loveless marriage, he realized, "That's it. It's not just something local but something larger. Americans would understand it." From its beautifully simple first line, "Every summer Lin Kong returned to Goose Village to divorce his wife, Shuyu," the reader is spellbound by the army doctor's attempts to extricate himself from his ill-fated, arranged marriage.

In artful, clear prose, *Waiting,* whose time frame approximately parallels the two decades of the Cultural Revolution, is both a commentary on the confining restrictions of China's past and the suffocating edicts imposed by Chairman Mao. The principal characters in the novel—Lin Kong, the physician; Shuyu, his long-suffering wife; and Manna Wu, his equally unhappy, though chaste, mistress—are all victims of a society in which they have no control nor voice. Nevertheless, they adhere to its tenets in what becomes a pantomime that fulfills duty and obligation but leaves their souls bereft.

Lin Kong is forced by filial duty to marry a simple peasant because she is devoted in attending to his ailing parents. His wife, Shuyu, is an embarrassment to him, especially in this new egalitarian society where she visibly manifests one of the crueler symbols of China's ancient past: bound feet. Despite his wife's good nature and simple devotion, she is also illiterate and homely. Lin is so ashamed of her that he chooses to leave Shuyu behind when he goes to work at the military hospital in Muji City. There he meets Manna Wu, the head nurse, with whom he gradually falls in love. Because of an obscure law, Lin must be separated from his wife for eighteen years before he can be granted a divorce without his wife's permission.

At the hospital, the lovers are thwarted in consummating their love because the party forbids members of the opposite sex to be seen together outside the compound, so in essence, Lin and Manna are platonic comrades. "Just a moment's pleasure," Lin Kong warns Manna Wu, "will ruin our lives for good." Nevertheless, the couple is subjected to gossip and speculation.

Every year, Lin returns dutifully to Shuyu and asks for a divorce, and every year she agrees and then tearfully refuses at the last minute. As time passes, Manna becomes increasingly fearful that she will become an old maid, while Lin retreats into a world of solitude with a secret collection of forbidden books. What Lin Kong never seems to realize is that during all of those years, when he returns home to ask for a divorce and Shuyu refuses, the couples' love changes and then wanes. After eighteen years, Manna and Lin are finally able to marry, and they become the parents of twin sons; however, during childbirth it is discovered that Manna has a heart defect that has left her weak and dying. Lin turns to Shuyu to help him and his new family, and he is

finally able to appreciate his first wife for all of her virtues. The novel ends with a bittersweet poignancy and the haunting questions of who has been waiting for whom and what they have been waiting for. Ironically, the much-maligned Shuyu emerges as a noble heroine, who, though no longer married to her husband, is at last appreciated by him.

Ron Breines, in a special to Tokyo's *Daily Yomiuri,* wrote: "*Waiting* is a simple book on the surface, but [it is also] profound and complex. It is a book about the loss of potential, the ease of acceptance of others' power, the difficulty of being decisive about anything at all and the missed opportunities that always pass procrastinators by." And though the novel firmly established Jin as the darling of the literati and of an increasingly appreciative American reading public—*Waiting* won the National Book Award in 1999—his reception in his homeland was much more tentative. At first it seemed as if the Chinese government was going to allow the book to be published in translation on the Mainland, and Jin was hopeful that his parents and siblings would finally be able to read something he had written. In the end, however, the Beijing Publishing Group withdrew its plans after a literary journal accused the book of portraying China as oppressive and primitive. In an interview with Judy Stoffman of the *Toronto Star,* Jin remarked, "The publisher got scared" and "said this was a kind of conspiracy, a disgrace to the Chinese."

THE BRIDEGROOM

During the year that followed the success of *Waiting,* Jin received a Guggenheim Fellowship and published his third collection of short stories, *The Bridegroom.* Set in the 1980s in Muji City, the memory of the Cultural Revolution hangs like a pall. Although the characters in these stories have managed to survive, they have grown wary and suspicious of the ever-present paternalistic regime that subjects its citizens to the vagaries of corrupt officials who can ruin a person's life on a whim. Jodi Daynard of the *Boston Globe* wrote that Jin's China is a place "where the scramble to meet basic needs supplants any loftier human goals. Husbands choose wives according to their apartment options. Virgins trade their virtue for a good meal."

In the much-anthologized opening story, "Saboteur," a mild-mannered college professor, Mr. Chiu, is returning home from his honeymoon. As he waits at a train station with his bride, a police officer tosses the remains of a cup of tea on his feet. Mr. Chiu is unwilling to tolerate this personal affront and demands an apology. An argument ensues until the police officers arrest Mr. Chiu. For his umbrage, he has been charged with sabotage. What follows is the transformation of a human soul when Mr. Chiu is thrown in jail and suffers one indignity after another. The protagonist, a loyal party member, is an idealist. At first he believes that his status as a scholar and comrade will give him leverage as he fights the false charges against him. But as the days pass and everyone who can assist him proves inept, Mr. Chiu, who suffers from hepatitis, becomes increasingly concerned with his health as his liver begins to swell. Finally, after he is bullied into confessing to a lesser crime, Mr. Chiu casts his principles aside. When he is freed from jail, Mr. Chiu has become physically ugly, a manifestation of his soul's decay that mirrors his actions. On the way home, Mr. Chiu stops by four restaurants, eating and drinking from public cups and bowls, and spreading his disease. In the wake of his revenge, Mr. Chiu *has* become a saboteur. His retaliation against a government that has wronged him has left eight hundred people sick and six dead.

Another story in the collection, "After Cowboy Chicken Came to Town," details the confusion and frustration of workers in a newly opened, Western-style fast food restaurant. Hongwen, a young man who goes to work every day in a uniform that symbolizes the bland conformity of corporate America, is pleased with his job, especially the fact that he makes more money than his father. This smugness, however, is temporary. When Hongwen discovers that his Chinese manager, who has been educated in America, is paid much more than he, in American currency no less, Hongwen and his fellow workers go on strike only to be fired. While the work-

ers are employed by a capitalist corporation, they do not have the privileges of workers of a capitalistic society. Again, this story reveals a sense of outrage and points at the travesties of a totalitarian regime. Despite China's supposed embrace of a free-market economy, Hongwen discovers that he is still subjected to the tyranny of his government and the arbitrary nature of those who make rules without representation.

The capstone of the collection and its title piece, "The Bridegroom," is Jin writing at his best, with sly observations that are hilarious and tragic at the same time. Mr. Cheng, a kindhearted man, is the narrator of the story. When a dear friend dies, Mr. Cheng inherits his homely, dull daughter, Beina, who becomes his ward. Although Mr. Cheng likes the girl well enough, his greatest concern is whether or not he will be able to marry her off, a feat he has serious doubts about accomplishing. Surprisingly, he is able to find a bridegroom, the stunningly handsome Baowen, who is the best-looking man in the factory where he works. Of their union, Mr. Cheng wonders, "Did he really like her fleshy face, which often reminded me of a blowfish?" Despite everyone's doubts about the couple, they seem compatible and happy. Mr. Cheng is even amazed at the home the pair has created together. Hopeful, but mistrustful of the long-term success of this marriage, Mr. Cheng is wary that Baowen cannot be fulfilled in such an unequal union, and he eyes with suspicion every woman at the factory who flirts with the bridegroom. As the story unfolds, the reason for the marriage becomes clear after Baowen is arrested at a club called Men's World, a homosexual salon. Baowen proves himself to be noble and unflinching as his world crashes around him. When confronted by Mr. Cheng, he admits that he and Beina have a platonic marriage, something that his wife's guardian cannot understand. When Mr. Cheng urges Beina to denounce her husband, he becomes angry when she refuses to do so, even when Baowen's "crime" is made public and he is sent to a mental institution to be "cured" of his homosexuality. Throughout his ordeal, never once does Baowen deny who he is, nor does he promise to forgo sexual relations with men. The ending of the story is poignant and tragic, as Beina is left alone, sullied by her relationship with Baowen and abandoned by those who have mocked her, first for her homeliness and now for her unconsummated marriage. Baowen, although willing to pay any price to remain true to himself, will probably spend the rest of his life in prison. His crime: daring to assert his individuality in a society that demands conformity.

While many critics praised Jin's precise, unadorned prose, even going as far as to call him a "Chinese Hemingway," as his readership grew, so did the inevitable comparisons of Jin to writers for whom English was not their first language, especially Vladimir Nabokov (Russia) and Joseph Conrad (the Ukraine). Claire Messud for the *New York Times Book Review* deemed the aforementioned "supreme stylists, whose conversion implied a willed mastery. ... Ha Jin, on the other hand, writes spare prose, with a limited vocabulary: his works read as if he had written them in Chinese and merely undertaken the translations himself." Even with her misgivings, Messud concluded her article with praise, lauding Jin's "eye for detail, his great storytelling talent."

WRECKAGE

Despite his prolific output and numerous awards, Jin continued to teach in Emory University's Creative Writing Program and travel the country. No engagement seemed too insignificant or too small. During a presentation at the Treasure Coast Literary Society, Jin answered questions from the audience. When asked about writing in English, he responded, "English is a messy language. ... It spreads in every direction, but it is for everyone." Jin also took time to discuss his forthcoming book, a poetry collection entitled *Wreckage* that he hoped would put some "ghosts to rest." He claimed, "If you carry too much baggage, you can't go far." Often savage in imagery and foreboding and dark in content, *Wreckage* seems to be about Jin's troubled bond with his homeland as he praises China's glorious past and laments its current shame. Arranged chronologically, the collection provides a sweeping view of China's history, starting with the legendary founding of

the Yellow River culture by Yu the Great. The poems are linear in their construction and read like condensed stories or miniature fables. As Jin ponders the sins and inequities of China's history, a recurrent theme is the brutal treatment of women. In "Human Pig" a concubine is tortured and tossed into an outhouse pit. In "A Young Girl's Lament" he recounts the horrors of foot binding where "the toes curl in like dead caterpillars." Perhaps too shocking in content for a general readership, *Wreckage* was reviewed less than his last few books. Jeffrey Twitchel-Waas accused Jin of being "caught in the dilemma of being a Chinese writing in English, who understandably sees his role as a truth teller but has cut himself off from the readers to whom these truths matter most." Of course he failed to mention that Jin's alienation from this audience with whom he shares this past is not of Jin's own making, nor did he seem to take into account the sadness, bitterness, and anger that might have shaped the poems in *Wreckage.*

THE CRAZED

In 2001, after a short sabbatical, Ha Jin left Emory. The following year, he was recruited by his longtime mentor and friend Leslie Epstein to teach in Boston University's Creative Writing Program. Despite his claim that he wanted to put his "ghosts to rest," Jin's next novel, *The Crazed,* is testimony that he was unable to do so. The backdrop for the novel is the Tiananmen Square Massacre and those horrible days when the citizens of his homeland were so tragically suppressed for daring to give voice to their discontent. In a review for *Commonweal,* Valerie Sayers wrote that *The Crazed* is "focused on an inevitable plot march that will end in Tiananmen Square."

The protagonist, Jian Wan, is a graduate student in literature who is preparing for his doctoral examinations. The Chinese university he attends is located in Shanning, a dry and dusty, polluted town in the northwest. He is engaged to his beloved mentor's daughter, Meimei, and everything in his life seems to be on course until Dr. Yang, his future father-in-law, has a stroke. Because Meimei is in Beijing at the university and his wife is in Tibet on a veterinary mission, Jian Wan and another student are the only ones who are able to attend to the professor.

The bulk of the novel takes place in Dr. Yang's hospital room as he rants, raves, and reminisces about everything from his early hopes and ambitions, to his persecution under the Cultural Revolution and even his sexual indiscretions. The plot is one that is difficult to execute because the story line is propelled by Dr. Yang's lapses in and out of consciousness as he vacillates between life and death. The professor speaks in monologues where "sometimes he talks like an imbecile and sometimes he speaks like a sage." Most scathing of all are the indictments Yang makes of academia, a world he reveals as filled with petty bickering and bitter power struggles. The professor laments that he is really nothing more than a clerk.

At first Jian Wan is horrified and disbelieving, but gradually he comes to accept the professor's diatribes as truth. Heeding his mentor's warnings, Jian Wan forsakes his examinations. When Dr. Yang dies and Wan discovers that his fiancée is carrying on with another man, he is left alone and disillusioned. As students from his university are boarding the train to the capital city so that they can take part in the protests at Tiananmen Square, Wan joins them. When China erupts in madness, images of the past and present "crazed," the events of Dr. Yang's memory and the current upheaval in Beijing, collide.

Although *Waiting* was compared to a doleful Chekhovian tale, *The Crazed* did not receive such eloquent praise. Sarah A. Smith of London's *Guardian* wrote, "If this novel fails to live up to the promise of its predecessor, it is perhaps because it falls prey to the problem that faces much diaspora literature—the need to explain the motherland, rather than just to write." Other reviewers felt that the plot was too implausible and, thus, the novel was plodding. A writer for the *Hindu* stated: "The narration at times is faulty and since politics directly affects the psyche of

the characters, the portrayal is also distorted. ... The creative distance between literature and life is at times lacking and hence it becomes contrived at places. The style of narration, though generally elegant and poetic, is prosaic, formal and often clichéd."

WAR TRASH

After *The Crazed* was published, there was a slight lull in Ha Jin's production. Maybe after having written six books in six years he was no longer driven by fear. Jin was secure in his teaching position at Boston University, and he had established himself as a writer of merit on a global scale. Three years passed before his third novel, *War Trash,* was published. In 2005 the book was nominated for the Pulitzer Prize, and it earned Jin's second PEN/Faulkner Award. Marcia Davis wrote in the *Washington Post* that although the writer was pleased at being the recipient of so many awards, Jin was "not fooled either, not caught up in the flash and glitter of the literati life or any idea that winning awards ... means more than a moment of recognition. That is not his style."

Jin was persuaded by his wife to write *War Trash* because he often talked about the Korean War, a conflict that tends to be overlooked in history. For Jin, however, this era has a personal resonance. His father was a soldier in the war, and Jin recalls that when he was a boy, he often listened to stories about that time in his father's life. When Jin became a young man and joined the army, he came to know the area well while he was stationed in the forbidding zone where China, North Korea, and the former Soviet Union intersect.

Originally the novel was intended to be a short story collection to satisfy his contract with Zoland Press, which was now floundering economically because it could not compete with the larger, more commercial and financially prosperous publishing houses. Then the work evolved into what Jin anticipated becoming a short novel, but as he stated in an interview with Rob Thomas for the *Capital Times,* "Once I started, I couldn't stop."

The novel is told from the perspective of Yu Yuan, a seventy-three-year-old veteran who is visiting his grandchildren in America. He is inspired to record his story for them, and the novel takes the form of a fictional memoir. Yu Yuan recounts his experiences as a Chinese soldier who is held as a captive during the Korean War. A drafted "volunteer" of Mao's Army, Yu Yuan is sent to fight the onslaught of American imperialism on the Korean Peninsula. Idealistic, Yu Yuan reluctantly embraces his mission because he believes China's borders must be protected. Soon, however, he begins to realize the horrible truth, that he and his comrades are mere fodder as they are marched into disaster, chiefly because of the incompetence of their generals. When the soldiers are abandoned, and with no other recourse, they must resort to guerrilla warfare to survive.

Eventually Yu Yuan is captured by the Americans, and as he endures a succession of POW camps, he is caught between the Communist soldiers and the pro-Nationalists who are urging the prisoners to relocate to Taiwan. The bulk of the novel focuses on Yuan's two years in these camps, where he is a witness to the brutal treatment of the prisoners at the hands of the Americans, the South Koreans, and even each other. Because Yu Yuan speaks English, he is forced into the role of mediator, when all he really wants to do is avoid taking sides and be sent home to his family and his girlfriend. As a result, no matter which faction is in control, Yuan cooperates. In the end, his primary allegiance is to himself. When Yuan and his comrades are finally returned to China, they are received as "war trash" for letting themselves be captured. Yu Yuan writes, "We were all discharged dishonourably. ... We had become the dregs of society."

While David Anthony Durham, one of the judges of the PEN/Faulkner Award, called *War Trash* a book of "enormous political and personal complicity, wrung through with emotion that somehow manages to be both melancholy and clear-eyed," other readers noted several problems with the text. Some asserted that the book reads

as if Jin is writing it with the goal of incorporating as much research into it as he can. Todd Hoffman of Montreal's *Gazette* wrote, "Facts, or more specifically, Ha's transparent fidelity to them is one of the major problems with the novel. Characters make choices and events unfold for, seemingly, no other purpose than to incorporate things Ha uncovered in his research." Other writers complained that the book ended too abruptly. Tracy Wilson stated, "And when he is released for the last time, the book simply ends, with only a page or two of detail about what happens to him. ... It leaves little room for hope and none for joy." In addition, it seemed that the farther Jin removed himself from the "exotic" nature of his homeland, as portrayed in the dreamlike, poetic *Waiting,* the more frequently his ability to write in English became the target of criticism. Julia Lovell of London's *Guardian* took swipes at the writer's skill in rendering dialogue, claiming it read like "clumsy translations from the Chinese." She further concludes, "While Ha Jin's dark, brutish subject matter is never less than fascinating, the language in which he tells it is still not nearly perfect enough. If he is to realise his full potential as a literary craftsman, he will have to sharpen up his linguistic act first."

A FREE LIFE

While Ha Jin was traveling the literary circuit and giving readings from *War Trash,* he continued to be generous in granting interviews to members of the press. By this time he was already approximately a year into his next novel, one about a Chinese American immigrant. Rob Thomas of *Madison Capital Times* asked Jin if he thought he would ever return to China as the setting for his work. The writer responded,

> *War Trash* is actually a kind of transitional book that's set outside China, a step toward the United States. I have lived in the States for 20 years, so the American experience feels closer to my heart. So, in that sense, it's natural. On the other hand, it's not natural, because everything is a challenge, even the language.
>
> (p. 7A)

In 2007 Ha Jin published the aforementioned novel, *A Free Life,* a massive tome almost seven hundred pages long. From its opening paragraph, the autobiographical nature of the book is readily apparent. The story line begins in the aftermath of the Tiananmen Square Massacre; the protagonist, Nan Wu, is in a doctoral program at Brandeis University, studying political science (although what he really wants to be is a poet); he and his wife, Pingping, are living in the Boston area, where the pair works a series of odd jobs to support themselves (Nan Wu works as a security guard at a factory and only quits the job when the company is moved); and they must go to California to retrieve their only child, a son, Taotao, who has miraculously been granted his exit papers from China, despite the insanity that was occurring during that time; and when the boy arrives, he recognizes his mother but not his father. When asked by Doug Most of the *Boston Globe* if this novel is really his autobiography, Jin responded with a laugh, and then replied, "He [Nan Wu] returns to China. ... I never returned. I'm really more fortunate than this guy." Jin further elaborates that the idea for *A Free Life* came from a friend of his who told him about a graduate student she had once met who managed a Chinese restaurant but really wanted to be a poet.

While Jin and his protagonist for *A Free Life* do indeed take divergent career paths, Nan Wu's restaurant, the Golden Wok, is in Atlanta, where Jin spent time as a college professor at Emory University. The bulk of the novel centers on Wu and his nuclear family as they adjust to the life of immigrants and discover that freedom has a price. The pair works endlessly at the Golden Wok. They are uneasy with a mortgage, a concept that was unknown to them in the China they grew up in, and they are motivated by the fear that if they do not pay off their house, it will be taken away from them. As Taotao grows into adulthood, he also strays away from them in his embrace of American culture. Underlying the entire span of the novel, as Richard Wallace of the *Seattle Times* wrote, "is the struggle of an artist to find his voice in a strange language, to

free himself from his own doubt and fear." The epilogue of *A Free Life* contains Nan's poetry journal and his poems. Most thought-provoking and heartbreaking of all, and probably the most reminiscent of not only Nan Wu's experiences of what it is to be an immigrant in the United States but also Ha Jin's, is "Homeland."

Although some reviewers considered *A Free Life* to be a ponderous novel, lacking a compelling plot, that is bogged down by minutiae, Donna Seaman in her review for the *Los Angeles Times* claimed that the brevity of the chapters makes them "vivid and brimming with feeling, and the moment-by-moment pace makes visceral the toil and anxiety of Nan and Pingping's disciplined lives."

As a writer, Ha Jin has been compared to Anton Chekhov, Nikolai Gogol, Ernest Hemingway, Nabokov, and Conrad, but the most apt analogy may be to John Steinbeck, that "proletariat" writer Ha Jin was first allowed to read as a young man who begrudgingly accepted being assigned English as a major when the universities in China were reopened. Art Winslow of the *Chicago Tribune* writes, "If likened to an American novelist, Ha Jin may bear the closest resemblance to John Steinbeck, both in his relatively simple, straightforward prose and in his novelistic eye."

Although Ha Jin signed a contract for five of his less controversial books to be published in China, not one had been printed by early 2008. Ha Jin is doubtful that they ever will be. His birth country's loss is the larger world's gain. Through his poetry, short stories, and novels, Ha Jin has provided insight into a China that few of us will ever know, giving the ordinary people of his homeland and their struggles in China and the United States a quiet dignity and haunting resonance. Although Ha Jin, as a writer, has ostensibly left the country of his birth behind, his legacy will remain through his art. When asked by Emily Parker of the *Wall Street Journal Asia* who will now tell the story of China, Ha Jin's answer was uniquely American: "I want to be an individual," he declared. "I want to be an independent man."

Selected Bibliography

WORKS OF HA JIN

Poetry

Between Silences: A Voice from China. Chicago: University of Chicago Press, 1990.

Facing Shadows. Brooklyn, N.Y.: Hanging Loose Press, 1996.

Wreckage. Brooklyn, N.Y.: Hanging Loose Press, 2001.

"Ways of Talking." Poetry Out Loud: National Recitation Project (http://www.poetryoutloud.org).

Short Stories

Ocean of Words: Army Stories. Cambridge, Mass.: Zoland Books, 1996.

Under the Red Flag. Athens: University of Georgia Press, 1997.

Quiet Desperation. New York: Pantheon, 2000.

The Bridegroom. New York: Pantheon, 2000.

Novels

In the Pond. Cambridge, Mass.: Zoland Books, 1998.

Waiting. New York: Pantheon, 1999.

The Crazed. New York: Pantheon, 2002.

War Trash. New York: Pantheon, 2004.

A Free Life. New York: Pantheon, 2007.

Nonfiction

The Writer as Migrant. Chicago: University of Chicago Press, 2008.

CRITICAL AND BIOGRAPHICAL STUDIES

"Book Award Author Changes His Perspective." *Palm Beach Post* (Martin-St. Lucie), March 16, 2001, p. IE.

Breines, Ron. "Waiting for Nothing to Happen." *Daily Yomiuri* (Tokyo), April 2, 2000, p. 1.

Dault, Julia. "'My First Drafts Are Always Awful': Pulitzer Nominee Gives No-Nonsense Advice to Writers." *National Post* (Don Mills, Ontario), July 20, 2005, p. B1.

Davis, Marcia. "Work of Heart." *Washington Post,* May 14, 2005, p. C01.

Franscell, Ron. "Hemingway 'Heir' Chinese Expatriate." *Denver Post,* November 15, 1999, p. F05.

Freeman, John. "A Sad Farewell to China." *Houston Chronicle,* December 19, 2004, p. 20.

Geyh, Paula. "Ha Jin." In *Dictionary of Literary Biography.* Vol. 244: *American Short-Story Writers Since World War II.* Fourth series. Edited by Patrick Meanor and Joseph McNicholas. Detroit: Gale, 2001. Pp. 192–201.

Granath, Jack. "Ha Jin and the Western Tradition (of Chinese Poetry)." *Carnelian* 2, no. 2 (April 2002). Available online (http://www.sidewalkpress.net/carnelian/Past/onthesepremisesapr2002.html).

Greenberg, Susan H. "Lessons in English." *Newsweek* (International ed.), October 29, 2007.

"Ha Jin's Fiction." *Hindu* (Chennai), February 2, 2003, p. 1.

Kieppel, Fredric. "Chinese Tales Resonate with Ordinary Life Quietly Told." *Commercial Appeal* (Memphis), October 8, 2000, p. H13.

Ludlow, Andrea. "Raw Experiences Help 'Make' Writer." *Deseret Morning News* (Salt Lake City), October 31, 2004, p. E01.

McElhatton, Heather. "Ha Jin Weds East to West in Brilliant Tales of Change." *Star Tribune* (Minneapolis), October 8, 2000, p. 16F.

Mehegan, David. "Cambridge's Zoland Books to Stop the Presses." *Boston Globe,* November 14, 2001, p. C5.

Morris, Anne. "China's Chekhov?" *Austin American Statesman,* October 30, 2000, p. D1.

Most, Doug. "American Inexperience." *Boston Globe,* September 3, 2006, p. 24.

Nieves, Felipe. "Writer Brings Homeland Theme to America." *Plain Dealer* (Cleveland), May 5, 2006, p. E1.

O'Briant, Don. "*Waiting* Is Worthwhile for Award Finalist Jin." *Atlanta Journal-Constitution,* October 14, 1999, p. D2.

Smith, Wendy. "Coming to America." *Publishers Weekly,* September 17, 2007, pp. 29–30.

Stoffman, Judy. "Author Finds Chinese Essence in English." *Toronto Star,* November 13, 2000, p. D01.

Sturr, Robert D. "Ha Jin." In *Dictionary of Literary Biography.* Vol. 292: *Twenty-First-Century American Novelists.* Edited by Lisa Abney and Suzanne Disheroon-Green. Farmington Hills, Mich.: Gale, 2004. Pp. 187–193.

"Waiting for Nothing to Happen." *Daily Yomiuri* (Tokyo), April 2, 2000, p. 1.

Wallace, Richard. "New Land, New Life." *Seattle Times,* November 11, 2007, p. J10.

Weaver, Teresa K. "A Master Storyteller." *Atlanta Journal-Constitution,* May 12, 2002, p. F4.

Yee, Amy. "Stories from *Under the Red Flag.*" *Asian Wall Street Journal,* November 13, 1998, p. 15.

BOOK REVIEWS

Allen, Frank. *Library Journal,* June 1, 2001, p. 170. (Review of *Wreckage.*)

Chin, Mei. Review of *In the Pond. New York Times Book Review,* January 31, 1999, p. 16.

Daynard, Jodi. "Ha Jin Explores Souls Under a Heavy Thumb." *Boston Globe,* October 22, 2000, p. C1. (Review of *The Bridegroom.*)

Domini, John. "Soldiers' Stories." *Oregonian* (Portland), June 23, 1996, p E03. (Review of *Ocean of Words.*)

Feeley, Gregory. "Love on Hold." *Washington Post,* January 9, 2000, p. X03. (Review of *Waiting.*)

Foran, Charles. "Chinese Voice, American Accent." *National Post* (Don Mills, Ontario; National edition), November 13, 2004, p. RB11.

Gray, Paul. "Divorce, Chinese-Style." *Time,* November 8, 1999, p. 144. (Review of *Under the Red Flag.*)

Harris, Michael. "Universal Longing in Totalitarian State." *Los Angeles Times,* October 3, 2000, p. 3. (Review of *The Bridegroom.*)

Hoffman, Todd. "Lonely Men Are Held Captive in Desperate Circumstances." *Gazette* (Montreal), December 11, 2004, p. H6. (Review of *War Trash.*)

Igloria, Luisa A. "Ha Jin's Short Stories Speak from the Soul." *Virginian-Pilot* (Norfolk, Va.), January 14, 2001, p. E3. (Review of *The Bridegroom.*)

Kinkley, Jeffrey C. *World Literature Today,* spring 1999, p. 390. (Review of *In the Pond.*)

Leung, K. C. *World Literature Today,* autumn 1997, pp. 861–862. (Review of *Facing Shadows.*)

Lovell, Julia. "Fighting for Mao." *Guardian,* (London), November 12, 2005, p. 17.

Mazur, Gail. *Ploughshares,* spring 1991, pp. 230–231. (*Review of Between Silences.*)

Messud, Claire. "Tiger-Fighter Meets Cowboy Chicken." *New York Times Book Review,* October 22, 2000, p. 9. (Review of *The Bridegroom.*)

Robinson, Bill. "The Crazed." *MostlyFiction* (http://www.mostlyfiction.com/world/jin.htm), October 12, 2002.

Park, Ed. Review of *In the Pond. Village Voice,* December 29, 1998, p. 131.

Perry, Phyllis Alesia. "Chinese Hero Makes Ripples in *Pond.*" *Atlanta Journal-Constitution,* January 10, 1999, p. L11. (Review of *In the Pond.*)

Sayers, Valerie. "The Road to Tiananmen." *Commonweal,* February 14, 2003, pp. 17–18. (Review of *The Crazed.*)

Scharf, Michael. *Publishers Weekly,* June 4, 2001, p. 78. (Review of *Wreckage.*)

Seaman, Donna. "The Art of Liberation." *Los Angeles Times,* November 25, 2007, p. R8. (Review of *A Free Life.*)

Skube, Michael. "Award-Winner Ha Jin's Gift in the Details." *Atlanta Journal-Constitution,* October 8, 2000, p. D3. (Review of *The Bridegroom.*)

Smith, Sarah A. "Saturday Review: Fiction." *Guardian* (London), November 30, 2002, p. 27. (Review of *The Crazed.*)

Steinberg, Sybil S. *Publishers Weekly,* October 12, 1998, pp. 58–59. (Review of *In the Pond.*)

Szatmary, Peter. "The Long Goodbye: Writer Ha Jin Assesses China by Way of Romantic Triangle." *Houston Chronicle,* December 5, 1999, p. 15. (Review of *Waiting.*)

Thomas, Rob. "Seeing War from Other Side." *Madison Capital Times,* September 30, 2005, p. 7A. (Review of *War Trash.*)

Twitchell-Waas, Jeffrey. *World Literature Today,* winter 2002. p. 109. (Review of *Wreckage.*)

Wilson, Tracy. "Too Realistic." *Winston-Salem Journal,* December 26, 2004, p. 28. (Review of *War Trash.*)

Winslow, Art. "Coming to America." *Chicago Tribune,* November 10, 2007, p. 3. (Review of *A Free Life.*)

Wong, Timothy C. *World Literature Today,* autumn 1997, p. 862. (Review of *Ocean of Words: Army Stories.*)

Interviews

Freeman, John. "Author Interview: Ha Jin." *St. Petersburg Times,* October 10, 2004, p. 5P.

Garner, Dwight. "Interview: 'Somehow I Couldn't Stop.'" *New York Times Book Review,* October 10, 2004, p. 9.

"Individualism Arrives in China." *New Perspective Quarterly* 20, no. 1:13–21 (winter 2003).

Parker, Emily. "The Journal Interview with Ha Jin: Who Will Tell the Story of China?" *Wall Street Journal Asia* (Hong Kong), September 25, 2006, p. 14.

Skube, Michael. "A Conversation with Novelist Ha Jin. "*Atlanta Journal-Constitution,* November 15, 1999, p. E1.

Weich, Dave. "Interview with Ha Jin." Powells.com (http://www.powells.com), February 2, 2000.

JON KRAKAUER

(1954—)

Susan Butterworth

JON KRAKAUER IS a journalist with a point of view, a reporter who tells his story as he sees it, whether or not it is the story the subject wants to tell or the public wants to hear. For this reason, his nonfiction books have been controversial and have received strong, not always favorable reactions. He told Robert Boynton, "I want to provoke people, to expose readers to unsettling truths" (p. 166). Krakauer is a researcher; he spends hours in libraries and archives; he conducts hundreds of interviews. At the same time, he speculates about causes. He is interested in the question "Why?": What motivates people to do extreme things, like walk into the wilds of the Alaskan wilderness with not much more than a sack of rice and a rifle or climb Mount Everest in spite of the well-documented dangers? Why would an otherwise personable and religious man kill a young mother and her child and feel no remorse for the murder? His speculation has led him to write about immoderation, or, as he calls it in his 2003 volume, *Under the Banner of Heaven,* the "territory of the extreme" (p. xxiii).

A CLIMBING OBSESSION

Jon Krakauer was born April 12, 1954, in Brookline, Massachusetts, the third of five children. His father, Lewis Krakauer, was a physician and his mother was an art teacher. His family moved to Corvallis, Oregon, when he was two years old. Young Krakauer began mountain climbing at the age of eight. In the author's note to *Eiger Dreams* (1990), he writes:

> I trace the roots of my own obsession back to 1962. I was a fairly ordinary kid growing up in Corvallis, Oregon. My father was a sensible, rigid parent who constantly badgered his five children to study calculus and Latin, keep their noses to the grindstone, fix their sights early and unflinchingly on careers in medicine or law. Inexplicably, on the occasion of my eighth birthday this strict taskmaster presented me with a pint-size ice axe and took me on my first climb. In retrospect I can't imagine what the old man was thinking; if he'd given me a Harley and a membership in the Hell's Angels he couldn't have sabotaged his paternal aspirations any more effectively.
>
> (pp. x–xi)

That first climb, an attempt on Oregon's ten-thousand-foot South Sister, was in the company of Willi Unsoeld, a close friend of Krakauer senior, and his son Regon. A few months later, Unsoeld departed for Nepal to make the first ascent of Mount Everest's West Ridge with fellow mountaineer Tom Hornbein in May of 1963. This feat, and the lure of the world's highest mountain, inspired young Krakauer's imagination, and would culminate in his own 1996 ascent of Mount Everest, chronicled in the best-selling *Into Thin Air* (1997).

Growing up in Corvallis Oregon, Krakauer found himself "in the happy company of Latter-day Saints" (*Under the Banner of Heaven,* p. 333). The town had a wide community of Latter-day Saints (the religious group commonly known as Mormons), who would become the subject of *Under the Banner of Heaven: A Story of Violent Faith* (2003). "Saints were my childhood friends and playmates, my teachers, my athletic coaches," he wrote in that volume (pp. 333–334). Krakauer played tennis for Corvallis High School, graduating in 1972. By this time, climbing had become his primary interest, essentially his obsession. His father, Lewis Krakauer, was a doctor who had graduated from elite Williams College and Harvard Medical School. When he was sent to New England to interview at similar elite colleges, Krakauer discovered the recently opened experimental school Hampshire College, which

had an outdoors program. He applied and was accepted. He and his father didn't speak to each other for two years, a fact that led him to some insight into the life and motivation of Christopher McCandless, the young man whose story he would tell in *Into the Wild* (1996).

While at Hampshire, he met David Roberts, a professor and climbing writer, who interested him in climbing in Alaska. In 1974, still a student, Krakauer climbed the Alaskan Arrigetch Peaks in the Brooks Range with a group of seven friends, ascending three peaks that had previously been unexplored. Pioneering a new route up the peak called the Moose's Tooth was the subject of his senior thesis. As a result, the American Alpine Club asked Krakauer to write about the climbs for its journal. He describes this first Alaskan expedition as a pivotal event in his life, intensifying his preoccupation with climbing. He credits David Roberts with teaching him how to write.

Krakauer graduated from Hampshire College with a bachelor's degree in Environmental Studies in December 1975. For the next eight years, he indulged his obsession, becoming a climbing bum, working just enough as a carpenter and commercial fisherman in Colorado, Seattle, and Alaska to finance the next climb. In 1977, he met his future wife, Linda Mariam Moore, a student at the University of Colorado at Denver and a fellow climber. Also in 1977, he made a solo climb of the Devil's Thumb in the Stikine Icecap region of Alaska, which he later wrote about for the British magazine *Mountain,* in his essay collection *Eiger Dreams,* and in *Into the Wild.* "Eventually," writes Krakauer in the introduction to his 1990 collection, *Eiger Dreams,* this life "began to wear thin":

> I found myself lying awake nights, reliving all the close scrapes I'd had on the heights. Sawing joists in the rain at some muddy construction site, my thoughts would increasingly turn to college classmates who were raising families, investing in real estate, buying lawn furniture, assiduously amassing wealth.
>
> I resolved to quit climbing, and said as much to the woman with whom I was involved at the time. She was so taken aback by this announcement that she agreed to marry me.
>
> (pp. xi–xii)

Krakauer and Linda Moore were married in 1980 and have been married ever since. However, his resolve to quit climbing proved to be easier said than done.

> My abstinence lasted barely a year, and when it ended it looked for a while like the connubial arrangement was going to end with it. Against all odds, I somehow managed to stay married *and* keep climbing. No longer, however, did I feel compelled to push things right to the brink, to see God on every pitch, to make each climb more radical than the last. Today I feel like an alcoholic who's managed to make the switch from week-long whiskey benders to a few beers on Saturday night. I've slipped happily into alpine mediocrity.
>
> (p. xii)

The title and lead article of *Eiger Dreams* appeared in *Outside* magazine in March 1985; in recounting the decision to abandon a climb of the legendary North Face of the Eiger, the piece would appear to corroborate Krakauer's description of himself as a more cautious man than the rash youth who had made the first solo ascent of Alaska's Devil's Thumb at the age of twenty-three. Nevertheless these words were written several years before the Mount Everest expedition that was as life-threatening as anything Krakauer had previously done.

FREELANCE JOURNALISM

Krakauer made a major life change in the early 1980s: he became a freelance writer, becoming especially well-known for writing about climbing and outdoor subjects. Recently married, with the construction industry in recession, he contemplated applying to law school. David Roberts, his friend and climbing partner, had recently left academia to become an editor and freelance writer, and Roberts convinced Krakauer that journalism would be more rewarding than carpentry.

Krakauer dove in headfirst, determined to learn as he worked. His models included the stylish nonfiction writers Tracy Kidder and John

McPhee. He bought a book on how to become a magazine writer and learned to write an effective query letter. He followed the book's advice to send out a quota of ten queries a week, and he began to receive assignments. He said in his interview with Boynton: "My first query to *Outside* magazine resulted in an assignment on spec, as did my first query to *Rolling Stone.* It took a few tries to get into *Smithsonian,* but eventually I started getting assignments there, too" (p. 165). He sold his first article to a national magazine in 1981; in November 1983 he abandoned part-time work as a carpenter and became a full-time writer. Although he wrote assignments on various topics—architecture, natural history, and popular culture—mountaineering stories continued to be his trademark. By 1995, Krakauer had written sixty articles for *Outside.*

Krakauer's first book was a collection of magazine articles originally written for *Outside* and *Smithsonian. Eiger Dreams: Ventures Among Men and Mountains,* published in 1990, introduced the theme that would preoccupy him through his next two books: what drives men to take the risks that climbing dangerous peaks demands? Opening with the disclaimer that his risk-taking has diminished as his writing life has blossomed, the collection begins with the essay "Eiger Dreams," a story of caution, and ends with "The Devil's Thumb," the story of his reckless youthful solo summit of the remote Alaskan peak.

Another piece in the collection, "A Bad Summer on K2," which was cowritten with Greg Child and first appeared in *Outside* in 1987, foreshadows the disastrous spring of 1996 on Mount Everest and raises the question of whether attempting to save the lives of climbing companions in desperate conditions is heroism or senseless sentimentality. It is impossible to pass judgment on those in "an unimaginably desperate situation," he writes (p. 160). With the summit of K2 within reach, "you might be inclined to take a few more chances than you normally would," one K2 adventurer tells him, reflecting on the psychology of the high-altitude climber (p. 160).

The story is a litany of bad weather, warnings not heeded, death from exposure, lack of oxygen, falls, and cumulative exhaustion. The mountains are littered with abandoned oxygen cylinders and bodies. Over and over again, climbers leave their friends behind, in such bad condition that they know they will never see them alive again. The collection showcases Krakauer's singular appeal as an adventure writer, his dramatic writing, his sense of place, and the authority his personal experience as a climber gives to his work.

INTO THE WILD

In late 1992, *Outside* asked Krakauer to write an article about Christopher McCandless, a young man whose body had been found in the Alaskan wilderness north of Mount McKinley. Young McCandless was from a well-to-do family, a college graduate who had given away his money, abandoned his car, taken the name Alexander Supertramp, and hitchhiked to Alaska. An idealist, a dreamer, he had rejected the advantages of his upbringing and decided to live off the land, alone. He failed. His body was found four months after he walked away from his last human contact. He had starved to death.

Krakauer flew to Alaska and retraced McCandless's last journey, taking photos of the landscape and of the abandoned bus that had been McCandless's camp and where he had died. He interviewed McCandless's friends and family members and read the young man's postcards and journals. Working on a tight deadline, Krakauer wrote a nine-thousand-word article that appeared in the January 1993 issue of the magazine. The article was a finalist for a National Magazine Award. It also drew a record amount of mail, more than the magazine had ever received about a single story. Readers reacted strongly to McCandless's story, whether they sympathized with his idealism or thought he was a reckless and selfish fool. There were those who felt he had meant to leave the world behind and die, that the journey into the Alaskan wilderness was essentially suicide.

Additional information came to light as a result of the article's publication, including this letter addressed "To Whom It May Concern" and received by the *Outside* office:

> I would like to get a copy of the magazine that carried the story of the young man (Alex McCandless) dying in Alaska. I would like to write the one that investigated the incident.
>
> (*Into the Wild,* pp. 47–48)

The writer of the letter had driven McCandless from Salton City, California, to Grand Junction, Colorado, in March 1992 and left him there to hitchhike to South Dakota. The letter poignantly continues:

> ". ... he always carried enough rice in his backpack + he had arctic clothes + plenty of money. ... Please do not make these facts available to anybody till I know more about his death for he was not just the common wayfarer. Please believe me."
>
> (*Into the Wild,* pp. 47–48)

Krakauer contacted the writer of the letter and spent more than a year retracing McCandless's path across the United States, uncovering new information, interviewing the people who had sheltered him during his journey. He was drawn to McCandless's story, to his spiritual quest. He saw parallels between McCandless's and his own life, between his own solo attempt on the Devil's Thumb and McCandless's desire to challenge the wilderness alone. Krakauer writes: "In trying to understand McCandless, I inevitably came to reflect on other, larger subjects as well: the grip wilderness has on the American imagination, the allure high-risk activities hold for young men of a certain mind, the complicated, highly charged bond that exists between fathers and sons" (*Into the Wild,* author's note, n.p.).

As a journalist, Krakauer had spent much of his career minimizing his authorial presence. But he felt compelled to respond to those who condemned young McCandless as an unprepared, arrogant, and irresponsible boy who had selfishly caused his family indescribable pain. In the book Krakauer would write about McCandless' journey, *Into the Wild,* Krakauer inserts his own experience on the Devil's Thumb in an attempt to shed light on the motivations of a young man who had not lived to speak for himself. What Krakauer presents is an idea of a rite of passage and a connection with nature that is missing from the lives of young males in contemporary America. In an age when there is no more uncharted territory, an age of privilege and materialism, he presents McCandless' and his own dangerous undertakings as a spiritual journey. A desire for transformation, an ascetic longing, is the motivation, and the desire to court danger and take risks is a response to a privileged upbringing and especially to a competitive and complicated relationship with a strong-willed father.

> "The fact that I survived my Alaska adventure and McCandless did not survive his was largely a matter of chance; had I not returned from the Stikine Ice Cap in 1977, people would have been quick to say of me—as they now say of him—that I had a death wish." And as Krakauer points out, to a young man death is an abstract concept; youth is incapable of appreciating "its terrible finality or the havoc it could wreak on those who'd entrusted the deceased with their hearts."
>
> (*Into the Wild,* p. 155)

Krakauer's account of McCandless's last weeks and days is painstakingly researched and affectingly written. *Into the Wild* became a best seller. In addition to its exploration of the rites of passage of the young American male in the twentieth century, the book is significant for its effect on the reader. Some have been inspired by the idealism of the young man and the call of the wilderness. Many have been saddened and some have been angered by the pain he caused his family and the futility of his death just when, from the evidence of his journals, he seems to have reached an epiphany in his spiritual journey, the idea that connection is essential to the human spirit. Many, including much of the Alaskan outdoors community, expressed outrage at his inexperience and unpreparedness, seeing it as a foolhardy arrogance.

INTO THIN AIR

In his 1987 essay "A Bad Summer on K2," Krakauer had clearly and specifically asked some central questions about the risks of high-altitude climbing: "Should a civilized society continue to condone, much less celebrate, an activity in which there appears to be a growing acceptance of death as a likely outcome?" (*Eiger Dreams,* p.

161). In 1996, he would have the opportunity to explore this question more thoroughly. The experience of climbing Mount Everest would prove to be a seminal event in his life and his writing career.

By 1995, Mount Everest, the world's tallest peak, had become an object of some disdain from the serious climbing community. The reason was the mountain's increasing commercialization. Commercial guided expeditions had made it possible for relatively inexperienced climbers with an abundance of money to reach the summit, under conditions that, while rigorous, nevertheless had some aspects of a luxury cruise. Guides and sherpas blazed the trail, carried the weight, set up camp, and provided the oxygen canisters that made the climb possible. Clients were even brought tea in their sleeping bags in the morning. The trail had become littered with trash, abandoned tents, oxygen bottles, and even the frozen dead bodies of climbers who had paid the ultimate price for their attempt on Everest.

In March 1995, *Outside*'s editors asked Krakauer to join a guided Everest expedition and spend two months at base camp writing about the controversies attending the commercialization of the mountain. For Krakauer, however, the offer unearthed his buried adolescent dreams of actually climbing Everest. He thought it would be unbearably frustrating to be so close and not be able to climb Everest himself. He thus persuaded the editors of *Outside* to cover the $65,000 fee that one of the more reputable guide services would charge, and send him to the summit of Everest. He also asked for a year's postponement so that he could get in shape for the arduous climb.

Some serious soul-searching followed. Krakauer had done some difficult climbing in Alaska, Canada, Colorado, and South America when he was considerably younger. He had presumably already completed his own rites of passage. In 1995 he was forty-one years old, married to a woman he loved, and had a successful writing career. Furthermore, he had no experience with extreme high altitude such as that of Mount Everest. He was aware that the mountain had claimed the lives of one in four of those who had reached its summit. Nevertheless, he writes, "boyhood dreams die hard," and when his editor called him in February 1996 and told him there was a place available for him with New Zealand guide Rob Hall's Adventure Consultants expedition, "I said yes without even pausing to catch my breath" (*Into Thin Air,* p. 26).

Krakauer reached the summit of Everest on 10 May 1996, but what he reported was shocking and devastating. The cost was great, too great for Krakauer or his readers to absorb without subsequent reflection. Four of Krakauer's five teammates who made it to the summit of Everest died in a storm that arrived while they were still on the peak. Nine climbers in total died by the time Krakauer had descended the mountain. What went wrong would be the subject of an article in the September 1996 issue of *Outside* and of the full-length book that followed: *Into Thin Air: A Personal Account of the Mount Everest Disaster* (1997).

Mount Everest was crowded in April 1996. No fewer than fifteen expeditions were present on the mountain, some experienced and prepared, some far less so. Krakauer describes in some detail the members and guides of several of these expeditions: Rob Hall, Andy Harris, Mike Groom, Doug Hansen, Beck Weathers, and Yasuko Namba of the Adventure Consultants expedition; the flamboyant Scott Fischer, Anatoli Boukreev, Neal Beidleman, Sandy Hill Pittman, Charlotte Fox, and Tim Madsen of the rival Mountain Madness expedition; the less-experienced members of the Taiwanese National Expedition; the uncooperative leadership and internal strife of the South African expedition; the role of the IMAX team in the rescue after the storm; all are players in the drama. A number of these players would lose their lives as a result of a series of small but critical unfortunate decisions.

After an arduous trek to base camp and a series of hikes to higher camps designed to acclimate the clients to the altitude, Rob Hall judged his group ready to attempt the summit. There is a small window of time when it is possible to reach the summit of Everest, between the hurricane season and the monsoon season. Conditions must be perfect. By the time the climber is

within reach of the summit, he or she has been living in conditions of limited oxygen for some time, conditions that are physically life-threatening and that affect the climber's judgment and decision-making ability. The optimal date in 1996 was May 10th; the day deemed meteorologically ideal for the summit attempt. Thus all the expeditions on the Nepalese side of the mountain wanted to summit on that day, and in spite of Rob Hall's attempt to coordinate the various expeditions, a bottleneck occurred, causing dangerous delays.

Guided climbs are commercial ventures; some decisions would be made on the basis of commercial success, getting as many clients to the top as possible. Hall, wise and experienced, had explained the importance of sticking to a predetermined turnaround time. No matter how badly a client wanted to make the summit, or how badly a guide wanted to get his client to the top, getting down the mountain after hours of supreme exertion with minimal oxygen was the true test—in fact, a matter of life or death.

According to Hall, in attempting the summit, "Sticking to your predetermined turn-around time—that was the most important rule on the mountain. ... Our turn-around time, he said, would probably be 1 p.m., and no matter how close we were to the top, we were to abide by it. With enough determination, any bloody idiot can get up this hill," Hall said. "The trick is to get back down alive" ("Into Thin Air" in *The Best American Sports Writing of the Century,* p. 643). This statement would turn out to be the heartbreaking truth.

Krakauer himself summitted Everest shortly after 1 p.m. just after the guide Anatoli Boukreev of the Mountain Madness expedition and just before his friend and guide Andy Harris of Adventure Consultants. Beginning his descent, he encountered a traffic jam of more than a dozen climbers from three expeditions, all still on their way up. Suffering from anoxia—oxygen deprivation—and already behind schedule, at least Krakauer was on his way down. These other climbers, including the head guides Rob Hall and Scott Fischer, were still on their way up. And in such close proximity to the summit, they were not about to turn back.

Unfortunately, the few seemingly benign clouds drifting below the summit would rapidly develop into a rogue storm. With no visibility and blizzard conditions, the seriously weakened and oxygen-deprived climbers would be unable to reach the safety of camp, and several, including the head guides Rob Hall and Scott Fischer, would die. Those who lived, Krakauer among them, would be severely traumatized.

Krakauer felt particularly responsible for the death of his companion, a junior guide named Andy Harris. The two men had become close over the course of the expedition and had begun the descent together. In hindsight, Krakauer realized that his friend's behavior had shown signs of severe oxygen deprivation. Deprived of oxygen himself, and slipping into the role of client with a guide, he failed to heed the signs. "Given what unfolded over the hours that followed," he writes, "the ease with which I abdicated responsibility—my utter failure to consider that Andy might have been in serious trouble—was a lapse that's likely to haunt me for the rest of my life" (*Into Thin Air,* p. 188). Krakauer continued down alone. The worsening weather and fresh snow had obliterated the trail. The wind chill was in excess of seventy below zero Fahrenheit, Krakauer was out of oxygen, and far beyond ordinary exhaustion. Finally coming within sight of the camp, only one obstacle remained: one ice slope between Krakauer and the safety of the tents, only intermittently visible through the blizzard. At this point, Krakauer sat down to rest, and Andy Harris, frozen and stumbling, caught up with him. Harris slid down the ice slope and walked toward the camp. Shortly afterward, Krakauer reached his tent and collapsed into his sleeping bag, thinking he and Harris were safe.

He had told another one of his companions that he'd seen Harris arrive safely, and word had been radioed to Harris's female partner in New Zealand. But in the morning, it was discovered that Harris was not in camp. He appeared to have lost his way within forty or fifty feet of the tents and fallen over the four-thousand-foot Lhotse

Face. Now his partner would have to receive an unthinkable phone call: a mistake had been made. Harris was missing and presumed dead. Krakauer was devastated at the loss of his friend and for causing his partner such pain.

While Krakauer slept in his tent, deadly and horrifying events were unfolding on the mountain. Both expedition leaders, Scott Fischer of Mountain Madness and Rob Hall of Adventure Consultants, along with a client, Doug Hansen, were trapped on the mountain, too weak and oxygen deprived to make the descent in the storm. Rob Hall, weak and unlikely to live, spoke to his wife in New Zealand via radio and satellite phone. The report of the phone call is heartbreaking. "I love you. Sleep well, my sweetheart. Please don't worry too much," were his last words (*Into Thin Air,* p. 235). Rescue attempts failed. All three men died. A group made up of clients Sandy Hill Pittman, Charlene Fox, Tim Madsen, Beck Weathers, Yasuko Namba, and the Mountain Madness guide Neal Beidleman was lost, wandering in the blizzard in desperate straits. During a slight break in the storm, Beidleman managed to get to camp and send Anatoli Boukreev to the rescue. Pittman, Fox, and Madsen were saved, but Weathers and Namba were left for dead. Yet later, Weathers stumbled into camp, his hands frozen solid, his survival dramatic and miraculous.

The ordeal wasn't over. The survivors, most of them in very poor condition, still had to climb down to base camp and then walk out to the nearest village where helicopter transport was possible. Their grief, and the grief of the Tibetan Sherpas who had been their constant companions, was devastating.

Arriving home in Seattle, Krakauer wrote the contracted article for *Outside* in five weeks. The seventeen-thousand-word article appeared in the September 1996 issue of the magazine. Krakauer's assignment had been to write about the commercialization of climbing Mount Everest. In speculating about the causes of the deadly events that occurred, Krakauer angered a number of people. He theorizes about the motives of the guides Hall and Fischer, neither of whom was alive to refute his speculation but whose surviving loved ones were deeply hurt. The commercial motivation, the desire to get as many paying clients to the summit as possible, may have contributed to excessive risk-taking and to ignoring the prespecified turnaround time. Krakauer's depiction of the guide Anatoli Boukreev is not flattering; Krakauer doesn't see him as a team player, although he credits him with heroism in the rescue of Pittman, Madsen, and Fox.

The very nature of the commercial expedition as opposed to the traditional climbing team, Krakauer feels, contributed to the sum of a number of smaller decisions and events that led up to the tragedy. He writes frankly:

> We were a team in name only, I'd sadly come to realize. ... Each client was in it for himself or herself, pretty much. And I was no different. ... To my mind, the rewards of climbing come from its emphasis on self-reliance, on making critical decisions and dealing with the consequences, on personal responsibility. When you become a client, I discovered, you give up all that. For safety's sake, the guide always calls the shots. ... Passivity on the part of the clients had thus been encouraged throughout our expedition.
>
> ("Into Thin Air," pp. 645–646)

Krakauer speculates about the role that using supplemental oxygen has in encouraging climbers who are not qualified for extreme high altitude climbing. He proposes forbidding the use of supplemental oxygen as a means of limiting future disasters. He also speculates about the role the presence of the socialite and magazine editor Sandy Hill Pittman had in decisions that were made on Everest in May 1996. It is possible that valuable energy was expended on Pittman, a particularly high-profile client who might have provided valuable publicity to Scott Fischer had she succeeded in reaching the summit. John Trombold, writing in *Popular Culture Review* in 1999, reads *Into Thin Air* as social criticism, referring to what he calls the hubris of the wealthy, the nature of guided climbing as accessible only to a privileged social class. This reading is neither flattering to nor popular with the wealthy clients of the Everest expeditions.

Krakauer's own role as a journalist, he felt, may have contributed to dangerous risk-taking on

the part of the two head guides as well. Simply having a journalist present, knowing that the events and results of the expedition would be reported in a prominent national outdoor magazine, is likely to have influenced their decisions.

The article that Krakauer wrote about the disaster on Everest is intense in its immediacy, written quickly and appearing so soon after the event. Some of the information, such as the crowding on the mountain and the bottleneck at the Hillary Step and the extreme effects of oxygen deprivation, is eye-opening. The emotional effect is powerful. Reactions were strong and varied, just as they had been to his article about Chris McCandless three years earlier. Krakauer felt that he had written an honest account of the events, but speculating about causes is often controversial or at the least unpopular. However, Krakauer's point of view is authoritative because of his own experience as a climber and as an acknowledged risk taker.

The reactions to the article, the desire to complete the tale that he had not been able to tell thoroughly even in seventeen thousand words, and new information that he uncovered led him to write a more detailed account, which appeared as *Into Thin Air* in 1997. The most compelling new information that distinguishes the book from the original article concerns the death of Andy Harris. Krakauer originally reported that Harris had safely reached camp, then determined that he had lost his way in the blizzard and fallen to his death. Krakauer describes his guilt about not realizing the extent of his friend's anoxic difficulty, his regret about not staying with Harris and somehow helping him back to camp, and his horror about the mistake he had made, causing Harris's partner in New Zealand unimaginable pain.

In July 1996, after the *Outside* article had gone to press, Krakauer was able to interview Martin Adams, a client on the Mountain Madness expedition. He uncovered two facts that shed light on Harris's death. Adams reported an encounter with an anonymous climber not far from the camp at the height of the storm. Then he slid down the ice face, he said, and stumbled to the tent. Krakauer writes: "As Adams described his encounter with the anonymous climber, and then sliding down the ice, my mouth went dry and the hairs on the back of my neck suddenly bristled" (*Into Thin Air,* p. 220). It hadn't been Harris that Krakauer had encountered. It had been Adams. "And if Andy had never arrived at Camp Four after reaching the summit, what in the name of God had happened to him?" (p. 220).

The answer emerged in an interview with Lopsang Jangbu Sherpa, the head climbing Sherpa of Fischer's expedition, also conducted in July 1996. Lopsang reported seeing Harris on the South Summit on the evening of 10 May, at about the time Krakauer thought he'd seen him near Camp Four. In light of the new evidence that he gained in the time between publishing the article and publishing the book, Krakauer revisits his assumptions about how Andy Harris died, and ultimately surmises that Harris must have turned back up the Hillary Step to bring oxygen to Rob Hall and the client Doug Hansen. It now seems likely that Harris died attempting to rescue his teammates. Nothing further is known about how his life ended, nor about Hansen's death. Their bodies were never found.

REACTION TO INTO THIN AIR

Krakauer's book came under intense scrutiny both as memoir and as journalism, as other climbers who had been on the mountain at the time of the tragedy contributed their own recollections and interpretations of the same events. Anatoli Boukreev wrote and published his own account of events in a book titled *The Climb* (1997). Boukreev was portrayed as the consummate climber and hero by Mountain Madness client Lene Gammelgaard, whose book *Climbing High: A Woman's Account of Surviving the Everest Tragedy* was published in Denmark in 1996 and translated into English in 1999. The American edition ends with a tribute to Boukreev, who died in an avalanche in the Himalaya on Christmas Day 1997.

In September 2006, ten years after Krakauer's article about the 1996 Mount Everest disaster, *Outside* published a follow-up special section

called "Return to Thin Air: The Everest Disaster Ten Years Later." The death toll on the mountain in 2006 had also been shockingly high. Krakauer's controversial book was still being debated. Charlene Fox and Sandy Hill Pittman had been rescued together by Anatoli Boukreev, yet the two women expressed opposing viewpoints on the accuracy of Krakauer's reporting. Fox was quoted as saying: "I'm glad that Krakauer's book stood out as the most popular and definitive statement regarding the events because he truly tried to get the facts straight" (p. 82). Pittman is referring to Krakauer when she writes: "There was really only one writer who made scapegoats and pointed fingers and placed blame. That's the writer who got the most airplay." Pittman continues: "Of all the coverage, Anatoli Boukreev's book *The Climb* got the story best ... at least I recognized what he wrote as being the same trip I was on" (p. 84). Jan Arnold, Rob Hall's widow, responds to a question about how Hall's actions were reported in *Into Thin Air*: "It was a mixture. There were some very critical words used—words such as hubris—and I think that was misdirected at Rob. Yet overall the book ends up respecting Rob" (p. 81).

Whatever the reactions of those involved in the Everest expeditions of 1996, the public loved *Into Thin Air.* It is the ultimate adventure narrative, the chronicle of a dream pursued even as far as death. Kristin Jacobson, writing in the journal *Genre,* defines the American adrenaline narrative as travel and nature writing with an element of heightened risk. The perilous outdoor adventure fascinates readers, who are eager to vicariously experience the physical journey as well as the deeper spiritual and emotional aspects of the experience.

As a notable example of the literary adrenaline narrative, *Into Thin Air* like *Into the Wild* refers to and quotes directly from other adventure tales, placing it in a literary tradition. The author's identity plays an important role in the narrative: Krakauer's own accomplishments and exploits as an experienced climber who has summitted Everest and lived to tell the tale. With vivid descriptive language, a powerful writing style, a clear sequence of events based on observation and interview, and clear explanation of technical terms, the book is as well-crafted as it is compelling in its drama.

AFTER EVEREST

As a freelance writer, Krakauer had always been a hard worker, turning out article after article to pay the rent. By 1996, he had made a name for himself as an outdoor adventure writer and was a contributing editor of *Outside* magazine. Although he characterizes himself as a slow writer, when he signed the contract to write a book about the Everest disaster, he had already committed to an expedition to Antarctica that was leaving only three months later. On 1 December 1996, immediately after finishing the manuscript of *Into Thin Air,* Krakauer departed on a project to film his ascent of a peak in Antarctica for the National Geographic production *Explorer.* He returned to Antarctica in 2001 to narrate a documentary for the PBS *Nova* series.

With two best-selling adventure books in two years, however, Krakauer's financial status was now secure. *Into Thin Air* made him something of a celebrity for a time. Publicity appearances and readings were well attended. However Krakauer is known as an intensely private, even reclusive, man. He stepped out of the limelight fairly quickly, declining offers to make advertising appearances. In 1998, Krakauer and his wife moved from Seattle to Boulder, Colorado.

With the financial success of *Into Thin Air,* Krakauer was able to support humanitarian work, including the Central Asia Institute, run by the climber Greg Mortenson. Mortensen had been nursed back to health by Pakistani villagers following a failed attempt on K2, and he resolved to help the remote region by building schools. Krakauer's support of the idea of one man with a little money making a difference in a remote mountain region seems in harmony with his self-effacing character, his experience as a climber, and his desire that something good might come from the Everest disaster.

Following the move to Boulder, Krakauer was able to regain some of the equilibrium that

had been so shaken by his experience on Everest, to do some solo climbing in the Rockies, and to do an annual summer climb with his old friend Tom Hornbein, who was then in his seventies and chairman of the board of Central Asia Institute.

He also edited a series of books for Random House that was reissued as the Modern Library Exploration Series. As a self-taught nonfiction writer, Krakauer had read widely not only the contemporary works of such writers as Tracy Kidder and John McPhee but also a broad range of nonfiction writers in the genres of historic adventure and exploration. He had drawn from these books for the epigraphs heading each chapter of *Into the Wild* and *Into Thin Air.* For the Exploration Series, he was able to select from among these little-known, often-forgotten classics and write a new introduction for each work. The series includes Francis Parkman's *La Salle and the Discovery of the Great West* (1999), Roland Huntford's *The Last Place on Earth: Scott and Amundsen's Race to the South Pole* (1999), and Valerian Albanov's *In the Land of the White Death: A Epic Story of Survival in the Siberian Arctic* (2000), all of which Krakauer consider as inspiration for his own work.

UNDER THE BANNER OF HEAVEN

Finally free from the necessity of writing for magazines and able to pursue projects of his own choice, Krakauer decided to approach the idea of fanatics, or individuals drawn to extremes, from a new angle. Both *Into the Wild* and *Into Thin Air* had been narratives with elements of the spiritual journey. The emotional toll of the Everest experience had been agonizing; Krakauer decided to write a meditation on the nature of faith and doubt. In the author's remarks at the end of *Under the Banner of Heaven* (2003), Krakauer writes: "The genesis for this book was a desire to grasp the nature of religious belief. Because I've spent most of my life in the West, in the happy company of Latter-day Saints, I decided to narrow my subject to a more manageable scope by examining belief more or less exclusively through the lens of Mormonism" (p. 333). He writes that he intended to explore the questions: "How does a critical mind reconcile scientific and historical truth with religious doctrine? How does one sustain belief when confronted with facts that appear to refute it?" (p. 334). Krakauer began to research both the paradox of faith and doubt and the history of the Mormon Church: the Church of Jesus Christ of Latter-day Saints (LDS).

He spent the next three years traveling to Mormon sacred sites, interviewing dozens of Mormons, visiting archives, and reading. Krakauer said in an interview that he enjoys research more than writing. A subject needs to "have [him] by the throat," he says (in Boynton, p. 162), in order to inspire him to invest the necessary time and energy in the writing. "A sense of place—a familiarity with the particulars of the landscape in question—is always important to me, so I buy lots of maps," he continues (Boynton, p. 163).

While researching his planned book about Mormon faith, he stumbled across the place that would provide the focus for his book: Colorado City, Utah. Stopping for gas "in the middle of nowhere" (Boynton, p. 159), he noticed the women and girls wearing distinctive nineteenth-century costume and decided to drive into the nearby town. A National Park Service ranger told him that Colorado City is the home of the nation's largest community of Mormon fundamentalists, practitioners of polygamy.

He found his central character, Dan Lafferty, by a similar twist of fate. Following his original theme of faith and doubt, he wrote to Mark Hofmann, a Mormon who had lost his faith and was serving a prison sentence for forgery and a cover-up bombing that had killed two people. Hofmann declined the interview, but his cellmate Dan Lafferty wrote back that he was a fanatical believer and would be happy to talk to a journalist. Dan Lafferty was serving a life sentence for a brutal ritual execution of a mother and child. This murder would become the central event of the developing book.

Under the Banner of Heaven is a masterful work of detailed research and reporting, part true-crime, part history of the Mormon Church, part

exploration of a faith carried to extreme ends. Unlike the previous two books, it is written entirely in the traditional journalistic third person; the writer's presence is not revealed until the author's remarks at the end.

The narrative opens with the bloody murder of twenty-four-year-old Brenda Lafferty and her baby daughter in a suburb of Provo, Utah, in the summer of 1984. The chief suspects in the ritualistic killing were her brothers-in-law Ron and Dan Lafferty, religious fundamentalists who believed that a revelation from God had commanded them to kill the young woman and her child. Arrested, tried, and convicted of the crime, the two men were completely without remorse, maintaining that what they had done was God's will. The purpose of the book, stated in the prologue, is "to cast some light on Rafferty and his ilk" (p. xxiii). Krakauer asks: "How could an apparently sane, avowedly pious man kill a blameless woman and her baby so viciously, without the barest flicker of emotion? Whence did he derive the moral justification? What filled him with such certitude?" (p. xxi).

The book that follows is a gripping account of a uniquely indigenous American religion with a definite recorded history from its inception. Krakauer traces the history of the Mormon Church from its beginnings to the split between the mainstream Mormon Church and the conservative fundamentalist sects who believe that the doctrine of plural marriage or polygamy is a necessary part of the road to salvation. The mainstream LDS Church renounced the doctrine of polygamy in the face of popular and government opposition at the end of the nineteenth century, and the church has since excommunicated some prominent fundamentalist practitioners who in turn see this renunciation as a betrayal of a crucial concept of their faith.

Krakauer sees this aspect of the LDS church as reflecting an uneasy relationship with its history. The mainstream church is eager to portray polygamy as a long-abandoned custom practiced by a handful of early Mormons who had been specifically commanded by God to take multiple wives. Nevertheless Joseph Smith, the religion's founder, married at least thirty-three women, and there are somewhere between thirty thousand and one hundred thousand Mormon fundamentalists practicing polygamy in Canada, Mexico, and the western United States at the beginning of the twenty-first century. Many of these plural wives, under the absolute rule of their husbands and the patriarchs of their church, are as young as fourteen years old.

After an overview of the background and history of the LDS Church and the related fundamentalist movement, Krakauer introduces Colorado City, an isolated municipality of unusually large homes on the Arizona–Utah border, governed with an iron hand by an elderly prophet known as Uncle Rulon. Uncle Rulon is married to an estimated seventy-five women and is the father of sixty-five children. He demands perfect obedience.

Krakauer proceeds to weave together a variety of related threads: the abduction of fourteen-year-old Elizabeth Smart from her Salt Lake City home in 2002; the story of Joseph Smith and the early history of the Mormon Church; descriptions of life in fundamentalist Mormon communities in Canada and Mexico and the women who have rebelled or escaped from them; a profile of an excommunicated former Mormon fundamentalist named DeLoy Bateman; the saga of the Rafferty family; ideas about divine revelation and a group that calls itself the School of the Prophets. Ultimately he arrives at the trial of Ron Lafferty and some big questions. Ron had attempted to kill himself while awaiting trial. Was Ron mentally competent to stand trial? The state of Utah determined that he was indeed competent. If Ron wasn't insane, what was he? Krakauer considers a diagnosis of narcissistic personality disorder, but not all narcissists are prophets or murderers. Why had the religious beliefs of the Rafferty brothers turned them into killers?

At the end of the book, Ron is awaiting death by firing squad and Dan, sentenced to life in prison, is certain that he is a prophet and that the Day of Judgment, when he will be released from prison and his true role revealed to all, is approaching soon. The final scene of the narrative, however, contains a conversation with DeLoy

Bateman, the former fundamentalist who has lost his faith. In his case, reason seems to have won the battle with faith. The certainty of Dan Lafferty juxtaposed with DeLoy Bateman's loss of faith emphasizes Krakauer's original theme, the contrast between faith and doubt.

Under the Banner of Heaven seems to be a radical departure from his previous material and style, but once again Krakauer is concerned with motivation. When his book editor was lukewarm about the new book, looking for another piece of adventure writing, Krakauer switched publishers. Reactions to the book were mixed. Some reviewers felt that he had neglected the positive aspects of Mormonism; some criticized his presentation of faith and reason as mutually exclusive. The public was fascinated with the subject, and *Under the Banner of Heaven* became his third best seller.

The LDS church leaders were particularly upset by the book. Krakauer had written about the particular vitality of the Mormon Church, characterizing it as growing and strong. About polygamy and the twenty-first-century church, he writes: "The Mormons have gained so much by abandoning polygamy that it is hard to imagine LDS authorities ever bringing it back by design" (*Under the Banner of Heaven,* p. 322). As the Mormon Church grows less peculiar, more normal and middle-American, Krakauer theorizes, the fundamentalist movement, ironically, will grow as well, drawing from the increasing numbers of mainstream Mormons who wish to return to the original vision of the founder Joseph Smith.

Leaders of the mainstream church were dismayed. The LDS Church has worked long and hard to emphasize its separation from the fundamentalist Mormons who are the focus of Krakauer's story. A lengthy rebuttal of Krakauer's book, published collectively as "Church Response to Jon Krakauer's *Under the Banner of Heaven*" on 27 June 2003, two weeks before the book's publication, turns on this distinction; Krakauer "by extrapolation tars every Mormon with the same brush," asserts the director of media relations for the LDS Church. "The story of Ron and Dan Lafferty is a story that should be told, but told in a way that emphasizes repeatedly the vital distinctions between mainline Latter-day Saint believers and those who have gone beyond the mark, been severed from the faith, and violated the standards of both church and state," writes an eminent Brigham Young University professor in the same statement.

"I didn't realize how rankled they would become about it," Krakauer said in his interview with Robert Boynton (p. 158). Indeed, while the church leaders accuse him of inaccuracies and oversimplifications, Krakauer certainly makes it clear that the fundamentalists are outside the mainstream church and condemned by it. In the Boynton interview, Krakauer admits that "the journalist never has *any intention* of telling the story your subject wants told. Your job is to tell the story as you see it" (p. 167).

Shortly after *Under the Banner of Heaven* was published, Krakauer met a young man in Utah who had been raised as a member of the fundamentalist LDS sect that he had written about. Tom Sam had been ejected from the community at the age of thirteen and forced to fend for himself. Krakauer took him under his wing and brought him to Colorado, where he and his wife, Linda, a landscape designer, live what Krakauer calls an ordinary life. Tom Sam had stopped going to school in the eighth grade. As their foster son, he has been able to continue his education and is a full-time college student.

LITERARY JOURNALISM

One of the qualities that distinguishes all of Krakauer's writing is its sense of place. Krakauer's fourth book of nonfiction, set partly in Iraq and Afghanistan, is scheduled to be published by Doubleday in late 2009. While the book will be in the third person that he finds most comfortable, he has traveled to the stark remote mountainous corners of Afghanistan so that he can see the setting with his own eyes.

Another quality that clearly places Krakauer in the genre of literary journalism is his extensive research and detailed reporting. *Into the Wild* and *Under the Banner of Heaven* each took three years to research. He filled nine notebooks with

details while on the Everest expedition. In each case he conducted dozens of interviews. He says that he contacts everyone who has any connection to the story; in this way he uncovers new threads. In the case of both *Into the Wild* and *Into Thin Air,* continuing the interview process after the magazine articles were sent to press uncovered new compelling information that led to the full-length book. In the case of *Under the Banner of Heaven,* the interview with Dan Rafferty was not originally intended to be a part of the story. In addition to interviews, Krakauer plumbs bookstores and archives, diaries, letters, court records, and transcripts of radio transmissions.

The role of speculation raises Krakauer's work from reportorial journalism to the level of New Journalism or creative nonfiction. Inserting his own voice to ask questions and consider causes, even in the third person as in *Under the Banner of Heaven,* he crosses the conventional boundaries between nonfiction and fiction. Referring to the insertion of his personal experience and speculation about Chris McCandless's motives in *Into the Wild,* Krakauer acknowledges his debt to the New Journalists: "Tom Wolfe and the other pioneers of New Journalism broke the ground that allowed me to write a book like *Into the Wild,* which ... does have some quirks that don't seem quite so weird and quirky in the wake of the New Journalists. In that sense I'm indebted to Wolfe's bold innovations" (Boynton, p. 180).

Structure is another quality that distinguishes Krakauer's writing style: Krakauer's full-length nonfiction is not presented in chronological order. Each of Krakauer's three major books opens with an extreme occurrence—*Into the Wild* with Christopher McCandless's death, *Into Thin Air* with the disaster on Mount Everest, *Under the Banner of Heaven* with the gruesome murder of a young mother and her child—and backtracks to the circumstances that lead up to the event. The structure of each book emphasizes the focus on causes that is the trademark of Krakauer's work. Krakauer is primarily a storyteller, and it is this trademark structure, opening with the most dramatic aspect of the story, that grips the reader from the first page. "For example, in *Into the Wild* (which I like better than anything else I've ever written)," he states in *The New New Journalism,* "people have told me I was crazy to start the book with Chris McCandless's death. Doing so gave away the 'ending,' and utterly scrambled the chronology. But in my view it was a powerful and effective way to bring readers into the story" (Boynton, p. 175).

The use of scenes to propel a nonfiction narrative is another device that characterizes Krakauer's work as literary journalism. Krakauer sifts through his extensive notes and chooses the most interesting scenes or incidents, then shapes the material into a structure that will emphasize his ideas and at the same time move the narrative forward. Then he works from his detailed outline. Writing a book like this, he says, is like rock climbing. "When you embark on a really big climb ... the enormity of the undertaking can be paralyzing. So a climber breaks down the ascent into rope-lengths, or pitches. If you can ... focus on each of these pitches to the exclusion of all the scary pitches that still lie above, climbing ... suddenly isn't such an intimidating prospect. ... By following an outline I can focus on the chapter that's in front of me. ... It makes writing a book less terrifying" (Boynton, p. 176).

Selected Bibliography

WORKS OF JON KRAKAUER

Eiger Dreams: Ventures Among Men and Mountains. New York: Lyons & Burford, 1990.

Into the Wild. New York: Villard Books, 1996.

Into Thin Air: A Personal Account of the Mount Everest Disaster. New York: Villard Books, 1997.

Under the Banner of Heaven: A Story of Violent Faith. New York: Doubleday, 2003.

CRITICAL AND BIOGRAPHICAL STUDIES

Boynton, Robert S. "Jon Krakauer." In his *The New New Journalism: Conversations with America's Best Nonfiction Writers on Their Craft.* New York: Vintage, 2005.

Bryant, Mark. "Everest One Year Later: False Summit." *Outside* (http://outside.away.com/magazine/0597/9705krakauer.html), May 1997.

Cahill, Tim. "Travel." *New York Times Book Review,* June 10, 1990, p. 48.

Church of Jesus Christ of Latter-day Saints. "Church Response to Jon Krakauer's *Under the Banner of Heaven." Newsroom: The Official Resource for News Media, Opinion Leaders, and the Public.* (http://newsroom.lds.org/ldsnewsroom/eng), June 27, 2003. (Official website of the Church of Jesus Christ of Latter-day Saints.)

Clash, James M. "Review of *Into Thin Air.*" *Forbes,* May 19, 1997, p. 291.

Fimrite, Ron. "Review of *Into Thin Air.*" *Sports Illustrated,* May 12, 1997, p. 18.

Jacobson, Kristin J. "Desiring Natures: The American Adrenaline Narrative." *Genre* 35, no. 2:355–382 (summer 2002).

Krakauer, Jon. "Into Thin Air" from *Outside,* 1996. In *The Best American Sports Writing of the Century.* Halberstam, David, ed. Boston, New York: Houghton Mifflin, 1999, pp. 630–667.

Marshall, John. "Lofty Pursuits Jon Krakauer Reappears out of 'Thin Air' with a Determined Sense of Direction." *Seattle Post-Intelligencer,* October 29, 2001.

McNamee, Thomas. "Adventures of Alexander Supertramp." *New York Times Book Review,* March 3, 1996, p. 29.

Plummer, William. "Everest's Shadow." *People,* June 2, 1997, pp. 53–57.

"Return to Thin Air: The Everest Disaster Ten Years Later, 1996–2006." *Outside,* September 2006, pp. 71–91.

Scott, Alastair. "Review of *Into Thin Air.*" *New York Times Book Review,* May 18, 1998, p. G11.

Trombold, John. "High and Low in the Himalayas: Jon Krakauer's *Into Thin Air.*" *Popular Culture Review* 10, no. 2:89–100 (August 1, 1999).

NELLA LARSEN

(1891—1964)

Whitney Womack Smith

LARGELY FORGOTTEN FOR nearly a half century, Nella Larsen is now hailed as one of the most intriguing and important figures of the Harlem Renaissance arts movement. Her novels, long out of print, have been reissued by major presses and regularly appear on the syllabi for African American literature, women's literature, and American modernism courses. In her small body of work—comprising just two novels and a handful of short stories and reviews—Larsen explored the complex intersections of race, gender, class, and sexuality in the early twentieth century. Her nuanced representations of the color line, racial passing, and multiracial identity in her fiction no doubt emerged from her own position as a the daughter of a white mother and black father. Her marginalized place within her family and in U.S. society is reflected in the feelings of her alienated characters.

Living and working as a librarian in Harlem during the early 1920s, Larsen witnessed the flowering of African American arts and letters that came to be known as the Harlem Renaissance. W. E. B. Du Bois hailed her first novel, *Quicksand,* which appeared in 1928, as "the best piece of fiction that Negro America has produced since the heyday of [Charles] Chesnutt" (quoted in Thadious Davis, *Nella Larsen,* p. 280). Her second novel, *Passing,* published in 1929, received similar critical, if not commercial, success, and Larsen was regarded by her peers as one of the leading novelists of the Harlem Renaissance. Her burgeoning literary career was cut short by accusations of plagiarism regarding her 1930 short story "Sanctuary." Although she was able to convince her editors of her original authorship, she never published another word and disappeared from the literary world for the last thirty years of her life. In the 1970s Larsen's works began to be reprinted as part of the recovery project championed by feminist and African American scholars seeking to unearth neglected writers and reshape the literary canon. Since then, interest in Larsen's life and works has resulted in multiple editions of her novels, three major biographies, several book-length studies, and scores of articles. Once an obscure footnote, Larsen is now canonical.

LIFE ON THE COLOR LINE

For much of the twentieth century Larsen's life was shrouded in mystery. One of earliest Larsen scholars, Arthur B. Davis, notes how little was known when he wrote in 1974, only ten years after Larsen's death: "When was she born? ... When did she die? ... We simply do no know, and there is no card for her in the morgue of the *New York Times.* There are no terminal dates for her in the card catalog of the Library of Congress" (p. 95). In 1980, Mary Helen Washington dubbed Larsen the "mystery woman" of the Harlem Renaissance (p. 44). It seems Larsen encouraged some of this mystery with her reluctance to share details about her life, perhaps in part to protect herself and her interracial family in a society controlled by the color line. At the time of her death she had no connections to the literary world. She left behind few letters, no diaries, no memoirs, and no descendents She was also known by many names throughout her life, including Nellie Walker, Nellye Larson, Nellie Larsen, Nellie Marian Larsen, and Nella Larsen Imes. Larsen's biographers have struggled to pin down even the most basic facts about her origins, leading to vastly different accounts of her life in various sources. The most accurate and definitive version of Larsen's life story is George

Hutchinson's *In Search of Nella Larsen: A Biography of the Color Line* (2006), which exposes many of the myths and erasures present in earlier publications. (All quotes from Hutchinson in this essay are from this volume, unless otherwise noted.)

We know from her birth certificate that she was born Nellie Walker on 13 April 1891 in Chicago's second ward, a notorious area of rooming houses, saloons, and brothels. Her parents are listed as Mary Hanson Walker, a twenty-two-year-old white woman, and Peter Walker, a "colored" man. The infant Nellie Walker is categorized as colored. There is no clear evidence that Mary and Peter were legally married, although they were issued a marriage license in 1890. Part of a large wave of Scandinavian immigration, Mary Hanson had moved from Denmark to Chicago as a teenager in 1886 and worked as a dressmaker. Little is know of Peter Walker, aside from the fact that his occupation is listed as "cook" on Nellie's birth certificate. During her lifetime, Larsen claimed that her father was a black man from the Danish West Indies (now the U.S. Virgin Islands) who abandoned the family after her birth and soon died. There is no record of his death, indeed no record of a Peter Walker in Chicago at all after 1891.

By 1892, Mary was living with a white man named Peter Larsen. The biographer Thadious Davis has speculated that Peter Walker and Peter Larsen may have been the same person. The name change, she argues, was a ruse that enabled Nella's light-skinned father to cross the color line and "pass" as a white man. More recently George Hutchinson has questioned this hypothesis, showing that Peter Larsen was five years older than Peter Walker and lived and worked in the same neighborhood. Had Peter Walker wanted to pass into white society, he surely would have moved to an area where he was not known. Hutchinson has also found records that show a Peter Larsen who was born in 1867, emigrated from Denmark to the United States in 1880s, and worked as a streetcar driver.

Her mother's remarriage significantly affected Nella Larsen's life and her sense of connection to and acceptance by her family. Certainly it saved her mother from a future of misery and poverty as a single woman with a mixed-race child. In 1892, Mary and Peter Larsen had a daughter, Annie, who is listed in official documents as white, leaving Nella as the only black member of her family. In the 1910 census, the Larsen family lists only one child, Anna, effectively erasing Nella. In the 1890s Chicago saw increased racial segregation and little acceptance for interracial families. The Larsen family's frequent moves were likely due in part to Nella's race. Nella and Anna later attended separate public schools, perhaps to keep their relationship as half-sisters a secret. It must have been clear to Nella from an early age that she stood apart from her family and would follow a very different path than her white sister.

For some time during Nella's childhood, Mary returned to Denmark with her daughters; records reveal their return to the United States in 1898, just after Nella turned seven, but there is no record of their departure. Her time in Denmark, probably in Askov in western Denmark, would have been a significant change from life on the color line in Chicago. Many Danish people would have never seen a dark-skinned person, and Larsen was likely an object of curiosity. This trip influenced her earliest publications, which were stories and games for children. She writes in the introduction to "Playtime: Danish Fun," which she penned in 1920 for a monthly children's magazine, the *Brownies' Book,* "Dear Children, These are some games which I learned in Denmark, from the little Danish children. I hope you will play them and like them as I did" (quoted in Hutchinson, p. 128).

Larsen's family sought out educational opportunities for her. Her formal education began when she was eight, later than was normal at the time. In the biographical sketch she wrote for Alfred A. Knopf, the house that published her novels, she described the pupils of the school she attended as the "children of German or Scandinavian parents," making it likely that Larsen was among the few nonwhite students (quoted in Hutchinson, p. 221). In 1905 she graduated from eighth grade and was enrolled in Wendell Phillips High School, the largest high school in

Chicago. It was not typical for working-class girls to attend high school at this time; in fact, Nella's own sister did not receive a high school education. Although the school was integrated, there were concerns about racial mixing and calls to segregate the lunchroom and social gatherings. The school had a rigorous curriculum, and the English courses stressed modern literature and creative writing, especially fiction writing and autobiography. Perhaps sensing the limited opportunities for Nella, and the problems faced by a family with a multiracial child, the Larsens enrolled Nellie Marie Larsen in the Normal Preparatory (high school) course at Fisk University in 1907. From this point on, Larsen was largely isolated from her immediate family. Located in Nashville, Fisk University was founded by the American Missionary Association after the Civil War as a school for former slaves. It served as the training ground for many African American leaders, including W. E. B. Du Bois (1868–1963; class of 1888). Fisk must have been a culture shock for Nella, who had always lived in white or mixed-race societies and had never traveled to the South. The school promoted the ideology of racial uplift, an attempt to create a positive black identity through education and public service. In her later fiction, Larsen is sharply critical of what she saw as the hypocrisy and racism grounded in the notion of racial uplift. Nella stayed only one year at Fisk, and it was speculated by earlier biographers that she left because her family cut her off financially. More recent documents show that she, along with several other students, were not invited to return the following year for protesting Fisk's strict dress codes and rules for moral conduct. She never received a high school diploma.

In 1908, Larsen left not just the South but also the entire United States, returning to her mother's family in Denmark. In her biographical statement for Knopf, Larsen stated that she lived for three years in Denmark. Her biographer Thadious Davis later questioned this claim and suggested that Larsen created this story out of whole cloth, perhaps to cover an illicit relationship or illegitimate child. More recently, George Hutchinson has located passenger manifests that prove she did travel to and from Copenhagen, and it is likely she spent a significant amount of time there between the summer of 1908 and April 1912, when she began nursing school in New York City. In *Quicksand,* the protagonist Helga Crane similarly moves in with her Danish relatives. Her description of her voyages and experiences in Denmark are our best insight into Larsen's experiences, since no letters or diaries exist from this time in her life. As Hutchinson notes, Larsen's physical descriptions of Copenhagen and details about Danish life and manners in *Quicksand* "could only derive from extended residence there" (p. 69). In later applications, Larsen claimed that she attended the high school in Askov and audited courses at the University of Copenhagen.

In 1912, just weeks after returning from Europe, the twenty-one-year-old Larsen began training as a nurse. She enrolled in the Lincoln Hospital and Home Training School for Nurses in the Bronx. Overseen by the Board of Regents system of the University of the State of New York, Lincoln was among the best and most influential nursing programs for African American women and was considered on par with white nursing programs. While most black nurses were trained in all-black hospitals, Lincoln's doctors and most of the hospital patients were white, while the affiliated nursing home was all black. In 1915, Larsen graduated and passed the R.N. exam with honor under the name Nellie Marian Larsen. Afterward she briefly worked as head nurse in one of Lincoln's ward and as an assistant superintendent with the nursing school.

Later that year, Larsen returned to the South to take the position of head nurse of the John Andrew Memorial Hospital and Nurse Training School at the internationally renowned Tuskegee Institute (now Tuskegee University) in Alabama. Founded in 1881, Tuskegee rose to prominence under the leadership of Booker T. Washington (1856–1915), who promoted practical application of education and vocational training as a means of uplifting African Americans. Tuskegee was unique because it was not only attended by African American students but also run entirely by African American professors and

administrators. Washington was still head of Tuskegee when Larsen was hired, but he died a few months after she began work. It's not known exactly why Larsen—a northern city dweller—chose to move to the rural South, with its open racism and Jim Crow laws. Hutchinson speculates that it may have been idealism and a desire to contribute to the black community. Larsen became quickly disillusioned with the nursing program, which was not up to the professional standards of Lincoln, and with Tuskegee in general. Once again, the semiautobiographical novel *Quicksand* provides insight into Larsen's experiences. The protagonist Helga takes a teaching position at the fictional southern black school Naxos, clearly based on Tuskegee and described as hypocritical and oppressive. She describes the school as a knife "ruthlessly cutting all to a pattern, the white man's pattern" (*Quicksand and Passing,* p. 4; all quotations from Larsen's novels are from this 1996 edition). Larsen later described her departure from Tuskegee in the biographical sketch for Knopf: "her dislike of conditions there, and the school authorities' dislike of her appearance and manner were both so intense that after a year they parted with mutual disgust and relief" (quoted in Hutchinson, p. 222). She resigned as head nurse in October 1916.

Larsen moved back to New York City, where she was to remain for most of her days. She returned to Lincoln Hospital, where she supervised nurses and taught nursing history before taking a position with the New York City Health Department as a public health nurse. She earned the second highest score that year on the civil service examination and began working in the Bronx, a predominantly white area. Public health was a relatively new branch of nursing that focused on "wellness, prevention, hygiene, and education for the entire population" (Hutchinson, p. 114). Public health nurses were particularly important in containing contagious diseases, including typhoid, polio, sexually transmitted diseases, and influenza. Larsen worked for the Health Department during the influenza pandemic of 1918–1919, which affected more than half a million New Yorkers.

In 1918 Larsen met Elmer S. Imes, who was only the second African American in the United States to earn a doctorate in physics. Educated at Fisk University and the University of Michigan, Imes had a long family history of education and good connections, similar to the character James Vayle in *Quicksand.* Imes moved to New York City in 1918 to take a position as a research physicist and assumed a position among the black bourgeoisie in the city. Little is known about their courtship, but Elmer Imes and Nella Marian Larsen applied for a marriage license in April 1919 and married the following month at the Union Theological Seminary, with Imes's brother officiating. Larsen took her husband's surname but retained her maiden name as her middle name.

Within a year the Imeses moved from Staten Island to 129th Street in Harlem, arriving at the dawn of the period that came to be known as the New Negro Movement or Harlem Renaissance. These terms describe the period from the end of World War I through the 1930s that witnessed a blossoming of African American cultural and intellectual life. Black writers, artists, dancers, and musicians asserted their right to express themselves on their own terms and black culture assumed new prominence, both nationally and internationally. For the first time, mainstream white publishers sought out African American writers and white critics took note. Among the best remembered writers of the period are James Weldon Johnson, Claude McKay, Jean Toomer, Countee Cullen, Jessie Redmon Fauset, Wallace Thurman, Alain Locke, Zora Neale Hurston, and Nella Larsen herself. In Harlem, the Imeses belonged to an active social circle of black artists and intellectuals and were members of the Fisk Club, to which W. E. B. Du Bois also belonged. In 1920, Larsen's first published work appeared in the *Brownies' Book,* a children's magazine published by the National Association for the Advancement of Colored People (NAACP) in 1920–1921. The *Brownies' Book* also included poems and stories by such Harlem Renaissance luminaries as Langston Hughes and Jessie Fauset. The stories "Playtime: Danish Fun" and "Playtime: Three Scandinavian Stories" are based on

Danish games and tales Larsen learned in Denmark during her childhood. Thadious Davis notes that these stories emphasize her Danish heritage and European experiences, thereby "stressing her place within a particular group of African Americans for whom such backgrounds inferred class position and social prominence" (*Nella Larsen,* p. 141). While both are short pieces, they mark Larsen's first foray into writing for a national audience.

While still working as a public health nurse, Larsen became involved with the 135th Street Branch of the New York Public Library (NYPL), now known as the Countee Cullen Branch. Larsen's move into librarianship was due perhaps to her literary ambitions, a desire to escape the grueling work of a nurse, or an effort to take a position that was better suited to the wife of a prominent scientist. In the 1920s, the 135th Street Branch was headed by the influential and progressive white librarian Ernestine Rose, who sponsored programs at the library highlighting black culture and literature. Larsen became a substitute assistant librarian at the branch and volunteered as secretary to the executive committee that organized the first exhibition of Negro art in New York City. Held at the 135th Street Branch in fall 1921, the exhibition marked a major milestone for the Harlem Renaissance, displaying visual arts as well as rare books by African Americans owned by collectors like Arthur A. Schomburg. A noted bibliophile, Schomburg later donated his collection to the 135th Street Branch, creating a major research center for the study of African American literature.

In 1922, Larsen officially took the post of junior assistant librarian, an entry-level job that came with a significantly lower salary than her job as a public health nurse. Her supervisor, Ernestine Rose, was committed to breaking down racial barriers in librarianship and encouraged Larsen to apply to the library school of the NYPL. While the school allowed African Americans to attend some courses, they were not allowed in the diploma program that led to becoming a certified librarian. The library school required at least a high school diploma, something Larsen, despite all her education, never had obtained. She changed the dates she attended Wendell Phillips and Fisk to make it appear she had graduated and took the examinations in history, current events, general information, literature, and foreign languages required of those applicants without university training. Larsen was accepted in 1922, and she and Elmer moved to Jersey City, perhaps because of their decreased income. She graduated in 1923, becoming the first black woman to graduate from library school in the United States, and took a position at the Seward Park Branch that served the largely Jewish Lower East Side of Manhattan.

In the mid–1920s Larsen began writing in earnest. She had returned to Harlem to take the position of head of the children's room at the 135th Street Branch, but she reduced her hours to half time in early 1925, presumably to devote herself to her writing. On 1 January 1926 she quit the library, only returning for a few months in 1929. During this period she developed important relationships with Walter White and Carl Van Vechten. White was a writer and worked for the NAACP; he later became the first black president of the organization. With his blond hair and blue eyes, White could have easily passed in white society, but he identified with his black heritage. He was a major promoter of black culture and arts, and he helped Larsen make connections with the black literati. Van Vechten was a white writer and photographer who championed black artists in the white community. He was a regular at black Harlem clubs and soirees when such racial mixing was viewed suspiciously by both blacks and whites. He is certainly the model for the character Hugh Wentworth in Larsen's second novel, *Passing.* Van Vechten used his experiences in Harlem to write the controversial book *Nigger Heaven* (1926), which focuses on the sensational and exotic aspects of Harlem nightlife. Du Bois called the novel "an affront to the hospitality of black folk and the intelligence of white" (quoted in Hutchinson, p. 220). Despite sharp criticisms of the book by other Harlem Renaissance figures, Larsen applauded the novel. Van Vechten encouraged Larsen's writing and introduced her to his editors at the publishing

house Alfred A. Knopf. He is also responsible for most of the photographs we have of Larsen.

In 1926, Larsen published her first two major short stories in *Young's Realistic Stories Magazine,* a monthly pulp fiction magazine with a primarily white female audience. Both stories appeared under the pseudonym Allen Semi, Nella Imes spelled backward. Larsen's nom de plume disguised not only her gender but also her racial identity. It is interesting that Larsen's first major stories do not focus on racial issues, especially when there was such contemporary interest in stories about black life by black writers. "The Wrong Man," which appeared in January 1926, is the story of Julia Romley, a young woman whose race is not revealed, although presumably she is white. Although she now lives a comfortable married life, Julia came from an impoverished background and had an affair with the man who paid for her education, a fact she has kept a secret from her husband. Like many of Larsen's heroines, Julia lives what seems to be a good life, but beneath the surface she is unhappy, restless, and fearful that it could all be taken away from her if her secret is revealed. The story is also a passing narrative, addressing class instead of race. In the startling climax, Julia reveals her secret to a man she thinks is her earlier lover but who turns out to be the "wrong man" and a friend of her husband.

In April of that same year *Young's* published Larsen's story "Freedom." Another psychological study, "Freedom" is told from the perspective of a man who had left his mistress, only to learn years later she had died in childbirth the very day he left: "Dead in childbirth, they had told him, both his mistress and the child she had borne him. She had been dead on that spring day when, resentful and angry at her influence on his life, he had reached toward freedom—to find only a mirage; for he saw quite plainly now he would never be free. It was she who escaped him" (*Complete Fiction,* p. 16). Like Julia in "The Wrong Man," the protagonist of this story appears calm and controlled in public, but he suffers from his secret obsession with the unnamed woman and in the end commits suicide. These 1926 stories display Larsen's interest in psychological realism and explore themes she develops more fully in her novels: sexual subjugation and the economic and emotional dependency of women on men.

QUICKSAND

Two years later, in 1928, *Quicksand,* Larsen's first novel, was published by Knopf. The original title, "Cloudy Amber," perhaps a reference to the mulatto heroine's skin color, was changed at the suggestion of Van Vechten to *Quicksand,* which suggests danger and disappearance. Larsen's debut novel is in many ways a thinly veiled autobiography, following the life of Helga Crane, the daughter of a Danish mother and a black father, who struggles to find her place in U.S. and European society. The novel explores and in many ways undermines the archetypal "tragic mulatto." The figure of the tragic mulatto appears in literature as early as 1842 in Lydia Maria Child's story "The Quadroons" and continues to be found in literature and film well into the twentieth century. Shunned by both black and white worlds, the tragic mulatto is usually depicted as a self-loathing, depressed, alcoholic, even suicidal victim. Larsen includes as an epigraph an excerpt from Langston Hughes's poem "Cross" that describes the dilemma of the mulatto.

Quicksand departs from the usual tragic mulatto narrative of a rich white father and an exploited black mother. Like Larsen's own parents, Helga's father is black and her mother is white, and her mother later remarries a white man. Helga describes this remarriage as one of social and economic necessity: "That second marriage, to a man of her race, but not of her own kind—so passionately, so instinctively resented by Helga even at the trivial age of six—she now understood as grievous necessity. Even foolish, despised women must have food and clothing; even unloved little Negro girls must somehow be provided for" (p. 23). Helga is effectively disowned by her white family and seeks her place in the black world of Naxos, a prominent college for African Americans in a small southern community, clearly based on the Tuskegee Institute.

The name Naxos has multiple meanings. Naxos is one of the Greek Cycladic islands in the Aegean Sea. In Greek mythology, Theseus abandoned Ariadne on Naxos, and the island comes to represent loneliness and exile. Deborah McDowell also notes in *Quicksand and Passing* that Naxos is an anagram of Saxon, perhaps meant to imply that this great black institution was in fact striving to obtain the approval of whites or fit into white models. This notion is emphasized in the first chapter, when the students and faculty of Naxos are forced to listen to "the banal, the patronizing, and even the insulting remarks of one of the renowned white preachers of the state" (p. 2). In his sermon, the preacher applauds the "Naxos Negroes" for knowing their place as the "hewers of wood and drawers of water" (p. 3).

Naxos is not a warm and welcoming environment for Helga, who lacks the family connections and credentials necessary to be accepted fully in the black elite. Like Helga, Larsen always struggled to feel accepted in black society because of her "low" background and interracial parents. The dean of Naxos is described as "a woman from one of the 'first families'—a great 'race' woman'" while in contrast Helga is "a despised mulatto" (p. 18). When the novel opens, Helga is unhappily engaged to fellow teacher, James Vayle, who offers her the family pedigree she lacks. Helga chafes against the rigid rules and restrictive atmosphere of Naxos, much as Larsen herself did at Fisk and Tuskegee, symbolized by the dress code that calls for the students and faculty to wear somber, dark colors. Helga, in contrast, has a wardrobe of brightly colored, well-tailored clothes in sensual fabrics. Dress and fashion are recurring motifs in Larsen's fiction. Restless and frustrated, Helga impulsively resigns her position and breaks her engagement. The school's idealistic principal, Dr. Robert Anderson, encourages her to stay and play a role in the school's racial uplift movement. He explains that the school, and the black community, need women with her "dignity and breeding," perhaps a reference to her mulatto appearance and European background. Helga replies, "The joke is on you, Dr. Anderson. My father was a gambler who deserted my mother, a white immigrant. It is even uncertain that they were married," before walking out the door (p. 21).

Helga then takes the first of many journeys in the novel, traveling by train from Naxos back to her hometown of Chicago. With only meager savings, she stays at the YWCA and plans to contact her mother's brother, Peter, her one relative in the United States who acknowledges her. When Helga arrives at her uncle Peter's grand North Side home, she is turned away by his new wife: "Mr. Nilssen has been very kind to you, supported you, sent you to school. But you mustn't expect anything else. And you mustn't come here any more. It—well, frankly, it isn't convenient. I'm sure an intelligent girl like yourself can understand" (p. 28). Rejected by the white world, Helga turns back to the black world by taking the position of private secretary to Mrs. Hayes-Rore, a noted "race woman" and lecturer who takes Helga with her on a speaking trip to Harlem. Helga finds she must perform a sort of reverse "passing" in Harlem by denying her Danish heritage and pledging her allegiance to the "race." She forms a friendship with Mrs. Hayes-Rore's niece, Anne Grey, who abhors interracial relationships and race mixing at parties and in clubs in Harlem.

Helga finds herself again facing an internal struggle over her place along the color line. When her estranged uncle Peter sends a letter terminating their relationship and includes a check for $5,000 in lieu of an inheritance, she uses the money to escape Harlem and flee to her mother's family in Denmark. In many works by African American writers, Europe is constructed as a haven, free from the racism that permeated American society. Larsen resists this usual depiction of Europe by revealing its subtler but nonetheless insidious forms of racism, as well as addressing the class prejudices and sexism that permeate Danish society. In contrast to her white American relatives, the Dahls welcome Helga with open arms, but she soon realizes that they mean to use her to advance their social climbing. Helga find herself consumed by Europeans fascinated by exotic black culture, much like the performers in the minstrel show she attends at the circus in Copenhagen. When she walks down

the street she is met with stares and whispers of "*sorte,*" Danish for black, by people who have rarely seen someone of her race. Her relatives treat her as an exotic commodity, dressing her in risqué frocks and jewels that she never would have worn in the United States. The outfits make her feel like a "veritable savage" (p. 69), and she compares her position to that of a "new and strange species of pet dog being proudly exhibited" (p. 70).

The Dahls act as her brokers in the marriage market, hoping she will form an alliance that will benefit them. She catches the eye of a noted painter, Axel Olsen, who attempts to capture the "true Helga Crane" in a portrait. While the portrait is much admired and sought after by European collectors, Helga hates the representation, which is described by her maid as a "bad, wicked" picture (p. 89). After Helga ignores Olsen's repeated attempts to initiate an affair, he proposes, but only after noting that she has "the soul of a prostitute, You sell yourself to the highest buyer" (p. 87). Helga states sharply, "I'm not for sale. Not to you. Not to any white man. I don't at all care to be owned" (p. 87). She bases her refusal on racial grounds, though it is clear that Helga does not want to be controlled by any man, black or white: "It isn't just you, not just personal, you understand. It's deeper, broader than that ... if we were married, you might come to be ashamed of me, to hate me, to hate all dark people. My mother did that" (p. 88).

Following a familiar pattern, Helga runs from a difficult position, fleeing Europe after the botched engagement, returning to Harlem, and reembracing her black identity. She returns to attend the wedding of her friend Anne Grey and Dr. Anderson, the former Naxos principal. Although Helga had said repeatedly she never meant to live again in the United States, with its racial strife, her voyage back turns out to be a permanent move. After the wedding, Dr. Anderson and Helga share a passionate kiss that sparks desire in Helga. When Dr. Anderson later rejects her, Helga suffers a sort of nervous breakdown and wanders the streets of Harlem in a rainstorm. Soaked to the skin, she wanders into a storefront Pentecostal church during services. The enthusiastic worshippers gather round her, assuming she is a prostitute, a "scarlet 'oman," who needs to be saved (p. 112). Helga, who had previously rejected religion, finds calm and happiness in the service and catches the eye of the Reverend Pleasant Green. Helga makes what would be in another novel a noble gesture of self-sacrifice to the racial uplift movement by impulsively marrying the righteous, if somewhat repugnant, Green and becoming a preacher's wife in rural Alabama. One child follows another, and by the end of the book she is the mother of four. Earlier in the novel Helga had rejected motherhood, stating, "Why add any more unwanted, tortured Negroes to America? Why *do* Negroes have children? Surely it must be sinful" (p. 103). Rather than find contentment in her new roles as mother and leader of black folk, Helga feels lost and unsatisfied. Indeed, the women she is supposed to uplift look at this city woman, struggling to cope with running a household and raising young children, with pity. This life leaves Helga, with her refined aesthetic sense, "no time for the pursuit of beauty" or for personal fulfillment (p. 124). The novel ends with Helga longing for escape, but she finds herself pregnant with a fifth child before she's fully recovered from her fourth. Unwilling to abandon her children and lacking the strength to leave, Helga is stuck in a quagmire of her own making.

Quicksand put Larsen on the literary map and received positive notices from black and white reviewers. In a glowing review, Du Bois asserts that the novel "stands easily with Jessie Fauset's 'There is Confusion,' in its subtle comprehension of the curious cross currents that swirl about the black American" (quoted in Thadious Davis, *Nella Larsen,* p. 280). *Quicksand* departs from earlier Harlem Renaissance novels, though, since it is not overtly a "problem novel," with a clear political agenda and goal of racial uplift. This was noted by the reviewer Arthur Huff Fauset, who states, "For the first time, perhaps, a Negro author has succeeded in writing a novel about colored characters in which the propaganda motive is decidedly absent" (quoted in Thadious Davis *Nella Larsen,* p. 279). In the end, Helga does not suffer the usual fate of the

tragic mulatto nor is she transformed through racial uplift. As David Levering Lewis notes, Helga is "not a tragic mulatto but a mulatto who is tragic for reasons that are both sociological and existential" (p. xxxiv). Based on the success of *Quicksand,* Larsen won the William E. Harmon Foundation Bronze Award for Distinguished Achievement Among Negroes in Literature (the novelist Claude McKay took the Gold Award for the novel *Home to Harlem*). The award included a $100 honorarium, a bronze medal, and recognition at a ceremony held at the Mother AME Zion Church in Harlem. She was also feted by the Women's Auxiliary of the NAACP. Soon after the publication of the novel, she and Elmer moved into the Dunbar apartment complex, home of many of the most famous figures of the Harlem Renaissance. *Quicksand* transformed Larsen from a librarian with literary aspirations to a respected writer and helped pave the way for the publication of her next novel, *Passing.*

PASSING

Larsen completed *Passing* in August 1928, and it was published by Knopf in April 1929, just thirteen months after *Quicksand.* As Thadious Davis notes, "She wanted to finish the book for Knopf while interest in her work was high enough to secure good sales" (*Nella Larsen,* p. 285). The novel went through three editions, selling a respectable if not remarkable three to four thousand copies that year. Knopf suggested Larsen change the original title, the more inflammatory "Nig," to *Passing.* "Nig" is the ironic nickname given to the character Clare Kendry, and it may also have been an allusion to Carl Van Vechten's *Nigger Heaven.* Indeed, the novel is dedicated to Van Vechten and his wife Fania Marinoff. Van Vechten also wrote a glowing blurb for the cover, which describes the book as a "strangely provocative story, superbly told. The sensational implications of *Passing* should make this book one of the most widely discussed on the Spring list."

A central question of the novel involves the ethics of racial passing, defined as "the movement of a person who is legally or socially designated black into a white racial category or white social identity" (Davis, Introduction to *Passing,* p. viii). Certainly passing was not a new phenomenon in the United States, and there are many examples of light-skinned slaves passing for white to escape chattel slavery. In 1896, the U.S. Supreme Court ruled on the case of *Plessy v. Ferguson,* codifying the notion of the color line. Blacks who could pass as whites were able to obtain opportunities and privileges otherwise legally denied. Although no accurate statistics exist, it is estimated that between ten thousand and thirty thousand African Americans were passing during the 1920s and 1930s, effectively disappearing from black society and remaking themselves in the white world. At this same time, many white Americans were "hell-bent on holding people to strict racial categories and extending segregation's legal and economic reach by making a movement across racial lines seem both undesirable and unnaturall" (Kaplan, "Nella Larsen's Erotics of Race," p. xv). Passing is an act of defiance, revealing that supposedly rigid racial boundaries are permeable and fluid and that identity is in fact constructed. "This hazardous business of passing," as Larsen describes it in her novel, entails "breaking away from all that was familiar and friendly to take one's chance in another environment, not entirely strange, perhaps, but certainly not entirely friendly" (p. 157). With this novel, Larsen joined a growing tradition of passing literature, including James Weldon Johnson's *The Autobiography of an Ex-Colored Man* (1912), Walter White's *Flight* (1926), and Jessie Redmon Fauset's *Plum Bun* (1928), which was published just a few months before Larsen's novel.

Larsen's book is not a formulaic tale about racial passing but a complex exploration of social class, black female subjectivity, female friendships, and female sexuality and desire. *Passing* chronicles the fraught relationship of Irene Redfield and Clare Bellew, two light-skinned black women who were friends in childhood but chose very different paths in their adult lives. As many critics have noted, these characters act as psychological doubles. Clare, who came from a working-class background, left the black world to pass

and has married a rich white man who is unaware of her true racial background. In contrast, the middle-class Irene is an avowed "race woman," an active member of the Negro Welfare League, and the wife of a dark-skinned professional man. Although she has chosen allegiance to her race, Irene is not above passing for convenience. On a summer day in Chicago, for instance, she seeks refuge from the heat at an all-white hotel. She does not worry about being exposed because "white people were so stupid about such things. ... They always took her for an Italian, a Spaniard, a Mexican, even a gipsy. Never, when she was alone, had they even remotely seemed to suspect that she was a Negro" (p. 150). In this scene and throughout the novel, Larsen explores how race is constructed and performed. While most passing narratives focus primarily on the inner turmoil of the passer, Larsen's novel explores the psychology of Irene, the woman who keeps the passer's secret and struggles with her own race, class, and sexual identity.

Passing is divided into three sections, much like acts of a play: "Encounter," "Re-Encounter," and "Finale." The novel begins with Irene holding a letter from Clare. Irene describes the letter as "mysterious," "slightly furtive," "flaunting," even dangerous, much like Clare herself. In the letter Clare writes "I am lonely, so lonely ... in this pale life of mine" and reaches out to Irene, her link to the black world (p. 145). The letter prompts Irene to recall two incidents involving Clare. The first is a flashback to her childhood in Chicago's South Side, when young Irene Westover witnessed Clare Kendry being abused by her working-class, alcoholic, mulatto father. Bob Kendry is angry because Clare has used some of the money she earned as a dressmaker's assistant to buy fabric to make herself a red Christmas dress. Much like Helga Crane, Clare is drawn to fine fabrics and beauty. She wants more than her working-class status provides, later telling Irene, "You had all the things I wanted and never had had. It made me all the more determined to get them, and others" (p. 159). After Clare's father dies in a saloon fight when she is fifteen, she is sent away to live with her white aunts. Although they are devout Christians, they can't "forgive the tar-brush" and treat Clare like a degraded servant (p. 159). When she decides to pass as white and marry a white man at age eighteen, Clare is not so much denying the black community as escaping from her oppressive white relatives and her lower-class status.

Irene's second, longer memory is of her chance meeting with Clare in Chicago two years earlier, which rekindled their relationship. Irene, who now lives in New York City, is visiting the city of her birth when she encounters Clare on the Drayton Hotel's exclusive rooftop restaurant, both women passing for white. She initially does not recognize the "white" woman at the next table, with blond hair, "dark, almost black eyes and that wide mouth like a scarlet flower" (p. 148). Irene finds herself both attracted to and repulsed by this woman, who she fears could expose her passing and embarrass her publicly. The mystery woman eventually introduces herself as Clare Kendry, now Clare Bellew. In the twelve years since they last saw each other, Clare has married a successful white businessman, Jack Bellew. Clare notes that passing is a "a frightfully easy thing to do. If one's the type, all that's needed is a little nerve" (p. 158) and that white people aren't nearly as obsessed with knowing one's family and pedigree as black people are. Although Irene tries to resist Clare's advances to renew their friendship, she agrees to come to visit the next day. There she meets another old schoolmate, Gertrude, another light-skinned woman who has also married a white man, a Chicago butcher, who is aware of Gertrude's racial identity. Class-conscious Irene clearly judges Gertrude, as much for marrying outside her race as for marrying a working-class man. While the three women take tea, Jack Bellew enters in what is one of the novel's most arresting scenes. Unaware of the racial background of the three women, the racist Bellew cracks jokes about his wife's complexion, which he says is "gettin' darker and darker," and he uses the pet name "Nig" for her (p. 170). When Clare asks whether it would really matter if she turned out to be "one or two per cent coloured," he replies, "No niggers in my family. Never have been and never will be" (p. 171). Clearly taken aback,

Irene represses her rage and indignation and keeps Clare's dangerous secret from Bellew. The next day she destroys a note from Clare and resolves to put Clare out of her mind forever.

Part 2 jumps back to present-day New York City, as Irene ponders this latest communication from Clare. While Irene feels duty bound to Clare by the ties of race, she also resents Clare's intrusion into her life. Irene is the wife of a successful doctor, the mother of two sons, and a society matron who does charity work to uplift the race. As Thadious Davis notes, although Irene does not pass all the time, she is clearly attracted to whiteness, and in her black bourgeois life adopts "white values, standards of beauty, and behavior" (Introduction, p. xx). But there are cracks beneath the seemingly perfect surface of Irene's privileged existence. Her husband, Brian, is deeply dissatisfied with life in racist America, and longs to move to Brazil to escape the color line. When Irene forbids him to talk to their sons about racism and lynching, he states, "I wanted to get them out of this hellish place years ago. But you wouldn't let me. I gave up the idea because you objected" (p. 232). Irene refuses to risk her comfortable social position by moving to a foreign country. The marriage is also a sexless one, and Brian bitterly comments that sex is a "grand joke" (p. 189). Irene's repressed sexuality stands in contrast to Clare's open and sensual nature.

Irene views Clare's presence in her life as a dangerous threat to her sense of security. Indeed, Clare later states that "to get the things I want badly enough, I'd do anything, hurt anybody, throw anything away. Really, 'Rene, I'm not safe" (p. 210). After Irene doesn't respond to the letter, Clare shows up at the Redfield house and invites herself to the Negro Welfare League dance that Irene is organizing. While the event is attended by some other white people, including the famed novelist Hugh Wentworth, Clare is nonetheless flirting with danger by attending a public event in Harlem. She arrives at the dance in a dress of "shining black taffeta," symbolic of her reconnection with her black heritage, and freely dances with both white men and black men. Throughout the novel, Larsen includes discussions about what exactly race is and how it is "read." At the party Clare's race is a matter of much speculation. Hugh Wentworth notes how difficult it is to tell "the sheep from the goats" (p. 206). Irene notes that "there are ways [to identify race]. But they're not definite or tangible" (p. 206). In this section Irene is increasingly attracted by Clare, who is repeatedly described in sensual, erotic terms. Deborah McDowell suggests that Irene's lesbian attraction to Clare represents yet another threat to her identity as a black, married, middle-class woman. It also gives the term "passing" another connotation. As Thadious Davis notes, "'to pass' has come into common usage as a general descriptive verb indicative of masking of disguising any aspect of identity ... particularly gay or lesbian sexuality" (Introduction, p. xxx).

In "Finale," Irene becomes convinced that Brian and Clare are having an affair, despite a lack of concrete evidence. Seething with rage, Irene believes an affair jeopardizes the safe, bourgeois life and identity she has created. While she has the power to reveal Clare's secret, Irene is torn between race loyalty and a desire to crush Clare. In the end, Irene does not have to choose. By chance, Jack Bellew encounters Irene and an obviously black friend walking arm in arm on the street; this revelation of Irene's race inevitably leads Jack to question Clare's race, too. She considers warning Clare, but ultimately takes no action. Irene fears that Bellew will seek an annulment or divorce, which would, she imagines, free Clare to marry Brian. Larsen alludes to the sensational Rhinelander case of 1925, in which the New York millionaire Kip Rhinelander, under pressure from his family, sued his wife Alice Jones for annulment on the grounds of fraud, that she had deceived him by passing as white. Although she won the case, Alice Jones was humiliated during the very public trial, forced to disrobe so the jury could decide whether Rhinelander could have been deceived about her race. A divorce would cause a scandal, but Clare has made it clear to Irene that she is ready to walk away from her marriage, even from her daughter. In the novel's final scene, Jack bursts into a Harlem party and declares, "So you're a nigger, a damned dirty nigger" (p. 238). Clare does not

seem upset by the revelation of her secret or by her husband's explosive statement; in fact, she has a faint smile on her lips. In the next moment she is dead, having "fallen" from the sixth-floor window. Larsen creates ambiguity in the ending, suggesting Clare's death could have been suicide, homicide, or a terrible accident, "death by misadventure" as the authorities label it. But Irene's wish for Clare's death in the penultimate chapter, as well as the fact that she grabs Clare's arm just before the fall, strongly suggests that she is complicit in Clare's death. Further, Irene is worried not that Clare has died from the fall but that she might still be alive. By implying that Clare was murdered, Larsen revises the traditional ending of the tragic mulatto story, in which the protagonist usually dies by her own hand.

With the publication of *Passing,* Larsen became one of the chief literary voices of the Harlem Renaissance and was at the height of her career. She once again received a positive review from W. E. B. Du Bois: "Nella Larsen's 'Passing' is one of the finest novels of the year. If it did not treat a forbidden subject—the inter-marriage of a stodgy middle-class white man to a very beautiful and selfish octoroon—it would have an excellent chance to be hailed, selected, and recommended" ("Passing," p. 97). Du Bois even claims in the same review that "if the American Negro renaissance gives us many more books like this, with its sincerity, its simplicity, and charm, we can soon with equanimity drop the word 'Negro'" (p. 98). Other reviews praised the novel's economy and characterization, as well as its psychological exploration of passing. After the book's publication, Larsen was the guest of honor at a tea hosted by Blanche Knopf and was asked to be the featured speaker at "Authors' Night" at the St. George Playhouse in Brooklyn. Buoyed by her successes, Larsen applied for a prestigious Guggenheim Fellowship for creative writing. Her application requested funding for travel in France and Spain in preparation for a new novel on the "difference in intellectual and physical freedom for the Negro" throughout Europe (quoted in Hutchinson, p. 340). But this was also a time of great flux in Larsen's life. Her husband left his research job in New York and accepted the position of head of the Physics Department at Fisk University, with a substantial $5,000 annual salary. Larsen was not pleased with the thought of moving back to the segregated South and relinquishing her life in Harlem and identity as a New York writer. The move would also mean a return to the very school that expelled her as a teenager for not conforming to its rigid rules. Although she was offered a position at the new Fisk library, Larsen delayed a move and stayed in New York.

THE "SANCTUARY" CONTROVERSY AND THE END OF LARSEN'S LITERARY CAREER

In January 1930, at the height of her literary career, Larsen's story "Sanctuary" appeared in *Forum* magazine, a prestigious journal of literature and current events with wide circulation. The January issue also included articles by Eleanor Roosevelt and E. B. White. Larsen was the first black writer to be included in its pages, a clear indication of her new status in the literary world, and she was paid $200 for the story. "Sanctuary" is markedly different from *Quicksand and Passing.* Charles Larson notes that "nowhere else in her published work has Larsen made such an emphatic statement about blackness" (*Invisible Darkness,* p. 95). "Sanctuary" is set exclusively in the South and uses black dialect, not seen in Larsen's other works. In the story, Jim Hammer, a black man, seeks refuge at the home of a black woman named Annie Poole after shooting a man. Annie agrees to harbor him but later is horrified to learn from the sheriff that Jim's victim was her own son Obadiah. Rather than turn Jim over to the authorities, Annie tells the sheriff, "No, Ah ain't sees nobody pass. Not yet" (*Complete Fiction,* p. 26). She chooses loyalty to her race over a desire to see her son's death avenged.

Readers of *Forum* quickly sent in letters claiming that "Sanctuary" was a plagiarized version of the story "Mrs. Adis" by the popular British writer Sheila Kaye-Smith. "Mrs. Adis" had appeared in the American periodical *Century Magazine* in 1922 and had been reprinted in a collected volume of Kaye-Smith's short stories in 1926. Indeed the two stories have remarkably

similar plots, descriptions, and dialogue. Entire sentences are nearly identical. Set in Sussex, "Mrs. Adis" is the story of an older working-class woman who gives sanctuary to Peter Crouch, a young man who has committed murder. While out poaching, he believes he has shot a gamekeeper. As in "Sanctuary," Peter appeals to the woman through his friendship with her son. In the same ironic twist, it turns out the shooting victim is Mrs. Adis's son, Tom. When the gamekeepers come looking for Peter, Mrs. Adis keeps his location a secret, choosing class allegiances over a desire for justice or revenge.

Soon the Harlem literary world was abuzz with gossip about the scandal. Harold Jackman wrote Countee Cullen to share the "literary dirt" (Hutchinson, p. 345). Larsen submitted multiple drafts to the editors of *Forum* to demonstrate the originality of the story. In the April edition, the journal expressed its support of Larsen, stating that the similarities were an "extraordinary" coincidence. The issue includes "The Author's Explanation" by Larsen, in which she explains that the germ of the story came from a tale told to her by a patient at Lincoln Hospital during her nursing days. Her friend Carl Van Vechten publicly supported her throughout the storm. Larsen's critics have struggled to make sense of this episode, especially since as a librarian she would have been aware of the concept of plagiarism and its consequences. In addition, Larsen was an avid reader of contemporary fiction and a librarian at the NYPL when "Mrs. Adis" was published, making it likely she would have encountered the story. It has been suggested that perhaps that she read or heard others discussing the story and later unconsciously rewrote it, believing it was of her own invention. Others have speculated that "Sanctuary" was intended to be a conscious adaptation of Kaye-Smith's story, replacing issues of class with issues of race. In postmodern literature there are other examples of such literary retellings and revisions, including Jean Rhys's *Wide Sargasso Sea* (1966). If it was meant to be a retelling, why did Larsen neglect to acknowledge her debt or continue to deny it when confronted by the readers and editors of *Forum*? As Kelli Larson and others have argued, "Sanctuary" is in fact the superior story, more fully developed than "Mrs. Adis," with less melodrama and increased psychological depth. This very public humiliation seems to have shaken Larsen's confidence in her writing and damaged her reputation. It was to be her last published work.

Just months after the "Sanctuary" controversy, Larsen became the first African American woman, and only the fourth African American, to be awarded the Guggenheim Fellowship, which she had applied for in November 1929. The fellowship, which came with a $2,500 stipend, offered Larsen the opportunity to escape from the gossip of Harlem and from her crumbling marriage. Elmer had moved alone to Nashville to assume his new position as head of the Physics Department, with the idea that Larsen would eventually follow. Almost immediately, Elmer began an affair with a white woman, Ethel Gilbert, Fisk's popular and powerful director of Publicity and Finance. When Larsen confronted him about the affair, Elmer persuaded her to put off a decision about a divorce until after her travels, hoping to avoid a public scandal that could jeopardize his place at Fisk. Larsen had an adventurous two years abroad in which she traveled throughout Europe and northern Africa, often with her friend Dorothy Peterson. She also socialized with a variety of European and expatriate artists and had a brief affair with an unnamed "English–Scotsman." During her fellowship, she worked on a novel titled "Mirage," which was rejected by Knopf in late 1931. The novel focused on a love triangle of white characters, a daring decision for a black author. It was generally assumed that black writers only had the authority to write about their "own" kind, and Larsen's novel would have been an attempt to break through the inherent racism of the literary world.

With her return to the United States, Larsen was forced to face the wreckage of her marriage and make decisions about her future. She moved to Nashville, but by this time Elmer's affair with Edith was an open secret and the marriage wrecked beyond repair. Larsen was suffering from a nervous depression and even made

suicidal gestures. She turned down a job at Fisk and spent her time in Nashville working on a revision of "Mirage" titled "Fall Fever," as well as another novel, "Adrian and Evadne," coauthored with her friend Edward Donahoe, who may have also had a romantic interest in Larsen. Her divorce was finalized in 1933, and Larsen was awarded alimony of $150 per month, sufficient to grant her financial independence. She moved back to New York to an apartment in the East Village and initially rejoined her circle of New York acquaintances, including Dorothy Peterson and Carl Van Vechten. In November 1934, she attended Van Vechten's party for Gertrude Stein and Alice B. Toklas, who were visiting from France. But by the mid–1930s she began to withdraw from her literary friends and act erratically, and there have been suspicions that Larsen became dependent on alcohol or drugs. There are no extant manuscripts or evidence that Larsen continued to write during this time.

When Elmer's alimony checks stopped after his death from cancer in 1941, Larsen went back to her first profession: nursing. As George Hutchinson has noted, her decision to end her writing career and return to nursing has been read by critics as a "disappearance or retreat, motivated by a lack of courage or dedication" (p. 465). Larsen, known as Mrs. Imes, began working as a staff nurse at Gouverneur Hospital in 1944, during a nursing shortage caused by World War II. By all accounts she was an excellent nurse, witnessed by her quick promotion from staff nurse to a chief nurse and night supervisor and her record of substantial pay raises. In 1962, she became night supervisor of the psychiatric ward at the large modern Metropolitan Hospital. It was discovered in 1963 that she had passed the mandatory retirement age of seventy, and she was forced to leave nursing. She lived for less than a year after her retirement, dying of congestive heart failure in her Second Avenue apartment around 30 March 1964. Her apartment was robbed soon after her death, and what papers she left were taken, and later lost, by a former nursing colleague. Although Larsen had not had a relationship with her family for over half a century, her white half-sister Anna Larsen Gardner eventually inherited the bulk of Larsen's $36,000 estate. Larsen received only a brief death notice in the *New York Times,* with no acknowledgement of her literary output. She is buried in the Cypress Hills Cemetery in Brooklyn, in an unmarked grave.

At the time of her death, Larsen's work was largely forgotten and out of fashion with African American intellectuals, who found her texts apolitical and not sufficiently focused on issues of black identity. In the 1970s she was reclaimed by black feminists, who saw in her work the precursors of "womanism," a racially conscious feminism. Larsen has been acknowledged as a sort of literary foremother to such writers who emerged later in the twentieth century such as Gloria Naylor, Alice Walker, and Toni Morrison. Since the 1980s, Larsen's writing has garnered an impressive amount of scholarship, especially given her limited body of work. Larsen's interest in the intersections of race, gender, class, and sexuality make her particularly appealing to contemporary critics of women's literature, African American literature, modernism, psychoanalysis, and queer theory. The publication of George Hutchinson's biography in 2006 has led to further critical attention for this fascinating and enigmatic writer.

Selected Bibliography

WORKS OF NELLA LARSEN

EDITIONS

Quicksand. New York: Knopf, 1928.

Passing. New York: Knopf, 1929.

Quicksand and Passing. Edited by Deborah E. McDowell. New Brunswick, N.J.: Rutgers UP, 1986.

The Complete Fiction of Nella Larsen: "Passing," "Quicksand," and the Stories. Edited by Charles Larson. New York: Anchor, 2001.

PUBLICATIONS IN MAGAZINES AND JOURNALS

"Playtime: Three Scandinavian Games." *Brownies Book,* June 1920, pp. 191–192.

"Playtime: Danish Fun." *Brownies' Book,* July 1920, p. 219.

Review of *Certain People of Importance,* by Kathleen Norris. *Messenger* 5: 713 (1923).

"Correspondence." *Opportunity* 4: 295 (1926).

Review of *Black Sadie,* by T. Bowyer Campbell. *Opportunity* 7: 24 (1929).

"Sanctuary." *Forum* 83: 15-18 (January 1930).

"The Author's Explanation." *Forum* (Supp. 4) 83: 41–42 (April 1930).

CRITICAL AND BIOGRAPHICAL STUDIES

Bennett, Juda. *The Passing Figure: Racial Confusion in Modern American Literature.* New York: Peter Lang, 1996.

Bennett, Michael, and Vanessa D. Dickerson. *Recovering the Black Female Body: Self-Representations by African American Women.* New Brunswick, N.J.: Rutgers University Press, 2001.

Berg, Allison. *Mothering the Race: Women's Narratives of Reproduction, 1890–1930.* Urbana: University of Illinois Press, 2002.

Blackmer, Corinne E. "The Veils of the Law: Race and Sexuality in Nella Larsen's *Passing.*" *College Literature* 22.3:50–67 (1995).

Blackmore, David L. "'That Unreasonable Restless Feeling': The Homosexual Subtexts of Nella Larsen's *Passing.*" *African American Review* 26.3:475–84 (1992).

Bone, Robert. *The Negro Novel in America.* New Haven: Yale University Press, 1965.

Brickhouse, Anna. "Nella Larsen and the Intertextual Geography of *Quicksand.*" *African American Review* 35. 4:533–60 (2001).

Brody, Jennifer DeVere. "Clare Kendry's 'True' Colors: Race and Class Conflict in Nella Larsen's *Passing.*" *Callaloo: A Journal of African American and African Arts and Letters* 15.4:1053–65 (1992).

Butler, Judith. "Passing, Queering: Nella Larsen's Psychoanalytic Challenge." In *Female Subjects in Black and White: Race, Psychoanalysis, Feminism.* Ed. Elizabeth Abel, Barbara Christian, and Helene Moglen. Berkeley, CA: University of California Press, 1997. Pp. 266–84.

Carby, Hazel. *Reconstructing Womanhood.* New York: Oxford University Press, 1987.

Carr, Brian. "Paranoid Interpretation, Desire's Nonobject, and Nella Larsen's *Passing.*" *PMLA* 119.2:282–95 (2004).

Caughie, Pamela L. "'Not Entirely Strange, ... Not Entirely Friendly': Passing and Pedagogy." *College English* 54. 7:775–93 (1992).

Christian, Barbara. *Black Women Novelists: The Development of a Tradition, 1892–1976.* Westport, Conn.: Greenwood Press, 1980.

Cutter, Martha J. "Sliding Significations: Passing as a Narrative and Textual Strategy in Nella Larsen's Fiction." In *Passing and the Fictions of Identity.* Ed. Elaine K. Ginsberg. Durham, NC: Duke University Press, 1996. Pp. 75–100.

Davis, Arthur P. *From the Dark Tower: Afro-American Writers, 1900–1960.* Washington, D.C.: Howard University Press, 1974.

Davis, Thadious M. Introduction to *Passing,* by Nella Larsen. Edited by Thadious Davis. New York: Penguin, 1997. Pp. vii–xxxii.

———. "Nella Larsen." In *Dictionary of Literary Biography* Vol. 51: *Afro-American Writers from the Harlem Renaissance to 1940.* Detroit: Gale Research Co. 1987. Pp. 182–192.

———. *Nella Larsen, Novelist of the Harlem Renaissance: A Woman's Life Unveiled.* Baton Rouge: Louisiana State University Press, 1994.

duCille, Ann. *Coupling Convention: Sex, Text, and Tradition in Black Women's Fiction.* New York: Oxford University Press, 1993.

Ginsberg, Elaine K., ed. *Passing and the Fictions of Identity.* Durham, NC: Duke University Press, 1996.

Haviland, Beverly. "Passing from Paranoia to Plagiarism: The Abject Authorship of Nella Larsen." *MFS: Modern Fiction Studies* 43.2:295–318 (1997).

Hostetler, Ann E. "The Aesthetics of Race and Gender in Nella Larsen's *Quicksand.*" *PMLA* 105.1:35–46 (1990).

Hutchinson, George. *In Search of Nella Larsen: A Biography of the Color Line.* Cambridge, Mass.: Belknap Press, Harvard University Press, 2006.

———. "Nella Larsen and the Veil of Race." *American Literary History* 9.2:329–49 (1997).

———. "Subject to Disappearance: Interracial Identity in Nella Larsen's *Quicksand.*" In *Temples for Tomorrow: Looking Back at the Harlem Renaissance.* Ed. Geneviève Fabre and Michel Feith. Bloomington, IN: Indiana University Press, 2001. Pp. 177–92.

Johnson, Barbara. *The Feminist Difference: Literature, Psychoanalysis, Race, and Gender.* Cambridge, Mass.: Harvard University Press, 1998.

Kaplan, Carla. "Nella Larsen's Erotics of Race." Introduction to *Passing.* Edited by Carla Kaplan. New York: Norton, 2007. Pp. ix–xxvii.

Kramer, Victor A., and Robert A. Russ. *Harlem Renaissance Re-Examined.* Rev. and expanded ed. Troy, N.Y.: Whitson Pub., 1997.

Larson, Charles R.. Introduction to *The Complete Fiction of Nella Larsen.* New York: Anchor Books, 2001. Pp. xi–xxii.

———. *Invisible Darkness: Jean Toomer & Nella Larsen.* Iowa City: University of Iowa Press, 1993.

Larson, Kelli. "Surviving the Taint of Plagiarism: Nella Larsen's 'Sanctuary' and Sheila Kaye-Smith's 'Mrs. Adis.'" *Journal of Modern Literature* 30, no. 4:82–104 (2007).

Lewis, David Levering, ed. Introduction to *The Portable Harlem Renaissance Reader.* New York: Viking, 1994. Pp. xiii–xli.

McDonald, C. Ann. "Nella Larsen (1891–1964)." In *American Women Writers, 1900–1945: A Bio-Bibliographical Critical Sourcebook.* Ed. Laurie Champion. Westport, CT: Greenwood, 2000. Pp. 182–91.

McDowell, Deborah E. *"The Changing Same": Black Women's Literature, Criticism, and Theory.* Bloomington, Ind.: Indiana University Press, 1995.

———. Introduction to *Quicksand and Passing,* by Nella Larsen. New Brunswick, NJ: Rutgers University Press, 1996. Pp. ix–xxxvii.

McLendon, Jacquelyn Y. *The Politics of Color in the Fiction of Jessie Fauset and Nella Larsen.* Charlottesville: University Press of Virginia, 1995.

Sherrard-Johnson, Cherene. "'A Plea for Color': Nella Larsen's Iconography of the Mulatta." *American Literature* 76.4:833–69 (2004).

Tate, Claudia. *Psychoanalysis and Black Novels: Desire and the Protocols of Race.* New York: Oxford University Press, 1998.

Wall, Cheryl A. "Passing for What? Aspects of Identity in Nella Larsen's Novels." *Black American Literature Forum* 20.1–2:97–111 (1986).

———. *Women of the Harlem Renaissance.* Bloomington: Indiana University Press, 1995.

Washington, Mary Helen. "Nella Larsen: Mystery Woman of the Harlem Renaissance." *Ms.* December 1980, pp. 44–50.

Wiegman, Robyn. *American Anatomies: Theorizing Race and Gender.* Durham, NC: Duke University Press, 1995.

Young, John K. *Black Writers, White Publishers: Marketplace Politics in Twentieth Century African American Literature.* Jackson: University Press of Mississippi, 2006.

BOOK REVIEWS

Du Bois, W. E. B. "Passing." 1929. Reprinted in *Passing.* Edited by Carla Kaplan. New York: Norton, 2007. Pp. 97–98.

———. "Two Novels." *Crisis* 35: 202 (June 1928).

Fauset, Arthur Huff. Review of *Quicksand,* by Nella Larsen. *Black Opals* 1:19 (June 1928).

JONATHAN LETHEM

(1964—)

Bert Almon

JONATHAN ALLEN LETHEM, a prolific and influential writer, was born in Manhattan at St. Vincent's Hospital in Greenwich Village on February 19, 1964. He has observed that his place of birth is often assumed to be Brooklyn, where two of his most important novels, *Motherless Brooklyn* (1999) and *Fortress of Solitude* (2003) are set. He grew up in an artistic and bohemian milieu in Brooklyn: his father, Richard Brown Lethem, is a distinguished painter, and his mother, Judith Frank, was a folksinger and political activist. Elements of their lives were used in the creation of the parents of the protagonist of Lethem's *Fortress of Solitude.* The death of his political activist mother from a brain tumor when he was fourteen years old had an enormous impact and reverberates in much of his fiction. She gave him a typewriter not long before she died and even watched *Star Wars* with him (he saw the movie twenty-one times!), though her taste was for art films. His younger siblings have artistic vocations: his sister, Mara, is a photographer, and his brother, Blake, is well-known graffiti artist (pseudonym: KEO) and scene painter who has contributed covers to several of Jonathan Lethem's books. Lethem has won an impressive number of awards, including a 2005 MacArthur Foundation award for $500,000.

A reader who wishes to learn about Lethem's life (especially his childhood in Brooklyn) and his preoccupations might begin with his essay collection, *The Disappointment Artist* (2005), particularly the work called "Lives of the Bohemians." He also operates an elaborate website (Jonathan.Lethem.com), which provides an extensive bibliography, links to published and unpublished writing, and links to a variety of websites that range from the profound to the zany.

Lethem's childhood is intertwined with his work, though not in a literal way. In 1968 the family moved from West Broadway in Manhattan to a red brick house on Dean Street in the Gowanus district of Brooklyn. Gowanus was a racially mixed neighborhood (mostly African American and Puerto Rican). In the 1970s it moved into a period of gentrification, a process that Lethem sees as a destructive one. The district was renamed Boerum Hill, to give it a classy sound harking back to the early Dutch settlers. His parents, his mother in particular, were utopians dreaming of racial harmony, and they sent him to the local public school, where he was one of the very few white students. He was bullied daily, an experience he has recounted several times and treated at length in *The Fortress of Solitude.* Rather than making him a racist, the ordeal gave him a drive toward racial understanding. He was raised as a Quaker.

He eventually attended the High School of Music & Art in Manhattan, a specialized school now known as LaGuardia Arts. His ambition was to become a painter, a vocation that he took up in imitation of his father, but he did edit his own little magazine, the *Literary Exchange,* and wrote *Heroes,* an unpublished novel. He entered Bennington College in 1982, where his classmates included Bret Easton Ellis, Jill Eisenstadt, and Donna Tartt, who also became distinguished writers. He was not prepared for the class divisions in the college and felt poorly motivated. He dropped out after one semester and then tried again the following year. He never completed a degree at Bennington or anywhere else. Ironically, he was able to give the commencement address at Bennington in 2005. One of his most important experiences at the college was his hosting of a showing of John Ford's *The Searchers,* a

movie that none of his classmates liked, according to his essay "Defending *The Searchers* (Scenes in the Life of an Obsession)." The film would inspire his fourth novel, *Girl in Landscape* (1998).

In 1984 he hitchhiked from Denver to California, a journey reflected in the settings of his dystopian novel *Amnesia Moon* (1995) and wound up in the Bay area. In the July 6, 2000, issue of *Rolling Stone* he recalled his journey in an essay called "Hitchhiking Is Illegal in Nevada." He worked in Berkeley at Pegasus Books (1985–1990) and Moe's Books (1990–1994), and he regards Moe's (an antiquarian shop) as part of his apprenticeship. His first two marriages, to the writer Shelley Jackson and the Canadian film producer Julia Rosenberg, both ended in divorce. In 2004 he married the filmmaker Amy Barrett and they have a son, Everett, born in 2007. Having returned to New York in 1996, he and his family live in a small brownstone house a few blocks from his childhood home in Brooklyn, where he has been a vocal opponent of gentrification and redevelopment plans for the area.

EARLY WORK

Jonathan Lethem is a writer with a remarkable range of influences. The fashionable term "intertexuality" applies very well to his work. His interviews cite an astonishing number of books, songs, and materials from popular culture that he acknowledges as models. His reading ranges from pulp science fiction to sophisticated novels by Iris Murdoch, Anthony Powell, Charles Dickens, John Barth, and Don DeLillo. His reading in thrillers includes Ross Macdonald and Raymond Chandler. His taste in science fiction ranges from the pulps (which he considers folk art) to major writers such as J. G. Ballard and Philip K. Dick. The rise of the latter from the category of pulp writer to the summit of the Library of America is largely Lethem's doing. He draws heavily on nonliterary sources, including comic books (which play a huge role in his work, especially in his masterpiece, *Fortress of Solitude*) and many varieties of rock and roll. Music is central to his work as well. The modern writer whose sensibility most approximates Lethem's is the poet T. S. Eliot, whose mind was an echo chamber in which everything he read and heard was likely to get into the poems—Dante and John Webster, but also music hall songs and Australian ballads.

Lethem's musical tastes affect his fiction. Not music hall songs but our equivalent: hip-hop, rhythm and blues, indie rock—all kinds of contemporary popular music (but not classical music). In an interview with the science fiction critic Fiona Kelleghan, Lethem said that each of his novels has a "sound track," a song or album that he was listening to while writing. His intertexuality is perhaps comparable to "sampling," the technique of interpolating quotations (as jazz musicians used to call it) from familiar songs into a new creation. Not surprisingly, Lethem has published attacks on the use of copyright law against samplers. Nor is the notion of sole authorship sacred to him: several of his books are collaborations with others.

Some of his interests can be symbolized by the tattoo he wears on his upper left arm. According to one interviewer, Heidi Benson, it is three inches long and depicts "a spray-can shooting a fan of reddish-pink paint." Benson notes that it is appropriate for someone who grew up in inner-city Brooklyn, but it also bears the word "UBIK" in block letters, and *Ubik* is the title of a novel by Philip K. Dick in which it is a spray that reverses entropy. Lethem's work preserves much that is in danger of disappearance, especially in a world where urban renewal projects sweep away entire neighborhoods and their intricate texture of relations. And popular culture has a remarkably short shelf life. Art reverses entropy, at least within the world created by the artist.

Lethem's interest in so many genres has led him to break the barriers between them. In an interview with the editors of the *Indiana Review,* he said that "one of my aesthetics is an aesthetic of rupturing genres, of playing with genres and reformatting my own narrative impulse, which is similar to the garb or the furniture of a very different kind of storytelling each time out." It is not unusual for authors to mix genres—Shakes-

peare mixed comedy, tragedy, and history in his *Henry IV* cycle—but Lethem is interested in less prestigious genres: detective stories, science fiction and fantasy, the comic book. As he said to Lorin Stein in the *Paris Review,* "I stitched together a notion—I'd be the American Calvino, but nourished by scruffy roots."

Lethem's first novel, *Gun, with Occasional Music* (1994), is a prime example of crossing genres. By the time of its publication, he had published several stories in the science fiction genre. The novel mixes the conventions of hard-boiled detective stories and science fiction. In a superb essay, "From Dick to Lethem: The Dickian Legacy, Postmodernism, and Avant-Pop in Jonathan Lethem's *Amnesia Moon,*" Umberto Rossi traces Lethem's relationship to American "avant-pop writing," work that mixes the procedures of high modernist art with genre writing. There are many writers nourishing any book by Lethem. The principal influences are, on the detective side, the hard-boiled detective fiction of Raymond Chandler and (to a lesser extent) Ross Macdonald and, on the science fiction side, the novels of Philip K. Dick, especially *Do Androids Dream of Electric Sheep?,* a work that mixes the detective and science fiction genres. The obvious literary precedent is William S. Burroughs's *Nova Express,* a kind of intergalactic crime thriller with powerful social satire. Lethem seems never to have cited Burroughs as a source for his work, but in his youth he was taken with the Beats, including Jack Kerouac and Burroughs.

Raymond Chandler's hero Philip Marlowe worked in Los Angeles. Lethem catches the world-weary tone of Chandler's work and the tendency to craft witty dialogue and unusual metaphors. Indeed, the protagonist, Conrad Metcalf, is proud of his metaphors. He also uses terms out of noir detective stories, like "dame." Metcalf lives in an Oakland of the future, in which consumerist capitalism has turned dictatorial. Lethem has suggested that the science fiction writers of the 1950s envisioned such changes (he mentions Dick, C. M. Kornbluth and Frederik Pohl as good examples), and the dystopian America of the novel owes as much to them as to George Orwell and Aldous Huxley. Order is kept by an office of the Grand Inquisition, and the police are known as inquisitors. All citizens carry a karma card, and infractions deduct points from their karma accounts. A negative balance of zero carries not the death penalty but the deep freeze: a term in suspended animation. Orwell's *1984* envisions a world in which language is engineered by the rulers into Newspeak, with a vocabulary that makes the discourses of freedom impossible. In Metcalf's world, the news has been reduced to pictures without captions, even more ominous. The chief means of social control is the legal use of free addictive drugs. Huxley's Soma from *Brave New World* is a literary precedent. The drugs in Metcalf's America have names like "Regrettol," "Believol," "Avoidol," and "Acceptol." They all contain "Addictol" to keep the users dependent.

Much of the setting seems a grungy extension of the present. The most frightening dystopian world is one that seems a modest extrapolation of our own, not one set far away in time or space. The author has said that the novel is an extrapolation from 1958, which gives it a Cold War atmosphere. There are few gadgets: a gun that plays mood music, an antigravity pen (a new invention in the world of the novel), a "slavebox" that controls the mind of a victim in whose scalp it is buried, a method of mind control very familiar in science fiction. (The more gadgets included in a science fiction novel, the more likely the reader decades later is to wonder why the writer failed to anticipate the Internet, e-mail, and iPods.)

The most exotic additions are the "evolved" beings, whose mental development has been accelerated by a treatment invented by Dr. Twostrand (an obvious reference to the structure of DNA). The most sinister development is the accelerated development of humans, resulting in "babyheads" with enormous bald craniums and permanently immature attitudes in spite of their large brains. The characters include evolved animals too: an intelligent sheep, a talking kitten, a humanized ape, and a hit-man kangaroo named (appropriately) Joey Castle, a goon who can do great damage with his teeth and legs. The kangaroo was suggested by a passage from Ray-

mond Chandler's last novel, *Playback*: "There was nothing to it. The *Super Chief* was on time, as it almost always is, and the subject was as easy to spot as a kangaroo in a dinner jacket."

The presence of a thug who happens to be a kangaroo is part of the camp atmosphere of the book and leads to such lines as "You sent a kangaroo to do a man's job." The drollery includes places like the Lost Muse Café and odd character names: Teleprompter, Testafer, Angwine, Phoneblum, and an evolved ape and private detective named Surface. The plot is complex to the point of absurdity and involves double-crosses, murdered witnesses, crime syndicates, and other apparatus of detective novels. The convolutions of the plot are true to the spirit of Chandler. When *The Big Sleep* was being filmed by Howard Hawks, neither Hawks nor the scriptwriter, William Faulkner, could figure out who killed one character. The legend is that they consulted Chandler, who did not know either. The last few chapters of *Gun, with Occasional Music* are full of plot turns and rough justice administered by the cynical but ultimately moral detective. The book is a young novelist's bravura performance. It won the Locus Award for Best First Novel and the Crawford Award for Best First Fantasy Novel and was also nominated for the Nebula Award, one of the most important science fiction prizes.

Lethem's second novel, *Amnesia Moon* (1995), is a whole set of possible futures experienced by one protagonist, aptly named Chaos, although his name in this deeply ambiguous text may actually be Everett Moon. In an interview with Ron Hogan, Lethem observed of his *Amnesia Moon* period: "I had this need to see my characters living in the most godawful dystopias." Chaos passes through a series of dystopias as he moves from Hatfork, Wyoming, through the desert Southwest (Arizona, Utah, and Nevada), ending up in San Francisco. These societies are perhaps a set of communities left over after a mysterious apocalypse. They are projections of the minds of Chaos and a few other characters, reflecting their fears and desires. Umberto Rossi's article "From Dick to Lethem" points out the sources for this conception, two novels by Philip K. Dick, *Eye in the Sky* (1957) and *The Man in the High Castle* (1962). Such fragments of societies give the novelist a chance to satirize various strands in the consumerist society—the influence of Lethem's science fiction masters is clear. His fictional models, he told Thomas Stolmar and Alexander Laurence, include Philip K. Dick's *Dr. Bloodmoney,* George Stewart's *Earth Abides,* and Orwell's *1984.* He sees this book as an extrapolation from 1978.

Hatfork is ruled by a villain named Kellogg and his Food Rangers. The corporate allusion is obvious. Kellogg has a monopoly on the scarce food supplies in a region where nothing grows, and that gives him control of the community. He runs the entire area out of "Little America," a reference to the enormous service station empire whose little penguin signs are posted everywhere in Wyoming, Montana, and Utah. At the beginning of the novel, Chaos lives in a movie theater, an apt metaphor for a universe in which reality is a projection, a simulacrum created by dreamers. After a clash with Kellogg, Chaos goes on a typical science fiction quest through the desert landscape accompanied by a fur-covered mutant girl, Melinda. On his hitchhiking trip to California, which simultaneously parodies Jack Kerouac's *On the Road* and the post-apocalyptic *Road Warrior* films, Chaos constantly forgets who he is and starts life anew in each town. (Lethem is fascinated by memory and in 2000 edited *The Vintage Book of Amnesia,* a collection of stories and essays.) Chaos comes first to The Green, a bizarre version of the Emerald City in *The Wizard of Oz,* in which everyone is blind. The city is ruled by a mysterious figure, Elaine. Other communities include the McDonaldonians, the last inhabitants of post-apocalypse Las Vegas (who are half-starved because even though they endlessly turn out hamburgers, company rules dictate that they cannot eat them) and the people of Vacaville, where people's status in society is determined by their luck and all the politicians are celebrities—the president is a game show host. The source for these passages is a pair of novels by Dick, *The Game Players of Titan* and *Solar Lottery,* which also depict societies ruled by luck. Rossi suggests in "From Dick to

Lethem" that the madman named Lucky who has created Vacaville is modeled on Philip K. Dick himself, a man who had frequent mental breakdowns.

In San Francisco, Chaos encounters a society that seems a parody of the hippie period. He learns what may be the truth about his experiences: after an apocalyptic "break," people have become receptive to dreams and find themselves FSRs ("finite subjective realities") created by the strongest dreamers. At the end of the novel, Chaos/Moon may have returned to a normal reality shared with a makeshift family he has acquired along the road, though the ending is ambiguous: he and his group are being shadowed by a helicopter.

In his insightful essay "Enclosed Dreams, Highways and Labyrinths: Jonathan Lethem's *Amnesia Moon,*" Rossi suggests that the book is a satire on Reaganomics, the free enterprise policies of Ronald Reagan, first as governor of California and then as president of the United States. As for the novel's fragmented form, Lethem revealed in his interview with Ron Hogan that the book was made up of pieces from his time at Bennington to just before he submitted it, and in his *Paris Review* interview with Lorin Stein he speaks of it as a "an anthology of my apprentice work," "made out of failed short stories." The fragmentary method works very well, especially as the fragments are vivid. Failed stories, successful novel.

Lethem's next book, *The Wall of the Sky, the Wall of the Eye* (1996), which collected seven of his stories, won the World Fantasy Award for 1997. The stories show remarkable psychological insight. The best known is "The Happy Man," a powerful study of pedophilia. The title character has become a "migratory." In a sense he has died, but his body remains on earth, working and living with his family. His soul is absent most of the time in a kind of hell, an alternate reality constructed from his traumatic memories. He returns to his body occasionally and unpredictably. The fantasy situation lets Lethem dramatize the self-alienation of a sexual abuse victim, and the hell narratives are based on the character's memories of being abused by his uncle Frank. Each narrative is a surreal nightmare realized with extraordinary vividness.

Lethem's interview with Fiona Kelleghan contains revealing comments by the author on the stories in the collection. He explores his fondness for "concretizing metaphors," making something literal out of a figurative situation. A superb example is "The Hardened Criminals," a story in which living criminals are "hardened" and used to construct a prison. The work is horrifying in its meticulous details. Another story, "Forever, Said the Duck," deals with characters who have an orgy in a virtual reality. Lethem points out to Kelleghan that in the years that he lived in the Bay area, there was much utopian talk about the possibilities of virtual realities. He is skeptical about such claims, and the world of "Forever, Said the Duck" is a sterile world of superficial orgies.

A story nominated for the Nebula Award, "Five Fucks," presents a love triangle whose basic situation—a woman has a sexual encounter with a stranger called E., suffers a strange amnesia, and seeks help from a detective to find the man—recurs in different versions. The detective's name mutates from Pupkiss to McPupkiss. The next-to-last version is a parody of *Frankenstein* and takes place in the village of Pupkinstein, and in the final story, the characters have been reduced to three primitive beings in a pale blue sea. One of them is called Pupfish. A less interesting story, "Vanilla Dunk," is based on the premise that basketball players in a future time can take on the skills of the great players of the past by wearing an "exosuit." The story probes into racism in America: What happens when a racist uses the skills of the great black player Michael Jordan to advance a show business career as "Vanilla Dunk" (an obvious play on the white rapper who called himself Vanilla Ice)? The story is exceedingly long. The descriptions of basketball games are ingenious but not at all like actually watching the sport being played.

Two richly imaginative stories are "Light and the Sufferer" and "Sleepy People." The first story describes a man who is trying to help his junkie brother. Not only does he fail, but an alien being, the Sufferer, tries to intervene in the brother's

life but also cannot succeed. In "Sleepy People," set in a disintegrating society torn by civil war and subject to marauding gangs called "dinosaurs," a woman finds and begins to take care of a man suffering from a strange sleepwalking malady. Kelleghan suggested to Lethem in their interview that the sleeper is a concretized metaphor, a way of talking about people who "sleepwalk" through their lives. Lethem, skeptical about this interpretation, responded by saying that it was an attempt to display sympathy for women. Presumably he refers to the frequent complaint that men can never achieve emotional intimacy. The woman in the story has sexual relations with the sleeping man, but a truly emotional relationship is impossible.

In *As She Climbed Across the Table* (1997), Lethem creates a satire on academic life. Unlike so many writers today, he has never held an academic job. His three semesters at Bennington College were at an avant-garde arts school, not at a major research university like the fictional one in his novel, North California at Beauchamp. He freely acknowledges that he got the campus atmosphere from two of Don DeLillo's novels, *White Noise* and *Ratner's Star,* plus some details about campus parties imitated from Malcolm Bradbury's *The History Man.* He quietly acknowledged DeLillo's influence by naming a character Robert Soft after DeLillo's Robert Softly in *Ratner's Star.* One of the most important sources, one not likely to be recognized by a contemporary reader, is John Barth's early novel *The End of the Road.* Lethem has been a strong admirer of Barth's work. In *The End of the Road,* a campus novel, there is a love triangle involving a married couple and an emotionally atrophied man, Jacob Horner, who attracts the woman by his frustrating emptiness. The triangle in Lethem's novel is among Alice Coombs, a physicist; Philip Engstrand, an anthropologist who studies neurosis in scientists; and a kind of bubble in space-time created in a laboratory experiment by Professor Soft meant to replicate the Big Bang.

The flaw in the universe, which rests on a steel table, is nicknamed "Lack" because it has no observable characteristics. However, when things are passed into its area, they are either accepted—and disappear—or rejected, whereupon they pass unaffected through it. Alice becomes obsessed with it. It is, after all, an absolute paradigm of the detached being, a kind of analogue for emotionally unavailable men. Various satirical figures become involved in the study of Lack, including a brilliantly conceived pair of blind mathematicians, Evan (white) and Garth (African American), who have a powerfully symbiotic existence. They are brought in the laboratory to observe the anomaly. The uncertainty principle dictates that observers modify what they observe. Garth has eyes that function perfectly, but his brain cannot interpret what he "sees," making him the perfect nonobserving observer who will see what is really there. This conceit is perhaps no less absurd than a personified nothingness like Lack. Other characters include De Tooth, the campus deconstructionist, whose name probably is meant to suggest Paul de Man. In one amusing scene, his literary jargon causes Professor Soft to vomit.

It becomes apparent that the space-time anomaly has taken on the qualities of Alice Coombs: the one pattern in its behavior is to accept what she likes and reject what she does not like. She attempts to enter it, but she does not like herself; hence, she is rejected. The jealous Engstrand decides to enter Lack, and it accepts him. He finds himself in a set of plural universes spun off by Lack, something like the finite subjective realities in *Amnesia Moon.* One speculation about the Big Bang is that it might have generated an enormous or even infinite number of realities. The worlds he enters are generated by Alice's mind, by his own, and by Garth's and Evan's, who turn out to have gone into Lack before him. Their universe is one entirely without light. At the end of the novel, Engstrand has become pure thought. From his vantage point as a pure consciousness within Lack, he sees that Alice is going to try to enter once again. She strips off her clothes and climbs onto the table. Her eyes glisten with love: clearly, she will now be reunited with Engstrand, who is now merged with Lack.

Lethem realized in the course of his *Paris Review* interview (published six years after the

novel) that he had unconsciously echoed the ending of Barth's *End of the Road,* which concludes with the woman in the love triangle lying naked on a steel table after her death from a botched abortion. But there is no tragedy in Lethem's novel: the tone would not support such a conclusion. The novel is a bagatelle, though an enjoyable one.

He was much more emotionally invested in *Girl in Landscape* (1998). He says in the *Paris Review* interview that "my first real book is *Girl in Landscape.* That's the first conceived after I was a published writer, the first not written by a gifted, and giddy, amateur." He speaks of beginning to trust his emotional instincts. Genre writing, whether in the form of westerns, science fiction, or detective novels, is often limited by its conventions. In *Girl,* Lethem turned his obsession with John Wayne's role in *The Searchers* into a serious work of art, probing the emotions as well as social issues. The three previous novels showed giddiness indeed, an intoxication with his ability to play with and combine genres. The grief felt by his protagonist, Pella Marsh, after her mother's death from brain cancer, is clearly a reflection of the fate of Lethem's mother: the image of a dead or absent mother colors this novel and is a major emotional element in the novels that succeed it.

The novel is a rewriting of themes from John Ford's important and problematic western film *The Searchers* (1956). In "Defending *The Searchers,*" collected in *The Disappointment Artist,* Lethem describes his complicated relationship with the movie over the years. While at Bennington College, he ran a showing of it to the students on campus. The work was booed and laughed at, and during an interval when the film broke and had to be spliced together, he rose and attempted to defend the movie, though he himself was unclear about its meaning. His fellow students were not receptive to a western in which both the Indians and John Wayne appeared to be evil. For years after, he tried to understand the film.

In it, John Wayne's character, Ethan Edwards, spends five years pursuing the Comanches who killed his brother, sister-in-law, nephew, and a niece and carried off another niece. He not only wants revenge, he also intends to kill his niece because she will have been tainted by marriage with an Indian. Naturally, the students at Bennington were appalled by the story. The film has had a long road to achieving status as a classic. Edwards, whose life and doings before the story begins are left obscure, shows an astonishing knowledge of the Comanches and their ways, facts that are also left unexplained. Ford managed to touch on very sensitive themes for white Americans: racism, horror at miscegenation, the pursuit of violence—especially with firearms. Lethem considers it to be a problematic but vital work of art. It occurred to him to write a novel giving the point of view of the kidnap victim, who was played by Natalie Wood.

At its best, the western genre can indeed explore themes of race, violence, the role of the hero, the ambiguous advance of civilization. Lethem was not about to write a straight western. Rather, he sets his version of the story on an imaginary new frontier, a distant planet being colonized rather haphazardly by refugees from a polluted earth where the decline of the ozone layer has made life outside shelters almost impossible. By implication, he is harking back to the original and mostly haphazard settlement of America by British colonists who came for diverse reasons and slowly formed institutions. Clashes of the colonists with the original inhabitants generally ended badly for the latter. Books and films have often dwelled on the problematic character of powerful individuals who could be forces for good or perpetrators of atrocities. The settlement of America, and especially of the western frontier, is evoked by what Lethem has called his "Southern Gothic Western."

The narrative focuses on the Marsh family. Clement, the father and a failed mayor of New York, follows the American tradition of (in Huckleberry Finn's phrase) "lighting out for the territory," the American zone of the Planet of the Archbuilders. His wife, Caitlin, dies of brain cancer before the journey begins. His children, Pella, who has just entered puberty, and her younger siblings, David and Raymond, accompany him. The Archbuilders are remnants of a very high civilization that created a world in

which the climate is always temperate and food grows underground with no need to cultivate it: it is only necessary to dig it up. They created an Eden, to use the archetype that so appealed to the Puritan settlers and which haunts American literature, as scholars such as R. W. B. Lewis (*The American Adam,* 1955) have shown. Inevitable questions arise: Will this paradise be destroyed by those enter it? Will the settlers adapt to the land or ravage it? Will they massacre the original inhabitants? Can they build a viable community and overcome the forces of pioneering egoism?

The relationship to the land is extremely important in the novel. There are viruses on the planet that alter ways of thinking, and the settlers have been given antiviral drugs to protect themselves. The deceased mother had suggested that it would be important to adapt to the new environment, and the Marsh family follows her suggestion and refuses the drugs, which distresses the settlers. A lesbian couple has decided to do the same, which gives them a double stigma. The viruses cause the Archbuilders to develop a mysterious condition called "witnessing," which is explained in the course of the novel after Pella develops it herself, a kind of clairvoyant ability to roam the landscape as an observing consciousness. She is on her way to becoming a part of the landscape (hence the title of the novel) rather than a conqueror or exploiter. The landscape itself is an altered version of the Monument Valley setting of *The Searchers,* with pollen storms instead of dust storms. It also harks back, according to Lethem's interview in the *Paris Review,* to something "stolen" unconsciously from Philip Dick's *Martian Time-Slip* (1964): "extremely vivid images of lonely children digging in the Martian desert." Carl Abbott has written an interesting study, "Homesteading on the Extraterrestrial Frontier," with commentary on interplanetary homesteading novels by Ray Bradbury, Robert Heinlein, Jonathan Lethem, Kim Stanley Robinson, and Molly Gloss. It is a curious literary phenomenon: the American frontier being recapitulated on other planets.

Efram Nugent, the John Wayne figure, is the looming presence in the novel, quite literally: he stands out against the big sky that gives Lethem's extraterrestrial landscape its flavor of a western film. He is first glimpsed wearing a hat and has a powerful stride, fitting the western hero image very well. He is an early settler in the valley where the Marshes begin their homesteading. He knows an Archbuilder language and models the interior of his house on the interiors of the massive ruins that fill the landscape. But his garden is a very earthlike enclosure, and he has a rifle in his kitchen. He has a split in his attitudes: he respects the ancient Archbuilder civilization but has deep contempt for their decadent descendents, whom he suspects of miscegenistic desire for sexual relations with humans. At the same time, he can help them entomb a dead Archbuilder—who was killed because of alleged sexual contact with the painter Hugh Merrow—in mud, a process that turns the individual into a monument in the landscape. This ritual suggests that the Archbuilders are truly at one with their environment.

The question implied in many westerns is whether or not settlers can become a cohesive society. Pella sees the community as a "might-be town." Efram Nugent is skeptical. After all, he is the man whose masculine force and knowledge give him enormous power. His natural antagonist should be Clement Marsh, the failed politician, but Marsh refuses that role, saying that he wants to be just a member of the community. When public feeling turns against the local Archbuilders and mob rule threatens, the only person to stand up to Nugent is the young girl Pella.

Pella is the key figure. Lethem was influenced by fictional works about tomboys. In his *Paris Review* exchange, he says: "I was reading Carson McCullers and Shirley Jackson and I was thinking about the teenage girl as archetype. The tomboy. Also Charles Portis's *True Grit.*" (John Wayne starred in the film made from *True Grit* in 1969, a western about a girl who disguises herself as a boy in order to pursue her father's killer.) Pella's entry into sexual maturity (she's described as *pretentious* with womanhood) creates a powerful tension in the novel. She is ambivalent about Nugent, fearing him but feeling sexual attraction. He in turn spies on her and holds mocking

conversations with her. He knows that, in the terminology of the western, she has "gone native" and learned to roam the land in a shamanistic identification with the "household deer," intangible but visible creatures who are found everywhere.

The crisis comes over that question of miscegenation that also drove *The Searchers.* The Archbuilders are sexually ambiguous beings that have humanoid features and qualities of insects at the same time. Lethem has carefully made them difficult to visualize and thinks that readers who complain about not being able to "see" them are missing the point. They are meant to be alien, not mere variations on human beings. They have large black eyes, in homage no doubt to the rather old-fashioned BEM (bug-eyed monster) genre of science fiction. They are fascinated by human utterances and play odd riffs on them that make it clear that their intelligence is not quite commensurable with our own. They choose odd names for themselves: "Crouching Kneel," "Lonely Dumptruck," "Gelatinous Stand," as if they scavenge through the English language. Creating their speech testifies to Lethem's skill. He reveals in his *Paris Review* interview that he was inspired by E. M. Forster's *A Passage to India,* in which the bemused Indian characters do not know what to make of the behavior of the British who rule them. Everything changes in Forster's novel when an Indian is accused of raping an Englishwoman.

In a similar plot development, the settlers come to suspect the aliens of carrying on interspecies sex and even molesting children. One, Truth Renowned, dies when Hugh Merrow's house is burned down. Merrow himself is driven out of town, if we can speak of a town. The engine behind the rule of lynch law is Efram, who is a homophobe as well as a hater of the aliens: he dislikes the lesbian couple. Lethem's extrapolated future has perhaps a little more homophobia than we might expect. There is a showdown between Pella and Efram when Hiding Kneel is accused of attacking a child and beaten. Pella has no hope of defeating Efram by force, so she plays the sex card, accusing him of molesting her. He knocks her down, looms over her, and she feels absolutely helpless against his masculine force. In the movie, Ethan Edwards comes very close to killing his niece at the end but suddenly relents. In the novel, a young man, a proto-Efram, shoots him with his own rifle.

The violent events help to disperse the bedraggled community. But Pella, confident in her new maturity, puts up a sign naming the town she plans to create: *Caitlin.* In the conventional western, women play a civilizing role, through institutions like marriage and the church, but they do not take such leading roles. After finishing this complex work the reader should go back to one of its epigraphs, from John Wayne himself: "Screw ambiguity. Perversion and corruption masquerade as ambiguity. I don't trust ambiguity." But as D. H. Lawrence pointed out, we have to trust the tale, not the teller. Both *The Searchers* and *Girl in Landscape* are shot through with complicated human motives about the land, about power, about community, about sexuality.

A TURNING POINT

With *Motherless Brooklyn* (1999), winner of the National Book Critics Circle Award, Jonathan Lethem entered the mainstream. However, he did not give up his interest in genre writing, and this remarkable noir detective story also received the Golden Dagger Award for crime fiction. The book has a most unlikely hero, or antihero, Lionel Essrog, who suffers from Tourette's syndrome, a neurological ailment that causes compulsive physical and verbal behavior, including in many cases an uncontrollable use of obscene language. The inspiration for the novel was Oliver Sacks's writings on Tourette's, supplemented with other reading and a film about Tourette's called *Twitch and Shout.* From his reading, and his cultivation of what he calls Tourettic tendencies in himself, he created a powerful representation of the thoughts and behaviors of a sufferer. His fullest discussion of the syndrome and its role in his novel comes in an online dialogue in "Book World Live," a transcription of a February 2005 online interview with Lethem by fans "calling in" via the Internet. At one point he says:

> Of course, after publication I was drawn very quickly into the Tourette's community—which is one of great solidarity and strong advocacy. They'd liked the book (lucky me, since I hadn't written it meaning to please anyone knowledgeable), and wanted me to participate in various public benefits and forums. I made some friends who taught me that some of what I thought I'd invented for Lionel was more real than I'd known.

His narrator, Lionel Essrog, was a foundling child and hired with three other boys out of an orphanage by Frank Minna, who runs a car service and moving company in Brooklyn as a cover for his detective agency. Minna likes to refer to his employees as "motherless Brooklyn." Much of the work is done for The Clients, elderly mobsters known as Mr. Matricardi and Mr. Rockaforte. When Minna is murdered, Lionel searches for the killer, his boss having been his benefactor and his only parental figure. Minna was a verbally abusive parent, certainly, given to calling Essrog a "free human freakshow." However, Minna also observed once that Lionel was so crazy that people thought he was stupid. Lionel himself says that Tourette's sufferers are in some ways invisible, easily ignored as damaged people.

The plot of the novel grows progressively more clichéd, commentators have observed, with a mysterious international conspiracy of a group of Japanese Zen monks who also belong to a criminal corporate organization. The superslick and villainous head of one of the group's Zen centers turns out to be the improbably sophisticated brother of the small-time semi-hoodlum Frank Minna. There are some camp gags: Frank Minna's widow, Julia, is a girl from Nantucket, calling to mind the most famous of dirty limericks. There is a James Bond flavor, with Lionel pursued by an apparently indestructible giant of a hit man who summons up Oddjob in Ian Fleming's *Goldfinger.* Albert Mobilio in the *New York Times* is one of several critics who complained about this "go-round with the hard-boiled genre." The solution to the mystery has to be delivered in thirteen pages of explanation by Julia to Lionel. The real interest lies not in the convolutions of the plot but in the convolutions of Lionel's speech and behavior.

What makes the novel indelible is the poetry of Lionel's verbal flights. "Poetry" is not too strong a term. Ronald Schleifer's article "The Poetics of Tourette Syndrome: Language, Neurobiology, and Poetry," shows strong similarities between the poetic process and the Tourette's process, between the verbal fireworks of poems and the verbal explosions of Tourette's. The malady makes it possible for Lethem to create a dazzling verbal surface. Lionel's speech is full of puns, chains of accidental associations, bits of onomatopoeia, and distorted echoes of what is said to him. His own name can segue from Liable Guesscog to Final Escrow to Ironic Pissclam. And his physical behavior is also disruptive. Tourette's is often linked to obsessive-compulsive behavior, and Lionel tends to repeat actions helplessly, with a drive toward doing them an odd number of times.

What keeps the novel from being an ignoble display of Lionel as a freak is Lethem's empathy and compassion. We feel with the character because we learn what it is to be Lionel Essrog. Lionel solves his mystery, gets revenge, and even manages to kill the giant hit man, but his drive for love ends in failure. He has a sexual encounter with Kimmery, a vacuous Zen student, but the woman he loves, Frank Minna's widow, Julia (the girl from Nantucket), dismisses him with language as brutal as the notorious limerick. Still, he has a role in life. Minna's detective agency masquerading as a car service becomes a car service masquerading as a detective agency. Lionel Essrog is motherless in Brooklyn but not homeless.

With *Motherless Brooklyn,* Jonathan Lethem finally brought his hometown into his writing. His earlier works had been set in California and the West, or, in the case of *Girl in Landscape,* on a distant planet with resemblances to the West. But some minor works came between the two Brooklyn novels. One, *Kafka Americana* (1999), was a collaboration with Carter Scholz, who wrote two of the stories and collaborated with Lethem on another. Lethem was sole author of two of the stories. They deal with fantasy situations or with possible alternate lives for Franz Kafka, imagining him in Hollywood writing for

Frank Capra (in the collaborative story, "Receding Horizons") or as an American painter put on trial like the protagonist in the great writer's novel *The Trial.* Lethem's work in the collection, solo and collaborative, is not among his finest achievements.

He collaborated again, this time with two writers, James Patrick Kelly and John Kessel, on a science fiction spoof, *Ninety Percent of Everything* (2001), which was a finalist for the Nebula Award. The science fiction writer Theodore Sturgeon formulated what is known humorously as Sturgeon's law. When someone said to Sturgeon that ninety percent of science fiction is shit, he replied, "ninety percent of everything is shit." In the collaborative novel, published online as a Microsoft Reader eBook, aliens burrowing to the center of the earth produce vast quantities of excrement, which contains rare gems. The situation is, in a way, a concretization of a metaphor, giving substance to Sturgeon's claim: some percentage of the dross must be valuable. One other minor work from 2001 is worth mentioning, a novella titled *This Shape We're In.* It has a carefully elaborated setting, for the characters are cells in a human body, and their environment is described in detail as they might experience it. The novella was collected with other stories in *Men and Cartoons* in 2004.

FORTRESS OF SOLITUDE

In his sixth novel, *Fortress of Solitude* (2003), Jonathan Lethem did what many novelists do in their first work: used his own life as a source, though there are significant differences between his life and the story of his protagonist, Dylan Ebdus. The title of the novel reflects his pop culture interests but has resonances of its own. In the Superman comics, the caped hero has a retreat somewhere in the distant arctic, a refuge where he can reflect on his adventures and consider the trophies of his triumphs. It also has a room of mementos of the people important to him, and, mostly importantly, the capital of Krypton, his home planet, shrunk small enough to fit in a bottle. It is full of living people, but though he can communicate with them and even shrink himself to visit, he has not been able to restore it to full size. In a perceptive discussion in the online magazine *Salon,* Peter Kurth draws the obvious conclusion: the novel contains a miniaturized version of part of Lethem's past, visible but not literally accessible. Dylan uses the metaphor himself near the end of the novel, of his desire to "sculpt statues of my lost friends, life's real actors, in my Fortress of Solitude."

The title also refers to the study of Dylan's painter father, Abraham Ebdus, who often isolates himself from his family to work on a film that he is painting, frame by frame, year after year, abstracting reality into pure forms. He abandoned ordinary painting and the art world at the height of his career. The house is filled with extraordinary nudes of his wife, Rachel, which indicates to the reader that he has isolated himself from his wife's physical reality for a lonely task. The marriage eventually ends with the disappearance of Rachel, a loss that reflects the disappearance—by death—of the novelist's own mother. No commentator seems to have commented on the resemblance of the name "Ebdus" to "Oedipus." There is indeed a conflict of loyalties in Dylan's mind, a kind of triangle, with a mother who often treats him like a chum and a father who loves him but is aloof. To support himself and his son, Abraham agrees to paint science fiction covers for paperbacks. They incorporate elements of modern style, but for a serious painter, commercial art—especially for the pulps—is a shameful pursuit. Abraham is rather chagrined when he wins a Hugo Award for science fiction illustration. In an excellent interview conducted by Sarah Anne Johnson, Lethem revealed that he made use of the career of Ed Emshwiller (1925–1990), an experimental filmmaker who also created science fiction covers.

The novel begins in the early 1970s, when Dylan's parents move into the Gowanus area of Brooklyn, newly renamed Boerum Hill. The real-life author of the change, and of the gentrification process that eventually swept away a complex neighborhood for trendy shops and yuppie housing, was an elderly woman, Helen Buckler (1894–1988). In the novel, she is turned into a character named Isabel Vendle, whose

apartment and attitudes reflect those of Charles Dickens's Miss Havisham in *Great Expectations,* an identification confirmed by the author. Dylan runs errands for her, making him the Pip figure, a naive young man. Magwitch, the frightening but ultimately kind convict, is probably represented by Barrett Rude Junior, the washed-up soul singer who moves next door to Dylan along with his son, Mingus, and treats them both generously. Lethem has said that Charles Dickens is his greatest influence. The character of Vendle reflects other characters besides Miss Havisham: An interview on the Random House website reveals the way that Lethem's imagination mines and refines his sources:

> A woman named Helen Buckler coined the name of the neighborhood. She lived on my block when I was a kid. But the Isabel Vendle character is sourced in Dickens' Mrs. Havisham [*sic*], and in characters from the Orson Welles film of Booth Tarkington's THE MAGNIFICENT AMBERSONS, and in characters from Paula Fox's novels, and in the character Agatha Harkness from Marvel's FANTASTIC FOUR comic book—as much, or more, than she is a portrait of Helen Buckler. My imagination tends to do that, again and again—to color in the outlines of an apparent depiction with a chaotic scribble of outside influences, imagined and real.

Not only books but also a film about a book, not only high art but also comic books: a mind that is rich and strange.

The neighborhood at the time the Ebdus family arrives is ethnically rich, with African Americans and Puerto Ricans most abundant. The Solver sisters, blonde and beautiful, who become a lifelong symbol of unattainable WASP beauty (a bit like Daisy in *The Great Gatsby*) are part of the gentrification wave, but they move away very soon and Dylan finds that his usual playmates are Marilla and Henry, both African Americans. All the children play typical New York games like stickball with the legendary "Spaldeen," a ball sold by the Spalding Company—it was the core of a tennis ball. Lethem has been rightly praised for his skill in depicting the mores of childhood.

Some of the children Dylan meets become permanent fixtures of his life, giving the novel a relatively small cast of characters who disappear and resurface. One, Robert Woolfolk, is a permanent antagonist. Another, Arthur Lomb, a hanger-on and apparent physical and moral weakling, plays an important role late in the book. He winds up a rich landlord. Young is modeled on Widmerpool, a laughable youth in Anthony Powell's twelve-volume series *A Dance to the Music of Time* (a series that Isabel Vendle reads in Lethem's book). Widmerpool, like Arthur, steadily rises in the world for all his apparent fecklessness, becoming a life peer and university chancellor before his life collapses in a series of catastrophes. Lethem's novel is a strange counterpart to Powell's story of the unfolding lives of a cluster of pupils at a school modeled on Eton: there is a great social and cultural difference between Eton College and Ebdus' Public School 38.

The most important friend is Mingus Rude, who moves into the neighborhood with his soul-singer father, Barrett, just before Dylan starts school in Boerum Hill. Mingus is a million-dollar baby, "bought" by his black father from his white wife in the divorce settlement. The boys' first names of course reflect the respective musical worlds of their parents: Charles Mingus (jazz) and Bob Dylan (folk music). (Lethem has discussed his own long involvement with Bob Dylan's music in "The Genius of Bob Dylan," an interview and profile in *Rolling Stone.*) Barrett appears crude but, like his neighbor Abraham, is an important artist, though in a different tradition. The mature Dylan Ebdus will write lengthy liner notes for the retrospective CD set covering Bob Dylan's career.

Dylan's parents see him as a utopian social experiment: a white child in an almost entirely black school. But the experiment is nothing but misery for Dylan, who finds himself constantly bullied and "yoked"—placed in a headlock and then relieved of any money he carries. Mingus Rude's friendship gives him some limited protection. It almost turns into a physical relationship. The critic Leslie Fiedler suggested repeatedly that at the core of American literature lies the symbol of a deep bond between two individuals, one black and one white, a process of reconciliation expressed in a homoerotic (but

not explicitly sexual) relationship. John Leonard pointed out the Fiedler parallel in his incisive survey of *Men and Cartoons, The Disappointment Artist,* and *The Fortress of Solitude.*

Mingus also shares Dylan's profound love of comic books and has a vast supply thanks to his generous father. He also expands Dylan's musical knowledge, supplementing the folk and folk rock passions of the Ebdus parents with a knowledge of rhythm and blues and soul music. Dylan eventually becomes a scholar in fields like hip-hop. He will be drawn to African American life, and at the start of the third section of the book, we witness the breakup of his relationship with a black graduate student, who believes that to him she is only a symbol of Negritude.

Mingus also initiates Dylan into the new world of graffiti creation. Mingus's signature is DOSE, a moniker borrowed from Lethem's brother Blake, who more often signed himself KEO. Lethem is very good at revealing the attitudes that lead young men, usually African American, to assert their presence and their skills on public buildings. At one point in their ramblings, they encounter an unconscious drunk, a black man named Aaron X. Doily. It is with the appearance of this derelict deep in the novel that the narrative shifts from brilliant realism to problematic magic realism, for Doily is a rather low-grade superhero. His ring enables him to fly, but he is not very good at it. He turns the ring over to the boys, and for some time they use it in turn for larks and pranks and attempted good deeds, with Mingus wearing a homemade outfit as "Aeroman." They are not very good superheroes either. The ring eventually provides the denouement of the novel and a means of removing the villainous Robert Woolfolk. Not all readers find that the magic ring is a satisfactory plot device in a novel marked by superb depiction of a genuine Brooklyn milieu.

The first section of the book comes to an end in the summer of 1981, when Mingus kills his demented preacher grandfather, who had been threatening Barrett Rude with a pistol. The sequence seems based on the story of the rhythm and blues singer Marvin Gaye, who was actually murdered by his deranged father. Mingus serves time in jail, and descends into a hell of drug use and criminality to support his habit. The second section is a relatively brief odd interlude, the story of Barrett Rude Junior and the Distinctions. It is a fine imitation of extended liner notes and helps to explain Barrett's tortured soul.

The third section, "Prisonaires," is a complex structure beginning in September 1999, with a number of flashbacks to fill in the eighteen years that have passed, during which Dylan has been expelled from a school very much like the Bennington his creator attended. During the present of the section, Dylan breaks up with his girlfriend, pitches the story of a black music group (the Prisonaires) to a producer in Hollywood, and finds out something about his mother's life after she deserted her family. But her trail ends with her flight from justice in 1979 after an armed robbery. He also tries to help Mingus escape from jail by offering him the magic ring, which has lost its powers of flight and has instead begun conferring invisibility on the wearer. Mingus, who sees the coming end to his latest prison sentence, refuses, but suggests that it be given to the obnoxious Robert Woolfolk, who is in the same prison. Woolfolk thinks that the ring will make him fly, and in a grotesquely amusing scene, he jumps to his death from a prison tower.

For Lethem, the prison scenes were the most difficult to write and caused the most anxiety: the problem was to convince readers that he knows what a prison is like. He relied on Malcolm Braly's *On the Yard* (1967) for atmosphere and detail, and the scenes are convincing, though the prison break subplot seems out of a thriller, not a serious bildungsroman. (In 2002 Lethem wrote an introduction for a new edition of Braly's prison novel.)

The most powerful scenes in the conclusion are surely the descriptions of Dylan's return to visit his old neighborhood. His visit is something like Superman's trips to the miniaturized capital of Krypton. Dylan is disturbed by the proliferation of fashionable shops and restaurants. Gentrification has transformed his home, ambivalent about it though he has been. At the end, when Dylan drives away from Gary, Indiana, where he learned the story of his mother's life through

1979 from the man she ran away with, Isabel Vendle's nephew, he reflects that "a gentrification was the scar left by a dream, Utopia the show which always closed on opening night" (p. 510). In a long passage comparable to F. Scott Fitzgerald's elegy for the promise of America at the end of *The Great Gatsby,* he laments the loss of "middle spaces," the utopian moments when experience seems to have a meaning. Although loss is a major theme in the novel, Lethem, like the entropy-reversing spray Ubik, has managed to preserve the vanishing in his art. The disappointment in the novel can be summed up by Gertrude Stein's marvelous phrase from *The Geographical History of America*: "What is the use of being a little boy if you are going to grow up to be a man?" After such an interesting childhood, Dylan's adult life seems anticlimactic. He becomes, not a novelist like his creator, but a writer on pop music. Lethem edited *Da Capo: Best Music Writing 2002,* and he sometimes writes on pop music, but he has done far more than that.

MEN AND CARTOONS

In 2004 Lethem published his second collection of stories, *Men and Cartoons.* Most of the work was recent, though "The Spray" dates to 1998. It was issued in a Vintage edition the next year with two additional stories, "Interview with the Crab" and "This Shape We're In." "Interview with the Crab" and "Super Goat Man" deal with washed-up public figures. The crab, a genuine but larger-than-life crustacean, is interviewed about his role on a successful sitcom. Lethem sends up the media machines that thrive on celebrities, even the ones out of vogue. The rather overlong "Super Goat Man" imagines a world in which there are real superheroes, and a rather minor one takes up a job at a college modeled on Bennington. The campus comedy harks back to *As She Climbed Across the Table.* Many of the stories involve comic books or science fiction plots. Jay McInerney, writing in the *New York Times,* points out that the gimmickry in many of the stories is transcended by Lethem's compassion for his characters, making him a "lovable dystopianist" and showing that "he has the will and the ability to seduce and emotionally engage the reader even as he celebrates the artificiality of narrative conventions." John Leonard dismissed it in "Welcome to New Dork," published in the *New York Review of Books,* as a "grab bag of his stories" and found a pattern of characters refusing adult responsibilities in favor of "the masked dreams of pop culture."

The collection of essays in *The Disappointment Artist* (2005) shows how deep those youthful dreams ran for Lethem. He covers some of his early obsessions with *Star Wars,* science fiction, and comic books. "The Beards" is a fine essay about his relationships with substitute fathers after his family life began to fray and then disintegrate with the death of his mother. As Leonard shrewdly observed in "Welcome to New Dork," Lethem's long and brilliant essay on Edward Dahlberg, who spent his life grieving for his mother, tells us covertly about Lethem's own grief, a subject that he confronts more directly in "13, 1977, 21," ostensibly an essay about seeing *Star Wars* twenty-one times when he was thirteen years old. But the obsession with the movie was related to his loneliness as the product of a broken home, as the cliché has it. He proves his credentials as a Brooklynite by writing a kind of ode to a subway station in "Speak, Hoyt-Schermerhorn" and his skill as a film critic with "Two or Three Things I Dunno About John Cassavetes." He might also have included his quick but perceptive response to the 9/11 attacks in the *New York Times,* "9 Failures of the Imagination." His collection of essays is a little more than half as long as *Men and Cartoons,* but it is far weightier. He continues to write on his obsessions, as shown by a 2006 essay on Philip K. Dick, "Phil in the Marketplace," published in the *Virginia Quarterly Review.*

Jonathan Lethem and Christopher Sorrentino, another novelist, published a humorous book about the New York Mets in 2006, using the names Ivan Felt and Harris Conklin respectively. *Believeniks!* supplied elaborate academic personas for its supposed authors on the dust jacket. The work is a rollicking exchange of letters, some in unusual literary forms, following the

progress—or lack of it—of the Mets' disastrous 2005 season. The book was definitely not a best seller, which seems appropriate enough. Another unusual project was published in 2008: Lethem cowrote the text (with Karl Rusnak) for a revival of one of his favorite comic book series, *Omega the Unknown,* from Marvel Comics.

The 2006 publication *How We Got Insipid* appeared under strange conditions. Lethem's usual publisher permitted Subterranean Press to issue a limited press run (fifteen hundred copies of the deluxe edition, and twenty-six copies of a signed traycased version at $225). The book has a dust jacket and frontispiece by Lethem's brother, Blake. The volume contains two stories, "How We Got in Town and Out Again" (the satire on virtual reality published in 1996), and "The Insipid Profession of Jonathan Horneboom." The Horneboom story is a parody of a story by the great master of science fiction Robert Heinlein, "The Unpleasant Profession of Jonathan Hoag" (1942). The resemblance between the stories is fanciful. Lethem's story uses magic realism to satirize artists who sell out: Horneboom finds that a mysterious bird image appears in his bland paintings. He enlists a detective named Harriet M. Welch to help him solve the mystery: she is the children's character Harriet the Spy, grown up. The surrealists André Breton and Paul Éluard appear in the story, and the bird figure turns out to be an incarnation of Horneboom's real father, the surrealist Max Ernst.

The story of Horneboom is minor, but the book has an important afterword in which Lethem discusses his art. He is, he says, an "instinctive novelist," hence the length of most of his stories: "When I began writing stories I tended to produce what I'd call 'short novellas,' like these two. Another way to describe this form, which usually involved a greater number of situations, characters, and motifs than the short story is usually thought capable of containing, is as a compacted novel." He says that these stories "introduce dangerously much material in dangerously compacted form, then hurry to a conclusion." For all his distrust of these stories, they constitute an interesting form in themselves. Henry James spoke of the "blesséd *nouvelle,*" and Lethem's accursed novellas have at their best a compulsion of their own as they rush to the end.

YOU DON'T LOVE ME YET

The next novel, *You Don't Love Me Yet* (2007) actually suffers from thinness, something unknown in Lethem's work before. He wanted a change of pace after writing substantial novels set in Brooklyn. This one takes place in Los Angeles. He made a visit to gather atmosphere. A chance trip to the zoo gave him a subplot about the "liberation" of a depressed kangaroo, the second kangaroo to appear in his work. The book, set in 1988, deals with an indie rock group with a very small reputation. The reader learns quite a lot about that world, which the novel takes very seriously, and also about conceptual art, which it sees quite satirically. The title comes from a song by the indie rock cult figure Roky Erickson.

The protagonist of the novel, Lucinda Hoekke (perhaps a pun on "hokey") belongs to a nameless indie band and works at an art gallery run by Falmouth (his utterances make the meaning of the name quite obvious). Other characters include the other band members, Matthew Plangent, Denise Urban, and Bedwin Greenish. The names are as stylized as those in Restoration drama, and the action is as sparkling and cynical as any play from the 1660s. Lethem's acknowledged model was the intellectual comedy in Iris Murdoch's novels, though he was surprised to find his publisher claiming that the model was Jane Austen's *Emma,* a work he had not read in many years. The gallery has a kind of installation, a complaints line, with young women taking calls and giving generic replies. Lucinda becomes intrigued with one caller, whose complaints are full of phrases (like "Monster Eyes") that she feeds to the group's songwriter, Bedwin, who has been suffering from writer's block. Lucinda meets and has an affair with her complainer, Carl Vogelsong ("bird song"), who discovers that his remarks have been appropriated. He is able to force himself into the group. Their song "Monster Eyes" gains local fame, and they get an invitation to appear on Fancher Autumnbreast's im-

mensely influential radio show. But Vogelsong clearly does not belong with the group, and they lose their chance.

The reviews of the book were almost entirely negative. Zach Baron in the *Village Voice* was typical, complaining about the deafness of nuance in writing about the band. David Kamp in the *New York Times* said the book was only for the Lethem completist. "It's just a strange experience, watching someone of his powers and years—an accomplished 43-year-old novelist, applying his skills to what seems like first-novel material." The thinness of the Los Angeles setting, which Lethem does not know very well, came in for heavy criticism. Lethem knows Brooklyn as thoroughly as Joyce knew Dublin, but he clearly wanted a break, a diversion. The Canadian novelist Ian McGillis was a rare voice of praise, seeing few flaws in the novel but admittedly writing from the point of view of "an indie-rock geek."

Some of the reviewers did link the novel to Lethem's major intervention in the questions of copyright and plagiarism through a long article, "The Ecstasy of Influence," published in *Harper's Magazine* in February 2007. The body of the essay makes an eloquent case for intellectual freedom and the kind of artistic ferment generated by the free exchange of ideas. Collage, according to the essay, was the art form of the twentieth century, as evidenced in works such as T. S. Eliot's *The Waste Land.* Publishers and corporate holders of copyright have steadily discouraged the use of copyrighted material even under the "fair use" doctrine. The superb twist comes at the end of the article, where Lethem reveals that the entire essay is a collage of other people's words, which he then identifies at length. Lethem's own practice has involved brilliant intertextuality and a constant appropriation of themes, conventions, and even characters out of other people's work.

Lethem has dramatized his concerns by making some of his song lyrics (including "Monster Eyes") freely available to composers and music groups, and his website has offered a number of his short stories to anyone who wants to make a film or play from one. The fee is one dollar. The relevant section of the website is entitled "The Promiscuous Materials Project." He posts audio files of the songs on the site. He offered the rights to film *You Don't Love Me Yet* for a fee of just 2 percent of the total budget, payable only if and when the film finds distribution, and selected the filmmaker Greg Marcks to undertake the project. Before the end of 2007, six songs based on his lyrics had been recorded, and two short films based on his stories were under way. Lethem speaks of the influence of the open source movement (Linux operating systems are a good example) and of Lewis Hyde's book *The Gift,* which suggests that culture is nourished by things freely given. The Promiscuous Materials Project even caught the attention of *Forbes* magazine, where in a discussion with Devon Pendleton, Lethem revealed that in 1999 he was paid $600,000 for the rights to *Motherless Brooklyn* by Edward Norton. The film has not yet been made.

Lethem's other intervention in contemporary affairs was more local. He wrote an open letter to the famous architect Frank Gehry, deploring his role in the major development project Atlantic Yards, right next to Boerum Hill. "The subject of my letter is the ill-conceived and out-of-scale flotilla of skyscrapers you propose to build on a series of sites between Atlantic Avenue and Dean Street in Brooklyn, in your partnership with a developer named Bruce Ratner and his firm, Forest City Ratner Companies." The project is gentrification on a staggering scale and has been encouraged by public agencies at several levels. Lethem made his feeling about gentrification clear in *Fortress of Solitude* and numerous interviews. It is not surprising that he took extreme exception to a plan beyond the dreams of Helen Buckler and her fictional avatar, Isabel Vendle. In 2006 he published a limited edition book, *Patchwork Planet* (available only at Brooklyn's BookCourt store), a portrait of Brooklyn with illustrations by the photographer Kate Milford.

Jonathan Lethem has written a powerful body of work. In 2005 the John D. and Catherine T. MacArthur Foundation awarded him a $500,000 fellowship. The foundation's website sums up his

achievement this way: "By orchestrating such allusions to popular genres within his fiction, Lethem heightens emotional engagement with his characters, blurs boundaries across a broad spectrum of cultural creations, and expands the frontier of American fiction." These are well-chosen words. Lethem continues to blur boundaries between genres, a way in which to extend the territory of American fiction.

Selected Bibliography

WORKS OF JONATHAN LETHEM

FICTION

Gun, with Occasional Music. San Diego: Harcourt Brace, 1994.

Amnesia Moon. San Diego: Harcourt Brace, 1995.

The Wall of the Sky, the Wall of the Eye: Stories. San Diego: Harcourt Brace, 1996.

As She Climbed Across the Table. New York: Doubleday, 1997.

Girl in Landscape. New York: Doubleday, 1998.

Motherless Brooklyn. New York: Doubleday, 1999.

With Carter Scholz. *Kafka Americana.* Burton, Mich.: Subterranean Press, 1999.

With James Patrick Kelly and John Kessel. *Ninety Percent of Everything.* Fictionwise (e-book), 2001.

This Shape We're In. San Francisco: McSweeney's Books, 2001.

The Fortress of Solitude. New York: Doubleday: 2003.

Men and Cartoons: Stories. New York: Doubleday, 2004.

How We Got Insipid. Burton, Mich.: Subterranean Press, 2006.

Believeniks! 2005: The Year We Wrote a Book About the Mets. As "Harris Conklin," with "Ivan Felt" (Chris Sorrentino). New York: Doubleday, 2006.

With Kate Milford. *Patchwork Planet.* Brooklyn, N. Y.: Soft Skull Press, 2006.

You Don't Love Me Yet. New York: Doubleday, 2007.

Omega: The Unknown. With Karl Rusnak. New York: Marvel Comics, 2008.

ESSAYS

"Monstrous Acts and Little Murders." *Salon* (http://ww.salon.com/jan97/jackson970106.html), January 1997.

"A Note on Influence, and John Barth's *The End of the Road.*" *Boldtype* (http://www.randomhouse.com/boldtype/0397/lethem/), March 1997.

"Body, Landscape, Symptom." *Boldtype* (http://www.randomhouse.com/boldtype/0598/lethem/essay.html), May 1998.

"Rushdie's *Ground*: The Moronic Verses." *Village Voice,* April 21–27, 1999. Available online (http://www.villagevoice.com/books/9916,lethem,5024,10.html).

"Hitchhiking Is Illegal in Nevada." *Rolling Stone,* July 6, 2000, pp. 88–90.

"9 Failures of the Imagination." *New York Times Magazine,* September 23, 2001, Section 6, p. 62.

"Stop Making Sense." *Rolling Stone,* October 25, 2001, pp. 84–85.

The Disappointment Artist and Other Essays. New York: Doubleday, 2005.

"The Writing Life." *Washington Post,* February 6, 2005, p. BW05.

"Bennington Commencement Address 6/05." Available online (http//www.jonathanlethem.com/bennington.html).

"Phil in the Marketplace." *Virginia Quarterly Review* 82, no. 4:24–30 (fall 2006).

"Brooklyn's Trojan Horse: What's Wrong with the Buildings Frank Gehry Wants to Put in My Neighborhood?" *Slate* (http://www.slate.com/id/2143634/), June 19, 2006.

"The Ecstasy of Influence." *Harper's,* February 2007, pp. 58–71.

"We Happy Fakes." *Guardian,* September 1, 2007, pp. 12–13.

INTERVIEWS BY LETHEM

"Noah Baumbach." *Bomb,* fall 2005, pp. 32–37.

"The Genius of Bob Dylan: An Intimate Conversation." *Rolling Stone,* September 7, 2006, pp. 74–80, 128.

EDITED VOLUMES

The Vintage Book of Amnesia: An Anthology of Writing on the Subject of Memory Loss. New York: Vintage, 2000.

Da Capo: Best Music Writing 2002: The Year's Finest Writing on Rock, Pop, Jazz, Country, & More. New York: Da Capo Press. (Edited with an introduction.)

Philip K. Dick: Five Novels of the 1960s & 70s. New York: Library of America, 2008.

CRITICAL AND BIOGRAPHICAL STUDIES

Abbott, Carl. "Homesteading on the Extraterrestrial Frontier." *Science Fiction Studies* 32:240–263 (July 2005).

Baron, Zach. "Steal this Band." *Village Voice,* March 1, 2007. Available online (http://www.villagevoice.com/books/0710,baron,75948,10.html).

Eskin, Blake. "Brooklyn Dodger." *Nextbook: A Gateway to Jewish Literature, Culture & Ideas* (http://www.nextbook.org/cultural/feature.html?id=91), October 22, 2003.

Kravitz, Bennett. "The Culture of Disease or the Dis-Ease of Culture in *Motherless Brooklyn* and *Eve's Apple.*" *Journal of American Culture* 26, no. 2:171–179 (June 2003).

Leonard, John. "Welcome to New Dork." *New York Review of Books,* April 7, 2005, pp. 31–32.

Mari, Christopher, and Dan Firrincili. "Jonathan Lethem." *Current Biography* 67, no. 3:74–80 (March 2006).

O'Brien, Paul. "Article 10." *Ninth Art* (http://www.ninthart.com/display.php?article=1058), June 20, 2005.

Pendleton, Devon. "Go Ahead, Steal Me." *Forbes.com* (http://www.forbes.com/forbes/2007/0702/106.html), July 7, 2007.

Rossi, Umberto. "From Dick to Lethem: The Dickian Legacy, Postmodernism, and Avant-Pop in Jonathan Lethem's *Amnesia Moon.*" *Science Fiction Studies* 29, no. 1:15–33 (March 2002).

———. "Enclosed Dreams, Highways and Labyrinths: Jonathan Lethem's *Amnesia Moon.*" In *America Today: Highways and Labyrinths.* Edited by Gigliola Nocera. Siracusa: Italy: Grafià: 2003. Pp. 255–263.

Schleifer, Ronald. "The Poetics of Tourette Syndrome: Language, Neurobiology, and Poetry." *New Literary History* 32, no. 3:563–584 (2001).

Siegel, Jacob. "Back to the Fortress of Brooklyn and the Millions of Destroyed Men Who Are My Brothers." *New Partisan* (http://www.newpartisan.com/jacobsiegel), April 18, 2005.

Wood, James. "Spaldeen Dreams." *New Republic* 220.15 / 16:38–44 (October 9, 2003).

Reviews

Bradshaw, Peter. "Flight of Fancy: Jonathan Lethem's Novel About Growing Up in Brooklyn During the 1970s Is Thrilling but Also Eccentric." *New Statesman,* January 19, 2004, pp. 51–52.

Getlin, Josh. "Jonathan Lethem's Improbable Serenade." *Los Angeles Times,* March 11, 2007, p. F12.

Heim, Joe. "Who Wrote the Book of Love?" *Washington Post,* March 18, 2007, p. BW07.

Kamp, David. "With the Band." *New York Times Book Review,* March 18, 2007, p. 12.

Kurth, Peter. "The Dreamer of Brooklyn." *Salon* (http://dir.salon.com/story/books/feature/2003/09/12/lethem/index.html), September 12, 2003.

McGillis, Ian. "Poised on the Brink of Stardom." *Montreal Gazette,* March 17, 2007, p. J3.

McInerey, Jay. "*Men and Cartoons*: The Superhero Next Door." *New York Times Book Review,* November 7, 2004, p. 14.

Mobilio, Albert. "What Makes Him Tic?" *New York Times,* October 17, 1999, sec. 7, p. 7.

Munson, Sam. "Born in the U.S.A." *Commentary,* November 2003, pp. 68–72.

Wood, James. "Spaldeen Dreams." *New Republic,* October 13, 2003, pp. 15–16.

Interviews

Adams, Tim. "Straight Outta Brooklyn." *Observer* (http://books.guardian.co.uk/departments/generalfiction/story/0,6000,1106351,00.html), December 14, 2003.

Benfer, Amy. "Writing in the Free World." *Salon* (http://www.salon.com/books/feature/2007/03/25/lethem_interview/index_np.html), March 25, 2000.

Bemis, Alec Hanley. "Chapter and Verse: Rick Moody, Jonathan Lethem and John Darnielle on the Crossbreeding of Literature and Pop." *LA Weekly,* February 28, 2006. Available online (http://www.laweekly.com/general/features/chapter-and-verse/12765/).

Benson, Heidi. "Jonathan Lethem Finds Utopias Lost in New Novel." *San Francisco Chronicle,* October 6, 2003, p. D1.

Birnbaum, Robert. "Birnbaum v. Jonathan Lethem." *Morning News* (http://www.themorningnews.org/archives/personalities/birnbaum_v_jonathan_lethem.php), 2005.

"Book World Live." Washingtonpost.com (http://www.washingtonpost.com/wp-dyn/articles/A60748-2005Feb3.html), February 8, 2005.

Burke, Richard. "Man Out of Time: An Interview with Jonathan Lethem." *Bloomsbury Review* 16, no. 3:5–6 (May–June 1996).

Cardwell, Diane. "Untangling the Knots of a Brooklyn Childhood." *New York Times,* September 16, 2003, p. E1.

"A Conversation with Jonathan Lethem." *Indiana Review* 22, no. 2:31–42 (fall 2000).

Dellinger, Matt. "Out of Brooklyn." *New Yorker Online Only* (http://www.newyorker.com/archive/2003/07/28/030728on_onlineonly01), July 28, 2003.

DeNiro, Alan. "The Blue Sky for American Fiction: An Interview with Jonathan Lethem." *Gadfly Online* (http://www.gadflyonline.com/archive/June99/archive-lethem.html), June 1999.

Hogan, Ron. "Jonathan Lethem: The Beatrice Interview 1995." *Beatrice* (http://www.beatrice.com/interviews/lethem/).

"In Conversation with Jonathan Lethem about *Fortress of Solitude.*" Random House website (http://www.randomhouse.com/features/jonathanlethem/fortressq_a.html).

Jackson, Shelley. "*Paradoxa* Interview with Jonathan Lethem: 'Involuntary Deconstructionism.' " *Paradoxa* 16:62–75 (2001).

Johnson, Sarah Anne. "Discovering the Story Word by Word." In her *The Very Telling: Conversations with*

American Writers. Hanover, N.H.: University Press of New England, 2006. Pp. 121–142.

Kelleghan, Fiona. "Private Hells and Radical Doubts: An Interview with Jonathan Lethem." *Science Fiction Studies* 25:225–240 (July 1998).

Kelley, Rich. "The Library of America Interviews Jonathan Lethem about Philip K. Dick." Available online (http://www.loa.org/images/pdf/lethem_interview.pdf), May 23, 2007.

Laurence, Alexander. "A Conversation with Bret Easton Ellis, Jonathan Lethem, and Joseph Clark." *Free Williamsburg* (http://www.freewilliamsburg.com/still_fresh/may/ellis.html), May 2000.

Newitz, Annalee. "Copy this Book—Jonathan Lethem on Life as a Copyfighter." *Wired* (http://www.wired.com/culture/culturereviews/news/2007/04/lethemprofile), April 19, 2007.

Press, Joy. "Brooklyn Belongs to Me." *Village Voice*. September 8, 2003. Available online (http://www.villagevoice.com/news/0337,press,46870,1.html).

Smith, Frank. "Key to the Fortress: An Interview with Jonathan Lethem." *Ninth Art* (http://www.ninthart.cm/printdisplay.php?article=702), November 24, 2003.

Smith, Zack. "Jonathan Lethem." *Independent Weekly* (http://www.indyweek.com/gyrobase/Content?oid=oid%3A46925), March 21, 2007.

Stein, Lorin. "Who Killed Brooklyn?" *Salon* (http://www.salon.com/books/feature/1999/09/23/brooklyn/print.html), September 23, 1999.

———. "Jonathan Lethem: The Art of Fiction CLXXVII." *Paris Review* 166:219–251 (summer 2003).

Warner, Toby. "Interview with Jonathan Lethem." *Boldtype* (http://www.boldtype.com/issues/may2005/index.html#feature), May 2005.

Weissman, Larry. "An Interview with Jonathan Lethem." *Boldtype* (http://www.randomhouse.com/boldtype/0598/lethem/interview.html), May 1998.

Welch, Dave. "Jonathan Lethem Takes the Long Way Home." Powells.com (http://www.powells.com/authors/lethem.html), September 23, 2003.

Wild, Peter. "Jonathan Lethem." *Bookmunch* (http://www.bookmunch.co.uk/view.php?id=1270), July 1, 2005.

Zeitchik, Steven. "A Brooklyn of the Soul." *Publishers Weekly,* September 15, 2003, pp. 37–38.

ALICE McDERMOTT

(1953—)

Paul Johnston

ALICE MCDERMOTT WAS born in Brooklyn, New York, on June 27, 1953, the third and last child (and only daughter) of Mildred Lynch McDermott and William J. McDermott. While she was still an infant, her family moved from Brooklyn to Elmont, Long Island, where she grew up. Hers was a middle-class childhood, her father a business representative for Con Edison and her mother a secretary and homemaker. Her parents were both first-generation Irish American Catholics, and her community as she grew up was largely Catholic. She attended a Catholic elementary school in Elmont, St. Boniface, and then a Catholic high school, Sacred Heart Academy, in nearby Hempstead. This world, the world of the generation of Irish Catholics who made the move from Brooklyn to Long Island in the decade or so after the Second World War, would provide the milieu of much of her writing.

McDermott describes herself as an indifferent student in elementary school and high school, telling an interviewer that she chose to attend the Oswego campus of the State University of New York because of its reputation as a party school. While there, though, she found she had both an interest in and a talent for writing fiction. She studied writing with Paul Briand, who encouraged her to take writing seriously. Following her graduation from Oswego with a BA degree in 1975, she found a job not as a writer but as a clerk-typist at Vanguard Press, the prominent vanity press in New York City, a job that would provide her with the setting for her first novel, *A Bigamist's Daughter* (1982). But such a vicarious job on the periphery of the world of writing and publishing did not satisfy her interest in writing, and she applied for and was awarded a scholarship in the master's program in fiction writing at the University of New Hampshire.

At the University of New Hampshire she studied with Mark Smith, who encouraged her to begin submitting short stories for publication. She placed her first story in *Ms.* magazine the summer following her graduation with an MA degree from UNH in 1978. While celebrating her first success with friends, she met the man who would become her husband, David Armstrong. They married the following summer, on June 16, 1979, after she had spent a year teaching at UNH. Two more of her stories were published that summer, one in *Ms.* and another in *Seventeen.* She and David moved to New York, where she began work on the novel that would become *A Bigamist's Daughter.* After moving around the country in response to David's education and work as a researcher in neuroscience, the couple settled in Bethesda, Maryland, to raise their three children, two sons and a daughter. McDermott has followed *A Bigamist's Daughter* with five more novels: *That Night* (1987), which was nominated for a Pulitzer Prize and a National Book Award and was made into a movie; *At Weddings and Wakes* (1992), also nominated for a Pulitzer; *Charming Billy* (1998), which won a National Book Award; *Child of My Heart* (2002); and *After This* (2006).

A Bigamist's Daughter drew on McDermott's own upbringing as an Irish American Catholic. In the novels since then, she has continued to focus on the Irish American Catholic generation who, like her own parents, moved from Brooklyn to the suburbs of Long Island in the years after World War II. This choice, far from confining McDermott, has allowed her to explore many aspects of American culture: the movement of middle-class America from the communal life of cities to the more isolating life of the suburbs, the experience of an ethnic minority as it has

moved into mainstream American culture, and the changing experience of faith in America. Though McDermott cites Flannery O'Connor in referring to the "Catholic décor" of her novels, there is as well a deeper meditation on matters of faith and spirituality, the added dimension of life that intimate acquaintance with religious belief entails. The role of memory and storytelling both in fiction and in life is a central concern. At the core of her novels is a belief in the interest of ordinary lives and ordinary events, the sorrows of life and the moments of transcendence of sorrow. Her novels tend to be brief, written as much as poetry as fiction, with a lyrical sense of language, stories in which the past intrudes on the present and in some sense is more real than the present. Her writing is quietly experimental in its handling of voice and time—"if you're trying to replicate memories or how people talk about memories," she explained to Mary Jo Dangel in a 2001 interview, "it's never chronological and it's seldom well-organized"—but with a sureness of description and metaphor that allows the reader to follow her confidently and with pleasure.

A BIGAMIST'S DAUGHTER

In her first novel, *A Bigamist's Daughter,* McDermott quickly establishes many of the concerns that she will return to in later works: the relationship between life and fiction; the intrusion of memory and the past into the present; the resonances of religious upbringing in later life; the loneliness and sadness of life, conveyed often with sardonic humor. Like the novels to follow, *A Bigamist's Daughter* is experimental in its point of view, written primarily in third person, present tense, but interspersed with chapters told by the novel's main character in the first person, past tense. Less is gained by these switches in point of view than McDermott may have hoped: in both points of view the reader sees the world from the main character's perspective; moreover, the past is brought in as much in the third-person chapters as in the first-person chapters because the third-person-present voice often itself switches to the past tense to cover the same ground. *A Bigamist's Daughter* is also mildly postmodern, as is appropriate for a first novel by a writer trained in a university creative writing program. McDermott writes a fiction which is itself about the writing of a fiction: her novel about a bigamist's daughter contains within it a novel about a bigamist which is without an ending, and the search for it will eventually bring both novels to their conclusions simultaneously.

A Bigamist's Daughter's main character, Elizabeth Connelly, has much in common with McDermott. She grows up on Long Island after her family's move from Brooklyn; she attends Catholic schools and is a young adolescent when the Beatles come on the scene; she attends college just outside of Rochester, New York; after graduation she finds herself in Manhattan, where she has a job with a vanity press. Unlike McDermott at Vanguard Press, however, Elizabeth is not a clerk-typist but editor in chief at the fictional Vista Books. It is not her job to read and evaluate manuscripts or to edit them but rather to get from Vista's hapless clients their signatures on contracts and their checks. She doesn't bother to read the manuscripts, relying instead in her conversations with the authors on the outlines and heartfelt letters they have submitted along with their manuscripts. The job's demands, she soon realizes, constitute "the only talent she'd developed in college—how to look as if you're listening and sound as if you've done all the reading." To Elizabeth and her coworkers, Vista Books seems

> not, in truth, a vanity publisher where real people spend real money to publish the books they'd spent years of their lives to write, but a half-hour situation comedy about a vanity publisher, where the authors were character actors or walk-ons or special guest stars and the regular cast of actor/workers vied each week for the best lines.
>
> (p. 93)

Into this world comes Tupper Daniels, a young man from a wealthy southern family that has sent him to good schools (Andover, Vanderbilt) and indulged his desire to be a writer, setting him up with an office in the family house. His manuscript is a novel about a bigamist, large sections of which (if not the whole thing) he seems to have memorized and from which he quotes at length when it seems appropriate to the conversation. (Elizabeth occasionally worries, as she nods her

head, that he might just be making these up to see if she has actually read his manuscript.) His manuscript has just one problem: it has no ending, and Tupper hopes that Elizabeth, as a professional editor, can help him find one. Though, or perhaps because, Elizabeth has been celibate for the past year, she soon takes Tupper to bed, all the while hoping that he will soon find an ending to his story so that she can get his signature on a contract and then drop him. She shares aspects of the relationship with her two confidantes, Ann, her secretary and a divorcée, and Joanne, her childhood best friend who has recently married.

Interwoven with this story are three other stories, all from the past: the story of Elizabeth's childhood life with her mother and father, her father more often absent on unknown "business" than at home; the life of her mother after her father's death, which appears to be a total turnabout from her married life; and Elizabeth's own time with a lover with whom she lived before coming to New York and taking up her present single life. It is soon apparent that these past relationships are more important, both to Elizabeth and to the novel, than her present life. These stories are told in part in the first-person past-tense chapters and in part as past-tense intrusions into the third-person present-tense main narrative. These latter intrusions into the present tense are the novel's true core, as Elizabeth's memories are more real to her than the life she presently lives, placing limits on her possibilities for love and happiness. That all people suffer from similar limitations is made clear, moreover, by the present relationships of Ann, who continually thinks of the present in terms of the fictions she constructs about her past marriage, and by Joanne's marriage, which is diminished by the exaggerated ideas of love and marriage she developed as a young Catholic girl.

Tupper Daniels's fictional manuscript, of which the reader gets significant chunks when he recites aloud, thus appears in the midst of numerous other fictions, including *A Bigamist's Daughter* itself. However inferior this fictional manuscript might be (the novelist Anne Tyler, reviewing *A Bigamist's Daughter* for the *New York Times,* finds it to be better than one might expect amid the other manuscripts received by Vista), it still has the power of fiction. "She is almost beginning to believe him," McDermott's novel opens, ironically reminding us of the power of fiction to draw us in. "There is something about this book," Elizabeth muses, "the image of that man, the bigamist, as Tupper Daniels talked him into existence." Elizabeth too has a man, her father, that she almost talks and remembers into existence, though perhaps not his real existence, and McDermott too has a character, Elizabeth, like herself but not the same, whom she writes into existence.

The possibility of reinventing oneself, free from memory and the past, seems to be present throughout the book as well, primarily in the new life of Elizabeth's mother. Dolores Connelly, once Elizabeth is on her own, completely leaves behind the life she had lived on Long Island and moves to Maine. She leaves behind not only the neighborhood where she had been a pious widow active in her church, but the church as well, erasing from her life every vestige of Catholicism. She erases from her life most vestiges of motherhood as well. She takes up with a man, her landlord, who could not be more different from Elizabeth's father, beginning with being always home, always a companion to Dolores. Even her body undergoes changes, becoming more lean and wiry. But in the end it may all be an illusion, a facade that fails, as Dolores seeks to be reconciled with the church and dies with her absent husband's name on her lips.

The so-often absent husband/father has had an effect on both the wife and the daughter, an effect at the heart of the novel, whether he was actually a bigamist or not. Following his death but before she moves to Maine, Elizabeth tells us in her first-person narrative, her mother became

> very active in our church, probably because it provided her with enough holy days and conferences and missions and bazaars and meetings to absorb her need for expectations, something to look forward to, just as hopeless crushes and later, hopeless love affairs, absorbed mine. It was a need my father had established in both of us.
>
> (p. 26)

In keeping with this, when Elizabeth chooses a lover to move in with, he is a man apparently in

love with another woman. When Elizabeth goes so far as to buy herself a wedding ring, it is with the knowledge that she will never have him to herself.

But even deeper at the core of *A Bigamist's Daughter* is another father figure, one she shares with other girls raised as she was in the Catholic Church: God. The religious element of *A Bigamist's Daughter* is established in its opening scene, as Elizabeth doodles during her interview with Tupper Daniels, "This is the day the Lord hath made," and then wonders, "Remnants of Catholic brainwashing or God trying to get a message to her?" Though the second possibility is presented ironically, the ambiguity of God's presence persists throughout the novel. Elizabeth wonders if the nuns of her school find "my mother's devotion to a man who was seldom there similar to their own calling." And just as Elizabeth grew up devoted to a father who is too often away, did she also grow up with a God who is too often away? Is this what she expects of love, of devotion? When she finally leaves for a life on the road, blessing authors with a visit before disappearing from their lives, whose bigamist's daughter is she? Her father's or God's?

THAT NIGHT

From its title onward, *That Night* is an exercise in storytelling and mythmaking, not just for McDermott but for the inhabitants of the lower-middle-class suburb where the fight that opens the novel is set. In the days and weeks after the fight, the middle-aged men who defended their own from a hoodlum gang meet to elevate the muddled fight into a battle that left them and their neighborhood victorious. Their wives, meantime, gradually make the unremarkable girl who occasions the fight into a romantic beauty. Most fully, the novel's narrator, a ten-year-old girl that night but now a woman in her thirties, makes the story into a meditation on love, youth, birth and death, parenthood, marriage, unfulfillment, the suburban American dream, and four generations of Americans.

The event of that night is both melodramatic and archetypal: a boy, Rick, backed by other boys, stands before the house, his girlfriend Sheryl's house, closed against him like a medieval fortress, and cries out her name only to find that she is not there; for Sheryl, in the manner of the times, has been "sent away" to Ohio to give birth to their child. When he and his friends, clad in leather and armed with chains, lay siege to the house, they are met by men armed with snow shovels and baseball bats. Everything that follows is an exploration of the causes, meaning, and consequences of the ensuing fight. The narrative does not move forward from the confrontation; rather it expands outward, gradually taking in the hours, days, and even years both before and after, as the world grows from a suburban street to a nearby pool hall and shopping mall to the wider world of which the suburb is only a part.

Like McDermott's handling of time in the novel, her handling of point of view is also unorthodox but done with such skill that its experimental nature is hardly noticed. A blend of first-person memory and reconstruction, childish understanding and mature reflection, acknowledged invention and speculation, and omniscient third-person narration ostensibly still in the voice of a narrator who could not possibly have access to the interior thoughts and private actions she reports, the novel and its author are both content to give us what can only be a fiction, however much it is grounded in an actual event and an actual summer of childhood impressions. The narrator has some insight into Sheryl's feeling for Rick because Sheryl spoke to her of her feelings as they played Barbie together one afternoon. But of Rick's feelings, the narrator at one point admits: "What Rick thought of all this I can only guess. I tend to imagine he was somewhat confused but nevertheless thrilled by it all. No one before had ever loved him enough" (p. 74). Yet from then on the narrator describes not only Rick's thoughts and feelings but his actions, conversations, and family life with utter sureness, leaving the reader to remember that not only is all this made up but so much else is as well—the thoughts of Sheryl's principal as he drives Sheryl home the day, some years before, when her father died, the late-night conversations in the house of

Sheryl's aunt and uncle the same night as the fight, the conversation between Rick and his lawyer at the jailhouse in the days to come. (The narrator only sees Rick once more after he is taken away, and that is years later, with only the briefest conversation between them.) Yet the narrator cannot share conversations that took place in her house because she could not make them out through the walls. McDermott expertly gives us both the imagination of the adult and the experience of the child.

What sets *That Night* apart from so many similar stories, from *Romeo and Juliet* to today's teen movies, are the feelings McDermott attributes not just to Sheryl and Rick but to even the most peripheral characters: not love itself, but need—the need to love, the need to be loved, the need to hold at bay feelings of loss and emptiness and meaninglessness. "I mean, how logical is it," Sheryl asks the narrator as they dress her Barbie, "for you to love somebody and then they just die, like you never existed?" (pp. 71–72). Not love, but the need to exist drives both Sheryl and Rick in their different ways. For Rick it is not love that stands him in front of Sheryl's house but the need to be loved. While the men of the street need to defend the ordered life they have made coming back from the violence of the Second World War, their wives need what Rick needs, they need to at least feel what he feels. As they call to their fighting husbands, the narrator reflects, from the emptiness of her own supposedly different, liberated life, "their thin voices were plaintive, even angry, as if this clumsy battle were the last disappointment they could bear, or as if, it seems to me now, they had begun to echo, even take up, that lovesick boy's bitter cry" (p. 5).

The lack of fulfillment the narrator here suggests in the lives of the generation of postwar suburban housewives is one of the submerged themes of *That Night*. Transplanted from the urban neighborhoods of their own childhoods to this isolated world of perfect houses (one family actually lives, hyperbolically, in their well-finished basement so as not mess up their house), women's lives become focused on their identification as mothers, all straining to have children, sometimes unsuccessfully, as a stay against nonexistence, even as Sheryl becomes pregnant with no need or desire to be a mother. It is a world where a knock at the door after dinner is as startling, and as welcome, as the intrusion of a burglar. But the suburb as a place of superficiality and boredom is not McDermott's chief interest, as it has been for so many before her (and probably after her). The suburb is rather the stage of the narrator's childhood, with all that that entails:

> Enough, too much, has already been said about the boredom of the suburbs, especially in the early sixties, and I suppose there was a kind of boredom in those predictable summer evenings. I suppose boredom had something to do with the violent, melodramatic way the men later rushed to Sheryl's mother's aid. But I remember those nights as completely interesting, full of flux; the street itself a stage lined with doors, the play rife with arrivals and departures, offstage battles, adorable children, unexpected soliloquies. ...
>
> (p. 11)

The world of ten-year-olds is exciting whatever the desire of their fathers to have it be unremarkable and without incident. Thus, when the three cars of hoodlums roars up on the lawn of Sheryl's house, even as the narrator's father is thinking "*This is serious ... this is insane,*" the narrator can say, "I remember only that my ten-year-old heart was stopped by the beauty of it all" (p. 3).

On its surface, *That Night* is the story of two generations, the first generation of suburban parents in America and their children, represented by Rick and Sheryl. But there are two additional generations important, if only implicitly, to the novel. Behind the door to Sheryl's house is not only her mother but her grandmother as well, an immigrant from the old country, who came to the teeming urban world of the old neighborhoods, now changing in their ethnic makeup, a generation for whom all is again becoming foreign as neighbors with the accents of home disappear. And younger than any of these is the generation of the narrator, only six years younger than Sheryl and thus ostensibly a part of the same generation but decidedly not. Sheryl's is the generation of Elvis and hoods in black leather jackets. The narrator's generation will be that of

the Beatles and boys in long hair, a generation whose girls will not "get in trouble" and be sent to relatives but rather the generation of the pill and abortion, McDermott's own generation. Their lives will be different, freer than those of either postwar parents or their first children, a generation whose own troubles are only mentioned obliquely as the narrator mentions her own failed marriage and her aborted child, a generation for whom love and birth and death will take on different meanings than for those involved in the drama of that night in the early 1960s.

Religion plays a smaller—almost nonexistent—role in *That Night* than in any of McDermott's other novels. But the lawn of Sheryl's house is not the only scene where something is happening that night. Far away in Ohio, where Sheryl has been sent to live with relatives, a greater drama is more quietly unfolding, a drama in which miracle, if not institutional religion, plays a role. While Rick desperately tries to hang onto the love that Sheryl has given him (and which he will eventually give up on), Sheryl moves instead in the direction of her father in her suicide attempt. Like *A Bigamist's Daughter, That Night* is a story of a daughter with an absent father. But this time the intervention of something divine, conspicuously absent in *A Bigamist's Daughter,* is not absent, and *That Night* concludes with an affirmation of life, an intrusion of the miraculous into the mundane that is finally the life of all.

AT WEDDINGS AND WAKES

The first paragraph of *At Weddings and Wakes* is a single sentence 129 words long. It neither lingers nor rushes as it sets in motion the trip from the suburbs of Long Island to an apartment in Brooklyn, first by bus and then by subway, that opens the novel. Nor is this expansiveness an aberration: the two sentences that follow, which together constitute the second paragraph, are 53 words and 48 words long respectively. This expansiveness, though—more in the mode of Henry James than William Faulkner (the entire novel might be thought of as Henry James done by a miniaturist or a jeweler)—serves not as a reinforcement of the novel's overall mood but as relief from its narrowness of vision. The majority of the novel takes place within the confines of the small Brooklyn apartment, inhabited by an old woman and three middle-aged stepdaughters. The trip from Long Island is made, as it is made twice a week throughout the summer, by a fourth stepdaughter, the only one to have married, and her three children.

The style of the narrative is intensely visual. The reader does not so much read as see the three children follow their white-gloved mother up the stairs of the apartment building, all holding their hands an inch above the rail, just as she does. Much, though not all, of the third-person narrative is told from the viewpoint of the three children, as in Henry James's *What Maisie Knew,* by turns interested, bored, restless, only partly comprehending of the adult world of unhappiness and smoldering anger and resentment in which they find themselves. In part they endure this world through the good treatment they enjoy on the sly from their one aunt—Aunt May—who seems determined to be happy; in part they endure it by shutting it out or explaining it to themselves as somehow normal. But although the world of *At Weddings and Wakes* is presented through the eyes and impressions of the children, the novel is not primarily interested in them. The reader is given only one or two glimpses of them at an age old enough to show the effects of their childhood, and these conceal more than they reveal. Rather, the novel is primarily interested in the adult world of loss, grief, bitterness, and the accommodations made or not made to these eternal facts of life.

There is not much of a story. Aunt May, in middle age, falls in love with the apartment's mailman and marries him, only to die three days later. Around this simple story are placed other marriages and other deaths, as well as births and children leaving, or not leaving, home. The story is compelling not for its events but for the way it is revealed, not linearly but as if it is a many-faceted jewel to be looked at from different angles until the whole is seen. The reader first learns of Aunt May's marriage and death before either happens in the novel, through a flash-

forward in which the youngest of the three children tells the nun who is her grade school teacher "the saddest thing in the world." The child, Maryanne, has her own reason for telling this story to the nun, and it is not entirely clear at this early point in the novel that it is true. But as the novel provides glimpses of the progress of the courtship, the reader comes to know it is true, and this knowledge gives the courtship, and all the rest of the unhappiness, loss, and oppressive family life, an added poignancy.

The unhappiness of three of the four sisters is their most prized possession, handed down to them by their fiercely unhappy stepmother. Lucy, the mother of three children, is not a woman in an unhappy marriage but an unhappy woman in a marriage that is no worse than most and better than many. Her husband is patient, thoughtful, and quietly fun-loving. He does not even mind the unhappiness of all these women his marriage has brought into his life, looking at it as a kind of balance to his own easygoing nature. The trip Lucy takes into the city twice a week in summer and as frequently as possible at other times is both a trip into the past and a trip into a timeless present. This timelessness gives glimpses of eternity, from the eternity of a child's bored afternoon to the eternity of what the novel calls "the lives of the dead." In this eternity, from which May escapes in her earlier life into a nunnery and now into a middle-age marriage but from which Lucy never wishes to escape even though she has moved out and started a family of her own, bitterness and loss never end, however ephemeral love and hope prove to be.

Catholicism, largely absent from *That Night* after being an important presence in *A Bigamist's Daughter,* returns in the opening sentence of *At Weddings and Wakes*—the front door of the house on Long Island, the reader is told, "served as backdrop for every Easter, First Holy Communion, confirmation, and graduation photo in the family album"—and remains throughout the novel (p. 1). Not only is May a former nun, the children too have desires for a vocation, whether as priest or nun. The bread the mother buys in Brooklyn as they approach the family apartment is, she tells her children, "the kind of bread ... that Christ ate at the Last Supper" (p. 12). May, thinking of the unexpected happiness of her requited love, finds herself "saying a short, silly prayer of thanks and then wondering if in order to bestow such a blessing—this blessing of romance, middle-aged romance at that—God was not sometimes as foolish, as childish, in his love for us as we are when we first discover our love for one another" (p. 68). Like the reader's foreknowledge of May's death, the presence of this religious undercurrent adds another dimension to *At Weddings and Wakes,* whose very title evokes religious ceremonies as central to life. This added invisible dimension, Flannery O'Connor observed in an essay titled "The Church and the Fiction Writer," must never come at the expense of the truth of the human situation, and this truth, so beautifully observed but also so often weighted down with anger and grief and regret, is the goal of the novel, as it is the goal of all of McDermott's writing.

This added dimension is hinted at in a strange story, unrelated to anything else in the novel, told on the school playground by one of Bobby's classmates. It is presented by McDermott without comment, and it is so curious that reviewers and critics have passed over it in silence. One day shortly after Christmas as a woman is coming down the stairs of her house in Queens, she sees through her small stained-glass window a man sitting in the neighbor's bay window. She at first thinks nothing of it but over the next few days she continues to see the man in the same place and the same position even when she knows the house is empty. She shows her neighbor, who also can see the mysterious figure. A policeman is called and then a priest. Both can see the figure clearly through the stained-glass window, but from no other vantage point. The priest finally declares that no exorcism is needed, though before leaving he blesses the house. A second priest advises the woman to replace the stained glass with regular glass, but as he is leaving he realizes his knuckle is bleeding where the light of the window had made a red stain across his hand. He wipes the blood from his split knuckle away with a laugh, after making the sign of the cross. When the woman then declares that she

will not live with this, the priest tells her "You live with far worse. ... We all do."

At Weddings and Wakes is more specific in its demographics than *That Night.* The family is Irish Catholic; the grandmother, like the sisters' father and mother, came from Ireland with no money and few prospects. Much of the family's bitterness has its origin in these difficult times. Much else as well is evocative of Irish families in America. In an interview conducted by Carol Burns in 2003, McDermott recalls a reading at which an audience member asks if the family is hers. Before she can answer, another member of the audience shouts "No, it's mine." But it is also a novel about families in general. At May's wedding, a cousin—the daughter of the stepmother's only true child, kicked out at age eighteen because he could not control his drinking—asks Lucy's daughters, "Aren't you glad you only have to see your relatives at weddings and wakes?" (p. 194). This family with its bitter mother and more bitter grandmother, its alcoholic aunt and aloof aunt and friendly aunt, its patient, generous-minded father, is all the family the three children know, but their lives are nevertheless rich with the intense impressions children form of the world around them, the intense impressions McDermott so masterfully evokes.

CHARMING BILLY

Charming Billy begins in the aftermath of the funeral of its title character, Billy Lynch. The guests who come first to an out-of-the-way Bronx restaurant for lunch and then later to Billy's house for the wake are mostly relatives, with a scattering of friends and neighbors. They all love to tell stories of Billy, sometimes furtively when speaking of the unrequited love that had been the center of his life before his marriage to Maeve, a plain woman whose knowledge of Billy's early love is unclear even to the guests who know her well. They also talk of Billy's alcoholism, which killed him and which, like his religious faith, is somehow tied to his love for Eva, the Irish girl, though how much of his alcoholism is unrequited love and how much is disease is a matter of some disagreement both among the guests and in the novel itself as it fills in the story of Billy's life. At the end of the first chapter, as the last guests are leaving the wake, the reader learns from Dennis Lynch, Billy's cousin and best friend, that at the heart of the story of Billy is a lie that only he knows.

Lies, love, and faith are central to *Charming Billy,* as are the progress of alcoholism, redemption, and the communal life of the Irish in America. The point of view is problematic, as it is in all of McDermott's novels. It is told by Dennis's daughter, a character at most on the periphery of the story for most of the novel, though she becomes important to the novel's symbolic structure at the end. As in McDermott's earlier novels, *Charming Billy* moves freely through time, from the days of Dennis's father, a bus driver who helps innumerable Irish countrymen come to America, to the summer when Dennis and Billy were young men just back from the Second World War, to the nights when, older, Dennis would help Maeve get drunken Billy into the house or off the floor and into bed. None of this, nor any of the numerous deaths and marriages of characters both central and peripheral, is presented chronologically; rather, scenes are visited and revisited, all the time revealing a little bit more. Unlike the narrator of *That Night,* who freely acknowledges that she is at times inventing her narrative, the narrator of *Charming Billy* simply disappears for long stretches of the narrative, leaving the reader to surmise that she has learned much of what she writes from her father, but also that she, like the mourners at Billy's funeral, is adding to the legend of charming Billy with details she has created herself. "This is the woman's role in a family," McDermott explained to Dinitia Smith of *The New York Times,* "to put the histories together."

Billy's alcoholism is presented as a part of Irish American life. His father-in-law is also an alcoholic, as is his Irish priest and various of his uncles and cousins. Though most at the wake shake their heads at the disease that has killed Billy, Dan Lynch, another cousin who is also no stranger to Quinlan's bar, insists that calling it a disease diminishes Billy's memory, that it is better to think of Billy as one among those in life

who stay "loyal to their own feelings" rather than behaving as the workaday world thinks they should. Throughout the novel, Dan Lynch more than any other character clings to the belief that human troubles and tribulations have meaning, that they are not just the result of accident or disease. Whatever the truth of alcoholism, though, the more important question is how those who love the alcoholic, those who love Billy, are to respond to it. And like the question of the alcoholism itself, McDermott provides no easy answer, showing instead the love itself, despite its failure to help.

Love, and the question of whether love can make a difference in this world of loss and disappointment and death, has been a question that McDermott has explored before, particularly in the character of Sheryl in *That Night.* It is a question that haunts the characters of *Charming Billy* as well. Does everyone's love for Billy make any difference in the end? Does Billy's love for Eva—the Irish girl—make any difference? Does Dennis's love for his wife dying of cancer make any difference? Despite the novel's frequent suggestion that the answer may be no, it ends in affirmation of the efficacy of love, but not before it has fully and honestly plumbed the evidence to the contrary. To come to its affirmation, *Charming Billy* must bring to completion not only the story of Billy but also the story of a house.

Billy meets Eva while working with Dennis on a small house owned by Dennis's stepfather out in the Hamptons, the other end of Long Island from their native Queens, the two of them just back from the war. Even this small house, a leftover from the days before the Hamptons became the summer home of Manhattan's wealthy, is to Billy and Dennis an experience of heaven, with its openness and its access to the ocean. But even more heavenly are the big houses all around. It is a world that neither had ever known existed, did not know of as they had "been locked into the adventure and the tedium of the war" (p. 65). For Billy it becomes a dream, particularly when he meets Eva there, the sister of a housekeeper for one of the wealthy families, just over from Ireland for the summer. In what McDermott acknowledges is a nod to F. Scott Fitzgerald's "fresh, green breast of the new world," this world of wealth and beauty is for Billy "this golden future, the Eden," something to believe in, something to look forward to, a place where he will be with Eva, heaven (p. 77).

But it all becomes a lie when Eva, back in Ireland, takes the money Billy has sent to her to bring her back over and marries another man. Dennis, the only one in Billy's world who knows the truth, does not tell him, but instead tells him that Eva is dead. Lies and deception, more than drinking, as much as love, are at the heart of *Charming Billy.* So too is a larger question, a religious question. Is heaven—not the figurative heaven of the Hamptons, but the heaven of Catholic faith—real? Or is it and all that goes with it—God, Christ, prayer—a deception, a lie Catholics tell themselves to get through the despair they would otherwise be left with? Though Billy will not speak of his loneliness after his marriage, for to do so would betray the woman he married, does he nevertheless think, as he drinks, of "the world where that loneliness existed, the world where change and cruelty, separation and loss, pity and sorrow refused to be forgotten, or forgiven, the world seen as it should be, through a veil of tears" (p. 186). A world where love makes no difference. A world, finally, where faith is always placed in a lie, not just by Billy but by everyone, a world no redemption, just illusion. After his wife's death from cancer, even before Billy's death, Dennis "cannot convince himself ... that heaven was any more than a well-intentioned deception," like his deception of Billy (p. 211).

But there is more to Billy's story, and more to the story of the house he and Dennis were fixing up when Billy and Eva meet. Billy, we learn, does not die ignorant of the truth. He does not die with faith simply in a lie, though he does die still with faith. On a visit to Ireland to "take the pledge" to stop drinking, he visits Eva's hometown and finds her still alive. But though he thus comes to know that all he'd had faith in was a lie, he doesn't return to America in anger or disillusionment. He speaks about the deception only with Dennis, over whisky at the house out in the Hamptons, where he had refused to go all

the years after he thought the love he had met there was dead. But to all outward appearances, and perhaps inwardly as well, he keeps his religious faith, stays true to his vision of heaven to come. And in a final affirmation, the house that he had thought was heaven comes symbolically to be an affirmation of redemption, as the narrator marries a boy she meets while visiting the house with her father, a boy whose life, like hers, is entangled with the house. And Dennis, eight years after the death of Billy, takes Maeve, Billy's widow, there as his wife. Faith is not faith in a lie after all but faith in the redemptive power of love in an often disappointing and lonely world.

CHILD OF MY HEART

In interviews, McDermott is regularly asked about her writing process as a novelist who is also the mother of three children. Somewhat surprisingly, she often works on two novels simultaneously, despite the other demands on her time and attention, so that if she becomes stuck with one she can turn to other. Her novels take a long time to write, despite their relatively brief two hundred pages or so, reflecting the complex and exquisite craftsmanship of each novel, with their finely wrought sentences, multiple points of view, and intricate time sequences. An exception, though, is *Child of My Heart.* Begun after the 9/11 attacks of 2001, it was published the next year. And unlike McDermott's earlier novels, both the narrative point of view and the time sequence are relatively straightforward. In addition, *Child of My Heart* is written without chapter divisions, as if it came out all in one stream.

Yet much links *Child of My Heart* to McDermott's other work, not least of which is its tone of "wry sorrow," as one reviewer put it. The sorrow outweighs the wryness, finally, as may be appropriate for a novel written in the wake of 9/11. And though the narrative is much more straightforward, the narrator—Theresa, a woman looking back at the summer she was fifteen years old—is very much involved in shaping memory and transforming it into something other than a mere record of events, in this case not just the transformation of family memories into family stories but the transformation of life into art through an act of the imagination. *Child of My Heart* is also concerned with the relationship between youth and adulthood, the relationship between the girl and the woman, the boy and the man. It is also, most poignantly, a novel of "the inevitable, insufferable loss buried like a dark jewel at the heart of every act of love" (*Child of My Heart,* p. 242).

In explaining how *Child of My Heart* came to be written in the aftermath of 9/11, McDermott says "Maybe it was just a lament in response to what we were all feeling; this is the way my lament took form" (p. 242). The setting, the beaches of eastern Long Island, is much the same as the setting where Billy meets Eva in *Charming Billy,* but it is also the setting of many of the photos McDermott saw of those who lost their lives in the World Trade Center on 9/11, pictures of happier times that have come to sadness. As a lament, *Child of My Heart* is haunted by death from beginning to end and is, finally, the saddest of McDermott's novels, unredeemed by miracle or revelation. Yet it is also the brightest of her novels, for Theresa is more full of life than any previous character. She is rich in imagination and rich in the capability to make her imaginative life real. One of the novel's pleasures is Theresa's competence at life, something she has to a greater degree than do the adults around her, though they do not prove completely without competence of their own when the crisis finally comes.

Theresa makes for herself a world of great sensual, which is not to say sexual, delight. On a summer morning, after her middle-class parents have gone to work (with one exception, the other houses of their neighborhood are wealthy vacation homes), Theresa takes a peach from its bowl and sits down on the porch steps with her summer reading book—Thomas Hardy's *Return of the Native.* She is surrounded with lilacs and dahlias still wet with dew, and after finishing her peach she shakes the lilacs to wash the peach juice from her fingers and lips. "The dew was cold, despite the sunshine that had already begun to hit the leaves, and I lifted my hair and bent under the branches to fell it on the back of my

neck" (p. 34). This summer Theresa will share her summer, with all of its life, with her young cousin Daisy, consciously named by McDermott after the Daisys of Fitzgerald's *The Great Gatsby* and Henry James's *Daisy Miller.* The relationship between the two girls is another of the novel's pleasures, the younger girl looking up to the older girl so determined to bring to her the fullness of life.

Theresa tells Daisy stories of lollipop trees and of an uncle who sees ghosts and of her own memory of heaven before she was born, stories Daisy half takes for truth. They sing together as well, the story of the boy who never returns, "whose fate is still unlearned." All of these stories involve in one way or another the deaths of children, as does *Child of My Heart* itself. The narrator presents herself as uncomprehending of Daisy's leukemia, though she sees the bruises and the paleness that are its chief signs. Nevertheless, in telling the story Theresa continually hints at Daisy's and everybody's mortality, creating a strong undercurrent to the celebration of life that is the story's surface. But the underlying mortality does not negate the surface vivacity of Theresa's world. Yes, her summer book is *The Return of the Native,* with its doomed Eustacia Vye. And yes, she retells the story of Macduff from *Macbeth* with the deaths of his children—"all my pretty ones." But she also invokes *A Midsummer Night's Dream,* which is equally true: tragedy and comedy, death and life, are both true. The fact that Theresa attempts to deny the reality of death does not invalidate her competence for life, any more than the tragedy of the World Trade Center attack invalidates the lives of those who died. Rather, it makes those lives more poignant.

The world of *Child of My Heart* is a world of children and small animals. (The one large animal—a stray dog—is in its wild willfulness a threat to this world.) Adults are present too, but their lives are only glimpsed, unimportant except to the extent they provide children or pets for Theresa to take care of; important, that is, in their absences and irresponsibility and inadequacy. One exception is an aged artist who employs Theresa to look after his toddler daughter, the product of his fourth marriage to a much younger woman who in her anger at his philandering spends most of her time in the city, if not out of the country entirely. But though he too is absent and irresponsible and inadequate as a parent, he is something else as well. He is an artist, and as such he is interesting to Theresa, herself an artist, a storyteller and transformer of life. His studio is where he works, and this is the first Theresa has heard of art being work and not just play. When Theresa first sees him, he is working on an abstract drawing, tossing away draft after draft, though Theresa cannot see how they differ. (Such is McDermott's exquisite art that we easily picture her similarly working over her sentences.) She at first cannot understand his art, preferring his one work of realism, a portrait of his daughter and her mother. But eventually she comes to recognize his art as an attempt to remake the world anew, that like herself he is up against the world of death and wishes to defy it. As many critics have noted and McDermott confirms, *Child of My Heart* is about its own art, about the power of art and the imagination to transform the world. Theresa's art differs from the artist's, yet is like it. It is not abstract and unrecognizable, but neither is it the real world. So too is McDermott's art in this novel: not bound to the realism of her earlier works but rather a remarkably vivid midsummer's dream of innocence and the worm in the bud.

The artist is not just an artist striving for immortality, however ineffectually, through his art and his philandering. He is also the one, out of all the fathers who are interested in their beautiful fifteen-year-old babysitter, that Theresa chooses for her first sexual experience. Her narration of this event is curiously elliptical and muted, compared to the novel's many other sensual experiences. The reader can hardly be sure it has happened, except for one phrase about her body after the experience, "some pain at my center, a dark, sharp jewel of it" (p. 227). The phrase returns at the novel's end, when the narrator speaks of the coming disappointing adulthood of one of the neighborhood waifs, in which he "would be plagued all his life ... by the inevitable, insufferable loss buried like a dark jewel at the

heart of every act of love" (p. 242). So too will be the adult life of Theresa in this ultimately sad novel of growing up, symbolized both by her experience of death and by her sexual experience.

Religion plays a small and, for once, largely negative role in *Child of My Heart.* Catholicism is not wholly absent from Theresa's imagination. Considering that she is older than her human charges, she remarks early that "I would naturally be worshipped and glorified." But when absolution comes at the end of the novel for her shortcomings, for her failure to tell anyone when she observes Daisy's bruises, it is only a false absolution based on Theresa's ability to turn her storytelling skills into outright deception. It is an unexpectedly bleak ending for a novel more full of charm than any that has preceded it.

AFTER THIS

Though *Child of My Heart* does not take up Catholicism nearly to the degree its predecessor, *Charming Billy,* does—the narrator of *Child of My Heart* declares only that "God and I ... weren't seeing eye to eye" and lets it go at that—McDermott's sixth novel, *After This,* again takes up a number of topical and timeless topics of Catholicism and religion. Two characters are faced with unwanted pregnancies, one heeding the teachings of the nuns at their Catholic high school and one not. The changes in church architecture that came about in the 1960s leave older parishioners alienated and their children derisive. A young man back from Vietnam leaves the church in search of meaningful religious experience, joining first an ashram and then a group of Krishnas and then a kibbutz before winding up in the basement of his old church in Long Island, attending AA meetings. Another boy looks for a lost Eden in the sexual revolution, but lies in bed remembering his Catholic prayers:

> To thee do we cry, poor banished children of Eve, to thee so we send up our sighs, mourning and weeping in this valley of tears. Turn then, most gracious advocate, thine eyes of mercy toward us, and after this our exile show us unto the blessed fruit of they womb. ...
>
> (p. 184)

He wonders if these words (the source of the novel's title—"and after this our exile") are a joke or are "the precise definition" of everything he wants (p. 184).

After This is the story of a family that loses a son/brother to the war in Vietnam. Whether it is more interested in the parents' generation or in the generation that is, after all, McDermott's own is finally a moot point as the novel's center of gravity gradually shifts from one generation to the next. The parents' generation is one that McDermott has written about extensively before, but her own generation, in its coming of age in the late 1960s and early 1970s, is one that until now she has avoided. She has written of her own generation as young adults in the 1980s or as youngsters in the late 1950s and early 1960s, but except for glimpses in *A Bigamist's Daughter,* this is the first time she has written of them facing their own war, the sexual revolution, and the social upheaval that accompanied these events.

The structure and narrative point of view of *After This* appears at first glance to be McDermott's most conventional so far. The story of the Keane family unfolds entirely in chronological order, and the omniscient third-person narrative moves from the consciousness of one character to another as McDermott's intentions demand. A standard nineteenth-century novel could be described in much the same terms. But in its refusal, as in the best of her earlier novels, to develop any story beyond the ordinary events of ordinary lives, it remains challenging and unconventional. And whereas the circular structures and foreshadowings of *That Night, At Weddings and Wakes,* and *Charming Billy* create a kind of suspense of their own as the reader waits for secrets to be revealed or explanations given, the strict chronological ordering of *After This* deprives the reader of even that interest. The novel is rather a series of vignettes—a woman emerging from church; two boys playing army on a beach dune; a woman giving birth in her living room with only a passerby to help; a boy only a year out of high school taking his younger sister for a ride in his car the day he is to report for military service; a mother and daughter waiting in line at the World's Fair to see the *Pietà*;

two high school girls visiting a clinic where one is to have an abortion; college students in a bar Halloween night, the girls seeing who can draw the most sexual attention, the boys seeing who can be the most outrageous in defiance of social norms. What holds the reader's attention is not suspense or the desire to find out what happens next—as often as not, McDermott skips what happens next—but McDermott's power of precise and evocative description, a power she shares with Virginia Woolf. Only gradually is the reader's emotional involvement with the characters' fates evoked.

McDermott's take on the Vietnam War is central to *After This,* though no scene actually takes place there. The only war scene is one remembered from John Keane's time in the European theater of the Second World War, in which a young man named Jacob who is at the front only one day is killed. As if to fulfill a promise, or to bring him back to life, John Keane names his first child Jacob, and he is the first of his two sons to become old enough for the draft. When his birthday is drawn early in the draft lottery as the war is winding down, the Keanes's neighbor, who has already had a son go to the war and return, tells John "Shoot him in the foot. Break his legs before you let him go" (p. 57). Even the nuns, otherwise socially conservative, think it a useless war. It is what the future becomes for Jacob, who in his childhood days of world's fairs and modern churches domed like spaceships thought his future would be "part Buck Rogers, part James Bond," but who instead finds a future of needless destruction.

But Jacob is not the only child lost to the Keanes, though his loss is the most complete and most tragic. Lost too are his brother and older sister, as surely as the old church is lost, though John Keane himself helps raise the money for the modern, abstract building that will replace it. In what is possibly the novel's weakest scene, we see Michael Keane in a bar run by a man old enough to be his father but without having ever grown up, who instead smokes marijuana, wears a pony tail, and beds willing girls the age of Michael's sister Annie. Annie meanwhile, while studying abroad, gives up on her dreams just as she has given up on seeing her brother come home from the war, drops out of college, and moves in with a graduate student.

The youngest child, Clare, seems to be the only one not lost, as she retains an innocence "that belonged, perhaps, to an earlier time," but also "an air of innocence that in this day and age—even the Sisters said it—seemed to indicate a lack of depth" (p. 254). And it is perhaps just this innocence that leads her into the reenactment of a story more typical of the pre–Beatles era of *That Night.* But she is not sent away and she declines to give up her child to adoption. Rather, she will marry the hapless father and move in with her family. Understandably, her mother, having lost her three older children in different ways, exclaims "How much more can I take?" But in the structure of *After This,* the coming child cannot be looked at as just one more grief for the Keanes. Her child is also new life, a promise of continuation "after this" loss of Eden that *After This* presents. It is a gift from God, as the Sisters have so often said when warning their girls against the sin of abortion.

Loss and redemption do not sum up *After This,* however. Love, often in the guise of charity (in the Christian sense) or compassion or pity, is the feeling the novel finally evokes. Pietà, the name of the Michelangelo statue of the dead Christ in the lap of Mary that Mary Keane and Annie stand in line to see, is the Italian word for all these things, reminding us that piety has its origin in love and compassion. The word "pity" is repeated a number of times as Mary and Annie observe all the others standing with them in line in the heat. It is the feeling that prompts a neighbor to work in a mental hospital after he comes back from the Second World War. It is love and compassion and pity, however sometimes begrudged, that unites the Keanes with Pauline, Mary's annoying friend from her days in the typing pool before her marriage. Charity—love, compassion, pity—remains after much else is lost in *After This,* not compassion and pity for this character or that character, but pity and compassion for the human race which, after its expulsion from the garden, suffers so much pain and loss.

CONCLUSION

Because Alice McDermott is for the most part a slow and careful writer who sets herself new narrative challenges each time she writes, it is difficult to make predictions about where she will go after *After This*. She has affirmed that she will continue to write of women, that she will write of Irish Catholicism, that she will continue to write of Brooklyn and Queens and Long Island, but in what ways remains to be seen. In a review essay in the Catholic magazine *Commonweal* in December 2007 she gives some hints, though. She praises books that write of the invisible world even as they engage with realism, much as her own do. She also praises fictions that are in some sense about themselves, about the human power to remember and imagine and create. In a recent interview with Julee Newberger, she adds that the goal of her next novel, like those she's already written, will be "to convey, however briefly, the pain and sweetness of life." These characteristics well summarize her work so far, and should give a good idea of where her work will go from here.

Selected Bibliography

WORKS OF ALICE MCDERMOTT

NOVELS

A Bigamist's Daughter. New York: Random House, 1982.

That Night. New York: Farrar, Straus and Giroux, 1987.

At Weddings and Wakes. New York: Farrar, Straus and Giroux, 1992.

Charming Billy. New York: Farrar, Straus and Giroux, 1998.

Child of My Heart. New York: Farrar, Straus and Giroux, 2002.

After This. New York: Farrar, Straus and Giroux, 2006.

SHORT STORIES

"Simple Truth." *Ms.,* July 1978, pp. 73–75.

"Romantic Reruns." *Seventeen,* June 1979, pp. 150–151.

"Small Losses." *Ms.,* August 1979, pp. 60–62.

"Deliveries." *Redbook,* July 1980, pp. 29ff.

"Summer Folk." *Ms.,* April 1981, pp. 69ff.

"She Knew What She Wanted." *Redbook,* February 1986, pp. 44ff.

"Robert of the Desert." *Savvy Woman,* July 1989, pp. 62ff.

"Enough." *New Yorker,* April 10, 2000, p. 82ff.

NONFICTION

"Not a Love Story." *Mademoiselle,* February 1982, pp. 90ff.

"Books and Babies." In *Women, Creativity, and the Arts: Critical and Autobiographical Perspectives.* Edited by Diane Apostolos-Cappadona and Lucinda Ebersole. New York: Continuum, 1997. Pp. 196–198.

"Bend Sinister: A Handbook for Writers." In *Sewanee Writers on Writing.* Edited by Wyatt Prunty. Baton Rouge: Louisiana State University Press, 2000. Pp. 125–137.

"Confessions of A Reluctant Catholic." *Commonweal,* February 11, 2000, p. 40.

"Too Happy for Words." In *The Writing Life: Writers on How They Think and Work.* Edited by Marie Arana. New York: Public Affairs, 2003. Pp. 74–77.

"Christmas Critics." *Commonweal,* December 2007, pp. 26–27.

CRITICAL AND BIOGRAPHICAL STUDIES

Acocella, Joan. "The Children's Hour: A Novel of Loss." *New Yorker,* November 11, 2002.

Acocella, Joan. "Heaven's Gate." *New Yorker,* September 11, 2006, p. 83.

Atwood, Margaret. "Castle of the Imagination." *New York Review of Books,* January 16, 2003. Reprinted in her *Writing with Intent: Essays, Reviews, Personal Prose, 1983–2005.* New York: Carroll & Graf, 2005.

Carden, Mary P. "Making Love, Making History: (Anti) Romance in Alice McDermott's *At Weddings and Wakes* and *Charming Billy.*" In *Doubled Plots: Romance and History.* Edited by Susan Strehle and Mary Paniccia Carden. Jackson: University Press of Mississippi, 2003. Pp. 3–23.

Fanning, Charles. *The Irish Voice in America: 250 Years of Irish American Fiction.* 2d ed. Lexington: University Press of Kentucky, 2000.

Klinkenborg, Verlyn. "Grief That Lasts Forever." *New York Times Book Review,* April 12, 1992, p. 3.

Smith, Dinitia. "Arts in America: A Book Award Dark Horse, but Not to Her Faithful." *New York Times,* November 24, 1998, pp. E1–2.

Towers, Robert. "All-American Novels." *New York Review of Books,* January 21, 1988, pp. 26–27.

Tyler, Anne. "Novels by Three Emerging Writers." *New York Times Book Review,* February 21, 1982, pp 1, 28–29.

INTERVIEWS

Burns, Carol, host. "Off the Page: Alice McDermott." *Washingtonpost.com* (http://www.washingtonpost.com/

wp-dyn/articles/A31756-2003Aug22.html), October 2, 2003. (Transcript of online discussion.)

Dangel, Mary Jo. "Charming Alice McDermott: Award Winning Novelist." *St. Anthony Messenger* (http://www.americancatholic.org/messenger/May2001/feature1.asp), May 2001.

Newberger, Julee. "Alice McDermott: Interview." *Failbetter.com* (http://www.failbetter.com/22/McDermottInterview.php), fall 2006.

Reilly, Charlie. "An Interview with Alice McDermott." *Contemporary Literature* 46, no. 4:557–578 (2005).

Weich, Dave. "Alice McDermott, Child at Heart." *Powells.com* (http://www.powells.com/authors/mcdermott.html), 2002.

MARILYN NELSON

(1946—)

Kim Bridgford

SINCE THE BEGINNING of her career Marilyn Nelson (also known as Marilyn Nelson Waniek, pronounced *Von-yek*) has been interested in issues of family, history (both personal and public), and community. However, the way in which she has illustrated those themes has changed. Starting out as a free-verse poet, Nelson has evolved into a new formalist poet who uses the tools of rhyme and meter to give her ideas resonance. She has also brought her work out of the adult arena and into the children's arena, introducing sophisticated ideas and poetic forms to a younger audience. Many would argue that her book *The Fields of Praise* (1997) as well as her children's books *Carver: A Life in Poems* (2001), *Fortune's Bones: The Manumission Requiem* (2004), *A Wreath for Emmett Till* (2005), and *Miss Crandall's School for Young Ladies & Little Misses of Color* (2007, written with Elizabeth Alexander) bring her preoccupations to a culmination.

As one of the most accomplished members of the new formalist movement, she has used the tools of form to highlight issues of race and gender. As the founder of Soul Mountain, a retreat space with an emphasis on writers of color, and as a former Connecticut poet laureate, she has put her ideas about community into practice and encouraged the next generation to do the same. While she tells young people to write for members of their own community, she emphasizes the importance of an enduring tradition: "Write for them, of course, but don't write only for your peers, your homeys, members of your poetry workshop. What will you say to someone who comes across a dusty journal in the basement of a library someplace in the future, opens the pages, and finds your words?" (quoted in Ellis, p. 631). She goes on to emphasize that point in her essay "Owning the Masters": "Owning the masters of our tradition, 'signifying,' paying due homage, gives us a way to escape the merely personal, puts us in dialogue with great thoughts of the past, and teaches us transparency. For the greatest masters of our tradition sought not to see their own eyes, but to see through them" (p. 17). Nelson's work embodies this sense of re-vision.

LIFE

Marilyn Nelson was born on 26 April 1946. As Nelson says in an essay in the *Contemporary Authors: Autobiography Series,* "In the Southern and black tradition, I like to start telling of myself by telling who my people are." Her father, Melvin M. Nelson, was a navigator, one of the Tuskegee Airmen, and her mother, Johnnie Mitchell Nelson, was a teacher. Nelson has two siblings, Jennifer (1948) and Melvin Jr. (1956); her youngest sibling, Peter Michael (1958), who had Down syndrome, died when he was three. In the same autobiographical essay, Nelson writes of the support her parents gave her:

> Mama, with her proud stories of her family, gave us roots; Daddy, who used to drive us out into the country at night, park the car, and point out constellations and name stars, gave us wings. They encouraged us to dream big, and they had confidence in our ability to be what we dreamed. My sister, Jennifer, is an actor/director; our brother, Mel, is a musician/composer. These are my people, and this is where I start.
>
> (p. 273)

Because her father was in the military, Nelson lived all over the United States: from Texas to Maine to California. As the children of an officer, Nelson and her siblings were usually the only African American children in their

neighborhoods. Yet her father's achievement as a navigator, his sense of magic in his profession, affected them in other ways. Once, when the family was traveling near the Grand Canyon, her father stopped after traveling all night, and Nelson says,

> We awoke to that grandeur at dawn. Daddy was like that. He loved the sound of rain on the car's roof at night. ... Rain sounds like wren's wings beating against a parked car's roof at night. Or like a cascade of coins made of moonlight. ... Daddy could pull coins out of our ears. I remember thinking as a young child that as long as he could do that, we would never be poor.
>
> (p. 276)

Nelson was an intellectual child, with an early interest in books and in writing. When she was in third grade and living in Kansas, she exhausted the school library. Her teacher gave her high school books to read. Later, when she was in sixth grade and lived in Maine, she lived near the library and again read nearly everything in it. She says in the *Contemporary Authors* essay that her teacher "Mrs. Gray predicted that I'd grow up to be a famous writer." Although she continued to excel, her interests became increasingly dominated by issues of justice and civil rights. She did still enjoy writing, however, and in 1965, when she announced to a group at a community project "that I like to read and write poems," she was told, "Baby, you gone have a hard time." Nelson earned a B.A. from the University of California (1968), an M.A. from the University of Pennsylvania (1970), and a Ph.D. from the University of Minnesota (1979). While in graduate school, she joined the critical discussion of the role that race plays in defining a literary tradition. Acknowledging the suffering at the core of African American literature, she writes in a 1975 essay "The Space Where Sex Should Be: Toward a Definition of the Black Literary Tradition" that "it is the fact of oppression that distinguishes this literature from all others." Emphasizing the way in which this tradition is both transformative and political, she says that "the Black American writer strives to demonstrate to white America that his Negro individuality is as much a kind of personhood as any colorless [white] identity." Such a conflict trumps any discussion of gender: "in the space where sex should be is instead the awful confrontation of Black self with white self, and the Black self with white society." The subject of her doctoral thesis, "The Schizoid Nature of the Implied Author in Twentieth-Century American Ethnic Novels," suggests the way in which one has to navigate a psychic space as an outsider, an issue of enduring concern for Nelson. In a publication based on her thesis, she goes on to say that "the duality of cultures thus produces a duality of personality—'a divided self'—in the marginal man" ("The Schizoid Implied Authors," p. 22). Because of her concern with this psychic space and history, she is often allied with Rita Dove, six years her junior, and she is seen as a role model for up-and-coming writers of color, such as A. Van Jordan, whose *M-a-c-n-o-l-i-a* (2004) is a volume of poetry that chronicles the story of an African American girl, MacNolia Cox, who was prevented from winning the national spelling bee because of racism. Increasingly, Nelson would be concerned with acknowledging a wide enough swath of experience for black writers. In a 1981 essay in the journal *MELUS* (published by the Society for the Study of Multi-Ethnic Literature of the United States), "Comments/Questions," she cites Ntozake Shange as saying, "What ... do we do with the experience of a Black raised on a farm in Indiana?" (p. 3). Nelson goes on to ask, "Has the Black Aesthetic finally enabled the Black writer to imagine a reader like herself?" (p. 4). Nelson has made her career as an English professor, teaching at such schools as Lane Community College, Reed College, St. Olaf College, and (since 1978) the University of Connecticut. She has been twice married and divorced: to Erdmann F. Waniek (1970–1979), using the name Marilyn Nelson Waniek until 1995; and to Roger R. Wilkenfeld (1979–1998). With Wilkenfeld she has two children, Jacob (1980) and Dora (1986).

Nelson's honors include National Endowment of the Arts fellowships (1981, 1990), a Fulbright teaching fellowship (1995); the Poets' Prize (1999); a Guggenheim Fellowship (2001), Coretta Scott King Honors for *Carver: A Life in Poems, Fortune's Bones: The Manumission Re-*

quiem, and *A Wreath for Emmett Till*; and a Lifetime Achievement Award at the Connecticut Book Awards (2006). She was Connecticut State poet laureate for the period 2001–2006.

FOR THE BODY

For the Body, Nelson's first collection of poems, was published in 1978, when she was thirty-two. Kirkland C. Jones emphasizes in the *Dictionary of Literary Biography* that "the *body* of the title becomes a metaphor for the individual, the family, and the extended family." Paul Griffith states in a separate volume of the *Dictionary of Literary Biography* that "*For the Body* is dedicated to reconstituting the self, to unifying the fragments that structure the poet's consciousness. The synecdochic assemblage of parts and 'bodies' chronicles pain, frustrations, pleasures, attainments, experiences, and values that conflict, shape, and sustain the self."

Key to understanding the book is the framing poem, "Dedication." Here Nelson underscores the importance of each part of the body, from the heart; to the brain; to the hands, "feet, belly, legs"; to the whole body. Although the heart and brain are of paramount importance, they cannot perform their functions without "our proletariat, / our common man (p. 1). In the end, it comes down to the experience of the body and its intensity, whether"riding its pain and pleasure"(p. 1), or"living like a beacon / out into death (p. 1). Most of the poems are written in free verse and deal with issues of family and history, like "Mama I Remember," chronicling the loss her mother has borne through life, and "I Am You Again," describing the experience of a black child in an all-white classroom (as Nelson explains in the notes at the end of her 1997 collection *The Fields of Praise,* the poem is not about her own experience but that of one of her students). One especially poignant stanza in "I Am You Again" has Nelson revisiting the classroom with her student.

Yet one can also see Nelson's interest in form in such poems as "Churchgoing" (an imitation of Philip Larkin) and in "The Perfect Couple." While the former addresses issues of faith in a dialectic of two different religious traditions—Lutheran and African American spiritual—the latter is a dialectic of self. Nelson's work continually deals with struggle in a range of contexts, and she would increasingly turn to form to highlight that struggle, or, as Christian Wiman puts it in "An Idea of Order," "a thematic line—between aesthetic beauty as a source of power and beauty as power's object—which it walks in form." At the same time, there is an appealing conversational quality to the free-verse poems, and a poem such as "Emily Dickinson's Defunct" uses both a colloquial free verse and a sparkling wit to give the poem power.

MAMA'S PROMISES

Mama's Promises (1985) addresses the multiple roles that women must play in their lives, and it functions as well as a tribute to mothers. Jones notes that the poems "appeal to both adult and adolescent readers," who find her direct style appealing. Yet in her essay for *Contemporary Authors,* Nelson herself says that she wishes the book to "be read as a book of black feminist theology." It is, indeed, a matriarchal book. In her notes at the end of *The Fields of Praise,* Nelson points out that "I had originally intended 'Mama' of my second book ... to be not only myself, my mother, and other mothers ... but also the Divine Mother, the feminine face of God."

Part of the struggle of the book is finding how life's circumstances can surprise us. As Nelson writes in the brief poem "A Strange Beautiful Woman," we can meet ourselves, face to face, with a certain astonishment. In "Cover Photograph," she says, "I want to be remembered / with a simple name, like Mama" (p. 4), but she goes on in other poems to discuss the complications of motherhood. For example, in "Levitation with Baby," she misses her appointment with the Muse because there are so many preparations for her son she has to make first. Meanwhile, the Muse passes her by, and visits the man next door.

Many of the poems focus on what we learn from experience. In thinking of past friendships,

for example, she admits in "Sleepless Nights" that "we used to tell each other erotic stories / at slumber parties when I was about ten" (p. 25), but real life delivers a different message: "We never dreamed of the face-making / self-reconstruction from scratch / we'd be engaged in or most of our lives" (p. 25). Yet there is a solidarity in women sharing each other's experience, making each other laugh. Because "Confessional Poem" also teases with its title, it is difficult to know whether the central figure is the lonely self, a friend, or both. In it a friend visits another friend to make her laugh, arriving in a fat lady suit and doing a strip tease. In response, the young mother, friend, or author would follow suit in unabandoned joy.

THE HOMEPLACE

Nelson's *The Homeplace*—published in 1990 and a finalist for the National Book Award as well as winner of the Anisfield–Wolf Award for Race Relations—bears obvious comparison to Rita Dove's *Thomas and Beulah* (1986), as Kevin Walzer, among others, has noted. The book, which is a mixture of traditional and free-verse forms, brings Nelson's emphasis on personal history to a culmination. Walzer says in *The Ghost of Tradition* that

> it stands as Nelson's finest collection largely through its formal dexterity and thematic coherence. ... Certainly when one writes a family history, one is enmeshed in a "long tradition"; Nelson's use of form and narrative therefore becomes especially appropriate in *The Homeplace*. The book is an unusual achievement, especially because it was not strongly anticipated by her earliest work.
>
> (p. 102)

What Walzer means by this is that the book is more thematically centered than Nelson's earlier work and that the writer has matured.

The book, by including photographs and poems, shows the interweaving of both actual history and the author's take on that history. The book traces Nelson's genealogy, with her mother as the pivotal figure, since most of the history explored in the book comes through her. There is poignancy in that the volume was written following Johnnie Mitchell Nelson's years with Alzheimer's and her eventual death. It becomes, then, both a way to remember and a remembrance. Yet, as Nelson herself points out in her *Contemporary Authors* essay, the book became larger than her own personal experience: "I planned to write a book in Mama's memory, just for the family, but gradually, as far-flung relatives and local historians, black and white, eagerly gave me anecdotes and information, the book 'jest growed.'"

The cover includes a photograph of Nelson's mother, and later in the book there is a rare photograph of Nelson's father boarding an airplane. Other photographs include those of her maternal great-grandfather, her grandmother, and "the homeplace" itself in Hickman, Kentucky, a house owned by her maternal side since the late 1800s. As Nelson illustrates in "The House on Moscow Street," history is made up both of the people and the texture of the experience, and she attempts to recapture them both. This texture may be joyful, and it may be painful; but it must be reclaimed, not lost, or defined by somebody else.

Kirkland C. Jones points out that in *The Homeplace,* the poet "tackles the difficult subject of miscegenation and the so-called cultural bastardy that results from mingling the blood of white slave owners with the book of the slaves." The collection is, he says, "an intergenerational work, starting with a re-creation of Waniek's great-great-grandmother Diverne, whose son was sired by a young Confederate Army officer. Diverne sends her powerful spirit through the generations." The structured forms in particular, by the juxtaposition of tradition and colloquial speech, provide a framework that heightens the cataclysms of history, as the Shakespearean sonnet does in "Annunciation." In "Annunciation," Nelson uses a mixture of the Shakespearean and Italian sonnet to accentuate that cataclysm. In the "Balance"—Italian in development, Shakespearean in rhyme scheme—she underscores this juxtaposition in a sextet.

As an advocate of traditional forms, Christian Wiman praises Nelson's poem "Balance" as a way of illustrating "a kind of closure that

compromises itself. There is a discrepancy between the finality with which the poem concludes and the possibility of disorder which it contains." Like Wiman, Jones praises Nelson's sonnets, saying that "the voices of Waniek's characters, most in dramatic monologues, come out clear and true, and the experiences she recreates are vivid." Yet Leslie Ullman is quick to emphasize Nelson's skill with both free-verse and traditional forms: "Her easy movement between poems in form and seemingly 'found' dramatic monologues suggests that her own background as an African-American poet is a rich patchwork of traditions, and that her clearly organic sense of self and family history has moved her neither to embrace nor eschew current Formalist concerns" (p. 182).

While there are only two sections to the book, the long section "The Homeplace" and the much shorter section "Wings," the first section is further divided by photographs and delineations of Nelson's genealogy in order to emphasize the shifting of generations. There are poems throughout the book that illustrate acts of racial violence, yet simultaneously there is a sense of achievement as the generations acquire personal power and peace. For example, in the Homeplace section, the villanelle "Daughters, 1900" illustrates the pleasure of watching five daughters in the circle of family, while the free-verse poem "Hurrah, Hurrah" shows the bravery of active duty abroad (although it is not appreciated at home). "The Ballad of Aunt Geneva," reminiscent of the Sadie side of Gwendolyn Brooks's well-known ballad "Sadie and Maud," shows how Geneva claims power in her world.

The last part of the first section is framed by Nelson's mother, Johnnie Mitchell Nelson. In "The Fortune Spill," Nelson writes touchingly about the meeting of her parents: "*I'll be a man up in the sky,* / he confides. She blurts out, *Hello, Jesus!* And they die / with laughter" (p. 37). From her perspective in the future, Nelson writes, "And I watch from this distant balcony / as they fall for each other, and for me" (p. 37).

The last section, "Wings," is appropriately framed by a photograph of Nelson's father boarding a plane. The poems in this section, such as "Porter," show Nelson's pride in being connected to the history of the Tuskegee Airmen, through her father's achievement. Although there are still daily indignities (like one of the Tuskegee Airmen being asked by a white woman to carry her luggage, even though he is a lieutenant colonel in the air force), there is a remarkable sense of history, and even sense of humor, that transcends. (After all, he says, he accepted the tip!) Thus, Nelson gains a new way of appreciation.

PARTIAL TRUTH

The beautiful chapbook *Partial Truth,* published in 1992 by the Kutenai Press in Willington, Connecticut, traces the dissolution of Nelson's first marriage. Because of their intimacy, some of the book's sonnets were published under a pseudonym, Lynn Nelson, when they first appeared in the *New Virginia Review*; eventually, the poems won a Pushcart Prize, and the chapbook was published under Nelson's real name.

Made up of fourteen sonnets—one short of a sonnet redouble or sonnet magistrale—the book demonstrates Nelson's relatively early interest in the sonnet series and the way in which the individual sonnets could be used to cumulative effect. This strategy would find its culmination, on an individual level, in *A Wreath for Emmett Till* and, on a collaborative level, in *Miss Crandall's School for Young Ladies & Little Misses of Color.* It is one of her most personal books. Griffith calls it "Nelson's most disturbing evocation of intense situations and states of mind" and says that "the sonnet form allows the poet to go deeply into her moods and perceptions while ordering and controlling the intensity of spiritual anguish." Nelson herself feels that they are her most accomplished sonnets of that period; *Partial Truth,* she says in the essay for *Contemporary Authors,* is "a beautiful book; it even smells good. The rest of my sonnets are gathering dust."

The book traces the difficulty of a racially mixed marriage and the sense of inadequacy felt by the woman in the relationship, who is black. In a touching take on Elizabeth Barrett

Browning's "How Do I Love Thee?" Nelson's "How Did I Love Him?" makes a catalogue of all of the things she cherishes about her beloved, from "his detailed and profuse / remembered past" to "the thin potato soup, / the push-meat sandwiches after the war" While this poem is grounded in literal details, it is filled with idealized love.

Partial Truth goes on to recount a range of betrayals, from a relationship with another woman to a request for the speaker to have an abortion or else the relationship will end. In staying in the relationship, the speaker finds she has betrayed herself. As she says in "Frogs,"

> I loved him: That's the thing I can't forgive.
> Feet in the stirrups, riding on my back,
> I loved him. Even as my world went black.

This betrayal in the love relationship radiates out into other relationships. In "Sisters," Nelson doesn't understand why white feminist colleagues would not see her as a part of the group, but then she looks back on childhood fights she has witnessed:

> We were all sisters, feminists, I thought,
> forgetting what those cat-fights should have taught.
> I was too well brought-up, too middle class
> to call a heifer out, and whup her ass.

Those poem foreshadows a shift of attitude that would find full expression in *She-Devil Circus*. Ultimately Nelson needs a change in relationships, and her last poem in the collection, "Recurrent Dream," spells out that change. Her father appears to her, and she tells him that she doesn't require his help. More persistent is "Love's ghost." This presence is more difficult to escape, and yet by the end of the series, Nelson is ready: "My love, I'm grown. Let go."

MAGNIFICAT

While *Partial Truth* was a brave poem to write in terms of personal relationships, *Magnificat* (1994) shows a different kind of courage, by linking religious truth to romantic truth. Nelson's most openly religious book, *Magnificat* traces a "what if" relationship. Nelson speculates about a man she was attracted to twenty years before he eventually took holy orders. She and her second husband, Roger Wilkenfeld, tracked him down. Nelson writes in the essay for *Contemporary Authors,* "When we found him, he wrote to us that he had finished a doctorate at Cambridge University, worked for several years, then felt the call. After seven years in a monastery he had left, with the blessings of his Father Abbot, to live as a hermit and build a new monastery." The Henri Cartier-Bresson drawing reproduced on the front cover, *Jacob Wrestling with the Angel,* illuminates the struggle of the book. As Andrew Hudgins says on the back cover, "In *Magnificat,* Marilyn Nelson Waniek follows the spiritual path from *eros* to *agape* with the joyful stride of George Herbert." While Michael Weaver is mostly laudatory in his appraisal of the collection for *African American Review,* he questions the ultimate effect of the volume:

> Waniek explores her own unattainable love to see if it is indeed unsurpassable. It is a love for a man who is committed to God, a man who became priest, a man who is indeed fallible. *Magnificat* is a valiant attempt by Waniek to move from her earlier poems of family and community to the *a capella* hymn of the lyrical voice singing its 'self'. ... This book has wonderful moments, but Waniek has more passageways to negotiate before she touches that most intense pitch.
>
> (p. 504)

Magnificat takes its title from the biblical Mary's praise of God, after realizing she is carrying his child. As Weaver points out, "It is at once a painfully singular moment in Christianity and the incomparable joy of a woman who has experienced the ecstasy of love with a Being more capable of love in all its manifestations than any man. In African-American spiritual experience, it is often said God is love" (p. 504). Nelson's book, then, is a book of monumental love.

In "Lost and Found" Nelson delineates the struggle between the outer world and the religious world in an examination of the experience of monks. Yet, she herself has no peace in the paradox. Ultimately, she resigns to live with this difficult combination, and find it holy.

The middle section of the book, "Plain Songs," moves along a range of moods, and

hungers. From a poem about eating too much, "Matins," to one about preserving moments, "Tell Me a Story," to hungering for longing itself, "Enigma Variations," the section explores what it means to be a human being. The style of the section emphasizes this theme: short bursts of poetry, similar to pangs of desire.

The "Abba Jacob" poems that follow are also in small bursts of poetry and serve almost as Zen koans. The poems tend to end with Abba Jacob's pronouncement on a particular situation, like a plant bearing fruit or the emotional balance of people in hell. "The Bread of Desire" sums up the paradoxes implicit in the poems: "The world balanced / on impossible truth" (p. 35). This balancing act prepares the groundwork for "A Canticle for Abba Jacob," which is an unabashed love poem in twelve sections.

Although, as Weaver notes, it can be difficult to bring the disparate pieces of the book together (p. 505), Nelson does unite her present and her past. When her son dreams of flying (like his grandfather, the Tuskegee Airman), Nelson extends this metaphor to include the flight to God. Nelson offers to us, and to God, her love for Abba Jacob.

THE FIELDS OF PRAISE

In reviewing Nelson's 1997 collection of new and selected poems, *The Fields of Praise,* Marilyn Hacker has said that "the energy and wit of these poems, even their occasional frank (comic) claustrophobia, has its source in feminist writing ... largely white, but including the earlier work of Lucille Clifton and Toi Derricotte as well as Nelson, for all of whom the perception of childbirth and childrearing as events with histories ... was the center of a worldview (pp. 17–18). Miller Williams, writing in *African American Review,* finds the power of the book less in Nelson's feminism than in her individual voice. He says that"reading her poems is remarkably like sitting in a porch swing listening to a cousin who pays attention tell about a trip to the city, except that we hear instead about being transported to a slave market (p. 179). In his praise for the book, he stresses,

> I don't know anything more important to say about ... [the poems] than this: If I were handed an unsigned sheaf of her work that I hadn't read, I'd know she was the poet. This is what we mean by voice. She writes like no one else, and her poems are well-wrought, and they say things that matter. No poet can want for more than for those three things to be true.
>
> (p. 180)

In addition to recognizing Nelson's voice, readers of her earlier work will recognize many of the poems themselves. However, in a daring move she has reorganized her poems along many of the themes that have preoccupied her: "Mama and Daddy," "Homeplace," "Hermitage," and "Still Faith," a section of completely new poems. By choosing this method of organization, Nelson emphasizes the fluid nature of her self and the way in which her interests transcend time, place, and history. Notable new poems include "Thus Far by Faith" in the "Homeplace" section and a sequence of what Nelson calls "unbuttoned sonnets" in the "Still Faith" section. "Thus Far by Faith" is a sonnet crown that looks ahead to "A Wreath for Emmett Till," although "Wreath" would extend the crown to fifteen sonnets. The crown illustrates what it means to be a slave and have faith, as in the first sonnet, "Sermon in the Cotton Field":

> *But old Satan roars*
> *louder, sometimes, than Master. He say, Hate*
> *the whip-hand and the yoke: Why be a fool?*
> *The Lord hisself were tempted, Brother Mule.*
>
> (p. 99)

Later, in the fourth sonnet, Aunt Sally thinks about her freedom: "the peace of hours like these, / and wages, now, for every house she cleans" (p. 100). Within the structure of this sonnet, its inhabitants find hope, and freedom. The last sonnet of the crown, "Easter Sermon, 1866," honors both the difficulties and the rewards of the situation. Like so many of Nelson's poems, this one ends with hope.

Two of the "unbuttoned sonnets," "No No, Bad Daddy" and "No Worst," highlight both the themes announced in the titles and their looser sonnet shape. While Nelson typically uses form to offset the subject matter of her poems (as

Richard Wilbur says, "the strength of the genie comes of his being confined in a bottle" [p. 1031]), here the subject matter spills out of the grid—and intense subject matter it is. "No No, Bad Daddy" uses a rope as a way to hold in secrets and encapsulate violence. Since Nelson is ultimately a poet of love, she wrestles with issues of evil in "No Worst": "But how love the woman who holds a child's head / under the bath water? How love the man who stuffs / a wadded sock into his daughter's sobbing mouth?" (p. 185). In addressing these issues in contemporary sonnets, she calls to mind the *Unholy Sonnets* of Mark Jarman, another strong American poet of faith. As Marilyn Hacker sums up,

> Underlying the personal/political and the historical/ narrative there is, from Nelson's earliest work on, a theme of spiritual quest structuring the poems: a search for the divine in the quotidian, balanced by a meditation on the nature of evil in a spectrum that goes from childish betrayals and individual bad faith to the authorship and agency of the Middle Passage and the Final Solution.
>
> (p. 18)

SHE-DEVIL CIRCUS

The seven poems in Nelson's (2001) chapbook *She-Devil Circus* pick up where *Partial Truth* left off. These poems, though, have more of an in-your-face attitude than those in *Partial Truth.* By turning romantic love poems on their head, these become love poems about a journey to self. Ironically, these rebellious sonnets are showcased in the elegant Aralia chapbook series; their message is that it is better to be true to the self than to be nice.

At first the attitude is relatively innocuous: taking a sensuous attitude toward food, as in "Asparagus," where the speaker learns "to slurp" it. The speaker delights in this new way of eating, "smug as a new billionaire." Yet, as the poems progress, the attitude has to do with self, in terms of being confident about being smart and being loved. For example, in "What I Knew" the speaker feels insecure around a "smug European intellect" and old fears are brought to the surface: "The insecurity I'd felt in school— / where I thought I got A's for being black." In "My Monkey," the speaker, worrying about weight gain, looks in the mirror and wonders how she can be loved, then faces a larger fear: "a monkey on my back / which whispered, 'You ain't beautiful. You black.'"

Yet the poems begin to erupt. In "She-Devil" the speaker leaves her significant other at a party, and later when he says, "I love you" she says that "all I could say was, 'Yeah? Well, whoopdidoo.'" In "Nice Girl," she realizes that she has always been "a wind-up Marilyn who smiled and smiled." This niceness has worked to her detriment. In a memorable couplet, she says, "That's why / it took so fucking long to say goodbye." If she hadn't been so nice, she reasons, she would have left sooner.

THE CACHOEIRA TALES

The Cachoeira Tales and Other Poems (2005) is an homage to Chaucer in a range of ways: in its dramatic and motley range of characters, its focus on journey, and its exploration of pilgrimage. In *Poetry* magazine, D. H. Tracy takes issue with the style, calling the poem "a Chaucer pastiche," and saying that "the couplets' fidelity is to clarity rather than grace." Ultimately Tracy decides that the poem "could use a good dousing in the particular."

While Nelson's book is mostly about a trip to Brazil that she undertakes using the money from a Guggenheim Fellowship, it is also about other journeys—one a taxi ride, the other a trip to a village named Triolet. If there is a unifying theme in the book, it is the difficulty of a first-world consciousness meeting third-world poverty. Yet in the midst of this realization there is the celebration of the moment and the celebration of family and community.

The book contains three sections, the first being Nelson's poem "Faster than Light," which introduces the theme of travel and randomness; suddenly Nelson is communing with a taxi driver. Nelson is the listener and the prophet, calling herself sarcastically "*Miss William Blake*" and wondering about the importance of her art in the

journey of the universe: "My poems: a handful of dust / trying to get back to supernova. / Like every longing, everything alive" (p. 3).

"Triolets for Triolet," which was also published as a chapbook by Curbstone in 2001, emphasizes both journey and community. Using the French poetic form of the triolet to give voice to this village by the same name in Mauritius, Nelson explores issues of the tension of the difference between first- and third-world experience. She writes in the introduction to this section, "As the villagers and I exchanged smiles, theirs shyly respectful of the rich black university professor from a distant world they could not dream of ever being able to visit, I felt both our differences and our affinity, as descendents of African slaves" (p. 7). Nelson uses the power of repetition and prayer to explore the world of Triolet (both the form and the place):

> Walk through the winding streets of Triolet,
> in two-room cement houses, whose tin roofs
> seem one bright blaze from satellites miles away.
> Walk through the winding streets of Triolet.
>
> (p. 9)

And she goes on to talk about the citizens of Triolet, their place in the world:

> Without their history, people stumble
> in Triolet, trying not to remember
> that they are poor, unalphabeted, black
> and historyless.
>
> (p. 9)

Section 6 gives a voice to people who typically do not have one, and its first few lines emphasize the attempt to find connection:

> Who talk like me? Who dye elect despise?
> Who patois, out day home, invite guffaw
> and swallow rage? Mask, except foe day eyes,
> who talk like me? Who dye elect despise?
>
> (p. 10)

Nelson continues her motif of journey with "The Cachoiera Tales." While this imitation of the *Canterbury Tales* emphasizes mostly the first-world group that goes to Brazil, the poem also addresses issues of inequity—AIDS, poverty, racial injustice. An air of celebration about the journey begins the poem, as the unexpected gift of the fellowship makes the trip possible. Tracy believes that "the pilgrims' characterization is Nelson's strongest achievement in the book." At the beginning of the poem the lilting, sing-song nature of the presentation also emphasizes this.

Since Nelson is a master of forms, she uses them both to amuse and to highlight more painful moments. Rather than moving from one member of the group to another, as Chaucer does, Nelson uses this strategy only as a starting point, speaking many of the poems from her own perspective. A couplet like "by making 'Danny's House' in Washington, D.C. / home to programs on AIDS and HIV" (p. 15) can be used to one effect, and to another in "From the far side of the hall, a loud halloo / called our attention. Harmonia and Moreen! / Moreen in peach, Harmonia in aubergine" (p. 25).

Ultimately the group, which has shared jazz, food, drink, and conversation with each other, ends up at Cachoeria, where a black sisterhood lives. The sisters themselves are not at home, but the speaker is tantalized by the notion of pilgrimage, the end of the journey.

POETRY TRANSLATIONS

In the 1970s, when Nelson was teaching in Denmark, she became friends with Inge Pedersen, ten years her senior. Later, when Pedersen turned to poetry following the death of her son, a new collaborative relationship developed, and Nelson wished to translate her friend's Danish into English. In 2001, when Nelson received a residency to spend time at Henrich Böll's house on an Irish island, the collaboration began to come to fruition. As Nelson writes, "There we sat every morning in Böll's workspace, a light, cool, sparsely furnished room, discussing our poems and our thoughts about translation. ... We completed the manuscript during the fall of 2004, when she and her husband spent two weeks at my home in Connecticut" (p. 9). The resulting translations, *The Thirteenth Month* (2005), won the American Scandinavian Foundation (ASF) Translation prize.

Although there is a seriousness to *The Thirteenth Month* and a conversational style that harkens to Nelson's earlier work, there is also a playfulness that is characteristic of Nelson; one can see how the collaboration is a good match. In the first poem, "Towards Morning," for example, these lines make one think of poems like "Emily Dickinson's Defunct": "scram / or you're dead meat / I snarl at all / the small rodents in my heart" (p. 13).

Yet there is a somber peacefulness to the poems as well, as noted in "Respite":

and the clouds fly
in the mirror
because no one I love
died last night
nor was anyone found last night
white and outstretched
in their beds.

(p. 15)

The poems acknowledge both warmth and loss, love and death; and the following passage from "Wound" sums up this paradox:

And from the train Europe looks like
a brittle romantic poem
in which the lakes close
their black moon-
lost eyes and trickling
roses can be lying in the ground
around a perfectly ordinary house.

(p. 36)

The poem "Mourning Doves" acknowledges the loss of Pedersen's son, when the speaker asks the mourning doves of the son's whereabouts. However, a sense of beauty ultimately triumphs. As Pedersen writes in "Grief Has Stamped,"

Grief has stamped
a rose
a strange courage
on my mouth.

(p. 40)

One is reminded of Nelson's "Dedication" in the emphasis on the physical to make one's way through life, dependent on "our proletariat, / our common man." And ultimately, as Pedersen says in her poem "Winter Trees," she wants her body to be "Plain, no unneeded weight, whistled through by the wind, simple as haiku" (p. 51).

Nelson's interest in children's poetry can be traced back to her work in translating the work of Halfdan Rasmussen (1915–2002), one of Denmark's most well-known children's poets. Although her own children's work would ultimately become more serious, there remains a playfulness and directness in her poetry that reflects the humorousness for which Rasmussen was beloved. In their introduction to *Hundreds of Hens and Other Poems for Children by Halfdan Rasmussen* (1982), Nelson and her cotranslator, Pamela Espeland, write that Rasmussen "does not idealize the children about whom he writes. Instead, he makes them real." It is not difficult to see what appeals to Nelson about Rasmussen:

The elf puts on his winter coat,
puts his winter hat on,
finds muffler for his throat
in his drawer—puts that on,
packs his pockets full of mice
and then, before he goes,
puts on an empty ice-cream cone
to insulate his nose.

The following two stanzas from "Here Inside My Forehead" further illustrate the perfect match between Nelson and Rasmussen, through both wit and word play:

Here inside my forehead
lives a little man.
He can eat canned peaches
still inside the can.
....
He can spit long distances
and say words that are horrid.
But he only does these things
here, inside my forehead.

For Nelson, there is appeal in being "that old owl who writes silly poems with invisible ink," the mythical, magical figure of the writer.

Nelson dedicated another translation of Rasmussen's poetry for children, *The Ladder* (2006), to Rasmussen's "memory and, to his daughter, Iben Nagel Rasmussen." As someone whose life spanned nearly the entire twentieth century, Rasmussen had certainly seen a great

deal and responded wittily to life's absurdities. *The Ladder* comments both on the magical nature of storytelling and the inventiveness of language and circumstance.

The personified ladder, which is built by a carpenter, is a way for people to go higher than they'd dreamed and to walk into the heavens. Since some of the book's pages contain folded-over extensions that can be opened vertically, the ladder literally moves closer to the sky. After enabling a cast of characters, including a chauffeur-driven limousine and a marching band, to go off into the clouds, the ladder gets tired and must reevaluate its circumstances. When it is struck by lightning, everyone comes running home down the zigzag stair steps made by the lightning. In the end, the carpenter takes his ladder elsewhere.

ORIGINAL WORK FOR CHILDREN

The Cat Walked Through the Casserole and Other Poems for Children (1984), also in collaboration with Pamela Espeland, is a book of original poems that nods to Rasmussen's playful style. There is an unexpectedness to some of the stanzaic arrangements that is new for Nelson. For example, in the title poem, "The Cat Walked Through the Casserole," the reader does not know what will come next, both in language and in theme:

The cat walked through the casserole
And tracked it on the floor
When we all rushed outside to see
The ambulance next door.
    So the cat had to go.

These are also poems with attitude. While the speaker in "If Grown-Ups Were Smart" confronts a gorilla at the zoo, the speaker in "If I Could Do Whatever I Wanted" threatens to "drill a dentist's molars" and "make all the farmers eat spinach." "Blue Tattoo" emphasizes this perspective, desiring a tattoo, a broken arm, and a plastic tooth: "Our mother thinks it's horrible, / But I think it's fantastic" (This poem in its delight in all things forbidden suggests Gwendolyn Brooks's "A Song in the Front Yard.").

The book is also not afraid to take on serious subjects. For example, "Father Fitzgerald" takes on the subject of the soul, and the speaker has big questions:

Is it like a stomach, or a heart?
Does it float inside me like a tiny cloud?
When I cry, or lie, or forget to say my prayers,
Does it squinch its eyes up tight and groan out loud?

And in "Daffodils," a nod to William Wordsworth, the speaker knows that Grandmother is not in the sky, but

Grandmother turned into daffodils.
They're blooming all over her grave.
Whenever we visit on Saturdays,
As soon as they see me, they wave.

LIVES IN POEMS: HISTORY FOR YOUNG PEOPLE

It is with *Carver: A Life in Poems* that Nelson brought her simple style and themes of race, suffering, and transformation to one of the most striking life stories of the nineteenth and twentieth centuries. With its success as both a Newbery Honor Book and a Coretta Scott King Honor winner, *Carver: A Life in Poems* changed the course of Nelson's career. Although this book was in free verse rather than cast as a series of sonnets like *A Wreath for Emmett Till* and *Miss Crandall's School for Young Ladies,* Nelson's strengths flourish in making an homage to, and bringing to life, the extraordinary journey of George Washington Carver as an African American, an inventor, and a person. The epitaph of Carver (1864–1943) sums up the life of this extraordinary American: "He could have added fortune to fame, but caring for neither, he found happiness and honor in being helpful to the world."

Response to the book and to its unusual undertaking, of using poetry to write a biography, was uniformly positive, with Betty Adcock in the *Southern Review* calling the book "ambitious." and "meticulous" and, because the book appeals to both adult and younger audiences, pointing to the fact that "like George Washington Carver's life ... this verse biography stands in two worlds.

In both, it stands as poetry of subtlety and grace." David Mason states in the *Hudson Review* that he also appreciates the accomplishment of the book and the importance of the homage to Carver, but he wishes the writing were in meter and not in free verse, hoping that Nelson "will return to this material in another form, moving it beyond the implications that mere truth allows."

By framing the book with quotations by Albert Einstein, Leo Tolstoy, and Carver himself, Nelson claims a rightful place for Carver. While honoring Carver's achievement, she also frames his humility in light of his greatness—the enduring paradox of Carver's life. As Carver says (quoted on the book's epigraph page), "A personal relationship with the Great Creator of all things is the only foundation for the abundant life. The farther we get away from self, the greater life will be." Apart from his faith, education was the primary motivator in Carver's life. In pursuing his dream he had to navigate the white world in order to attain the best education possible. To pay for his expenses, he had to take in washing. Nelson uses a multiplicity of voices who attempt to come to terms with Carver. Because he does not fit into the preconceptions people have about his race, he is a mystery. In the poem "Washboard Wizard," the speaker pays respect to Carver and grapples with his achievement in light of the community's prejudice.

Nelson's homage to Carver shows the way in which he was such a role model of elegance, intelligence, and goodness that people had to accept him for who he was, not who they expected him to be. Finally getting a chance to attend college, Carver went to Simpson College and then Iowa State. "Green-Thumb Boy," spoken in the voice of Dr. L. H. Pammel, emphasizes the way in which Carver approaches life and his education, wearing a flower in his lapel even in winter, and its positive effect on others. In addition to being an accomplished scientist, Carver was also a teacher and painter, bringing about transformation in the world around him. Such achievements could incite envy and prejudice, but Carver persevered, attempting to do good in the world, and from all walks of life he received admiration. Nelson's letter "From an Alabama Farmer" emphasizes how Carver changed lives.

Nelson draws attention to the working relationship that Carver had with Booker T. Washington, who hired Carver at the Tuskegee Institute. Although not all of Carver's endeavors were successful at Tuskegee—his work with the poultry farm, for example—he became well known for his use of the peanut and became spoken of in the same breath as Washington. Carver was so upset when Washington died that people said he appeared to lose faith in his ambitions. But Carver never did lose his faith, and Marilyn Nelson stresses the importance of Carver's legacy by linking Carver with her own father, one of the Tuskegee Airmen, a story of faith in a different sense. Adcock writes that "the poem [about Nelson's father] is a touching and powerful ending for his story of struggle and faith, failure and triumph. Nelson brings us Carver's life with careful research, craftsmanship, and her characteristic affirmative humor, along with the serious appreciation such a life deserves. Young people should know this story. So should the rest of us." Nelson's "sky-roaring victory roll" (p. 96) speaks to the triumph inherent in Carver's steady, awe-inspiring achievements. Through his belief in God and in himself, he taught people to fly.

Fortune's Bones: The Manumission Requiem (2004), is another biography told in poems. Fortune was a slave whose identity had been mistaken for that of a Revolutionary war figure—and whose skeleton was affectionately spoken of as Larry—and this volume is a way for Nelson to reclaim history and to make young people aware of its importance. As a Connecticut resident, she used the poem as a way to reframe Connecticut history, specifically in the town of Waterbury.

The book is an homage to Fortune, whose bones, rather than being buried, were boiled and used as a medical model by his owner, Dr. Preserved Porter. It received the 2005 Lion and the Unicorn Award for Excellence in Poetry. The book was selected because, said the judges, the poems it presents "are perfect for reading aloud and profoundly moving. ... The language is textured, the poems are formally compelling, and

the content is politically, historically, and socially relevant. It's accessible to the engaged child reader without being condescending; and, external to the poetry, the book is wonderful to handle. Simply put, it's an excellent book of poetry" (p. 427). The collection was praised for its musicality; Nelson in her author's note says that "I'm setting grief side by side with joy. I'm trying to imitate a traditional New Orleans brass band jazz funeral. ... What was a dirge for the dead becomes a celebration of life" (p. 9). The book was also bestowed with a Coretta Scott King Honor.

David Mason found the book difficult to categorize, given that it was a children's book, but he also found the book praiseworthy for adult readers. Mason finally settled on calling it an "illustrated libretto," since the book has been set to music. Ultimately he calls the collection a "strangely powerful little book, more suggestive of outrage than voluable about it." Saying that he was tempted at first to compare the book with *Carver: A Life in Poems,* he finds a more suitable comparison in *The Homeplace,* and it is true that Nelson's concerns pervade her poems rather than being compartmentalized. Yet ultimately the issue is not the body of the poem but its spirit, as it is for Fortune. As Theodore Rosengarten writes in the *New York Times,* "By elevating him from a curiosity to the subject of a frighteningly honest work of art, Marilyn Nelson endows Fortune with life both in and out of time, releasing him from the shackles of his master's intentions."

The poem that serves as "Preface" takes up the theme of cost on a range of levels that Fortune bore as a slave: emotional, physical, and literal costs. It is his bones that bear the burden finally, and they need to be reclaimed and renamed. As she does in *Carver: A Life in Poems,* Nelson uses a multiplicity of voices to shed light on the life of her poem's subject. One particularly moving poem is from the perspective of Fortune's wife, Dinah, who is given the task of dusting his bones. In "Dinah's Lament," this grim duty gains poignancy. Dinah is lonely, with only the bones of her husband for comfort.

By contrast, Dr. Porter sees Fortune's bones as an opportunity to learn. After dismantling the body of Fortune, Porter boils him and later labels the bones with their anatomical names. While Porter acknowledges in "On Abrigador Hill" that the bones of his former slave will now serves the advancement, he has a sense of worshipfulness about the bones that is ironic, and also somewhat sexual. Both Dinah and Dr. Porter speak of a bones in terms of marriage; yet, while Dinah sees Fortune's identity in the bones, Dr. Porter sees Fortune's service extended through the marriage of the mind to the discoveries of science. In other words, Dinah sees Fortune as a person while Dr. Porter uses the metaphor of a person. Flynn, Hager, and Thomas go further, saying that Dr. Porter "describes his dissection of Fortune, with utter disregard for Fortune's humanity."

After Nelson uses a range of voices to speak about perspectives on Fortune's bones, Fortune himself speaks. In "Not My Bones," he distinguishes between his identity and his physical form, what remains of his body. When he dies, he gains freedom. Although the debate continues as to whether Fortune's bones should be buried to honor him as a person or whether they should be displayed in the museum, so as to honor his place in history, Nelson ends the book with a sense of community and religiosity through her poem "Sanctus."

In *A Wreath for Emmett Till* (2005), Nelson prefaces her sonnet magistrale, or heroic crown of sonnets, with a note about what inspired her to write the poem. She took as a challenge writing a poem about the 1955 lynching of the teenage Emmett Till for people of Till's same age group. She also decided to write this poem in a structured form, the sonnet, which is often used for love, and it is her love poem for Emmett Till. Nelson, who in her dedication says that she wrote the book "for innocence murdered. For innocence alive," said of the experience, "I wrote this poem with my heart in my mouth and tears in my eyes, breathless with anticipation and surprise." For those unfamiliar with the case, she gives a brief narrative at the end of the book. In short, Emmett Till at fourteen years old—he had left Chicago and was visiting family in the South—was accused of making a sexually motivated gesture at a white woman: whistling. He was later found dead—having been tortured, shot, and

thrown into a river. During his funeral, his casket was open for viewing, so that people could see the results of racism. Those accused of lynching him were found innocent, and his violent death galvanized people to demand their civil rights.

The discussion surrounding this book, which won both a Coretta Scott King Honor and a Michael L. Printz Award for Excellence in Young Adult Writing, centered around two issues—history and poetic form, particularly with regard to the young adult audience. R. S. Gwynn writes in the *Hudson Review* that "read strictly as poetry, Nelson's new poem is a stunning success. ... But read as history, *A Wreath for Emmett Till* raises more questions than it answers, leading me to quibble with Nelson's approach to her subject and to her intended audience" (p. 675). Gwynn cites information from the *Chicago Tribune* newspaper and the television news program *60 Minutes* to suggest that, while Nelson does base her poem on fact, she poeticizes and mythologizes, linking Till's case with other more heinous crimes (p. 676). He wonders if her audience will connect with "an iconic Till," musing that "Nelson may have missed an even greater opportunity to honor his memory by defending Bobo Till's right to be exactly who he was" (p. 677). Responding with a letter to the *Hudson Review,* Nelson took issue with Gwynn's assessment, saying that "lacking the gift of clairvoyance, I was not able to include information published after my poem was written, or after the book was published. And anyway, I don't see why anyone should care whether my poem attributes the lynching to a gang of five, or eight, or twelve" (p. 182). She found Gwynn's parsing the difference between lynching and "d[ying] at the hands of racists for a social indiscretion" disingenuous (p. 182). In terms of the difficulty of the book, Nelson writes that "the young adult designation is a marketing decision, not a choice to trivialize or condescend, and certainly not a decision to write easy poetry with which 'today's youth' can thoughtlessly 'connect.' They have video games for that" (p. 183).

Ironically, the book, in being cited as an honor book for the 2006 *Lion and Unicorn* Award for Excellence in North American Poetry, an award given for children's poetry, was criticized not for its poetry, but for its illustrations. The judges found it "supremely condescending to think that young people need to be spared the actual images" and said they would have preferred instead the documentary style approach of real photographs, not "garish and busy" drawings.

The first line of each of the book's first fourteen Petrarchan sonnets is repeated in the last, and fifteenth sonnet, and also forms an acrostic: "RIP EMMETT L. TILL." The poem addresses its own purpose, its meaning to the author, and its role in documenting history. For example, in the first sonnet, the speaker asks, "What should my wreath for Emmett Till denote?" In this questioning, the author also plays on words, where the word "wreath" means both the sonnets (also called a crown) and a wreath on the grave of Emmett Till. In the next two stanzas she uses a tree, as long-living natural entity, to be the witness for Till's lynching. There are seasons that trees bear in their rings, as well as seasons of violence. In sonnet 4, Nelson addresses the irony of Till's stutter being misinterpreted as a whistle, and she uses this sonnet as well as the next to show his mother's good intentions in sending him off to relatives, then mourning the horror of his death. In sonnet 5 Nelson compares the boy's mother to Mary, the mother of Christ, and wonders if, faced with the choice of her role in history, she would have chosen it:

> If sudden loving light proclaimed you blest
> would you bow your head in humility,
> your healed heart overflow in gratitude?
> Would you say yes, like the mother of Christ?
> Or would you say no to your destiny,
> mother of a boy martyr, if you could?

The speaker herself says that she would save him, and fantasizes about how that could be done. In stanza 6, she says, "I'd put you in a parallel universe, / give you a better fate. There is none worse." She does not want his memory to be forgotten, and so in stanza 7, she marks it: "Let America remember what he taught." If he has to die, she would prefer an acknowledged heroic death, like that of a firefighter dying on September 11th. The next two sonnets attempt to move the horrors of history to the world of fantasy. She

wants flowers for his memory and chooses "wildflowers" in stanza 10, saying, "I cling to the faith / that innocence lives on, that a blind soul / can see again. That miracles do exist." While stanza 11 acknowledges the complicated history of America, stanza 12 finds its bloody history reflected in flowers. The next two stanzas gather up the themes and players of the poem—from the wildflowers to America itself—and gather up readers to join this cast and "bear witness to atrocity." By working through all of these phases of the poem—from questioning, to horror, to acknowledgement, to acceptance—Nelson can allow Till to "rest in peace" and she can rest too.

Nelson's 2007 book, *Miss Crandall's School for Young Ladies & Little Misses of Color,* continues her work on honoring African American history and Connecticut history and, appropriately enough, given the topic of the book, returns to collaboration. Nelson's partner in this venture was Elizabeth Alexander, a Pulitzer Prize finalist in poetry, an essayist, and a professor of African American history at Yale. The two alternated sonnets in this tribute to the white Quaker schoolteacher Prudence Crandall (1803–1890), who risked her life so that African American girls would have an education. In their authors' notes, the two poets explain that they chose the sonnet form both because it is traditionally about love and because there is a rich African American tradition surrounding the sonnet, with such famous practitioners as Countee Cullen (1903–1946) and Gwendolyn Brooks (1917–2000) (p. 46). The book is ultimately about community—in both its positive and negative forms. Crandall and the girls form their own community, while the town of Canterbury, Connecticut, uses every means possible—from intimidation, to poisoning, to fire—to shut down the school.

In the introduction to the volume, Alexander and Nelson describe how the townspeople of Canterbury were, at first, excited to have Crandall as a schoolteacher in their town. As a Quaker, Crandall believed in the power of education and in the equality of all humankind. These tenets were fine, while the students were all white. But, when Crandall accepted her first African American student, the situation changed dramatically. Twenty-four African American girls took up the call to gain a first-rate education, but the community at large rebelled, finally driving Crandall and her students away. In 1984, when the school became a museum, the Ku Klux Klan protested its existence. Yet, as Alexander and Nelson write, the school "remains a place where anyone can discover the story of Prudence Crandall and a group of courageous young women ... together braved extreme resistance for the simple, just wish to teach and to learn" (p. 8).

Typically paired throughout the volume, the sonnets by the two poets are signed with the initials of each author, since they don't necessarily fall in the same order each time. Nelson's tend to be more strictly formal; Alexander's are a more conversational "take" on the form. Each pairing emphasizes the same theme. For example, the first two sonnets focus on the importance of knowledge. While Nelson's emphasizes book knowledge, Alexander's emphasizes life knowledge. Thus, while the two are in conversation with the subject matter and with the voices in the poems, they are also in conversation with each other. The book traces not only the development of the girls as students and individuals, but the development of community anger, Crandall and the girls' resilience, and the final disbandment of the school.

One particularly interesting juxtaposition is the sonnet "We," by Alexander, with "All-Night Melodies," by Nelson. The first emphasizes the townspeople's devilish expectations of the African American students, through the point of view of the girls. By contrast, Miss Crandall and the school community have a gentle, prayerful space. The moods of the poems shift as the dynamics in the outside and inside communities shift. While in "Etymology," Nelson emphasizes the outside, Alexander emphasizes the inside. This strategy, both for theme and reflection, provides an effective dialogue throughout the volume.

At the end of the book, though, the two poets write two pairs of poems. Because the schoolhouse is set ablaze, fire is an important motif in the poem. Nelson juxtaposes her poem "Open Secret," about the power of love, against another

of her poems, "Arson at Midnight," about the power of hate. Alexander's poems, with their emphasis on works, show the struggle to bring about justice. Crandall married and moved away after being forced to close her school, but she never forgot her brave students. Nelson and Alexander want to make sure that others do not forget this courageous schoolhouse community.

THE FREEDOM BUSINESS

In continuing her theme of witness and remembrance, Marilyn Nelson's 2008 venture, *The Freedom Business,* is literally the story of Venture Smith, who was "the first man to document both his capture from Africa and life as an American slave" (front cover). Nelson intersperses poems in a range of forms—whose versatility mirrors Venture Smith's own amazing adaptability to circumstances—with Venture's own narrative, published in 1798. The side-by-side presentation, with Venture's slave narrative on the left side and Nelson's poetic take on the right, serves as a counterpoint of voices, a collaboration that speaks across the span of years. This historical collaboration is underscored by Deborah Muirhead's impressionistic artwork. As Muirhead writes, "In creating art work for *The Freedom Business,* my main goal was not to illustrate the narrative or the poems but to create images that continue on the path of reawakening this eighteenth-century story" (p. 71). In this "reawakening," the three artists illuminate the issue of cost, in both monetary and human terms.

The book traces Venture Smith's story from his childhood in Africa to the end of this life in the United States, after he has freed himself and has family and has amassed a fortune in land and other holdings. Notable in his narrative is a matter-of-factness about his circumstances, whether they are unfair or not. In his unflinching acceptance, he is reminiscent of another of Nelson's subjects, George Washington Carver. In a modest and direct way, he shows us his view of the situation, and thus Nelson's first poem, "Witness," is the thematic key to the whole book. While the poem specifically expounds upon Venture's heritage, it provides a frame for the quiet nobility that underscores the volume.

While throughout her *oeuvre* Nelson shows her skill as a practitioner of varied forms, this volume, perhaps, shows her greatest range. This experimentation is illustrated in a range of ways. She plays with spacing in the sonnet; she writes conversational sestinas; and she writes direct and powerful free verse. She even includes an imitation of Robert Frost. This stylistic playfulness, while emphasizing the difficult odds of Venture's life, is used to underscore the human capacity for inventiveness in the midst of restriction. At the same time, while hope is the ultimate message of the book, Nelson can use "her side"—both the literal page and her position from a later vantage point in history—to underscore the cruelty of slavery, when Venture takes it simply as the set of circumstances with which he is faced. In "Pestilence," for example, while Nelson takes his point of view, it is clear that she finds Venture's spiritual capacity for metamorphosis remarkable.

It is ironic that Venture Smith, whose true name was Broteer Furro, finds in his new name the clue to his own survival, his entrepreneurial nature, and that, while his name is stolen from him, he takes the name *Venture* to another level, by owning it and himself. In the poem "Farm Garden" Nelson emphasizes Venture Smith's achievement. As Nelson writes in the preface, "I hope our words will speak to you and fill you with the courage needed to hold faith, as Venture Smith did, in our common humanity, and to stand with him against the forces of spiritual blindness and cruelty." In this statement, she invites the reader both to read Venture Smith's story and take on his courage, difficult in any time period. By the end of the book, just like Venture's holdings, they hold even more value.

ASSESSMENT

Marilyn Nelson has claimed a place for herself since the 1970s as one of the most important voices and one of the most skilled practitioners of the new formalist movement. In addition, she has brought a playfulness and a prayerfulness to contemporary poetry, by enjoying the wit of

wordplay and by acknowledging painful histories, both personal and public, that had hitherto not been given a place in the canon. She has also physically given a place to writers of color through Soul Mountain and has been a public voice through her role as the Connecticut poet laureate. There is about Marilyn Nelson both the workaday bravery of one of the girls going to Prudence Crandall's school and the sense of joyfulness that comes from George Washington Carver's discoveries. If she is not literally flying, she has certainly taken on her mother's love of history and her father's wings. As Nelson said when receiving the Lifetime Achievement Award from the Connecticut Center for the Book, "Poets are dreamers and live in the imagination. ... It's odd to be honored for being blessed" (Goldberg). Ultimately she provides the vehicle for the twenty-four girls attending Prudence Crandall's school to walk up Halfdan Rasmussen's ladder, into the sky. Marilyn Nelson shows in both her philosophy and her words the power of collaboration.

Selected Bibliography

WORKS OF MARILYN NELSON

POETRY

For the Body. Baton Rouge: Louisiana State University Press, 1978.

The Cat Walked Through the Casserole: And Other Poems for Children. With Pamela Espeland. Minneapolis: Carolrhoda Books, 1984.

Mama's Promises. Baton Rouge: Louisiana State University, 1985.

The Homeplace. Baton Rouge: Louisiana State University Press, 1990.

Partial Truth. Willington, Conn.: Kutenai Press, 1992.

Magnificat. Baton Rouge: Louisiana State University Press, 1994.

The Fields of Praise: New and Selected Poems. Baton Rouge: Louisiana State University Press, 1997.

Carver: A Life in Poems. Ashville, N.C.: Front Street, 2001.

She-Devil Circus. West Chester, Pa.: Aralia, 2001.

Triolets for Triolet. Willimantic, Conn.: Curbstone Press, 2001.

Fortune's Bones: The Manumission Requiem. Ashville, N.C.: Front Street, 2004.

The Cachoeira Tales and Other Poems. Baton Rouge: Louisiana State University Press, 2005.

A Wreath for Emmett Till. Boston: Houghton Mifflin, 2005.

Miss Crandall's School for Young Ladies & Little Misses of Color. With Elizabeth Alexander. Honesdale, Pa.: Wordsong, 2007.

The Freedom Business. Honesdale, PA: Wordsong, 2008.

ESSAYS, REVIEWS, UNCOLLECTED ARTICLES, AND OTHER WORK

"The Schizoid Implied Authors of Two Jewish-American Novels." *MELUS 7,* no. 1: 21–38 (1980).

"Comments/Questions." *MELUS 8,* no. 3: 3–4 (1981).

"Review: Black Silence, Black Songs." *Callaloo* 17: 156–163 (1983).

"A Black Rainbow: Modern Afro-American Poetry." With Rita Dove. In *Poetry After Modernism.* Edited by Robert McDowell. Ashland, Ore.: Story Line, 1990. Pp. 217–275.

"The Gender of Grace." *Southern Review* 27: 405–419 (1993).

"Marilyn Nelson." In *Contemporary Authors: Autobiography Series.* Vol. 23. Edited by Shelly Andrew. Detroit: Gale, 1996. Pp. 247–267.

"Owning the Masters." In *After New Formalism: Poets on Form, Narrative, and Tradition.* Edited by Annie Finch. Ashland, Ore.: Story Line Press, 1999. Pp. 8–17.

"Sense of Discovery." In *New Expansive Poetry: Theory, Criticism, History.* Edited by R. S. Gwynn. Ashland, Ore.: Story Line Press, 1999. p. 181.

"Aborigine in the Citadel." *Hudson Review* 11: 543–553 (2001).

"Abracadabra, Alakazam, Pax, Salaam, Shalom, Amen." *Horn Book Magazine* 78: 41–46 (2002).

"Letter to the Editor." *Hudson Review* 59, no. 2: 182–183 (2006). (Response to a review of *A Wreath for Emmett Till.* Printed with "R. S. Gwynn Replies.")

The Thirteenth Month. Introduction with twelve poems in the original Danish by Inge Pedersen and twelve translations by Marilyn Nelson. *Scandinavian Review* 93, no. 3: 15+ (2006).

VOLUMES EDITED AND TRANSLATED BY NELSON

Literary Sex Roles, by Pil Dahlerup. Translated from the Danish. Minneapolis: Minnesota Women in Higher Education, 1975.

Hundreds of Hens and Other Poems for Children, by Halfdan Rasmussen. Translated from the Danish, with Pamela Espeland. Minneapolis: Black Willow Press, 1982.

"Hecuba" in *Euripides, 1: Medea, Hecuba, Andromache, The Bacchae,* edited by David R. Slavitt and Palmer

Bovie. Translated from the Greek. Philadelphia: University of Pennsylvania Press, 1998.

Rumors of Troy: Poems Inspired by "The Iliad." Edited by Nelson. Boston: Longman, 2001.

The Thirteenth Month, by Inge Pedersen. Translated from the Danish. Oberlin, Ohio: Oberlin College Press, 2005.

The Ladder, by Halfdan Rasmussen. Translated from the Danish. Cambridge, Mass.: Candlewick Press, 2006.

CRITICAL AND BIOGRAPHICAL STUDIES

Adcock, Betty. "Getting Serious." *Southern Review* 39, no. 3:650 (2003). (Review of *Carver: A Life in Poems.*)

Ellis, Thomas Sayers. "An Excerpt from Quotes Community: Notes for Black Poets." *Callaloo* 27, no. 3:631–645 (summer 2004).

Flynn, Richard, Kelly Hager, and Joseph Thomas. "It Could Be Verse: The 2005 *Lion and Unicorn* Award for Excellence in Poetry." *The Lion and the Unicorn.* 29.3:427+.

Galbus, Julia A. Review of *M-a-c-n-o-l-i-a,* by A. Van Jordan. *African American Review* 40, no. 3:595–596 (2006).

Goldberg, Carole. "Poet's 'Blessed' Life Honored at Connecticut Book Awards." *HartfordInfo.org* (http://www.hartfordinfo.org/issues/documents/artsandculture/htfd_courant_120406.asp), 4 December 2006.

Griffith, Paul. "Marilyn Nelson." In *Dictionary of Literary Biography.* Vol. 282, *New Formalist Poets.* Edited by Jonathan Barron and Bruce Meyer. Detroit: Gale, 2003. Pp. 233–240.

Gwynn, R. S. "Histories and Mysteries." Review of *A Wreath for Emmett Till. The Hudson Review* 58, no. 4:675–677 (2006).

Hacker, Marilyn. "Double Vision." *Women's Review of Books* 15, no. 8:17–18 (1998). (Review of *The Fields of Praise: New and Selected Poems.*)

Jones, Kirkland C. "Marilyn Nelson Waniek." In *Dictionary of Literary Biography.* Vol. 120, *American Poets Since World War II, Third Series.* Edited by R. S. Gwynn. Detroit: Gale, 1992. Pp. 311–315.

"Marilyn Nelson." In *Contemporary Authors Online.* Detroit: Gale, 2007.

Martin, Herbert Woodward. Review of *Carver: A Life in Poems. African American Review,* 36, no. 2:345–349 (summer 2002).

Mason, David. "The Passionate Pursuit of the Real." *Hudson Review* 58, no. 2:319+ (summer 2005). (Review of *Fortune's Bones: The Manumission Requiem.*)

———. "Stories and Lines." *Hudson Review* 55, no. 4:671+ (winter 2003). (Review of *Carver: A Life in Poems.*)

Rosengarten, Theodore. "'A Dream of Freedom' and 'Fortune's Bones': American in Black and White." *New York Times* (www.nytimes.com/2004/11/14/books/review/14ROSENGA.html), 14 November 2004.

Thomas, Joseph T., Jr., JonArno Lawson, and Richard Flynn. "'It Don't Mean a Thing (If It Ain't Got That Swing)': The 2006 *Lion and the Unicorn* Award for Excellence in North American Poetry." *Lion and the Unicorn* 30, no. 3:383–397 (2006).

Tracy, D. H. Review of *The Cachoeira Tales and Other Poems. Poetry* 188, no. 2:164–166 (May 2006).

Ullman, Leslie. "Solitaries and Storytellers, Magicians and Pagans: Five Poets in the World." *Kenyon Review* 13, no. 2:179–193 (spring 1991). (Review of *The Homeplace.*)

Walzer, Kevin. "Bold Colors: Jarman, Nelson, Peacock, Turner." In his *The Ghost of Tradition: Expansive Poetry and Postmodernism.* Ashland, Ore.: Story Line, 1998. Pp. 85–121.

Weaver, Michael S. Review of *Magnificat. African American Review* 30, no. 3:504–506 (1996).

Wilbur, Richard. As quoted in "Richard Wilbur." In *The Norton Anthology of Modern Poetry.* Eds. Richard Ellmann and Robert O'Clair. New York: Norton, 1988. Pp. 1030–32.

Williams, Miller. Review of *Fields of Praise: New and Selected Poems. African American Review* 33, no. 1:179–181 (1999).

Wiman, Christian. "An Idea of Order." *Poetry* 173, no. 3:241–253 (1999).

JANISSE RAY

(1962—)

Joan Wylie Hall

JANISSE RAY CELEBRATES the wildness of nature and pleads for the preservation of the landscape in three books of literary nonfiction and in scores of poems and essays. Reviewers compared her award-winning memoir *Ecology of a Cracker Childhood* (1999) to such naturalist classics as Rachel Carson's *Silent Spring,* Annie Dillard's *Pilgrim at Tinker Creek,* and even Henry David Thoreau's *Walden.* Ray has lectured on environmental issues in many settings, from small-town libraries and university writers' workshops to conferences of the Nature Conservancy. Audiences describe these presentations as intense, compelling, and personal. Although Ray has spent several years in Montana and Vermont, the South is the homeland to which she always returns. The title of her essay "On the Bosom of This Grave and Wasted Land I Will Lay My Head" reflects her affection for the ravaged terrain of the South, the place of her birth and the inspiration for her career as a writer and an activist.

Ray refers to many American naturalists and nature authors in her work, from John James Audubon to Kathleen Norris and Rick Bass. Although the genre was long dominated by men (Thoreau, William Bartram, John Burroughs, John Muir, Ernest Thompson Seton, and Aldo Leopold, for example), Ray is one of many contemporary female literary naturalists. In a variety of forms, Pattiann Rogers, Terry Tempest Williams, Barbara Kingsolver, Louise Erdrich, Joy Harjo, Gretel Ehrlich, Linda Hogan, and many other women record their closeness to the land. Lorraine Anderson, editor of *Sisters of the Earth: Women's Prose and Poetry About Nature* (1991), concludes in her preface to that volume that "there is no such thing as a woman's view of nature"; but she describes a "feminine way of being in relationship to nature" that is more characteristic of women than of men in Western civilization. "This way is caring rather than controlling; it seeks harmony rather than mastery; it is characterized by humility rather than arrogance, by appreciation rather than acquisitiveness," says Anderson. Ray's *Ecology of a Cracker Childhood, Wild Card Quilt: Taking a Chance on Home* (2003), and *Pinhook: Finding Wholeness in a Fragmented Land* (2005) all reflect these positive qualities. At the same time, the three volumes record an environmental activism that increasingly draws the author from the role of domestic southern daughter that her parents, especially her father, had envisioned for her.

BIOGRAPHY

Janisse Ray was born in Baxley, seat of Appling County, Georgia, on February 2, 1962, to Franklin Delano Ray, Sr., and Lee Ada Branch Ray. The spelling of her unusual first name comes from a nurse's error on her birth certificate. Ray's namesakes were her twin cousins Janet and Janice, whom her sister Kay called "the two Janneices." In "Child of Pine," the opening chapter of *Ecology of a Cracker Childhood,* Ray describes the creation stories her parents invented for each of their four children. Kay, the oldest, was discovered in the garden in a cabbage; the youngest two, Franklin ("Dell") Delano, Jr., and Steve, were found under a grapevine and next to a huckleberry bush. Her mother and father said they were looking for a missing ewe when they came upon Janisse, the second child, crying in a palmetto clump under a pine tree. Winter was "half undone" on that dark Candlemas evening, the sort of night the pipes could freeze, "and if the fig tree wasn't covered with quilts, it would

be knocked back to the ground." So vivid is her retelling of the event that readers are quickly drawn into the family myth.

Janisse was delighted by her father's whimsy and his powerful storytelling, but Frank Ray's junkyard business embarrassed the young Rays. After she read the work of the anthropologist Claude Levi-Strauss years later, she recognized her father in the definition of a *bricoleur,* the term for a folk genius who turns castoffs to new use, even to art. "Daddy's was an amazing triad of traits—frugality, creativity, and mechanical ingenuity—so that as I grew," says Ray, "our estate grew. Junk bred junk." Frank Ray was a high school dropout, but he learned mathematics from his grandfather as a young surveyor and attended business school in Baxley. A lover of knowledge, he read encyclopedias at night and gave coins to his children for answering the scientific and historical questions with which he quizzed them daily.

Ray came to realize that "His game is understanding and order, two things denied him early on" by her grandfather Charlie Joe Ray, nicknamed "Iron Man." Hospitalized in Milledgeville for what was probably bipolar disorder, Charlie Ray escaped from the state mental hospital and paid erratic visits home to his wife and eight children. Janisse's grandmother Clyo Ray, "strong-willed and independent," was working at a Baxley café to support the family when she finally told her abusive husband to leave. Grandpa Charlie fled to Florida, leaving Granny Ray as a single parent. When his son Frank was eighteen, the restless Charlie Ray suggested that they establish a wrecking yard in Baxley, and the younger man displayed an unusual talent for buying and selling. The partnership was short lived, but the son bought his father's share of the business. "Salvaging completely suited him," says Ray.

Frank Ray's drive to fix things extended to the family's spiritual life. When the children were small, he started a church, but because he had received no divine call to preach, he found a more satisfying religious home in the Apostolic Church. For years, he took his family to distant services held by African American congregations, an experience that was extremely unusual for rural southern whites in the 1960s and early 1970s. "We had been taught that the color of a person's skin was not a measure of his or her heart, but in church we stuck out like sore thumbs," says Janisse Ray. Restricted by her fundamentalist parents from watching television, inviting friends to visit, cutting her hair, wearing makeup, participating in sports, or dressing immodestly, Janisse felt different from her classmates and spent hours playing in the junkyard with her siblings. In their imagination, abandoned cars became schoolrooms and obstacle courses. Although she was an excellent and attentive student, in the rusting vehicles she mimicked "our worst teachers, saying things we dared not say in real school." And risky leaps from the hood of one junked car to another were "good practice for my life."

Because Lee Ada Ray so capably mended the children's injuries from shattered glass and sharp metal, Janisse was deeply frightened when her mother failed to heal her husband Frank during the most traumatic event of the author's childhood. Like Grandpa Charlie, Frank Ray fell victim to serious mental illness. The onslaught was sudden and mysterious, and the result was a three-year period of frequent hospitalizations in Milledgeville. Not only her father's sickness, but religion, too, became a source of terror to the sensitive child. "When I was growing up," she says, "the world about me was subverted by the world of the soul, the promise of a future after death." Haunted by her small lies and minor acts of disobedience, she was afraid to fall asleep at night, worried she might die in a state of sin. "For me, the chance to be simply a young mammal roaming the woods did not exist."

Yet nature became her source of wonder and solace, beginning with a 4-H project when Janisse was in fifth grade. "I attribute the opening of my heart to one clump of pitcher plants that still survives on the backside of my father's junkyard," says Ray. The plant taught her to love rain and to hate artificial flowers; from the "columns of dead insects" in its stem, she learned "the glory of purpose no matter how small." Her club project turned into a personal search for a "*man-*

era de ser, a way of being—no, not for a way of being but of being able to be. I was looking for a patch of ground that supported the survival of rare, precious, and endangered biota within my own heart." Beside the junkyard that she operated with her husband, Janisse's hardworking mother kept a garden; but Frank Ray had no interest in hiking, fishing, hunting, or other interactions with the nearby woods and fields. It was Lucia Godfrey, Janisse's fifth- and sixth-grade science teacher, who encouraged her to look closely at nature and to study its vital lessons: "Evolve. Adapt. Survive." Ray recalls that she sat in the front row of Mrs. Godfrey's class, absorbing her words "as if this knowledge might deliver all of us from pain."

On her Grandpa Charlie's occasional visits home, he taught Janisse to fish, and he once led her and her siblings to his secret spot in the woods where huckleberries grew. Ray describes a long walk "through air inundated with the long-summer smell of pine, alcoholic and comforting, until we came to a gabble of shrubs thick with purple berries." The remarkable scene remains for her a vision of "plenitude" and a "mythic terra incognita." Orphaned at fourteen, Charlie knew the wilderness like no one else, according to Ray. Trees and wetlands were the refuge to which he turned "for safety and comfort and for shelter and food." She has always regretted that he never shared his keen understanding with her and with her father, "fenced as it was by Grandpa's anguish." Between the two men, she says, "the thread of nature" was somehow lost. Janisse Ray left home at age eighteen to seek and to mend the broken thread.

As a teenager, Ray openly questioned her parents' religious fundamentalism and their daily attempts to regulate her dress, her books, and her behavior. At North Georgia College in Dahlonega, a mountain town near the Chattahoochee National Forest, she was initially "tortured by my lack of experience and by my newness." But her two years in the Appalachian foothills, six hours from Baxley, provided "a stepping-stone into myself." Ray says she "dived recklessly and surely into the world" as a freshman, "not because it was a form of rebellion, as people might think, but as a form of healing and survival." By working in the school cafeteria, she supplemented her tuition scholarship and maintained financial independence. Because North Georgia College required military training of all male students, regulations were strict, though not nearly as rigid as the rules of the Ray household. Aiming to fit in with the other coeds, Janisse was an intramurals cheerleader and attended Mardi Gras. "I always wound up with the wild crowd, the liquor drinkers and risk takers. It was what I had to do," she writes in the "Leaving" chapter of *Ecology of a Cracker Childhood.* She went night-rappelling and skydiving, camped and collected specimens with a feminist friend for field botany class, learned to swim and to fiddle. Her father wanted her to become a teacher, but the book-loving Ray knew she wanted to write instead.

Determined to learn "life" in addition to the usual academic offerings, Ray says she "researched beekeeping, chickens and goats, organic gardening, homesteading in Alaska, the peace corps, recycling." James Dickey's visit to campus was a highlight of her time in Dahlonega. Ray persuaded him to accept a modest honorarium, and more than a thousand people attended the reading by the author of *Deliverance,* a best-selling novel (adapted for film) about a canoe trip that turns violent in rural Georgia. The next morning, Ray and her friends hiked in the wilderness with the poet. "He talked to the locals we met like a starving man, old men and women fishing the creek with corn kernels," she says, "and all day he seemed happy." In her memoir, Ray quotes from Dickey's "Cherrylog Road," a poem set in a southern junkyard reminiscent of her father's.

After two years at North Georgia College, Ray transferred to the urban and much larger Florida State University, where she majored in creative writing and graduated in 1984. Interviewed by the *New York Times* book reviewer Anne Raver on the publication of *Ecology of a Cracker Childhood,* Ray described her attraction to Tallahassee's "hippie culture." She designed and built her own small house in the country from recycled windows and telephone poles.

After the dissolution of her marriage to a woodworker, Ray lived in the tin-roofed home with her small son, Silas Ausable. Ray's father had disowned her in her early twenties, but Silas's birth increased her parents' tolerance of her unconventional ways and ended their three-year refusal to communicate with her. Struggling to support herself and her child while writing, Ray kept a large garden, did farmwork, and washed her clothes in a nearby stream. Yet, Ray was also composing poetry and studying under Wendell Berry, a naturalist and author whose work was very familiar to her. In the acknowledgments for *Wild Card Quilt,* Ray pays her mentor high praise, remarking that she "was blessed to discover Wendell Berry's books when I was not yet grown, and his great thinking and sound character have inspired and guided me every day on this earth: I owe him an unsayable debt." When Silas was still a toddler, Ray traveled to South America with him to teach English. In an interview with Sidney I. Dobrin and Christopher J. Keller, Ray said that during her time in the Andes she realized that she had to combine her dedication to writing with her love of nature in an "overarching attempt to find wholeness."

Ray moved to Missoula, Montana, to enroll in graduate school and in 1997 completed the MFA degree in Creative Writing at the University of Montana. Her poems and essays had already appeared in many publications, ranging from *Midwifery Today* and *Florida Wildlife* to *Orion* and the *Katuah Journal.* Ray's poetry chapbook, *Naming the Unseen* (1996), won the University of Montana's Merriam-Frontier Award, honoring H. G. Merriam, a longtime professor, and the journal he founded. *Frontier,* produced at the university from 1920 to 1939, was notable for printing early work by young authors, including the environmentalist Wallace Stegner. Themes and images from Ray's chapbook reappear in the memoir *Ecology of a Cracker Childhood,* which she began in Montana and completed after she returned to Baxley, Georgia, in the summer of 1997. Winner of the American Book Award, the Southeastern Booksellers Association Book Award for Nonfiction, and other honors, this is her best-known volume. The book was widely reviewed; and many nature writers, including Wendell Berry, Bill McKibben, and Jim Kilgo, praised the skillful alternation of family history with the history of Georgia's longleaf pines.

Wild Card Quilt likewise integrates events of the author's home life with her growth as a naturalist. This second memoir, however, also reflects Ray's increasing activism on behalf of endangered species. Near the end of *Ecology of a Cracker Childhood,* she says she first heard the word "environmentalism" as a new student at North Georgia College. By the time she published *Wild Card Quilt,* she was involved in Altamaha Riverkeeper, as a founding board member; the Nature Conservancy of Georgia; POGO (Pinhook Swamp, Osceola National Forest, Greater Okefenokee) Coalition; and other organizations committed to saving regional ecosystems. Several chapters of *Wild Card Quilt* portray Ray's efforts to preserve nearby Moody Forest from destruction, but her action in south Georgia was not confined to nature. As the mother of a nine-year-old, she also struggled to save a small local elementary school and to help her son adjust to a radically different culture than the one he knew in Montana. On many fronts, including race relations, Ray was dedicated to recovering a sense of community in Baxley.

Although she continued to write in the first person in *Pinhook: Finding Wholeness in a Fragmented Land,* this third nonfiction volume is not so much a memoir as a record of the struggle to preserve a wild, mysterious corridor near the Georgia-Florida border. Ray began the book in Sitka, Alaska, during a writing residency at the Island Institute in April 2003. She completed the work while teaching at the University of Mississippi as the 2003–2004 John and Renée Grisham Visiting Writer-in-Residence, the first nonfiction author to hold an award typically made to fiction writers. Ray was joined in Oxford, Mississippi, by her husband Raven Burchard, a political activist whom she met at the Florida Folk Festival in 2001. In 2004 the couple moved to Brattleboro, Vermont, to be close to Silas while he attended high school in the town where his father lives. Both in Mississippi and Vermont, Ray and Burchard (who changed his legal name to Waters)

continued their social activism and their support of the local economy. They planted gardens and bought food from area farmers; wrote letters and guest columns in local papers; demonstrated against racial prejudice and the war in Iraq; participated in nearby academic and cultural communities; bought a hybrid vehicle but walked and bicycled as much as possible. Ray was a public radio commentator in Vermont, as she has been in Georgia. Unity College in Maine awarded her an honorary doctorate in 2007.

In January 2008 Ray and Waters returned to Baxley. Although Ray has conducted workshops, taught college classes, lectured, and read her work throughout the country, she is now reluctant to add to the depletion of fuel resources by flying to such events. She is pursuing new means of activism, including filmmaking and weekly columns on the environment for Georgia newspapers. In 2007 she established Wildfire, a small press for southern nature writing; one of her first projects was an anthology of local narratives on Moody Forest, the wilderness Ray describes in *Wild Card Quilt.* Long fascinated with flight in nature, she began to study trapeze. In collaboration with the aerialist Susan Murphy of Canopy Studio in Athens, Georgia, she developed the spring 2008 show "Water Body." Ray's first published fiction, a story titled "Pilgrimage," appeared in *Georgia Review* in 2007, when she was revising the manuscript of her first novel. Several of her poems have appeared in periodicals and anthologies since the publication of her chapbook; in 2008, she was working on a second poetry collection, along with a nonfiction book on American life.

NAMING THE UNSEEN

Ray's prize-winning chapbook, *Naming the Unseen,* was published by the University of Montana in 1996, a year before she received the university's MFA degree in Creative Writing. Bound with twine and printed on recycled paper in a limited edition, the slim volume physically conveys the message of conservation voiced in several of Ray's verses. Two black-and-white photographs frame the twenty-one poems. On the title page, a water view with lush vegetation is identified as "Slave Canal." "Slave Canal" is also the name of the collection's first poem, which thanks the enslaved diggers of this Florida waterway for their "impossible labor." A photographic portrait of a dramatically shaped plant appears at the end of the chapbook, captioned only with the Latin phrase "*Sarracenia flava.*" The poem "Say All" describes a pinewoods tree frog crouching over "the mouth of pitcher plant *flava.*" And in *Ecology of a Cracker Childhood,* Ray credits a junkyard pitcher plant with opening her heart: "I know it now to be the hooded species, *Sarracenia minor,* that sends the red bonnets of its traps knee-high out of soggy ground. In spring it blooms loose, yellow, exotic tongues." Like the hooded *Sarracenia minor,* the more open *Sarracenia flava* is a New World plant that grows in the southeastern United States, far from the mountains of Montana.

Further proclaiming her closeness to her southern birthplace, Ray dedicates *Naming the Unseen* "For the people I love, and the land." Beneath the inscription, she reproduces a hand-drawn map of southern Georgia and northern Florida. This "Map of the Coastal Plains from the Altamaha to the Gulf of Mexico" bears several place names and sketches of animals that Ray cites in such poems as "Aucilla: Underground River," "Okefenokee Swamp," and "Indigo Snake." Quoting the South Carolina novelist and memoirist Pat Conroy, the epigraph for the chapbook embodies one of Ray's central themes: "Geography is my wound." In "Slave Canal," Ray links the tragedy of slavery to the tragedy of the "long gash" the enslaved were forced to inflict on the landscape to ease the transport of cotton to the sea. "The earth has claimed that long scar," she says; and the water "lilts in sorrow that cannot be / washed away, nor undone." Even though the poet celebrates the palms and alligators, the magnolias and the bog frogs that surround her as she runs the canal, she cannot forget "the dead, five hundred strong," who "row us / forward." As Ray underscores in *Ecology of a Cracker Childhood,* the past leaves bruises that are generations deep.

Other poems mourn other wounds. "What Happened to Georgia" pictures Big Sandy Creek, muddied by the "orange pigment" of "eroding flatwoods" that have been "cut & turned, cut & turned." Repeating the phrase, Ray hints at the relentless mechanism of the state's timber mills; but the lumber industry is not the only travesty against the land. Millions of metric tons of kaolin, or "white clay," are extracted annually in Georgia to make paper, plastics, and other products. When Ray says that the "wide white eyes of the kaolin mines, / ... stare up / out of Wilkinson County," her image suggests a blinded land and its blind people. The poem's first stanza ends with a cruel scene of rape and murder. Razor in hand, "kneeling over Georgia, / with all her beauty, we take her down / to nerves and ends." By using the word "we" instead of "they," the poet acknowledges her relationship with those who wield the instrument of torture.

Progressively, as Ray presents a succession of abuses in the poem, the land becomes more and more human, and the people lose their humanity. Georgians share the curse of "some evil / born into all of us." Her "kin," says Ray, were stained by "*slavery, / fundamentalism, ignorance, fear.*" Yet those who leave to distance themselves from Georgia's sad history "are the people she calls home." Unexpectedly, "What Happened to Georgia" ends with a grand vision that evokes God's promise to Noah after the Flood. From a dock "where willow hangs and bottlebush / blooms," the poet beholds a rainbow and its watery double: a "perfect circle, / hoop of frail ribbons, their colors bright / and whole." Those who watch, says Ray, are "held holy / in the iris" of the circle's "fleeting eye, / its marriage of love and squander." The careful positioning of the words "whole" and "holy" offsets the emptiness of "squander."

In "Bone Deposit," the poem that follows, Ray speaks in the imperative, committing herself to help remedy the waste, even after death: "Put my bones in Georgia / that made them." Depositing her "unruly flesh" in Georgian soil will restore a measure of calcium, phosphorous, and "holy manganese"—"holy," perhaps, because the chemical is a free element, or possibly because of the etymological similarity between "manganese" and "magnet." Ray echoes her mention of Georgia's pull in the previous poem, now wondering "what hauls me back" with a compulsion "to feel her soil." The pun in the title "Bone Deposit" is evident in Ray's close, where she speaks of the "debt that will be freed" when her skeleton merges with the earth.

With its fourteen lines and its financial imagery, "Bone Deposit" inevitably recalls Shakespeare's sonnets of love and loss. Even though several lines in the poem are ten syllables long, Ray's rhythms are much more varied than Shakespeare's iambic pentameter. Whitman's free verse, fluctuating in line and stanza length, frequently patterned by parallel syntax, is a more pervasive literary heritage throughout *Naming the Unseen.* Whitman comes especially to mind in Ray's title poem, with its many catalogs of bird species, its energetic verbs, and its thrice-repeated rejoinder "Imagine if." Ray's buzzard "lavishly swirls," much as Whitman's spotted hawk "swoops" at the end of *Song of Myself.* Apostrophes in "Bird Banding with the Biologists" ("Oh cardinal," "Oh kinglet, Oh oriole") are both Whitmanesque and Keatsian.

Yet, the literary ancestors whom Ray explicitly names in the chapbook are not forefathers but foremothers. Visiting Dahlonega after a ten-year absence from the north Georgia town, Ray relates an encounter with her "snake-tongued" college English teacher, Edith Creed, in the poem "The Return." For Ray, the epithet is no insult; in "Indigo Snake," the muscular "heavy purple scarf" of a snake reminds her of a free-spirited midwife who loves purple skirts and shawls. Ray would like to dedicate a book to Ms. Creed to thank her for introducing Kate Chopin, Flannery O'Connor, and other

> southern women who braved insanity,
> village idiothood & their own deaths
> to pen our horrendous & well-tilled kin.
>
> (p. 22)

Ms. Creed "served them up on crucial lips," says Ray, who follows in this tradition of outspoken southern women: teachers like Edith Creed and writers like Chopin, O'Connor, Marjorie Kinnan

Rawlings, Marjory Stoneman Douglas, and Dorothy Allison.

ECOLOGY OF A CRACKER CHILDHOOD

In 1996, the year she won the Merriam-Frontier Award for *Naming the Unseen,* Janisse Ray also received the Writers Conferences & Festivals Nonfiction Award, as well as first place in the *Camas* Nature Writing competition sponsored by the University of Montana's graduate student journal. Like most chapbooks, *Naming the Unseen* had a limited printing, and most of her other poetry has appeared in literary journals and in regional anthologies. Several of her essays, on the other hand, have been published by nationally known magazines and science journals, including *Orion, Sierra, National Geographic Traveler, Audubon,* and even *O: The Oprah Magazine.* With *Ecology of a Cracker Childhood,* Ray established her reputation as an author of literary nonfiction that attracts many audiences.

Her aim was to call attention to the vanishing longleaf pine ecosystem, and the volume was received foremost as a significant contribution to American nature writing. James Tuten, in a review for *Environmental History,* says *Ecology of a Cracker Childhood* "demonstrates that the Muir branch of environmental writing is alive and well." In *Mississippi Quarterly*'s "Ecocritical Essays" issue, Jay Watson compares Ray's book to Larry Brown's novel *Joe* for exploring "how economic exigencies work to shape Southern responses to the environment." Caren J. Town is more concerned with gender issues than with the environment in *The New Southern Girl: Female Adolescence in the Works of 12 Women Authors;* she compares Ray with Lee Smith, Anne Tyler, Tina McElroy Ansa, Jill McCorkle, and others who tell contemporary coming-of-age stories. Other scholars and reviewers have commented on Ray's activism for endangered species, her lyrical prose, her focus on the rural South, her debunking of class stereotypes, and her appeal as a memoirist.

By alternating chapters about her family with segments on the imperiled longleaf, Ray emphasizes the relationship between the land and the people, much as she does in several *Naming the Unseen* poems. The book cover juxtaposes a painting of majestic trees rising in a blue sky with a gray-toned photograph of a junkyard. Standing between the porch of her house and a vista of dilapidated cars, Janisse Ray's mother, Lee Ada Ray, poses on a small plot of grass with an infant and a small girl. Ray told Dobrin and Keller that she wrote *Ecology of a Cracker Childhood* for her fellow southerners, to remind them "that culture is inextricably tied to the landscape. For Southerners to recognize that, knowing how much most of us value where we came from, the land, and our sense of place, we wouldn't be so quick to have it destroyed. That was my hope." Ray's memoir has been especially popular in the South, and in 2002 the Georgia Center for the Book selected it as "The Book Every Georgian Should Read."

Although the arrangement of chapters highlights the bonds between southern culture and southern landscapes, Ray had a second reason for structuring the volume as a combination of personal history and environmental history. The interviewer Rebecca Lauck Cleary summarizes: "She knew no one was going to read a book about a pine tree, but she figured she had an interesting childhood which might captivate them." First-person accounts by Harry Crews, Dorothy Allison, Rick Bragg, and other southerners who grew up in poor white families had reached best-seller status, and Ray's memories of her junkyard youth are equally moving. The journalist Tony Horwitz is unusual for criticizing her strategy for integrating these memories into a larger design. Her "insistence on alternating chapters," he argues, "dilutes the impact of her memoir and makes it as choppy as a clear-cut forest." Horwitz wants to know more about Ray's development as a writer; the personal sections, he says, are more like "a family album that flips between generations. It is often hard to keep track of the cast, or what decade we're in."

Ray does provide visual cues, bookending her text with twelve black-and-white photographs of four generations of her family. Captions in Ray's handwriting personalize the book from the

start. A view of two smiling girls with a go-cart in the junkyard is labeled "Me and Kay." Ray's two-page family tree traces the layers of her paternal and maternal lines all the way back to Daniel Johnson, whom she identifies as *"resident of Appling in the first census in 1820."* Johnson's daughter married Wilson Baxley, *"for whom the town was named."* Like the roots of the adult longleaf pine, Ray's roots in Appling County are old and deep. But, as Horwitz indicates, *Ecology of a Cracker Childhood* does not proceed in a linear fashion. Readers learn about these earlier generations in bits and pieces; and sometimes Ray circles back to family members whom she introduced earlier, modifying the reader's initial perception.

Reviewers of the sequel, *Wild Card Quilt,* compare that book to a quilt sewn from variegated material, and Ray's first memoir makes a similar impact. Not only does she alternate the story of the pines with the story of the Rays, but, within the two narratives, the sequence of chapters has a random quality. Because Ray does not number them, each section appears to stand on its own as an independent essay. In fact, she published some of the chapters, with minor adjustments, as journal articles. This fragmented presentation mirrors Ray's concern that fragmentation threatens rural landscapes and communities, but patterns of kinship, in homes and in the wilderness, emerge from the collected segments of the book. And, much as the family tree imposes a measure of order on the family chapters, the longleaf narrative also has a visual icon: an elegantly drawn pinecone at the head of each nature segment. *Ecology of a Cracker Childhood* does not end at the final chapter. Many of the plants and animals named throughout the book reappear in sobering columns in Ray's appendixes of recently extinct species, endangered species, and species proposed for endangered status. Lest the reader fear that all is lost, however, Ray provides a final appendix of longleaf resources in several southern states.

Her epigraph for the book comes from Iain Crichton Smith, a twentieth-century poet of the Scottish Highlands: *"Words rise out of the country."* While Smith criticized the forced displacement of Scots from their rural homes in the eighteenth century and the resulting cultural changes, Ray looks back into Georgia's history to understand the destructive pressures experienced by her land and its people. Ray's words, like Smith's, rise out of her country. Moreover, as she explains in the chapter titled "Crackers," the ancestors of many poor white Georgians came from the Scotch-English borderland, as well as the Scottish Highlands and parts of Wales and Ireland. "Peril was an old companion for the Borderlanders," she says, and peril is the condition of their often maligned American descendants, even after two hundred years on the new continent. As a girl, Ray was embarrassed by the judgmental stares of tourists passing through Baxley on their way to Florida. When she was in college, her affluent Florida boyfriend broke off their relationship after cutting short his visit to her junkyard home. In her memoir, Ray proudly claims a Cracker heritage. At the same time, she weeps at the thought that, in their struggle to survive, her profligate forefathers fished, hunted, and logged the beautiful wilderness to its ruin.

Much as Walt Whitman emphasizes his generations-old American heritage at the beginning of *Leaves of Grass,* Ray's introduction to *Ecology of a Cracker Childhood* stresses her long history in Appling County: "I was born from people who were born from people who were born from people who were born here." Settling in southeastern Georgia's coastal plains, the early Crackers were "surrounded by a singing forest of tall and widely spaced pines whose history they did not know, whose stories were untold." Ray tells the stories of people but also the stories of these forests; her task is crucial because the singing has fallen almost silent in the two centuries since the Crackers's arrival. Over these years, the native Creek Indians disappeared along with great portions of their habitat. Recalling the skeletal and wound imagery of her chapbook poems, Ray says the memory of the lost wilderness is "scrawled on my bones, so that I carry the landscape inside like an ache." Unlike those ancestors who did not grasp the depth of their relationship to nature, Ray knows that "The story of who I am cannot be severed from the story of

the flatwoods." She rejects the sharp razor of destruction.

The second chapter title, *"Below the Fall Line,"* is italicized, as are all segment headings in Ray's nature narrative. Like the pinecone emblem, italics distinguish the history of the longleaf from the family history and suggest the preeminence of the nature chapters. Ray begins the forest's account by contrasting past and present landscapes in south Georgia. "My homeland is about as ugly as a place gets," says the junkyard daughter and "child of pine"; yet "It wasn't always this way." Walking through virgin forest, the first immigrants encountered a scene of "sublimity" and "majesty." According to Ray, who has seen the tiny sylvan remnant, "Nothing is more beautiful, nothing more mysterious, nothing more breathtaking, nothing more surreal." In many cases, these splendid ecosystems have been replaced with inferior slash-pine plantations, sown for harvesting.

At an early point in *Ecology of a Cracker Childhood,* the author bolsters lyrical passion with harsh facts. Citing forest historians, she says about 2 million acres of longleaf remain in the southeastern range. The number sounds very small compared to the original 85 million acres of longleaf in this territory; and fewer than 10,000 acres, or less than 0.001 percent of the original acreage, are virgin forest. Virgin longleaf has vanished in Virginia, Louisiana, Texas, and South Carolina. "Apocalyptic," Ray concludes. Not only the longleaf forest but all of nature, from air to earth and water, is vulnerable. "The rivers that have been lifelines are polluted by radioactive waste," she says. Near the end of the volume, Ray summarizes her argument for environmental action: "Culture springs from the actions of people in a landscape, and what we, especially Southerners, are watching is a daily erosion of unique folkways as our native ecosystems and all their inhabitants disappear."

Coming immediately after her "Iron Man" segment on the fierce and undependable Grandpa Charlie, the *"Forest Beloved"* chapter is central to Ray's argument that the loss of the land diminishes the people as well. Although Grandpa Charlie's love for the wilderness is his main redeeming quality in *Ecology of a Cracker Childhood,* he makes his small children fear nature when he takes them on an interminable coon hunt, only to pretend they are lost in the dark and in danger of attack by wild animals. Ray's father Frank never seems to recover from the trauma. Although he has an urge to repair wounded creatures, he views them much as he views broken machinery. For him, nature is "superfluous. Nature got in the way," like the toad he accidentally crushes on the way to his tractor. In contrast, Janisse Ray speaks of the longleaf as "heart pine" and describes the rare thrill of hearing its song when the flattened tree crowns contain the wind. Her references to limbs of people and limbs of trees underscore the intimate relationship between them. Pine needles resemble "a piano player's fingers"; they stand upright at the end of a branch, "like a bride holds her bouquet." The whole longleaf ecosystem is, for Ray, a welcoming place: wiregrass and other ground cover comprise a "comforter laid on the land." The longleaf communicates with the visitor who sits and leans against it: "The trunk is your spine, the nerve centers reaching into other worlds, below ground and above. You stand and press your body into the ancestral and enduring, arms wide."

In embracing the longleaf, Ray reaches out to an intricate network of plants and animals. She devotes chapters to the indigo snake, Bachman's sparrow, and the flatwoods salamander. Only gradually does the reader come to understand the extent of the network and the interdependence of its members. Near the midpoint of the book, the *"Longleaf Clan"* chapter is brief in length but strong in impact. Ray's catalogs of longleaf creatures read like a litany of saints or heroes: *"Southern hognose snake. Arogos skipper. Carter's noctuid moth. Bachman's sparrow. Short-tailed snake."* Ray explains some of the complex relationships within the clan. The gopher tortoise's burrow shelters the eastern diamondback rattlesnake in cold weather; on warmer days, diamondbacks lie in wait on the trails of small mammals. Rabbits, rats, and squirrels are their prey, and the female diamondback has as many as twenty-one live young in the fall

birthing season. "As Southern forests are logged," Ray concludes, "these species of flora and fauna, in ways as varied as their curious adaptations to life in the southeastern plains, suffer. All face loss of place."

A few chapters later, Ray reveals that diamondbacks are hardly the only guests in the gopher tortoise's burrow. In the *"Keystone"* segment, the tortoise seems to underpin the whole longleaf world. In describing it as "an ancient tortoise of great tolerance," Ray puns on the creature's tolerance for adverse conditions. Tolerant in its hospitality too, the gopher burrows "in sandhills, flatwoods, and other upland habitat, sharing its hole with more than three hundred species of vertebrates and arthropods." These range from armadillos and three types of scarab beetle to the tineid moth, "whose larvae feed on the tortoises' fecal pellets as well as decaying plant material." To the more obvious reasons for creatures to seek asylum (fleeing predators and weather extremes), Ray adds that the long and deep burrows provide a life-saving escape from fires that periodically renew the longleaf forest. These fires are as necessary as the burrows to the longleaf system, which evolved over millennia in response to the fire's challenge.

In suppressing fire to protect man-made environments, people disrupt nature's elaborate chain, Ray explains. Allowed to flourish, sumac, brambles, and other ground species crowd out the herbaceous plants on which the keystone tortoise depends for its diet. When the keystone is shaken, the rest of the ecosystem trembles. The gopher tortoise becomes such a dignified and essential figure of Ray's narrative that the reader shares her shock when she comes upon a spray-painted tortoise scrambling in a tall-sided wagon at the Baxley fruit stand, beneath the July sun. "Because it was an elder in terms of gopher tortoises," says Ray, "its predicament seemed even more of an abomination." The "beefy, red-faced" captor refuses to let her relocate his victim to an area with burrows; but the man knows her father and finally lets Frank Ray remove the suffering tortoise.

More than once in *Ecology of a Cracker Childhood,* Frank Ray rescues hurting creatures. Ironically, he himself is a major center of pain in the family chapters. Although Janisse Ray affirms several times that she and her siblings were deeply loved by both parents, she also records an unforgettable scene in which her father whips her and her brothers with his leather belt. He blames them for not intervening when an older neighbor boy suddenly stomps a turtle to death in front of the "horrified and mesmerized" siblings. Ray describes the "agonizing" sting, "pain on top of pain," as the belt raises welts on her skin. She was never paddled in school, she says, but her strategies for blocking out the impact of her father's lashings indicate physical punishment was not uncommon at home. "Even a child knows that flogging diminishes the human spirit and seeks to avoid that reduction," she remarks. She understands that her father "meant well," but she adds that she "vowed never to hit a child, not even my own." Ray repeats the sentiment in *Wild Card Quilt* when she tells Silas's new teacher in Baxley that she did not raise her son with physical punishment, and "he may not be hit" at school.

For the Ray children, their father's unbending rules are worse than the lashings. Forbidden to celebrate Christmas, Janisse and her brothers "skulk" to a small cedar they decorate in a pine grove; and the boys "furtively" open the presents she made for them. Because Frank Ray supervises his daughters' reading so closely, the girls hide library books under their clothes. "We weren't allowed to socialize outside of school," Ray says, "so classmates didn't come home with us, and we didn't go to other kids' houses. The junkyard, then, was all we knew." In those ten acres of junk, childhood accidents are frequent, but the Rays have no insurance and cannot afford visits to the emergency room. "More than that, however," Ray adds, "Daddy tried to live a life of faith, which relied on miracles of God over those of doctors." Frank Ray's religious fanaticism is so tangled with his mental disorder that the young Janisse distrusts fundamentalism and fears for her own sanity. While her father craves the presence of the Holy Spirit, she dreads the possibility: "I had seen people filled with something they said was the Holy Ghost, except it was sickness,

mental illness, and I had no desire to let any such spirit steer my boat." When her father steps through his bedroom window while praying loudly, Janisse feels bewildered and confused. "I was frightened by an unbidden and uncontrollable illness that might pounce at any time and leap away with me in its claws."

The tomboyish Ray also resents her father's "canon," which "restricted daughters to the household and made them mistresses of domesticity and which prohibited an intemperate tramping about." In the family chapters of *Ecology of a Cracker Childhood,* her grandmothers and her mother are her main sources of comfort. All three women are highly domestic, but domesticity does not define them fully. Ray praises Granny Clyo's independence, Grandmama Beulah's easygoing ways, and Lee Ada's wisdom. At the center of her memoir, she names chapters after each of them: "Clyo," "Beulahland," and "Mama." In spite of her poor health, Granny Clyo Ray picks cotton, cooks in restaurants, and even bootlegs whiskey until treasury agents sign a warrant against her in 1945. Yielding to authority is a rare event in the life of this single mother of eight, and she stubbornly rejects her doctors' advice, as she had rejected Grandpa Charlie's violence years earlier. "To her dying day Clyo did the telling, not the following, of orders," says the admiring Ray. Like Granny Ray, Grandmama Branch is a mother of several children and a good cook; Ray prints her recipes for buttermilk pie and biscuit pudding. Janisse's grandfather Branch dies when she is five, but the Branch family farm remains a place of nature, abundance, and freedom for the Ray grandchildren. A lover of birds and flowers, Beulah Branch has a less conventional attraction to televised wrestling; and she lets Janisse and her siblings watch with her, ignoring Frank Ray's disapproval. On the farm, the children eat candy, read comics, play with their Uncle Percy, and escape the regimen of home. Ray associates her grandmother with a nearby juke joint named Beulahland. When her father says the name means heaven, Janisse decides that "Grandmama's name fit her then."

Lee Ada Branch Ray's relatively comfortable family background is a revelation in these middle chapters. The "Mama" segment opens with the surprising fact that "My mother was a beauty queen," but Janisse Ray quickly identifies Lee Ada as a typical young woman of the 1950s, who lacked any real ambition for a career, despite her enrollment in business school. Lee Ada would have shared the common conviction that "Woman came from man, intended as a helpmate for him, and her job was to be a good wife and a good mother." At eighteen she eloped with the dashing Frank Ray because her parents "were vocal in their condemnation" of the romance. Their love was so strong, according to Janisse Ray, that she sometimes was envious; yet she did not take her mother as her model. "As I reached womanhood, when I was first hot for equality, justice, and freedom," says Ray, "virtue meant no more to me than cow dung." She later modified her opinion so drastically that she now describes Lee Ada Ray as the "most steadfast, generous, and honorable person I have ever known, wise in her unassuming way, and because of this, she approached sainthood." Ray nevertheless concludes the "Mama" chapter with a decisive: "On these terms I did not want to be a saint."

Caren J. Town points out that "Ray has chosen not to follow her mother's model, although in her passionate plea to save the pine forest ecosystem, she takes on her shoulders an even larger burden, sacrificing herself to protect the environment instead of just her family." From start to finish, *Ecology of a Cracker Childhood* portrays its author as the "child of pine." Prophetically, Ray imagines a "blessed day" on which the separated narratives of longleaf and family will come together, when her "quest," as described by Thomas L. McHaney, will be fulfilled. Looking to the future, she yokes the double claims on her heart, dedicating the book "For my son Silas and for the land." And in her final chapter, *"There Is a Miracle for You If You Keep Holding On,"* Ray envisions a descendant ("my granddaughter's granddaughter") whose girlhood is more of a wholeness with nature than hers ever was: "she bears the new forest about her, the forest so grand." In this distant child, and in the restoration of the wilderness, says Ray, "I will lay to rest this implacable longing."

WILD CARD QUILT

In *Wild Card Quilt: Taking a Chance on Home,* Janisse Ray returns to Baxley, Georgia, to live in her late grandmother Beulah's farmhouse, seventeen years after she left for college. Although she makes occasional reference to the years that have passed, Ray's focus is her increasing environmental activism through the late 1990s and her ongoing efforts to strengthen communities, including her hometown. In contrast to the lovely Vermont village where her son Silas would rather live, Baxley is not "aesthetically pleasing by any stretch of the eye," but it is not "artless" either. "Ours," says Ray, "is a folk art." Fittingly, the endpapers for *Wild Card Quilt* reproduce a primitive style drawing of the home place, including seven simple outbuildings and several large trees, one with a tire swing; clothes hang on the line, and smoke rises from the chimneys. The quilt in the book title, a collaboration between Ray and her mother, is a vivid expression of the folk impulse. And the Florida Folk Festival, with its ballads and homemade ice cream, is the place where Ray, after a long period of loneliness and self-questioning, meets Raven, "the man I'd dreamed and prayed into being." This sequel to *Ecology of a Cracker Childhood* concludes with the completion of the quilt, Ray's marriage to her fellow nature lover, and the planting of a thousand longleaf seedlings. Emily Bowles suggests that *Wild Card Quilt* "reworks the language and codes of domestic fiction" to "accommodate a self produced by activism, environmentalism, and integrity."

Ray does not repeat the alternating chapter structure of her first memoir, and Bowles observes that the "storied lives of Ray, her family, and members of her community" follow a "somewhat more linear narrative trajectory" in *Wild Card Quilt.* The "somewhat" is an important qualifier since the thirty-nine segments are not numbered, and they hold together much more loosely than the parallel nature and family sections of *Ecology of a Cracker Childhood.* Several chapters—among them, "Syrup-Boiling," "The Picture-Taker," "Heroic Vegetables," "A Natural Almanac," and "Cypress Lake"—could easily be repositioned without disrupting the surrounding essays. On the other hand, some chapters are firmly linked. "Milton," "Bird Dreams," and "The Bread Man Still Stops in Osierfield" comprise a three-part sequence on the conservationist Milton Hopkins, who perfectly "represents the Southern landscape, with its deep pine flatwoods grace."

Elsewhere in the book, the pairing of chapters highlights themes. For instance, Ray's omnipresent motif of loss and recovery is underscored by her juxtaposition of chapters titled "Despair" and "Angels, Arise." In "Despair," the 1998 Election Day failure of a preservation amendment almost drives Ray into permanent exile from the South. "Angels, Arise" is primarily an entertaining history of Georgia's *Market Bulletin,* but the piece opens with a summer moonlit garden scene that counters the wintry mood of "Despair." Relating the heirloom plant ads from the *Bulletin* to her own 1980s heirloom garden, Ray portrays a natural abundance far removed from nature's bleak prospects in the preceding essay. Much as Alice Walker emphasizes the artistic impulse of her mother's beautiful plantings in the essay "In Search of Our Mothers' Gardens," Ray fondly recalls that her Florida garden was "living art, a verdant jumble." There is poetry in the very names of her moon-and-stars watermelon, unicorn plant, velvet bean, and globe amaranth.

The elaborate garden built lovingly with her early "sweetheart" in north Florida does not survive the end of their brief marriage, however. Ray relates: "For many years to follow I had no garden—no time for one, no plot of land, no energy. I wandered far from the happy young woman among flowers who kept bees." Here, and throughout *Wild Card Quilt,* Ray links thriving environments to thriving relationships. Self-sufficiency is a lesser value to her than co-sufficiency, the best means to survival in the longleaf ecosystem and in Baxley, as well. This second memoir records Ray's successful integration into several communities, from a local writing group to the Altamaha Riverkeeper, an organization formed to protect a crucial Georgia waterway. She praises individuals who devote long hours to strengthening natural and human networks. While Milton Hopkins is the preeminent example, there are many others, including

Ray's friends Sandy and Stan Brobston, returnees like herself. Their very reason for coming back to Baxley is to be close to a family member, and after his death, these "two kind-hearted, educated, hopeful people who care" stay on, joining the arts council, fighting against litter ("a terrible problem in the region"), volunteering at the hospital gift shop to raise money for essential equipment. The Brobstons, says Ray, are "vital assets to our community; they are not expendable." She calls for more southerners to respond to local needs with equal "courage and tenacity."

As in *Ecology of a Cracker Childhood,* Ray is most passionately involved with family and wilderness communities. Prizing wholeness as she does, she regrets that religion is such a divisive force in her conversations with her fundamentalist father. "Perhaps he, too, is looking for common threads to bind things together," she reflects after Frank Ray interrupts a mother-daughter quilting session to harangue Janisse for not believing in the existence of hell. "But his tools draw more blood than our pins and needles." Over the same period that Ray stitches colorful patterned squares with her mother, she encourages both parents to reach out to their estranged older daughter Kay. Again adopting a sewing metaphor, Ray says of the nineteen-year silence between parents and child: "We humans have proven that kinship is not inviolable, that it can be broken and broken again, and that to build it back we must set to mending." In hopes of finally bringing the family together, Ray organizes a big reunion, taking on the role of her grandmother Beulah, whom she characterizes as "the family's glue." The disappointment of Kay's last-hour decision not to come "turned my mouth metallic," Ray says. Thus, her sister's attendance at Ray's wedding to Raven Burchard in the final chapter of *Wild Card Quilt* adds heightened significance to the ceremony beside the Suwannee River. In a book about literal and figurative mending and stitching, Kay's gift of a pine tree quilt is a culminating symbol of the newlyweds' firm ties. On a label sewn to this work of art, Kay affirms: "It honors their love for each other and their love of nature. ... Let it be a warm reminder of that commitment."

Ray's commitment to the longleaf pine is a constant in her two memoirs, but *Wild Card Quilt* gives a detailed account of one particular battle to save the wildness. In the "Moody Swamp" chapter, she relates her 1992 trip to a "mythic" part of Appling County that she had heard about as a girl. With an ornithologist friend, Ray visits the heart-pine home of the elderly Miss Elizabeth Moody and her brother Wade, heirs to the wilderness property. Walking beneath old-growth pines, Ray realizes that "this wood was a miracle, a monument"; Creek Indians had stood here two hundred years before, and "the signature of longleaf pine" is upon "our Cracker history." Because the red-cockaded woodpecker colony at Moody Swamp is one sign of a viable ecosystem, Ray suddenly sees "how I belonged." "If a landscape could be returned to function, so could a family, and a community," she reasons. "I could be returned to a life rooted in the fullness of place." The epiphany remains with her through the next five years in Florida and Montana and through the difficult first months of her return to Baxley. When the Nature Conservancy of Georgia finally outbids seven timber companies, the long struggle to preserve Moody Swamp comes to a thrilling conclusion. "Now it has been saved forever," says Ray, who had prayed, fasted monthly, and even "fashioned an altar" from a tobacco sack found on the Moody place. In her devotion to the wilderness, Ray adapts her father's terminology of sacrifice and redemption.

The search for wholeness that leads Ray home also encompasses Baxley's African American community. On Martin Luther King, Jr., Day, her mother worries when Ray announces her plans to march in the local parade. "The statement I was making was simply one of solidarity," she says. In Baxley, she adds, she has seen whites avoid a grocery store aisle where they spotted a biracial couple. "The people shopping told me so. They'd rather not be that close, they said." As if in defiance of such prejudice, Ray hitches a ride home from the parade on a Harley-Davidson motorcycle with a young black biker named Vegas. In a later chapter, "Toward the

Promised Land," she participates in a Christmas candle-lighting service at the First African Missionary Baptist Church at the invitation of Dr. Juanita Nails, a fellow member of the Baxley arts council. Ray believes social change starts with such friendships, and she deplores the obstacles that make such relationships difficult. "Powerfully I have felt the deep wound that divides races here in the South," she says. Ray is proud when her son Silas steps on a black tile in the Altamaha Elementary cafeteria to indicate his own solidarity with African Americans after white children invent a racist game. Standing in a large circle with worshippers at the First African Missionary Baptist Church, she wishes for more white residents to join the emblematic ring. "Every day we move toward reconciliation is a step toward the promised land," she concludes.

In her review of *Wild Card Quilt,* Emily Bowles remarks that "Ray subtly interweaves issues of community, environment, politics, gender, familial obligation, creativity, authorship, education, craft, and beauty into a story of self-production." Throughout the book, Ray develops as an author, researcher, and public speaker. In "Long Road Home," the first chapter, she hopes her grandmother's house will be "a quiet abode where I could write." Yet, she wonders if, back in the constricting world of her childhood, she can "find a voice where I had not had one." Among a long series of questions, Ray asks: "Could I be a tongue for a whittled and beleaguered landscape?" The imagery recalls a related tension in *Ecology of a Cracker Childhood,* where she strains to hear the music of the vanishing longleaf: "It falters, a great tongue chopped in pieces." Both memoirs are the fruits of Ray's return to the South. In finding her voice, she speaks, in the same breath, for herself and the wilderness.

PINHOOK: FINDING WHOLENESS IN A FRAGMENTED LAND

Ray's working title for her third book of nonfiction was "Wild America," but the title *Pinhook: Finding Wholeness in a Fragmented Land* identifies the American wilderness that embodies her most emphatic argument against fragmentation. Like the black bears that range between north Florida and southern Georgia, Ray crosses the two state borders repeatedly in this narrative. On her journeys, she observes members of various human and natural communities who strengthen her resolve to forge wholeness. From the country store regulars she greets in Taylor, Florida, to the spiders at work on her hike through Pinhook Swamp, Ray finds models of connection. The Pinhook Swamp Purchase Unit pictured on Ray's frontispiece map is the epitome of bridges. Linking Osceola National Forest to Okefenokee National Wildlife Refuge, the 170,000-acre Pinhook "models a large contiguous conservation corridor for the nation. O to O. O2O," says Ray in the "Lay of the Land" chapter. As she explains at the start of the book, she did not write *Pinhook* "simply to describe this particular place ... but to tell you its story, the sad and happy of it. Because it is the back of a turtle, this story, on which many things can ride." The restoration of Pinhook would secure one of the South's rare wild places and protect the water supply of millions of people. Beyond these positive consequences, an intact Pinhook would also serve as a powerful image of wholeness, intimacy, and community. Leading lives of wholeness, says Ray, involves *"rejoining ourselves to others"* but also *"returning ourselves to wildness: relearning."* Pinhook Swamp teaches life-saving lessons.

Of Ray's three books of literary nonfiction, *Pinhook* has the loosest structure. The volume's twenty-eight segments include three chantlike poems: "Native Blessing," "Voice from the Wilderness," and "Psalm for Pinhook." These highly rhetorical verses evoke the language of myth, legend, and sacred texts. Near the beginning of the book, "Native Blessing" asks that we "put our minds together" and thank "Mother Earth, Elder Brother Sun, Grandmother / Moon, Sister Stars. Families. Safe Journeys." The other two poems appear near the end of *Pinhook,* shortly before and shortly after Ray describes her climactic arrival at the center of the mysterious swamp in the "Noah's Island" chapter. With its

many sentence fragments and its emotional intensity, the prose of "Noah's Island" is somewhere between poetry and the prose of the other essay-chapters. In short bursts, Ray recounts her slow journey through the tangled growth: "Me walking with binoculars, backpack, pad and pencil. The gun in its holster against my ribs. Marking me. Embarrassing me. An imprinted fear." Thomas McHaney's comparison of Janisse Ray to Faulkner's Isaac McCaslin of *Go Down, Moses* is even more pertinent to this scene than to *Ecology of a Cracker Childhood.* The breathlessness of Ray's sentences reflects her awe as she approaches the heart of the great wilderness: "Center of Pinhook. Everything Pinhook is, is here." Pinhook contains the formidable and the dainty: bears, alligators, bobcats, raccoons, "dog hobble, sweet bay magnolia, wax myrtle," and "lavender flowers of smooth meadow beauty. So fragile the petals fall if you brush them." At the end of the chapter, Ray runs back to the road as night falls; only then does she quit gasping. "I can breathe" is her final thought.

Ray's stylistic inventiveness is seen in a different way in the pairing of the chapters "Silence" and "Red Wolves." Ray considers that silence can have many sources, from wisdom to sleepiness; but the silence of Pinhook is ominous to her because sounds that should be there are missing. Silence is "the sound of death, of annihilation"; noise, on the other hand, is celebratory, says Ray. The "Silence" essay ends with an italicized meditation on the importance of saving Pinhook for the future: *"Could it mean your great-grandchildren may hear a red wolf calling or a panther cry? Two great sounds denied to me."* As she does at the end of *Ecology of a Cracker Childhood,* Ray looks beyond present fragmentation to a distant generation of fulfillment. She spells out the length of the wait more precisely in the two short statements that comprise the whole of the "Red Wolves" chapter. The first sentence clarifies that one of the two great sounds has been absent for decades: "The last red wolf was heard near Pinhook Swamp about 1915." After a gap on a page that is mainly blank, Ray emphasizes the emptiness with a simple phrase: "The end." In "Naming the Unseen," the title poem of her chapbook, Ray describes a friend who has suffered a hearing loss: "The man who devoted his life to birds / can no longer hear them sing." As she walks with him, watching for sandhill cranes, hawks, and Acadian flycatchers, Ray reflects somberly: "Imagine if the woods were silent as a photograph." Her portrait of Pinhook in the chapter "Hundreds of Senses" insists on the preciousness of each sense we recognize, along with scores of channels of perception to which we are oblivious. Capitalizing the five familiar sense organs, Ray writes a vibrant series of paragraphs on Pinhook's appeal to eyes, ears, mouth, skin, and nose, only to add: "Wouldn't I wish all my senses to be keener?"

Ray presents several examples of lives lived close to the Georgia-Florida wilderness. In the chapter "Meeting Johnny," her friend Johnny Dame speaks of the "indescribable comfort" of sleeping on the earth, looking at the stars; this naturalist and nature artist spent 140 nights outside in 2004. "If three hurricanes hadn't crossed his area of Florida that fall, the figure would have been 180, he said." A beekeeper named Mike, in "Connoisseur of Honey," sells honey made from gallberry, a shrub that grows in Pinhook; he loves bear meat and hunted bears before the ban in Florida. The segment titled "Silas Mann's Story" records Ray's interview with an elderly man who has spent a lifetime near Pinhook. Following upon several chapters of Ray's own first-person narrative, the opening catches the reader off guard: "Back when I were a young man, I was in Pinhook a lot. This was in the '40s and '50s." Mann talks about cutting trees with his wife to build a log cabin: "Those were some of the happiest days of my life." Married for "sixty-seven years and nineteen days" when she died, he tells Ray he lost his best friend with her death. Silas Mann is not involved in the campaign to save Pinhook, but his comments on population growth and changes to the land give urgency to the cause. Moreover, his poignant remarks on missing his wife underscore the companionship Ray and her husband Raven share throughout the book. With Raven, she marvels at a half-inch frog and visits a gallery to see Johnny

Dame's wildlife art. They are together on the spring morning she first sees Pinhook; chapters later, they eat Mike's honey as they camp at the swamp and experience the "flavor" of Pinhook: "wild yet demure, strong yet delicate, exotic yet plain. Homespun."

The struggle to reclaim this wild home continues, but Ray describes great progress toward preserving the Pinhook Corridor. Like *Ecology of a Cracker Childhood* and *Wild Card Quilt, Pinhook* concludes with an image of wholeness. *"Fragmentation,"* Ray says in the opening chapter, *"is what happens when a glass platter falls."* "A Vision" is the name of the final chapter, and here she predicts that "When the last tract of land is added that makes the Pinhook puzzle a beautiful platter again, it will become a land bridge in a sea of civilization. Over which our progeny may someday cross." A drawing of a heron in flight heads each chapter of *Pinhook,* and, in her vision, Ray shares a bird's-eye view of an intact Okefenokee-Pinhook-Osceola corridor. There is room for people in this vista because, as she says earlier in the volume, *"Part of being fully human requires engagement with our places."* Human *"intimacy with a wild place"* requires a deliberate decision, however: *"By choice we can ignore or honor this connection."* Honoring the connection is Ray's abiding theme.

Selected Bibliography

WORKS OF JANISSE RAY

NONFICTION

Ecology of a Cracker Childhood. Minneapolis: Milkweed Editions, 1999.

Wild Card Quilt: Taking a Chance on Home. Minneapolis: Milkweed Editions, 2003.

Between Two Rivers: Stories from the Red Hills to the Gulf. Edited by Ray, Susan Cerulean, and Laura Newton. Tallahassee, Fla.: Red Hills Writers Project, 2004.

Pinhook: Finding Wholeness in a Fragmented Land. White River Junction, Vt.: Chelsea Green Publishing, 2005.

POETRY AND SHORT STORY

Naming the Unseen. Missoula: University of Montana, 1996. (Poetry chapbook.)

"Pilgrimage." *Georgia Review* 61, no. 3: 587–601 (fall 2007). (Short story.)

ESSAYS

"Cumberland Island National Seashore, Georgia." In *American Safari.* Edited by Judith Dunham. Discovery Travel Adventures. London: Discovery Communications, 1999. Pp. 78–83.

"Everglades National Park, Florida." In *American Safari.* Edited by Judith Dunham. Discovery Travel Adventures. London: Discovery Communications, 1999. Pp. 84–93.

"Whither Thou Goest." In *The Woods Stretched for Miles: New Nature Writing from the South.* Edited by John Lane and Gerald Thurmond. Athens: University of Georgia Press, 1999. Pp. 203–213.

"How the Heart Opens." *Natural History* 109, no. 5:84 (June 2000).

"The Faith of Deer." In *American Nature Writing 2000.* Edited by John Murray. Corvallis: Oregon State University Press, 2000. Pp. 77–85.

"Weaving the World." *Audubon* 104, no. 1:46–47 (January–February 2002).

"On the Bosom of This Grave and Wasted Land I Will Lay My Head." *Orion,* spring 2002, pp. 108–115.

"Up Against Openings." In *The Roadless Yaak: Reflections and Observations About One of Our Last Great Wild Places.* Edited by Rick Bass. Guilford, Conn.: Lyons Press, 2002. Pp. 51–59.

"Belize: A Record of Life." *Heartstone* 4, no. 1:94–103 (spring 2003).

"The Fabric of Their Lives." *O: The Oprah Magazine,* May 2003, pp. 170, 172, 174.

"Singing for My Life." *Oxford Town,* December 11–17, 2003, p. 11.

"Deep in the Georgia Woods." *Sierra* 89, no. 2:42–43 (March–April 2004).

"Delta Defender." *Sierra* 89, no. 3:26–30 (May–June 2004).

"Beyond Capitalism." In *Where We Stand: Voices of Southern Dissent.* Edited by Anthony Dunbar. Montgomery, Ala.: NewSouth Books, 2004. Pp. 103–120.

"Reasons." In *Elemental South: An Anthology of Southern Nature Writing.* Edited by Dorinda G. Dallmeyer. Athens: University of Georgia Press, 2004. Pp. 131–132.

"Earth Work." *Washington Post,* April 22, 2005, p. WE26.

"Singing the World Back." *Ecological Restoration* 23, no. 2:110–114 (June 2005).

"Syrup Boiling." In *Cornbread Nation 3: Foods of the Mountain South.* Edited by Ronni Lundy. Chapel Hill: University of North Carolina Press, 2005. Pp. 144–148.

"Mr. Roy's Market." In *Where the Mountain Stands Alone: Stories of Place in the Monadnock Region.* Edited by Howard Mansfield. Hanover, N.H.: University Press of New England, 2006. Pp. 318–325.

"Grown in Vermont." *Orion* (http://www.orionmagazine.org/index.php/articles/article/303/), May–June 2007.

"Altar Call for True Believers." *Orion*, September–October 2007, pp. 58–63.

"Changing Sex." In *Courage for the Earth: Writers, Scientists, and Activists Celebrate the Life and Writing of Rachel Carson*. Edited by Peter Matthiessen. Boston: Houghton Mifflin, 2007. Pp. 109–128.

"Bleeding Fields: Rural Exodus and Reinhabitation of the Southlands (A Personal Narrative)." Agrarian Studies Symposium, Yale University (http://www.yale.edu/agrarianstudies/papers/15bleeding.pdf), 2007.

CRITICAL AND BIOGRAPHICAL STUDIES

Bowles, Emily. "'It Would Ever Seem to Me a Dowry': Human Ecology and Domestic Economies in Janisse Ray's *Wild Card Quilt*." *South Atlantic Review* 70, no. 1:1–20 (winter 2005).

Drew, Julie. "Making Arguments: A Response to Janisse Ray." In *Writing Environments*. Edited by Sidney I. Dobrin and Christopher J. Keller. Albany: State University of New York Press, 2005. Pp. 137–142.

McHaney, Thomas L. "The Ecology of Uncle Ike: Teaching *Go Down, Moses* with Janisse Ray's *Ecology of a Cracker Childhood*." In *Faulkner and the Ecology of the South: Faulkner and Yoknapatawpha, 2003*. Edited by Joseph R. Urgo and Ann J. Abadie. Jackson: University Press of Mississippi, 2005. Pp. 98–114.

Milkweed Editions. "Janisse Ray, *Ecology of a Cracker Childhood*: A Reading Guide" (http://www.milkweed.org/downloads/rgEcology.pdf).

Otto, Eric. "Ecocomposition, Active Writing, and Natural Ecosystems." In *Writing Environments*. Edited by Sidney I. Dobrin and Christopher J. Keller. Albany: State University of New York Press, 2005. Pp. 143–148.

Purcell, Kim. "Janisse Ray." *The New Georgia Encyclopedia* (http://www.georgiaencyclopedia.org). (A succinct survey of Ray's life and her three nonfiction books, this article was updated in 2005.)

"Ray, Janisse." In *Contemporary Authors, New Revision Series*. Vol. 191. Detroit: Gale, 2001. P. 318.

Robertson, Sarah. "Junkyard Tales: Poverty and the Southern Landscape in Janisse Ray's *Ecology of a Cracker Childhood*." In *Poverty and Progress in the U.S. South Since 1920*. Edited by Suzanne W. Jones and Mark Newman. Amsterdam: VU University Press, 2006. Pp. 167–175.

Town, Caren J. " 'Odd How Things Are and Then They Aren't': Janisse Ray's Identity of Loss." In *The New Southern Girl: Female Adolescence in the Works of 12 Women Authors*. Jefferson, N.C.: McFarland, 2004. Pp. 115–127.

Watson, Jay. "Economics of a Cracker Landscape: Poverty as an Environmental Issue in Two Southern Writers." *Mississippi Quarterly* 55, no. 4:497–513 (fall 2002).

Book Reviews

Adair, Jordon. Review of *Wild Card Quilt: Taking a Chance on Home*. *INDY: The Independent Weekly* (Raleigh, Durham, Chapel Hill, N.C.) (http://www.indyweek.com/gyrobase/Content?oid=oid%3A19499), May 7, 2003.

Bowles, Emily. Review of *Wild Card Quilt: Taking a Chance on Home*. *Southern Scribe* (http://www.southernscribe.com/reviews/biography-memoir/wild_card_quilt.htm), 2003.

Brody, James. "Candle Pine: A Review of *Ecology of a Cracker Childhood* by Janisse Ray." *Human Nature Review* 3:309–12 (2003). Available online (http://www.human-nature.com/nibbs/03/ray.html).

Carden, Gary. "The Ghosts of Trees: Odd Paradoxes Arise from a Bleak Childhood." *Smoky Mountain News* (Waynesville, N.C.) (http://www.smokymountainnews.com/issues/04_02/04_17_02/books_carden.html), April 17, 2002. (Review of *Ecology of a Cracker Childhood*.)

Delaney-Lehman, Maureen. Review of *Wild Card Quilt*. *Library Journal*, May 15, 2003, p. 98.

Horwitz, Tony. "In Praise of the Blue-Tailed Mole Skink." *New York Times Book Review*, January 9, 2000, p. 16. (Review of *Ecology of a Cracker Childhood*.)

Lehman, Maureen. Review of *Pinhook: Finding Wholeness in a Fragmented Land*. *Library Journal*, May 1, 2005, p. 113.

Paulson, Michael. Review of *Ecology of a Cracker Childhood*. *Georgia Review* 54, no. 1:178–179 (spring 2000).

Raver, Anne. "Human Nature; A Georgia Daughter's Lullaby of the Pines." *New York Times*, April 27, 2000, p. F1. (Review of *Ecology of a Cracker Childhood*.)

Seaman, Donna. Review of *Wild Card Quilt*. *Booklist*, April 15, 2003, p. 1446.

Slocum, Beth. "Georgia on Her Mind." *Ruminator Review* 14:23 (summer 2003). (Review of *Wild Card Quilt*.)

Tuten, James. Review of *Ecology of a Cracker Childhood*. *Environmental History* 8, no. 4:694–695 (October 2003).

Williams, Susan Millar. "Home, Difficult Home." *Women's Review of Books*, July 2003, p. 22. (Review of *Wild Card Quilt*.)

Interviews

Chaddha, Rima. "Janisse Ray Speaks on Books, Upbringing." *Daily Mississippian*, February 5, 2004, p. 14.

Cleary, Rebecca Lauck. "Writer-in-Residence Thankful for Time in Oxford." *Oxford Town*, February 5–11, 2004, pp. 10, 15.

Cuthbertson, Jennifer G. "Janisse Ray: Connecting Lives and Landscape Through Story." *Arts & Letters: Journal of Contemporary Culture* 11:35–42 (spring 2004).

Dllonardo, Mary Jo. "Talking with ... Author Janisse Ray." *Atlanta,* July 2003, p. 58.

Dobrin, Sidney I., and Christopher J. Keller. "Writing with Intent: An Interview with Janisse Ray." In *Writing Environments.* Edited by Sidney I. Dobrin and Christopher J. Keller. Albany: State University of New York Press, 2005. Pp. 121–136.

Graham, Benjamin. "Wild Card Cracker." *Mountaineer On-Line* (Green Mountain College, Poultney, Vt.) (http://campus.greenmtn.edu/mountaineer/2004_Oct/Graham_cracker.asp), October 2004.

Jones, Jeremy. "To Protect and Uphold Life." *Southern Nature Writers: Writing and Thinking About the Southern Landscape.* Southern Nature Project (http://www.southernnature.org/profile_interview.php?ID=15), January 2007.

O'Connor, Kevin. "Love and Winter: Amid the Green Mountains, a Writer Finds Georgia on Her Mind." *Rutland Herald* (Rutland, Vt.) (http://www.rutlandherald.com/apps/pbcs.dll/article?AID=/20060115/NEWS/601150365/-1/realvermonter), January 15, 2006.

CONRAD RICHTER

(1890—1968)

David R. Johnson

AT THE TIME of his death in 1968, Conrad Richter was at the height of his literary reputation, his novels both popular and critical successes. Approximately every two years a new Richter novel would appear, and reviews in major newspapers and news magazines would again pronounce him one of America's most accomplished historical novelists, perhaps its best at portraying frontier life. His novel *The Town* was awarded the Pulitzer Prize for Fiction in 1950; in 1961 his *Waters of Kronos* won the National Book Award. Among other awards and acknowledgments were the 1942 Gold Medal of the Associated Libraries of New York University, a special medal in 1947 from the Ohioana Library Association for *The Awakening Land,* and honorary degrees from a number of colleges and universities. Though only two of Richter's novels sold largely, most appeared on best-seller lists for major cities. By the end of his career, novels by Richter had been translated into over thirty languages.

This literary prominence was accomplished despite Richter's career-long refusal to promote himself or his works. A modest, shy man with a near-phobia about appearing in public, Richter declined all offers to read from his work on college campuses, to be interviewed on radio or television, or even to appear at bookstores for signings. A member of PEN and the National Institute of Arts and Letters, Richter rarely attended their meetings and dinners or otherwise consorted with his literary peers. Nonetheless Richter was well regarded by fellow novelists, a number of whom wrote highly laudatory reviews of his works, and loyal readers awaited the publication of his next novel.

Richter's first novels are about the settling of frontier America, most prominently a trilogy of novels chronicling the lives of the earliest settlers into wilderness of Ohio and three novels fictionalizing frontier life in the American Southwest. These novels are historical fiction but of a special kind; unlike historical romances, his stories are not set against a backdrop of the major events and actors in history. And though Richter assiduously researched the times of his novels and the lives of people who lived through them, he has little in common with writers of historical fiction whose primary aim is to get all the details right. Richter's novels are re-creations of particular moments in the past and of the ordinary people living within those times. His novels seldom mention recognizable figures from history or particular historical events. Richter's special genius was to immerse himself in primary historical materials and, from his own feeling for the life within those documents, to re-create that life so evocatively that readers would participate in the experience, sharing the sensations of his characters.

As a storyteller, Richter was not an experimentalist. Following the models of the realists who preceded him and notably Willa Cather, whose work he especially admired, Richter presents his stories episodically and linearly, relying primarily upon first-person narration, limited omniscience, and interior monologue. Typically his first-person narrators are reminiscing in old age, and the stories they recount carry a major Richter theme, a regret for the lost times of pioneering and admiration for the people who lived through them. Readers admired his psychological portrayals of characters, though critical commentators sometimes remarked on their lack of complexity, misunderstanding a Richter tenet that interior human motivations are seldom truly knowable, even to those most intimate with each other. In Richter's novels the actions of charac-

ters, though always prepared for and invested with emotional reality, are often not wholly explainable in psychological terms.

If not an experimentalist, Richter has been widely lauded as a stylist. His stories are told economically, in a restrained realism that is taut but flexible, graceful without being literary. In several novels he effectively uses archaisms and the idiomatic language of early settlers to create an immediacy of experience—language conveying the tensions of the story, the surface details for what Richter called, in the introduction of *Early Americana,* an "underlying pattern" of "endless, small authenticities." Few writers have as effectively crafted dialogue to give authentic voices to their characters.

EARLY LIFE AND WORK

Conrad Michael Richter was born on October 13, 1890, to John Absalom and Charlotte Esther (Henry) Richter, who lived in Pine Grove, Pennsylvania, a small town at the western edge of the state's anthracite region. There, for ten years he lived a secure childhood within a close community of family and friends, an especially beneficial environment for an often ill, sensitive, and shy child. That life changed in 1900 when Richter's father sold his general store to pursue the Lutheran ministry. Thereafter, Richter, his parents, and two younger brothers moved frequently from one country parish to another, and the family would never again achieve the financial security of Richter's earlier life. The consequences for the young Conrad were considerable, including his rejection as an adolescent of his father's church and faith and his deep-set, conflicted resentment against his father for carrying the family and especially his mother into a life of penury. There was as well the difference in personalities between Richter and his father: John Richter was hearty and gregarious, while his oldest son was never comfortable in gatherings larger than his own family and friends. Reconciling these differences was for Richter a lifetime task, resulting in two late novels, both autobiographical, *The Waters of Kronos* and *A Simple Honorable Man.*

Richter's one opportunity to attend college came as a scholarship offer to study for the ministry. In what would be an early decisive act, he declined and, at the age of sixteen, accepted a clerk's job taking him far from home. Within a year he suffered what he later called a nervous breakdown, the first of two he would experience while living apart from his family. In today's terminology, what Richter experienced would likely have been diagnosed as a major depressive episode, but whatever the terminology, Richter was unquestionably forced to spend months recuperating in his parent's home. During that time, he first attempted to pursue an ambition to write stories for the magazines he had read avidly since childhood. This early apprenticeship, halting and unproductive, continued over several years as he worked as a newspaper reporter and editor, then as a private secretary in Cleveland. There his efforts finally led to acceptances, first scripts for silent films, then stories of no special merit, derivative and formulaic, with one notable exception. "Brothers of No Kin" accomplishes a surprising sophistication in narrative method and tone as its narrator ponders how it could be that Ebenezer Straint, an unbending religious crank, when confronted with the imminent death of a childhood friend who has lived profligately, would pray to take upon himself the sins of his friend. This exceptional story was chosen by Edwin O'Brien of the *Boston Evening Transcript* as the best story of 1914.

Shortly after completing "Brothers of No Kin," Richter again slipped into depression. While recuperating at his father's parsonage in Reading, Pennsylvania, Richter met Harvena Maria Achenbach of Pine Grove and immediately began an ardent courtship, spurring him to attempt, with insufficient success, to write stories for a living. They were married in 1916, immediately after Richter secured a job as manager of the Handy Book Company, a small publishing house he purchased in 1926 and renamed the Good Books Corporation. Over the next decade writing stories was an evening and weekend endeavor, the occasional sales a source of extra income. Some of these stories sold for substantial

sums, but none repeated the artistic achievement of "Brothers of No Kin."

Richter's primary interests during these years were in writing nature essays, reading all he could find about nervous disorders, and, most significantly, pursuing his own unitary theory of life's meaning. Unable to accept the gloomy tenets of his father's church, he created for himself an alternative vision of a God-centered universe—a theory of the evolution of human consciousness based on his own explanation of energy depletion and the body's recovery from stress to achieve increased energy levels. Through this process humans are able to grow to ever-higher levels of "understanding," by which Richter meant the imaginative ability to empathize with others. The goal, according to Richter in *Human Vibration* (1925), the first of what would be three books about this theory, was the ascent of human consciousness toward an ultimate understanding of God. Richter's theory also was an attempt to explain and otherwise come to terms with his own nervous affliction and acute shyness.

In 1924 Richter published a collection of his stories as *Brothers of No Kin.* Reviews were not kind, except to acknowledge the clear superiority of the title story. But Richter's aspirations for his stories were not high. As he noted in a letter (January 15, 1924) to his agent, they were written "only to furnish a little entertainment, and perhaps a stray ray or two of human warmth." With the extra income Richter bought a used Model-T Ford and in 1924 made the down payment on Pine Tree Farm, ten miles north of Harrisburg, Pennsylvania, where Richter hoped his wife could recover from pulmonary tuberculosis.

It is unlikely that Richter's occasional stories would have led to his later accomplishments had his wife's illness not become life threatening. Forced to the warmer and drier climate of New Mexico, in the spring of 1928 Richter sold his publishing company and farm and relocated to Albuquerque, where Harvena entered a sanitarium and Richter set up housekeeping with his eleven-year-old daughter. For Richter, life in the Southwest was an exile: though the days were brilliantly sunny, the desert landscape seemed barren and inhospitable, the houses and outlying ranches unkempt and unprosperous. The stock market collapse in 1929 made a bad situation disastrous. Richter's funds from the sale of his business and Pine Tree Farm were invested in stocks purchased on margin, and with the crash that margin disappeared virtually overnight, leaving Richter owing almost as much as his remaining stocks were worth at their depressed prices. His one source of income was his story writing—during a time when magazines were buying fewer stories and paying reduced sums.

From the fall of 1929 until the spring of 1934 Conrad Richter undertook a second, more stringent apprenticeship in story writing. Desperate for any income, he wrote "pulp" westerns for as little as a cent a word. No longer able to afford a sanitarium for his wife, he nursed Harvena himself, working days while she napped and nights after his wife and daughter were asleep. To find material for stories to sell to better magazines, Richter mined the area libraries and newspaper archives and visited surviving early settlers, recording in notebooks their stories and colorful language. This research and Richter's growing sensibility for the landscape and people of the Southwest led finally to the sale of "Early Marriage" to the *Saturday Evening Post,* the first of a series of stories set in the frontier West but not a "western" as magazine readers and moviegoers had come to expect. "Early Marriage" recounts the experience of a young woman who, despite threats of an Indian uprising, travels over two hundred miles of barren land to arrive on time for her wedding. In a later story, "New Home," a young woman waits stoically when her husband fails to return from his several-day ride to register their homestead. The danger in these and the stories to follow is latent, beneath the surface of the landscape, and the language of Richter's telling is taut, spare, yet evocative of the intense wariness of these characters toward the land they have come to make their own.

A painstakingly slow writer, Richter wrote only six stories during 1934, all exploring the lives of frontier women. All six sold to the *Saturday Evening Post* or its sister publication, the *Ladies Home Journal.* In 1935 Richter

introduced stories of men's experiences as well, and these stories are equally recognizable as distinctly Richter's vision—each an authentic experience of ordinary people who settled the vast, seemingly empty, and often inhospitable desert of the American Southwest. By the end of 1935 Richter had a sufficient number of stories to collect in book form. This he entitled *Early Americana,* the title of the collection's most memorable story. Like all Richter's book-length works for the remainder of his life, *Early Americana* was published by Alfred A. Knopf.

NOVELS OF THE SOUTHWEST: THE SEA OF GRASS, TACEY CROMWELL, *AND* THE LADY

Encouraged by his publisher and agent, Richter next attempted a novel, *The Sea of Grass.* Written as a three-part serial for the *Saturday Evening Post,* this novella entwines three tales within an overarching story of the conflict between a cattle baron and the homesteaders who want to plow up and fence in his grazing lands. In the first section Colonel James Brewton's young bride, Lutie, arrives in Salt Fork, New Mexico Territory. Unprepared for the lonely existence in what to her is a terrifyingly wild landscape, Lutie creates a social life imitating that which she left in St. Louis, leading to rumors that her favorite dance partner, Brice Chamberlain, the attorney for the homesteaders and Brewton's bitter enemy, has become her lover and the father of her third child. Brewton refuses to countenance the whispers until Lutie announces her intention to leave. Climaxing the first part is Brewton's attempt to confront his archenemy at the train station as Lutie boards the train for Denver. When Chamberlain, seeing Brewton, turns away from the train, Lutie departs from Salt Fork and disappears from the lives of her husband and three young children.

The second is Colonel Brewton's section, telling of the devastation to the range by nesters and their advocate Chamberlain, who uses his Washington connections to thwart Brewton's attempts to protect the land. Lutie reappears only in the final scenes of the third section, which focuses on her younger son, Brock. Indulged by his father and deserted by his mother, Brock grows into the best and worst of his impulsive nature, willfulness unmitigated by any self-restraint. Rebelling against his father, Brock moves to Salt Fork and even takes the name Chamberlain, a choice Chamberlain encourages as an additional insult to the cattle baron. When Brock's recklessness leads to murder and his own fatal wounding, word that he is dying in a nester's cabin sends Chamberlain quickly away by train; it is Brewton who rides across the ruined prairie to his son's side.

Throughout this novel of public and private conflicts, Jim Brewton, the first tamer of the desert land and its implacable defender against the farming that will ruin it, keeps faith with his vision and his family, despite the defections of his wife and youngest son. As the years pass his arrogant and ruthless visage shows the evidence of his stubborn resistance to change. When Lutie returns for her son's funeral she finds the Colonel haggard and spent, but undefeated. The tombstone he orders reads "Brock Brewton, Son of Lutie and James Brewton." And about his returned wife he says to his nephew: "She's one in a thousand, Hal. No one will ever be like her."

Hal Brewton narrates the novel retrospectively, from his old age. Looking back on events that occurred in his youth and early manhood, he acknowledges his nostalgia for the frontier life that has vanished from the New Mexico territory and his admiration for the heroic first settlers like Brewton. There is as well his attraction to the poise and sophistication Lutie brings to Salt Fork. An orphan living among men at Jim Brewton's ranch—the first of several orphans who will narrate Richter novels—Hal falls immediately under her thrall. Even in old age, remembering his uncle's defense of his range and his wife's honor, Hal does not connect Lutie's betrayal and desertion of her family with the second wave of settlers. Civilization has come to Salt Fork because of the accomplishments of pioneers like Brewton who preceded it. Though the demise of the cattle barons is a natural evolution, an inevitable progress, the second wave brings a generation of lesser men and women.

Not surprisingly, *The Sea of Grass* reintroduces several themes and motifs of *Early Americana*'s frontier stories: the larger-than-life shadows of the wilderness's first pioneers; the degeneration that comes with easier times; the inevitable losses that result because of the passage of time. It also introduced Richter's readers to other themes and motifs with which they would become familiar: the plight of lost, abandoned, or orphaned children; the visitation of suffering on others who have not themselves sinned; the restless unease of those who live without some guiding faith or purpose; and the mixed consequences of altruism. There is as well Richter's perspective on romantic love and marriage, here represented in the complex relationship of two people whose choices are indecipherable in usual romantic terms. James and Lutie Brewton are two of Richter's most memorable characters. In different ways they are each larger than life, something Metro-Goldwyn-Mayer Studio apparently recognized when it assigned to the film version of *The Sea of Grass* its two major stars, Spencer Tracy and Katharine Hepburn.

In 1942 Richter returned to the Southwest for another novella, *Tacey Cromwell,* this time to the picturesque and raucous Brewery Gulch, with its miners' houses perched on the canyon's steep hillsides, in the town of Bisbee, Arizona. Again the narrator is remembering past events of a bygone time, and again the narrator is an orphan. Nugget Oldaker has come to live with Tacey Cromwell, a reformed madam, and her common-law husband Gaye Oldaker, a gambler from Tacey's former sporting house and Nugget's half brother. When a miner's death leaves a young girl, Seely Dowdon, an orphan, the residents of Brewery Gulch are happy to have Tacey take in the child. However, a resident from the other side of town, Quality Hill, steps in to take both children from Tacey because she is a woman living with a man not her husband. For Nugget, the foster home turns out well enough, but for Seely, adopted by Rudith Watrous, the daughter of the town's richest man, the change spells disaster.

A major issue of the novel is the contrast of Tacey's strict discipline and Rudith Watrous's indulgence of the wild and self-destructive Seely. A second issue is the social difference in the treatment of Tacey and Gaye; both have the same unsavory past, but Tacey remains an untouchable as Gaye is welcomed into the community—the citizens of Quality Hill ignoring that Gaye is weak and Tacey strong, he selfish and she giving, and he morally spineless except when propped up by his former mistress. In its depiction of human nature *Tacey Cromwell* is Richter's darkest book, contrasting the boisterous vitality of Brewery Gulch to the constricted lives of the socially correct residents of Quality Hill. As a community, Quality Hill is a closed, repressive system, close in spirit to the novels of Richter's neighbor from Pottsville, John O'Hara, where social conventions become weapons for the ambitious and vindictive. To live in that world requires wariness and a shrewd sense of human nature, and it requires self-discipline to guard one's thoughts and feelings. Tacey has these things, and she also has the qualities that most of Richter's heroines possess: the will to persevere despite hardship, and the generosity of spirit to keep alive, through long separations, her love for Nugget, Seely, and even the indolent Gaye.

Richter's final novel of the Southwest, *The Lady,* appeared as a four-part serial in the *Saturday Evening Post* in 1957. Again the narrator is remembering in old age events he witnessed in childhood, when taken in as an orphan. Like Lutie Brewton in *The Sea of Grass,* Doña Ellen Johnson y Campo is an aristocratic, charismatic woman. But unlike Lutie, Doña Ellen has grown up on the high desert and is entirely at home on the vast holdings of the Johnson y Campo family. As heir to an estate that has been claimed and held by forebears strong enough to impose their own order upon huge tracts of land, she accepts as an unquestioned right her authority to defend her property by whatever force is necessary.

When a cattleman is shot to death while maliciously driving his herd across her land, destroying her garden, Doña Ellen's neighbors believe she fired the shot even when her brother takes responsibility. Although her brother is found innocent in court, her rash act ultimately brings on the murder of her brother and the disappearance and presumed death of her husband and son.

For Doña Ellen these terrible losses initiate a spiritual journey, bringing her to accept her personal culpability. Attempting to change the circumstances that brought on the original enmity and killing, she is made more vulnerable to the predations of the man responsible for the loss of her brother, husband, and son. In the novel's crisis, Doña Ellen chooses not to pursue her vengeance against her enemy but to leave him to a higher justice. The choice is difficult, requiring a self-discipline she has never before been asked to command; and the result, as is usual in Richter's novels, is a psychic growth in inner strength and "understanding."

THE OHIO TRILOGY: THE TREES, THE FIELDS, *AND* THE TOWN

Before *The Sea of Grass* appeared in the *Saturday Evening Post* during the fall of 1937, Richter had accepted a $15,000 offer from Metro-Goldwyn-Mayer for the movie rights to his novel, releasing him from debt for the first time since October 1929. Following the book's publication in February 1938, reviews were favorable, lauding Richter's novel as a promising beginning, and sales were those of a modest best seller. The reviews arrived just as Richter completed a four-month assignment writing scripts for MGM, an exasperating experience for a writer who had never before attempted to craft stories by committee. Despite his reservations, Richter accepted a second contract the following fall; though out of debt, he needed funds to research and write his next major project, a trilogy of novels about a family migrating from the farmlands of Pennsylvania into the dense virgin forests of Ohio. As Richter's journal entries from the second Hollywood experience indicate, Richter's disgust at the unreality of Hollywood's films catalyzed his determination to write something utterly different from that "fiction" and even from the plot protocols he was obliged to observe to sell stories to the *Saturday Evening Post.*

For a writer as hesitant and cautious of his success as Richter, his decision to write *The Trees* was remarkable. His story took him away from his expertise writing about the southwestern frontier to a distinctly different wilderness experience, a family homesteading in the primeval forest of Ohio. *The Trees* is a novel of discrete incidents, told omnisciently but primarily through the consciousness of the novel's central character, Sayward Luckett, the narrative interlacing limited omniscience and interior monologue. Chapters do not move sequentially toward a traditional climax but are rather a series of individual experiences, ordinary events brought into sharp focus, as in Richter's earlier stories of the Southwest, by his careful use of historical detail. Narrated in language reflecting the untutored speech of the earliest settlers, together the chapters accrete into an intimately felt sense of life as Sayward and her family would have lived it. Richter's narrative language is at its most poetic in passages where Sayward is acutely aware of the forest world, experiencing there a sense of menace, of things lurking, but also the ephemeral intimations of an organic unity with nature.

As the novel begins, Worth Luckett is guiding his family out of the farmland of Pennsylvania and into the virgin forests of Ohio, choosing a cabin site deep in the twilit depths, where no sunshine reaches the ground. There his wife, Jary, sickens and dies of the "slow fever," tuberculosis, leaving Sayward, oldest of five children, as housekeeper and caregiver for her brothers and sisters. When Worth, her father, does not return from a hunting foray, "Saird" again accepts what providence has given her to do. As the seasons pass she grows to a sturdy young woman who has cleared enough land to begin rudimentary farming, welcomed new neighbors, turned down marriage proposals, and seen the marriage, then abandonment and emotional collapse, of her sister Genny. Most heartrending of all, she has experienced the loss of Sulie, the youngest, who disappears into the dark forest one afternoon and is never found.

The first novel of the trilogy ends with Sayward's strange marriage to "the solitary," Portius Wheeler, a dissolute Massachusetts lawyer living as a hermit in an ill-made, ill-kept cabin. What begins as a cruel joke by others on a drunken Wheeler ends in Sayward's offer to

marry him—an offer to which a sober Portius acquiesces. The next day finds Sayward and Portius both taking axes to the trees that enclose and obstruct their cabin, an unromantic marriage of oddly yoked partners that would outlast the dark woods surrounding them.

Richter's second novel was published to critical acclaim, reviewers commending Sayward's memorable portrayal, the lyrical quality of the novel's telling, the rich use of folklore and historical detail, and Richter's mastery of a narrative voice evoking an authentic feel of pioneer speech. The novel would be a finalist for the Pulitzer Prize for Fiction for 1941 and, as a Book of the Month Club selection, *The Trees* became Richter's largest-selling novel in hardback and among the most financially rewarding. When MGM offered $25,000 for the film rights, Richter rejected the offer for fear that a Hollywood version of his novel would wreck any chance for him to continue Sayward's story.

Richter returned in 1944 to the story of the Luckett family. Like *The Trees, The Fields* is episodic, and again the narration relies upon the idiom of the original settlers. There is no central conflict, no primary obstruction, no crisis leading to a climax. Incidents play out over seasons, with Richter's rich evocation making the land itself a major character. Sayward continues to be the central consciousness, the story told primarily in her voice as she and her family attend to the slow, arduous work of clearing their land and raising first crops. In the twenty years following her marriage, Sayward gives birth to eight children. More settlers arrive and become neighbors, the trading outpost becomes a settlement, and a sawmill is built on the river, the beginnings of industrial development.

In five central chapters the narrative perspective shifts to Sayward's oldest two sons. From the eyes of Resolve and Guerdon, their lawyer father, Portius, cuts an increasingly impressive figure as the backwoods "improvement" surrounding their cabin becomes the settlement of Moonshine Church and finally the incorporated town of Americus. But despite the sons' admiring thoughts about their father, they understand that their mother, Sayward, is the rock upon which the family is built. After years of heavy labor, she has become a tall, thick, imposing woman. Still in her own mind a "woodsy," barely able to write her name, she is nonetheless the unquestioned head of the family. Even the eloquent and educated Portius defers to her.

In a thematically significant and especially poignant chapter, Sayward struggles through the anguish of a humiliating discovery. After eight children, Sayward has refused to sleep any longer with Portius, thinking to save herself another lying in and recuperation. In time Portius has an affair with the schoolmarm, and when Mistress Bartram marries the scoundrel Jake Tench, only Sayward does not know that Bartram is with child and the child's father is Portius. When the truth is revealed to her, Sayward takes her straining nerves to the fields, tasking herself to plow behind her oxen—slow, dull creatures, imperturbably plodding. Forced to settle herself to their pace, Sayward gradually regains her composure and in essence achieves a Richterian "understanding." As much as she blames Portius for his betrayal, she blames herself as well for willfully cheating God, putting her own preferences ahead of His: "That was her secret sin. You couldn't cheat God and live. Sooner or later His word would catch up with you." And the sign of her sin is that empty place in the ages of her children, a place filled elsewhere, a baby in another mother's arms.

Critics have repeatedly commented on Richter's talent for communicating the numinousness of the natural world and his mastery of a narrative style that weaves the sound of pioneer speech into his narrator's voice. In "The Cherry Yoke," the novel's penultimate chapter, he accomplishes just such an evocation as Sayward fights against her anger and anguish, drawing comfort from her land and slowly gathering the self control and higher understanding that for Richter are the goals of human evolution. In her own language, Sayward is "broke to the yoke now. She had fought against it. She had yawed around and fouled it. But it did no good in the end." It is an important lesson for the strong-willed Sayward, one she will learn again in the third volume of the trilogy. Although her relation-

ship with Portius is forever changed by his infidelity, Sayward returns to his bed and, in time, gives birth to two more children.

Like most Richter novels, *The Fields* was a modest best seller, selling 14,000 initial copies. Reviews were mixed but primarily positive, again lauding Richter's talent in bringing the historical record of pioneering so evocatively to life. Unsatisfied by these sales, Richter began *The Town,* the third part of his trilogy, promising himself that this novel would have more plot and more action. The novel Richter finished three years later was his longest and most traditionally plotted, carrying the chronicle of "westering" to its conclusion, with Americus a thriving center of commerce and industry. Though artistically less successful than the first two, the novel does make more explicit the messages underlying all three in its portrayal of contrasting perspectives and values.

Several narrative streams run through *The Town.* One has to do with the growth and departure from home of Sayward's children and the gradual dispersal, then death, of her oldest friends and relatives. A second traces the expansion of the town, its growing pains as it transforms from rural life and values to more citified ways. The evolving town and the "modern" notions of its inhabitants are part of a third stream, with Sayward, as she ages, voicing more and more insistently Richter's belief that easier times make for softer, less interesting people. Another is the continuation of Sayward's evolving response toward trees—the enemy of her first years in the forest, obstructions to be cut down and grubbed out over years, even decades. In the final years of her life Sayward's perspective on trees has changed so completely that Americus seems to her barren without them, and she has saplings planted around her house and protects them in her will.

The most prominent stream concerns Sayward's youngest child, Chancey. Born "sickly" and not expected to live, he is nursed through early illnesses by Sayward and watched over fretfully throughout his childhood. Because he has a weak heart, Chancey spends his early life sitting by a window while his siblings play outside. Forced into inactivity, he receives much more completely than they the sights and sounds of the outside, experiencing the natural world with all his senses. Sitting by his window, Chancey also daydreams of a world where he runs and plays with children like himself, who understand him without his even speaking. In adolescence Chancey discovers a soul mate in Rosa Tench, who is equally sensitive to nature's marvels and escapes like Chancey into her own imaginary world. But Rosa is Chancey's half sister, from his father's adulterous affair in *The Fields,* and both families try to keep the two apart. When Chancey discovers their kinship and separates from her, Rosa's despair leads to her taking her own life. In his own anguish Chancey seeks out and rejects what to him are only callous pieties offered by several different religions and from his atheist father's "religion" of the body of the law. He does find some comfort in the curious ranting of an addled old man, Johnny Appleseed, who preaches something about the unity of all in God and gives Chancey two pages torn from a book by Emanuel Swedenborg.

Intensely aware of Chancey's suffering, Sayward offers her son no advice, having discovered that too often her acts to help others only make matters worse. It is a lesson she has suffered greatly to learn. Having overprotected Chancey throughout his childhood, she watches him grow into a priggish, prideful young man who turns from his family and places all his energies into publishing a pacifist newspaper. There he writes solemn editorials attacking his older brother Resolve, who has become Ohio's governor, and espousing everything "modern" that promises people more comfort and ease. These are virtually ignored by the townspeople except his mother.

Intermittently throughout *The Town* are interior monologues from the minds of Sayward, Chancey, Rosa, and others, as they respond to the natural world surrounding them. The final two chapters are the interior thoughts of Sayward, then Chancey. In "The Witness Tree," Sayward is in her eighties, too old to live alone but refusing to leave the huge house she had been outfoxed by Portius into building. There she lives

an inward life, slipping from the present to reveries of lost times and lost friends—memories affirming her belief that the hard times of the earliest settlers delivered benefits that following generations could not understand. Chancey's chapter is less celebratory. As his mother's health deteriorates and she lies unconscious, he discovers that she has been the anonymous donor who has supported his press. For Chancey, the revelation turns inside out his cynical assumptions about the unenlightened selfishness underlying the apparent generosities of the early settlers like his mother. But he cannot ask her why she has underwritten a newspaper directly attacking her ideas. She is no longer reachable. The novel ends with what would become a characteristic Richter manner for his later novels: Chancey stands over his mother's unconscious body, uncertain where to turn.

The Town was awarded the Pulitzer Prize for Fiction in 1950, a prize generally recognized to be for the whole chronicle of Sayward's life. Reviews were again laudatory, describing the three works collectively as a "distinguished achievement." When Knopf published the trilogy as a single volume titled *The Awakening Land,* the praise from reviewers was even higher, most notably that of Isaac Bashevis Singer, who wrote in *Life* magazine (September 30, 1966) that "one can scarcely believe that talent and research alone could have created this vast panorama of American life," and pronounced *The Awakening Land* to be "a great novel in any literature," and "a literary edifice that will endure."

SERIALS FOR THE POST

During the years writing the three novels of *The Awakening Land,* Richter several times put aside what he considered his important books to write novellas to sell as serials to the *Saturday Evening Post.* These shorter novels Richter thought of as lesser work, necessary to acquire the capital for major projects like the trilogy, but nonetheless needing to be crafted well out of pride in his workmanship and his reputation. *Tacey Cromwell* had been the first of these. When the *Post* turned down the story of a reformed madam as unsuitable for its audience, Richter immediately followed *Tacey Cromwell* with a novella about the American Revolution. A four-part serial published during the summer of 1943, *The Free Man* again demonstrates Richter's thorough research of primary materials, though to less effect.

Written during the early days of American participation in World War II and intended to be a patriotic story about the high but justified cost of freedom, the novel is the story of Henry Dellicker, a German immigrant tricked into signing papers of indenture. After an effectively realized first section, the Atlantic crossing, the novel slips into historical romance uncharacteristic of Richter. Once in Philadelphia, Henry is persecuted by the haughty and imperious Amity Bayley, niece of his master. Rebelling, he escapes and hides above Pennsylvania's Blue Mountain, where he lives safely as Henry Free until his patriotism leads him to enlist in General Washington's army. That choice takes him back to Philadelphia and to his arrest and further humiliation by the vindictive Amity, but all ends well when the two settle their differences and marry. Implausible even for historical romance, *The Free Man* is a disappointing novel, Richter's weakest. Even so, there are well-captured scenes of the shipboard experience and of life in Pennsylvania Dutch settlements north of Blue Mountain. Thematically, it shares with other novels Richter's belief that humans evolve spiritually from hardship endured.

A third novella written for the *Saturday Evening Post,* begun as Richter revised *The Fields,* would be for Richter an experiment. By making the setting of *Always Young and Fair* a fictional representation of his hometown of Pine Grove, Pennsylvania, Richter hoped to replace much of his usual historical research with memories from his own childhood and adolescence. Published as a single-issue, abridged novel in the *Post,* then by Alfred Knopf in 1946, *Always Young and Fair* is closest to *The Sea of Grass* in its depiction of strong-willed and enigmatically motivated characters and of what in Richter novels are often vexed human relations of love and marriage. But whereas *The Sea*

of Grass affirms a way of life and regrets its passing, *Always Young and Fair,* even with its celebration of small-town life, exposes the emptiness of its primary characters' lives.

Lucy Markle and Will Grail live in turn-of-the-century America and suffer from the twentieth-century woes of alienation and displacement. Having promised herself to a man who does not return from the Spanish-American War, Lucy refuses to abandon the memory of the dead soldier she did not love to marry Will Grail, the man she does love. As a love story, *Always Young and Fair* has something of the foreboding inevitability of *Ethan Frome,* Edith Wharton's starkly naturalistic novel, which Richter had read and been powerfully moved by just before beginning to write his story of Pine Grove. The flux of feeling between Lucy Markle and Will Grail creates an unsettling tale of frustrated love and engagement between two people who, because they are alive, cannot be constant and, because they are "modern," have nothing fixed upon which to orient themselves.

NONFICTION: THE MOUNTAIN ON THE DESERT

Richter never abandoned his plans to write another nonfiction book about his theories of a unitary, coherent, comprehendible meaning of life. Following the publication of *The Town,* Richter took up again the project of explaining his theories. Put aside several times, the book he finally published in 1955, *The Mountain on the Desert,* is a series of conversations between an ascetic weaver of rugs and four students who visit him at his mountain hermitage. The weaver Michael's message is that all life is the gathering and expending of energy; that human consciousness expands and rises toward "God" only by increasing its capacity for energy release, thereby shedding lower orders of understanding; and that higher levels of energy release are obtained only by self-imposed stoicism or, for those without self-discipline, hardships imposed by fate. As Michael explains, it is human nature to crave ease, but growth comes only through experiences that strain energy resources. The goal of Michael's regimen is to create God-like levels of understanding, in its ultimate form a sympathetic identification with all living things. Understood rightly, according to Michael, hate is only the raw material of love. When the book was finally published—reluctantly by Alfred Knopf—there was almost no critical response. In time several academic scholars would puzzle out the relationships between Richter's theories and his novels, with interesting insights. But for Richter the lack of any first response to what to him was unquestionably his most important work was exceedingly painful, a humiliation he did not easily overcome.

THE LIGHT IN THE FOREST

In 1952 Richter put a draft of *The Mountain on the Desert* aside to write another serial for the *Saturday Evening Post.* From historical accounts he knew that not all settler's children returned from Indian captivity were happily reunited with their families. From this kernel and Richter's usual historical research came *The Light in the Forest,* Richter's best known and most widely read novel. This is the story of fifteen-year-old John Butler, renamed True Son by his Indian foster parents, who after eleven years among the Tuscaroras is forced by a peace treaty to return to his white family in western Pennsylvania. True Son resists, as do other children raised in Indian families, including the wife of Little Crane. True Son's friend Half Arrow and Little Crane follow along with the returning militia as far as Fort Pittsburgh. There they are turned back, and True Son and Little Crane's wife continue on to their families in Paxton Township—famous for the Paxton Boys who savagely attacked Indian villages, killing all including children. There John Butler resists his family's efforts to re-acculturate him. Even the clothes he is given are uncomfortable to wear, emblems of a people who have done evil to Indians, and he is puzzled by white ways—imprisoning themselves in dark houses instead of living in the free air, building huge barns to store possessions, instead of sharing with one's neighbors, as Indians do. At a family gathering John angrily confronts his uncle Wilse

Owens, who has participated in the Paxton Boys' massacres of Indian women and children.

When Half Arrow appears and takes John to the body of Little Crane, murdered while trying to visit his wife, the two boys confront Wilse Owens with the murder, wounding him before escaping together back to their Indian village. When True Son joins his father and the Tuscorora braves in avenging the murder of Little Crane, he witnesses the savagery he had accused his Uncle Wilse of perpetrating, his fellow warriors murdering defenseless women and children. Ordered to decoy a riverboat of settlers to shore, True Son refuses, leaving him an outcast from both white and Indian families, alienated from both his worldly fathers. "Who then is my father?" True Son asks. At novel's end he is alone at a ford carrying him to the land of the white settlers. He cannot return to his Indian village; he cannot go forward into a white world where he is now an enemy.

Once again Richter had fashioned an ending that was not what he termed, derogatorily, "fiction." As he had throughout his career as a novelist, Richter resisted concluding his stories with either a wedding or a funeral. At the insistence of the *Saturday Evening Post,* Richter had acquiesced in rewriting the final chapters of *The Sea of Grass,* making clearer where Lutie had been for fifteen years, but he declined to answer the question of what the prospects were for the Colonel and Lutie Brewton to continue their lives together. Equally indefinite is the conclusion of *Tacey Cromwell,* where Tacey's "family" is temporarily reunited but with no hint of what the next day will bring. And at the conclusion of *The Town,* Sayward's youngest child, Chancey, remains alone and perplexed at the bedside of his dying mother. Chancey's circumstance comes closest to that of True Son, who also finds himself alone and friendless, not knowing where to turn.

Because *The Light in the Forest* presents sympathetically and realistically the strife between American Indians and the early European settlers, the novella has remained for decades on the assigned reading lists for many school districts. Until his death more than a decade after the novel's publication, Richter received letters from school classes asking what happened to True Son. In 1966 Richter answered that question in *A Country of Strangers,* a companion novel to *The Light in the Forest,* choosing for his main character a white woman raised by Indians who has taken an Indian husband and borne him a child. Told she must be returned, Stone Girl and her husband plot to hide her far away from the "Yengues," a journey that takes her and her child to the far shore of Lake Erie, then north to Lake Ontario. Only after she learns of the death of her husband does she agree to be returned to her parents' home along the Susquehanna. But there an impostor has taken her place, and her efforts to reunite with her family are rejected by her father and younger sister, who are unable to understand her behavior and misconstrue her efforts to save her sister's life—actions that cost Stone Girl the life of her own child. Left with no home, husband, or child, she accepts the offer of True Son, who has appeared at her white father's house during an Indian uprising. Together they travel westward, away from the farm fields of white civilization and into the dark forests of the Tuscaroras.

As they depart, Stone Girl pauses before turning forever from the family that has rejected her. The novel concludes with what is a rare Richter poem, unquestionably his best, an imitation of and tribute to Old English alliterative poetry. Looking back for a last time, Stone Girl remembers the chant of an old man from her village. The novel's title appears in the poem's second line:

> I am the wanderer. I am the exile,
> Banished to live in a country of strangers. ...
>
> (p. 168)

THE UNFINISHED "FAMILY" TRILOGY: THE WATERS OF KRONOS *AND* A SIMPLE HONORABLE MAN

From the sale of Pine Tree Farm in 1928 until 1950, when Richter purchased a home in Pine Grove, he and his wife lived as nomads—often moving several times a year, renting furnished

houses in the Southwest, California, and Pennsylvania, and tourist cabins in Florida. They moved for Harvena's health but also for the energizing effect Richter believed new scenery had on his writing. Once the Pine Grove home was purchased, Richter and Harvena chose to spend all but the coldest months of each year there. Again living in the town of his childhood, Richter began to contemplate a trilogy of autobiographical novels drawing even more directly upon his childhood memories than had *Always Young and Fair.*

The Waters of Kronos begins that trilogy. Commentators on Richter's novels have remarked that he is one of America's most autobiographical novelists. The accuracy of this description rests almost entirely on *The Water of Kronos* and the novel following it, *A Simple Honorable Man.* In *The Waters of Kronos* virtually every character is identifiable from Richter's own family and his childhood in Pine Grove. Names have changed, but relationships to John Donner, the protagonist, are identical to those of family members and friends to Conrad Richter, novelist. Like Richter, John Donner is a successful novelist, modest of his accomplishments and embarrassed by fame.

Although orphanage and questions of fatherhood have occurred frequently in Richter's work, in *The Waters of Kronos* he writes with the thinnest of fictional veils about the distance separating him from his father, their difference in personality and demeanor, and his lifelong suspicion that he was not his father's son. And he confronts more directly than before in his novels and stories his own persistent struggle because he could not, like his father, abandon himself entirely into Christianity. The resulting novel is a haunting book, Richter at his best in creating the sights, sounds, and sensations of small-town life in rural Pennsylvania. Because the progress of the novel is a spiritual quest, a journey into the past in search of reasons to hope for a future, the descriptions resonate with the deep, desperate longing of a dying man to return to his parents' home and his childhood.

The Waters of Kronos returns to a narrative device from an earlier story, "Dr. Hanray's Second Chance," in which an elderly scientist is transported into his own childhood. There he warns himself as a boy not to follow the educational path he took, leading to the Manhattan Project and the atomic bomb. In *The Waters of Kronos* the aging novelist John Donner, ill and preparing for death, journeys to the hometown of his childhood to visit the graves of his parents. But the relocated graves are no longer in the quiet valley through which the Kronos River once flowed. The river has been dammed, and the churches, stores, and houses of Unionville are buried deep beneath the waters. Taking a path that should lead to the water's edge, John Donner encounters a wagon loaded with anthracite creaking down an old road. Accepting a ride from the silent teamster, he descends magically into the Unionville of his childhood, where it is 1899 and the town is busy preparing for the funeral of John Donner's grandfather, the town's most prominent minister.

Though the seventy-year-old John Donner steps eagerly into the streets of his childhood, he quickly discovers that he cannot reach back from his old age to again become a part of that life. At his father's store his father impatiently turns away the old and apparently addled man. Attempting to visit his favorite aunt, Donner is again rebuffed. Unable to make himself known to anyone, Donner places his hopes on his mother, Valeria Donner, who he believes will surely recognize him. But at the funeral her face is covered by a black veil, and at the funeral dinner afterward she is hidden behind others at the table.

As the novel ends Donner is lying ill in the other half of the double house of his childhood. There the young Johnny Donner visits him, carrying a message from his mother. Seeing the fright in the young boy's eyes, Donner raises himself to look in the bureau mirror and confronts the specter from his own childhood nightmares. It is not the spirit of his father, as he has thought; rather the demon is the image of his own decaying and death, the reality of his mortality. The only hope against this slow dissolution is the survival of the soul after earthly death, and that is what John Donner longs for as he awaits his mother. She has promised to visit him and "she had never told him a falsehood yet."

The Waters of Kronos was published in 1960 to excellent reviews and in 1961 was awarded the National Book Award for fiction. Though the award did not lead to sales beyond Richter's usual numbers, it did spur Richter to undertake immediately the second book of his planned trilogy. The award apparently also spurred several academic critics to approach Richter with plans to write about his stories and novels. Reluctantly Richter allowed himself to be interviewed and patiently answered lists of questions sent to him by mail. On receiving copies of their work, Richter offered polite replies. About what he had been sent, Richter wrote in his journal, in typically modest fashion, "They all misunderstand me. I write simply about people I admire, principally those who have the vision to accept their life and its hardships as something given to grapple with and try to overcome for both temporary and permanent benefits" (November 9, 1963).

The permanent benefits Richter refers to are spiritual, the psychic evolution that is the subject of *The Mountain on the Desert.* As Richter's characters like Sayward and Doña Ellen struggle to accept hardships as things they must learn to bear, they achieve a raised consciousness, a higher order of "understanding." In *A Simple Honorable Man* the Reverend Harry Donner has an equally sustaining vision. If at times he is distressed by the pain and consequent suffering that inhabit the lives of his parishioners, these troubles do not affect his faith. Nor does he question why people dedicated to God's work are so often thwarted by bedeviling circumstances. The answers to these questions await him in the hereafter. That conclusion is less satisfying for his son Johnny, who asks why there are so few earthly rewards for simple honorable men like his father. And what of the pastor's wife, his mother—relegated to a life of poverty, kept from her family and friends as Harry Donner moves from one poor parish to another?

Visiting the churches of his father's ministry, John Donner puzzles over his father's seemingly unrewarding life as a servant of God. At a country church he listens as an organ is played by the tuner who has completed his work, beauty emanating from the small church, empty except for the tuner, the music dissipating "into the air, unheard, unacknowledged." But if the seemingly wasted music is symbolic for John Donner of his father's life among unremarkable people in obscure parishes, his conclusion was not shared by the novel's reviewers. With few exceptions these passed over the novel's lax narrative structure and emphasized Richter's success in accomplishing the difficult task of creating in fiction an insightful, uplifting, and entertaining psychological portrait of a good man.

THE LAST NOVELS

Following *A Simple Honorable Man,* Richter tried repeatedly to write the concluding novel of his trilogy. Tentatively entitled "River to the Sea" and, more explicitly, "The Search for Meaning," each time Richter returned to the manuscript he found himself suffering nighttime attacks of heart arrhythmia that forced him to put aside his chapters. During the times when he was unable to work on "River to the Sea," Richter completed his last two novels, both of which he thought of as his "lesser work." The first was a comic novel based on the hillside farming families he had known when living at Pine Tree Farm, the second a fictional portrait of a prominent Pine Grove character, the last vestige of the town's nineteenth-century aristocracy.

In *The Grandfathers* two families dispute which has the right to claim the young, comely Chariter Murdock, the daughter of an unmarried women, as one of their own. This is another portrait of a strong-willed woman, calm in the face of confusion. In this novel, however, the alarms and upsets are comic, Richter creating again the special expressiveness of country people whose speech had been the model for the Ohio trilogy. Just old enough to be thinking about marriage, Chariter Murdock is curious to discover the identity of her father, a secret her mother has kept from her. She also must deal with her discovery that the man she plans to wed is conniving to cohabit rather than marry. Born out of wedlock and surrounded by siblings and cousins who are also the offspring of illegitimate relation-

ships, Chariter sets for herself a different standard. Though the novel is a collection of comic vignettes, its heroine has the recognizable characteristics of other Richter heroines: practical and resolute, Chariter intuitively understands what is right for her and perseveres. She will not be diverted.

Though Richter's one attempt at a comic novel met with some success, both with reviewers and book buyers, it is not one of his more accomplished novels. Nor would be his next and last, *The Aristocrat,* written as his health declined and published just before his death. Again stymied by "River to the Sea," Richter put aside his notebooks about his own life and took up a notebook full of epigrammatic quotes from a favorite dinner companion, Augusta Filbert. From these he created Alexandra Morley, the last of Uniontown's Victorians, who holds forth about the encroachments of most things modern. Many of the novel's incidents were taken from events well known to Richter and others in Pine Grove. Instilling life into these anecdotes were the pithy and often tart quips of Miss Alexandra and her commentaries on earlier life in Uniontown, the behavior of current residents, and the striking difference between the two. The novel offers Richter's last portrait of a strong-hearted woman.

CONCLUSION

Conrad Richter's career as a novelist began late. Though he had written a number of short stories for magazines during the first decade of his marriage and written desperately to support his family during the early years of the Great Depression, his first attempt to write a novel was not undertaken until 1936. When *The Sea of Grass* was published in 1937, Richter was forty-seven years old. Thereafter until his death on October 30, 1968, at the age of seventy-eight, Richter produced fourteen novels, a book for children, *Over the Blue Mountain* (1967), and a nonfiction work on his philosophical theories. In addition to the eight stories collected in *Early Americana,* Richter wrote another eleven stories, all published in the *Post* or *Atlantic Monthly,* and several nonfiction articles.

Richter thought himself to be an exceptionally slow writer, and most of his novels were shorter works—novellas. As a novelist he was best at the condensation and unity of effect that can be achieved within this shorter form, falling between the short story and the fully developed novel. The best of Richter's novels are, by consensus, his first, *The Sea of Grass,* the first two of his Ohio trilogy, *The Trees* and *The Fields,* and *The Waters of Kronos.* All these demonstrate Richter's most notable accomplishments as a novelist: his use of particular historical detail to communicate a felt sense of a distinct place and time, and his ability to place within these environments sharply drawn, complex characters who are believably real for readers. The most memorable of these are Sayward Luckett and Portius Wheeler of the Ohio trilogy, Harry Donner of *A Simple Honorable Man,* Jim and Lutie Brewton of *The Sea of Grass,* and, to a lesser extent, Doña Ellen of *The Lady.*

Despite excellent reviews and attempts by admirers such as Isaac Bashevis Singer to attract critics and readers to Richter's work, Richter's novels have received little attention from the academy. Following the National Book Award, there was modest interest by academic critics, resulting in a number of articles in professional journals and three book-length studies. All are useful for initial study of Richter's work, and especially noteworthy is Clifford Edwards' *Conrad Richter's Ohio Trilogy,* the best extended discussion of Richter's theories and their relationship to his stories and novels.

The inattention of academic scholars is in part due to Richter's classification as a writer of historical novels, a genre not held in high regard among literary scholars. Perhaps more importantly, Richter was not an experimenter in form or subject matter, nor engaged except peripherally in exploring the modernist woes of alienation and loss of faith, and thus his work has not attracted the interest of the formalist critics of his own time or of the diverse schools of criticism that have followed. Although Richter is not regarded as a major figure in twentieth-century American literature, he rightfully has a place and continues to have a readership. Most of his novels

remain available in paperback, and readers continue to be attracted to his fictional portrayals of earlier times.

Selected Bibliography

WORKS BY CONRAD RICHTER

Novels

The Sea of Grass. New York: Knopf, 1937.

The Trees. New York: Knopf, 1940.

Tacey Cromwell. New York: Knopf, 1942.

The Free Man. New York: Knopf, 1943.

The Fields. New York: Knopf, 1946.

Always Young and Fair. New York: Knopf, 1947.

The Town. New York: Knopf, 1950.

The Light in the Forest. New York: Knopf, 1953.

The Lady. New York: Knopf, 1957.

The Waters of Kronos. New York: Knopf, 1960.

A Simple Honorable Man. New York: Knopf, 1962.

The Grandfathers. New York: Knopf, 1964.

A Country of Strangers. New York: Knopf, 1966.

The Awakening Land. New York: Knopf, 1966. (First publication of the trilogy *The Trees, The Fields, The Town* in one volume.)

Over the Blue Mountain. New York: Knopf, 1967. Illustrated by Herbert Danska. (Juvenile novella.)

The Aristocrat. New York: Knopf, 1968.

Short Story Collections

Brothers of No Kin and Other Stories. New York: Hinds, Hayden & Eldridge, 1924.

Early Americana and Other Stories. New York: Knopf, 1936.

The Rawhide Knot and Other Stories. New York: Knopf, 1978.

Nonfiction

Human Vibration: The Underlying Mechanics of Life and Mind. Harrisburg. Penn.: Handy Book Corporation, 1925.

Principles in Bio-Physics: The Underlying Process Controlling Life Phenomena and Inner Evolution. Harrisburg, Penn.: Good Books Corporation, 1927.

The Mountain on the Desert: A Philosophical Journey. New York: Knopf, 1955.

Selected Articles

"Individualists Under the Shade Trees." In *A Vanishing America.* Edited by Thomas C. Wheeler. New York: Holt, Rinehart, and Winston, 1964. Pp. 34–42.

"New Mexico Was Our Fate." *New Mexico Magazine,* March 1957, pp. 2–21, 45, 47.

"Pennsylvania." *Holiday,* October 1955, pp. 98–112.

"That Early American Quality." *Atlantic,* September 1950, pp. 26–30.

"Three Towns I Love." *Holiday,* December 1953, pp. 54–58, 94, 96, 98, 100, 103–105.

"Valley From the Past." *Country Beautiful,* April 1963, pp. 8–13.

CRITICAL AND BIOGRAPHICAL STUDIES

Barnard, Kenneth J. "Presentation of the West in Conrad Richter's Trilogy." *Northwest Ohio Quarterly* 29, no. 4:224–234 (1957).

Barnes, Robert J. *Conrad Richter.* Austin, Tex.: Steck-Vaughn, 1968.

Carpenter, Frederic I. "Conrad Richter's Pioneers: Reality and Myth." *College English* 12, no 2:77–83 (1950).

Edwards, Clifford D. *Conrad Richter's Ohio Trilogy: Its Ideas, Themes, and Relationship to Literary Tradition.* The Hague: Mouton, 1970.

Flanagan, John T. "Folklore in the Novels of Conrad Richter." *Midwest Folklore* 2:5–15 (spring 1952).

———. "Conrad Richter: Romancer of the Southwest." *Southwest Review* 43:189–196 (1958).

Gaston, Edwin W., Jr. *Conrad Richter.* New Haven, Conn.: Twayne, 1965; updated ed., Boston: Twayne, 1989.

Johnson, David R. *Conrad Richter: A Writer's Life.* University Park: Pennsylvania State University Press, 2001.

Kohler, Dayton. "Conrad Richter: Early Americana." *College English* 8, no. 5:221–227 (1947).

Lahood, Marvin J. "*The Light in the Forest*: History or Fiction." *English Journal* 55, no. 3:298–304 (1966).

———. "Conrad Richter and Willa Cather: Some Similarities." *Xavier University Studies* 9, no. 1:33–46 (1970).

———. "Conrad Richter's Pennsylvania Trilogy." *Susquehanna University Studies* 8, no. 2:5–13 (1968).

———. *Conrad Richter's America.* The Hague: Mouton, 1975.

McCullough, David. "Cross the Blue Mountain." *Country Journal,* February 1977, pp. 63–67.

Meldrum, Barbara. "Conrad Richter's Southwestern Ladies." In *Women, Women Writers, and the West.* Troy, N.Y.: Whitson, 1978.

Milton, John R. "The Novel of the American West." *South Dakota Review* 2, no. 1:56–76 (1964).

Pierce, T. M. "Conrad Richter." *New Mexico Quarterly* 20, no. 3:371–373 (1950).

Schmaier, Maurice D. "Conrad Richter's *The Light in the Forest*: An Ethnohistorical Approach to Fiction." *Ethnohistory* 7, no. 4:327–398 (1960).

Sutherland, Bruce. "Conrad Richter's Americana." *New Mexico Quarterly* 15, no. 1:413–422 (1945).

PAPERS

Conrad Richter's manuscripts, writing notebooks, journals, and letters are to be found primarily at Paterno Library, The Pennsylvania State University, and Firestone Library, Princeton University. Other manuscript holdings are to be found at The American Academy of Arts and Letters; Mugar Library, Boston University; the University of California at Los Angeles Library; and Toppan Library, University of Wyoming.

PAUL WILLIAM RYAN

(1906—1947)

Joseph G. Ramsey

BORN ON JULY 7, 1906 in San Francisco shortly after the great earthquake and fire of that year, Paul William Ryan led a tumultuous but short life as a "people's artist." A prolific creative writer, activist, radio personality, and labor reporter, Ryan grew to prominence, particularly on the West Coast, during the fifteen years leading up to his premature death in August 1947. He was best known under his pseudonyms "Mike Quin" and, later, "Robert Finnegan." Ryan worked relentlessly to bring often radical social messages to working-class audiences in particular, through a variety of forms and genres, including journalism, poetry, satire, short stories, political pamphlets, and paperback pulp fiction. Yet despite his considerable, if short-lived, influence and his furious productivity—and in part thanks to the legacies of the cold war—Paul Ryan is a virtually lost writer today. Nonetheless, as a homegrown, overtly pro-Communist writer who worked in innovative ways to reach a popular American audience, Paul Ryan represents something of a "missing link" in American twentieth-century literature and culture, one that is worthy of reconsideration.

From 1933 to his death in 1947, Paul Ryan emerged as a significant figure in at least two distinct but overlapping cultural fields: proletarian literature (including short stories, poems, and reportage) and hard-boiled crime fiction. In a biographical sketch that introduces *On the Drumhead: A Selection from the Writing of Mike Quin* (1948), Harry Carlisle, Ryan's editor and comrade, estimates that "during the fourteen years of his career as a labor journalist, editor, columnist, magazine writer, novelist, radio commentator, and pamphleteer, [Ryan] wrote on the average of a million words a year," an astounding count by any standard. Furthermore, as Carlisle notes, "although the vast bulk of his writing was produced under the space limitations and time pressure of daily columns and radio programs, which denies the leisure for the sort of writing he ultimately wished to produce," Ryan "worked within the means available to the labor movement for the expression of its ideas, but always sought to extend [those means]" (p. xix).

Ryan's overtly political works exemplify the suppressed richness of the traditions of working-class and social protest literature, while his more subtly and suggestively politicized pulp novels suggest for us the generally ignored critical potential embedded in a subgenre of fiction—1950s hard-boiled detective fiction—whose conservative, even reactionary tendencies (represented by authors such as Mickey Spillane) have been well documented. Taken together, Paul Ryan's work as "Mike Quin" and "Robert Finnegan" connects and complicates 1930s radical proletarian writing and 1950s pulp fiction, in ways that have yet to be appreciated, despite recent critical acknowledgments, by Alan Wald among others, that popular and pulp fiction was perhaps the most significant venue for American left-wing writers in the period following the World War II. His prose and poetry constitute a sustained, varied, suppressed, partisan engagement with mid-twentieth-century U.S. popular and mass culture that is of interest for literary, historical, and political reasons.

EARLY YEARS

The son of an Irish traveling salesman, who seems to have all but disappeared when Paul was a child, and a dressmaker of Irish, French, and Jewish ancestry, Paul Ryan grew up in a working-class Irish neighborhood, known as "South of the

Slot," in San Francisco. Paul's mother had come from a pioneer family that had settled in Wisconsin and that counted a Chippewa Indian in its distant genealogy. Paul had two siblings: a brother, Ralph, and a sister, Alice, with whom he seems to have remained close. Paul also boasted of a maternal grandmother who had been an organizer for the militant Knights of Labor and who remained something of a working-class firebrand even late in life. A gown-maker for "ladies," she reportedly referred to her wealthy clients collectively as "Mrs. Richbitch," and she appears to have been stood up for Paul against several exploitative childhood employers.

Paul penned his first verse around age ten, and he continued to write constantly, if often between shifts, throughout a youth interrupted by work. Ashamed to let most of his family know of his literary inclinations, Paul did, however, share his work with his sister. Already Ryan's early poems took on a political edge. As he wrote, from the cusp of U.S. entry into World War I: "A thousand mothers sit in grief / Without a soul to bring relief" (*Drumhead,* p. xxii). During the influenza pandemic that followed the war, Paul worked for a druggist delivering medicine and penned lines describing the air in 1919 as "dirty with death" (ibid.). Leaving school altogether at fifteen, Ryan went to work to help support the family, first at a department store, then as a poolroom attendant at a local YMCA, and eventually at a stock and bond house. Hoping to "better himself," he enrolled in a business correspondence course, which Ryan credited with teaching him the importance of conciseness in writing. With his business-writing skills fine-tuned, Ryan worked for two years in an insurance firm, for a man he described later as having a "brain like an adding machine" (*On the Drumhead,* p. xxiv), and eventually he rose to the rank of a department manager. He moved into an apartment of his own at age sixteen, and he soon became close friends with Fritz Orton, a boy from a wealthy family who went on to study philosophy at Stanford University. At Stanford, Orton would sneak Ryan into lectures and class discussions on campus, allowing him glimpses of "higher knowledge," which, however, seem to have left Ryan relatively unimpressed.

At age nineteen, in what would amount to a major turning point in his early life, Paul Ryan headed out to sea, seeking "experience" to aid his writing. This experience, from 1925 to 1929, placed him in close contact with hard physical labor and the harsh working conditions of the modern ship, which undercut his whimsical romantic notions about "sea life." Work at sea also placed Ryan in an international and multiracial environment; he traveled through Latin America and the islands of the South Pacific, and he reportedly met at least one sailor who took offense at the racism implied by Joseph Conrad's title to his 1897 novella, *Nigger of the Narcissus.* Paul further encountered the often-radical political culture of maritime workers, including at least one outspoken member of the "Wobblies," the anarcho-syndicalist Industrial Workers of the World (IWW). Indeed, despite his firm affiliation with the Communist party, much of Ryan's later work as "Mike Quin" can be read as continuing in the tradition of the famous, and martyred, IWW poet and songwriter Joe Hill, whose lyrics (collected in editions of the *Little Red Song Book* that first appeared in 1909) remained popular throughout this period. Ryan later put his experience and knowledge of the maritime industry to use and pay tribute to the militancy of maritime workers throughout his writings.

Soon after Paul returned to shore, in 1929, the stock market crashed, bringing on the Great Depression and precipitating a rise in unemployment and poverty throughout California and beyond. While at first maintaining a satirical perspective on the horridly ironic spectacle of formerly wealthy businessmen leaping to their deaths and thus becoming embodied social critics of the system that they had so staunchly defended, Ryan's disaffection with the workings of business—and with the literary establishment—grew through his experiences working at a Hollywood bookstore. Here he reportedly saw some people "spend more for one order than the book salesman made in a month" (*Drumhead,* p. xxv). While working amid the shadows of Hollywood, Ryan grew frustrated at his difficulties in finding

a publisher for his already voluminous prose and verse. He also grew increasingly aware of the unemployment and social inequality that surrounded him. Getting away from Hollywood during a late-night drinking-and-storytelling session at a Los Angeles tavern, Paul Ryan was apparently hailed as "Mike Quin" by a retired maritime worker, who mistook him for an old friend, and he embraced the name as his new pseudonym.

In Hollywood, Ryan became involved in the local John Reed Club. One of dozens spread across the country, and sponsored by the Communist Party of the United States (CPUSA), these writer-activist-social clubs were named after the famous bohemian revolutionary and martyr John Reed (1887–1920), author of a 1919 account of the Bolshevik revolution, *Ten Days That Shook the World.* The clubs were seen by Party organizers as a means of encouraging, cultivating, and organizing a new generation of "proletarian literature," and they developed a significant following during the early 1930s, in particular among emerging and working-class writers. Ryan produced a number of works for the John Reed Club and its organ, the *Partisan*, including the 1933 pamphlet *And We Are Millions,* about growing unemployment. Reportedly, during this period Ryan developed the habit of going directly to and talking with working people to gather material for his writing, sitting in courtrooms to watch unemployed young men prosecuted for "vagrancy" and visiting railroad stations and fruit orchards to meet with striking Mexican workers. Paul Ryan was deeply shaped by the ways that the economic conditions of the Depression increasingly brought forth militant and collective responses from working people.

Through actively engaging the rising tide of labor activism and witnessing the often-repressive responses of the state, as well as through conversation with Marxists at the John Reed Club, Ryan became radicalized, and he assumed the persona of "Mike Quin": a tough, no-nonsense, witty Irish radical commentator, poet, and reporter, who declared his sympathies openly with socialism, Communism, and the rank-in-file activism of the working class. Like many writers of his generation, Ryan became further convinced that spontaneous working-class resistance to the ravages of capitalism, while absolutely necessary, was inadequate to the task of radical social transformation; conscious political organization seemed to him necessary. Thus he became active in the largest and most visible radical organization in the United States at the time, the Communist Party of the United States, and he remained committed to the CPUSA from 1932 until his death in 1947. The question of how to negotiate the "twisted" field of a profit-driven book industry while still reaching a mass audience with progressive, radical, and often socialist political messages hence became the central task for "Mike Quin" in the days ahead. Contrary to the musings of those radical intellectuals concerned with developing the "proletarian novel," however, Ryan seems to have decided that the best way for him to reach a broad audience of workers might be not through the book-length efforts that had occupied his youth as a writer but rather through a variety of shorter and more accessible literary works, often disseminated through local newspapers. As the longtime Communist activist and leader Elizabeth Gurley Flynn put it after meeting him in 1940, Mike Quin's "words are simple, salty, plain proletarian language, but as workers really do talk, not the exaggerated or vulgar 'proletarian lingo' some writers affect" (p. xxxii). When word spread that the San Francisco–area maritime workers, organized into the International Longshoreman's Association, had gone out on strike in a major confrontation with their employers, Paul Ryan rushed back to the city of his birth, and "Mike Quin" threw himself into literary labor defending the developing labor movement, covering the pitched battles in the streets, and reporting the escalating class struggle that culminated in the General Strike in 1934, the largest citywide work stoppage in U.S. history.

"MIKE QUIN": POET OF THE WATERFRONT

During the 1930s and 1940s, under the "fighting" Irish name of "Mike Quin," Ryan became a popular left-wing activist-writer associated with the radical wing of the labor movement. Through the radical papers—the *Western Worker* (in which

he wrote a regular column titled "Seeing Red") and the Communist daily *People's World*—and the independent rank-and-file publication the *Waterfront Worker,* Quin issued a diverse array of short works ranging from journalism, editorials, poetry, short fiction, satire, allegory, and dramatic sketches to full pamphlets on pro-union, antiracist, antifascist, antiwar, and socialist themes. He wrote about and in support of the labor struggle in 1934, and he later joined the maritime strike committee during another strike in 1935–1936, helping the workers to win hearts and minds among the general public. Many of his shorter writings, originally appearing in various newspapers, were collected in three "Mike Quin" books issued by his political allies; all are now out of print. First came *Dangerous Thoughts* (1940), then *More Dangerous Thoughts* (1941), followed by the posthumously published *On the Drumhead* (1948), a "representative sample" edited by Harry Carlisle. Quin's book-length participant history of the San Francisco General Strike of 1934, *The Big Strike* was not published until 1949, following his death. This delay seems in part to have been the result of political resistance from the commercial press, although one publisher of cheap paperbacks did offer to issue the text earlier if Quin could guarantee a sale of one hundred thousand copies—a tall order for such a radical book. The text lay finished but unpublished for nearly a decade, although it was "rented" by *Fortune* magazine and by the novelist Charles Norris (lesser-known brother to the famous American novelist and literary naturalist Frank Norris), who was then working on a novel about the San Francisco struggle and so required realistic descriptions of the recent events.

"Now essentially a forgotten writer," Cary Nelson has written in *Repression and Recovery* (1989), Quin was "the quintessential Communist party poet ... ready to produce a poem about almost any current cause" (p. 24). Indeed, it seems that "Mike Quin" could be counted on to churn out poems of immediate political value; he wrote poems in opposition to the conviction of the Scottsboro Boys on false rape charges, in support of the antifascist cause of the Republicans in the Spanish Civil War, and to declare that "The Yanks Aren't Coming" during the period of the Nazi-Soviet Nonaggression Pact during World War II. Continuing the thrust of *And We Are Millions,* Quin penned "The Man in the Rain," which chillingly examined the haunting, disciplinary effects that the specter of unemployment and homelessness exerted on even the employed sectors of the working class. He also wrote poems to rally workers to support the "Win the War" effort in World War II, after the notorious shift of the Communist party line following the Nazi invasion of the Soviet Union. Quin's appeal extended beyond narrow CP circles, however. He gained a wide and committed following up and down the West Coast, and even across the country, for his clarity and humor, as well as his pull-no-punches radical politics. As the lifelong labor activist Steve Nelson recalls in his 1981 political autobiography, *Steve Nelson, American Radical,* Mike Quin was "a really unusual human being."

> Slim with big horn-rimmed glasses and a serious appearance that concealed a rapier wit, his prose was like poetry. ... We worked together on little pamphlets like *Why Socialism for Maritime Workers?* He bowled me over with his capacity to make things convincing and clear. ... Without using a lot of legal jargon, he put complex courtroom maneuverings into everyday language. [His] radio hour was like religion all over the waterfront. People would gather around a radio and listen to Mike's crisp, machine-gun diction. There was no waste of words, no crazy embellishments or phony put-ons—but a working-class approach with a good measure of sarcasm.
>
> (pp. 257–258)

Similarly appreciating Quin's ability to put complex truths in "everyday language," in 1940, the novelist Theodore Dreiser wrote Quin a personal letter praising his *Dangerous Thoughts* for its "truly startling and illuminating intellectual force." He likened Quin "in spots," to "Rabelais, Voltaire, and Thomas Paine" (*Drumhead,* p. xxxii). Upon Ryan's death in 1947, the *People's World* referred to Quin as "a people's writer, a people's artist" because he "transmuted his ... quest for a better world into wit and fantasy and satire and verse and dialogue ... to break through the barriers of words and ideas that have been created to divide the American working class and

its conscious vanguard, to reach the great mass of our people in words to which they would listen."

While there is no denying Cary Nelson's double-edged characterization of Quin as "the quintessential Communist party poet," such labeling potentially blinds us to the fact that as a Communist writer in the 1930s and 1940s, Quin was not just a hack obeying Party directives but instead was an engaged "labor intellectual." As such he mediated between workers' struggles and middle-class artists and intellectuals, between populism and internationalism, between the colloquial and the radical, between the proletarian public sphere and commercial mass culture.

EARLY FICTION AND POETRY

Paul Ryan's early story "The Sacred Thing" was selected and reprinted by Edward J. O'Brien in his *Best Short Stories of 1934* and appeared in *Scribner's Magazine* in 1935. It features a cop who ashamedly confesses to his wife how he accidentally kicked over a dead man during his stressful day's "work" of forcing vagrants and bums off of park benches. This story already suggests Quin's lifelong concern for the effects of state violence, both its physical effects upon the poor and homeless victims and its psychological impact on the frontline perpetrators of repression. Throughout his writings, Paul William Ryan, as "Mike Quin" and as "Robert Finnegan" continued to confront the question of state violence—and hence the specter of fascism lurking in the wings of capitalist "normalcy"—from both sides of the policeman's nightstick.

"Shirts of a Single Color," published in August 1938 by Ryan under his own name in *Direction* magazine, similarly depicts everyday American life as saturated with violence and haunted by the specter of fascism. The tale focuses on Jim, an unemployed man who is attracted to the opportunity for aggression embodied in American anti-Communist vigilantism. Sitting at the table and eating "like an ogre," as the story opens, Jim "tore the buns violently, buttered the jagged halves in two swipes, crammed food into his mouth, and chewed vigorously" (*Drumhead,* p. 72). Jim then asks his wife, Helen, to dig out his old gray shirt and black tie. Lured by the promises of a local "big shot" sponsor, as well as the appeal of a uniform and his admiration for the exemplary "guts" of fascists in Germany and Italy, Jim refuses to listen to Helen's reasoned questioning. Such early work registers Ryan's awareness of both the political vulnerability of desperate Depression-era American masculinity and of the way in which right-wing ideologies and institutions could continue to expand while the U.S. government remained officially "neutral" toward fascism abroad.

Quin's 1933 story "Mexican Hands," written for the John Reed Club publication, *Partisan,* had also concerned itself with the state as it extends its hand toward the unemployed. This time however, the hand of the state is ostensibly more benevolent, "helping" the Mexican workers on their way "home" across the US border. Against detailed depictions of the work-ravaged and weather-beaten hands of Julio and Maria Herrera and hundreds of other Mexican deportees, Quin contrasts the palms of the immigration officials "handing out the wages of the poor. A banana for a life's labor. Two sandwiches for building a bridge. An orange for an arm torn off in a threshing machine. A cookie for years in the mines. A bag of beans for years in the fields" (*Drumhead,* p. 16).

Quin remained interested in exposing and satirizing the role of the state, not only in its explicit aggression but also in its charitable "concern" for the poor and working-class. In the poem, "Investigation," the speaker—seemingly a working-class mother—addresses the reader with the collective pronoun "we":

We know the investigation men
Who call and never come back again
It must be holy; it must be nice
To enter homes and count the lice.

They are so kind in considerations,
They've made so many investigations.
They look at the stove and the sagging beds,
And count the children, and shake their heads.

Where were we born? How much do we weigh?
Where do we work? How much does it pay?
They write it down on a paper sheet
Their writing is so clean and neat.

I am told they file it in fireproof files
In buildings of glistening, colored tiles.
And our empty stomachs and broken hearts
Are traced on new statistical charts.

Ah, the men with dollars, so many times,
Have peeped in our dreary world of dimes,
And I hear that people in brand new clothes,
Meet in the cities to speak of our woes.

And one of them said that my child was weak,
That its twisted bones and its pale white cheek,
Could be cured with food and warmth and sun,
And that something drastic must be done.

That our social system had gone amiss,
And things could never go on like this.
And I know it is true, what the gentleman said,
For he never came back—and my child is dead.

(*Drumhead,* p. 18)

Contrasting the shelter and kind treatment given to the *files* of the working poor to the neglect and exploitation of poor *people,* the poem suggests the degree to which even the socially conscious "investigators" and intellectual "gentlemen" are part of the system that has here "gone amiss." On one level, Quin's maternal, collective speaker ironically levels the "investigations" of social workers and government sociologists to mere "peeping"; these men snatch information for their "fireproof files" and "statistical charts," only to leave the suffering poor and their children to fend—or to die—on their own. Still, on another more subtle and ironic level, as the poignant closing line of the poem emphasizes, it is the very fact that the liberal investigators' theoretically correct sociological knowledge fails to translate into a social practice that would save the speaker's child—that the self-styled experts know of the crisis and yet do nothing—that finally condemns the present social system. In this way the speaker confirms the social worker's assertion that "something drastic must be done" but on a level that suggests the need to go beyond the realm of mere social work.

Quin's provocative 1934 poem "They Shall Not Die," written upon hearing the news that two of the Scottsboro Boys had been convicted of rape and condemned to be electrocuted to death in Alabama (in what many saw and denounced as tantamount to a "legal lynching"), returns us again to the spectacle of direct state and class coercion. The poem demonstrates that even a text produced for the most immediate, and Party-championed cause, could yield Quin intricate and powerful results. As he writes midway through the poem:

If the world martyred Negroes rose
From long-forgotten graves;
If the dark soil burst and issued forth
Its hoard of murdered slaves;

If they marched their broken bodies past
In ghastly black parade
Before the men who struck them down
That fortunes might be made;

The sea of lash-torn human Negro flesh,
Rope-strangled throats, gouged eyes,
Charred bodies, bullet-ridden forms
Would shock the very skies.

As the poem continues:

Too long the trees of Southern hate
Such bloody fruit have borne
As Negroes strangled on bosses' ropes
For parasites to scorn.

Too oft through balmy Southern air
The awful, sickening smell
Of burning human flesh
Floats like the breath of Hell.

(*Drumhead,* pp. 28–29)

Anticipating the famous refrain of Billie Holiday's 1939 song "Strange Fruit," Quin's poem poses the Scottsboro case as a question of class interest to Americans. Closing with the call for black and white to unite and fight behind the slogan not only that "THOSE NINE BOYS SHALL NOT DIE!" but also that "OUR SONS SHALL NOT BE KILLED!" Quin's speaker urges the reader to move beyond liberal sympathy for the innocent black victims of southern racial terrorism and state violence to political, class,

and indeed familial "blood" identification with the Scottsboro boys and those in similar situations. It is a "class" enemy Quin writes, who "pulls lynching ropes"—a trope which suggests not only the direct mob lynching of African Americans (and others) but the master puppeteer's manipulation of white workers into racist false consciousness. The speaker's question: "Who profits ... from keeping men in chains?" thus signifies doubly, suggesting the material *and* ideological components of ruling-class domination. According to the Marxist theory to which Paul William Ryan held, this ruling class profited not only economically from chaining black labor but also politically by dividing workers against each other along racial lines.

MORE DANGEROUS THOUGHTS

Following the success of *Dangerous Thoughts,* and the continued popularity of his newspaper columns, Mike Quin's *More Dangerous Thoughts* was published in 1941. This came during the period of Communist party agitation against U.S. intervention in what was soon to become World War II, a period that extended from the Nazi-Soviet Nonaggression Pact of September 1939 to the German invasion of the Soviet Union in 1941. To many observers, this turn represented a serious, and even shameful, turn away from the militant antifascism of the Popular Front period, 1935–1939, when the CPUSA had played a leading role in opposing fascist forces at home and abroad. Quin's text often takes aim at war, its promoters and profiteers, as well as against bellicose notions of "Americanism." Opening and closing with essays pitched against those who would lead the United States into the growing world conflict, *More Dangerous Thoughts* is certainly open to accusations of being an example of crass Communist or "Stalinist" political-literary expediency. Yet with strikingly few exceptions, Quin's antiwar writings reveal a complexity, humor, irony, and radical insight worthy of renewed attention.

Quin's sketch "The Patriotic Thing," for instance, explores the irony of a desperately impoverished old man relying for survival on the street sale of "God Bless America" banners to tight-fisted city passersby. When the would-be buyer-haggler accuses the vendor of overcharging him for the cheaply constructed item, the salesman professes that it's not his fault, but that "it's the system that's wrong," forcing him to overpay for the banner from the manufacturers in the first place. This then prompts the customer to accuse the vendor of a lack of patriotism: "If you don't like the American system, why don't you get the hell out of here and go to some other country?" (p. 37). On a similarly sarcastic-patriotic note, Quin's poem "The Glorious Fourth" revels in the irony of "Senator Screwball," who on Independence Day is standing "up there beside Old Glory, / blowing off his mouth like a damned old Tory." Quin later directly addresses the infamous Congressman Martin Dies, the originator of the red-baiting investigations of the House Committee on Un-American Activities, with a limerick titled "Probe":

> Once Congressman Dies, it is said,
> When retiring, looked under his bed.
> He bellowed like thunder
> On spying thereunder
> A chamber pot colored bright red.
>
> (p. 87)

The humorous leveling of the infamous and much-feared public official by the limerick form itself, with its colloquial associations with obscenity and vulgarity, is doubled by the "probing" placement of Martin Dies alone in bed, presumably in nightclothes, and far from the "chamber" with which he is generally associated. In five simple lines Quin seeks to reduce to ridiculousness the (re)emergent propaganda of the "red scare" by puncturing the abstract monstrosities invoked by anti-Communist politicians with images of "redness" drawn from the everyday and the mundane. Quin's posthumously published "Farewell" statement (to be examined below) attempts a similar reduction of anti-Communist rhetoric to embodied absurdity, when he writes that "any idea which is any good for the workingman will come wearing red flannel underwear." (One is left to wonder what pithy poetic pranks Quin would have played on Joseph

McCarthy, had he lived to see the Senator's rise in the 1950s.)

A SIMPLE, SENTIMENTAL, AND TRADITIONAL LITERARY RADICALISM

Often Quin deploys the seemingly traditional, sentimental tropes of newborn babies or animals in order to critique the modern world of business, greed, and war. Particularly interesting is the short prose piece "The Subversive Element," which examines a racially diverse nursery of newborn babies who reflect aloud on their recent and involuntary entry into what they have heard is a dangerous and callous "adult" world of war and competition, a world that "will love and cherish us until we get big, then will kick our behinds or kill us in a war" (*More Dangerous Thoughts,* p. 45). Against the harsh, narrow ethics of the grown-ups, the newborns—led by a brown-skinned babe—pledge to "stick together" and to resist the "big people" and their ways. And yet, frustratingly, at the end of the story the newborns remain dependent on the adults to change their wet diapers and can only communicate with the grown-ups by crying. The poem thus suggests that while the "subversive element" may inhere in "human nature," that natural element itself is insufficient to bring about the social transformation for which it, nonetheless, cries. In lyric form, Quin's postwar poem "The Diaper Brigade" similarly explores the relationship between the present and future generations, conjuring imagined youth-to-come to criticize the present.

Mike Quin's prose and poetry frequently deploy seemingly "simple" or "traditional" rhyme and rhythm schemes to bear his ideas and images. As Cary Nelson has pointed out with respect to other American writers of the early twentieth century, the specter of such poetic "conservatism" and popular "simplicity," since the rise of New Criticism in the 1950s, has frequently been conjured so as to disqualify much radical poetry from inclusion in the canon of modern American literature. Contrary, however, to the "melodramatic" literary history that commonly pits an outmoded, sentimental, or even reactionary "traditional" poetry against the cutting edge of an emergent experimental poetic modernism, as Nelson notes, "traditional forms continued to do vital cultural work throughout this period. Far from being preeminently genteel, poetry in traditional forms was a frequent vehicle for sharply focused social commentary. Poets were thus often quite successful at making concise, paradigmatic statements about social life" (p. 23). In keeping with and extending this comment, Mike Quin's "simple" and "traditional" poems are filled with wit, humor, pathos, irony, and wordplay, as well as incisive social critique, revolutionary injunction, and prophecy.

Quin's explicit partisanship of course seems to be yet another reason for his marginalization in the postwar New Critical canon. As Cary Nelson has written, "If we have lost [radical poets], it is partly because [their] poetry does not generally display the surface indecision and ambivalence that many critics since the 1950s have deemed a transcendent, unquestionable literary and cultural value" (p. 44). Indeed, most of Ryan's work as "Mike Quin" rejects, or challenges the reader to move beyond, indecision and ambivalence.

For a striking example of Quin's innovative combination of the genteel and the partisan, consider his poem "A Lesson for the Ill Clothed and Ill Fed." Here Quin's poetic model is quite explicitly taken from traditional British literature. Specifically he appropriates the formal structures of Shakespeare's famous eulogy from *Julius Caesar.* Subtitled with "(Apologies to William Shakespeare)," the poem revises Mark Anthony's famous dramatic speech for the dead Caesar in a distinctly partisan, postwar direction. As Quin hails his readers:

> Friends, veterans, workingmen, clean out your ears;
> I come to bury the New Deal not to praise it.
> The failures of great causes live after them;
> The good intentions are oft interred with their bones.
>
> So let it be with this one. The noble Republicans
> Have said the New Deal was communistic;
> If so, then it hath died partly by its own hand,
> For sternly did the New Dealers denounce communism;

Thus showering blows upon their own heads.

(*Drumhead,* pp. 208–209)

Proceeding then to review valued social programs, as well as the anti-Communist, pro-business aspects of the New Deal, Quin admits, again closely echoing Shakespearean phraseology, that the Deal "was my friend, in spite of grievous faults. / But Republicans say it was communistic; And Republicans are honorable men" (p. 209). Repeating the ironic "honorable men" refrain at various points in relation to "[Harry] Truman" and to "bankers," Quin comes quickly to one of his central insights:

I speak not to disprove what Republicans say,
But here I am to speak what I do know.
The virtues of the New Deal which we loved,
Were those things communistic, more or less.
The weaknesses from which the New Deal died
Were compromising steps by which it sought
To shield and to conciliate the brutal enemy it fought.

(p. 209)

As Quin draws the lessons out for readers:

now lies [The New Deal] there
Mute evidence of the awful fate in store
For all brave knights who charge the forts of greed
Still swearing loyalty to the foe they fight.

(p. 209)

And continues:

Mute testimony of what sad end befalls
Those who challenge capitalism, yet contend
They are capitalism's defender, and loyal friend.
The fate of causes essentially socialistic
Which swear by the God they're anti-communistic

(p. 209)

More often than progressive parodies of Shakespeare, Quin deploys the tropes of fairy tales and folk imagery, populist historical allusions, and sarcasm. For instance, in "The Woman in the Shoe," he revises the traditional nursery rhyme in a distinctly activist direction:

There was an old woman
Who lived in a shoe.
She had so many children
She didn't know what to do.
She gave them red banners
And slogans to yell,
And they marched to the Mayor
And raised plenty of hell.

(*More Dangerous Thoughts,* p. 72)

Quin's rewriting of this Mother Goose rhyme recalls the observations of historians such as Robin Kelley, Mark Naison, and Cary Nelson, who each have found that many radical writer-activists of the early to mid-twentieth century set their work to familiar, traditional patterns and melodies—for instance black church hymns in the Deep South. They did so not only in order to assure that their songs could be sung and remembered by those who could not read music but also "to empty out the conservative, sentimental, or patriotic values of the existing songs [or rhymes] while replacing them with radical impulses" (Cary Nelson, p. 61). In the traditional Mother Goose version of "The Old Woman Who Lived in a Shoe," the last lines read: "She gave them some broth without any bread, then whipped them all soundly and sent them to bed." Revising the pessimistic domestic closure of the traditional lyric, Quin suggests not only that the old woman in the shoe can become a picket leader but that the children, who are generally taken to constitute the old woman's subjection, could, with a "red" shift of political approach, amplify rather than negate her power and agency. Indeed, this revised "old woman in a shoe" may recall Mike Quin's own grandmother, whom he describes in *More Dangerous Thoughts* as "a magnificent and powerful woman who struck fear in the hearts of bill collectors. Many a time I have seen her chase them down the stairs, beating them over the head with a broom. As a girl she was a volunteer worker for the Knights of Labor. ... She knew you could only tackle ... these things by organization" (p. 126). Indeed, Ryan routinely deployed the domestic, privatized, feminized work of "housekeeping" as his metaphor for revolution, that ultimate "public sphere" transformation.

Quin seems to have had little faith in the existing American public sphere of his day, which seemed to him closed off to the American working class. As his early and bluntly titled poem "Three Percent Own All the Wealth" puts it:

America is the space between the cracks
In the pavement,
and the space between the railroad ties,
and the rest of it is fenced and owned,
by the top hat guys.

(*More Dangerous,* p. 111)

Yet while poetically dramatizing the vanishing of "America" and the exclusion of working-class people from increasingly privatized public space, Mike Quin simultaneously illuminated, anticipated, and worked to build the cultural and political possibilities of the new civic space of what could be called a proletarian public sphere.

BEYOND "DUBIOUS RESPECTABILITY"

In *The Big Strike,* "Mike Quin" dramatically documents the labor struggles on the early-twentieth-century San Francisco waterfront, the historic General Strike of 1934, and the militant organization of West Coast longshoremen under the leadership of the Australian-born Communist Harry Bridges. Written alongside the events it details—Quin was a participant as well as an observer of West Coast labor struggles—the book emphasizes the importance of rank-and-file activism in the worker's struggle. When *The Big Strike* was finally published by Olema Press in 1949, with the help of Ryan's wife and fellow writer, Mary King O'Donnell, the domestic political climate for the book could hardly have been more hostile. The passage of the Taft-Hartley Act in 1947, for instance, had made Communist leadership in U.S. labor unions, as well as the powerful tactics of the sympathy strike and the secondary boycott—each of which play "starring roles" in *The Big Strike*—illegal and officially "un-American." The Taft-Hartley Act precipitated the 1949 expulsion of a number of the most militant—and often Communist-led—unions in the Congress of Industrial Organizations (CIO), including Bridges' International Longshoremen's and Warehousemen's Union (ILWU)—another "star" in Quin's contemporary drama. In the view of many labor historians, this act precipitated the general sapping, and internal division, of the American labor movement. Cold-war anti-Communism rapidly took on other forms as well; 1947 saw the revival of the House Un-American Activities Committee (HUAC) under the command of Parnell Thomas, as well as Truman's Executive Order requiring loyalty checks on hundreds of thousands of federal employees. In 1948 a dozen leaders of the U.S. Communist party were arrested and convicted of conspiracy under the 1940 Smith Act, which had criminalized the organization, based on the claim that its print literature "advocated the violent overthrow of the government."

The Big Strike recounts a range of historical events: from the history of corporate-government collusion and corruption that established the modern American maritime industry during World War I; to the early-twentieth-century labor struggles and contract conflicts that led to the citywide and then regional strikes of the 1930s; to the open debates of striker mass meetings; to the unfolding of violent street confrontations between workers, hired strikebreakers, replacement "scabs," police, and national guardsmen; to the backroom discussions and contract negotiations between politicians, employers, and labor leaders; to the widespread state repression that followed the Great Strike itself, of which Quin's own newspaper office was a target. Yet while the dramatic events surrounding 1934 provide the plot and framework for the book, *The Big Strike* extends well beyond "sheer reportage." It is by turns a work of incisive cultural critique and of left-wing sensationalism, a text that plays upon and subverts prevailing contemporary mass discourses of the "waterfront" and the "underworld." The writing practice of *The Big Strike* was perhaps best formulated in Quin's column on "Journalism" (which appears in *Dangerous Thoughts*):

> Apathy; a dulled sense of reality; tired, rut-flowing minds that scarcely distinguish between what they read in the papers and what they see in the movies; an illusion of detachment; a weary sense of fatality that accepts life as an inexplicable scenario written by God Almighty, directed by Wall Street, and in which the ordinary man is a lost and impotent, unimportant extra. ... That is the blanket of fog through which the modern journalist must cleave. ... The whole technique of the commercial press is to make the "ordinary man" feel that he is an unimpor-

tant extra in the scenario of life. We've got to make him realize that he is important, all powerful, and that he can write his own scenario.

(pp. 63-64)

Combining documentary, sensational, and didactic aesthetics, *The Big Strike* is concerned with putting working-class people back at the center of how we narrate contemporary history and politics, as well as with dramatizing the terror of right-wing attacks on those who seek to do just that. Quin himself experienced this terror, not only while covering police riots during the strike but when his own offices at the *Western Worker* were raided by antiunion vigilantes.

In 1941, Mike Quin turned down an offer to join the board of the popular New York–based pro-Communist paper, the *Daily Worker,* and he continued working in California, now in support of the United States war effort. Significantly, Mike Quin continued to find new ways of popularizing progressive ideas as the director of the CIO's radio campaigns in California during the years 1943–1945. In this capacity he became the "CIO reporter on the Air," offering daily "Facts to Fight Fascism" and shaping the union's "Labor on the March" series, while on his own time traveling to do local radio support for worker campaigns throughout California. He worked furiously and constantly under deadline pressure, often at the expense of his health.

THE PULP FICTION OF "ROBERT FINNEGAN"

After World War II, as the left-wing unions for which he was a militant advocate were coming under increased (often anti-Communist) assault, under the name "Robert Finnegan," Ryan launched yet another successful, if short-lived, career, as an author of hard-boiled crime and detective fiction. In just the two years before his death at age forty, he turned out three pulp novels, *The Lying Ladies* (1946), *The Bandaged Nude (*1946), and *Many a Monster* (1948). Indicative of their popular success is that each of the novels was carried by a major publisher (Simon & Schuster) and each reissued by mass commercial publishers shortly after Ryan's death. Even to his final days, however, while his pulp writing helped pay the bills in Olema, California, Ryan kept up more explicitly radical political writing as "Mike Quin," often publishing three columns per week in the Communist *People's World* and the ILWU *Dispatcher.* According to Harry Carlisle, until advanced cancer exhausted and crippled him utterly, Quin continued to speak, to write, and to plan future projects; in addition to his own unfinished autobiography, in his final days he was drafting a play on the life of Karl Marx (*Drumhead,* p. xxxv). Carlisle appears to have written off Ryan's "Finnegan" fiction as merely a moneymaking venture that Ryan devised to support his continued "writing for the people" as Mike Quin. However, an examination of the pulp texts that Ryan actually produced reveals that in the years following World War II, he was experimenting with innovative and sophisticated ways of weaving his left-wing politics into this notoriously conservative but massively popular fiction form.

In *The Lying Ladies* (1946), Paul William Ryan, writing as "Robert Finnegan," appropriates the mass-cultural form of the hard-boiled novel as a site for radical reflections on the state of US mass culture and society. The title's focus on female falsehood, however, while typical of the postwar subgenre, is misleading. For in *The Lying Ladies,* while pursuing the case of a single murder, Robert Finnegan's serial pulp hero, newspaper reporter, and amateur detective, Dan Banion, unearths duplicity, hypocrisy, crime, corruption, and murder entangling not just the "ladies" but virtually every realm of "respectable" middle-American society, all while working *against* rather than *with* local state authorities. While Banion's task in *The Lying Ladies* is never to investigate the crimes of state directly, elite opportunism, commonplace corruption, and, more disturbingly, the fascistic tendencies of the police-and-propaganda structure the novel, garnering attention in most every chapter.

The plot of *The Lying Ladies* centers on the efforts of Dan Banion to prove the innocence of an unemployed vagrant, Ralph Flavin, whom local police, politicians, and press alike contend is guilty of the "fiendish" daylight murder of Esther Berglan, a young maid working for one of the

wealthy families in town. As will become a recurring trope in the later pulp novels, Finnegan's Dan Banion champions the cause of the underdog, coming to the defense of a man considered to be utterly depraved by police, press, and respectable opinion alike. Found unconscious beside the road, and later picked up by police for having a bloodied pocket knife and stolen jewelry in his possession, Flavin was on his way to California in search of a job. A friendless outsider, stopping in the town of Hamilton to beg work for food, Flavin is also an aspiring poet, whose pocket notepad of love-and-sex-themed lyrics police interpret as still more proof of his predatory sexual perversion. Yet it is these same poems that quickly win Banion to Flavin's cause; he is particularly impressed by the two-line lyric, "In narrow caves of conscience called themselves / Too many live alone like frightened elves" (p. 33), a line that speaks to the novel's theme of the destructive impact of isolating individualism and moral hypocrisy.

Gradually, after becoming identified—and targeted—as a supporter of Flavin, Banion gathers a string of allies, locals who similarly suspect Ralph's innocence. These include Tom and Amy Regan, the local working couple who first found Flavin passed out beside the road and fed him at their home, only to have him subsequently taken away by the police, and Shirley La Rue, a discontented prostitute who helps Banion to investigate her boss, the madam Beth Ridgley, and who uses the case as a chance to escape her profession.

Published in 1946, following World War II, and concurrent with the American paperback boom—as well as the stirrings of the next cold war and red scare—the novel is set in 1938, on the edge of the Nazi's military aggression in Europe. The year takes on textual meaning through background radio reports and newspaper headlines that position the action against the backdrop of the Western capitalist powers' infamous appeasement of the Nazis via the Munich "peace treaty" over Czechoslovakia. Banion predicts the fascist war clouds ahead, while the powers-that-be—specifically the police chief and would-be governor, Earl Grimes, and Vance Dalbert, the publisher and editor of the major commercial area newspaper—discount the threat posed by emerging European fascism, accusing Dan of being "alarmist" (p. 42). By situating the detective plot against the specter of creeping fascism in prewar Europe, and by foregrounding the established powers' lack of concern about—and even complicity with—the rise of 1930s fascism, Finnegan alerts readers to the possibility that fascism may yet be creeping still in the postwar United States. Further he suggests that if fascism is to be stopped it will take the initiative of everyday "little people" working independently of the "powers that be."

Further, on the margins of its central story line *The Lying Ladies* examines the quasi-fascist elements within Patterson County, where the town of Hamilton is located. These elements, including politicians and newspaper editors, seek to turn events to their own cynical advantage, as a way of boosting their newspaper sales and political ambitions. Thus County Attorney Grimes, Sheriff Horgan, and the newspaper publisher Vance Dalbert are eager to scapegoat the murder onto a convenient "outside fanatic" and "fiend" like Flavin and, further, to blame the alleged "crime wave" on the coddling of the poor by the liberal New Deal.

The Lying Ladies does not acknowledge or affirm the role played by leading radicals in the progressive 1930s struggle in the way that "Mike Quin" does in *The Big Strike*. It does however imply that Dan Banion has a reputation for having once been a political idealist, even a "red" radical. In keeping with hard-boiled conventions, little to no personal history—no flashbacks—are provided; only suggestive glimpses appear: "'Red told me about you," one character chides Banion, multiply signaling his former "redness": "He said you're the swellest guy who ever walked, bar none. ... But you're a screwball ... you still believe in Santa Claus" (p. 82).

What truly distinguishes *The Lying Ladies* from standard pulp fare, however, is the cumulative social critique that Banion's investigation yields with respect to dominant institutions and ideologies. While ceaselessly pursuing its isolated murder mystery and "solving its own problems"

(in Raymond Chandler's phrase), *The Lying Ladies* brings attention to many other problems as well, social problems that cannot be resolved individually by Banion, let alone by the state authorities. With the help of Shirley and the Regans, Banion discovers a web of deceit, corruption, blackmail, and murder implicating everyone from the late state attorney general Hibley to the Hibley gardener, Otis Farnsworth. Altogether, it's "an appalling picture of life on planet earth" (p. 168), according to Banion. He will—according to convention—eventually find his murderer(s), but his unsolicited investigation links the web of criminality not just to intrusive, exceptional *individuals*—where the dominant institutional discourse of the police, the politicians, and the commercial press prefer to locate it—but to the inequities, instabilities, and injustices of American "business society" itself. As Tom Regan quips near novel's end, "If we investigate any further the whole county may land in the penitentiary" (p. 230).

Through an intertextual strategy, *The Lying Ladies* further encourages readers to see through the sensational and anti-Communist demonization of ragged-looking, poor, and "foreign" threats to the community in the press. Banion himself is constantly picking up newspapers, effectively reading long, politically loaded editorial passages into the novel. Such innovative pulp intertexts draw our attention to America's homegrown propaganda apparatus, suggesting the potentially fascistic cultural tendencies and structures at work in middle-American Patterson County, without ever literally breaking the "realistic" linear flow of the detective action.

THE BANDAGED NUDE

In *The Bandaged Nude* (1947), Paul Ryan's second pulp effort as "Robert Finnegan," we find that although the setting and year has changed, many of Finnegan's socially critical themes remain. The novel is set just after World War II, in and around the various districts of San Francisco, far removed from the prewar middle-American setting for *Lying Ladies.* Dan Banion remains a professional newspaper reporter, with an amateur nose for detective work and a hunger for justice. This time Banion's case regards a murdered war veteran and artist, Kent Kipper, a painter who has been cut down in the midst of his own postwar political-artistic transition. Kipper, whom Banion meets once at a bar prior to his death, appears to have been poisoned by a mysterious substance that has left his lips an eerie green. In an intriguing narrative twist, Banion learns of Kipper's killing through his inside police sources; he then takes it upon himself to investigate Kipper's life and acquaintances before his death by murder is officially reported in the newspapers the following day. Inquiring after the deceased Kipper as if he were still living, Banion discovers more than a few parallels between Kipper's life and his own, and he gets to know a number of Kipper's friends, rivals, ex-lovers, and, eventually, his killer.

Finnegan here explores the tragedy of an artist trying to survive in the "cold, cold" world of postwar America. Young Kent Kipper, we learn, before being murdered, had been reflecting aloud about how "a guy needs a world to live in" (p. 7) and how he is committed to "mak[ing] some sense of things" (p. 7). Banion grows to feel what he calls "comradeship" with this late artist. "How could anyone hope to lead a serene life in a disorderly world?" Banion reflects. "Kipper had put it in an interesting way. You need a world to live in. You need an environment" (p. 63). The pervasive deadness and disorder that characterizes Banion's own postwar environment is suggested by the names of the taverns where much of Banion's investigating occurs—the Wreck, the Crow, the Pearl Harbor—as well as the veterans' "welcome home" sign, which has weathered down from reading "Well Done" to merely "... Done."

The drive to "make some sense" of the "cold, cold, cold" world of postwar America is what links Banion and the murder victim. In fact, Banion and Kipper had already bonded early in the novel, just before the murder, through reflecting on their common experiences as veterans of World War II. "Yet," as Victor Cohen has pointed out, "unlike [Mickey] Spillane's [Mike] Hammer, whose experiences in the war are valorized (and

in effect, validate his violent excesses), the veterans of Ryan's novels take no such salvation from their time in the army" (p. 18). Indeed, Kipper's postwar paintings focus on the suffering of civilians, and especially children. As Cohen emphasizes, this contrasts starkly with the glorification of the sacrifice and violence of World War II American soldiers in Spillane's fiction. Mike Hammer, in *I, the Jury* (1947), recalls the heroics of his recently murdered army brother-in-arms, Jack Williams, so as to license his violent, misogynist, and xenophobic crusade of revenge to find and punish Williams' killer. In Banion's (and Kipper's) recurring demand for an "orderly environment" and "a world to live in" without "war and depression" we can thus detect the mournful residue of Quin's radicalism. Finnegan's cloaking of these quasi-political reflections may render them somewhat ambiguous but not invisible.

Developing Finnegan's pulp reflections further, *The Bandaged Nude* calls attention to how the major postwar newspapers marginalize what he sees as the most important stories relating to people's everyday lives. The papers that Dan Banion surveys play up grotesque spectacles, including but not limited to the story of Kipper's "green-lipped" death. As Dan Banion reads the morning paper, he notes that stories about strikes, price gauging, and troops clamoring for transport home, as well as debates about the atom bomb, are all subordinated to the coverage of the sensational "Green Lip Murders." That Banion and the novel's author himself are participating in and making their living off this sensational public shift even while decrying it adds a dark irony to this pulp text.

Just a few years prior, Mike Quin had written along similar lines in his column on "Journalism." "Unable to gain entrance to the public main through the door," he wrote, the capitalist press was "trying to climb [into workers' heads] through the sewer. Hideous sex crimes force every other consideration into the background. At the least rumor of a rape, editors clear their front pages and send batteries of photographers rushing to the scene like peeping toms" (*Dangerous Thoughts,* p. 63). Continuing, he insists: "Look at the magazine racks. Good heavens above! Raped, stripped and murdered; photographed, painted and drawn; buxom, half-draped figures being whipped, attacked, kidnapped and strangled. That's where your sex crimes are manufactured. Lurid pictures like these dangled in front of thousands of men bug-eyed with sex starvation" (*Dangerous Thoughts,* pp. 63-64). Against this lurid sensationalism in the commercial press, "Mike Quin" had taken a clear stance. Now, however, as "Robert Finnegan," Ryan takes a more sly and subversive approach.

MANY A MONSTER

Published shortly after Paul Ryan's death from cancer in 1948, and reissued in 1949, *Many a Monster,* Finnegan's final pulp novel, again takes as its point of departure the public demonizing of a seemingly innocent man. Rogan Lochmeister, a mentally traumatized Jewish veteran of World War II, stands accused of a sensational series of brutal murders. Rogan has been labeled by the press as "Gus the Grue" after the gruesome form in which his supposed female victims have been found. As was the case in *The Lying Ladies,* from the early pages of the novel it becomes clear that Rogan is a victim of circumstances and scapegoating: he has been traumatized by the war, and now he is being railroaded by the police and the press, who are attempting to explain the sadistic crimes in their midst. Published at a time when the "red menace" was becoming a stock figure of popular paranoia, Banion's crusade to exonerate Rogan thus takes on the feel of a critique of newspaper hysteria generally.

Dan Banion opens this novel as a writer at odds and often in conflict with his commercial employers. Arguing with his chief editor, Rolf Burgess, at the *Journal* in the book's opening scene, Banion rips the prurient sensationalism of his employer's headlines. "To Burgess ... newspaper publishing was a business. Business came first and the writhing chaos of human existence which comprised the news was only raw material from which to realize a return of the publisher's investment." In contrast, "To Dan Banion the

news itself was a passion, and the newspaper was a kind of necessary nuisance" (p. 6). The conflict between Banion and Burgess soon comes to a head after Burgess rewrites Banion's first article on the "lady-killer," undermining his reporter's interpretation. Burgess claims that in juicing up Banion's piece and retaining Lochmeister as the unquestioned villain, he is only being a "shrewd" businessman. Banion responds that "a lot of shrewd heads fell at Nuremberg" (p. 52), drawing parallels between cynical American business operatives playing with others' lives and Nazi collaborators. Banion quits and operates as a freelance journalist for the rest of the novel.

Representing an alternative to such cynical postwar society—literally living beneath it—is Souzas Tsvirka, a Lithuanian immigrant janitor who resides in the basement of Lochsmeister's old apartment. As Finnegan describes, "He had built bookshelves of orange boxes. Dan roved an eye over the titles and concluded that Souzas Tsvirka was an advanced social thinker ... bookshelves crammed with volumes that yearned and argued for the brotherhood of man" (pp. 52–53). To these unspecified volumes, Souzas offers some more personal political advice:

> My fadder says to me "keep your mout shut and you stay out of trouble." ... My fadder kept his mout shut all his life and all his life he was in trouble. One day dey [the coassacks] killed him. And as he lay dere dying, he cursed dem wit all his breath. But it was too late. ... But I learned de lesson, and I keep my mout shut never. It means nudding to stand erect when you words are crawling. ... We shall drink to men who speak bravely.
>
> (p. 53)

Embodying an underground culture of multiethnic working-class solidarity, Souzas supports Banion in his renegade quest to prove Lochmeister's innocence.

On the opposite end of the political spectrum, but similarly marking *Many a Monster* as another politically self-conscious pulp novel, stand the White Knights of the Flaming Torch, a racist and anti-Semitic vigilante terror organization on the order of the Ku Klux Klan, who suddenly interrupt the flow of the detective plot midway through the book. The White Knights capture the "meddling" Banion, to torture him into revealing where "that Jew rapist" (p. 109). Lochmeister is hiding; Dan of course refuses. At one point, the White Knights command, "Get down on your knees and kiss the flag" (p. 108), prompting him to reply with macho antifascist patriotism that echoes Souzas Tsvirka. "'That flag,' Dan said, 'is the symbol of men who fought erect in order that other men could live erect. Any man who crawls on his knees to kiss it is insulting everything it stands for" (p. 108). Following this patriotic speech, Banion's antifascism takes a violent, hypermasculine form as Dan shoots down and kills seven White Knights in an improbable, superheroic escape. When a fellow reporter tries to restrain him from outright killing the goons, reminding him that "you're not in uniform now, you know," Banion replies, "My kind of uniform doesn't come off" (p. 112). Banion's violent tough-guy authenticity could be confused with Spillane's Mike Hammer, except that the targets of his self-righteous aggression are racists rather than, say, Communists.

Despite the several continuities through Ryan's "Robert Finnegan" series, significant differences emerge in this last novel. For instance, unlike in *The Lying Ladies,* where Banion remains in stark opposition to the entrenched authorities, in *Many a Monster* Banion appears able to win a number of police and newspaperman to his antifascist crusade. Perhaps the most remarkable shift here, however, is that, where in *Lying Ladies,* Banion remains allied with both the Regans and Shirley, in this last posthumously published novel Banion's closest partner on the case, Myrtle Wyler, turns out to be not only a cross-dressing turncoat but the actual murderer, a cold-blooded killer who has framed the innocent Rogan Lochmeister. (Her name, with its evocations of "wily" and "muddle," suggests her untrustworthiness from the start.) Early on Myrtle seems to be Banion's most trustworthy ally in this battle against the fascist supporter Braddock and his allies. Yet as she takes an increasingly assertive role in the undercover investigation, Banion begins treating her more and more harshly, forcing her back into a passive role, even

physically roughing her up, until, in a sudden revelation, Dan's sexist cruelty and suspicion are proven to have been retroactively "justified." Within just the last few dozen pages of the novel, Myrtle Wyler suddenly becomes the "monster" of the text, responsible, we learn, for *all* the book's many murders. Thus while on one level *Many a Monster* indicates that the "real" threat is posed by right-wing organizations in the United States, on another level the text's climax displaces such anxieties—and even this antifascist energy—onto the figure of a "misbehaving" woman, the mobile, malleable, and masculine Myrtle. Freeing the innocent Lochmeister, in a sense Finnegan replaces one "monstrous" scapegoat with another.

In this context, Tsvirka's closing toast "to all men who speak and act with boldness," takes on a vexed and contradictory meaning rather more disturbing than the quasi-socialist wisdom he shares in his first meeting with Banion. His outspoken call to act and speak "erect" in the service of the "brotherhood of men" can now be read simultaneously as misogyny, the strangling of the public female voice, the reestablishing of a stable (working-class) male-dominated gender order. Myrtle's morphing into a murdering monster reminds us of the "dangerous thoughts" and conventions of hard-boiled fiction. Sexist tropes that float through Finnegan's earlier novels here come to the foreground in a disturbing manner. In his overtly political "writing for the people" as Mike Quin, however, Ryan often targeted sexist and misogynist ideas quite directly—for instance his columns "The Bothersome Sex and O'Brien" and "The Family and Socialism," affirm women's rights to equality and self-determination in the workplace and at home in the postwar era. Indeed, the back cover of Quin's *More Dangerous Thoughts* sported strong endorsements from the left-wing women's activist-writers Ruth McKenney and Anna Louise Strong, alongside those from Clifford Odets and Millen Band.

When "Mike Quin" died on August 14, 1947, succumbing after a long and painful struggle with cancer, the CIO Council of San Francisco honored him with a moment of silence. Harry Bridges read aloud Quin's "Farewell to My Union Brothers" to a packed house of the union rank-and-file. The late "voice of the waterfront" characteristically left his readers with two pieces of advice. First, he admonished:

> Always remember that everything you ever gained you gained by standing together; by standing shoulder to shoulder under the slogan that an injury to one is an injury to all—no matter if a longshoreman's or warehouseman's skin is dark or light, and no matter what his creed.
>
> (p. xxxix)

Furthermore, he added,

> As for the Red Scare, remember that any idea which is any good for the working men will come wearing red flannel underwear. Even the mild social reforms by which the late President Roosevelt attempted to make some of America's great abundance available to ordinary families were decried by the money-hogs as the wildest communism.
>
> (p. xxxix)

Soon after, Bridges provided the foreword to Quin's posthumously published history of the 1934 San Francisco General Strike, writing, "The ILWU and the whole CIO on the West Coast would not be the organizations they are today had it not been for the contributions of Mike Quin" (*The Big Strike,* p. xii). While the ILWU, the American labor movement, and the political and cultural landscape of the United States look drastically different today than it did in Bridges' day, Paul William Ryan's diverse body of work deserves reconsideration, both as a representative of all-but-forgotten literary, cultural, and political movements and as a bearer of varied and vexed "dangerous thoughts" that may yet continue to resonate in the twenty-first century.

Selected Bibliography

WORKS OF PAUL WILLIAM RYAN

As "Robert Finnegan"

The Lying Ladies. New York: Simon & Schuster, 1946.

Bandaged Nude. New York: Simon & Schuster, 1947.

Many a Monster. New York: Simon & Schuster, 1948.

As "Mike Quin"

Ashcan the M-Plan: The Yanks Are Not Coming. San Francisco: Maritime Federation of the Pacific Coast, 1939.

Dangerous Thoughts. San Francisco: People's World, 1940.

The Enemy Within. San Francisco: People's World, 1941.

More Dangerous Thoughts. San Francisco: People's World, 1941.

On the Drumhead: A Selection from the Writing of Mike Quin. Edited by Harry Carlisle. San Francisco: Pacific Publishing Foundation, 1948.

The Big Strike. Olema, Calif.: Olema Press, 1949.

CRITICAL AND BIOGRAPHICAL STUDIES

Booker, M. Keith. *The Modern American Novel of the Left: A Research Guide.* Westport, Conn.: Greenwood Press, 1999.

Cohen, Victor. "Heroes for Sale." Ph.D. dissertation, Carnegie-Mellon University, 2006.

Davis, Mike. *Prisoners of the American Dream: Politics and Economy in the History of the U.S. Working Class.* New York: Verso, 1986.

Denning, Michael. *The Cultural Front: The Laboring of American Culture in the Twentieth Century.* New York: Verso, 1997.

Haut, Woody. *Pulp Culture: Hardboiled Fiction and the Cold War.* New York: Serpent's Tail, 1995.

Kelley, Robin. *Hammer and Hoe: Alabama Communists During the Great Depression.* Chapel Hill: University of North Carolina Press, 1990.

Lichtenstein, Nelson. *Labor's War at Home: The CIO in World War II.* Cambridge, U.K.: Cambridge University Press, 1982.

Mandel, Ernest. *Delightful Murder: A Social History of the Crime Story.* Minneapolis: University of Minnesota Press, 1986.

Naison, Mark. *Communists in Harlem During the Depression.* New York: Grove Press, 1984.

Nelson, Cary. *Repression and Recovery: Modern American Poetry and the Politics of Cultural Memory, 1910–1945.* Madison: University of Wisconsin Press, 1989.

Nelson, Steve. *Steve Nelson, American Radical.* Pittsburgh, Pa.: University of Pittsburgh Press, 1981.

Nyman, Jopi. *Men Alone: Masculinity, Individualism, and Hard-Boiled Fiction.* Amsterdam and Atlanta: Rodopi, 1997.

O'Brien, Geoffrey. *Hardboiled America: The Lurid Years of Paperbacks.* New York: Van Nostrand Reinhold, 1981.

Shaub, Thomas. *American Fiction in the Cold War.* Madison: University of Wisconsin Press, 1991.

Smith, Erin. *Hard-Boiled: Working-Class Readers and Pulp Magazines.* Philadelphia: Temple University Press, 2000.

Wald, Alan. *Exiles from a Future Time: The Forging of the Mid-Twentieth Century Literary Left.* Chapel Hill: University of North Carolina Press, 2002.

———. *Trinity of Passion: The Literary Left and the Antifascist Crusade.* Chapel Hill: University of North Carolina Press, 2007.

———. "The Urban Landscape of Marxist Noir." *Crime Time,* December 26, 2002, pp. 81–89.

———. *Writing from the Left: New Essays on Radical Culture and Politics.* New York: Verso, 1994.

Weigand, Kate. *Red Feminism: American Communism and the Making of Women's Liberation.* Baltimore, Md.: Johns Hopkins University Press, 2001.

Worpole, Ken. *Dockers and Detectives.* London: Verso, 1983.

BUDD SCHULBERG

(1914—)

Tom Cerasulo

IN A PROLIFIC writing career spanning many decades, Seymour Wilson ("Budd") Schulberg has published short stories, plays, book reviews, essays, screenplays, and sports journalism, but his greatest contribution to American literary culture has remained his role as a native informant on the inner workings of Hollywood and his examination of the place of the writer within the film industry. A highly skilled screenwriter and a serviceable novelist in the social realist, muckraking tradition of Upton Sinclair and John Steinbeck, Budd Schulberg has looked at institutional corruption in prizefighting, unions, television broadcasting, and politics. His best–known documentary novel, however, remains his debut novel, in which he takes on the world he knows best. During the 1930s, when many East Coast literary authors were moving west to work in the movie studios, Schulberg, the son of a studio pioneer, aspired to head east to write the Hollywood exposé *What Makes Sammy Run?* (1941).

Appearing in *Liberty* magazine in October 1937, the story "What Makes Sammy Run?"—Schulberg's first professional publication and the basis for the novel to come—provides a rich introduction to the profession of authorship in Hollywood, a theme Schulberg has returned to again and again in his writing. Sammy Glick, the antihero of "What Makes Sammy Run?" is a writer-producer who produces almost no writing. His radio columns are plagiarized; he is invited to Hollywood on the merits of someone else's script, and he moves up the screenwriting ladder by slightly altering the details of a recent movie. Instead of keeping quiet, Sammy boasts about it: "I used exactly the same construction as *Five-Star Final,* scene for scene, only I changed the characters, and I made it funny" (*What Makes Sammy Run?* 1990 ed., p. 298).

Sammy demonstrates that creative ownership in the film industry can be obtained through means other than artistry. Glick is a mediocre writer, but a genius at marketing himself. By end of the story, every movie he works on instantly becomes a Sammy Glick movie. As he leapfrogs from newspaper copyboy to radio columnist to screenwriter to Hollywood producer, his determination overrides his lack of originality. Who needs talent when you have tenacity? Sammy's star is on the rise, and his friend-enemy, a genteel playwright named Al, hitches a ride and serves as his biographer. Appropriately, Al's last name is "Manners." When his drama column loses space to Sammy's radio column, a blatant metaphor of art being swallowed up by mass culture, razor-sharp sarcasm is the only weapon he uses in retaliation. But his irony is no match for Sammy's iron will.

Schulberg's story is insider's literature written from an outsider's point of view. In the novel, Al Manners will go through a complex moral struggle regarding artistic integrity, once he's in Hollywood, but the end of the short story finds him quickly capitulated to Sammy's worldview. He realizes that the future of film authorship is Sammy Glick: "My agent tells me I may go to work for him next week, and I'd still rather have my name on a Sammy Glick production than any picture in town" (p. 299). But if it's a "Sammy Glick production," it has already been branded with someone else's mark of ownership—Sammy Glick's. Sammy, and Sammy alone, will decide who will get screen credit. Couple this with the fact that Sammy is an admitted plagiarist, and Al's chances for seeing his name written on screen look slim indeed. With this story, Schul-

berg, a Hollywood favorite son, begins his career-long examination of the movie industry's effect on the American writer.

EARLY YEARS

Budd Schulberg was born on March 27, 1914 in New York City. His movie executive father, Benjamin P. Schulberg, soon moved the family to Los Angeles, where the film industry had gradually been relocating. The senior Schulberg, who would rise to become head of production at Paramount before falling from grace fast and hard, was arguably the most intelligent producer in town. An aggressive businessman, a philanderer, and a compulsive gambler, B. P. was nonetheless a highly cultured man.

Literature was held in the highest regard in the Schulberg home. In an interview with Kurt Vonnegut in the *Paris Review* in 2001, Budd Schulberg recounts that Sunday afternoons at their Hollywood mansion would find B. P. reading Charles Dickens, Herman Melville, Leo Tolstoy, and Fyodor Dostoyevsky to his children. Schulberg's mother, Adeline, who would later become a literary agent, paid the children a quarter for every book they read. "Sonya, my youngest sister, said in our house the typewriter stood where a piano might be in other homes," said Schulberg. "We'd just sit down at the typewriter and run off a couple of scales—stories" (p. 97). In this way, Budd Schulberg was encouraged to be a writer in the way that other parents pushed their offspring toward professions in finance, medicine, or law.

Moving Pictures: Memoirs of a Hollywood Prince (1981), Schulberg's autobiography of his childhood and adolescence, expresses his eagerness to live the literary life. Throughout his career, Schulberg has maintained a fascination for the 1920s and a yearning for kinship with other authors. In his 1983 volume *Writers in America,* he writes about the lost, tight-knit literary community of the Lost Generation:

> In the Jazz Age it was still literary etiquette for a young man of promise to send politely inscribed copies of his new book to Edith Wharton, T. S. Eliot, or other established literary figures of his day. There was every sort of exchange, from F. Scott Fitzgerald's genteel tea-time encouragement from Edith Wharton and Eliot, to his Long Island drinking bouts with Ring Lardner.
>
> (pp. 15–16)

A speech impediment led Schulberg to become a good listener and pushed him even further toward the quiet pastimes of reading and writing. But he was also getting a top-notch education in the family business. While still a child, he began honing his gift for plot structure by sitting in on his father's script sessions and story conferences. At seventeen he worked as a publicist at Paramount, churning out semifictional narratives about the early lives of the stars.

After attending Los Angeles High School and Deerfield Academy, Schulberg enrolled at Dartmouth. He edited the school paper and graduated cum laude with a degree in sociology in 1936. Schulberg then returned to Hollywood, a newly minted Communist, and took a job with a family friend, the producer David O. Selznick. After a short time as a reader of scripts, he was promoted to junior screenwriter. Schulberg's first assignment was to work, uncredited, on the script for the 1937 film *A Star Is Born,* a self-reflexive Hollywood work about Hollywood. The film graphs the narrative geometry of a female star on her way up and a male on his way down.

After Dorothy Parker had submitted her draft of the picture, Selznick had then brought in Schulberg and Ring Lardner—at a bargain basement $25 a week apiece—to tighten up the story. Parker's strength was dialogue. Schulberg excelled at plot and structure. According to Tom Schatz, Schulberg took out a scene that had Norman Maine, an alcoholic star on the decline, driving drunk and killing a motorist. The junior writer convinced Selznick that such a plot point would steer the film toward being a "social problem" picture. Not all of Schulberg's suggestions were implemented, however. He also felt that the opening scene, set in the rural Midwest, caused the movie to get off to a slow start. But Selznick kept it in, and he was right to do so. Christopher Ames posits in *Movies About the Movies* (1997) that the film's beginning establishes Hollywood as the last frontier, a homeland El Dorado, and

the epicenter of the American Dream. He writes: "These scenes in the Dakota wilds not only establish Esther's naiveté and the long reach of Hollywood, but also introduce the resonant metaphor of moviemakers as pioneers" (p. 28).

In many ways, *A Star Is Born* is a derivative work. It shares the same basic plot as Theodore Dreiser's *Sister Carrie* (1900), as well as several other naturalistic novels, and the films *The Blue Angel* (1930) and Selznick's own *What Price Hollywood?* (1932)—not to mention the rocky Hollywood marriage of Al Jolson and Ruby Keeler—chart exactly the same axis. But Selznick, one of many models used to create the character Sammy Glick, had a vision of what the movie could be and should be. In the *Paris Review* Schulberg describes how the final shooting script was put together:

> I'll be damned if I didn't see it with my own eyes: David Selznick with a scissors taking the three screenplays, cutting them apart, literally cutting out two lines here and five lines there, making his own David Selznick screenplay, and the goddamn thing was one of the best Hollywood movies of all time, *A Star Is Born.* It worked.
>
> (pp. 132–133)

Reportedly, the film's famous last line, "This is Mrs. Norman Maine," was written by Schulberg, though others have also claimed credit. Once his draft was submitted, he was quickly shuffled to another Selznick project, the 1937 comedy *Nothing Sacred.* His name doesn't appear on that film either. Another screenwriter might have thrown a fit, but it didn't worry Schulberg much.

Because he was born into the movies, he seems to have understood atavistically some of the things about film writing that took other authors years to realize. Film was a visual medium, and it was a producer's medium. In *Writers in America,* Schulberg reflects: "Since I had been brought up in the place, I had no illusions about it. I had learned from intelligent producers, like Irving Thalberg, David Selznick, and my own father, that even the wisest of them looked upon the screenwriter as low man on the totem pole" (p. 113). Movie producers divided up labor in such a way that the guiding vision behind individual films remained their own, as did legal ownership of the scripts. Screen credits were sometimes withheld out of spite or granted to friends and lovers on a whim. Multiple writers were often assigned to the same script, a policy that infuriated many "name" authors.

There was a traditional Hollywood belief that someday a system would be figured out to do away with writers entirely. The cliché "time is money" was a perfect fit for the Hollywood studio system, where the assembly-line mode of production fostered an atmosphere of constant crisis. Shooting couldn't start until the writers were finished, so the writers could never be finished fast enough. Part of what rankled screenwriters about those in the front office was that so many of the executives believed that they could do the writer's job faster and better than the writer could. After all, weren't writers a dime a dozen? Since the late 1910s and early 1920s, the studios had been deluged with movie ideas and original stories from amateurs and professionals alike. In *Moving Pictures* Schulberg writes, "'They came pouring in, mostly in illegible scrawls,' B. P. would tell me, 'written on everything from postcards to butcher paper. Everybody who paid his nickel to see one of our shows thought it was easy money to dash off a movie'" (pp. 16–17). Designing costumes and building sets and composing the film score were jobs for specialists, but the writer's specialization wasn't seen as being very special. If a movie was a hit, the producer would take the credit. If it bombed, usually the script was blamed.

As an insider, Schulberg knew that working hard on scripts was commendable, but becoming attached to them was a mistake. The writer under the Hollywood studio system was more of an advisor than a creator. Unlike the poet, the screenwriter didn't begin typing because he had something to say. He usually started typing because a novel needed to be adapted for the silver screen or because the bosses wanted to capitalize on a recent successful film. Schulberg learned as a kid that the screenwriter was more of a craftsman than an artist; more of a carpenter than an architect. Scripts weren't written in Hollywood; they were assembled. With so many writers behind each film, Schulberg has said, "It

was like laying linoleum, different people working on different little squares" (quoted in Fine, pp. 117–118).

By paying Schulberg a junior writer's salary of $25 a week to add his squares and making him pay his dues, Selznick thought he was grooming his young employee to be a producer. Selznick had been B. P. Schulberg's assistant at Paramount, and he assumed the dynasty would continue with the young Schulberg working for him, and his own son eventually working for Schulberg.

But in 1937, Schulberg's primary interest wasn't the movies. He wanted to publish fiction. When Schulberg reminded Selznick of this, his disappointed boss responded by saying: "But I felt that if I kept you with me long enough sooner or later your producer's blood would begin to assert itself" (quoted in Fine, p. 111). Following the "write what you know" creed, the producer's son Budd Schulberg would write a case study about the film industry. After a few more years writing short stories and working on scripts, including 1938's *Little Orphan Annie,* a film on which he received his first screen credit, he left Hollywood in 1939 and moved to Vermont to write his novel.

WHAT MAKES SAMMY RUN? *AND THE 1940s*

Like *A Star Is Born,* Schulberg's 1941 novel *What Makes Sammy Run?* introduces us to workers in Hollywood and examines the effort that goes into creating films that look effortless. Over the years, the novel has often been read as an indictment of the movies. Yet, it ultimately allows for a marriage between art and commerce. Al Manheim is a literary man who comes to appreciate the film medium. The producer Fineman tells him the story of a famous playwright charged with writing a film scene establishing that a husband is tiring of his marriage. Twenty pages of brilliant dialogue later the scene is no closer to being finished. An old hand is brought in, "one of the few men left in the business who got his training in the Mack Sennett two-reel comedy school" of silent films, and the next day the scene looks like this:

> INT. ELEVATOR MEDIUM SHOT
>
> Husband and wife in evening clothes. Husband wearing top hat.
>
> REVERSE ANGLE
>
> As elevator door opens and classy dame enters.
>
> CLOSE SHOT HUSBAND AND WIFE
>
> Get husband's reaction to new dame. Removes hat with flourish.
>
> Wife looks from dame to husband's hat to husband. Then glares at him as we
>
> CUT TO:
>
> (pp. 159–160)

Without a word of dialogue, the scene is set. Inspired by the anecdote, Al is eager to get working on a new screenplay. "The most exciting way ever invented to tell a story is with a moving-picture camera," Kit Sargent, a respected eastern author and successful screenwriter, tells him (p. 160).

Under the influence of the story's love interest, Kit, Al begins to understand the reasons why a creative artist might be drawn to Hollywood and, more importantly, would want to stay there. It's not always all about the money, as Al explains:

> The trouble with Hollywood is that too many people who won't leave are ashamed to be there. But when a moving picture is right, it socks the eye and the ear and the solar plexus all at once and that is a hell of a temptation for any writer. I felt that when I went back for the fourth time to see *The Informer.* And one afternoon when I happened to catch a revival of the Murnau-Jannings masterpiece, *The Last Laugh.* And even when I saw one of my own jobs, a stinker if there ever was one, but with one scene in it that sang because I happened to stumble onto real picture technique. That is what held Kit there. Hollywood may be full of phonies, mediocrities, dictators, and good men who have lost their way, but there is something that draws you there that you should not be ashamed of.
>
> (pp. 233–234)

Schulberg reminds the reader that you're not required to check your integrity and your artistic aspirations at the studio gates. With its deep pockets and global reach, Hollywood during the studio era was a magnet for genius—Germany's F. W. Murnau included. At perhaps no other time in history did so many talented people engaged in the same enterprise reside in so small an area.

What Makes Sammy Run? points toward the fact that just because a piece of work is the product of a bureaucratic organization doesn't automatically mean it lacks quality or merit. After all, a ballet company divides up labor, too. Monetary interest doesn't preclude creative merit, and mass production doesn't necessarily lead to inferior products. *What Makes Sammy Run?* shows that artists boiling with creative passion do reside in Hollywood—and can thrive there. But, the novel warns, the good guys have to stick together.

Schulberg was a key member of the Screen Writers Guild, and *What Makes Sammy Run?* presents a wide spectrum of writers' responses to unionization and, by extension, their view of themselves as workers and citizens, as professionals and proletariats, and as artists. Al jokes with Kit before a union meeting that he likes seeing other people, "but one at a time, not all bunched together" (p. 130). While the intellectuals Kit and Al align themselves with the "little guys" of the SWG and opportunists like Sammy cozy up to the powerful and highly paid screenwriters of the house union, Screen Playwrights (here called "the Association of Photodramatists"), the aesthete Pancake scoffs at the notion of authors getting together to organize "like a bunch of plumbers" (p. 136). When talk surfaces of a plan to have Hollywood screenwriters align themselves with the Author's League of America, a former movie extra who has risen to respected writer argues that "no bunch of Broadway snobs" are "going to sit around the Algonquin" and give him orders (p. 132). Another red-baiting writer wants to kick out all "the goddam parlor pinks" (p. 137). The producers take this lack of consensus as a sign of weakness and try to break up the SWG through institutional pressures like graylists and stapling resignation forms to paychecks. When Al refuses to quit the union, the studio lets him go without needing to tell him why. His agent says that if there were a blacklist, he'd certainly be on it: "But they don't need anything like that in this chummy little business. All it takes is a couple of big shots happening to mention it over a poker game—or a meeting at Chasen's and passing the word along. That's why you should have played ball" (p. 191).

In the short-story version of the novel, Al devolves into a money-hungry hack, but here Schulberg leaves him at the end of the book just as we found him in the beginning: moral, passive, and intellectual. We feel Al's disgust as he watches Sammy Glick's Machiavellian slither up the corporate ladder, but we can also understand why he's fascinated by him. How far and how fast can Sammy go? Can anything stop him? Will he get his comeuppance? Sammy is a much more intriguing character than the one-dimensional narrator, Al. Hollywood is a Darwinian jungle to Sammy Glick, and he sees himself as the fastest and the fittest. Manheim chronicles the carnage, and in the process the reader is given a complete tour of the studio system as Glick tears his way through it. Sammy uses Max Weber's terrible trio—charisma, bureaucracy, and force—to cement his power and feed his megalomania. In a reversal of the typical Hollywood novel, Sammy isn't the writer as Hollywood victim; he's the writer as Hollywood victimizer. After chewing up other screenwriters, he graduates to preying upon weak and aging executives like the book lover Fineman, a stand-in for Schulberg's dethroned father.

From the moment they meet in the New York newspaper office, Glick views Manheim as a chump, but the older writer possesses the education, carriage, and taste that the boy wants to imitate. Sammy isn't satisfied with being a lowly radio columnist. Radio, although popular, lacks the glamour of film and the highbrow cachet of the stage. Using Al, Sammy looks to acquire a literary reputation that will increase his cultural capital, which he can then trade in for money and power. Once in Hollywood, as he moves from lowly screenwriter to powerful producer,

Sammy wants to mentor Al and make him wise up. But Manheim doesn't want to be tutored by the younger writer; he only wants to learn from him. In Al's final analysis, Glick represents greed gone wild. Unlike Horatio Alger's heroes with their pluck and luck, Glick uses shrewd deceit and cold opportunism in his quest for the American Dream. In this way, he's the spiritual godson of Theodore Dreiser's Frank Cowperwood of *The Financier* (1912). To Al, Sammy's story is "a blueprint of a way of life that was paying dividends in America in the first half of the twentieth century" (p. 276). It's paying dividends in the first half of the twenty-first century as well. In his afterword to the 1990 reprint of the noel, Schulberg bemoaned that many of today's fiscal-minded college students regard the text as more of a how-to manual than a cautionary tale: "The book I had written as an angry exposé of Sammy Glick was becoming a character reference: How to succeed in America when really trying!" (p. 326). In the end, *What Makes Sammy Run?* isn't anti-Hollywood; it's anticapitalism.

Glick's rise to producer is quick and savage, but what goes up must come down, and so, eventually, Schulberg makes sure Sammy is punished. The two things Glick can't buy, fake, or steal are gentility and an awareness of high culture. Like many an ethnic movie gangster before him and after him, he marries a WASP princess. But Laurette Harrington is a beautiful woman without mercy. At a party she mentions Gainsborough's picture *Blue Boy,* and Sammy asks if a foreign studio put it out. After stringing him along a bit, it's finally revealed she's talking about a painting. Laurette laughs at his expense, and Sammy can't conceal his embarrassment. Later she cuckolds him, and Sammy is left to wander aimlessly through the rooms of his huge, Xanadu-like mansion. In portions of these last chapters, especially when Al goes to the Jewish ghetto to uncover Sammy's origins, discovering that "what makes Sammy run" is fear of becoming like his weak father, the plot can lapse into schmaltz, but the majority of Schulberg's book is a solid documentary novel, narrated by a pitch-perfect participant-observer.

Still smarting from the poor sales of *The Day of the Locust,* Nathanael West's 1939 Hollywood novel, the Random House publisher Bennett Cerf had told his author Schulberg not to expect too much, since "the problem is that people who read novels have no interest in Hollywood, and people who go to the movies don't read books" (quoted in Schulberg's 1990 afterword to *What Makes Sammy Run?,* p. 321). Despite this, the novel was an instant best seller and a critical darling, named "Best First Novel of the Year" by the *New York Times.* His highbrow writer friends and fellow screenwriters Dorothy Parker and F. Scott Fitzgerald provided Schulberg with blurbs for *What Makes Sammy Run?* Both endorsements arrived too late for the first printing and only appeared on later runs. The front jacket copy quoted Fitzgerald, who called the novel "a grand book, utterly fearless with a great deal of beauty side by side with the most bitter satire." Parker, quoted on the back jacket, said of the novel: "It has understanding, pity, savagery, courage and sometimes a strange high beauty. It is written with a pace that rushes you along with it, and a sureness that comes only of great skill." Later, Parker would rise to the book's defense regarding accusations that it was anti-Semitic, claiming, "Those who hail us Jews as brothers must allow us to have our villains, the same, alas, as any other race" (quoted in the 1990 introduction to *What Makes Sammy Run?,* p. xv). But Hollywood's power brokers felt betrayed by one of their own. Sam Goldwyn banned Schulberg from his lot. Metro-Goldwyn-Mayer's Louis B. Mayer wanted him deported.

Heat from the studios would have been bad enough, but the Communist Party was also incensed at Schulberg. He had not received permission to print the book, and even with the narrator's name changed from Al Manners to Al Manheim—so that the story's most positive character would be Jewish, as was its less-appealing title character—the Party still found the story anti-Semitic. In addition, the Communists denounced the book as too realistic, too depressing, and too decadent. It did not focus enough on the positive force of the workers. Schulberg recalls that one reviewer, under pres-

sure from the Party, even retracted a positive review of the novel, claiming that, upon further inspection, "The book was elitist in that it only dealt with the writers; it didn't deal with the grips or the electricians, the workers" ("The Hollywood Years," p. 128). Despite the fact that the book repeatedly makes the point that writers *are* workers, Schulberg did not argue. He left the Party and left Hollywood.

Yet, even after his "banishment" in 1941, Schulberg never really left moviemaking. In 1943, helping out his father, a once-mighty captain of the industry who now couldn't find a job in the studios, he helped script *City Without Men,* a film about the women left behind when men go to prison. That same year, Schulberg worked on the screenplay for *Government Girl,* the story of a wartime secretary, directed by Dudley Nichols. As a navy lieutenant during World War II and a member of John Ford's documentary unit, he also pitched in to make propaganda films for the armed services. A film he worked on, *December 7,* won the 1944 Oscar for Best Documentary Short Subject. He also did some rewrites on the 1945 film *They Were Expendable.* After the war, Schulberg was awarded the Army Commendation Ribbon for gathering photographic evidence of Nazi war crimes, evidence that was used in the Nuremberg trials. He then went back to his true passion, writing novels.

Schulberg's second novel, 1947's *The Harder They Fall,* exposes the seamy side of yet another segment of the entertainment industry—professional sports. Instead of morally bankrupt movie producers, the book focuses on crooked boxing promoters. Based on the career of the Italian prizefighter Primo Carnera, the novel depicts the financial exploitation and physical decline of a brawny peasant at the hands of his ruthless managers. As in *Sammy,* the narrator is a genteel writer—in this case a sportswriter slumming it as a boxing publicist—who finds himself in a nest of vipers.

Eddy's job is to promote his boss Nick's latest discovery, a South American heavyweight named Toro. Since Toro has a soft punch and glass jaw, Eddy has to lie about his talent. He also has to ignore the fact that Toro's unbeaten record is the result of Nick fixing the fights. Toro doesn't realize that he's being set up to take a beating at the hands of the heavyweight champ. Once he's released from the hospital, he'll be used as a punching bag for other boxers on their way up. Eddy finds a conscience in the book's final pages, but it is too late:

> I know the goddam trouble with me, I thought. Enough brains to see it and not enough guts to stand up to it. Thousands of us, millions of us, corrupted, rootless, career-ridden, good hearts and yellow bellies, living out our lives for the easy buck, the soft berth, indulging ourselves in the illusion that we can deal in filth without becoming the thing we touch.
>
> (1995 ed., p. 343)

As in *Sammy,* Schulberg, a boxing aficionado, doesn't condemn an entire industry, just those racketeering opportunists who treat boxers like cattle to be bought, slaughtered, and sold.

THE DISENCHANTED

Schulberg's third novel, *The Disenchanted,* published in 1950, is a retrospective look at his own early screenwriting career and literary apprenticeship. It retains the boilerplate structure and themes of his first two novels and of those to follow: a bully works the system and dominates others, all of whom are too afraid or self-interested to stand up to him. Here again, the picture of American culture revealed is one that has institutionalized practices which reward the exploitation of the weak. But the novels also hold out hope that an individual—better yet, a writer—strong enough to resist can make a difference.

Like *What Makes Sammy Run? The Disenchanted* doesn't condemn Hollywood; it tries to come to terms with it. Both novels satirize the film industry, sometimes even savagely. But they also carefully examine studio society and American society at large, trying to figure out the writer's place within both. Instead of revenge tracts, they are sites of negotiation.

As in *Sammy,* a movie producer serves as the stock villain in *The Disenchanted.* Schulberg has often told the story of being stunned when Walter

Wanger, a producer with United Artists, announced to him in 1939 that he was pairing him with Fitzgerald to write *Winter Carnival,* a romantic comedy set at an Ivy League college. Schulberg had thought Fitzgerald was dead. The disastrous screenwriting trip to Dartmouth that followed can be outlined as follows: Fitzgerald got drunk on the plane, stayed drunk in New Hampshire despite Schulberg's attempts to babysit him, caught a huge cold, acted like a fool at a meeting with faculty and students that Wanger had arranged for the purpose of showing him off, got himself and Schulberg fired when it was revealed no work on the script had been done, and wound up attached to an IV in the hospital. This anecdote forms the basis for *The Disenchanted,* a 1950 novel that looks back at the 1930s. Scott Fitzgerald gets poured into the character of Manley Halliday, a drunken novelist whose best days are long behind him.

In greater detail than *What Makes Sammy Run?* had, the novel attempts to sketch the cultural history of the western migration of literary writers to Hollywood. As Richard Fine explains in *West of Eden: Writers in Hollywood 1928–1940* (1993), when the Depression hobbled Broadway and the New York publishing industry in the 1930s, the American film industry, with its need for spoken dialogue, allowed starving playwrights, literary journalists, and novelists to transform themselves into screenwriters with a paycheck. But this new role came with a price. Accepting a studio contract put authors into a structure and hierarchy where time, function, and productivity were measured and used to gauge success.

But movie producers believed that the product was too expensive to be left in the hands of effete, dillydallying artists, and writers who smelled of the highbrow were often paired with industry insiders or junior apprentices. Therefore, Budd Schulberg, the son of a movie mogul—and therefore both neophyte and old hand—had been called upon to babysit for Fitzgerald. While Fitzgerald was picking the brain of Schulberg for the character of Cecilia in the novel that was published posthumously in 1941 as *The Last Tycoon,* Schulberg was sizing up Fitzgerald for what would become *The Disenchanted.*

Fitzgerald's 1920 debut novel, *This Side of Paradise,* ends with a train trip where Amory defends his generation to a middle-aged businessman; *The Disenchanted* offers an artistic debate, begun on a plane, between the 1920s romantic individualism of Manley Halliday and the 1930s social commitment of Shep Stearns: Halliday wants to leave Hollywood and escape back into his boozy, poetic nostalgia for the Jazz Age; Stearns wants to push cinema into the hands of the revolution and create a realist art form made by the people for the people. Much of the early part of the novel is given over to Stearns's attempts to nudge his older partner toward the political left. Halliday is endowed with an amplified version of Fitzgerald's character flaws, biography, and appearance, yet Schulberg has always claimed—never very convincingly—that Manley Halliday isn't based on Scott Fitzgerald. Before we even meet Halliday, *The Disenchanted* prepares us for what is to come. Schulberg rolls out part of Henry James's subordinating preface to *The Lesson of the Master* (1909) as the novel's epigraph. It reads:

> The wondrous figure of that genius had long haunted me, and circumstances into which I needn't here enter had within a few years contributed much to making it vivid. ... More interesting still than the man—for the dramatist at any rate—is the S. T. Coleridge TYPE; so what I was to do was merely to recognise the type, to borrow it, to re-embody and freshly place it; an ideal under the law of which I could but cultivate a free hand. I proceeded to do so; I reconstructed the scene and the figures—I had my own idea, which required, to express itself, a new set of relations—though, when all is said, it had assuredly taken the recorded, transmitted person, the image embalmed in literary history, to fertilise my fancy. ... Therefore let us have here as little as possible about its "'being" Mr. This or Mrs. That. If it adjusts itself with the least truth to its new life it can't possibly be either.

Schulberg maintains that Mr. Halliday isn't Mr. Fitzgerald, but he has also expressed pride that *The Disenchanted* helped spark "the popular revival of Scott's work that happily goes on and on" (quoted in Beck, p. 27).

Rather than inciting a "popular revival of Scott's work," however, the book actually fuels the myth of F. Scott Fitzgerald as movie-industry casualty. Tom Dardis writes: "The tradition of seeing Fitzgerald in Hollywood as a *suffering* man, a *failed* man, really began with Budd Schulberg's novel of 1950, *The Disenchanted*" (p. 17). During the time Schulberg was composing the novel, Arthur Mizener was putting together the first major biography of Fitzgerald, and the two compared notes. As a result, both works—one fiction and the other nonfiction—are plots of decline. Despite the fact that the tail end of *The Disenchanted* ultimately reveals the older writer to be a productive artist who is still relevant, the bulk of the narrative is Shep's weekend walk with a zombie. Halliday refuses to let go of his death grip on the past, and throughout the novel he is referred to using terms such as "specter," "ghost," and "shadow." Listening to Halliday's constant self-analysis of his selfish mistakes, Shep thinks to himself, is "like having a corpse suddenly rise and deliver his own funeral oration, or, worse, perform his own autopsy" (p. 184).

At the beginning of *The Disenchanted,* Shep thinks Halliday is dead. He then proceeds to treat him as a relic during the trip and finally sees him dead at the end. In this way, Schulberg has it both ways. Nostalgia for the writers of the 1920s coexists with an Oedipal relief that they are fading away. Still, the novel tries to retain a sort of subjective distance. Unlike Schulberg's first two books, *The Disenchanted* is written from a Jamesian, third-person-limited point of view. The capitalist joys of Halliday's early career are sung in flashback chapters titled "Old Business." These discordant attempts to mimic Fitzgerald's lyrical style alternate with more sober, grittier chapters depicting Halliday's decline during the Depression.

The novel examines the pressure to compromise that Hollywood places on artists. Julian Blumberg, the shy, boyish, and principled screenwriter Sammy continually victimizes in *What Makes Sammy Run?* shows up briefly here as a middle-aged hack who has abandoned his idealism and literary aspirations. But, as a very tipsy Halliday points out, Hollywood and its capitalist ethic of success isn't the only drain on the American writer's talent—so is early success itself:

> Oh, I read Granville Hicks too. Trouble with all our writers is they never read Marx. Poe, Melville, Dickinson, all of 'em frustrated 'cause they didn't worship Marx. Booshwah. Banana oil. Baloney. Reason's economic, all right. But more complicated. Writer starts as rebel. Hits out at his own roots. Spoon River. Sauk Center. Pottsville country club—wherever it is. Book's a success—writer's like a race-horse—moves up in class. Gets money—goes away—New York—Europe—starts writing things he doesn't know—shoulda stayed home. Stayed put. Should stood in bed. That's trouble with 'merican writers. Most of 'em. Success uproots 'em. Isolates 'em. Europe, a book is a book, a leaf o' literature. America, a book's a commodity, even the honest book, if it *clicks,* if it *goes over big.*
>
> (pp. 183–184)

The *Disenchanted* reflects that working in Hollywood not only made authors further question their professional roles; it also deepened their anxiety about their cultural roles. Although Shep and Halliday have many heated arguments about the writer's vocation, the true antagonist of the book is the producer Victor Milgrim. Among many Hollywood executives, a dismissal of high culture was often paired with a reverence for the cultural prestige it carried, a tension that runs throughout *Sammy* as well. Milgrim brings Halliday to Dartmouth in order to show him off and borrow some of his literary capital. In the absence of possessing artistic credibility, many film executives settled for possessing the possessors of this quality. We are reminded of Jack Warner's claim to visitors that he had bought America's best writer, William Faulkner, "for peanuts" (quoted in Hamilton, p. 200). Although Milgrim is not as ruthless a class striver as Sammy, his depiction as a man of culture, as someone who should know better, holds him up for greater scorn. He is neither interested in art nor money, just in appearing to have both. He is most interested in stasis. For Schulberg, there are few greater sins than not believing in anything.

As the book goes on, the progressive Stearns comes to change his mind about the nostalgic Halliday. His pity and disgust turn to respect and

admiration. On the plane Shep is angry at Halliday's politics, and during the trip he resents him for blowing the assignment, but after reading the master's novel-in-progress he has an epiphany:

> Then it hit him hard: how was it possible for Manley Halliday to write this well in 1939?
>
> After all, Shep knew why Manley Halliday hadn't published in nearly a decade: because he was defeatist, an escapist, cut off from "vital issues," from "The People," a disillusioned amanuensis of a dying order. ... If poor, old Halliday, aware of himself and all his own friends in their own neurotic little world, could do what he promised to do in this new work, wouldn't Shep have to re-examine his own standards? Maybe ideology wasn't the literary shibboleth he had believed in so dogmatically.
>
> (p. 368)

Writing a book about the 1920s and 1930s from a perch in the 1950s, Schulberg can safely have the character of Shep Stearns become disenchanted with the vulgar Marxism of the 1930s and grow to appreciate the timeless artistry of a forgotten writer-competitor who looks an awful lot like F. Scott Fitzgerald.

But is the competition over? In *Writers in America,* Schulberg recalls his reaction to Fitzgerald's *The Last Tycoon*:

> It was almost as if I had written the book and then Scott had filtered it through his more tempered and sophisticated imagination. It is still the most uncanny experience I've ever had with another man's work. ... Scott had channeled off into his book some of my energy, some of my emotion and special insights into Hollywood. The sneak thief of vicarious experience that every writer has to be had taken possession of Scott—probably from our very first meeting.
>
> (pp. 150–151)

RETURN TO HOLLYWOOD

In 1950, the year *The Disenchanted* was published, Louis B. Mayer—who had wanted the novelist deported for *What Makes Sammy Run?*—approached Schulberg about bringing Sammy Glick to the screen. This seemed like a sudden change in Mayer's attitude, but the mogul was losing his power at MGM and needed a hit film to rekindle his career. When Schulberg turned down the project, Mayer and the studio simply appropriated many of the book's elements and built them into *The Bad and the Beautiful* (1952), the story of a talented—albeit ruthless—producer trying to regain his footing in Hollywood. But the studio system, which Mayer had helped create, was on its last legs in the 1950s. Independent production was taking over. In this climate, Budd Schulberg was about make an impressive film industry comeback of his own. *On the Waterfront* (1954) and *A Face in the Crowd* (1957), projects done in close collaboration with the director Elia Kazan, allowed him to achieve much greater cinematic success than he had in the 1930s and 1940s.

Both films were adapted solely by Schulberg from his own original stories—something that was rarely allowed under the studio system, with its distrust of meddlesome writers, at its height. Therefore, while Schulberg may not be the "auteur" of these movies, his mark on them can clearly be seen. In a manner that wasn't possible under the factory-like conditions of the studio system, a Taylorized filmmaking process where the screenwriter stopped working when the project began shooting, Kazan and Schulberg collaborated every step of the way—from preproduction, to production, to post-production—to create these movies.

Kazan approached Schulberg in the early 1950s about doing a film about corruption on the New Jersey docks. It would film on location, strive for a gritty realism, and pull no punches. In what seemed like a radical break from the old studio system, Schulberg as a screenwriter would be given complete authority over the script. Kazan told him: "Budd, if you'll do this I promise to treat it with the same respect I would give to a Tennessee Williams play or an Arthur Miller play or a Bill Inge play. I'll advise or argue with you, but I won't change anything. It'll be your play. I won't change a line of dialogue unless you agree" (quoted in Schulberg, "The Art of Fiction," p. 111).

Viewing himself as a novelist who occasionally wrote for the movies, Schulberg began

developing the material as a screenplay and a book simultaneously, angling to have the two projects released at the same time. But the novel took longer than expected, and getting the film financed was more difficult than Kazan and Schulberg had hoped. No longer tethered to studios, actors had the luxury of being picky, and Marlon Brando, the star of 1951's *A Streetcar Named Desire,* directed by Kazan, was waffling about doing the picture. But when he signed on, the film got the green light.

Elia Kazan may have sworn not to interfere with the script, but the producer Sam Spiegel had made no such promises. Spiegel made Schulberg's blood boil by whispering conspiratorially in Kazan's ear during story conferences and trying to take a red pen to some of the dialogue. Despite being barred from the set, throughout filming the producer used a barrage of telephone calls to play the director and writer off of each other, trying to drive a wedge between them and gain control over the picture from his booth at Manhattan's 21 Club. One day Schulberg's wife awoke in the middle to the night to find her husband shaving in the bathroom. When she asked him where he was going, he answered "I'm driving to New York ... to kill Sam Spiegel" (quoted in Fraser-Cavassoni, p. 314).

In hindsight, however, Schulberg had to admit that the producer had improved the screenplay. He admits in the foreword to Joanna Rapf's 2003 Cambridge Film Handbook for *On the Waterfront*:

> To give Spiegel his due, he hammered for tighter structure, and stronger (and what came to be total) focus on my main character. Precious scenes that added texture and complexity were jettisoned to the purpose of keeping it moving. The film asks "And then? And then? And then?" Often with a pang of regret I had to admit that in the interest of relentless storytelling, my pet sidebars had to go.
>
> (p. xvi)

Schulberg, Kazan, Brando, and Spiegel all received Academy Awards for *On the Waterfront,* and all deserve a piece of the credit for the movie's success. But, as usual in a collaborative art, how large a share each ultimately deserves is a subject of debate. With echoes of the attribution controversy over the "This is Mrs. Norman Maine" line of *A Star Is Born,* Brando claimed in the years before his death that he improvised the "I coulda been a contender" speech, one of the most famous monologues in film history.

The published shooting script proves that while Schulberg can't take credit for Brando's performance, or Leonard Bernstein's score, or the confining and threatening city created by Kazan in collaboration with the film's cinematographer Boris Kaufman and art director Richard Day, he is certainly responsible for *On the Waterfront*'s tight structure and Terry Malloy's nuanced characterization. In fact, read side by side with Shulberg's subsequent novel, titled *Waterfront* (1955), the screenplay emerges as the better-crafted piece of work.

As F. Scott Fitzgerald learned, script writing and novel writing are different skills, and what plays on the page doesn't always play in front of the camera. Obviously, the reverse also holds true, as can be demonstrated by Schulberg's misguided novelization of *Waterfront.* Schulberg's strength was for screenwriting, not for lyrical prose fiction. He excelled at giving structure to scripts, something his friends Fitzgerald and Nathanael West struggled with. More important, as a Hollywood insider, he knew the complicated process of how movies actually get made—what would work and what wouldn't, what was possible and what wasn't. He was able to write directly *to* the screen instead of blindly *for* the screen.

The priest's pomposity and moralism, the one weakness of the movie, is amplified in the book version. The novel concentrates more on Father Barry than it does on Terry, and the split focus and sloppy access to consciousness further hurt the book, leading it to wander and get bogged down in Christian allegory. In the script and on the screen (and looking at both reveals just how dependent they are on each other) Terry rightfully emerges as the more complex and more interesting character. Terry is both sinner and saint; he is both brutal and sensitive; he is a loner who is trying to make a connection to others. Terry's inner turmoil is what drives the narrative. Brando may have brought the character to life,

but the DNA is right there on the pages of Schulberg's script.

His murderous urges toward Sam Spiegel aside, Budd Schulberg ended up enjoying his *On the Waterfront* experience—a collaboration that wouldn't have been possible under the script-by-committee system during the height of the studio era. Schulberg told Vonnegut in the *Paris Review* that working with Kazan made him begin "to feel, Jesus, you can do the same thing in film that you can do in a book. You can really write what you want to write without any studio interference" (p. 111).

But could a writer author a film like he could author a book? During this same time, the mid-1950s, the "auteur theory" began gaining currency in France. Just when writers were in a position to be the guiding vision behind films, American directors—regarded during the studio era as little more than a bunch of interchangeable hired hands—were being proclaimed authors. Still, Kazan always gave Schulberg much of the credit for the movie, and the look and feel of *On the Waterfront* demonstrates the close collaboration between writer and director that went on during every stage of production. Both of their marks are all over the picture.

The movie has also been popularly read as Kazan and Schulberg's justification of their 1951 testimony as friendly witnesses before the House Committee on Un-American Activities. If it is, it offers the pair a shaky defense. Snitching on gangsters who murder isn't the same thing as snitching on leftist screenwriters who hold political beliefs. Perhaps Schulberg felt, like Shep Stearns of the *Disenchanted,* that turning his back on the ideology and the "literary shibboleth" of 1930s Marxism was a way of demonstrating that he had left his youthful indiscretions behind.

Whether or not Schulberg needed to testify at all is a bone of contention. Dorothy Parker invoked the First Amendment to the committee, and many others pleaded the Fifth. Bennett Cerf told Schulberg it wouldn't matter to Random House whether he testified or not (Beck, p. 45). Perhaps Schulberg could have been blacklisted in the film industry, but this is doubtful. He had been getting out of jams his entire adult life. Rich and powerful friends and relations certainly played a part in this, but another part is that Schulberg, like many American authors, perhaps overstates the "danger" of his beliefs and actions. He very seldom works without a net. For example, he was fired from *Winter Carnival* for being in cahoots with Fitzgerald, but in his retelling he often elides the part where his father's influence gets him rehired. He was persona non grata in Hollywood for *What Makes Sammy Run?* but his "banishment" appears not to have lasted very long. Membership in the Communist Party kept Dorothy Parker from being granted government clearance to go overseas as a war correspondent during World War II, but this same pink mark on Schulberg's record curiously didn't prevent him from getting a commission in the U.S. Navy. To hear Schulberg tell it, however, he is more sinned against than sinning. For instance, he has made the claim (recounted by his biographer, Nicholas Beck) that Ernest Hemingway and John Wayne both tried to pick fistfights with him. Without backing down, Schulberg somehow managed to avoid these beatings.

Along these lines, *On the Waterfront* contains Schulberg's familiar trope of the powerful bully who eventually gets foiled. The backstabbing producer Sammy Glick, the social climbing producer Victor Milgrim in *The Disenchanted, Waterfront*'s gangster boss Johnny Friendly, the fight promoter Nick Benko in *The Harder They Fall,* and the singing fascist Lonesome Rhodes in *A Face in the Crowd* all crumble, their inner rot revealed. *What Makes Sammy Run?* and *The Disenchanted* had exposed the film business, and *The Harder They Fall* had taken a swing at the business of professional sports. Schulberg's next project, 1957's *A Face in the Crowd,* looks at a third segment of the American entertainment industry—television.

The film is based on Schulberg's story "Your Arkansas Traveler" from the 1953 collection *Some Faces in the Crowd.* Partnering up again with Kazan, Schulberg was even more involved in the shaping of this film than he had been for *On the Waterfront.* In addition to the original story and the original script, he also wrote lyrics for the movie's songs. Kazan's introduction to

the film's published script, released before the movie, notes that once again Schulberg was on set each day of shooting and once again the director promised to be hands-off. In an attempt to make the script more reader-friendly for the layperson, Schulberg's preface to the screenplay for *A Face in the Crowd* includes his definitions of basic motion-picture terms like "long shot" and "fade-in." This glossary, coupled with the fact that the script was published before the film was even released, is Schulberg's attempt to make a case for the screenplay as a stand-alone piece of art. But as with the script for *On the Waterfront,* blueprints, no matter how impressive, only fulfill their promise when we see the objects built from them. A screenplay is always a draft; the film is the finished text.

A Face in the Crowd deviates from the rest of Budd Schulberg's oeuvre in terms of its treatment of the business world. *What Makes Sammy Run?* and *The Disenchanted* are both solidly pro-film but staunchly critical of the film industry. *On the Waterfront* is all for organized labor but speaks out against organized crime within the union. Schulberg had his own stable of prizefighters and served as the boxing editor of *Sports Illustrated,* and while the film version of *The Harder They Fall* calls for the sport to be banned, the source novel merely pleads for the sweet science to be cleaned up a little bit. *A Face in the Crowd,* on the other hand, reads like an argument for the elimination of television. Other Schulberg works about work call for "the people" to rise up, organize, seize the reins of production, and trample down corruption. In *A Face in the Crowd,* the people have all been narcoticized by their televisions. Lonesome Rhodes (Andy Griffith), a charming hobo turned right-wing demagogue and point man for an arch-conservative senator, has used the idiot box to fool all of the people all of the time.

Rhodes is exposed as a fraud when Marcia Jefferies (Patricia Neal), the woman who gave him his start, flips on his microphone as he begins joking about how dumb his audience is. Marcia follows the character trajectory of *Sammy*'s Kit Sargent: she's a strong, intelligent woman who finally wakes up and realizes she's in love with a complete heel, which sends her into the arms of a more genteel partner. The pipe-smoking, glasses-wearing television writer Mel Miller (Walter Matthau)—the "man without a face" whom Rhodes derides as "Vanderbilt '44"—is a more smug and more impotent version of *Sammy*'s Al Manners. Like Al, he wears his lack of success as a badge of honor.

With its fear of mass culture and warnings about homegrown fascism, *A Face in the Crowd* seems closer to the pessimism of Nathanael West than to the progressivism of Budd Schulberg. Kit and Al and Shep seek to transform the cinema into an art form for the masses. They work toward this end. For Marcia and Mel, however, it's enough to be smugly right about TV being a tool of mass hypnosis. Why bother rolling up your sleeves and doing something about it? It's hopeless anyway. After the film's climatic scene, which finds Lonesome Rhodes alone with his laugh-track machine, Mel tells Marcia that they haven't destroyed Rhodes; the cracker-barrel philosopher will be back on a small market station in no time, selling snake oils like Vitajex and grinning his way back into the nation's living rooms.

In 1958, after forming a production company with his brother Stuart, Schulberg wrote and produced the Warner Bros. film *Wind Across the Everglades,* the story of a warden in the Florida Everglades who tries to stop the slaughter of baby eagles. When director Nicholas Ray suffered a nervous breakdown, Schulberg shot the last scenes himself. Critics didn't find the overly earnest performances convincing, and the movie could not find a public.

Despite the failure of *Wind Across the Everglades,* the films *On the Waterfront* and *A Face in the Crowd* have cemented Schulberg a prominent place in cinema history. The result of this today is that his renown as a screenwriter has perhaps unfairly eclipsed his importance as a prose writer.

LATER CAREER

As Manley Halliday makes clear in *The Disenchanted,* an author can only be a first-time novel-

ist with huge promise once, and Schulberg's subsequent novels, while healthy sellers, have never reached the same level of critical acclaim as *What Makes Sammy Run?* A 1969 melodrama about a Latin American dictator and the human costs of political oppression, *Sanctuary V,* did not receive good reviews. *Everything That Moves,* published in 1980, uses short, filmic chapters to map the career of a character much like the teamster boss Jimmy Hoffa. In his selfish drive to control trucking, boat docks, and airfreight—"everything that moves"—the main character leaves behind the spirit of brotherhood that had drawn him into union activism in the first place. Like Schulberg's earlier novels, these books have been criticized for their one-note flat characters, ready-made plots, and dollops of superficial Marxism.

But both novels, like *The Harder They Fall* before them, warn of the damage that results when the will to power goes unchecked and good men stand around and do nothing. Despite Schulberg's stylistic flaws, there is much to admire in the search for social justice we find in his work. The commitment to activism found in Schulberg's novels has also been reflected in his life. In 1965, after a riot tore apart the Watts neighborhood in Los Angeles, Schulberg founded the Watts Writer Workshop to give an artistic outlet to the devastated community. The result was the collection *From the Ashes* (1967). Schulberg has taught writing at Columbia University, Hofstra University, Dartmouth, Southampton College, and Valley Forge General Hospital. He has also served as chairman of the Frederick Douglass Creative Arts Center in New York City and on the advisory board of the Center for the Book at the Library of Congress.

Among the most versatile of authors, Schulberg has also written successfully for the stage and smaller screen. Along with Harvey Breit, he adapted *The Disenchanted* into a 1958 off-Broadway play. With his brother Stuart he wrote the dramatization and libretto for the 1959 NBC broadcast of *What Makes Sammy Run?* And Schulberg's nonfiction writing career has also enjoyed its highlights. He has contributed to magazines such as *Sports Illustrated, Esquire, Harper's, Playboy,* and *Saturday Review. Loser and Still Champion: Muhammad Ali,* published in 1972, reflects Schulberg's lifelong study of the sweet science. *The Four Seasons of Success* (1972) examines the highs and lows—but mainly the lows—in the careers of several American authors, most notably Nathanael West, John Steinbeck, and F. Scott Fitzgerald. *Swan Watch* (1975), as its title indicates, draws from Schulberg's observations of a family of birds. Schulberg's autobiography, *Moving Pictures: Memoirs of a Hollywood Prince,* which covers his privileged childhood, was published in 1981. *Writers in America,* an expanded revision of *The Four Seasons of Success,* was released in 1983.

ASSESSMENT

Not only will literary history remember Budd Schulberg as an important practitioner of the Hollywood novel, having written two of its most representative examples, but he also remains the foremost authority on the subgenre and its authors. He has written introductions to reprints of Hollywood novels and has provided numerous quotes and sound bites. Biographers and film historians have been eager to hear him reminisce. In the twenty-first century, Schulberg continues to dole out stories perpetuating the tale of Fitzgerald as Hollywood failure. In 2001, he told the *Paris Review* that Fitzgerald was seen as "marginal" in Hollywood and that he was "pathetic, really, because he thought he could be as good a screenwriter as he *had been* a novelist" (pp. 120, 124; emphasis added). Grumbling about the lack of respect his own writing gets from literary critics, Schulberg said in the same interview:

> Scott Fitzgerald often wished that after *Gatsby* he had never done anything but just stuck to his last. Sometimes at night I feel that way. I have a little bit of that feeling, that I probably would be more respected as a novelist if I had just stayed on that track. Instead, I have this sort of fatal problem of versatility. Because I was raised in such a writing atmosphere, it got so I could write anything. I could write a movie; I could write a novel; I could write a play, I could even write lyrics, which I did for *A Face in the Crowd.* Always there were these differ-

ent strings, so many different ones. I was sort of cursed with versatility.

(p. 111)

Despite his "fatal problem" and talk of being "cursed," over a long career and long life Budd Schulberg has used his documentary powers, coupled with his insider point of view, to vitally examine the impact of the entertainment industry's success ethic on humanity in general and on American writers in particular.

Selected Bibliography

WORKS OF BUDD SCHULBERG

BOOKS

What Makes Sammy Run? New York: Random House 1941. Reprint, New York: Vintage, 1990. (With an introduction and an afterword by Schulberg.)

The Harder They Fall. New York: Random House, 1947.

The Disenchanted. New York: Random House, 1950.

Some Faces in the Crowd. New York: Random House, 1953.

Waterfront. New York: Random House, 1955.

A Face in the Crowd: A Play for the Screen. New York: Random House, 1957.

Across the Everglades: A Play for the Screen. New York: Random House, 1958.

The Disenchanted: A Drama in Three Acts, with Harvey Breit. New York: Random House, 1959.

What Makes Sammy Run? A New Musical. With Stuart Schulberg. New York: Random House, 1964.

From the Ashes: Voices of Watts. Edited and with an introduction by Schulberg. New York: New American Library, 1967.

Sanctuary V. New York: New American Library, 1969.

Loser and Still Champion: Muhammad Ali. Garden City, N.J.: Doubleday, 1972.

The Four Seasons of Success. Garden City, N.J.: Doubleday, 1972. Revised edition published as *Writers in America: The Four Seasons of Success.* New York: Stein & Day, 1983.

Swan Watch. New York: Delacorte, 1975.

Everything That Moves. Garden City, N.J.: Doubleday, 1980.

On the Waterfront: A Screenplay. Carbondale: Southern Illinois University Press, 1980.

Moving Pictures: Memoirs of a Hollywood Prince. New York: Stein & Day, 1981.

On the Waterfront: The Final Shooting Script. New York: Samuel French, 1988.

Love, Action, Laughter, and Other Sad Tales. New York: Random House, 1989.

Sparring with Hemingway: And Other Legends of the Fight Game. Chicago: Ivan R. Dee, 1995.

SCREENPLAY WORK

Nothing Sacred. Directed by William Wellman. United Artists. 1937.

A Star Is Born. Directed by William Wellman. United Artists. 1937.

Little Orphan Annie. Directed by Ben Holmes. Paramount. 1938.

Winter Carnival. Directed by Charles Reisner. United Artists. 1939.

Foreign Correspondent. Directed by Alfred Hitchcock. United Artists. 1940.

Weekend for Three. Directed by Irving Reis. RKO. 1941.

City Without Men. Directed by Sidney Salkow. Columbia. 1943.

Government Girl. Directed by Dudley Nichols. RKO. 1943.

The Nazi Plan. Directed by George Stevens. Nuremberg War Crimes Tribunal. 1945.

On the Waterfront. Directed by Elia Kazan. Columbia. 1954.

A Face in the Crowd. Directed by Elia Kazan. Warner Bros. 1957.

Wind Across the Everglades. Directed by Nicholas Ray and (uncredited) Budd Schulberg. Warner Bros. 1958.

CRITICAL AND BIOGRAPHICAL STUDIES

Beck, Nicholas. *Budd Schulberg.* Lanham, Md.: Scarecrow Press, 2001.

Breit, Harvey. "A Talk with Mr. Schulberg." *New York Times Book Review,* November 5, 1950, p. 28.

Eisinger, Chester. *Fiction of the Forties.* Chicago: University of Chicago Press, 1967.

Lyman, Rick. "The Long Run of Sammy Glick." *New York Times,* May 7, 2000.

Rapf, Joanna, ed. *On the Waterfront: The Cambridge Film Handbook.* New York: Cambridge University Press, 2003. (Includes a foreword by Schulberg.)

Schulberg, Budd. "Old Scott." *Esquire,* January 1961, pp. 97–101.

———. "Two Conversations." *Paris Review,* no. 160:90–127 (winter 2001). (Interviews with Schulberg: "The Art of Fiction" and "The Hollywood Years.")

Schwartz, Nancy Lynn. *The Hollywood Writers' Wars.* New York: Knopf, 1982.

Wells, Walter. *Tycoons and Locusts.* Carbondale: Southern Illinois University Press, 1969.

Wilson, Edmund. *The Boys in the Back Room.* San Francisco: Colt Press, 1941.

Papers

The majority of Schulberg's papers are deposited at Princeton University's Harvey S. Firestone Memorial Library. Other Schulberg materials are housed at Dartmouth College's Rauner Special Collections Library and Baker Library.

Further Reading

Ames, Christopher. *Movies About the Movies.* Lexington: University Press of Kentucky, 1997.

Bernstein, Walter. *Inside Out: A Memoir of the Blacklist.* New York: Knopf, 1996.

Brando, Marlon. *Brando: Songs My Mother Taught Me.* New York: Random House, 1994.

Dardis, Tom. *Some Time in the Sun.* New York: Scribners, 1976.

Dickstein, Morris. "What Price Hollywood: Dreams and Nightmares of the Great Depression." *Common Review* 1, no. 3:22–31 (spring 2002).

Fine, Richard. *West of Eden: Writers in Hollywood 1928–1940.* Washington, D.C.: Smithsonian Institution Press, 1993.

Fitzgerald, F. Scott. *The Love of the Last Tycoon: A Western.* Edited by Matthew Bruccoli. Cambridge, U.K.: Cambridge University Press, 1993.

Fraser–Cavassoni, Natasha. "Spiegel's Mighty Shadow." *Vanity Fair,* April 2003, pp. 304–322.

Gabler, Neal. *An Empire of Their Own: How the Jews Invented Hollywood.* New York: Crown, 1988.

Hamilton, Ian. *Writers in Hollywood, 1915–1951.* New York: Harper & Row, 1990.

Kazan, Elia. *A Life.* New York: Knopf, 1988.

Navasky, Victor. *Naming Names.* New York: Viking, 1980.

Schatz, Thomas. *The Genius of the System.* New York: Metro, 1988.

SUSAN WARNER

(1819—1885)

Laurie Ousley

SUSAN WARNER'S CONTRIBUTION to American literary history is an important one: upon the publication of her first novel, *The Wide, Wide World,* made available in time for the 1850 Christmas season and published under the pseudonym Elizabeth Wetherell, she became the nation's first best-selling author. George Haven Putnam put these sales figures into context years later in his memoir of his father, George Palmer Putnam, Warner's publisher: "The sale of *The Wide, Wide World* had ... reached the fiftieth thousand, a sale for which the community of at that time (the country contained ... about twenty five millions of people) was as noteworthy as would be a sale to-day of two hundred and fifty thousand." Furthermore, the novel came to such popularity not primarily through advertising (other than its notice of publication) or reviews by the usual leaders of literary sensibilities but through readers' individual recommendations. In *Female Prose Writers of America* (1851), John Seely Hart writes that the novel sold by word of mouth alone, reaching "a circulation then considered almost unprecedented. ... It was one of the most signal instances in recent times of a popularity reaching almost to fame, springing up spontaneously, and entirely in advance of all the usual organs of public opinion." *The Wide, Wide World* sold well in both the United States and in Britain, where it was fairly consistently in print until the 1950s, and was translated into French, German, Polish, and Dutch, among other languages.

The popularity of *The Wide, Wide World,* as well as Warner's later works, was long lasting. Translations, in fact, appeared in the Netherlands through the nineteenth and into the twentieth century, according to Yvonne Wellink. Wellink notes that translations appeared periodically over a span of years, the novel eventually being simplified for child readers and the translations of later editions removing much of the religious text of the novel, leaving it a very different story. In "The Most Popular Novels in America," printed in the *Forum,* Hamilton W. Mabie indicates that *The Wide, Wide World* was still being requested by 44 percent of library patrons and *Queechy* by 25 percent in December 1893. "Even years later," writes James D. Hart in *The Popular Book: A History of America's Literary Taste* (1950), the novel "continued to attract weeping readers at home and abroad, readers as different as Martha Finley Farquharson, author of Elsie Dinsmore's endless saga, and Vincent van Gogh, the great Dutch painter."

This introduction of the best seller to the literary marketplace changed the publishing business dramatically, as Ellen D. Kolba points out in "Stories for Sale," leading to a vast expansion in the number of American publishers. The success of this book also changed the way that the next, *Queechy* (1852), was both printed and marketed. According to Ezra Greenspan, in *George Palmer Putnam: Representative American Publisher,* the first run of *The Wide, Wide World* consisted of just 750 copies and was advertised "rather lightly," but the first run of *Queechy* consisted of 7,000 copies and was advertised aggressively, capitalizing on the author's name recognition and the success of the first. Additionally, as Kolba argues and Mary Kelley aptly demonstrates in *Private Woman, Public Stage: Literary Domesticity in Nineteenth-Century America* (1984), the advent of this best seller written by an unknown woman opened the market to women's fiction. Indeed, Putnam expanded his list to include many of the popular women writers of the day, as did other firms such as Ticknor and Fields, Harper, Lippincott, and Peterson.

For most of her contemporary reviewers, Warner's acclaim was earned both for her talents as a local colorist as well as for her depictions of religious themes. Both John S. Hart and Caroline Kirkland, a writer contemporary to Warner, praise the religion of the novels, Hart asserting that "We know no work of fiction in which real religion, as it is understood by Evangelical Christians, is exhibited with such truth and force." From the outset, the novel was included in church and Sunday school libraries, beginning with that of the Baptist Sunday school following an 1850 convention in Providence, Rhode Island.

In an 1865 review in the *Nation,* Henry James notes Warner's skill as a local colorist, and a July 1860 review of *Say and Seal* in *Atlantic Monthly* claims that

> Miss Warner's books have always a genuine flavor of originality, and an acute, living appreciation of Yankee character, that give them a right to rank, unchallenged, as real and valuable novels ... they have the real essence of the New England character.

Kirkland concurs, arguing that Warner's first two novels "paint human nature in its American type" ("Novels and Novelists," *North American Review,* January 1853). Three decades later, Edward G. Salmon asserted in an October 1886 article in *Nineteenth Century* titled "What Girls Read" that "Miss Wetherell knew how to write stories true in every particular to nature, and to pourtray [*sic*] character at once real and ideal."

Clearly, Warner is important for her unprecedented popularity, and for some time she was studied merely because she was popular in the period that canonical writers were working—Nathaniel Hawthorne, Ralph Waldo Emerson, Henry David Thoreau, and Herman Melville were Warner's contemporaries. Throughout most of the twentieth century, scholars considered Warner's writing beneath their concern, considering her works only when discussing popular literature of the period and generally for the purpose of derision. Even her physical appearance did not escape criticism. Note, for example, James D. Hart's comment in *The Popular Book*: "One look at her spare equine face distinguished by a pair of eyes set not quite evenly in her head, a thin determined mouth, and hair brushed tightly behind large ears proclaimed her a spinster by nature." (The nature of this comment is, of course, distinctly misogynist.) Much of this criticism makes use of Nathaniel Hawthorne's famous complaint to his friend and publisher William Ticknor in a letter of January 19, 1855, about the "d—d mob of scribbling women" who prove that America's poor literary taste is responsible for his own failure to sell books. "What is the mystery of these innumerable editions of the Lamplighter, and other books neither better nor worse?" he continues, "worse they could not be, and better they need not be, when they sell by 100,000."

The feminist movement changed literary scholarship a good deal, and the study of women's literature, often deemed (or dismissed as) "domestic" or "sentimental" became legitimized for the purpose of serious study. In 1978 Ann Douglas (whose work is decidedly not feminist) and Nina Baym brought scholarly attention to the work of women writers of the nineteenth century. In *The Feminization of American Culture,* Douglas argued that the women writers of the period worked with clergy, serving to feminize or weaken American culture and values. While Douglas's work is largely a polemic against the popular women writers and the clergy of the nineteenth century in order to serve the canonical writers of the period, she did bring an attention to Warner and her contemporaries that they had not enjoyed in some time. Baym's important feminist study of nineteenth-century women writers, *Woman's Fiction: A Guide to Novels By and About Women in America, 1820–1870,* attempts to understand the books and the ideology of the writers, outlining the conventions of popular women's fiction of the fifty-year period under consideration, devoting a chapter to Susan and Anna Warner and Maria Cummins. Baym's text, in which she described Warner's first three novels in some detail, brought legitimacy both to Warner and her contemporaries as well as to the scholarly study of them. Jane Tompkins continued the work of explicating sentimental and domestic fiction in "The Other American Renaissance," revised and later republished in *Sensational Designs: The Cultural Work*

of American Fiction, 1790–1860 (1985), a chapter devoted to delineating the social and political contexts of the sentimental novel, *The Wide, Wide World* in particular, demonstrating its connections with religious tract literature as well as its participation in republican heritage. Critics such as Joanne Dobson have worked to explicate the ideology and aesthetics of Warner and her contemporaries since the advent of Baym's and Tompkins's landmark studies. Now that the study of sentimental and domestic literature has been legitimized, the criticism is significantly more nuanced, although few have addressed the aesthetics of the literature in any depth and the number of texts actually studied remains fairly small.

EARLY LIFE

Born July 11, 1819, in New York, Susan Bogert Warner was the eldest surviving daughter of Henry Whiting Warner and Anna Marsh Bartlett Warner. Anna was a wealthy socialite from Long Island and Henry a successful lawyer in New York, born, however, in Canaan, New York, close to the border of Massachusetts. According to Mabel Baker, a former Constitution Island Association historian, both Henry and Anna could boast of ancestry from the founding of the nation, Henry claiming a relation to William Bradford, who arrived on the *Mayflower,* and Anna to Robert Bartlett, who was a passenger on one of the ships that arrived in Plymouth just three years later, the *Anne & the Little James.* Anna made social debuts in Newport, Providence, and New York. Henry was a writer himself, publishing on political matters in *An Inquiry into the Moral and Religious Character of the American Government* (1838) and *The Liberties of America* (1853) and reportedly working on a thesaurus and various papers on the law. Susan's younger sister Anna, who became a lifetime companion and occasional collaborator, was born on August 31, 1824. Upon his wife's death in 1828, Henry's sister Frances, Aunt Fanny, moved in with the family, where she remained until her death in 1885. The family was prosperous, associating with the upper echelons of New York society and living in the most fashionable areas of the city, finally in a mansion on St. Mark's Place.

Susan's youth is lovingly described in some detail with the assistance of Susan's journals in Anna's biography of her sister, *Susan Warner ("Elizabeth Wetherell")* (Putnam, 1909). Young Susan appears to have been somewhat willful and even spoiled; indeed, Anna titles one chapter on Susan's childhood "The Little Queen." The loss of three infants led the Warner parents to dote excessively on their eldest daughter, as Anna indicates. Susan was very well educated and spent a good deal of time in reading and study, as documented in her extant journals, letters, and in Anna's biography. Susan studied Greek, Latin, French, German, and Italian, history, classic literature, the natural sciences, and geography, as well as painting, drawing, singing, and piano. Her education was thorough and was intended to prepare her for a good marriage. If the family fortune had not been lost, Susan and Anna would have married into established New York families and lived comfortable, luxurious lives, not likely writing themselves into literary history.

Thomas Warner, Henry's brother, was appointed chaplain and professor of geography, history, and ethics at West Point in 1834, and it was through Thomas that Henry came to purchase Constitution Island, then known as Martelaer's Rock, an island in the Hudson River across from the U.S. Military Academy at West Point. The property was intended to become a country estate and fashionable hotel, but Henry had just begun the construction before the family began its long decline into poverty in the Panic of 1837. As a result of Henry's continued speculations and a series of lawsuits with his neighbors on the island, the family never recovered any semblance of its previous prosperity. Anna's account of the times, along with Mabel Baker's historiography in *The Warner Family and the Warner Books,* indicates that Thomas could have helped the family in the litigation, because he was the only witness on Henry's side of a key transaction, but he moved to France rather than help his brother, even deserting his own wife in the process. Neither Susan nor Anna, however, leave evidence that they blame their uncle for their financial

burdens, although there are certainly questions about what occurred and it seems that Thomas could have helped them considerably.

The Warners's decline was an extended one, beginning with leaving their fashionable mansion in New York and their subsequent isolation from society, to the loss of all of their servants, one by one, and, finally in 1846, to a permanent move to the island and a permanent struggle for financial well-being. As Mary Kelley and others point out, Susan continued her education after the loss of the family's wealth and her tutors, although she did so while taking on the daily work formerly done by the servants. The sisters chopped their own wood and sewed and cooked for themselves and their family, marking a significant change in their circumstances. Susan, a good deal older than Anna, had a more difficult time with the transition than her sister; as Anna writes in *Susan Warner,* "for my sister in the bloom of her young womanhood, it must have been hard. ... I think it tried my sister more than anyone guessed."

It was in the midst of this extended financial downfall that Aunt Fanny suggested that Susan write as a means of earning some much-needed income. Anna recounts the origin of *The Wide, Wide World* in *Susan Warner*: "Aunt Fanny spoke. 'Sue, I believe if you would try, you could write a story.' Whether she added 'that would sell' I am not sure; but of course that was what she meant." Upon its completion, Henry began to seek a publisher, meeting rejection after rejection from many New York publishing houses. George Haven Putnam recalled in his memoir of his father that, without the interjection of his grandmother, the novel would likely have remained unpublished:

> Father had the manuscript at his home on Staten Island, where his mother, an earnest Christian woman, happened to be visiting him. He handed the manuscript to her for an opinion. Her report was, in substance: "George, if you never publish another book, you must make 'The Wide, Wide World' available to your fellow men. ... Whatever the business difficulties, I feel sure that Providence will take care of this book."
>
> (pp. 25–26)

Although she never became wealthy or even lived in ease, Warner earned a healthy income on the royalties of *The Wide, Wide World.* G. P. Putnam remarked on the sales of the novel in a letter (February 10, 1853) to Nathaniel Hawthorne: "This year Miss Warner received from us for six months' sales $4500." This income went toward the debts incurred by the mortgage and the lawsuits but never served to bring the family financial security, although they were finally able to purchase furnishings to replace some of those sold at an 1849 sheriff's auction to satisfy outstanding debts. Indeed, the sisters sold their later copyrights outright, although always wishing the necessity for doing so were not there. For *A Red Wallflower* (1884) Susan was paid by the printed page, $1.75 for 664 pages, according to Baker.

Before *The Wide, Wide World* found its publisher, Warner entered an essay contest, the winner of which would win fifty dollars and publication in the *Ladies' Wreath.* Warner, writing as Wetherell, won the prize and the publication of *American Female Patriotism.* Henry spent all but the family's last two cents to go to New York City to collect the prize money. Upon his return, he brought the first copy of *The Wide, Wide World* itself along with its first reviews, as well as necessary supplies such as lamp oil and tea. Susan describes the volume in her journal: "a most elegant volume, gilt most ornamentally on the sides and back, and with gilt edges." In the essay that was intended to respond to the question "How may an American woman best show her patriotism?" Warner depicts a scene in which a woman poses the same question to her husband to write for a fictional contest of the same nature. The wife, Laura, is reading of the contest in the newspaper and fancies that, if she wins, she might be able to purchase a French hat her husband had denied her. The substance of the response is revealed through the conversation with her husband and sister-in-law, Theresa, in the midst of waiting for dinner to be announced—a homely scene similar to those in Warner's other work. The answer to the question is recapped at the end of the essay, as the dinner bell is rung:

> "Oh, well enough. But stop, before we go down, I should like to make sure of my points—at present

> they are all in confusion. Let me see. In the first place I was to bring up my sons to be patriots; Mr. St. John, I leave that to you, sir; it is astonishing how much humbug there is in the world! Secondly—"
>
> "No, *firstly,* Laura, your former head stands by itself, and you now enter upon your qualifications for the duty."
>
> "Well, firstly, I am to be an American; that is, in other words—no matter what. Secondly, I am to be Christian; thirdly,—"
>
> "An enlightened patriot."
>
> "And fourthly,—was there a 'fourthly'?"
>
> "And, fourthly, a *woman.*"
>
> (p. 327)

This final exchange leaves out a good deal of the discussion contained within, about the importance of staying true to one's national identity by eschewing foreign customs, the importance of women's education, particularly in history, an emphasis on Christian and Republican principles, arguing for a meritocracy based on "mind and manners." Laura, in learning the answer to the question of how an American woman may best show her patriotism, learns that she is not particularly patriotic herself and demonstrates this in her summation. *American Female Patriotism* illustrates Warner's rhetorical strategy. She poses the question at hand in a way that engages her reader, disarming her so that she may address her own actions rather than putting her on the defensive, by presenting a protagonist who also has defects that must be addressed. As Warner's heroines undergo their conversion experiences and learn of their many Christian duties, the reader is engaged in the activities and education along with her. This rhetorical device is one of the elements of her writing that has led scholars to deem the writing instructional, in the manner of training manuals, and an element to which her readers clearly responded.

A note on the Warner sisters' own patriotism and the importance of American history to them is warranted here because it is present in their daily lives on Constitution Island and in a good deal of their writing as well. Above the mantel in the room in which Susan and Anna wrote early each morning, when it was too cool to write outside, was a Gilbert Stuart painting of Washington, and the room was constructed of an old Revolutionary War fort. Remnants of fortifications from the war were scattered throughout the grounds, as Anna noted to Olivia Egleston Phelps Stokes, family friend and biographer:

> Miss Anna pointed out to me remains of fortifications on the Island, and told me of the old days when the Island was fortified during the Revolutionary War and the American forces had connected the island with West Point by a chain to prevent the English fleet passing up the river, and the discovery of Arnold's treachery in removing a link from this chain. On the part of the property known as "Washingon's Parade Ground" Washington's bodyguard was mustered out in 1793.
>
> (*Susan Warner,* p. 16)

Although the Warners went through many periods of near-destitution, they never sold their portrait of Washington. Out of desperation, Susan apparently wrote to Putnam to inquire into the possibility of its sale, but the issue was not pursued. An offer was made to Anna for the painting in 1897, and though she was, as usual, in need of the money, she refused. Later, she wrote to a friend: "I can dispose of other things, but that portrait my sister and I agreed should go to the academy." The portrait remained over the mantle until Anna's death in 1915 when it was bequeathed to the cadets. Today a reprint of the portrait hangs in the place of the original, which is now in the Cadet Library at West Point. It is appropriate, then, as a descendant of men who fought in the Continental Army, writing in a room of a fort once occupied by George Washington, and writing under his portrait, that Susan would choose female patriotism as the subject of her first published work. American history is a subject many of her heroines discuss, as patriotism is an important part of their development as women. In *Family, Kinship, and Sympathy in Nineteenth-Century America,* Cindy Weinstein notes that the American Revolution is repeatedly employed in Warner's first novel as a means of asserting the heroine's right to choose her own family.

THE WIDE, WIDE WORLD

The Wide, Wide World details the growth and Christian development of Ellen Montgomery. At the outset of the novel, Ellen lives closely with her pious but very ill mother. Her father, Captain Montgomery, is a worldly businessman, cold and domineering, who has little interaction with the family other than to interrupt the close warmth of mother and daughter. When the Captain's business fails, he takes a position in Europe, intending to take his dying wife with him, sending his daughter to live with his sister, Miss Fortune Emerson. Mrs. Montgomery begins to prepare Ellen for their imminent separation, providing her with what she sees are necessities—a stocked writing desk, a work box, clothing, and a Bible. More importantly, she begins to transfer the love and devotion Ellen has for her to a love and devotion to Christ, believing that this is what will protect and guide her daughter after their separation. After the day of shopping, Ellen lays her head on her mother's breast, listening to her heartbeat:

> She was thinking how very, very precious was the heart she could feel beating where her cheek lay—she thought it was greater happiness to lie there than anything in life could be—she thought she had rather even die so, on her mother's breast, than live long without her in the world—she felt that in earth or in heaven there was nothing so dear.
>
> (p. 38)

Ellen appears to know that loving her mother more than anything "in heaven" is problematic because "Suddenly she broke the silence": "Mamma, what does it mean, 'He that loveth father or mother more than me is not worthy of me'?" What follows is a catechism that will be repeated until their separation—soon to follow—and is intended to secure Ellen's connection to Christ and, therefore, to a Christian community.

Although it takes Ellen some time to become a Christian, she never forgets the lessons her mother began to teach her; as she remembers when she learns of her mother's death, "I think I am changed." It was with this simple thought that she knows that she and her mother are closer now than they ever had been: "There seemed to be a link of communion between her mother and her that was wanting before. The promise, written and believed in by the one, realized and rejoiced in by the other, was a dear something in common, though one had in the mean while been removed to heaven, and the other was still a lingerer on the earth. Ellen bound the words upon her heart." It is this communion that the unconverted cannot know, and it is this Christian community that is promoted by this and other of Susan's novels. Throughout all of her trials, Ellen always obtains the assistance of a member of this community that is always present in Ellen's life.

Once Ellen has left her home and is on the voyage to her Aunt's farm, she meets the first Christian who comforts and guides her, illustrating the realization of her mother's hope that her daughter will be cared for in her absence. The gentleman, in fact, continues the lesson begun by Mrs. Montgomery, very much in the same language:

> And patient and kind as your mother is, the Lord Jesus is kinder and more patient still. In all your life so far, Ellen, you have not loved or obeyed him; and yet he loves you, and is ready to be your friend. Is he not even to-day taking away your dear mother for the very purpose that he may draw you gently to himself and fold you in his arms, as he has promised to do with his lambs? He knows you can never be happy anywhere else.
>
> (p. 73)

As in the *Patriotism* essay, many of these lessons occur in dialog, Ellen and the reader reasoning logically through biblical text and its demands. Ellen's training in obedience continues in this fashion, under many different circumstances throughout the novel, until she is a fully-fashioned Christian woman.

Once Ellen reaches her Aunt Fortune's farm (the setting is drawn from Susan's childhood memories of the Whiting farm in Canaan) she must learn the culture and labor of a working farm. At the farm there is abundance, but no luxury. The aptly named Miss Fortune is cold and miserly, certainly not the warm, loving guardian for which Ellen had hoped. The farm setting provides Warner with many opportunities to illustrate rural farm life (one of her real talents as a writer that has not gone unappreciated), including the scenes of working in the buttery,

cooking over the hearth, the "bee" for which the community is invited to the farm to help Aunt Fortune with the harvest work, followed by a party. During her time on the farm, Ellen's spiritual and Christian growth must continue, learning to break her own will and obey. Although Ellen experiences a constant struggle with obedience to Christ and her elders, she inspires and converts many, including her aunt's future husband, Mr. Van Brunt. Ellen's struggle continues over several years, taking her through various households, and finally to Scotland.

Near Miss Fortune's farm live the Humphreys, a minister and his daughter, Alice. Alice and her father provide a good deal of comfort and instruction to Ellen, and they eventually take her in to live with them. John Humphreys, a minister-in-training and Ellen's future husband, is away at school when she is adopted as a member of the family. Captain Montgomery takes charge of Ellen again after Alice's death, sending her to live with her mother's family in Scotland. The Lindsays test Ellen's self-control and powers of obedience as they challenge her religious convictions as well as her American identity. One of Ellen's first conversations with the Lindsays concerns Americans and the American Revolution. Her aunt, Lady Keith, expresses her disdain over "backwoods" American speech: "But it is extraordinary ... how after living among a parcel of thick-headed and thicker-tongued Yankees she [Ellen] could come out and speak pure English in a clear voice;—it is an enigma to me." Mr. Lindsay remarks, "your aunt does not like" Americans, explaining, "Don't you know that they are a parcel of rebels who have broken loose from all loyalty and fealty, that no Briton has any business to like?" Ellen defends her nation's honor, and proceeds to explain that George Washington was "a great deal better than some saints," disagreeing that the Americans are rebels; the account Ellen gives of her study of history illustrates that recommended in *American Female Patriotism,* and she impresses them with her overall education. Ellen's challenge is to find a means of obeying her Scottish family without losing her moral and political principles or her allegiance to the Humphreys. Of their opinion of her religion she states to herself: "They think religion is a strange melancholy thing. ... I must not give them reason to think so—I must let my rushlight burn bright—I must take care—I never had more need!" Eventually John Humphreys visits Ellen, makes his intention to marry her clear, but leaves her to stay with the Lindsays until she is of age:

> Three or four more years of Scottish discipline wrought her no ill; they did but serve to temper and beautify her Christian character; and then, to her unspeakable joy, she went back to spend her life with the friends and guardians she best loved, and to be to them, still more than she had been to her Scottish relations, "the light of the eyes."
>
> (p. 569)

The novel ended here until the publication of Mabel Baker's *Light in the Morning,* which includes the final chapter as an appendix. Jane Tompkins's 1987 edition of the novel also includes the final chapter. This final chapter depicts Ellen touring her new home, the Humphreys's home, which John has made ready for her. His preparations predict the sort of role she will fulfill as minister's wife.

A good deal of what is written about *The Wide, Wide World* examines the position of the mother or the maternal in the novel, and even more concentrates on the nature of power. Indeed, as Jennifer Mason points out in her introduction to "Animal Bodies: Corporeality, Class, and Subject Formation in *The Wide, Wide World,*" most of the substantial number of critics who analyze Ellen's riding lessons read them as "violent, dehumanizing." Mason, however, rereads these lessons in the context of the practice and language of nineteenth-century equestrianism, finding that Ellen actually "attains power *over* other kinds of women who fail to meet the standards that she does."

Warner's conversion marked an important change in her life and directed her activities as well as her presentation of religion in her writing. In 1841 Susan and Anna became members of the Mercer Street Presbyterian Church under the guidance of the Reverend Thomas Harvey Skinner. As directed by the church, the sisters participated in frequent and lengthy church

services, attended lectures at the church on Thursday evenings, distributed tracts, participated in sewing circles, collected for missions door to door, and worked to convert others. This wish to bring others to Christ is a central part of *The Wide, Wide World,* and many readers saw it as such.

Warner's correspondence shows the relationship she had with her readers, indicating her position as theological authority. (Her later work, *The Law and the Testimony* of 1853, cemented that authority, as marked by its purchase by the library of the Union Theological Seminary.) In a letter to Susan of March 7, 1851, John S. Hart, author of *Female Prose Writers of America,* wrote that he read *The Wide, Wide World* to his family, "the only book save the Bible that I have so read for a twelvemonth and as I proceeded with the story, we sent you many a hearty 'God bless you' for its beautiful [truth] sentiments. ... I feel as if I owe you a debt of gratitude." Hart wrote again (May 2, 1852) after reading *Queechy,* telling her that the two novels have "done me good. They have made me a wiser and better man—more strengthened to duty, more reconciled to suffering." In the Hart home, he said, the novel was placed next to the Bible, indicating both the impact and function of the book within the household. Many such letters from readers are housed in Special Collections at the Military Academy at West Point and at the Constitution Island Association. In a letter dated February 9, 1879, many years after publication of the book, Mrs. Ella Blake of Viroque, Wisconsin, wrote, "I was but a little girl, and the character of Ellen Montgomery made so great an impression on me as to lead me, I humbly trust, from darkness to light." Mrs. Blake gave a copy to her young daughter and hoped it would influence her in the same way. She also reported that she had lost her home in a fire, and one of the few books she could salvage from the rubble was her cherished copy of *The Wide, Wide World,* implying that the book was sanctioned by God himself. In her letter of July 16, 1880, Louise Brine of New York City stated clearly her use of *The Wide, Wide World*: "When I feel angry or out of temper I read in the book and find out how Ellen fought against temptations, and I am instantly put aright in tune again and feel good desires; when I want to hear some good advice I go to Alice and take the lesson she gives to Ellen myself." Gertrude Stanwood of Sicamore Grove, Virginia, wrote to request a sequel, writing "we need to learn from you how to preserve the purity of the child, in the worldly life of a woman. ... Guide us by the light of Ellen's example through them" (June 12, [year illegible]). Many other letters from readers relate such reactions to *The Wide, Wide World* and Warner's other works, some of them arguing theological points, some relating conversion experiences, some disagreeing vehemently, but it is clear that the readers considered Warner a religious authority.

After the great success of *The Wide, Wide World,* Susan and Anna began work on a series titled *Ellen Montgomery's Bookshelf,* a collection that included *Mr. Rutherford's Children* (1853), *Carl Krinken: His Christmas Stocking* (1853), *Casper and His Friends* (1856), *Hard Maple* (1859), and *Sybil and Chryssa* (1869). Although Susan is often credited with *Mr. Rutherford's Children* and *Carl Krinken,* she wrote in a letter (April 2, 1857) to D. Appleton & Company in New York:

> But the 'Wide, Wide World,' 'Queechy,' & 'The Hills of the Shatemuc,' are all that I have to do with, except about half of 'Karl Krinken.' 'Dollars & Cents'—'My Brother's Keeper'—'Mr. Rutherford's Children'—&c. are my sister's.

QUEECHY, THE HILLS OF THE SHATEMUC, *AND* SAY AND SEAL

Warner began *Queechy,* her second novel, upon the acceptance of *The Wide, Wide World,* and it sold briskly upon its publication in the United States, Australia, England, France, and Sweden. *Queechy* was published in 1852, the same year as Anna's *Dollars and Cents,* bringing the Warners some more relief from their burdens, enough so that they could purchase some clothing and even a horse for recreation. The novel was so popular and the residents of Canaan so impressed with their portrayal in the novel, that they

renamed Whiting Pond, named so after the Warner ancestors, to Queechy Lake.

Fleda Ringgan, the heroine of *Queechy,* like Ellen, is an orphan, and much of the novel is set in a place much like the Whiting farm at Canaan. Fleda lives a pleasant pastoral life with her grandfather, Elzevir Ringgan, an earnest Christian and Revolutionary War veteran. Grandfather dies just before the farm is repossessed (he had been cheated). Fortunately, her elder cousin Rossitur arrives to invite her to live at the home of her Aunt Lucy, Uncle Rolf, and cousin Hugh in France. With nowhere to go, Fleda travels to France accompanied by Rossitur and his friend, Guy Carleton, *Queechy*'s hero. Carleton, an Englishman, is so impressed with Fleda that his conversion begins upon their meeting and continues on the voyage overseas. Fleda and the Rossiturs live in France in some luxury for a number of years before Uncle Rolf has financial difficulties and they move back to the States. After further losses, Uncle Rolf appeals to a friend who owns a farm—Queechy—and the family returns to Fleda's early home where they attempt to run the farm. As in *The Wide, Wide World,* the work of the farm is described in significant detail, from the kitchen to the fields and the surrounding community. It is in no way idealized, although it is a rich portrayal of nineteenth-century farm life. While the domestic is a large part of the lives of the characters and is skillfully drawn, it is not portrayed through a sentimental lens; in fact, it is quite the opposite. If anything, the portrayals of Aunt Fortune and the very hard work on her farm and that at Queechy provide a good portrait of what Warner respected but clearly wished she could avoid. Indeed, Edward Halsey Foster asserts in *Susan and Anna Warner* that Warner had a real aversion to rural New England and its people.

Aunt Lucy and Uncle Rolf prove to be of very little help, and the burden of the establishment falls onto the shoulders of Fleda and Hugh. After Uncle Rolf causes the family real discomfort and distress, he leaves for the West in search of fortune and never returns, which is a relief to the family. Uncle Rolf does continue to cause problems for the family, even from afar, but Fleda, with some help, manages to make this right as well. The work on the farm is difficult, but Fleda's Christian sensibilities help her to manage the gardens, fields, kitchen, family, and servants well—in fact, Fleda is declared "the best farmer in the state" by one of her neighbors, because the farm is so successful. Hugh, always unhealthy, grows ill and eventually dies under the strain, but his death is the beginning of Aunt Lucy's conversion. Finally, Guy Carleton returns and, in spite of the interference of many people, he and Fleda marry and move to his estate in England.

As Edward Halsey Foster points out, "Susan's primary object in *Queechy* was to outline the distinction between aristocracy of virtue and manners (represented by her heroine) and an aristocracy of wealth and birth." Certainly Fleda is a model ruler—and a successful one—as a result of her Christian principles:

> The farming plan succeeded beyond Fleda's hopes; thanks not more to her wisdom than to the nice tact with which the wisdom was brought into play. ... But Fleda's delicate handling stood her yet more in stead than her strength. Earl Douglass was sometimes unmanageable, and held out in favour of an old custom or a prevailing opinion in spite of all the weight of testimony and light of discovery that could be brought to bear upon him. Fleda would let the thing go. But seizing her opportunity another time she would ask him to try the experiment, on a piece of the ground; so pleasantly and skillfully that Earl could do nothing but shut his mouth and obey. ... And as Fleda always forgot to remind him that she had been right and he wrong, he forgot it too, and presently took to the new way kindly.
>
> (*Queechy,* vol. 2, p. 1)

One without Fleda's principles, with just a consciousness of wealth and superior birth, does not experience as much success as does Fleda. The example of the character aristocratic by wealth and birth is, of course, Uncle Rossitur, who only insults and alienates those workers on whom he must depend (as he is utterly ignorant of farming and housekeeping), including his family. The lesson in identifying the man who is superior because he is a good Christian is an important one because, as Aunt Miriam puts it, "So much security has any woman in a man without religion!"—words Fleda later remembers.

Women must place their fate in the hands of the men they must marry—they have no choice in fathers or brothers, but there is a choice in husbands—and they cannot count on just and gentle handling from gentlemen not ruled by Christian principles. Fleda has learned this lesson from her experiences with her Uncle Rolf, whose unprincipled mind and manners lead him to mistreat family and servants when he refuses to accept his humbled position. Instead, he insists upon privileges he believes are due him as a member of a privileged class—although he is no longer a member of that class. *Queechy,* however, instructs the reader that class should be determined by Christian merit, an idea that had been part of American culture since before the Revolution. Because Carleton is a good Christian—although English—he will make a good husband for Fleda, and, Warner hints, American influence taken to the other side of the Atlantic will bring salvation to the decaying aristocracy of England.

The Hills of the Shatemuc (1856) was also well received, reportedly selling ten thousand copies on the first day of its sale. The story of *Hills* is based on the youth of Henry and Thomas Warner, the material largely culled from family history and letters written by Henry, Thomas, and their father. Winthrop, the character based on young Henry Warner, is affectionate and somewhat idealized while his brother Rufus, based on Thomas, is less sympathetic, marking a difference from the portrayals of him in the Warners's journals and letters. This novel, like the previous ones, is somewhat, although not entirely, autobiographical. The portraits of her male characters are of overly idealized, impossibly good men or of irresponsible heels who subject their wives, daughters, and sisters to moral and economic penury. Although the Landholm boys are born into a farming family, their father is in the New York state legislature, and they both envision a life entirely away from the farm. The brothers are very different from one another: Winthrop is patient and disciplined; Rufus is rash and somewhat shiftless. Both men are highly regarded but for very different reasons: Winthrop because he is dependable and has strong moral principles and Rufus because he is charming and witty. Winthrop works his way through college, studies law, and then opens a successful office, while Rufus becomes an engineer. While in "Manahatta," Manhattan, the brothers come to be acquainted with the Hayes family. Elizabeth, the eldest daughter and a spoiled socialite, has taken charge of her widowed father's home. Mr. Hayes's ward, Rose, lives with them, and is Elizabeth's constant and unwelcome companion. Elizabeth reluctantly develops a respect for Winthrop, marking the beginning of her Christian education—Winthrop, like Fleda, is a model of Christian and republican principles. Mr. Hayes, much to Elizabeth's mortification and everyone else's surprise, marries Rose. Winthrop consoles Elizabeth, and after the family has lost its fortune and Mr. Hayes dies, this consolation becomes a conversion narrative. Once Elizabeth has lost her fortune, become her young stepmother's guardian, and moved to the Landholm farm, she undergoes her conversion, and finally she and Winthrop marry.

Warner's next novel, *Say and Seal* (1860), is a collaboration with Anna, and its tone is very much Anna's contribution. Edward Halsey Foster credits *Say and Seal* as a fully accomplished work of local color, providing "one of the earliest literary descriptions of a complete New England settlement." The community is thoroughly developed at all levels of social rank, preserving small but important distinctions, including in their speech. Religious instruction is an important part of this work as well, but the development of the community really makes it a *tour de force.* Of course, the most famous feature of the novel is the hymn "Jesus Loves Me," which is still printed and sung today.

LATER WORKS

Warner's work published after 1853 is seldom addressed by literary scholars—indeed, few have given attention to publications other than her first—although it has much to offer those interested in women's and children's literature as well as the "cultural work" and social problem fiction of the period. Mabel Baker does address the later

works of both Susan and Anna in *The Warner Family and the Warner Books* (1971), but not in significant depth. Sondra Smith Gates is one of the few to have investigated these later works, considering Warner's Sunday school novels in "The Edge of Possibility: Susan Warner and the World of Sunday School Fiction." Gates asserts that Warner exerted an influence with her publishers that other writers of the genre were unable to claim, that the novels were distinctly Methodist in their theological underpinnings, particularly in their adherence to the doctrine of perfectionism, and that the novels distinctly participated in teaching the social gospel. Indeed, in a letter to Warner, Peter Carter, one of the brothers of the Robert Carter & Brothers publishing firm, described his reading of the 1863 *Golden Ladder* series (illustrating the Beatitudes), questioning their teaching "the Methodist doctrine of *perfection,*" stating, "I was sorry to see this in so nice a little book—." Peter Carter's objections to the religious teachings of these children's books did not prevent Robert Carter & Bros. from becoming the Warners's primary publishers for the remainder of their careers, with the exception of their return to Putnam with *Wych Hazel* and *The Gold of Chickaree* in 1876 and 1877.

In 1863 Susan and Anna did convert to Methodism, and the doctrinal debates in which they likely participated were much a part of *The Old Helmet* (1864), and, as Jane Weiss notes in her study of Susan Warner, the sisters' extant journals of the period document that conversion and the social and theological breaks that ensued. The doctrine of holiness and the ensuing perfection were very much a part of Methodism of the nineteenth century. The Warners, while staying with the prominent Hudson Valley Methodist Catharine Livingston Garrettson in Rhinebeck, New York, in 1863, became very much attracted to the church and its warmth. The Calvinism that Sharon Kim convincingly sees in *The Wide, Wide World* was no longer a part of Susan's religious faith as she wrote her later works, which accounts for her very different heroines as well as the much-expanded lessons of the later novels. Indeed, on January 2, 1863, Susan Warner wrote in her journal, "Read Mr. Calvin's Life and Times (stupid)." In "Puritan Realism: *The Wide, Wide World* and *Robinson Crusoe,*" Kim argues that *The Wide, Wide World* is part of the Puritan literary tradition, demonstrating that generic elements of sentimentalism are intertwined with realism. While Ellen's focus in *The Wide, Wide World* is almost entirely on disciplining herself—leading Marianne Noble, for instance, to label the book "masochistic" and the feminist scholars who recovered Warner's work to struggle to find some way to explain and accommodate it—the later works do see a fairly expansive world and far fewer tears than are cried by Ellen and Fleda. Warner's journal of the period marks an enjoyment of the sermons and of the atmosphere of the church, finding it intellectually stimulating as well as comforting and hopeful.

The Old Helmet, "The Helmet of Salvation" in its working title, is set in England, Australia, and the Fiji Islands and has a heroine who is a dissenter, disobeying her parents, her community, and her childhood religious instruction in order to become a Methodist missionary in Fiji. Warner never traveled to any of these places, finding her instruction about them from travel books and her stereoscope, which leads the local color aspect of the novel to be somewhat deemphasized. She was much criticized for inaccuracy of the house she describes in the islands and the clothing in which she outfits her heroine. Weiss notes that the story is based loosely on the life of Catharine Livingston Garrettson, with whom the sisters were staying when Susan began the novel. The "Note to the Reader" indicates a source: "The incidents and testimonies given in this work as matters of fact, are not drawn from imagination, but reported from excellent authority, though I have used my own words. And in the cases of reported words of third parties, the words stand unchanged, without any meddling." Certainly, however, in *The Old Helmet* the world becomes significantly wider and more hopeful. The emphasis of much of the literary criticism of *The Wide, Wide World* is about its insistence on discipline, its harshness, and the severely limited role it defines for women; and it seems that Warner herself rejected it at least on some level in the 1860s.

The Warners continued to write throughout the Civil War, writing more novels and briefly publishing a bimonthly story paper, the *Little American* (October 1862–December 1864). Although Susan did not address the war directly in her writing, she did address the injustice of slavery in *Daisy* (1868), the sequel to *Melbourne House.* In this novel, written in the first person, fourteen-year-old Daisy attempts to help the slaves on her parents' plantation. She eventually takes her slave Margaret north across the Mason-Dixon Line, purposely freeing her. When questioned, she enters into an argument about the inalienable rights of slaves, explaining to Dr. Sanford that "nobody *can* belong to anybody—in that way, nobody can give anybody a *right* to anybody else—in that way." Daisy proceeds to explain to the reader, if not to the doctor, the doctrine that supports her view of Christian duty:

> "Daisy, you must not take it on your heart that you have to teach all the ignorant and help all the distressed that come in your way; because simply you cannot do it."
>
> "I looked up at him. I could not tell him what I thought, because he would not, I feared, understand it. Christ came to do just such work, and his servants must have it on their heart to do just the same."
>
> (American Libraries, p. 145)

This scene and the ideology it clearly explicates—that the Christian must emulate the model of Christ in the domestic sphere and in the world—is the lesson modeled in many of these later novels. Shortly after *Daisy*'s publication, Bertha, a freed slave, arrived at the Warner home on Constitution Island where she lived until she passed away several years after Anna. African American characters appear in quite a few of Susan's novels. In the late 1990s, Susan L. Robeson discovered a previously unpublished scene from *The Wide, Wide World* that includes Ellen interacting with a young African American girl in New York. (See "Ellen Montgomery's Other Friend: Race Relations in an Expunged Episode of Warner's *Wide, Wide World.*")

The three novels published by Putnam in the 1870s, marking a temporary return to her first publishing house and a moderate resurgence of popularity, further illustrate Warner's new doctrine fairly well. These three novels, as part of their illustration of Christian morality, present the Christian as working on behalf of social justice, particularly against the crimes of capitalism and industrialization. *Wych Hazel* and *The Gold of Chickaree,* both published in 1876, portray the coming of age of Miss Kennedy, the Wych Hazel of the title. Hazel is a very wealthy young socialite, an orphan under the guardianship of both Mr. Falkirk and Mr. Rollo. She is young and willful and determines at the outset of *Wych Hazel,* "I *must* go and seek my fortune!" It is this declaration that leads her back to her ancestral home in the Catskills in time for the summer, when it was fashionable to travel to the area. Hazel leads a life of parties and dancing, bridling occasionally under the rule of her guardians, particularly Mr. Rollo, the young hero. Like other of Warner's heroes, Rollo is masterful and, through the course of the two books, becomes a model Christian. Hazel's parents, friends of Rollo's parents and guardians, hoped that Hazel and he would marry and made provisions to secure this marriage in their will. Like many other of Warner's heroines, Hazel must undergo a conversion to Christianity, but she does so with the pressure of Rollo's good example as well as the real desire to be a good person, something Rollo models particularly well. Additionally, the conversion is not a painful or tearful one—but the difficulty for the young heroine lies in what she clearly understands as forfeiture of her independence. Rollo does limit her movement in some ways in order to keep her safe (he restricts her from driving alone through New York City, for instance), but he reassures her several times after their marriage that she has room to have her own will. He assures her that she has more power now that they are married because she has the weight of his authority behind her. The Christian doctrine to which they prescribe limits her in terms of her use of money more than anything. Christians are set up in opposition to society, especially high society, again returning to Foster's summation of *Queechy,* that Warner argues on behalf of an aristocracy of manners as opposed to one of birth and wealth. The doctrine

here serves to define the wealthy as stewards of property to be used for the purpose of lightening the burdens of the lower classes. Indeed, as Gates argues, these later novels are very much a part of the social gospel movement beginning in the 1870s. The later novels, according to Gates, "treat important theological and social issues with gravity and directness because, like other evangelicals of her day, Warner believed children to be Christianity's last, best hope." As Hazel develops from adolescence into adulthood, she demonstrates that hope for the future of society.

Once Rollo and Wych Hazel undergo their conversions, they immediately embark upon social reform. Indeed, Hazel's conversion experience effectively begins with the recognition of the poverty and misery of workers in a local textile mill. Rollo has actually purchased the mill and details some of his reforms, explaining how he has raised the workers' salaries, allowed for paid sick days, provided medical care, and begun construction of good and aesthetically pleasing housing as well as of a community center where he will provide education for both the children and the adults, beginning, essentially, a thoroughly Owenite mill reform. Hazel suggests that he also provide day care and Christmas celebrations, among other things. Hazel and Rollo spend their honeymoon planning the comfort they will provide their mill hands as well as sending care packages to the families of poor clergy. Much of the sequel, *The Gold of Chickaree,* is dedicated to instruction about "economy," proposing a Christian alternative to capitalism in order to alleviate the suffering of those casualties of industrialization. These later works, in short, are very different from Warner's first three novels.

Henry Warner's death on February 20, 1875, had an immediate impact on the family. He had been rather demanding, after falling in 1872 and remaining in bed and in a wheelchair for the last years of his life. Susan, Anna, and Fanny spent a good deal of time and energy on his needs. Apparently none of the three women attended his funeral in Canaan, and neither Susan nor Anna wrote a eulogy for their father. Indeed, Baker points out that Susan did not even note his death in her journal, and "silence from Susan who habitually recorded every incident in her life which might suggest some deviation from its crushing routine says more with her silence about her reaction to Henry's death than she might have in a half-dozen pages rehearsing her grief." Susan, who years before had become the primary breadwinner for the family, wrote in her journal several years before of her trials with her father: "Very weary, weary in mind and body. I giving orders to Ellis about the walks—and Father giving other orders—and I countermanding or objecting, and then Father very displeased or disturbed. I am very wrong—I must be—I consider my own pleasure." Jane Weiss notes, "Although some degree of infirmity must have come naturally with age, there is some evidence to suggest that his infirmities had non-physical causes. The Warner House Collection includes an impressive array of glass bottles from Henry's collection of patent medicines, which included among their ingredients generous doses of opium, cocaine derivatives, and alcohol."

After Henry's death, winters were spent in Highland Falls, just outside the military academy, and the sisters began rebuilding their ties with the community at West Point, as Baker reports in *Light in the Morning.* Although there was no explicit break between the family and their neighbors, it appears that Henry's death allowed for communication that had not existed for many years. Susan began participating in Bible readings with some of the officers' wives at West Point and she was eventually asked to include cadets. Susan was pleased and thus began her real connection with West Point. The remainder of Susan's life, with a hiatus of just a year, was spent in those Bible classes and on her writing. In 1885 Susan had a stroke or cerebral hemorrhage and lost consciousness. She died two weeks later on March 17. The U.S. secretary of war granted permission for Susan to be buried in the cemetery at West Point, overlooking the island. Aunt Fanny died six months later. Anna lived on with Bertha, and before her death on January 22, 1915, she bequeathed the island to the United States government and the Gilbert Stuart portrait of Washington to West Point.

In the past few years, many of Warner's books have returned to print by presses that serve scholarship by digitally preserving historical texts, such as BiblioBazaar and Kessinger Publishing, as well as by Christian presses, such as Lamplighter Publishing. Additionally, as of this writing, most of Warner's books are available on the Internet. It is possible, then, that Warner might again enjoy a readership that will look to her for the lessons in religion that her first readers so appreciated, in addition to the scholars who have been her primary readers for the past decades.

Selected Bibliography

WORKS OF SUSAN WARNER

Novels and Other Original Works

The Wide, Wide World. As Elizabeth Wetherell. 2 vols. New York: Putnam, 1851; London: J. Nisbet, 1851; Wright American Fiction (http://www.letrs.indiana.edu/web/w/wright2/); Celebration of Women Writers (http://digital.library.upenn.edu/women/warner-susan/wide/wide.html); Project Gutenberg (http://www.gutenberg.org/etext/18689); American Libraries (http://www.archive.org/details/widewideworldby00warnrich). Previously unpublished final chapter included in *The Wide, Wide World.* Afterword by Jane Tompkins. New York: Feminist Press, 1987. Edited materials published as appendix in Susan L. Roberson, "Ellen Montgomery's Other Friend: Race Relations in an Expunged Episode of Warner's *Wide, Wide World.*" *ESQ: A Journal of the American Renaissance* 45:1–31 (1999).

American Female Patriotism: A Prize Essay. As Elizabeth Wetherell. New York: E. H. Fletcher, 1852.

Queechy. As Elizabeth Wetherell. 2 vols. New York: Putnam, 1852; London: Nisbet, 1852; Paperbackshop.Co.UK–Echo Library, 2006; Michigan Making of America website (http://quod.lib.umich.edu/m/moa/); Wright American Fiction (http://www.letrs.indiana.edu/web/w/wright2/); Project Gutenberg (http://www.gutenberg.org/etext/18686); American Libraries, vol. 1 (http://www.archive.org/details/queechyby01warnrich), vol. 2 (http://www.archive.org/details/queechby02warnrich).

Carl Krinken: His Christmas Stocking. By Susan and Anna Warner, anonymous. New York: Putnam, 1854 [i.e., 1853]; London: Nisbet, 1854.

The Hills of the Shatemuc. As the author of "The Wide, Wide World." 2 vols. London: Sampson Low, 1856; New York: Appleton, 1856; Charleston, S.C.: Bibliobazaar, 2007; Michigan Making of America (http://quod.lib.umich.edu/m/moa/); Wright American Fiction (http://www.letrs.indiana.edu/web/w/wright2/); Project Gutenberg (http://www.gutenberg.org/etext/16918). Republished as *Rufus and Winthrop; or, The Hills of the Shatemuc,* London: Simpkin, Marshall, 1857; as *Rest; or, The Hills of the Shatemuc,* London: Milner & Sowerby, 1860; as *Hope's Little Hand,* London: Routledge, 1877; as *Hope and Rest,* London: Ward, Lock, 1890.

Say and Seal. By Susan Warner and Anna Warner, as the author of "Wide, Wide World," and the author of "Dollars and Cents." 2 vols. London: Bentley, 1860; Philadelphia: Lippincott, 1860; American Libraries (http://www.archive.org/details/sayandseal00warnrich); Wright American Fiction (http://www.letrs.indiana.edu/web/w/wright2/).

The Golden Ladder: Stories Illustrative of the Eight Beatitudes. By Susan Warner and Anna Warner, as the author of "The Wide, Wide World." London: Nisbet, 1863 [i.e., 1862]; New York: Randolph, n.d. Republished in 8 vols. as *The Two School Girls and Other Tales.* By Susan Warner, anonymous. New York: Carlton & Porter, Sunday-School Union, 1862 [i.e., 1863]; London: Routledge, 1864.

Althea. "Blessed Are They That Mourn: For They Shall Be Comforted." By Susan Warner and Anna Warner, anonymous. New York: Carlton & Porter, Sunday-School Union, 1862 [i.e., 1863]. Republished as *The Widow and Her Daughter.* London: Routledge, 1864.

Gertrude and Her Cat. "Blessed Are the Meek: For They Shall Inherit the Earth." New York: Carlton & Porter, Sunday-School Union, 1862 [i.e., 1863]. Republished as *Gertrude and Her Bible.* London: Routledge, 1864.

The Rose in the Desert. "Blessed Are They Which Do Hunger and Thirst After Righteousness: For They Shall See God." By Susan Warner and Anna Warner, anonymous. New York: Carlton & Porter, Sunday-School Union, 1862, [i.e., 1863]; London: Routledge, 1864.

The Little Black Hen. "Blessed Are the Merciful: For They Shall Obtain Mercy." By Susan Warner and Anna Warner, anonymous. New York: Carlton & Porter, Sunday-School Union, 1862 [i.e., 1863]; London: Routledge, 1864.

Martha's Hymn. "Blessed Are the Pure in Heart: For They Shall See God." By Susan Warner, anonymous. New York: Carlton & Porter, Sunday-School Union, 1862 [i.e., 1863]. Republished as *Martha and Her Kind Friend Rachel.* London: Routledge, 1864.

The Carpenter's House. "Blessed Are the Peacemakers: For They Shall Be Called the Children of God." By Susan Warner, anonymous. New York: Carlton & Porter, Sunday-School Union, 1862 [i.e., 1863]. Republished as *The Carpenter's Daughter,* London: Routledge, 1864; Project Gutenberg (http://www.gutenberg.org/etext/18689). Republished as *Little Nettie; or, Home Sunshine.* London: Warne, 1872.

The Prince in Disguise. "Blessed Are They Which Are Persecuted for Righteousness' Sake. For Theirs Is the Kingdom of Heaven." By Anna Warner, anonymous. New York: Carlton & Porter, Sunday-School Union, 1862 [i.e., 1863].

The Old Helmet. 2 vols. New York: Carter, 1864 [i.e., 1863]; London: Nisbet, 1863; Wright American Fiction (http://www.letrs.indiana.edu/web/w/wright2/); American Libraries, vol. 1 (http://www.archive.org/details/oldhelmet01warniala), vol. 2 (http://www.archive.org/details/oldhelmet02warniala).

Melbourne House. As the author of "The Wide, Wide World." 2 vols. New York: Carter, 1864; London: Nisbet, 1864; Michigan Making of America (http://quod.lib.umich.edu/m/moa/); Wright American Fiction (http://www.letrs.indiana.edu/web/w/wright2/); Project Gutenberg (http://www.gutenberg.org/etext/18686); American Libraries (http://www.archive.org/details/melbournehouse00warniala).

The Word. Walks from Eden. As the author of "The Wide, Wide World." New York: Carter, 1866 [i.e., 1865]; London: Nisbet, 1865.

The Word. The House of Israel. A Sequel to "Walks from Eden." New York: Carter, 1867; London: Nisbet, 1867.

Daisy: Continued from "Melbourne House." As the author of "The Wide, Wide World." 2 vols. Philadelphia: Lippincott, 1868; London: Nisbet 1868; Wright American Fiction (http://www.letrs.indiana.edu/web/w/wright2/); Project Gutenberg (http://www.gutenberg.org/etext/18687); American Libraries (http://www.archive.org/details/daisy00warniala) and (http://www.archive.org/details/daisybyauthor00warnrich).

Daisy in the Field. As the author of "The Wide, Wide World." London: Nisbet, 1869. Republished as *Daisy. Continued from "Melbourne House."* As the author of "The Wide, Wide World." Philadelphia: Lippincott, 1869; Project Gutenberg (http://www.gutenberg.org/etext/18688).

"What She Could." As the author of "The Wide, Wide World." New York: Carter, 1871; London: Nisbet, 1871; American Libraries (http://www.archive.org/details/whatshecould00warniala). Republished as *What She Could; and, Opportunities, a Sequel.* London: Nisbet, 1871; American Libraries (http://www.archive.org/details/whatshecould00warnrich).

Opportunities. A Sequel to "What She Could." As the author of "The Wide, Wide World." New York: Carter, 1871; London: Nisbet, 1871; American Libraries (http://www.archive.org/details/opportunitiesseq00warniala). Republished with *"What She Could."* London: Nisbet, 1871.

The House in Town. A Sequel to "Opportunities." As the author of "The Wide, Wide World." New York: Carter, 1872 [i.e., 1871]; London: Nisbet, 1871; American Libraries (http://www.archive.org/details/houseintown00warniala).

Lessons on the Standard Bearers of the Old Testament. Third Grade for Older Classes. New York: Randolph, 1872; London: Nisbet, 1873.

"Trading." Finishing the Story of "The House in Town." New York: Carter, 1873 [i.e., 1872]; London: Nisbet, 1873; American Libraries (http://www.archive.org/details/tradingfinishing00warnrich).

The Little Camp on Eagle Hill. London: Nisbet, 1873; New York: Carter, 1874. Republished as *Giving Honour.* London: Nisbet, 1876.

Willow Brook: A Sequel to "The Little Camp on Eagle Hill." as the author of "The Wide, Wide World." New York: Carter, 1874; London: Nisbet, 1874.

Sceptres and Crowns. As the author of "The Wide, Wide World." Nashville: Publishing House of the Methodist Episcopal Church, South, Barber, and Smith, 1874; London: Routledge, 1875. Republished with *The Flag of Truce.* London: Nisbet, 1875.

The Flag of Truce. As the author of "The Wide, Wide World." New York: Carter, 1875. Republished with *Sceptres and Crowns.* London: Nisbet, 1875.

Giving Trust. As the author of "The Wide, Wide World." London: Nisbet, 1875.

The Rapids of Niagara. As the author of "The Wide, Wide World." New York: Carter, 1876; American Libraries (http://www.archive.org/details/rapidsofniagara00warniala).

Wych Hazel. By Susan Warner and Anna Warner, as the author of "The Wide, Wide World." London: Nisbet, 1876; New York: Putnam, 1876; Charleston, S.C.: Bibliobazaar, 2007; Project Gutenberg (http://www.gutenberg.org/etext/17800); American Libraries (http://www.openlibrary.org/details/wychhazel00warniala).

The Gold of Chickaree. By Susan Warner and Anna Warner. New York: Putnam, 1876; London: Nisbet, 1876; Project Gutenberg (http://www.gutenberg.org/etext/23584).

Pine Needles. As the author of "The Wide, Wide World." London: Nisbet, 1877; New York: Carter, 1877. Republished as *Needles and Old Yarns,* London: Simpkin, 1878; as *Pine Needles and Old Yarns,* Wakefield, U.K.: Nicholson, 1878; American Libraries (http://www.archive.org/details/pineneedlesstory00warnrich).

Diana. New York: Putnam, 1877; London: Nisbet, 1877; Whitefish, Mont.: Kessinger, 2007; American Libraries (http://www.archive.org/details/dianaanovel00warniala).

The Kingdom of Judah. As the author of "The Wide, Wide World." New York: Carter, 1878; London: Nisbet, 1878.

The King's People. 5 vols. New York: Carter, 1878. (Comprises *Walks from Eden, The House of Israel, The Kingdom of Judah,* and *The Broken Walls of Jerusalem,* all by Susan Warner, and *The Star of Jacob,* by Anna Warner.)

The Broken Walls of Jerusalem and the Rebuilding of Them. As the author of "The Wide, Wide World." New York: Carter, 1879; London: Nisbet, 1879.

My Desire. As the author of "The Wide, Wide World." New York: Carter, 1879; London: Nisbet, 1879; American Libraries (http://www.archive.org/details/mydesire00warnrich).

The End of a Coil. As the author of "The Wide, Wide World." New York: Carter, 1880; London: Nisbet, 1880; American Libraries (http://www.archive.org/details/endofcoil00warniala).

The Letter of Credit. As the author of "The Wide, Wide World." London: Nisbet, 1881; New York: Carter, 1882; American Libraries (http://www.archive.org/details/letterofcredit00warniala).

Nobody. London: Nisbet, 1882; New York: Carter, 1883; American Libraries (http://www.archive.org/details/nobodywarner00warniala).

Stephen, M.D. As the author of "The Wide, Wide World." New York: Carter, 1883; London: Nisbet, 1883; American Libraries (http://www.archive.org/details/stephenmd00warniala).

A Red Wallflower. As the author of "The Wide, Wide World." New York: Carter, 1884; London: Nisbet, 1884.

Daisy Plains. Begun by Susan Warner and completed by Anna Warner, as the author of "The Wide, Wide World." New York: Carter, 1885; London: Nisbet, 1885.

OTHER WORKS

"How May an American Woman Best Show Her Patriotism?" In *Ladies Wreath: An Illustrated Annual.* Edited by Mrs. S. T. Martyn. New York: J. M. Fletcher, 1851.

The Law and the Testimony. Extracts from the Bible arranged by Susan Warner and Anna Warner. New York: Carter, 1853. Republished as *The Law and the Testimony: Christian Doctrine.* London: Nisbet, 1853.

Little American. Bimonthly story paper by Susan Warner and Anna Warner. October 1862–December 1864.

JOURNALS AND LETTERS

Stokes, Olivia Egleston Phelps. *Letters and Memories of Susan and Anna Bartlett Warner.* New York: Putnam, 1925.

Weiss, Jane. " 'Many Things Take My Time': The Journals of Susan Warner." Ph.D. dissertation, City University of New York, 1996.

PAPERS

The Constitution Island Association Archives is the primary location of Susan Warner's papers, which include correspondence, manuscripts, journals, scrapbooks, financial documents, Sunday school notes. Special Collections at the Cadet Library of the United States Military Academy at West Point houses a fairly large collection of correspondence. The Huntington Library houses the original manuscript of *The Wide, Wide World.*

BIBLIOGRAPHIES

Baker, Mabel. *The Warner Family and The Warner Books.* West Point, N.Y.: Constitution Island Association, 1971.

Sanderson, Dorothy Hurlbut. *They Wrote for a Living: A Bibliography of the Works of Susan Bogert Warner and Anna Bartlett Warner.* West Point, N.Y.: Constitution Island Association, 1976.

CRITICAL AND BIOGRAPHICAL STUDIES

Ackmann, Martha. "Legacy Guide to American Women Writers' Homes (II)." *Legacy* 2, no. 1:10–12 (1985).

Argersinger, Jana L. "Family Embraces: The Unholy Kiss and Authorial Relations in *The Wide, Wide World.*" *American Literature* 74:251–285 (June 2002).

———. "Susan Warner (1819–1885)." In *Writers of the American Renaissance: An A-to-Z Guide.* Edited by Denise D. Knight. Westport, Conn.: Greenwood, 2003. Pp. 384–391.

Ashworth, Suzanne M. "Susan Warner's *The Wide, Wide World,* Conduct Literature, and Protocols of Female Reading in Mid-Nineteenth-Century America." *Legacy* 17, no. 2:14–164 (2000).

Baker, Mabel. *The Warner Family and the Warner Books.* West Point, N.Y.: Constitution Island Association Press, 1971.

———. *Light in the Morning: Memories of Susan and Anna Warner.* West Point, N.Y.: Constitution Island Association Press, 1978. (Includes previously unpublished final chapter of *The Wide, Wide World.*)

Ball, David M. "Toward an Archaeology of American Modernism: Reconsidering Prestige and Popularity in the American Renaissance." *ESQ: A Journal of the American Renaissance* 49, no. 13:161–177 (2003).

Ball, Kevin. "Converting Her Readers: Susan Warner's Modeling of Reading in *The Wide, Wide World.*" *Reader: Essays in Reader-Oriented Theory, Criticism, and Pedagogy* 46:7–31 (spring 2002).

Bauermeister, Erica R. "*The Lamplighter, The Wide, Wide World,* and *Hope Leslie*: The Recipes for Nineteenth-Century American Women's Novels." *Legacy* 8, no. 1:17–28 (1991).

Baym, Nina. *Woman's Fiction: A Guide to Novels By and About Women in America, 1820–1870.* Ithaca, N.Y.: Cornell University Press, 1978.

Blair, Andrea. "Landscape in Drag: The Paradox of Feminine Space in Susan Warner's *The Wide, Wide World.*" In *The Greening of Literary Scholarship: Literature, Theory, and the Environment.* Edited by Steven Rosendale. Foreword by Scott Slovic. Iowa City: University of Iowa Press, 2002. Pp. 111–130.

Brusky, Sarah. "Beyond the Ending of Maternal Absence in *A New England-Tale, The Wide, Wide World,* and *St. Elmo.*" *ESQ: A Journal of the American Renaissance* 46, no. 3:149–176 (2000).

SUSAN WARNER

Calabro, John A. "Susan Warner and Her Bible Classes." *Legacy* 4, no. 2:45–52 (fall 1987).

Campbell, Donna M. "Sentimental Conventions and Self-Protection: Little Women and *The Wide, Wide World.*" *Legacy* 11, no. 2:118–129 (1994).

Chantell, Claire. "The Limits of the Mother at Home in *The Wide, Wide World* and *The Lamplighter.*" *Studies in American Fiction* 30:131–153 (autumn 2002).

Constitution Island Association. "Susan and Anna Warner: 'The Bronte Sisters of America.'" In *Constitution Island: Compiled for the Meeting of the Garden Club of America.* Newburgh, N.Y: Moore Printing for the Constitution Island Association, 1936. Pp. 9–15.

Damon-Bach, Lucinda L. "To Be a 'Parlor Soldier': Susan Warner's Answer to Emerson's 'Self-Reliance' Publication." In *Separate Spheres No More: Gender Convergence in American Literature, 1830–1930.* Edited by Monika M. Elbert. Tuscaloosa: University of Alabama Press, 2000. Pp. 29–49.

Dobson, Joanne. "The Hidden Hand: Subversion of Cultural Ideology in Three Mid-Nineteenth-Century American Women's Novels." *American Quarterly* 38, no. 2:223–242 (summer 1986).

———. "'Read the Bible and Sew More': Domesticity and the Woman's Novel in Mid-Nineteenth Century America." *Amerikastudien/American Studies* 36, no. 1:24–30 (1991).

Foster, Edward Halsey. *Susan and Anna Warner.* Boston: Twayne, 1978.

Gates, Sondra Smith. "Edge of Possibility: Susan Warner and the World of Sunday School Fiction." *Arizona Quarterly* 60:1–31 (winter 2004).

Goshgarian, G. M. *To Kiss the Chastening Rod: Domestic Fiction and Sexual Ideology in the American Renaissance.* Ithaca, N.Y.: Cornell University Press, 1992.

Greenspan, Ezra. *George Palmer Putnam: Representative American Publisher.*University Park: Pennsylvania State University Press, 2000.

Harris, Susan K. *19th-Century American Women's Novels: Interpretive Strategies.* New York: Cambridge University Press, 1990.

Hart, John Seely. *The Female Prose Writers of America* (1852). 5th ed. Philadelphia: E. H. Butler, 1866.

Hiatt, Mary P. "Susan Warner's Subtext: The Other Side of Piety." *Journal of Evolutionary Psychology* 8:250–261 (August 1987).

Hovet, Grace Ann, and Theodore R. Hovet. "Identity Development in Susan Warner's *The Wide, Wide World*: Relationship, Performance, and Construction." *Legacy* 8, no. 1:3–16 (1991).

———. "Tableaux Vivants: Masculine Vision and Feminine Reflections in Novels by Warner, Alcott, Stowe, and Wharton." *American Transcendental Quarterly* 7:335–356 (December 1993).

Kelley, Mary. *Private Woman, Public Stage: Literary Domesticity in Nineteenth-Century America.* New York: Oxford University Press, 1984.

Kim, Sharon. "Puritan Realism: The Wide, Wide World and Robinson Crusoe." *American Literature* 75:783–811 (December 2003).

Kolba, Ellen D. "Stories for Sale." *English Journal* 69:37–40 (October 1980).

MacDonald, Ruth K. "Susan Bogert Warner (Elizabeth Wetherell)." In *Dictionary of Literary Biography.* Vol. 42: *American Writers for Children Before 1900.* Edited by Glenn E. Estes. Detroit: Gale, 1985. Pp. 362–367.

Marks, Pamela. "The Good Provider in Romance Novels." In *Romantic Conventions.* Edited by Anne K. Kaler and Rosemary E. Johnson-Kurek. Bowling Green, Ky.: Bowling Green State University Popular Press, 1999. Pp. 10–22.

Mason, Jennifer. "Animal Bodies: Corporeality, Class, and Subject Formation in *The Wide, Wide World.*" *Nineteenth-Century Literature* 54:503–533 (March 2000).

Myer-Frazier, Petra. "Music, Novels, and Women: Nineteenth-Century Prescriptions for an Ideal Life." *Women and Music: A Journal of Gender and Culture* 10:45–59 (2006).

Myers, D. G. "The Canonization of Susan Warner." *New Criterion* 7:73–78 (December 1988).

Naranjo-Huebl, Linda. "'Take, Eat': Food Imagery, the Nurturing Ethic, and Christian Identity in *The Wide, Wide World, Uncle Tom's Cabin,* and *Incidents in the Life of a Slave Girl.*" *Christianity and Literature* 56:597–631 (summer 2007).

Nguyen, Phong. "Naming the Trees: Literary Onomastics in Susan Warner's The Wide, Wide World." *Studies in American Fiction* 34:33–52 (spring 2006).

Noble, Marianne. "An Ecstasy of Apprehension: The Gothic Pleasures of Sentimental Fiction." In *American Gothic: New Interventions in a National Narrative.* Edited by Robert K. Martin and Eric Savoy. Iowa City: University of Iowa Press, 1998. Pp. 163–182.

———. *The Masochistic Pleasures of Sentimental Literature.* Princeton, N.J.: Princeton University Press, 2000.

Oates, Joyce Carol. "Pleasure, Duty, Redemption Then and Now: Susan Warner's *Diana.*" In *American Literature* 59: 422–427 (October 1987). Reprinted in her *(Woman) Writer: Occasions and Opportunities.* New York: Dutton, 1988. Pp. 190–197.

O'Connell, Catharine. " 'We Must Sorrow': Silence, Suffering, and Sentimentality in Susan Warner's *The Wide, Wide World.*" *Studies in American Fiction* 25:21–39 (spring 1997).

Olin, Stephen Henry. *A Visit to Constitution Island: Address Before the Martlaer's Rock Association. June 13, 1917.*

Ousley, Laurie. "The Power of Piety in Susan Warner's

Republic." In *Northeast Regional Meeting of the Conference on Christianity and Literature.* Edited by Joan F. Hallisey and Mary-Anne Vetterling. Weston, Mass.: Regis College, 1996. Pp. 97–101.

———. "Susan Bogert Warner." In *Dictionary of Literary Biography.* Vol. 239: *American Women Prose Writers, 1820–1870.* Edited by Katharine Rodier and Amy E. Hudock. Detroit: Gale, 2001. Pp. 338–347.

Overmeyer, Grace. "Hudson River Bluestockings—The Warner Sisters of Constitution Island." *New York History,* April 1859, pp. 137–158.

Parris, Brandy. "'Feeling Right': Domestic Emotional Labor in *The Wide, Wide World.*" *Arizona Quarterly* 61:31–66 (winter 2005).

Putnam, George Haven. "The Warner Sisters and the Literary Associations of the Hudson River Valley: Address Delivered at the Annual Meeting, September 23, 1922." In *Fourth Report and Year Book of the Martelaer's Rock Association, 1920–1923.* Highland Falls, N.Y.: Book Hill Press, 1923. Pp. 16–33.

Quay, Sara E. "Homesickness in Susan Warner's *The Wide, Wide World.*" *Tulsa Studies in Women's Literature* 18:39–58 (spring 1999).

Roberson, Susan L. "Ellen Montgomery's Other Friend: Race Relations in an Expunged Episode of Warner's *Wide, Wide World.*" *ESQ: A Journal of the American Renaissance* 45, no. 1:1–31 (1999). (The appendix to this article includes a scene with a young African American girl edited out of *The Wide, Wide World.*)

Rowe, John Carlos. "Religious Transnationalism in the American Renaissance: Susan Warner's *Wide, Wide World.*" *ESQ: A Journal of the American Renaissance* 49, nos. 1–3:45–57 (2003).

Schnog, Nancy. "Inside the Sentimental: The Psychological Work of *The Wide, Wide World.*" *Genders* 4:11–25 (March 1989).

Seelye, John. *Jane Eyre's American Daughters: From* The Wide, Wide World *to* Anne of Green Gables. *A Study of Marginalized Maidens and What They Mean.* Newark: University of Delaware Press, 2005.

Silverman, Gillian. "'The Polishing Attrition': Reading, Writing, and Renunciation in the Work of Susan Warner." *Studies in American Fiction* 33:3–28 (spring 2005).

Smith, Henry Nash. "The Scribbling Women and the Cosmic Success Story." *Critical Inquiry* 1:47–70 (September 1974).

Stern, Madeline B., and Leona Rostenberg. "Susan Bogert Warner." In *Dictionary of Literary Biography.* Vol. 3: *Antebellum Writers in New York and the South.* Edited by Joel Myerson. Detroit: Gale, 979. Pp. 348–349.

Stewart, Veronica. "The Wild Side of *The Wide, Wide World.*" *Legacy* 11, no. 1:1–16 (1994).

———. "Mothering a Female Saint: Susan Warner's Dialogic Role in *The Wide, Wide World.*" *Essays in Literature* 22:59–74 (spring 1995).

Stone, Susan M. "Susan Warner." In *Dictionary of Literary Biography.* Vol. 250: *Antebellum Writers in New York.* Second series. Edited by Kent P. Ljungquist. Detroit: Gale. Pp. 338–347.

Tompkins, Jane. "Legacy Profile: Susan Warner (1819–1885)." *Legacy* 2, no. 1:1, 14–15 (1985).

———. "The Other American Renaissance." In *The American Renaissance Reconsidered.* Edited by Walter Benn Michaels and Donald E. Pease. Baltimore: Johns Hopkins University Press 1985. Pp. 34–57.

———. *Sensational Designs: The Cultural Work of American Fiction, 1790–1860.* New York: Oxford University Press, 1985.

———. Afterword to *The Wide, Wide World.* New York: Feminist Press, 1987.

Trubey, Elizabeth Fekete. "Imagined Revolution: The Female Reader and *The Wide, Wide World.*" *Modern Language Studies* 31:57–74 (fall 2001).

Warner, Anna. *Susan Warner ("Elizabeth Wetherell").* New York: Putnam, 1909.

Weiss, Jane. "Susan Warner (1819–1885)." In *Nineteenth-Century American Women Writers: A Bio-Bibliographical Critical Sourcebook.* Edited by Denise D. Knight and Emmanuel S. Nelson. Westport, Conn.: Greenwood, 1997. Pp. 452–462.

Weinstein, Cindy. *Family, Kinship, and Sympathy in Nineteenth-Century American Literature.* New York: Cambridge University Press, 2004. (See chapter 5, "Love American Style: *The Wide, Wide World.*")

Wellink, Yvonne. "American Sentimental Bestsellers in Holland in the Nineteenth Century." In *Something Understood: Studies in Anglo-Dutch Literary Translation.* Edited by Bart Westerweel and Theo D'haen. Atlanta, Ga.: Rodopi, 1990. Pp. 271–289.

White, Isabelle. "Anti-Individualism, Authority, and Identity: Susan Warner's Contradictions in *The Wide, Wide World.*" *American Studies* 31:31–41 (fall 1990).

Williams, Cynthia Schoolar. "Susan Warner's *Queechy* and the Bildungsroman Tradition." *Legacy* 7, no. 2:3–16 (1990).

Williams, Susan S. "Widening the World: Susan Warner, Her Readers, and the Assumption of Authorship." *American Quarterly* 42:565–586 (December 1990).

Dissertations

Balaam, Peter. "'Misery's Mathematics': Mourning, Compensation and Reality in Emerson, Warner, and Melville." Princeton University, 2000.

Cruea, Susan. "Romancing the Ladies: Hawthorne's Response to the Woman Movement." Bowling Green State University, 2004.

Damon-Bach, Lucinda Linfield. "'The Joy of Untamed Spirits and Undiminished Strength': Catherine Sedgwick's

and Susan Warner's Revisionary Romances." State University of New York–Buffalo, 1996.

Gandolfo, Maria Christina. "Compelled to Write: Crisis and Self-Constitution in the Work of Susan Warner, Edith Wharton, and Anne Sexton." Lehigh University, 1993.

Gates, Sondra Smith. "The Virtuous Poor in Domestic Fiction by Catharine Maria Sedgwick and Susan Warner, 1822–1877." University of Michigan, 2001.

Goshgarian, G. M. "To Kiss the Chastening Rod: Sex in American Domestic Fiction of the 1850s." Dissertation Abstracts International 49:8:2220A (February 1989).

Le Purnine, Marjorie. "Therapeutic Pieties: Sentimental Prescriptions for Surviving Loss in Mid-Nineteenth-Century America." Boston University, 2005.

Mason, Jennifer Adrienne. "Creatures: Animality, Cultural Power, and American Literature, 1850–1901." University of Texas–Austin, 2001.

O'Connell, Catherine Elizabeth. "Chastening the Rod: Sentimental Strategies in Three Antebellum Novels by Women." University of Michigan, 1992.

Papazian, Gretchen Diane. "Hunger Pangs: Emotion and the Nineteenth-Century American Novel Publication." University of Wisconsin–Milwaukee. 1998.

Perin, Joshua Baynard. "Agriculture and Authorship in Nineteenth-Century America." Yale University, 2003.

Quay, Sara Elisabeth. "Objects of Affection: Counter Cultures of Consumerism in American Fiction." Brandeis University, 1996.

Wall, Mary Grace. "'Advice in Every Shape': Nineteenth-Century American Women's Writing and the Discourse of Advice." University of Virginia, 1998.

DOROTHY WEST

(1907—1998)

Whitney Womack Smith

WHEN DOROTHY WEST died on August 16, 1998, at age ninety-one, her obituaries noted that she was the last surviving member of the historic explosion of black arts in the 1920s and 1930s known as the Harlem Renaissance movement. Younger than most of her Harlem Renaissance contemporaries, West was nicknamed "the Kid" by Langston Hughes (1902–1967). West came from a privileged background and grew up among Boston's black elite. She began publishing stories at age fourteen and at the age of eighteen won *Opportunity* magazine's national story competition. In the 1930s she edited *Challenge,* and later *New Challenge,* literary magazines devoted to fulfilling the promise of the Harlem Renaissance and providing a forum for young black writers, including Richard Wright (1908–1960) and Ralph Ellison (1914–1994).

When her first novel, *The Living Is Easy,* appeared in 1948, the Harlem Renaissance was over, which may explain why West's work is often left out of critical discussions of the period. In the early 1940s she took a position with the Federal Writers' Project sponsored by the Works Projects Administration. After World War II, West moved to her family's cottage on the Massachusetts island, Martha's Vineyard, where she lived the rest of her life. For decades it was widely assumed that West had left the literary world. In fact, she continued writing, publishing frequently in the New York *Daily News* into the 1960s and writing regular columns for the *Vineyard Gazette* into the 1990s. In the interviews she granted to scholars and journalists and in the PBS documentary about her life, *As I Remember It* (1991), West frequently mentioned a novel in progress. It was former first lady Jacqueline Kennedy Onassis, also a resident of Martha's Vineyard and an editor at Doubleday, who encouraged West to complete her second novel, *The Wedding.* Both *The Wedding* and a collection of short pieces, *The Richer, the Poorer: Sketches and Reminiscences,* were published in 1995. *The Wedding* became a best seller and was adapted into a popular television miniseries on the ABC network in 1998. Produced by Oprah Winfrey and starring Halle Berry, the film introduced millions of viewers to Dorothy West. At the end of her life, West found herself suddenly famous. While there has been renewed critical attention to West since the 1990s, no full-length biography or critical study of her work has yet been published. Studies of West have focused largely on her representations of middle-class black life, black women, family relationships and dynamics, the Great Migration, place and region, and the politics of skin color and the caste system in the black community.

FROM BOSTON TO HARLEM

Dorothy West was born in Boston, Massachusetts, on June 2, 1907, the only child of Isaac Christopher West and Rachel Pease Benson West. Isaac West was born a slave in Virginia in 1860. An industrious boy, Isaac ("Ike") worked from an early age and saved enough money by age ten to open a restaurant and boardinghouse in Richmond, Virginia. Like many southern blacks in the late nineteenth century, Isaac migrated to Massachusetts seeking wider opportunities, eventually settling in Springfield. A savvy, self-educated entrepreneur, Isaac West started a successful fruit import business on South Market Street across from Boston's Faneuil Hall that earned him the nickname the "Black Banana King." Isaac is likely the inspiration for the self-made man Bart Judson in *The Living is Easy.* Dorothy's mother

was also originally a southerner, born to former slaves in rural Camden, South Carolina. Certainly the Benson clan was large, and various biographical sketches claim Rachel was one of eighteen, nineteen, or even twenty-two children. As a teenager, the light-skinned Rachel moved to Springfield, Massachusetts, at the urging of a teacher. Dreaming of a career on the stage, she took singing lessons but her ambitions were never fulfilled. Rachel worked as a companion to an elderly woman when she met Isaac, who was eighteen years her senior. West's memories of her mother paint a portrait of a confident, passionate, flamboyant, and sometimes volatile woman who was a master storyteller. Rachel undoubtedly sparked Dorothy's love of stories, and she also becomes the inspiration for many of the female characters in Dorothy's fiction. Both Isaac and Rachel West were determined to join Boston's new black bourgeoisie. The couple moved to a four-story home at 478 Brookline Street. The large house was often filled with members of their extended family; a family joke was that "if we lived in the Boston Museum, we'd still need one more room" ("Rachel," collected in *The Richer, the Poorer,* p. 167). The Wests were among the first affluent black families to purchase property at Oak Bluffs, a black resort community on the exclusive island of Martha's Vineyard. Dorothy later recalled her idyllic childhood summers at Oak Bluffs, where "nobody ... called you 'nigger'" (*As I Remember It*).

Isaac and Rachel West valued arts and education and sought out the best opportunities for their only child. When she was just a toddler, Dorothy took private dancing, music, and deportment classes with Bessie Trotter, the sister of Monroe Trotter, the Harvard-educated editor of Boston's black paper the *Guardian.* By West's own account, she was a precocious child:

> When I was a child of 4 or 5, listening to the conversation of my mother and her sisters, I would sometimes intrude on their territory with a solemnly stated opinion that would jerk their heads in my direction, then send them into roars of uncontrollable laughter ... the first adult who caught her breath would speak for them all and say, 'That's no child. That's a little sawed-off woman.' That was to become a self-fulfilling prophecy.
>
> ("Remembrance," in *The Richer, the Poorer,* p. 201)

Her mother petitioned the public schools to accept Dorothy at age four, when she was already working at the second-grade level. By the age of seven she was determined to become a writer. Her parents encouraged this ambition, and Isaac told his young daughter, "'Your little head is for books and mine is for buying and selling and buying bananas'" (McDowell, p. 286). As a girl she wrote stories that she shared with her cousins, part of the large extended family that lived with the Wests. West, who shared her father's darker skin, later noted that she spent much of her time alone indoors reading and writing in order "not to mark her lighter-skinned cousins with her public presence" (Rayson, p. 37). Dorothy completed elementary school at Martin School, where she was often subjected to racist remarks. At the age of ten she passed the examination to enter Boston's prestigious Girls' Latin School. West later recalled that at the Latin School, "All the other students were white, middle-class girls. I don't know whether they liked me or not, but they were polite" (Dålsgard, p. 35). She finished her senior year at Brighton High School.

West's literary career began when she was just fourteen and her story "Promise and Fulfillment" won the contest for best story of the week in the *Boston Post.* She began to enter—and win—the contest regularly. West recalled that "eight times out of ten or seven times out of ten, I got the $10 prize [first prize] and contributed to the family pot. When I got the $2 or $5 prize, everybody in the family was indignant" (McDowell, p. 288). She cited an eclectic group of writers as her early influences, including Shakespeare, Goethe, Dostoevsky, Sinclair Lewis, and Edith Wharton, as well as the popular novelist Fannie Hurst. In an interview, she recalled the impact of reading Dostoevsky's *Crime and Punishment*: "My eyes filled with tears and I remember thinking, 'This is genius. Now I know what genius is.' Dostoevsky became my master" (McDowell, p. 288). Interestingly, she does not cite any black authors.

In 1925, Eugene Gordon, the short story editor at the *Boston Post,* invited Dorothy to join his black writers' group, the Saturday Evening Quill Club. That same year, Dorothy and her cousin Helene Johnson submitted entries for the literary contest sponsored by *Opportunity* magazine, the organ of the National Urban League. West's submission, "The Typewriter," shared second prize with Zora Neale Hurston's story "Muttsy," while Helene's poems won three honorable mentions. The judges included such literary luminaries as Robert Frost, Carl Van Doren, Jean Toomer, and Blanch Colton William, who later taught and mentored West. *Opportunity* promoted the Harlem Renaissance by holding lavish banquets to honor the contest winners and introduce their work to influential white patrons and publishers. The cousins traveled alone to attend the ceremony in 1926, staying at the Harlem YWCA on 137th Street. In 1926 Harlem was a dynamic place, filled with black artists and intellectuals. As the story goes, Dorothy and Helene were so shocked by the number of black people in the streets that they assumed it must be for a parade. The Harlem Renaissance was at its height, with the publications of such groundbreaking texts as Alain Locke's *The New Negro* (1925) and Langston Hughes's "The Negro Artist and the Racial Mountain" (1926). At the banquet, Dorothy and Helene were introduced to some of the most important writers of the day, including Hurston, Hughes, Countee Cullen, Wallace Thurman, Carl Van Vechten, and West's childhood favorite, Fannie Hurst. Hurst later helped West get her first literary agent.

"The Typewriter" (collected in *The Richer, the Poorer*) tells the story of a middle-aged black man who has been beaten down by life. When he migrated to an urban center in the North as a young man, pursuing the American Dream, he imagined that someday he would have an office job and sit behind a "real mahogany desk" (p. 11). Now, more than thirty years later, he returns home from his job as a janitor in a downtown office building to face the complaints of tenants in the apartment house where he acts as the maintenance man. His nagging wife and noisy daughters provide little solace. When his daughter Millie needs a rental typewriter to practice her secretarial skills, her father has to find a way to pay for it out of his meager paycheck. At first he is annoyed and longs to escape the "tack, tack, tack," but his attitude changes when Millie asks him to dictate business letters. He invents the persona of J. Lucius Jones, a wealthy stock trader, who corresponds with such captains of industry as J. P. Morgan and Henry Ford. He soon begins to dictate their replies, inventing an imaginary world of mergers and acquisitions to replace his real world of drudgery; as he goes about his janitorial duties, he composes letters about billion-dollar deals. This persona brings him confidence and self-esteem, which is shattered when he returns home one day to find the typewriter gone. Millie has been offered a secretarial job and no longer needs to practice at home, so the typewriter has been sent back. The protagonist's shock and horror at the loss of the typewriter leads to his death: "He clutched at his heart and felt, almost, the jagged edges drive into his hand ... He could not move, nor utter a sound. He could not pray, nor curse. Against that wall of silence J. Lucius Jones crashed and died" (p. 17). *Opportunity* published the story in its June 1926 issue, and it was reprinted in the Dodd Mead volume *The Best Short Stories of 1926,* edited by Edward O'Brien.

KEEPING THE HARLEM RENAISSANCE ALIVE

Although she returned home after the *Opportunity* ceremony and may have briefly attended Boston University, West was determined to join the thriving artistic community in Harlem. Helene accompanied her, and the pair stayed at the YWCA. When Zora Neale Hurston was awarded a fellowship, Dorothy and Helene, with financial assistance from Isaac West, sublet Hurston's apartment and led a bohemian life. Dorothy West briefly attended creative writing classes at Columbia University through its Extension Division, where she studied under Blanch Colton Williams and Dorothy Scarborough. Williams believed "the short story is the literary medium that supersedes all others in America," and she encouraged West to pursue the genre (quoted in Mitchell and Davis, p. 20). Scarbor-

ough pushed West to complete a novel she began in 1927 titled "Five Sheaves"; her literary agent was not able to interest publishers, and the manuscript has been lost.

West continually struggled to place her work. While the Harlem Renaissance had sparked a sort of "Negro vogue" among some whites, most magazines were cautious about offending racist readers and instituted race quotas, only publishing one or two stories per issue, sometimes per year, by black writers. Black women writers labored under a double prejudice. Over the years *Collier's, Ladies' Home Journal,* and other mainstream publications rejected West's submissions. In 1926, West's story "Hannah Byde" appeared in the *Messenger,* a magazine started by the black labor activist and economist A. Philip Randolph to introduce socialist thought to black readers. "Hannah Byde" is a naturalistic portrait of a desperately unhappy woman who is "crushed by environment, looking dully down the stretch of drab tomorrows" (*Where the Wild Grape Grows,* p. 79). Trapped in a cramped apartment and tied to a husband she doesn't love, Hannah wishes for change, even death, to escape from her miserable existence. Although her husband, George, thinks Hannah is "jes' nervous," she makes a botched attempt at suicide on New Year's Eve (p. 80). When she is found alive, her doctor informs her she is pregnant. In the end, trapped by a stifling marriage and an unwanted child, Hannah is resigned to her fate.

In the late 1920s, West's Boston mentor, Eugene Gordon, included two of West's stories in his acclaimed literary annual *Saturday Evening Quill.* "An Unimportant Man" (collected in *The Richer, the Poorer*) appeared in the first issue in 1928 and is another story of thwarted ambitions. The protagonist, Zeb, longs to be a lawyer and a member of the bourgeoisie, but he fails the bar exam and works as a cook. He is determined that his daughter will not squander her life, so he takes control of her education, thus repeating the pattern his mother began and dooming Essie to an unhappy life. When the story was reprinted in *Copy,* a collection of works by Columbia University's writing students, Dorothy included a biographical statement: "I have no ability nor desire to be other than a writer, though the fact is I whistle beautifully" (quoted in Ferguson, *Dictionary of Literary Biography,* p. 189).

The other story selected by Gordon, "Prologue to a Life" (collected in *Where the Wild Grape Grows*), recounts the lives of Luke Kane and Lily Bemis, who in their physical appearance match West's parents: Luke is dark with blue eyes, Lily is light-skinned. Sharon L. Jones sees Luke and Lily Kane in "Prologue to a Life" as the prototype for the Judsons in West's later novel *The Living Is Easy.* Luke sees Lily, with her beauty and fair skin, as an asset for his social climbing; Lily, despite her lack of love for Luke, marries him. Their life in a fine Brookline home in Boston is shattered when their beloved light-skinned twin sons drown. Lily's spirit is broken by her loss of identity as a mother, especially as the mother of sons, and she sinks into a deep depression. She is distraught when she finds herself pregnant again, and sickened when she gives birth to a daughter with her father's dark skin, who will face the double prejudice of class and race. Lily dies just after the birth. Many critics also note the clear influence of Dostoevsky on these early stories. West grafts Dostoevsky's bleak portraits of urban life and existential despair onto a black landscape.

During the late 1920s, West developed significant relationships with most of the major figures of the Harlem Renaissance. Langston Hughes jokingly called her "the Kid" and later became a romantic interest for West. Hurston called her "little sister" and influenced her representations of the South and folk life. Carl Van Vechten, the white champion of the Harlem Renaissance and author of the controversial novel *Nigger Heaven* (1926), gave her literary advice and included her in his social circle. Claude McKay (1890–1948) was a mentor who frequently invited her to his apartment to meet serious writers and later professed his love for her. Countee Cullen (1903–1946) shared her middle-class background and became a great friend. Although he was homosexual, he proposed to West, but she refused, explaining in an interview, "if I had married him, I would have had to go

south, where he was going to teach. I didn't want to be one of those women who sat around and drank tea. I was not that person at all" (quoted in Kenney, p. 11).

West formed a special relationship with Wallace Thurman (1902–1934), the former editor of the *Messenger* and the founder of the radical magazine *Fire!! A Quarterly Devoted to the Younger Negro Artists.* He invited West to the infamous parties at his studio apartment, nicknamed Niggerati Manor, where she drank bootleg liquor and took part in conversations with Harlem's avant-garde. In 1927, in need of money, Thurman and West took bit parts in the original Broadway production of *Porgy,* a dramatization of the 1924 novel by DuBose Heyward, directed by Rouben Mamoulian. (The play was adapted by George Gershwin in 1935 into the popular opera *Porgy and Bess.*) West and many well-known figures of the Harlem Renaissance were models for characters in Thurman's novel *Infants of the Spring* (1932). In 1970, West remembered Thurman, who died years earlier from tuberculosis and alcoholism at the age of thirty-two, in the memoir "The Elephant's Dance" (collected in *The Richer, the Poorer*). West describes the prejudice he faced within the black community: "He hated Negro society, and since dark skins have never been the fashion among Negro upper classes, the feeling was occasionally mutual" (p. 219). Thurman's *The Blacker the Berry: A Novel of Negro Life* (1929) examines the color-caste system among blacks, a topic West takes up in her later fiction.

Seeking adventure and a break from racist American society, West traveled abroad. Her parents separated in 1927 and her father's business faltered, so she no longer had anyone to subsidize her lifestyle. She applied for a position at the Theater Guild, which led to being hired for the London cast of *Porgy.* During the trip, West spent time with the flamboyant actress Edna Lewis Thomas, a member of the "glamorous gay and bisexual subculture in Harlem" (Mitchell and Davis, p. 26). West had hoped to stay in Europe longer, but the play did not go over well with British audiences.

While volunteering at the Fellowship of Youth and Peace Reconciliation in New York City, West learned of a proposed venture to make a film about American race relations titled "Black and White" in the Soviet Union. West, Langston Hughes, and Henry Lee Moon were among twenty-two Americans who sailed for Russia in June 1932 to take part in the picture. Russia fascinated West, who wrote in a letter to her mother that "there are more people in Moscow than anywhere in the world, I think" (*Where the Wild Grape Grows,* p. 188). The Americans were discouraged to find the script did not reflect the realities of black life, and Hughes attempted a rewrite. Plans for the film were eventually scrapped; West always believed the Russians pulled the plug because they were concerned American companies would withdraw support if they produced a film depicting the United States in a negative light.

From her correspondence, we learn that during her time in Russia, West was involved in a love triangle involving the artist Mildred Jones and Hughes, whom West called "Lang." Verner Mitchell and Cynthia Davis suggest that West was involved in her first lesbian relationship with Jones. West never discussed her relationships with women openly; as Mitchell and Davis note, West was always evasive and discreet in discussions of her personal life. While still involved with Jones, West professed her love to Langston Hughes. In May 1933 she wrote a marriage proposal to Hughes, telling him that she wanted to give him a "dark son" or "brown daughter," then would set him free "to have adventures to the last of your life" (*Where the Wild Grape Grows,* pp. 195, 194). The two never married; in fact, West never married or had the child she so desired. West maintained friendships with Hughes and Jones, both of whom later contributed to *Challenge* magazine. While most critics have viewed West as apolitical, her time in Russia opened her eyes to the hypocrisy of the Soviet system and made her resistant to the increasing interest in Communism among black intellectuals in the 1930s and 1940s.

West saw her return to the United States in 1933 as the end of her youth, although she was

only twenty-five years old. Her beloved father had died while she was abroad. Her beloved Harlem Renaissance movement had waned with the Great Depression. West was determined to find a way to keep the creative spirit of the movement alive. In a letter to the novelist James Weldon Johnson, who was an influential professor at Fisk University, West stated, "It occurred to me that I could make up for so much wasted by some way finding space for young dark throats to sing heard songs" (*Where the Wild Grape Grows,* p. 198). Using the $300 she earned from the failed Russian venture, West founded a magazine titled *Challenge* in 1934. With this magazine, West attempted to connect the ideas of the older guard of the Harlem Renaissance with the new generation of black writers and thinkers. She struggled to find new voices, however, and the first two issues contain works by established black writers, all friends of West: Johnson, Hughes, Cullen, Hurston, McKay, Arna Bontemps, and West's cousin Helene Johnson. In fact, her initial plan had been to publish the magazine monthly, which was revised to quarterly because of the poor quality of the submissions. West published some of her own work in *Challenge,* including the story "The Five-Dollar Bill," under the pseudonym Mary Christopher, taken from her paternal grandmother's first name and her father's middle name. Like many of West's stories, "The Five-Dollar Bill" (collected in *The Richer, the Poorer*) is written from the perspective of an innocent child and deals with themes of money and materialism. Young Judy witnesses her parents' deteriorating marriage and her mother's affair with a college man. Her mother's selfishness and greed lead her to steal money from her daughter—the five-dollar bill—to give to her lover. Judy had earned the money by selling reproductions of famous paintings; when she submits the money, she will receive a motion picture projector, which she hopes will help the family's finances. Judy fears she will be sent to jail for not sending the money, and the ending is one of sadness and loss: "Very few parents profit by childhood experiences. When they look back they do not really remember. They see through a sentimental haze. For childhood is full of unrequited love, and suffering, and tears" (p. 25).

Challenge evolved to include an increasing number of younger writers and to take a more political stance, largely in response to the Chicago Group, a loose network of leftist black intellectuals who believed that *Challenge* was too "pink," or tame, and should publish more proletarian literature. In her editorial for the June 1936 issue, West acknowledges the need for the journal to be more political: "We would like to print more articles of protest. We have daily contact with the underprivileged. We know their suffering and soul weariness" (quoted in Ferguson, p. 192). West was also influenced by her friend and longtime companion Marian Minus, a graduate of Fisk University who had done doctoral work at the University of Chicago. While in Chicago, Minus joined the South Side Writers' Group, a radical group of artists including Margaret Walker and Richard Wright that had links to the Communist party. West and Minus had met in New York in the early 1930s and the two began an intimate relationship. When Minus returned to New York in 1937, she urged West to move *Challenge* radically to the left and allow Wright to edit a special issue articulating the message of the Chicago Group.

The proposed issue turned into a short-lived new journal—*New Challenge*—that was coedited by West and Minus, with Wright as associate editor. Wright had recently moved to New York from Chicago and was the Harlem editor for the Communist paper the *Daily Worker.* Like many small magazines, *New Challenge* had trouble attracting sufficient numbers of subscribers and advertising dollars. It also faced major ideological conflicts between West and Wright. The magazine folded after just one issue. But that single 1937 issue is memorable for the publication of Wright's manifesto "Blueprint for Negro Writing." In this scathing piece, Wright critiques the Harlem Renaissance as the "result of a liaison between inferiority-complexed Negro 'geniuses' and burnt-out white Bohemians with money" (p. 195). In this movement, "Negro writing ... has been confined to humble novels, poems, and plays, prim and decorous ambassadors who went

a-begging to white America" (p. 194). Wright argues for greater freedom and social realism in black writing. This essay appeared just one year before his influential story collection *Uncle Tom's Children* (1938); the book helped him to win a Guggenheim fellowship to complete his first novel, *Native Son* (1940). *New Challenge* was also the forum for Ralph Ellison's first work, a review of E. Walters Turpin's *These Low Grounds* titled "Creative and Cultural Lag."

After the end of *Challenge* and *New Challenge,* West and Minus looked for new ways to support themselves. They moved together to an apartment on West 110th Street in 1938, and West took a job as a welfare investigator in Harlem. This position gave her writing a more sociological perspective and inspired the story "Mammy," which appeared in *Opportunity* in October 1940. Set during the Depression, "Mammy" (collected in *The Richer, the Poorer*) tells the story of a black relief investigator who is torn between loyalty to her race and the obligations of her job. As a black elevator operator tells her, "With white folks needin' jobs, us niggers got to eat dirt to hang on" (p. 48). Bound by the rules of the welfare system, the caseworker is forced to deny an old black woman's welfare relief application. Old "Mammy" is forced to return to the home of Mrs. Coleman, the racist white employer who views her as a possession.

In the early 1940s West was part of the Federal Writers' Project, a Works Progress Administration (WPA) initiative created in 1935 to provide money and creative outlets for writers, editors, and historians during the Depression era. The Federal Writers' Project provided a forum for a number of prominent black writers, including Bontemps, Hurston, McKay, and Ellison. Among the major contributions of the Federal Writers' Project was the collection of oral histories of former slaves and rural blacks. West interviewed her maternal aunts from Camden, South Carolina, and recorded their stories in "Quilting" and "Blackberrying." Much like Alice Walker's later essay "In Search of Our Mothers' Gardens," these personal narratives describe how many black women found creative outlets through domestic arts. These and some others of West's previously unpublished WPA stories are collected in *Where the Wild Grape Grows: Selected Writings, 1930–1950.*

In 1940 West also began writing for the New York *Daily News,* which published over thirty of her stories over the next twenty years. In an interview late in life, West stated that she was likely the first black writer to be published by the *Daily News,* a daily tabloid with a largely white circulation. Some of her black peers were critical of her for publishing in this forum. She was paid $400, a significant sum, for her first story for the *Daily News.* Titled "Jack in the Pot" and renamed "Jackpot" by the editor at the *Daily News,* it has become one of West's most anthologized stories. Although the assumption is that West's fiction focuses exclusively on the black middle class, "Jack in the Pot" (collected in *The Richer, the Poorer*) is among a number of her stories that chronicle the lives of the poor and underprivileged. The formerly middle-class Mrs. Edmunds is now on welfare after her husband lost his stationery business in the Great Depression. At the beginning of the story she wins $55 in a movie-house drawing. She is torn over whether to spend the money on herself and her family, who have suffered years of poverty and unemployment, or to use it to help others in even greater need. When Mrs. Edmunds learns that her poor neighbor needs $50 to pay for the funeral of his dead baby, she can't bring herself to give away all of the money. Instead she spends a dollar to buy the child a dress to be buried in—only to learn that the family, unable to afford a burial, had to donate the body for medical experimentation. Mrs. Edmunds's guilt over her decision leads her to put the money away, swearing she will not use it for her own pleasure, only for "burial money."

After "Jack in the Pot," West began to publish regularly in the *Daily News,* receiving $50 for each story. These compact stories reveal West's eye for detail and narrative economy. "The Penny" (1941; collected in *The Richer, the Poorer*) also contains themes of money, poverty, and class-consciousness. Again set in an unnamed northern center during the Depression, "The Penny" focuses on a young black boy whose

father, for the first time in a long time, is able to give his son a penny to spend as he wishes. The excited boy trips on a curb, falls on his face, and drops his penny in the gutter. When a patronizing middle-class black woman, Miss Hester Halsey, finds him in the street, she assumes that his bruised face must be the result of child abuse in an impoverished, dysfunctional home. He tells Miss Hester what she wants to hear when she offers him a shiny penny, and they both get what they want: the boy has his candy money and Miss Halsey can continue to feel superior to her poor brethren. The race of the characters is never specifically identified in many of West's stories for the *Daily News,* including "The Maple Tree" and "Fluff and Mr. Ripley" (which are also collected in *The Richer, the Poorer*). West recalled, "For their sake, and for my sake because I had to eat, I never mentioned the word 'black'" (Dålsgard, p. 37).

THE LIVING IS EASY

In the mid-1940s, West moved permanently to her family's summer cottage on Martha's Vineyard, which she called "the home of my heart" (*Dorothy West's Martha's Vineyard,* p. 5). West lived with her mother and her aunt Carrie, who had suffered a stroke. West has said that she sought to escape the noise and distractions of the city, but the move was also likely due to the difficulties of earning enough money to support herself in New York. West continued a relationship with Marian Minus for several more years, and Minus was a visitor on the island. The summer cottage was not truly fitted for year-round living, and West recalled dealing with frozen water pipes and other inconveniences before the house was winterized. For several years she worked in earnest to complete her autobiographical novel, *The Living Is Easy.* The title is from "Summertime," the famous Gershwin song from *Porgy and Bess.* Although her passion was for short fiction, West recognized the constraints of the literary marketplace: "I probably would not have written *The Living* or started the other novels had it not been for the fact that stories don't sell. I love short stories; I think they are the most perfect literary form. A novel goes on forever and is a more difficult form to control" (McDowell, p. 302). In 1945 she sent Countee Cullen six chapters of *The Living Is Easy.* She completed the novel in 1948, and her agent, George Bye, sold the manuscript to Houghton Mifflin.

Although it is dedicated to West's father, *The Living Is Easy* is truly the story of her mother, Rachel, renamed Cleo Jericho Judson. West breaks with tradition by making Cleo a complex, unlikable, unsympathetic, and mesmerizing black female character. As Mary Helen Washington has noted, black women writers have often been so sensitive to the degraded images of black women in literature and society that they have taken a "sacred-cow attitude" toward their black female characters (*Black-Eyed Susans,* p. xxxi). Cleo is a black woman who migrates from the South to Boston, determined to break into the small circle of black Boston society by using whatever means necessary. In fact, her calculating ways have led Ann duCille to dub Cleo "the Scarlett O'Hara of black fiction" (p. 112). Although she is light-skinned, Cleo is not a tragic mulatto but rather is a woman with a strength and spirit very unlike that usual stereotypically passive figure. Nor does she possess the moral stature and selfless devotion to racial uplift of the light-skinned female characters in such novels as Frances E. W. Harper's *Iola Leroy* (1892) or Pauline Hopkins's *Contending Forces* (1900). Even as a child, Cleo is described as a "hell-raiser" who connives to get what she wants (p. 23). She blackmails her younger sisters to get their penny candy and headbutts a boy in the groin to win a fight. She identifies with the stories of her strong foremothers, including her great-grandmother Patsy. After her white slave mistress admonished her for burning a pan of biscuits, Patsy "walked out of that kitchen and down to the river. When they fished her out by her long black hair, her soul had got free and she didn't have to listen to anybody's lip forever after" (p. 91). When Miss Josephine, a visiting northern white spinster, notices the lively teenage Cleo, she offers to take her North. Cleo's mother readily agrees, fearing her beauty will lead to "wantonness" (p. 24).

In Boston, Cleo uses her cunning and good looks to achieve her goal of upward social mobility. She catches the eye of one of Boston's wealthiest black men, Bart Judson. A former slave, Bart migrated North after Emancipation to seek the American Dream. He has become the wealthy owner of a successful produce business specializing in bananas, just like West's father Isaac. Their meeting, with Cleo running into Bart while riding a bicycle, is reminiscent of the meeting of Lily and Luke in West's early short story "Prologue to a Life." Cleo accepts Bart's proposal not out of love but instead out of a desire to escape the home of her white benefactress and the wandering eye of a young white man. She also hopes that Bart, twenty-three years her senior, will leave her a rich young widow. After the wedding, Cleo resists Bart's sexual advances, only conceiving a child five years later, when "her body's hunger broke down her controlled resistance" (p. 35). Their only child, Judy (a name that recurs in West's fiction), is a plain girl who inherits her father's "cocoa-brown skin" (p. 39). Judy's appearance is a disappointment to Cleo, who values light skin and Anglo features as markers of class and status. Cleo seeks to mold Judy into her image of a "little Boston lady" who has fine clothes, impeccable manners, and private tutors.

Bart Judson's money funds Cleo's ambitious social striving, which eventually takes a toll on her entire extended family. She uses her bargaining skills to rent a house in the previously all-white area of Brookline for only $25 a month. West depicts both the black bourgeois exodus from urban centers and the middle-class white flight from the inner ring of suburbs; the Brookline homeowner is putting the grand house up for rent to escape the influx of Irish immigrants. In one of her many schemes, Cleo tells Bart that the rent is $45, pocketing the extra money to send to her three sisters, Lily, Charity, and Serena. She manipulates each sister into traveling North with her children to visit, and then she never lets them leave. Once they are under her roof, Cleo systematically destroys their marriages, since she believes their husbands are all too far down the socioeconomic ladder. Although she comes from a poor, southern background, Cleo harbors prejudices against working-class blacks and the new wave of black migrants to Boston. According to Sharon L. Jones, West is contending that "elitism among the black bourgeoisie serves as a denial of one's heritage" (*Rereading the Harlem Renaissance,* p. 137). Cleo attempts to control the lives of her husband, daughter, sisters, nieces and nephews, and even the members of the Binney family, one of first families of the black elite, now fallen on hard times. In *The Negro Novel in America,* Robert Bone compared Cleo's ability to manipulate and inflict pain to Shakespeare's notorious villain Iago. Bart's business eventually collapses, both from Cleo's constant drain on his capital and his inability to compete with large supermarkets that undercut his produce prices. Again, this mirrors Isaac West's own experiences, when his business failed during the Great Depression. In the end, Bart leaves Boston for New York to try to remake his life. Only then does Cleo show any emotion for her husband, finally treating him with the affection and tenderness she denied him throughout their marriage. In the end, Cleo faces the terrifying question, "Who is there now to love me best? Who?" (p. 347).

The Living Is Easy was met with generally positive reviews in the both black and white press. In a review for the NAACP magazine *Crisis,* Henry Lee Moon noted that that West had "enlarged the canvas of Negro fiction" by presenting a portrait of Boston's black community. *Opportunity,* however, was more critical of the text, claiming it is "narrow in scope" and lacks a "balanced insight." The *New York Times* reviewer Seymour Krim applauded the novel's "abundant and special woman's energy" (all reviews quoted in Ferguson, *Dictionary of Literary Biography,* p. 194). In 1965, Robert Bone included *The Living Is Easy* is his list of important contemporary "negro novels," critiquing its uneven narrative structure but labeling it a "diamond in the rough" (p. 190). *Ladies' Home Journal,* a popular monthly women's magazine, considered serializing *The Living Is Easy,* which would have given the novel broader exposure and greater commercial success. It also

would have crossed the color line that was still entrenched in the publishing world. As West noted in an interview, the editors were enthusiastic, but the magazine's board of directors vetoed the idea, probably because they "feared the loss of advertising revenues by serializing a novel by a Black woman about Black people" (McDowell, p. 296). As Cynthia Davis notes, white American readers preferred texts that "reinforced stereotypes of black people as poor and powerless" and were not ready for West's portrait of Cleo, beautiful, wealthy, and powerful (p. 13). With its portrait of bourgeois black life, *The Living Is Easy* did not fit comfortably into the white literary imagination or into the new black aesthetic emerging in the 1940s and 1950s, with such protest texts as Ann Petry's *The Street* (1946) and Richard Wright's *Native Son* (1940) and *Black Boy* (1945).

A new generation of readers discovered *The Living Is Easy* when the Feminist Press, as part of its mission to recover lost women's voices, reissued the novel in 1982, with an afterword by Adelaide Cromwell Gulliver. This new edition brought Dorothy West back onto the literary circuit, with invitations to speak at colleges and universities, and led to a critical reevaluation of West's body of work. Scholars now read West's novel both in the context of the Harlem Renaissance and beyond, including the ways the novel participates in the larger literary conversation about the American Dream and how it enhances our understanding of the African American women's literary tradition. West's resistance to and revision of stereotypes of black life, along with her representations of strong black women, black family dynamics, and color consciousness are seen as forerunners for the works of such later black women writers as Maya Angelou, Gloria Naylor, Alice Walker, and Toni Morrison. In 2001, the *Langston Hughes Review* celebrated the fiftieth anniversary of the publication of *The Living Is Easy* with a special issue guest edited by Sharon L. Jones.

LATER WRITINGS AND THE WEDDING

Over the years, West worked a variety of jobs on Martha's Vineyard. She took a position at the *Vineyard Gazette,* Martha Vineyard's weekly newspaper of record since 1846, not long after the publication of *The Living Is Easy.* She worked for two years as a file clerk, then took a position as a cashier at the popular Harborside Inn restaurant. Even with her day (and sometimes evening) jobs, she continued to write, completing about fifty pages of a new novel titled *Where the Wild Grape Grows.* Like her first novel, it is based on the life of Rachel West, focusing on her later years. West submitted it to Houghton Mifflin, but although the editor claimed it was beautifully written, the publishing house passed on the book. West believed it was because Houghton Mifflin assumed a book about middle-class blacks wouldn't sell. The fragment is now available in Mitchell and Davis's collection, *Where the Wild Grape Grows.*

West soon found another forum for her writing. When the *Vineyard Gazette*'s local bird-watching columnist left, West took column over, using the byline "The Highland Waterboy." Her regular pieces on the birds and wildlife of the island were often meditations on the connection between human beings and nature. In late 1968, she began writing a column for the paper titled "Cottagers' Corner." The Cottagers are a sorority of black women who own homes on Martha's Vineyard, and the column reported on the social activities of their circle. In 1973, she began the weekly "Oak Bluffs" column, which appeared nearly every Friday for the next twenty years. In "Oak Bluffs," she reported more broadly about the happenings and events of the community's black and white citizens, including local arts events, library open houses, famous visitors to the island, and stories about the island's many animals. Her contributions to the paper also included memories of her many years on the island, reflections on the natural world, and even musings on growing old. In "The Inroads of Time" (1984; collected in *Where the Wild Grape Grows*), West describes looking at a picture from her trip to Moscow, more than a half-century earlier, and not being able to recognize herself. She finally realizes that the smiling girl in the front row is herself: "Then I gave a little gasp, not so much of dismay as disbelief. I was looking at myself. Though that

face was familiar, I could not juxtapose it with mine and see the slightest resemblance. I remember saying softly, Now I am that girl's mother. And now, so many more years later, I am that girl's grandmother" (p. 176). In an interview, West stated that the *Gazette* allowed her to "write freely about Black people, my family, my childhood" (McDowell, p. 301).

West's second novel was published nearly a half century after her first. West began *The Wedding* decades earlier, receiving a Mary Roberts Rinehart Foundation grant to support her writing and even submitting chapters to Harper and Row in the late 1960s. West worried her story about bourgeois black life would not be welcomed by the radical Black Arts movement of the 1960s. In an interview, West explained how this anxiety prevented her from finishing the novel: "It coincided with the Black Revolution, when many Blacks believed that middle-class Blacks were Uncle Toms ... I feared that some Black reviewer would give *The Wedding* a bad review because it was a book about Black professional people" (McDowell, p. 298). Her columns and vignettes in the *Gazette* drew the attention of Martha's Vineyard resident Jacqueline Kennedy Onassis, the widow of former President John F. Kennedy and an editor at the major New York publishing house Doubleday. When she learned that West was sitting on a manuscript for an unpublished novel, she began to make regular trips across the island to meet with West during the 1990s. Thus began a productive editorial relationship and unlikely friendship between the two women. When *The Wedding* was published by Doubleday in 1995, West dedicated it to Onassis, who had died the year before: "To the memory of my editor, Jacqueline Kennedy Onassis. Though there was never such a mismatched pair in appearance, we were perfect partners." There was, though, a controversy surrounding Doubleday's treatment of the book. When initial galleys were printed in 1994, they included an ending that West had not written. With the help of the literary critic Henry Louis Gates Jr., an agent, and a lawyer, West was able to get Doubleday to scrap the unauthorized conclusion and allow her to write a new ending for the novel.

Like *The Living Is Easy, The Wedding* addresses the aspirations, snobbery, class-consciousness, and inner conflicts among well-to-do blacks in the 1950s. *The Wedding* takes place on Martha's Vineyard in a fictional neighborhood called "the Oval," where members of the East Coast's black elite own summer homes; it is clearly based on West's own area in Oak Bluffs. This small, insular enclave, consisting of only a "baker's dozen" of houses, is hidden at the end of a rutted, winding road. This location gives the "Ovalites," as they are known, a sense of being "as exclusive as the really exclusive—the really rich, the really powerful—who also live at the end of impressively bad roads to discourage the curious" (p. 3). The Ovalites value light skin, which is read as "a marker of gentility and aristocratic background" (Jones, *Rereading the Harlem Renaissance,* p. 142). This prejudice hearkens back to "blue vein societies" that sprung up after Emancipation, designed to promote an elite of light-skinned blacks; for membership, a person had to be pale enough so that the blue veins on the underside of the wrist were visible. During the summer, an outsider penetrates the rarified world of the Oval. Old Addie Bannister, the local invalid, rents her cottage to Lute McNeil, a "nut-brown," nouveau riche furniture maker and seller, and his three "honey-colored" daughters by three different white mothers. His marriages to white women have not given him the status that he wants; he now seeks it among the black elite who emulate white society.

The Coles are the first family of the Oval and live in a mansion affectionately called a "cottage," complete with black servants. Ironically, their grand home once belonged to the family of Miss Amy Norton, the white spinster schoolteacher who brought Isaac Coles from the South and paid for his education in the North. In just two generations, the Coles family has gone from being poor southern blacks to members of elite northern black society. Dr. Clark Coles is a graduate of Harvard Medical School, a skilled diagnostician whose practice attracts white patients. His wife, Corrine Coles, is the college-educated daughter of an influential black college president

and now a top society matron. Their eldest daughter, Liz, followed in her father's footsteps in medicine before leaving work for full-time motherhood; their youngest daughter, Shelby, is a famed beauty. The Coleses "came closest to being as real as their counterparts" among Martha's Vineyard's white society (p. 3). Dr. and Mrs. Coles's seemingly perfect facade conceals a loveless union, kept together purely for appearances. Clark is in love with his brown-skinned nurse, while Corrine has not-so-secret affairs with dark men. The family's class and race snobbery had caused Liz to elope with her dark-skinned husband. Although Liz's husband, Linc, is a doctor, in keeping with the Coles family tradition, his skin color marks him as an outsider. Much of the novel consists of Clark's and Corrine's family histories, traced from Reconstruction to World War II. These lengthy flashbacks, comprising more than half the novel, explain how the families acquired their money, class status, and light skin. As Susan Kenney notes, the Coles have a "family tree of many colors—copper, ebony, butternut, golden, bronze, brown, tan, rose-pink, and more." The various tales of race intermixing, both coerced and voluntary, provide a compelling history of American race relations and raise questions about what constitutes "blackness" and "whiteness."

The novel opens with preparations for Shelby's lavish wedding. With her "rose-pink skin, golden hair and dusk-blue eyes," Shelby could effortlessly "pass" as white (p. 4). When she once wandered away from the Oval during her childhood, the local white authorities were unable to find her because they insisted on looking for a "black" child, not believing the young girl they found could actually be "colored." Although Shelby could have "her pick of the best of breed in her own race," she has chosen a white man. Her fiancé, Meade, is a jazz musician, which the Ovalites consider a "frivolous occupation without office, title, or foreseeable future" (p. 4). While lightness is privileged in the Oval, so too is loyalty to one's race. The Ovalites object to Meade not just because of his whiteness but also because of his socioeconomic class and career choices. Likewise, Meade's parents object to the union and have threatened to boycott the wedding. The only person who approves of the match is Gram, Shelby's white maternal great-grandmother who lives with the family. Gram, the daughter of the wealthy southern planter Colonel Lance Shelby, was left impoverished after the Civil War. Her daughter, Josephine, sought to escape the world of genteel southern whites, clinging to memories of past glory while starving in the present, by marrying Hannibal, the son of one of the former slaves of the Xanadu plantation owned by Gram's family. Following the Great Migration, Hannibal had migrated North for a college education. When Josephine suffered a nervous breakdown after giving birth to her daughter, Corrine, Gram moved North. In addition to raising her granddaughter, Gram reluctantly acts as a sort of surrogate wife to Hannibal, helping him advance his career as a professor and later as a college president. Gram, who has lived among blacks for more than half her life, still harbors racial prejudices and hopes to be buried in a "white-only graveyard of her kith and kin" (p. 29). She refuses to hold Liz's daughter, Laurie, because she is dark-skinned. Gram believes that Shelby's union with a white man, and the white children they will produce, will finally purge the blackness from her bloodline and return her family to whiteness.

The question becomes whether or not Shelby's marriage to Meade will go off as planned. She is pressured by her family, including her father and sister, who accuses her of not giving any black men a chance. In addition, she is also subject to the advances of the dangerous player Lute McNeil, who sees marriage to Shelby as his ticket into black bourgeoisie society. He longs for status and power, which his marriages to white women have not brought him; indeed his current wife, Della, has kept the union a secret from her Beacon Hill family. When he realizes these white women don't fulfill his social-climbing desires, he physically and mentally abuses and discards them, while keeping their

offspring. Ironically, he truly loves his children, especially Tina, the middle child who longs for maternal love and seeks surrogate mothers among the women of the Oval. With Tina's story, West returns to her recurrent theme of the suffering of childhood. Lute's lease on Addie Bannister's house brings him into proximity to the black elite but not into its fold, symbolized by the fact that he is not invited to Shelby's wedding. On the eve of the wedding, Lute meets Shelby on the beach and attempts to seduce her. He plants seeds of doubt in her mind about intermarriage: "You're on the brink of turning your back on your family, your community, your race, all for some white-bread fantasy ... He's slumming, that what's he's doing. He's just looking for something exotic. Oh, he's hot for you now, but once he has had his fill of your hot black blood he'll cool, all right" (p. 222). When Lute's wife Della show up the next morning and threatens to spoil his well-laid plans, he tries to get her off the island, leading to the tragic accident that kills his beloved daughter Tina. The death of this young, mixed-race girl brings Lute's drive to acquire social position and the Ovalites's bigotry into sharp relief. In the end, Gram overcomes her prejudice and holds the dark-skinned Laurie, finally realizing, "Color was a false distinction; love was not" (p. 240).

The Wedding met with almost unanimous critical praise, bringing West the recognition that had largely eluded her throughout her career. The trade journal *Publishers Weekly* gave *The Wedding* a starred review, declaring it a triumph. Writing for the *Washington Post,* Elizabeth Benedict praises the "psychological and historic richness" of West's characters and her ability to be "wickedly eloquent about the costs of living in a world where the shadings of one's skin are more important than the bonds between blood relatives" (Yarrow, p. A29). Susan Kenney concludes in the *New York Times* that "you have only to read the first page to know that you are in the hands of a writer, pure and simple. At the end, it's as though we've been invited not so much to a wedding as to a full-scale opera, only to find that one great artist is belting out all the parts. She brings down the house." The success of *The Wedding* led Doubleday to release *The Richer, the Poorer* in the same year, a collection of some of West's best early short stories (such as "The Typewriter" and "Jack in the Pot"), columns for the *Vineyard Gazette,* and reminiscences about her family, including "Rachel" and "Fond Memories of a Black Childhood."

In February 1998, a two-part miniseries adapted from *The Wedding* aired on the ABCnetwork as part of the "Oprah Winfrey Presents" series. The influential talk show host Oprah Winfrey has long been involved with bringing the works of black women writers to the screen, and she said that she was particularly interested in producing *The Wedding* as a television movie because it "shows a world that most people have rarely seen, a world where black families are all highly educated, very successful, living in Martha's Vineyard" (Yarrow, p. A29). The film adaptation made some alterations to West's novel: Shelby, as played by Halle Berry, was no longer so light she could pass for white; Lute's violence was tempered; and Tina survived the accident. Shelby and Meade's wedding occurred on screen, while the novel ended before the wedding took place.

At West's ninetieth birthday celebration in 1997, First Lady Hillary Rodham Clinton declared her a "national treasure" (Yarrow, p. A29). West died just over a year later, on August 16, 1998, at the New England Medical Center in Boston. Several hundred mourners, including the civil rights legal scholar Lani Guinier and the artist Anna Deveare Smith, gathered at the Union Chapel in Oak Bluffs to remember the last surviving Harlem Renaissance writer. West's extraordinary career in literature and journalism spanned over seventy years. The venerable writer published in every decade from the 1920s to the 1990s, and she was working on a new book, a history of Oak Bluffs, at the time of her death. "I'm always surprised when someone tells me they've read one of my stories somewhere," West told *Ms.* magazine "I didn't know that if you wrote a story, it could last forever" (De Veaux, p. 73). Through her work, West's memory and legacy live on.

Selected Bibliography

WORKS OF DOROTHY WEST

EDITIONS

The Living Is Easy. Boston: Houghton Mifflin, 1948. Reprint, with an afterword by Adelaide Cromwell Gulliver, Old Westbury, N.Y.: Feminist Press, 1982.

The Richer, the Poorer: Stories, Sketches, Reminiscences. New York Doubleday, 1995. (With an introduction by Mary Helen Washington.)

The Wedding. New York: Doubleday, 1995. (Produced as a two-part miniseries for ABC television, *Oprah Winfrey Presents: The Wedding.* Directed by Charles Burnett. Harpo Films, 1998.)

Dorothy West's Martha's Vineyard: Stories, Essays, and Reminiscences by Dorothy West Writing in the "Vineyard Gazette." Edited by James Robert Saunders and Renae Nadine Shackelford. Jefferson, N.C.: McFarland, 2001.

Where the Wild Grape Grows: Selected Writings, 1930–1950. Edited by Verner D. Mitchell and Cynthia Davis. Amherst: University of Massachusetts Press, 2005. (Includes an introduction by the editors.)

UNCOLLECTED FICTION AND OTHER WORKS

"Papa's Place." *New York Daily News,* 8 September 1941, p. 28.

"Bessie." *New York Daily News,* 3 November 1941, p. 50.

"Mother's Love." *New York Daily News,* 21 April 1942, p. 32.

"The Puppy." *New York Daily News,* 9 May 1942, p. 24.

"A Boy in the House." *New York Daily News,* 24 August 1944, p. 6.

"Mrs. Carmody." *New York Daily News,* 15 April 1946, p. 6.

"Skippy." *New York Daily News,* 29 April 1946, p. 52.

"A Matter of Money." *New York Daily News,* 15 May 1946, p. 52.

"Wives and Women." *New York Daily News,* 7 March 1947, p. 6.

"The Letters." *New York Daily News,* 14 August 1947, p. 6.

"Made for Each Other." *New York Daily News,* 25 August 1949, p. 8.

"The Lean and the Plenty." *New York Daily News,* 6 March 1957, p. 20.

"Homecoming." *New York Daily News,* 17 April 1957, p. 8.

"Summer Setting." *New York Daily News,* 21 May 1957, p. 20.

"The Blue Room." *New York Daily News,* 28 December 1957, pp. K3, 16.

"Interlude." *New York Daily News,* 5 June 1958, p. 40.

"The Summer of Wonderful Silence." *New York Daily News,* 2 August 1958, p. B3.

"The Long Wait." *New York Daily News,* 2 November 1959, p. 8.

"A Writer's Remembrance." *Essence,* August 1995, pp. 4+.

PAPERS

Dorothy West's papers are held at the Schlesinger Library, Radcliffe Institute, Harvard University.

CRITICAL AND BIOGRAPHICAL STUDIES

Barnes, Paula C. "Dorothy West: Harlem Renaissance Writer?" In *New Voices on the Harlem Renaissance: Essays on Race, Gender, and Literary Discourse.* Edited by Australia Tarver and Paula C. Barnes. Madison, N.J.: Fairleigh Dickinson University Press, 2005. Pp. 99–124.

Bone, Robert A. *The Negro Novel in America.* (Rev. ed.) New Haven, CT: Yale Univ. Press, 1965.

Champion, Laurie. "Dorothy West (1907–1998)." In *American Women Writers, 1900–1945: A Bio-Bibliographical Critical Sourcebook.* Edited by Champion. Westport, Conn.: Greenwood, 2000. Pp. 357–362.

———. "Social Class Distinctions in Dorothy West's *The Richer, the Poorer.*" *Langston Hughes Review* 16, nos. 1–2:39–49 (1999–2001).

Daniel, Walter C. "*Challenge Magazine*: An Experiment That Failed." *College Language Association Journal* 26:494–503 (1976).

Davis, Cynthia. "The Living Ain't Easy: Signifying the American Dream." *Langston Hughes Review* 16, nos. 1–2:12–18 (1999–2001).

De Veaux, Alexis. "Bold Type: Renaissance Woman." *Ms.* May–June 1995, p. 73.

duCille, Ann. *The Coupling Convention: Sex, Text, and Tradition in Black Women's Fiction.* New York: Oxford University Press, 1993.

Ferguson, Sally H. "Dorothy West." In *Dictionary of Literary Biography: Afro-American Women.* Vol. 76. Edited by Trudier Harris and Thadious Harris. Detroit: Gale, 1988. Pp. 187–195.

Griffin, Farah Jasmine. *"Who Set You Flowin'?": The African American Migration Narrative.* New York: Oxford University Press, 1995.

Harrison, Naomi. "Dorothy West: A Bibliography." *Bulletin of Bibliography* 56, no. 4:181–187 (1999).

Hutchinson, George. *The Harlem Renaissance in Black and White.* Cambridge, Mass.: Belknap Press, Harvard University Press, 1995.

Jimoh, A. Yemisi. "Dorothy West." In *Contemporary African American Novelists: A Bio-Bibliographical Critical Sourcebook.* Edited by Emmanuel S. Nelson. Westport, Conn.: Greenwood, 1999. Pp 475–481.

Jones, Sharon L. "The Bourgeois Blues: African American Literary Aesthetics in Dorothy West's *The Living is*

Easy." *Langston Hughes Review* 16, nos. 1–2:12–18 (2001).

———. "Dorothy West: Bibliography." *Langston Hughes Review* 16, nos. 1–2:109 (1999–2001).

———. *Rereading the Harlem Renaissance: Race, Class, and Gender in the Fiction of Jessie Fauset, Zora Neale Hurston, and Dorothy West.* Westport, Conn.: Greenwood, 2002.

Kenney, Susan. "Shades of Difference." *New York Times Book Review,* February 12, 1995, sec. 7, p. 11.

Kramer, Victor A., ed. *The Harlem Renaissance Re-Examined.* New York: AMS Press, 1987.

Mitchell, Verner, and Cynthia Davis. "Dorothy West and Her Circle." In *Where the Wild Grape Grows.* Edited by Mitchell and Davis. Amherst: University of Massachusetts Press, 2005. Pp. 3–48.

Muther, Elizabeth. "The Racial Subject of Suspense in Dorothy West's *The Wedding.*" *Narrative* 7, no. 2:194–212 (1999).

Rayson, Ann. "Sexuality, Color, and Class in Dorothy West's *The Wedding.*" *Langston Hughes Review* 16, nos. 1–2:32–38 (2001).

Rodgers, Lawrence R. "Dorothy West's *The Living Is Easy* and the Ideal of Southern Folk Community." *African American Review* 26, no. 1:161–172 (1992).

———. Introduction. In *Black-Eyed Susans: Classic Stories By and About Black Women.* Garden City, N.Y.: Anchor Books, 1975. Pp. ix–xxxii.

Wilks, Jennifer. "New Women and New Negroes: Archetypal Womanhood in *The Living Is Easy.*" *African American Review* 39, no. 4:569–579 (2005).

Wright, Richard. "Blueprint for Negro Writing." In *The Portable Harlem Renaissance Reader.* Edited by David Levering Lewis. New York: Penguin, 1994. Pp. 194–205.

Yarrow, Andrew L. "Dorothy West, a Harlem Renaissance Writer, Dies at 91." *New York Times,* August 19, 1998, p. A29. (Obituary.)

INTERVIEWS

Dålsgard, Katrine. "Alive and Well and Living on the Island of Martha's Vineyard: An Interview with Dorothy West." *Langston Hughes Review* 12, no. 2:28–44 (1993).

Guinier, Genii. "Interview with Dorothy West, May 6, 1978." In *The Black Women's Oral History Project.* Vol 10. Edited by Ruth Edmonds Hill. Westport, Conn.: Meckler, 1991. Pp. 143–223.

McDowell, Deborah E. "Conversations with Dorothy West." In *The Harlem Renaissance Re-Examined.* Edited by Victor Kramer. New York: AMS, 1987. Pp. 265–282.

Mekuria, Salem. *As I Remember It: A Portrait of Dorothy West.* Videotaped interviews, directed and produced by Mekuria, 1991.

Roses, Lorraine. "Interviews with Black Women Writers: Dorothy West at Oak Bluffs, Massachusetts, July 1984." *SAGE: A Scholarly Journal on Black Women* 2, no. 1:47–49 (1985).

ROBERT WRIGLEY

(1951—)

Richard Wakefield

ROBERT WRIGLEY WAS born on February 27, 1951, to Arvil William Wrigley, a coal miner, and Betty Ann Feutsch Wrigley, a church librarian. Although he is identified with the West, especially Idaho, Wrigley spent his first eighteen years in East St. Louis, Illinois, where the economy depended on coal mining; Wrigley broke a family tradition when he chose not to work in the mines.

Drafted in 1971, during the Vietnam War, he was discharged as a conscientious objector after four months. This turning point increased his alienation from his father, a theme that informs many of his poems. In 1974 Wrigley earned his B.A. from Southern Illinois University, where he also edited the literary magazine *Sou'wester.* He then enrolled in the M.F.A. program (completed in 1976) at the University of Montana and joined the staff of the journal *CutBank.* His teachers included Madeline DeFrees and Richard Hugo.

Wrigley had married Vana Berry in 1971. They were married ten years and had a son, Philip, in 1977. By the time of his divorce Wrigley was teaching at Lewis-Clark State College in Lewiston, Idaho, where he stayed for over twenty years. In 1983 he married Kim Barnes, a noted writer of memoirs about her life in Idaho. A daughter, Jordan, was born in 1987, and a son, Jace, in 1989. In 1999 Wrigley began teaching at the University of Idaho, where he remains.

Wrigley has received many awards for his work, including an appointment as Idaho writer-in-residence, two appointments as the Richard Hugo Distinguished Poet in Residence at the University of Montana, two Pushcart Prizes, a Guggenheim Fellowship, and others. One of the most significant recognitions was for his 1999 collection *Reign of Snakes,* which won the 2000 Kingsley Tufts Poetry Award, carrying a cash prize of $50,000.

In addition to the influence of other poets, especially his teacher Richard Hugo, Wrigley cites the importance of music to his poetry. As a teenager he sang and played guitar, and his taste in music includes jazz and blues. He has said that he often listens to music while he writes.

The poem "Finding a Bible in an Abandoned Cabin," which appeared in the winter 2007 issue of *Hudson Review* (the poem is not yet collected) presents many of Wrigley's characteristics. "First comes music," Wrigley once told Sarah Kennedy, adding: "The sound of things." Note that he says things, not merely *words,* as if all language were onomatopoeic.

In this lyric, Wrigley narrates an instant of observation. He establishes nature's primacy as he stands in a ruined cabin and describes the dust on the cover of a Bible he has found as "plush as a moth's wing," a natural simile applied to a human artifact.

Although reticent about orthodox religious claims, he suggests their possibility, as if his religious beliefs are stirred but not awakened. For example, he observes that "everywhere else but this spot was sodden / beneath the roof's unraveling shingles." The Bible has been spared from the rain. By some special providence? He makes no such claim, but he feels "that back-of-the-neck lick of chill," the stirring of vestigial beliefs. He will later refer to the book as a "box," a sort of cabin within the cabin; we are invited to wonder if, just as the scrap of intact roof has protected the Bible, the Bible itself has preserved some message for him.

The book opens "like a blasted bird," something both natural and violated. If this speaker expects an omen, his simile alludes to the ancient

practice of augury by studying the entrails of birds. Inside he finds "familiar and miraculous inks." Like nature, the book is something he knows well but that still seems extraordinary, although the downward movement from "miraculous" to "inks" (instead of, say, to "words" or "verses," which would attribute miraculous power to the text itself) suggests that any miracles here are more earthly than divine.

The book has not been spared nearly as much as first appeared. In five lines of description the speaker recapitulates the book's deterioration, the return of the paper to its natural elements, beginning with those "familiar and miraculous inks" and then describing the insect-damaged pages as "filaments and dust," then as "thoroughfares of worms" and as "a silage of silverfish husks." Finally, the pages have decayed to "perfect wordless lace." As the cabin protected the book from rain, so the book has protected the vermin from predators.

The last word of the poem, "lace," perfectly describes the insect-damaged remnants. It also works a turn on the earlier figurative language, in which the book, an artifact, was described in natural terms; now, the leavings of the insects, a natural phenomenon, are described as lace, a human creation.

Given Wrigley's emphasis on "the sound of things," we note that "lace" rhymes with "grace," a word that doesn't appear in the poem but is invoked by the Bible and its (at-first) apparent preservation. In an earlier line the word "miraculous" modified not something exalted but something ordinary, "ink." Here, "wordless" is poised to be figurative, to describe an ineffable (albeit verbal) scriptural message. One would not be surprised to hear "grace" in this context, and the sound of "lace" hints at it. However, "wordless" turns out to be literal. No words remain on the damaged pages: "wordless" points toward "grace" but does not insist upon it. The line evokes a word that isn't present, just as the experience evokes beliefs that are never referred to directly.

This turn on "lace" is only one example of Wrigley's use of sound. Among many examples of alliteration and assonance, the first three words of the poem, "Under dust plush," repeat vowels and consonants in a way that is ornamental in itself but that also plays on the unspoken word "hush," as if we are being "hushed" upon entering a holy place, which the poem suggests this abandoned cabin is.

In using "Finding a Bible in an Abandoned Cabin" as an introduction to Wrigley's poetry, we should look at its form. Although Wrigley does not obey strict metrical rules, his lines tend toward traditional iambic pentameter. Many of them, in fact, have exactly ten syllables, and almost all of them have between eight and eleven. However, the accented and unaccented syllables don't necessarily alternate. Each of the first two lines can be read as having five accents, but the accented syllables are often adjacent to one another or separated by two unaccented syllables:

UNder DUST PLUSH as a MOTH'S WING,
the BOOK'S LEATHer COVer still DARKly SHONE
(*The Hudson Review,* p. 620)

Other lines have only four accents, some six. While Wrigley's metrics are more conventional than those of many contemporary poets, he certainly doesn't conform to any rigid rules. Instead, his meter vaguely echoes traditional form. Such an echo seems apt in this poem, where old teachings are present as gentle pressures on the speaker's sensibilities rather than as insistent pushes.

"Finding a Bible in an Abandoned Cabin" shows signs of having been composed with attention to how it appears on the page. Comprising twelve lines divided into two stanzas, the poem looks something like the two orthogonal objects it describes, a cabin and a Bible. Indeed, the stanza break comes midsentence, even midclause: "the book // opened." As the book opens, so does the poem, now looking like the opened covers of the book itself.

THE SINKING OF CLAY CITY

Although Robert Wrigley broke with family tradition when he didn't work in the Illinois coal mines, the experiences of that underground labor pervade many of his earlier poems. The poems in *The Sinking of Clay City* (1979), his first book,

which is dedicated to Wrigley's grandfather, a coal miner, look at the effects of mining on the miners and at the economic devastation that followed the mines' closing. The decline of the coal industry in the second quarter of the twentieth century gave Wrigley opportunities his forebears lacked, but it scarred towns and families.

The observations and sensations of a miner's life are particularly vivid because Wrigley contrasts them with the sensibility of a man enamored of open air and natural splendor. In "From Lumaghi Mine," he speaks in the voice of a miner writing to his father from within the mine, telling his experience of perpetual night. This persona is a man living Wrigley's alternative life, the one he rejected. This is the man he avoided becoming, and by casting his poem as a letter to his father he explains his own decision to pursue a different life.

The "letter" begins "Dear Father," a traditional gesture of endearment but also an acknowledgement of distance. After the salutation, four words, punctuated as a sentence, lack a verb and so are a grammatical fragment. The phrase cannot describe action, and because verbs have tense, it also cannot give the scene a temporal location—it is timeless: "Eleven days without sunlight." The sun's movement is our most primitive way of marking time, but this place cuts him off from that rhythm and thus from time itself. The lack of temporal markers feels normal, even preferable, he says, telling his father that the outside world now seems "too bright." The dim, narrow beam of the miner's headlamp illuminates the equally narrow world in which he works.

He describes the dark, circumscribed life by telling how the features underground have replaced those of the sunlit world. The "sculptures" on the walls (gouges made by the miners' tools) are now his "constellations"; the startlingly white cuticles of his hands resemble "fireflies." Descending before dawn, laboring in the dark until after sunset, he says, he has "learned how not to see."

Later he says his "eyes / are as black as anthracite"—becoming what they reflect. If he saw the sun again it would "ignite them / and they would burn for days." This last word of the poem, "days," harks back to the beginning: "Eleven days without sunlight." The burning that the sun would ignite in his eyes is the figurative heat and blaze of desire. One glimpse of the sun would make him yearn for more. He knows he cannot inhabit two worlds, one light and one dark. Writing in the persona of a man who has chosen the second, he explains why in reality he chose the first.

In the same collection, as a coda to "From Lumaghi Mine," "Coroner's Report" graphically describes the lungs of a miner's corpse. This is the fate Wrigley fled, a life and death in which the passions are squelched.

MOON IN A MASON JAR

Wrigley had been living and teaching in Idaho for two years before the publication of *The Sinking of Clay City,* but that book shows little influence of the western landscape with which he would become identified. While *Moon in a Mason Jar,* published in 1986, after he had been a resident of Idaho for almost a decade, continues to look back to Wrigley's earlier life, it also relishes the Idaho landscape. (There had also been a 1982 chapbook, *The Glow,* from which many poems are carried over into *Moon in a Mason Jar.*)

However, the long poem "Moonlight: Chickens on a Road" veers far from the West to recount the aftermath of a fatal car accident in the Ozarks. On a winding mountain road, an automobile and a farm truck have collided on an early November evening. The only survivor is a boy who has suffered a broken arm but has extricated himself from the wreckage where his family remains "knotted in the snarl of metal and glass." He sees that his mother's hair has been "set free of its pincurls."

He gazes upon the farmer who was driving the truck, "looking dead, half in / and half out of his windshield." The live chickens that were crated in the truck are also loosed from the wreckage. Stunned, the boy walks in circles barefoot through the broken glass, and gradually the chickens begin to follow him, "as though they believed / me some savior." It is an absurd

scene, a sardonic joke: As the boy goes "ambling barefoot through the jeweled debris" he is "towing a cloud around a scene / of death."

The last lines transcend the absurdity, or translate it into a profound realization. The boy and the chickens are enacting a primal urge. As they circle they are

> coming round and round
> like a dream, or a mountain road,
> like a pincurl, like pulse, like life.
>
> (*Earthly Meditations,* p. 37)

The bizarre procession connects all the pieces of the event—the boy, the minute detail of his mother's curls, the animals, the place. This stunning vision of harmony in apparent chaos is a hallmark of Wrigley's work.

Moon in a Mason Jar also includes poems that reflect Wrigley's fascination with music. "Torch Songs" celebrates the sultry, sexually charged music that he likens to "the paths we followed / into the sexual forest, the witch's spellbound cabin." If "sexual forest" seems too insistent, the metaphor of the witch's cabin evokes the vague sexuality of fairy tales and the seductive nature of this music he calls "the plod of the human heart."

"Star Dust," taking its name from a familiar song by Hoagy Carmichael (although the song title is usually printed as one word, "Stardust"), describes a man listening alone to "Dorsey and Sinatra on the phonograph," feeling "melancholy, a nameless / yearning." His yearning, however, is not for a lost romance like the one in the song, but for the love his parents shared

> years ago,
> huddled on the old Ford's hood, wrapped
> in a woolen blanket
>
> (*Earthly Meditations,* p. 42)

He longs for the past, when such love was possible and music like the song he is listening to "rang the perfect omen."

The poem shifts between perfect and slant rhymes, as if the man wants to express his reverie in the rhymed lyrics of a song but cannot do so consistently. The opening line plays off the clichés of Tin Pan Alley: "That crooning they spooned for, all the moons in June." And the rhymes sometimes seem to lead the man's thoughts as much as they reflect them. At one point, for example, the word "know" at the end of a line suggests the rhyme "ago," and that word evoking the past turns him more forcefully toward the memories, imagined or real, of his parents' love.

In titling his poem with a variation on the song title—"Star Dust" instead of "Stardust"—Wrigley may intend a shift of emphasis. The song title puts the accent on the first syllable, "star," while the poem title makes them nearly equal (in metrical terms, a spondee). Dust is given sonic weight equal to that of the star. As in "Finding a Bible in an Abandoned Cabin," in which the transcendent message of the holy text weighed equally with the insect-damaged paper, in "Star Dust" the high and low points of human experience are closely linked.

The major poem in *Moon in a Mason Jar* is "The Glow," originally published in a chapbook. The long narrative describes a beehive that dominates an old elm tree in a school playground: "even the woodpecker," we are told,

> flew away wild in swoops
> from the dark swarm
> the hive hauled out to halt him.
>
> (*Earthly Meditations,* p. 46)

The children, of course, have learned not to approach at all, and their exclamations can be heard in the "aw-aw" assonance of "hauled ... halt."

When the intense rain shatters classroom windows, the children are gathered in the cafeteria, but one boy sneaks out to check on the hive. He lives near enough the school to have observed the growth of the hive, so close that his "bedroom window caught every morning / the bees' first early dronings." As he approaches, the trunk breaks and the tree crashes around him "like a prehistoric bird." But instead of being crushed, he is

> suddenly swaddled in tree.
> All around him leaves and branches
> closed in.
>
> (*Earthly Meditations,* pp. 49–50)

The hive splashes him with honey and comb fragments, "gold and pearl all across him," in addition to his cuts from the twigs and branches.

Dazed, he wanders inside. No one has noticed his absence until he enters, drenched from the rain and "his face a smear of small bleeding cuts / and drops of honey." In the stunned faces of the students and teachers, the boy senses that they see something more than merely the battered survivor of a mishap, and that sensation persists long after:

> he will feel the glow of gold
> they have seen around him, hear the whirr
> they heard that day, as bees
> came to life in his matted hair.
>
> (*Earthly Meditations,* p. 51)

There are many beautiful sonic effects throughout this poem, as in all of Wrigley's writing, including the alliteration and assonance in those lines quoted above: "feel" and "seen"; "hear," "whirr," "heard," and "hair." The lines, arranged into twenty nine-line stanzas, tend to be short and without metrical regularity, rarely more than ten syllables and sometimes as few as four or five, giving the narrative strong momentum. The urgency of the boy's desire to check on the beehive is conveyed partly through these shorter lines, and the frequent enjambments likewise lead the reader rapidly from line to line and stanza to stanza. Here, for example, the boy sees the others staring at him:

> peering up at the miracle of him,
> not knowing whether
> the look in his eyes
> was terror or the transfix
> of high wind and venom.
>
> (*Earthly Meditations,* p. 51)

The middle three of these five lines have no end stops, and the line breaks are placed within grammatical units, as between a subject and verb ("look ... / was terror") or between a noun and a prepositional phrase ("the transfix / of high wind and venom"). With no place for the eye to rest, the lines urge the reader rapidly forward.

The poem hints that the people staring at the boy are witnessing a miracle, not merely his survival, but his changed sense of himself. Wrigley uses religious allusions to suggest the power of the transformation. His new sense of himself "will not go away / for years and years // of his life," and he is "someone partly other / than human"; he is "as chosen and blessed as any survivor." The "glow of gold" is nothing less than a halo; he is wet, as if baptized. Now "partly other / than human," he is elevated, like someone newly baptized.

There are subtle parallels between "The Glow" and "Moonlight: Chickens on the Road." Each is about a boy transformed by an accident. Each reassembles the fragments of a catastrophe into something transcendent. Like "Finding a Bible in an Abandoned Cabin," both find higher truth by scrutinizing something natural (the chickens, the bees and their honey) and close at hand. And they also, like many of Wrigley's poems, refuse to name the higher truth, instead letting the story convey it, ineffable but accessible through the senses.

With one exception, these features appear in "The Owl," also from *Moon in a Mason Jar.* In this poem, the speaker names the transcendent truth that he experiences, even if the circumstances rob the name of some of its certainty. Late at night a boy sits amidst "the musky aroma" of the family outhouse, when through "the door's / slim crack" he sees an owl swoop across the yard. "I knew it was God," he says, as "it flew across / the still world, silent as a star." Then with "a flash / of talon" it descends and seizes the boy's year-old cat. He runs inside and lies awake in fear.

Now a grown man, he thinks of how far his childhood world is from the one in which his own children live, and even now, he says, "I lie in my bed and listen, remembering." He doesn't disavow his childish conviction that the owl was God, but neither does he reassert it in the present tense.

"Since that day," he says, he has wondered how the three pieces came together: the boy in the outhouse, the cat, the owl. It suggests the trinity, although he doesn't explicitly say so and it doesn't map tidily onto the Christian Trinity. However, when he describes the owl's flight as

"winging effortless as breath," the simile alludes to "spirit," the Latin word for breath, identified with one part of the Trinity and with the vital force with which God animates Adam in the biblical book of Genesis.

Other literary allusions work here as well. Robert Frost's "Design," in which a man sees an albino spider capture a white moth that has settled on a white flower, ends with a series of questions as the speaker wonders what brought the three together, concluding in favor (but only slightly so) of a design by a force he names only "darkness." Like Frost's speaker, Wrigley's narrator wonders about the coincidence, if such it is, that brought together the three actors in this drama. As a boy, he says, he "knew just enough of darkness / and nightsounds" to know the owl was God; as a man he has only the recollection of that knowledge. Now he has a dream that takes him "away on great white wingbeats, / regular as moonrise, nightly as letting go." Sleep, death, and transcendence are associated through his experience, but their precise relation is left unresolved.

WHAT MY FATHER BELIEVED

The title poem of Wrigley's 1991 collection *What My Father Believed,* published the year he turned forty, speaks from the complicated multiple perspectives of a man looking ahead to middle age and back at youth. As a teacher, he also looks at the students from whom he finds himself as alienated as his father felt from him.

Written in slant rhyme ("things" is rhymed with "killing," for example, and "gone" with "along") and in lines that tend toward five accents but that vary from three to six, "What My Father Believed" acknowledges the rules of formal verse without strictly obeying them. It is as if his recollection of his father organizes itself in ways reminiscent of old rules, recognizing but not obeying his father's stricter code. In fact, as he remembers himself at the age of twenty arguing with his father about the Vietnam War, he also remembers his father's breach of decorum as he, the father, in frustration "muttered" the word "fuck," the first time the son heard him say it. Twenty years later, with this deft and understated use of poetic form, the narrator hints that he is a little more amenable to the broader rules that he rejected when he was "a fool of twenty."

The first line of the poem presents striking ambiguities that convey the narrator's ambivalence: "Man of his age, he believed in the things / built by men." Because there is no article before "Man," this is not *a* man we're being told of, but rather the generic "Man." The lack of an article also promotes the word to first position and thus to being capitalized, as it often is when used generically. In addition, "his age" can mean the father's chronological age, presumably not far from the narrator's age; it can also mean the cultural era that shaped him. In this sense, too, the narrator is like his father, not only of a certain chronological age but also the product of his times.

The poet also observes his students, who respond to stories of his "father's...faith" with "boredom / and blankness." The beliefs that the young man rebelled against don't ignite a flicker of interest in the today's youth. Part of the problem seems to be that "the truth / I was so eager to embrace is constantly told"—presumably the "truth" about the Vietnam War—and so is not controversial to the twenty-year-olds of 1991. The teacher finds that his students "scold / us both as naïve and thoughtless." The poem ends, "My father believed in the nation, I in my father, / a man of whom those students had not the slightest notion." The internal slant rhyme of "nation" and "notion" mimics the slippage from old beliefs, as something as substantial as a "nation" becomes as evanescent as a "notion."

Much of "What My Father Believed" is autobiographical. At forty, Wrigley was teaching at a college in Idaho; at twenty, after having been drafted into the army during the Vietnam War, he applied for and finally received conscientious objector status and was discharged after less than a year. Wrigley tells the story of this episode in the poem "C.O.," included in the same collection, where he writes, "I was twenty years old and could not tell / if I was a coward or a man of conviction."

Two important literary influences inform "What My Father Believed" as well. Richard Hugo, a poet and teacher who "had an enormous effect" on Wrigley (as he told Sarah Kennedy), had served as a bombardier in the army air force during World War II, having enlisted for what Hugo himself, in his autobiography *The Real West Marginal Way* (New York: Norton, 1986), called "the cheapest kind of personal romantic reasons" and then discovering himself, before each mission, crippled with "panic in my belly [that] was physiologically real." Similarly, James Dickey, whom Wrigley credits with teaching him "how to loop the story through the lens of the language" (quoted in Kennedy) also served in World War II and often wrote about it. There is no record that either Hugo or Dickey concerned himself with Wrigley's earlier abortive military career, but each was also a "Man of his age" to whom the middle-aged Wrigley needs to explain himself.

"His Father's Whistle," another poem in *What My Father Believed,* expresses a longing for reassurance, predictability. A boy lies awake listening for the sounds of his father coming home, especially "his father's whistle among night sounds." The boy is afraid of the dark and "of all / he did not know," but with the sound of his father's whistle "there would come an order / like the one a melody imposed upon silence."

A poem, too, imposes an order upon silence. Rhyme and meter satisfy some of the need for the reassurance of pattern. But even though that need persists into adulthood, the grown-up cannot rest quite so comfortably. The adult still longs for the old order that once comforted him, but he can no longer accept it uncritically. In his growth from the child lying awake in the dark to the man writing a poem, he cannot gloss over his rebellion against his "father's faith," as he put it in "What My Father Believed." Hence his poetry echoes old rules but does not strictly obey them.

Among the most striking examples of Wrigley's adapting of old forms to new uses in this collection is "Ravens at Deer Creek." A man out skiing sees ravens "circle and swoop" above some trees where, he surmises, there must be something dead. "In the mountains / in winter, it's true: death is a joyful flame," he says, and he contemplates how these birds, perhaps the very ones to which he has given bread crumbs outside his window, would keep watch and await his death if he were injured out here.

The poem begins with unobtrusive sound repetitions: the alliteration of the terminal words of lines one and three, "fir" and "others," and of lines two and four, "swoop" and "scraps." The repeated sounds in lines five through eight are just as subtle: "mountains" / "celebration," "flame" / "come." But thereafter many of the rhymes are perfect: "birds" / "words," "hot" / "not," "night" / "white," and so on, up until the last rhyme pair, "wise" and "eyes." Having described the birds as expressing "pure celebration" with their "caws and cartwheels," he mimics their sounds, especially with the repeated gutturals. As his end rhymes move from slant to perfect, the sound grows more insistent, as if he is approaching the ravens (or they him). Where the first few lines end with sounds befitting the quiet of the winter setting, with the birds still at a distance, by the poem's end the birds are very close and very loud: they will approach his dying form, he says, like

> angels down Jacob's ladder, wise
> to the moon, and waiting for me, simple as sin,
> that they may know the delicacy of my eyes.
>
> (*Earthly Meditations,* p. 77)

The sardonic play on "delicacy" is a masterful stroke that is only preparation for the way Wrigley emphasizes the key word, "eyes," at the very conclusion and gives it even more weight by pairing it with a perfect rhyme.

This use of form is all in the service of the poem's larger purpose. Among the many ways Wrigley accomplishes this is his reference to Jacob's ladder, which in Genesis 28:12 is a stairway on which the sleeping Jacob sees God's messengers ascending and descending. Wrigley's use of the image here is a characteristic trope. These messengers are not literal "angels," but rather ravens. As in so many of his poems, Wrigley combines traditional religious imagery with features of the natural world, especially of the woods and mountains of Idaho.

In "Finding a Bible in an Abandoned Cabin," insects rewrote the Bible into the language of nature; here, ravens descend Jacob's ladder to bring a message. That message is not translatable into ordinary speech, but it means that this man, like all creatures, is part of the natural world, ultimately to be consumed by it, and yet may be fulfilled by that condition rather than reduced by it. In Robert Frost's poem "The Most of It," a man observes something swimming across a lake toward him and prepares himself for some message. What finally appears is a moose that shakes the water off itself and then disappears into the trees. "And that was all," Frost's poem concludes, leaving the speaker (and the reader) to ponder whether "all" means "a little" or "everything." In "Ravens at Deer Creek," the birds bring a similar ambiguous message.

IN THE BANK OF BEAUTIFUL SINS

Two poems in the 1995 collection *In the Bank of Beautiful Sins* offer particularly clear examples of Wrigley's characteristic ways of combining the sacred and the worldly. "A Cappella" (the title is Italian for "in the style of the church" and in music nomenclature designates a song sung without instrumental accompaniment) is a long narrative about a boy who sings in Sunday school choir and discovers a passage to the church attic, where he can look down at the congregation, "the righteous and the wretched," and where he also has access to the pipes for the church organ. One Easter Sunday, as a prank to deflate the pompous hellfire preacher, he rearranges the pipes (which will cause the organ keys to sound the wrong notes) and then, undetected, rushes back to join the choir as it processes into the sanctuary.

The person most grievously injured by the prank, however, is the organist, Lucius Hart, "aging, kindly, / effeminate," who goes "apoplectic / at the first chord" and runs to investigate. The boy wonders if the preacher will "blame the Jews or the Catholics" for "the debacle," but in the event he

> only stood
> at the pulpit, his head to one side,
> chin slightly up. He looked like Jesus.
>
> (*Earthly Meditations*, p. 91)

After the "wave of chatter" of the congregation quiets, he closes his eyes and sings "of God, / from Whom all blessings flowed." The choir and the congregation join in the a cappella hymn. The effect is so powerful that "even those of us who had vowed / never to give in, gave in," believing at least for the moment in "real wings." Later, the boy suspects that the preacher knows who committed the sabotage, but he is never upbraided or even accused.

The prank disrupts the service, but it has the ironic effect of revivifying the message the service was intended to convey, and forgiveness—the preacher's forgiveness of the vandal—is by no means the least part of that message. The preacher even tells the boy that his "gift" is "music," although he had earlier thought that the boy might someday be a preacher himself. It's a wonderfully ironic observation that this boy who tried to ruin the music of the Easter service decides he will "find another way to make [his] peace with music." Poetry is that way.

"About Language" also traces an unexpected turn by which something sacred arises from an unlikely source, in this case, something literally profane. In this poem, the narrator's three-year-old daughter has learned to "mimic" her father's words of "adult exasperation," his profanity. The poem begins with her imitation of a complaint she has heard from him: "Damn the rain anyway." The narrator's wife has "warned [him] about language." Overhearing the child, she directs a look of disapproval at him.

The poem is set in western Oregon, where "the rain / blows endlessly in from the sea," so there is plenty of opportunity for the child to hear her father's imprecations about the weather. Their only recreation on this rainy day is for the little girl to play in the garage while her father works on the family car—a task that provides more opportunity for the child to hear intemperate language as his wrench slips and he bloodies his knuckles. What stop him this time are his daughter's questions. She asks the name of each tool as she holds it toward him. Four lines comprise nothing but the names of tools:

Standard screwdriver, sparkplug socket,
diagonals, crimper, clamp, ratchet, torque wrench,
deep throw 12-millimeter socket, crescent,
point gauge, black tape, rasp—

(*Earthly Meditations,* p. 94)

These lines are a bravura performance. The names of the tools are pure sound, full of alliteration, assonance, and rhythm; the sequence ends (as Wrigley tells Kennedy) with "strong, single syllables." Presented for his daughter's delectation, the words become music. They are at the same time pure "things," each sound representing a real object that the little girl can hold. The words are "the sound of things" to which Wrigley referred in his *Poetry Daily* interview.

These words that are celebrated as pure sound and yet remain inextricably connected to mundane "things" are the prelude to the poem's conclusion about language. The inventory of the tool kit is interrupted by the honking of Canada geese. "I pick her up and rush out, pointing, / headed for the pasture and the clearest view," he says, and they are in time to see the geese "rising from the lake, through rain / and the shambles of late morning fog." As they watch "vee after vee of calling Canadas," he gives her another word, telling her, "they're geese." The little girl's words end the poem: "She says bye-bye geese; she says wow; she says Jesus."

Like the boy in "The Owl," from *Moon in a Mason Jar,* the girl has found the word to embody this transcendent moment. Her awe turns the profanity she learned from her father back to its original purpose, an expression of awe, a holy word. This is perhaps the signature trope of Wrigley's most powerful writing, as in "Finding a Bible in an Abandoned Cabin." "About Language" is about how in language we sometimes find, even stumble upon, the link between our inner world to the wonders outside. Just as the birds take flight, so does language.

In "The Bramble," a poem about (among other things) finding two human skeletons in an old car that has been overgrown with brambles, Wrigley makes a similar turn. The brambles are many things in this poem, but in the first line they are a "cathedral of thorns." As the speaker pushes through them, he says,

My arms are crosshatched with scratches
and purpled by juice, my back flayed
like a flagellant's

(*Earthly Meditations,* p. 95)

It may be too ingenious to see the crosshatching as an allusion to the Christian cross and the purple juice to the wine of the Eucharist, but there is no confusion about the imagery of the cathedral and the flagellant (one who inflicts suffering upon himself out of religious conviction). Although the speaker's discovery of the skeletons is the dominant scene, Wrigley again connects the sensual world of nature with the transcendent world of spirit. Like Emily Dickinson in her famous poem "Some keep the Sabbath going to Church" (number 324 in the editor Thomas H. Johnson's numbering), Wrigley reinterprets Christian conventions into a religion of nature.

"Poetry" explores the mysterious and intensely physical forces of love and sex, but here too Wrigley acknowledges a spiritual dimension. As he longs for his wife, both emotionally and physically, he says,

I'd pledge myself
to Jesus to see the light on her face
that I might generate inside her.

(*Earthly Meditations,* p. 104)

The line break after "myself" suggests the slightest pause as the speaker gropes for a commitment proportionate to his desire, and of course in traditional Christian belief there is no greater commitment than to Christ. In a poem about love and sex, the phrase "generate inside her" takes multiple meanings: he imagines that his presence might create in her the same intense emotional response that he feels to her; he also imagines the physical act of love, literally "inside her," and he finds in the word "generate" the literal root "gener-," from the Latin for "descent" and "birth," also the source of the title of the first book of the Hebrew Bible, Genesis.

The phrase is an example of Wrigley's use of what may be termed mixed diction, of words from seemingly disparate language registers. In "Poetry" as in most of his poetry, Wrigley chooses his words predominantly from the vocabulary for the physical world, hence largely

from words with Anglo-Saxon roots: "crows," "bees," "wind." But he frequently moves beyond the word horde of early English and uses words of Latin, French, or Greek origin, almost always as a signal of another level of significance. His turns from earth to spirit are reflected in these changes of register.

REIGN OF SNAKES

The long title poem from Wrigley's 1999 collection, *Reign of Snakes,* comprises nine sections, each given its own title: "Revival," "Confession," "The Fall," "Catechism," "Fellowship," "Deliverance," "Glossolalia," "Paradise," and "Resurrection." As the titles indicate, the poem explores the powerful and familiar imagery of the snake, but not abstractly. Instead, each part relates an experience that ramifies into an unstated theme, all nine of them finally intertwining like the "fist of snakes as big as man" that he describes in "Revival." The knot of wintering reptiles, immersed in "approximate sleep," seems to uncoil as the poem itself uncoils.

In "Revival" a man on a long automobile journey stops at a revival meeting. Tired, he means only to take advantage of the free iced tea the revivalists offer. But as he prepares to leave, having sat through the hymns led by the "graying, hortatory praisemaster" and the condemnatory sermon of the praisemaster's "stern wife," he stops, fascinated by the sight of their "pale, thin son" who holds a live rattlesnake above his head and dances; with his eyes "sublimely closed," he prepares to kiss the head of the snake.

The rest of "Reign of Snakes" is a series of recollections that each touch, albeit indirectly, on this scene. The speaker recalls himself, much younger, killing a corn snake with a rake, then later episodes in which he "hacked rattlesnakes to bloody hunks." He remembers his grandfather's pointing to a blacksnake "high on the scaly bark / of a cemetery silver maple," a sign, his grandfather tells him, "of evil buried near."

In the third section, "The Fall," the poet wonders at the seeming ubiquity of snakes, both imagery and real. "Why snakes? Always snakes?" he asks, and the next scene is a pool hall and tattoo parlor described in reptilian imagery: "that long narrow room, nearly dark," into which "phosphorescent fixtures [are] shedding / a skin of light."

The name of the place, appropriately, is "Snake's Uptown Pool Hall and Tattoo Parlor," and the eponymous proprietor bears elaborate tattoos that he displays as he sits behind the counter "naked to the waist." He is marked with

> a cathedral expanse of tattoos: twenty or more
> curvaceous women wearing nothing
> but strategically placed snakes.
>
> (*Earthly Meditations,* p. 113)

The speaker's age isn't specified, but he is young enough to depend on a bicycle for transportation and to be buying "a Slim Jim, a soda"—early adolescence. Staring at the man's art work, his fascination makes the boy snakelike himself: He imagines how his own "pupils must have loomed above my lips" and he reports that he "could not stop making" a "hiss." When Snake breaks the spell by asking, "You like my serpents, boy?" the boy flees and hears the man's laughter behind him.

"The Fall" recapitulates the traditional biblical fall. Sex and snakes recall chapter 3 of Genesis, where a snake (or serpent) tempts Adam and Eve, leading to their exile from Eden. Theologians debate whether the specific temptation, to eat the forbidden fruit, represents the discovery of sexuality, but that common interpretation is supported by Adam and Eve's sudden shame in their nakedness.

The boy's shame sends him running not merely from the "long narrow room" but from his earlier, innocent self. Whatever Eden of youthful simplicity he inhabited, it is as lost as the garden from which Adam and Eve were exiled.

The title of the next section, "Catechism," denotes a formalized series of questions and answers on religious doctrine (especially Catholic doctrine). The poem begins with the words of "Giuseppe 'Big Joe' Truccano," a small-time hoodlum, who tells the narrator, "You want to

taste what's good, you got to lick / what's evil." Big Joe lords his wealth and privilege over the speaker and the "half dozen jittery alcoholics" haunting a bar on a Sunday morning. The sound of "dueling church bells" fills the air, an ironic accompaniment to this scene of degradation and ill-gotten wealth. But the real lesson is not the wisdom of Big Joe's words.

Rather, we see Big Joe, despite his claim that "every week I go down / on my knees and do the penance / the sin-shifter says I should," come to a horrific end foreshadowed by his hissing sibilants of "sin-shifter says I should." Big Joe's body is found "armless, legless, / battered, even the genitals gone," identifiable only by his treasured St. Christopher medal that has been partly "melted / under a blowtorch blast." Divested of all appendages, he is now snakelike. In a final allusion to the Eden story, we learn that the corpse was found "in the tall grass / of some abandoned orchard, beneath a barren tree."

The title of part seven, "Glossolalia," is the technical term for the phenomenon commonly called "speaking in tongues." This is an unintelligible language spoken under the influence of the Holy Spirit, according to some churches. Likewise, in this section, long and seemingly nonsensical sequences of words form serpentine lines that flow without caesuras or stops until the periods that conclude each of the three stanzas.

As the lines mimic writhing serpents, the words evoke a dizzying array of elongated or slithery objects. Some also refer to other sections of the poem, for example, "Rake ravaged hoed up buried in air / and blasphemed blackberry transits"—an echo of the beginning of section two, "Confession," where the poet recalls that "As a boy I flogged a corn snake to death / with the limber end of a leaf rake" and that he has since "hacked rattlesnakes to bloody hunks." Here, those "bloody hunks" reassemble into nightmare scenes. The poem itself is as involuted, as tangled as the writhing masses of snakes.

The sinuous lines, however, are really neither nonsense nor nightmare. The repeated images suggest that beyond logic and grammar lies an identity of snake, tongue, phallus, blackberry vine—and the poetic line itself. As in "Finding a Bible in an Abandoned Cabin," these earthly objects become transcendent: "speed of blood needy foil and oil / slick agent of doom snake man mask of God." The chthonic lines twist and contort into an image of divinity.

Fittingly for a poem incorporating so much religious imagery and experience, "Reign of Snakes" concludes with a section titled "Resurrection." Although this resurrection is manifestly earthly, the separation of earthiness and holiness is called into question.

"Resurrection" opens with a description of a canyon in summer, where the ancient lava flows cooled into "caves and gaps, subterranean chambers," ideal habitat for "field mice and shrews, pack rats / and meadow voles" However, the creatures for which the place is best are snakes, and for the very reason that it suits shrews and rats so well. This Eden for small mammals has a serpent—it is, ironically, the serpent's Eden.

The scene shifts to winter, the snakes and prey stilled by cold. Now, because the snow eases travel across the broken terrain, the canyon is more hospitable to human beings. Only "snow-hidden trip wires— / fallen fences, a blackberry's creeping vines" impede the narrator. In the context of the longer poem of which this section is a part, however, those wires and vines have an ominous familiarity: like the coiling, snake-like objects in "Glossolalia," they trip the speaker out of complacency.

Undeterred by metaphorical snakes, he is instead stopped by a real one that seems

> fabulous, a sweet trick of fate,
> a frigid day in February and a full-grown rattlesnake
> curled into a comma in the middle of the just plowed
> road.
>
> (*Earthly Meditations,* p. 121)

Doubting his own eyes, he thinks of what else it might be: "Ice-ghost," he muses, or perhaps a "curve of rock / or stubbed-off branch." Picking it up, he says, "I cannot / believe my eyes, my hands." This poet with snakes so much on his mind isn't prepared for a real snake in such an unlikely setting. As in all the best poetry, however, imagination and reality meld together.

He takes the snake home and puts it in a burlap bag that he sets on the hearth. Relaxing with a cup of tea and a cigar, he watches as his dog and cats investigate the awakening creature in the bag; they leap in alarm as it rouses and sounds its "dim clack-clack." This section and the entire sequence conclude,

Call it Sunday, a day of rest.
I blow a huge, undulant ring of smoke
and wait.

(*Earthly Meditations,* p. 122)

In this microcosm of creation, the poet is God contemplating His work. It is not farfetched to hear an allusion to Genesis 2:2, where God rests after his six days labor; the "undulant ring of smoke" also obliquely recalls the Gospel of John: "In the beginning was the word." The "ring of smoke" is like a coiled snake and is also a "word" breathed into the world by the creator.

Carried over from *Reign of Snakes* and providing the title for Wrigley's volume of new and selected poems, "Earthly Meditations" is divided into five titled sections, each subdivided into three numbered parts. The poem is rich in literary tradition and also in particularized experience.

Meditations as a literary form extend back at least to Marcus Aurelius in the second century C.E., the last major Stoic philosopher, whose *Meditations* contemplate the order of the natural world and man's relationship to it. In the New World, the Puritan poet Anne Bradstreet wrote a series of meditations celebrating nature primarily as evidence and expression of divine providence.

The traditional motif is deductive: the writer begins with philosophical or theological principles and then ponders the way those principles are embodied in nature. Wrigley, however, qualifying his meditations with the word "earthly," works in the other direction, inductively, from particulars to principles. Yet his division of each major section into three subsections mimics the traditional structure of sermons, which often begin with an explication of a Bible passage, move to analysis of its themes, and conclude with a discussion of how those themes applied to daily life. Of course, Wrigley's scripture is nature itself.

The first section, "The Afterlife," opens with an image of loss: "Spring, and the first full crop of dandelions gone / to smoke." This borrows from the tradition of *ubi sunt* (derived from the Latin for the first words of the phrase "Where are they now, those who went before us?"). Wrigley reads the image of transience like a scripture passage foretelling his own fate.

I would enter the sky through the soil
myself, sing up the snail bowers
and go on the lam with the roots

(*Earthly Meditations,* p. 135)

he says, expressing a desire distinct from Anne Bradstreet's yearning for Christian resurrection and much closer to Walt Whitman's declaration at the conclusion of "Song of Myself," where Whitman says, "I bequeath myself to the dirt to grow from the grass I love." The "sky" that Wrigley would "enter" is not Bradstreet's heaven, but rather Whitman's literal sky into which the dandelion seeds have dispersed.

Later in the same section the poet shifts his attention to a river, but still in the *ubi sunt* mood. Marcus Aurelius wrote that "time is a river of passing events, and strong is its current; no sooner is a thing brought to sight than it is swept by and another takes its place, and this too will be swept away." Eschewing such abstraction, Wrigley makes a similar observation that is all the stronger for its specificity: "Where the river will be next week, / a puddle two trout go savagely dying in." His gospel is earthly: "Notice the bland, Darwinian sand," he writes, "bone wrack / and tree skin."

When he recounts a dream in which he heard "a lowly chirruped chorus / of amens," the line break mimics the speaker's hesitation as he ponders the metaphor that will convey his reverence for the sounds of nature. These ordinary sounds are "lowly," yet holy. The heartbeat of hesitation at the line break is the moment in which he resolves to identify earth with heaven. In the second subsection of this first part of the poem (as revised for his 2006 volume *Earthly Meditations*), he sees himself as Siddhartha (the

given name of Buddha) seeking wisdom as he sits by a river, as Buddha is said to have done. The wisdom Wrigley finds is physical, natural, like the sound of the "chorus," but translated into divinity.

Still, he tells us, he was only "*near* believing" (italics added) that

> we are angels,
> blue muck engenders a heaven,
> this rush toward oblivion is the afterlife of all.
>
> (*Earthly Meditations*, p. 136)

The qualifier, "near," works in two ways. He may be unable to believe completely; he may, on the other hand, be physically near the site where belief is possible. The participle "believing" then asserts that belief is a process analogous to the river's flow, something unfolding continuously, unstoppable.

Through the next three major sections of the poem as published in his 2006 volume, Wrigley continues to compose a paean, a hymn to nature, out of language from the disparate registers of science and religion. In the last part of the third section ("Meditation at Bedrock Canyon") he even ponders the distance of his own speech (or song) from that of the world he observes, asking,

> What language speaks
> that widowed cow across the way,
> mouthing down the last supple bloom in sight?
>
> (*Earthly Meditations*, p. 143)

He may be asking what "language" the cow speaks, oblivious yet intimately a part of nature, but he is also asking what language can adequately describe the creature, preserve her, or even call her into existence, as Christian doctrine claims the words of God created the world and the words of Adam named it.

Seeking language to create the natural world seems grandiose, even hubristic. But the concluding meditation, "The Name," represents the speaker as a literal creator not merely of words but of life (or as a cocreator). "The Name" begins with a dizzying change of scene from a wide perspective on the natural world to a sharply delineated glimpse of a child *in utero* seen through an ultrasound. This too is a vision of nature, but a nature normally hidden. He sees "a heart speck / flickering in the ultrasound." He invents language for the revealed tissues, including those of the fetus itself and of the womb in which it is embedded: "the smear of flesh, swirl of home." "Home" is an apt and unexpected locution for *womb* and is even a slant rhyme for it.

> Ignition, parturition, pairs of arms and eyes,
> all that delicate, permeable skin. You're in,
> and that's the sin. All the rest is dying.
>
> (*Earthly Meditations*, p. 147)

The language has shimmered with multiplicity, the words interconnected by sound and connotation as much as by logic or denotation. Now, that complexity ascends to even higher sonic richness:

The rhyme of "ignition" and "parturition" evokes the traditional association of fire and life, and the word "sin" sonically combines "skin" and "in." These words within words mirror the interiority of the fetus in the womb.

The last clause, "All the rest is dying," may be a claim that everything not in the process of coming into life is inevitably leaving it. It may play on the multiple meanings of "rest," claiming that to be passive is to slide toward death.

"Earthly Meditations" concludes with the child's birth. The crying infant is addressed as "tiny fossicker"—in Australian slang, a "fossicker" is someone who seeks gems in detritus. The poem offers no formal name for the child; this nickname predicts for the child a lifetime enterprise like his father's, a quest for what is precious in the places to which others are oblivious. Fittingly for a poem that is about the complexity of natural connections, the newborn child lies at both culmination of one search (his father's) and the beginning of another (his own).

The poem ends with the image of the delicate, vulnerable spot on the child's head where the skull bones have not yet fused, "the fontanel springs" where the pulse is visible. "All the worlds revolve in your name," the poet declares, "the word at last we all are known by." That "word," notwithstanding the "tiny fossicker" a few lines earlier, remains unsaid. And yet it has been implied throughout the five sections and

fifteen subsections of the poems: the child's name is this array of interconnecting, overlaid images. "Earthly Meditations" is Wrigley's *tour de force* treatise on the mysterious power of language to create an identity between our selves and the world outside ourselves.

LIVES OF THE ANIMALS

Although the 2003 collection *Lives of the Animals* speaks in a variety of tones, it continues Wrigley's major themes and emphasizes one that has previously been one among many. Especially prominent here is mutability, in particular the changes associated with age and death. Several poems dwell on the speaker's awareness of his advancing age. His vision seems drawn more strongly than before to images of decay. But the sense of redemption not *from* but *through* nature remains as strong as ever. We continue to see traditional religious language and imagery brought into harmony with the natural world at the same time that the speaker discovers or explores his own harmony with nature.

"The Church of Omnivorous Light" works a turn on the almost universal association of light with spiritual development; indeed, "enlightenment" so often denotes religious awakening that we can forget that it is a metaphor. But the modifier, "omnivorous," suggests a light that is aggressive, all-consuming, and perhaps sinister. By revealing a scene emblematic of his own inevitable fate, this light will consume any chance the speaker may have had to maintain bland optimism.

The poem begins with a scene reminiscent of the opening of "Ravens at Deer Creek," from the 1991 collection *What My Father Believed.* The commotion of birds over a dead animal has drawn the narrator's attention, but whereas in the earlier poem he focused on the birds and left the dead animal offstage, so to speak, in "The Church of Omnivorous Light" the illumination includes the corpse. It is a deer that has been "gutted out" by a hunter, and by depicting only one part in detail, "the severed esophagus," Wrigley uses synecdoche to imply the rest. In a poem weighted with figurative language, even this one brutally realistic detail is rendered in terms of something seemingly far distant: the esophagus is said to look "like a deaf man's antique horn." In a poem largely about vision, this simile suggests that the butchered organ might speak to us despite our customary deafness.

But most of the figurative language translates the scene into a religious service. This "church" into which the poet has stumbled resounds with the "fundamental squawking" of "little Pentecostal magpies, diminutive / raven priests." It is as though he has "strayed / out of Hawthorne into Cotton Mather," he says, that is, out of the reserved skepticism that characterized the nineteenth-century Romantics and into unrestrained dogmatism of the seventeenth-century Puritans. Complementing the birds are the bears, bobcats, and wolves (although all are present only as tracks in the snow), which are the "deacons." For the animals that have come to feed on it, the corpse is a "sweet eucharist of luck."

Although Wrigley typically writes in the first person, "The Church of Omnivorous Light" is in the second person, "you," and in the conditional mood, "would," rather than the indicative, "are." These two grammatical choices universalize the experience, transforming it from an anecdote to an allegory. Not merely one man who happens upon this religious "service," the narrator is a stand-in for us all. "You'd want to go," he says, "but you'd want to stay; / you'd want a way to say your part in the service / going on." To "say your part" is to recognize and enact our role in this ritual of death, decay, and scavenging. We are simultaneously observers, partakers, and the "sweet eucharist."

The poem ends with the birds and other animals returning after having been frightened away by the man. They are "the brethren," he says, using the archaic plural of "brother": these creatures feeding on the corpse are our spiritual as well as our biological brothers, linked to us as our coparticipants in a religious rite and as our natural counterparts.

They appear to be attired in "surplice and cassock," the vestments of a church service, but

they are also animated by literal hunger. They are, the poet says,

hopeful too,
that something might yet come and open
your coarse, inexplicable soul to their sight.
(*Earthly Meditations,* p. 154)

The omnivorous light, then, is the light in which nature sees us and also the light in which nature makes us see ourselves. In that light we see truth more profound than any revealed through conventional religion: we are wholly natural and, in a sense, holy as well.

The unexpected word "inexplicable" is an example of Wrigley's eclectic diction. Abstract, especially in this context of concrete nouns, it denotes something unexplainable, as the soul is traditionally thought to be, but in its etymology it suggests something that can't be unfolded from its context. In this poem, the soul cannot be understood apart from the flesh.

Images of decay dominate in these poems, but decay is balanced with transcendence. In "Horseflies," for example, the narrator recalls volunteering as a boy to douse a dead horse with kerosene and set it afire. The stench of the rotting flesh engulfs him "like water," permeating even "into the tear ducts / and taste buds," into "the last dark tendrils / of my howling, agonized hair." He sets the carcass aflame and witnesses the horse's resurrection when a "billion flies [become] airborne / exactly in the shape / of the horse itself." Although the vision lasts only "a brief quivering / instant" before the flies disperse, it is a glimpse of something beyond death. The title puns on this vision: these are literal horseflies, but the horse also "flies," if only for the duration of "a pulse thump."

In "The Other World" the poet finds the carcass of a buck and reads its biography in the wounds it bears, "the mangled ear / and the twisted, hindering leg." He imagines the creature as it "struck now and then / a pose against the wind," as if it had possessed human vanity. Against that vanity he posits "a line of tiny ants" feeding on the remains: "[T]hey carry him / bit by gnawn bit / into another world." Working purely by instinct, these ants, like the flies in "Horseflies," are nevertheless the agents of deliverance.

"Clemency" explicitly addresses a more orthodox God than Wrigley's poems usually do, but only in passing. The primary focus remains on this world. As he feeds his livestock on a February day that feels like "a sudden, unearthly spring," the speaker praises the animals: a horse, a toad, birds. "Unearthly" this day may be, but his attention lingers on this earth. At first, only as an exclamation does he turn to God: "God above me, / I am halfway through this field, a feeding, the season, my life." Then, suddenly aware that what is precious is also fleeting, he prays, asking for "ten thousand more afternoons / like this."

He even welcomes ordinarily unwelcome creatures, "the unkilled fleas, scintillant / and fat." In his reverent mood he can find something praiseworthy even in them, as he imagines one of the fleas

among
the rumpled bedclothes to catch us there,
my lover and me, and marry us done.
(*Earthly Meditations,* p. 167)

Here he observes his threefold connection: to nature (the flea, among other things), to another human being (his lover), and to literature—specifically, to John Donne's seventeenth-century poem "The Flea," even punning on his predecessor's name. (In Donne's poem, a man attempts to seduce a woman by pointing out to her that their "two bloods" are already intimately "mingled" in a flea that has bitten both of them.)

The title, "Clemency," evokes divine mercy, the very mercy for which the poet prays. He asks that his time in nature be prolonged, but his title suggests that he is aware that he has no special claim on more life. Yet he has seen that nature does sometimes grant clemency. His opening lines depicted a toad "croaking dead center in a hoof print"—by chance, or by some divine clemency, the horse's hoof descended in precisely the place that would spare the toad (an image reminiscent of the "The Glow," in *Moon in a Mason Jar,* in which a tree crashes *around* a boy but does not crush him). The poet asks that the

weight of nature likewise fall in such a way as to spare him, at least for a while.

Selected Bibliography

WORKS OF ROBERT WRIGLEY

The Sinking of Clay City. Port Townsend, Wash.: Copper Canyon, 1979.

The Glow. Missoula, Mont: Owl Creek Press, 1982.

Moon in a Mason Jar. Urbana: University of Illinois Press, 1986. Reprinted with *What My Father Believed* as *Moon in a Mason Jar & What My Father Believed: Two Volumes of Poetry,* 1998.

In the Dark Pool. Lewiston, Idaho; Confluence Press, 1987.

What My Father Believed. Urbana: University of Illinois Press, 1991. Reprinted with *Moon in a Mason Jar* as *Moon in a Mason Jar & What My Father Believed: Two Volumes of Poetry,* 1998.

In the Bank of Beautiful Sins. New York: Penguin, 1995.

Reign of Snakes. New York: Penguin, 1999.

Lives of the Animals. New York: Penguin, 2003.

Earthly Meditations. New York: Penguin, 2006.

"Delicious." *Georgia Review,* 502–503 (fall–winter 2006).

"Finding a Bible in an Abandoned Cabin." *Hudson Review* 59, no. 4: (winter 2007).

CRITICAL AND BIOGRAPHICAL STUDIES

Bedient, Calvin. Review of *In the Bank of Beautiful Sins. Southern Review* 33:183–141 (winter 1977).

Browning, M. K. "Robert Wrigley's Canon—Earlier Works." *Connections,* no. 2:33–37 (spring 2000).

———. "Robert Wrigley's Canon—Poems and Parables." *Connections,* no. 3:29–36 (summer 2000).

Chappell, Fred. "Family Matters." *Georgia Review* 45, no. 4:767 (winter 1991). (Review of *Moon in a Mason Jar.*)

Cramer, Steven. Review of *What My Father Believed. Poetry,* no. 161:171–176 (December 1992).

Kennedy, Sarah. "An Interview with Robert Wrigley." *Sou'wester* (February 24, 2004) (http://www.cstone.net/˜poems/essawrig.htm).

Levy, Buddy. "Writing Their Way Home: An Interview with Kim Barnes and Robert Wrigley." *Poets & Writers* 27, no. 3:26–31 (May–June 1999).

McFarland, Ron. Review of *Moon in a Mason Jar. Northwest Review* 25, no. 2:152–156 (1987).

———. Review of *Reign of Snakes. Northwest Review* 38, no. 1:128–133 (2000).

———. "Robert Wrigley." In *Dictionary of Literary Biography.* Vol. 256. Edited by Richard H. Cracroft. Detroit: Gale, 2002. Pp. 334–340.

Wakefield, Richard. "Poems in Crossing Chasms." *Seattle Times,* November 5, 2006, p. K-8. (Review of *Earthly Meditations.)*

Cumulative Index

Arabic numbers printed in bold-face type refer to extended treatment of a subject.

A

"A" (Zukofsky), **Supp. III Part 2:** 611, 612, 614, 617, 619, 620, 621, 622, 623, 624, 626, 627, 628, 629, 630, 631; **Supp. IV Part 1:** 154; **Supp. XVI:** 287

Aal, Katharyn, **Supp. IV Part 1:** 332

Aaron, Daniel, **IV:** 429; **Supp. I Part 2:** 647, 650

Aaron's Rod (Lawrence), **Supp. I Part 1:** 255

Abacus (Karr), **Supp. XI: 240–242,** 248, 254

Abádi-Nagy, Zoltán, **Supp. IV Part 1:** 280, 289, 291

"Abandoned House, The" (L. Michaels), **Supp. XVI:** 214

"Abandoned Newborn, The" (Olds), **Supp. X:** 207

"Abba Jacob" (Nelson), **Supp. XVIII:** 177

Abbey, Edward, **Supp. VIII:** 42; **Supp. X:** 24, 29, 30, 31, 36; **Supp. XIII: 1–18; Supp. XIV:** 179

Abbey's Road (Abbey), **Supp. XIII:** 12

Abbott, Carl, **Supp. XVIII:** 142

Abbott, Edith, **Supp. I Part 1:** 5

Abbott, George, **Supp. IV Part 2:** 585

Abbott, Grace, **Supp. I Part 1:** 5

Abbott, Jack Henry, **Retro. Supp. II:** 210

Abbott, Jacob, **Supp. I Part 1:** 38, 39

Abbott, Lyman, **III:** 293

Abbott, Sean, **Retro. Supp. II:** 213

ABC of Color, An: Selections from Over a Half Century of Writings (Du Bois), **Supp. II Part 1:** 186

ABC of Reading (Pound), **III:** 468, 474–475

"Abdication, An" (Merrill), **Supp. III Part 1:** 326

Abel, Lionel, **Supp. XIII:** 98

Abel, Sam, **Supp. XIII:** 199

Abelard, Peter, **I:** 14, 22

Abeles, Sigmund, **Supp. VIII:** 272

Abercrombie, Lascelles, **III:** 471; **Retro. Supp. I:** 127, 128

Abernathy, Milton, **Supp. III Part 2:** 616

Abernon, Edgar Vincent, Viscount d', **Supp. XVI:** 191

Abhau, Anna. *See* Mencken, Mrs. August (Anna Abhau)

"Abide with Me" (Hoffman), **Supp. XVIII:** 86

"Ability" (Emerson), **II:** 6

Abingdon, Alexander, **Supp. XVI:** 99

Abish, Walter, **Supp. V:** 44

"Abishag" (Glück), **Supp. V:** 82

"Abortion, The" (Sexton), **Supp. II Part 2:** 682

"Abortions" (Dixon), **Supp. XII:** 153

"About C. D. Wright" (Colburn), **Supp. XV:** 341

"About Hospitality" (Jewett), **Retro. Supp. II:** 131

"About Kathryn" (Dubus), **Supp. VII:** 91

"About Language" (Wrigley), **Supp. XVIII:** 300–301

"About Looking Alone at a Place: Arles" (M. F. K. Fisher), **Supp. XVII:** 89, 91

About the House (Auden), **Supp. II Part 1:** 24

About Town: "The New Yorker" and the World It Made (Yagoda), **Supp. VIII:** 151

"Above Pate Valley" (Snyder), **Supp. VIII:** 293

Above the River (Wright), **Supp. III Part 2:** 589, 606

"Abraham" (Schwartz), **Supp. II Part 2:** 663

Abraham, Nelson Algren. *See* Algren, Nelson

Abraham, Pearl, **Supp. XVII:** 49

"Abraham Davenport" (Whittier), **Supp. I Part 2:** 699

"Abraham Lincoln" (Emerson), **II:** 13

Abraham Lincoln: The Prairie Years (Sandburg), **III:** 580, 587–589, 590

Abraham Lincoln: The Prairie Years and the War Years (Sandburg), **III:** 588, 590

Abraham Lincoln: The War Years (Sandburg), **III:** 588, 589–590; **Supp. XVII:** 105

"Abraham Lincoln Walks at Midnight" (Lindsay), **Supp. I Part 2:** 390–391

"Abram Morrison" (Whittier), **Supp. I Part 2:** 699

Abramovich, Alex, **Supp. X:** 302, 309

Abrams, M. H., **Supp. XVI:** 19

Abridgment of Universal Geography, An: Together with Sketches of History (Rowson), **Supp. XV:** 243

"Absalom" (Rukeyser), **Supp. VI:** 278–279

Absalom, Absalom! (Faulkner), **II:** 64, 65–67, 72, 223; **IV:** 207; **Retro. Supp. I:** 75, 81, 82, 84, 85, 86, 87, 88, 89, 90, 92, 382; **Supp. V:** 261; **Supp. X:** 51; **Supp. XIV:** 12–13

"Absence of Mercy" (Stone), **Supp. V:** 295

"Absentee, The" (Levertov), **Supp. III Part 1:** 284

Absentee Ownership (Veblen), **Supp. I Part 2:** 642

"Absent-Minded Bartender" (X. J. Kennedy), **Supp. XV:** 159

"Absent Thee from Felicity Awhile" (Wylie), **Supp. I Part 2:** 727, 729

"Absolution" (Fitzgerald), **Retro. Supp. I:** 108

"Absolution" (Sobin), **Supp. XVI:** 289

"Abuelita's Ache" (Mora), **Supp. XIII:** 218

Abysmal Brute, The (London), **II:** 467

"Academic Story, An" (Simpson), **Supp. IX:** 279–280

"Academic Zoo, The: Theory——in Practice" (Epstein), **Supp. XIV:** 107–108, 109

"A Capella" (Wrigley), **Supp. XVIII:** 300

"Accident" (Minot), **Supp. VI: 208–209**

"Accident, The" (Southern), **Supp. XI:** 295

"Accident, The" (Strand), **Supp. IV Part 2:** 624

Accident/A Day's News (Wolf), **Supp. IV Part 1:** 310

Accidental Tourist, The (Tyler), **Supp. IV Part 2:** 657, 668–669; **Supp. V:** 227

Accordion Crimes (Proulx), **Supp. VII:** 259–261

"Accountability" (Dunbar), **Supp. II Part 1:** 197, 204

"Account of the Method of Drawing Birds" (Audubon), **Supp. XVI:** 12

"Accusation, The" (Wright), **Supp. III Part 2:** 595

"Accusation of the Inward Man, The" (Taylor), **IV:** 156

"Accusing Message from Dead Father" (Karr), **Supp. XI:** 244

Ace, Goodman, **Supp. IV Part 2:** 574

Achievement in American Poetry (Bogan), **Supp. III Part 1:** 63–64

Acker, Kathy, **Supp. XII:1–20**

Ackerman, Diane, **Supp. XIII:** 154

"Acknowledgment" (Lanier), **Supp. I Part 1:** 364

Ackroyd, Peter, **Supp. V:** 233; **Supp. XVII:** 180

"Acquaintance in the Heavens, An" (Dillard), **Supp. VI:** 34

"Acquainted with the Night" (Frost), **II:** 155; **Retro. Supp. I:** 137

Across Spoon River (Masters), **Supp. I Part 2:** 455, 457, 459, 460, 466, 474–475, 476
Across the Layers: Poems Old and New (Goldbarth), **Supp. XII:** 181, **187–189**
Across the River and into the Trees (Hemingway), **I:** 491; **II:** 255–256, 261; **Retro. Supp. I:** 172, **184–185**
"Actfive" (MacLeish), **III:** 18–19, 22
Actfive and Other Poems (MacLeish), **III:** 3, 17–19, 21
Action (Shepard), **Supp. III Part 2:** 446
Active Anthology (Pound), **Supp. III Part 2:** 617
Active Service (Crane), **I:** 409
Acton, Patricia Nassif, **Supp. X:** 233
Actual, The (Bellow), **Retro. Supp. II:** 33
"Actual Experience, Preferred Narratives" (Julier), **Supp. IV Part 1:** 211
Acuff, Roy, **Supp. V:** 335
Ada (Nabokov), **Retro. Supp. I:** 265, 266, 270, 276–277, 278, 279
"Ada" (Stein), **IV:** 43
"Adagia" (Stevens), **IV:** 78, 80, 88, 92
"Adam" (Hecht), **Supp. X:** 62
"Adam" (W. C. Williams), **Retro. Supp. I:** 422, 423
"Adam and Eve" (Eugene), **Supp. X:** 204
"Adam and Eve" (Shapiro), **Supp. II Part 2:** 708, 712
"Adamantine Practice of Poetry, The" (Wright), **Supp. XV:** 341–342, 343–344
Adam Bede (Eliot), **II:** 181
Adamé, Leonard, **Supp. XIII:** 316
Adam & Eve & the City (W. C. Williams), **Retro. Supp. I:** 423
"Adamic Purity as Double Agent" (Whalen-Bridge), **Retro. Supp. II:** 211–212
Adams, Althea. *See* Thurber, Mrs. James (Althea Adams)
Adams, Annie. *See* Fields, Annie Adams
Adams, Brooks, **Supp. I Part 2:** 484
Adams, Charles, **Supp. I Part 2:** 644
Adams, Charles Francis, **I:** 1, 4; **Supp. I Part 2:** 484
Adams, Franklin P., **Supp. I Part 2:** 653; **Supp. IX:** 190; **Supp. XV:** 294, 297
Adams, Henry, **I: 1–24,** 111, 243, 258; **II:** 278, 542; **III:** 396, 504; **IV:** 191, 349; **Retro. Supp. I:** 53, 59; **Retro. Supp. II:** 207; **Supp. I Part 1:** 299–300, 301, 314; **Supp. I Part 2:** 417, 492, 543, 644; **Supp. II Part 1:** 93–94, 105; **Supp. III Part 2:** 613; **Supp. IV Part 1:** 31, 208
Adams, Henry B., **Supp. I Part 1:** 369
Adams, James Truslow, **Supp. I Part 2:** 481, 484, 486
Adams, J. Donald, **IV:** 438
Adams, John, **I:** 1; **II:** 103, 301; **III:** 17, 473; **Supp. I Part 2:** 483, 506, 507, 509, 510, 511, 517, 518, 520, 524
Adams, John Luther, **Supp. XII:** 209
Adams, John Quincy, **I:** 1, 3, 16–17; **Supp. I Part 2:** 685, 686
Adams, Léonie, **Supp. I Part 2:** 707; **Supp. IX:** 229; **Supp. V:** 79; **Supp. XVII:** 75
Adams, Luella, **Supp. I Part 2:** 652
Adams, Mrs. Henry (Marian Hooper), **I:** 1, 5, 10, 17–18
Adams, Noah, **Supp. XVII:** 218
Adams, Phoebe, **Supp. IV Part 1:** 203; **Supp. VIII:** 124
Adams, Samuel, **Supp. I Part 2:** 516, 525
Adams, Timothy Dow, **Supp. XVI:** 67, 69
Ada; or Ardor (Nabokov), **III:** 247
"Ad Castitatem" (Bogan), **Supp. III Part 1:** 50
Adcock, Betty, **Supp. XVIII:** 181–182, 182
Addams, Jane, **Supp. I Part 1: 1–26; Supp. XI:** 200, 202
Addams, John Huy, **Supp. I Part 1:** 2
"Addendum" (Wright), **Supp. V:** 339
Addiego, John, **Supp. XII:** 182
Adding Machine, The (Rice), **I:** 479
Adding Machine, The: Selected Essays (Burroughs), **Supp. III Part 1:** 93, 97
Addison, Joseph, **I:** 8, 105, 106–107, 108, 114, 131, 300, 304; **III:** 430
"Addressed to a Political Shrimp, or, Fly upon the Wheel" (Freneau), **Supp. II Part 1:** 267
"Address to My Soul" (Wylie), **Supp. I Part 2:** 729
"Address to the Devil" (Jarman), **Supp. XVII:** 114
Address to the Government of the United States on the Cession of Louisiana to the French, An (Brown), **Supp. I Part 1:** 146
"Address to the Scholars of New England" (Ransom), **III:** 491
"Address with Exclamation Points, A" (Simic), **Supp. VIII:** 283
"Adjutant Bird, The" (Banks), **Supp. V:** 5
Adkins, Nelson F., **II:** 20
Adler, Alfred, **I:** 248
Adler, Betty, **III:** 103
Adler, George J., **III:** 81
Adler, Renata, **Supp. X:** 171
Admiral of the Ocean Sea: A Life of Christopher Columbus (Morison), **Supp. I Part 2:** 486–488
"Admirals" (Chabon), **Supp. XI:** 72
"Admonition, An" (Brodsky), **Supp. VIII:** 33
"Adolescence" (Bidart), **Supp. XV:** 32
"Adolescence" (Dove), **Supp. IV Part 1:** 245
"Adolescence" (Olds), **Supp. X:** 211
"Adolescence II" (Dove), **Supp. IV Part 1:** 242, 244–245
Adolescent's Christmas, An: 1944 (C. Bly), **Supp. XVI:** 31–32
"Adolf Eichmann" (Carruth), **Supp. XVI:** 47
"Adonais" (Shelley), **II:** 516, 540
Adorno, Theodor, **Supp. I Part 2:** 645, 650; **Supp. IV Part 1:** 301
"Adrienne Rich: The Poetics of Change" (Gelpi), **Supp. I Part 2:** 554
"Adultery" (Banks), **Supp. V:** 15
"Adultery" (Dubus), **Supp. VII:** 85
Adultery and Other Choices (Dubus), **Supp. VII:** 83–85
Adulthood Rites (O. Butler), **Supp. XIII:** 63, **64–65**
Adult Life of Toulouse Lautrec by Henri Toulouse Lautrec, The (Acker), **Supp. XII:** 5, 6, **8–9**
Adventure (London), **II:** 466
Adventures in Ancient Egypt (Goldbarth), **Supp. XII:** 191
Adventures in Value (Cummings), **I:** 430
"Adventures of a Book Reviewer" (Cowley), **Supp. II Part 1:** 137, 142
Adventures of Augie March, The (Bellow), **I:** 144, 147, 149, 150, 151, 152–153, 154, 155, 157, 158–159, 164; **Retro. Supp. II:** 19, 20, **22–23,** 24, 30; **Supp. VIII:** 234, 236–237
Adventures of a Young Man (Dos Passos), **I:** 488, 489, 492
Adventures of Captain Bonneville (Irving), **II:** 312
Adventures of Harry Franco, The: A Tale of the Great Panic (Briggs), **Supp. XVIII:** 1, 2, 5–8
Adventures of Huckleberry Finn, The (Twain), **I:** 307, 506; **II:** 26, 72, 262, 266–268, 290, 418, 430; **III:** 101, 112–113, 357, 554, 558, 577; **IV:** 198, 201–204, 207; **Retro. Supp. I:** 188; **Retro. Supp. II:** 121; **Supp. I Part 1:** 247; **Supp. IV Part 1:** 247, 257; **Supp. IV Part 2:** 502; **Supp. V:** 131; **Supp. VIII:** 198; **Supp. X:** 230; **Supp. XII:** 16; **Supp. XVI:** 222
Adventures of Jimmy (Broughton), **Supp. XV:** 146
Adventures of Roderick Random, The (Smollett), **I:** 134
Adventures of the Letter I (Simpson), **Supp. IX:** 266, **273–274**
Adventures of Tom Sawyer, The (Twain), **II:** 26; **III:** 223, 572, 577; **IV:** 199–200, 203, 204; **Supp. I Part 2:** 456, 470; **Supp. XVI:** 66
Adventures While Preaching the Gospel of Beauty (Lindsay), **Supp. I Part 2:** 374, 376, 381, 382–384, 389, 399
Adventures with Ed (Loeffler), **Supp. XIII:** 1
Advertisements for Myself (Mailer), **III:** 27, 35–38, 41–42, 45, 46; **Retro. Supp. II:** 196, 199, 200, 202, 203, 212; **Supp. IV Part 1:** 90, 284; **Supp. XIV:** 157
"Advertisements for Myself on the Way Out" (Mailer), **III:** 37
"Advice to a Prophet" (Wilbur), **Supp. III Part 2:** 555–557
Advice to a Prophet and Other Poems (Wilbur), **Supp. III Part 2:** 554–558
"Advice to a Raven in Russia" (Barlow), **Supp. II Part 1:** 65, 74, 80, 83
"Advice to Players" (Bidart), **Supp. XV:** 35

Advice to the Lovelorn (film), **Retro. Supp. II:** 328
Advice to the Privileged Orders, Part I (Barlow), **Supp. II Part 1:** 80
"Aeneas and Dido" (Brodsky), **Supp. VIII:** 24–25
"Aeneas at Washington" (Tate), **IV:** 129
Aeneid (Virgil), **I:** 396; **II:** 542; **III:** 124; **Supp. XV:** 23
Aeneus Tacticus, **I:** 136
Aerial View (Barabtarlo), **Retro. Supp. I:** 278
"Aeria the Evanescent" (Sobin), **Supp. XVI:** 292
Aeschylus, **I:** 274, 433; **III:** 398; **IV:** 358, 368, 370; **Retro. Supp. I:** 65; **Supp. I Part 2:** 458, 494
Aesop, **I:** 387; **II:** 154, 169, 302; **III:** 587
Aesthetic (Croce), **III:** 610
"Aesthetics" (Mumford), **Supp. II Part 2:** 476
"Aesthetics of Silence, The" (Sontag), **Supp. III Part 2:** 459
"Aesthetics of the Shah" (Olds), **Supp. X:** 205
"Affair at Coulter's Notch, The" (Bierce), **I:** 202
Affaire de viol, Une (C. Himes). *See Case of Rape, A* (C. Himes)
"Affair of Outposts, An" (Bierce), **I:** 202
Affliction (Banks), **Supp. V:** 15, 16
Affluent Society, The (Galbraith), **Supp. I Part 2:** 648
Afghanistan Picture Show, An: or, How I Saved the World (Vollmann), **Supp. XVII:** 226, **228–229,** 233
"Aficionados, The" (Carver), **Supp. III Part 1:** 137
"Afloat" (Beattie), **Supp. V:** 29
Afloat and Ashore (Cooper), **I:** 351, 355
Africa, Its Geography, People, and Products (Du Bois), **Supp. II Part 1:** 179
Africa, Its Place in Modern History (Du Bois), **Supp. II Part 1:** 179
"Africa, to My Mother" (D. Diop), **Supp. IV Part 1:** 16
African American Writers (Smith, ed.), **Supp. XIII:** 115, 127
"African Book" (Hemingway), **II:** 259
"African Chief, The" (Bryant), **Supp. I Part 1:** 168
"African Fragment" (Brooks), **Supp. III Part 1:** 85
African Queen, The (film), **Supp. XI:** 17
"African Roots of War, The" (Du Bois), **Supp. II Part 1:** 174
African Silences (Matthiessen), **Supp. V:** 203
African Treasury, An (Hughes, ed.), **Supp. I Part 1:** 344
"Afrika Revolution" (Baraka), **Supp. II Part 1:** 53
"AFRO-AMERICAN LYRIC" (Baraka), **Supp. II Part 1:** 59
After (Bukiet), **Supp. XVII:** 43, **44–45**
After All: Last Poems (Matthews), **Supp. IX:** 155, **167–169**
After and Before the Lightning (Ortiz), **Supp. IV Part 2:** 513
"After a Party" (Salinas), **Supp. XIII:** 327
"After Apple-Picking" (Frost), **Retro. Supp. I:** 126, 128
"After Arguing against the Contention That Art Must Come from Discontent" (Stafford), **Supp. XI:** 327
After Confession: Poetry as Autobiography (Harris), **Supp. XIV:** 269
After Confession: Poetry as Autobiography (K. Sontag and D. Graham), **Supp. XV:** 104
"After Cowboy Chicken Came to Town" (Jin), **Supp. XVIII:** 97–98
"After Disappointment" (Jarman), **Supp. XVII:** 118–119
After Experience (Snodgrass), **Supp. VI:** 314–316, 317
"After great pain, a formal feeling comes" (Dickinson), **Retro. Supp. I:** 37
"After Hearing a Waltz by Bartók" (Lowell), **II:** 522
"After Henry" (Didion), **Supp. IV Part 1:** 211
After Henry (Didion), **Supp. IV Part 1:** 195, 196, 199, 207, 208, 211
"After Holbein" (Wharton), **IV:** 325; **Retro. Supp. I:** 382
After Ikkyu and Other Poems (Harrison), **Supp. VIII:** 42
"After-Image" (Bierds), **Supp. XVII:** 31–32
"After-Image" (Caldwell), **I:** 309
After-Images: Autobiographical Sketches (Snodgrass), **Supp. VI:** 314, **319–323,** 324, 326–327
After I's (Zukofsky), **Supp. III Part 2:** 628, 629
Afterlife (Monette), **Supp. X:** 153
Afterlife (Updike), **Retro. Supp. I:** 322
Afterlife, The (Levis), **Supp. XI:** 259, **260–264**
"After Magritte" (McClatchy), **Supp. XII:** 264
"After Making Love" (Dunn), **Supp. XI:** 153
"Aftermath" (Longfellow), **II:** 498
Aftermath (Longfellow), **II:** 490
After New Formalism (A. Finch, ed.), **Supp. XVII:** 74
"Afternoon" (Ellison), **Supp. II Part 1:** 238
"Afternoon at MacDowell" (Kenyon), **Supp. VII:** 159
"Afternoon Miracle, An" (O. Henry), **Supp. II Part 1:** 390
Afternoon of a Faun (Hearon), **Supp. VIII: 63–64**
Afternoon of an Author: A Selection of Uncollected Stories and Essays (Fitzgerald), **II:** 94
"Afternoon of a Playwright" (Thurber), **Supp. I Part 2:** 620
Afternoon of the Unreal (Salinas), **Supp. XIII:** 311, **316–318**
"Afternoon with the Old Man, An" (Dubus), **Supp. VII:** 84
"After Punishment Was Done with Me" (Olds), **Supp. X:** 213
"After Reading *Barely and Widely,*" (Zukofsky), **Supp. III Part 2:** 625, 631
"After Reading 'In the Clearing' for the Author, Robert Frost" (Corso), **Supp. XII:** 130
"After Reading *Mickey in the Night Kitchen* for the Third Time before Bed" (Dove), **Supp. IV Part 1:** 249
"After Reading Tu Fu, I Go Outside to the Dwarf Orchard" (Wright), **Supp. V:** 343
"After Reading Wang Wei, I Go Outside to the Full Moon" (Wright), **Supp. V:** 343
After Shocks, Near Escapes (Dobyns), **Supp. XIII: 80–82**
"After Song, An" (W. C. Williams), **Retro. Supp. I:** 413
After Strange Gods (Eliot), **I:** 588
After Such Knowledge: Memory, History, and the Legacy of the Holocaust (E. Hoffman), **Supp. XVI:** 152–153, **158–161**
"After the Alphabets" (Merwin), **Supp. III Part 1:** 356
"After the Argument" (Dunn), **Supp. XI:** 149
"After the Baptism" (C. Bly), **Supp. XVI:** 40
"After the Burial" (Lowell), **Supp. I Part 2:** 409
"After the Curfew" (Holmes), **Supp. I Part 1:** 308
"After the Death of John Brown" (Thoreau), **IV:** 185
"After the Denim" (Carver), **Supp. III Part 1:** 144
"After the Dentist" (Swenson), **Supp. IV Part 2:** 645
After the Fall (A. Miller), **III:** 148, 149, 156, 161, 162, 163–165, 166
"After the Fire" (Merrill), **Supp. III Part 1:** 328
"After the Flood" (Sanders), **Supp. XVI:** 274–275
After the Fox (film), **Supp. IV Part 2:** 575
After the Genteel Tradition (Cowley), **Supp. II Part 1:** 143
"After the Heart's Interrogation" (Komunyakaa), **Supp. XIII:** 120
After the Lost Generation: A Critical Study of the Writers of Two Wars (Aldridge), **Supp. IV Part 2:** 680
"After the Night Office——Gethsemani Abbey" (Merton), **Supp. VIII:** 195–196
"After the Persian" (Bogan), **Supp. III Part 1:** 64
"After the Pleasure Party" (Melville), **III:** 93
"After the Resolution" (Dunn), **Supp. XI:** 151
After the Stroke (Sarton), **Supp. VIII:** 264
"After the Surprising Conversions" (Lowell), **I:** 544, 545; **II:** 550; **Retro. Supp. II:** 187

"After 37 Years My Mother Apologizes for My Childhood" (Olds), **Supp. X:** 208
After This (McDermott), **Supp. XVIII:** 155, **166–167**
Afterthoughts (L. P. Smith), **Supp. XIV:** 339, 345
"Afterthoughts on the Rosenbergs" (Fiedler), **Supp. XIII:** 99
"After Twenty Years" (Rich), **Supp. I Part 2:** 559–560
"Afterwake, The" (Rich), **Supp. I Part 2:** 553
"Afterward" (Wharton), **Retro. Supp. I:** 372
"After Working Long" (Kenyon), **Supp. VII:** 170
"After Yitzl" (Goldbarth), **Supp. XII:** 186
"After You, My Dear Alphonse" (Jackson), **Supp. IX:** 119
"After Your Nap" (B. Kelly), **Supp. XVII:** 124
"Again" (Dixon), **Supp. XII:** 157
"Again, Kapowsin" (Hugo), **Supp. VI:** 141
"Against" (Goldbarth), **Supp. XII:** 193
"Against Decoration" (Karr), **Supp. XI:** 248
"Against Epiphanies" (C. Baxter), **Supp. XVII:** 20
"Against Interpretation" (Sontag), **Supp. III Part 2:** 456–458, 463
Against Interpretation (Sontag), **Supp. III Part 2:** 451, 455; **Supp. XIV:** 15
"Against Modernity" (Ozick), **Supp. V:** 272
"Against Nature" (Karr), **Supp. XI:** 243
Against Nature (Updike), **Retro. Supp. I:** 323
Against the Cold (Bynner), **Supp. XV:** 51
"Against the Crusades" (Stern), **Supp. IX:** 300
Against the Current: As I Remember F. Scott Fitzgerald (Kroll Ring), **Supp. IX:** 63
Agamben, Giorgio, **Supp. XVI:** 289
Agapida, Fray Antonio (pseudonym). *See* Irving, Washington
"Agassiz" (Lowell), **Supp. I Part 2:** 414, 416
Agassiz, Louis, **II:** 343; **Supp. I Part 1:** 312; **Supp. IX:** 180
Ãge cassant, L' (Char; Sobin, trans.), **Supp. XVI:** 282
"Aged Wino's Counsel to a Young Man on the Brink of Marriage, The" (X. J. Kennedy), **Supp. XV:** 156
Agee, Emma, **I:** 26
Agee, James, **I: 25–47,** 293; **IV:** 215; **Supp. IX:** 109; **Supp. XIV:** 92; **Supp. XV:** 143
"Agent, The" (Wilbur), **Supp. III Part 2:** 557–561
Age of Anxiety, The (Auden), **Supp. II Part 1:** 2, 19, 21
"Age of Conformity, The" (Howe), **Supp. VI:** 117
Age of Grief, The: A Novella and Stories (Smiley), **Supp. VI:** 292, **299–301**
Age of Innocence, The (Wharton), **IV:** 320–322, 327–328; **Retro. Supp. I:** 372, 374, **380–381; Supp. IV Part 1:** 23
Age of Longing, The (Koestler), **I:** 258
Age of Reason, The (Paine), **Supp. I Part 2:** 503, 515–517, 520
"Age of Strolling, The" (Stern), **Supp. IX:** 297
"Ages, The" (Bryant), **Supp. I Part 1:** 152, 155, 166, 167
"Aging" (Jarrell), **II:** 388
Aging and Gender in Literature (George), **Supp. IV Part 2:** 450
"Agio Neró" (Mora), **Supp. XIII:** 224
"Agitato ma non Troppo" (Ransom), **III:** 493
"Agnes of Iowa" (Moore), **Supp. X:** 165, 178
Agnes of Sorrento (Stowe), **Supp. I Part 2:** 592, 595–596
Agnon, S. Y., **Supp. V:** 266
"Agosta the Winged Man and Rasha the Black Dove" (Dove), **Supp. IV Part 1:** 246–247
Agrarian Justice (Paine), **Supp. I Part 2:** 517–518
"Agricultural Show, The" (McKay), **Supp. X:** 139
Agrippa: A Book of the Dead (W. Gibson), **Supp. XVI:** 125
Agua Fresca: An Anthology of Raza Poetry (Rodríguez, ed.), **Supp. IV Part 2:** 540
Agua Santa/Holy Water (Mora), **Supp. XIII: 222–225**
Agüero Sisters, The (García), **Supp. XI: 185–190**
Aguiar, Sarah Appleton, **Supp. XIII:** 30
Ah, Wilderness! (O'Neill), **III:** 400–401; **Supp. IV Part 2:** 587
Ah, Wilderness!: The Frontier in American Literature (Humphrey), **Supp. IX:** 104
Ahearn, Barry, **Retro. Supp. I:** 415
Ahearn, Frederick L., Jr., **Supp. XI:** 184
Ahearn, Kerry, **Supp. IV Part 2:** 604
Ahmed Arabi Pasha, **I:** 453
Ahnebrink, Lars, **III:** 328
Ah Sin (Harte), **Supp. II Part 1:** 354–355
"Ah! Sun-flower" (Blake), **III:** 19
AIDS and Its Metaphors (Sontag), **Supp. III Part 2:** 452, 466–468
Aids to Reflection (Coleridge), **II:** 10
Aiieeeee! An Anthology of Asian-American Writers (The Combined Asian Resources Project), **Supp. X:** 292
Aiken, Conrad, **I: 48–70,** 190, 211, 243; **II:** 55, 530, 542; **III:** 458, 460; **Retro. Supp. I:** 55, 56, 57, 58, 60, 62; **Supp. X:** 50, 115; **Supp. XV:** 144, 297, 298, 302, 306, 309; **Supp. XVII:** 135
"Aim Was Song, The" (Frost), **Retro. Supp. I:** 133
Ainsworth, Linda, **Supp. IV Part 1:** 274
Ainsworth, William, **III:** 423
Air-Conditioned Nightmare, The (H. Miller), **III:** 186
Airing Dirty Laundry (Reed), **Supp. X:** 241
"Air Plant, The" (Crane), **I:** 401
Air Raid: A Verse Play for Radio (MacLeish), **III:** 21
"Airs above the Ground" (Sarton), **Supp. VIII:** 261
Air Tight: A Novel of Red Russia. See We the Living (Rand)
Air Up There, The (film, Glaser), **Supp. XVII:** 9
"Airwaves" (Mason), **Supp. VIII:** 146
Airways, Inc. (Dos Passos), **I:** 482
"A is for Dining Alone" (M. F. K. Fisher), **Supp. XVII:** 86
Aitken, Robert, **Supp. I Part 2:** 504
Akhmadulina, Bella, **Supp. III Part 1:** 268
Akhmatova, Anna, **Supp. III Part 1:** 268, 269; **Supp. VIII:** 20, 21, 25, 27, 30
Akhmatova Translations, The (Kenyon), **Supp. VII:** 160
"Akhnilo" (Salter), **Supp. IX:** 260
Akins, Zoë, **Supp. XVI:** 187
Aksenev, Vasily P., **Retro. Supp. I:** 278
"Al Aaraaf" (Poe), **III:** 426–427
Al Aaraaf, Tamerlane, and Minor Poems (Poe), **III:** 410
"Alain Locke and Cultural Pluralism" (Kallen), **Supp. XIV:** 197
"Alain Locke: Bahá'í Philosopher" (Buck), **Supp. XIV:** 199
Alain Locke: Faith and Philosophy (Buck), **Supp. XIV:** 200
Alarçon, **Supp. XVII:** 74
Alarcón, Justo, **Supp. IV Part 2:** 538, 539, 540
À la Recherche du Temps Perdu (Proust), **IV:** 428
"Alarm" (X. J. Kennedy), **Supp. XV:** 163
"Alastor" (Shelley), **Supp. I Part 2:** 728
"Alatus" (Wilbur), **Supp. III Part 2:** 563
"Alba" (Creeley), **Supp. IV Part 1:** 150
Albee, Edward, **I: 71–96,** 113; **II:** 558, 591; **III:** 281, 387; **IV:** 4, 230; **Retro. Supp. II:** 104; **Supp. VIII:** 331; **Supp. XIII:** 196, 197
Albers, Joseph, **Supp. IV Part 2:** 621
Alberti, Rafael, **Supp. XV:** 75
Albright, Margery, **Supp. I Part 2:** 613
"Album, The" (Morris), **III:** 220
Alcestiad, The (Wilder), **IV:** 357, 374
"Alchemist, The" (Bogan), **Supp. III Part 1:** 50
"Alchemist in the City, The" (Hopkins), **Supp. IV Part 2:** 639
Alchymist's Journal, The (Connell), **Supp. XIV:** 80
"Alcmena" (Winters), **Supp. II Part 2:** 801
Alcott, Abba. *See* Alcott, Mrs. Amos Bronson (Abigail May)
Alcott, Amos Bronson, **II:** 7, 225; **IV:** 172, 173, 184; **Retro. Supp. I:** 217; **Supp. I Part 1:** 28, 29–32, 35, 39, 41, 45; **Supp. II Part 1:** 290; **Supp. XVI:** 84, 89
Alcott, Anna. *See* Pratt, Anna

Alcott, Louisa May, **IV:** 172; **Supp. I Part 1: 28–46; Supp. IX:** 128; **Supp. XV:** 338; **Supp. XVI:** 84
Alcott, May, **Supp. I Part 1:** 41
Alcott, Mrs. Amos Bronson (Abigail May), **IV:** 184; **Supp. I Part 1:** 29, 30, 31, 32, 35
Alcuin: A Dialogue (Brown), **Supp. I Part 1:** 126–127, 133
Alden, Hortense. *See* Farrell, Mrs. James T. (Hortense Alden)
Alden, John, **I:** 471; **II:** 502–503
"Alder Fork, The" (Leopold), **Supp. XIV:** 186
Aldington, Mrs. Richard. *See* Doolittle, Hilda
Aldington, Perdita, **Supp. I Part 1:** 258
Aldington, Richard, **II:** 517; **III:** 458, 459, 465, 472; **Retro. Supp. I:** 63, 127; **Supp. I Part 1:** 257–262, 270
Aldo Leopold: His Life and Work (Meine), **Supp. XIV:** 179
"Aldo Leopold's Intellectual Heritage" (Nash), **Supp. XIV:** 191–192
Aldon, Raymond, **Supp. XV:** 297
Aldrich, Thomas Bailey, **II:** 400; **Supp. II Part 1:** 192; **Supp. XIV:** 45; **Supp. XVIII:** 4
Aldrich, Tom, **Supp. I Part 2:** 415
Aldridge, John W., **Supp. I Part 1:** 196; **Supp. IV Part 1:** 286; **Supp. IV Part 2:** 680, 681; **Supp. VIII:** 189; **Supp. XI:** 228
Aleck Maury Sportsman (Gordon), **II:** 197, 200, 203–204
Alegría, Claribel, **Supp. IV Part 1:** 208
Aleichem, Sholom, **IV:** 3, 10; **Supp. IV Part 2:** 585
"Alert Lovers, Hidden Sides, and Ice Travelers: Notes on Poetic Form and Energy" (Dunn), **Supp. XI:** 153
"Aleš Debeljak" (Simic), **Supp. VIII:** 279
"Alex" (Oliver), **Supp. VII:** 232
Alexander, Doris, **Supp. XVII:** 99
Alexander, Elizabeth, **Supp. XVIII:** 171, 185, 186
Alexander, George, **II:** 331
Alexander, Michael, **Retro. Supp. I:** 293
"Alexander Crummell Dead" (Dunbar), **Supp. II Part 1:** 207, 208–209
Alexander's Bridge (Cather), **I:** 313, 314, 316–317, 326; **Retro. Supp. I:** 1, 6, 7, 8
Alexander the Great, **IV:** 322
"Alexandra" (Cather), **Retro. Supp. I:** 7, 9, 17
Alexandrov, V. E., **Retro. Supp. I:** 270
Alexie, Sherman, **Supp. XVIII:** 58
Algonquin Round Table, **Supp. IX:** 190, 191, 197
Algren, Nelson, **I:** 211; **Supp. IX: 1–18; Supp. V:** 4; **Supp. XII:** 126; **Supp. XIII:** 173; **Supp. XIV:** 3; **Supp. XVII:** 161
Alhambra, The (Irving), **II:** 310–311
Ali, Agha Shahid, **Supp. XVII:** 74
Alias Grace (Atwood), **Supp. XIII:** 20, **31–32**
Alice (film; Allen), **Supp. XV:** 2, 11
"Alice Doane's Appeal" (Hawthorne), **II:** 227
Alice in Wonderland (Carroll), **Supp. I Part 2:** 622
Alice's Adventures in Wonderland (Carroll), **Supp. XVI:** 261
"Alicia and I Talking on Edna's Steps" (Cisneros), **Supp. VII:** 64
"Alicia Who Sees Mice" (Cisneros), **Supp. VII:** 60
Alien 3 (screenplay, W. Gibson), **Supp. XVI:** 120, 124
"Ali in Havana" (Talese), **Supp. XVII:** 207, 208
Alison, Archibald, **Supp. I Part 1:** 151, 159
Alison's House (Glaspell), **Supp. III Part 1:** 182, 188, 189
Alive (screenplay, Shanley), **Supp. XIV:** 316
Alive and Writing: Interviews with American Authors of the 1980s (McCaffery and Gregory), **Supp. X:** 260
"Alki Beach" (Hugo), **Supp. VI:** 135
"Alla Breve Loving" (Wright), **Supp. XV:** 340
Alla Breve Loving (Wright), **Supp. XV:** 339, 340
"All Around the Town" (Benét), **Supp. XI:** 48, 58
All at Sea (Lardner), **II:** 427
"All Boy" (Rawlings), **Supp. X:** 222
Allegiances (Stafford), **Supp. XI: 322–323,** 329
"Allegory of the Cave" (Dunn), **Supp. XI:** 150
Allegro, Johnny (film, Tetzloff), **Supp. XVII:** 62
"Allegro, L'" (Milton), **Supp. XIV:** 8
Allen, Brooke, **Supp. VIII:** 153
Allen, Dick, **Supp. IX:** 279
Allen, Donald, **Supp. VIII:** 291; **Supp. XIII:** 112
Allen, Frank, **Supp. XI:** 126; **Supp. XII:** 186
Allen, Frederick Lewis, **Supp. I Part 2:** 655
Allen, Gay Wilson, **IV:** 352; **Supp. I Part 2:** 418
Allen, Paula Gunn. *See* Gunn Allen, Paula
Allen, Walter, **I:** 505; **III:** 352; **Supp. IV Part 2:** 685; **Supp. IX:** 231
Allen, Woody, **Supp. I Part 2:** 607, 623; **Supp. IV Part 1:** 205; **Supp. X:** 164; **Supp. XI:** 307; **Supp. XV: 1–18; Supp. XVII:** 48
"Aller et Retour" (Barnes), **Supp. III Part 1:** 36
Aller Retour New York (H. Miller), **III:** 178, 182, 183
Allessandrini, Goffredo, **Supp. IV Part 2:** 520
Alleys of Eden, The (R. O. Butler), **Supp. XII:** 62, **62–64,** 68
All God's Children Need Traveling Shoes (Angelou), **Supp. IV Part 1:** 2, 9–10, 12–13, 17
All God's Chillun Got Wings (O'Neill), **III:** 387, 391, 393–394
All Gone (Dixon), **Supp. XII:** 148, 149
"All Hallows" (Glück), **Supp. V:** 82
"All I Can Remember" (Jackson), **Supp. IX:** 115
"Alligators, The" (Updike), **IV:** 219
Allingham, John Till, **Supp. XV:** 243
"ALL IN THE STREET" (Baraka), **Supp. II Part 1:** 53
Allison, Dorothy, **Supp. XVIII:** 195
"All I Want" (Tapahonso), **Supp. IV Part 2:** 508
"All Little Colored Children Should Play the Harmonica" (Patchett), **Supp. XII:** 309
"All Mountains" (Doolittle), **Supp. I Part 1:** 271
All My Friends Are Going to Be Strangers (McMurtry), **Supp. V:** 224, 228, 229
"All My Pretty Ones" (Sexton), **Supp. II Part 2:** 681–682
All My Pretty Ones (Sexton), **Supp. II Part 2:** 678, 679–683
"All My Sad Captains" (Jewett), **Retro. Supp. II:** 134
All My Sons (A. Miller), **III:** 148, 149, 150, 151–153, 154, 155, 156, 158, 159, 160, 164, 166
"All Night, All Night" (Schwartz), **Supp. II Part 2:** 665
All Night Long (Caldwell), **I:** 297
"All-Night Melodies" (Nelson), **Supp. XVIII:** 185
"All Our Lost Children: Trauma and Testimony in the Performance of Childhood" (Pace), **Supp. XI:** 245
"All Out" (Hecht), **Supp. X:** 72
All Over (Albee), **I:** 91–94
"Allowance" (Minot), **Supp. VI:** 206, 207–208
"Alloy" (Rukeyser), **Supp. VI:** 279
"All Parrots Speak" (Bowles), **Supp. IV Part 1:** 89
Allport, Gordon, **II:** 363–364
All Quiet on the Western Front (Remarque), **Supp. IV Part 1:** 380, 381
"ALL REACTION IS DOOMED-!-!-!" (Baraka), **Supp. II Part 1:** 59
"All Revelation" (Frost), **II:** 160–162
All Shot Up (C. Himes), **Supp. XVI:** 143, 144
"All Souls'" (Gioia), **Supp. XV:** 117
"All Souls" (Wharton), **IV:** 315–316; **Retro. Supp. I:** 382
"All Souls' Night" (Yeats), **Supp. X:** 69
All Souls' Rising (Bell), **Supp. X:** 12, **13–16,** 17
"All-Star Literary Vaudeville" (Wilson), **IV:** 434–435
Allston, Washington, **II:** 298
All Stories Are True (Wideman), **Supp. X:** 320
"All That Is" (Wilbur), **Supp. III Part 2:** 563
"All the Bearded Irises of Life: Confessions of a Homospiritual" (Walker), **Supp. III Part 2:** 527
"All the Beautiful Are Blameless" (Wright), **Supp. III Part 2:** 597

ALL: The Collected Poems, 1956–1964 (Zukofsky), **Supp. III Part 2:** 630
ALL: The Collected Short Poems, 1923–1958 (Zukofsky), **Supp. III Part 2:** 629
All the Conspirators (Isherwood), **Supp. XIV:** 156, 159, 160
All the Dark and Beautiful Warriors (Hansberry), **Supp. IV Part 1:** 360, 374
All the Days and Nights: The Collected Stories (Maxwell), **Supp. VIII:** 151, 158, 169
"All the Dead Dears" (Plath), **Retro. Supp. II:** 246; **Supp. I Part 2:** 537
All the Good People I've Left Behind (Oates), **Supp. II Part 2:** 510, 522, 523
"All the Hippos Were Boiled in Their Tanks" (Burroughs and Kerouac), **Supp. III Part 1:** 94
All the King's Men (Warren), **I:** 489; **IV:** 243, 248–249, 252; **Supp. V:** 261; **Supp. VIII:** 126; **Supp. X:** 1; **Supp. XVIII:** 77, 79
All the Little Live Things (Stegner), **Supp. IV Part 2:** 599, 604, 605, 606, 609–610, 611, 613
All the Pretty Horses (film), **Supp. VIII:** 175
All the Pretty Horses (McCarthy), **Supp. VIII:** 175, **182–183,** 188
All the Sad Young Men (Fitzgerald), **II:** 94; **Retro. Supp. I:** 108
"All the Time in the World" (Dubus), **Supp. VII:** 91
"All the Way to Flagstaff, Arizona" (Bausch), **Supp. VII:** 47, 49
"All This and More" (Karr), **Supp. XI:** 243
All Tomorrow's Parties (W. Gibson), **Supp. XVI:** 119, 121, 123, 124, **130**
"All Too Real" (Vendler), **Supp. V:** 189
All Trivia: Triva, More Trivia, Afterthoughts, Last Words (L. P. Smith), **Supp. XIV:** 339
All-True Travels and Adventures of Lidie Newton (Smiley), **Supp. VI:** 292, **305–307**
All We Need of Hell (Crews), **Supp. XI:** **114**
Almack, Edward, **Supp. IV Part 2:** 435
al-Maghut, Muhammad, **Supp. XIII:** 278
"Almanac" (Swenson), **Supp. IV Part 2:** 641
Almanac of the Dead (Silko), **Supp. IV Part 2:** 558–559, 560, 561, 570–571
Almon, Bert, **Supp. IX:** 93
"Almost" (Untermeyer), **Supp. XV:** 304
Almost Revolution, The (Priaulx and Ungar), **Supp. XI:** 228
Alnilam (Dickey), **Supp. IV Part 1:** 176, 186, 188–189
"Alone" (Levine), **Supp. V:** 184, 185, 186
"Alone" (Poe), **Retro. Supp. II:** 266
"Alone" (Singer), **IV:** 15
"Alone" (Winters), **Supp. II Part 2:** 786, 811
Aloneness (Brooks), **Supp. III Part 1:** 85, 86
Alone with America (Corso), **Supp. XII:** 131
Alone with America (Howard), **Supp. IX:** 326
"Along America's Edges" (Sobin), **Supp. XVI:** 288
"Along the Color Line" (Du Bois), **Supp. II Part 1:** 173
Along the Illinois (Masters), **Supp. I Part 2:** 472
"Alphabet" (Nye), **Supp. XIII:** 283
Alphabet, An (Doty), **Supp. XI:** 120
Alphabet for Gourmets, An (M. F. K. Fisher), **Supp. XVII:** 86, 87, 92
Alphabet of Grace, The (Buechner), **Supp. XII:** 52
"Alphabet of My Dead, An" (Pinsky), **Supp. VI:** 235, 250
"Alphabet of Subjects, An" (Zukofsky), **Supp. III Part 2:** 624
"Alpine Christ, The" (Jeffers), **Supp. II Part 2:** 415, 419
Alpine Christ and Other Poems, The (Jeffers), **Supp. II Part 2:** 419
"Alpine Idyll, An" (Hemingway), **II:** 249; **Retro. Supp. I:** 176
Al Que Quiere! (W. C. Williams), **Retro. Supp. I:** 414, 416, **417,** 428
Alraune (Ewers; Endore, trans.), **Supp. XVII:** 54
Alsop, Joseph, **II:** 579
"Altar, The" (Herbert), **Supp. IV Part 2:** 646
"Altar, The" (MacLeish), **III:** 4
"Altar Boy" (Fante), **Supp. XI:** 160, 164
"Altar of the Dead, The" (James), **Retro. Supp. I:** 229
"Altars in the Street, The" (Levertov), **Supp. III Part 1:** 280
Alter, Robert, **Supp. XII:** 167
Altgeld, John Peter, **Supp. I Part 2:** 382, 455
Althea (Masters), **Supp. I Part 2:** 455, 459
Altick, Richard, **Supp. I Part 2:** 423
Altieri, Charles, **Supp. VIII:** 297, 303
Altman, Robert, **Supp. IX:** 143
"Alto" (C. Frost), **Supp. XV:** 101
"Altra Ego" (Brodsky), **Supp. VIII:** 31–32
A Lume Spento (Pound), **Retro. Supp. I:** 283, 285
"Aluminum House" (F. Barthelme), **Supp. XI:** 26
Alvares, Mosseh, **Supp. V:** 11
Alvarez, A., **Supp. I Part 2:** 526, 527; **Supp. II Part 1:** 99; **Supp. IX:** 248
Alvarez, Julia, **Supp. VII:** **1–21;** **Supp. XI:** 177; **Supp. XVII:** 71, 112
"Always a Rose" (L.-Y. Lee), **Supp. XV:** 215, 216
"Always in Good Humor" (Adams), **Supp. XV:** 294
Always Outnumbered, Always Outgunned (Mosley), **Supp. XIII:** 242
"Always the Stories" (Ortiz), **Supp. IV Part 2:** 499, 500, 502, 504, 512
Always the Young Strangers (Sandburg), **III:** 577–578, 579
Always Young and Fair (Richter), **Supp. XVIII:** **215–216**
Amadeus (Shaffer), **Supp. XIV:** 330
"Amahl and the Night Visitors: A Guide to the Tenor of Love" (Moore), **Supp. X:** 167
"Am and Am Not" (Olds), **Supp. X:** 212
"Amanita, The" (Francis), **Supp. IX:** 81
Amaranth (Robinson), **III:** 509, 510, 512, 513, 522, 523
Amazing Adele, The (Barillet and Grédy; Loos, trans.), **Supp. XVI:** 194
Amazing Adventures of Kavalier and Clay, The (Chabon), **Supp. XI:** 68, 76, **77–80**
Amazing Science Fiction Stories, **Supp. XVI:** 121
Amazons: An Intimate Memoir by the First Woman to Play in the National Hockey League (DeLillo), **Supp. VI:** 2
Ambassador of Peace, An (Abernon), **Supp. XVI:** 191
Ambassadors, The (H. James), **II:** 320, 333–334, 600; **III:** 517; **IV:** 322; **Retro. Supp. I:** 215, 218, 219, 220, 221, **232–233**
Ambelain, Robert, **Supp. I Part 1:** 260, 273, 274
"Ambition Bird, The" (Sexton), **Supp. II Part 2:** 693
Ambition: The Secret Passion (Epstein), **Supp. XIV:** 113–114
Ambler, Eric, **III:** 57
Ambrose Holt and Family (Glaspell), **Supp. III Part 1:** 175, 181, 184, 187, 188
"Ambrose Seyffert" (Masters), **Supp. I Part 2:** 464
"Ambush" (Komunyakaa), **Supp. XIII:** 122
Amen Corner, The (Baldwin), **Retro. Supp. II:** 5, 7; **Supp. I Part 1:** 48, 51, 54, 55, 56
America (Benét), **Supp. XI:** 46, 47, 51
"America" (Ginsberg), **Supp. II Part 1:** 58–59, 317
"America" (song), **IV:** 410
"America, America!" poem) (Schwartz), **Supp. II Part 2:** 665
"America, Commerce, and Freedom" (Rowson and Reinagle), **Supp. XV:** 240
"America, Seen Through Photographs, Darkly" (Sontag), **Supp. III Part 2:** 464
"America! America!" (story) (Schwartz), **Supp. II Part 2:** 640, 658–659, 660
America and Americans (Steinbeck), **IV:** 52
"America and the Vidal Chronicles" (Pease), **Supp. IV Part 2:** 687
America as a Civilization (Lerner), **III:** 60
"America Independent" (Freneau), **Supp. II Part 1:** 261
America Is Worth Saving (Dreiser), **Retro. Supp. II:** 96

American, The (James), **I:** 226; **II:** 326–327, 328, 331, 334; **IV:** 318; **Retro. Supp. I:** 220, **221,** 228, 376, 381
Americana (DeLillo), **Supp. VI:** 2, **3,** 5, 6, 8, 13, 14
American Adam, The (R. W. B. Lewis), **II:** 457–458; **Supp. XIII:** 93
American Almanac (Leeds), **II:** 110
American Anthem (Doctorow and Suares), **Supp. IV Part 1:** 234
"American Apocalypse" (Gunn Allen), **Supp. IV Part 1:** 325
American Aristocracy (film), **Supp. XVI:** 185–186
American Blood, (Nichols), **Supp. XIII:** 268
American Blues (T. Williams), **IV:** 381, 383
American Buffalo (Mamet), **Supp. XIV:** 239, 241, 242, 244–245, 246, 254, 255
American Caravan: A Yearbook of American Literature (Mumford, ed.), **Supp. II Part 2:** 482
American Cause, The (MacLeish), **III:** 3
American Childhood, An (Dillard), **Supp. VI: 19–21,** 23, 24, 25, 26, 30, 31
"American Childhood in the Dominican Republic, An" (Alvarez), **Supp. VII:** 2, 5
American Child Supreme, An: The Education of a Liberation Ecologist (Nichols), **Supp. XIII:** 256, 257, 258, 264, 265, 266, 267, 268, 269
American Claimant, The (Twain), **IV:** 194, 198–199
American Crisis I (Paine), **Supp. I Part 2:** 508
American Crisis II (Paine), **Supp. I Part 2:** 508
American Crisis XIII (Paine), **Supp. I Part 2:** 509
"American Critic, The" (J. Spingarn), **I:** 266
American Culture, Canons, and the Case of Elizabeth Stoddard (Smith and Weinauer), **Supp. XV:** 270
American Daughter, An (Wasserstein), **Supp. XV: 330–332,** 333
American Democrat, The (Cooper), **I:** 343, 346, 347, 353
American Desert (Everett), **Supp. XVIII: 62–63**
American Diary (Webb), **Supp. I Part 1:** 5
American Drama since World War II (Weales), **IV:** 385
American Dream, An (Mailer), **III:** 27, 33–34, 35, 39, 41, 43, 44; **Retro. Supp. II:** 203, **204–205**
American Dream, The (Albee), **I:** 74–76, 77, 89, 94
"American Dreams" (Simpson), **Supp. IX:** 274
American Earth (Caldwell), **I:** 290, 308
"American Emperors" (Poirier), **Supp. IV Part 2:** 690
American Exodus, An (Lange and Taylor), **I:** 293
American Experience, The (Parkes), **Supp. I Part 2:** 617–618
American Express (Corso), **Supp. XII:** 129
"American Express" (Salter), **Supp. IX:** 260–261
"American Fear of Literature, The" (Lewis), **II:** 451
American Female Patriotism (S. Warner as Wetherell), **Supp. XVIII: 260–261,** 262, 263
American Fictions (Hardwick), **Supp. X:** 171
American Fictions, 1940–1980 (Karl), **Supp. IV Part 1:** 384
"American Financier, The" (Dreiser), **II:** 428
American Folkways (book series), **I:** 290
American Heroine: The Life and Legend of Jane Addams (Davis), **Supp. I Part 1:** 1
American Historical Novel, The (Leisy), **Supp. II Part 1:** 125
"American Horse" (Erdrich), **Supp. IV Part 1:** 333
American Humor (Rourke), **IV:** 339, 352
American Hunger (Wright), **Supp. IV Part 1:** 11
American Indian Anthology, An (Tvedten, ed.), **Supp. IV Part 2:** 505
"American Indian Women: At the Center of Indigenous Resistance in Contemporary North America" (Jaimes and Halsey), **Supp. IV Part 1:** 331
"American in England, An" (Wylie), **Supp. I Part 2:** 707
American Jitters, The: A Year of the Slump (Wilson), **IV:** 427, 428
American Journal (Hayden), **Supp. II Part 1:** 367
American Journey: The Times of Robert F. Kennedy (Plimpton, ed.), **Supp. XVI:** 245
"American Land Ethic, An" (Momaday), **Supp. IV Part 2:** 488
American Landscape, The, **Supp. I Part 1:** 157
American Language, The (Mencken), **II:** 289, 430; **III:** 100, 104, 105, 108, 111, 119–120
American Language, The: Supplement One (Mencken), **III:** 111
American Language, The: Supplement Two (Mencken), **III:** 111
"American Letter" (MacLeish), **III:** 13
"American Liberty" (Freneau), **Supp. II Part 1:** 257
American Literary History (Harrison), **Supp. VIII:** 37
American Mercury, **Supp. XI:** 163, 164
American Mind, The (Commager), **Supp. I Part 2:** 650
American Moderns: Bohemian New York and the Creation of a New Century (Stansell), **Supp. XVII:** 106
American Moderns: From Rebellion to Conformity (Geismar), **Supp. IX:** 15; **Supp. XI:** 223
"American Names" (Benét), **Supp. XI:** 47
American Nature Writers (Elder, ed.), **Supp. IX:** 25
American Nature Writers (Winter), **Supp. X:** 104
American Negro, The (W. H. Thomas), **Supp. II Part 1:** 168
American Notebooks, The (Hawthorne), **II:** 226
American Novel Since World War II, The (Klein, ed.), **Supp. XI:** 233
Americano, The (film), **Supp. XVI:** 185
"American Original, An: Learning from a Literary Master" (Wilkinson), **Supp. VIII:** 164, 165, 168
American Ornithology (Wilson), **Supp. XVI:** 4, 6
American Pastoral (P. Roth), **Retro. Supp. II:** 279, 289, **292–293; Supp. XI:** 68
American Places (Porter, Stegner and Stegner), **Supp. IV Part 2:** 599
"American Poet" (Shapiro), **Supp. II Part 2:** 701
"American Poetry" (Simpson), **Supp. IX:** 272
American Poetry, 1922: A Miscellany (Untermeyer, ed.), **Supp. XV:** 306
"American Poetry and American Life" (Pinsky), **Supp. VI:** 239–240
American Poetry from the Beginning to Whitman (Untermeyer, ed.), **Supp. XV:** 310
American Poetry since 1900 (Untermeyer, ed.), **Supp. XV:** 306
American Poetry since 1945: A Critical Survey (Stepanchev), **Supp. XI:** 312
American Poetry since 1960 (Mesic), **Supp. IV Part 1:** 175
American Poets since World War II Dictionary of Literary Biography (Gwynn, ed.), **Supp. XV:** 343
American Primer, An (Boorstin), **I:** 253
American Primer, An (Whitman), **IV:** 348
"American Primitive" (W. J. Smith), **Supp. XIII:** 333
American Primitive: Poems (Oliver), **Supp. VII:** 234–237, 238
American Procession, An: The Major American Writers from 1830–1930—the Crucial Century (Kazin), **Supp. VIII: 105–106,** 108
"American Prose Writers" articles (Briggs), **Supp. XVIII:** 11
American Radio Company, The (radio show, Keillor), **Supp. XVI:** 176–177
"American Realist Playwrights, The" (McCarthy), **II:** 562
American Register, or General Repository of History, Politics, and Science, The (Brown, ed.), **Supp. I Part 1:** 146
American Renaissance (Matthiessen), **I:** 259–260; **III:** 310; **Supp. XIII:** 93
"American Rendezvous, An" (Beauvoir), **Supp. IX:** 4
American Scene, The (James), **II:** 336; **III:** 460; **Retro. Supp. I:** 232, 235
American Scenes (Kozlenko, ed.), **IV:** 378
"American Scholar, The" (Emerson), **I:** 239; **II:** 8, 12–13; **Retro. Supp. I:** 62,

74–75, 149, 298; **Retro. Supp. II:** 155; **Supp. I Part 2:** 420; **Supp. IX:** 227, 271; **Supp. XIV:** 104
Americans in England; or, Lessons for Daughters (Rowson), **Supp. XV:** 240
"American Soldier, The" (Freneau), **Supp. II Part 1:** 269
American Songbag, The (Sandburg), **III:** 583
"American Student in Paris, An" (Farrell), **II:** 45
"American Sublime, The" (Stevens), **IV:** 74
"American Tar, The; or, The Press Gang Defeated" (Rowson and Taylor), **Supp. XV:** 238
"American Temperament, The" (Locke), **Supp. XIV:** 211
American Tragedy, An (Dreiser), **I:** 497, 498, 499, 501, 502, 503, 511–515, 517, 518, 519; **III:** 251; **IV:** 35, 484; **Retro. Supp. II:** 93, 95, **104–108; Supp. XVII:** 155
"American Triptych" (Kenyon), **Supp. VII:** 165
"American Use for German Ideals" (Bourne), **I:** 228
"American Village, The" (Freneau), **Supp. II Part 1:** 256
American Village, The (Freneau), **Supp. II Part 1:** 256, 257
America's Coming-of-Age (Brooks), **I:** 228, 230, 240, 245, 258; **IV:** 427
America's Humor: From Poor Richard to Doonesbury (Blair and Hill), **Retro. Supp. II:** 286
"America's Part in World Peace" (Locke), **Supp. XIV:** 208
America's Rome (Vance), **Supp. IV Part 2:** 684
America: The Story of a Free People (Commager and Nevins), **I:** 253
America Was Promises (MacLeish), **III:** 16, 17
"Amerika" (Snyder), **Supp. VIII:** 301
Ames, Christopher, **Supp. XVIII:** 242–243
Ames, Fisher, **Supp. I Part 2:** 486
Ames, Lois, **Supp. I Part 2:** 541, 547
Ames, William, **IV:** 158
Ames Stewart, Beatrice, **Supp. IX:** 200
Amichai, Yehuda, **Supp. XI:** 267
Amidon, Stephen, **Supp. XI:** 333
Amiel, Henri F., **I:** 241, 243, 250
Amis, Kingsley, **IV:** 430; **Supp. IV Part 2:** 688; **Supp. VIII:** 167; **Supp. XIII:** 93; **Supp. XV:** 117
Amis, Martin, **Retro. Supp. I:** 278
Ammons, A. R., **Supp. III Part 2:** 541; **Supp. IX:** 41, 42, 46; **Supp. VII: 23–38; Supp. XII:** 121; **Supp. XV:** 115; **Supp. XVII:** 242
Ammons, Elizabeth, **Retro. Supp. I:** 364, 369; **Retro. Supp. II:** 140
Amnesia Moon (Lethem), **Supp. XVIII:** 136, **138–139**
"Among Children" (Levine), **Supp. V:** 192
Among Friends (M. F. K. Fisher), **Supp. XVII:** 89, 90–91, 92
Among My Books (Lowell), **Supp. I Part 2:** 407
"Among School Children" (Yeats), **III:** 249; **Supp. IX:** 52; **Supp. XIV:** 8
"Among the Hills" (Whittier), **Supp. I Part 2:** 703
Among the Isles of Shoals (Thaxter), **Supp. XIII:** 152
"Among Those Present" (Benét), **Supp. XI:** 53
"Amoral Moralist" (White), **Supp. I Part 2:** 648
Amory, Cleveland, **Supp. I Part 1:** 316
Amory, Fred, **Supp. III Part 1:** 2
Amos (biblical book), **II:** 166
Amran, David, **Supp. XIV:** 150
"Am Strand von Tanger" (Salter), **Supp. IX:** 257
"AMTRAK" (Baraka), **Supp. II Part 1:** 60
Amy and Isabelle (Strout), **Supp. X:** 86
"Amy Lowell of Brookline, Mass." (Scott), **II:** 512
Amy Lowell: Portrait of the Poet in Her Time (Gregory), **II:** 512
"Amy Wentworth" (Whittier), **Supp. I Part 2:** 694, 696
Anabase (Perse), **III:** 12
"Anabasis (I)" (Merwin), **Supp. III Part 1:** 342, 346
"Anabasis (II)" (Merwin), **Supp. III Part 1:** 342, 346
Anagrams: A Novel (Moore), **Supp. X:** 163, 164, 167, **169–171,** 172
Analects (Confucius), **Supp. IV Part 1:** 14
Analects, The (Pound, trans.), **III:** 472
Analogy (J. Butler), **II:** 8
"Analysis of a Theme" (Stevens), **IV:** 81
Anarchiad, The, A Poem on the Restoration of Chaos and Substantial Night, in Twenty Four Books (Barlow), **Supp. II Part 1:** 70
Anarchist Woman, An (Hapgood), **Supp. XVII:** 102–103
Anatomy Lesson, and Other Stories, The (Connell), **Supp. XIV:** 84, 87, 89
"Anatomy Lesson, The" (Connell), **Supp. XIV:** 84, 86, 87
Anatomy Lesson, The (P. Roth), **Retro. Supp. II:** 286, 290; **Supp. III Part 2:** 422–423, 425
"Anatomy Lesson of Dr. Nicholaas Tulp, Amsterdam, 1632, The" (Bierds), **Supp. XVII:** 27–28
Anatomy of Criticism (Frye), **Supp. XIII:** 19; **Supp. XIV:** 15
Anatomy of Melancholy (Burton), **III:** 78; **Supp. XVII:** 229
Anatomy of Nonsense, The (Winters), **Supp. II Part 2:** 811, 812
Anaya, Rudolfo A., **Supp. IV Part 2:** 502; **Supp. XIII:** 213, 220
"Ancestor" (A. Finch), **Supp. XVII:** 72
Ancestors (Maxwell), **Supp. VIII:** 152, 168
"Ancestors, The" (Tate), **IV:** 128
Ancestral Voice: Conversations with N. Scott Momaday (Woodard), **Supp. IV Part 2:** 484, 485, 486, 489, 493
"Anchorage" (Harjo), **Supp. XII:** 220–221
Ancient Child, The: A Novel (Momaday), **Supp. IV Part 2:** 488, 489–491, 492, 493
"Ancient Egypt/Fannie Goldbarth" (Goldbarth), **Supp. XII:** 191–192
Ancient Evenings (Mailer), **Retro. Supp. II:** 206, 210, 213
Ancient Law, The (Glasgow), **II:** 179–180, 192
Ancient Musics (Goldbarth), **Supp. XII:** 191–192
"Ancient Semitic Rituals for the Dead" (Goldbarth), **Supp. XII:** 191–192
"Ancient World, The" (Doty), **Supp. XI:** 122
& (And) (Cummings), **I:** 429, 431, 432, 437, 445, 446, 448
Andersen, Hans Christian, **I:** 441; **Supp. I Part 2:** 622
Anderson, Charles R., **Supp. I Part 1:** 356, 360, 368, 371, 372
Anderson, Frances, **I:** 231
Anderson, Guy, **Supp. X:** 264, 265
Anderson, Henry J., **Supp. I Part 1:** 156
Anderson, Irwin M., **I:** 98–99
Anderson, Jon, **Supp. V:** 338
Anderson, Judith, **III:** 399
Anderson, Karl, **I:** 99, 103
Anderson, Lorraine, **Supp. XVIII:** 189
Anderson, Margaret, **I:** 103; **III:** 471
Anderson, Margaret Bartlett, **III:** 171
Anderson, Mary Jane. *See* Lanier, Mrs. Robert Sampson (Mary Jane Anderson)
Anderson, Maxwell, **III:** 159
Anderson, Mrs. Irwin M., **I:** 98–99
Anderson, Mrs. Sherwood (Tennessee Mitchell), **I:** 100; **Supp. I Part 2:** 459, 460
Anderson, Quentin, **Retro. Supp. I:** 392
Anderson, Robert, **Supp. I Part 1:** 277; **Supp. V:** 108
Anderson, Sally, **Supp. XIII:** 95
Anderson, Sherwood, **I: 97–120,** 211, 374, 375, 384, 405, 423, 445, 480, 487, 495, 506, 518; **II:** 27, 38, 44, 55, 56, 68, 250–251, 263, 271, 289, 451, 456–457; **III:** 220, 224, 382–383, 453, 483, 545, 576, 579; **IV:** 27, 40, 46, 190, 207, 433, 451, 482; **Retro. Supp. I:** 79, 80, 177; **Supp. I Part 2:** 378, 430, 459, 472, 613; **Supp. IV Part 2:** 502; **Supp. IX:** 14, 309; **Supp. V:** 12, 250; **Supp. VIII:** 39, 152; **Supp. XI:** 159, 164; **Supp. XII:** 343; **Supp. XV:** 298; **Supp. XVI:** 17, 20; **Supp. XVII:** 105
Anderson, T. J., **Supp. XIII:** 132
Anderssen, A., **III:** 252
"And Hickman Arrives" (Ellison), **Retro. Supp. II:** 118, 126; **Supp. II Part 1:** 248
And in the Hanging Gardens (Aiken), **I:** 63
"And It Came to Pass" (Wright), **Supp. XV:** 348

And I Worked at the Writer's Trade (Cowley), **Supp. II Part 1:** 137, 139, 141, 143, 147, 148
Andorra (Cameron), **Supp. XII:** 79, 81, **88–91**
"——and Other Poets" (column; Untermeyer), **Supp. XV:** 294
"*——and Other Poets*" (Untermeyer), **Supp. XV:** 297
Andral, Gabriel, **Supp. I Part 1:** 302
Andre, Michael, **Supp. XII:** 117–118, 129, 132, 133–134
Andre's Mother (McNally), **Supp. XIII:** 206
Andress, Ursula, **Supp. XI:** 307
"Andrew Jackson" (Masters), **Supp. I Part 2:** 472
Andrews, Bruce, **Supp. IV Part 2:** 426
Andrews, Roy Chapman, **Supp. X:** 172
Andrews, Tom, **Supp. XI:** 317
Andrews, Wayne, **IV:** 310
Andrews, William L., **Supp. IV Part 1:** 13
Andreyev, Leonid Nikolaevich, **I:** 53; **II:** 425
Andria (Terence), **IV:** 363
"Andromache" (Dubus), **Supp. VII:** 84
"And Summer Will Not Come Again" (Plath), **Retro. Supp. II:** 242
"And That Night Clifford Died" (Levine), **Supp. V:** 195
And the Band Played On (Shilts), **Supp. X:** 145
"And the Moon Be Still as Bright" (Bradbury), **Supp. IV Part 1:** 106
"And the Sea Shall Give up Its Dead" (Wilder), **IV:** 358
And Things That Go Bump in the Night (McNally), **Supp. XIII: 196–197,** 205, 208
And to Think That I Saw It on Mulberry Street (Geisel), **Supp. XVI:** 100, 101, 104
"And *Ut Pictura Poesis* Is Her Name" (Ashbery), **Supp. III Part 1:** 19
And We Are Millions (Ryan), **Supp. XVIII:** 225
"Anecdote and Storyteller" (Howe), **Supp. VI:** 127
"Anecdote of the Jar" (Stevens), **IV:** 83–84
"Anemone" (Rukeyser), **Supp. VI:** 281, 285
"Angel, The" (Buck), **Supp. II Part 1:** 127
"Angel and Unicorn and Butterfly" (Everwine), **Supp. XV:** 76
Angela's Ashes (McCourt), **Supp. XII: 271–279,** 283, 285
"Angel at the Grave, The" (Wharton), **IV:** 310; **Retro. Supp. I:** 365
"Angel Butcher" (Levine), **Supp. V:** 181
Angel City (Shepard), **Supp. III Part 2:** 432, 445
"Angel Is My Watermark!, The" (H. Miller), **III:** 180
Angell, Carol, **Supp. I Part 2:** 655
Angell, Katharine Sergeant. *See* White, Katharine
Angell, Roger, **Supp. I Part 2:** 655; **Supp. V:** 22; **Supp. VIII:** 139
Angel Landing (Hoffman), **Supp. X: 82–83**
"Angel Levine" (Malamud), **Supp. I Part 2:** 431, 432, 433–434, 437
Angel of Bethesda, The (Mather), **Supp. II Part 2:** 464
"Angel of the Bridge, The" (Cheever), **Supp. I Part 1:** 186–187
"Angel of the Odd, The" (Poe), **III:** 425
Angelo Herndon Jones (Hughes), **Retro. Supp. I:** 203
"Angel on the Porch, An" (Wolfe), **IV:** 451
Angelou, Maya, **Supp. IV Part 1: 1–19; Supp. XI:** 20, 245; **Supp. XIII:** 185; **Supp. XVI:** 259
"Angel Poem, The" (Stern), **Supp. IX:** 292
Angels and Earthly Creatures (Wylie), **Supp. I Part 2:** 709, 713, 724–730
Angels in America: A Gay Fantasia on National Themes (Kushner), **Supp. IX:** 131, 134, **141–146**
"Angels of the Love Affair" (Sexton), **Supp. II Part 2:** 692
"Angel Surrounded by Paysans" (Stevens), **IV:** 93
Angel That Troubled the Waters, The (Wilder), **IV:** 356, 357–358
"Anger" (Creeley), **Supp. IV Part 1:** 150–152
Anger (Sarton), **Supp. VIII: 256**
"Anger against Children" (R. Bly), **Supp. IV Part 1:** 73
Angle of Ascent (Hayden), **Supp. II Part 1:** 363, 367, 370
"Angle of Geese" (Momaday), **Supp. IV Part 2:** 485
Angle of Geese and Other Poems (Momaday), **Supp. IV Part 2:** 487, 491
Angle of Repose (Stegner), **Supp. IV Part 2:** 599, 605, 606, 610–611
"*Angle of Repose* and the Writings of Mary Hallock Foote: A Source Study" (Williams-Walsh), **Supp. IV Part 2:** 611
Anglo-Saxon Century, The (Dos Passos), **I:** 474–475, 483
Angoff, Charles, **III:** 107
"Angola Question Mark" (Hughes), **Supp. I Part 1:** 344
Angry Wife, The (Sedges), **Supp. II Part 1:** 125
"Angry Women Are Building: Issues and Struggles Facing American Indian Women Today" (Gunn Allen), **Supp. IV Part 1:** 324
"Animal, Vegetable, and Mineral" (Bogan), **Supp. III Part 1:** 66
"Animal Acts" (Simic), **Supp. VIII:** 278
Animal and Vegetable Physiology Considered with Reference to Natural Theology (Roget), **Supp. I Part 1:** 312
"Animal Bodies: Corporeality, Class, and Subject Formation in *The Wide, Wide World*" (Mason), **Supp. XVIII:** 263
Animal Dreams (Kingsolver), **Supp. VII:** 199, 204–207
Animal Magnetism (Prose), **Supp. XVI:** 251, 260
"Animals, The" (Merwin), **Supp. III Part 1:** 348
"Animals Are Passing from Our Lives" (Levine), **Supp. V:** 181, 182
Animals in That Country, The (Atwood), **Supp. XIII:** 20, 33
Animals of the Soul: Sacred Animals of the Oglala Sioux (Brown), **Supp. IV Part 2:** 487
"Animals You Eat, The" (X. J. Kennedy), **Supp. XV:** 169
"Animula" (Eliot), **Retro. Supp. I:** 64
Anita Loos Rediscovered (M. A. Loos), **Supp. XVI:** 196
Ankor Wat (Ginsberg), **Supp. II Part 1:** 323
"Annabelle" (Komunyakaa), **Supp. XIII:** 117
"Annabel Lee" (Poe), **Retro. Supp. I:** 273; **Retro. Supp. II:** 266
Anna Christie (O'Neill), **III:** 386, 389, 390
Anna Karenina (Tolstoy), **I:** 10; **II:** 290; **Retro. Supp. I:** 225; **Supp. V:** 323
"*Anna Karenina*" (Trilling), **Supp. III Part 2:** 508
"Anna Who Was Mad" (Sexton), **Supp. II Part 2:** 692
"Ann Burlak" (Rukeyser), **Supp. VI:** 280
"Anne" (Davis), **Supp. XVI:** 91, 92
"Anne" (Oliver), **Supp. VII:** 232
"Anne at the Symphony" (Shields), **Supp. VII:** 310
"Anne Bradstreet's Poetic Voices" (Requa), **Supp. I Part 1:** 107
Anne Sexton: The Artist and Her Critics (McClatchy), **Supp. XII:** 253
"Ann from the Street" (Dixon), **Supp. XII:** 146–147
"Ann Garner" (Agee), **I:** 27
"Anniad, The" (Brooks), **Supp. III Part 1:** 77, 78
Annie (musical), **Supp. IV Part 2:** 577
Annie Allen (Brooks), **Supp. III Part 1:** 76–79
Annie Dillard Reader, The (Dillard), **Supp. VI:** 23
Annie Hall (film; Allen), **Supp. IV Part 1:** 205; **Supp. XV:** 1, 2, 4, 5, **6–7,** 14
Annie John (Kincaid), **Supp. VII:** 184–186, 193
Annie Kilburn, a Novel (Howells), **II:** 275, 286, 287
"Annihilation" (X. J. Kennedy), **Supp. XV:** 168
Anniversary (Shields), **Supp. VII:** 320, 322, 323, 324
"Annunciation" (Nelson), **Supp. XVIII:** 174
"Annunciation, The" (Le Sueur), **Supp. V:** 130
Ann Vickers (Lewis), **II:** 453
"A No-Account Creole, A" (Chopin), **Retro. Supp. II:** 64
"Anodyne" (Komunyakaa), **Supp. XIII:** 130

Another America/Otra America (Kingsolver), **Supp. VII:** 207–209
"Another Animal" (Swenson), **Supp. IV Part 2:** 639
Another Animal: Poems (Swenson), **Supp. IV Part 2:** 639–641, 649
Another Antigone (Gurney), **Supp. V:** 97, 98, 100, 101, 102, 105
"Another August" (Merrill), **Supp. III Part 1:** 326
"Another Beer" (Matthews), **Supp. IX:** 158
Another Country (Baldwin), **Retro. Supp. II: 9–11,** 14; **Supp. I Part 1:** 51, 52, 56–58, 63, 67, 337; **Supp. II Part 1:** 40; **Supp. VIII:** 349
"Another Language" (Jong), **Supp. V:** 131
Another Mother Tongue: Gay Words, Gay Worlds (Grahn), **Supp. IV Part 1:** 330
"Another Night in the Ruins" (Kinnell), **Supp. III Part 1:** 239, 251
"Another Old Woman" (W. C. Williams), **Retro. Supp. I:** 423
Another Part of the Forest (Hellman), **Supp. I Part 1:** 282–283, 297
Another Republic: 17 European and South American Writers (Strand, trans.), **Supp. IV Part 2:** 630
Another Roadside Attraction (Robbins), **Supp. X:** 259, 261, 262, 263, 264, 265–266, **267–269,** 274, 275, 277, 284
Another Side of Bob Dylan (album, Dylan), **Supp. XVIII:** 25
"Another Spring Uncovered" (Swenson), **Supp. IV Part 2:** 644
Another Thin Man (film), **Supp. IV Part 1:** 355
Another Time (Auden), **Supp. II Part 1:** 15
Another Turn of the Crank (Berry), **Supp. X:** 25, 35
"Another upon the Same" (Taylor), **IV:** 161
"Another Voice" (Wilbur), **Supp. III Part 2:** 557
"Another Wife" (Anderson), **I:** 114
Another Woman (film; Allen), **Supp. XV:** 11
Another You (Beattie), **Supp. V:** 29, 31, 33–34
Anouilh, Jean, **Supp. I Part 1:** 286–288, 297
Ansa, Tina McElroy, **Supp. XVIII:** 195
Ansky, S., **IV:** 6
Ansky, Shloime, **Supp. IX:** 131, 138
"Answer, The" (Jeffers), **Supp. III Part 2:** 423
Answered Prayers: The Unfinished Novel (Capote), **Supp. III Part 1:** 113, 125, 131–132; **Supp. XVI:** 245
"Answering the Deer: Genocide and Continuance in the Poetry of American Indian Women" (Gunn Allen), **Supp. IV Part 1:** 322, 325
"Answer of Minerva, The: Pacifism and Resistance in Simone Weil" (Merton), **Supp. VIII:** 204
Antaeus (Wolfe), **IV:** 461
"Ante-Bellum Sermon, An" (Dunbar), **Supp. II Part 1:** 203–204
Antheil, George, **III:** 471, 472; **IV:** 404
Anthem (Rand), **Supp. IV Part 2:** 523
Anthology of Holocaust Literature (Glatstein, Knox, and Margoshes, eds.), **Supp. X:** 70
Anthology of Twentieth-Century Brazilian Poetry, An (Bishop and Brasil, eds.), **Retro. Supp. II:** 50; **Supp. I Part 1:** 94
Anthon, Kate, **I:** 452
Anthony, Andrew, **Supp. XVI:** 235, 245, 246
Anthony, Saint, **III:** 395
Anthony, Susan B., **Supp. XI:** 200
"Anthropologist as Hero, The" (Sontag), **Supp. III Part 2:** 451
"Anthropology of Water, The" (Carson), **Supp. XII: 102–103**
Anthropos: The Future of Art (Cummings), **I:** 430
Antichrist (Nietzsche), **III:** 176
"Anti-Father" (Dove), **Supp. IV Part 1:** 246
"Anti-Feminist Woman, The" (Rich), **Supp. I Part 2:** 550
Antigone (Sophocles), **Supp. I Part 1:** 284; **Supp. X:** 249
Antin, David, **Supp. VIII:** 292; **Supp. XII:** 2, 8
Antin, Mary, **Supp. IX:** 227; **Supp. XVI:** 148, 149
Anti-Oedipus: Capitalism and Schizophrenia (Deleuze and Guattari), **Supp. XII:** 4
Antiphon, The (Barnes), **Supp. III Part 1:** 43–44
"Antiquities" (Mather), **Supp. II Part 2:** 452
"Antiquity of Freedom, The" (Bryant), **Supp. I Part 1:** 168
"Antislavery Tocsin, An" (Douglass), **Supp. III Part 1:** 171
Antoine, Andre, **III:** 387
Antonioni, Michelangelo, **Supp. IV Part 1:** 46, 47, 48
Antony and Cleopatra (Shakespeare), **I:** 285
"Antony on Behalf of the Play" (Burke), **I:** 284
"An trentiesme de mon Eage, L'" (MacLeish), **III:** 9
"Ants" (R. Bly), **Supp. IV Part 1:** 71
Anxiety of Influence, The (Bloom), **Supp. XIII:** 46
"Any City" (Untermeyer), **Supp. XV:** 296
"Any Object" (Swenson), **Supp. IV Part 2:** 640
"Any Porch" (Parker), **Supp. IX:** 194
Anything Else (film; Allen), **Supp. XV:** 2, 11
"Anywhere Out of This World" (Baudelaire), **II:** 552
Any Woman Can't (Wasserstein), **Supp. XV:** 322
Any Woman's Blues (Jong), **Supp. V:** 115, 123, 126
Anzaldúa, Gloria, **Supp. IV Part 1:** 330; **Supp. XIII:** 223
"Aphorisms on Society" (Stevens), **Retro. Supp. I:** 303
"Apiary IX" (C. Frost), **Supp. XV:** 106
"Apisculptures" (Bierds), **Supp. XVII:** 29
Apollinaire, Guillaume, **I:** 432; **II:** 529; **III:** 196; **IV:** 80; **Retro. Supp. II:** 326; **Supp. XV:** 182
Apologies to the Iroquois (Wilson), **IV:** 429
"Apology" (C. Frost), **Supp. XV:** 103
"Apology, An" (Malamud), **Supp. I Part 2:** 435, 437
"Apology for Bad Dreams" (Jeffers), **Supp. II Part 2:** 427, 438; **Supp. XVII:** 112
"Apology for Crudity, An" (Anderson), **I:** 109
Apology for Poetry (Sidney), **Supp. II Part 1:** 105
"Apostle of the Tules, An" (Harte), **Supp. II Part 1:** 356
"Apostrophe to a Dead Friend" (Kumin), **Supp. IV Part 2:** 442, 451, 452
"Apostrophe to a Pram Rider" (White), **Supp. I Part 2:** 678
"Apostrophe to Man (on reflecting that the world is ready to go to war again)" (Millay), **III:** 127
"Apostrophe to Vincentine, The" (Stevens), **IV:** 90
"Apotheosis" (Kingsolver), **Supp. VII:** 208
"Apotheosis of Martin Luther King, The" (Hardwick), **Supp. III Part 1:** 203–204
Appalachia (Wright), **Supp. V:** 333, 345
"Appalachian Book of the Dead III" (Wright), **Supp. V:** 345
"Appeal to Progressives, An" (Wilson), **IV:** 429
Appeal to Reason (Paine), **I:** 490
Appeal to the World, An (Du Bois), **Supp. II Part 1:** 184
Appearance and Reality (Bradley), **I:** 572
"Appendix to 'The Anniad'" (Brooks), **Supp. III Part 1:** 77
Apple, Max, **Supp. VIII:** 14; **Supp. XVII: 1–11,** 49–50
Apple, Sam, **Supp. XVII:** 8
"Apple, The" (Kinnell), **Supp. III Part 1:** 250
Applebaum, Anne, **Supp. XVI:** 153
Applegarth, Mabel, **II:** 465, 478
"Apple of Discord, The" (Humphrey), **Supp. IX:** 109
"Apple Peeler" (Francis), **Supp. IX:** 82
"Apple Rind" (C. Frost), **Supp. XV:** 102
Appleseed, Johnny (pseudonym). *See* Chapman, John (Johnny Appleseed)
Appleton, Nathan, **II:** 488
Appleton, Thomas Gold, **Supp. I Part 1:** 306; **Supp. I Part 2:** 415
"Apple Tree, The" (McCarriston), **Supp. XIV:** 263, 268
"Applicant, The" (Plath), **Retro. Supp. II:** 252; **Supp. I Part 2:** 535, 544, 545

"Application, The" (Neugeboren), **Supp. XVI:** 219, 220, 225
"Applications of the Doctrine" (Hass), **Supp. VI: 100–101**
Appointment, The (film), **Supp. IX:** 253
Appointment in Samarra (O'Hara), **III:** 361, 363–364, 365–367, 371, 374, 375, 383
Appreciation of Sarah Orne Jewett (Cary), **Retro. Supp. II:** 132
"Approaches, The" (Merwin), **Supp. III Part 1:** 350
"Approaching Artaud" (Sontag), **Supp. III Part 2:** 470–471
"Approaching Prayer" (Dickey), **Supp. IV Part 1:** 175
Approach to Literature, An: A Collection of Prose and Verse with Analyses and Discussions (Brooks, Warren, and Purser), **Su pp. XIV:**4
"Approach to Thebes, The" (Kunitz), **Supp. III Part 1:** 265–267
Approach to Vedanta, An (Isherwood), **Supp. XIV:** 157, 163, 164
"Appropriation of Cultures, The" (Everett), **Supp. XVIII:** 66
"Après-midi d'un faune, L'" (Mallarmé), **III:** 8
"April" (Bierds), **Supp. XVII:** 29
"April" (W. C. Williams), **Retro. Supp. I:** 422
"April" (Winters), **Supp. II Part 2:** 788
April, Steve. *See* Lacy, Ed
"April Galleons" (Ashbery), **Supp. III Part 1:** 26
April Galleons (Ashbery), **Supp. III Part 1:** 26
April Hopes (Howells), **II:** 285, 289
"April Lovers" (Ransom), **III:** 489–490
"April Showers" (Wharton), **Retro. Supp. I:** 361
"April Today Main Street" (Olson), **Supp. II Part 2:** 581
April Twilights (Cather), **I:** 313; **Retro. Supp. I:** 5
"Apt Pupil" (King), **Supp. V:** 152
Arabian Nights, **I:** 204; **II:** 8; **Supp. I Part 2:** 584, 599; **Supp. IV Part 1:** 1
"Arabic Coffee" (Nye), **Supp. XIII:** 276
"Araby" (Joyce), **I:** 174; **Supp. VIII:** 15
Aragon, Louis, **I:** 429; **III:** 471; **Retro. Supp. II:** 85, 321
Arana-Ward, Marie, **Supp. VIII:** 84
Ararat (Glück), **Supp. V:** 79, 86–87
Arbre du voyageur, L' (W. J. Smith; Haussmann, trans.), **Supp. XIII:** 347
Arbus, Diane, **Supp. XII:** 188
Arbuthnott, John (pseudonym). *See* Henry, O.
"Arc, The" (Bidart), **Supp. XV:** 25–26, 27
Archaeologist of Morning (Olson), **Supp. II Part 2:** 557
"Archaic Maker, The" (Merwin), **Supp. III Part 1:** 357
"Archaic Torso of Apollo" (Rilke), **Supp. XV:** 148
"Archaischer Torso Apollos" (Rilke), **Supp. XVII:** 244
"Archbishop, The" (Gioia), **Supp. XV:** 126, 127
Archer (television show), **Supp. IV Part 2:** 474
Archer, William, **IV:** 131; **Retro. Supp. I:** 228
Archer at Large (Macdonald), **Supp. IV Part 2:** 473
Archer in Hollywood (Macdonald), **Supp. IV Part 2:** 474
"Archetype and Signature: The Relationship of Poet and Poem" (Fiedler), **Supp. XIII:** 101
"Archibald Higbie" (Masters), **Supp. I Part 2:** 461
"Architect, The" (Bourne), **I:** 223
Architect, The (Briggs and Ranlett), **Supp. XVIII:** 3
Arctic Dreams (Lopez), **Supp. V:** 211
Arctic Refuge: A Circle of Testimony (Haines), **Supp. XII:** 205
"Arcturus" (Connell), **Supp. XIV:** 88
Arendt, Hannah, **II:** 544; **Retro. Supp. I:** 87; **Retro. Supp. II:** 28, 117; **Supp. I Part 2:** 570; **Supp. IV Part 1:** 386; **Supp. VIII:** 98, 99, 100, 243; **Supp. XII:** 166–167
Arensberg, Walter, **IV:** 408; **Retro. Supp. I:** 416
Aren't You Happy for Me? (Bausch), **Supp. VII:** 42, 51, 54
Areopagitica (Milton), **Supp. I Part 2:** 422
"Are You a Doctor?" (Carver), **Supp. III Part 1:** 139–141
"Are You Mr. William Stafford? (Stafford), **Supp. XI:** 317
Argall: The True Story of Pocahontas and Captain John Smith (Vollmann), **Supp. XVII:** 225, 226, 231, 232, 233
"Argonauts of 49, California's Golden Age"(Harte), **Supp. II Part 1:** 353, 355
"Arguments of Everlasting"(B. Kelly), **Supp. XVII:** 129
"Arguments with the Gestapo Continued: II" (Wright), **Supp. XV:** 344
"Arguments with the Gestapo Continued: Literary Resistance" (Wright), **Supp. XV:** 344
Aria da Capo (Millay), **III:** 137–138
Ariadne's Thread: A Collection of Contemporary Women's Journals (Lifshin, ed.), **Supp. XVI:** 37–38
"Ariel" (Plath), **Supp. I Part 2:** 542, 546
Ariel (Plath), **Retro. Supp. II: 250–255; Supp. I Part 2:** 526, 539, 541; **Supp. V:** 79
"Ariel Poems" (Eliot), **I:** 579
Ariosto, Ludovico, **Supp. XV:** 175
"Ariosto: Critical Notice of His Life and Genius" (Hunt), **Supp. XV:** 175
Arise, Arise (Zukofsky), **Supp. III Part 2:** 619, 629
Aristides. *See* Epstein, Joseph
"Aristocracy" (Emerson), **II:** 6
Aristocracy and Justice (More), **I:** 223
Aristocrat, The (Richter), **Supp. XVIII:** 220
Aristophanes, **I:** 436; **II:** 577; **Supp. I Part 2:** 406
Aristotle, **I:** 58, 265, 280, 527; **II:** 9, 12, 198, 536; **III:** 20, 115, 145, 157, 362, 422, 423; **IV:** 10, 18, 74–75, 89; **Supp. I Part 1:** 104, 296; **Supp. I Part 2:** 423; **Supp. IV Part 1:** 391; **Supp. IV Part 2:** 526, 530; **Supp. X:** 78; **Supp. XI:** 249; **Supp. XII:** 106; **Supp. XIV:** 242–243
Aristotle Contemplating the Bust of Homer (Rembrandt), **Supp. IV Part 1:** 390, 391
"Arkansas Traveller" (Wright), **Supp. V:** 334
"Arm, The" (X. J. Kennedy), **Supp. XV:** 169
"Armadillo, The" (Bishop), **Supp. I Part 1:** 93
Armadillo in the Grass (Hearon), **Supp. VIII: 58–59**
"Armageddon" (Ransom), **III:** 489, 492
Armah, Aiy Kwei, **Supp. IV Part 1:** 373
Armies of the Night, The (Mailer), **III:** 39–40, 41, 42, 44, 45, 46; **Retro. Supp. II:** 205, 206–207, 208; **Supp. IV Part 1:** 207; **Supp. XIV:** 49, 162
"Arm in Arm" (Simpson), **Supp. IX:** 267–268
Arminius, Jacobus, **I:** 557
Armitage, Shelley, **Supp. IV Part 2:** 439
Arm of Flesh, The (Salter), **Supp. IX:** 251
"Armor" (Dickey), **Supp. IV Part 1:** 179
Armored Attack (film), **Supp. I Part 1:** 281
Arms, George W., **Supp. I Part 2:** 416–417
Armstrong, George, **Supp. I Part 2:** 386
Armstrong, Louis, **Retro. Supp. II:** 114
"'Arm the Paper Arm': Kenneth Koch's Postmodern Comedy" (Chinitz), **Supp. XV:** 180, 185
"Army" (Corso), **Supp. XII:** 117, 127
Army Brat (W. J. Smith), **Supp. XIII:** 331, 347
Arna Bontemps Langston Hughes: Letters 1925–1967 (Nichols), **Retro. Supp. I:** 194
Arner, Robert D., **Retro. Supp. II:** 62
Arnold, Edwin T., **Supp. VIII:** 189
Arnold, George W., **Supp. I Part 2:** 411
Arnold, Marilyn, **Supp. IV Part 1:** 220
Arnold, Matthew, **I:** 222, 228, 275; **II:** 20, 110, 338, 541; **III:** 604; **IV:** 349; **Retro. Supp. I:** 56, 325; **Supp. I Part 2:** 416, 417, 419, 529, 552, 602; **Supp. IX:** 298; **Supp. XIV:** 11, 335
Arnold, Thurman, **Supp. I Part 2:** 645
Aronson, Steven M. L., **Supp. V:** 4
Around about America (Caldwell), **I:** 290
"Arrangement in Black and White" (Parker), **Supp. IX:** 198
"Arrival at Santos" (Bishop), **Retro. Supp. II:** 46; **Supp. IX:** 45–46
"Arrival of the Bee Box, The" (Plath), **Retro. Supp. II:** 255
Arrivistes, The: Poem 1940–1949 (Simpson), **Supp. IX:** 265, **267–268**

Arrogance (J. Scott), **Supp. XVII: 186–188,** 189, 191, 192, 194
"Arrow" (Dove), **Supp. IV Part 1:** 250
Arrowsmith (Lewis), **I:** 362; **II:** 445–446, 449
"Arsenal at Springfield, The" (Longfellow), **Retro. Supp. II:** 168
"Arson at Midnight" (Nelson), **Supp. XVIII:** 186
"Arson Plus" (Hammett), **Supp. IV Part 1:** 343
"Ars Poetica" (Dove), **Supp. IV Part 1:** 250
"Ars Poetica" (Dunn), **Supp. XI:** 154
"Ars Poetica" (MacLeish), **III:** 9–10
"Ars Poetica" (X. J. Kennedy), **Supp. XV:** 154
"*Ars Poetica:* A Found Poem" (Kumin), **Supp. IV Part 2:** 455
"Ars Poetica; or, Who Lives in the Ivory Tower" (McGrath), **Supp. X:** 117
"Ars Poetica: Some Recent Criticism" (Wright), **Supp. III Part 2:** 603
"Art" (Emerson), **II:** 13
"Art and Neurosis" (Trilling), **Supp. III Part 2:** 502
Art and Technics (Mumford), **Supp. II Part 2:** 483
Art & Ardor: Essays (Ozick), **Supp. V:** 258, 272
Art as Experience (Dewey), **I:** 266
Art by Subtraction (Reid), **IV:** 41
Art de toucher le clavecin, L' (Couperin), **III:** 464
Artemis to Actaeon and Other Verse (Wharton), **Retro. Supp. I:** 372
Arte of English Poesie (Puttenham), **Supp. I Part 1:** 113
Arthur, Anthony, **Supp. IV Part 2:** 606
Arthur Mervyn; or, Memoirs of the Year 1793 (Brown), **Supp. I Part 1:** 137–140, 144
"Article of Faith" (Sobin), **Supp. XVI:** 291
Articles of Light & Elation (Sobin), **Supp. XVI:** 291
Articulation of Sound Forms in Time (Howe), **Supp. IV Part 2:** 419, 431–433
"Artificer" (X. J. Kennedy), **Supp. XV:** 160
"Artificial Nigger, The" (O'Connor), **III:** 343, 351, 356, 358; **Retro. Supp. II:** 229, 232
Artist, The: A Drama without Words (Mencken), **III:** 104
"Artist of the Beautiful, The" (Hawthorne), **Retro. Supp. I:** 149
Artistry of Grief (Torsney), **Retro. Supp. I:** 224
"Artists' and Models' Ball, The" (Brooks), **Supp. III Part 1:** 72
"Art of Disappearing, The" (Nye), **Supp. XIII:** 287
Art of Eating, The (M. F. K. Fisher), **Supp. XVII:** 87, 90, 91
Art of Fiction, The (Gardner), **Supp. VI:** 73
"Art of Fiction, The" (H. James), **Retro. Supp. I:** 226; **Retro. Supp. II:** 223
Art of Hunger, The (Auster), **Supp. XII:** 22
"Art of Keeping Your Mouth Shut, The" (Heller), **Supp. IV Part 1:** 383
"Art of Literature and Commonsense, The" (Nabokov), **Retro. Supp. I:** 271
Art of Living and Other Stories, The (Gardner), **Supp. VI:** 72
"Art of Love, The" (Koch), **Supp. XV:** 182
Art of Love, The (Koch), **Supp. XV:** 182
"Art of Poetry, The" (Koch), **Supp. XV:** 182
Art of Poetry, The (Koch), **Supp. XV:** 175–176, 178, 188
"Art of Poetry, The" (McClatchy), **Supp. XII:** 262
"Art of Romare Bearden, The" (Ellison), **Retro. Supp. II:** 123
"Art of Storytelling, The" (Simpson), **Supp. IX:** 277
Art of Sylvia Plath, The (Newman), **Supp. I Part 2:** 527
Art of the Moving Picture, The (Lindsay), **Supp. I Part 2:** 376, 391–392, 394; **Supp. XVI:** 185
Art of the Novel (H. James), **Retro. Supp. I:** 227
"Art of Theodore Dreiser, The" (Bourne), **I:** 235
Art of the Personal Essay, The (Lopate, comp.), **Supp. XIII:** 280–281; **Supp. XVI:** 266
Art of the Self, The: Essays a Propos "Steps" (Kosinski), **Supp. VII:** 222
Arts and Sciences (Goldbarth), **Supp. XII: 184–186**
"Art's Bread and Butter" (Benét), **Retro. Supp. I:** 108
Arvin, Newton, **I:** 259; **II:** 508; **Retro. Supp. I:** 19, 137
Asali, Muna, **Supp. XIII:** 121, 126
Asbury, Herbert, **Supp. IV Part 1:** 353
Ascent of F6, The (Auden), **Supp. II Part 1:** 11, 13
Ascent to Truth, The (Merton), **Supp. VIII:** 208
Asch, Nathan, **Supp. XV:** 133, 134
Asch, Sholem, **IV:** 1, 9, 11, 14; **Retro. Supp. II:** 299
Ascherson, Neal, **Supp. XII:** 167
"As Close as Breathing" (Jarman), **Supp. XVII:** 120
As Does New Hampshire and Other Poems (Sarton), **Supp. VIII:** 259
"As Evening Lays Dying" (Salinas), **Supp. XIII:** 319
"As Flowers Are" (Kunitz), **Supp. III Part 1:** 265
"Ash" (Sobin), **Supp. XVI:** 284–285
Ashbery, John, **Retro. Supp. I:** 313; **Supp. I Part 1:** 96; **Supp. III Part 1: 1–29; Supp. III Part 2:** 541; **Supp. IV Part 2:** 620; **Supp. IX:** 52; **Supp. VIII:** 272; **Supp. XI:** 139; **Supp. XIII:** 85; **Supp. XV:** 176, 177, 178, 188, 250
"Ashes" (Levine), **Supp. V:** 188
"Ashes of the Beacon" (Bierce), **I:** 209
Ashes: Poems Old and New (Levine), **Supp. V:** 178, 188–189
Ashford, Margaret Mary (Daisy), **II:** 426
"Ash Wednesday" (Eliot), **Supp. IV Part 2:** 436
Ash Wednesday (Eliot), **I:** 570, 574–575, 578–579, 580, 582, 584, 585; **Retro. Supp. I:** 64
"Ash Wednesday" (Garrett), **Supp. VII:** 109–110
"Ash Wednesday" (Merton), **Supp. VIII:** 199
Asian American Authors (Hsu and Palubinskas, eds.), **Supp. X:** 292
Asian American Heritage: An Anthology of Prose and Poetry (Wand), **Supp. X:** 292
Asian Figures (Mervin), **Supp. III Part 1:** 341
Asian Journal of Thomas Merton, The (Merton), **Supp. VIII:** 196, 206, 208
"Asian Peace Offers Rejected without Publication" (R. Bly), **Supp. IV Part 1:** 61
"Asides on the Oboe" (Stevens), **Retro. Supp. I:** 305
"As I Ebb'd with the Ocean of Life" (Whitman), **IV:** 342, 345–346; **Retro. Supp. I:** 404, 405
As I Lay Dying (Faulkner), **II:** 60–61, 69, 73, 74; **IV:** 100; **Retro. Supp. I:** 75, 82, 84, 85, 86, 88, 89, 91, 92; **Supp. IV Part 1:** 47; **Supp. IX:** 99, 103, 251; **Supp. VIII:** 37, 178; **Supp. XIV:** 24
"As I Lay with My Head in Your Lap, Camerado" (Whitman), **IV:** 347
Asimov, Isaac, **Supp. IV Part 1:** 116; **Supp. XVI:** 122
Asinof, Eliot, **II:** 424
As I Remember It (PBS documentary), **Supp. XVIII:** 277
Asirvatham, Sandy, **Supp. XVI:** 249
"As Is the Daughter, So Is Her Mother" (Patchett), **Supp. XII:** 310
"As It Was in the Beginning" (Benét), **Supp. XI:** 56
"As I Walked Out One Evening" (Auden), **Supp. II Part 1:** 13; **Supp. XV:** 126
"As I Went Down by Havre de Grace" (Wylie), **Supp. I Part 2:** 723
"Ask Me" (Stafford), **Supp. XI:** 326–327
Ask Me Tomorrow (Cozzens), **I:** 365–367, 379
Ask the Dust (Fante), **Supp. XI:** 159, 160, 166, **167–169,** 172, 173, 174
Ask Your Mama (Hughes), **Supp. I Part 1:** 339, 341–342
Ask Your Mama: 12 Moods for Jazz (Hughes), **Retro. Supp. I:** 210, 211
As Little Children (R. P. Smith), **Supp. XIV:** 333
"As One Put Drunk into the Packet Boat" (Ashbery), **Supp. III Part 1:** 18
"Asparagus" (Nelson), **Supp. XVIII:** 178
"Aspects of Robinson" (Kees), **Supp. XV:** 134
Aspects of the Novel (Forster), **Retro. Supp. I:** 232; **Supp. VIII:** 155

"Aspen and the Stream, The" (Wilbur), **Supp. III Part 2:** 555, 556
"Aspern Papers, The" (James), **Retro. Supp. I:** 219, 227, 228
Aspern Papers, The (James), **Supp. V:** 101, 102
Asphalt Georgics (Carruth), **Supp. XVI:** 54
Asphalt Jungle (film, Huston), **Supp. XIII:** 174
"Asphodel" (Welty), **IV:** 265, 271
"Asphodel, That Greeny Flower" (W. C. Williams), **Retro. Supp. I:** 429
"Aspic and Buttermilk" (Olds), **Supp. X:** 213
Asquith, Herbert Henry, **Retro. Supp. I:** 59
"Ass" (Cisneros), **Supp. VII:** 67
Assante, Armand, **Supp. VIII:** 74
Assassins, The (Oates), **Supp. II Part 2:** 512, 517–519
"Assault" (Millay), **III:** 130–131
"Assemblage of Husbands and Wives, An" (Lewis), **II:** 455–456
Assembly (O'Hara), **III:** 361
As She Climbed Across the Table (Lethem), **Supp. XVIII: 140–141,** 148
Assignment, Wildlife (LaBastille), **Supp. X: 99,** 104
"Assimiliation in Recent American Jewish Autobiographies" (Krupnick), **Supp. XVI:** 153
Assistant, The (Malamud), **Supp. I Part 2:** 427, 428, 429, 431, 435, 441–445, 451; **Supp. XVI:** 220
Assommoir, L' (Zola), **II:** 291; **III:** 318
Assorted Prose (Updike), **IV:** 215–216, 218; **Retro. Supp. I:** 317, 319, 327
Astaire, Adele, **Supp. XVI:** 187
*As They Were (*M. F. K. Fisher), **Supp. XVII:** 88, 89, 91
Astor, Mary, **Supp. IV Part 1:** 356; **Supp. XII:** 173
Astoria, or, Anecdotes of an Enterprise beyond the Rocky Mountains (Irving), **II:** 312
"Astounding News by Electric Express via Norfolk! The Atlantic Crossed in Three Days Signal Triumph of Mr. Monck's Flying-Machine ..." (Poe), **III:** 413, 420
Astraea (Holmes), **III:** 82
Astro, Richard, **Supp. I Part 2:** 429, 445
"Astrological Fricassee" (H. Miller), **III:** 187
Astrophil and Stella (Sidney), **Supp. XIV:** 128
"As Weary Pilgrim" (Bradstreet), **Supp. I Part 1:** 103, 109, 122
"As We Know" (Ashbery), **Supp. III Part 1:** 21–22
As We Know (Ashbery), **Supp. III Part 1:** 9, 21–25
Aswell, Edward C., **IV:** 458, 459, 461
"Asylum, The" (Carruth), **Supp. XVI:** 48–49
"As You Like It" (Chopin), **Supp. I Part 1:** 217
As You Like It (Shakespeare), **Supp. I Part 1:** 308
"At a Bar in Charlotte Amalie" (Updike), **IV:** 214
"At a Lecture" (Brodsky), **Supp. VIII:** 33
"At a March against the Vietnam War" (R. Bly), **Supp. IV Part 1:** 61
"At a Reading" (McClatchy), **Supp. XII:** 256–257
"Atavism of John Tom Little Bear, The" (O. Henry), **Supp. II Part 1:** 410
"At Chênière Caminada" (Chopin), **Supp. I Part 1:** 220
"At Chinese Checkers" (Berryman), **I:** 182
Atchity, Kenneth John, **Supp. XI:** 227
At Eighty-Two (Sarton), **Supp. VIII:** 264
"At Every Gas Station There Are Mechanics" (Dunn), **Supp. XI:** 144
At Fault (Chopin), **Retro. Supp. II:** 57, 60, **62–63; Supp. I Part 1:** 207, 209–211, 220
At Heaven's Gate (Warren), **IV:** 243, 247–248, 251
Atheism Refuted: in a Discourse to Prove the Existence of God (Paine), **Supp. I Part 2:** 517
"Athénaïse" (Chopin), **Retro. Supp. II:** 66, 67; **Supp. I Part 1:** 219–220
Atherton, Gertrude, **I:** 199, 207–208
Athey, Jean L., **Supp. XI:** 184
At Home: Essays, 1982–1988 (Vidal), **Supp. IV Part 2:** 682, 687, 688
"At Home With" (column; Leland), **Supp. XV:** 69
"At Kino Viejo, Mexico" (Ríos), **Supp. IV Part 2:** 541
Atkinson, Brooks, **IV:** 288; **Supp. IV Part 2:** 683
"Atlantis" (Doty), **Supp. XI:** 127–128
Atlantis (Doty), **Supp. XI:** 121, **126–129**
Atlas, James, **Supp. V:** 233; **Supp. XV:** 25
Atlas, The (Vollmann), **Supp. XVII:** 226, 227
Atlas Shrugged (Rand), **Supp. IV Part 2:** 517, 521, 523, 524–526, 528, 531
At Liberty (T. Williams), **IV:** 378
"At Melville's Tomb" (H. Crane), **I:** 393; **Retro. Supp. II:** 76, 78, 80, 82
"At Mother Teresa's" (Nye), **Supp. XIII:** 276
At Night the Salmon Move (Carver), **Supp. III Part 1:** 142
"At North Farm" (Ashbery), **Supp. III Part 1:** 1–2
At Paradise Gate (Smiley), **Supp. VI:** 292, **293–294**
"At Paso Rojo" (Bowles), **Supp. IV Part 1:** 87
At Play in the Fields of the Lord (Matthiessen), **Supp. V:** 199, 202, 204–206, 212
"At Play in the Paradise of Bombs" (Sanders), **Supp. XVI:** 272–273, 274, 277
"At Pleasure By" (Pinsky), **Supp. VI:** 245
At Risk (Hoffman), **Supp. X:** 87
"At Sea" (Hemingway), **II:** 258
"At Shaft 11" (Dunbar), **Supp. II Part 1:** 212
"At Slim's River" (Haines), **Supp. XII:** 208–209
"At St. Croix" (Dubus), **Supp. VII:** 83, 87
At Sundown (Whittier), **Supp. I Part 2:** 704
"At Sunset" (Simic), **Supp. VIII:** 282
Attebery, Brian, **Supp. IV Part 1:** 101
"At That Time, or The History of a Joke" (Paley), **Supp. VI:** 229–230
At the Back of the North Wind (Macdonald), **Supp. XIII:** 75
"At the Birth of an Age" (Jeffers), **Supp. II Part 2:** 432
"At the Bomb Testing Site" (Stafford), **Supp. XI:** 317–318, 321, 323
At the Bottom of the River (Kincaid), **Supp. VII:** 182–184, 185
"At the 'Cadian Ball" (Chopin), **Retro. Supp. II:** 64, 65, 68
"At the Chelton-Pulver Game" (Auchincloss), **Supp. IV Part 1:** 27
"At the Drugstore" (Taylor), **Supp. V:** 323
At the Edge of the Body (Jong), **Supp. V:** 115, 130
At the End of the Open Road (Simpson), **Supp. IX:** 265, 269, **271–273,** 277
At the End of This Summer: Poems 1948–1954, **Supp. XII:** 211
"At the End of War" (Eberhart), **I:** 522–523
"At the Executed Murderer's Grave" (Wright), **Supp. III Part 2:** 595, 597
"At the Fishhouses" (Bishop), **Retro. Supp. II:** 45; **Supp. I Part 1:** 90, 92
"At the Grave of My Guardian Angel: St. Louis Cemetery, New Orleans" (Levis), **Supp. XI:** 268–269
"At the Gym" (Doty), **Supp. XI:** 135
"At the Indian Store" (McCarriston), **Supp. XIV:** 271
"At the Lake" (Oliver), **Supp. VII:** 244
"At the Landing" (Welty), **IV:** 265–266; **Retro. Supp. I:** 348
"At the Last" (Bynner), **Supp. XV:** 44
"At the Last Rites for Two Hot Rodders" (X. J. Kennedy), **Supp. XV:** 166
"At the Premiere" (Keillor), **Supp. XVI:** 167
At the Root of Stars (Barnes), **Supp. III Part 1:** 34
"At the Slackening of the Tide" (Wright), **Supp. III Part 2:** 597
"At the Tomb of Walt Whitman" (Kunitz), **Supp. III Part 1:** 262
"At the Tourist Centre in Boston" (Atwood), **Supp. XIII:** 33
"At the Town Dump" (Kenyon), **Supp. VII:** 167
"At the Worcester Museum" (Pinsky), **Supp. VI:** 251
"Atticus Finch and the Mad Dog: Harper Lee's *To Kill a Mockingbird*" (Jones), **Supp. VIII:** 128
"Atticus Finch——Right and Wrong" (Freedman), **Supp. VIII:** 127–128

"Attic Which Is Desire, The" (W. C. Williams), **Retro. Supp. I:** 422
"At Times in Flight: A Parable" (H. Roth), **Supp. IX:** 234
Attitudes toward History (Burke), **I:** 274
Atwan, Robert, **Supp. XVI:** 273, 277
At Weddings and Wakes (McDermott), **Supp. XVIII:** 155, **160–162,** 166
"At White River" (Haines), **Supp. XII:** 208–209
Atwood, Margaret, **Supp. IV Part 1:** 252; **Supp. V:** 119; **Supp. XI:** 317; **Supp. XIII: 19–39,** 291, 306
"Atwood's Gorgon Touch" (Davey), **Supp. XIII:** 33
"Aubade" (McCarriston), **Supp. XIV:** 271
"Aubade: November" (McCarriston), **Supp. XIV:** 261–262
"Aubade of an Early Homo Sapiens" (C. Frost), **Supp. XV:** 97–98
"Aubade: Opal and Silver" (Doty), **Supp. XI:** 129
"Au Bal Musette" (Van Vechten), **Supp. II Part 2:** 735
Auchincloss, Hugh D., **Supp. IV Part 2:** 679
Auchincloss, Louis, **I:** 375; **III:** 66; **Retro. Supp. I:** 370, 373; **Supp. IV Part 1: 21–38**
"Auction" (Simic), **Supp. VIII:** 278
"Auction, The" (Crane), **I:** 411
"Auction Model 1934" (Z. Fitzgerald), **Supp. IX:** 61
Auden, W. H., **I:** 71, 381, 539; **II:** 367, 368, 371, 376, 586; **III:** 17, 134, 269, 271, 292, 476–477, 504, 527, 530, 542, 615; **IV:** 136, 138, 240, 430; **Retro. Supp. I:** 430; **Retro. Supp. II:** 183, 242, 244, 323; **Supp. I Part 1:** 270; **Supp. I Part 2:** 552, 610; **Supp. II Part 1: 1–28; Supp. III Part 1:** 2, 3, 14, 26, 60, 61, 64, 341; **Supp. III Part 2:** 591, 595; **Supp. IV Part 1:** 79, 84, 136, 225, 302, 313; **Supp. IV Part 2:** 440, 465; **Supp. IX:** 94, 287, 288; **Supp. V:** 337; **Supp. VIII:** 19, 21, 22, 23, 30, 32, 155, 190; **Supp. X:** 35, 57, 59, 115–116, 117, 118–119; **Supp. XI:** 243, 244; **Supp. XII:** 253, 264–265, 266, 269–270; **Supp. XIV:** 156, 158, 160, 162, 163; **Supp. XV:** 74, 117–118, 139, 144, 186
"Auden's OED" (McClatchy), **Supp. XII:** 264–265
"Audition" (Alvarez), **Supp. VII:** 10
Audubon, John James, **III:** 210; **IV:** 265; **Supp. IX:** 171; **Supp. XVI: 1–14**
Audubon, John Woodhouse, **Supp. XVI:** 10
Audubon, Maria Rebecca, **Supp. XVI:** 11
Audubon, Victor Gifford, **Supp. XVI:** 10
Audubon and His Journals (M. Audubon, ed.), **Supp. XVI:** 11, 12
Audubon Reader, The: The Best Writings of John James Audubon (Sanders, ed.), **Supp. XVI:** 269
Auer, Jane. *See* Bowles, Jane
Auerbach, Eric, **III:** 453
Auerbach, Nina, **Supp. I Part 1:** 40
"August" (Oliver), **Supp. VII:** 235
"August" (Rich), **Supp. I Part 2:** 564
"August 1968" (Auden), **Supp. II Part 1:** 25
"August Darks, The" (Clampitt), **Supp. IX:** 43, **50–51,** 52
Augustine, Saint, **I:** 279, 290; **II:** 537; **III:** 259, 270, 292, 300; **IV:** 69, 126; **Retro. Supp. I:** 247; **Supp. VIII:** 203; **Supp. XI:** 245; **Supp. XIII:** 89
August Snow (Price), **Supp. VI:** 264
"Au Jardin" (Pound), **III:** 465–466
Aunt Carmen's Book of Practical Saints (Mora), **Supp. XIII: 227–229**
"Aunt Cynthy Dallett" (Jewett), **II:** 393
"Aunt Gladys" (Karr), **Supp. XI:** 241
"Aunt Imogen" (Robinson), **III:** 521
"Aunt Jemima of the Ocean Waves" (Hayden), **Supp. II Part 1:** 368, 379
"Aunt Jennifer's Tigers" (Rich), **Supp. XV:** 252
Aunt Jo's Scrapbooks (Alcott), **Supp. I Part 1:** 43
"Aunt Mary" (Oliver), **Supp. VII:** 232
"Aunt Mary" (Stowe), **Supp. I Part 2:** 587
"Aunt Moon's Young Man" (Hogan), **Supp. IV Part 1:** 400
"Aunt Rectita's Good Friday" (X. J. Kennedy), **Supp. XV:** 166
"Aunt Sarah" (Lowell), **II:** 554
"Aunt Sue's Stories" (Hughes), **Retro. Supp. I:** 197, 199
"Aunt Violet's Canadian Honeymoon/ 1932" (Shields), **Supp. VII:** 311
"Aunt Violet's Things" (Shields), **Supp. VII:** 311–312
"Aurelia: Moon Jellies" (Mora), **Supp. XIII:** 224
Aurora Leigh (E. Browning), **Retro. Supp. I:** 33; **Supp. XI:** 197
Aurora Means Dawn (Sanders), **Supp. XVI:** 268
"Auroras of Autumn, The" (Stevens), **Retro. Supp. I:** 311, 312; **Supp. III Part 1:** 12
Auroras of Autumn, The (Stevens), **Retro. Supp. I:** 297, 300, **309–312**
Auschwitz: the Nazis and the "Final Solution" (television documentary), **Supp. XVII:** 40
Auslander, Joseph, **Supp. XIV:** 120
"Auspex" (Frost), **Retro. Supp. I:** 122
"Auspex" (Lowell), **Supp. I Part 2:** 424
Austen, Jane, **I:** 130, 339, 375, 378; **II:** 272, 278, 287, 568–569, 577; **IV:** 8; **Retro. Supp. I:** 354; **Supp. I Part 1:** 267; **Supp. I Part 2:** 656, 715; **Supp. IV Part 1:** 300; **Supp. IX:** 128; **Supp. VIII:** 125, 167; **Supp. XII:** 310; **Supp. XV:** 338
Auster, Paul, **Supp. XII: 21–39; Supp. XIV:** 292
"Austerities" (Simic), **Supp. VIII:** 277
Austerities (Simic), **Supp. VIII: 276–278,** 283
Austin, Mary Hunter, **Retro. Supp. I:** 7; **Supp. IV Part 2:** 503; **Supp. X:** 29; **Supp. XIII:** 154
"Authentic Unconscious, The" (Trilling), **Supp. III Part 2:** 512
Author and Agent: Eudora Welty and Diarmuid Russell (Kreyling), **Retro. Supp. I:** 342, 345, 347, 349–350
"Author at Sixty, The" (Wilson), **IV:** 426
"Author of 'Beltraffio,' The" (James), **Retro. Supp. I:** 227
"Author's Explanation, The" (Larsen), **Supp. XVIII:** 131
"Author's House" (Fitzgerald), **Retro. Supp. I:** 98
"Author's Reflections, An: Willie Loman, Walter Younger, and He Who Must Live" (Hansberry), **Supp. IV Part 1:** 370
"Author to Her Book, The" (Bradstreet), **Supp. I Part 1:** 119; **Supp. V:** 117–118; **Supp. XV:** 125–126
"Autobiographical Note" (H. Miller), **III:** 174–175
"Autobiographical Notes" (Baldwin), **Supp. I Part 1:** 54
"Autobiographical Notes" (Holmes), **Supp. I Part 1:** 301
"Autobiographic Chapter, An" (Bourne), **I:** 236
Autobiography (Franklin), **II:** 102, 103, 108, 121–122, 302
Autobiography (James), **I:** 462
"Autobiography" (MacLeish), **III:** 20
Autobiography (Van Buren), **III:** 473
Autobiography (W. C. Williams), **Supp. I Part 1:** 254
Autobiography (Zukofsky), **Supp. III Part 2:** 627
"Autobiography in the Shape of a Book Review" (Bynner), **Supp. XV:** 40
"Autobiography of a Confluence, The" (Gunn Allen), **Supp. IV Part 1:** 321
Autobiography of Alice B. Toklas, The (Stein), **IV:** 26, 30, 35, 43; **Supp. IV Part 1:** 11, 81
Autobiography of an Ex-Colored Man, The (Johnson), **Supp. II Part 1:** 33, 194; **Supp. XVIII:** 127
Autobiography of a Schizophrenic Girl (Renée), **Supp. XVI:** 64, 66
Autobiography of a Thief, The (Hapgood), **Supp. XVII:** 96, 101–102
Autobiography of Benjamin Franklin (Franklin), **Supp. IV Part 1:** 5
Autobiography of LeRoi Jones, The (Baraka), **Retro. Supp. I:** 411
Autobiography of Malcolm X (Little), **Supp. I Part 1:** 66; **Supp. X:** 27; **Supp. XIII:** 264
Autobiography of Mark Twain, The (Twain), **IV:** 209
Autobiography of My Mother, The (Kincaid), **Supp. VII:** 182, 188–190, 191, 192, 193
Autobiography of Red: A Novel in Verse (Carson), **Supp. XII:** 97, **106–110**
Autobiography of Upton Sinclair, The (Sinclair), **Supp. V:** 276, 282
Autobiography of W. E. B. Du Bois, The (Du Bois), **Supp. II Part 1:** 159, 186

Autobiography of William Carlos Williams, The (W. C. Williams), **Retro. Supp. I:** 51, 428
Autocrat of the Breakfast-Table, The (Holmes), **Supp. I Part 1:** 306–307
"Automatic Gate, The" (Southern), **Supp. XI:** 294
"Automotive Passacaglia" (H. Miller), **III:** 186
"Autopsy Room, The" (Carver), **Supp. III Part 1:** 137
"Auto Wreck" (Shapiro), **Supp. II Part 2:** 706
"Autre Temps" (Wharton), **IV:** 320, 324
"Autumn Afternoon" (Farrell), **II:** 45
"Autumnal" (Eberhart), **I:** 540–541
"Autumn Begins in Martins Ferry, Ohio" (Wright), **Supp. III Part 2:** 599
"Autumn Courtship, An" (Caldwell), **I:** 309
Autumn Garden, The (Hellman), **Supp. I Part 1:** 285–286, 290
"Autumn Garden, The: Mechanics and Dialectics" (Felheim), **Supp. I Part 1:** 297
"Autumn Holiday, An" (Jewett), **II:** 391; **Retro. Supp. II:** 140–141
"Autumn Musings" (Harte), **Supp. II Part 1:** 336
"Autumn Within" (Longfellow), **II:** 499
"Autumn Woods" (Bryant), **Supp. I Part 1:** 164
"Au Vieux Jardin" (Aldington), **Supp. I Part 1:** 257
"Aux Imagistes" (W. C. Williams), **Supp. I Part 1:** 266
Avakian, Aram, **Supp. XI:** 294, 295, 309
"Ave Atque Vale" (Bynner), **Supp. XV:** 49
Avedon, Richard, **Supp. I Part 1:** 58; **Supp. V:** 194; **Supp. X:** 15
Aveling, Edward, **Supp. XVI:** 85
"Avenue" (Pinsky), **Supp. VI:** 248
Avenue Bearing the Initial of Christ into the New World: Poems 1946–1964 (Kinnell), **Supp. III Part 1:** 235, 239–241
"Avenue of the Americas" (Simic), **Supp. VIII:** 278
"Average Torture" (Karr), **Supp. XI:** 243
Avery, John, **Supp. I Part 1:** 153
"Avey" (Toomer), **Supp. IX:** 317
Avon's Harvest (Robinson), **III:** 510
Awake and Sing! (Odets), **Supp. II Part 2:** 530, 531, 536–538, 550; **Supp. IV Part 2:** 587
Awakening, The (Chopin), **Retro. Supp. I:** 10; **Retro. Supp. II:** 57, 59, 60, 67, **68–71,** 73; **Supp. I Part 1:** 200, 201, 202, 211, 220–225; **Supp. V:** 304; **Supp. VIII:** 198; **Supp. XII:** 170
Awakening Land, The (Richter), **Supp. XVIII:** 207, 215
Awful Rowing Toward God, The (Sexton), **Supp. II Part 2:** 694–696
Awiakta, Marilou, **Supp. IV Part 1:** 319, 335
Awkward Age, The (James), **II:** 332; **Retro. Supp. I:** 229, **230–231**
Axe Handles (Snyder), **Supp. VIII: 303–305**
Axel's Castle: A Study in the Imaginative Literature of 1870 to 1930 (Wilson), **I:** 185; **II:** 577; **IV:** 428, 431, 438, 439, 443; **Supp. VIII:** 101
"Ax-Helve, The" (Frost), **Retro. Supp. I:** 133
Azikewe, Nnamdi, **Supp. IV Part 1:** 361
"Aztec Angel" (Salinas), **Supp. XIII:** 314
Aztec Treasure House, The: New and Selected Essays (Connell), **Supp. XIV:** 80, 97

B

Babbitt (Lewis), **II:** 442, 443–445, 446, 447, 449; **III:** 63–64, 394; **IV:** 326
Babbitt, Irving, **I:** 247; **II:** 456; **III:** 315, 461, 613; **IV:** 439; **Retro. Supp. I:** 55; **Supp. I Part 2:** 423
Babcock, Elisha, **Supp. II Part 1:** 69
Babel, Isaac, **IV:** 1; **Supp. IX:** 260; **Supp. XII:** 308–309; **Supp. XVII:** 41
Babel, Isaak, **Supp. XIV:** 83, 84
Babel to Byzantium (Dickey), **Supp. IV Part 1:** 177, 185
Babeuf, François, **Supp. I Part 2:** 518
"Babies, The" (Strand), **Supp. IV Part 2:** 625
Babouk (Endore), **Supp. XVII: 56–57,** 61, 64
Baby, Come on Inside (Wagoner), **Supp. IX: 335**
"Baby, The" (Barthelme), **Supp. IV Part 1:** 49
Baby Doll (T. Williams), **IV:** 383, 386, 387, 389, 395
"Baby Face" (Sandburg), **III:** 584
"Babylon Revisited" (Fitzgerald), **II:** 95; **Retro. Supp. I:** 109
"Baby or the Botticelli, The" (Gass), **Supp. VI:** 92
"Baby Pictures of Famous Dictators" (Simic), **Supp. VIII:** 276
"Baby's Breath" (Bambara), **Supp. XI:** 15, 16
"Babysitter, The" (Coover), **Supp. V:** 43–44
"Baby Villon" (Levine), **Supp. V:** 182
Bacall, Lauren, **Supp. IV Part 1:** 130
"Baccalaureate" (MacLeish), **III:** 4
Bacchae, The (Euripides), **Supp. VIII:** 182
Bach, Johann Sebastian, **Supp. I Part 1:** 363; **Supp. III Part 2:** 611, 612, 619
Bachardy, Don, **Supp. XIV:** 166, 170, 172, 173
Bache, Richard, **Supp. I Part 2:** 504
Bachelard, Gaston, **Supp. XIII:** 225; **Supp. XVI:** 292
Bachelor Girls (Wasserstein), **Supp. XV: 327–328,** 332
Bachman, John, **Supp. XVI:** 10, 11
Bachmann, Ingeborg, **Supp. IV Part 1:** 310; **Supp. VIII:** 272
Bachofen, J. J., **Supp. I Part 2:** 560, 567
Back Bog Beast Bait (Shepard), **Supp. III Part 2:** 437, 438
Backbone (C. Bly), **Supp. XVI: 34–36,** 37, 40, 41
Back Country, The (Snyder), **Supp. VIII: 296–299**
"Back fom the Argentine" (Leopold), **Supp. XIV:** 186
"Background with Revolutionaries" (MacLeish), **III:** 14–15
Back in The World (Wolff), **Supp. VII:** 345
Back in the World (Wolff), **Supp. VII:** 344
"Backlash Blues, The" (Hughes), **Supp. I Part 1:** 343
"Backlash of Kindness, A" (Nye), **Supp. XIII:** 285, 286
Back to China (Fiedler), **Supp. XIII: 102–103**
Back to Methuselah (Shaw), **IV:** 64
"Backwacking: A Plea to the Senator" (Ellison), **Retro. Supp. II:** 126; **Supp. II Part 1:** 248
Backward Glance, A (Wharton), **Retro. Supp. I:** 360, 363, 366, 378, 380, 382
"Backward Glance o'er Travel'd Roads, A" (Whitman), **IV:** 348
Bacon, Francis, **II:** 1, 8, 11, 15–16, 111; **III:** 284; **Retro. Supp. I:** 247; **Supp. I Part 1:** 310; **Supp. I Part 2:** 388; **Supp. IX:** 104; **Supp. XIV:** 22, 210
Bacon, Helen, **Supp. X:** 57
Bacon, Leonard, **II:** 530
Bacon, Roger, **IV:** 69
"Bacterial War, The" (Nemerov), **III:** 272
Bad and the Beautiful, The (film), **Supp. XVIII:** 250
Bad Boy Brawly Brown (Mosley), **Supp. XIII:** 237, 239, 240–241
Bad Boys (Cisneros), **Supp. VII:** 58
"Bad Dream" (Taylor), **Supp. V:** 320
Badè, William Frederic, **Supp. IX:** 178
"Bad Fisherman, The" (Wagoner), **Supp. IX:** 328
Bad for Each Other (film), **Supp. XIII:** 174
"Badger" (Clare), **II:** 387
Badger, A. G., **Supp. I Part 1:** 356
Bad Government and Silly Literature (C. Bly), **Supp. XVI:** 37, 38, 40
Badlands (film; Malick), **Supp. XV:** 351
"Bad Lay" (McCarriston), **Supp. XIV:** 267
Badley, Linda, **Supp. V:** 148
Bad Man, A (Elkin), **Supp. VI: 47**
Bad Man Ballad (Sanders), **Supp. XVI:** 268
Bad Man Blues: A Portable George Garrett (Garrett), **Supp. VII:** 111
"Bad Music, The" (Jarrell), **II:** 369
"Bad Summer on K2, A" (Krakauer and Child), **Supp. XVIII:** 107, 108
"Bad Woman, A" (Fante), **Supp. XI:** 165
Baeck, Leo, **Supp. V:** 260
Baecker, Diann L., **Supp. VIII:** 128
Baer, William, **Supp. XIII:** 112, 118, 129
Baez, Joan, **Supp. IV Part 1:** 200; **Supp. VIII:** 200, 202; **Supp. XVIII:** 24, 25–26, 27
Bag of Bones (King), **Supp. V:** 139, 148, 151
"Bagpipe Music" (MacNeice), **Supp. X:** 117

"Bahá'í Faith: Only Church in World That Does Not Discriminate" (Locke), **Supp. XIV:** 200
"Bahá'u'lláh in the Garden of Ridwan" (Hayden), **Supp. II Part 1:** 370, 378
Bahr, David, **Supp. XV:** 66
"Bailbondsman, The" (Elkin), **Supp. VI:** 49, **50,** 58
Bailey, Gamaliel, **Supp. I Part 2:** 587, 590
Bailey, Peter, **Supp. XVI:** 69
Bailey, William, **Supp. IV Part 2:** 631, 634
Bailey's Café (Naylor), **Supp. VIII: 226–228**
Bailyn, Bernard, **Supp. I Part 2:** 484, 506
Bair, Deirdre, **Supp. X:** 181, 186, 187, 188, 192, 194, 195, 196, 197
Baird, Linnett, **Supp. XII:** 299
Baird, Peggy, **I:** 385, 401
Bakan, David, **I:** 59
Baker, Carlos, **II:** 259
Baker, David, **Supp. IX:** 298; **Supp. XI:** 121, 142, 153; **Supp. XII:** 175, 191–192
Baker, George Pierce, **III:** 387; **IV:** 453, 455
Baker, Gladys, **Supp. XIV:** 121
Baker, Houston A., Jr., **Retro. Supp. II:** 121; **Supp. IV Part 1:** 365; **Supp. X:** 324
Baker, Kevin, **Supp. XIV:** 96
Baker, Mabel, **Supp. XVIII:** 259, 263, 266–267, 269
Baker, Nicholson, **Supp. XIII: 41–57**
Baker, Robert, **Supp. XVI:** 288, 290
Bakerman, Jane S., **Supp. IV Part 2:** 468
Bakhtin, Mikhail, **Retro. Supp. II:** 273; **Supp. IV Part 1:** 301; **Supp. X:** 120, 239
Bakst, Léon, **Supp. IX:** 66
Bakunin, Mikhail Aleksandrovich, **IV:** 429
Balakian, Jan, **Supp. XV:** 327
"Balance" (Bierds), **Supp. XVII:** 31
"Balance" (Nelson), **Supp. XVIII:** 174–175
Balbo, Ned, **Supp. XVII:** 120
Balbuena, Bernado de, **Supp. V:** 11
Balch, Emily Greene, **Supp. I Part 1:** 25
Balcony, The (Genet), **I:** 84
Bald Soprano, The (Ionesco), **I:** 74
Baldwin, David, **Supp. I Part 1:** 47, 48, 49, 50, 51, 54, 65, 66
Baldwin, James, **Retro. Supp. II: 1–17; Supp. I Part 1: 47–71,** 337, 341; **Supp. II Part 1:** 40; **Supp. III Part 1:** 125; **Supp. IV Part 1:** 1, 10, 11, 163, 369; **Supp. V:** 201; **Supp. VIII:** 88, 198, 235, 349; **Supp. X:** 136, 324; **Supp. XI:** 288, 294; **Supp. XIII:** 46, 111, 181, 186, 294; **Supp. XIV:** 54, 71, 73, 306; **Supp. XVI:** 135, 141, 143; **Supp. XVIII:** 25
Baldwin, Samuel, **Supp. I Part 1:** 48
Balitas, Vincent D., **Supp. XVI:** 222
Balkian, Nona, **Supp. XI:** 230
Ball, Gordon, **Supp. XIV:** 148
Ball, John, **Supp. XV:** 202
"Ballad: Between the Box Cars" (Warren), **IV:** 245
"Ballade" (MacLeish), **III:** 4
"Ballade at Thirty-Five" (Parker), **Supp. IX:** 192
"Ballade for the Duke of Orléans" (Wilbur), **Supp. III Part 2:** 556
"Ballade of Broken Flutes, The" (Robinson), **III:** 505
"Ballade of Meaty Inversions" (White), **Supp. I Part 2:** 676
"Ballad of a Thin Man" (song, Dylan), **Supp. XVIII:** 30, 31
"Ballad of Aunt Geneva, The" (Nelson), **Supp. XVIII:** 175
"Ballad of Billie Potts, The" (Warren), **IV:** 241–242, 243, 253
"Ballad of Carmilhan, The" (Longfellow), **II:** 505
"ballad of chocolate Mabbie, the" (Brooks), **Supp. IV Part 1:** 15
"Ballad of Dead Ladies, The" (Villon), **Retro. Supp. I:** 286
Ballad of Dingus Magee, The (Markson), **Supp. XVII:** 139, 141
"Ballad of East and West" (Kipling), **Supp. IX:** 246
"Ballad of Jesse Neighbours, The" (Humphrey), **Supp. IX:** 100
"Ballad of Jesus of Nazareth, A" (Masters), **Supp. I Part 2:** 459
"Ballad of John Cable and Three Gentlemen" (Merwin), **Supp. III Part 1:** 342
"Ballad of Larry and Club" (Jarman), **Supp. XVII:** 115
"Ballad of Nat Turner, The" (Hayden), **Supp. II Part 1:** 378
"Ballad of Pearl May Lee, The" (Brooks), **Supp. III Part 1:** 74, 75
"Ballad of Remembrance, A" (Hayden), **Supp. II Part 1:** 368, 372, 373
Ballad of Remembrance, A (Hayden), **Supp. II Part 1:** 367
"Ballad of Ruby, The" (Sarton), **Supp. VIII:** 259–260
"Ballad of Sue Ellen Westerfield, The" (Hayden), **Supp. II Part 1:** 364
"Ballad of the Brown Girl, The" (Cullen), **Supp. IV Part 1:** 168
Ballad of the Brown Girl, The (Cullen), **Supp. IV Part 1:** 167, 168, 169–170, 173
"Ballad of the Children of the Czar, The" (Schwartz), **Supp. II Part 2:** 649
"Ballad of the Girl Whose Name Is Mud" (Hughes), **Retro. Supp. I:** 205
"Ballad of the Goodly Fere," **III:** 458
"Ballad of the Harp-Weaver" (Millay), **III:** 135
"Ballad of the Sad Cafe, The" (McCullers), **II:** 586, 587, 588, 592, 595, 596–600, 604, 605, 606
"Ballad of the Sixties" (Sarton), **Supp. VIII:** 259
"Ballad of Trees and the Master, A" (Lanier), **Supp. I Part 1:** 370
"Ballad of William Sycamore, The" (Benét), **Supp. XI:** 44, 47
Ballads and Other Poems (Longfellow), **II:** 489; **III:** 412, 422; **Retro. Supp. II:** 157, 168
Ballads for Sale (Lowell), **II:** 527
"Ballads of Lenin" (Hughes), **Supp. I Part 1:** 331
Ballantyne, Sheila, **Supp. V:** 70
Ballard, J. G., **Supp. XVI:** 123, 124; **Supp. XVIII:** 136
Ballard, Josephine. *See* McMurtry, Josephine
"Ballena" (Mora), **Supp. XIII:** 224
"Ballet in Numbers for Mary Ellen, A" (Karr), **Supp. XI:** 241
"Ballet of a Buffoon, The" (Sexton), **Supp. II Part 2:** 693
"Ballet of the Fifth Year, The" (Schwartz), **Supp. II Part 2:** 650
"Ball Game, The" (Creeley), **Supp. IV Part 1:** 140
"Balloon Hoax, The" (Poe), **III:** 413, 420
"Balm of Recognition, The: Rectifying Wrongs through Generations" (E. Hoffman, lecture), **Supp. XVI:** 155
Balo (Toomer), **Supp. III Part 2:** 484
Balsan, Consuelo, **IV:** 313–314
Balthus, **Supp. IV Part 2:** 623
Balthus Poems, The (Dobyns), **Supp. XIII:** 87
Baltimore, Lord, **I:** 132
Balzac, Honoré de, **I:** 103, 123, 339, 376, 474, 485, 499, 509, 518; **II:** 307, 322, 324, 328, 336, 337; **III:** 61, 174, 184, 320, 382; **IV:** 192; **Retro. Supp. I:** 91, 217, 218, 235; **Retro. Supp. II:** 93; **Supp. I Part 2:** 647; **Supp. XVI:** 72
Bambara, Toni Cade, **Supp. XI: 1–23**
Banana Bottom (McKay), **Supp. X:** 132, **139–140**
Bananas (film; Allen), **Supp. XV:** 3, 4
Bancal, Jean, **Supp. I Part 2:** 514
Bancroft, George, **I:** 544; **Supp. I Part 2:** 479
Band, Millen, **Supp. XVIII:** 238
Bandaged Nude, The (Ryan as Finnegan), **Supp. XVIII:** 233, **235–236**
Band of Angels (Warren), **IV:** 245, 254–255
Bang the Drum Slowly (Harris), **II:** 424–425
Banjo: A Story without a Plot (McKay), **Supp. X:** 132, **138–139**
"Banjo Song, A" (Dunbar), **Supp. II Part 1:** 197
Bankhead, Tallulah, **IV:** 357; **Supp. IV Part 2:** 574
"Banking Potatoes" (Komunyakaa), **Supp. XIII:** 126
"Bank of England Restriction, The" (Adams), **I:** 4
Banks, Joanne Trautmann, **Supp. XIII:** 297
Banks, Russell, **Supp. IX:** 153; **Supp. V: 1–19,** 227; **Supp. X:** 85; **Supp. XI:** 178; **Supp. XII:** 295, 309, 343
"Banned Poem" (Nye), **Supp. XIII:** 282
Bannon, Barbara, **Supp. XI:** 228
"Banyan" (Swenson), **Supp. IV Part 2:** 651, 652

"Baptism" (Olsen). *See* "O Yes" (Olsen)
Baptism, The (Baraka), **Supp. II Part 1:** 40, 41–42, 43
Baptism of Desire (Erdrich), **Supp. IV Part 1:** 259
Barabtarlo, Gennady, **Retro. Supp. I:** 278
Baraka, Imamu Amiri (LeRoi Jones), **Retro. Supp. I:** 411; **Retro. Supp. II:** 280; **Supp. I Part 1:** 63; **Supp. II Part 1: 29–63,** 247, 250; **Supp. III Part 1:** 83; **Supp. IV Part 1:** 169, 244, 369; **Supp. VIII:** 295, 329, 330, 332; **Supp. X:** 324, 328; **Supp. XIII:** 94; **Supp. XIV:** 125, 144
"Bar at the Andover Inn, The" (Matthews), **Supp. IX:** 168
"Barbados" (Marshall), **Supp. XI:** 281
"Barbara Frietchie" (Whittier), **Supp. I Part 2:** 695–696
Barbarella (film), **Supp. XI:** 293, **307–308**
"Barbarian Status of Women, The" (Veblen), **Supp. I Part 2:** 636–637
Barbarous Coast, The (Macdonald), **Supp. IV Part 2:** 472, 474
Barbary Shore (Mailer), **III:** 27, 28, 30–31, 33, 35, 36, 40, 44; **Retro. Supp. II: 199–200,** 207; **Supp. XIV:** 162
Barber, David, **Supp. IV Part 2:** 550; **Supp. XII:** 188–189
Barber, Rowland, **Supp. IV Part 2:** 581
Barber, Samuel, **Supp. IV Part 1:** 84
"Barclay of Ury" (Whittier), **Supp. I Part 2:** 693
Barcott, Bruce, **Supp. XVII:** 32
Bard of Savagery, The: Thorstein Veblen and Modern Social Theory (Diggins), **Supp. I Part 2:** 650
"Barefoot Boy, The" (Whittier), **Supp. I Part 2:** 691, 699–700
Barefoot in the Park (Simon), **Supp. IV Part 2:** 575, 578–579, 586, 590
"Bare Hills, The" (Winters), **Supp. II Part 2:** 790
Bare Hills, The (Winters), **Supp. II Part 2:** 786, 788
Barely and Widely (Zukofsky), **Supp. III Part 2:** 627, 628, 635
Barenblat, Rachel, **Supp. XIII:** 274
Barfield, Owen, **III:** 274, 279
"Bargain Lost, The" (Poe), **III:** 411
Barillas, William, **Supp. XIV:** 177
Barillet, Pierre, **Supp. XVI:** 194
Barker, Arthur, **Supp. XIII:** 167
Barker, Clive, **Supp. V:** 142
"Barking Man" (Bell), **Supp. X:** 9
Barking Man and Other Stories (Bell), **Supp. X: 9**
Barksdale, Richard, **Retro. Supp. I:** 202, 205; **Supp. I Part 1:** 341, 346
Barlow, Joel, **Supp. I Part 1:** 124; **Supp. I Part 2:** 511, 515, 521; **Supp. II Part 1: 65–86,** 268
Barlow, Ruth Baldwin (Mrs. Joel Barlow), **Supp. II Part 1:** 69
"B.A.R. Man, The" (Yates), **Supp. XI:** 341
Barnaby Rudge (Dickens), **III:** 421
Barnard, Frederick, **Supp. I Part 2:** 684
Barnard, Rita, **Retro. Supp. II:** 324
Barn Blind (Smiley), **Supp. VI: 292–293**
"Barn Burning" (Faulkner), **II:** 72, 73; **Supp. IV Part 2:** 682
Barnes, Djuna, **Supp. III Part 1: 31–46; Supp. IV Part 1:** 79, 80; **Supp. XVI:** 282
Barnes, Kim, **Supp. XVIII:** 293
Barnett, Claudia, **Supp. XV:** 323, 330, 334
Barnett, Samuel, **Supp. I Part 1:** 2
Barnstone, Tony, **Supp. XIII:** 115, 126
Barnstone, Willis, **Supp. I Part 2:** 458
Barnum, P. T., **Supp. I Part 2:** 703
Baroja, Pío, **I:** 478
Baron, Zach, **Supp. XVIII:** 150
"Baroque Comment" (Bogan), **Supp. III Part 1:** 56, 58
"Baroque Sunburst, A" (Clampitt), **Supp. IX:** 49
"Baroque Wall-Fountain in the Villa Sciarra, A" (Wilbur), **Supp. III Part 2:** 553
Barr, Robert, **I:** 409, 424
Barracks Thief, The (Wolff), **Supp. VII:** 344–345
Barren Ground (Glasgow), **II:** 174, 175, 178, 179, 184–185, 186, 187, 188, 189, 191, 192, 193, 194; **Supp. X:** 228
Barrés, Auguste M., **I:** 228
Barresi, Dorothy, **Supp. XV:** 100, 102
Barrett, Amy, **Supp. XVIII:** 136
Barrett, E. B., **Supp. XV:** 309
Barrett, Elizabeth, **Supp. IV Part 2:** 430
Barrett, George, **Supp. IX:** 250
Barrett, Ralph, **Supp. I Part 2:** 462
Barrier of a Common Language: An American Looks at Contemporary British Poetry (Gioia), **Supp. XV:** 112, **116–117**
"Barroco: An Essay" (Sobin), **Supp. XVI:** 291
Barron, Jonathan, **Supp. IX:** 299
Barrow, John, **II:** 18
Barrus, Clara, **I:** 220
Barry, Iris, **Supp. XIII:** 170
Barry, Philip, **Retro. Supp. I:** 104; **Supp. IV Part 1:** 83; **Supp. V:** 95
Barstow, Elizabeth Drew. *See* Stoddard, Elizabeth
Bartas, Seigneur du, **IV:** 157
Barth, John, **I: 121–143; Supp. I Part 1:** 100; **Supp. III Part 1:** 217; **Supp. IV Part 1:** 48, 379; **Supp. IX:** 208; **Supp. V:** 39, 40; **Supp. X:** 263, 301, 302, 307; **Supp. XI:** 309; **Supp. XII:** 29, 289, 316; **Supp. XIII:** 41, 101, 104; **Supp. XVII:** 183; **Supp. XVIII:** 136, 140, 141
Barth, Karl, **III:** 40, 258, 291, 303, 309; **IV:** 225; **Retro. Supp. I:** 325, 326, 327
Barth, Robert C., **Supp. XV:** 169
Barthé, Richmond, **Retro. Supp. II:** 115
Barthelme, Donald, **Supp. IV Part 1: 39–58,** 227; **Supp. V:** 2, 39, 44; **Supp. VIII:** 75, 138; **Supp. X:** 263; **Supp. XI:** 25; **Supp. XII:** 29; **Supp. XIII:** 41, 46; **Supp. XVI:** 206
Barthelme, Frederick, **Supp. XI: 25–41**
Barthelme, Peter, **Supp. XI:** 25
Barthelme, Steven, **Supp. XI:** 25, 27, 37
Barthes, Roland, **Supp. IV Part 1:** 39, 119, 126; **Supp. XIII:** 83; **Supp. XVI:** 285, 294; **Supp. XVII:** 244
Bartholomew and the Oobleck (Geisel), **Supp. XVI:** 104
"Bar Time" (B. Collins), **Supp. XVII:** 245
"Bartleby, the Scrivener; A Story of Wall-Street" (Melville), **III:** 88–89; **Retro. Supp. I:** 255
Bartleby in Manhattan and Other Essays (Hardwick), **Supp. III Part 1:** 204, 210
"Bartleby the Scrivener" (Melville), **Supp. XVIII:** 4
Bartlet, Phebe, **I:** 562
Bartlett, Lee, **Supp. VIII:** 291
Bartlett, Mary Dougherty, **Supp. IV Part 1:** 335
Barton, Bruce, **III:** 14; **Retro. Supp. I:** 179
Barton, Priscilla. *See* Morison, Mrs. Samuel Eliot (Priscilla Barton)
Barton, Ralph, **Supp. XVI:** 195
Barton, Rev. William E., **Retro. Supp. I:** 179
Bartov, Omer, **Supp. XVI:** 153–154
Bartram, John, **Supp. I Part 1:** 244
Bartram, William, **II:** 313; **Supp. IX:** 171; **Supp. X:** 223
Barzun, Jacques, **Supp. XIV:** 54
"Basement" (Bambara), **Supp. XI:** 5
Basement Tapes, The (album, Dylan), **Supp. XVIII:** 27, 30, 32
"Base of All Metaphysics, The" (Whitman), **IV:** 348
"Base Stealer, The" (Francis), **Supp. IX:** 82
Bashevis, Isaac. *See* Singer, Isaac Bashevis
Basil Stories, The (Fitzgerald), **Retro. Supp. I:** 109
Basin and Range (McPhee), **Supp. III Part 1:** 309
"Basin of Eggs, A" (Swenson), **Supp. IV Part 2:** 645
"Basket, The" (Lowell), **II:** 522
"Basketball and Beefeaters" (McPhee), **Supp. III Part 1:** 296
"Basketball and Poetry: The Two Richies" (Dunn), **Supp. XI:** 140
"Basketball Player" (L. Michaels), **Supp. XVI:** 209
Baskin, Leonard, **Supp. X:** 58, 71; **Supp. XV:** 348
Bass, Rick, **Supp. XIV:** 227; **Supp. XVI: 15–29**
Basso, Hamilton, **Retro. Supp. I:** 80
Bastard, The (Caldwell), **I:** 291, 292, 308
"Bat, The" (Kenyon), **Supp. VII:** 168
Bataille, Georges, **Supp. VIII:** 4; **Supp. XII:** 1
"Batard" (London), **II:** 468–469
Bate, W. J., **II:** 531
Bates, Arlo, **Retro. Supp. I:** 35
Bates, Blanche, **Supp. XVI:** 182
Bates, Kathy, **Supp. XIII:** 207
Bates, Lee, **Retro. Supp. II:** 46
Bates, Milton J., **Supp. XII:** 62

Bates, Sylvia Chatfield, **II:** 586
Bateson, Gregory, **Supp. XV:** 146
"Bath, The" (Carver), **Supp. III Part 1:** 144, 145
"Bath, The" (Snyder), **Supp. VIII:** 302
Bathwater Wine (Coleman), **Supp. XI:** 83, 90, **91**
"Batter my heart, three person'd God" (Donne), **Supp. I Part 2:** 726; **Supp. XVII:** 119
"Battle, The" (Simpson), **Supp. IX:** 268–269
Battlefield Where the Moon Says I Love You, The (Stanford), **Supp. XV:** 345
Battle-Ground, The (Glasgow), **II:** 175, 176, 177, 178, 193
"Battle Hymn of the Republic" (Sandburg), **III:** 585
"Battle Hymn of the Republic, The" (Howe), **III:** 505
"Battle Hymn of the Republic, The" (Updike), **Retro. Supp. I:** 324
Battle of Angels (T. Williams), **IV:** 380, 381, 383, 385, 386, 387
"Battle of Lovell's Pond, The" (Longfellow), **II:** 493
Battle of the Atlantic, The (Morison), **Supp. I Part 2:** 490
"Battle of the Baltic, The" (Campbell), **Supp. I Part 1:** 309
"Battle of the Bunker, The" (Snodgrass), **Supp. VI:** 319–320
"***Battle of the Century!!!, The***" (Goldbarth), **Supp. XII:** 193
Battle-Pieces and Aspects of the War (Melville), **II:** 538–539; **III:** 92; **IV:** 350; **Retro. Supp. I:** 257
"Battler, The" (Hemingway), **II:** 248; **Retro. Supp. I:** 175
"Baudelaire" (Schwartz), **Supp. II Part 2:** 663
Baudelaire, Charles, **I:** 58, 63, 384, 389, 420, 569; **II:** 543, 544–545, 552; **III:** 137, 141–142, 143, 409, 417, 418, 421, 428, 448, 466, 474; **IV:** 74, 79, 80, 87, 211, 286; **Retro. Supp. I:** 56, 90; **Retro. Supp. II:** 261, 262, 322, 326; **Supp. I Part 1:** 271; **Supp. III Part 1:** 4, 6, 105; **Supp. XIII:** 77, 284
Baudelaire, Charles-Pierre, **Supp. XV:** 165
Baudrillard, Jean, **Supp. IV Part 1:** 45
Bauer, Dale, **Retro. Supp. I:** 381
Bauer, Douglas, **Supp. XII:** 290
Baum, L. Frank, **Supp. I Part 2:** 621; **Supp. IV Part 1:** 101, 113; **Supp. XII:** 42
Baumann, Walter, **III:** 478
Bausch, Richard, **Supp. VII: 39–56; Supp. XVII:** 21
Bawer, Bruce, **Supp. IX:** 135; **Supp. VIII:** 153; **Supp. X:** 187
Baxter, Charles, **Supp. XII:** 22; **Supp. XIV:** 89, 92; **Supp. XVII: 13–24**
Baxter, John, **Supp. XI:** 302
Baxter, Richard, **III:** 199; **IV:** 151, 153; **Supp. I Part 2:** 683
"Baxter's Procrustes" (Chesnutt), **Supp. XIV:** 76
"Bay City Blues" (Chandler), **Supp. IV Part 1:** 129
Baylies, William, **Supp. I Part 1:** 153
Baym, Nina, **Supp. IV Part 2:** 463; **Supp. X:** 229; **Supp. XVI:** 92; **Supp. XVIII:** 258, 259
Bayou Folk (Chopin), **Retro. Supp. II: 64–65,** 73; **Supp. I Part 1:** 200, 216, 218
Baziotes, William, **Supp. XV:** 144
Beach, Anna Hampstead, **Supp. XVII:** 75
Beach, Joseph Warren, **I:** 309, 500; **II:** 27; **III:** 319
Beach, Sylvia, **IV:** 404; **Retro. Supp. I:** 109, 422
"Beach Women, The" (Pinsky), **Supp. VI:** 241
"Beaded Pear, The" (Simpson), **Supp. IX:** 276
Beagle, Peter, **Supp. X:** 24
Beam, Jeffrey, **Supp. XII:** 98
Beaman, E. O., **Supp. IV Part 2:** 604
Bean, Michael, **Supp. V:** 203
Bean, Robert Bennett, **Supp. II Part 1:** 170
Bean Eaters, The (Brooks), **Supp. III Part 1:** 79–81
Be Angry at the Sun (Jeffers), **Supp. II Part 2:** 434
"Beanstalk Country, The" (T. Williams), **IV:** 383
Bean Trees, The (Kingsolver), **Supp. VII:** 197, 199–201, 202, 207, 209
"Bear" (Hogan), **Supp. IV Part 1:** 412
"Bear, The" (Faulkner), **II:** 71–72, 73, 228; **IV:** 203; **Supp. IV Part 2:** 434; **Supp. IX:** 95; **Supp. X:** 30; **Supp. XIV:** 32
Bear, The (Faulkner), **Supp. VIII:** 184
"Bear, The" (Kinnell), **Supp. III Part 1:** 244
"Bear, The" (Momaday), **Supp. IV Part 2:** 480, 487
Bear and His Daughter: Stories (Stone), **Supp. V:** 295, 308
Beard, Charles, **I:** 214; **IV:** 429; **Supp. I Part 2:** 481, 490, 492, 632, 640, 643, 647
Beard, James, **I:** 341; **Supp. XVII:** 89, 90
Beard, Mary, **Supp. I Part 2:** 481
"Bearded Oaks" (Warren), **IV:** 240
Bearden, Romare, **Retro. Supp. I:** 209; **Supp. VIII:** 337, 342
"Beard of Bees, A" (X. J. Kennedy), **Supp. XV:** 171
Beardon, Romare, **Supp. XV:** 144
"Beards, The" (Lethem), **Supp. XVIII:** 148
Beardsley, Aubrey, **II:** 56; **IV:** 77
Beaser, Robert, **Supp. XV:** 259
"Beast" (Swenson), **Supp. IV Part 2:** 639
"Beast & Burden, The: Seven Improvisations" (Komunyakaa), **Supp. XIII:** 120, 121
Beast God Forgot to Invent, The (Harrison), **Supp. VIII:** 37, 46, **51–52**
Beast in Me, The (Thurber), **Supp. I Part 2:** 615
"Beast in the Jungle, The" (James), **I:** 570; **II:** 335; **Retro. Supp. I:** 235; **Supp. V:** 103–104
Beast in View (Rukeyser), **Supp. VI:** 272, 273, 279, 280
Beasts of Bethlehem, The (X. J. Kennedy), **Supp. XV:** 163
"Beat! Beat! Drums!" (Whitman), **III:** 585
Beat Down to Your Soul: What Was the Beat Generation? (Charters, ed.), **Supp. XIV:** 152
Beaton, Cecil, **Supp. XVI:** 191
"Beatrice Palmato" (Wharton), **Retro. Supp. I:** 379
Beats, The (Krim, ed.), **Supp. XV:** 338
Beattie, Ann, **Supp. V: 21–37; Supp. XI:** 26; **Supp. XII:** 80, 139, 294
Beatty, General Sam, **I:** 193
Beaty, Jerome, **Supp. IV Part 1:** 331
"Beau Monde of Mrs. Bridge, The" (Connell), **Supp. XIV:** 88, 89
Beaumont, Francis, **Supp. I Part 2:** 422
"Beauties of Santa Cruz, The" (Freneau), **Supp. II Part 1:** 260
Beautiful and Damned, The (Fitzgerald), **II:** 88, 89–91, 93, 263; **Retro. Supp. I: 103–105,** 105, 106, 110; **Supp. IX:** 56, 57
"Beautiful Changes, The" (Wilbur), **Supp. III Part 2:** 549, 550
Beautiful Changes, The (Wilbur), **Supp. III Part 2:** 544–550
"Beautiful Child, A" (Capote), **Supp. III Part 1:** 113, 125
"Beautiful & Cruel" (Cisneros), **Supp. VII:** 63, 67
"Beautiful Woman Who Sings, The" (Gunn Allen), **Supp. IV Part 1:** 326
"Beauty" (Emerson), **II:** 2, 5
"Beauty" (Sanders), **Supp. XVI:** 277
"Beauty" (Wylie), **Supp. I Part 2:** 710
"Beauty and the Beast" (Dove), **Supp. IV Part 1:** 245
"Beauty and the Beast" (fairy tale), **IV:** 266; **Supp. X:** 88
"Beauty and the Shoe Sluts" (Karr), **Supp. XI:** 250
Beauty of the Husband, The: A Fictional Essay in Twenty-Nine Tangos (Carson), **Supp. XII: 113–114**
Beauty's Punishment (Rice), **Supp. VII:** 301
Beauty's Release: The Continued Erotic Adventures of Sleeping Beauty (Rice), **Supp. VII:** 301
Beauvoir, Simone de, **IV:** 477; **Supp. I Part 1:** 51; **Supp. III Part 1:** 200–201, 208; **Supp. IV Part 1:** 360; **Supp. IX:** 4
"Be Careful" (Zach; Everwine, trans.), **Supp. XV:** 86
Be Careful How You Live (Lacy), **Supp. XV:** 203–204
"Because I could not stop for Death——" (Dickinson), **Retro. Supp. I: 38–40,** 41, 43, 44

"Because It Happened" (Goldbarth), **Supp. XII:** 192
"Because of Libraries We Can Say These Things" (Nye), **Supp. XIII:** 283
"Because You Mentioned the Spiritual Life" (Dunn), **Supp. XI:** 154
Bech: A Book (Updike), **IV:** 214; **Retro. Supp. I:** 329, 335
Beck, Dave, **I:** 493
Beck, Jack, **Supp. IV Part 2:** 560
Beck, Nicholas, **Supp. XVIII:** 252
Becker, Carl, **Supp. I Part 2:** 492, 493
Becker, Paula. *See* Modersohn, Mrs. Otto (Paula Becker)
Beckett, Samuel, **I:** 71, 91, 142, 298, 461; **III:** 387; **IV:** 95; **Retro. Supp. I:** 206; **Supp. IV Part 1:** 297, 368–369; **Supp. IV Part 2:** 424; **Supp. V:** 23, 53; **Supp. XI:** 104; **Supp. XII:** 21, 150–151; **Supp. XIII:** 74; **Supp. XIV:** 239; **Supp. XVII:** 185
Beckett, Tom, **Supp. IV Part 2:** 419
Beckford, William, **I:** 204
Beckonings (Brooks), **Supp. III Part 1:** 85
"Becky" (Toomer), **Supp. III Part 2:** 481, 483; **Supp. IX:** 312
Becoming a Man: Half a Life Story (Monette), **Supp. X:** 146, 147, 149, 151, 152, **155–157**
"Becoming a Meadow" (Doty), **Supp. XI:** 124–125
"Becoming and Breaking: Poet and Poem" (Ríos), **Supp. IV Part 2:** 539
Becoming Canonical in American Poetry (Morris), **Retro. Supp. I:** 40
Becoming Light: New and Selected Poems (Jong), **Supp. V:** 115
Bécquer, Gustavo Adolfo, **Supp. XIII:** 312
"Bed, The" (Dixon), **Supp. XII:** 154
Beddoes, Thomas Lovell, **III:** 469; **Retro. Supp. I:** 285
Bedichek, Roy, **Supp. V:** 225
Bedient, Calvin, **Supp. IX:** 298; **Supp. XII:** 98
"Bed in the Sky, The" (Snyder), **Supp. VIII:** 300
Bednarik, Joseph, **Supp. VIII:** 39
"Bedrock" (Proulx), **Supp. VII:** 253
"Bee, The" (Lanier), **Supp. I Part 1:** 364
Beecher, Catharine, **Supp. I Part 2:** 581, 582–583, 584, 586, 588, 589, 591, 599; **Supp. X:** 103; **Supp. XI:** 193
Beecher, Charles, **Supp. I Part 2:** 588, 589
Beecher, Edward, **Supp. I Part 2:** 581, 582, 583, 584, 588, 591
Beecher, Harriet. *See* Stowe, Harriet Beecher
Beecher, Henry Ward, **II:** 275; **Supp. I Part 2:** 581; **Supp. XI:** 193; **Supp. XVIII:** 4
Beecher, Lyman, **Supp. I Part 2:** 580–581, 582, 583, 587, 588, 599; **Supp. XI:** 193
Beecher, Mrs. Lyman (Roxanna Foote), **Supp. I Part 2:** 580–581, 582, 588, 599
Beeching, Jack, **Supp. X:** 114, 117, 118, 123, 125, 126
"Beehive" (Toomer), **Supp. IX:** 317
"Bee Hunt, The" (Irving), **II:** 313
"Beekeeper's Daughter, The" (Plath), **Retro. Supp. II:** 246–247
"Bee Meeting, The" (Plath), **Retro. Supp. II:** 254–255
Bee Poems (Plath), **Retro. Supp. II:** 254–255
Beer, John, **Supp. XVII:** 239
Beer, Thomas, **I:** 405
Beerbohm, Max, **III:** 472; **IV:** 436; **Supp. I Part 2:** 714
"Beer in the Sergeant Major's Hat, or The Sun Also Sneezes" (Chandler), **Supp. IV Part 1:** 121
"Bees Bees Bees" (J. Scott), **Supp. XVII:** 188, 190
Beethoven, Ludwig van, **II:** 536; **III:** 118; **IV:** 274, 358; **Supp. I Part 1:** 363; **Supp. VIII:** 103
Beet Queen, The (Erdrich), **Supp. IV Part 1:** 259, 260, 264–265, 266, 273, 274, 275
Befo' de War: Echoes in Negro Dialect (Gordon), **Supp. II Part 1:** 201
"Before" (Goldbarth), **Supp. XII:** 175
"Before" (Snyder), **Supp. VIII:** 301
Before Adam (London), **II:** 466
"Before Disaster" (Winters), **Supp. II Part 2:** 801, 815
Before Disaster (Winters), **Supp. II Part 2:** 786, 800
"Before I Knocked" (D. Thomas), **III:** 534
Beforelife, The (F. Wright), **Supp. XVII:** 240, 245–246
"Before March" (MacLeish), **III:** 15
Before My Life Began (Neugeboren), **Supp. XVI: 224–225**
"Before the Altar" (Lowell), **II:** 516
"Before the Birth of one of her children" (Bradstreet), **Supp. I Part 1:** 118
"Before the Sky Darkens" (Dunn), **Supp. XI:** 155
"Begat" (Sexton), **Supp. II Part 2: 693**
Beggar on Horseback (Kaufman and Connelly), **III:** 394
"Beggar Said So, The" (Singer), **IV:** 12
Beggars in the House of Plenty (Shanley), **Supp. XIV:** 316, **327–328**
Beggar's Opera, The (Gay), **Supp. I Part 2:** 523
Begiebing, Robert, **Retro. Supp. II:** 210
Begin Again (Paley), **Supp. VI:** 221
"Beginning and the End, The" (Jeffers), **Supp. II Part 2:** 420–421, 424
"Beginning of Decadence, The" (Jeffers), **Supp. II Part 2:** 420
"Beginning of Enthusiasm, The" (Salinas), **Supp. XIII:** 327–328
Beginning of Wisdom, The (Benét), **I:** 358; **Supp. XI:** 44
Be Glad You're Neurotic (Bisch), **Supp. I Part 2:** 608
"Begotten of the Spleen" (Simic), **Supp. VIII:** 277
"Behaving Like a Jew" (Stern), **Supp. IX: 290–291,** 294
"Behavior" (Emerson), **II:** 2, 4
Behavior of Titans, The (Merton), **Supp. VIII:** 201
Behind a Mask (Alcott), **Supp. I Part 1:** 36–37, 43–44
"Behind a Wall" (Lowell), **II:** 516
Behind the Movie Camera (radio show), **Supp. XV:** 147
"Behold the Key" (Malamud), **Supp. I Part 2:** 437
Behrendt, Stephen, **Supp. X:** 204
Behrman, S. N., **Supp. V:** 95
Beidler, Peter G., **Supp. IV Part 2:** 557
Beidler, Philip D., **Supp. XII:** 69
Beige Dolorosa (Harrison), **Supp. VIII:** 40, 51
Beiles, Sinclair, **Supp. XII:** 129
Beiliss, Mendel, **Supp. I Part 2:** 427, 446, 447, 448
"Being a Constellation" (A. Finch), **Supp. XVII:** 72
"Being a Lutheran Boy-God in Minnesota" (R. Bly), **Supp. IV Part 1:** 59, 67
Being and Race (Johnson), **Supp. VI:** 193, 199
Being and Time (Heidegger), **Supp. VIII:** 9
Being Busted (Fiedler), **Supp. XIII:** 95, 102, 104
Being John Malkovich (Kaufman), **Supp. XV:** 16
Being Perfect (Quindlen), **Supp. XVII:** 167, 179
Being There (Kosinski), **Supp. VII:** 215, 216, 222–223
Beiswanger, George, **Retro. Supp. II:** 220
Belasco, David, **Supp. XVI:** 182
Bel Canto (Patchett), **Supp. XII:** 307, 310, **320–322**
"Beleaguered City, The" (Longfellow), **II:** 498
Belfry of Bruges, The, and Other Poems (Longfellow), **II:** 489; **Retro. Supp. II:** 157, 168
"Belief" (Levine), **Supp. V:** 186, 190
"Beliefs of Writers, The" (Doctorow), **Supp. IV Part 1:** 235–236
Believeniks! (Lethem and Sorrentino), **Supp. XVIII:** 148–149
"Believers" (C. Baxter), **Supp. XVII:** 21
Believers (C. Baxter), **Supp. XVII:** 20–21, 22
"Believers, The/Los Creyentes" (Kingsolver), **Supp. VII:** 208
Belinda (Rice), **Supp. VII:** 301–302
"Belinda's Petition" (Dove), **Supp. IV Part 1:** 245
"Belita" (Ríos), **Supp. IV Part 2:** 541
Belitt, Ben, **Supp. XII:** 260
Bell, Clive, **IV:** 87
Bell, Daniel, **Supp. I Part 2:** 648
Bell, George Kennedy Allen, **Retro. Supp. I:** 65
Bell, Madison Smartt, **Supp. X: 1–20; Supp. XVII:** 236
Bell, Marvin, **Supp. IX:** 152; **Supp. V:** 337, 339; **Supp. XI:** 316
Bell, Michael, **Retro. Supp. II:** 139

Bell, Pearl, **Supp. XI:** 233
Bell, Quentin, **Supp. I Part 2:** 636
Bell, Whitfield J., Jr., **II:** 123
Bellafante, Gina, **Supp. VIII:** 85
Bellamy, Edward, **II:** 276; **Supp. I Part 2:** 641; **Supp. XI:** 200, 203
Bellarosa Connection, The (Bellow), **Retro. Supp. II:** 31, 32
"Belle Dollinger" (Masters), **Supp. I Part 2:** 463
Belleforest, François de, **IV:** 370
"Belle Zoraïde, La" (Chopin), **Supp. I Part 1:** 215–216
Bell Jar, The (Plath), **Retro. Supp. II:** 242, **249–250; Supp. I Part 2:** 526, 527, 529, 531–536, 539, 540, 541, 542, 544
Belloc, Hilary, **III:** 176; **IV:** 432
Bellow, Saul, **I:** 113, 138–139, **144–166,** 375, 517; **II:** 579; **III:** 40; **IV:** 3, 19, 217, 340; **Retro. Supp. II: 19–36,** 118, 279, 307, 324; **Supp. I Part 2:** 428, 451; **Supp. II Part 1:** 109; **Supp. IV Part 1:** 30; **Supp. IX:** 212, 227; **Supp. V:** 258; **Supp. VIII:** 98, 176, 234, 236–237, 245; **Supp. XI:** 64, 233; **Supp. XII:** 159, 165, 170, 310; **Supp. XIII:** 106; **Supp. XV:** 143; **Supp. XVI:** 208; **Supp. XVIII:** 90
Bellows, George, **Supp. XV:** 295
"Bells, The" (Poe), **III:** 593; **Retro. Supp. II:** 266; **Supp. I Part 2:** 388
"Bells, The" (Sexton), **Supp. II Part 2:** 673
"Bells for John Whiteside's Daughter" (Ransom), **III:** 490
"Bells of Lynn, The" (Longfellow), **II:** 498
"Bells of San Blas, The" (Longfellow), **II:** 490–491, 493, 498
"Bell Tower, The" (Melville), **III:** 91
"Belly, The" (Dobyns), **Supp. XIII:** 87
"Belonging Kind, The" (W. Gibson and J. Shirley), **Supp. XVI:** 123
Beloved (Morrison), **Supp. III Part 1:** 364, 372–379; **Supp. IV Part 1:** 13–14; **Supp. V:** 259; **Supp. VIII:** 343; **Supp. XIII:** 60
Beloved Lady: A History of Jane Addams' Ideas on Reform and Peace (Farrell), **Supp. I Part 1:** 24
Beloved Stranger, The (Bynner), **Supp. XV:** 44, 50
Benchley, Robert, **I:** 48, 482; **II:** 435; **III:** 53; **Supp. IX:** 190, 195, 204
Benda, W. T., **Retro. Supp. I:** 13
Bend Sinister (Nabokov), **III:** 253–254; **Retro. Supp. I:** 265, 266, 270
"Beneath the Sidewalk" (Dunn), **Supp. XI:** 145
"Beneath the Smooth Skin of America" (Sanders), **Supp. XVI:** 275
Benedict, Elizabeth, **Supp. XVIII:** 289
Benedict, Ruth, **Supp. IX:** 229
Benefactor, The (Sontag), **Supp. III Part 2:** 451, 455, 468, 469
"Benefit Performance" (Malamud), **Supp. I Part 2:** 431
Benét, Laura, **Supp. XI:** 44
Benét, Rosemary, **Supp. XI:** 44, 51
Benét, Stephen Vincent, **I:** 358; **II:** 177; **III:** 22; **IV:** 129; **Supp. XI: 43–61**
Benét, William Rose, **II:** 530; **Retro. Supp. I:** 108; **Supp. I Part 2:** 709; **Supp. XI:** 43, 44; **Supp. XIV:** 119, 122, 129
Ben Franklin's Wit and Wisdom (Franklin), **II:** 111
Ben-Hur (film), **Supp. IV Part 2:** 683
Benigna Machiavelli (Gilman), **Supp. XI:** 201, 208
Benitez, R. Michael, **Retro. Supp. II:** 264
Benito Cereno (Lowell), **II:** 546; **Retro. Supp. II:** 181
"Benito Cereno" (Melville), **III:** 91; **Retro. Supp. I:** 255; **Retro. Supp. II:** 188; **Supp. XVII:** 185
Benito's Dream Bottle (Nye), **Supp. XIII:** 278
"Bênitou's Slave, The" (Chopin), **Retro. Supp. II:** 64
Benjamin, Walter, **Supp. IX:** 133; **Supp. XVI:** 290, 291
Benjamin Franklin (Van Doren), **Supp. I Part 2:** 486
"Benjamin Pantier" (Masters), **Supp. I Part 2:** 461
Bennett, Anne Virginia, **II:** 184
Bennett, Arnold, **I:** 103; **II:** 337; **Supp. XVI:** 190
Bennett, Elizabeth, **Supp. VIII:** 58
Bennett, Patrick, **Supp. V:** 225
Bennett, Paula, **Retro. Supp. I:** 29, 33, 42
Bennett, William, **Supp. VIII:** 245
Benson, Heidi, **Supp. XVIII:** 136
Benson, Jackson J., **Supp. IV Part 2:** 613
Benson, Martin, **Supp. XVIII:** 38
Benstock, Shari, **Retro. Supp. I:** 361, 368, 371, 382
Bentham, Jeremy, **I:** 279; **Supp. I Part 2:** 635
Bentley, Eric R., **IV:** 396
Bentley, Nelson, **Supp. IX:** 324
Bentley, Richard, **III:** 79, 86
Benton, Robert, **Supp. IV Part 1:** 236
"Bent Tones" (Wright), **Supp. XV:** 346
Benveniste, Emile, **Supp. XVI:** 292
Benzel, Jan, **Supp. XVI:** 112
Beowulf, **Supp. II Part 1:** 6; **Supp. XVII:** 70, 73
Beran, Carol, **Supp. XIII:** 25
"Berck-Plage" (Plath), **Retro. Supp. II:** 253–254
Bercovitch, Sacvan, **Retro. Supp. I:** 408; **Retro. Supp. II:** 325, 330; **Supp. I Part 1:** 99; **Supp. I Part 2:** 659
Berdyaev, Nikolai, **I:** 494; **III:** 292
"Bereaved Apartments" (Kingsolver), **Supp. VII:** 203
"Bereavement in their death to feel" (Dickinson), **Retro. Supp. I:** 43, 44
"Berenice" (Poe), **III:** 415, 416, 425; **Retro. Supp. II:** 270
Bérénice (Racine), **II:** 573
Berenson, Bernard, **Retro. Supp. I:** 381; **Supp. IV Part 1:** 314; **Supp. XIV:** 335, 336, 337; **Supp. XVII:** 99
Berg, James, **Supp. XIV:** 157, 159
Berg, Stephen, **Supp. IV Part 1:** 60
Berger, Alan, **Supp. XVII:** 39
Berger, Charles, **Retro. Supp. I:** 311
Berger, John, **Supp. XVI:** 284
Berger, Roger, **Supp. XIII:** 237
Berger, Thomas, **III:** 258; **Supp. XII:** 171
Bergman, Ingmar, **I:** 291; **Supp. XV:** 7, 8, 12
Bergson, Henri, **I:** 224; **II:** 163, 165, 166, 359; **III:** 8, 9, 488, 619; **IV:** 86, 122, 466, 467; **Retro. Supp. I:** 55, 57, 80; **Supp. IV Part 1:** 42
Berkeley, Anthony, **Supp. IV Part 1:** 341
Berkeley, George, **II:** 10, 349, 357, 480, 554
Berkman, Leonard, **Supp. XV:** 321
Berkowitz, Gerald, **Supp. IV Part 2:** 590
Berlin Alexanderplatz (Döblin), **Supp. XV:** 137
Berlin Stories (Isherwood), **Supp. IV Part 1:** 82; **Supp. XIV:** 155, 156, 161, 162, 164, 165
Berlioz, Hector, **Supp. XV:** 33
Berlyne, Daniel E., **Supp. I Part 2:** 672
Berman, Alexander, **Supp. XVII:** 103
Bernard Clare (Farrell), **II:** 38, 39
Bernard of Clairvaux, Saint, **I:** 22; **II:** 538
Bernays, Thekla, **Retro. Supp. II:** 65
Berne, Suzanne, **Supp. XII:** 320
Berne, Victoria (pseudonym). *See* Fisher, M. F. K.
Berneis, Peter, **IV:** 383
Bernhard, Brendan, **Supp. XIV:** 163
Bernhardt, Sarah, **I:** 484; **Retro. Supp. I:** 377
Bernice (Glaspell), **Supp. III Part 1:** 179
"Bernice Bobs Her Hair" (Fitzgerald), **II:** 88; **Retro. Supp. I:** 103
Bernstein, Aline, **IV:** 455, 456
Bernstein, Andrea, **Supp. IX:** 146
Bernstein, Charles, **Supp. IV Part 2:** 421, 426
Bernstein, Elizabeth, **Supp. XII:** 318
Bernstein, Leonard, **I:** 28; **Supp. I Part 1:** 288, 289; **Supp. IV Part 1:** 83, 84
Bernstein, Melvin, **Supp. XIV:** 41, 46
Bernstein, Michael André, **Retro. Supp. I:** 427
Bernstein, Richard, **Supp. IX:** 253, 262; **Supp. XII:** 113; **Supp. XIV:** 33
Berrett, Jesse, **Supp. XIII:** 241, 242
Berrigan, Ted, **Supp. XIV:** 150
"Berry" (Hughes), **Supp. I Part 1:** 329, 330
Berry, Faith, **Retro. Supp. I:** 194, 201
Berry, Walter, **IV:** 313–314, 326
Berry, Wendell, **Supp. VIII:** 304; **Supp. X: 21–39; Supp. XII:** 202; **Supp. XIII:** 1–2; **Supp. XIV:** 179; **Supp. XVI:** 39, 56; **Supp. XVIII:** 192
"Berry Feast, A" (Snyder), **Supp. VIII:** 289, 297
Berryman, John, **I: 167–189,** 405, 441–442, 521; **II:** 554; **III:** 273; **IV:** 138, 430; **Retro. Supp. I:** 430; **Retro. Supp. II:** 175, 178; **Supp. I Part 2:** 546; **Supp. II Part 1:** 109; **Supp. III Part 2:** 541, 561, 595, 596, 603; **Supp.**

IV Part 2: 620, 639; **Supp. IX:** 152; **Supp. V:** 179–180, 337; **Supp. XI:** 240; **Supp. XV:** 93; **Supp. XVII:** 111
Berryman, Mrs. John, **I:** 168–169
Berryman's Sonnets (Berryman), **I:** 168, 175–178
"Berry Territory" (Snyder), **Supp. VIII:** 304
Berthoff, Warner, **Supp. I Part 1:** 133
Bertolucci, Bernardo, **Supp. IV Part 1:** 94
"Bertrand Hume" (Masters), **Supp. I Part 2:** 463–464
"Best, the Most, The" (Carruth), **Supp. XVI:** 59
Best American Essays 1987, The (G. Talese and R. Atwan, eds.), **Supp. XVI:** 273
Best American Essays 1988, The (Dillard, ed.), **Supp. VIII:** 272
Best American Essays 1989, The (Wolff, ed.), **Supp. XVII:** 208
Best American Essays 1993, The (J. Epstein, ed.), **Supp. XVI:** 275
Best American Essays 1997, The (Frazier, ed.), **Supp. VIII:** 272; **Supp. XVII:** 207
Best American Essays 1999, The (E. Hoagland and R. Atwan, eds.), **Supp. XVI:** 277
Best American Essays for College Students, The (R. Atwan, ed.), **Supp. XVI:** 273
Best American New Voices 2001 (C. Baxter, ed.), **Supp. XVII:** 22
Best American Poetry, The: 1988 (Ashbery, ed.), **Supp. III Part 1:** 26
Best American Short Stories, **I:**174; **II:** 587; **III:** 443; **Supp. IV Part 1:** 102, 315; **Supp. IX:** 114; **Supp. X:** 301
Best American Short Stories, 1915–1050, The, **Supp. IX:** 4
Best American Short Stories 1965, The (Foley, ed.), **Supp. XVI:** 225
Best American Short Stories 1982, The (Gardner, ed.), **Supp. XVII:** 16
Best American Short Stories 1983, The (A. Tyler, ed.), **Supp. XVI:** 37
Best American Short Stories 1986, The (Carver, ed.), **Supp. XVII:** 17
Best American Short Stories 1988, The (Helprin, ed.), **Supp. XVI:** 16
Best American Short Stories 1989, The (Atwood, ed.), **Supp. XVII:** 18
Best American Short Stories 1991, The (Adams and Kenison, eds.), **Supp. XVI:** 256
Best American Short Stories 2001, The (Kenison and Kingsover, eds.), **Supp. XVI:** 24
Best American Short Stories of 1942, The, **Supp. V:** 316
Best American Short Stories of 1944, The, **Supp. IX:** 119
Best American Short Stories of the Century (Updike, ed.), **Supp. X:** 163
Best American Short Stories of the Eighties, The (Ravenal, ed.), **Supp. IV Part 1:** 93
Best American Sports Writing of the Century, The (Halberstam, ed.), **Supp. XVII:** 204
"Best China Saucer, The" (Jewett), **Retro. Supp. II:** 145–146
Bester, Alfred, **Supp. XVI:** 123
Best Hour of the Night, The (Simpson), **Supp. IX: 277–279**
Bestiaire, Le (Apollinaire), **IV:** 80
Bestiary, A (Wilbur), **Supp. III Part 2:** 552
"Bestiary for the Fingers of My Right Hand" (Simic), **Supp. VIII:** 274, 275
Best Man, The: A Play About Politics (Vidal), **Supp. IV Part 2:** 683
"Best of Everything, The" (Yates), **Supp. XI:** 341
Best of Plimpton (Plimpton), **Supp. XVI:** 238, 239, 240
Best Short Plays, The (Mayorga), **IV:** 381
Best Short Stories, The (O'Brien, ed.), **I:** 289
Best Short Stories by Negro Writers, The (Hughes, ed.), **Supp. I Part 1:** 345
Best Short Stories of 1926, The (O'Brien, ed.), **Supp. XVIII:** 279
Best Short Stories of 1934 (O'Brien, ed.), **Supp. XVIII:** 227
Best That Ever Did It, The (Lacy), **Supp. XV:** 201–202
Best Times, The: An Informal Memoir (Dos Passos), **I:** 475, 482
Best Words, Best Order: Essays on Poetry (Dobyns), **Supp. XIII:** 74, **76–78,** 87
Best Years of Our Lives, The (film; Wyler), **Supp. XV:** 195
"BETANCOURT" (Baraka), **Supp. II Part 1:** 33, 34
Bête humaine, La (Zola), **III:** 316, 318
"Bethe" (Hellman), **Supp. I Part 1:** 293
Bethea, David, **Supp. VIII:** 27
Bethel Merriday (Lewis), **II:** 455
Bethke, Bruce, **Supp. XVI:** 121
Bethlehem in Broad Daylight (Doty), **Supp. XI:** 121, **122–123**
Bethune, Mary McLeod, **Retro. Supp. I:** 197; **Supp. I Part 1:** 333
Bethurum, Dorothy, **IV:** 121
"Betrayal" (Lanier), **Supp. I Part 1:** 364
"Betrothed" (Bogan), **Supp. III Part 1:** 49–51
Bettelheim, Bruno, **Supp. I Part 2:** 622; **Supp. X:** 77, 84; **Supp. XIV:** 126; **Supp. XVI:** 33
Better Days (Price), **Supp. VI:** 264
Better Sort, The (James), **II:** 335
"Better Things in Life, The" (Loos), **Supp. XVI:** 194
Betty Leicester (Jewett), **II:** 406
Betty Leicester's Christmas (Jewett), **II:** 406; **Retro. Supp. II:** 145
"Between Angels" (Dunn), **Supp. XI:** 150
Between Angels (Dunn), **Supp. XI: 149–159**
Between Fantoine and Agapa (Pinget), **Supp. V:** 39
"Between Memory and History: A Writer's Voice" (Kreisler), **Supp. XVI:** 155
Between Silences: A Voice from China (Jin), **Supp. XVIII:** 91, 92, 93
"Between the Porch and the Altar" (Lowell), **II:** 540–541
"Between the World and Me" (Wright), **Supp. II Part 1:** 228
Between Time and Timbuktu (Vonnegut), **Supp. II Part 2:** 753, 759
Bevis, Howard L., **Supp. I Part 2:** 611
Bevis, John, **Supp. I Part 2:** 503
"Bewitched" (Wharton), **IV:** 316
Bewley, Marius, **I:** 336
Beyle, Marie Henri. *See* Stendhal
Beyond (Goldbarth), **Supp. XII:** 192
Beyond Black Bear Lake (LaBastille), **Supp. X:** 95, **99–102,** 108
"Beyond Charles River to the Acheron" (Lowell), **II:** 541
Beyond Criticism (Shapiro), **Supp. II Part 2:** 703, 711
Beyond Culture (Trilling), **Supp. III Part 2:** 508–512
Beyond Desire (Anderson), **I:** 111
Beyond Document: The Art of Nonfiction Film (Warren, ed.), **Supp. IV Part 2:** 434
Beyond Good and Evil (Nietzsche), **Supp. IV Part 2:** 519
"Beyond Harm" (Olds), **Supp. X:** 210
"Beyond the Alps" (Lowell), **II:** 547, 550
"Beyond the Bayou" (Chopin), **Supp. I Part 1:** 215
Beyond the Horizon (O'Neill), **III:** 389
Beyond the Hundredth Meridian: John Wesley Powell and the Second Opening of the West (Stegner), **Supp. IV Part 2:** 599, 603–604, 611
"Beyond the Kittery Bridge" (Hatlen), **Supp. V:** 138
Beyond the Law (film) (Mailer), **Retro. Supp. II:** 205
"Beyond the Sea (at the sanatorium)" (Salinas), **Supp. XIII:** 325
Beyond the Wall: Essays from the Outside (Abbey), **Supp. XIII:** 13
Beyond the Writers' Workshop: New Ways to Write Creative Nonfiction (C. Bly), **Supp. XVI:** 41
Beyond Tragedy (Niebuhr), **III:** 300–303
Bezner, Kevin, **Supp. XII:** 202
B. F.'s Daughter (Marquand), **III:** 59, 65, 68, 69
Bhagavad Gita, **III:** 566; **IV:** 183
"Biafra: A People Betrayed" (Vonnegut), **Supp. II Part 2:** 760
Bianchi, Martha Dickinson, **I:** 470; **Retro. Supp. I:** 35, 37, 38
Bible, **I:** 191, 280, 414, 421, 490, 506; **II:** 6, 12, 15, 17, 108, 231, 237, 238, 252, 267, 302; **III:** 28, 199, 308–309, 341, 343, 350, 356, 402, 492, 519, 565, 577; **IV:** 11, 13, 42, 57, 60, 67, 152, 153, 154, 155, 164, 165, 296, 337, 341, 367, 369, 370, 371, 438; **Retro. Supp. I:** 91; **Supp. I Part 1:** 4, 6, 63, 101, 104, 105, 113, 193, 369; **Supp. I Part 2:** 388, 433, 494, 515, 516, 517, 583, 584, 587, 589, 653, 689, 690, 691; **Supp. IV Part 1:** 284;

Supp. IX: 246; **Supp. VIII:** 20; **Supp. XIV:** 225. *See also* names of biblical books; New Testament; Old Testament
Biblia Americana (Mather), **Supp. II Part 2:** 442
Biblical Dialogues between a Father and His Family (Rowson), **Supp. XV:** 245–246
"Bibliography of the King's Book, A, or, Eikon Basilike" (Howe), **Supp. IV Part 2:** 435
Bibliography of the King's Book, A; or, Eikon Basilike (Almack), **Supp. IV Part 2:** 435
Bickel, Freddy. *See* March, Fredric
Bidart, Frank, **Retro. Supp. II:** 48, 50, 52, 182, 183, 184; **Supp. XV: 19–37; Supp. XVIII:** 91,92
Bid Me to Live (Doolittle), **Supp. I Part 1:** 258, 260, 268, 269, 270
"*Bien* Pretty" (Cisneros), **Supp. VII:** 70
"Bienvenidos" (Mora), **Supp. XIII:** 220
Bierce, Albert, **I:** 191, 209
Bierce, Ambrose, **I: 190–213,** 419; **II:** 74, 264, 271; **IV:** 350; **Retro. Supp. II:** 72
Bierce, Day, **I:** 195, 199
Bierce, General Lucius Verus, **I:** 191
Bierce, Helen, **I:** 210
Bierce, Leigh, **I:** 195, 198, 208
Bierce, Marcus, **I:** 190, 191
Bierce, Mrs. Ambrose, **I:** 194–195, 199
Bierce, Mrs. Marcus, **I:** 190, 191
Bierds, Linda, **Supp. XVII: 25–37**
Biffle, Kent, **Supp. V:** 225
"Bi-Focal" (Stafford), **Supp. XI:** 318, 321
Bigamist's Daughter, A (McDermott), **Supp. XVIII:** 155, **156–158,** 160, 166
Big as Life (Doctorow), **Supp. IV Part 1:** 231, 234
"Big Bite" (Mailer), **Retro. Supp. II:** 204
"Big Blonde" (Parker), **Supp. IX:** 189, 192, 193, 195, 196, 203
Big Bozo, The (Glaspell), **Supp. III Part 1:** 182
Bigelow, Gordon, **Supp. X:** 222, 227, 229
Bigelow, Jacob, **Supp. I Part 1:** 302
Bigelow Papers, Second Series, The (Lowell), **Supp. I Part 2:** 406, 415–416
Bigelow Papers, The (Lowell), **Supp. I Part 2:** 406, 407, 408, 410, 411–412, 415, 417, 424
Big Fix, The (Lacy), **Supp. XV:** 204–205
Bigfoot Dreams (Prose), **Supp. XVI:** 253–254
Big Funk, The: A Casual Play (Shanley), **Supp. XIV:** 316, **327**
Big Gold Dream, The (C. Himes), **Supp. XVI:** 143, 144
"Bight, The" (Bishop), **Retro. Supp. II:** 38, 45
Big Hunger: Stories 1932–1959 (Fante), **Supp. XI:** 160
Big Knife, The (Odets), **Supp. II Part 2:** 546, 547, 548
Big Knockover, The (Hammett), **Supp. I Part 1:** 292; **Supp. IV Part 1:** 344, 345, 356
Big Laugh, The (O'Hara), **III:** 362, 373–375
Big Man (Neugeboren), **Supp. XVI:** 219, **220,** 221, 225
Big Money, The (Dos Passos), **I:** 482, 483, 486–487, 489; **Supp. I Part 2:** 646, 647
"Big Picture" (Everett), **Supp. XVIII:** 66
Big Picture (Everett), **Supp. XVIII:** 54, 66
"Big Rock Candy Figgy Pudding Pitfall, The" (Didion), **Supp. IV Part 1:** 195
Big Rock Candy Mountain, The (Stegner), **Supp. IV Part 2:** 596, 597, 598, 599, 600, 603, 604, 605, 606–607, 608, 610–611
Bigsby, C. W. E. (Christopher), **Supp. IX:** 137, 140; **Supp. XV:** 332
Big Sea, The (Hughes), **Retro. Supp. I:** 195, 197, 199, 201, 204; **Supp. I Part 1:** 322, 332, 333; **Supp. II Part 1:** 233–234
Big Sky, The (Mora), **Supp. XIII:** 221
Big Sleep, The (Chandler), **Supp. IV Part 1:** 122–125, 127, 128, 134
Big Sleep, The (film), **Supp. IV Part 1:** 130; **Supp. XVIII:** 148
Big Strike, The (Ryan as Quin), **Supp. XVIII:** 226,**232–233**
Big Sur (Kerouac), **Supp. III Part 1:** 230
Big Sur and the Oranges of Hieronymous Bosch (H. Miller), **III:** 189–190
Big Town, The (Lardner), **II:** 426, 429
"Big Two-Hearted River" (Hemingway), **II:** 249; **Retro. Supp. I:** 170–171; **Supp. IX:** 106; **Supp. XIV:** 227, 235
"Big Wind" (Roethke), **III:** 531
"Big Winner Rises Late, The" (Dunn), **Supp. XI:** 146
"Bilingual Christmas" (Mora), **Supp. XIII:** 216–217
"Bilingual Sestina" (Alvarez), **Supp. VII:** 10
"Bill" (Winters), **Supp. II Part 2:** 792
"Bill, The" (Malamud), **Supp. I Part 2:** 427, 430, 434
"Billie Holiday" (Carruth), **Supp. XVI:** 50
Billings, Gladys. *See* Brooks, Mrs. Van Wyck
Billings, Josh, **Supp. XVIII:** 1, 4
Bill of Rites, a Bill of Wrongs, a Bill of Goods, A (Morris), **III:** 237
"Bill's Beans" (Nye), **Supp. XIII:** 283
"Billy" (Gordon), **Supp. IV Part 1:** 306
"Billy" (McCarriston), **Supp. XIV:** 265
Billy Bathgate (Doctorow), **Supp. IV Part 1:** 217, 219, 222, 224, 227, 229–231, 231, 232, 233, 238
Billy Bathgate (film), **Supp. IV Part 1:** 236
Billy Budd, Sailor (Melville), **III:** 40, 93–95; **IV:** 105; **Retro. Supp. I:** 249, **258–260**
Billy Phelan's Greatest Game (W. Kennedy), **Supp. VII:** 131, 132, 134, 135, 142–147, 149, 151, 153, 155
Billy the Kid, **Supp. IV Part 2:** 489, 490, 492
Biloxi Blues (Simon), **Supp. IV Part 2:** 576, 577, 584, 586–587, 590
"Bimini" (Hemingway), **II:** 258
Bingham, Anne, **Supp. XV:** 239
Bingham, Millicent Todd, **I:** 470; **Retro. Supp. I:** 36
Bingo Palace, The (Erdrich), **Supp. IV Part 1:** 259, 260, 261, 263–264, 265, 266–267, 268–269, 270, 271–273, 274, 275
"Binsey Poplars" (Hopkins), **Supp. I Part 1:** 94; **Supp. IV Part 2:** 639
Binswanger, Ludwig, **Supp. XV:** 26
Biographia Literaria (Coleridge), **II:** 10; **Retro. Supp. I:** 308
"Biography" (Francis), **Supp. IX:** 77
"Biography" (Pinsky), **Supp. VI:** 235, 236, 239, 241, **243,** 249, 250
Biography and Poetical Remains of the Late Margaret Miller Davidson (Irving), **II:** 314
"Biography in the First Person" (Dunn), **Supp. XI:** 144
"Biography of an Armenian Schoolgirl" (Nye), **Supp. XIII:** 275, 280
"Biography of a Story" (Jackson), **Supp. IX:** 113
Biondi, Joann, **Supp. XI:** 103
"Biopoetics Sketch for *Greenfield Review*" (Harjo), **Supp. XII:** 216
"Birchbrook Mill" (Whittier), **Supp. I Part 2:** 699
"Birches" (Frost), **II:** 154; **Retro. Supp. I:** 132; **Supp. XIII:** 147
Bird, Alan, **Supp. I Part 1:** 260
Bird, Gloria, **Supp. XII:** 216
Bird, Isabella, **Supp. X:** 103
Bird, Robert M., **III:** 423
"Bird, The" (Simpson), **Supp. IX:** 269–270
"Bird, the Bird, the Bird, The" (Creeley), **Supp. IV Part 1:** 149
"Bird Banding with the Biologists" (Ray), **Supp. XVIII:** 194
"Bird came down the Walk, A" (Dickinson), **Retro. Supp. I:** 37
"Bird Frau, The" (Dove), **Supp. IV Part 1:** 245
"Bird in Hand" (screen story) (West and Ingster), **Retro. Supp. II:** 330
Bird Kingdom of the Mayas (LaBastille), **Supp. X:** 96
Birds and Beasts (W. J. Smith), **Supp. XIII:** 346
Bird's Nest, The (Jackson), **Supp. IX: 124–125**
Birds of America (McCarthy), **II:** 579–583; **Supp. X:** 177
Birds of America (Moore), **Supp. X:** 163, 165, 167, 168, 171, **177–179**
Birds of America, The (Audubon), **Supp. XVI: 5–6,** 7, 9, 10, 12, 13
"Birds of Killingsworth, The" (Longfellow), **Retro. Supp. II:** 164
Birds of North America (Audubon Society), **Supp. X:** 177
"Birds of Vietnam, The" (Carruth), **Supp. XVI:** 55

"Bird-Witted" (Moore), **III:** 214
Birkerts, Sven, **Supp. IV Part 2:** 650; **Supp. V:** 212; **Supp. VIII:** 85; **Supp. X:** 311
Birkhead, L. M., **III:** 116
"Birmingham Sunday" (Hughes), **Supp. I Part 1:** 343
Birnbaum, Henry, **Supp. XII:** 128
Birnbaum, Robert, **Supp. X:** 13; **Supp. XVI:** 75
Birney, James G., **Supp. I Part 2:** 587, 588
Birstein, Ann, **Supp. VIII:** 100
"Birthday, A" (Untermeyer), **Supp. XV:** 296
Birthday Basket for Tía, A (Mora), **Supp. XIII:** 221
"Birthday Cake" (Carruth), **Supp. XVI:** 59
"Birthday Cake for Lionel, A" (Wylie), **Supp. I Part 2:** 721
"Birthday Girl: 1950" (McCarriston), **Supp. XIV:** 261
"Birthday of Mrs. Pineda, The" (Ríos), **Supp. IV Part 2:** 542, 546
"Birthday Poem, A" (Hecht), **Supp. X:** 64
"Birthday Present, A" (Plath), **Supp. I Part 2:** 531
"Birthmark, The" (Ellison), **Retro. Supp. II:** 116; **Supp. II Part 1:** 237–238
"Birth-mark, The" (Hawthorne), **Retro. Supp. I:** 152
Birth-mark, The: Unsettling the Wilderness in American Literary History (Howe), **Supp. IV Part 2:** 422, 431, 434
Birth of a Nation, The (film), **Supp. I Part 1:** 66
Birth of the Poet, The (Gordon), **Supp. XII:** 7
Birth of Tragedy, The (Nietzsche), **Supp. IV Part 1:** 105, 110; **Supp. IV Part 2:** 519; **Supp. VIII:** 182
"Birth of Venus, The" (Botticelli), **IV:** 410
"Birth of Venus, The" (Rukeyser), **Supp. VI:** 281
"Birthplace Revisited" (Corso), **Supp. XII:** 123
"Birthright" (McKay), **Supp. X:** 136
Bisch, Louis E., **Supp. I Part 2:** 608
Bisco, John, **Supp. XVIII:** 11
"B is for Bachelors" (M. F. K. Fisher), **Supp. XVII:** 86
Bishop, Elizabeth, **Retro. Supp. I:** 140, 296, 303; **Retro. Supp. II: 37–56,** 175, 178, 189, 233, 234, 235; **Supp. I Part 1: 72–97,** 239, 320, 326; **Supp. III Part 1:** 6, 7, 10, 18, 64, 239, 320, 326; **Supp. III Part 2:** 541, 561; **Supp. IV Part 1:** 249, 257; **Supp. IV Part 2:** 439, 626, 639, 641, 644, 647, 651, 653; **Supp. IX:** 40, 41, 45, 47, 48; **Supp. V:** 337; **Supp. X:** 58; **Supp. XI:** 123, 136; **Supp. XIII:** 115, 348; **Supp. XV:** 20–21, 100, 101, 112, 119, 249, 251; **Supp. XVII:** 36, 76
Bishop, James, Jr., **Supp. XIII:** 1, 5, 6, 7, 9, 11, 15
Bishop, John Peale, **I:** 432, 440; **II:** 81, 85, 86–87, 91, 209; **IV:** 35, 140, 427; **Retro. Supp. I:** 109; **Supp. I Part 2:** 709
Bishop, John W., **Supp. I Part 1:** 83
Bishop, Judith, **Supp. XVI:** 295
Bishop, Morris, **Supp. I Part 2:** 676
Bishop, William Thomas, **Supp. I Part 1:** 83
"Bishop Orders His Tomb at St. Praxed's Church, The" (R. Browning), **Supp. XV:** 127
"Bishop's Beggar, The" (Benét), **Supp. XI:** 56
"Bismarck" (Chapman), **Supp. XIV:** 52, 53
Bismark, Otto von, **Supp. I Part 2:** 643
"Bistro Styx, The" (Dove), **Supp. IV Part 1:** 250–251
Bitov, Andrei, **Retro. Supp. I:** 278
Bits of Gossip (Davis), **Supp. XVI:** 82–83, 84, 85, 89
"Bitter Drink, The" (Dos Passos), **Supp. I Part 2:** 647
"Bitter Farce, A" (Schwartz), **Supp. II Part 2:** 640, 657–658
"Bitter Pills for the Dark Ladies" (Jong), **Supp. V:** 118
Bitterroot (Burke), **Supp. XIV:** 34, 35
Bitter Victory (Hardy; Kinnell, trans.), **Supp. III Part 1:** 235
Bitzer, G. W. "Billy," **Supp. XVI:** 183
Bixby, Horace, **IV:** 194
Bjorkman, Frances Maule, **Supp. V:** 285
Bjorkman, Stig, **Supp. XV:** 6
Björnson, Björnstjerne, **II:** 275
Black 100, The (Salley), **Supp. XIV:** 195
Blackamerican Literature, 1760-Present (R. Miller), **Supp. X:** 324
Black American Literature Forum, **Supp. XI:** 86, 92, 93
Black and Blue (Quindlen), **Supp. XVII:** 166, **176–178**
"Black and Tan" (Bell), **Supp. X:** 9
Black Armour (Wylie), **Supp. I Part 2:** 708, 709, 712–714, 729
"Black Art" (Baraka), **Supp. II Part 1:** 49, 50–51, 59, 60
"Black Art, The" (Sexton), **Supp. II Part 2:** 682
"Black Ball, The" (Ellison), **Retro. Supp. II:** 124
Black Bart and the Sacred Hills (Wilson), **Supp. VIII:** 330, 331
Black Beetles in Amber (Bierce), **I:** 204, 209
"Blackberries" (Komunyakaa), **Supp. XIII:** 126
"Blackberry Eating" (Kinnell), **Supp. III Part 1:** 250
"Blackberrying" (D. West), **Supp. XVIII:** 283
Blackberry Winter (Warren), **IV:** 243, 251, 252
Black Betty (Mosley), **Supp. XIII:** 237, **Supp. XIII:** 240, 243
"Black Birch in Winter, A" (Wilbur), **Supp. III Part 2:** 561
Black Boy (Wright), **IV:** 477, 478, 479, 480–482, 488, 489, 494; **Retro. Supp. II:** 117; **Supp. II Part 1:** 235–236; **Supp. IV Part 1:** 11; **Supp. XVIII:** 286
"Black Boys and Native Sons" (Howe), **Retro. Supp. II:** 112
Blackburn, Alex, **Supp. XIII:** 112
Blackburn, William, **IV:** 100
"Black Buttercups" (Clampitt), **Supp. IX:** 42
Black Cargo, The (Marquand), **III:** 55, 60
Black Cargoes: A History of the Atlantic Slave Trade (Cowley), **Supp. II Part 1:** 140
"Black Cat, The" (Poe), **III:** 413, 414, 415; **Retro. Supp. II:** 264, 267, 269, 270
Black Cherry Blues (Burke), **Supp. XIV:** 30
"Black Christ, The" (Cullen), **Supp. IV Part 1:** 170, 171–172
Black Christ and Other Poems, The (Cullen), **Supp. IV Part 1:** 166, 170
"Black Cottage, The" (Frost), **Retro. Supp. I:** 128
"BLACK DADA NIHILISMUS" (Baraka), **Supp. II Part 1:** 39, 41
"Black Death" (Hurston), **Supp. VI:** 153
"Black Dog, Red Dog" (Dobyns), **Supp. XIII:** 89
Black Dog, Red Dog (Dobyns), **Supp. XIII:** 87, **88–89**
"Black Earth" (Moore), **III:** 197, 212
Blacker the Berry, The: A Novel of Negro Life (Thurman), **Supp. XVIII:** 281
Black Fire (Jones and Neal, eds.), **Supp. X:** 324, 328
Black Fire: An Anthology of Afro American Writing (Baraka, ed.), **Supp. II Part 1:** 53
Black Flame, The (Du Bois), **Supp. II Part 1:** 159, 185–186
Black Folk, Then and Now: An Essay in the History and Sociology of the Negro Race (Du Bois), **Supp. II Part 1:** 159, 178, 183, 185
"Black Fox, The" (Whittier), **Supp. I Part 2:** 692
Black Freckles (Levis), **Supp. XI:** 257, 271
"Black Gang," **IV:** 406, 407
Black Genius (Mosley, ed.), **Supp. XIII:** 246
"Black Hood, The" (Francis), **Supp. IX:** 83, 91
Black House, The (Theroux), **Supp. VIII:** 319
Black Humor (Johnson), **Supp. VI:** 187, 199
Black Image in the White Mind, The (Fredrickson), **Supp. I Part 2:** 589
"Black Is My Favorite Color" (Malamud), **Supp. I Part 2:** 437
"Black Jewel, The" (Merwin), **Supp. III Part 1:** 355
Black Lamb and Grey Falcon (R. West), **Supp. XVI:** 152
"Blacklegs" (B. Kelly), **Supp. XVII:** 131

Black Light (Kinnell), **Supp. III Part 1:** 235, 243
"Blacklist and the Cold War, The" (Kramer), **Supp. I Part 1:** 295
Black Literature in America (Baker), **Supp. X:** 324
Black Magic, A Pictorial History of the Negro in American Entertainment (Hughes), **Supp. I Part 1:** 345
Black Magic: Collected Poetry 1961–1967 (Baraka), **Supp. II Part 1:** 45, 49–50
"Blackmailers Don't Shoot" (Chandler), **Supp. IV Part 1:** 121–122
Black Manhattan (Johnson), **Supp. IV Part 1:** 169
Black Mass, A (Baraka), **Supp. II Part 1:** 46, 48–49, 56, 57
"Black Mesa, The" (Merrill), **Supp. III Part 1:** 328
Black Metropolis (Cayton and Drake), **IV:** 475, 486, 488
Black Misery (Hughes), **Supp. I Part 1:** 336
Blackmur, Helen Dickson (Mrs. R. P. Blackmur), **Supp. II Part 1:** 90
Blackmur, Richard P., **I:** 50, 63, 67, 280, 282, 386, 455, 472; **II:** 320, 537; **III:** 194, 208, 462, 478, 497; **Supp. II Part 1: 87–112,** 136; **Supp. II Part 2:** 543, 643; **Supp. XII:** 45
Black Music (Baraka), **Supp. II Part 1:** 47, 51
Black Nativity (Hughes), **Retro. Supp. I:** 196
Black No More (Schuyler), **Supp. XVI:** 142
Black on Black: "Baby Sister" and Selected Writings (C. Himes), **Supp. XVI:** 145
"Blackout" (Hay), **Supp. XIV:** 121
"Black Panther" (Hughes), **Retro. Supp. I:** 211
"Black Petal" (L.-Y. Lee), **Supp. XV:** 224–225
Black Power (Wright), **IV:** 478, 488, 494
"Black Rainbow, A: Modern Afro-American Poetry" (Dove and Waniek), **Supp. IV Part 1:** 244
Black Reconstruction (Du Bois), **Supp. II Part 1:** 159, 162, 171, 182
Black Riders and Other Lines, The (Crane), **I:** 406, 419
Black Riviera, The (Jarman), **Supp. XVII:** 109, 110, **115–116**
"Black Rook in Rainy Weather" (Plath), **Supp. I Part 2:** 543, 544
Blacks (Brooks), **Supp. III Part 1:** 69, 72, 86, 87
Blacks, The (Genet), **Supp. IV Part 1:** 8
Black Skin, White Masks (Fanon), **Retro. Supp. II:** 118
Black Sleuth, The (J. Bruce), **Supp. XVI:** 143
Black Spear, The (Hayden), **Supp. II Part 1:** 375
Black Spring (H. Miller), **III:** 170, 175, 178, 180–182, 183, 184; **Supp. X:** 187
"Black Stone Lying on a White Stone" (Vallejo), **Supp. XIII:** 324
Black Sun (Abbey), **Supp. XIII:** 4, **8–9,** 17
"Black Swan" (B. Kelly), **Supp. XVII:** 130–131
"Black Swan, The" (Jarrell), **II:** 382
Black Swan, The (Merrill), **Supp. III Part 1:** 319, 320
"Black Tambourine" (Crane), **I:** 387–388; **II:** 371
"Black Tuesday" (Swenson), **Supp. IV Part 2:** 646
Black Voices (Chapman), **IV:** 485
"Blackwater Mountain" (Wright), **Supp. V:** 335, 340
"Black Wedding, The" (Singer), **IV:** 12–13
Blackwell, Alice Stone, **Supp. XI:** 195, 197
Blackwell, Elizabeth, **Retro. Supp. II:** 146
Black Woman, The (Bambara, ed.), **Supp. XI:** 1
"Black Workers" (Hughes), **Retro. Supp. I:** 202
"Black Writer and the Southern Experience, The" (Walker), **Supp. III Part 2:** 521
Black Zodiac (Wright), **Supp. V:** 333, 344, 345
Blade Runner (film), **Supp. XI:** 84
Blaine, Anita McCormick, **Supp. I Part 1:** 5
Blaine, Nell, **Supp. XV:** 179
Blair, Hugh, **II:** 8, 17; **Supp. I Part 2:** 422
Blair, Robert, **Supp. I Part 1:** 150
Blair, Walter, **II:** 20; **Retro. Supp. II:** 286
Blaisdell, Gus, **Supp. XIV:** 87
Blake, William, **I:** 381, 383, 389, 390, 398, 447, 476, 525, 526, 533; **II:** 321; **III:** 5, 19, 22, 195, 196, 197, 205, 485, 528, 540, 544–545, 567, 572; **IV:** 129; **Retro. Supp. II:** 76, 300; **Supp. I Part 1:** 80; **Supp. I Part 2:** 385, 514, 517, 539, 552, 708; **Supp. V:** 208, 257, 258; **Supp. VIII:** 26, 99, 103; **Supp. X:** 120; **Supp. XII:** 45; **Supp. XIV:** 344; **Supp. XVI:** 282; **Supp. XVII:** 119
Blakely, Barbara, **Supp. XIII:** 32
Blanc, Marie Thérèse, **Retro. Supp. II:** 135
Blanc-Bentzon, Mme. Thérèse, **II:** 405
Blanchard, Paula, **Retro. Supp. II:** 131, 133–134, 135
Blanchot, Maurice, **Supp. XVI:** 288
Blancs, Les (Hansberry), **Supp. IV Part 1:** 359, 364, 365, 369, 372–374
Blancs, Les: The Collected Last Plays of Lorraine Hansberry (Nemiroff, ed.), **Supp. IV Part 1:** 365, 368, 374
"'Blandula, Tenulla, Vagula'" (Pound), **III:** 463; **Supp. V:** 336, 337, 345
Blankenship, Tom, **IV:** 193
Blanshard, Rufus A., **I:** 67
Blauvelt, William Satake, **Supp. V:** 171, 173
Blavatsky, Elena Petrovna, **III:** 176
"Blazing in Gold and Quenching in Purple" (Dickinson), **Retro. Supp. I:** 30
Bleak House (Dickens), **II:** 291; **Supp. IV Part 1:** 293
Blechman, Burt, **Supp. I Part 1:** 290
"Bleeder" (Dobyns), **Supp. XIII:** 88
"Bleeding" (Swenson), **Supp. IV Part 2:** 646–647
"Blessed Is the Man" (Moore), **III:** 215
"Blessed Man of Boston, My Grandmother's Thimble, and Fanning Island, The" (Updike), **IV:** 219
"Blessing, A" (Wright), **Supp. III Part 2:** 600, 606
Blessing on the Moon, A (Skibell), **Supp. XVII:** 48
Blessings (Quindlen), **Supp. XVII:** 167, **178–179**
"Blessing the Animals" (Komunyakaa), **Supp. XIII:** 129–130
"Blessing the Children" (Hogan), **Supp. IV Part 1:** 401
Bless Me, Ultima (Anya), **Supp. XIII:** 220
Blew, Mary Clearman, **Supp. XIV:** 227
Bligh, S. M., **I:** 226
Blind Assassin, The (Atwood), **Supp. XIII:** 20, **32**
Blind Bow-Boy, The (Van Vechten), **Supp. II Part 2:** 737, 740–742
Blind Date (Kosinski), **Supp. VII:** 215, 224–225
Blind Lion, The (Gunn Allen), **Supp. IV Part 1:** 324
"Blind Man's Holiday" (O. Henry), **Supp. II Part 1:** 401
Blind Man with a Pistol (C. Himes), **Supp. XVI:** 143, 144
Blindness and Insight (de Man), **Retro. Supp. I:** 67
"Blind Poet, The: Sidney Lanier" (Warren), **Supp. I Part 1:** 371, 373
"Blind Tom" (Davis), **Supp. XVI:** 89, 90
Blithedale Romance, The (Hawthorne), **II:** 225, 231, 239, 241–242, 271, 282, 290; **IV:** 194; **Retro. Supp. I:** 63, 149, 152, 156–157, **162–163; Supp. I Part 2:** 579; **Supp. II Part 1:** 280; **Supp. VIII:** 153, 201
Blitzstein, Marc, **Supp. I Part 1:** 277
Blix (Norris), **III:** 314, 322, 327, 328, 333
Blixen, Karen Denisen Baroness. *See* Dinesen, Isak
"Blizzard in Cambridge" (Lowell), **II:** 554
Blok, Aleksandr Aleksandrovich, **IV:** 443
Blonde Bait (Lacy), **Supp. XV:** 204
Blonde on Blonde (album, Dylan), **Supp. XVIII:** 20, 27, 30
Blondin, Antoine, **Supp. XVI:** 230
"Blood" (Hoffman), **Supp. XVIII:** 86
"Blood" (Singer), **IV:** 15, 19
Blood, Tin, Straw (Olds), **Supp. X: 212–215**
Blood and Guile (Hoffman), **Supp. XVIII: 83–84**
Blood and Guts in High School (Acker), **Supp. XII:** 5, 6, **11–12**

"Blood Bay, The" (Proulx), **Supp. VII:** 262–263
"Blood-Burning Moon" (Toomer), **Supp. III Part 2:** 483; **Supp. IX:** 314–315
"Bloodchild" (O. Butler), **Supp. XIII:** 61, **69–70**
Bloodchild and Other Stories (O. Butler), **Supp. XIII:** 69
"Blood Donor" (Hay), **Supp. XIV:** 121
Blood for a Stranger (Jarrell), **II:** 367, 368–369, 370–371, 375, 377
Blood Issue (Crews), **Supp. XI:** 103
Bloodlines (Wright), **Supp. V:** 332, 335, 340
Blood Meridian; or, The Evening Redness in the West (McCarthy), **Supp. VIII:** 175, 177, **180–182,** 188, 190
"Blood of the Conquistadores, The" (Alvarez), **Supp. VII:** 7
"Blood of the Lamb, The" (hymn), **Supp. I Part 2:** 385
Blood of the Martyr (Crane), **I:** 422
"Blood of the Martyrs, The" (Benét), **Supp. XI:** 56, 58
Blood of the Prophets, The (Masters), **Supp. I Part 2:** 458, 459, 461
Blood on the Forge (Attaway), **Supp. II Part 1:** 234–235
Blood on the Tracks (album, Dylan), **Supp. XVIII:** 20, 27, 30
"Blood Relatives" (Apple), **Supp. XVII:** 6
"Blood Returns, The" (Kingsolver), **Supp. VII:** 209
"Bloodshed" (C. Ozick), **Supp. XVII:** 43
Bloodshed and Three Novellas (Ozick), **Supp. V:** 259–260, 261, 266–268
"Blood Stains" (Francis), **Supp. IX:** 86
Bloody Crossroads, The: Where Literature and Politics Meet (Podhoretz), **Supp. VIII: 241–242**
Bloom, Alice, **Supp. IV Part 1:** 308
Bloom, Allan, **Retro. Supp. II:** 19, 30, 31, 33–34
Bloom, Claire, **Retro. Supp. II:** 281; **Supp. IX:** 125
Bloom, Harold, **Retro. Supp. I:** 67, 193, 299; **Retro. Supp. II:** 81, 210, 262; **Supp. IV Part 2:** 620, 689; **Supp. IX:** 146, 259; **Supp. V:** 178, 272; **Supp. VIII:** 180; **Supp. XII:** 261; **Supp. XIII:** 46, 47; **Supp. XIV:** 14; **Supp. XV:** 134; **Supp. XVII:** 70, 141
Bloom, Larry, **Supp. XIII:** 133
Bloom, Leopold, **I:** 27, 150; **III:** 10
Bloom, Lynn Z., **Supp. IV Part 1:** 6
Bloomfield, Leonard, **I:** 64
Bloomingdale Papers, The (Carruth), **Supp. XVI:** 48–50
"Blossom and Fruit" (Benét), **Supp. XI:** 52–53
Blotner, Joseph, **Retro. Supp. I:** 88
Blouin, Lenora, **Supp. VIII:** 266
"Blowin' in the Wind" (song, Dylan), **Supp. XVIII:** 24, 25, 26, 29
Blue Angel (Prose), **Supp. XVI:** 249, 259–260
Blue Angel, The (film), **Supp. XVIII:** 243
"Blue Battalions, The" (Crane), **I:** 419–420
"Bluebeard" (Barthelme), **Supp. IV Part 1:** 47
"Bluebeard" (Millay), **III:** 130
"Blueberries" (Frost), **Retro. Supp. I:** 121, 128
Blue Calhoun (Price), **Supp. VI:** 265–266
Blue City (Macdonald, under Millar), **Supp. IV Part 2:** 466–467
Blue Dahlia, The (Chandler), **Supp. IV Part 1:** 130
Blue Estuaries, The: Poems, 1923–1968 (Bogan), **Supp. III Part 1:** 48, 57, 66
Blue Hammer, The (Macdonald), **Supp. IV Part 2:** 462
"Blue Hotel, The" (Crane), **I:** 34, 415–416, 423
"Blue Hour, The" (Komunyakaa), **Supp. XIII:** 130
Blue in the Face (Auster), **Supp. XII:** 21
Blue Jay's Dance, The: A Birth Year (Erdrich), **Supp. IV Part 1:** 259–260, 265, 270, 272
"Blue Juniata" (Cowley), **Supp. II Part 1:** 144
Blue Juniata: Collected Poems (Cowley), **Supp. II Part 1:** 140
Blue Light (Mosley), **Supp. XIII: 245–247,** 248, 249
"Blue Light Lounge Sutra for the Performance Poets at Harold Park Hotel" (Komunyakaa), **Supp. XIII:** 125
"Blue Meridian" (Toomer), **Supp. III Part 2:** 476, 487; **Supp. IX:** 320
"Blue Moles" (Plath), **Supp. I Part 2:** 539
Blue Mountain Ballads (music) (Bowles), **Supp. IV Part 1:** 84
Blue Movie (Southern), **Supp. XI:** 309
"Blue Notes" (Matthews), **Supp. IX:** 169
Blue Pastures (Oliver), **Supp. VII:** 229–230, 245
"Blueprint for Negro Writing" (Wright), **Supp. XVIII:** 282–283
"Blueprints" (Kingsolver), **Supp. VII:** 203
Blue Rhine, Black Forest (Untermeyer), **Supp. XV:** 310
"Blue Ribbon at Amesbury, A" (Frost), **Retro. Supp. I:** 138
"Blues Ain't No Mockin Bird" (Bambara), **Supp. XI:** 3
"Blues Chant Hoodoo Rival" (Komunyakaa), **Supp. XIII:** 117, 118
"Blues for Another Time" (Dunn), **Supp. XI:** 148
"Blues for Jimmy" (McGrath), **Supp. X:** 116
"Blues for John Coltraine, Dead at 41" (Matthews), **Supp. IX:** 157
Blues for Mister Charlie (Baldwin), **Retro. Supp. II:** 8; **Supp. I Part 1:** 48, 61–62, 63
"Blues for Warren" (McGrath), **Supp. X:** 116
Blues If You Want (Matthews), **Supp. IX:** 155, **163–165**
"Blues I'm Playing, The" (Hughes), **Retro. Supp. I:** 204
"Blue Sky, The" (Snyder), **Supp. VIII:** 306
"Blues on a Box" (Hughes), **Retro. Supp. I:** 208
"Blues People" (Ellison), **Retro. Supp. II:** 124
Blues People: Negro Music in White America (Baraka), **Retro. Supp. II:** 124; **Supp. II Part 1:** 30, 31, 33–35, 37, 41, 42, 53
Bluest Eye, The (Morrison), **Supp. III Part 1:** 362, 363–367, 379; **Supp. IV Part 1:** 2, 253; **Supp. VIII:** 213, 214, 227; **Supp. XI:** 4, 91
Bluestone, George, **Supp. IX:** 7, 15
Blue Swallows, The (Nemerov), **III:** 269, 270, 271, 274–275, 278, 284, 286–288
"Blue Tattoo" (Nelson and Espeland), **Supp. XVIII:** 181
Blue Voyage (Aiken), **I:** 53, 56
Blum, Gustav, **Supp. XV:** 194
Blum, Morgan, **I:** 169
Blum, W. C (pseudonym). *See* Watson, James Sibley, Jr.
Blumenthal, Nathaniel. *See* Branden, Nathaniel
Blumenthal, Sidney, **Supp. VIII:** 241
Blunt, Wilfrid Scawen, **III:** 459
Bly, Carol, **Supp. XVI: 31–43**
Bly, Robert, **I:** 291; **Supp. III Part 2:** 599; **Supp. IV Part 1: 59–77,** 177; **Supp. IV Part 2:** 623; **Supp. IX:** 152, 155, 265, 271, 290; **Supp. V:** 332; **Supp. VIII:** 279; **Supp. X:** 127; **Supp. XI:** 142; **Supp. XIII:** 284; **Supp. XV:** 74, 176; **Supp. XVI:** 32, 36, 39, 177, 212, 230; **Supp. XVII:** 243, 244
"B Negative" (X. J. Kennedy), **Supp. XV: 156–157**
"Boarder, The" (Simpson), **Supp. IX:** 269
Boarding House Blues (Farrell), **II:** 30, 43, 45
Boas, Franz, **I:** 214; **Supp. I Part 2:** 641; **Supp. IX:** 329; **Supp. VIII:** 295; **Supp. XIV:** 199, 209, 210
"Boat, The" (Oliver), **Supp. VII:** 247
"Boat, The" (Sexton), **Supp. II Part 2:** 692
Boating Party, The (Renoir), **Supp. XII:** 188
"Boat of Quiet Hours, The" (Kenyon), **Supp. VII:** 168
Boat of Quiet Hours, The (Kenyon), **Supp. VII:** 167–169, 171
"Bob and Spike" (Wolfe), **Supp. III Part 2:** 580
"Bob Dylan's 115th Dream" (song, Dylan), **Supp. XVIII:** 25
Bobrowski, Johannes, **Supp. XV:** 78
Bob the Gambler (F. Barthelme), **Supp. XI:** 30, 31, 32, 34–35, 36–37
Boccaccio, Giovanni, **III:** 283, 411; **IV:** 230
Bocock, Maclin, **Supp. X:** 79
Bodelson, Anders, **Supp. XVI:** 33
Bodenheim, Maxwell, **II:** 42, 530; **Retro. Supp. I:** 417; **Supp. I Part 1:** 257
"Bodies" (Oates), **Supp. II Part 2:** 520

"Bodies and Souls: The Haitian Revolution and Madison Smartt Bell's *All Souls' Rising*" (Trouillot), **Supp. X:** 14
Bodies of Work: Essays (Acker), **Supp. XII:** 7
Bodily Harm (Atwood), **Supp. XIII: 25–27**
Bodley Head Jack London (London), **II:** 483
Body (Crews), **Supp. XI: 108–109**
"Body, The" (Heldreth), **Supp. V:** 151
Body and Soul (Conroy), **Supp. XVI:** 63, **72–74,** 77
"Body and Soul: A Meditation" (Kumin), **Supp. IV Part 2:** 442, 452
Body and Soul: Essays on Poetry (Jarman), **Supp. XVII:** 110, **111–112**
"Body and Soul: Parts of a Life" (Jarman), **Supp. XVII:** 112, 113
Body and the Song, The (Bishop), **Retro. Supp. II:** 40
"Body Bright" (Sanders), **Supp. XVI:** 276
Body of Martin Aquilera, The (Everett), **Supp. XVIII:** 57
Body of Poetry, The: Essays on Women, Form, and the Poetic Self (A. Finch), **Supp. XVII:** 69–70, **77–78**
Body of This Death: Poems (Bogan), **Supp. III Part 1:** 47, 49–52, 58
"Body of Waking" (Rukeyser), **Supp. VI:** 279
Body of Waking (Rukeyser), **Supp. VI:** 274, 281
"Body on Fire, the Soul in Flight, The" (Jarman), **Supp. XVII:** 111, 112
Body Rags (Kinnell), **Supp. III Part 1:** 235, 236, 243–245, 250, 253, 254
"Body's Curse, The" (Dobyns), **Supp. XIII:** 87
"Body's Weight, The" (Dobyns), **Supp. XIII:** 89
Body Traffic (Dobyns), **Supp. XIII:** 87, 89
"'Body with the Lamp Lit Inside, The'" (Mills), **Supp. IV Part 1:** 64
Boehm, David, **Supp. XVII:** 58
Boehme, Jakob, **I:** 10
Bogan, Louise, **I:** 169, 185; **Retro. Supp. I:** 36; **Supp. I Part 2:** 707, 726; **Supp. III Part 1: 47–68; Supp. IX:** 229; **Supp. VIII:** 171, 265; **Supp. X:** 58, 102; **Supp. XIII:** 347; **Supp. XIV:** 129; **Supp. XVII:** 75
Bogan, Major Benjamin Lewis, **IV:** 120
Bogart, Humphrey, **Supp. I Part 2:** 623; **Supp. IV Part 1:** 130, 356
Bogdanovich, Peter, **Supp. V:** 226
Bogey Man, The (Plimpton), **Supp. XVI:** 241
Boggs, Francis W., **Supp. XVI:** 182
"Bohemian, The" (Hapgood), **Supp. XVII:** 103
"Bohemian, The" (Harte), **Supp. II Part 1:** 339
"Bohemian Girl, The" (Cather), **Retro. Supp. I:** 7
"Bohemian Hymn, The" (Emerson), **II:** 19
"Boids and Beasties" (Geisel), **Supp. XVI:** 100
Boissevain, Eugen, **III:** 124
Boit, Edward, **Retro. Supp. I:** 366
Bojorquez, Jennifer, **Supp. XII:** 318
Boker, George, **Supp. XV:** 269
"Bold Words at the Bridge" (Jewett), **II:** 394
Boleslavsky, Richard, **Supp. XIV:** 240, 243
Boleyn, Anne, **Supp. I Part 2:** 461
Bolick, Katie, **Supp. XVI:** 167
Bolivar, Simon, **Supp. I Part 1:** 283, 284, 285
Bolonik, Kera, **Supp. XVIII:** 60
Bolton, Guy, **Supp. I Part 1:** 281
Bolts of Melody: New Poems of Emily Dickinson (Todd and Bingham, eds.), **I:** 470; **Retro. Supp. I:** 36
"Bomb" (Corso), **Supp. XII:** 117, 124, 125–126, 127
Bombeck, Erma, **Supp. XVII:** 168
Bombs Away (Steinbeck), **IV:** 51–52
"Bona and Paul" (Toomer), **Supp. IX:** 307, 318–319
Bonaparte, Marie, **III:** 418; **Retro. Supp. II:** 264, 266
"Bon-Bon" (Poe), **III:** 425
Bond, The (N. Boyce), **Supp. XVII:** 99, 100
Bondsman, The (Massinger), **Supp. XV:** 238
Bone, Robert, **Supp. IX:** 318–319; **Supp. XI:** 283; **Supp. XVIII:** 285
Bone by Bone (Matthiessen), **Supp. V:** 199, 212, 213, 214
"Bone Deposit" (Ray), **Supp. XVIII:** 194
Boners (Abingdon). *See Schoolboy Howlers* (Abingdon)
"Bones" (Goldbarth), **Supp. XII: 173–174**
"Bones and Jewels" (Monette), **Supp. X:** 159
"Bones and Shells" (Sanders), **Supp. XVI:** 271–272
"Bones of a House" (Cowley). *See* "Blue Juniata"
Bonetti, Kay, **Supp. VIII:** 47, 152, 159, 160, 165, 168, 170, 223; **Supp. XII:** 61; **Supp. XIV:** 232, 234
Bonfire of the Vanities, The (Wolfe), **Supp. III Part 2:** 584–586
Bonheur, Rosa, **Supp. XV:** 276
Bonhoeffer, Dietrich, **Supp. VIII:** 198
Boni, Charles, **Supp. XIV:** 288
Boni and Liveright, **Retro. Supp. I:** 59, 80, 178
Bonicelli, Vittorio, **Supp. XI:** 307
Bonifacius (Mather), **Supp. II Part 2:** 461, 464
Bonnefoy, Yves, **Supp. III Part 1:** 235, 243
Bonner, Robert, **Retro. Supp. I:** 246
Bonneville, Mme. Marguerite, **Supp. I Part 2:** 520, 521
Bonneville, Nicolas de, **Supp. I Part 2:** 511, 518, 519
Bonney, William. *See* Billy the Kid
Bontemps, Arna, **Retro. Supp. I:** 194, 196, 203; **Supp. I Part 1:** 325; **Supp. IV Part 1:** 170; **Supp. IX:** 306, 309; **Supp. XVIII:** 282
Book, A (Barnes), **Supp. III Part 1:** 36, 39, 44
Book about Myself, A (Dreiser), **I:** 515; **Retro. Supp. II:** 104
"Book as a Container of Consciousness, The" (Gass), **Supp. VI:** 92
Booker, Keith, **Supp. XV:** 197
"Bookies, Beware!" (Heller), **Supp. IV Part 1:** 383
Book of American Negro Poetry, The (Johnson), **Supp. IV Part 1:** 165, 166
Book of Americans, A (Benét), **Supp. XI:** 46, 47, 51
Book of Beb, The (Buechner), **Supp. XII:** 53
Book of Breeething, The (Burroughs), **Supp. III Part 1:** 97, 103
Book of Burlesques, A (Mencken), **III:** 104
Book of Common Prayer, A (Didion), **Supp. IV Part 1:** 196, 198, 203–205, 207, 208
Book of Daniel, The (Doctorow), **Supp. IV Part 1:** 218, 219, 220–222, 227, 231, 237–238, 238; **Supp. V:** 45
Book of Dreams (Kerouac), **Supp. III Part 1:** 225
"Book of Ephraim, The" (Merrill), **Supp. III Part 1:** 330–334
Book of Folly, The (Sexton), **Supp. II Part 2:** 691, 692–694
Book of Gods and Devils, The (Simic), **Supp. VIII: 281**
Book of Guys, The (Keillor), **Supp. XVI:** 177
"Book of Hours of Sister Clotilde, The" (Lowell), **II:** 522
Book of Jamaica, The (Banks), **Supp. V:** 11, 12, 16
"Book of Life" (Bidart), **Supp. XV:** 23
Book of Living Verse, The; English and American Poetry from the Thirteenth Century to the Present Day (Untermeyer, ed.), **Supp. XV:** 310
Book of Love, A (Vildrac; Bynner, trans.), **Supp. XV:** 50
Book of Lyrics (Bynner), **Supp. XV:** 51
"Book of Medicines, The" (Hogan), **Supp. IV Part 1:** 412, 413
Book of Medicines, The (Hogan), **Supp. IV Part 1:** 397, 410, 411–414
"Book of Memory, The" (Auster), **Supp. XII:** 21–22
Book of My Nights (L.-Y. Lee), **Supp. XV:** 215, **223–226**
Book of Negro Folklore, The (Hughes, ed.), **Supp. I Part 1:** 345
Book of Nightmares, The (Kinnell), **Supp. III Part 1:** 235, 236, 243, 244, 246–254
Book of Prefaces, A (Mencken), **III:** 99–100, 105
Book of Repulsive Women, The (Barnes), **Supp. III Part 1:** 33
Book of Roses, The (Parkman), **Supp. II Part 2:** 597, 598

Book of the Body, The (Bidart), **Supp. XV:** 21, **25–27**
"Book of the Dead, The" (Rukeyser), **Supp. VI:** 272, 278, 279; **Supp. XV:** 349
"Book of the Grotesque, The" (Anderson), **I:** 106
Book of the Homeless, The (Wharton), **Retro. Supp. I:** 377
Book of the Hopi (Waters), **Supp. X:** 124
Book of Tobit (Bible), **Supp. XII:** 54
Book of Verses, A (Masters), **Supp. I Part 2:** 458
Book of Yaak, The (Bass), **Supp. XVI: 18–19**
"Book of Yolek, The" (Hecht), **Supp. X:** 69, **70–71**
"Books Considered" (Bloom), **Supp. I Part 1:** 96
Books in My Life, The (H. Miller), **II:** 176, 189
"Books/P,L,E, The" (Goldbarth), **Supp. XII:** 190
Bookviews, **Supp. XI:** 216
"Book World Live," **Supp. XVIII:** 143–144
"Boom" (Nemerov), **III:** 278
Boom! (T. Williams), **IV:** 383
"Boom Town" (Wolfe), **IV:** 469
Boom Town (Wolfe), **IV:** 456
Boone, Daniel, **II:** 207; **III:** 444; **IV:** 192, 193
Boorstin, Daniel, **I:** 253
Booth, Charles, **Supp. I Part 1:** 13
Booth, General William, **Supp. I Part 2:** 384, 386
Booth, John Wilkes, **III:** 588
Booth, Philip, **I:** 522; **Supp. IX:** 269; **Supp. XI:** 141; **Supp. XIII:** 277; **Supp. XV:** 92
Borah, William, **III:** 475
Borden, Lizzie, **II:** 5
Borderlands/La Frontera: The New Mestiza (Anzaldúa), **Supp. XIII:** 223
Borders (Mora), **Supp. XIII:** 213, **215–217**
Border Trilogy (McCarthy), **Supp. VIII:** 175, 182
Borel, Pétrus, **III:** 320
Borges, Jorge Luis, **I:** 123, 135, 138, 140, 142; **Supp. III Part 2:** 560; **Supp. IV Part 2:** 623, 626, 630; **Supp. V:** 238; **Supp. VIII:** 15, 348, 349; **Supp. XII:** 21, 147; **Supp. XV:** 34; **Supp. XVI:** 201, 206; **Supp. XVII:** 47
"Borges and I" (Bidart), **Supp. XV:** 34, 35
"Borinken Blues" (Komunyakaa), **Supp. XIII:** 117
"Born a Square: The Westerner's Dilemma" (Stegner), **Supp. IV Part 2:** 595; **Supp. V:** 224
"Born Bad" (Cisneros), **Supp. VII:** 62
Borrowed Time: An AIDS Memoir (Monette), **Supp. X:** 145, 146, 147, 152, 154, 155
"Bosque del Apache Wildlife Refuge" (Mora), **Supp. XIII:** 218
Boss Dog, The: A Story of Provence (M. F. K. Fisher), **Supp. XVII:** 91
"Boston" (Hardwick), **Supp. III Part 1:** 201
Boston (Sinclair), **Supp. V:** 282, 288–289
Boston, B. H., **Supp. XIII:** 312
Boston Adventure (Stafford), **Retro. Supp. II:** 177, 178
"Boston Common" (Berryman), **I:** 172
"Boston Hymn" (Emerson), **II:** 13, 19
Bostonians, The (H. James), **I:** 9; **II:** 282; **IV:** 202; **Retro. Supp. I:** 216, 225
Boston Marriage (Mamet), **Supp. XIV:** 247
"Boston Nativity, The" (Lowell), **II:** 538
Boswell, James, **IV:** 431; **Supp. I Part 2:** 656
Boswell: A Modern Comedy (Elkin), **Supp. VI:** 42, **44–45**, 57
Bosworth, Patricia, **Supp. IV Part 2:** 573, 591
"Bothersome Sex and O'Brien, The" (Ryan as Quin), **Supp. XVIII:** 238
Botticelli (McNally), **Supp. XIII:** 197
Botticelli, Sandro, **IV:** 410; **Retro. Supp. I:** 422
"Botticellian Trees, The" (W. C. Williams), **Retro. Supp. I:** 422
"Bottle of Milk for Mother, A" (Algren), **Supp. IX:** 3
"Bottle of Perrier, A" (Wharton), **IV:** 316
"Bottles" (Kenyon), **Supp. VII:** 171
"Bottom Line, The" (Elkin), **Supp. VI:** 52, **53**
Bottom: On Shakespeare (Zukofsky), **Supp. III Part 2:** 622, 624, 625, 626, 627, 629
Boucher, Anthony, **Supp. IV Part 2:** 473; **Supp. XV:** 203, 205
Boukreev, Anatoli, **Supp. XVIII:** 112
Boulanger, Nadia, **Supp. IV Part 1:** 81
"Boulot and Boulette" (Chopin), **Supp. I Part 1:** 211
Boulton, Agnes, **III:** 403
Bound East for Cardiff (O'Neill), **III:** 388
Bound for Glory (Guthrie), **Supp. XVIII:** 23
"Bouquet, The" (Stevens), **IV:** 90
"Bouquet of Roses in Sunlight" (Stevens), **IV:** 93
Bourdin, Henri L., **Supp. I Part 1:** 251
Bourgeois Poet, The (Shapiro), **Supp. II Part 2:** 701, 703, 704, 713, 714–716
Bourget, James, **IV:** 319
Bourget, Paul, **II:** 325, 338; **IV:** 311, 315; **Retro. Supp. I:** 224, 359, 373
Bourjaily, Vance, **III:** 43; **Supp. IX:** 260
Bourke-White, Margaret, **I:** 290, 293, 295, 297
Bourne, Charles Rogers, **I:** 215
Bourne, Mrs. Charles Rogers, **I:** 215
Bourne, Randolph, **I: 214–238**, 243, 245, 246–247, 251, 259; **Supp. I Part 2:** 524; **Supp. XV:** 141, 298, 301
Bowden, Charles, **Supp. XIII:** 17
Bowditch, Nathaniel, **Supp. I Part 2:** 482
Bowen, Barbara, **Supp. IX:** 311
Bowen, Elizabeth, **Retro. Supp. I:** 351; **Supp. IV Part 1:** 299; **Supp. IX:** 128; **Supp. VIII:** 65, 165, 251, 265
Bowen, Francis, **Supp. I Part 2:** 413
Bowen, Henry, **Supp. XVIII:** 4
Bowen, Louise de Koven, **Supp. I Part 1:** 5
Bowen, Michael, **Supp. VIII:** 73
Bowers, John, **Supp. XI:** 217–218
"Bowlers Anonymous" (Dobyns), **Supp. XIII:** 86
Bowles, Emily, **Supp. XVIII:** 200, 202
Bowles, Jane (Jane Auer), **II:** 586; **Supp. IV Part 1:** 89, 92
Bowles, Paul, **I:** 211; **II:** 586; **Supp. II Part 1:** 17; **Supp. IV Part 1: 79–99**
Bowles, Samuel, **I:** 454, 457; **Retro. Supp. I:** 30, 32, 33
"Bowl of Blood, The" (Jeffers), **Supp. II Part 2:** 434
"Bowls" (Moore), **III:** 196
Bowman, James, **I:** 193
"Bows to Drouth" (Snyder), **Supp. VIII:** 303
Box, Edgar (pseudonym). *See* Vidal, Gore
Box and Quotations from Chairman Mao Tse-tung (Albee), **I:** 89–91, 94
Box Garden, The (Shields), **Supp. VII:** 314–315, 320
"Box Seat" (Toomer), **Supp. III Part 2:** 484; **Supp. IX:** 316, 318
Boy, A (Ashbery), **Supp. III Part 1:** 5
Boyce, Horace, **II:** 136
Boyce, Neith, **Supp. XVII:** 96, 97, 98–99, 100, 106
Boyd, Brian, **Retro. Supp. I:** 270, 275
Boyd, Janet L., **Supp. X:** 229
Boyd, Nancy (pseudonym). *See* Millay, Edna St. Vincent
Boyd, Thomas, **I:** 99; **IV:** 427
Boyesen, H. H., **II:** 289
"Boyhood" (Farrell), **II:** 28
"Boy in France, A" (Salinger), **III:** 552–553
Boy in the Water (Dobyns), **Supp. XIII:** 75, **84**
Boyle, Kay, **IV:** 404
Boyle, T. C. (Thomas Coraghessan), **Supp. VIII: 1–17**
Boyle, Thomas John. *See* Boyle, T. C.
Boynton, H. W., **Supp. IX:** 7
Boynton, Percy Holmes, **Supp. I Part 2:** 415
Boynton, Robert, **Supp. XVII:** 209; **Supp. XVIII:** 105, 107, 116
"Boy on a Train" (Ellison), **Retro. Supp. II:** 124
"Boy Riding Forward Backward" (Francis), **Supp. IX:** 82
"Boys and Girls" (Cisneros), **Supp. VII:** 59–60
Boy's Froissart, The (Lanier), **Supp. I Part 1:** 361
Boy's King Arthur, The (Lanier), **Supp. I Part 1:** 361
Boy's Mabinogion, The (Lanier), **Supp. I Part 1:** 361
"Boys of '29, The" (Holmes), **Supp. I Part 1:** 308
Boys of '76, The (Coffin), **III:** 577
Boy's Percy, The (Lanier), **Supp. I Part 1:** 361
Boy's Town (Howells), **I:** 418

Boy's Will, A (Frost), **II:** 152, 153, 155–156, 159, 164, 166; **Retro. Supp. I:** 124, 127, 128, 131; **Retro. Supp. II:** 168
"Boy Up a Tree" (Hoffman), **Supp. XVIII:** 86
"Boy Who Wrestled with Angels, The" (Hoffman), **Supp. X:** 90
"Boy with One Shoe, The" (Jewett), **Retro. Supp. II:** 132
"Brace, The" (Bausch), **Supp. VII:** 48
Bracebridge Hall, or, The Humorists (Irving), **I:** 339, 341; **II:** 308–309, 313
Bracher, Frederick, **I:** 378, 380; **Supp. I Part 1:** 185
Brackenridge, Hugh Henry, **Supp. I Part 1:** 124, 127, 145; **Supp. II Part 1:** 65
Brackett, Leigh, **Supp. IV Part 1:** 130
Bradbury, John M., **I:** 288–289; **IV:** 130, 135
Bradbury, Malcolm, **Supp. VIII:** 124; **Supp. XVIII:** 140
Bradbury, Ray, **Supp. I Part 2:** 621–622; **Supp. IV Part 1: 101–118; Supp. XVI:** 122; **Supp. XVII:** 41
Braddon, Mary E., **Supp. I Part 1:** 35, 36
Bradfield, Scott, **Supp. VIII:** 88
Bradford, Gamaliel, **I:** 248, 250
Bradford, Roark, **Retro. Supp. I:** 80
Bradford, William, **Retro. Supp. II:** 161, 162; **Supp. I Part 1:** 110, 112; **Supp. I Part 2:** 486, 494
Bradlee, Ben, **Supp. V:** 201
Bradley, Bill, **Supp. VIII:** 47
Bradley, F. H., **Retro. Supp. I:** 57, 58
Bradley, Francis Herbert, **I:** 59, 567–568, 572, 573
Bradshaw, Barbara, **Supp. XIII:** 313
Bradstreet, Anne, **I:** 178–179, 180, 181, 182, 184; **III:** 505; **Retro. Supp. I:** 40; **Supp. I Part 1: 98–123,** 300; **Supp. I Part 2:** 484, 485, 496, 546, 705; **Supp. V:** 113, 117–118; **Supp. XIII:** 152; **Supp. XIV:** 128; **Supp. XVIII:** 304
Bradstreet, Elizabeth, **Supp. I Part 1:** 108, 122
Bradstreet, Mrs. Simon. *See* Bradstreet, Anne
Bradstreet, Simon, **I:** 178; **Supp. I Part 1:** 103, 110, 116
Brady, Alice, **III:** 399
Brady, Matthew, **Supp. XVIII:** 4
"Bragdowdy and the Busybody, The" (Thurber), **Supp. I Part 2:** 617
Bragg, Rick, **Supp. XVIII:** 195
"Brahma" (Emerson), **II:** 19, 20
Brahms, Johannes, **III:** 118, 448
"Braiding" (L.-Y. Lee), **Supp. XV:** 214
"Brain and the Mind, The" (James), **II:** 346
Brainard, Joe, **Supp. XV:** 33
"Brain Damage" (Barthelme), **Supp. IV Part 1:** 44
"Brain to the Heart, The" (Komunyakaa), **Supp. XIII:** 120
Braithewaite, W. S., **Retro. Supp. I:** 131
Braithwaite, William Stanley, **Supp. IX:** 309; **Supp. XV:** 296–297, 301–302, 305, 306
Brakhage, Stan, **Supp. XII:** 2
Braly, Malcolm, **Supp. XVIII:** 147
"Bramble, The" (Wrigley), **Supp. XVIII:** 301
Brame, Gloria, **Supp. XV:** 113
Bramer, Monte, **Supp. X:** 152
Branch Will Not Break, The (Wright), **Supp. III Part 2:** 596, 598–601; **Supp. IV Part 1:** 60; **Supp. IX:** 159
Brancusi, Constantin, **III:** 201; **Retro. Supp. I:** 292
Brande, Dorothea, **Supp. I Part 2:** 608
Branden, Nathaniel, **Supp. IV Part 2:** 526, 528
"Brand-Name Blues" (Kaufmann), **Supp. XI:** 39
Brand New Life, A (Farrell), **II:** 46, 48
Brando, Marlon, **II:** 588; **Supp. IV Part 2:** 560; **Supp. XVIII:** 251
Brandon, Henry, **Supp. I Part 2:** 604, 612, 618
Brandt, Alice, **Supp. I Part 1:** 92
Brandt, Carl, **Supp. XI:** 45
Brant, Sebastian, **III:** 447, 448
Braque, Georges, **III:** 197; **Supp. IX:** 66
Brashford, Jake, **Supp. X:** 252
Brasil, Emanuel, **Supp. I Part 1:** 94
"Brasília" (Plath), **Supp. I Part 2:** 544, 545
"Brass Buttons" (McCoy), **Supp. XIII:** 161
"Brass Candlestick, The" (Francis), **Supp. IX:** 89
Brass Check, The (Sinclair), **Supp. V:** 276, 281, 282, 284–285
"Brass Ring, The" (Carver), **Supp. III Part 1:** 137
"Brass Spittoons" (Hughes), **Supp. I Part 1:** 326–327
Brats (X. J. Kennedy), **Supp. XV:** 163
Brautigan, Richard, **III:** 174; **Supp. VIII:** 42, 43; **Supp. XII:** 139; **Supp. XVI:** 172
Brave Cowboy, The (Abbey), **Supp. XIII:** 4–5
Brave Men (Pyle), **Supp. XVII:** 61
Brave New World (Huxley), **II:** 454; **Supp. XIII:** 29; **Supp. XVIII:** 137
"Brave New World" (MacLeish), **III:** 18
Bravery of Earth, A (Eberhart), **I:** 522, 524, 525, 526, 530
"Brave Tailors of Maida, The" (Talese), **Supp. XVII:** 208
"Brave Words for a Startling Occasion" (Ellison), **Retro. Supp. II:** 118
Braving the Elements (Merrill), **Supp. III Part 1:** 320, 323, 325–327, 329
Bravo, The (Cooper), **I:** 345–346, 348
"Bravura" (Francis), **Supp. IX:** 90
Brawley, Benjamin, **Supp. I Part 1:** 327, 332
Brawne, Fanny, **I:** 284; **II:** 531
Braxton, Joanne, **Supp. IV Part 1:** 12, 15
Brazil (Bishop), **Retro. Supp. II:** 45; **Supp. I Part 1:** 92
"Brazil" (Marshall), **Supp. XI:** 281
Brazil (Updike), **Retro. Supp. I:** 329, 330, 334
"Brazil, January 1, 1502" (Bishop), **Retro. Supp. II:** 47
Braziller, George, **Supp. X:** 24
Brazzi, Rossano, **Supp. IV Part 2:** 520
"Bread" (Dickey), **Supp. IV Part 1:** 182
"Bread" (Olds), **Supp. X:** 206
"Bread Alone" (Wylie), **Supp. I Part 2:** 727
Bread in the Wilderness (Merton), **Supp. VIII:** 197, 208
"Bread of Desire, The" (Nelson), **Supp. XVIII:** 177
Bread of Idleness, The (Masters), **Supp. I Part 2:** 460
"Bread of This World, The" (McGrath), **Supp. X:** 119, 127
Bread of Time, The (Levine), **Supp. V:** 180
Bread without Sugar (Stern), **Supp. IX: 297–298**
"Break, The" (Sexton), **Supp. II Part 2:** 689
Breakfast at Tiffany's (Capote), **Supp. III Part 1:** 113, 117, 119–121, 124, 126
Breakfast of Champions (Vonnegut), **Supp. II Part 2:** 755, 759, 769, 770, 777–778
Breaking and a Death, A (Kees), **Supp. XV:** 145
Breaking and Entering (X. J. Kennedy), **Supp. XV:** 153, **160–162**
Breaking Hard Ground (D. Hunter), **Supp. XVI:** 38
Breaking Ice (McMillan, ed.), **Supp. XIII:** 182–183
"Breaking Open" (Rukeyser), **Supp. VI:** 286
Breaking Open (Rukeyser), **Supp. VI:** 274, 281
Breaking Ranks: A Political Memoir (Podhoretz), **Supp. VIII: 239–241,** 245
"Breaking the Code of Silence: Ideology and Women's Confessional Poetry" (Harris), **Supp. XIV:** 269
"Breaking Up of the Winships, The" (Thurber), **Supp. I Part 2:** 616
Breast, The (P. Roth), **Retro. Supp. II:** 287–288; **Supp. III Part 2:** 416, 418
"Breast, The" (Sexton), **Supp. II Part 2:** 687
"Breasts" (Simic), **Supp. VIII:** 275
"Breath" (Levine), **Supp. V:** 185
Breathe No More, My Lady (Lacy), **Supp. XV:** 203
Breathing Lessons (Tyler), **Supp. IV Part 2:** 669–670
Breathing the Water (Levertov), **Supp. III Part 1:** 274, 283, 284
"Breath of Life, The" (C. Baxter), **Supp. XVII:** 23
Breath's Burials (Sobin), **Supp. XVI: 288–289**
Breaux, Zelia, **Retro. Supp. II:** 114
Brecht, Bertolt, **I:** 60, 301; **III:** 161, 162; **IV:** 394; **Supp. I Part 1:** 292; **Supp. II Part 1:** 10, 26, 56; **Supp. IV Part**

1: 359; **Supp. IX:** 131, 133, 140; **Supp. X:** 112; **Supp. XIII:** 206, 286; **Supp. XIV:** 162; **Supp. XVIII:** 33
Breen, Joseph I., **IV:** 390
Breines, Ron, **Supp. XVIII:** 97
Breit, Harvey, **I:** 433; **III:** 575; **Retro. Supp. II:** 230; **Supp. XVIII:** 254
Bremer, Fredrika, **Supp. I Part 1:** 407
Brendan: A Novel (Buechner), **Supp. XII:** 53
Brennan, Matthew, **Supp. XV:** 113, 125
Brent, Linda, **Supp. IV Part 1:** 12, 13
Brentano, Franz, **II:** 350; **Supp. XIV:** 198, 199
Brer Rabbit (tales), **Supp. IV Part 1:** 11, 13; **Supp. XIV:** 88
Breslin, James E. B., **Retro. Supp. I:** 430
Breslin, John B., **Supp. IV Part 1:** 308
Breslin, Paul, **Supp. VIII:** 283
Bresson, Robert, **Supp. IV Part 1:** 156
"Bresson's Movies" (Creeley), **Supp. IV Part 1:** 156–157
Breton, André, **III:** 425; **Supp. XIII:** 114; **Supp. XVII:** 244
Brett, George, **II:** 466; **Supp. V:** 286
Brevoort, Henry, **II:** 298
Brew, Kwesi, **Supp. IV Part 1:** 10, 16
Brewer, Gaylord, **Supp. XV:** 330
"Brewing of Soma, The" (Whittier), **Supp. I Part 2:** 704
Brewsie and Willie (Stein), **IV:** 27
Brewster, Martha, **Supp. I Part 1:** 114
"Brewsterville Croesus, A" (Briggs), **Supp. XVIII:** 16
Brewsterville letters (Briggs), **Supp. XVIII:** 1, 5, **15–16**
"Brian Age 7" (Doty), **Supp. XI:** 136
Briand, Paul, **Supp. XVIII:** 155
"Briar Patch, The" (Warren), **IV:** 237
Briar Rose (Coover), **Supp. V:** 52
"Briar Rose (Sleeping Beauty)" (Sexton), **Supp. II Part 2:** 690
Brice, Fanny, **II:** 427
"Brick, The" (Nye), **Supp. XIII:** 276
"Bricklayer in the Snow" (Fante), **Supp. XI:** 164–165
"Brick Layer's Lunch Hour, The" (Ginsberg), **Supp. II Part 1:** 318
Brickman, Marshall, **Supp. XV:** 5
"Bricks, The" (Hogan), **Supp. IV Part 1:** 413
"Bridal Ballad, The" (Poe), **III:** 428
Bridal Dinner, The (Gurney), **Supp. V:** 109, 110
"Bride Comes to Yellow Sky, The" (Crane), **I:** 34, 415, 416, 423
"Bridegroom, The" (Jin), **Supp. XVIII:** 98
Bridegroom, The (Jin), **Supp. XVIII: 97–98**
"Bride in the 30's, A" (Auden), **Supp. II Part 1:** 9
Bride of Lammermoor (Scott), **II:** 291
Bride of Samoa (film), **Supp. IV Part 1:** 82
"Bride of the Innisfallen, The" (Welty), **IV:** 278–279; **Retro. Supp. I:** 353
Bride of the Innisfallen, The (Welty), **IV:** 261, 275–279
Bride of the Innisfallen, The, and Other Stories (Welty), **Retro. Supp. I:** 352–353, 355
Brides of the South Wind: Poems 1917–1922 (Jeffers), **Supp. II Part 2:** 419
Bridge, Horatio, **II:** 226
"BRIDGE, THE" (Baraka), **Supp. II Part 1:** 32, 36
Bridge, The (H. Crane), **I:** 62, 109, 266, 385, 386, 387, 395–399, 400, 402; **IV:** 123, 341, 418, 419, 420; **Retro. Supp. I:** 427; **Retro. Supp. II:** 76, 77, 81, 83, **84–87;** **Supp. IX:** 306; **Supp. V:** 342
Bridge, The (Talese), **Supp. XVII:** 202, 203, 208
Bridge at Remagen, The (film), **Supp. XI:** 343
"Bridge Burners, The" (Van Vechten), **Supp. II Part 2:** 733
Bridge of San Luis Rey, The (Wilder), **I:** 360; **IV:** 356, 357, 360–363, 365, 366
Bridge of Years, The (Sarton), **Supp. VIII:** 253
"Bridges" (Kingsolver), **Supp. VII:** 208
Bridges, Harry, **I:** 493; **Supp. XVIII:** 238
Bridges, Lloyd, **Supp. XV:** 202
Bridges, Robert, **II:** 537; **III:** 527; **Supp. I Part 2:** 721; **Supp. II Part 1:** 21; **Supp. XIV:** 336, 341, 342, 343
"Bridging" (Apple), **Supp. XVII:** 5
Bridgman, P. W., **I:** 278
"Bridle, The" (Carver), **Supp. III Part 1:** 138
"Brief and Blameless Outline of the Ontogeny of Crow, A" (Wright), **Supp. XV:** 347
"Brief Début of Tildy, The" (O. Henry), **Supp. II Part 1:** 408
"Brief Encounters on the Inland Waterway" (Vonnegut), **Supp. II Part 2:** 760
Briefings (Ammons), **Supp. VII:** 29
"Brief Interviews with Hideous Men" (Wallace), **Supp. X:** 309
Brief Interviews with Hideous Men (Wallace), **Supp. X: 308–310**
"Briefly It Enters, and Briefly Speaks" (Kenyon), **Supp. VII:** 174
Briffault, Robert, **Supp. I Part 2:** 560, 567
"Brigade de Cuisine" (McPhee), **Supp. III Part 1:** 307–308
Brigadier and the Golf Widow, The (Cheever), **Supp. I Part 1:** 184–185, 192
Briggs, Charles F., **Supp. I Part 2:** 411
Briggs, Charles Frederick, **Supp. XVIII: 1–18**
brigham, besmilr, **Supp. XV:** 349
"Bright and Morning Star" (Wright), **IV:** 488
Bright Book of Life: American Novelists and Storytellers from Hemingway to Mailer (Kazin), **Supp. VIII:** 102, 104
Bright Center of Heaven (Maxwell), **Supp. VIII: 153–155,** 164
"Brightness from the North" (B. Kelly), **Supp. XVII:** 131
Brighton Beach Memoirs (Simon), **Supp. IV Part 2:** 576, 577, 584, 586–587, 590
Bright Procession (Sedges), **Supp. II Part 1:** 125
Bright Room Called Day, A (Kushner), **Supp. IX:** 133, **138–141,** 142
Brillat-Savarin, Jean Anthelme, **Supp. XVII:** 82, 86, 87
"Brilliance" (Doty), **Supp. XI:** 124, 128
"Brilliant Leaves" (Gordon), **II:** 199
"Brilliant Sad Sun" (W. C. Williams), **Retro. Supp. I:** 422
"Bringing Back the Trumpeter Swan" (Kumin), **Supp. IV Part 2:** 454
Bringing It All Back Home (album, Dylan), **Supp. XVIII:** 20, 25, 26, 30
Bringing It All Back Home (McNally), **Supp. XIII:** 197–198
Bringing the Devil to His Knees (C. Baxter), **Supp. XVII:** 22
"Bringing the Strange Home" (Dunn), **Supp. XI:** 141
"Bring the Day!" (Roethke), **III:** 536
Brinkley, Douglas, **Supp. XIII:** 9
Brinkmeyer, Robert H., Jr., **Supp. XI:** 38
Brinnin, John Malcolm, **IV:** 26, 27, 28, 42, 46; **Supp. XV:** 139
Brissot, Jacques Pierre, **Supp. I Part 2:** 511
"Britain's Negro Problem in Sierra Leone" (Du Bois), **Supp. I Part 1:** 176
"British Guiana" (Marshall), **Supp. XI:** 281–282
"British Poets, The" (Holmes), **Supp. I Part 1:** 306
"British Prison Ship, The" (Freneau), **Supp. II Part 1:** 261
Brittan, Gordon G., Jr., **Supp. XIV:** 234
Britten, Benjamin, **II:** 586; **Supp. II Part 1:** 17; **Supp. IV Part 1:** 84
Broadwater, Bowden, **II:** 562
Broadway, Broadway (McNally). *See It's Only a Play* (McNally)
Broadway, J. William, **Supp. V:** 316
Broadway Bound (Simon), **Supp. IV Part 2:** 576, 577, 584, 586–587, 590
Broadway Danny Rose (film; Allen), **Supp. XV:** 9
"Broadway Sights" (Whitman), **IV:** 350
Broccoli, Albert R. "Cubby," **Supp. XI:** 307
Bröck, Sabine, **Supp. XI:** 275, 277, 278
Brodhead, Richard, **Retro. Supp. II:** 139; **Supp. XIV:** 61
Brodkey, Harold, **Supp. VIII:** 151; **Supp. X:** 160
Brodskii, Iosif Alexsandrovich. *See* Brodsky, Joseph
Brodsky, Joseph, **Supp. VIII: 19–35;** **Supp. X:** 65, 73; **Supp. XV:** 134, 135, 256
Brody, Alter, **Supp. XV:** 302, 307
Brodyar, Anatole, **Supp. XIV:** 106
"Brokeback Mountain" (Proulx), **Supp. VII:** 264–265
"Broken Balance, The" (Jeffers), **Supp. II Part 2:** 426
"Broken Field Running" (Bambara), **Supp. XI:** 10, 11

Broken Frieze, The (Everwine), **Supp. XV:** 74, 75, 89
Broken Ground, The (Berry), **Supp. X:** 30
"Broken Home, The" (Merrill), **Supp. III Part 1:** 319, 325
"Broken Oar, The" (Longfellow), **Retro. Supp. II:** 169
"Broken Promise" (MacLeish), **III:** 15
Broken Span, The (W. C. Williams), **IV:** 419; **Retro. Supp. I:** 424
"Broken Tower, The" (H. Crane), **I:** 385, 386, 400, 401–402; **Retro. Supp. II:** 89, 90
"Broken Vessels" (Dubus), **Supp. VII:** 90
Broken Vessels (Dubus), **Supp. VII:** 90–91; **Supp. XI:** 347
"Broker" (H. Roth), **Supp. IX:** 234
Bromfield, Louis, **IV:** 380
"Brompton Cocktail" (Mamet), **Supp. XIV:** 252
Bromwich, David, **Retro. Supp. I:** 305; **Supp. XII:** 162
"Broncho That Would Not Be Broken, The" (Lindsay), **Supp. I Part 2:** 383
Bronk, William, **Supp. XV:** 115
Brontë, Anne, **Supp. IV Part 2:** 430
Brontë, Branwell, **I:** 462
Brontë, Charlotte, **I:** 458; **II:** 175; **Supp. IV Part 2:** 430; **Supp. IX:** 128; **Supp. XII:** 104, 303; **Supp. XV:** 338; **Supp. XVI:** 158
Brontë, Emily, **I:** 458; **Retro. Supp. I:** 43; **Supp. IV Part 2:** 430; **Supp. IX:** 128; **Supp. X:** 78, 89; **Supp. XV:** 338
"Bronze" (Francis), **Supp. IX:** 76
"Bronze" (Merrill), **Supp. III Part 1:** 336
Bronze Booklets on the History, Problems, and Cultural Contributions of the Negro series, **Supp. XIV:** 202
"Bronze Buckaroo, The" (Baraka), **Supp. II Part 1:** 49
"Bronze Horses, The" (Lowell), **II:** 524
"Bronze Tablets" (Lowell), **II:** 523
Bronzeville Boys and Girls (Brooks), **Supp. III Part 1:** 79
"Bronzeville Mother Loiters in Mississippi, A. Meanwhile, a Mississippi Mother Burns Bacon" (Brooks), **Supp. III Part 1:** 80
"Brooch, The" (Singer), **IV:** 20
Brook, Peter, **Retro. Supp. II:** 182
Brooke, Rupert, **II:** 82; **III:** 3
Brook Evans (Glaspell), **Supp. III Part 1:** 182–185
"Brooking Likeness" (Glück), **Supp. V:** 85
"Brooklyn" (Marshall), **Supp. XI:** 281, 282
Brooks, Cleanth, **I:** 280, 282; **III:** 517; **IV:** 236, 279; **Retro. Supp. I:** 40, 41, 90; **Retro. Supp. II:** 235; **Supp. I Part 2:** 423; **Supp. III Part 2:** 542; **Supp. IX:** 153, 155; **Supp. V:** 316; **Supp. X:** 115, 123; **Supp. XIV:** **1–20**
Brooks, David, **Supp. IV Part 2:** 623, 626, 630; **Supp. VIII:** 232
Brooks, Gwendolyn, **Retro. Supp. I:** 208; **Supp. III Part 1:** **69–90;** **Supp. IV Part 1:** 2, 15, 244, 251, 257; **Supp. XI:** 1, 278; **Supp. XIII:** 111, 112, 296; **Supp. XIV:** 73; **Supp. XVIII:** 175, 181, 185
Brooks, Mel, **Supp. IV Part 1:** 390; **Supp. IV Part 2:** 591
Brooks, Mrs. Van Wyck (Eleanor Kenyon Stimson), **I:** 240, 245, 250, 252
Brooks, Mrs. Van Wyck (Gladys Billings), **I:** 258
Brooks, Paul, **Supp. IX:** 26, 31, 32
Brooks, Phillips, **II:** 542; **Retro. Supp. II:** 134; **Supp. XIII:** 142
Brooks, Van Wyck, **I:** 106, 117, 215, 222, 228, 230, 231, 233, 236, **239–263,** 266, 480; **II:** 30, 271, 285, 309, 337, 482; **III:** 394, 606; **IV:** 171, 312, 427, 433; **Retro. Supp. II:** 46, 137; **Supp. I Part 2:** 423, 424, 650; **Supp. II Part 1:** 137; **Supp. VIII:** 98, 101; **Supp. XIV:** 11; **Supp. XV:** 298, 301
Broom of the System, The (Wallace), **Supp. X:** 301, **302–305,** 310
"Brooms" (Simic), **Supp. VIII:** 275
Brosnan, Jim, **II:** 424–425
Brother Carl (Sontag), **Supp. III Part 2:** 452
"Brother Death" (Anderson), **I:** 114
Brotherhood of the Grape, The (Fante), **Supp. XI:** 160, **171–172**
"Brothers" (Anderson), **I:** 114
Brothers, The (F. Barthelme), **Supp. XI:** 25, 28, 29, 30, 32–33
Brothers and Keepers (Wideman), **Supp. X:** 320, 321–322, 323, **325–327,** 328, 329–330, 331, 332
Brothers Ashkenazi, The (Singer), **IV:** 2
Brothers Karamazov, The (Dostoevsky), **II:** 60; **III:** 146, 150, 283; **Supp. IX:** 102, 106; **Supp. XI:** 172; **Supp. XII:** 322
"Brothers of No Kin" (Richter), **Supp. XVIII:** 208
Brothers of No Kin (Richter), **Supp. XVIII:** 209
Brother to Dragons: A Tale in Verse and Voices (Warren), **IV:** 243–244, 245, 246, 251, 252, 254, 257
Broughton, James, **Supp. XV:** 146
Broughton, Rhoda, **II:** 174; **IV:** 309, 310
Broun, Heywood, **I:** 478; **II:** 417; **IV:** 432; **Supp. IX:** 190
Broussais, François, **Supp. I Part 1:** 302
Browder, Earl, **I:** 515
Brower, David, **Supp. X:** 29
Brower, Reuben, **Supp. XV:** 20
Brown, Alice, **II:** 523; **Retro. Supp. II:** 136
Brown, Andrew, **Supp. XVI:** 150
Brown, Ashley, **Retro. Supp. II:** 48; **Supp. I Part 1:** 79, 80, 82, 84, 92
Brown, Charles Brockden, **I:** 54, 211, 335; **II:** 74, 267, 298; **III:** 415; **Supp. I Part 1:** **124–149;** **Supp. II Part 1:** 65, 292
Brown, Clifford, **Supp. V:** 195
Brown, Deborah, **Supp. XVII:** 75
Brown, Dee, **Supp. IV Part 2:** 504
Brown, Elijah, **Supp. I Part 1:** 125
Brown, George Douglas, **III:** 473
Brown, Harry, **Supp. IV Part 2:** 560
Brown, Harvey, **Supp. XIV:** 148
Brown, John, **II:** 13; **IV:** 125, 126, 172, 237, 249, 254; **Supp. I Part 1:** 345; **Supp. VIII:** 204
Brown, Joseph Epes, **Supp. IV Part 2:** 487
Brown, Larry, **Supp. XVIII:** 195
Brown, Leonard, **Supp. IX:** 117
Brown, Mary Armitt, **Supp. I Part 1:** 125
Brown, Mrs. Charles Brockden (Elizabeth Linn), **Supp. I Part 1:** 145, 146
Brown, Percy, **II:** 20
Brown, Robert E., **Supp. X:** 12
Brown, Scott, **Supp. XI:** 178
Brown, Slater, **IV:** 123; **Retro. Supp. II:** 79
Brown, Solyman, **Supp. I Part 1:** 156
Brown, Sterling, **Retro. Supp. I:** 198; **Supp. IV Part 1:** 169; **Supp. XIV:** 202
Brown, Tina, **Supp. XVI:** 176–177
Brown, Wesley, **Supp. V:** 6
Brown Decades, The (Mumford), **Supp. II Part 2:** 475, 478, 491–492
Brown Dog (Harrison), **Supp. VIII:** 51
Brown Dog of the Yaak: Essays on Art and Activism (Bass), **Supp. XVI:** 22
"Brown Dwarf of Rügen, The" (Whittier), **Supp. I Part 2:** 696
Browne, Charles Farrar, **II:** 289; **IV:** 193, 196; **Supp. XVIII:** 1, 4
Browne, Roscoe Lee, **Supp. VIII:** 345
Browne, Thomas, **II:** 15–16, 304; **III:** 77, 78, 198, 487; **IV:** 147; **Supp. IX:** 136; **Supp. XII:** 45; **Supp. XVI:** 292
Browne, William, **Supp. I Part 1:** 98
Brownell, W. C., **II:** 14
Brownell, William Crary, **Retro. Supp. I:** 365, 366
Browner, Stephanie P., **Supp. XVIII:** 17
Brown Girl, Brownstones (Marshall), **Supp. XI:** 275, 276, **278–280,** 282
Brownies' Book, The (Hughes), **Supp. I Part 1:** 321
Browning, Elizabeth Barrett, **I:** 458, 459; **Retro. Supp. I:** 33, 43; **Supp. XVIII:** 175–176
Browning, Robert, **I:** 50, 66, 103, 458, 460, 468; **II:** 338, 478, 522; **III:** 5, 8, 467, 469, 484, 511, 521, 524, 606, 609; **IV:** 135, 245, 366, 416; **Retro. Supp. I:** 43, 55, 217; **Retro. Supp. II:** 188, 190; **Supp. I Part 1:** 2, 6, 79, 311; **Supp. I Part 2:** 416, 468, 622; **Supp. III Part 1:** 5, 6; **Supp. IV Part 2:** 430; **Supp. X:** 65; **Supp. XV:** 92, 250, 275
Brownmiller, Susan, **Supp. X:** 252
"Brown River, Smile" (Toomer), **Supp. IV Part 1:** 16
Brownstone Eclogues and Other Poems (Aiken), **I:** 65, 67
Brown: The Last Discovery of America (Rodriguez), **Supp. XIV:** 297, 298, 300, **305–309,** 310, 311–312
Broyard, Anatole, **Supp. IV Part 1:** 39; **Supp. VIII:** 140; **Supp. X:** 186; **Supp. XI:** 348; **Supp. XVI:** 213

Bruccoli, Matthew, **Retro. Supp. I:** 98, 102, 105, 114, 115, 359; **Supp. IV Part 2:** 468, 470
Bruce, John Edward, **Supp. XVI:** 143
Bruce, Lenny, **Supp. VIII:** 198
Bruce, Virginia, **Supp. XII:** 173
Bruce-Novoa, Juan, **Supp. VIII:** 73, 74
Bruchac, Joseph, **Supp. IV Part 1:** 261, 319, 320, 321, 322, 323, 325, 328, 398, 399, 403, 408, 414; **Supp. IV Part 2:** 502, 506
Brueghel, Pieter, **I:** 174; **Supp. I Part 2:** 475
Brueghel, Pieter, the Elder, **Retro. Supp. I:** 430
Bruell, Edwin, **Supp. VIII:** 126
Brugh, Spangler Arlington. *See* Taylor, Robert
"Bruja: Witch" (Mora), **Supp. XIII:** 214, 220, 221, **Supp. XIII:** 222
Brulé, Claude, **Supp. XI:** 307
Brumer, Andy, **Supp. XIII:** 88
Brunner, Emil, **III:** 291, 303
"Brush Fire" (J. Wright), **Supp. XVII:** 241
Brustein, Robert, **Supp. VIII:** 331
Brutus, **IV:** 373, 374; **Supp. I Part 2:** 471
"Brutus and Antony" (Masters), **Supp. I Part 2:** 472
"Bryan, Bryan, Bryan, Bryan" (Lindsay), **Supp. I Part 2:** 394, 395, 398
Bryan, George, **Retro. Supp. II:** 76
Bryan, Sharon, **Supp. IX:** 154
Bryan, William Jennings, **I:** 483; **IV:** 124; **Supp. I Part 2:** 385, 395–396, 455, 456
Bryant, Austin, **Supp. I Part 1:** 152, 153
Bryant, Frances, **Supp. I Part 1:** 153
Bryant, Louise, **Supp. X:** 136
Bryant, Mrs. William Cullen (Frances Fairchild), **Supp. I Part 1:** 153, 169
Bryant, Peter, **Supp. I Part 1:** 150, 151, 152, 153. *See also* George, Peter
Bryant, William Cullen, **I:** 335, 458; **II:** 311; **III:** 81; **IV:** 309; **Retro. Supp. I:** 217; **Retro. Supp. II:** 155; **Supp. I Part 1: 150–173,** 312, 362; **Supp. I Part 2:** 413, 416, 420; **Supp. IV Part 1:** 165; **Supp. XIII:** 145
Bryer, Jackson R., **Supp. IV Part 2:** 575, 583, 585, 586, 589, 591; **Supp. XIII:** 200, **Supp. XIII:** 205
Bryher, Jackson R. (pseudonym). *See* Ellerman, Winifred
"Bubbs Creek Haircut" (Snyder), **Supp. VIII:** 306
Buber, Martin, **II:** 228; **III:** 45, 308, 528; **IV:** 11; **Supp. I Part 1:** 83, 88; **Supp. XVI:** 291
Buccaneers, The (Wharton), **IV:** 327; **Retro. Supp. I:** 382
Buchanan Dying (Updike), **Retro. Supp. I:** 331, 335
Buchbinder, David, **Supp. XIII:** 32
Buchwald, Art, **Supp. XII:** 124–125; **Supp. XVI:** 110–111
Buchwald, Emilie, **Supp. XVI:** 35, 36
Buck, Dudley, **Supp. I Part 1:** 362
Buck, Gene, **II:** 427
Buck, Pearl S., **Supp. II Part 1: 113–134; Supp. XIV:** 274
"Buckdancer's Choice" (Dickey), **Supp. IV Part 1:** 191
Buckdancer's Choice (Dickey), **Supp. IV Part 1:** 176, 177, 178, 180
Bucke, Richard Maurice, **Retro. Supp. I:** 407
"Buck Fever" (Humphrey), **Supp. IX:** 109
"Buck in the Snow, The" (Millay), **III:** 135
Buckley, Christopher, **Supp. IX:** 169; **Supp. XI:** 257, 329; **Supp. XV:** 76–77, 86
Buckley, James, Jr., **Supp. XVII:** 220
Buckminster, Joseph, **Supp. II Part 1:** 66–67, 69
Bucknell, Katherine, **Supp. XIV:** 170
Bucolics (Auden), **Supp. II Part 1:** 21, 24
Budd, Louis J., **IV:** 210
Buddha, **I:** 136; **II:** 1; **III:** 173, 179, 239, 567; **Supp. I Part 1:** 363; **Supp. I Part 2:** 397
"Buddha's Last Instruction, The" (Oliver), **Supp. VII:** 239
Budding Prospects: A Pastoral (Boyle), **Supp. VIII: 8–9**
Buechner, Frederick, **III:** 310; **Supp. XII: 41–59**
Buell, Lawrence, **Supp. IX:** 29; **Supp. V:** 209; **Supp. XV:** 269, 282
"Buffalo, The" (Moore), **III:** 215
"Buffalo Bill." *See* Cody, William
Buffalo Girls (McMurtry), **Supp. V:** 229
Buffalo Girls (screenplay) (McMurtry), **Supp. V:** 232
Buffett, Jimmy, **Supp. VIII:** 42
Buffon, Comte de, **II:** 101
Buford, Fanny McConnell, **Retro. Supp. II:** 117
Bugeja, Michael, **Supp. X:** 201
Bugged for Murder (Lacy), **Supp. XV:** 205
"Buglesong" (Stegner), **Supp. IV Part 2:** 606
"Buick" (Shapiro), **Supp. II Part 2:** 705
"Builders" (Yates), **Supp. XI: 342–343**
Builders, The (Glasgow), **II:** 183–184, 193
"Builders, The" (Hay), **Supp. XIV:** 125
Builders of the Bay Colony (Morison), **Supp. I Part 2:** 484–485
"Builders of the Bridge, The" (Mumford), **Supp. II Part 2:** 475
"Building" (Snyder), **Supp. VIII:** 305
"Building, Dwelling, Thinking" (Heidegger), **Retro. Supp. II:** 87
Building a Character (Stanislavsky), **Supp. XIV:** 243
"Building of the Ship, The" (Longfellow), **II:** 498; **Retro. Supp. II:** 159, 167, 168
"Build Soil" (Frost), **Retro. Supp. I:** 138, 139
"Build Soil" (Snyder), **Supp. VIII:** 304
Build-Up, The (W. C. Williams), **Retro. Supp. I:** 423
Bukiet, Melvin Jules, **Supp. XVII: 39–51**
Bukowski, Charles, **Supp. III Part 1:** 147; **Supp. XI:** 159, 161, 172, 173; **Supp. XVII:** 245
Bulgakov, Mikhail, **Supp. XIV:** 97
"Bulgarian Poetess, The" (Updike), **IV:** 215, 227; **Retro. Supp. I:** 329
Bull, Ole, **II:** 504
"Bulldozer, The" (Francis), **Supp. IX:** 87
"Bullet in the Brain" (Wolff), **Supp. VII:** 342–343
Bullet Park (Cheever), **Supp. I Part 1:** 185, 187–193, 194, 195
Bullets over Broadway (film; Allen), **Supp. XV:** 12, **12–13**
Bullfight, The (Mailer), **Retro. Supp. II:** 205
Bullins, Ed, **Supp. II Part 1:** 34, 42
Bullock, Sandra, **Supp. X:** 80
"Bull-Roarer, The" (Stern), **Supp. IX:** 297
"Bully, The" (Dubus), **Supp. VII:** 84
"Bulsh" (X. J. Kennedy), **Supp. XV:** 161
Bultmann, Rudolf, **III:** 309
Bulwark, The (Dreiser), **I:** 497, 506, 516–517; **Retro. Supp. II:** 95, 96, 105, 108
Bulwer-Lytton, Edward George, **IV:** 350
"Bums in the Attic" (Cisneros), **Supp. VII:** 62
Bunche, Ralph, **Supp. I Part 1:** 343; **Supp. XIV:** 202
"Bunchgrass Edge of the World, The" (Proulx), **Supp. VII:** 263
Bunge, Nancy, **Supp. XVII:** 218
"Bunner Sisters, The" (Wharton), **IV:** 317
Bunting, Basil, **Retro. Supp. I:** 422; **Supp. III Part 2:** 616, 620, 624; **Supp. XIV:** 286
Buñuel, Luis, **III:** 184; **Retro. Supp. II:** 337
Bunyan, John, **I:** 445; **II:** 15, 104, 228; **IV:** 80, 84, 156, 437; **Supp. I Part 1:** 32
Burana, Lily, **Supp. XI:** 253
Burbank, Luther, **I:** 483
Burbank, Rex, **IV:** 363
Burchfield, Alice, **Supp. I Part 2:** 652, 660
Burden of Proof, The (Turow), **Supp. XVII: 216–217,** 218
Burden of Southern History, The (Woodward), **Retro. Supp. I:** 75
Burdens of Formality, The (Lea, ed.), **Supp. X:** 58
Burger, Gottfried August, **II:** 306
Burgess, Anthony, **Supp. IV Part 1:** 227; **Supp. IV Part 2:** 685; **Supp. V:** 128
Burgh, James, **Supp. I Part 2:** 522
"Burglar of Babylon, The" (Bishop), **Retro. Supp. II:** 47; **Supp. I Part 1:** 93
Burgum, E. B., **IV:** 469, 470
Buried Child (Shepard), **Supp. III Part 2:** 433, 447, 448; **Supp. XIV:** 327
"Buried Lake, The" (Tate), **IV:** 136
Burke, Edmund, **I:** 9; **III:** 310; **Supp. I Part 2:** 496, 511, 512, 513, 523; **Supp. II Part 1:** 80; **Supp. XVII:** 236
Burke, James Lee, **Supp. XIV: 21–38**
Burke, Kenneth, **I: 264–287,** 291; **III:** 497, 499, 546; **IV:** 123, 408; **Retro.**

Supp. I: 297; **Retro. Supp. II:** 117, 120; **Supp. I Part 2:** 630; **Supp. II Part 1:** 136; **Supp. IX:** 229; **Supp. VIII:** 105; **Supp. XIV:** 3
Burley, Justin, **Supp. XVI:** 158
"Burly Fading One, The" (Hayden), **Supp. II Part 1:** 366
"Burned" (Levine), **Supp. V:** 186, 192
"Burned Diary, The" (Olds), **Supp. X:** 215
Burnett, Allison, **Supp. XVII:** 22
Burnett, David, **Supp. XI:** 299
Burnett, Frances Hodgson, **Supp. I Part 1:** 44
Burnett, Whit, **III:** 551; **Supp. XI:** 294
Burney, Fanny, **Supp. XV:** 232
Burnham, James, **Supp. I Part 2:** 648
Burnham, John Chynoweth, **I:** 59
"Burning, The" (Welty), **IV:** 277–278; **Retro. Supp. I:** 353
Burning Angel (Burke), **Supp. XIV:** 30, 32
Burning Bright (Steinbeck), **IV:** 51, 61–62
"Burning Bush" (Untermeyer), **Supp. XV:** 309
Burning Bush (Untermeyer), **Supp. XV: 309**
Burning Bush, The (H. and G. Herczeg), **Supp. XVII:** 62
"Burning Chrome" (W. Gibson), **Supp. XVI:** 117, 120, 123, 124, 128
Burning Chrome (W. Gibson), **Supp. XVI:** 118, 122, **128**
Burning City (Benét), **Supp. XI:** 46, 58
Burning Daylight (London), **II:** 474, 481
Burning Down the House: Essays on Fiction (C. Baxter), **Supp. XVII:** 13, 20, 21
Burning House, The (Beattie), **Supp. V:** 29
"Burning Ladder, The" (Gioia), **Supp. XV:** 118
Burning Mystery of Anna in 1951, The (Koch), **Supp. XV:** 182–183
"Burning of Paper Instead of Children, The" (Rich), **Supp. I Part 2:** 558
Burning the Days: Recollections (Salter), **Supp. IX:** 245, 246, 248, 260, **261–262**
"Burning the Small Dead" (Snyder), **Supp. VIII:** 298
Burns, Carol, **Supp. XVIII:** 162
Burns, David, **III:** 165–166
Burns, Ken, **Supp. XIV:** 14
Burns, Michael, **Supp. XV:** 339
Burns, Robert, **II:** 150, 306; **III:** 592; **IV:** 453; **Supp. I Part 1:** 158; **Supp. I Part 2:** 410, 455, 683, 685, 691, 692; **Supp. IX:** 173; **Supp. XII:** 171; **Supp. XIII:** 3; **Supp. XVIII:** 82
Burnshaw, Stanley, **Retro. Supp. I:** 298, 303; **Supp. III Part 2:** 615
"Burn the Cities" (West), **Retro. Supp. II:** 338
"Burnt Norton" (Eliot), **Retro. Supp. I:** 66; **Supp. XV:** 216
Burnt Norton (Eliot), **I:** 575, 580–581, 582, 584, 585; **III:** 10
Burnt-Out Case, A (Greene), **Supp. VIII:** 4
"Burnt-out Spa, The" (Plath), **Retro. Supp. II:** 246
Burn Witch Burn (A. Merritt), **Supp. XVII:** 58
Burr, Aaron, **I:** 7, 549, 550; **II:** 300; **IV:** 264; **Supp. I Part 2:** 461, 483
Burr: A Novel (Vidal), **Supp. IV Part 2:** 677, 682, 684, 685, 687, 688, 689, 691
Burr Oaks (Eberhart), **I:** 533, 535
Burroughs, Edgar Rice, **Supp. IV Part 1:** 101
Burroughs, John, **I:** 220, 236, 506; **IV:** 346; **Supp. IX:** 171
Burroughs, William S., **III:** 45, 174, 258; **Supp. II Part 1:** 320, 328; **Supp. III Part 1: 91–110,** 217, 226; **Supp. IV Part 1:** 79, 87, 90; **Supp. XI:** 297, 308; **Supp. XII:** 1, 3, 118, 121, 124, 129, 131, 136; **Supp. XIV:** 137, 140–141, 143–144, 150; **Supp. XVI:** 123, 135; **Supp. XVII:** 225; **Supp. XVIII:** 137
Burrow, Trigant, **Supp. II Part 1:** 6
Burrows, Ken, **Supp. V:** 115
Burson, Claudia, **Supp. XV:** 343
Burstein, Janet, **Supp. XVII:** 41, 44, 48
Burt, Stephen, **Supp. XV:** 341, 342, 345, 347, 351; **Supp. XVII:** 18, 246
Burt, Steve, **Supp. V:** 83
Burtis, Thomson, **Supp. XIII:** 163
Burton, Robert, **II:** 535; **III:** 77, 78; **Supp. I Part 1:** 349
Burton, William Evans, **III:** 412
"Burying Ground by the Ties" (MacLeish), **III:** 14
Bury My Heart at Wounded Knee (Brown), **Supp. IV Part 2:** 504
Bury the Dead (Shaw), **IV:** 381
"Bus Along St. Clair: December, A" (Atwood), **Supp. XIII:** 33
Busch, Frederick, **Supp. X:** 78; **Supp. XII:** 343; **Supp. XVII:** 175
Bush, Barney, **Supp. XII:** 218, 222
Bush, Douglas, **Supp. I Part 1:** 268; **Supp. XIV:** 10
"Busher Comes Back, The" (Lardner), **II:** 422
"Busher's Letters Home, A" (Lardner), **II:** 418–419, 421
"Business and Poetry" (Gioia), **Supp. XV:** 113, 115
"Business Deal" (West), **IV:** 287
"Business Man, A" (Jewett), **Retro. Supp. II:** 132
Business of Memory, The: The Art of Remembering in an Age of Forgetting (C. Baxter, ed.), **Supp. XVII:** 21
"Business Trip" (Hoffman), **Supp. XVIII:** 86
Buss, Helen M., **Supp. IV Part 1:** 12
Butcher, Margaret Just, **Supp. XIV:** 203
"Butcher, The" (Southern), **Supp. XI:** 294
"Butcher Shop" (Simic), **Supp. VIII:** 273
But Gentlemen Marry Brunettes (Loos), **Supp. XVI:** 190–191
Butler, Benjamin, **I:** 457
Butler, Dorothy. *See* Farrell, Mrs. James T. (Dorothy Butler)
Butler, Elizabeth, **Supp. I Part 1:** 260
Butler, Ethel, **Supp. XIV:** 125
Butler, Hugo, **Supp. XVII:** 63
Butler, James D., **Supp. IX:** 175
Butler, Joseph, **II:** 8, 9
Butler, Judith, **Supp. XII:** 6
Butler, Maud. *See* Falkner, Mrs. Murray C. (Maud Butler)
Butler, Nicholas Murray, **I:** 223; **Supp. I Part 1:** 23; **Supp. III Part 2:** 499
Butler, Octavia, **Supp. XIII: 59–72**
Butler, Robert Olen, **Supp. XII: 61–78,** 319
Butler, Samuel, **II:** 82, 86; **IV:** 121, 440; **Supp. VIII:** 171
Butler-Evans, Elliot, **Retro. Supp. II:** 121
"But Only Mine" (Wright), **Supp. III Part 2:** 595
Butscher, Edward, **Supp. I Part 2:** 526
Butter Battle Book, The (Geisel), **Supp. XVI:** 110
"Buttercups" (Lowell), **Retro. Supp. II:** 187
Butterfield, R. W., **I:** 386
Butterfield, Stephen, **Supp. IV Part 1:** 3, 11
Butterfield 8 (O'Hara), **III:** 361
"Butterflies Under Persimmon" (Jarman), **Supp. XVII:** 120
Butterfly (Harvey), **Supp. XIII:** 184
"Butterfly, The" (Brodksy), **Supp. VIII:** 26
"Butterfly and the Traffic Light, The" (Ozick), **Supp. V:** 263, 265
Butterfly Stories (Vollmann), **Supp. XVII:** 226
"Butterfly-toed Shoes" (Komunyakaa), **Supp. XIII:** 126
Butter Hill and Other Poems (Francis), **Supp. IX:** 88, 89
Buttons, Red, **Supp. IV Part 2:** 574
Buttrick, George, **III:** 301; **Supp. XII:** 47–48
"But What Is the Reader to Make of This?" (Ashbery), **Supp. III Part 1:** 25
Butz, Earl, **Supp. X:** 35
"Buz" (Alcott), **Supp. I Part 1:** 43
By Avon River (Doolittle), **Supp. I Part 1:** 272
"By Blue Ontario's Shore" (Whitman), **Retro. Supp. I:** 399, 400
"By Disposition of Angels" (Moore), **III:** 214
"By Earth" (Olds), **Supp. X:** 214
"By Fire" (Olds), **Supp. X:** 214
Bygones (Untermeyer), **Supp. XV:** 304, **308–309,** 312, 313
By Land, By Sea (Hoffman), **Supp. XVIII:** 86
By Land and by Sea (Morison), **Supp. I Part 2:** 492
By-Line: Ernest Hemingway (Hemingway), **II:** 257–258
By Love Possessed (Cozens), **I:** 358, 365, 372–374, 375, 376, 377, 378, 379

"By Morning" (Swenson), **Supp. IV Part 2:** 642
"By Night" (Francis), **Supp. IX:** 76
Bynner, Witter, **II:** 513, 527; **Supp. XIII:** 347; **Supp. XV: 39–54**
Byrd, William, **Supp. IV Part 2:** 425
Byrne, Donn, **IV:** 67
Byron, George Gordon, Lord, **I:** 343, 568, 577; **II:** 135, 193, 296, 301, 303, 310, 315, 331, 566; **III:** 82, 137, 170, 409, 410, 412, 469; **IV:** 245, 435; **Supp. I Part 1:** 150, 312, 349; **Supp. I Part 2:** 580, 591, 683, 685, 719; **Supp. XIII:** 139; **Supp. XVI:** 188, 203, 206, 210
"Byron's Cain" (L. Michaels), **Supp. XVI:** 203
"Bystanders" (Matthews), **Supp. IX:** 160
By the Bias of Sound (Sobin), **Supp. XVI:** 281
By the North Gate (Oates), **Supp. II Part 2:** 504
"By the Waters of Babylon" (Benét), **Supp. XI:** 56, 58
By the Waters of Manhattan (Reznikoff), **Supp. XIV:** 288, 293, 294
By the Waters of Manhattan: An Annual (Reznikoff), **Supp. XIV:** 277, 280, 289
By the Waters of Manhattan: Selected Verse (Reznikoff), **Supp. XIV:** 281, 291
By the Well of Living and Seeing and the Fifth Book of the Maccabees (Reznikoff), **Supp. XIV:** 281
By the Well of Living and Seeing: New and Selected Poems 1918–1973 (Reznikoff), **Supp. XIV:** 281, 287–288, 295
By Way of Orbit (O'Neill), **III:** 405

C
"C 33" (H. Crane), **I:** 384; **Retro. Supp. II:** 76
Cabala, The (Wilder), **IV:** 356, 358–360, 369, 374
Cabaret (film), **Supp. XIV:** 155, 162
Cabaret (play), **Supp. XIV:** 162; **Supp. XVII:** 45
Cabbages and Kings (O. Henry), **Supp. II Part 1:** 394, 409
Cabell, James Branch, **II:** 42; **III:** 394; **IV:** 67, 359, 360; **Retro. Supp. I:** 80; **Supp. I Part 2:** 613, 714, 718, 721; **Supp. X:** 223
"Cabin, The" (Carver), **Supp. III Part 1:** 137, 146
Cabin, The: Reminiscence and Diversions (Mamet), **Supp. XIV:** 240
Cabinet of Dr. Caligari, The (film), **Retro. Supp. I:** 268
Cable, George Washington, **II:** 289; **Retro. Supp. II:** 65; **Supp. I Part 1:** 200; **Supp. II Part 1:** 198; **Supp. XIV:** 63
Cables to the Ace; or, Familiar Liturgies of Misunderstanding (Merton), **Supp. VIII:** 208
Cabot, James, **II:** 14; **IV:** 173
Cabot, John, **Supp. I Part 2:** 496, 497
Cachoeira Tales and Other Poems, The (Nelson), **Supp. XVIII: 178–179**
"Cachoiera Tales, The" (Nelson), **Supp. XVIII:** 179
Cactus Flower (Barillet and Grédy), **Supp. XVI:** 194
"Caddy's Diary, A" (Lardner), **II:** 421–422
"Cadence" (Dubus), **Supp. VII:** 84–85
Cadieux, Isabelle, **Supp. XIII:** 127
"Cadillac Flambé" (Ellison), **Retro. Supp. II:** 119, 126; **Supp. II Part 1:** 248
Cadillac Jack (McMurtry), **Supp. V:** 225
Cadillac Jukebox (Burke), **Supp. XIV:** 32
Cadle, Dean, **Supp. I Part 2:** 429
Cady, Edwin H., **II:** 272
"Caedmon" (Garrett), **Supp. VII:** 96–97
Caesar, Julius, **II:** 12, 502, 561–562; **IV:** 372, 373
Caesar, Sid, **Supp. IV Part 2:** 574, 591
"Cafeteria, The" (Singer), **Retro. Supp. II:** 316
Cage, John, **Supp. IV Part 1:** 84; **Supp. V:** 337, 341
"Cage and the Prairie: Two Notes on Symbolism, The" (Bewley), **Supp. I Part 1:** 251
Cage of Spines, A (Swenson), **Supp. IV Part 2:** 641–642, 647
Cagney, James, **Supp. IV Part 1:** 236; **Supp. XIII:** 174
Cagney, William, **Supp. XIII:** 174
Cahalan, James, **Supp. XIII:** 1, 2, 3, 4, 12
Cahan, Abraham, **Supp. IX:** 227; **Supp. XIII:** 106
Cahill, Tim, **Supp. XIII:** 13
Cain, James M., **III:** 99; **Supp. IV Part 1:** 130; **Supp. XI:** 160; **Supp. XIII:** 159, 165
Cairns, Huntington, **III:** 103, 108, 114, 119
Cairo! Shanghai! Bombay! (Williams and Shapiro), **IV:** 380
Cake (Bynner), **Supp. XV:** 50
Cakes and Ale (Maugham), **III:** 64
Calabria, Frank, **Supp. XIII:** 164
Calamity Jane (Martha Jane Canary), **Supp. V:** 229–230; **Supp. X:** 103
"Calamus" (Whitman), **IV:** 342–343; **Retro. Supp. I:** 52, 403, 404, 407
Calasso, Roberto, **Supp. IV Part 1:** 301
Calderón, Hector, **Supp. IV Part 2:** 544
Caldwell, Christopher, **Supp. IV Part 1:** 211
Caldwell, Erskine, **I:** 97, 211, **288–311; IV:** 286; **Supp. IV Part 2:** 601
Caldwell, Mrs. Erskine (Helen Lannegan), **I:** 289
Caldwell, Mrs. Erskine (Margaret Bourke-White), **I:** 290, 293–295, 297
Caldwell, Mrs. Erskine (Virginia Fletcher), **I:** 290
Caldwell, Reverend Ira Sylvester, **I:** 289, 305
Caldwell, Zoe, **Supp. XIII:** 207
Caleb Williams (Godwin), **III:** 415
"Calendar" (Creeley), **Supp. IV Part 1:** 158
Calendar of Saints for Unbelievers, A (Wescott), **Supp. XIV:** 342
Calendars (A. Finch), **Supp. XVII: 76–77**
Calhoun, John C., **I:** 8; **III:** 309
"Caliban in the Coal Mines" (Untermeyer), **Supp. XV:** 296
"California" (Carruth), **Supp. XVI:** 56
"California" (Didion), **Supp. IV Part 1:** 195
"California, This Is Minnesota Speaking" (Dunn), **Supp. XI:** 146
California and Oregon Trail, The (Parkman), **Supp. I Part 2:** 486
"California Hills in August" (Gioia), **Supp. XV:** 118–119
Californians (Jeffers), **Supp. II Part 2:** 415, 418, 420
"California Oaks, The" (Winters), **Supp. II Part 2:** 798
"California Plush" (Bidart), **Supp. XV:** 23
"California Republic" (Didion), **Supp. IV Part 1:** 205
"California Requiem, A" (Gioia), **Supp. XV:** 126
California Suite (film), **Supp. IV Part 2:** 589
California Suite (Simon), **Supp. IV Part 2:** 581, 582
"Caligula" (Lowell), **II:** 554
Callahan, John F., **Retro. Supp. II:** 119, 126, 127
"Call at Corazón" (Bowles), **Supp. IV Part 1:** 82, 87
Calle, Sophia, **Supp. XII:** 22
"Called Back" (Kazin), **Supp. VIII:** 104
Calley, Captain William, **II:** 579
Calley, John, **Supp. XI:** 305
Callicott, J. Baird, **Supp. XIV:** 184
Calligrammes (Apollinaire), **I:** 432
"Calling Jesus" (Toomer), **Supp. III Part 2:** 484
Calling Myself Home (Hogan), **Supp. IV Part 1:** 397, 399, 400, 401, 413
Call It Experience (Caldwell), **I:** 290–291, 297
"Call It Fear" (Harjo), **Supp. XII:** 220
Call It Sleep (H. Roth), **Supp. IX:** 227, 228, **229–231; Supp. VIII:** 233; **Supp. XIII:** 106
"Call Letters: Mrs. V. B." (Angelou), **Supp. IV Part 1:** 15
Call Me Ishmael (Olson), **Supp. II Part 2:** 556
Call Me Shakespeare (Endore), **Supp. XVII:** 65
Call of the Gospel, The (Mather), **Supp. II Part 2:** 448
Call of the Wild, The (London), **II:** 466, 470–471, 472, 481
"Call of the Wild, The" (Snyder), **Supp. VIII:** 301
"Calloway's Code" (O. Henry), **Supp. II Part 1:** 404
"Call to Arms" (Mumford), **Supp. II Part 2:** 479

Call to Arms, The (film), **Retro. Supp. I:** 325
Calmer, Ned, **Supp. XI:** 219
Calvert, George H., **Supp. I Part 1:** 361
Calverton, V. F., **Supp. VIII:** 96
Calvin, John, **II:** 342; **IV:** 160, 490
Calvino, Italo, **Supp. IV Part 2:** 623, 678
Cambridge Edition of the Works of F. Scott Fitzgerald, The (Bruccoli, ed.), **Retro. Supp. I:** 115
Cambridge Film Handbook for *On the Waterfront* (Rapf), **Supp. XVIII:** 251
"Cambridge Thirty Years Ago" (Lowell), **Supp. I Part 2:** 419
Cambridge University Press, **Retro. Supp. I:** 115
"Camellia Sabina" (Moore), **III:** 208, 215
"Cameo Appearance" (Simic), **Supp. VIII:** 283
Camera Obscura (Nabokov), **III:** 255
Cameron, Elizabeth, **I:** 10, 17
Cameron, Kenneth W., **II:** 16
Cameron, Peter, **Supp. XII: 79–95**
Cameron, Sharon, **Retro. Supp. I:** 43; **Retro. Supp. II:** 40
Camerson, Don, **I:** 10, 17
Camino, Léon Felipe, **Retro. Supp. II:** 89
Camino Real (T. Williams), **IV:** 382, 385, 386, 387, 388, 391, 392, 395, 398
Camões, Luiz Vaz de, **II:** 133; **Supp. I Part 1:** 94
"Camouflaging the Chimera" (Komunyakaa), **Supp. XIII: 122–123**
Camp, James, **Supp. XV:** 165
Camp, Walter, **II:** 423
Campana, Dino, **Supp. V:** 337
Campbell (Hale), Janet, **Supp. IV Part 2:** 503
Campbell, Alan, **Supp. IV Part 1:** 353; **Supp. IX:** 196, 198, 201
Campbell, Alexander, **Supp. I Part 2:** 381, 395
Campbell, Donna, **Retro. Supp. II:** 139
Campbell, Helen, **Supp. XI:** 200, 206
Campbell, James, **Supp. XII:** 127
Campbell, James Edwin, **Supp. II Part 1:** 202
Campbell, Joanna (pseudonym). *See* Bly, Carol
Campbell, Joseph, **I:** 135; **IV:** 369, 370; **Supp. IX:** 245
Campbell, Lewis, **III:** 476
Campbell, Thomas, **II:** 8, 303, 314; **III:** 410; **Supp. I Part 1:** 309, 310
Campbell, Virginia, **Supp. XIII:** 114
"Campers Leaving: Summer 1981" (Kenyon), **Supp. VII:** 169
"Camp Evergreen" (Kenyon), **Supp. VII:** 168
"Camping in Madera Canyon" (Swenson), **Supp. IV Part 2:** 649
Campion, Thomas, **I:** 439; **Supp. VIII:** 272
Campo, Rafael, **Supp. XVII:** 112
Camus, Albert, **I:** 53, 61, 292, 294, 494; **II:** 57, 244; **III:** 292, 306, 453; **IV:** 6, 211, 236, 442, 487; **Retro. Supp. I:** 73; **Retro. Supp. II:** 20; **Supp. I Part 2:** 621; **Supp. VIII:** 11, 195, 241; **Supp. XI:** 96; **Supp. XIII:** 74, 165, 233, 247; **Supp. XVII:** 137
Camuto, Christopher, **Supp. V:** 212–213
Canada Fragrant with Resin, **Supp. XVI:** 149
"Canadian Mosaic, The" (Beran), **Supp. XIII:** 25
"Canadians and Pottawatomies" (Sandburg), **III:** 592–593
"Can a Good Wife Be a Good Sport?" (T. Williams), **IV:** 380
"Canal, The: A Poem on the Application of Physical Science to Political Economy" (Barlow), **Supp. II Part 1:** 73
Canary, Martha Jane. *See* Calamity Jane (Martha Jane Canary)
"Canary for One, A" (Hemingway), **Retro. Supp. I:** 170, 189
Canary in a Cat House (Vonnegut), **Supp. II Part 2:** 758
"Canary in Bloom" (Dove), **Supp. IV Part 1:** 248
Canby, Henry Seidel, **IV:** 65, 363
"Cancer" (McClatchy), **Supp. XII:** 266
"Cancer Match, The" (Dickey), **Supp. IV Part 1:** 182
"Cancíon y Glosa" (Merwin), **Supp. III Part 1:** 342
Candide (Hellman), **I:** 28; **Supp. I Part 1:** 288–289, 292
Candide (Voltaire), **Supp. I Part 1:** 288–289; **Supp. XI:** 297; **Supp. XVI:** 189
Candide (Voltaire; Wilbur, trans.), **Supp. III Part 2:** 560
Candle in the Cabin, The (Lindsay), **Supp. I Part 2:** 398, 400
"Candles" (Plath), **Retro. Supp. II:** 248, 257
Candles in Babylon (Levertov), **Supp. III Part 1:** 283
Candles in the Sun (T. Williams), **IV:** 381
Candles of Your Eyes, The (Purdy), **Supp. VII:** 278
Candy (Southern), **Supp. XI:** 297, **298–299,** 305
"Candy-Man Beechum" (Caldwell), **I:** 309
Cane (Toomer), **Supp. III Part 2:** 475, 481–486, 488; **Supp. IV Part 1:** 164, 168; **Supp. IX:** 305, 306, 307, **308–320**
"Cane in the Corridor, The" (Thurber), **Supp. I Part 2:** 616
Canfield, Cass, **Supp. I Part 2:** 668
Canfield, Dorothy, **Retro. Supp. I:** 4, 11, 14, 18. *See also* Fisher, Dorothy Canfield
Can Grande's Castle (Lowell), **II:** 518, 524
"Canicula di Anna" (Carson), **Supp. XII: 101–102**
"Canis Major" (Frost), **Retro. Supp. I:** 137
Cannery Row (Steinbeck), **IV:** 50, 51, 64–65, 66, 68
Cannibal Galaxy, The (Ozick), **Supp. V:** 270
Cannibals and Christians (Mailer), **III:** 38–39, 40, 42; **Retro. Supp. II:** 203, 204, 205
Canning, George, **I:** 7, 8
Canning, Richard, **Supp. X:** 147
Cannon, Jimmy, **II:** 424
Cannon, Steve, **Retro. Supp. II:** 111
Cannon between My Knees, A (Gunn Allen), **Supp. IV Part 1:** 324
Canolle, Jean, **Supp. XVI:** 194
"Canonization, The" (Donne), **Supp. XIV:** 8
"Can Poetry Matter?" (Gioia), **Supp. XV:** 113, 114
Can Poetry Matter?: Essays on Poetry and American Culture (Gioia), **Supp. XV:** 112, **113–115**
"Canso" (Merwin), **Supp. III Part 1:** 344
Can Such Things Be? (Bierce), **I:** 203, 204, 205, 209
Canterbury Tales (Chaucer), **II:** 504; **III:** 411; **IV:** 65
"Canto Amor" (Berryman), **I:** 173
Canto I (Pound), **III:** 469, 470; **Retro. Supp. I:** 286
Canto II (Pound), **III:** 470
Canto III (Pound), **III:** 470
Canto IV (Pound), **III:** 470
Canto VIII (Pound), **III:** 472
Canto IX (Pound), **III:** 472
Canto X (Pound), **III:** 472
Canto XIII (Pound), **III:** 472
Canto XXXIX (Pound), **III:** 468
Canto LXV (Pound), **Retro. Supp. I:** 292
Canto LXXXI (Pound), **III:** 459; **Retro. Supp. I:** 293
Cantor, Lois, **Supp. IV Part 1:** 285
Cantos (Pound), **I:** 482; **III:** 13–14, 17, 457, 462, 463, 466, 467, 469–470, 472–473, 474, 475, 476, 492; **Retro. Supp. I:** 284, 292, **292–293,** 293, 427; **Supp. I Part 1:** 272; **Supp. II Part 1:** 5; **Supp. II Part 2:** 420, 557, 564, 644; **Supp. IV Part 1:** 153; **Supp. V:** 343, 345; **Supp. VIII:** 305; **Supp. XIV:** 55, 96; **Supp. XV:** 349
"Cantus Planis" (Pound), **III:** 466
Cantwell, Robert, **Retro. Supp. I:** 85; **Supp. VIII:** 96; **Supp. XIII:** 292
"Can You Carry Me" (O'Hara), **III:** 369
Canzoneri, Robert, **IV:** 114, 116
Canzoni (Pound), **Retro. Supp. I:** 286, 288, 413
"Cap" (Shaw), **Supp. IV Part 1:** 345
"Cape Breton" (Bishop), **Supp. I Part 1:** 92; **Supp. IX:** 45
Cape Cod (Thoreau), **II:** 540
"Cape Cod, Rome, and Jerusalem" (Chapman), **Supp. XIV:** 55
Capitalism: The Unknown Ideal (Rand), **Supp. IV Part 2:** 518, 527, 531, 532
Caponi, Gena Dagel, **Supp. IV Part 1:** 95
Capote, Truman, **Supp. I Part 1:** 291, 292; **Supp. III Part 1: 111–133; Supp. III Part 2:** 574; **Supp. IV Part 1:** 198, 220; **Supp. VIII:** 105; **Supp. XII:** 43, 249; **Supp. XV:** 146; **Supp. XVI:** 245–246; **Supp. XVII:** 236
Capouya, Emile, **Supp. I Part 1:** 50

Cappetti, Carla, **Supp. IX:** 4, 8
Capra, Frank, **Supp. XVI:** 102
Capra, Fritjof, **Supp. X:** 261
Capron, Marion, **Supp. IX:** 193
"Capsule History of Conservation, A" (Stegner), **Supp. IV Part 2:** 600
"Captain Carpenter" (Ransom), **III:** 491
Captain Craig (Robinson), **III:** 508, 523; **Supp. II Part 1:** 192
"Captain Jim's Friend" (Harte), **Supp. II Part 1:** 337
"Captain Jones's Invitation" (Freneau), **Supp. II Part 1:** 261
"Captain's Son, The" (Taylor), **Supp. V:** 314, 325, 327
"Captain's Wife, The" (Salter), **Supp. IX:** 261
"Capt Christopher Levett (of York)" (Olson), **Supp. II Part 2:** 576, 577
Captive Israel (Reznikoff), **Supp. XIV:** 283
"Captivity and Restoration of Mrs. Mary Rowlandson, The" (Howe), **Supp. IV Part 2:** 419, 431, 434
"Captivity of the Fly" (MacLeish), **III:** 19
"Captured Goddess, The" (Lowell), **II:** 520
Caputi, Jane, **Supp. IV Part 1:** 334, 335
Caputo, Philip, **Supp. XI:** 234
Capuzzo, Michael, **Supp. XIII:** 254
Car (Crews), **Supp. XI: 110–111**
Carabi, Angels, **Supp. VIII:** 223; **Supp. XII:** 215
"Caramels" (Zinberg), **Supp. XV:** 195
"Caravaggio: Swirl & Vortex" (Levis), **Supp. XI:** 258, 269
Caravan (Bynner), **Supp. XV:** 50
Carby, Hazel B., **Supp. IV Part 1:** 13
"Carcassonne" (Faulkner), **Retro. Supp. I:** 81
Card, Antha E., **Supp. I Part 2:** 496
Cárdenas, Lupe, **Supp. IV Part 2:** 538, 539, 540
Cardinale, Anthony, **Supp. XVII:** 239
Cardinale, Ernesto, **Supp. XII:** 225
"Cardinal Ideograms" (Swenson), **Supp. IV Part 2:** 645
"Cards" (Beattie), **Supp. V:** 31
"Career Woman" (Hay), **Supp. XIV:** 131
Carefree (film, Sandrich), **Supp. XVII:** 59
"Careful" (Carver), **Supp. III Part 1:** 138
Careful and Strict Enquiry into the Modern Prevailing Notions of That Freedom of Will, Which Is Supposed to be Essential to Moral Agency, Vertue and Vice, Reward and Punishment, Praise and Blame, A (Edwards), **I:** 549, 557, 558, 562
Carel: A Poem and Pilgrimage in the Holy Land (Melville), **III:** 92–93
"Carentan O Carentan" (Simpson), **Supp. IX:** 267
Carew, Thomas, **IV:** 453
Carey, Gary, **Supp. XVI:** 186
Carey, Mathew, **Supp. XV:** 238
"Car Games" (Conroy), **Supp. XVI:** 72
Cargill, Oscar, **Supp. II Part 1:** 117
Caribbean as Columbus Saw It (Morison and Obregon), **Supp. I Part 2:** 488
"Caribou Kitchen" (A. Finch), **Supp. XVII:** 76–77
Caribou Rising: Defending the Porcupine Herd, Gwich-'in Culture, and the Arctic National Wildlife Refuge (Bass), **Supp. XVI:** 27–28, 28
Carl, K. A., **III:** 475
Carleton, George W., **Supp. XVIII:** 4
Carlisle, Harry, **Supp. XVIII:** 223, 233
Carl Krinken: His Christmas Stocking (S. and A. Warner), **Supp. XVIII:** 264
"Carlos Who Died, and Left Only This, The" (Ríos), **Supp. IV Part 2:** 547
Carlotta (empress of Mexico), **Supp. I Part 2:** 457
Carl Sandburg (Golden), **III:** 579
Carlson, Susan L., **Supp. XV:** 323
Carlyle, Thomas, **I:** 103, 279; **II:** 5, 7, 11, 15–16, 17, 20, 145, 315; **III:** 82, 84, 85, 87; **IV:** 169, 182, 338, 350; **Retro. Supp. I:** 360, 408; **Supp. I Part 1:** 2, 349; **Supp. I Part 2:** 410, 422, 482, 485, 552
"Carma" (Toomer), **Supp. III Part 2:** 481–483; **Supp. IX:** 312–313
"Carmen de Boheme" (Crane), **I:** 384
Carmen Jones (film), **Supp. I Part 1:** 66
Carmina Burana, **Supp. X:** 63
Carnegie, Andrew, **I:** 483; **IV:** 192; **Supp. I Part 2:** 639, 644; **Supp. V:** 285
Carnegie, Dale, **Supp. I Part 2:** 608
"Carnegie Hall: Rescued" (Moore), **III:** 215
Carne-Ross, D. S., **Supp. I Part 1:** 268, 269
Carnes, Mark C., **Supp. X:** 14
"Carnets" poems (Sobin), **Supp. XVI:** 286–287
Carnovsky, Morris, **III:** 154
"Carol for Carolyn, A" (A. Finch), **Supp. XVII:** 74, 75
Caroling Dusk: An Anthology of Verse by Negro Poets (Cullen), **Supp. IV Part 1:** 166, 169
"Carol of Occupations" (Whitman), **I:** 486
"Carolyn Kizer and the Chain of Women" (A. Finch), **Supp. XVII:** 74–75
Carolyn Kizer: Perspectives on Her Life and Work (A. Finch), **Supp. XVII: 74–75**
"Carpe Diem" (Frost), **Supp. XII:** 303
"Carpe Noctem, if You Can" (Thurber), **Supp. I Part 2:** 620
Carpenter, Dan, **Supp. V:** 250
Carpenter, David, **Supp. VIII:** 297
Carpenter, Frederic I., **II:** 20
Carpentered Hen and Other Tame Creatures, The (Updike), **IV:** 214; **Retro. Supp. I:** 320
Carpenter's Gothic (Gaddis), **Supp. IV Part 1:** 288, 289–291, 293, 294
Carr, Dennis W., **Supp. IV Part 2:** 560
Carr, Elias, **Supp. XIV:** 57
Carr, Rosemary. *See* Benét, Rosemary
Carrall, Aaron, **Supp. IV Part 2:** 499
Carrel, Alexis, **IV:** 240
"Carrell/Klee/and Cosmos's Groom" (Goldbarth), **Supp. XII:** 183
"Carriage from Sweden, A" (Moore), **III:** 212
Carrie (King), **Supp. V:** 137
Carried Away (Harrison), **Supp. VIII:** 39
Carrier of Ladders (Merwin), **Supp. III Part 1:** 339, 346, 350–352, 356, 357
"Carriers of the Dream Wheel" (Momaday), **Supp. IV Part 2:** 481
Carriers of the Dream Wheel: Contemporary Native American Poetry (Niatum, ed.), **Supp. IV Part 2:** 484, 505
Carrington, Carroll, **I:** 199
"Carrion Spring" (Stegner), **Supp. IV Part 2:** 604
Carroll, Charles, **Supp. I Part 2:** 525
Carroll, Lewis, **I:** 432; **II:** 431; **III:** 181; **Supp. I Part 1:** 44; **Supp. I Part 2:** 622, 656; **Supp. XVI:** 103
"Carrots, Noses, Snow, Rose, Roses" (Gass), **Supp. VI:** 87
Carrouges, Michel, **Supp. IV Part 1:** 104
"Carrousel, The" (Rilke), **III:** 558
Carruth, Hayden, **Supp. IV Part 1:** 66; **Supp. IX:** 291; **Supp. VIII:** 39; **Supp. XIII:** 112; **Supp. XIV:** 273–274; **Supp. XVI: 45–61**
Carruth, Joe-Anne McLaughlin, **Supp. XVI:** 47
"Carry" (Hogan), **Supp. IV Part 1:** 412
"Carrying On" (Dunn), **Supp. XI:** 145
Cars of Cuba (García), **Supp. XI:** 190
Carson, Anne, **Supp. XII: 97–116; Supp. XV:** 252
Carson, Johnny, **Supp. IV Part 2:** 526
Carson, Rachel, **Supp. IX: 19–36; Supp. V:** 202; **Supp. X:** 99; **Supp. XVI:** 36
Carson, Tom, **Supp. XI:** 227
Cart, Michael, **Supp. X:** 12
Carter, Elliott, **Supp. III Part 1:** 21
Carter, Hodding, **Supp. XIV:** 2
Carter, Jared, **Supp. XVII:** 110
Carter, Jimmy, **Supp. I Part 2:** 638; **Supp. XIV:** 107
Carter, Marcia, **Supp. V:** 223
Carter, Mary, **Supp. IV Part 2:** 444
Carter, Peter, **Supp. XVIII:** 267
Carter, Stephen, **Supp. XI:** 220
Cartesian Sonata and Other Novellas (Gass), **Supp. VI: 92–93**
Cartier, Jacques, **Supp. I Part 2:** 496, 497
Cartier-Bresson, Henri, **Supp. VIII:** 98
"Cartographies of Silence" (Rich), **Supp. I Part 2:** 571–572
Cartwright, Louis, **Supp. XIV:** 147, 149, 151
Carver, Raymond, **Supp. III Part 1: 135–151; Supp. IV Part 1:** 342; **Supp. V:** 22, 23, 220, 326; **Supp. VIII:** 15; **Supp. X:** 85, 167; **Supp. XI:** 26, 65, 116, 153; **Supp. XII:** 79, 139, 289, 294
Carver: A Life in Poems (Nelson), **Supp. XVIII:** 171, 172, **181–182,** 183
Cary, Alice, **Retro. Supp. II:** 145; **Supp. XV:** 273
Cary, Phoebe, **Supp. XV:** 273
Cary, Richard, **Retro. Supp. II:** 132, 137

"Casabianca" (Bishop), **Retro. Supp. II:** 42; **Supp. I Part 1:** 86
Casablanca (film), **Supp. VIII:** 61; **Supp. XV:** 14
Casanova: His Known and Unknown Life (Endore), **Supp. XVII:** 54
Case of Rape, A (C. Himes), **Supp. XVI:** 143
Case of the Crushed Petunias, The (T. Williams), **IV:** 381
Case of the Officers of Excise (Paine), **Supp. I Part 2:** 503–504
Casey, John, **Supp. X:** 164
Cash, Arthur, **Supp. IV Part 1:** 299
Cashman, Nellie, **Supp. X:** 103
Casiero, Robert, **Supp. XIV:** 167
Casino Royale (film), **Supp. XI: 306–307**
Caskey, William, **Supp. XIV:** 166
"Cask of Amontillado, The" (Poe), **II:** 475; **III:** 413; **Retro. Supp. II:** 268, 269, 270, 273
Caso, Frank, **Supp. XVIII:** 95
Casper, Robert N., **Supp. XV:** 339, 347
Casper and His Friends (S. and A. Warner), **Supp. XVIII:** 264
Cassada (Salter), **Supp. IX: 251–252**
Cassady, Carolyn, **Supp. XIV:** 150
Cassady, Neal, **Supp. II Part 1:** 309, 311; **Supp. XIV:** 137, 144
"Cassandra Southwick" (Whittier), **Supp. I Part 2:** 693
Cassell, Verlin, **Supp. XI:** 315
Cassill, Ronald Verlin, **Supp. XVIII:** 72
Cassill, R. V., **Supp. V:** 323
Cassirer, Ernst, **I:** 265; **IV:** 87, 89
Cass Timberlane (Lewis), **II:** 455–456
Cast a Cold Eye (McCarthy), **II:** 566
Castaway (Cozzens), **I:** 363, 370, 374, 375, 379
"Caste in America" (Du Bois), **Supp. II Part 1:** 169
Castiglione, Baldassare, **I:** 279; **III:** 282
"Castilian" (Wylie), **Supp. I Part 2:** 714
Castillo, Ana, **Supp. XI:** 177
"Castle in Lynn, A" (McCarriston), **Supp. XIV:** 265, 268
"Castles and Distances" (Wilbur), **Supp. III Part 2:** 550
Castle Sinister (Marquand), **III:** 58
Cast of Thousands (Loos), **Supp. XVI:** 192, 193, 195
Castro, Fidel, **II:** 261, 434
Cast the First Stone (C. Himes), **Supp. XVI:** 135, 137–138
"Casual Incident, A" (Hemingway), **II:** 44
"Cat, The" (Matthews), **Supp. IX: 157–158**
Cat, You Better Come Home (Keillor), **Supp. XVI:** 177
"Catbird Seat, The" (Thurber), **Supp. I Part 2:** 623
"Catch" (Francis), **Supp. IX:** 82
Catch-22 (Heller), **III:** 558; **Supp. IV Part 1:** 379, 380, 381–382, 383, 384–386, 387, 390, 391, 392, 393, 394; **Supp. V:** 244, 248; **Supp. XII:** 167–168
Catcher in the Rye, The (Salinger), **I:** 493; **III:** 551, 552, 553–558, 567, 571; **Retro. Supp. I:** 102; **Retro. Supp. II:** 222, 249; **Supp. I Part 2:** 535; **Supp. V:** 119; **Supp. VIII:** 242; **Supp. XI:** 65; **Supp. XVII:** 2
"Catching Frogs" (Kenyon), **Supp. VII:** 170
Catching the Mermother (A. Finch), **Supp. XVII:** 72
catechism of d neoamerican hoodoo church (Reed), **Supp. X:** 240, 241
Catered Affair, The (film), **Supp. IV Part 2:** 683
"Cathay" (Goldbarth), **Supp. XII:** 185, 186
Cathay (Pound), **II:** 527; **Retro. Supp. I:** 289
"Cathedral" (Carver), **Supp. III Part 1:** 144–145
Cathedral (Carver), **Supp. III Part 1:** 144–146; **Supp. XII:** 139
Cathedral, The (Lowell), **Supp. I Part 2:** 407, 416–417
Cather, Willa, **I: 312–334,** 405; **II:** 51, 96, 177, 404, 412; **III:** 453; **IV:** 190; **Retro. Supp. I: 1–23,** 355, 382; **Retro. Supp. II:** 71, 136; **Supp. I Part 2:** 609, 719; **Supp. IV Part 1:** 31; **Supp. VIII:** 101, 102, 263; **Supp. X:** 103; **Supp. XIII:** 253; **Supp. XIV:** 112; **Supp. XV:** 40, 51; **Supp. XVI:** 226; **Supp. XVIII:** 207
Catherine, Saint, **II:** 211
Catherine II, **Supp. I Part 2:** 433
Catholic Art and Culture (Watkin), **Retro. Supp. II:** 187
"Catholic Novelist in the Protestant South, The" (O'Connor), **Retro. Supp. II:** 223, 224
"Cathy Queen of Cats" (Cisneros), **Supp. VII:** 59
Cat Inside, The (Burroughs), **Supp. III Part 1:** 105
Cat in the Hat, The (Geisel), **Supp. XVI:** 106–107, 112
Cat in the Hat Come Back, The (Geisel), **Supp. XVI:** 107
"Cat in the Hat for President, The" (Coover), **Supp. V:** 44, 46–47
Cat in The Hat Songbook, The (Geisel), **Supp. XVI:** 104
Cato, **II:** 114, 117
Cat on a Hot Tin Roof (T. Williams), **II:** 190; **IV:** 380, 382, 383, 386, 387, 389, 390, 391, 394, 395, 397–398
"Cat People: What Dr. Seuss Really Taught Us" (Menand), **Supp. XVI:** 106
Cat's Cradle (Vonnegut), **Supp. II Part 2:** 758, 759, 767–768, 770, 771, 772; **Supp. V:** 1
Cat's Eye (Atwood), **Supp. XIII: 29–30**
"Cat's Meow, A" (Brodsky), **Supp. VIII:** 31
Cat's Quizzer, The (Geisel), **Supp. XVI:** 111
"Catterskill Falls" (Bryant), **Supp. I Part 1:** 160
"Cattle Car Complex" (T. Rosenbaum), **Supp. XVII:** 48
Catullus, **Supp. XII:** 2, 13, **112; Supp. XV:** 23, 27, 35, 36
Catullus (Gai Catulli Veronensis Liber) (Zukofsky), **Supp. III Part 2:** 625, 627, 628, 629
Catullus, Gaius Valerius, **I:** 381; **Supp. I Part 1:** 261; **Supp. I Part 2:** 728
"Catullus: *Carmina*" (Carson), **Supp. XII: 112**
"Catullus: Excrucior" (Bidart), **Supp. XV:** 32, 35
"Cat Walked Through the Casserole, The" (Nelson and Espeland), **Supp. XVIII: 181**
Cat Walked Through the Casserole and Other Poems for Children (Nelson and Espeland), **Supp. XVIII:** 181
"Cat Who Aspired to Higher Things, The" (X. J. Kennedy), **Supp. XV:** 163
Caudwell, Christopher, **Supp. X:** 112
"Caul, The" (Banks), **Supp. V:** 10–11
Cause for Wonder (Morris), **III:** 232–233
"Causerie" (Tate), **IV:** 129
Causes and Consequences (Chapman), **Supp. XIV:** 41, 49, 51
"Causes of American Discontents before 1768, The" (Franklin), **II:** 120
Causley, Charles, **Supp. XV:** 117
Cavafy, Constantine P., **Supp. IX:** 275; **Supp. XI:** 119, 123
Cavalcade of America, The (radio program), **III:** 146
Cavalcanti (Pound, opera), **Retro. Supp. I:** 287
Cavalcanti, Guido, **I:** 579; **III:** 467; **Supp. III Part 2:** 620, 621, 622, 623
Cavalieri, Grace, **Supp. IV Part 2:** 630, 631
"Cavalry Crossing the Ford" (Whitman), **IV:** 347
"Cave, The" (Bass), **Supp. XVI:** 23
Cave, The (Warren), **IV:** 255–256
Cavell, Stanley, **Retro. Supp. I:** 306–307, 309
Cavender's House (Robinson), **III:** 510
Caviare at the Funeral (Simpson), **Supp. IX:** 266, **276–277**
"Cawdor" (Jeffers), **Supp. II Part 2:** 431
Caxton, William, **III:** 486
Cayton, Horace, **IV:** 475, 488
Cazamian, Louis, **II:** 529
Celan, Paul, **Supp. X:** 149; **Supp. XII:** 21, 110–111; **Supp. XVI:** 284–285, 288; **Supp. XVII:** 241
"Celebrated Jumping Frog of Calaveras County, The" (Twain), **IV:** 196
Celebrated Jumping Frog of Calaveras County, The, and Other Sketches (Twain), **IV:** 197
Celebration (Crews), **Supp. XI:** 103, **108**
Celebration at Dark (W. J. Smith), **Supp. XIII:** 332
"Celebration for June 24th" (McGrath), **Supp. X:** 116
Celebration of the Sound Through (Sobin), **Supp. XVI:** 284–285

Celebrations after the Death of John Brennan (X. J. Kennedy), **Supp. XV:** 165
Celebrity (film; Allen), **Supp. XV:** 11
"Celery" (Stein), **IV:** 43
"Celestial Games" (Conroy), **Supp. XVI:** 72
"Celestial Globe" (Nemerov), **III:** 288
Celestial Navigation (Tyler), **Supp. IV Part 2:** 662–663, 671
"Celestial Railroad, The" (Hawthorne), **Retro. Supp. I:** 152; **Supp. I Part 1:** 188
Celibate Season, A (Shields), **Supp. VII:** 323, 324
Cellini (Shanley), **Supp. XIV:** 316, **329–330**
"Cemetery at Academy, California" (Levine), **Supp. V:** 182
Cemetery Nights (Dobyns), **Supp. XIII:** 85, 87, 89
"Censors As Critics: *To Kill a Mockingbird* As a Case Study" (May), **Supp. VIII:** 126
"Census-Taker, The" (Frost), **Retro. Supp. I:** 129
"Centaur, The" (Swenson), **Supp. IV Part 2:** 641
Centaur, The (Updike), **IV:** 214, 216, 217, 218, 219–221, 222; **Retro. Supp. I:** 318, 322, 324, 331, 336
"Centennial Meditation of Columbia, The" (Lanier), **Supp. I Part 1:** 362
Centeno, Agusto, **IV:** 375
"Centipede" (Dove), **Supp. IV Part 1:** 246
"Central Man, The" (Bloom), **Supp. IV Part 2:** 689
"Central Park" (Lowell), **II:** 552
Central Park (Wasserstein and Drattel), **Supp. XV:** 333
Central Park West (Allen), **Supp. XV:** 13
Century of Dishonor, A (Jackson), **Retro. Supp. I:** 31
"Cerebral Snapshot, The" (Theroux), **Supp. VIII:** 313
"Ceremonies" (Rukeyser), **Supp. VI:** 279
Ceremony (Silko), **Supp. IV Part 1:** 274, 333; **Supp. IV Part 2:** 557–558, 558–559, 559, 561–566, 570; **Supp. XVIII:** 59
Ceremony (Wilbur), **Supp. III Part 2:** 550–551
"Ceremony, The" (Harjo), **Supp. XII:** 230
"Ceremony, The——Anatomy of a Massacre" (E. Hoffman, play), **Supp. XVI:** 160
Ceremony in Lone Tree (Morris), **III:** 229–230, 232, 238, 558
Ceremony of Brotherhood, A (Anaya and Ortiz, eds.), **Supp. IV Part 2:** 502
Cerf, Bennett, **III:** 405; **IV:** 288; **Retro. Supp. II:** 330; **Supp. XIII:** 172
"Certain Attention to the World, A" (Haines), **Supp. XII:** 201
Certain Distance, A (Francis), **Supp. IX:** 85
"Certain Music, A" (Rukeyser), **Supp. VI:** 273
Certain Noble Plays of Japan (Pound), **III:** 458
Certain People (Wharton), **Retro. Supp. I:** 382
"Certain Poets" (MacLeish), **III:** 4
"Certain Testimony" (Bausch), **Supp. VII:** 48
Certificate, The (Singer), **IV:** 1; **Retro. Supp. II: 314–315**
"Cerulean" (Everett), **Supp. XVIII:** 66
Cervantes, Lorna Dee, **Supp. IV Part 2:** 545
Cervantes, Miguel de, **I:** 130, 134; **II:** 8, 272, 273, 276, 289, 302, 310, 315; **III:** 113, 614; **IV:** 367; **Retro. Supp. I:** 91; **Supp. I Part 2:** 406; **Supp. V:** 277; **Supp. XIII:** 17
Césaire, Aimé, **Supp. X:** 132, 139; **Supp. XIII:** 114
"Cesarean" (Kenyon), **Supp. VII:** 173
Cézanne, Paul, **II:** 576; **III:** 210; **IV:** 26, 31, 407; **Supp. V:** 333, 341–342
Chabon, Michael, **Supp. XI: 63–81; Supp. XVI:** 259
Chaboseau, Jean, **Supp. I Part 1:** 260
Chaikin, Joseph, **Supp. III Part 2:** 433, 436–437
"Chain, The" (Kumin), **Supp. IV Part 2:** 452
Chainbearer, The (Cooper), **I:** 351, 352–353
"Chain of Love, A" (Price), **Supp. VI: 258–259,** 260
Chains of Dew (Glaspell), **Supp. III Part 1:** 181
Challacombe, Robert Hamilton, **III:** 176
"Challenge" (Untermeyer), **Supp. XV:** 296
Challenge (Untermeyer), **Supp. XV:** 296, 303
Chalmers, George, **Supp. I Part 2:** 514, 521
"Chambered Nautilus, The" (Holmes), **Supp. I Part 1:** 254, 307, 312–313, 314
Chamberlain, John, **Supp. I Part 2:** 647; **Supp. IV Part 2:** 525
Chamberlain, Neville, **II:** 589; **Supp. I Part 2:** 664
Chamber Music (Joyce), **III:** 16
Chambers, Richard, **Supp. III Part 2:** 610, 611, 612
Chambers, Whittaker, **Supp. III Part 2:** 610; **Supp. IV Part 2:** 526; **Supp. XV:** 143
Chameleon (C. Baxter), **Supp. XVII:** 14–15
"Champ, The" (Zinberg), **Supp. XV:** 193
"Champagne Regions" (Ríos), **Supp. IV Part 2:** 553
"Champion" (Lardner), **II:** 420–421, 428, 430
Champion, Laurie, **Supp. VIII:** 128
Champollion-Figeac, Jean Jacques, **IV:** 426
"Chance" (Doolittle), **Supp. I Part 1:** 271
Chance, Frank, **II:** 418
Chance Acquaintance, A (Howells), **II:** 278
"Chanclas" (Cisneros), **Supp. VII:** 61
Chandler, Raymond, **Supp. III Part 1:** 91; **Supp. IV Part 1: 119–138,** 341, 344, 345; **Supp. IV Part 2:** 461, 464, 469, 470, 471, 472, 473; **Supp. XI:** 160, 228; **Supp. XII:** 307; **Supp. XIII:** 159, 233; **Supp. XIV:** 21; **Supp. XV:** 119; **Supp. XVI:** 122; **Supp. XVII:** 137; **Supp. XVIII:** 136,137, 137–138
Chaney, "Professor" W. H., **II:** 463–464
Chang, Leslie C., **Supp. IV Part 1:** 72
"Change, The: Kyoto-Tokyo Express" (Ginsberg), **Supp. II Part 1:** 313, 329
Changed Man, A (Prose), **Supp. XVI:** 261–262
Changeling (Middleton), **Retro. Supp. I:** 62
"Changeling, The" (Lowell), **Supp. I Part 2:** 409
"Changeling, The" (Whittier), **Supp. I Part 2:** 697
Change of World, A (Rich), **Supp. I Part 2:** 551, 552
"Changes of Mind" (Baker), **Supp. XIII:** 52
"Change the Joke and Slip the Yoke" (Ellison), **Retro. Supp. II:** 118
Changing Light at Sandover, The (Merrill), **Supp. III Part 1:** 318, 319, 323, 327, 332, 335–336; **Supp. XII:** 269–270; **Supp. XV:** 264
"Changing Same, The" (Baraka), **Supp. II Part 1:** 47, 51, 53
Changing the Bully Who Rules the World: Reading and Thinking about Ethics (C. Bly), **Supp. XVI:** 32, **39–40,** 41
Chanler, Mrs. Winthrop, **I:** 22; **IV:** 325
Channing, Carol, **IV:** 357
Channing, Edward, **Supp. I Part 2:** 479–480
Channing, Edward Tyrrel, **Supp. I Part 1:** 155; **Supp. I Part 2:** 422
Channing, William Ellery, **I:** 336; **II:** 224, 495; **IV:** 172, 173, 176, 177; **Retro. Supp. I:** 54; **Supp. I Part 1:** 103; **Supp. I Part 2:** 589
Channing, William Henry, **IV:** 178; **Supp. II Part 1:** 280, 285
Chanson de Roland, La, **I:** 13
"Chanson un Peu Naïve" (Bogan), **Supp. III Part 1:** 50–51
"Chanteuse" (Doty), **Supp. XI:** 119
"Chant for May Day" (Hughes), **Supp. I Part 1:** 331
Chants (Mora), **Supp. XIII: 214–215**
Chaos (Dove), **Supp. IV Part 1:** 243
"Chaperone, The" (Van Vechten), **Supp. II Part 2:** 728
Chaplin, Charles Spencer, **I:** 27, 32, 43, 386, 447; **III:** 403; **Supp. I Part 2:** 607; **Supp. IV Part 1:** 146; **Supp. IV Part 2:** 574
"Chaplinesque" (H. Crane), **Retro. Supp. II:** 79
"Chapman" (Rukeyser), **Supp. VI:** 273
Chapman, Abraham, **IV:** 485
Chapman, George, **Supp. I Part 2:** 422
Chapman, John (Johnny Appleseed), **Supp. I Part 2:** 397

Chapman, John Jay, **IV:** 436; **Supp. XIV: 39–56**
Chapman, Stephen, **Supp. XIII:** 12
Chappell, Fred, **Supp. IV Part 1:** 69; **Supp. XI:** 317; **Supp. XVIII:** 87
Chapters in a Mythology: The Poetry of Sylvia Plath (Kroll), **Supp. I Part 2:** 541–543
Chapters on Erie (Adams and Adams), **Supp. I Part 2:** 644
Chapter Two (Simon), **Supp. IV Part 2:** 575, 586
"Chapter VI" (Hemingway), **II:** 252
Char, René, **Supp. XVI:** 282; **Supp. XVII:** 244
"Character" (Emerson), **II:** 6
"Character of Presidents, The" (Doctorow), **Supp. IV Part 1:** 224
"Character of Socrates, The" (Emerson), **II:** 8–9
Character of the Poet, The (Simpson), **Supp. IX:** 273, 275, 278
"Characters in Fiction" (McCarthy), **II:** 562
"Charades" (Moore), **Supp. X:** 178
"Charge It" (Fante), **Supp. XI:** 164–165
Charlatan, The (Singer), **IV:** 1
"Charles" (Jackson), **Supp. IX:** 125
Charles, Larry, **Supp. XVIII:** 21
"Charles Baxter, August Kleinzahler, Adrienne Rich: Contemporary Stevensians and the Problem of 'Other Lives'" (S. Burt), **Supp. XVII:** 18–19
Charles Goodnight: Cowman and Plainsman (Haley), **Supp. V:** 226
Charles Simic: Essays on the Poetry (Weigl), **Supp. VIII:** 269
Charles the Bold, Duke of Burgundy, **III:** 487
Charleville, Victoria Verdon, **Supp. I Part 1:** 200–201, 205, 206, 210
Charley's Aunt (B. Thomas), **II:** 138
Charlie Chan Is Dead: An Anthology of Contemporary Asian American Fiction (Hagedorn), **Supp. X:** 292
"Charlie Christian Story, The" (Ellison), **Retro. Supp. II:** 121
"Charlie Howard's Descent" (Doty), **Supp. XI:** 122
Charlotte: A Tale of Truth (Rowson), **Supp. I Part 1:** 128; **Supp. XV: 234–235,** 238. *See also Charlotte Temple* (Rowson)
Charlotte's Daughter; or, The Three Orphans (Rowson), **Supp. XV: 246**
Charlotte's Web (White), **Supp. I Part 2:** 655, 656, 658, 667, 670
Charlotte Temple (Rowson), **Supp. XV:** 229, **238–239**. *See also Charlotte: A Tale of Truth* (Rowson)
Charm, The (Creeley), **Supp. IV Part 1:** 139, 141, 144, 149–150
Charmed Life, A (McCarthy), **II:** 571–574
Charming Billy (McDermott), **Supp. XVIII:** 155, **162–164,** 166
Charms for the Easy Life (Gibbons), **Supp. X:** 45, **47–48**
Charnel Rose, The (Aiken), **I:** 50, 57, 62
Charon's Cosmology (Simic), **Supp. VIII: 276–278**
Charterhouse, The (Percy), **Supp. III Part 1:** 388
Charvat, William, **II:** 244
Charyn, Jerome, **Supp. XVII:** 5
Chase, Mary Ellen, **Retro. Supp. II:** 243, 245
Chase, Richard, **IV:** 202, 443; **Retro. Supp. I:** 40, 395
Chase, Salmon P., **Supp. I Part 2:** 584
Chase, Stuart, **Supp. I Part 2:** 609
Chase, The (Foote), **Supp. I Part 1:** 281
"Chaste Land, The" (Tate), **IV:** 122
Château, The (Maxwell), **Supp. VIII:** 152, 160, **165–167,** 168, 169
Chatham, Russell, **Supp. VIII:** 40
Chatterdon, The Black Death, and Meriwether Lewis (Reznikoff), **Supp. XIV:** 288
Chatterton, Thomas, **Supp. I Part 1:** 349; **Supp. I Part 2:** 410, 716
Chatterton, Wayne, **Supp. IX:** 2, 4, 11–12
Chatwin, Bruce, **Supp. VIII:** 322
Chaucer, Geoffrey, **I:** 131; **II:** 11, 504, 516, 542, 543; **III:** 283, 411, 473, 492, 521; **Retro. Supp. I:** 135, 426; **Supp. I Part 1:** 356, 363; **Supp. I Part 2:** 422, 617; **Supp. V:** 259; **Supp. XII:** 197; **Supp. XVII:** 70
Chauncy, Charles, **I:** 546–547; **IV:** 147
Chavez, César, **Supp. V:** 199
Chávez, Denise, **Supp. IV Part 2:** 544; **Supp. XI:** 316
Chavez, Lydia, **Supp. VIII:** 75
Chavkin, Allan, **Supp. IV Part 1:** 259
Chavkin, Nancy Feyl, **Supp. IV Part 1:** 259
Chayefsky, Paddy, **Supp. XI:** 306
Cheang, Shu Lea, **Supp. XI:** 20
"Cheat Takes Over" (Leopold), **Supp. XIV:** 189
"Cheers" (Carver), **Supp. III Part 1:** 138
Cheetham, James, **Supp. I Part 2:** 521
Cheever, Benjamin Hale, **Supp. I Part 1:** 175
Cheever, David W., **Supp. I Part 1:** 304
Cheever, Ezekiel, **Supp. I Part 1:** 174, 193
Cheever, Federico, **Supp. I Part 1:** 175
Cheever, Fred, **Supp. I Part 1:** 174
Cheever, Frederick L., **Supp. I Part 1:** 174
Cheever, John, **Retro. Supp. I:** 116, 333, 335; **Supp. I Part 1: 174–199; Supp. IX:** 114, 208; **Supp. V:** 23, 95; **Supp. VIII:** 151; **Supp. XI:** 65, 66, 99; **Supp. XII:** 140; **Supp. XIV:** 93; **Supp. XV:** 119, 142
Cheever, Mary Liley, **Supp. I Part 1:** 174
Cheever, Mrs. John (Mary Winternitz), **Supp. I Part 1:** 175
Cheever, Susan. *See* Cowley, Susan Cheever (Susan Cheever)
Cheever Evening, A (Gurney), **Supp. V:** 95
Chekhov, Anton, **I:** 52, 90; **II:** 27, 38, 44, 49, 198, 542; **III:** 362, 467; **IV:** 17, 53, 359, 446; **Retro. Supp. I:** 5, 355; **Retro. Supp. II:** 299; **Supp. I Part 1:** 196; **Supp. II Part 1:** 6; **Supp. IV Part 2:** 585; **Supp. IX:** 260, 265, 274; **Supp. V:** 265; **Supp. VIII:** 153, 332; **Supp. XI:** 66; **Supp. XII:** 94, 307; **Supp. XIII:** 79; **Supp. XIV:** 87, 242; **Supp. XV:** 320, 329; **Supp. XVIII:** 102
"Chekhov's Sense of Writing as Seen Through His Letters" (Dobyns), **Supp. XIII:** 77–78
"Chemin de Fer" (Bishop), **Retro. Supp. II:** 41; **Supp. I Part 1:** 80, 85, 86
Cheney, Brainard, **Retro. Supp. II:** 229
Chenzira, Ayoka, **Supp. XI:** 19
Chéri (Colette; stage adaptation, Loos), **Supp. XVI:** 194
Cherkovski, Neeli, **Supp. XII:** 118, 132, 134
Chernyshevski, Nikolai, **III:** 261, 262, 263; **Retro. Supp. I:** 269
Cherokee Lottery, The: A Sequence of Poems (W. J. Smith), **Supp. XIII: 340–344**
Cherry (Karr), **Supp. XI:** 239, **251–254**
"Cherrylog Road" (Dickey), **Supp. XVIII:** 191
Cherry Orchard, The (Chekhov), **IV:** 359, 426; **Supp. VIII:** 153
Cheslock, Louis, **III:** 99, 118, 119
Chesnutt, Charles Waddell, **Supp. II Part 1:** 174, 193, 211; **Supp. IV Part 1:** 257; **Supp. XIV: 57–78**
"Chess House, The" (Dixon), **Supp. XII:** 139
Chessman, Caryl, **Supp. I Part 2:** 446
Chester, Alfred, **Retro. Supp. II:** 111, 112; **Supp. X:** 192
Chesterfield, Lord, **II:** 36
Chesterton, Gilbert Keith, **I:** 226; **IV:** 432
Cheuse, Alan, **Supp. IV Part 2:** 570
Chevigny, Bell Gale, **Supp. XI:** 283
"Chicago" (Sandburg), **III:** 581, 592, 596; **Supp. III Part 1:** 71
Chicago (Shepard), **Supp. III Part 2:** 439
Chicago: City on the Make (Algren), **Supp. IX:** 1, 3
"*Chicago Defender* Sends a Man to Little Rock, The" (Brooks), **Supp. III Part 1:** 80–81
"Chicago Hamlet, A" (Anderson), **I:** 112
Chicago Loop (Theroux), **Supp. VIII:** 324
"Chicago Picasso, The" (Brooks), **Supp. III Part 1:** 70–71, 84
Chicago Poems (Sandburg), **III:** 579, 581–583, 586
"Chicano/Borderlands Literature and Poetry" (Ríos), **Supp. IV Part 2:** 537, 538, 542, 545
Chick, Nancy, **Supp. IV Part 1:** 1
"Chickamauga" (Bierce), **I:** 201
"Chickamauga" (Wolfe), **IV:** 460
"Chickamauga" (Wright), **Supp. V:** 334
Chickamauga (Wright), **Supp. V:** 333, 343–344
"Chiefly about War Matters" (Hawthorne), **II:** 227; **Retro. Supp. I:** 165
"Child" (Plath), **Supp. I Part 2:** 544

Child, Greg, **Supp. XVIII:** 107
Child, Julia, **Supp. XVII:** 89, 90
Child, Lydia Maria, **Supp. XIII:** 141; **Supp. XVIII:** 11
"Child, The" (Ríos), **Supp. IV Part 2:** 543
"Child by Tiger, The" (Wolfe), **IV:** 451
"Childhood" (Wright), **Supp. V:** 341
Childhood, A: The Biography of a Place (Crews), **Supp. XI:** 102–103, 245
"Childhood, When You Are in It ..." (Kenyon), **Supp. VII:** 160, 170
"Childhood Sketch" (Wright), **Supp. III Part 2:** 589
"Child Is Born, A" (Benét), **Supp. XI:** 46
"Child Is the Meaning of This Life, The" (Schwartz), **Supp. II Part 2:** 659–660
"Childlessness" (Merrill), **Supp. III Part 1:** 323
"Childless Woman" (Plath), **Supp. I Part 2:** 544
Child-Life (Whittier and Larcom, eds.), **Supp. XIII:** 142
Child-Life in Prose (Whittier and Larcom, eds.), **Supp. XIII:** 142
Childlike Life of the Black Tarantula, The (Acker), **Supp. XII:** 4, 6, **7–8**
"Child Margaret" (Sandburg), **III:** 584
"Child of Courts, The" (Jarrell), **II:** 378, 379, 381
Child of God (McCarthy), **Supp. VIII: 177–178**
Child of My Heart (McDermott), **Supp. XVIII:** 155, **164–166**
"CHILD OF THE THIRTIES" (Baraka), **Supp. II Part 1:** 60
"Child on Top of a Greenhouse" (Roethke), **III:** 531
Children (Gurney), **Supp. V:** 95, 96
"Children" (Stowe), **Supp. I Part 2:** 587
"Children, The" (Jarman), **Supp. XVII:** 116
Children, The (Wharton), **IV:** 321, 326; **Retro. Supp. I:** 381
"Children, the Sandbar, That Summer" (Rukeyser), **Supp. VI:** 274
Children and Others (Cozzens), **I:** 374
Children Is All (Purdy), **Supp. VII:** 277, 278, 282
"Children of Adam" (Whitman), **IV:** 342; **Retro. Supp. I:** 403, 405
Children of Job, The: American Second-Generation Witnesses to the Holocaust (A. Berger), **Supp. XVII:** 39
Children of Light (Stone), **Supp. V:** 304–306
Children of Light and the Children of Darkness, The (Niebuhr), **III:** 292, 306, 310
Children of the Frost (London), **II:** 469, 483
Children of the Holocaust (H. Epstein), **Supp. XVII:** 48
"Children of the Lord's Supper, The" (Tegnér), **Retro. Supp. II:** 155, 157
Children of the Market Place (Masters), **Supp. I Part 2:** 471
"Children on Their Birthdays" (Capote), **Supp. III Part 1:** 114, 115
"Children Selecting Books in a Library" (Jarrell), **II:** 371
Children's Hour, The (Hellman), **Supp. I Part 1:** 276–277, 281, 286, 297
"Children's Rhymes" (Hughes), **Supp. I Part 1:** 340
Childress, Mark, **Supp. X:** 89
Child's Garden of Verses, A (Stevenson), **Supp. IV Part 1:** 298, 314; **Supp. XIII:** 75
"Child's Nature, A" (Jin), **Supp. XVIII:** 93
"Child's Reminiscence, A" (Whitman), **IV:** 344
Childwold (Oates), **Supp. II Part 2:** 519–520
Chill, The (Macdonald), **Supp. IV Part 2:** 473
Chills and Fever (Ransom), **III:** 490, 491–492, 493
Chilly Scenes of Winter (Beattie), **Supp. V:** 21, 22, 23, 24, 26, 27
Chime of Words, A: The Letters of Logan Pearsall Smith (Tribble, ed.), **Supp. XIV:** 348–349
Chimera (C. Frost), **Supp. XV:** 94, 95, 100
"Chimes for Yahya" (Merrill), **Supp. III Part 1:** 329
Chin, Frank, **Supp. V:** 164, 172
Chin, Mei, **Supp. XVIII:** 95
"China" (Johnson), **Supp. VI: 193–194**
"Chinaman's Hat" (Kingston), **Supp. V:** 169
China Men (Kingston), **Supp. V:** 157, 158, 159, 160, 161, 164–169; **Supp. X:** 292; **Supp. XV:** 220
China Trace (Wright), **Supp. V:** 332, 340, 341, 342
Chinese Classics (Legge), **III:** 472
Chinese Materia Medica (P. Smith), **III:** 572
"Chinese Nightingale, The" (Lindsay), **Supp. I Part 2:** 392–393, 394
Chinese Nightingale and Other Poems, The (Lindsay), **Supp. I Part 2:** 392
Chinese Siamese Cat, The (Tan), **Supp. X:** 289
Chinese Translations, The (Bynner), **Supp. XV:** 47, 52
Chinitz, David, **Supp. XV:** 180, 185
"Chinoiseries" (Lowell), **II:** 524–525
Chip (Untermeyer), **Supp. XV:** 310
Chirico, Giorgio de, **Supp. III Part 1:** 14
Chirico, Miriam M., **Supp. XV:** 323
"Chiron" (Winters), **Supp. II Part 2:** 801
"Chloroform Jags" (J. Scott), **Supp. XVII:** 189
Chodorov, Jerome, **IV:** 274
"Choice, The" (Karr), **Supp. XI:** 251
"Choice of Profession, A" (Malamud), **Supp. I Part 2:** 437
Chomei, Kamo No, **IV:** 170, 171, 184
Chomsky, Noam, **Supp. IV Part 2:** 679
Choosing not Choosing (Cameron), **Retro. Supp. I:** 43
Chopin, Felix, **Supp. I Part 1:** 202
Chopin, Frédéric, **Supp. I Part 1:** 363
Chopin, Jean, **Supp. I Part 1:** 206
Chopin, Kate, **II:** 276; **Retro. Supp. I:** 10, 215; **Retro. Supp. II: 57–74; Supp. I Part 1: 200–226; Supp. V:** 304; **Supp. X:** 227; **Supp. XVIII:** 194
"Choral: The Pink Church" (W. C. Williams), **Retro. Supp. I:** 428
"Chord" (Merwin), **Supp. III Part 1:** 356
"Chords and Dischords" (column; Untermeyer), **Supp. XV:** 294
Choruses from Iphigenia in Aulis (Doolittle, trans.), **Supp. I Part 1:** 257, 268, 269
"Chosen Blindness" (Karr), **Supp. XI:** 251
Chosen Country (Dos Passos), **I:** 475, 490–491
Chosen Place, The Timeless People, The (Marshall), **Supp. XI:** 275, 276, **282–284**
Chosön (Lowell), **II:** 513
Choukri, Mohamed, **Supp. IV Part 1:** 92
Chovteau, Mane Thérèse, **Supp. I Part 1:** 205
Chrisman, Robert, **Supp. IV Part 1:** 1
Christabel (Coleridge), **Supp. IV Part 2:** 465
"Christ for Sale" (Lowell), **II:** 538
Christian, Graham, **Supp. XII:** 193
Christian Dictionary, A (Wilson), **IV:** 153
"Christian in World Crisis, The" (Merton), **Supp. VIII:** 203
Christianity and Power Politics (Niebuhr), **III:** 292, 303
"Christianity and the Survival of Creation" (Berry), **Supp. X:** 30
"Christian Minister, The" (Emerson), **II:** 10
Christian Philosopher, The (Mather), **Supp. II Part 2:** 463–464
Christian Realism and Practical Problems (Niebuhr), **III:** 292, 308
"Christian Roommates, The" (Updike), **IV:** 226–227; **Retro. Supp. I:** 319, 323
Christiansen, Carrie, **I:** 210
Christian's Secret of a Happy Life, The (H. W. Smith), **Supp. XIV:** 333–334
Christie, Agatha, **Supp. IV Part 1:** 341; **Supp. IV Part 2:** 469
Christine (King), **Supp. V:** 139, 148
"Christ Light, The" (Chopin), **Retro. Supp. II:** 61
"Christmas, or the Good Fairy" (Stowe), **Supp. I Part 2:** 586
"Christmas 1944" (Levertov), **Supp. III Part 1:** 274
"Christmas Banquet, The" (Hawthorne), **II:** 227
Christmas Card, A (Theroux), **Supp. VIII:** 322
Christmas Carol, A (Dickens), **Retro. Supp. I:** 196; **Supp. I Part 2:** 409–410; **Supp. X:** 252, 253
"Christmas Eve at Johnson's Drugs N Goods" (Bambara), **Supp. XI:** 11–12
"Christmas Eve in the Time of War: A Capitalist Meditates by a Civil War Monument" (Lowell), **II:** 538
"Christmas Eve under Hooker's Statue" (Lowell), **II:** 539–540

"Christmas Gift" (Warren), **IV:** 252–253
"Christmas Greeting, A" (Wright), **Supp. III Part 2:** 601
"Christmas Hymn, A" (Wilbur), **Supp. III Part 2:** 557
Christmas Memory, A (Capote), **Supp. III Part 1:** 118, 119, 129
"Christmass Poem" (West), **Retro. Supp. II:** 338
Christmas Story (Mencken), **III:** 111
"Christmas to Me" (Lee), **Supp. VIII:** 113
Christographia (Taylor), **IV:** 164–165
"*Christ on the Cross*/Nuestro Señor Crucificado" (Mora), **Supp. XIII:** 229
Christopher, Mary (pseudonym). *See* West, Dorothy
Christopher and His Kind: 1929–1939 (Isherwood), **Supp. XIV:** 157, 163, 164, 171
"Christopher Cat" (Cullen), **Supp. IV Part 1:** 173
Christopher Columbus, Mariner (Morison), **Supp. I Part 2:** 488
Christopher Isherwood: A Critical Biography (Finney), **Supp. XIV:** 158
Christophersen, Bill, **Supp. IX:** 159, 167; **Supp. XI:** 155; **Supp. XIII:** 87
"Christ's Passion" (Karr), **Supp. XI:** 251
Christus: A Mystery (Longfellow), **II:** 490, 493, 495, 505–507; **Retro. Supp. II:** 161, 165, 166
"Chroma" (F. Barthelme), **Supp. XI:** 31
Chroma (F. Barthelme), **Supp. XI:** 30, 33, 34
"Chronicle of Race Relations, A" (Du Bois), **Supp. II Part 1:** 182
Chronicle of the Conquest of Granada (Irving), **II:** 310
Chronicles: Volume One (Dylan), **Supp. XVIII:** 20, 21, 23, 24, 28, **32–33**
"Chronologues" (Goldbarth), **Supp. XII:** 183, 184
"Chrysanthemums, The" (Steinbeck), **IV:** 53
"Chrysaor" (Longfellow), **II:** 498
Chu, Louis, **Supp. X:** 291
Chuang, Hua, **Supp. X:** 291
Chuang-Tzu, **Supp. VIII:** 206
"Chunk of Amethyst, A" (R. Bly), **Supp. IV Part 1:** 72
Church, Margaret, **IV:** 466
"Church and the Fiction Writer, The" (O'Connor), **Retro. Supp. II:** 223, 233; **Supp. XVIII:** 161
"Churchgoing" (Nelson), **Supp. XVIII:** 173
Churchill, Charles, **Supp. XV:** 232
Churchill, Winston, **I:** 9, 490; **Supp. I Part 2:** 491
Church of Dead Girls, The (Dobyns), **Supp. XIII:** 75, **83–84**
"Church of Omnivorous Light, The" (Wrigley), **Supp. XVIII:** 306–307
"Church Porch, The" (Herbert), **IV:** 153
Church Psalmody, Selected from Dr. Watts and Other Authors (Mason and Greene, ed.), **I:** 458
Ciannic, Saint, **II:** 215
Ciano, Edda, **IV:** 249
Ciardi, John, **I:** 169, 179, 535; **III:** 268; **Supp. IV Part 1:** 243; **Supp. IV Part 2:** 639; **Supp. IX:** 269, 324; **Supp. XII:** 119
Cicada (Haines), **Supp. XII: 206–207**
"Cicadas" (Wilbur), **Supp. III Part 2:** 549
Cicero, **I:** 279; **II:** 8, 14–15; **III:** 23; **Supp. I Part 2:** 405
Cider House Rules, The (Irving), **Supp. VI:** 164, **173–175**
"Cigales" (Wilbur), **Supp. III Part 2:** 549
"Cigarette" (L. Michaels), **Supp. XVI:** 214
Cimarron, Rose (Burke), **Supp. XIV:** 22, 35
"Cimetière Marin, Le" (Valéry), **IV:** 91–92
Cimino, Michael, **Supp. X:** 126
Cincinnati Kid, The (film), **Supp. XI: 306**
"Cinderella" (Jarrell), **II:** 386
"Cinderella" (Perrault), **IV:** 266, 267
"Cinderella" (Sexton), **Supp. II Part 2:** 691
"Cinema, The" (Salter), **Supp. IX:** 257
Cinema of Tony Richardson, The: Essays and Interviews (Phillips), **Supp. XI:** 306
Cinthio, **IV:** 370
Ciolkowski, Laura, **Supp. XVI:** 24
CIOPW (Cummings), **I:** 429
"Circe" (Welty), **Retro. Supp. I:** 353
Circle Game, The (Atwood), **Supp. XIII:** 20, 33
"Circle in the Fire, A" (O'Connor), **III:** 344–345, 349–350, 351, 353, 354; **Retro. Supp. II:** 229, 232
"Circle of Breath" (Stafford), **Supp. XI:** 318, 322
"Circles" (Emerson), **I:** 455, 460
"Circles" (Lowell), **II:** 554
"Circus, The" (Porter), **III:** 443, 445
"Circus Animals' Desertion" (Yeats), **I:** 389
"Circus in the Attic" (Warren), **IV:** 253
Circus in the Attic, The (Warren), **IV:** 243, 251–253
"Circus in Three Rings" (Plath), **Retro. Supp. II:** 243; **Supp. I Part 2:** 536
Circus of Needs, A (Dunn), **Supp. XI: 147–148**
"Cirque d'Hiver" (Bishop), **Supp. I Part 1:** 85
Cisneros, Sandra, **Supp. IV Part 2:** 544; **Supp. VII: 57–73; Supp. XI:** 177; **Supp. XVII:** 71
Cities of the Interior (Nin), **Supp. X:** 182
Cities of the Plain (McCarthy), **Supp. VIII:** 175, **186–187**
Cities of the Red Night (Burroughs), **Supp. III Part 1:** 106
"Citizen Cain" (Baraka), **Supp. II Part 1:** 49
Citizen Kane (film), **Retro. Supp. I:** 115; **Supp. V:** 251; **Supp. XI:** 169
"Citizen of the World" (Goldsmith), **II:** 299
"City" (Francis), **Supp. IX:** 87
City and the Pillar, The (Vidal), **Supp. IV Part 2:** 677, 680–681; **Supp. XIV:** 170
"*City and the Pillar, The,* as Gay Fiction" (Summers), **Supp. IV Part 2:** 680–681
"City Articles" series (Briggs), **Supp. XVIII:** 12
"City Boy" (L. Michaels), **Supp. XVI:** 203–204
City Boy (L. Michaels), **Supp. XVI:** 212
City in History, The (Mumford), **Supp. II Part 2:** 495
"City in the Sea, The" (Poe), **III:** 411; **Retro. Supp. II:** 274
"City in Which I Love You, The" (L.-Y. Lee), **Supp. XV:** 215, **217–218**
City in Which I Love You, The (L.-Y. Lee), **Supp. XV:** 212, **215–220**
City Life (Barthelme), **Supp. IV Part 1:** 44, 47
"City of Change, A" (Bynner), **Supp. XV:** 45
City of Glass (Auster), **Supp. XII:** 22, **24–26**
City of God, The (St. Augustine), **IV:** 126
City of the Living and Other Stories, The (Stegner), **Supp. IV Part 2:** 599, 609, 613
City of Words: American Fiction 1950–1970 (T. Tanner), **Supp. XVI:** 69
City of Your Final Destination, The (Cameron), **Supp. XII:** 79, 82, **91–94**
"City on a Hill" (Lowell), **II: 552**
"City Person Encountering Nature, A" (Kingston), **Supp. V:** 170
"City Planners, The" (Atwood), **Supp. XIII:** 33
City Without Men (film), **Supp. XVIII:** 247
City Without Walls (Auden), **Supp. II Part 1:** 24
Civil Disobedience (Thoreau), **IV:** 185; **Supp. I Part 2:** 507
Civilization in the United States (Stearns), **I:** 245
"Civil Rights" (Lanier), **Supp. I Part 1:** 357
Cixous, Hélène, **Supp. X:** 102; **Supp. XIII:** 297; **Supp. XV:** 347
Claiborne, Craig, **Supp. XVII:** 89
Claiborne, William, **I:** 132
Claiming of Sleeping Beauty, The (Rice), **Supp. VII:** 301
Clampitt, Amy, **Supp. IX: 37–54; Supp. X:** 120; **Supp. XI:** 249; **Supp. XV:** 251, 256
Clancy's Wake, At (Crane), **I:** 422
"Clandeboye" (Leopold), **Supp. XIV:** 189
Clara Howard; or, The Enthusiasm of Love (Brown), **Supp. I Part 1:** 145
Clara's Ole Man (Bullins), **Supp. II Part 1:** 42
Clare, John, **II:** 387; **III:** 528; **Supp. XVI:** 295
Clarel: A Poem and Pilgrimage in the Holy Land (Melville), **Retro. Supp. I:** 257

Clarissa (Richardson), **II:** 111; **Supp. I Part 2:** 714; **Supp. V:** 127; **Supp. XV:** 231
Clark, Alex, **Supp. XII:** 307
Clark, Charles, **I:** 470
Clark, Eleanor. *See* Warren, Mrs. Robert Penn (Eleanor Clark)
Clark, Francis Edward, **II:** 9
Clark, Geoffrey, **Supp. XI:** 342
Clark, Harry Hayden, **Supp. I Part 2:** 423
Clark, John Bates, **Supp. I Part 2:** 633
Clark, Kenneth, **Supp. XIV:** 342, 348
Clark, Lewis Gaylord, **Supp. XVIII:** 4, 7, 8
Clark, Thomas, **Supp. III Part 2:** 629; **Supp. IV Part 1:** 140, 145, 147
Clark, Walter, **Supp. XI:** 315
Clark, William, **III:** 14; **IV:** 179, 283
Clark, Willis Gaylord, **Supp. I Part 2:** 684
Clarke, James Freeman, **Supp. II Part 1:** 280
Clarke, John, **Supp. IV Part 1:** 8
Clarke, John J., **III:** 356
Clarke, Samuel, **II:** 108
Clark Lectures, **Retro. Supp. I:** 65
Clash by Night (Odets), **Supp. II Part 2:** 531, 538, 544–546, 550, 551
Classical Tradition, The (Highet), **Supp. I Part 1:** 268
Classic Ballroom Dances (Simic), **Supp. VIII:** 271, **276–278,** 283
Classics and Commercials: A Literary Chronicle of the Forties (Wilson), **IV:** 433
"CLASS STRUGGLE" (Baraka), **Supp. III Part 1:** 55
"Claude Glass, The: 1890" (Bierds), **Supp. XVII:** 27
Claudel, Paul, **I:** 60
Claudelle Inglish (Caldwell), **I:** 304
Clavel, Marcel, **I:** 343
"CLAY" (Baraka), **Supp. II Part 1:** 54
Clay, Henry, **I:** 8; **Supp. I Part 2:** 684, 686
Clay's Ark (O. Butler), **Supp. XIII:** 63
Clayton, John J., **Supp. IV Part 1:** 238
"Clean, Well Lighted Place, A" (Hemingway), **Retro. Supp. I:** 181
"Clear, with Light Variable Winds" (Lowell), **II:** 522
"Clear Days" (White), **Supp. I Part 2:** 664, 665
Clearing (Berry), **Supp. X:** 22
"Clearing, A" (Simpson), **Supp. IX:** 280
"Clearing, The" (Kenyon), **Supp. VII:** 174
"Clearing the Title" (Merrill), **Supp. III Part 1:** 336
"Clearing Up the Question of Stesichoros' Blinding by Helen" (Carson), **Supp. XII:** 107–108
"Clear Morning" (Glück), **Supp. V:** 88
"Clearness" (Wilbur), **Supp. III Part 2:** 544, 550
"Clear Night" (Wright), **Supp. V:** 341
Clear Pictures: First Loves, First Guides (Price), **Supp. VI:** 253, 254, 255, 256, 265
Clear Springs (Mason), **Supp. VIII:** 134–136, 137–138, 139, 147
Cleary, Rebecca Lauck, **Supp. XVIII:** 195
Cleaver, Eldridge, **Retro. Supp. II:** 12; **Supp. IV Part 1:** 206; **Supp. X:** 249
"Cleaving, The" (L.-Y. Lee), **Supp. XV:** 215, **218–220**
Cleland, John, **Supp. V:** 48, 127
Clemenceau, Georges, **I:** 490
"Clemency" (Wrigley), **Supp. XVIII:** 307–308
Clemens, Jane, **I:** 247
Clemens, Mrs. Samuel Langhorne (Olivia Langdon), **I:** 197, 208, 247; **Supp. I Part 2:** 457
Clemens, Orion, **IV:** 193, 195
Clemens, Samuel Langhorne. *See* Twain, Mark
Clemens, Susie, **IV:** 208
Clementine Recognitions (novel), **Supp. IV Part 1:** 280
Clements, Colin Campbell, **Supp. XVI:** 190
Clemons, Walter, **Supp. IV Part 1:** 305, 307
Cleopatra, **III:** 44; **IV:** 373; **Supp. I Part 1:** 114
"Clepsydra" (Ashbery), **Supp. III Part 1:** 10–15
"Clerks, The" (Robinson), **III:** 517–518
Cleveland, Carol, **Supp. IX:** 120, 125
Cleveland, Ceil, **Supp. V:** 222
Cleveland, Grover, **II:** 126, 128, 129, 130, 137, 138; **Supp. I Part 2:** 486
"Clever Magician Carrying My Heart, A" (Salinas), **Supp. XIII:** 323
"Cliff, The" (C. Baxter), **Supp. XVII:** 16–17
Clifford, Craig, **Supp. IX:** 99
Clift, Montgomery, **III:** 161
Clifton, Lucille, **Supp. XVIII:** 177
Climate of Monastic Prayer, The (Merton), **Supp. VIII:** 205, 207
Climb, The (Boukreev), **Supp. XVIII:** 112
"Climber, The" (Mason), **Supp. VIII:** 140–141
Climbing High: A Woman's Account of Surviving the Everest Tragedy (Gammelgaard), **Supp. XVIII:** 112
"Climbing the Tower" (Crews), **Supp. XI:** 102
Clinton, De Witt, **I:** 338
"Clipped Wings" (H. Miller), **III:** 176–177
Clive, Robert, **Supp. I Part 2:** 505
Clock Winder, The (Tyler), **Supp. IV Part 2:** 661–662, 670
Clock Without Hands (McCullers), **II:** 587–588, 604–606
Clockwork Orange, A (Burgess), **Supp. XIII:** 29
Clorindy (Cook), **Supp. II Part 1:** 199
"Close, The" (Jarman), **Supp. XVII:** 113
"Close Calls" (Wolff), **Supp. VII:** 332–333
"Closed Book, A" (Mosley), **Supp. XIII:** 237
Close Range: Wyoming Stories (Proulx), **Supp. VII:** 261–265
Closest Possible Union, The (J. Scott), **Supp. XVII: 185–186,** 188, 191
Close the Book (Glaspell), **Supp. III Part 1:** 179
"Close the Book" (Lowell), **II:** 554
Close to Shore: A True Story of Terror in an Age of Innocence (Capuzzo), **Supp. XIII:** 254
Closet Writing & Gay Reading: The Case of Melville's Pierre (Creech), **Retro. Supp. I:** 254
Closing Circle, The (Commoner), **Supp. XIII:** 264
Closing of the American Mind, The (Bloom), **Retro. Supp. II:** 19, 30, 31
"Closing of the Rodeo, The" (W. J. Smith), **Supp. XIII:** 332
Closing Time (Heller), **Supp. IV Part 1:** 382, 386, 391–394
Closset, Marie, **Supp. VIII:** 251, 265
"Cloud, The" (Shelley), **Supp. I Part 2:** 720
"Cloud and Fame" (Berryman), **I:** 173
Cloud Forest, The: A Chronicle of the South American Wilderness (Matthiessen), **Supp. V:** 202, 204
"Cloud on the Way, The" (Bryant), **Supp. I Part 1:** 171
"Cloud River" (Wright), **Supp. V:** 341
"Clouds" (Levine), **Supp. V:** 184
Cloudsplitter (Banks), **Supp. V:** 16
"Clover" (Lanier), **Supp. I Part 1:** 362–364
Clover and Other Poems (Lanier), **Supp. I Part 1:** 362
"Clown" (Corso), **Supp. XII:** 127
Clown in the Belfry, The: Writings on Faith and Fiction (Buechner), **Supp. XII:** 53
Cluck, Julia, **Supp. I Part 2:** 728
Clum, John M., **Supp. XIII: 200,** 201, 209
Cluny, Hugo, **IV:** 290
Clurman, Harold, **I:** 93; **IV:** 381, 385
Clytus, Radiclani, **Supp. XIII:** 128, **Supp. XIII:** 129, 132
"C.O." (Wrigley), **Supp. XVIII:** 298
"Coal: Beginning and End" (Winters), **Supp. II Part 2:** 791
Coale, Howard, **Supp. XIII:** 15
"Coals" (Hoffman), **Supp. XVIII:** 86
"Coast, The" (column), **Supp. IV Part 1:** 198
"Coast Guard's Cottage, The" (Wylie), **Supp. I Part 2:** 723
Coast of Trees, A (Ammons), **Supp. VII:** 24, 34
"Coast-Range Christ, The" (Jeffers), **Supp. II Part 2:** 414, 419
"Coast-Road, The" (Jeffers), **Supp. II Part 2:** 425
"Coat, The" (Everwine), **Supp. XV:** 80
Coates, Joseph, **Supp. VIII:** 80
Coates, Robert, **I:** 54; **IV:** 298
"Coatlicue's Rules: Advice from an Aztec Goddess" (Mora), **Supp. XIII:** 223
"Coats" (Kenyon), **Supp. VII:** 172
Cobb, Lee J., **III:** 153

Cobb, Ty, **III:** 227, 229
Cobbett, William, **Supp. I Part 2:** 517; **Supp. XV:** 237
"Cobbler Keezar's Vision" (Whittier), **Supp. I Part 2:** 699
"Cobweb, The" (Carver), **Supp. III Part 1:** 148
Cobwebs From an Empty Skull (Bierce), **I:** 195
Coccimiglio, Vic, **Supp. XIII:** 114
"Cock-a-Doodle-Doo!" (Melville), **III:** 89
"Cockayne" (Emerson), **II:** 6
"Cock-Crow" (Gordon), **II:** 219
Cock Pit (Cozzens), **I:** 359, 378, 379
Cockpit (Kosinski), **Supp. XII:** 21
Cockpit: A Novel (Kosinski), **Supp. VII:** 215, 223–224, 225
"Cock Robin Takes Refuge in the Storm House" (Snodgrass), **Supp. VI:** 319
Cocktail Hour, The (Gurney), **Supp. V:** 95, 96, 100, 101, 103, 105, 108
Cocktail Hour and Two Other Plays: Another Antigone and *The Perfect Party* (Gurney), **Supp. V:** 100
Cocktail Party, The (Eliot), **I:** 571, 582–583; **III:** 21; **Retro. Supp. I:** 65; **Supp. V:** 101, 103
Cocteau, Jean, **III:** 471; **Retro. Supp. I:** 82, 378; **Supp. IV Part 1:** 82; **Supp. XVI:** 135
"Coda: Wilderness Letter" (Stegner), **Supp. IV Part 2:** 595
"Code, The" (Frost), **Retro. Supp. I:** 121, 128
Codman, Florence, **Supp. II Part 1:** 92, 93
Codman, Ogden, Jr., **Retro. Supp. I:** 362, 363
Cody, William ("Buffalo Bill"), **I:** 440; **III:** 584; **Supp. V:** 230
Coffey, Michael, **Supp. V:** 243; **Supp. XV:** 65
Coffey, Warren, **III:** 358
Coffin, Charles, **III:** 577
Cogan, David J., **Supp. IV Part 1:** 362
Coghill, Nevill, **Supp. II Part 1:** 4; **Supp. XIV:** 13
Cohan, George M., **II:** 427; **III:** 401
Cohen, Edward M., **Supp. XVI:** 212
Cohen, Esther, **Supp. XV:** 323
Cohen, Hettie, **Supp. II Part 1:** 30
Cohen, Marty, **Supp. X:** 112
Cohen, Norman J., **Supp. IX:** 132, 143
Cohen, Rosetta, **Supp. XV:** 257
Cohen, Sarah Blacher, **Supp. V:** 273
Cohen, Victor, **Supp. XVIII:** 235, 236
"Coherent Decentering: Towards a New Model of the Poetic Self" (A. Finch), **Supp. XVII:** 76
"Coin" (Goldbarth), **Supp. XII:** 187
Coindreau, Maurice, **III:** 339
Coiner, Constance, **Supp. XIII:** 297, 302
Coit, Lille Hitchcock, **Supp. X:** 103
"Coitus" (Pound), **III:** 466
Colburn, Nadia Herman, **Supp. XV:** 339, 341, 347
"Cold, The" (Kenyon), **Supp. VII:** 164
"Cold, The" (Winters), **Supp. II Part 2:** 790–791, 809, 811
"Cold-blooded Creatures" (Wylie), **Supp. I Part 2:** 729
Colden, Cadwallader, **Supp. I Part 1:** 250
"Colder the Air, The" (Bishop), **Supp. I Part 1:** 86
Cold Feet (Harrison), **Supp. VIII:** 39
Cold Frame (C. Frost), **Supp. XV:** 93, 96
"Cold Ground Was My Bed Last Night" (Garrett), **Supp. VII:** 100
Cold Ground Was My Bed Last Night (Garrett), **Supp. VII:** 98
"Cold Night, The" (W. C. Williams), **Retro. Supp. I:** 418
"Cold Plunge into Skin Diving, A" (Knowles), **Supp. XII:** 241
Cold Spring, A (Bishop), **Retro. Supp. II:** 45
Cold Springs Harbor (Yates), **Supp. XI:** 348
Cold War American Poetry, **Supp. V:** 182
Cold War and the Income Tax, The (Wilson), **IV:** 430
Cole, Goody, **Supp. I Part 2:** 696–697
Cole, Lester, **Retro. Supp. II:** 329
Cole, Nat King, **Retro. Supp. I:** 334; **Supp. X:** 255
Cole, Thomas, **Supp. I Part 1:** 156, 158, 171
"Coleman" (Karr), **Supp. XI:** 244
Coleman, Wanda, **Supp. XI: 83–98**
Coleridge, Samuel Taylor, **I:** 283, 284, 447, 522; **II:** 7, 10, 11, 19, 71, 169, 273, 301, 502, 516, 549; **III:** 77, 83–84, 424, 461, 488, 523; **IV:** 74, 173, 250, 349, 453; **Retro. Supp. I:** 65, 308; **Supp. I Part 1:** 31, 311, 349; **Supp. I Part 2:** 376, 393, 422; **Supp. IV Part 2:** 422, 465; **Supp. IX:** 38, 50; **Supp. V:** 258; **Supp. XIII:** 139; **Supp. XIV:** 21–22; **Supp. XV:** 250
Coles, Katharine, **Supp. IV Part 2:** 630
Colette, **Supp. VIII:** 40, 171
Colette, Sidonie-Gabrielle, **Supp. XVI:** 193–194
"Coliseum, The" (Poe), **III:** 411
Collage of Dreams (Spencer), **Supp. X:** 196
"Collapse of Tomorrow, The" (Mumford), **Supp. II Part 2:** 482
"Collected by a Valetudinarian" (E. Stoddard), **Supp. XV:** 286–287
Collected Earlier Poems (Hecht), **Supp. X:** 58, 59
Collected Earlier Poems (W. C. Williams), **Retro. Supp. I:** 414, 428
Collected Earlier Poems 1940–1960 (Levertov), **Supp. III Part 1:** 273, 275
Collected Essays (Tate), **IV:** 133–134
Collected Essays of Ralph Ellison, The (Ellison), **Retro. Supp. II:** 119
Collected Essays of Robert Creeley, The (Creeley), **Supp. IV Part 1:** 153, 154
Collected Later Poems (W. C. Williams), **Retro. Supp. I:** 428
Collected Plays (A. Miller), **III:** 158
Collected Plays, 1974–1983 (Gurney), **Supp. V:** 99
Collected Poems (Aiken), **I:** 50
Collected Poems (Burke), **I:** 269
Collected Poems (Cummings), **I:** 430, 439, 441
Collected Poems (Doolittle), **Supp. I Part 1:** 264–267, 269
Collected Poems (Frost), **Retro. Supp. I:** 136
Collected Poems (Kees; Justice, ed.), **Supp. XV:** 134
Collected Poems (Lindsay), **Supp. I Part 2:** 380, 387, 392, 396–397, 400
Collected Poems (Lowell), **Supp. XV:** 20
Collected Poems (Markson), **Supp. XVII:** 143
Collected Poems (Moore), **III:** 194, 215
Collected Poems (Price), **Supp. VI:** 267
Collected Poems (Simpson), **Supp. IX:** 279
Collected Poems (W. C. Williams), **IV:** 415; **Retro. Supp. I:** 430
Collected Poems (Winters), **Supp. II Part 2:** 791, 810
Collected Poems (Wright), **Supp. III Part 2:** 602
Collected Poems (Yeats), **Supp. XV:** 152
Collected Poems, 1923–1953 (Bogan), **Supp. III Part 1:** 64
Collected Poems, 1936–1976 (Francis), **Supp. IX:** 77, 80, **87**
Collected Poems, The (Stevens), **III:** 273; **IV:** 75, 76, 87, 93; **Retro. Supp. I:** 296, 309
Collected Poems 1909–1935 (Eliot), **I:** 580; **Retro. Supp. I:** 66
Collected Poems 1909–1962 (Eliot), **I:** 583
Collected Poems 1917–1952 (MacLeish), **III:** 3, 4, 19
Collected Poems 1921–1931 (W. C. Williams), **Retro. Supp. I:** 422; **Supp. XIV:** 285
Collected Poems 1930–1960 (Eberhart), **I:** 522, 525–526, 540, 541
Collected Poems: 1939–1989 (W. J. Smith), **Supp. XIII:** 332, 340, 343, 345
Collected Poems: 1940–1978 (Shapiro), **Supp. II Part 2:** 703, 717
Collected Poems: 1951–1971 (Ammons), **Supp. VII:** 24, 26–29, 32, 33
Collected Poems: 1956–1976 (Wagoner), **Supp. IX:** 323, **328–329**
Collected Poems of Amy Clampitt, The (Clampitt), **Supp. IX:** 37, 44, 53
Collected Poems of George Garrett (Garrett), **Supp. VII:** 109
Collected Poems of Hart Crane, The (Crane), **I:** 399–402
Collected Poems of James Agee, The (Fitzgerald, ed.), **I:** 27–28
Collected Poems of James T. Farrell, The (Farrell), **II:** 45
Collected Poems of Langston Hughes, The (Rampersad and Roessel, ed.), **Retro. Supp. I:** 194, 196, 212
Collected Poems of Muriel Rukeyser, The (Rukeyser), **Supp. VI:** 274
Collected Poems of Thomas Merton, The, **Supp. VIII:** 207, 208

Collected Poetry (Auden), **Supp. II Part 1:** 18
Collected Prose (Wright), **Supp. III Part 2:** 596
Collected Prose, The (Bishop), **Retro. Supp. II:** 51
Collected Recordings (W. C. Williams), **Retro. Supp. I:** 431
Collected Shorter Poems, 1946–1991 (Carruth), **Supp. XVI:** 47
Collected Short Stories, The (Wharton), **Retro. Supp. I:** 362, 363, 366
Collected Sonnets (Millay), **III:** 136–137
Collected Stories, 1939–1976 (Bowles), **Supp. IV Part 1:** 92
Collected Stories, The (Paley), **Supp. VI:** 218
Collected Stories, The (Price), **Supp. VI:** 266
Collected Stories, The (Theroux), **Supp. VIII:** 318
Collected Stories, The (Wharton), **Retro. Supp. I:** 361
Collected Stories of Eudora Welty, The (Welty), **Retro. Supp. I:** 355
Collected Stories of Isaac Bashevis Singer (Singer), **Retro. Supp. II: 307–308**
Collected Stories of Katherine Anne Porter (Porter), **III:** 454
Collected Stories of Peter Taylor (Taylor), **Supp. V:** 314, 320, 323–324, 325, 326
Collected Stories of Richard Yates, The, **Supp. XI:** 349
Collected Stories of Wallace Stegner (Stegner), **Supp. IV Part 2:** 599, 605
Collected Stories of William Faulkner (Faulkner), **II:** 72; **Retro. Supp. I:** 75
Collected Stories of William Humphrey, The (Humphrey), **Supp. IX:** 106
Collected Works (Bierce), **I:** 204, 208–210
Collected Works of Buck Rogers in the 25th Century, The (Bradbury), **Supp. IV Part 1:** 101
Collected Writings, The (Z. Fitzgerald; Bruccoli, ed.), **Supp. IX:** 65, 68
Collecting the Animals (Everwine), **Supp. XV:** 73, 75, **78–81,** 85, 88
Collection of Epigrams, **II:** 111
Collection of Poems, on American Affairs, and a Variety of Other Subjects ... (Freneau), **Supp. II Part 1:** 274
Collection of Select Aphorisms and Maxims (Palmer), **II:** 111
"Collectors" (Carver), **Supp. III Part 1:** 141–142
Collette, **Supp. XVII:** 86
Collier, Michael, **Supp. XVII:** 23, 110
Collingwood, R. G., **I:** 278
Collins, Billy, **Supp. XI:** 143; **Supp. XIV:** 123; **Supp. XVII:** 245
Collins, Doug, **Supp. V:** 5
Collins, Eddie, **II:** 416
Collins, Richard, **Supp. XI:** 171
Collins, Wilkie, **Supp. I Part 1:** 35, 36; **Supp. IV Part 1:** 341
Collins, William, **Supp. I Part 2:** 714
Collinson, Peter, **II:** 114
Collinson, Peter (pseudonym). *See* Hammett, Dashiell
Colloff, Pamela, **Supp. XIII:** 281
Colloque Sentimental (ballet), **Supp. IV Part 1:** 83
"Colloquy" (Kees), **Supp. XV:** 133
"Colloquy in Black Rock" (Lowell), **II:** 535; **Retro. Supp. II:** 178
"Colloquy of Monos and Una, The" (Poe), **III:** 412
Colonel's Dream, The (Chesnutt), **Supp. XIV:** 63, 75–76
Colônia, Regina, **Retro. Supp. II:** 53
Color (Cullen), **Supp. IV Part 1:** 164, 166, 167, 168
"Colorado" (Beattie), **Supp. V:** 27
Color and Democracy: Colonies and Peace (Du Bois), **Supp. II Part 1:** 184, 185
Color Curtain, The (Wright), **IV:** 478, 488
"Colored Americans" (Dunbar), **Supp. II Part 1:** 197
"Color Line, The" (Douglass), **Supp. III Part 1:** 163–165
Color Line, The (W. B. Smith), **Supp. II Part 1:** 168
Color of a Great City, The (Dreiser), **Retro. Supp. II:** 104
Color of Darkness (Purdy), **Supp. VII:** 271
Color Purple, The (Walker), **Supp. III Part 2:** 517, 518, 520, 525–529, 532–537; **Supp. VIII:** 141; **Supp. X:** 252, 330
Color Schemes (Cheang; film), **Supp. XI:** 20
"Colors of Night, The" (Momaday), **Supp. IV Part 2:** 490
"Colors without Objects" (Swenson), **Supp. IV Part 2:** 645
"Color: The Unfinished Business of Democracy" (Locke), **Supp. XIV:** 202, 207
"Colossus, The" (Plath), **Retro. Supp. II:** 250
Colossus, The (Plath), **Retro. Supp. II: 245–247; Supp. I Part 2:** 529, 531, 536, 538, 540; **Supp. V:** 79; **Supp. XI:** 317
Colossus of Maroussi, The (H. Miller), **III:** 178, 185–186
"Colt, The" (Stegner), **Supp. IV Part 2:** 600
Coltelli, Laura, **Supp. IV Part 1:** 323, 330, 335, 409; **Supp. IV Part 2:** 493, 497, 559
Colter: The True Story of the Best Dog I Ever Had (Bass), **Supp. XVI:** 23
Coltrane, John, **Supp. VIII:** 197
Colum, Mary, **I:** 246, 252, 256; **Supp. I Part 2:** 708, 709
Columbiad, The (Barlow), **Supp. II Part 1:** 67, 72, 73, 74, 75–77, 79
Columbia History of the American Novel, **Supp. XV:** 270
Columbia Literary History of the United States, **Supp. XV:** 270
"Columbian Ode" (Dunbar), **Supp. II Part 1:** 199
"Columbia U Poesy Reading——1975" (Corso), **Supp. XII:** 134
Columbus, Christopher, **I:** 253; **II:** 6, 310; **III:** 8; **Supp. I Part 2:** 397, 479, 480, 483, 486–488, 491, 495, 497, 498
"Columbus to Ferdinand" (Freneau), **Supp. II Part 1:** 255
Comanche Moon (McMurtry), **Supp. V:** 232
"Come, Break With Time" (Bogan), **Supp. III Part 1:** 52
Come Along with Me (Jackson), **Supp. IX:** 117, 118, 122
Come Back, Charleston Blue (film), **Supp. XVI:** 144
Comeback, The (Gurney), **Supp. V:** 97
"Come Back to the Raft Ag'in, Huck Honey!" (Fiedler), **Supp. XIII:** 93, **96–97,** 101
Come Blow Your Horn (Simon), **Supp. IV Part 2:** 574, 575, 577, 578, 586, 587, 591
"Come Dance with Me in Ireland" (Jackson), **Supp. IX:** 119
"Comedian as the Letter C, The" (Stevens), **IV:** 84–85, 88; **Retro. Supp. I:** 297, 301, 302
"Comedy Cop" (Farrell), **II:** 45
"Comedy's Greatest Era" (Agee), **I:** 31
"Come In" (Frost), **Retro. Supp. I:** 139
"Come On, Baby" (Zinberg), **Supp. XV:** 195
"Come on Back" (Gardner), **Supp. VI:** 73
"Come Out into the Sun" (Francis), **Supp. IX:** 82
Come Out into the Sun: Poems New and Selected (Francis), **Supp. IX: 82–83**
"Come out the Wilderness" (Baldwin), **Supp. I Part 1:** 63
Comer, Anjanette, **Supp. XI:** 305
Comer, Cornelia, **I:** 214
"Come Shining: The Spiritual South" (exhibition; Luster), **Supp. XV:** 350
Come with Me: Poems for a Journey (Nye), **Supp. XIII:** 279
"Comforts of Home, The" (O'Connor), **III:** 349, 351, 355; **Retro. Supp. II:** 237
Comic Artist, The (Glaspell and Matson), **Supp. III Part 1:** 182
"Comic Imagination of the Young Dickens, The" (Wright), **Supp. III Part 2:** 591
"Comic Textures and Female Communities 1937 and 1977: Clare Boothe and Wendy Wasserstein" (Carlson), **Supp. XV:** 323
Comic Tragedies (Alcott), **Supp. I Part 1:** 33
"Coming Close" (Levine), **Supp. V:** 192
Coming Forth by Day of Osiris Jones, The (Aiken), **I:** 59
"Coming Home" (Gordon), **Supp. IV Part 1:** 309
"Coming Home to Vermont" (McCarriston), **Supp. XIV:** 269
"Coming in From the Cold" (Walker), **Supp. III Part 2:** 526
"Coming into Eighty" (Sarton), **Supp. VIII:** 262

Coming into Eighty (Sarton), **Supp. VIII:** 262
Coming into the Country (McPhee), **Supp. III Part 1:** 298, 301–306, 309, 310
Coming Into Writing (Cixous), **Supp. X:** 102
Coming of Age in Mississippi (Moody), **Supp. IV Part 1:** 11
Comings Back (Goldbarth), **Supp. XII:** 180
"Coming to Canada—Age Twenty Two" (Shields), **Supp. VII:** 311
Coming to Canada: Poems (Shields), **Supp. VII:** 311–312
"Coming to the Morning" (Merwin), **Supp. III Part 1:** 356
"Coming to This" (Strand), **Supp. IV Part 2:** 627
Comiskey, Charles, **II:** 422
Commager, Henry Steele, **I:** 253; **Supp. I Part 1:** 372; **Supp. I Part 2:** 484, 647, 650
Command the Morning (Buck), **Supp. II Part 1:** 125
"Commencement Address, A" (Brodsky), **Supp. VIII:** 31
"Commencement Day Address, The" (Schwartz), **Supp. II Part 2:** 660
Commentaries (Caesar), **II:** 502, 561
"Commentary" (Auden), **Supp. II Part 1:** 13
"Comment on Curb" (Hughes), **Supp. I Part 1:** 340
"Comments/Questions" (Nelson), **Supp. XVIII:** 172
"Commerce" (Nye), **Supp. XIII:** 281
Commins, Saxe, **Retro. Supp. I:** 73; **Retro. Supp. II:** 337
Commodity of Dreams & Other Stories, A (Nemerov), **III:** 268–269, 285
Common Carnage (Dobyns), **Supp. XIII:** 87
"Common Ground, A" (Levertov), **Supp. III Part 1:** 277
"Common Life, The" (Auden), **Supp. IV Part 1:** 302, 313
Common Room, A: Essays 1954–1987 (Price), **Supp. VI:** 264–265, 267
Commons, John, **Supp. I Part 2:** 645
Common Sense (Paine), **II:** 117; **Supp. I Part 1:** 231; **Supp. I Part 2:** 505, 506–508, 509, 513, 516, 517, 521
"Communication" (Dobyns), **Supp. XIII:** 91
"Communion" (Dubus), **Supp. VII:** 91
Communion (Mora), **Supp. XIII: 217–219**
Communist Manifesto, The (Marx), **II:** 463
"Community Life" (Moore), **Supp. X:** 178
"Community of Glaciers, The" (Bass), **Supp. XVI:** 23
Comnes, Gregory, **Supp. IV Part 1:** 283, 284, 291
"Companions, The" (Nemerov), **III:** 269, 278, 287
Company of Poets, A (Simpson), **Supp. IX:** 265, 275
Company of Women, The (Gordon), **Supp. IV Part 1:** 302–304, 304, 306, 313
Company She Keeps, The (McCarthy), **II:** 562, 563–566
"Comparisons of Wonder" (Jarman), **Supp. XVII:** 114
Compass Flower, The (Merwin), **Supp. III Part 1:** 353, 357
"Compassionate Friendship" (Doolittle), **Supp. I Part 1:** 257, 258, 259, 260, 271
"Compatibility" (C. Frost), **Supp. XV:** 103
"Compendium" (Dove), **Supp. IV Part 1:** 248
"Complaint" (W. C. Williams), **Retro. Supp. I:** 418
"Complete Birth of the Cool, The" (Wright), **Supp. XV:** 343, 344
Complete Collected Poems of William Carlos Williams, 1906–1938, The (W. C. Williams), **Retro. Supp. I:** 424
"Complete Destruction" (W. C. Williams), **IV:** 413
"Complete Life of John Hopkins, The" (O. Henry), **Supp. II Part 1:** 405
Complete Poems (Frost), **II:** 155, 164
Complete Poems (Reznikoff), **Supp. XIV:** 281
Complete Poems (Sandburg), **III:** 590–592, 594, 596
Complete Poems, The (Bishop), **Retro. Supp. II:** 49; **Supp. I Part 1:** 72, 82, 94
Complete Poems, The (Bradbury), **Supp. IV Part 1:** 105
Complete Poems, The: 1927–1979 (Bishop), **Retro. Supp. II:** 51
Complete Poems of Emily Dickinson, The (Bianchi and Hampson, eds.), **Retro. Supp. I:** 35
Complete Poems of Emily Dickinson, The (Johnson, ed.), **I:** 470
Complete Poems of Frederick Goddard Tuckerman, The (Momaday), **Supp. IV Part 2:** 480
Complete Poems of Hart Crane, **Retro. Supp. II:** 81
Complete Poems to Solve, The (Swenson), **Supp. IV Part 2:** 652
Complete Poetical Works (Hulme), **III:** 464
Complete Poetical Works (Longfellow), **Retro. Supp. II:** 154
Complete Poetical Works (Lowell), **II:** 512, 516–517
Complete Poetical Works of Amy Lowell, The, **Supp. XV:** 295–296
Complete Stories (O'Connor), **Supp. X:** 1
Complete Tragedies, The: Euripedes II, **Supp. XV:** 50
"Complete with Starry Night and Bourbon Shots" (Goldbarth), **Supp. XII:** 192–193
Complete Works of Kate Chopin, The (Seyersted, ed.), **Supp. I Part 1:** 212, 225
Complete Works of the Gawain-Poet (Gardner), **Supp. VI:** 64, 65
"Complex Histories, Contested Memories: Some Reflections on Remembering Difficult Pasts" (E. Hoffman, lecture), **Supp. XVI:** 155
"Complicated Thoughts About a Small Son" (White), **Supp. I Part 2:** 678
"Compliments of the Season" (O. Henry), **Supp. II Part 1:** 392, 399
"Compline" (Auden), **Supp. II Part 1:** 23
"Composition as Explanation" (Stein), **IV:** 27, 28
Composition as Explanation (Stein), **IV:** 32, 33, 38
"Compounding *of* Consciousness" (James), **II:** 358–359
Comprehensive Bibliography (Hanneman), **II:** 259
Compton-Burnett, Ivy, **I:** 93; **II:** 580
"Comrade Laski, C.P.U.S.A. [M.L.]" (Didion), **Supp. IV Part 1:** 200
Comstock, Anthony, **Retro. Supp. II:** 95
Comus (Milton), **II:** 12; **Supp. I Part 2:** 622
Conan Doyle, Arthur. *See* Doyle, Arthur Conan
Conceptions of Reality in Modern American Poetry (Dembo), **Supp. I Part 1:** 272
"Concept of Character in Fiction, The" (Gass), **Supp. VI:** 85, **86**
Concept of Dread, The (Kierkegaard), **III:** 305
Concerning Children (Gilman), **Supp. XI:** 206
"Concerning Mold upon the Skin, Etc." (J. Scott), **Supp. XVII:** 188
"Concerning Necessity" (Carruth), **Supp. XVI:** 57
"Concerning Some Recent Criticism of His Work" (Doty), **Supp. XI:** 131
Concerning the End for Which God Created the World (Edwards), **I:** 549, 557, 559
Concerto for Two Pianos, Winds, and Percussion (Bowles), **Supp. IV Part 1:** 83
Conchologist's First Book, The (Poe), **III:** 412
Conclusive Evidence (Nabokov), **III:** 247–250, 252
"Concord Hymn" (Emerson), **II:** 19
"Concrete Universal, The: Observations on the Understanding of Poetry" (Ransom), **III:** 480
Concurring Beasts (Dobyns), **Supp. XIII:** 76
Condensed Novels and Other Papers (Harte), **Supp. II Part 1:** 342
"Condition, The" (Karmi; Everwine, trans.), **Supp. XV:** 78
Condition of Man, The (Mumford), **Supp. II Part 2:** 483, 484, 486, 495–496, 498
"Condolence" (Parker), **Supp. IX:** 191
"Condominium, The" (Elkin), **Supp. VI:** 49, **50–51,** 55, 56
Condon, Charles R., **Supp. XIII:** 163

Condor and the Cows, The: A South American Travel Diary (Isherwood and Caskey), **Supp. XIV:** 166
"Condor and the Guests, The" (Connell), **Supp. XIV:** 86
Condorcet, Marquis de, **Supp. I Part 2:** 511
Conduct of Life, The (Emerson), **II:** 1–5, 8
Conduct of Life, The (Mumford), **Supp. II Part 2:** 485, 496–497
"Conductor of Nothing, The" (Levine), **Supp. V:** 189
"Conference Male, The" (Mora), **Supp. XIII:** 218
"Confessional" (Bidart), **Supp. XV:** 29–30, 31
"Confessional Poem" (Nelson), **Supp. XVIII:** 174
Confession de Claude, La (Zola), **I:** 411
"Confession of a House-Breaker, The" (Jewett), **Retro. Supp. II:** 146–147
Confession of Jereboam O. Beauchamp, The (pamphlet), **IV:** 253
Confessions (Augustine), **I:** 279; **Supp. XVI:** 288
Confessions (Rousseau), **I:** 226
Confessions of a Barbarian: Selections from the Journals of Edward Abbey, 1951–1989 (Abbey; Petersen, ed.), **Supp. XIII:** 2, 4
"Confessions of a Latina Author" (Mora), **Supp. XIII:** 221
Confessions of Nat Turner, The (Styron), **IV:** 98, 99, 105, 113–117; **Supp. X:** 16, 250
Confetti (Mora), **Supp. XIII:** 221
Confidence (James), **II:** 327, 328
Confidence-Man, The (Melville), **III:** 91; **Retro. Supp. I:** 255–256, 257; **Retro. Supp. II:** 121; **Supp. XIV:** 49
Confidence Man, The (Van Vechten), **Supp. II Part 2:** 737
Confidential Clerk, The (Eliot), **I:** 570, 571–572, 583, 584; **Retro. Supp. I:** 65
Confident Years, 1885–1915, The (Brooks), **I:** 257, 259; **Supp. I Part 2:** 650
"Configurations" (Ammons), **Supp. VII:** 28
Confronting the Horror: The Novels of Nelson Algren (Giles), **Supp. IX:** 11, 15
Confucius, **II:** 1; **III:** 456, 475; **Supp. IV Part 1:** 14
Confusion (Cozzens), **I:** 358, 359, 377, 378
Congo (film), **Supp. IV Part 1:** 83
Congo (screenplay, Shanley), **Supp. XIV:** 316
"Congo, The" (Lindsay), **Supp. I Part 2:** 388–389, 392, 395
Congo and Other Poems, The (Lindsay), **Supp. I Part 2:** 379, 382, 389, 390, 391
"Congress of the Insomniacs, The" (Simic), **Supp. VIII:** 281–282
Congreve, William, **III:** 195; **Supp. V:** 101; **Supp. XVIII:** 12
Coningsby (Disraeli), **II:** 127
Conjectures of a Guilty Bystander (Merton), **Supp. VIII:** 197, 206, 207
Conjugal Bliss: A Comedy of Marital Arts (Nichols), **Supp. XIII:** 269
"Conjugation of the Paramecium, The" (Rukeyser), **Supp. VI:** 271
"Conjuration" (Wilbur), **Supp. III Part 2:** 551
Conjure (recording), **Supp. X:** 241
Conjure (Reed), **Supp. X:** 240, 242
Conjure-Man Dies, The (R. Fisher), **Supp. XVI:** 143
Conjure Woman, The (Chesnutt), **Supp. II Part 1:** 193; **Supp. XIV:** 57, **58–61,** 62, 63
Conklin, Grof, **Supp. I Part 2:** 672
Conkling, Hilda, **II:** 530
Conkling, Roscoe, **III:** 506
Conley, Robert J., **Supp. V:** 232
Conley, Susan, **Supp. XIII:** 111, 112
Connaroe, Joel, **Supp. IV Part 2:** 690
"Connecticut Lad, A" (White), **Supp. I Part 2:** 677
"Connecticut Valley" (Cowley), **Supp. II Part 1:** 141–142
Connecticut Yankee in King Arthur's Court, A (Twain), **I:** 209; **II:** 276; **IV:** 205
Connell, Evan S., **Supp. XIV: 79–100**
Connell, Norreys (pseudonym). *See* O'Riordan, Conal Holmes O'Connell
Connelly, Marc, **III:** 394; **Supp. I Part 2:** 679; **Supp. IX:** 190
Connery, Thomas B., **Supp. XVII:** 106
Connoisseur, The (Connell), **Supp. XIV:** 87
"Connoisseur of Chaos" (Stevens), **IV:** 89; **Retro. Supp. I:** 306
Connolly, Cyril, **Supp. XIV:** 158, 343, 348
Connors, Elizabeth. *See* Lindsay, Mrs. Vachel (Elizabeth Connors)
Conover, Roger, **Supp. I Part 1:** 95
Conquering Horse (Manfred), **Supp. X:** 126
"Conqueror Worm, The" (Poe), **Retro. Supp. II:** 261
Conquest of Canaan (Dwight), **Supp. I Part 1:** 124
Conquistador (MacLeish), **III:** 2, 3, 13–14, 15
Conrad, Alfred, **Retro. Supp. II:** 245
Conrad, Alfred H., **Supp. I Part 2:** 552
Conrad, David, **Supp. I Part 2:** 552
Conrad, Jacob, **Supp. I Part 2:** 552
Conrad, Joseph, **I:** 123, 343, 394, 405, 409, 415, 421, 485, 506, 575–576, 578; **II:** 58, 73, 74, 91, 92, 144, 263, 320, 338, 595; **III:** 28, 102, 106, 328, 464, 467, 491, 512; **IV:** 476; **Retro. Supp. I:** 80, 91, 106, 108, 231, 274, 377; **Retro. Supp. II:** 222; **Supp. I Part 1:** 292; **Supp. I Part 2:** 621, 622; **Supp. IV Part 1:** 197, 341; **Supp. IV Part 2:** 680; **Supp. V:** 249, 251, 262, 298, 307, 311; **Supp. VIII:** 4, 310; **Supp. XIV:** 112; **Supp. XVI:** 158, 212; **Supp. XVIII:** 98, 102
Conrad, Paul, **Supp. I Part 2:** 552
Conrad, Peter, **Supp. IV Part 2:** 688
"Conrad Aiken: From Savannah to Emerson" (Cowley), **Supp. II Part 1:** 43
Conrad Richter's Ohio Trilogy (Edwards), **Supp. XVIII:** 220
Conroy, Frank, **Supp. VIII:** 145; **Supp. XI:** 245; **Supp. XVI: 63–78**
Conroy, Pat, **Supp. XVIII:** 193
Conscience with the Power and Cases thereof (Ames), **IV:** 158
"Conscientious Objector, The" (Shapiro), **Supp. II Part 2:** 710
"Consciousness and Dining" (Harrison), **Supp. VIII:** 46
"Conscription Camp" (Shapiro), **Supp. II Part 2:** 705
"Consejos de Nuestra Señora de Guadalupe: Counsel from the Brown Virgin" (Mora), **Supp. XIII:** 224
"Conservation Esthetic" (Leopold), **Supp. XIV:** 179, 181, 186, 189–190
"Conserving Natural and Cultural Diversity: The Prose and Poetry of Pat Mora" (Murphy), **Supp. XIII:** 214
Considerable Town, A (M. F. K. Fisher), **Supp. XVII:** 90
"Considerations by the Way" (Emerson), **II:** 2, 5
Consider the Oyster (M. F. K. Fisher), **Supp. XVII:** 84, 87
Considine, Bob, **II:** 424
"Consolation" (Bausch), **Supp. VII:** 48
"Consolations" (Stafford), **Supp. XI:** 329
"Conspiracy of History, The: E. L. Doctorow's *The Book of Daniel*" (Levine), **Supp. IV Part 1:** 221
Conspiracy of Kings, The (Barlow), **Supp. II Part 1:** 80
Conspiracy of Pontiac, The (Parkman), **Supp. II Part 2:** 590, 595, 596, 599–600
Constab Ballads (McKay), **Supp. X:** 131, 133
Constance (Kenyon), **Supp. VII:** 170–172
Constancy (N. Boyce), **Supp. XVII:** 100
Construction of Boston, The (Koch), **Supp. XV:** 187
"Constructive Work" (Du Bois), **Supp. II Part 1:** 172
"Consumer's Report" (X. J. Kennedy), **Supp. XV:** 161–162
"Consumption" (Bryant), **Supp. I Part 1:** 169–170
"Contagiousness of Puerperal Fever, The" (Holmes), **Supp. I Part 1:** 303–304
"Contemplation in a World of Action" (Merton), **Supp. VIII:** 204
"Contemplation of Poussin" (Sarton), **Supp. VIII:** 261
"Contemplations" (Bradstreet), **Supp. I Part 1:** 112, 113, 119–122
Contemporaries (Kazin), **Supp. VIII:** 102, **103–104**
Contemporary American Playwrights (Bigsby), **Supp. XV:** 332
Contemporary American Poetry (Poulin, ed.), **Supp. IX:** 272; **Supp. XI:** 259
Contending Forces (Hopkins), **Supp. XVIII:** 284

"Contentment" (Holmes), **Supp. I Part 1:** 307
"Contest, The" (Paley), **Supp. VI:** 223, 230, 231
"Contest for Aaron Gold, The" (P. Roth), **Supp. III Part 2:** 403
Continental Drift (Banks), **Supp. V:** 13–14, 16, 227
Continental Op, The (Hammett), **Supp. IV Part 1:** 344
Continuity of American Poetry, The (Pearce), **Supp. I Part 1:** 111; **Supp. I Part 2:** 475
Continuous Harmony, A: Essays Cultural and Agricultural (Berry), **Supp. X:** 33
Continuous Life, The (Strand), **Supp. IV Part 2:** 630, 631–633
Contoski, Victor, **Supp. XII:** 181
"Contract" (Lardner), **II:** 432
"Contraption, The" (Swenson), **Supp. IV Part 2:** 643
"Contrariness of the Mad Farmer, The" (Berry), **Supp. X:** 35
"Contrition" (Dubus), **Supp. VII:** 84
"Control Burn" (Snyder), **Supp. VIII:** 301
"Control Is the Mainspring" (Komunyakaa), **Supp. XIII:** 122, 124
"Controlling the 'Sloppiness of Things' in Frank Conroy's *Stop-Time*" (Strychacz), **Supp. XVI:** 69–70
Control of Nature, The (McPhee), **Supp. III Part 1:** 310–313
"Conventional Wisdom, The" (Elkin), **Supp. VI: 52–53**
"Convergence" (Ammons), **Supp. VII:** 28
"Convergence of the Twain, The" (Hardy), **Supp. VIII:** 31, 32
Conversation (Aiken), **I:** 54
Conversation at Midnight (Millay), **III:** 138
"Conversation of Eiros and Charmion, The" (Poe), **III:** 412
"Conversation on Conversation" (Stowe), **Supp. I Part 2:** 587
"Conversations in Moscow" (Levertov), **Supp. III Part 1:** 282
Conversations on Some of the Old Poets (Lowell), **Supp. I Part 2:** 405
Conversations with Byron (Blessington), **Retro. Supp. II:** 58
Conversations with Eudora Welty (Prenshaw, ed.), **Retro. Supp. I:** 339, 340, 341, 342, 343, 352, 354
"Conversations with Helmholtz" (Allen), **Supp. XV:** 15
Conversations with Ishmael Reed (Dick and Singh, eds.), **Supp. X:** 244
Conversations with James Baldwin (Standley and Pratt, eds.), **Retro. Supp. II:** 6
Conversations with Richard Wilbur (Wilbur), **Supp. III Part 2:** 542–543
"Conversation with My Father, A" (Paley), **Supp. VI:** 220
"Conversion of the Jews, The" (P. Roth), **Retro. Supp. II:** 281; **Supp. III Part 2:** 404, 406
Convict, The: Stories (Burke), **Supp. XIV:** 25
"Convicta et Combusta" (J. Scott), **Supp. XVII:** 189
Conway, Jill, **Supp. I Part 1:** 19
Coode, John, **I:** 132
Cook, Bruce, **Supp. XII:** 130, 131, 133–134
Cook, Captain James, **I:** 2
Cook, Eleanor, **Retro. Supp. I:** 311
Cook, Elisha, **Supp. IV Part 1:** 356
Cook, Elizabeth Christine, **II:** 106
Cook, Mercer, **Supp. IV Part 1:** 368
Cooke, Alistair, **III:** 113, 119, 120
Cooke, Delmar G., **II:** 271
Cooke, Grace MacGowan, **Supp. V:** 285
Cooke, Philip Pendleton, **III:** 420
Cooke, Rose Terry, **II:** 401; **Retro. Supp. II:** 51, 136, 138; **Supp. XIII:** 152
"Cookie" (Taylor), **Supp. V:** 320
"Cookies, The" (Nye), **Supp. XIII:** 281
Cooking of Provincial France, The (M. F. K. Fisher), **Supp. XVII:** 89
Cook-Lynn, Elizabeth, **Supp. IV Part 1:** 325
Coolbrith, Ina, **I:** 193, 196
"Coole Park" (Yeats), **Supp. VIII:** 155, 159
"Coole Park and Ballylee" (Yeats), **Supp. VIII:** 156
Cooley, John, **Supp. V:** 214
Cooley, Peter, **Supp. XIII:** 76
Coolidge, Calvin, **I:** 498; **II:** 95; **Supp. I Part 2:** 647
Cooling Time: An American Poetry Vigil (Wright), **Supp. XV:** 353
"Cool Million, A" (screen story) (West and Ingster), **Retro. Supp. II:** 330
Cool Million, A (West), **III:** 425; **IV:** 287, 288, 297–299, 300; **Retro. Supp. II:** 321, 322–323, 328, **335–337**
"Cool Tombs" (Sandburg), **III:** 554
Coon, Ross, **IV:** 196
Cooney, Seamus, **Supp. XIV:** 289
"Coon Hunt" (White), **Supp. I Part 2:** 669
Co-op (Sinclair), **Supp. V:** 290
Cooper, Bernard, **Supp. XI:** 129
Cooper, Gary, **Supp. IV Part 2:** 524
Cooper, James Fenimore, **I:** 211, 257, **335–357; II:** 74, 277, 295–296, 302, 306, 309, 313, 314; **III:** 51; **IV:** 205, 333; **Retro. Supp. I:** 246; **Retro. Supp. II:** 160; **Supp. I Part 1:** 141, 155, 156, 158, 171, 372; **Supp. I Part 2:** 413, 495, 579, 585, 652, 660; **Supp. IV Part 1:** 80; **Supp. IV Part 2:** 463, 469; **Supp. V:** 209–210; **Supp. VIII:** 189; **Supp. XIV:** 227; **Supp. XVIII:** 4
Cooper, Jane, **Supp. XV:** 259
Cooper, Mrs. James Fenimore (Susan A. De Lancey), **I:** 338, 351, 354
Cooper, Mrs. William, **I:** 337
Cooper, Rand Richards, **Supp. XVI:** 74
Cooper, Susan Fenimore, **I:** 337, 354
Cooper, William, **I:** 337–338, 351
Coover, Robert, **Supp. IV Part 1:** 388; **Supp. V: 39–55; Supp. XII:** 152; **Supp. XIV:** 96; **Supp. XVII:** 6
Copacetic (Komunyakaa), **Supp. XIII: 116–118,** 126
Cope, Wendy, **Supp. XV:** 117
Copland, Aaron, **II:** 586; **Supp. I Part 1:** 281; **Supp. III Part 2:** 619; **Supp. IV Part 1:** 79, 80–81, 84
Coplas de Don Jorge Manrique (Longfellow, trans.), **II:** 488, 492
Coppée, François Edouard Joachim, **II:** 325
Copperhead, The (Frederic), **II:** 134–135
Copper Sun (Cullen), **Supp. IV Part 1:** 167, 168
Coppola, Francis Ford, **Supp. XI:** 171, 172; **Supp. XII:** 75
Coprolites (Goldbarth), **Supp. XII: 177–178,** 180, 183
Coral and Captive Israel (Reznikoff), **Supp. XIV:** 288
"Coral Ring, The" (Stowe), **Supp. I Part 2:** 586
"Cora Unashamed" (Hughes), **Supp. I Part 1:** 329, 330
"Corazón del Corrido" (Mora), **Supp. XIII:** 225
Corban Ephphata (Li Lin Lee), **Supp. XV:** 225
Corbett, Gentlemen Jim, **II:** 416
Corbett, William, **Supp. XI:** 248; **Supp. XVI:** 286, 295
Corbière, Jean Antoine, **II:** 354–355, 528
Cordiall Water, A: A garland of Odd & Old Receipts to Assuage the Ills of Man and Beast (M. F. K. Fisher), **Supp. XVII:** 88, 90
Cording, Robert, **Supp. IX:** 328; **Supp. XII:** 184
Core, George, **Supp. XVIII:** 86
Corelli, Marie, **III:** 579
Corey, Lewis, **Supp. I Part 2:** 645
"Corinna's Going a-Maying" (Herrick), **Supp. XIV:** 8, 9
"Coriolan" (Eliot), **I:** 580
"Coriolanus and His Mother" (Schwartz), **Supp. II Part 2:** 643, 644–645
"Corkscrew" (Hammett), **Supp. IV Part 1:** 345, 347
Corkum, Gerald, **I:** 37
"Corky's Brother" (Neugeboren), **Supp. XVI:** 225
Corky's Brother (Neugeboren), **Supp. XVI:** 225
Corliss, Richard, **Supp. VIII:** 73
Corman, Cid, **Supp. III Part 2:** 624, 625, 626, 627, 628; **Supp. IV Part 1:** 144; **Supp. VIII:** 292; **Supp. XV:** 74, 153
"Corn" (Lanier), **Supp. I Part 1:** 352, 353, 354, 356–361, 364, 366
Corn, Alfred, **Supp. IX:** 156; **Supp. XV:** 250
Corneille, Pierre, **Supp. I Part 2:** 716; **Supp. IX:** 131
Cornell, Esther, **I:** 231
Cornell, Katherine, **IV:** 356
"Corners" (Dunn), **Supp. XI:** 148
Cornhuskers (Sandburg), **III:** 583–585
"Corn-Planting, The" (Anderson), **I:** 114
"Coroner's Report" (Wrigley), **Supp. XVIII:** 295

"Corporal of Artillery" (Dubus), **Supp. VII:** 84, 85
"Corpse Plant, The" (Rich), **Supp. I Part 2:** 555
Corpus Christi (McNally), **Supp. XIII: 205–206,** 209
Corradi, Juan, **Supp. IV Part 1:** 208
"Correspondences" (Baudelaire), **I:** 63
"Corrido de Gregorio Cortez" (Mora), **Supp. XIII:** 225
"Corrigenda" (Komunyakaa), **Supp. XIII:** 115, 116
Corruption City (McCoy), **Supp. XIII:** 175
Corso, Gregory, **Supp. II Part 1:** 30; **Supp. IV Part 1:** 90; **Supp. XII: 117–138; Supp. XIV:** 150; **Supp. XVI:** 135
"Corsons Inlet" (Ammons), **Supp. VII:** 25–26
Corsons Inlet (Ammons), **Supp. VII:** 25–26, 28–29, 36
Cortázar, Julio, **Retro. Supp. I:** 278
"Cortège for Rosenbloom" (Stevens), **IV:** 81
Cortez, Hernando, **III:** 2
Coser, Lewis, **Supp. I Part 2:** 650
Cosgrave, Patrick, **Retro. Supp. II:** 185
Cosmic Optimism: A Study of the Interpretation of Evolution by American Poets from Emerson to Robinson (Conner), **Supp. I Part 1:** 73
"Cosmological Eye, The" (H. Miller), **III:** 183
Cosmological Eye, The (H. Miller), **III:** 174, 184
"Cosmos" (Beattie), **Supp. V:** 35
"Cost, The" (Hecht), **Supp. X:** 62–63
Costello, Bonnie, **Retro. Supp. II:** 40
Costner, Kevin, **Supp. VIII:** 45
"Cost of Living, The" (Malamud), **Supp. I Part 2:** 429, 437
Cott, Jonathan, **Supp. XVI:** 104, 106
"Cottagers' Corner" column (D. West), **Supp. XVIII:** 286
"Cottage Street, 1953" (Wilbur), **Supp. III Part 2:** 543, 561
"Cottagette, The" (Gilman), **Supp. XI:** 207
Cotten, Joseph, **Supp. IV Part 2:** 524
Cotter, James Finn, **Supp. X:** 202
Cotton, John, **Supp. I Part 1:** 98, 101, 110, 111, 116
Cotton, Joseph, **Supp. XII:** 160
Cotton, Seaborn, **Supp. I Part 1:** 101
Cotton Comes to Harlem (C. Himes), **Supp. XVI:** 143, 144
Cotton Comes to Harlem (film, O. Davis), **Supp. XVI:** 144
"Cotton Song" (Toomer), **Supp. IX:** 312
Couch, W. T., **Supp. X:** 46
Coughlin, Ruth Pollack, **Supp. VIII:** 45
Coulette, Henri, **Supp. V:** 180; **Supp. XIII:** 312; **Supp. XV:** 74, 75
Coultrap-McQuin, Susan, **Supp. XVI:** 85, 92
"Council of State, A" (Dunbar), **Supp. II Part 1:** 211, 213
"Count Dracula" (Allen), **Supp. XV:** 15
"Countee Cullen at 'The Heights'" (Tuttleton), **Supp. IV Part 1:** 166
Counterfeiters, The (Gide), **Supp. IV Part 1:** 80; **Supp. IV Part 2:** 681
"Countering" (Ammons), **Supp. VII:** 28
Counterlife, The (P. Roth), **Retro. Supp. II:** 279, 280, 291; **Supp. III Part 2:** 424–426
Counter-Statement (Burke), **I:** 270–272; **IV:** 431
"Countess, The" (Whittier), **Supp. I Part 2:** 691, 694
Count Frontenac and New France Under Louis XIV (Parkman), **Supp. II Part 2:** 607, 609–610
"Counting Small-Boned Bodies" (R. Bly), **Supp. IV Part 1:** 62
"Counting the Children" (Gioia), **Supp. XV: 122–123**
"Counting the Mad" (Justice), **Supp. VII:** 117
Count of Monte Cristo, The (Dumas), **III:** 386, 396; **Supp. XVII:** 64, 216
"Countries We Live In, The" (Zach; Everwine, trans.), **Supp. XV:** 87
"Country Boy in Boston, The" (Howells), **II:** 255
Country By-Ways (Jewett), **II:** 402
Country Doctor, A (Jewett), **II:** 391, 392, 396, 404–405; **Retro. Supp. II:** 131, 141, 146
"Country Full of Swedes" (Caldwell), **I:** 297, 309
Country Girl, The (Odets), **Supp. II Part 2:** 546, 547, 548–549
"Country House" (Kumin), **Supp. IV Part 2:** 446
"Country Husband, The" (Cheever), **Supp. I Part 1:** 184, 189
"Country Marriage" (C. Frost), **Supp. XV:** 99
Countrymen of Bones (R. O. Butler), **Supp. XII:** 62, **65–66**
"Country Mouse, The" (Bishop), **Retro. Supp. II:** 37, 38, 51
Country Music: Selected Early Poems (Wright), **Supp. V:** 332, 335, 338, 342
Country of a Thousand Years of Peace, The (Merrill), **Supp. III Part 1:** 321, 322, 331
"Country of Elusion, The" (O. Henry), **Supp. II Part 1:** 407
Country Of Language, The (Sanders), **Supp. XVI:** 277
Country of Marriage, The (Berry), **Supp. X:** 33
Country of Strangers, A (Richter), **Supp. XVIII:** 217
Country of the Pointed Firs, The (Jewett), **II:** 392, 399, 405, 409–411; **Retro. Supp. I:** 6; **Retro. Supp. II:** 134, 136, 139, 140, 141, 145, 146, 147; **Supp. VIII:** 126; **Supp. XIII:** 152
"Country Printer, The" (Freneau), **Supp. II Part 1:** 269
"Country Wife, The" (Gioia), **Supp. XV:** 120
Count Your Bullets (film), **Supp. XVII:** 141
Count Zero (W. Gibson), **Supp. XVI:** 19, **126–127,** 129
Coup, The (Updike), **Retro. Supp. I:** 331, 334, 335
"Coup de Grâce, The" (Bierce), **I:** 202
Couperin, François, **III:** 464
"Couple, The" (Olds), **Supp. X:** 206
"Couple of Hamburgers, A" (Thurber), **Supp. I Part 2:** 616
"Couple of Nuts, A" (Z. Fitzgerald), **Supp. IX:** 58, 71, 72
Couples (Updike), **IV:** 214, 215, 216, 217, 227, 229–230; **Retro. Supp. I:** 320, 327, 330; **Supp. XII:** 296
Cournos, John, **III:** 465; **Supp. I Part 1:** 258
"Course in Creative Writing, A" (Stafford), **Supp. XI:** 327
"Course of a Particular, The" (Stevens), **Retro. Supp. I:** 312
"Coursier de Jeanne d'Arc, Le" (McCarriston), **Supp. XIV:** 267–268
Courtier, The (Castiglione), **III:** 282
"'Courtin,' The" (Lowell), **Supp. I Part 2:** 415
"Courting of Sister Wisby, The" (Jewett), **Retro. Supp. II:** 134, 135, 146
"Courting the Famous Figures at the Grotto of Improbable Thought" (B. Kelly), **Supp. XVII:** 127–128
"Courtship" (Dove), **Supp. IV Part 1:** 248
"Courtship, Diligence" (Dove), **Supp. IV Part 1:** 248
Courtship of Miles Standish, The (Longfellow), **II:** 489, 502–503; **Retro. Supp. II:** 155, **161–162,** 163, 166, 168
"Cousin Aubrey" (Taylor), **Supp. V:** 328
Cousine Bette (Balzac), **Retro. Supp. II:** 98
Couturier, Maurice, **Supp. IV Part 1:** 44
Covarrubias, Miguel, **Supp. XVI:** 187
"Covered Bridges" (Kingsolver), **Supp. VII:** 203
"Cover Photograph" (Nelson), **Supp. XVIII:** 173
Cowan, Lester, **III:** 148
Cowan, Louise, **IV:** 120, 125
Coward, Noel, **Retro. Supp. I:** 65; **Supp. I Part 1:** 332; **Supp. V:** 101; **Supp. XV:** 329
"Cowardice" (Theroux), **Supp. VIII:** 313
Cowboy Mouth (Shepard), **Supp. III Part 2:** 441–442
"Cowboys" (Salter). *See* "Dirt" (Salter)
Cowboys (Shepard), **Supp. III Part 2:** 432
Cowboys #2 (Shepard), **Supp. III Part 2:** 437, 438
Cowell, Henry, **Supp. IV Part 1:** 80, 82
Cowen, Wilson Walker, **Supp. IV Part 2:** 435
Cowie, Alexander, **IV:** 70
"Cow in Apple Time, The" (Frost), **II:** 154; **Retro. Supp. I:** 131
Cowl, Jane, **IV:** 357
Cowley, Abraham, **III:** 508; **IV:** 158; **Supp. I Part 1:** 357

Cowley, Malcolm, **I:** 246, 253, 254, 255, 256, 257, 283, 385; **II:** 26, 57, 94, 456; **III:** 606; **IV:** 123; **Retro. Supp. I:** 73, 91, 97; **Retro. Supp. II:** 77, 83, 89, 221, 330; **Supp. I Part 1:** 174; **Supp. I Part 2:** 609, 610, 620, 647, 654, 678; **Supp. II Part 1:** 103, **135–156; Supp. VIII:** 96; **Supp. XV:** 142
Cowley, Marguerite Frances Baird (Mrs. Malcolm Cowley), **Supp. I Part 2:** 615; **Supp. II Part 1:** 138, 139
Cowley, Muriel Maurer (Mrs. Malcolm Cowley), **Supp. II Part 1:** 139
Cowley, Susan Cheever (Susan Cheever), **Supp. I Part 1:** 175; **Supp. IX:** 133
Cowper, William, **II:** 17, 304; **III:** 508, 511; **Supp. I Part 1:** 150, 151, 152; **Supp. I Part 2:** 539
"Cow Wandering in the Bare Field, The" (Jarrell), **II:** 371, 388
Cox, Martha Heasley, **Supp. IX:** 2, 4, 11–12
Cox, Sidney, **Retro. Supp. I:** 131
Cox, Stephen, **Supp. IV Part 2:** 523, 524
Coxey, Jacob, **II:** 464
"Coxon Fund, The" (James), **Retro. Supp. I:** 228
"Coy Mistress" (A. Finch), **Supp. XVII:** 72
Coyne, Patricia, **Supp. V:** 123
"Coyote Ortiz: *Canis latrans latrans* in the Poetry of Simon Ortiz" (P. C. Smith), **Supp. IV Part 2:** 509
Coyote's Daylight Trip (Gunn Allen), **Supp. IV Part 1:** 320, 324
Coyote Was Here (Ortiz), **Supp. IV Part 2:** 499
Cozzens, James Gould, **I: 358–380; II:** 459
Crabbe, George, **II:** 304; **III:** 469, 508, 511, 521
"Crab-Boil" (Dove), **Supp. IV Part 1:** 249
"Cracked Looking-Glass, The" (Porter), **III:** 434, 435, 446
"Cracker Chidlings" (Rawlings), **Supp. X:** 224, 228
Cracks (Purdy), **Supp. VII:** 277–278
"Crack-Up, The" (Fitzgerald), **I:** 509; **Retro. Supp. I:** 113, 114
Crack-Up, The (Fitzgerald), **II:** 80; **III:** 35, 45; **Retro. Supp. I:** 113, 115; **Supp. IX:** 61; **Supp. V:** 276
"Crack-up of American Optimism, The: Vachel Lindsay, the Dante of the Fundamentalists" (Viereck), **Supp. I Part 2:** 403
Cradle Will Rock, The (Blitzstein), **Supp. I Part 1:** 277, 278
Craft of Fiction, The (Lubbock), **I:** 504; **Supp. VIII:** 165
Craft of Peter Taylor, The (McAlexander, ed.), **Supp. V:** 314
Craig, Gordon, **III:** 394
Crain, Jane Larkin, **Supp. V:** 123; **Supp. XII:** 167, 168
Cram, Ralph Adams, **I:** 19
Cramer, Stephen, **Supp. XI:** 139
Cramer, Steven, **Supp. XV:** 26
Crandall, Reuben, **Supp. I Part 2:** 686
Crane, Agnes, **I:** 406
Crane, Edmund, **I:** 407
Crane, Hart, **I:** 61, 62, 97, 109, 116, 266, **381–404; II:** 133, 215, 306, 368, 371, 536, 542; **III:** 260, 276, 453, 485, 521; **IV:** 122, 123–124, 127, 128, 129, 135, 139, 140, 141, 341, 380, 418, 419; **Retro. Supp. I:** 427; **Retro. Supp. II: 75–91; Supp. I Part 1:** 86; **Supp. II Part 1:** 89, 152; **Supp. III Part 1:** 20, 63, 350; **Supp. IX:** 38, 229, 320; **Supp. V:** 342; **Supp. VIII:** 39; **Supp. X:** 115, 116, 120; **Supp. XI:** 123, 131; **Supp. XII:** 198; **Supp. XV:** 138
Crane, Jonathan, Jr., **I:** 407
Crane, Jonathan Townley, **I:** 406
Crane, Luther, **I:** 406
Crane, Milton, **Supp. XV:** 144
Crane, Mrs. Jonathan Townley, **I:** 406
Crane, Nellie, **I:** 407
Crane, R. S., **Supp. I Part 2:** 423
Crane, Stephen, **I:** 34, 169–170, 201, 207, 211, **405–427,** 477, 506, 519; **II:** 58, 144, 198, 262, 263, 264, 276, 289, 290, 291; **III:** 314, 317, 334, 335, 454, 505, 585; **IV:** 207, 208, 256, 350, 475; **Retro. Supp. I:** 231, 325; **Retro. Supp. II:** 97, 123; **Supp. I Part 1:** 314; **Supp. III Part 2:** 412; **Supp. IV Part 1:** 350, 380; **Supp. IV Part 2:** 680, 689, 692; **Supp. IX:** 1, 14; **Supp. VIII:** 98, 105; **Supp. X:** 223; **Supp. XI:** 95; **Supp. XII:** 50; **Supp. XIV:** 21, 50, 51, 227; **Supp. XVII:** 71, 228; **Supp. XVIII:** 74, 75
Crane, William, **I:** 407
Cranford (Gaskell), **Supp. IX:** 79
Crashaw, William, **IV:** 145, 150, 151, 165
"Crash Report" (McGrath), **Supp. X:** 116
Crater, The (Cooper), **I:** 354, 355
Cratylus (Plato), **II:** 10
"Craven Street Gazette" (Franklin), **II:** 119
"Crawdad, The" (F. Wright), **Supp. XVII:** 244
Crawdad Creek (Sanders), **Supp. XVI:** 269
Crawford, Brad, **Supp. XI:** 133
Crawford, Eva, **I:** 199
Crawford, F. Marion, **III:** 320
Crawford, Joan, **Supp. I Part 1:** 67
Crawford, Kathleen, **I:** 289
"Crayon House" (Rukeyser), **Supp. VI:** 273
Crayon Miscellany, The (Irving), **II:** 312–313
Crazed, The (Jin), **Supp. XVIII: 99–100**
"Crazy about her Shrimp" (Simic), **Supp. VIII:** 282
"Crazy Cock" (H. Miller), **III:** 177
"Crazy Gypsy" (Salinas), **Supp. XIII:** 313–314
Crazy Gypsy (Salinas), **Supp. XIII:** 311, **313–315,** 316
Crazy Horse, **Supp. IV Part 2:** 488, 489
Crazy Horse (McMurtry), **Supp. V:** 233
Crazy Horse in Stillness (Heyen), **Supp. XIII:** 344
"Crazy in the Stir" (C. Himes), **Supp. XVI:** 137
Crazy Kill, The (C. Himes), **Supp. XVI:** 143
Creating a Role (Stanislavsky), **Supp. XIV:** 243
"Creation, According to Coyote, The" (Ortiz), **Supp. IV Part 2:** 505
Creation: A Novel (Vidal), **Supp. IV Part 2:** 677, 685, 688
"Creation of Anguish" (Nemerov), **III:** 269
"Creation Story" (Gunn Allen), **Supp. IV Part 1:** 325
"Creative and Cultural Lag" (Ellison), **Retro. Supp. II:** 116; **Supp. II Part 1:** 229
"Creative and Cultural Lag" (Wllison), **Supp. XVIII:** 283
Creative Criticism (Spingarn), **I:** 266
"Creative Democracy" (Locke), **Supp. XIV:** 208
Creative Present, The (Balkian and Simmons, eds.), **Supp. XI:** 230
Creatures in an Alphabet (illus. Barnes), **Supp. III Part 1:** 43
"Credences of Summer" (Stevens), **IV:** 93–94
"Credo" (Bynner), **Supp. XV:** 50
"Credo" (Du Bois), **Supp. II Part 1:** 169
"Credo" (Jeffers), **Supp. II Part 2:** 424
"Credos and Curios" (Thurber), **Supp. I Part 2:** 606, 613
Creech, James, **Retro. Supp. I:** 254
"Creed for Americans, A" (Benét), **Supp. XI:** 52
"Creed of a Beggar, The" (Lindsay), **Supp. I Part 2:** 379
Creekmore, Hubert, **II:** 586
Creeley, Robert, **Retro. Supp. I:** 411; **Supp. II Part 1:** 30; **Supp. III Part 1:** 2; **Supp. III Part 2:** 622, 626, 629; **Supp. IV Part 1: 139–161,** 322, 325; **Supp. XI:** 317; **Supp. XIII:** 104, 112; **Supp. XIV:** 150; **Supp. XVI:** 283
Creelman, James Ashmore, **Supp. XVI:** 186–187
"Cremona Violin, The" (Lowell), **II:** 523
"Crêpe de Chine" (Doty), **Supp. XI:** 128
"Cressy" (Harte), **Supp. II Part 1:** 354, 356
"Cretan Woman, The" (Jeffers), **Supp. II Part 2:** 435
Crèvecoeur, Michel-Guillaume Jean de, **I:** 229; **Supp. I Part 1: 227–252**
Crèvecoeur's Eighteenth-Century Travels in Pennsylvania and New York (Adams), **Supp. I Part 1:** 251
Crevel, René, **Supp. XIV:** 343
Crewe-Jones, Florence, **Supp. XVII:** 58
Crewe Train (Macaulay), **Supp. XII:** 88
Crews, Harry, **Supp. X:** 11, 12; **Supp. XI: 99–117,** 245; **Supp. XVIII:** 195
Crichton, Michael, **Supp. XIV:** 316
Crick, Philip, **Supp. XVI:** 289
"Crickets" (R. O. Butler), **Supp. XII:** 71

Criers and Kibitzers, Kibitzers and Criers (Elkin), **Supp. VI: 45–46,** 57
Crime and Punishment (Dostoevsky), **II:** 60, 130; **IV:** 484; **Supp. IV Part 2:** 525; **Supp. VIII:** 282; **Supp. XII:** 281; **Supp. XVII:** 155; **Supp. XVIII:** 278
Crime at Scottsboro, The (Endore), **Supp. XVII:** 59
Crimes and Misdemeanors (film; Allen), **Supp. XV:** 1, 2, **11,** 12
Crisis papers (Paine), **Supp. I Part 2:** 508–509, 510
"Criteria of Negro Arts" (Du Bois), **Supp. II Part 1:** 181
"Critiad, The" (Winters), **Supp. II Part 2:** 794, 799
Critical Anthology A (Untermeyer), **Supp. XV:** 310
Critical Essays on Charlotte Perkins Gilman (Karpinski, ed.), **Supp. XI:** 201
Critical Essays on Peter Taylor (McAlexander), **Supp. V:** 319, 320, 323–324
Critical Essays on Robert Bly (Davis), **Supp. IV Part 1:** 64, 69
Critical Essays on Wallace Stegner (Arthur), **Supp. IV Part 2:** 606
Critical Fable, A (Lowell), **II:** 511–512, 527, 529–530
Critical Guide to Leaves of Grass, A (J. Miller), **IV:** 352
Critical Response to Joan Didion, The (Felton), **Supp. IV Part 1:** 210
Critical Temper of Alain Locke, The: A Selection of His Essays on Art and Culture (Stewart, ed.), **Supp. XIV:** 196, **210–211,** 213
"Critic as Artist, The" (Wilde), **Supp. X:** 189
Criticism and Fiction (Howells), **II:** 288
Criticism and Ideology (Eagleton), **Retro. Supp. I:** 67
Criticism in the Borderlands (Calderón and Saldívar, eds.), **Supp. IV Part 2:** 544
"Critics, The" (Jong), **Supp. V:** 119
"Critics and Connoisseurs" (Moore), **III:** 209
Critic's Notebook, A (Howe), **Supp. VI:** 126–128
"Critic's Task, The" (Kazin), **Supp. VIII:** 103
"Critic Who Does Not Exist, The" (Wilson), **IV:** 431
"Critique de la Vie Quotidienne" (Barthelme), **Supp. IV Part 1:** 50
Critique of Pure Reason (Kant), **Supp. XVI:** 184
Croce, Benedetto, **I:** 58, 255, 265, 273, 281; **III:** 610
Crockett, Davy, **II:** 307; **III:** 227; **IV:** 266; **Supp. I Part 2:** 411
Crofter and the Laird, The (McPhee), **Supp. III Part 1:** 301–302, 307
Croly, Herbert, **I:** 229, 231, 235; **IV:** 436
Cromwell, Oliver, **IV:** 145, 146, 156; **Supp. I Part 1:** 111
Cronin, A. J., **Supp. XVII:** 59
Cronin, Dr. Archibald, **III:** 578
Cronin, Justin, **Supp. X:** 10
Crooke, Dr. Helkiah, **Supp. I Part 1:** 98, 104
Crooks, Alan, **Supp. V:** 226
Crooks, Robert, **Supp. XIII:** 237
"Crop, The" (O'Connor), **Retro. Supp. II:** 223–225
Crosby, Caresse, **I:** 385; **III:** 473; **Retro. Supp. II:** 85; **Supp. XII:** 198
Crosby, Harry, **I:** 385; **Retro. Supp. II:** 85
"Cross" (Hughes), **Supp. I Part 1:** 325; **Supp. XVIII:** 124
Crossan, John Dominic, **Supp. V:** 251
"Cross Country Snow" (Hemingway), **II:** 249
Cross Creek (Rawlings), **Supp. X:** 223, 226, 228, **231–232,** 233, 234, 235
Cross Creek Cookery (Rawlings), **Supp. X:** 233
Crossing, The (McCarthy), **Supp. VIII:** 175, **184–186**
"Crossing, The" (Swenson), **Supp. IV Part 2:** 644
"Crossing Brooklyn Ferry" (Whitman), **IV:** 333, 340, 341; **Retro. Supp. I:** 389, 396, 397, 400–401
"Crossing into Poland" (Babel), **Supp. XIV:** 84
Crossings (Chuang), **Supp. X:** 291
"Crossings" (Hogan), **Supp. IV Part 1:** 412
Crossing the Water (Plath), **Retro. Supp. II:** 248; **Supp. I Part 2:** 526, 538
Crossing to Safety (Stegner), **Supp. IV Part 2:** 599, 606, 612, 613–614
"Cross of Snow, The" (Longfellow), **II:** 490; **Retro. Supp. II:** 169–170
"Crossover" (O. Butler), **Supp. XIII:** 61
"Cross-Roads, The" (Lowell), **II:** 523
"Crossroads of the World Etc." (Merwin), **Supp. III Part 1:** 347, 348
Cross-Section (Seaver), **IV:** 485
Cross the Border, Close the Gap (Fiedler), **Supp. XIII:** 104
"Cross Ties" (X. J. Kennedy), **Supp. XV:** 158
Cross Ties (X. J. Kennedy), **Supp. XV:** 165, **166–167**
"Croup" (Karr), **Supp. XI:** 243
Crouse, Russel, **III:** 284
"Crow" (Hogan), **Supp. IV Part 1:** 405
Crow (Hughes), **Supp. XV:** 347, 348
"Crow, The" (Creeley), **Supp. IV Part 1:** 148–149
Crow and the Heart,The (Carruth), **Supp. XVI:** 47–48
"Crowded Street, The" (Bryant), **Supp. I Part 1:** 168
Crowder, A. B., **Supp. XI:** 107
"Crow Jane" (Baraka), **Supp. II Part 1:** 38
Crowninshield, Frank, **III:** 123; **Supp. IX:** 201
Crown of Columbus (Erdrich and Dorris), **Supp. IV Part 1:** 260
"Crows, The" (Bogan), **Supp. III Part 1:** 50, 51
Crucial Instances (Wharton), **Retro. Supp. I:** 365, 367
Crucible, The (A. Miller), **III:** 147, 148, 155, 156–158, 159, 166; **Supp. XIII:** 206
"Crucifix in the Filing Cabinet" (Shapiro), **Supp. II Part 2:** 712
"Crude Foyer" (Stevens), **Retro. Supp. I:** 310
"Cruel and Barbarous Treatment" (McCarthy), **II:** 562, 563
"Cruel Mother, The" (B. Kelly), **Supp. XVII:** 126
Cruise of the Dazzler, The (London), **II:** 465
Cruise of the Snark, The (London), **II:** 476–477
"Cruising with the Beach Boys" (Gioia), **Supp. XV:** 118
"'Crumbling Idols' by Hamlin Garland" (Chopin), **Supp. I Part 1:** 217
"Crusade of the Excelsior, The" (Harte), **Supp. II Part 1:** 336, 354
"Crusoe in England" (Bishop), **Retro. Supp. II:** 50; **Supp. I Part 1:** 93, 95, 96; **Supp. III Part 1:** 10, 18
Cry, the Beloved Country (Paton), **Supp. VIII:** 126
Cryer, Dan, **Supp. VIII:** 86, 88; **Supp. XII:** 164
Crying of Lot 49, The (Pynchon), **Supp. II Part 2:** 618, 619, 621, 630–633
"Crying Sisters, The" (Rand), **Supp. IV Part 2:** 524
"Crying Wolf" (C. Frost), **Supp. XV:** 101
Cryptogram, The (Mamet), **Supp. XIV:** 240, 247, 255
"Crystal, The" (Aiken), **I:** 60
"Crystal, The" (Lanier), **Supp. I Part 1:** 364, 370
"Crystal Cage, The" (Kunitz), **Supp. III Part 1:** 258
"Crytal" (Sobin), **Supp. XVI:** 283
Cry to Heaven (Rice), **Supp. VII:** 300–301
"Cuba" (Hemingway), **II:** 258
"Cuba Libre" (Baraka), **Supp. II Part 1:** 33
Cudjoe, Selwyn, **Supp. IV Part 1:** 6
"Cudjo's Own Story of the Last American Slaver" (Hurston), **Supp. VI:** 153
Cudlipp, Thelma, **I:** 501
Cudworth, Ralph, **II:** 9, 10
"Cuentista" (Mora), **Supp. XIII:** 224
"Cuento de agua santa, Un" (Mora), **Supp. XIII:** 224
Cujo (King), **Supp. V:** 138–139, 143, 149, 152
Cukor, George, **Supp. XVI:** 192
Cullen, Countee, **Retro. Supp. I:** 207; **Retro. Supp. II:** 114; **Supp. I Part 1:** 49, 325; **Supp. III Part 1:** 73, 75, 76; **Supp. IV Part 1: 163–174; Supp. IX:** 306, 309; **Supp. X:** 136, 140; **Supp. XIII:** 186; **Supp. XVIII:** 122,131, 185, 279, 280, 282, 284
"Cultivation of Christmas Trees, The" (Eliot), **I:** 579
"Cult of the Best, The" (Arnold), **I:** 223
"Cultural Exchange" (Hughes), **Supp. I Part 1:** 341

"Cultural Pluralism: A New Americanism" (Locke), **Supp. XIV:** 195
"Cultural Relativism and Ideological Peace" (Locke), **Supp. XIV:** 202, 212
"Culture" (Emerson), **III:** 2, 4
"Culture, Self, and Style" (Gass), **Supp. VI:** 88
"Culture and Religion" (Olds), **Supp. X:** 214
Culture of Cities, The (Mumford), **Supp. II Part 2:** 492, 494–495
Cummings, E. E., **I:** 44, 48, 64, 105, 176, **428–450,** 475, 477, 482, 526; **III:** 20, 196, 476; **IV:** 384, 402, 415, 427, 433; **Retro. Supp. II:** 178, 328; **Supp. I Part 2:** 622, 678; **Supp. III Part 1:** 73; **Supp. IV Part 2:** 637, 641; **Supp. IX:** 20; **Supp. XV:** 312, 338
Cummings, Robert, **Supp. IV Part 2:** 524
Cummins, James, **Supp. XVII:** 74
Cunard, Lady, **III:** 459
Cunningham, J. V., **Supp. XV:** 169
Cunningham, Merce, **Supp. IV Part 1:** 83; **Supp. XV:** 187
Cunningham, Michael, **Supp. XII:** 80; **Supp. XV: 55–71**
Cup of Gold (Steinbeck), **IV:** 51, 53, 61–64, 67
"Cupola, The" (Bogan), **Supp. III Part 1:** 53
"Curandera" (Mora), **Supp. XIII:** 214, 222
Curé de Tours, Le (Balzac), **I:** 509
Cure for Dreams, A: A Novel (Gibbons), **Supp. X: 45–47,** 48, 50
Curie, Marie, **IV:** 420, 421; **Supp. I Part 2:** 569
Curie, Pierre, **IV:** 420
Curiosa Americana (Mather), **Supp. II Part 2:** 463
Curiosities (Matthews), **Supp. IX:** 151, 152
"Curious Case of Sidd Finch, The" (Plimpton), **Supp. XVI:** 244
"Curious Shifts of the Poor" (Dreiser), **Retro. Supp. II:** 97
"Currents and Counter-Currents in Medical Science" (Holmes), **Supp. I Part 1:** 305
"Curried Cow" (Bierce), **I:** 200
Curry, Professor W. C., **IV:** 122
Curse of the Jade Scorpion, The (film; Allen), **Supp. XV:** 11
Curse of the Starving Class (Shepard), **Supp. III Part 2:** 433, 447–448
Curse of the Werewolf, The (film), **Supp. XVII:** 56
"Curse on a Thief, A" (X. J. Kennedy), **Supp. XV:** 171
"Curtain, The" (Chandler), **Supp. IV Part 1:** 122
Curtain Calls: British and American Women and the Theater, 1660–1820 (Saar), **Supp. XV:** 237
"Curtain of Green, A" (Welty), **IV:** 263–264
Curtain of Green, A (Welty), **IV:** 261–264, 268, 283
Curtain of Green and Other Stories, A (Welty), **Retro. Supp. I:** 343, 344, 345, 346, 347, 355
Curtain of Trees (opera), **Supp. IV Part 2:** 552
"Curtain Raiser, A" (Stein), **IV:** 43, 44
"Curtains" (Cisneros), **Supp. VII:** 66
Curtin, John, **Supp. IX:** 184
Curtis, George William, **Supp. I Part 1:** 307; **Supp. XVIII:** 3, 14
Curve (Goldbarth), **Supp. XII:** 181
Curve of Binding Energy, The (McPhee), **Supp. III Part 1:** 301
Curzon, Mary, **III:** 52
Cushing, Caleb, **Supp. I Part 2:** 684, 686
Cushman, Howard, **Supp. I Part 2:** 652
Cushman, Stephen, **Retro. Supp. I:** 430
"Custard Heart, The" (Parker), **Supp. IX:** 201
Custer, General George, **I:** 489, 491
Custer Died for Your Sins (Deloria), **Supp. IV Part 1:** 323; **Supp. IV Part 2:** 504
"Custom House, The" (Hawthorne), **II:** 223; **Retro. Supp. I:** 147–148, 157
Custom of the Country, The (Wharton), **IV:** 318; **Retro. Supp. I:** 374, **375–376**
"Cut" (Plath), **Retro. Supp. II:** 253
"Cut-Glass Bowl, The" (Fitzgerald), **II:** 88
Cutting, Bronson, **III:** 600
Cutting Lisa (Everett), **Supp. XVIII: 56**
"Cuttings, *later*" (Roethke), **III:** 532
"Cyberpunk" (Bethke), **Supp. XVI:** 121
Cyberspace trilogy (W. Gibson). *See* Sprawl trilogy (W. Gibson)
"Cycles, The" (Pinsky), **Supp. VI:** 250–252
Cynic's Word Book, The (Bierce), **I:** 197, 205, 208, 209, 210
Cynthia Ozick (Lowin), **Supp. V:** 273
Cynthia Ozick's Comic Art (Cohen), **Supp. V:** 273
Cynthia Ozick's Fiction (Kauvar), **Supp. V:** 273

D

Da Capo: Best Music Writing 2002 (Lethem, ed.), **Supp. XVIII:** 148
Dacey, Philip, **Supp. IV Part 1:** 70
Dacier, André, **II:** 10
"Dad" (Cullen), **Supp. IV Part 1:** 167
"Daddy" (Plath), **Retro. Supp. II:** 250–251; **Supp. I Part 2:** 529, 542, 545, 546; **Supp. II Part 2:** 688
"Daemon, The" (Bogan), **Supp. III Part 1:** 58, 61
"Daemon Lover, The" (Jackson), **Supp. IX:** 116–117
"Daffodils" (Nelson and Espeland), **Supp. XVIII:** 181
"Daffodils" (Wordsworth), **Supp. XIII:** 284
"Daffy Duck in Hollywood" (Ashbery), **Supp. III Part 1:** 18
D'Agata, John, **Supp. XII:** 97, 98
Dago Red (Fante), **Supp. XI:** 160, 169
Dahl, Roald, **Supp. IX:** 114
Dahlberg, Edward, **I:** 231; **Retro. Supp. I:** 426; **Supp. III Part 2:** 624; **Supp. XIV:** 148; **Supp. XVIII:** 148
Dahlberg, R'lene, **Supp. XIV:** 148
Daiches, David, **Retro. Supp. II:** 243; **Supp. I Part 2:** 536
"Daily Horoscope" (Gioia), **Supp. XV:** 119
Daily Horoscope (Gioia), **Supp. XV:** 112, **118–121,** 126
Daily Modernism (Podnieks), **Supp. X:** 189
Dain Curse, The (Hammett), **Supp. IV Part 1:** 348
"Daisies" (Glück), **Supp. V:** 88
"Daisy" (Oates), **Supp. II Part 2:** 523
Daisy (S. and A. Warner), **Supp. XVIII:** 268
Daisy-Head Mayzie (Geisel), **Supp. XVI:** 112
"Daisy Miller" (H. James), **II:** 325, 326, 327, 329; **IV:** 316
Daisy Miller (H. James), **Retro. Supp. I:** 216, 220, 222, 223, 228, 231; **Supp. XVIII:** 165
Dale, Charlie, **Supp. IV Part 2:** 584
Dali, Salvador, **II:** 586; **Supp. IV Part 1:** 83; **Supp. XIII:** 317
Dalibard, Thomas-François, **II:** 117
"Dallas-Fort Worth: Redband and Mistletoe" (Clampitt), **Supp. IX:** 45
"Dalliance of Eagles, The" (Whitman), **IV:** 348
Dalva (Harrison), **Supp. VIII:** 37, 45, 46, **48–49**
Daly, Carroll John, **Supp. IV Part 1:** 343, 345
Daly, John, **II:** 25, 26
Daly, Julia Brown, **II:** 25, 26
"Dalyrimple Goes Wrong" (Fitzgerald), **II:** 88
"Dam, The" (Rukeyser), **Supp. VI:** 283
Damas, Leon, **Supp. X:** 139
Damascus Gate (Stone), **Supp. V:** 308–311
Damballah (Wideman), **Supp. X:** 319, 320, 321, 322, 323, 326, 327, 331, 333–334
Damnation of Theron Ware, The (Frederic), **II:** 140–143, 144, 146, 147; **Retro. Supp. I:** 325
Damned If I Do (Everett), **Supp. XVIII:** 66
"Damned Thing, The" (Bierce), **I:** 206
Damon, Matt, **Supp. VIII:** 175
Damon, S. Foster, **I:** 26; **II:** 512, 514, 515
"Damon and Vandalia" (Dove), **Supp. IV Part 1:** 252
Dana, H. W. L., **I:** 225
Dana, Richard Henry, **I:** 339, 351; **Supp. I Part 1:** 103, 154, 155; **Supp. I Part 2:** 414, 420
Dana, Richard Henry, Jr., **III:** 81
Dana, Robert, **Supp. V:** 178, 180
"Dana Gioia and Fine Press Printing" (Peich), **Supp. XV:** 117
"Dance, The" (Crane), **I:** 109
"Dance, The" (Roethke), **III:** 541

"Dance, The" (W. C. Williams), **Supp. XVII:** 113
Dance of Death, The (Auden), **Supp. II Part 1:** 10
Dance of Death, The (Bierce and Harcourt), **I:** 196
Dance of the Sleepwalkers (Calabria), **Supp. XIII:** 164
"Dance of the Solids, The" (Updike), **Retro. Supp. I:** 323
"Dancer" (Hoffman), **Supp. XVIII:** 86
Dances with Wolves (film), **Supp. X:** 124
Dance to the Music of Time, A (Powell), **Supp. XVIII:** 146
Dancing After Hours (Dubus), **Supp. VII:** 91
Dancing Bears, The (Merwin), **Supp. III Part 1:** 343–344
Dancing on the Stones (Nichols), **Supp. XIII:** 256, 257, 259, 267, 269
"Dancing the Jig" (Sexton), **Supp. II Part 2:** 692
Dandelion Wine (Bradbury), **Supp. IV Part 1:** 101, 109–110
Dandurand, Karen, **Retro. Supp. I:** 30
"Dandy Frightening the Squatters, The" (Twain), **IV:** 193–194
Dangel, Mary Jo, **Supp. XVIII:** 156
Dangerous Crossroads (film), **Supp. XIII:** 163
Dangerous Moonlight (Purdy), **Supp. VII:** 278
"Dangerous Road Before Martin Luther King" (Baldwin), **Supp. I Part 1:** 52
"Dangerous Summer, The" (Hemingway), **II:** 261
Dangerous Thoughts (Ryan as Quin), **Supp. XVIII:** 226
"Dangers of Authorship, The" (Blackmur), **Supp. II Part 1:** 147
Dangling Man (Bellow), **I:** 144, 145, 147, 148, 150–151, 153–154, 158, 160, 161, 162, 163; **Retro. Supp. II:** 19, 20–21, 22, 23; **Supp. VIII:** 234
Daniel (biblical book), **Supp. I Part 1:** 105
Daniel (film), **Supp. IV Part 1:** 236
Daniel, Arnaut, **III:** 467
Daniel, Robert W., **III:** 76
Daniel, Samuel, **Supp. I Part 1:** 369
Daniel Deronda (Eliot), **I:** 458
Daniels, Kate, **Supp. XVII:** 112
Danielson, Linda, **Supp. IV Part 2:** 569
D'Annunzio, Gabriele, **II:** 515
Danny and the Deep Blue Sea: An Apache Dance (Shanley), **Supp. XIV:** 315, **318–319,** 320, 321, 323, 324
Danny O'Neill pentalogy (Farrell), **II:** 35–41
Danse Macabre (King), **Supp. IV Part 1:** 102; **Supp. V:** 144
"Danse Russe" (W. C. Williams), **IV:** 412–413
"Dans le Restaurant" (Eliot), **I:** 554, 578
Dans l'ombre des cathédrales (Ambelain), **Supp. I Part 1:** 273
Dante Alighieri, **I:** 103, 136, 138, 250, 384, 433, 445; **II:** 8, 274, 278, 289, 490, 492, 493, 494, 495, 504, 508, 524, 552; **III:** 13, 77, 124, 182, 259, 278, 448, 453, 467, 533, 607, 609, 610–612, 613; **IV:** 50, 134, 137, 138, 139, 247, 437, 438; **Retro. Supp. I:** 62, 63, 64, 66, 360; **Retro. Supp. II:** 330; **Supp. I Part 1:** 256, 363; **Supp. I Part 2:** 422, 454; **Supp. III Part 2:** 611, 618, 621; **Supp. IV Part 2:** 634; **Supp. V:** 277, 283, 331, 338, 345; **Supp. VIII:** 27, 219–221; **Supp. X:** 120, 121, 125; **Supp. XII:** 98; **Supp. XV:** 254; **Supp. XVII:** 227, 241
Danziger, Adolphe, **I:** 199–200
Dar (Nabokov), **III:** 246, 255
D'Arcy, Randall, **Supp. XVII:** 76
Dardis, Tom, **Supp. XVIII:** 249
"Dare's Gift" (Glasgow), **II:** 190
Dark Angel, The (Bolton), **Supp. I Part 1:** 281
"Dark Angel Travels With Us to Canada and Blesses Our Vacation, The" (Dunn), **Supp. XI:** 146
Dark Carnival (Bradbury), **Supp. IV Part 1:** 102
Darker (Strand), **Supp. IV Part 2:** 619, 626–628
Darker Face of the Earth, The (Dove), **Supp. IV Part 1:** 255–257
Dark Green, Bright Red (Vidal), **Supp. IV Part 2:** 677
Dark Half, The (King), **Supp. V:** 141
Dark Harbor: A Poem (Strand), **Supp. IV Part 2:** 633–634
"Dark Hills, The" (Robinson), **III:** 523
Dark Horses (X. J. Kennedy), **Supp. XV: 167–170**
Dark Laughter (Anderson), **I:** 111, 116; **II:** 250–251
"Darkling Alphabet, A" (Snodgrass), **Supp. VI:** 323
Darkling Child (Merwin and Milroy), **Supp. III Part 1:** 346
"Darkling Summer, Ominous Dusk, Rumorous Rain" (Schwartz), **Supp. II Part 2:** 661
"Darkling Thrush" (Hardy), **Supp. IX:** 40
"Dark Men, The" (Dubus), **Supp. VII:** 86
Dark Mirrors (Sobin), **Supp. XVI:** 295
Dark Mountains, The (Hoffman), **Supp. XVIII: 76–77**
Darkness and the Light, The (Hecht), **Supp. X:** 58
"Darkness on the Edge of Town" (O'Brien), **Supp. V:** 246
Darkness under the Trees/Walking behind the Spanish (Salinas), **Supp. XIII:** 311, **319–324**
"Dark Night" (St. John of the Cross), **Supp. XV:** 30
Dark Night of the Soul, The (St. John of the Cross), **I:** 1, 585
"Dark Ones" (Dickey), **Supp. IV Part 1:** 182
Dark Princess: A Romance (Du Bois), **Supp. II Part 1:** 179, 181–182
Dark Room, The (T. Williams), **IV:** 381
"Dark Summer" (Bogan), **Supp. III Part 1:** 51, 53
Dark Summer: Poems (Bogan), **Supp. III Part 1:** 52–53, 57
"Dark Tower, The" (column), **Supp. IV Part 1:** 168, 170
Dark Tower, The: The Gunslinger (King), **Supp. V:** 152
Dark Tower IV, The: Wizard and Glass (King), **Supp. V:** 139
Dark Tunnel, The (Macdonald, under Millar), **Supp. IV Part 2:** 465, 466
"Dark TV Screen" (Simic), **Supp. VIII:** 282
"Dark Voyage, The" (McLay), **Supp. XIII:** 21
"Dark Walk, The" (Taylor), **Supp. V:** 320–321, 322, 326
Darkwater: Voices from Within the Veil (Du Bois), **Supp. II Part 1:** 178, 180, 183
Dark Waves and Light Matter (Goldbarth), **Supp. XII:** 176, 193
Dark World (Carruth), **Supp. XVI:** 55
"Darling" (Nye), **Supp. XIII:** 283–284
"Darling, The" (Chekhov), **Supp. IX:** 202
Darling-Darling (Barillet and Grédy; Loos, trans.), **Supp. XVI:** 194
Darnell, Linda, **Supp. XII:** 173
Darragh, Tina, **Supp. IV Part 2:** 427
Darreu, Robert Donaldson, **Supp. II Part 1:** 89, 98, 102
Darrow, Clarence, **Supp. I Part 1:** 5; **Supp. I Part 2:** 455
Darwin, Charles, **I:** 457; **II:** 323, 462, 481; **III:** 226, 231; **IV:** 69, 304; **Retro. Supp. I:** 254; **Retro. Supp. II:** 60, 65; **Supp. I Part 1:** 368; **Supp. IX:** 180; **Supp. XI:** 203; **Supp. XVI:** 13
"Darwin in 1881" (Schnackenberg), **Supp. XV:** 253, 254, 258
Daryush, Elizabeth, **Supp. V:** 180
Dash, Julie, **Supp. XI:** 17, 18, 20
Dashell, Alfred, **Supp. X:** 224
"DAS KAPITAL" (Baraka), **Supp. II Part 1:** 55
Datlow, Ellen, **Supp. XVI:** 123
"Datum Centurio" (Wallace), **Supp. X:** 309
Daudet, Alphonse, **II:** 325, 338
"Daughter" (Caldwell), **I:** 309
"Daughter in the House" (X. J. Kennedy), **Supp. XV:** 160
Daughter of Earth (Smedly), **Supp. XIII:** 295
Daughter of the Snows, A (London), **II:** 465, 469–470
"Daughters" (Anderson), **I:** 114
Daughters (Marshall), **Supp. XI:** 275, 276, 277, **286–288,** 289, 290
"Daughters, 1900" (Nelson), **Supp. XVIII:** 175
Daughters, I Love You (Hogan), **Supp. IV Part 1:** 397, 399, 401
"Daughters of Invention" (Alvarez), **Supp. VII:** 9
Daughters of the Dust (Dash; film), **Supp. XI:** 17, 18
Daumier, Honoré, **IV:** 412
Dave, R. A., **Supp. VIII:** 126

Davenport, Abraham, **Supp. I Part 2:** 699
Davenport, Gary, **Supp. IX:** 98
Davenport, Guy, **Supp. XIV:** 96
Davenport, Herbert J., **Supp. I Part 2:** 642
Davenport, James, **I:** 546
Daves, E. G., **Supp. I Part 1:** 369
Davey, Frank, **Supp. XIII:** 33
"David" (Garrett), **Supp. VII:** 109–110
"David" (Gordon), **Supp. IV Part 1:** 298–299
"David and Agnes, a Romance" (Keillor), **Supp. XVI:** 175
David Copperfield (Dickens), **I:** 458; **II:** 290; **Retro. Supp. I:** 33; **Supp. XVI:** 65, 72
"David Crockett's Other Life" (Nye), **Supp. XIII:** 282
Davideis (Cowley), **IV:** 158
David Harum (Westcott), **I:** 216
"David Lynch Keeps His Head" (Wallace), **Supp. X:** 314
David Show, The (Gurney), **Supp. V:** 97
Davidson, Cathy, **Supp. XV:** 238
Davidson, Donald, **I:** 294; **III:** 495, 496; **IV:** 121, 122, 124, 125, 236; **Supp. II Part 1:** 139; **Supp. XIV:** 2
Davidson, John, **Retro. Supp. I:** 55
Davidson, Michael, **Supp. VIII:** 290, 293, 294, 302–303
Davidson, Sara, **Supp. IV Part 1:** 196, 198, 203
Davidsz de Heem, Jan, **Supp. XI:** 133
Davie, Donald, **III:** 478; **Supp. IV Part 2:** 474; **Supp. V:** 331; **Supp. X:** 55, 59; **Supp. XVII:** 111, 112, 121
Davies, Arthur, **III:** 273
Davies, Marion, **Supp. XVI:** 186
Davies, Sir John, **III:** 541
Da Vinci, Leonardo, **I:** 274; **II:** 536; **III:** 210
Davis, Allen F., **Supp. I Part 1:** 1, 7
Davis, Allison, **Supp. I Part 1:** 327
Davis, Angela, **Supp. I Part 1:** 66; **Supp. X:** 249
Davis, Arthur B., **Supp. XVIII:** 119
Davis, Bette, **I:** 78; **Supp. I Part 1:** 67
Davis, Bill, **Supp. XIII:** 267
Davis, Christina, **Supp. XV:** 264
Davis, Cynthia, **Supp. XVIII:** 281, 286
Davis, Donald, **Supp. XIII:** 93
Davis, Elizabeth Gould, **Supp. I Part 2:** 567
Davis, George, **II:** 586
Davis, Glover, **Supp. V:** 180, 182, 186
Davis, Jefferson, **II:** 206; **IV:** 122, 125, 126
Davis, Jordan, **Supp. XV:** 178, 181, 186, 188
Davis, Katie, **Supp. VIII:** 83
Davis, L. J., **Supp. XI:** 234
Davis, Lydia, **Supp. XII:** 24; **Supp. XVII:** 21
Davis, Marcia, **Supp. XVIII:** 91, 100
Davis, Mary H., **Supp. XVIII:** 77
Davis, Miles, **Supp. XV:** 346
Davis, Ossie, Jr., **Supp. IV Part 1:** 362; **Supp. XVI:** 144
Davis, Rebecca Harding, **Supp. I Part 1:** 45; **Supp. XIII:** 292, 295, 305; **Supp. XVI: 79–96**
Davis, Richard Harding, **III:** 328; **Supp. II Part 1:** 393; **Supp. XVI:** 85
Davis, Robert Gorham, **II:** 51; **IV:** 108
Davis, Stuart, **IV:** 409; **Supp. XV:** 295
Davis, Thadious, **Supp. XVIII:** 120, 121, 123, 127, 129
Davis, Thulani, **Supp. XI:** 179; **Supp. XIII:** 233, 234, 239
Davis, William V., **Supp. IV Part 1:** 63, 64, 68, 69, 70
Davy's Lake (M. Finch), **Supp. XVII:** 69
Dawn (Dreiser), **I:** 498, 499, 503, 509, 515, 519
Dawn (O. Butler), **Supp. XIII:** 63, **64**
"Dawnbreaker" (Hayden), **Supp. II Part 1:** 370
Dawn Patrol, The (film), **Supp. XIV:** 81
"Dawn Patrol: A Review of the Literature of the Negro for 1948" (Locke), **Supp. XIV:** 211
Dawson, Edward, **IV:** 151
Dawson, Emma, **I:** 199
Dawson, Ruth, **Supp. XI:** 120
Day, Dorothy, **II:** 215; **Supp. I Part 2:** 524; **Supp. X:** 142
Day, Georgiana, **Supp. I Part 2:** 585
Day, Richard, **Supp. XVIII:** 251
Dayan, Joan, **Retro. Supp. II:** 270
Day Book, A (Creeley), **Supp. IV Part 1:** 155
"Daybreak" (Kinnell), **Supp. III Part 1:** 250
"Daybreak Blues" (Kees), **Supp. XV:** 133
"Daybreak in Alabama" (Hughes), **Retro. Supp. I:** 211; **Supp. I Part 1:** 344
Day by Day (Lowell), **Retro. Supp. II:** 184, 186, 191
"Day-Care Field Trip: Aquarium" (Karr), **Supp. XI:** 243
"Day-Dream, A" (Bryant), **Supp. I Part 1:** 160
"Day-Dream of a Grocer, The" (Twain), **Supp. XVIII:** 9
"Day for Poetry and Song, A" (Douglass), **Supp. III Part 1:** 172
Day Late and a Dollar Short, A (McMillan), **Supp. XIII:** 184, **Supp. XIII:** 185, **191–192**
"Day longs for the evening, The" (Levertov), **Supp. III Part 1:** 274
Daynard, Jodi, **Supp. XVIII:** 97
Day of a Stranger (Merton), **Supp. VIII:** 203
"Day of Days, A" (James), **II:** 322
Day of Doom (Wigglesworth), **IV:** 147, 155, 156
Day of the Body (C. Frost), **Supp. XV:** 93, **98–100,** 106
Day of the Locust, The (West), **I:** 298; **IV:** 288, 299–306; **Retro. Supp. II:** 321, 323, 324, 329, **337–338; Supp. II Part 2:** 626; **Supp. XI:** 296; **Supp. XII:** 173; **Supp. XIII:** 170; **Supp. XIV:** 328; **Supp. XVIII:** 246
"Day on the Big Branch, A" (Nemerov), **III:** 275–276
"Day on the Connecticut River, A" (Merrill), **Supp. III Part 1:** 336
Day Room, The (DeLillo), **Supp. VI:** 4
"Days" (Emerson), **II:** 19, 20
"Days and Nights" (Koch), **Supp. XV:** 179, 180
"Days and Nights: A Journal" (Price), **Supp. VI:** 265
Days Before, The (Porter), **III:** 433, 453
Days in the Yellow Leaf (Hoffman), **Supp. XVIII:** 75
"Days of 1935" (Merrill), **Supp. III Part 1:** 325, 328
"Days of 1941 and '44" (Merrill), **Supp. III Part 1:** 336
"Days of 1964" (Merrill), **Supp. III Part 1:** 328, 352
"Days of 1971" (Merrill), **Supp. III Part 1:** 328
"Days of 1981" (Doty), **Supp. XI:** 123
"Days of Awe: The Birth of Lucy Jane" (Wasserstein), **Supp. XV:** 332
"Days of Edward Hopper" (Haines), **Supp. XII:** 210
"Days of Heaven" (Bass), **Supp. XVI:** 20
Days of Obligation: An Argument with My Mexican Father (Rodriguez), **Supp. XIV:** 298, 300, **302–305,** 307, 310
Days of Our Lives (soap opera), **Supp. XI:** 83
Days of Our Lives Lie in Fragments: New and Old Poems (Garrett), **Supp. VII:** 109–110, 111
Days of the Phoenix (Brooks), **I:** 266
Days of Wine and Roses (J. P. Miller), **Supp. XIII:** 262
Days: Tangier Journal, 1987–1989 (Bowles), **Supp. IV Part 1:** 94
Days to Come (Hellman), **Supp. I Part 1:** 276, 277–278
Days without End (O'Neill), **III:** 385, 391, 397
"Day's Work, A" (Capote), **Supp. III Part 1:** 120
"Day's Work, A" (Porter), **III:** 443, 446
"Day the Presidential Candidate Came to Ciudad Tamaulipas, The" (Caldwell), **I:** 309
Day the World ended, The (Coover), **Supp. V:** 1
"Day with Conrad Green, A" (Lardner), **II:** 428–429, 430
"Deacon's Masterpiece, The" (Holmes), **Supp. I Part 1:** 302, 307
"Dead, The" (Joyce), **I:** 285; **III:** 343
Dead and the Living, The (Olds), **Supp. X:** 201, **204–206,** 207
"Dead Body, The" (Olds), **Supp. X:** 210
"Dead by the Side of the Road, The" (Snyder), **Supp. VIII:** 301
"Dead Doe" (B. Kelly), **Supp. XVII:** 128–129
Dead End (Kingsley), **Supp. I Part 1:** 277, 281
Dead Father, The (Barthelme), **Supp. IV Part 1:** 43, 47, 50–51
"Dead Fiddler, The" (Singer), **IV:** 20

Dead Fingers Talk (Burroughs), **Supp. III Part 1:** 103
"Dead Hand" series (Sinclair), **Supp. V:** 276, 277, 281
"Dead Languages, The" (Humphrey), **Supp. IX:** 109
Dead Lecturer, The (Baraka), **Supp. II Part 1:** 31, 33, 35–37, 49
Deadline at Dawn (Odets), **Supp. II Part 2:** 546
"Dead-Lock and Its Key, A" (E. Stoddard), **Supp. XV:** 286
"Dead Loon, The" (Bynner), **Supp. XV:** **44–45**
Deadly Affair, A (Lacy), **Supp. XV:** 205–206
Deadly is the Female (film), **Supp. XVII:** 62
Dead Man's Walk (McMurtry), **Supp. V:** 231, 232
Dead Man's Walk (screenplay; McMurtry and Ossana), **Supp. V:** 231
Dead Man Walking (opera libretto, McNally), **Supp. XIII:** 207
"Dead Reckoning" (Jarman), **Supp. XVII:** 113
"Dead Soldier's Talk, The" (Jin), **Supp. XVIII:** 92
Dead Souls (Gogol), **I:** 296
"Dead Souls on Campus" (Kosinski), **Supp. VII:** 222
"Dead Wingman, The" (Jarrell), **II:** 374
"Dead Yellow Women" (Hammett), **Supp. IV Part 1:** 345
Dead Zone, The (King), **Supp. V:** 139, 143, 144, 148, 152
Dean, James, **I:** 493
Dean, Man Mountain, **II:** 589
Deane, Silas, **Supp. I Part 2:** 509, 524
"Dean of Men" (Taylor), **Supp. V:** 314, 323
Dean's December, The (Bellow), **Retro. Supp. II:** 30–31
"Dear Adolph" (Benét), **Supp. XI:** 46
"Dear America" (Ortiz), **Supp. IV Part 2:** 503
"Dearest M—" (Carruth), **Supp. XVI:** 59
"Dear Judas" (Jeffers), **Supp. II Part 2:** 431–432, 433
Dear Juliette (Sarton), **Supp. VIII:** 265
Dear Lovely Death (Hughes), **Retro. Supp. I:** 203; **Supp. I Part 1:** 328
"Dear Villon" (Corso), **Supp. XII:** 135
"Dear World" (Gunn Allen), **Supp. IV Part 1:** 321
Death (Allen), **Supp. XV:** 3
"Death" (Corso), **Supp. XII:** 127
"Death" (Lowell), **II:** 536
"Death" (Mailer), **III:** 38
"Death" (W. C. Williams), **Retro. Supp. I:** 422
"Death" (West), **IV:** 286
"Death and Absence" (Glück), **Supp. V:** 82
Death and Taxes (Parker), **Supp. IX:** 192
"Death and the Child" (Crane), **I:** 414
"Death as a Society Lady" (Hecht), **Supp. X:** 71–72
Death before Bedtime (Vidal as Box), **Supp. IV Part 2:** 682
"Death Be Not Proud" (Donne), **Supp. XVI:** 158
"Death by Water" (Eliot), **I:** 395, 578
Death Comes for the Archbishop (Cather), **I:** 314, 327, 328–330; **Retro. Supp. I:** 16–18, 21; **Supp. XIII:** 253
Death in the Afternoon (Hemingway), **II:** 253; **IV:** 35; **Retro. Supp. I:** 182; **Supp. VIII:** 182; **Supp. XVI:** 205
"Death in the Country, A" (Benét), **Supp. XI:** 53–54
Death in the Family, A (Agee), **I:** 25, 29, 42, 45
Death in the Fifth Position (Vidal as Box), **Supp. IV Part 2:** 682
"Death in the Woods" (Anderson), **I:** 114, 115
Death in the Woods and Other Stories (Anderson), **I:** 112, 114, 115
Death in Venice (Mann), **III:** 231; **Supp. IV Part 1:** 392; **Supp. V:** 51
"Death in Viet Nam" (Salinas), **Supp. XIII:** 315
"Death in Winter" (C. Frost), **Supp. XV:** 98
Death Is a Lonely Business (Bradbury), **Supp. IV Part 1:** 102, 103, 111–112, 115
"Death Is Not the End" (Wallace), **Supp. X:** 309
Death Kit (Sontag), **Supp. III Part 2:** 451, 468–469
Death Likes It Hot (Vidal as Box), **Supp. IV Part 2:** 682
"*Death*/Muerta" (Mora), **Supp. XIII:** 228
Death Notebooks, The (Sexton), **Supp. II Part 2:** 691, 694, 695
"Death of a Jazz Musician" (W. J. Smith), **Supp. XIII:** 334
Death of a Kinsman, The (Taylor), **Supp. V:** 324, 326
"Death of an Old Seaman" (Hughes), **Retro. Supp. I:** 199
"Death of a Pig" (White), **Supp. I Part 2:** 665–668
Death of a Salesman (A. Miller), **I:** 81; **III:** 148, 149, 150, 153–154, 156, 157, 158, 159, 160, 163, 164, 166; **IV:** 389; **Supp. IV Part 1:** 359; **Supp. XIV:** 102, 239, 254, 255; **Supp. XV:** 205
"Death of a Soldier, The" (Stevens), **Retro. Supp. I:** 299, 312. *see also* "Lettres d'un Soldat" (Stevens)
"Death of a Soldier, The" (Wilson), **IV:** 427, 445
"Death of a Toad" (Wilbur), **Supp. III Part 2:** 550
"Death of a Traveling Salesman" (Welty), **IV:** 261; **Retro. Supp. I:** 344
"Death of a Young Son by Drowning" (Atwood), **Supp. XIII:** 33
Death of Bessie Smith, The (Albee), **I:** 76–77, 92
Death of Billy the Kid, The (Vidal), **Supp. IV Part 2:** 683
Death of Cock Robin, The (Snodgrass), **Supp. VI:** 315, **317–319**, 324
Death of Dreams, A (Hoffman), **Supp. XVIII:** 79
"Death of General Wolfe, The" (Paine), **Supp. I Part 2:** 504
"Death of Halpin Frayser, The" (Bierce), **I:** 205
"Death of Justina, The" (Cheever), **Supp. I Part 1:** 184–185
Death of Life, The (Barnes), **Supp. III Part 1:** 34
Death of Malcolm X, The (Baraka), **Supp. II Part 1:** 47
"Death of Marilyn Monroe, The" (Olds), **Supp. X:** 205
"Death of Me, The" (Malamud), **Supp. I Part 2:** 437
"Death of Slavery, The" (Bryant), **Supp. I Part 1:** 168–169
"Death of St. Narcissus, The" (Eliot), **Retro. Supp. I:** 291
"Death of the Ball Turret Gunner, The" (Jarrell), **II:** 369–370, 372, 374, 375, 376, 378
"Death of the Fathers, The" (Sexton), **Supp. II Part 2:** 692
"Death of the Flowers, The" (Bryant), **Supp. I Part 1:** 170
Death of the Fox (Garrett), **Supp. VII:** 99, 101–104, 108
"Death of the Hired Man, The" (Frost), **III:** 523; **Retro. Supp. I:** 121, 128; **Supp. IX:** 261
"Death of the Kapowsin Tavern" (Hugo), **Supp. VI:** 137, 141
Death of the Kapowsin Tavern (Hugo), **Supp. VI:** 133–135
"Death of the Lyric, The: The Achievement of Louis Simpson" (Jarman and McDowell), **Supp. IX:** 266, 270, 276
"Death of Venus, The" (Creeley), **Supp. IV Part 1:** 143, 144–145
"Death on All Fronts" (Ginsberg), **Supp. II Part 1:** 326
"Deaths" (Dunn), **Supp. XI:** 147
"Death Sauntering About" (Hecht), **Supp. X:** 72
Deaths for the Ladies (and Other Disasters) (Mailer), **Retro. Supp. II:** 203
Death's Jest-Book (Beddoes), **Retro. Supp. I:** 285
Death Song (McGrath), **Supp. X:** 127
"Death the Carnival Barker" (Hecht), **Supp. X:** 72
"Death the Film Director" (Hecht), **Supp. X:** 72
"Death the Judge" (Hecht), **Supp. X:** 72
"Death the Mexican Revolutionary" (Hecht), **Supp. X:** 72
"Death the Oxford Don" (Hecht), **Supp. X:** 72
"Death the Painter" (Hecht), **Supp. X:** 72
Death the Proud Brother (Wolfe), **IV:** 456
"Death to Van Gogh's Ear!" (Ginsberg), **Supp. II Part 1:** 320, 322, 323
"Death Warmed Over!" (Bradbury), **Supp. IV Part 1:** 104–105, 112
Débâcle, La (Zola), **III:** 316
"Debate with the Rabbi" (Nemerov), **III:** 272
Debeljak, Aleš, **Supp. VIII:** 272

De Bellis, Jack, **Supp. I Part 1:** 366, 368, 372
DeBoer-Langworthy, Carol, **Supp. XVII:** 98, 99, 100
De Bosis, Lauro, **IV:** 372
"Debriefing" (Sontag), **Supp. III Part 2:** 468–470
Debs, Eugene, **I:** 483, 493; **III:** 580, 581; **Supp. I Part 2:** 524; **Supp. IX:** 1, 15
Debt to Pleasure, The (Lanchester), **Retro. Supp. I:** 278
Debussy, Claude, **Retro. Supp. II:** 266; **Supp. XIII:** 44
Decameron (Boccaccio), **III:** 283, 411; **Supp. IX:** 215
"Deceased" (Hughes), **Retro. Supp. I:** 208
"December" (Oliver), **Supp. VII:** 245
"December 1, 1994" (Stern), **Supp. IX:** 299
December 7 (film, Ford), **Supp. XVIII:** 247
"December Eclogue" (Winters), **Supp. II Part 2:** 794
Deception (P. Roth), **Retro. Supp. II:** 291; **Supp. III Part 2:** 426–427
"Deceptions" (Dobyns), **Supp. XIII:** 77
De Chiara, Ann. *See* Malamud, Mrs. Bernard (Ann de Chiara)
De Chirico, Giorgio, **Supp. XIII:** 317
"Decided Loss, A" (Poe), **II:** 411
"Decisions to Disappear" (Dunn), **Supp. XI:** 144
"Decisive Moment, The" (Auster), **Supp. XIV:** 292
Decker, James A., **Supp. III Part 2:** 621
Declaration of Gentlemen and Merchants and Inhabitants of Boston, and the Country Adjacent, A (Mather), **Supp. II Part 2:** 450
"Declaration of Paris, The" (Adams), **I:** 4
Declaration of the Rights of Man and the Citizen, **Supp. I Part 2:** 513, 519
Declaration of Universal Peace and Liberty (Paine), **Supp. I Part 2:** 512
Decline and Fall (Waugh), **Supp. I Part 2:** 607; **Supp. XV:** 142
Decline and Fall of the English System of Finance, The (Paine), **Supp. I Part 2:** 518
Decline and Fall of the Roman Empire, The (Gibbons), **Supp. III Part 2:** 629
"Decline of Book Reviewing, The" (Hardwick), **Supp. III Part 1:** 201–202
Decline of the West, The (Spengler), **I:** 270; **IV:** 125
Deconstructing Harry (film; Allen), **Supp. XV:** 12, **13**
"Décor" (X. J. Kennedy), **Supp. XV:** 171
"Decoration Day" (Jewett), **II:** 412; **Retro. Supp. II:** 138
Decoration of Houses, The (Wharton and Codman), **IV:** 308; **Retro. Supp. I:** 362, 363–364, 366
"Decoy" (Ashbery), **Supp. III Part 1:** 13–14
"De Daumier-Smith's Blue Period" (Salinger), **III:** 560–561
"Dedication" (Nelson), **Supp. XVIII:** 173, 180
"Dedication and Household Map" (Erdrich), **Supp. IV Part 1:** 272
"Dedication Day" (Agee), **I:** 34
"Dedication for a Book" (Hay), **Supp. XIV:** 125
"Dedication for a Book of Criticism" (Winters), **Supp. II Part 2:** 801
"Dedication in Postscript, A" (Winters), **Supp. II Part 2:** 801
Dedications and Other Darkhorses (Komunyakaa), **Supp. XIII:** 112, **113–114**
"Dedication to Hunger" (Glück), **Supp. V:** 83
"Dedication to My Wife, A" (Eliot), **I:** 583
Dee, Ruby, **Supp. IV Part 1:** 362
Deeds of Utmost Kindness (Gander), **Supp. XV:** 340
"Deep Breath at Dawn, A" (Hecht), **Supp. X:** 58
Deeper into Movies: The Essential Kael Collection from '69 to '72 (Kael), **Supp. IX:** 253
"Deeper Wisdom, The" (Hay), **Supp. XIV:** 129
Deep Green Sea (R. O. Butler), **Supp. XII:** 62, **74**
Deephaven (Jewett), **II:** 398–399, 400, 401, 410, 411; **Retro. Supp. II:** 133, 134, 135, 136, 137, 138, 140, 141, 143, 144
"Deep Sight and Rescue Missions" (Bambara), **Supp. XI:** 18–19
Deep Sightings and Rescue Missions: Fiction, Essays, and Conversations (Bambara), **Supp. XI:** 1, 3, **14–20**
Deep Sleep, The (Morris), **III:** 224–225
Deep South (Caldwell), **I:** 305, 309, 310
Deepstep Come Shining (Wright), **Supp. XV:** 337, 341, 344, **349–350,** 351, 353
"Deep Water" (Marquand), **III:** 56
"Deep Woods" (Nemerov), **III:** 272–273, 275
"Deer at Providencia, The" (Dillard), **Supp. VI:** 28, 32
"Deer Dancer" (Harjo), **Supp. XII:** 224–225
"Deer Ghost" (Harjo), **Supp. XII:** 225
Deer Park, The (Mailer), **I:** 292; **III:** 27, 31–33, 35–36, 37, 39, 40, 42, 43, 44; **Retro. Supp. II: 200–202,** 205, 207, 211
Deer Park, The: A Play (Mailer), **Retro. Supp. II:** 205
Deer Pasture, The (Bass), **Supp. XVI:** 15, 16, 23
Deerslayer, The (Cooper), **I:** 341, 349, 350, 355; **Supp. I Part 1:** 251
"Defence of Poesy, The" (Sidney), **Supp. V:** 250
"Defence of Poetry" (Longfellow), **II:** 493–494
"Defender of the Faith" (P. Roth), **Retro. Supp. II:** 281; **Supp. III Part 2:** 404, 407, 420
"Defending *The Searchers* (Scenes in the Life of an Obsession)" (Lethem), **Supp. XVIII:** 136,141
"Defenestration in Prague" (Matthews), **Supp. IX:** 168
Defenestration of Prague (Howe), **Supp. IV Part 2:** 419, 426, 429–430
Defense, The (Nabokov), **III:** 251–252; **Retro. Supp. I:** 266, 268, **270–272**
"Defense of Poetry" (Francis), **Supp. IX:** 83–84
Defiant Ones, The (film), **Supp. I Part 1:** 67
"Defining the Age" (Davis), **Supp. IV Part 1:** 64
"Definition" (Ammons), **Supp. VII:** 28
Defoe, Daniel, **I:** 204; **II:** 104, 105, 159, 304–305; **III:** 113, 423; **IV:** 180; **Supp. I Part 2:** 523; **Supp. V:** 127
De Forest, John William, **II:** 275, 280, 288, 289; **IV:** 350
DeFrees, Madeline, **Supp. XVIII:** 293
Degas, Brian, **Supp. XI:** 307
Degler, Carl, **Supp. I Part 2:** 496
"Degrees of Fidelity" (Dunn), **Supp. XI:** 148, 156
Deguy, Michel, **Supp. XV:** 178
De Haven, Tom, **Supp. XI:** 39; **Supp. XII:** 338–339
Deitch, Joseph, **Supp. VIII:** 125
"Dejection" (Coleridge), **II:** 97
DeJong, Constance, **Supp. XII:** 4
DeJong, David Cornel, **I:** 35
Dekker,Thomas, **Supp. XVII:** 232
de Kooning, Willem, **Supp. XII:** 198; **Supp. XV:** 177, 178
Delacroix, Henri, **I:** 227
De La Mare, Walter, **III:** 429; **Supp. II Part 1:** 4; **Supp. XVII:** 69
Delamotte, Eugenia C., **Supp. XI:** 279
De Lancey, James, **I:** 338
De Lancey, Mrs. James (Anne Heathcote), **I:** 338
De Lancey, Susan A. *See* Cooper, Mrs. James Fenimore
De Lancey, William Heathcote, **I:** 338, 353
Delano, Amasa, **III:** 90
Delattre, Roland A., **I:** 558
De Laurentiis, Dino, **Supp. XI:** 170, 307
De la Valdéne, Guy, **Supp. VIII:** 40, 42
De l'éducation d'un homme sauvage (Itard), **Supp. I Part 2:** 564
"Delft" (Goldbarth), **Supp. XII:** 189
Delft: An Essay-Poem (Goldbarth), **Supp. XII:** 187
Delicate Balance, A (Albee), **I:** 86–89, 91, 93, 94
"Delicate Balance, The" (Hay), **Supp. XIV:** 122
Delicate Balance, The (Hay), **Supp. XIV:** 121, 122, 124, 129, 133–134
"Delicate Prey, The" (Bowles), **Supp. IV Part 1:** 86
Delicate Prey and Other Stories, The (Bowles), **Supp. IV Part 1:** 86–87
Délie (Scève), **Supp. III Part 1:** 11
DeLillo, Don, **Retro. Supp. I:** 278; **Retro. Supp. II:** 279; **Supp. IX:** 212;

Supp. VI: 1–18; Supp. XI: 68; **Supp. XII:** 21, 152; **Supp. XVII:** 183; **Supp. XVIII:** 136, 140
DeLisle, Anne, **Supp. VIII:** 175
Deliverance (Dickey), **Supp. IV Part 1:** 176, 186–188, 190; **Supp. X:** 30
Deliverance, The (Glasgow), **II:** 175, 176, 177–178, 181
"Delivering" (Dubus), **Supp. VII:** 87
Dell, Floyd, **I:** 103, 105; **Supp. I Part 2:** 379; **Supp. XV:** 295; **Supp. XVII:** 96
Della Francesca, Piero, **Supp. XV:** 262
"Della Primavera Trasportata al Morale" (W. C. Williams), **Retro. Supp. I:** 419, 422
DeLoria, Philip J., **Supp. XIV:** 306
Deloria, Vine, Jr., **Supp. IV Part 1:** 323; **Supp. IV Part 2:** 504
"Delta Autumn" (Faulkner), **II:** 71
"Delta Factor, The" (Percy), **Supp. III Part 1:** 386
Delta of Venus: Erotica (Nin), **Supp. X:** 192, 195
Delta Wedding (Welty), **IV:** 261, 268–271, 273, 281; **Retro. Supp. I:** 349–350, 351
Delusions (Berryman), **I:** 170
De Man, Paul, **Supp. XVII:** 70
de Man, Paul, **Retro. Supp. I:** 67
DeMarinis, Rick, **Supp. XIV:** 22
DeMars, James, **Supp. IV Part 2:** 552
Dembo, L. S., **I:** 386, 391, 396, 397, 398, 402; **III:** 478; **Supp. I Part 1:** 272; **Supp. XIV:** 277, 282, 288, 290
"Dementia Translucida" (Bierds), **Supp. XVII:** 33
Demetrakopoulous, Stephanie A., **Supp. IV Part 1:** 12
DeMille, Cecil B., **Supp. IV Part 2:** 520; **Supp. XV:** 42
Demme, Jonathan, **Supp. V:** 14
Democracy (Adams), **I:** 9–10, 20; **Supp. IV Part 1:** 208
Democracy (Didion), **Supp. IV Part 1:** 198, 208–210
"Democracy" (Lowell), **Supp. I Part 2:** 419
Democracy and Education (Dewey), **I:** 232
Democracy and Other Addresses (Lowell), **Supp. I Part 2:** 407
Democracy and Social Ethics (Addams), **Supp. I Part 1:** 8–11
Democracy in America (Tocqueville), **Retro. Supp. I:** 235; **Supp. XIV:** 306
Democratic Vistas (Whitman), **IV:** 333, 336, 348–349, 351, 469; **Retro. Supp. I:** 408; **Supp. I Part 2:** 456
Democritus, **I:** 480–481; **II:** 157; **III:** 606; **Retro. Supp. I:** 247
"Demon Lover, The" (Rich), **Supp. I Part 2:** 556
"Demonstrators, The" (Welty), **IV:** 280; **Retro. Supp. I:** 355
DeMott, Benjamin, **Supp. IV Part 1:** 35; **Supp. V:** 123; **Supp. XIII:** 95; **Supp. XIV: 106**
DeMott, Robert, **Supp. VIII:** 40, 41
Demuth, Charles, **IV:** 404; **Retro. Supp. I:** 412, 430
"Demystified Zone" (Paley), **Supp. VI:** 227
Denmark Vesey (opera) (Bowles), **Supp. IV Part 1:** 83
Denney, Joseph Villiers, **Supp. I Part 2:** 605
Denney, Reuel, **Supp. XII:** 121
Dennie, Joseph, **II:** 298; **Supp. I Part 1:** 125
Denniston, Dorothy Hamer, **Supp. XI:** 276, 277
"Den of Lions" (Plath), **Retro. Supp. II:** 242
"Dental Assistant, The" (Simpson), **Supp. IX:** 280
Den Uyl, Douglas, **Supp. IV Part 2:** 528, 530
"Deodand, The" (Hecht), **Supp. X:** 65
"Departing" (Cameron), **Supp. XII:** 81
"Departure" (Glück), **Supp. V:** 89
"Departure" (Plath), **Supp. I Part 2:** 537
"Departure, The" (Freneau), **Supp. II Part 1:** 264
"Departure from Hydra, The" (Koch), **Supp. XV:** 180–181
Departures (Justice), **Supp. VII:** 124–127
Departures and Arrivals (Shields), **Supp. VII:** 320, 322
"Depressed by a Book of Bad Poetry, I Walk Toward an Unused Pasture and Invite the Insects to Join Me" (Wright), **Supp. III Part 2:** 600
"Depressed Person, The" (Wallace), **Supp. X:** 309
"Depression Days" (Mora), **Supp. XIII:** 224–225
De Puy, John, **Supp. XIII:** 12
D'Erasmo, Stacey, **Supp. IX:** 121
Derby, J. C., **Supp. XVIII:** 4
De Reilhe, Catherine, **Supp. I Part 1:** 202
De Rerum Natura (Lucretius), **II:** 162
"De Rerum Virtute" (Jeffers), **Supp. II Part 2:** 424
De Rioja, Francisco, **Supp. I Part 1:** 166
"Derivative Sport in Tornado Alley" (Wallace), **Supp. X:** 314
Derleth, August, **Supp. I Part 2:** 465, 472
Deronda, Daniel, **II:** 179
Derricotte, Toi, **Supp. XVIII:** 177
Derrida, Jacques, **Supp. IV Part 1:** 45; **Supp. XV:** 215, 224; **Supp. XVI:** 285, 288
Deruddere, Dominique, **Supp. XI:** 173
Der Wilde Jäger (Bürger), **II:** 306
Derzhavin, Gavrila Romanovich, **Supp. VIII:** 27
Desai, Anita, **Supp. XVI:** 156, 157, 158
De Santis, Christopher, **Retro. Supp. I:** 194
Descartes, René, **I:** 255; **III:** 618–619; **IV:** 133
Descendents, The (Glasgow), **II:** 173, 174–175, 176
Descending Figure (Glück), **Supp. V:** 83–84
"Descending Theology: Christ Human" (Karr), **Supp. XI:** 251
"Descending Theology: The Garden" (Karr), **Supp. XI:** 251
"Descent, The" (W. C. Williams), **Retro. Supp. I:** 428, 429
"Descent from the Cross" (Eliot), **Retro. Supp. I:** 57, 58
"Descent in the Maelström, A" (Poe), **Retro. Supp. II:** 274
"Descent into Proselito" (Knowles), **Supp. XII:** 237
"Descent into the Maelström, A" (Poe), **III:** 411, 414, 416, 424
"Descent of Man" (Boyle), **Supp. VIII:** 14
Descent of Man (Boyle), **Supp. VIII:** 1, 12–13
Descent of Man, The (Darwin), **Supp. XIV:** 192
Descent of Man, The (Wharton), **IV:** 311; **Retro. Supp. I:** 367
Descent of Man and Other Stories, The (Wharton), **Retro. Supp. I:** 367
Descent of Winter, The (W. C. Williams), **Retro. Supp. I:** 419, 428
De Schloezer, Doris, **III:** 474
"Description" (Doty), **Supp. XI:** 126
"Description of the great Bones dug up at Clavarack on the Banks of Hudsons River A.D. 1705, The" (Taylor), **IV:** 163, 164
"Description without Place" (Stevens), **Retro. Supp. I:** 422
"Desert" (Hughes), **Retro. Supp. I:** 207
"Deserted Cabin" (Haines), **Supp. XII:** 203
Deserted Village, The (Goldsmith), **II:** 304
Desert Is My Mother, The/El desierto es mi madre (Mora), **Supp. XIII:** 214, 221
"Desert Music, The" (W. C. Williams), **Retro. Supp. I:** 428, 429
Desert Music, The (W. C. Williams), **IV:** 422; **Retro. Supp. I:** 428, 429
"Desert Places" (Frost), **II:** 159; **Retro. Supp. I:** 121, 123, 129, 138, 299; **Supp. XIV:** 229
Desert Rose, The (McMurtry), **Supp. V:** 225, 231
Desert Solitaire (Abbey), **Supp. X:** 30; **Supp. XIII: 7–8,** 12; **Supp. XIV:** 177, 179
"Design" (Frost), **II:** 158, 163; **Retro. Supp. I:** 121, 126, 138, 139; **Supp. IX:** 81; **Supp. XVII:** 132; **Supp. XVIII:** 298
"Designated National Park, A" (Ortiz), **Supp. IV Part 2:** 509
"Designs on a Point of View" (Everwine), **Supp. XV:** 76
Des Imagistes (Pound), **II:** 513; **Supp. I Part 1:** 257, 261, 262
Desire (album, Dylan), **Supp. XVIII:** 28
"Desire" (Beattie), **Supp. V:** 29
Desire (Bidart), **Supp. XV: 32–34,** 35
"Desire" (Everwine), **Supp. XV:** 85
"Désirée's Baby" (Chopin), **Retro. Supp. II:** 64, 65; **Supp. I Part 1:** 213–215
Desire under the Elms (O'Neill), **III:** 387, 390

"Desolate Field, The" (W. C. Williams), **Retro. Supp. I:** 418
"Desolation, A" (Ginsberg), **Supp. II Part 1:** 313
Desolation Angels (Kerouac), **Supp. III Part 1:** 218, 225, 230
"Desolation Is a Delicate Thing" (Wylie), **Supp. I Part 2:** 729
"Desolation Row" (song, Dylan), **Supp. XVIII:** 30
Despair (Nabokov), **Retro. Supp. I:** 270, 274
"Despisals" (Rukeyser), **Supp. VI:** 282
Des Pres, Terrence, **Supp. X:** 113, 120, 124
"Destiny and the Lieutenant" (McCoy), **Supp. XIII:** 171
"Destruction of Kreshev, The" (Singer), **IV:** 13; **Retro. Supp. II:** 307
Destruction of the European Jews, The (Hilberg), **Supp. V:** 267
"Destruction of the Goetheanum, The" (Salter), **Supp. IX:** 257
"Destruction of the Long Branch, The" (Pinsky), **Supp. VI:** 239, 240, 243–244, 245, 247, 250
Destructive Element, The (Spender), **Retro. Supp. I:** 216
"Detail & Parody for the poem 'Paterson'" (W. C. Williams), **Retro. Supp. I:** 424
Detmold, John, **Supp. I Part 2:** 670
Detour at Night (Endore), **Supp. XVII:** 64
Deuce, The (R. O. Butler), **Supp. XII:** 62, **69–70,** 72
Deus Lo Volt! (Connell), **Supp. XIV:** 80, 81, 95
Deuteronomy (biblical book), **II:** 166
Deutsch, Andre, **Supp. XI:** 297, 301
Deutsch, Babette, **Supp. I Part 1:** 328, 341
Deutsch, Michel, **Supp. IV Part 1:** 104
Deutsche, Babette, **Supp. XV:** 305
"Devaluation Blues: Ruminations on Black Families in Crisis" (Coleman), **Supp. XI:** 87
Devane, William, **Supp. XI:** 234
"Development of the Literary West" (Chopin), **Retro. Supp. II:** 72
"Development of the Modern English Novel, The" (Lanier), **Supp. I Part 1:** 370–371
DeVeriante (Herbert of Cherbury), **II:** 108
"Devil and Daniel Webster, The" (Benét), **III:** 22; **Supp. XI:** 45–46, 47, 50–51, 52
Devil and Daniel Webster and Other Writings, The (Benét), **Supp. XI:** 48
"Devil and Tom Walker, The" (Irving), **II:** 309–310
Devil At Large, The: Erica Jong on Henry Miller (Jong), **Supp. V:** 115, 131
Devil-Doll, The (film, Browning), **Supp. XVII:** 58–59
Devil Finds Work, The (Baldwin), **Retro. Supp. II:** 14; **Supp. I Part 1:** 48, 52, 66–67
Devil in a Blue Dress (Mosley), **Supp. XIII:** 237, 239
"Devil in Manuscript, The" (Hawthorne), **II:** 226; **Retro. Supp. I:** 150–151
Devil in Paradise, A (H. Miller), **III:** 190
"Devil in the Belfry, The" (Poe), **III:** 425; **Retro. Supp. II:** 273
"Devil Is a Busy Man, The" (Wallace), **Supp. X:** 309
Devil's Dictionary, The (Bierce), **I:** 196, 197, 205, 208, 209, 210
Devil's Stocking, The (Algren), **Supp. IX:** 5, 16
"Devil's Thumb, The" (Krakauer), **Supp. XVIII:** 107
Devil's Tour, The (Karr), **Supp. XI:** 240, **242–244**
Devil Tree, The (Kosinski), **Supp. VII:** 215, 222, 223
"Devising" (Ammons), **Supp. VII:** 28
De Voto, Bernard, **I:** 247, 248; **II:** 446; **Supp. IV Part 2:** 599, 601
"Devout Meditation in Memory of Adolph Eichmann, A" (Merton), **Supp. VIII:** 198, 203
De Vries, Peter, **Supp. I Part 2:** 604
Dewberry, Elizabeth, **Supp. XII:** 62, 72
Dewey, John, **I:** 214, 224, 228, 232, 233, 266, 267; **II:** 20, 27, 34, 229, 361; **III:** 112, 294–295, 296, 303, 309–310, 599, 605; **IV:** 27, 429; **Supp. I Part 1:** 3, 5, 7, 10, 11, 12, 24; **Supp. I Part 2:** 493, 641, 647, 677; **Supp. IX:** 179; **Supp. V:** 290; **Supp. XIV:** 3; **Supp. XV:** 41
Dewey, Joseph, **Supp. IX:** 210
Dewey, Thomas, **IV:** 161
Dexter, Peter, **Supp. XIV:** 221
De Young, Charles, **I:** 194
Dhairyam, Sagari, **Supp. IV Part 1:** 329, 330
Dharma Bums, The (Kerouac), **Supp. III Part 1:** 230, 231; **Supp. VIII:** 289, 305
"D. H. Lawrence" (Bynner), **Supp. XV:** 46
D. H. Lawrence: An Unprofessional Study (Nin), **Supp. X:** 182–183
D. H. Lawrence: The World of the Major Novels (Sanders), **Supp. XVI:** 267
D'Houdetot, Madame, **Supp. I Part 1:** 250
"Diabetes" (Dickey), **Supp. IV Part 1:** 182
Diaghilev, Sergei, **Supp. I Part 1:** 257
Dial (publication), **I:** 58, 109, 115, 116, 215, 231, 233, 245, 261, 384, 429; **II:** 8, 430; **III:** 194, 470, 471, 485; **IV:** 122, 171, 427; **Retro. Supp. I:** 58; **Retro. Supp. II:** 78; **Supp. I Part 2:** 642, 643, 647; **Supp. II Part 1:** 168, 279, 291; **Supp. II Part 2:** 474; **Supp. III Part 2:** 611
"Dialectics of Love, The" (McGrath), **Supp. X:** 116
"Dialogue" (Rich), **Supp. I Part 2:** 560
Dialogue, A (Baldwin and Giovanni), **Supp. I Part 1:** 66
"Dialogue Between Franklin and the Gout" (Franklin), **II:** 121
"Dialogue Between General Wolfe and General Gage in a Wood near Boston, A" (Paine), **Supp. I Part 2:** 504
"Dialogue between Old England and New" (Bradstreet), **Supp. I Part 1:** 105–106, 110–111, 116
"Dialogue between the Writer and a Maypole Dresser, A" (Taylor), **IV:** 155
Dialogues (Bush, ed.), **III:** 4
Dialogues in Limbo (Santayana), **III:** 606
"Dialogue: William Harvey; Joan of Arc" (Goldbarth), **Supp. XII:** 178
"Diamond as Big as the Ritz, The" (Fitzgerald), **II:** 88–89
Diamond Cutters and Other Poems, The (Rich), **Supp. I Part 2:** 551, 552, 553
"Diamond Guitar, A" (Capote), **Supp. III Part 1:** 124
"Diana and Persis" (Alcott), **Supp. I Part 1:** 32, 41
"Diaper Brigade, The" (Ryan as Quin), **Supp. XVIII:** 230
Diaries of Charlotte Perkins Gilman (Knight, ed.), **Supp. XI:** 201
Diary of a Chambermaid, The (film; Renoir), **Supp. XVI:** 193
Diary of Anaïs Nin, The (1931–1974), **Supp. X:** 181, 185–189, 191, 192, 193, 195
Diary of a Rapist, The: A Novel (Connell), **Supp. XIV:** 80, 82, 94
Diary of a Yuppie (Auchincloss), **Supp. IV Part 1:** 31, 32–33
Diary of "Helena Morley," The (Bishop, trans.), **Retro. Supp. II:** 45, 51; **Supp. I Part 1:** 92
Díaz del Castillo, Bernál, **III:** 13, 14
Dick, Philip K., **Supp. XVI:** 123; **Supp. XVIII:** 136, 137, 138, 139, 142
Dickens, Charles, **I:** 152, 198, 505; **II:** 98, 179, 186, 192, 271, 273–274, 288, 290, 297, 301, 307, 316, 322, 559, 561, 563, 577, 582; **III:** 146, 247, 325, 368, 411, 421, 426, 572, 577, 613–614, 616; **IV:** 21, 192, 194, 211, 429; **Retro. Supp. I:** 33, 91, 218; **Retro. Supp. II:** 204; **Supp. I Part 1:** 13, 34, 35, 36, 41, 49; **Supp. I Part 2:** 409, 523, 579, 590, 622, 675; **Supp. IV Part 1:** 293, 300, 341; **Supp. IV Part 2:** 464; **Supp. IX:** 246; **Supp. VIII:** 180; **Supp. XI:** 277; **Supp. XII:** 335, 337; **Supp. XIII:** 233; **Supp. XV:** 62; **Supp. XVI:** 63, 65–66, 72–73, 202; **Supp. XVIII:** 7, 136, 146
Dickey, James, **I:** 29, 535; **III:** 268; **Retro. Supp. II:** 233; **Supp. III Part 1:** 354; **Supp. III Part 2:** 541, 597; **Supp. IV Part 1: 175–194; Supp. V:** 333; **Supp. X:** 30; **Supp. XI:** 312, 317; **Supp. XV:** 115, 348; **Supp. XVIII:** 191, 299
Dick Gibson Show, The (Elkin), **Supp. VI:** 42, **48–49**
Dickie, Margaret, **Retro. Supp. II:** 53, 84
Dickinson, Donald, **Retro. Supp. I:** 206, 212
Dickinson, Edward, **I:** 451–452, 453

Dickinson, Emily, **I:** 384, 419, 433, **451–473; II:** 272, 276, 277, 530; **III:** 19, 194, 196, 214, 493, 505, 508, 556, 572, 576; **IV:** 134, 135, 331, 444; **Retro. Supp. I: 25–50; Retro. Supp. II:** 39, 40, 43, 45, 50, 76, 134, 155, 170; **Supp. I Part 1:** 29, 79, 188, 372; **Supp. I Part 2:** 375, 546, 609, 682, 691; **Supp. II Part 1:** 4; **Supp. III Part 1:** 63; **Supp. III Part 2:** 600, 622; **Supp. IV Part 1:** 31, 257; **Supp. IV Part 2:** 434, 637, 641, 643; **Supp. IX:** 37, 38, 53, 87, 90; **Supp. V:** 79, 140, 332, 335; **Supp. VIII:** 95, 104, 106, 108, 198, 205, 272; **Supp. XII:** 226; **Supp. XIII:** 153, 339; **Supp. XIV:** 45, 127–128, 133, 261, 284; **Supp. XV:** 287, 303, 309; **Supp. XVI:** 288; **Supp. XVII:** 71, 73, 74, 75, 132; **Supp. XVIII:** 301

Dickinson, Gilbert, **I:** 469

Dickinson, Goldsworthy Lowes, **Supp. XIV:** 336

Dickinson, Lavinia Norcross, **I:** 451, 453, 462, 470

Dickinson, Mrs. Edward, **I:** 451, 453

Dickinson, Mrs. William A. (Susan Gilbert), **I:** 452, 453, 456, 469, 470

Dickinson, William Austin, **I:** 451, 453, 469

Dickinson and the Strategies of Reticence (Dobson), **Retro. Supp. I:** 29, 42

Dickson, Helen. *See* Blackmur, Helen Dickson

Dickstein, Morris, **Supp. XIII:** 106

"Dick Whittington and His Cat," **Supp. I Part 2:** 656

"DICTATORSHIP OF THE PROLETARIAT, THE" (Baraka), **Supp. II Part 1:** 54

Dictionary of Literary Biography (Barron and Meyer, eds.), **Supp. XVIII:** 173

Dictionary of Literary Biography (Gwynn, ed.), **Supp. XVIII:** 173

Dictionary of Literary Biography (Kibler, ed.), **Supp. IX:** 94, 109; **Supp. XI:** 297

Dictionary of Literary Biography (Knight), **Supp. XIV:** 144

Dictionary of Literary Biography (Sicher, ed.), **Supp. XVII:** 41

Dictionary of Modern English Usage, A (Fowler), **Supp. I Part 2:** 660

"Dictum: For a Masque of Deluge" (Merwin), **Supp. III Part 1:** 342–343

"Didactic Poem" (Levertov), **Supp. III Part 1:** 280

Diderot, Denis, **II:** 535; **IV:** 440; **Supp. XVI:** 293; **Supp. XVII:** 145

Did I Ever Tell You How Lucky You Are? (Geisel), **Supp. XVI:** 109

Didion, Joan, **Retro. Supp. I:** 116; **Retro. Supp. II:** 209; **Supp. I Part 1:** 196, 197; **Supp. III Part 1:** 302; **Supp. IV Part 1: 195–216; Supp. XI:** 221; **Supp. XII:** 307

Dido, **I:** 81

"Did You Ever Dream Lucky?" (Ellison), **Supp. II Part 1:** 246

"Die-Hard, The" (Benét), **Supp. XI:** 54–55, 56

Diehl, Digby, **Supp. IV Part 1:** 204

Dien Cai Dau (Komunyakaa), **Supp. XIII:** 121, **122–124,** 125, 131, 132

Dies, Martin, **Supp. XVIII:** 229

"Dies Irae" (Lowell), **II:** 553

Die Zeit Ohne Beispiel, (Goebbels), **III:** 560

Difference Engine, The (W. Gibson and B. Sterling), **Supp. XVI:** 121, 124, **128–129**

Different Drummer, A (Larkin; film), **Supp. XI:** 20

Different Fleshes (Goldbarth), **Supp. XII:** 181–182, 188

Different Hours (Dunn), **Supp. XI:** 139, 142, 143, 155

Different Seasons (King), **Supp. V:** 148, 152

"Different Ways to Pray" (Nye), **Supp. XIII:** 275

Different Ways to Pray (Nye), **Supp. XIII:** 274, 275, 277, 285, 287

"Difficulties of a Statesman" (Eliot), **I:** 580

"Difficulties of Modernism and the Modernism of Difficulty" (Poirier), **Supp. II Part 1:** 136

Diff'rent (O'Neill), **III:** 389

DiGaetani, John L., **Supp. XIII:** 200

"Digging" (Sanders), **Supp. XVI:** 272

"Digging in the Garden of Age I Uncover a Live Root" (Swenson), **Supp. IV Part 2:** 649

Diggins, John P., **Supp. I Part 2:** 650

"Dignity of Life, The" (C. Bly), **Supp. XVI:** 34, 36–37

Digregorio, Charles, **Supp. XI:** 326

"Dilemma of Determinism, The" (James), **II:** 347–348, 352

"Dilemma of the Negro Writer, The" (speech, C. Himes), **Supp. XVI:** 140

"Dilettante, The" (Wharton), **IV:** 311, 313

"Dilettante, The: A Modern Type" (Dunbar), **Supp. II Part 1:** 199

Dillard, Annie, **Supp. VI: 19–39; Supp. VIII:** 272; **Supp. X:** 31; **Supp. XIII:** 154

Dillard, R. H. W., **Supp. XII:** 16

Dillman, Bradford, **III:** 403; **Supp. XII:** 241

Dillon, Brian, **Supp. X:** 209

Dillon, George, **III:** 141; **Supp. III Part 2:** 621

Dillon, Millicent, **Supp. IV Part 1:** 95

Dilsaver, Paul, **Supp. XIII:** 112

Dilthey, Wilhelm, **I:** 58

Dime-Store Alchemy: The Art of Joseph Cornell, **Supp. VIII:** 272

"Diminuendo" (Dunn), **Supp. XI:** 152–153

"Dimout in Harlem" (Hughes), **Supp. I Part 1:** 333

"Dinah's Lament" (Nelson), **Supp. XVIII:** 183

Dinesen, Isak, **IV:** 279; **Supp. VIII:** 171; **Supp. XVI:** 250

Dining Room, The (Gurney), **Supp. V:** 105–106

"Dinner at———, A" (O. Henry), **Supp. II Part 1:** 402

"Dinner at Sir Nigel's" (Bowles), **Supp. IV Part 1:** 94

Dinner at the Homesick Restaurant (Tyler), **Supp. IV Part 2:** 657, 667–668

"Dinner at Uncle Borris's" (Simic), **Supp. VIII:** 272

Dinner Bridge (Lardner), **II:** 435

Dinosaur Tales (Bradbury), **Supp. IV Part 1:** 103

"Diogenes Invents a Game" (Karr), **Supp. XI:** 240–241

"Diogenes Tries to Forget" (Karr), **Supp. XI:** 241

Dionysis in Doubt (Robinson), **III:** 510

Diop, Birago, **Supp. IV Part 1:** 16

Diop, David, **Supp. IV Part 1:** 16

Di Piero, W. S., **Supp. XVII:** 241

Di Prima, Diane, **Supp. III Part 1:** 30; **Supp. XIV:** 125, 144, 148, 150

Direction of Poetry, The: An Anthology of Rhymed and Metered Verse Written in the English Language since 1975 (Richman, ed.), **Supp. XV:** 250, 251

Direction of Poetry, The: Rhymed and Metered Verse Written in the English Language since 1975 (Richman), **Supp. XI:** 249

"Directive" (Bishop), **Retro. Supp. II:** 42

"Directive" (Frost), **III:** 287; **Retro. Supp. I:** 140; **Supp. VIII:** 32, 33

"Dire Cure" (Matthews), **Supp. IX:** 168

"Dirge" (Dunbar), **Supp. II Part 1:** 199

"Dirge without Music" (Millay), **III:** 126

"Dirt" (Salter), **Supp. IX:** 257, 260, 261

"Dirt and Desire: Essay on the Phenomenology of Female Pollution in Antiquity" (Carson), **Supp. XII: 111**

Dirty Dingus Magee (film), **Supp. XVII:** 139

"Dirty English Potatoes" (X. J. Kennedy), **Supp. XV:** 165

"Dirty Memories" (Olds), **Supp. X:** 211

Dirty Story (Shanley), **Supp. XIV:** 316, 331

"Dirty Word, The" (Shapiro), **Supp. II Part 2:** 710

Disappearance of the Jews, The (Mamet), **Supp. XIV:** 249–250, 250–251, 252, 254

Disappearances (Auster), **Supp. XII:** 23

"Disappearances" (Hogan), **Supp. IV Part 1:** 401

"Disappeared, The" (C. Baxter), **Supp. XVII:** 19

Disappearing Acts (McMillan), **Supp. XIII:** 182, 183, **188–189,** 192

Disappearing Ink: Poetry at the End of Print Culture (Gioia), **Supp. XV:** 112

"Disappointment, The" (Creeley), **Supp. IV Part 1:** 143

"Disappointment and Desire" (R. Bly), **Supp. IV Part 1:** 71

Disappointment Artist, The (Lethem), **Supp. XVIII:** 135, 141, **148**

"Discards" (Baker), **Supp. XIII:** 53, 55–56

Discerning the Signs of the Times (Niebuhr), **III:** 300–301, 307–308
"Disciple of Bacon, The" (Epstein), **Supp. XII:** 163–164
"Discordants" (Aiken), **I:** 65
Discourse on Method (Descartes), **I:** 255
"Discourtesies" (Kirsch), **Supp. XV:** 341
"Discovering Theme and Structure in the Novel" (Schuster), **Supp. VIII:** 126
"Discovery" (Freneau), **Supp. II Part 1:** 258
"Discovery of the Madeiras, The" (Frost), **Retro. Supp. I:** 139
"Discovery of What It Means to Be an American, The" (Baldwin), **Supp. I Part 1:** 54–55
Discovery! The Search for Arabian Oil (Stegner), **Supp. IV Part 2:** 599
"Discrete Series" (Zukofsky), **Supp. III Part 2:** 616
"Discretions of Alcibiades" (Pinsky), **Supp. VI:** 241
"Disease, The" (Rukeyser), **Supp. VI:** 279
Disenchanted, The (play, Schulberg and Breit), **Supp. XVIII:** 254
Disenchanted, The (Schulberg), **II:** 98; **Retro. Supp. I:** 113; **Supp. XVIII: 247–250,** 253
Disenchantments: An Anthology of Modern Fairy Tale Poetry (Mieder), **Supp. XIV:** 126
"Dish of Green Pears, A" (Ríos), **Supp. IV Part 2:** 552
"Disillusion and Dogma" (Untermeyer), **Supp. XV:** 306
Dismantling the Silence (Simic), **Supp. VIII: 273–274,** 275, 276
Disney, Walt, **III:** 275, 426
"Disney of My Mind" (Chabon), **Supp. XI:** 63
Dispatches (Herr), **Supp. XI:** 245
"Displaced Person, The" (O'Connor), **III:** 343–344, 350, 352, 356; **Retro. Supp. II:** 229, 232, 236
"Disposal" (Snodgrass), **Supp. VI:** 314
Dispossessed, The (Berryman), **I:** 170, 172, 173, 174, 175, 176, 178
"Disquieting Muses, The" (Plath), **Supp. I Part 2:** 538
Disraeli, Benjamin, **II:** 127
Dissent (Didion), **Supp. IV Part 1:** 208
"Dissenting Opinion on Kafka, A" (Wilson), **IV:** 437–438
Dissent in Three American Wars (Morison, Merk, and Freidel), **Supp. I Part 2:** 495
Dissertation on Liberty and Necessity, Pleasure and Pain, A (Franklin), **II:** 108
Dissertations on Government; the Affairs of the Bank: and Paper Money (Paine), **Supp. I Part 2:** 510
"Distance" (Carver), **Supp. III Part 1:** 146
"Distance" (Everwine), **Supp. XV:** 85
"Distance" (Paley), **Supp. VI:** 222
"Distance, The" (Karr), **Supp. XI:** 241
"Distance from the Sea, A" (Kees), **Supp. XV:** 147
"Distance Nowhere" (Hughes), **Retro. Supp. I:** 207
"Distant Episode, A" (Bowles), **Supp. IV Part 1:** 84–85, 86, 90
Distant Episode, A: The Selected Stories (Bowles), **Supp. IV Part 1:** 79
Distinguished Guest, The (Miller), **Supp. XII: 299–301**
Distortions (Beattie), **Supp. V:** 21, 23, 24, 25, 27
"Distrest Shepherdess, The" (Freneau), **Supp. II Part 1:** 258
District of Columbia (Dos Passos), **I:** 478, 489–490, 492
Disturber of the Peace (Manchester), **III:** 103
Disturbing the Peace (Yates), **Supp. XI:** 345, 346
"Diver, The" (Hayden), **Supp. II Part 1:** 368, 372, 373
"Divided Life of Jean Toomer, The" (Toomer), **Supp. III Part 2:** 488
Divina Commedia (Longfellow, trans.), **II:** 490, 492, 493
"Divine Collaborator" (Simic), **Supp. VIII:** 282
Divine Comedies (Merrill), **Supp. III Part 1:** 324, 329–332
Divine Comedy (Dante), **I:** 137, 265, 400, 446; **II:** 215, 335, 490, 492, 493; **III:** 13, 448, 453; **Supp. V:** 283, 331, 338, 345; **Supp. X:** 253; **Supp. XIV:** 6
"Divine Image, The" (Blake), **Supp. V:** 257
Divine Pilgrim, The (Aiken), **I:** 50, 55
Divine Tragedy, The (Longfellow), **II:** 490, 500, 505, 506, 507; **Retro. Supp. II:** 165, 166
Divine Weekes and Workes (Sylvester, trans.), **Supp. I Part 1:** 104
Divine Weeks (Du Bartas), **IV:** 157–158
Diving into the Wreck: Poems 1971–1972 (Rich), **Supp. I Part 2:** 550, 559–565, 569; **Supp. XV:** 252
"Diving Past African Violets" (A. Finch), **Supp. XVII:** 72
Diving Rock on the Hudson, A (H. Roth), **Supp. IX:** 236, **237–238**
"Divinity in Its Fraying Fact, A" (Levis), **Supp. XI:** 271
"Divinity School Address" (Emerson), **II:** 12–13
"Divisions upon a Ground" (Hecht), **Supp. X:** 58
"Divorce" (Karr), **Supp. XI:** 244
Divorced in America: Marriage in an Age of Possibility (Epstein), **Supp. XIV:** 113
Dix, Douglas Shields, **Supp. XII:** 14
Dixie City Jam (Burke), **Supp. XIV:** 32
Dixon, Ivan, **Supp. IV Part 1:** 362
Dixon, Stephen, **Supp. XII: 139–158**
Dixon, Terrell F., **Supp. XVI:** 21
Dixon, Thomas, Jr., **Supp. II Part 1:** 169, 171, 177
Djinn (Robbe-Grillet), **Supp. V:** 48
D'Lugoff, Burt, **Supp. IV Part 1:** 362, 370
Do, Lord, Remember Me (Garrett), **Supp. VII:** 98–100, 110
"Doaksology, The" (Wolfe), **IV:** 459
Do Androids Dream of Electric Sheep? (Dick), **Supp. XVIII:** 137
Dobie, J. Frank, **Supp. V:** 225; **Supp. XIII:** 227
Döblin, Alfred, **Supp. XV:** 137
Dobriansky, Lev, **Supp. I Part 2:** 648, 650
Dobrin, Sidney I., **Supp. XVIII:** 192, 195
Dobson, Joanne, **Retro. Supp. I:** 29, 31, 42; **Supp. XVIII:** 259
Dobyns, Stephen, **Supp. XIII: 73–92**
"Docking at Palermo" (Hugo), **Supp. VI:** 137–138
"Dock Rats" (Moore), **III:** 213
"Dock-Witch, The" (Ozick), **Supp. V:** 262, 264
"Doc Mellhorn and the Pearly Gates" (Benét), **Supp. XI:** 55
"Doctor, The" (Dubus), **Supp. VII:** 80–81
"Doctor and the Doctor's Wife, The" (Hemingway), **II:** 248; **Retro. Supp. I:** 174, 175
Doctor Breen's Practice, a Novel (Howells), **I:** 282
Doctor Faustus (Mann), **III:** 283
Doctor Jazz (Carruth), **Supp. XVI:** 47, 59
"Doctor Jekyll" (Sontag), **Supp. III Part 2:** 469
"Doctor Leavis and the Moral Tradition" (Trilling), **Supp. III Part 2:** 512–513
Doctor Martino and Other Stories (Faulkner), **II:** 72; **Retro. Supp. I:** 84
"Doctor of the Heart, The" (Sexton), **Supp. II Part 2:** 692
Doctorow, E. L., **Retro. Supp. I:** 97; **Supp. III Part 2:** 590, 591; **Supp. IV Part 1: 217–240; Supp. V:** 45; **Supp. XVI:** 73; **Supp. XVII:** 183
Doctor Sax (Kerouac), **Supp. III Part 1:** 220–222, 224–227
Doctor Sleep (Bell), **Supp. X: 9–11**
"Doctors' Row" (Aiken), **I:** 67
Doctor's Son and Other Stories, The (O'Hara), **III:** 361
Doctor Stories, The (W. C. Williams), **Retro. Supp. I:** 424
"Doctor's Wife, The" (Ozick), **Supp. V:** 262, 265
Doctor Zhivago (Pasternak), **IV:** 434, 438, 443
"Documentary" (Simic), **Supp. VIII:** 282
Dodd, Elizabeth, **Supp. V:** 77
Dodd, Wayne, **Supp. IV Part 2:** 625
Dodson, Owen, **Supp. I Part 1:** 54
Dodsworth (Lewis), **II:** 442, 449–450, 453, 456
Doenitz, Karl, **Supp. I Part 2:** 491
Does Civilization Need Religion? (Niebuhr), **III:** 293–294
"Does 'Consciousness' Exist?" (James), **II:** 356
"Does Education Pay?" (Du Bois), **Supp. II Part 1:** 159
"Dog" (B. Kelly), **Supp. XVII:** 126
Dog (Shepard), **Supp. III Part 2:** 434
"Dog Act, The" (Komunyakaa), **Supp. XIII:** 114–115

"Dog and the Playlet, The" (O. Henry), **Supp. II Part 1:** 399
Dog Beneath the Skin, The (Auden), **Supp. II Part 1:** 10
"Dog Creek Mainline" (Wright), **Supp. V:** 340
"Dogfight" (W. Gibson and Swanwick), **Supp. XVI:** 128
Dog in the Manger, The (Vega; Merwin, trans.), **Supp. III Part 1:** 341, 347
Dogs Bark, but the Caravan Rolls On (Conroy), **Supp. XVI:** 63, 70, 74, **75–76**
Dogs Bark, The: Public People and Private Places (Capote), **Supp. III Part 1:** 120, 132
Dog Soldiers (Stone), **Supp. V:** 298, 299–301
"Dog Stories" (Prose), **Supp. XVI:** 256
Dog & the Fever, The (Quevedo), **Retro. Supp. I:** 423
"Dogtown Letters, The" (Jarman and R. McDowell), **Supp. XVII:** 111
"Dogwood, The" (Levertov), **Supp. III Part 1:** 276
"Dogwood Tree, The: A Boyhood" (Updike), **IV:** 218; **Retro. Supp. I:** 318, 319
Doig, Ivan, **Supp. XIV:** 227
"Doing Battle with the Wolf" (Coleman), **Supp. XI:** 87–88
Doing Literary Business: American Women Writers in the Nineteenth Century (Coultrap-McQuin), **Supp. XVI:** 85
Doings and Undoings (Podhoretz), **Supp. VIII: 236–237**
"Do-It-Yourself" (C. Baxter), **Supp. XVII:** 14–15
Dolan, Jill, **Supp. XV:** 327
"Dolce Far' Niente" (Humphrey), **Supp. IX:** 106
Dolci, Carlo, **III:** 474–475
Dollars and Cents (A. Warner), **Supp. XVIII:** 264
"Dollhouse, The" (Haines), **Supp. XII:** 204
Dollmaker's Ghost, The (Levis), **Supp. XI:** 259, 260, **264–268**
Doll's House, A (Ibsen), **III:** 523; **IV:** 357; **Supp. XVI:** 182
Dolmetsch, Arnold, **III:** 464
Dolores Claiborne (King), **Supp. V:** 138, 141, 147, 148, 149–150, 152
"Dolph Heyliger" (Irving), **II:** 309
Dolphin, The (Lowell), **Retro. Supp. II:** 183, 186, 188, **190–191; Supp. XII:** 253–254
"Dolphins" (Francis), **Supp. IX:** 83
Dome of Many-Coloured Class, A (Lowell), **II:** 515, 516–517
Domesday Book (Masters), **Supp. I Part 2:** 465, 466–469, 471, 473, 476
"Domestic Economy" (Gilman), **Supp. XI:** 206
"Domestic Manners" (Hardwick), **Supp. III Part 1:** 211
"Dominant White, The" (McKay), **Supp. X:** 134
Dominguez, Robert, **Supp. VIII:** 83
Dominique, Jean. *See* Closset, Marie
Donahoe, Edward, **Supp. XVIII:** 132
Donahue, Phil, **Supp. IV Part 2:** 526; **Supp. X:** 311
Doña Perfecta (Galdós), **II:** 290
Dong, Stella, **Supp. XVI:** 222
Don Juan (Byron), **Supp. XV:** 259
"DON JUAN IN HELL" (Baraka), **Supp. II Part 1:** 33
Donkey of God, The (Untermeyer), **Supp. XV:** 310
"Donna mi Prega" (Cavalcanti), **Supp. III Part 2:** 620, 621, 622
Donn-Byrne, Brian Oswald. *See* Byrne, Donn
Donne, John, **I:** 358–359, 384, 389, 522, 586; **II:** 254; **III:** 493; **IV:** 83, 88, 135, 141, 144, 145, 151, 156, 165, 331, 333; **Retro. Supp. II:** 76; **Supp. I Part 1:** 80, 364, 367; **Supp. I Part 2:** 421, 424, 467, 725, 726; **Supp. III Part 2:** 614, 619; **Supp. IX:** 44; **Supp. VIII:** 26, 33, 164; **Supp. XII:** 45, 159; **Supp. XIII:** 94, 130; **Supp. XIV:** 122; **Supp. XV:** 92, 251; **Supp. XVI:** 158, 204; **Supp. XVIII:** 35, 39, 50–51, 307
Donne's Sermons: Selected Passages (L. P. Smith, ed.), **Supp. XIV:** 342
Donoghue, Denis, **I:** 537; **Supp. IV Part 1:** 39; **Supp. VIII:** 105, 189
Donohue, H. E. F., **Supp. IX:** 2, 3, 15, 16
"Do Not Weep Maiden, For War Is Kind" (Crane), **Supp. XVIII:** 75
Donovan, Josephine, **Retro. Supp. II:** 138, 139, 147
Don Quixote (Cervantes), **I:** 134; **II:** 291, 434; **III:** 113, 614; **Supp. I Part 2:** 422; **Supp. IX:** 94
Don Quixote: Which Was a Dream (Acker), **Supp. XII:** 5, **12–14**
Don't Ask (Levine), **Supp. V:** 178
Don't Ask Questions (Marquand), **III:** 58
Don't Bet on the Prince: Contemporary Feminist Fairy Tales in North America and England (Zipes), **Supp. XIV:** 126
Don't Drink the Water (Allen), **Supp. XV:** 3, **14**
Don't Look Back (film, Pennebaker), **Supp. XVIII:** 19
"Don't Shoot the Warthog" (Corso), **Supp. XII:** 123
"Don't Tell Mother" (Wasserstein), **Supp. XV:** 319
"Don't Think Twice, It's All Right" (song, Dylan), **Supp. XVIII:** 24
"Don't Worry About the Kids" (Neugeboren), **Supp. XVI:** 226
Don't Worry About the Kids (Neugeboren), **Supp. XVI:** 226
Don't You Want to Be Free? (Hughes), **Retro. Supp. I:** 203; **Supp. I Part 1:** 339
"Doodler, The" (Merrill), **Supp. III Part 1:** 321
Doolan, Moira, **Retro. Supp. II:** 247
Doolittle, Hilda (H. D.), **II:** 517, 520–521; **III:** 194, 195–196, 457, 465; **IV:** 404, 406; **Retro. Supp. I:** 288, 412, 413, 414, 415, 417; **Supp. I Part 1: 253–275; Supp. I Part 2:** 707; **Supp. III Part 1:** 48; **Supp. III Part 2:** 610; **Supp. IV Part 1:** 257; **Supp. V:** 79; **Supp. XV:** 43, 249, 301, 302; **Supp. XVII:** 77
Doolittle, Thomas, **IV:** 150
"Doomed by Our Blood to Care" (Orfalea), **Supp. XIII:** 278
"Doomsday" (Plath), **Retro. Supp. II:** 242
Doomsters, The (Macdonald), **Supp. IV Part 2:** 462, 463, 472, 473
"Door, The" (Creeley), **Supp. IV Part 1:** 145, 146, 156–157
"Door, The" (White), **Supp. I Part 2:** 651, 675–676
"Door in the Dark, The" (Frost), **II:** 156
Door in the Hive, A (Levertov), **Supp. III Part 1:** 283, 284
"Door of the Trap, The" (Anderson), **I:** 112
"Doors" (Hoffman), **Supp. XVIII:** 86–87
Doors (Hoffman), **Supp. XVIII:** 86–87
"Doors, Doors, Doors" (Sexton), **Supp. II Part 2:** 681
Doors, The, **Supp. X:** 186
"Doorways into the Depths" (Sanders), **Supp. XVI:** 272
Doreski, William, **Retro. Supp. II:** 185
Dorfman, Ariel, **Supp. IX:** 131, 138
Dorfman, Joseph, **Supp. I Part 2:** 631, 647, 650
Dorman, Jen, **Supp. XI:** 240
Dorn, Edward, **Supp. IV Part 1:** 154
"Dorothea Dix, Samaritan" (J. Scott), **Supp. XVII:** 189
Dorr, Julia, **Supp. XV:** 286
Dorris, Michael, **Supp. IV Part 1:** 260, 272
Dos Passos, John, **I:** 99, 288, 374, 379, **474–496,** 517, 519; **II:** 74, 77, 89, 98; **III:** 2, 28, 29, 70, 172, 382–383; **IV:** 340, 427, 433; **Retro. Supp. I:** 105, 113, 187; **Retro. Supp. II:** 95, 196; **Supp. I Part 2:** 646; **Supp. III Part 1:** 104, 105; **Supp. V:** 277; **Supp. VIII:** 101, 105; **Supp. XIV:** 24; **Supp. XV:** 135, 137, 182; **Supp. XVII:** 105, 107
"Dos Passos: Poet Against the World" (Cowley), **Supp. II Part 1:** 143, 145
Dostoevsky, Fyodor, **I:** 53, 103, 211, 468; **II:** 60, 130, 275, 320, 587; **III:** 37, 61, 155, 174, 176, 188, 189, 267, 272, 283, 286, 354, 357, 358, 359, 467, 571, 572; **IV:** 1, 7, 8, 17, 21, 50, 59, 106, 110, 128, 134, 285, 289, 476, 485, 491; **Retro. Supp. II:** 20, 204, 299; **Supp. I Part 1:** 49; **Supp. I Part 2:** 445, 466; **Supp. IV Part 2:** 519, 525; **Supp. VIII:** 175; **Supp. X:** 4–5; **Supp. XI:** 161; **Supp. XII:** 322; **Supp. XVI:** 63; **Supp. XVII:** 225; **Supp. XVIII:** 278, 280
Doty, Mark, **Supp. IX:** 42, 300; **Supp. XI: 119–138**
Doty, M. R. *See* Dawson, Ruth; Doty, Mark
Double, The (Dostoevsky), **Supp. IX:** 105

"Double, The" (Levis), **Supp. XI:** 260, **261–263**
Double, The (Rank), **Supp. IX:** 105
Double Agent, The (Blackmur), **Supp. II Part 1:** 90, 108, 146
Double Axe, The (Jeffers), **Supp. II Part 2:** 416, 434
Doubleday, Frank, **I:** 500, 502, 515, 517; **III:** 327
Doubleday, Mrs. Frank, **I:** 500
Double Down (F. and S. Barthelme), **Supp. XI:** 27, 34, 35, 36–38
Double Dream of Spring, The (Ashbery), **Supp. III Part 1:** 11–13
Double Fold: Libraries and the Assault on Paper (Baker), **Supp. XIII:** 52, 56
Double Game (Calle), **Supp. XII:** 22
"Double Gap, The" (Auchincloss), **Supp. IV Part 1:** 33
"Double-Headed Snake of Newbury, The" (Whittier), **Supp. I Part 2:** 698
Double Honeymoon (Connell), **Supp. XIV:** 80, 87
Double Image, The (Levertov), **Supp. III Part 1:** 274, 276
"Double Image, The" (Sexton), **Supp. II Part 2:** 671, 677–678
Double Indemnity (film), **Supp. IV Part 1:** 130
"Double Limbo" (Komunyakaa), **Supp. XIII:** 132
Double Man, The (Auden), **Supp. III Part 1:** 16; **Supp. X:** 118
"Double Ode" (Rukeyser), **Supp. VI:** 282–283, 286
Double Persephone (Atwood), **Supp. XIII:** 19
Doubles in Literary Psychology (Tymms), **Supp. IX:** 105
Double Vision: American Thoughts Abroad (Knowles), **Supp. XII:** 249
"Doubt on the Great Divide" (Stafford), **Supp. XI:** 322
Dougherty, Steve, **Supp. X:** 262
Douglas, Aaron, **Supp. I Part 1:** 326
Douglas, Alfred, **Supp. X:** 151
Douglas, Ann, **Supp. XII:** 136; **Supp. XVIII:** 258
Douglas, Claire, **III:** 552
Douglas, George (pseudonym). *See* Brown, George Douglas
Douglas, Kirk, **Supp. XIII:** 5–6
Douglas, Lloyd, **IV:** 434
Douglas, Marjory Stoneman, **Supp. XVIII:** 195
Douglas, Melvyn, **Supp. V:** 223
Douglas, Michael, **Supp. XI:** 67
Douglas, Paul, **III:** 294
Douglas, Stephen A., **III:** 577, 588–589; **Supp. I Part 2:** 456, 471
Douglas, William O., **III:** 581
Douglass, Frederick, **Supp. I Part 1:** 51, 345; **Supp. I Part 2:** 591; **Supp. II Part 1:** 157, 195, 196, 292, 378; **Supp. III Part 1: 153–174; Supp. IV Part 1:** 1, 2, 13, 15, 256; **Supp. VIII:** 202; **Supp. XVIII:** 16
Douglass Pilot, The (Baldwin, ed.), **Supp. I Part 1:** 49
Dove, Belle, **I:** 451
Dove, Rita, **Supp. IV Part 1: 241–258; Supp. XVII:** 71, 110; **Supp. XVIII:** 172, 174
"Dover Beach" (Arnold), **Retro. Supp. I:** 325
Dow, Lorenzo, **IV:** 265
Dowd, Douglas, **Supp. I Part 2:** 645, 650
"Do We Understand Each Other?" (Ginsberg), **Supp. II Part 1:** 311
Dowie, William, **Supp. V:** 199
Do with Me What You Will (Oates), **Supp. II Part 2:** 506, 515–517
Dowling, Eddie, **IV:** 394
Down and Out (Shanley), **Supp. XIV:** 317
"Down at City Hall" (Didion), **Supp. IV Part 1:** 211
"Down at the Cross" (Baldwin), **Retro. Supp. II:** 1, 2, 7, 12, 13, 15; **Supp. I Part 1:** 60, 61
"Down at the Dinghy" (Salinger), **III:** 559, 563
"Down by the Station, Early in the Morning" (Ashbery), **Supp. III Part 1:** 25
Downhill Racer (film), **Supp. IX:** 253
"Down in Alabam" (Bierce), **I:** 193
Downing, Ben, **Supp. XII:** 175, 189, 190–191
Downing, Major Jack (pseudonym). *See* Smith, Seba
Down in My Heart (Stafford), **Supp. XI:** 313, 315
Down Mailer's Way (Solotaroff), **Retro. Supp. II:** 203
"Down the Highway" (song, Dylan), **Supp. XVIII:** 24
Down the Rabbit Hole: Adventures and Misadventures in the Realm of Children's Literature (Lanes), **Supp. XVI:** 104
Down There on a Visit (Isherwood), **Supp. XIV:** 159, 161, 164, **168–169,** 170, 171
Down the River (Abbey), **Supp. XIII:** 12–13
"Down the River with Henry Thoreau" (Abbey), **Supp. XIII:** 12–13
Down These Mean Streets (P. Thomas), **Supp. XIII:** 264
Down the Starry River (Purdy), **Supp. VII:** 278
"Downward Path to Wisdom, The" (Porter), **III:** 442, 443, 446
"Down Where I Am" (Hughes), **Supp. I Part 1:** 344
Dowson, Ernest C., **I:** 384
Doyle, Arthur Conan, **Retro. Supp. I:** 270; **Supp. IV Part 1:** 128, 341; **Supp. IV Part 2:** 464, 469; **Supp. XI:** 63
Doyle, C. W., **I:** 199
"Draba" (Leopold), **Supp. XIV:** 186
Drabble, Margaret, **Supp. IV Part 1:** 297, 299, 305
Drabelle, Dennis, **Supp. XIII:** 13
Drach, Ivan, **Supp. III Part 1:** 268
Dracula (film), **Supp. IV Part 1:** 104; **Supp. XVII:** 57
"Draft Horse, The" (Frost), **Retro. Supp. I:** 141
"Draft Lyrics for *Candide*" (Agee), **I:** 28
Draft of XVI Cantos, A (Pound), **III:** 472; **Retro. Supp. I:** 292
Draft of XXX Cantos, A (Pound), **III:** 196; **Retro. Supp. I:** 292
Drafts &Fragments (Pound), **Retro. Supp. I:** 293
Dragon Country (T. Williams), **IV:** 383
Dragon Seed (Buck), **Supp. II Part 1:** 124
Dragon's Teeth (Sinclair), **Supp. V:** 290
Drake, Benjamin, **Supp. I Part 2:** 584
Drake, Daniel, **Supp. I Part 2:** 584
Drake, Sir Francis, **Supp. I Part 2:** 497
Drake, St. Clair, **IV:** 475
Drake, William, **Supp. XV:** 295
Dramatic Duologues (Masters), **Supp. I Part 2:** 461
Drattel, Deborah, **Supp. XV:** 333
Drat These Brats (X. J. Kennedy), **Supp. XV:** 163
"Draught" (Cowley), **Supp. II Part 1:** 141, 142
Drayton, Michael, **IV:** 135; **Retro. Supp. II:** 76
"Dr. Bergen's Belief" (Schwartz), **Supp. II Part 2:** 650
Dr. Bloodmoney (Dick), **Supp. XVIII:** 138
"Dreadful Has Already Happened, The" (Strand), **Supp. IV Part 2:** 627
"Dream, A" (Ginsberg), **Supp. II Part 1:** 312
"Dream, A" (Tate), **IV:** 129
"Dream, The" (Hayden), **Supp. II Part 1:** 368, 377
Dream at the End of the World, The: Paul Bowles and the Literary Renegades in Tangier (Green), **Supp. IV Part 1:** 95
"Dream Avenue" (Simic), **Supp. VIII:** 282
"Dream Boogie" (Hughes), **Retro. Supp. I:** 208; **Supp. I Part 1:** 339–340
"Dreambook Bestiary" (Komunyakaa), **Supp. XIII:** 120
Dreamer (Johnson), **Supp. VI:** 186, **196–199**
dreamer examines his pillow, the (Shanley), **Supp. XIV:** 315, **327**
"Dreamer in a Dead Language" (Paley), **Supp. VI:** 217
Dreaming in Cuban (García), **Supp. XI:** 178, **179–185,** 190
"Dreaming of Hair" (L.-Y. Lee), **Supp. XV:** 214
"Dreaming the Breasts" (Sexton), **Supp. II Part 2:** 692
"Dream Interpreted, The" (Paine), **Supp. I Part 2:** 505
Dream Jumbo (Longo), **Supp. XVI:** 124
Dream Keeper, The (Hughes), **Supp. I Part 1:** 328, 332, 333, 334
Dream Keeper and Other Poems, The (Hughes), **Retro. Supp. I:** 201, 202
Dreamland (Baker), **Supp. XIV:** 96
"Dream-Land" (Poe), **Retro. Supp. II:** 274

Dream Life of Balso Snell, The (West), **IV:** 286, 287, 288–290, 291, 297; **Retro. Supp. II:** 321, 322, 327, 328, **330–332**
Dream of a Common Language, The: Poems, 1974–1977 (Rich), **Supp. I Part 2:** 551, 554, 569–576
Dream of Arcadia: American Writers and Artists in Italy (Brooks), **I:** 254
Dream of Governors, A (Simpson), **Supp. IX:** 265, **269–270**
"Dream of Italy, A" (Masters), **Supp. I Part 2:** 458
"Dream of Mourning, The" (Glück), **Supp. V:** 84
"Dream of the Blacksmith's Room, A" (R. Bly), **Supp. IV Part 1:** 73
"Dream of the Cardboard Lover" (Haines), **Supp. XII:** 204
Dream of the Golden Mountains, The (Cowley), **Supp. II Part 1:** 139, 141, 142, 144
"Dream Pang, A" (Frost), **II:** 153
"Dreams About Clothes" (Merrill), **Supp. III Part 1:** 328–329
Dreams from Bunker Hill (Fante), **Supp. XI:** 160, 166, **172–173**
"Dreams of Adulthood" (Ashbery), **Supp. III Part 1:** 26
"Dreams of Glory on the Mound" (Plimpton), **Supp. XVI:** 238–239
"Dreams of Math" (Kenyon), **Supp. VII:** 160–161
"Dreams of the Animals" (Atwood), **Supp. XIII:** 33
"Dream Variations" (Hughes), **Retro. Supp. I:** 198; **Supp. I Part 1:** 323
"Dream Vision" (Olsen), **Supp. XIII:** 295–296
Dream Work (Oliver), **Supp. VII:** 234–235, 236–238, 240
Dred: A Tale of the Great Dismal Swamp (Stowe), **Supp. I Part 2:** 592
Dreiser, Theodore, **I:** 59, 97, 109, 116, 355, 374, 375, 475, 482, **497–520; II:** 26, 27, 29, 34, 38, 44, 74, 89, 93, 180, 276, 283, 428, 444, 451, 456–457, 467–468; **III:** 40, 103, 106, 251, 314, 319, 327, 335, 453, 576, 582; **IV:** 29, 35, 40, 135, 208, 237, 475, 482, 484; **Retro. Supp. I:** 325, 376; **Retro. Supp. II: 93–110,** 114, 322; **Supp. I Part 1:** 320; **Supp. I Part 2:** 461, 468; **Supp. III Part 2:** 412; **Supp. IV Part 1:** 31, 236, 350; **Supp. IV Part 2:** 689; **Supp. IX:** 1, 14, 15, 308; **Supp. V:** 113, 120; **Supp. VIII:** 98, 101, 102; **Supp. XI:** 207; **Supp. XIV:** 111; **Supp. XVII:** 95, 96–97, 105, 155; **Supp. XVIII:** 1, 6, 76, 226
"Drenched in Light" (Hurston), **Supp. VI:** 150–151
Dresser, Paul, **Retro. Supp. II:** 94, 103
Dress Gray (teleplay), **Supp. IV Part 2:** 683
Dress Gray (Truscott), **Supp. IV Part 2:** 683
"Dressing for Dinner" (Ríos), **Supp. IV Part 2:** 548
Dressing Up for the Carnival (Shields), **Supp. VII:** 328
Drew, Bettina, **Supp. IX:** 2, 4
Drew, Elizabeth, **Retro. Supp. II:** 242, 243
Drexler, Eric, **Supp. XVI:** 121
Dreyfus, Alfred, **Supp. I Part 2:** 446
"Dr. Hanray's Second Chance" (Richter), **Supp. XVIII:** 218
Drift and Mastery (Lippmann), **I:** 222–223
"Driftwood" (C. Frost), **Supp. XV:** 106–107
"Drinker, The" (Lowell), **II:** 535, 550
"Drinking Cold Water" (Everwine), **Supp. XV:** 80–81
"Drinking from a Helmet" (Dickey), **Supp. IV Part 1:** 180
Drinking Gourd, The (Hansberry), **Supp. IV Part 1:** 359, 365–367, 374
Drinks before Dinner (Doctorow), **Supp. IV Part 1:** 231, 234–235
Drive, He Said (Larner), **Supp. XVI:** 220
"Drive Home, The" (Banks), **Supp. V:** 7
"Driver" (Merrill), **Supp. III Part 1:** 331
"Driving Through Minnesota During the Hanoi Bombings" (R. Bly), **Supp. IV Part 1:** 61; **Supp. XVII:** 243
"Driving through Oregon" (Haines), **Supp. XII:** 207
"Driving toward the Lac Qui Parle River" (R. Bly), **Supp. IV Part 1:** 61
"Dr. Jack-o'-Lantern" (Yates), **Supp. XI:** 340–341
Dr. Jekyll and Mr. Hyde (film), **Supp. XVII:** 57
"Drone" (Coleman), **Supp. XI:** 85–86
"Drowned Man, The: Death between Two Rivers" (McGrath), **Supp. X:** 116
"Drowning 1954" (Keillor), **Supp. XVI:** 172
Drowning Pool, The (film), **Supp. IV Part 2:** 474
Drowning Pool, The (Macdonald), **Supp. IV Part 2:** 470, 471
Drowning Season, The (Hoffman), **Supp. X: 82**
Drowning with Others (Dickey), **Supp. IV Part 1:** 176, 178, 179
"Drowsy Day, A" (Dunbar), **Supp. II Part 1:** 198
Dr. Seuss. *See* Geisel, Theodor Seuss (Dr. Seuss)
Dr. Seuss and Mr. Geisel (J. and N. Morgan), **Supp. XVI:** 103
Dr. Seuss Goes to War: The World War II Editorial Cartoons of Theodor Seuss Geisel (Minear), **Supp. XVI:** 101
Dr. Seuss's ABC (Geisel), **Supp. XVI:** 99
Dr. Strangelove; or, How I Learned to Stop Worrying and Love the Bomb (film), **Supp. XI:** 293, **301–305**
Drugiye Berega (Nabokov), **III:** 247–250, 252
"Drug Shop, The, or Endymion in Edmonstoun" (Benét), **Supp. XI:** 43
"Drug Store" (Shapiro), **Supp. II Part 2:** 705
"Drugstore in Winter, A" (Ozick), **Supp. V:** 272
Drukman, Steven, **Supp. XIII:** 195, 197, 202
"Drum" (Hogan), **Supp. IV Part 1:** 413
"Drum, The" (Alvarez), **Supp. VII:** 7
"Drumlin Woodchuck, A" (Frost), **II:** 159–160; **Retro. Supp. I:** 138
Drummond, William, **Supp. I Part 1:** 369
Drummond de Andrade, Carlos, **Supp. IV Part 2:** 626, 629, 630
Drum-Taps (Whitman), **IV:** 346, 347, 444; **Retro. Supp. I:** 406
"Drunken Fisherman, The" (Lowell), **II:** 534, 550
"Drunken Sisters, The" (Wilder), **IV:** 374
"Drunk in the Furnace, The" (Merwin), **Supp. III Part 1:** 346
Drunk in the Furnace, The (Merwin), **Supp. III Part 1:** 345–346
Druten, John van, **Supp. XIV:** 162
"Dr. Williams' Position" (Pound), **Supp. XVII:** 226–227
Dryden, John, **II:** 111, 542, 556; **III:** 15; **IV:** 145; **Retro. Supp. I:** 56; **Supp. I Part 1:** 150; **Supp. I Part 2:** 422; **Supp. IX:** 68; **Supp. XIV:** 5; **Supp. XV:** 258
Drye, Captain Frank, **Retro. Supp. II:** 115
"Dry Salvages, The" (Eliot), **Retro. Supp. I:** 66
Dry Salvages, The (Eliot), **I:** 581
"Dry September" (Faulkner), **II:** 72, 73
Dry Sun, Dry Wind (Wagoner), **Supp. IX:** 323, 324
D'Souza, Dinesh, **Supp. X:** 255
"Dual" (Goldbarth), **Supp. XII:** 188
"Dual Curriculum" (Ozick), **Supp. V:** 270
"Dualism" (Reed), **Supp. X:** 242
Duane's Depressed (McMurtry), **Supp. V:** 233
Du Bartas, Guillaume, **Supp. I Part 1:** 98, 104, 111, 118, 119
Duberman, Martin, **Supp. I Part 2:** 408, 409
"Dubin's Lives" (Malamud), **Supp. I Part 2:** 451
Dubious Honors (M. F. K. Fisher), **Supp. XVII:** 91
"Dubliners" (J. Joyce), **Supp. XVI:** 41
Dubliners (Joyce), **I:** 130, 480; **III:** 471; **Supp. VIII:** 146
Du Bois, Nina Gomer (Mrs. W. E. B. Du Bois), **Supp. II P art 1:** 158; **Supp. XIV:** 200
Du Bois, Shirley Graham (Mrs. W. E. B. Du Bois), **Supp. II Part 1:** 186
Du Bois, W. E. B., **I:** 260; **Supp. I Part 1:** 5, 345; **Supp. II Part 1:** 33, 56, 61, **157–189,** 195; **Supp. IV Part 1:** 9, 164, 170, 362; **Supp. X:** 133, 134, 137, 139, 242; **Supp. XIII:** 185, **Supp. XIII:** 186, 233, 238, 243, 244, 247; **Supp. XIV:** 54, 69, 72, 201, 202; **Supp. XVI:** 135; **Supp. XVIII:** 119, 122, 126, 130
Dubreuil, Jean, **Supp. IV Part 2:** 425
Dubus, Andre, **Supp. VII: 75–93; Supp. XI:** 347,**Supp. XI:** 349; **Supp. XIV:** 21

Duchamp, Marcel, **IV:** 408; **Retro. Supp. I:** 416, 417, 418, 430; **Supp. IV Part 2:** 423, 424; **Supp. XII:** 124; **Supp. XV:** 157
"Duchess at Prayer, The" (Wharton), **Retro. Supp. I:** 365
Duchess of Malfi, The (Webster), **IV:** 131
Duck Soup (film), **Supp. IV Part 1:** 384
Duck Variations, The (Mamet), **Supp. XIV:** 239, 240, 249
Dudley, Anne. *See* Bradstreet, Anne
Dudley, Joseph, **III:** 52
Dudley, Thomas, **III:** 52; **Supp. I Part 1:** 98, 99, 110, 116
"Duet, With Muffled Brake Drums" (Updike), **Retro. Supp. I:** 319
Duet for Cannibals (Sontag), **Supp. III Part 2:** 452, 456
Duffey, Bernard, **Supp. I Part 2:** 458, 471
Duffus, R. L., **Supp. I Part 2:** 650
Duffy, Martha, **Supp. IV Part 1:** 207
Duffy, William, **Supp. XVI:** 32
Du Fu (Tu Fu), **Supp. XV:** 217
Dufy, Raoul, **I:** 115; **IV:** 80
Dugan, Alan, **Supp. XIII:** 76
Dugan, James, **Supp. XV:** 197
Duhamel, Marcel, **Supp. XVI:** 135, 143
Dujardin, Edouard, **I:** 53
"Duke de l'Omelette, The" (Poe), **III:** 411, 425
"Duke in His Domain, The" (Capote), **Supp. III Part 1:** 113, 126
Duke of Deception, The (G. Wolff), **Supp. II Part 1:** 97; **Supp. XI:** 246
"Duke's Child, The" (Maxwell), **Supp. VIII:** 172
"Dulce et Decorum Est" (Owen), **Supp. XVIII:** 92
"Dulham Ladies, The" (Jewett), **II:** 407, 408; **Retro. Supp. II:** 143
Duluth (Vidal), **Supp. IV Part 2:** 677, 685, 689, 691–692
Dumas, Alexandre, **III:** 386; **Supp. XVII:** 64
"Dumb Oax, The" (Lewis), **Retro. Supp. I:** 170
"Dummy, The" (Sontag), **Supp. III Part 2:** 469
"Dump Ground, The" (Stegner), **Supp. IV Part 2:** 601
Dunbar, Alice Moore (Mrs. Paul Laurence Dunbar), **Supp. II Part 1:** 195, 200, 217
Dunbar, Paul Laurence, **Supp. I Part 1:** 320; **Supp. II Part 1:** 174, **191–219; Supp. III Part 1:** 73; **Supp. IV Part 1:** 15, 165, 170; **Supp. X:** 136; **Supp. XI:** 277; **Supp. XIII:** 111
Duncan, Harry, **Supp. XV:** 75
Duncan, Isadora, **I:** 483; **Supp. XV:** 42, 50
Duncan, Robert, **Retro. Supp. II:** 49; **Supp. III Part 2:** 625, 626, 630, 631; **Supp. VIII:** 304; **Supp. XVI:** 282–283
Dunciad, The (Pope), **I:** 204
Dunford, Judith, **Supp. VIII:** 107
Dunlap, William, **Supp. I Part 1:** 126, 130, 137, 141, 145
Dunn, Stephen, **Supp. XI: 139–158**
Dunne, Finley Peter, **II:** 432
Dunne, John Gregory, **Supp. IV Part 1:** 197, 198, 201, 203, 207
"Dunnet Shepherdess, A" (Jewett), **II:** 392–393; **Retro. Supp. II:** 139
Dunning, Stephen, **Supp. XIV:** 126
Dunning, William Archibald, **Supp. II Part 1:** 170; **Supp. XIV:** 48
Dunnock, Mildred, **III:** 153
Dunster, Henry, **Supp. I Part 2:** 485
"Duo Tried Killing Man with Bacon" (Goldbarth), **Supp. XII:** 176
Dupee, F. W., **I:** 254; **II:** 548; **Supp. IX:** 93, 96; **Supp. VIII:** 231
DuPlessis, Rachel Blau, **Supp. IV Part 2:** 421, 426, 432; **Supp. XVI:** 284
Duplicate Keys (Smiley), **Supp. VI:** 292, **294–296**
Duplications, The (Koch), **Supp. XV:** 181, 183, 186
Durable Fire, A (Sarton), **Supp. VIII:** 260
Durand, Asher, B., **Supp. I Part 1:** 156, 157
Durand, Régis, **Supp. IV Part 1:** 44
"Durango Suite" (Gunn Allen), **Supp. IV Part 1:** 326
"Durations" (Matthews), **Supp. IX:** 152–153, 154
Dürer, Albrecht, **III:** 212; **Supp. XII:** 44
Durham, David Anthony, **Supp. XVIII:** 100
"During Fever" (Lowell), **II:** 547
Durkheim, Émile, **I:** 227; **Retro. Supp. I:** 55, 57; **Supp. I Part 2:** 637, 638
Durrell, Lawrence, **III:** 184, 190; **IV:** 430; **Supp. X:** 108, 187; **Supp. XVI:** 294
Dürrenmatt, Friedrich, **Supp. IV Part 2:** 683
Duse, Eleonora, **II:** 515, 528
Dusk and Other Stories (Salter), **Supp. IX: 260–261**
Dusk of Dawn: An Essay Toward an Autobiography of a Race Concept (Du Bois), **Supp. II Part 1:** 159, 183, 186
"Dusting" (Alvarez), **Supp. VII:** 4
"Dusting" (Dove), **Supp. IV Part 1:** 247, 248
"Dusting" (Schnackenberg), **Supp. XV:** 256
"Dust of Snow" (Frost), **II:** 154
Dust Tracks on a Road (Hurston), **Supp. IV Part 1:** 5, 11; **Supp. VI:** 149, 151, 158–159
"Dusty Braces" (Snyder), **Supp. VIII:** 302
Dutchman (Baraka), **Supp. II Part 1:** 38, 40, 42–44, 54, 55
"Dutch Nick Massacre, The" (Twain), **IV:** 195
"Dutch Picture, A" (Longfellow), **Retro. Supp. II:** 171
Dutton, Charles S., **Supp. VIII:** 332, 342
Dutton, Clarence Earl, **Supp. IV Part 2:** 598
Duvall, Robert, **Supp. V:** 227
"Duwamish" (Hugo), **Supp. VI:** 136
"Duwamish, Skagit, Hoh" (Hugo), **Supp. VI:** 136–137
"Duwamish No. 2" (Hugo), **Supp. VI:** 137
Duyckinck, Evert, **III:** 77, 81, 83, 85; **Retro. Supp. I:** 155, 247, 248; **Supp. I Part 1:** 122, 317
Duyckinck, George, **Supp. I Part 1:** 122
"Dvonya" (Simpson), **Supp. IX:** 274
Dwellings: A Spiritual History of the Living World (Hogan), **Supp. IV Part 1:** 397, 410, 415–416, 417
Dwight, Sereno E., **I:** 547
Dwight, Timothy, **Supp. I Part 1:** 124; **Supp. I Part 2:** 516, 580; **Supp. II Part 1:** 65, 69
Dworkin, Andrea, **Supp. XII:** 6
Dwyer, Jim, **Supp. XVI:** 16, 19
Dybbuk, A, or Between Two Worlds: Dramatic Legend in Four Acts (Kushner), **Supp. IX:** 138
Dybbuk, The (Ansky), **IV:** 6
Dyer, Geoff, **Supp. X:** 169
Dyer, R. C., **Supp. XIII:** 162
Dying Animal, The (P. Roth), **Retro. Supp. II:** 288
"Dying Elm, The" (Freneau), **Supp. II Part 1:** 258
"Dying Indian, The" (Freneau), **Supp. II Part 1:** 262
"Dying Man, The" (Roethke), **III:** 540, 542, 543–545
Dylan, Bob, **Supp. VIII:** 202; **Supp. XIII:** 114, 119; **Supp. XV:** 349, 350; **Supp. XVIII: 19–34**
Dylan's Visions of Sin (Ricks), **Supp. XVIII:** 20
Dynamo (O'Neill), **III:** 396
"Dysfunctional Narratives: Or, 'Mistakes Were Made'" (C. Baxter), **Supp. XVII:** 20
"Dysfunctional Nation" (Karr), **Supp. XI:** 245
Dyson, A. E., **Retro. Supp. II:** 247
Dyson, Freeman, **Supp. XVII:** 42

E

"Each and All" (Emerson), **II:** 19
Each in His Season (Snodgrass), **Supp. VI:** 324, 327
"Each Like a Leaf" (Swenson), **Supp. IV Part 2:** 644
Eads, Martha Greene, **Supp. XVIII:** 49
Eager, Allen, **Supp. XI:** 294
"Eagle, The" (Tate), **IV:** 128
"Eagle and the Mole, The" (Wylie), **Supp. I Part 2:** 710, 711, 713, 714, 729
Eagle as Wide as the World, The (X. J. Kennedy), **Supp. XV:** 162, 164
"Eagle Poem" (Harjo), **Supp. XII:** 224, 226
"Eagles" (Dickey), **Supp. IV Part 1:** 186
Eagle's Mile, The (Dickey), **Supp. IV Part 1:** 178, 185–186
"Eagle That Is Forgotten, The" (Lindsay), **Supp. I Part 2:** 382, 387
Eagleton, Terry, **Retro. Supp. I:** 67
Eakin, Paul John, **Supp. VIII:** 167, 168; **Supp. XIII:** 225; **Supp. XVI:** 70
Eakins, Thomas, **Supp. XIV:** 338

Eames, Roscoe, **II:** 476
"Earl: My Life with a Louse" (Keillor), **Supp. XVI:** 176
"Earl Painter" (Banks), **Supp. V:** 14–15
"Early Adventures of Ralph Ringwood, The" (Irving), **II:** 314
Early Americana (Richter), **Supp. XVIII:** 208, 210, 211, 220
Early Ayn Rand, The: A Selection of Her Unpublished Fiction (Rand), **Supp. IV Part 2:** 520
Early Dark (Price), **Supp. VI:** 262
Early Diary of Anaïs Nin, The, **Supp. X:** 184, 192
Early Elkin (Elkin), **Supp. VI: 42–43,** 45
"Early Evenin' Blues" (Hughes), **Retro. Supp. I:** 205
"Early History of a Seamstress" (Reznikoff), **Supp. XIV:** 277, 289
"Early History of a Sewing-Machine Operator" (Reznikoff), **Supp. XIV:** 277
Early History of a Sewing-Machine Operator (Reznikoff), **Supp. XIV:** 289
"Early History of a Writer" (Reznikoff), **Supp. XIV:** 278, 290
"Early in the Morning" (L.-Y. Lee), **Supp. XV:** 214
Early Lectures of Ralph Waldo Emerson, The (Emerson), **II:** 11
Early Lives of Melville, The (Sealts), **Retro. Supp. I:** 257
"Early Marriage" (Richter), **Supp. XVIII:** 209
Early Martyr and Other Poems, An (W. C. Williams), **Retro. Supp. I:** 423
"Early Morning: Cape Cod" (Swenson), **Supp. IV Part 2:** 641
"Early Spring between Madison and Bellingham" (R. Bly), **Supp. IV Part 1:** 71
Earnhardt, Dale, **Supp. XII:** 310
Earnshaw, Doris, **Supp. IV Part 1:** 310
"Earth" (Bryant), **Supp. I Part 1:** 157, 164, 167
"Earth, The" (Sexton), **Supp. II Part 2:** 696
Earth Abides (Stewart), **Supp. XVIII:** 138
"Earth and Fire" (Berry), **Supp. X:** 27
Earth as Air, The: An Ars Poetica (Sobin), **Supp. XVI: 285–286**
"Earth Being" (Toomer), **Supp. IX:** 320
"Earthly Care a Heavenly Discipline" (Stowe), **Supp. I Part 2:** 586
"Earthly City of the Jews, The" (Kazin), **Retro. Supp. II:** 286
"Earthly Meditations" (Wrigley), **Supp. XVIII:** 304–306
Earthly Meditations (Wrigley), **Supp. XVIII:** 304–305
Earthly Possessions (Tyler), **Supp. IV Part 2:** 665–666, 671
Earth Power Coming (Ortiz, ed.), **Supp. IV Part 2:** 502
"Earth's Holocaust" (Hawthorne), **II:** 226, 231, 232, 242; **III:** 82; **Retro. Supp. I:** 152
Earth Without You, The (F. Wright), **Supp. XVII:** 243
"East Coker" (Eliot), **Retro. Supp. I:** 66; **Supp. VIII:** 195, 196
East Coker (Eliot), **I:** 580, 581, 582, 585, 587
"Easter" (Toomer), **Supp. III Part 2:** 486
"Easter, an Ode" (Lowell), **II:** 536
"Easter Morning" (Ammons), **Supp. VII:** 34
"Easter Morning" (Clampitt), **Supp. IX:** 45
"Easter Ode, An" (Dunbar), **Supp. II Part 1:** 196
Easter Parade, The (Yates), **Supp. XI:** 346, 349
"Easter Sermon, 1866" (Nelson), **Supp. XVIII:** 177
"Easter Sunday: Recollection" (Gunn Allen), **Supp. IV Part 1:** 322
"Easter Wings" (Herbert), **Supp. IV Part 2:** 646
"East European Cooking" (Simic), **Supp. VIII:** 277
East Is East (Boyle), **Supp. VIII:** 1–3
Eastlake, William, **Supp. XIII:** 12
East Lynne (Wood), **Supp. I Part 1:** 35, 36; **Supp. I Part 2:** 459, 462; **Supp. XVI:** 182
Eastman, Elaine Goodale, **Supp. X:** 103
Eastman, Max, **Supp. III Part 2:** 620; **Supp. X:** 131, 134, 135, 137; **Supp. XV:** 295; **Supp. XVI:** 185; **Supp. XVII:** 96
East of Eden (Steinbeck), **IV:** 51, 56–57, 59
"East of the Sun and West of the Moon" (Merwin), **Supp. III Part 1:** 344
Easton, Alison, **Retro. Supp. II:** 143, 144, 145
Easton, Bret Ellis, **Supp. XI:** 65
Easton, Robert, **Supp. IV Part 2:** 461, 474
East Wind (Lowell), **II:** 527
East Wind: West Wind (Buck), **Supp. II Part 1:** 114–115
Easy Rawlins mysteries, **Supp. XIII:** 236, **237–241,** 242
Easy Rider (film), **Supp. XI:** 293, **308,** 309
Eat a Bowl of Tea (Chu), **Supp. X:** 291
"Eating" (Bass), **Supp. XVI:** 23–24
"Eating Alone" (L.-Y. Lee), **Supp. XV:** 214
Eating Naked (Dobyns), **Supp. XIII: 78–79**
"Eating Out" (L. Michaels), **Supp. XVI:** 209
"Eating Poetry" (Strand), **Supp. IV Part 2:** 626
"Eating the Whole" (C. Frost), **Supp. XV:** 101
"Eating Together" (L.-Y. Lee), **Supp. XV:** 214
"Eating with My Fingers" (C. Frost), **Supp. XV:** 97
Eaton, Edith, **Supp. X:** 291
Eaton, Peggy, **Supp. I Part 2:** 461
Eaton, Winnifred, **Supp. X:** 291
"Eatonville Anthology, The" (Hurston), **Supp. VI:** 152
Eat the Document (film, Pennebaker), **Supp. XVIII:** 19, 26, 27, 28
"Ebb and Flow, The" (Taylor), **IV:** 161
"Ebenezer Marsh, 1725" (Schnackenberg), **Supp. XV:** 256
Eben Holden (Bacheller), **I:** 216
Eberhardt, Isabelle, **Supp. IV Part 1:** 92
Eberhart, Mrs., **I:** 521–522, 530
Eberhart, Richard, **I: 521–543; II:** 535–536; **III:** 527; **IV:** 416; **Retro. Supp. II:** 176, 178; **Supp. I Part 1:** 83; **Supp. XII:** 119
Eble, Kenneth E., **Supp. I Part 1:** 201
Eccentricities of a Nightingale (T. Williams), **IV:** 382, 385, 397, 398
Ecclesiastica Historia Integram Ecclesiae (Taylor), **IV:** 163
"Echart" (Sobin), **Supp. XVI:** 289
"Echo, The" (Bowles), **Supp. IV Part 1:** 84, 86, 87
Echoes inside the Labyrinth (McGrath), **Supp. X:** 127
Eckehart, Meister, **Supp. XV:** 225
Eckhart, Maria, **Supp. V:** 212
Eclipse (Hogan), **Supp. IV Part 1:** 397, 400, 402
Eclipse, a Nightmare (Montalembert), **Supp. XV:** 349
Eclogues (Virgil), **Supp. VIII:** 31
"Ecologue" (Ginsberg), **Supp. II Part 1:** 326
"Ecologues of These States 1969–1971" (Ginsberg), **Supp. II Part 1:** 325
Ecology of a Cracker Childhood (Ray), **Supp. XVIII:** 189, 191, 192, 193, **195–199,** 201, 202, 204
"Economics of Negro Emancipation in the United States, The" (Du Bois), **Supp. II Part 1:** 174
"Economic Theory of Women's Dress, The" (Veblen), **Supp. I Part 2:** 636
Economy of the Unlost: Reading Simonides of Keos with Paul Celan (Carson), **Supp. XII:** 110–111
Ecotactics: The Sierra Club Handbook for Environmental Activists (Mitchell and Stallings, eds.), **Supp. IV Part 2:** 488
"Ecstasy" (Bierds), **Supp. XVII:** 34
"Ecstasy" (Olds), **Supp. X:** 206
"Ecstasy of Influence, The" (Lethem), **Supp. XVIII:** 150
"Ecstatic" (Komunyakaa), **Supp. XIII:** 131
Edda, **Supp. X:** 114
Eddy, Mary Baker, **I:** 583; **III:** 506
Edel, Leon, **I:** 20; **II:** 338–339; **Retro. Supp. I:** 218, 224, 231
Edelberg, Cynthia, **Supp. IV Part 1:** 155
"Eden and My Generation" (Levis), **Supp. XI:** 270
Edenbaum, Robert, **Supp. IV Part 1:** 352
Eden Tree (Bynner), **Supp. XV:** 42, 51
Eder, Richard, **Supp. XII:** 189; **Supp. XV:** 62, 187, 259, 261
Edgar Huntly; or, Memoirs of a Sleep-Walker (Brown), **Supp. I Part 1:** 140–144, 145
"Edge" (Plath), **Retro. Supp. II:** 256; **Supp. I Part 2:** 527, 547

Edge, Mary E., **II:** 316
"Edge of Possibility, The: Susan Warner and the World of Sunday School Fiction" (Gates), **Supp. XVIII:** 267
"Edge of the Great Rift, The" (Theroux), **Supp. VIII:** 325
Edge of the Sea, The (Carson), **Supp. IX:** 19, **25–31,** 32
Edgers, Geoff, **Supp. XV:** 113
Edgeworth, Maria, **II:** 8; **Supp. XV:** 231
Edible Woman, The (Atwood), **Supp. XIII:** 19, 20, **20–21**
"Edict by the King of Prussia, An" (Franklin), **II:** 120
Edie: An American Biography (Stein), **Supp. XVI:** 245
Edison, Thomas A., **I:** 483; **Supp. I Part 2:** 392
Edith Wharton (Joslin), **Retro. Supp. I:** 376
Edith Wharton: A Biography (Lewis), **Retro. Supp. I:** 362
Edith Wharton: A Woman in Her Time (Auchincloss), **Retro. Supp. I:** 370
Edith Wharton: Matters of Mind and Spirit (Singley), **Retro. Supp. I:** 373
Edith Wharton's Argument with America (Ammons), **Retro. Supp. I:** 364
Edith Wharton's Brave New Politics (Bauer), **Retro. Supp. I:** 381
Edith Wharton's Letters from the Underworld (Waid), **Retro. Supp. I:** 360
Edith Wharton: Traveller in the Land of Letters (Goodwyn), **Retro. Supp. I:** 370
"Editing and Glosses" (Reznikoff), **Supp. XIV:** 283
Editing of Emily Dickinson, The (Franklin), **Retro. Supp. I:** 41
"Editor and the Schoolma'am, The" (Frederic), **II:** 130
"Editor's Easy Chair" (Howells), **II:** 276
"Editor's Study, The" (Howells), **II:** 275, 276, 285
"Editor Whedon" (Masters), **Supp. I Part 2:** 463
Edlin, Mari, **Supp. X:** 266
Edman, Irwin, **III:** 605
Edmond (Mamet), **Supp. XIV:** 241, 248, 249, 250
Edmundson, Mark, **Retro. Supp. II:** 262
Edsel (Shapiro), **Supp. II Part 2:** 703, 704, 717–719
Edson, Margaret, **Supp. XVIII: 35–52**
Edson, Russell, **Supp. VIII:** 279
"Educated American Woman, An" (Cheever), **Supp. I Part 1:** 194
"Education, An" (Ozick), **Supp. V:** 267
Education and Living (Bourne), **I:** 252
"Education by Poetry" (Frost), **Supp. XV:** 215
"Education of a Storyteller, The" (Bambara), **Supp. XI:** 20
Education of Black People, The (Du Bois), **Supp. II Part 1:** 186
Education of Harriet Hatfield, The (Sarton), **Supp. VIII: 257–258**
Education of Henry Adams, The (Adams), **I:** 1, 5, 6, 11, 14, 15–18, 19, 20–21, 111; **II:** 276; **III:** 504; **Retro. Supp. I:** 53, 59; **Supp. IX:** 19; **Supp. XIV:** 299
*Education of H*y*m*a*n K*a*p*l*a*n, The* (Rosten), **Supp. XVII:** 9
"Education of Mingo, The" (Johnson), **Supp. VI:** 193, 194
"Education of Norman Podhoretz, The" (Goldberg), **Supp. VIII:** 238
Education of Oscar Fairfax, The (Auchincloss), **Supp. IV Part 1:** 25, 36
"Education of the Poet" (Glück), **Supp. V:** 78, 80
Education sentimentale (Flaubert), **III:** 315
"Education the Imagination" (Koch), **Supp. XV:** 175–176, 177
Edwards, Clifford, **Supp. XVIII:** 220
Edwards, Eli. *See* McKay, Claude
Edwards, Esther, **I:** 545
Edwards, John, **I:** 478
Edwards, Jonathan, **I: 544–566; II:** 432; **Retro. Supp. II:** 187; **Supp. I Part 1:** 301, 302; **Supp. I Part 2:** 552, 594, 700; **Supp. IV Part 2:** 430; **Supp. VIII:** 205
Edwards, Sarah, **I:** 545
Edwards, Thomas, **Supp. XV:** 20
Edwards, Thomas R., **Supp. XVI:** 207
Edwards, Timothy, **I:** 545
Edwards-Yearwood, Grace, **Supp. VIII:** 81
"Edwin Arlington Robinson" (Cowley), **Supp. II Part 1:** 144
Edwin Arlington Robinson (Winters), **Supp. II Part 2:** 812
Edwin Booth (play), **Supp. IV Part 1:** 89
E. E. Cummings (Marks), **I:** 438
E. E. Cummings: A Miscellany (Cummings), **I:** 429, 441
E. E. Cummings: A Miscellany, Revised (Cummings), **I:** 429
"Effects of Analogy" (Stevens), **Retro. Supp. I:** 297
Effluences from the Sacred Caves; More Selected Essays and Reviews (Carruth), **Supp. XVI:** 46
"Effort at Speech between Two People" (Rukeyser), **Supp. VI:** 276, 284
"Efforts of Affection" (Moore), **III:** 214
"Efforts of Affection: A Memoir of Marianne Moore" (Bishop), **Retro. Supp. II:** 52
"Egg, The" (Anderson), **I:** 113, 114
"Egg, The" (Snyder), **Supp. VIII:** 302
Eggleston, George Cary, **Supp. XVIII:** 15
"Eggplant Epithalamion, The" (Jong), **Supp. V:** 119
"Eggs" (Olds), **Supp. X:** 206
"Eggshell" (Stern), **Supp. IX:** 299
Egoist, The (Meredith), **II:** 186
Egorova, Lubov, **Supp. IX:** 58
"Egotism, or the Bosom Sergent" (Hawthorne), **II:** 227, 239
"Egyptian Pulled Glass Bottle in the Shape of a Fish, An" (Moore), **III:** 195, 213
Ehrenfels, Christian von, **Supp. XIV:** 198
Ehrenpreis, Irvin, **Supp. XII:** 128
Ehrenreich, Barbara, **Supp. XVII:** 210
Ehrlich, Gretel, **Supp. XIV:** 227; **Supp. XVIII:** 189
Eichmann, Adolf, **Supp. XII:** 166
Eichmann in Jerusalem (Arendt), **Retro. Supp. II:** 28; **Supp. VIII:** 243; **Supp. XII:** 166
"Eichmann in New York: The New York Intellectuals and the Hannah Arendt Controversy" (Rabinbach), **Supp. XII:** 166
"Eidolon" (Warren), **IV:** 239
"Eiger Dreams" (Krakauer), **Supp. XVIII:** 107
Eiger Dreams: Ventures Among Men and Mountains (Krakauer), **Supp. XVIII:** 105, 106, 107
Eight Cousins (Alcott), **Supp. I Part 1:** 29, 38, 42, 43
18 Poems from the Quechua (Strand, trans.), **Supp. IV Part 2:** 630
"18 West 11th Street" (Merrill), **Supp. III Part 1:** 323, 328
1876: A Novel (Vidal), **Supp. IV Part 2:** 677, 684, 688, 689, 691, 692
"Eighth Air Force" (Jarrell), **II:** 373–374, 377
Eight Harvard Poets, **I:** 429, 475
"Eighth Day, The" (Apple), **Supp. XVII:** 6, 50
"Eighth Ditch, The" (Baraka), **Supp. II Part 1:** 40
"'80s Pastoral: Frederick Barthelme's *Moon Deluxe* Ten Years On" (Peters), **Supp. XI:** 39
Eight Men (Wright), **IV:** 478, 488, 494
80 Flowers (Zukofsky), **Supp. III Part 2:** 631
Eikon Basilike, The, **Supp. IV Part 2:** 435
Eileen (Masters), **Supp. I Part 2:** 460
Eimi (Cummings), **I:** 429, 433, 434, 439–440
"Einstein" (MacLeish), **III:** 5, 8, 10–11, 18–19
Einstein, Albert, **I:** 493; **III:** 8, 10, 21, 161; **IV:** 69, 375, 410, 411, 421; **Retro. Supp. I:** 63; **Supp. I Part 2:** 609, 643; **Supp. III Part 2:** 621; **Supp. V:** 290; **Supp. XII:** 45
Eiseley, Loren, **III:** 227–228
Eisenhower, Dwight D., **I:** 136, 376; **II:** 548; **III:** 215; **IV:** 75; **Supp. I Part 1:** 291; **Supp. III Part 2:** 624; **Supp. V:** 45
Eisenstadt, Jill, **Supp. XVIII:** 135
Eisenstein, Sergei, **I:** 481
Eisinger, Chester E., **I:** 302; **II:** 604; **Supp. IX:** 15
Eisner, Douglas, **Supp. X:** 155
Elam, Angela, **Supp. XI:** 290
El Bernardo (Balbuena), **Supp. V:** 11
Elbert, Sarah, **Supp. I Part 1:** 34, 41
Elder, Donald, **II:** 417, 426, 435, 437; **Supp. XV:** 137

Elder, John, **Supp. IX:** 25
Elder, Lonne, III, **Supp. IV Part 1:** 362
Elder, Richard, **Supp. XII:** 172
"Elder Sister, The" (Olds), **Supp. X:** 205–206
Elder Statesman, The (Eliot), **I:** 572, 573, 583; **Retro. Supp. I:** 53, 65
E. L. Doctorow (Harter and Thompson), **Supp. IV Part 1:** 217
Eldredge, Kay, **Supp. IX:** 254, 259
Eldridge, Florence, **III:** 154, 403; **IV:** 357
Eleanor of Aquitaine, **III:** 470
Eleanor of Guienne, **I:** 14
"Elect, The" (Taylor), **Supp. V:** 323
"Elections, Nicaragua, 1984" (Kingsolver), **Supp. VII:** 208
Elective Affinities (Goethe; Bogan and Mayer, trans.), **Supp. III Part 1:** 63
Electra (Euripides), **III:** 398
Electra (Sophocles), **III:** 398; **IV:** 370; **Supp. IX:** 102
"Electra on Azalea Path" (Plath), **Supp. I Part 2:** 538
"Electrical Storm" (Bishop), **Supp. I Part 1:** 93
"Electrical Storm" (Hayden), **Supp. II Part 1:** 370
"Electric Arrows" (Proulx), **Supp. VII:** 256
"Electricity Saviour" (Olds), **Supp. X:** 215
Electric Kool-Aid Acid Test, The (Wolfe), **Supp. III Part 2:** 575–577, 582–584; **Supp. XI:** 239
Electric Lady, The (film), **Supp. XI:** 309
Elegant Extracts (Knox), **II:** 8
"Elegant Tom Dillar" (Briggs), **Supp. XVIII:** 17
Elegiac Feelings American (Corso), **Supp. XII: 131–134**
"Elegiac Fragments" (Everwine), **Supp. XV:** 89
"Elegies" (Rukeyser), **Supp. VI:** 272
Elegies (Rukeyser), **Supp. VI:** 273
"Elegies for Paradise Valley" (Hayden), **Supp. II Part 1:** 363
"Elegy" (Bidart), **Supp. XV:** 25, 29
Elegy (Levis), **Supp. XI:** 257, 259, 261, **271–272**
"Elegy" (Merwin), **Supp. III Part 1:** 351
"Elegy" (Stafford), **Supp. XI:** 322
"Elegy" (Tate), **IV:** 128
"Elegy, for the U.S.N. Dirigible, Macon, An" (Winters), **Supp. II Part 2:** 810
"Elegy Ending in the Sound of a Skipping Rope" (Levis), **Supp. XI:** 271–272
"Elegy for 41 Whales Beached in Florence, Oregon, June 1979" (Bierds), **Supp. XVII:** 27
"Elegy for D. H. Lawrence, An" (W. C. Williams), **Retro. Supp. I:** 421
"Elegy for My Father" (Strand), **Supp. IV Part 2:** 628
"Elegy for My Mother" (Wagoner), **Supp. IX:** 330
"Elegy for Redondo Beach" (Jarman), **Supp. XVII:** 112, 113
Elegy for September, An (Nichols), **Supp. XIII:** 268
"Elegy for Thelonious" (Komunyakaa), **Supp. XIII:** 118
"Elegy for the U.S.N. Dirigible, Macon, A" (Winters), **Supp. II Part 2:** 810
"Elegy of Last Resort" (Nemerov), **III:** 271
"Elegy with a Thimbleful of Water in the Cage" (Levis), **Supp. XI:** 272
"Elegy Written in a Country Churchyard" (Gray), **Supp. XIV:** 8
Elegy Written in a Country Churchyard (Gray), **I:** 68
"Elementary Scene, The" (Jarrell), **II:** 387, 388, 389
"Elements" (Frank), **Supp. X:** 213
Elements of Style, The (Strunk), **Supp. I Part 2:** 670
"Elenita, Cards, Palm, Water" (Cisneros), **Supp. VII:** 64
"Eleonora" (Poe), **III:** 412
Eleothriambos (Lee), **IV:** 158
"Elephants" (Moore), **III:** 203
"Elephant's Dance, The" (D. West), **Supp. XVIII:** 281
"Elevator, The" (Dixon), **Supp. XII:** 154
"Elevator Boy" (Hughes), **Retro. Supp. I:** 200; **Supp. I Part 1:** 326
"Eleven" (Cisneros), **Supp. VII:** 69
Eleven Essays in the European Novel (Blackmur), **Supp. II Part 1:** 91, 111
Eleven Kinds of Loneliness (Yates), **Supp. XI: 340–343,** 349
Eleven Poems on the Same Theme (Warren), **IV:** 239–241
"Eleven Times a Poem" (Corso), **Supp. XII:** 132, 133
El Greco (Doménikos Theotokópoulos), **I:** 387; **III:** 212
"El-Hajj Malik El-Shabazz" (Hayden), **Supp. II Part 1:** 379
"Eli, the Fanatic" (P. Roth), **Supp. III Part 2:** 407–408
Eliade, Mircea, **Supp. XVI:** 292
Eliot, Charles W., **I:** 5; **II:** 345; **Supp. I Part 2:** 479; **Supp. IX:** 94
Eliot, Charles William, **Retro. Supp. I:** 55
Eliot, George, **I:** 375, 458, 459, 461, 467; **II:** 179, 181, 191–192, 275, 319, 324, 338, 577; **IV:** 311, 322; **Retro. Supp. I:** 218, 220, 225; **Supp. I Part 1:** 370; **Supp. I Part 2:** 559, 579; **Supp. IV Part 1:** 31, 297; **Supp. IV Part 2:** 677; **Supp. IX:** 38, 43, 51; **Supp. V:** 258; **Supp. XI:** 68; **Supp. XII:** 335; **Supp. XIV:** 344
Eliot, T. S., **I:** 48, 49, 52, 59, 60, 64, 66, 68, 105, 107, 215–216, 236, 243, 256, 259, 261, 266, 384, 386, 395, 396, 399, 403, 430, 433, 441, 446, 475, 478, 479, 482, 521, 522, 527, **567–591; II:** 65, 96, 158, 168, 316, 371, 376, 386, 529, 530, 532, 537, 542, 545; **III:** 1, 4, 5, 6, 7–8, 9, 10, 11, 14, 17, 20, 21, 23, 26, 34, 174, 194, 195–196, 205–206, 220, 236, 239, 269, 270–271, 277–278, 301, 409, 428, 435, 436, 453, 456–457, 459–460, 461–462, 464, 466, 471, 476, 478, 485, 488, 492, 493, 498, 504, 509, 511, 517, 524, 527, 539, 572, 575, 586, 591, 594, 600, 613; **IV:** 27, 74, 82, 83, 95, 122, 123, 127, 129, 134, 138, 140, 141, 191, 201, 237, 331, 379, 402, 403, 418, 419, 420, 430, 431, 439, 442, 491; **Retro. Supp. I: 51–71,** 74, 80, 89, 91, 171, 198, 210, 283, 289, 290, 292, 296, 298, 299, 311, 324, 359, 411, 413, 414, 416, 417, 420, 428; **Retro. Supp. II:** 79, 178, 189, 262, 326; **Supp. I Part 1:** 257, 264, 268, 270, 274, 299; **Supp. I Part 2:** 387, 423, 455, 536, 554, 624, 659, 721; **Supp. II Part 1:** 1, 4, 8, 20, 30, 91, 98, 103, 136, 314; **Supp. III Part 1:** 9, 10, 26, 31, 37, 41, 43, 44, 48, 62–64, 73, 91, 99–100, 105–106, 273; **Supp. III Part 2:** 541, 611, 612, 617, 624; **Supp. IV Part 1:** 40, 47, 284, 380, 404; **Supp. IV Part 2:** 436; **Supp. IX:** 158–159, 229; **Supp. V:** 79, 97, 101, 338, 343, 344; **Supp. VIII:** 19, 21, 93, 102, 105, 182, 195, 205, 290, 292; **Supp. X:** 59, 115, 119, 124, 187, 324; **Supp. XI:** 242; **Supp. XII:** 45, 159, 198, 308; **Supp. XIII:** 77, 104, 115, 332, 341–342, 344, 346; **Supp. XIV:** 5, 13, 107, 287, 290, 306, 347; **Supp. XV:** 20, 51, 139, 177, 181, 186, 216, 218, 250, 251, 258, 298, 302, 303, 306, 307; **Supp. XVI:** 158–159, 204, 207, 282; **Supp. XVII:** 36, 71, 75, 111, 240; **Supp. XVIII:** 136
Eliot's Early Years (Gordon), **Retro. Supp. I:** 55
"Elizabeth" (Longfellow), **I:** 502
"Elizabeth, 1905" (Schnackenberg), **Supp. XV:** 253, 256
Elizabeth Appleton (O'Hara), **III:** 362, 364, 375–377
"Elizabeth Bishop (1911–1979)" (Merrill), **Retro. Supp. II:** 53
"Elizabeth Bishop in Brazil" (Brown), **Supp. I Part 1:** 96
"Elizabeth Bishop's *North & South*" (Lowell), **Retro. Supp. II:** 40–41
"Elizabeth Gone" (Sexton), **Supp. II Part 2:** 674, 681
Elizabeth Stoddard and the Boundaries of Bourgeois Culture (Mahoney), **Supp. XV:** 270
Elk Heads on the Wall (Ríos), **Supp. IV Part 2:** 540
Elkin, Stanley, **Supp. VI: 41–59**
"Elk Song" (Hogan), **Supp. IV Part 1:** 406
Ella in Bloom (Hearon), **Supp. VIII: 70–71**
Elledge, Jim, **Supp. XIII:** 88
Ellen Foster: A Novel (Gibbons), **Supp. X:** 41, **42–44,** 46, 47, 49, 50
Ellen Montgomery's Bookshelf (S. and A. Warner), **Supp. XVIII:** 264
Ellen Rogers (Farrell), **II:** 42–43
"Ellen's Dream" (Gioia), **Supp. XV:** 128
"Ellen West" (Bidart), **Supp. XV: 26–27**
Eller, Ernest, **Supp. I Part 2:** 497
Ellerman, Winifred, **Supp. I Part 1:** 258–259. *See also* McAlmon, Mrs. Robert (Winifred Ellerman)

"*El libro de la sexualidad*" (Simic), **Supp. VIII:** 283
Ellington, Duke, **Retro. Supp. II:** 115; **Supp. IV Part 1:** 360; **Supp. IX:** 164
Elliot, Charles, **Supp. V:** 161
Elliot, George P., **Supp. XV:** 92
Elliott, George B., **III:** 478
"Ellipsis" (C. Frost), **Supp. XV:** 107
Ellis, Albert, **Supp. IV Part 2:** 527
Ellis, Anne, **Supp. XVI:** 38
Ellis, Bret Easton, **Supp. XII:** 81; **Supp. XVIII:** 135
Ellis, Brett Easton, **Supp. X:** 7
Ellis, Charles, **Supp. I Part 1:** 99
Ellis, Havelock, **II:** 276
Ellis, John Harvard, **Supp. I Part 1:** 103
Ellis, Katherine, **IV:** 114
Ellison, Harlan, **Supp. XIII:** 61
Ellison, Ralph, **IV:** 250, 493; **Retro. Supp. II:** 3, **111–130; Supp. II Part 1:** 33, **221–252; Supp. IV, Part 1:** 374; **Supp. IX:** 114, 316; **Supp. VIII:** 105, 245; **Supp. X:** 324; **Supp. XI:** 18, 92, 275; **Supp. XIII:** 186, 233, 305; **Supp. XIV:** 306; **Supp. XV:** 194; **Supp. XVI:** 135, 139; **Supp. XVIII:** 59, 61, 62, 277, 283
Ellmann, Maud, **Supp. IV Part 1:** 302
Ellmann, Richard, **Supp. VIII:** 105; **Supp. XV:** 74
Ellroy, James, **Supp. XIV:** 26
Elman, Richard, **Supp. V:** 40
"Elmer" (Faulkner), **Retro. Supp. I:** 79, 80
Elmer Gantry (Lewis), **I:** 26, 364; **II:** 447–449, 450, 455
Elmer the Great (Lardner), **II:** 427
"Elms" (Glück), **Supp. V:** 85
Eloges (Perse), **Supp. XIII:** 344
"Eloquence of Grief, An" (Crane), **I:** 411
"El Río Grande" (Mora), **Supp. XIII:** 224
"*El* Round up" (Alvarez), **Supp. VII:** 11
"El Salvador: Requiem and Invocation" (Levertov), **Supp. III Part 1:** 284
Elsasser, Henry, **I:** 226
"Elsa Wertman" (Masters), **Supp. I Part 2:** 462–463
Elsie John and Joey Martinez: Two Stories (Huncke), **Supp. XIV:** 148
Elsie Venner (Holmes), **Supp. I Part 1:** 243, 315–316
Elton, Charles, **Supp. XIV:** 192
Éluard, Paul, **III:** 528; **Supp. IV Part 1:** 80; **Supp. XVII:** 244
Elvins, Kells, **Supp. III Part 1:** 93, 101
Ely, Richard T., **Supp. I Part 1:** 5; **Supp. I Part 2:** 640, 645
"Emancipation. A Life Fable" (Chopin), **Retro. Supp. II:** 59; **Supp. I Part 1:** 207–208
"Emancipation in the British West Indies" (Emerson), **II:** 13
"Emancipation Proclamation, The" (Emerson), **II:** 13
Emanuel, James, **Supp. I Part 1:** 346
Embargo, The (Bryant), **Supp. I Part 1:** 152–153
Embarrassments (James), **Retro. Supp. I:** 229
Embezzler, The (Auchincloss), **Supp. IV Part 1:** 24, 30–31
"Embroidery, The" (C. Frost), **Supp. XV:** 97
"Emerald" (Doty), **Supp. XI:** 131
"Emerald, The" (Merrill), **Supp. III Part 1:** 328
"Emergence of Flight from Aristotle's Mud, The" (Goldbarth), **Supp. XII:** 190
"Emergency Haying" (Carruth), **Supp. XVI:** 55
"Emergency Room" (Mora), **Supp. XIII:** 218
"Emerging Voices: The Teaching of Writing" (Mora), **Supp. XIII:** 220
Emerson, and Other Essays (Chapman), **Supp. XIV:** 41–44
Emerson, Ellen, **Supp. I Part 1:** 33
Emerson, John, **Supp. XVI:** 185, 186, 190, 192
Emerson, Ralph Waldo, **I:** 98, 217, 220, 222, 224, 228, 239, 246, 251, 252, 253, 257, 260, 261, 283, 386, 397, 402, 424, 433, 444, 447, 455, 458, 460–461, 463, 464, 485, 561; **II: 1–24,** 49, 92, 127–128, 169, 170, 226, 233, 237, 273–274, 275, 278, 289, 295, 301, 313, 315, 336, 338, 344, 402, 491, 503; **III:** 53, 82, 171, 174, 260, 277, 409, 424, 428, 453, 454, 507, 576–577, 606, 614; **IV:** 60, 167, 169, 170, 171, 172, 173–174, 176, 178, 183, 186, 187, 192, 201, 202, 211, 335, 338, 340, 342, 350; **Retro. Supp. I:** 34, 53, 54, 57, 62, 74–75, 76, 125, 148–149, 152–153, 159, 217, 250, 298, 392, 400, 403; **Retro. Supp. II:** 96, 113, 135, 142, 155, 207, 262; **Supp. I Part 1:** 2, 28–29, 31, 33, 188, 299, 308–309, 317, 358, 365, 366, 368; **Supp. I Part 2:** 374, 383, 393, 407, 413, 416, 420, 422, 474, 482, 580, 582, 602, 659, 679; **Supp. II Part 1:** 280, 288; **Supp. III Part 1:** 387; **Supp. IV Part 2:** 439, 597, 619; **Supp. IX:** 38, 90, 175, 176, 181; **Supp. V:** 118; **Supp. VIII:** 42, 105, 106, 108, 198, 201, 204, 205, 292; **Supp. X:** 42, 45, 121, 223; **Supp. XI:** 203; **Supp. XIII:** 141, 145, 233, 246, **Supp. XIII:** 247; **Supp. XIV:** 41–44, 46, 54, 104, 177; **Supp. XV:** 219, 224; **Supp. XVI:** 84; **Supp. XVII:** 42, 236
"Emerson and the Essay" (Gass), **Supp. VI:** 88
"Emerson the Lecturer" (Lowell), **Supp. I Part 2:** 420, 422
Emerson-Thoreau Award, **Retro. Supp. I:** 67
Emery, Clark, **III:** 478
E. M. Forster (Trilling), **Supp. III Part 2:** 496, 501, 504
"Emigre in Autumn, An" (Gioia), **Supp. XV:** 120
"Emily Dickinson and Class" (Erkkila), **Retro. Supp. I:** 42–43
Emily Dickinson Editorial Collective, **Retro. Supp. I:** 47
Emily Dickinson in Southern California (X. J. Kennedy), **Supp. XV: 164–165**
"Emily Dickinson's Defunct" (Nelson), **Supp. XVIII:** 173
Emily Dickinson: Woman Poet (Bennett), **Retro. Supp. I:** 42
Eminent Victorians (Strachey), **Supp. I Part 2:** 485
Emma (Austen), **Supp. XVIII:** 149
"Emma and Eginhard" (Longfellow), **III:** 505
"Emma Enters a Sentence of Elizabeth Bishop's" (Gass), **Supp. VI:** 93
Emperor Jones, The (O'Neill), **II:** 278; **III:** 391, 392
Emperor of Haiti (Hughes), **Supp. I Part 1:** 339
"Emperor of Ice Cream, The" (Stevens), **IV:** 76, 80–81
"Emperors" (Dunn), **Supp. XI:** 155
"Emperor's New Clothes, The" (Anderson), **I:** 441
"Empire" (Ford), **Supp. V:** 69
Empire: A Novel (Vidal), **Supp. IV Part 2:** 677, 684, 686, 690
"Empire Builders" (MacLeish), **III:** 14
Empire Falls (Russo), **Supp. XII: 339–343**
Empire of Summer, The (Doty), **Supp. XI:** 120
Empire of the Senseless (Acker), **Supp. XII:** 5, **6, 14–16**
"Empires" (Simic), **Supp. VIII:** 282
"Emporium" (Shapiro), **Supp. II Part 2:** 705
Empress of the Splendid Season (Hijuelos), **Supp. VIII: 86–89**
Empson, William, **I:** 522, 533; **II:** 536; **III:** 286, 497, 498, 499; **IV:** 136, 431; **Retro. Supp. I:** 263; **Retro. Supp. II:** 253; **Supp. XVI:** 190
"Empty Hills, The" (Winters), **Supp. II Part 2:** 792, 793, 796
Empty Mirror, Early Poems (Ginsberg), **Supp. II Part 1:** 308, 311, 313–314, 319, 329
"Empty Room" (Hughes), **Supp. I Part 1:** 337
"Empty Threat, An" (Frost), **II:** 159
Emshwiller, Ed, **Supp. XVIII:** 145
"Encantadas, The" (Melville), **III:** 89; **Supp. XVIII:** 4
Enchanter, The (Nabokov), **Retro. Supp. I:** 266
"Enclosed Dreams, Highways and Labyrinths: Jonathan Lethem's *Amnesia Moon*" (Rossi), **Supp. XVIII:** 139
"Encomium Twenty Years Later" (Tate), **I:** 381
"Encounter, The" (Pound), **III:** 466
"Encounter in April" (Sarton), **Supp. VIII:** 259
Encounter in April (Sarton), **Supp. VIII:** 259
"Encountering the Sublime" (McClatchy), **Supp. XII:** 261
"Encounter on the Seine: Black Meets Brown" (Baldwin), **Retro. Supp. II:** 2
Encounters with Chinese Writers (Dillard), **Supp. VI:** 19, 23, 31

Encounters with the Archdruid (McPhee), **Supp. III Part 1:** 292–294, 301; **Supp. X:** 30
Encyclopedia of Scotland, The (A. Finch), **Supp. XVII: 70–71**
"End, The" (Olds), **Supp. X:** 205
"Endangered Species" (Mora), **Supp. XIII:** 219–220
Endecott and the Red Cross (Lowell), **II:** 545
Endgame (Beckett), **Supp. XIII:** 196
"Endgame" (Tan), **Supp. X:** 290
"Endicott and the Red Cross" (Hawthorne), **Retro. Supp. II:** 181, 187–188
"End of Books, The" (Coover), **Supp. V:** 53
End of Education, The (Postman), **Supp. XI:** 275
"End of Season" (Warren), **IV:** 239–240
"End of Something, The" (Hemingway), **II:** 248
End of the Affair, The (Greene), **Supp. XI:** 99
End of the Age of Innocence, The (Price), **Retro. Supp. I:** 377
"End of the Line, The" (Jarrell), **III:** 527
"End of the Rainbow, The" (Jarrell), **II:** 386
End of the Road (film), **Supp. XI:** 309
End of the Road, The (Barth), **I:** 121, 122, 126–131; **Supp. XI:** 309; **Supp. XVIII:** 140, 141
"End of the World, The" (Gioia), **Supp. XV:** 126
"End of the World, The" (MacLeish), **III:** 8
Endor (Nemerov), **III:** 269, 270, 279
Endore, Guy, **Supp. XVII: 53–67**
"Ends" (Dixon), **Supp. XII:** 153
End to Innocence, An: Essays on Culture and Politics (Fiedler), **Supp. XIII: 98–99**
Endure: The Diaries of Charles Walter Stetson (Stetson), **Supp. XI:** 196
"Enduring Chill, The" (O'Connor), **III:** 349, 351, 357; **Retro. Supp. II:** 236
Enduring Vision of Norman Mailer, The (Leeds), **Retro. Supp. II:** 204
Endymion (Keats), **IV:** 405; **Retro. Supp. I:** 412
End Zone (DeLillo), **Supp. VI:** 2, 3, 4, 10, 11, 12
Enemies (Hapgood and N. Boyce), **Supp. XVII:** 100
Enemies: A Love Story (Singer), **IV:** 1; **Retro. Supp. II: 310–311**
Enemy, The: Time (T. Williams), **IV:** 391
Enemy of the People, An (adapt. Miller), **III:** 154–156
"Energy Vampire" (Ginsberg), **Supp. II Part 1:** 326
"Enforcement of the Slave Trade Laws, The" (Du Bois), **Supp. II Part 1:** 161
"Engaging the Past" (Bell), **Supp. X:** 17
Engel, Bernard F., **I:** 532
Engels, Friedrich, **IV:** 429, 443–444; **Supp. I Part 1:** 13
Engineer of Beasts, The (Sanders), **Supp. XVI:** 270
Engineer of Moonlight (DeLillo), **Supp. VI:** 4
Engineers and the Price System, The (Veblen), **I:** 475–476; **Supp. I Part 2:** 638, 642, 648
Engines of Creation: the Coming Era of Nanotechnology (Drexler), **Supp. XVI:** 121
"England" (Moore), **III:** 203, 207, 214
Engle, Paul, **III:** 542; **Retro. Supp. II:** 220, 221; **Supp. V:** 337; **Supp. XI:** 315; **Supp. XIII:** 76; **Supp. XVIII:** 72
English, Zoë, **Supp. XVI:** 293
English Elegy, The: Studies in the Genre from Spenser to Yeats (Sacks), **Supp. IV Part 2:** 450
English Hours (James), **II:** 337; **Retro. Supp. I:** 235
English Language, The (L. P. Smith), **Supp. XIV:** 341
Englishmen of Letters (James), **II:** 327
English Notebooks, The (Hawthorne), **II:** 226, 227–228
English Novel, The (Lanier), **Supp. I Part 1:** 371
English Poets, The: Lessing, Rousseau (Lowell), **Supp. I Part 2:** 407
English Prosody and Modern Poetry (Shapiro), **Supp. II Part 2:** 710
English Traits (Emerson), **II:** 1, 5, 6–7, 8
"English Writers on America" (Irving), **II:** 308
Engstrand, Stuart, **Supp. I Part 1:** 51
"Enigma Variations" (Nelson), **Supp. XVIII:** 177
"Enoch and the Gorilla" (O'Connor), **Retro. Supp. II:** 225
"Enormous Changes at the Last Minute" (Paley), **Supp. VI:** 226, 232
Enormous Changes at the Last Minute (Paley), **Supp. VI:** 218
"Enormous Radio, The" (Cheever), **Supp. I Part 1:** 175–177, 195
Enormous Radio and Other Stories, The (Cheever), **Supp. I Part 1:** 175–177
Enormous Room, The (Cummings), **I:** 429, 434, 440, 445, 477
"Enough for a Lifetime" (Buck), **Supp. II Part 1:** 127
Enough Rope (Parker), **Supp. IX:** 189, 192
Enquiry Concerning Political Justice (Godwin), **Supp. I Part 1:** 126, 146
Entered From the Sun (Garrett), **Supp. VII:** 105–106, 107–109
"Entering the Kingdom" (Oliver), **Supp. VII:** 234
Entertaining Strangers (Gurney), **Supp. V:** 98, 99
Enter without Desire (Lacy), **Supp. XV:** 201
Entrance: Four Chicano Poets, **Supp. XIII:** 316
Entrance to Porlock, The (Buechner), **Supp. XII:** 52
Entries (Berry), **Supp. X:** 23
"Entropy" (Pynchon), **Supp. II Part 2:** 619, 621
Entry in an Unknown Hand (F. Wright), **Supp. XVII:** 240, 244, 245
Environmental Imagination, The (Buell), **Supp. IX:** 29; **Supp. V:** 209
"Envoys, The" (Merrill), **Supp. III Part 1:** 326
"Envy; or, Yiddish in America" (Ozick), **Supp. V:** 263, 265–266
"Eolian Harp, The" (Coleridge), **I:** 284
"Eototo" (Sobin), **Supp. XVI:** 283–284
"Ephemera, The" (Franklin), **II:** 121
Ephesians (biblical book), **Supp. I Part 1:** 117
Epictetus, **III:** 566
"Epicurean, The" (Auchincloss), **Supp. IV Part 1:** 25
Epicurus, **I:** 59
"Epigram" (Lowell), **II:** 550
"Epilogue" (Lowell), **Retro. Supp. II:** 191
"Epimanes" (Poe), **III:** 411
"Epimetheus" (Longfellow), **II:** 494
"Epiphany" (X. J. Kennedy), **Supp. XV:** 166, 167
"Epipsychidion" (Shelley), **Supp. I Part 2:** 718
Episode in Palmetto (Caldwell), **I:** 297, 307
"Epistle" (L.-Y. Lee), **Supp. XV:** 212
Epistle to a Godson (Auden), **Supp. II Part 1:** 24
"Epistle to Be Left in the Earth" (MacLeish), **III:** 13
"Epistle to George William Curtis" (Lowell), **Supp. I Part 2:** 416
"Epistle to Léon-Paul Fargue" (MacLeish), **III:** 15
"Epitaph Ending in And, The" (Stafford), **Supp. XI:** 321–322
Epitaph for a Dead Beat (Markson), 139; **Supp. XVII: 136–138,** 141
Epitaph for a Desert Anarchist (Bishop), **Supp. XIII:** 1
Epitaph for a Tramp (Markson), **Supp. XVII:** 136, 137, 139 142
"Epitaph for Fire and Flower" (Plath), **Supp. I Part 2:** 537
"Epitaph for the Race of Man" (Millay), **III:** 127–128
"Epithalamium" (Auden), **Supp. II Part 1:** 15
"Epstein" (P. Roth), **Retro. Supp. II:** 281; **Supp. III Part 2:** 404, 406–407, 412, 422
Epstein, Helen, **Supp. XVII:** 47
Epstein, Jason, **Supp. VIII:** 233
Epstein, Joseph, **Supp. IV Part 2:** 692; **Supp. VIII:** 236, 238; **Supp. XIV: 101–117; Supp. XVI:** 230, 275
Epstein, Leslie, **Supp. XII: 159–174; Supp. XVIII:** 92, 99
Epstein, Philip, **Supp. XII:** 159
"Equal in Paris" (Baldwin), **Retro. Supp. II:** 3; **Supp. I Part 1:** 52
"Equals" (Untermeyer), **Supp. XV:** 304
"Equations of the Light" (Gioia), **Supp. XV:** 125
"Equilibrists, The" (Ransom), **III:** 490, 494

"Equipment for Pennies" (H. Roth), **Supp. IX:** 233
Erasmus, Desiderius, **Supp. XV:** 258
Erasure (Everett), **Supp. XVIII:** 54, 60, **61–62**
"Erat Hora" (Pound), **III:** 463; **Retro. Supp. I:** 413
Erdrich, Louise, **Supp. IV Part 1: 259–278,** 333, 404; **Supp. X:** 290; **Supp. XVIII:** 189
"Erectus" (Karr), **Supp. XI:** 243
"Ere Sleep Comes Down to Soothe the Weary Eyes" (Dunbar), **Supp. II Part 1:** 199, 207–208
Erikson, Erik, **I:** 58, 214, 218
Erisman, Fred, **Supp. VIII:** 126
Erkkila, Betsy, **Retro. Supp. I:** 42
"Ernest: or Parent for a Day" (Bourne), **I:** 232
Ernst, Max, **Retro. Supp. II:** 321
"Eros" (Komunyakaa), **Supp. XIII:** 130
"Eros and Anteros" (E. Stoddard), **Supp. XV:** 283
Eros and Civilization (Marcuse), **Supp. XII:** 2
"Eros at Temple Stream" (Levertov), **Supp. III Part 1:** 278–279
Eros the Bittersweet (Carson), **Supp. XII:** 97, **98–99**
"Eros Turannos" (Robinson), **III:** 510, 512, 513–516, 517, 518
"Eroticism in Women" (Nin), **Supp. X:** 195
"Errand" (Carver), **Supp. III Part 1:** 149
Erskine, Albert, **IV:** 261; **Retro. Supp. II:** 117
Erskine, John, **I:** 223; **Supp. X:** 183; **Supp. XIV:** 120
Erstein, Hap, **Supp. IV Part 2:** 589, 590
"Escape" (MacLeish), **III:** 4
Escape Artist, The (Wagoner), **Supp. IX:** 324, **334–335**
Escher, M. C., **Supp. XII:** 26; **Supp. XVI:** 102
"Escudilla" (Leopold), **Supp. XIV:** 188
Eshleman, Clayton, **Supp. XVI:** 284
"Eskimo Love" (Apple), **Supp. XVII:** 5
Espeland, Pamela, **Supp. XVIII:** 180, 181
Espen, Hal, **Supp. X:** 15
Espey, John, **III:** 463, 468, 478
Esposito, Scott, **Supp. XVII:** 234
Essais (Renouvier), **II:** 344–345
Essay Concerning Human Understanding, An (Locke), **I:** 554; **II:** 8, 348–349
Essay on American Poetry (Brown), **Supp. I Part 1:** 156
"Essay on Aristocracy" (Paine), **Supp. I Part 2:** 515
"Essay on Friendship, An" (McClatchy), **Supp. XII:** 258–259
"Essay on Love" (Carruth), **Supp. XVI:** 56
Essay on Man (Pope), **II:** 111; **Supp. I Part 2:** 516
"Essay on Marriage" (Carruth), **Supp. XVI:** 48
Essay on Our Changing Order (Veblen), **Supp. I Part 2:** 629, 642
"Essay on Poetics" (Ammons), **Supp. VII:** 29–31
Essay on Projects (Defoe), **II:** 104
"Essay on Psychiatrists" (Pinsky), **Supp. VI:** 237, 238, 241, 242, 249, 250
Essay on Rime (Shapiro), **I:** 430; **Supp. II Part 2:** 702, 703, 708–711
"Essay on Sanity" (Dunn), **Supp. XI:** 147
"Essay on the Character of Robespierre" (Paine), **Supp. I Part 2:** 515
Essay on the Chinese Written Character (Fenollosa), **III:** 474
"Essay on What I Think About Most" (Carson), **Supp. XII: 111–112**
Essays (Emerson), **II:** 1, 7, 8, 12–13, 15, 21
Essays, Speeches, and Public Letters by William Faulkner (Meriweather, ed.), **Retro. Supp. I:** 77
Essays in Anglo-Saxon Law (Adams), **I:** 5
Essays in London (James), **II:** 336
Essays in Radical Empiricism (James), **II:** 355, 356–357
Essays on Norman Mailer (Lucid), **Retro. Supp. II:** 195
Essays on the Nature and Principles of Taste (Alison), **Supp. I Part 1:** 151
Essays to Do Good (Mather), **II:** 104; **Supp. II Part 2:** 461, 467
"Essay: The Love of Old Houses" (Doty), **Supp. XI:** 136
"Essay Toward a Point of View, An" (Brooks), **I:** 244
"Essence, Absence, and Sobin's *Venus Blue*" (English), **Supp. XVI:** 293
Essential Haiku, The (Hass), **Supp. VI:** 102
Essential Keats (Levine, ed.), **Supp. V:** 179
"Essential Oils——are wrung" (Dickinson), **I:** 471; **Retro. Supp. I:** 43, 46
"Essentials" (Toomer), **Supp. III Part 2:** 486
Essentials: A Philosophy of Life in Three Hundred Definitions and Aphorisms (Toomer), **Supp. III Part 2:** 486
Essentials: Definitions and Aphorisms (Toomer), **Supp. IX:** 320
"Essentials of Spontaneous Prose" (Kerouac), **Supp. III Part 1:** 227–228
"Estate Sale" (Nye), **Supp. XIII:** 283
Estess, Sybil, **Supp. IV Part 2:** 449, 452
Esther (Adams), **I:** 9–10, 20
"Esther" (Toomer), **Supp. IX:** 313–314
"Esthétique du Mal" (Stevens), **IV:** 79; **Retro. Supp. I:** 300, 311, 312
"Estoy-eh-muut and the Kunideeyahs (Arrowboy and the Destroyers)" (film), **Supp. IV Part 2:** 560
Estrada, Genaro, **Retro. Supp. II:** 89
Estray, The (Longfellow, ed.), **Retro. Supp. II:** 155
Esty, William, **III:** 358
"Etching, An" (Masters), **Supp. I Part 2:** 458
"Eternal Goodness, The" (Whittier), **Supp. I Part 2:** 704
Eternal Spring, The (N. Boyce), **Supp. XVII:** 100
"Eternity, An" (W. C. Williams), **Retro. Supp. I:** 423
"Eternity Is Now" (Roethke), **III:** 544–545
"Ethan Brand" (Hawthorne), **II:** 227
Ethan Frome (Wharton), **IV:** 316–317, 327; **Retro. Supp. I:** 372–373; **Supp. IX:** 108; **Supp. XVIII:** 216
Ethics (Spinoza), **IV:** 12; **Retro. Supp. II:** 300
"Ethics of Culture, The" (Locke), **Supp. XIV:** 211
"Ethnics of Frank Costello, The" (Talese), **Supp. XVII:** 202
Etulain, Richard, **Supp. IV Part 2:** 597, 601, 604, 606, 607, 608, 610, 611
"Etymology" (Nelson), **Supp. XVIII:** 185
Euclid, **III:** 6, 620
"Euclid Alone Has Looked on Beauty Bare" (Millay), **III:** 133
Eugene, Frank, **Supp. X:** 204
Eugene Onegin (Pushkin), **III:** 246, 263
Eugene Onegin (Pushkin; Nabokov, trans.), **Retro. Supp. I:** 266, 267, 272
Eugénie, Empress, **IV:** 309
Eugénie Grandet (Balzac), **II:** 328
"Eugénie Grandet" (Barthelme), **Supp. IV Part 1:** 47
"Eulogy for Richard Hugo (1923–1982)" (Wagoner), **Supp. IX:** 330–331
"Eulogy on the Flapper" (Z. Fitzgerald), **Supp. IX:** 71
Eumenides (Aeschylus), **Retro. Supp. I:** 65
"E Unibus Pluram: Television and U.S. Fiction" (Wallace), **Supp. X:** 315–316
"Euphemisms" (Matthews), **Supp. IX: 167–168**
Eureka (Poe), **III:** 409, 424, 428–429
Eurekas (Goldbarth), **Supp. XII:** 181
Euripides, **I:** 325; **II:** 8, 282, 543; **III:** 22, 145, 398; **IV:** 370; **Supp. I Part 1:** 268, 269, 270; **Supp. I Part 2:** 482; **Supp. V:** 277
"Euripides and Professor Murray" (Eliot), **Supp. I Part 1:** 268
"Euripides——A Playwright" (West), **IV:** 286; **Retro. Supp. II:** 326
"Europe" (Ashbery), **Supp. III Part 1:** 7–10, 13, 18
European Discovery of America, The: The Northern Voyages (Morison), **Supp. I Part 2:** 496–497
European Discovery of America, The: The Southern Voyages (Morison), **Supp. I Part 2:** 497
Europeans, The (H. James), **I:** 452; **II:** 327, 328; **Retro. Supp. I:** 216, 220
Europe Central (Vollmann), **Supp. XVII:** 225, 226, 227, 229, 231, **233–235,** 236
"Europe! Europe!" (Ginsberg), **Supp. II Part 1:** 320, 322
Europe of Trusts, The: Selected Poems (Howe), **Supp. IV Part 2:** 420, 422, 426
Europe without Baedeker (Wilson), **IV:** 429

Eurydice in the Underworld (Acker), **Supp. XII:** 7
Eustace, Saint, **II:** 215
Eustace Chisholm and the Works (Purdy), **Supp. VII:** 273–274, 279–280
"Euthanasia" (Tate), **IV:** 122
Eva-Mary (McCarriston), **Supp. XIV:** 259, 260, **263–268**
"Evangeline" (Dixon), **Supp. XII:** 153
Evangeline (Longfellow), **II:** 489, 501–502; **Retro. Supp. II:** 155, **156–159,** 162, 164; **Supp. I Part 2:** 586
Evanier, David, **Supp. XVI:** 212
Evans, Alice, **Supp. XVII:** 71, 72
Evans, Mary Ann. *See* Eliot, George
Evans, Oliver, **Supp. IV Part 1:** 85, 91
Evans, Sandy, **Supp. XIII:** 129
Evans, Walker, **I:** 36, 38, 293; **Retro. Supp. II:** 85
Eve (A. Finch), **Supp. XVII: 72–74**
"Eve" (W. C. Williams), **Retro. Supp. I:** 423
Even Cowgirls Get the Blues (Robbins), **Supp. X:** 259, 260, 261, 262–263, 264, 266, **269–271,** 272, 274, 277, 284; **Supp. XIII:** 11
"Evening" (Carver), **Supp. III Part 1:** 148
Evening (Minot), **Supp. VI:** 204–205, 208, **213–215**
"Evening at a Country Inn" (Kenyon), **Supp. VII:** 167
"Evening in a Sugar Orchard" (Frost), **Retro. Supp. I:** 133
"Evening in Nuevo Leon, An" (Caldwell), **I:** 309
"Evening in the Sanitarium" (Bogan), **Supp. III Part 1:** 61
"Evening of the 4th of July, The" (Kees), **Supp. XV:** 140, 142
"Evening on the Cote d'Azur" (Yates), **Supp. XI:** 349
Evening Performance, An: New and Selected Short Stories (Garrett), **Supp. VII:** 109
"Evenings at Home" (Hardwick), **Supp. III Part 1:** 195–196
"Evening's at Seven, The" (Thurber), **Supp. I Part 2:** 616
"Evening Star" (Bogan), **Supp. III Part 1:** 56
Evening Star, The (McMurtry), **Supp. V:** 230
Evening Star, The (screenplay) (McMurtry), **Supp. V:** 232
"Evening Sun" (Kenyon), **Supp. VII:** 168
"Evening Sun Turned Crimson, The" (Huncke), **Supp. XIV:** 137–138, 139
Evening Sun Turned Crimson, The (Huncke), **Supp. XIV:** 140, 149–150
"Evening Wind, The" (Bryant), **Supp. I Part 1:** 164
"Evening without Angels" (Stevens), **Retro. Supp. I:** 302
Evening with Richard Nixon, An (Vidal), **Supp. IV Part 2:** 683
"Even Sea, The" (Swenson), **Supp. IV Part 2:** 641
Even Stephen (Perelman and West), **Retro. Supp. II:** 328
"Event, An" (Wilbur), **Supp. III Part 2:** 547, 554
"Event, The" (Dove), **Supp. IV Part 1:** 242, 247–248
"Eventide" (Brooks), **Supp. III Part 1:** 73
"Eventide" (Purdy), **Supp. VII:** 270
"Event Itself, The" (Carruth), **Supp. XVI:** 47
Eve of Saint Agnes, The (Keats), **II:** 82, 531
"Eve of St. Agnes, The" (Clampitt), **Supp. IX:** 40
"Ever a Bridegroom: Reflections on the Failure of Texas Literature" (McMurtry), **Supp. V:** 225
Everett, Alexander Hill, **Supp. I Part 1:** 152
Everett, Percival, **Supp. XVIII: 53–67**
Everlasting Story of Nory, The (Baker), **Supp. XIII:** 52, **Supp. XIII: 53–55**
Ever-Present Past, The (Hamilton), **Supp. XVI:** 196
Evers, Medgar, **IV:** 280; **Retro. Supp. II:** 13; **Supp. I Part 1:** 52, 65
Everwine, Peter, **Supp. V:** 180; **Supp. XIII:** 312; **Supp. XV: 73–90**
"Everybody's Protest Novel" (Baldwin), **Retro. Supp. II:** 4; **Supp. I Part 1:** 50, 51
"Everybody's Reading Li Po' Silk-screened on a Purple T-Shirt" (Komunyakaa), **Supp. XIII:** 120
Everybody's Story: Writing by Older Minnesotans (C. Bly, ed.), **Supp. XVI:** 38
"Everybody Was Very Nice" (Benét), **Supp. XI:** 53
"Every-Day Girl, A" (Jewett), **Retro. Supp. II:** 132
"Everyday Use" (Walker), **Supp. III Part 2:** 534
"Every-Day Work" (Jewett), **Retro. Supp. II:** 132
Everyone Says I Love You (film; Allen), **Supp. XV:** 11
Every Pleasure (Goldbarth), **Supp. XII:** 181
Every Soul Is a Circus (Lindsay), **Supp. I Part 2:** 384, 394, 399
"Everything Is a Human Being" (Walker), **Supp. III Part 2:** 527
Everything Is Illuminated (Foer), **Supp. XII:** 169
"Everything Stuck to Him" (Carver), **Supp. III Part 1:** 143
Everything That Moves (Schulberg), **Supp. XVIII:** 254
"Everything That Rises Must Converge" (O'Connor), **III:** 349, 352, 357; **Retro. Supp. II:** 236
Everything That Rises Must Converge (O'Connor), **III:** 339, 348–349, 350–351; **Retro. Supp. II:** 235, **236–237**
Everything You Always Wanted to Know about Sex (film; Allen), **Supp. XV:** 4–5, 13
Eve's Diary (Twain), **IV:** 208–209
"Eve Speaks" (Untermeyer), **Supp. XV:** 300
"Eve the Fox" (Gunn Allen), **Supp. IV Part 1:** 331
"Evidence" (Harjo), **Supp. XII:** 219
Evidence of the Senses, The (Kelley), **Supp. IV Part 2:** 529
Evidence of Things Not Seen, The (Baldwin), **Retro. Supp. II:** 15
"Evil Seekers, The" (Sexton), **Supp. II Part 2:** 696
"Evolution" (Swenson), **Supp. IV Part 2:** 639
Evolving the Idol: The Poetry of Gustaf Sobin (Crick), **Supp. XVI:** 289
Ewing, Jon, **Supp. X:** 253
Ewings, The (O'Hara), **III:** 383
"Examination at the Womb Door" (Hughes), **Supp. XV:** 347
"Examination of the Hero in a Time of War" (Stevens), **Retro. Supp. I:** 305–306, 308
"Excavation of Troy" (MacLeish), **III:** 18
Excellent Becomes the Permanent, The (Addams), **Supp. I Part 1:** 25
"Excelsior" (Longfellow), **Retro. Supp. II:** 169
"Excerpts from Swan Lake" (Cameron), **Supp. XII:** 80, **84**
"Excerpts from the Epistemology Workshops" (Rand), **Supp. IV Part 2:** 529
"Excess of Charity" (Wylie), **Supp. I Part 2:** 720
"Exchange, The" (Swenson), **Supp. IV Part 2:** 644
"Excitement, The" (Jarman), **Supp. XVII:** 120–121
"Exclusive" (Olds), **Supp. X:** 206
"Excrement Poem, The" (Kumin), **Supp. IV Part 2:** 448
"Excursion" (Garrett), **Supp. VII:** 100
Excursions (Thoreau), **IV:** 188
"Excursion to Canada, An" (Thoreau), **Supp. XVIII:** 4
"Excursus of Reassurance in Begonia Time, An" (Carruth), **Supp. XVI:** 58
Executioner's Song, The (Mailer), **Retro. Supp. II:** 108, 209
Exercises in History, Chronology, and Biography, in Question and Answer (Rowson), **Supp. XV:** 245
Ex-Friends: Falling Out with Allen Ginsberg, Lionel and Diana Trilling, Lillian Hellman, Hannah Arendt, and Norman Mailer (Podhoretz), **Supp. VIII:** 239, **242–244**
"Exhausted Bug, The" (R. Bly), **Supp. IV Part 1:** 73
"Exhortation" (Bogan), **Supp. III Part 1:** 58
"Exhortation" (McKay), **Supp. X:** 135
"Exile" (Gass), **Supp. VI:** 92
"Exile" (Oates), **Supp. II Part 2:** 523
Exile, The (Buck), **Supp. II Part 1:** 119, 131
"Exiles, The" (Bradbury), **Supp. IV Part 1:** 113
"Exiles, The" (Whittier), **Supp. I Part 2:** 692–693
Exiles and Fabrications (Scott), **II:** 512

Exile's Daughter, The (Spencer), **Supp. II Part 1:** 121
"Exile's Departure, The" (Whittier), **Supp. I Part 2:** 683
Exiles from Paradise: Zelda and Scott Fitzgerald (Mayfield), **Supp. IX:** 65
"Exile's Letter" (Karr), **Supp. XI:** 241
Exile's Return (Cowley), **Supp. III Part 1:** 136, 138, 140, 141, 144, 147, 148
"Exile's Return, The" (Lowell), **II:** 539; **Retro. Supp. II:** 187
"Existences" (Stafford), **Supp. XI:** 324
Existentialism from Dostoevsky to Sartre (W. Kaufmann), **Supp. XVII:** 137
Exit into History (Hoffman), **Supp. XVI:** 148, 150, **151–153**
Exit to Eden (Rampling), **Supp. VII:** 301–302
Exley, Frederick, **Supp. XVII:** 135
Exley, Frederick, **Supp. XVI:** 69
Exodus (biblical book), **IV:** 300
Exodus (Uris), **Supp. IV Part 1:** 379
"Exorcism" (Snodgrass), **Supp. VI:** 314
"Exorcism, An" (Malamud), **Supp. I Part 2:** 435
Exorcist, The (film), **Supp. I Part 1:** 66
"Expanses" (Dickey), **Supp. IV Part 1:** 186
"Ex Parte" (Lardner), **II:** 432
"Expatiation on the Combining of Weathers at Thirty-seventh and Indiana Where the Southern More or Less Crosses th e Dog, The" (Carruth), **Supp. XVI:**51–52
"Expectant Father Compares His Wife to a Rabbit, An" (White), **Supp. I Part 2:** 678
"Expedition to the Pole, An" (Dillard), **Supp. VI:** 32, 34
"Expelled" (Cheever), **Supp. I Part 1:** 174, 186
Expense of Greatness, The (Blackmur), **Supp. II Part 1:** 90, 107
Expense of Vision, The (Holland), **Retro. Supp. I:** 216
"Expensive Gifts" (Miller), **Supp. XII:** 294
"Expensive Moment, The" (Paley), **Supp. VI:** 222, **227–228,** 230
Expensive People (Oates), **Supp. II Part 2:** 509, 510–511
"Experience" (Emerson), **Supp. XIV:** 42
"Experience and Fiction" (Jackson), **Supp. IX:** 121
"Experience and the Objects of Knowledge in the Philosophy of F. H. Bradley" (Eliot), **I:** 572; **Retro. Supp. I:** 59
Experience of Literature, The (Trilling), **Supp. III Part 2:** 493
"Experiences and Principles of an Historian" (Morison), **Supp. I Part 2:** 492
Experimental Death Unit # 1 (Baraka), **Supp. II Part 1:** 46
"Experimental Life, The" (Bourne), **I:** 217, 220
"Experiment in Misery, An" (S. Crane), **I:** 411; **Retro. Supp. II:** 97
Experiments and Observations on Electricity (Franklin), **II:** 102, 114–115
"Expiation" (Hoffman), **Supp. XVIII:** 86
"Expiation" (Wharton), **Retro. Supp. I:** 367
"Explaining Evil" (Gordon), **Supp. IV Part 1:** 310
"Explanation" (Stevens), **IV:** 79
Explanation of America, An (Pinsky), **Supp. VI:** 237, **241–243**
Exploding Gravy (X. J. Kennedy), **Supp. XV:** 163
"Exploit" (Wharton), **IV:** 324
"Exploration in the Great Tuolumne Cañon" (Muir), **Supp. IX:** 181
"Explorer, The" (Brooks), **Supp. III Part 1:** 79–80
"Exploring the Magalloway" (Parkman), **Supp. II Part 2:** 591
Expositor's Bible, The (G. A. Smith), **III:** 199
Expressions of Sea Level (Ammons), **Supp. VII:** 24, 28, 36
Extract from Captain Stormfeld's Visit to Heaven (Twain), **IV:** 209–210
Extracts from Adam's Diary (Twain), **IV:** 208–209
"Exulting, The" (Roethke), **III:** 544
"Eye, The" (Bowles), **Supp. IV Part 1:** 93
Eye, The (Nabokov), **III:** 251
Eye-Beaters, Blood, Victory, Madness, Buckhead and Mercy, The (Dickey), **Supp. IV Part 1:** 178, 182–183
"Eye for an Eye, An" (Humphrey), **Supp. IX:** 108
"Eye in the Rock, The" (Haines), **Supp. XII:** 208, 209
Eye in the Sky (Dick), **Supp. XVIII:** 138
"Eye-Mote, The" (Plath), **Retro. Supp. II:** 246, 247
"Eye of Paris, The" (H. Miller), **III:** 183–184
Eye of the Poet, The: Six Views of the Art and Craft of Poetry (Citino, ed.), **Supp. XIII:** 115
"Eye of the Rock, The" (Haines), **Supp. XII:** 208
"Eye of the Story, The" (Porter), **IV:** 279
Eye of the Story, The: Selected Essays and Reviews (Welty), **Retro. Supp. I:** 339, 342, 344, 345, 346, 351, 354, 355, 356
"Eyes, The" (Wharton), **IV:** 315
"Eyes like They Say the Devil Has" (Ríos), **Supp. IV Part 2:** 543, 544
Eyes of the Dragon, The (King), **Supp. V:** 139, 152
Eyes of the Heart: A Memoir of the Lost and Found (Buechner), **Supp. XII:** 53
"Eyes of Zapata" (Cisneros), **Supp. VII:** 70
"Eyes to See" (Cozzens), **I:** 374
Eye-to-Eye (Nye), **Supp. XIII:** 274
Eysturoy, Annie O., **Supp. IV Part 1:** 321, 322, 323, 328
Ezekiel (biblical book), **II:** 541
Ezekiel, Mordecai, **Supp. I Part 2:** 645
"Ezra Pound" (Bynner), **Supp. XV:** 49
"Ezra Pound: His Cantos" (Zukofsky), **Supp. III Part 2:** 612, 619, 622
Ezra Pound's Mauberley (Espey), **III:** 463
"Ezra Pound's Very Useful Labors" (Schwartz), **Supp. II Part 2:** 644

F

Faas, Ekbert, **Supp. VIII:** 292
"Fabbri Tape, The" (Auchincloss), **Supp. IV Part 1:** 21–22
Faber, Geoffrey, **Retro. Supp. I:** 63
Faber Book of Movie Verse, The (French and Wlaschin, eds.), **Supp. XVI:** 294
"Fable" (Merwin), **Supp. III Part 1:** 343
"Fable" (Wylie), **Supp. I Part 2:** 714
Fable, A (Faulkner), **II:** 55, 73; **Retro. Supp. I:** 74
"Fable, A" (Glück), **Supp. V:** 86
"Fable, The" (Winters), **Supp. II Part 2:** 792, 793, 796
"Fable for Critics, A" (Lowell), **Supp. XVIII:** 3, 8
Fable for Critics, A (Lowell), **Supp. I Part 2:** 406, 407–408, 409, 412–413, 416, 420, 422
"Fable of the War, A" (Nemerov), **III:** 272
Fables (Gay), **II:** 111
Fables and Distances: New and Selected Essays (Haines), **Supp. XII:** 197, 199, 207–208, 211
Fables for Our Time (Thurber), **Supp. I Part 2:** 610
Fables of Identity: Studies in Poetic Mythology (Frye), **Supp. X:** 80
Fables of La Fontaine, The (Moore), **III:** 194, 215
"Fables of Representation: Poetry of the New York School" (Hoover), **Supp. XV:** 179
"Fables of the Fallen Guy" (Rosaldo), **Supp. IV Part 2:** 544
"Fables of the Moscow Subway" (Nemerov), **III:** 271
Fabulators, The (Scholes), **Supp. V:** 40
Fabulous Small Jews (Epstein), **Supp. XIV:** 112
Face against the Glass, The (Francis), **Supp. IX: 80–81**
Face in the Crowd, A (film, Kazan), **Supp. XVIII:** 252–253
Face of Time, The (Farrell), **II:** 28, 34, 35, 39
Faces of Jesus, The (Buechner), **Supp. XII:** 53
Face to the Wind (film), **Supp. XVII:** 141
Fachinger, Petra, **Supp. XVI:** 153
"Facing It" (Komunyakaa), **Supp. XIII:** 117, 124, 125
Facing Shadows (Jin), **Supp. XVIII:** 92, **93**
"Facing West from California's Shores" (Jeffers), **Supp. II Part 2:** 437–438
"Fact in Fiction, The" (McCarthy), **II:** 562
"Facts" (Levine), **Supp. V:** 193
"Facts" (Oliver), **Supp. VII:** 231–232
"Facts" (Snyder), **Supp. VIII:** 301
"Facts, The" (Lardner), **II:** 431

Facts, The: A Novelist's Autobiography (P. Roth), **Retro. Supp. II:** 280, 291; **Supp. III Part 2:** 401, 405, 417, 426
"Facts and Traditions Respecting the Existence of Indigenous Intermittent Fever in New England" (Holmes), **Supp. I Part 1:** 303
"Facts in the Case of M. Valdemar, The" (Poe), **III:** 416
Faderman, Lillian, **Retro. Supp. II:** 135; **Supp. XIII:** 313
Fadiman, Clifton, **II:** 430, 431, 443, 591–592; **Supp. IX:** 8; **Supp. XVI:** 100, 106; **Supp. XVII:** 87, 90
Fading, My Parmacheene Belle (J. Scott), **Supp. XVII: 184–185,** 188
"Fado" (McClatchy), **Supp. XII:** 265–266
Faerie Queene, The (Spenser), **III:** 487; **IV:** 253; **Supp. XIV:** 6; **Supp. XV:** 181
Faery, Rebecca Blevins, **Retro. Supp. I:** 374
Fagan, Kathy, **Supp. V:** 180; **Supp. XV:** 73
Fahrenheit 451 (Bradbury), **Supp. IV Part 1:** 101, 102, 104, 107–109, 110, 113; **Supp. XIII:** 29
"Failure" (Gioia), **Supp. XV:** 125
"Failure" (Zach; Everwine, trans.), **Supp. XV:** 86
"Failure of David Barry, The" (Jewett), **Retro. Supp. II:** 132
Fainlight, Ruth, **Supp. XV:** 261, 264
Faint Perfume (Gale), **Supp. I Part 2:** 613
Fair, Bryan K., **Supp. VIII:** 128
Fairbanks, Douglas, **Supp. XVI:** 185, 186
Fairchild, Frances. *See* Bryant, Mrs. William Cullen (Frances Fairchild)
Fairchild, Hoxie, **Supp. XIV:** 120
Fairfield, Flora (pseudonym). *See* Alcott, Louisa May
Fairly Conventional Woman, A (Shields), **Supp. VII:** 312, 316, 318
"Fairly Sad Tale, A" (Parker), **Supp. IX:** 192
Fair Warning (R. O. Butler), **Supp. XII:** 62, **75–76**
Faith (Goldbarth), **Supp. XII:** 181, **182–183**
Faith and History (Niebuhr), **III:** 308
Faith and the Good Thing (Johnson), **Supp. VI:** 187, **188–190,** 191, 193, 194, 196
Faith for Living (Mumford), **Supp. II Part 2:** 479–480
Faithful Narrative of the Surprising Works of God in the Conversion of Many Hundred Souls in Northampton, and the Neighboring Towns and Villages of New-Hampshire in New-England, A (Edwards), **I:** 545, 562
"Faith Healer" (Komunyakaa), **Supp. XIII:** 117
"Faith in a Tree" (Paley), **Supp. VI:** 217–218, 224, 230
"Faith in Search of Understanding" (Updike), **Retro. Supp. I:** 327
"Faith of an Historian" (Morison), **Supp. I Part 2:** 492
Faker's Dozen, A (Bukiet), **Supp. XVII:** 47
Falcoff, Mark, **Supp. VIII:** 88
Falcon (Hammett), **Supp. IV Part 1:** 351
Falconer (Cheever), **Supp. I Part 1:** 176, 193–195, 196
Falconer, A. F., **Supp. XIV:** 2
"Falcon of Ser Federigo, The" (Longfellow), **II:** 505
Falk, Peter, **Supp. XI:** 174
Falkner, Dean, **II:** 55
Falkner, John, **II:** 55
Falkner, Mrs. Murray C. (Maud Butler), **II:** 55
Falkner, Murray, **II:** 55
Falkner, Murray C., **II:** 55
Falkner, William C., **II:** 55
"Fall" (Francis), **Supp. IX:** 76
"Fall, The" (Bass), **Supp. XVI:** 25
"Fall 1961" (Lowell), **II:** 550
"Fallen Western Star: The Decline of San Francisco as a Literary Region" (Gioia), **Supp. XV:** 112, **115–116**
"Fallen Western Star" Wars, The: A Debate about Literary California (Foley, ed.), **Supp. XV:** 112, 116
"Fall in Corrales" (Wilbur), **Supp. III Part 2:** 556
"Falling" (Dickey), **Supp. IV Part 1:** 182
Falling (Dickey), **Supp. IV Part 1:** 178, 181–182
"Falling Asleep over the Aeneid" (Lowell), **II:** 542; **Retro. Supp. II:** 188
Falling in Place (Beattie), **Supp. V:** 28–29
"Falling into Holes in Our Sentences" (R. Bly), **Supp. IV Part 1:** 71
"Fall Journey" (Stafford), **Supp. XI:** 322
Fall of America, The: 1965–1971 (Ginsberg), **Supp. II Part 1:** 323, 325, 327; **Supp. XV:** 264
Fall of Eve, The (Loos), **Supp. XVI:** 187
Fall of the City, The: A Verse Play for Radio (MacLeish), **III:** 20
"Fall of the House of Usher, The" (Poe), **III:** 412, 414, 415, 419; **Retro. Supp. II:** 270
Fall of the Magicians, The (Kees), **Supp. XV:** 144
Fallows, James, **Supp. VIII:** 241
Fall Quarter (Kees), **Supp. XV:** 141
Fall & Rise (Dixon), **Supp. XII:** 147–148, 148, 153, 157
"Falls, The" (Olds), **Supp. X:** 215
"Falls Fight, The" (Howe), **Supp. IV Part 2:** 431–432
Falon, Janet Ruth, **Supp. IV Part 2:** 422
"False Dawn" (Wharton), **Retro. Supp. I:** 381
"False Documents" (Doctorow), **Supp. IV Part 1:** 220, 236
"False Leads" (Komunyakaa), **Supp. XIII:** 116
Fame and Obscurity: Portraits by Gay Talese (Talese), **Supp. XVII:** 202, 203, 204
Fame & Folly: Essays (Ozick), **Supp. V:** 272
"Familiar Epistle to a Friend, A" (Lowell), **Supp. I Part 2:** 416
Familiar Territory: Observations on American Life (Epstein), **Supp. XIV: 106**
"Family" (Sanders), **Supp. XVI:** 276
"Family" (Wilson), **IV:** 426
Family, Kinship, and Sympanthy in Nineteenth-Century America (Weinstein), **Supp. XVIII:** 261
"Family Affair, A" (Chopin), **Retro. Supp. II:** 71
"Family and Socialism, The" (Ryan as Quin), **Supp. XVIII:** 238
Family Arsenal, The (Theroux), **Supp. VIII:** 322
Family Chronicle: An Odyssey from Russia to America (Reznikoff), **Supp. XIV:** 277, 288, 289
"Family History" (Mora), **Supp. XIII:** 217
"Family History, A" (Davis), **Supp. XVI:** 82
Family Life (Banks), **Supp. V:** 7
"Family Matters" (Alvarez), **Supp. VII:** 10
Family Moskat, The (Singer), **IV:** 1, 17, 20, 46; **Retro. Supp. II:** 304
"Family of Little Feet, The" (Cisneros), **Supp. VII:** 61
Family Party, A (O'Hara), **III:** 362
Family Pictures (Brooks), **Supp. III Part 1:** 69, 85, 86
Family Pictures (Miller), **Supp. XII:** 291, **295–297,** 299
"Family Reunion" (X. J. Kennedy), **Supp. XV:** 169
Family Reunion, The (Eliot), **I:** 570–571, 572, 581, 584, 588; **Retro. Supp. I:** 62, 65
"Family Secrets" (Kingsolver), **Supp. VII:** 208
"Family Sideshow, The" (Karr), **Supp. XI:** 245
"Family Ties" (Mora), **Supp. XIII:** 215
"Family Tree" (Komunyakaa), **Supp. XIII:** 117–118, 126
"Family Wasserstein, The" (Hoban), **Supp. XV:** 319, 325
Famous American Negroes (Hughes), **Supp. I Part 1:** 345
"Famous Gilson Bequest, The" (Bierce), **I:** 204
Famous Negro Music Makers (Hughes), **Supp. I Part 1:** 345
"Famous New York Trials" (Ellison), **Supp. II Part 1:** 230
Fanatics, The (Dunbar), **Supp. II Part 1:** 213–214
Fancher, Edwin, **Retro. Supp. II:** 202
Fancher, Lou, **Supp. XVI:** 177
"Fancy and Imagination" (Poe), **III:** 421
"Fancy Flights" (Beattie), **Supp. V:** 25
"Fancy's Show Box" (Hawthorne), **II:** 238
"Fancy Woman, The" (Taylor), **Supp. V:** 316–317, 319, 323
"Fang" (Goldbarth), **Supp. XII:** 190

Fanny: Being the True History of the Adventures of Fanny Hackabout-Jones (Jong), **Supp. V:** 115, 127
Fanny Hill (Cleland), **Supp. V:** 48, 127
Fan of Swords, The (al-Maghut), **Supp. XIII:** 278
Fanon, Frantz, **Retro. Supp. II:** 118; **Supp. X:** 131, 141
Fanshawe (Hawthorne), **II:** 223–224; **Retro. Supp. I:** 149, 151
Fan's Notes, A (Exley), **Supp. XVI:** 69
"Fantasia on 'The Nut-Brown Maid'" (Ashbery), **Supp. III Part 1:** 19
"Fantasia on the Relations between Poetry and Photography" (Strand), **Supp. IV Part 2:** 631
"Fantastic Fables" (Bierce), **I:** 209
Fante, John, **Supp. XI: 159–176**
Faraday, Michael, **I:** 480–481
"Far and Away" (Jarman), **Supp. XVII:** 115
Far and Away (Jarman), **Supp. XVII:** 110, 115
"Farewell" (Emerson), **II:** 13
"Farewell" (Ryan as Quin), **Supp. XVIII:** 229
Farewell, My Lovely (Chandler), **Supp. IV Part 1:** 122, 125–126, 127, 128, 130
"Farewell, My Lovely!" (White), **Supp. I Part 2:** 661–663, 665
"Farewell Performance" (Merrill), **Supp. III Part 1:** 336–337
Farewell-Sermon Preached at the First Precinct in Northampton, after the People's Publick Rejection of their Minister, A (Edwards), **I:** 548, 562
"Farewell Sweet Dust" (Wylie), **Supp. I Part 2:** 727–728
Farewell to Arms, A (Hemingway), **I:** 212, 421, 476, 477; **II:** 68–69, 248–249, 252–253, 254, 255, 262, 265; **Retro. Supp. I:** 171, 178, **180–182,** 187, 189; **Retro. Supp. II:** 108; **Supp. IV Part 1:** 380–381, 381; **Supp. VIII:** 179; **Supp. XII:** 241–242
"Farewell to Miles" (Berryman), **I:** 173
"Farewell to My Union Brothers" (Ryan as Quin), **Supp. XVIII:** 238
Farewell to Reform (Chamberlain), **Supp. I Part 2:** 647
Farewell to Sport (Gallico), **Supp. XVI:** 238
"Farewell to the Middle Class" (Updike), **Retro. Supp. I:** 321
"Far Field, The" (Roethke), **III:** 537, 540
Far Field, The (Roethke), **III:** 528, 529, 539, 545, 547–548
Far-Flung (Cameron), **Supp. XII:** 81
Far from the Madding Crowd (Hardy), **II:** 291
Faris, Athénaíse Charleville, **Supp. I Part 1:** 204
Farley, Abbie, **I:** 458
Farley, Harriet, **Supp. XIII:** 140
"Farm, The" (Creeley), **Supp. IV Part 1:** 155
Farmer (Harrison), **Supp. VIII:** 39, **44–45**
Farmer, Frances, **Supp. XV:** 196–197
Farmer, Richard, **Supp. XIV:** 2
"Farmer and the Fox, The" (Leopold), **Supp. XIV:** 188
"Farmers' Daughters, The" (W. C. Williams), **Retro. Supp. I:** 423
Farmers Hotel, The (O'Hara), **III:** 361
"Farmer's Sorrow, A" (Jewett), **Retro. Supp. II:** 132
"Farmer's Wife, The" (Sexton), **Supp. II Part 2:** 676
"Farm Garden" (Nelson), **Supp. XVIII:** 186
"Farm Implements and Rutabagas in a Landscape" (Ashbery), **Supp. III Part 1:** 13
Farming: A Hand Book (Berry), **Supp. X:** 31, 35
"Farm on the Great Plains, The" (Stafford), **Supp. XI:** 322
Farnol, Jeffrey, **Supp. I Part 2:** 653
Far North (Shepard), **Supp. III Part 2:** 433, 435
"Far Northern Birch, The" (Francis), **Supp. IX:** 90
Farnsworth, Elizabeth, **Supp. XI:** 139
"Farrago" (Kees), **Supp. XV:** 145
Farrand, Max, **II:** 122
Farrar, Geraldine, **Retro. Supp. I:** 10
Farrar, John, **II:** 191; **Supp. XI:** 47
Farrell, Barry, **Supp. XIV:** 142
Farrell, James Francis, **II:** 25, 26
Farrell, James T., **I:** 97, 288, 475, 508, 517, 519; **II: 25–53,** 416, 424; **III:** 28, 114, 116, 118, 119, 317, 382; **IV:** 211, 286; **Retro. Supp. II:** 196, 327; **Supp. I Part 2:** 679; **Supp. VIII:** 96, 97; **Supp. XIV:** 3; **Supp. XV:** 141
Farrell, John, **II:** 26
Farrell, John C., **Supp. I Part 1:** 24
Farrell, Kate, **Supp. XV:** 187–188,**Supp. XV:** 190
Farrell, Kevin, **II:** 26
Farrell, Mary, **II:** 25
Farrell, Mrs. James T. (Dorothy Butler), **II:** 26
Farrell, Mrs. James T. (Hortense Alden), **II:** 26, 27, 45, 48
"Far Rockaway" (Schwartz), **Supp. II Part 2:** 649
Farrow, Mia, **Supp. XV:** 8, 10
Far Side of the Dollar, The (Macdonald), **Supp. IV Part 2:** 473
Farther Off from Heaven (Humphrey), **Supp. IX:** 93, 96, 101, **103–104,** 105, 109
Far Tortuga (Matthiessen), **Supp. V:** 201, 206–207
"Fascinating Fascism" (Sontag), **Supp. III Part 2:** 465
"Fascination of Cities, The" (Hughes), **Supp. I Part 1:** 325
Fashion, Power, Guilt and the Charity of Families (Shields), **Supp. VII:** 323
Fasman, Jonathan, **Supp. V:** 253
Fast, Howard, **Supp. I Part 1:** 295
Fast, Jonathan, **Supp. V:** 115
Fast and Loose (Wharton), **Retro. Supp. I:** 361
"Faster than Light" (Nelson), **Supp. XVIII:** 178–179
"Fastest Runner on Sixty-first Street, The" (Farrell), **II:** 45
"Fat" (Carver), **Supp. III Part 1:** 141
Fatal Interview (Millay), **III:** 128–129, 130
"Fatality" (Bausch), **Supp. VII:** 54
Fatal Lady (film), **Supp. XIII:** 166
"Fate" (Emerson), **II:** 2–3, 4, 16; **Supp. XIV:** 42
"Fate" (Koch), **Supp. XV:** 183
"Fate" (Mailer), **Retro. Supp. II:** 207
"Fate of Pleasure, The" (Trilling), **Supp. III Part 2:** 510
Fate of the Jury, The (Masters), **Supp. I Part 2:** 466, 468, 469
"Fat Girl, The" (Dubus), **Supp. VII:** 84, 85
"Father" (Levine), **Supp. V:** 188
"Father" (Sanders), **Supp. XVI:** 277
"Father" (Walker), **Supp. III Part 2:** 522
"Father, The" (Carver), **Supp. III Part 1:** 137, 140
Father, The (Olds), **Supp. X: 209–211**
"Father Abraham" (Faulkner), **Retro. Supp. I:** 81, 82
Fatheralong: A Meditation on Fathers and Sons, Race and Society (Wideman), **Supp. X:** 320, 332–333, 334, 335
"Father and Daughter" (Eberhart), **I:** 539
Father and Glorious Descendant (Lowe), **Supp. X:** 291
"Father and Son" (Eberhart), **I:** 539
Father and Son (Farrell), **II:** 34, 35, 290, 291
Father and Son (Gosse), **Supp. VIII:** 157
"Father and Son" (Hughes), **Retro. Supp. I:** 204; **Supp. I Part 1:** 329, 339
"Father and Son" (Kunitz), **Supp. III Part 1:** 262
"Father and Son" (Schwartz), **Supp. II Part 2:** 650
Father Bombo's Pilgrimage to Mecca (Freneau), **Supp. II Part 1:** 254
"Father Fitzgerald" (Nelson and Espeland), **Supp. XVIII:** 181
"Father Guzman" (Stern), **Supp. IX: 293,** 296
"Father out Walking on the Lawn, A" (Dove), **Supp. IV Part 1:** 246
"Fathers" (Creeley), **Supp. IV Part 1:** 157–158
Fathers, The (Tate), **IV:** 120, 127, 130, 131–133, 134, 141; **Supp. X:** 52
Fathers and Crows (Vollmann), **Supp. XVII:** 226, 231–232
"Fathers and Sons" (Hemingway), **II:** 249, 265–266; **Retro. Supp. I:** 175
"Father's Body, The" (Dickey), **Supp. IV Part 1:** 176
"Father's Story, A" (Dubus), **Supp. VII:** 88
"Father's Voice" (Stafford), **Supp. XI:** 322
"Fat Lady, The" (Carruth), **Supp. XVI:** 48
"Fat Man, Floating" (Dunn), **Supp. XI:** 144
Faulkner, Barry, **Supp. XV:** 41

Faulkner, William, **I:** 54, 97, 99, 105, 106, 115, 117, 118, 123, 190, 204–205, 211, 288, 289, 291, 292, 297, 305, 324, 374, 378, 423, 480, 517; **II:** 28, 51, **54–76,** 131, 174, 194, 217, 223, 228, 230, 259, 301, 306, 431, 458–459, 542, 594, 606; **III:** 45, 70, 108, 164, 218, 220, 222, 236–237, 244, 292, 334, 350, 382, 418, 453, 454, 482, 483; **IV:** 2, 4, 33, 49, 97, 98, 100, 101, 120, 131, 203, 207, 211, 217, 237, 257, 260, 261, 279, 280, 352, 461, 463; **Retro. Supp. I: 73–95,** 215, 339, 347, 356, 379, 382; **Retro. Supp. II:** 19, 221, 326; **Supp. I Part 1:** 196, 197, 242, 372; **Supp. I Part 2:** 450, 621; **Supp. III Part 1:** 384–385, 396; **Supp. IV Part 1:** 47, 130, 257, 342; **Supp. IV Part 2:** 434, 463, 468, 502, 677, 682; **Supp. IX:** 20, 95; **Supp. V:** 58, 59, 138, 210, 226, 237, 261, 262, 334–336; **Supp. VIII:** 37, 39, 40, 104, 105, 108, 175, 176, 180, 181, 183, 184, 188, 189, 215; **Supp. X:** 44, 228; **Supp. XI:** 92, 247; **Supp. XII:** 16, 289, 310, 313; **Supp. XIII:** 100, 169; **Supp. XIV:** 1, 12–13, 21, 24, 93, 306; **Supp. XV:** 92, 135, 338; **Supp. XVI:** 148, 189; **Supp. XVII:** 225; **Supp. XVIII:** 76, 84, 90, 148, 249
Faulkner: A Collection of Critical Essays (Warren), **Retro. Supp. I:** 73
Faulkner at Nagano (Jelliffe, ed.), **I:** 289; **II:** 63, 65
Faulkner-Cowley File, The: Letters and Memories 1944–1962 (Cowley, ed.), **Retro. Supp. I:** 73, 92; **Supp. II Part 1:** 140, 141
"Faun" (Plath), **Supp. I Part 2:** 537
"Fauna" (Jeffers), **Supp. II Part 2:** 415
Fauset, Arthur Huff, **Supp. XVIII:** 126
Fauset, Jessie, **Supp. I Part 1:** 321, 325; **Supp. IV Part 1:** 164
Fauset, Jessie Redmon, **Supp. XVIII:** 122,127
Faust (Goethe), **I:** 396; **II:** 489; **III:** 395; **Supp. II Part 1:** 16; **Supp. IX:** 141
Faust, Clarence H., **II:** 20
Faute de l'Abbé Mouret, La (Zola), **III:** 322
Favor Island (Merwin), **Supp. III Part 1:** 346, 347
"Favrile" (Doty), **Supp. XI:** 131
Fay, Bernard, **IV:** 41
"Fear, The" (Frost), **Retro. Supp. I:** 128
"Fear & Fame" (Levine), **Supp. V:** 192
"Fearful Child, The" (C. Frost), **Supp. XV:** 96
Fearful Child, The (C. Frost), **Supp. XV:** 96, 97, 106
Fearing, Kenneth, **Supp. XV:** 138
"Fearless" (Mosley), **Supp. XIII:** 241
Fearless Jones (Mosley), **Supp. XIII: 241–242**
Fear of Fifty: A Midlife Memoir (Jong), **Supp. V:** 114, 115, 116, 131
Fear of Flying (Jong), **Supp. V:** 113, 115, 116, 119–123, 124, 129
"Feast, The" (Kinnell), **Supp. III Part 1:** 239, 250
Feast of All Saints, The (Rice), **Supp. VII:** 299–301
Feast of Love, The (C. Baxter), **Supp. XVII:** 13, 21–22
Feast of Love, The (film, R. Benton), **Supp. XVII:** 22
Feast of Snakes, A (Crews), **Supp. XI:** 102, **107–108**
"Feast of Stephen, The" (Hecht), **Supp. X:** 63–64
"Featherbed for Critics, A" (Blackmur), **Supp. II Part 1:** 93, 151
Feather Crowns (Mason), **Supp. VIII: 146–147**
"Feathers" (Carver), **Supp. III Part 1:** 145
Feathers (Van Vechten), **Supp. II Part 2:** 736, 749
"Feathers, The" (Hogan), **Supp. IV Part 1:** 416
"February" (Ellison), **Supp. II Part 1:** 229
"February 14th" (Levine), **Supp. V:** 194
"February in Sydney" (Komunyakaa), **Supp. XIII:** 125
February in Sydney (Komunyakaa), **Supp. XIII: 124–125,** 129
"February: Thinking of Flowers" (Kenyon), **Supp. VII:** 171
"Feces" (McClatchy), **Supp. XII:** 266, 267–268
Fechner, Gustav, **II:** 344, 355, 358, 359, 363
Feder, Lillian, **IV:** 136; **Supp. XVI:** 49, 50
Federal Arts Project, **Supp. III Part 2:** 618
Federigo, or, The Power of Love (Nemerov), **III:** 268, 276, 282, 283–284, 285
"Fedora" (Chopin), **Supp. I Part 1:** 220
Fedorko, Kathy A., **Retro. Supp. I:** 361, 374
"Feeling and Precision" (Moore), **III:** 206
"Feeling of Effort, The" (James), **II:** 349
"Feel Like a Bird" (Swenson), **Supp. IV Part 2:** 639
"Feel Me" (Swenson), **Supp. IV Part 2:** 647
Feeney, Mary, **Supp. IX:** 152, 154
Feinstein, Sascha, **Supp. XIII:** 125
Feldman, Charles K., **Supp. XI:** 307
Fellini, Federico, **Supp. XII:** 172; **Supp. XV:** 8
"Fellow Citizens" (Sandburg), **III:** 553
Fellows, John, **Supp. I Part 2:** 520
"Felo de Se" (Wylie), **Supp. I Part 2:** 727, 729
Felton, Sharon, **Supp. IV Part 1:** 210
"Female Author" (Plath), **Retro. Supp. II:** 243
"Female Frailty" (Freneau), **Supp. II Part 1:** 258
"Female Laughter and Comic Possibilities: *Uncommon Women and Others*" (Chirico), **Supp. XV:** 323
Female Patriot, The; or, Nature's Rights (Rowson), **Supp. XV:** 237–238
Female Prose Writers of America (Hart), **Supp. XVIII:** 257, 264
"Female Voice in *To Kill a Mockingbird*, The: Narrative Strategies in Film and Novel" (Shakelford), **Supp. VIII:** 129
"Feminine Landscape of Leslie Marmon Silko's *Ceremony*, The" (Gunn Allen), **Supp. IV Part 1:** 324
Feminism and the Politics of Literary Reputation: The Example of Erica Jong (Templin), **Supp. V:** 116
"Feminismo" (Robbins), **Supp. X:** 272
"Feminist Criticism in the Wilderness" (Showalter), **Supp. X:** 97
Feminization of American Culture, The (Douglas), **Supp. XVIII:** 258
"Fence, The" (Oliver), **Supp. VII:** 232
"Fence Posts" (Snyder), **Supp. VIII:** 304
Fences (Wilson), **Supp. VIII:** 329, 330, 331, **334–337,** 350
Fenick, Elizabeth, **Retro. Supp. II:** 221
"Fenimore Cooper's Literary Offenses" (Twain), **IV:** 204–205
Fennell, Frank L., **Supp. XVII:** 177–178
Fenollosa, Ernest, **III:** 458, 465, 466, 474, 475, 477; **Retro. Supp. I:** 289; **Supp. IV Part 1:** 154
Fenollosa, Mrs. Ernest, **III:** 458
"Fenstad's Mother" (C. Baxter), **Supp. XVII:** 18
Fenton, Charles, **Supp. XI:** 43
Fenton, James, **Supp. XV:** 117
Ferdinand: Including "It Was" (Zukofsky), **Supp. III Part 2:** 630
"Fergus" (Bourne), **I:** 229
Ferguson, James, **Supp. I Part 2:** 503
Ferguson, Otis, **Supp. IX:** 7
Ferguson, William, **Supp. XII:** 189
Ferguson Affair, The (Macdonald), **Supp. IV Part 2:** 473
Fergusson, Francis, **I:** 265, 440; **Supp. XV:** 20
Ferlinghetti, Lawrence, **Supp. IV Part 1:** 90; **Supp. VIII:** 290, 292; **Supp. XII:** 121, 125; **Supp. XIII:** 275
Fermata, The (Baker), **Supp. XIII: 49–52,** 54
"Fern" (Toomer), **Supp. III Part 2:** 481; **Supp. IX:** 313
Fern, Fanny, **Retro. Supp. I:** 246; **Supp. V:** 122
Fernández, Enrique, **Supp. VIII:** 73
Fernandez, Ramon, **Retro. Supp. I:** 302, 303; **Supp. XVI:** 214
"Fern-Beds in Hampshire Country" (Wilbur), **Supp. III Part 2:** 558
"Fern Hill" (D. Thomas), **IV:** 93
"Fern-Life" (Larcom), **Supp. XIII:** 143
Ferragammo, Salvatore, **Supp. XVI:** 192
Ferreo, Guglielmo, **Supp. I Part 2:** 481
Fessenden, Thomas Green, **II:** 300
Fessier, Michael, **Supp. XIII:** 164
"Festival Aspect, The" (Olson), **Supp. II Part 2:** 585
"Festival of Regrets, The" (Wasserstein), **Supp. XV:** 333
Fetching the Dead (Sanders), **Supp. XVI:** 269
Fêtes galantes (Verlaine), **IV:** 79
"Fetish" (McClatchy), **Supp. XII:** 256
Fetterley, Judith, **Retro. Supp. II:** 139
"Feud" (Zinberg), **Supp. XV:** 195

"Fever" (Carver), **Supp. III Part 1:** 145
"Fever 103°" (Plath), **Supp. I Part 2:** 541
Fever Pitch (Hornby), **Supp. XII:** 286
Fever: Twelve Stories (Wideman), **Supp. X:** 320
"Few Don'ts by an Imagiste, A" (Pound), **III:** 465; **Retro. Supp. I:** 288; **Supp. I Part 1:** 261–262
"Few Stray Comments on the Cultivation of the Lyric, A" (Sobin), **Supp. XVI:** 285
"Few Words of Introduction, A" (McNally), **Supp. XIII:** 198–199
Fiamengo, Janice, **Supp. XIII:** 35
Fiber (Bass), **Supp. XVI:** 22
"*Fiber:* A Post-Pastoral Georgic" (Gifford), **Supp. XVI:** 22
Ficke, Arthur Davison, **Supp. XIII:** 347; **Supp. XV:** 40, 42, 43, 46, 48, 49
"Fiction" (Stafford), **Supp. XI:** 327
"Fiction: A Lens on Life" (Stegner), **Supp. IV Part 2:** 595, 596, 600
Fictional World of William Hoffman, The (Frank, ed.), **Supp. XVIII:** 74, 79, 80, 87
Fiction and the Figures of Life (Gass), **Supp. VI:** 85
Fiction of Joseph Heller, The (Seed), **Supp. IV Part 1:** 391
Fiction of Paule Marshall, The (Denniston), **Supp. XI:** 276
Fiction of the Forties (Eisinger), **I:** 302; **II:** 604
Fictions in Autobiography: Studies in the Art of Self-Invention (Eakin), **Supp. XVI:** 70
"Fiction Writer and His Country, The" (O'Connor), **III:** 342; **Retro. Supp. II:** 223, 225; **Supp. II Part 1:** 148
Fidelity (Glaspell), **Supp. III Part 1:** 177
Fiedler, Leslie A., **II:** 27; **III:** 218; **Retro. Supp. II:** 280, 324; **Supp. II Part 1:** 87; **Supp. IV Part 1:** 42, 86; **Supp. IX:** 3, 227; **Supp. X:** 80; **Supp. XIII: 93–110; Supp. XIV:** 11; **Supp. XVIII:** 146
Fiedler on the Roof: Essays on Literature and Jewish Identity (Fiedler), **Supp. XIII:** 106–107
"Fie! Fie! Fi-Fi!" (Fitzgerald), **Retro. Supp. I:** 100
Field, Eugene, **Supp. II Part 1:** 197
Field, John, **IV:** 179
"Field Events" (Bass), **Supp. XVI:** 19
"Field Full of Black Cats, A" (C. Frost), **Supp. XV:** 101
Field Guide, (Hass), **Supp. VI:** 97–98, **99–101,** 102, 103, 106
Field Guide to Contemporary Poetry and Poetics (Friebert and Young, eds.), **Supp. XI:** 270
"Field Guide to the Western Birds" (Stegner), **Supp. IV Part 2:** 609
Fielding, Henry, **I:** 134; **II:** 302, 304–305; **III:** 61; **Supp. I Part 2:** 421, 422, 656; **Supp. IV Part 2:** 688; **Supp. IX:** 128; **Supp. V:** 127; **Supp. XI:** 277; **Supp. XVIII:** 2, 7
Fielding, Richard, **Supp. XV:** 232
"Field-larks and Blackbirds" (Lanier), **Supp. I Part 1:** 355
"Field of Honor" (Hay), **Supp. XIV:** 120–121, 129–130
Field of Honor (Hay), **Supp. XIV:** 120–121, 125, 130
Field of Vision, The (Morris), **III:** 226–228, 229, 232, 233, 238
"Field Report" (Corso), **Supp. XII:** 124, **136**
"Fields" (Wright), **Supp. XV:** 342
Fields, Annie Adams, **II:** 401, 402, 403–404, 406, 412; **IV:** 177; **Retro. Supp. II:** 134, 135, 142; **Supp. I Part 1:** 317; **Supp. XVI:** 84, 88
Fields, James T., **II:** 274, 279, 402–403; **Retro. Supp. II:** 135; **Supp. I Part 1:** 317; **Supp. XIII:** 150; **Supp. XVI:** 84, 88
Fields, Joseph, **IV:** 274
Fields, Mrs. James T., **Supp. XIV:** 44, 46. *See* Fields, Annie Adams
Fields, The (Richter), **Supp. XVIII: 213–214,** 220
Fields, W. C., **II:** 427; **IV:** 335
"Fields at Dusk, The" (Salter), **Supp. IX:** 260
Fields of Praise, The (Nelson), **Supp. XVIII:** 171, 173, **177–178**
Fields of Wonder (Hughes), **Retro. Supp. I:** 206, 207; **Supp. I Part 1:** 333–334
Fierce Invalids Home from Hot Climates (Robbins), **Supp. X:** 267, 276–277, **282–285**
Fiery Chariot, The (Hurston), **Supp. VI:** 155–156
15 Poems (Banks), **Supp. V:** 5
"Fifteenth Farewell" (Bogan), **Supp. III Part 1:** 51, 58
"Fifth Avenue, Uptown" (Baldwin), **Supp. I Part 1:** 52
"Fifth Avenue——Spring Afternoon" (Untermeyer), **Supp. XV:** 296
Fifth Book of Peace, The (Kingston), **Supp. V:** 173
Fifth Chinese Daughter (Wong), **Supp. X:** 291
Fifth Column, The (Hemingway), **II:** 254, 258; **Retro. Supp. I:** 184
"Fifth Column of the Fencerow" (Leopold), **Supp. XIV:** 185
Fifth Decad of Cantos, The (Pound), **Retro. Supp. I:** 292
"Fifth Movement: *Autobiography*" (Zukofsky), **Supp. III Part 2:** 611
"Fifth Sunday" (Dove), **Supp. IV Part 1:** 252
Fifth Sunday (Dove), **Supp. IV Part 1:** 251, 252–253
50 Poems (Cummings), **I:** 430, 440, 442–443, 444–445, 446
Fifty Best American Short Stories (O'Brien), **III:** 56
"Fifty Dollars" (Elkin), **Supp. VI: 43–44**
"55 Miles to the Gas Pump" (Proulx), **Supp. VII:** 264
55 Poems (Zukofsky), **Supp. III Part 2:** 611, 621
"Fifty Grand" (Hemingway), **II:** 250, 424; **Retro. Supp. I:** 177
"Fifty Suggestions" (Poe), **Retro. Supp. II:** 266
"52 Oswald Street" (Kinnell), **Supp. III Part 1:** 251
Fifty Years Among Authors, Editors, and Publishers (Derby), **Supp. XVIII:** 4
"Fifty Years Among the Black Folk" (Du Bois), **Supp. II Part 1:** 169
"Fifty Years of American Poetry" (Jarrell), **Retro. Supp. I:** 52
Fight, The (Mailer), **Retro. Supp. II:** 207, 208
Fight Back: For the Sake of the People, For the Sake of the Land (Ortiz), **Supp. IV Part 2:** 497, 498, 499, 503, 510–512, 514
"Fighters, The" (Zinberg), **Supp. XV:** 193
Fight for Freedom (Hughes), **Supp. I Part 1:** 345
Fighting Angel (Buck), **Supp. II Part 1:** 119, 131
Fighting France; From Dunkerque to Belfort (Wharton), **Retro. Supp. I:** 377, 378
Fightin': New and Collected Stories (Ortiz), **Supp. IV Part 2:** 513
"Figlia che Piange, La" (Eliot), **I:** 570, 584; **III:** 9
Figliola, Samantha, **Supp. V:** 143
"Figure a Poem Makes, The" (Frost), **Retro. Supp. I:** 139
"Figured Wheel, The" (Pinsky), **Supp. VI:** 243, 244, 245, 246
Figured Wheel, The: New and Collected Poems (Pinsky), **Supp. VI:** 247–248
"Figure in the Carpet, The" (James), **Retro. Supp. I:** 228, 229
"Figure in the Doorway, The" (Frost), **Retro. Supp. I:** 138
Figures from the Double World (McGrath), **Supp. X: 118–119**
"Figures in the Clock, The" (McCarthy), **II:** 561–562
Figures Made Visible in the Sadness of Time (Everwine), **Supp. XV:** 75, 88
Figures of Time (Hayden), **Supp. II Part 1:** 367
"Filling Out a Blank" (Wagoner), **Supp. IX:** 324
Fillmore, Millard, **III:** 101
Film Flam: Essays on Hollywood (McMurtry), **Supp. V:** 228
Films of Ayn Rand, The (Cox), **Supp. IV Part 2:** 524
Filo, John, **Supp. XII:** 211
Filson, John, **Retro. Supp. I:** 421
Final Beast, The (Buechner), **Supp. XII: 49–51**
"Finale" (Longfellow), **II:** 505, 506–507
"Final Fear" (Hughes), **Supp. I Part 1:** 338
Final Harvest: Emily Dickinson's Poems (Johnson, ed.), **I:** 470, 471
Final Payments (Gordon), **Supp. IV Part 1:** 297, 299, 300–302, 304, 306, 314
"Final Report, A" (Maxwell), **Supp. VIII:** 169
"Final Soliloquy of the Interior Paramour" (Stevens), **Retro. Supp. I:** 312

Final Solution, The (Reitlinger), **Supp. XII:** 161
Financier, The (Dreiser), **I:** 497, 501, 507, 509; **Retro. Supp. II:** 94, 101–102, 105; **Supp. XVIII:** 246
Finch, Annie, **Supp. XVII: 69–79**
Finch, Henry Leroy, **Supp. XVII:** 69
Finch, Margaret Rockwell, **Supp. XVII:** 69
Finch, Robert, **Supp. XIV:** 186–187
Find a Victim (Macdonald), **Supp. IV Part 2:** 467, 472, 473
Fin de Chéri, La (Colette; stage adaptation, Loos), **Supp. XVI:** 194
"Fin de Saison Palm Beach" (White), **Supp. I Part 2:** 673
"Finding a Bible in an Abandoned Cabin" (Wrigley), **Supp. XVIII: 293–294,** 296, 297, 300, **301,** 303
Finding a Form (Gass), **Supp. VI:** 91–92, 93
"Finding a Girl in America" (Dubus), **Supp. VII:** 87
Finding a Girl in America (Dubus), **Supp. VII:** 85–88
"Finding Beads" (Hogan), **Supp. IV Part 1:** 400
"Finding of Zach, The" (Dunbar), **Supp. II Part 1:** 212
Findings and Keepings: Analects for an Autobiography (Mumford), **Supp. II Part 2:** 483
Finding the Center: Narrative Poetry of the Zuni Indians (Tedlock), **Supp. IV Part 2:** 509
Finding the Islands (Merwin), **Supp. III Part 1:** 353, 357
"Finding the Place: A Migrant Childhood" (Stegner), **Supp. IV Part 2:** 597
"Find the Woman" (Macdonald, under Millar), **Supp. IV Part 2:** 466
Fine, David, **Supp. XI:** 160
Fine, Richard, **Supp. XVIII:** 248
Fine Clothes to the Jew (Hughes), **Retro. Supp. I:** 200, 201, 203, 205; **Supp. I Part 1:** 326–328
"Fine Old Firm, A" (Jackson), **Supp. IX:** 120
Fine Preserving (Plagemann), **Supp. XVII:** 91
Fine Preserving: M. F. K. Fisher's Annotated Edition of Catherine Plagemann's Cookbook (Plagemann; M. F. K. Fisher, ed.), **Supp. XVII:** 91
Finer Grain, The (James), **II:** 335
Fine Writing (L. P. Smith), **Supp. XIV:** 347
"Finis" (X. J. Kennedy), **Supp. XV:** 169
Finished Man, The (Garrett), **Supp. VII:** 96, 97–98
Fink, Mike, **IV:** 266
Finley, John H., **II:** 418
Finn, David, **Supp. VIII:** 106–107
Finnegan, Robert (pseudonym). *See* Ryan, Paul William
Finnegans Wake (Joyce), **III:** 7, 12, 14, 261; **IV:** 182, 369–370, 418, 421; **Supp. I Part 2:** 620; **Supp. II Part 1:** 2; **Supp. XIII:** 191; **Supp. XVIII:** 32
Finney, Brian, **Supp. XIV:** 158, 160, 161, 165, 166, 167, 169
"Finnish Rhapsody" (Ashbery), **Supp. III Part 1:** 26
Finster, Howard, **Supp. XV:** 349
Firbank, Ronald, **IV:** 77, 436
"Fire" (Hughes), **Supp. I Part 1:** 327
"Fire and Cloud" (Wright), **IV:** 488
"Fire and Ice" (Frost), **II:** 154; **Retro. Supp. I:** 133
Fire and Ice (Stegner), **Supp. IV Part 2:** 598, 607–608
"Fire and the Cloud, The" (Hurston), **Supp. VI:** 158
"Fire and the Hearth, The" (Faulkner), **II:** 71
Firebird (Doty), **Supp. XI:** 119–120, 121, **132–133,** 134
"Firebombing, The" (Dickey), **Supp. IV Part 1:** 180–181, 187, 189–190
"Fireborn Are at Home in Fire, The" (Sandburg), **III:** 591
"Fire Chaconne" (Francis), **Supp. IX:** 87
Firecrackers (Van Vechten), **Supp. II Part 2:** 740, 742–744, 749
Fire: From "A Journal of Love," the Unexpurgated Diary of Anaïs Nin, 1934–1937, **Supp. X:** 184, 185, 189, 194, 195
"Fireman, The" (Bass), **Supp. XVI:** 24
Fireman's Wife and Other Stories, The (Bausch), **Supp. VII:** 48, 54
"Fire Next Time, The" (Baldwin). *See* "Down at the Cross" (Baldwin)
Fire Next Time, The (Baldwin), **Retro. Supp. II:** 5, 8, 9; **Supp. I Part 1:** 48, 49, 52, 60–61
"Fire of Driftwood, The" (Longfellow), **II:** 499; **Retro. Supp. II:** 159, 168
"Fire of Life" (McCullers), **II:** 585
Fire on the Mountain (Abbey), **Supp. XIII:** 6
"Fire Poem" (Merrill), **Supp. III Part 1:** 321
"Fires" (Bass), **Supp. XVI:** 20
"Fires" (Carver), **Supp. III Part 1:** 136–139, 147
Fire Screen, The (Merrill), **Supp. III Part 1:** 319, 325–329
"Fire Season" (Didion), **Supp. IV Part 1:** 199
"Fire Sequence" (Winters), **Supp. II Part 2:** 791, 796, 800
Fire Sermon (Morris), **III:** 238–239
"Fire Sermon, The" (Eliot), **Retro. Supp. I:** 60–61
Fires: Essays, Poems, Stories (Carver), **Supp. III Part 1:** 136, 140, 142, 146–147
Fireside Travels (Lowell), **Supp. I Part 2:** 407, 419–420
Firestarter (King), **Supp. IX:** 114; **Supp. V:** 140, 141, 144
"fire the bastards" (Green), **Supp. IV Part 1:** 285
"Fire-Truck, A" (Wilbur), **Supp. III Part 2:** 556
"Fireweed" (Clampitt), **Supp. IX: 44–45**
"Firewood" (Banks), **Supp. V:** 15
"Fireworks" (Ford), **Supp. V:** 69
"Fireworks" (Shapiro), **Supp. II Part 2:** 707
Fireworks: A History and Celebration (Plimpton), **Supp. XVI:** 245
Fir-Flower Tablets (Lowell), **II:** 512, 526–527
Firkins, Oscar W., **II:** 271; **Supp. XV:** 297, 309
"Firmament, The" (Bryant), **Supp. I Part 1:** 162
Firmat, Gustavo Pérez, **Supp. VIII:** 76, 77, 79; **Supp. XI:** 184
"First American, The" (Toomer), **Supp. III Part 2:** 480, 487
"First Birth" (Olds), **Supp. X:** 212
First Book of Africa, The (Hughes), **Supp. I Part 1:** 344–345
First Book of Jazz, The (Hughes), **Supp. I Part 1:** 345
First Book of Negroes, The (Hughes), **Supp. I Part 1:** 345
First Book of Rhythms, The (Hughes), **Supp. I Part 1:** 345
First Book of the West Indies, The (Hughes), **Supp. I Part 1:** 345
Firstborn (Glück), **Supp. V:** 80, 81, 82, 84
"Firstborn" (Wright), **Supp. V:** 340
"First Chaldaic Oracle" (Carson), **Supp. XII: 111**
"First Communion" (Fante), **Supp. XI:** 160
"First Confession" (X. J. Kennedy), **Supp. XV: 154–155**
"First Day of School, The" (Gibbons), **Supp. X:** 41, 42
"First Death in Nova Scotia" (Bishop), **Supp. I Part 1:** 73
"First Formal" (Olds), **Supp. X:** 212
First Four Books of Poems, The (Glück), **Supp. V:** 81, 83
"First Grade" (Stafford), **Supp. XI:** 328
First Hand (Bierds), **Supp. XVII:** 32, 34–36
"First Hawaiian Bank" (Nye), **Supp. XIII:** 278
"First Heat" (Taylor), **Supp. V:** 323
"First Hour of the Night, The" (Bidart), **Supp. XV: 30–32**
"First Hunters and the Last, The" (Sobin), **Supp. XVI:** 292
"First Job, The" (Cisneros), **Supp. VII:** 62
"1st Letter on Georges" (Olson), **Supp. II Part 2:** 578
First Light (C. Baxter), **Supp. XVII:** 15, **17–18,** 19, 22
First Light (Preston), **Supp. XVII:** 18
First Light (Wagoner), **Supp. IX:** 330
"First Love" (Welty), **IV:** 264; **Retro. Supp. I:** 347
First Love: A Lyric Sequence (Untermeyer), **Supp. XV:** 295
First Man, The (O'Neill), **III:** 390
First Manifesto (McGrath), **Supp. X:** 115
"First Meditation" (Roethke), **III:** 545–546
"First Noni Daylight, The" (Harjo), **Supp. XII:** 219

"First Passover" (Longfellow), **II:** 500–501
"First Person Female" (Harrison), **Supp. VIII:** 40, 41, 48
"First Place, The" (Wagoner), **Supp. IX:** 328
First Poems (Buechner), **Supp. XII:** 45
First Poems (Merrill), **Supp. III Part 1:** 318–321, 323
First Poems 1946–1954 (Kinnell), **Supp. III Part 1:** 235, 238–239
"First Praise" (W. C. Williams), **Retro. Supp. I:** 413
First Principles (Spencer), **Supp. I Part 1:** 368
"First Ride and First Walk" (Goldbarth), **Supp. XII:** 182–183
"First Seven Years, The" (Malamud), **Supp. I Part 2:** 431
"First Sex" (Olds), **Supp. X:** 208
"First Snow in Alsace" (Wilbur), **Supp. III Part 2:** 545, 546, 559
"First Song" (Kinnell), **Supp. III Part 1:** 239
"First Spade in the West, The" (Fiedler), **Supp. XIII:** 103
"First Steps" (McClatchy), **Supp. XII:** 256
First There Is the Need (Reznikoff), **Supp. XIV:** 291
"First Things First" (Auden), **Supp. II Part 1:** 13
"First Thought, Best Thought" (Ginsberg), **Supp. II Part 1:** 327
"First Time I Saw Paris, The" (Fante), **Supp. XI:** 174
"First Travels of Max" (Ransom), **III:** 490–491
"First Tycoon of Teen, The" (Wolfe), **Supp. III Part 2:** 572
"First Views of the Enemy" (Oates), **Supp. II Part 2:** 508
"First Wife, The" (Buck), **Supp. II Part 1:** 127
First Words before Spring (Untermeyer), **Supp. XV:** 310
"First World War" (White), **Supp. I Part 2:** 665
"Fish" (F. Barthelme), **Supp. XI:** 26
"Fish" (Levis), **Supp. XI:** 259–260
Fish, Stanley, **Supp. IV Part 1:** 48; **Supp. XIV:** 14, 15
"Fish, The" (Bishop), **Supp. XV:** 100, 102
"Fish, The" (Moore), **III:** 195, 197, 209, 211, 213–214
"Fish, The" (Oliver), **Supp. VII:** 236
"Fish, The/Lago Chapala" (Everwine), **Supp. XV:** 82–83
"Fish and Shadow" (Pound), **III:** 466
Fishburne, Laurence, **Supp. VIII:** 345
"Fish Cannery" (Fante), **Supp. XI:** 167
Fisher, Alexander Metcalf, **Supp. I Part 2:** 582
Fisher, Alfred, **Retro. Supp. II:** 243
Fisher, Craig, **Supp. V:** 125
Fisher, Dorothy Canfield, **Retro. Supp. I:** 21, 133; **Supp. II Part 1:** 117. *See also* Canfield, Dorothy
Fisher, Mary, **Supp. I Part 2:** 455
Fisher, M. F. K., **Supp. XVII: 81–93**
Fisher, Phillip, **Retro. Supp. I:** 39
Fisher, Rudolph, **Retro. Supp. I:** 200; **Supp. I Part 1:** 325; **Supp. X:** 139; **Supp. XVI:** 143
Fisher, Vardis, **Supp. IV Part 2:** 598
Fisher King, The (Marshall), **Supp. XI:** 275–276, **288–290**
"Fisherman, The" (Merwin), **Supp. II Part 1:** 346
"Fisherman and His Wife, The" (Welty), **IV:** 266
"Fisherman from Chihuahua, The" (Connell), **Supp. XIV:** 86
"Fishing" (Harjo), **Supp. XII:** 227–228
"Fish in the Stone, The" (Dove), **Supp. IV Part 1:** 245, 257
"Fish in the unruffled lakes" (Auden), **Supp. II Part 1:** 8–9
"Fish R Us" (Doty), **Supp. XI:** 135
Fisk, James, **I:** 4, 474
Fiske, John, **Supp. I Part 1:** 314; **Supp. I Part 2:** 493
"Fit Against the Country, A" (Wright), **Supp. III Part 2:** 591–592, 601
Fitch, Clyde, **Supp. IV Part 2:** 573
Fitch, Elizabeth. *See* Taylor, Mrs. Edward (Elizabeth Fitch)
Fitch, James, **IV:** 147
Fitch, Noël Riley, **Supp. X:** 186, 187
Fitts, Dudley, **I:** 169, 173; **Supp. I Part 1:** 342, 345; **Supp. XIII:** 346
FitzGerald, Edward, **Supp. I Part 2:** 416; **Supp. III Part 2:** 610
Fitzgerald, Ella, **Supp. XIII:** 132
Fitzgerald, F. Scott, **I:** 107, 117, 118, 123, 188, 221, 288, 289, 358, 367, 374–375, 382, 423, 476, 482, 487, 495, 509, 511; **II: 77–100**, 257, 263, 272, 283, 415, 416, 417–418, 420, 425, 427, 430, 431, 432, 433, 434, 436, 437, 450, 458–459, 482, 560; **III:** 2, 26, 35, 36, 37, 40, 44, 45, 69, 106, 244, 284, 334, 350–351, 453, 454, 471, 551, 552, 572; **IV:** 27, 49, 97, 101, 126, 140, 191, 222, 223, 287, 297, 427, 471; **Retro. Supp. I:** 1, 74, **97–120**, 178, 180, 186, 215, 359, 381; **Retro. Supp. II:** 257, 321, 326, 328; **Supp. I Part 1:** 196, 197; **Supp. I Part 2:** 622; **Supp. III Part 2:** 409, 411, 585; **Supp. IV Part 1:** 123, 197, 200, 203, 341; **Supp. IV Part 2:** 463, 468, 607, 689; **Supp. IX:** 15, 20, 55, 57–63, 199; **Supp. V:** 23, 95, 226, 251, 262, 276, 313; **Supp. VIII:** 101, 103, 106, 137; **Supp. X:** 225; **Supp. XI:** 65, 221, 334; **Supp. XII:** 42, 173, 295; **Supp. XIII:** 170, 263; **Supp. XV:** 135; **Supp. XVI:** 64, 75, 191, 192, 294; **Supp. XVIII:** 148, 246, 248, 251, 254
Fitzgerald, Robert, **I:** 27–28; **III:** 338, 348; **Retro. Supp. II:** 179, 221, 222, 223, 228, 229; **Supp. IV Part 2:** 631; **Supp. XV:** 112, 249
Fitzgerald, Zelda (Zelda Sayre), **I:** 482; **II:** 77, 79, 82–85, 88, 90–91, 93, 95; **Supp. IV Part 1:** 310; **Supp. IX: 55–73; Supp. X:** 172. *See also* Sayre, Zelda
"Fitzgerald's Tragic Sense" (Schorer), **Retro. Supp. I:** 115
"Fitzgerald: The Romance of Money" (Cowley), **Supp. II Part 1:** 143
5 Detroits (Levine), **Supp. V:** 178
Five Came Back (West), **IV:** 287
Five Corners (screenplay, Shanley), **Supp. XIV:** 316
"Five-Dollar Bill, The" (D. West as Mary Christopher), **Supp. XVIII:** 282
"Five Dollar Guy, The" (W. C. Williams), **Retro. Supp. I:** 423
Five Easy Pieces (film), **Supp. V:** 26
"Five Elephants" (Dove), **Supp. IV Part 1:** 244–245
"Five Fucks" (Lethem), **Supp. XVIII:** 139
Five Groups of Verse (Reznikoff), **Supp. XIV:** 279, 282
500 Hundred Hats of Bartholomew Cubbins, The (Geisel), **Supp. XVI:** 100
Five Hundred Scorpions (Hearon), **Supp. VIII:** 57, 65, **66**
Five Indiscretions (Ríos), **Supp. IV Part 2:** 545–547
Five Men and Pompey (Benét), **Supp. XI:** 43, 44
Five Plays (Hughes), **Retro. Supp. I:** 197, 209
"Five Psalms" (Jarman), **Supp. XVII:** 120
Five Temperaments (Kalstone), **Retro. Supp. II:** 40
5,000 Fingers of Dr. T, The (film), **Supp. XVI:** 103
Five Young American Poets, **I:** 170; **II:** 367
Fixer, The (Malamud), **Supp. I Part 2:** 428, 435, 445, 446–448, 450, 451
Fjellestad, Danuta Zadworna, **Supp. XVI:** 150
Flaccus, Kimball, **Retro. Supp. I:** 136
Flacius, Matthias, **IV:** 163
"Flagellant's Song" (X. J. Kennedy), **Supp. XV:** 165
Flag for Sunrise, A (Stone), **Supp. V:** 301–304
Flag of Childhood, The: Poems from the Middle East (Nye, ed.), **Supp. XIII:** 280
"Flag of Summer" (Swenson), **Supp. IV Part 2:** 645
Flagons and Apples (Jeffers), **Supp. II Part 2:** 413, 414, 417–418
Flags in the Dust (Faulkner), **Retro. Supp. I:** 81, 82, 83, 86, 88
Flamel, Nicolas, **Supp. XII:** 178

Flaming Corsage, The (W. Kennedy), **Supp. VII:** 133, 153–156
Flammarion, Camille, **Supp. I Part 1:** 260
Flanagan, John T., **Supp. I Part 2:** 464, 465, 468
Flanner, Janet, **Supp. XVI:** 195
"Flannery O'Connor: Poet to the Outcast" (Sister Rose Alice), **III:** 348
Flappers and Philosophers (Fitzgerald), **II:** 88; **Retro. Supp. I:** 103; **Supp. IX:** 56
Flash and Filigree (Southern), **Supp. XI:** 295, **296–297**
"Flashcards" (Dove), **Supp. IV Part 1:** 250
Flash Fiction: Seventy-two Very Short Stories (J. Thomas, ed.), **Supp. XVI:** 268
Flatt, Lester, **Supp. V:** 335
Flaubert, Gustave, **I:** 66, 123, 130, 272, 312, 314, 315, 477, 504, 506, 513, 514; **II:** 182, 185, 194, 198–199, 205, 209, 230, 289, 311, 316, 319, 325, 337, 392, 401, 577, 594; **III:** 196, 207, 251, 315, 461, 467, 511, 564; **IV:** 4, 29, 31, 37, 40, 134, 285, 428; **Retro. Supp. I:** 5, 215, 218, 222, 225, 235, 287; **Supp. III Part 2:** 411, 412; **Supp. XI:** 334; **Supp. XIV:** 87, 336
"Flavia and Her Artists" (Cather), **Retro. Supp. I:** 5
Flavoring of New England, The (Brooks), **I:** 253, 256
Flavor of Man, The (Toomer), **Supp. III Part 2:** 487
Flaxman, Josiah, **Supp. I Part 2:** 716
"Flea, The" (Donne), **Supp. XVIII:** 307
"Flèche d'Or" (Merrill), **Supp. III Part 1:** 328
Flecker, James Elroy, **Supp. I Part 1:** 257
"Flee on Your Donkey" (Sexton), **Supp. II Part 2:** 683, 685
Fleming, Ian, **Supp. XI:** 307
Fleming, Rene, **Supp. XII:** 321
Fleming, Robert E., **Supp. XVII:** 155
Flesch, Rudolf, **Supp. XVI:** 105, 106
Flesh and Blood (Cunningham), **Supp. XV: 63–65**
Flesh and Blood (play; Cunnigham and Gaitens), **Supp. XV:** 65
"Fleshbody" (Ammons), **Supp. VII:** 27
Fletcher, H. D., **II:** 517, 529
Fletcher, John, **Supp. IV Part 2:** 621
Fletcher, John Gould, **I:** 243; **II:** 517, 529; **III:** 458; **Supp. I Part 1:** 263; **Supp. I Part 2:** 422; **Supp. XV:** 298, 302, 306, 307, 308
Fletcher, Phineas, **Supp. I Part 1:** 369
Fletcher, Virginia. *See* Caldwell, Mrs. Erskine (Virginia Fletcher)
Fleurs du mal, Les (Beaudelaire; Millay and Dillon, trans.), **III:** 141–142
"Flight" (Bierds), **Supp. XVII:** 36
"Flight" (Updike), **IV:** 218, 222, 224; **Retro. Supp. I:** 318
Flight (White), **Supp. XVIII:** 127
"Flight, The" (Haines), **Supp. XII:** 204–205
"Flight, The" (Roethke), **III:** 537–538
Flight among the Tombs (Hecht), **Supp. X:** 58, **71–74**
"Flight for Freedom" (McCoy), **Supp. XIII:** 170
"Flight from Byzantium" (Brodsky), **Supp. VIII:** 30–31
"Flight of Besey Lane, The" (Jewett), **Retro. Supp. II:** 139
Flight of the Rocket, The (Fitzgerald), **II:** 89
Flights of the Harvest-Mare (Bierds), **Supp. XVII:** 26–27
Flight to Canada (Reed), **Supp. X:** 240, **249–252**
Flinn, Mary, **Supp. XVII:** 110
Flint, F. S., **II:** 517; **III:** 459, 464, 465; **Retro. Supp. I:** 127; **Supp. I Part 1:** 261, 262
Flint, R. W., **Supp. XVI:** 47, 49, 57
"Flitting Flies" (X. J. Kennedy), **Supp. XV:** 166, **167**
Flivver King, The (Sinclair), **Supp. V:** 290
Floating House, The (Sanders), **Supp. XVI:** 269
Floating Light Bulb, The (Allen), **Supp. XV:** 2, 3, 13
Floating Opera, The (Barth), **I:** 121, 122–126, 127, 129, 130, 131
"Floating Poem, Unnumbered, The" (Rich), **Supp. I Part 2:** 572–573
"Floating Trees" (Wright), **Supp. XV:** 348
Flood (Matthews), **Supp. IX:** 154, **160–161**
Flood (Warren), **IV:** 252, 256–257
"Flood of Years, The" (Bryant), **Supp. I Part 1:** 159, 170, 171; **Supp. I Part 2:** 416
"Floor and the Ceiling, The" (W. J. Smith), **Supp. XIII:** 345, 346
"Floor Plans" (Komunyakaa), **Supp. XIII:** 114
"Floral Decorations for Bananas" (Stevens), **IV:** 8
Florida (Acker), **Supp. XII:** 5
"Florida" (Bishop), **Retro. Supp. II:** 43
"Florida Road Workers" (Hughes), **Retro. Supp. I:** 203
"Florida Sunday, A" (Lanier), **Supp. I Part 1:** 364, 366
"Flossie Cabanis" (Masters), **Supp. I Part 2:** 461–462
"Flowchart" (Ashbery), **Supp. III Part 1:** 26
Flow Chart (Ashbery), **Supp. VIII:** 275
Flower, Fruit, and Thorn Pieces (Richter), **Supp. XVI:** 182
Flower-de-Luce (Longfellow), **II:** 490
Flower Fables (Alcott), **Supp. I Part 1:** 33
"Flower-Fed Buffaloes, The" (Lindsay), **Supp. I Part 2:** 398
"Flower Garden" (Jackson), **Supp. IX:** 119
"Flower-gathering" (Frost), **II:** 153
"Flower Herding on Mount Monadnock" (Kinnell), **Supp. III Part 1:** 242
Flower Herding on Mount Monadnock (Kinnell), **Supp. III Part 1:** 235, 239, 241–244
"Flowering Death" (Ashbery), **Supp. III Part 1:** 22
"Flowering Dream, The" (McCullers), **II:** 591
"Flowering Judas" (Porter), **III:** 434, 435–436, 438, 441, 445, 446, 450–451
Flowering Judas and Other Stories (Porter), **III:** 433, 434
Flowering of New England, The (Brooks), **IV:** 171–172; **Supp. VIII:** 101
Flowering of the Rod (Doolittle), **Supp. I Part 1:** 272
Flowering Peach, The (Odets), **Supp. II Part 2:** 533, 547, 549–550
"Flowering Plum" (Glück), **Supp. V:** 82
"Flowers for Marjorie" (Welty), **IV:** 262
"Flowers of the Fallow" (Larcom), **Supp. XIII:** 143, 145–146
"Flowers Well if anybody" (Dickinson), **Retro. Supp. I:** 30
"Fluff and Mr. Ripley" (D. West), **Supp. XVIII:** 284
"Fly, The" (Kinnell), **Supp. III Part 1:** 249
"Fly, The" (Shapiro), **Supp. II Part 2:** 705
"Fly, The" (Simic), **Supp. VIII:** 278
Flye, Father James Harold, **I:** 25, 26, 35–36, 37, 42, 46; **IV:** 215
"Fly in Buttermilk, A" (Baldwin), **Retro. Supp. II:** 8
"Flying High" (Levertov), **Supp. III Part 1:** 284
"Flying Home" (Ellison), **Retro. Supp. II:** 117, **125–126; Supp. II Part 1:** 235, 238–239
"Flying Home" (Kinnell), **Supp. III Part 1:** 250
"Flying Home" and Other Stories (Ellison), **Retro. Supp. II:** 119, 124
"Flying Home from Utah" (Swenson), **Supp. IV Part 2:** 645
"Flying over Clouds" (Gioia), **Supp. XV:** 118
"Flying to Hanoi" (Rukeyser), **Supp. VI:** 279
Flynn, Elizabeth Gurley, **Supp. XVIII:** 225
Flynn, Richard, **Supp. XVII:** 115; **Supp. XVIII:** 183
Fly-Truffler, The (Sobin), **Supp. XVI: 294–295,** 296
Foata, Anne, **Supp. XI:** 104
Focillon, Henri, **IV:** 90
Focus (A. Miller), **III:** 150–151, 156
Foer, Jonathan Safran, **Supp. XII:** 169
Foerster, Norman, **I:** 222; **Supp. I Part 2:** 423, 424; **Supp. IV Part 2:** 598
"Fog" (Sandburg), **III:** 586
"Fog Galleon" (Komunyakaa), **Supp. XIII:** 127
"Foggy Lane, The" (Simpson), **Supp. IX:** 274
Folded Leaf, The (Maxwell), **Supp. III Part 1:** 62; **Supp. VIII: 159–162**
Folding Star, The (Hollinghurst), **Supp. XIII:** 52

Foley, Jack, **Supp. X:** 125; **Supp. XV:** 112, 116; **Supp. XVII:** 77
Foley, Martha, **II:** 587; **Supp. XVI:** 225
Folks from Dixie (Dunbar), **Supp. II Part 1:** 211–212
Folkways (Sumner), **III:** 102
Follain, Jean, **Supp. IX:** 152, 154
Follett, Wilson, **I:** 405; **Supp. XIII:** 173
Follower of Dusk (Salinas), **Supp. XIII:** 326
Following the Equator (Twain), **II:** 434; **IV:** 208
Follow Me Home (Hoffman), **Supp. XVIII:** 86
Folly (Minot), **Supp. VI:** 205, 208, **210–213**
Folly of Others, The (N. Boyce), **Supp. XVII:** 100
Folsom, Charles, **Supp. I Part 1:** 156
Folsom, Ed, **Retro. Supp. I:** 392
Folson, Marcia McClintock, **Retro. Supp. II:** 139
Fonda, Henry, **Supp. I Part 1:** 67; **Supp. IV Part 1:** 236
Fonda, Jane, **III:** 284; **Supp. XI:** 307
Fonda, Peter, **Supp. VIII:** 42; **Supp. XI:** 293, 308
"Fond Memories of a Black Childhood" (D. West), **Supp. XVIII:** 289
Foner, Eric, **Supp. I Part 2:** 523
Fong and the Indians (Theroux), **Supp. VIII:** 314, 315, **316–317**
Fontanne, Lynn, **III:** 397
Food and Drink (Untermeyer), **Supp. XV:** 310
Fool for Love (Shepard), **Supp. III Part 2:** 433, 447, 448
Fools (Simon), **Supp. IV Part 2:** 584–585
Fool's Progress, The: An Honest Novel (Abbey), **Supp. XIII:** 4, **13–15**
Foot Book, The (Geisel), **Supp. XVI:** 108
Foote, Horton, **Supp. I Part 1:** 281; **Supp. VIII:** 128, 129
Foote, Mary Hallock, **Retro. Supp. II:** 72; **Supp. IV Part 2:** 611
Foote, Roxanna. *See* Beecher, Mrs. Lyman (Roxanna Foote)
Foote, Samuel, **Supp. I Part 2:** 584
Foote, Stephanie, **Retro. Supp. II:** 139
"Foot Fault" (pseudonym). *See* Thurber, James
Footing on This Earth, A (Hay), **Supp. XIV:** 125, 126, 130
"Footing up a Total" (Lowell), **II:** 528
"Footnote to Howl" (Ginsberg), **Supp. II Part 1:** 316–317
"Footnote to Weather Forecasts, A" (Brodsky), **Supp. VIII:** 32
Footprints (Hearon), **Supp. VIII: 69–70**
Footprints (Levertov), **Supp. III Part 1:** 272, 281
"Footsteps of Angels" (Longfellow), **II:** 496
For a Bitter Season: New and Selected Poems (Garrett), **Supp. VII:** 99–100
"For a Dead Kitten" (Hay), **Supp. XIV:** 119–120
"For a Dead Lady" (Robinson), **III:** 508, 513, 517
"For a Ghost Who Once Placed Bets in the Park" (Levis), **Supp. XI:** 265
"For a Lamb" (Eberhart), **I:** 523, 530, 531
"For All" (Snyder), **Supp. VIII:** 304
"For All Tuesday Travelers" (Cisneros), **Supp. VII:** 67–68
"For a Lost Child" (Stafford), **Supp. XI:** 329
"For a Marriage" (Bogan), **Supp. III Part 1:** 52
"For an Emigrant" (Jarrell), **II:** 371
"For Anna Akmatova" (Lowell), **II:** 544
"For Anna Mae Pictou Aquash, Whose Spirit Is Present Here and in the Dappled Stars" (Harjo), **Supp. XII:** 225
"For Anne, at a Little Distance" (Haines), **Supp. XII:** 207
"For Annie" (Poe), **III:** 427; **Retro. Supp. II:** 263
"For a Southern Man" (Cisneros), **Supp. VII:** 67
"For Bailey" (Angelou), **Supp. IV Part 1:** 15
Forbes, Malcolm, **Supp. IV Part 1:** 94
"Forbidden, The" (Glück), **Supp. XIV:** 269
"For Bill Nestrick (1940–96)" (Bidart), **Supp. XV:** 35
For Bread Alone (Choukri), **Supp. IV Part 1:** 92
Force of Spirit, The (Sanders), **Supp. XVI:** 277–278
Forché, Carolyn, **Supp. IV Part 1:** 208
Ford, Arthur, **Supp. IV Part 1:** 140
Ford, Ford Madox, **I:** 288, 405, 409, 417, 421, 423; **II:** 58, 144, 198, 257, 263, 265, 517, 536; **III:** 458, 464–465, 470–471, 472, 476; **IV:** 27, 126, 261; **Retro. Supp. I:** 127, 177, 178, 186, 231, 286–287, 418; **Supp. II Part 1:** 107; **Supp. III Part 2:** 617; **Supp. VIII:** 107; **Supp. XIV:** 3
Ford, Harrison, **Supp. VIII:** 323
Ford, Harry, **Supp. V:** 179; **Supp. XIII:** 76
Ford, Henry, **I:** 295, 480–481; **III:** 292, 293; **Supp. I Part 1:** 21; **Supp. I Part 2:** 644; **Supp. III Part 2:** 612, 613; **Supp. IV Part 1:** 223; **Supp. V:** 290
Ford, John, **Supp. I Part 2:** 422; **Supp. III Part 2:** 619; **Supp. XVIII:** 247
Ford, Richard, **Supp. IV Part 1:** 342; **Supp. V:** 22, **57–75**
Ford, Webster (pseudonym). *See* Masters, Edgar Lee
"Fording and Dread" (Harrison), **Supp. VIII:** 41
"Ford Madox Ford" (Lowell), **II:** 547; **Retro. Supp. II:** 188
"For Dudley" (Wilbur), **Supp. III Part 2:** 558
Fordyce, David, **II:** 113
Foregone Conclusion, A (Howells), **II:** 278–279, 282
"Foreign Affairs" (Kunitz), **Supp. III Part 1:** 265
"Foreigner, A" (Bynner), **Supp. XV:** 46
"Foreigner, The" (Jewett), **II:** 409–410; **Retro. Supp. II:** 133, 142
"Foreigners" (Jarman), **Supp. XVII:** 113
"Foreign Shores" (Salter), **Supp. IX:** 260
Forensic and the Navigators (Shepard), **Supp. III Part 2:** 439
Foreseeable Future, The (Price), **Supp. VI:** 265
Foreseeable Futures (Matthews), **Supp. IX:** 155, **163,** 169
"For Esmé with Love and Squalor" (Salinger), **III:** 560
"Forest" (Simic), **Supp. VIII:** 273
Forest, Jean-Claude, **Supp. XI:** 307
Forester's Letters (Paine), **Supp. I Part 2:** 508
"Forest Hymn, A" (Bryant), **Supp. I Part 1:** 156, 162, 163, 164, 165, 170
"Forest in the Seeds, The" (Kingsolver), **Supp. VII:** 203
"Forest of the South, The" (Gordon), **II:** 199, 201
Forest of the South, The (Gordon), **II:** 197
Forest without Leaves (Adams and Haines), **Supp. XII:** 209
"Forever, Said the Duck" (Lethem), **Supp. XVIII:** 139
"Forever and the Earth" (Bradbury), **Supp. IV Part 1:** 102
"Forever in That Year" (Carruth), **Supp. XVI:** 51
"Forever Young" (Jarman and R. McDowell), **Supp. XVII:** 111
"For Fathers of Girls" (Dunn), **Supp. XI:** 146
"For/From Lew" (Snyder), **Supp. VIII:** 303
"For Garrison Keillor, Fantasy Is a Lot More Fun then Reality" (Letofsky), **Supp. XVI:** 167
"For George Santayana" (Lowell), **II:** 547
Forgotten Helper, The: A Story for Children (Moore), **Supp. X:** 175
"Forgotten in an Old Notebook" (F. Wright), **Supp. XVII:** 244
Forgotten Village, The (Steinbeck), **IV:** 51
"For Grizzel McNaught (1709–1792)" (A. Finch), **Supp. XVII:** 72
Forgue, Guy J., **III:** 118, 119
For Her Dark Skin (Everett), **Supp. XVIII:** 56, 60
"FOR HETTIE" (Baraka), **Supp. II Part 1:** 32
"FOR HETTIE IN HER FIFTH MONTH" (Baraka), **Supp. II Part 1:** 32, 38
"For Homer" (Corso), **Supp. XII:** 135
"For I'm the Boy" (Barthelme), **Supp. IV Part 1:** 47
"For Jessica, My Daughter" (Strand), **Supp. IV Part 2:** 629
"For John, Who Begs Me not to Enquire Further" (Sexton), **Supp. II Part 2:** 676
"For Johnny Pole on the Forgotten Beach" (Sexton), **Supp. II Part 2:** 675
"For Joy to Leave Upon" (Ortiz), **Supp. IV Part 2:** 508

"Fork" (Simic), **Supp. VIII:** 275
For Lancelot Andrewes (Eliot), **Retro. Supp. I:** 64
For Lizzie and Harriet (Lowell), **Retro. Supp. II:** 183, 186, 190
"Forlorn Hope of Sidney Lanier, The" (Leary), **Supp. I Part 1:** 373
"For Love" (Creeley), **Supp. IV Part 1:** 145
For Love (Creeley), **Supp. IV Part 1:** 139, 140, 142–145, 147–149, 150, 154
For Love (Miller), **Supp. XII: 297–299,** 299
For Love of Imabelle (C. Himes), **Supp. XVI:** 135, 143, 144
"Formal Elegy" (Berryman), **I:** 170
Formal Feeling Comes, A (A. Finch, ed.), **Supp. XVII: 71–72**
"Formalist Criticism: Its Principles and Limits" (Burke), **I:** 282
Forman, Milos, **Supp. IV Part 1:** 236
"Form and Function of the Novel, The" (Goldbarth), **Supp. XII:** 183
"For Marse Chouchoute" (Chopin), **Retro. Supp. II:** 60
"For Mary Ann Youngren" (Bidart), **Supp. XV:** 29
"Format and Form" (A. Rich), **Supp. XVII:** 74
"Formation of a Separatist, I" (Howe), **Supp. IV Part 2:** 427
"Form Is Emptiness" (Baraka), **Supp. II Part 1:** 51
"For Mr. Death Who Stands with His Door Open" (Sexton), **Supp. II Part 2:** 695
Forms of Discovery (Winters), **Supp. II Part 2:** 812, 813
Forms of Fiction, The (Gardner and Dunlap), **Supp. VI:** 64
"For My Children" (Karr), **Supp. XI:** 254
"For My Daughter" (Kees), **Supp. XV:** 141, 147
"For My Daughter" (Olds), **Supp. X:** 206
"For My Lover, Returning to His Wife" (Sexton), **Supp. II Part 2:** 688
"For Night to Come" (Stern), **Supp. IX:** 292
"For Once, Then, Something" (Frost), **II:** 156–157; **Retro. Supp. I:** 126, 133, 134
"For Peg: A Remnant of Song Still Distantly Sounding" (Carruth), **Supp. XVI:** 54
"For Pot-Boiling" (Hay), **Supp. XIV:** 128
"For Radicals" (Bourne), **I:** 221
"For Rainer Gerhardt" (Creeley), **Supp. IV Part 1:** 142–143, 147
Forrestal, James, **I:** 491; **Supp. I Part 2:** 489
Forrester, Fanny, **Supp. XVIII:** 13
"For Richard After All" (Kingsolver), **Supp. VII:** 208
"For Sacco and Vanzetti" (Kingsolver), **Supp. VII:** 208
"Forsaken Merman" (Arnold), **Supp. I Part 2:** 529
For Spacious Skies (Buck), **Supp. II Part 1:** 131
Forster, E. M., **I:** 292; **IV:** 201; **Retro. Supp. I:** 59, 232; **Supp. III Part 2:** 503; **Supp. IX:** 128; **Supp. V:** 258; **Supp. VIII:** 155, 171; **Supp. XII:** 79, 81; **Supp. XIV:** 159, 160, 163; **Supp. XV:** 62; **Supp. XVI:** 236; **Supp. XVIII:** 143
Forster, John, **II:** 315
Fort, Paul, **II:** 518, 528, 529; **Retro. Supp. I:** 55
"For the Ahkoond" (Bierce), **I:** 209
For the Body (Nelson), **Supp. XVIII:** 173
For the Century's End: Poems 1990–1999 (Haines), **Supp. XII: 211–213**
"For the Dedication of the New City Library, Boston" (Holmes), **Supp. I Part 1:** 308
"For the Fallen" (Levine), **Supp. V:** 188
For the Health of the Land: Previously Unpublished Essays and Other Writings (Leopold), **Supp. XIV:** 183
"For the Last Wolverine" (Dickey), **Supp. IV Part 1:** 182
"For the Lovers of the Absolute" (Simic), **Supp. VIII:** 278–279
"For the Man Cutting the Grass" (Oliver), **Supp. VII:** 235
"For the Marriage of Faustus and Helen" (H. Crane), **I:** 395–396, 399, 402; **Retro. Supp. II:** 78–79, 82
"For the Meeting of the National Sanitary Association, 1860" (Holmes), **Supp. I Part 1:** 307
For the New Intellectual (Rand), **Supp. IV Part 2:** 521, 526–527, 527, 532
"For the New Railway Station in Rome" (Wilbur), **Supp. III Part 2:** 554
"For the Night" (Kenyon), **Supp. VII:** 163
"For Theodore Roethke: 1908–1963" (Lowell), **II:** 554
"For the Poem *Patterson*" (W. C. Williams), **Retro. Supp. I:** 424
"For the Poets of Chile" (Levine), **Supp. V:** 188
"FOR THE REVOLUTIONARY OUTBURST BY BLACK PEOPLE" (Baraka), **Supp. II Part 1:** 55
"For the Sleepless" (Dunn), **Supp. XI:** 145
For the Time Being (Auden), **Supp. II Part 1:** 2, 17, 18
For the Time Being (Dillard), **Supp. VI:** 23, 27, 29, 32, **34–35**
"For the Twentieth Century" (Bidart), **Supp. XV:** 35
"For the Union Dead" (Lowell), **II:** 551; **Retro. Supp. II:** 189
For the Union Dead (Lowell), **II:** 543, 550–551, 554, 555; **Retro. Supp. II:** 181, 182, 186, 189; **Supp. X:** 53
"For the Walking Dead" (Komunyakaa), **Supp. XIII:** 121
"For the West" (Snyder), **Supp. VIII:** 299
"For the Word Is Flesh" (Kunitz), **Supp. III Part 1:** 262–264
"Fortress, The" (Glück), **Supp. V:** 82
"Fortress, The" (Sexton), **Supp. II Part 2:** 682
Fortress of Solitude, The (Lethem), **Supp. XVIII:** 135, 136, **145–148,** 150
Fortune, T. Thomas, **Supp. II Part 1:** 159
Fortune's Bones: The Manumission Requiem (Nelson), **Supp. XVIII:** 171, 172–173, 182–183
Fortune's Daughter (Hoffman), **Supp. X:** 77, 85
"Fortune Spill, The" (Nelson), **Supp. XVIII:** 175
45 Mercy Street (Sexton), **Supp. II Part 2:** 694, 695, 697
Forty Poems Touching on Recent American History (Bly, ed.), **Supp. IV Part 1:** 61
42nd Parallel, The (Dos Passos), **I:** 482, 484–485
Forty Stories (Barthelme), **Supp. IV Part 1:** 47, 49, 53, 54
For Whom the Bell Tolls (Hemingway), **II:** 249, 254–255, 261; **III:** 18, 363; **Retro. Supp. I:** 115, 176–177, 178, **184,** 187; **Supp. XVII:** 229
Foscolo, Ugo, **II:** 543
Foss, Sam Walter, **Supp. II Part 1:** 197
"Fossils, The" (Kinnell), **Supp. III Part 1:** 244
Foster, Edward, **Supp. IV Part 2:** 431, 434; **Supp. XVI:** 281, 293
Foster, Edward Halsey, **Supp. XII:** 120, 129, 130, 135; **Supp. XVIII:** 265, 268
Foster, Emily, **II:** 309
Foster, Hannah, **Supp. XV:** 234
Foster, John Wilson, **Supp. XIII:** 32–33
Foster, Phil, **Supp. IV Part 2:** 574
Foster, Richard, **Supp. XV:** 269
Foster, Stephen, **Supp. I Part 1:** 100–101; **Supp. I Part 2:** 699
Foucault, Michel, **Supp. VIII:** 5; **Supp. XII:** 98; **Supp. XV:** 344; **Supp. XVI:** 285
"Founder, The" (Stern), **Supp. IX:** 297
Founding of Harvard College, The (Morison), **Supp. I Part 2:** 485
"Fountain, The" (Bryant), **Supp. I Part 1:** 157, 165, 166, 168
Fountain, The (O'Neill), **III:** 391
Fountain and Other Poems, The (Bryant), **Supp. I Part 1:** 157
Fountainhead, The (film), **Supp. IV Part 2:** 524
Fountainhead, The (Rand), **Supp. IV Part 2:** 517, 521–523, 525, 531
Fountainhead, The: A Fiftieth Anniversary Celebration (Cox), **Supp. IV Part 2:** 523
"Fountain Piece" (Swenson), **Supp. IV Part 2:** 641
4-H Club (Shepard), **Supp. III Part 2:** 439
"Four Ages of Man, The" (Bradstreet), **Supp. I Part 1:** 111, 115
Four American Indian Literary Masters (Velie), **Supp. IV Part 2:** 486
"Four Beasts in One; the Homo Cameleopard" (Poe), **III:** 425
Four Black Revolutionary Plays (Baraka), **Supp. II Part 1:** 45; **Supp. VIII:** 330
"Four Brothers, The" (Sandburg), **III:** 585

Four Dogs and a Bone and the Wild Goose (Shanley), **Supp. XIV:** 316, **328–329**
"Four Evangelists, The" (Komunyakaa), **Supp. XIII:** 131
"Four for Sir John Davies" (Roethke), **III:** 540, 541
"Four Girls, The" (Alvarez), **Supp. VII:** 7
"Four Horse Songs" (Harjo), **Supp. XII:** 220
"400-Meter Free Style" (Kumin), **Supp. IV Part 2:** 442
Fourier, Charles, **II:** 342
"Four in a Family" (Rukeyser), **Supp. VI:** 272
Four in Hand: A Quartet of Novels (Warner), **Supp. VIII:** 164
"Four Lakes' Days" (Eberhart), **I:** 525
"Four Meetings" (James), **II:** 327
Four Million, The (O. Henry), **Supp. II Part 1:** 394, 408
"Four Monarchyes" (Bradstreet), **Supp. I Part 1:** 105, 106, 116
"Four Mountain Wolves" (Silko), **Supp. IV Part 2:** 561
Four of a Kind (Marquand), **III:** 54, 55
"Four of the Horsemen (Hypertense and Stroke, Coronary Occlusion and Cerebral Insult)" (Karr), **Supp. XI:** 250
"Four Poems" (Bishop), **Supp. I Part 1:** 92
"Four Preludes on Playthings of the Wind" (Sandburg), **III:** 586
Four Quartets (Eliot), **I:** 570, 576, 580–582, 585, 587; **II:** 537; **III:** 539; **Retro. Supp. I:** 66, 67; **Supp. II Part 1:** 1; **Supp. IV Part 1:** 284; **Supp. V:** 343, 344; **Supp. VIII:** 182, 195; **Supp. XIII:** 344; **Supp. XIV:** 167; **Supp. XV:** 216, 260, 266
Four Saints in Three Acts (Stein), **IV:** 30, 31, 33, 43, 44–45
"Four Seasons" (Bradstreet), **Supp. I Part 1:** 112–113
Four Seasons of Success, The (Schulberg), **Supp. XVIII:** 254
"Four Sides of One Story" (Updike), **Retro. Supp. I:** 328
"Four Skinny Trees" (Cisneros), **Supp. VII:** 64
"14: In A Dark Wood: Wood Thrushes" (Oliver), **Supp. VII:** 244
"14 Men Stage Head Winter 1624/ 25" (Olson), **Supp. II Part 2:** 574
14 Stories (Dixon), **Supp. XII:** 141, **145–147**
Fourteen Hundred Thousand (Shepard), **Supp. III Part 2:** 439
Fourteen Sisters of Emilio Montez O'Brien, The (Hijuelos), **Supp. VIII: 82–85**
Fourteen Stories (Buck), **Supp. II Part 1:** 126
"Fourteenth Ward, The" (H. Miller), **III:** 175
Fourth Book of Peace, The (Kingston), **Supp. V:** 173
"Fourth Down" (Marquand), **III:** 56
Fourth Group of Verse, A (Reznikoff), **Supp. XIV:** 282, 284
"Fourth of July in Maine" (Lowell), **II:** 535, 552–553
Fourth Wall, The (Gurney), **Supp. V:** 109–110
Fowler, Douglas, **Supp. IV Part 1:** 226, 227
Fowler, Gene, **Supp. VIII:** 290
Fowler, Henry Watson, **Supp. I Part 2:** 660
Fowler, Singrid, **Supp. VIII:** 249, 258
Fowler, Virginia C., **Supp. VIII:** 224
Fox, Alan, **Supp. XIII:** 120
Fox, Dixon Ryan, **I:** 337
Fox, Joe, **Supp. IX:** 259, 261
Fox, John, **Supp. XIII:** 166
Fox, Linda C., **Supp. XIII:** 217–218
Fox, Ruth, **Supp. I Part 2:** 619
"Fox, The" (Levine), **Supp. V:** 181, 189
Fox-Genovese, Elizabeth, **Supp. IV Part 1:** 286
Fox in Socks (Geisel), **Supp. XVI:** 108, 112
"Fox Night" (Jarman), **Supp. XVII:** 120
"Fox of Peapack, The" (White), **Supp. I Part 2:** 677
Fox of Peapack, The (White), **Supp. I Part 2:** 676, 677–678
Foye, Raymond, **Supp. XIV:** 150
Fraenkel, Michael, **III:** 178, 183
"Fragging" (Komunyakaa), **Supp. XIII:** 123
Fragile Beauty, A: John Nichols' Milagro Country: Text and Photographs from His Life and Work (Nichols), **Supp. XIII:** 268
"Fragility" (Shields), **Supp. VII:** 318
"Fragment" (Ashbery), **Supp. III Part 1:** 11, 13, 14, 19, 20
"Fragment" (Lowell), **II:** 516
"Fragment" (Ortiz), **Supp. IV Part 2:** 507
"Fragment of a Meditation" (Tate), **IV:** 129
"Fragment of an Agon" (Eliot), **I:** 579–580
"Fragment of a Prologue" (Eliot), **I:** 579–580
"Fragment of New York, 1929" (Eberhart), **I:** 536–537
"Fragments" (Emerson), **II:** 19
"Fragments for Fall" (Salinas), **Supp. XIII:** 320–321
"Fragments of a Hologram Rose" (W. Gibson), **Supp. XVI:** 122, 123, 128
"Fragments of a Liquidation" (Howe), **Supp. IV Part 2:** 426
Fragonard, Jean Honoré, **III:** 275; **IV:** 79
Fraiman, Susan, **Supp. IV Part 1:** 324
"Frame for Poetry, A" (W. J. Smith), **Supp. XIII:** 333
France, Anatole, **IV:** 444; **Supp. I Part 2:** 631; **Supp. XIV:** 79
France and England in North America (Parkman), **Supp. II Part 2:** 596, 600–605, 607, 613–614
Franchere, Hoyt C., **II:** 131
Franchiser, The (Elkin), **Supp. VI: 51–52,** 58
Franciosi, Robert, **Supp. XIV:** 283
Francis, Lee, **Supp. IV Part 2:** 499
Francis, Richard, **Supp. XV:** 121
Francis, Robert, **Supp. IX: 75–92**
Francis of Assisi, Saint, **III:** 543; **IV:** 69, 375, 410; **Supp. I Part 2:** 394, 397, 441, 442, 443
Franco, Francisco, **II:** 261
Franco, Harry (pseudonym). *See* Briggs, Charles Frederick
Franconia (Fraser), **Retro. Supp. I:** 136
"Franconia" tales (Abbott), **Supp. I Part 1:** 38
Frank, Anne, **Supp. X:** 149; **Supp. XVII:** 39
Frank, Frederick S., **Retro. Supp. II:** 273
Frank, James M., **Supp. XIV:** 1
Frank, Jerome, **Supp. I Part 2:** 645
Frank, Joseph, **II:** 587
Frank, Mary, **Supp. X:** 213
Frank, Robert, **Supp. XI:** 295; **Supp. XII:** 127; **Supp. XIV:** 150
Frank, Waldo, **I:** 106, 109, 117, 229, 236, 245, 259, 400; **Retro. Supp. II:** 77, 79, 83; **Supp. IX:** 308, 309, 311, 320; **Supp. XV:** 298
Frank, W. L., Jr., **Supp. XVIII:** 77
Frankel, Charles, **III:** 291
Frankel, Haskel, **Supp. I Part 2:** 448
Frankenberg, Lloyd, **I:** 436, 437, 445, 446; **III:** 194
Frankenheimer, John, **Supp. XI:** 343
Frankenstein (film), **Supp. IV Part 1:** 104; **Supp. XVII:** 57
Frankenstein (Gardner), **Supp. VI:** 72
Frankenstein (Shelley), **Supp. XII:** 79
Frankfurter, Felix, **I:** 489
"Frankie" (Keillor), **Supp. XVI:** 167
Frankie and Johnny (film), **Supp. XIII:** 206
Frankie and Johnny in the Clair de Lune (McNally), **Supp. XIII: 200,** 201
Franklin, Benjamin, **II:** 6, 8, 92, **101–125,** 127, 295, 296, 302, 306; **III:** 74, 90; **IV:** 73, 193; **Supp. I Part 1:** 306; **Supp. I Part 2:** 411, 503, 504, 506, 507, 510, 516, 518, 522, 524, 579, 639; **Supp. VIII:** 202, 205; **Supp. XIII:** 150; **Supp. XIV:** 306; **Supp. XVIII:** 12
Franklin, Cynthia, **Supp. IV Part 1:** 332
Franklin, Ruth, **Supp. XVI:** 160
Franklin, R. W., **Retro. Supp. I:** 29, 41, 43, 47
Franklin, Sarah, **II:** 122
Franklin, Temple, **II:** 122
Franklin, William, **II:** 122; **Supp. I Part 2:** 504
Franklin Evans (Whitman), **Retro. Supp. I:** 393
"Frank O'Connor and *The New Yorker*" (Maxwell), **Supp. VIII:** 172
Franks, Lucinda, **Supp. XIII:** 12
"Frank Sinatra Has a Cold" (Talese), **Supp. XVII:** 203
"Frank Stanford of the Mulberry Family: An Arkansas Epilogue" (Wright), **Supp. XV:** 339–340
"Franny" (Salinger), **III:** 564, 565–566

Franny and Zooey (Salinger), **III:** 552, 564–567; **IV:** 216; **Supp. XIII:** 263
Franzen, Jonathan, **Retro. Supp. II:** 279
Fraser, G. S., **Supp. XII:** 128; **Supp. XIV:** 162
Fraser, Joe, **III:** 46
Fraser, Marjorie Frost, **Retro. Supp. I:** 136
Frayn, Michael, **Supp. IV Part 2:** 582
Frazee, E. S., **Supp. I Part 2:** 381
Frazee, Esther Catherine. *See* Lindsay, Mrs. Vachel Thomas (Esther Catherine Frazee)
Frazer, Sir James G., **I:** 135; **II:** 204; **III:** 6–7; **IV:** 70; **Retro. Supp. I:** 80; **Supp. I Part 1:** 18; **Supp. I Part 2:** 541
Frazier, Ian, **Supp. VIII:** 272
"Freak Show, The" (Sexton), **Supp. II Part 2:** 695
Freaks: Myths and Images of the Secret Self (Fiedler), **Supp. XIII:** 106, 107
Freddy's Book (Gardner), **Supp. VI: 72**
Frederic, Harold, **I:** 409; **II: 126–149,** 175, 276, 289; **Retro. Supp. I:** 325
"Frederick Douglass" (Dunbar), **Supp. II Part 1:** 197, 199
"Frederick Douglass" (Hayden), **Supp. II Part 1:** 363
Frederick the Great, **II:** 103; **Supp. I Part 2:** 433
Fredrickson, George M., **Supp. I Part 2:** 589
"Free" (O'Hara), **III:** 369
Free, and Other Stories (Dreiser), **Retro. Supp. II:** 104
Free Agents (Apple), **Supp. XVII: 5–6**
Free Air (Lewis), **II:** 441
Freedman, Monroe H., **Supp. VIII:** 127
Freedman, Richard, **Supp. V:** 244
"Freedom" (Larsen), **Supp. XVIII:** 124
"Freedom" (White), **Supp. I Part 2:** 659
"Freedom, New Hampshire" (Kinnell), **Supp. III Part 1:** 238, 239, 251
"Freedom and Discipline" (Carruth), **Supp. XVI:** 50
Freedom Business, The (Nelson), **Supp. XVIII: 186**
Freedom Is the Right to Choose: An Inquiry into the Battle for the American Future (MacLeish), **III:** 3
"Freedom's a Hard-Bought Thing" (Benét), **Supp. XI:** 47, 48
"Freedom's Plow" (Hughes), **Supp. I Part 1:** 346
"Free Fantasia: Tiger Flowers" (Hayden), **Supp. II Part 1:** 363, 366
Freeing of the Dust, The (Levertov), **Supp. III Part 1:** 281–282
"Free Lance, The" (Mencken), **III:** 104, 105
Free-Lance Pallbearers, The (Reed), **Supp. X:** 240, **242–243,** 244
Free Life, A (Jin), **Supp. XVIII: 101–102**
Freeloaders, The (Lacy), **Supp. XV:** 204
"Free Man" (Hughes), **Supp. I Part 1:** 333
Freeman, Chris, **Supp. XIV:** 157, 159
Freeman, Douglas Southall, **Supp. I Part 2:** 486, 493
Freeman, John, **Supp. XVIII:** 90
Freeman, Joseph, **II:** 26; **Supp. I Part 2:** 610
Freeman, Mary E. Wilkins, **II:** 401; **Supp. IX:** 79
Freeman, Mary Wilkins, **Retro. Supp. II:** 51, 136, 138
Freeman, Morgan, **Supp. XII:** 317
Freeman, Suzanne, **Supp. X:** 83
Free Man, The (Richter), **Supp. XVIII:** 215
"Free Man's Worship, A" (Russell), **Supp. I Part 2:** 522
Freewheelin' Bob Dylan, The (album, Dylan), **Supp. XVIII:** 20, 24, 29
Freilicher, Jane, **Supp. XV:** 178
Freinman, Dorothy, **Supp. IX:** 94
Frémont, John Charles, **Supp. I Part 2:** 486
Fremont-Smith, Eliot, **Supp. XIII:** 263
Fremstad, Olive, **I:** 319; **Retro. Supp. I:** 10
French, Warren, **Supp. XII:** 118–119
French Chef, The (television program), **Supp. XVII:** 89
French Connection, The (film), **Supp. V:** 226
French Leave (X. J. Kennedy), **Supp. XV:** 165
French Poets and Novelists (James), **II:** 336; **Retro. Supp. I:** 220
"French Scarecrow, The" (Maxwell), **Supp. VIII:** 169, 170
French Ways and Their Meaning (Wharton), **IV:** 319; **Retro. Supp. I:** 378
Freneau, Eleanor Forman (Mrs. Philip Freneau), **Supp. II Part 1:** 266
Freneau, Philip M., **I:** 335; **II:** 295; **Supp. I Part 1:** 124, 125, 127, 145; **Supp. II Part 1:** 65, **253–277**
Frenzy (Everett), **Supp. XVIII: 59–60**
Frescoes for Mr. Rockefeller's City (MacLeish), **III:** 14–15
"Fresh Air" (Koch), **Supp. XV:** 181, 185
Fresh Air Fiend: Travel Writings, 1985–2000 (Theroux), **Supp. VIII:** 325
Fresh Brats (X. J. Kennedy), **Supp. XV:** 163
"Freshman" (Sanders), **Supp. XVI:** 277
Freud, Sigmund, **I:** 55, 58, 59, 66, 67, 135, 241, 242, 244, 247, 248, 283; **II:** 27, 370, 546–547; **III:** 134, 390, 400, 418, 488; **IV:** 7, 70, 138, 295; **Retro. Supp. I:** 80, 176, 253; **Retro. Supp. II:** 104; **Supp. I Part 1:** 13, 43, 253, 254, 259, 260, 265, 270, 315; **Supp. I Part 2:** 493, 527, 616, 643, 647, 649; **Supp. IV Part 2:** 450; **Supp. IX:** 102, 155, 161, 308; **Supp. VIII:** 103, 196; **Supp. X:** 193, 194; **Supp. XII:** 14–15; **Supp. XIII:** 75; **Supp. XIV:** 83; **Supp. XV:** 219; **Supp. XVI:** 157–158, 161, 292
"Freud and Literature" (Trilling), **Supp. III Part 2:** 502–503
Freudian Psychology and Veblen's Social Theory, The (Schneider), **Supp. I Part 2:** 650
Freudian Wish and Its Place in Ethics, The (Holt), **I:** 59
"Freud's Room" (Ozick), **Supp. V:** 268
Freud: The Mind of the Moralist (Sontag and Rieff), **Supp. III Part 2:** 455
"Freud: Within and Beyond Culture" (Trilling), **Supp. III Part 2:** 508
"Friday Morning Trial of Mrs. Solano, The" (Ríos), **Supp. IV Part 2:** 538, 548
Frieburger, William, **Supp. XIII:** 239
Friede, Donald, **Supp. XVII:** 85, 86, 87, 90
Friedenberg, Edgar Z., **Supp. VIII:** 240
Friedman, Bruce Jay, **I:** 161; **Supp. IV Part 1:** 379
Friedman, Lawrence S., **Supp. V:** 273
Friedman, Milton, **Supp. I Part 2:** 648
Friedman, Norman, **I:** 431–432, 435, 439
Friedman, Stan, **Supp. XII:** 186
Friedmann, Georges, **Supp. I Part 2:** 645
"Fried Sausage" (Simic), **Supp. VIII:** 270
Friend, Julius, **Retro. Supp. I:** 80
Friend, The (Coleridge), **II:** 10
"Friend Husband's Latest" (Sayre), **Retro. Supp. I:** 104
"Friendly Debate between a Conformist and a Non-Conformist, A" (Wild), **IV:** 155
"Friendly Neighbor" (Keillor), **Supp. XVI:** 172
Friend of the Earth (Boyle), **Supp. VIII:** 12, 16
"Friend of the Fourth Decade, The" (Merrill), **Supp. III Part 1:** 327
"Friends" (Beattie), **Supp. V:** 23, 27
"Friends" (Paley), **Supp. VI:** 219, 226
"Friends" (Sexton), **Supp. II Part 2:** 693
Friend's Delight, The (Bierce), **I:** 195
"Friends from Philadelphia" (Updike), **Retro. Supp. I:** 319
"Friendship" (Emerson), **Supp. II Part 1:** 290
Friends: More Will and Magna Stories (Dixon), **Supp. XII:** 148, 149
"Friends of Heraclitus, The" (Simic), **Supp. VIII:** 284
"Friends of Kafka, The" (Singer), **Retro. Supp. II:** 308
"Friends of the Family, The" (McCarthy), **II:** 566
"Friend to Alexander, A" (Thurber), **Supp. I Part 2:** 616
"Frigate Pelican, The" (Moore), **III:** 208, 210–211, 215
"Frill, The" (Buck), **Supp. XIV:** 274
"Fringe, The" (Bass), **Supp. XVI:** 19
Frobenius, Leo, **III:** 475; **Supp. III Part 2:** 620
Froebel, Friedrich, **Supp. XIV:** 52–53
Frog (Dixon), **Supp. XII:** 151
"Frog Dances" (Dixon), **Supp. XII:** 151
"Frog Pond, The" (Kinnell), **Supp. III Part 1:** 254
"Frogs" (Nelson), **Supp. XVIII:** 176

"Frog Takes a Swim" (Dixon), **Supp. XII:** 152
Frohock, W. M., **I:** 34, 42
Frolic of His Own, A (Gaddis), **Supp. IV Part 1:** 279, 291, 292–294
"From a Mournful Village" (Jewett), **Retro. Supp. II:** 146
"From an Alabama Farm" (Nelson), **Supp. XVIII:** 182
"From an Old House in America" (Rich), **Supp. I Part 2:** 551, 565–567
From Another World (Untermeyer), **Supp. XV:** 293, 303, 310–311, 313
"From a Roadside Motel" (F. Wright), **Supp. XVII:** 245
"From a Survivor" (Rich), **Supp. I Part 2:** 563
From A to Z (musical review; Allen), **Supp. XV:** 3, 13
From a Writer's Notebook (Brooks), **I:** 254
From Bauhaus to Our House (Wolfe), **Supp. III Part 2:** 580, 581, 584
From Bondage (H. Roth), **Supp. IX:** 236, **238–240**
"From *Chants* to *Borders* to *Communion*" (Fox), **Supp. XIII:** 217–218
"From Chicago" (Anderson), **I:** 108–109
From Death to Morning (Wolfe), **IV:** 450, 456, 458
"From Dick to Lethem: The Dickian Legacy, Postmodernism, and Avant-Pop in Jonathan Lethem's *Amnesia Moon*" (Rossi), **Supp. XVIII:** 137, 138–139
"From Discord, a Wife Makes a Nice New Life——Too Nice" (Linfield), **Supp. XVII:** 177
"From Feathers to Iron" (Kunitz), **Supp. III Part 1:** 261
"From Fifth Avenue Up" (Barnes), **Supp. III Part 1:** 33, 44
"From Gorbunov and Gorchakov" (Brodsky), **Supp. VIII:** 26
"From Grand Canyon to Burbank" (H. Miller), **III:** 186
"From Hell to Breakfast," **Supp. IX:** 326–327
From Here to Eternity (film), **Supp. XI:** 221
From Here to Eternity (Jones), **I:** 477; **Supp. XI:** 215, 216, 217, 218, **219–221,** 223, 224, 226, 229, 230, 231, 232, 234
From Here to Eternity (miniseries), **Supp. XI:** 234
From Jordan's Delight (Blackmur), **Supp. II Part 1:** 91
"From Lumaghi Mine" (Wrigley), **Supp. XVIII:** 295
Fromm, Erich, **I:** 58; **Supp. VIII:** 196
From Morn to Midnight (Kaiser), **I:** 479
"From Native Son to Invisible Man" (Locke), **Supp. IX:** 306
"From Pico, the Women: A Life" (Creeley), **Supp. IV Part 1:** 149
From Ritual to Romance (Weston), **II:** 540; **III:** 12; **Supp. I Part 2:** 439
"From Room to Room" (Kenyon), **Supp. VII:** 159, 163–165
From Room to Room (Kenyon), **Supp. VII:** 163–165, 166, 167
From Sand Creek: Rising in this Heart Which Is Our America (Ortiz), **Supp. IV Part 2:** 512–513
"From Sea Cliff, March" (Swenson), **Supp. IV Part 2:** 649
"From the Antigone" (Yeats), **III:** 459
From the Ashes: Voices of Watts (Schulberg, ed.), **Supp. XVIII:** 254
From the Barrio: A Chicano Anthology (Salinas and Faderman, eds.), **Supp. XIII:** 313
"From the Childhood of Jesus" (Pinsky), **Supp. VI:** 244–245, 247
"From the Corpse Woodpiles, From the Ashes" (Hayden), **Supp. II Part 1:** 370
"From the Country to the City" (Bishop), **Supp. I Part 1:** 85, 86
"From the Cupola" (Merrill), **Supp. III Part 1:** 324–325, 331
"From the Dark Side of the Earth" (Oates), **Supp. II Part 2:** 510
"From the Diary of a New York Lady" (Parker), **Supp. IX:** 201
"From the Diary of One Not Born" (Singer), **IV:** 9
"From the East, Light" (Carver), **Supp. III Part 1:** 138
From the First Nine: Poems 1946–1976 (Merrill), **Supp. III Part 1:** 336
"From the Flats" (Lanier), **Supp. I Part 1:** 364
From the Flower Courtyard (Everwine), **Supp. XV:** 75
From the Heart of Europe (Matthiessen), **III:** 310
From the Meadow: Selected and New Poems (Everwine), **Supp. XV:** 75, **88–89**
"From the Memoirs of a Private Detective" (Hammett), **Supp. IV Part 1:** 343
"From the Nursery" (Kenyon), **Supp. VII:** 171
"From the Poets in the Kitchen" (Marshall), **Supp. XI:** 277
From the Terrace (O'Hara), **III:** 362
"From the Thirties: Tillie Olsen and the Radical Tradition" (Rosenfelt), **Supp. XIII:** 296, 304
"From Trollope's Journal" (Bishop), **Retro. Supp. II:** 47
"Front, A" (Jarrell), **II:** 374
Front, The (film), **Supp. I Part 1:** 295
"Front and the Back Parts of the House, The" (Maxwell), **Supp. VIII:** 169
Frontier Eden (Bigelow), **Supp. X:** 227
"Frontiers of Culture" (Locke), **Supp. XIV:** 213
"Front Lines" (Snyder), **Supp. VIII:** 301
Frost, A. B., **Retro. Supp. II:** 72
Frost, Carol, **Supp. XV: 91–109**
Frost, Isabelle Moodie, **II:** 150, 151
Frost, Jeanie, **II:** 151
Frost, Richard, **Supp. XV:** 92
Frost, Robert, **I:** 26, 27, 60, 63, 64, 171, 229, 303, 326, 418; **II:** 55, 58, **150–172,** 276, 289, 388, 391, 471, 523, 527, 529, 535; **III:** 5, 23, 67, 269, 271, 272, 275, 287, 453, 510, 523, 536, 575, 581, 591; **IV:** 140, 190, 415; **Retro. Supp. I:** 67, **121–144,** 276, 287, 292, 298, 299, 311, 413; **Retro. Supp. II:** 40, 47, 50, 146, 178, 181; **Supp. I Part 1:** 80, 242, 263, 264; **Supp. I Part 2:** 387, 461, 699; **Supp. II Part 1:** 4, 19, 26, 103; **Supp. III Part 1:** 63, 74–75, 239, 253; **Supp. III Part 2:** 546, 592, 593; **Supp. IV Part 1:** 15; **Supp. IV Part 2:** 439, 445, 447, 448, 599, 601; **Supp. IX:** 41, 42, 75, 76, 80, 87, 90, 266, 308; **Supp. VIII:** 20, 30, 32, 98, 100, 104, 259, 292; **Supp. X:** 64, 65, 66, 74, 120, 172; **Supp. XI:** 43, 123, 150, 153, 312; **Supp. XII:** 130, 241, 303, 307; **Supp. XIII:** 143, 147, 334–335; **Supp. XIV:** 42, 122, 222, 229; **Supp. XV:** 21, 51, 65, 96, 212, 215, 250, 256, 293, 296, 299, 301, 302, 306, 348; **Supp. XVII:** 36, 110, 115–116; **Supp. XVIII:** 298, 300
Frost, William Prescott, **II:** 150–151
"Frost: A Dissenting Opinion" (Cowley), **Supp. II Part 1:** 143
Frost: A Time to Talk (Francis), **Supp. IX:** 76, **85–86**
"Frost at Midnight" (Coleridge), **Supp. X:** 71
"Frost Flowers" (Kenyon), **Supp. VII:** 168
"Frost: He Is Sometimes a Poet and Sometimes a Stump-Speaker" (News-Week), **Retro. Supp. I:** 137
Frothingham, Nathaniel, **I:** 3
Frothingham, Octavius B., **IV:** 173
"Frozen City, The" (Nemerov), **III:** 270
"Frozen Fields, The" (Bowles), **Supp. IV Part 1:** 80
"Fruit Garden Path, The" (Lowell), **II:** 516
"Fruit of the Flower" (Cullen), **Supp. IV Part 1:** 167
Fruit of the Tree, The (Wharton), **IV:** 314–315; **Retro. Supp. I:** 367, **370–371,** 373
"Fruit of Travel Long Ago" (Melville), **III:** 93
Fruits and Vegetables (Jong), **Supp. V:** 113, 115, 117, 118, 119
Frumkes, Lewis Burke, **Supp. XII:** 335–336
Fry, Christopher, **Supp. I Part 1:** 270
Fry, Roger, **Supp. XIV:** 336
Frye, Joanne, **Supp. XIII:** 292, 296, 298, 302
Frye, Northrop, **Supp. I Part 2:** 530; **Supp. II Part 1:** 101; **Supp. X:** 80; **Supp. XIII:** 19; **Supp. XIV:** 11, 15; **Supp. XVI:** 149, 156
Fryer, Judith, **Retro. Supp. I:** 379
F. Scott Fitzgerald: A Critical Portrait (Piper), **Supp. IX:** 65
"F. S. F., 1896–1996, R.I.P." (Doctorow), **Retro. Supp. I:** 97
Fuchs, Daniel, **Supp. XIII:** 106
Fuchs, Miriam, **Supp. IV Part 1:** 284

Fuehrer Bunker, The (Snodgrass), **Supp. VI:** 314, 315–317, 319–321
"Fuel" (Nye), **Supp. XIII:** 283
Fuel (Nye), **Supp. XIII:** 277, **282–284**
Fuertes, Gloria, **Supp. V:** 178
Fugard, Athol, **Supp. VIII:** 330; **Supp. XIII:** 205
Fugitive Group, The (Cowan), **IV:** 120
Fugitive Kind, The (T. Williams), **IV:** 381, 383
Fugitives, The (group), **IV:** 122, 124, 125, 131, 237, 238
Fugitives, The: A Critical Account (Bradbury), **IV:** 130
"Fugitive Slave Law, The" (Emerson), **II:** 13
Fugitive's Return (Glaspell), **Supp. III Part 1:** 182–184
Fuller, B. A. G., **III:** 605
Fuller, Hiram, **Supp. XVIII:** 12,14
Fuller, Jesse "Lonecat," **Supp. XV:** 147
Fuller, Margaret, **I:** 261; **II:** 7, 276; **IV:** 172; **Retro. Supp. I:** 155–156, 163; **Retro. Supp. II:** 46; **Supp. I Part 2:** 524; **Supp. II Part 1: 279–306; Supp. IX:** 37; **Supp. XVIII:** 3, 11, 12, 16
Fuller, Thomas, **II:** 111, 112
Fullerton Street (Wilson), **Supp. VIII:** 331
"Full Fathom Five" (Plath), **Supp. I Part 2:** 538
Full Measure: Modern Short Stories on Aging (D. Sennett, ed.), **Supp. XVI:** 37
Full Monty, The (musical, McNally), **Supp. XIII:** 207
"Full Moon" (Hayden), **Supp. II Part 1:** 370
Full Moon and Other Plays (Price), **Supp. VI:** 266
"Full Moon and You're Not Here" (Cisneros), **Supp. VII:** 71–72
"Full Moon: New Guinea" (Shapiro), **Supp. II Part 2:** 707
"Fullness of Life, The" (Wharton), **Retro. Supp. I:** 363
Full of Life (Fante), **Supp. XI:** 160
Full of Life (film), **Supp. XI:** 170
Full of Lust and Good Usage (Dunn), **Supp. XI: 145–147**
"Full Summer" (Olds), **Supp. X:** 212
Fulton, Robert, **Supp. I Part 2:** 519; **Supp. II Part 1:** 73
Function of Criticism, The (Winters), **Supp. II Part 2:** 812, 813
"Fundamentalism" (Tate), **IV:** 125
"Fundamental Project of Technology, The" (Kinnell), **Supp. III Part 1:** 253
"Funeral of Bobò, The" (Brodsky), **Supp. VIII:** 27, 28
"Funnel" (Sexton), **Supp. II Part 2:** 675
"Furious Seasons, The" (Carver), **Supp. III Part 1:** 137
Furious Seasons and Other Stories (Carver), **Supp. III Part 1:** 142, 143, 146
"Furious Versions" (L.-Y. Lee), **Supp. XV: 215–217,** 218, 220
"Furnished Room, The" (Hayden), **Supp. II Part 1:** 386–387, 394, 397, 399, 406, 408
"Furor Scribendi" (O. Butler), **Supp. XIII:** 70
Furors Die (Hoffman), **Supp. XVIII: 80–81**
Fur Person, The (Sarton), **Supp. VIII: 264–265**
Further Adventures with You (Wright), **Supp. XV:** 339, 342**, 343–345**
Further Fables for Our Time (Thurber), **Supp. I Part 2:** 612
"Further in Summer than the Birds" (Dickinson), **I:** 471
Further Poems of Emily Dickinson (Bianchi and Hampson, ed.), **Retro. Supp. I:** 35
Further Range, A (Frost), **II:** 155; **Retro. Supp. I:** 132, 136, 137, 138, 139
"Fury of Aerial Bombardment, The" (Eberhart), **I:** 535–536
"Fury of Flowers and Worms, The" (Sexton), **Supp. II Part 2:** 694
"Fury of Rain Storms, The" (Sexton), **Supp. II Part 2:** 695
Fury of the Jungle (film), **Supp. XIII:** 163
Fussell, Paul, **Supp. V:** 241
"Future, if Any, of Comedy, The" (Thurber), **Supp. I Part 2:** 620
Future is Ours, Comrade, The: Conversations with the Russians (Kosinski), **Supp. VII:** 215
Futureland: Nine Stories of an Imminent World (Mosley), **Supp. XIII: 247–249**
"Future Life, The" (Bryant), **Supp. I Part 1:** 170
Future Punishment of the Wicked, The (Edwards), **I:** 546

G
"Gabriel" (Rich), **Supp. I Part 2:** 557
Gabriel, Ralph H., **Supp. I Part 1:** 251
Gabriel, Trip, **Supp. V:** 212
Gabriel Conroy (Harte), **Supp. II Part 1:** 354
"Gabriel's Truth" (Kenyon), **Supp. VII:** 166
Gaddis, William, **Supp. IV Part 1: 279–296; Supp. IV Part 2:** 484; **Supp. IX:** 208; **Supp. V:** 52; **Supp. X:** 301, 302
Gadiot, Pud, **Supp. XI:** 295
Gain (Powers), **Supp. IX:** 212, **220–221**
Gaines, Ernest, **Supp. X:** 250
Gaines, Ernest J., **Supp. X:** 24
Gaines, James R., **Supp. IX:** 190
Gaitens, Peter, **Supp. XV:** 65
Galamain, Ivan, **Supp. III Part 2:** 624
Galassi, Jonathan, **Supp. XVIII:** 92
Galatea 2.2 (Powers), **Supp. IX:** 212, **219–220**
"Galatea Encore" (Brodsky), **Supp. VIII:** 31
Galbraith, John Kenneth, **Supp. I Part 2:** 645, 650
Galdós, Benito Pérez. *See* Pérez Galdós, Benito
Gale, Zona, **Supp. I Part 2:** 613; **Supp. VIII:** 155
"Gale in April" (Jeffers), **Supp. II Part 2:** 423
Galignani, Giovanni Antonio, **II:** 315
Galileo Galilei, **I:** 480–481; **Supp. XII:** 180; **Supp. XIII:** 75
Gallagher, Tess, **Supp. XVI:** 36; **Supp. XVII:** 110
Gallant, Mavis, **Supp. VIII:** 151
Gallatin, Albert, **I:** 5
"Gallery" (Goldbarth), **Supp. XII:** 188
"Gallery of Real Creatures, A" (Thurber), **Supp. I Part 2:** 619
Gallico, Paul, **Supp. XVI:** 238
Gallows Songs (Snodgrass), **Supp. VI:** 317
Gallup, Donald, **III:** 404, 478
Galsworthy, John, **III:** 70, 153, 382
Galton Case, The (Macdonald), **Supp. IV Part 2:** 463, 473, 474
"Gal Young 'Un" (Rawlings), **Supp. X:** 228
"Gambler, the Nun, and the Radio, The" (Hemingway), **II:** 250
"Gambler's Wife, The" (Dunbar), **Supp. II Part 1:** 196
Gambone, Philip, **Supp. XII:** 81
"Gambrel Roof, A" (Larcom), **Supp. XIII:** 144
"Game at Salzburg, A" (Jarrell), **II:** 384, 389
Game Management (Leopold), **Supp. XIV:** 182
"Game of Catch, A" (Wilbur), **Supp. III Part 2:** 552
Game Players of Titan, The (Dick), **Supp. XVIII:** 138
"Games in Frank Conroy's *Stop-Time*" (T. Adams), **Supp. XVI:** 67
"Games Two" (Wilbur), **Supp. III Part 2:** 550
Gammelgaard, Lene, **Supp. XVIII:** 112
"Gamut, The" (Angelou), **Supp. IV Part 1:** 15
Gander, Forrest, **Supp. XV:** 339, 340, 342
Gandhi, Indira, **Supp. X:** 108
Gandhi, Mahatma, **III:** 179, 296–297; **IV:** 170, 185, 367; **Supp. VIII:** 203, 204; **Supp. X:** 27
Gandhi on Non-Violence (Merton, ed.), **Supp. VIII:** 204–205
"Gang of Mirrors, The" (Simic), **Supp. VIII:** 283
Gansevoort, Guert, **III:** 94
Gansevoort, Peter, **III:** 92
"Gap" (Bierds), **Supp. XVII:** 35–36
Garabedian, Michael, **Supp. XIII:** 115
Garbage (Ammons), **Supp. VII:** 24, 35–36
Garbage (Dixon), **Supp. XII:** 147, 148
Garbage Man, The (Dos Passos), **I:** 478, 479, 481, 493
Garber, Frederick, **Supp. IX:** 294–295
Garbo, Greta, **Supp. I Part 2:** 616
García, Cristina, **Supp. VIII:** 74; **Supp. XI: 177–192**
García Lorca, Federico. *See* Lorca, Federico García
"García Lorca: A Photograph of the Granada Cemetery, 1966" (Levis), **Supp. XI:** 264

García Márquez, Gabriel, **Supp. V:** 244; **Supp. VIII:** 81, 82, 84, 85; **Supp. XII:** 147, 310, 316, 322; **Supp. XIII:** 226; **Supp. XVII:** 45
"Garden" (Marvell), **IV:** 161; **Supp. XVI:** 204
"Garden, The" (Glück), **Supp. V:** 83
"Garden, The" (Strand), **Supp. IV Part 2:** 629
"Garden Among Tombs" (B. Kelly), **Supp. XVII:** 126
"Garden by Moonlight, The" (Lowell), **II:** 524
"Gardener Delivers a Fawn, The" (C. Frost), **Supp. XV:** 99
Gardener's Son, The (McCarthy), **Supp. VIII:** 187
"Gardenias" (Doty), **Supp. XI:** 122
"Gardenias" (Monette), **Supp. X:** 159
"Garden Lodge, The" (Cather), **I:** 316, 317
Garden of Adonis, The (Gordon), **II:** 196, 204–205, 209
Garden of Earthly Delights, A (Oates), **Supp. II Part 2:** 504, 507–509
"Garden of Eden" (Hemingway), **II:** 259
Garden of Eden, The (Hemingway), **Retro. Supp. I:** 186, **187–188**
"Garden of Flesh, Garden of Stone" (B. Kelly), **Supp. XVII:** 128
"Garden of the Moon, The" (Doty), **Supp. XI:** 122
"Garden of the Trumpet Tree, The" (B. Kelly), **Supp. XVII:** 131
"Gardens, The" (Oliver), **Supp. VII:** 236
"Gardens of Mont-Saint-Michel, The" (Maxwell), **Supp. VIII:** 169
"Gardens of the Villa D'Este, The" (Hecht), **Supp. X:** 59
"Gardens of Zuñi, The" (Merwin), **Supp. III Part 1:** 351
Gardiner, Judith Kegan, **Supp. IV Part 1:** 205
Gardner, Erle Stanley, **Supp. IV Part 1:** 121, 345
Gardner, Isabella, **IV:** 127
Gardner, John, **Supp. I Part 1:** 193, 195, 196; **Supp. III Part 1:** 136, 142, 146; **Supp. VI: 61–76**
Gardons, S. S. *See* Snodgrass, W. D.
"Gare de Lyon" (M. F. K. Fisher), **Supp. XVII:** 91
Garfield, John, **Supp. XII:** 160
Garibaldi, Giuseppe, **I:** 4; **II:** 284
Garibay, Angel M., **Supp. XV:** 77
Garland, Hamlin, **I:** 407; **II:** 276, 289; **III:** 576; **Retro. Supp. I:** 133; **Retro. Supp. II:** 72; **Supp. I Part 1:** 217; **Supp. IV Part 2:** 502; **Supp. XVIII:** 6
Garland Companion, The (Zverev), **Retro. Supp. I:** 278
Garments the Living Wear (Purdy), **Supp. VII:** 278–279, 280–281
Garner, Dwight, **Supp. X:** 202; **Supp. XVIII:** 89
Garnett, Edward, **I:** 405, 409, 417; **III:** 27
Garrett, George, **Supp. XVIII:** 74, 75
Garrett, George P., **Supp. I Part 1:** 196; **Supp. VII: 95–113; Supp. X:** 3, 7; **Supp. XI:** 218
Garrigue, Jean, **Supp. XII:** 260
Garrison, Deborah, **Supp. IX:** 299
Garrison, Fielding, **III:** 105
Garrison, William Lloyd, **Supp. I Part 2:** 524, 588, 683, 685, 686, 687; **Supp. XIV:** 54
"Garrison of Cape Ann, The" (Whittier), **Supp. I Part 2:** 691, 694
Garry Moore Show (television show), **Supp. IV Part 2:** 575
"Garter Motif" (White), **Supp. I Part 2:** 673
Gartner, Zsuzsi, **Supp. X:** 276
Garvey, Marcus, **Supp. III Part 1:** 175, 180; **Supp. IV Part 1:** 168; **Supp. X:** 135, 136
Gas (Kaiser), **I:** 479
Gas-House McGinty (Farrell), **II:** 41–42
Gaskell, Elizabeth, A., **Supp. I Part 2:** 580
Gasoline (Corso), **Supp. XII:** 118, **121–123,** 134
Gass, William, **Supp. XVII:** 183
Gass, William H., **Supp. IX:** 208; **Supp. V:** 44, 52, 238; **Supp. VI: 77–96; Supp. XII:** 152; **Supp. XIV:** 305
Gassner, John, **IV:** 381; **Supp. I Part 1:** 284, 292
"Gas Stations" (Apple), **Supp. XVII:** 4
Gastronomical Me, The (M. F. K. Fisher), **Supp. XVII:** 84, 85, 87, 91, 92
Gates, David, **Supp. V:** 24; **Supp. XIII:** 93; **Supp. XVI:** 73, 74
Gates, Elmer, **I:** 515–516
Gates, Henry Louis, Jr., **Retro. Supp. I:** 194, 195, 203; **Supp. X:** 242, 243, 245, 247; **Supp. XVIII:** 287
Gates, Lewis E., **III:** 315, 330
Gates, Sondra Smith, **Supp. XVIII:** 267, 269
"Gates, The" (Rukeyser), **Supp. VI:** 286
Gates, The (Rukeyser), **Supp. VI:** 271, 274, 281
Gates, Tudor, **Supp. XI:** 307
Gates of Ivory, the Gates of Horn, The (McGrath), **Supp. X:** 118
Gates of Wrath, The; Rhymed Poems (Ginsberg), **Supp. II Part 1:** 311, 319
"Gathering of Dissidents, A" (Applebaum), **Supp. XVI:** 153
Gathering of Fugitives, A (Trilling), **Supp. III Part 2:** 506, 512
Gathering of Zion, The: The Story of the Mormon Trail (Stegner), **Supp. IV Part 2:** 599, 602–603
Gather Together in My Name (Angelou), **Supp. IV Part 1:** 2, 3, 4–6, 11
Gathorne-Hardy, Robert, **Supp. XIV:** 344, 347, 348, 349
Gaudier-Brzeska, Henri, **III:** 459, 464, 465, 477
Gauguin, Paul, **I:** 34; **IV:** 290; **Supp. IV Part 1:** 81; **Supp. XII:** 128
"Gauley Bridge" (Rukeyser), **Supp. VI:** 278
Gauss, Christian, **II:** 82; **IV:** 427, 439–440, 444
Gautier, Théophile, **II:** 543; **III:** 466, 467; **Supp. I Part 1:** 277
Gay, John, **II:** 111; **Supp. I Part 2:** 523; **Supp. XIV:** 337
Gay, Peter, **I:** 560
Gay, Sydney Howard, **Supp. I Part 1:** 158; **Supp. XVIII:** 3
Gay, Walter, **IV:** 317
Gayatri Prayer, The, **III:** 572
"Gay Chaps at the Bar" (Brooks), **Supp. III Part 1:** 74, 75
Gaylord, Winfield R., **III:** 579–580
Gay Talese Reader, The: Portraits & Encounters (Talese), **Supp. XVII:** 202, 208
"Gazebo" (Carver), **Supp. III Part 1:** 138, 144, 145
Gazer Within, The, and Other Essays by Larry Levis, **Supp. XI:** 270
Gazzara, Ben, **Supp. VIII:** 319
Gazzo, Michael V., **III:** 155
"Geese Gone Beyond" (Snyder), **Supp. VIII:** 304
"Gegenwart" (Goethe), **Supp. II Part 1:** 26
Geisel, Theodor Seuss (Dr. Seuss), **Supp. X:** 56; **Supp. XVI: 97–115**
Geismar, Maxwell, **II:** 178, 431; **III:** 71; **Supp. IX:** 15; **Supp. XI:** 223
Gelb, Arthur, **IV:** 380
Gelbart, Larry, **Supp. IV Part 2:** 591
Gelder, Robert Van, **Supp. XIII:** 166
Gelfant, Blanche, **Supp. XVII:** 161
Gelfant, Blanche H., **II:** 27, 41
Gelfman, Jean, **Supp. X:** 3
Gellhorn, Martha. *See* Hemingway, Mrs. Ernest (Martha Gellhorn)
Gelpi, Albert, **Supp. I Part 2:** 552, 554, 560
Gelpi, Barbara, **Supp. I Part 2:** 560
Gemini: an extended autobiographical statement on my first twenty-five years of being a black poet (Giovanni), **Supp. IV Part 1:** 11
"Gen" (Snyder), **Supp. VIII:** 302
"Gender Norms" (Radinovsky), **Supp. XV:** 285
"Gender of Sound, The" (Carson), **Supp. XII: 106**
"Genealogy" (Komunyakaa), **Supp. XIII:** 129
"General Aims and Theories" (Crane), **I:** 389
General Died at Dawn, The (Odets), **Supp. II Part 2:** 546
"General Gage's Confession" (Freneau), **Supp. II Part 1:** 257
"General Gage's Soliloquy" (Freneau), **Supp. II Part 1:** 257
General History of the Robberies and Murders of the Most Notorious Pyrates from Their First Rise and Settlement in the Island of New Providence to the Present Year, A (Johnson), **Supp. V:** 128
"General William Booth Enters into Heaven" (Lindsay), **Supp. I Part 2:** 374, 382, 384, 385–388, 389, 392, 399

General William Booth Enters into Heaven and Other Poems (Lindsay), **Supp. I Part 2:** 379, 381, 382, 387–388, 391
"Generations of Men, The" (Frost), **Retro. Supp. I:** 128; **Supp. XIII:** 147
Generous Man, A (Price), **Supp. VI:** 259, 260, 261
Genesis (biblical book), **I:** 279; **II:** 540; **Retro. Supp. I:** 250, 256; **Supp. XII:** 54
"Genesis" (Stegner), **Supp. IV Part 2:** 604
Genesis: Book One (Schwartz), **Supp. II Part 2:** 640, 651–655
Genet, Jean, **I:** 71, 82, 83, 84; **Supp. IV Part 1:** 8; **Supp. XI:** 308; **Supp. XII:** 1; **Supp. XIII:** 74; **Supp. XVII:** 95
"Genetic Expedition" (Dove), **Supp. IV Part 1:** 249, 257
"Genetics of Justice" (Alvarez), **Supp. VII:** 19
"Genial Host, The" (McCarthy), **II:** 564
"Genie in the Bottle, The" (Wilbur), **Supp. III Part 2:** 542
"Genius, The" (MacLeish), **III:** 19
Genius and Lust: A Journey through the Major Writings of Henry Miller (Mailer), **Retro. Supp. II:** 208
"Genius Child" (Hughes), **Retro. Supp. I:** 203
"Genius of Bob Dylan, The" (Lethem), **Supp. XVIII:** 146
"Genius," The (Dreiser), **I:** 497, 501, 509–511, 519; **Retro. Supp. II:** 94–95, **102–103,** 104, 105
"Genteel Tradition in American Philosophy, The" (Santayana), **I:** 222
"Gentle Communion" (Mora), **Supp. XIII:** 218–219
Gentle Crafter, The (O. Henry), **Supp. II Part 1:** 410
"Gentle Lena, The" (Stein), **IV:** 37, 40
Gentleman Caller, The (T. Williams), **IV:** 383
"Gentleman from Cracow, The" (Singer), **IV:** 9
"Gentleman of Bayou Têche, A" (Chopin), **Supp. I Part 1:** 211–212
"Gentleman of Shalott, The" (Bishop), **Supp. I Part 1:** 85, 86
Gentleman's Agreement (Hobson), **III:** 151
Gentlemen Prefer Blondes (Loos; musical adaptation), **Supp. XVI:** 193
Gentlemen Prefer Blondes: The Illuminating Diary of a Professional Lady (Loos), **Supp. XVI:** 181, 183, 186, **188–189**
Gentlemen Prefer "Books" (J. Yeats), **Supp. XVI:** 190
Gentry, Marshall Bruce, **Supp. IV Part 1:** 236
"Genuine Man, The" (Emerson), **II:** 10
Geo-Bestiary (Harrison), **Supp. VIII:** 53
"Geode" (Frost), **II:** 161
Geographical History of America, The (Stein), **IV:** 31, 45; **Supp. XVIII:** 148
Geography and Plays (Stein), **IV:** 29–30, 32, 43, 44
Geography III (Bishop), **Retro. Supp. II:** 50; **Supp. I Part 1:** 72, 73, 76, 82, 93, 94, 95
Geography of a Horse Dreamer (Shepard), **Supp. III Part 2:** 432
Geography of Home, The: California's Poetry of Place (Bluckey and Young, eds.), **Supp. XIII:** 313
Geography of Lograire, The (Merton), **Supp. VIII:** 208
Geography of the Heart (Johnson), **Supp. XI:** 129
"Geometric Poem, The" (Corso), **Supp. XII:** 132, 133–134
George, Diana Hume, **Supp. IV Part 2:** 447, 449, 450
George, Henry, **II:** 276; **Supp. I Part 2:** 518
George, Jan, **Supp. IV Part 1:** 268
George, Lynell, **Supp. XIII:** 234–235, 237, 249
George, Peter, **Supp. XI:** 302, 303, 304
George and the Dragon (Shanley), **Supp. XIV:** 315
George Bernard Shaw: His Plays (Mencken), **III:** 102
George Mills (Elkin), **Supp. VI: 53–54**
George Palmer Putnam: Representative American Publisher (Greenspan), **Supp. XVIII:** 257
"George Robinson: Blues" (Rukeyser), **Supp. VI:** 279
George's Mother (Crane), **I:** 408
"George Thurston" (Bierce), **I:** 202
George Washington Crossing the Delaware (Koch), **Supp. XV:** 186
Georgia Boy (Caldwell), **I:** 288, 305–306, 308, 309, 310
"Georgia Dusk" (Toomer), **Supp. IX:** 309
"Georgia: Invisible Empire State" (Du Bois), **Supp. II Part 1:** 179
"Georgia Night" (Toomer), **Supp. III Part 2:** 481
Georgia Scenes (Longstreet), **II:** 70, 313; **Supp. I Part 1:** 352
Georgics (Virgil), **Retro. Supp. I:** 135; **Supp. XVI:** 22
Georgoudaki, Ekaterini, **Supp. IV Part 1:** 12
Gerald McBoing-Boing (film), **Supp. XVI:** 102
"Geraldo No Last Name" (Cisneros), **Supp. VII:** 60–61
Gerald's Game (King), **Supp. V:** 141, 148–150, 151, 152
Gerald's Party (Coover), **Supp. V:** 49–50, 51, 52
Gérando, Joseph Marie de, **II:** 10
"Geranium" (O'Connor), **Retro. Supp. II:** 221, 236
Gerber, Dan, **Supp. VIII:** 39
Gerhardt, Rainer, **Supp. IV Part 1:** 142
"German Girls! The German Girls!, The" (MacLeish), **III:** 16
"German Refugee, The" (Malamud), **Supp. I Part 2:** 436, 437
"Germany's Reichswehr" (Agee), **I:** 35
Germinal (Zola), **III:** 318, 322
Gernsback, Hugo, **Supp. IV Part 1:** 101
"Gernsback Continuum, The" (W. Gibson), **Supp. XVI:** 123, 128
"Gerontion" (Eliot), **I:** 569, 574, 577, 578, 585, 588; **III:** 9, 435, 436; **Retro. Supp. I:** 290; **Supp. XV:** 341; **Supp. XVI:** 158–159
Gerry, Elbridge, **Supp. I Part 2:** 486
"Gerry's Jazz" (Komunyakaa), **Supp. XIII:** 125
Gershwin, Ira, **Supp. I Part 1:** 281
"Gert" (Monette), **Supp. X:** 158
Gertrude of Stony Island Avenue (Purdy), **Supp. VII:** 281–282
Gertrude Stein (Sprigge), **IV:** 31
Gertrude Stein: A Biography of Her Work (Sutherland), **IV:** 38
"Gertrude Stein and the Geography of the Sentence" (Gass), **Supp. VI:** 87
Gesell, Silvio, **III:** 473
"Gestalt at Sixty" (Sarton), **Supp. VIII:** 260
"Gesture toward an Unfound Renaissance, A" (Stafford), **Supp. XI:** 323
Getlin, Josh, **Supp. V:** 22; **Supp. VIII:** 75, 76, 78, 79
"Getting Along" (Larcom), **Supp. XIII:** 144
"Getting Along with Nature" (Berry), **Supp. X:** 31–32
"Getting Away from Already Pretty Much Being Away from It All" (Wallace), **Supp. X:** 314–315
"Getting Born" (Shields), **Supp. VII:** 311
Getting Even (Allen), **Supp. XV:** 3, 14, 15
"Getting Lucky" (L. Michaels), **Supp. XVI:** 205, 209
"Getting Out of Jail on Monday" (Wagoner), **Supp. IX:** 327
"Getting There" (Plath), **Supp. I Part 2:** 539, 542
"Getting to the Poem" (Corso), **Supp. XII:** 135
Getty, J. Paul, **Supp. X:** 108
Getty, Norris, **Supp. XV:** 136–137, 138, 139, 142, 143, 145, 146
Gettysburg, Manila, Acoma (Masters), **Supp. I Part 2:** 471
"Gettysburg: July 1, 1863" (Kenyon), **Supp. VII:** 172
Ghachem, Malick, **Supp. X:** 17
"Ghazals: Homage to Ghalib" (Rich), **Supp. I Part 2:** 557
Ghost, The (Crane), **I:** 409, 421
"Ghost Chant, et alii" (Komunyakaa), **Supp. XIII:** 114
Ghost in the Music, A (Nichols), **Supp. XIII:** 267
"Ghostlier Demarcations, Keener Sounds" (Vendler), **Supp. I Part 2:** 565
"Ghostly Father, I Confess" (McCarthy), **II:** 565–566
Ghostly Lover, The (Hardwick), **Supp. III Part 1:** 194–196, 208, 209
Ghost of Meter, The (A. Finch), **Supp. XVII:** 71, 73
"Ghost of the Buffaloes, The" (Lindsay), **Supp. I Part 2:** 393
Ghost of Tradition, The (Walzer), **Supp. XVIII:** 174

Ghosts (Auster), **Supp. XII:** 22, **24, 26–27**
Ghosts (Ibsen), **III:** 152
Ghosts (Wharton), **IV:** 316, 327
Ghost Town (Coover), **Supp. V:** 52–53
Ghost Trio, The (Bierds), **Supp. XVII:** 29, **30**
Ghost Writer, The (P. Roth), **Retro. Supp. II:** 22, 290, 291; **Supp. III Part 2:** 420–421; **Supp. XVII:** 43
Giachetti, Fosco, **Supp. IV Part 2:** 520
"Giacometti" (Wilbur), **Supp. III Part 2:** 551
Giacometti, Alberto, **Supp. VIII:** 168, 169
Giacomo, Padre, **II:** 278–279
Giant's House, The: A Romance (McCracken), **Supp. X:** 86
"Giant Snail" (Bishop), **Retro. Supp. II:** 49
Giant Weapon, The (Winters), **Supp. II Part 2:** 810
"Giant Woman, The" (Oates), **Supp. II Part 2:** 523
Gibbon, Edward, **I:** 4, 378; **IV:** 126; **Supp. I Part 2:** 503; **Supp. III Part 2:** 629; **Supp. XIII:** 75; **Supp. XIV:** 97
Gibbons, James, **Supp. XVII:** 228
Gibbons, Kaye, **Supp. X: 41–54; Supp. XII:** 311
Gibbons, Reginald, **Supp. X:** 113, 124, 127; **Supp. XV:** 105
Gibbons, Richard, **Supp. I Part 1:** 107
"Gibbs" (Rukeyser), **Supp. VI:** 273
Gibbs, Barbara, **Supp. IV Part 2:** 644
Gibbs, Wolcott, **Supp. I Part 2:** 604, 618; **Supp. VIII:** 151
"GIBSON" (Baraka), **Supp. II Part 1:** 54
Gibson, Charles Dana, **Supp. X:** 184
Gibson, Graeme, **Supp. XIII:** 20
Gibson, Wilfrid W., **Retro. Supp. I:** 128
Gibson, William, **Supp. XVI: 117–133**
Giddins, Gary, **Supp. XIII:** 245
Gide, André, **I:** 271, 290; **II:** 581; **III:** 210; **IV:** 53, 289; **Supp. I Part 1:** 51; **Supp. IV Part 1:** 80, 284, 347; **Supp. IV Part 2:** 681, 682; **Supp. VIII:** 40; **Supp. X:** 187; **Supp. XIV:** 24, 348; **Supp. XVII:** 242
Gideon Planish (Lewis), **II:** 455
Gielgud, John, **I:** 82; **Supp. XI:** 305
Gierow, Dr. Karl Ragnar, **III:** 404
Gifford, Bill, **Supp. XI:** 38
Gifford, Terry, **Supp. XVI:** 22
"Gift, The" (Creeley), **Supp. IV Part 1:** 153
"Gift, The" (Doolittle), **Supp. I Part 1:** 267
Gift, The (Hyde), **Supp. XVIII:** 150
"Gift, The" (Jarman), **Supp. XVII:** 116
"Gift, The" (L.-Y. Lee), **Supp. XV:** 213, 214
Gift, The (Nabokov), **III:** 246, 255, 261–263; **Retro. Supp. I:** 264, 266, **268–270,** 273, 274–275, 278
"Gift from the City, A" (Updike), **Retro. Supp. I:** 320
"Gift of God, The" (Robinson), **III:** 512, 517, 518–521, 524
Gift of the Black Folk, The: The Negroes in the Making of America (Du Bois), **Supp. II Part 1:** 179
"Gift of the Magi, The" (O. Henry), **Supp. II Part 1:** 394, 406, 408
"Gift of the *Osuo,* The" (Johnson), **Supp. VI:** 194
"Gift of the Prodigal, The" (Taylor), **Supp. V:** 314, 326
"Gift Outright, The" (Frost), **II:** 152; **Supp. IV Part 1:** 15
Gigi (Colette; stage adaptation, Loos), **Supp. XVI:** 193
"Gigolo" (Plath), **Retro. Supp. II:** 257
"G.I. Graves in Tuscany" (Hugo), **Supp. VI:** 138
"Gila Bend" (Dickey), **Supp. IV Part 1:** 185–186
Gilbert, Jack, **Supp. IX:** 287
Gilbert, Peter, **Supp. IX:** 291, 300
Gilbert, Roger, **Supp. XI:** 124
Gilbert, Sandra M., **Retro. Supp. I:** 42; **Retro. Supp. II:** 324; **Supp. IX:** 66; **Supp. XV:** 270
Gilbert, Susan. *See* Dickinson, Mrs. William A.
Gilbert and Sullivan, **Supp. IV Part 1:** 389
Gil Blas (Le Sage), **II:** 290
Gilded Age, The (Twain), **III:** 504; **IV:** 198
"Gilded Lapse of Time, A" (Schnackenberg), **Supp. XV:** 257
Gilded Lapse of Time, A (Schnackenberg), **Supp. XV:** 258, **260–263**
"Gilded Six-Bits, The" (Hurston), **Supp. VI:** 154–155
Gilder, R. W., **Retro. Supp. II:** 66; **Supp. I Part 2:** 418
Gildersleeve, Basil, **Supp. I Part 1:** 369
Giles, H. A., **Retro. Supp. I:** 289
Giles, James R., **Supp. IX:** 11, 15; **Supp. XI:** 219, 223–224, 228, 234
"Giles Corey of the Salem Farms" (Longfellow), **II:** 505, 506; **Retro. Supp. II:** 166, 167
Giles Goat-Boy (Barth), **I:** 121, 122–123, 129, 130, 134, 135–138; **Supp. V:** 39
Gill, Brendan, **Supp. I Part 2:** 659, 660
Gillespie, Nick, **Supp. XIV:** 298, 311
Gillette, Chester, **I:** 512
Gilligan, Carol, **Supp. XIII:** 216
Gillis, Jim, **IV:** 196
Gillis, Steve, **IV:** 195
Gilman, Charlotte Perkins, **Supp. I Part 2:** 637; **Supp. V:** 121, 284, 285; **Supp. XI: 193–211; Supp. XIII:** 295, 306; **Supp. XVI:** 84
Gilman, Daniel Coit, **Supp. I Part 1:** 361, 368, 370
Gilman, Richard, **IV:** 115; **Supp. IV Part 2:** 577; **Supp. XIII:** 100
Gilmore, Eddy, **Supp. I Part 2:** 618
Gilmore, Mikal, **Supp. XVI:** 123, 124
Gilpin, Charles, **III:** 392
Gilpin, Dewitt, **Supp. XV:** 197
Gilpin, Laura, **Retro. Supp. I:** 7
Gilpin, Sam, **Supp. V:** 213
Gilpin, William, **Supp. IV Part 2:** 603
"Gil's Furniture Bought & Sold" (Cisneros), **Supp. VII:** 61–62, 64
"Gimcrackery" articles (Briggs), **Supp. XVIII:** 8–9
"Gimpel the Fool" (Singer), **IV:** 14; **Retro. Supp. II:** 22, 307
Gimpel the Fool and Other Stories (Singer), **IV:** 1, 7–9, 10, 12
"Gin" (Levine), **Supp. V:** 193
"Gingerbread House, The" (Coover), **Supp. V:** 42–43
Gingerbread Lady, The (Simon), **Supp. IV Part 2:** 580, 583–584, 588
Gingerich, Willard, **Supp. IV Part 2:** 510
Gingertown (McKay), **Supp. X:** 132, 139
Gingold, Hermione, **Supp. XV:** 13
Gingrich, Arnold, **Retro. Supp. I:** 113; **Supp. XVII:** 88
Ginna, Robert, **Supp. IX:** 259
Ginsberg, Allen, **I:** 183; **Retro. Supp. I:** 411, 426, 427; **Retro. Supp. II:** 280; **Supp. II Part 1:** 30, 32, 58, **307–333; Supp. III Part 1:** 2, 91, 96, 98, 100, 222, 226; **Supp. III Part 2:** 541, 627; **Supp. IV Part 1:** 79, 90, 322; **Supp. IV Part 2:** 502; **Supp. IX:** 299; **Supp. V:** 168, 336; **Supp. VIII:** 239, 242–243, 289; **Supp. X:** 120, 204; **Supp. XI:** 135, 297; **Supp. XII:** 118–119, 121–122, 124, 126, 130–131, 136, 182; **Supp. XIV:** 15, 53, 54, 125, 137, 141, 142, 143–144, 148, 150, 269, 280, 283; **Supp. XV:** 134, 177, 263; **Supp. XVI:** 123, 135; **Supp. XVII:** 138, 243; **Supp. XVIII:** 20, 27, 29, 30
Gioia, Dana, **Supp. IX:** 279; **Supp. XII:** 209; **Supp. XIII:** 337; **Supp. XV: 111–131,** 251; **Supp. XVII:** 69, 72, 112
Giono, Jean, **Supp. XVI:** 135
Giotto di Bondone, **Supp. I Part 2:** 438; **Supp. XI:** 126
Giovani, Regula, **Supp. XV:** 270
Giovanni, Nikki, **Supp. I Part 1:** 66; **Supp. II Part 1:** 54; **Supp. IV Part 1:** 11; **Supp. VIII:** 214
Giovanni's Room (Baldwin), **Retro. Supp. II:** 5, 6, **6–7,** 8, 10; **Supp. I Part 1:** 51, 52, 55–56, 57, 60, 63, 67; **Supp. III Part 1:** 125
Giovannitti, Arturo, **I:** 476; **Supp. XV:** 299, 301, 302, 307
"Giraffe" (Swenson), **Supp. IV Part 2:** 651
Giraldi, Giovanni Battista. *See* Cinthio
"Girl" (Kincaid), **Supp. VII:** 182–183
"Girl, The" (Olds), **Supp. X:** 207
"Girl Friend Poems" (Wright), **Supp. XV:** 349
"Girl from Lynn Bathes Horse!!" (McCarriston), **Supp. XIV:** 266
"Girl from Red Lion, P.A., A" (Mencken), **III:** 111
Girl in Glass, The: Love Poems (W. J. Smith), **Supp. XIII:** 335
Girl in Landscape (Lethem), **Supp. XVIII:** 136, **141–143**

"Girl in the Grave, The" (McCoy), **Supp. XIII:** 170
Girl Like I, A (Loos), **Supp. XVI:** 181, 183, 184, 187, 194, 196
"Girl of the Golden West" (Didion), **Supp. IV Part 1:** 195, 208, 211
Girl of the Golden West, The (Puccini), **III:** 139
"Girl on a Scaffold" (C. Frost), **Supp. XV:** 98
"Girl on the Baggage Truck, The" (O'Hara), **III:** 371–372
Girls at Play (Theroux), **Supp. VIII:** 314, 315, 316, **317**
"Girls at the Sphinx, The" (Farrell), **II:** 45
Girl Sleuth, The: A Feminist Guide (Mason), **Supp. VIII:** 133, 135, **139,** 142
"Girl's Story, A" (Bambara), **Supp. XI:** 10–11
"Girl the Prince Liked, The" (Z. Fitzgerald), **Supp. IX:** 71
Girl Who Loved Tom Gordon, The (King), **Supp. V:** 138, 152
"Girl with Curious Hair" (Wallace), **Supp. X:** 306
Girl with Curious Hair (Wallace), **Supp. X:** 301, **305–308**
"Girl with Silver Eyes, The" (Hammett), **Supp. IV Part 1:** 344, 345
"Girl with Talent, The" (Z. Fitzgerald), **Supp. IX:** 71
Girodias, Maurice, **III:** 171; **Supp. XI:** 297
Giroux, Robert, **Retro. Supp. II:** 177, 229, 235; **Supp. IV Part 1:** 280; **Supp. VIII:** 195; **Supp. XV:** 146
Gish, Dorothy, **Retro. Supp. I:** 103
Gish, Lillian, **Supp. XVI:** 184
Gissing, George, **II:** 138, 144
Gittings, Robert, **II:** 531
"Given" (C. Frost), **Supp. XV:** 96
"Give Us Back Our Country" (Masters), **Supp. I Part 2:** 472
"Give Way, Ye Gates" (Roethke), **III:** 536
"Give Your Heart to the Hawks" (Jeffers), **Supp. II Part 2:** 433
"Giving Blood" (Updike), **IV:** 226; **Retro. Supp. I:** 332
Giving Good Weight (McPhee), **Supp. III Part 1:** 307
"Giving in to You" (X. J. Kennedy), **Supp. XV:** 160
"Giving Myself Up" (Strand), **Supp. IV Part 2:** 627
G. K. the DJ (Keillor), **Supp. XVI:** 171
Glackens, William, **Retro. Supp. II:** 103
Gladden, Washington, **III:** 293; **Supp. I Part 1:** 5
Gladstone, William Ewart, **Supp. I Part 2:** 419
"Gladys Poem, The" (Alvarez), **Supp. VII:** 10
"Glance at German 'Kultur,' A" (Bourne), **I:** 228
Glance Away, A (Wideman), **Supp. X:** 320
"Glance from the Bridge, A" (Wilbur), **Supp. III Part 2:** 551
Glance toward Shakespeare, A (Chapman), **Supp. XIV:** 44
Glanville-Hicks, Peggy, **Supp. IV Part 1:** 84
Glare (Ammons), **Supp. VII:** 35–36
Glasgow, Cary, **II:** 173, 182
Glasgow, Ellen, **II: 173–195; IV:** 328; **Supp. X:** 228, 234
Glasmon, Kubec, **Supp. XIII:** 166
Glaspell, Susan, **Supp. III Part 1: 175–191; Supp. X:** 46; **Supp. XVII:** 99
"Glass" (Francis), **Supp. IX:** 80
Glass, Irony, and God (Carson), **Supp. XII:** 97, **104–106**
"Glass Ark, The" (Komunyakaa), **Supp. XIII:** 129
Glass Bees, The (Jünger; Bogan and Mayer, trans.), **Supp. III Part 1:** 63
"Glass Blower of Venice" (Malamud), **Supp. I Part 2:** 450
"Glass Essay, The" (Carson), **Supp. XII: 104–105**
"Glass Face in the Rain, A: New Poems" (Stafford), **Supp. XI: 327–328**
Glass Key, The (Hammett), **Supp. IV Part 1:** 351–353
"Glass Meadows" (Bausch), **Supp. VII:** 53–54
Glass Menagerie, The (T. Williams), **I:** 81; **IV:** 378, 379, 380, 382, 383, 385, 386, 387, 388, 389, 390, 391, 392, 393–394, 395, 398; **Supp. IV Part 1:** 84
"Glass Mountain, The" (Barthelme), **Supp. IV Part 1:** 47
"Glass Tent, The" (Everwine), **Supp. XV:** 76
Glatstein, Jacob, **Supp. X:** 70
Glazer, Nathan, **Supp. VIII:** 93, 243
"Gleaners, The" (Merwin), **Supp. III Part 1:** 346
Gleanings in Europe (Cooper), **I:** 346
Gleason, Ralph J., **Supp. IX:** 16
Glenday, Michael, **Retro. Supp. II:** 210
Glengarry Glen Ross (film), **Supp. XIV:** 242
Glengarry Glen Ross (Mamet), **Supp. XIV:** 239, 240, 242, 245, 246, 250, 254, 255
Glimcher, Arne, **Supp. VIII:** 73
"Glimpses" (Jones), **Supp. XI:** 218
Glimpses of the Moon, The (Wharton), **II:** 189–190; **IV:** 322–323; **Retro. Supp. I:** 381
"Glimpses of Vietnamese Life" (Levertov), **Supp. III Part 1:** 282
Glisson, J. T., **Supp. X:** 234
Gloria Mundi (Frederic), **II:** 144–145
Gloria Naylor (Fowler), **Supp. VIII:** 224
"Glorious Fourth, The" (Ryan as Quin), **Supp. XVIII:** 229
Glorious Ones, The (Prose), **Supp. XVI:** 251
Glory of Hera, The (Gordon), **II:** 196–197, 198, 199, 217–220
Glory of the Conquered, The (Glaspell), **Supp. III Part 1:** 176
Glossary of Literary Terms (Abrams), **Supp. XVI:** 19
Glotfelty, Cheryll, **Supp. IX:** 25
"Glow, The" (Wrigley), **Supp. XVIII:** 296–297, 307
Glow, The (Wrigley), **Supp. XVIII:** 295
Gluck, Christoph Willibald, **II:** 210, 211
Glück, Louise, **Supp. V: 77–94; Supp. VIII:** 272; **Supp. X:** 209; **Supp. XIV:** 269; **Supp. XV:** 19, 252; **Supp. XVII:** 241
"Glutton, The" (Shapiro), **Supp. II Part 2:** 705
"Glutton for Punishment, A" (Yates), **Supp. XI:** 341
Glyph (Everett), **Supp. XVIII: 60–61**
Gnädiges Fräulein, The (T. Williams), **IV:** 382, 395, 398
Gnomes and Occasions (Nemerov), **III:** 269
Gnomologia (Fuller), **II:** 111
"Gnothis Seauton" (Emerson), **II:** 11, 18–19
Go (Holmes), **Supp. XIV:** 144
"Goal of Intellectual Men, The" (Eberhart), **I:** 529–530
Go-Between, The (Hartley), **Supp. I Part 1:** 293
Gobineau, Joseph Arthur de, **Supp. XIV:** 209
God (Allen), **Supp. XV:** 3
God and the American Writer (Kazin), **Supp. VIII: 108–109**
Godard, Jean-Luc, **Supp. I Part 2:** 558
Godbey (Masters), **Supp. I Part 2:** 472
God Bless You, Mr. Rosewater (Vonnegut), **Supp. II Part 2:** 758, 767, 768–769, 771, 772
Goddess Abides, The (Buck), **Supp. II Part 1:** 129, 131–132
Gödel, Kurt, **Supp. IV Part 1:** 43
Godfather (Puzo), **Supp. IV Part 1:** 390
Godfires (Hoffman), **Supp. XVIII: 81–82**
"God in the Doorway" (Dillard), **Supp. VI:** 28
"God is a distant-stately Lover" (Dickinson), **I:** 471
Godkin, E. L., **II:** 274
God Knows (Heller), **Supp. IV Part 1:** 386, 388–389
God Made Alaska for the Indians (Reed), **Supp. X:** 241
God of His Fathers, The (London), **II:** 469
God of Vengeance (Asch), **IV:** 11
"Go Down, Moses" (Faulkner), **II:** 71–72
Go Down, Moses (Faulkner), **Retro. Supp. I:** 75, 82, 85, 86, 88, 89, 90, 92; **Supp. XVIII:** 203
Go Down, Moses (Hayden), **Supp. II Part 1:** 365
Go Down, Moses and Other Stories (Faulkner), **II:** 71; **Supp. X:** 52
"Go Down Death A Funeral Sermon" (Johnson), **Supp. IV Part 1:** 7
"God Rest Ye Merry, Gentlemen" (Hemingway), **IV:** 122
Godric (Buechner), **Supp. XII:** 53
Gods, The (Goldbarth), **Supp. XII:** 189, 190
Gods Arrive, The (Wharton), **IV:** 326–327; **Retro. Supp. I:** 382

"God Save the Rights of Man" (Freneau), **Supp. II Part 1:** 268
"Godsildren" (Swenson), **Supp. IV Part 2:** 645
"God's Christ Theory" (Carson), **Supp. XII: 106**
God's Country (Everett), **Supp. XVIII: 57–58,** 64, 65
God's Country and My People (Morris), **III:** 238
Gods Determinations touching his Elect: and the Elects Combat in their Conversion, and Coming up to God in Christ together with the Comfortable Effects thereof (Taylor), **IV:** 155–160, 165
God-Seeker, The (Lewis), **II:** 456
God's Favorite (Simon), **Supp. IV Part 2:** 575, 586, 588, 590
God's Little Acre (Caldwell), **I:** 288, 289, 290, 297, 298–302, 305–306, 309, 310
God's Man: A Novel in Wood Cuts (Ward), **I:** 31
"Gods of Winter, The" (Gioia), **Supp. XV:** 117
Gods of Winter, The (Gioia), **Supp. XV:** 112, **121–125**
"God's Peace in November" (Jeffers), **Supp. II Part 2:** 420
God's Silence (F. Wright), **Supp. XVII:** 240, 246–247
"God Stiff" (Carson), **Supp. XII: 106**
God's Trombones (Johnson), **Supp. II Part 1:** 201
"God's Youth" (Untermeyer), **Supp. XV:** 296
"God the Father and the Empty House" (McCarriston), **Supp. XIV:** 273
Godwin, William, **II:** 304; **III:** 415; **Supp. I Part 1:** 126, 146; **Supp. I Part 2:** 512, 513–514, 522, 709, 719
God without Thunder (Ransom), **III:** 495–496, 499
Goebbels, Josef, **III:** 560
Goebel, Irma, **Supp. X:** 95
Goen, C. C., **I:** 560
Goethe, Johann Wolfgang von, **I:** 181, 396, 587–588; **II:** 5, 6, 320, 344, 488, 489, 492, 502, 556; **III:** 395, 453, 607, 612, 616; **IV:** 50, 64, 173, 326; **Retro. Supp. I:** 360; **Retro. Supp. II:** 94; **Supp. I Part 2:** 423, 457; **Supp. II Part 1:** 26; **Supp. III Part 1:** 63; **Supp. IX:** 131, 308; **Supp. X:** 60; **Supp. XI:** 169; **Supp. XVIII:** 278
Go for the Body (Lacy), **Supp. XV:** 201, 204
Gogol, Nikolai, **I:** 296; **IV:** 1, 4; **Retro. Supp. I:** 266, 269; **Supp. VIII:** 14; **Supp. XVII:** 45; **Supp. XVIII:** 102
Going, William T., **Supp. VIII:** 126
Going After Cacciato (O'Brien), **Supp. V:** 237, 238, 239, 244–246, 248, 249
Going All the Way (Wakefield), **Supp. VIII:** 43
"Going Critical" (Bambara), **Supp. XI:** 14
Going Down (Markson), **Supp. XVII:** 136, 138, **139–140,** 141, 142–143, 144, 145
Going for the Rain (Ortiz), **Supp. IV Part 2:** 499, 505–508, 509, 514
"Going Home by Last Night" (Kinnell), **Supp. III Part 1:** 244
"Going Home in America" (Hardwick), **Supp. III Part 1:** 205
"Going North" (Salinas), **Supp. XIII:** 316
"Going Places" (L. Michaels), **Supp. XVI:** 203
Going Places (L. Michaels), **Supp. XVI:** 201, **203–206**
Going South (Lardner and Buck), **II:** 427
Going To and Fro and Walking Up and Down (Reznikoff), **Supp. XIV:** 280, 282, 284, 285
"Going to Meet the Man" (Baldwin), **Retro. Supp. II:** 8, 9; **Supp. I Part 1:** 62–63
Going to Meet the Man (Baldwin), **Supp. I Part 1:** 60, 62–63
"Going to Naples" (Welty), **IV:** 278; **Retro. Supp. I:** 352, 353
"Going to Shrewsbury" (Jewett), **II:** 393
"Going to the Bakery" (Bishop), **Supp. I Part 1:** 93
Going-to-the-Stars (Lindsay), **Supp. I Part 2:** 398
Going-to-the-Sun (Lindsay), **Supp. I Part 2:** 397–398
Going to the Territory (Ellison), **Retro. Supp. II:** 119, 123–124
"Going towards Pojoaque, A December Full Moon/72" (Harjo), **Supp. XII:** 218
"Going Under" (Dubus), **Supp. VII:** 83
"Gold" (Francis), **Supp. IX:** 82
Gold (O'Neill), **III:** 391
Gold, Michael, **II:** 26; **IV:** 363, 364, 365; **Retro. Supp. II:** 323; **Supp. I Part 1:** 331; **Supp. I Part 2:** 609; **Supp. XIV:** 288
Goldbarth, Albert, **Supp. XII: 175–195**
Goldbarth's Book of Occult Phenomena (Goldbarth), **Supp. XII:** 181
Goldberg, S. L., **Supp. VIII:** 238
"Gold Bug, The" (Poe), **III:** 410, 413, 419, 420
Gold Bug Variations, The (Powers), **Supp. IX:** 210, 212, **216–217,** 219
Gold Cell, The (Olds), **Supp. X: 206–209**
Gold Diggers, The (Monette), **Supp. X:** 153
Golde, Miss (Mencken's Secretary), **III:** 104, 107
Golden, Harry, **III:** 579, 581; **Supp. VIII:** 244
Golden, Mike, **Supp. XI:** 294, 295, 297, 299, 303
Golden Age, The (Gurney), **Supp. V:** 101–103
Golden Apples (Rawlings), **Supp. X: 228–229,** 230, 234
Golden Apples, The (Welty), **IV:** 261, 271–274, 281, 293; **Retro. Supp. I:** 341, 342, 343, **350–351,** 352, 355
Golden Apples of the Sun, The (Bradbury), **Supp. IV Part 1:** 102, 103
Golden Book of Springfield, The (Lindsay), **Supp. I Part 2:** 376, 379, 395, 396
Golden Bough, The (Frazer), **II:** 204, 549; **III:** 6–7; **Supp. I Part 1:** 18; **Supp. IX:** 123; **Supp. X:** 124
Golden Bowl, The (James), **II:** 320, 333, 335; **Retro. Supp. I:** 215, 216, 218–219, 232, **234–235,** 374
Golden Boy (Odets), **Supp. II Part 2:** 538, 539, 540–541, 546, 551
Golden Calves, The (Auchincloss), **Supp. IV Part 1:** 35
Golden Day, The (Mumford), **Supp. II Part 2:** 471, 475, 477, 483, 484, 488–489, 493
Golden Fleece, The (Gurney), **Supp. V:** 97
Golden Gate, The (Seth), **Supp. XVII:** 117
Golden Grove, The: Selected Passages from the Sermons and Writings of Jeremy Taylor (L. P. Smith), **Supp. XIV:** 345
"Golden Heifer, The" (Wylie), **Supp. I Part 2:** 707
"Golden Honeymoon, The" (Lardner), **II:** 429–430, 431
Golden Journey, The (W. J. Smith and Bogan, comps.), **Supp. XIII:** 347
Golden Ladder series (S. and A. Warner), **Supp. XVIII:** 267
"Golden Lads" (Marquand), **III:** 56
Golden Legend, The (Longfellow), **II:** 489, 490, 495, 505, 506, 507; **Retro. Supp. II:** 159, 165, 166
Golden Mean and Other Poems, The (Tate and Wills), **IV:** 122
"Golden Retrievals" (Doty), **Supp. XI:** 132
Golden Shakespeare, The: An Anthology (L. P. Smith), **Supp. XIV:** 349
Goldensohn, Lorrie, **Retro. Supp. II:** 51
"Golden State" (Bidart), **Supp. XV:** 23, 24, 25
Golden State (Bidart), **Supp. XV:** 21, **23–25**
Golden States (Cunningham), **Supp. XV:** 55, **56–59,** 63
Golden Treasury of Best Songs and Lyrical Poems in the English Language (Palgrave), **Retro. Supp. I:** 124
Golden Treasury of the Best Songs and Lyrical Poems in the English Language (Palgrave), **Supp. XIV:** 340
Golden Whales of California and Other Rhymes in the American Language, The (Lindsay), **Supp. I Part 2:** 394–395, 396
"Goldfish Bowl, The" (Francis), **Supp. IX:** 78
Goldin Boys, The (Epstein), **Supp. XIV:** 112
Golding, Arthur, **III:** 467, 468
Golding, William, **Supp. IV Part 1:** 297
Goldini, Carlo, **II:** 274
Goldkorn Tales (Epstein), **Supp. XII: 163–164**
Goldman, Albert, **Supp. XI:** 299

Goldman, Emma, **III:** 176, 177; **Supp. I Part 2:** 524; **Supp. XVII:** 96, 103, 104
Goldman, William, **Supp. IV Part 2:** 474
"Gold Mountain Stories" project (Kingston), **Supp. V:** 164
Gold of Chickaree, The (S. and A. Warner), **Supp. XVIII:** 267, 268, 269
Goldring, Douglas, **III:** 458
Goldsmith, Oliver, **II:** 273, 282, 299, 304, 308, 314, 315, 514; **Retro. Supp. I:** 335; **Supp. I Part 1:** 310; **Supp. I Part 2:** 503, 714, 716; **Supp. XVIII:** 12
Gold Standard and the Logic of Naturalism, The (Michaels), **Retro. Supp. I:** 369
Goldstein, Rebecca, **Supp. XVII:** 44
Goldwater, Barry, **I:** 376; **III:** 38
Goldwyn, Samuel, **Retro. Supp. II:** 199; **Supp. I Part 1:** 281
Golem, The (Leivick), **IV:** 6
"Goliardic Song" (Hecht), **Supp. X:** 63
"Go Like This" (Moore), **Supp. X:** 165
Goll, Ivan, **Supp. III Part 1:** 235, 243–244; **Supp. III Part 2:** 621
Goncharova, Natalya, **Supp. IX:** 66
Goncourt, Edmond de, **II:** 325, 328; **III:** 315, 317–318, 321; **Retro. Supp. I:** 226
Goncourt, Jules de, **II:** 328; **III:** 315, 317–318, 321
Gone Fishin' (Mosley), **Supp. XIII: 235–236,** 240
"Gone to War" (E. Stoddard), **Supp. XV:** 282
"Gone West" (Rodriguez), **Supp. XIV:** 308
Gone with the Wind (film), **Retro. Supp. I:** 113
Gone with the Wind (Mitchell), **II:** 177; **Retro. Supp. I:** 340
Gongora y Argote, Luis de, **II:** 552
Gonzalez, David, **Supp. VIII:** 85
Gooch, Brad, **Supp. XII:** 121
Good, George, **Supp. XI:** 306
"Good, the Plaid, and the Ugly, The" (Wasserstein), **Supp. XV:** 327
"Good and Not So Good, The" (Dunn), **Supp. XI:** 141
"Good Anna, The" (Stein), **IV:** 37, 40, 43
Good As Gold (Heller), **Supp. IV Part 1:** 386, 388, 394
Good as I Been to You (album, Dylan), **Supp. XVIII:** 28
Good Boys and Dead Girls and Other Essays (Gordon), **Supp. IV Part 1:** 309–310
"Good-by and Keep Cold" (Frost), **Retro. Supp. I:** 135
"Good-bye" (Emerson), **II:** 19
"Goodbye, Christ" (Hughes), **Retro. Supp. I:** 202, 203
"Goodbye, Columbus" (P. Roth), **Supp. III Part 2:** 401, 404, 408–409, 411
Goodbye, Columbus (P. Roth), **Retro. Supp. II:** 280, 281, 290; **Supp. III Part 2:** 403–406; **Supp. XIV:** 112
Goodbye, Columbus and Five Short Stories (P. Roth), **Retro. Supp. II:** 279
"Goodbye, Goldeneye" (Swenson), **Supp. IV Part 2:** 651
"Goodbye, Mr. Chipstein" (Epstein), **Supp. XIV:** 103, 108
"Goodbye, My Brother" (Cheever), **Supp. I Part 1:** 175, 177, 193
"Goodbye and Good Luck" (Paley), **Supp. VI:** 219, 223
Goodbye Girl, The (film), **Supp. IV Part 2:** 589
Goodbye Girl, The (musical), **Supp. IV Part 2:** 576, 588
Goodbye Girl, The (Simon), **Supp. IV Part 2:** 575
Goodbye Look, The (Macdonald), **Supp. IV Part 2:** 473, 474
"Good-Bye My Fancy" (Whitman), **IV:** 348
"Goodbye to All That" (Didion), **Supp. IV Part 1:** 197
Goodbye to All That (Graves), **I:** 477
Goodbye to Berlin (Isherwood), **Supp. XIV:** 159, 161, 162, 169
"Good-Bye to the Mezzogiorno" (Auden), **Supp. II Part 1:** 19
"Goodbye to the Poetry of Calcium" (Wright), **Supp. III Part 2:** 599
"Good Company" (Matthews), **Supp. IX:** 160
"Good Country People" (O'Connor), **III:** 343, 350, 351, 352, 358; **Retro. Supp. II:** 229, 232
Good Day to Die, A (Harrison), **Supp. VIII: 42–44,** 45, 47
Good Doctor, The (Simon), **Supp. IV Part 2:** 575, 585
Good Earth, The (Buck), **Supp. I Part 1:** 49; **Supp. II Part 1:** 115–175, 118, 125, 132
Good European, The (Blackmur), **Supp. II Part 1:** 91
Good Evening Mr. & Mrs. America, and All the Ships at Sea (Bausch), **Supp. VII:** 41, 47, 52
"Good Friday" (Jarman), **Supp. XVII:** 116
Good Gray Poet, The (O'Connor), **Retro. Supp. I:** 407
Good Health and How We Won It (Sinclair), **Supp. V:** 285–286
Good Hearts (Price), **Supp. VI:** 259, 265
"Good Job Gone, A" (Hughes), **Retro. Supp. I:** 204
Good Journey, A (Ortiz), **Supp. IV Part 2:** 497, 499, 503, 505, 509–510, 514
Good Luck in Cracked Italian (Hugo), **Supp. VI:** 133, 137–138
Goodman, Allegra, **Supp. XII:** 159; **Supp. XVI:** 205
Goodman, Ellen, **Supp. XVI:** 103
Goodman, Jenny, **Supp. XV:** 343, 344
Goodman, Paul, **I:** 218, 261; **III:** 39; **Supp. I Part 2:** 524; **Supp. VIII:** 239–240
Goodman, Philip, **III:** 105, 108
Goodman, Walter, **Supp. IV Part 2:** 532
"Good Man Is Hard to Find, A" (O'Connor), **III:** 339, 344, 353; **Retro. Supp. II:** 230–231
Good Man Is Hard to Find, A (O'Connor), **III:** 339, 343–345
Good Man Is Hard to Find and Other Stories, A (O'Connor), **Retro. Supp. II:** 229, **230–232**
Good Morning, America (Sandburg), **III:** 592–593
"Good Morning, Major" (Marquand), **III:** 56
Good Morning, Midnight (Rhys), **Supp. III Part 1:** 43
"Good Morning, Revolution" (Hughes), **Retro. Supp. I:** 201, 203
Good Morning Revolution: Uncollected Writings of Social Protest (Hughes), **Retro. Supp. I:** 194, 201, 202, 209
Good Mother, The (Miller), **Supp. XII:** 289, **290–294,** 299, 301
Good News (Abbey), **Supp. XIII: 11–12**
"Good News from New-England" (Johnson), **Supp. I Part 1:** 115
Good News of Death and Other Poems (Simpson), **Supp. IX:** 265, **268–269**
Good Night, Willie Lee, I'll See You in the Morning (Walker), **Supp. III Part 2:** 520, 531
"Good Oak" (Leopold), **Supp. XIV:** 185, 187, 191
"Good Old Times, The: New York Fifty Years Ago" (Briggs), **Supp. XVIII:** 15
Goodrich, Samuel G., **Supp. I Part 1:** 38
Good Scent from a Strange Mountain, A (R. O. Butler), **Supp. XII:** 62, **70–72**
Good School, A (Yates), **Supp. XI:** 334, **346–347,** 348, 349
"*Good Shepherdess, The*/La Buena Pastora" (Mora), **Supp. XIII:** 228–229
Good Will (Smiley), **Supp. VI:** 292, **299–300**
Goodwin, K. L., **III:** 478
Goodwin, Stephen, **Supp. V:** 314, 316, 322, 323, 325
"Good Word for Winter, A" (Lowell), **Supp. I Part 2:** 420
Goodwyn, Janet, **Retro. Supp. I:** 370
"Goophered Grapevine, The" (Chesnutt), **Supp. XIV:** 57, **58–61**
"Goose Fish, The" (Nemerov), **III:** 272, 284
"Goose Pond" (Kunitz), **Supp. III Part 1:** 262
Goose-Step, The (Sinclair), **Supp. V:** 276
Gordimer, Nadine, **Supp. XV:** 251
Gordon, Ambrose, **Supp. XV:** 144
Gordon, A. R., **III:** 199
Gordon, Caroline, **II: 196–222,** 536, 537; **III:** 454, 482; **IV:** 123, 126–127, 139, 282; **Retro. Supp. II:** 177, 222, 229, 233, 235; **Supp. II Part 1:** 139
Gordon, Charles G., **I:** 454
Gordon, Don, **Supp. X:** 119
Gordon, Eugene, **Supp. II Part 1:** 170; **Supp. XVIII:** 280
Gordon, Fran, **Supp. XIII:** 111
Gordon, James Morris, **II:** 197
Gordon, Lois, **Supp. IV Part 1:** 48; **Supp. V:** 46
Gordon, Lyndall, **Retro. Supp. I:** 55

Gordon, Mary, **Supp. IV Part 1: 297–317**
Gordon, Neil, **Supp. XVI:** 156
Gordon, Peter, **Supp. XII:** 3–4, 4–5, 8
Gordon, Ruth, **IV:** 357
Gore, Thomas Pryor, **Supp. IV Part 2:** 679
Gorey, Edward, **IV:** 430, 436
"Gorilla, My Love" (Bambara), **Supp. XI:** 2, 3–4
Gorilla, My Love (Bambara), **Supp. XI:** 1, **2–7**
Gorki, Maxim, **I:** 478; **II:** 49; **III:** 402; **IV:** 299; **Supp. I Part 1:** 5, 51
Gorney, Cynthia, **Supp. XVI:** 112
Gorra, Michael, **Supp. V:** 71
Goslings, The (Sinclair), **Supp. V:** 276, 281
Go South to Sorrow (Rowan), **Supp. XIV:** 306
Gospel According to Joe, The (Gurney), **Supp. V:** 99
"Gospel According to Saint Mark, The" (Gordon), **Supp. IV Part 1:** 310
Gospel according to the Son (Mailer), **Retro. Supp. II:** 213
"Gospel for the Twentieth Century, The" (Locke), **Supp. XIV:** 206
"Gospel of Beauty, The" (Lindsay), **Supp. I Part 2:** 380, 382, 384, 385, 391, 396
Gospel Singer, The (Crews), **Supp. XI:** 102, **109**
Gosse, Edmund, **II:** 538; **IV:** 350; **Supp. VIII:** 157
"Gossip" (Conroy), **Supp. XVI:** 71–72
Gossips, Gorgons, and Crones: The Fates of the Earth (Caputi), **Supp. IV Part 1:** 335
Go Tell It on the Mountain (Baldwin), **Retro. Supp. II:** 1, 2, 3, **4–5,** 7, 14; **Supp. I Part 1:** 48, 49, 50, 51, 52, 53–54, 55, 56, 57, 59, 61, 63, 64, 67; **Supp. II Part 1:** 170
Gotera, Vince, **Supp. XIII:** 115, 116, 119, 121, 127
Gothic Revival, The: An Essay on the History of Taste (Clark), **Supp. XIV:** 348
Gothic Writers (Thomson, Voller, and Frank, eds.), **Retro. Supp. II:** 273
"Go to the Devil and Shake Yourself" (song), **Supp. I Part 2:** 580
"Go to the Shine That's on a Tree" (Eberhart), **I:** 523
Go to the Widow-Maker (Jones), **Supp. XI:** 214, **225–226,** 227, 229, 233
Gottfried, Martin, **Supp. IV Part 2:** 584
Gotthelf, Allan, **Supp. IV Part 2:** 528
Gottlieb, Adolph, **Supp. XV:** 144
Gottlieb, Morton, **Supp. XVI:** 196
Gottlieb, Robert, **Supp. IV Part 2:** 474
"Gottschalk and the Grande Tarantelle" (Brooks), **Supp. III Part 1:** 86–87
Gottschalk and the Grande Tarantelle (Brooks), **Supp. III Part 1:** 86
Gould (Dixon), **Supp. XII:** 152, **153**
Gould, Edward Sherman, **I:** 346
Gould, Janice, **Supp. IV Part 1:** 322, 327; **Supp. XII:** 229
Gould, Jay, **I:** 4
Gould, Joe, **Supp. XV:** 143
Gourd Dancer, The (Momaday), **Supp. IV Part 2:** 481, 487, 491, 493
Gourmont, Remy de, **I:** 270, 272; **II:** 528, 529; **III:** 457, 467–468, 477; **Retro. Supp. I:** 55
Gouverneurs de la Rosée (Roumain), **Supp. IV Part 1:** 360, 367
Government Girl (film, Nichols), **Supp. XVIII:** 247
"Governors of Wyoming, The" (Proulx), **Supp. VII:** 264
Goyen, William, **Supp. V:** 220
Grabhorn, Janet, **Supp. XV:** 142
"Grace" (Dubus), **Supp. VII:** 91
"Grace" (Harjo), **Supp. XII:** 224
Grace Notes (Dove), **Supp. IV Part 1:** 248–250, 252
Grade, Chaim, **Supp. XVII:** 41
"Graduation" (Dubus), **Supp. VII:** 84
Grady, Henry W., **Supp. I Part 1:** 370
Graeber, Laurel, **Supp. V:** 15
Graham, Billy, **I:** 308
Graham, David, **Supp. XV:** 104
Graham, Don, **Supp. XI:** 252, 254
Graham, Jorie, **Supp. IX:** 38, 52; **Supp. X:** 73; **Supp. XII:** 209; **Supp. XIII:** 85; **Supp. XVII:** 110, 111, 133, 240, 241, 242
Graham, Martha, **Supp. XI:** 152
Graham, Maryemma, **Retro. Supp. I:** 201, 204
Graham, Nan, **Supp. XII:** 272
Graham, Sheilah, **II:** 94; **Retro. Supp. I:** 97, 113–114, 115; **Supp. IX:** 63
Graham, Shirley, **Supp. I Part 1:** 51
Graham, Stephen, **Supp. I Part 2:** 397
Graham, Tom (pseudonym). *See* Lewis, Sinclair
Grahn, Judy, **Supp. IV Part 1:** 325, 330
"Grain Field" (Crapsey), **Supp. XVII:** 77
Grainger, Percy, **Supp. I Part 2:** 386
Grain of Mustard Seed, A (Sarton), **Supp. VIII: 259–260,** 263
Gramar (Lowth), **II:** 8
Grammar of Motives, A (Burke), **I:** 272, 275, 276–278, 283, 284
Granados, Gabriel Bernal, **Supp. XV:** 350
Granath, Jack, **Supp. XVIII:** 93
Granberry, Edwin, **I:** 288
Grand Canyon, Inc. (Everett), **Supp. XVIII:** 66
Grand Design, The (Dos Passos), **I:** 489–490
"Grande Malade, The" (Barnes), **Supp. III Part 1:** 36
"Grandfather" (Dunn), **Supp. XI:** 147
"Grandfather and Grandson" (Singer), **Retro. Supp. II:** 307
Grandfathers, The (Richter), **Supp. XVIII: 219–220**
"Grandfather's Blessing" (Alvarez), **Supp. VII:** 2
"Grand Forks" (Bierds), **Supp. XVII:** 34
"Grand Forks" (Simpson), **Supp. IX:** 280–281
"Grand Inquisitor" (Dostoevsky), **IV:** 106
Grandissimes (Cable), **II:** 291
"Grand-Master Nabokov" (Updike), **Retro. Supp. I:** 317
"Grand Miracle, The" (Karr), **Supp. XI:** 251
"Grandmother" (Gunn Allen), **Supp. IV Part 1:** 320, 325
"Grandmother in Heaven" (Levine), **Supp. V:** 186
"Grandmother of the Sun: Ritual Gynocracy in Native America" (Gunn Allen), **Supp. IV Part 1:** 328
Grandmothers of the Light: A Medicine Woman's Sourcebook (Gunn Allen, ed.), **Supp. IV Part 1:** 332, 333–334
"Grandmother Songs, The" (Hogan), **Supp. IV Part 1:** 413
"Grandpa and the Statue" (A. Miller), **III:** 147
"Grandparents" (Lowell), **II:** 550
"Grandsire Bells, The" (Bierds), **Supp. XVII:** 28–29
"Grandstand Complex, The" (McCoy), **Supp. XIII:** 166
Grange, Red, **II:** 416
Granger's Index to Poetry (anthology), **Retro. Supp. I:** 37, 39
Grant, Lee, **Supp. XIII:** 295
Grant, Madison, **Supp. II Part 1:** 170
Grant, Richard, **Supp. X:** 282
Grant, Ulysses S., **I:** 4, 15; **II:** 542; **III:** 506, 584; **IV:** 348, 446; **Supp. I Part 2:** 418
Grantwood, **Retro. Supp. I:** 416, 417
"Grapes, The" (Hecht), **Supp. X:** 65–66
"Grape Sherbet" (Dove), **Supp. IV Part 1:** 246
Grapes of Wrath, The (Steinbeck), **I:** 301; **III:** 589; **IV:** 51, 53–55, 59, 63, 65, 67, 68, 69; **Supp. V:** 290; **Supp. XI:** 169; **Supp. XIV:** 181; **Supp. XV:** 351
"Grapevine, The" (Ashbery), **Supp. III Part 1:** 4
"Grass" (Sandburg), **III:** 584
Grass, Günter, **Supp. VIII:** 40
"Grasse: The Olive Trees" (Wilbur), **Supp. III Part 2:** 550
Grass Harp, The (Capote), **Supp. III Part 1:** 114–117, 123
Grass Still Grows, The (A. Miller), **III:** 146
Gratitude to Old Teachers (R. Bly), **Supp. IV Part 1:** 73
Graupner, Gottlieb, **Supp. XV:** 240, 244
"Grave, A" (Moore), **III:** 195, 202, 208, 213
Grave, The (Blair), **Supp. I Part 1:** 150
"Grave, The" (Porter), **III:** 433, 443, 445–446
"Grave, The" (Winters), **Supp. II Part 2:** 795, 796
"Graven Image" (O'Hara), **III:** 320
Grave of the Right Hand, The (Wright), **Supp. V:** 332, 338, 339
"Grave Piece" (Eberhart), **I:** 533
Graves, Billy, **Supp. I Part 2:** 607
Graves, John, **Supp. V:** 220
Graves, Morris, **Supp. X:** 264
Graves, Peter, **Supp. IV Part 2:** 474
Graves, Rean, **Supp. I Part 1:** 326
Graves, Robert, **I:** 437, 477, 523; **Supp. I Part 2:** 541; **Supp. IV Part 1:** 280, 348; **Supp. IV Part 2:** 685

Graveyard for Lunatics, A (Bradbury), **Supp. IV Part 1:** 102, 114–116

Gravity's Rainbow (Pynchon), **Supp. II Part 2:** 617, 618–619, 621–625, 627, 630, 633–636; **Supp. IV Part 1:** 279; **Supp. V:** 44; **Supp. XIV:** 49; **Supp. XVII:** 236

Gray, Cecil, **Supp. I Part 1:** 258

Gray, Francine Du Plessix, **Supp. V:** 169

Gray, James, **III:** 207; **Supp. I Part 2:** 410

Gray, Jeffrey, **Supp. XV:** 27

Gray, Paul, **Supp. IV Part 1:** 305; **Supp. IV Part 2:** 639; **Supp. XVI:** 74; **Supp. XVIII:** 94

Gray, Thomas, **I:** 68; **Supp. I Part 1:** 150; **Supp. I Part 2:** 422, 716

Gray, Thomas A., **Supp. I Part 2:** 710

"Gray Heron, The" (Kinnell), **Supp. III Part 1:** 250

"Gray Mills of Farley, The" (Jewett), **Retro. Supp. II:** 132, 144

"Gray Poem" (Everwine), **Supp. XV:** 81

Grayson, Charles, **Supp. XIII:** 171

"Gray Squirrel" (Francis), **Supp. IX:** 90

"Gray Wolf's H 'ant, The" (Chesnutt), **Supp. XIV:** 60

Grealy, Lucy, **Supp. XII:** 310

"Greasy Lake" (Boyle), **Supp. VIII:** 15

Greasy Lake (Boyle), **Supp. VIII: 14–15**

"Great Adventure of Max Breuck, The" (Lowell), **II:** 522

Great American Novel, The (P. Roth), **Retro. Supp. II:** 283, 288–289; **Supp. III Part 2:** 414–416

Great American Short Novels (Phillips, ed.), **Supp. VIII:** 156

Great Battles of the World (Crane), **I:** 415

"Great Carousel, The" (Untermeyer), **Supp. XV:** 296

Great Christian Doctrine of Original Sin Defended, The ... (Edwards), **I:** 549, 557, 559

Great Circle (Aiken), **I:** 53, 55, 57

"Great Class-Reunion Bazaar, The" (Theroux), **Supp. VIII:** 312

Great Day, The (Hurston), **Supp. VI:** 154

Great Days (Barthelme), **Supp. IV Part 1:** 39

Great Days, The (Dos Passos), **I:** 491

Great Digest (Pound, trans.), **III:** 472

"Great Elegy for John Donne" (Brodsky), **Supp. VIII:** 21, 23

Greater Inclination, The (Wharton), **Retro. Supp. I:** 363, **364–365,** 366

"Greater Torment, The" (Blackmur), **Supp. II Part 1:** 92

Greatest Hits 1969–1996 (Salinas), **Supp. XIII:** 311

"Greatest Thing in the World, The" (Mailer), **Retro. Supp. II:** 196

Great Expectations (Acker), **Supp. XII:** 5, **9–11**

Great Expectations (Dickens), **III:** 247; **Supp. I Part 1:** 35; **Supp. XVI:** 73; **Supp. XVIII:** 146

"Great Expectations, No Satisfaction" (D. Gates), **Supp. XVI:** 73

"Great Figure, The" (W. C. Williams), **IV:** 414

"Great Fillmore Street Buffalo Drive, The" (Momaday), **Supp. IV Part 2:** 493

Great Gatsby, The (Fitzgerald), **I:** 107, 375, 514; **II:** 77, 79, 83, 84, 85, 87, 91–93, 94, 96, 98; **III:** 244, 260, 372, 572; **IV:** 124, 297; **Retro. Supp. I:** 98, 105, **105–108,** 110, 114, 115, 335, 359; **Retro. Supp. II:** 107, 201; **Supp. II Part 2:** 626; **Supp. III Part 2:** 585; **Supp. IV Part 2:** 468, 475; **Supp. IX:** 57, 58; **Supp. X:** 175; **Supp. XI:** 65, 69, 334; **Supp. XVI:** 64, 75; **Supp. XVIII:** 76, 148, 165

Great Gatsby, The (Fitzgerald) (Modern Library), **Retro. Supp. I:** 113

Great God Brown, The (O'Neill), **III:** 165, 391, 394–395

Great Goodness of Life: A Coon Show (Baraka), **Supp. II Part 1:** 47

Great Inclination, The (Wharton), **IV:** 310

"Great Infirmities" (Simic), **Supp. VIII:** 277

Great Jones Street (DeLillo), **Supp. VI:** 2, 3, 8–9, 11, 12

"Great Lawsuit, The: Man *versus* Men: Woman *versus* Women" (Fuller), **Retro. Supp. I:** 156; **Supp. II Part 1:** 292

"Great Men and Their Environment" (James), **II:** 347

"Great Mississippi Bubble, The" (Irving), **II:** 314

Great Railway Bazaar, The: By Train through Asia (Theroux), **Supp. VIII:** 318, 319, **320–321,** 322

"Great Scott" (Conroy), **Supp. XVI:** 75, 77

"Great Sleigh-Ride of Brewsterville, The" (Briggs), **Supp. XVIII:** 16

Great Stories of Suspense (Millar, ed.), **Supp. IV Part 2:** 474

Great Topics of the World (Goldbarth), **Supp. XII:** 187, 189, 191

Great Valley, The (Masters), **Supp. I Part 2:** 465

Great World and Timothy Colt, The (Auchincloss), **Supp. IV Part 1:** 25, 31, 32

Grédy, Jean-Pierre, **Supp. XVI:** 194

"Greek Boy, The" (Bryant), **Supp. I Part 1:** 168

Greek Mind/Jewish Soul: The Conflicted Art of Cynthia Ozick (Strandberg), **Supp. V:** 273

"Greek Partisan, The" (Bryant), **Supp. I Part 1:** 168

"Greeks, The" (McCarriston), **Supp. XIV:** 271

Greeley, Horace, **II:** 7; **IV:** 197, 286–287

Green, Ashbel, **Supp. IV Part 2:** 474

Green, Henry, **IV:** 279; **Retro. Supp. I:** 354; **Supp. III Part 1:** 3; **Supp. XI:** 294–295, 296, 297; **Supp. XII:** 315

Green, Jack, **Supp. IV Part 1:** 284–285

Green, Martin, **Supp. I Part 1:** 299

Green, Michelle, **Supp. IV Part 1:** 95

"Green Automobile, The" (Ginsberg), **Supp. II Part 1:** 322

Greenberg, Clement, **Supp. XV:** 141, 143, 144, 145

Greenberg, Eliezer, **Supp. I Part 2:** 432

Greenberg, Jonathan, **Supp. XII:** 285

Greenberg, Samuel, **I:** 393

Green Bough, A (Faulkner), **Retro. Supp. I:** 84

Green Centuries (Gordon), **II:** 196, 197–207, 209

"Green Crab's Shell, A" (Doty), **Supp. XI:** 126

"Green Door, The" (O. Henry), **Supp. II Part 1:** 395

Greene, A. C., **Supp. V:** 223, 225

Greene, Graham, **I:** 480; **II:** 62, 320; **III:** 57, 556; **Retro. Supp. I:** 215; **Supp. I Part 1:** 280; **Supp. IV Part 1:** 341; **Supp. IX:** 261; **Supp. V:** 298; **Supp. XI:** 99,**Supp. XI:** 104; **Supp. XIII:** 233; **Supp. XVIII:** 79

Greene, Helga, **Supp. IV Part 1:** 134, 135

Greene, J. Lee, **Retro. Supp. II:** 121

Greene, Nathanael, **Supp. I Part 2:** 508

Greene, Richard Tobias, **III:** 76

Greene, Robert, **Supp. XVII:** 232

Green Eggs and Ham (Geisel), **Supp. XVI:** 108, 109

"Greene-ing of the Portables, The" (Cowley), **Supp. II Part 1:** 140

"Greenest Continent, The" (Stevens), **Retro. Supp. I:** 304

Greenfeld, Josh, **III:** 364

Green Hills of Africa (Hemingway), **II:** 253; **Retro. Supp. I:** 182, 186

Greening of America, The (C. Reich), **Supp. XVII:** 3

"Green Lagoons, The" (Leopold), **Supp. XIV:** 188

"Green Lampshade" (Simic), **Supp. VIII:** 283

Greenlanders, The (Smiley), **Supp. VI:** 292, **296–298,** 299, 305, 307

Greenlaw, Edwin A., **IV:** 453

"Greenleaf" (O'Connor), **III:** 350, 351; **Retro. Supp. II:** 233, 237

Greenman, Walter F., **I:** 217, 222

Green Memories (Mumford), **Supp. II Part 2:** 474, 475, 479, 480–481

"Green Pasture, The" (Leopold), **Supp. XIV:** 184

Green Pastures, The (Connelly), **Supp. II Part 1:** 223

"Green Red Brown and White" (Swenson), **Supp. IV Part 2:** 639

"Green River" (Bryant), **Supp. I Part 1:** 155, 164

Green Shadows, White Whale (Bradbury), **Supp. IV Part 1:** 102, 103, 116

"Green Shirt, The" (Olds), **Supp. X:** 209

"Greensleeves" (Jarman), **Supp. XVII:** 113

Greenslet, Ferris, **I:** 19; **Retro. Supp. I:** 9, 10, 11, 13; **Retro. Supp. II:** 41

Greenspan, Alan, **Supp. IV Part 2:** 526

Greenspan, Ezra, **Supp. XVIII:** 257

Greenstreet, Sydney, **Supp. IV Part 1:** 356

"Green Thought, A" (L. Michaels), **Supp. XVI:** 204

"Green-Thumb Boy" (Nelson), **Supp. XVIII:** 182
Greenwald, Ted, **Supp. IV Part 2:** 423
Green Wall, The (Wright), **Supp. III Part 2:** 591, 593, 595
Green Wave, The (Rukeyser), **Supp. VI:** 273, 280
"Green Ways" (Kunitz), **Supp. III Part 1:** 265
Green with Beasts (Merwin), **Supp. III Part 1:** 340, 344–346
Greenwood, Grace, **Supp. XIII:** 141
Gregerson, Linda, **Supp. IV Part 2:** 651; **Supp. X:** 204–205; **Supp. XI:** 142
"Gregorio Valdes" (Bishop), **Retro. Supp. II:** 51
Gregory, Alyse, **I:** 221, 226, 227, 231
Gregory, Horace, **II:** 512; **Supp. III Part 2:** 614, 615; **Supp. IX:** 229; **Supp. XV:** 143
Gregory, Lady Isabella Augusta, **III:** 458
Gregory, Sinda, **Supp. X:** 260, 268
Grendel (Gardner), **Supp. VI:** 63, **67,** 68, 74
Grenstone Poems (Bynner), **Supp. XV:** 44
"Gretel in Darkness" (Glück), **Supp. V:** 82
Gretta (Caldwell), **I:** 301, 302
Greuze, Jean Baptiste, **Supp. I Part 2:** 714
Grey, Zane, **Supp. XIII:** 5
"Grief Has Stamped" (Pedersen; Nelson, trans.), **Supp. XVIII:** 180
Grieg, Michael, **Supp. XV:** 133, 148
Griffin, Bartholomew, **Supp. I Part 1:** 369
Griffin, John Howard, **Supp. VIII:** 208
Griffin, Merv, **Supp. IV Part 2:** 526
Griffith, Albert J., **Supp. V:** 325
Griffith, D. W., **I:** 31, 481–482; **Retro. Supp. I:** 103, 325; **Supp. XI:** 45; **Supp. XVI:** 183, 184
Griffith, Paul, **Supp. XVIII:** 173, 175
Griffiths, Clyde, **I:** 511
Grile, Dod (pseudonym). *See* Bierce, Ambrose
Grimm, Herman, **II:** 17
Grimm brothers, **II:** 378; **III:** 101, 491, 492; **IV:** 266; **Supp. I Part 2:** 596, 622; **Supp. X:** 78, 84, 86
Grinnell, George Bird, **Supp. XVI:** 13
Gris, Juan, **I:** 442; **Retro. Supp. I:** 430
Griswold, Rufus Wilmot, **III:** 409, 429; **Retro. Supp. II:** 261, 262; **Supp. XV:** 277, 278; **Supp. XVI:** 8, 10–11
Grogg, Sam, Jr., **Supp. IV Part 2:** 468, 471
Gromer, Crystal, **Supp. XII:** 297
Gronlund, Laurence, **II:** 276
Grooms, Red, **Supp. XV:** 178
"Groping for Trouts" (Gass), **Supp. VI:** 87
Grosholz, Emily, **Supp. XII:** 185
Gross, Terry, **Supp. XVI:** 167
"*Grosse Fuge*" (Doty), **Supp. XI:** 126–127
Grossman, Allen, **Retro. Supp. II:** 83; **Supp. XVIII:** 91
Grosz, George, **III:** 172; **IV:** 438; **Retro. Supp. II:** 321; **Supp. X:** 137
"Grotesque in Modern Fiction, The" (E. Hoffman, Ph.D. dissertation), **Supp. XVI:** 147
"Groundhog, The" (Eberhart), **I:** 523, 530–532, 533
"Ground on Which I Stand, The" (Wilson), **Supp. VIII:** 331
"Ground Swell" (Jarman), **Supp. XVII:** 118
Group, The (McCarthy), **II:** 570, 574–578
"Group of Two, A" (Jarrell), **II:** 368
Group Therapy (Hearon), **Supp. VIII: 64–65**
"Grove" (Goldbarth), **Supp. XII:** 176
Groves of Academe, The (McCarthy), **II:** 568–571
Growing into Love (X. J. Kennedy), **Supp. XV:** 153, **158–160**
Growing Pains (J. S. Untermeyer), **Supp. XV:** 303
"Growing Season, The" (Caldwell), **I:** 309
Growing Up Gay: A Literary Anthology (Singer, ed.), **Supp. IV Part 1:** 330
"Growing Up Good in Maycomb" (Shaffer), **Supp. VIII:** 128
"Grown-Up" (Jewett), **Retro. Supp. II:** 134
"Growth" (Lowell), **II:** 554
"Growth and Decay in Recent Verse" (Untermeyer), **Supp. XV:** 299
Growth of the American Republic, The (Morison and Commager), **Supp. I Part 2:** 484
"Growtown Buggle, The" (Jewett), **Retro. Supp. II:** 132
Gruenberg, Louis, **III:** 392
Grumbach, Doris, **II:** 560
"Gryphon" (C. Baxter), **Supp. XVII:** 14, 17
"Guacamaja" (Leopold), **Supp. XIV:** 188–189
Guardian Angel, The (Holmes), **Supp. I Part 1:** 315–316
Guard of Honor (Cozzens), **I:** 370–372, 375, 376–377, 378, 379
Guardsman, The (Molnar), **Supp. XVI:** 187
Guare, John, **Supp. XIII:** 196, 207
Gubar, Susan, **Retro. Supp. I:** 42; **Retro. Supp. II:** 324; **Supp. IX:** 66; **Supp. XV:** 270
Guerard, Albert, Jr., **Supp. X:** 79; **Supp. XIII:** 172
Guérin, Maurice de, **I:** 241
"Guerrilla Handbook, A" (Baraka), **Supp. II Part 1:** 36
Guess and Spell Coloring Book, The (Swenson), **Supp. IV Part 2:** 648
Guess Who's Coming to Dinner (film), **Supp. I Part 1:** 67
Guest, Judith, **Supp. XVI:** 36
Guest, Val, **Supp. XI:** 307
Guest Book (Bynner), **Supp. XV:** 51
"Guests of Mrs. Timms, The" (Jewett), **II:** 408; **Retro. Supp. II:** 135
Guevara, Martha, **Supp. VIII:** 74
"Guevara ...Guevara" (Salinas), **Supp. XIII:** 312–313, 315
"Guided Tours of Hell" (Prose), **Supp. XVI:** 257
Guided Tours of Hell (Prose), **Supp. XVI:** 257, 261
Guide for the Perplexed (Maimonides), **Supp. XVII:** 46
Guide in the Wilderness, A (Cooper), **I:** 337
"Guide to Dungeness Spit, A" (Wagoner), **Supp. IX:** 325–326, 329
Guide to Ezra Pound's Selected Cantos' (Kearns), **Retro. Supp. I:** 292
Guide to Kulchur (Pound), **III:** 475
Guide to the Ruins (Nemerov), **III:** 269, 270–271, 272
Guillén, Nicolás, **Retro. Supp. I:** 202; **Supp. I Part 1:** 345
Guillevic, Eugene, **Supp. III Part 1:** 283
"Guilty Man, The" (Kunitz), **Supp. II Part 1:** 263
Guilty of Everything: The Autobiography of Herbert Huncke (Huncke), **Supp. XIV:** 138, 140, 141, 150
Guilty Pleasures (Barthelme), **Supp. IV Part 1:** 44, 45, 53
Guinness, Alec, **Retro. Supp. I:** 65
Gulag Archipelago, The (Solzhenitsyn), **Supp. XVII:** 229
"Gulf, The" (Dunn), **Supp. XI:** 149
Gulistan (Saadi), **II:** 19
Gullible's Travels (Lardner), **II:** 426, 427
Gulliver, Adelaide Cromwell, **Supp. XVIII:** 286
Gulliver's Travels (Swift), **I:** 209, 348, 366; **II:** 301; **Supp. I Part 2:** 656; **Supp. XI:** 209; **Supp. XVI:** 110
"Gulls" (Hayden), **Supp. II Part 1:** 367
"Gulls, The" (Nemerov), **III:** 272
"Gun, The" (Dobyns), **Supp. XIII:** 88
Gun, with Occasional Music (Lethem), **Supp. XVIII: 137–138**
Günderode: A Translation from the German (Fuller), **Supp. II Part 1:** 293
Gundy, Jeff, **Supp. XI:** 315; **Supp. XVI:** 46, 265, 275
Gunn, Thom, **Supp. IX:** 269
Gunn, Thomas, **Supp. V:** 178
Gunn Allen, Paula, **Supp. IV Part 1: 319–340,** 404; **Supp. IV Part 2:** 499, 502, 557, 568; **Supp. XII:** 218
"Gunnar's Sword" (C. Bly), **Supp. XVI:** 34, 35, 37, 42
"Guns as Keys; and the Great Gate Swings" (Lowell), **II:** 524
Gurdjieff, Georges, **Supp. IX:** 320; **Supp. V:** 199
Gurganus, Allan, **Supp. XII:** 308–309, 310
Gurko, Leo, **III:** 62
Gurney, A. R., **Supp. IX:** 261; **Supp. V: 95–112**
Gurney, Mary (Molly) Goodyear, **Supp. V:** 95
Gussow, Mel, **Supp. IX:** 93; **Supp. XII:** 325, 328, 341
Gustavus Vassa, the African (Vassa), **Supp. IV Part 1:** 11

Gusto, Thy Name Was Mrs. Hopkins: A Prose Rhapsody (Francis), **Supp. IX:** 89
Gute Mensch von Sezuan, Der (Brecht), **Supp. IX:** 138
Gutenberg, Johann, **Supp. I Part 2:** 392
Guthrie, A. B., **Supp. X:** 103
Guthrie, Woody, **Supp. XVIII:** 23
Gutman, Herbert, **Supp. I Part 1:** 47
Guttenplan, D. D., **Supp. XI:** 38
"Gutting of Couffignal, The" (Hammett), **Supp. IV Part 1:** 345
Guy Domville (James), **II:** 331; **Retro. Supp. I:** 228
"Gwendolyn" (Bishop), **Retro. Supp. II:** 51
Gwynn, R. S., **Supp. XVIII:** 184
Gypsy Ballads (Hughes, trans.), **Supp. I Part 1:** 345
Gypsy's Curse, The (Crews), **Supp. XI:** **110**
"Gyroscope, The" (Rukeyser), **Supp. VI:** 271
Gysin, Brion, **Supp. XII:** 129

H
Haardt, Sara. *See* Mencken, Mrs. H. L. (Sara Haardt)
Habakkuk (biblical book), **III:** 200, 347
Habibi (Nye), **Supp. XIII:** 273, **279**
"Habit" (James), **II:** 351
Habitations of the Word (Gass), **Supp. VI:** 88
Hacker, Marilyn, **Supp. XV:** 250; **Supp. XVII:** 71, 76, 112; **Supp. XVIII:** 177, 178
Hackett, David, **Supp. XII:** 236
Hadda, Janet, **Retro. Supp. II:** 317
Haeckel, Ernst Heinrich, **II:** 480
Haegert, John, **Supp. XVI:** 69
Hafif, Marcia, **Supp. IV Part 2:** 423
Hagar's Daughter (P. Hopkins), **Supp. XVI:** 143
Hagedorn, Jessica, **Supp. X:** 292
Hagen, Beulah, **Supp. I Part 2:** 679
Hager, Kelly, **Supp. XVIII:** 183
Haggard, Rider, **III:** 189
Hagoromo (play), **III:** 466
Hagstrum, Jean, **Supp. XV:** 74
"Hail Mary" (Fante), **Supp. XI:** 160, 164
Haines, George, IV, **I:** 444
Haines, John, **Supp. XII:** **197–214**
"Hair" (Corso), **Supp. XII:** 117, 126, 127
"Hair, The" (Carver), **Supp. III Part 1:** 137
"Haircut" (Lardner), **II:** 430, 436
"Hair Dressing" (Untermeyer), **Supp. XV:** 304, 305
Hairpiece: A Film for Nappy-Headed People (Chenzira; film), **Supp. XI:** 19–20
"Hairs" (Cisneros), **Supp. VII:** 59
Hairs/Pelitos (Cisneros), **Supp. VII:** 58
Hairy Ape, The (O'Neill), **III:** 391, 392, 393
"Haïta the Shepherd" (Bierce), **I:** 203
Haldeman, Anna, **Supp. I Part 1:** 2
Hale, Edward Everett, **Supp. I Part 2:** 584; **Supp. XI:** 193, 200
Hale, John Parker, **Supp. I Part 2:** 685
Hale, Nancy, **Supp. VIII:** 151, 171
Haley, Alex, **Supp. I Part 1:** 47, 66
Haley, J. Evetts, **Supp. V:** 226
"Half a Century Gone" (Lowell), **II:** 554
Half-a-Hundred: Tales by Great American Writers (Grayson, ed.), **Supp. XIII:** 171
Half Asleep in Frog Pajamas (Robbins), **Supp. X:** 259, **279–282**
Half Breed, The (film), **Supp. XVI:** 185
Half-Century of Conflict, A (Parkman), **Supp. II Part 2:** 600, 607, 610
"Half Deity" (Moore), **III:** 210, 214, 215
"Half Hour of August" (Ríos), **Supp. IV Part 2:** 552
Half-Lives (Jong), **Supp. V:** 115, 119
Half Moon Street: Two Short Novels (Theroux), **Supp. VIII:** 322, 323
Half of Paradise (Burke), **Supp. XIV:** 22, 24
Half-Past Nation Time (Johnson), **Supp. VI:** 187
"Half-Skinned Steer, The" (Proulx), **Supp. VII:** 261–262
"Half Sonnets" (Jarman), **Supp. XVII:** 115
Half Sun Half Sleep (Swenson), **Supp. IV Part 2:** 645–646
Halfway (Kumin), **Supp. IV Part 2:** 441–442
"Halfway" (Rich), **Supp. I Part 2:** 553
Halfway Home (Monette), **Supp. X:** 154
Halfway to Silence (Sarton), **Supp. VIII:** 261
Half You Don't Know, The: Selected Stories (Cameron), **Supp. XII:** 79, 80, 81
Haliburton, Thomas Chandler, **II:** 301; **IV:** 193; **Supp. I Part 2:** 411
Halifax, Lord, **II:** 111
Hall, Daniel, **Supp. XII:** 258
Hall, Donald, **I:** 567; **III:** 194; **Supp. IV Part 1:** 63, 72; **Supp. IV Part 2:** 621; **Supp. IX:** 269; **Supp. XIV:** 82, 126; **Supp. XV:** 21, 153, 176; **Supp. XVI:** 39, 230, 235
Hall, James, **II:** 313; **Supp. I Part 2:** 584, 585
Hall, James Baker, **Supp. X:** 24
Hall, Timothy L., **Supp. VIII:** 127, 128
Halleck, Fitz-Greene, **Supp. I Part 1:** 156, 158
"Hallelujah: A Sestina" (Francis), **Supp. IX:** 82
"Hallelujah on the Bum" (Abbey), **Supp. XIII:** 2
"Haller's Second Home" (Maxwell), **Supp. VIII:** 169
Halliday, Mark, **Supp. XV:** 19, 20, 21, 23, 25, 27, 30
Hallock, Rev. Moses, **Supp. I Part 1:** 153
Hall of Mirrors, A (Stone), **Supp. V:** 295, 296–299, 300, 301
"Hallowe'en" (Huncke), **Supp. XIV:** 145
"Halloween Party, The" (Chabon), **Supp. XI:** 72
Halloween Tree, The (Bradbury), **Supp. IV Part 1:** 102, 112–113
Hallwas, John E., **Supp. I Part 2:** 454
Halpern, Daniel, **Supp. IV Part 1:** 94–95, 95
Halsey, Theresa, **Supp. IV Part 1:** 330, 331
"Halt in the Desert, A" (Brodsky), **Supp. VIII:** 24
"Halves" (Dunn), **Supp. XI:** 149
Hamburg, Victoria, **Supp. XVI:** 126
Hamerik, Asger, **Supp. I Part 1:** 356
Hamill, Sam, **Supp. X:** 112, 125, 126, 127
Hamilton, Alexander, **I:** 485; **Supp. I Part 2:** 456, 483, 509
Hamilton, Alice, **Supp. I Part 1:** 5
Hamilton, David, **Supp. IX:** 296
Hamilton, Edith, **Supp. XVI:** 196
Hamilton, Lady Emma, **II:** 524
Hamilton, Hamish, **Supp. I Part 2:** 617
Hamilton, Walton, **Supp. I Part 2:** 632
Hamilton Stark (Banks), **Supp. V:** 8, 9–10, 11
"Hamlen Brook" (Wilbur), **Supp. III Part 2:** 564
"Hamlet" (Laforgue), **I:** 573; **III:** 11
Hamlet (Miller and Fraenkel), **III:** 178, 183
Hamlet (Shakespeare), **I:** 53, 183, 205, 377, 586–587; **II:** 158, 531; **III:** 7, 11, 12, 183; **IV:** 116, 131, 227; **Supp. I Part 1:** 369; **Supp. I Part 2:** 422, 457, 471; **Supp. IV Part 2:** 612; **Supp. IX:** 14
Hamlet, The (Faulkner), **II:** 69–71, 73, 74; **IV:** 131; **Retro. Supp. I:** 82, 91, 92; **Supp. IX:** 103; **Supp. VIII:** 178; **Supp. XI:** 247
"Hamlet and His Problems" (Eliot), **I:** 586–587
Hamlet of A. MacLeish, The (MacLeish), **III:** 11–12, 14, 15, 18
Hamlin, Eva, **Retro. Supp. II:** 115
"Hammer" (Bidart), **Supp. XV:** 35
Hammer, Adam, **Supp. XIII:** 112
Hammer, Langdon, **Retro. Supp. II:** 45, 53; **Supp. X:** 65
"Hammer Man, The" (Bambara), **Supp. XI:** 4–5
Hammett, Dashiell, **IV:** 286; **Retro. Supp. II:** 327; **Supp. I Part 1:** 286, 289, 291, 292, 293, 294, 295; **Supp. III Part 1:** 91; **Supp. IV Part 1:** 120, 121, **341–357; Supp. IV Part 2:** 461, 464, 468, 469, 472, 473; **Supp. IX:** 200; **Supp. XI:** 228; **Supp. XIII:** 159; **Supp. XIV:** 21; **Supp. XVII:** 137
Hammond, John, **Supp. XVIII:** 24
Hammond, Karla, **Supp. IV Part 2:** 439, 442, 448, 637, 640, 644, 648
Hampl, Patricia, **Supp. IX:** 291; **Supp. XI:** 126; **Supp. XVII:** 21
Hampson, Alfred Leete, **Retro. Supp. I:** 35–36, 38
"Hamrick's Polar Bear" (Caldwell), **I:** 309–310
Hamsun, Knut, **Supp. VIII:** 40; **Supp. XI:** 161, 167; **Supp. XII:** 21, 128
Hancock, John, **Supp. I Part 2:** 524
Hancock, Wade, **Supp. XVI:** 34
Handbook of North American Indians (Sando), **Supp. IV Part 2:** 510

Handcarved Coffins: A Nonfiction Account of an American Crime (Capote), **Supp. III Part 1:** 131
Handel, Georg Friedrich, **III:** 210; **IV:** 369
"Handfasting" (Wright), **Supp. XV:** 343
"Handfuls" (Sandburg), **III:** 584
"Handle with Care" (Fitzgerald), **Retro. Supp. I:** 114
Handley, William R., **Supp. XVIII:** 58
Handmaid's Tale, The (Atwood), **Supp. XIII:** 19, 20, **27–29**
"Hand of Emmagene, The" (Taylor), **Supp. V:** 314, 325–326
Hand of the Potter, The: A Tragedy in Four Acts (Dreiser), **Retro. Supp. II:** 104; **Supp. XVII:** 96
"Hands" (Anderson), **I:** 106, 107
"Hands" (Mora), **Supp. XIII:** 215
Hands of Orlac, The (M. Renard; Crewe-Jones, trans.), **Supp. XVII:** 58
"Hand to Mouth" (Auster), **Supp. XII:** 31
Hand to Mouth (Auster), **Supp. XII:** 21
Handy, Lowney, **Supp. XI:** 217, 220, 221, 225
Handy, W. C., **Supp. VIII:** 337
Handy Guide for Beggars, A (Lindsay), **Supp. I Part 2:** 376–378, 380, 382, 399
Hanging Garden, The (Wagoner), **Supp. IX: 338–339**
"Hanging Gardens of Tyburn, The" (Hecht), **Supp. X:** 58
"Hanging of the Crane, The" (Longfellow), **Retro. Supp. II:** 169, 171
Hanging On (Conroy), **Supp. XVI:** 69
"Hanging Pictures in Nanny's Room" (Kenyon), **Supp. VII:** 164
"Hanging the Wash" (Alvarez), **Supp. VII:** 4
"Hangman, The" (Sexton), **Supp. II Part 2:** 680, 691
Hangover Mass (X. J. Kennedy), **Supp. XV:** 165
Hangsaman (Jackson), **Supp. IX:** 116, 123, **124**
Hanh, Thich Nhat, **Supp. V:** 199
Hanks, Lucy, **III:** 587
Hanks, Nancy. *See* Lincoln, Mrs. Thomas (Nancy Hanks)
Hanley, Lynne T., **Supp. IV Part 1:** 208
Hanna, Mark, **Supp. I Part 2:** 395
Hannah, Barry, **Supp. X:** 285
Hannah and Her Sisters (film; Allen), **Supp. XV:** 9, **10–11**
"Hannah Armstrong" (Masters), **Supp. I Part 2:** 461
"Hannah Binding Shoes" (Larcom), **Supp. XIII:** 141, 143
"Hannah Byde" (D. West), **Supp. XVIII:** 280
Hannah's House (Hearon), **Supp. VIII:** 58, **60–61**
Hanneman, Audre, **II:** 259
Hannibal Lecter, My Father (Acker), **Supp. XII:** 6
Hanoi (McCarthy), **II:** 579
Hansberry, Lorraine, **Supp. IV Part 1: 359–377; Supp. VIII:** 329
Hanscom, Leslie, **Supp. XI:** 229
"Hansel and Gretel" (Prose), **Supp. XVI:** 256, 258
Hansen, Erik, **Supp. V:** 241
Hansen, Harry, **IV:** 366
Han-shan, **Supp. VIII:** 292
Hanson, Curtis, **Supp. XI:** 67
Han Suyin, **Supp. X:** 291
Hanzlicek, C. G., **Supp. XV:** 73
Hapgood, Hutchins, **Supp. XVII: 95–108**
Hapgoods, The: Three Earnest Brothers (Marcaccio), **Supp. XVII:** 106
"Happenings: An Art of Radical Juxtaposition" (Sontag), **Supp. III Part 2:** 456
"Happenstance" (Komunyakaa), **Supp. XIII:** 130
Happenstance (Shields), **Supp. VII:** 315–318, 320, 323, 324, 326
Happersberger, Lucien, **Supp. I Part 1:** 51
"Happiest I've Been, The" (Updike), **IV:** 219
Happily Ever After (Quindlen), **Supp. XVII:** 167
"Happiness" (Oliver), **Supp. VII:** 236
"Happiness" (Sandburg), **III:** 582–583
Happiness of Getting It Down Right, The (Steinman, ed.), **Supp. VIII:** 172
"Happy Birthday" (Bambara), **Supp. XI:** 4
Happy Birthday (Loos), **Supp. XVI:** 193
Happy Birthday, Wanda June (Vonnegut), **Supp. II Part 2:** 759, 776–777
Happy Birthday of Death, The (Corso), **Supp. XII: 127–129**
Happy Childhood, A (Matthews), **Supp. IX:** 155, 160, **161–163**
Happy Days (Beckett), **Retro. Supp. I:** 206
Happy Days, 1880–1892 (Mencken), **III:** 100, 111, 120
"Happy End" (Simic), **Supp. VIII:** 276–277
"Happy Failure, The" (Melville), **III:** 90
Happy Families Are All Alike (Taylor), **Supp. V:** 322–323, 325
Happy Isles of Oceania, The: Paddling the Pacific (Theroux), **Supp. VIII:** 324
"Happy Journey to Trenton and Camden, The" (Wilder), **IV:** 366
"Happy Man, The" (Lethem), **Supp. XVIII:** 139
"Happy Marriage, The" (MacLeish), **III:** 15–16
Happy Marriage and Other Poems, The (MacLeish), **III:** 4
"Happy To Be Here" (Keillor), **Supp. XVI:** 168
Happy to Be Here (Keillor), **Supp. XVI:** 165, 171
"Hapworth 16, 1924" (Salinger), **III:** 552, 571–572
"Harbor Lights" (Doty), **Supp. XI:** 122
Harcourt, Alfred, **II:** 191, 451–452; **III:** 587; **Retro. Supp. I:** 131; **Supp. XV:** 308
Harcourt, Brace, **Retro. Supp. I:** 83
Harcourt, T. A., **I:** 196
Hard Candy, a Book of Stories (T. Williams), **IV:** 383
"Hardcastle Crags" (Plath), **Supp. I Part 2:** 537
"Hard Daddy" (Hughes), **Retro. Supp. I:** 200
"Hardened Criminals, The" (Lethem), **Supp. XVIII:** 139
Harder They Fall, The (Schulberg), **Supp. XV:** 194, 201
Hard Facts (Baraka), **Supp. II Part 1:** 54, 55, 58
Hard Freight (Wright), **Supp. V:** 332, 339–340
Hard Hours, The (Hecht), **Supp. X:** 57, **59–62,** 63, 64
Hardie, Kier, **Supp. I Part 1:** 5
Harding, Walter, **IV:** 177, 178
Harding, Warren G., **I:** 486; **II:** 253, 433; **Supp. I Part 1:** 24
"Hard Kind of Courage, The" (Baldwin), **Supp. I Part 1:** 52
Hard Maple (S. and A. Warner), **Supp. XVIII:** 264
"Hard Rain's A-Gonna Fall, A" (song, Dylan), **Supp. XVIII:** 26, 29
"Hard Time Keeping Up, A" (Ellison), **Retro. Supp. II:** 124
Hard Times (Dickens), **Supp. I Part 2:** 675
"Hard Times in Elfland, The" (Lanier), **Supp. I Part 1:** 365
Hardwick, Elizabeth, **II:** 543, 554, 566; **Retro. Supp. II:** 179, 180, 183, 184, 190, 221, 228–229, 245; **Supp. I Part 1:** 196; **Supp. III Part 1: 193–215; Supp. IV Part 1:** 299; **Supp. V,** 319; **Supp. X,** 171; **Supp. XII:** 209; **Supp. XIV:** 89
"Hard Work 1956" (Dunn), **Supp. XI:** 147
Hardy, Barbara, **Supp. I Part 2:** 527
Hardy, Oliver, **Supp. I Part 2:** 607; **Supp. IV Part 2:** 574
Hardy, René, **Supp. III Part 1:** 235
Hardy, Thomas, **I:** 59, 103, 292, 317, 377; **II:** 181, 184–185, 186, 191–192, 271, 275, 372, 523, 542; **III:** 32, 453, 485, 508, 524; **IV:** 83, 135, 136; **Retro. Supp. I:** 141, 377–378; **Supp. I Part 1:** 217; **Supp. I Part 2:** 429, 512; **Supp. II Part 1:** 4, 26; **Supp. IX:** 40, 78, 85, 108, 211; **Supp. VIII:** 32; **Supp. X:** 228; **Supp. XI:** 311; **Supp. XIII:** 294, **Supp. XIII:** 130; **Supp. XIV:** 24; **Supp. XV:** 170; **Supp. XVIII:** 74
Harjo, Joy, **Supp. IV Part 1:** 325, 404; **Supp. IV Part 2:** 499, 507; **Supp. XII: 215–234; Supp. XVIII:** 189
"Harlem" (Hughes), **Retro. Supp. I:** 194, 204; **Supp. I Part 1:** 340; **Supp. VIII:** 213
Harlem, Mecca of the New Negro (Locke), **Supp. XIV:** 201
"Harlem Dancer, The" (McKay), **Supp. X:** 134

Harlem Gallery (Tolson), **Retro. Supp. I:** 208, 209, 210
Harlem Glory: A Fragment of Aframerican Life (McKay), **Supp. X:** 132, **141–142**
Harlem: Negro Metropolis (McKay), **Supp. X:** 132, 141, 142
"Harlem Runs Wild" (McKay), **Supp. X:** 140
Harlem Shadows (McKay), **Supp. X:** 131–132, 136
Harlem Underground (Lacy), **Supp. XV:** 206
"Harlequin of Dreams, The" (Lanier), **Supp. I Part 1:** 365
Harlot's Ghost (Mailer), **Retro. Supp. II:** 211–212
Harlow, Jean, **IV:** 256; **Retro. Supp. I:** 110
"Harm" (C. Frost), **Supp. XV:** 101
Harmon, William, **Retro. Supp. I:** 37; **Supp. XI:** 248
"Harmonic" (F. Barthelme), **Supp. XI:** 26
Harmonium (Stevens), **III:** 196; **IV:** 76, 77, 78, 82, 87, 89, 92; **Retro. Supp. I:** 296, 297, 299, **300–302,** 301, 302
"Harmony of the Gospels" (Taylor), **IV:** 149
"Harmony of the World" (C. Baxter), **Supp. XVII:** 16
Harmony of the World (C. Baxter), **Supp. XVII:** 16–17
Harnett, Vincent, **Supp. XV:** 198
Harper (film), **Supp. IV Part 2:** 473
Harper, Donna, **Retro. Supp. I:** 194, 195, 209
Harper, Frances E. Watkins, **Supp. II Part 1:** 201–202; **Supp. XVIII:** 284
Harper, Gordon Lloyd, **Retro. Supp. II:** 23
Harper, Michael, **Supp. XV:** 74
Harper, Michael S., **Retro. Supp. II:** 116, 123
Harper, William Rainey, **Supp. I Part 2:** 631
Harper's Anthology of 20th Century Native American Poetry (Niatum, ed.), **Supp. IV Part 1:** 331
"Harriet" (Lowell), **II:** 554
Harrigan, Edward, **II:** 276; **III:** 14
Harrington, Michael, **I:** 306
Harrington, Ollie, **Supp. XVI:** 142–143
Harris, Celia, **Retro. Supp. I:** 9
Harris, George, **II:** 70
Harris, Joel Chandler, **III:** 338; **Supp. I Part 1:** 352; **Supp. II Part 1:** 192, 201; **Supp. XIV:** 61
Harris, Judith, **Supp. XIV:** 269
Harris, Julie, **II:** 587, 601; **Supp. IX:** 125
Harris, Leonard, **Supp. XIV:** 196, 211–212
Harris, MacDonald, **Supp. XI:** 65
Harris, Marie, **Supp. IX:** 153
Harris, Peter, **Supp. X:** 206, 207
Harris, Susan K., **Supp. XV:** 269
Harris, Thomas, **Supp. XIV:** 26
Harris, Victoria Frenkel, **Supp. IV Part 1:** 68, 69
Harrison, Colin, **Supp. XIV:** 26
Harrison, Hazel, **Retro. Supp. II:** 115
Harrison, Jim, **Supp. VIII: 37–56**
Harrison, Kathryn, **Supp. X:** 191
Harrison, Ken, **Supp. IX:** 101
Harrison, Oliver (pseudonym). *See* Smith, Harrison
Harry: A Portrait (N. Boyce), **Supp. XVII:** 104
Harryhausen, Ray, **Supp. IV Part 1:** 115
Harryman, Carla, **Supp. XV:** 344
"Harry of Nothingham" (Hugo), **Supp. VI:** 146–147
"Harry's Death" (Carver), **Supp. III Part 1:** 146
"Harsh Judgment, The" (Kunitz), **Supp. III Part 1:** 264
Hart, Albert Bushnell, **Supp. I Part 2:** 479, 480, 481
Hart, Bernard, **I:** 241, 242, 248–250, 256
Hart, Henry, **Retro. Supp. II:** 187; **Supp. XIV:** 97
Hart, James D., **Supp. XVIII:** 257
Hart, John Seely, **Supp. XVIII:** 257, 258, 264
Hart, Lorenz, **III:** 361
Hart, Moss, **Supp. IV Part 2:** 574; **Supp. XV:** 329
Hart, Pearl, **Supp. X:** 103
"Hart Crane" (Tate), **I:** 381
"Hart Crane and Poetry: A Consideration of Crane's Intense Poetics with Reference to 'The Return'" (Grossman), **Retro. Supp. II:** 83
Harte, Anna Griswold, **Supp. II Part 1:** 341
Harte, Bret, **I:** 193, 195, 203; **II:** 289; **IV:** 196; **Retro. Supp. II:** 72; **Supp. II Part 1: 335–359,** 399; **Supp. XV:** 115
Harte, Walter Blackburn, **I:** 199
Harter, Carol C., **Supp. IV Part 1:** 217
Hartley, David, **III:** 77
Hartley, Lois, **Supp. I Part 2:** 459, 464–465
Hartley, L. P., **Supp. I Part 1:** 293
Hartley, Marsden, **IV:** 409, 413; **Retro. Supp. I:** 430; **Supp. X:** 137; **Supp. XV:** 298
Hartman, Geoffrey, **Supp. IV Part 1:** 119; **Supp. XII:** 130, 253
Harum, David, **II:** 102
"Harvard" (Lowell), **II:** 554
Harvard College in the Seventeenth Century (Morison), **Supp. I Part 2:** 485
"Harvesters of Night and Water" (Hogan), **Supp. IV Part 1:** 412
"Harvest Song" (Toomer), **Supp. III Part 2:** 483
Harvill Book of 20th Century Poetry in English, **Supp. X:** 55
"Harv Is Plowing Now" (Updike), **Retro. Supp. I:** 318
Haselden, Elizabeth Lee, **Supp. VIII:** 125
Hass, Robert, **Supp. VI: 97–111; Supp. VIII:** 24, 28; **Supp. XI:** 142, 270; **Supp. XIV:** 83, 84
Hassam, Childe, **Retro. Supp. II:** 136
Hassan, Ihab, **IV:** 99–100, 115; **Supp. XI:** 221
Hasse, Henry, **Supp. IV Part 1:** 102
Hasty-Pudding, The (Barlow), **Supp. II Part 1:** 74, 77–80
Hatful of Rain, A (Gazzo), **III:** 155
Hatlen, Burton, **Supp. V:** 138, 139–140
"Hattie Bloom" (Oliver), **Supp. VII:** 232
Haunch, Paunch, and Jowl (Ornitz), **Supp. IX:** 227
"Haunted Landscape" (Ashbery), **Supp. III Part 1:** 22
Haunted Merchant, The (Briggs), **Supp. XVIII:** 2, 8
"Haunted Mind" (Simic), **Supp. VIII:** 282
"Haunted Mind, The" (Hawthorne), **II:** 230–231
"Haunted Oak, The" (Dunbar), **Supp. II Part 1:** 207, 208
"Haunted Palace, The" (Poe), **III:** 421
"Haunted Valley, The" (Bierce), **I:** 200
Haunting, The (film), **Supp. IX:** 125
Haunting of Hill House, The (Jackson), **Supp. IX:** 117, 121, 126
Hauptmann, Gerhart, **III:** 472
Haussmann, Sonja, **Supp. XIII:** 331, **Supp. XIII:** 347
"Havanna vanities come to dust in Miami" (Didion), **Supp. IV Part 1:** 210
Haven, Cynthia, **Supp. XV:** 252, 264
Haven's End (Marquand), **III:** 55, 56, 63, 68
"Have You Ever Tried to Enter the Long Black Branches" (Oliver), **Supp. VII:** 247
"Having Been Interstellar" (Ammons), **Supp. VII:** 25
"Having It Out With Melancholy" (Kenyon), **Supp. VII:** 171
"Having Lost My Sons, I Confront the Wreckage of the Moon: Christmas, 1960" (Wright), **Supp. III Part 2:** 600
"Having Snow" (Schwartz), **Supp. II Part 2:** 652
Hawai'i One Summer (Kingston), **Supp. V:** 157, 160, 166, 169–170
"Hawk, The" (Francis), **Supp. IX:** 81
Hawke, David Freeman, **Supp. I Part 2:** 511, 516
Hawkes, John, **I:** 113; **Retro. Supp. II:** 234; **Supp. III Part 1:** 2; **Supp. IX:** 212; **Supp. V:** 40; **Supp. XVII:** 183
Hawkins, William, **II:** 587
Hawk in the Rain, The (Hughes), **Retro. Supp. II:** 244; **Supp. I Part 2:** 537, 540
Hawk Is Dying, The (Crews), **Supp. XI: 111**
Hawk Moon (Shepard), **Supp. III Part 2:** 445
Hawks, Howard, **Supp. IV Part 1:** 130; **Supp. XVIII:** 148
"Hawk's Cry in Autumn, The" (Brodsky), **Supp. VIII:** 29
"Hawk's Shadow" (Glück), **Supp. V:** 85
Hawk's Well, The (Yeats), **III:** 459–460
Hawley, Adelaide, **Supp. XIV:** 207
Hawley, Joseph, **I:** 546
Hawthorne (James), **II:** 372–378; **Retro. Supp. I:** 220, **223–224**

"Hawthorne" (Longfellow), **Retro. Supp. II:** 169
"Hawthorne" (Lowell), **II:** 550
Hawthorne, Julian, **II:** 225; **Supp. I Part 1:** 38; **Supp. XV:** 274
Hawthorne, Mrs. Nathaniel (Sophia Peabody), **II:** 224, 244; **III:** 75, 86
Hawthorne, Nathaniel, **I:** 106, 204, 211, 340, 355, 363, 384, 413, 458, 561–562; **II:** 7, 8, 40, 60, 63, 74, 89, 127–128, 138, 142, 198, **223–246,** 255, 259, 264, 267, 272, 274, 277, 281, 282, 295, 307, 309, 311, 313, 322, 324, 326, 402, 408, 446, 501, 545; **III:** 51, 81–82, 83, 84, 85, 87, 88, 91, 92, 113, 316, 359, 412, 415, 421, 438, 453, 454, 507, 565, 572; **IV:** 2, 4, 167, 172, 179, 194, 333, 345, 453; **Retro. Supp. I:** 1, 53, 59, 62, 63, 91, **145–167,** 215, 218, 220, 223, 248–249, 252, 257, 258, 330, 331, 365; **Retro. Supp. II:** 136, 142, 153, 156–157, 158, 159, 187, 221; **Supp. I Part 1:** 38, 188, 197, 317, 372; **Supp. I Part 2:** 420, 421, 545, 579, 580, 582, 587, 595, 596; **Supp. III Part 2:** 501; **Supp. IV Part 1:** 80, 127, 297; **Supp. IV Part 2:** 463, 596; **Supp. IX:** 114; **Supp. V:** 152; **Supp. VIII:** 103, 105, 108, 153, 201; **Supp. X:** 78; **Supp. XI:** 51, 78; **Supp. XII:** 26; **Supp. XIII:** 102; **Supp. XIV:** 48; **Supp. XV:** 269, 272, 282; **Supp. XVI:** 83, 84, 157; **Supp. XVII:** 42; **Supp. XVIII:** 258, 260
Hawthorne, Rose, **II:** 225
Hawthorne, Una, **II:** 225
"Hawthorne and His Mosses" (Melville), **Retro. Supp. I:** 254; **Supp. XIV:** 48
"Hawthorne Aspect [of Henry James], The" (Eliot), **Retro. Supp. I:** 63
"Hawthorne in Solitude" (Cowley), **Supp. II Part 1:** 143
Hay, John, **I:** 1, 10, 12, 14–15; **Supp. I Part 1:** 352
Hay, Mrs. John, **I:** 14
Hay, Sara Henderson, **Supp. XIV: 119–135**
Hayakawa, S. I., **I:** 448; **Supp. I Part 1:** 315; **Supp. XV:** 176
Hayden, Robert, **Supp. II Part 1: 361–383; Supp. IV Part 1:** 169; **Supp. XIII:** 115, 127; **Supp. XIV:** 119, 123
Hayden, Sterling, **Supp. XI:** 304
Haydn, Hiram, **IV:** 100, 358
Hayduke Lives! (Abbey), **Supp. XIII: 16**
Hayek, Friedrich A. von, **Supp. IV Part 2:** 524
Hayes, Helen, **Supp. XVI:** 193, 195
Hayes, Ira, **Supp. IV Part 1:** 326
Hayes, Richard, **Supp. V:** 320
Hayes, Rutherford B., **Supp. I Part 2:** 419
Haygood, Wil, **Supp. VIII:** 79
Hayne, Paul Hamilton, **Supp. I Part 1:** 352, 354, 355, 360, 372
Haynes, Todd, **Supp. XVIII:** 23
Hayward, Florence, **Retro. Supp. II:** 65
Hayward, John, **Retro. Supp. I:** 67
Haywood, "Big" Bill, **I:** 483; **Supp. V:** 286
Hazard, Grace, **II:** 530
Hazard of Fortunes, A (Howells), **Retro. Supp. II:** 288
Hazard of New Fortunes, A (Howells), **II:** 275, 276, 286–297, 290
Hazel, Robert, **Supp. VIII:** 137, 138
Hazen, General W. B., **I:** 192, 193
Hazlitt, Henry, **Supp. IV Part 2:** 524
Hazlitt, William, **I:** 58, 378; **II:** 315
Hazmat (McClatchy), **Supp. XII: 265–270**
Hazo, Samuel, **I:** 386; **Supp. XIV:** 123, 124
Hazzard, Shirley, **Supp. VIII:** 151
H.D. *See* Doolittle, Hilda
"He" (Porter), **III:** 434, 435
"Head and Shoulders" (Fitzgerald), **Retro. Supp. I:** 101
"Head-Hunter, The" (O. Henry), **Supp. II Part 1:** 403
"Headless Hawk, The" (Capote), **Supp. III Part 1:** 124
Headlines (T. Williams), **IV:** 381
Headlong Hall (Peacock), **Supp. I Part 1:** 307
Headmaster, The (McPhee), **Supp. III Part 1:** 291, 294, 298
"Head of Joaquín Murrieta, The" (Rodriguez), **Supp. XIV:** 303
Headsman, The (Cooper), **I:** 345–346
"Headwaters" (Momaday), **Supp. IV Part 2:** 486
Healy, Eloise Klein, **Supp. XI:** 121, 124, 126, 127, 129, 137
Healy, Tim, **II:** 129, 137
Heaney, Sally, **Supp. XVII:** 241
Heaney, Seamus, **Retro. Supp. II:** 245; **Supp. IX:** 41, 42; **Supp. X:** 67, 122; **Supp. XI:** 249; **Supp. XV:** 256
"Heard through the Walls of the Race-track Glen Motel" (X. J. Kennedy), **Supp. XV:** 170
Hearn, Lafcadio, **I:** 211; **II:** 311
Hearon, Shelby, **Supp. VIII: 57–72**
Hearst, Patty, **Supp. IV Part 1:** 195
Hearst, William Randolph, **I:** 198, 207, 208; **IV:** 298
Heart and Perimeter (Bierds), **Supp. XVII: 28–29**
"Heart and the Lyre, The" (Bogan), **Supp. III Part 1:** 65
"Heartbeat" (Harjo), **Supp. XII:** 221–222
Heartbreak Kid, The (film), **Supp. IV Part 2:** 575, 589
Heart for the Gods of Mexico, A (Aiken), **I:** 54
"Hear the Nightingale Sing" (Gordon), **II:** 200
Hear the Wind Blow (Sanders), **Supp. XVI:** 268
Heart is a Lonely Hunter, The (McCullers), **II:** 586, 588–593, 604, 605
Heart of a Woman, The (Angelou), **Supp. IV Part 1:** 2, 5, 7–9, 9, 14, 17
"Heart of Darkness" (Conrad), **I:** 575, 578; **II:** 595; **Supp. XVI:** 212
Heart of Darkness (Conrad), **Retro. Supp. II:** 292; **Supp. V:** 249, 311; **Supp. VIII:** 4, 316
Heart of Darkness (Didion), **Supp. IV Part 1:** 207
Heart of Happy Hollow, The (Dunbar), **Supp. II Part 1:** 214
Heart of Knowledge, The: American Indians on the Bomb (Gunn Allen and Caputi, eds.), **Supp. IV Part 1:** 334–335
"Heart of Knowledge, The: Nuclear Themes in Native American Thought and Literature" (Caputi), **Supp. IV Part 1:** 335
"Heart of the Park, The" (O'Connor), **Retro. Supp. II:** 225
Heart of the West (O. Henry), **Supp. II Part 1:** 410
"Hearts, The" (Pinsky), **Supp. VI:** 245–247, 248
"'Hearts and Flowers'" (MacLeish), **III:** 8
"Hearts and Heads" (Ransom), **Supp. I Part 1:** 373
"Heart's Graveyard Shift, The" (Komunyakaa), **Supp. XIII:** 120
Heart-Shape in the Dust (Hayden), **Supp. II Part 1:** 365, 366
"Heart's Needle" (Snodgrass), **Supp. VI: 311–313,** 320
Heart's Needle (Snodgrass), **I:** 400
"Hearts of Oak" (Rowson), **Supp. XV:** 243
"Heart Songs" (Proulx), **Supp. VII:** 254
Heart Songs and Other Stories (Proulx), **Supp. VII:** 252–256, 261
Heart to Artemis, The (Bryher), **Supp. I Part 1:** 259
Heartwood (Burke), **Supp. XIV:** 35
Heath Anthology of American Literature, The, **Supp. IX:** 4; **Supp. XV:** 270, 313
Heathcote, Anne. *See* De Lancey, Mrs. James
"Heathen Chinee, The" (Harte), **Supp. II Part 1:** 350–351, 352
Heathen Days, 1890–1936 (Mencken), **III:** 100, 111
Heath-Stubbs, John, **Supp. XV:** 153
Heat's On, The (C. Himes), **Supp. XVI:** 143, 144
"Heaven" (Dunn), **Supp. XI:** 154
"Heaven" (Levine), **Supp. V:** 182
"Heaven" (Patchett), **Supp. XII:** 309
Heaven and Earth: A Cosmology (Goldbarth), **Supp. XII: 187**
"Heaven and Earth in Jest" (Dillard), **Supp. VI:** 24, 28
"Heaven as Anus" (Kumin), **Supp. IV Part 2:** 448
Heavenly Conversation, The (Mather), **Supp. II Part 2:** 460
"Heavenly Feast, The" (Schnackenberg), **Supp. XV:** 257, 259
Heavens (Untermeyer), **Supp. XV:** 306
Heavens and Earth (Benét), **Supp. XI:** 44
Heaven's Coast (Doty), **Supp. XI:** 119, 121, **129–130,** 134

Heaven's Prisoners (Burke), **Supp. XIV:** 23, 29
"Heavy Angel, The" (Everwine), **Supp. XV:** 80
"Heavy Bear Who Goes with Me, The" (Schwartz), **Supp. II Part 2:** 646
"He Came Also Still" (Zukofsky), **Supp. III Part 2:** 612
Hecht, Anthony, **IV:** 138; **Supp. III Part 2:** 541, 561; **Supp. X: 55–75; Supp. XII:** 269–270; **Supp. XV:** 251, 256
Hecht, Ben, **I:** 103; **II:** 42; **Supp. I Part 2:** 646; **Supp. XI:** 307; **Supp. XIII:** 106
Hecht, S. Theodore, **Supp. III Part 2:** 614
Heckewelder, John, **II:** 503
"Hedge Island" (Lowell), **II:** 524
Hedges, William I., **II:** 311–312
"He 'Digesteth Harde Yron'" (Moore), **Supp. IV Part 2:** 454
Hedin, Robert, **Supp. XII:** 200, 202
Hedylus (Doolittle), **Supp. I Part 1:** 259, 270
"Heel & Toe To the End" (W. C. Williams), **Retro. Supp. I:** 430
Heffernan, Michael, **Supp. XII:** 177
"HEGEL" (Baraka), **Supp. II Part 1:** 53
Hegel, Georg Wilhelm Friedrich, **I:** 265; **II:** 358; **III:** 262, 308–309, 480, 481, 487, 607; **IV:** 86, 333, 453; **Supp. I Part 2:** 633, 635, 640, 645; **Supp. XVI:** 289
"Hegemony of Race, The" (Du Bois), **Supp. II Part 1:** 181
Hegger, Grace Livingston. *See* Lewis, Mrs. Sinclair (Grace Livingston Hegger)
"He Had Spent His Youth Dreaming" (Dobyns), **Supp. XIII:** 90
Heidegger, Martin, **II:** 362, 363; **III:** 292; **IV:** 491; **Retro. Supp. II:** 87; **Supp. V:** 267; **Supp. VIII:** 9; **Supp. XVI:** 283, 288
Heidenmauer, The (Cooper), **I:** 345–346
Heidi Chronicles, The (Wasserstein), **Supp. IV Part 1:** 309; **Supp. XV:** 319, **325–327**
"Height of the Ridiculous, The" (Holmes), **Supp. I Part 1:** 302
Heilbroner, Robert, **Supp. I Part 2:** 644, 648, 650
Heilbrun, Carolyn G., **Supp. IX:** 66; **Supp. XI:** 208; **Supp. XIV:** 161, 163
Heilman, Robert Bechtold, **Supp. XIV:** 11, 12
Heilpern, John, **Supp. XIV:** 242
Heim, Michael, **Supp. V:** 209
Heine, Heinrich, **II:** 272, 273, 277, 281, 282, 387, 544; **IV:** 5; **Supp. XV:** 293, 299; **Supp. XVI:** 188
Heineman, Frank, **Supp. III Part 2:** 619
Heinlein, Robert, **Supp. IV Part 1:** 102; **Supp. XVI:** 122; **Supp. XVIII:** 149
Heinz, Helen. *See* Tate, Mrs. Allen (Helen Heinz)
Heiress, The (film), **Retro. Supp. I:** 222
"Heirs" (Nye), **Supp. XIII:** 284
"He Is Not Worth the Trouble" (Rowson), **Supp. XV:** 240
"He Knew" (C. Himes), **Supp. XVI:** 137
"Helas" (Creeley), **Supp. IV Part 1:** 150, 158
Helburn, Theresa, **IV:** 381
Heldreth, Leonard, **Supp. V:** 151
"Helen" (Lowell), **II:** 544
"Helen, Thy Beauty Is to Me" (Fante), **Supp. XI:** 169
"Helen: A Courtship" (Faulkner), **Retro. Supp. I:** 81
"Helen I Love You" (Farrell), **II:** 28, 45
Helen in Egypt (Doolittle), **Supp. I Part 1:** 260, 272, 273, 274; **Supp. XV:** 264
Helen Keller: Sketch for a Portrait (Brooks), **I:** 254
"Helen of Tyre" (Longfellow), **II:** 496
Heliodora (Doolittle), **Supp. I Part 1:** 266
"Helix" (Sobin), **Supp. XVI:** 283
Hellbox (O'Hara), **III:** 361
Heller, Joseph, **III:** 2, 258; **IV:** 98; **Retro. Supp. II:** 324; **Supp. I Part 1:** 196; **Supp. IV Part 1: 379–396; Supp. V:** 244; **Supp. VIII:** 245; **Supp. XI:** 307; **Supp. XII:** 167–168; **Supp. XV:** 322; **Supp. XVII:** 139
Hellman, Lillian, **I:** 28; **III:** 28; **Supp. I Part 1: 276–298; Supp. IV Part 1:** 1, 12, 83, 353, 355, 356; **Supp. IX:** 196, 198, 200–201, 204; **Supp. VIII:** 243
Hellmann, Lillian, **Retro. Supp. II:** 327
Hello (Creeley), **Supp. IV Part 1:** 155, 157
"Hello, Hello Henry" (Kumin), **Supp. IV Part 2:** 446
"Hello, Stranger" (Capote), **Supp. III Part 1:** 120
Hello Dolly! (musical play), **IV:** 357
Hellyer, John, **Supp. I Part 2:** 468
Helm, Bob, **Supp. XV:** 147
Helm, Levon, **Supp. XVIII:** 26
Helmets (Dickey), **Supp. IV Part 1:** 175, 178, 180
"Helmsman, The" (Doolittle), **Supp. I Part 1:** 266
"Help" (Barth), **I:** 139
"Help Her to Believe" (Olsen). *See* "I Stand There Ironing" (Olsen)
"Helsinki Window" (Creeley), **Supp. IV Part 1:** 158
Hemenway, Robert E., **Supp. IV Part 1:** 6
Hemingway, Dr. Clarence Edwards, **II:** 248, 259
Hemingway, Ernest, **I:** 28, 64, 97, 99, 105, 107, 117, 150, 162, 190, 211, 221, 288, 289, 295, 367, 374, 378, 421, 423, 445, 476, 477, 478, 482, 484–485, 487, 488, 489, 491, 495, 504, 517; **II:** 27, 44, 51, 58, 68–69, 78, 90, 97, 127, 206, **247–270,** 289, 424, 431, 456, 457, 458–459, 482, 560, 600; **III:** 2, 18, 20, 35, 36, 37, 40, 61, 108, 220, 334, 363, 364, 382, 453, 454, 471–472, 476, 551, 575, 576, 584; **IV:** 27, 28, 33, 34, 35, 42, 49, 97, 108, 122, 126, 138, 190, 191, 201, 216, 217, 257, 297, 363, 404, 427, 433, 451; **Retro. Supp. I:** 74, 98, 108, 111, 112, 113, 115, **169–191,** 215, 292, 359, 418; **Retro. Supp. II:** 19, 24, 30, 68, 115, 123; **Supp. I Part 2:** 621, 658, 678; **Supp. II Part 1:** 221; **Supp. III Part 1:** 146; **Supp. III Part 2:** 617; **Supp. IV Part 1:** 48, 102, 123, 197, 236, 342, 343, 344, 348, 350, 352, 380–381, 383; **Supp. IV Part 2:** 463, 468, 502, 607, 679, 680, 681, 689, 692; **Supp. IX:** 16, 57, 58, 94, 106, 260, 262; **Supp. V:** 237, 240, 244, 250, 336; **Supp. VIII:** 40, 101, 105, 179, 182, 183, 188, 189, 196; **Supp. X:** 137, 167, 223, 225; **Supp. XI:** 214, 221; **Supp. XIII:** 96, 255, 270; **Supp. XIV:** 24, 83; **Supp. XV:** 69, 135; **Supp. XVI:** 203, 205–206, 208, 210, 233, 236–237, 281–282; **Supp. XVII:** 4, 105, 107, 137, 228, 229; **Supp. XVIII:** 74, 90, 102
Hemingway, Mrs. Ernest (Hadley Richardson), **II:** 257, 260, 263
Hemingway, Mrs. Ernest (Martha Gellhorn), **II:** 260
Hemingway, Mrs. Ernest (Mary Welsh), **II:** 257, 260
Hemingway, Mrs. Ernest (Pauline Pfeiffer), **II:** 260
"Hemingway in Paris" (Cowley), **Supp. II Part 1:** 144
"Hemingway Story, A" (Dubus), **Supp. VII:** 91
"Hemingway: The Old Lion" (Cowley), **Supp. II Part 1:** 143
"Hemp, The" (Benét), **Supp. XI:** 44
"Henchman, The" (Whittier), **Supp. I Part 2:** 696
Henderson, Alice Corbin, **Supp. I Part 2:** 387; **Supp. XV:** 302–303
Henderson, Darwin L., **Supp. XIII:** 213, 221–222
Henderson, Jane, **Supp. VIII:** 87
Henderson, Katherine, **Supp. IV Part 1:** 203, 207
Henderson, Linda. *See* Hogan, Linda
Henderson, Robert W., **Supp. VIII:** 124
Henderson, Stephen, **Supp. IV Part 1:** 365
Henderson, the Rain King (Bellow), **I:** 144, 147, 148, 152, 153, 154, 155, 158, 160, 161, 162–163; **Retro. Supp. II:** 19, **24–25,** 30
"Hen Flower, The" (Kinnell), **Supp. III Part 1:** 247–248
Henie, Sonja, **Supp. XII:** 165
Henle, James, **II:** 26, 30, 38, 41; **Supp. IX:** 2
Hennesy, Dale, **Supp. XV:** 5
Henri, Robert, **IV:** 411; **Supp. I Part 2:** 376
Henry, Arthur, **I:** 515; **Retro. Supp. II:** 97
Henry, DeWitt, **Supp. XI:** 342
Henry, O., **I:** 201; **III:** 5; **Supp. I Part 2:** 390, 462; **Supp. II Part 1: 385–412; Supp. XV:** 40
Henry, Robert, **Retro. Supp. II:** 103
Henry, William A., III, **Supp. IV Part 2:** 574
Henry and June (film), **Supp. X:** 186

Henry and June: From the Unexpurgated Diary of Anaïs Nin, **Supp. X:** 184, 185, 187, 194
Henry Holt and Company, **Retro. Supp. I:** 121, 131, 133, 136
Henry IV (Shakespeare), **III:** 166; **Supp. VIII:** 164
"Henry James, Jr." (Howells), **II:** 289; **Retro. Supp. I:** 220
"Henry James and the Art of Teaching" (Rowe), **Retro. Supp. I:** 216
"Henry Manley, Living Alone, Keeps Time" (Kumin), **Supp. IV Part 2:** 451
"Henry Manley Looks Back" (Kumin), **Supp. IV Part 2:** 451
"Henry Manley" poems (Kumin), **Supp. IV Part 2:** 446
Henry Miller Reader, The (Durrell, ed.), **III:** 175, 190
"Henry's Confession" (Berryman), **I:** 186
Henry VIII (Shakespeare), **Supp. IX:** 235
Henslee, **Supp. IV Part 1:** 217
Henson, Josiah, **Supp. I Part 2:** 589
Hentoff, Margot, **Supp. IV Part 1:** 205
Hentz, Caroline Lee, **Supp. I Part 2:** 584
Henze, Hans Werner, **Supp. II Part 1:** 24
"He of the Assembly" (Bowles), **Supp. IV Part 1:** 90
Hepburn, Katharine, **Supp. IX:** 189; **Supp. XI:** 17
Heraclitus, **II:** 1, 163; **IV:** 86
Herakles: A Play in Verse (MacLeish), **III:** 21, 22
Herald of the Autochthonic Spirit (Corso), **Supp. XII:** 134–136
He Ran All the Way (film), **Supp. XVII:** 63
Herberg, Will, **III:** 291
Herbert, Edward, **II:** 11
Herbert, Francis (pseudonym). *See* Bryant, William Cullen
Herbert, George, **II:** 12; **IV:** 141, 145, 146, 151, 153, 156, 165; **Retro. Supp. II:** 40; **Supp. I Part 1:** 80, 107, 108, 122; **Supp. IV Part 2:** 646; **Supp. XV:** 92, 212, 251
Herbert, Zbigniew, **Supp. VIII:** 20
Herbert Huncke Reader, The (Schafer, ed.), **Supp. XIV:** 137, 138, 139, 140, 145, 147, 150, 151–152
Herbert of Cherbury, Lord, **II:** 108
"Herbert White" (Bidart), **Supp. XV:** 24, 27
Herbst, Josephine, **Retro. Supp. II:** 325, 328; **Supp. XIII:** 295
"Her Choice" (Larcom), **Supp. XIII:** 144
"Her Dead Brother" (Lowell), **Retro. Supp. II:** 188
"Her Dream Is of the Sea" (Ríos), **Supp. IV Part 2:** 546
"Here" (Kenyon), **Supp. VII:** 164
Here and Beyond (Wharton), **Retro. Supp. I:** 382
Here and Now (Levertov), **Supp. III Part 1:** 275, 276
"Here and There" (Wallace), **Supp. X:** 305–306
Here Comes the Mystery Man (Sanders), **Supp. XVI:** 269
Heredia, Juanita, **Supp. XI:** 185, 190
Heredity and Variation (Lock), **Retro. Supp. I:** 375
"Here Inside My Forehead" (Rasmussen; Nelson and Espeland, trans.), **Supp. XVIII:** 180
Here is Your War (Pyle), **Supp. XVII:** 61
Here Let Us Feast (M. F. K. Fisher), **Supp. XVII:** 86, 87
Here Lies (Parker), **Supp. IX:** 192
Here on Earth (Hoffman), **Supp. X:** 77, 89
Heresy and the Ideal: On Contemporary Poetry (Baker), **Supp. XI:** 142
"Here to Learn" (Bowles), **Supp. IV Part 1:** 93
"Here to Yonder" (Hughes), **Retro. Supp. I:** 205
"Her Father's Letters" (Milburn), **Supp. XI:** 242
Herford, Reverend Brooke, **I:** 471
Hergesheimer, Joseph, **Supp. I Part 2:** 620; **Supp. XVI:** 187
"Heritage" (Cullen), **Supp. IV Part 1:** 164–165, 168, 170, 171
"Heritage" (Hogan), **Supp. IV Part 1:** 413
"Her Kind" (Sexton), **Supp. II Part 2:** 687
Herland (Gilman), **Supp. XI:** 208–209
Herman, Florence. *See* Williams, Mrs. William Carlos (Florence Herman)
Herman, Jan, **Supp. XIV:** 150–151
Herman, William (pseudonym). *See* Bierce, Ambrose
"Her Management" (Swenson), **Supp. IV Part 2:** 642
"Herman Melville" (Auden), **Supp. II Part 1:** 14
Herman Melville (Mumford), **Supp. II Part 2:** 471, 476, 489–491
"Hermes of the Ways" (Doolittle), **Supp. I Part 1:** 266
Hermetic Definition (Doolittle), **Supp. I Part 1:** 271, 272, 273, 274
"Hermitage, The" (Haines), **Supp. XII:** 205–206
"Hermit and the Wild Woman, The" (Wharton), **Retro. Supp. I:** 372
Hermit and the Wild Woman, The (Wharton), **IV:** 315; **Retro. Supp. I:** 371
"Hermit Meets the Skunk, The" (Kumin), **Supp. IV Part 2:** 447
Hermit of 69th Street, The: The Working Papers or Norbert Kosky (Kosinski), **Supp. VII:** 215, 216, 223, 226–227
"Hermit of Saba, The" (Freneau), **Supp. II Part 1:** 259
"Hermit Picks Berries, The" (Kumin), **Supp. IV Part 2:** 447
Hermit's Story, The (Bass), **Supp. XVI:** 23–24
"Hermit Thrush, A" (Clampitt), **Supp. IX:** 40
Hernández, Miguel, **Supp. V:** 194; **Supp. XIII:** 315, 323
Herne, James A., **II:** 276; **Supp. II Part 1:** 198
Hernton, Calvin, **Supp. X:** 240
"Hero, The" (Moore), **III:** 200, 211, 212
Hero, The (Raglan), **I:** 135
Hérodiade (Mallarmé), **I:** 66
Herodotus, **Supp. I Part 2:** 405
Heroes, The (Ashbery), **Supp. III Part 1:** 3
Hero in America, The (Van Doren), **II:** 103
"Heroines of Nature: Four Women Respond to the American Landscape" (Norwood), **Supp. IX:** 24
"Heron, The" (Roethke), **III:** 540–541
"Her One Bad Eye" (Karr), **Supp. XI:** 244
"Her Own People" (Warren), **IV:** 253
"Her Quaint Honour" (Gordon), **II:** 196, 199, 200
Herr, Michael, **Supp. XI:** 245
Herrick, Robert, **II:** 11, 18, 444; **III:** 463, 592; **IV:** 453; **Retro. Supp. I:** 319; **Retro. Supp. II:** 101; **Supp. I Part 2:** 646; **Supp. XIII:** 334; **Supp. XIV:** 8, 9; **Supp. XV:** 155
Herrmann, John, **Retro. Supp. II:** 328
Herron, George, **Supp. I Part 1:** 7
"Hers" (column, Prose), **Supp. XVI:** 254
Herschel, Sir John, **Supp. I Part 1:** 314
"Her Sense of Timing" (Elkin), **Supp. VI:** 56, 58
Hersey, John, **IV:** 4; **Supp. I Part 1:** 196; **Supp. XVI:** 105–106
"Her Sweet turn to leave the Homestead" (Dickinson), **Retro. Supp. I:** 44
Herzog (Bellow), **I:** 144, 147, 149, 150, 152, 153, 154, 155, 156, 157, 158, 159–160; **Retro. Supp. II:** 19, **26–27**; **Supp. IV Part 1:** 30
Hesford, Walter A., **Supp. XV:** 215, 217, 218
"He/She" (Dunn), **Supp. XI:** 149
"Hesitation Blues" (Hughes), **Retro. Supp. I:** 211
Hesse, Hermann, **Supp. V:** 208
Hester, Carolyn, **Supp. XVIII:** 24
"Hetch Hetchy Valley" (Muir), **Supp. IX:** 185
He Who Gets Slapped (Andreyev), **II:** 425
"He Who Spits at the Sky" (Stegner), **Supp. IV Part 2:** 605
"He Will Not Leave a Note" (Ríos), **Supp. IV Part 2:** 548
Hewitt, James, **Supp. XV:** 240
Hewlett, Maurice, **I:** 359
Heyen, William, **Supp. XIII:** 285, 344; **Supp. XV:** 212
"Hey! Hey!" (Hughes), **Supp. I Part 1:** 327–328
Hey Rub-a-Dub-Dub (Dreiser), **I:** 515; **II:** 26; **Retro. Supp. II:** 104, 105, 108
"Hey Sailor, What Ship?" (Olsen), **Supp. XIII:** 293, 294, 298, **299**
Heyward, DuBose, **Supp. XVIII:** 281
Hiawatha (Longfellow), **Supp. I Part 1:** 79; **Supp. III Part 2:** 609, 610
"Hibernaculum" (Ammons), **Supp. VII:** 26–27
Hichborn, Mrs. Philip. *See* Wylie, Elinor
Hichborn, Philip, **Supp. I Part 2:** 707, 708

"Hic Jacet" (W. C. Williams), **Retro. Supp. I:** 414
Hickok, James Butler ("Wild Bill"), **Supp. V:** 229, 230
Hicks, Granville, **I:** 254, 259, 374; **II:** 26; **III:** 342, 355, 452; **Supp. I Part 1:** 361; **Supp. I Part 2:** 609; **Supp. IV Part 1:** 22; **Supp. IV Part 2:** 526; **Supp. VIII:** 96, 124; **Supp. XII:** 250; **Supp. XIII:** 263
Hicok, Bethany, **Retro. Supp. II:** 39
"Hidden" (Nye), **Supp. XIII:** 283
"Hidden Gardens" (Capote), **Supp. III Part 1:** 125
Hidden Law, The (Hecht), **Supp. X:** 58
"Hidden Name and Complex Fate" (Ellison), **Supp. II Part 1:** 245
Hidden Wound, The (Berry), **Supp. X:** 23, 25, 26–27, 29, 34, 35
"Hide-and-Seek" (Francis), **Supp. IX:** 81
"Hiding" (Minot), **Supp. VI:** 203, 206
Hiding Place (Wideman), **Supp. X:** 320, 321, 327, 329, 331–332, 333
Hienger, Jorg, **Supp. IV Part 1:** 106
Higgins, George, **Supp. IV Part 1:** 356
Higginson, Thomas Wentworth, **I:** 451–452, 453, 454, 456, 458, 459, 463, 464, 465, 470; **Retro. Supp. I:** 26, 31, 33, 35, 39, 40; **Supp. I Part 1:** 307, 371; **Supp. IV Part 2:** 430
"High Bridge above the Tagus River at Toledo, The" (W. C. Williams), **Retro. Supp. I:** 429
"High Dive: A Variant" (Kumin), **Supp. IV Part 2:** 442
"High Diver" (Francis), **Supp. IX:** 82
"Higher Keys, The" (Merrill), **Supp. III Part 1:** 335–336
Higher Learning in America, The (Veblen), **Supp. I Part 2:** 630, 631, 641, 642
Highet, Gilbert, **Supp. I Part 1:** 268
High Noon (film), **Supp. V:** 46
"High on Sadness" (Komunyakaa), **Supp. XIII:** 114
"High School Senior" (Olds), **Supp. X:** 212
Highsmith, Patricia, **Supp. IV Part 1:** 79, 94, 132
"High Tide" (Marquand), **III:** 56
High Tide in Tucson: Essays from Now or Never (Kingsolver), **Supp. VII:** 198, 201, 209
"High-Toned Old Christian Woman, A" (Stevens), **Retro. Supp. I:** 301
"Highway, The" (Merwin), **Supp. III Part 1:** 346
Highway 61 Revisited (album, Dylan), **Supp. XVIII:** 20, 27, 30, 32
"Highway 61 Revisited" (song, Dylan), **Supp. XVIII:** 30
"Highway 99E from Chico" (Carver), **Supp. III Part 1:** 136
High Window, The (Chandler), **Supp. IV Part 1:** 127–129, 130, 131
Hijuelos, Oscar, **Supp. IV Part 1:** 54; **Supp. VIII: 73–91**
Hike and the Aeroplane (Lewis), **II:** 440–441
Hilberg, Raul, **Supp. V:** 267
Hildebrand, Al, **III:** 118
Hiler, Hilaire, **Retro. Supp. II:** 327; **Supp. III Part 2:** 617
"Hill, A" (Hecht), **Supp. X:** 59–60, 63
Hill, Abram, **Supp. XV:** 194
Hill, Hamlin, **Retro. Supp. II:** 286
Hill, James J., **Supp. I Part 2:** 644
Hill, Joe, **I:** 493; **Supp. XVIII:** 224
Hill, Lee, **Supp. XI:** 293, 294, 297, 299, 301, 305, 307
Hill, Patti, **I:** 289
Hill, Peggy, **Supp. XIII:** 163
"Hill, The" (Strand), **Supp. IV Part 2:** 627
"Hill, The" (Toomer), **Supp. III Part 2:** 486
Hill, Vernon, **Supp. I Part 2:** 397
"Hillcrest" (Robinson), **III:** 504
Hill-Lubin, Mildred A., **Supp. IV Part 1:** 13
Hillman, Sidney, **Supp. I Part 1:** 5
Hillringhouse, Mark, **Supp. IX:** 286, 288, 299
"Hills Beyond, The" (Wolfe), **IV:** 460
Hills Beyond, The (Wolfe), **IV:** 450, 451, 460, 461
Hillside and Seaside in Poetry (Larcom, ed.), **Supp. XIII:** 142
"Hillside Thaw, A" (Frost), **Retro. Supp. I:** 133
"Hills Like White Elephants" (Hemingway), **Retro. Supp. I:** 170
Hills of the Shatemuc, The (S. Warner), **Supp. XVIII:** 266
"Hill-Top View, A" (Jeffers), **Supp. II Part 2:** 417
"Hill Wife, The" (Frost), **II:** 154; **Retro. Supp. I:** 131
Hillyer, Catherine, **Supp. XV:** 244
Hillyer, Robert, **I:** 475; **Supp. IX:** 75; **Supp. XIV:** 11
Hilton, James, **Supp. XIII:** 166
"Hiltons' Holiday, The" (Jewett), **II:** 391; **Retro. Supp. II:** 134
Him (Cummings), **I:** 429, 434–435
Himes, Chester, **Retro. Supp. II:** 117; **Supp. I Part 1:** 51, 325; **Supp. XIII:** 233
Himes, Chester Bomar, **Supp. XVI: 135–146**
Himes, Norman, **Supp. V:** 128
"Him with His Foot in His Mouth" (Bellow), **Retro. Supp. II:** 34
Him with His Foot in His Mouth and Other Stories (Bellow), **Retro. Supp. II:** 31
Hinchman, Sandra K., **Supp. IV Part 1:** 210
Hindemith, Paul, **IV:** 357; **Supp. IV Part 1:** 81
Hindsell, Oliver, **Supp. XIII:** 162
Hindus, Milton, **Supp. XIV:** 288, 291, 292, 293
Hines, Suzanne, **Supp. XIV:** 151
Hinge Picture (Howe), **Supp. IV Part 2:** 423–424
"Hinterlands" (W. Gibson), **Supp. XVI:** 123, 128
"Hippies: Slouching towards Bethlehem" (Didion), **Supp. IV Part 1:** 200
Hippolytus (Euripides), **II:** 543; **Supp. I Part 1:** 270
Hippolytus Temporizes (Doolittle), **Supp. I Part 1:** 270
"Hips" (Cisneros), **Supp. VII:** 61, 62
"Hipster's Hipster" (Ginsberg), **Supp. XIV:** 141
Hirsch, Edward, **Supp. XV:** 78, 225; **Supp. XVII:** 23
Hirsch, Edward D., **Supp. IX:** 262; **Supp. V:** 177; **Supp. XIV:** 15
Hirsch, Sidney, **Supp. XIV:** 1. *See* Mttron-Hirsch, Sidney
Hirschfeld, Jane, **Supp. XVII:** 241
Hirschorn, Clive, **Supp. IV Part 2:** 577, 579
Hirson, Roger, **Supp. XI:** 343
"His Bride of the Tomb" (Dunbar), **Supp. II Part 1:** 196
"His Chest of Drawers" (Anderson), **I:** 113, 114
"His Father's Whistle" (Wrigley), **Supp. XVIII:** 299
"His Last Day" (C. Himes), **Supp. XVI:** 137
"His Lover" (Dubus), **Supp. VII:** 86
"His Music" (Dunn), **Supp. XI:** 149
"His Own Key" (Ríos), **Supp. IV Part 2:** 543
His Picture in the Papers (film; Emerson), **Supp. XVI:** 185
His Religion and Hers (Gilman), **Supp. XI:** 209
Hiss, Alger, **Supp. XV:** 143
"Hiss, Chambers, and the Age of Innocence" (Fiedler), **Supp. XIII:** 99
"His Shield" (Moore), **III:** 211
"His Story" (Cisneros), **Supp. VII:** 67
His Thought Made Pockets & the Plane Buckt (Berryman), **I:** 170
"His Three Women" (Gioia), **Supp. XV:** 119–120
Histoire comparée des systèmes de philosophie (Gérando), **II:** 10
Historical and Moral View of the Origin and Progress of the French Revolution (Wollstonecraft), **Supp. I Part 1:** 126
"Historical Conceptualization" (Huizinga), **I:** 255
Historical Evidence and the Reading of Seventeenth-Century Poetry (Brooks), **Supp. XIV:** 11
"Historical Interpretation of Literature, The" (Wilson), **IV:** 431, 433, 445
Historical Jesus, The: The Life of a Mediterranean Jewish Peasant (Crossan), **Supp. V:** 251
"Historical Value of Crèvecoeur's *Voyage* ...," (Adams), **Supp. I Part 1:** 251
"History" (Emerson), **II:** 13, 15
"History" (Hughes), **Supp. I Part 1:** 344
History (Lowell), **Retro. Supp. II:** 183, 190
"History" (Simic), **Supp. VIII:** 279
"History, Myth, and the Western Writer" (Stegner), **Supp. IV Part 2:** 596, 601
"History among the Rocks" (Warren), **IV:** 252
History as a Literary Art (Morison), **Supp. I Part 2:** 493

"History as Fate in E. L. Doctorow's Tale of a Western Town" (Arnold), **Supp. IV Part 1:** 220
"History Is the Memory of Time" (Olson), **Supp. II Part 2:** 574
"History Lessons" (Komunyakaa), **Supp. XIII:** 126
History Man, The (Bradbury), **Supp. XVIII:** 140
"History of a Literary Movement" (Nemerov), **III:** 270
"History of a Literary Radical, The" (Bourne), **I:** 215, 235, 236
History of a Radical: Essays by Randolph Bourne (Brooks), **I:** 245
"History of Buttons, The" (Goldbarth), **Supp. XII:** 187
History of English Literature (Taine), **III:** 323
History of English Prosody (Saintsbury), **Supp. XV:** 181
History of Fortus, The (Emerson), **II:** 8
History of Henry Esmond, The (Thackeray), **II:** 91, 130
History of Modern Poetry, A (Perkins), **Supp. I Part 2:** 475; **Supp. XV:** 185
History of My Heart (Pinsky), **Supp. VI:** 243, 244, 245
History of New York, from the Beginning of the World to the End of the Dutch Dynasty, A (Irving), **II:** 300–303, 304, 310
History of Pendennis, The (Thackeray), **II:** 291
"History of Red, The" (Hogan), **Supp. IV Part 1:** 411
"History of Rodney, The" (Bass), **Supp. XVI:** 20
History of Roxbury Town (Ellis), **Supp. I Part 1:** 99
History of the African-American People (Proposed) by Strom Thurmond, The (Everett and Kincaid), **Supp. XVIII:** 62, **63–64**
History of the Conquest of Mexico (Prescott), **Retro. Supp. I:** 123
History of the Conquest of Peru (Morison, ed.), **Supp. I Part 2:** 494
History of the Dividing Line betwixt Virginia and North Carolina (Byrd), **Supp. IV Part 2:** 425
History of the Life and Voyages of Christopher Columbus, A (Irving), **II:** 310, 314
History of the Navy of the United States of America (Cooper), **I:** 347
History of the Rise and Fall of the Slave-power in America (Wilson), **Supp. XIV:** 48, 49
History of the United States of America during the Administrations of Thomas Jefferson and James Madison (Adams), **I:** 6–9, 10, 20, 21
History of the Work of Redemption, A (Edwards), **I:** 560
History of United States Naval Operations in World War II (Morison), **Supp. I Part 2:** 490–492
History of Womankind in Western Europe, The, **Supp. XI:** 197
"History Through a Beard" (Morison), **Supp. I Part 2:** 490
His Toy, His Dream, His Rest (Berryman), **I:** 169, 170, 183, 184–186
"His Words" (Roethke), **III:** 544
Hitchcock, Ada. *See* MacLeish, Mrs. Archibald (Ada Hitchcock)
Hitchcock, Alfred, **IV:** 357; **Supp. IV Part 1:** 132; **Supp. VIII:** 177
Hitchcock, George, **Supp. X:** 127; **Supp. XVII:** 110
"Hitch Haiku" (Snyder), **Supp. VIII:** 297
"Hitch-Hikers, The" (Welty), **IV:** 262
"Hitchhiking Is Illegal in Nevada" (Lethem), **Supp. XVIII:** 136
Hitchins, Christopher, **Supp. VIII:** 241
Hitler, Adolf, **I:** 261, 290, 492; **II:** 146, 454, 561, 565, 592; **III:** 2, 3, 110, 115, 140, 156, 246, 298, 446; **IV:** 5, 17, 18, 298, 372; **Supp. I Part 2:** 431, 436, 446, 664; **Supp. V:** 290
Hitler, Wendy, **III:** 404
Hitler Lives? (film), **Supp. XVI:** 102
Hix, H. L., **Supp. XV:** 114
H. L. Mencken, a Portrait from Memory (Angoff), **III:** 107
"H. L. Mencken Meets a Poet in the West Side Y.M.C.A." (White), **Supp. I Part 2:** 677
H. L. Mencken: The American Scene (Cairns), **III:** 119
H. M. Pulham, Esquire (Marquand), **II:** 482–483; **III:** 58, 59, 65, 68–69
Hnizdovsky, Jacques, **Supp. XIII:** 346
"Hoadley's Test Case in Indiana" (Neugeboren), **Supp. XVI:** 219
Hoagland, Edward, **Supp. XIV:** 80; **Supp. XVI:** 277
"Hoarder, The" (Sexton), **Supp. II Part 2:** 692
"Hoarfrost" (C. Baxter), **Supp. XVII:** 15
Hoban, Phoebe, **Supp. XV:** 319, 325
Hobb, Gormley, **I:** 203
Hobbes, Thomas, **I:** 277; **II:** 9, 10, 540; **III:** 306; **IV:** 88; **Supp. XII:** 33; **Supp. XIV:** 5, 7
Hobson, Geary, **Supp. IV Part 1:** 321; **Supp. IV Part 2:** 502
Hobson, J. A., **I:** 232
Hobson, John A., **Supp. I Part 2:** 650
Hobson, Laura Z., **III:** 151
Hocking, Agnes, **Supp. VIII:** 251
Hocking, William Ernest, **III:** 303
Hodges, Campbell B., **Supp. XIV:** 8
Hodgson, Captain Joseph, **III:** 328
Hoffa, Jimmy, **I:** 493
Hoffenberg, Mason, **Supp. XI:** 294, 297, 299, 305
Hoffer, Eric, **Supp. VIII:** 188
Hoffman, Abbie, **Supp. XIV:** 150
Hoffman, Alice, **Supp. X: 77–94; Supp. XIII:** 13
Hoffman, Allen, **Supp. XVII:** 42, 44
Hoffman, Daniel, **Retro. Supp. II:** 265
Hoffman, Daniel G., **I:** 405; **II:** 307; **Supp. XI:** 152
Hoffman, Dustin, **Supp. IV Part 1:** 236
Hoffman, E. T. A., **Supp. XVI:** 157
Hoffman, Eva, **Supp. XVI: 147–164**
Hoffman, Frederick J., **I:** 60, 67; **II:** 443; **IV:** 113
Hoffman, Josiah Ogden, **II:** 297, 300
Hoffman, Matilda, **II:** 300, 314
Hoffman, Paul, **Supp. XV:** 141–142
Hoffman, Todd, **Supp. XVIII:** 101
Hoffman, William, **Supp. XVIII: 69–88**
Hoffman, William M., **Supp. X:** 153
Hoffmann, E. T. A., **III:** 415
Hofmann, Hans, **Supp. XV:** 144
Ho for a Hat (W. J. Smith), **Supp. XIII:** 346
Hofstadter, Richard, **Supp. VIII:** 98, 99, 108
Hogan, Linda, **Supp. IV Part 1:** 324, 325, **397–418; Supp. XVIII:** 189
Hogan, Randolph, **Supp. XVI:** 252–253
Hogan, Ron, **Supp. XVIII:** 138, 139
Hogarth, William, **Supp. XII:** 44
Hogg, James, **I:** 53; **Supp. I Part 1:** 349; **Supp. IX:** 275
Hoggart, Richard, **Supp. XIV:** 299
Hohne, Karen, **Supp. V:** 147
Hojoki (Chomei), **IV:** 170
Holbrook, David, **Supp. I Part 2:** 526–527, 546
Holcroft, Thomas, **Supp. I Part 2:** 514
Holden, Jonathan, **Supp. XI:** 143
Holden, Raymond, **Supp. XIV:** 121–122
Holden, William, **Supp. XI:** 307
Hölderlin, Friedrich, **Supp. XVI:** 48
"Holding On" (Levine), **Supp. V:** 184
Holding the Line: Women in the Great Arizona Mine Strike of 1983 (Kingsolver), **Supp. VII:** 197, 201–202, 204
"Holding the Mirror Up to Nature" (Nemerov), **III:** 275, 276
"Hold Me" (Levine), **Supp. V:** 186
Hold the Press (film), **Supp. XIII:** 163
Hold with the Hares (Zinberg), **Supp. XV:** 197–198,**Supp. XV:** 203
"Hole in the Floor, A" (Wilbur), **Supp. III Part 2:** 556–557
Holiday (Barry), **Retro. Supp. I:** 104
"Holiday" (Porter), **III:** 454
Holiday, Billie, **Supp. I Part 1:** 80; **Supp. IV Part 1:** 2, 7
Holinshed, Raphael, **IV:** 370
Holland, Josiah, **Supp. I Part 2:** 420
Holland, Laurence Bedwell, **Retro. Supp. I:** 216
Holland, Mrs. Theodore, **I:** 453, 455, 465
Holland, Theodore, **I:** 453
Holland, William, **IV:** 381
Hollander, John, **Supp. III Part 2:** 541; **Supp. IV Part 2:** 642; **Supp. IX:** 50, 153, 155; **Supp. XII:** 254, 255, 260; **Supp. XV:** 256; **Supp. XVII:** 112
Holley, Marietta, **Supp. XIII:** 152
Hollinghurst, Alan, **Supp. XIII:** 52
Hollis, Thomas Brand, **Supp. I Part 2:** 514
Hollow Men, The (Eliot), **I:** 574, 575, 578–579, 580, 585; **III:** 586; **Retro. Supp. I:** 63, 64
"Hollow Tree, A" (R. Bly), **Supp. IV Part 1:** 64, 66
Hollyberrys at the Shore, The, **Supp. X:** 42

"Hollywood!" (Vidal), **Supp. IV Part 2:** 688

Hollywood: American Movie-City (Rand, unauthorized), **Supp. IV Part 2:** 519

Hollywood: A Novel of America in the 1920s (Vidal), **Supp. IV Part 2:** 677, 684, 686, 688, 690, 691

Hollywood Ending (film; Allen), **Supp. XV:** 11

Hollywood on Trial (film), **Supp. I Part 1:** 295

Holmes, Abiel, **Supp. I Part 1:** 300, 301, 302, 310

Holmes, John, **I:** 169; **Supp. II Part 1:** 87; **Supp. IV Part 2:** 440–441; **Supp. XIV:** 119

Holmes, John Clellon, **Supp. XII:** 118; **Supp. XIV:** 144, 150

Holmes, Mrs. Abiel (Sarah Wendell), **Supp. I Part 1:** 300

Holmes, Mrs. Oliver Wendell (Amelia Jackson), **Supp. I Part 1:** 303

Holmes, Oliver Wendell, **I:** 487; **II:** 225, 273–274, 402, 403; **III:** 81–82, 590, 591–592; **IV:** 429, 436; **Retro. Supp. II:** 155; **Supp. I Part 1:** 103, 243, 254, **299–319; Supp. I Part 2:** 405, 414, 415, 420, 593, 704, 705; **Supp. XI:** 194

Holmes, Oliver Wendell, Jr., **I:** 3, 19; **Supp. IV Part 2:** 422

Holmes, Steven J., **Supp. IX:** 172, 177

Holmes, Ted, **Supp. V:** 180

Holmes, William Henry, **Supp. IV Part 2:** 603–604

Holocaust (Reznikoff), **Supp. XIV:** 281, **291–293**

Holocaust in American Life, The (Novick), **Supp. XVI:** 154

Holt, Edwin E., **I:** 59

Holt, Felix, **II:** 179

Holt, Henry, **II:** 348; **III:** 587

Holt, Patricia, **Supp. XIV:** 89

Holtby, Winifred, **Supp. I Part 2:** 720

Holy Ghostly, The (Shepard), **Supp. III Part 2:** 437–438, 447

"Holy Innocents, The" (Lowell), **II:** 539

Holy Sonnets (Donne), **IV:** 145; **Supp. I Part 1:** 367; **Supp. III Part 2:** 619; **Supp. XIII:** 130–131; **Supp. XVIII:** 50–51

"Holy Terror, A" (Bierce), **I:** 203

"Holy Terror, The" (Maxwell), **Supp. VIII:** 169

Holy the Firm (Dillard), **Supp. VI:** 23, **29,** 30, 31, 32

Holy War, The (Bunyan), **IV:** 156

"Homage to Arthur Rimbaud" (Wright), **Supp. V:** 339

Homage to Baudelaire (Duncan, ed.), **Supp. XV:** 75

Homage to Catalonia (Orwell), **Supp. XVII:** 229

"Homage to Che Guevara" (Banks), **Supp. V:** 5

Homage to Clio (Auden), **Supp. II Part 1:** 24

"Homage to Elizabeth Bishop" (Ivask, ed.), **Supp. I Part 1:** 96

"Homage to Ezra Pound" (Wright), **Supp. V:** 339

Homage to Frank O'Hara (Ashbery), **Supp. III Part 1:** 2–3

"Homage to Franz Joseph Haydn" (Hecht), **Supp. X:** 69

"Homage to Hemingway" (Bishop), **IV:** 35

Homage to Mistress Bradstreet (Berryman), **I:** 168, 169, 170–171, 172, 174, 175, 178–183, 184, 186

"Homage to Paul Cézanne" (Wright), **Supp. V:** 341–342

"Homage to Sextus Propertius" (Pound), **III:** 462, 476; **Supp. III Part 2:** 622

Homage to Sextus Propertius (Pound), **Retro. Supp. I:** 290

"Homage to Shakespeare" (Cheever), **Supp. I Part 1:** 180

"Homage to the Empress of the Blues" (Hayden), **Supp. II Part 1:** 379

"Homage to the Memory of Wallace Stevens" (Justice), **Supp. VII:** 126

Homage to Theodore Dreiser (Warren), **I:** 517

Homans, Margaret, **Supp. X:** 229

"Home" (Hughes), **Supp. I Part 1:** 329, 330

"Home" (Mora), **Supp. XIII:** 217

Home (Updike), **Retro. Supp. I:** 320

"Home, Home on the Strange" (J. D. Reed), **Supp. XVI:** 174

"Home, Sweet Home" (Fante), **Supp. XI:** 164, 165

Home, The (Gilman), **Supp. XI: 206–207**

"Home, The" (Jarman), **Supp. XVII:** 116

"Home after Three Months Away" (Lowell), **II:** 547

Home and Colonial Library (Murray), **Retro. Supp. I:** 246

Home as Found (Cooper), **I:** 348, 349, 350, 351

Home at the End of the World, A (Cunningham), **Supp. XV: 59–62,** 63

"Home Away from Home, A" (Humphrey), **Supp. IX:** 101

Home Book of Shakespeare Quotations (Stevenson), **Supp. XIV:** 120

"Home Burial" (Frost), **Retro. Supp. I:** 124, 125, 128, **129–130; Supp. VIII:** 31

"Home Burial" (R. Frost), **Supp. XV:** 159

Homecoming (Alvarez), **Supp. VII:** 1, 3–5, 9

"Homecoming" (Carruth), **Supp. XVI:** 55

"Homecoming" (McGrath), **Supp. X:** 116

"Homecoming, The" (Gioia), **Supp. XV:** 123, 124

Homecoming, The (Wilson), **Supp. VIII:** 330

Homecoming Game, The (Nemerov), **III:** 268, 282, 284–285

"Home during a Tropical Snowstorm I Feed My Father Lunch" (Karr), **Supp. XI:** 241–242, 248

Home Economics (Berry), **Supp. X:** 28, 31–32, 35, 36, 37

Home from the Hill (film), **Supp. IX:** 95

Home from the Hill (Humphrey), **Supp. IX:** 93, 95, **96–98,** 104, 106, 109

"Home Grown" (Vital), **Supp. XVI:** 160

"Homeland" (Merwin), **Supp. III Part 1:** 351

Homeland and Other Stories (Kingsolver), **Supp. VII:** 199, 202–204, 207

Home on the Range (Baraka), **Supp. II Part 1:** 47

Home Place, The (Morris), **III:** 221, 222, 232

Homeplace, The (Nelson), **Supp. XVIII: 174–175**

Homer, **I:** 312, 433; **II:** 6, 8, 133, 302, 543, 544, 552; **III:** 14, 21, 278, 453, 457, 473, 567; **IV:** 54, 371; **Retro. Supp. I:** 59; **Supp. I Part 1:** 158, 283; **Supp. I Part 2:** 494; **Supp. X:** 36, 120, 122; **Supp. XIV:** 21; **Supp. XVII:** 70, 227

Homer, Louise, **Retro. Supp. I:** 10

"Home Range" (Leopold), **Supp. XIV:** 184, 185

"Homesick Blues" (Hughes), **Supp. I Part 1:** 327

Home: Social Essays (Baraka), **Supp. II Part 1:** 45, 61

"Homesteading on the Extraterrestrial Frontier" (Abbott), **Supp. XVIII:** 142

Home to Harlem (McKay), **Supp. X:** 132, 137–138, **138–139; Supp. XVIII:** 127

Homeward Bound (Cooper), **I:** 348

"Homeward Star, The" (Palmer), **Supp. XV:** 81–82

Homewood trilogy (Wideman), **Supp. X:** 319

"Homework" (Cameron), **Supp. XII:** 80, **83,** 84

"Homily" (Tate), **IV:** 121–122

"Homme Moyen Sensuel, L'" (Pound), **III:** 462

Homme révolté, L' (Camus), **III:** 306

"Homoeopathy and Its Kindred Delusions" (Holmes), **Supp. I Part 1:** 303–304, 305

Homo Ludens (Huizinga), **II:** 416–417, 425

"Homosexual Villain, The" (Mailer), **III:** 36

"Homo Will Not Inherit" (Doty), **Supp. XI:** 128

Hone and Strong Diaries of Old Manhattan, The (Auchincloss, ed.), **Supp. IV Part 1:** 23

"Honey" (Beattie), **Supp. V:** 33

"Honey" (Wright), **Supp. III Part 2:** 589

"Honey, We'll Be Brave" (Farrell), **II:** 45

"Honey and Salt" (Sandburg), **III:** 594

Honey and Salt (Sandburg), **III:** 594–596

"Honey Babe" (Hughes), **Supp. I Part 1:** 334

"Honey Tree, The" (Oliver), **Supp. VII:** 236

Hong, Maxine. *See* Kingston, Maxine Hong

Hongo, Garrett, **Supp. X:** 292; **Supp. XIII:** 114; **Supp. XVII:** 112

"Honkytonk" (Shapiro), **Supp. II Part 2:** 705
"Honky Tonk in Cleveland, Ohio" (Sandburg), **III:** 585
Honorable Men (Auchincloss), **Supp. IV Part 1:** 23
Honor Thy Father (Talese), **Supp. XVII:** 204–205, 210
Hood, Tom, **I:** 195
"Hoodoo in America" (Hurston), **Supp. VI:** 153–154
"Hook" (Wright), **Supp. III Part 2:** 604
Hook, Sidney, **I:** 265; **Supp. IV Part 2:** 527; **Supp. VIII:** 96, 100; **Supp. XIV:** 3
Hooker, Adelaide. *See* Marquand, Mrs. John P. (Adelaide Hooker)
Hooker, Isabella Beecher, **Supp. XI:** 193
Hooker, Samuel, **IV:** 162, 165
Hooker, Thomas, **II:** 15–16; **IV:** 162
Hooper, Marian. *See* Adams, Mrs. Henry (Marian Hooper)
Hoosier Holiday, A (Dreiser), **Retro. Supp. II:** 104
Hoover, Herbert, **Supp. I Part 2:** 638
Hoover, J. Edgar, **Supp. XIII:** 170
Hoover, Paul, **Supp. XV:** 179
"Hope" (Jarrell), **II:** 389
"Hope" (Matthews), **Supp. IX:** 163
Hope, A. D., **Supp. XIII:** 347
Hope, Lynn, **Supp. II Part 1:** 38
"Hope Atherton's Wanderings" (Howe), **Supp. IV Part 2:** 432
Hope of Heaven (O'Hara), **III:** 361
"Hop-Frog" (Poe), **Retro. Supp. II:** 264, 268, 269
Hopkin, Pauline, **Supp. XVI:** 143
Hopkins, Anne Yale, **Supp. I Part 1:** 100, 102, 113
Hopkins, Gerard Manley, **I:** 171, 179, 397, 401, 522, 525, 533; **II:** 537; **III:** 197, 209, 523; **IV:** 129, 135, 141, 421; **Retro. Supp. II:** 40; **Supp. I Part 1:** 79, 81, 94; **Supp. III Part 2:** 551; **Supp. IV Part 1:** 178; **Supp. IV Part 2:** 637, 638, 639, 641, 643; **Supp. IX:** 39, 42; **Supp. V:** 337; **Supp. X:** 61, 115; **Supp. XIII:** 294; **Supp. XIV:** 83; **Supp. XV:** 250, 347; **Supp. XVI:** 282; **Supp. XVII:** 241; **Supp. XVIII:** 78, 79
Hopkins, L. A., **I:** 502
Hopkins, Lemuel, **Supp. II Part 1:** 70
Hopkins, Miriam, **IV:** 381; **Supp. I Part 1:** 281
Hopkins, Pauline, **Supp. XVIII:** 284
Hopkins, Samuel, **I:** 547, 549
Hopkins, Vivian, **II:** 20
Hopkinson, Francis, **Supp. I Part 2:** 504
Hopper (Strand), **Supp. IV Part 2:** 632
Hopper, Dennis, **Supp. XI:** 293, 308
Hopper, Edward, **IV:** 411, 413; **Supp. IV Part 2:** 619, 623, 631, 634
Hopwood, Avery, **Supp. IV Part 2:** 573
Horace, **II:** 8, 154, 169, 543, 552, 568; **III:** 15; **IV:** 89; **Supp. I Part 2:** 423; **Supp. IX:** 152; **Supp. X:** 65; **Supp. XII:** 258, 260, 262
Horae Canonicae (Auden), **Supp. II Part 1:** 21
"Horatian Ode" (Marvell), **IV:** 135
"Horatian Ode upon Cromwell's Return from Ireland" (Marvell), **Supp. XIV:** 10
Horgan, Paul, **Supp. XV:** 46, 49, 52
Horkheimer, Max, **Supp. I Part 2:** 645; **Supp. IV Part 1:** 301
Horn, Dara, **Supp. XVII:** 50
Horn, Mother, **Supp. I Part 1:** 49, 54
Hornby, Nick, **Supp. XII:** 286
"Horn of Plenty" (Hughes), **Retro. Supp. I:** 210; **Supp. I Part 1:** 342
Horovitz, Israel, **Supp. XV:** 321
Horowitz, James. *See* Salter, James
Horowitz, Mark, **Supp. V:** 219, 231
"Horse, The" (Levine), **Supp. V:** 182
"Horse, The" (Wright), **Supp. III Part 2:** 592, 601
Horse Eats Hay (play), **Supp. IV Part 1:** 82
Horse Feathers (film), **Supp. IV Part 1:** 384
"Horseflies" (Wrigley), **Supp. XVIII:** 307
Horse Has Six Legs, The (Simic), **Supp. VIII:** 272
"Horselaugh on Dibber Lannon" (Fante), **Supp. XI:** 164
Horseman, Pass By (McMurtry), **Supp. V:** 220–221, 224
"Horses" (Doty), **Supp. XI:** 122
Horses and Men (Anderson), **I:** 112–113, 114
"Horses and Men in Rain" (Sandburg), **III:** 584
"Horse Show, The" (W. C. Williams), **Retro. Supp. I:** 423
Horses Make a Landscape More Beautiful (Walker), **Supp. III Part 2:** 521, 533
"Horse Thief" (Caldwell), **I:** 310
"Horsie" (Parker), **Supp. IX:** 193
Horton, Philip, **I:** 383, 386, 387, 393, 441; **Supp. XV:** 138
Horton Hatches the Egg (Geisel), **Supp. XVI:** 100, 112
Horton Hears a Who! (Geisel), **Supp. XVI:** 102
Horwitz, Tony, **Supp. XVIII:** 195–196
Hosea (biblical book), **II:** 166
Hospers, John, **Supp. IV Part 2:** 528
Hospital, Janette Turner, **Supp. IV Part 1:** 311–302
Hospital Sketches (Alcott), **Supp. I Part 1:** 34, 35
Hostages to Fortune (Humphrey), **Supp. IX:** 96, **104–106,** 109
"Hot Dog" (Stern), **Supp. IX: 298–299**
"Hotel Bar" (McClatchy), **Supp. XII:** 269
Hotel Dwellers, The (Lacy), **Supp. XV:** 205
Hotel Insomnia (Simic), **Supp. VIII:** 280, **281–282**
Hotel Lambosa and Other Stories (Koch), **Supp. XV:** 186
Hotel New Hampshire, The (Irving), **Supp. VI:** 163, 164, **172–173,** 177, 179
"Hot-Foot Hannibal" (Chesnutt), **Supp. XIV:** 60
"Hot Night on Water Street" (Simpson), **Supp. IX:** 269, 270
"Hot Time, A" (Gunn Allen), **Supp. IV Part 1:** 333
Houdini, Harry, **IV:** 437
"Hound of Heaven" (Thompson), **Retro. Supp. I:** 55
"Hourglass, The" (Kees), **Supp. XV:** 147
"Hour in Chartres, An" (Bourne), **I:** 228
Hours, The (Cunningham), **Supp. XII:** 80; **Supp. XV: 65–68**
"Hours before Eternity" (Caldwell), **I:** 291
House, Bridge, Fountain, Gate (Kumin), **Supp. IV Part 2:** 448, 449, 451, 454
House, Edward, **Supp. I Part 2:** 643
"House, The" (Merrill), **Supp. III Part 1:** 323
House at Pooh Corner, The (Milne), **Supp. IX:** 189
House Behind the Cedars, The (Chesnutt), **Supp. XIV: 69–71**
Houseboat Days (Ashbery), **Supp. III Part 1:** 18–20
Housebreaker of Shady Hill and Other Stories, The (Cheever), **Supp. I Part 1:** 184
"House by the Sea, The" (E. Stoddard), **Supp. XV:** 277
House by the Sea, The (Sarton), **Supp. VIII:** 264
House Divided, A (Buck), **Supp. II Part 1:** 118
"House Divided, The/La Casa Divida" (Kingsolver), **Supp. VII:** 207
"House Guest" (Bishop), **Retro. Supp. II:** 49; **Supp. I Part 1:** 93
Household Saints (film), **Supp. XVI:** 256
Household Saints (Prose), **Supp. XVI:** 252–253, 254, 261
"House in Athens, The" (Merrill), **Supp. III Part 1:** 323
House in the Uplands, A (Caldwell), **I:** 297, 301, 306
"House in Turk Street, The" (Hammett), **Supp. IV Part 1:** 344
"House in Winter, The" (Sarton), **Supp. VIII:** 259
"Housekeeping" (Alvarez), **Supp. VII:** 3–5, 10
"Housekeeping for Men" (Bourne), **I:** 231
House Made of Dawn (Momaday), **Supp. IV Part 1:** 274, 323, 326; **Supp. IV Part 2:** 479, 480, 481–484, 485, 486, 504, 562
Houseman, John, **Supp. IV Part 1:** 173
House of Dust, The: A Symphony (Aiken), **I:** 50
House of Earth trilogy (Buck), **Supp. II Part 1:** 118, 123
House of Five Talents, The (Auchincloss), **Supp. IV Part 1:** 21, 25–27
"House of Flowers" (Capote), **Supp. III Part 1:** 123
House of Games (Mamet), **Supp. XIV:** 243

House of Houses (Mora), **Supp. XIII:** 213, 215, 218, 219, 223–224, **225–227,** 228, 229
House of Incest (Nin), **Supp. III Part 1:** 43; **Supp. X:** 187, 190, 193
House of Life, The: Rachel Carson at Work (Brooks), **Supp. IX:** 26
House of Light (Oliver), **Supp. VII:** 238–240
House of Mirth, The (Wharton), **II:** 180, 193; **IV:** 311–313, 314, 316, 318, 323, 327; **Retro. Supp. I:** 360, 366, 367, **367–370,** 373, 380
"House of Mist, The" (Rand), **Supp. IV Part 2:** 524
"House of My Own, A" (Cisneros), **Supp. VII:** 64
"House of Night, The" (Freneau), **Supp. II Part 1:** 259, 260
"House of Representatives and Me, The" (Conroy), **Supp. XVI:** 75
House of the Far and Lost, The (Wolfe), **IV:** 456
"House of the Injured, The" (Haines), **Supp. XII:** 203
House of the Prophet, The (Auchincloss), **Supp. IV Part 1:** 31
House of the Seven Gables (Hawthorne), **I:** 106; **II:** 60, 224, 225, 231, 237, 239, 240–241, 243, 244; **Retro. Supp. I:** 63, 149, **160–162,** 163, 164; **Supp. I Part 2:** 579
House of the Solitary Maggot, The (Purdy), **Supp. VII:** 274–275
"House on 15th S.W., The" (Hugo), **Supp. VI:** 140
"House on Main Street, The" (B. Kelly), **Supp. XVII:** 127
"House on Mango Street, The" (Cisneros), **Supp. VII:** 59
House on Mango Street, The (Cisneros), **Supp. VII:** 58, 59–64, 65, 66, 67, 68, 72
House on Marshland, The (Glück), **Supp. V:** 81–83, 84
"House on Moscow Street, The" (Nelson), **Supp. XVIII:** 174
"House on the Heights, A" (Capote), **Supp. III Part 1:** 120
"House on the Hill, The" (Robinson), **III:** 505, 524
"Houses" (Hogan), **Supp. IV Part 1:** 402
"Houses, The" (Merwin), **Supp. III Part 1:** 354
"Houses of the Spirit" (Karr), **Supp. XI:** 250
"House Sparrows" (Hecht), **Supp. X: 68**
House That Tai Maing Built, The (Lee), **Supp. X:** 291
"House Unroofed by the Gale" (Tu Fu), **II:** 526
"House Where Mark Twain Was Born, The" (Masters), **Supp. I Part 2:** 472
"Housewife" (Sexton), **Supp. II Part 2:** 682
Housman, A. E., **III:** 15, 136, 606; **Supp. II Part 1:** 4; **Supp. IV Part 1:** 165; **Supp. XV:** 40–41
Houston Trilogy (McMurtry), **Supp. V:** 223–225
How"(Ginsberg), **Supp. XIV:** 142, 143
"How"(Moore), **Supp. X:** 167
"How About This?"(Carver), **Supp. III Part 1:** 141
"How Annandale Went Out"(Robinson), **III:** 513
Howard, Ben, **Supp. XVI:** 54
Howard, Gerald, **Supp. XII:** 21
Howard, Jane, **Retro. Supp. I:** 334
Howard, June, **Retro. Supp. II:** 139
Howard, Leon, **Supp. I Part 2:** 408, 422, 423
Howard, Maureen, **Supp. XII:** 285; **Supp. XVII:** 183
Howard, Richard, **Retro. Supp. II:** 43; **Supp. IV Part 2:** 624, 626, 640; **Supp. IX:** 324, 326; **Supp. VIII:** 273; **Supp. X:** 152; **Supp. XI:** 317; **Supp. XII:** 254; **Supp. XIII:** 76; **Supp. XV:** 23, 24
Howard, Vilma, **Retro. Supp. II:** 111, 112
Howards, J. Z., **Supp. VIII:** 178
Howards End (Forster), **Supp. XII:** 87
Howarth, Cora, **I:** 408, 409
Howbah Indians (Ortiz), **Supp. IV Part 2:** 513
"How Black Sees Green and Red"(McKay), **Supp. X:** 136
"How David Did Not Care"(R. Bly), **Supp. IV Part 1:** 73
"How Did I Love Him?"(Nelson), **Supp. XVIII:** 176
"How Do I Love Thee?"(Browning), **Supp. XVIII:** 176
Howe, E.W., **I:** 106
Howe, Florence, **Supp. XIII:** 295, 306
Howe, Harriet, **Supp. XI:** 200, 201
Howe, Irving, **IV:** 10; **Retro. Supp. I:** 369; **Retro. Supp. II:** 112, 286; **Supp. I Part 2:** 432; **Supp. II Part 1:** 99; **Supp. IX:** 227; **Supp. VI: 113–129; Supp. VIII:** 93, 232; **Supp. X:** 203, 245; **Supp. XII:** 160; **Supp. XIII:** 98; **Supp. XVII:** 50
Howe, Irving, **Supp. XIV:** 103–104, 104
Howe, James Wong, **Supp. I Part 1:** 281; **Supp. V:** 223
Howe, Julia Ward, **III:** 505; **Retro. Supp. II:** 135
Howe, M. A. DeWolfe, **I:** 258; **II:** 406; **Supp. XIV:** 54
Howe, Mary Manning, **Supp. IV Part 2:** 422
Howe, Samuel, **Supp. I Part 1:** 153
Howe, Susan, **Retro. Supp. I:** 33, 43; **Supp. IV Part 2: 419–438; Supp. XVI:** 284
Howell, Chris, **Supp. XIII:** 112
Howell, James, **II:** 111
Howells, Margaret, **II:** 271
Howells, Mrs. William Dean (Elinor Mead), **II:** 273
Howells, William C., **II:** 273
Howells, William Dean, **I:** 109, 192, 204, 210, 211, 254, 355, 407, 411, 418, 459, 469; **II:** 127–128, 130, 131, 136, 137, 138, 140, **271–294,** 322, 331–332, 338, 397–398, 400, 415, 444, 451, 556; **III:** 51, 118, 314, 327–328, 461, 576, 607; **IV:** 192, 202, 342, 349; **Retro. Supp. I:** 220, 334, 362, 378; **Retro. Supp. II:** 93, 101, 135, 288; **Supp. I Part 1:** 306, 318, 357, 360, 368; **Supp. I Part 2:** 414, 420, 645–646; **Supp. II Part 1:** 198, 352; **Supp. IV Part 2:** 678; **Supp. VIII:** 98, 101, 102; **Supp. XI:** 198, 200; **Supp. XIV:** 45–46; **Supp. XV:** 269, 274, 285, 287; **Supp. XVIII:** 6
Howells, Winifred, **II:** 271
"Howells as Anti-Novelist"(Updike), **Retro. Supp. I:** 334
Howells: His Life and World (Brooks), **I:** 254
Hower, Edward, **Supp. XII:** 330, 343
Howes, Barbara, **Supp. XIII:** 331
How Good Is David Mamet, Anyway? (Heilpern), **Supp. XIV:** 242
"How I Became a Shadow"(Purdy), **Supp. VII:** 269
"How I Came to Vedanta"(Isherwood), **Supp. XIV:** 164
"How I Learned to Sweep"(Alvarez), **Supp. VII:** 4
"How I Spent My Forties"(Wasserstein), **Supp. XV:** 325, 330, 332
"How It Began"(Stafford), **Supp. XI:** 327
"How It Feels to Be Colored Me"(Hurston), **Supp. VI:** 152
"How It Is"(Everwine), **Supp. XV:** 79, 86
"How I Told My Child About Race"(Brooks), **Supp. III Part 1:** 78
"How I Went to the Mines"(Harte), **Supp. II Part 1:** 336
"How I Write"(Welty), **IV:** 279, 280
"How Jonah Did Not Care"(R. Bly), **Supp. IV Part 1:** 73
Howl (Ginsberg), **Retro. Supp. I:** 426; **Supp. III Part 1:** 92; **Supp. IV Part 1:** 90; **Supp. V:** 336; **Supp. VIII:** 290; **Supp. XIV:** 15, 126, 157; **Supp. XVIII:** 20, 29
Howl and Other Poems (Ginsberg), **Supp. II Part 1:** 308, 317–318, 319; **Supp. X:** 123
Howlett, William, **Retro. Supp. I:** 17
Howl: Original Draft Facsimile, Transcript and Variant Versions (Gimsberg), **Supp. XIV:** 142
"How Many Midnights"(Bowles), **Supp. IV Part 1:** 86–87
"How Many Nights"(Kinnell), **Supp. III Part 1:** 245–246
How Much? (Blechman), **Supp. I Part 1:** 290
"How Much Are You Worth"(Salinas), **Supp. XIII:** 325–326
"How Much Earth"(Levine), **Supp. V:** 184
How Much Earth: The Fresno Poets (Buckley, Oliveira, and Williams, eds.), **Supp. XIII:** 313
"How Not to Forget"(Bartov), **Supp. XVI:** 153–154
"How Poetry Comes to Me"(Corso), **Supp. XII:** 122
"How Poetry Comes to Me"(Snyder), **Supp. VIII:** 305

How Reading Changed My Life (Quindlen), **Supp. XVII:** 167, 179–180
"How She Came By Her Name: An Interview with Louis Massiah"(Bambara), **Supp. XI:** 20
"How Soon Hath Time"(Ransom), **IV:** 123
How Stella Got Her Groove Back (McMillan), **Supp. XIII:** 185, **190–191**
How the Alligator Missed Breakfast (Kinney), **Supp. III Part 1:** 235, 253
"How the Devil Came Down Division Street"(Algren), **Supp. IX:** 3
How the García Girls Lost Their Accents (Alvarez), **Supp. VII:** 3, 5–9, 11, 15, 17, 18
How the Grinch Stole Christmas! (Geisel), **Supp. XVI:** 102
How the Other Half Lives (Riis), **I:** 293
"How the Saint Did Not Care"(R. Bly), **Supp. IV Part 1:** 73
"How the Women Went from Dover"(Whittier), **Supp. I Part 2:** 694, 696, 697
"How To"(Carruth), **Supp. XVI:** 51
"How to Be an Other Woman"(Moore), **Supp. X:** 165, 167, 168
"How to Become a Writer"(Moore), **Supp. X:** 167, 168
"How to Be Happy: Another Memo to Myself"(Dunn), **Supp. XI:** 145
How To Cook a Wolf (M. F. K. Fisher), **Supp. XVII:** 84–85, 87
How to Develop Your Personality (Shellow), **Supp. I Part 2:** 608
How to Know God: The Yoga Aphorisms of Patanjali (Isherwood and Prabhavananda)), **Supp. XIV:** 164
"How To Like It"(Dobyns), **Supp. XIII:** **85–86**
"How to Live on $36,000 a Year"(Fitzgerald), **Retro. Supp. I:** 105
"How to Live. What to Do"(Stevens), **Retro. Supp. I:** 302
"How Tom is Doin'"(Kees), **Supp. XV:** 143
How to Read (Pound), **Supp. VIII:** 291
How to Read a Novel (Gordon), **II:** 198
How to Save Your Own Life (Jong), **Supp. V:** 115, 123–125, 130
"How to Study Poetry"(Pound), **III:** 474
"How to Talk to Your Mother"(Moore), **Supp. X:** 167, 172
How to Win Friends and Influence People (Carnegie), **Supp. I Part 2:** 608
How to Worry Successfully (Seabury), **Supp. I Part 2:** 608
How to Write (Stein), **IV:** 32, 34, 35
"How to Write a Blackwood Article"(Poe), **III:** 425; **Retro. Supp. II:** 273
"How to Write a Memoir Like This"(Oates), **Supp. III Part 2:** 509
"How to Write Like Somebody Else"(Roethke), **III:** 540
How to Write Short Stories (Lardner), **II:** 430, 431
"How Vincentine Did Not Care"(R. Bly), **Supp. IV Part 1:** 73
How We Became Human: New and Selected Poems (Harjo), **Supp. XII:** **230–232**
"How We Danced"(Sexton), **Supp. II Part 2:** 692
How We Got Insipid (Lethem), **Supp. XVIII:** 149
"How We Got in Town and Out Again"(Lethem), **Supp. XVIII:** 149
"How You Sound??"(Baraka), **Supp. II Part 1:** 30
Hoy, Philip, **Supp. X:** 56, 58
Hoyer, Linda Grace (pseudonym). *See* Updike, Mrs. Wesley
Hoyt, Constance, **Supp. I Part 2:** 707
Hoyt, Elinor Morton. *See* Wylie, Elinor
Hoyt, Henry (father), **Supp. I Part 2:** 707
Hoyt, Henry (son), **Supp. I Part 2:** 708
Hoyt, Henry Martyn, **Supp. I Part 2:** 707
Hsu, Kai-yu, **Supp. X:** 292
Hsu, Ruth Y., **Supp. XV:** 212
Hubba City (Reed), **Supp. X:** 241
Hubbard, Elbert, **I:** 98, 383
Hubbell, Jay B., **Supp. I Part 1:** 372
"Hubbub, The"(Ammons), **Supp. VII:** 35
Huber, François, **II:** 6
Huckins, Olga, **Supp. IX:** 32
Huckleberry Finn (Twain). *See Adventures of Huckleberry Finn, The* (Twain)
Hud (film), **Supp. V:** 223, 226
Hudgins, Andrew, **Supp. X:** 206; **Supp. XVII:** 111, 112; **Supp. XVIII:** 176
Hudson, Henry, **I:** 230
"Hudsonian Curlew, The"(Snyder), **Supp. VIII:** 302
Hudson River Bracketed (Wharton), **IV:** 326–327; **Retro. Supp. I:** 382
Huebsch, B. W., **III:** 110
Hueffer, Ford Madox, **Supp. I Part 1:** 257, 262. *See also* Ford, Ford Madox
Hug Dancing (Hearon), **Supp. VIII:** **67–68**
Huge Season, The (Morris), **III:** 225–226, 227, 230, 232, 233, 238
"Hugging the Jukebox"(Nye), **Supp. XIII:** 276
Hugging the Jukebox (Nye), **Supp. XIII:** **275–276,** 277
Hughes, Brigid, **Supp. XVI:** 247
Hughes, Carolyn, **Supp. XII:** 272, 285
Hughes, Frieda, **Supp. I Part 2:** 540, 541
Hughes, Glenn, **Supp. I Part 1:** 255
Hughes, H. Stuart, **Supp. VIII:** 240
Hughes, James Nathaniel, **Supp. I Part 1:** 321, 332
Hughes, Ken, **Supp. XI:** 307
Hughes, Langston, **Retro. Supp. I: 193–214; Retro. Supp. II:** 114, 115, 117, 120; **Supp. I Part 1: 320–348; Supp. II Part 1:** 31, 33, 61, 170, 173, 181, 227, 228, 233, 361; **Supp. III Part 1:** 72–77; **Supp. IV Part 1:** 15, 16, 164, 168, 169, 173, 243, 368; **Supp. IX:** 306, 316; **Supp. VIII:** 213; **Supp. X:** 131, 136, 139, 324; **Supp. XI:** 1; **Supp. XIII:** 75, 111, 132, 233; **Supp. XVI:** 135, 138; **Supp. XVIII:** 90, 277, 279, 280, 281, 282
Hughes, Nicholas, **Supp. I Part 2:** 541
Hughes, Robert, **Supp. X:** 73
Hughes, Ted, **IV:** 3; **Retro. Supp. II:** 244, 245, 247, 257; **Supp. I Part 2:** 536, 537, 538, 539, 540, 541; **Supp. XV:** 117, 347, 348
Hughes, Thomas, **Supp. I Part 2:** 406
"Hugh Harper"(Bowles), **Supp. IV Part 1:** 94
Hughie (O'Neill), **III:** 385, 401, 405
Hugh Selwyn Mauberley (Pound), **I:** 66, 476; **III:** 9, 462–463, 465, 468; **Retro. Supp. I: 289–290,** 291, 299; **Supp. XIV:** 272
Hugo, Richard, **Supp. IX:** 296, 323, 324, 330; **Supp. VI: 131–148; Supp. XI:** 315, 317; **Supp. XII:** 178; **Supp. XIII:** 112, 113, 133; **Supp. XVIII:** 293, 299
Hugo, Victor, **II:** 290, 490, 543; **Supp. IV Part 2:** 518; **Supp. IX:** 308
Hui-neng, **III:** 567
Huis Clos (Sartre), **Supp. IV Part 1:** 84
Huizinga, Johan, **I:** 225; **II:** 416–417, 418, 425
Hulbert, Ann, **Supp. XI:** 38–39
Hull, Lynda, **Supp. XI:** 131
Hulme, Thomas E., **I:** 68, 69, 475; **III:** 196, 209, 463–464, 465; **IV:** 122; **Supp. I Part 1:** 261, 262; **Supp. XV:** 43
Human, All Too Human (Nietzsche), **Supp. X:** 48
"Human Culture"(Emerson), **II:** 11–12
Human Factor, The (Greene), **Supp. V:** 298
"Human Figures"(Doty), **Supp. XI:** 123–124
"Human Geography"(Jarman), **Supp. XVII:** 116
"Human Immortality"(James), **II:** 353–354
"Human Life"(Emerson), **II:** 11–12
"Human Pig"(Jin), **Supp. XVIII:** 99
Human Rights, Human Wrongs: The Oxford Amnesty Lectures, 2001, **Supp. XVI:** 155
Human Stain, The (P. Roth), **Retro. Supp. II:** 279, 289, 294–295
"Human Things"(Nemerov), **III:** 279
"Human Universe"(Olson), **Supp. II Part 2:** 565, 567
Human Universe (Olson), **Supp. II Part 2:** 571
Human Vibration (Richter), **Supp. XVIII:** 209
Human Wishes (Hass), **Supp. VI:** 105–106, 107
Human Work (Gilman), **Supp. XI:** 206
Humbert, Humbert, **Supp. X:** 283
Humble Inquiry into the Rules of the Word of God, An, Concerning the Qualifications Requisite to a Complete Standing and Full Communion in the Visible Christian Church (Edwards), **I:** 548
Humboldt, Alexander von, **III:** 428

Humboldt's Gift (Bellow), **Retro. Supp. II:** 19, 28–29, 34; **Supp. XIII:** 320
Hume, David, **I:** 125; **II:** 349, 357, 480; **III:** 618
Humes, Harold, **Supp. V:** 201; **Supp. XIV:** 82
Humes, H. L."Doc,"**Supp. XI:** 294
"Humility"(Hoffman), **Supp. XVIII:** 86
"Hummingbirds, The"(Welty), **IV:** 273
Humphrey, William, **Supp. IX: 93–112; Supp. XV:** 353
Humphreys, Christmas, **Supp. V:** 267
Humphreys, David, **Supp. II Part 1:** 65, 69, 70, 268
Humphreys, Josephine, **Supp. XII:** 311
Humphries, Rolfe, **III:** 124; **Retro. Supp. I:** 137
Hunchback of Notre Dame, The (film), **Supp. IV Part 1:** 101
Hunches in Bunches (Geisel), **Supp. XVI:** 111
Huncke, Herbert, **Supp. XII:** 118; **Supp. XIV: 137–153**
Huncke's Journal (Huncke), **Supp. XIV:** 139, 144, 145, 146
Hundred Camels in the Courtyard, A (Bowles), **Supp. IV Part 1:** 90
"Hundred Collars, A" (Frost), **Retro. Supp. I:** 128; **Supp. XIII:** 147
Hundred Secret Senses, The (Tan), **Supp. X:** 289, 293, 295, 297, 298, 299
Hundreds of Hens and Other Poems for Children by Halfdan Rasmussen (Nelson and Espeland, trans.), **Supp. XVIII:** 180
Hundred White Daffodils, A: Essays, Interviews, Newspaper Columns, and One Poem (Kenyon), **Supp. VII:** 160–162, 165, 166, 167, 174
Huneker, James, **III:** 102
Hunger (Hamsun), **Supp. XI:** 167
"Hunger" (Hogan), **Supp. IV Part 1:** 411
"Hunger ..." (Rich), **Supp. I Part 2:** 571
"Hungerfield" (Jeffers), **Supp. II Part 2:** 416–417, 436
Hungerfield and Other Poems (Jeffers), **Supp. II Part 2:** 422
Hunger of Memory: The Education of Richard Rodriguez (Rodriguez), **Supp. XIV:** 297, 298, **298–302,** 310
Hungry Ghosts, The (Oates), **Supp. II Part 2:** 504, 510
Hungry Hearts (Prose), **Supp. XVI:** 253
Hunnewell, Susannah, **Supp. VIII:** 83
Hunt, Harriot K., **Retro. Supp. II:** 146
Hunt, Leigh, **II:** 515–516; **Supp. XV:** 175
Hunt, Richard Morris, **IV:** 312
Hunt, Robert, **Supp. XV:** 42, 49, 52
Hunt, William, **II:** 343
"Hunter" (Bierds), **Supp. XVII:** 30
Hunter, Dianna, **Supp. XVI:** 38
Hunter, Dr. Joseph, **II:** 217
Hunter, J. Paul, **Supp. IV Part 1:** 332
Hunter, Kim, **Supp. I Part 1:** 286
"Hunter of Doves" (Herbst), **Retro. Supp. II:** 325
"Hunter of the West, The" (Bryant), **Supp. I Part 1:** 155
Hunters, The (film), **Supp. IX:** 250
Hunters, The (Salter), **Supp. IX:** 246, **249–250**
Hunters and Gatherers (Prose), **Supp. XVI:** 257
"Hunters in the Snow" (Brueghel), **I:** 174; **Retro. Supp. I:** 430
"Hunters in the Snow" (Wolff), **Supp. VII:** 339–340
"Hunter's Moon——Eating the Bear" (Oliver), **Supp. VII:** 234
"Hunter's Vision, The" (Bryant), **Supp. I Part 1:** 160
Hunting for Hope: A Father's Journey (Sanders), **Supp. XVI:** 276–277, 278
"Hunting Is Not Those Heads on the Wall" (Baraka), **Supp. II Part 1:** 45
Huntington, Collis P., **I:** 198, 207
"Hunt in the Black Forest, The" (Jarrell), **II:** 379–380
Huntley, Jobe, **Supp. I Part 1:** 339
"Hurrah, Hurrah" (Nelson), **Supp. XVIII:** 175
Hurray Home (Wideman), **Supp. X:** 320
"Hurricane, The" (Crane), **I:** 401
"Hurricane, The" (Freneau), **Supp. II Part 1:** 262
"Hurry Kane" (Lardner), **II:** 425, 426, 427
"Hurry up Please It's Time" (Sexton), **Supp. II Part 2:** 694, 695
Hurst, Fannie, **Supp. XVIII:** 278, 279
Hurston, Zora Neale, **Retro. Supp. I:** 194, 198, 200, 201, 203; **Supp. I Part 1:** 325, 326, 332; **Supp. II Part 1:** 33; **Supp. IV Part 1:** 5, 11, 12, 164, 257; **Supp. VI: 149–161; Supp. VIII:** 214; **Supp. X:** 131, 139, 232, 242; **Supp. XI:** 85; **Supp. XIII:** 185, 233, 236, 295, 306; **Supp. XVIII:** 122, 279, 280, 282
Hurt, John, **Supp. XIII:** 132
Husbands and Wives (film; Allen), **Supp. XV: 12**
Husband's Story, The (Shields), **Supp. VII:** 316. *See also* "Happenstance" (Shields)
Husserl, Edmund, **II:** 362, 363; **IV:** 491; **Supp. IV Part 1:** 42, 43
Hussey, Jo Ella, **Supp. XII:** 201
Hustler, The (film), **Supp. XI:** 306
Huston, John, **I:** 30, 31, 33, 35; **II:** 588; **III:** 161; **Supp. IV Part 1:** 102, 116, 355; **Supp. XI:** 307; **Supp. XIII:** 174
"Huswifery" (Taylor), **IV:** 161; **Supp. I Part 2:** 386
"Hut, The" (Sobin), **Supp. XVI:** 284–285
Hutchens, John K., **Supp. IX:** 276
Hutcheson, Francis, **I:** 559
Hutchins, Patricia, **III:** 478
Hutchinson, Abigail, **I:** 562
Hutchinson, Anne, **Supp. I Part 1:** 100, 101, 113; **Supp. IV Part 2:** 434; **Supp. VIII:** 202, 205
Hutchinson, George, **Supp. XVIII:** 119–120, 121, 132
Hutton, James, **Supp. IX:** 180
Huxley, Aldous, **II:** 454; **III:** 281, 428, 429–430; **IV:** 77, 435; **Supp. I Part 2:** 714; **Supp. XIV:** 3, 164; **Supp. XVI:** 189, 192; **Supp. XVIII:** 137
Huxley, Julian, **Supp. VIII:** 251; **Supp. X:** 108
Huxley, Juliette, **Supp. VIII:** 251, 265
Huxley, Thomas, **III:** 102, 108, 113, 281; **Retro. Supp. II:** 60, 65, 93
Huxley, Thomas Henry, **Supp. I Part 1:** 368
Huysmans, Joris Karl (Charles Marie Georges), **I:** 66; **III:** 315; **IV:** 286; **Retro. Supp. II:** 326
"*Hwame, Koshkalaka,* and the Rest: Lesbians in American Indian Cultures" (Gunn Allen), **Supp. IV Part 1:** 330
Hwang, David Henry, **Supp. X:** 292
"Hyacinth Drift" (Rawlings), **Supp. X: 226–227**
Hyde, Lewis, **Supp. XVIII:** 150
"Hydrangeas" (C. Frost), **Supp. XV:** 106
"Hydras, The" (Merwin), **Supp. III Part 1:** 349
Hydriotaphia, The; or, Death of Dr. Browne: An Epic Farce about Death and Primitive Capital Accumulation (Kushner), **Supp. IX:** 133, **136–138**
"Hydriotaphia; or, Urne-Buriall" (Browne), **Supp. IX:** 136–137
Hyman, Stanley Edgar, **I:** 129, 264, 363, 377, 379; **Retro. Supp. II:** 118; **Supp. IX:** 113, 114, 117, 118, 121, 122, 128
Hymen (Doolittle), **Supp. I Part 1:** 266
"Hymie's Bull" (Ellison), **Retro. Supp. II:** 124; **Supp. II Part 1:** 229
"Hymn Books" (Emerson), **II:** 10
"HYMN FOR LANIE POO" (Baraka), **Supp. II Part 1:** 31, 37
"Hymn from a Watermelon Pavilion" (Stevens), **IV:** 81
"Hymn of the Sea, A" (Bryant), **Supp. I Part 1:** 157, 163, 165
"Hymns of the Marshes" (Lanier), **Supp. I Part 1:** 364
"Hymn to Death" (Bryant), **Supp. I Part 1:** 169, 170
"Hymn to Earth" (Wylie), **Supp. I Part 2:** 727–729
"Hymn to the Night" (Longfellow), **Supp. I Part 2:** 409
Hynes, Jennifer, **Supp. XV:** 207
Hynes, Samuel, **Supp. XIV:** 159
Hyperion (Longfellow), **II:** 488, 489, 491–492, 496; **Retro. Supp. II:** 58, 155–156
"Hypocrite Auteur" (MacLeish), **III:** 19
"Hypocrite Swift" (Bogan), **Supp. III Part 1:** 55
"Hysteria" (Eliot), **I:** 570

I

I (Dixon), **Supp. XII:** 141, 155, **156–157**
I, etcetera (Sontag), **Supp. III Part 2:** 451–452, 469
I, Governor of California and How I Ended Poverty (Sinclair), **Supp. V:** 289
I, the Jury (Spillane), **Supp. XVIII:** 236

"I, Too" (Hughes), **Retro. Supp. I:** 193, 199; **Supp. I Part 1:** 320
I Accuse! (film), **Supp. IV Part 2:** 683
"I Almost Remember" (Angelou), **Supp. IV Part 1:** 15
"'I Always Wanted You to Admire My Fasting'; or, Looking at Kafka"(P. Roth), **Retro. Supp. II:** 282
I am a Camera (Druten), **Supp. XIV:** 162
"I am a cowboy in the boat of Ra" (Reed), **Supp. X:** 242
"I Am a Dangerous Woman" (Harjo), **Supp. XII:** 216, 219
"I Am Alive" (Momaday), **Supp. IV Part 2:** 489
I Am a Sonnet (Goldbarth), **Supp. XII:** 181
"I Am a Writer of Truth" (Fante), **Supp. XI:** 167
"'I Am Cherry Alive,' the Little Girl Sang" (Schwartz), **Supp. II Part 2:** 663
"I Am Dying, Meester?" (Burroughs), **Supp. III Part 1:** 98
I Am Elijah Thrush (Purdy), **Supp. VII:** 274
"I Am in Love" (Stern), **Supp. IX:** 295
"I Am Not Flattered" (Francis), **Supp. IX:** 78
I Am! Says the Lamb (Roethke), **III:** 545
"I Am You Again" (Nelson), **Supp. XVIII:** 173
"I and My Chimney" (Melville), **III:** 91
I and Thou (Buber), **III:** 308
"I Apologize" (Komunyakaa), **Supp. XIII:** 120, **Supp. XIII:** 121
I Apologize for the Eyes in My Head (Komunyakaa), **Supp. XIII: 119–121,** 126
"I Believe I Shall Die an Impenetrable Secret": The Writings of Elizabeth Barstow Stoddard (Giovani), **Supp. XV:** 270
Ibsen, Henrik, **II:** 27, 276, 280, 291–292; **III:** 118, 145, 148, 149, 150, 151, 152, 154–155, 156, 161, 162, 165, 511, 523; **IV:** 397; **Retro. Supp. I:** 228; **Retro. Supp. II:** 94; **Supp. IV Part 2:** 522; **Supp. XIV:** 89; **Supp. XVII:** 100
"I Came Out of the Mother Naked" (R. Bly), **Supp. IV Part 1:** 62–63, 68
I Can Lick 30 Tigers Today! and Other Stories (Geisel), **Supp. XVI:** 108
"I Cannot Forget with What Fervid Devotion" (Bryant), **Supp. I Part 1:** 154
I Can Read with My Eyes Shut! (Geisel), **Supp. XVI:** 111
"I Can't Stand Your Books: A Writer Goes Home" (Gordon), **Supp. IV Part 1:** 314
"Icarium Mare" (Wilbur), **Supp. III Part 2:** 563
"Icarus in Winter" (C. Frost), **Supp. XV:** 94
Icarus's Mother (Shepard), **Supp. III Part 2:** 446
"Ice" (Bambara), **Supp. XI:** 16
"Iceberg, The" (Merwin), **Supp. III Part 1:** 345
Ice-Cream Headache, The, and Other Stories (Jones), **Supp. XI:** 215, 227
Ice Fire Water: A Leib Goldkorn Cocktail (Epstein), **Supp. XII: 164–166**
"Ice Fisherman, The" (C. Baxter), **Supp. XVII:** 15
"Ice House, The" (Gordon), **II:** 201
Iceman Cometh, The (O'Neill), **I:** 81; **III:** 151, 385, 386, 401, 402–403; **Supp. VIII:** 345; **Supp. XVI:** 193; **Supp. XVII:** 103
"Ice Palace, The" (Fitzgerald), **II:** 83, 88; **Retro. Supp. I:** 103
Ice-Shirt, The (Vollmann), **Supp. XVII:** 226, 231, 232, 233
"Ice Storm, The" (Ashbery), **Supp. III Part 1:** 26
"Ice-Storm, The" (Pinsky), **Supp. VI:** 247–248
"Ichabod" (Whittier), **Supp. I Part 2:** 687, 689–690; **Supp. XI:** 50
"Icicles" (Francis), **Supp. IX:** 83
"Icicles" (Gass), **Supp. VI:** 83
Ickes, Harold, **Supp. I Part 1:** 5
Iconographs (Swenson), **Supp. IV Part 2:** 638, 646–648, 651
"Icosaphere, The" (Moore), **III:** 213
"I Could Believe" (Levine), **Supp. V:** 189
"I Could Take" (Carruth), **Supp. XVI:** 56
"I Cry, Love! Love!" (Roethke), **III:** 539–540
Ida (Stein), **IV:** 43, 45
"Idea, The" (Carver), **Supp. III Part 1:** 143
"Idea, The" (Strand), **Supp. IV Part 2:** 631
Ideal Husband (Wilde), **II:** 515
Idea of Florida in the American Literary Imagination, The (Rowe), **Supp. X:** 223
"Idea of Ice, The" (C. Baxter), **Supp. XVII:** 15
"Idea of Order, An" (Wiman), **Supp. XVIII:** 173
"Idea of Order at Key West, The" (Stevens), **IV:** 89–90; **Retro. Supp. I:** 302, 303, 313
Ideas of Order (Stevens), **Retro. Supp. I:** 296, 298, **302–303,** 303, 305
"Identity Theft: True Memory, False Memory, and the Holocaust" (R. Franklin), **Supp. XVI:** 160
Ideograms in China (Michaux; Sobin, trans.), **Supp. XVI:** 288
"Ideographs" (Olds), **Supp. X:** 205
Ides of March, The (Wilder), **IV:** 357, 372
"I Did Not Learn Their Names" (Ellison), **Retro. Supp. II:** 124
"I Died with the First Blow & Was Reborn Wrong" (Coleman), **Supp. XI:** 91
"Idiom of a Self, The" (Pinsky), **Supp. VI:** 240
"Idiot, The" (Crane), **I:** 401
Idiot, The (Dostoevsky), **I:** 468
"Idiots First" (Malamud), **Supp. I Part 2:** 434–435, 437, 440–441
"Idiot Wind" (song, Dylan), **Supp. XVIII:** 30
I Don't Need You Any More (A. Miller), **III:** 165
Idoru (W. Gibson), **Supp. XVI:** 119, 124, **129–130**
"I Dream I'm the Death of Orpheus" (Rich), **Supp. I Part 2:** 557–558
I Dreamt I Became a Nymphomaniac! Imagining (Acker), **Supp. XII:** 4, 6, **8,** 11
Idylls of the King (Tennyson), **III:** 487; **Supp. I Part 2:** 410; **Supp. XIII:** 146
Idyl of Work, An (Larcom), **Supp. XIII:** 139, 142, 146–147, 150
"If" (Creeley), **Supp. IV Part 1:** 158
If Beale Street Could Talk (Baldwin), **Retro. Supp. II:** 13–14; **Supp. I Part 1:** 48, 59–60, 67
If Blessing Comes (Bambara), **Supp. XI:** 1
I Feel a Little Jumpy around You (Nye and Janeczko, eds.), **Supp. XIII:** 280
"I felt a Funeral, in my Brain" (Dickinson), **Retro. Supp. I:** 38
"If Grown-Ups Were Smart" (Nelson and Espeland), **Supp. XVIII:** 181
If He Hollers Let Him Go (C. Himes), **Supp. XVI:** 135, 138–139, 142
"If I Could Be Like Wallace Stevens" (Stafford), **Supp. XI:** 327
"If I Could Do Whatever I Wanted" (Nelson and Espeland), **Supp. XVIII:** 181
"If I Could Only Live at the Pitch That Is Near Madness" (Eberhart), **I:** 523, 526–527
If I Die in a Combat Zone (O'Brien), **Supp. V:** 238, 239, 240, 245
"If I Had My Way" (Creeley), **Supp. IV Part 1:** 157
"If I Might Be" (Chopin), **Retro. Supp. II:** 61
"I Find the Real American Tragedy" (Dreiser), **Retro. Supp. II:** 105
If I Ran the Circus (Geisel), **Supp. XVI:** 105
If I Ran the Zoo (Geisel), **Supp. XVI:** 104–105
If It Die (Gide), **I:** 290
"If It Were Not for You" (Carruth), **Supp. XVI:** 57
"If I Were a Man" (Gilman), **Supp. XI:** 207
"If I Were the Wind" (Leopold), **Supp. XIV:** 184
If Morning Ever Comes (Tyler), **Supp. IV Part 2:** 658–659
If Mountains Die: A New Mexico Memoir (Nichols), **Supp. XIII:** 255, 257, 267
I Forgot to Go to Spain (Harrison), **Supp. VIII:** 39, **52–53**
If the River Was Whiskey (Boyle), **Supp. VIII: 15–16**
"If They Knew Yvonne" (Dubus), **Supp. VII:** 81
"If We Had Bacon" (H. Roth), **Supp. IX:** 232, 234
"If We Had Known" (Francis), **Supp. IX:** 78
"If We Must Die" (McKay), **Supp. IV Part 1:** 3; **Supp. X:** 132, 134

"If We Take All Gold" (Bogan), **Supp. III Part 1:** 52
If You Call This a Cry Song (Carruth), **Supp. XVI:** 56
If You Want to Write (Ueland), **Supp. XVII:** 13
I Gaspiri (Lardner), **II:** 435
"I Gather the Limbs of Osiris" (Pound), **Retro. Supp. I:** 287
"I Give You Back" (Harjo), **Supp. XII:** 223
Ignatius of Loyola, **IV:** 151; **Supp. XI:** 162
Ignatow, David, **Supp. XIII:** 275
"Ignis Fatuus" (Tate), **IV:** 128
"I Go Back to May 1937" (Olds), **Supp. X:** 207
I Go Dreaming Serenades (Salinas), **Supp. XIII:** 316
I Got the Blues (Odets), **Supp. II Part 2:** 530
Iguana Killer, The (Ríos), **Supp. IV Part 2:** 542–544
"I Had Eight Birds Hatcht in One Nest" (Bradstreet), **Supp. I Part 1:** 102, 115, 117, 119
"I had no time to Hate" (Dickinson), **Retro. Supp. I:** 44–45, 46
I Had Trouble in Getting to Solla Sollew (Geisel), **Supp. XVI:** 108, 109
"I Have a Rendezvous with Life" (Cullen), **Supp. IV Part 1:** 168
"I Have Increased Power" (Ginsberg), **Supp. II Part 1:** 313
"I Have Seen Black Hands" (Wright), **Supp. II Part 1:** 228
"I Hear an Army" (Joyce), **Supp. I Part 1:** 262
"I heard a Fly buzz when I died" (Dickinson), **Retro. Supp. I:** 38
"I Heard Immanuel Singing" (Lindsay), **Supp. I Part 2:** 379
"I Hear It Was Charged against Me" (Whitman), **IV:** 343
"I Held a Shelley Manuscript" (Corso), **Supp. XII:** 128
"I Held His Name" (Ríos), **Supp. IV Part 2:** 547
I Knew a Phoenix (Sarton), **Supp. VIII:** 249, 251–252
"I Know a Man" (Creeley), **Supp. IV Part 1:** 147–148, 149
I Know Some Things: Stories about Childhood by Contemporary Writers (Moore, ed.), **Supp. X:** 175
"I Know Why the Caged Bird Cannot Read" (Prose), **Supp. XVI:** 259
I Know Why the Caged Bird Sings (Angelou), **Supp. IV Part 1:** 2–4, 5, 7, 11, 12, 13, 14, 15, 17; **Supp. XVI:** 259
"Ikon: The Harrowing of Hell" (Levertov), **Supp. III Part 1:** 284
Ile (O'Neill), **III:** 388
"I Let Him Take Me" (Cisneros), **Supp. VII:** 71
Iliad (Bryant, trans.), **Supp. I Part 1:** 158
Iliad (Homer), **II:** 470; **Supp. IV Part 2:** 631; **Supp. IX:** 211; **Supp. X:** 114
Iliad (Pope, trans.), **Supp. I Part 1:** 152
Iliad, The (Homer), **Supp. XVII:** 117
"I like to see it lap the Miles" (Dickinson), **Retro. Supp. I:** 37
"I Live Up Here" (Merwin), **Supp. III Part 1:** 349
"Illegal Alien" (Mora), **Supp. XIII:** 215
"Illegal Days, The" (Paley), **Supp. VI:** 222
"Illegibility" (F. Wright), **Supp. XVII:** 244
Illig, Joyce, **Retro. Supp. II:** 20
"Illinois" (Masters), **Supp. I Part 2:** 458
"Illinois Bus Ride" (Leopold), **Supp. XIV:** 189
Illinois Poems (Masters), **Supp. I Part 2:** 472
"Illinois Village, The" (Lindsay), **Supp. I Part 2:** 381
"Ill-Lit" (F. Wright), **Supp. XVII:** 245
Ill-Lit: Selected & New Poems (F. Wright), **Supp. XVII:** 245
Illness as Metaphor (Sontag), **Supp. III Part 2:** 452, 461, 466
I'll Take My Stand ("Twelve Southerners"), **II:** 196; **III:** 496; **IV:** 125, 237; **Supp. X:** 25, 52–53; **Supp. XIV:** 3
"I'll Take You to Tennessee" (Connell), **Supp. XIV:** 82
Illumination (Frederic), **II:** 141
Illumination Night (Hoffman), **Supp. X:** 85, **86,** 88, 89
Illusion comique, L' (Corneille), **Supp. IX:** 138
"Illusion of Eternity, The" (Eberhart), **I:** 541
"Illusion of Fiction in Frank Conroy's *Stop-Time,* The" (R. Ramsey), **Supp. XVI:** 69
Illusions (Dash; film), **Supp. XI:** 20
"Illusions" (Emerson), **II:** 2, 5, 14, 16
Illustrated Man, The (Bradbury), **Supp. IV Part 1:** 102, 103, 113
Illustrations of Political Economy (Martineau), **Supp. II Part 1:** 288
"I Look at My Hand" (Swenson), **Supp. IV Part 2:** 638, 647
I Love Gootie: My Grandmother's Story (Apple), **Supp. XVII: 9–10**
I Love Myself When I Am Laughing ...: A Zora Neale Hurston Reader (Walker), **Supp. III Part 2:** 531, 532
"I'm a Fool" (Anderson), **I:** 113, 114, 116; **Supp. I Part 2:** 430
Image and Idea (Rahv), **Supp. II Part 1:** 146
Image and the Law, The (Nemerov), **III:** 268, 269–271, 272
"Images" (Hass), **Supp. VI:** 103
"Images and 'Images'" (Simic), **Supp. VIII:** 274
"Images for Godard" (Rich), **Supp. I Part 2:** 558
"Images of Walt Whitman" (Fiedler), **IV:** 352
"Imaginary Friendships of Tom McGrath, The" (Cohen), **Supp. X:** 112
"Imaginary Iceberg, The" (Bishop), **Retro. Supp. II:** 42; **Supp. I Part 1:** 86, 88
"Imaginary Jew, The" (Berryman), **I:** 174–175
Imaginary Letters (Pound), **III:** 473–474
Imaginary Paintings (C. Baxter), **Supp. XVII:** 18–19
"Imaginary Prisons" (Schnackenberg), **Supp. XV:** 257, 258
Imagination and Fancy; or, Selections from the English Poets, illustrative of those first requisites of their art; with markings of the best passages, critical notices of the writers, and an essay in answer to the question'What is Poetry?' (Hunt), **II:** 515–516
"Imagination as Value" (Stevens), **Retro. Supp. I:** 298
"Imagination of Disaster, The" (Gordon), **Supp. IV Part 1:** 306
"Imagine a Day at the End of Your Life" (Beattie), **Supp. V:** 33
Imagined London: A Tour of the World's Greatest Fictional City (Quindlen), **Supp. XVII:** 167, 180
"Imagine Kissing Pete" (O'Hara), **III:** 372; **Supp. VIII:** 156
Imaging Robert: My Brother, Madness, and Survival (Neugeboren), **Supp. XVI:** 225, **226–229**
"Imagining How It Would Be to Be Dead" (Eberhart), **I:** 533
Imagining Los Angeles: A City in Fiction (Fine), **Supp. XI:** 160
"Imagining Their Own Hymns" (B. Kelly), **Supp. XVII:** 126–127
"Imagining the Midwest" (Sanders), **Supp. XVI:** 275–276
Imagining the Worst: Stephen King and the Representations of Women (Lant and Thompson), **Supp. V:** 141
"Imagisme" (Pound), **Retro. Supp. I:** 288
Imagistes, Des: An Anthology of the Imagists (Pound, ed.), **III:** 465, 471; **Retro. Supp. I:** 288
Imago (O. Butler), **Supp. XIII:** 63, **65–66**
"Imago" (Stevens), **IV:** 74, 89
Imagoes (Coleman), **Supp. XI:** 89–90
I Married a Communist (P. Roth), **Retro. Supp. II:** 289, 293–294
I Married an Angel (film), **Supp. XVI:** 193
"I May, I Might, I Must" (Moore), **III:** 215
"I'm Crazy" (Salinger), **III:** 553
"I'm Here" (Roethke), **III:** 547
Imitations (Lowell), **II:** 543, 544–545, 550, 555; **Retro. Supp. II:** 181, 187
"Imitations of Drowning" (Sexton), **Supp. II Part 2:** 684, 686
"Immaculate Man" (Gordon), **Supp. IV Part 1:** 311
"Immanence of Dostoevsky, The" (Bourne), **I:** 235
"Immigrants" (Mora), **Supp. XIII:** 216
"Immigrant Story, The" (Paley), **Supp. VI:** 230

"Immobile Wind, The" (Winters), **Supp. II Part 2:** 788, 811

Immobile Wind, The (Winters), **Supp. II Part 2:** 786

"Immolatus" (Komunyakaa), **Supp. XIII:** 126

"Immoral Proposition, The" (Creeley), **Supp. IV Part 1:** 144

"Immortal Autumn" (MacLeish), **III:** 13

"Immortality Ode" (Nemerov), **III:** 87

Immortality Ode (Wordsworth), **II:** 17; **Supp. I Part 2:** 673

"Immortal Woman, The" (Tate), **IV:** 130, 131, 137

"I'm Not Ready to Die Yet" (Harjo), **Supp. XII:** 231

I'm Not There (film, Haynes), **Supp. XVIII:** 23

"I'm on My Way" (Salinas), **Supp. XIII:** 320

"Impasse" (Hughes), **Supp. I Part 1:** 343

Imperative Duty, An, a Novel (Howells), **II:** 286

Imperial Eyes: Travel Writing and Transculturation (Pratt), **Retro. Supp. II:** 48

Imperial Germany and the Industrial Revolution (Veblen), **Supp. I Part 2:** 642, 643

Imperial Way, The: By Rail from Peshawar to Chittagong (Theroux), **Supp. VIII:** 323

"Implosions" (Rich), **Supp. I Part 2:** 556

"Imp of the Perverse, The" (Poe), **III:** 414–415; **Retro. Supp. II:** 267

Impolite Interviews, **Supp. XI:** 293

"Importance of Artists' Biographies, The" (Goldbarth), **Supp. XII:** 183, 184, 191

Importance of Being Earnest, The (Wilde), **Supp. XIV:** 324, 339

"Important Houses, The" (Gordon), **Supp. IV Part 1:** 315

"Impossible Indispensability of the Ars Poetica, The" (Carruth), **Supp. XVI:** 57

"Impossible to Tell" (Pinsky), **Supp. VI:** 247, 248

"Imposter, The" (West), **Retro. Supp. II:** 322, 327

"Impressionism and Symbolism in *Heart of Darkness*" (Watt), **Supp. VIII:** 4

"Impressions of a European Tour" (Bourne), **I:** 225

"Impressions of a Plumber" (H. Roth), **Supp. IX:** 228, 234

"Impressions of Europe, 1913–1914" (Bourne), **I:** 225

"I'm Walking behind the Spanish" (Salinas), **Supp. XIII:** 323–324

"I/Myself" (Shields), **Supp. VII:** 311

"In Absence" (Lanier), **Supp. I Part 1:** 364

"In Absentia" (Bowles), **Supp. IV Part 1:** 94

"In a Cab" (Untermeyer), **Supp. XV:** 296

Inada, Lawson Fusao, **Supp. V:** 180

"In a Dark Room, Furniture" (Nye), **Supp. XIII:** 274

"In a Dark Time" (Roethke), **III:** 539, 547, 548

"In a Disused Graveyard" (Frost), **Retro. Supp. I:** 126, 133

In a Dusty Light (Haines), **Supp. XII:** 207

"In a Garden" (Lowell), **II:** 513

"In a Hard Intellectual Light" (Eberhart), **I:** 523

"In a Hollow of the Hills" (Harte), **Supp. II Part 1:** 354

In America (Sontag), **Supp. XIV:** 95–96

"In Amicitia" (Ransom), **IV:** 141

In a Narrow Grave: Essays on Texas (McMurtry), **Supp. V:** 220, 223

"Inanna" (A. Finch), **Supp. XVII:** 72

"In Another Country" (Hemingway), **I:** 484–485; **II:** 249

In April Once (Percy), **Retro. Supp. I:** 341

"In a Prominent Bar in Secaucus One Day" (X. J. Kennedy), **Supp. XV:** 154, 155–156

In A Shallow Grave (Purdy), **Supp. VII:** 272

"In a Station of the Metro" (Pound), **Retro. Supp. I:** 288; **Supp. I Part 1:** 265; **Supp. XIV:** 284–285

"In a Strange Town" (Anderson), **I:** 114, 115

"In Athens Once" (Rodriguez), **Supp. XIV:** 303

In Battle for Peace: The Story of My 83rd Birthday (Du Bois), **Supp. II Part 1:** 185

In Bed One Night & Other Brief Encounters (Coover), **Supp. V:** 49, 50

"In Bertram's Garden" (Justice), **Supp. VII:** 117

"In Blackwater Woods" (Oliver), **Supp. VII:** 244, 246

In Black & Whitey (Lacy), **Supp. XV:** 206–207

"In Broad Daylight" (Jin), **Supp. XVIII:** 94

In Broken Country (Wagoner), **Supp. IX:** 330

"In California" (Simpson), **Supp. IX:** 271

"In Camp" (Stafford), **Supp. XI:** 329

"Incant against Suicide" (Karr), **Supp. XI:** 249

"In Celebration of My Uterus" (Sexton), **Supp. II Part 2:** 689

"Incendiary, The" (Rowson), **Supp. XV:** 234

"In Certain Places and Certain Times There Can Be More of You" (Dunn), **Supp. XI:** 144

Incest: From "A Journal of Love," the Unexpurgated Diary of Anaïs Nin, 1932–1934 (Nin), **Supp. X:** 182, 184, 185, 187, 191

"In Chandler Country" (Gioia), **Supp. XV:** 119

Inchbald, Elizabeth, **II:** 8

"In Cheever Country" (Gioia), **Supp. XV:** 119

Inchiquin, the Jesuit's Letters (Ingersoll), **I:** 344

"Incident" (Cullen), **Supp. IV Part 1:** 165, 166

Incidental Numbers (Wylie), **Supp. I Part 2:** 708

Incidentals (Sandburg), **III:** 579

Incident at Vichy (A. Miller), **III:** 165, 166

Incidents in the Life of a Slave Girl (Brent), **Supp. IV Part 1:** 13

Incidents in the Life of a Slavegirl (Jacobs), **Supp. XVI:** 85

"Incipience" (Rich), **Supp. I Part 2:** 559

"In Clare" (McCarriston), **Supp. XIV:** 270–271

Including Horace (Untermeyer), **Supp. XV:** 301, 303–304

In Cold Blood: A True Account of a Multiple Murder and Its Consequences (Capote), **Retro. Supp. II:** 107–108; **Supp. I Part 1:** 292; **Supp. III Part 1:** 111, 117, 119, 122, 123, 125–131; **Supp. III Part 2:** 574; **Supp. IV Part 1:** 220; **Supp. XIV:** 162

"In Cold Hell, in Thicket" (Olson), **Supp. II Part 2:** 558, 563–564, 566, 572, 580

In Cold Hell, in Thicket (Olson), **Supp. II Part 2:** 571

"Incomparable Light, The" (Eberhart), **I:** 541

Incorporative Consciousness of Robert Bly, The (Harris), **Supp. IV Part 1:** 68

In Country (Mason), **Supp. VIII:** 133, **142–143,** 146

"Incredible Survival of Coyote, The" (Snyder), **Supp. VIII:** 297

"Increment" (Ammons), **Supp. VII:** 28

In Defense of Ignorance (Shapiro), **Supp. II Part 2:** 703, 704, 713–714

In Defense of Reason (Winters), **Supp. I Part 1:** 268

In Defense of Women (Mencken), **III:** 109

Independence Day (film), **Supp. X:** 80

Independence Day (Ford), **Supp. V:** 57, 62–63, 67–68

"Independent Candidate, The, a Story of Today" (Howells), **II:** 277

"Indestructible Mr. Gore, The" (Vidal), **Supp. IV Part 2:** 679

Index of American Design, **Supp. III Part 2:** 618

"India" (Rodriguez), **Supp. XIV:** 302

"Indian at the Burial-Place of His Fathers, An" (Bryant), **Supp. I Part 1:** 155–156, 167–168

"Indian Burying Ground, The" (Freneau), **Supp. II Part 1:** 264, 266

"Indian Camp" (Hemingway), **II:** 247–248, 263; **Retro. Supp. I:** 174–175, 176, 177, 181; **Supp. XVI:** 208

Indian Country (Matthiessen), **Supp. V:** 211

"Indian Country" (McCarriston), **Supp. XIV:** 271

"Indian Country" (Simpson), **Supp. IX:** 274

Indian Earth (Bynner), **Supp. XV:** 46

"Indian Girls" (McCarriston), **Supp. XIV:** 272–273

"Indian Manifesto" (Deloria), **Supp. IV Part 1:** 323

"Indian Names" (Sigourney), **Retro. Supp. II:** 47
"Indian Student, The" (Freneau), **Supp. II Part 1:** 264
"Indian Student, The" (Simpson), **Supp. IX:** 280
Indian Summer (Howells), **II:** 275, 279–281, 282
Indian Summer (Knowles), **Supp. XII:** 249, 250
"Indian Uprising, The" (Barthelme), **Supp. IV Part 1:** 44
Indifferent Children, The (Auchincloss), **Supp. IV Part 1:** 25
Indiscretions (Pound), **Retro. Supp. I:** 284
"Indispensability of the Eyes, The" (Olds), **Supp. X:** 202
"In Distrust of Merits" (Moore), **III:** 201, 214
"Individual and the State, The" (Emerson), **II:** 10
Individualism, Old and New (Dewey), **Supp. I Part 2:** 677
"In Dreams Begin Responsibilities" (Schwartz), **Supp. II Part 2:** 641, 649, 654
In Dreams Begin Responsibilities (Schwartz), **Supp. II Part 2:** 642, 645–650
In Dubious Battle (Steinbeck), **IV:** 51, 55–56, 59, 63
"In Durance" (Pound), **Retro. Supp. I:** 285
"Industry of Hard Kissing, The" (Ríos), **Supp. IV Part 2:** 547
"In Duty Bound" (Gilman), **Supp. XI:** 196–197
"I Need, I Need" (Roethke), **III:** 535–536
"I Need Help" (Stern), **Supp. IX:** 290
"Inés in the Kitchen" (García), **Supp. XI:** 190
"I never saw a Moor" (Dickinson), **Retro. Supp. I:** 37
I Never Told Anybody: Teaching Poetry Writing in a Nursing Home (Koch), **Supp. XV:** 190
"I Never Will Be Married, I'd Rather Be Excus'd" (Rowson), **Supp. XV:** 240
Inevitable Exiles (Kielsky), **Supp. V:** 273
"Inevitable Trial, The" (Holmes), **Supp. I Part 1:** 318
"Inexhaustible Hat, The" (Wagoner), **Supp. IX:** 327
"In Extremis" (Berry), **Supp. X:** 23
"Infancy" (Wilder), **IV:** 375
"Infant Boy at Midcentury" (Warren), **IV:** 244–245, 252
Infante, Guillermo Cabrera, **Retro. Supp. I:** 278
"Infant Sea Turtles" (F. Wright), **Supp. XVII:** 245
Infants of the Spring (Thurman), **Supp. XVIII:** 281
Inferno (Dante), **IV:** 139; **Supp. V:** 338; **Supp. VIII:** 219–221
Inferno of Dante, The (Pinsky), **Supp. VI:** 235, 248
"Infidelity" (Komunyakaa), **Supp. XIII:** 130
Infidels (album, Dylan), **Supp. XVIII:** 28
"Infiltration of the Universe" (MacLeish), **III:** 19
Infinite Jest: A Novel (Wallace), **Supp. X:** 301, **310–314**
"Infinite Reason, The" (MacLeish), **III:** 19
"Infirmity" (Lowell), **II:** 554
"Infirmity" (Roethke), **III:** 548
In Five Years Time (Haines), **Supp. XII:** 206
"In Flower" (Snodgrass), **Supp. VI:** 325
"Influence of Landscape upon the Poet, The" (Eliot), **Retro. Supp. I:** 67
"In Football Season" (Updike), **IV:** 219
Informer, The (film), **Supp. III Part 2:** 619
Ingersoll, Charles J., **I:** 344
Ingersoll, Robert Green, **Supp. II Part 1:** 198
Ingraham, Lloyd, **Supp. XVI:** 184
Ingster, Boris, **Retro. Supp. II:** 330
Inhabitants, The (Morris), **III:** 221–222
"Inheritance and Invention in Li-Young Lee's Poetry" (Xiaojing), **Supp. XV:** 214
"Inheritance of Tools, The" (Sanders), **Supp. XVI:** 273
Inheritors (Glaspell), **Supp. III Part 1:** 175, 179–181, 186, 189
"In Honor of David Anderson Brooks, My Father" (Brooks), **Supp. III Part 1:** 79
"Inhumanist, The" (Jeffers), **Supp. II Part 2:** 423, 426
"In Illo Tempore" (Karr), **Supp. XI:** 242
"In Interims: Outlyer" (Harrison), **Supp. VIII:** 38
"Initial" (F. Wright), **Supp. XVII:** 243
"Injudicious Gardening" (Moore), **III:** 198
"Injustice" (Paley), **Supp. VI:** 220
Injustice Collectors, The (Auchincloss), **Supp. IV Part 1:** 25
Ink, Blood, Semen (Goldbarth), **Supp. XII:** 181, 183
Ink Truck, The (W. Kennedy), **Supp. VII:** 132, 133–138, 140, 141, 149, 152
In Life Sentences: Literary Essays (Epstein), **Supp. XIV:** 112
"In Limbo" (Wilbur), **Supp. III Part 2:** 544, 561
In Limestone Country (Sanders), **Supp. XVI:** 272
In Love and Trouble: Stories of Black Women (Walker), **Supp. III Part 2:** 520, 521, 530, 531, 532
In Mad Love and War (Harjo), **Supp. XII: 224–226**
"In Memoriam" (Emerson), **II:** 13
"In Memoriam" (Hay), **Supp. XIV:** 122, 127
"In Memoriam" (Tennyson), **Retro. Supp. I:** 325; **Supp. I Part 2:** 416
In Memoriam: 1933 (Reznikoff), **Supp. XIV:** 280, 285
In Memoriam to Identity (Acker), **Supp. XII:** 5, **16–18**
"In Memory of Arthur Winslow" (Lowell), **II:** 541, 547, 550; **Retro. Supp. II:** 187
"In Memory of Congresswoman Barbara Jordan" (Pinsky), **Supp. VI:** 250
"In Memory of Joe Brainard" (Bidart), **Supp. XV:** 33
"In Memory of My Feelings" (O'Hara), **Supp. XV:** 215–216
"In Memory of W. B. Yeats" (Auden), **Supp. VIII:** 19, 30; **Supp. XI:** 243, 244
"In Memory of W. H. Auden" (Stern), **Supp. IX:** 288
"In Mercy on Broadway" (Doty), **Supp. XI:** 132
In Morocco (Wharton), **Retro. Supp. I:** 380; **Supp. IV Part 1:** 81
Inmost Leaf, The: A Selection of Essays (Kazin), **Supp. VIII:** 102, 103
In Motley (Bierce), **I:** 209
In My Father's Court (Singer), **IV:** 16–17; **Retro. Supp. II: 301–302**
"In My Life" (Dubus), **Supp. VII:** 81
Inner Landscape (Sarton), **Supp. VIII:** 259
Inner Room, The (Merrill), **Supp. III Part 1:** 336
"In Nine Sleep Valley" (Merrill), **Supp. III Part 1:** 328
Innocents, The: A Story for Lovers (Lewis), **II:** 441
Innocents Abroad, The; or, The New Pilgrim's Progress (Twain), **II:** 275, 434; **IV:** 191, 196, 197–198
Innocents at Cedro, The: A Memoir of Thorstein Veblen and Some Others (Duffus), **Supp. I Part 2:** 650
"In Off the Cliffs of Moher" (McCarriston), **Supp. XIV:** 270
In Old Plantation Days (Dunbar), **Supp. II Part 1:** 214
In Ole Virginia (Page), **Supp. II Part 1:** 201
In Orbit (Morris), **III:** 236
In Other Words (Swenson), **Supp. IV Part 2:** 650–652
In Our Terribleness (Some elements and meaning in black style) (Baraka), **Supp. II Part 1:** 52, 53
In Our Time (Hemingway), **I:** 117; **II:** 68, 247, 252, 263; **IV:** 42; **Retro. Supp. I:** 170, 173, 174, 178, 180; **Supp. IX:** 106
"In Our Time" (Wolfe), **Supp. III Part 2:** 584
"Inpatient" (Kenyon), **Supp. VII:** 169
In Pharaoh's Army: Memories of the Lost War (Wolff), **Supp. VII:** 331–334, 335, 338
"In Plaster" (Plath), **Supp. I Part 2:** 540
"In Prague, in Montmartre" (Bierds), **Supp. XVII:** 27
"In Praise of Johnny Appleseed" (Lindsay), **Supp. I Part 2:** 397
"In Praise of Limestone" (Auden), **Supp. II Part 1:** 20–21; **Supp. VIII:** 23
In Pursuit of a Vanishing Star (Sobin), **Supp. XVI: 294**

In Quest of the Ordinary (Cavell), **Retro. Supp. I:** 307
Inquiry into the Moral and Religious Character of the American Government, An (H. Warner), **Supp. XVIII:** 259
Inquiry into the Nature of Peace, An (Veblen), **Supp. I Part 2:** 642
Inquisitor, The (Rowson), **Supp. XV: 232,** 238
In Radical Pursuit (Snodgrass), **Supp. VI:** 312, 316, 318
In Reckless Ecstasy (Sandburg), **III:** 579
In Recognition of William Gaddis (Kuehl and Moore), **Supp. IV Part 1:** 279
"In Retirement" (Malamud), **Supp. I Part 2:** 437
"In Retrospect" (Angelou), **Supp. IV Part 1:** 15
"Inroads of Time, The" (D. West), **Supp. XVIII:** 286–287
In Russia (A. Miller), **III:** 165
"In Sabine" (Chopin), **Supp. I Part 1:** 213
"In School-Days" (Whittier), **Supp. I Part 2:** 699–700
"Inscription for the Entrance to a Wood" (Bryant), **Supp. I Part 1:** 154, 155, 161–162
Inscriptions, 1944–1956 (Reznikoff), **Supp. XIV:** 281
In Search of Bisco (Caldwell), **I:** 296
In Search of Nella Larsen: A Biography of the Color Line (Hutchinson), **Supp. XVIII:** 120
"In Search of Our Mothers' Gardens" (Walker), **Supp. III Part 2:** 520–532, 524, 525, 527, 529, 532–533, 535, 536; **Supp. IX:** 306; **Supp. XVIII:** 200, 283
"In Search of Thomas Merton" (Griffin), **Supp. VIII:** 208
"In Search of Yage" (Burroughs), **Supp. III Part 1:** 98
"Insertion of Self into a Space of Borderless Possibilities, The" (Fjellestad), **Supp. XVI:** 150
"In Shadow" (Crane), **I:** 386
"In Sickness and in Health" (Auden), **Supp. II Part 1:** 15
"In Sickness and in Health" (Humphrey), **Supp. IX:** 94
Inside His Mind (A. Miller), **III:** 154
"Inside Norman Mailer" (Apple), **Supp. XVII:** 3, 4
"Insider Baseball" (Didion), **Supp. IV Part 1:** 211
Inside Sports magazine, **Supp. V:** 58, 61
"Insipid Profession of Jonathan Horneboom, The" (Lethem), **Supp. XVIII:** 149
"In So Many Dark Rooms" (Hogan), **Supp. IV Part 1:** 400
"Insomnia" (Bishop), **Supp. I Part 1:** 92
"Insomniac" (Plath), **Supp. I Part 2:** 539
"Inspiration for Greatness" (Caldwell), **I:** 291
"Instability of Race Types, The" (Boas), **Supp. XIV:** 209
"Installation #6" (Beattie), **Supp. V:** 33
Instinct of Workmanship and the State of the Industrial Arts, The (Veblen), **Supp. I Part 2:** 642
Instincts of the Herd in Peace and War, The (Trotter), **I:** 249
Institute (Calvin), **IV:** 158, 160
"Instruction Manual, The" (Ashbery), **Supp. III Part 1:** 6–7, 10, 12
"Instructions for the Afternoon" (Gioia), **Supp. XV:** 120
"Instruction to Myself" (Brooks), **Supp. III Part 1:** 87
Instrument, The (O'Hara), **III:** 362, 364
"In Such Times, Ties Must Bind" (Nye), **Supp. XIII:** 286
"Insurance and Social Change" (Stevens), **Retro. Supp. I:** 297
Insurgent Mexico (Reed), **I:** 476
In Suspect Terrain (McPhee), **Supp. III Part 1:** 309, 310
"In Tall Grass" (Sandburg), **III:** 585
"Integer Vitae" (Horace), **Supp. XV:** 304
Intellectual History, An (Senghor), **Supp. X:** 139
"Intellectual Pre-Eminence of Jews in Modern Europe, The" (Veblen), **Supp. I Part 2:** 643–644
Intellectual Things (Kunitz), **Supp. III Part 1:** 260, 262–264
Intellectual versus the City, The (White), **I:** 258
"In Temporary Pain" (Bynner), **Supp. XV:** 41–42
Intentions (Wilde), **Retro. Supp. I:** 56
"Interest in Life, An" (Paley), **Supp. VI:** 222, 224–225
Interest of Great Britain Considered, with Regard to Her Colonies and the Acquisition of Canada and Guadeloupe, The (Franklin), **II:** 119
Interior Landscapes (Vizenor), **Supp. IV Part 1:** 262
Interiors (film; Allen), **Supp. IV Part 1:** 205; **Supp. XV:** 1, **7,** 10
Interlocking Lives (Koch), **Supp. XV:** 185
"Interlude" (A. Lowell), **Retro. Supp. II:** 46
Interlunar (Atwood), **Supp. XIII:** 35
"Intermezzo" (Schnackenberg), **Supp. XV:** 254
"In Terms of the Toenail: Fiction and the Figures of Life" (Gass), **Supp. VI:** 85
"International Episode, An" (James), **II:** 327
International Workers Order, **Retro. Supp. I:** 202
Interpretation of Christian Ethics, An (Niebuhr), **III:** 298–300, 301, 302
"Interpretation of Dreams, The" (Matthews), **Supp. IX:** 162–163
Interpretation of Music of the XVIIth and XVIIIth Centuries, The (Dolmetsch), **III:** 464
Interpretations and Forecasts: 1922–1972 (Mumford), **Supp. II Part 2:** 481
Interpretations of Poetry and Religion (Santayana), **III:** 611
Interpreters and Interpretations (Van Vechten), **Supp. II Part 2:** 729, 733–734
"Interrogate the Stones" (MacLeish), **III:** 9
Interrogations at Noon (Gioia), **Supp. XV:** 112, **125–127,** 128, 129
"Interrupted Conversation, An" (Van Vechten), **Supp. II Part 2:** 735
Intersect: Poems (Shields), **Supp. VII:** 310–311
Interstate (Dixon), **Supp. XII:** 140, 152–153, 153, 156
"Interview" (Hay), **Supp. XIV:** 132
"Interview, The" (Thurber), **Supp. I Part 2:** 616
"Interview With a Lemming" (Thurber), **Supp. I Part 2:** 603
"Interview with Peter Everwine, An" (Veinberg and Buckley), **Supp. XV:** 76–77
"Interview with the Crab" (Lethem), **Supp. XVIII:** 148
"Interview with the Vampire" (Rice), **Supp. VII:** 288
Interview with the Vampire (Rice), **Supp. VII:** 287, 288–291, 297–298, 303
Interzone (Burroughs), **Supp. IV Part 1:** 90
"In the Absence of Bliss" (Kumin), **Supp. IV Part 2:** 453
"In the Afternoon" (Dunn), **Supp. XI:** 146
"In the Alley" (Elkin), **Supp. VI: 46–47**
In the American Grain (W. C. Williams), **Retro. Supp. I:** 420–421
In the American Tree (Silliman), **Supp. IV Part 2:** 426
In the Bank of Beautiful Sins (Wrigley), **Supp. XVIII: 300–302**
In the Bar of a Tokyo Hotel (T. Williams), **IV:** 382, 386, 387, 391, 393
In the Beauty of the Lilies (Updike), **Retro. Supp. I:** 322, 325, 326, 327, 333
"In the Beeyard" (Bierds), **Supp. XVII:** 29
"In the Beginning" (Quindlen), **Supp. XVII:** 166
"In the Beginning ..." (Simic), **Supp. VIII:** 270, 271
In the Belly of the Beast: Letters from Prison (Abbott), **Retro. Supp. II:** 210
"In the Black Museum" (Nemerov), **III:** 275
"In the Bodies of Words" (Swenson), **Supp. IV Part 2:** 651
"In the Cage" (Gass), **Supp. VI:** 85
"In the Cage" (James), **II:** 332; **Retro. Supp. I:** 231
In the Cage (James), **Retro. Supp. I:** 229
"In the Cage" (Lowell), **Retro. Supp. II:** 187
"In the Cave at Lone Tree Meadow" (Haines), **Supp. XII:** 212
"In the City Ringed with Giants" (Kingsolver), **Supp. VII:** 209
"In the Clearing" (Brodsky), **Supp. VIII:** 32

In the Clearing (Frost), **II:** 153, 155, 164; **Retro. Supp. I:** 121, 122, 141
"In the Closet of the Soul" (Walker), **Supp. III Part 2:** 526
"In the Confidence of a Story-Writer" (Chopin), **Retro. Supp. II:** 66–67; **Supp. I Part 1:** 217
In the Country of Last Things (Auster), **Supp. XII:** 23, **29–30,** 31, 32
"In the Courtyard of the Isleta Missions" (R. Bly), **Supp. IV Part 1:** 71
"In the Dark" (Levine), **Supp. V:** 194
"In the Dark New England Days" (Jewett), **Retro. Supp. II:** 139
"In the Days of Prismatic Colour" (Moore), **III:** 205, 213
In the Electric Mist with Confederate Dead (Burke), **Supp. XIV:** 30, 31–32
"In the Field" (Wilbur), **Supp. III Part 2:** 558
"In the First Stanza" (C. Kizer), **Supp. XVII:** 75
"In the Fleeting Hand of Time" (Corso), **Supp. XII:** 122–123
"In the Footsteps of Gutenberg" (Mencken), **III:** 101
"In the Forest" (Simpson), **Supp. IX:** 270
"In the Forties" (Lowell), **II:** 554
In the Garden of the North American Martyrs (Wolff), **Supp. VII:** 341–342
In the Garret (Van Vechten), **Supp. II Part 2:** 735
"In the Grove: The Poet at Ten" (Kenyon), **Supp. VII:** 160
"In the Hall of Mirrors" (Merrill), **Supp. III Part 1:** 322
In the Harbor (Longfellow), **II:** 491
In the Heart of the Heart of the Country (Gass), **Supp. VI: 82–83,** 84, 85, 93
In the Heat of the Night (Ball), **Supp. XV:** 202
In the Heat of the Night (film), **Supp. I Part 1:** 67
In the Hollow of His Hand (Purdy), **Supp. VII:** 278–280
In the House of Light (Everwine, trans.), **Supp. XV:** 73, 75, **76–78,** 82
In the Lake of the Woods (O'Brien), **Supp. V:** 240, 243, 250–252
In the Land of the White Death: A Epic Story of Survival in the Siberian Arctic (Albanov), **Supp. XVIII:** 114
"In the Last Days" (Everwine), **Supp. XV:** 88, 89
"In the Loyal Mountains" (Bass), **Supp. XVI:** 20
In the Loyal Mountains (Bass), **Supp. XVI: 19–20**
"In the Mecca" (Brooks), **Supp. III Part 1:** 70, 83–84
In the Mecca (Brooks), **Supp. III Part 1:** 74
In the Midst of Life (Bierce), **I:** 200–203, 204, 206, 208, 212
"In the Miro District" (Taylor), **Supp. V:** 323
In the Miro District and Other Stories (Taylor), **Supp. V:** 325–326
In the Money (W. C. Williams), **Retro. Supp. I:** 423
"In the Motel" (X. J. Kennedy), **Supp. XV:** 163
"In the Naked Bed, in Plato's Cave" (Schwartz), **Supp. II Part 2:** 646–649
In the Name of the Neither (Sobin), **Supp. XVI:** 291
"In the Night" (Kincaid), **Supp. VII:** 183
In the Night Season: A Novel (Bausch), **Supp. VII:** 52–53
"In the Old Neighborhood" (Dove), **Supp. IV Part 1:** 241, 257
"In the Old World" (Oates), **Supp. II Part 2:** 503, 504
"In the Park" (Huncke), **Supp. XIV:** 139
"In the Pit" (Proulx), **Supp. VII:** 255, 261
In the Pond (Jin), **Supp. XVIII: 95–96**
In the Presence of the Sun (Momaday), **Supp. IV Part 2:** 489, 490, 491–493, 493
"In the Quiet Night" (Li Po), **Supp. XV:** 47
"In the Realm of the Fisher King" (Didion), **Supp. IV Part 1:** 211
"In the Red Room" (Bowles), **Supp. IV Part 1:** 93
"In the Region of Ice" (Oates), **Supp. II Part 2:** 520
In the Room We Share (Simpson), **Supp. IX:** 279
"In These Dissenting Times" (Walker), **Supp. III Part 2:** 522
"In the Shadow of Gabriel, A.D.1550" (Frederic), **II:** 139
In the Spirit of Crazy Horse (Matthiessen), **Supp. V:** 211
"In the Subway" (Untermeyer), **Supp. XV:** 296
In the Summer House (Jane Bowles), **Supp. IV Part 1:** 83, 89
In the Tennessee Country (Taylor), **Supp. V:** 328
"In the Thick of Darkness" (Salinas), **Supp. XIII:** 325
"In the Time of the Blossoms" (Mervin), **Supp. III Part 1:** 352
In the Time of the Butterflies (Alvarez), **Supp. VII:** 1, 12–15, 18
"In the Tube" (Jarman), **Supp. XVII:** 121
"In the Tunnel Bone of Cambridge" (Corso), **Supp. XII:** 120–121
"In the Upper Pastures" (Kumin), **Supp. IV Part 2:** 453
In the Valley (Frederic), **II:** 133–134, 136, 137
"In the Village" (Bishop), **Retro. Supp. II:** 38; **Supp. I Part 1:** 73, 74–75, 76, 77, 78, 88
"In the Waiting Room" (Bishop), **Retro. Supp. II:** 50; **Supp. I Part 1:** 81, 94, 95; **Supp. IV Part 1:** 249
"In the Ward: The Sacred Wood" (Jarrell), **II:** 376, 377
In the Western Night: Collected Poems 1965–90 (Bidart), **Supp. XV:** 19, **30–32**
"In the White Night" (Beattie), **Supp. V:** 30–31
"In the Wind My Rescue Is" (Ammons), **Supp. VII:** 25
In the Winter of Cities (T. Williams), **IV:** 383
"In the X-Ray of the Sarcophagus of Tapero" (Goldbarth), **Supp. XII:** 191
"In the Yard" (Swenson), **Supp. IV Part 2:** 647
In the Zone (O'Neill), **III:** 388
In This, Our Life (film), **Supp. I Part 1:** 67
"In This Country, but in Another Language, My Aunt Refuses to Marry the Men Everyone Wants Her To" (Paley), **Supp. VI:** 225
In This Hung-up Age (Corso), **Supp. XII: 119–120,** 129
In This Our Life (Glasgow), **II:** 175, 178, 189
In This Our World (Gilman), **Supp. XI:** 196, 200, 202
"In Those Days" (Jarrell), **II:** 387–388
"In Time of War" (Auden), **Supp. II Part 1:** 8, 13
"Into Egypt" (Benét), **Supp. XI:** 56, 57–58
Intolerance (film; Griffith), **Supp. XVI:** 184
"Into My Own" (Frost), **II:** 153; **Retro. Supp. I:** 127
"Into the Night Life ..." (H. Miller), **III:** 180, 184
"Into the Nowhere" (Rawlings), **Supp. X:** 220
"Into the Stone" (Dickey), **Supp. IV Part 1:** 179
Into the Stone (Dickey), **Supp. IV Part 1:** 178
Into the Stone and Other Poems (Dickey), **Supp. IV Part 1:** 176
Into the Wild (Krakauer), **Supp. XVIII:** 106, **107–108,** 116, 117
Into Thin Air (Krakauer), **Supp. XVII:** 210
Into Thin Air: A Personal Account of the Mount Everest Disaster (Krakauer), **Supp. XVIII:** 105, **109–113,** 117
In Touch: The Letters of Paul Bowles (J. Miller, ed.), **Supp. IV Part 1:** 95
"Intoxicated, The" (Jackson), **Supp. IX:** 116
"Intrigue" (Crane), **I:** 419
"Introducing the Fathers" (Kumin), **Supp. IV Part 2:** 452
Introductio ad Prudentiam (Fuller), **II:** 111
"Introduction to a Haggadah" (Paley), **Supp. VI:** 219
Introduction to Objectivist Epistemology (Rand), **Supp. IV Part 2:** 527, 528–529
Introduction to Objectivist Epistemology 2nd ed. (Rand), **Supp. IV Part 2:** 529
Introduction to Poetry, An (Gioia and X. J. Kennedy), **Supp. XV:** 113, 153
"Introduction to Some Poems, An" (Stafford), **Supp. XI:** 311, 324
Introduction to the Geography of Iowa, The (Doty), **Supp. XI:** 120
"Introduction to the Hoh" (Hugo), **Supp. VI:** 136–137

"Introduction to *The New Writing in the USA*" (Creeley), **Supp. IV Part 1:** 153–154
"Introduction to William Blake, An" (Kazin), **Supp. VIII:** 103
Introitus (Longfellow), **II:** 505, 506–507
"Intruder, The" (Dubus), **Supp. VII:** 76–78, 91
Intruder, The (Maeterlinck), **I:** 91
Intruder in the Dust (Faulkner), **II:** 71, 72; **Supp. XVI:** 148
"Invaders, The" (Haines), **Supp. XII:** 205
Invasion of Privacy: The Cross Creek Trial of Marjorie Kinnan Rawlings (Acton), **Supp. X:** 233
Inventing Memory: A Novel of Mothers and Daughters (Jong), **Supp. V:** 115, 129
Inventing the Abbotts (Miller), **Supp. XII: 294–295**
"Invention of God in a Mouthful of Milk, The" (Karr), **Supp. XI:** 250
Invention of Solitude, The (Auster), **Supp. XII:** 21–22
"Inventions of the March Hare" (Eliot), **Retro. Supp. I:** 55
Inventions of the March Hare (Eliot), **Retro. Supp. I:** 55–56, 58
"Inventory" (Parker), **Supp. IX:** 192
"Inverted Forest, The" (Salinger), **III:** 552, 572
"Investigation" (Ryan as Quin), **Supp. XVIII:** 227–228
"Investigations of a Dog" (Kafka), **IV:** 438
"Investiture, The" (Banks), **Supp. V:** 7
"Investiture at Cecconi's" (Merrill), **Supp. III Part 1:** 336
Invisible Company, The (Sanders), **Supp. XVI:** 270–271
Invisible Man (Ellison), **IV:** 493; **Retro. Supp. II:** 3, 12, 111, 112, 113, 117, 119, **120–123,** 125; **Supp. II Part 1:** 40, 170, 221, 224, 226, 227, 230, 231–232, 235, 236, 241–245; **Supp. IX:** 306; **Supp. X:** 242; **Supp. XI:** 18, 92; **Supp. XVIII:** 59
Invisible: Poems (Nye), **Supp. XIII:** 277
Invisible Spectator, An (Sawyer-Lauçanno), **Supp. IV Part 1:** 95
Invisible Swords (Farrell), **II:** 27, 46, 48–49
Invisible Worm, The (Millar), **Supp. IV Part 2:** 465
Invitation to a Beheading (Nabokov), **III:** 252–253, 254, 257–258; **Retro. Supp. I:** 265, 270, 273
"Invitation to the Country, An" (Bryant), **Supp. I Part 1:** 160
"Invocation" (McKay), **Supp. X:** 134
"Invocation" (Untermeyer), **Supp. XV:** 296
"Invocation to Kali" (Sarton), **Supp. VIII:** 260
"Invocation to the Social Muse" (MacLeish), **III:** 15
"In Weather" (Hass), **Supp. VI: 102–103**
"In Your Fugitive Dream" (Hugo), **Supp. VI:** 143
"In Your Good Dream" (Hugo), **Supp. VI:** 143–144
"Iola, Kansas" (Clampitt), **Supp. IX: 45–46**
Iola Leroy (Harper), **Supp. XVIII:** 284
Ion (Doolittle, trans.), **Supp. I Part 1:** 269, 274
Ion (Plato), **I:** 523
"Ione" (Dunbar), **Supp. II Part 1:** 199
Ionesco, Eugène, **I:** 71, 74, 75, 84, 295; **II:** 435; **Supp. VIII:** 201
"I Only Am Escaped Alone to Tell Thee" (Nemerov), **III:** 272, 273–274
"I Opened All the Portals Wide" (Chopin), **Retro. Supp. II:** 71
I Ought to Be in Pictures (Simon), **Supp. IV Part 2:** 584
Iphigenia in Tauris (Euripedes), **Supp. XV:** 42, 50
I Promessi Sposi (Manzoni), **II:** 291
"Irascibles, The" (Kees), **Supp. XV:** 145–146
"I Remember" (Sexton), **Supp. II Part 2:** 680
"Irenicon" (Shapiro), **Supp. II Part 2:** 704
Irigaray, Luce, **Supp. XII:** 6
Iris (Jarman), **Supp. XVII:** 110, **116–117**
"Iris by Night" (Frost), **Retro. Supp. I:** 132
"Irises" (L.-Y. Lee), **Supp. XV:** 214–215
Irish Stories of Sarah Orne Jewett, The (Jewett), **Retro. Supp. II:** 142
Irish Triangle, An (Barnes), **Supp. III Part 1:** 34
"Iron Characters, The" (Nemerov), **III:** 279, 282
"Iron Hans" (Sexton), **Supp. II Part 2:** 691
Iron Heel, The (London), **II:** 466, 480
Iron John: A Book about Men (R. Bly), **Supp. IV Part 1:** 59, 67; **Supp. XVI:** 177
"Iron Table, The" (Jane Bowles), **Supp. IV Part 1:** 82–83
"Iron Throat, The" (Olsen), **Supp. XIII:** 292, 297, 299
Ironweed (W. Kennedy), **Supp. VII:** 132, 133, 134, 135, 142, 144, 145–147, 148, 150, 153
"Irony as Art: The Short Fiction of William Humphrey" (Tebeaux), **Supp. IX:** 109
"Irony Is Not Enough: Essay on My Life as Catherine Deneuve" (Carson), **Supp. XII: 112–113**
Irony of American History, The (Niebuhr), **III:** 292, 306–307, 308
"Irrational Element in Poetry, The" (Stevens), **Retro. Supp. I:** 298, 301
"Irrevocable Diameter, An" (Paley), **Supp. VI:** 231–232
Irvine, Lorna, **Supp. XIII:** 26
Irving, Ebenezer, **II:** 296
Irving, John, **Supp. VI: 163–183; Supp. X:** 77, 85
Irving, John Treat, **II:** 296
Irving, Peter, **II:** 296, 297, 298, 299, 300, 303
Irving, Sir Henry, **IV:** 350
Irving, Washington, **I:** 211, 335, 336, 339, 343; **II: 295–318,** 488, 495; **III:** 113; **IV:** 309; **Retro. Supp. I:** 246; **Supp. I Part 1:** 155, 157, 158, 317; **Supp. I Part 2:** 377, 487, 585; **Supp. II Part 1:** 335; **Supp. IV Part 1:** 380; **Supp. XVIII:** 12
Irving, William, **II:** 296
Irving, William, Jr., **II:** 296, 297, 298, 299, 303
Irwin, Mark, **Supp. XII:** 21, 22, 24, 29
Irwin, William Henry, **Supp. II Part 1:** 192
Is 5 (Cummings), **I:** 429, 430, 434, 435, 440, 445, 446, 447
"Isaac and Abraham" (Brodsky), **Supp. VIII:** 21
"Isaac and Archibald" (Robinson), **III:** 511, 521, 523
"Isabel Sparrow" (Oliver), **Supp. VII:** 232
Isaiah (biblical book), **Supp. I Part 1:** 236; **Supp. I Part 2:** 516
"Isaiah Beethoven" (Masters), **Supp. I Part 2:** 461
"I Saw in Louisiana a Live-Oak Growing" (Whitman), **I:** 220
"I Shall Be Released" (Dylan), **Supp. XV:** 349
I Shall Spit on Your Graves (film), **Supp. I Part 1:** 67
Isherwood, Christopher, **II:** 586; **Supp. II Part 1:** 10, 11, 13; **Supp. IV Part 1:** 79, 82, 102; **Supp. XI:** 305; **Supp. XIV: 155–175; Supp. XVI:** 194
Isherwood Century, The (Berg and Freeman), **Supp. XIV:** 157, 159
Isherwood's Fiction (Schwerdt), **Supp. XIV:** 155
Ishiguro, Kazuo, **Supp. VIII:** 15
Ishi Means Man (Merton), **Supp. VIII:** 208
"Ishmael's Dream" (Stern), **Supp. IX:** 287
I Should Have Stayed Home (McCoy), **Supp. XIII:** 167, **168–170,** 171
"I Should Worry" (Kees), **Supp. XV:** 140
"I Sigh in the Afternoon" (Salinas), **Supp. XIII:** 318
"I Sing the Body Electric" (Whitman), **Retro. Supp. I:** 394, 395
"Isis: Dorothy Eady, 1924" (Doty), **Supp. XI:** 122
"Is It O.K. to Be a Luddite?" (Pynchon), **Supp. XVI:** 128
"Is It True?" (Hughes), **Supp. I Part 1:** 342
I: Six Nonlectures (Cummings), **I:** 430, 433, 434
"Island" (Hughes), **Supp. I Part 1:** 340
Island Garden, An (Thaxter), **Retro. Supp. II:** 136; **Supp. XIII:** 152
Island Holiday, An (Henry), **I:** 515
"Island of the Fay, The" (Poe), **III:** 412, 417
"Islands, The" (Hayden), **Supp. II Part 1:** 373
"Island Sheaf, An" (Doty), **Supp. XI:** 136
Islands in the Stream (Hemingway), **II:** 258; **Retro. Supp. I:** 186

Isn't It Romantic (Wasserstein), **Supp. XV: 323–325,** 327
Is Objectivism a Religion? (Ellis), **Supp. IV Part 2:** 527
"Isolation of Modern Poetry, The" (Schwartz), **Supp. II Part 2:** 644
"Israel" (Reznikoff), **Supp. XIV:** 283
Israel Potter, or Fifty Years of Exile (Melville), **III:** 90; **Supp. XVIII:** 4
"Israfel" (Poe), **III:** 411
Is Sex Necessary? (Thurber and White), **Supp. I Part 2:** 607, 612, 614, 653
"Issues, The" (Olds), **Supp. X:** 205
"I Stand Here Ironing" (Olsen), **Supp. XIII:** 292, 294, 296, 298, 300, 305
I Stole a Million (West), **IV:** 287
"Is Verse a Dying Technique?" (Wilson), **IV:** 431
It (Creeley), **Supp. IV Part 1:** 157, 158
IT (King), **Supp. V:** 139, 140, 141, 146–147, 151, 152
"It" (Olds), **Supp. X:** 208
Italian American Reconciliation: A Folktale (Shanley), **Supp. XIV:** 315, **324–326,** 328, 330
Italian Backgrounds (Wharton), **Retro. Supp. I:** 370
Italian Hours (James), **I:** 12; **II:** 337; **Retro. Supp. I:** 235
Italian Journeys (Howells), **II:** 274
"Italian Morning" (Bogan), **Supp. III Part 1:** 58
Italian Villas and Their Gardens (Wharton), **IV:** 308; **Retro. Supp. I:** 361, 367
Italie, Hillel, **Supp. XV:** 128
It All Adds Up: From the Dim Past to the Uncertain Future (Bellow), **Retro. Supp. II:** 32
"It Always Breaks Out" (Ellison), **Retro. Supp. II:** 126; **Supp. II Part 1:** 248
Itard, Jean-Marc Gaspard, **Supp. I Part 2:** 564
"I taste a liquor never brewed" (Dickinson), **Retro. Supp. I:** 30, 37
It Came from Outer Space (film), **Supp. IV Part 1:** 102
It Can't Happen Here (Lewis), **II:** 454
"It Don't Mean a Thing If It Ain't Got That Swing" (Matthews), **Supp. IX: 164–165**
I Tell You Now (Ortiz), **Supp. IV Part 2:** 500
"Ithaca" (Glück), **Supp. V:** 89
It Happened One Night (Capra), **Supp. XV:** 197
It Has Come to Pass (Farrell), **II:** 26
"I think to live May be a Bliss" (Dickinson), **Retro. Supp. I:** 44
I Thought of Daisy (Wilson), **IV:** 428, 434, 435
"Itinerary of an Obsession" (Kumin), **Supp. IV Part 2:** 450
"It Is a Strange Country" (Ellison), **Supp. II Part 1:** 238
"It Is Dangerous to Read Newspapers" (Atwood), **Supp. XIII:** 33
"It Must Be Abstract" (Stevens), **IV:** 95; **Retro. Supp. I:** 307
"It Must Change" (Stevens), **Retro. Supp. I:** 300, 307, 308
"It Must Give Pleasure" (Stevens), **Retro. Supp. I:** 307, 308, 309
"'It Out-Herods Herod. Pray You, Avoid It'" (Hecht), **Supp. X:** 62, 64
"It's All Over Now, Baby Blue" (song, Dylan), **Supp. XVIII:** 30
It's Loaded, Mr. Bauer (Marquand), **III:** 59
"It's Nation Time" (Baraka), **Supp. II Part 1:** 53
It's Nation Time (Baraka), **Supp. II Part 1:** 52, 53
It's Only a Play (McNally), **Supp. XIII:** 198
It Was (Zukofsky), **Supp. III Part 2:** 630
It Was the Nightingale (Ford), **III:** 470–471
"It Was When" (Snyder), **Supp. VIII:** 300
Ivanhoe (Scott), **I:** 216; **Supp. I Part 2:** 410
Ivens, Bryna, **Supp. XV:** 311, 312
Ivens, Joris, **I:** 488; **Retro. Supp. I:** 184
"Iverson Boy, The" (Simpson), **Supp. IX:** 280
"Ives" (Rukeyser), **Supp. VI:** 273, 283
Ives, George H., **Supp. I Part 1:** 153
Ivory Grin, The (Macdonald), **Supp. IV Part 2:** 471, 472
Ivory Tower, The (James), **II:** 337–338
"Ivory Tower, The: Louis Untermeyer as Critic" (Aiken), **Supp. XV:** 298
"Ivy Winding" (Ammons), **Supp. VII:** 33
"I Wandered Lonely as a Cloud" (Wordsworth), **Retro. Supp. I:** 121–122; **Supp. X:** 73; **Supp. XIV:** 184
"I want, I want" (Plath), **Retro. Supp. II:** 246
"I Wanted to Be There When My Father Died" (Olds), **Supp. X:** 210
"I Want to Be a Father Like the Men" (Cisneros), **Supp. VII:** 71
"I Want to Be Miss America" (Alvarez), **Supp. VII:** 18
"I Want to Know Why" (Anderson), **I:** 114, 115, 116; **II:** 263
"I Want You Women Up North To Know" (Olsen), **Supp. XIII:** 292, 297
"I Was Born in Lucerne" (Levine), **Supp. V:** 181, 189
"I Was Really Very Hungry" (M. F. K. Fisher), **Supp. XVII:** 91
"I Went into the Maverick Bar" (Snyder), **Supp. VIII:** 301
"I Will Lie Down" (Swenson), **Supp. IV Part 2:** 640
I Will Say Beauty (C. Frost), **Supp. XV:** 96, **105–107**
I Wonder As I Wander (Hughes), **Retro. Supp. I:** 196, 203; **Supp. I Part 1:** 329, 332–333
I Would Have Saved Them If I Could (L. Michaels), **Supp. XVI:** 203, 205, **206–210**
"Iyani: It goes this Way" (Gunn Allen), **Supp. IV Part 1:** 321
"I years had been from home" (Dickinson), **I:** 471
Iyer, Pico, **Supp. V:** 215
Izzo, David Garrett, **Supp. XIV:** 155, 156, 159, 160, 161, 163, 169, 171

J

"Jachid and Jechidah" (Singer), **IV:** 15
Jack and Jill (Alcott), **Supp. I Part 1:** 42
"Jack and the Beanstalk" (Hay), **Supp. XIV:** 124
"Jack in the Pot" (D. West), **Supp. XVIII:** 283
Jack Kelso (Masters), **Supp. I Part 2:** 456, 471–472
Jacklight (Erdrich), **Supp. IV Part 1:** 259, 270
Jack London, Hemingway, and the Constitution (Doctorow), **Supp. IV Part 1:** 220, 222, 224, 232, 235
Jackman, Harold, **Supp. XVIII:** 131
Jackpot (Caldwell), **I:** 304
"Jack Schmidt, Arts Administrator" (Keillor), **Supp. XVI:** 171
"Jack Schmidt on the Burning Sands" (Keillor), **Supp. XVI:** 171
Jackson, Amelia. *See* Holmes, Mrs. Oliver Wendell (Amelia Jackson)
Jackson, Andrew, **I:** 7, 20; **III:** 473; **IV:** 192, 248, 298, 334, 348; **Supp. I Part 2:** 456, 461, 473, 474, 493, 695
Jackson, Blyden, **Supp. I Part 1:** 337
Jackson, Charles, **Supp. I Part 1:** 303
Jackson, George, **Supp. I Part 1:** 66
Jackson, Helen Hunt, **I:** 459, 470; **Retro. Supp. I:** 26, 27, 30–31, 32, 33
Jackson, James, **Supp. I Part 1:** 302, 303
Jackson, J. O., **III:** 213
Jackson, Joe, **Supp. I Part 2:** 441
Jackson, Katherine Gauss, **Supp. VIII:** 124
Jackson, Lawrence, **Retro. Supp. II:** 113, 115
Jackson, Melanie, **Supp. X:** 166
Jackson, Michael, **Supp. VIII:** 146
Jackson, Richard, **II:** 119; **Supp. IX:** 165
Jackson, Shelley, **Supp. XVIII:** 136
Jackson, Shirley, **Supp. IX: 113–130**
Jackson, Thomas J. ("Stonewall"), **IV:** 125, 126
"Jackson Square" (Levertov), **Supp. III Part 1:** 276
"Jackstraws" (Simic), **Supp. VIII: 283**
Jackstraws (Simic), **Supp. VIII:** 280, 282–283
Jack Tier (Cooper), **I:** 354, 355
"Jacob" (Garrett), **Supp. VII:** 109–110
"Jacob" (Schwartz), **Supp. II Part 2:** 663
Jacob, Max, **Supp. XV:** 178, 182
"Jacob and the Indians" (Benét), **Supp. XI:** 47–48
Jacobs, Harriet, **Supp. XVI:** 85
Jacobs, Rita D., **Supp. XII:** 339
Jacobsen, Josephine, **Supp. XIII:** 346; **Supp. XIV:** 260
"Jacob's Ladder" (Rawlings), **Supp. X:** 224, 228
"Jacob's Ladder, The" (Levertov), **Supp. III Part 1:** 278

Jacob's Ladder, The (Levertov), **Supp. III Part 1:** 272, 276–278, 281
Jacobson, Dale, **Supp. X:** 112
Jacobson, Kristin, **Supp. XVIII:** 113
Jacobson, Leslie, **Supp. XV:** 323
Jacoby, Russell, **Supp. IV Part 2:** 692
"Jacquerie, The" (Lanier), **Supp. I Part 1:** 355, 356, 360, 364, 370
Jacques le fataliste (D. Diderot), **Supp. XVII:** 145
Jade Mountain, The: A Chinese Anthology, Being Three Hundred Poems of the T'ang Dynasty (Bynner, trans.), **II:** 527; **Supp. XV:** 46, 47, 48
Jafsie and John Henry: Essays on Hollywood, Bad Boys, and Six Hours of Perfect Poker (Mamet), **Supp. XIV:** 252
Jaguar Totem (LaBastille), **Supp. X:** 99, 106, **107–109**
Jailbird (Vonnegut), **Supp. II Part 2:** 760, 779–780
Jaimes, M. Annette, **Supp. IV Part 1:** 330, 331
Jain, Manju, **Retro. Supp. I:** 53, 58
Jake's Women (Simon), **Supp. IV Part 2:** 576, 588
"Jakie's Mother" (Fante), **Supp. XI:** 164
Jakobson, Roman, **Supp. IV Part 1:** 155
"Jamaica Kincaid's New York" (Kincaid), **Supp. VII:** 181
James, Alice, **I:** 454; **Retro. Supp. I:** 228, 235
James, A. Lloyd, **Supp. XIV:** 343
James, Caryn, **Supp. X:** 302, 303
James, Etta, **Supp. X:** 242
James, Henry, **I:** 4, 5, 9, 10, 12, 15, 16, 20, 52, 93, 109, 211, 226, 228, 244, 246, 251, 255, 258, 259, 336, 363, 374, 375, 379, 384, 409, 429, 436, 439, 452, 454, 459, 461–462, 463, 464, 485, 500, 504, 513, 514, 517–518, 571; **II:** 38, 58, 60, 73, 74, 95, 138, 140, 144, 147, 196, 198, 199, 228, 230, 234, 243, 259, 267, 271, 272, 275, 276, 278, 281, 282, 283, 284, 285, 286, 287, 288, 290, 306, 309, 316, **319–341,** 398, 404, 410, 415, 427, 444, 542, 544, 547–548, 556, 600; **III:** 44, 51, 136, 194–195, 199, 206, 208, 218, 228–229, 237, 281, 319, 325, 326, 334, 409, 453, 454, 457, 460, 461, 464, 511, 522, 576, 607; **IV:** 8, 27, 34, 37, 40, 53, 58, 73, 74, 134, 168, 172, 182, 198, 202, 285, 308, 309, 310, 311, 314, 316, 317, 318, 319, 321, 322, 323, 324, 328, 347, 352, 359, 433, 439, 476; **Retro. Supp. I:** 1, 8, 53, 56, 59, 108, 112, **215–242,** 272, 283, 284, 362, 366, 367, 368, 371, 373, 374, 375, 376, 377, 378, 379; **Retro. Supp. II:** 93, 135, 136, 203, 223; **Supp. I Part 1:** 35, 38, 43; **Supp. I Part 2:** 414, 454, 608, 609, 612–613, 618, 620, 646; **Supp. II Part 1:** 94–95; **Supp. III Part 1:** 14, 200; **Supp. III Part 2:** 410, 412; **Supp. IV Part 1:** 31, 35, 80, 127, 197, 349, 353; **Supp. IV Part 2:** 613, 677, 678, 682, 689, 693; **Supp. IX:** 121; **Supp. V:** 97, 101, 103, 258, 261, 263, 313; **Supp. VIII:** 98, 102, 156, 166, 168; **Supp. XI:** 153; **Supp. XIII:** 102; **Supp. XIV:** 40, 110, 112, 335, 336, 348, 349; **Supp. XV:** 41; **Supp. XVII:** 5, 47; **Supp. XVIII:** 160, 258
James, Henry (father), **II:** 7, 275, 321, 337, 342–344, 364; **IV:** 174; **Supp. I Part 1:** 300
James, Henry (nephew), **II:** 360
James, Horace, **Supp. XIV:** 57
James, William, **I:** 104, 220, 224, 227, 228, 255, 454; **II:** 20, 27, 165, 166, 276, 321, 337, **342–366,** 411; **III:** 303, 309, 509, 599, 600, 605, 606, 612; **IV:** 26, 27, 28–29, 31, 32, 34, 36, 37, 43, 46, 291, 486; **Retro. Supp. I:** 57, 216, 227, 228, 235, 295, 300, 306; **Supp. I Part 1:** 3, 7, 11, 20; **Supp. XIV:** 40, 50, 197, 199, 212, 335; **Supp. XVII:** 97
James, William (grandfather), **II:** 342
James Baldwin: The Legacy (Troupe, ed.), **Retro. Supp. II:** 15
James Baldwin——The Price of the Ticket (film), **Retro. Supp. II:** 2
James Dickey and the Politics of Canon (Suarez), **Supp. IV Part 1:** 175
"James Dickey on Yeats: An Interview" (Dickey), **Supp. IV Part 1:** 177
James Hogg: A Critical Study (Simpson), **Supp. IX:** 269, 276
James Jones: A Friendship (Morris), **Supp. XI:** 234
James Jones: An American Literary Orientalist Master (Carter), **Supp. XI:** 220
"James Jones and Jack Kerouac: Novelists of Disjunction" (Stevenson), **Supp. XI:** 230
James Jones: Reveille to Taps (television documentary), **Supp. XI:** 234
Jameson, F. R., **Supp. IV Part 1:** 119
Jameson, Sir Leander Starr, **III:** 327
James Shore's Daughter (Benét), **Supp. XI:** 48
"James Thurber" (Pollard), **Supp. I Part 2:** 468
"James Whitcomb Riley (From a Westerner's Point of View)" (Dunbar), **Supp. II Part 1:** 198
Jammes, Francis, **II:** 528; **Retro. Supp. I:** 55
"Jan, the Son of Thomas" (Sandburg), **III:** 593–594
Jan. 31 (Goldbarth), **Supp. XII:** 177, **178–179,** 180
Janeczko, Paul, **Supp. XIII:** 280
Jane Eyre (Brontë), **Supp. XVI:** 158
Janet, Pierre, **I:** 248, 249, 252; **Retro. Supp. I:** 55, 57
Jane Talbot: A Novel (Brown), **Supp. I Part 1:** 145–146
"Janet Waking" (Ransom), **III:** 490, 491
"Janice" (Jackson), **Supp. IX:** 117
Janowitz, Tama, **Supp. X:** 7
Jantz, Harold S., **Supp. I Part 1:** 112
"January" (Barthelme), **Supp. IV Part 1:** 54
January Man, The (screenplay, Shanley), **Supp. XIV:** 316
"January Thaw" (Leopold), **Supp. XIV:** 183–184
"Janus" (Beattie), **Supp. V:** 31
Janzen, Jean, **Supp. V:** 180
"Japanese Beetles" (X. J. Kennedy), **Supp. XV:** 161, 165
Japanese by Spring (Reed), **Supp. X:** 241, **253–255**
Japanese Cooking: A Simple Art (Tsuji), **Supp. XVII:** 90
"Japan's Young Dreams" (Geisel), **Supp. XVI:** 102
Jara, Victor, **Supp. IV Part 2:** 549
Jarman, Mark, **Supp. IV Part 1:** 68; **Supp. IX:** 266, 270, 276; **Supp. XII:** 209; **Supp. XV:** 251; **Supp. XVIII:** 178
Jarmon, Mark, **Supp. XVII: 109–122**
Jarrell, Mrs. Randall (Mary von Schrader), **II:** 368, 385
Jarrell, Randall, **I:** 167, 169, 173, 180; **II: 367–390,** 539–540; **III:** 134, 194, 213, 268, 527; **IV:** 352, 411, 422; **Retro. Supp. I:** 52, 121, 135, 140; **Retro. Supp. II:** 44, 177, 178, 182; **Supp. I Part 1:** 89; **Supp. I Part 2:** 552; **Supp. II Part 1:** 109, 135; **Supp. III Part 1:** 64; **Supp. III Part 2:** 541, 550; **Supp. IV Part 2:** 440; **Supp. IX:** 94, 268; **Supp. V:** 315, 318, 323; **Supp. VIII:** 31, 100, 271; **Supp. XI:** 311, 315; **Supp. XII:** 121, 260, 297; **Supp. XV:** 93, 153; **Supp. XVII:** 111
Jarry, Alfred, **Retro. Supp. II:** 326; **Supp. XV:** 177–178, 182, 188
Jarvis, John Wesley, **Supp. I Part 2:** 501, 520
Jaskoski, Helen, **Supp. IV Part 1:** 325
"Jasmine" (Komunyakaa), **Supp. XIII:** 132
"Jason" (Hecht), **Supp. X:** 62
"Jason" (MacLeish), **III:** 4
Jason and Medeia (Gardner), **Supp. VI:** 63, **68–69**
Jaspers, Karl, **III:** 292; **IV:** 491
Jay, William, **I:** 338
Jayber Crow (Berry), **Supp. X:** 28, 34
"Jaz Fantasia" (Sandburg), **III:** 585
"Jazz Age Clerk, A" (Farrell), **II:** 45
Jazz Country: Ralph Ellison in America (Porter), **Retro. Supp. II:** 127
"Jazzonia" (Hughes), **Supp. I Part 1:** 324
Jazz Poetry Anthology, The (Komunyakaa and Feinstein, eds.), **Supp. XIII:** 125
"Jazztet Muted" (Hughes), **Supp. I Part 1:** 342
J. B.: A Play in Verse (MacLeish), **II:** 163, 228; **III:** 3, 21–22, 23; **Supp. IV Part 2:** 586
"Jealous" (Ford), **Supp. V:** 71
Jealousies, The: A Faery Tale, by Lucy Vaughan Lloyd of China Walk, Lambeth (Keats), **Supp. XII:** 113
"Jean Harlow's Wedding Night" (Wasserstein), **Supp. XV:** 328
Jean Huguenot (Benét), **Supp. XI:** 44
"Jeff Briggs's Love Story" (Harte), **Supp. II Part 1:** 355

Jeffers, Robinson, **I:** 66; **III:** 134; **Retro. Supp. I:** 202; **Supp. II Part 2: 413–440; Supp. IX:** 77; **Supp. VIII:** 33, 292; **Supp. X:** 112; **Supp. XI:** 312; **Supp. XV:** 113, 114, 115; **Supp. XVII:** 111, 112, 117

Jeffers, Una Call Kuster (Mrs. Robinson Jeffers), **Supp. II Part 2:** 414

Jefferson, Blind Lemon, **Supp. VIII:** 349

Jefferson, Thomas, **I:** 1, 2, 5, 6–8, 14, 485; **II:** 5, 6, 34, 217, 300, 301, 437; **III:** 3, 17, 18, 294–295, 306, 310, 473, 608; **IV:** 133, 243, 249, 334, 348; **Supp. I Part 1:** 146, 152, 153, 229, 230, 234, 235; **Supp. I Part 2:** 389, 399, 456, 474, 475, 482, 507, 509, 510, 511, 516, 518–519, 520, 522; **Supp. X:** 26; **Supp. XIV:** 191

Jefferson and/or Mussolini (Pound), **Retro. Supp. I:** 292

"Jefferson Davis as a Representative American" (Du Bois), **Supp. II Part 1:** 161

J-E-L-L-O (Baraka), **Supp. II Part 1:** 47

"Jelly-Bean, The" (Fitzgerald), **II:** 88

"Jellyfish, A" (Moore), **III:** 215

Jemie, Onwuchekwa, **Supp. I Part 1:** 343

Jenkins, J. L., **I:** 456

Jenkins, Kathleen, **III:** 403

Jenkins, Susan, **IV:** 123

Jenks, Deneen, **Supp. IV Part 2:** 550, 554

Jennie Gerhardt (Dreiser), **I:** 497, 499, 500, 501, 504–505, 506, 507, 519; **Retro. Supp. II:** 94, **99–101**

"Jennie M'Grew" (Masters), **Supp. I Part 2:** 468

Jennifer Lorn (Wylie), **Supp. I Part 2:** 709, 714–717, 718, 721, 724

"Jenny Garrow's Lover" (Jewett), **II:** 397

"Jerboa, The" (Moore), **III:** 203, 207, 209, 211–212

Jeremiah, **Supp. X:** 35

Jeremy's Version (Purdy), **Supp. VII:** 274

"Jericho" (Lowell), **II:** 536

"Jersey City Gendarmerie, Je T'aime" (Lardner), **II:** 433

Jersey Rain (Pinsky), **Supp. VI:** 235, **247–250**

"Jerusalem" (Nye), **Supp. XIII:** 287

Jerusalem the Golden (Reznikoff), **Supp. XIV:** 280, 285, 286

Jessup, Richard, **Supp. XI:** 306

"Je Suis Perdu" (Taylor), **Supp. V:** 314, 321–322

Jesuits in North America in the Seventeenth Century, The (Parkman), **Supp. II Part 2:** 597, 603–605

Jesus, **I:** 27, 34, 68, 89, 136, 552, 560; **II:** 1, 16, 197, 198, 214, 215, 216, 218, 219, 239, 373, 377, 379, 537, 538, 539, 549, 569, 585, 591, 592; **III:** 39, 173, 179, 270, 291, 296–297, 300, 303, 305, 307, 311, 339, 340, 341, 342, 344, 345, 346, 347, 348, 352, 353, 354, 355, 436, 451, 489, 534, 564, 566, 567, 582; **IV:** 51, 69, 86, 107, 109, 117, 137, 138, 141, 144, 147, 149, 150, 151, 152, 155, 156, 157, 158, 159, 163, 164, 232, 241, 289, 293, 294, 296, 331, 364, 392, 396, 418, 430; **Supp. I Part 1:** 2, 54, 104, 107, 108, 109, 121, 267, 371; **Supp. I Part 2:** 379, 386, 458, 515, 580, 582, 583, 587, 588, 683; **Supp. V:** 280

"Jesus Asleep" (Sexton), **Supp. II Part 2:** 693

"Jesus of Nazareth, Then and Now" (Price), **Supp. VI:** 268

"Jesus Papers, The" (Sexton), **Supp. II Part 2:** 693

"Jesus Raises Up the Harlot" (Sexton), **Supp. II Part 2:** 693

Jetée, La (film), **Supp. IV Part 2:** 436

"Jeune Parque, La" (Valéry), **IV:** 92

"Jew as Writer/The Writer as Jew, The: Reflections on Literature and Identity" (Apple), **Supp. XVII:** 1, 9

"Jewbird, The" (Malamud), **Supp. I Part 2:** 435

"Jewboy, The" (P. Roth), **Supp. III Part 2:** 412

Jewett, Caroline, **II:** 396

Jewett, Dr. Theodore Herman, **II:** 396–397, 402

Jewett, Katharine, **Retro. Supp. II:** 46

Jewett, Mary, **II:** 396, 403

Jewett, Rutger, **Retro. Supp. I:** 381

Jewett, Sarah Orne, **I:** 313; **II: 391–414; Retro. Supp. I:** 6, 7, 19; **Retro. Supp. II:** 51, 52, **131–151,** 156; **Supp. I Part 2:** 495; **Supp. IX:** 79; **Supp. VIII:** 126; **Supp. XIII:** 153

Jewett, Theodore Furber, **II:** 395

"Jew for Export, The" (Mamet), **Supp. XIV:** 251–252

Jew in the American Novel, The (Fiedler), **Supp. XIII:** 106

"Jewish Graveyards, Italy" (Levine), **Supp. V:** 190

"Jewish Hunter, The" (Moore), **Supp. X:** 163, 165, **174**

Jewison, Norman, **Supp. XI:** 306; **Supp. XIV:** 316

Jews of Shklov (Schneour), **IV:** 11

Jews without Money (Gold), **Supp. XIV:** 288–289

JFK (film), **Supp. XIV:** 48

Jig of Forslin, The: A Symphony (Aiken), **I:** 50, 51, 57, 62, 66

"Jig Tune: Not for Love" (McGrath), **Supp. X:** 116

"Jihad" (McClatchy), **Supp. XII:** 266

"Jilting of Granny Weatherall, The" (Porter), **III:** 434, 435, 438

Jim Crow's Last Stand (Hughes), **Retro. Supp. I:** 205

Jiménez, Juan Ramón, **Supp. XIII:** 315, 323

Jimmie Higgins (Sinclair), **Supp. V:** 288

"Jimmy Harlow" (X. J. Kennedy), **Supp. XV:** 170

Jimmy's Blues (Baldwin), **Retro. Supp. II:** 8, 9, 15

Jim's Book: A Collection of Poems and Short Stories (Merrill), **Supp. III Part 1:** 319

Jin, Ha, **Supp. XVIII: 89–104**

Jitney (Wilson), **Supp. VIII:** 330, 331, 351

Jitterbug Perfume (Robbins), **Supp. X:** 273, **274–276,** 279

Joachim, Harold, **Retro. Supp. I:** 58

Joan, Pope, **IV:** 165

Joanna and Ulysses (Sarton), **Supp. VIII: 254–255**

Joan of Arc, **IV:** 241; **Supp. I Part 1:** 286–288; **Supp. I Part 2:** 469

Joans, Ted, **Supp. IV Part 1:** 169

Job (biblical book), **II:** 165, 166–167, 168; **III:** 21, 199, 512; **IV:** 13, 158; **Supp. I Part 1:** 125

Job, The (Burroughs and Odier), **Supp. III Part 1:** 97, 103

Job, The: An American Novel (Lewis), **II:** 441

"Job History" (Proulx), **Supp. VII:** 262

Jobim, Antonio Carlos, **Supp. IV Part 2:** 549

"Job of the Plains, A" (Humphrey), **Supp. IX:** 101

"Jody Rolled the Bones" (Yates), **Supp. XI:** 335, 341

"Joe" (Alvarez), **Supp. VII:** 7–8

Joe (Brown), **Supp. XVIII:** 195

Joe Hill: A Biographical Novel (Stegner), **Supp. IV Part 2:** 599

"Joe Louis: The King as a Middle-Aged Man" (Talese), **Supp. XVII:** 202

Joe Turner's Come and Gone (Wilson), **Supp. VIII:** 334, **337–342,** 345

Joe versus the Volcano (screenplay, Shanley), **Supp. XIV:** 316

"Joey Martiney" (Huncke), **Supp. XIV:** 149

Johannes in Eremo (Mather), **Supp. II Part 2:** 453

John (biblical book), **I:** 68; **Supp. XV:** 222, 224

"John" (Shields), **Supp. VII:** 310–311

"John, John Chinaman" (Buck), **Supp. II Part 1:** 128

John Addington Symonds: A Biographical Study (Brooks), **I:** 240, 241

John Barleycorn (London), **II:** 467, 481

John Brown (Du Bois), **Supp. II Part 1:** 171–172

"John Brown" (Emerson), **II:** 13

"John Brown" (Lindsay), **Supp. I Part 2:** 393

John Brown's Body (Benét), **II:** 177; **Supp. XI:** 45, 46, 47, **56–57**

John Brown: The Making of a Martyr (Warren), **IV:** 236

John Bull in America; or, The New Munchausen (Paulding), **I:** 344

"John Burke" (Olson), **Supp. II Part 2:** 579, 580

"John Burns of Gettysburg" (Harte), **Supp. II Part 1:** 343

"John Carter" (Agee), **I:** 27

"John Coltrane: Where Does Art Come From?" (Baraka), **Supp. II Part 1:** 60

John Deth: A Metaphysical Legend and Other Poems (Aiken), **I:** 61

"John Endicott" (Longfellow), **II:** 505, 506; **Retro. Supp. II:** 165–166, 167

"John Evereldown" (Robinson), **III:** 524

John Fante Reader, The (Cooper, ed.), **Supp. XI:** 174
John Fante: Selected Letters, 1932–1981 (Cooney, ed.), **Supp. XI:** 170
"John Gardner: The Writer As Teacher" (Carver), **Supp. III Part 1:** 136, 146–147
John Gaunt (Davis), **Supp. XVI:** 89
John Jay Chapman and His Letters (Howe), **Supp. XIV:** 54
John Keats (Lowell), **II:** 530–531
"John Kinsella's Lament for Mrs. Mary Moore" (Yeats), **Supp. XVII:** 144
"John Lamar" (Davis), **Supp. XVI:** 89–90
John Lane, **Retro. Supp. I:** 59
"John L. Sullivan" (Lindsay), **Supp. I Part 2:** 394, 395
"John Marr" (Melville), **III:** 93
John Marr and Other Sailors (Melville), **III:** 93; **Retro. Supp. I:** 257
John Muir: A Reading Bibliography (Kimes and Kimes), **Supp. IX:** 178
Johnny Appleseed and Other Poems (Lindsay), **Supp. I Part 2:** 397
"Johnny Bear" (Steinbeck), **IV:** 67
"Johnny Mnemonic" (W. Gibson), **Supp. XVI:** 122, 123–125, 128, 131
"Johnny Panic and the Bible of Dreams" (Plath), **Retro. Supp. II:** 245
"Johnny Ray" (Ríos), **Supp. IV Part 2:** 543
John of the Cross (Saint), **I:** 585; **Supp. IV Part 1:** 284; **Supp. XV:** 223; **Supp. XVII:** 112
John Paul Jones: A Sailor's Biography (Morison), **Supp. I Part 2:** 494–495
"John Redding Goes to Sea" (Hurston), **Supp. VI:** 150
Johns, George Sibley, **Retro. Supp. II:** 65
Johns, Orrick, **Retro. Supp. II:** 71
John Sloan: A Painter's Life (Brooks), **I:** 254
"John Smith Liberator" (Bierce), **I:** 209
Johnson, Alexandra, **Supp. X:** 86
Johnson, Alvin, **I:** 236; **Supp. XV:** 304
Johnson, Ben, **Retro. Supp. I:** 56
Johnson, Buffie, **Supp. IV Part 1:** 94
Johnson, Charles, **Supp. I Part 1:** 325; **Supp. V:** 128; **Supp. VI: 185–201; Supp. X:** 239; **Supp. XIII:** 182
Johnson, Charles S., **Supp. IX:** 309
Johnson, Claudia Durst, **Supp. VIII:** 126–127
Johnson, Diane, **Supp. XIII:** 127
Johnson, Dianne, **Retro. Supp. I:** 196
Johnson, Eastman, **IV:** 321
Johnson, Edward, **IV:** 157; **Supp. I Part 1:** 110, 115
Johnson, Fenton, **Supp. XI:** 129
Johnson, Georgia Douglas, **Supp. IV Part 1:** 164
Johnson, Helene, **Supp. XVIII:** 282
Johnson, James Weldon, **Retro. Supp. II:** 114; **Supp. I Part 1:** 324, 325; **Supp. II Part 1:** 33, 194, 200, 202–203, 206–207; **Supp. III Part 1:** 73; **Supp. IV Part 1:** 7, 11, 15, 16, 164, 165, 166, 169; **Supp. X:** 42, 136, **246; Supp. XVIII:** 122; **Supp. XVIII:** 127, 282
Johnson, Joyce, **Supp. XIV:** 150
Johnson, Kent, **Supp. XV:** 347
Johnson, Lady Bird, **Supp. IV Part 1:** 22
Johnson, Lyndon B., **I:** 254; **II:** 553, 582; **Retro. Supp. II:** 27
Johnson, Marguerite. *See* Angelou, Maya
Johnson, Maurice, **Supp. XV:** 136, 137, 138
Johnson, Michael K., **Supp. XVIII:** 59, 64
Johnson, Mordecai, **Supp. XIV:** 202
Johnson, Nunnally, **Supp. IV Part 1:** 355
Johnson, Pamela Hansford, **IV:** 469
Johnson, Rafer, **Supp. I Part 1:** 271
Johnson, Reed, **Supp. IV Part 2:** 589
Johnson, Richard, **Supp. XIII:** 132
Johnson, Robert, **Supp. IV Part 1:** 146; **Supp. VIII:** 15, 134
Johnson, Robert K., **Supp. IV Part 2:** 573, 584
Johnson, Robert Underwood, **Supp. IX:** 182, 184, 185
Johnson, Samuel, **II:** 295; **III:** 491, 503; **IV:** 452; **Retro. Supp. I:** 56, 65; **Supp. I Part 1:** 33; **Supp. I Part 2:** 422, 498, 503, 523, 656; **Supp. IV Part 1:** 34, 124; **Supp. XI:** 209; **Supp. XII:** 159; **Supp. XIII:** 55, 347; **Supp. XVI:** 204; **Supp. XVII:** 1
Johnson, Sarah Anne, **Supp. XVIII:** 145
Johnson, Steve, **Supp. XVI:** 177
Johnson, Thomas H., **I:** 470–471; **IV:** 144, 158; **Retro. Supp. I:** 26, 28, 36, 39, 40, 41, 43
Johnson, Walter, **II:** 422
Johnson, Willard "Spud," **Supp. XV:** 42, 46
"Johnson Girls, The" (Bambara), **Supp. XI:** 7
Johnsrud, Harold, **II:** 562
Johnston, Basil, **Supp. IV Part 1:** 269
Johnston, Mary, **II:** 194
Johnston, Robert M., **Supp. I Part 1:** 369
"John Sutter" (Winters), **Supp. II Part 2:** 810
John's Wife (Coover), **Supp. V:** 51–52
John the Baptist, **I:** 389; **II:** 537, 591
John Wesley Harding (album, Dylan), **Supp. XVIII:** 27
John XXIII, Pope, **Supp. I Part 2:** 492
Jolas, Eugène, **Retro. Supp. II:** 85, 328; **Supp. IV Part 1:** 80
Jolie Blon's Bounce (Burke), **Supp. XIV:** 26, 33–34
Jolly (Mamet), **Supp. XIV:** 240, 254
"Jolly Corner, The" (James), **I:** 571; **Retro. Supp. I:** 235
"Jonah" (Lowell), **II:** 536
Jonah's Gourd Vine (Hurston), **Supp. VI:** 149, 155
"Jonathan Edwards" (Holmes), **Supp. I Part 1:** 302, 315
"Jonathan Edwards in Western Massachusetts" (Lowell), **II:** 550
Jonathan Troy (Abbey), **Supp. XIII:** 4, 13
Jones, Anne, **Supp. X:** 8
Jones, Carolyn, **Supp. VIII:** 128
Jones, Chuck, **Supp. XVI:** 102
Jones, David, **Supp. XVII:** 241
Jones, Derek Anson, **Supp. XVIII:** 38, 39
Jones, Edith Newbold. *See* Wharton, Edith
Jones, E. Stanley, **III:** 297
Jones, Everett LeRoi. *See* Baraka, Imamu Amiri
Jones, George Frederic, **IV:** 309
Jones, Grover, **Supp. XIII:** 166
Jones, Harry, **Supp. I Part 1:** 337
Jones, Howard Mumford, **I:** 353; **Supp. IV Part 2:** 606; **Supp. XIV:** 11
Jones, James, **III:** 40; **IV:** 98; **Supp. XI: 213–237**
Jones, James Earl, **Supp. VIII:** 334; **Supp. XI:** 309
Jones, Jennifer, **Supp. IV Part 2:** 524
Jones, John Paul, **II:** 405–406; **Supp. I Part 2:** 479, 480, 494–495
Jones, Kirkland C., **Supp. XVIII:** 173, 174, 175
Jones, LeRoi. *See* Baraka, Imamu Amiri
Jones, Louis B., **Supp. XVI:** 41
Jones, Lucretia Stevens Rhinelander, **IV:** 309
Jones, Madison, **Retro. Supp. II:** 235; **Supp. X:** 1
Jones, Major (pseudonym). *See* Thompson, William T.
Jones, Malcolm, **Supp. V:** 219
Jones, Mildred, **Supp. XVIII:** 281
Jones, Robert Edmond, **III:** 387, 391, 394, 399
Jones, Sharon L., **Supp. XVIII:** 280, 285, 286
Jones, Tommy Lee, **Supp. V:** 227
"Jones's Private Argyment" (Lanier), **Supp. I Part 1:** 352
"Jones's *The Thin Red Line:* The End of Innocence" (Michel-Michot), **Supp. XI:** 224–225
Jong, Allan, **Supp. V:** 115
Jong, Erica, **Supp. V: 113–135**
Jong-Fast, Molly Miranda, **Supp. V:** 115
Jonson, Ben, **I:** 58, 358; **II:** 11, 16, 17, 18, 436, 556; **III:** 3, 463, 575–576; **IV:** 395, 453; **Retro. Supp. II:** 76; **Supp. I Part 2:** 423; **Supp. IV Part 2:** 585
Jonsson, Thorsten, **Retro. Supp. I:** 73
Joplin, Janis, **Supp. IV Part 1:** 206; **Supp. XI:** 239
Joplin, Scott, **Supp. IV Part 1:** 223
Jordan, A. Van, **Supp. XVIII:** 172
Jordan, Barbara, **Supp. VIII:** 63; **Supp. XI:** 249
Jordan, June, **Supp. XII:** 217
Jordan, Marie, **Supp. XV:** 224
Jo's Boys (Alcott), **Supp. I Part 1:** 32, 35, 40–41, 42
Joseph Heller (Ruderman), **Supp. IV Part 1:** 380
"Josephine Has Her Day" (Thurber), **Supp. I Part 2:** 606
Josephine Stories, The (Fitzgerald), **Retro. Supp. I:** 109

"Joseph Martinez" (Huncke), **Supp. XIV:** 149
"Joseph Pockets" (Stern), **Supp. IX:** 292
Josephson, Matthew, **I:** 259
"José's Country" (Winters), **Supp. II Part 2:** 789, 790
Joshua (biblical book), **Supp. I Part 2:** 515
Joslin, Katherine, **Retro. Supp. I:** 376
Journal (Emerson), **Supp. I Part 1:** 309
"Journal" (L. Michaels), **Supp. XVI:** 213
Journal (Thoreau), **IV:** 175
Journal (Woolman), **Supp. VIII:** 202
"Journal for My Daughter" (Kunitz), **Supp. III Part 1:** 268
Journal of Arthur Stirling, The (Sinclair), **Supp. V:** 280
"Journal of a Solitary Man, The" (Hawthorne), **II:** 226
Journal of a Solitude (Sarton), **Supp. VIII:** 256, 262–263
Journal of My Other Self (Rilke), **Retro. Supp. II:** 20
Journal of the Fictive Life (Nemerov), **III:** 267, 268, 269, 272, 273, 274, 280–281, 284–285, 286, 287
Journal of the Plague Year, A (Defoe), **III:** 423
"Journal of the Year of the Ox, A" (Wright), **Supp. V:** 343
Journals (Thoreau), **Supp. I Part 1:** 299
Journals and Other Documents on the Life and Voyages of Christopher Columbus (Morison, ed.), **Supp. I Part 2:** 494
Journals of Ralph Waldo Emerson, The (Emerson), **II:** 8, 17, 21
Journals of Susanna Moodie, The: Poems (Atwood), **Supp. XIII:** 33
"Journey, A" (Wharton), **Retro. Supp. I:** 364
"Journey, The" (Winters), **Supp. II Part 2:** 795
"Journey, The" (Wright), **Supp. III Part 2:** 605–606
"Journey, the Arrival and the Dream, The" (Gioia), **Supp. XV:** 120
"Journey, The: For Jane at Thirteen" (Kumin), **Supp. IV Part 2:** 442
Journey and Other Poems, The (Winters), **Supp. II Part 2:** 786, 794, 795, 796, 799, 800, 801
Journey Around My Room: The Autobiography of Louise Bogan——A Mosaic (Bogan), **Supp. III Part 1:** 47, 48, 52, 53
Journey Down, The (Bernstein), **IV:** 455
Journey Home, The (Abbey), **Supp. XIII:** 2, 12
Journeyman (Caldwell), **I:** 297, 302–304, 307, 309
Journey of Tai-me, The (Momaday), **Supp. IV Part 2:** 485
"Journey of the Magi" (Eliot), **Retro. Supp. I:** 64
Journey to a War (Auden and Isherwood), **Supp. II Part 1:** 13; **Supp. XIV:** 156, 158, 162
Journey to Love (W. C. Williams), **IV:** 422; **Retro. Supp. I:** 429
Journey to My Father; Isaac Bashevis Singer (Zamir), **Retro. Supp. II:** 317
"Journey to Nine Miles" (Walker), **Supp. III Part 2:** 527
"Journey to the Interior" (W. J. Smith), **Supp. XIII:** 339, 340
Journey with Genius: Recollections and Reflections Concerning the D. H. Lawrences (Bynner), **Supp. XV:** 46
Jowett, Benjamin, **Supp. XIV:** 335
"Joy" (Moore), **Supp. X:** 174
"Joy" (Singer), **IV:** 9; **Retro. Supp. II:** 307
Joyce, Cynthia, **Supp. X:** 194, 195, 196
Joyce, James, **I:** 53, 105, 108, 130, 174, 256, 285, 377, 395, 475–476, 478, 480, 483, 576; **II:** 27, 42, 58, 73, 74, 198, 209, 264, 320, 569; **III:** 7, 16, 26–27, 45, 174, 181, 184, 261, 273, 277, 343, 396, 398, 465, 471, 474; **IV:** 32, 73, 85, 95, 103, 171, 182, 211, 286, 370, 412, 418, 419, 428, 434, 456; **Retro. Supp. I:** 59, 63, 75, 80, 89, 91, 108, 109, 127, 287, 290, 292, 334, 335, 420; **Retro. Supp. II:** 221, 326; **Supp. I Part 1:** 257, 262, 270; **Supp. I Part 2:** 437, 546, 613, 620; **Supp. II Part 1:** 136; **Supp. III Part 1:** 35, 36, 65, 225, 229; **Supp. III Part 2:** 611, 617, 618; **Supp. IV Part 1:** 40, 47, 80, 227, 300, 310; **Supp. IV Part 2:** 424, 677; **Supp. IX:** 211, 229, 235, 308; **Supp. V:** 261, 331; **Supp. VIII:** 14, 40, 103; **Supp. X:** 115, 137, 194, 324; **Supp. XI:** 66; **Supp. XII:** 139, 151, 165, 191, 289; **Supp. XIV:** 83; **Supp. XVI:** 41, 189, 282; **Supp. XVII:** 44
Joy Comes in the Morning (J. Rosen), **Supp. XVII:** 50
Joy Luck Club, The (Tan), **Supp. X:** 289, 291, 293, 294, 296, 297, 298, 299
"Joy of Sales Resistance, The" (Berry), **Supp. X:** 36
J R (Gaddis), **Supp. IV Part 1:** 279, 280, 285–289, 291, 294; **Supp. IV Part 2:** 484
"Juan's Song" (Bogan), **Supp. III Part 1:** 50
Jubilate Agno (Smart), **Supp. IV Part 2:** 626
Judah, Hettie, **Supp. XIII:** 246
Judah the Pious (Prose), **Supp. XVI:** 249, 250, 262
"Judas Maccabaeus" (Longfellow), **II:** 506; **Retro. Supp. II:** 165, 167
Judd, Sylvester, **II:** 290; **Supp. I Part 2:** 420
Judd Rankin's Daughter (Glaspell), **Supp. III Part 1:** 186–188
Jude the Obscure (Hardy), **Supp. I Part 1:** 217
"Judgement Day" (O'Connor), **III:** 349, 350; **Retro. Supp. II:** 236
Judgment Day (Farrell), **II:** 29, 31, 32, 34, 39
"Judgment of Paris, The" (Merwin), **Supp. III Part 1:** 350
Judgment of Paris, The (Vidal), **Supp. IV Part 2:** 680, 682
"Judgment of the Sage, The" (Crane), **I:** 420
Judith (Farrell), **II:** 46, 48
"Judith" (Garrett), **Supp. VII:** 109–110
"Juggernaut" (Bass), **Supp. XVI:** 16–17
"Jug of Sirup, A" (Bierce), **I:** 206
"Jugurtha" (Longfellow), **II:** 499
"Juice or Gravy" (P. Roth), **Retro. Supp. II:** 279
"Juke Box Love Song" (Hughes), **Retro. Supp. I:** 209
"Julia" (Hellman), **Supp. I Part 1:** 280, 293
"Julia Miller" (Masters), **Supp. I Part 2:** 461
Julian (Vidal), **Supp. IV Part 2:** 677, 684–685, 685, 689
Julian the Apostate, **Retro. Supp. I:** 247
"Julian Vreden" (Bowles), **Supp. IV Part 1:** 94
Julie and Romeo (Ray), **Supp. XII:** 308, 310
Julien, Isaac, **Supp. XI:** 19
Julie; ou, La nouvelle Héloïse (Rousseau), **Supp. XVI:** 184
Julier, Laura, **Supp. IV Part 1:** 211
Julip (Harrison), **Supp. VIII: 51**
Julius Caesar (Shakespeare), **I:** 284
"July Midnight" (Lowell), **II:** 521
Jumel, Madame, **Supp. I Part 2:** 461
Jumping Out of Bed (R. Bly), **Supp. IV Part 1:** 71
"Jump-Up Day" (Kingsolver), **Supp. VII:** 203
"June 1940" (Kees), **Supp. XV:** 141
"June Light" (Wilbur), **Supp. III Part 2:** 545
June Moon (Lardner and Kaufman), **II:** 427
"June Recital" (Welty), **IV:** 272–273
"Juneteenth" (Ellison), **Retro. Supp. II:** 119, 126; **Supp. II Part 1:** 248
Juneteenth (Ellison), **Retro. Supp. II:** 119, 124, **126–128**
"June the Third" (Gander), **Supp. XV:** 340
Jung, Carl, **I:** 58, 135, 241, 248, 252, 402; **III:** 400, 534, 543; **Supp. I Part 2:** 439; **Supp. IV Part 1:** 68, 69; **Supp. VIII:** 45; **Supp. X:** 193; **Supp. XV:** 214
Junger, Ernst, **Supp. III Part 1:** 63
Jungle, The (Sinclair), **III:** 580; **Supp. V:** 281–284, 285, 289
Jungle Lovers (Theroux), **Supp. VIII:** 314, 315, 316, **317**
"Junior Addict" (Hughes), **Supp. I Part 1:** 343
"Juniper" (Francis), **Supp. IX:** 79
"Junk" (Wilbur), **Supp. III Part 2:** 556
Junker, Howard, **Supp. XV:** 116
Junkie: Confessions of an Unredeemed Drug Addict (Burroughs), **Supp. III Part 1:** 92, 94–96, 101
Junky (Burroughs), **Supp. XIV:** 143
Juno and the Paycock (O'Casey), **Supp. IV Part 1:** 361
"Jupiter Doke, Brigadier General" (Bierce), **I:** 204

Jupiter Laughs (A. Cronin), **Supp. XVII:** 59
Jurgen (Cabell), **III:** 394; **IV:** 286; **Retro. Supp. I:** 80; **Supp. I Part 2:** 718
Jusserand, Jules, **II:** 338
Just above My Head (Baldwin), **Retro. Supp. II:** 14–15
"Just a Little One" (Parker), **Supp. IX:** 191
Just and the Unjust, The (Cozzens), **I:** 367–370, 372, 375, 377, 378, 379
Just an Ordinary Day (Jackson), **Supp. IX:** 120
Just Before Dark: Collected Nonfiction (Harrison), **Supp. VIII:** 41, 45, 46, 53
"Just Before the War with the Eskimos" (Salinger), **III:** 559
"Just Boys" (Farrell), **II:** 45
"Just for the Thrill: An Essay on the Difference Between Women and Men" (Carson), **Supp. XII: 103–104**
"Justice" (Hughes), **Supp. I Part 1:** 331
"Justice, A" (Faulkner), **Retro. Supp. I:** 83
Justice, Donald, **Retro. Supp. I:** 313; **Supp. III Part 2:** 541; **Supp. V:** 180, 337, 338, 341; **Supp. VII: 115–130; Supp. XI:** 141, 315; **Supp. XIII:** 76, 312; **Supp. XV:** 74, 93, 118, 119, 134; **Supp. XVII:** 110, 120, 246
Justice and Expediency (Whitter), **Supp. I Part 2:** 686
"Justice Denied in Massachusetts" (Millay), **III:** 140
Justice for Salcido (Endore), **Supp. XVII:** 63
Justice of Gold in the Damnation of Sinners, The (Edwards), **I:** 559
"Justice to Feminism" (Ozick), **Supp. V:** 272
"Just Like a Woman" (Dylan), **Supp. XV:** 350
"Just Like Job" (Angelou), **Supp. IV Part 1:** 15
Just Whistle: A Valentine (Wright), **Supp. XV: 346–348**
Just Wild About Harry (H. Miller), **III:** 190
Juvenal, **II:** 8, 169, 552

K

"K, The" (Olson), **Supp. II Part 2:** 558, 563, 569
Kabir, **Supp. IV Part 1:** 74
"Kabnis" (Toomer), **Supp. III Part 2:** 481, 484; **Supp. IX:** 309, 310, **319–320**
Kachel, Elsie. *See* Stevens, Mrs. Wallace (Elsie Kachel)
"Kaddish" (Ginsberg), **Supp. II Part 1:** 319, 327
Kaddish and Other Poems, 1958–1960 (Ginsberg), **Supp. II Part 1:** 309, 319–320; **Supp. XIV:** 269
Kael, Pauline, **Supp. IX:** 253; **Supp. XV:** 147, 148
Kafka, Franz, **II:** 244, 565, 569; **III:** 51, 253, 418, 566, 572; **IV:** 2, 113, 218, 437–439, 442; **Retro. Supp. II:** 20, 221, 282; **Supp. I Part 1:** 197; **Supp. III Part 1:** 105; **Supp. III Part 2:** 413; **Supp. IV Part 1:** 379; **Supp. IV Part 2:** 623; **Supp. VIII:** 14, 15, 103; **Supp. XII:** 21, 37, 98, 168; **Supp. XIII:** 305; **Supp. XVI:** 17, 201, 206, 209; **Supp. XVII:** 244
Kafka Americana (Lethem and Scholtz), **Supp. XVIII:** 144–145
Kaganoff, Penny, **Supp. XI:** 122
Kagan's Superfecta (A. Hoffman), **Supp. XVII:** 42
Kahane, Jack, **III:** 171, 178
Kahn, Otto, **I:** 385; **IV:** 123; **Retro. Supp. II:** 81, 84, 85
Kahn, R. T., **Supp. XI:** 216
"Kai, Today" (Snyder), **Supp. VIII:** 300
Kaiser, Georg, **I:** 479
Kaiser, Henry, **Supp. I Part 2:** 644
Kakutani, Michiko, **Supp. IV Part 1:** 196, 201, 205, 211, 212; **Supp. V:** 63; **Supp. VIII:** 81, 84, 86, 88, 141; **Supp. X:** 171, 301, 302, 310, 314; **Supp. XI:** 38, 179; **Supp. XII:** 165, 171, 172, 299; **Supp. XVI:** 71; **Supp. XVII:** 6
Kalem, T. E., **Supp. IV Part 2:** 585
Kalevala (Finnish epic), **II:** 503, 504; **Retro. Supp. II:** 155
Kalevala (Lönnrot), **Retro. Supp. II:** 159, 160
Kalfus, Ken, **Supp. XVII:** 50
Kalki: A Novel (Vidal), **Supp. IV Part 2:** 677, 682, 685, 691, 692
Kallen, Horace, **I:** 229; **Supp. I Part 2:** 643; **Supp. XIV:** 195, 197, 198
Kallman, Chester, **II:** 586; **Supp. II Part 1:** 15, 17, 24, 26
"Kallundborg Church" (Whittier), **Supp. I Part 2:** 696
Kalstone, David, **Retro. Supp. II:** 40
Kamel, Rose, **Supp. XIII:** 306
Kamera Obskura (Nabokov), **III:** 255
Kamhi, Michelle Moarder, **Supp. IV Part 2:** 529, 530
Kaminsky, Wally, **Supp. XVIII:** 72
Kamp, David, **Supp. XVIII:** 150
Kandy-Kolored Tangerine-Flake Streamline Baby, The (Wolfe), **Supp. III Part 2:** 569, 573–576, 580, 581
Kane, Julie, **Supp. XVII:** 78
Kane, Lesley, **Supp. XIV:** 250
Kanellos, Nicolás, **Supp. VIII:** 82; **Supp. XIII:** 213
Kanin, Garson, **Supp. IV Part 2:** 574
"Kansas City Coyote" (Harjo), **Supp. XII:** 219, 222
"Kansas Emigrants, The" (Whittier), **Supp. I Part 2:** 687
Kant, Immanuel, **I:** 61, 277, 278; **II:** 10–11, 362, 480, 580–581, 582, 583; **III:** 300, 480, 481, 488, 612; **IV:** 90; **Supp. I Part 2:** 640; **Supp. IV Part 2:** 527; **Supp. XIV:** 198, 199; **Supp. XVI:** 184
Kanter, Hal, **IV:** 383
Kapital, Das (Marx), **III:** 580
Kaplan, Abraham, **I:** 277
Kaplan, Justin, **I:** 247–248; **Retro. Supp. I:** 392
Kaplan, Steven, **Supp. V:** 238, 241, 243, 248
Karate Is a Thing of the Spirit (Crews), **Supp. XI: 112–113**
Karbo, Karen, **Supp. X:** 259, 262
"Karintha" (Toomer), **Supp. IX:** 311
Karl, Frederick R., **Supp. IV Part 1:** 384
Karl Shapiro's America (film), **Supp. II Part 2:** 703
Karmi, T., **Supp. XV:** 78, 88
Karr, Mary, **Supp. XI: 239–256; Supp. XIII:** 285; **Supp. XV:** 223; **Supp. XVI:** 63, 70, 77; **Supp. XVII:** 242
Kasabian, Linda, **Supp. IV Part 1:** 206
Kasper, Catherine, **Supp. XVI:** 294–295
Kate Chopin (Toth), **Retro. Supp. II:** 71
Kate Chopin: A Critical Biography (Seyersted), **Retro. Supp. II:** 65; **Supp. I Part 1:** 225
Kate Chopin and Edith Wharton: An Annotated Bibliographical Guide to Secondary Sources (Springer), **Supp. I Part 1:** 225
Kate Chopin and Her Creole Stories (Rankin), **Retro. Supp. II:** 57; **Supp. I Part 1:** 200, 225
"Kate Chopin's *The Awakening* in the Perspective of Her Literary Career" (Arms), **Supp. I Part 1:** 225
Kate Vaiden (Price), **Supp. VI:** 264, 265
"Käthe Kollwitz" (Rukeyser), **Supp. VI:** 283, 284
Katherine and Jean (Rice), **Supp. VII:** 288
"Kathleen" (Whittier), **Supp. I Part 2:** 693
Kathleen and Frank: The Autobiography of a Family (Isherwood), **Supp. XIV:** 158, 171
Kathy Goes to Haiti (Acker), **Supp. XII:** 5
Katz, Alex, **Supp. XV:** 185
Katz, Jonathan, **Supp. XII:** 179
Katz, Steve, **Supp. V:** 44
Katz, Steven T., **Supp. XVI:** 154
Kauffman, Carol, **Supp. XI:** 295
Kauffmann, Stanley, **III:** 452; **Supp. I Part 2:** 391; **Supp. XVI:** 74
Kaufman, Boris, **Supp. XVIII:** 251
Kaufman, Charlie, **Supp. XV:** 16
Kaufman, George S., **II:** 427, 435, 437; **III:** 62, 71–72, 394; **Retro. Supp. II:** 327; **Supp. IV Part 2:** 574; **Supp. IX:** 190; **Supp. XV:** 329
Kaufmann, James, **Supp. XI:** 39
Kaufmann, Walter, **Supp. XVII:** 137
Kauvar, Elaine M., **Supp. V:** 273
Kavanaugh (Longfellow), **I:** 458; **II:** 489, 491; **Retro. Supp. II:** 156; **Supp. I Part 2:** 420
Kaveney, Roz, **Supp. XI:** 39
Kawabata, Yasunari, **Supp. XV:** 186
Kaye-Smith, Sheila, **Supp. XVIII:** 130–131
Kazan, Elia, **III:** 153, 163; **IV:** 383; **Supp. I Part 1:** 66, 295; **Supp. XVI:** 193; **Supp. XVIII:** 250–251, 252
Kazin, Alfred, **I:** 248, 417, 419, 517; **II:** 177, 459; **IV:** 236; **Retro. Supp. II:** 206, 243, 246, 286; **Supp. I Part 1:** 195, 196, 294, 295, 296; **Supp. I Part 2:** 536, 631, 647, 650, 678, 679, 719;

Supp. II Part 1: 143; Supp. IV Part 1: 200, 382; Supp. IX: 3, 227; Supp. V: 122; Supp. VIII: 93–111; Supp. XIII: 98, 106; Supp. XIV: 11; Supp. XV: 142
Keach, Stacey, Supp. XI: 309
Keane, Sarah, Supp. I Part 1: 100
Kearns, Cleo McNelly, Retro. Supp. I: 57
Kearns, George, Retro. Supp. I: 292
Keating, AnnLouise, Supp. IV Part 1: 330
Keaton, Buster, I: 31; Supp. I Part 2: 607; Supp. IV Part 2: 574
Keaton, Diane, Supp. XV: 5
Keats, John, I: 34, 103, 284, 314, 317–318, 385, 401, 448; II: 82, 88, 97, 214, 368, 512, 516, 530–531, 540, 593; III: 4, 10, 45, 122, 133–134, 179, 214, 237, 272, 275, 469, 485, 523; IV: 360, 405, 416; Retro. Supp. I: 91, 301, 313, 360, 395, 412; Supp. I Part 1: 82, 183, 266, 267, 312, 349, 362, 363, 365; Supp. I Part 2: 410, 422, 424, 539, 552, 675, 719, 720; Supp. III Part 1: 73; Supp. IV Part 1: 123, 168, 325; Supp. IV Part 2: 455; Supp. IX: 38, 39, 45; Supp. VIII: 41, 273; Supp. XI: 43, 320; Supp. XII: 9, 113, 255; Supp. XIII: 131, 281; Supp. XIV: 274; Supp. XV: 92; Supp. XVII: 76, 112
Keats, John (other), Supp. IX: 190, 195, 200
"Keela, the Outcast Indian Maiden" (Welty), IV: 263
Keeley, Mary Paxton, Supp. XV: 136
"Keen Scalpel on Racial Ills" (Bruell), Supp. VIII: 126
"Keep A-Inchin' Along" (Van Vechten), Supp. III Part 2: 744
Keeping (Goldbarth), Supp. XII: 179–180, 180
"Keeping Informed in D.C." (Nemerov), III: 287
Keeping Slug Woman Alive: A Holistic Approach to American Indian Texts (Sarris), Supp. IV Part 1: 329
"'Keeping Their World Large'" (Moore), III: 201–202
Keeping the Night (Everwine), Supp. XV: 75, 81–85, 86
"Keeping Things Whole" (Strand), Supp. IV Part 2: 624
Keep It Simple: A Defense of the Earth (Nichols), Supp. XIII: 268
Kees, Weldon, Supp. X: 118; Supp. XII: 198; Supp. XV: 113, 114, 115, 133–149
Keillor, Garrison, Supp. XII: 343; Supp. XIII: 274; Supp. XVI: 165–179
Keillor, Gary Edward. *See* Keiller, Garrison
Keith, Brian, Supp. IV Part 2: 474
Keith, Minor C., I: 483
Kelleghan, Fiona, Supp. XVIII: 136, 139, 140
Keller, A. G., III: 108
Keller, Christopher J., Supp. XVIII: 192, 195
Keller, Helen, I: 254, 258
Keller, Lynn, Supp. IV Part 2: 423; Supp. V: 78, 80
Kelley, David, Supp. IV Part 2: 528, 529
Kelley, Florence, Supp. I Part 1: 5, 7
Kelley, Mary, Supp. XVIII: 257, 260
Kelley, Robin, Supp. XVIII: 231
Kellogg, Paul U., Supp. I Part 1: 5, 7, 12
Kellogg, Reverend Edwin H., III: 200
Kelly, II: 464
Kelly, Brigit Pegeen, Supp. XVII: 123–134
Kelly, Emmett, Supp. XI: 99, 106
Kelly, James Patrick, Supp. XVIII: 145
Kelly, Walt, Supp. XI: 105
Kelly, William, Supp. XV: 75, 88
Kelsh, Nick, Supp. XVII: 167, 179
Kemble, Fanny, Retro. Supp. I: 228
Kemble, Gouverneur, II: 298
Kemble, Peter, II: 298
Kempton, Murray, Supp. VIII: 104
Kempton-Wace Letters, The (London and Strunsky), II: 465
Kennan, George F., Supp. VIII: 241
Kennedy, Albert J., Supp. I Part 1: 19
Kennedy, Arthur, III: 153
Kennedy, Burt, Supp. IV Part 1: 236
Kennedy, J. Gerald, Retro. Supp. II: 271
Kennedy, John F., I: 136, 170; II: 49, 152–153; III: 38, 41, 42, 234, 411, 415, 581; IV: 229; Supp. I Part 1: 291; Supp. I Part 2: 496; Supp. VIII: 98, 104, 203; Supp. XII: 132
Kennedy, John Pendleton, II: 313
Kennedy, Mrs. John F., I: 136
Kennedy, Robert, Supp. V: 291
Kennedy, Robert F., I: 294; Supp. I Part 1: 52; Supp. XI: 343
Kennedy, Sarah, Supp. XVIII: 293, 299, 301
Kennedy, William, Supp. VII: 131–157; Supp. XVII: 135
Kennedy, X. J., Supp. V: 178, 182; Supp. XV: 113, 151–173
Kenner, Hugh, III: 475, 478; IV: 412; Supp. I Part 1: 255; Supp. IV Part 2: 474; Supp. XV: 147
"Kenneth Koch's 'Serious Moment'" (Spurr), Supp. XV: 183
Kenneth Millar/Ross Macdonald: A Checklist (Bruccoli), Supp. IV Part 2: 464, 469, 471
Kenney, Susan, Supp. XVIII: 288, 289
Kenny, Maurice, Supp. IV Part 2: 502
Kent, George, Supp. IV Part 1: 11
Kent, Rockwell, Supp. XV: 41
Kenton, Maxwell. *See* Burnett, David; Hoffenberg, Mason; Southern, Terry
"Kent State, May 1970" (Haines), Supp. XII: 211
Kenyatta, Jomo, Supp. X: 135
Kenyon, Jane, Supp. VII: 159–177; Supp. VIII: 272
Keogh, Tom, Supp. XVI: 230
Kepler, Johannes, III: 484; IV: 18
Keppel, Frederick P., I: 214
"Kéramos" (Longfellow), II: 494; Retro. Supp. II: 167, 169
Kéramos and Other Poems (Longfellow), II: 490
Kerim, Ussin, Supp. IX: 152
Kermode, Frank, IV: 133; Retro. Supp. I: 301
Kern, Jerome, II: 427
Kerouac, Jack, III: 174; Retro. Supp. I: 102; Supp. II Part 1: 31, 307, 309, 318, 328; Supp. III Part 1: 91–94, 96, 100, 217–234; Supp. IV Part 1: 90, 146; Supp. IX: 246; Supp. V: 336; Supp. VIII: 42, 138, 289, 305; Supp. XII: 118, 121, 122, 123, 126, 131, 132; Supp. XIII: 275, 284; Supp. XIV: 137, 138, 141, 142, 143–144; Supp. XV: 134, 221; Supp. XVI: 123; Supp. XVII: 135, 138
Kerr, Deborah, Supp. XI: 307
Kerr, Orpheus C. (pseudonym). *See* Newell, Henry
Kerr, Walter, Supp. IV Part 2: 575, 579
Kerridge, Richard, Supp. XVI: 26
Kesey, Ken, III: 558; Supp. III Part 1: 217; Supp. V: 220, 295; Supp. X: 24, 265; Supp. XI: 104
Kessel, John, Supp. XVIII: 145
Kesten, Stephen, Supp. XI: 309
Ketchup (Shanley), Supp. XIV: 315
Kevane, Bridget, Supp. XI: 185, 190
"Key, The" (Welty), IV: 262
"Keys" (Nye), Supp. XIII: 281
Key to Uncle Tom's Cabin, A (Stowe), Supp. I Part 2: 580
"Key West" (H. Crane), I: 400
Key West (H. Crane), Retro. Supp. II: 84
Key West: An Island Sheaf (Crane), I: 385, 399–402
Khrushchev, Nikita, I: 136
Kiang Kang-hu, Supp. XV: 45, 47
Kick for a Bite, A (Cobbett), Supp. XV: 237
"Kicking the Candles Out" (Jarman), Supp. XVII: 113
Kid, The (Aiken), I: 61
Kid, The (Chaplin), I: 386
Kidder, Tracy, Supp. III Part 1: 302; Supp. XVIII: 106, 114
Kidman, Nicole, Supp. X: 80
"Kidnapping in the Family, A" (Fante), Supp. XI: 164
"Kid's Guide to Divorce, The" (Moore), Supp. X: 167, 172
Kidwell, Clara Sue, Supp. IV Part 1: 333
Kielsky, Vera Emuma, Supp. V: 273
Kiely, Brendan, Supp. XVII: 75
Kieran, John, II: 417
Kierkegaard, Søren Aabye, II: 229; III: 292, 305, 309, 572; IV: 438, 491; Retro. Supp. I: 326; Retro. Supp. II: 222; Supp. V: 9; Supp. VIII: 7–8
Kiernan, Robert F., Supp. IV Part 2: 684
Kieseritsky, L., III: 252
Kilgo, Jim, Supp. XVIII: 192
"Kilim" (McClatchy), Supp. XII: 258
"Killed at Resaca" (Bierce), I: 202
"Killed at the Ford" (Longfellow), Retro. Supp. II: 170–171

Killens, John Oliver, **Supp. IV Part 1:** 8, 369
"Killer in the Rain" (Chandler), **Supp. IV Part 1:** 122
"Killers, The" (Hemingway), **II:** 249; **Retro. Supp. I:** 188, 189
Killing Mister Watson (Matthiessen), **Supp. V:** 212, 214
"Killing of a State Cop, The" (Ortiz), **Supp. IV Part 2:** 499
Killing of Sister George, The (Marcus), **Supp. I Part 1:** 277
"Killings" (Dubus), **Supp. VII:** 85–86
"Killing the Plants" (Kenyon), **Supp. VII:** 167, 168
Kilmer, Joyce, **Supp. I Part 2:** 387; **Supp. XV:** 294
Kilpatrick, James K., **Supp. X:** 145
Kilvert, Francis, **Supp. VIII:** 172
Kim (Kipling), **Supp. X:** 230
Kim, Alfred, **Supp. XI:** 140
Kim, Sharon, **Supp. XVIII:** 267
Kimball, J. Golden, **Supp. IV Part 2:** 602
Kimbrough, Mary Craig. *See* Sinclair, Mary Craig (Mary Craig Kimbrough)
Kimes, Maymie B., **Supp. IX:** 178
Kimes, William F., **Supp. IX:** 178
"Kin" (Welty), **IV:** 277; **Retro. Supp. I:** 353
Kinard, Agnes Dodds, **Supp. XIV:** 122, 123, 127
Kincaid, Jamaica, **Supp. VII: 179–196**
Kincaid, James, **Supp. XVIII:** 62, 63
"Kindness" (Dunn), **Supp. XI:** 149, 150
"Kindness" (Nye), **Supp. XIII:** 285
"Kindness" (Plath), **Retro. Supp. II:** 256
Kind of Order, A Kind of Folly, A: Essays and Conversations (Kunitz), **Supp. III Part 1:** 262, 268
Kindred (O. Butler), **Supp. XIII: 59–60,** 69
"Kind Sir: These Woods" (Sexton), **Supp. II Part 2:** 673
Kinds of Love (Sarton), **Supp. VIII: 253–254,** 256
Kinfolk (Buck), **Supp. II Part 1:** 126
King, Alexander, **IV:** 287
King, Carole, **Supp. XII:** 308
King, Clarence, **I:** 1
King, Ernest, **Supp. I Part 2:** 491
King, Fisher, **II:** 425
King, Francis, **Supp. XIV:** 155, 156, 166, 169
King, Grace, **Retro. Supp. II:** 136
King, Martin Luther, Jr., **Retro. Supp. II:** 12, 13; **Supp. XVIII:** 24
King, Michael, **Supp. XII:** 182
King, Queen, Knave (Nabokov), **III:** 251; **Retro. Supp. I:** 270
King, Starr, **Supp. II Part 1:** 341, 342
King, Stephen, **Supp. IV Part 1:** 102, 104; **Supp. IV Part 2:** 467; **Supp. IX:** 114; **Supp. V: 137–155; Supp. XIII:** 53
King, Tabitha (Mrs. Stephen King), **Supp. V:** 137
King, The (Barthelme), **Supp. IV Part 1:** 47, 52
King Coffin (Aiken), **I:** 53–54, 57
"King David" (Benét), **Supp. XI:** 44
"King David" (Reznikoff), **Supp. XIV:** 283
Kingdom and the Power, The (Talese), **Supp. XVII:** 202, 203, 204, 210
Kingdom by the Sea, The: A Journey around Great Britain (Theroux), **Supp. VIII:** 323
Kingdom of Earth (T. Williams), **IV:** 382, 386, 387, 388, 391, 393, 398
"Kingdom of Earth, The" (T. Williams), **IV:** 384
Kingfisher, The (Clampitt), **Supp. IX:** 38
"Kingfishers, The" (Olson), **Supp. II Part 2:** 557, 558–563, 582
King Jasper (Robinson), **III:** 523
King Kong (film), **Supp. IV Part 1:** 104; **Supp. XVII:** 58
King Lear (Shakespeare), **I:** 538; **II:** 540, 551; **Retro. Supp. I:** 248; **Supp. IV Part 1:** 31, 36; **Supp. IX:** 14; **Supp. XI:** 172; **Supp. XV:** 349
King Leopold's Soliloquy (Twain), **IV:** 208
King My Father's Wreck, The (Simpson), **Supp. IX:** 266, 267, 270, 275, 276
King of Babylon Shall Not Come Against You, The (Garrett), **Supp. VII:** 110–111; **Supp. X:** 3
"King of Folly Island, The" (Jewett), **II:** 394; **Retro. Supp. II:** 132, 133
King of Kings (film), **Supp. IV Part 2:** 520
King of Paris (Endore), **Supp. XVII:** 64
"King of the Bingo Game" (Ellison), **Retro. Supp. II:** 117, 125; **Supp. II Part 1:** 235, 238, 240–241
"King of the Cats, The" (Benét), **Supp. XI:** 49–50
"King of the Clock Tower" (Yeats), **III:** 473
"King of the Desert, The" (O'Hara), **III:** 369
King of the Fields, The (Singer), **Retro. Supp. II:** 317
King of the Jews (Epstein), **Supp. XII:** 161, **166–170,** 172
King of the Mountain (Garrett), **Supp. VII:** 96, 97
"King of the River" (Kunitz), **Supp. III Part 1:** 263, 267–268
"King of the Sea" (Marquand), **III:** 60
"King over the Water" (Blackmur), **Supp. II Part 1:** 107
"King Pandar" (Blackmur), **Supp. II Part 1:** 92, 102
"King Pest" (Poe), **Retro. Supp. II:** 273
Kingsblood Royal (Lewis), **II:** 456
Kingsbury, John, **Supp. I Part 1:** 8
"King's Daughters, Home for Unwed Mothers, 1948" (Stanford), **Supp. XV:** 345
King's Henchman, The (Millay), **III:** 138–139
Kingsley, Sidney, **Supp. I Part 1:** 277, 281
King's Mare, The (Canolle; Loos, trans.), **Supp. XVI:** 194
"King's Missive, The" (Whittier), **Supp. I Part 2:** 694
Kingsolver, Barbara, **Supp. VII: 197–214; Supp. XIII:** 16; **Supp. XVIII:** 189
King's Stilts, The (Geisel), **Supp. XVI:** 100, 104
Kingston, Earll, **Supp. V:** 160
Kingston, Maxine Hong, **Supp. IV Part 1:** 1, 12; **Supp. V: 157–175,** 250; **Supp. X:** 291–292; **Supp. XI:** 18, 245
"King Volmer and Elsie" (Whittier), **Supp. I Part 2:** 696
Kinmont, Alexander, **Supp. I Part 2:** 588–589
Kinnaird, John, **Retro. Supp. I:** 399
Kinnell, Galway, **Supp. III Part 1: 235–256; Supp. III Part 2:** 541; **Supp. IV Part 2:** 623; **Supp. V:** 332; **Supp. VIII:** 39; **Supp. XI:** 139; **Supp. XII:** 241; **Supp. XV:** 212; **Supp. XVI:** 53
Kinsey, Alfred, **IV:** 230; **Supp. XIV:** 140
Kinsgton, Maxine Hong, **Supp. XV:** 220, 223
Kinzie, Mary, **Supp. XII:** 181
"Kipling" (Trilling), **Supp. III Part 2:** 495
Kipling, Rudyard, **I:** 421, 587–588; **II:** 271, 338, 404, 439; **III:** 55, 328, 508, 511, 521, 524, 579; **IV:** 429; **Supp. IV Part 2:** 603; **Supp. X:** 255
Kirby, David, **Supp. XIII:** 89
Kirkland, Caroline, **Supp. XVIII:** 258
Kirkland, David, **Supp. XVI:** 186
Kirkland, Jack, **I:** 297
Kirkpatrick, Jeane, **Supp. VIII:** 241
Kirkus, Virginia, **Supp. XV:** 198
Kirkwood, Cynthia A., **Supp. XI:** 177, 178, 179
Kirp, David L., **Supp. XI:** 129
Kirsch, Adam, **Supp. XV:** 251, 260, 264, 266, 341, 347, 350–351
Kirstein, Lincoln, **Supp. II Part 1:** 90, 97; **Supp. IV Part 1:** 82, 83
Kiss, The (Harrison), **Supp. X:** 191
"Kiss, The" (Sexton), **Supp. II Part 2:** 687
"Kiss Away" (C. Baxter), **Supp. XVII:** 20
Kissel, Howard, **Supp. IV Part 2:** 580
Kiss Hollywood Good-by (Loos), **Supp. XVI:** 190, 195
Kissinger, Henry, **Supp. IV Part 1:** 388; **Supp. XII:** 9, 14
Kiss of the Spider Woman, the Musical (McNally), **Supp. XIII:** 207, **Supp. XIII:** 208
Kiss Tomorrow Good-bye (McCoy), **Supp. XIII:** 170, **172–173,** 174
"Kit and Caboodle" (Komunyakaa), **Supp. XIII:** 115
Kit Brandon: A Portrait (Anderson), **I:** 111
Kitchen, Judith, **Supp. IV Part 1:** 242, 245, 252; **Supp. IX:** 163; **Supp. XI:** 312, 313, 315, 317, 319, 320, 326, 329; **Supp. XV:** 215, 219
"Kitchenette" (Brooks), **Retro. Supp. I:** 208
Kitchen God's Wife, The (Tan), **Supp. X:** 289, 292, 293, 294–295, 296–297, 298–299

"Kitchen Terrarium: 1983" (McCarriston), **Supp. XIV:** 270
Kit O'Brien (Masters), **Supp. I Part 2:** 471
Kittel, Frederick August. *See* Wilson, August
Kittredge, Charmian. *See* London, Mrs. Jack (Charmian Kittredge)
Kittredge, William, **Supp. VIII:** 39; **Supp. XI:** 316; **Supp. XII:** 209; **Supp. XIII:** 16
"Kitty Hawk" (Frost), **II:** 164; **Retro. Supp. I:** 124, 141
Kizer, Carolyn, **Supp. XVII:** 71, 72, 73, 74
Klein, Joe, **Supp. XII:** 67–68
Klein, Marcus, **Supp. I Part 2:** 432; **Supp. XI:** 233
Kleist, Heinrich von, **Supp. IV Part 1:** 224
Kline, Franz, **Supp. XII:** 198
Kline, George, **Supp. VIII:** 22, 28
Klinghoffer, David, **Supp. XVI:** 74
Klinkowitz, Jerome, **Supp. IV Part 1:** 40; **Supp. X:** 263; **Supp. XI:** 347
Knapp, Adeline, **Supp. XI:** 200
Knapp, Friedrich, **III:** 100
Knapp, Samuel, **I:** 336
Knapp, Samuel Lorenzo, **Supp. XV:** 246
Kneel to the Rising Sun (Caldwell), **I:** 304, 309
"Knees/Dura-Europos" (Goldbarth), **Supp. XII:** 185
"Knife" (Simic), **Supp. VIII:** 275
Knight, Arthur, **Supp. XIV:** 144
Knight, Etheridge, **Supp. XI:** 239
"Knight in Disguise, The" (Lindsay), **Supp. I Part 2:** 390
Knightly Quest, The (T. Williams), **IV:** 383
Knight's Gambit (Faulkner), **II:** 72
Knish, Anne. *See* Ficke, Arthur Davison
"Knit One, Purl Two" (K. Snodgrass), **Supp. XVI:** 42
"Knock" (Dickey), **Supp. IV Part 1:** 182
Knocked Out Loaded (album, Dylan), **Supp. XVIII:** 28
"Knocking Around" (Ashbery), **Supp. III Part 1:** 22
"Knocking on Three, Winston" (Epstein), **Supp. XIV:** 109
Knock on Any Door (film, Ray), **Supp. XVII:** 150
Knock on Any Door (W. Motley), 158; **Supp. XVII: 150–155,** 159, 160
Knockout Artist, The (Crews), **Supp. XI: 113–114**
Knoll, Robert E., **Supp. XV:** 118
Knopf, Alfred A., **III:** 99, 105, 106, 107; **Retro. Supp. I:** 13, 19, 317; **Supp. I Part 1:** 324, 325, 327; **Supp. IV Part 1:** 125, 354; **Supp. XIII:** 172
Knopf, Blanche, **Supp. I Part 1:** 324, 325, 327, 328, 332, 341; **Supp. IV Part 1:** 128, 346, 348; **Supp. XIII:** 169
"Knot, The" (Rich), **Supp. I Part 2:** 555
Knotts, Kristina, **Supp. XIII:** 238
"Knowing, The" (Olds), **Supp. X:** 215
"Knowledge Forwards and Backwards" (Stern), **Supp. IX:** 296
Knowles, John, **Supp. IV Part 2:** 679; **Supp. XII: 235–250**
Knox, Frank, **Supp. I Part 2:** 488, 489
Knox, Israel, **Supp. X:** 70
Knox, Vicesimus, **II:** 8
Knoxville: Summer of 1915 (Agee), **I:** 42–46
Knudson, R. Rozanne, **Supp. IV Part 2:** 648
Kober, Arthur, **Supp. I Part 1:** 292
Koch, Frederick, **IV:** 453
Koch, John, **Supp. VIII:** 88
Koch, Kenneth, **Supp. XV: 175–192**
Koch, Vivienne, **III:** 194; **IV:** 136, 140; **Retro. Supp. I:** 428, 430
"Kochinnenako in Academe: Three Approaches to Interpreting a Keres Indian Tale" (Gunn Allen), **Supp. IV Part 1:** 329
"Kodachromes of the Island" (Hayden), **Supp. II Part 1:** 367, 380
Koestler, Arthur, **I:** 258; **Supp. I Part 2:** 671
Kokkinen, Eila, **Supp. XIV:** 146, 148
Kolba, Ellen D., **Supp. XVIII:** 257
Kolbenheyer, Dr. Frederick, **Supp. I Part 1:** 207
Kolodny, Annette, **Supp. X:** 97, 103, 229
"Komodo" (C. Frost), **Supp. XV:** 95
Komunyakaa, Yusef, **Supp. XIII: 111–136**
Konigsberg, Allan Stewart. *See* Allen, Woody
Kon-Tiki (Heyerdahl), **II:** 477
Koopman, Harry Lyman, **Retro. Supp. I:** 40
Ko; or, A Season on Earth (Koch), **Supp. XV:** 175, 180, 181, 183, 186
Kooser, Ted, **Supp. XV:** 113, 115
Kootz, Samuel, **Supp. XV:** 144
Kora and Ka (Doolittle), **Supp. I Part 1:** 270
Kora in Hell (W. C. Williams), **Retro. Supp. I:** 416, **417–418,** 419, 430, 431
Korb, Rena, **Supp. XI:** 2
Korczak, Janosz, **Supp. X:** 70
Kornblatt, Joyce Reiser, **Supp. XV:** 62
Kort, Amy, **Supp. XIII:** 148
Kosinski, Jerzy, **Supp. VII: 215–228; Supp. XII:** 21
"Kostas Tympakianakis" (Merrill), **Supp. III Part 1:** 326
Koteliansky, S. S., **Supp. VIII:** 251, 265
Kowloon Tong (Theroux), **Supp. VIII:** 325
Kozlenko, William, **IV:** 378, 381
Krabbenhoft, Ken, **Supp. XVII:** 112
Kraft, James, **Supp. XV:** 40, 41, 42, 43, 52
Krakauer, Jon, **Supp. XVII:** 210; **Supp. XVIII: 105–118**
Kramer, Dale, **Supp. I Part 2:** 669
Kramer, Hilton, **III:** 537; **Supp. I Part 1:** 295, 296; **Supp. VIII:** 239; **Supp. XV:** 113
Kramer, Lawrence, **Supp. IV Part 1:** 61, 65, 66; **Supp. IX:** 291
Kramer, Peter D., **Supp. XVI:** 229
Kramer, Stanley, **II:** 421, 587
Krapp's Last Tape (Beckett), **I:** 71; **III:** 387; **Retro. Supp. I:** 206
Krassner, Paul, **Supp. IV Part 1:** 385; **Supp. XI:** 293
Krauth, Leland, **Supp. XVIII:** 58
Kreisler, Harry, **Supp. XVI:** 155
Kreitman, Esther, **IV:** 2
"Kremlin of Smoke" (Schnackenberg), **Supp. XV:** 257–258
Kreymborg, Alfred, **II:** 530; **III:** 465; **IV:** 76; **Retro. Supp. I:** 417; **Supp. XV:** 301, 306
Krim, Seymour, **Supp. XV:** 338; **Supp. XVI:** 217; **Supp. XVIII:** 285
Kristeva, Julia, **Supp. XII:** 6
Kristofferson, Kris, **Supp. XIII:** 119
Kristol, Irving, **Supp. VIII:** 93, 244; **Supp. XIII:** 98
Krivak, Andrew, **Supp. XVII:** 242
Kroll, Jack, **Supp. IV Part 2:** 590
Kroll, Judith, **Supp. I Part 2:** 541–543, 544, 546
Kroll Ring, Frances. *See* Ring, Frances Kroll
Krondorfer, Björn, **Supp. XVI:** 160
Krook, Dorothea, **Retro. Supp. II:** 243
Kropotkin, Peter, **I:** 493; **Supp. I Part 1:** 5; **Supp. IV Part 2:** 521
Kruif, Paul de, **II:** 446
Krupat, Arnold, **Supp. IV Part 2:** 500
Krupnick, Mark, **Supp. XVI:** 153
Krutch, Joseph Wood, **II:** 459; **III:** 425; **IV:** 70, 175
Kublai Khan, **III:** 395
"Kubla Khan" (Coleridge), **Supp. XIII:** 131, 283
Kubrick, Stanley, **Supp. IV Part 1:** 392; **Supp. XI:** 293,**Supp. XI:** 301, 302–303
Kuehl, John, **Supp. IV Part 1:** 279, 284, 285, 287
Kuehl, Linda, **Supp. IV Part 1:** 199
"Kugelmass Episode, The" (Allen), **Supp. XV:** 15, 16
Kukachin, Princess, **III:** 395
"Ku Klux" (Hughes), **Retro. Supp. I:** 205
Kulshrestha, Chirantan, **Retro. Supp. II:** 21
Kumin, Maxine, **Supp. IV Part 2: 439–457; Supp. XIII:** 294; **Supp. XVII:** 71, 75–76
Kundera, Milan, **Supp. VIII:** 241
Kunitz, Stanley, **I:** 179, 180, 181, 182, 521; **II:** 545; **Supp. III Part 1: 257–270; Supp. V:** 79; **Supp. XI:** 259; **Supp. XIII:** 341
Kuo, Helena, **Supp. X:** 291
Kuropatkin, General Aleksei Nikolaevich, **III:** 247–248
Kurth, Peter, **Supp. XVIII:** 145
Kurzy of the Sea (Barnes), **Supp. III Part 1:** 34
Kushner, Tony, **Supp. IX: 131–149**
Kussy, Bella, **IV:** 468
Kuttner, Henry, **Supp. IV Part 1:** 102
Kuzma, Greg, **Supp. XV:** 118

L

LaBastille, Anne, **Supp. X: 95–110**
"Labours of Hercules, The" (Moore), **III:** 201
La Bruyère, Jean de, **I:** 58
La Bufera e Altro (Montale), **Supp. V:** 337
Labyrinth of Love (Untermeyer), **Supp. XV:** 312
Labyrinth of Solitude, The (Paz), **Supp. XIII:** 223
Lacan, Jacques, **Supp. IV Part 1:** 45; **Supp. VIII:** 5; **Supp. XII:** 98
La Casa en Mango Street (Cisneros), **Supp. VII:** 58–59
Lachaise, Gaston, **I:** 434
"Lackawanna" (Merwin), **Supp. III Part 1:** 350
Lackawanna Elegy (Goll; Kinnell, trans.), **Supp. III Part 1:** 235, 243–244
Laclède, Pierre, **Supp. I Part 1:** 205
"Lacquer Prints" (Lowell), **II:** 524–525
Lacy, Ed, **Supp. XV: 193–210**
Ladder, The (Rasmussen; Nelson, trans.), **Supp. XVIII:** 180–181
Ladder of Years (Tyler), **Supp. IV Part 2:** 657, 671–672
Ladders to Fire (Nin), **Supp. X:** 185
"Ladies" (Coleman), **Supp. XI:** 93
Ladies Almanack (Barnes), **Supp. III Part 1:** 37–39, 42
"Ladies in Spring" (Welty), **IV:** 276–277; **Retro. Supp. I:** 353
Lady, The (Richter), **Supp. XVIII: 211–212,** 220
Lady Audley's Secret (Braddon), **Supp. I Part 1:** 35, 36
"Lady Barberina" (James), **Retro. Supp. I:** 227
"Lady Bates" (Jarrell), **II:** 380–381
Lady Chatterley's Lover (Lawrence), **III:** 170; **IV:** 434; **Supp. XVI:** 267
Lady from Louisiana (film, Vorhaus), **Supp. XVII:** 59
"Lady from Redhorse, A" (Bierce), **I:** 203
Lady in Kicking Horse Reservoir, The (Hugo), **Supp. VI:** 134, **138–139**
"Lady in the Lake, The" (Chandler), **Supp. IV Part 1:** 129
Lady in the Lake, The (Chandler), **Supp. IV Part 1:** 127, 129–130
Lady in the Lake, The (film), **Supp. IV Part 1:** 130
"Lady in the Pink Mustang, The" (Erdrich), **Supp. IV Part 1:** 270
"Lady Is Civilized, The" (Taylor), **Supp. V:** 315
Lady Is Cold, The (White), **Supp. I Part 2:** 653
"Lady Lazarus" (Plath), **Retro. Supp. II:** 250, 251, 255; **Supp. I Part 2:** 529, 535, 542, 545
Lady of Aroostook, The (Howells), **II:** 280
"Lady of Bayou St. John, A" (Chopin), **Retro. Supp. II:** 58
"Lady of the Lake, The" (Malamud), **Supp. I Part 2:** 437
Lady Oracle (Atwood), **Supp. XIII:** 21, **23–24**
Lady Sings the Blues (film), **Supp. I Part 1:** 67
"Lady's Maid's Bell, The" (Wharton), **IV:** 316
"Lady Wentworth" (Longfellow), **II:** 505
"Lady with a Lamp" (Parker), **Supp. IX:** 193
"Lady with the Heron, The" (Merwin), **Supp. III Part 1:** 343
La Farge, John, **I:** 1, 2, 20; **II:** 322, 338; **Retro. Supp. I:** 217
La Farge, Oliver, **Supp. IV Part 2:** 503
Lafayette, Marquis de, **I:** 344, 345; **II:** 405–406; **Supp. I Part 2:** 510, 511, 683
"La Figlia che Piange" (Eliot), **Retro. Supp. I:** 63
La Follette, Robert, **I:** 483, 485, 492; **III:** 580
La Fontaine, Jean de, **II:** 154; **III:** 194; **IV:** 80
Laforgue, Jules, **I:** 386, 569, 570, 572–573, 575, 576; **II:** 528; **III:** 8, 11, 466; **IV:** 37, 79, 80, 122; **Retro. Supp. I:** 55, 56; **Supp. XIII:** 332, 335, 346; **Supp. XV:** 165
La Gallienne, Eva, **Supp. VIII:** 251
"Lager Beer" (Dunbar), **Supp. II Part 1:** 193
"La Gringuita: On Losing a Native Language" (Alvarez), **Supp. VII:** 18
Laguna Woman (Silko), **Supp. IV Part 2:** 557, 560–561
Laing, R. D., **Supp. I Part 2:** 527
La kabbale pratique (Ambelain), **Supp. I Part 1:** 273
"Lake, The" (Bradbury), **Supp. IV Part 1:** 101
Lake, The (play), **Supp. IX:** 189
Lakeboat (Mamet), **Supp. XIV:** 240–241
"Lake Chelan" (Stafford), **Supp. XI:** 321
Lake Effect Country (Ammons), **Supp. VII:** 34, 35
"Lake Isle of Innisfree" (Yeats), **Retro. Supp. I:** 413
"Lake Return" (Wright), **Supp. XV:** 345
Lake Wobegon Days (Keillor), **Supp. XVI:** 165, 166, **173–174**
Lake Wobegon Summer 1956 (Keillor), **Supp. XVI:** 178
Lalic, Ivan V., **Supp. VIII:** 272
L'Alouette (Anouilh), **Supp. I Part 1:** 286–288
Lamantia, Philip, **Supp. VIII:** 289
Lamb, Charles, **III:** 111, 207; **Supp. VIII:** 125
Lamb, Wendy, **Supp. IV Part 2:** 658
Lambardi, Marilyn May, **Retro. Supp. II:** 45–46
"Lament" (Wilbur), **Supp. III Part 2:** 550
"Lamentations" (Glück), **Supp. V:** 83, 84
"Lament for Dark Peoples" (Hughes), **Retro. Supp. I:** 199
"Lament for Saul and Jonathan" (Bradstreet), **Supp. I Part 1:** 111
"Lament-Heaven" (Doty), **Supp. XI:** 125
"Lament of a New England Mother, The" (Eberhart), **I:** 539
Laments for the Living (Parker), **Supp. IX:** 192
"Lame Shall Enter First, The" (O'Connor), **III:** 348, 351, 352, 355, 356–357, 358; **Retro. Supp. II:** 237
Lamia (Keats), **II:** 512; **III:** 523
La Motte-Fouqué, Friedrich Heinrich Karl, **III:** 77, 78
L'Amour, Louis, **Supp. XIII:** 5
Lamp for Nightfall, A (Caldwell), **I:** 297
Lamplit Answer, The (Schnackenberg), **Supp. XV:** 251, 254, **256–260**
"Lance" (Nabokov), **Retro. Supp. I:** 266
Lancelot (Percy), **Supp. III Part 1:** 384, 395–396
Lancelot (Robinson), **III:** 513, 522
Lanchester, John, **Retro. Supp. I:** 278
"Land" (Emerson), **II:** 6
"Land Aesthetic, The" (Callicott), **Supp. XIV:** 184
Landau, Deborah, **Supp. XI:** 122, 123
"Land beyond the Blow, The" (Bierce), **I:** 209
"Land Ethic, The" (Leopold), **Supp. XIV:** 179, 180, 183, 191, 192
Landfall (Wagoner), **Supp. IX:** 330
"Landing in Luck" (Faulkner), **Retro. Supp. I:** 85
"Landing on the Moon" (Swenson), **Supp. IV Part 2:** 643
"Landings" (Hoffman), **Supp. XVIII:** 86
"Landing Under Water, I See Roots" (A. Finch), **Supp. XVII:** 76
Landlord at Lion's Head, The (Howells), **II:** 276, 287–288
Landmarks of Healing: A Study of House Made of Dawn (Scarberry-García), **Supp. IV Part 2:** 486
Land of Little Rain, The (Dillard), **Supp. VI: 27–28**
Land of the Free U.S.A. (MacLeish), **I:** 293; **III:** 16–17
Land of Unlikeness (Lowell), **II:** 537–538, 539, 547; **Retro. Supp. II:** 177, 178, **184–185**
Landor, Walter Savage, **III:** 15, 469; **Supp. I Part 2:** 422
"Landscape" (Sarton), **Supp. VIII:** 259
"Landscape as a Nude" (MacLeish), **III:** 14
Landscape at the End of the Century (Dunn), **Supp. XI:** 139, 143, **150–151**
"Landscape Chamber, The" (Jewett), **II:** 408–409
"Landscape for the Disappeared" (Komunyakaa), **Supp. XIII:** 120, 126
Landscape in American Poetry (Larcom), **Supp. XIII:** 142
"Landscape Painter, A" (James), **II:** 322; **Retro. Supp. I:** 219
"Landscape Symbolism in Kate Chopin's *At Fault*" (Arner), **Retro. Supp. II:** 62
"Landscape: The Eastern Shore" (Barth), **I:** 122
"Landscape with Boat" (Stevens), **Retro. Supp. I:** 306
"Landscape with the Fall of Icarus" (Brueghel), **Retro. Supp. I:** 430

Land's End: A Walk through Provincetown (Cunningham), **Supp. XV:** 69
Land That Drank the Rain, The (Hoffman), **Supp. XVIII:** 76, 80, 81, 82
"Land Where There Is No Death, The" (Benét), **Supp. XI:** 56
Lane, Ann, **Supp. XI:** 195, 208
Lane, Cornelia. *See* Anderson, Mrs. Sherwood
Lane, Homer, **Supp. II Part 1:** 6; **Supp. XIV:** 160
Lane, Nathan, **Supp. XIII:** 207
Lane, Rose Wilder, **Supp. IV Part 2:** 524
Lanes, Selma G., **Supp. XVI:** 104, 107
Lang, Andrew, **Retro. Supp. I:** 127
Lang, Violet, **Supp. XII:** 119
Langdon, Olivia. *See* Clemens, Mrs. Samuel Langhorne (Olivia Langdon)
Lange, Carl Georg, **II:** 350
Lange, Dorothea, **I:** 293; **Supp. XIV:** 181
Langland, Joseph, **III:** 542
Langston Hughes, American Poet (Walker), **Supp. III Part 2:** 530–531
Langston Hughes and the "Chicago Defender": Essays on Race, Politics, and Culture (De Santis, ed.), **Retro. Supp. I:** 194
Langston Hughes: Modern Critical Views (Bloom, ed.), **Retro. Supp. I:** 193
Langston Hughes Reader, The (Hughes), **Retro. Supp. I:** 202; **Supp. I Part 1:** 345
Langston Hughes: The Poet and His Critics (Barksdale), **Retro. Supp. I:** 202
"Language, Visualization and the Inner Library" (Shepard), **Supp. III Part 2:** 436, 438, 449
"Language and the Writer" (Bambara), **Supp. XI:** 18
Language As Gesture (Blackmur), **Supp. II Part 1:** 108
Language as Symbolic Action (Burke), **I:** 275, 282, 285
Language Book, The (Andrews and Bernstein), **Supp. IV Part 2:** 426
Language in Thought and Action (Hayakawa), **I:** 448
"Language of Being and Dying, The" (Gass), **Supp. VI:** 91
"Language of Home, The" (Wideman), **Supp. X:** 320, 323–324
Language of Life, The (Moyers, television series), **Supp. XIII:** 274, 276
Language of the American South, The (Brooks), **Supp. XIV:** 14
"Language of the Brag, The" (Olds), **Supp. X:** 204
"Language We Know, The" (Ortiz), **Supp. IV Part 2:** 500
Lanier, Clifford, **Supp. I Part 1:** 349, 350, 353, 355, 356, 371
Lanier, James F. D., **Supp. I Part 1:** 350
Lanier, Lyle H., **Supp. X:** 25
Lanier, Mrs. Robert Sampson (Mary Jane Anderson), **Supp. I Part 1:** 349
Lanier, Mrs. Sidney (Mary Day), **Supp. I Part 1:** 351, 355, 357, 361, 362, 364, 370, 371
Lanier, Robert Sampson, **Supp. I Part 1:** 349, 351, 355, 356, 361
Lanier, Sidney, **IV:** 444; **Supp. I Part 1: 349–373; Supp. I Part 2:** 416; **Supp. IV Part 1:** 165
"Lanier as Poet" (Parks), **Supp. I Part 1:** 373
"Lanier's Reading" (P. Graham), **Supp. I Part 1:** 373
"Lanier's Use of Science for Poetic Imagery" (Beaver), **Supp. I Part 1:** 373
Lannegan, Helen. *See* Caldwell, Mrs. Erskine
Lannin, Paul, **II:** 427
Lanny Budd novels (Sinclair), **Supp. V:** 290
Lant, Kathleen Margaret, **Supp. V:** 141
Lanthenas, François, **Supp. I Part 2:** 515
Laotzu, **III:** 173, 189, 567; **Supp. XV:** 39, 46, 48
"Lapis Lazuli" (Yeats), **I:** 532; **III:** 40
Laplace, Pierre Simon de, **III:** 428
Lapouge, M. G., **Supp. I Part 2:** 633
Lappa, Katherine, **Supp. XV:** 176
Laqueur, Thomas, **Supp. XVI:** 154
Larbaud, Valery, **IV:** 404; **Supp. XIII:** 332; **Supp. XIV:** 338
Larcom, Lucy, **Retro. Supp. II:** 145; **Supp. XIII: 137–157**
Larcom's Poetical Works (Larcom), **Supp. XIII:** 142
Lardner, John, **II:** 437
Lardner, Ring, **I:** 487; **II:** 44, 91, 259, 263, **415–438; III:** 566, 572; **IV:** 433; **Retro. Supp. I:** 105; **Retro. Supp. II:** 222; **Supp. I Part 2:** 609; **Supp. IX:** 200; **Supp. XVI:** 189
Lardner, Ring, Jr., **Supp. XI:** 306
"Lardner, Shakespeare and Chekhov" (Matthews), **II:** 430
"Large Bad Picture" (Bishop), **Retro. Supp. II:** 43; **Supp. I Part 1:** 73, 80–82, 85, 86, 89, 90
"Large Coffee" (Lardner), **II:** 437
Large Glass, or The Bride Stripped Bare by Her Bachelors, Even (Duchamp), **Supp. IV Part 2:** 423, 424
Largo (Handel), **IV:** 369
Lark, The (Hellman), **Supp. I Part 1:** 286–288, 297
Larkin, Philip, **Supp. I Part 2:** 536; **Supp. XI:** 243, 249; **Supp. XIII:** 76, 85; **Supp. XV:** 117, 251; **Supp. XVII:** 110; **Supp. XVIII:** 173
Larkin, Sharon Alile, **Supp. XI:** 20
Larmore, Phoebe, **Supp. X:** 266
Larner, Jeremy, **Supp. XVI:** 220
La Rochefoucauld, François de, **I:** 279; **II:** 111; **Supp. XIV:** 130
"La Rose des Vents" (Wilbur), **Supp. III Part 2:** 550
Larry's Party (Shields), **Supp. VII:** 324, 326–327
Larsen, Nella, **Supp. I Part 1:** 325, 326; **Supp. IV Part 1:** 164; **Supp. XVIII: 119–134**
Larson, Charles, **Supp. IV Part 1:** 331
Larson, Clinton, **Supp. XI:** 328
Larson, Kelli, **Supp. XVIII:** 131
"Larval Stage of a Bookworm" (Mencken), **III:** 101
La Salle and the Discovery of the Great West (Parkman), **Supp. II Part 2:** 595, 598, 605–607; **Supp. XVIII:** 114
Lasch, Christopher, **I:** 259
Lasher (Rice), **Supp. VII:** 299–300
Lask, Thomas, **III:** 576; **Supp. XVI:** 250
Laski, Harold, **Supp. I Part 2:** 632, 643
Lassalle, Ferdinand, **IV:** 429
Lasser, Louise, **Supp. XV:** 4
"Last Acts" (Olds), **Supp. X:** 210
Last Adam, The (Cozzens), **I:** 362–363, 364, 368, 375, 377, 378, 379
Last Analysis, The (Bellow), **I:** 152, 160, 161; **Retro. Supp. II:** 26
Last and Lost Poems of Delmore Schwartz (Phillips, ed.), **Supp. II Part 2:** 661, 665
Last Avant-Garde, The: The Making of the New York School of Poets (Lehman), **Supp. XV:** 178–179, 187
Last Beautiful Days of Autumn, The (Nichols), **Supp. XIII:** 254, 255, 267, 269
Last Blue (Stern), **Supp. IX: 299–300**
Last Carousel, The (Algren), **Supp. IX:** 16
"Last Child" (X. J. Kennedy), **Supp. XV:** 162, 165
"Last Day in the Field, The" (Gordon), **II:** 200
"Last Day of the Last Furlough" (Salinger), **III:** 552–553
"Last Days of Alice" (Tate), **IV:** 129
"Last Days of August, The" (Nye), **Supp. XIII:** 284
"Last Days of John Brown, The" (Thoreau), **IV:** 185
Last Days of Louisiana Red, The (Reed), **Supp. X:** 240, **248–249**
Last Decade, The (Trilling), **Supp. III Part 2:** 493, 499
"Last Demon, The" (Singer), **IV:** 15, 21
Last Exit to Brooklyn (Selby), **Supp. III Part 1:** 125
Last Flower, The (Thurber), **Supp. I Part 2:** 610
"Last Frontier" (McCarriston), **Supp. XIV:** 272
Last Gentleman, The (Percy), **Supp. III Part 1:** 383–388, 392–393
"Last Good Country, The" (Hemingway), **II:** 258–259
Last Good Time, The (Bausch), **Supp. VII:** 45–46
"Last Hiding Places of Snow, The" (Kinnell), **Supp. III Part 1:** 252
"Last Hours, The" (Dunn), **Supp. XI:** 141
Last House: Reflections, Dreams, and Observations, 1943–1991 (M. F. K. Fisher), **Supp. XVII:** 92
Last Husband and Other Stories, The (Humphrey), **Supp. IX:** 94
"Last Jew in America, The" (Fiedler), **Supp. XIII:** 103
Last Jew in America, The (Fiedler), **Supp. XIII:** 103
Last Laugh, Mr. Moto (Marquand), **III:** 57

"Last Leaf, The" (Holmes), **Supp. I Part 1:** 302, 309
"Last Leaf, The" (Porter), **III:** 444
"Last Look at the Lilacs" (Stevens), **IV:** 74
Last Man, The (Kees), **Supp. XV:** 142, 143, 145
"Last May" (Dixon), **Supp. XII: 143**
"Last Mermother, The" (A. Finch), **Supp. XVII:** 72
"Last Mohican, The" (Malamud), **Supp. I Part 2:** 437–438, 450, 451
"Lastness" (Kinnell), **Supp. III Part 1:** 248–249
"Last Night" (Olds), **Supp. X:** 212
"Last Night at Tía's" (Alvarez), **Supp. VII:** 5
Last Night of Summer, The (Caldwell), **I:** 292–293
Last of Mr. Norris, The (Isherwood), **Supp. XIV:** 161
"Last of the Brooding Miserables, The" (Karr), **Supp. XI:** 250
"Last of the Caddoes, The" (Humphrey), **Supp. IX:** 101
"Last of the Gold Star Mothers, The" (C. Bly), **Supp. XVI:** 34, 35, 36
"Last of the Legions, The" (Benét), **Supp. XI:** 56, 57
Last of the Mohicans, The (Cooper), **I:** 341, 342, 349
Last of the Red Hot Lovers (Simon), **Supp. IV Part 2:** 575, 583, 589
"Last of the Valerii, The" (James), **II:** 327; **Retro. Supp. I:** 218
"Last One, The" (Merwin), **Supp. III Part 1:** 355
Last Picture Show, The (film), **Supp. V:** 223, 226
Last Picture Show, The (McMurtry), **Supp. V:** 220, 222–223, 233
Last Place on Earth, The: Scott and Amundsen's Race to the South Pole (Huntford), **Supp. XVIII:** 114
Last Puritan, The (Santayana), **III:** 64, 600, 604, 607, 612, 615–617
"Last Ride Together, The" (Browning), **I:** 468
"Last River, The" (Kinnell), **Supp. III Part 1:** 236
Last Song, The (Harjo), **Supp. XII:** 218
"Last Song for the Mend-It Shop" (Nye), **Supp. XIII:** 283
"Last Tango in Fresno" (Salinas), **Supp. XIII:** 318
Last Tycoon, The: An Unfinished Novel (Fitzgerald), **II:** 84, 98; **Retro. Supp. I:** 109, 114, **114–115; Retro. Supp. II:** 337; **Supp. IV Part 1:** 203; **Supp. IX:** 63; **Supp. XII:** 173; **Supp. XIII:** 170; **Supp. XVIII:** 248, 250
"Last WASP in the World, The" (Fiedler), **Supp. XIII:** 103
Last Watch of the Night: Essays Too Personal and Otherwise (Monette), **Supp. X:** 147, 148, 153, **157–159**
"Last Word, The" (column, Quindlen), **Supp. XVII:** 165, 167, 170
Last Word, The: Letters between Marcia Nardi and William Carlos Williams (O'Neil, ed.), **Retro. Supp. I:** 427
"Last Words" (Levine), **Supp. V:** 190
"Last Words" (Olds), **Supp. X:** 210
Last Worthless Evening, The (Dubus), **Supp. VII:** 87–88
"Las Vegas (What?) Las Vegas (Can't Hear You! Too Noisy) Las Vegas!!!!" (Wolfe), **Supp. III Part 2:** 572
"Late" (Bogan), **Supp. III Part 1:** 53
"Late Air" (Bishop), **Supp. I Part 1:** 89
"Late Autumn" (Sarton), **Supp. VIII:** 261
"Late Bronze, Early Iron: A Journey Book" (Sobin), **Supp. XVI:** 290
Late Child, The (McMurtry), **Supp. V:** 231
"Late Conversation" (Doty), **Supp. XI:** 122
"Late Encounter with the Enemy, A" (O'Connor), **III:** 345; **Retro. Supp. II:** 232
Late Fire, Late Snow (Francis), **Supp. IX: 89–90**
Late George Apley, The (Marquand), **II:** 482–483; **III:** 50, 51, 52, 56–57, 58, 62–64, 65, 66
Late George Apley, The (Marquand and Kaufman), **III:** 62
"Late Hour" (Everwine), **Supp. XV:** 85
Late Hour, The (Strand), **Supp. IV Part 2:** 620, 629–630
"Lately, at Night" (Kumin), **Supp. IV Part 2:** 442
"Late Moon" (Levine), **Supp. V:** 186
"Late Night Ode" (McClatchy), **Supp. XII:** 262–263
Later (Creeley), **Supp. IV Part 1:** 153, 156, 157
Later Life (Gurney), **Supp. V:** 103, 105
La Terre (Zola), **III:** 316, 322
Later the Same Day (Paley), **Supp. VI:** 218
Late Settings (Merrill), **Supp. III Part 1:** 336
"Late Sidney Lanier, The" (Stedman), **Supp. I Part 1:** 373
"Late Snow & Lumber Strike of the Summer of Fifty-Four, The" (Snyder), **Supp. VIII:** 294
"Latest Freed Man, The" (Stevens), **Retro. Supp. I:** 306
"Latest Injury, The" (Olds), **Supp. X:** 209
Latest Literary Essays and Addresses (Lowell), **Supp. I Part 2:** 407
"Late Subterfuge" (Warren), **IV:** 257
"Late Supper, A" (Jewett), **Retro. Supp. II:** 137
"Late Victorians" (Rodriguez), **Supp. XIV:** 303–304
"Late Walk, A" (Frost), **II:** 153; **Retro. Supp. I:** 127
Latham, Edyth, **I:** 289
Lathrop, George Parsons, **Supp. I Part 1:** 365
Lathrop, H. B., **Supp. III Part 2:** 612
Lathrop, Julia, **Supp. I Part 1:** 5
Latière de Trianon, La (Wekerlin), **II:** 515
"La Tigresse" (Van Vechten), **Supp. II Part 2:** 735, 738
Latimer, Hugh, **II:** 15
Latimer, Margery, **Supp. IX:** 320
La Traviata (Verdi), **III:** 139
"Latter-Day Warnings" (Holmes), **Supp. I Part 1:** 307
La Turista (Shepard), **Supp. III Part 2:** 440
Lauber, John, **Supp. XIII:** 21
Laud, Archbishop, **II:** 158
"Lauds" (Auden), **Supp. II Part 1:** 23
"Laughing Man, The" (Salinger), **III:** 559
Laughing to Keep From Crying (Hughes), **Supp. I Part 1:** 329–330
"Laughing with One Eye" (Schnackenberg), **Supp. XV:** 253
Laughlin, James, **III:** 171; **Retro. Supp. I:** 423, 424, 428, 430, 431; **Supp. VIII:** 195; **Supp. XV:** 140; **Supp. XVI:** 284
Laughlin, Jay, **Supp. II Part 1:** 94
Laughlin, J. Laurence, **Supp. I Part 2:** 641
Laughter in the Dark (Nabokov), **III:** 255–258; **Retro. Supp. I:** 270
Laughter on the 23rd Floor (Simon), **Supp. IV Part 2:** 575, 576, 588, 591–592
"Launcelot" (Lewis), **II:** 439–440
"Laura Dailey's Story" (Bogan), **Supp. III Part 1:** 52
Laurel, Stan, **Supp. I Part 2:** 607; **Supp. IV Part 2:** 574
Laurel and Hardy Go to Heaven (Auster), **Supp. XII:** 21
Laurence, Alexander, **Supp. XVIII:** 138
Laurence, Dan H., **II:** 338–339
Laurens, John, **Supp. I Part 2:** 509
Lauter, Paul, **Supp. XV:** 313
Lautréamont, Comte de, **III:** 174
Law, John, **Supp. XI:** 307
Law and Order (television), **Supp. XVII:** 153
Law and the Testimony, The (S. and A. Warner), **Supp. XVIII:** 264
Lawd Today (Wright), **IV:** 478, 492
Law for the Lion, A (Auchincloss), **Supp. IV Part 1:** 25
"Law Lane" (Jewett), **II:** 407
"Law of Nature and the Dream of Man, The: Ruminations of the Art of Fiction" (Stegner), **Supp. IV Part 2:** 604
Lawrence, D. H., **I:** 291, 336, 377, 522, 523; **II:** 78, 84, 98, 102, 264, 517, 523, 532, 594, 595; **III:** 27, 33, 40, 44, 46, 172, 173, 174, 178, 184, 229, 261, 423, 429, 458, 546–547; **IV:** 138, 339, 342, 351, 380; **Retro. Supp. I:** 7, 18, 203, 204, 421; **Retro. Supp. II:** 68; **Supp. I Part 1:** 227, 230, 243, 255, 257, 258, 263, 329; **Supp. I Part 2:** 546, 613, 728; **Supp. II Part 1:** 1, 9, 20, 89; **Supp. IV Part 1:** 81; **Supp. VIII:** 237; **Supp. X:** 137, 193, 194; **Supp. XII:** 172; **Supp. XIV:** 310; **Supp. XV:** 45, 46, 158, 254; **Supp. XVI:** 267
Lawrence, Frieda, **Supp. XV:** 46
Lawrence, Rhoda, **Supp. I Part 1:** 45

Lawrence, Seymour, **Supp. IX:** 107; **Supp. XI:** 335, 346, 348
Lawrence, T. E., **Supp. XIV:** 159
Lawrence of Arabia (Aldington), **Supp. I Part 1:** 259
Lawrence of Arabia (film), **Supp. I Part 1:** 67
Laws (Plato), **Supp. IV Part 1:** 391
Laws of Ice, The (Price), **Supp. VI:** 264
Laws of Our Fathers, The (Turow), **Supp. XVII: 218–219**
Lawson, John Howard, **I:** 479, 482
Lawton Girl, The (Frederic), **II:** 132–133, 144
Layachi, Larbi (Driss ben Hamed Charhadi), **Supp. IV Part 1:** 92, 93
Layard, John, **Supp. XIV:** 160
Lay Down My Sword and Shield (Burke), **Supp. XIV:** 22, 25, 34
"Layers, The" (Kunitz), **Supp. III Part 1:** 260, 266–267
"Layers, The: Some Notes on 'The Abduction'" (Kunitz), **Supp. III Part 1:** 266
"Lay-mans Lamentation, The" (Taylor), **IV:** 162–163
Lay of the Land, The: Metaphor as Experience and History in American Life and Letters (Kolodny), **Supp. X:** 97
"Layover" (Hass), **Supp. VI:** 109
"Lay Preacher" (Dennie), **Supp. I Part 1:** 125
Layton, Irving, **Supp. XII:** 121
Lazarillo de Tormes (Mendoza), **III:** 182
Lazar Malkin Enters Heaven (S. Stern), **Supp. XVII:** 42
Lazarus Laughed (O'Neill), **III:** 391, 395–396
Lazer, Hank, **Supp. IX:** 265
Lea, Luke, **IV:** 248
Leacock, Stephen, **Supp. IV Part 2:** 464
"LEADBELLY GIVES AN AUTOGRAPH" (Baraka), **Supp. II Part 1:** 49
Leaflets: Poems, 1965–1968 (Rich), **Supp. I Part 2:** 551, 556–557
"League of American Writers, The: Communist Organizational Activity among American Writers 1929–1942" (Wolfe), **Supp. III Part 2:** 568
League of Brightened Philistines and Other Papers, The (Farrell), **II:** 49
Leaning Forward (Paley), **Supp. VI:** 221
"Leaning Tower, The" (Porter), **III:** 442, 443, 446–447
Leaning Tower and Other Stories, The (Porter), **III:** 433, 442, 443–447
"Leap, The" (Dickey), **Supp. IV Part 1:** 182
"Leaping Up into Political Poetry" (R. Bly), **Supp. IV Part 1:** 61, 63
Leap Year (Cameron), **Supp. XII:** 79–80, 81, **85–86,** 88
Lear, Edward, **III:** 428, 536; **Supp. XVI:** 103
Lear, Linda, **Supp. IX:** 19, 22, 25, 26
Learned Ladies, The (Molière; Wilbur, trans.), **Supp. III Part 2:** 560
"Learning a Dead Language" (Merwin), **Supp. III Part 1:** 345
Learning a Trade: A Craftsman's Notebooks, 1955–1997 (Price), **Supp. VI:** 254, 255, 267
Learning to Love: Exploring Solitude and Freedom (Merton), **Supp. VIII:** 200
"Learning to Read" (Harper), **Supp. II Part 1:** 201–202
"Learning to Speak" (Everwine), **Supp. XV:** 79
Leary, Lewis, **III:** 478
Leary, Paris, **Supp. IV Part 1:** 176
Leary, Timothy, **Supp. X:** 265; **Supp. XIV:** 150
Least Heat Moon, William, **Supp. V:** 169
Leather-Stocking Tales, The (Cooper), **I:** 335
Leatherwood God, The (Howells), **II:** 276, 277, 288
"Leaves" (Updike), **Retro. Supp. I:** 323, 329, 335
Leaves and Ashes (Haines), **Supp. XII:** 206
Leaves from the Notebook of a Tamed Cynic (Niebuhr), **III:** 293
Leaves of Grass (1856) (Whitman), **Retro. Supp. I:** 399–402
Leaves of Grass (1860) (Whitman), **Retro. Supp. I:** 402–405
"Leaves of Grass" (Whitman), **IV:** 463
Leaves of Grass (Whitman), **II:** 8; **IV:** 331, 332, 333, 334, 335, 336, 340, 341–342, 348, 350, 405, 464; **Retro. Supp. I:** 387, 388, 389, 390, **392–395,** 406, 407, 408; **Retro. Supp. II:** 93; **Supp. I Part 1:** 365; **Supp. I Part 2:** 416, 579; **Supp. III Part 1:** 156; **Supp. IX:** 265; **Supp. V:** 170; **Supp. VIII:** 275; **Supp. X:** 120; **Supp. XIV:** 334; **Supp. XV:** 218; **Supp. XVIII:** 4
Leaves of the Tree, The (Masters), **Supp. I Part 2:** 460
"Leaving" (Hogan), **Supp. IV Part 1:** 400
"Leaving" (Wilbur), **Supp. III Part 2:** 563
"Leaving, The" (B. Kelly), **Supp. XVII:** 127, 132
Leaving a Doll's House: A Memoir (C. Bloom), **Retro. Supp. II:** 281
Leaving Another Kingdom: Selected Poems (Stern), **Supp. IX:** 296
"Leaving Brooklyn" (Neugeboren), **Supp. XVI:** 226
Leaving Cheyenne (McMurtry), **Supp. V:** 220, 221–222, 224, 229
Leaving Home (Keillor), **Supp. XVI:** 175
"Leaving the Island" (Olds), **Supp. X:** 214
"Leaving the Yellow House" (Bellow), **Retro. Supp. II:** 27, 32
"Leaving Town" (Kenyon), **Supp. VII:** 163
Leavis, F. R., **I:** 522; **III:** 462–463, 475, 478; **Retro. Supp. I:** 67; **Retro. Supp. II:** 243; **Supp. I Part 2:** 536; **Supp. VIII:** 234, 236, 245
"Leavis-Snow Controversy, The" (Trilling), **Supp. III Part 2:** 512
Leavitt, David, **Supp. VIII:** 88
Le Braz, Anatole, **Supp. XIII:** 253
Lecker, Robert, **Supp. XIII:** 21
LeClair, Thomas, **Supp. IV Part 1:** 286
LeClair, Tom, **Supp. V:** 53; **Supp. XII:** 152
Le Conte, Joseph, **II:** 479; **III:** 227–228
"Lecture, The" (Singer), **IV:** 21
"LECTURE PAST DEAD CATS" (Baraka), **Supp. II Part 1:** 52
Lectures in America (Stein), **IV:** 27, 32, 33, 35, 36, 41, 42
"Lectures on Poetry" (Bryant), **Supp. I Part 1:** 159, 161
Lectures on Rhetoric (Blair), **II:** 8
"Leda and the Swan" (Yeats), **III:** 347; **Supp. IX:** 52
Ledger (Fitzgerald), **Retro. Supp. I:** 109, 110
Lee (Masters), **Supp. I Part 2:** 471
Lee, Don, **Supp. XII:** 295; **Supp. XVII:** 13, 14, 15, 16
Lee, Don L. *See* Madhubuti, Haki R.
Lee, Gypsy Rose, **II:** 586; **III:** 161; **Supp. IV Part 1:** 84
Lee, Harper, **Supp. VIII: 113–131**
Lee, Harriett, **Supp. XV:** 230
Lee, James Kyun-Jin, **Supp. XV:** 213
Lee, James W., **Supp. IX:** 94, 97, 109
Lee, James Ward, **Supp. VIII:** 57
Lee, Li Lin, **Supp. XV:** 211, 212
Lee, Li-Young, **Supp. XV: 211–228; Supp. XVII:** 241
Lee, Robert E., **II:** 150, 206; **IV:** 126; **Supp. I Part 2:** 471, 486
Lee, Samuel, **IV:** 158
Lee, Spike, **Retro. Supp. II:** 12; **Supp. XI:** 19; **Supp. XIII:** 179, 186; **Supp. XVI:** 144
Lee, Virginia Chin-lan, **Supp. X:** 291
Leeds, Barry, **Retro. Supp. II:** 204
Leeds, Daniel, **II:** 110
Leeds, Titan, **II:** 110, 111
Leeming, David, **Retro. Supp. II:** 4, 10
"Lees of Happiness, The" (Fitzgerald), **II:** 88
Left Out in the Rain: New Poems 1947–1985 (Snyder), **Supp. VIII:** 305
"Legacy" (Dunn), **Supp. XI:** 148
"Legacy" (Komunyakaa), **Supp. XIII:** 132
"Legacy of Aldo Leopold, The" (Stegner), **Supp. XIV:** 193
Legacy of Fear, A (Farrell), **II:** 39
"Legacy of the Ancestral Arts, The" (Locke), **Supp. XIV:** 201
Legacy of the Civil War, The: Meditations on the Centennial (Warren), **IV:** 236
"Legal Alien" (Mora), **Supp. XIII:** 215
"Legal Tender Act, The" (Adams), **I:** 5
Légende de la mort, La (Le Braz), **Supp. XIII:** 253
"Legend of Duluoz, The" (Kerouac), **Supp. III Part 1:** 218, 226, 227, 229
"Legend of Lillian Hellman, The" (Kazin), **Supp. I Part 1:** 297
"Legend of Monte del Diablo, The" (Harte), **Supp. II Part 1:** 339
"Legend of Paper Plates, The" (Haines), **Supp. XII:** 204

"Legend of Sammtstadt, A" (Harte), **Supp. II Part 1:** 355
"Legend of Sleepy Hollow, The" (Irving), **II:** 306–308
Legends (Lowell), **II:** 525–526
Legends of New England (Whittier), **Supp. I Part 2:** 684, 692
Legends of the Fall (Harrison), **Supp. VIII:** 38, 39, **45–46,** 48
Legends of the West (Hall), **II:** 313
Léger, Fernand, **Retro. Supp. I:** 292
Legge, James, **III:** 472
Leggett, William, **Supp. I Part 1:** 157
"Legion, The" (Karr), **Supp. XI:** 243
Legs (W. Kennedy), **Supp. VII:** 133, 134, 138–142, 143, 151
Le Guin, Ursula K., **Supp. IV Part 1:** 333
Lehan, Richard, **Retro. Supp. II:** 104
Lehman, David, **Supp. IX:** 161; **Supp. XIII:** 130; **Supp. XV:** 178–179, 180, 187, 190
Lehmann, John, **Retro. Supp. II:** 243; **Supp. XIV:** 158, 159
Lehmann, Paul, **III:** 311
Lehmann-Haupt, Christopher, **Retro. Supp. II:** 291; **Supp. IV Part 1:** 205, 209, 306; **Supp. IX:** 95, 103; **Supp. XVI:** 73, 210, 294, 295
Lehrer, Jim, **Supp. XVIII:** 39
Leiber, Fritz, **Supp. XVI:** 123
Leibling, A. J., **Supp. XIV:** 112
Leibniz, Gottfried Wilhelm von, **II:** 103; **III:** 428
Leibowitz, Herbert A., **I:** 386; **Supp. XV:** 78
Leich, Roland, **Supp. XIV:** 123
Leithauser, Brad, **Retro. Supp. I:** 133; **Supp. XV:** 250; **Supp. XVII:** 112
Leitz, Robert, **Supp. XIV:** 62
Leivick, H., **IV:** 6
Lekachman, Robert, **Supp. I Part 2:** 648
Leland, Charles, **Supp. II Part 1:** 193
Leland, Charles Godfrey, **I:** 257
Leland, John, **Supp. XV:** 69
Lem, Stanislaw, **Supp. IV Part 1:** 103
"Le marais du cygne" (Whittier), **Supp. I Part 2:** 687
Lemay, Harding, **Supp. IX:** 98; **Supp. VIII:** 125
Lemercier, Eugène, **Retro. Supp. I:** 299
"Lemorne *versus* Huell" (E. Stoddard), **Supp. XV:** 270, 273, 283
Le Morte D'Arthur Notes (Gardner), **Supp. VI:** 65, 66
Lenin, V. I., **I:** 366, 439, 440; **III:** 14–15, 262, 475; **IV:** 429, 436, 443–444; **Supp. I Part 2:** 647
"Lenore" (Poe), **III:** 411
"Lenox Avenue: Midnight" (Hughes), **Retro. Supp. I:** 198
Leonard, Elmore, **Supp. IV Part 1:** 356; **Supp. X:** 5; **Supp. XIV:** 26
Leonard, John, **Supp. IV Part 1:** 24; **Supp. IV Part 2:** 474; **Supp. V:** 164, 223–224; **Supp. XI:** 13; **Supp. XVIII:** 147, 148
Leonardo da Vinci, **Supp. XII:** 44
León-Portilla, Miguel, **Supp. XV:** 77
Leontiev, Constantine, **Supp. XIV:** 98
Leopard, The (Lampedusa), **Supp. XII:** 13–14
Leopardi, Giacomo, **II:** 543
"Leopard Man's Story, The" (London), **II:** 475
Leopard's Mouth Is Dry and Cold Inside, The (Levis), **Supp. XI:** 258
Leopold, Aldo, **Supp. V:** 202; **Supp. X:** 108; **Supp. XIV: 177–194**
"Leper's Bell, the" (Komunyakaa), **Supp. XIII:** 118
Lerman, Leo, **Supp. X:** 188; **Supp. XVI:** 194
Lerner, Max, **III:** 60; **Supp. I Part 2:** 629, 630, 631, 647, 650, 654
"Lesbos" (Plath), **Retro. Supp. II:** 254
Lesesne, Teri, **Supp. XIII:** 277
LeSieg, Theo (pseudonym). *See* Geisel, Theodor Seuss (Dr. Seuss)
Leskov, Nikolai, **IV:** 299
Leslie, Alfred, **Supp. XII:** 127
Les Misérables (Hugo), **II:** 179; **Supp. I Part 1:** 280
"Less and Less Human, O Savage Spirit" (W. Stevens), **Supp. XVI:** 64
Lesser, Wendy, **Supp. IV Part 2:** 453; **Supp. XII:** 297; **Supp. XVI:** 201
Lessing, Gotthold, **Supp. I Part 2:** 422
"Lesson, The" (Bambara), **Supp. XI:** 5–6
"Lesson, The" (Dunbar), **Supp. II Part 1:** 199
"Lesson, The" (Olsen), **Supp. XIII:** 297
"Lesson for the Ill Clothed and Ill Fed, A" (Ryan as Quin), **Supp. XVIII:** 230–231
"Lesson of the Master, The" (James), **Retro. Supp. I:** 227
Lesson of the Master, The (James), **Supp. XVIII:** 248
Lesson of the Masters: An Anthology of the Novel from Cervantes to Hemingway (Cowley-Hugo, ed.), **Supp. II Part 1:** 140
"Lesson on Concealment, A" (Brown), **Supp. I Part 1:** 133
"Lessons" (Epstein), **Supp. XII:** 163
"Lessons of the Body" (Simpson), **Supp. IX:** 267
Less than One (Brodsky), **Supp. VIII:** 22, 29–31
Lester, Jerry, **Supp. IV Part 2:** 574
Lester, Ketty, **Supp. XV:** 133, 147
Le Style Apollinaire (Zukofsky), **Supp. III Part 2:** 616
Le Sueur, Meridel, **Supp. V:** 113, 130; **Supp. XII:** 217
"Let America Be America Again" (Hughes), **Retro. Supp. I:** 202; **Supp. I Part 1:** 331
Let Evening Come (Kenyon), **Supp. VII:** 160, 169–171
Lethem, Jonathan, **Supp. IX:** 122; **Supp. XVIII: 135–153**
Let It Come Down (Bowles), **Supp. IV Part 1:** 87
"Let Me Be" (Levine), **Supp. V:** 181, 189
"Let Me Begin Again" (Levine), **Supp. V:** 181, 189
"Let No Charitable Hope" (Wylie), **Supp. I Part 2:** 713–714, 729
Let No Man Write My Epitaph (film, Leacock), **Supp. XVII:** 150, 158
Let No Man Write My Epitaph (W. Motley), **Supp. XVII:** 150, **158–160**
Let Noon Be Fair (W. Motley), **Supp. XVII: 161**
Letofsky, Irv, **Supp. XVI:** 167
"Let one Eye his watches keep/While the Other Eye doth sleep" (Fletcher), **Supp. IV Part 2:** 621
Let's Balance the Books (radio show; Untermeyer), **Supp. XV:** 311
"Letter ..." (Whittier), **Supp. I Part 2:** 687
"Letter, A" (Bogan), **Supp. III Part 1:** 54
"Letter, May 2, 1959" (Olson), **Supp. II Part 2:** 579, 580
"Letter, Much Too Late" (Stegner), **Supp. IV Part 2:** 613
"Letter, The" (Gioia), **Supp. XV:** 120
"Letter, The" (Malamud), **Supp. I Part 2:** 435–436
"Letter about Money, Love, or Other Comfort, If Any, The" (Warren), **IV:** 245
Letter Addressed to the People of Piedmont, on the Advantages of the French Revolution, and the Necessity of Adopting Its Principles in Italy, A (Barlow), **Supp. II Part 1:** 80, 81
"Letter for Marion, A" (McGrath), **Supp. X:** 116
"Letter from Aldermaston" (Merwin), **Supp. III Part 1:** 347
"Letter from a Region in My Mind" (Baldwin). *See* "Down at the Cross"
Letter from Li Po, A (Aiken), **I:** 68
"Letter from 'Manhattan'" (Didion), **Supp. IV Part 1:** 205
"Letter from the Country" (column, C. Bly), **Supp. XVI:** 33
"Letter from the End of the Twentieth Century" (Harjo), **Supp. XII:** 227
Letter from the End of the Twentieth Century (Harjo), **Supp. XII:** 223
"Letter on Céline" (Kerouac), **Supp. III Part 1:** 232
Letters (Cato), **II:** 114
Letters (Landor), **Supp. I Part 2:** 422
Letters (White), **Supp. I Part 2:** 651, 653, 675, 680
Letters (Wolfe), **IV:** 462
Letters and Leadership (Brooks), **I:** 228, 240, 245, 246
"Letters for the Dead" (Levine), **Supp. V:** 186
Letters from an American Farmer (Crèvecoeur), **Supp. I Part 1:** 227–251
"Letters from Maine" (Sarton), **Supp. VIII:** 261
Letters from Maine (Sarton), **Supp. VIII: 261**
"Letters from My Father" (R. O. Butler), **Supp. XII:** 71
Letters from the Country (C. Bly), **Supp. XVI: 33–34,** 35, 37
Letters from the Earth (Twain), **IV:** 209

Letters from the East (Bryant), **Supp. I Part 1:** 158
"Letters from the Ming Dynasty" (Brodsky), **Supp. VIII:** 28
Letters of a Traveller (Bryant), **Supp. I Part 1:** 158
Letters of a Traveller, Second Series (Bryant), **Supp. I Part 1:** 158
Letters of Emily Dickinson, The (Johnson and Ward, eds.), **I:** 470; **Retro. Supp. I:** 28
Letters of William James (Henry James, ed.), **II:** 362
Letters on Various Interesting and Important Subjects ... (Freneau), **Supp. II Part 1:** 272
Letters to a Niece (Adams), **I:** 22
Letters to a Young Poet (Rilke), **Supp. XIII:** 74; **Supp. XV:** 93
"Letters to Dead Imagists" (Sandburg), **I:** 421
"Letters Written on a Ferry While Crossing Long Island Sound" (Sexton), **Supp. II Part 2:** 683
"Letter to Abbé Raynal" (Paine), **Supp. I Part 2:** 510
Letter to a Man in the Fire: Does God Exist or Does He Care? (Price), **Supp. VI:** 267–268
"Letter to American Teachers of History, A" (Adams), **I:** 19
Letter to an Imaginary Friend (McGrath), **Supp. X:** 111, 112–113, 116, **119–125**
"Letter to a Reader" (Sanders), **Supp. XVI:** 266, 267, 268, 269, 275
"Letter to a Young Contributor" (Higginson), **Retro. Supp. I:** 31
"Letter to a Young Writer" (Price), **Supp. VI:** 267
"Letter to Bell from Missoula" (Hugo), **Supp. VI:** 142–143
"Letter to E. Franklin Frazier" (Baraka), **Supp. II Part 1:** 49
"Letter to Elaine Feinstein" (Olson), **Supp. II Part 2:** 561
"Letter to Freddy" (music) (Bowles), **Supp. IV Part 1:** 82
"Letter to Garber from Skye" (Hugo), **Supp. VI:** 146
"Letter to George Washington" (Paine), **Supp. I Part 2:** 517
"Letter to His Brother" (Berryman), **I:** 172, 173
Letter to His Countrymen, A (Cooper), **I:** 346, 347, 349
"Letter to Kizer from Seattle" (Hugo), **Supp. VI:** 142
Letter to Lord Byron (Auden), **Supp. II Part 1:** 11
"Letter to Lord Byron" (Mumford), **Supp. II Part 2:** 494
"Letter to Matthews from Barton Street Flats" (Hugo), **Supp. VI:** 133
"Letter to Minnesota" (Dunn), **Supp. XI:** 146
"Letter to Mr." (Poe), **III:** 411
"Letter Too Late to Vallejo" (Salinas), **Supp. XIII:** 313, 324
"Letter to Sister Madeline from Iowa City" (Hugo), **Supp. VI:** 142–143
"Letter to Soto" (Salinas), **Supp. XIII:** 325
"Letter to the Lady of the House" (Bausch), **Supp. VII:** 48
"Letter to the Rising Generation, A" (Comer), **I:** 214
"Letter to Walt Whitman" (Doty), **Supp. XI:** 135–136
"Letter to Wendell Berry, A" (Stegner), **Supp. IV Part 2:** 600
"Letter Writer, The" (Singer), **IV:** 20–21
"Let the Air Circulate" (Clampitt), **Supp. IX:** 45
"Letting Down of the Hair, The" (Sexton), **Supp. II Part 2:** 692
Letting Go (P. Roth), **Retro. Supp. II:** 282, 283; **Supp. III Part 2:** 403, 404, 409–412
"Letting the Puma Go" (Dunn), **Supp. XI:** 149
"Lettres d'un Soldat" (Stevens), **Retro. Supp. I:** 299
Let Us Go into the Starry Night (Shanley), **Supp. XIV:** 317
Let Us Now Praise Famous Men (Agee and Evans), **I:** 25, 27, 35, 36–39, 42, 45, 293
Let Your Mind Alone! (Thurber), **Supp. I Part 2:** 608
Leutze, Emanuel, **Supp. X:** 307
Levels of the Game (McPhee), **Supp. III Part 1:** 292, 294, 301
Levertov, Denise, **Retro. Supp. I:** 411; **Supp. III Part 1: 271–287; Supp. III Part 2:** 541; **Supp. IV Part 1:** 325; **Supp. VIII:** 38, 39; **Supp. XVI:** 39, 40
Levi, Primo, **Supp. X:** 149; **Supp. XVII:** 48
Leviathan (Auster), **Supp. XII:** 27, **33–34**
"Leviathan" (Lowell), **II:** 537, 538
"Leviathan" (Merwin), **Supp. III Part 1:** 345
Levin, Harry, **Supp. I Part 2:** 647
Levin, Jennifer, **Supp. X:** 305
Lévinas, Emmanuel, **Supp. XVI:** 290, 291
Levine, Ellen, **Supp. V:** 4; **Supp. XI:** 178
Levine, Paul, **Supp. IV Part 1:** 221, 224
Levine, Philip, **Supp. III Part 2:** 541; **Supp. IX:** 293; **Supp. V: 177–197,** 337; **Supp. XI:** 123, 257, 259, 267, 271, 315; **Supp. XIII:** 312; **Supp. XV:** 73, 74, 212
Levine, Rosalind, **Supp. XII:** 123
Levine, Sherry, **Supp. XII:** 4
Le Violde Lucrèce (Obey), **IV:** 356
Levis, Larry, **Supp. IX:** 299; **Supp. V:** 180; **Supp. XI: 257–274; Supp. XIII:** 312; **Supp. XV:** 73; **Supp. XVII:** 110
Lévi-Strauss, Claude, **Supp. I Part 2:** 636; **Supp. IV Part 1:** 45; **Supp. IV Part 2:** 490; **Supp. XVIII:** 190
Levitation: Five Fictions (Ozick), **Supp. V:** 268–270
"Levitation with Baby" (Nelson), **Supp. XVIII:** 173
Levitt, Saul, **Supp. XV:** 197
Levy, Alan, **Supp. IV Part 2:** 574, 589
Levy, G. Rachel, **Supp. I Part 2:** 567
Lévy-Bruhl, Lucien, **Retro. Supp. I:** 57
Levy Mayer and the New Industrial Era (Masters), **Supp. I Part 2:** 473
Lewes, George Henry, **II:** 569
Lewin, Albert, **Supp. XIV:** 279, 293
Lewis, C. Day, **III:** 527
Lewis, David Levering, **Supp. XVIII:** 127
Lewis, Dr. Claude, **II:** 442
Lewis, Edith, **I:** 313; **Retro. Supp. I:** 19, 21, 22
Lewis, Edwin, J., **II:** 439, 442
Lewis, Jerry, **Supp. IV Part 2:** 575; **Supp. X:** 172
Lewis, John L., **I:** 493
Lewis, Lilburn, **IV:** 243
Lewis, Lorene, **Supp. IV Part 2:** 596, 597
Lewis, Lucy, **IV:** 243
Lewis, Maggie, **Supp. V:** 23
Lewis, Meriwether, **II:** 217; **III:** 14; **IV:** 179, 243, 283
Lewis, Merrill, **Supp. IV Part 2:** 596, 597
Lewis, Michael, **II:** 451, 452; **Supp. XVII:** 210
Lewis, Mrs. Sinclair (Dorothy Thompson), **II:** 449–450, 451, 453
Lewis, Mrs. Sinclair (Grace Livingston Hegger), **II:** 441
Lewis, Robert Q., **Supp. IV Part 2:** 574
Lewis, R. W. B., **I:** 386, 561; **II:** 457–458; **Retro. Supp. I:** 362, 367; **Supp. I Part 1:** 233; **Supp. XIII:** 93
Lewis, Sinclair, **I:** 116, 212, 348, 355, 362, 374, 378, 487, 495; **II:** 27, 34, 74, 79, 271, 277, 306, **439–461,** 474; **III:** 28, 40, 51, 60, 61, 63–64, 66, 70, 71, 106, 394, 462, 572, 606; **IV:** 53, 326, 366, 455, 468, 475, 482; **Retro. Supp. I:** 332; **Retro. Supp. II:** 95, 108, 197, 322; **Supp. I Part 2:** 378, 613, 709; **Supp. IV Part 2:** 678; **Supp. IX:** 308; **Supp. V:** 278; **Supp. X:** 137; **Supp. XVII:** 41; **Supp. XVIII:** 278
Lewis, Wyndham, **III:** 458, 462, 465, 470; **Retro. Supp. I:** 59, 170, 292; **Supp. III Part 2:** 617
Lexicon Tetraglotton (Howell), **II:** 111
"Leyenda" (Mora), **Supp. XIII:** 214
Leyte (Morison), **Supp. I Part 2:** 491
"Liar, The" (Baraka), **Supp. II Part 1:** 36
"Liars, The" (Sandburg), **III:** 586
Liars' Club, The: A Memoir (Karr), **Supp. XI:** 239, 240, 241, 242, **244–248,** 252, 254; **Supp. XVI:** 70
"Liar's Dice" (C. Frost), **Supp. XV:** 94, 107
Liar's Dice (C. Frost), **Supp. XV:** 93, 96
Liars in Love (Yates), **Supp. XI:** 348, 349
Libation Bearers, The (Aeschylus), **III:** 398; **Supp. IX:** 103
Li Bay. *See* Li Po
Libby, Anthony, **Supp. XIII:** 87
Libera, Padre, **II:** 278

Liberal Imagination, The (Trilling), **III:** 308; **Retro. Supp. I:** 97, 216; **Supp. II Part 1:** 146; **Supp. III Part 2:** 495, 498, 501–504
Liberation (J. Scott), **Supp. XVII:** 192, **194–196**
"Liberation" (Winters), **Supp. II Part 2:** 791
Liber Brunenesis (yearbook), **IV:** 286
Liberties, The (Howe), **Supp. IV Part 2:** 426–428, 430, 432
Liberties of America, The (H. Warner), **Supp. XVIII:** 259
Liberty Jones (play), **Supp. IV Part 1:** 83
"Liberty Tree" (Paine), **Supp. I Part 2:** 505
Libra (DeLillo), **Supp. VI:** 2, **4, 5,** 6, **7,** 9, 10, 12, 13, 14, 16
Library for Juana, A (Mora), **Supp. XIII:** 218
Library of America, **Retro. Supp. I:** 2
"Library of Babel, The" (J. Borges), **Supp. XVII:** 47
"Library of Law, A" (MacLeish), **III:** 4
"Library of Moloch, The" (Bukiet), **Supp. XVII:** 47, 49
"Librettos for Eros" (Gander), **Supp. XV:** 340
Lice, The (Merwin), **Supp. III Part 1:** 339, 341–342, 346, 348, 349, 355
Lichtenberg, Georg Christoph, **Supp. XIV:** 339
Lichtenstein, Roy, **Supp. I Part 2:** 665; **Supp. XV:** 186
"Liddy's Orange" (Olds), **Supp. X:** 209
Lieberman, Laurence, **Supp. XI:** 323–324
Liebestod (Wagner), **I:** 284, 395
Liebling, A. J., **IV:** 290; **Supp. VIII:** 151; **Supp. XVI:** 167
Lie Down in Darkness (Styron), **IV:** 98, 99, 100–104, 105, 111; **Supp. XI:** 343
Lie of the Mind, A (Shepard), **Supp. III Part 2:** 433, 435, 441, 447–449
"Lies" (Haines), **Supp. XII:** 204
Lies (Hoffman), **Supp. XVIII: 78–79**
Lies Like Truth (Clurman), **IV:** 385
Lieutenant, The (Dubus), **Supp. VII:** 78
"Life" (Wharton), **Retro. Supp. I:** 372
Life along the Passaic River (W. C. Williams), **Retro. Supp. I:** 423
Life Among the Savages (Jackson), **Supp. IX:** 115, **125**
Life and Gabriella (Glasgow), **II:** 175, 176, 182–183, 184, 189
"Life and I" (Wharton), **Retro. Supp. I:** 360, 361, 362
"Life and Letters" (Epstein), **Supp. XIV:** 104–105
Life and Letters of Harrison Gray Otis, Federalist, 1765–1848, The (Morison), **Supp. I Part 2:** 480–481
Life and Letters of Sir Henry Wotton (L. P. Smith), **Supp. XIV:** 340–341
Life and Times of Frederick Douglass, Written by Himself, The (Douglass), **Supp. III Part 1:** 155, 159–163
Life and Writings of Horace McCoy, The (Wolfson), **Supp. XIII:** 172, 174
"Life as a Visionary Spirit" (Eberhart), **I:** 540, 541
"Life at Angelo's, A" (Benét), **Supp. XI:** 53
Life at Happy Knoll (Marquand), **III:** 50, 61
Life Before Man (Atwood), **Supp. XIII: 24–25**
"Life Cycle of Common Man" (Nemerov), **III:** 278
"Lifecycle Stairmaster" (Karr), **Supp. XI:** 250
Life Estates (Hearon), **Supp. VIII: 68–69**
Life for Life's Sake (Aldington), **Supp. I Part 1:** 256
Life Full of Holes, A (Layachi), **Supp. IV Part 1:** 92
"Lifeguard" (Updike), **IV:** 226; **Retro. Supp. I:** 325
"Lifeguard, The" (Dickey), **Supp. IV Part 1:** 179–180
"Life in the 30s" (column, Quindlen), **Supp. XVII:** 165, 167–169
Life in the Clearings (Shields), **Supp. VII:** 313
"Life in the Country: A City Friend Asks, 'Is It Boring?'" (Paley), **Supp. VI:** 231
Life in the Forest (Levertov), **Supp. III Part 1:** 282–283
Life in the Iron Mills (Davis), **Supp. XIII:** 292, 295, 299, 305; **Supp. XVI:** 79–82, **85–88,** 91
Life in the Iron Mills and Other Stories (T. Olson, ed.), **Supp. XVI:** 83
Life in the Theatre, A (Mamet), **Supp. XIV:** 241, 255
Life Is a Miracle: An Essay Against Modern Superstition (Berry), **Supp. X:** 35
"Life Is Fine" (Hughes), **Supp. I Part 1:** 334, 338
"Life Is Motion" (Stevens), **IV:** 74
Life of Albert Gallatin, The (Adams), **I:** 6, 14
Life of an Ordinary Woman, The: Anne Ellis (A. Ellis), **Supp. XVI:** 38
Life of Dryden (Johnson), **Retro. Supp. II:** 223
Life of Emily Dickinson, The (Sewall), **Retro. Supp. I:** 25
Life of Forms, The (Focillon), **IV:** 90
Life of Franklin Pierce (Hawthorne), **Retro. Supp. I:** 163
Life of George Cabot Lodge, The (Adams), **I:** 21
Life of George Washington (Irving), **II:** 314, 315–316
Life of Henry James (Edel), **Retro. Supp. I:** 224
"Life of Irony, The" (Bourne), **I:** 219
"Life of Lincoln West, The" (Brooks), **Supp. III Part 1:** 86
Life of Mary, The (Rilke; F. Wright, trans.), **Supp. XVII:** 244
Life of Michelangelo (Grimm), **II:** 17
"Life of Nancy, The" (Jewett), **Retro. Supp. II:** 133, 144
Life of Oliver Goldsmith, The, with Selections from His Writings (Irving), **II:** 315
Life of Phips (Mather), **Supp. II Part 2:** 451, 452, 459
Life of Poetry, The (Rukeyser), **Supp. VI:** 271, 273, 275–276, 282, 283, 286
Life of Samuel Johnson (Boswell), **Supp. I Part 2:** 656
Life of Savage (Johnson), **Supp. I Part 2:** 523
Life of the Drama, The (Bentley), **IV:** 396
"Life of the Mind, The" (Kees), **Supp. XV:** 140
Life of the Right Reverend Joseph P. Machebeuf, The (Howlett), **Retro. Supp. I:** 17
Life of Thomas Paine, author of Rights of Men, With a Defence of his Writings (Chalmers), **Supp. I Part 2:** 514
Life of Thomas Paine, The (Cobbett), **Supp. I Part 2:** 517
"Life of Towne, The" (Carson), **Supp. XII: 102**
"Life on Beekman Place, A" (Naylor), **Supp. VIII:** 214
"Life on the Black List" (Endore), **Supp. XVII:** 63
Life on the Hyphen: The Cuban-American Way (Firmat), **Supp. VIII:** 76; **Supp. XI:** 184
Life on the Mississippi (Twain), **I:** 209; **IV:** 198, 199; **Supp. I Part 2:** 440
"Life on the Rocks: The Galápagos" (Dillard), **Supp. VI:** 32
"Life Stories, East and West" (E. Hoffman), **Supp. XVI:** 157
Life Story (Baker), **II:** 259
"Life Studies" (Lowell), **Retro. Supp. II:** 188
Life Studies (Lowell), **I:** 400; **II:** 384, 386, 543, 546–550, 551, 555; **Retro. Supp. II:** 180, 185, 186, 188, 189, 191; **Supp. I Part 2:** 543; **Supp. XI:** 240, 244, 250, 317; **Supp. XII:** 255; **Supp. XIV:** 15; **Supp. XV:** 252
"Life Styles in the Golden Land" (Didion), **Supp. IV Part 1:** 200
"Life That Is, The" (Bryant), **Supp. I Part 1:** 169
"Life Work" (Stafford), **Supp. XI:** 329–330
"Life You Save May Be Your Own, The" (O'Connor), **III:** 344, 350, 354; **Retro. Supp. II:** 229, 230, 233
Lifshin, Lyn, **Supp. XVI:** 37
"Lifting, The" (Olds), **Supp. X:** 210
"Ligeia" (Poe), **III:** 412, 414; **Retro. Supp. II:** 261, 270, 271, 275
Liggett, Walter W., **Supp. XIII:** 168
Light, James F., **IV:** 290; **Retro. Supp. II:** 325
Light, Kate, **Supp. XVII:** 109
"Light and the Sufferer" (Lethem), **Supp. XVIII:** 139–140
Light around the Body, The (R. Bly), **Supp. IV Part 1:** 61–62, 62; **Supp. XVII:** 243
"Light Comes Brighter, The" (Roethke), **III:** 529–530

"Light from Above" (Eberhart), **I:** 541
Light in August (Faulkner), **II:** 63–64, 65, 74; **IV:** 207; **Retro. Supp. I:** 82, 84, 85, 86, 89, 92; **Supp. XIV:** 12
Light in the Forest, The (Richter), **Supp. XVIII: 216–217**
Light in the Morning (Baker), **Supp. XVIII:** 263, 269
"Light Man, A" (James), **II:** 322; **Retro. Supp. I:** 219
"Lightning" (Barthelme), **Supp. IV Part 1:** 53
"Lightning" (Bynner), **Supp. XV:** 44
"Lightning" (Oliver), **Supp. VII:** 235
"Lightning, The" (Swenson), **Supp. IV Part 2:** 645
"Lightning Rod Man, The" (Melville), **III:** 90; **Supp. XVIII:** 4
"Light of the World, The" (Hemingway), **II:** 249
"Lights in the Windows" (Nye), **Supp. XIII:** 280
Light Verse and Satires (Bynner), **Supp. XV:** 52
Light Years (Salter), **Supp. IX: 257–259**
"LIKE, THIS IS WHAT I MEANT!" (Baraka), **Supp. II Part 1:** 59
"Like All the Other Nations" (Paley), **Supp. VI:** 220
"Like a Rolling Stone" (song, Dylan), **Supp. XVIII:** 20, 30
"Like Decorations in a Nigger Cemetery" (Stevens), **IV:** 74, 79; **Retro. Supp. I:** 305
Like Ghosts of Eagles (Francis), **Supp. IX:** 86
"Like Life" (Moore), **Supp. X:** 163, 165, **172–173**
Like Life: Stories (Moore), **Supp. X:** 163, **171–175,** 177, 178
"Like Talk" (Mills), **Supp. XI:** 311
"Like the New Moon I Will Live My Life" (R. Bly), **Supp. IV Part 1:** 71
Li'l Abner (Capp), **IV:** 198
"Lilacs" (Lowell), **II:** 527
"Lilacs, The" (Wilbur), **Supp. III Part 2:** 557–558
"Lilacs for Ginsberg" (Stern), **Supp. IX:** 299
Liliom (Molnar), **Supp. XVI:** 187
Lilith's Brood (O. Butler), **Supp. XIII:** 63
Lillabulero Press, **Supp. V:** 4, 5
Lillian Hellman (Adler), **Supp. I Part 1:** 297
Lillian Hellman (Falk), **Supp. I Part 1:** 297
Lillian Hellman: Playwright (Moody), **Supp. I Part 1:** 280
Lillo, George, **II:** 111, 112
"Lily Daw and the Three Ladies" (Welty), **IV:** 262
Lima, Agnes de, **I:** 231, 232
"Limbo: Altered States" (Karr), **Supp. XI:** 249–250
"Lime Orchard Woman, The" (Ríos), **Supp. IV Part 2:** 548
Lime Orchard Woman, The (Ríos), **Supp. IV Part 2:** 538, 547–550, 553
Limitations (Turow), **Supp. XVII: 222–223**
"Limits" (Emerson), **II:** 19
Lincoln, Abraham, **I:** 1, 4, 30; **II:** 8, 13, 135, 273, 555, 576; **III:** 576, 577, 580, 584, 587–590, 591; **IV:** 192, 195, 298, 347, 350, 444; **Supp. I Part 1:** 2, 8, 26, 309, 321; **Supp. I Part 2:** 379, 380, 382, 385, 390, 397, 399, 418, 424, 454, 456, 471, 472, 473, 474, 483, 579, 687; **Supp. IX:** 15; **Supp. VIII:** 108; **Supp. XIV:** 73
Lincoln, Kenneth, **Supp. IV Part 1:** 329; **Supp. IV Part 2:** 507
Lincoln, Mrs. Thomas (Nancy Hanks), **III:** 587
Lincoln, Thomas, **III:** 587
Lincoln: A Novel (Vidal), **Supp. IV Part 2:** 677, 684, 685, 688, 689–690, 691, 692
"Lincoln Relics, The" (Kunitz), **Supp. III Part 1:** 269
Lincoln: The Man (Masters), **Supp. I Part 2:** 471, 473–474
Lindbergh, Charles A., **I:** 482
"Linden Branch, The" (MacLeish), **III:** 19, 20
Linden Hills (Naylor), **Supp. VIII:** 214, 218, **219–223**
Linderman, Lawrence, **Supp. IV Part 2:** 579, 583, 585, 589
Lindner, April, **Supp. XV:** 111, 119
Lindsay, Howard, **III:** 284
Lindsay, John, **Supp. I Part 2:** 374
Lindsay, Mrs. Vachel (Elizabeth Connors), **Supp. I Part 2:** 398, 399, 473
Lindsay, Mrs. Vachel Thomas (Esther Catherine Frazee), **Supp. I Part 2:** 374, 375, 384–385, 398
Lindsay, Olive, **Supp. I Part 2:** 374, 375, 392
Lindsay, Vachel, **I:** 384; **II:** 263, 276, 530; **III:** 5, 505; **Retro. Supp. I:** 133; **Supp. I Part 1:** 324; **Supp. I Part 2: 374–403,** 454, 473, 474; **Supp. III Part 1:** 63, 71; **Supp. XV:** 293, 297, 299, 301, 306; **Supp. XVI:** 184–185
Lindsay, Vachel Thomas, **Supp. I Part 2:** 374, 375
Lindsey, David, **Supp. XIV:** 26
"Line, The" (Olds), **Supp. X:** 206
Lineage of Ragpickers, Songpluckers, Elegiasts, and Jewelers, A (Goldbarth), **Supp. XII:** 191
"Line of Least Resistance, The" (Wharton), **Retro. Supp. I:** 366
Line Out for a Walk, A: Familiar Essays (Epstein), **Supp. XIV: 107**
"Liner Notes for the Poetically Unhep" (Hughes), **Retro. Supp. I:** 210
"Lines After Rereading T. S. Eliot" (Wright), **Supp. V:** 343
"Lines Composed a Few Miles Above Tintern Abbey" (Wordsworth), **Supp. III Part 1:** 12
"Lines for an Interment" (MacLeish), **III:** 15
"Lines for My Father" (Cullen), **Supp. IV Part 1:** 167
"Lines from Israel" (Lowell), **II:** 554
"Lines from Pietro Longhi" (Sobin), **Supp. XVI:** 289
"Lines on Revisiting the Country" (Bryant), **Supp. I Part 1:** 164
"Lines Suggested by a Tennessee Song" (Agee), **I:** 28
"Line-Storm Song, A" (Frost), **Retro. Supp. I:** 127
"Lines Written at Port Royal" (Freneau), **Supp. II Part 1:** 264
"Lines Written in an Asylum" (Carruth), **Supp. XVI:** 48
"Lines Written in Manassas," **Supp. XV:** 99–100
"Line Written in the Dark Illegible Next Day" (F. Wright), **Supp. XVII:** 242
Linfield, Susie, **Supp. XVII:** 169, 177
Lingeman, Richard, **Supp. X:** 82
Linn, Elizabeth. *See* Brown, Mrs. Charles Brockden (Elizabeth Linn)
Linn, John Blair, **Supp. I Part 1:** 145
Linnaeus, Carolus, **II:** 6; **Supp. I Part 1:** 245
"Linnets" (Levis), **Supp. XI:** 260, 261
"Linoleum Roses" (Cisneros), **Supp. VII:** 63, 66
Linotte: 1914–1920 (Nin), **Supp. X:** 193, 196, 197
Linschoten, Hans, **II:** 362, 363, 364
"Lion" (B. Kelly), **Supp. XVII:** 133
"Lion and Honeycomb" (Nemerov), **III:** 275, 278, 280
Lion and the Archer, The (Hayden), **Supp. II Part 1:** 366, 367
Lion and the Honeycomb, The (Blackmur), **Supp. II Part 1:** 91
Lion Country (Buechner), **Supp. XII:** 52, 53
Lionel Lincoln (Cooper), **I:** 339, 342
"Lion for Real, The" (Ginsberg), **Supp. II Part 1:** 320
Lionhearted, The: A Story about the Jews of Medieval England (Reznikoff), **Supp. XIV:** 280, 289
Lion in the Garden (Meriweather and Millgate), **Retro. Supp. I:** 91
"Lionizing" (Poe), **III:** 411, 425
"Lions, Harts, and Leaping Does" (Powers), **III:** 356
Lions and Shadows: An Education in the Twenties (Isherwood), **Supp. XIV:** 158, 159, 160, 162
"Lions in Sweden" (Stevens), **IV:** 79–80
Lipman, William R., **Supp. XIII:** 170
Li Po, **Supp. XI:** 241; **Supp. XII:** 218; **Supp. XV:** 47, 217
Lippmann, Walter, **I:** 48, 222–223, 225; **III:** 291, 600; **IV:** 429; **Supp. I Part 2:** 609, 643; **Supp. VIII:** 104
Lips Together, Teeth Apart (McNally), **Supp. XIII: 201–202,** 208, 209
Lipsyte, Robert, **Supp. XVI:** 220
Lipton, James, **Supp. IV Part 2:** 576, 577, 579, 583, 586, 588
Lipton, Lawrence, **Supp. IX:** 3
Lisbon Traviata, The (McNally), **Supp. XIII:** 198, **199–200,** 201, 204, 208
Lisicky,Paul, **Supp. XI:** 120, 131, 135
"Lisp, The" (Olds), **Supp. X:** 211

Listen, Ruben Fontanez (Neugeboren), **Supp. XVI: 220–221**
"Listeners, The" (de la Mare), **Supp. XVII:** 69
"Listeners and Readers: The Unforgetting of Vachel Lindsay" (Trombly), **Supp. I Part 2:** 403
"Listening" (Paley), **Supp. VI:** 218, 231, 232
"Listening" (Stafford), **Supp. XI:** 321, 322
Listening to Prozac (P. Kramer), **Supp. XVI:** 229
"Listening to the Desert" (Henderson), **Supp. XIII:** 221–222
"Listening to the Mockingbird" (Woodard), **Supp. VIII:** 128
Listening to Your Life: Daily Meditations with Frederick Buechner (Buechner), **Supp. XII:** 53
Listen to the Desert/Oye al desierto (Mora), **Supp. XIII:** 221
"Listen to the People" (Benét), **Supp. XI:** 51–52
Liston, Sonny, **III:** 38, 42
Li T'ai-po, **II:** 526
"Litany" (Ashbery), **Supp. III Part 1:** 21–22, 25, 26
"Litany" (Sandburg), **III:** 593
"Litany, The" (Gioia), **Supp. XV:** 125, 126
"Litany for Dictatorships" (Benét), **Supp. XI:** 46, 58
"Litany for Survival, A" (Lorde), **Supp. XII:** 220
"Litany of the Dark People, The" (Cullen), **Supp. IV Part 1:** 170, 171
"Litany of the Heroes" (Lindsay), **Supp. I Part 2:** 397
"Litany of Washington Street, The" (Lindsay), **Supp. I Part 2:** 376, 398–399
Literary Anthropology (Trumpener and Nyce), **Retro. Supp. I:** 380
Literary Art and Activism of Rick Bass, The (Weltzien), **Supp. XVI:** 20–21
"Literary Blacks and Jews" (Ozick), **Supp. V:** 272
"Literary Career of Elizabeth Barstow Stoddard, The" (Matlack), **Supp. XV:** 269
Literary Criticism: A Short History (Brooks and Wimsatt), **Supp. XIV:** 12
"Literary Criticism of Georg Lukács, The" (Sontag), **Supp. III Part 2:** 453
Literary Essays of Thomas Merton, The, **Supp. VIII:** 207
"Literary Folk As They Came and Went with Ourselves" (E. Stoddard), **Supp. XV:** 274
Literary Friends and Acquaintance (Howells), **Supp. I Part 1:** 318; **Supp. XV:** 287
"Literary Heritage of Tennyson, The" (Locke), **Supp. XIV:** 197
Literary History of the United States (Spiller et al., ed.), **Supp. I Part 1:** 104; **Supp. II Part 1:** 95
"Literary Importation" (Freneau), **Supp. II Part 1:** 264
"Literary Life of America, The" (Brooks), **I:** 245
Literary Outlaw: The Life and Times of William S. Burroughs (Morgan), **Supp. XIV:** 141
Literary Situation, The (Cowley), **Supp. II Part 1:** 135, 140, 144, 146, 147, 148
"Literary Worker's Polonius, The" (Wilson), **IV:** 431, 432
"Literature" (Emerson), **II:** 6
Literature (X. J. Kennedy), **Supp. XV:** 153
Literature and American Life (Boynton), **Supp. I Part 2:** 415
Literature and Life (Howells), **Supp. XIV:** 45–46
Literature and Morality (Farrell), **II:** 49
"Literature and Place: Varieties of Regional Experience" (Erisman), **Supp. VIII:** 126
"Literature as a Symptom" (Warren), **IV:** 237
"Literature in Low Life" (Hapgood), **Supp. XVII:** 103
"Literature of Exhaustion, The" (Barth), **Supp. IV Part 1:** 48
"Lithuanian Nocturne" (Brodsky), **Supp. VIII:** 29
"Lit Instructor" (Stafford), **Supp. XI:** 321
Littauer, Kenneth, **Retro. Supp. I:** 114
Little Big Man (Berger), **Supp. XII:** 171
Little Big Man (film), **Supp. X:** 124
Littlebird, Harold, **Supp. IV Part 2:** 499
Littlebird, Larry, **Supp. IV Part 2:** 499, 505
Little Birds: Erotica (Nin), **Supp. X:** 192, 195
"Little Brown Baby" (Dunbar), **Supp. II Part 1:** 206
"Little Brown Jug" (Baraka), **Supp. II Part 1:** 51
"Little Clown, My Heart" (Cisneros), **Supp. VII:** 71
"Little Cosmic Dust Poem" (Haines), **Supp. XII:** 209–210
"Little Country Girl, A" (Chopin), **Retro. Supp. II:** 71
"Little Curtis" (Parker), **Supp. IX:** 193
Little Disturbances of Man, The (Paley), **Supp. VI:** 218
"Little Dog" (Hughes), **Supp. I Part 1:** 329
Little Dorrit (Dickens), **Supp. I Part 1:** 35
"Little Edward" (Stowe), **Supp. I Part 2:** 587
"Little Elegy" (X. J. Kennedy), **Supp. XV:** 155
Little Essays Drawn from the Writings of George Santayana (L. P. Smith), **Supp. XIV:** 342
"Little Expressionless Animals" (Wallace), **Supp. X:** 305
"Little Fable" (Hay), **Supp. XIV:** 131
Littlefield, Catherine, **Supp. IX:** 58
Little Foxes, The (Hellman), **Supp. I Part 1:** 276, 278–279, 281, 283, 297
"Little Fred, the Canal Boy" (Stowe), **Supp. I Part 2:** 587
"Little French Mary" (Jewett), **II:** 400
Little Friend, Little Friend (Jarrell), **II:** 367, 372, 375–376
"Little Gidding" (Eliot), **I:** 582, 588; **II:** 539; **Retro. Supp. I:** 66
"Little Girl, My Stringbean, My Lovely Woman" (Sexton), **Supp. II Part 2:** 686
"Little Girl, The" (Paley), **Supp. VI:** 222, **228–229**
"Little Girl Tells a Story to a Lady, A" (Barnes), **Supp. III Part 1:** 36
"Little Goose Girl, The" (Grimm), **IV:** 266
Little Ham (Hughes), **Retro. Supp. I:** 203; **Supp. I Part 1:** 328, 339
Little King, The (Bynner), **Supp. XV:** 42, 50
Little Lady of the Big House, The (London), **II:** 481–482
Little Liar, The (film; Ingraham), **Supp. XVI:** 184–185
"Little Lion Face" (Swenson), **Supp. IV Part 2:** 651
"Little Lobelia's Song" (Bogan), **Supp. III Part 1:** 66
"Little Local Color, A" (Henry), **Supp. II Part 1:** 399
Little Lord Fauntleroy (Burnett), **Retro. Supp. I:** 188; **Supp. XVI:** 182
"Little Lyric" (Hughes), **Supp. I Part 1:** 334
Little Man, Little Man (Baldwin), **Supp. I Part 1:** 67
"Little Man at Chehaw Station, The" (Ellison), **Retro. Supp. II:** 123
Little Me (musical), **Supp. IV Part 2:** 575
Little Men (Alcott), **Supp. I Part 1:** 32, 39, 40
"Little Morning Music, A" (Schwartz), **Supp. II Part 2:** 662–663
Little Ocean (Shepard), **Supp. III Part 2:** 447
"Little Old Girl, A" (Larcom), **Supp. XIII:** 144
"Little Old Spy" (Hughes), **Supp. I Part 1:** 329
Little Orphan Annie (film), **Supp. XVIII:** 244
"Little Owl Who Lives in the Orchard" (Oliver), **Supp. VII:** 239
"Little Peasant, The" (Sexton), **Supp. II Part 2:** 690
"Little Rapids, The" (Swenson), **Supp. IV Part 2:** 645
Little Red Song Book (Hill), **Supp. XVIII:** 224
Little Regiment and Other Episodes of the American Civil War, The (Crane), **I:** 408
Little River: New and Selected Poems (McCarriston), **Supp. XIV: 269–272**
"Little Road not made of Man, A" (Dickinson), **Retro. Supp. I:** 44
Little Sister, The (Chandler), **Supp. IV Part 1:** 122, 130, 131–132
"Little Sleep's-Head Sprouting Hair in the Moonlight" (Kinnell), **Supp. III Part 1:** 247

"Little Snow White" (Grimm), **IV:** 266
"Little Testament of Bernard Martin, Aet. 30" (Mumford), **Supp. II Part 2:** 472, 473, 474
"Little Things" (Olds), **Supp. X:** 208
Little Tour in France (James), **II:** 337
Little Women (Alcott), **Supp. I Part 1:** 28, 29, 32, 35, 37, 38, 39–40, 41, 43, 44; **Supp. IX:** 128
Little Yellow Dog, A (Mosley), **Supp. XIII:** 237, 241
"Liturgy and Spiritual Personalism" (Merton), **Supp. VIII:** 199
Litz, A. Walton, **Retro. Supp. I:** 306
"Liu Ch'e" (Pound), **III:** 466
"Live" (Sexton), **Supp. II Part 2:** 684, 686
Live from Baghdad (screenplay, Shanley), **Supp. XIV:** 316
Live from Golgotha (Vidal), **Supp. IV Part 2:** 677, 682, 691, 692
Live Now and Pay Later (Garrett), **Supp. VII:** 111
"Live-Oak with Moss" (Whitman), **Retro. Supp. I:** 403
Live or Die (Sexton), **Supp. II Part 2:** 670, 683–687
Liveright, Horace, **Retro. Supp. I:** 80, 81, 83; **Supp. I Part 2:** 464
Lives (Plutarch), **II:** 5, 104
Lives of a Cell, The (L. Thomas), **Retro. Supp. I:** 322, 323
Lives of Distinguished American Naval Officers (Cooper), **I:** 347
"Lives of Gulls and Children, The" (Nemerov), **III:** 271, 272
Lives of the Animals (Wrigley), **Supp. XVIII: 306–308**
Lives of the Artists (Vasari), **Supp. I Part 2:** 450
"Lives of the Bohemians" (Lethem), **Supp. XVIII:** 135
Lives of the Muses, The: Nine Women and the Artists They Inspired (Prose), **Supp. XVI:** 250, 260
"Lives of the Poets" (Doctorow), **Supp. IV Part 1:** 234
Lives of the Poets (Doctorow), **Supp. IV Part 1:** 234
"Lives of the——Wha'?, The" (Goldbarth), **Supp. XII:** 191
"Living" (Wright), **Supp. XV:** 345
Living, The (Dillard), **Supp. VI:** 23
"Living at Home" (Gordon), **Supp. IV Part 1:** 311
Living by Fiction (Dillard), **Supp. VI:** 23, 31, **32,** 33
Living by the Word (Walker), **Supp. III Part 2:** 521, 522, 526, 527, 535
Living End, The (Elkin), **Supp. VI: 54,** 58
"Living in the Flatlands" (Carruth), **Supp. XVI:** 54
Living Is Easy, The (D. West), **Supp. XVIII:** 277, 280, **284–286,** 287
"Living Like Weasels" (Dillard), **Supp. VI:** 26, 33
Living Novel, The (Hicks), **III:** 342
Living of Charlotte Perkins Gilman, The (Gilman), **Supp. XI:** 193, 209
Living off the Country: Essays on Poetry and Place (Haines), **Supp. XII:** 199, 203, 207
"Living on a Giant" (X. J. Kennedy), **Supp. XV:** 163
Living Out Loud (Quindlen), **Supp. XVII:** 166, **167–169**
Living Reed, The (Buck), **Supp. II Part 1:** 129–130
Livingston, Myra Cohn, **Supp. XV:** 153, 162
Living Theater, **Retro. Supp. I:** 424
"Living There" (Dickey), **Supp. IV Part 1:** 182–183
Living the Spirit: A Gay American Indian Anthology (Roscoe, ed.), **Supp. IV Part 1:** 330
"Living with a Peacock" (O'Connor), **III:** 350
"Livvie" (Welty), **IV:** 265; **Retro. Supp. I:** 348–349
"Livvie Is Back" (Welty), **Retro. Supp. I:** 351
Livy, **II:** 8
Lizzie (film), **Supp. IX:** 125
"Llantos de La Llorona: Warnings from the Wailer" (Mora), **Supp. XIII:** 217, 224
"L'Lapse" (Barthelme), **Supp. IV Part 1:** 45–47, 48
Lloyd, Henry Demarest, **Supp. I Part 1:** 5
Lloyd George, Harold, **I:** 490
"LMFBR" (Snyder), **Supp. VIII:** 302
"Loam" (Sandburg), **III:** 584–585
"Loan, The" (Malamud), **Supp. I Part 2:** 427, 428, 431, 437
Loberer, Eric, **Supp. XV:** 339
"Local" (McCarriston), **Supp. XIV:** 270
Local Color (Capote), **Supp. III Part 1:** 120
"Local Color" (London), **II:** 475
"Local Family Keeps Son Happy" (Keillor), **Supp. XVI:** 168, 169
"Local Girls" (Hoffman), **Supp. X:** 90
Local Girls (Hoffman), **Supp. X:** 77, **90–91,** 92
Local Men (Whitehead), **Supp. XV:** 339
Local Time (Dunn), **Supp. XI:** 143, **148–149**
Lock, Helen, **Supp. XIII:** 233, 237–238
Lock, Robert H., **IV:** 319; **Retro. Supp. I:** 375
Locke, Alain, **Retro. Supp. II:** 115; **Supp. I Part 1:** 323, 325, 341; **Supp. II Part 1:** 53, 176, 182, 228, 247; **Supp. IV Part 1:** 170; **Supp. IX:** 306, 309; **Supp. X:** 134, 137, 139; **Supp. XIV: 195–219; Supp. XVIII:** 122
Locke, Duane, **Supp. IX:** 273
Locke, John, **I:** 554–555, 557; **II:** 15–16, 113–114, 348–349, 480; **III:** 294–295; **IV:** 149; **Supp. I Part 1:** 130, 229, 230; **Supp. I Part 2:** 523
Locke, Sondra, **II:** 588
"Locked House, A" (Snodgrass), **Supp. VI:** 323
Locked Room, The (Auster), **Supp. XII:** 22, 24, **27–28**
Locket, The (Masters), **Supp. I Part 2:** 460
"Locksley Hall" (Tennyson), **Supp. IX:** 19
Lockwood Concern, The (O'Hara), **III:** 362, 364, 377–382
"Locus" (Ammons), **Supp. VII:** 28
"Locus" (Hayden), **Supp. II Part 1:** 361–362, 381
"Locusts, the Plaza, the Room, The" (Kees), **Supp. XV:** 141
Loden, Barbara, **III:** 163
Lodge, Henry Cabot, **I:** 11–12, 21
Lodge, Mrs. Henry Cabot, **I:** 11–12, 19
Lodge, Thomas, **IV:** 370
Loeb, Gerald, **Supp. IV Part 2:** 523
Loeb, Jacques, **I:** 513; **Retro. Supp. II:** 104; **Supp. I Part 2:** 641
Loeffler, Jack, **Supp. XIII:** 1, 3, 12, 14, 16
Lofty Dogmas (A. Finch, M. Kumin and D. Brown, eds.), **Supp. XVII:** 75–76
"Log" (Merrlll), **Supp. III Part 1:** 328
Logan, Rayford W., **Supp. II Part 1:** 171, 194; **Supp. XIV:** 73
Logan, William, **Supp. X:** 201, 213; **Supp. XI:** 131, 132; **Supp. XII:** 98, 107, 113, 184; **Supp. XV:** 212, 226, 251, 257, 260–261, 262,**Supp. XV:** 263, 266
Log Book of "The Loved One," The, **Supp. XI:** 306
Logenbach, James, **Supp. XVII:** 183
"Logging and Pimping and 'Your Pal, Jim'" (Maclean), **Supp. XIV:** 229
Logue, Christopher, **Supp. XIV:** 82
Lohengrin (Wagner), **I:** 216
Lohrfinck, Rosalind, **III:** 107, 117
Lolita (Nabokov), **III:** 246, 247, 255, 258–261; **Retro. Supp. I:** 263, 264, 265, 266, 269, 270, **272–274,** 275; **Supp. V:** 127, 252; **Supp. VIII:** 133; **Supp. XVI:** 294
"Lolita" (Parker), **Supp. IX:** 193
Lolly Dinks' Doings (E. Stoddard), **Supp. XV:** 273,**Supp. XV:** 286
Lombardi, Marilyn May, **Retro. Supp. II:** 40
London, Eliza, **II:** 465
London, Jack, **I:** 209; **II:** 264, 440, 444, 451, **462–485; III:** 314, 580; **Supp. IV Part 1:** 236; **Supp. IX:** 1, 14; **Supp. V:** 281; **Supp. XIII:** 312; **Supp. XIV:** 227; **Supp. XV:** 115; **Supp. XVI:** 181; **Supp. XVIII:** 90
London, John, **II:** 464, 465
London, Mrs. Jack (Bessie Maddern), **II:** 465, 466, 473, 478
London, Mrs. Jack (Charmian Kittredge), **II:** 466, 468, 473, 476, 478, 481
London, Scott, **Supp. XIV:** 301, 307, 311
London Embassy, The (Theroux), **Supp. VIII:** 323
London Fields (Amis), **Retro. Supp. I:** 278
"London Letter" (column; Eliot), **Supp. XV:** 306
London Magazine (Plath), **Supp. I Part 2:** 541

London Snow: A Christmas Story (Theroux), **Supp. VIII:** 322
London Suite (Simon), **Supp. IV Part 2:** 576, 581, 582, 588
London: The Biography (Ackroyd), **Supp. XVII:** 180
Lonely Are the Brave (film), **Supp. XIII:** 6
"Lonely Coast, A" (Proulx), **Supp. VII:** 264
Lonely Crusade (C. Himes), **Supp. XVI:** 135, 139–140
Lonely for the Future (Farrell), **II:** 46, 47
Lonely Impulse of Delight, A (Shanley), **Supp. XIV:** 317–318
"Lonely Street, The" (W. C. Williams), **IV:** 413
"Lonely Worker, A" (Jewett), **Retro. Supp. II:** 132
Lonergan, Wayne, **Supp. I Part 1:** 51
Lonesome Dove (McMurtry), **Supp. V:** 226–228, 231, 232, 233
Lonesome Traveler (Kerouac), **Supp. III Part 1:** 219, 225
"Lonesome Whistle Blowing" (Skow), **Supp. XVI:** 174
"Lone Striker, A" (Frost), **Retro. Supp. I:** 136, 137
Long, Ada, **Supp. V:** 178
Long, Haniel, **Supp. XV:** 46, 49
Long, Huey, **I:** 489; **II:** 454; **IV:** 249; **Supp. IV Part 2:** 679; **Supp. XIV:** 14
Long, Ray, **II:** 430; **III:** 54
Long after Midnight (Bradbury), **Supp. IV Part 1:** 102
Long Ago in France: The Years in Dijon (M. F. K. Fisher), **Supp. XVII:** 91
Long and Happy Life, A (Price), **Supp. VI:** 258, **259–260,** 262, 264, 265
Long Approach, The (Kumin), **Supp. IV Part 2:** 452–453, 453
Long Christmas Dinner, The (Wilder), **IV:** 357, 365; **Supp. V:** 105
Long Christmas Dinner and Other Plays (Wilder), **IV:** 365–366
Long Day's Dying, A (Buechner), **Supp. XII: 45–47**
Long Day's Journey into Night (O'Neill), **III:** 385, 401, 403–404; **Supp. IV Part 1:** 359; **Supp. XIV:** 327
Long Desire, A (Connell), **Supp. XIV:** 79, 80, 97
"Long Distance" (Stafford), **Supp. XI:** 329
"Long-Distance Runner, The" (Paley), **Supp. VI:** 221–222, 228, 230
Long Dream, The (Wright), **IV:** 478, 488, 494
"Long Embrace, The" (Levine), **Supp. V:** 187
"Long Enough" (Rukeyser), **Supp. VI:** 274
"Longest Night of My Life, The" (Nichols), **Supp. XIII:** 269
Longfellow, Henry Wadsworth, **I:** 458, 471; **II:** 274, 277, 295–296, 310, 313, 402, **486–510; III:** 269, 412, 421, 422, 577; **IV:** 309, 371; **Retro. Supp. I:** 54, 123, 150, 155, 362; **Retro. Supp. II: 153–174; Supp. I Part 1:** 158, 299, 306, 317, 362, 368; **Supp. I Part 2:** 405, 406, 408, 409, 414, 416, 420, 586, 587, 602, 699, 704; **Supp. II Part 1:** 291, 353; **Supp. III Part 2:** 609; **Supp. IV Part 1:** 165; **Supp. IV Part 2:** 503; **Supp. XII:** 260; **Supp. XIII:** 141; **Supp. XIV:** 120; **Supp. XVIII:** 4
"Long Feud" (Untermeyer), **Supp. XV:** 309
Long Feud: Selected Poems (Untermeyer), **Supp. XV:** 312
"Long Fourth, A" (Taylor), **Supp. V:** 313
Long Fourth and Other Stories, A (Taylor), **Supp. V:** 318–319
Long Gay Book, A (Stein), **IV:** 42
Long Goodbye, The (Chandler), **Supp. IV Part 1:** 120, 122, 132–134, 135
Long Goodbye, The (T. Williams), **IV:** 381
"Long Hair" (Snyder), **Supp. VIII:** 300
Longing for Home, The: Recollections and Reflections (Buechner), **Supp. XII:** 53
Longinus, Dionysius Cassius, **I:** 279
"Long-Legged House, The" (Berry), **Supp. X:** 21, 24–25, 27, 31
Long Live Man (Corso), **Supp. XII:** 129–130, 132
Long Love, The (Sedges), **Supp. II Part 1:** 125
Long Made Short (Dixon), **Supp. XII:** 152
Long March, The (Styron), **IV:** 97, 99, 104–107, 111, 113, 117
"Long Night, The" (Bambara), **Supp. XI:** 9
"Long Novel, A" (Ashbery), **Supp. III Part 1:** 6
Longo, Robert, **Supp. XVI:** 124
Long Patrol, The (Mailer), **III:** 46
"Long Point Light" (Doty), **Supp. XI:** 127
Long Road of Woman's Memory, The (Addams), **Supp. I Part 1:** 17–18
"Long Run, The" (Wharton), **IV:** 314
Long Season, The (Brosnan), **II:** 424, 425
"Long Shadow of Lincoln, The: A Litany" (Sandburg), **III:** 591, 593
Longshot O'Leary (McGrath), **Supp. X:** 117
"Long Shower, The" (Francis), **Supp. IX:** 90
"Long Stemmed Roses" (Jarman), **Supp. XVII:** 115
Longstreet, Augustus B., **II:** 70, 313; **Supp. I Part 1:** 352; **Supp. V:** 44; **Supp. X:** 227
"Long Summer" (Lowell), **II:** 553–554
"Long Term" (Dunn), **Supp. XI:** 149
Longtime Companion (film), **Supp. X:** 146, 152
Long Valley, The (Steinbeck), **IV:** 51
Long Voyage Home, The (O'Neill), **III:** 388
"Long Wail, A" (Crews), **Supp. XI:** 101
"Long Walk, The" (Bogan), **Supp. III Part 1:** 61
Long Walks and Intimate Talks (Paley), **Supp. VI:** 221
Long Way from Home, A (McKay), **Supp. X:** 132, 140
Lönnrot, Elias, **Retro. Supp. II:** 159
Looby, Christopher, **Supp. XIII:** 96
Look, Stranger! (Auden), **Supp. II Part 1:** 11
"Look, The" (Olds), **Supp. X:** 210
Look at the Harlequins (Nabokov), **Retro. Supp. I:** 266, 270
"Look for My White Self" (Ammons), **Supp. VII:** 25
Look Homeward, Angel (Wolfe), **II:** 457; **IV:** 450, 452, 453, 454, 455–456, 461, 462, 463, 464, 468, 471; **Supp. XI:** 216
"Looking" (Sanders), **Supp. XVI:** 277
"Looking a Mad Dog Dead in the Eyes" (Komunyakaa), **Supp. XIII:** 114
"Looking at Each Other" (Rukeyser), **Supp. VI:** 280, 285–286
"Looking at Kafka" (P. Roth), **Supp. III Part 2:** 402
"Looking at Women" (Sanders), **Supp. XVI:** 274
"Looking Back" (Harjo), **Supp. XII:** 218
"Looking Back" (Merwin), **Supp. III Part 1:** 352
"Looking Back at Girlhood" (Jewett), **Retro. Supp. II:** 131, 133
Looking Backward (Bellamy), **II:** 276; **Supp. I Part 2:** 641; **Supp. XI:** 200
"Looking for a Ship" (McPhee), **Supp. III Part 1:** 312–313
"Looking for Dragon Smoke" (R. Bly), **Supp. IV Part 1:** 60
Looking for Holes in the Ceiling (Dunn), **Supp. XI:** 139, **143–145**
Looking for Langston (Julien; film), **Supp. XI:** 19, 20
Looking for Luck (Kumin), **Supp. IV Part 2:** 453, 454–455
"Looking for Mr. Green" (Bellow), **Retro. Supp. II:** 27
"Looking for the Buckhead Boys" (Dickey), **Supp. IV Part 1:** 182, 183
"Looking Forward to Age" (Harrison), **Supp. VIII:** 49
"Looking from Inside My Body" (R. Bly), **Supp. IV Part 1:** 71
"Looking Glass, The" (Wharton), **Retro. Supp. I:** 382
"Lookout's Journal" (Snyder), **Supp. VIII:** 291
"Looks Like They'll Never Learn" (McCoy), **Supp. XIII:** 166
"Look to Thy Heart ..." (Hay), **Supp. XIV:** 130
Loon, Hendrik Willem van, **Supp. XVI:** 185
Loon Lake (Doctorow), **Supp. IV Part 1:** 219, 222, 224–227, 230, 231, 232, 233
"Loon Point" (O'Brien), **Supp. V:** 237
Loos, Adolf, **Supp. XVI:** 187
Loos, Anita, **Supp. XVI: 181–199**
Loos, Mary Anita, **Supp. XVI:** 196
"Loosestrife" (Dunn), **Supp. XI:** 154
Loosestrife (Dunn), **Supp. XI: 152–154**
"Loose Woman" (X. J. Kennedy), **Supp. XV:** 159

Loose Woman: Poems (Cisneros), **Supp. VII:** 58, 71–72
Lopate, Edward, **Supp. XVI:** 266
Lopate, Philip, **Supp. XII:** 184; **Supp. XIII:** 280–281; **Supp. XVI:** 230
Lopatnikoff, Nikolai, **Supp. XIV:** 123
Lopez, Barry, **Supp. IV Part 1:** 416; **Supp. V:** 211; **Supp. X:** 29, 31; **Supp. XIII:** 16; **Supp. XIV:** 227
Lopez, Rafael, **Supp. IV Part 2:** 602
Lorax, The (Geisel), **Supp. XVI:** 109–110
Lorca, Federico García, **IV:** 380; **Supp. I Part 1:** 345; **Supp. IV Part 1:** 83; **Supp. VIII:** 38, 39; **Supp. XIII:** 315, 323, 324; **Supp. XV:** 186
Lord, Judge Otis P., **I:** 454, 457, 458, 470
Lorde, Audre, **Supp. I Part 2:** 550, 571; **Supp. IV Part 1:** 325; **Supp. XI:** 20; **Supp. XII:** 217, 220; **Supp. XIII:** 295; **Supp. XVII:** 71
Lord Jim (Conrad), **I:** 422; **II:** 26; **Retro. Supp. II:** 292; **Supp. I Part 2:** 623; **Supp. IV Part 2:** 680; **Supp. V:** 251
"Lord of Hosts" (Pinsky), **Supp. VI:** 244
Lord of the Flies (W. Golding), **Supp. XVI:** 65
Lord of the Rings (Tolkien), **Supp. V:** 140
Lords of Misrule, The (X. J. Kennedy), **Supp. XV:** 154, **170–171**
Lords of the Housetops (Van Vechten), **Supp. II Part 2:** 736
Lord's Prayer, **I:** 579
Lord Timothy Dexter of Newburyport, Mass. (Marquand), **III:** 55
Lord Weary's Castle (Lowell), **II:** 538, 542–551; **Retro. Supp. II:** 178, **186–187**, 188; **Supp. XV:** 252
"Lorelei" (Plath), **Retro. Supp. II:** 246; **Supp. I Part 2:** 538
"Lorenzo" (Bynner), **Supp. XV:** 46, 50
Lorimer, George Horace, **II:** 430; **Retro. Supp. I:** 101, 113
Lorre, Peter, **Supp. IV Part 1:** 356
"Los Alamos" (Momaday), **Supp. IV Part 2:** 482
"Los Angeles, 1980" (Gunn Allen), **Supp. IV Part 1:** 325
"Los Angeles Days" (Didion), **Supp. IV Part 1:** 211
"Loser, The" (Talese), **Supp. XVII:** 202, 208
Loser and Still Champion: Muhammad Ali (Schulberg), **Supp. XVIII:** 254
Losey, Joseph, **IV:** 383
"Losing a Language" (Merwin), **Supp. III Part 1:** 356
Losing Battles (Welty), **IV:** 261, 281–282; **Retro. Supp. I:** 341, 352, **353–354**
"Losing the Marbles" (Merrill), **Supp. III Part 1:** 337
"Losing Track of Language" (Clampitt), **Supp. IX:** 38, 40
"Losses" (Jarrell), **II:** 375–376
Losses (Jarrell), **II:** 367, 372, 373–375, 376, 377, 380–381
Lossky, N. O., **Supp. IV Part 2:** 519
"Loss of Breath" (Poe), **III:** 425–426
"Loss of My Arms and Legs, The" (Kingsolver), **Supp. VII:** 208
"Loss of the Creature, The" (Percy), **Supp. III Part 1:** 387
"Lost" (Wagoner), **Supp. IX:** 328
"Lost, The/Los Perdidos" (Kingsolver), **Supp. VII:** 208
"Lost and Found" (Levine), **Supp. V:** 188
"Lost and Found" (Nelson), **Supp. XVIII:** 176
"Lost Bodies" (Wright), **Supp. V:** 342
"Lost Boy, The" (Wolfe), **IV:** 451, 460, 466–467
"Lost Decade, The" (Fitzgerald), **II:** 98
Lost Galleon and Other Tales, The (Harte), **Supp. II Part 1:** 344
Lost Get-Back Boogie, The (Burke), **Supp. XIV:** 22, 25
"Lost Girls, The" (Hogan), **Supp. IV Part 1:** 406–407
Lost Grizzlies, The: A Search for Survivors in the Wilderness of Colorado (Bass), **Supp. XVI:** 25, 26
Lost Highway (film), **Supp. X:** 314
Lost Illusions (Balzac), **I:** 500
"Lost in Nostalgia: The Autobiographies of Eva Hoffman and Richard Rodriguez" (Fachinger), **Supp. XVI:** 153
Lost in the Bonewheel Factory (Komunyakaa), **Supp. XIII: 114–115,** 116
Lost in the Cosmos: The Last Self-Help Book (Percy), **Supp. III Part 1:** 397
Lost in the Funhouse (Barth), **I:** 122, 135, 139; **Supp. X:** 307
"Lost in the Whichy Thicket" (Wolfe), **Supp. III Part 2:** 573, 574
Lost in Translation (E. Hoffman), **Supp. XVI:** 147, **148–151**, 153, 154, 159
"Lost in Translation" (Hass), **Supp. VIII:** 28
"Lost in Translation" (Merrill), **Supp. III Part 1:** 324, 329–330
Lost in Yonkers (film), **Supp. IV Part 2:** 588
Lost in Yonkers (Simon), **Supp. IV Part 2:** 576, 577, 584, 587–588, 590–591
"Lost Jerusalem" (Untermeyer), **Supp. XV:** 307
Lost Lady, A (Cather), **I:** 323–325, 327; **Retro. Supp. I: 15–16,** 20, 21, 382
"Lost Lover, A" (Jewett), **II:** 400–401, 402; **Retro. Supp. II:** 137
"Lost Loves" (Kinnell), **Supp. III Part 1:** 237, 245
Lost Man's River (Matthiessen), **Supp. V:** 212, 213, 214, 215
"Lost on September Trail, 1967" (Ríos), **Supp. IV Part 2:** 540
Lost Puritan (Mariani), **Retro. Supp. II:** 189
Lost Roads Project, The: A Walk-In Book of Arkansas (exhibition; Wright and Luster), **Supp. XV:** 337, 348
"Lost Sailor, The" (Freneau), **Supp. II Part 1:** 264
"Lost Son, The" (Roethke), **III:** 536, 537–539, 542
Lost Son, The (Roethke), **III:** 529, 530–532, 533
"Lost Sons" (Salter), **Supp. IX:** 260
Lost Souls (Singer). *See* Meshugah (Singer)
Lost Weekend, The (Jackson), **Supp. XIII:** 262
"Lost World, A" (Ashbery), **Supp. III Part 1:** 9
"Lost World, The" (Chabon), **Supp. XI:** 72–73
Lost World, The (Jarrell), **II:** 367, 368, 371, 379–380, 386, 387
"Lost World, The" cycle (Chabon), **Supp. XI: 71–73**
"Lost World of Richard Yates, The: How the Great Writer of the Age of Anxiety Disappeared from Print" (O'Nan), **Supp. XI:** 348
"Lost Young Intellectual, The" (Howe), **Supp. VI:** 113, **115–116**
Lost Zoo, The: (A Rhyme for the Young, But Not Too Young) (Cullen), **Supp. IV Part 1:** 173
Loti, Pierre, **II:** 311, 325; **Supp. IV Part 1:** 81
"Lot of People Bathing in a Stream, A" (Stevens), **IV:** 93
Lotringer, Sylvère, **Supp. XII:** 4
"Lot's Wife" (Nemerov), **III:** 270
"Lottery, The" (Jackson), **Supp. IX:** 113, 114, 118, 120, **122–123**
Lottery, The; or, The Adventures of James Harris (Jackson), **Supp. IX:** 113, 115, 116, 124, 125
Lotze, Hermann, **III:** 600
Loud and Clear (Quindlen), **Supp. XVII:** 167, **170–172**
"Louie, His Cousin & His Other Cousin" (Cisneros), **Supp. VII:** 60
Louis, Joe, **II:** 589; **Supp. IV Part 1:** 360
Louis, Pierre Charles Alexandre, **Supp. I Part 1:** 302, 303
"Louisa, Please Come Home" (Jackson), **Supp. IX:** 122
Louis Lambert (Balzac), **I:** 499
"Louis Simpson and Walt Whitman: Destroying the Teacher" (Lazer), **Supp. IX:** 265
"Louis Zukofsky: *All: The Collected Short Poems, 1923–1958*" (Creeley), **Supp. IV Part 1:** 154
"Lounge" (Francis), **Supp. IX:** 83
Lounsberry, Barbara, **Supp. XVII:** 208
Lounsbury, Thomas R., **I:** 335
Louter, Jan, **Supp. XI:** 173
"Love" (Olson), **Supp. II Part 2:** 571
"Love" (Paley), **Supp. VI:** 219, 222, 230
Love, Deborah, **Supp. V:** 208, 210
Love Alone: 18 Elegies for Rog (Monette), **Supp. X:** 146, 154
Love Always (Beattie), **Supp. V:** 29, 30, 35
Love among the Cannibals (Morris), **III:** 228, 230–231
"Love Among the Ruins" (Mosley), **Supp. XIII:** 247
Love and Death (film; Allen), **Supp. XV:** 2, **5–6,** 7, 11
Love and Death in the American Novel (Fiedler), **Supp. XIII:** 93, 96, **99–101,** 104

Love and Exile (Singer), **Retro. Supp. II: 302–304,** 315
Love and Fame (Berryman), **I:** 170
Love and Friendship (Bloom), **Retro. Supp. II:** 31, 33–34
"Love and How to Cure It" (Wilder), **IV:** 365
Love and Scorn: New and Selected Poems (C. Frost), **Supp. XV:** 95, 96, 100, 103–105, 106
Love and Theft (album, Dylan), **Supp. XVIII:** 28, 31
"Love and the Hate, The" (Jeffers), **Supp. II Part 2:** 434–435
Love and Will (Dixon), **Supp. XII:** 148, 149
Love and Work (Price), **Supp. VI:** 261
"Love Calls Us to the Things of This World" (Wilbur), **Supp. III Part 2:** 544, 552–553
Love Course, The (Gurney), **Supp. V:** 98
Loved One, The (film), **Supp. XI: 305–306,** 307
Loved One, The (Waugh), **Supp. XI:** 305
Love Expert, The (film; Kirkland), **Supp. XVI:** 186
Love Feast (Buechner), **Supp. XII:** 52
Love for Love (Congreve), **Supp. XVIII:** 12
"Love Fossil" (Olds), **Supp. X:** 203
Love in Buffalo (Gurney), **Supp. V:** 96
"Love——In Other Words" (Lee), **Supp. VIII:** 113
"Love in the Air" (Jin), **Supp. XVIII:** 93–94
"Love in the Morning" (Dubus), **Supp. VII:** 91
Love in the Ruins: The Adventures of a Bad Catholic at a Time near the End of the World (Percy), **Supp. III Part 1:** 385, 387, 393–394, 397–398
Love in the Western World (de Rougemont), **Retro. Supp. I:** 328
"Love Is a Deep and a Dark and a Lonely" (Sandburg), **III:** 595
Lovejoy, Elijah P., **Supp. I Part 2:** 588
Lovejoy, Owen R., **Supp. I Part 1:** 8
Lovejoy, Thomas, **Supp. X:** 108
Lovelace, Richard, **II:** 590
"Love Letter (Schnackenberg), **Supp. XV:** 258–259
Love Letters (film), **Supp. IV Part 2:** 524
Love Letters (Gurney), **Supp. V:** 105, 108–109
Love Letters, The (Massie), **Supp. IV Part 2:** 524
Love Letters and Two Other Plays: The Golden Age and *What I Did Last Summer* (Gurney), **Supp. V:** 100
"Love Lies Sleeping"(Bishop), **Retro. Supp. II:** 42
"Love Life"(Mason), **Supp. VIII: 145–146**
Love Life (Mason), **Supp. VIII:** 145–146
Lovell, Julia, **Supp. XVIII:** 101
"Lovely Lady, The"(Lawrence), **Supp. I Part 1:** 329
Lovely Lady, The (Lawrence), **Retro. Supp. I:** 203
Love Me (Keillor), **Supp. XVI:** 178
Love Medicine (Erdrich), **Supp. IV Part 1:** 259, 260, 261, 263, 265, 266, 267–268, 270, 271, 274–275; **Supp. X:** 290
Love Medicine (expanded version) (Erdrich), **Supp. IV Part 1:** 263, 273, 274, 275
"Love Minus Zero/No Limit"(song, Dylan), **Supp. XVIII:** 31
"Love Nest, The"(Lardner), **II:** 427, 429
Love Nest, The, and Other Stories (Lardner), **II:** 430–431, 436
Lovenheim, Barbara, **Supp. X:** 169
"Love of Elsie Barton: A Chronicle, The"(Warren), **IV:** 253
Love of Landry, The (Dunbar), **Supp. II Part 1:** 212
"Love of Morning, The"(Levertov), **Supp. III Part 1:** 284
Love of the Last Tycoon, The: A Western. See Last Tycoon, The
"Love on the Bon Dieu"(Chopin), **Supp. I Part 1:** 213
Love Poems (Sexton), **Supp. II Part 2:** 687–689
Love Poems of May Swenson, The (Swenson), **Supp. IV Part 2:** 652, 653
"Love Poet"(Agee), **I:** 28
"Lover"(Hoffman), **Supp. XVIII:** 87
"Love Ritual"(Mora), **Supp. XIII:** 215
Loveroot (Jong), **Supp. V:** 115, 130
"Lovers, The"(Berryman), **I:** 174
"Lovers, The"(Buck), **Supp. II Part 1:** 128
"Lover's Garden, A" (Ginsberg), **Supp. II Part 1:** 311
"Lovers of the Poor, The" (Brooks), **Supp. III Part 1:** 81, 85
Lovers Should Marry (Martin), **Supp. IV Part 1:** 351
"Lover's Song" (Yeats), **Supp. I Part 1:** 80
"Love Rushes By" (Salinas), **Supp. XIII:** 326–327
"Love's Ghost" (Nelson), **Supp. XVIII:** 176
Lovesick (Stern), **Supp. IX: 295–296**
Love's Labour's Lost (Shakespeare), **III:** 263
Love's Old Sweet Song (Saroyan), **Supp. IV Part 1:** 83
"Love Song of J. Alfred Prufrock, The" (Eliot), **I:** 52, 66, 569–570; **III:** 460; **Retro. Supp. I:** 55, 56, 57, 60; **Supp. II Part 1:** 5; **Supp. XIII:** 346
"Lovesong of J. Alfred Prufrock, The" (T. S. Eliot), **Supp. XVI:** 150
"Love Song of St. Sebastian" (Eliot), **Retro. Supp. I:** 57
Love's Pilgrimage (Sinclair), **Supp. V:** 286
"Love the Wild Swan" (Jeffers), **Supp. VIII:** 33
Love to Mamá: A Tribute to Mothers (Mora, ed.), **Supp. XIII:** 221
Lovett, Robert Morss, **II:** 43
"Love-Unknown" (Herbert), **Supp. I Part 1:** 80
Love! Valor! Compassion! (film), **Supp. XIII:** 206
Love! Valour! Compassion! (McNally), **Supp. XIII:** 199, **203–204,** 208, 209
"Love *versus* Law" (Stowe), **Supp. I Part 2:** 585–586
Love with a Few Hairs (Mrabet), **Supp. IV Part 1:** 92
Loving a Woman in Two Worlds (R. Bly), **Supp. IV Part 1:** 66, 67, 68–69, 71, 72
"Loving Shepherdess, The" (Jeffers), **Supp. II Part 2:** 432
"Loving the Killer" (Sexton), **Supp. II Part 2:** 688
Lovin' Molly (film), **Supp. V:** 223, 226
Lowe, John, **Supp. XIII:** 238
Lowe, Pardee, **Supp. X:** 291
Lowell, Abbott Lawrence, **I:** 487; **II:** 513; **Supp. I Part 2:** 483
Lowell, Amy, **I:** 231, 384, 405, 475, 487; **II:** 174, **511–533,** 534; **III:** 465, 581, 586; **Retro. Supp. I:** 131, 133, 288; **Retro. Supp. II:** 46, 175; **Supp. I Part 1:** 257–259, 261–263, 265, 266; **Supp. I Part 2:** 465, 466, 707, 714, 729; **Supp. XIV:** 128; **Supp. XV:** 43, 293, 295, 297, 298, 299, 300, 301, 303, 306
Lowell, Blanche, **Supp. I Part 2:** 409
Lowell, Harriet, **II:** 553, 554
Lowell, James Russell, **I:** 216, 458; **II:** 273, 274, 289, 302, 320, 402, 529, 530, 532, 534, 551; **III:** 409; **IV:** 129, 171, 175, 180, 182–183, 186; **Retro. Supp. I:** 228; **Retro. Supp. II:** 155, 175, 326; **Supp. I Part 1:** 168, 299, 300, 303, 306, 311, 312, 317, 318, 362; **Supp. I Part 2: 404–426; Supp. II Part 1:** 197, 291, 352; **Supp. XV:** 278, 279; **Supp. XVI:** 84; **Supp. XVIII:** 2–3, 4, 8, 12
Lowell, Mrs. James Russell (Maria White), **Supp. I Part 2:** 405, 406, 414, 424
Lowell, Percival, **II:** 513, 525, 534
Lowell, Robert, **I:** 172, 381, 382, 400, 442, 521, 544–545, 550; **II:** 371, 376, 377, 384, 386–387, 532, **534–557; III:** 39, 44, 142, 508, 527, 528–529, 606; **IV:** 120, 138, 402, 430; **Retro. Supp. I:** 67, 140, 411; **Retro. Supp. II:** 27, 40, 44, 46, 48, 50, **175–193,** 221, 228–229, 235, 245; **Supp. I Part 1:** 89; **Supp. I Part 2:** 538, 543, 554; **Supp. III Part 1:** 6, 64, 84, 138, 147, 193, 194, 197–202, 205–208; **Supp. III Part 2:** 541, 543, 555, 561, 599; **Supp. IV Part 2:** 439, 620, 637; **Supp. IX:** 325; **Supp. V:** 81, 179, 180, 315–316, 337, 344; **Supp. VIII:** 27, 100, 271; **Supp. X:** 53, 58; **Supp. XI:** 146, 240, 244, 250, 317; **Supp. XII:** 253–254, 255; **Supp. XIII:** 76; **Supp. XIV:** 15, 126, 269; **Supp. XV:** 20, 22, 93, 184, 249, 251, 253, 340; **Supp. XVII:** 239
Lowell, Rose, **Supp. I Part 2:** 409
"Lowell in the Classrom" (Vendler), **Retro. Supp. II:** 191
Lowenthal, Michael, **Supp. XII:** 82
Lower Depths, The (Gorki), **III:** 402

"Lower the Standard" (Shapiro), **Supp. II Part 2:** 715
Lowes, John Livingston, **II:** 512, 516, 532; **IV:** 453, 455
Lowin, Joseph, **Supp. V:** 273
"Low-Lands" (Pynchon), **Supp. II Part 2:** 620, 624
Lowle, Percival, **Supp. I Part 2:** 404
Lownsbrough, John, **Supp. IV Part 1:** 209, 211
Lowry, Malcolm, **Supp. XVII:** 135, 136
Lowth, Richard, **II:** 8
Loy, Mina, **III:** 194
Loy, Myrna, **Supp. IV Part 1:** 355
"Loyal Woman's No, A" (Larcom), **Supp. XIII:** 142, 143–144
"Luani of the Jungle" (Hughes), **Supp. I Part 1:** 328
Lubbock, Percy, **I:** 504; **II:** 337; **IV:** 308, 314, 319, 322; **Retro. Supp. I:** 366, 367, 373; **Supp. VIII:** 165
Lubin, Isidor, **Supp. I Part 2:** 632
Lubow, Arthur, **Supp. VIII:** 310
Lucas, Victoria (pseudonym). *See* Plath, Sylvia
Luce, Dianne C., **Supp. VIII:** 189
Lucid, Robert F., **Retro. Supp. II:** 195, 204
"Lucid Eye in Silver Town, The" (Updike), **IV:** 218
"Lucid Walking" (A. Finch), **Supp. XVII:** 72
"Lucinda Matlock" (Masters), **Supp. I Part 2:** 461, 465
"Luck" (Dunn), **Supp. XI:** 149
Luck of Barry Lyndon, The (Thackeray), **II:** 290
"Luck of Roaring Camp, The" (Harte), **Supp. II Part 1:** 335, 344, 345–347
"Luck of the Bogans, The" (Jewett), **Retro. Supp. II:** 142
Lucky Life (Stern), **Supp. IX: 290–291**
Lucretius, **I:** 59; **II:** 162, 163; **III:** 600, 610–611, 612; **Supp. I Part 1:** 363
Lucy (Kincaid), **Supp. VII:** 180, 185, 186, 187–188, 194
Lucy, Saint, **II:** 211
Lucy Gayheart (Cather), **I:** 331; **Retro. Supp. I:** 19
"Lucy Tavish's Journey" (E. Stoddard), **Supp. XV:** 286
Lucy Temple (Rowson). *See Charlotte's Daughter; or, The Three Orphans*
Ludlow, Andrea, **Supp. XVIII:** 90
Ludvigson, Susan, **Supp. IV Part 2:** 442, 446, 447, 448, 451
Lueders, Edward, **Supp. XVI:** 265
"Luggage" (Bidart), **Supp. XV:** 35
Luhan, Mabel Dodge, **Retro. Supp. I:** 7; **Supp. XV:** 46, 50
Lu Ji, **Supp. VIII:** 303
Luke (biblical book), **III:** 606
"Luke Havergal" (E. A. Robinson), **Supp. XVII:** 69
"Luke Havergal" (Robinson), **III:** 524
Lukeman, Gary, **Supp. XV:** 221
Luks, George, **IV:** 411; **Retro. Supp. II:** 103
"Lullaby" (Auden), **Supp. II Part 1:** 9
"Lullaby" (Bishop), **Supp. I Part 1:** 85
"Lullaby" (Everwine), **Supp. XV:** 89
"Lullaby" (Silko), **Supp. IV Part 2:** 560, 568–569
"Lullaby for Amy" (Jarman), **Supp. XVII:** 113, 121
"Lullaby of Cape Cod" (Brodsky), **Supp. VIII:** 27–28
Lullaby Raft (Nye), **Supp. XIII:** 278
Lullaby Raft (Nye, album), **Supp. XIII:** 274
Lullaby: The Comforting of Cock Robin (Snodgrass), **Supp. VI:** 324
"Lulls" (Walker), **Supp. III Part 2:** 525
"Lulu" (Wedekind), **Supp. XII:** 14
Lulu on the Bridge (film), **Supp. XII:** 21
Lulu's Library (Alcott), **Supp. I Part 1:** 43
"Lumber" (Baker), **Supp. XIII:** 55, 56
"Lumens, The" (Olds), **Supp. X:** 209
Lume Spento, A (Pound), **III:** 470
Lumet, Sidney, **Supp. IV Part 1:** 236; **Supp. IX:** 253
Luminous Debris: Reflecting on Vestige in Provence and Languedoc (Sobin), **Supp. XVI: 291–293,** 293–294
"Lumumba's Grave" (Hughes), **Supp. I Part 1:** 344
"Luna, Luna" (Mora), **Supp. XIII:** 217
Lupercal (Hughes), **Retro. Supp. II:** 245; **Supp. I Part 2:** 540
Lupton, Mary Jane, **Supp. IV Part 1:** 7
Luria, Isaac, **IV:** 7
Lurie, Alison, **Supp. X:** 166; **Supp. XVI:** 103, 111–112
Lust and Other Stories (Minot), **Supp. VI:** 205
Luster, Deborah, **Supp. XV:** 337,**Supp. XV:** 353, 348, 349, 350
Lustgarten, Edith, **III:** 107
Lustra (Pound), **Retro. Supp. I:** 289, 290
Luther, Martin, **II:** 11–12, 506; **III:** 306, 607; **IV:** 490
"Luther on Sweet Auburn" (Bambara), **Supp. XI:** 16–17
Lux, Thomas, **Supp. XI:** 270
Luxury Girl, The (McCoy), **Supp. XIII:** 163
Lyall, Sarah, **Supp. XIII:** 247
Lycidas (Milton), **II:** 540; **IV:** 347; **Retro. Supp. I:** 60; **Retro. Supp. II:** 186; **Supp. I Part 1:** 370; **Supp. IX:** 41
Lycographia (Paullini), **Supp. XVII:** 55
"Lydia and Marian" (Rowson), **Supp. XV:** 234
Lydon, Susan, **Supp. XII:** 170
Lyell, Charles, **Supp. IX:** 180
Lyell, Frank H., **Supp. VIII:** 125
Lyford, Harry, **Supp. I Part 2:** 679
"Lying" (Wilbur), **Supp. III Part 2:** 547, 562
"Lying and Looking" (Swenson), **Supp. IV Part 2:** 652
"Lying in a Hammock at William Duffy's Farm in Pine Island, Minnesota" (Wright), **Supp. III Part 2:** 589, 599, 600
"Lying in the Pollen and Water" (C. Frost), **Supp. XV:** 96
Lying Ladies, The (Ryan as Finnegan), **Supp. XVIII: 233–235,** 237
Lyles, Lois F., **Supp. XI:** 7, 8
Lyly, John, **III:** 536; **Supp. I Part 1:** 369
Lynch, Anne, **Supp. XV:** 273
Lynch, Doris, **Supp. XVI:** 294
Lynchburg (Gander), **Supp. XV:** 340
"Lynched Man, The" (Karr), **Supp. XI:** 241
Lynchers, The (Wideman), **Supp. X:** 320
"Lynching, The" (McKay), **Supp. I Part 1:** 63
"Lynching of Jube Benson, The" (Dunbar), **Supp. II Part 1:** 214
"Lynching Song" (Hughes), **Supp. I Part 1:** 331
Lynd, Staughton, **Supp. VIII:** 240
Lynn, Kenneth, **Supp. XIII:** 96–97
Lynn, Kenneth S., **Supp. XIV:** 103
Lynn, Vera, **Supp. XI:** 304
Lyon, Kate, **I:** 409; **II:** 138, 143, 144
Lyon, Thomas, **Supp. IX:** 175
"Lyonnesse" (Plath), **Supp. I Part 2:** 541
Lyons, Bonnie, **Supp. V:** 58; **Supp. VIII:** 138
Lyotard, Jean-François, **Supp. IV Part 1:** 54
Lyrical Ballads (Wordsworth), **III:** 583; **IV:** 120; **Supp. IX:** 274; **Supp. XI:** 243; **Supp. XV:** 21
Lyrics of Love and Laughter (Dunbar), **Supp. II Part 1:** 207
Lyrics of Lowly Life (Dunbar), **Supp. II Part 1:** 197, 199, 200, 207
Lyrics of the Hearthside (Dunbar), **Supp. II Part 1:** 206
Lytal, Tammy, **Supp. XI:** 102
Lytle, Andrew, **IV:** 125; **Retro. Supp. II:** 220, 221, 235; **Supp. II Part 1:** 139; **Supp. X:** 1, 25; **Supp. XI:** 101
Lytton of Knebworth. *See* Bulwer-Lytton, Edward George

M

Mabie, Hamilton W., **Supp. XVIII:** 257
McAlexander, Hubert H., **Supp. V:** 314, 319, 320, 323
McAlmon, Mrs. Robert (Winifred Ellerman), **III:** 194. *See also* Ellerman, Winifred
McAlmon, Robert, **IV:** 404; **Retro. Supp. I:** 418, 419, 420; **Retro. Supp. II:** 328; **Supp. I Part 1:** 259; **Supp. III Part 2:** 614
McAninch, Jerry, **Supp. XI:** 297, 298
Macaulay, Catherine, **Supp. I Part 2:** 522
Macaulay, Rose, **Supp. XII:** 88; **Supp. XIV:** 348
Macaulay, Thomas, **II:** 15–16; **III:** 113, 591–592
Macauley, Robie, **Retro. Supp. II:** 228; **Supp. X:** 56
Macbeth (Shakespeare), **I:** 271; **IV:** 227; **Retro. Supp. I:** 131; **Supp. I Part 1:** 67; **Supp. I Part 2:** 457; **Supp. IV Part 1:** 87; **Supp. XIV:** 8
Macbeth (silent film), **Supp. XVI:** 184
MacBeth, George, **Retro. Supp. II:** 250
McCafferty, Larry, **Supp. XVII:** 227

McCaffery, Larry, **Supp. IV Part 1:** 217, 227, 234; **Supp. V:** 53, 238; **Supp. VIII:** 13, 14; **Supp. X:** 260, 268, 301, 303, 307; **Supp. XVI:** 117
McCarriston, Linda, **Supp. X:** 204; **Supp. XIV: 259–275**
McCarthy, Charles Joseph, Jr. *See* McCarthy, Cormac
McCarthy, Cormac, **Supp. VIII: 175–192; Supp. XII:** 310; **Supp. XVII:** 185
McCarthy, Eugene, **Retro. Supp. II:** 182
McCarthy, Joseph, **I:** 31, 492; **II:** 562, 568; **Supp. I Part 1:** 294, 295; **Supp. I Part 2:** 444, 611, 612, 620; **Supp. XV:** 198, 311–312
McCarthy, Mary, **II: 558–584; Supp. I Part 1:** 84; **Supp. IV Part 1:** 209, 297, 310; **Supp. VIII:** 96, 99, 100; **Supp. X:** 177; **Supp. XI:** 246; **Supp. XIV:** 3; **Supp. XV:** 142; **Supp. XVI:** 64, 70; **Supp. XVII:** 43
McCay, Maura, **Supp. XII:** 271, 276
McClanahan, Ed, **Supp. X:** 24
McClanahan, Thomas, **Supp. XII:** 125–126
McClatchy, J. D., **Supp. XII: 253–270; Supp. XV:** 185, 257, 258
McClellan, John L., **I:** 493
McClung, Isabelle, **Retro. Supp. I:** 5
McClure, John, **Retro. Supp. I:** 80
McClure, Michael, **Supp. II Part 1:** 32; **Supp. VIII:** 289; **Supp. XVI:** 283
McClure, S. S., **I:** 313; **II:** 465; **III:** 327; **Retro. Supp. I:** 5, 6, 9; **Supp. XV:** 40
McCombs, Judith, **Supp. XIII:** 33
McConagha, Alan, **Supp. XVI:** 166
McConnell, Frank, **Supp. X:** 260, 274
McCorkle, Jill, **Supp. X:** 6
McCourt, Frank, **Supp. XII: 271–287**
McCoy, Horace, **Supp. XIII: 159–177**
McCracken, Elizabeth, **Supp. X:** 86; **Supp. XII:** 310, 315–316, 321
McCrae, Fiona, **Supp. XVIII:** 60, 62
McCullers, Carson, **I:** 113, 190, 211; **II: 585–608; IV:** 282, 384, 385, 386; **Retro. Supp. II:** 324; **Supp. II Part 1:** 17; **Supp. IV Part 1:** 31, 84; **Supp. IV Part 2:** 502; **Supp. VIII:** 124; **Supp. XII:** 309; **Supp. XIV:** 120; **Supp. XV:** 338
McCullers, Reeves, **III:** 585, 586, 587
McDavid, Raven I., **III:** 120; **Supp. XIV:** 14
McDermott, Alice, **Supp. XII:** 311; **Supp. XVIII: 155–169**
McDermott, John J., **II:** 364
MacDiarmid, Hugh, **Supp. X:** 112
Macdonald, C. G., **Supp. XVII:** 73–74
Macdonald, Dwight, **I:** 233, 372, 379; **III:** 39; **Supp. V:** 265; **Supp. XIV:** 340; **Supp. XV:** 140
McDonald, E. J., **Supp. I Part 2:** 670
Macdonald, George, **Supp. XIII:** 75
MacDonald, Jeanette, **II:** 589
Macdonald, Ross, **Supp. IV Part 1:** 116, 136; **Supp. IV Part 2: 459–477; Supp. XIII:** 233; **Supp. XVIII:** 137,136
MacDonald, Ruth K., **Supp. XVI:** 102
MacDougall, Ruth Doan, **Supp. XV:** 58; **Supp. XVI:** 174
MacDowell, Edward, **I:** 228; **III:** 504, 508, 524
McDowell, Frederick P. W., **II:** 194
McDowell, Mary, **Supp. I Part 1:** 5
McDowell, Robert, **Supp. IX:** 266, 270, 276, 279
MacDowell, Robert, **Supp. XI:** 249
McDowell, Robert, **Supp. XVII:** 109, 110, 111
McDowell. Deborah, **Supp. XVIII:** 125, 129
McElderry, Margaret K., **Supp. XV:** 162
McElrath, Joseph, **Supp. XIV:** 62
McElroy, Joseph, **Supp. IV Part 1:** 279, 285
McEuen, Kathryn, **II:** 20
McEwen, Arthur, **I:** 206
McFarland, Ron, **Supp. IX:** 323, 327, 328, 333
McGann, Jerome, **Retro. Supp. I:** 47
McGill, Meredith, **Supp. XVIII:** 17
McGillis, Ian, **Supp. XVIII:** 150
MacGillivray, William, **Supp. XVI:** 8
McGovern, Edythe M., **Supp. IV Part 2:** 573, 582, 585
McGovern, George, **III:** 46
MacGowan, Christopher, **Retro. Supp. I:** 430
MacGowan, Kenneth, **III:** 387, 391
McGrath, Douglas, **Supp. XV:** 12
McGrath, Joseph, **Supp. XI:** 307, 309
McGrath, Patrick, **Supp. IX:** 113
McGrath, Thomas, **Supp. X: 111–130**
"McGrath on McGrath" (McGrath), **Supp. X:** 119, 120
McGuane, Thomas, **Supp. V:** 53, 220; **Supp. VIII:** 39, 40, 42, 43
MacGuffin, The (Elkin), **Supp. VI: 55–56**
McGuiness, Daniel, **Supp. XV:** 261
Machado y Ruiz, Antonio, **Supp. XIII:** 315, 323
Machan, Tibor, **Supp. IV Part 2:** 528
McHaney, Thomas, **Supp. XVIII:** 199,203
Machen, Arthur, **IV:** 286
Machiavelli, Niccolò, **I:** 485
"Machine-Gun, The" (Jarrell), **II:** 371
"Machine Song" (Anderson), **I:** 114
McHugh, Vincent, **Supp. XV:** 147
McInerney, Jay, **Supp. X:** 7, 166; **Supp. XI:** 65; **Supp. XII:** 81; **Supp. XVIII:** 148
"Mac in Love" (Dixon), **Supp. XII: 142**
McIntire, Holly, **Supp. V:** 338
McIntosh, Maria, **Retro. Supp. I:** 246
Mack, Maynard, **Supp. XIV:** 12
Mackail, John William, **Supp. I Part 1:** 268; **Supp. I Part 2:** 461
McKay, Claude, **Supp. I Part 1:** 63; **Supp. III Part 1:** 75, 76; **Supp. IV Part 1:** 3, 79, 164; **Supp. IX:** 306; **Supp. X: 131–144; Supp. XI:** 91; **Supp. XVII:** 74; **Supp. XVIII:** 122, 127, 280, 282
McKay, Donald, **Supp. I Part 2:** 482
McKee, Elizabeth, **Retro. Supp. II:** 221, 222
McKee, Ellen, **Retro. Supp. II:** 67
McKenney, Eileen, **IV:** 288; **Retro. Supp. II:** 321, 330
McKenney, Ruth, **IV:** 288; **Retro. Supp. II:** 321; **Supp. XVIII:** 238
MacKenzie, Agnes, **I:** 199
Mackenzie, Captain Alexander, **III:** 94
Mackenzie, Compton, **II:** 82; **Retro. Supp. I:** 100, 102
McKenzie, Geraldine, **Supp. XII:** 107
MacKenzie, Margaret, **I:** 199
McKibben, Bill, **Supp. XVIII:** 192
McKinley, William, **I:** 474; **III:** 506; **Supp. I Part 2:** 395–396, 707
MacKinnon, Catharine, **Supp. XII:** 6
MacLachlan, Suzanne L., **Supp. XII:** 300,**Supp. XII:** 299
McLaverty, Michael, **Supp. X:** 67
McLay, Catherine, **Supp. XIII:** 21
Maclean, Alasdair, **Supp. V:** 244
Maclean, Norman, **Supp. XIV: 221–237; Supp. XVI:** 98
MacLeish, Archibald, **I:** 283, 293, 429; **II:** 165, 228; **III: 1–25,** 427; **Supp. I Part 1:** 261; **Supp. I Part 2:** 654; **Supp. IV Part 1:** 359; **Supp. IV Part 2:** 586; **Supp. X:** 120; **Supp. XIV:** 11
MacLeish, Kenneth, **III:** 1
MacLeish, Mrs. Archibald (Ada Hitchcock), **III:** 1
McLennan, Gordon Lawson, **Supp. IX:** 89
McLeod, A. W., **Supp. I Part 1:** 257
McLuhan, Marshall, **Supp. IV Part 2:** 474
McLure, Michael, **Supp. XIV:** 150
Macmahon, Arthur, **I:** 226
McMahon, Helen, **Supp. IV Part 2:** 579
McMichael, George, **Supp. VIII:** 124
McMichael, Morton, **Supp. I Part 2:** 707
McMichaels, James, **Supp. XIII:** 114
McMillan, James B., **Supp. VIII:** 124
McMillan, Terry, **Supp. XIII: 179–193**
McMullan, Jim, **Supp. XIV:** 124
McMurtry, Josephine, **Supp. V:** 220
McMurtry, Larry, **Supp. V: 219–235; Supp. X:** 24; **Supp. XI:** 172
McNally, Terrence, **Supp. XIII: 195–211**
McNamer, Deirdre, **Supp. XI:** 190
McNeese, Gretchen, **Supp. V:** 123
MacNeice, Louis, **II:** 586; **III:** 527; **Supp. II Part 1:** 17, 24; **Supp. IV Part 2:** 440; **Supp. X:** 116; **Supp. XIII:** 347
McNeil, Claudia, **Supp. IV Part 1:** 360, 362
M-a-c-n-o-l-i-a (Jordan), **Supp. XVIII:** 172
McPhee, John, **Supp. III Part 1: 289–316; Supp. X:** 29, 30; **Supp. XVIII:** 106–107, 114
MacPherson, Aimee Semple, **Supp. V:** 278
McPherson, Dolly, **Supp. IV Part 1:** 2, 3, 4, 6, 8, 11, 12
McPherson, James Allen, **Retro. Supp. II:** 126
Macpherson, Jay, **Supp. XIII:** 19
MacPherson, Kenneth, **Supp. I Part 1:** 259

McPhillips, Robert, **Supp. XV:** 119, 250, 251, 252, 264, 266
McQuade, Molly, **Supp. IX:** 151, 163; **Supp. VIII:** 277, 281
McQueen, Steve, **Supp. XI:** 306
Macrae, John, **I:** 252–253
McRobbie, Angela, **Supp. IV Part 2:** 691
MacShane, Frank, **Supp. IV Part 2:** 557; **Supp. XI:** 214, 216
"MacSwiggen" (Freneau), **Supp. II Part 1:** 259
McTaggart, John, **I:** 59
McTeague (Norris), **III:** 314, 315, 316–320, 322, 325, 327–328, 330, 331, 333, 335; **Retro. Supp. II:** 96; **Supp. IX:** 332
McWilliams, Carey, **Supp. XI:** 169
Madama Butterfly (Puccini), **III:** 139
"Madam and the Minister" (Hughes), **Supp. I Part 1:** 335
"Madam and the Wrong Visitor" (Hughes), **Supp. I Part 1:** 335
"Madame and Ahmad" (Bowles), **Supp. IV Part 1:** 93
"Madame Bai and the Taking of Stone Mountain" (Bambara), **Supp. XI:** 14–15
Madame Bovary (Flaubert), **II:** 185; **Retro. Supp. I:** 225; **Retro. Supp. II:** 70; **Supp. XI:** 334
"Madame Célestin's Divorce" (Chopin), **Supp. I Part 1:** 213
Madame Curie (film), **Retro. Supp. I:** 113
"Madame de Mauves" (James), **II:** 327; **Retro. Supp. I:** 218, 220
Madame de Treymes (Wharton), **IV:** 314, 323; **Retro. Supp. I:** 376
"Madam's Calling Cards" (Hughes), **Retro. Supp. I:** 206
Madden, David, **Supp. IV Part 1:** 285
Maddern, Bessie. *See* London, Mrs. Jack (Bessie Maddern)
Mad Dog Black Lady (Coleman), **Supp. XI: 85–89,** 90
Mad Dog Blues (Shepard), **Supp. III Part 2:** 437, 438, 441
Maddox, Lucy, **Supp. IV Part 1:** 323, 325
Mad Ducks and Bears: Football Revisited (Plimpton), **Supp. XVI:** 243
Mademoiselle Coeur-Brisé (Sibon, trans.), **IV:** 288
Mademoiselle de Maupin (Gautier), **Supp. I Part 1:** 277
"Mad Farmer, Flying the Flag of Rough Branch, Secedes from the Union, The" (Berry), **Supp. X:** 35
"Mad Farmer Manifesto, The: The First Amendment" (Berry), **Supp. X:** 35
"Mad Farmer's Love Song, The" (Berry), **Supp. X:** 35
Madheart (Baraka), **Supp. II Part 1:** 47
Madhouse, The (Farrell), **II:** 41
Madhubuti, Haki R. (Don L. Lee), **Supp. II Part 1:** 34, 247; **Supp. IV Part 1:** 244
Madison, Dolley, **II:** 303
Madison, James, **I:** 1, 2, 6–9; **II:** 301; **Supp. I Part 2:** 509, 524
"Madison Smartt Bell: *The Year of Silence*" (Garrett), **Supp. X:** 7
Mad Love (film, Freund), **Supp. XVII:** 58
"Madman, A" (Updike), **Retro. Supp. I:** 320
"Madman's Song" (Wylie), **Supp. I Part 2:** 711, 729
Madonick, Michael, **Supp. XVII:** 123
"Madonna" (Lowell), **II:** 535–536
"Madonna of the Evening Flowers" (Lowell), **II:** 524
"Madonna of the Future, The" (James), **Retro. Supp. I:** 219
"Mad Song" (Gioia), **Supp. XV:** 128
Madwoman in the Attic, The (Gilbert and Gubar), **Retro. Supp. I:** 42; **Supp. IX:** 66
"Maelzel's Chess-Player" (Poe), **III:** 419, 420
"Maestria" (Nemerov), **III:** 275, 278–279
Maeterlinck, Maurice, **I:** 91, 220
"Magazine-Writing Peter Snook" (Poe), **III:** 421
Magdeburg Centuries (Flacius), **IV:** 163
Magellan, Ferdinand, **Supp. I Part 2:** 497
Maggie: A Girl of the Streets (S. Crane), **I:** 407, 408, 410–411, 416; **IV:** 208; **Retro. Supp. II:** 97, 107; **Supp. XVII:** 228
Maggie Cassidy (Kerouac), **Supp. III Part 1:** 220–221, 225, 227, 229, 232
"Maggie of the Green Bottles" (Bambara), **Supp. XI:** 2–3
"Maggie's Farm" (song, Dylan), **Supp. XVIII:** 25, 26
"Magi" (Plath), **Supp. I Part 2:** 544–545
"Magi, The" (Garrett), **Supp. VII:** 97
"Magic" (Porter), **III:** 434, 435
"Magic Barrel, The" (Malamud), **Supp. I Part 2:** 427, 428, 431, 432–433
Magic Barrel, The (Malamud), **Supp. I Part 2:** 427, 428, 430–434
Magic Christian, The (film), **Supp. XI:** 309
Magic Christian, The (Southern), **Supp. XI:** 297, **299–301,** 309
Magic City (Komunyakaa), **Supp. XIII: 125–127,** 128, 131
"Magic Flute, The" (Epstein), **Supp. XII:** 165
Magic Flute, The (Mozart), **III:** 164
Magician of Lublin, The (Singer), **IV:** 6, 9–10; **Retro. Supp. II: 308–309**
Magician's Assistant, The (Patchett), **Supp. XII:** 307, 310, **317–320,** 322
"Magician's Wife, The" (Gordon), **Supp. IV Part 1:** 306
Magic Journey, The (Nichols), **Supp. XIII:** 266–267
Magic Kingdom, The (Elkin), **Supp. VI:** 42, **54–55,** 56, 58
"Magic Mirror, The: A Study of the Double in Two of Doestoevsky's Novels" (Plath), **Supp. I Part 2:** 536
Magic Mountain, The (Mann), **III:** 281–282; **Supp. IV Part 2:** 522; **Supp. XII:** 321; **Supp. XVII:** 137
Magic Tower, The (Willams), **IV:** 380
Magnaghi, Ambrogio, **Supp. XVI:** 286
Magnalia Christi Americana (Mather), **II:** 302; **Supp. I Part 1:** 102; **Supp. I Part 2:** 584; **Supp. II Part 2:** 441, 442, 452–455, 460, 467, 468; **Supp. IV Part 2:** 434
Magnificat (Nelson), **Supp. XVIII: 176–177**
"Magnificent Little Gift" (Salinas), **Supp. XIII:** 318
"Magnifying Mirror" (Karr), **Supp. XI:** 240
Magpie, The (Baldwin, ed.), **Supp. I Part 1:** 49
Magpie's Shadow, The (Winters), **Supp. II Part 2:** 786, 788
"Magpie's Song" (Snyder), **Supp. VIII:** 302
Magritte, René, **Supp. IV Part 2:** 623
Mahan, Albert Thayer, **Supp. I Part 2:** 491
"Mahatma Joe" (Bass), **Supp. XVI:** 19
"Mahogany Tree, The" (M. F. K. Fisher), **Supp. XVII:** 88
Mahomet and His Successors (Irving), **II:** 314
Mahoney, Jeremiah, **IV:** 285
Mahoney, Lynn, **Supp. XV:** 270
"Maiden in a Tower" (Stegner), **Supp. IV Part 2:** 613
"Maiden Without Hands" (Sexton), **Supp. II Part 2:** 691
"Maid of St. Philippe, The" (Chopin), **Retro. Supp. II:** 63
"Maid's Shoes, The" (Malamud), **Supp. I Part 2:** 437
Mailer, Fanny, **III:** 28
Mailer, Isaac, **III:** 28
Mailer, Norman, **I:** 261, 292, 477; **III: 26–49,** 174; **IV:** 98, 216; **Retro. Supp. II:** 182, **195–217,** 279; **Supp. I Part 1:** 291, 294; **Supp. III Part 1:** 302; **Supp. IV Part 1:** 90, 198, 207, 236, 284, 381; **Supp. IV Part 2:** 689; **Supp. VIII:** 236; **Supp. XI:** 104, 218, 222, 229; **Supp. XIV:** 49, 53, 54, 111, 162; **Supp. XVII:** 225, 228, 236; **Supp. XVIII:** 19–20
"Maimed Man, The" (Tate), **IV:** 136
Maimonides, Moses, **Supp. XVII:** 46–47
Main Currents in American Thought: The Colonial Mind, 1625–1800 (Parrington), **I:** 517; **Supp. I Part 2:** 484
"Maine Roustabout, A" (Eberhart), **I:** 539
"Maine Speech" (White), **Supp. I Part 2:** 669–670
Maine Woods, The (Thoreau), **IV:** 188
Mains d'Orlac, Les (M. Renard), **Supp. XVII:** 58
Main Street (Lewis), **I:** 362; **II:** 271, 440, 441–442, 447, 449, 453; **III:** 394
Maitland, Margaret Todd, **Supp. XVI:** 292
"Majorat, Das" (Hoffman), **III:** 415
Major Barbara (Shaw), **III:** 69
"Major Chord, The" (Bourne), **I:** 221
Majors and Minors (Dunbar), **Supp. II Part 1:** 197, 198
"Major's Tale, The" (Bierce), **I:** 205

Make Believe (J. Scott), **Supp. XVII: 191–192,** 193, 194, 195
Make-Believe Town: Essays and Remembrances (Mamet), **Supp. XIV:** 240, 251
Make It New (Pound), **III:** 470
Makers and Finders (Brooks), **I:** 253, 254, 255, 257, 258
Makers of the Modern World (Untermeyer), **Supp. XV:** 312
"Making a Change" (Gilman), **Supp. XI:** 207
"Making a Living" (Sexton), **Supp. II Part 2:** 695
"Making Changes" (L. Michaels), **Supp. XVI:** 204
"Making Do" (Hogan), **Supp. IV Part 1:** 406
Making Face, Making Soul: Haciendo Caras, Creative and Critical Perspectives by Feminists of Color (Anzaldúa, ed.), **Supp. IV Part 1:** 330
Making It (Podhoretz), **Supp. VIII:** 231, 232, 233, **237–238,** 239, 244
"Making Light of Auntie" (X. J. Kennedy), **Supp. XV:** 163
"Making of a Marginal Farm, The" (Berry), **Supp. X:** 22
Making of Americans, The (Stein), **IV:** 35, 37, 40–42, 45, 46; **Supp. III Part 1:** 37
"Making of Ashenden, The" (Elkin), **Supp. VI:** 49, 50
"Making of a Soldier USA, The" (Simpson), **Supp. IX:** 270
"Making of Garrison Keillor, The" (McConagha), **Supp. XVI:** 166"
"Making of Paths, The" (Stegner), **Supp. IV Part 2:** 614
"Making of Poems, The" (W. J. Smith), **Supp. XIII:** 348
Making of the Modern Mind (Randall), **III:** 605
Making the Light Come: The Poetry of Gerald Stern (Somerville), **Supp. IX:** 296–297
"Making Up Stories" (Didion), **Supp. IV Part 1:** 196, 203, 205
Making Your Own Days: The Pleasures of Reading and Writing Poetry (Koch), **Supp. XV:** 188
Malady of the Ideal, The: Oberman, Maurice de Guérin, and Amiel (Brooks), **I:** 240, 241, 242
Malamud, Bernard, **I:** 144, 375; **II:** 424, 425; **III:** 40, 272; **IV:** 216; **Retro. Supp. II:** 22, 279, 281; **Supp. I Part 2: 427–453; Supp. IV Part 1:** 297, 382; **Supp. IX:** 114, 227; **Supp. V:** 257, 266; **Supp. XIII:** 106, 264, 265, 294; **Supp. XVI:** 220
Malamud, Mrs. Bernard (Ann de Chiara), **Supp. I Part 2:** 451
Malanga, Gerard, **Supp. III Part 2:** 629
Malaquais, Jean, **Retro. Supp. II:** 199
Malatesta, Sigismondo de, **III:** 472, 473
Malcolm (Purdy), **Supp. VII:** 270–273, 277
"Malcolm Cowley and the American Writer" (Simpson), **Supp. II Part 1:** 147
Malcolm Lowry's "Volcano": Myth Symbol Meaning (Markson), **Supp. XVII:** 142, 144
"MALCOLM REMEMBERED (FEB. 77)" (Baraka), **Supp. II Part 1:** 60
Malcolm X, **Retro. Supp. II:** 12, 13; **Supp. I Part 1:** 52, 63, 65, 66; **Supp. IV Part 1:** 2, 10; **Supp. VIII:** 330, 345; **Supp. X:** 240; **Supp. XIV:** 306
Malcolm X (film), **Retro. Supp. II:** 12
"Maldrove" (Jeffers), **Supp. II Part 2:** 418
Male, Roy, **II:** 239
Male Animal, The (Thurber), **Supp. I Part 2:** 605, 606, 610–611
"Malediction upon Myself" (Wylie), **Supp. I Part 2:** 722
Malefactors, The (Gordon), **II:** 186, 199, 213–216; **IV:** 139
"Malest Cornifici Tuo Catullo" (Ginsberg), **Supp. II Part 1:** 315
Malick, Terrence, **Supp. XI:** 234; **Supp. XV:** 351
Malin, Irving, **I:** 147; **Supp. XVI:** 71–72
"Malinche's Tips: Pique from Mexico's Mother" (Mora), **Supp. XIII:** 223
"Mallard" (C. Frost), **Supp. XV:** 98, 99
Mallarmé, Stéphane, **I:** 66, 569; **II:** 529, 543; **III:** 8, 409, 428; **IV:** 80, 86; **Retro. Supp. I:** 56; **Supp. I Part 1:** 261; **Supp. II Part 1:** 1; **Supp. III Part 1:** 319–320; **Supp. III Part 2:** 630; **Supp. XIII:** 114; **Supp. XV:** 158; **Supp. XVI:** 282, 285
Mallia, Joseph, **Supp. XII:** 26, 29, 37
Mallon, Thomas, **Supp. IV Part 1:** 200, 209
Maloff, Saul, **Supp. VIII:** 238
Malory, Thomas, **II:** 302; **III:** 486; **IV:** 50, 61; **Supp. IV Part 1:** 47
"Mal Paso Bridge" (Jeffers), **Supp. II Part 2:** 415, 420
Malraux, André, **I:** 33–34, 127, 509; **II:** 57, 376; **III:** 35, 310; **IV:** 236, 247, 434; **Retro. Supp. I:** 73; **Retro. Supp. II:** 115–116, 119; **Supp. II Part 1:** 221, 232
Maltese Falcon, The (film), **Supp. IV Part 1:** 342, 353, 355
Maltese Falcon, The (Hammett), **IV:** 286; **Supp. IV Part 1:** 345, 348–351
Mama (McMillan), **Supp. XIII:** 182, **187–188**
"Mama and Daughter" (Hughes), **Supp. I Part 1:** 334
Mama Day (Naylor), **Supp. VIII: 223–226,** 230
"Mama I Remember" (Nelson), **Supp. XVIII:** 173
Mama Poc: An Ecologist's Account of the Extinction of a Species (LaBastille), **Supp. X:** 99, **104–105,** 106
Mama's Bank Account (K. Forbes), **Supp. XVII:** 9
Mama's Promises (Nelson), **Supp. XVIII: 173–174**
"Mama Still Loves You" (Naylor), **Supp. VIII:** 214
Mambo Hips and Make Believe (Coleman), **Supp. XI: 94–96**
Mambo Kings, The (film), **Supp. VIII:** 73, 74
Mambo Kings Play Songs of Love, The (Hijuelos), **Supp. VIII:** 73–74, **79–82**
"Ma'me Pélagie" (Chopin), **Retro. Supp. II:** 64
Mamet, David, **Supp. XIV: 239–258,** 315
"Mamie" (Sandburg), **III:** 582
Mammedaty, Novarro Scott. *See* Momaday, N. Scott
"Mammon and the Archer" (O. Henry), **Supp. II Part 1:** 394, 408
Mammonart (Sinclair), **Supp. V:** 276–277
"Mammy" (D. West), **Supp. XVIII:** 283
"Mamouche" (Chopin), **Retro. Supp. II:** 66
Mamoulian, Rouben, **Supp. XVIII:** 281
"Man" (Corso), **Supp. XII:** 130
"Man" (Herbert), **II:** 12
"Man Against the Sky, The" (Robinson), **III:** 509, 523
"Man and a Woman Sit Near Each Other, A" (R. Bly), **Supp. IV Part 1:** 71
Man and Boy (Morris), **III:** 223, 224, 225
"Man and the Snake, The" (Bierce), **I:** 203
"Man and Woman" (Caldwell), **I:** 310
Manassas (Sinclair), **Supp. V:** 280, 281, 285
"Man Bring This Up Road" (T. Williams), **IV:** 383–384
"Man Carrying Thing" (Stevens), **IV:** 90
Manchester, William, **III:** 103
"Man Child, The" (Baldwin), **Supp. I Part 1:** 63
Man Could Stand Up, A (Ford), **I:** 423
"Mandarin's Jade" (Chandler), **Supp. IV Part 1:** 125
Mandel, Charlotte, **Supp. XVI:** 57
Mandelbaum, Maurice, **I:** 61
Mandelstam, Osip, **Retro. Supp. I:** 278; **Supp. III Part 1:** 268; **Supp. VIII:** 21, 22, 23, 27; **Supp. XIII:** 77; **Supp. XV:** 254, 261, 263
"Mandelstam: The Poem as Event" (Dobyns), **Supp. XIII:** 78
"Mandolin" (Dove), **Supp. IV Part 1:** 247
"Mandoline" (Verlaine), **IV:** 79
"Man Eating" (Kenyon), **Supp. VII:** 173
"Man Feeding Pigeons" (Clampitt), **Supp. IX: 49–50,** 52
Manfred, Frederick, **Supp. X:** 126
Man From Limbo, The (Endore), **Supp. XVII:** 55
"Mango Says Goodbye Sometimes" (Cisneros), **Supp. VII:** 64
Manhattan (film; Allen), **Supp. IV Part 1:** 205; **Supp. XV:** 5, **7–8,** 13
"Manhattan Dawn" (Justice), **Supp. VII:** 117
"Manhattan: Luminism" (Doty), **Supp. XI:** 135
Manhattan Murder Mystery (film; Allen), **Supp. XV:** 5, 11

Manhattan Transfer (Dos Passos), **I:** 26, 475, 478, 479, 480, 481, 482–484, 487; **II:** 286; **Supp. I Part 1:** 57
"Mania" (Lowell), **II:** 554
"Manic in the Moon, The" (Thurber), **Supp. I Part 2:** 620
Manikin, The (J. Scott), **Supp. XVII: 189–191,** 192, 194
"Man in Black" (Plath), **Supp. I Part 2:** 538
Man in Prehistory (Chard), **Supp. XII:** 177–178
Man in the Black Coat Turns, The (R. Bly), **Supp. IV Part 1:** 66–68, 71, 73
"Man in the Brooks Brothers Shirt, The" (McCarthy), **II:** 563–564
"Man in the Drawer, The" (Malamud), **Supp. I Part 2:** 437
Man in the Flying Lawn Chair and Other Excursions and Observations, The (Plimpton), **Supp. XVI:** 234
Man in the Gray Flannel Suit, The (Wilson), **Supp. IV Part 1:** 387
Man in the High Castle, The (Dick), **Supp. XVIII:** 138
Man in the Middle, The (Wagoner), **Supp. IX:** 324, **332–333**
"Man in the Rain, The" (Ryan as Quin), **Supp. XVIII:** 226
Mankiewicz, Herman, **Supp. XVI:** 189
Mankiewicz, Joseph, **Retro. Supp. I:** 113
Mankowitz, Wolf, **Supp. XI:** 307
"Man Made of Words, The" (Momaday), **Supp. IV Part 2:** 481, 484–485, 486, 487, 488
Man-Made World, The (Gilman), **Supp. XI:** 207
"Man-Moth, The" (Bishop), **Retro. Supp. II:** 42; **Supp. I Part 1:** 85–87, 88
Mann, Charles, **Retro. Supp. II:** 40
Mann, Erika, **Supp. II Part 1:** 11
Mann, Seymour (Samuel Weisman), **Supp. V:** 113
Mann, Thomas, **I:** 271, 490; **II:** 42, 539; **III:** 231, 281–282, 283; **IV:** 70, 73, 85; **Supp. IV Part 1:** 392; **Supp. IV Part 2:** 522; **Supp. IX:** 21; **Supp. V:** 51; **Supp. XI:** 275; **Supp. XII:** 173, 310, 321; **Supp. XIV:** 87; **Supp. XVII:** 137
Mannerhouse (Wolfe), **IV:** 460
Manner Music, The (Reznikoff), **Supp. XIV: 293–295**
"Manners" (Bishop), **Supp. I Part 1:** 73
"Manners" (Emerson), **II:** 4, 6
"Manners, Morals, and the Novel" (Trilling), **Supp. III Part 2:** 502, 503
Mannheim, Karl, **I:** 279; **Supp. I Part 2:** 644
Manning, Frederic, **III:** 459
Manning, Robert, **Supp. IX:** 236
Mannix, Daniel P., **Supp. II Part 1:** 140
Man Nobody Knows, The (B. Barton), **Retro. Supp. I:** 179
Mano, D. Keith, **Supp. XVI:** 250
Mano, Guy Levis, **Supp. XVI:** 282
"Man of Letters as a Man of Business, The" (Howells), **Supp. XIV:** 45–46
"Man of No Account, The" (Harte), **Supp. II Part 1:** 339
"Man of the Crowd, The" (Poe), **III:** 412, 417; **Retro. Supp. I:** 154
Man on Spikes (Asinof), **II:** 424
Man on Stage (Dixon), **Supp. XII:** 141, **154–155**
"Man on the Dump, The" (Stevens), **IV:** 74; **Retro. Supp. I:** 306
"Man on the Train, The" (Percy), **Supp. III Part 1:** 387
Manor, The (Singer), **IV:** 6, 17–19
Manrique, Jorge, **Retro. Supp. II:** 154
Mansart Builds a School (Du Bois), **Supp. II Part 1:** 185–186
Man's Fate (Malraux), **I:** 127; **Retro. Supp. II:** 121
"Man's Fate A Film Treatment of the Malraux Novel" (Agee), **I:** 33–34
Mansfield, June, **Supp. X:** 183, 194
Mansfield, Katherine, **III:** 362, 453
Mansfield, Stephanie, **Supp. IV Part 1:** 227
Man's Hope (Malraux), **IV:** 247
Mansion, The (Faulkner), **II:** 73; **Retro. Supp. I:** 74, 82
Man's Nature and His Communities (Niebuhr), **III:** 308
Manson, Charles, **Supp. IV Part 1:** 205
"Man Splitting Wood in the Daybreak, The" (Kinnell), **Supp. III Part 1:** 254
"Man's Pride" (Jeffers), **Supp. II Part 2:** 417
"Man's Story, The" (Anderson), **I:** 114
Man's Woman, A (Norris), **III:** 314, 322, 328, 329, 330, 332, 333
Man That Corrupted Hadleyburg, The (Twain), **I:** 204; **IV:** 208
"Man That Was Used Up, The" (Poe), **III:** 412, 425
"Mantis" (Zukofsky), **Supp. III Part 2:** 617
"'Mantis': An Interpretation" (Zukofsky), **Supp. III Part 2:** 617–618
Man to Send Rain Clouds, The (Rosen, ed.), **Supp. IV Part 2:** 499, 505, 513
"Man to Send Rain Clouds, The" (Silko), **Supp. IV Part 2:** 559
Mantrap (Lewis), **II:** 447
Manuductio Ad Ministerium (Mather), **Supp. II Part 2:** 465–467
"Manuelzinho" (Bishop), **Retro. Supp. II:** 47–48
Manuscript Books of Emily Dickinson, The (Franklin, ed.), **Retro. Supp. I:** 29, 41
"Man Waiting for It to Stop, A" (Dunn), **Supp. XI:** 144
"Man Who Became a Woman, The" (Anderson), **I:** 114
"Man Who Carries the Desert Around Inside Himself, The: For Wally" (Komunyakaa), **Supp. XIII:** 125
"Man Who Closed Shop, The" (Dunn), **Supp. XI:** 149
Man Who Gave Up His Name, The (Harrison), **Supp. VIII:** 45, 52
Man Who Had All the Luck, The (A. Miller), **III:** 148, 149, 164, 166
"Man Who Knew Belle Star, The" (Bausch), **Supp. VII:** 46
"Man Who Knew Coolidge, The" (Lewis), **II:** 449
Man Who Knew Coolidge, The: Being the Soul of Lowell Schmaltz, Constructive and Nordic Citizen (Lewis), **II:** 450
"Man Who Lived Underground, The" (Wright), **IV:** 479, 485–487, 492; **Retro. Supp. II:** 121
Man Who Lived Underground, The (Wright), **Supp. II Part 1:** 40
"Man Who Makes Brooms, The" (Nye), **Supp. XIII:** 276
"Man Who Studied Yoga, The" (Mailer), **III:** 35–36; **Retro. Supp. II:** 200
"Man Who Wanted to Win, The" (McCoy), **Supp. XIII:** 161
Man Who Was There, The (Morris), **III:** 220–221
"Man Who Writes Ants, The" (Merwin), **Supp. III Part 1:** 348
"Man with a Family" (Humphrey), **Supp. IX:** 94
Man without a Country, The (Hale), **I:** 488
"Man with the Blue Guitar, The" (Stevens), **I:** 266; **IV:** 85–87; **Retro. Supp. I: 303–305,** 306, 307, 309
Man with the Blue Guitar and Other Poems, The (Stevens), **IV:** 76; **Retro. Supp. I:** 303, 422
Man with the Golden Arm, The (Algren), **Supp. IX:** 1, 3, **9–11,** 14, 15; **Supp. V:** 4
Man with the Golden Arm, The (film), **Supp. IX:** 3
"Man with the Golden Beef, The" (Podhoretz), **Supp. IX:** 3
"Man with the Hoe, The" (Markham), **Supp. XV:** 115
Many a Monster (Ryan as Finnegan), **Supp. XVIII:** 233, **236–238**
Manyan Letters (Olson), **Supp. II Part 2:** 571
Many Circles (Goldbarth), **Supp. XII:** 193
"Many Handles" (Sandburg), **III:** 594
"Many Happy Returns" (Auden), **Supp. II Part 1:** 15
Many Loves (W. C. Williams), **Retro. Supp. I:** 424
"Many Mansions" (H. Roth), **Supp. IX:** 233, 234
Many Marriages (Anderson), **I:** 104, 111, 113
"Many of Our Waters: Variations on a Poem by a Black Child" (Wright), **Supp. III Part 2:** 602
"Many Swans" (Lowell), **II:** 526
"Many Thousands Gone" (Baldwin), **Retro. Supp. II:** 4; **Supp. I Part 1:** 51
"Many Wagons Ago" (Ashbery), **Supp. III Part 1:** 22
"Many-Windowed House, A" (Cowley), **Supp. II Part 1:** 137
Many-Windowed House, A (Cowley), **Supp. II Part 1:** 141, 143
Mao II (DeLillo), **Supp. VI:** 2, 4, **5,** 6, **7,** 8, 9, 14, 16

"Map, The" (Bishop), **Retro. Supp. II:** 41; **Supp. I Part 1:** 72, 82, 85–88, 93
"Map, The" (Strand), **Supp. IV Part 2:** 623–624
"Maple Leaf, The" (Joplin), **Supp. IV Part 1:** 223
"Maple Tree, The" (D. West), **Supp. XVIII:** 284
Map of Another Town: A Memoir of Provence (M. F. K. Fisher), **Supp. XVII:** 88, 89, 92
"Map of Montana in Italy, A" (Hugo), **Supp. VI:** 139
"Maps" (Hass), **Supp. VI:** 103–104
Mapson, Jo-Ann, **Supp. IV Part 2:** 440, 454
Map to the Next World, A: Poems and Tales (Harjo), **Supp. XII: 228–230**
"Mara" (Jeffers), **Supp. II Part 2:** 434
Ma Rainey's Black Bottom (Wilson), **Supp. VIII:** 331, **332–334,** 346, 349, 350
Marat, Jean Paul, **IV:** 117; **Supp. I Part 2:** 514, 515, 521
"Marathon" (Glück), **Supp. V:** 85
Marble Faun, The (Faulkner), **II:** 55, 56; **Retro. Supp. I:** 79
Marble Faun, The; or, The Romance of Monte Beni (Hawthorne), **II:** 225, 239, 242–243, 290, 324; **IV:** 167; **Retro. Supp. I:** 63, 149, 163, **164–165; Supp. I Part 1:** 38; **Supp. I Part 2:** 421, 596; **Supp. XIII:** 102
Marbles (Brodsky), **Supp. VIII:** 26–27
Marcaccio, Michael, **Supp. XVII:** 97, 106
"March" (W. C. Williams), **Retro. Supp. I:** 418
March, Alan, **Supp. XVI:** 242
March, Fredric, **III:** 154, 403; **IV:** 357; **Supp. X:** 220
Marchalonis, Shirley, **Supp. XIII:** 138, 140, 141, 143, 147–148
"Marché aux Oiseaux" (Wilbur), **Supp. III Part 2:** 550
"Märchen, The" (Jarrell), **II:** 378–379
March Hares (Frederic), **II:** 143–144
Marching Men (Anderson), **I:** 99, 101, 103–105, 111
"Marching Music" (Simic), **Supp. VIII:** 281
"Marcia" (Davis), **Supp. XVI:** 91–92
Marcks, Greg, **Supp. XVIII:** 150
Marco Millions (O'Neill), **III:** 391, 395
Marcosson, Isaac, **III:** 322
Marcus, Greil, **Supp. XVIII:** 30, 53
Marcus, Steven, **Retro. Supp. II:** 196, 200
Marcus Aurelius, **II:** 1; **III:** 566; **Supp. XVIII:** 304
Marcuse, Herbert, **Supp. I Part 2:** 645; **Supp. VIII:** 196; **Supp. XII:** 2
Mardi and a Voyage Thither (Melville), **I:** 384; **II:** 281; **III:** 77–79, 84, 87, 89; **Retro. Supp. I:** 247, 254, 256
Margaret (Judd), **II:** 290
"Margaret Fuller, 1847" (Clampitt), **Supp. IX:** 43
"Marginalia" (Wilbur), **Supp. III Part 2:** 544
Margin of Hope, A: An Intellectual Autobiography (Howe), **Supp. VI:** 113–114, 117, 125, 128
"Margins of Maycomb, The: A Rereading of *To Kill a Mockingbird*" (Phelps), **Supp. VIII:** 128
Margoshes, Samuel, **Supp. X:** 70
"Margrave" (Jeffers), **Supp. II Part 2:** 426
Margret Howth (Davis), **Supp. XVI:** 81, 83, 84, **88–89**
Margret Howth: A Story of Today (J. Yellin, ed.), **Supp. XVI:** 88
"Maria Concepción" (Porter), **III:** 434–435, 451
Mariani, Paul L., **Retro. Supp. I:** 412, 419; **Retro. Supp. II:** 189
Marianne Moore Reader, (Moore), **III:** 199
Marie Antoinette (film), **Retro. Supp. I:** 113
Marie Laveau (Prose), **Supp. XVI:** 251
Mariella Gable, Sister, **III:** 339, 355
"Marijuana and a Pistol" (C. Himes), **Supp. XVI:** 137
"Marijuana Notation" (Ginsberg), **Supp. II Part 1:** 313
Marilyn: A Biography (Mailer), **Retro. Supp. II:** 208
"Marin" (Cisneros), **Supp. VII:** 60, 61
Marin, Jay, **Retro. Supp. II:** 325
"Marina" (Eliot), **I:** 584, 585; **Retro. Supp. I:** 64
"Marine Surface, Low Overcast" (Clampitt), **Supp. IX: 47–48**
Marinetti, Tommaso, **Retro. Supp. I:** 59
Marionettes, The (Faulkner), **Retro. Supp. I:** 79
Maritain, Jacques, **I:** 402
Maritime Compact (Paine), **Supp. I Part 2:** 519
Maritime History of Massachusetts, 1783–1860, The (Morison), **Supp. I Part 2:** 481–483
Marjolin, Jean-Nicolas, **Supp. I Part 1:** 302
Marjorie Kinnan Rawlings: Sojourner at Cross Creek (Silverthorne), **Supp. X:** 220, 234
"Mark, The" (Bogan), **Supp. III Part 1:** 52
Marker, Chris, **Supp. IV Part 2:** 434, 436
"Market" (Hayden), **Supp. II Part 1:** 368, 369
Marketplace, The (Frederic), **II:** 145–146
Markham, Edwin, **I:** 199, 207; **Supp. XV:** 115
Markings (Hammarskjold), **Supp. II Part 1:** 26
Mark of the Vampire (film, Browning), **Supp. XVII:** 58
Markopoulos, Gregory, **Supp. XII:** 2
Markowick-Olczakova, Hanna, **Supp. X:** 70
Marks, Alison, **Supp. I Part 2:** 660
Marks, Barry A., **I:** 435, 438, 442, 446
Markson, David, **Supp. XVII: 135–147**
Mark Twain in Eruption (Twain), **IV:** 209
Mark Twain's America (De Voto), **I:** 248
Mark Twain's Autobiography (Twain), **IV:** 209
Marley, Bob, **Supp. IX:** 152
Marlowe, Christopher, **I:** 68, 368, 384; **II:** 590; **III:** 259, 491; **Retro. Supp. I:** 127; **Retro. Supp. II:** 76; **Supp. I Part 2:** 422
"Marlowe Takes on the Syndicate" (Chandler), **Supp. IV Part 1:** 135
Marne, The (Wharton), **IV:** 319, 320; **Retro. Supp. I:** 378
Marquand, John, **Supp. XI:** 301
Marquand, J. P., **I:** 362, 375; **II:** 459, 482–483; **III: 50–73,** 383; **Supp. I Part 1:** 196; **Supp. IV Part 1:** 31; **Supp. V:** 95
Marquand, Mrs. John P. (Adelaide Hooker), **III:** 57, 61
Marquand, Mrs. John P. (Christina Sedgwick), **III:** 54, 57
Marquand, Philip, **III:** 52
Marquis, Don, **Supp. I Part 2:** 668
"Marriage" (Corso), **Supp. XII:** 117, 124, **127–128**
"Marriage" (Moore), **III:** 198–199, 213
Marriage (Moore), **III:** 194
"Marriage, A" (Untermeyer), **Supp. XV:** 305
Marriage A-la-Mode (Dryden), **Supp. IX:** 68
Marriage and Other Science Fiction (Goldbarth), **Supp. XII:** 189, 190
"Marriage in the Sixties, A" (Rich), **Supp. I Part 2:** 554
"Marriage of Heaven and Hell, The" (Blake), **III:** 544–545; **Supp. VIII:** 99
"Marriage of Phaedra, The" (Cather), **Retro. Supp. I:** 5
Marrow of Tradition, The (Chesnutt), **Supp. XIV:** 63, **71–75,** 76
Marryat, Captain Frederick, **III:** 423
"Marrying Absurd" (Didion), **Supp. IV Part 1:** 200
"Marrying Iseult?" (Updike), **Retro. Supp. I:** 329
Marrying Man (Simon), **Supp. IV Part 2:** 588
"Marrying the Hangman" (Atwood), **Supp. XIII:** 34
Marry Me: A Romance (Updike), **Retro. Supp. I:** 329, 330, 332
"Mars and Hymen" (Freneau), **Supp. II Part 1:** 258
Marsden, Dora, **III:** 471; **Retro. Supp. I:** 416
Marsena (Frederic), **II:** 135, 136–137
Marsh, Edward, **Supp. I Part 1:** 257, 263
Marsh, Fred T., **Supp. IX:** 232
Marsh, Mae, **Supp. I Part 2:** 391
Marshall, George, **III:** 3
Marshall, John, **Supp. I Part 2:** 455; **Supp. XVI:** 117
Marshall, Paule, **Supp. IV Part 1:** 8, 14, 369; **Supp. XI:** 18, **275–292; Supp. XIII:** 295
Marshall, Tod, **Supp. XV:** 224; **Supp. XVII:** 25, 26, 29, 32
"Marshall Carpenter" (Masters), **Supp. I Part 2:** 463

"Marshes of Glynn, The" (Lanier), **Supp. I Part 1:** 364, 365–368, 370, 373
"'Marshes of Glynn, The': A Study in Symbolic Obscurity" (Ross), **Supp. I Part 1:** 373
Marsh Island, A (Jewett), **II:** 405; **Retro. Supp. II:** 134
"Marshland Elegy" (Leopold), **Supp. XIV:** 187, 189
"Mars Is Heaven!" (Bradbury), **Supp. IV Part 1:** 103, 106
Marsman, Henrik, **Supp. IV Part 1:** 183
Marston, Ed, **Supp. IV Part 2:** 492
Marta y Maria (Valdes), **II:** 290
"Martha's Lady" (Jewett), **Retro. Supp. II:** 140, 143
Marthe, Saint, **II:** 213
Martial, **II:** 1, 169; **Supp. IX:** 152
Martian Chronicles, The (Bradbury), **Supp. IV Part 1:** 102, 103, 106–107
Martian Time-Slip (Dick), **Supp. XVIII:** 142
Martin, Benjamin, **Supp. I Part 2:** 503
Martin, Charles, **Supp. XVII:** 112
Martin, Dick, **Supp. XII:** 44
Martin, Jay, **I:** 55, 58, 60, 61, 67; **III:** 307; **Retro. Supp. II:** 326, 327, 329; **Supp. XI:** 162
Martin, John, **Supp. XI:** 172
Martin, Judith, **Supp. V:** 128
Martin, Nell, **Supp. IV Part 1:** 351, 353
Martin, Reginald, **Supp. X:** 247, 249
Martin, Stephen-Paul, **Supp. IV Part 2:** 430
Martin, Tom, **Supp. X:** 79
Martin du Gard, Roger, **Supp. I Part 1:** 51
Martineau, Harriet, **Supp. II Part 1:** 282, 288, 294; **Supp. XVIII:** 7
Martin Eden (London), **II:** 466, 477–481
Martinelli, Sheri, **Supp. IV Part 1:** 280
Martínez, Guillermo, **Supp. XIII:** 313
Martini, Adrienne, **Supp. XVIII:** 35
Mart'nez, Rafael, **Retro. Supp. I:** 423
Martone, John, **Supp. V:** 179
Marty (Chayefsky), **Supp. XV:** 205
"Martyr, The" (Porter), **III:** 454
Martz, Louis L., **IV:** 151, 156, 165; **Supp. I Part 1:** 107; **Supp. XIV:** 12
Marvell, Andrew, **IV:** 135, 151, 156, 161, 253; **Retro. Supp. I:** 62, 127; **Retro. Supp. II:** 186, 189; **Supp. I Part 1:** 80; **Supp. XII:** 159; **Supp. XIV:** 10; **Supp. XVI:** 204
"Marvella, for Borrowing" (Ríos), **Supp. IV Part 2:** 551
"Marvelous Sauce, The," **Supp. XVII:** 189
Marx, Eleanor, **Supp. XVI:** 85
Marx, Karl, **I:** 60, 267, 279, 283, 588; **II:** 376, 462, 463, 483, 577; **IV:** 429, 436, 443–444, 469; **Retro. Supp. I:** 254; **Supp. I Part 2:** 518, 628, 632, 633, 634, 635, 639, 643, 645, 646; **Supp. III Part 2:** 619; **Supp. IV Part 1:** 355; **Supp. IX:** 133; **Supp. VIII:** 196; **Supp. X:** 119, 134; **Supp. XIII:** 75
Marx, Leo, **Supp. I Part 1:** 233
"Marxism and Monastic Perpectives" (Merton), **Supp. VIII:** 196
Mary (Nabokov), **Retro. Supp. I: 267–268,** 270, 277
"Mary Karr, Mary Karr, Mary Karr, Mary Karr" (Harmon), **Supp. XI:** 248
Maryles, Daisy, **Supp. XII:** 271
Mary Magdalene, **I:** 303
Mary; or, The Test of Honour (Rowson), **Supp. XV: 233,** 236
"Mary O'Reilly" (Anderson), **II:** 44
"Mary Osaka, I Love You" (Fante), **Supp. XI:** 169
"Mary's Song" (Plath), **Supp. I Part 2:** 541
"Mary Winslow" (Lowell), **Retro. Supp. II:** 187
Marzynski, Marian, **Supp. XVI:** 153
Masefield, John, **II:** 552; **III:** 523
Masked and Anonymous (film, Dylan and Charles), **Supp. XVIII:** 21, 28
Mask for Janus, A (Merwin), **Supp. III Part 1:** 339, 341, 342
Maslin, Janet, **Supp. XVI:** 213
Maslow, Abraham, **Supp. I Part 2:** 540
Mason, Bobbie Ann, **Supp. VIII: 133–149; Supp. XI:** 26; **Supp. XII:** 294, 298, 311
Mason, Charlotte, **Supp. XIV:** 201
Mason, David, **Supp. V:** 344; **Supp. XV:** 116, 251; **Supp. XVII:** 109, 110, 112, 121; **Supp. XVIII:** 182, 183
Mason, Jennifer, **Supp. XVIII:** 263
Mason, Lowell, **I:** 458
Mason, Marsha, **Supp. IV Part 2:** 575, 586
Mason, Otis Tufton, **Supp. I Part 1:** 18
Mason, Walt, **Supp. XV:** 298
Mason & Dixon (Pynchon), **Supp. XVII:** 232
"Mason Jars by the Window" (Ríos), **Supp. IV Part 2:** 548
Masque of Mercy, A (Frost), **II:** 155, 165, 167–168; **Retro. Supp. I:** 131, 140
"Masque of Mummers, The" (MacLeish), **III:** 18
"Masque of Pandora, The" (Longfellow), **Retro. Supp. II:** 167
Masque of Pandora, The, and Other Poems (Longfellow), **II:** 490, 494, 506; **Retro. Supp. II:** 169
Masque of Poets, A (Lathrop, ed.), **Retro. Supp. I:** 31; **Supp. I Part 1:** 365, 368
Masque of Reason, A (Frost), **II:** 155, 162, 165–167; **Retro. Supp. I:** 131, 140; **Retro. Supp. II:** 42
"Masque of the Red Death, The" (Poe), **III:** 412, 419, 424; **Retro. Supp. II:** 262, 268–269
"Masquerade" (Banks), **Supp. V:** 7
Massachusetts, Its Historians and Its History (Adams), **Supp. I Part 2:** 484
"Massachusetts 1932" (Bowles), **Supp. IV Part 1:** 94
"Massachusetts to Virginia" (Whittier), **Supp. I Part 2:** 688–689
"Massacre and the Mastermind, The" (Bausch), **Supp. VII:** 49
"Massacre at Scio, The" (Bryant), **Supp. I Part 1:** 168
"Massacre of the Innocents, The" (Simic), **Supp. VIII:** 282
Masses and Man (Toller), **I:** 479
"Masseur de Ma Soeur, Le" (Hecht), **Supp. X:** 58
Massey, Raymond, **Supp. IV Part 2:** 524
"Mass Eye and Ear: The Ward" (Karr), **Supp. XI:** 244
"Mass for the Day of St. Thomas Didymus" (Levertov), **Supp. III Part 1:** 283
Massie, Chris, **Supp. IV Part 2:** 524
Massing, Michael, **Supp. IV Part 1:** 208
Massinger, Philip, **Supp. I Part 2:** 422; **Supp. XV:** 238
Master Builder, The (Ibsen), **Supp. IV Part 2:** 522
Master Class (McNally), **Supp. XIII: 204–205,** 208
"Masterful" (Matthews), **Supp. IX: 161–162**
Mastering the Art of French Cooking (Child), **Supp. XVII:** 89
"Master Misery" (Capote), **Supp. III Part 1:** 117
Master of Dreams: A Memoir of Isaac Bashevis Singer (Telushkin), **Retro. Supp. II:** 317
"Master of Secret Revenges, The" (Gass), **Supp. VI:** 93
Master of the Crossroads (Bell), **Supp. X: 16–17**
"'Masterpiece of Filth, A': Portrait of Knoxville Forgets to Be Fair" (Howards), **Supp. VIII:** 178
Masterpieces of American Fiction, **Supp. XI:** 198
"Master Player, The" (Dunbar), **Supp. II Part 1:** 200
Masters, Edgar Lee, **I:** 106, 384, 475, 480, 518; **II:** 276, 529; **III:** 505, 576, 579; **IV:** 352; **Retro. Supp. I:** 131; **Supp. I Part 2:** 378, 386, 387, **454–478; Supp. III Part 1:** 63, 71, 73, 75; **Supp. IV Part 2:** 502; **Supp. IX:** 308; **Supp. XIV:** 282–283; **Supp. XV:** 256, 293, 297, 301, 306
Masters, Hardin W., **Supp. I Part 2:** 468
Masters, Hilary, **Supp. IX:** 96
Masters of Sociological Thought (Coser), **Supp. I Part 2:** 650
Masters of the Dew (Roumain), **Supp. IV Part 1:** 367
"Masters of War" (song, Dylan), **Supp. XVIII:** 24
Matchmaker, The (Wilder), **IV:** 357, 369, 370, 374
Mate of the Daylight, The, and Friends Ashore (Jewett), **II:** 404; **Retro. Supp. II:** 146–147
Materassi, Mario, **Supp. IX:** 233
Mather, Cotton, **II:** 10, 104, 302, 506, 536; **III:** 442; **IV:** 144, 152–153, 157; **Supp. I Part 1:** 102, 117, 174, 271; **Supp. I Part 2:** 584, 599, 698; **Supp. II Part 2: 441–470; Supp. IV Part 2:** 430, 434
Mather, Increase, **II:** 10; **IV:** 147, 157; **Supp. I Part 1:** 100
Mathews, Cornelius, **III:** 81; **Supp. I Part 1:** 317
Mathews, Shailer, **III:** 293

"Matinees" (Merrill), **Supp. III Part 1:** 319, 327
"Matins" (C. Frost), **Supp. XV:** 105
"Matins" (Glück), **Supp. V:** 88
"Matins" (Nelson), **Supp. XVIII:** 177
Matisse, Henri, **III:** 180; **IV:** 90, 407; **Supp. I Part 2:** 619; **Supp. IX:** 66; **Supp. VIII:** 168; **Supp. X:** 73, 74
"Matisse: Blue Interior with Two Girls–1947" (Hecht), **Supp. X: 73–74**
"Matisse: The Red Studio" (Snodgrass), **Supp. VI:** 316–317
Matlack, James, **Supp. XV:** 269, 271, 286
Matlock, Lucinda, **Supp. I Part 2:** 462
Matrimaniac, The (film), **Supp. XVI:** 185, 186
Matrix Trilogy, The (film), **Supp. XVI:** 271
Matson, Harold, **Supp. XIII:** 164, 166, 167, 169, 172
Matson, Peter, **Supp. IV Part 1:** 299
Matson, Suzanne, **Supp. VIII:** 281
Matters of Fact and Fiction: Essays 1973–1976 (Vidal), **Supp. IV Part 2:** 687
Matthew (biblical book), **IV:** 164; **Supp. XV:** 222
Matthew Arnold (Trilling), **Supp. III Part 2:** 500–501
Matthews, Jackson, **Supp. XVI:** 282
Matthews, T. S., **II:** 430; **Supp. XV:** 142
Matthews, William, **Supp. IX: 151–170; Supp. V:** 4, 5; **Supp. XIII:** 112
Matthiessen, F. O., **I:** 254, 259–260, 517; **II:** 41, 554; **III:** 310, 453; **IV:** 181; **Retro. Supp. I:** 40, 217; **Retro. Supp. II:** 137; **Supp. IV Part 2:** 422; **Supp. XIII:** 93; **Supp. XIV:** 3
Matthiessen, Peter, **Supp. V: 199–217,** 332; **Supp. XI:** 231, 294; **Supp. XIV:** 82; **Supp. XVI:** 230
Mattingly, Garrett, **Supp. IV Part 2:** 601
Mattu, Ravi, **Supp. XVI:** 124
"Maud Island" (Caldwell), **I:** 310
Maud Martha (Brooks), **Supp. III Part 1:** 74, 78–79, 87; **Supp. XI:** 278
"Maud Muller" (Whittier), **Supp. I Part 2:** 698
Maugham, W. Somerset, **III:** 57, 64; **Supp. IV Part 1:** 209; **Supp. X:** 58; **Supp. XIV:** 161
Maule's Curse: Seven Studies in the History of American Obscurantism (Winters), **Supp. II Part 2:** 807–808, 812
"Mau-mauing the Flak Catchers" (Wolfe), **Supp. III Part 2:** 577
Maupassant, Guy de, **I:** 309, 421; **II:** 191–192, 291, 325, 591; **IV:** 17; **Retro. Supp. II:** 65, 66, 67, 299; **Supp. I Part 1:** 207, 217, 223, 320; **Supp. XIV:** 336
"Maurice Barrès and the Youth of France" (Bourne), **I:** 228
Maurier, George du, **II:** 338
Maurras, Charles, **Retro. Supp. I:** 55
Maus II: And Here My Troubles Began (A. Speigelman), **Supp. XVII:** 48
Mauve Gloves & Madmen, Clutter & Vine (Wolfe), **Supp. III Part 2:** 581
Maverick, Augustus, **Supp. XVIII:** 4
Maverick in Mauve (Auchincloss), **Supp. IV Part 1:** 26
"Mavericks, The" (play) (Auchincloss), **Supp. IV Part 1:** 34
"Mavericks, The" (story) (Auchincloss), **Supp. IV Part 1:** 32
"Max" (H. Miller), **III:** 183
Max and the White Phagocytes (H. Miller), **III:** 178, 183–184
Maximilian (emperor of Mexico), **Supp. I Part 2:** 457–458
Maximilian: A Play in Five Acts (Masters), **Supp. I Part 2:** 456, 457–458
"Maximus, to Gloucester" (Olson), **Supp. II Part 2:** 574
"Maximus, to himself" (Olson), **Supp. II Part 2:** 565, 566, 567, 569, 570, 572
Maximus Poems, The (Olson), **Retro. Supp. I:** 209; **Supp. II Part 2:** 555, 556, 563, 564–580, 584; **Supp. VIII:** 305; **Supp. XV:** 170, 264, 349; **Supp. XVI:** 287
Maximus Poems 1–10, The (Olson), **Supp. II Part 2:** 571
Maximus Poems IV, V, VI (Olson), **Supp. II Part 2:** 555, 580, 582–584
Maximus Poems Volume Three, The (Olson), **Supp. II Part 2:** 555, 582, 584–585
"Maximus to Gloucester, Letter 19 (A Pastoral Letter)" (Olson), **Supp. II Part 2:** 567
"Maximus to Gloucester, Sunday July 19" (Olson), **Supp. II Part 2:** 580
"Maximus to himself June 1964" (Olson), **Supp. II Part 2:** 584
Maxwell, Glyn, **Supp. XV:** 252, 253, 260, 261, 263, 264
Maxwell, William, **Supp. I Part 1:** 175; **Supp. III Part 1:** 62; **Supp. VIII: 151–174; Supp. XVII:** 23
May, Abigail (Abba). *See* Alcott, Mrs. Amos Bronson (Abigail May)
May, Jill, **Supp. VIII:** 126
"May 24, 1980" (Brodsky), **Supp. VIII:** 28
"May 1968" (Olds), **Supp. X:** 211–212
"Mayan Warning" (Mora), **Supp. XIII:** 214
Maybe (Hellman), **Supp. IV Part 1:** 12
"Maybe" (Oliver), **Supp. VII:** 239
"Maybe, Someday" (Ritsos), **Supp. XIII:** 78
May Blossom (Belasco), **Supp. XVI:** 182
"Mayday" (Faulkner), **Retro. Supp. I:** 80
"May Day" (Fitzgerald), **II:** 88–89; **Retro. Supp. I:** 103
"May Day Dancing, The" (Nemerov), **III:** 275
"May Day Sermon to the Women of Gilmer County, Georgia, by a Woman Preacher Leaving the Baptist Church" (Dickey), **Supp. IV Part 1:** 182
Mayer, Elizabeth, **Supp. II Part 1:** 16; **Supp. III Part 1:** 63
Mayer, John, **Retro. Supp. I:** 58
Mayer, Louis B., **Supp. XII:** 160; **Supp. XVIII:** 250
Mayes, Wendell, **Supp. IX:** 250
Mayfield, Sara, **Supp. IX:** 65
Mayflower, The (Stowe), **Supp. I Part 2:** 585, 586
Mayle, Peter, **Supp. XVI:** 295
Maynard, Joyce, **Supp. V:** 23
Maynard, Tony, **Supp. I Part 1:** 65
Mayo, Robert, **III:** 478
Mayorga, Margaret, **IV:** 381
"Maypole of Merrymount, The" (Hawthorne), **II:** 229
May Sarton: Selected Letters 1916–1954, **Supp. VIII:** 265
"May Sun Sheds an Amber Light, The" (Bryant), **Supp. I Part 1:** 170
"May Swenson: The Art of Perceiving" (Stanford), **Supp. IV Part 2:** 637
"Maze" (Eberhart), **I:** 523, 525–526, 527
Mazel (R. Goldstein), **Supp. XVII:** 44
Mazur, Gail, **Supp. XVIII:** 92
Mazurkiewicz, Margaret, **Supp. XI:** 2
Mazzini, Giuseppe, **Supp. I Part 1:** 2, 8; **Supp. II Part 1:** 299
M Butterfly (Hwang), **Supp. X:** 292
McCorkle, Jill, **Supp. XVIII:** 195
McElligot's Pool (Geisel), **Supp. XVI:** 104
McLean, Carolyn (pseudonym). *See* Bly, Carol
Mc. Names starting with Mc are alphabetized as if spelled Mac.
"M. Degas Teaches Art & Science at Durfee Intermediate School, Detroit, 1942" (Levine), **Supp. V:** 181, 193
"Me, Boy Scout" (Lardner), **II:** 433
Me, Vashya! (T. Williams), **IV:** 381
Mead, Elinor. *See* Howells, Mrs. William Dean (Elinor Mead)
Mead, George Herbert, **II:** 27, 34; **Supp. I Part 1:** 5; **Supp. I Part 2:** 641
Mead, Margaret, **Supp. I Part 1:** 49, 52, 66; **Supp. IX:** 229
Mead, Taylor, **Supp. XV:** 187
Meade, Frank, **Retro. Supp. II:** 114
Meade, Marion, **Supp. IX:** 191, 193, 194, 195
Meadow, Lynne, **Supp. XIII:** 198
"Meadow House" (Carruth), **Supp. XVI:** 48
Meadowlands (Glück), **Supp. V:** 88–90
"Mean, Mrs." (Gass), **Supp. VI:** 83
"Me and the Mule" (Hughes), **Supp. I Part 1:** 334
"Meaningless Institution, A" (Ginsberg), **Supp. II Part 1:** 313
"Meaning of a Literary Idea, The" (Trilling), **Supp. III Part 2:** 498
"Meaning of Birds, The" (C. Smith), **Supp. X:** 177
"Meaning of Death, The, An After Dinner Speech" (Tate), **IV:** 128, 129
"Meaning of Life, The" (Tate), **IV:** 137
"Meaning of Simplicity, The" (Ritsos), **Supp. XIII:** 78
Mean Spirit (Hogan), **Supp. IV Part 1:** 397, 404, 407–410, 415, 416–417
Mearns, Hughes, **III:** 220
"Measure" (Hass), **Supp. VI: 99–100,** 101

"Measuring My Blood" (Vizenor), **Supp. IV Part 1:** 262
Meatyard, Gene, **Supp. X:** 30
Me: By Jimmy (Big Boy) Valente (Keillor), **Supp. XVI:** 177
Mechan, Dennis B., **Supp. XVI:** 267–268
Mechanic, The (Bynner and DeMille), **Supp. XV:** 42, 50
"Mechanism" (Ammons), **Supp. VII:** 28
"Mechanism in Thought and Morals" (Holmes), **Supp. I Part 1:** 314
Mecom, Mrs. Jane, **II:** 122
"Meddlesome Jack" (Caldwell), **I:** 309
Medea (Jeffers), **Supp. II Part 2:** 435
Medea and Some Poems, The (Cullen), **Supp. IV Part 1:** 169, 173
"Me Decade and the Third Great Awakening, The" (Wolfe), **Supp. III Part 2:** 581
"Médecin Malgré Lui, Le" (W. C. Williams), **IV:** 407–408
"Medfield" (Bryant), **Supp. I Part 1:** 157
Medical History of Contraception, A (Himes), **Supp. V:** 128
"Medicine Song" (Gunn Allen), **Supp. IV Part 1:** 326
Médicis, Marie de, **II:** 548
Medina (McCarthy), **II:** 579
"Meditation, A" (Eberhart), **I:** 533–535
"Meditation 1.6" (Taylor), **IV:** 165
"Meditation 1.20" (Taylor), **IV:** 165
"Meditation 2.68A" (Taylor), **IV:** 165
"Meditation 2.102" (Taylor), **IV:** 150
"Meditation 2.112" (Taylor), **IV:** 165
"Meditation 20" (Taylor), **IV:** 154–155
"Meditation 40" (Second Series) (Taylor), **IV:** 147
"Meditation at Lagunitas" (Hass), **Supp. VI:** 104–105
"Meditation at Oyster River" (Roethke), **III:** 537, 549
Meditations (Descartes), **III:** 618
Meditations (Marcus Aurelius), **Supp. XVIII:** 304
"Meditations for a Savage Child" (Rich), **Supp. I Part 2:** 564–565
Meditations from a Movable Chair (Dubus), **Supp. VII:** 91
"Meditations in a Swine Yard" (Komunyakaa), **Supp. XIII:** 131
"Meditations of an Old Woman" (Roethke), **III:** 529, 540, 542, 543, 545–547, 548
Meditations on the Insatiable Soul (R. Bly), **Supp. IV Part 1:** 72–73
Meditative Poems, The (Martz), **IV:** 151
"Mediterranean, The" (Tate), **IV:** 129
"Medium of Fiction, The" (Gass), **Supp. VI:** 85–86
"Medley" (Bambara), **Supp. XI:** 9
"Medusa" (Bogan), **Supp. III Part 1:** 50, 51
Meehan, Thomas, **Supp. IV Part 2:** 577–578, 586, 590
Meek, Martha, **Supp. IV Part 2:** 439, 440, 441, 442, 445, 447, 448
Meeker, Richard K., **II:** 190
Meese, Elizabeth, **Supp. XIII:** 297
"Meeting, The" (F. Wright), **Supp. XVII:** 245
"Meeting and Greeting Area, The" (Cameron), **Supp. XII: 84–85**
Meeting by the River, A (Isherwood), **Supp. XIV:** 164, **170–171,** 172
"Meeting-House Hill" (Lowell), **II:** 522, 527
"Meeting in the Kitchen, The" (Schnackenberg), **Supp. XV:** 256
"Meeting South, A" (Anderson), **I:** 115
"Meeting the Mountains" (Snyder), **Supp. VIII:** 300
Meeting Trees (Sanders), **Supp. XVI:** 269
Meet Me at the Morgue (Macdonald), **Supp. IV Part 2:** 472
Mehta, Sonny, **Supp. XI:** 178
Meine, Curt, **Supp. XIV:** 179
Meiners, R. K., **IV:** 136, 137, 138, 140
Meinong, Alexius, **Supp. XIV:** 198, 199
Meisner, Sanford, **Supp. XIV:** 240, 242
Meister, Charles W., **II:** 112
"Melancholia" (Dunbar), **Supp. II Part 1:** 194
"Melanctha" (Stein), **IV:** 30, 34, 35, 37, 38–40, 45
"Melancthon" (Moore), **III:** 212, 215
Melbourne House (S. and A. Warner), **Supp. XVIII:** 268
Meliboeus Hipponax (Lowell). *See Biglow Papers, The* (Lowell)
Melinda and Melinda (Allen), **Supp. XV:** 16
Mellaart, James, **Supp. I Part 2:** 567
Mellard, James, **Supp. IV Part 1:** 387
Mellon, Andrew, **III:** 14
Melnick, Jeffrey, **Supp. X:** 252
Melnyczuk, Askold, **Supp. IV Part 1:** 70
Melodrama Play (Shepard), **Supp. III Part 2:** 440–441, 443, 445
Melodramatists, The (Nemerov), **III:** 268, 281–283, 284
Melting-Pot, The (Zangwill), **I:** 229
Melville, Allan, **III:** 74, 77
Melville, Gansevoort, **III:** 76
Melville, Herman, **I:** 104, 106, 211, 288, 340, 343, 348, 354, 355, 561–562; **II:** 27, 74, 224–225, 228, 230, 232, 236, 255, 259, 271, 272, 277, 281, 295, 307, 311, 319, 320, 321, 418, 477, 497, 539–540, 545; **III:** 29, 45, 70, **74–98,** 359, 438, 453, 454, 507, 562–563, 572, 576; **IV:** 57, 105, 194, 199, 202, 250, 309, 333, 345, 350, 380, 444, 453; **Retro. Supp. I:** 54, 91, 160, 215, 220, **243–262; Retro. Supp. II:** 76; **Supp. I Part 1:** 147, 238, 242, 249, 309, 317, 372; **Supp. I Part 2:** 383, 495, 579, 580, 582, 602; **Supp. IV Part 2:** 463, 613; **Supp. V:** 279, 281, 298, 308; **Supp. VIII:** 48, 103, 104, 105, 106, 108, 156, 175, 181, 188; **Supp. XI:** 83; **Supp. XII:** 282; **Supp. XIII:** 294, 305; **Supp. XIV:** 48, 227; **Supp. XV:** 287; **Supp. XVII:** 42, 185; **Supp. XVIII:** 1, 4, 6, 7, 9
Melville, Maria Gansevoort, **III:** 74, 77, 85
Melville, Mrs. Herman (Elizabeth Shaw), **III:** 77, 91, 92
Melville, Thomas, **III:** 77, 79, 92; **Supp. I Part 1:** 309
Melville, Whyte, **IV:** 309
Melville Goodwin, USA (Marquand), **III:** 60, 65–66
Melville's Marginalia (Cowen), **Supp. IV Part 2:** 435
"Melville's Marginalia" (Howe), **Supp. IV Part 2:** 435
Member of the Wedding, The (McCullers), **II:** 587, 592, 600–604, 605, 606; **Supp. VIII:** 124
"Meme Ortiz" (Cisneros), **Supp. VII:** 60
Memmon (song cycle) (Bowles), **Supp. IV Part 1:** 82
Memnoch the Devil (Rice), **Supp. VII:** 289, 290, 294, 296–299
"Memoir" (Untermeyer), **II:** 516–517
"Memoir, A" (Koch), **Supp. XV:** 184
"Memoirist's Apology, A" (Karr), **Supp. XI:** 245, 246
Memoir of Mary Ann, A (O'Connor), **III:** 357
Memoir of Thomas McGrath, A (Beeching), **Supp. X:** 114, 118
Memoirs of Arii Taimai (Adams), **I:** 2–3
"Memoirs of Carwin, the Biloquist" (Brown), **Supp. I Part 1:** 132
Memoirs of Hecate County (Wilson), **IV:** 429
Memoirs of Margaret Fuller Ossoli (Fuller), **Supp. II Part 1:** 280, 283, 285
"Memoirs of Stephen Calvert" (Brown), **Supp. I Part 1:** 133, 144
Memorabilia (Xenophon), **II:** 105
Memorable Providences (Mather), **Supp. II Part 2:** 458
Memorial, The: Portrait of a Family (Isherwood), **Supp. XIV:** 156, 159, 160–161
"Memorial Day" (Cameron), **Supp. XII:** 80, **82–83**
"Memorial for the City" (Auden), **Supp. II Part 1:** 20
"Memorial Rain" (MacLeish), **III:** 15
"Memorial to Ed Bland" (Brooks), **Supp. III Part 1:** 77
"Memorial Tribute" (Wilbur), **Supp. IV Part 2:** 642
"Memories" (Whittier), **Supp. I Part 2:** 699
Memories of a Catholic Girlhood (McCarthy), **II:** 560–561, 566; **Supp. XI:** 246; **Supp. XVI:** 64, 70
"Memories of East Texas" (Karr), **Supp. XI:** 239
"Memories of Uncle Neddy" (Bishop), **Retro. Supp. II:** 38; **Supp. I Part 1:** 73, 93
"Memories of West Street and Lepke" (Lowell), **II:** 550
"Memory" (Epstein), **Supp. XII:** 163
"Memory" (Everwine), **Supp. XV:** 82
"Memory, A" (Welty), **IV:** 261–262; **Retro. Supp. I:** 344–345
"Memory, The" (Gioia), **Supp. XV:** 119
Memory Gardens (Creeley), **Supp. IV Part 1:** 141, 157

Memory of Murder, A (Bradbury), **Supp. IV Part 1:** 103
Memory of Old Jack, The (Berry), **Supp. X:** 34
Memory of Two Mondays, A (A. Miller), **III:** 153, 156, 158–159, 160, 166
"Memo to Non-White Peoples" (Hughes), **Retro. Supp. I:** 209
Men, Women and Ghosts (Lowell), **II:** 523–524
Menaker, Daniel, **Supp. VIII:** 151
Menand, Louis, **Supp. XIV:** 40, 197; **Supp. XVI:** 106, 107
Men and Angels (Gordon), **Supp. IV Part 1:** 304–305, 306, 308
Men and Brethen (Cozzens), **I:** 363–365, 368, 375, 378, 379
Men and Cartoons (Lethem), **Supp. XVIII:** 145, **148**
"Men and Women" (R. Bly), **Supp. IV Part 1:** 72
"Men at Forty" (Justice), **Supp. VII:** 126–127
Mencius (Meng-tzu), **IV:** 183
Mencken, August, **III:** 100, 108
Mencken, August, Jr., **III:** 99, 109, 118–119
Mencken, Burkhardt, **III:** 100, 108
Mencken, Charles, **III:** 99
Mencken, Gertrude, **III:** 99
Mencken, H. L., **I:** 199, 210, 212, 235, 245, 261, 405, 514, 515, 517; **II:** 25, 27, 42, 89, 90, 91, 271, 289, 430, 443, 449; **III: 99–121,** 394, 482; **IV:** 76, 432, 440, 475, 482; **Retro. Supp. I:** 1, 101; **Retro. Supp. II:** 97, 98, 102, 265; **Supp. I Part 2:** 484, 629–630, 631, 647, 651, 653, 659, 673; **Supp. II Part 1:** 136; **Supp. IV Part 1:** 201, 314, 343; **Supp. IV Part 2:** 521, 692, 693; **Supp. XI:** 163–164, 166; **Supp. XIII:** 161; **Supp. XIV:** 111; **Supp. XV:** 297, 301, 303; **Supp. XVI:** 187–188, 189; **Supp. XVII:** 106
Mencken, Mrs. August (Anna Abhau), **III:** 100, 109
Mencken, Mrs. H. L. (Sara Haardt), **III:** 109, 111
"Men Deified Because of Their Cruelty" (Simic), **Supp. VIII:** 282
Mendelbaum, Paul, **Supp. V:** 159
Mendele, **IV:** 3, 10
Mendelief, Dmitri Ivanovich, **IV:** 421
Mendelsohn, Daniel, **Supp. X:** 153, 154; **Supp. XV:** 257, 258, 261, 266
"Mending Wall" (Frost), **II:** 153–154; **Retro. Supp. I:** 128, 130; **Supp. X:** 64
Men from the Boys, The (Lacy), **Supp. XV:** 202, 205
Men in the Off Hours (Carson), **Supp. XII: 111–113**
"Men in the Storm, The" (Crane), **I:** 411
"Men Loved Wholly Beyond Wisdom" (Bogan), **Supp. III Part 1:** 50
"Men Made Out of Words" (Stevens), **IV:** 88
Men Must Act (Mumford), **Supp. II Part 2:** 479
Mennes, John, **II:** 111
Mennoti, Gian Carlo, **Supp. IV Part 1:** 84
Men of Brewster Place, The (Naylor), **Supp. VIII:** 213, **228–230**
"Men of Color, to Arms!" (Douglass), **Supp. III Part 1:** 171
Men of Good Hope: A Story of American Progressives (Aaron), **Supp. I Part 2:** 650
Mens' Club, The (film), **Supp. XVI:** 212–213
Men's Club, The (L. Michaels), **Supp. XVI:** 206, **210–212**
"Menstruation at Forty" (Sexton), **Supp. II Part 2:** 686
"Mental Hospital Garden, The" (W. C. Williams), **Retro. Supp. I:** 428
Mental Radio (Sinclair), **Supp. V:** 289
Mentoria; or, The Young Lady's Friend (Rowson), **Supp. XV: 233–234,** 238
"Men We Carry in Our Minds, The" (Sanders), **Supp. XVI:** 273
Men Who Made the Nation, The (Dos Passos), **I:** 485
Men Without Women (Hemingway), **II:** 249; **Retro. Supp. I:** 170, 176; **Supp. IX:** 202
"Merced" (Rich), **Supp. I Part 2:** 563
"Mercedes" (E. Stoddard), **Supp. XV:** 278
"Mercedes Hospital" (Bishop), **Retro. Supp. II:** 51
"Mercenary, A" (Ozick), **Supp. V:** 267
Merchant of Venice, The (Shakespeare), **IV:** 227; **Supp. XIV:** 325
Mercury Theatre, **Retro. Supp. I:** 65
Mercy, Pity, Peace, and Love (Ozick), **Supp. V:** 257, 258
Mercy, The (Levine), **Supp. V:** 194–195
Mercy of a Rude Stream (H. Roth), **Supp. IX:** 231, 234, **235–242**
Mercy Philbrick's Choice (Jackson), **Retro. Supp. I:** 26, 27, 33
Mercy Street (Sexton), **Supp. II Part 2:** 683, 689
Meredith, George, **II:** 175, 186; **Supp. IV Part 1:** 300
Meredith, Mary. *See* Webb, Mary
Meredith, William, **II:** 545; **Retro. Supp. II:** 181
"Merely to Know" (Rich), **Supp. I Part 2:** 554
"Mère Pochette" (Jewett), **II:** 400
"Merger II, The" (Auchincloss), **Supp. IV Part 1:** 34
"Mericans" (Cisneros), **Supp. VII:** 69
"Merida, 1969" (Matthews), **Supp. IX:** 151
"Meridian" (Clampitt), **Supp. IX: 48–49**
Meridian (Walker), **Supp. III Part 2:** 520, 524, 527, 528, 531–537
Mérimée, Prosper, **II:** 322
Meriweather, James B., **Retro. Supp. I:** 77, 91
Meriwether, James B., **Retro Supp. I:** 77, 91
"Meriwether Connection, The" (Cowley), **Supp. II Part 1:** 142
Merker, Kim K., **Supp. XI:** 261; **Supp. XV:** 75, 77
"Merlin" (Emerson), **II:** 19, 20
Merlin (Robinson), **III:** 522
"Merlin Enthralled" (Wilbur), **Supp. III Part 2:** 544, 554
"Mermother" (A. Finch), **Supp. XVII:** 72
Merril, Judith, **Supp. XVI:** 123
Merrill, Christopher, **Supp. XI:** 329
Merrill, James, **Retro. Supp. I:** 296; **Retro. Supp. II:** 53; **Supp. III Part 1: 317–338; Supp. III Part 2:** 541, 561; **Supp. IX:** 40, 42, 48, 52; **Supp. X:** 73; **Supp. XI:** 123, 131, 249; **Supp. XII:** 44, 254, 255, 256, 261–262, 269–270; **Supp. XIII:** 76, 85; **Supp. XV:** 249, 250, 253; **Supp. XVII:** 123
Merrill, Mark (pseudonym). *See* Markson, David
Merrill, Robert, **Retro. Supp. II:** 201
Merrill, Ronald, **Supp. IV Part 2:** 521
Merritt, Abraham, **Supp. XVII:** 58
Merritt, Theresa, **Supp. VIII:** 332
"Merry-Go-Round" (Hughes), **Retro. Supp. I:** 194, 205; **Supp. I Part 1:** 333
Merry-Go-Round, The (Van Vechten), **Supp. II Part 2:** 734, 735
Merry Month of May, The (Jones), **Supp. XI: 227–228**
Merry Widow, The (Lehar), **III:** 183
Merton, Thomas, **III:** 357; **Supp. VIII: 193–212**
Merwin, W. S., **Supp. III Part 1: 339–360; Supp. III Part 2:** 541; **Supp. IV Part 2:** 620, 623, 626; **Supp. IX:** 152, 155, 290; **Supp. V:** 332; **Supp. XIII:** 274, 277; **Supp. XV:** 222, 342
Meryman, Richard, **Supp. IV Part 2:** 579, 583
Meshugah (Singer), **Retro. Supp. II: 315–316**
Mesic, Michael, **Supp. IV Part 1:** 175
Mesic, Penelope, **Supp. X:** 15
"Message in the Bottle, The" (Percy), **Supp. III Part 1:** 388
Message in the Bottle, The (Percy), **Supp. III Part 1:** 387–388, 393, 397
"Message of Flowers and Fire and Flowers, The" (Brooks), **Supp. III Part 1:** 69
Messengers Will Come No More, The (Fiedler), **Supp. XIII:** 103
Messerli, Douglas, **Supp. XVI:** 293
Messiah (Vidal), **Supp. IV Part 2:** 677, 680, 681–682, 685, 691, 692
"Messiah, The" (Wasserstein), **Supp. XV:** 328
Messiah of Stockholm, The (Ozick), **Supp. V:** 270–271; **Supp. XVII:** 42
Messud, Claire, **Supp. XVIII:** 98
Metamorphic Tradition in Modern Poetry (Quinn), **IV:** 421
Metamorphoses (Ovid), **II:** 542–543; **III:** 467, 468
Metamorphoses (Pound, trans.), **III:** 468–469
Metamorphosis (Ovid), **Supp. XV:** 33; **Supp. XVI:** 20

Metamorphosis, The (Kafka), **IV:** 438; **Retro. Supp. II:** 287–288; **Supp. VIII:** 3
"Metamorphosis and Survival" (Woodcock), **Supp. XIII:** 33
"Metaphor as Mistake" (Percy), **Supp. III Part 1:** 387–388
Metaphor & Memory: Essays (Ozick), **Supp. V:** 272
"Metaphors of a Magnifico" (Stevens), **IV:** 92
Metaphysical Club, The (Menand), **Supp. XIV:** 40, 197
"Metaphysical Poets, The" (Eliot), **I:** 527, 586
"Metaphysics" (Ginsberg), **Supp. II Part 1:** 313
Metcalf, Paul, **Supp. XIV:** 96
"Meteor, The" (Bradbury), **Supp. IV Part 1:** 102
Methinks the Lady...(Endore), **Supp. XVII:** 61–62
Metress, Christopher P., **Supp. V:** 314
Metrical History of Christianity, The (Taylor), **IV:** 163
Metropolis, The (Sinclair), **Supp. V:** 285
"Metterling Lists, The" (Allen), **Supp. XV:** 15
"Metzengerstein" (Poe), **III:** 411, 417
Mew, Charlotte, **Retro. Supp. II:** 247
Mewshaw, Michael, **Supp. V:** 57; **Supp. X:** 82
"Mexican Hands" (Ryan as Quin), **Supp. XVIII:** 227
"Mexico" (Lowell), **II:** 553, 554
"Mexico, Age Four" (Salinas), **Supp. XIII:** 315
Mexico City Blues (Kerouac), **Supp. III Part 1:** 225, 229
"Mexico Is a Foreign Country: Five Studies in Naturalism" (Warren), **IV:** 241, 252
"Mexico's Children" (Rodriguez), **Supp. XIV:** 302
Meyer, Donald B., **III:** 298
Meyer, Ellen Hope, **Supp. V:** 123
Meyers, Jeffrey, **Retro. Supp. I:** 124, 138; **Retro. Supp. II:** 191
Meynell, Alice, **Supp. I Part 1:** 220
Mezey, Robert, **Supp. IV Part 1:** 60; **Supp. V:** 180; **Supp. XIII:** 312; **Supp. XV:** 74
Mezzanine, The (Baker), **Supp. XIII: 41–43,** 44, 45, 48, 55
"Mezzo Cammin" (Longfellow), **II:** 490
"Mi Abuelo" (Ríos), **Supp. IV Part 2:** 541
Miami (Didion), **Supp. IV Part 1:** 199, 210
Miami and the Siege of Chicago (Mailer), **Retro. Supp. II:** 206
"Michael" (Wordsworth), **III:** 523
Michael, Magali Cornier, **Supp. XIII:** 32
"Michael Angelo: A Fragment" (Longfellow), **II:** 490, 494, 495, 506; **Retro. Supp. II:** 167
"Michael Egerton" (Price), **Supp. VI:** 257–258, 260
Michael Kohlhaas (Kleist), **Supp. IV Part 1:** 224
Michaels, Leonard, **Supp. XVI: 201–215**
Michaels, Walter Benn, **Retro. Supp. I:** 115, 369, 379
Michael Scarlett (Cozens), **I:** 358–359, 378
Michaux, Henri, **Supp. XVI:** 288
Michelangelo, **I:** 18; **II:** 11–12; **III:** 124; **Supp. I Part 1:** 363; **Supp. XVII:** 112
Michel-Michot, Paulette, **Supp. XI:** 224–225
Michelson, Albert, **IV:** 27
Mickelsson's Ghosts (Gardner), **Supp. VI:** 63, **73–74**
Mickiewicz, Adam, **Supp. II Part 1:** 299
"Mid-Air" (Conroy), **Supp. XVI:** 69, 71
Midair (Conroy), **Supp. XVI:** 63, **71–72**
Mid-American Chants (Anderson), **I:** 109, 114
"Midas" (Winters), **Supp. II Part 2:** 801
"Mid-August at Sourdough Mountain Lookout" (Snyder), **Supp. VIII:** 292–293
Midcentury (Dos Passos), **I:** 474, 475, 478, 490, 492–494; **Supp. I Part 2:** 646
Mid-Century American Poets, **III:** 532
"Mid-Day" (Doolittle), **Supp. I Part 1:** 266–267
"Middle Age" (Lowell), **II:** 550
"Middleaged Man, The" (Simpson), **Supp. IX:** 274–275
Middle Ages, The (Gurney), **Supp. V:** 96, 105, 108
Middlebrook, Diane Wood, **Supp. IV Part 2:** 444, 451
"Middle Daughter, The" (Kingsolver), **Supp. VII:** 209
Middlemarch (Eliot), **I:** 457, 459; **II:** 290, 291; **Retro. Supp. I:** 225; **Supp. I Part 1:** 174; **Supp. IX:** 43; **Supp. XI:** 68; **Supp. XII:** 335
Middle of My Tether, The: Familiar Essays (Epstein), **Supp. XIV: 106–107**
"Middle of Nowhere, The" (Wagoner), **Supp. IX:** 327–328
Middle of the Journey, The (Trilling), **Supp. III Part 2:** 495, 504–506
"Middle of the Way" (Kinnell), **Supp. III Part 1:** 242
"Middle Passage" (Hayden), **Supp. II Part 1:** 363, 375–376
Middle Passage (Johnson), **Supp. VI: 194–196,** 198, 199; **Supp. XIII:** 182
"Middle Toe of the Right Foot, The" (Bierce), **I:** 203
Middleton, Thomas, **Retro. Supp. I:** 62
"Middle Years, The" (James), **Retro. Supp. I:** 228, 272
Middle Years, The (James), **II:** 337–338; **Retro. Supp. I:** 235
"Midnight" (Dunn), **Supp. XI:** 147
"Midnight Consultations, The" (Freneau), **Supp. II Part 1:** 257
Midnight Cry, A (Mather), **Supp. II Part 2:** 460
"Midnight Gladness" (Levertov), **Supp. III Part 1:** 284–285
"Midnight Magic" (Mason), **Supp. VIII:** 146
Midnight Magic: Selected Stories of Bobbie Ann Mason (Mason), **Supp. VIII:** 148
Midnight Mass (Bowles), **Supp. IV Part 1:** 93
"Midnight Postscript" (F. Wright), **Supp. XVII:** 245, 246
"Midnight Show" (Shapiro), **Supp. II Part 2:** 705
"Midpoint" (Updike), **Retro. Supp. I:** 321, 323, 327, 330, 335
Midpoint and Other Poems (Updike), **IV:** 214
"Midrash on Happiness" (Paley), **Supp. VI:** 217
"Midsummer in the Blueberry Barrens" (Clampitt), **Supp. IX:** 40–41
"Midsummer Letter" (Carruth), **Supp. XVI:** 47
Midsummer Night's Dream, A (Shakespeare), **Supp. I Part 1:** 369–370; **Supp. X:** 69
Midsummer Night's Sex Comedy, A (film; Allen), **Supp. XV:** 8
"Midwest" (Stafford), **Supp. XI:** 317
"Midwest Poetics" (C. Baxter), **Supp. XVII:** 18
Mieder, Wolfgang, **Supp. XIV:** 126
Mies van der Rohe, Ludwig, **Supp. IV Part 1:** 40
Mighty Aphrodite (film; Allen), **Supp. XV:** 11
"Mighty Fortress, A" (Leopold), **Supp. XIV:** 185
"Mighty Lord, The (Rowson), **Supp. XV:** 243
"Migration, The"(Tate), **IV:** 130
Mihailovitch, Bata, **Supp. VIII:** 272
Miklitsch, Robert, **Supp. IV Part 2:** 628, 629
Mila 18 (Uris), **Supp. IV Part 1:** 379
Milagro Beanfield War, The (film), **Supp. XIII:** 267
Milagro Beanfield War, The (Nichols), **Supp. XIII:** 253, **265–266**
Milburn, Michael, **Supp. XI:** 239, 242
Milch, David, **Supp. XI:** 348
Miles, Barry, **Supp. XII:** 123
Miles, Jack, **Supp. VIII:** 86
Miles, Josephine, **Supp. XIII:** 275
Miles, Julie, **I:** 199
Miles, Kitty, **I:** 199
Milestone, Lewis, **Supp. I Part 1:** 281
Miles Wallingford (Cooper). *See Afloat and Ashore* (Cooper)
Milford, Kate, **Supp. XVIII:** 150
Milford, Nancy, **II:** 83; **Supp. IX:** 60
Milhaud, Darius, **Supp. IV Part 1:** 81
Miligate, Michael, **IV:** 123, 130, 132
"Militant Nudes"(Hardwick), **Supp. III Part 1:** 210–211
"Milk Bottles"(Anderson), **I:** 114
Milk Train Doesn't Stop Here Anymore, The (T. Williams), **IV:** 382, 383, 384, 386, 390, 391, 392, 393, 394, 395, 398
Mill, James, **II:** 357
Mill, John Stuart, **III:** 294–295; **Supp. XI:** 196; **Supp. XIV:** 22
Millar, Kenneth. *See* Macdonald, Ross

Millar, Margaret (Margaret Sturm), **Supp. IV Part 2:** 464, 465
Millay, Cora, **III:** 123, 133–134, 135–136
Millay, Edna St. Vincent, **I:** 482; **II:** 530; **III: 122–144; IV:** 433, 436; **Retro. Supp. II:** 48; **Supp. I Part 2:** 707, 714, 726; **Supp. IV Part 1:** 168; **Supp. IV Part 2:** 607; **Supp. IX:** 20; **Supp. V:** 113; **Supp. XIV:** 120, 121, 122, 127; **Supp. XV:** 42, 46, 51, 250, 293, 307; **Supp. XVII:** 69, 75, 96
Millennium Approaches (Kushner), **Supp. IX:** 141, 142, 145
Miller, Arthur, **I:** 81, 94; **III: 145–169; Supp. IV Part 1:** 359; **Supp. IV Part 2:** 574; **Supp. VIII:** 334; **Supp. XIII:** 127; **Supp. XIV:** 102, 239; **Supp. XVI:** 194
Miller, Brown, **Supp. IV Part 1:** 67
Miller, Carol, **Supp. IV Part 1:** 400, 405, 409, 410, 411
Miller, Henry, **I:** 97, 157; **III:** 40, **170–192; IV:** 138; **Retro. Supp. II:** 327; **Supp. I Part 2:** 546; **Supp. V:** 119, 131; **Supp. X:** 183, 185, 187, 194, 195; **Supp. XIII:** 1, 17
Miller, Henry (actor), **Supp. XVI:** 182
Miller, Herman, **Supp. I Part 2:** 614, 617
Miller, James E., Jr., **IV:** 352
Miller, Jeffrey, **Supp. IV Part 1:** 95
Miller, J. Hillis, **Supp. IV Part 1:** 387
Miller, Joaquin, **I:** 193, 195, 459; **Supp. II Part 1:** 351
Miller, John Duncan, **Supp. I Part 2:** 604
Miller, Jonathan, **Retro. Supp. II:** 181
Miller, Laura, **Supp. XIII:** 48
Miller, Marilyn, **Supp. XVI:** 187
Miller, Matt, **Supp. XV:** 211
Miller, Matthew, **Supp. XVI:** 47, 51
Miller, Mrs. Arthur (Ingeborg Morath), **III:** 162–163
Miller, Mrs. Arthur (Marilyn Monroe), **III:** 161, 162–163
Miller, Mrs. Arthur (Mary Grace Slattery), **III:** 146, 161
Miller, Orilla, **Supp. I Part 1:** 48
Miller, Perry, **I:** 546, 547, 549, 550, 560; **IV:** 186; **Supp. I Part 1:** 31, 104; **Supp. I Part 2:** 484; **Supp. IV Part 2:** 422; **Supp. VIII:** 101
Miller, R. Baxter, **Retro. Supp. I:** 195, 207
Miller, Robert Ellis, **II:** 588
Miller, Ruth, **Supp. X:** 324
Miller, Stuart, **Supp. XVI:** 242
Miller, Sue, **Supp. X:** 77, 85; **Supp. XI:** 190; **Supp. XII: 289–305**
Miller of Old Church, The (Glasgow), **II:** 175, 181
"Miller's Tale"(Chaucer), **III:** 283
Miller Williams and the Poetry of the Particular (Burns), **Supp. XV:** 339
Millett, Kate, **Supp. X:** 193, 196
Millgate, Michael, **Retro. Supp. I:** 91
Mill Hand's Lunch Bucket (Bearden), **Supp. VIII:** 337
Millier, Brett C., **Retro. Supp. II:** 39
Milligan, Bryce, **Supp. XIII:** 274, 275, 277
Millions of Strange Shadows (Hecht), **Supp. X:** 57, **62–65**
"Million Young Workmen, 1915, A" (Sandburg), **III:** 585
Millroy the Magician (Theroux), **Supp. VIII:** 325
Mills, Alice, **Supp. XIII:** 233
Mills, Benjamin Fay, **III:** 176
Mills, C. Wright, **Supp. I Part 2:** 648, 650
Mills, Florence, **Supp. I Part 1:** 322
Mills, Ralph J., Jr., **III:** 530; **Supp. IV Part 1:** 64; **Supp. XI:** 311
Mills, Tedi López, **Supp. XVI:** 281
"Mills of the Kavanaughs, The" (Lowell), **II:** 542–543
Mills of the Kavanaughs, The (Lowell), **II:** 542–543, 546, 550; **III:** 508; **Retro. Supp. II:** 178, 179, 188
Milne, A. A., **Supp. IX:** 189
Milne, A. J. M., **I:** 278
Milosz, Czeslaw, **Supp. III Part 2:** 630; **Supp. VIII:** 20, 22; **Supp. XI:** 267, 312; **Supp. XVII:** 241
Miltner, Robert, **Supp. XI:** 142
Milton, Edith, **Supp. VIII:** 79; **Supp. X:** 82
Milton, John, **I:** 6, 138, 273, 587–588; **II:** 11, 15, 113, 130, 411, 540, 542; **III:** 40, 124, 201, 225, 274, 468, 471, 486, 487, 503, 511; **IV:** 50, 82, 126, 137, 155, 157, 241, 279, 347, 422, 461, 494; **Retro. Supp. I:** 60, 67, 127, 360; **Retro. Supp. II:** 161, 295; **Supp. I Part 1:** 124, 150, 370; **Supp. I Part 2:** 412, 422, 491, 501, 522, 622, 722, 724; **Supp. IV Part 2:** 430, 634; **Supp. VIII:** 294; **Supp. X:** 22, 23, 36; **Supp. XII:** 180; **Supp. XIV:** 5, 7
Milton, John R., **Supp. IV Part 2:** 503
Milton and His Modern Critics (L. P. Smith), **Supp. XIV:** 347
"Milton by Firelight" (Snyder), **Supp. II Part 1:** 314; **Supp. VIII:** 294
"Miltonic Sonnet, A" (Wilbur), **Supp. III Part 2:** 558
Mimesis (Auerbach), **III:** 453
"Mimnermos and the Motions of Hedonism" (Carson), **Supp. XII: 99–100**
"Mimnermos Interviews, The" (Carson), **Supp. XII: 100–101**
Mims, Edwin, **Supp. I Part 1:** 362, 364, 365, 371
"Mind" (Wilbur), **Supp. III Part 2:** 554
"Mind, The" (Kinnell), **Supp. III Part 1:** 245
Mind Breaths: Poems 1972–1977 (Ginsberg), **Supp. II Part 1:** 326
Mindfield: New and Selected Poems (Corso), **Supp. XII: 136**
"Mind in the Modern World" (Trilling), **Supp. III Part 2:** 512
"Mind Is Shapely, Art Is Shapely" (Ginsberg), **Supp. II Part 1:** 327
Mindlin, Henrique, **Supp. I Part 1:** 92
Mind of My Mind (O. Butler), **Supp. XIII:** 62, 63
Mind of Primitive Man, The (Boas), **Supp. XIV:** 209
"Mind-Reader, The" (Wilbur), **Supp. III Part 2:** 561–562
Mind-Reader, The (Wilbur), **Supp. III Part 2:** 560–562
Mindwheel (Pinsky), **Supp. VI:** 235
Minear, Richard H., **Supp. XVI:** 101, 102
"Mined Country" (Wilbur), **Supp. III Part 2:** 546–548
"Mine Own John Berryman" (Levine), **Supp. V:** 179–180
Miner, Bob, **Supp. V:** 23
Miner, Earl, **III:** 466, 479
Miner, Madonne, **Supp. XIII:** 29
"Minerva Writes Poems" (Cisneros), **Supp. VII:** 63–64, 66
Mingus, Charles, **Supp. IX:** 152
"Mingus in Diaspora" (Matthews), **Supp. IX:** 166
"Mingus in Shadow" (Matthews), **Supp. IX:** 168–169
Ming Yellow (Marquand), **III:** 56
"Minimal, The" (Roethke), **III:** 531–532
Minimus Poems, The (X. J. Kennedy), **Supp. XV:** 169–170
"Mini-novela: *Rosa y sus espinas"* (Mora), **Supp. XIII:** 218
"Minions of Midas, The" (London), **II:** 474–475
Minister's Charge, The, or The Apprenticeship of Lemuel Barber (Howells), **II:** 285–286, 287
"Minister's Wooing, The" (Stowe), **Supp. I Part 2:** 592–595
Minister's Wooing, The (Stowe), **II:** 541
"Ministration of Our Departed Friends, The" (Stowe), **Supp. I Part 2:** 586–587
"Minneapolis Poem, The" (Wright), **Supp. III Part 2:** 601–602
Minnesota Grain Show, The (radio, Keillor), **Supp. XVI:** 170
"Minnesota Transcendentalist" (Peseroff), **Supp. IV Part 1:** 71
Minnie, Temple, **II:** 344
Minority Report: H. L. Mencken's Notebooks (Mencken), **III:** 112
Minor Pleasures of Life, The (Macaulay), **Supp. XIV:** 348
"Minor Poems" (Eliot), **I:** 579
"Minor Poet" (Hay), **Supp. XIV:** 127
"Minor Topics" (Howells), **II:** 274
Minot, Susan, **Supp. VI: 203–215**
"Minotaur Loves His Labyrinth, The" (Simic), **Supp. VIII:** 270, 279, 281
"Minstrel Man" (Hughes), **Supp. I Part 1:** 325
Mint (Nye), **Supp. XIII:** 277
"Minting Time" (Sarton), **Supp. VIII:** 259
"Mint Snowball" (Nye), **Supp. XIII:** 278, 284
Mint Snowball (Nye), **Supp. XIII:** 277–278, **284–285**
"Mint Snowball II" (Nye), **Supp. XIII:** 284, 285
Mintzlaff, Dorothy, **Supp. XV:** 153
Minus, Marian, **Supp. XVIII:** 282
Minutes to Go (Corso, Gysin, Beiles and Burroughs), **Supp. XII:** 129

Mirabell: Books of Number (Merrill), **Supp. III Part 1:** 332–334
"Miracle" (Carver), **Supp. III Part 1:** 139–140
"Miracle for Breakfast, A" (Bishop), **Retro. Supp. II:** 43
"Miracle of Lava Canyon, The" (Henry), **Supp. II Part 1:** 389, 390
Miracle of Mindfulness, The: A Manual on Meditation (Thich Nhat Hanh), **Supp. V:** 199–200
Mirage (Masters), **Supp. I Part 2:** 459, 470, 471
"Mirages, The" (Hayden), **Supp. II Part 1:** 373
"Miranda" (Buck), **Supp. II Part 1:** 128
Miranda, Carmen, **Supp. XII:** 165
Miranda, Francisco de, **Supp. I Part 2:** 522
"Miranda Over the Valley" (Dubus), **Supp. VII:** 81–83
"Miriam" (Capote), **Supp. III Part 1:** 117, 120, 122
"Miriam" (Whittier), **Supp. I Part 2:** 691, 703
"Miriam Tazewell" (Ransom), **Supp. X:** 58
"Mirror" (Merrill), **Supp. III Part 1:** 322
"Mirror" (Plath), **Retro. Supp. II:** 248–249, 257
"Mirror, The" (Glück), **Supp. V:** 83
"Mirroring Evil: Nazi Images/Recent Art" (Epstein), **Supp. XII:** 166
Mirrors (Creeley), **Supp. IV Part 1:** 156
Mirrors and Windows (Nemerov), **III:** 269, 275–277
"Mirrors of Chartres Street" (Faulkner), **II:** 56
Misanthrope, The (Molière; Wilbur, trans.), **Supp. III Part 2:** 552, 560
Miscellaneous Poems (Rowson), **Supp. XV:** 243
Miscellaneous Works of Mr. Philip Freneau, Containing His Essays and Additional Poems (Freneau), **Supp. II Part 1:** 263, 264, 266
Miscellany of American Poetry, A (Untermeyer, ed.), **Supp. XV:** 305, 310
Misery (King), **Supp. V:** 140, 141, 142, 147–148, 151, 152
Mises, Ludwig von, **Supp. IV Part 2:** 524
Misfits, The (A. Miller), **III:** 147, 149, 156, 161–162, 163
"Misogamist, The" (Dubus), **Supp. VII:** 86–87
Misread City, The: New Literary Los Angeles (Gioia and Timberg, eds.), **Supp. XV:** 116
Misrepresentations Corrected, and Truth Vindicated, in a Reply to the Rev. Mr. Solomon Williams's Book (Edwards), **I:** 549
Miss Crandall's School for Young Ladies & Little Misses of Color (Nelson and Alexander), **Supp. XVIII:** 171, 175, 181, **185–186**
Miss Doll, Go Home (Markson), **Supp. XVII:** 138
"Miss Ella" (Z. Fitzgerald), **Supp. IX:** 57, 59, **71–72**
"Miss Emily and the Bibliographer" (Tate), **Supp. II Part 1:** 103
"Miss Furr and Miss Skeene" (Stein), **IV:** 29–30
"Missing Child" (Simic), **Supp. VIII:** 282
"Missing in Action" (Komunyakaa), **Supp. XIII:** 123, 124
Missing/Kissing: Missing Marisa, Kissing Christine (Shanley), **Supp. XIV:** 316
Missing Link (X. J. Kennedy), **Supp. XV:** 165
"Mission of Jane, The" (Wharton), **Retro. Supp. I:** 367
"Missions, The" (Rodriguez), **Supp. XIV:** 303
Mission to Moscow (film), **Supp. I Part 1:** 281
"Mississippi" (Bass), **Supp. XVI:** 17
"Mississippi" (Faulkner), **Retro. Supp. I:** 77
"Mississippi" (Simpson), **Supp. IX:** 271
"Miss Kate in H-1" (Twain), **IV:** 193
Miss Leonora When Last Seen (Taylor), **Supp. V:** 323
Miss Lonelyhearts (West), **I:** 107; **II:** 436; **III:** 357; **IV:** 287, 288, 290–297, 300, 301, 305, 306; **Retro. Supp. II:** 321, 322, 325, 328, **332–335**
Miss Mamma Aimee (Caldwell), **I:** 308, 309, 310
"Miss Mary Pask" (Wharton), **IV:** 316; **Retro. Supp. I:** 382
"Miss McEnders" (Chopin), **Retro. Supp. II:** 67
"Missoula Softball Tournament" (Hugo), **Supp. VI:** 132
Miss Ravenel's Conversion from Secession to Loyalty (De Forest), **IV:** 350
"Miss Tempy's Watchers" (Jewett), **II:** 401; **Retro. Supp. II:** 139
"Miss Terriberry to Wed in Suburbs" (Updike), **Retro. Supp. I:** 335
"Miss Urquhart's Tiara" (Jarman), **Supp. XVII:** 116
"Mist, The" (King), **Supp. V:** 144
"Mistaken Charity, A" (Freeman), **Retro. Supp. II:** 138
"Mister Brother" (Cunningham), **Supp. XV:** 68
"Mister Toussan" (Ellison), **Retro. Supp. II:** 124–125; **Supp. II Part 1:** 238
"Mistress of Sydenham Plantation, The" (Jewett), **Retro. Supp. II:** 141
Mitchell, Burroughs, **Supp. XI:** 218, 222, 227
Mitchell, Dr. S. Weir, **IV:** 310
Mitchell, Margaret, **II:** 177
Mitchell, Roger, **Supp. IV Part 1:** 70; **Supp. XV:** 213, 215
Mitchell, Tennessee. *See* Anderson, Mrs. Sherwood (Tennessee Mitchell)
Mitchell, Verner, **Supp. XVIII:** 281, 286
Mitchell, Wesley C., **Supp. I Part 2:** 632, 643
Mitch Miller (Masters), **Supp. I Part 2:** 456, 466, 469–471, 474, 475, 476
Mitchum, Robert, **Supp. IX:** 95, 250
Mitgang, Herbert, **Supp. IV Part 1:** 220, 226, 307; **Supp. VIII:** 124
"Mixed Sequence" (Roethke), **III:** 547
Miyazawa Kenji, **Supp. VIII:** 292
Mizener, Arthur, **II:** 77, 81, 84, 94; **IV:** 132; **Supp. XVIII:** 249
Mizner, Addison, **Supp. XVI:** 191
Mizner, Wilson, **Supp. XVI:** 191, 195
Mladenoff, Nancy, **Supp. X:** 176
"M'liss: An Idyl of Red Mountain" (Harte), **Supp. II Part 1:** 339
"Mnemonic Devices" (Goldbarth), **Supp. XII:** 183
"Mobile in Back of the Smithsonian, The" (Swenson), **Supp. IV Part 2:** 646
Mobilio, Albert, **Supp. VIII:** 3; **Supp. XVIII:** 144
Moby Dick (film), **Supp. IV Part 1:** 102, 116
Moby Dick; or, The Whale (Melville), **I:** 106, 354; **II:** 33, 224–225, 236, 539–540; **III:** 28–29, 74, 75, 77, 81, 82, 83–86, 87, 89, 90, 91, 93, 94, 95, 359, 453, 556; **IV:** 57, 199, 201, 202; **Retro. Supp. I:** 160, 220, 243, 244, 248, **249–253,** 254, 256, 257, 335; **Retro. Supp. II:** 121, 186, 275; **Supp. I Part 1:** 249; **Supp. I Part 2:** 579; **Supp. IV Part 2:** 613; **Supp. V:** 281; **Supp. VIII:** 106, 188, 198
Mock, John, **Supp. XIII:** 174
"Mocking-Bird, The" (Bierce), **I:** 202
"Mock Orange" (Glück), **Supp. V:** 84–85
Modarressi, Mitra, **Supp. IV Part 2:** 657
Models of Misrepresentation: On the Fiction of E. L. Doctorow (Morris), **Supp. IV Part 1:** 231
Model World and Other Stories, A (Chabon), **Supp. XI:** 66
Modern American and British Poetry (Untermeyer, ed.), **Supp. XV:** 306
Modern American Poetry (Untermeyer, ed.), **Supp. XV:** 293, 303, 306, 312
Modern American Verse (Untermeyer), **Supp. XV:** 301
Modern Brazilian Architecture (Bishop, trans.), **Supp. I Part 1:** 92
Modern British Poetry (Untermeyer, ed.), **Supp. XV:** 305, 308, 312
Modern Fiction Studies, **Supp. V:** 238
Modern Fiction Studies (Haegert), **Supp. XVI:** 69
Modern Instance a Novel, A (Howells), **II:** 275, 279, 282–283, 285
Modern Library, The, **Retro. Supp. I:** 112, 113
Modern Mephistopheles, A (Alcott), **Supp. I Part 1:** 37–38
Modern Poetic Sequence, The (Rosenthal), **Supp. V:** 333
"Modern Poetry" (Crane), **I:** 390
Modern Poetry and the Tradition (Brooks), **Supp. XIV: 5–7**
"Modern Race Creeds and Their Fallacies" (Locke), **Supp. XIV:** 210
Modern Rhetoric, with Readings (Brooks and Warren), **Supp. XIV:** 11
"Modern Sorcery" (Simic), **Supp. VIII:** 283

Modern Times (album, Dylan), **Supp. XVIII:** 28, 31, 33
"Modern Times" (Zukofsky), **Supp. III Part 2:** 624
Modern Writer, The (Anderson), **I:** 117
Modersohn, Mrs. Otto (Paula Becker), **Supp. I Part 2:** 573–574
Modersohn, Otto, **Supp. I Part 2:** 573
"Modes of Being" (Levertov), **Supp. III Part 1:** 282
Modest Enquiry into the Nature and Necessity of a Paper-Currency, A (Franklin), **II:** 108–109
"Modest Proposal, A" (Swift), **I:** 295; **Retro. Supp. II:** 287
"Modest Proposal with Feline Feeling, A" (Neugeboren), **Supp. XVI:** 219
"Modest Self-Tribute, A" (Wilson), **IV:** 431, 432
Moeller, Philip, **III:** 398, 399
"Moench von Berchtesgaden, Der" (Voss), **I:** 199–200
Moers, Ellen, **Retro. Supp. II:** 99
Moe's Villa and Other Stories (Purdy), **Supp. VII:** 270, 280
Mogen, David, **Supp. IV Part 1:** 106
Mohammed, **I:** 480; **II:** 1
Mohawk (Russo), **Supp. XII: 326–328**
Moir, William Wilmerding, **Supp. V:** 279
Moldaw, Carol, **Supp. XV:** 264; **Supp. XVII:** 127, 130
"Moles" (Oliver), **Supp. VII:** 235
Molesworth, Charles, **Supp. IV Part 1:** 39; **Supp. VIII:** 292, 306
Molière (Jean-Baptiste Poquelin), **III:** 113; **Supp. I Part 2:** 406; **Supp. III Part 2:** 552, 560; **Supp. IV Part 2:** 585; **Supp. V:** 101
"Molino Rojo, El" (Ríos), **Supp. IV Part 2:** 544
Moll Flanders (Defoe), **Supp. V:** 127; **Supp. XIII:** 43
"Molloch in State Street" (Whittier), **Supp. I Part 2:** 687
"Moll Pitcher" (Whittier), **Supp. I Part 2:** 684
"Molly Brant, Iroquois Matron" (Gunn Allen), **Supp. IV Part 1:** 331
Molnar, Ferenc, **Supp. XVI:** 187
"Moloch" (H. Miller), **III:** 177
Momaday, N. Scott, **Supp. IV Part 1:** 274, 323, 324, 404; **Supp. IV Part 2: 479–496,** 504, 557, 562; **Supp. XII:** 209; **Supp. XVIII:** 58
"'Momentary Stay against Confusion,' A: Frank Conroy's *Stop-Time*" (T. Adams), **Supp. XVI:** 69
Moment of Untruth (Lacy), **Supp. XV:** 206, 207
Moments of the Italian Summer (Wright), **Supp. III Part 2:** 602
"Momus" (Robinson), **III:** 508
Monaghan, Pat?/, **Supp. XI:** 121
Monaghan, Patricia?/, **Supp. XVII:** 76, 123, 127, 129
Mona Lisa Overdrive (W. Gibson), **Supp. XVI:** 119, 120, **127–128**
"Mon Ami" (Bourne), **I:** 227
Monet, Claude, **Retro. Supp. I:** 378
"Monet's 'Waterlilies'" (Hayden), **Supp. II Part 1:** 361–362
Monette, Paul, **Supp. X: 145–161**
Money (Amis), **Retro. Supp. I:** 278
"Money" (Matthews), **Supp. IX:** 166
"Money" (Nemerov), **III:** 287
Money, Money, Money (Wagoner), **Supp. IX:** 324, **333–334**
Moneyball: The Art of Winning an Unfair Game (M. Lewis), **Supp. XVII:** 210
Moneychangers, The (Sinclair), **Supp. V:** 285
Money Writes! (Sinclair), **Supp. V:** 277
Monica, Saint, **IV:** 140
Monikins, The (Cooper), **I:** 348, 354
Monk, Thelonious, **Supp. XVIII:** 62
Monk and the Hangman's Daughter, The (Bierce), **I:** 199–200, 209
"Monkey Garden, The" (Cisneros), **Supp. VII:** 63
"Monkey Puzzle, The" (Moore), **III:** 194, 207, 211
Monkeys (Minot), **Supp. VI:** 203–205, **206–210**
"Monkeys, The" (Moore), **III:** 201, 202
Monkey Wrench Gang, The (Abbey), **Supp. VIII:** 42; **Supp. XIII: 9–11,** 16
"Monk of Casal-Maggiore, The" (Longfellow), **II:** 505
"Monocle de Mon Oncle, Le" (Stevens), **IV:** 78, 84; **Retro. Supp. I:** 301; **Supp. III Part 1:** 20; **Supp. X:** 58
"Monolog from a Mattress" (Untermeyer), **Supp. XV:** 307
Monro, Harold, **III:** 465; **Retro. Supp. I:** 127; **Supp. XV:** 296
Monroe, Harriet, **I:** 235, 384, 390, 393; **III:** 458, 581, 586; **IV:** 74; **Retro. Supp. I:** 58, 131; **Retro. Supp. II:** 82, 83; **Supp. I Part 1:** 256, 257, 258, 262, 263, 267; **Supp. I Part 2:** 374, 387, 388, 464, 610, 611, 613, 614, 615, 616; **Supp. XIV:** 286; **Supp. XV:** 43, 299, 302
Monroe, James, **Supp. I Part 2:** 515, 517
Monroe, Lucy, **Retro. Supp. II:** 70
Monroe, Marilyn, **III:** 161, 162–163
Monroe's Embassy; or, the Conduct of the Government in Relation to Our Claims to the Navigation of the Mississippi (Brown), **Supp. I Part 1:** 146
"Monsoon Season" (Komunyakaa), **Supp. XIII:** 122
Monsour, Leslie, **Supp. XV:** 125
"Monster, The" (Crane), **I:** 418
Monster, The, and Other Stories (Crane), **I:** 409
Montage of a Dream Deferred (Hughes), **Retro. Supp. I:** 194, **208–209; Supp. I Part 1:** 333, 339–341
Montagu, Ashley, **Supp. I Part 1:** 314
"Montaigne" (Emerson), **II:** 6
Montaigne, Michel de, **II:** 1, 5, 6, 8, 14–15, 16, 535; **III:** 600; **Retro. Supp. I:** 247; **Supp. XIV:** 105
Montale, Eugenio, **Supp. III Part 1:** 320; **Supp. V:** 337–338; **Supp. VIII:** 30; **Supp. XV:** 112
Montalembert, Hughes de, **Supp. XV:** 349
"Montana Memory" (Maclean), **Supp. XIV:** 221
"Montana; or the End of Jean-Jacques Rousseau" (Fiedler), **Supp. XIII: 97–98**
"Montana Ranch Abandoned" (Hugo), **Supp. VI:** 139
"Mont Blanc" (Shelley), **Supp. IX:** 52
Montcalm, Louis Joseph de, **Supp. I Part 2:** 498
Montcalm and Wolfe (Parkman), **Supp. II Part 2:** 596, 609, 610, 611–613
Montemarano, Nicholas, **Supp. XVI:** 227
Montgomery, Benilde, **Supp. XIII:** 202
Montgomery, Robert, **Supp. I Part 2:** 611; **Supp. IV Part 1:** 130
Month of Sundays, A (Updike), **Retro. Supp. I:** 325, 327, 329, 330, 331, 333, 335
Monti, Luigi, **II:** 504
Montoya, José, **Supp. IV Part 2:** 545
"Montrachet-le-Jardin" (Stevens), **IV:** 82
Mont-Saint-Michel and Chartres (Adams), **I:** 1, 9, 12–14, 18, 19, 21; **Supp. I Part 2:** 417
Montserrat (Hellman), **Supp. I Part 1:** 283–285
Montserrat (Robles), **Supp. I Part 1:** 283–285
"Monument, The" (Bishop), **Supp. I Part 1:** 89
Monument, The (Strand), **Supp. IV Part 2:** 629, 630
"Monument in Utopia, A" (Schnackenberg), **Supp. XV:** 261, 263
"Monument Mountain" (Bryant), **Supp. I Part 1:** 156, 162
"Monument to After-Thought Unveiled, A" (Frost), **Retro. Supp. I:** 124
Moo (Smiley), **Supp. VI:** 292, **303–305**
Moods (Alcott), **Supp. I Part 1:** 33, 34–35, 43
Moody, Anne, **Supp. IV Part 1:** 11
Moody, Mrs. William Vaughn, **I:** 384; **Supp. I Part 2:** 394
Moody, Richard, **Supp. I Part 1:** 280
Moody, William Vaughn, **III:** 507; **IV:** 26
"Moon" (A. Finch), **Supp. XVII:** 77
Moon, Henry Lee, **Supp. XVIII:** 281, 285
"Moon and the Night and the Men, The" (Berryman), **I:** 172
"Moon Deluxe" (F. Barthelme), **Supp. XI:** 26, 27, 33, 36
Mooney, Tom, **I:** 505
"Moon-Face" (London), **II:** 475
Moon-Face and Other Stories (London), **II:** 483
"Moon Flock" (Dickey), **Supp. IV Part 1:** 186
Moon for the Misbegotten, A (O'Neill), **III:** 385, 401, 403, 404
Moon in a Mason Jar (Wrigley), **Supp. XVIII: 295–298**
Moon Is a Gong, The (Dos Passos). *See Garbage Man, The* (Dos Passos)
Moon Is Down, The (Steinbeck), **IV:** 51
Moon Lady, The (Tan), **Supp. X:** 289

"Moonlight Alert" (Winters), **Supp. II Part 2:** 801, 811, 815
"Moonlight: Chickens on a Road" (Wrigley), **Supp. XVIII:** 295–296, 297
"Moonlit Night" (Reznikoff), **Supp. XIV:** 285–286
Moon of the Caribbees, The (O'Neill), **III:** 388
Moon Palace (Auster), **Supp. XII:** 22, 27, **30–32**
"Moonshine" (Komunyakaa), **Supp. XIII:** 127, 128
"Moon Solo" (Laforgue), **Supp. XIII:** 346
Moonstruck (screenplay, Shanley), **Supp. XIV:** 315, 316, **321–324**
"Moon upon her fluent Route, The" (Dickinson), **I:** 471
Moony's Kid Don't Cry (T. Williams), **IV:** 381
Moore, Arthur, **Supp. I Part 1:** 49
Moore, Dr. Merrill, **III:** 506
Moore, George, **I:** 103
Moore, Hannah, **Supp. XV:** 231
Moore, John Milton, **III:** 193
Moore, Lorrie, **Supp. VIII:** 145; **Supp. X: 163–180**
Moore, Marianne, **I:** 58, 285, 401, 428; **III: 193–217,** 514, 592–593; **IV:** 74, 75, 76, 91, 402; **Retro. Supp. I:** 416, 417; **Retro. Supp. II:** 39, 44, 48, 50, 82, 178, 179, 243, 244; **Supp. I Part 1:** 84, 89, 255, 257; **Supp. I Part 2:** 707; **Supp. II Part 1:** 21; **Supp. III Part 1:** 58, 60, 63; **Supp. III Part 2:** 612, 626, 627; **Supp. IV Part 1:** 242, 246, 257; **Supp. IV Part 2:** 454, 640, 641; **Supp. XIV:** 124, 130; **Supp. XV:** 306, 307; **Supp. XVII:** 131
Moore, Marie Lorena. *See* Moore, Lorrie
Moore, Mary Tyler, **Supp. V:** 107
Moore, Mary Warner, **III:** 193
Moore, Steven, **Supp. IV Part 1:** 279, 283, 284, 285, 287; **Supp. XII:** 151; **Supp. XVII:** 230, 231, 232
Moore, Sturge, **III:** 459
Moore, Thomas, **II:** 296, 299, 303; **Supp. IX:** 104; **Supp. X:** 114
Moore, Virginia, **Supp. XV:** 308
Moorehead, Caroline, **Supp. XIV:** 337
Moorepack, Howard, **Supp. XV:** 199
"Moorings" (Hoffman), **Supp. XVIII:** 87
Moos, Malcolm, **III:** 116, 119
"Moose, The" (Bishop), **Retro. Supp. II:** 50; **Supp. I Part 1:** 73, 93, 94, 95; **Supp. IX:** 45, 46
"Moose Wallow, The" (Hayden), **Supp. II Part 1:** 367
"Moquihuitzin's Answer" (Everwine), **Supp. XV:** 78
Mora, Pat, **Supp. XIII: 213–232**
"Moral Bully, The" (Holmes), **Supp. I Part 1:** 302
"Moral Character, the Practice of Law, and Legal Education" (Hall), **Supp. VIII:** 127
"Moral Equivalent for Military Service, A" (Bourne), **I:** 230
"Moral Equivalent of War, The" (James), **II:** 361; **Supp. I Part 1:** 20
"Moral Imperatives for World Order" (Locke), **Supp. XIV:** 207, 213
Moralités Légendaires (Laforgue), **I:** 573
"Morality and Mercy in Vienna" (Pynchon), **Supp. II Part 2:** 620, 624
"Morality of Indian Hating, The" (Momaday), **Supp. IV Part 2:** 484
"Morality of Poetry, The" (Wright), **Supp. III Part 2:** 596–597, 599
Moral Man and Immoral Society (Niebuhr), **III:** 292, 295–297
"Morals Is Her Middle Name" (Hughes), **Supp. I Part 1:** 338
"Morals of Chess, The" (Franklin), **II:** 121
"Moral Substitute for War, A" (Addams), **Supp. I Part 1:** 20
"Moral Theology of Atticus Finch, The" (Shaffer), **Supp. VIII:** 127
"Moral Thought, A" (Freneau), **Supp. II Part 1:** 262
Moran, Thomas, **Supp. IV Part 2:** 603–604
Moran of the Lady Letty (Norris), **II:** 264; **III:** 314, 322, 327, 328, 329, 330, 331, 332, 333
Morath, Ingeborg. *See* Miller, Mrs. Arthur (Ingeborg Morath)
Moravia, Alberto, **I:** 301
Moré, Gonzalo, **Supp. X:** 185
More, Henry, **I:** 132
More, Paul Elmer, **I:** 223–224, 247; **Supp. I Part 2:** 423
Moreau, Gustave, **I:** 66
"More Blues and the Abstract Truth" (Wright), **Supp. XV:** 345
More Boners (Abingdon), **Supp. XVI:** 99
More Conversations with Eudora Welty (Prenshaw, ed.), **Retro. Supp. I:** 340, 341, 342, 343, 344, 352, 353, 354
More Dangerous Thoughts (Ryan as Quin), **Supp. XVIII:** 226, **229–230,** 231, 238
More Die of Heartbreak (Bellow), **Retro. Supp. II:** 31, 33, 34
"More Girl Than Boy" (Komunyakaa), **Supp. XIII:** 117
"More Light! More Light! (Hecht), **Supp. X:** 60
"Morella"(Poe), **III:** 412; **Retro. Supp. II:** 270
"More Love in the Western World"(Updike), **Retro. Supp. I:** 327–328, 329
"Morels"(W. J. Smith), **Supp. XIII: 336–339**
Moreno, Gary, **Supp. XV:** 5
"More Observations Now"(Conroy), **Supp. XVI:** 75
"More of a Corpse Than a Woman"(Rukeyser), **Supp. VI:** 280
"More Pleasant Adventures"(Ashbery), **Supp. III Part 1:** 1
More Poems to Solve (Swenson), **Supp. IV Part 2:** 640, 642, 648
More Stately Mansions (O'Neill), **III:** 385, 401, 404–405
"More Than Human"(Chabon), **Supp. XI:** 71–72
More Triva (L. P. Smith), **Supp. XIV:** 339
Morgan, Edmund S., **IV:** 149; **Supp. I Part 1:** 101, 102; **Supp. I Part 2:** 484
Morgan, Edwin, **Supp. IV Part 2:** 688
Morgan, Emanuel. *See* Bynner, Witter
Morgan, Henry, **II:** 432; **IV:** 63
Morgan, Jack, **Retro. Supp. II:** 142
Morgan, J. P., **I:** 494; **III:** 14, 15
Morgan, Judith, **Supp. XVI:** 103
Morgan, Neil, **Supp. XVI:** 103
Morgan, Robert, **Supp. V:** 5
Morgan, Robin, **Supp. I Part 2:** 569
Morgan, Ted, **Supp. XIV:** 141
Morgan's Passing (Tyler), **Supp. IV Part 2:** 666–667, 668, 669
Morgenthau, Hans, **III:** 291, 309
Morgesons, The (E. Stoddard), **Supp. XV:** 270, 273, 274, 278, **279–282,** 283
Morgesons and Other Writings, Published and Unpublished, The (Buell and Zagarell), **Supp. XV:** 269
Moricand, Conrad, **III:** 190
Morison, Mrs. Samuel Eliot (Elizabeth Shaw Greene), **Supp. I Part 2:** 483
Morison, Mrs. Samuel Eliot (Priscilla Barton), **Supp. I Part 2:** 493, 496, 497
Morison, Samuel Eliot, **Supp. I Part 2: 479–500**
"Morituri Salutamus"(Longfellow), **II:** 499, 500; **Retro. Supp. II:** 169; **Supp. I Part 2:** 416
"Moriturus"(Millay), **III:** 126, 131–132
Morley, Christopher, **III:** 481, 483, 484; **Supp. I Part 2:** 653; **Supp. IX:** 124
Morley, Edward, **IV:** 27
Morley, Lord John, **I:** 7
Mormon Country (Stegner), **Supp. IV Part 2:** 598, 601–602
"Morning, The"(Updike), **Retro. Supp. I:** 329
"Morning after My Death, The"(Levis), **Supp. XI:** 260, 263–264
"Morning Arrives"(F. Wright), **Supp. XVII:** 244
Morning for Flamingos, A (Burke), **Supp. XIV:** 30, 31, 32
"Morning Glory"(Merrill), **Supp. III Part 1:** 337
Morning Glory, The (R. Bly), **Supp. IV Part 1:** 63–65, 66, 71
"Morning Imagination of Russia, A" (W. C. Williams), **Retro. Supp. I:** 428
Morning in Antibes (Knowles), **Supp. XII:** 249
Morning in the Burned House (Atwood), **Supp. XIII:** 20, 35
Morning Is Near Us, The (Glaspell), **Supp. III Part 1:** 184–185
Morning Noon and Night (Cozzens), **I:** 374, 375, 376, 377, 379, 380
"Morning of the Day They Did It, The" (White), **Supp. I Part 2:** 663
"Morning Prayers" (Harjo), **Supp. XII:** 231
"Morning Roll Call" (Anderson), **I:** 116
"Mornings in a New House" (Merrill), **Supp. III Part 1:** 327

Mornings Like This (Dillard), **Supp. VI:** 23, 34
"Morning Song" (Plath), **Retro. Supp. II:** 252
Morning Watch, The (Agee), **I:** 25, 39–42
"Morning with Broken Window" (Hogan), **Supp. IV Part 1:** 405
Morrell, Ottoline, **Retro. Supp. I:** 60
Morris, Bernard E., **Supp. XV:** 154, 169
Morris, Christopher D., **Supp. IV Part 1:** 231, 236
Morris, George Sylvester, **Supp. I Part 2:** 640
Morris, Gouverneur, **Supp. I Part 2:** 512, 517, 518
Morris, Lloyd, **III:** 458
Morris, Robert, **Supp. I Part 2:** 510
Morris, Timothy, **Retro. Supp. I:** 40
Morris, William, **II:** 323, 338, 523; **IV:** 349; **Supp. I Part 1:** 260, 356; **Supp. XI:** 202
Morris, Willie, **Supp. XI:** 216, 231, 234
Morris, Wright, **I:** 305; **III:** **218–243,** 558, 572; **IV:** 211
Morrison, Charles Clayton, **III:** 297
Morrison, Jim, **Supp. IV Part 1:** 206
Morrison, Toni, **Retro. Supp. II:** 15, 118; **Supp. III Part 1: 361–381; Supp. IV Part 1:** 2, 13, 14, 250, 253, 257; **Supp. V:** 169, 259; **Supp. VIII:** 213, 214; **Supp. X:** 85, 239, 250, 325; **Supp. XI:** 4, 14, 20, 91; **Supp. XII:** 289, 310; **Supp. XIII:** 60, 185; **Supp. XVI:** 143; **Supp. XVII:** 183
"Morro Bay" (Jeffers), **Supp. II Part 2:** 422
Morrow, W. C., **I:** 199
Morse, Jedidiah, **Supp. XV:** 243
Morse, Robert, **Supp. XI:** 305
Morse, Samuel F. B., **Supp. I Part 1:** 156
Mortal Acts, Mortal Words (Kinnell), **Supp. III Part 1:** 235, 236, 237, 249–254
Mortal Antipathy, A (Holmes), **Supp. I Part 1:** 315–316
"Mortal Enemies" (Humphrey), **Supp. IX:** 109
"Mortal Eternal" (Olds), **Supp. X:** 214
Mortal No, The (Hoffman), **IV:** 113
Morte D'Arthur, Le (Malory), **Supp. IV Part 1:** 47
Mortmere Stories, The (Isherwood and Upward), **Supp. XIV:** 159
Morton, David, **Supp. IX:** 76
Morton, Jelly Roll, **Supp. X:** 242
"Mosaic of the Nativity: Serbia, Winter 1993" (Kenyon), **Supp. VII:** 173
Mosby's Memoirs and Other Stories (Bellow), **Retro. Supp. II:** 27
Moscow under Fire (Caldwell), **I:** 296
Moser, Barry, **Supp. XIV:** 223
Moses (Untermeyer), **Supp. XV: 309**
Moses, Man of the Mountain (Hurston), **Supp. VI:** 149, 158, 160
"Moses on Sinai" (Untermeyer), **Supp. XV:** 300
Mosle, Sara, **Supp. XI:** 254
Mosley, Walter, **Supp. XIII: 233–252; Supp. XVI:** 143
Mosquito Coast, The (film), **Supp. VIII:** 323
Mosquito Coast, The (Theroux), **Supp. VIII:** 321, **322–323**
Mosquitos (Faulkner), **II:** 56; **Retro. Supp. I:** 79, 81
Moss, Howard, **III:** 452; **Supp. IV Part 2:** 642; **Supp. IX:** 39; **Supp. XIII:** 114; **Supp. XV:** 143, 152
Moss, Stanley, **Supp. XI:** 321
Moss, Thylias, **Supp. XI:** 248
Mosses from an Old Manse (Hawthorne), **I:** 562; **II:** 224; **III:** 82, 83; **Retro. Supp. I:** 157, 248
"Moss of His Skin" (Sexton), **Supp. II Part 2:** 676
Most, Doug, **Supp. XVIII:** 101
"Most Extraordinary Case, A" (James), **II:** 322; **Retro. Supp. I:** 218
Most Likely to Succeed (Dos Passos), **I:** 491
"Most of It, The" (Frost), **Retro. Supp. I:** 121, 125, 129, 139; **Supp. XVIII:** 300
"Most Popular Novels in America, The" (Mabie), **Supp. XVIII:** 257
Motel Chronicles (Shepard), **Supp. III Part 2:** 445
"Mother" (Paley), **Supp. VI: 222–223**
"Mother" (Snyder), **Supp. VIII:** 298
Mother (Whistler), **IV:** 369
Mother, The (Buck), **Supp. II Part 1:** 118–119
"Mother and Jack and the Rain" (Sexton), **Supp. II Part 2:** 686
"Mother and Son" (Tate), **IV:** 128, 137–138
Mother Courage and Her Children (Brecht), **III:** 160; **Supp. IX:** 140; **Supp. XII:** 249
"Mother Earth: Her Whales" (Snyder), **Supp. VIII:** 302
"Motherhood" (Swenson), **Supp. IV Part 2:** 645
Mother Hubbard (Reed), **Supp. X:** 241
Motherless in Brooklyn (Lethem), **Supp. XVIII:** 135, **143–144**
Mother Love (Dove), **Supp. IV Part 1:** 250–251, 254
"Mother Marie Therese" (Lowell), **Retro. Supp. II:** 188
Mother Night (Vonnegut), **Supp. II Part 2:** 757, 758, 767, 770, 771
"Mother Rosarine" (Kumin), **Supp. IV Part 2:** 442
"Mothers and Daughters in the Fiction of the New Republic" (Davidson), **Supp. XV:** 238
Mother's Recompense, The (Wharton), **IV:** 321, 324; **Retro. Supp. I:** 382
"Mother's Tale, A" (Agee), **I:** 29–30
"Mother's Things" (Creeley), **Supp. IV Part 1:** 141
"Mother's Voice" (Creeley), **Supp. IV Part 1:** 156
Mother to Daughter, Daughter to Mother (Olsen, ed.), **Supp. XIII:** 295
"Mother Tongue" (Simic), **Supp. VIII:** 283
"Mother to Son" (Hughes), **Retro. Supp. I:** 199, 203; **Supp. I Part 1:** 321–322, 323
Motherwell, Robert, **Supp. XV:** 145
"Mother Writes to the Murderer, The: A Letter" (Nye), **Supp. XIII:** 276
"Motion, The" (Olson), **Supp. II Part 2:** 571
Motion of History, The (Baraka), **Supp. II Part 1:** 55, 56
"Motive for Metaphor, The" (Stevens), **IV:** 89; **Retro. Supp. I:** 310
Motiveless Malignity (Auchincloss), **Supp. IV Part 1:** 31
Motley, John Lothrop, **Supp. I Part 1:** 299; **Supp. I Part 2:** 479
Motley, Willard, **Supp. XVII: 149–163**
"Motor Car, The" (White), **Supp. I Part 2:** 661
Motor-Flight Through France (Wharton), **I:** 12; **Retro. Supp. I:** 372
Mott, Michael, **Supp. VIII:** 204, 208
Mottetti: Poems of Love: The Motets of Eugenio Montale (Montale; Gioia, trans.), **Supp. XV:** 112, **127–128**
"Mountain, The" (Frost), **Retro. Supp. I:** 121
"Mountain Hermitage, The: Pages from a Japanese Notebook" (Passin), **Supp. XIII:** 337
Mountain Interval (Frost), **II:** 154; **Retro. Supp. I:** 131, 132, 133
"Mountain Lion" (Hogan), **Supp. IV Part 1:** 412
"Mountain Music" essays (Sanders), **Supp. XVI:** 276–277
Mountain on the Desert, The (Richter), **Supp. XVIII:** 216, 219
Mountainous Journey, A (Tuqan), **Supp. XIII:** 278
Mountains, The (Wolfe), **IV:** 461
Mountains and Rivers without End (Snyder), **Supp. VIII:** 295, **305–306**
"Mountains grow unnoticed, The" (Dickinson), **Retro. Supp. I:** 46
Mountains of California, The (Muir), **Supp. IX:** 183
"Mountain Whippoorwill, The" (Benét), **Supp. XI:** 44–45, 46, 47
"Mount-Joy: or Some Passages Out of the Life of a Castle-Builder" (Irving), **II:** 314
"Mount Venus" (Wright), **Supp. XV:** 346
"Mourners, The" (Malamud), **Supp. I Part 2:** 431, 435, 436–437
Mourners Below (Purdy), **Supp. VII:** 274, 280
"Mourning and Melancholia" (Freud), **Supp. IV Part 2:** 450; **Supp. XVI:** 161
Mourning Becomes Electra (O'Neill), **III:** 391, 394, 398–400
"Mourning Doves" (Pedersen; Nelson, trans.), **Supp. XVIII:** 180
"Mourning Poem for the Queen of Sunday" (Hayden), **Supp. II Part 1:** 379–380
"Mouse Elegy" (Olds), **Supp. X:** 209
Mouse Is Born, A (Loos), **Supp. XVI:** 193

"Mouse Roulette Wheel, The" (C. Bly), **Supp. XVI:** 34
"Mouth of Brass" (Humphrey), **Supp. IX:** 101
Moveable Feast, A (Hemingway), **II:** 257; **Retro. Supp. I:** 108, 171, **186–187**
Movement, The: Documentary of a Struggle for Equality (Student Nonviolent Coordinating Committee), **Supp. IV Part 1:** 369
"Move over Macho, Here Comes Feminismo" (Robbins), **Supp. X:** 272
"Move to California, The" (Stafford), **Supp. XI:** 318, 321
"Movie" (Shapiro), **Supp. II Part 2:** 707
Movie at the End of the World, The (McGrath), **Supp. X:** 127
Moviegoer, The (Percy), **Supp. III Part 1:** 383–385, 387, 389–392, 394, 397
"Movie Magazine, The: A Low 'Slick'" (Percy), **Supp. III Part 1:** 385
Movies (Dixon), **Supp. XII:** 147
Movies About the Movies (Ames), **Supp. XVIII:** 242–243
"Moving Around" (Matthews), **Supp. IX:** 155
"Moving Finger, The" (Wharton), **Retro. Supp. I:** 365
Moving On (McMurtry), **Supp. V:** 223–224
Moving Pictures: Memoirs of a Hollywood Prince (Schulberg), **Supp. XVIII:** 242, 243, 254
Moving Target, The (Macdonald), **Supp. IV Part 2:** 462, 463, 467, 470, 471, 473, 474
Moving Target, The (Merwin), **Supp. III Part 1:** 346, 347–348, 352, 357
"Mowbray Family, The" (Farrell and Alden), **II:** 45
"Mowing" (Frost), **II:** 169–170; **Retro. Supp. I:** 127, 128
"Moxan's Master" (Bierce), **I:** 206
Moxley, Jennifer, **Supp. XVII:** 70
Moyers, Bill, **Supp. IV Part 1:** 267; **Supp. VIII:** 331; **Supp. XI:** 126, 132; **Supp. XII:** 217; **Supp. XIII:** 274, 276; **Supp. XV:** 212
Moynihan, Daniel Patrick, **Retro. Supp. II:** 123; **Supp. VIII:** 241
"Mozart" (C. Frost), **Supp. XV:** 94
Mozart, Wolfgang Amadeus, **I:** 479, 588; **IV:** 74, 358; **Supp. IV Part 1:** 284
"Mozart and the Gray Steward" (Wilder), **IV:** 358
Mrabet, Mohammed, **Supp. IV Part 1:** 92, 93
Mr. and Mrs. Baby and Other Stories (Strand), **Supp. IV Part 2:** 631
"Mr. and Mrs. Fix-It" (Lardner), **II:** 431
Mr. Arcularis (Aiken), **I:** 54, 56
"Mr. Big" (Allen), **Supp. XV:** 15
Mr. Bridge (Connell), **Supp. XIV:** 80, 82, 93
Mr. Brown Can Moo! Can You? (Geisel), **Supp. XVI:** 104
"Mr. Bruce" (Jewett), **II:** 397; **Retro. Supp. II:** 134, 143
"Mr. Burnshaw and the Statue" (Stevens), **Retro. Supp. I:** 298, 303
"Mr. Carson Death on His Nights Out" (McGrath), **Supp. X:** 118
Mr. Clemens and Mark Twain (Kaplan), **I:** 247–248
"Mr. Coffee and Mr. Fixit" (Carver), **Supp. III Part 1:** 145
"Mr. Cornelius Johnson, Office-Seeker" (Dunbar), **Supp. II Part 1:** 211, 213
"Mr. Costyve Duditch" (Toomer), **Supp. III Part 2:** 486
"Mr. Dajani, Calling from Jericho" (Nye), **Supp. XIII:** 286–287
"Mr. Edwards and the Spider" (Lowell), **I:** 544; **II:** 550; **Retro. Supp. II:** 187
Mr. Field's Daughter (Bausch), **Supp. VII:** 47–48, 51–52
"Mr. Flood's Party" (Robinson), **III:** 512
"Mr. Forster's Pageant" (Maxwell), **Supp. VIII:** 172
"Mr. Frost's Chickens" (Oliver), **Supp. VII:** 232–233
Mr. Hodge and Mr. Hazard (Wylie), **Supp. I Part 2:** 708, 709, 714, 721–724
"Mr. Hueffer and the Prose Tradition" (Pound), **III:** 465
Mr. Ives' Christmas (Hijuelos), **Supp. VIII: 85–86**
"Mr. Longfellow and His Boy" (Sandburg), **III:** 591
"Mr. Luna and History" (Ríos), **Supp. IV Part 2:** 551
"Mr. Mitochondria" (Stollman), **Supp. XVII:** 50
Mr. Moto Is So Sorry (Marquand), **III:** 57, 58
Mr. Norris Changes Trains (Isherwood), **Supp. XIV:** 161
"Mr. Preble Gets Rid of His Wife" (Thurber), **Supp. I Part 2:** 615
"Mr. Rolfe" (Wilson), **IV:** 436
Mr. Rutherford's Children (S. and A. Warner), **Supp. XVIII:** 264
"Mrs. Adis" (Kaye-Smith), **Supp. XVIII:** 130–131
Mrs. Albert Grundy: Observations in Philistia (Frederic), **II:** 138–139
Mr. Sammler's Planet (Bellow), **I:** 144, 147, 150, 151, 152, 158; **Retro. Supp. II:** 19, 28, 30
"Mrs. Bilingsby's Wine" (Taylor), **Supp. V:** 323
Mrs. Bridge: A Novel (Connell), **Supp. XIV:** 79, 80, 81, 82, **89–94,** 95
"Mrs. Cassidy's Last Year" (Gordon), **Supp. IV Part 1:** 306
Mrs. Dalloway (Woolf), **Supp. IV Part 1:** 299; **Supp. VIII:** 5; **Supp. XV:** 55, 65–66
"Mr. Shelley Speaking" (Wylie), **Supp. I Part 2:** 719
"Mrs. Jellison" (Hay), **Supp. XIV:** 123
"Mrs. Krikorian" (Olds), **Supp. X:** 211
"Mrs. Maecenas" (Burke), **I:** 271
"Mrs. Mandrill" (Nemerov), **III:** 278
"Mrs. Manstey's View" (Wharton), **Retro. Supp. I:** 362, 363
"Mrs. Mobry's Reason" (Chopin), **Retro. Supp. II:** 61
Mr. Spaceman (R. O. Butler), **Supp. XII:** 62, **74–75**
Mrs. Reynolds (Stein), **IV:** 43
Mrs. Stevens Hears the Mermaids Singing (Sarton), **Supp. VIII:** 252–253, **256–257**
Mrs. Ted Bliss (Elkin), **Supp. VI: 56,** 58
"Mrs. Turner Cutting the Grass" (Shields), **Supp. VII:** 319–320
"Mrs. Walpurga" (Rukeyser), **Supp. VI:** 273
"Mr. Thompson's Prodigal" (Harte), **Supp. II Part 1:** 354
Mr. Vertigo (Auster), **Supp. XII: 34–35,** 36
"Mr. Whittier" (Scott), **Supp. I Part 2:** 705
Mr. Wilson's War (Dos Passos), **I:** 485
"MS. Found in a Bottle" (Poe), **III:** 411, 416; **Retro. Supp. II:** 274
"Ms. Lot" (Rukeyser), **Supp. VI:** 281
Ms. Magazine, **Supp. V:** 259
Mttron-Hirsch, Sidney, **III:** 484–485
"Muchas Gracias Por Todo" (Nye), **Supp. XIII:** 282–283
"Much Madness is divinest Sense" (Dickinson), **Retro. Supp. I:** 37–38
"Muck-A-Muck" (Harte), **Supp. II Part 1:** 342
"Mud Below, The" (Proulx), **Supp. VII:** 262
Mudge, Alden, **Supp. XIV:** 35
Mudrick, Marvin, **Retro. Supp. II:** 289
"Mud Season" (Kenyon), **Supp. VII:** 167–168
Mueller, Lisel, **Supp. I Part 1:** 83, 88; **Supp. XIV:** 268
Muggli, Mark, **Supp. IV Part 1:** 207
Muhammad, Elijah, **Supp. I Part 1:** 60
Muir, Edwin, **I:** 527; **II:** 368; **III:** 20
Muir, John, **Supp. IX:** 33, **171–188; Supp. VIII:** 296; **Supp. X:** 29; **Supp. XIV:** 177, 178, 181
Muirhead, Deborah, **Supp. XVIII:** 186
Mujica, Barbara, **Supp. VIII:** 89
Mulatto (Hughes), **Retro. Supp. I:** 197, 203; **Supp. I Part 1:** 328, 339
Mulching of America, The (Crews), **Supp. XI:** 107
Muldoon, William, **I:** 500–501
Mule Bone (Hughes and Hurston), **Retro. Supp. I:** 194, 203; **Supp. VI:** 154
Mules and Men (Hurston), **Supp. VI:** 149, 153, 154, 160
Mulford, Prentice, **I:** 193
Mulligan, Robert, **Supp. VIII:** 128, 129
Mulligan Stew (Sorrentino), **Supp. XII:** 139
Mullins, Eustace, **III:** 479
Mullins, Priscilla, **II:** 502–503
"Multiplication of Wool, The" (Sanders), **Supp. XVI:** 268
Multitudes, Multitudes (Clampitt), **Supp. IX:** 39
Mumbo Jumbo (Reed), **Supp. X:** 240, 242, **245–248,** 251

Mumford, Lewis, **I:** 245, 250, 251, 252, 259, 261; **II:** 271, 473–474; **Supp. I Part 2:** 632, 638; **Supp. II Part 2: 471–501**
Mumford, Sophia Wittenberg (Mrs. Lewis Mumford), **Supp. II Part 2:** 474, 475
Mummy, The (film), **Supp. IV Part 1:** 104; **Supp. XVII:** 57
"Mundus et Infans" (Auden), **Supp. II Part 1:** 15
"Munich, 1938" (Lowell), **II:** 554
"Munich Mannequins, The" (Plath), **Retro. Supp. II:** 256
"Municipal Report, A" (Henry), **Supp. II Part 1:** 406–407
Munro, Alice, **Supp. IX:** 212; **Supp. X:** 290; **Supp. XII:** 289–290, 310
Munsey, Frank, **I:** 501
Munson, Gorham, **I:** 252, 388, 432; **Retro. Supp. II:** 77, 78, 79, 82, 83; **Supp. I Part 2:** 454
Münsterberg, Hugo, **Supp. XIV:** 197
Murakami, Haruki, **Supp. XVI:** 124
"Murano" (Doty), **Supp. XI:** 131
Murasaki, Lady, **II:** 577
Muratori, Fred, **Supp. XVI:** 281
Muray, Nicholas, **Supp. I Part 2:** 708
Murder, My Sweet (film), **Supp. IV Part 1:** 130
"Murderer Guest, The" (Gordon), **Supp. IV Part 1:** 306
"Murderers" (L. Michaels), **Supp. XVI:** 207–208
Murder in Mount Holly (Theroux), **Supp. VIII:** 315–316
Murder in the Cathedral (Eliot), **I:** 571, 573, 580, 581; **II:** 20; **Retro. Supp. I:** 65; **Retro. Supp. II:** 222
Murder of Lidice, The (Millay), **III:** 140
"Murders in the Rue Morgue, The" (Poe), **III:** 412, 416, 419–420; **Retro. Supp. II:** 271, 272
Murdoch, Iris, **Supp. VIII:** 167; **Supp. XVIII:** 136,149
Murnau, F. W., **Supp. XV:** 128
Murphy, Jacqueline Shea, **Retro. Supp. II:** 143
Murphy, Patrick, **Supp. XIII:** 214
Murphy, Richard, **Retro. Supp. II:** 250
Murray, Albert, **Retro. Supp. II:** 119, 120
Murray, Edward, **I:** 229
Murray, G. E., **Supp. X:** 201; **Supp. XI:** 143, 155
Murray, Gilbert, **III:** 468–469
Murray, Jan, **Supp. IV Part 2:** 574
Murray, John, **II:** 304; **III:** 76, 79; **Retro. Supp. I:** 246
Murray, Judith Sargent, **Supp. XV:** 236–237
Murray, Margaret A., **Supp. V:** 128
Murrell, John A., **IV:** 265
Mursell, James L., **Supp. I Part 2:** 608
"Muse" (Ammons), **Supp. VII:** 29
"Muse, Postmodern and Homeless, The" (Ozick), **Supp. V:** 272
"Musée des Beaux Arts" (Auden), **Retro. Supp. I:** 430; **Supp. II Part 1:** 14
"Muse of Aboutness, The" (Baker), **Supp. XVI:** 288
Muses Are Heard, The (Capote), **Supp. III Part 1:** 126
"Muses of Terrence McNally, The" (Zinman), **Supp. XIII:** 207–208
"Muse's Tragedy, The" (Wharton), **Retro. Supp. I:** 364
Museum (Dove), **Supp. IV Part 1:** 245–247, 248
"Museum" (Hass), **Supp. VI:** 107
Museums and Women (Updike), **Retro. Supp. I:** 321
"Museum Vase" (Francis), **Supp. IX:** 83
"Mushrooms" (Plath), **Retro. Supp. II:** 246; **Supp. I Part 2:** 539
"Music" (Oliver), **Supp. VII:** 236
Music After the Great War (Van Vechten), **Supp. II Part 2:** 732
Music and Bad Manners (Van Vechten), **Supp. II Part 2:** 733
"Music for a Farce" (Bowles), **Supp. IV Part 1:** 83
Music for Chameleons (Capote), **Supp. III Part 1:** 120, 125–127, 131, 132
"Music for Museums?" (Van Vechten), **Supp. II Part 2:** 732
"Music for the Movies" (Van Vechten), **Supp. II Part 2:** 733
"Music from Spain" (Welty), **IV:** 272
"Music Like Dirt" (Bidart), **Supp. XV:** 35
Music Like Dirt (Bidart), **Supp. XV:** 35
Music of Chance, The (Auster), **Supp. XII:** 21, 23, **32–33**
"Music of Prose, The" (Gass), **Supp. VI:** 92
Music of Spain, The (Van Vechten), **Supp. II Part 2:** 734, 735
"Music of the Spheres" (Epstein), **Supp. XII:** 165
"Music School" (B. Kelly), **Supp. XVII:** 124
"Music School, The" (Updike), **Retro. Supp. I:** 326, 329, 335
Music School, The (Updike), **IV:** 214, 215, 219, 226, 227; **Retro. Supp. I:** 320, 328, 329, 330
"Music Swims Back to Me" (Sexton), **Supp. II Part 2:** 673
Muske, Carol, **Supp. IV Part 2:** 453–454
"Mussel Hunter at Rock Harbor" (Plath), **Supp. I Part 2:** 529, 537
Musset, Alfred de, **I:** 474; **II:** 543
Mussolini, Benito, **III:** 115, 473, 608; **IV:** 372, 373; **Supp. I Part 1:** 281, 282; **Supp. I Part 2:** 618; **Supp. V:** 290; **Supp. XVI:** 191
"Mustafa Ferrari" (X. J. Kennedy), **Supp. XV:** 170–171
"Must the Novelist Crusade?" (Welty), **IV:** 280
"Mutability of Literature, The" (Irving), **II:** 308
"Mutation of the Spirit" (Corso), **Supp. XII:** 132, 133
Mute, The (McCullers), **II:** 586
Mutilated, The (T. Williams), **IV:** 382, 386, 393
Mutiny of the Elsinore, The (London), **II:** 467
"Muttsy" (Hurston), **Supp. XVIII:** 279
"My Adventures as a Social Poet" (Hughes), **Retro. Supp. I:** 194, 207
"My Alba" (Ginsberg), **Supp. II Part 1:** 320, 321
My Alexandria (Doty), **Supp. XI:** 119, 120, 121, **123–125,** 130
My Ántonia (Cather), **I:** 321–322; **Retro. Supp. I:** 1, 3, 4, **11–13,** 14, 17, 18, 22; **Supp. IV Part 2:** 608; **Supp. XVI:** 226
"My Appearance" (Wallace), **Supp. X:** 306–307
My Argument with the Gestapo: A Macaronic Journal (Merton), **Supp. VIII:** 207; **Supp. XV:** 344
"My Arkansas" (Angelou), **Supp. IV Part 1:** 15
"My Aunt" (Holmes), **Supp. I Part 1:** 302, 310
"My Beginnings" (Simpson), **Supp. IX:** 273
My Bondage and My Freedom (Douglass), **Supp. III Part 1:** 155, 173
My Brother (Kincaid), **Supp. VII:** 191–193
"My Brother Paul" (Dreiser), **Retro. Supp. II:** 94
"My Brothers the Silent" (Merwin), **Supp. III Part 1:** 349–350
"My Brother's Work" (Dunn), **Supp. XI:** 147
"My Brother Takes a Hammer to the Mirror" (F. Wright), **Supp. XVII:** 244
"My Butterfly" (Frost), **II:** 151; **Retro. Supp. I:** 124
"My Children, and a Prayer for Us" (Ortiz), **Supp. IV Part 2:** 507
"My Confession" (McCarthy), **II:** 562
"My Confessional Sestina" (Gioia), **Supp. XV:** 123
My Country and My People (Yutang), **Supp. X:** 291
"My Country 'Tis of Thee" (Reznikoff), **Supp. III Part 2:** 616
My Days of Anger (Farrell), **II:** 34, 35–36, 43
"My Dear Republican Mother" (C. Bly), **Supp. XVI:** 31–32
My Death My Life by Pier Paolo Pasolini (Acker), **Supp. XII:** 7
My Dog Stupid (Fante), **Supp. XI:** 160, **170–171**
My Emily Dickinson (Howe), **Retro. Supp. I:** 33, 43; **Supp. IV Part 2:** 430–431
"My English" (Alvarez), **Supp. VII:** 2
Myers, Linda A., **Supp. IV Part 1:** 10
"My Extended Family" (Theroux), **Supp. VIII:** 311
"My Father" (L. Michaels), **Supp. XVI:** 214
"My Father" (Sterne), **IV:** 466
"My Father at Eighty-Five" (R. Bly), **Supp. IV Part 1:** 73
"My Father Is a Simple Man" (Salinas), **Supp. XIII:** 324
"My Father: October 1942" (Stafford), **Supp. XI:** 323

"My Fathers Came From Kentucky" (Lindsay), **Supp. I Part 2:** 395
"My Father's Friends" (Maxwell), **Supp. VIII:** 171
"My Father's Ghost" (Wagoner), **Supp. IX:** 330
"My Father's God" (Fante), **Supp. XI:** 160, 174
"My Father's House" (L.-Y. Lee), **Supp. XV:** 225
"My Father's Love Letters" (Komunyakaa), **Supp. XIII:** 127
"My Father Speaks to me from the Dead" (Olds), **Supp. X:** 210
"My Father's Telescope" (Dove), **Supp. IV Part 1:** 246, 248
"My Father with Cigarette Twelve Years Before the Nazis Could Break His Heart" (Levine), **Supp. V:** 194
"My Favorite Murder" (Bierce), **I:** 205
My Favorite Plant: Writers and Gardeners on the Plants They Love (Kincaid), **Supp. VII:** 193–194
"My Fifty-Plus Years Celebrate Spring" (Salinas), **Supp. XIII:** 327
"My First Book" (Harte), **Supp. II Part 1:** 343
My First Summer in the Sierra (Muir), **Supp. IX:** 172, 173, **178–181,** 183, 185; **Supp. XIV:** 177
"My Fountain Pen" (McClatchy), **Supp. XII:** 254, 260
My Friend, Henry Miller (Perlès), **III:** 189
My Friend, Julia Lathrop (Addams), **Supp. I Part 1:** 25
"My Friend, Walt Whitman" (Oliver), **Supp. VII:** 245
"My Garden Acquaintance" (Lowell), **Supp. I Part 2:** 420
My Garden [Book]: (Kincaid), **Supp. VII:** 193–194
"My Grandfather" (Lowell), **II:** 554
"My Grandmother's Love Letters" (H. Crane), **Retro. Supp. II:** 78
"My Grandson, Home at Last" (Angelou), **Supp. IV Part 1:** 13
My Green Hills of Jamaica (McKay), **Supp. X:** 132, 142
My Guru and His Disciple (Isherwood), **Supp. XIV:** 157, 164, 172
My Heart's in the Highlands (Saroyan), **Supp. IV Part 1:** 83
"My High School Reunion" (Kingston), **Supp. V:** 169
"My Indigo" (L.-Y. Lee), **Supp. XV:** 214
"My Kinsman, Major Molineux" (Hawthorne), **II:** 228, 229, 237–239, 243; **Retro. Supp. I:** 153–154, 158, 160, 161; **Retro. Supp. II:** 181, 187; **Supp. XVI:** 157
My Kinsman, Major Molineux (Lowell), **II:** 545–546
"My Last Afternoon with Uncle Devereux Winslow" (Lowell), **II:** 547–548; **Retro. Supp. II:** 189
"My Last Drive" (Hardy), **Supp. VIII:** 32
"My Last Duchess" (Browning), **Supp. XV:** 121
"My Life" (Strand), **Supp. IV Part 2:** 627
My Life, Starring Dara Falcon (Beattie), **Supp. V:** 31, 34–35
My Life a Loaded Gun: Dickinson, Plath, Rich, and Female Creativity (Bennett), **Retro. Supp. I:** 29
My Life and Hard Times (Thurber), **Supp. I Part 2:** 607, 609
My Life as a Man (P. Roth), **Retro. Supp. II:** 281, 286, 289; **Supp. III Part 2:** 401, 404, 405, 417–418
"My Life as a P.I.G., or the True Adventures of Smokey the Cop" (Abbey), **Supp. XIII:** 3
"My life closed twice before its close" (Dickinson), **Retro. Supp. I:** 38
"My Life had stood a Loaded Gun" (Dickinson), **Retro. Supp. I:** 42, 43, 45, 46; **Supp. IV Part 2:** 430
My Life of Absurdity (C. Himes), **Supp. XVI:** 145
"My Life with Medicine" (Nye), **Supp. XIII:** 282
"My Life with *Playboy*" (Plimpton), **Supp. XVI:** 246
"My Life with R. H. Macy" (Jackson), **Supp. IX:** 118
"My Little Utopia" (Simic), **Supp. VIII:** 283
My Lives and How I Lost Them (Cullen), **Supp. IV Part 1:** 173
"My Lord Bag of Rice" (C. Bly), **Supp. XVI:** 40
My Lord Bag of Rice: New and Selected Stories (C. Bly), **Supp. XVI:** 41
"My Lost City" (Fitzgerald), **Retro. Supp. I:** 102
"My Lost Youth" (Longfellow), **II:** 487, 499; **Retro. Supp. II:** 168
My Love Affair with America: The Cautionary Tale of a Cheerful Conservative (Podhoretz), **Supp. VIII:** 232, 233, 237, **244–246**
"My Lover Has Dirty Fingernails" (Updike), **Retro. Supp. I:** 332, 333
"My Lucy Friend Who Smells Like Corn" (Cisneros), **Supp. VII:** 68–69
"My Mammogram" (McClatchy), **Supp. XII:** 263–264
"My Man Bovanne" (Bambara), **Supp. XI:** 2
"My Mariner" (Larcom), **Supp. XIII:** 147
My Mark Twain (Howells), **II:** 276
"My Metamorphosis" (Harte), **Supp. II Part 1:** 339
"My Moby Dick" (Humphrey), **Supp. IX:** 95
"My Monkey" (Nelson), **Supp. XVIII:** 178
My Mortal Enemy (Cather), **I:** 327–328; **Retro. Supp. I:** 16–17; **Supp. I Part 2:** 719
My Mother, My Father and Me (Hellman), **Supp. I Part 1:** 290–291
"My Mother and My Sisters" (Ortiz), **Supp. IV Part 2:** 499
My Mother: Demonology (Acker), **Supp. XII:** 6
"My Mother Is Speaking from the Desert" (Gordon), **Supp. IV Part 1:** 309, 314
"My Mother's Goofy Song" (Fante), **Supp. XI:** 164
"My Mother's Memoirs, My Father's Lie, and Other True Stories" (Banks), **Supp. V:** 15
"My Mother's Nipples" (Hass), **Supp. VI:** 109
"My Mother's Story" (Kunitz), **Supp. III Part 1:** 259
"My Mother Then and Now" (Wasserstein), **Supp. XV:** 327
"My Mother with Purse the Summer They Murdered the Spanish Poet" (Levine), **Supp. V:** 194
My Movie Business: A Memoir (Irving), **Supp. VI:** 164
"My Name" (Cisneros), **Supp. VII:** 60
"My Negro Problem——And Ours" (Podhoretz), **Supp. VIII: 234–236**
"My New Diet" (Karr), **Supp. XI:** 241
"My Old Man" (Hemingway), **II:** 263
My Other Life (Theroux), **Supp. VIII:** 310, 324
"My Own Story" (E. Stoddard), **Supp. XV:** 273, 279, 283
My Own True Name: New and Selected Poems for Young Adults, 1984–1999 (Mora), **Supp. XIII:** 222
"My Parents Have Come Home Laughing" (Jarman), **Supp. XVII:** 113
"My Passion for Ferries" (Whitman), **IV:** 350
"My People" (Hughes), **Retro. Supp. I:** 197; **Supp. I Part 1:** 321–322, 323
"My Philosophy" (Allen), **Supp. XV:** 15
"My Playmate" (Whittier), **Supp. I Part 2:** 699–700
"My Priests" (Monette), **Supp. X:** 159
Myra Breckinridge (Vidal), **Supp. IV Part 2:** 677, 685–686, 689, 691
"My Raptor" (A. Finch), **Supp. XVII:** 72
"My Recollections of S. B. Fairchild" (Jackson), **Supp. IX:** 118–119
"My Religion" (Carson), **Supp. XII: 105–106**
"My Road to Hell Was Paved" (Patchett), **Supp. XII:** 310–311
Myron (Vidal), **Supp. IV Part 2:** 677, 685, 686, 691
"My Roomy" (Lardner), **II:** 420, 421, 428, 430
"My Sad Self" (Ginsberg), **Supp. II Part 1:** 320
My Secret History (Theroux), **Supp. VIII:** 310, 324
"Myself" (Audubon), **Supp. XVI:** 1–2, 5, 12
"My Shoes" (Simic), **Supp. VIII:** 275
"My Side of the Matter" (Capote), **Supp. III Part 1:** 114, 115
My Silk Purse and Yours: The Publishing Scene and American Literary Art (Garrett), **Supp. VII:** 111; **Supp. X:** 7
My Sister Eileen (McKenney), **IV:** 288; **Retro. Supp. II:** 321
My Sister's Hand in Mine: The Collected Works of Jane Bowles, **Supp. IV Part 1:** 82–83

"My Son" (Strand), **Supp. IV Part 2:** 629
My Son, John (film), **Supp. I Part 1:** 67
"My Son, the Murderer" (Malamud), **Supp. I Part 2:** 437
"My Son the Man" (Olds), **Supp. X:** 212
"My Speech to the Graduates" (Allen), **Supp. XV:** 16
"Mysteries of Caesar, The" (Hecht), **Supp. X:** 73
"Mysteries of Eleusis, The" (Hardwick), **Supp. III Part 1:** 195
Mysteries of Pittsburgh, The (Chabon), **Supp. XI:** 65, 68, **69–71**
"Mysterious Case of R, The" (Conroy), **Supp. XVI:** 72
Mysterious Stranger, The (Twain), **IV:** 190–191, 210
Mystery, A (Shields). *See Swann* (Shields)
"Mystery, The" (Dunbar), **Supp. II Part 1:** 199, 210
"Mystery, The" (Glück), **Supp. V:** 91
Mystery and Manners (O'Connor), **Retro. Supp. II:** 230
"'Mystery Boy' Looks for Kin in Nashville" (Hayden), **Supp. II Part 1:** 366, 372
"Mystery of Coincidence, The" (Conroy), **Supp. XVI:** 74
"Mystery of Heroism, A" (Crane), **I:** 414
"Mystery of Marie Rogêt, The" (Poe), **III:** 413, 419; **Retro. Supp. II:** 271
"Mystic" (Plath), **Retro. Supp. II:** 257; **Supp. I Part 2:** 539, 541
"Mystical Poet, A" (Bogan), **Retro. Supp. I:** 36
"Mystic of Sex, The——A First Look at D. H. Lawrence" (Nin), **Supp. X:** 188
"Mystic Vision in 'The Marshes of Glynn'" (Warfel), **Supp. I Part 1:** 366, 373
"Mystification" (Poe), **III:** 425
My Study Windows (Lowell), **Supp. I Part 2:** 407
"My Teacher" (Conroy), **Supp. XVI:** 75
"Myth" (Rukeyser), **Supp. VI:** 281–282
Myth of Sisyphus, The (Camus), **I:** 294; **Supp. XIII:** 165
"Myth of the Isolated Artist, The" (Oates), **Supp. II Part 2:** 520
Myth of the Machine, The (Mumford), **Supp. II Part 2:** 476, 478, 482, 483, 493, 497
Mythology and the Romantic Tradition in English Poetry (Bush), **Supp. I Part 1:** 268
Myths and Texts (Snyder), **Supp. VIII: 295–296**
"Myths of Bears, The" (Bass), **Supp. XVI:** 19, 20
"My *Tocaya*" (Cisneros), **Supp. VII:** 69
My Uncle Dudley (Morris), **I:** 305; **III:** 219–220
"My Uncle's Favorite Coffee Shop" (Nye), **Supp. XIII:** 283
"My Weariness of Epic Proportions" (Simic), **Supp. VIII:** 276
"My Wicked Wicked Ways" (Cisneros), **Supp. VII:** 58, 64–66
My Wicked Wicked Ways (Cisneros), **Supp. VII:** 58, 64–68, 71
"My Word-house" (Mora), **Supp. XIII:** 219, 225
My Works and Days (Mumford), **Supp. II Part 2:** 475, 477, 481
My World and Welcome to It (Thurber), **Supp. I Part 2:** 610

N

Nabokov, Peter, **Supp. IV Part 2:** 490
Nabokov, Véra, **Retro. Supp. I:** 266, 270
Nabokov, Vladimir, **I:** 135; **III: 244–266,** 283, 286; **Retro. Supp. I: 263–281,** 317, 335; **Supp. I Part 1:** 196; **Supp. II Part 1:** 2; **Supp. IV Part 1:** 135; **Supp. IX:** 152, 212, 261; **Supp. V:** 127, 237, 251, 252, 253; **Supp. VIII:** 105, 133, 138; **Supp. X:** 283; **Supp. XI:** 66; **Supp. XII:** 310; **Supp. XIII:** 46, 52; **Supp. XVI:** 148, 294; **Supp. XVIII:** 98, 102
Nabokov's Dozen (Nabokov), **Retro. Supp. I:** 266
Nabokov's Garden: A Guide to Ada (Mason), **Supp. VIII:** 138
Naca, Kristin, **Supp. XIII:** 133
Nadeau, Robert, **Supp. X:** 261, 270
Nadel, Alan, **Supp. IV Part 1:** 209
Naipaul, V. S., **Supp. IV Part 1:** 297; **Supp. VIII:** 314; **Supp. X:** 131; **Supp. XIV:** 111
Naison, Mark, **Supp. XVIII:** 231
Naked and the Dead, The (Mailer), **I:** 477; **III:** 26, 27, 28–30, 31, 33, 35, 36, 44; **Retro. Supp. II: 197–199; Supp. IV Part 1:** 381; **Supp. XI:** 218
Naked Babies (Quindlen and Kelsh), **Supp. XVII:** 167, 179
Naked in Garden Hills (Crews), **Supp. XI:** 102, **110**
Naked Lunch (Burroughs), **Supp. III Part 1:** 92–95, 97–105; **Supp. IV Part 1:** 90
"Naked Nude" (Malamud), **Supp. I Part 2:** 450
Naked Poetry (Berg and Mezey, eds.), **Supp. IV Part 1:** 60
Naked Poetry (Levine), **Supp. V:** 180
Naked Revenge (film), **Supp. XVII:** 141
Namedropping: Mostly Literary Memoirs (Coover), **Supp. V:** 40
"Name in the Papers" (Hughes), **Supp. I Part 1:** 330
Name Is Archer, The (Macdonald, under Millar), **Supp. IV Part 2:** 466
"Name Is Burroughs, The" (Burroughs), **Supp. III Part 1:** 93
Name Is Fogarty, The: Private Papers on Public Matters (Farrell), **II:** 49
"Names" (Carruth), **Supp. XVI:** 54, 56
Names, The (DeLillo), **Supp. VI:** 3, 10, 13, 14
Names, The (Momaday), **Supp. IV Part 2:** 479, 480, 483, 486, 487, 488, 489
Names and Faces of Heroes, The (Price), **Supp. VI:** 258, 260
Names of the Lost, The (Levine), **Supp. V:** 177–178, 179, 187–188
"Naming for Love" (Carruth), **Supp. XVI:** 48
"Naming Myself" (Kingsolver), **Supp. VII:** 208
"Naming of Names, The" (Sanders), **Supp. XVI:** 268
Naming of the Beasts, The (Stern). *See Rejoicings: Selected Poems, 1966–1972* (Stern)
"Naming the Unseen" (Ray), **Supp. XVIII:** 203
Naming the Unseen (Ray), **Supp. XVIII:** 192, **193–195**
Nana (Zola), **III:** 321
"Nancy Culpepper" (Mason), **Supp. VIII:** 141
Nancy Drew stories, **Supp. VIII:** 133, 135, 137, 142
"Nancy Knapp" (Masters), **Supp. I Part 2:** 461
"Naomi Shihab Nye: U.S. Mideast-History a Harbinger of 9-11?" (Nye), **Supp. XIII:** 286
"Naomi Trimmer" (X. J. Kennedy), **Supp. XV:** 170
"Nap, The" (Banks), **Supp. V:** 7
"Napoleon" (Emerson), **II:** 6
Napoleon I, **I:** 6, 7, 8, 474; **II:** 5, 309, 315, 321, 523; **Supp. I Part 1:** 153; **Supp. I Part 2:** 518, 519
Narcissa and Other Fables (Auchincloss), **Supp. IV Part 1:** 21, 34
"Narcissus as Narcissus" (Tate), **IV:** 124
"Narcissus Leaves the Pool" (Epstein), **Supp. XIV:** 110
Narcissus Leaves the Pool: Familiar Essays (Epstein), **Supp. XIV:** 110
Nardal, Paulette, **Supp. X:** 139
Nardi, Marcia, **Retro. Supp. I:** 426, 427
Narration (Stein), **IV:** 27, 30, 32, 33, 36
Narrative of a Four Months' Residence among the Natives of a Valley of the Marquesas Islands (Melville), **III:** 76
Narrative of Arthur Gordon Pym, The (Poe), **III:** 412, 416; **Retro. Supp. II:** 265, **273–275; Supp. XI:** 293
Narrative of the Life of Frederick Douglass, an American Slave, Written by Himself (Douglass), **Supp. III Part 1:** 154–159, 162, 165; **Supp. IV Part 1:** 13; **Supp. VIII:** 202
"Narrativity Scenes" (Wright), **Supp. XV:** 345
Narrenschiff, Das (Brant), **III:** 447
"Narrow Fellow in the Grass, A" (Dickinson), **Retro. Supp. I:** 30, 37
Narrow Heart, A: Portrait of a Woman (Gordon), **II:** 197, 217
Narrow Rooms (Purdy), **Supp. VII:** 274
Nasby, Petroleum, **Supp. XVIII:** 1
Nash, Roderick, **Supp. IX:** 185; **Supp. XIV:** 191–192
Nash, Susan Smith, **Supp. XVI:** 274
Nash, Thomas, **Supp. III Part 1:** 387–388
Nashe, Thomas, **I:** 358; **Supp. XVII:** 232
Nashville (film), **Supp. IX:** 143
Nashville Skyline (album, Dylan), **Supp. XVIII:** 27
Nason, Elias, **Supp. XV:** 242

Nasser, Gamal Abdel, **IV:** 490
Natalie Mann (Toomer), **Supp. III Part 2:** 484–486
Nathan, George Jean, **II:** 91; **III:** 103, 104, 106, 107; **IV:** 432; **Supp. IV Part 1:** 343; **Supp. IX:** 56–57; **Supp. XIII:** 161
"Nathanael West" (Herbst), **Retro. Supp. II:** 325
Nathanael West: The Art of His Life (Martin), **Retro. Supp. II:** 325
Nathan Coulter (Berry), **Supp. X:** 24, 33
"Nationalist, The" (Anderson), **I:** 115
"Nation Is Like Ourselves, The" (Baraka), **Supp. II Part 1:** 53
"Native, The" (Olds), **Supp. X:** 215
"Native American Attitudes to the Environment" (Momaday), **Supp. IV Part 2:** 481, 491
Native American Renaissance (Lincoln), **Supp. IV Part 2:** 507
Native American Testimony (Nabokov, ed.), **Supp. IV Part 2:** 490
"Native Blessing" (Ray), **Supp. XVIII:** 202
"Native Hill, A" (Berry), **Supp. X:** 21
Native in a Strange Land: Trials & Tremors (Coleman), **Supp. XI: 84–85,** 87
Native of Winby and Other Tales, A (Jewett), **II:** 396; **Retro. Supp. II:** 138
Native Son (Wright), **IV:** 476, 477, 478, 479, 481, 482–484, 485, 487, 488, 491, 495; **Retro. Supp. II:** 107, 116; **Supp. I Part 1:** 51, 64, 67, 337; **Supp. II Part 1:** 170, 235–236; **Supp. IX:** 306; **Supp. XIV:** 73; **Supp. XVII:** 155; **Supp. XVIII:** 283, 286
"Native Trees" (Merwin), **Supp. III Part 1:** 355
Natorp, Paul, **Supp. XIV:** 198
Natural, The (Malamud), **II:** 424, 425; **Retro. Supp. II:** 288; **Supp. I Part 2:** 438–441, 443
"*Natural, The:* Malamud's World Ceres" (Wasserman), **Supp. I Part 2:** 439
"Natural History" (Olds), **Supp. X:** 210
"Natural History Note" (Hay), **Supp. XIV:** 124, 130
"Natural History of Some Poems, A" (Harrison), **Supp. VIII:** 53
"Natural History of the Dead" (Hemingway), **II:** 206; **Retro. Supp. I:** 176
"Naturally Superior School, A" (Knowles), **Supp. XII:** 235, 240–241
"Natural Method of Mental Philosophy" (Emerson), **II:** 14
"Natural Resources" (Rich), **Supp. I Part 2:** 575
Natural Selection (F. Barthelme), **Supp. XI:** 2, 28, 32, 33
"Nature" (Emerson), **Retro. Supp. I:** 250; **Supp. I Part 2:** 383; **Supp. III Part 1:** 387; **Supp. IX:** 178
Nature (Emerson), **I:** 463; **II:** 1, 8, 12, 16; **IV:** 171, 172–173
"Nature, Inc." (Lewis), **II:** 441
Nature and Destiny of Man, The (Niebuhr), **III:** 292, 303–306, 310
"Nature and Life" (Emerson), **II:** 19
"Nature and Nurture: When It Comes to Twins, Sometimes It's Hard to Tell the Two Apart" (Bausch), **Supp. VII:** 40
"Nature-Metaphors" (Lanier), **Supp. I Part 1:** 352
Nature Morte (Brodsky), **Supp. VIII:** 25
Nature of Evil, The (James), **II:** 343
Nature of Peace, The (Veblen), **Supp. I Part 2:** 642
Nature of True Virtue, The (Edwards), **I:** 549, 557–558, 559
Nature: Poems Old and New (Swenson), **Supp. IV Part 2:** 652
Nature's Economy: A History of Ecological Ideas (Worster), **Supp. IX:** 19
Nausea (Sartre), **Supp. VIII:** 7
"Navajo Blanket, A" (Swenson), **Supp. IV Part 2:** 649
Navarette, Don Martín de, **II:** 310
Navarro, Ramon, **Supp. IV Part 1:** 206
Navigator, The (film), **I:** 31
Naylor, Gloria, **Supp. VIII: 213–230**
Naylor, Paul Kenneth, **Supp. IV Part 2:** 420
Nazimova, **III:** 399
Neal, Larry, **Retro. Supp. II:** 112, 128; **Supp. X:** 324, 328
Neal, Lawrence P., **Supp. II Part 1:** 53
Neal, Patricia, **Supp. I Part 1:** 286; **Supp. IV Part 2:** 524; **Supp. V:** 223
Neale, Walter, **I:** 192, 208
Nearer the Moon: From "A Journal of Love," the Unexpurgated Diary of Anaïs Nin, 1937–1939, **Supp. X:** 184, 185
Near-Johannesburg Boy and Other Poems, The (Brooks), **Supp. III Part 1:** 86
Near Klamath (Carver), **Supp. III Part 1:** 137
"Near Perigord" (Pound), **Retro. Supp. I:** 289, 290
Near the Ocean (Lowell), **II:** 543, 550, 551–553, 554, 555; **Retro. Supp. II:** 182, 186, 189–190
"Near View of the High Sierra, A" (Muir), **Supp. IX:** 183
Nebeker, Helen, **Supp. IX:** 122
"Nebraska Blizzard" (F. Wright), **Supp. XVII:** 247
Necessary Angel, The (Stevens), **IV:** 76, 79, 89, 90
Necessities of Life: Poems, 1962–1965 (Rich), **Supp. I Part 2:** 553, 555
"Necrological" (Ransom), **III:** 486–489, 490, 492
Ned Christie's War (Conley), **Supp. V:** 232
"Need for a Cultural Base to Civil Rites & Bpower Mooments, The" (Baraka), **Supp. II Part 1:** 48
"Need for Christian Preaching, The" (Buechner), **Supp. XII:** 49
Needful Things (King), **Supp. V:** 139, 146
"Needle" (Simic), **Supp. VIII:** 275
"Needle Trade" (Reznikoff), **Supp. XIV:** 277, 289
"Need of Being Versed in Country Things, The" (Frost), **II:** 154; **Retro. Supp. I:** 133, 135
Neel, Philippe, **Supp. XIV:** 338
Neelakantappa, Tara, **Supp. XV:** 104–105
Neeley, Barbara, **Supp. XVI:** 143
"Negative Capability" (Komunyakaa), **Supp. XIII:** 131
Negligible Tales (Bierce), **I:** 209
"Negotiating the Darkness, Fortified by Poets' Strength" (Karr), **Supp. XI:** 254; **Supp. XIII:** 285
Negotiating with the Dead (Atwood), **Supp. XIII:** 20, 35
Negritude movement, **Supp. X:** 131, 139
"Negro" (Hughes), **Supp. I Part 1:** 321–322
Negro, The (Du Bois), **Supp. II Part 1:** 178, 179, 185
Negro, The: The Southerner's Problem (Page), **Supp. II Part 1:** 168
Negro and His Music, The (Locke), **Supp. XIV:** 202
"Negro Artisan, The" (Du Bois), **Supp. II Part 1:** 166
"Negro Artist and the Racial Mountain, The" (Hughes), **Retro. Supp. I:** 200, 207; **Supp. I Part 1:** 323, 325; **Supp. IV Part 1:** 169
Negro Art: Past and Present (Locke), **Supp. XIV:** 202
"Negro Assays the Negro Mood, A" (Baldwin), **Supp. I Part 1:** 52
"Negro Citizen, The" (Du Bois), **Supp. II Part 1:** 179
"Negro Dancers" (Hughes), **Retro. Supp. I:** 199; **Supp. I Part 1:** 324
Negroes in America, The (McKay), **Supp. X:** 132, 136
"Negroes of Farmville, Virginia, The: A Social Study" (Du Bois), **Supp. II Part 1:** 166
Negro Family, The: The Case for National Action (Moynihan), **Retro. Supp. II:** 123
"Negro Farmer, The" (Du Bois), **Supp. II Part 1:** 167
"Negro Ghetto" (Hughes), **Supp. I Part 1:** 331
Negro in America, The (Locke), **Supp. XIV:** 208
Negro in American Civilization, The (Du Bois), **Supp. II Part 1:** 179
Negro in American Culture, The (Locke and Butcher), **Supp. XIV:** 202–203
Negro in Art, The: A Pictorial Record of the Negro Artist and of the Negro Theme in Art (Locke), **Supp. XIV:** 202
"Negro in Large Cities, The" (Du Bois), **Supp. II Part 1:** 169
"Negro in Literature and Art, The" (Du Bois), **Supp. II Part 1:** 174
Negro in New York, The (Ellison), **Supp. II Part 1:** 230
"Negro in the Black Belt, The: Some Social Sketches" (Du Bois), **Supp. II Part 1:** 166
"Negro in the Three Americas, The" (Locke), **Supp. XIV:** 211

"Negro in the Well, The" (Caldwell), **I:** 309
"Negro Love Song, A" (Dunbar), **Supp. II Part 1:** 204
"Negro Martyrs Are Needed" (C. Himes), **Supp. XVI:** 138
Negro Mother, The (Hughes), **Supp. I Part 1:** 328
Negro Mother and Other Dramatic Recitations, The (Hughes), **Retro. Supp. I:** 203
Negro Novel in America, The (Bone), **Supp. IX:** 318–319; **Supp. XVIII:** 285
Negro Publication Society of America, **Retro. Supp. I:** 205
"Negro Renaissance, The: Jean Toomer and the Harlem of the 1920s" (Bontemps), **Supp. IX:** 306
"Negro Schoolmaster in the New South, A" (Du Bois), **Supp. II Part 1:** 168
"Negro's Contribution to American Culture, The" (Locke), **Supp. XIV:** 210, 211
"Negro Sermon, A: Simon Legree" (Lindsay), **Supp. I Part 2:** 393
"Negro Sings of Rivers, The" (Hughes), **Supp. IV Part 1:** 16
"Negro Speaks of Rivers, The" (Hughes), **Retro. Supp. I:** 199; **Supp. I Part 1:** 321
"Negro Spirituals, The (Locke), **Supp. XIV:** 201
"Negro Takes Stock, The"(Du Bois), **Supp. II Part 1:** 180
"Negro Theatre, The"(Van Vechten), **Supp. II Part 2:** 735
"Negro Voter Sizes Up Taft, A" (Hurston), **Supp. VI:** 160
"Negro Writer and His Roots, The: Toward a New Romanticism" (Hansberry), **Supp. IV Part 1:** 364
"Negro Youth Speaks" (Locke), **Supp. XIV:** 201
"Nehemias Americanus" (Mather), **Supp. II Part 2:** 453
Nehru, Jawaharlal, **IV:** 490
"Neighbor" (Hugo), **Supp. VI:** 135–136
"Neighbors" (Carver), **Supp. III Part 1:** 135, 139, 141; **Supp. XI:** 153
"Neighbors" (Hogan), **Supp. IV Part 1:** 405
"Neighbors, The" (Hay), **Supp. XIV:** 126
"Neighbour Rosicky" (Cather), **I:** 331–332
Neil Simon (Johnson), **Supp. IV Part 2:** 573
"Neil Simon's Jewish-Style Comedies" (Walden), **Supp. IV Part 2:** 584, 591
"Neil Simon: Toward Act III?" (Walden), **Supp. IV Part 2:** 591
Neilson, Heather, **Supp. IV Part 2:** 681
Neiman, Gilbert, **Supp. XV:** 140
"Neither Out Far Nor In Deep" (Frost), **I:** 303; **Retro. Supp. I:** 121, 138
"Nellie Clark" (Masters), **Supp. I Part 2:** 461
Nelson, Alice Dunbar, **Supp. XVII:** 75
Nelson, Cary, **Supp. XVIII:** 226, 227, 230, 231
Nelson, Ernest, **I:** 388
Nelson, Howard, **Supp. IV Part 1:** 66, 68
Nelson, Lord Horatio, **II:** 524
Nelson, Lynn (pseudonym). *See* Nelson, Marilyn
Nelson, Marilyn, **Supp. XVII:** 74, 112; **Supp. XVIII: 171–188**
Nelson, Shirley, **Supp. XII:** 293
Nelson, Steve, **Supp. XVIII:** 226
Nelson Algren (Cox and Chatterton), **Supp. IX:** 11–12
Nelson Algren: A Life on the Wild Side (Drew), **Supp. IX:** 2
Nemerov, David, **II:** 268
Nemerov, Howard, **III: 267–289; IV:** 137, 140; **Supp. III Part 2:** 541; **Supp. IV Part 2:** 455, 650; **Supp. IX:** 114
Nemiroff, Robert Barron, **Supp. IV Part 1:** 360, 361, 365, 369, 370, 374
Neoconservative Criticism: Norman Podhoretz, Kenneth S. Lynn, and Joseph Epstein (Winchell), **Supp. VIII:** 241; **Supp. XIV:** 103
"Neo-Hoodoo Manifesto, The" (Reed), **Supp. X:** 242
Neon Rain, The (Burke), **Supp. XIV:** 22, 24, 26–27, 28–29, 30
Neon Vernacular (Komunyakaa), **Supp. XIII:** 121, **127–128,** 131
Neon Wilderness, The (Algren), **Supp. IX:** 3, 4
Neo-Slave Narratives (Rushdy), **Supp. X:** 250
Nepantla: Essays from the Land in the Middle (Mora), **Supp. XIII:** 213, **219–221,** 227
Nephew, The (Purdy), **Supp. VII:** 271, 273, 282
"Nereids of Seriphos, The" (Clampitt), **Supp. IX:** 41
Nericcio, William, **Supp. XIV:** 304–305
Neruda, Pablo, **Supp. I Part 1:** 89; **Supp. IV Part 2:** 537; **Supp. IX:** 157, 271; **Supp. V:** 332; **Supp. VIII:** 272, 274; **Supp. X:** 112; **Supp. XI:** 191; **Supp. XII:** 217; **Supp. XIII:** 114, 315, 323
Nesbit, Edith, **Supp. VIII:** 171
Nesbitt, Robin, **Supp. VIII:** 89
Nesting Ground, The (Wagoner), **Supp. IX:** 324, **325–326**
Nest of Ninnies, A (Ashbery and Schuyler), **Supp. III Part 1:** 3; **Supp. XV:** 178
Nets to Catch the Wind (Wylie), **Supp. I Part 2:** 709, 710–712, 714
Nettleton, Asahel, **I:** 458
"Net to Snare the Moonlight, A" (Lindsay), **Supp. I Part 2:** 387
Neubauer, Carol E., **Supp. IV Part 1:** 9
Neugeboren, Jacob Mordecai. *See* Neugeboren, Jay
Neugeboren, Jay, **Supp. XVI: 217–231**
Neugroschel, Joachim, **Supp. IX:** 138
Neuhaus, Richard John, **Supp. VIII:** 245
Neumann, Erich, **Supp. I Part 2:** 567; **Supp. IV Part 1:** 68, 69
Neuromancer (W. Gibson), **Supp. XII:** 15; **Supp. XVI:** 117, 119–120, 122, 124, **125–126,** 127, 129, 131
Neurotica: Jewish Writers on Sex (Bukiet, ed.), **Supp. XVII:** 48
"Neurotic America and the Sex Impulse" (Dreiser), **Retro. Supp. II:** 105
Neutra, Richard, **Supp. XVI:** 192
"Never Bet the Devil Your Head" (Poe), **III:** 425; **Retro. Supp. II:** 273
Never Come Morning (Algren), **Supp. IX:** 3, **7–9**
Never in a Hurry: Essays on People and Places (Nye), **Supp. XIII:** 273, **280–282,** 286
"Never Marry a Mexican" (Cisneros), **Supp. VII:** 70
"Never Room with a Couple" (Hughes), **Supp. I Part 1:** 330
"Nevertheless" (Moore), **III:** 214
Nevins, Allan, **I:** 253; **Supp. I Part 2:** 486, 493
"Nevsky Prospekt" (Olds), **Supp. X:** 205
New Adam, The (Untermeyer), **Supp. XV:** 304, 305
New Addresses (Koch), **Supp. XV:** 177, 184
"New Age of the Rhetoricians, The" (Cowley), **Supp. II Part 1:** 135
New American Cyclopedia, **Supp. XVIII:** 4
New American Literature, The (Pattee), **II:** 456
New American Novel of Manners, The (Klinkowitz), **Supp. XI:** 347
"New American Ode, The" (Wright), **Supp. XV:** 346
New American Poetry, 1945–1960 (Allen, ed.), **Supp. XIII:** 112
New American Poetry, The (Allen, ed.), **Supp. VIII:** 291, 292
"New American Writer, A" (W. C. Williams), **Retro. Supp. II:** 335
New and Collected Poems (Reed), **Supp. X:** 241
New and Collected Poems (Wilbur), **Supp. III Part 2:** 562–564
New and Selected Poems (Nemerov), **III:** 269, 275, 277–279
New and Selected Poems (Oliver), **Supp. VII:** 240–241, 245
New and Selected Poems (Wagoner), **Supp. IX: 326–327**
New and Selected Poems (W. J. Smith), **Supp. XIII:** 332
New and Selected Poems: 1974–1994 (Dunn), **Supp. XI: 151–152**
New and Selected Things Taking Place (Swenson), **Supp. IV Part 2:** 648–650, 651
"New Art Gallery Society, The" (Wolfe), **Supp. III Part 2:** 580
Newberger, Julee, **Supp. XVIII:** 168
"New Capitalist Tool, The" (Wasserstein), **Supp. XV:** 328
Newcomb, Ralph, **Supp. XIII:** 12
Newcomb, Robert, **II:** 111
New Conscience and an Ancient Evil, A (Addams), **Supp. I Part 1:** 14–15, 16

"New Conservatism in American Poetry, The" (Wakoski), **Supp. XVII:** 112
"New Conservatives, The: Intellectuals in Retreat" (Epstein), **Supp. XIV:** 103
New Criticism, The (Ransom), **III:** 497–498, 499, 501
"New Day, A" (Levine), **Supp. V:** 182
Newdick, Robert Spangler, **Retro. Supp. I:** 138
Newdick's Season of Frost (Newdick), **Retro. Supp. I:** 138
New Dictionary of Quotations, A (Mencken), **III:** 111
New Directions Anthology in Prose and Poetry (Laughlin, ed.), **Supp. XVI:** 284
"New Directions in Poetry" (D. Locke), **Supp. IX:** 273
"New Dog, The: Variations on a Text by Jules Laforgue" (C. Frost), **Supp. XV:** 98
Newell, Henry, **IV:** 193
"New England" (Lowell), **II:** 536
"New England" (Robinson), **III:** 510, 524
"New England Bachelor, A" (Eberhart), **I:** 539
"New Englander, The" (Anderson), **I:** 114
New England Girlhood, A (Larcom), **Supp. XIII:** 137, 142, 143, 144, **147–154**
New England: Indian Summer (Brooks), **I:** 253, 256
New England Local Color Literature (Donovan), **Retro. Supp. II:** 138
"New England Sabbath-Day Chace, The" (Freneau), **Supp. II Part 1:** 273
New-England Tale, A (Sedgwick), **I:** 341
New England Tragedies, The (Longfellow), **II:** 490, 505, 506; **Retro. Supp. II:** 165, 167
New Era in American Poetry, The (Untermeyer, ed.), **Supp. XV:** 301, 303, 306
Newer Ideals of Peace (Addams), **Supp. I Part 1:** 11–12, 15, 16–17, 19, 20–21
New Feminist Criticism, The: Essays on Women, Literature, and Theory (Showalter), **Supp. X:** 97
"New Folsom Prison" (Matthews), **Supp. IX:** 165
New Formalism, The: A Critical Introduction (McPhillips), **Supp. XV:** 250, 251, 252, 264
New Found Land: Fourteen Poems (MacLeish), **III:** 12–13
"New Hampshire, February" (Eberhart), **I:** 536
New Hampshire: A Poem with Notes and Grace Notes (Frost), **II:** 154–155; **Retro. Supp. I:** 132, 133, 135
New Hard-Boiled Writers (Panek), **Supp. XIV:** 27
"New Home" (Richter), **Supp. XVIII:** 209
New Industrial State, The (Galbraith), **Supp. I Part 2:** 648
"New Journalism, The" (Wolfe), **Supp. III Part 2:** 571
New Journalism, The (Wolfe and Johnson, eds.), **Supp. III Part 2:** 570, 579–581, 583, 586
New Left, The: The Anti-Industrial Revolution (Rand), **Supp. IV Part 2:** 527
"New Letters from Thomas Jefferson" (Stafford), **Supp. XI:** 324
New Letters on the Air: Contemporary Writers on Radio, **Supp. X:** 165, 169, 173
"New Life" (Glück), **Supp. V:** 90
New Life, A (Malamud), **Supp. I Part 2:** 429–466
"New Life, The" (Bynner), **Supp. XV:** 44
"New Life at Kyerefaso" (Sutherland), **Supp. IV Part 1:** 9
"New Light on Veblen" (Dorfman), **Supp. I Part 2:** 650
Newman, Charles, **Supp. I Part 2:** 527, 546–548
Newman, Edwin, **Supp. IV Part 2:** 526
Newman, Judie, **Supp. IV Part 1:** 304, 305
Newman, Paul, **Supp. IV Part 2:** 473, 474
New Man, The (Merton), **Supp. VIII:** 208
"New Medea, The" (Howells), **II:** 282
New Mexico trilogy (Nichols), **Supp. XIII:** 269
New Morning (album, Dylan), **Supp. XVIII:** 27, 33
"New Mother" (Olds), **Supp. X:** 206
"New Mothers, The" (Shields), **Supp. VII:** 310
New Music (Price), **Supp. VI:** 264, 265
"New Mutants, The" (Fiedler), **Supp. XIII:** 104
"New Name for Some Old Ways of Thinking, A" (James), **II:** 353
New Native American Novel, The: Works in Progress (Bartlett), **Supp. IV Part 1:** 335
"New Natural History, A" (Thurber), **Supp. I Part 2:** 619
"New Negro, The" (Locke), **Supp. XIV:** 201
New Negro, The (Locke, ed.), **Supp. II Part 1:** 176; **Supp. IX:** 309; **Supp. X:** 137
New Negro, The: An Interpretation (Locke, ed.), **Retro. Supp. I:** 199; **Supp. IV Part 1:** 170; **Supp. XIV:** 195, 201–202
New Negro for a New Century, A (Washington, Wood, and Williams), **Supp. XIV:** 201
New New Journalism, The (R. Boynton), **Supp. XVII:** 209
"New Nomads, The" (E. Hoffman), **Supp. XVI:** 161
"New Orleans" (Carruth), **Supp. XVI:** 50
New Orleans Sketches (Faulkner), **Retro. Supp. I:** 80
New Path to the Waterfall, A (Carver), **Supp. III Part 1:** 138–140, 147, 149
"New Poem, The" (Wright), **Supp. V:** 339, 340
"New Poems" (MacLeish), **III:** 19
"New Poems" (Oliver), **Supp. VII:** 240
New Poems 1960 (Bynner), **Supp. XV:** 51
New Poems: 1980–88 (Haines), **Supp. XII: 209–210**
New Poetry, The (Monroe and Henderson, eds.), **Supp. I Part 2:** 387
"New Poetry Handbook, The" (Strand), **Supp. IV Part 2:** 626
New Poetry of Mexico (Strand, trans.), **Supp. IV Part 2:** 630
New Poets of England and America (Hall, Pack, and Simpson, eds.), **Supp. IV Part 2:** 621
"Newport of Anchuria" (Henry), **Supp. II Part 1:** 409
New Princeton Encyclopedia of Poetry and Poetics (Preminger and Brogan, eds.), **Supp. XV:** 250
"*New Republic* Moves Uptown, The" (Cowley), **Supp. II Part 1:** 142
"New Rose Hotel" (W. Gibson), **Supp. XVI:** 120, 122, 124
"News, The" (McClatchy), **Supp. XII:** 269
"New Season" (Levine), **Supp. V:** 188
New Seeds of Contemplation (Merton), **Supp. VIII:** 200, 208
News from the Glacier: Selected Poems 1960–1980 (Haines), **Supp. XII:** 207, 208–209
"News Item" (Parker), **Supp. IX:** 190
New Song, A (Hughes), **Retro. Supp. I:** 202; **Supp. I Part 1:** 328, 331–332
"New South, The" (Lanier), **Supp. I Part 1:** 352, 354, 370
New Southern Girl, The: Female Adolescence in the Works of 12 Women Authors (Town), **Supp. XVIII:** 195
Newspaper Days, 1899–1906 (Mencken), **III:** 100, 102, 120
"New Spirit, The" (Ashbery), **Supp. III Part 1:** 14, 15
New Spoon River, The (Masters), **Supp. I Part 2:** 461–465, 473
New Star Chamber and Other Essays, The (Masters), **Supp. I Part 2:** 455–456, 459
New Tales of the Vampires (Rice), **Supp. VII:** 290
New Testament, **I:** 303, 457, 458; **II:** 167; **III:** 305; **IV:** 114, 134, 152; **Retro. Supp. I:** 58, 140, 360; **Supp. I Part 1:** 104, 106; **Supp. I Part 2:** 516; **Supp. XVII:** 155. *See also* names of New Testament books
New Testament, A (Anderson), **I:** 101, 114
"New Theory of Thorstein Veblen, A" (Galbraith), **Supp. I Part 2:** 650
Newton, Benjamin Franklin, **I:** 454
Newton, Huey P., **Supp. I Part 1:** 66; **Supp. IV Part 1:** 206
Newton, Isaac, **I:** 132, 557; **II:** 6, 103, 348–349; **III:** 428; **IV:** 18, 149
Newton, Sarah Emily, **Supp. XV:** 234
"New-Wave Format, A" (Mason), **Supp. VIII:** 141, 143, 147
New West of Edward Abbey, The (Ronald), **Supp. XIII:** 4

New Wolves, The: The Return of the Mexican Wolf to the American Southwest (Bass), **Supp. XVI:** 26–27
New Woman's Survival Sourcebook, The (Rennie and Grimstead, eds.), **Supp. I Part 2:** 569
New World, The (Bynner), **Supp. XV:** 41, 42
New World, The: Tales (Banks), **Supp. V:** 8, 9, 10
New World Naked, A (Mariani), **Retro. Supp. I:** 419
New Worlds of Literature (Beaty and Hunter, eds.), **Supp. IV Part 1:** 331
New World Writing (Updike), **IV:** 217
New Year Letter (Auden), **Supp. II Part 1:** 14, 16
"New Year's Day" (Wharton), **Retro. Supp. I:** 381
"New Year's Eve" (Schwartz), **Supp. II Part 2:** 640, 656–657
New Year's Eve/1929 (Farrell), **II:** 43
"New Year's Eve 1968" (Lowell), **II:** 554
"New Year's Gift, The" (Stowe), **Supp. I Part 2:** 587
"New York" (Capote), **Supp. III Part 1:** 122
"New York" (Moore), **III:** 196, 198, 202, 206
"New York 1965" (Bowles), **Supp. IV Part 1:** 94
New York: A Serendipiter's Journey (Talese), **Supp. XVII:** 202, 203
New York City Arts Project, **Supp. III Part 2:** 618
"New York City in 1979"(Acker), **Supp. XII:** 5
New York Edition, **Retro. Supp. I:** 235
"New York Edition" (James), **II:** 336, 337
"New York Gold Conspiracy, The" (Adams), **I:** 4
New York Hat, The (film; Griffith), **Supp. XVI:** 183
New York Intellectuals, **Supp. VIII:** 93
"New York Intellectuals, The" (Howe), **Supp. VI:** 120
"New York Is a City of Things Unnoticed" (Talese), **Supp. XVII:** 202, 209
New York Jew (Kazin), **Supp. VIII:** 95, **97–100**
"New York Theater: Isn't It Romantic" (Wasserstein), **Supp. XV:** 320
New York Trilogy, The (Auster), **Supp. XII:** 21, **24–28**
Next (McNally), **Supp. XIII:** 197
"Next in Line, The" (Bradbury), **Supp. IV Part 1:** 102
Next Room of the Dream, The (Nemerov), **III:** 269, 275, 278, 279–280, 284
"Next Time I Crossed the Line into Oklahoma, The" (Wright), **Supp. XV:** 345
Next-to-Last Things: New Poems and Essays (Kunitz), **Supp. III Part 1:** 257–259, 261, 262, 265, 266, 268
"'Next to Reading Matter'" (Henry), **Supp. II Part 1:** 399
Nexus (H. Miller), **III:** 170, 187, 188, 189
Niatum, Duane, **Supp. IV Part 1:** 331; **Supp. IV Part 2:** 505
Nice and Noir (Schwartz), **Supp. XIV:** 23
"Nice Girl" (Nelson), **Supp. XVIII:** 178
Nice Jewish Boy, The (P. Roth), **Supp. III Part 2:** 412
Nicholas II, Tsar, **Supp. I Part 2:** 447
Nichols, Charles, **Retro. Supp. I:** 194
Nichols, Dudley, **Supp. XVIII:** 247
Nichols, John Treadwell, **Supp. XIII: 253–272**
Nichols, Luther, **Supp. X:** 265
Nichols, Mike, **Supp. IV Part 1:** 234; **Supp. IV Part 2:** 577
Nicholson, Colin, **Supp. VIII:** 129
Nicholson, Harold, **Supp. XIV:** 163
Nicholson, Jack, **Supp. V:** 26; **Supp. VIII:** 45; **Supp. XI:** 308
Nicholson, John, **Supp. XVI:** 293
Nick Adams Stories, The (Hemingway), **II:** 258; **Retro. Supp. I:** 174
"Nick and the Candlestick" (Plath), **Supp. I Part 2:** 544
Nickel and Dimed: On (Not) Getting By in America (Ehrenreich), **Supp. XVII:** 210
Nickel Mountain: A Pastoral Novel (Gardner), **Supp. VI:** 63, 64, 68, **69**
"Nicodemus" (Keillor), **Supp. XVI:** 167
Nicoll, Allardyce, **III:** 400
Nicoloff, Philip, **II:** 7
Niebuhr, Gustav, **III:** 292
Niebuhr, H. Richard, **I:** 494
Niebuhr, Lydia, **III:** 292
Niebuhr, Reinhold, **III: 290–313; Supp. I Part 2:** 654
Niedecker, Lorine, **Supp. III Part 2:** 616, 623; **Supp. XIV:** 287
Nielsen, Ed, **Supp. IX:** 254
Nielson, Dorothy, **Supp. I Part 2:** 659
Nietzsche, Friedrich Wilhelm, **I:** 227, 283, 383, 389, 396, 397, 402, 509; **II:** 7, 20, 27, 42, 90, 145, 262, 462, 463, 577, 583, 585; **III:** 102–103, 113, 156, 176; **IV:** 286, 491; **Supp. I Part 1:** 254, 299, 320; **Supp. I Part 2:** 646; **Supp. IV Part 1:** 104, 105–106, 107, 110, 284; **Supp. IV Part 2:** 519; **Supp. V:** 277, 280; **Supp. VIII:** 11, 181, 189; **Supp. X:** 48; **Supp. XII:** 98; **Supp. XIV:** 339
Nieves, Felipe, **Supp. XVIII:** 90
Niflis, N. Michael, **Supp. IV Part 1:** 175
Nigger Heaven (Van Vechten), **Supp. II Part 2:** 739, 744–746; **Supp. XVIII:** 123, 127
"Nigger Jeff" (Dreiser), **Retro. Supp. II:** 97
Nigger of the "Narcissus," The (Conrad), **II:** 91; **Retro. Supp. I:** 106; **Supp. XVIII:** 224
"NIGGY THE HO" (Baraka), **Supp. II Part 1:** 54
"Night, Death, Mississippi" (Hayden), **Supp. II Part 1:** 369
'Night, Mother (Norman), **Supp. VIII:** 141
"Night above the Avenue" (Merwin), **Supp. III Part 1:** 355
"Night among the Horses, A" (Barnes), **Supp. III Part 1:** 33–34, 39, 44
Night at the Movies, A, or, You Must Remember This: Fictions (Coover), **Supp. V:** 50–51
"Night at the Opera, A" (Matthews), **Supp. IX:** 167
"Night before the Sentence Is Carried Out, The" (Wright), **Supp. XV:** 341
"Nightbird" (Komunyakaa), **Supp. XIII:** 132
"Night-Blooming Cereus, The" (Hayden), **Supp. II Part 1:** 367
Night-Blooming Cereus, The (Hayden), **Supp. II Part 1:** 367, 373
Night-Born, The (London), **II:** 467
"Nightbreak" (Rich), **Supp. I Part 2:** 556
Night Dance (Price), **Supp. VI:** 264
"Night Dances, The" (Plath), **Supp. I Part 2:** 544
"Night Dream, The" (MacLeish), **III:** 15
"Night Ferry" (Doty), **Supp. XI:** 124
"Nightfishing" (Schnackenberg), **Supp. XV:** 254
"Night I Met Little Floyd, The" (Wright), **Supp. XV:** 345–346
"Night in Acadie, A" (Chopin), **Retro. Supp. II:** 66
Night in Acadie, A (Chopin), **Retro. Supp. II: 66–67**, 73; **Supp. I Part 1:** 200, 219, 220, 224
"Night in June, A" (W. C. Williams), **Retro. Supp. I:** 424
"Night in New Arabia, A" (Henry), **Supp. II Part 1:** 402
Night in Question, The: Stories (Wolff), **Supp. VII:** 342–344
"Night Journey" (Roethke), **Supp. III Part 1:** 260
Night Light (Justice), **Supp. VII:** 126–127
"Nightmare" (Kumin), **Supp. IV Part 2:** 442
"Nightmare Factory, The" (Kumin), **Supp. IV Part 2:** 445, 453
Nightmare Factory, The (Kumin), **Supp. IV Part 2:** 444–447, 451
Nightmare on Main Street (Poe), **Retro. Supp. II:** 262
"Nightmare" poems (Benét), **Supp. XI:** 46, 58
"Night Mirror" (L.-Y. Lee), **Supp. XV:** 225
Night Music (Odets), **Supp. II Part 2:** 541, 543, 544
"Night of First Snow" (R. Bly), **Supp. IV Part 1:** 71
Night of January 16th (Rand), **Supp. IV Part 2:** 527
"Night of the Iguana, The" (T. Williams), **IV:** 384
Night of the Iguana, The (T. Williams), **IV:** 382, 383, 384, 385, 386, 387, 388, 391, 392, 393, 394, 395, 397, 398
"Night of the Living Beanfield: How an Unsuccessful Cult Novel Became an Unsuccessful Cult Film in Only Fourteen Years, Eleven Nervous Breakdowns, and $20 Million" (Nichols), **Supp. XIII:** 267

Night Rider (Warren), **IV:** 243, 246–247
Nights (Doolittle), **Supp. I Part 1:** 270, 271
Nights and Days (Merrill), **Supp. III Part 1:** 319, 320, 322–325
"Nights and Days" (Rich), **Supp. I Part 2:** 574
"Night's for Cryin,' The" (C. Himes), **Supp. XVI:** 137
"Night Shift" (Plath), **Supp. I Part 2:** 538
"Night-Side" (Oates), **Supp. II Part 2:** 523
Night-Side (Oates), **Supp. II Part 2:** 522
"Night Sketches: Beneath an Umbrella" (Hawthorne), **II:** 235–237, 238, 239, 242
"Night Sport" (Hoffman), **Supp. XVIII:** 86, 87
"Night-Sweat" (Lowell), **II:** 554
"Night-Talk" (Ellison), **Retro. Supp. II:** 126; **Supp. II Part 1:** 248
Night Thoughts (Young), **III:** 415
Night Traveler, The (Oliver), **Supp. VII:** 233
"Night Watch" (Gioia), **Supp. XV:** 117
"Night Watch, The" (Wright), **Supp. V:** 339
"Night We All Had Grippe, The" (Jackson), **Supp. IX:** 118
Nightwood (Barnes), **Supp. III Part 1:** 31, 32, 35–37, 39–43
Night World and the Word Night, The (F. Wright), **Supp. XVII:** 240, 244–245
"Nihilist as Hero, The" (Lowell), **II:** 554; **Retro. Supp. II:** 190
Nijinsky, Vaslav, **Supp. XV:** 28–29
Nikolai Gogol (Nabokov), **Retro. Supp. I:** 266
Niles, Thomas, **Retro. Supp. I:** 35
Niles, Thomas, Jr., **Supp. I Part 1:** 39
Nilsson, Christine, **Supp. I Part 1:** 355
Nilsson, Harry, **Supp. XI:** 309
Nilsson, Jenny Lind, **Supp. XVI:** 177
Nimitz, Chester, **Supp. I Part 2:** 491
"Nimram" (Gardner), **Supp. VI:** 73
Nims, John Frederick, **III:** 527; **Supp. XVII:** 112
Nin, Anaïs, **III:** 182, 184, 190; **Supp. III Part 1:** 43; **Supp. IV Part 2:** 680; **Supp. X: 181–200**
"9" (Oliver), **Supp. VII:** 244
"9 Failures of the Imagination" (Lethem), **Supp. XVIII:** 148
"Nine from Eight" (Lanier), **Supp. I Part 1:** 352–354
Nine Headed Dragon River: Zen Journals 1969–1982 (Matthiessen), **Supp. V:** 199
Ninemile Wolves,The (Bass), **Supp. XVI:** 24–25, 26
"Nine Nectarines" (Moore), **III:** 203, 209, 215
Nine Plays (Reznikoff), **Supp. XIV:** 288
"Nine Poems for the Unborn Child" (Rukeyser), **Supp. VI:** 280–281, 284
Nine Stories (Nabokov), **Retro. Supp. I:** 266
Nine Stories (Salinger), **III:** 552, 558–564
"19 Hadley Street" (Schnackenberg), **Supp. XV:** 253
19 Necromancers from Now (Reed), **Supp. X:** 240
"19 Varieties of Gazelle" (Nye), **Supp. XIII:** 286
19 Varieties of Gazelle (Nye), **Supp. XIII:** 275, **286–288**
1984 (Orwell), **Supp. XIII:** 29; **Supp. XVIII:** 137, 138
"1940" (Stafford), **Supp. XI:** 328–329
"1945–1985: Poem for the Anniversary" (Oliver), **Supp. VII:** 237
1919 (Dos Passos), **I:** 482, 485–486, 487, 489, 490, 492
"1975" (Wright), **Supp. V:** 341
"1910" (Mora), **Supp. XIII:** 215
"1938" (Komunyakaa), **Supp. XIII:** 114
"1939" (Taylor), **Supp. V:** 316
"1933" (Levine), **Supp. V:** 188
1933 (Levine), **Supp. V:** 185–187
"Nineteenth New York, The" (Doctorow), **Supp. IV Part 1:** 232
"1929" (Auden), **Supp. II Part 1:** 6
"1926" (Kees), **Supp. XV:** 135
"90 North" (Jarrell), **II:** 370, 371
90 Trees (Zukofsky), **Supp. III Part 2:** 631
95 Poems (Cummings), **I:** 430, 433, 435, 439, 446, 447
"91 Revere Street" (Lowell), **II:** 547; **Retro. Supp. II:** 188; **Supp. XI:** 240
Ninety Percent of Everything (Lethem, Kelly and Kessel), **Supp. XVIII:** 145
"Nine Years Later" (Brodsky), **Supp. VIII:** 32
"Nirvana" (Lanier), **Supp. I Part 1:** 352
Nirvana Blues, The (Nichols), **Supp. XIII:** 266, 267
Nishikigi (play), **III:** 466
Niven, David, **Supp. XI:** 307
Nixon (film), **Supp. XIV:** 48
Nixon, Richard M., **I:** 376; **III:** 38, 46; **Supp. I Part 1:** 294, 295; **Supp. V:** 45, 46, 51; **Supp. XII:** 14; **Supp. XIV:** 306
"NJ Transit" (Komunyakaa), **Supp. XIII:** 132
Nketia, J. H., **Supp. IV Part 1:** 10
Nketsia, Nana, **Supp. IV Part 1:** 2, 10
Nkize, Julius, **Supp. IV Part 1:** 361
Nkrumah, Kwame, **I:** 490, 494; **Supp. IV Part 1:** 361; **Supp. X:** 135
Noailles, Anna de, **IV:** 328
Noa Noa (Gauguin), **I:** 34
Nobel Lecture (Singer), **Retro. Supp. II:** 300
"No Better Than a 'Withered Daffodil'" (Moore), **III:** 216
Noble, David W., **Supp. I Part 2:** 650
Noble, Marianne, **Supp. XVIII:** 267
"Noble Rider and the Sound of Words, The" (Stevens), **Retro. Supp. I:** 299
Noble Savage, The (Coover), **Supp. V:** 40
"No Bobolink reverse His Singing" (Dickinson), **Retro. Supp. I:** 45
Nobodaddy (MacLeish), **III:** 5–6, 8, 10, 11, 18, 19, 20
"Nobodaddy" (W. Blake), **Supp. XVII:** 245
"Nobody in Hollywood" (Bausch), **Supp. VII:** 54
"Nobody Knows My Name" (Baldwin), **Retro. Supp. II:** 8; **Supp. I Part 1:** 52
Nobody Knows My Name (Baldwin), **Supp. XIII:** 111
Nobody Knows My Name: More Notes of a Native Son (Baldwin), **Retro. Supp. II:** 6, 8; **Supp. I Part 1:** 47, 52, 55
"Nobody knows this little Rose" (Dickinson), **Retro. Supp. I:** 30
"Nobody Said Anything" (Carver), **Supp. III Part 1:** 141
Nobody's Fool (Russo), **Supp. XII:** 326, **331–335,** 340
"No Change of Place" (Auden), **Supp. II Part 1:** 5
"Noche Triste, La" (Frost), **Retro. Supp. I:** 123
Nock, Albert Jay, **I:** 245; **Supp. IV Part 2:** 521, 524
"No Coward Soul Is Mine" (Brontë), **I:** 458
"No Crime in the Mountains" (Chandler), **Supp. IV Part 1:** 129
"Nocturne" (Komunyakaa), **Supp. XIII:** 126
"Nocturne" (MacLeish), **III:** 8
"Nocturne in a Deserted Brickyard" (Sandburg), **III:** 586
Nocturne of Remembered Spring (Aiken), **I:** 50
No Direction Home (documentary film, Scorsese), **Supp. XVIII:** 22, 23, 29
No Direction Home (Shelton), **Supp. XVIII:** 21
"No Door" (Wolfe), **IV:** 456
No Door (Wolfe), **IV:** 451–452, 456
"No Epitaph" (Carson), **Supp. XII: 111**
No Exit (Sartre), **I:** 82, 130; **Supp. XIV:** 320
No Exit (Sartre; Bowles, trans.), **Supp. IV Part 1:** 84
No Gifts from Chance (Benstock), **Retro. Supp. I:** 361
"No-Good Blues" (Komunyakaa), **Supp. XIII:** 130
No Hero (Marquand), **III:** 57
No! In Thunder (Fiedler), **Supp. XIII:** 101
"Noiseless Patient Spider" (Whitman), **III:** 555; **IV:** 348; **Supp. IV Part 1:** 325
Noises Off (Frayn), **Supp. IV Part 2:** 582
Noi vivi. See *We the Living* (film)
"No Lamp Has Ever Shown Us Where to Look" (MacLeish), **III:** 9
Nolan, Sidney, **Retro. Supp. II:** 189
No Laughing Matter (Heller and Vogel), **Supp. IV Part 1:** 384, 389
No Love Lost, a Romance of Travel (Howells), **II:** 277
No Man Is an Island (Merton), **Supp. VIII:** 207
No Mother to Guide Her (Loos), **Supp. XVI:** 194

No Name in the Street (Baldwin), **Retro. Supp. II:** 13, 14; **Supp. I Part 1:** 47, 48, 52, 65–66, 67
No Nature: New and Selected Poems (Snyder), **Supp. VIII: 305**
Nonconformist's Memorial, The (Howe), **Supp. IV Part 2:** 434, 435–436
Nonconformity (Algren), **Supp. IX:** 15
None but the Lonely Heart (film), **Supp. II Part 2:** 546
"Nones" (Auden), **Supp. II Part 1:** 22–23
Nones (Auden), **Supp. II Part 1:** 21
None Shall Look Back (Gordon), **II:** 205–207, 208
"No No, Bad Daddy" (Nelson), **Supp. XVIII:** 177, 178
Nonverbal Communication: Notes on the Visual Perception of Human Relations (Kees and Ruesch), **Supp. XV:** 147
"Noon" (Bryant), **Supp. I Part 1:** 157
"No One Remembers" (Levine), **Supp. V:** 187
"Noon Walk on the Asylum Lawn" (Sexton), **Supp. II Part 2:** 673
"Noon Wine" (Porter), **III:** 436, 437–438, 442, 446
"No Pain Whatsoever" (Yates), **Supp. XI:** 341
"No Place for You, My Love" (Welty), **IV:** 278, 279; **Retro. Supp. I:** 353
No Plays of Japan, The (Waley), **III:** 466
No Pockets in a Shroud (McCoy), **Supp. XIII: 166–168,** 171, 172, 173, 174
"No Poem So Fine" (Francis), **Supp. IX:** 83
Norcross, Frances, **I:** 456, 462
Norcross, Louise, **I:** 456, 462
Nordyke, Lewis, **Supp. XIII:** 5
No Relief (Dixon), **Supp. XII:** 139, **142–143**
No Resting Place (Humphrey), **Supp. IX:** 94, **106–108**
Norfolk Poems, The (Carruth), **Supp. XVI:** 47, 48
Norma (Bellini), **IV:** 309
Norma Ashe (Glaspell), **Supp. III Part 1:** 175, 186–187
"Normal Motor Adjustments" (Stein and Solomons), **IV:** 26
Norman, Charles, **III:** 479
Norman, Gurney, **Supp. X:** 24
Norman, Marsha, **Supp. VIII:** 141
Norman Mailer (Poirier), **Retro. Supp. II:** 207–208
Norman Mailer: Modern Critical Views (Bloom), **Retro. Supp. II:** 205
Norman Mailer Revisited (Merrill), **Retro. Supp. II:** 201
Norna; or, The Witch's Curse (Alcott), **Supp. I Part 1:** 33
Norris, Charles, **III:** 320; **Retro. Supp. I:** 100; **Supp. XVIII:** 226
Norris, Frank, **I:** 211, 355, 500, 506, 517, 518, 519; **II:** 89, 264, 276, 289, 307; **III:** 227, **314–336,** 596; **IV:** 29; **Retro. Supp. I:** 100, 325; **Retro. Supp. II:** 96, 101; **Supp. III Part 2:** 412; **Supp. IX:** 14, 15; **Supp. VIII:** 101, 102; **Supp. XV:** 115
"North" (Hugo), **Supp. VI:** 135
North, Milou (pseudonym), **Supp. IV Part 1:** 260. *See also* Dorris, Michael; Erdrich, Louise
North, Sir Thomas, **IV:** 370
"North American Sequence" (Roethke), **I:** 171–172, 183; **III:** 529, 545, 547, 548
"North Beach" (Snyder), **Supp. VIII:** 289
"North Country Sketches" (McClatchy), **Supp. XII:** 256
"Northeast Playground" (Paley), **Supp. VI:** 226–227, 229
Northern Lights (O'Brien), **Supp. V:** 237, 239, 241–244, 250
"Northern Motive" (Levine), **Supp. V:** 195
Northfield Poems (Ammons), **Supp. VII:** 29
"Northhanger Ridge" (Wright), **Supp. V:** 335, 340
"North Haven" (Bishop), **Retro. Supp. II:** 50
"North Labrador" (Crane), **I:** 386
North of Boston (Frost), **II:** 152, 153–154, 527; **Retro. Supp. I:** 121, 125, 127, **128–130,** 131; **Supp. I Part 1:** 263; **Supp. XIII:** 146
North of Jamaica (Simpson), **Supp. IV Part 2:** 448; **Supp. IX:** 275, 276
North of the Danube (Caldwell), **I:** 288, 290, 293, 294, 309, 310
Northrup, Cyrus, **Supp. I Part 1:** 350
North Sea (Jarman), **Supp. XVII:** 110, 113
"North Sea Undertaker's Complaint, The" (Lowell), **II:** 550
North & South (Bishop), **Retro. Supp. II: 41–43; Supp. I Part 1:** 72, 84, 85, 89
North Star, The (Hellman), **Supp. I Part 1:** 281
Northup, Solomon, **Supp. XIV:** 32
"North Winter" (Carruth), **Supp. XVI:** 53
Norton, Charles Eliot, **I:** 223, 568; **II:** 279, 322–323, 338; **Retro. Supp. I:** 371; **Retro. Supp. II:** 135; **Supp. I Part 1:** 103; **Supp. I Part 2:** 406, 479
Norton, Jody, **Supp. VIII:** 297
Norton, John, **Supp. I Part 1:** 99, 110, 112, 114
Norton Anthology of African American Literature, The, **Supp. X:** 325
Norton Anthology of American Literature, **Supp. X:** 325; **Supp. XV:** 270
Norton Anthology of Literature by Women (Gilbert and Gubar, eds.), **Supp. XV:** 270
Norton Anthology of Modern Poetry, The, **Supp. XI:** 259; **Supp. XV:** 258
Norton Anthology of Poetry, The, **Supp. XVIII:** 20
Norton Anthology of Short Fiction, The, **Supp. IX:** 4
Norton Book of Personal Essays, The, **Supp. XIV:** 105
Norton Lectures, **Retro. Supp. I:** 65
Norwood, Vera, **Supp. IX:** 24
No Safe Harbour (Porter), **III:** 447
Nosferatu: An Opera Libretto (Gioia), **Supp. XV:** 112, **128**
"Nosferatu's Serenade" (Gioia), **Supp. XV:** 128
No Siege Is Absolute (Char; version of F. Wright), **Supp. XVII:** 244
"No Snake" (A. Finch), **Supp. XVII:** 72
"No Speak English" (Cisneros), **Supp. VII:** 63
"Nostalgia of the Lakefronts" (Justice), **Supp. VII:** 118, 119, 120
"Nostalgic Mood" (Farrell), **II:** 45
No Star Is Lost (Farrell), **II:** 34, 35, 44
Nostrandt, Jeanne, **Supp. XVIII:** 80–81
Nostromo (Conrad), **II:** 600; **IV:** 245
"Nosty Fright, A" (Swenson), **Supp. IV Part 2:** 651
Not about Nightingales (T. Williams), **IV:** 381
"Not a Womb in the House" (Quindlen), **Supp. XVII:** 166, 171
Not Dancing (Dunn), **Supp. XI:** 143, **148**
"Note about *Iconographs,* A" (Swenson), **Supp. IV Part 2:** 646
Notebook (Lowell), **Retro. Supp. II:** 186, 190; **Supp. V:** 343
Notebook 1967–68 (Lowell), **II:** 553–555; **Retro. Supp. II:** 182, 186, 190
Notebook of Malte Laurids Brigge, The (Rilke), **III:** 571
Notebooks (Fitzgerald), **Retro. Supp. I:** 110
"Note on Abraham Lincoln" (Vidal), **Supp. IV Part 2:** 688
"Note on Commercial Theatre" (Hughes), **Retro. Supp. I:** 207
"Note on Ezra Pound, A" (Eliot), **Retro. Supp. I:** 290
"Note on Lanier's Music, A" (P. Graham), **Supp. I Part 1:** 373
Note on Literary Criticism, A (Farrell), **II:** 26, 49
"Note on Poetry, A" (Doolittle), **Supp. I Part 1:** 254, 267–268
"Note on Realism, A" (Anderson), **I:** 110
"Note on the Limits of 'History' and the Limits of 'Criticism,' A" (Brooks), **Supp. XIV:** 11
"Note on the Poetry of Love, A" (Untermeyer), **Supp. XV:** 304
"Note on the Truth of the Tales, A" (Vollmann), **Supp. XVII:** 230
"Notes" (Dove), **Supp. IV Part 1:** 246
"Notes for a Moving Picture: The House" (Agee), **I:** 33, 34
"Notes for an Autobiography" (Van Vechten), **Supp. II Part 2:** 749
"Notes for a Novel About the End of the World" (Percy), **Supp. III Part 1:** 393
"Notes for a Preface" (Sandburg), **III:** 591, 596–597
"NOTES FOR A SPEECH" (Baraka), **Supp. II Part 1:** 33
Notes for the Green Box (Duchamp), **Supp. IV Part 2:** 423
Notes from a Bottle Found on the Beach at Carmel (Connell), **Supp. XIV:** 80, 87, 96, 97
Notes from a Sea Diary: Hemingway All the Way (Algren), **Supp. IX:** 16

"Notes from the Childhood and Girlhood" (Brooks), **Supp. III Part 1:** 77
"Notes from the River" (Stern), **Supp. IX:** 285, 287, 294, 295
Notes from Underground (Dostoevsky), **III:** 571; **IV:** 485; **Retro. Supp. II:** 121
"Notes of a Faculty Wife" (Jackson), **Supp. IX:** 126
"Notes of a Native Daughter" (Didion), **Supp. IV Part 1:** 196, 197, 200, 201
"Notes of a Native Son" (Baldwin), **Supp. I Part 1:** 50, 54
Notes of a Native Son (Baldwin), **Retro. Supp. II:** 1, 2, 3, 5, 6; **Supp. I Part 1:** 50, 52, 54; **Supp. IV Part 1:** 163
Notes of a Son and Brother (James), **II:** 337; **Retro. Supp. I:** 235
"Notes on a Departure" (Trilling), **Supp. III Part 2:** 498
"Notes on Babbitt and More" (Wilson), **IV:** 435
"Notes on Camp" (Sontag), **Supp. XIV:** 167
"Notes on 'Camp'" (Sontag), **Supp. III Part 2:** 455–456
Notes on Democracy (Mencken), **III:** 104, 107–108, 109, 116, 119
"Notes on Free Verse" (Dobyns), **Supp. XIII:** 77
"Notes on 'Layover'" (Hass), **Supp. VI:** 109
Notes on Novelists (James), **II:** 336, 337; **Retro. Supp. I:** 235
"Notes on Nukes, Nookie, and Neo-Romanticism" (Robbins), **Supp. X:** 272
"Notes on Poetry" (Eberhart), **I:** 524, 527–528, 529
"Notes on the Craft of Poetry" (Strand), **Supp. IV Part 2:** 626
"Notes on the Decline of Outrage" (Dickey), **Supp. IV Part 1:** 181
"Notes on the New Formalism" (Gioia), **Supp. XV:** 113, 114–115
"Notes on the Novel-as-Autobiography" (P. Bailey), **Supp. XVI:** 69
Notes on the State of Virginia (1781–1782) (Jefferson), **Supp. XIV:** 191
"Notes to Be Left in a Cornerstone" (Benét), **Supp. XI:** 46, 58
"Notes toward a Supreme Fiction" (Stevens), **IV:** 87–89; **Retro. Supp. I:** 300, 306, **306–309,** 311; **Supp. I Part 1:** 80
"Notes towards a Poem That Can Never Be Written" (Atwood), **Supp. XIII:** 34–35
No Thanks (Cummings), **I:** 430, 431, 432, 436, 437, 441, 443, 446
"Nothing" (C. Frost), **Supp. XV:** 94
"Nothing Big" (Komunyakaa), **Supp. XIII:** 121
Nothing for Tigers (Carruth), **Supp. XVI:** 47, 48, 50
"Nothing Gold Can Stay" (Frost), **Retro. Supp. I:** 133
"Nothing in Heaven Functions as It Ought" (X. J. Kennedy), **Supp. XV:** 158–159
Nothing Makes You Free: Writings by Descendants of Jewish Holocaust Survivors (Bukiet, ed.), **Supp. XVII: 39–40,** 48–49
"Nothing Missing" (O'Hara), **III:** 369
Nothing Personal (Baldwin), **Supp. I Part 1:** 58, 60
Nothing Sacred (film), **Supp. XVIII:** 243
"Nothing Song, The" (Snodgrass), **Supp. VI:** 326
"Nothing Stays Put" (Clampitt), **Supp. IX:** 42
"Nothing Will Yield" (Nemerov), **III:** 279
No Third Path (Kosinski), **Supp. VII:** 215
"Not Ideas About the Thing but the Thing Itself" (Stevens), **IV:** 87
Notions of the Americans: Picked up by a Travelling Bachelor (Cooper), **I:** 343–345, 346
"Not-Knowing" (Barthelme), **Supp. IV Part 1:** 48
"Not Leaving the House" (Snyder), **Supp. VIII:** 300
"'Not Marble nor the Gilded Monument'" (MacLeish), **III:** 12
"Not My Bones" (Nelson), **Supp. XVIII:** 183
Not Now But Now (M. F. K. Fisher), **Supp. XVII:** 86, 90
"Not Quite Social" (Frost), **II:** 156
"Not Sappho, Sacco" (Rukeyser), **Supp. VI:** 277
"Not Sixteen" (Anderson), **I:** 114
"Not Slightly" (Stein), **IV:** 44
Not So Deep as a Well (Parker), **Supp. IX:** 192
"Not Somewhere Else, but Here" (Rich), **Supp. I Part 2:** 552, 573
Not-So-Simple Neil Simon (McGovern), **Supp. IV Part 2:** 573
Not So Simple: The "Simple" Stories by Langston Hughes (Harper), **Retro. Supp. I:** 194, 209
"Not the Point" (Cameron), **Supp. XII: 83**
"Not They Who Soar" (Dunbar), **Supp. II Part 1:** 199
Not This Pig (Levine), **Supp. V:** 178, 181, 182–183
Not to Eat; Not for Love (Weller), **III:** 322
Not Without Laughter (Hughes), **Retro. Supp. I:** 197, 198, 201; **Supp. I Part 1:** 328, 332
Nouvelle Héloïse, La (Rousseau), **Supp. XV:** 232
Nova Express (Burroughs), **Supp. III Part 1:** 93, 103, 104; **Supp. XVIII:** 137
Novel, The (Bulwer), **Retro. Supp. II:** 58
"Novel as a Function of American Democracy, The" (Ellison), **Retro. Supp. II:** 124
"Novel Démeublé, The" (Cather), **Retro. Supp. I:** 15
Novel History: Historians and Novelists Confront America's Past (and Each Other) (Carnes), **Supp. X:** 14
Novella (Goethe; Bogan and Mayer, trans.), **Supp. III Part 1:** 63
Novellas and Other Writings (Wharton), **Retro. Supp. I:** 360
"Novel of the Thirties, A" (Trilling), **Supp. III Part 2:** 499
Novels and Other Writings (Bercovitch), **Retro. Supp. II:** 325
Novels and Tales of Henry James, The (James), **Retro. Supp. I:** 232
"Novel-Writing and Novel-Reading" (Howells), **II:** 276, 290
"November" (Larcom), **Supp. XIII:** 143
"November Cotton Flower" (Toomer), **Supp. IX:** 312
November Twenty Six Nineteen Sixty Three (Berry), **Supp. X:** 24
"Novices" (Moore), **III:** 200–201, 202, 213
Novick, Peter, **Supp. XVI:** 154–155
"Novogodnee" ("New Year's Greetings") (Tsvetayeva), **Supp. VIII:** 30
"Novotny's Pain" (P. Roth), **Supp. III Part 2:** 403
"No Voyage" (Oliver), **Supp. VII:** 231
No Voyage and Other Poems (Oliver), **Supp. VII:** 230–231, 232
Now and Another Time (Hearon), **Supp. VIII:** 58, **61–62**
Now and Then (Buechner), **Supp. XII:** 49, 53
"Now and Then, America" (Mora), **Supp. XIII:** 217
"Nowhere" (J. Scott), **Supp. XVII:** 189
Nowhere Is a Place: Travels in Patagonia (Theroux and Chatwin), **Supp. VIII:** 322
"Now I Am Married" (Gordon), **Supp. IV Part 1:** 299
"Now I Lay Me" (Hemingway), **II:** 249; **Retro. Supp. I:** 175
"Now I Lay Me" (Olds), **Supp. X:** 208
"Now Is the Air Made of Chiming Balls" (Eberhart), **I:** 523
"No Word" (Kunitz), **Supp. III Part 1:** 263
"No Worst" (Nelson), **Supp. XVIII:** 177, 178
Now Sheba Sings the Song (Angelou), **Supp. IV Part 1:** 16
"Now That We Live" (Kenyon), **Supp. VII:** 165
"Now the Servant's Name Was Malchus" (Wilder), **IV:** 358
"Now We Know" (O'Hara), **III:** 368–369
NOW with Bill Moyers (television), **Supp. XIII:** 286
Noyes, Alfred, **IV:** 434
Nuamah, Grace, **Supp. IV Part 1:** 10
"Nuances of a Theme by Williams" (Stevens), **Retro. Supp. I:** 422
Nuclear Age, The (O'Brien), **Supp. V:** 238, 243, 244, 246–248, 249, 251
"Nuclear Arms and Morality" (Sanders), **Supp. XVI:** 266
Nude Croquet (Fiedler), **Supp. XIII:** 103
"Nude Descendig a Staircase" (X. J. Kennedy), **Supp. XV:** 168

"Nude Descending a Staircase" (Duchamp), **IV:** 408; **Retro. Supp. I:** 416
Nude Descending a Staircase (X. J. Kennedy), **Supp. XV:** 153, **154–157**
Nugent, Bruce, **Retro. Supp. I:** 200
Nugent, Elliot, **Supp. I Part 2:** 606, 611, 613
Nuggets and Dust (Bierce), **I:** 195
"Nullipara" (Olds), **Supp. X:** 209
Number One (Dos Passos), **I:** 489
"Numbers, Letters" (Baraka), **Supp. II Part 1:** 50
Nunc Dimittis (Brodsky), **Supp. VIII:** 25–26, 28
"Nun No More, A" (Fante), **Supp. XI:** 160
"Nun's Priest's Tale" (Chaucer), **III:** 492
Nunzio, Nanzia, **IV:** 89
Nuptial Flight, The (Masters), **Supp. I Part 2:** 460, 471
"Nuptials" (Tate), **IV:** 122
"Nurse Whitman" (Olds), **Supp. X:** 203
Nurture (Kumin), **Supp. IV Part 2:** 453–454, 455
Nussbaum, Emily, **Supp. XI:** 143
Nussbaum, Felicity A., **Supp. X:** 189
Nutcracker, The (Tchaikovsky), **Retro. Supp. I:** 196
"Nux Postcoenatica" (Holmes), **Supp. I Part 1:** 303
Nyce, James M., **Retro. Supp. I:** 380
Nye, Naomi Shihab, **Supp. XI:** 316; **Supp. XIII: 273–290**
Nyerere, Julius, **Supp. X:** 135
"Nympholepsy" (Faulkner), **Retro. Supp. I:** 81

O
"Ö" (Dove), **Supp. IV Part 1:** 245
Oak and Ivy (Dunbar), **Supp. II Part 1:** 98
"Oak Bluffs" column (D. West), **Supp. XVIII:** 286
Oak Openings, The (Cooper), **I:** 354, 355
Oandasan, Bill, **Supp. IV Part 2:** 499
Oasis, The (McCarthy), **II:** 566–568
Oates, Joyce Carol, **Supp. II Part 2: 503–527; Supp. IV Part 1:** 205; **Supp. IV Part 2:** 447, 689; **Supp. V:** 323; **Supp. XI:** 239; **Supp. XII:** 343; **Supp. XIII:** 306; **Supp. XIV:** 26, 109
"Oath, The" (Tate), **IV:** 127
Obbligati (Hecht), **Supp. X:** 57
Ober, Harold, **Retro. Supp. I:** 101, 103, 105, 110, 113
Oberndorf, Clarence P., **Supp. I Part 1:** 315
Obey, André, **IV:** 356, 375
"Obit" (Lowell), **II:** 554
"Objective Value of a Social Settlement, The" (Addams), **Supp. I Part 1:** 4
"Objective Woman, The" (Jong), **Supp. V:** 119
Objectivist Anthology, An, **Supp. XIV:** 287
"Objectivist Ethics, The" (Rand), **Supp. IV Part 2:** 530–532
"Objectivists" Anthology, An (Zukofsky), **Supp. III Part 2:** 613, 615
Object Lessons (Quindlen), **Supp. XVII: 173–174**
"Objects" (Wilbur), **Supp. III Part 2:** 545–547
Oblique Prayers (Levertov), **Supp. III Part 1:** 283
"Oblivion" (Justice), **Supp. VII:** 121
Oblivion Seekers, The (Eberhardt), **Supp. IV Part 1:** 92
"Oblong Box, The" (Poe), **III:** 416
Obregon, Maurice, **Supp. I Part 2:** 488
O'Briant, Don, **Supp. X:** 8
O'Brien, Edward, **Supp. XV:** 140
O'Brien, Edward J., **I:** 289; **III:** 56; **Supp. XVIII:** 227
O'Brien, Edwin, **Supp. XVIII:** 208
O'Brien, Fitzjames, **I:** 211
O'Brien, Geoffrey, **Supp. IV Part 2:** 471, 473
O'Brien, John, **Supp. V:** 48, 49; **Supp. X:** 239, 244
O'Brien, Tim, **Supp. V: 237–255; Supp. XI:** 234; **Supp. XVII:** 14
"Obscene Poem, An" (Creeley), **Supp. IV Part 1:** 150
Obscure Destinies (Cather), **I:** 331–332; **Retro. Supp. I:** 19
"Observation Relative to the Intentions of the Original Founders of the Academy in Philadelphia" (Franklin), **II:** 114
"Observations" (Dillard), **Supp. VI:** 34
Observations (Moore), **III:** 194, 195–196, 197, 199, 203, 205, 215
"Observations Now" (Conroy), **Supp. XVI:** 75
Observations: Photographs by Richard Avedon: Comments by Truman Capote, **Supp. III Part 1:** 125–126
O Canada: An American's Notes on Canadian Culture (Wilson), **IV:** 429–430
"O Carib Isle!" (Crane), **I:** 400–401
O'Casey, Sean, **III:** 145; **Supp. IV Part 1:** 359, 361, 364
"Occidentals" (Ford), **Supp. V:** 71–72
"Occultation of Orion, The" (Longfellow), **Retro. Supp. II:** 168
"Occurrence at Owl Creek Bridge, An" (Bierce), **I:** 200–201; **II:** 264
"Ocean 1212-W" (Plath), **Supp. I Part 2:** 528
"Ocean of Words" (Jin), **Supp. XVIII:** 94
Ocean of Words: Army Stories (Jin), **Supp. XVIII:** 89, 92, **93–94**
O'Connell, Nicholas, **Supp. IX:** 323, 325, 334
O'Connor, Edward F., Jr., **III:** 337
O'Connor, Flannery, **I:** 113, 190, 211, 298; **II:** 606; **III: 337–360; IV:** 4, 217, 282; **Retro. Supp. II:** 179, **219–239,** 272, 324; **Supp. I Part 1:** 290; **Supp. III Part 1:** 146; **Supp. V:** 59, 337; **Supp. VIII:** 13, 14, 158; **Supp. X:** 1, 26, 69, 228, 290; **Supp. XI:** 104; **Supp. XIII:** 294; **Supp. XIV:** 93; **Supp. XV:** 338; **Supp. XVI:** 219; **Supp. XVII:** 43, 114; **Supp. XVIII:** 156, 161, 194
O'Connor, Frank, **III:** 158; **Retro. Supp. II:** 242; **Supp. I Part 2:** 531; **Supp. VIII:** 151, 157, 165, 167, 171; **Supp. XV:** 74
O'Connor, Richard, **II:** 467
O'Connor, T. P., **II:** 129
O'Connor, William, **IV:** 346; **Retro. Supp. I:** 392, 407
O'Connor, William Van, **III:** 479; **Supp. I Part 1:** 195
"Octascope" (Beattie), **Supp. V:** 27, 28
"Octaves" (Robinson), **Supp. III Part 2:** 593
"Octet" (Wallace), **Supp. X:** 309
October (Isherwood), **Supp. XIV:** 157, 164
"October" (Oliver), **Supp. VII:** 241
"October" (Swenson), **Supp. IV Part 2:** 649
"October, 1866" (Bryant), **Supp. I Part 1:** 169
"October 1913" (McCarriston), **Supp. XIV:** 266
"October and November" (Lowell), **II:** 554
"October in the Railroad Earth" (Kerouac), **Supp. III Part 1:** 225, 227, 229
October Light (Gardner), **Supp. VI:** 63, **69–71,** 72
"October Maples, Portland" (Wilbur), **Supp. III Part 2:** 556
"Octopus, An" (Moore), **III:** 202, 207–208, 214
"Octopus, The" (Merrill), **Supp. III Part 1:** 321
Octopus, The (Norris), **I:** 518; **III:** 314, 316, 322–326, 327, 331–333, 334, 335
"O Daedalus, Fly Away Home" (Hayden), **Supp. II Part 1:** 377–378
"OD and Hepatitis Railroad or Bust, The" (Boyle), **Supp. VIII:** 1
Odd Couple, The (1985 version, Simon), **Supp. IV Part 2:** 580
Odd Couple, The (film), **Supp. IV Part 2:** 589
Odd Couple, The (Simon), **Supp. IV Part 2:** 575, 579–580, 585, 586; **Supp. XVII:** 8
Odd Jobs (Updike), **Retro. Supp. I:** 334
Odd Mercy (Stern), **Supp. IX: 298–299**
"Odds, The" (Hecht), **Supp. X:** 64–65
"Odds, The" (Salinas), **Supp. XIII:** 321
"Ode" (Emerson), **II:** 13
"Ode (Intimations of Immortality)" (Matthews), **Supp. IX:** 162
"Ode" (Sobin), **Supp. XVI:** 284–285
"Ode" (X. J. Kennedy), **Supp. XV:** 160
"Ode for Memorial Day" (Dunbar), **Supp. II Part 1:** 199
"Ode for the American Dead in Asia" (McGrath), **Supp. X:** 119
"Ode: For the Budding of Islands" (Sobin), **Supp. XVI:** 287
"Ode Inscribed to W. H. Channing" (Emerson), **Supp. XIV:** 46
"Ode: Intimations of Immortality" (Wordsworth), **Supp. I Part 2:** 729; **Supp. III Part 1:** 12; **Supp. XIV:** 8

"Ode: My 24th Year" (Ginsberg), **Supp. II Part 1:** 312
"Ode on a Grecian Urn" (Keats), **I:** 284; **III:** 472; **Supp. XII:** 113; **Supp. XIV:** 8, 9–10; **Supp. XV:** 100
"Ode on Human Destinies" (Jeffers), **Supp. II Part 2:** 419
"Ode on Indolence" (Keats), **Supp. XII:** 113
"Ode on Melancholy" (Keats), **Retro. Supp. I:** 301
"Ode Recited at the Harvard Commemoration" (Lowell), **II:** 551
Ode Recited at the Harvard Commemoration (Lowell), **Supp. I Part 2:** 416–418, 424
"Ode Secrète" (Valéry), **III:** 609
"Odes of Estrangement" (Sobin), **Supp. XVI:** 289
"Odes to Natural Processes" (Updike), **Retro. Supp. I:** 323
"Ode to a Nightingale" (Keats), **II:** 368; **Retro. Supp. II:** 261; **Supp. IX:** 52
"Ode to Autumn" (Masters), **Supp. I Part 2:** 458
"Ode to Cervantes" (Salinas), **Supp. XIII:** 324
"Ode to Coit Tower" (Corso), **Supp. XII:** 122
"Ode to Ethiopia" (Dunbar), **Supp. II Part 1:** 199, 207, 208, 209
"Ode to Fear" (Tate), **IV:** 128
Ode to Harvard and Other Poems, An (Bynner), **Supp. XV:** 41, 44
"Ode to Meaning" (Pinsky), **Supp. VI: 249–250,** 251
"Ode to Night" (Masters), **Supp. I Part 2:** 458
"Ode to Our Young Pro-Consuls of the Air" (Tate), **IV:** 135
"Ode to the Austrian Socialists" (Benét), **Supp. XI:** 46, 58
"Ode to the Confederate Dead" (Tate), **II:** 551; **IV:** 124, 133, 137; **Supp. X:** 52
"Ode to the Johns Hopkins University" (Lanier), **Supp. I Part 1:** 370
"Ode to the Maggot" (Komunyakaa), **Supp. XIII:** 130
"Ode to the Mexican Experience" (Salinas), **Supp. XIII:** 316–317
"Ode to the Virginian Voyage" (Drayton), **IV:** 135
"Ode to the West Wind" (Shelley), **Retro. Supp. I:** 308; **Supp. I Part 2:** 728; **Supp. IX:** 52; **Supp. XII:** 117; **Supp. XIV:** 271–272; **Supp. XV:** 221
"Ode to Walt Whitman" (Benét), **Supp. XI:** 52
Odets, Clifford, **Supp. I Part 1:** 277, 295; **Supp. I Part 2:** 679; **Supp. II Part 2: 529–554; Supp. IV Part 2:** 587; **Supp. V:** 109; **Supp. VIII:** 96; **Supp. XVIII:** 238
Odier, Daniel, **Supp. III Part 1:** 97
"Odi et Amo" (Catullus), **Supp. XV:** 27, 32, 35
O'Donnell, George Marion, **II:** 67
O'Donnell, Mary King, **Supp. XVIII:** 232
O'Donnell, Thomas F., **II:** 131
"Odor of Verbena" (Faulkner), **II:** 66
O'Doul, Lefty, **II:** 425
"Odysseus to Telemachus" (Brodsky), **Supp. VIII:** 25
Odyssey (Bryant, trans.), **Supp. I Part 1:** 158
Odyssey (Homer), **III:** 14, 470; **Retro. Supp. I:** 286, 290; **Retro. Supp. II:** 121; **Supp. I Part 1:** 185; **Supp. IV Part 2:** 631; **Supp. IX:** 211; **Supp. X:** 114; **Supp. XIV:** 191; **Supp. XVII:** 117
"Odyssey of a Wop, The" (Fante), **Supp. XI:** 164, 165
Oedipus Rex (Sophocles), **I:** 137; **III:** 145, 151, 152, 332; **Supp. I Part 2:** 428
Oedipus Tyrannus (Sophocles), **II:** 203; **Supp. XV:** 265
Oehlschlaeger, Fritz, **Supp. IX:** 123
"Of Alexander Crummell" (Du Bois), **Supp. II Part 1:** 170
O'Faoláin, Seán, **Supp. II Part 1:** 101
Of a World That Is No More (Singer), **IV:** 16
"Of Booker T. Washington and Others" (Du Bois), **Supp. II Part 1:** 168
"Of Bright & Blue Birds & the Gala Sun" (Stevens), **IV:** 93
"Of Christian Heroism" (Ozick), **Supp. V:** 272
"Of Dying Beauty" (Zukofsky), **Supp. III Part 2:** 610
"Of 'Father and Son'" (Kunitz), **Supp. III Part 1:** 262
Offenbach, Jacques, **II:** 427
"Offering for Mr. Bluehart, An" (Wright), **Supp. III Part 2:** 596, 601
"Offerings" (Mason), **Supp. VIII:** 141
"Official Piety" (Whittier), **Supp. I Part 2:** 687
"Off-Shore Pirates, The" (Fitzgerald), **II:** 88
Off the Beaten Path (Proulx), **Supp. VII:** 261
Off the Beaten Path: Stories of Place, **Supp. XVI:** 22
"Off the Cuff" (Simpson), **Supp. IX:** 278
Off the Map (Levine), **Supp. V:** 178
O'Flaherty, George, **Supp. I Part 1:** 202, 205–206
O'Flaherty, Kate. *See* Chopin, Kate
O'Flaherty, Thomas, **Supp. I Part 1:** 202, 203–204, 205
O'Flaherty, Thomas, Jr., **Supp. I Part 1:** 202
"Of Maids and Other Muses" (Alvarez), **Supp. VII:** 11
"Of Margaret" (Ransom), **III:** 491
Of Mice and Men (Steinbeck), **IV:** 51, 57–58
"Of Modern Poetry" (Stevens), **IV:** 92
Of Plymouth Plantation (Bradford), **Retro. Supp. II:** 161, 162
Of Plymouth Plantation (Morison, ed.), **Supp. I Part 2:** 494
"Ofrenda for Lobo" (Mora), **Supp. XIII:** 224
"Often" (Kenyon), **Supp. VII:** 171
"Often, in Dreams, He Moved through a City" (Dobyns), **Supp. XIII:** 90
"Of the Coming of John" (Du Bois), **Supp. II Part 1:** 170
"Of the Culture of White Folk" (Du Bois), **Supp. II Part 1:** 175
Of the Farm (Updike), **IV:** 214, 217, 223–225, 233; **Retro. Supp. I:** 318, 329, 332
"Of the Four-Winged Cherubim as Signature" (Sobin), **Supp. XVI:** 287
"Of 'The Frill'" (McCarriston), **Supp. XIV:** 274
"Of the Passing of the First-Born" (Du Bois), **Supp. II Part 1:** 170
"Of the Sorrow Songs" (Du Bois), **Supp. II Part 1:** 170
"Of the Wings of Atlanta" (Du Bois), **Supp. II Part 1:** 170
Of This Time, Of This Place (Trilling), **Supp. III Part 2:** 498, 504
Of Time and the River (Wolfe), **IV:** 450, 451, 452, 455, 456, 457, 458, 459, 462, 464–465, 467, 468, 469
Of Woman Born: Motherhood as Experience and Institution (Rich), **Supp. I Part 2:** 554, 567–569
Of Women and Their Elegance (Mailer), **Retro. Supp. II:** 209
Ogden, Archie, **Supp. XIII:** 174
Ogden, Henry, **II:** 298
Ogden, Uzal, **Supp. I Part 2:** 516
"Oh, Fairest of the Rural Maids" (Bryant), **Supp. I Part 1:** 169
"Oh, Immobility, Death's Vast Associate" (Dobyns), **Supp. XIII:** 89
"Oh, Joseph, I'm So Tired" (Yates), **Supp. XI:** 348
Oh, the Places You'll Go! (Geisel), **Supp. XVI:** 111
Oh, the Thinks You can Think! (Geisel), **Supp. XVI:** 111
"O'Halloran's Luck" (Benét), **Supp. XI:** 47
O'Hara, Frank, **Supp. XII:** 121; **Supp. XV:** 93, 176, 177, 178, 179–180, 182, 186, 187, 215–216
O'Hara, J. D., **Supp. IV Part 1:** 43; **Supp. V:** 22; **Supp. XVI:** 221
O'Hara, John, **I:** 375, 495; **II:** 444, 459; **III:** 66, **361–384; IV:** 59; **Retro. Supp. I:** 99, 112; **Supp. I Part 1:** 196; **Supp. II Part 1:** 109; **Supp. IV Part 1:** 31, 383; **Supp. IV Part 2:** 678; **Supp. IX:** 208; **Supp. V:** 95; **Supp. VIII:** 151, 156
O'Hehir, Andrew, **Supp. XII:** 280
O. Henry Biography (C. A. Smith), **Supp. II Part 1:** 395
"Ohio Pagan, An" (Anderson), **I:** 112, 113
Ohio trilogy (Richter), **Supp. XVIII:** 212–215
Oh Mercy (album, Dylan), **Supp. XVIII:** 28, 33
Oh Say Can You Say? (Geisel), **Supp. XVI:** 111
Oil! (Sinclair), **Supp. V:** 276, 277–279, 282, 288, 289
Oil Notes (Bass), **Supp. XVI:** 17

"Oil Painting of the Artist as the Artist" (MacLeish), **III:** 14
O'Keeffe, Georgia, **Supp. IX:** 62, 66
"Oklahoma" (Levis), **Supp. XI:** 267
Oktenberg, Adrian, **Supp. XVII:** 76
"Old, Old, Old, Old Andrew Jackson" (Lindsay), **Supp. I Part 2:** 398
"Old Amusement Park, An" (Moore), **III:** 216
"Old Angel Midnight" (Kerouac), **Supp. III Part 1:** 229–230
"Old Apple Dealer, The" (Hawthorne), **II:** 227, 233–235, 237, 238
"Old Apple-Tree, The" (Dunbar), **Supp. II Part 1:** 198
"Old Army Game, The" (Garrett), **Supp. VII:** 100–101
"Old Aunt Peggy" (Chopin), **Retro. Supp. II:** 64
"Old Barn at the Bottom of the Fogs, The" (Frost), **Retro. Supp. I:** 138
Old Beauty and Others, The (Cather), **I:** 331
Old Bruin: Commodore Matthew C. Perry, 1794–1858 (Morison), **Supp. I Part 2:** 494–495
"Old Cracked Tune, An" (Kunitz), **Supp. III Part 1:** 264
Old Curiosity Shop, The (Dickens), **I:** 458; **Supp. I Part 2:** 409
Oldest Killed Lake in North America, The (Carruth), **Supp. XVI:** 51
"Oldest Man, The" (M. F. K. Fisher), **Supp. XVII:** 91
"Old Farmer, The" (Jeffers), **Supp. II Part 2:** 418
Old-Fashioned Girl, An (Alcott), **Supp. I Part 1:** 29, 41, 42
"Old Father Morris" (Stowe), **Supp. I Part 2:** 586
"Old Flame, The" (Lowell), **II:** 550
"Old Florist" (Roethke), **III:** 531
"Old Folsom Prison" (Matthews), **Supp. IX:** 165
"Old Forest, The" (Taylor), **Supp. V:** 313, 321, 323, 326
Old Forest, The (Taylor), **Supp. V:** 320, 321, 326, 327
Old Forest and Other Stories (Taylor), **Supp. V:** 326
Old Friends and New (Jewett), **II:** 402; **Retro. Supp. II:** 137, 140
Old Glory, The (Lowell), **II:** 543, 545–546, 555; **Retro. Supp. II:** 188
Old Helmet, The (S. and A. Warner), **Supp. XVIII:** 267
"Old Homestead, The" (Dunbar), **Supp. II Part 1:** 198
"Old Iron" (Nye), **Supp. XIII:** 276
"Old Ironsides" (Holmes), **Supp. I Part 1:** 302
"Old Lady We Saw, An" (Shields), **Supp. VII:** 310–311
"Old Love" (Singer), **Retro. Supp. II:** 307
"Old McGrath Place, The" (McGrath), **Supp. X:** 114
"Old Maid, The" (Wharton), **Retro. Supp. I:** 381, 382
"Old Man" (Faulkner), **II:** 68, 69
Old Man and the Sea, The (Hemingway), **II:** 250, 256–257, 258, 265; **III:** 40; **Retro. Supp. I:** 180, **185,** 186
"Old Man Drunk" (Wright), **Supp. III Part 2:** 595
"Old Man Feeding Hens" (Francis), **Supp. IX:** 78
"Old Man on the Hospital Porch" (Ríos), **Supp. IV Part 2:** 546–547
Old Man Rubbing His Eyes (R. Bly), **Supp. IV Part 1:** 65
"Old Manse, The" (Hawthorne), **II:** 224
"Old Man's Winter Night, An" (Frost), **Retro. Supp. I:** 126, 131
Old Man Who Love Cheese, The (Keillor), **Supp. XVI:** 177
"Old Man with a Dog" (Wright), **Supp. XV:** 346
"Old Meeting House, The" (Stowe), **Supp. I Part 2:** 586
"Old Memory, An" (Dunbar), **Supp. II Part 1:** 198
"Old Men, The" (McCarthy), **II:** 566
"Old Men Pitching Horseshoes" (X. J. Kennedy), **Supp. XV:** 166
Old Money (Wasserstein), **Supp. XV: 333–334**
"Old Morgue, The" (Prose), **Supp. XVI:** 250
Old Morning Program, The (radio show, Keillor). *See Prairie Home Companion, A* (radio show, Keillor)
"Old Mortality" (Porter), **III:** 436, 438–441, 442, 445, 446
"Old Mrs. Harris" (Cather), **I:** 332; **Retro. Supp. I:** 19
Old Neighborhood, The (Mamet), **Supp. XIV:** 240, 241, 242, 249–250, 251, 252, 254
Old New York (Wharton), **IV:** 322; **Retro. Supp. I:** 381
"Ol' Doc Hyar" (Campbell), **Supp. II Part 1:** 202
Old One-Two, The (Gurney), **Supp. V:** 98
"Old Order, The" (Porter), **III:** 443, 444–445, 451
"Old Osawatomie" (Sandburg), **III:** 584
Old Patagonia Express, The: By Train through the Americas (Theroux), **Supp. VIII:** 322
"Old People, The" (Faulkner), **II:** 71–72
"Old Poet Moves to a New Apartment 14 Times, The" (Zukofsky), **Supp. III Part 2:** 628
Old Possum's Book of Practical Cats (Eliot), **Supp. XIII:** 228, 344
"Old Red" (Gordon), **II:** 199, 200, 203
Old Red and Other Stories (Gordon), **II:** 157
Old Régime in Canada, The (Parkman), **Supp. II Part 2:** 600, 607, 608–609, 612
Old Religion, The (Mamet), **Supp. XIV:** 253
Olds, Sharon, **Supp. X: 201–217; Supp. XI:** 139, 142, 244; **Supp. XII:** 229; **Supp. XIV:** 265; **Supp. XVII:** 114, 240
"Old Saws" (Garrett), **Supp. VII:** 96–97
Old Testament, **I:** 109, 181, 300, 328, 401, 410, 419, 431, 457, 458; **II:** 166, 167, 219; **III:** 270, 272, 348, 390, 396; **IV:** 41, 114, 152, 309; **Retro. Supp. I:** 122, 140, 249, 311, 360; **Retro. Supp. II:** 299; **Supp. I Part 1:** 60, 104, 106, 151; **Supp. I Part 2:** 427, 515, 516; **Supp. IX:** 14. *See also* names of Old Testament books
"Old Things, The" (James), **Retro. Supp. I:** 229
"Old Times on the Mississippi" (Twain), **IV:** 199
Oldtown Folks (Stowe), **Supp. I Part 2:** 587, 596–598
"Old Town of Berwick, The" (Jewett), **Retro. Supp. II:** 132
"Old Trails" (Robinson), **III:** 513, 517
"Old Tyrannies" (Bourne), **I:** 233
"Old West" (Bausch), **Supp. VII:** 48
"Old Whorehouse, An" (Oliver), **Supp. VII:** 235
"Old Woman" (Pinsky), **Supp. VI:** 238
"Old Woman of Beare, The" (X. J. Kennedy), **Supp. XV:** 156
"Old Word, The" (Simic), **Supp. VIII:** 282
"Old-World Landowners" (Gogol), **Supp. XV:** 262
Oldys, Francis. *See* Chalmers, George
Oleanna (Mamet), **Supp. XIV:** 239, 241, 245, 248, 250
Olendorf, Donna, **Supp. IV Part 1:** 196
"Olga Poems, The" (Levertov), **Supp. III Part 1:** 279–281
"Olive Groves of Thasos, The" (Clampitt), **Supp. IX: 51–52**
Oliver, Bill, **Supp. VIII:** 138
Oliver, Mary, **Supp. VII: 229–248; Supp. X:** 31; **Supp. XVI:** 39; **Supp. XVII:** 111, 240
Oliver, Sydney, **I:** 409
Oliver Goldsmith: A Biography (Irving), **II:** 315
Oliver Twist (Dickens), **I:** 354; **Supp. IV Part 2:** 464
"Olivia" (Salinas), **Supp. XIII:** 316
Olivieri, David (pseudonym), **Retro. Supp. I:** 361. *See also* Wharton, Edith
Ollive, Samuel, **Supp. I Part 2:** 503
Olmsted, Frederick Law, **Supp. I Part 1:** 355
Olsen, Lance, **Supp. IV Part 1:** 54; **Supp. IV Part 2:** 623
Olsen, Tillie, **Supp. V:** 114, 220; **Supp. XIII: 291–309; Supp. XVI:** 83, 90
Olson, Charles, **Retro. Supp. I:** 209; **Supp. II Part 1:** 30, 328; **Supp. II Part 2: 555–587; Supp. III Part 1:** 9, 271; **Supp. III Part 2:** 542, 624; **Supp. IV Part 1:** 139, 144, 146, 153, 154, 322; **Supp. IV Part 2:** 420, 421, 423, 426; **Supp. VIII:** 290, 291; **Supp. XII:** 2, 198; **Supp. XIII:** 104; **Supp. XIV:** 96; **Supp. XV:** 177
Olson, Ray, **Supp. XVII:** 111, 112, 119
"Ol' Tunes, The" (Dunbar), **Supp. II Part 1:** 197
"O Lull Me, Lull Me" (Roethke), **III:** 536–537

Omar Khayyam, **Supp. I Part 1:** 363
O'Meally, Robert, **Retro. Supp. II:** 112
Omega the Unknown (comic book series), **Supp. XVIII:** 149
"Omen" (Komunyakaa), **Supp. XIII:** 126, 127
Omensetter's Luck (Gass), **Supp. VI: 80–82,** 87
Omeros (Walcott), **Supp. XV:** 264
"Ominous Baby, An" (Crane), **I:** 411
Ommateum, with Doxology (Ammons), **Supp. VII:** 24–26, 27, 28, 36
"Omnibus Jaunts and Drivers" (Whitman), **IV:** 350
Omoo: A Narrative of Adventures in the South Seas (Melville), **III:** 76–77, 79, 84; **Retro. Supp. I:** 247
O My Land, My Friends (H. Crane), **Retro. Supp. II:** 76
"On Abrigador Hill" (Nelson), **Supp. XVIII:** 183
"On a Certain Condescension in Foreigners" (Lowell), **Supp. I Part 2:** 419
"On a Certain Engagement South of Seoul" (Carruth), **Supp. XVI:** 47
"On a Child Who Lived One Minute" (X. J. Kennedy), **Supp. XV:** 152, 155
"On Acquiring Riches" (Banks), **Supp. V:** 5
On a Darkling Plain (Stegner), **Supp. IV Part 2:** 598, 607
On a Fire on the Moon (Mailer), **Retro. Supp. II:** 206
"On a Hill Far Away" (Dillard), **Supp. VI:** 28
"On a Honey Bee, Drinking from a Glass and Drowned Therein" (Freneau), **Supp. II Part 1:** 273
"On a Monument to a Pigeon" (Leopold), **Supp. XIV:** 187–188
"On a Mountainside" (Wagoner), **Supp. IX:** 332
O'Nan, Stewart, **Supp. XI:** 348
"On an Old Photograph of My Son" (Carver), **Supp. III Part 1:** 140
"Onan's Soliloquy" (X. J. Kennedy), **Supp. XV:** 165
"On a Proposed Trip South" (W. C. Williams), **Retro. Supp. I:** 413
Onassis, Jacqueline Kennedy, **Supp. XVIII:** 287
"On a Tree Fallen across the Road" (Frost), **Retro. Supp. I:** 134
"On a View of Pasadena from the Hills" (Winters), **Supp. II Part 2:** 795, 796–799, 814
"On a Visit to a Halfway House after a Long Absence" (Salinas), **Supp. XIII:** 325
"On a Windy Night" (Dixon), **Supp. XII:** 155
On Becoming a Novelist (Gardner), **Supp. VI:** 64
"On Being an American" (Toomer), **Supp. III Part 2:** 479
"On Being Asked to Write a Poem against the War in Vietnam" (Carruth), **Supp. XVI:** 55–56
"On Being a Woman" (Parker), **Supp. IX:** 201
On Being Blue (Gass), **Supp. VI:** 77, 78, 86, 94; **Supp. XIV:** 305
"On Being Too Inhibited" (Hay), **Supp. XIV:** 130
On Beyond Zebra! (Geisel), **Supp. XVI:** 105
"On Burroughs' Work" (Ginsberg), **Supp. II Part 1:** 320
Once (Walker), **Supp. III Part 2:** 519, 522, 530
Once at Antietam (Gaddis), **Supp. IV Part 1:** 285
"Once by the Pacific" (Frost), **II:** 155; **Retro. Supp. I:** 122, 137
"Once More, the Round" (Roethke), **III:** 529
Once More around the Block: Familiar Essays (Epstein), **Supp. XIV: 107**
"Once More to the Lake" (White), **Supp. I Part 2:** 658, 668, 673–675
"On Certain Political Measures Proposed to Their Consideration" (Barlow), **Supp. II Part 1:** 82
"Once There Was Light" (Kenyon), **Supp. VII:** 171–172
Ondaatje, Michael, **Supp. IV Part 1:** 252
"On Dining Alone" (M. F. K. Fisher), **Supp. XVII:** 83
On Distant Ground (R. O. Butler), **Supp. XII:** 62, **66–68,** 69, 74
"1 January 1965" (Brodsky), **Supp. VIII:** 23–24
O'Neale, Sondra, **Supp. IV Part 1:** 2
"One A.M. with Voices" (X. J. Kennedy), **Supp. XV:** 157
"One Arm" (T. Williams), **IV:** 383
One Arm, and Other Stories (T. Williams), **IV:** 383
"One Art" (Bell), **Supp. X:** 2
"One Art" (Bishop), **Retro. Supp. II:** 50; **Supp. I Part 1:** 72, 73, 82, 93, 94–95, 96; **Supp. XV:** 126
One Art (Bishop), **Retro. Supp. II:** 51
"One Art: The Poetry of Elizabeth Bishop, 1971–1976" (Schwartz), **Supp. I Part 1:** 81
One Big Self: Prisoners of Louisiana (Wright and Luster), **Supp. XV:** 337, 344, 350**, 351–353**
"One Blessing had I than the rest" (Dickinson), **Retro. Supp. I:** 45
"One Body" (Hass), **Supp. VI:** 106
One Boy's Boston, 1887–1901 (Morison), **Supp. I Part 2:** 494
"One Coat of Paint" (Ashbery), **Supp. III Part 1:** 26
"One Dash-Horses" (Crane), **I:** 416
One Day (Morris), **III:** 233–236
One Day, When I Was Lost (Baldwin), **Retro. Supp. II:** 13; **Supp. I Part 1:** 48, 66, 67
"One Dead Friend" (Kumin), **Supp. IV Part 2:** 441
One Fish Two Fish Red Fish Blue Fish (Geisel), **Supp. XVI:** 108
One Flew Over the Cuckoo's Nest (Kesey), **III:** 558
"One for the Rose" (Levine), **Supp. V:** 181, 190
One for the Rose (Levine), **Supp. V:** 178, 179, 181, 187, 189–191
"One Friday Morning" (Hughes), **Supp. I Part 1:** 330
"One Holy Night" (Cisneros), **Supp. VII:** 69–70
"One Home" (Stafford), **Supp. XI:** 321
100 Faces of Death, The, Part IV (Boyle), **Supp. VIII:** 16
"$106,000 Blood Money" (Hammett), **Supp. IV Part 1:** 345, 346
$106,000 Blood Money (Hammett), **Supp. IV Part 1:** 345
One Hundred Days in Europe (Holmes), **Supp. I Part 1:** 317
158-Pound Marriage, The (Irving), **Supp. VI:** 163, 164, **167–170**
O'Neil, Elizabeth Murrie, **Retro. Supp. I:** 427
O'Neill, Brendan, **Supp. XII:** 286
O'Neill, Eugene, **I:** 66, 71, 81, 94, 393, 445; **II:** 278, 391, 427, 585; **III:** 151, 165, **385–408; IV:** 61, 383; **Retro. Supp. II:** 82, 104; **Supp. III Part 1:** 177–180, 189; **Supp. IV Part 1:** 359; **Supp. IV Part 2:** 587, 607; **Supp. V:** 277; **Supp. VIII:** 332, 334; **Supp. XIV:** 239, 320, 328; **Supp. XVI:** 193; **Supp. XVII:** 96, 99–100, 103, 105, 107
"One Is a Wanderer" (Thurber), **Supp. I Part 2:** 616
One L (Turow), **Supp. XVII: 214,** 215, 217
"One Last Look at the Adige: Verona in the Rain" (Wright), **Supp. III Part 2:** 603
One Life (Rukeyser), **Supp. VI:** 273, 281, 283
One Life at a Time, Please (Abbey), **Supp. XIII:** 13
One Man in His Time (Glasgow), **II:** 178, 184
"One Man's Fortunes" (Dunbar), **Supp. II Part 1:** 211, 212–213
One Man's Initiation (Dos Passos), **I:** 476–477, 479, 488
"One Man's Meat" (White), **Supp. I Part 2:** 655
One Man's Meat (White), **Supp. I Part 2:** 654, 669, 676
"One Moment on Top of the Earth" (Nye), **Supp. XIII:** 282
One More July: A Football Dialogue with Bill Curry (Plimpton), **Supp. XVI:** 243
"One More Song" (Lindsay), **Supp. I Part 2:** 400–401
"One More Thing" (Carver), **Supp. III Part 1:** 138, 144
"One More Time" (Gordon), **II:** 200
One Nation (Stegner), **Supp. IV Part 2:** 599, 608
"One-Night Homecoming" (X. J. Kennedy), **Supp. XV:** 167
"ONE NIGHT STAND" (Baraka), **Supp. II Part 1:** 32
"One of Our Conquerors" (Bourne), **I:** 223

One of Ours (Cather), **I:** 322–323; **Retro. Supp. I:** 1, 3, **13–15,** 20
"One of the Missing" (Bierce), **I:** 201–202
"One of the Rooming Houses of Heaven" (Doty), **Supp. XI:** 131
"One of the Smallest" (Stern), **Supp. IX:** 299–300
"One of Us" (Fante), **Supp. XI:** 165
"One Out of Twelve: Writers Who Are Women in Our Century" (Olsen), **Supp. XIII:** 294
"One Part Humor, 2 Parts Whining" (Kakutani), **Supp. XI:** 38
"One Person" (Wylie), **Supp. I Part 2:** 709, 724–727
"One Sister have I in our house" (Dickinson), **Retro. Supp. I:** 34
"One Song, The" (Strand), **Supp. IV Part 2:** 619
"One Summer in Spain" (Coover), **Supp. V:** 40
One That Got Away, The (Everett), **Supp. XVIII:** 54
One Thousand Avant-Garde Plays (Koch), **Supp. XV:** 187
One Time, One Place: Mississippi in the Depression, a Snapshot Album (Welty), **Retro. Supp. I:** 339, 343, 344
1 x 1 (One Times One) (Cummings), **I:** 430, 436, 438–439, 441, 446, 447, 448
"One Touch of Nature" (McCarthy), **II:** 580
One Train (Koch), **Supp. XV:** 177, 184
"One Trip Abroad" (Fitzgerald), **II:** 95
One True Thing (film), **Supp. XVII:** 176
One True Thing (Quindlen), **Supp. XVII:** 166, **174–176**
"One Way" (Creeley), **Supp. IV Part 1:** 150–151
One Way or Another (Cameron), **Supp. XII:** 81
One-Way Ticket (Hughes), **Retro. Supp. I:** 206, 207, 208; **Supp. I Part 1:** 333–334
One Way to Heaven (Cullen), **Supp. IV Part 1:** 170, 172
"One Way to Spell Man" (Stegner), **Supp. IV Part 2:** 601
One Way to Spell Man (Stegner), **Supp. IV Part 2:** 595, 598, 601, 609
One Whose Eyes Open When You Close Your Eyes, The (F. Wright), **Supp. XVII:** 240, 243
"One Who Skins Cats, The" (Gunn Allen), **Supp. IV Part 1:** 331
"One Who Went Forth to Feel Fear" (Grimms), **Supp. X:** 86
"One Winter I Devise a Plan of My Own" (Ríos), **Supp. IV Part 2:** 549
One Winter Night in August (X. J. Kennedy), **Supp. XV:** 154, 162
One Writer's Beginnings (Welty), **Retro. Supp. I:** 339, 340, 341, 343, 344, 355–356
"One Year" (Olds), **Supp. X:** 210
"On First Looking Out through Juan de la Cosa's Eyes" (Olson), **Supp. II Part 2:** 565, 566, 570, 579
"On First Opening *The Lyric Year*" (W. C. Williams), **Retro. Supp. I:** 414
"On Freedom's Ground" (Wilbur), **Supp. III Part 2:** 562
On Glory's Course (Purdy), **Supp. VII:** 275–276, 279, 280
On Grief and Reason (Brodsky), **Supp. VIII: 31–32**
"On Hearing a Symphony of Beethoven" (Millay), **III:** 132–133
"On Hearing the Airlines Will Use a Psychological Profile to Catch Potential Skyjackers" (Dunn), **Supp. XI:** 144–145
On Human Finery (Bell), **Supp. I Part 2:** 636
"On *Imagerie:* Esther Williams, 1944" (Sobin), **Supp. XVI:** 294
"On Imminence: An Essay" (Sobin), **Supp. XVI:** 291
On Liberty (Mill), **Supp. XI:** 196
"On Looking Alone at a Place" (M. F. K. Fisher), **Supp. XVII:** 91
"On Looking at a Copy of Alice Meynell's Poems, Given Me, Years Ago, by a Friend" (Lowell), **II:** 527–528
"On Lookout Mountain" (Hayden), **Supp. II Part 1:** 380
Only a Few of Us Left (Marquand), **III:** 55
"Only Animal, The" (F. Wright), **Supp. XVII:** 245
"Only a Pawn in Their Game" (song, Dylan), **Supp. XVIII:** 24
"Only Bar in Dixon, The" (Hugo), **Supp. VI:** 140, 141
Only Dark Spot in the Sky, The (Dove), **Supp. IV Part 1:** 244
"Only Good Indian, The" (Humphrey), **Supp. IX:** 101
Only in America (Golden), **Supp. VIII:** 244
"Only in the Dream" (Eberhart), **I:** 523
"Only Path to Tomorrow, The" (Rand), **Supp. IV Part 2:** 524
"Only Rose, The" (Jewett), **II:** 408
"Only Son of the Doctor, The" (Gordon), **Supp. IV Part 1:** 305, 306
"Only the Cat Escapes," **Supp. XII:** 150–151
"Only the Dead Know Brooklyn" (Wolfe), **IV:** 451
Only When I Laugh (Simon), **Supp. IV Part 2:** 575
On Moral Fiction (Gardner), **Supp. VI:** 61, **71,** 72, 73
"On Morality" (Didion), **Supp. IV Part 1:** 196
"On My Own" (Levine), **Supp. V:** 181, 189–190
"On My Own Work" (Wilbur), **Supp. III Part 2:** 541–542
On Native Grounds: An Interpretation of Modern American Prose Literature (Kazin), **I:** 517; **Supp. I Part 2:** 650; **Supp. VIII:** 93, 96–97, 98, **100–102**
"On Not Being a Dove" (Updike), **Retro. Supp. I:** 323
"On Open Form" (Merwin), **Supp. III Part 1:** 347–348, 353
On Photography (Sontag), **Supp. III Part 2:** 451, 458, 462–465
"On Political Poetry" (R. Bly), **Supp. IV Part 1:** 61
On Politics: A Carnival of Buncombe (Moos, ed.), **III:** 116
"On Pretentiousness" (Kushner), **Supp. IX:** 131–132
"On Quitting a Little College" (Stafford), **Supp. XI:** 321
"On Reading Eckerman's Conversations with Goethe" (Masters), **Supp. I Part 2:** 458
On Reading Shakespeare (L. P. Smith), **Supp. XIV:** 345–346
"On Reading to Oneself" (Gass), **Supp. VI:** 88, 89
On Revolution (Arendt), **Retro. Supp. I:** 87
"On Seeing Larry Rivers' *Washington Crossing the Delaware* at the Museum of Modern Art" (O'Hara), **Supp. XV:** 186
"On Seeing Red" (Walker), **Supp. III Part 2:** 527
"On Social Plays" (A. Miller), **III:** 147, 148, 159
"On Steinbeck's Story 'Flight'" (Stegner), **Supp. IV Part 2:** 596
"On Style" (Sontag), **Supp. III Part 2:** 456–459, 465–466
"On Suicide" (Hay), **Supp. XIV:** 130, 132
"On Teaching the Young Laurel to Shoot" (Bynner), **Supp. XV:** 50
"On the Antler" (Proulx), **Supp. VII:** 252–253
"On the Banks of the Wabash" (Paul Dresser), **Retro. Supp. II:** 94
"On the Beach, at Night" (Whitman), **IV:** 348
"On the Bosom of This Grave and Wasted Land I Will Lay My Head" (Ray), **Supp. XVIII:** 189
On the Boundary (Tillich), **Retro. Supp. I:** 326
"On the Building of Springfield" (Lindsay), **Supp. I Part 2:** 381
"On the Coast of Maine" (Hayden), **Supp. II Part 1:** 381
On the Contrary: Articles of Belief (McCarthy), **II:** 559, 562
"On the Death of a Friend's Child" (Lowell), **Supp. I Part 2:** 409
"On the Death of Senator Thomas J. Walsh" (Winters), **Supp. II Part 2:** 802, 806
"On the Death of Yeats" (Bogan), **Supp. III Part 1:** 59
"On the Death of Zhukov" (Brodsky), **Supp. VIII:** 27
"On the Disadvantages of Central Heating" (Clampitt), **Supp. IX:** 41, 47, 52
On the Drumhead: A Selection from the Writing of Mike Quin (Carlisle, ed.), **Supp. XVIII:** 223, 226
"On the Edge" (Levine), **Supp. V:** 181–182

On the Edge and Over (Levine), **Supp. V:** 178, 180–182, 186
On the Edge of the Great Rift: Three Novels of Africa (Theroux), **Supp. VIII:** 316
"On the Eve of the Feast of the Immaculate Conception, 1942" (Lowell), **II:** 538; **Retro. Supp. II:** 185
"On the Eyes of an SS Officer" (Wilbur), **Supp. III Part 2:** 548
"On the Fall of General Earl Cornwallis" (Freneau), **Supp. II Part 1:** 261
"On the Folly of Writing Poetry" (Freneau), **Supp. II Part 1:** 263
On the Frontier (Auden and Isherwood), **Supp. II Part 1:** 13; **Supp. XIV:** 163
On the Great Atlantic Rainway: Selected Poems, 1950–1988 (Koch), **Supp. XV:** 177
"On the Island" (Stern), **Supp. IX:** 290
"On the Late Eclipse" (Bryant), **Supp. I Part 1:** 152
On the Laws of the Poetic Art (Hecht), **Supp. X:** 58
"On the Marginal Way" (Wilbur), **Supp. III Part 2:** 558, 559
On the Mesa (Nichols), **Supp. XIII:** 268
"On the Moon and Matriarchal Consciousness" (Neumann), **Supp. IV Part 1:** 68
"On the Morning after the Sixties" (Didion), **Supp. IV Part 1:** 205, 206
On the Motion and Immobility of Douve (Bonnefoy; Kinnell, trans.), **Supp. III Part 1:** 235
"On the Murder of Lieutenant José del Castillo by the Falangist Bravo Martinez, July 12, 1936" (Levine), **Supp. V:** 187
"On the Night of a Friend's Wedding" (Robinson), **III:** 524
"On the Occasion of a Poem: Richard Hugo" (Wright), **Supp. III Part 2:** 596
On the Occasion of My Last Afternoon (Gibbons), **Supp. X:** 46, **50–53**
On the Origin of Species (Darwin), **Supp. XIV:** 192
"On the Parapet" (Tanner), **Retro. Supp. II:** 205
"On the Platform" (Nemerov), **III:** 287
On the Poetry of Philip Levine: Stranger to Nothing (Levis), **Supp. XI:** 257
"On the Powers of the Human Understanding" (Freneau), **Supp. II Part 1:** 274
On the Prejudices, Predilections, and Firm Beliefs of William Faulkner (Brooks), **Supp. XIV:** 13
"On the Pulse of Morning" (Angelou), **Supp. IV Part 1:** 15–17
"On the Railway Platform" (Jarrell), **II:** 370
"On the Rainy River" (O'Brien), **Supp. V:** 250
On the Rebound: A Story and Nine Poems (Purdy), **Supp. VII:** 276–277
"On the Religion of Nature" (Freneau), **Supp. II Part 1:** 275
"On the River" (Dunbar), **Supp. II Part 1:** 193
"On the River" (Levine), **Supp. V:** 193
On the River Styx and Other Stories (Matthiessen), **Supp. V:** 212
On the Road (Kerouac), **Retro. Supp. I:** 102; **Supp. III Part 1:** 92, 218, 222–224, 226, 230–231; **Supp. V:** 336; **Supp. X:** 269; **Supp. XIII:** 275; **Supp. XIV:** 138, 150; **Supp. XV:** 221; **Supp. XVIII:** 20, 138
"On the Road Home" (Stevens), **Retro. Supp. I:** 306
On the Road with the Archangel (Buechner), **Supp. XII:** 54
On These I Stand: An Anthology of the Best Poems of Countee Cullen (Cullen), **Supp. IV Part 1:** 173
"On the Skeleton of a Hound" (Wright), **Supp. III Part 2:** 593
"On the Street: Monument" (Gunn Allen), **Supp. IV Part 1:** 326
"On the Subway" (Olds), **Supp. X:** 207
"On the System of Policy Hitherto Pursued by Their Government" (Barlow), **Supp. II Part 1:** 82
"On the Teaching of Modern Literature" (Trilling), **Supp. III Part 2:** 509–510
"On the Uniformity and Perfection of Nature" (Freneau), **Supp. II Part 1:** 275
"On the Universality and Other Attributes of the God of Nature" (Freneau), **Supp. II Part 1:** 275
"On the Use of Trisyllabic Feet in Iambic Verse" (Bryant), **Supp. I Part 1:** 156
On the Waterfront (film, Kazan), **Supp. XVIII: 250–251,** 252, 253
On the Way toward a Phenomenological Psychology: The Psychology of William James (Linschoten), **II:** 362
"On the Way to Work" (Dunn), **Supp. XI:** 149–150
"On the Wide Heath" (Millay), **III:** 130
"On the Writing of Novels" (Buck), **Supp. II Part 1:** 121
On the Yard (Braly), **Supp. XVIII:** 147
On This Island (Auden), **Supp. II Part 1:** 11
"On Time" (O'Hara), **III:** 369–370
"Ontological Episode of the Asylum" (Carruth), **Supp. XVI:** 48, 50
"Ontology of the Sentence, The" (Gass), **Supp. VI:** 77
"On Top" (Leopold), **Supp. XIV:** 188
"On Top" (Snyder), **Supp. VIII:** 304
"On Translating Akhmatova" (Kunitz), **Supp. III Part 1:** 268
"On Waking to Old Debts" (Keillor), **Supp. XVI:** 167
On William Stafford: The Worth of Local Things (Andrews, ed.), **Supp. XI:** 311, 312, 317, 321, 324, 326
"On Writing" (Carver), **Supp. III Part 1:** 142–143
"On Writing" (Nin), **Supp. X:** 182
Opatoshu, Joseph, **IV:** 9
"Open Boat, The" (Crane), **I:** 408, 415, 416–417, 423; **Retro. Supp. I:** 325; **Supp. XIV:** 51
Open Boat and Other Stories (Crane), **I:** 408
Open Heart: A Patient's Story of Life-Saving Medicine and Life-Giving Friendship (Neugeboren), **Supp. XVI:** 217, **229–230**
"Open House" (Roethke), **III:** 529
Open House (Roethke), **III:** 529–530, 540
"Opening, An" (Swenson), **Supp. IV Part 2:** 639
Opening of the Field, The (Duncan), **Supp. III Part 2:** 625
Opening the Hand (Merwin), **Supp. III Part 1:** 341, 353, 355
"Open Letter" (Roethke), **III:** 532, 534
"Open Letter to Surrealists Everywhere, An" (H. Miller), **III:** 184
Open Meeting, The (Gurney), **Supp. V:** 98
Open Net (Plimpton), **Supp. XVI:** 241
"Open Road, The" (Dreiser), **II:** 44
Open Sea, The (Masters), **Supp. I Part 2:** 471
Open Season: Sporting Adventures (Humphrey), **Supp. IX:** 95
"Open Secret" (Nelson), **Supp. XVIII:** 185
"Open the Gates" (Kunitz), **Supp. III Part 1:** 264–265, 267
"Opera Company, The" (Merrill), **Supp. III Part 1:** 326
"Operation, The" (Sanders), **Supp. XVI:** 266
"Operation, The" (Sexton), **Supp. II Part 2:** 675, 679
Operation Shylock: A Confession (P. Roth), **Retro. Supp. II:** 279, 280, 291
Operation Sidewinder (Shepard), **Supp. III Part 2:** 434–435, 439, 446–447
Operations in North African Waters (Morison), **Supp. I Part 2:** 490
Operation Wandering Soul (Powers), **Supp. IX:** 212, **217–219**
Opffer, Emil, **Retro. Supp. II:** 80
"Opinion" (Du Bois), **Supp. II Part 1:** 173
Opinionator, The (Bierce), **I:** 209
Opinions of Oliver Allston (Brooks), **I:** 254, 255, 256
O Pioneers! (Cather), **I:** 314, 317–319, 320; **Retro. Supp. I:** 1, 5, 6, **7–9,** 10, 13, 20; **Retro. Supp. II:** 136
Oppen, George, **IV:** 415; **Supp. III Part 2:** 614, 615, 616, 626, 628; **Supp. XIV:** 285, 286, 287; **Supp. XVI:** 282, 283; **Supp. XVII:** 243
Oppenheim, James, **I:** 106, 109, 239, 245; **Supp. XV:** 294, 296, 298, 299, 301, 302, 307, 313
Oppenheimer, J. Robert, **I:** 137, 492
Oppenheimer, Judy, **Supp. IX:** 115, 116, 118, 120, 126
"Opportunity for American Fiction, An" (Howells), **Supp. I Part 2:** 645–646
Opposing Self, The (Trilling), **Supp. III Part 2:** 506–507
"Opposition" (Lanier), **Supp. I Part 1:** 368, 373

Opticks: A Poem in Seven Sections (Goldbarth), **Supp. XII:** 177, **178**
"Optimist's Daughter, The" (Welty), **IV:** 280–281
Optimist's Daughter, The (Welty), **IV:** 261, 280; **Retro. Supp. I:** 339, 355
Options (O. Henry), **Supp. II Part 1:** 410
Opus Posthumous (Stevens), **IV:** 76, 78
Opus Posthumous (W. Stevens), **Supp. XVII:** 241
Oracle at Stoneleigh Court, The (Taylor), **Supp. V:** 328
Orage, Alfred, **III:** 473
Orange, Max (pseudonym). *See* Heller, Joseph
Orange Fish, The (Shields), **Supp. VII:** 318, 320, 323, 328
Oranges (McPhee), **Supp. III Part 1:** 298–299, 301, 309
"Oranging of America, The" (Apple), **Supp. XVII:** 3–4, 6
Oranging of America and Other Short Stories, The (Apple), **Supp. XVII:** 1–2, **3–4,** 7, 8
Oration Delivered at Washington, July Fourth, 1809 (Barlow), **Supp. II Part 1:** 80, 83
Orations and Addresses (Bryant), **Supp. I Part 1:** 158
Orators, The (Auden), **Supp. II Part 1:** 6, 7, 11, 18–19
Orb Weaver, The (Francis), **Supp. IX:** **81–82**
"Orchard" (Doolittle), **Supp. I Part 1:** 263–264, 265, 266
"Orchard" (Eberhart), **I:** 539
"Orchard, The" (B. Kelly), **Supp. XVII:** 133
Orchard, The (B. Kelly), **Supp. XVII:** 123, 127, **130–133**
Orchard Keeper, The (McCarthy), **Supp. VIII: 175–176**
Orchestra (Davies), **III:** 541
"Orchids" (Roethke), **III:** 530–531
"Or Consider Prometheus" (Clampitt), **Supp. IX:** 44
Ordeal of Mansart, The (Du Bois), **Supp. II Part 1:** 185–186
Ordeal of Mark Twain, The (Brooks), **I:** 240, 247, 248; **II:** 482
"Order of Insects" (Gass), **Supp. VI:** 83
Order Out of Chaos (McPherson), **Supp. IV Part 1:** 2, 12
"Ordinary Afternoon in Charlottesville, An" (Wright), **Supp. V:** 344
"Ordinary Days" (Dunn), **Supp. XI:** 151
"Ordinary Evening in New Haven, An" (Stevens), **IV:** 91–92; **Retro. Supp. I:** 297, 300, 311, 312
Ordinary Heroes (Turow), **Supp. XVII:** **221–222,** 223
Ordinary Love (Smiley), **Supp. VI:** 292, **299–300**
Ordinary Love; and Good Will: Two Novellas (Smiley), **Supp. VI:** 292, **299–300**
Ordinary Miracles (Jong), **Supp. V:** 115, 130–131
"Ordinary Time: Virginia Woolf and Thucydides on War" (Carson), **Supp. XII: 111**
"Ordinary Women, The" (Stevens), **IV:** 81
Ordways, The (Humphrey), **Supp. IX:** 95, **98–100,** 109; **Supp. XV:** 353
"Oread" (Doolittle), **II:** 520–521; **Supp. I Part 1:** 265–266
Oregon Message, An (Stafford), **Supp. XI: 328–329**
Oregon Trail, The (Parkman), **II:** 312; **Supp. II Part 2:** 592, 595–596, 598, 606
Oresteia (Aeschylus), **Supp. IX:** 103
"Orestes at Tauris" (Jarrell), **II:** 376, 377
Orfalea, Gregory, **Supp. XIII:** 278
Orfeo ed Euridice (Gluck), **II:** 210, 211
Orff, Carl, **Supp. X:** 63
"Organizer's Wife, The" (Bambara), **Supp. XI:** 8–9
"Organmeister: Hasse After Marienkirche" (Bierds), **Supp. XVII:** 34
"Orgy" (Rukeyser), **Supp. VI:** 280
Orgy, The (Rukeyser), **Supp. VI:** 274, 283
"Orientation of Hope, The" (Locke), **Supp. XIV:** 212–213
Orient Express (Dos Passos), **I:** 480
"Orient Express, The" (Jarrell), **II:** 382, 383–384
Origen, Adamantius, **IV:** 153
"Origin" (Harjo), **Supp. XII:** 219
Original Child Bomb: Points for Meditation to Be Scratched on the Walls of a Cave (Merton), **Supp. VIII:** 203
Original Essays on the Poetry of Anne Sexton (George), **Supp. IV Part 2:** 450
"Original Follies Girl, The" (Z. Fitzgerald), **Supp. IX:** 71
Original Light (Goldbarth), **Supp. XII:** 181, **183–184,** 188
Original of Laura, The (Nabokov), **Retro. Supp. I:** 266
"Original Sin" (Jeffers), **Supp. II Part 2:** 426
"Original Sin" (Warren), **IV:** 245
"Origin of Extermination in the Imagination, The" (Gass), **Supp. VI:** 89
Origin of Species, The (Darwin), **II:** 173, 462; **Supp. XVI:** 13
Origin of the Brunists, The (Coover), **Supp. V:** 39, 41, 52
"Origins and History of Consciousness" (Rich), **Supp. I Part 2:** 570
"Origins of a Nonfiction Writer" (Talese), **Supp. XVII:** 208
"Origins of a Poem" (Levertov), **Supp. III Part 1:** 273
"Origins of the Beat Generation, The" (Kerouac), **Supp. III Part 1:** 231
Origo, Iris, **IV:** 328
"O'Riley's Late-Bloomed Little Son" (X. J. Kennedy), **Supp. XV:** 159
"Orion" (Rich), **Supp. I Part 2:** 557
O'Riordan, Conal Holmes O'Connell, **III:** 465
Orlacs Hände (film, Weine), **Supp. XVII:** 58
Orlando (V. Woolf), **Supp. XVII:** 86
Orlando (Woolf), **Supp. I Part 2:** 718; **Supp. VIII:** 263; **Supp. XII:** 9
Orlando Furioso (Ariosto), **Supp. XV:** 175
Orlovsky, Peter, **Supp. XII:** 121, 126; **Supp. XIV:** 150; **Supp. XVIII:** 27
Ormonde, Czenzi, **Supp. IV Part 1:** 132
Ormond; or, The Secret Witness (Brown), **Supp. I Part 1:** 133–137
Ornament and Crime (Loos), **Supp. XVI:** 187
Orne, Sarah. *See* Jewett, Sarah Orne
Ornithological Biography; or, An Account of the Habits of the Birds of the United States of America, and Interspersed with Delineations of American Scenery and Manners (Audubon), **7–10**
Ornithological Biography; or, An Account of the Habits of the Birds of the United States of America, and Interspersed with Delin eations of American Scenery and Manners (Audubon), **Supp. XVI:**13
Ornitz, Samuel, **Supp. IX:** 227; **Supp. XIII:** 166
Orphan Angel, The (Wylie), **Supp. I Part 2:** 707, 709, 714, 717, 719–721, 722, 724
Orphan's Tale, An (Neugeboren), **Supp. XVI:** 222, 223
"Orpheus (1)" (Atwood), **Supp. XIII:** 35
"Orpheus (2)" (Atwood), **Supp. XIII:** 35
Orpheus (Rukeyser), **Supp. VI:** 273
"Orpheus" (Winters), **Supp. II Part 2:** 801
"Orpheus, Eurydice, Hermes" (Rilke), **Supp. VIII:** 31, 32
"Orpheus Alone" (Strand), **Supp. IV Part 2:** 632
Orpheus Descending (T. Williams), **IV:** 380, 381, 382, 385, 386, 387, 389, 391–392, 395, 396, 398
Orr, Peter, **Supp. I Part 2:** 538, 540, 543
Ortega y Gasset, José, **I:** 218, 222; **Supp. IV Part 2:** 521
Ortiz, Simon J., **Supp. IV Part 1:** 319, 404; **Supp. IV Part 2: 497–515,** 557; **Supp. XII:** 217, 218
O'Ruddy, The (Crane), **I:** 409, 424
Orwell, George, **I:** 489; **II:** 454, 580; **Supp. I Part 2:** 523, 620; **Supp. II Part 1:** 143; **Supp. IV Part 1:** 236; **Supp. V:** 250; **Supp. VIII:** 241; **Supp. XIV:** 112, 158; **Supp. XVII:** 228, 229; **Supp. XVIII:** 137, 138
Osborn, Dwight, **III:** 218–219, 223
"Osborn Look, The" (Morris), **III:** 221
Osgood, Frances, **Supp. XVII:** 75
Osgood, J. R., **II:** 283
O'Shea, Kitty, **II:** 137
O'Shea, Milo, **Supp. XI:** 308
"Oshkikwe's Baby" (traditional Chippewa story), **Supp. IV Part 1:** 333
Oshogay, Delia, **Supp. IV Part 1:** 333
Ossana, Diana, **Supp. V:** 230–231, 232
Ossian, **Supp. I Part 2:** 491
Ossip, Kathleen, **Supp. X:** 201

Ostanovka v Pustyne (A halt in the wilderness) (Brodsky), **Supp. VIII:** 21
Oster, Judith, **Supp. XVI:** 151
Ostriker, Alicia, **Supp. I Part 2:** 540; **Supp. IV Part 2:** 439, 447, 449; **Supp. X:** 207, 208; **Supp. XI:** 143; **Supp. XV:** 251
Ostrom, Hans, **Retro. Supp. I:** 195
Oswald, Lee Harvey, **III:** 234, 235
Oswald II (DeLillo), **Supp. VI:** 16
Oswald's Tale (Mailer), **Retro. Supp. II:** 212–213
O Taste and See (Levertov), **Supp. III Part 1:** 278–279, 281
Othello (Shakespeare), **I:** 284–285
"Other, The" (Sexton), **Supp. II Part 2:** 692
Other America, The (Harrington), **I:** 306
"Other American Renaissance, The" (Tompkins), **Supp. XVIII:** 258
Other Destinies: Understanding the American Indian Novel (Owens), **Supp. IV Part 1:** 404
"Other Frost, The" (Jarrell), **Retro. Supp. I:** 121
Other Gods: An American Legend (Buck), **Supp. II Part 1:** 123, 130–131
Other House, The (James), **Retro. Supp. I:** 229
"Other League of Nations, The" (Ríos), **Supp. IV Part 2:** 552
"Other Margaret, The" (Trilling), **Supp. III Part 2:** 504–505
"Other Miller, The" (Wolff), **Supp. VII:** 343–344
"Other Mothers" (Paley), **Supp. VI:** 225
"Other Night at Columbia, The" (Trilling), **Supp. XII:** 126
"Other Robert Frost, The" (Jarrell), **Retro. Supp. I:** 135
Others (Shields), **Supp. VII:** 310
Other Side, The (Gordon), **Supp. IV Part 1:** 299, 306, 307–309, 310–311
Other Side, The/El Otro Lado (Alvarez), **Supp. VII:** 9–12
"Other Side of the River, The" (Wright), **Supp. V:** 335
Other Side of the River, The (Wright), **Supp. V:** 332–333, 342
"Other Tradition, The" (Ashbery), **Supp. III Part 1:** 15, 18
"Other Two, The" (Wharton), **Retro. Supp. I:** 367
Other Voices, Other Rooms (Capote), **Supp. III Part 1:** 113–118, 121, 123–124
"Other War, The" (Cowley), **Supp. II Part 1:** 144
"Otherwise" (Kenyon), **Supp. VII:** 172, 174
Otherwise: New and Selected Poems (Kenyon), **Supp. VII:** 167, 172–174
Otherwise Than Being; or, Beyond Essence (Lévinas), **Supp. XVI:** 290, 291
"Other Woman, The" (Anderson), **I:** 114
"Other World, The" (Wrigley), **Supp. XVIII:** 307
Otho the Great: A Tragedy in Five Acts (Keats), **Supp. XII:** 113
Otis, Harrison Gray, **Supp. I Part 2:** 479–481, 483, 486, 488
Otis, James, **III:** 577; **Supp. I Part 2:** 486; **Supp. XV:** 229
O to Be a Dragon (Moore), **III:** 215
Otto, Rudolf, **Supp. XVII:** 243
"Ouija" (McClatchy), **Supp. XII:** 269–270
Oupensky, Peter, **Supp. XIV:** 188
Our America (Frank), **I:** 229; **Supp. IX:** 308
Our America (Michaels), **Retro. Supp. I:** 379
"Our Assistant's Column" (Twain), **IV:** 193
"Our Bourgeois Literature" (Sinclair), **Supp. V:** 281
Our Brains and What Ails Them (Gilman), **Supp. XI:** 207
Our Century (Wilder), **IV:** 374
"Our Christmas Party" (E. Stoddard), **Supp. XV:** 273, 278
Our Country (Strong), **Supp. XIV:** 64
"Our Countrymen in Chains!" (Whittier), **Supp. I Part 2:** 688
"Our Cultural Humility" (Bourne), **I:** 223, 228
Our Depleted Society (Seymour), **Supp. XIII:** 264
"Our Dust" (Wright), **Supp. XV:** 345, 346
"Our Father Who Drowns the Birds" (Kingsolver), **Supp. VII:** 208–209
"Our First House" (Kingston), **Supp. V:** 169
Our Gang (P. Roth), **Retro. Supp. II:** 287; **Supp. III Part 2:** 414; **Supp. IV Part 1:** 388
"Our Good Day" (Cisneros), **Supp. VII:** 60
Our Ground Time Here Will Be Brief (Kumin), **Supp. IV Part 2:** 450–452
Our House in the Last World (Hijuelos), **Supp. VIII:** 73, **76–79,** 87, 88
"Our Lady" (A. Finch), **Supp. XVII:** 77
"*Our Lady of the Annunciation*/Nuestra Señora de Anunciación" (Mora), **Supp. XIII:** 217, 224, 228
"Our Lady of Troy" (MacLeish), **III:** 3, 20
"Our Limitations" (Holmes), **Supp. I Part 1:** 314
"Our Martyred Soldiers" (Dunbar), **Supp. II Part 1:** 193
"Our Master" (Whittier), **Supp. I Part 2:** 704
"Our Mother Pocahontas" (Lindsay), **Supp. I Part 2:** 393
Our Mr. Wrenn: The Romantic Adventures of a Gentle Man (Lewis), **II:** 441
Our National Parks (Muir), **Supp. IX:** 181, 184
Our New York: A Personal Vision in Words and Photographs (Kazin), **Supp. VIII: 106–107**
"Our Old Aunt Who Is Now in a Retirement Home" (Shields), **Supp. VII:** 310
Our Old Home: A Series of English Sketches (Hawthorne), **II:** 225; **Retro. Supp. I:** 163
"Our Own Movie Queen" (Z. Fitzgerald), **Supp. IX:** 71
"Our River Now" (L.-Y. Lee), **Supp. XV:** 224, 225
Ourselves to Know (O'Hara), **III:** 362, 365
"Our Story Begins" (Wolff), **Supp. VII:** 345
Our Town (Wilder), **IV:** 357, 364, 365, 366, 368–369
"Our Unplanned Cities" (Bourne), **I:** 229, 230
Our Wonder World, **Retro. Supp. I:** 341
Ouspensky, P. D., **I:** 383
"Out" (Harjo), **Supp. XII:** 219
"'Out, Out'" (Frost), **Retro. Supp. I:** 131
"Outcast" (McKay), **Supp. X:** 135
"Outcasts of Poker Flats, The" (Harte), **Supp. II Part 1:** 345, 347–348
Outcroppings (Harte), **Supp. II Part 1:** 343
Out Cry (T. Williams), **IV:** 383, 393
Outcry, The (James), **Retro. Supp. I:** 235
"Outdoor Shower" (Olds), **Supp. X:** 214
Outerbridge Reach (Stone), **Supp. V:** 306–308
Outer Dark (McCarthy), **Supp. VIII: 176–177**
Outermost Dream, The: Essays and Reviews (Maxwell), **Supp. VIII: 171–172**
"Outing, The" (Baldwin), **Supp. I Part 1:** 63
"Out Like a Lamb" (Dubus), **Supp. VII:** 91
"Outline of an Autobiography" (Toomer), **Supp. III Part 2:** 478
Outlyer and Ghazals (Harrison), **Supp. VIII:** 41
"Out of Business" (Mora), **Supp. XIII:** 217
Out of My League (Plimpton), **Supp. XVI:** 233, 239
"Out of Nowhere into Nothing" (Anderson), **I:** 113
"Out of Season" (Hemingway), **II:** 263
"Out of the Cradle Endlessly Rocking" (Whitman), **IV:** 342, 343–345, 346, 351; **Retro. Supp. I:** 404, 406
"Out of the Deeps" (E. Stoddard), **Supp. XV:** 286
"Out of the Hospital and Under the Bar" (Ellison), **Retro. Supp. II:** 118–119; **Supp. II Part 1:** 246
"Out of the Rainbow End" (Sandburg), **III:** 594–595
"Out of the Sea, Early" (Swenson), **Supp. IV Part 2:** 645
"Out of the Snow" (Dubus), **Supp. VII:** 91
Out of the Stars (Purdy), **Supp. VII:** 281–282
Outre-Mer: A Pilgrimage beyond the Sea (Longfellow), **II:** 313, 491; **Retro. Supp. II:** 155, 165
"Outside" (Stafford), **Supp. XI:** 318

Outside, The (Glaspell), **Supp. III Part 1:** 179, 187
Outsider, The (Wright), **IV:** 478, 481, 488, 491–494, 495
Out West (Shanley), **Supp. XIV:** 317
"Out with the Old" (Yates), **Supp. XI:** 342
"Ouzo for Robin" (Merrill), **Supp. III Part 1:** 326
"Oval Portrait, The" (Poe), **III:** 412, 415; **Retro. Supp. II:** 270
"Oven Bird, The" (Frost), **Retro. Supp. I:** 131; **Supp. XI:** 153
"Over 2,000 Illustrations and a Complete Concordance" (Bishop), **Retro. Supp. II:** 45; **Supp. I Part 1:** 90–91
"Over by the River" (Maxwell), **Supp. VIII:** 169, 170
"Overgrown Pasture, The" (Lowell), **II:** 523
"Overheard through the Walls of the Invisible City" (Bidart), **Supp. XV:** 32
"Over Kansas" (Ginsberg), **Supp. II Part 1:** 320
Overland to the Islands (Levertov), **Supp. III Part 1:** 275, 276
"Overnight Pass" (X. J. Kennedy), **Supp. XV:** 168
Overreachers, The (Talese), **Supp. XVII:** 202
"Over-Soul, The" (Emerson), **II:** 7
Over the Blue Mountain (Richter), **Supp. XVIII:** 220
"Over the Hill" (Dubus), **Supp. VII:** 76, 79–80
Overtime (Gurney), **Supp. V:** 104
"Overwhelming Question, An" (Taylor), **Supp. V:** 323
Ovid, **I:** 62; **II:** 542–543; **III:** 457, 467, 468, 470; **Retro. Supp. I:** 63; **Supp. IV Part 2:** 634; **Supp. XII:** 264
"Ovid's Farewell" (McClatchy), **Supp. XII:** 257–258
Owen, David, **II:** 34
Owen, Maureen, **Supp. IV Part 2:** 423
Owen, Wilfred, **II:** 367, 372; **III:** 524; **Supp. X:** 146; **Supp. XVII:** 245; **Supp. XVIII:** 92
Owens, Hamilton, **III:** 99, 109
Owens, Louis, **Supp. IV Part 1:** 404
"O Where Are You Going?" (Auden), **Supp. X:** 116
"Owl, The" (Wrigley), **Supp. XVIII:** 297–298, 301
Owl in the Attic, The (Thurber), **Supp. I Part 2:** 614
Owl in the Mask of the Dreamer, The: Collected Poems (Haines), **Supp. XII:** 211
"Owl in the Sarcophagus, The" (Stevens), **Retro. Supp. I:** 300
"Owl's Clover" (Stevens), **IV:** 75
Owl's Clover (Stevens), **Retro. Supp. I:** 298, **303–304**
Owl's Insomnia, Poems by Rafael Alberti, The (Strand, trans.), **Supp. IV Part 2:** 630
Owlstone Crown, The (X. J. Kennedy), **Supp. XV:** 162, **164**
"Owl Who Was God, The" (Thurber), **Supp. I Part 2:** 610
Owning Jolene (Hearon), **Supp. VIII: 66–67**
"Owning the Masters" (Nelson), **Supp. XVIII:** 171
Oxford Anthology of American Literature, The, **III:** 197; **Supp. I Part 1:** 254
Oxford Book of American Verse (Matthiessen, ed.), **Retro. Supp. I:** 40
Oxford Book of Children's Verse in America, The (Hall, ed.), **Supp. XIV:** 126
Oxford Companion to Twentieth-Century Poetry (Hamilton, ed.), **Supp. XVII:** 243
Oxford History of the American People, The (Morison), **Supp. I Part 2:** 495–496
Oxford History of the United States, 1783–1917, The (Morison), **Supp. I Part 2:** 483–484
"Oxford Town" (song, Dylan), **Supp. XVIII:** 24
Oxherding Tale (Johnson), **Supp. VI: 190–192,** 193, 194, 196
Oxley, William, **Supp. XV:** 125
"O Yes" (Olsen), **Supp. XIII:** 294, 298, **299–300,** 301
"O Youth and Beauty!" (Cheever), **Retro. Supp. I:** 335
"Oysters" (Sexton), **Supp. II Part 2:** 692
"Ozark Odes" (Wright), **Supp. XV:** 346
Ozick, Cynthia, **Supp. V: 257–274; Supp. VIII:** 141; **Supp. X:** 192; **Supp. XVII:** 42, 43, 49, 50
O-Zone (Theroux), **Supp. VIII:** 323–324

P

Pace, Patricia, **Supp. XI:** 245
Pacernik, Gary, **Supp. IX:** 287, 291
"Pacific Distances" (Didion), **Supp. IV Part 1:** 211
"Pacific Village" (M. F. K. Fisher), **Supp. XVII:** 83
Pack, Robert, **Supp. IV Part 2:** 621
"Packed Dirt, Churchgoing, a Dying Cat, a Traded Cat" (Updike), **IV:** 219
"Packing Mother's Things" (C. Frost), **Supp. XV:** 97
Paddock, Joe, **Supp. XVI:** 36
Paddock, Nancy, **Supp. XVI:** 36
Padel, Ruth, **Supp. XII:** 107
Padgett, Ron, **Supp. XV:** 190
Pafko at the Wall (DeLillo), **Supp. VI:** 4
"Pagan Prayer" (Cullen), **Supp. IV Part 1:** 170
"Pagan Rabbi, The" (Ozick), **Supp. V:** 262, 264, 265; **Supp. XVII:** 43
Pagan Rabbi and Other Stories, The (Ozick), **Supp. V:** 260, 261, 263–265
Pagan Spain (Wright), **IV:** 478, 488, 495
Page, Geraldine, **Supp. XV:** 7
Page, Kirby, **III:** 297
Page, Thomas Nelson, **II:** 174, 176, 194; **Supp. XIV:** 61
Page, Walter Hines, **II:** 174, 175; **Supp. I Part 1:** 370
Page, William, **Supp. XVIII:** 2, 11
"Pages from Cold Point" (Bowles), **Supp. IV Part 1:** 85, 86, 87
Paid on Both Sides: A Charade (Auden), **Supp. II Part 1:** 6, 18–19
Paige, Satchel, **Supp. I Part 1:** 234
Paige, T. D. D., **III:** 475
Pain, Joseph, **Supp. I Part 2:** 502
Paine, Albert Bigelow, **I:** 249
Paine, Thomas, **I:** 490; **II:** 117, 302; **III:** 17, 148, 219; **Retro. Supp. I:** 390; **Supp. I Part 1:** 231; **Supp. I Part 2: 501–525; Supp. XI:** 55
"Pain has an Element of Blank" (Dickinson), **Retro. Supp. I:** 44
"Paint and Powder" (Z. Fitzgerald), **Supp. IX:** 71
Painted Bird, The (Kosinski), **Supp. VII:** 215–217, 219–221, 222, 227
Painted Desert (F. Barthelme), **Supp. XI:** 28–29, 32
Painted Dresses (Hearon), **Supp. VIII: 63**
"Painted Head" (Ransom), **III:** 491, 494; **Supp. II Part 1:** 103, 314
Painted Word, The (Wolfe), **Supp. III Part 2:** 580–581, 584; **Supp. XV:** 143
"Painter, The" (Ashbery), **Supp. III Part 1:** 5–6, 13
Painter Dreaming in the Scholar's House, The (Nemerov), **III:** 269
"Painters" (Rukeyser), **Supp. VI:** 281
"Painting a Mountain Stream" (Nemerov), **III:** 275
"Pair a Spurs" (Proulx), **Supp. VII:** 263–264
"Pair of Bright Blue Eyes, A" (Taylor), **Supp. V:** 321
"Pajamas" (Olds), **Supp. X:** 206
Pakula, Alan, **Supp. XIII:** 264
Palace at 4 A.M. (Giacometti), **Supp. VIII:** 169
"Palantine, The" (Whittier), **Supp. I Part 2:** 694, 696
Palatella, John, **Retro. Supp. II:** 48
Pale Fire (Nabokov), **III:** 244, 246, 252, 263–265; **Retro. Supp. I:** 264, 265, 266, 270, 271, 272, 276, 278, 335; **Supp. V:** 251, 253
"Pale Horse, Pale Rider" (Porter), **III:** 436, 437, 441–442, 445, 446, 449
Pale Horse, Pale Rider: Three Short Novels (Porter), **III:** 433, 436–442; **Supp. VIII:** 157
"Pale Pink Roast, The" (Paley), **Supp. VI:** 217
"Pale Rider" (B. Kelly), **Supp. XVII:** 132–133
Paley, Grace, **Supp. IX:** 212; **Supp. VI: 217–233; Supp. X:** 79, 164; **Supp. XII:** 309
Paley, William, **II:** 9
Palgrave, Francis Turner, **Retro. Supp. I:** 124; **Supp. XIV:** 340
Palgrave's Golden Treasury (Palgrave), **IV:** 405
Palimpsest (Doolittle), **Supp. I Part 1:** 259, 268, 269, 270–271
Palimpsest (Vidal), **Supp. X:** 186
"Palingenesis" (Longfellow), **II:** 498
Pal Joey (O'Hara), **III:** 361, 367–368

"Pal Joey" stories (O'Hara), **III:** 361
Pallbearers Envying the One Who Rides (Dobyns), **Supp. XIII:** 89
"Palm, The" (Merwin), **Supp. III Part 1:** 355
Palmer, Charles, **II:** 111
Palmer, Elihu, **Supp. I Part 2:** 520
Palmer, George Herbert, **Supp. XIV:** 197
Palmer, Michael, **Supp. IV Part 2:** 421; **Supp. XVI:** 284; **Supp. XVII:** 240
Palmer, Samuel, **Supp. XV:** 81
Palmerston, Lord, **I:** 15
Palm-of-the-Hand-Stories (Kawabata), **Supp. XV:** 186
"Palo Alto: The Marshes" (Hass), **Supp. VI:** 100
Palpable God, A: Thirty Stories Translated from the Bible with an Essay on the Origins and Life of Narrative (Price), **Supp. VI:** 262, 267
Palubinskas, Helen, **Supp. X:** 292
Pamela (Richardson), **Supp. V:** 127
Pamela's First Musical (Wasserstein), **Supp. XV:** 333
Panache de bouquets (Komunyakaa; Cadieux, trans.), **Supp. XIII:** 127
Pan-African movement, **Supp. II Part 1:** 172, 175
Pandaemonium (Epstein), **Supp. XII:** 161, **172–173**
"Pandora" (Adams), **I:** 5
Pandora: New Tales of Vampires (Rice), **Supp. VII:** 295
Panek, LeRoy, **Supp. XIV:** 27
"Pangolin, The" (Moore), **III:** 210
Panic: A Play in Verse (MacLeish), **III:** 2, 20
Panic in Needle Park (film), **Supp. IV Part 1:** 198
Pantagruel (Rabelais), **II:** 112
"Pantaloon in Black" (Faulkner), **II:** 71
Panther and the Lash, The (Hughes), **Retro. Supp. I:** 204, 211; **Supp. I Part 1:** 342–344, 345–346
"Panthers, The" (Southern), **Supp. XI:** 295
"Pan *versus* Moses" (Ozick), **Supp. V:** 262
"Paolo Castelnuovo" (Everwine), **Supp. XV:** 83–84
"Papa and Mama Dance, The" (Sexton), **Supp. II Part 2:** 688
"Papa Who Wakes Up Tired in the Dark" (Cisneros), **Supp. VII:** 62
Pape, Greg, **Supp. V:** 180; **Supp. XIII:** 312; **Supp. XV:** 73
"Paper Dolls Cut Out of a Newspaper" (Simic), **Supp. VIII:** 282
"Paper House, The" (Mailer), **III:** 42–43
Paper Lion (film, March), **Supp. XVI:** 242
Paper Lion: Confessions of a Last-String Quarterback (Plimpton), **Supp. XVI: 242–243**
Papernick, Jon, **Supp. XVII:** 50
Papers on Literature and Art (Fuller), **Supp. II Part 1:** 292, 299
Papini, Giovanni, **Supp. XVI:** 195
Papp, Joseph, **Supp. IV Part 1:** 234
"Paprika Johnson" (Barnes), **Supp. III Part 1:** 33
"Par" (Bausch), **Supp. VII:** 54
"Parable in the Later Novels of Henry James" (Ozick), **Supp. V:** 257
"Parable of the Gift" (Glück), **Supp. V:** 89
"Parable of the Hostages" (Glück), **Supp. V:** 89
"Parable of the King" (Glück), **Supp. V:** 89
Parable of the Sower (O. Butler), **Supp. XIII: 66–67,** 69
Parable of the Talents (O. Butler), **Supp. XIII:** 61,**Supp. XIII:** 66, **67–69**
"Parable of the Trellis" (Glück), **Supp. V:** 89
Parachutes & Kisses (Jong), **Supp. V:** 115, 123, 125–126, 129
"Parade of Painters" (Swenson), **Supp. IV Part 2:** 645
"Paradigm, The" (Tate), **IV:** 128
Paradise (Barthelme), **Supp. IV Part 1:** 52
"Paradise" (Doty), **Supp. XI:** 123
Paradise Lost (Milton), **I:** 137; **II:** 168, 549; **IV:** 126; **Supp. XII:** 173, 297; **Supp. XV:** 181
Paradise Lost (Odets), **Supp. II Part 2:** 530, 531, 538–539, 550
"Paradise of Bachelors and the Tartarus of Maids, The" (Melville), **III:** 91
Paradise of Bombs, The (Sanders), **Supp. XVI:** 265, 272–273
Paradise Poems (Stern), **Supp. IX: 293–294,** 295
Paradiso (Dante), **Supp. IX:** 50
"Paradoxes and Oxymorons" (Ashbery), **Supp. III Part 1:** 23–24
Paradox of Progressive Thought, The (Noble), **Supp. I Part 2:** 650
Paragon, The (Knowles), **Supp. XII:** 249
"Paragraphs" (Carruth), **Supp. XVI:** 52–53
"Parameters" (Dunn), **Supp. XI:** 154
"Paraphrase" (Crane), **I:** 391–392, 393
"Pardon, The" (Wilbur), **Supp. III Part 2:** 544, 550
Paredes, Américo, **Supp. XIII:** 225
Paredes, Raymund A., **Supp. XIII:** 320, 321
"Parentage" (Stafford), **Supp. XI:** 321, 322
Parentheses: An Autobiographical Journey (Neugeboren), **Supp. XVI:** 217, 218, 219, 221, 226
"Parents" (F. Barthelme), **Supp. XI:** 34
"Parents Taking Shape" (Karr), **Supp. XI:** 243
"Parents' Weekend: Camp Kenwood" (Kenyon), **Supp. VII:** 169
Pareto, Vilfredo, **II:** 577
Paretsky, Sara?/, **Supp. XIV:** 26
Paretsky, Sarah?/, **Supp. IV Part 2:** 462
Parini, Jay, **Supp. X:** 17
"Paris" (Stern), **Supp. IX:** 300
"Paris, 7 A.M." (Bishop), **Retro. Supp. II:** 41, 42; **Supp. I Part 1:** 85, 89
Paris France (Stein), **IV:** 45
Park, Robert, **IV:** 475
"Park Bench" (Hughes), **Supp. I Part 1:** 331–332
"Park City" (Beattie), **Supp. V:** 35
Park City (Beattie), **Supp. V:** 24, 35–36
Parker, Charlie, **Supp. I Part 1:** 59; **Supp. X:** 240, 242, 246; **Supp. XIII:** 129
Parker, Dorothy, **Retro. Supp. II:** 327; **Supp. IV Part 1:** 353; **Supp. IX:** 62, 114, **189–206; Supp. X:** 164; **Supp. XI:** 28; **Supp. XVIII:** 242, 246, 252
Parker, Emily, **Supp. XVIII:** 102
Parker, Idella, **Supp. X:** 232, 234–235
Parker, Muriel, **Supp. IX:** 232
Parker, Patricia, **Supp. XV:** 242
Parker, Robert B., **Supp. IV Part 1:** 135, 136
Parker, Theodore, **Supp. I Part 1:** 38; **Supp. I Part 2:** 518
Parker, Thomas, **Supp. I Part 1:** 102
"Parker's Back" (O'Connor), **III:** 348, 352, 358
Parkes, Henry Bamford, **Supp. I Part 2:** 617
Park-Fuller, Linda, **Supp. XIII:** 297
Parkman, Francis, **II:** 278, 310, 312; **IV:** 179, 309; **Supp. I Part 2:** 420, 479, 481–482, 486, 487, 493, 498; **Supp. II Part 2: 589–616**
Parkman Reader, The (Morison, ed.), **Supp. I Part 2:** 494
Parks, Gordon, Sr., **Supp. XI:** 17
Parks, Larry, **Supp. I Part 1:** 295
Parks, Rosa, **Supp. I Part 1:** 342
"Park Street Cemetery, The" (Lowell), **II:** 537, 538
Par le Détroit (cantata) (Bowles), **Supp. IV Part 1:** 82
Parliament of Fowls, The (Chaucer), **III:** 492
Parmenides (Plato), **II:** 10
Parnassus (Emerson), **II:** 8, 18
Parnell, Charles Stewart, **II:** 129, 137
Parole (film), **Supp. XIII:** 166
Parole Fixer (film), **Supp. XIII:** 170
Parrington, Vernon Louis, **I:** 254, 517, 561; **III:** 335, 606; **IV:** 173; **Supp. I Part 2:** 484, 640
Parrish, Dillwyn, **Supp. XVII:** 83–84, 90
Parrish, Robert, **Supp. XI:** 307
"Parrot, The" (Merrill), **Supp. III Part 1:** 320
"Parsley" (Dove), **Supp. IV Part 1:** 245, 246
Parson, Annie, **Supp. I Part 2:** 655
Parsons, Elsie Clews, **I:** 231, 235
Parsons, Ian, **Supp. IX:** 95
Parsons, Louella, **Supp. XII:** 173
Parsons, Talcott, **Supp. I Part 2:** 648
Parsons, Theophilus, **II:** 396, 504; **Retro. Supp. II:** 134; **Supp. I Part 1:** 155
"Parthian Shot, The" (Hammett), **Supp. IV Part 1:** 343
Partial Payments: Essays on Writers and Their Lives (Epstein), **Supp. XIV:** 111
Partial Portraits (James), **II:** 336
Partial Truth (Nelson), **Supp. XVIII: 175–176,** 178
Parties (Van Vechten), **Supp. II Part 2:** 739, 747–749

"Parting" (Kunitz), **Supp. III Part 1:** 263
"Parting Gift" (Wylie), **Supp. I Part 2:** 714
"Parting Glass, The" (Freneau), **Supp. II Part 1:** 273
"Partings" (Hogan), **Supp. IV Part 1:** 413
Partington, Blanche, **I:** 199
Partisans (Matthiessen), **Supp. V:** 201
"Partner, The" (Roethke), **III:** 541–542
Partners, The (Auchincloss), **Supp. IV Part 1:** 31, 34
"Part of a Letter" (Wilbur), **Supp. III Part 2:** 551
Part of Speech, A (Brodsky), **Supp. VIII:** 22
"Part of the Bee's Body Embedded in the Flesh, The" (C. Frost), **Supp. XV:** 105, 107
"Part of the Story" (Dobyns), **Supp. XIII:** 79
Parton, Sara, **Retro. Supp. I:** 246
Partridge, Jeffrey F., **Supp. XV:** 219
Partridge, John, **II:** 110, 111
"Parts of a Journal" (Gordon), **Supp. IV Part 1:** 310
Parts of a World (Stevens), **Retro. Supp. I: 305–306,** 307, 309, 313
"Party, The" (Dunbar), **Supp. II Part 1:** 198, 205–206
"Party, The" (Taylor), **Supp. V:** 315
Party at Jack's, The (Wolfe), **IV:** 451–452, 469
"Party Down at the Square, A" (Ellison), **Retro. Supp. II:** 124
Pascal, Blaise, **II:** 8, 159; **III:** 292, 301, 304, 428; **Retro. Supp. I:** 326, 330
"Paskudnyak" (Pilcer), **Supp. XVII:** 50
"Pass, The" (Neugeboren), **Supp. XVI:** 225
"Passage" (Crane), **I:** 391
"Passage in the Life of Mr. John Oakhurst, A" (Harte), **Supp. II Part 1:** 353–354
"Passages" (Duncan), **Supp. XVI:** 287
"Passages from a Relinquished Work" (Hawthorne), **Retro. Supp. I:** 150
Passages toward the Dark (McGrath), **Supp. X:** 126, 127
"Passage to India" (Whitman), **IV:** 348
Passage to India, A (Forster), **II:** 600; **Supp. XVIII:** 143
Passaro, Vince, **Supp. X:** 167, 302, 309, 310
"Passenger Pigeons" (Jeffers), **Supp. II Part 2:** 437
Passin, Herbert, **Supp. XIII:** 337
Passing (Larsen), **Supp. XVIII:** 119, 123, **127–130**
"Passing Beauty" (C. Frost), **Supp. XV:** 97
"Passing of Grandison, The" (Chesnutt), **Supp. XIV:** 62, **66–69**
"Passing of Sister Barsett, The" (Jewett), **Retro. Supp. II:** 138–139, 143
"Passing Show, The" (Bierce), **I:** 208
"Passing Through" (Kunitz), **Supp. III Part 1:** 265
"Passion, The" (Barnes), **Supp. III Part 1:** 36
"Passion, The" (Merwin), **Supp. III Part 1:** 343
Passionate, Accurate Story, The: Making Your Heart's Truth into Literature (C. Bly), **Supp. XVI: 41–42**
"Passionate Pilgrim, A" (James), **II:** 322, 323–324; **Retro. Supp. I:** 218
Passionate Pilgrim, A (James), **II:** 324; **Retro. Supp. I:** 219
Passion Play (Kosinski), **Supp. VII:** 215, 225–226
Passions of Uxport, The (Kumin), **Supp. IV Part 2:** 444
"Passive Resistance" (McKay), **Supp. X:** 133
Passport to the War (Kunitz), **Supp. III Part 1:** 261–264
Passwords (Stafford), **Supp. XI: 329–330**
"Past, The" (Bryant), **Supp. I Part 1:** 157, 170
"Past, The" (Kinnell), **Supp. III Part 1:** 254
Past, The (Kinnell), **Supp. III Part 1:** 235, 253–254
Past and Present (Carlyle), **Supp. I Part 2:** 410
Pasternak, Boris, **II:** 544
"Pastiches et Pistaches" (Van Vechten), **Supp. II Part 2:** 732
"Past Is the Present, The" (Moore), **III:** 199–200
"Pastoral" (Carver), **Supp. III Part 1:** 137, 146
"Pastoral" (Dove), **Supp. IV Part 1:** 249
"Pastoral Hat, A" (Stevens), **IV:** 91
"Pastor Dowe at Tacaté" (Bowles), **Supp. IV Part 1:** 87
Pastorela (ballet) (Kirstein), **Supp. IV Part 1:** 83
Pastorius, Francis Daniel, **Supp. I Part 2:** 700
"Pasture Poems" (Kumin), **Supp. IV Part 2:** 446
Pastures of Heaven, The (Steinbeck), **IV:** 51
Patch, Jerry, **Supp. XVIII:** 38
Patchen, Kenneth, **Supp. III Part 2:** 625
Patchett, Ann, **Supp. XII: 307–324**
Patchwork Planet (Lethem), **Supp. XVIII:** 150
Pater, Walter, **I:** 51, 272, 476; **II:** 27, 338; **III:** 604; **IV:** 74; **Retro. Supp. I:** 56, 79; **Retro. Supp. II:** 326; **Supp. I Part 2:** 552; **Supp. IX:** 66
Paterna (Mather), **Supp. II Part 2:** 451
"Paterson" (Ginsberg), **Supp. II Part 1:** 314–315, 321, 329
Paterson (W. C. Williams), **I:** 62, 446; **IV:** 418–423; **Retro. Supp. I:** 209, 284, 413, 419, 421, **424–428,** 428, 429, 430; **Retro. Supp. II:** 321, 328; **Supp. II Part 2:** 557, 564, 625; **Supp. VIII:** 275, 305; **Supp. XIV:** 96; **Supp. XV:** 264, 349
Paterson, Book Five (W. C. Williams), **IV:** 422–423
Paterson, Book One (W. C. Williams), **IV:** 421–422
Paterson, Isabel, **Supp. IV Part 2:** 524
Paterson, Part Three (W. C. Williams), **IV:** 420–421
Pat Garrett and Billy the Kid (film, Peckinpah), **Supp. XVIII:** 27
"Path, The" (Bryant), **Supp. I Part 1:** 169
Pathfinder, The (Cooper), **I:** 349, 350, 355
Pat Hobby Stories, The (Fitzgerald), **Retro. Supp. I:** 114
"Pathos of Low Life, The" (Hapgood), **Supp. XVII:** 103
"Patience of a Saint, The" (Humphrey), **Supp. IX:** 106
Patinkin, Mandy, **Supp. IV Part 1:** 236
Paton, Alan, **Supp. VIII:** 126
"Patria Mia" (Pound), **Retro. Supp. I:** 284
Patria Mia (Pound), **III:** 460–461; **Retro. Supp. I:** 284
"Patriarch, The" (Alvares), **Supp. V:** 11
Patrimony: A True Story (P. Roth), **Retro. Supp. II:** 279, 280, 291; **Supp. III Part 2:** 427
Patriot, The (Buck), **Supp. II Part 1:** 122–123
Patriot, The (Connell), **Supp. XIV:** 94–95
Patriotic Gore: Studies in the Literature of the American Civil War (Wilson), **III:** 588; **IV:** 430, 438, 443, 445–445, 446; **Supp. VIII:** 100
"Patriotic Thing, The" (Ryan as Quin), **Supp. XVIII:** 229
"Patriots, The/Los Patriotas" (Kingsolver), **Supp. VII:** 209
Patron Saint of Liars, The (Patchett), **Supp. XII:** 307, 310, **311–314,** 317
Pattee, Fred L., **II:** 456
Patten, Gilbert, **II:** 423
Patten, Simon, **Supp. I Part 2:** 640
Patternmaster (O. Butler), **Supp. XIII:** 61, 62, 63
Patternmaster Series (O. Butler), **Supp. XIII: 62–63**
Pattern Recognition (W. Gibson), **Supp. XVI:** 124, **130–131**
"Patterns" (Lowell), **II:** 524
Patterson, Floyd, **III:** 38
Patterson, William M., **Supp. I Part 1:** 265
Patton, General George, **III:** 575; **Supp. I Part 2:** 664
"Patty-Cake, Patty-Cake...A Memoir" (Apple), **Supp. XVII:** 7
Paul, Saint, **I:** 365; **II:** 15, 494; **IV:** 122, 154, 164, 335; **Retro. Supp. I:** 247; **Supp. I Part 1:** 188
Paul, Sherman, **I:** 244; **IV:** 179
"Paula Becker to Clara Westhoff" (Rich), **Supp. I Part 2:** 573–574
"Paula Gunn Allen" (Ruppert), **Supp. IV Part 1:** 321
Paul Bowles: Romantic Savage (Caponi), **Supp. IV Part 1:** 95
Paulding, James Kirke, **I:** 344; **II:** 298, 299, 303; **Supp. I Part 1:** 157
Paul Jones (Hapgood), **Supp. XVII:** 100–101

Paul Marchand, F.M.C. (Chesnutt), **Supp. XIV:** 76
"Paul Monette: The Brink of Summer's End" (film), **Supp. X:** 152
"Paul Revere" (Longfellow), **II:** 489, 501
"Paul Revere's Ride" (Longfellow), **Retro. Supp. II:** 163
"Paul's Case" (Cather), **I:** 314–315; **Retro. Supp. I:** 3, 5
Paulsen, Friedrich, **III:** 600
"Pauper Witch of Grafton, The" (Frost), **Retro. Supp. II:** 42
"Pause by the Water, A" (Merwin), **Supp. III Part 1:** 354
"Pavane for the Nursery, A" (W. J. Smith), **Supp. XIII:** 335
"Pavement, The" (Olson), **Supp. II Part 2:** 571
Pavilion of Women (Buck), **Supp. II Part 1:** 125–126
"Pawnbroker, The" (Kumin), **Supp. IV Part 2:** 442, 443–444, 451
Pawnbroker, The (Wallant), **Supp. XVI:** 220
"Paying Dues" (Bass), **Supp. XVI:** 16
Payne, Daniel, **Supp. V:** 202
Payne, John Howard, **II:** 309
Paz, Octavio, **Supp. III Part 2:** 630; **Supp. VIII:** 272; **Supp. XI:** 191; **Supp. XIII:** 223
P. D. Kimerakov (Epstein), **Supp. XII:** 160, **162**
Peabody, Elizabeth, **Retro. Supp. I:** 155–156, 225
Peabody, Francis G., **III:** 293; **Supp. I Part 1:** 5
Peabody, Josephine Preston, **III:** 507
Peaceable Kingdom, The (Prose), **Supp. XVI:** 256–257
Peace and Bread in Time of War (Addams), **Supp. I Part 1:** 21, 22–23
"Peace Between Black and White in the United States" (Locke), **Supp. XIV:** 205
Peace Breaks Out (Knowles), **Supp. XII:** 249
"Peace March, The" (Simpson), **Supp. IX:** 279
"Peace of Cities, The" (Wilbur), **Supp. III Part 2:** 545
"Peaches——Six in a Tin Box, Sarajevo" (Cisneros), **Supp. VII:** 67
Peacock, Doug, **Supp. VIII:** 38; **Supp. XIII:** 12
Peacock, Gibson, **Supp. I Part 1:** 360
Peacock, Molly, **Supp. XVII:** 74
"Peacock, The" (Merrill), **Supp. III Part 1:** 320
Peacock, Thomas Love, **Supp. I Part 1:** 307; **Supp. VIII:** 125
"Peacock Room, The" (Hayden), **Supp. II Part 1:** 374–375
Pearce, Richard, **Supp. IX:** 254
Pearce, Roy Harvey, **II:** 244; **Supp. I Part 1:** 111, 114; **Supp. I Part 2:** 475
Pearl, The (Steinbeck), **IV:** 51, 62–63
Pearlman, Daniel, **III:** 479
Pearlman, Mickey, **Supp. XIII:** 293, 306
Pearl of Orr's Island, The (Stowe), **Supp. I Part 2:** 592–593, 595
"Pearls" (A. Finch), **Supp. XVII:** 72
Pears, Peter, **II:** 586; **Supp. IV Part 1:** 84
Pearson, Drew, **Supp. XIV:** 126
Pearson, Norman Holmes, **Supp. I Part 1:** 259, 260, 273
"Pear Tree" (C. Frost), **Supp. XV:** 105
"Peasants' Way O' Thinkin'" (McKay), **Supp. X:** 133
Pease, Donald E., **Supp. IV Part 2:** 687
Peck, Gregory, **Supp. VIII:** 128, 129; **Supp. XII:** 160, 173
Peckinpah, Sam, **Supp. XI:** 306; **Supp. XVIII:** 27
"Peck of Gold, A" (Frost), **II:** 155
Peculiar Treasures: A Biblical Who's Who (Buechner), **Supp. XII:** 53
"Pedal Point" (Francis), **Supp. IX:** 87
Pedersen, Inge, **Supp. XVIII:** 179
"Pedersen Kid, The" (Gass), **Supp. VI:** 83
"Pedigree, The" (Creeley), **Supp. IV Part 1:** 150
Peebles, Melvin Van, **Supp. XI:** 17; **Supp. XVI:** 144
"Peed Onk" (Moore). *See* "People Like That Are the Only People Here: Canonical Babbling in Peed Onk" (Moore)
"Peeler, The" (O'Connor), **Retro. Supp. II:** 225
Peich, Michael, **Supp. XV:** 113, 117
Peikoff, Leonard, **Supp. IV Part 2:** 520, 526, 529
Peirce, Charles Sanders, **II:** 20, 352–353; **III:** 599; **Supp. I Part 2:** 640; **Supp. III Part 2:** 626
Pelagius, **III:** 295
"Pelican, The" (Merrill), **Supp. III Part 1:** 320
"Pelican, The" (Wharton), **IV:** 310; **Retro. Supp. I:** 364
Pellacchia, Michael, **Supp. XIII:** 16
Peltier, Leonard, **Supp. V:** 212
"Pen and Paper and a Breath of Air" (Oliver), **Supp. VII:** 245
Pence, Amy, **Supp. XV:** 211, 223
"Pencil, The" (Chandler), **Supp. IV Part 1:** 135
Pencillings by the Way (Willis), **II:** 313; **Supp. XVIII:** 12
"Pencils" (Sandburg), **III:** 592
Pendleton, Devon, **Supp. XVIII:** 151
"Pendulum" (Bradbury and Hasse), **Supp. IV Part 1:** 102
"Penelope's Song" (Glück), **Supp. V:** 89
Penhally (Gordon), **II:** 197, 199, 201–203, 204
"Penis" (McClatchy), **Supp. XII:** 266–267
Penitent, The (Singer), **Retro. Supp. II: 309–310,** 313
Penn, Robert, **I:** 489
Penn, Sean, **Supp. XI:** 107
Penn, Thomas, **II:** 118
Penn, William, **Supp. I Part 2:** 683
Pennebaker, D. A., **Supp. XVIII:** 19, 26
"Pennsylvania Pilgrim, The" (Whittier), **Supp. I Part 2:** 700
"Pennsylvania Planter, The" (Freneau), **Supp. II Part 1:** 268
Penny, Rob, **Supp. VIII:** 330
"Penny, The" (D. West), **Supp. XVIII:** 283–284
Penrod (Tarkington), **III:** 223
"Penseroso, Il" (Milton), **Supp. XIV:** 8
Pentagon of Power, The (Mumford), **Supp. II Part 2:** 498
Pentimento (Hellman), **Supp. I Part 1:** 280, 292–294, 296; **Supp. IV Part 1:** 12; **Supp. VIII:** 243
"Peonies at Dusk" (Kenyon), **Supp. VII:** 171
People, The (Glaspell), **Supp. III Part 1:** 179
People, Yes, The (Sandburg), **III:** 575, 589, 590, 591
"PEOPLE BURNING, THE" (Baraka), **Supp. II Part 1:** 49
"People in Hell Just Want a Drink of Water" (Proulx), **Supp. VII:** 263
"People Like That Are the Only People Here: Canonical Babbling in Peed Onk" (Moore), **Supp. X:** 168, **178–179**
People Live Here: Selected Poems 1949–1983 (Simpson), **Supp. IX:** 269, 277
"People Next Door, The" (Simpson), **Supp. IX:** 279
People of the Abyss, The (London), **II:** 465–466
"People on the Roller Coaster, The" (Hardwick), **Supp. III Part 1:** 196
People Shall Continue, The (Ortiz), **Supp. IV Part 2:** 510
"People's Surroundings" (Moore), **III:** 201, 202, 203
"People *v.* Abe Lathan, Colored, The" (Caldwell), **I:** 309
"Peppermint Lounge Revisited, The" (Wolfe), **Supp. III Part 2:** 571
Pepys, Samuel, **Supp. I Part 2:** 653
"Perch'io non spero di tornar giammai" (Cavalcanti), **Supp. III Part 2:** 623
Percy, Thomas, **Supp. XIV:** 2
Percy, Walker, **Supp. III Part 1: 383–400; Supp. IV Part 1:** 297; **Supp. V:** 334; **Supp. X:** 42; **Supp. XIV:** 21
Percy, William, **Supp. V:** 334
Percy, William Alexander, **Retro. Supp. I:** 341
Peregrin, Tony, **Supp. XV:** 69
"Peregrine" (Wylie), **Supp. I Part 2:** 712–713, 714
Perelman, Bob, **Supp. XII:** 23
Perelman, S. J., **IV:** 286; **Retro. Supp. I:** 342; **Retro. Supp. II:** 321, 322, 325, 326, 327, 336; **Supp. IV Part 1:** 353; **Supp. XI:** 66
Perestroika (Kushner), **Supp. IX:** 141, 142, 145
Péret, Benjamin, **Supp. VIII:** 272
Peretz, Isaac Loeb, **IV:** 1, 3; **Retro. Supp. II:** 299
Pérez Galdós, Benito, **II:** 275
Perfect Analysis Given by a Parrot, A (T. Williams), **IV:** 395
"Perfect Couple, The" (Nelson), **Supp. XVIII:** 173

"Perfect Day for Bananafish, A" (Salinger), **III:** 563–564, 571
Perfect Ganesh, A (McNally), **Supp. XIII: 202–203,** 208, 209
"Perfect Knight, The" (Chandler), **Supp. IV Part 1:** 120
Perfect Party, The (Gurney), **Supp. V:** 100, 105, 106–107
"Perfect Things" (F. Barthelme), **Supp. XI:** 30, 33–34
"Performance, The" (Dickey), **Supp. IV Part 1:** 178–179, 181
"Perfume" (Mora), **Supp. XIII:** 218
"Perhaps the World Ends Here" (Harjo), **Supp. XII:** 228, 231
Perhaps Women (Anderson), **I:** 114
Pericles (Shakespeare), **I:** 585; **Supp. III Part 2:** 624, 627, 629
Period of Adjustment (T. Williams), **IV:** 382, 386, 387, 388, 389, 390, 392, 393, 394, 397
"Period Pieces from the Mid-Thirties" (Agee), **I:** 28
"Periphery" (Ammons), **Supp. VII:** 28
Perkins, David, **Supp. I Part 2:** 459, 475; **Supp. XV:** 185
Perkins, Maxwell, **I:** 252, 289, 290; **II:** 87, 93, 95, 252; **IV:** 452, 455, 457, 458, 461, 462, 463, 469; **Retro. Supp. I:** 101, 105, 108, 109, 110, 113, 114, 178; **Supp. IX:** 57, 58, 60, 232; **Supp. X:** 219, 224, 225, 229, 230, 233; **Supp. XI:** 218, 227
Perlès, Alfred, **III:** 177, 183, 187, 189
Perloff, Marjorie, **Supp. I Part 2:** 539, 542; **Supp. IV Part 1:** 68; **Supp. IV Part 2:** 420, 424, 432
Permanence and Change (Burke), **I:** 274
Permanent Errors (Price), **Supp. VI:** 261
"Permanent Traits of the English National Genius" (Emerson), **II:** 18
Permit Me Voyage (Agee), **I:** 25, 27
"Perosa Canavese" (Everwine), **Supp. XV:** 84
Perrault, Charles, **IV:** 266; **Supp. I Part 2:** 622
Perrin, Noel, **Supp. XVI:** 34
Perrins, Carol. *See* Frost, Carol
Perry, Anne, **Supp. V:** 335
Perry, Bliss, **I:** 243
Perry, Donna, **Supp. IV Part 1:** 322, 327, 335
Perry, Dr. William, **II:** 395, 396
Perry, Edgar A., **III:** 410
Perry, Lincoln, **Supp. V:** 24, 33
Perry, Matthew C., **Supp. I Part 2:** 494–495
Perry, Patsy Brewington, **Supp. I Part 1:** 66
Perry, Phyllis Alesia, **Supp. XVIII:** 96
Perry, Ralph Barton, **I:** 224; **II:** 356, 362, 364; **Supp. XIV:** 197
Perse, St.-John, **III:** 12, 13, 14, 17; **Supp. III Part 1:** 14; **Supp. IV Part 1:** 82; **Supp. XIII:** 344; **Supp. XV:** 178
"Persephone in Hell" (Dove), **Supp. IV Part 1:** 250, 251
"Persimmons" (L.-Y. Lee), **Supp. XV:** 211, 213
"Persistence of Desire, The" (Updike), **IV:** 222–223, 228
"Persistence of Poetry, The" (Bynner), **Supp. XV:** 49
"Persistences" (Hecht), **Supp. X: 68–69**
Person, Place, and Thing (Shapiro), **Supp. II Part 2:** 702, 705
Personae of Ezra Pound (Pound), **III:** 458
Personae: The Collected Poems (Pound), **Retro. Supp. I:** 285, 286; **Supp. I Part 1:** 255; **Supp. XVII:** 32
"Personal" (Stern), **Supp. IX:** 299
"Personal and Occasional Pieces" (Welty), **Retro. Supp. I:** 355
"Personal and the Individual, The" (L. Michaels), **Supp. XVI:** 201
Personal Injuries (Turow), **Supp. XVII: 219–220,** 221, 223
"Personalities" (column, Briggs), **Supp. XVIII:** 15
Personal Narrative (Edwards), **I:** 545, 552, 553, 561, 562; **Supp. I Part 2:** 700
Personal Recollection of Joan of Arc (Twain), **IV:** 208
"Personals" (Didion), **Supp. IV Part 1:** 200
"Personism" (O'Hara), **Supp. XV:** 181
Persons and Places (Santayana), **III:** 615
Persons in Hiding (film), **Supp. XIII:** 170
Persons in Hiding (Hoover), **Supp. XIII:** 170
Person Sitting in Darkness, A (Twain), **IV:** 208
"Perspective" (Francis), **Supp. IX:** 78
"Perspective: Anniversary D-Day" (Karr), **Supp. XI:** 241
Perspectives by Incongruity (Burke), **I:** 284–285
"Perspectives: Is It Out of Control?" (Gleason), **Supp. IX:** 16
Perspectives on Cormac McCarthy (Arnold and Luce, eds.), **Supp. VIII:** 189
Pertes et Fracas (McCoy), **Supp. XIII:** 175
"Peruvian Child" (Mora), **Supp. XIII:** 218
Peseroff, Joyce, **Supp. IV Part 1:** 71
"Pestilence" (Nelson), **Supp. XVIII:** 186
"Peter" (Cather), **Retro. Supp. I:** 4
"Peter" (Moore), **III:** 210, 212
Peter, Saint, **III:** 341, 346; **IV:** 86, 294
Peterkin, Julia, **Supp. I Part 1:** 328
"Peter Klaus" (German tale), **II:** 306
Peter Pan (Barrie), **Supp. XV:** 319
"Peter Parley" works (Goodrich), **Supp. I Part 1:** 38
"Peter Pendulum" (Poe), **III:** 425
"Peter Quince at the Clavier" (Stevens), **IV:** 81, 82
Peter Rabbit tales, **Retro. Supp. I:** 335
Peters, Cora, **Supp. I Part 2:** 468
Peters, Jacqueline, **Supp. XII:** 225
Peters, Margot, **Supp. VIII:** 252
Peters, Robert, **Supp. XIII:** 114
Peters, S. H. (pseudonym). *See* Henry, O.
Peters, Timothy, **Supp. XI:** 39
"Peter's Avocado" (Rodriguez), **Supp. XIV:** 308–309
Petersen, David, **Supp. XIII:** 2
Petersen, Donald, **Supp. V:** 180; **Supp. XV:** 74, 92
Peterson, Dorothy, **Supp. XVIII:** 131, 132
Peterson, Houston, **I:** 60
Peterson, Roger Tory, **Supp. V:** 202
Peterson, Virgilia, **Supp. IV Part 1:** 30
Peter Whiffle: His Life and Works (Van Vechten), **Supp. II Part 2:** 728–729, 731, 735, 738–741, 749
"Petey and Yotsee and Mario" (H. Roth), **Supp. IX:** 234
"Petition, A" (Winters), **Supp. II Part 2:** 785
"'Pet Negro' System, The" (Hurston), **Supp. VI:** 159
"Petra and Its Surroundings" (Frost), **Retro. Supp. I:** 124
Petrarch, **I:** 176; **II:** 590; **III:** 4
"Petrarch, Shakespeare, and the Blues" (C. Frost), **Supp. XV:** 92, 104, 105
"Petrified Man" (Welty), **IV:** 262; **Retro. Supp. I:** 345, 351
"Petrified Man, The" (Twain), **IV:** 195
"Petrified Woman, The" (Gordon), **II:** 199
Petronius, **III:** 174, 179
Petry, Ann, **Supp. VIII:** 214; **Supp. XI:** 6, 85; **Supp. XVIII:** 286
Pet Sematary (King), **Supp. V:** 138, 143, 152
Pettengill, Richard, **Supp. VIII:** 341, 345, 348
Pettingell, Phoebe, **Supp. XV:** 251, 256–257, 262
Pettis, Joyce, **Supp. XI:** 276, 277, 278, 281
Pfaelzer, Jean, **Supp. XVI:** 88, 90
Pfaff, Timothy, **Supp. V:** 166
Pfeil, Fred, **Supp. XIV:** 36
Pfister, Karin, **IV:** 467, 475
Phaedo (Plato), **II:** 10
Phaedra (Lowell and Barzun, trans.), **II:** 543–544
"Phantasia for Elvira Shatayev" (Rich), **Supp. I Part 2:** 570
Phantasms of War (Lowell), **II:** 512
"Phantom of the Movie Palace, The" (Coover), **Supp. V:** 50–51
Phantom Ship, The (Marryat), **Supp. XVII:** 55
"Pharaoh, The" (Kenyon), **Supp. VII:** 172
Pharr, Mary, **Supp. V:** 147
"Phases" (E. Stoddard), **Supp. XV:** 273
"Phases" (Stevens), **Retro. Supp. I:** 299
Phases of an Inferior Planet (Glasgow), **II:** 174–175
"Pheasant, The" (Carver), **Supp. III Part 1:** 146
Pheloung, Grant, **Supp. XI:** 39
Phelps, Elizabeth Stuart, **Retro. Supp. II:** 146; **Supp. XIII:** 141; **Supp. XVI:** 80
Phelps, Teresa Godwin, **Supp. VIII:** 128
"Phenomena and Laws of Race Contacts, The" (Locke), **Supp. XIV:** 210

"Phenomenology of Anger, The" (Rich), **Supp. I Part 2:** 562–563, 571
Phenomenology of Moral Experience, The (Mandelbaum), **I:** 61
"Phenomenology of *On Moral Fiction*" (Johnson), **Supp. VI:** 188
Phidias, **Supp. I Part 2:** 482
Philadelphia Fire (Wideman), **Supp. X:** 320, 334
Philadelphia Negro, The (Du Bois), **Supp. II Part 1:** 158, 163–164, 166
Philbrick, Thomas, **I:** 343
"Phil in the Marketplace" (Lethem), **Supp. XVIII:** 148
Philip, Jim, **Supp. XII:** 136
Philip, Prince, **Supp. X:** 108
"Philip of Pokanoket" (Irving), **II:** 303
Philippians (biblical book), **IV:** 154
"Philippine Conquest, The" (Masters), **Supp. I Part 2:** 456
"Philip Roth Reconsidered" (Howe), **Retro. Supp. II:** 286
"Philistinism and the Negro Writer" (Baraka), **Supp. II Part 1:** 39, 44
Phillips, Adam, **Supp. XII:** 97–98
Phillips, David Graham, **II:** 444; **Retro. Supp. II:** 101
Phillips, Gene D., **Supp. XI:** 306
Phillips, Jayne Anne, **Supp. XIV:** 21
Phillips, J. O. C., **Supp. I Part 1:** 19
Phillips, Robert, **Supp. XIII:** 335, 344
Phillips, Wendell, **Supp. I Part 1:** 103; **Supp. I Part 2:** 524
Phillips, Willard, **Supp. I Part 1:** 154, 155
Phillips, William, **Supp. VIII:** 156
Phillips, William L., **I:** 106
"Philosopher, The" (Farrell), **II:** 45
Philosopher of the Forest (pseudonym). *See* Freneau, Philip
Philosophes classiques, Les (Taine), **III:** 323
"Philosophical Cobbler, The" (Sanders), **Supp. XVI:** 268
"Philosophical Concepts and Practical Results" (James), **II:** 352
"Philosophical Investigation of Metaphor, A" (Gass), **Supp. VI:** 79
Philosophical Transactions (Watson), **II:** 114
"Philosophy, Or Something Like That" (P. Roth), **Supp. III Part 2:** 403
"Philosophy and Its Critics" (James), **II:** 360
"Philosophy and the Form of Fiction" (Gass), **Supp. VI:** 85
"Philosophy for People" (Emerson), **II:** 14
"Philosophy in Warm Weather" (Kenyon), **Supp. VII:** 168
"Philosophy Lesson" (Levine), **Supp. V:** 195
Philosophy of Alain Locke, The: Harlem Renaissance and Beyond (Harris, ed.), **Supp. XIV:** 196, 211–212
"Philosophy of Composition, The" (Poe), **III:** 416, 421; **Retro. Supp. II:** 266, 267, 271
Philosophy of Friedrich Nietzsche, The (Mencken), **III:** 102–103
"Philosophy of Handicap, A" (Bourne), **I:** 216, 218
"Philosophy of History" (Emerson), **II:** 11–12
Philosophy of Literary Form, The (Burke), **I:** 275, 281, 283, 291
Philosophy of the Human Mind, The (Stewart), **II:** 8
Philosophy: Who Needs It (Rand), **Supp. IV Part 2:** 517, 518, 527, 533
Philoxenes, **Supp. VIII:** 201
"Phineas" (Knowles), **Supp. XII:** 238–240
Phineas: Six Stories (Knowles), **Supp. XII:** 249
"Phocion" (Lowell), **II:** 536
Phoenix and the Turtle, The (Shakespeare), **I:** 284
"Phoenix Lyrics" (Schwartz), **Supp. II Part 2:** 665
"Phone Booths, The" (Jarman), **Supp. XVII:** 112–113
"Phony War Films" (Jones), **Supp. XI:** 217, 232
"Photograph: Migrant Worker, Parlier, California, 1967" (Levis), **Supp. XI:** 272
"Photograph of a Child on a Vermont Hillside" (Kenyon), **Supp. VII:** 168
"Photograph of My Mother as a Young Girl" (Gioia), **Supp. XV:** 119
"Photograph of the Girl" (Olds), **Supp. X:** 205
"Photograph of the Unmade Bed" (Rich), **Supp. I Part 2:** 558
Photographs (Welty), **Retro. Supp. I:** 343
"Photographs, The" (Barthelme), **Supp. IV Part 1:** 53
"Photography" (Levine), **Supp. V:** 194
Phyrrho, **Retro. Supp. I:** 247
"Physical Universe" (Simpson), **Supp. IX:** 278
"Physicist We Know, A" (Shields), **Supp. VII:** 310
"Physics and Cosmology in the Fiction of Tom Robbins" (Nadeau), **Supp. X:** 270
Physiologie du goût (Brillat-Savarin), **Supp. XVII:** 82, 86
Physiology of Taste, The; or, Meditations on Transcendent Gastronomy (Brillat-Savarin; M. F. K. Fisher, trans.), **Supp. XVII:** 86, 87, 91
"Physiology of Versification, The: Harmonies of Organic and Animal Life" (Holmes), **Supp. I Part 1:** 311
Physique de l'Amour (Gourmont), **III:** 467–468
Piaf, Edith, **Supp. IV Part 2:** 549
Piaget, Jean, **Supp. XIII:** 75
"Piano" (Lawrence), **Supp. XV:** 254
"Piano Fingers" (Mason), **Supp. VIII:** 146
Piano Lesson, The (Bearden), **Supp. VIII:** 342
Piano Lesson, The (Wilson), **Supp. VIII: 342–345**
Piatt, James, **Supp. I Part 2:** 420
Piatt, John J., **II:** 273
Piazza, Ben, **Supp. XIII:** 163
Piazza, Paul, **Supp. XIV:** 157, 160, 171
"Piazza de Spagna, Early Morning" (Wilbur), **Supp. III Part 2:** 553
Piazza Tales (Melville), **III:** 91
Picabia, Francis, **Retro. Supp. I:** 416; **Retro. Supp. II:** 331
Picasso (Stein), **IV:** 28, 32, 45
Picasso, Pablo, **I:** 429, 432, 440, 442, 445; **II:** 602; **III:** 197, 201, 470; **IV:** 26, 31, 32, 46, 87, 407, 436; **Retro. Supp. I:** 55, 63; **Supp. IV Part 1:** 81; **Supp. IX:** 66
Piccione, Anthony, **Supp. XV:** 212
"Piccola Comedia" (Wilbur), **Supp. III Part 2:** 561
Pickard, Samuel T., **Supp. I Part 2:** 682
Picked-Up Pieces (Updike), **Retro. Supp. I:** 320, 322, 323, 335
Picker, Lauren, **Supp. VIII:** 78, 83
Picker, Tobias, **Supp. XII:** 253
Pickford, Mary, **Retro. Supp. I:** 325; **Supp. I Part 2:** 391
"Picking and Choosing" (Moore), **III:** 205
Picnic Cantata (music) (Bowles), **Supp. IV Part 1:** 89
"Picnic Remembered" (Warren), **IV:** 240
Pictorial History of the Negro in America, A (Hughes), **Supp. I Part 1:** 345
"Picture, The" (Olson), **Supp. II Part 2:** 574
Picture Bride (Son), **Supp. X:** 292
"Picture I Want, The" (Olds), **Supp. X:** 209
Picture of Dorian Gray, The (Wilde), **Supp. IX:** 105
"Picture of Little J. A. in a Prospect of Flowers, A" (Ashbery), **Supp. III Part 1:** 3
Picture Palace (Theroux), **Supp. VIII:** 322
"Pictures at an Extermination" (Epstein), **Supp. XII:** 161
"Pictures from an Expedition" (Duffy), **Supp. IV Part 1:** 207
Pictures from an Institution (Jarrell), **II:** 367, 385
"Pictures from Brueghel" (W. C. Williams), **Retro. Supp. I:** 419
Pictures from Brueghel (W. C. Williams), **Retro. Supp. I:** 429–431
"Pictures of Columbus, the Genoese, The" (Freneau), **Supp. II Part 1:** 258
Pictures of Fidelman: An Exhibition (Malamud), **Supp. I Part 2:** 450–451
"Pictures of the Artist" (Malamud), **Supp. I Part 2:** 450
Pictures of the Floating World (Lowell), **II:** 521, 524–525
Pictures of Travel (Heine), **II:** 281
Picturesque America; or, the Land We Live In (Bryant, ed.), **Supp. I Part 1:** 158
"Picturesque Ghetto, The" (Hapgood), **Supp. XVII:** 101
"Picturesque: San Cristóbal de las Casas" (Mora), **Supp. XIII:** 218
Picture This (Heller), **Supp. IV Part 1:** 386, 388, 390–391

Picturing Will (Beattie), **Supp. V:** 29, 31–32, 34
"Pie" (X. J. Kennedy), **Supp. XV:** 170
"Piece, A" (Creeley), **Supp. IV Part 1:** 155, 156
"Piece of Moon, A" (Hogan), **Supp. IV Part 1:** 407
Piece of My Heart, A (Ford), **Supp. V:** 57, 58–61, 62
Piece of My Mind, A: Reflections at Sixty (Wilson), **IV:** 426, 430, 438, 441
"Piece of News, A" (Welty), **IV:** 263; **Retro. Supp. I:** 345, 346
Pieces (Creeley), **Supp. IV Part 1:** 155
Pieces and Pontifications (Mailer), **Retro. Supp. II:** 209–210
Pieces of the Frame (McPhee), **Supp. III Part 1:** 293
Pierce, Franklin, **II:** 225, 226, 227; **III:** 88; **Retro. Supp. I:** 150, 163, 164, 165
Pierce, Frederick, **Retro. Supp. I:** 136
Piercy, Josephine K., **Supp. I Part 1:** 103
"Pierian Handsprings" (column, Untermeyer), **Supp. XV:** 294
Pierpont, Claudia Roth, **Supp. X:** 192, 193, 196
Pierre et Jean (Maupassant), **I:** 421
Pierre: or The Ambiguities (Melville), **III:** 86–88, 89; **IV:** 194; **Retro. Supp. I:** 249, 253–254, 256; **Supp. I Part 2:** 579
Pierrepont, Sarah. *See* Edwards, Sarah
Pierrot qui pleure et Pierrot qui rit (Rostand), **II:** 515
Pig Cookies (Ríos), **Supp. IV Part 2:** 537, 550, 552–554
"Pigeon Feathers" (Updike), **Retro. Supp. I:** 318, 322, 323
Pigeon Feathers (Updike), **IV:** 214, 218, 219, 221–223, 226
"Pigeons" (Rilke), **II:** 544
"Pigeon Woman" (Swenson), **Supp. IV Part 2:** 644
Pigs in Heaven (Kingsolver), **Supp. VII:** 197, 199, 209–210
Pike County Ballads, The (Hay), **Supp. I Part 1:** 352
Piket, Vincent, **Supp. IV Part 1:** 24
Pilar San-Mallafre, Maria del, **Supp. V:** 40
Pilcer, Sonya, **Supp. XVII:** 50
"Pilgrim" (Freneau), **Supp. I Part 1:** 125
"Pilgrimage" (Ray), **Supp. XVIII:** 193
"Pilgrimage" (Sontag), **Supp. III Part 2:** 454–455
"Pilgrimage, The" (Maxwell), **Supp. VIII:** 169, 171
Pilgrimage of Festus, The (Aiken), **I:** 50, 55, 57
Pilgrimage of Henry James, The (Brooks), **I:** 240, 248, 250; **IV:** 433
Pilgrim at Tinker Creek (Dillard), **Supp. VI:** 22, **23–26,** 28, 29, **30–31,** 34; **Supp. XVIII:** 189
"Pilgrim Makers" (Lowell), **II:** 541
Pilgrim's Progress (Bunyan), **I:** 92; **II:** 15, 168, 572; **Supp. I Part 1:** 32, 38; **Supp. I Part 2:** 599
Pili's Wall (Levine), **Supp. V:** 178, 183–184
"Pillar of Fire" (Bradbury), **Supp. IV Part 1:** 113–114
Pillars of Hercules, The: A Grand Tour of the Mediterranean (Theroux), **Supp. VIII:** 325
"Pillow" (L.-Y. Lee), **Supp. XV:** 224
Pilot, The (Cooper), **I:** 335, 337, 339, 342–343, 350
"Pilot from the Carrier, A" (Jarrell), **II:** 374
"Pilots, Man Your Planes" (Jarrell), **II:** 374–375
"Pilots, The" (Levertov), **Supp. III Part 1:** 282
"Pimp's Revenge, A" (Malamud), **Supp. I Part 2:** 435, 450, 451
Pinball (Kosinski), **Supp. VII:** 215, 226
Pinchot, Gifford, **Supp. IX:** 184; **Supp. XIV:** 178
Pindar, **I:** 381; **II:** 543; **III:** 610
"Pine" (Dickey), **Supp. IV Part 1:** 183
Pine Barrens, The (McPhee), **Supp. III Part 1:** 298–301, 309
"Pineys, The" (Stern), **Supp. IX:** 288, 296
Pinget, Robert, **Supp. V:** 39
Pinhook: Finding Wholeness in a Fragmented Land (Ray), **Supp. XVIII:** 189, 192, 202–204
"Pink Dog" (Bishop), **Retro. Supp. II:** 48
Pinker, James B., **I:** 409; **Retro. Supp. I:** 231
Pinkerton, Jan, **Supp. V:** 323–324
"Pink Moon——The Pond" (Oliver), **Supp. VII:** 234
Pinktoes (C. Himes), **Supp. XVI: 142**
Pinocchio in Venice (Coover), **Supp. V:** 40, 51
Pinsker, Sanford, **Retro. Supp. II:** 23; **Supp. IX:** 293, 327; **Supp. V:** 272; **Supp. XI:** 251, 254, 317
Pinsky, Robert, **Retro. Supp. II:** 50; **Supp. IX:** 155, 158; **Supp. VI: 235–251; Supp. XIII:** 277, 285
Pinter, Harold, **I:** 71; **Supp. XIII:** 20, 196; **Supp. XIV:** 239; **Supp. XVI:** 207
Pinto, Ferdinand Mendes (pseudonym). *See* Briggs, Charles Frederick
Pinto and Sons (Epstein), **Supp. XII:** 170, **171–172**
Pinto letters (Briggs), **Supp. XVIII:** 3, **12–13**
Pioneers, The (Cooper), **I:** 336, 337, 339, 340–341, 342, 348; **II:** 313
Pioneers of France in the New World (Parkman), **Supp. III Part 2:** 599, 602
"Pioneers! O Pioneers!" (Whitman), **Retro. Supp. I:** 8
"Pioneer's Vision, The" (Larcom), **Supp. XIII:** 140
Pious and Secular America (Niebuhr), **III:** 308
Pipe Night (O'Hara), **III:** 361, 368
Piper, Dan, **Supp. IX:** 65
Pipers at the Gates of Dawn: The Wisdom of Children's Literature (Cott), **Supp. XVI:** 104
"Piper's Rocks" (Olson), **Supp. IV Part 1:** 153
"Pipistrelles" (B. Kelly), **Supp. XVII:** 129–130
Pipkin, Charles W., **Supp. XIV:** 3
Pippa Passes (Browning), **IV:** 128
Piquion, René, **Supp. I Part 1:** 346
Pirandello, Luigi, **Supp. IV Part 2:** 576, 588
Piranesi, Giovanni Battista, **Supp. XV:** 258
Pirate, The (Robbins), **Supp. XII:** 6
Pirate, The (Scott), **I:** 339
Pirates of Penzance, The (Gilbert and Sullivan), **IV:** 386
Pisan Cantos, The (Pound), **III:** 476; **Retro. Supp. I:** 140, 283, 285, 293; **Supp. III Part 1:** 63; **Supp. V:** 331, 337; **Supp. XIV:** 11; **Supp. XV:** 351
Piscator, Erwin, **IV:** 394
Pissarro, Camille, **I:** 478
"Pissing off the Back of the Boat into the Nevernais Canal" (Matthews), **Supp. IX:** 160–161
Pistol, The (Jones), **Supp. XI:** 219, **223–224,** 227, 234
Pit, The (Norris), **III:** 314, 322, 326–327, 333, 334
"Pit, The" (Roethke), **III:** 538
"Pit and the Pendulum, The" (Poe), **III:** 413, 416; **Retro. Supp. II:** 264, 269–270, 273
"Pitcher" (Francis), **Supp. IX:** 82
"Pitcher, The" (Dubus), **Supp. VII:** 87
Pitchford, Nicola, **Supp. XII:** 13
"Pits, The" (D. Graham), **Supp. XI:** 252, 254
Pitt, William, **Supp. I Part 2:** 510, 518
"Pittsburgh" (Carruth), **Supp. XVI:** 58
"Pity Me" (Wylie), **Supp. I Part 2:** 729
Pity the Monsters (Williamson), **Retro. Supp. II:** 185
Pius II, Pope, **III:** 472
Pius IX, Pope, **II:** 79
"Piute Creek" (Snyder), **Supp. VIII:** 293
Pixley, Frank, **I:** 196
Pizer, Donald, **III:** 321; **Retro. Supp. II:** 100, 199
"Place (Any Place) to Transcend All Places, A" (W. C. Williams), **Retro. Supp. I:** 422
"Place" (Hoffman), **Supp. XVIII:** 86
"Place at the Outskirts" (Simic), **Supp. VIII:** 282
Place Called Estherville, A (Caldwell), **I:** 297, 307
Place Called Freedom, A (Sanders), **Supp. XVI:** 269
Place for My Head, A (Hoffman), **Supp. XVIII:** 76
"Place in Fiction" (Welty), **IV:** 260, 279
Place of Dead Roads, The (Burroughs), **Supp. III Part 1:** 196
Place of Love, The (Shapiro), **Supp. II Part 2:** 702, 706
"Place of Poetry, The" (Stevens), **Retro. Supp. I:** 304

Place of Science in Modern Civilization and Other Essays, The (Veblen), **Supp. I Part 2:** 629, 642
"Place of Trumpets, The" (B. Kelly), **Supp. XVII:** 127
Place on Earth, A (Berry), **Supp. X:** 33–34, 36
Places Left Unfinished at the Time of Creation (Santos), **Supp. XIII:** 274
"Places to Look for Your Mind" (Moore), **Supp. X:** 174–175
"Place They'd Never Seen, A: The Theater" (Wasserstein), **Supp. XV:** 332
"Place to Live, A" (Levertov), **Supp. III Part 1:** 281
"Place to Stand, A" (Price), **Supp. VI:** 258
Place to Stand, A (Wagoner), **Supp. IX:** 324
Placi, Carlo, **IV:** 328
Plagemann, Catherine, **Supp. XVII:** 91
"Plagiarist, The" (Singer), **IV:** 19
"Plain Language from Truthful James" (Harte). *See* "Heathen Chinee, The"
"Plain Sense of Things, The" (Stevens), **Retro. Supp. I:** 298, 299, 307, 312
"Plain Song" (Carruth), **Supp. XVI:** 54
Plain Song (Harrison), **Supp. VIII: 38–39**
"Plain Song for Comadre, A" (Wilbur), **Supp. III Part 2:** 554
"Plain Talk." *See Common Sense* (Paine)
Plaint of a Rose, The (Sandburg), **III:** 579
Plain Truth: Or, Serious Considerations on the Present State of the City of Philadelphia, and Province of Pennsylvania (Franklin), **II:** 117–119
Plainwater: Essays and Poetry (Carson), **Supp. XII:** 97, **99–104**
Plan B (C. Himes), **Supp. XVI:** 143, 144
"Planchette" (London), **II:** 475–476
"Planetarium" (Rich), **Supp. I Part 2:** 557
Planet News: 1961–1967 (Ginsberg), **Supp. II Part 1:** 321
Planet Waves (album, Dylan), **Supp. XVIII:** 27
"Plantation a beginning, a" (Olson), **Supp. II Part 2:** 573
Plant Dreaming Deep (Sarton), **Supp. VIII:** 250, 263
Plante, David, **Supp. IV Part 1:** 310
"Planting a Sequoia" (Gioia), **Supp. XV:** 111, 112, 117**, 121–122**
Planting a Sequoia (Gioia), **Supp. XV:** 117
"Plants Fed On By Fawns" (B. Kelly), **Supp. XVII:** 133
Plarr, Victor, **III:** 459, 477
Plath, James, **Retro. Supp. I:** 334
Plath, Sylvia, **Retro. Supp. II:** 181, **241–260; Supp. I Part 2: 526–549,** 554, 571; **Supp. III Part 2:** 543, 561; **Supp. IV Part 2:** 439; **Supp. V:** 79, 81, 113, 117, 118, 119, 344; **Supp. X:** 201, 202, **203,** 215; **Supp. XI:** 146, 240, 241, 317; **Supp. XII:** 217, 308; **Supp. XIII:** 35, 76, 312; **Supp. XIV:** 269; **Supp. XV:** 123, 148, 184, 252, 253, 340; **Supp. XVII:** 239
Plath, Warren, **Supp. I Part 2:** 528
Plato, **I:** 224, 279, 383, 389, 485, 523; **II:** 5, 8, 10, 15, 233, 346, 391–392, 591; **III:** 115, 480, 600, 606, 609, 619–620; **IV:** 74, 140, 333, 363, 364; **Retro. Supp. I:** 247; **Retro. Supp. II:** 31; **Supp. I Part 2:** 595, 631; **Supp. IV Part 1:** 391; **Supp. IV Part 2:** 526; **Supp. X:** 78
"Plato" (Emerson), **II:** 6
"Platonic Relationship, A" (Beattie), **Supp. V:** 22
Platonic Scripts (Justice), **Supp. VII:** 115
Platonov, Dmitri, **Supp. VIII:** 30
Platt, Anthony M., **Supp. I Part 1:** 13–14
"Platte River" (Bass), **Supp. XVI:** 20
Platte River (Bass), **Supp. XVI:** 19
Plausible Prejudices: Essays on American Writing (Epstein), **Supp. XIV:** 111
Plautus, Titus Maccius, **IV:** 155; **Supp. III Part 2:** 630
Play and Other Stories, The (Dixon), **Supp. XII:** 148, 149
Playback (Chandler), **Supp. IV Part 1:** 134–135; **Supp. XVIII:** 138
Playback (script) (Chandler), **Supp. IV Part 1:** 131
"Play Ball!" (Francis), **Supp. IX:** 89
Playboy of the Western World, The (Synge), **Supp. III Part 1:** 34
Play Days (Jewett), **Retro. Supp. II:** 135
Play Days: A Book of Stories for Children (Jewett), **II:** 401–402
Player Piano (Vonnegut), **Supp. II Part 2:** 756, 757, 760–765
Players (DeLillo), **Supp. VI:** 3, 6, 8, 14
"Players, The" (W. J. Smith), **Supp. XIII:** 340, 343
"Playground, The" (Bradbury), **Supp. IV Part 1:** 104
Playing in the Dark (Morrison), **Retro. Supp. II:** 118; **Supp. XIII:** 185–186
Play in Poetry (Untermeyer), **Supp. XV:** 310
"Playin with Punjab" (Bambara), **Supp. XI:** 6
Play It Again Sam (Allen), **Supp. XV:** 2, 3, 14
Play It as It Lays (Didion), **Supp. IV Part 1:** 198, 201–203, 203, 211
Play It as It Lays (film), **Supp. IV Part 1:** 198
"Plays and Operas Too" (Whitman), **IV:** 350
Plays of Negro Life: A Source-Book of Native American Drama (Locke and Gregory), **Supp. XIV:** 202
Plays: Winesburg and Others (Anderson), **I:** 113
"Playthings" (Komunyakaa), **Supp. XIII:** 126
"Playtime: Danish Fun" (Larsen), **Supp. XVIII:** 120, 122–123
"Playtime: Three Scandinavian Stories" (Larsen), **Supp. XVIII:** 122–123
Playwright's Voice, The (Savran), **Supp. XIII:** 209; **Supp. XV:** 321
Plaza Suite (Simon), **Supp. IV Part 2:** 575, 581–582, 583, 589
Pleading Guilty (Turow), **Supp. XVII: 218,** 219
"Plea for Captain Brown, A" (Thoreau), **IV:** 185
"Please" (Komunyakaa), **Supp. XIII:** 122
"Please Don't Kill Anything" (A. Miller), **III:** 161
"Please Don't Take My Sunshine Away" (Conroy), **Supp. XVI:** 69
Pleasure Dome (Frankenberg), **I:** 436
Pleasure Dome (Komunyakaa), **Supp. XIII:** 113, 121, **131–133**
Pleasure of Hope, The (Emerson), **II:** 8
"Pleasure of Ruins, The" (McClatchy), **Supp. XII:** 256
"Pleasures of Formal Poetry, The" (Bogan), **Supp. III Part 1:** 51
"Pleasures of Peace, The" (Koch), **Supp. XV:** 180
"Plea to the Protestant Churches, A" (Brooks), **Supp. XIV:** 4
Plimpton, George, **Supp. IV Part 1:** 386; **Supp. IX:** 256; **Supp. V:** 201; **Supp. VIII:** 82, 157; **Supp. XI:** 294; **Supp. XIV:** 82; **Supp. XVI: 233–248**
Pliny the Elder, **Supp. XVI:** 292
Pliny the Younger, **II:** 113
"Ploesti Isn't Long Island" (Zinberg), **Supp. XV:** 195
"Plot against the Giant, The" (Stevens), **IV:** 81
Plotinus, **Supp. XV:** 33; **Supp. XVI:** 291
Plough and the Stars, The (O'Casey), **III:** 159
"Ploughing on Sunday" (Stevens), **IV:** 74
Plowing the Dark (Powers), **Supp. IX:** 212–213, **221–224**
Plum Bun (Fauset), **Supp. XVIII:** 127
Plumed Serpent, The (Lawrence), **Supp. XV:** 46
"Plumet Basilisk, The" (Moore), **III:** 203, 208, 215
Plumly, Stanley, **Supp. IV Part 2:** 625
Plummer, Amanda, **Supp. IV Part 1:** 236
Plunder (serial movie), **Supp. IV Part 2:** 464
Plunket, Robert, **Supp. XV:** 68
"Plunkville Patriot" (O'Henry), **Supp. II Part 1:** 389
"Pluralism and Ideological Peace" (Locke), **Supp. XIV:** 202, 212
"Pluralism and Intellectual Democracy" (Locke), **Supp. XIV:** 202, 208, 212
Pluralistic Universe, A (James), **II:** 342, 348, 357–358
Plutarch, **II:** 5, 8, 16, 555; **Retro. Supp. I:** 360; **Supp. XVI:** 292
Plymell, Charles, **Supp. XIV:** 149
Plymell, Pam, **Supp. XIV:** 149
Pnin (Nabokov), **III:** 246; **Retro. Supp. I:** 263, 265, 266, 275, 335
"Po' Boy Blues" (Hughes), **Supp. I Part 1:** 327
Pocahontas, **I:** 4; **II:** 296; **III:** 584
"Pocahontas to Her English Husband, John Rolfe" (Gunn Allen), **Supp. IV Part 1:** 331

Podhoretz, Norman, **IV:** 441; **Retro. Supp. II:** 323; **Supp. IV Part 1:** 382; **Supp. IX:** 3; **Supp. VIII:** 93, **231–247; Supp. XIV:** 103
Podnieks, Elizabeth, **Supp. X:** 189, 190, 191, 192
"Pod of the Milkweed" (Frost), **Retro. Supp. I:** 141
Poe, Edgar Allan, **I:** 48, 53, 103, 190, 194, 200, 210, 211, 261, 340, 459; **II:** 74, 77, 194, 255, 273, 295, 308, 311, 313, 421, 475, 482, 530, 595; **III:** 259, **409–432,** 485, 507, 593; **IV:** 123, 129, 133, 141, 187, 261, 345, 350, 432, 438, 439, 453; **Retro. Supp. I:** 41, 273, 365, 421; **Retro. Supp. II:** 102, 104, 160, 164, 220, **261–277,** 322; **Supp. I Part 1:** 36, 309; **Supp. I Part 2:** 376, 384, 385, 388, 393, 405, 413, 421, 474, 682; **Supp. II Part 1:** 385, 410; **Supp. III Part 2:** 544, 549–550; **Supp. IV Part 1:** 80, 81, 101, 128, 341, 349; **Supp. IV Part 2:** 464, 469; **Supp. IX:** 115; **Supp. VIII:** 105; **Supp. X:** 42, 78; **Supp. XI:** 85, 293; **Supp. XIII:** 100, 111; **Supp. XVI:** 294; **Supp. XVIII:** 3, 11
Poe, Edgar Allen, **Supp. XV:** 275
Poe Abroad: Influence, Reputation, Affinities (Vines), **Retro. Supp. II:** 261
"Poem" (Bishop), **Retro. Supp. II:** 40; **Supp. I Part 1:** 73, 76–79, 82, 95
"Poem" (Harrison), **Supp. VIII:** 38
"Poem" (Justice), **Supp. VII:** 125
"Poem" (Kunitz), **Supp. III Part 1:** 263
"Poem" (Wright), **Supp. III Part 2:** 590
"Poem About George Doty in the Death House, A" (Wright), **Supp. III Part 2:** 594–595, 597–598
"Poem about People" (Pinsky), **Supp. VI: 240–241,** 244, 248
"Poem as Mask, The" (Rukeyser), **Supp. VI:** 281, 285
"Poem Beginning 'The'" (Zukofsky), **Supp. III Part 2:** 610, 611, 614
"Poem Catching Up with an Idea" (Carruth), **Supp. XVI:** 56
"Poem for a Birthday" (Plath), **Supp. I Part 2:** 539
"POEM FOR ANNA RUSS AND FANNY JONES, A" (Baraka), **Supp. II Part 1:** 58
"Poem for Black Hearts, A" (Baraka), **Supp. II Part 1:** 50
"POEM FOR DEEP THINKERS, A" (Baraka), **Supp. II Part 1:** 55
"Poem for D. H. Lawrence" (Creeley), **Supp. IV Part 1:** 141
"Poem for Dorothy, A" (Merwin), **Supp. III Part 1:** 342
"Poem for Hemingway and W. C. Williams" (Carver), **Supp. III Part 1:** 147
"Poem for my Son" (Kumin), **Supp. IV Part 2:** 442
"Poem for People Who Are Understandably Too Busy to Read Poetry" (Dunn), **Supp. XI:** 147
"Poem for Someone Killed in Spain, A" (Jarrell), **II:** 371
"Poem for the Blue Heron, A" (Oliver), **Supp. VII:** 235–236
"Poem for Two Voices" (Everwine), **Supp. XV:** 89
"Poem For Willie Best, A" (Baraka), **Supp. II Part 1:** 36
"Poem in Prose" (Bogan), **Supp. III Part 1:** 58
"Poem in Which I Refuse Contemplation" (Dove), **Supp. IV Part 1:** 249
"Poem Is a Walk, A" (Ammons), **Supp. VII:** 36
"Poem Like a Grenade, A" (Haines), **Supp. XII:** 204
"Poem of Flight, The" (Levine), **Supp. V:** 189
"Poem of Liberation, The" (Stern), **Supp. IX:** 292
Poem of the Cid (Merwin, trans.), **Supp. III Part 1:** 347
"Poem of the Forgotten" (Haines), **Supp. XII:** 202–203
"Poem on the Memorable Victory Obtained by the Gallant Captain Paul Jones" (Freneau), **Supp. II Part 1:** 261
"Poem out of Childhood" (Rukeyser), **Supp. VI:** 272, 277
"Poem Read at the Dinner Given to the Author by the Medical Profession" (Holmes), **Supp. I Part 1:** 310–311
Poems (Auden), **Supp. II Part 1:** 6
Poems (Berryman), **I:** 170
Poems (Bryant), **II:** 311; **Supp. I Part 1:** 155, 157
Poems (Cummings), **I:** 430, 447
Poems (Eliot), **I:** 580, 588; **IV:** 122; **Retro. Supp. I:** 59, 291
Poems (Emerson), **II:** 7, 8, 12–13, 17
Poems (E. Stoddard), **Supp. XV:** 274
Poems (Holmes), **Supp. I Part 1:** 303
Poems (Koch), **Supp. XV:** 179
Poems (Lowell), **Supp. I Part 2:** 405
Poems (Moore), **III:** 194, 205, 215
Poems (Poe), **III:** 411
Poems (Reznikoff), **Supp. XIV:** 282, 283, 284, 285
Poems (Tate), **IV:** 121
Poems (W. C. Williams), **Retro. Supp. I:** 412–413, 416, 424
Poems (Winters), **Supp. II Part 2:** 809, 810
Poems (W. J. Smith), **Supp. XIII:** 332
Poems (Wordsworth), **I:** 468
Poems, 1909–1925 (Eliot), **Retro. Supp. I:** 64
Poems, 1924–1933 (MacLeish), **III:** 7, 15
Poems, 1943–1956 (Wilbur), **Supp. III Part 2:** 554
Poems, The (Freneau), **Supp. II Part 1:** 263
Poems 1918–1975: The Complete Poems of Charles Reznikoff (Cooney, ed.), **Supp. XIV:** 289
Poems 1940–1953 (Shapiro), **Supp. II Part 2:** 703, 711
Poems 1947–1954 (Kees), **Supp. XV:** 147
Poems: 1947–1957 (W. J. Smith), **Supp. XIII:** 333
Poems 1957–1967 (Dickey), **Supp. IV Part 1:** 178, 181
Poems about God (Ransom), **III:** 484, 486, 491; **IV:** 121
"Poems about Painting" (Snodgrass), **Supp. VI:** 316
Poems and Essays (Ransom), **III:** 486, 490, 492
Poems and New Poems (Bogan), **Supp. III Part 1:** 60–62
"Poems and Places" (Haines), **Supp. XII:** 203
Poems and Poetry of Europe, The (Longfellow, ed.), **Retro. Supp. II:** 155
Poems by Emily Dickinson (Todd and Higginson, eds.), **I:** 469, 470; **Retro. Supp. I:** 35, 39
Poems by Emily Dickinson, Second Series (Todd and Higginson, eds.), **I:** 454; **Retro. Supp. I:** 35
Poems by Emily Dickinson, The (Bianchi and Hampson, eds.), **Retro. Supp. I:** 35
Poems by Emily Dickinson, Third Series (Todd, ed.), **Retro. Supp. I:** 35
Poems by James Russell Lowell, Second Series (Lowell), **Supp. I Part 2:** 406, 409
Poems by Sidney Lanier, (Lanier), **Supp. I Part 1:** 364
Poems from Black Africa (Hughes, ed.), **Supp. I Part 1:** 344
"Poems I Have Lost, The" (Ortiz), **Supp. IV Part 2:** 507
Poems: North & South–A Cold Spring, (Bishop), **Supp. I Part 1:** 83, 89
Poems of a Jew (Shapiro), **Supp. II Part 2:** 703, 712–713
Poems of Anna Akhmatova, The (Kunitz and Hayward, trans.), **Supp. III Part 1:** 269
Poems of Emily Dickinson, The (Bianchi and Hampson, eds.), **Retro. Supp. I:** 35
Poems of Emily Dickinson, The (Johnson, ed.), **I:** 470
Poems of François Villon (Kinnell, trans.), **Supp. III Part 1:** 235, 243, 249
"Poems of Our Climate, The" (Stevens), **Retro. Supp. I:** 313
Poems of Philip Freneau, Written Chiefly during the Late War (Freneau), **Supp. II Part 1:** 261
Poems of Places (Longfellow, ed.), **II:** 490; **Retro. Supp. II:** 155; **Supp. I Part 1:** 368
Poems of Stanley Kunitz, The (Kunitz), **Supp. III Part 1:** 258, 263, 264, 266, 268
"Poems of These States" (Ginsberg), **Supp. II Part 1:** 323, 325
Poems of Two Friends (Howells and Piatt), **II:** 273, 277
"POEM SOME PEOPLE WILL HAVE TO UNDERSTAND, A" (Baraka), **Supp. II Part 1:** 49

Poems on Slavery (Longfellow), **II:** 489; **Retro. Supp. II:** 157, 168; **Supp. I Part 2:** 406
Poems on Various Subjects (Rowson), **Supp. XV:** 232
Poem Spoken at the Public Commencement at Yale College, in New Haven; September 1, 1781, A (Barlow), **Supp. II Part 1:** 67–68, 74, 75
Poems to Solve (Swenson), **Supp. IV Part 2:** 642
Poems Written and Published during the American Revolutionary War (Freneau), **Supp. II Part 1:** 273, 274
Poems Written between the Years 1768 and 1794 (Freneau), **Supp. II Part 1:** 269
"Poem That Took the Place of a Mountain" (Olson), **Supp. II Part 2:** 582
"Poem to My First Lover" (Olds), **Supp. X:** 206
"Poem to the Reader" (Olds), **Supp. X:** 213
"Poem with No Ending, A" (Levine), **Supp. V:** 186, 190
"Poem You Asked For, The" (Levis), **Supp. XI:** 259–260
Poe Poe Poe Poe Poe Poe Poe (Hoffman), **Retro. Supp. II:** 265
Poesía Náhuatl, **Supp. XV:** 77
Poésies 1917–1920 (Cocteau), **Retro. Supp. I:** 82
"Poesis: A Conceit" (Sobin), **Supp. XVI:** 288
"Poet, The" (Dunbar), **Supp. II Part 1:** 207, 209–210
"Poet, The" (Emerson), **II:** 13, 19, 20, 170
"Poet, The" (Ortiz), **Supp. IV Part 2:** 505
"Poet and His Book, The" (Millay), **III:** 126, 138
"Poet and His Public, The" (Jarrell), **Supp. I Part 1:** 96
"Poet and His Song, The" (Dunbar), **Supp. II Part 1:** 199
"Poet and the Person, The" (Kinard), **Supp. XIV:** 127
"Poet and the World, The" (Cowley), **Supp. II Part 1:** 145
"Poet as Anti-Specialist, The" (Swenson), **Supp. IV Part 2:** 638, 643
"Poet as *Curandera*" (Mora), **Supp. XIII:** 214, 220
"Poet as Hero, The: Keats in His Letters" (Trilling), **Supp. III Part 2:** 506–507
"Poet as Religious Moralist, The" (Larson), **Supp. XI:** 328
"Poet at Seven, The" (Rimbaud), **II:** 545
Poet at the Breakfast-Table, The (Holmes), **Supp. I Part 1:** 313–314
"Poète contumace, Le" (Corbiere), **II:** 384–385
"Poet for President, A" (Mora), **Supp. XIII:** 220–221
Poetic Achievement of Ezra Pound, The (Alexander), **Retro. Supp. I:** 293
Poetic Diction: A Study in Meaning (Barfield), **III:** 274, 279
"Poetic Principle, The" (Poe), **III:** 421, 426; **Retro. Supp. II:** 266
"Poetics" (Ammons), **Supp. VII:** 29–30
Poetics (Aristotle), **III:** 422; **Supp. XI:** 249; **Supp. XIII:** 75; **Supp. XIV:** 243; **Supp. XV:** 265
Poetics of Space, The (Bachelard), **Supp. XIII:** 225; **Supp. XVI:** 292
"Poetics of the Periphery: Literary Experimentalism in Kathy Acker's *In Memoriam to Identity*" (Acker), **Supp. XII:** 17
"Poetics of the Physical World, The" (Kinnell), **Supp. III Part 1:** 239
"Poetics of Tourette Syndrome, The: Language, Neurobiology, and Poetry" (Schleifer), **Supp. XVIII:** 144
Poet in the World, The (Levertov), **Supp. III Part 1:** 271, 273, 278, 282
"Poet or the Growth of a Lit'ry Figure" (White), **Supp. I Part 2:** 676
Poetry (Barber), **Supp. IV Part 2:** 550
"Poetry" (Moore), **III:** 204–205, 215
"Poetry" (Nye), **Supp. XIII:** 282
"Poetry" (Wrigley), **Supp. XVIII:** 301–302
"Poetry, Community and Climax" (Snyder), **Supp. VIII:** 290
"Poetry: A Metrical Essay" (Holmes), **Supp. I Part 1:** 310
"Poetry and Belief in Thomas Hardy" (Schwartz), **Supp. II Part 2:** 666
Poetry and Criticism (Nemerov, ed.), **III:** 269
"Poetry and Drama" (Eliot), **I:** 588
Poetry and Fiction: Essays (Nemerov), **III:** 269, 281
"Poetry and Place" (Berry), **Supp. X:** 22, 28, 31, 32
Poetry and Poets (Lowell), **II:** 512
"Poetry and Religion" (Jarman), **Supp. XVII:** 111
Poetry and the Age (Jarrell), **IV:** 352; **Retro. Supp. I:** 121; **Supp. II Part 1:** 135
"Poetry and the Primitive: Notes on Poetry as an Ecological Survival Technique" (Snyder), **Supp. VIII:** 291, 292, 299, 300
"Poetry and the Public World" (MacLeish), **III:** 11
Poetry and the World (Pinsky), **Supp. VI:** 236, 239, 244, 247
Poetry and Truth (Olson), **Supp. II Part 2:** 583
"Poetry As a Way of Life" (Bishop interview), **Retro. Supp. II:** 53
"Poetry as Survival" (Harrison), **Supp. VIII:** 45
Poetry for Students (Taibl), **Supp. XV:** 255
"Poetry for the Advanced" (Baraka), **Supp. II Part 1:** 58
Poetry Handbook, A (Oliver), **Supp. VII:** 229, 245
"Poetry of Barbarism, The" (Santayana), **IV:** 353
Poetry of Chaucer, The (Gardner), **Supp. VI: 63**
Poetry of Meditation, The (Martz), **IV:** 151; **Supp. I Part 1:** 107
Poetry of Mourning: The Modern Elegy from Hardy to Heaney (Ramazani), **Supp. IV Part 2:** 450
Poetry of Stephen Crane, The (Hoffman), **I:** 405
Poetry of the Negro 1746–1949, The (Hughes, ed.), **Supp. I Part 1:** 345
Poetry Reading against the Vietnam War, A (Bly and Ray, eds.), **Supp. IV Part 1:** 61, 63
"Poetry Wreck, The" (Shapiro), **Supp. II Part 2:** 717
Poetry Wreck, The: Selected Essays (Shapiro), **Supp. II Part 2:** 703, 704, 717
"Poets" (X. J. Kennedy), **Supp. XV:** 158
Poet's Alphabet, A: Reflections on the Literary Art and Vocation (Bogan), **Supp. III Part 1:** 55, 64
Poets and Poetry of America (Griswold), **Supp. XV:** 277
Poet's Choice (Engle and Langland, eds.), **III:** 277, 542
Poets of the Old Testament, The (Gordon), **III:** 199
Poets of Today (Wheelock, ed.), **Supp. IV Part 2:** 639
Poets on Poetry (Nemerov, ed.), **III:** 269
"Poet's Tact, and a Necessary Tactlessness, The" (C. Frost), **Supp. XV:** 94–95
"Poet's View, A" (Levertov), **Supp. III Part 1:** 284
"Poet's Voice, The" (Oliver), **Supp. VII:** 245
"Poet Turns on Himself, The" (Dickey), **Supp. IV Part 1:** 177, 181, 185
Poganuc People (Stowe), **Supp. I Part 2:** 581, 596, 599–600
Pogo (comic strip), **Supp. XI:** 105
Poincaré, Raymond, **IV:** 320
"Point, The" (Hayden), **Supp. II Part 1:** 373
"Point at Issue!, A" (Chopin), **Retro. Supp. II:** 61; **Supp. I Part 1:** 208
"Point of Age, A" (Berryman), **I:** 173
Point of No Return (Marquand), **III:** 56, 59–60, 65, 67, 69
Point Reyes Poems (R. Bly), **Supp. IV Part 1:** 71
"Points" (Hoffman), **Supp. XVIII:** 86
Points for a Compass Rose (Connell), **Supp. XIV:** 79, 80, 96
"Point Shirley" (Plath), **Supp. I Part 2:** 529, 538
Points in Time (Bowles), **Supp. IV Part 1:** 93
"Points West" (column), **Supp. IV Part 1:** 198
Poirier, Richard, **I:** 136, 239; **III:** 34; **Retro. Supp. I:** 134; **Retro. Supp. II:** 207–208; **Supp. I Part 2:** 660, 665; **Supp. IV Part 2:** 690
Poison Pen (Garrett), **Supp. VII:** 111
Poisonwood Bible, The (Kingsolver), **Supp. VII:** 197–198, 202, 210–213
Poitier, Sidney, **Supp. IV Part 1:** 360, 362

"Polar Bear" (Heller), **Supp. IV Part 1:** 383
"Polar Seas and Sir John Franklin, The" (Briggs), **Supp. XVIII:** 14
Pole, Rupert, **Supp. X:** 185
"Pole Star" (MacLeish), **III:** 16
Po Li, **Supp. I Part 1:** 262
Police (Baraka), **Supp. II Part 1:** 47
"Police" (Corso), **Supp. XII:** 117, 127
"Police Court Saturday Morning" (X. J. Kennedy), **Supp. XV:** 170
"Police Dreams" (Bausch), **Supp. VII:** 47
Politian (Poe), **III:** 412
"Political and Practical Conceptions of Race, The" (Locke), **Supp. XIV:** 209–210
Political Essays (Lowell), **Supp. I Part 2:** 407
Political Fable, A (Coover), **Supp. V:** 44, 46, 47, 49, 51
"Political Fables" (Mather), **Supp. II Part 2:** 450
"Political Interests" (Stevens), **Retro. Supp. I:** 295
"Political Litany, A" (Freneau), **Supp. II Part 1:** 257
"Political Pastoral" (Frost), **Retro. Supp. I:** 139
"Political Poem" (Baraka), **Supp. II Part 1:** 36
Politics (Acker), **Supp. XII:** 3, 4
Politics (Macdonald), **I:** 233–234
"Politics" (Paley), **Supp. VI:** 217
"Politics, Structure, and Poetic Development" (McCombs), **Supp. XIII:** 33
"Politics and the English Language" (Orwell), **Retro. Supp. II:** 287; **Supp. I Part 2:** 620
Politics and the Novel (Howe), **Supp. VI:** 113
"Politics and the Personal Lyric in the Poetry of Joy Harjo and C. D. Wright" (Goodman), **Supp. XV:** 344
"Politics of Ethnic Authorship, The: Li-Young Lee, Emerson, and Whitman at the Banquet Table" (Partridge), **Supp. XV:** 219
"Politics of Silence, The" (Monette), **Supp. X:** 148
Polito, Robert, **Supp. XVIII:** 33
Politt, Katha, **Supp. XII:** 159
Polk, James, **Supp. XIII:** 20
Polk, James K., **I:** 17; **II:** 433–434
Pollack, Sydney, **Supp. XIII:** 159
"Pollen" (Nye), **Supp. XIII:** 284
Pollitt, Katha, **Supp. X:** 186, 191, 193; **Supp. XVI:** 39
Pollock, Jackson, **IV:** 411, 420; **Supp. XV:** 145, 177, 178
"Polly" (Chopin), **Retro. Supp. II:** 72
Polo, Marco, **III:** 395
Polybius, **Supp. I Part 2:** 491
"Polydore" (Chopin), **Retro. Supp. II:** 66
"Pomegranate" (Glück), **Supp. V:** 82
"Pomegranate Seed" (Wharton), **IV:** 316; **Retro. Supp. I:** 382
Ponce de Leon, Luis, **III:** 391
"Pond, The" (Nemerov), **III:** 272
"Pond at Dusk, The" (Kenyon), **Supp. VII:** 168
Ponder Heart, The (Welty), **IV:** 261, 274–275, 281; **Retro. Supp. I:** 351–352
"Ponderosa Pine" (Huncke), **Supp. XIV:** 146
Ponsot, Margaret, **Supp. XVII:** 241
"Pony" (Sanders), **Supp. XVI:** 277
Poodle Springs (Parker and Chandler), **Supp. IV Part 1:** 135
Poodle Springs Story, The (Chandler), **Supp. IV Part 1:** 135
"Pool, The" (Doolittle), **Supp. I Part 1:** 264–265
Poole, Ernest, **II:** 444
"Pool Lights" (F. Barthelme), **Supp. XI:** 25, 26–27, 36
"Pool Room in the Lions Club" (Merwin), **Supp. III Part 1:** 346
"Poor Black Fellow" (Hughes), **Retro. Supp. I:** 204
"Poor Bustard, The" (Corso), **Supp. XII:** 134
"Poor but Happy" (Mamet), **Supp. XIV:** 252, 253
Poore, Charles, **III:** 364
Poor Fool (Caldwell), **I:** 291, 292, 308
Poorhouse Fair, The (Updike), **IV:** 214, 228–229, 232; **Retro. Supp. I:** 317, 320
"Poor Joanna" (Jewett), **II:** 394
"Poor Man's Pudding and Rich Man's Crumbs" (Melville), **III:** 89–90
"Poor Richard" (James), **II:** 322
Poor Richard's Almanac (undated) (Franklin), **II:** 112
Poor Richard's Almanac for 1733 (Franklin), **II:** 108, 110
Poor Richard's Almanac for 1739 (Franklin), **II:** 112
Poor Richard's Almanac for 1758 (Franklin), **II:** 101
Poor White (Anderson), **I:** 110–111
"Poor Working Girl" (Z. Fitzgerald), **Supp. IX:** 71
Popa, Vasko, **Supp. VIII:** 272
Pope, Alexander, **I:** 198, 204; **II:** 17, 114; **III:** 263, 267, 288, 517; **IV:** 145; **Retro. Supp. I:** 335; **Supp. I Part 1:** 150, 152, 310; **Supp. I Part 2:** 407, 422, 516, 714; **Supp. II Part 1:** 70, 71; **Supp. X:** 32, 36; **Supp. XII:** 260; **Supp. XV:** 258
Pope-Hennessy, James, **Supp. XIV:** 348
"Pope's Penis, The" (Olds), **Supp. X:** 207
"Poplar, Sycamore" (Wilbur), **Supp. III Part 2:** 549
Popo and Fifina (Hughes and Bontemps), **Retro. Supp. I:** 203
"Poppies" (Oliver), **Supp. VII:** 240
"Poppies in July" (Plath), **Supp. I Part 2:** 544
"Poppies in October" (Plath), **Supp. I Part 2:** 544
"Poppycock" (Francis), **Supp. IX:** 87
"Poppy Seed" (Lowell), **II:** 523
Popular Book, The: A History of America's Literary Taste (Hart), **Supp. XVIII:** 257, 258
Popular Culture (Goldbarth), **Supp. XII: 186**
Popular History of the United States (Gay), **Supp. I Part 1:** 158
"Popular Songs" (Ashbery), **Supp. III Part 1:** 6
"Populist Manifesto" (Ferlinghetti), **Supp. VIII:** 290
"Porcelain Bowl" (Glück), **Supp. V:** 83
Porcher, Frances, **Retro. Supp. II:** 71
Porco, Mike, **Supp. XVIII:** 24
"Porcupine, The" (Kinnell), **Supp. III Part 1:** 244
Porcupine's Kiss, The (Dobyns), **Supp. XIII: 89–90**
Porgy and Bess (film), **Supp. I Part 1:** 66
Porgy and Bess (play), **Supp. IV Part 1:** 6
"Porphyria's Lover" (Browning), **II:** 522
Portable Beat Reader, The (Charters, ed.), **Supp. XIV:** 152
Portable Blake, The (Kazin, ed.), **Supp. VIII:** 103
Portable Faulkner, The (Cowley, ed.), **II:** 57, 59; **Retro. Supp. I:** 73
Portable Paul and Jane Bowles, The (Dillon), **Supp. IV Part 1:** 95
Portable Veblen, The (Veblen), **Supp. I Part 2:** 630, 650
"Porte-Cochere" (Taylor), **Supp. V:** 320
"Porter" (Hughes), **Supp. I Part 1:** 327
"Porter" (Nelson), **Supp. XVIII:** 175
Porter, Bern, **III:** 171
Porter, Cole, **Supp. IX:** 189
Porter, Eliot, **Supp. IV Part 2:** 599
Porter, Fairfield, **Supp. XV:** 178
Porter, Herman W., **Supp. I Part 1:** 49
Porter, Horace, **Retro. Supp. II:** 4, 127
Porter, Jacob, **Supp. I Part 1:** 153
Porter, Katherine Anne, **I:** 97, 385; **II:** 194, 606; **III: 433–455,** 482; **IV:** 26, 138, 246, 261, 279, 280, 282; **Retro. Supp. I:** 354; **Retro. Supp. II:** 233, 235; **Supp. IV Part 1:** 31, 310; **Supp. IX:** 93, 94, 95, 98, 128; **Supp. V:** 225; **Supp. VIII:** 156, 157; **Supp. X:** 50; **Supp. XIII:** 294; **Supp. XIV:** 3; **Supp. XV:** 338
Porter, Noah, **Supp. I Part 2:** 640
Porter, William Sydney. *See* Henry, O.
Porteus, Beilby, **Supp. I Part 1:** 150
"Portland Going Out, The" (Merwin), **Supp. III Part 1:** 345
Portnoy's Complaint (P. Roth), **Retro. Supp. II: 282–286,** 291; **Supp. III Part 2:** 401, 404, 405, 407, 412–414, 426; **Supp. V:** 119, 122; **Supp. XI:** 140; **Supp. XVII:** 8, 43
Port of Saints (Burroughs), **Supp. III Part 1:** 106
"Portrait" (Dixon), **Supp. XII:** 154
"Portrait, A" (Parker), **Supp. IX:** 192–193
"Portrait, The" (Kunitz), **Supp. III Part 1:** 263
"Portrait, The" (Wharton), **Retro. Supp. I:** 364
"Portrait d'une Femme" (Pound), **Retro. Supp. I:** 288

Portrait in Brownstone (Auchincloss), **Supp. IV Part 1:** 21, 23, 27, 31
"Portrait in Georgia" (Toomer), **Supp. IX:** 314
"Portrait in Greys, A" (W. C. Williams), **Retro. Supp. I:** 416
"Portrait of a Girl in Glass" (T. Williams), **IV:** 383
"Portrait of a Jewelry Drummer" (Untermeyer), **Supp. XV:** 299–300
"Portrait of a Lady" (Eliot), **I:** 569, 570, 571, 584; **III:** 4; **Retro. Supp. I:** 55, 56, 62
Portrait of a Lady, The (James), **I:** 10, 258, 461–462, 464; **II:** 323, 325, 327, 328–329, 334; **Retro. Supp. I:** 215, 216, 217, 219, 220, 223, **224–225,** 232, 233, 381
"Portrait of an Artist" (P. Roth), **Supp. III Part 2:** 412
Portrait of an Eye: Three Novels (Acker), **Supp. XII:** 6, **7–9**
"Portrait of an Invisible Man" (Auster), **Supp. XII:** 21
"Portrait of a Supreme Court Judge" (Untermeyer), **Supp. XV:** 299
Portrait of Bascom Hawkes, A (Wolfe), **IV:** 451–452, 456
Portrait of Edith Wharton (Lubbock), **Retro. Supp. I:** 366
Portrait of Logan Pearsall Smith, Drawn from His Letters and Diaries, A (Russell, ed.), **Supp. XIV:** 349
Portrait of Picasso as a Young Man (Mailer), **Retro. Supp. II:** 213
"Portrait of the Artist as an Old Man, A" (Humphrey), **Supp. IX:** 109
Portrait of the Artist as a Young Man, A (Joyce), **I:** 475–476; **III:** 471, 561; **Retro. Supp. I:** 127; **Retro. Supp. II:** 4, 331; **Supp. IX:** 236; **Supp. XIII:** 53, 95
"Portrait of the Artist with Hart Crane" (Wright), **Supp. V:** 342
"Portrait of the Intellectual as a Yale Man" (McCarthy), **II:** 563, 564–565
"Portrait of the Self ..., A" (Sobin), **Supp. XVI:** 288
Portraits and Elegies (Schnackenberg), **Supp. XV:** 249, **253–256**
"Port Town" (Hughes), **Retro. Supp. I:** 199
Portuguese Voyages to America in the Fifteenth Century (Morison), **Supp. I Part 2:** 488
"Po' Sandy" (Chesnutt), **Supp. XIV:** 60
Poseidon Adventure, The (film), **Supp. XII:** 321
Poseidon Adventure, The (Gallico), **Supp. XVI:** 238
"Poseidon and Company" (Carver), **Supp. III Part 1:** 137
"Positive Obsession" (O. Butler), **Supp. XIII:** 70
Poss, Stanley, **Supp. XIV:** 166
"Possessions" (H. Crane), **I:** 392–393; **Retro. Supp. II:** 78
Possible World, A (Koch), **Supp. XV:** 184
Postal Inspector (film), **Supp. XIII:** 166
Postcards (Proulx), **Supp. VII:** 249, 256–258, 262
"Postcolonial Tale, A" (Harjo), **Supp. XII:** 227
"Posthumous Letter to Gilbert White" (Auden), **Supp. II Part 1:** 26
"Post-Larkin Triste" (Karr), **Supp. XI:** 242–243
Postlethwaite, Diana, **Supp. XII:** 317–318; **Supp. XVI:** 176
"Postlude" (W. C. Williams), **Retro. Supp. I:** 415
Postman, Neil, **Supp. XI:** 275
Postman Always Rings Twice, The (Cain), **Supp. XIII:** 165–166
Postman Always Rings Twice, The (film), **Supp. XIV:** 241
"Postmortem Guide, A" (Dunn), **Supp. XI:** 155
Postrel, Virginia, **Supp. XIV:** 298, 311
"Postscript" (Du Bois), **Supp. II Part 1:** 173
"Postscript" (Nye), **Supp. XIII:** 287
"Potato" (Wilbur), **Supp. III Part 2:** 545
"Potatoes' Dance, The" (Lindsay), **Supp. I Part 2:** 394
Pot of Earth, The (MacLeish), **III:** 5, 6–8, 10, 12, 18
"Pot Roast" (Strand), **Supp. IV Part 2:** 629
Pot Shots at Poetry (Francis), **Supp. IX: 83–84**
Potter, Beatrix, **Supp. I Part 2:** 656; **Supp. XVI:** 100
Potter, Stephen, **IV:** 430
Potter's House, The (Stegner), **Supp. IV Part 2:** 598, 606
Poulenc, Francis, **Supp. IV Part 1:** 81
Poulin, Al, Jr., **Supp. IX:** 272; **Supp. XI:** 259
Pound, Ezra, **I:** 49, 58, 60, 66, 68, 69, 105, 236, 243, 256, 384, 403, 428, 429, 475, 476, 482, 487, 521, 578; **II:** 26, 55, 168, 263, 316, 371, 376, 513, 517, 520, 526, 528, 529, 530; **III:** 2, 5, 8, 9, 13–14, 17, 174, 194, 196, 278, 430, 453, **456–479,** 492, 504, 511, 523, 524, 527, 575–576, 586, 590; **IV:** 27, 28, 407, 415, 416, 433, 446; **Retro. Supp. I:** 51, 52, 55, 58, 59, 63, 82, 89, 127, 140, 171, 177, 178, 198, 216, **283–294,** 298, 299, 359, 411, 412, 413, 414, 417, 418, 419, 420, 423, 426, 427, 430, 431; **Retro. Supp. II:** 178, 183, 189, 326; **Supp. I Part 1:** 253, 255–258, 261–268, 272, 274; **Supp. I Part 2:** 387, 721; **Supp. II Part 1:** 1, 8, 20, 30, 91, 136; **Supp. III Part 1:** 48, 63, 64, 73, 105, 146, 225, 271; **Supp. III Part 2:** 542, **609–617,** 619, 620, 622, 625, 626, 628, 631; **Supp. IV Part 1:** 153, 314; **Supp. IX:** 291; **Supp. V:** 331, 338, 340, 343, 345; **Supp. VIII:** 39, 105, 195, 205, 271, 290, 291, 292, 303; **Supp. X:** 24, 36, 112, 120, 122; **Supp. XII:** 97; **Supp. XIV:** 11, 55, 83, 272, 284, 286, 287, 347; **Supp. XV:** 20, 42, 43, 51, 93, 161, 181, 297, 298, 299, 301, 302, 306; **Supp. XVI:** 47, 282; **Supp. XVII:** 111, 226–227
Pound, Louise, **Retro. Supp. I:** 4; **Supp. XV:** 137
Pound, T. S., **I:** 428
"Pound Reweighed" (Cowley), **Supp. II Part 1:** 143
Powell, Anthony, **Supp. XVIII:** 136, 146
Powell, Betty, **Retro. Supp. II:** 140
Powell, Dawn, **Supp. IV Part 2:** 678, 682
Powell, Dick, **Supp. IX:** 250
Powell, John Wesley, **Supp. IV Part 2:** 598, 604, 611
Powell, Lawrence Clark, **III:** 189
Powell, William, **Supp. IV Part 1:** 355
"Power" (Corso), **Supp. XII:** 117, 126, 127, **128**
"Power" (Emerson), **II:** 2, 3
"Power" (Rich), **Supp. I Part 2:** 569
"Power and Light" (Dickey), **Supp. IV Part 1:** 182
Power and the Glory, The (Greene), **III:** 556
"Powerhouse" (Welty), **Retro. Supp. I:** 343, 346
"Power Never Dominion" (Rukeyser), **Supp. VI:** 281
"Power of Fancy, The" (Freneau), **Supp. II Part 1:** 255
Power of Myth, The (Campbell), **Supp. IX:** 245
"Power of Prayer, The" (Lanier), **Supp. I Part 1:** 357
"Power of Stories, The" (Sanders), **Supp. XVI:** 278
"Power of Suggestion" (Auchincloss), **Supp. IV Part 1:** 33
Power of Sympathy, The (Brown), **Supp. II Part 1:** 74
Power Politics (Atwood), **Supp. XIII:** 20, 33–34, 35
Powers, J. F., **Supp. V:** 319; **Supp. XVII:** 43
Powers, Kim, **Supp. VIII:** 329, 340
Powers, Richard, **Supp. IX: 207–225; Supp. XVII:** 183
Powers of Attorney (Auchincloss), **Supp. IV Part 1:** 31, 32, 33
"Powers of Darkness" (Wharton), **Retro. Supp. I:** 379
Powys, John Cowper, **Supp. I Part 2:** 454, 476; **Supp. IX:** 135
Poynton, Jerome, **Supp. XIV:** 147, 150
Practical Agitation (Chapman), **Supp. XIV:** 41
Practical Criticism: A Study of Literary Judgment (Richards), **Supp. XIV:** 3, 16
Practical Magic (film), **Supp. X:** 80
Practical Magic (Hoffman), **Supp. X:** 78, 82, **88–89**
"Practical Methods of Meditation, The" (Dawson), **IV:** 151
Practical Navigator, The (Bowditch), **Supp. I Part 2:** 482
Practice of Perspective, The (Dubreuil), **Supp. IV Part 2:** 425

Practice of Reading, The (Donoghue), **Supp. VIII:** 189
Pragmatism: A New Name for Some Old Ways of Thinking (James), **II:** 352
"Pragmatism's Conception of Truth" (James), **Supp. XIV:** 40
Prague Orgy, The (P. Roth), **Retro. Supp. II:** 280
"Praire, The" (Clampitt), **Supp. IX:** 42
"Prairie" (Sandburg), **III:** 583, 584
Prairie, The (Cooper), **I:** 339, 342
"Prairie Birthday" (Leopold), **Supp. XIV:** 185
Prairie Home Companion, A (Keillor, radio program), **Supp. XIII:** 274; **Supp. XVI:** 169–171, 173–178
Prairie Home Morning Show, A (Keillor, radio program), **Supp. XVI:** 171
"Prairie Life, A Citizen Speaks" (Dunn), **Supp. XI:** 145
"Prairies, The" (Bryant), **Supp. I Part 1:** 157, 162, 163, 166
Praise (Hass), **Supp. VI:** 104–105, 106
"Praise for an Urn" (Crane), **I:** 388
"Praise for Sick Women" (Snyder), **Supp. VIII:** 294
"Praise in Summer" (Wilbur), **Supp. III Part 2:** 546–548, 560, 562
"Praise of a Palmtree" (Levertov), **Supp. III Part 1:** 284
"Praise of the Committee" (Rukeyser), **Supp. VI:** 278
"Praises, The" (Goldbarth), **Supp. XII:** 185
"Praises, The" (Olson), **Supp. II Part 2:** 558, 560, 563, 564
Praises and Dispraises (Des Pres), **Supp. X:** 120
Praisesong for the Widow (Marshall), **Supp. IV Part 1:** 14; **Supp. XI:** 18, 276, 278, **284–286,** 287
"Praise to the End!" (Roethke), **III:** 529, 532, 539
Prajadhipok, King of Siam, **I:** 522
Prater Violet (Isherwood), **Supp. XIV: 164–166,** 169–170, 171
Pratt, Anna (Anna Alcott), **Supp. I Part 1:** 33
Pratt, Louis H., **Retro. Supp. II:** 6
Pratt, Mary Louise, **Retro. Supp. II:** 48
Pratt, Parley, **Supp. IV Part 2:** 603
"Prattler" (newspaper column), **I:** 207
"Prattler, The" (Bierce), **I:** 196
"Prayer" (Gioia), **Supp. XV:** 117
"Prayer" (Olds), **Supp. X:** 204
"Prayer" (Toomer), **Supp. IX:** 318
"Prayer, A" (Kushner), **Supp. IX: 134**
"Prayer for Columbus" (Whitman), **IV:** 348
"Prayer for My Daughter" (Yeats), **II:** 598
"Prayer for My Grandfather to Our Lady, A" (Lowell), **II:** 541–542
"Prayer for my Son" (C. Frost), **Supp. XV:** 98–99
"Prayer for Our Daughters" (Jarman), **Supp. XVII:** 120
Prayer for Owen Meany, A (Irving), **Supp. VI:** 164, 165, 166, **175–176**
"PRAYER FOR SAVING" (Baraka), **Supp. II Part 1:** 52–53
"Prayer in Spring, A" (Frost), **II:** 153, 164
"Prayer on All Saint's Day" (Cowley), **Supp. II Part 1:** 138, 153
Prayers for Dark People (Du Bois), **Supp. II Part 1:** 186
"Prayer to Hermes" (Creeley), **Supp. IV Part 1:** 156, 157
"Prayer to Masks" (Senghor), **Supp. IV Part 1:** 16
"Prayer to the Child of Prague" (Salinas), **Supp. XIII:** 327
"Prayer to the Good Poet" (Wright), **Supp. III Part 2:** 603
"Prayer to the Pacific" (Silko), **Supp. IV Part 2:** 560
"Pray without Ceasing" (Emerson), **II:** 9–10
Praz, Mario, **IV:** 430
"Preacher, The" (Whittier), **Supp. I Part 2:** 698–699
Preacher and the Slave, The (Stegner), **Supp. IV Part 2:** 599, 608, 609
Precaution (Cooper), **I:** 337, 339
"Preconceptions of Economic Science, The" (Veblen), **Supp. I Part 2:** 634
Predecessors, Et Cetera (Clampitt), **Supp. IX:** 37
"Predicament, A" (Poe), **Retro. Supp. II:** 273
Predilections (Moore), **III:** 194
Prefaces and Prejudices (Mencken), **III:** 99, 104, 106, 119
Preface to a Twenty Volume Suicide Note.... (Baraka), **Supp. II Part 1:** 31, 33–34, 51, 61
"Preference" (Wylie), **Supp. I Part 2:** 713
"Prejudice against the Past, The" (Moore), **IV:** 91
Prejudices (Mencken), **Supp. I Part 2:** 630
Prejudices: A Selection (Farrell, ed.), **III:** 116
Prejudices: First Series (Mencken), **III:** 105
"Preliminary Remarks on the Poetry in the First Person" (Wright), **Supp. XV:** 339
Prelude, A: Landscapes, Characters and Conversations from the Earlier Years of My Life (Wilson), **IV:** 426, 427, 430, 434, 445
Prelude, The (Wordsworth), **III:** 528; **IV:** 331, 343; **Supp. I Part 2:** 416, 676; **Supp. XI:** 248
Prelude and Liebestod (McNally), **Supp. XIII:** 201
"Preludes" (Eliot), **I:** 573, 576, 577; **Retro. Supp. I:** 55; **Supp. IV Part 2:** 436
Preludes for Memnon (Aiken), **I:** 59, 65
Preludes from Memnon (Aiken), **Supp. X:** 50
"Prelude to an Evening" (Ransom), **III:** 491, 492–493
Prelude to Darkness (Salinas), **Supp. XIII:** 311, **318–319,** 320
"Prelude to the Present" (Mumford), **Supp. II Part 2:** 471
"Premature Burial, The" (Poe), **III:** 415, 416, 418; **Retro. Supp. II:** 270
Preminger, Otto, **Supp. IX:** 3, 9
"Premonition" (Hay), **Supp. XIV:** 122
"Premonitions of the Bread Line" (Komunyakaa), **Supp. XIII:** 114, 115
Prenshaw, Peggy Whitman, **Supp. X:** 229
"Preparations" (Silko), **Supp. IV Part 2:** 560
Preparatory Meditations (Taylor), **IV:** 145, 148, 149, 150, 152, 153, 154–155, 164, 165
"Prepare" (Carruth), **Supp. XVI:** 59
Prepositions: The Collected Critical Essays of Louis Zukofsky (Zukofsky), **Supp. III Part 2:** 630
Prescott, Anne, **Supp. IV Part 1:** 299
Prescott, Orville, **Supp. IV Part 2:** 680; **Supp. XI:** 340
Prescott, Peter, **Supp. X:** 83
Prescott, Peter S., **Supp. XVI:** 212
Prescott, William, **Retro. Supp. I:** 123
Prescott, William Hickling, **II:** 9, 310, 313–314; **IV:** 309; **Supp. I Part 2:** 414, 479, 493, 494
"Prescription of Painful Ends" (Jeffers), **Supp. II Part 2:** 424
"Presence, The" (Gordon), **II:** 199, 200
"Presence, The" (Kumin), **Supp. IV Part 2:** 445, 455
Presence and Desire: Essays on Gender, Sexuality, Performance (Dolan), **Supp. XV:** 327
"Presence of Others, The" (Kenyon), **Supp. VII:** 164
Presences (Taylor), **Supp. V:** 325
"Present Age, The" (Emerson), **II:** 11–12
Present Danger, The: Do We Have the Will to Reverse the Decline of American Power? (Podhoretz), **Supp. VIII:** 241
Present for Young Ladies, A (Rowson), **Supp. XV:** 245
"Present Hour" (Sandburg), **III:** 593–594
Present Philosophical Tendencies (Perry), **I:** 224
"Present State of Ethical Philosophy, The" (Emerson), **II:** 9
"Present State of Poetry, The" (Schwartz), **Supp. II Part 2:** 666
"Preservation of Innocence" (Baldwin), **Supp. I Part 1:** 51
"Preserving Wildness" (Berry), **Supp. X:** 28, 29, 32
"President and Other Intellectuals, The" (Kazin), **Supp. VIII:** 104
Presidential Papers, The (Mailer), **III:** 35, 37–38, 42, 45; **Retro. Supp. II:** 203, 204, 206
"Presidents" (Merwin), **Supp. III Part 1:** 351
Presnell, Robert, Sr., **Supp. XIII:** 166
Pressley, Nelson, **Supp. XVIII:** 37–38
"PRES SPOKE IN A LANGUAGE" (Baraka), **Supp. II Part 1:** 60
Presumed Innocent (Turow), 217; **Supp. XVII:** 214–216, 223

"Pretext, The" (Wharton), **Retro. Supp. I:** 371
Pretty Boy Floyd (McMurtry), **Supp. V:** 231
"Pretty Girl, The" (Dubus), **Supp. VII:** 87–88
"Pretty Mouth and Green My Eyes" (Salinger), **III:** 560
"Previous Condition" (Baldwin), **Supp. I Part 1:** 51, 55, 63
"Previous Tenant, The" (Simpson), **Supp. IX:** 278–279
Priaulx, Allan, **Supp. XI:** 228
Price, Alan, **Retro. Supp. I:** 377
Price, Reynolds, **Supp. IX:** 256, 257; **Supp. VI: 253–270**
Price, Richard, **II:** 9; **Supp. I Part 2:** 522
Price, The (A. Miller), **III:** 165–166
"Price of the Harness, The" (Crane), **I:** 414
Pricksongs & Descants; Fictions (Coover), **Supp. V:** 39, 42, 43, 49, 50
"Pride" (Hughes), **Supp. I Part 1:** 331
Pride and Prejudice (Austen), **II:** 290
Prideaux, Tom, **Supp. IV Part 2:** 574, 590
"Priesthood, The" (Winters), **Supp. II Part 2:** 786
Priestly, Joseph, **Supp. I Part 2:** 522
Primary Colors, The (A. Theroux), **Supp. VIII:** 312
"Primary Ground, A" (Rich), **Supp. I Part 2:** 563
"Prime" (Auden), **Supp. II Part 1:** 22
"Primer Class" (Bishop), **Retro. Supp. II:** 38, 51
Primer for Blacks (Brooks), **Supp. III Part 1:** 85
"Primer for the Nuclear Age" (Dove), **Supp. IV Part 1:** 246
Primer of Ignorance, A (Blackmur), **Supp. II Part 1:** 91
Primitive, The (C. Himes), **Supp. XVI:** 139, **141–142**
"Primitive Black Man, The" (Du Bois), **Supp. II Part 1:** 176
"Primitive Like an Orb, A" (Stevens), **IV:** 89; **Retro. Supp. I:** 309
Primitive People (Prose), **Supp. XVI:** 255, 256, 257
"Primitive Singing" (Lindsay), **Supp. I Part 2:** 389–390
Primitivism and Decadence (Winters), **Supp. II Part 2:** 786, 803–807, 812
Prince, Richard, **Supp. XII:** 4
"Prince, The" (Jarrell), **II:** 379
"Prince, The" (Winters), **Supp. II Part 2:** 802
Prince and the Pauper, The (Twain), **IV:** 200–201, 206
Prince Hagen (Sinclair), **Supp. V:** 280
Prince of a Fellow, A (Hearon), **Supp. VIII:** 58, **62–63**
Princess, The (Tennyson), **Supp. I Part 2:** 410
Princess and the Goblins, The (Macdonald), **Supp. XIII:** 75
Princess Casamassima, The (James), **II:** 276, 291; **IV:** 202; **Retro. Supp. I:** 216, 221, 222, 225, **226–227**
"Princess Casamassima, The" (Trilling), **Supp. III Part 2:** 502, 503
Princess of Arcady, A (Henry), **Retro. Supp. II:** 97
"Principles" (Du Bois), **Supp. II Part 1:** 172
Principles of Literary Criticism (Richards), **I:** 274; **Supp. I Part 1:** 264; **Supp. XIV:** 3
Principles of Psychology, The (James), **II:** 321, 350–352, 353, 354, 357, 362, 363–364; **IV:** 28, 29, 32, 37
Principles of Psychology, The (W. James), **Supp. XVII:** 97
Principles of Zoölogy (Agassiz), **Supp. I Part 1:** 312
Prior, Matthew, **II:** 111; **III:** 521
Prior, Sir James, **II:** 315
"Prison, The" (Malamud), **Supp. I Part 2:** 431, 437
Prisoner of Second Avenue, The (Simon), **Supp. IV Part 2:** 583, 584
Prisoner of Sex, The (Mailer), **III:** 46; **Retro. Supp. II:** 206
Prisoner of Zenda, The (film), **Supp. I Part 2:** 615
Prisoner's Dilemma (Powers), **Supp. IX:** 212, **214–216**, 221
Prison Memoirs of an Anarchist (A. Berkman), **Supp. XVII:** 103–104
Pritchard, William, **Supp. XVI:** 71
Pritchard, William H., **Retro. Supp. I:** 131, 141; **Supp. IV Part 1:** 285; **Supp. IV Part 2:** 642; **Supp. XI:** 326
Pritchett, V. S., **II:** 587; **Supp. II Part 1:** 143; **Supp. VIII:** 171; **Supp. XIII:** 168
"Privatation and Publication" (Cowley), **Supp. II Part 1:** 149
Private Contentment (Price), **Supp. VI:** 263
"Private History of a Campaign That Failed" (Twain), **IV:** 195
Private Life of Axie Reed, The (Knowles), **Supp. XII:** 249
"Private Man Confronts His Vulgarities at Dawn, A" (Dunn), **Supp. XI:** 146
Private Memoirs and Confessions of a Justified Sinner, The (Hogg), **Supp. IX:** 276
"Private Property and the Common Wealth" (Berry), **Supp. X:** 25
Private Snafu series (Geisel), **Supp. XVI:** 102
"Private Theatricals" (Howells), **II:** 280
Private Women, Public Stage: Literary Domesticity in Nineteenth-Century America (Kelley), **Supp. XVIII:** 257
Privilege, The (Kumin), **Supp. IV Part 2:** 442–444, 451
Prize Stories 1918: The O. Henry Awards, **Supp. XVI:** 16
"Probe" (Ryan as Quin), **Supp. XVIII:** 229
"Probing the Dark" (Komunyakaa), **Supp. XIII:** 131
"Problem from Milton, A" (Wilbur), **Supp. III Part 2:** 550
"Problem of Anxiety, The" (Koch), **Supp. XV:** 183
"Problem of Being, The" (James), **II:** 360
Problem of Classification in the Theory of Value, The (Locke), **Supp. XIV:** 199
"Problem of Housing the Negro, The" (Du Bois), **Supp. II Part 1:** 168
"Problem of the Religious Novel, The" (Isherwood), **Supp. XIV:** 172
Problems and Other Stories (Updike), **Retro. Supp. I:** 322, 329
"Problem Solving" (Goldbarth), **Supp. XII:** 185
"Procedures for Underground" (Atwood), **Supp. XIII:** 33
Procedures for Underground (Atwood), **Supp. XIII:** 33
Processional (Lawson), **I:** 479
"Procession at Candlemas, A" (Clampitt), **Supp. IX:** 41
Proclus, **Retro. Supp. I:** 247
"Prodigal" (Ammons), **Supp. VII:** 29
"Prodigal" (Hoffman), **Supp. XVIII:** 86
"Prodigal, The" (Bishop), **Supp. I Part 1:** 90, 92
Prodigal Parents, The (Lewis), **II:** 454–455
"Prodigy" (Simic), **Supp. VIII:** 278
Producers, The (film, M. Brooks), **Supp. XVII:** 45
"Proem" (Crane), **I:** 397
"Proem, The: By the Carpenter" (O. Henry), **Supp. II Part 1:** 409
"Professions for Women" (Woolf), **Supp. XIII:** 305
"Professor" (Hughes), **Supp. I Part 1:** 330
"Professor, The" (Bourne), **I:** 223
Professor at the Breakfast Table, The (Holmes), **Supp. I Part 1:** 313, 316
"Professor Clark's Economics" (Veblen), **Supp. I Part 2:** 634
Professor of Desire, The (P. Roth), **Retro. Supp. II:** 288; **Supp. III Part 2:** 403, 418–420
Professor's House, The (Cather), **I:** 325–336; **Retro. Supp. I:** 16
"Professor Veblen" (Mencken), **Supp. I Part 2:** 630
Proffer, Carl R., **Supp. VIII:** 22
Profile Makers, The (Bierds), **Supp. XVII:** 29, **30–32**, 33
"Profile of the Tenderloin Street Prostitute, A" (Vollmann), **Supp. XVII:** 230
Profits of Religion, The (Sinclair), **Supp. V:** 276
"Prognosis" (Warren), **IV:** 245
"Progress" (F. Wright), **Supp. XVII:** 247
"Progress Report" (Simic), **Supp. VIII:** 278
"Project for a Trip to China" (Sontag), **Supp. II Part 2:** 454, 469
"Project for *The Ambassadors*" (James), **Retro. Supp. I:** 229
"Projection" (Nemerov), **III:** 275

"Projective Verse" (Olson), **Supp. III Part 1:** 30; **Supp. III Part 2:** 555, 556, 557, 624; **Supp. IV Part 1:** 139, 153; **Supp. VIII:** 290
"Projector, The" (Baker), **Supp. XIII:** 53, 55
Prokofiev, Sergey Sergeyevich, **Supp. IV Part 1:** 81
"Prolegomena, Section 1" (Pound), **Supp. III Part 2:** 615–616
"Prolegomena, Section 2" (Pound), **Supp. III Part 2:** 616
"Prolegomenon to a Biography of Mailer" (Lucid), **Retro. Supp. II:** 195
Proletarian Literature in the United States (Hicks), **Supp. I Part 2: 609–610**
"Prologue" (MacLeish), **III:** 8, 14
"Prologue to a Life" (D. West), **Supp. XVIII:** 280
"Prologue to Our Time" (Mumford), **Supp. III Part 2:** 473
"Prometheus" (Longfellow), **II:** 494
Prometheus Bound (Lowell), **II:** 543, 544, 545, 555
Promise, The (Buck), **Supp. II Part 1:** 124
"Promise, The" (Olds), **Supp. X:** 213
"Promise and Fulfillment" (D. West), **Supp. XVIII:** 278
Promised Land, The (M. Antin), **Supp. IX:** 227; **Supp. XVI:** 148, 149
Promised Land, The (Porter), **III:** 447
Promised Lands (Sontag), **Supp. III Part 2:** 452
Promise of American Life, The (Croly), **I:** 229
"Promise of Blue Horses, The" (Harjo), **Supp. XII:** 228
Promise of Rest, The (Price), **Supp. VI:** 262, 266
Promises (Warren), **Supp. XIV:** 15
Promises, Promises (musical), **Supp. IV Part 2:** 575
Promises: Poems 1954–1956 (Warren), **IV:** 244–245, 249, 252
"Promise This When You Be Dying" (Dickinson), **Retro. Supp. I:** 44, 46
Proof, The (Winters), **Supp. II Part 2:** 786, 791, 792–794
Proofs and Theories: Essays on Poetry (Glück), **Supp. V:** 77, 79, 92; **Supp. XIV:** 269
"Propaganda of History, The" (Du Bois), **Supp. II Part 1:** 182
Propertius, Sextus, **III:** 467; **Retro. Supp. II:** 187; **Supp. XII:** 2
Property Of: A Novel (Hoffman), **Supp. X:** 77, 79, **80–82**
"Prophecy of Samuel Sewall, The" (Whittier), **Supp. I Part 2:** 699
Propheteers, The (Apple), **Supp. XVII: 6–7**
"Prophetic Pictures, The" (Hawthorne), **II:** 227
"Proportion" (Lowell), **II:** 525
"Proposal" (Carver), **Supp. III Part 1:** 149
Proposals Relating to the Education of Youth in Pensilvania (Franklin), **II:** 113
"Proposed New Version of the Bible" (Franklin), **II:** 110
Prose, Francine, **Supp. XII:** 333; **Supp. XVI: 249–264**
"Prose for Departure" (Merrill), **Supp. III Part 1:** 336
Prose Pieces (Bynner), **Supp. XV:** 52
"Prose Poem as an Evolving Form, The" (R. Bly), **Supp. IV Part 1:** 64
"Proserpina and the Devil" (Wilder), **IV:** 358
"Prosody" (Shapiro), **Supp. II Part 2:** 710
Prospect before Us, The (Dos Passos), **I:** 491
"Prospective Immigrants Please Note" (Rich), **Supp. I Part 2:** 555
Prospect of Peace, The (Barlow), **Supp. II Part 1:** 67, 68, 75
Prospects of Literature, The (L. P. Smith), **Supp. XIV:** 343
Prospects on the Rubicon (Paine), **Supp. I Part 2:** 510–511
Prospectus of a National Institution, to Be Established in the United States (Barlow), **Supp. II Part 1:** 80, 82
Prospice (Browning), **IV:** 366
"Protestant Easter" (Sexton), **Supp. II Part 2:** 684
"Prothalamion" (Schwartz), **Supp. II Part 2:** 649, 652
"Prothalamion" (Spenser), **Retro. Supp. I:** 62
Proud, Robert, **Supp. I Part 1:** 125
"Proud Farmer, The" (Lindsay), **Supp. I Part 2:** 381
Proud Flesh (Humphrey), **Supp. IX:** 94, 95, 96, **102–103,** 104, 105, 109
"Proud Flesh" (Warren), **IV:** 243
"Proud Lady" (Wylie), **Supp. I Part 2:** 711–712
Proulx, Annie, **Supp. VII: 249–267**
Proust, Marcel, **I:** 89, 319, 327, 377, 461; **II:** 377, 514, 606; **III:** 174, 181, 184, 244–245, 259, 471; **IV:** 32, 201, 237, 301, 312, 328, 359, 428, 431, 434, 439, 443, 466, 467; **Retro. Supp. I:** 75, 89, 169, 335; **Supp. III Part 1:** 10, 12, 14, 15; **Supp. IV Part 2:** 600; **Supp. IX:** 211; **Supp. VIII:** 103; **Supp. X:** 193, 194; **Supp. XII:** 289; **Supp. XIV:** 24, 83, 95; **Supp. XVI:** 295
Proverbs, **Supp. X:** 45
"Proverbs" (Jarman), **Supp. XVII:** 118
"Providence" (Komunyakaa), **Supp. XIII:** 132
"Provincetown Postcards" (F. Wright), **Supp. XVII:** 244
"Provincia deserta" (Pound), **Retro. Supp. I:** 289
"Provisional Remarks on Being / A Poet / of Arkansas" (Wright), **Supp. XV:** 337
Pruette, Lorine, **Supp. IV Part 2:** 522
Prufrock and Other Observations (Eliot), **I:** 569–570, 571, 573, 574, 576–577, 583, 584, 585; **Retro. Supp. I:** 59, 62
"Prufrock's Perivigilium" (Eliot), **Retro. Supp. I:** 57
Pryor, Richard, **Supp. XIII:** 343
Pryse, Marjorie, **Retro. Supp. II:** 139, 146
"Psalm" (Ginsberg), **Supp. II Part 1:** 312
"Psalm" (Simic), **Supp. VIII:** 282
"Psalm and Lament" (Justice), **Supp. VII:** 116, 117–118, 120–122, 124
"Psalm for Pinhook" (Ray), **Supp. XVIII:** 202
"Psalm of Life, A" (Longfellow), **II:** 489, 496; **Retro. Supp. II:** 164, 168, 169; **Supp. I Part 2:** 409
"Psalm of the West" (Lanier), **Supp. I Part 1:** 362, 364
"Psalm: Our Fathers" (Merwin), **Supp. III Part 1:** 350
Psalms (biblical book), **I:** 83; **II:** 168, 232; **Retro. Supp. I:** 62; **Supp. I Part 1:** 125
Psalms, Hymns, and Spiritual Songs of the Rev. Isaac Watts, The (Worcester, ed.), **I:** 458
Psychiatric Novels of Oliver Wendell Holmes, The (Oberndorf), **Supp. I Part 1:** 315
"Psychology and Form" (Burke), **I:** 270
Psychology: Briefer Course (James), **II:** 351–352
Psychology of Art (Malraux), **IV:** 434
Psychology of Insanity, The (Hart), **I:** 241–242, 248–250
Psychopathia Sexualis (Shanley), **Supp. XIV:** 316, **329**
Psychophysiks (Fechner), **II:** 358
"Pu-239" (Kalfus), **Supp. XVII:** 50
"Publication is the Auction" (Dickinson), **Retro. Supp. I:** 31
"Public Bath, The" (Snyder), **Supp. VIII:** 298
Public Burning, The (Coover), **Supp. IV Part 1:** 388; **Supp. V:** 44, 45, 46–47, 48, 51, 52; **Supp. XVII:** 6
"Public Burning of Julius and Ethel Rosenberg, The: An Historical Romance" (Coover), **Supp. V:** 44
"Public Figure" (Hay), **Supp. XIV:** 124
"Public Garden, The" (Lowell), **II:** 550
Public Good (Paine), **Supp. I Part 2:** 509–510
Public Poetry of Robert Lowell, The (Cosgrave), **Retro. Supp. II:** 185
"Public & Private" (column, Quindlen), **Supp. XVII:** 165, 167, 169–170
Public Speech: Poems (MacLeish), **III:** 15–16
Public Spirit (Savage), **II:** 111
"Puck" (Monette), **Supp. X:** 157–158
Pudd'nhead Wilson (Twain), **I:** 197
"Pudd'nhead Wilson's Calendar" (Twain), **I:** 197
"Pueblo Revolt, The" (Sando), **Supp. IV Part 2:** 510
Puella (Dickey), **Supp. IV Part 1:** 178, 185
Pulitzer, Alfred, **Retro. Supp. I:** 257
Pull Down Vanity (Fiedler), **Supp. XIII:** 103
Pullman, George, **Supp. I Part 1:** 9

"Pullman Car Hiawatha" (Wilder), **IV:** 365–366

Pull My Daisy (film), **Supp. XII:** 126–127

"Pulpit and the Pew, The" (Holmes), **Supp. I Part 1:** 302

"Pulse-Beats and Pen-Strokes" (Sandburg), **III:** 579

"Pump, The" (Humphrey), **Supp. IX:** 101

Pump House Gang, The (Wolfe), **Supp. III Part 2:** 575, 578, 580, 581

Punch, Brothers, Punch and Other Sketches (Twain), **IV:** 200

Punch: The Immortal Liar, Documents in His History (Aiken), **I:** 57, 61

Punishment Without Vengeance (Vega; Merwin, trans.), **Supp. III Part 1:** 341, 347

"Pupil" (F. Barthelme), **Supp. XI:** 26

"Pupil, The" (James), **II:** 331; **Retro. Supp. I:** 217, 219, 228

"Purchase" (Banks), **Supp. V:** 6

"Purchase of Some Golf Clubs, A" (O'Hara), **III:** 369

"Purdah" (Plath), **Supp. I Part 2:** 602

Purdy, Charles, **Supp. VIII:** 330

Purdy, James, **Supp. VII: 269–285**

Purdy, Theodore, **Supp. VIII:** 153

"Pure" (C. Frost), **Supp. XV:** 101–102

Pure (C. Frost), **Supp. XV:** 93, **101–102,** 104, 106

"Pure and the Good, The: On Baseball and Backpaking" (Maclean), **Supp. XIV:** 222

"Pure Good of Theory, The" (Stevens), **Retro. Supp. I:** 310

Purgatorio (Dante), **III:** 182

Puritan Family (Morgan), **Supp. I Part 1:** 101

"Puritanical Pleasures" (Hardwick), **Supp. III Part 1:** 213–214

Puritan Origins of the American Self, The (Bercovitch), **Supp. I Part 1:** 99

Puritan Pronaos, The: Studies in the Intellectual Life of New England in the Seventeenth Century (Morison), **Supp. I Part 2:** 485

"Puritan Realism: *The Wide, Wide World* and *Robinson Crusoe*" (Kim), **Supp. XVIII:** 267

Puritans, The (P. Miller), **Supp. VIII:** 101

"Puritan's Ballad, The" (Wylie), **Supp. I Part 2:** 723

"Purloined Letter, The" (Poe), **Retro. Supp. II:** 271, 272

Purple Cane Road (Burke), **Supp. XIV:** 32, 33

Purple Decades, The (Wolfe), **Supp. III Part 2:** 584

"Purple Hat, The" (Welty), **IV:** 264

Purple Rose of Cairo, The (film; Allen), **Supp. XV:** 1, **9–10,** 12, 14

Purser, John T., **Supp. XIV:** 4

"Pursuit of Happiness" (Simpson), **Supp. IX:** 279

"Pursuit of Happiness, The" (Ashbery), **Supp. III Part 1:** 23

Pursuit of the Prodigal, The (Auchincloss), **Supp. IV Part 1:** 25

Pushcart at the Curb, A (Dos Passos), **I:** 478, 479

"Pushcart Man" (Hughes), **Supp. I Part 1:** 330

Pushcart Prize, XIII, The (Ford), **Supp. V:** 58

Pushcart Prize VII, The (Hendeson, ed.), **Supp. XVII:** 16

Pushcart Prize XIV, The (Henderson, ed.), **Supp. XVII:** 18

Pushcart Prize XX, The (Henderson, ed.), **Supp. XVII:** 20

"Pushing 100" (Mora), **Supp. XIII:** 215

Pushkin, Aleksander, **III:** 246, 261, 262; **Retro. Supp. I:** 266, 269; **Supp. XVI:** 188

Pussy, King of the Pirates (Acker), **Supp. XII:** 6–7

"Pussycat and the Expert Plumber Who Was a Man, The" (A. Miller), **III:** 146–147

Pussycat Fever (Acker), **Supp. XII:** 6

Putnam, George Haven, **Supp. XVIII:** 257, 260

Putnam, George P., **II:** 314; **Supp. XVIII:** 3–4, 14, 260

Putnam, Phelps, **I:** 288

Putnam, Samuel, **II:** 26; **III:** 479; **Supp. III Part 2:** 615

"Put Off the Wedding Five Times and Nobody Comes to It" (Sandburg), **III:** 586–587

Puttenham, George, **Supp. I Part 1:** 113

Puttermesser Papers, The (Ozick), **Supp. V:** 269

"Putting on *Visit to a Small Planet*" (Vidal), **Supp. IV Part 2:** 683

"Put Yourself in My Shoes" (Carver), **Supp. III Part 1:** 139, 141

Put Yourself in My Shoes (Carver), **Supp. III Part 1:** 139

Putzi, Jennifer, **Supp. XV:** 284

Puzo, Mario, **Supp. IV Part 1:** 390

"Puzzle of Modern Society, The" (Kazin), **Supp. VIII:** 103

Pygmalion (Shaw), **Supp. XII:** 14

Pyle, Ernie, **III:** 148; **Supp. V:** 240; **Supp. XVII:** 61

Pylon (Faulkner), **II:** 64–65, 73; **Retro. Supp. I:** 84, 85

Pynchon, Thomas, **III:** 258; **Retro. Supp. I:** 278; **Retro. Supp. II:** 279, 324; **Supp. II Part 2:** 557, **617–638; Supp. III Part 1:** 217; **Supp. IV Part 1:** 53, 279; **Supp. IV Part 2:** 570; **Supp. IX:** 207, 208, 212; **Supp. V:** 40, 44, 52; **Supp. VIII:** 14; **Supp. X:** 260, 301, 302; **Supp. XI:** 103; **Supp. XII:** 289; **Supp. XIV:** 49, 53, 54, 96; **Supp. XVI:** 123, 128; **Supp. XVII:** 183, 225, 232, 236

Pyrah, Gill, **Supp. V:** 126

"Pyramid Club, The" (Doctorow), **Supp. IV Part 1:** 234

"Pyrography" (Ashbery), **Supp. III Part 1:** 18

Pythagoras, **I:** 332

Pythagorean Silence (Howe), **Supp. IV Part 2:** 426, 428–429

Q

"Qebehseneuf" (Goldbarth), **Supp. XII:** 186

"Quadroons, The" (Child), **Supp. XVIII:** 124

"Quai d'Orléans" (Bishop), **Supp. I Part 1:** 89

"Quail for Mr. Forester" (Humphrey), **Supp. IX:** 94

"Quail in Autumn" (W. J. Smith), **Supp. XIII:** 334–335, 339

"Quaker Graveyard in Nantucket, The" (Lowell), **II:** 54, 550; **Retro. Supp. II:** 178, 186–187

"Quake Theory" (Olds), **Supp. X:** 203

Qualey, Carlton C., **Supp. I Part 2:** 650

Quality of Hurt, The (C. Himes), **Supp. XVI:** 137, 145

"Quality of Wine" (Carruth), **Supp. XVI:** 59

"Quality Time" (Kingsolver), **Supp. VII:** 203

"Quandary" (F. Wright), **Supp. XVII:** 244

Quang-Ngau-chè, **III:** 473

Quarles, Francis, **I:** 178, 179

Quarry, The (Chesnutt), **Supp. XIV:** 76

"Quarry, The" (Nemerov), **III:** 272

Quarry, The: New Poems (Eberhart), **I:** 532, 539

Quartermain, Peter, **Supp. IV Part 2:** 423, 434

"Quaternions, The" (Bradstreet), **Supp. I Part 1:** 104–106, 114, 122

"Quatrains for Ishi" (Komunyakaa), **Supp. XIII:** 129

Queechy (S. Warner as Wetherell), **Supp. XVIII:** 257, **264–266**

"Queen Elizabeth and the Blind Girl or Music for the Dead Children" (B. Kelly), **Supp. XVII:** 124, 125

"Queen of the Blues" (Brooks), **Supp. III Part 1:** 75

Queen of the Damned, The (Rice), **Supp. VII:** 290, 292–293, 297, 299

Queen of the Mob (film), **Supp. XIII:** 170

"Queens of France" (Wilder), **IV:** 365

"Queen's Twin, The" (Jewett), **Retro. Supp. II:** 138

Queen's Twin, The, and Other Stories (Jewett), **Retro. Supp. II:** 140

Queen Victoria (Strachey), **Supp. I Part 2:** 485, 494; **Supp. XIV:** 342

Queer (Burroughs), **Supp. III Part 1:** 93–102

"Queer Beer" (Hansberry), **Supp. IV Part 1:** 374

"Quelques considérations sur la méthode subjective" (James), **II:** 345–346

"Question" (Swenson), **Supp. IV Part 2:** 640

"Question and Answer" (Hughes), **Retro. Supp. I:** 211

"Questioning Faces" (Frost), **Retro. Supp. I:** 141

"Question Mark in the Circle, The" (Stegner), **Supp. IV Part 2:** 597

"Questionnaire, The" (Snodgrass), **Supp. VI:** 318

"Question of Fidelity, A" (Beauvoir), **Supp. IX:** 4
"Question of Our Speech, The" (Ozick), **Supp. V:** 272
"Question of Simone de Beauvoir, The" (Algren), **Supp. IX:** 4
Questions for Ecclesiastes (Jarman), **Supp. XVII:** 109, 110, **118–119**
"Questions of Geography" (Hollander), **Supp. I Part 1:** 96
"Questions of Travel" (Bishop), **Retro. Supp. II:** 47
Questions of Travel (Bishop), **Retro. Supp. II: 46–48; Supp. I Part 1:** 72, 83, 92, 94
"Questions to Tourists Stopped by a Pineapple Field" (Merwin), **Supp. III Part 1:** 355
"Questions without Answers" (T. Williams), **IV:** 384
"Quest of the Purple-Fringed, The" (Frost), **Retro. Supp. I:** 139
Quest of the Silver Fleece, The (Du Bois), **Supp. II Part 1:** 176–178
Quevedo y Villegas, Francisco Gómez, **Retro. Supp. I:** 423
Quickly: A Column for Slow Readers (Mailer), **Retro. Supp. II:** 202
Quicksand (Larsen), **Supp. XVIII:** 119, 121, 122, **124–127**
Quicksand and Passing (Larsen; McDowell, ed.), **Supp. XVIII:** 125
"Quies," (Pound), **Retro. Supp. I:** 413
Quiet Days in Clichy (H. Miller), **III:** 170, 178, 183–184, 187
"Quiet Desperation" (Simpson), **Supp. IX:** 277–278
"Quiet of the Mind" (Nye), **Supp. XIII:** 284
"Quilting" (D. West), **Supp. XVIII:** 283
Quin, Mike (pseudonym). *See* Ryan, Paul William
Quincy, Edmund, **Supp. XVIII:** 4
Quindlen, Anna, **Supp. XVI:** 108; **Supp. XVII: 165–181**
Quinlan, Kathleen, **Supp. X:** 80
Quinn, John, **III:** 471
Quinn, Paul, **Supp. V:** 71
Quinn, Sister M. Bernetta, **III:** 479; **IV:** 421
Quinn, Vincent, **I:** 386, 401, 402; **Supp. I Part 1:** 270
"Quinnapoxet" (Kunitz), **Supp. III Part 1:** 263
Quinn's Book (W. Kennedy), **Supp. VII:** 133, 148–150, 153
Quintero, José, **III:** 403
Quintilian, **IV:** 123
Quinzaine for This Yule, A (Pound), **Retro. Supp. I:** 285
Quite Contrary: The Mary and Newt Story (Dixon), **Supp. XII: 144,** 153
Quod Erat Demonstrandum (Stein), **IV:** 34
Quo Vadis? (Sienkiewicz), **Supp. IV Part 2:** 518; **Supp. XVI:** 182

R

Raab, Max, **Supp. XI:** 309
"Rabbi, The" (Hayden), **Supp. II Part 1:** 363, 369
Rabbit, Run (Updike), **IV:** 214, 223, 230–234; **Retro. Supp. I:** 320, 325, 326, 327, 331, 333, 335; **Supp. XI:** 140; **Supp. XII:** 298; **Supp. XVI:** 220
"Rabbit, The" (Barnes), **Supp. III Part 1:** 34
Rabbit at Rest (Updike), **Retro. Supp. I:** 334
Rabbit Is Rich (Updike), **Retro. Supp. I:** 334
Rabbit novels (Updike), **Supp. V:** 269
Rabbit Redux (Updike), **IV:** 214; **Retro. Supp. I:** 332, 333
Rabbit's Umbrella, The (Plimpton), **Supp. XVI:** 244
"Rabbits Who Caused All the Trouble, The" (Thurber), **Supp. I Part 2:** 610
Rabelais, and His World (Bakhtin), **Retro. Supp. II:** 273
Rabelais, François, **I:** 130; **II:** 111, 112, 302, 535; **III:** 77, 78, 174, 182; **IV:** 68; **Supp. I Part 2:** 461
Rabelais and His World (Bakhtin), **Supp. X:** 120
Rabinbach, Anson, **Supp. XII:** 166
Rabinowitz, Paula, **Supp. V:** 161
"Race" (Emerson), **II:** 6
"Race Contacts and Inter-Racial Relations" (Locke), **Supp. XIV:** 211
"Race Contacts and Inter-Racial Relations: A Study in the Theory and Practice of Race" (lectures, Locke), **Supp. XIV:** 199, 209
Race Contacts and Interracial Relations: Lectures on the Theory and Practice of Race (Locke, Stewart, ed.), **Supp. XIV:** 196, **209–210**
"'RACE LINE' IS A PRODUCT OF CAPITALISM, THE" (Baraka), **Supp. II Part 1:** 61
"Race of Life, The" (Thurber), **Supp. I Part 2:** 614
"Race Problems and Modern Society" (Toomer), **Supp. III Part 2:** 486
Race Questions, Provincialism, and Other American Problems (Royce), **Supp. XIV:** 199
"Race Riot, Tulsa, 1921" (Olds), **Supp. X:** 205
Race Rock (Matthiessen), **Supp. V:** 201
"Races, The" (Lowell), **II:** 554
"Rachel" (D. West), **Supp. XVIII:** 289
Rachel Carson: Witness for Nature (Lear), **Supp. IX:** 19
Rachel River (film, Smolan), **Supp. XVI:** 36
"Racial Progress and Race Adjustment" (Locke), **Supp. XIV:** 210
Racine, Jean Baptiste, **II:** 543, 573; **III:** 145, 151, 152, 160; **IV:** 317, 368, 370; **Supp. I Part 2:** 716
"Radical" (Moore), **III:** 211
"Radical Chic" (Wolfe), **Supp. III Part 2:** 577–578, 584, 585
Radical Chic & Mau-mauing the Flak Catchers (Wolfe), **Supp. III Part 2:** 577–578
Radical Empiricism of William James, The (Wild), **II:** 362, 363–364
Radicalism in America, The (Lasch), **I:** 259
"Radical Jewish Humanism: The Vision of E. L. Doctorow" (Clayton), **Supp. IV Part 1:** 238
"Radically Condensed History of Postindustrial Life, A" (Wallace), **Supp. X:** 309
Radinovsky, Lisa, **Supp. XV:** 284, 285
"Radio" (O'Hara), **III:** 369
Radio Days (film; Allen), **Supp. XV:** 9
"Radio Pope" (Goldbarth), **Supp. XII:** 188, 192
Raditzer (Matthiessen), **Supp. V:** 201
Radkin, Paul, **Supp. I Part 2:** 539
"Rafaela Who Drinks Coconut & Papaya Juice on Tuesdays" (Cisneros), **Supp. VII:** 63
Rafelson, Bob, **Supp. XIV:** 241
Raffalovich, Marc-André, **Supp. XIV:** 335
"Raft, The" (Lindsay), **Supp. I Part 2:** 393
Rag and Bone Shop of the Heart, The: Poems for Men (Bly, Hillman, and Meade, eds.), **Supp. IV Part 1:** 67
Rage in Harlem (C. Himes). *See For Love of Imabelle* (C. Himes)
Rage to Live, A (O'Hara), **III:** 361
Raglan, Lord, **I:** 135
Rago, Henry, **Supp. III Part 2:** 624, 628, 629
"Ragtime" (Doctorow), **Supp. IV Part 1:** 234
Ragtime (Doctorow), **Retro. Supp. II:** 108; **Supp. IV Part 1:** 217, 222–224, 231, 232, 233, 234, 237, 238; **Supp. V:** 45
Ragtime (film), **Supp. IV Part 1:** 236
Ragtime (musical, McNally), **Supp. XIII:** 207
Rahaim, Liz, **Supp. XVII:** 2
Rahv, Philip, **Retro. Supp. I:** 112; **Supp. II Part 1:** 136; **Supp. IX:** 8; **Supp. VIII:** 96; **Supp. XIV:** 3; **Supp. XV:** 140
"Raid" (Hughes), **Retro. Supp. I:** 208
Raids on the Unspeakable (Merton), **Supp. VIII:** 201, 208
Rail, DeWayne, **Supp. XIII:** 312
"Rain and the Rhinoceros" (Merton), **Supp. VIII:** 201
Rainbow, The (Lawrence), **III:** 27
"Rainbows" (Marquand), **III:** 56
Rainbow Stories, The (Vollmann), **Supp. XVII:** 226, 227, 230, 231, 233
Rainbow Tulip, The (Mora), **Supp. XIII:** 221
"Rain Country" (Haines), **Supp. XII:** 210
"Rain-Dream, A" (Bryant), **Supp. I Part 1:** 164
Raine, Kathleen, **I:** 522, 527
"Rain Falling Now, The" (Dunn), **Supp. XI:** 147
"Rain in the Heart" (Taylor), **Supp. V:** 317, 319

Rain in the Trees, The (Merwin), **Supp. III Part 1:** 340, 342, 345, 349, 354–356
"Rainmaker, The" (Humphrey), **Supp. IX:** 101
Rainwater, Catherine, **Supp. V:** 272
"Rainy Day" (Longfellow), **II:** 498
"Rainy Day, The" (Buck), **Supp. II Part 1:** 127
"Rainy Mountain Cemetery" (Momaday), **Supp. IV Part 2:** 486
Rainy Mountain Christmas Doll (painting) (Momaday), **Supp. IV Part 2:** 493
"Rainy Season: Sub-Tropics" (Bishop), **Supp. I Part 1:** 93
"Raise High the Roof Beam, Carpenters" (Salinger), **III:** 567–569, 571
Raise High the Roof Beam, Carpenters; and Seymour: An Introduction (Salinger), **III:** 552, 567–571, 572
Raise Race Rays Raze: Essays Since 1965 (Baraka), **Supp. II Part 1:** 47, 52, 55
Raisin (musical), **Supp. IV Part 1:** 374
Raising Demons (Jackson), **Supp. IX: 125–126**
Raisin in the Sun, A (film: Columbia Pictures), **Supp. IV Part 1:** 360, 367
Raisin in the Sun, A (Hansberry), **Supp. IV Part 1:** 359, 360, 361, 362–364; **Supp. VIII:** 343
Raisin in the Sun, A (television film: American Playhouse), **Supp. IV Part 1:** 367, 374
Raisin in the Sun, A (unproduced screenplay) (Hansberry), **Supp. IV Part 1:** 360
Rajan, R., **I:** 390
"Rake, The" (Mamet), **Supp. XIV:** 240
Rake's Progress, The (opera), **Supp. II Part 1:** 24
Rakosi, Carl, **Supp. III Part 2:** 614, 615, 616, 617, 618, 621, 629; **Supp. XIV:** 286, 287
Ralegh, Sir Walter, **Supp. I Part 1:** 98
Raleigh, John Henry, **IV:** 366
Ralph, Brett, **Supp. XVII:** 245
Ramakrishna, Sri, **III:** 567
Ramakrishna and His Disciples (Isherwood), **Supp. XIV:** 164
Ramazani, Jahan, **Supp. IV Part 2:** 450
"Ramble of Aphasia, A" (O. Henry), **Supp. II Part 1:** 410
Ramey, Phillip, **Supp. IV Part 1:** 94
Rampersad, Arnold, **Retro. Supp. I:** 196, 200, 201, 204; **Supp. IV Part 1:** 244, 250
Rampling, Anne, **Supp. VII:** 201. *See also* Rice, Anne
Rampling, Charlotte, **Supp. IX:** 253
Ramsey, Priscilla R., **Supp. IV Part 1:** 15
Ramsey, Roger, **Supp. XVI:** 69
Ramsey, William, **Supp. XVIII:** 66
Ramus, Petrus, **Supp. I Part 1:** 104
Rand, Ayn, **Supp. I Part 1:** 294; **Supp. IV Part 2: 517–535**
Randall, Jarrell, 1914–1965 (Lowell, Taylor, and Warren, eds.), **II:** 368, 385
Randall, John H., **III:** 605
Randolph, John, **I:** 5–6
"Range-Finding" (Frost), **Retro. Supp. I:** 131
Range of the Possible (T. Marshall), **Supp. XVII:** 36
Rangoon (F. Barthelme), **Supp. XI:** 25
Rank, Otto, **I:** 135; **Supp. IX:** 105; **Supp. X:** 183, 185, 193
Ranke, Leopold von, **Supp. I Part 2:** 492
Rankin, Daniel, **Retro. Supp. II:** 57, 72; **Supp. I Part 1:** 200, 203, 225
Ranlett, William H., **Supp. XVIII:** 3
Ransohoff, Martin, **Supp. XI:** 305, 306
Ransom, John Crowe, **I:** 265, 301; **II:** 34, 367, 385, 389, 536–537, 542; **III:** 454, **480–502,** 549; **IV:** 121, 122, 123, 124, 125, 127, 134, 140, 141, 236, 237, 433; **Retro. Supp. I:** 90; **Retro. Supp. II:** 176, 177, 178, 183, 220, 228, 246; **Supp. I Part 1:** 80, 361; **Supp. I Part 2:** 423; **Supp. II Part 1:** 90, 91, 136, 137, 139, 318; **Supp. II Part 2:** 639; **Supp. III Part 1:** 318; **Supp. III Part 2:** 542, 591; **Supp. IV Part 1:** 217; **Supp. V:** 315, 331, 337; **Supp. X:** 25, 56, 58; **Supp. XIV:** 1
"Rape" (Coleman), **Supp. XI:** 89–90
"Rape, The" (Baraka), **Supp. II Part 1:** 40
Rape of Bunny Stuntz, The (Gurney), **Supp. V:** 109
"Rape of Philomel, The" (Shapiro), **Supp. II Part 2:** 720
"Rape of the Lock, The" (Pope), **Supp. XIV:** 8
Rapf, Joanna, **Supp. XVIII:** 251
Raphael, **I:** 15; **III:** 505, 521, 524; **Supp. I Part 1:** 363
"Rapist" (Dunn), **Supp. XI:** 144
Rap on Race, A (Baldwin and Mead), **Supp. I Part 1:** 66
"Rappaccini's Daughter" (Hawthorne), **II:** 229
"Rapunzel" (Sexton), **Supp. II Part 2:** 691
Rare & Endangered Species: A Novella & Short Stories (Bausch), **Supp. VII:** 51, 54
"Raree Show" (MacLeish), **III:** 9
Rascoe, Burton, **III:** 106, 115
Raskin, Jonah, **Supp. XV:** 116
"Raskolnikov" (Simic), **Supp. VIII:** 282
Rasmussen, Douglas, **Supp. IV Part 2:** 528, 530
Rasmussen, Halfdan, **Supp. XVIII:** 180
Rasselas (Johnson), **Supp. XI:** 209
Rathmann, Andrew, **Supp. XV:** 34
"Ration" (Baraka), **Supp. II Part 1:** 50
"Rationale of Verse, The" (Poe), **III:** 427–428; **Retro. Supp. II:** 266
Ratner, Rochelle, **Supp. XV:** 105
Ratner's Star (DeLillo), **Supp. VI:** 1, 2, 3, 4, 10, 12, 14; **Supp. XVIII:** 140
"Rat of Faith, The" (Levine), **Supp. V:** 192
Rattigan, Terence, **III:** 152
Raugh, Joseph, **Supp. I Part 1:** 286
Rauschenberg, Robert, **Supp. XV:** 187
Rauschenbusch, Walter, **III:** 293; **Supp. I Part 1:** 7
Ravelstein (Bellow), **Retro. Supp. II:** 19, **33–34**
Raven, Simon, **Supp. XII:** 241
Raven, The (film, Friedlander), **Supp. XVII:** 58
"Raven, The" (Poe), **III:** 413, 421–422, 426; **Retro. Supp. II:** 265, 266–267; **Supp. XVII:** 58
Raven, The, and Other Poems (Poe), **III:** 413
Ravenal, Shannon, **Supp. IV Part 1:** 93
"Raven Days, The" (Lanier), **Supp. I Part 1:** 351
Ravenna, Michael. *See* Welty, Eudora
"Ravens at Deer Creek" (Wrigley), **Supp. XVIII:** 299–300, 306
Raven's Road (Gunn Allen), **Supp. IV Part 1:** 330, 335
Raver, Anne, **Supp. XVIII:** 191
"Ravine, The" (Carruth), **Supp. XVI:** 53
Rawlings, Marjorie Kinnan, **Supp. X: 219–237; Supp. XVIII:** 194–195
Rawlins, C. L., **Supp. XVII:** 72, 73
Ray, David, **Supp. IV Part 1:** 61
Ray, Janisse, **Supp. XVIII: 189–206**
Ray, Jeanne Wilkinson, **Supp. XII:** 308, 310
Ray, John, **II:** 111, 112
Ray, Man, **IV:** 404; **Retro. Supp. I:** 416; **Supp. XII:** 124
Ray, Nicholas, **Supp. XVIII:** 253
Ray Bradbury Theatre, The (television show), **Supp. IV Part 1:** 103
Raymond, Henry J., **Supp. XVIII:** 4
"Razor's Edge, The" (Wasserstein), **Supp. XV:** 328
Reactionary Essays on Poetry and Ideas (Tate), **Supp. II Part 1:** 106, 146
Read, Deborah, **II:** 122
Read, Forrest, **III:** 478
Read, Herbert, **I:** 523; **II:** 372–373, 377–378; **Retro. Supp. I:** 54; **Supp. III Part 1:** 273; **Supp. III Part 2:** 624, 626
Read, William A., **Supp. XIV:** 4
Reade, Charles, **Supp. I Part 2:** 580
Reader, Constant. *See* Parker, Dorothy
Reader, Dennis J., **Supp. I Part 2:** 454
"Reader, The" (F. Wright), **Supp. XVII:** 246
Reader's Block (Markson), **Supp. XVII: 143–145,** 146
Reader's Encyclopedia, The: An Encyclopedia of World Literature and the Arts (W. Benét), **Supp. XI:** 44
Reader's Guide to William Gaddis's The Recognitions, A (Moore), **Supp. IV Part 1:** 283
Reader's Map of Arkansas (Wright), **Supp. XV:** 348
"Reader's Tale, A" (Doty), **Supp. XI:** 119, 120, 128, 129
"Reading" (Auden), **Supp. VIII:** 155
"Reading Group Guide," **Supp. XI:** 244–245
"Reading Lao Tzu Again in the New Year" (Wright), **Supp. V:** 343
"Reading Late of the Death of Keats" (Kenyon), **Supp. VII:** 169
"Reading Myself" (Lowell), **II:** 555

Reading Myself and Others (P. Roth), **Retro. Supp. II:** 282; **Supp. V:** 45
"Reading *Ode to the West Wind* 25 Years Later" (McCarriston), **Supp. XIV:** 271–272
"Reading of the Psalm, The" (Francis), **Supp. IX:** 79
"Reading Philosophy at Night" (Simic), **Supp. VIII:** 272
Reading Rilke: Reflections on the Problems of Translation (Gass), **Supp. VI:** 92, **93–94**
"Reading Rorty and Paul Celan One Morning in Early June" (Wright), **Supp. V:** 343
"Reading Sarcophagi: An Essay" (Sobin), **Supp. XVI:** 290
"Readings of History" (Rich), **Supp. I Part 2:** 554
"Reading the Signs, Empowering the Eye" (Bambara), **Supp. XI:** 17–18
Reading the Spirit (Eberhart), **I:** 525, 527, 530
"Ready Or Not" (Baraka), **Supp. II Part 1:** 50
Reagan, Ronald, **Supp. IV Part 1:** 224–225
"Real Bowery, The" (Hapgood), **Supp. XVII:** 103
"Real Class" (Vidal), **Supp. IV Part 1:** 35
Real Cool Killers, The (C. Himes), **Supp. XVI:** 143
Real Dope, The (Lardner), **II:** 422–423
"Real Estate" (Moore), **Supp. X:** 178
"Real Gone Guy, A" (McGrath), **Supp. X:** 117
"Real Horatio Alger Story, The" (Cowley), **Supp. II Part 1:** 143
"Realities" (MacLeish), **III:** 4
"Reality in America" (Trilling), **Supp. III Part 2:** 495, 502
"Reality! Reality! What Is It?" (Eberhart), **I:** 536
Reality Sandwiches, 1953–60 (Ginsberg), **Supp. II Part 1:** 315, 320
Real Life of Sebastian Knight, The (Nabokov), **III:** 246; **Retro. Supp. I:** 266, 269, 270, 274
"Really Good Jazz Piano, A" (Yates), **Supp. XI:** 342
Real Presence: A Novel (Bausch), **Supp. VII:** 42–43, 50
"Real Revolution Is Love, The" (Harjo), **Supp. XII:** 224, 225–226
"Real Thing, The" (H. James), **Retro. Supp. I:** 228; **Retro. Supp. II:** 223
"Real Two-Party System" (Vidal), **Supp. IV Part 2:** 679
Real West Marginal Way, The (Hugo), **Supp. VI:** 132, 134; **Supp. XVIII:** 299
"Real World around Us, The" (Carson), **Supp. IX:** 21
Reaper Essays, The (Jarman and McDowell), **Supp. IX:** 270; **Supp. XVII:** 110–111
"*Reaper* Interviews Jean Doh and Sean Dough, *The*" (Jarman and McDowell), **Supp. XVII:** 110
"Reapers" (Toomer), **Supp. III Part 2:** 481; **Supp. IX:** 312
"Reason and Race: A Review of the Literature of the Negro for 1946" (Locke), **Supp. XIV:** 206
"Reason for Moving, A" (Strand), **Supp. IV Part 2:** 624
"Reason for Stories, The: Toward a Moral Fiction" (Stone), **Supp. V:** 298, 300
Reasons for Moving (Strand), **Supp. IV Part 2:** 624–626, 626
"Reasons for Music" (MacLeish), **III:** 19
"Reasons of the Body" (Sanders), **Supp. XVI:** 274
Rebecca, or, The Fille de Chambre (Rowson), **Supp. XV:** 229, **235–236,** 238
Rebecca Harding Davis Reader, A (Pfaelzer, ed.), **Supp. XVI:** 88, 90
Rebel Angels: Twenty-five Poets of the New Formalism (Jarman and Mason, eds.), **Supp. XV:** 251; **Supp. XVII:** 109, 110, 112, 121
"Rebellion" (Lowell), **Retro. Supp. II:** 187
Rebel Powers (Bausch), **Supp. VII:** 41, 45–46, 49–51
Rebel without a Cause (film), **Supp. XII:** 9
"Rebirth of God and the Death of Man, The" (Fiedler), **Supp. XIII:** 108
Rebolledo, Tey Diana, **Supp. XIII:** 214
Recapitulation (Stegner), **Supp. IV Part 2:** 598, 600, 612–613
"Recapitulation, The" (Eberhart), **I:** 522
"Recapitulations" (Shapiro), **Supp. II Part 2:** 701, 702, 708, 710–711
"Receding Horizons" (Lethem and Scholtz), **Supp. XVIII:** 145
"Recencies in Poetry" (Zukofsky), **Supp. III Part 2:** 615
Recent Killing, A (Baraka), **Supp. II Part 1:** 55
"Recent Negro Fiction" (Ellison), **Supp. II Part 1:** 233, 235
"Recessional" (A. Finch), **Supp. XVII:** 70–71
"Recital, The" (Ashbery), **Supp. III Part 1:** 14
"Recitative" (H. Crane), **I:** 390; **Retro. Supp. II:** 78
Reckless Eyeballing (Reed), **Supp. X:** 241
Recognitions, The (Gaddis), **Supp. IV Part 1:** 279, 280–285, 286, 287, 288, 289, 291, 292, 294
Recollections (R. H. Stoddard), **Supp. XV:** 271
Recollections of Logan Pearsall Smith: The Story of a Friendship (Gathorne-Hardy), **Supp. XIV:** 344
"Reconciliation" (Whitman), **IV:** 347
"Reconstructed but Unregenerate" (Ransom), **III:** 496
"Reconstruction and Its Benefits" (Du Bois), **Supp. II Part 1:** 171
Recovering (Sarton), **Supp. VIII:** 264
Recovering the U.S. Hispanic Literary Heritage (Paredes), **Supp. XIII:** 320
"Recovery" (Dove), **Supp. IV Part 1:** 248
Rector of Justin, The (Auchincloss), **Supp. IV Part 1:** 21, 23, 27–30, 36
"Recurrent Dream" (Nelson), **Supp. XVIII:** 176
"RED AUTUMN" (Baraka), **Supp. II Part 1:** 55
Red Badge of Courage, The (Crane), **I:** 201, 207, 212, 405, 406, 407, 408, 412–416, 419, 421, 422, 423, 477, 506; **II:** 264; **III:** 317; **IV:** 350; **Retro. Supp. II:** 108; **Supp. IV Part 1:** 380; **Supp. XIV:** 51; **Supp. XVIII:** 75
Red Badge of Courage, The (S. Crane), **Supp. XVII:** 228
"Redbirds" (C. Frost), **Supp. XV:** 99
"Redbreast in Tampa" (Lanier), **Supp. I Part 1:** 364
"Red Brocade" (Nye), **Supp. XIII:** 288
Redburn: His First Voyage (Melville), **III:** 79–80, 84; **Retro. Supp. I:** 245, 247–248, 249; **Supp. XVIII:** 6
"Red Carpet for Shelley, A" (Wylie), **Supp. I Part 2:** 724
Red Channels (Harnett), **Supp. XV:** 198
"Red Clowns" (Cisneros), **Supp. VII:** 63
Red Coal, The (Stern), **Supp. IX: 291–292**
Red Coat, The (Shanley), **Supp. XIV:** 316–317
"Red Cross" (Hughes), **Retro. Supp. I:** 205
Red Cross (Shepard), **Supp. III Part 2:** 440, 446
Red Death, A (Mosley), **Supp. XIII:** 237, 239, 240
"Red Deer" (C. Frost), **Supp. XV:** 101
Redding, Saunders, **Supp. I Part 1:** 332, 333
Reddings, J. Saunders, **Supp. IV Part 1:** 164
"Red Dust" (Levine), **Supp. V:** 184
Red Dust (Levine), **Supp. V:** 178, 183–184, 188
"Redemption" (Gardner), **Supp. VI:** 72
"Redeployment" (Nemerov), **III:** 267, 272
Redfield, Robert, **IV:** 475
Redford, Robert, **Supp. IX:** 253, 259; **Supp. XIII:** 267; **Supp. XIV:** 223
Redgrave, Lynn, **Supp. V:** 107
Red Harvest (Hammett), **Supp. IV Part 1:** 346–348, 348; **Supp. IV Part 2:** 468
Red-Headed Woman (film), **Retro. Supp. I:** 110; **Supp. XVI:** 191
"Red Horse Wind over Albuquerque" (Harjo), **Supp. XII:** 219
Red Hot Vacuum, The (Solotaroff), **Retro. Supp. II:** 281
"Red Leaves" (Faulkner), **II:** 72
"Red Meat: What Difference Did Stesichoros Make?" (Carson), **Supp. XII:** 107
"Red Pawn" (Rand), **Supp. IV Part 2:** 520
Red Pony, The (Steinbeck), **IV:** 50, 51, 58, 70

Redrawing the Boundaries (Fisher), **Retro. Supp. I:** 39
Red Robins, The (Koch), **Supp. XV:** 185–186, 187
Red Roses for Bronze (Doolittle), **Supp. I Part 1:** 253, 268, 271
Red Rover, The (Cooper), **I:** 342–343, 355
"Red Silk Stockings" (Hughes), **Retro. Supp. I:** 200
Redskins, The (Cooper), **I:** 351, 353
"Red Star, Winter Orbit" (W. Gibson and B. Sterling), **Supp. XVI:** 123
Red Suitcase (Nye), **Supp. XIII:** 277, 278, 287
Red Wallflower, A (S. Warner), **Supp. XVIII:** 260
"Red Wheelbarrow, The" (W. C. Williams), **IV:** 411–412; **Retro. Supp. I:** 419, 430
"Red Wind" (Chandler), **Supp. IV Part 1:** 122
"Redwings" (Wright), **Supp. III Part 2:** 603
Reed, Edward Bliss, **Supp. XV:** 297, 298, 300
Reed, Ishmael, **Retro. Supp. II:** 111, 324–325; **Supp. II Part 1:** 34; **Supp. X: 239–257,** 331; **Supp. XIII:** 181, 182; **Supp. XVI:** 143
Reed, J. D., **Supp. XVI:** 174
Reed, John, **I:** 48, 476, 483; **Supp. X:** 136; **Supp. XV:** 295, 299; **Supp. XVII:** 96, 99, 100; **Supp. XVIII:** 225
Reed, Lou, **Retro. Supp. II:** 266
"Reedbeds of the Hackensack, The" (Clampitt), **Supp. IX:** 41
"Reed of Pan, A" (McCullers), **II:** 585
Reedy, Billy, **Retro. Supp. II:** 65, 67, 71, 73
Reedy, William Marion, **Supp. I Part 2:** 456, 461, 465
Reef, The (Wharton), **IV:** 317–318, 322; **Retro. Supp. I:** 372, **373–374**
Reena and Other Stories (Marshall), **Supp. XI:** 275, 277, 278
Reeve, F. D., **Supp. XV:** 344, 349
Reeve's Tale (Chaucer), **I:** 131
"Reflection from Anita Loos" (Empson), **Supp. XVI:** 190
"Reflections" (Carruth), **Supp. XVI:** 54
"Reflections" (Komunyakaa), **Supp. XIII:** 117
Reflections at Fifty and Other Essays (Farrell), **II:** 49
"Reflections by a Fire" (Sarton), **Supp. VIII:** 259
Reflections in a Golden Eye (McCullers), **II:** 586, 588, 593–596, 604; **IV:** 384, 396
Reflections of a Jacobite (Auchincloss), **Supp. IV Part 1:** 31
Reflections on a Gift of Watermelon Pickle (Dunning), **Supp. XIV:** 126
Reflections on Poetry and Poetics (Nemerov), **III:** 269
"Reflections on the Constitution of Nature" (Freneau), **Supp. II Part 1:** 274
"Reflections on the Death of the Reader" (Morris), **III:** 237
Reflections on the End of an Era (Niebuhr), **III:** 297–298
"Reflections on the Life and Death of Lord Clive" (Paine), **Supp. I Part 2:** 505
Reflections on the Revolution in France (Burke), **Supp. I Part 2:** 511, 512
Reflections: Thinking Part I (Arendt), **Supp. I Part 2:** 570
"Reflex Action and Theism" (James), **II:** 345, 363
"Refrains/Remains/Reminders" (Goldbarth), **Supp. XII:** 180–181, 181
"Refuge" (Kingsolver), **Supp. VII:** 208
"Refuge, A" (Goldbarth), **Supp. XII:** 190
Refugee Children: Theory, Research, and Services (Ahearn and Athey, eds.), **Supp. XI:** 184
"Refugees, The" (Jarrell), **II:** 371
"Refusal" (C. Frost), **Supp. XV:** 102
Regarding Wave (Snyder), **Supp. VIII: 299–300**
Regina (Epstein), **Supp. XII: 170–171**
"Regional Literature of the South" (Rawlings), **Supp. X:** 228
"Regional Writer, The" (O'Connor), **Retro. Supp. II:** 223, 225
Régnier, Henri de, **II:** 528–529
Regulators, The (King), **Supp. V:** 141
Rehder, Robert, **Supp. IV Part 1:** 69
Reichel, Hans, **III:** 183
Reichl, Ruth, **Supp. X:** 79, 85
Reich,Tova, **Supp. XVI:** 158
Reid, B. L., **II:** 41, 47
Reid, Thomas, **II:** 9; **Supp. I Part 1:** 151
"Reign of Snakes" (Wrigley), **Supp. XVIII:** 302–304
Reign of Snakes (Wrigley), **Supp. XVIII:** 293, **302–306**
Reign of Wonder, The (Tanner), **I:** 260
Rein, Yevgeny, **Supp. VIII:** 22
Reinagle, Alexander, **Supp. XV:** 238, 240
"Reincarnation" (Dickey), **Supp. IV Part 1:** 181–182
Reine des pommes, La (C. Himes). *See For Love of Imabelle* (C. Himes)
Reiner, Carl, **Supp. IV Part 2:** 591
Reinfeld, Linda, **Supp. IV Part 2:** 421
Reinhardt, Max, **Supp. XV:** 307
Reinventing the Enemy's Language: Contemporary Native Women's Writing of North America (Bird and Harjo, eds.), **Supp. XII:** 216, 217
Reisman, Jerry, **Supp. III Part 2:** 618
Reitlinger, Gerald, **Supp. XII:** 161
Reivers, The: A Reminiscence (Faulkner), **I:** 305; **II:** 57, 73; **Retro. Supp. I:** 74, 82, 91
"Rejoicings" (Stern), **Supp. IX:** 289–290
Rejoicings: Selected Poems, 1966–1972 (Stern), **Supp. IX: 289–290**
Relation of My Imprisonment, The (Banks), **Supp. V:** 8, 12–13
"Relations between Poetry and Painting, The" (Stevens), **Retro. Supp. I:** 312
Relations of the Alabama-Georgia Dialect to the Provincial Dialects of Great Britain, The (Brooks), **Supp. XIV:** 3
Relative Stranger, A (C. Baxter), **Supp. XVII:** 19, 22
"Relativity of Beauty, The" (Rawlings), **Supp. X:** 226
Relearning the Alphabet (Levertov), **Supp. III Part 1:** 280, 281
"Release" (C. Baxter), **Supp. XVII:** 15
"Release, The" (MacLeish), **III:** 16
Reles, Abe ("Kid Twist"), **Supp. IV Part 1:** 382
"Relevance of an Impossible Ethical Ideal, The" (Niebuhr), **III:** 298
"Religion" (Dunbar), **Supp. II Part 1:** 199
"Religion" (Emerson), **II:** 6
Religion of Nature Delineated, The (Wollaston), **II:** 108
Religious Rebel, A: The Letters of "H. W. S." (Mrs. Pearsall Smith) (L. P. Smith), **Supp. XIV:** 349
"Reluctance" (Frost), **II:** 153
Reluctantly: Autobiographical Essays (Carruth), **Supp. XVI:** 45–46, 50
Remains (Snodgrass), **Supp. VI:** 311, **313–314**
"Remains, The" (Strand), **Supp. IV Part 2:** 627
"Remarks on Color" (Wright), **Supp. XV:** 346
"Remarks on Spencer's *Definition of Mind as Correspondence*" (James), **II:** 345
Remarque, Erich Maria, **Retro. Supp. I:** 113; **Supp. IV Part 1:** 380
Rembrandt, **II:** 536; **IV:** 310; **Supp. IV Part 1:** 390, 391
"Rembrandt, The" (Wharton), **IV:** 310
"Rembrandt's Hat" (Malamud), **Supp. I Part 2:** 435, 437
Rembrandt Takes a Walk (Strand), **Supp. IV Part 2:** 631
"Rembrandt to Rembrandt" (Robinson), **III:** 521–522
Remembered Earth, The: An Anthology of Contemporary Native American Literature (Hobson, ed.), **Supp. IV Part 1:** 321
Remembered Yesterdays (Johnson), **Supp. IX:** 184
"Remembering" (Angelou), **Supp. IV Part 1:** 15
"Remembering Allen Tate" (Cowley), **Supp. II Part 1:** 153
"Remembering Barthes" (Sontag), **Supp. III Part 2:** 451, 471
"Remembering Guston" (Kunitz), **Supp. III Part 1:** 257
"Remembering James Laughlin" (Karr), **Supp. XI:** 242
Remembering Laughter (Stegner), **Supp. IV Part 2:** 598, 606, 607, 608, 611, 614
"Remembering Lobo" (Mora), **Supp. XIII:** 220, 227
"Remembering My Father" (Berry), **Supp. X:** 23
"Remembering that Island" (McGrath), **Supp. X:** 116
"Remembering the Children of Auschwitz" (McGrath), **Supp. X:** 127
"Remembering the Lost World" (Jarrell), **II:** 388

"Remembering the Sixties" (Simpson), **Supp. IX:** 279
Remember Me to Tom (T. Williams), **IV:** 379–380
"Remember the Moon Survives" (Kingsolver), **Supp. VII:** 209
Remember to Remember (H. Miller), **III:** 186
"Remembrance, A" (Gioia), **Supp. XV:** 112
Remembrance of Things Past (Proust), **Supp. IV Part 2:** 600; **Supp. XII:** 9; **Supp. XIII:** 44
Remembrance Rock (Sandburg), **III:** 590
Reminiscence, A (Ashbery), **Supp. III Part 1:** 2
Remnick, David, **Supp. XVI:** 246
"Remora" (Merrill), **Supp. III Part 1:** 326
"Removal" (White), **Supp. I Part 2:** 664–665
"Removal, The" (Merwin), **Supp. III Part 1:** 350, 351
Removed from Time (Matthews and Feeney), **Supp. IX:** 154
Remsen, Ira, **Supp. I Part 1:** 369
"Rémy de Gourmont, A Distinction" (Pound), **III:** 467
"Renaissance" (Carruth), **Supp. XVI:** 56
Renaissance in the South (Bradbury), **I:** 288–289
Renaldo and Clara (film, Dylan and Shepard), **Supp. XVIII:** 21, 28, 31
"Renaming the Kings" (Levine), **Supp. V:** 184
Renan, Joseph Ernest, **II:** 86; **IV:** 440, 444
Renard, Jules, **IV:** 79
"Renascence" (Millay), **III:** 123, 125–126, 128; **Supp. XV:** 42
Renault, Mary, **Supp. IV Part 2:** 685
"Rendezvous, The" (Kumin), **Supp. IV Part 2:** 455
René, Norman, **Supp. X:** 146, 152
Renée (anonymous author), **Supp. XVI:** 64, 66
"Renegade, The" (Jackson), **Supp. IX:** 120
Renewal of Life series (Mumford), **Supp. II Part 2:** 476, 479, 481, 482, 485, 495, 497
Renoir, Jean, **Supp. XII:** 259
Renouvrier, Charles, **II:** 344–345, 346
"Renunciation" (Banks), **Supp. V:** 10
Renza, Louis A., **Retro. Supp. II:** 142
"Repeating Dream" (Gander), **Supp. XV:** 340
Repent in Haste (Marquand), **III:** 59
Reperusals and Re-Collections (L. P. Smith), **Supp. XIV:** 346–347
"Repetitive Heart, The: Eleven Poems in Imitation of the Fugue Form" (Schwartz), **Supp. II Part 2:** 645–646
"Replacing Regionalism" (Murphy), **Retro. Supp. II:** 143
Replansky, Naomi, **Supp. X:** 119
"Reply to Mr. Wordsworth" (MacLeish), **III:** 19
"Report, A" (Jin), **Supp. XVIII:** 93
"Report from a Forest Logged by the Weyhaeuser Company" (Wagoner), **Supp. IX:** 328
"Report from North Vietnam" (Paley), **Supp. VI:** 227
Report from Part One (Brooks), **Supp. III Part 1:** 70, 72, 80, 82–85
Report from Part Two (Brooks), **Supp. III Part 1:** 87
Report on a Game Survey of the North Central States (Leopold), **Supp. XIV:** 182
"Report on the Barnhouse Effect" (Vonnegut), **Supp. II Part 2:** 756
"Report to Crazy Horse" (Stafford), **Supp. XI: 324–325**
"Repose of Rivers" (H. Crane), **I:** 393; **Retro. Supp. II:** 78, 81
"Repossession of a Heritage, The" (Zagarell), **Supp. XV:** 270, 281
"Representation and the War for Reality" (Gass), **Supp. VI:** 88
Representative Men (Emerson), **II:** 1, 5–6, 8
"Representing Far Places" (Stafford), **Supp. XI:** 321
Repression and Recovery (Nelson), **Supp. XVIII:** 226
"REPRISE OF ONE OF A. G.'S BEST POEMS" (Baraka), **Supp. II Part 1:** 59
"Reproducing Ourselves Is All Very Well" (E. Hoffman), **Supp. XVI:** 155
Republic (Plato), **I:** 485
"Republican Manifesto, A" (Paine), **Supp. I Part 2:** 511
Republic of Love, The (Shields), **Supp. VII:** 323–324, 326, 327
"Requa" (Olsen), **Supp. XIII:** 294, **302–303,** 304
Requa, Kenneth A., **Supp. I Part 1:** 107
"Requa I" (Olsen). *See* "Requa" (Olsen)
"Request for Offering" (Eberhart), **I:** 526
"Requiem" (Akhmatova), **Supp. VIII:** 20
"Requiem" (LaBastille), **Supp. X:** 105
Requiem for a Nun (Faulkner), **II:** 57, 72–73
Requiem for Harlem (H. Roth), **Supp. IX:** 235, 236, **240–242**
"Rescue, The" (Updike), **IV:** 214
"Rescued Year, The" (Stafford), **Supp. XI:** 322, 323
Rescued Year, The (Stafford), **Supp. XI: 321–322**
"Rescue with Yul Brynner" (Moore), **III:** 215
"Resemblance" (Bishop), **Supp. I Part 1:** 86
"Resemblance between a Violin Case and a Coffin, A" (T. Williams), **IV:** 378–379
"Reservations" (Taylor), **Supp. V:** 323
"Reserved Memorials" (Mather), **Supp. II Part 2:** 446, 449
"Resistance to Civil Government" (Thoreau), **Supp. X:** 27, 28
Resist Much, Obey Little (Berry), **Supp. XIII:** 2
"Resolution and Independence" (Wordsworth), **Supp. XV:** 346
Resources of Hope (R. Williams), **Supp. IX:** 146
"Respectable Place, A" (O'Hara), **III:** 369
"Respectable Woman, A" (Chopin), **Retro. Supp. II:** 66
"Respite" (Pedersen; Nelson, trans.), **Supp. XVIII:** 180
Responses (Wilbur), **Supp. III Part 2:** 541
"Response to a Rumor that the Oldest Whorehouse in Wheeling, West Virginia, Has Been Condemned" (Wright), **Supp. III Part 2:** 602
Restif de La Bretonne, Nicolas, **III:** 175
"Rest of Life, The" (Gordon), **Supp. IV Part 1:** 311
Rest of Life, The: Three Novellas (Gordon), **Supp. IV Part 1:** 310–312
Rest of the Way, The (McClatchy), **Supp. XII:** 255, **258–259**
Restoration comedy, **Supp. I Part 2:** 617
"Restraint" (F. Barthelme), **Supp. XI:** 26
"Result" (Emerson), **II:** 6
"Résumé" (Parker), **Supp. IX:** 189
Resurrection (Della Francesca), **Supp. XV:** 262
"Resurrection" (Harjo), **Supp. XII:** 224
"Resurrection" (Jin), **Supp. XVIII:** 94–95
Resurrection, The (Gardner), **Supp. VI:** 61, 63, **64–65,** 68, 69, 73, 74
"Retort" (Hay), **Supp. XIV:** 133
Retour amont (Char; Sobin, trans.), **Supp. XVI:** 282
Retrieval System, The (Kumin), **Supp. IV Part 2:** 449, 451, 452
"Retrievers in Translation" (Doty), **Supp. XI:** 132
"Retroduction to American History" (Tate), **IV:** 129
"Retrospects and Prospects" (Lanier), **Supp. I Part 1:** 352
"Return" (Corso), **Supp. XII:** 135
"Return" (Creeley), **Supp. IV Part 1:** 141, 145
"Return" (MacLeish), **III:** 12
"Return, The" (Bidart), **Supp. XV:** 32–33
"Return, The" (Pound), **Retro. Supp. I:** 288
"Return, The" (Ray), **Supp. XVIII:** 194
"Return, The" (Roethke), **III:** 533
"Return, The: Orihuela, 1965" (Levine), **Supp. V:** 194
"Return: An Elegy, The" (Warren), **IV:** 239
"Return: Buffalo" (Hogan), **Supp. IV Part 1:** 411
"Returning" (Komunyakaa), **Supp. XIII:** 122
"Returning a Lost Child" (Glück), **Supp. V:** 81
"Returning from the Enemy" (Harjo), **Supp. XII:** 229–230
"Returning the Borrowed Road" (Komunyakaa), **Supp. XIII:** 113, 133
"Return of Alcibiade, The" (Chopin), **Retro. Supp. II:** 58, 64
Return of Ansel Gibbs, The (Buechner), **III:** 310; **Supp. XII: 48**

"Return of Eros to Academe, The" (Bukiet), **Supp. XVII:** 47
"Return of Spring" (Winters), **Supp. II Part 2:** 791
Return of the Native, The (Hardy), **II:** 184–185, 186
Return of the Vanishing American, The (Fiedler), **Supp. XIII:** 103
Return to a Place Lit by a Glass of Milk (Simic), **Supp. VIII:** 274, 276, 283
"Return to Lavinia" (Caldwell), **I:** 310
"Return to Thin Air: The Everest Disaster Ten Years Later" *(Outside),* **Supp. XVIII:** 113
Reuben (Wideman), **Supp. X:** 320
Reuben and Rachel; or, Tales of Old Times (Rowson), **Supp. XV: 240–241**
Reunion (Mamet), **Supp. XIV:** 240, 247, 254
"Reunion in Brooklyn" (H. Miller), **III:** 175, 184
Reuther brothers, **I:** 493
"Reveille" (Kingsolver), **Supp. VII:** 208
"Reveille" (Untermeyer), **Supp. XV:** 300
"Reveille, The" (Harte), **Supp. II Part 1:** 342–343
Revelation (biblical book), **II:** 541; **IV:** 104, 153, 154; **Supp. I Part 1:** 105, 273
"Revelation" (O'Connor), **III:** 349, 353–354; **Retro. Supp. II:** 237
"Revelation" (Warren), **III:** 490
Revenge (Harrison), **Supp. VIII:** 39, 45
"Revenge of Hamish, The" (Lanier), **Supp. I Part 1:** 365
"Revenge of Hannah Kemhuff, The" (Walker), **Supp. III Part 2:** 521
"Revenge of Rain-in-the-Face, The" (Longfellow), **Retro. Supp. II:** 170
Reverberator, The (James), **Retro. Supp. I:** 227
"Reverdure" (Berry), **Supp. X:** 22
Reverdy, Pierre, **Supp. XV:** 178, 182
"Reverend Father Gilhooley" (Farrell), **II:** 45
Reverse Transcription (Kushner), **Supp. IX:** 138
Reversible Errors (Turow), **Supp. XVII: 220–221**
"Rev. Freemont Deadman" (Masters), **Supp. I Part 2:** 463
Reviewer's ABC, A (Aiken), **I:** 58
Review of Contemporary Fiction, 1990 (Tabbi, ed.), **Supp. XVII:** 143
"Revolt, against the Crepuscular Spirit in Modern Poetry" (Pound), **Retro. Supp. I:** 286
Revolutionary Petunias (Walker), **Supp. III Part 2:** 520, 522, 530
Revolutionary Road (Yates), **Supp. XI:** 334, **335–340**
"Revolutionary Symbolism in America" (Burke), **I:** 272
"Revolutionary Theatre, The" (Baraka), **Supp. II Part 1:** 42
Revolution in Taste, A: Studies of Dylan Thomas, Allen Ginsberg, Sylvia Plath, and Robert Lowell (Simpson), **Supp. IX:** 276
"Revolution in the Revolution in the Revolution" (Snyder), **Supp. VIII:** 300
Revon, Marcel, **II:** 525
"Rewaking, The" (W. C. Williams), **Retro. Supp. I:** 430
"Rewrite" (Dunn), **Supp. XI:** 147
Rexroth, Kenneth, **II:** 526; **Supp. II Part 1:** 307; **Supp. II Part 2:** 436; **Supp. III Part 2:** 625, 626; **Supp. IV Part 1:** 145–146; **Supp. VIII:** 289; **Supp. XIII:** 75; **Supp. XIV:** 287; **Supp. XV:** 140, 141, 146
Reynolds, Ann (pseudonym). *See* Bly, Carol
Reynolds, Clay, **Supp. XI:** 254
Reynolds, David, **Supp. XV:** 269
Reynolds, Sir Joshua, **Supp. I Part 2:** 716
Reynolds, Quentin, **IV:** 286
Reznikoff, Charles, **IV:** 415; **Retro. Supp. I:** 422; **Supp. III Part 2:** 615, 616, 617, 628; **Supp. XIV: 277–296**
"Rhapsodist, The" (Brown), **Supp. I Part 1:** 125–126
"Rhapsody on a Windy Night" (Eliot), **Retro. Supp. I:** 55
Rhetoric of Motives, A (Burke), **I:** 272, 275, 278, 279
Rhetoric of Religion, The (Burke), **I:** 275, 279
"Rhobert" (Toomer), **Supp. IX:** 316–317
"Rhododendrons" (Levis), **Supp. XI:** 260, 263
Rhubarb Show, The (radio, Keillor), **Supp. XVI:** 178
"Rhyme of Sir Christopher, The" (Longfellow), **II:** 501
Rhymes to Be Traded for Bread (Lindsay), **Supp. I Part 2:** 380, 381–382
Rhys, Ernest, **III:** 458
Rhys, Jean, **Supp. III Part 1:** 42, 43; **Supp. XVIII:** 131
"Rhythm & Blues" (Baraka), **Supp. II Part 1:** 37–38
Rhythms (Reznikoff), **Supp. XIV:** 279, 282, 283
Rhythms II (Reznikoff), **Supp. XIV:** 282, 283, 284
Ribalow, Harold, **Supp. IX:** 236
Ribbentrop, Joachim von, **IV:** 249
Ribicoff, Abraham, **Supp. IX:** 33
Ricardo, David, **Supp. I Part 2:** 628, 634
Rice, Allen Thorndike, **Retro. Supp. I:** 362
Rice, Anne, **Supp. VII: 287–306**
Rice, Elmer, **I:** 479; **III:** 145, 160–161
Rice, Mrs. Grantland, **II:** 435
Rice, Philip Blair, **IV:** 141
Rice, Stan, **Supp. XII:** 2
Rice, Tom, **Supp. XIV:** 125
Rich, Adrienne, **Retro. Supp. I:** 8, 36, 42, 47, 404; **Retro. Supp. II:** 43, 191, 245; **Supp. I Part 2:** 546–547, **550–578; Supp. III Part 1:** 84, 354; **Supp. III Part 2:** 541, 599; **Supp. IV Part 1:** 257, 325; **Supp. V:** 82; **Supp. VIII:** 272; **Supp. XII:** 217, 229, 255; **Supp. XIII:** 294; **Supp. XIV:** 126, 129; **Supp. XV:** 176, 252; **Supp. XVII:** 32, 74
Rich, Arnold, **Supp. I Part 2:** 552
Rich, Frank, **Supp. IV Part 2:** 585, 586; **Supp. V:** 106
Richard Cory (Gurney), **Supp. V:** 99–100, 105
"Richard Hunt's 'Arachne'" (Hayden), **Supp. II Part 1:** 374
Richard II (Shakespeare), **Supp. XVII:** 244
Richard III (Shakespeare), **Supp. I Part 2:** 422
Richards, David, **Supp. IV Part 2:** 576
Richards, Grant, **I:** 515
Richards, I. A., **I:** 26, 273–274, 279, 522; **III:** 498; **IV:** 92; **Supp. I Part 1:** 264, 265; **Supp. I Part 2:** 647
Richards, Ivor Armonstrong, **Supp. XIV:** 2–3, 16
Richards, Laura E., **II:** 396; **III:** 505–506, 507
Richards, Leonard, **Supp. XIV:** 48
Richards, Lloyd, **Supp. IV Part 1:** 362; **Supp. VIII:** 331
Richards, Rosalind, **III:** 506
Richards, Tad, **Supp. XVII:** 77
Richardson, Alan, **III:** 295
Richardson, Charles, **Supp. XVIII:** 14, 15
Richardson, Dorothy, **I:** 53; **II:** 320; **Supp. III Part 1:** 65
Richardson, Helen Patges, **Retro. Supp. II:** 95
Richardson, Henry Hobson, **I:** 3, 10
Richardson, Maurice, **Supp. XII:** 241
Richardson, Samuel, **I:** 134; **II:** 104, 111, 322; **Supp. IX:** 128; **Supp. V:** 127; **Supp. XV:** 232
Richardson, Tony, **Supp. XI:** 305, 306
"Richard Wright and Recent Negro Fiction" (Ellison), **Retro. Supp. II:** 116
"Richard Wright's Blues" (Ellison), **Retro. Supp. II:** 117, 124
"Richard Yates: A Requiem" (Lawrence), **Supp. XI:** 335
"Rich Boy, The" (Fitzgerald), **II:** 94; **Retro. Supp. I:** 98, 108
Richer, the Poorer, The: Sketches and Reminiscences (D. West), **Supp. XVIII:** 277, 289
"Riches" (Bausch), **Supp. VII:** 54
Richler, Mordecai, **Supp. XI:** 294, 297
Richman, Robert, **Supp. XI:** 249; **Supp. XV:** 120–121, 251
Richmond (Masters), **Supp. I Part 2:** 471
Richter, Conrad, **Supp. X:** 103; **Supp. XVIII: 207–222**
Richter, Jean Paul, **II:** 489, 492; **Supp. XVI:** 182
Rick Bass (Weltzien), **Supp. XVI:** 20
Rickman, Clio, **Supp. I Part 2:** 519
Ricks, Christopher, **Retro. Supp. I:** 56; **Supp. XVIII:** 20, 30, 32
Riddel, Joseph N., **IV:** 95
"Riddle, The" (Hay), **Supp. XIV:** 130
"Ride in an Omnibus, A" (Briggs), **Supp. XVIII:** 9, 16

"Riders to the Blood-Red Wrath" (Brooks), **Supp. III Part 1:** 82–83
Riders to the Sea (Synge), **III:** 157
Ridge, Lola, **Supp. IX:** 308; **Supp. XV:** 307
Riding, Alan, **Supp. XVI:** 294
Riding, Laura, **I:** 437
"Riding Out at Evening" (McCarriston), **Supp. XIV:** 262–263
Riding the Iron Rooster: By Train through China (Theroux), **Supp. VIII:** 324
Riesenberg, Felix, **I:** 360, 361
Riesman, David, **Supp. I Part 2:** 649, 650
"Rif, to Music, The" (Bowles), **Supp. IV Part 1:** 89
Riffs & Reciprocities (Dunn), **Supp. XI:** **154–155**
Rifles, The (Vollmann), **Supp. XVII:** 226, 233
Riggs, Marlon, **Supp. XI:** 19
Right Madness on Skye, The (Hugo), **Supp. VI:** 145–147
Rights of Man (Paine), **Supp. I Part 2:** 508, 511, 512–514, 516, 519, 523
"Rights of Woman" (Rowson), **Supp. XV:** 243
"Rights of Women, The" (Brown). *See Alcuin: A Dialogue* (Brown)
Right Stuff, The (Wolfe), **Supp. III Part 2:** 581–584
Right Thoughts in Sad Hours (Mather), **IV:** 144
Rigney, Barbara Hill, **Supp. VIII:** 215
"Rigorists" (Moore), **III:** 198
Riis, Jacob A., **I:** 293; **Supp. I Part 1:** 13; **Supp. XVII:** 101, 106
Riley, James Whitcomb, **I:** 205; **Supp. II Part 1:** 192, 193, 196, 197
Rilke, Rainer Maria, **I:** 445, 523; **II:** 367, 381, 382–383, 389, 543, 544; **III:** 552, 558, 563, 571, 572; **IV:** 380, 443; **Retro. Supp. II:** 20, 187; **Supp. I Part 1:** 264; **Supp. I Part 2:** 573; **Supp. III Part 1:** 239, 242, 246, 283, 319–320; **Supp. IV Part 1:** 284; **Supp. V:** 208, 343; **Supp. VIII:** 30, 40; **Supp. X:** 164; **Supp. XI:** 126; **Supp. XIII:** 74, 88; **Supp. XV:** 93, 212, 222,**Supp. XV:** 223, 225; **Supp. XVI:** 292; **Supp. XVII:** 244
Rilke on Love and Other Difficulties (Rilke), **Supp. X:** 164
"Rilke's Growth as a Poet" (Dobyns), **Supp. XIII:** 77
"Rimbaud" (Kerouac), **Supp. III Part 1:** 232
Rimbaud, Arthur, **I:** 381, 383, 389, 391, 526; **II:** 528, 543, 545; **III:** 23, 174, 189; **IV:** 286, 380, 443; **Retro. Supp. I:** 56; **Retro. Supp. II:** 187, 326; **Supp. III Part 1:** 14, 195; **Supp. IV Part 2:** 624; **Supp. VIII:** 39, 40; **Supp. XII:** 1, 16, 128, 255; **Supp. XIII:** 284; **Supp. XIV:** 338; **Supp. XVIII:** 23, 33
Rinehart, Stanley, **III:** 36
Ring, Frances Kroll, **Supp. IX:** 63, 64
Ring and the Book, The (Browning), **Supp. I Part 2:** 416, 468
Ring cycle (Wagner), **Supp. IV Part 1:** 392
Ringe, Donald, **I:** 339, 343; **Retro. Supp. II:** 270
"Ringing" (Bierds), **Supp. XVII:** 28
"Ringing the Bells" (Sexton), **Supp. II Part 2:** 672, 687
Ringle, Ken, **Supp. X:** 15
Ring of Heaven: Poems (Hongo), **Supp. X:** 292
Rink, The (musical, McNally), **Supp. XIII:** 207
Rio Lobo (film), **Supp. XVI:** 246
Ríos, Alberto Alvaro, **Supp. IV Part 2:** **537–556**
"Riot" (Brooks), **Supp. III Part 1:** 71, 84–85
Ripley, Ezra, **II:** 8; **IV:** 172
Rip-off Red, Girl Detective (Acker), **Supp. XII:** 3–4
Ripostes (Pound), **Retro. Supp. I:** 287–288, 413
Ripostes of Ezra Pound, The, Whereunto Are Appended the Complete Poetical Works of T. E. Hulme, with Prefatory Note (Pound), **III:** 458, 464, 465
"Riprap" (Snyder), **Supp. VIII:** 293–294
Riprap (Snyder), **Supp. VIII:** **292–294,** 295
"Rip Van Winkle" (Irving), **II:** 304–306; **Supp. I Part 1:** 185
Rischin, Moses, **Supp. XVII:** 101, 103, 106
Risco-Lozado, Eliezar, **Supp. XIII:** 313
Rise and Shine (Quindlen), **Supp. XVII:** 179
Rise of David Levinsky, The (Cahan), **Supp. IX:** 227; **Supp. XIII:** 106
Rise of Silas Lapham, The (Howells), **II:** 275, 279, 283–285; **IV:** 202; **Retro. Supp. II:** 93, 101
"Rise of the Middle Class" (Banks), **Supp. V:** 10
Rising and Falling (Matthews), **Supp. IX:** 154, **160**
"Rising Daughter, The" (Olds), **Supp. X:** 204
Rising from the Plains (McPhee), **Supp. III Part 1:** 309–310
Rising Glory of America, The (Brackenridge and Freneau), **Supp. I Part 1:** 124; **Supp. II Part 1:** 67, 253, 256, 263
"Rising of the Storm, The" (Dunbar), **Supp. II Part 1:** 199
Rising Sun in the Pacific, The (Morison), **Supp. I Part 2:** 490
Rising Up and Rising Down (Vollmann), **Supp. XVII:** 225, 226, **229–230,** 232, 233, 235–236
Risk Pool, The (Russo), **Supp. XII:** **328–331**
Ristovic, Aleksandar, **Supp. VIII:** 272
"Rita Dove: Identity Markers" (Vendler), **Supp. IV Part 1:** 247, 257
Ritchey, John, **Supp. XIV:** 122
"Rite of Passage" (Olds), **Supp. X:** 206
"Rites and Ceremonies" (Hecht), **Supp. X:** 61
"Rites of Spring, The" (Morris), **III:** 223
Ritivoi, Andreea Deciu, **Supp. XVI:** 148
Ritschl, Albrecht, **III:** 309, 604
Ritsos, Yannis, **Supp. X:** 112
"Ritsos and the Metaphysical Moment" (Dobyns), **Supp. XIII:** 78
Rittenhouse, David, **Supp. I Part 2:** 507
Rittenhouse, Jessie, **Supp. XV:** 295
"Ritual, The" (Jarman), **Supp. XVII:** 114
"Ritual and Renewal: Keres Traditions in the Short Fiction of Leslie Silko" (Ruoff), **Supp. IV Part 2:** 559
Ritz, The (film), **Supp. XIII:** 206
Ritz, The (McNally), **Supp. XIII:** 198
"Rival, The" (Plath), **Retro. Supp. II:** 254
Riven Rock (Boyle), **Supp. VIII:** 5–6
"River" (Ammons), **Supp. VII:** 28
"River, The" (O'Connor), **III:** 344, 352, 353, 354, 356; **Retro. Supp. II:** 229, 231–232
Rivera, Tomás, **Supp. XIII:** 216, 221
Riverbed (Wagoner), **Supp. IX:** **327–328**
"River Driftwood" (Jewett), **Retro. Supp. II:** 132, 133, 147
"River Jordan, The" (DeLillo), **Supp. VI:** 3, 4
River King, The (Hoffman), **Supp. X:** 78, 85, 90, **91–92**
"River Merchant's Wife: A Letter, The" (Pound), **III:** 463
"River Now, The" (Hugo), **Supp. VI:** 144
"River of Rivers in Connecticut, The" (Stevens), **Retro. Supp. I:** 313
River of the Mother of God and Other Essays by Aldo Leopold, The (Leopold), **Supp. XIV:** 180
"River Profile" (Auden), **Supp. II Part 1:** 26
"River Road" (Kunitz), **Supp. III Part 1:** 260
"River Runs Through It, A" (Maclean), **Supp. XIV:** 222–223, **223–229,** 233, 234, 235; **Supp. XVI:** 98
River Runs Through It and Other Stories, A (Maclean), **Supp. XIV:** 221, 223
Rivers, Larry, **Supp. III Part 1:** 3; **Supp. XV:** 177, 178, 186
Rivers and Mountains (Ashbery), **Supp. III Part 1:** 10, 26
Riverside Drive (Simpson), **Supp. IX:** **275–276**
Rivers to the Sea (Teasdale), **Supp. XV:** 295
River Styx, Ohio, and Other Poems, The (Oliver), **Supp. VII:** 231, 232
"River That Is East, The" (Kinnell), **Supp. III Part 1:** 241–242
"River Towns" (Masters), **Supp. I Part 2:** 473
Rives, Amélie, **II:** 194
Rivière, Jacques, **Retro. Supp. I:** 63
"Rivington's Last Will and Testament" (Freneau), **Supp. II Part 1:** 261
"Rivulet, The" (Bryant), **Supp. I Part 1:** 155, 162
Rix, Alice, **I:** 199
RL's Dream (Mosley), **Supp. XIII:** 234, **244–245,** 249
Roach, Max, **Supp. X:** 239

"Road, Roadsides, and the Disparate Frames of a Sequence" (Sobin), **Supp. XVI:** 288
Road Between, The (Farrell), **II:** 29, 38, 39–40
"Road Between Here and There, The" (Kinnell), **Supp. III Part 1:** 254
"Road Home, The" (Hammett), **Supp. IV Part 1:** 343
Road Home, The (Harrison), **Supp. VIII:** 37, 45, 48, **49–50,** 53
Roadless Yaak, The: Reflections and Observations about One of Our Last Great Wild Places (Bass, ed.), **Supp. XVI:** 23
"Road Not Taken, The" (R. Frost), **II:** 154; **Retro. Supp. I:** 131; **Supp. XI:** 150; **Supp. XV:** 127
Roadside Poems for Summer Travellers (Larcom, ed.), **Supp. XIII:** 142
Roads of Destiny (O. Henry), **Supp. II Part 1:** 410
Road through the Wall, The (Jackson), **Supp. IX:** 115, 118, 120, 123–124
"Road to Avignon, The" (Lowell), **II:** 516
"Road to Hell, The" (Fante), **Supp. XI:** 160
Road to Los Angeles, The (Fante), **Supp. XI:** 160, 166, 167, **168,** 172
Road to Many a Wonder, The (Wagoner), **Supp. IX:** 327, **336**
Road to the Temple, The (Glaspell), **Supp. III Part 1:** 175, 182, 186
Road to Wellville, The (Boyle), **Supp. VIII:** 6–8
Road to Xanadu, The (Lowes), **IV:** 453
"Roan Stallion" (Jeffers), **Supp. II Part 2:** 428–429
"Roast-beef" (Stein), **IV:** 43
Roast Leviatham (Untermeyer), **Supp. XV:** 307
"Roast Possum" (Dove), **Supp. IV Part 1:** 247, 248
Robards, Jason, Jr., **III:** 163, 403
Robb, Christina, **Supp. XV:** 251
Robbe-Grillet, Alain, **I:** 123; **IV:** 95; **Supp. IV Part 1:** 42; **Supp. V:** 47, 48
Robber Bride, The (Atwood), **Supp. XIII: 30–31**
Robber Bridegroom, The (Welty), **IV:** 261, 266–268, 271, 274; **Retro. Supp. I:** 347
Robbins, Harold, **Supp. XII:** 6
Robbins, Henry, **Supp. IV Part 1:** 198, 201, 210, 211
Robbins, Katherine Robinson, **Supp. X:** 264
Robbins, Thomas, **Supp. XV:** 271
Robbins, Tom, **Supp. IV Part 1:** 227; **Supp. VIII:** 14; **Supp. X: 259–288; Supp. XIII:** 11
"Robe, The" (Douglas), **IV:** 434
"Robert Bly" (Davis), **Supp. IV Part 1:** 70
Robert Bly (Sugg), **Supp. IV Part 1:** 68
"Robert Bly and the Trouble with America" (Mitchell), **Supp. IV Part 1:** 70
Robert Bly: An Introduction to the Poetry (Nelson), **Supp. IV Part 1:** 66
Robert Bly: The Poet and His Critics (Davis), **Supp. IV Part 1:** 63
Robert Coover: The Universal Fictionmaking Process (Gordon), **Supp. V:** 46
Robert Creeley (Ford), **Supp. IV Part 1:** 140
Robert Creeley and the Genius of the American Common Place (Clark), **Supp. IV Part 1:** 140
Robert Creeley's Poetry: A Critical Introduction (Edelberg), **Supp. IV Part 1:** 155
Robert Frost (Meyers), **Retro. Supp. I:** 138
Robert Lowell (Meyers), **Retro. Supp. II:** 191
Robert Lowell and the Sublime (Hart), **Retro. Supp. II:** 187
Robert Lowell's Shifting Colors (Doreski), **Retro. Supp. II:** 185
Robert Lowell: The First Twenty years (Staples), **Retro. Supp. II:** 187
Roberts, David, **Supp. XVIII:** 106
Roberts, Diane, **Supp. X:** 15
Roberts, J. M., **IV:** 454
Roberts, Leo, **II:** 449
Roberts, Margaret, **II:** 449; **IV:** 453, 454
Roberts, Matthew, **Retro. Supp. II:** 324
Roberts, Meade, **IV:** 383
Roberts, Michael, **I:** 527, 536
Roberts, Richard, **III:** 297
Roberts, Wally, **Supp. XI:** 119, 120, 126
Roberts, William, **Supp. XI:** 343
Roberts Brothers, **Retro. Supp. I:** 31, 35
Robertson, David, **Supp. VIII:** 305
Robertson, D. B., **III:** 311
Robertson, Nan, **Supp. IV Part 1:** 300
Robertson, William, **II:** 8
Robert the Devil (Merwin, trans.), **Supp. III Part 1:** 341, 346
Robeson, Paul, **III:** 392; **Supp. IV Part 1:** 360, 361; **Supp. X:** 137
Robeson, Susan L., **Supp. XVIII:** 268
Robespierre, Maximilien, **Supp. I Part 2:** 514, 515, 517
"Robinson" (Kees), **Supp. XV:** 143–144
Robinson, Christopher L., **Supp. XII:** 13, 14
Robinson, Dean, **III:** 506
Robinson, Edward, **III:** 505
Robinson, Edward G., **Supp. XI:** 306
Robinson, Edwin Arlington, **I:** 480; **II:** 388, 391, 529, 542; **III:** 5, **503–526,** 576; **Supp. I Part 2:** 699; **Supp. II Part 1:** 191; **Supp. III Part 1:** 63, 75; **Supp. III Part 2:** 592, 593; **Supp. IX:** 77, 266, 276, 308; **Supp. XV:** 256, 299, 300, 301, 306; **Supp. XVII:** 69
Robinson, Forrest G., **Supp. IV Part 2:** 597, 601, 604
Robinson, Herman, **III:** 506–507
Robinson, H. M., **IV:** 369, 370
Robinson, Jackie, **Supp. I Part 1:** 338
Robinson, James Harvey, **I:** 214; **Supp. I Part 2:** 492
Robinson, James K., **Supp. IX:** 328
Robinson, Margaret G., **Supp. IV Part 2:** 597, 601, 604
Robinson, Mary, **Supp. XI:** 26
Robinson, Sugar Ray, **Supp. IV Part 1:** 167
Robinson, Ted, **Supp. XIII:** 166
Robinson Crusoe (Defoe), **II:** 159; **III:** 113, 423; **IV:** 369; **Retro. Supp. II:** 274; **Supp. I Part 2:** 714; **Supp. IV Part 2:** 502
Robison, Mary, **Supp. V:** 22
Roblès, Emmanuel, **Supp. I Part 1:** 283
"Robstown" (Salinas), **Supp. XIII:** 315
Rochefort, Christina, **Supp. XVI:** 143
Rochefoucauld, Louis Alexandre, **Supp. I Part 2:** 510
"Rock" (Nye), **Supp. XIII:** 287
Rock (Wagoner), **Supp. IX:** 324, **334,** 335
Rock, Catherine, **Supp. XII:** 17
Rock, The (Eliot), **Retro. Supp. I:** 65
"Rock, The" (Stevens), **Retro. Supp. I:** 312
Rock, The (Stevens), **Retro. Supp. I:** 309, 312
Rockaway (Shanley), **Supp. XIV:** 315
"Rock Climbers, The" (Francis), **Supp. IX:** 82
Rock-Drill (Pound), **Retro. Supp. I:** 293
Rockefeller, John D., **I:** 273; **III:** 580; **Supp. I Part 2:** 486; **Supp. V:** 286
Rockefeller, Nelson, **III:** 14, 15
Rocket to the Moon (Odets), **Supp. II Part 2:** 541–543, 544
Rock Garden, The (Shepard), **Supp. III Part 2:** 432, 447
"Rocking Horse Winner, The" (Lawrence), **Supp. I Part 1:** 329
Rocking the Boat (Vidal), **Supp. IV Part 2:** 683
"Rockpile, The" (Baldwin), **Supp. I Part 1:** 63
Rock Springs (Ford), **Supp. V:** 57, 58–59, 68–69
Rocky Mountains, The: or, Scenes, Incidents, and Adventures in the Far West; Digested from the Journal of Captain E. L. E Bonneville, of the Army of the United States, and Illustrated from Various Other Sources (Irving), **II:** 312
Rodden, John, **Supp. XVI:** 63, 69, 72
Roderick, David, **Supp. XV:** 223
Roderick Hudson (James), **II:** 284, 290, 324, 326, 328; **Retro. Supp. I:** 219, **220–221,** 221, 226; **Supp. IX:** 142
Rodgers, Richard, **III:** 361
Rodgers, Ronald, **Supp. IV Part 2:** 503
Rodker, John, **III:** 470
Rodman, Selden, **Supp. I Part 1:** 83; **Supp. X:** 115
"Rodrigo Returns to the Land and Linen Celebrates" (Cisneros), **Supp. VII:** 68
Rodriguez, Randy A., **Supp. XIV:** 312
Rodriguez, Richard, **Supp. XIV: 297–313**
Roethke, Charles, **III:** 531
Roethke, Theodore, **I:** 167, 171–172, 183, 254, 285, 521; **III:** 273, **527–550; IV:** 138, 402; **Retro. Supp. II:** 178, 181, 246; **Supp. I Part 2:** 539; **Supp. III Part 1:** 47, 54, 56, 239, 253, 260–261,

350; **Supp. IV Part 2:** 626; **Supp. IX:** 323; **Supp. XV:** 140, 145, 212; **Supp. XVIII:** 90
"Roger Malvin's Burial" (Hawthorne), **II:** 243; **Retro. Supp. I:** 153
Rogers, Michael, **Supp. X:** 265, 266
Rogers, Pattiann, **Supp. XVIII:** 189
Rogers, Samuel, **II:** 303; **Supp. I Part 1:** 157
Rogers, Will, **I:** 261; **IV:** 388
Roger's Version (Updike), **Retro. Supp. I:** 325, 327, 330
Roget, Peter Mark, **Supp. I Part 1:** 312
"Rogue River Jet-Board Trip, Gold Beach, Oregon, July 4, 1977" (Carver), **Supp. III Part 1:** 140
"Rogue's Gallery" (McCarthy), **II:** 563
Roland de La Platière, Jean Marie, **II:** 554
Rôle du Nègre dans la culture des Amériques, La (Locke), **Supp. XIV:** 202
"Role of Society in the Artist, The" (Ammons), **Supp. VII:** 34
Rolfe, Alfred, **IV:** 427
"Roll, Jordan, Roll" (spiritual), **Supp. IV Part 1:** 16
"Roll Call" (Hoffman), **Supp. XVIII:** 86
"Roll Call" (Komunyakaa), **Supp. XIII:** 123
Rolle, Esther, **Supp. IV Part 1:** 367
Rollin, Charles, **II:** 113
Rolling Stones (O. Henry), **Supp. II Part 1:** 410
Rolling Thunder Logbook (Shepard), **Supp. III Part 2:** 433
Rolling Thunder Logbook, The (Shepard), **Supp. XVIII:** 31
"Rolling Up" (Simpson), **Supp. IX:** 265, 274, 280
Rollins, Howard E., Jr., **Supp. IV Part 1:** 236
Rollins, Hyder E., **Supp. IV Part 1:** 168
Rollins, Sonny, **Supp. V:** 195
"Rollo" tales (Abbott), **Supp. I Part 1:** 38
"Roma I" (Wright), **Supp. V:** 338
"Roma II" (Wright), **Supp. V:** 338
Romains, Jules, **I:** 227
Román, David, **Supp. XIII:** 208
"Romance and a Reading List" (Fitzgerald), **Retro. Supp. I:** 101
Romance of a Plain Man, The (Glasgow), **II:** 175, 180–181
"Romance of Certain Old Clothes, The" (James), **II:** 322; **Retro. Supp. I:** 218
"Roman Elegies" (Brodsky), **Supp. VIII:** 29
"Roman Fever" (Wharton), **Retro. Supp. I:** 382
"Roman Fountain" (Bogan), **Supp. III Part 1:** 56
"*Romanitas* of Gore Vidal, The" (Tatum), **Supp. IV Part 2:** 684
Romaniuk, Zbigniew, **Supp. XVI:** 154
Romano, John, **Supp. XV:** 253
"Roman Sarcophagus, A" (Lowell), **II:** 544
Roman Spring of Mrs. Stone, The (T. Williams), **IV:** 383, 385
"Romantic, The" (Bogan), **Supp. III Part 1:** 50
Romantic Comedians, The (Glasgow), **II:** 175, 186, 190, 194
Romantic Egoists, The (Auchincloss), **Supp. IV Part 1:** 25
"Romantic Egotist, The" (Fitzgerald), **Retro. Supp. I:** 100
Romantic Egotist, The (Fitzgerald), **II:** 82
"Romanticism and Classicism" (Hulme), **III:** 196
"Romanticism Comes Home" (Shapiro), **Supp. II Part 2:** 713
Romantic Manifesto, The: A Philosophy of Literature (Rand), **Supp. IV Part 2:** 521, 523, 527, 529–530
"Romantic Regionalism of Harper Lee, The" (Erisman), **Supp. VIII:** 126
"Rome" (W. C. Williams), **Retro. Supp. I:** 420
Rome Brothers, **Retro. Supp. I:** 393
Romeo and Juliet (Shakespeare), **Supp. V:** 252; **Supp. VIII:** 223
Romola (Eliot), **II:** 291; **IV:** 311
Romulus: A New Comedy (Vidal), **Supp. IV Part 2:** 683
Romulus der Grosse (Dürrenmatt), **Supp. IV Part 2:** 683
Ronald, Ann, **Supp. XIII:** 4, 5, 6, 7, 9, 11
"Rondel for a September Day" (White), **Supp. I Part 2:** 676
"Ron Narrative Reconstructions, The" (Coleman), **Supp. XI:** 83
Ronsard, Pierre de, **Supp. X:** 65; **Supp. XV:** 165
Rood, John, **IV:** 261
"Roof, the Steeple, and the People, The" (Ellison), **Retro. Supp. II:** 118, 126; **Supp. II Part 1:** 248
"Room" (Levertov), **Supp. III Part 1:** 282
Roomates (film, P. Yates), **Supp. XVII:** 8, 9
Roomates: My Grandfather's Story (Apple), **Supp. XVII:** 2, **7–9**
"Room at the Heart of Things, A" (Merrill), **Supp. III Part 1:** 337
Room Called Remember, A: Uncollected Pieces (Buechner), **Supp. XII:** 53
"Roomful of Hovings, A" (McPhee), **Supp. III Part 1:** 291, 294
Room of One's Own, A (Woolf), **Supp. IX:** 19; **Supp. V:** 127; **Supp. XIII:** 305
Room Rented by a Single Woman (Wright), **Supp. XV:** 340–341
Room Temperature (Baker), **Supp. XIII:** 41, **43–45,** 48, 50
Room to Swing (Lacy), **Supp. XV:** 202, 203, 205, 207
"Room Upstairs, The" (Gioia), **Supp. XV:** 120–121, 124
Roosevelt, Eleanor, **IV:** 371; **Supp. IV Part 2:** 679
Roosevelt, Franklin, **Supp. V:** 290
Roosevelt, Franklin Delano, **I:** 482, 485, 490; **II:** 553, 575; **III:** 2, 18, 69, 110, 297, 321, 376, 476, 580, 581; **Supp. I Part 2:** 488, 489, 490, 491, 645, 654, 655
Roosevelt, Kermit, **III:** 508
Roosevelt, Theodore, **I:** 14, 62; **II:** 130; **III:** 508; **IV:** 321; **Retro. Supp. I:** 377; **Supp. I Part 1:** 1, 21; **Supp. I Part 2:** 455, 456, 502, 707; **Supp. IX:** 184; **Supp. V:** 280, 282
Roosevelt After Inauguration And Other Atrocities (Burroughs), **Supp. III Part 1:** 98
"Roosters" (Bishop), **Retro. Supp. II:** 39, 43, 250; **Supp. I Part 1:** 89
Root, Abiah, **I:** 456
Root, Elihu, **Supp. IV Part 1:** 33
Root, Simeon, **I:** 548
Root, Timothy, **I:** 548
Rootabaga Stories (Sandburg), **III:** 583, 587
"Rootedness: The Ancestor as Foundation" (Morrison), **Supp. III Part 1:** 361
Roots in the Soil (film), **Supp. IV Part 1:** 83
"Rope" (Porter), **III:** 451
Rope, The (O'Neill), **III:** 388
Ropemakers of Plymouth, The (Morison), **Supp. I Part 2:** 494
"Ropes" (Nye), **Supp. XIII:** 276
"Rope's End, The" (Nemerov), **III:** 282
Roquelaure, A. N., **Supp. VII:** 301. *See also* Rice, Anne
Rorem, Ned, **Supp. IV Part 1:** 79, 84
Rorschach Test (F. Wright), **Supp. XVII:** 240, 245
"Rosa" (Ozick), **Supp. V:** 271
Rosa, Rodrigo Rey, **Supp. IV Part 1:** 92
Rosaldo, Renato, **Supp. IV Part 2:** 544
"Rosalia" (Simic), **Supp. VIII:** 278
Roscoe, Will, **Supp. IV Part 1:** 330
"Rose" (Dubus), **Supp. VII:** 88
Rose (L.-Y. Lee), **Supp. XV:** 211, **212–215,** 218
Rose, Alice, Sister, **III:** 348
Rose, Mickey, **Supp. XV:** 3
Rose, Philip, **Supp. IV Part 1:** 362
"Rose, The" (Roethke), **III:** 537
"Rose, The" (W. C. Williams), **Retro. Supp. I:** 419
Rose, Where Did You Get That Red?: Teaching Great Poetry to Children (Koch), **Supp. XV:** 189
"Rose for Emily, A" (Faulkner), **II:** 72; **Supp. IX:** 96
Rose in Bloom (Alcott), **Supp. I Part 1:** 42
"Rose-Johnny" (Kingsolver), **Supp. VII:** 203
Rose Madder (King), **Supp. V:** 141, 148, 150, 152
"Rose-Morals" (Lanier), **Supp. I Part 1:** 364
Rosen, Jonathan, **Supp. XVII:** 50
Rosen, Kenneth, **Supp. IV Part 2:** 499, 505, 513

Rosen, Norma, **Supp. XVII:** 49, 50
Rosenbaum, Alissa Zinovievna. *See* Rand, Ayn
Rosenbaum, Thane, **Supp. XVII:** 48
Rosenberg, Bernard, **Supp. I Part 2:** 650
Rosenberg, Harold, **Supp. XV:** 143
Rosenberg, Julia, **Supp. XVIII:** 136
Rosenberg, Julius and Ethel, **Supp. I Part 1:** 295; **Supp. I Part 2:** 532; **Supp. V:** 45
Rosenberg, Liz, **Supp. XV:** 251
Rosenbloom, Joel, **Supp. IV Part 2:** 527
Rosenfeld, Alvin H., **Supp. I Part 1:** 120
Rosenfeld, Isaac, **Supp. XII:** 160
Rosenfeld, Paul, **I:** 116, 117, 231, 245
Rosenfelt, Deborah, **Supp. XIII:** 296, 304
Rosenfield, Isaac, **IV:** 3
Rosengarten, Theodore, **Supp. XVIII:** 183
Rosenthal, Ira, **Supp. XIV:** 146–147
Rosenthal, Lois, **Supp. VIII:** 258
Rosenthal, M. L., **II:** 550; **III:** 276, 479; **Supp. V:** 333
Rosenthal, Peggy, **Supp. XVII:** 119
"Rose Pogonias" (Frost), **Retro. Supp. I:** 127
"Rose Red and Snow White" (Grimms), **Supp. X:** 82
"Roses" (Conroy), **Supp. XVI:** 72
"Roses" (Dove), **Supp. IV Part 1:** 246
"Roses and Skulls" (Goldbarth), **Supp. XII:** 192
"Roses for Lubbock" (Nye), **Supp. XIII:** 281
"Roses Only" (Moore), **III:** 195, 198, 200, 202, 215
Rose Tattoo, The (T. Williams), **IV:** 382, 383, 387, 388, 389, 392–393, 394, 397, 398
"Rosewood, Ohio" (Matthews), **Supp. IX:** 160
Rosinante to the Road Again (Dos Passos), **I:** 478
Roskies, David, **Supp. XVII:** 39, 44, 49–50
Roskolenko, Harry, **Supp. XV:** 179
Rosmersholm (Ibsen), **III:** 152
Rosmond, Babette, **II:** 432
Ross, Eleanor. *See* Taylor, Eleanor Ross
Ross, Harold, **Supp. I Part 1:** 174; **Supp. I Part 2:** 607, 617, 653, 654, 655, 660; **Supp. IX:** 190; **Supp. VIII:** 151, 170
Ross, Herbert, **Supp. XV:** 2
Ross, John F., **II:** 110
Ross, Lillilan, **Retro. Supp. II:** 198
Ross, Mitchell S., **Supp. IV Part 2:** 692; **Supp. X:** 260
Rossen, Robert, **Supp. XI:** 306
Rosset, Barney, **III:** 171
Rossetti, Christina, **Supp. XIV:** 128
Rossetti, Dante Gabriel, **I:** 433; **II:** 323; **Retro. Supp. I:** 128, 286; **Supp. I Part 2:** 552
Rossetti, William Michael, **Retro. Supp. I:** 407
Rossi, Umberto, **Supp. XVIII:** 137, 138–139
Rossini, Clare, **Supp. XVII:** 111
Rosskam, Edwin, **IV:** 477
Ross Macdonald (Bruccoli), **Supp. IV Part 2:** 468, 470
Rostand, Edmond, **II:** 515; **Supp. IV Part 2:** 518
Rosten, Leo, **Supp. XVII:** 9
Rosy Crucifixion, The (H. Miller), **III:** 170, 187, 188–189, 190
Rote Walker, The (Jarman), **Supp. XVII:** 110, **113–115**
Roth, Henry, **Supp. IV Part 1:** 314; **Supp. IX: 227–243; Supp. VIII:** 233; **Supp. XIII:** 106
Roth, Philip, **I:** 144, 161; **II:** 591; **Retro. Supp. II:** 22, **279–297; Supp. I Part 1:** 186, 192; **Supp. I Part 2:** 431, 441, 443; **Supp. II Part 1:** 99; **Supp. III Part 2: 401–429; Supp. IV Part 1:** 236, 379, 388; **Supp. IX:** 227; **Supp. V:** 45, 119, 122, 257, 258; **Supp. VIII:** 88, 236, 245; **Supp. XI:** 64, 68, 99, 140; **Supp. XII:** 190, 310; **Supp. XIV:** 79, 93, 111, 112; **Supp. XVI:** 206; **Supp. XVII:** 43, 48, 183; **Supp. XVIII:** 89
Roth, Rita, **Supp. XVI:** 112
Roth, William, **Supp. XV:** 142
Rothenberg, Jerome, **Supp. VIII:** 292; **Supp. XII:** 3
Rothermere, Lady Mary, **Retro. Supp. I:** 63
Rothko, Mark, **Supp. XV:** 144
Rothstein, Mervyn, **Supp. VIII:** 142
"Rouge High" (Hughes), **Supp. I Part 1:** 330
Rougemont, Denis de, **II:** 586; **IV:** 216; **Retro. Supp. I:** 328, 329, 330, 331
Roughing It (Twain), **II:** 312; **IV:** 195, 197, 198
Roughing It in the Bush (Shields), **Supp. VII:** 313
"Rough Outline" (Simic), **Supp. VIII:** 276
Rougon-Macquart, Les (Zola), **II:** 175–176
Roumain, Jacques, **Retro. Supp. I:** 202; **Supp. IV Part 1:** 360, 367
"Round, The" (Kunitz), **Supp. III Part 1:** 268
"Round Trip" (Dunn), **Supp. XI:** 148–149
Round Up (Lardner), **II:** 426, 430, 431
Rourke, Constance, **I:** 258; **IV:** 339, 352
Rourke, Milton, **Retro. Supp. II:** 89
Rousseau, Jean-Jacques, **I:** 226; **II:** 8, 343; **III:** 170, 178, 259; **IV:** 80, 173, 440; **Supp. I Part 1:** 126; **Supp. I Part 2:** 637, 659; **Supp. IV Part 1:** 171; **Supp. XI:** 245; **Supp. XVI:** 292
Roussel, Raymond, **Supp. III Part 1:** 6, 7, 10, 15, 16, 21; **Supp. XV:** 182
"Routes" (Everwine), **Supp. XV:** 82
"Route Six" (Kunitz), **Supp. III Part 1:** 258
Route Two (Erdrich and Dorris), **Supp. IV Part 1:** 260
"Routine Things Around the House, The" (Dunn), **Supp. XI:** 148
Rover Boys (Winfield), **III:** 146
Rovit, Earl, **IV:** 102
Rowan, Carl T., **Supp. XIV:** 306
Rowe, Anne E., **Supp. X:** 223
Rowe, John Carlos, **Retro. Supp. I:** 216
"Rowing" (Sexton), **Supp. II Part 2:** 696
"Rowing Endeth, The" (Sexton), **Supp. II Part 2:** 696
Rowlandson, Mary, **Supp. IV Part 2:** 430, 431
"Rows of Cold Trees, The" (Winters), **Supp. II Part 2:** 790–791, 800
Rowson, Susanna, **Supp. I Part 1:** 128; **Supp. XV: 229–248**
Roxanna Slade (Price), **Supp. VI:** 267
Roxie Hart (Watkins), **Supp. XVI:** 188
Royal Family, The (Vollmann), **Supp. XVII:** 226, 230, 233
"Royal Palm" (Crane), **I:** 401
Royce, Josiah, **I:** 443; **III:** 303, 600; **IV:** 26; **Retro. Supp. I:** 57; **Supp. XIV:** 197, 199; **Supp. XVII:** 97
Royster, Sarah Elmira, **III:** 410, 429
Royte, Elizabeth, **Supp. XV:** 59
Rózewicz, Tadeusz, **Supp. X:** 60
Ruas, Charles, **Supp. IV Part 1:** 383
Rubáiyát (Khayyám), **I:** 568
Rubáiyát of Omar Khayyam (Fitzgerald), **Supp. I Part 2:** 416; **Supp. III Part 2:** 610; **Supp. XV:** 156
"Rubber Life" (Prose), **Supp. XVI:** 256
Rub from Snub, A (Swanwick), **Supp. XV:** 237
Rubin, Louis, **Supp. I Part 2:** 672, 673, 679; **Supp. X:** 42
Rubin, Louis D., Jr., **IV:** 116, 462–463
Rubin, Stan, **Supp. XIV:** 307, 310
Rubin, Stan Sanvel, **Supp. IV Part 1:** 242, 245, 252
"Ruby Brown" (Hughes), **Supp. I Part 1:** 327
"Ruby Daggett" (Eberhart), **I:** 539
Rucker, Rudy, **Supp. X:** 302
Rudd, Hughes, **Supp. XII:** 141
"Rude Awakening, A" (Chopin), **Retro. Supp. II:** 64
Rudens (Plautus), **Supp. III Part 2:** 630
Ruderman, Judith, **Supp. IV Part 1:** 380
Rudge, Olga, **Supp. V:** 338
Rudikoff, Sonya, **Supp. XIV:** 113
Rueckert, William, **I:** 264
Ruesch, Jurgen, **Supp. XV:** 147
Rugby Chapel (Arnold), **Supp. I Part 2:** 416
"Rugby Road" (Garrett), **Supp. VII:** 100
Ruining the New Road (Matthews), **Supp. IX:** 154, **155–157**
"Ruins of Italica, The" (Bryant, trans.), **Supp. I Part 1:** 166
Rukeyser, Muriel, **Retro. Supp. II:** 48; **Supp. VI: 271–289; Supp. XV:** 349; **Supp. XVII:** 74
"Rule of Phase Applied to History, The" (Adams), **I:** 19
Rule of the Bone (Banks), **Supp. V:** 16
"Rules by Which a Great Empire May Be Reduced to a Small One" (Franklin), **II:** 120
Rules For the Dance: A Handbook for Reading and Writing Metrical Verse (Oliver), **Supp. VII:** 229, 247

Rules of the Game, The (film), **Supp. XII:** 259
Rulfo, Juan, **Supp. IV Part 2:** 549
Rumba (film, Gering), **Supp. XVII:** 57
Rumbaut, Rubén, **Supp. XI:** 184
Rumens, Carol, **Supp. XI:** 14; **Supp. XVI:** 212
Rumkowski, Chaim, **Supp. XII:** 168
Rummel, Mary Kay, **Supp. XIII:** 280
"Rumor and a Ladder" (Bowles), **Supp. IV Part 1:** 93
Rumors (Simon), **Supp. IV Part 2:** 582–583, 591
Rumpelstiltskin (Gardner), **Supp. VI:** 72
"Rumpelstiltskin" (Grimm), **IV:** 266
"Rumpelstiltskin" (Sexton), **Supp. II Part 2:** 690
"Runagate Runagate" (Hayden), **Supp. II Part 1:** 377
"Runes" (Nemerov), **III:** 267, 277–278
Run Man Run (C. Himes), **Supp. XVI:** 142, 143
"Running" (Wilbur), **Supp. III Part 2:** 558–559
Running Dog (DeLillo), **Supp. VI:** 3, 6, 8, 14
"Running in Church" (A. Finch), **Supp. XVII:** 72
"Running the Table" Conroy), **Supp. XVI:** 75
"Run of Bad Luck, A" (Proulx), **Supp. VII:** 253–254
Run of Jacks, A (Hugo), **Supp. VI:** 131, 133, 134, 135, 136
Run River (Didion), **Supp. IV Part 1:** 197, 199–200, 201
Ruoff, A. LaVonne Brown, **Supp. IV Part 1:** 324, 327; **Supp. IV Part 2:** 559
Rupert, Jim, **Supp. XII:** 215
Ruppert, James, **Supp. IV Part 1:** 321
Rural Hours (Cooper), **Supp. XIII:** 152
"Rural Route" (Wright), **Supp. V:** 340
"Rural South, The" (Du Bois), **Supp. II Part 1:** 174
Rush, Benjamin, **Supp. I Part 2:** 505, 507
Rushdie, Salman, **Supp. IV Part 1:** 234, 297
Rushdy, Ashraf, **Supp. X:** 250
Rushing, Jimmy, **Retro. Supp. II:** 113
Rusk, Dean, **II:** 579
Ruskin, John, **II:** 323, 338; **IV:** 349; **Retro. Supp. I:** 56, 360; **Supp. I Part 1:** 2, 10, 87, 349; **Supp. I Part 2:** 410
Rusnak, Karl, **Supp. XVIII:** 149
Russell, Ada Dwyer, **II:** 513, 527
Russell, Bertrand, **II:** 27; **III:** 605, 606; **Retro. Supp. I:** 57, 58, 59, 60; **Supp. I Part 2:** 522; **Supp. V:** 290; **Supp. XII:** 45; **Supp. XIV:** 337
Russell, Diarmuid, **Retro. Supp. I:** 342, 345, 346–347, 349–350
Russell, George, **Retro. Supp. I:** 342
Russell, Herb, **Supp. I Part 2:** 465–466
Russell, John, **Supp. XIV:** 344, 347, 348
Russell, Peter, **III:** 479
Russell, Richard, **Supp. XI:** 102
Russell, Sue, **Supp. IV Part 2:** 653
Russert, Margaret, **Supp. XVIII:** 62
Russert, Tim, **Supp. XII:** 272
Russia at War (Caldwell), **I:** 296
Russian Journal, A (Steinbeck), **IV:** 52, 63
Russo, Richard, **Supp. XI:** 349; **Supp. XII: 325–344**
"Rusty Autumn" (Swenson), **Supp. IV Part 2:** 640
Rutabaga-Roo: I've Got a Song and It's for You (Nye, album), **Supp. XIII:** 274
Ruth (biblical book), **Supp. I Part 2:** 516
Ruth, George Herman ("Babe"), **II:** 423; **Supp. I Part 2:** 438, 440
Ruth Hall (Fern), **Supp. V:** 122
Rutledge, Ann, **III:** 588; **Supp. I Part 2:** 471
Ruwe, Donelle R., **Supp. XII:** 215
Ryan, Paul William, **Supp. XVIII: 223–239**
Ryder (Barnes), **Supp. III Part 1:** 31, 36–38, 42, 43
"Ryder" (Rukeyser), **Supp. VI:** 273, 283
Rymer, Thomas, **IV:** 122

S

S. (Updike), **Retro. Supp. I:** 330, 331, 332, 333
S-1 (Baraka), **Supp. II Part 1:** 55, 57
Saadi, **II:** 19
Saar, Doreen Alvarez, **Supp. XV:** 237
"Sabbath, The" (Stowe), **Supp. I Part 2:** 587
"Sabbath Mom" (White), **Supp. I Part 2:** 671–672
Sabbaths (Berry), **Supp. X:** 31
Sabbath's Theater (P. Roth), **Retro. Supp. II:** 279, 288
Sabines, Jaime, **Supp. V:** 178
"Sabotage" (Baraka), **Supp. II Part 1:** 49, 53
"Saboteur" (Jin), **Supp. XVIII:** 97
Sacco, Nicola, **I:** 482, 486, 490, 494; **II:** 38–39, 426; **III:** 139–140; **Supp. I Part 2:** 446; **Supp. IX:** 199; **Supp. V:** 288–289
Sachs, Hanns, **Supp. I Part 1:** 259; **Supp. X:** 186
"Sacks" (Carver), **Supp. III Part 1:** 143–144
Sacks, Oliver, **Supp. XVIII:** 143
Sacks, Peter, **Supp. IV Part 2:** 450
Sackville-West, Vita, **Supp. VIII:** 263
"Sacrament of Divorce, The" (Patchett), **Supp. XII:** 309
"Sacraments" (Dubus), **Supp. VII:** 91
Sacred and Profane Memories (Van Vechten), **Supp. II Part 2:** 735, 749
"Sacred Chant for the Return of Black Spirit and Power" (Baraka), **Supp. II Part 1:** 51
"Sacred Factory, The" (Toomer), **Supp. IX:** 320
Sacred Fount, The (James), **II:** 332–333; **Retro. Supp. I:** 219, 228, 232
"Sacred Hoop, The: A Contemporary Perspective" (Gunn Allen), **Supp. IV Part 1:** 324
Sacred Hoop, The: Recovering the Feminine in American Indian Traditions (Gunn Allen), **Supp. IV Part 1:** 319, 320, 322, 324, 325, 328–330, 331, 333, 334
Sacred Journey, The (Buechner), **Supp. XII:** 42, 53
"Sacred Thing, The" (Ryan as Quin), **Supp. XVIII:** 227
Sacred Wood, The (Eliot), **IV:** 431; **Retro. Supp. I:** 59, 60; **Supp. I Part 1:** 268; **Supp. II Part 1:** 136, 146
"Sacrifice, The" (Bidart), **Supp. XV:** 29
Sacrifice, The (Bidart), **Supp. XV:** 22, **27–30,** 35
"Sacrifice, The" (Oates), **Supp. II Part 2:** 523
Sacrilege of Alan Kent, The (Caldwell), **I:** 291–292
"Sad Brazil" (Hardwick), **Supp. III Part 1:** 210
"Sad Dust Glories" (Ginsberg), **Supp. II Part 1:** 376
Sad Dust Glories: Poems Written Work Summer in Sierra Woods (Ginsberg), **Supp. II Part 1:** 326
Sade, Marquis de, **III:** 259; **IV:** 437, 442; **Supp. XII:** 1, 14–15
Sad Flower in the Sand, A (film), **Supp. XI:** 173
Sad Heart at the Supermarket, A (Jarrell), **II:** 386
"Sadie" (Matthiessen), **Supp. V:** 201
"Sadie and Maud" (Brooks), **Supp. XVIII:** 175
Sadness and Happiness (Pinsky), **Supp. VI:** 235, **237–241**
"Sadness of Brothers, The" (Kinnell), **Supp. III Part 1:** 237, 251
"Sadness of Days, The" (Salinas), **Supp. XIII:** 325
Sadness of Days, The: Selected and New Poems (Salinas), **Supp. XIII:** 311, **324–326**
"Sadness of Lemons, The" (Levine), **Supp. V:** 184
Sadoff, Ira, **Supp. XVII:** 241
"Sad Rite" (Karr), **Supp. XI:** 243
"Sad Strains of a Gay Waltz" (Stevens), **Retro. Supp. I:** 302
"Safe" (Gordon), **Supp. IV Part 1:** 299, 306
"Safe in their Alabaster Chambers" (Dickinson), **Retro. Supp. I:** 30
"Safe Subjects" (Komunyakaa), **Supp. XIII:** 118
"Safeway" (F. Barthelme), **Supp. XI:** 26, 27, 36
Saffin, John, **Supp. I Part 1:** 115
Saffy, Edna, **Supp. X:** 227
"Saga of Arturo Bandini" (Fante), **Supp. XI:** 159, **166–169**
"Saga of King Olaf, The" (Longfellow), **II:** 489, 505; **Retro. Supp. II:** 154, 155, 164
"Sage of Stupidity and Wonder, The" (Goldbarth), **Supp. XII:** 191
Sahl, Mort, **II:** 435–436
"Said" (Dixon), **Supp. XII:** 149–150
"Sailing after Lunch" (Stevens), **IV:** 73

"Sailing Home from Rapallo" (Lowell), **Retro. Supp. II:** 189

Sailing through China (Theroux), **Supp. VIII:** 323

"Sailing to Byzantium" (Yeats), **III:** 263; **Supp. VIII:** 30; **Supp. X:** 74; **Supp. XI:** 281

"Sail Made of Rags, The" (Nye), **Supp. XIII:** 277

"Sailors Lost at Sea" (Shields), **Supp. VII:** 318

"*St Anne*/Santa Ana" (Mora), **Supp. XIII:** 229

"*Saint Anthony of Padua*/San Antonio de Padua" (Mora), **Supp. XIII:** 228

"St. Augustine and the Bullfights" (Porter), **III:** 454

Sainte-Beuve, Charles Augustin, **IV:** 432

St. Elmo (Wilson), **Retro. Supp. I:** 351–352

"Saint Emmanuel the Good, Martyr" (Unamuno; Everwine, trans.), **Supp. XV:** 79

Sainte Vierge, La (Picabia), **Retro. Supp. II:** 331

Saint-Exupéry, Antoine de, **Supp. IX:** 247

"St. Francis Einstein of the Daffodils" (W. C. Williams), **IV:** 409–411

Saint-Gaudens, Augustus, **I:** 18, 228; **II:** 551

Saint-Gaudens, Homer, **Supp. XV:** 41

"St. George, the Dragon, and the Virgin" (R. Bly), **Supp. IV Part 1:** 73

St. George and the Godfather (Mailer), **III:** 46; **Retro. Supp. II:** 206, 208

Saint Jack (Theroux), **Supp. VIII:** 319

St. John, David, **Supp. V:** 180; **Supp. XI:** 270, 272; **Supp. XIII:** 312

St. John, Edward B., **Supp. IV Part 2:** 490

St. John, James Hector. *See* Crèvecoeur, Michel-Guillaume Jean de

"Saint John and the Back-Ache" (Stevens), **Retro. Supp. I:** 310

"Saint Judas" (Wright), **Supp. III Part 2:** 598–599

Saint Judas (Wright), **Supp. III Part 2:** **595–599**

St. Louis Woman (Bontemps and Cullen), **Supp. IV Part 1:** 170

St. Mawr (Lawrence), **II:** 595

Saint Maybe (Tyler), **Supp. IV Part 2:** 670–671

"Saint Nicholas" (Moore), **III:** 215

St. Petersburg (Biely), **Supp. XII:** 13

Saint-Phalle, Niki de, **Supp. XV:** 187

"St. Roach" (Rukeyser), **Supp. VI:** 286

"Saint Robert" (Dacey), **Supp. IV Part 1:** 70

Saintsbury, George, **IV:** 440; **Supp. XV:** 181

Saints' Everlasting Rest, The (Baxter), **III:** 199; **IV:** 151, 153

Saint-Simon, Claude Henri, **Supp. I Part 2:** 648

"St. Thomas Aquinas" (Simic), **Supp. VIII:** 281

Saks, Gene, **Supp. IV Part 2:** 577, 588

Salamun, Tomaz, **Supp. VIII:** 272

Salazar, Dixie, **Supp. V:** 180; **Supp. XV:** 73

Saldívar, José David, **Supp. IV Part 2:** 544, 545

Sale, Richard, **Supp. IV Part 1:** 379

Sale, Roger, **Supp. V:** 244

Saleh, Dennis, **Supp. V:** 182, 186

"Salem" (Lowell), **II:** 550

Salemi, Joseph, **Supp. IV Part 1:** 284

Salem's Lot (King), **Supp. V:** 139, 144, 146, 151

"Sale of the Hessians, The" (Franklin), **II: 120**

Salinas, Luis Omar, **Supp. IV Part 2:** 545; **Supp. V:** 180; **Supp. XIII: 311–330; Supp. XV:** 73

"Salinas Is on His Way" (Salinas), **Supp. XIII:** 317

"Salinas Sends Messengers to the Stars" (Salinas), **Supp. XIII:** 317

"Salinas Summering at the Caspian and Thinking of Hamlet" (Salinas), **Supp. XIII:** 320

"Salinas Wakes Early and Goes to the Park to Lecture Sparrows" (Salinas), **Supp. XIII:** 320

Salinger, Doris, **III:** 551

Salinger, J. D., **II:** 255; **III: 551–574; IV:** 190, 216, 217; **Retro. Supp. I:** 102, 116, 335; **Supp. IV Part 2:** 502; **Supp. V:** 23, 119; **Supp. VIII:** 151; **Supp. XI:** 2, 66; **Supp. XIV:** 93

Salisbury, Harrison, **Supp. I Part 2:** 664

Salle, David, **Supp. XII:** 4

Salley, Columbus, **Supp. XIV:** 195

"Sally" (Cisneros), **Supp. VII:** 63

"Sally's Choice" (E. Stoddard), **Supp. XV:** 282

Salmagundi; or, The Whim-Whams and Opinions of Launcelot Langstaff Esq., and Others (Irving), **II:** 299, 300, 304

Salmon, Edward G., **Supp. XVIII:** 258

Salome (Strauss), **IV:** 316

Salon (online magazine), **Supp. VIII:** 310; **Supp. X:** 202

Salt Eaters, The (Bambara), **Supp. XI:** 1, **12–14**

Salt Ecstasies, The (White), **Supp. XI:** 123

Salter, James, **Supp. IX: 245–263; Supp. XVI:** 237, 247

Salter, Mary Jo, **Supp. IV Part 2:** 653; **Supp. IX:** 37, 292; **Supp. XV:** 251, 253; **Supp. XVII:** 112

"Salt Garden, The" (Nemerov), **III:** 267–268

Salt Garden, The (Nemerov), **III:** 269, 272–275, 277

Salting the Ocean (Nye, ed.), **Supp. XIII:** 280

"Salt Lesson, The" (C. Frost), **Supp. XV:** 99

Salt Lesson, The (C. Frost), **Supp. XV:** 92, 96

"Salts and Oils" (Levine), **Supp. V:** 190

Saltzman, Arthur, **Supp. XIII:** 48

Saltzman, Harry, **Supp. XI:** 307

"Salut au Monde!" (Whitman), **Retro. Supp. I:** 387, 396, 400

"Salute" (MacLeish), **III:** 13

"Salute to Mister Yates, A" (Dubus), **Supp. XI:** 347, 349

Salvador (Didion), **Supp. IV Part 1:** 198, 207–208, 210

"Salvage" (Clampitt), **Supp. IX:** 41

Samain, Albert, **II:** 528

Same Door, The (Updike), **IV:** 214, 219, 226; **Retro. Supp. I:** 320

"Same in Blues" (Hughes), **Retro. Supp. I:** 208

"Samhain" (A. Finch), **Supp. XVII:** 72

Sam Lawson's Oldtown Fireside Stories (Stowe), **Supp. I Part 2:** 587, 596, 598–599

"Sa'm Pèdi" (Bell), **Supp. X:** 17

"Sampler, A" (MacLeish), **III:** 4

Sampoli, Maria, **Supp. V:** 338

Sampson, Edward, **Supp. I Part 2:** 664, 673

Sampson, Martin, **Supp. I Part 2:** 652

Sam's Legacy (Neugeboren), **Supp. XVI:** 221, 222

Samson Agonistes (Milton), **III:** 274

"Samson and Delilah" (Masters), **Supp. I Part 2:** 459

Samuel de Champlain: Father of New France (Morison), **Supp. I Part 2:** 496–497

Samuels, Charles Thomas, **Retro. Supp. I:** 334

"Samuel Sewall" (Hecht), **Supp. X:** 58

Sanborn, Franklin B., **IV:** 171, 172, 178

Sanborn, Kate, **Supp. XIII:** 152

Sanborn, Sara, **Supp. XIV:** 113

Sanchez, Carol Anne, **Supp. IV Part 1:** 335

Sanchez, Carol Lee, **Supp. IV Part 2:** 499, 557

Sanchez, Sonia, **Supp. II Part 1:** 34

Sanctified Church, The (Hurston), **Supp. VI:** 150

"Sanction of the Victims, The" (Rand), **Supp. IV Part 2:** 528

Sanctuary (Faulkner), **II:** 57, 61–63, 72, 73, 74, 174; **Retro. Supp. I:** 73, 84, 86–87, 87; **Supp. I Part 2:** 614; **Supp. XII:** 16

"Sanctuary" (Larsen), **Supp. XVIII:** 119, 130–131

Sanctuary (Wharton), **IV:** 311

"Sanctuary" (Wylie), **Supp. I Part 2:** 711

"Sanctuary, The" (Nemerov), **III:** 272, 274

Sanctuary V (Schulberg), **Supp. XVIII:** 254

"Sanctus" (Nelson), **Supp. XVIII:** 183

Sand, George, **II:** 322; **Retro. Supp. I:** 235, 372; **Supp. XV:** 275

"Sandalphon" (Longfellow), **II:** 498

Sandbox, The (Albee), **I:** 74–75, 89

Sandburg, Carl, **I:** 103, 109, 384, 421; **II:** 529; **III:** 3, 20, **575–598; Retro. Supp. I:** 133, 194; **Supp. I Part 1:** 257, 320; **Supp. I Part 2:** 387, 389, 454, 461, 653; **Supp. III Part 1:** 63, 71, 73, 75; **Supp. IV Part 1:** 169; **Supp. IV Part 2:** 502; **Supp. IX:** 1, 15, 308; **Supp. XIII:** 274, 277; **Supp. XV:** 293, 299, 300, 301, 302, 306

Sandburg, Helga, **III:** 583

Sandburg, Janet, **III:** 583, 584
Sandburg, Margaret, **III:** 583, 584
Sandburg, Mrs. Carl (Lillian Steichen), **III:** 580
Sand County Almanac and Sketches Here and There, A (Leopold), **Supp. XIV:** 177, 178, **182–192**
"Sand Dabs" (Oliver), **Supp. VII:** 245
"Sand Dunes" (Frost), **Retro. Supp. I:** 137; **Retro. Supp. II:** 41
Sander, August, **Supp. IX:** 211
Sanders, Scott Russell, **Supp. XVI: 265–280**
"Sandman, The" (Barthelme), **Supp. IV Part 1:** 47
Sandman's Dust (Bukiet), **Supp. XVII:** 40, 41
Sando, Joe S., **Supp. IV Part 2:** 510
Sandoe, James, **Supp. IV Part 1:** 131; **Supp. IV Part 2:** 470
Sandoz, Mari, **Supp. XV:** 141
Sandperl, Ira, **Supp. VIII:** 200
"Sand-Quarry and Moving Figures" (Rukeyser), **Supp. VI:** 271, 278
Sand Rivers (Matthiessen), **Supp. V:** 203
"Sand Roses, The" (Hogan), **Supp. IV Part 1:** 401
Sands, Diana, **Supp. IV Part 1:** 362
Sands, Robert, **Supp. I Part 1:** 156, 157
"Sands at Seventy" (Whitman), **IV:** 348
"Sandstone Farmhouse, A" (Updike), **Retro. Supp. I:** 318
Sandy Bottom Orchestra,The (Keillor and Nilsson), **Supp. XVI:** 177
Sanford, John, **IV:** 286, 287
San Francisco (film), **Supp. XVI:** 181, 192
"San Francisco Blues" (Kerouac), **Supp. III Part 1:** 225
Sangamon County Peace Advocate, The (Lindsay), **Supp. I Part 2:** 379
Sanger, Margaret, **Supp. I Part 1:** 19
Sansom, William, **IV:** 279
Sans Soleil (film), **Supp. IV Part 2:** 436
"Santa" (Sexton), **Supp. II Part 2:** 693
Santa Claus: A Morality (Cummings), **I:** 430, 441
"Santa Fé Trail, The" (Lindsay), **Supp. I Part 2:** 389
"Santa Lucia" (Hass), **Supp. VI:** 105–106
"Santa Lucia II" (Hass), **Supp. VI:** 105–106
Santayana, George, **I:** 222, 224, 236, 243, 253, 460; **II:** 20, 542; **III:** 64, **599–622; IV:** 26, 339, 351, 353, 441; **Retro. Supp. I:** 55, 57, 67, 295; **Retro. Supp. II:** 179; **Supp. I Part 2:** 428; **Supp. II Part 1:** 107; **Supp. X:** 58; **Supp. XIV:** 199, 335, 340, 342; **Supp. XVI:** 189; **Supp. XVII:** 97, 106
Santiago, Esmeralda, **Supp. XI:** 177
"Santorini: Stopping the Leak" (Merrill), **Supp. III Part 1:** 336
Santos, John Phillip, **Supp. XIII:** 274
Santos, Sherod, **Supp. VIII:** 270
Sapir, Edward, **Supp. VIII:** 295; **Supp. XVI:** 283
"Sapphics for Patience" (A. Finch), **Supp. XVII:** 72
Sapphira and the Slave Girl (Cather), **I:** 331; **Retro. Supp. I:** 2, **19–20**
Sappho, **II:** 544; **III:** 142; **Supp. I Part 1:** 261, 269; **Supp. I Part 2:** 458; **Supp. XII:** 98, 99; **Supp. XVII:** 74
"Sappho" (Wright), **Supp. III Part 2:** 595, 604
"Sara" (song, Dylan), **Supp. XVIII:** 28
"Sarah" (Schwartz), **Supp. II Part 2:** 663
Sarah; or, The Exemplary Wife (Rowson), **Supp. XV:** 242
"Saratoga" mysteries (Dobyns), **Supp. XIII:** 79–80
Sargent, John Singer, **II:** 337, 338
Saroyan, Aram, **Supp. XV:** 182
Saroyan, William, **III:** 146–147; **IV:** 393; **Supp. I Part 2:** 679; **Supp. IV Part 1:** 83; **Supp. IV Part 2:** 502; **Supp. XIII:** 280
Sarris, Greg, **Supp. IV Part 1:** 329, 330
Sarton, George, **Supp. VIII:** 249
Sarton, May, **Supp. III Part 1:** 62, 63; **Supp. VIII: 249–268; Supp. XIII:** 296; **Supp. XVII:** 71
Sartoris (Faulkner), **II:** 55, 56–57, 58, 62; **Retro. Supp. I:** 77, 81, 82, 83, 88
Sartor Resartus (Carlyle), **II:** 26; **III:** 82
Sartre, Jean-Paul, **I:** 82, 494; **II:** 57, 244; **III:** 51, 204, 292, 453, 619; **IV:** 6, 223, 236, 477, 487, 493; **Retro. Supp. I:** 73; **Supp. I Part 1:** 51; **Supp. IV Part 1:** 42, 84; **Supp. IX:** 4; **Supp. VIII:** 11; **Supp. XIII:** 74, 171; **Supp. XIV:** 24; **Supp. XVII:** 137
Sassone, Ralph, **Supp. X:** 171
Sassoon, Siegfried, **II:** 367; **Supp. XV:** 308
Satan in Goray (Singer), **IV:** 1, 6–7, 12; **Retro. Supp. II:** 303, **304–305**
"Satan Says" (Olds), **Supp. X:** 202; **Supp. XVII:** 114
Satan Says (Olds), **Supp. X:** 201, 202, **202–204,** 215
Satanstoe (Cooper), **I:** 351–352, 355
"Sather Gate Illumination" (Ginsberg), **Supp. II Part 1:** 329
"Satire as a Way of Seeing" (Dos Passos), **III:** 172
Satires of Persius, The (Merwin, trans.), **Supp. III Part 1:** 347
Satirical Rogue on Poetry, The (Francis). *See Pot Shots at Poetry* (Francis)
Satori in Paris (Kerouac), **Supp. III Part 1:** 231
"Saturday" (Salinas), **Supp. XIII:** 315
Saturday Night at the War (Shanley), **Supp. XIV:** 315
"Saturday Rain" (Kees), **Supp. XV:** 136
"Saturday Route, The" (Wolfe), **Supp. III Part 2:** 580
Satyagraha (Gandhi), **IV:** 185
"Satyr's Heart, The" (B. Kelly), **Supp. XVII:** 132
"Saul and Patsy" (C. Baxter), **Supp. XVII:** 17
Saul and Patsy (C. Baxter), **Supp. XVII:** 22–23
"Saul and Patsy Are Getting Comfortable in Michigan" (C. Baxter), **Supp. XVII:** 22
"Saul and Patsy Are in Labor" (C. Baxter), **Supp. XVII:** 20, 22
"Saul and Patsy Are Pregnant" (C. Baxter), **Supp. XVII:** 22
Saunders, Richard, **II:** 110
Savage, Augusta, **Retro. Supp. II:** 115
Savage, James, **II:** 111
Savage Holiday (Wright), **IV:** 478, 488
Savage in Limbo: A Concert Play (Shanley), **Supp. XIV:** 315, **319–321,** 323, 324
Savage Love (Shepard and Chaikin), **Supp. III Part 2:** 433
Savage Wilds (Reed), **Supp. X:** 241
Save Me, Joe Louis (Bell), **Supp. X:** 7, 10, **11–12**
Save Me the Waltz (Z. Fitzgerald), **II:** 95; **Retro. Supp. I:** 110; **Supp. IX:** 58, 59, 65, **66–68**
Savers, Michael, **Supp. XI:** 307
Saving Lives (Goldbarth), **Supp. XII:** 192
Saving Private Ryan (film), **Supp. V:** 249; **Supp. XI:** 234
Savings (Hogan), **Supp. IV Part 1:** 397, 404, 405, 406, 410
Savo, Jimmy, **I:** 440
Savran, David, **Supp. IX:** 145; **Supp. XIII:** 209; **Supp. XV:** 321
Sawyer-Lauçanno, Christopher, **Supp. IV Part 1:** 95
Saxon, Lyle, **Retro. Supp. I:** 80
"Say All" (Ray), **Supp. XVIII:** 193
Say and Seal (S. and A. Warner), **Supp. XVIII:** 258, 266
Saye and Sele, Lord, **Supp. I Part 1:** 98
Sayer, Mandy, **Supp. XIII:** 118
Sayers, Dorothy, **Supp. IV Part 1:** 341; **Supp. IV Part 2:** 464
Sayers, Valerie, **Supp. XI:** 253; **Supp. XVIII:** 99
"Sayings/For Luck" (Goldbarth), **Supp. XII:** 176
Say! Is This the U.S.A.? (Caldwell), **I:** 293, 294–295, 304, 309, 310
Saylor, Bruce, **Supp. XII:** 253
Sayre, Joel, **Supp. XIII:** 166
Sayre, Nora, **Supp. XII:** 119
Sayre, Zelda, **Retro. Supp. I:** 101, 102–103, 104, 105, 108, 109, 110, 113, 114. *See also* Fitzgerald, Zelda (Zelda Sayre)
"Say Yes" (Wolff), **Supp. VII:** 344
"Scales of the Eyes, The" (Nemerov), **III:** 272, 273, 277
Scalpel (McCoy), **Supp. XIII: 174–175**
Scalpel (screen treatment, McCoy), **Supp. XIII:** 174
Scandalabra (Zelda Fitzgerald), **Supp. IX:** 60, 61, 65, 67, **68–70**
"Scandal Detectives, The" (Fitzgerald), **II:** 80–81; **Retro. Supp. I:** 99
Scarberry-García, Susan, **Supp. IV Part 2:** 486
Scarborough, Dorothy, **Supp. XVIII:** 279–280
"Scarecrow, The" (Farrell), **II:** 45
"Scarf, A" (Shields), **Supp. VII:** 328

Scarlet Letter, The (Hawthorne), **II:** 63, 223, 224, 231, 233, 239–240, 241, 243, 244, 255, 264, 286, 290, 291, 550; **Retro. Supp. I:** 63, 145, 147, 152, **157–159,** 160, 163, 165, 220, 248, 330, 335; **Retro. Supp. II:** 100; **Supp. I Part 1:** 38; **Supp. II Part 1:** 386; **Supp. VIII:** 108, 198; **Supp. XII:** 11; **Supp. XVII:** 143
Scarlet Plague, The (London), **II:** 467
Scar Lover (Crews), **Supp. XI:** 103, 107, **114–115**
"Scarred Girl, The" (Dickey), **Supp. IV Part 1:** 180
Scates, Maxine, **Supp. XIV:** 264, 265, 274
"Scenario" (H. Miller), **III:** 184
"Scene" (Howells), **II:** 274
"Scene in Jerusalem, A" (Stowe), **Supp. I Part 2:** 587
"Scenes" (Shields), **Supp. VII:** 318
Scènes d'Anabase (chamber music) (Bowles), **Supp. IV Part 1:** 82
Scenes from American Life (Gurney), **Supp. V:** 95, 96, 105, 108
Scenes from Another Life (McClatchy), **Supp. XII: 255–256**
"Scenes of Childhood" (Merrill), **Supp. III Part 1:** 322, 323, 327
"Scented Herbage of My Breast" (Whitman), **IV:** 342–343
"Scent of a Woman's Ink" (Prose), **Supp. XVI:** 259
"Scent of Unbought Flowers, The" (Ríos), **Supp. IV Part 2:** 547
Scepticisms (Aiken), **I:** 58
Scève, Maurice, **Supp. III Part 1:** 11
Schad, Christian, **Supp. IV Part 1:** 247
Schafer, Benjamin G., **Supp. XIV:** 144
Schaller, George, **Supp. V:** 208, 210–211
Schapiro, Meyer, **II:** 30
Scharmann, Hermann Balthazar, **Supp. XII:** 41
Schary, Dore, **Supp. IV Part 1:** 365; **Supp. XIII:** 163
Schatz, Tom, **Supp. XVIII:** 242
Schaumbergh, Count de, **II:** 120
Scheele, Roy, **Supp. XVI:** 54
Scheffauer, G. H., **I:** 199
"Scheherazade" (Ashbery), **Supp. III Part 1:** 18
Scheick, William, **Supp. V:** 272
Schelberg, Budd, **Supp. XVIII: 241–256**
Scheler, Max, **I:** 58
Schelling, Friedrich, **Supp. I Part 2:** 422
Schenck, Joseph, **Supp. XVI:** 186
Schenk, Margaret, **I:** 199
Scheponik, Peter, **Supp. X:** 210
Scherer, Loline, **Supp. XIII:** 161
Schevill, James, **I:** 116
Schickel, Richard, **Supp. XV:** 1
Schilder, Paul, **Supp. I Part 2:** 622
Schiller, Andrew, **II:** 20
Schiller, Frederick, **Supp. V:** 290
Schiller, Johann Christoph Friedrich von, **I:** 224; **Supp. IV Part 2:** 519; **Supp. XVI:** 292
Schiller, Lawrence, **Retro. Supp. II:** 208, 212, 214
Schimmel, Harold, **Supp. V:** 336
"Schizoid Nature of the Implied Author in Twentieth-Century American Ethnic Novels, The" (Nelson), **Supp. XVIII:** 172
Schlegel, Augustus Wilhelm, **III:** 422, 424
Schlegell, David von, **Supp. IV Part 2:** 423
Schleiermacher, Friedrich, **III:** 290–291, 309
Schleifer, Ronald, **Supp. XVIII:** 144
Schlepping Through the Alps (S. Apple), **Supp. XVII:** 8
Schlesinger, Arthur, Jr., **III:** 291, 297–298, 309
Schmidt, Jon Zlotnik, **Supp. IV Part 1:** 2
Schmidt, Kaspar. *See* Stirner, Max
Schmidt, Michael, **Supp. X:** 55
Schmitt, Carl, **I:** 386–387
Schmitz, Neil, **Supp. X:** 243
Schnackenberg, Gjertrud, **Supp. XV: 249–268**
Schneider, Alan, **I:** 87
Schneider, Louis, **Supp. I Part 2:** 650
Schneider, Romy, **Supp. IV Part 2:** 549
Schneider, Steven, **Supp. IX:** 271, 274
Schnellock, Emil, **III:** 177
Schneour, Zalman, **IV:** 11
Schnitzler, Arthur, **Supp. XV:** 307; **Supp. XVI:** 187
Schoerke, Meg, **Supp. XVII:** 110
"Scholar Gypsy, The" (Arnold), **II:** 541
"Scholastic and Bedside Teaching" (Holmes), **Supp. I Part 1:** 305
Schöler, Bo, **Supp. IV Part 1:** 399, 400, 403, 407, 409; **Supp. IV Part 2:** 499
Scholes, Robert, **Supp. V:** 40, 42
Scholtz, Carter, **Supp. XVIII:** 144
Schomburg, Arthur, **Supp. X:** 134
Schoolboy Howlers (Abingdon), **Supp. XVI:** 99
Schoolcraft, Henry Rowe, **II:** 503; **Retro. Supp. II:** 160
"School Daze" (Bambara), **Supp. XI:** 19
School Daze (film), **Supp. XI:** 19, 20
"Schoolhouse" (Levis), **Supp. XI:** 258
"School of Giorgione, The" (Pater), **I:** 51
"School Play, The" (Merrill), **Supp. III Part 1:** 336
"Schooner Fairchild's Class" (Benét), **Supp. XI:** 55
Schopenhauer, Arthur, **III:** 600, 604; **IV:** 7; **Retro. Supp. I:** 256; **Retro. Supp. II:** 94; **Supp. I Part 1:** 320; **Supp. I Part 2:** 457; **Supp. X:** 187; **Supp. XVI:** 184
Schorer, Mark, **II:** 28; **III:** 71; **Retro. Supp. I:** 115; **Supp. IV Part 1:** 197, 203, 211; **Supp. XVI:** 206
Schott, Webster, **Supp. IX:** 257
Schotts, Jeffrey, **Supp. XII:** 193
Schrader, Mary von. *See* Jarrell, Mrs. Randall (Mary von Schrader)
Schreiner, Olive, **I:** 419; **Supp. XI:** 203
Schroeder, Eric James, **Supp. V:** 238, 244
Schubert, Bernard L., **Supp. XVII:** 58
Schubert, Franz Peter, **Supp. I Part 1:** 363
Schubnell, Matthias, **Supp. IV Part 2:** 486
Schulberg, Budd, **II:** 98; **Retro. Supp. I:** 113; **Supp. XIII:** 170; **Supp. XV:** 194; **Supp. XVIII: 241-256**
Schulberg, Stuart, **Supp. XVIII:** 253
Schulz, Bruno, **Supp. IV Part 2:** 623; **Supp. XVII:** 41
Schuman, William, **Supp. XII:** 253
Schumann, Dr. Alanson Tucker, **III:** 505
Schuster, Edgar H., **Supp. VIII:** 126
Schuyler, George S., **III:** 110; **Supp. XVI:** 142
Schuyler, James, **Supp. XV:** 177, 178
Schuyler, William, **Supp. I Part 1:** 211
Schwartz, Delmore, **I:** 67, 168, 188, 288; **IV:** 128, 129, 437; **Retro. Supp. II:** 29, 178; **Supp. II Part 1:** 102, 109; **Supp. II Part 2: 639–668; Supp. IX:** 299; **Supp. VIII:** 98; **Supp. XIII:** 320; **Supp. XIV:** 3; **Supp. XV:** 184
Schwartz, Leonard, **Supp. XVI:** 289
Schwartz, Lloyd, **Supp. I Part 1:** 81
Schwartz, Marilyn, **Supp. XII:** 126, 128, 130, 132
Schwartz, Richard B., **Supp. XIV:** 23, 27
Schweitzer, Albert, **Supp. IV Part 1:** 373
Schweitzer, Harold, **Supp. X:** 210
Schwerdt, Lisa M., **Supp. XIV:** 155, 171
Schwitters, Kurt, **III:** 197; **Retro. Supp. II:** 322, 331, 336; **Supp. IV Part 1:** 79
"Science" (Jeffers), **Supp. II Part 2:** 426
Science and Health with Key to the Scriptures (Eddy), **I:** 383
"Science Favorable to Virtue" (Freneau), **Supp. II Part 1:** 274
Science of English Verse, The (Lanier), **Supp. I Part 1:** 368, 369
"Science of the Night, The" (Kunitz), **Supp. III Part 1:** 258, 265
Sciolino, Martina, **Supp. XII:** 9
"Scissors" (C. Baxter), **Supp. XVII:** 19
Scopes, John T., **III:** 105, 495
"Scorched Face, The" (Hammett), **Supp. IV Part 1:** 344
"Scorn" (C. Frost), **Supp. XV:** 105
"Scorpion, The" (Bowles), **Supp. IV Part 1:** 84, 86
Scorsese, Martin, **Supp. IV Part 1:** 356; **Supp. XVIII:** 22
Scott, Anne Firor, **Supp. I Part 1:** 19
Scott, A. O., **Supp. X:** 301, 302; **Supp. XII:** 343
Scott, Evelyn, **Retro. Supp. I:** 73
Scott, George C., **III:** 165–166; **Supp. XI:** 304
Scott, George Lewis, **Supp. I Part 2:** 503, 504
Scott, Herbert, **Supp. V:** 180
Scott, Howard, **Supp. I Part 2:** 645
Scott, Joanna, **Supp. XVII: 183–197**
Scott, Lizabeth, **Supp. IV Part 2:** 524
Scott, Lynn Orilla, **Retro. Supp. II:** 12
Scott, Mark, **Retro. Supp. I:** 127
Scott, Nathan A., Jr., **II:** 27
Scott, Paul, **Supp. IV Part 2:** 690
Scott, Ridley, **Supp. XIII:** 268
Scott, Sir Walter, **I:** 204, 339, 341, 343, 354; **II:** 8, 17, 18, 217, 296, 301, 303, 304, 308; **III:** 415, 482; **IV:** 204, 453;

Retro. Supp. I: 99; **Supp. I Part 2:** 579, 580, 685, 692; **Supp. IV Part 2:** 690; **Supp. IX:** 175; **Supp. X:** 51, 114
Scott, Walter, **Supp. XVI:** 7, 13
Scott, Winfield Townley, **II:** 512; **Supp. I Part 2:** 705; **Supp. XV:** 51
Scottsboro boys, **I:** 505; **Supp. I Part 1:** 330
Scottsboro Limited (Hughes), **Retro. Supp. I:** 203; **Supp. I Part 1:** 328, 330–331, 332
Scoundrel Time (Hellman), **Supp. I Part 1:** 294–297; **Supp. IV Part 1:** 12; **Supp. VIII:** 243
Scrambled Eggs Super! (Geisel), **Supp. XVI:** 105
Scrambled Eggs & Whiskey: Poems, 1991–1995 (Carruth), **Supp. XVI:** 47
Scratch (MacLeish), **III:** 22–23
"Scratch Music" (Wright), **Supp. XV:** 343
"Scream, The" (Lowell), **II:** 550
"Screamer, The" (Coleman), **Supp. XI: 92–93**
"Screamers, The" (Baraka), **Supp. II Part 1:** 38
"Screen Guide for Americans" (Rand), **Supp. IV Part 2:** 524
"Screeno" (Schwartz), **Supp. II Part 2:** 660
Screens, The (Genet), **Supp. XII:** 12
Scribblers on the Roof: Contemporary American Jewish Fiction (Bukiet and Roskies, eds.), **Supp. XVII:** 39, 49–50
Scripts for the Pageant (Merrill), **Supp. III Part 1:** 332, 333, 335
Scrolls from the Dead Sea, The (Wilson), **IV:** 429
Scruggs, Earl, **Supp. V:** 335
Scudder, Horace Elisha, **II:** 400, 401; **Retro. Supp. II:** 67; **Supp. I Part 1:** 220; **Supp. I Part 2:** 410, 414
Scully, James, **Supp. XII:** 131
"Sculpting the Whistle" (Ríos), **Supp. IV Part 2:** 549
"Sculptor" (Plath), **Supp. I Part 2:** 538
"Sculptor's Funeral, The" (Cather), **I:** 315–316; **Retro. Supp. I:** 5, 6; **Supp. XV:** 40
Scum (Singer), **Retro. Supp. II:** 316–317
Scupoli, Lorenzo, **IV:** 156
"Scythe Song" (Lang), **Retro. Supp. I:** 128
Sea and the Mirror, The: A Commentary on Shakespeare's "The Tempest" (Auden), **Supp. II Part 1:** 2, 18
Sea around Us, The (Carson), **Supp. IX:** 19, **23–25**
Sea around Us, The (film), **Supp. IX:** 25
"Sea Birds Are Still Alive, The" (Bambara), **Supp. XI:** 8
Sea Birds Are Still Alive, The (Bambara), **Supp. XI:** 1, 4, **7–12**
"Sea-Blue and Blood-Red" (Lowell), **II:** 524
Seabrook, John, **Supp. VIII:** 157
"Sea Burial from the Cruiser Reve" (Eberhart), **I:** 532–533
Seabury, David, **Supp. I Part 2:** 608
"Sea Calm" (Hughes), **Retro. Supp. I:** 199
"Sea Chanty" (Corso), **Supp. XII:** 118
"Sea Dream, A" (Whitter), **Supp. I Part 2:** 699
"Seafarer, The" (Pound, trans.), **Retro. Supp. I:** 287
Seagall, Harry, **Supp. XIII:** 166
Sea Garden (Doolittle), **Supp. I Part 1:** 257, 259, 266, 269, 272
Seager, Allan, **IV:** 305
"Seagulls and Children" (C. Frost), **Supp. XV:** 95
"Sea Lily" (Doolittle), **Supp. I Part 1:** 266
Sea Lions, The (Cooper), **I:** 354, 355
Sealts, Merton M., Jr., **Retro. Supp. I:** 257
Seaman, Donna, **Supp. VIII:** 86; **Supp. X:** 1, 4, 12, 16, 213; **Supp. XV:** 65; **Supp. XVIII:** 102
"Séance, The" (Singer), **IV:** 20
Séance and Other Stories, The (Singer), **IV:** 19–21
Sea of Cortez (Steinbeck), **IV:** 52, 54, 62, 69
Sea of Grass, The (film), **Supp. XVIII:** 211
Sea of Grass, The (Richter), **Supp. XVIII: 210–211,** 215–216, 217, 220
"Sea Pieces" (Melville), **III:** 93
Searchers, The (film, Ford), **Supp. XVIII:** 57, 58, 135–136, 141
Searches and Seizures (Elkin), **Supp. VI: 49**
"Search for Southern Identity, The" (Woodward), **Retro. Supp. I:** 75
Search for the King, A: A Twelfth-Century Legend (Vidal), **Supp. IV Part 2:** 681
Searching for Caleb (Tyler), **Supp. IV Part 2:** 663–665, 671
"Searching for Poetry: Real *vs.* Fake" (B. Miller), **Supp. IV Part 1:** 67
Searching for Survivors (Banks), **Supp. V:** 7
"Searching for Survivors (I)" (Banks), **Supp. V:** 8
"Searching for Survivors (II)" (Banks), **Supp. V:** 7, 8
"Searching for the Ox" (Simpson), **Supp. IX:** 275, 280
Searching for the Ox (Simpson), **Supp. IX:** 266, **274–275**
"Searching in the Britannia Tavern" (Wagoner), **Supp. IX:** 327
Searching Wing, The, (Hellman), **Supp. I Part 1:** 277, 278, 281–282, 283, 292, 297
"Search Party, The" (Matthews), **Supp. IX: 156**
Searle, Ronald, **Supp. I Part 2:** 604, 605
Sea Road to the Indies (Hart), **Supp. XIV:** 97
"Seascape" (Bishop), **Retro. Supp. II:** 42–43
"Sea's Green Sameness, The" (Updike), **IV:** 217
Seaside and the Fireside, The (Longfellow), **II:** 489; **Retro. Supp. II:** 159, 168
Season in Hell, A (Rimbaud), **III:** 189
Seasons, The (Thomson), **II:** 304; **Supp. I Part 1:** 151
Seasons' Difference, The (Buechner), **Supp. XII: 47**
Seasons of Celebration (Merton), **Supp. VIII:** 199, 208
Seasons of the Heart: In Quest of Faith (Kinard, comp.), **Supp. XIV:** 127
"Seasons of the Soul" (Tate), **IV:** 136–140
Seasons on Earth (Koch), **Supp. XV: 183–184**
"Sea Surface Full of Clouds" (Stevens), **IV:** 82
"Sea Tides" (Hoffman), **Supp. XVIII:** 87
"Sea Treader" (Hoffman), **Supp. XVIII:** 87
"Sea Unicorns and Land Unicorns" (Moore), **III:** 202–203
Seaver, Richard, **Supp. XI:** 301
"Seaweed" (Longfellow), **II:** 498
Sea-Wolf, The (London), **II:** 264, 466, 472–473
Sebald, W. G., **Supp. XIV:** 96
Seckler, David, **Supp. I Part 2:** 650
"2nd Air Force" (Jarrell), **II:** 375
Second American Revolution and Other Essays (1976–1982), The (Vidal), **Supp. IV Part 2:** 679, 687, 688
Secondary Colors, The (A. Theroux), **Supp. VIII:** 312
Second Chance (Auchincloss), **Supp. IV Part 1:** 33
"Second Chances" (Hugo), **Supp. VI:** 144, 145
Second Coming, The (Percy), **Supp. III Part 1:** 383, 384, 387, 388, 396–397
"Second Coming, The" (Yeats), **III:** 294; **Retro. Supp. I:** 290, 311; **Supp. VIII:** 24; **Supp. XVI:** 159
Second Decade, The. See Stephen King, The Second Decade: "Danse Macabre" to "The Dark Half" (Magistrale)
Second Dune, The (Hearon), **Supp. VIII:** 58, **59–60**
Second Flowering, A: Works and Days of the Lost Generation (Cowley), **Retro. Supp. II:** 77; **Supp. II Part 1:** 135, 141, 143, 144, 147, 149
Second Growth (Stegner), **Supp. IV Part 2:** 599, 608
"Second Hour of the Night, The" (Bidart), **Supp. XV:** 32, **33–34**
Second Marriage (F. Barthelme), **Supp. XI:** 32, 33
"Second Marriage" (McCarriston), **Supp. XIV:** 262
Second Nature (Hoffman), **Supp. X:** 88, 89
Seconds, The (Bierds), **Supp. XVII: 33–34**
Second Set, The (Komunyakaa and Feinstein, eds.), **Supp. XIII:** 125
Second Sex, The (Beauvoir), **Supp. IV Part 1:** 360
Second Stone, The (Fiedler), **Supp. XIII:** 102
"Second Swimming, The" (Boyle), **Supp. VIII:** 13, 14

"Second Tree from the Corner" (White), **Supp. I Part 2:** 651
Second Tree from the Corner (White), **Supp. I Part 2:** 654
Second Twenty Years at Hull-House, The: September 1909 to September 1929, with a Record of a Growing World Consciousness (Addams), **Supp. I Part 1:** 24–25
Second Voyage of Columbus, The (Morison), **Supp. I Part 2:** 488
Second Words, (Atwood), **Supp. XIII:** 35
Second World, The (Blackmur), **Supp. II Part 1:** 91
Secret, The (E. Hoffman), **Supp. XVI:** 151, **155–158,** 161
"Secret, The" (Levine), **Supp. V:** 195
Secret Agent, The (Conrad), **Supp. IV Part 1:** 341
Secret Agent X-9 (Hammett), **Supp. IV Part 1:** 355
"Secret Courts of Men's Hearts, The: Code and Law in Harper Lee's *To Kill a Mockingbird*" (Johnson), **Supp. VIII:** 126
"Secret Dog, The" (Cameron), **Supp. XII: 83–84**
Secret Garden, The (Burnett), **Supp. I Part 1:** 44
"Secret Garden, The" (Hoffman), **Supp. XVIII:** 86
"Secret Gladness, A" (C. Frost), **Supp. XV:** 91
Secret Historie (J. Smith), **I:** 131
Secret History of the Dividing Line (Howe), **Supp. IV Part 2:** 424, 425–426
"Secret Integration, The" (Pynchon), **Supp. II Part 2:** 624
"Secret Life of Musical Instruments, The" (Wright), **Supp. XV:** 343
"Secret Life of Walter Mitty, The" (Thurber), **Supp. I Part 2:** 623; **Supp. XVI:** 233
"Secret Lion, The" (Ríos), **Supp. IV Part 2:** 543, 544
"Secret Ocean, The" (Jarman), **Supp. XVII:** 120
Secret of Poetry, The: Essays (Jarman), **Supp. XVII:** 110, 111, 120
"Secret of the Russian Ballet, The" (Van Vechten), **Supp. II Part 2:** 732
"Secret Prune" (Ríos), **Supp. IV Part 2:** 549
Secret River, The (Rawlings), **Supp. X:** 233
Secrets and Surprises (Beattie), **Supp. V:** 23, 27, 29
Secrets from the Center of the World (Harjo), **Supp. XII: 223–224**
"Secret Sharer, The" (Conrad), **Supp. IX:** 105
"Secret Sharer, The" (J. Conrad), **Supp. XVI:** 158
"Secret Society, A" (Nemerov), **III:** 282
Secrets of the Universe: Scenes from the Journey Home (Sanders), **Supp. XVI:** 273–274
Secular Journal of Thomas Merton, The, **Supp. VIII:** 206
"Security" (Stafford), **Supp. XI:** 329
Sedges, John (pseudonym). *See* Buck, Pearl S.
Sedgwick, Catherine Maria, **I:** 341; **Supp. I Part 1:** 155, 157
Sedgwick, Christina. *See* Marquand, Mrs. John P. (Christina Sedgwick)
Sedgwick, Ellery, **I:** 217, 229, 231; **III:** 54–55
Sedgwick, Henry, **Supp. I Part 1:** 156
Sedgwick, Robert, **Supp. I Part 1:** 156
Sedore, Timothy, **Supp. XIV:** 312
"Seduction and Betrayal" (Hardwick), **Supp. III Part 1:** 207
Seduction and Betrayal: Women and Literature (Hardwick), **Supp. III Part 1:** 194, 204, 206–208, 212, 213; **Supp. XIV:** 89
Seed, David, **Supp. IV Part 1:** 391
"Seed Eaters, The" (Francis), **Supp. IX:** 82
"Seed Leaves" (Wilbur), **Supp. III Part 2:** 558
"Seeds" (Anderson), **I:** 106, 114
Seeds of Contemplation (Merton), **Supp. VIII:** 199, 200, 207, 208
Seeds of Destruction (Merton), **Supp. VIII:** 202, 203, 204, 208
"Seeing Red" (column, Ryan as Quin), **Supp. XVIII:** 226
Seeing through the Sun (Hogan), **Supp. IV Part 1:** 397, 400, 401–402, 402, 413
"See in the Midst of Fair Leaves" (Moore), **III:** 215
"Seekers, The" (McGrath), **Supp. X:** 117
"Seeking a Vision of Truth, Guided by a Higher Power" (Burke), **Supp. XIV:** 21, 23
"See(k)ing the Self: Mirrors and Mirroring in Bicultural Texts" (Oster), **Supp. XVI:** 151
"Seele im Raum" (Jarrell), **II:** 382–383
"Seele im Raum" (Rilke), **II:** 382–383
"See Naples and Die" (Hecht), **Supp. X:** 69, 70
"Seen from the 'L'" (Barnes), **Supp. III Part 1:** 33
"See the Moon?" (Barthelme), **Supp. IV Part 1:** 42, 49–50, 50
Segal, D. (pseudonym). *See* Singer, Isaac Bashevis
Segal, George, **Supp. XI:** 343
Segal, Lore, **Supp. XVI:** 203
Segregation: The Inner Conflict in the South (Warren), **IV:** 237, 238, 246, 252
"**Se:* Hegel's Absolute and Heidegger's *Ereignis*" (Agamben), **Supp. XVI:** 289
Seidel, Frederick, **I:** 185
Seize the Day (Bellow), **I:** 144, 147, 148, 150, 151, 152, 153, 155, 158, 162; **Retro. Supp. II:** 19, **23–24,** 27, 32, 34; **Supp. I Part 2:** 428
Selby, Hubert, **Supp. III Part 1:** 125
Selby, John, **Retro. Supp. II:** 221, 222
Selden, John, **Supp. XIV:** 344
Seldes, Gilbert, **II:** 437, 445; **Retro. Supp. I:** 108
Selected Criticism: Prose, Poetry (Bogan), **Supp. III Part 1:** 64
Selected Essays (Eliot), **I:** 572
Selected Essays and Reviews (Carruth), **Supp. XVI:** 46
Selected Journals and Other Writings (Audubon), **Supp. XVI:** 10, 12, 13
Selected Letters (Bynner), **Supp. XV:** 52
Selected Letters (W. C. Williams), **Retro. Supp. I:** 430
Selected Letters, 1940–1956 (Kerouac), **Supp. XIV:** 137, 144
Selected Letters of Robert Frost (Thompson, ed.), **Retro. Supp. I:** 125
Selected Levis, The (Levis), **Supp. XI:** 257, 272
Selected Poems (Aiken), **I:** 69
Selected Poems (Ashbery), **Supp. III Part 1:** 25–26
Selected Poems (Brodsky), **Supp. VIII:** 22
Selected Poems (Brooks), **Supp. III Part 1:** 82–83
Selected Poems (Bynner), **Supp. XV:** 51, 52
Selected Poems (Corso), **Supp. XII:** 129
Selected Poems (Dove), **Supp. IV Part 1:** 241, 243, 250
Selected Poems (Frost), **Retro. Supp. I:** 133, 136
Selected Poems (Guillevic; Levertov, trans.), **Supp. III Part 1:** 283
Selected Poems (Hayden), **Supp. II Part 1:** 363, 364, 367
Selected Poems (Hughes), **Retro. Supp. I:** 202; **Supp. I Part 1:** 341, 345, 346
Selected Poems (Hugo), **Supp. VI:** 143
Selected Poems (Jarrell), **II:** 367, 370, 371, 374, 377, 379, 380, 381, 382, 384
Selected Poems (Justice), **Supp. VII:** 115
Selected Poems (Kinnell), **Supp. III Part 1:** 235, 253
Selected Poems (Levine, 1984), **Supp. V:** 178, 179
Selected Poems (Lowell), **II:** 512, 516; **Retro. Supp. II:** 184, 186, 188, 190
Selected Poems (Merton), **Supp. VIII:** 207, 208
Selected Poems (Moore), **III:** 193, 194, 205–206, 208, 215
Selected Poems (Pound), **Retro. Supp. I:** 289, 291
Selected Poems (Ransom), **III:** 490, 492
Selected Poems (R. Bly), **Supp. IV Part 1:** 60, 62, 65, 66, 68, 69–71
Selected Poems (Reznikoff), **Supp. XIV:** 288
Selected Poems (Rukeyser), **Supp. VI:** 274
Selected Poems (Sexton), **Supp. IV Part 2:** 449
Selected Poems (Strand), **Supp. IV Part 2:** 630
Selected Poems, 1923–1943 (Warren), **IV:** 241–242, 243
Selected Poems, 1928–1958 (Kunitz), **Supp. III Part 1:** 261, 263–265
Selected Poems, 1938–1988 (McGrath), **Supp. X:** 127

Selected Poems, 1963–1983 (Simic), **Supp. VIII:** 275
Selected Poems 1936–1965 (Eberhart), **I:** 541
Selected Poems: 1957–1987 (Snodgrass), **Supp. VI:** 314–315, 323, 324
Selected Poems 1965–1975 (Atwood), **Supp. XIII: 32–34**
Selected Poems II: Poems Selected and New, 1976–1986 (Atwood), **Supp. XIII:** 20, **34–35**
Selected Poems of Ezra Pound (Pound), **Supp. V:** 336
Selected Poems of Gabriela Mistral (Hughes, trans.), **Supp. I Part 1:** 345
Selected Poetry of Amiri Baraka/LeRoi Jones (Baraka), **Supp. II Part 1:** 58
Selected Poetry of Hayden Carruth, The (Carruth), **Supp. XVI:** 53
Selected Stories (Dubus), **Supp. VII:** 88–89
Selected Stories of Richard Bausch, The (Bausch), **Supp. VII:** 42
Selected Translations (Snodgrass), **Supp. VI:** 318, 324, **325–326**
Selected Verse of Margaret Haskins Durber, The (Keillor), **Supp. XVI:** 171
Selected Witter Bynner, The, **Supp. XV:** 52
Selected Works of Djuna Barnes, The (Barnes), **Supp. III Part 1:** 44
Selected Writings 1950–1990 (Howe), **Supp. VI:** 116–117, 118, 120
Selected Writings of John Jay Chapman, The (Barzun), **Supp. XIV:** 54
Select Epigrams from the Greek Anthology (Mackail), **Supp. I Part 2:** 461
"Selene Afterwards" (MacLeish), **III:** 8
"Self" (James), **II:** 351
Self and the Dramas of History, The (Niebuhr), **III:** 308
Self-Consciousness (Updike), **Retro. Supp. I:** 318, 319, 320, 322, 323, 324
"Self-Exposed, The" (X. J. Kennedy), **Supp. XV:** 159
Self-Help: Stories (Moore), **Supp. X:** 163, 166, **167–169,** 174, 175
Self-Interviews (Dickey), **Supp. IV Part 1:** 179
"Self-Made Man, A" (Crane), **I:** 420
"Self Pity" (C. Frost), **Supp. XV:** 93, 94, 101, 102, 104
Self Portrait (album, Dylan), **Supp. XVIII:** 27
"Self-Portrait" (Creeley), **Supp. IV Part 1:** 156
"Self-Portrait" (Mumford), **Supp. II Part 2:** 471
"Self-Portrait" (Wylie), **Supp. I Part 2:** 729
Self-Portrait: Ceaselessly into the Past (Millar, ed. Sipper), **Supp. IV Part 2:** 464, 469, 472, 475
"Self-Portrait in a Convex Mirror" (Ashbery), **Supp. III Part 1:** 5, 7, 9, 16–19, 22, 24, 26
"Self-Reliance" (Emerson), **II:** 7, 15, 17; **Retro. Supp. I:** 159; **Retro. Supp. II:** 155; **Supp. X:** 42, 45
Sélincourt, Ernest de, **Supp. I Part 2:** 676
Selinger, Eric, **Supp. XVI:** 47
Selinger, Eric Murphy, **Supp. XI:** 248
Sell, Henry, **Supp. XVI:** 188
Sellers, Isaiah, **IV:** 194–195
Sellers, Peter, **Supp. XI:** 301, 304, 306, 307, 309
Sellers, William, **IV:** 208
Seltzer, Mark, **Retro. Supp. I:** 227
Selznick, David O., **Retro. Supp. I:** 105, 113; **Supp. IV Part 1:** 353; **Supp. XVIII:** 242
Semi, Allen (pseudonym). *See* Larsen, Nella
"Semi-Lunatics of Kilmuir, The" (Hugo), **Supp. VI:** 145
"Semiotics/The Doctor's Doll" (Goldbarth), **Supp. XII:** 183–184
Semmelweiss, Ignaz, **Supp. I Part 1:** 304
Senancour, Étienne Divert de, **I:** 241
Sendak, Maurice, **Supp. IX:** 207, 208, 213, 214; **Supp. XVI:** 110
Seneca, **II:** 14–15; **III:** 77
Senghor, Leopold Sédar, **Supp. IV Part 1:** 16; **Supp. X:** 132, 139
Senier, Siobhan, **Supp. IV Part 1:** 330
"Senility" (Anderson), **I:** 114
"Senior Partner's Ethics, The" (Auchincloss), **Supp. IV Part 1:** 33
Senlin: A Biography (Aiken), **I:** 48, 49, 50, 52, 56, 57, 64
Sennett, Dorothy, **Supp. XVI:** 43
Sennett, Mack, **III:** 442
"Señora X No More" (Mora), **Supp. XIII:** 218
"Señor Ong and Señor Ha" (Bowles), **Supp. IV Part 1:** 87
Sensational Designs: The Cultural Work of American Fiction, 1790–1860 (Tompkins), **Supp. XVIII:** 258–259
Sense of Beauty, The (Santayana), **III:** 600
Sense of Life in the Modern Novel, The (Mizener), **IV:** 132
"Sense of Shelter, A" (Updike), **Retro. Supp. I:** 318
"Sense of the Meeting, The" (Conroy), **Supp. XVI:** 72
Sense of the Past, The (James), **II:** 337–338
"Sense of the Past, The" (Trilling), **Supp. III Part 2:** 503
"Sense of the Present, The" (Hardwick), **Supp. III Part 1:** 210
"Sense of the Sleight-of-Hand Man, The" (Stevens), **IV:** 93
"Sense of Where You Are, A" (McPhee), **Supp. III Part 1:** 291, 296–298
"Sensibility! O La!" (Roethke), **III:** 536
"Sensible Emptiness, A" (Kramer), **Supp. IV Part 1:** 61, 66
"Sensuality Plunging Barefoot Into Thorns" (Cisneros), **Supp. VII:** 68
"Sentence" (Barthelme), **Supp. IV Part 1:** 47
Sent for You Yesterday (Wideman), **Supp. X:** 320, 321
"Sentimental Education, A" (Banks), **Supp. V:** 10
"Sentimental Journey" (Oates), **Supp. II Part 2:** 522, 523
"Sentimental Journey, A" (Anderson), **I:** 114
Sentimental Journey, A (Sterne), **Supp. I Part 2:** 714
"Sentimental Journeys" (Didion), **Supp. IV Part 1:** 211
Sentimental Journey through France and Italy, A (Sterne), **Supp. XV:** 232
"Sentiment of Rationality, The" (James), **II:** 346–347
"Separate Flights" (Dubus), **Supp. VII:** 83
Separate Flights (Dubus), **Supp. VII:** 78–83
Separate Peace, A (Knowles), **Supp. IV Part 2:** 679; **Supp. XII: 241–249**
Separate Way (Reznikoff), **Supp. XIV:** 280
"Separating" (Updike), **Retro. Supp. I:** 321
"Separation, The" (Kunitz), **Supp. III Part 1:** 263
"Sepia High Stepper" (Hayden), **Supp. II Part 1:** 379
September (film; Allen), **Supp. XV:** 11
"September" (Komunyakaa), **Supp. XIII:** 130
"September 1, 1939" (Auden), **Supp. II Part 1:** 13; **Supp. IV Part 1:** 225; **Supp. VIII:** 30, 32; **Supp. XV:** 117–118
September 11, 2001: American Writers Respond (Heyen), **Supp. XIII:** 285
September Song (Humphrey), **Supp. IX:** 101, 102, **108–109**
"September Twelfth, 2001" (X. J. Kennedy), **Supp. XV:** 171
"Sept Vieillards, Les" (Millay, trans.), **III:** 142
Sequel to Drum-Taps (Whitman), **Retro. Supp. I:** 406
"Sequence, Sometimes Metaphysical" (Roethke), **III:** 547, 548
Sequence of Seven Plays with a Drawing by Ron Slaughter, A (Nemerov), **III:** 269
Sequoya, Jana, **Supp. IV Part 1:** 334
Seraglio, The (Merrill), **Supp. III Part 1:** 331
Seraphita (Balzac), **I:** 499
Seraph on the Suwanee (Hurston), **Supp. VI:** 149, 159–160
Serenissima: A Novel of Venice (Jong). *See Shylock's Daughter: A Novel of Love in Venice (Serenissima)* (Jong)
Sergeant, Elizabeth Shepley, **I:** 231, 236, 312, 319, 323, 328
Sergeant Bilko (television show), **Supp. IV Part 2:** 575
"Serious Talk, A" (Carver), **Supp. III Part 1:** 138, 144
Serly, Tibor, **Supp. III Part 2:** 617, 619
"Sermon by Doctor Pep" (Bellow), **I:** 151
Sermones (Horace), **II:** 154
"Sermon for Our Maturity" (Baraka), **Supp. II Part 1:** 53
"Sermon in the Cotton Field" (Nelson), **Supp. XVIII:** 177

Sermons and Soda Water (O'Hara), **III:** 362, 364, 371–373, 382
"Sermons on the Warpland" (Brooks), **Supp. III Part 1:** 84
"Serpent in the Wilderness, The" (Masters), **Supp. I Part 2:** 458
Servant of the Bones (Rice), **Supp. VII:** 298, 302
"Servant to Servants, A" (Frost), **Retro. Supp. I:** 125, 128; **Supp. X:** 66
Serve It Forth (M. F. K. Fisher), **Supp. XVII:** 83, 86, 87, 89, 92
Seshachari, Neila, **Supp. V:** 22
"Session, The" (Adams), **I:** 5
"Sestina" (Bishop), **Supp. I Part 1:** 73, 88
Set-angya, **Supp. IV Part 2:** 493
Seth, Vikram, **Supp. XVII:** 117
Seth's Brother's Wife (Frederic), **II:** 131–132, 137, 144
Set This House on Fire (Styron), **IV:** 98, 99, 105, 107–113, 114, 115, 117
Setting Free the Bears (Irving), **Supp. VI:** 163, **166–167,** 169–170
Setting the Tone (Rorem), **Supp. IV Part 1:** 79
Settle, Mary Lee, **Supp. IX:** 96
Settlement Horizon, The: A National Estimate (Woods and Kennedy), **Supp. I Part 1:** 19
"Settling the Colonel's Hash" (McCarthy), **II:** 559, 562
Setzer, Helen, **Supp. IV Part 1:** 217
"Seurat's Sunday Afternoon along the Seine" (Schwartz), **Supp. II Part 2:** 663–665
7 Years from Somehwere (Levine), **Supp. V:** 178, 181, 188–189
Seven against Thebes (Aeschylus; Bacon and Hecht, trans.), **Supp. X:** 57
Seven Ages of Man, The (Wilder), **IV:** 357, 374–375
Seven Deadly Sins, The (Wilder), **IV:** 357, 374–375
Seven Descents of Myrtle, The (T. Williams), **IV:** 382
"Seven Fat Brides, The" (P. Abraham), **Supp. XVII:** 50
Seven Guitars (Wilson), **Supp. VIII:** 331, **348–351**
Seven Lady Godivas, The (Geisel), **Supp. XVI:** 100, 103
Seven-League Crutches, The (Jarrell), **II:** 367, 372, 381, 382, 383–384, 389
Seven Mountains of Thomas Merton, The (Mott), **Supp. VIII:** 208
Seven-Ounce Man, The (Harrison), **Supp. VIII:** 51
"Seven Places of the Mind" (Didion), **Supp. IV Part 1:** 200, 210
Seven Plays (Shepard), **Supp. III Part 2:** 434
"Seven Stanzas at Easter" (Updike), **IV:** 215
Seven Storey Mountain, The (Merton), **Supp. VIII:** 193, 195, 198, 200, 207, 208
Seventh Heaven (Hoffman), **Supp. X:** 87, 89
"Seventh of March" (Webster), **Supp. I Part 2:** 687
"7000 Romaine, Los Angeles 38" (Didion), **Supp. IV Part 1:** 200
"Seventh Street" (Toomer), **Supp. IX:** 316
Seven Types of Ambiguity (Empson), **II:** 536; **IV:** 431
77 Dream Songs (Berryman), **I:** 168, 169, 170, 171, 174, 175, 183–188
73 Poems (Cummings), **I:** 430, 431, 446, 447, 448
Sevier, Jack, **IV:** 378
Sévigné, Madame de, **IV:** 361
Sewall, Richard, **Retro. Supp. I:** 25
Sewall, Samuel, **IV:** 145, 146, 147, 149, 154, 164; **Supp. I Part 1:** 100, 110
Sewell, Elizabeth, **Supp. XIII:** 344
"Sex" (Carruth), **Supp. XVI:** 58
Sex, Economy, Freedom and Community (Berry), **Supp. X:** 30, 36
"Sex Camp" (Mamet), **Supp. XIV:** 240
Sex Castle, The (Lacy), **Supp. XV:** 206
Sex & Character (Weininger), **Retro. Supp. I:** 416
"Sext" (Auden), **Supp. II Part 1:** 22
Sexton, Anne, **Retro. Supp. II:** 245; **Supp. I Part 2:** 538, 543, 546; **Supp. II Part 2: 669–700; Supp. III Part 2:** 599; **Supp. IV Part 1:** 245; **Supp. IV Part 2:** 439, 440–441, 442, 444, 447, 449, 451, 620; **Supp. V:** 113, 118, 124; **Supp. X:** 201, 202, 213; **Supp. XI:** 146, 240, 317; **Supp. XII:** 217, 253, 254, 256, 260, 261; **Supp. XIII:** 35, 76, 294, 312; **Supp. XIV:** 125, 126, 132, 269; **Supp. XV:** 123, 252, 340; **Supp. XVII:** 239
Sexual Behavior in the American Male (Kinsey), **Supp. XIII:** 96–97
Sexual Perversity in Chicago (Mamet), **Supp. XIV:** 239, 240, 246–247, 249
"Sexual Revolution, The" (Dunn), **Supp. XI:** 142
Sexus (H. Miller), **III:** 170, 171, 184, 187, 188
"Sex Without Love" (Olds), **Supp. X:** 206
Seyersted, Per E., **Retro. Supp. II:** 65; **Supp. I Part 1:** 201, 204, 211, 216, 225; **Supp. IV Part 2:** 558
Seyfried, Robin, **Supp. IX:** 324
Seymour, Miranda, **Supp. VIII:** 167
"Seymour: An Introduction" (Salinger), **III:** 569–571, 572
Shacochis, Bob, **Supp. VIII:** 80
"Shadow" (Creeley), **Supp. IV Part 1:** 158
"Shadow, The" (Lowell), **II:** 522
Shadow and Act (Ellison), **Retro. Supp. II:** 119; **Supp. II Part 1:** 245–246
"Shadow and Shade" (Tate), **IV:** 128
"Shadow and the Flesh, The" (London), **II:** 475
"Shadow A Parable" (Poe), **III:** 417–418
Shadow Country (Gunn Allen), **Supp. IV Part 1:** 322, 324, 325–326
Shadow Man, The (Gordon), **Supp. IV Part 1:** 297, 298, 299, 312–314, 315
Shadow of a Dream, The, a Story (Howells), **II:** 285, 286, 290
"Shadow of the Crime, The: A Word from the Author" (Mailer), **Retro. Supp. II:** 214
Shadow on the Dial, The (Bierce), **I:** 208, 209
"Shadow Passing" (Merwin), **Supp. III Part 1:** 355
Shadowplay (C. Baxter), **Supp. XVII:** 15, 19–20
Shadows (Gardner), **Supp. VI:** 74
Shadows and Fog (film; Allen), **Supp. XV:** 11
Shadows by the Hudson (Singer), **IV:** 1
Shadows of Africa (Matthiessen), **Supp. V:** 203
Shadows on the Hudson (Singer), **Retro. Supp. II: 311–313**
Shadows on the Rock (Cather), **I:** 314, 330–331, 332; **Retro. Supp. I:** 18
Shadow Train (Ashbery), **Supp. III Part 1:** 23–24, 26
"Shad-Time" (Wilbur), **Supp. III Part 2:** 563
Shaffer, Thomas L., **Supp. VIII:** 127, 128
Shaft (Parks; film), **Supp. XI:** 17
Shaftesbury, Earl of, **I:** 559
Shahn, Ben, **Supp. X:** 24
Shakedown for Murder (Lacy), **Supp. XV:** 203
Shakelford, Dean, **Supp. VIII:** 129
Shaker, Why Don't You Sing? (Angelou), **Supp. IV Part 1:** 16
Shakespear, Mrs. Olivia, **III:** 457; **Supp. I Part 1:** 257
"Shakespeare" (Emerson), **II:** 6
Shakespeare, William, **I:** 103, 271, 272, 284–285, 358, 378, 433, 441, 458, 461, 573, 585, 586; **II:** 5, 8, 11, 18, 72, 273, 297, 302, 309, 320, 411, 494, 577, 590; **III:** 3, 11, 12, 82, 83, 91, 124, 130, 134, 145, 153, 159, 183, 210, 263, 286, 468, 473, 492, 503, 511, 567, 575–576, 577, 610, 612, 613, 615; **IV:** 11, 50, 66, 127, 132, 156, 309, 313, 362, 368, 370, 373, 453; **Retro. Supp. I:** 43, 64, 91, 248; **Retro. Supp. II:** 114, 299; **Supp. I Part 1:** 79, 150, 262, 310, 356, 363, 365, 368, 369, 370; **Supp. I Part 2:** 397, 421, 422, 470, 494, 622, 716, 720; **Supp. II Part 2:** 624, 626; **Supp. IV Part 1:** 31, 83, 87, 243; **Supp. IV Part 2:** 430, 463, 519, 688; **Supp. IX:** 14, 133; **Supp. V:** 252, 280, 303; **Supp. VIII:** 160, 164; **Supp. X:** 42, 62, 65, 78; **Supp. XII:** 54–57, 277, 281; **Supp. XIII:** 111, 115, 233; **Supp. XIV:** 97, 120, 225, 245, 306; **Supp. XV:** 92; **Supp. XVIII:** 278
Shakespeare and His Forerunners (Lanier), **Supp. I Part 1:** 369
Shakespeare in Harlem (Hughes), **Retro. Supp. I:** 194, 202, 205, 206, 207, 208; **Supp. I Part 1:** 333, 334, 345
Shalit, Gene, **Supp. VIII:** 73
Shall We Gather at the River (Wright), **Supp. III Part 2:** 601–602; **Supp. XVII:** 241

"Shame" (Oates), **Supp. II Part 2:** 520
"Shame" (Wilbur), **Supp. III Part 2:** 556
"Shame and Forgetting in the Information Age" (C. Baxter), **Supp. XVII:** 21
"Shameful Affair, A" (Chopin), **Retro. Supp. II:** 61
Shamela (Fielding), **Supp. V:** 127
"Shampoo, The" (Bishop), **Retro. Supp. II:** 46; **Supp. I Part 1:** 92
Shange, Ntozake, **Supp. VIII:** 214; **Supp. XVII:** 70; **Supp. XVIII:** 172
Shank, Randy, **Supp. X:** 252
Shankaracharya, **III:** 567
Shanley, John Patrick, **Supp. XIV: 315–332**
Shannon, Sandra, **Supp. VIII:** 333, 348
"Shape of Flesh and Bone, The" (MacLeish), **III:** 18–19
Shape of Me and Other Stuff, The (Geisel), **Supp. XVI:** 111
Shape of the Journey, The (Harrison), **Supp. VIII:** 53
Shapes of Clay (Bierce), **I:** 208, 209
Shaping Joy, A: Studies in the Writer's Craft (Brooks), **Supp. XIV:** 13
Shapiro, David, **Supp. XII:** 175, 185
Shapiro, Dorothy, **IV:** 380
Shapiro, Karl, **I:** 430, 521; **II:** 350; **III:** 527; **Supp. II Part 2: 701–724; Supp. III Part 2:** 623; **Supp. IV Part 2:** 645; **Supp. X:** 116; **Supp. XI:** 315
Shapiro, Laura, **Supp. IX:** 120
Sharif, Omar, **Supp. IX:** 253
"Shark Meat" (Snyder), **Supp. VIII:** 300
Shatayev, Elvira, **Supp. I Part 2:** 570
Shaviro, Steven, **Supp. VIII:** 189
Shaw, Colonel Robert Gould, **II:** 551
Shaw, Elizabeth. *See* Melville, Mrs. Herman (Elizabeth Shaw)
Shaw, George Bernard, **I:** 226; **II:** 82, 271, 276, 581; **III:** 69, 102, 113, 145, 155, 161, 162, 163, 373, 409; **IV:** 27, 64, 397, 432, 440; **Retro. Supp. I:** 100, 228; **Supp. IV Part 1:** 36; **Supp. IV Part 2:** 585, 683; **Supp. IX:** 68, 308; **Supp. V:** 243–244, 290; **Supp. XI:** 202; **Supp. XII:** 94; **Supp. XIV:** 343; **Supp. XVII:** 100
Shaw, Irwin, **IV:** 381; **Supp. IV Part 1:** 383; **Supp. IX:** 251; **Supp. XI:** 221, 229, 231
Shaw, Joseph Thompson ("Cap"), **Supp. IV Part 1:** 121, 345, 351; **Supp. XIII:** 161
Shaw, Judge Lemuel, **III:** 77, 88, 91
Shaw, Peter, **Supp. XVI:** 70
Shaw, Sarah Bryant, **Supp. I Part 1:** 169
Shaw, Wilbur, Jr., **Supp. XIII:** 162
Shawl, The (Mamet), **Supp. XIV:** 245
"Shawl, The" (Ozick), **Supp. V:** 271–272
Shawl, The (Ozick), **Supp. V:** 257, 260, 271
Shawl and Prarie du Chien, The: Two Plays (Mamet), **Supp. XIV:** 243–244
Shawn, William, **Supp. VIII:** 151, 170
"Shawshank Redemption, The" (King), **Supp. V:** 148
She (Haggard), **III:** 189
Shearer, Flora, **I:** 199
"Sheaves, The" (Robinson), **III:** 510, 524
"She Came and Went" (Lowell), **Supp. I Part 2:** 409
"She-Devil" (Nelson), **Supp. XVIII:** 178
She-Devil Circus (Nelson), **Supp. XVIII:** 176, **178**
Sheed, Wilfrid, **IV:** 230; **Supp. XI:** 233
Sheeler, Charles, **IV:** 409; **Retro. Supp. I:** 430
"Sheep Child" (B. Kelly), **Supp. XVII:** 131–132
"Sheep Child, The" (Dickey), **Supp. XVII:** 131–132
Sheeper (Rosenthal), **Supp. XIV:** 147
Sheffer, Jonathan, **Supp. IV Part 1:** 95
"She Had Some Horses" (Harjo), **Supp. XII:** 215, 222
She Had Some Horses (Harjo), **Supp. XII: 220–223,** 231
"Shell, The" (Humphrey), **Supp. IX:** 94
Shelley, Percy Bysshe, **I:** 18, 68, 381, 476, 522, 577; **II:** 331, 516, 535, 540; **III:** 412, 426, 469; **IV:** 139; **Retro. Supp. I:** 308, 360; **Supp. I Part 1:** 79, 311, 349; **Supp. I Part 2:** 709, 718, 719, 720, 721, 722, 724, 728; **Supp. IV Part 1:** 235; **Supp. IX:** 51; **Supp. V:** 258, 280; **Supp. XII:** 117, 132, 136–137, 263; **Supp. XIV:** 271–272; **Supp. XV:** 92, 175, 182
Shellow, Sadie Myers, **Supp. I Part 2:** 608
"Shelter" (C. Baxter), **Supp. XVII:** 19
"Shelter" (Doty), **Supp. XI:** 132
Sheltered Life, The (Glasgow), **II:** 174, 175, 179, 186, 187–188
Sheltering Sky, The (Bowles), **Supp. IV Part 1:** 82, 84, 85–86, 87
Sheltering Sky, The (film), **Supp. IV Part 1:** 94, 95
Shelton, Frank, **Supp. IV Part 2:** 658
Shelton, Mrs. Sarah. *See* Royster, Sarah Elmira
Shelton, Richard, **Supp. XI:** 133; **Supp. XIII:** 7
Shelton, Robert, **Supp. XVIII:** 20; **Supp. XVIII:** 21, 22, 23, 24, 25, 26
Shenandoah (Schwartz), **Supp. II Part 2:** 640, 651–652
"Shenandoah" (Shapiro), **Supp. II Part 2:** 704
Shepard, Alice, **IV:** 287
Shepard, Harvey, **Supp. XVII:** 240
Shepard, Odell, **II:** 508; **Supp. I Part 2:** 418
Shepard, Sam, **Supp. III Part 2: 431–450; Supp. XVIII:** 21, 28, 31
Shepard, Thomas, **I:** 554; **IV:** 158
"Shepherd of Resumed Desire, The" (Wright), **Supp. XV:** 349
Sheppard Lee (Bird), **III:** 423
"She Remembers the Future" (Harjo), **Supp. XII:** 222
Sheridan, Richard Brinsley, **Retro. Supp. I:** 127
Sherlock, William, **IV:** 152
Sherman, Sarah Way, **Retro. Supp. II:** 145
Sherman, Stuart Pratt, **I:** 222, 246–247; **Supp. I Part 2:** 423
Sherman, Susan, **Supp. VIII:** 265
Sherman, Tom, **IV:** 446
Sherman, William T., **IV:** 445, 446
Sherwood, Robert, **II:** 435; **Supp. IX:** 190
Sherwood Anderson & Other Famous Creoles (Faulkner), **I:** 117; **II:** 56
Sherwood Anderson Reader, The (Anderson), **I:** 114, 116
Sherwood Anderson's Memoirs (Anderson), **I:** 98, 101, 102, 103, 108, 112, 116
Sherwood Anderson's Notebook (Anderson), **I:** 108, 115, 117
She Stoops to Conquer (Goldsmith), **II:** 514
Shestov, Lev, **Supp. VIII:** 20, 24
Shetley, Vernon, **Supp. IX:** 292; **Supp. XI:** 123
"She Wept, She Railed" (Kunitz), **Supp. III Part 1:** 265
"Shiddah and Kuziba" (Singer), **IV:** 13, 15
"Shield of Achilles, The" (Auden), **Supp. II Part 1:** 21, 25
Shield of Achilles, The (Auden), **Supp. II Part 1:** 21
Shields, Carol, **Supp. VII: 307–330**
Shifting Landscape: A Composite, 1925–1987 (H. Roth), **Supp. IX: 233–235**
Shifts of Being (Eberhart), **I:** 525
Shigematsu, Soiko, **Supp. III Part 1:** 353
Shihab, Aziz, **Supp. XIII:** 273
Shih-hsiang Chen, **Supp. VIII:** 303
Shiksa Goddess; or, How I Spent My Forties (Wasserstein), **Supp. XV:** 319, 320, 325, 332, 333
"Shiloh" (Mason), **Supp. VIII:** 140
Shiloh and Other Stories (Mason), **Supp. VIII:** 133, **139–141,** 143, 145
Shilts, Randy, **Supp. X:** 145
Shining, The (King), **Supp. V:** 139, 140, 141, 143–144, 146, 149, 151, 152
Shining Victory (film, Rapper), **Supp. XVII:** 60
Shinn, Everett, **Retro. Supp. II:** 103
"Ship of Death" (Lawrence), **Supp. I Part 2:** 728
Ship of Fools (Porter), **III:** 433, 447, 453, 454; **IV:** 138
Shipping News, The (Proulx), **Supp. VII:** 249, 258–259
"Ships" (O. Henry), **Supp. II Part 1:** 409
Ships Going into the Blue: Essays and Notes on Poetry (Simpson), **Supp. IX:** 275
Ship to America, A (Singer), **IV:** 1
"Shipwreck, The" (Merwin), **Supp. III Part 1:** 346
Shirley, John, **Supp. XVI:** 123, 128
"Shirt" (Pinsky), **Supp. VI: 236–237,** 239, 240, 241, 245, 247
"Shirt Poem, The" (Stern), **Supp. IX:** 292
"Shirts of a Single Color" (Ryan), **Supp. XVIII:** 227
"Shiva and Parvati Hiding in the Rain" (Pinsky), **Supp. VI:** 244
Shively, Charley, **Retro. Supp. I:** 391; **Supp. XII:** 181, 182

Shock of Recognition, The (Wilson), **II:** 530
Shock of the New, The (Hughes), **Supp. X:** 73
Shoe Bird, The (Welty), **IV:** 261; **Retro. Supp. I:** 353
Shoemaker of Dreams (Ferragammo), **Supp. XVI:** 192
"Shoes" (O. Henry), **Supp. II Part 1:** 409
"Shoes of Wandering, The" (Kinnell), **Supp. III Part 1:** 248
"Shooters, Inc." (Didion), **Supp. IV Part 1:** 207, 211
"Shooting, The" (Dubus), **Supp. VII:** 84, 85
"Shooting Niagara; and After?" (Carlyle), **Retro. Supp. I:** 408
"Shooting Script" (Rich), **Supp. I Part 2:** 558; **Supp. IV Part 1:** 257
Shooting Star, A (Stegner), **Supp. IV Part 2:** 599, 608–609
"Shooting Whales" (Strand), **Supp. IV Part 2:** 630
"Shopgirls" (F. Barthelme), **Supp. XI:** 26, 27, 33, 36
Shop Talk (P. Roth), **Retro. Supp. II:** 282
Shoptaw, John, **Supp. IV Part 1:** 247
Shore Acres (Herne), **Supp. II Part 1:** 198
Shorebirds of North America, The (Matthiessen), **Supp. V:** 204
"Shore House, The" (Jewett), **II:** 397
Shore Leave (Wakeman), **Supp. IX:** 247
"Shoreline Horses" (Ríos), **Supp. IV Part 2:** 553
Shores of Light, The: A Literary Chronicle of the Twenties and Thirties (Wilson), **IV:** 432, 433
Shorey, Paul, **III:** 606
Short Cuts (film), **Supp. IX:** 143
"Short End, The" (Hecht), **Supp. X:** 65
"Shorter View, The" (X. J. Kennedy), **Supp. XV:** 160, 168
Short Fiction of Norman Mailer, The (Mailer), **Retro. Supp. II:** 205
Short Friday and Other Stories (Singer), **IV:** 14–16
Short Guide to a Happy Life, A (Quindlen), **Supp. XVII:** 167, 179
"Short Happy Life of Francis Macomber, The" (Hemingway), **II:** 250, 263–264; **Retro. Supp. I:** 182; **Supp. IV Part 1:** 48; **Supp. IX:** 106
Short Night, The (Turner), **Supp. XV:** 201
Short Novels of Thomas Wolfe, The (Wolfe), **IV:** 456
Short Poems (Berryman), **I:** 170
"SHORT SPEECH TO MY FRIENDS" (Baraka), **Supp. II Part 1:** 35
Short Stories (Rawlings), **Supp. X:** 224
"Short Story, The" (Welty), **IV:** 279
Short Story Masterpieces, **Supp. IX:** 4
Short Studies of American Authors (Higginson), **I:** 455
"Short-timer's Calendar" (Komunyakaa), **Supp. XIII:** 125
Shosha (Singer), **Retro. Supp. II: 313–314**
Shostakovich, Dimitri, **IV:** 75; **Supp. VIII:** 21
Shot of Love (album, Dylan), **Supp. XVIII:** 28
"Shots" (Ozick), **Supp. V:** 268
Shotts, Jeffrey, **Supp. XV:** 103, 104
"Should Wizard Hit Mommy?" (Updike), **IV:** 221, 222, 224; **Retro. Supp. I:** 335
Shoup, Barbara, **Supp. XV:** 55, 59, 62, 69
"Shovel Man, The" (Sandburg), **III:** 553
Showalter, Elaine, **Retro. Supp. I:** 368; **Supp. IV Part 2:** 440, 441, 444; **Supp. X:** 97; **Supp. XVI:** 80, 92
"Shower of Gold" (Welty), **IV:** 271–272
"Shrike and the Chipmunks, The" (Thurber), **Supp. I Part 2:** 617
Shrimp Girl (Hogarth), **Supp. XII:** 44
"Shrine and the Burning Wheel, The" (Jarman), **Supp. XVII:** 116
"Shriveled Meditation" (X. J. Kennedy), **Supp. XV:** 170
Shropshire Lad, A (Housman), **Supp. XV:** 41
"Shrouded Stranger, The" (Ginsberg), **Supp. II Part 1:** 312
"Shroud of Color, The" (Cullen), **Supp. IV Part 1:** 166, 168, 170, 171
Shtetl (film; Marzynski), **Supp. XVI:** 153
Shtetl: The Life and Death of a Small Town and the World of Polish Jews (E. Hoffman), **Supp. XVI:** 152, **153–155**
Shuffle (L. Michaels), **Supp. XVI:** 202, 203, 213
Shuffle Along (musical), **Supp. I Part 1:** 322; **Supp. X:** 136
Shultz, George, **Supp. IV Part 1:** 234
Shurr, William, **Retro. Supp. I:** 43
Shuster, Joel, **Supp. XI:** 67
Shusterman, Richard, **Retro. Supp. I:** 53
"Shut a Final Door" (Capote), **Supp. III Part 1:** 117, 120, 124
Shut Up, He Explained (Lardner), **II:** 432
Shylock's Daughter: A Novel of Love in Venice (Serenissima) (Jong), **Supp. V:** 115, 127, 128–129
"Siasconset: How It Arose and What It Is" (Briggs), **Supp. XVIII:** 9
Siberian Village, The (Dove), **Supp. IV Part 1:** 255, 256
Sibley, Mulford Q., **Supp. I Part 2:** 524
"Sibling Mysteries" (Rich), **Supp. I Part 2:** 574
Siblings (Quindlen and Kelsh), **Supp. XVII:** 167, 179
Sibon, Marcelle, **IV:** 288
"Sicilian Emigrant's Song" (W. C. Williams), **Retro. Supp. I:** 413
Sicilian Miniatures (Sobin), **Supp. XVI:** 288
"Sick Wife, The" (Kenyon), **Supp. VII:** 173, 174
"'Sic transit gloria mundi'" (Dickinson), **Retro. Supp. I:** 30
Sid Caesar Show (television show), **Supp. IV Part 2:** 575
Siddons, Sarah, **II:** 298
Side Effects (Allen), **Supp. XV:** 3, 14, **15–16**
Side of Paradise, This (Fitgerald), **Supp. IX:** 56
Sidnee Poet Heroical, The (Baraka), **Supp. II Part 1:** 55
Sidney, Algernon, **II:** 114
Sidney, Mary, **Supp. I Part 1:** 98
Sidney, Philip, **II:** 470; **Supp. I Part 1:** 98, 111, 117–118, 122; **Supp. I Part 2:** 658; **Supp. II Part 1:** 104–105; **Supp. V:** 250; **Supp. XII:** 264; **Supp. XIV:** 128
Sidney, Sylvia, **Supp. I Part 1:** 67
Sidney Lanier: A Bibliographical and Critical Study (Starke), **Supp. I Part 1:** 371
Sidney Lanier: A Biographical and Critical Study (Starke), **Supp. I Part 1:** 371
Siegel, Barry, **Supp. XIV:** 82
Siegel, Catherine, **Supp. XII:** 126
Siegel, Jerry, **Supp. XI:** 67
"Siege of London, The" (James), **Retro. Supp. I:** 227
Siegle, Robert, **Supp. XII:** 8
Sienkiewicz, Henryk, **Supp. IV Part 2:** 518; **Supp. XVI:** 182
"Sierra Kid" (Levine), **Supp. V:** 180–181
Sigg, Eric, **Retro. Supp. I:** 53
"Sight" (Merwin), **Supp. III Part 1:** 356
"Sight in Camp in the Daybreak Gray and Dim, A" (Whitman), **II:** 373
Sights and Spectacles (McCarthy), **II:** 562
"Sights from a Steeple" (Hawthorne), **Retro. Supp. I:** 62
Sights Unseen (Gibbons), **Supp. X: 49–50**
"Signals" (Carver), **Supp. III Part 1:** 143
"Signature for Tempo" (MacLeish), **III:** 8–9
"Signed Confession of Crimes against the State" (Merton), **Supp. VIII:** 201
Signifying Monkey, The (Gates), **Supp. X:** 243
Signifying Monkey, The (Hughes), **Retro. Supp. I:** 195
"Signing, The (Dixon), **Supp. XII: 146**
Sign in Sidney Brustein's Window, The (Hansberry), **Supp. IV Part 1:** 359, 365, 369, 370–372
Sign of Jonas, The (Merton), **Supp. VIII:** 194–195, 195, 197, 200, 206, 207
"Sign of Saturn, The"(Olds), **Supp. X:** 206
Signs and Wonders (Bukiet), **Supp. XVII: 45–46**
Sigourney, Lydia, **Supp. I Part 2:** 684
Sikora, Malgorzata, **Retro. Supp. II:** 324
Silas Marner (Eliot), **II:** 26
Silberg, Richard, **Supp. XV:** 116
"Silence"(Moore), **III:** 212
"Silence"(Poe), **III:** 416
"Silence"(Sanders), **Supp. XVI:** 278
"Silence, A" (Clampitt), **Supp. IX:** 53
"Silence——A Fable" (Poe), **III:** 416
"Silence Before Harvest, The" (Merwin), **Supp. III Part 1:** 352

Silence Dogood Papers, The (Franklin), **II:** 106–107
Silence in the Snowy Fields (R. Bly), **Supp. IV Part 1:** 60–61, 62, 63, 65, 66, 72
Silence of History, The (Farrell), **II:** 46–47
Silence Opens, A (Clampitt), **Supp. IX: 53**
Silences (Olsen), **Supp. XIII:** 293, 294, 295, 296, **304–306**
"Silences: When Writers Don't Write" (Olsen), **Supp. XIII:** 294
Silencing the Past: Power and the Production of History (Trouillot), **Supp. X:** 14
"Silent in America" (Levine), **Supp. V:** 183
Silent Life, The (Merton), **Supp. VIII:** 208
Silent Partner, The (Odets), **Supp. II Part 2:** 539
"Silent Poem" (Francis), **Supp. IX:** 86
"Silent Season of a Hero, The" (Talese), **Supp. XVII:** 203–204
"Silent Slain, The" (MacLeish), **III:** 9
"Silent Snow, Secret Snow" (Aiken), **I:** 52
Silent Spring (Carson), **Supp. IX:** 19, 24, **31–34; Supp. V:** 202; **Supp. XIV:** 177; **Supp. XVI:** 36; **Supp. XVIII:** 189
Silhouettes of American Life (Davis), **Supp. XVI:** 85
"Silken Tent, The" (Frost), **Retro. Supp. I:** 138–139; **Supp. IV Part 2:** 448
Silko, Leslie Marmon, **Supp. IV Part 1:** 274, 319, 325, 333–334, 335, 404; **Supp. IV Part 2:** 499, 505, **557–572; Supp. V:** 169; **Supp. XI:** 18; **Supp. XII:** 217; **Supp. XVIII:** 58
Silliman, Ron, **Supp. IV Part 2:** 426; **Supp. XV:** 344; **Supp. XVII:** 70, 77
Silliman's Blog (R. Silliman), **Supp. XVII:** 70
Silman, Roberta, **Supp. X:** 6
Silverblatt, Michael, **Supp. XV:** 224
"Silver Crown, The" (Malamud), **Supp. I Part 2:** 434–435, 437; **Supp. V:** 266
"Silver Dish, The" (Bellow), **Retro. Supp. II:** 30
"Silver Filigree" (Wylie), **Supp. I Part 2:** 707
"Silver Lake" (B. Kelly), **Supp. XVII:** 130
Silvers, Phil, **Supp. IV Part 2:** 574
Silverthorne, Elizabeth, **Supp. X:** 220, 221, 222, 226, 234
"Silver To Have and to Hurl" (Didion), **Supp. IV Part 1:** 197
Simic, Charles, **Supp. V:** 5, 332; **Supp. VIII:** 39, **269–287; Supp. XI:** 317; **Supp. XV:** 179, 185
"Similar Cases" (Gilman), **Supp. XI:** 200, 202
Similitudes, from the Ocean and Prairie (Larcom), **Supp. XIII:** 141
Simmel, Georg, **Supp. I Part 2:** 644; **Supp. XVII:** 98
Simmons, Charles, **Supp. XI:** 230
Simmons, Maggie, **Retro. Supp. II:** 21
Simms, Michael, **Supp. XII:** 184
Simms, William Gilmore, **I:** 211
Simon, John, **Supp. IV Part 2:** 691
Simon, Neil, **Supp. IV Part 2: 573–594; Supp. XVII:** 8
"Simon Gerty" (Wylie), **Supp. I Part 2:** 713
Simonides, **Supp. XII:** 110–111
"Simon Ortiz" (Gingerich), **Supp. IV Part 2:** 510
Simon Ortiz (Wiget), **Supp. IV Part 2:** 509
Simonson, Lee, **III:** 396
"Simple Art of Murder, The" (Chandler), **Supp. IV Part 1:** 121, 341
"Simple Autumnal" (Bogan), **Supp. III Part 1:** 52–53
Simple Heart (Flaubert), **I:** 504
Simple Honorable Man, A (Richter), **Supp. XVIII:** 208, 218, **219,** 220
Simple Speaks his Mind (Hughes), **Retro. Supp. I:** 209; **Supp. I Part 1:** 337
Simple Stakes a Claim (Hughes), **Retro. Supp. I:** 209; **Supp. I Part 1:** 337
Simple's Uncle Sam (Hughes), **Retro. Supp. I:** 209; **Supp. I Part 1:** 337
Simple Takes a Wife (Hughes), **Retro. Supp. I:** 209; **Supp. I Part 1:** 337
Simple Truth, The (Hardwick), **Supp. III Part 1:** 199, 200, 208
Simple Truth, The (Levine), **Supp. V:** 178, 179, 193–194
"Simplicity" (Sanders), **Supp. XVI:** 276
Simply Heavenly (Hughes), **Retro. Supp. I:** 209; **Supp. I Part 1:** 338, 339
Simpson, Louis, **Supp. III Part 2:** 541; **Supp. IV Part 2:** 448, 621; **Supp. IX: 265–283,** 290; **Supp. VIII:** 39, 279; **Supp. XI:** 317; **Supp. XII:** 130; **Supp. XIII:** 337
Simpson, Mona, **Supp. XVI:** 206
"Sin" (C. Frost), **Supp. XV:** 96
Sinatra, Frank, **Supp. IX:** 3; **Supp. X:** 119; **Supp. XI:** 213
Sincere Convert, The (Shepard), **IV:** 158
Sincerely, Willis Wayde (Marquand), **III:** 61, 63, 66, 67–68, 69
Sincerity (Rowson), **Supp. XV:** 242
Sincerity and Authenticity (Trilling), **Supp. III Part 2:** 510–512
"Sincerity and Objectification: With Special Reference to the Work of Charles Reznikoff" (Zukofsky), **Supp. XIV:** 286
Sinclair, Mary Craig (Mary Craig Kimbrough), **Supp. V:** 275, 286, 287
Sinclair, Upton, **II:** 34, 440, 444, 451; **III:** 580; **Retro. Supp. II:** 95; **Supp. V: 275–293; Supp. VIII:** 11
Sinclair Lewis: An American Life (Schorer), **II:** 459
"Singapore" (Oliver), **Supp. VII:** 239, 240
Singer, Bennett L., **Supp. IV Part 1:** 330
Singer, Beth, **Supp. XIV:** 203
Singer, Isaac Bashevis, **I:** 144; **IV: 1–24; Retro. Supp. II:** 22, **299–320; Supp. IX:** 114; **Supp. XVIII:** 215, 220
Singer, Israel Joshua, **IV:** 2, 16, 17; **Retro. Supp. II:** 302; **Supp. XVII:** 41
Singer, Joshua, **IV:** 4
Singer, Rabbi Pinchos Menachem, **IV:** 16
Singin' and Swingin' and Gettin' Merry Like Christmas (Angelou), **Supp. IV Part 1:** 2, 5, 6–7, 9, 13, 14
"Singing & Doubling Together" (Ammons), **Supp. VII:** 34–35
Singing Jailbirds (Sinclair), **Supp. V:** 277
"Singing the Black Mother" (Lupton), **Supp. IV Part 1:** 7
Single Hound, The (Sarton), **Supp. VIII:** 251, 265
Single Hound, The: Poems of a Lifetime (Dickinson; Bianchi, ed.), **Retro. Supp. I:** 35
Single Man, A (Isherwood), **Supp. XIV:** 157, 164, **169–170,** 171
"Single Sonnet" (Bogan), **Supp. III Part 1:** 56–58
Singley, Carol, **Retro. Supp. I:** 373
Singular Family, A: Rosacoke and Her Kin (Price), **Supp. VI: 258–259,** 260
"Singular First Person, The" (Sanders), **Supp. XVI:** 274
Singularities (Howe), **Supp. IV Part 2:** 431
Sin in Their Blood (Lacy), **Supp. XV:** 200
"Sinister Adolescents, The" (Dos Passos), **I:** 493
Sinister Street (Mackenzie), **II:** 82
Sinking of Clay City, The (Wrigley), **Supp. XVIII: 294–295**
Sinners in the Hands of an Angry God (Edwards), **I:** 546, 552–553, 559, 562
Sinning with Annie, and Other Stories (Theroux), **Supp. VIII:** 318
"Sins of Kalamazoo, The" (Sandburg), **III:** 586
Sintram and His Companions (La Motte-Fouqué), **III:** 78
"Siope" (Poe), **III:** 411
"Sipapu: A Cultural Perspective" (Gunn Allen), **Supp. IV Part 1:** 323
Sipchen, Bob, **Supp. X:** 145
Sipper, Ralph B., **Supp. IV Part 2:** 475
"Sire" (Cisneros), **Supp. VII:** 62–63, 64
"Siren and Signal" (Zukofsky), **Supp. III Part 2:** 611, 612
Sirens of Titan, The (Vonnegut), **Supp. II Part 2:** 757, 758, 760, 765–767
"Sir Galahad" (Tennyson), **Supp. I Part 2:** 410
Sirin, V. (pseudonym), **Retro. Supp. I:** 266. *See also* Nabokov, Vladimir
Sir Vadia's Shadow: A Friendship across Five Continents (Theroux), **Supp. VIII:** 309, 314, 321, 325
"Sis" (F. Barthelme), **Supp. XI:** 26
"S is for Sad" (M. F. K. Fisher), **Supp. XVII:** 86
Sisley, Alfred, **I:** 478
Sissman, L. E., **Supp. X:** 69
"Sister" (Hughes), **Retro. Supp. I:** 208
Sister Age (M. F. K. Fisher), **Supp. XVII:** 88, 91

Sister Carrie (Dreiser), **I:** 482, 497, 499, 500, 501–502, 503–504, 505, 506, 515, 519; **III:** 327; **IV:** 208; **Retro. Supp. I:** 376; **Retro. Supp. II:** 93, **96–99; Supp. XVIII:** 76, 243
"Sister of the Minotaur" (Stevens), **IV:** 89; **Supp. IX:** 332
"Sisters" (Nelson), **Supp. XVIII:** 176
"Sisters, The" (Whittier), **Supp. I Part 2:** 696
Sister's Choice (Showalter), **Retro. Supp. I:** 368
Sisters of the Earth: Women's Prose and Poetry About Nature (Anderson, ed.), **Supp. XVIII:** 189
Sisters Rosensweig, The (Wasserstein), **Supp. XV:** 320, **328–330**
"Sisyphus" (Kumin), **Supp. IV Part 2:** 443, 444, 451
"Sitalkas" (Doolittle), **Supp. I Part 1:** 266
Sitney, P. Adams, **Supp. XII:** 2
Sitting Bull, **Supp. IV Part 2:** 492
"Sitting in a Rocking Chair Going Blind" (Komunyakaa), **Supp. XIII:** 114
Sitting In: Selected Writings on Jazz, Blues, and Related Topics (Carruth), **Supp. XVI:** 46
"Sitting Up Late with My Father, 1977" (F. Wright), **Supp. XVII:** 247
Sitti's Secrets (Nye), **Supp. XIII:** 278
Situation Normal (A. Miller), **III:** 148, 149, 156, 164
Situation of Poetry, The: Contemporary Poetry and Its Traditions (Pinsky), **Supp. VI: 237–238,** 239, 241, 242
Sitwell, Edith, **IV:** 77; **Supp. I Part 1:** 271
"Six Brothers" (Cisneros), **Supp. VII:** 67
Six Characters in Search of an Author (Pirandello), **Supp. IV Part 2:** 576
"Six Days: Some Rememberings" (Paley), **Supp. VI:** 226
"65290" (Leopold), **Supp. XIV:** 184–185
Six French Poets (Lowell), **II:** 528–529
"Six in All" (Bierds), **Supp. XVII:** 31
"Six Persons" (Baraka), **Supp. II Part 1:** 53
Six Sections from Mountains and Rivers without End (Snyder), **Supp. VIII:** 305
"Sixteen Months" (Sandburg), **III:** 584
1601, or Conversation as It Was by the Fireside in the Time of the Tudors (Twain), **IV:** 201
"Sixth-Month Song in the Foothills" (Snyder), **Supp. VIII:** 297
Sixties, The (magazine) (R. Bly), **Supp. IV Part 1:** 60; **Supp. IX:** 271
"Sixty" (Dunn), **Supp. XI:** 155
"Sixty Acres" (Carver), **Supp. III Part 1:** 141
"69 Hidebound Opinions, Propositions, and Several Asides from a Manila Folder concerning the Stuff of Poetry" (Wright), **Supp. XV:** 344–345
Sixty Stories (Barthelme), **Supp. IV Part 1:** 41, 42, 44, 47, 49, 50
63: Dream Palace (Purdy), **Supp. VII:** 270–271
"Six Variations" (Levertov), **Supp. III Part 1:** 277–278
"Six-Year-Old Boy" (Olds), **Supp. X:** 206
"Six Years Later" (Brodsky), **Supp. VIII:** 26, 28
"Size and Sheer Will" (Olds), **Supp. X:** 206
Size of Thoughts, The: Essays and Other Lumber (Baker), **Supp. XIII: 52–53,** 55, 56
Sizwe Bansi Is Dead (Fugard), **Supp. VIII:** 330
"Skagway" (Haines), **Supp. XII:** 206
"Skaters, The" (Ashbery), **Supp. III Part 1:** 10, 12, 13, 18, 25
"Skaters, The" (Jarrell), **II:** 368–369
Skau, Michael, **Supp. XII:** 129, 130, 132, 134
Skeeters Kirby (Masters), **Supp. I Part 2:** 459, 470, 471
Skeleton Crew (King), **Supp. V:** 144
"Skeleton in Armor, The" (Longfellow), **Retro. Supp. II:** 168
"Skeleton's Cave, The" (Bryant), **Supp. I Part 1:** 157
Skelton, John, **III:** 521
Skepticisms (Aiken), **Supp. XV:** 298, 302
Sketch Book of Geoffrey Crayon, Gent., The (Irving), **II:** 295, 303, 304–308, 309, 311, 491; **Supp. I Part 1:** 155
Sketches of Art (Jameson), **Retro. Supp. II:** 58
Sketches of Eighteenth Century America (Crèvecoeur), **Supp. I Part 1:** 233, 240–241, 250, 251
"Sketches of Female Biography" (Rowson), **Supp. XV:** 245
Sketches of Switzerland (Cooper), **I:** 346
Sketches Old and New (Twain), **IV:** 198
"Sketch for a Job-Application Blank" (Harrison), **Supp. VIII:** 38
Sketch of Old England, by a New England Man (Paulding), **I:** 344
Skibell, Joseph, **Supp. XVII:** 48
"Skier and the Mountain, The" (Eberhart), **I:** 528–529
"Skin-Boats: 1830, The" (Bierds), **Supp. XVII:** 28
Skinker, Mary Scott, **Supp. IX:** 20
Skinny Island (Auchincloss), **Supp. IV Part 1:** 33
Skinny Legs and All (Robbins), **Supp. X:** 267, 273, **276–279**
Skin of Our Teeth, The (Wilder), **IV:** 357, 358, 369–372; **Supp. IV Part 2:** 586
"Skins" (Wright), **Supp. V:** 340
Skins and Bones: Poems 1979–1987 (Gunn Allen), **Supp. IV Part 1:** 321, 331
"Skipper Ireson's Ride" (Whittier), **Supp. I Part 2:** 691, 693–694
"Skirmish at Sartoris" (Faulkner), **II:** 67
Skotheim, Robert Allen, **Supp. XVII:** 104
Skow, John, **Supp. V:** 213; **Supp. XVI:** 174
Skube, Michael, **Supp. XVIII:** 96
"Skunk Cabbage" (Oliver), **Supp. VII:** 235, 236
"Skunk Hour" (Lowell), **II:** 548–550; **Retro. Supp. II:** 188, 189; **Supp. XIV:** 269
Sky, The Stars, The Wilderness, The (Bass), **Supp. XVI:** 19, 20
"Sky Dance" (Leopold), **Supp. XIV:** 186
"Sky Line" (Taylor), **Supp. V:** 316
"Sky Line, The" (Mumford), **Supp. II Part 2:** 475
"Skyscraper" (Sandburg), **III:** 581–582
Sky's the Limit, The: A Defense of the Earth (Nichols), **Supp. XIII:** 268
"Sky Valley Rider" (Wright), **Supp. V:** 335, 340
Sky-Walk; or the Man Unknown to Himself (Brown), **Supp. I Part 1:** 127–128
"Slang in America" (Whitman), **IV:** 348
Slapstick (Vonnegut), **Supp. II Part 2:** 753, 754, 778
Slapstick Tragedy (T. Williams), **IV:** 382, 393
Slate, Lane, **Supp. IX:** 251, 253
Slattery, Mary Grace. *See* Miller, Mrs. Arthur (Mary Grace Slattery)
"Slaughterer, The" (Singer), **IV:** 19
Slaughterhouse-Five (Vonnegut), **Supp. II Part 2:** 755, 758–759, 760, 770, 772–776; **Supp. V:** 41, 244
Slave, The (Baraka), **Supp. II Part 1:** 42, 44, 56
Slave, The: A Novel (Singer), **IV:** 13; **Retro. Supp. II: 305–307**
"Slave Canal" (Ray), **Supp. XVIII:** 193
"Slave Coffle" (Angelou), **Supp. IV Part 1:** 16
"Slave on the Block" (Hughes), **Supp. I Part 1:** 329
Slave Power, The: The Free North and Southern Domination, 1780–1860 (Richards), **Supp. XIV:** 48
"Slave Quarters" (Dickey), **Supp. IV Part 1:** 181
"Slave's Dream, The" (Longfellow), **Supp. I Part 2:** 409
Slave Ship: A Historical Pageant (Baraka), **Supp. II Part 1:** 47–49, 53, 56–57
"Slave-Ships, The" (Whittier), **Supp. I Part 2:** 687–688
Slaves in Algiers; or, A Struggle for Freedom (Rowson), **Supp. XV: 236–237**
Slavs! Thinking about the Longstanding Problems of Virtue and Happiness (Kushner), **Supp. IX: 146**
Sledge, Eugene, **Supp. V:** 250
Sleek for the Long Flight (Matthews), **Supp. IX:** 154, 155, **157–158**
Sleep (Dixon), **Supp. XII:** 154
"Sleep, The" (Strand), **Supp. IV Part 2:** 627
Sleeper (film; Allen), **Supp. XV:** 5
"Sleeper, The" (Poe), **III:** 411
"Sleeper 1, The" (Hay), **Supp. XIV:** 132–133
"Sleeper 2, The" (Hay), **Supp. XIV:** 132–133
"Sleepers, The" (Whitman), **IV:** 336
"Sleepers in Jaipur" (Kenyon), **Supp. VII:** 172

Sleepers in Moon-Crowned Valleys (Purdy), **Supp. VII:** 274, 275
"Sleepers Joining Hands" (R. Bly), **Supp. IV Part 1:** 63, 73
Sleeping Beauty (Macdonald), **Supp. IV Part 2:** 474, 475
Sleeping Beauty, The (Carruth), **Supp. XVI:** 53, 57–58
"Sleeping Beauty Syndrome, The: The New Agony of Single Men" (Wasserstein), **Supp. XV:** 328
"Sleeping Fury, The" (Bogan), **Supp. III Part 1:** 58
Sleeping Fury, The: Poems (Bogan), **Supp. III Part 1:** 55–58
Sleeping Gypsy and Other Poems, The (Garrett), **Supp. VII:** 96–98
"Sleeping in the Forest" (Oliver), **Supp. VII:** 233–234
Sleeping in the Forest (Oliver), **Supp. VII:** 233
Sleeping in the Woods (Wagoner), **Supp. IX: 328**
Sleeping on Fists (Ríos), **Supp. IV Part 2:** 540
Sleeping on the Wing: An Anthology of Modern Poetry (Koch and Farrell, eds.), **Supp. XV:** 187–188
"Sleeping Standing Up" (Bishop), **Supp. I Part 1:** 85, 89, 93
"Sleeping with Animals" (Kumin), **Supp. IV Part 2:** 454
Sleeping with One Eye Open (Strand), **Supp. IV Part 2:** 621–624, 623, 628
Sleep in Thunder (Lacy), **Supp. XV:** 206
"Sleepless, The" (L.-Y. Lee), **Supp. XV:** 224
"Sleepless at Crown Point" (Wilbur), **Supp. III Part 2:** 561
Sleepless Nights (Hardwick), **Supp. III Part 1:** 193, 208–211
"Sleepless Nights" (Nelson), **Supp. XVIII:** 174
Sleepy Lagoon Mystery, The (Endore), **Supp. XVII:** 60
"Sleepy People" (Lethem), **Supp. XVIII:** 140
Sleight, Ken, **Supp. XIII:** 12
Slick, Sam (pseudonym). *See* Haliburton, Thomas Chandler
"Slick Gonna Learn" (Ellison), **Retro. Supp. II:** 116; **Supp. II Part 1:** 237–238
"Slight Rebellion off Madison" (Salinger), **III:** 553
"Slight Sound at Evening, A" (White), **Supp. I Part 2:** 672
"Slim Graves Show, The" (Keillor), **Supp. XVI:** 172
"Slim Greer" series (Hayden), **Supp. II Part 1:** 369
"Slim in Hell" (Hayden), **Supp. II Part 1:** 369
"Slim Man Canyon" (Silko), **Supp. IV Part 2:** 560
"Slip, Shift, and Speed Up: The Influence of Robinson Jeffers's Narrative Syntax" (Jarman), **Supp. XVII:** 111, 112
"Slippery Fingers" (Hammett), **Supp. IV Part 1:** 343
Slipping-Down Life, A (Tyler), **Supp. IV Part 2:** 660–661
Sloan, Jacob, **IV:** 3, 6
Sloan, John, **I:** 254; **IV:** 411; **Retro. Supp. II:** 103
Sloane, John, **Supp. XV:** 295
"Slob" (Farrell), **II:** 25, 28, 31
Slocum, Joshua, **Supp. I Part 2:** 497
Slonim, Véra. *See* Nabokov, Véra
Slouching towards Bethlehem (Didion), **Supp. IV Part 1:** 196, 197, 200–201, 202, 206, 210
Slovic, Scott, **Supp. XVI:** 277
"Slow Child with a Book of Birds" (Levis), **Supp. XI:** 268
"Slow Down for Poetry" (Strand), **Supp. IV Part 2:** 620
"Slow Pacific Swell, The" (Winters), **Supp. II Part 2:** 790, 793, 795, 796, 799
Slow Parade (Kees), **Supp. XV:** 137
Slow Train Coming (album, Dylan), **Supp. XVIII:** 28
"Slumgullions" (Olsen), **Supp. IV Part 1:** 54
Slumgullion Stew: An Edward Abbey Reader (Abbey), **Supp. XIII:** 4
"S & M" (Komunyakaa), **Supp. XIII:** 114
"Small" (C. Frost), **Supp. XV:** 102
Small, Albion, **Supp. I Part 1:** 5
"Small, Good Thing, A" (Carver), **Supp. III Part 1:** 145, 147
Small, Miriam Rossiter, **Supp. I Part 1:** 319
Small Boy and Others, A (James), **II:** 337, 547; **Retro. Supp. I:** 235
"Small but Urgent Request to the Unknowable" (Karr), **Supp. XI:** 243
Small Ceremonies (Shields), **Supp. VII:** 312–315, 320
Small Craft Warnings (T. Williams), **IV:** 382, 383, 384, 385, 386, 387, 392, 393, 396, 398
Small Place, A (Kincaid), **Supp. VII:** 186–187, 188, 191
"Small Rain, The" (Pynchon), **Supp. II Part 2:** 620
Small Room, The (Sarton), **Supp. VIII:** 252, **255–256**
Smalls, Bob, **II:** 128
Small Time Crooks (film; Allen), **Supp. XV:** 11
Small Town, A (Hearon), **Supp. VIII: 65–66**
"Small Vases from Hebron, The" (Nye), **Supp. XIII:** 283
"Small Vision, The" (Goldbarth), **Supp. XII:** 180
"Small Voice from the Wings" (Everwine), **Supp. XV:** 76
"Small Wire" (Sexton), **Supp. II Part 2:** 696
Small Worlds (A. Hoffman), **Supp. XVII:** 44
Smardz, Zofia, **Supp. XVI:** 155
Smart, Christopher, **III:** 534; **Supp. I Part 2:** 539; **Supp. IV Part 2:** 626
Smart, Joyce H., **Supp. XI:** 169
"Smart Cookie, A" (Cisneros), **Supp. VII:** 64
"Smashup" (Thurber), **Supp. I Part 2:** 616
Smedly, Agnes, **Supp. XIII:** 295
"Smelt Fishing" (Hayden), **Supp. II Part 1:** 367
"Smile of the Bathers, The" (Kees), **Supp. XV:** 145
"Smiles" (Dunn), **Supp. XI:** 151
Smiles, Samuel, **Supp. X:** 167
Smiley, Jane, **Supp. VI: 291–309; Supp. XII:** 73, 297; **Supp. XIII:** 127
Smith, Adam, **II:** 9; **Supp. I Part 2:** 633, 634, 639; **Supp. XVII:** 235
Smith, Annick, **Supp. XIV:** 223
Smith, Benjamin, **IV:** 148
Smith, Bernard, **I:** 260
Smith, Bessie, **Retro. Supp. I:** 343; **Supp. VIII:** 330
Smith, Charlie, **Supp. X:** 177
Smith, Dale, **Supp. XV:** 136, 138, 139
Smith, Dave, **Supp. V:** 333; **Supp. XI:** 152; **Supp. XII:** 178, 198
Smith, David, **Supp. XIII:** 246, 247
Smith, David Nichol, **Supp. XIV:** 2
Smith, Dinitia, **Supp. VIII:** 74, 82, 83; **Supp. XVIII:** 162
Smith, Elihu Hubbard, **Supp. I Part 1:** 126, 127, 130
Smith, George Adam, **III:** 199
Smith, Hannah Whitall, **Supp. XIV:** 333, 334, 338
Smith, Harrison, **II:** 61
Smith, Henry Nash, **IV:** 210; **Supp. I Part 1:** 233
Smith, Herbert F., **Supp. I Part 2:** 423
Smith, Iain Crichton, **Supp. XVIII:** 196
Smith, James, **II:** 111
Smith, Jedediah Strong, **Supp. IV Part 2:** 602
Smith, Jerome, **Supp. IV Part 1:** 369
Smith, Joe, **Supp. IV Part 2:** 584
Smith, John, **I:** 4, 131; **II:** 296
Smith, John Allyn, **I:** 168
Smith, Johnston (pseudonym). *See* Crane, Stephen
Smith, Kellogg, **Supp. I Part 2:** 660
Smith, Lamar, **II:** 585
Smith, Larry David, **Supp. XVIII:** 22
Smith, Lee, **Supp. XII:** 311; **Supp. XVIII:** 195
Smith, Logan Pearsall, **Supp. XIV: 333–351**
Smith, Lula Carson. *See* McCullers, Carson
Smith, Mark, **Supp. XVIII:** 155
Smith, Martha Nell, **Retro. Supp. I:** 33, 43, 46, 47
Smith, Mary Rozet, **Supp. I Part 1:** 5, 22
Smith, Mrs. Lamar (Marguerite Walters), **II:** 585, 587
Smith, Oliver, **II:** 586
Smith, Patricia Clark, **Supp. IV Part 1:** 397, 398, 402, 406, 408, 410; **Supp. IV Part 2:** 509; **Supp. XII:** 218
Smith, Patrick, **Supp. VIII:** 40, 41
Smith, Patti, **Supp. XII:** 136; **Supp. XIV:** 151

Smith, Porter, **III:** 572
Smith, Red, **II:** 417, 424
Smith, Robert McClure, **Supp. XV:** 270
Smith, Robert Pearsall, **Supp. XIV:** 333
Smith, Sarah A., **Supp. XVIII:** 99
Smith, Seba, **Supp. I Part 2:** 411
Smith, Sidonie Ann, **Supp. IV Part 1:** 11
Smith, Stevie, **Supp. V:** 84
Smith, Sydney, **II:** 295; **Supp. XIV:** 112
Smith, Thorne, **Supp. IX:** 194
Smith, Wendy, **Supp. XII:** 330, 335; **Supp. XVIII:** 89, 92
Smith, Wilford Bascom "Pitchfork," **Supp. XIII:** 168
Smith, William, **II:** 114
Smith, William Gardner, **Supp. XVI:** 142–143
Smith, William Jay, **Supp. XIII: 331–350**
Smoke (film), **Supp. XII:** 21
Smoke and Steel (Sandburg), **III:** 585–587, 592
"Smokers" (Wolff), **Supp. VII:** 340–341
Smokey Bites the Dust (film, C. Griffith), **Supp. XVII:** 9
"Smoking My Prayers" (Ortiz), **Supp. IV Part 2:** 503
"Smoking Room, The" (Jackson), **Supp. IX:** 116
"Smoky Gold" (Leopold), **Supp. XIV:** 186
Smolan, Sandy, **Supp. XVI:** 36
Smollett, Tobias G., **I:** 134, 339, 343; **II:** 304–305; **III:** 61; **Supp. XVIII:** 7
Smuggler's Bible, A (McElroy), **Supp. IV Part 1:** 285
Smuggler's Handbook, The (Goldbarth), **Supp. XII:** 181, 183
Smugglers of Lost Soul's Rock, The (Gardner), **Supp. VI: 70**
Smyth, Albert Henry, **II:** 123
"Snack Firm Maps New Chip Push" (Keillor), **Supp. XVI:** 168, 169
"Snail, The" (Hay), **Supp. XIV:** 124
"Snake, The" (Berry), **Supp. X:** 31
"Snake, The" (Crane), **I:** 420
"Snakecharmer" (Plath), **Supp. I Part 2:** 538
"Snakes, Mongooses" (Moore), **III:** 207
"Snakes of September, The" (Kunitz), **Supp. III Part 1:** 258
"Snapshot of 15th S.W., A" (Hugo), **Supp. VI:** 141
"Snapshot Rediscovered, A" (X. J. Kennedy), **Supp. XV:** 170
"Snapshots of a Daughter-in-Law" (Rich), **Supp. I Part 2:** 553–554
Snapshots of a Daughter-in-Law: Poems, 1954–1962 (Rich), **Supp. I Part 2:** 550–551, 553–554; **Supp. XII:** 255
Snaring the Flightless Birds (Bierds), **Supp. XVII:** 26
Sneetches and Other Stories, The (Geisel), **Supp. XVI:** 109
"Sneeze, The" (Chekhov), **Supp. IV Part 2:** 585
Snell, Ebenezer, **Supp. I Part 1:** 151
Snell, Thomas, **Supp. I Part 1:** 153
"Snob, The" (Shapiro), **Supp. II Part 2:** 705
Snobbery: The America Version (Epstein), **Supp. XIV:** 102, 114–115
Snodgrass, Kathleen, **Supp. XVI:** 42
Snodgrass, W. D., **I:** 400; **Retro. Supp. II:** 179; **Supp. III Part 2:** 541; **Supp. V:** 337; **Supp. VI: 311–328; Supp. XI:** 141, 315; **Supp. XIII:** 312; **Supp. XV:** 92, 153; **Supp. XVII:** 239
"Snow" (C. Baxter), **Supp. XVII:** 19
"Snow" (Frost), **Retro. Supp. I:** 133
"Snow" (Haines), **Supp. XII:** 212
"Snow" (Sexton), **Supp. II Part 2:** 696
Snow, C. P., **Supp. I Part 2:** 536
Snow, Hank, **Supp. V:** 335
Snow Ball, The (Gurney), **Supp. V:** 99
"Snow-Bound" (Whittier), **Supp. I Part 2:** 700–703
"Snow Bound at Eagle's" (Harte), **Supp. II Part 1:** 356
"Snowflakes" (Longfellow), **II:** 498
"Snow Goose, The" (Gallico), **Supp. XVI:** 238
Snow-Image and Other Twice Told Tales, The (Hawthorne), **II:** 237; **Retro. Supp. I:** 160
"Snowing in Greenwich Village" (Updike), **IV:** 226; **Retro. Supp. I:** 321
"Snow in New York" (Swenson), **Supp. IV Part 2:** 644
Snow Leopard, The (Matthiessen), **Supp. V:** 199, 207–211
"Snow Man, The" (Stevens), **IV:** 82–83; **Retro. Supp. I:** 299, 300, 302, 306, 307, 312
"Snowmass Cycle, The" (Dunn), **Supp. XI:** 152
Snow: Meditations of a Cautious Man in Winter (Banks), **Supp. V:** 6
Snow Poems, The (Ammons), **Supp. VII:** 32–34
"Snows of Kilimanjaro, The" (Hemingway), **II:** 78, 257, 263, 264; **Retro. Supp. I:** 98, 182; **Supp. XII:** 249
"Snows of Studiofiftyfour, The" (Plimpton), **Supp. XVI:** 245
"Snow Songs" (Snodgrass), **Supp. VI:** 324
"Snowstorm, The" (Oates), **Supp. II Part 2:** 523
"Snowstorm as It Affects the American Farmer, A" (Crèvecoeur), **Supp. I Part 1:** 251
Snow White (Barthelme), **Supp. IV Part 1:** 40, 47, 48–49, 50, 52; **Supp. V:** 39
"Snowy Mountain Song, A" (Ortiz), **Supp. IV Part 2:** 506
Snyder, Gary, **Supp. III Part 1:** 350; **Supp. IV Part 2:** 502; **Supp. V:** 168–169; **Supp. VIII:** 39, **289–307; Supp. XVI:** 283
Snyder, Mike, **Supp. XIV:** 36
"So-and-So Reclining on Her Couch" (Stevens), **IV:** 90
"Soapland" (Thurber), **Supp. I Part 2:** 619
Soares, Lota de Macedo, **Retro. Supp. II:** 44; **Supp. I Part 1:** 89, 94
"Sobbin' Women, The" (Benét), **Supp. XI:** 47
Sobin, Gustaf, **Supp. XVI: 281–298**
Social Ethics (Gilman), **Supp. XI:** 207
"Socialism and the Negro" (McKay), **Supp. X:** 135
"Socialism of the Skin, A (Liberation, Honey!)" (Kushner), **Supp. IX:** 135
Social Thought in America: The Revolt against Formalism (White), **Supp. I Part 2:** 648, 650
"Society, Morality, and the Novel" (Ellison), **Retro. Supp. II:** 118, 123–124
"Sociological Habit Patterns in Linguistic Transmogrification" (Cowley), **Supp. II Part 1:** 143
"Sociological Poet, A" (Bourne), **I:** 228
Socrates, **I:** 136, 265; **II:** 8–9, 105, 106; **III:** 281, 419, 606; **Supp. I Part 2:** 458; **Supp. XII:** 98
Socrates Fortlow stories (Mosley), **Supp. XIII: 242–243**
"So Forth" (Brodsky), **Supp. VIII:** 33
So Forth (Brodsky), **Supp. VIII:** 32–33
Soft Machine, The (Burroughs), **Supp. III Part 1:** 93, 103, 104
"Soft Mask" (Karr), **Supp. XI:** 243
Soft Side, The (James), **II:** 335; **Retro. Supp. I:** 229
"Soft Spring Night in Shillington, A" (Updike), **Retro. Supp. I:** 318, 319
"Soft Wood" (Lowell), **II:** 550–551
"So Help Me" (Algren), **Supp. IX:** 2
Soil and Survival: Land Stewardship and the Future of American Agriculture (C. Bly, J. Paddock and N. Paddock), **Supp. XVI:** 36–37
"Soirée in Hollywood" (H. Miller), **III:** 186
Sojourner, The (Rawlings), **Supp. X:** 233–234
"Sojourn in a Whale" (Moore), **III:** 211, 213
"Sojourns" (Didion), **Supp. IV Part 1:** 205
Solanus, Jane, **Supp. XVI:** 293
Solar Lottery (Dick), **Supp. XVIII:** 138
Solar Storms (Hogan), **Supp. IV Part 1:** 397, 410, 414–415
"Soldier, The" (Frost), **II:** 155
"Soldier Asleep at the Tomb" (Schnackenberg), **Supp. XV:** 262–263
Soldier Blue (film), **Supp. X:** 124
"Soldier of Fortune" (Wright), **Supp. XV:** 341
"Soldier's Home" (Hemingway), **Retro. Supp. I:** 189
Soldier's Joy (Bell), **Supp. X:** 7, **7–8,** 10, 11
Soldiers of the Storm (film), **Supp. XIII:** 163
Soldiers' Pay (Faulkner), **I:** 117; **II:** 56, 68; **Retro. Supp. I:** 80, 81
"Soldier's Testament, The" (Mumford), **Supp. II Part 2:** 473
"Soliloquy: Man Talking to a Mirror" (Komunyakaa), **Supp. XIII:** 116–117
"Solitary Confinement" (X. J. Kennedy), **Supp. XV:** 157

"Solitary Pond, The" (Updike), **Retro. Supp. I:** 323
So Little Time (Marquand), **III:** 55, 59, 65, 67, 69
"Solitude" (Maupassant), **Supp. I Part 1:** 223
Solo Faces (Salter), **Supp. IX: 259–260**
Solomon, Andy, **Supp. X:** 11
Solomon, Carl, **Supp. XIV:** 143, 150
Solomon, Charles, **Supp. VIII:** 82
Solomon, Henry, Jr., **Supp. I Part 2:** 490
Solomons, Leon, **IV:** 26
So Long, See You Tomorrow (Maxwell), **Supp. VIII:** 156, 160, 162, **167–169; Supp. XVII:** 23
"So Long Ago" (Bausch), **Supp. VII:** 41–42
Solotaroff, Robert, **Retro. Supp. II:** 203
Solotaroff, Theodore, **III:** 452–453; **Retro. Supp. II:** 281; **Supp. I Part 2:** 440, 445; **Supp. X:** 79; **Supp. XI:** 340; **Supp. XII:** 291
"Solstice" (Jeffers), **Supp. II Part 2:** 433, 435
"Solstice, The" (Merwin), **Supp. III Part 1:** 356
"Solus Rex" (Nabokov), **Retro. Supp. I:** 274
"Solutions" (McCarthy), **II:** 578
"Solving the Puzzle" (Dunn), **Supp. XI:** 152
Solzhenitsyn, Alexandr, **Retro. Supp. I:** 278; **Supp. VIII:** 241
"Some Afternoon" (Creeley), **Supp. IV Part 1:** 150–151
Some American People (Caldwell), **I:** 292, 294, 295, 296, 304, 309
"Some Ashes Drifting above Piedra, California" (Levis), **Supp. XI:** 264–265
"Some Aspects of the Grotesque in Southern Fiction" (O'Connor), **Retro. Supp. II:** 223, 224
"Somebody Always Grabs the Purple" (H. Roth), **Supp. IX:** 234
Somebody in Boots (Algren), **Supp. IX:** 3, **5–7,** 12
Somebody's Darling (McMurtry), **Supp. V:** 225
Some Came Running (film), **Supp. XI:** 213
Some Came Running (Jones), **Supp. XI:** 214, 215, 220, **222–223,** 226, 227, 232
Some Can Whistle (McMurtry), **Supp. V:** 229
"Some Children of the Goddess" (Mailer), **Retro. Supp. II:** 204
Someday, Maybe (Stafford), **Supp. XI: 323–325; Supp. XIII:** 281
"Some Dreamers of the Golden Dream" (Didion), **Supp. IV Part 1:** 200
Some Faces in the Crowd (Schulberg), **Supp. XVIII:** 252
"Some Foreign Letters" (Sexton), **Supp. II Part 2:** 674
"Some General Instructions" (Koch), **Supp. XV:** 182
"Some Good News" (Olson), **Supp. II Part 2:** 575, 576, 577
"Some Grass along a Ditch Bank" (Levis), **Supp. XI:** 266
"Some Greek Writings" (Corso), **Supp. XII:** 130
Some Honorable Men: Political Conventions, 1960–1972 (Mailer), **Retro. Supp. II:** 208
Some Imagist Poets (Lowell), **III:** 511, 518, 520; **Supp. I Part 1:** 257, 261
"Some keep the Sabbath going to Church" (Dickinson), **Retro. Supp. I:** 30; **Supp. XVIII:** 301
"Some Laughed" (L. Michaels), **Supp. XVI:** 207
"Some Like Indians Endure" (Gunn Allen), **Supp. IV Part 1:** 330
"Some Like Them Cold" (Lardner), **II:** 427–428, 430, 431; **Supp. IX:** 202
"Some Lines from Whitman" (Jarrell), **IV:** 352
"Some Matters Concerning the Occupant" (Keillor), **Supp. XVI:** 167
"Some Negatives: X. at the Chateau" (Merrill), **Supp. III Part 1:** 322
"Some Neglected Points in the Theory of Socialism" (Veblen), **Supp. I Part 2:** 635
"Some Notes for an Autobiographical Lecture" (Trilling), **Supp. III Part 2:** 493, 497, 500
"Some Notes on French Poetry" (R. Bly), **Supp. IV Part 1:** 61
"Some Notes on Miss L." (West), **IV:** 290–291, 295; **Retro. Supp. II:** 322
"Some Notes on Organic Form" (Levertov), **Supp. III Part 1:** 272, 279
"Some Notes on Teaching: Probably Spoken" (Paley), **Supp. VI:** 225
"Some Notes on the Gazer Within" (Levis), **Supp. XI:** 270
"Some Notes on Violence" (West), **IV:** 304; **Retro. Supp. II:** 322, 323
"Some Observations Now" (Conroy), **Supp. XVI:** 75
Some of the Dharma (Kerouac), **Supp. III Part 1:** 225
"Someone Is Buried" (Salinas), **Supp. XIII:** 324
"Someone Puts a Pineapple Together" (Stevens), **IV:** 90–91
"Someone's Blood" (Dove), **Supp. IV Part 1:** 245
"Someone Talking" (Harjo), **Supp. XII:** 219–220
"Someone Talking to Himself" (Wilbur), **Supp. III Part 2:** 557
"Someone to Watch Over Me" (Stern), **Supp. IX:** 300
Someone to Watch Over Me: Stories (Bausch), **Supp. VII:** 53
Some People, Places, & Things That Will Not Appear in My Next Novel (Cheever), **Supp. I Part 1:** 184–185
"Some Poets' Criticism and the Age" (Yenser), **Supp. XV:** 113–114
Some Problems of Philosophy: A Beginning of an Introduction to Philosophy (James), **II:** 360–361
"Some Questions You Might Ask" (Oliver), **Supp. VII:** 238–239
"Some Remarks on Humor" (White), **Supp. I Part 2:** 672
"Some Remarks on Rhythm" (Roethke), **III:** 548–549
Somers, Fred, **I:** 196
Somerville, Jane, **Supp. IX:** 289, 296–297
"Some Secrets" (Stern), **Supp. IX:** 286, 287, 288, 289, 295
Some Sort of Epic Grandeur (Bruccoli), **Retro. Supp. I:** 115, 359
"Something" (Oliver), **Supp. VII:** 236
Something Happened (Heller), **Supp. IV Part 1:** 383, 386–388, 389, 392
"*Something Happened:* The Imaginary, the Symbolic, and the Discourse of the Family" (Mellard), **Supp. IV Part 1:** 387
Something in Common (Hughes), **Supp. I Part 1:** 329–330
Something Inside: Conversations with Gay Fiction Writers (Gambone), **Supp. XII:** 81
"Something New" (Stern), **Supp. IX:** 290
"Something's Going to Happen" (Zinberg), **Supp. XV:** 196
"Something Spurious from the Mindinao Deep" (Stegner), **Supp. IV Part 2:** 605
Something to Declare (Alvarez), **Supp. VII:** 1, 2, 11, 17–19
"Something to Remember Me By (Bellow), **Retro. Supp. II:** 32
Something to Remember Me By (Bellow), **Retro. Supp. II:** 32
Something Wicked This Way Comes (Bradbury), **Supp. IV Part 1:** 101, 110–111
"Something Wild ..."(T. Williams), **IV:** 381
"Some Thoughts"(McNally), **Supp. XIII:** 207
"Some Thoughts on the Line"(Oliver), **Supp. VII:** 238
"Sometimes, Reading"(Stafford), **Supp. XI:** 314
"Sometimes I Wonder"(Hughes), **Supp. I Part 1:** 337
"Sometimes Mysteriously"(Salinas), **Supp. XIII:** 328
Sometimes Mysteriously (Salinas), **Supp. XIII:** 311, **326–328**
"Some Trees"(Ashbery), **Supp. III Part 1:** 2
Some Trees (Ashbery), **Supp. III Part 1:** 3–7, 12
"Some Views on the Reading and Writing of Short Stories"(Welty), **Retro. Supp. I:** 351
"Somewhere"(Nemerov), **III:** 279–280
"Somewhere Else"(Paley), **Supp. VI:** 227
"Somewhere in Africa"(Sexton), **Supp. II Part 2:** 684–685
"Somewhere Is Such a Kingdom"(Ransom), **III:** 492
"Somewhere near Phu Bai: (Komunyakaa), **Supp. XIII:** 123–124
"Some Words with a Mummy" (Poe), **III:** 425

"Some Yips and Barks in the Dark" (Snyder), **Supp. VIII:** 291
Sommers, Michael, **Supp. IV Part 2:** 581
Sommers, William, **I:** 387, 388
"Somnambulisma" (Stevens), **Retro. Supp. I:** 310
"So Much Summer" (Dickinson), **Retro. Supp. I:** 26, 44, 45
"So Much the Worse for Boston" (Lindsay), **Supp. I Part 2:** 398
"So Much Water So Close to Home" (Carver), **Supp. III Part 1:** 143, 146
Son, Cathy, **Supp. X:** 292
"Son, The" (Dove), **Supp. IV Part 1:** 245
"Sonata" (Schnackenberg), **Supp. XV:** 259
"Sonata for the Invisible" (Harjo), **Supp. XII:** 228
Sonata for Two Pianos (Bowles), **Supp. IV Part 1:** 83
Son at the Front, A (Wharton), **II:** 183; **IV:** 320; **Retro. Supp. I:** 378
Sondheim, Stephen, **Supp. XII:** 260; **Supp. XVI:** 194
Son Excellence Eugène Rougon (Zola), **III:** 322
"Song" (B. Kelly), **Supp. XVII:** 127
Song (B. Kelly), **Supp. XVII:** 123, **127–130**
"Song" (Bogan), **Supp. III Part 1:** 57
"Song" (Bryant). *See* "Hunter of the West, The"
"Song" (Dunbar), **Supp. II Part 1:** 199
"Song" (Ginsberg), **Supp. II Part 1:** 317
"Song" (Kenyon), **Supp. VII:** 169
"Song" (Rich), **Supp. I Part 2:** 560
"Song" (Wylie), **Supp. I Part 2:** 729
"Song, A" (Creeley), **Supp. IV Part 1:** 145
"Song, The" (Gioia), **Supp. XV:** 117
Song and Idea (Eberhart), **I:** 526, 529, 533, 539
"Song: Enlightenment" (X. J. Kennedy), **Supp. XV:** 169
"Song for Myself and the Deer to Return On" (Harjo), **Supp. XII:** 225
"Song for My Sixtieth Year" (Carruth), **Supp. XVI:** 54
"Song for Occupations, A" (Whitman), **Retro. Supp. I:** 394
"Song for Simeon, A" (Eliot), **Retro. Supp. I:** 64
"Song for the Coming of Smallpox" (Wagoner), **Supp. IX:** 329, 330
"Song for the End of Time" (Gioia), **Supp. XV:** 126–127
"Song for the First People" (Wagoner), **Supp. IX:** 328
"Song for the Last Act" (Bogan), **Supp. III Part 1:** 64
"Song for the Middle of the Night, A" (Wright), **Supp. III Part 2:** 594
"Song for the Rainy Season" (Bishop), **Supp. I Part 1:** 93–94, 96
"Song for the Romeos, A" (Stern), **Supp. IX:** 296
"Song for Woody" (song, Dylan), **Supp. XVIII:** 24
"Song from a Courtyard Window" (Gioia), **Supp. XV:** 119
"Song in the Front Yard, A" (Brooks), **Supp. XVIII:** 181
"Songline of Dawn" (Harjo), **Supp. XII:** 229
"Song: Love in Whose Rich Honor" (Rukeyser), **Supp. VI:** 285
"Song: Now That She Is Here" (Carruth), **Supp. XVI:** 59
"Song of Advent, A" (Winters), **Supp. II Part 2:** 789
"Song of a Man Who Rushed at the Enemy" (Wagoner), **Supp. IX:** 329, 330
"Song of Courage, A" (Masters), **Supp. I Part 2:** 458
Song of God, The: Bhagavad-Gita (Isherwood and Prabhavananda, trans.), **Supp. XIV:** 156, 157, 164
Song of Hiawatha, The (Longfellow), **II:** 501, 503–504; **Retro. Supp. II:** 155, **159–161,** 162, 163
"Song of Innocence, A" (Ellison), **Retro. Supp. II:** 126; **Supp. II Part 1:** 248
"Song of My Fiftieth Birthday, The" (Lindsay), **Supp. I Part 2:** 399
"Song of Myself" (Whitman), **II:** 544; **III:** 572, 584, 595; **IV:** 333, 334, 337–339, 340, 341, 342, 344, 348, 349, 351, 405; **Retro. Supp. I:** 388, 389, 395–399, 400; **Supp. IX:** 131, 136, 143, 328, 331; **Supp. V:** 122; **Supp. XIV:** 139; **Supp. XVIII:** 194, 304
Song of Russia (film), **Supp. I Part 1:** 281, 294; **Supp. XVII:** 60–61
"Song of Self" (Huncke), **Supp. XIV:** 138–139, 145
Song of Solomon (biblical book), **III:** 118; **IV:** 150
Song of Solomon (Morrison), **Supp. III Part 1:** 364, 368, 369, 372, 379; **Supp. XVIII:** 55
Song of Songs (biblical book), **II:** 538; **IV:** 153–154; **Supp. XV:** 221
"Song of the Answerer" (Whitman), **Retro. Supp. I:** 393, 399
"Song of the Chattahoochee, The" (Lanier), **Supp. I Part 1:** 365, 368
"Song of the Degrees, A" (Pound), **III:** 466
"Song of the Exposition" (Whitman), **IV:** 332
"Song of the Gavilan" (Leopold), **Supp. XIV:** 189
"Song of the Gourd" (Wright), **Supp. XV:** 348–349
"Song of the Greek Amazon" (Bryant), **Supp. I Part 1:** 168
Song of the Lark, The (Cather), **I:** 312, 319–321, 323; **Retro. Supp. I:** 1, 3, 7, **9–11,** 13, 19, 20
"Song of the Open Road" (McGrath), **Supp. X:** 127
"Song of the Open Road" (Whitman), **IV:** 340–341; **Retro. Supp. I:** 400; **Supp. IX:** 265
"Song of the Redwood Tree" (Whitman), **IV:** 348
"Song of the Scullery" (McCarriston), **Supp. XIV:** 272
"Song of the Sky Loom" (traditional Tewa poem), **Supp. IV Part 1:** 325
"Song of the Son" (Toomer), **Supp. III Part 2:** 482–483; **Supp. IX:** 313
"Song of the Sower, The" (Bryant), **Supp. I Part 1:** 169
"Song of the Stars" (Bryant), **Supp. I Part 1:** 163
"Song of the Swamp-Robin, The" (Frederic), **II:** 138
"Song of the Vermonters, The" (Whittier), **Supp. I Part 2:** 692
"Song of Three Smiles" (Merwin), **Supp. III Part 1:** 344
"Song of Wandering Aengus, The" (Yeats), **IV:** 271; **Retro. Supp. I:** 342, 350
"Song of Welcome" (Brodsky), **Supp. VIII:** 32
"Song on Captain Barney's Victory" (Freneau), **Supp. II Part 1:** 261
"Song/Poetry and Language-Expression and Perception" (Ortiz), **Supp. IV Part 2:** 500, 508
"Song: 'Rough Winds Do Shake the Darling Buds of May'" (Simpson), **Supp. IX:** 268
Songs and Satires (Masters), **Supp. I Part 2:** 465–466
Songs and Sonnets (L. P. Smith), **Supp. XIV:** 341
Songs and Sonnets (Masters), **Supp. I Part 2:** 455, 459, 461, 466
"Songs for a Colored Singer" (Bishop), **Supp. I Part 1:** 80, 85
Songs for a Summer's Day (A Sonnet Cycle) (MacLeish), **III:** 3
"Songs for Eve" (MacLeish), **III:** 19
Songs for Eve (MacLeish), **III:** 3, 19
"Songs for My Father" (Komunyakaa), **Supp. XIII:** 128
"Songs for Two Seasons" (C. Frost), **Supp. XV:** 95–96
Songs from This Earth on Turtle's Back: Contemporary American Indian Poetry (Bruchac, ed.), **Supp. IV Part 1:** 320, 328
"Songs of a Housewife" (Rawlings), **Supp. X:** 221–222
"Songs of Billy Bathgate, The" (Doctorow), **Supp. IV Part 1:** 230
Songs of Innocence (Blake), **Supp. I Part 2:** 708
Songs of Jamaica (McKay), **Supp. X:** 131, 133
"Songs of Maximus, The" (Olson), **Supp. II Part 2:** 567
"Songs of Parting" (Whitman), **IV:** 348
Songs of the Sierras (J. Miller), **I:** 459
Songs of Three Centuries (Whittier and Larcom, eds.), **Supp. XIII:** 142
"Song to David" (Smart), **III:** 534
"Song to No Music, A" (Brodsky), **Supp. VIII:** 26
Sonneschein, Rosa, **Retro. Supp. II:** 65
"Sonnet" (Rukeyser), **Supp. VI:** 284
"Sonnet Crown for Two Voices" (Bierds), **Supp. XVII:** 35
"Sonnets" (Carruth), **Supp. XVI:** 56
"Sonnets at Christmas" (Tate), **IV:** 135

Sonnets to Orpheus (Rilke), **Supp. XV:** 222
"Sonnet-To Zante" (Poe), **III:** 421
"Sonny's Blues" (Baldwin), **Retro. Supp. II:** 7, 8, 10, 14; **Supp. I Part 1:** 58–59, 63, 67; **Supp. XI:** 288
Son of Laughter, The: A Novel (Buechner), **Supp. XII:** 54
Son of Perdition, The (Cozzens), **I:** 359–360, 377, 378, 379
Son of the Circus, A (Irving), **Supp. VI:** 165, 166, **176–179**
"Son of the Gods, A" (Bierce), **I:** 202
Son of the Morning (Oates), **Supp. II Part 2:** 518, 519, 520–522
Son of the Morning Star: Custer and the Little Bighorn (Connell), **Supp. XIV:** 80, 82, 97
"Son of the Romanovs, A" (Simpson), **Supp. IX:** 273–274
Son of the Wolf, The (London), **II:** 465, 469
"Son of the Wolfman" (Chabon), **Supp. XI:** 76
"Sonrisas" (Mora), **Supp. XIII:** 216, 219
Sons (Buck), **Supp. II Part 1:** 117–118
Sons and Lovers (Lawrence), **III:** 27
Sontag, Kate, **Supp. XV:** 104
Sontag, Susan, **IV:** 13, 14; **Retro. Supp. II:** 279; **Supp. I Part 2:** 423; **Supp. III Part 2: 451–473; Supp. VIII:** 75; **Supp. XIV:** 14, 15, 95–96, 167; **Supp. XVI:** 201, 204, 206
"Soonest Mended" (Ashbery), **Supp. III Part 1:** 1, 13
"Sootfall and Fallout" (White), **Supp. I Part 2:** 671
Sophocles, **I:** 274; **II:** 291, 385, 577; **III:** 145, 151, 152, 153, 159, 398, 476, 478, 609, 613; **IV:** 291, 363, 368, 370; **Supp. I Part 1:** 153, 284; **Supp. I Part 2:** 491; **Supp. V:** 97; **Supp. VIII:** 332; **Supp. XV:** 265, 266
"Sophronsiba" (Bourne), **I:** 221
Sorcerer's Apprentice, The: Tales and Conjurations (Johnson), **Supp. VI: 192–193,** 194
"Sorcerer's Eye, The" (Nemerov), **III:** 283
Sordello (Browning), **III:** 467, 469, 470
"Sordid? Good God!" (Williams), **Retro. Supp. II:** 334
"Sorghum" (Mason), **Supp. VIII:** 146
Sorokin, Pitirim, **Supp. I Part 2:** 679
Sorrentino, Christopher, **Supp. XVIII:** 148
Sorrentino, Gilbert, **Retro. Supp. I:** 426; **Supp. IV Part 1:** 286; **Supp. XII:** 139
"Sorrow" (Komunyakaa), **Supp. XIII:** 119
Sorrow Dance, The (Levertov), **Supp. III Part 1:** 279–280, 283
"Sorrowful Guest, A" (Jewett), **Retro. Supp. II:** 137
Sorrows of Fat City, The: A Selection of Literary Essays and Reviews (Garrett), **Supp. VII:** 111
Sorrows of Young Werther, The (Goethe), **Supp. XI:** 169
Sorrows of Young Werther, The (Goethe; Bogan and Mayer, trans.), **Supp. III Part 1:** 63
"Sorting Facts; or, Nineteen Ways of Looking at Marker" (Howe), **Supp. IV Part 2:** 434, 436
"Sort of Song, A" (W. C. Williams), **Supp. XVII:** 243
"S O S" (Baraka), **Supp. II Part 1:** 50
"So Sassafras" (Olson), **Supp. II Part 2:** 574
"So There" (Creeley), **Supp. IV Part 1:** 157
Sotirov, Vasil, **Supp. IX:** 152
Soto, Gary, **Supp. IV Part 2:** 545; **Supp. V:** 180; **Supp. XI:** 270; **Supp. XIII:** 313, 315, 316, 320, 323; **Supp. XV:** 73
"Soto Thinking of the Ocean" (Salinas), **Supp. XIII:** 321
"Sotto Voce" (Kunitz), **Supp. III Part 1:** 265
Sot-Weed Factor, The (Barth), **I:** 122, 123, 125, 129, 130, 131–134, 135
Soul, The (Brooks), **I:** 244
Soul and Body of John Brown, The (Rukeyser), **Supp. VI:** 273
Soul Clap Hands and Sing (Marshall), **Supp. XI:** 276, 278, **280–282**
Soul Expeditions (Singer). *See* Shosha (Singer)
Soul Gone Home (Hughes), **Retro. Supp. I:** 203; **Supp. I Part 1:** 328
"Soul inside the Sentence, The" (Gass), **Supp. VI:** 88
Soul Is Here for Its Own Joy, The (Bly, ed.), **Supp. IV Part 1:** 74
Soul of Man under Socialism, The (Wilde), **Supp. IX:** 134–135
Soul of the Far East, The (Lowell), **II:** 513
Soul on Ice (Cleaver), **Retro. Supp. II:** 12, 13
"Souls Belated" (Wharton), **Retro. Supp. I:** 364
"Soul selects her own Society, The" (Dickinson), **Retro. Supp. I:** 37
Souls of Black Folk, The (Du Bois), **Supp. II Part 1:** 33, 40, 160, 168–170, 176, 183; **Supp. IV Part 1:** 164; **Supp. IX:** 305, 306; **Supp. X:** 133; **Supp. XIII:** 185, 238, 243
"Sound, The" (Olds), **Supp. X:** 214
"Sound and Fury" (O. Henry), **Supp. II Part 1:** 402
Sound and the Fury, The (Faulkner), **I:** 480; **II:** 55, 57, 58–60, 73; **III:** 237; **IV:** 100, 101, 104; **Retro. Supp. I:** 73, 75, 77, 82, **83–84,** 86, 88, 89, 90, 91, 92; **Supp. IX:** 103; **Supp. VIII:** 215; **Supp. X:** 44; **Supp. XII:** 33; **Supp. XIV:** 12; **Supp. XVII:** 138; **Supp. XVIII:** 84
"Sound Bites" (Alvarez), **Supp. VII:** 11
Sound I Listened For, The (Francis), **Supp. IX: 78–79,** 87
"Sound Mind, Sound Body" (Lowell), **II:** 554
"Sound of Distant Thunder, A" (Elkin), **Supp. VI: 42–43,** 44
"Sound of Light, The" (Merwin), **Supp. III Part 1:** 356
Sound of Mountain Water, The (Stegner), **Supp. IV Part 2:** 595, 596, 598, 600, 608
"Sound of Talking" (Purdy), **Supp. VII:** 270
Sounds of Poetry, The (Pinsky), **Supp. VI:** 236, 247, 248
Soupault, Philippe, **IV:** 288, 404; **Retro. Supp. II:** 85, 321, 324
"Source" (Doty), **Supp. XI:** 136
Source (Doty), **Supp. XI:** 121, **134–137**
"Source, The" (Olds), **Supp. X:** 211
"Source, The" (Porter), **III:** 443
Source of Light, The (Price), **Supp. VI: 262,** 266
"Sources of Soviet Conduct, The" (Kennan), **Supp. VIII:** 241
Sour Grapes (W. C. Williams), **Retro. Supp. I:** 418
"South" (Levis), **Supp. XI:** 266
"South, The" (Hughes), **Supp. I Part 1:** 321
"Southbound on the Freeway" (Swenson), **Supp. IV Part 2:** 643
South Dakota Guidebook, The (C. Baxter), **Supp. XVII:** 15
Southern, Terry, **Supp. IV Part 1:** 379; **Supp. V:** 40, 201; **Supp. XI: 293–310; Supp. XVI:** 230
"Southern Cross, The" (Wright), **Supp. V:** 338
Southern Cross, The (Wright), **Supp. V:** 332, 342
"Southerner's Problem, The" (Du Bois), **Supp. II Part 1:** 168
"Southern Girl" (Zelda Fitzgerald), **Supp. IX:** 71
"Southern Mode of the Imagination, A" (Tate), **IV:** 120
"Southern Romantic, A" (Tate), **Supp. I Part 1:** 373
"Southern Sojourn, A" (Hoffman), **Supp. XVIII:** 87
Southern Terry, **Supp. XIV:** 82
Southey, Robert, **II:** 304, 502; **Supp. I Part 1:** 154
South Moon Under (Rawlings), **Supp. X: 225–226,** 229, 233
South Pacific Affair (Lacy), **Supp. XV:** 206
Southpaw, The (Harris), **II:** 424–425
"South Sangamon" (Cisneros), **Supp. VII:** 66
Southwell, Robert, **IV:** 151
Southwick, Marcia, **Supp. XI:** 259
Southworth, E. D. E. N, **Retro. Supp. I:** 246
Souvenir of the Ancient World, Selected Poems of Carlos Drummond de Andrade (Strand, trans.), **Supp. IV Part 2:** 630
"Sow" (Plath), **Supp. I Part 2:** 537
"Sowing and Reaping in *Furors Die*" (Nostrandt), **Supp. XVIII:** 80–81
Space between Our Footsteps, The: Poems and Paintings from the Middle East (Nye, ed.), **Supp. XIII:** 280
"Space Quale, The" (James), **II:** 349

"Spaces Between, The" (Kingsolver), **Supp. VII:** 209
"Space Where Sex Should Be, The: Toward a Definition of the Black Literary Tradition" (Nelson), **Supp. XVIII:** 172
Spackman, Peter, **Supp. XVI:** 221
Spacks, Patricia, **Supp. XVI:** 251
"Spain" (Auden), **Supp. II Part 1:** 12–13, 14
"Spain in Fifty-Ninth Street" (White), **Supp. I Part 2:** 677
"Spanish-American War Play" (Crane), **I:** 422
Spanish Ballads (Merwin, trans.), **Supp. III Part 1:** 347
Spanish Bayonet (Benét), **Supp. XI:** 45, 47
Spanish Earth, The (film), **Retro. Supp. I:** 184
Spanish Papers and Other Miscellanies (Irving), **II:** 314
"Spanish Revolution, The" (Bryant), **Supp. I Part 1:** 153, 168
Spanish Student, The (Longfellow), **II:** 489, 506; **Retro. Supp. II:** 165
Spanking the Maid (Coover), **Supp. V:** 47, 48, 49, 52
Spargo, John, **Supp. I Part 1:** 13
"Spark, The" (Wharton), **Retro. Supp. I:** 381
"Sparkles from the Wheel" (Whitman), **IV:** 348
Sparks, Debra, **Supp. X:** 177
Sparks, Jared, **Supp. I Part 1:** 156
"Sparrow" (Berry), **Supp. X:** 31
Sparrow, Henry, **III:** 587
Sparrow, Mrs. Henry, **III:** 587
"Sparrow's Gate, The" (B. Kelly), **Supp. XVII:** 133
Spaulding, William, **Supp. XVI:** 106
"Spawning Run, The" (Humphrey), **Supp. IX:** 95
"Speak, Gay Memory" (Kirp), **Supp. XI:** 129
"Speak, Hoyt-Schermerhorn" (Lethem), **Supp. XVIII:** 148
Speak, Memory (Nabokov), **III:** 247–250, 252; **Retro. Supp. I:** 264, 265, 266, 267, 268, 277; **Supp. XVI:** 148
Speak, Memory (V. Nabokov), **Supp. XVII:** 47
Speaking and Language (Shapiro), **Supp. II Part 2:** 721
Speaking for Nature: How Literary Naturalists from Henry Thoreau to Rachel Carson Have Shaped America (Brooks), **Supp. IX:** 31
Speaking for Ourselves: American Ethnic Writing (Faderman and Bradshaw, eds.), **Supp. XIII:** 313
"Speaking of Accidents" (Everwine), **Supp. XV:** 88–89
Speaking of Accidents (Everwine), **Supp. XV:** 75, 88
"Speaking of Counterweights" (White), **Supp. I Part 2:** 669
Speaking of Literature and Society (Trilling), **Supp. III Part 2:** 494, 496, 499
"Speaking of Love" (Gioia), **Supp. XV:** 124–125
Speaking on Stage (Kolin and Kullman, eds.), **Supp. IX:** 145
Speaking on Stage: Interviews with Contemporary American Playwrights (Balakian), **Supp. XV:** 327
"Speaking Passions" (Kitchen), **Supp. XV:** 215
Speak What We Feel (Not What We Ought to Say): Reflections on Literature and Faith (Buechner), **Supp. XII:** 57
Spear, Roberta, **Supp. V:** 180; **Supp. XV:** 73
"Special Kind of Fantasy, A: James Dickey on the Razor's Edge" (Niflis), **Supp. IV Part 1:** 175
"Special Pleading" (Lanier), **Supp. I Part 1:** 364
"Special Problems in Teaching Leslie Marmon Silko's *Ceremony*" (Gunn Allen), **Supp. IV Part 1:** 333
Special Providence, A (Yates), **Supp. XI:** 342, **344–345**
"Special Time, a Special School, A" (Knowles), **Supp. XII:** 236
Special View of History, The (Olson), **Supp. II Part 2:** 566, 569, 572
Specimen Days (Whitman), **IV:** 338, 347, 348, 350; **Retro. Supp. I:** 408
Specimens of the American Poets, **Supp. I Part 1:** 155
"Spectacles, The" (Poe), **III:** 425
Spectator Bird, The (Stegner), **Supp. IV Part 2:** 599, 604, 606, 611–612
Spector, Robert, **Supp. XIII:** 87
Spectra: A Book of Poetic Experiments (Bynner and Ficke), **Supp. XV:** 43
"Spectre Bridegroom, The" (Irving), **II:** 304
"Spectre Pig, The" (Holmes), **Supp. I Part 1:** 302
"Speculating Woman" (X. J. Kennedy), **Supp. XV:** 168
"Speech Sounds" (O. Butler), **Supp. XIII:** 61, **70**
"Speech to a Crowd" (MacLeish), **III:** 16
"Speech to the Detractors" (MacLeish), **III:** 16
"Speech to the Young" (Brooks), **Supp. III Part 1:** 79, 86
"Speech to Those Who Say Comrade" (MacLeish), **III:** 16
Speedboat (Adler), **Supp. X:** 171
Speed of Darkness, The (Rukeyser), **Supp. VI:** 274, 281
Speed-the-Plow (Mamet), **Supp. XIV:** 241, 246, 249, 250, 251
Speilberg, Steven, **Supp. XI:** 234
"Spell" (Francis), **Supp. IX:** 87
Spelling Dictionary, A (Rowson), **Supp. XV:** 244
Spence, Thomas, **Supp. I Part 2:** 518
Spence + Lila (Mason), **Supp. VIII:** 133, **143–145**
Spencer, Edward, **Supp. I Part 1:** 357, 360
Spencer, Herbert, **I:** 515; **II:** 345, 462–463, 480, 483, 536; **III:** 102, 315; **IV:** 135; **Retro. Supp. II:** 60, 65, 93, 98; **Supp. I Part 1:** 368; **Supp. I Part 2:** 635
Spencer, Sharon, **Supp. X:** 185, 186, 195, 196
Spencer, Theodore, **I:** 433; **Supp. III Part 1:** 2
Spender, Natasha, **Supp. IV Part 1:** 119, 127, 134
Spender, Stephen, **II:** 371; **III:** 504, 527; **Retro. Supp. I:** 216; **Retro. Supp. II:** 243, 244; **Supp. I Part 2:** 536; **Supp. II Part 1:** 11; **Supp. IV Part 1:** 82, 134; **Supp. IV Part 2:** 440; **Supp. X:** 116
Spengler, Oswald, **I:** 255, 270; **II:** 7, 577; **III:** 172, 176; **Retro. Supp. II:** 324; **Supp. I Part 2:** 647
Spens, Sir Patrick, **Supp. I Part 2:** 404
Spenser, Edmund, **I:** 62; **III:** 77, 78, 89; **IV:** 155, 453; **Retro. Supp. I:** 62; **Supp. I Part 1:** 98, 152, 369; **Supp. I Part 2:** 422, 719
"Spenser's Ireland" (Moore), **III:** 211, 212
Sperry, Margaret, **Supp. IV Part 1:** 169
Sphere: The Form of a Motion (Ammons), **Supp. VII:** 24, 32, 33, 35, 36
"Sphinx" (Hayden), **Supp. II Part 1:** 373
"Spiced Plums" (Ríos), **Supp. IV Part 2:** 553
"Spider and the Ghost of the Fly, The" (Lindsay), **Supp. I Part 2:** 375
Spider Bay (Van Vechten), **Supp. II Part 2:** 746
"Spiders" (Schwartz), **Supp. II Part 2:** 665
Spider's House, The (Bowles), **Supp. IV Part 1:** 87–89, 90, 91
Spider Woman's Granddaughters: Traditional Tales and Contemporary Writing by Native American Women (Gunn Allen, ed.), **Supp. IV Part 1:** 320, 326, 332–333; **Supp. IV Part 2:** 567
Spiegel, Sam, **Supp. XVIII:** 251, 252
Spiegelman, Art, **Supp. XVII:** 48
Spiegelman, Willard, **Supp. XI:** 126
Spillane, Mickey, **Supp. IV Part 2:** 469, 472; **Supp. XV:** 200; **Supp. XVIII:** 236, 237
Spiller, Robert E., **I:** 241; **Supp. I Part 1:** 104
"Spillikins: Gregor Mendel at the Table" (Bierds), **Supp. XVII:** 34–35
Spillway (Barnes), **Supp. III Part 1:** 44
Spingarn, Amy, **Supp. I Part 1:** 325, 326
Spingarn, Joel, **I:** 266; **Supp. I Part 1:** 325
Spinoza, Baruch, **I:** 493; **II:** 590, 593; **III:** 600; **IV:** 5, 7, 11, 12, 17; **Retro. Supp. II:** 300; **Supp. I Part 1:** 274; **Supp. I Part 2:** 643; **Supp. XVI:** 184
"Spinoza of Market Street, The" (Singer), **IV:** 12–13; **Retro. Supp. II:** 307
"Spinster" (Plath), **Supp. I Part 2:** 536
"Spinster's Tale, A" (Taylor), **Supp. V:** 314–315, 316–317, 319, 323

Spiral of Memory, The: Interviews (Coltelli, ed.), **Supp. XII:** 215
Spires, Elizabeth, **Supp. X:** 8
"Spire Song" (Bowles), **Supp. IV Part 1:** 80
Spirit and the Flesh, The: Sexual Diversity in American Indian Culture (W. L. Williams), **Supp. IV Part 1:** 330
"Spirit Birth" (Cullen), **Supp. IV Part 1:** 168
Spirit in Man, The (Jung), **Supp. IV Part 1:** 68
"Spirit in Me, The" (Hoffman), **Supp. XVIII:** 87
Spirit of Culver (West), **IV:** 287
Spirit of Labor, The (Hapgood), **Supp. XVII:** 96, 99, 101–102
Spirit of Romance, The (Pound), **III:** 470; **Retro. Supp. I:** 286
Spirit of the Ghetto, The: Studies of the Jewish Quarter of New York (Hapgood), **Supp. XVII:** 96, 101, 103, 106
Spirit of Youth and the City Streets, The (Addams), **Supp. I Part 1:** 6–7, 12–13, 16, 17, 19
"Spirits" (Bausch), **Supp. VII:** 46–47
Spirits, and Other Stories (Bausch), **Supp. VII:** 46–47, 54
"Spirit Says, You Are Nothing, The" (Levis), **Supp. XI:** 265–266
Spiritual Conflict, The (Scupoli), **IV:** 156
Spiritual Exercises, The (Loyola), **IV:** 151; **Supp. XI:** 162
"Spiritual Manifestation, A" (Whittier), **Supp. I Part 2:** 699
"Spirituals and Neo-Spirituals" (Hurston), **Supp. VI:** 152–153
Spits, Ellen Handler, **Supp. XII:** 166
"Spitzbergen Tales" (Crane), **I:** 409, 415, 423
Spitzer, Philip, **Supp. XIV:** 21
"Spleen" (Eliot), **I:** 569, 573–574
Spleen de Paris, Le (Baudelaire), **Supp. XIV:** 337
Splendid Drunken Twenties, The (Van Vechten), **Supp. II Part 2:** 739–744
"Splinters" (Bukiet), **Supp. XVII:** 47
"Splittings" (Rich), **Supp. I Part 2:** 570–571
"Splitting Wood at Six Above" (Kumin), **Supp. IV Part 2:** 449
Spofford, Harriet Prescott, **Supp. XIII:** 143
Spoils of Poynton, The (James), **I:** 463; **Retro. Supp. I:** 229–230
Spoken Page, The (Nye), **Supp. XIII:** 274
"Spokes" (Auster), **Supp. XII:** 23
Spokesmen (Whipple), **II:** 456
Spook Sonata, The (Strindberg), **III:** 387, 392
Spooky Art, The: A Book about Writing (Mailer), **Retro. Supp. II:** 214
"Spoon, The" (Simic), **Supp. VIII:** 275
Spoon River Anthology (Masters), **I:** 106; **III:** 579; **Supp. I Part 2:** 454, 455, 456, 460–465, 466, 467, 471, 472, 473, 476; **Supp. IX:** 306; **Supp. XIV:** 282–283
Sport and a Pastime, A (Salter), **Supp. IX: 254–257; Supp. XVI:** 237
Sporting Club, The (McGuane), **Supp. VIII:** 43
Sport of the Gods, The (Dunbar), **Supp. II Part 1:** 193, 200, 207, 214–217
"Sportsman Born and Bred, A" (Plimpton), **Supp. XVI:** 241
Sportsman's Sketches, A (Turgenev), **I:** 106; **IV:** 277
Sportswriter, The (Ford), **Supp. V:** 57, 58, 62–67
"Spotted Horses" (Faulkner), **IV:** 260
Sprague, Morteza, **Retro. Supp. II:** 115
Spratling, William, **II:** 56; **Retro. Supp. I:** 80
Sprawl trilogy (W. Gibson), **Supp. XVI:** 117, 122, 124
"Spray, The" (Lethem), **Supp. XVIII:** 148
"Spray Paint King, The" (Dove), **Supp. IV Part 1:** 252–253
Spreading Fires (Knowles), **Supp. XII:** 249
Sprigge, Elizabeth, **IV:** 31
"Spring" (Millay), **III:** 126
"Spring" (Mora), **Supp. XIII:** 217
"Spring 1967" (Carruth), **Supp. XVI:** 55
"Spring and All" (W. C. Williams), **Retro. Supp. I:** 419
Spring and All (W. C. Williams), **Retro. Supp. I:** 412, 418, **418–420,** 427, 430, 431
"Spring Break-Up" (Carruth), **Supp. XVI:** 56
"Spring Bulletin" (Allen), **Supp. XV:** 15
Springer's Progress (Markson), **Supp. XVII: 141–142,** 143, 146
"Spring Evening" (Farrell), **II:** 45
"Spring Evening" (Kenyon), **Supp. VII:** 173
"Springfield Magical" (Lindsay), **Supp. I Part 2:** 379
Spring in New Hampshire and Other Poems (McKay), **Supp. X:** 131, 135
"Spring Notes from Robin Hill" (Carruth), **Supp. XVI:** 48
"Spring Pastoral" (Wylie), **Supp. I Part 2:** 707
"Spring Pools" (Frost), **II:** 155; **Retro. Supp. I:** 137
"Spring Snow" (Matthews), **Supp. IX:** 160
"SPRING SONG" (Baraka), **Supp. II Part 1:** 60
Springsteen, Bruce, **Supp. VIII:** 143
"Spring Strains" (W. C. Williams), **Retro. Supp. I:** 416
Spring Tides (Morison), **Supp. I Part 2:** 494
Springtime and Harvest (Sinclair), **Supp. V:** 280
Spruance, Raymond, **Supp. I Part 2:** 479, 491
"Spruce Has No Taproot, The" (Clampitt), **Supp. IX:** 41–42
"Spunk" (Hurston), **Supp. VI:** 150, 151–152
Spunk: The Selected Stories (Hurston), **Supp. VI:** 150
Spurr, David, **Supp. XV:** 183
Spy, The (Cooper), **I:** 335, 336, 337, 339, 340; **Supp. I Part 1:** 155
"Spy, The" (Francis), **Supp. IX:** 81
Spy, The (Freneau), **Supp. II Part 1:** 260
Spy in the House of Love, A (Nin), **Supp. X:** 186
Squanto, **Supp. I Part 2:** 486
"Square Business" (Baraka), **Supp. II Part 1:** 49
Square Root of Wonderful, The (McCullers), **II:** 587–588
"Squash in Blossom" (Francis), **Supp. IX:** 81
"Squatter on Company Land, The" (Hugo), **Supp. VI:** 133
"Squatter's Children" (Bishop), **Retro. Supp. II:** 47
"Squeak, Memory" (Bukiet), **Supp. XVII:** 47
Squeeze Play (Auster), **Supp. XII:** 21
Squires, Radcliffe, **IV:** 127; **Supp. XV:** 118
Squirrels (Mamet), **Supp. XIV:** 240
S.S. Gliencairn (O'Neill), **III:** 387, 388, 405
S.S. San Pedro (Cozzens), **I:** 360–362, 370, 378, 379
"Ssshh" (Olds), **Supp. X:** 215
"Stacking the Straw" (Clampitt), **Supp. IX:** 41
Stade, George, **Supp. IV Part 1:** 286
Staël, Madame de, **II:** 298
"Staff of Life, The" (H. Miller), **III:** 187
Stafford, Jean, **II:** 537; **Retro. Supp. II:** 177; **Supp. V:** 316
Stafford, William, **Supp. IV Part 1:** 72; **Supp. IV Part 2:** 642; **Supp. IX:** 273; **Supp. XI: 311–332; Supp. XIII:** 76, 274, 276, 277, 281, 283; **Supp. XIV:** 119, 123
"Stage All Blood, The" (MacLeish), **III:** 18
"Staggerlee Wonders" (Baldwin), **Retro. Supp. II:** 15
Stained White Radiance, A (Burke), **Supp. XIV:** 28, 31
Stalin, Joseph, **I:** 261, 490; **II:** 39, 40, 49, 564; **III:** 30, 298; **IV:** 372; **Supp. V:** 290
"Stalking the Billion-Footed Beast: A Literary Manifesto for the New Social Novel" (Wolfe), **Supp. III Part 2:** 586
Stallman, R. W., **I:** 405
Stamberg, Susan, **Supp. IV Part 1:** 201; **Supp. XII:** 193
Stamford, Anne Marie, **Supp. XII:** 162
Stanard, Mrs. Jane, **III:** 410, 413
Stand, The (King), **Supp. V:** 139, 140–141, 144–146, 148, 152
"Standard of Liberty, The" (Rowson), **Supp. XV:** 243
"Standard of Living, The" (Parker), **Supp. IX: 198–199**
Stander, Lionel, **Supp. I Part 1:** 289
"Standing and the Waiting, The" (M. F. K. Fisher), **Supp. XVII:** 83
Standing by Words (Berry), **Supp. X:** 22, 27, 28, 31, 32, 33, 35

"Standing Halfway Home" (Wagoner), **Supp. IX:** 324
Stand in the Mountains, A (Taylor), **Supp. V:** 324
Standish, Burt L. (pseudonym). *See* Patten, Gilbert
Standish, Miles, **I:** 471; **II:** 502–503
Standley, Fred L., **Retro. Supp. II:** 6
Stand Still Like the Hummingbird (H. Miller), **III:** 184
"Stand Up" (Salinas), **Supp. XIII:** 315
Stand with Me Here (Francis), **Supp. IX:** 76
Stanford, Ann, **Retro. Supp. I:** 41; **Supp. I Part 1:** 99, 100, 102, 103, 106, 108, 109, 113, 117; **Supp. IV Part 2:** 637
Stanford, Donald E., **II:** 217
Stanford, Frank, **Supp. XV:** 338, 339, 341, 342–343, 343, 345, 348, 350
Stanford, Ginny (Crouch), **Supp. XV:** 339
Stanford, Leland, **I:** 196, 198
Stanislavsky, Konstantin, **Supp. XIV:** 240, 243
"Stanley Kunitz" (Oliver), **Supp. VII:** 237
Stansell, Christine, **Supp. XVII:** 106
Stanton, Frank L., **Supp. II Part 1:** 192
Stanton, Robert J., **Supp. IV Part 2:** 681
"Stanzas from the Grande Chartreuse" (Arnold), **Supp. I Part 2:** 417
Stanzas in Meditation (Stein), **Supp. III Part 1:** 13
Staples, Hugh, **Retro. Supp. II:** 187
Star, Alexander, **Supp. X:** 310
Starbuck, George, **Retro. Supp. II:** 53, 245; **Supp. I Part 2:** 538; **Supp. IV Part 2:** 440; **Supp. XIII:** 76
Star Child (Gunn Allen), **Supp. IV Part 1:** 324
"Star Dust" (Wrigley), **Supp. XVIII:** 296
Stardust Memories (film; Allen), **Supp. XV:** 1, 4, **8,** 9, 13
"Stare, The" (Updike), **Retro. Supp. I:** 329
"Starfish, The" (R. Bly), **Supp. IV Part 1:** 72
"Staring at the Sea on the Day of the Death of Another" (Swenson), **Supp. IV Part 2:** 652
Star Is Born, A (film), **Supp. IV Part 1:** 198; **Supp. IX:** 198; **Supp. XVIII:** 242, 243
Stark, David, **Supp. XII:** 202
"Stark Boughs on the Family Tree" (Oliver), **Supp. VII:** 232
Starke, Aubrey Harrison, **Supp. I Part 1:** 350, 352, 356, 360, 362, 365, 370, 371
Starkey, David, **Supp. XII:** 180, 181
"Starlight" (Levine), **Supp. V:** 188
"Starlight Scope Myopia" (Komunyakaa), **Supp. XIII:** 123, 124
Starnino, Carmine, **Supp. XVII:** 74
"Star of the Nativity" (Brodsky), **Supp. VIII:** 33
Starr, Ellen Gates, **Supp. I Part 1:** 4, 5, 11
Starr, Jean. *See* Untermeyer, Jean Starr
Starr, Ringo, **Supp. XI:** 309
Star Rover, The (London), **II:** 467
"Starry Night, The" (Sexton), **Supp. II Part 2:** 681
"Stars" (Frost), **II:** 153
Stars, the Snow, the Fire, The: Twenty-five Years in the Northern Wilderness (Haines), **Supp. XII: 199–201,** 206, 209
Star Shines over Mt. Morris Park, A (H. Roth), **Supp. IX:** 227, 236, **236–237**
"Stars of the Summer Night" (Longfellow), **II:** 493
"Stars over Harlem" (Hughes), **Retro. Supp. I:** 207
"Star-Spangled" (García), **Supp. XI:** 177, 178
Star-Spangled Girl, The (Simon), **Supp. IV Part 2:** 579
"Star-Splitter, The" (Frost), **Retro. Supp. I:** 123, 133
Stars Principal (McClatchy), **Supp. XII: 256–258**
"Starting from Paumanok" (Whitman), **IV:** 333
Starting Out in the Thirties (Kazin), **Supp. VIII: 95–97**
"Starved Lovers" (MacLeish), **III:** 19
Starved Rock (Masters), **Supp. I Part 2:** 465
"Starving Again" (Moore), **Supp. X:** 163, 172, 175
"State, The" (Bourne), **I:** 233
State and Main (Mamet), **Supp. XIV:** 241
"Statement of Principles" (Ransom), **III:** 496
"Statement: Phillipa Allen" (Rukeyser), **Supp. VI:** 283–284
"Statements on Poetics" (Snyder), **Supp. VIII:** 291, 292
"Statement with Rhymes" (Kees), **Supp. XV:** 139
"State of the Art, The" (Elkin), **Supp. VI:** 52
"State of the Arts, The" (Wasserstein), **Supp. XV:** 332
State of the Nation (Dos Passos), **I:** 489
"State of the Union" (Vidal), **Supp. IV Part 2:** 678
Static Element, The: Selected Poems of Natan Zach (Everwine, trans.), **Supp. XV:** 73, 75, **85–88**
"Statue, The" (Berryman), **I:** 173
"Statue and Birds" (Bogan), **Supp. III Part 1:** 50
"Statues, The" (Schwartz), **Supp. II Part 2:** 654, 659
"Status Rerum" (Pound), **Supp. I Part 1:** 257
Stavans, Ilan, **Supp. XI:** 190
"Staying Alive" (Levertov), **Supp. III Part 1:** 281
Staying Alive (Wagoner), **Supp. IX:** 324, **326**
"Staying at Ed's Place" (Swenson), **Supp. IV Part 2:** 648
Staying Put: Making a Home in a Restless World (Sanders), **Supp. XVI:** 274–275
Stay Me, Oh Comfort Me: Journals and Stories, 1933–1941 (M. F. K. Fisher), **Supp. XVII:** 92
Stayton, Richard, **Supp. IX:** 133
Steadman, Goodman, **IV:** 147
"Steak" (Snyder), **Supp. VIII:** 301
Steal Away: Selected and New Poems (Wright), **Supp. XV:** 337, 340, 348, 350–351
Stealing Beauty (Minot), **Supp. VI:** 205
Stealing Glimpses (McQuade), **Supp. IX:** 151
Stealing the Language: The Emergence of Women's Poetry in America (Ostriker), **Supp. XV:** 251
"Stealing the Thunder: Future Visions for American Indian Women, Tribes, and Literary Studies" (Gunn Allen), **Supp. IV Part 1:** 331
"Steam Shovel Cut" (Masters), **Supp. I Part 2:** 468
Stearns, Harold, **I:** 245; **Supp. XVII:** 106
Stedman, Edmund Clarence, **Supp. I Part 1:** 372; **Supp. II Part 1:** 192; **Supp. XV:** 115, 269, 273, 274, 282, 286
Steele, Max, **Supp. XIV:** 82
Steele, Sir Richard, **I:** 378; **II:** 105, 107, 300; **III:** 430
Steele, Timothy, **Supp. XV:** 251; **Supp. XVII:** 112
Steenburgen, Mary, **Supp. IV Part 1:** 236
Steeple Bush (Frost), **II:** 155; **Retro. Supp. I:** 140; **Retro. Supp. II:** 42
"Steeple-Jack, The" (Moore), **III:** 212, 213, 215
"Steerage" (Goldbarth), **Supp. XII:** 187
Steers, Nina, **Retro. Supp. II:** 25
Steffens, Lincoln, **II:** 577; **III:** 580; **Retro. Supp. I:** 202; **Retro. Supp. II:** 101; **Supp. I Part 1:** 7; **Supp. XVII:** 98, 101, 106–107
Stegner, Page, **IV:** 114, 116; **Supp. IV Part 2:** 599
Stegner, Wallace, **Supp. IV Part 2: 595–618; Supp. V:** 220, 224, 296; **Supp. X:** 23, 24; **Supp. XIV:** 82, 193, 230, 233; **Supp. XVIII:** 192
"Stegner's Short Fiction" (Ahearn), **Supp. IV Part 2:** 604
Steichen, Edward, **III:** 580, 594–595
Steichen, Lillian. *See* Sandburg, Mrs. Carl (Lillian Steichen)
Steier, Rod, **Supp. VIII:** 269
Steiger, Rod, **Supp. XI:** 305
Stein, Gertrude, **I:** 103, 105, 476; **II:** 56, 251, 252, 257, 260, 262–263, 264, 289; **III:** 71, 454, 471–472, 600; **IV: 24–48,** 368, 375, 404, 415, 443, 477; **Retro. Supp. I:** 108, 170, 176, 177, 186, 418, 422; **Retro. Supp. II:** 85, 207, 326, 331; **Supp. I Part 1:** 292; **Supp. III Part 1:** 13, 37, 225, 226; **Supp. III Part 2:** 626; **Supp. IV Part 1:** 11, 79, 80, 81, 322; **Supp. IV Part 2:** 468; **Supp. IX:** 55, 57, 62, 66; **Supp. V:** 53; **Supp. XII:** 1, 139; **Supp. XIV:** 336; **Supp. XVI:** 187; **Supp. XVII:** 98, 105, 107; **Supp. XVIII:** 148

Stein, Jean, **Supp. XVI:** 245
Stein, Karen F., **Supp. XIII:** 29, 30
Stein, Leo, **IV:** 26; **Supp. XIV:** 336; **Supp. XV:** 298
Stein, Lorin, **Supp. XII:** 254; **Supp. XVIII:** 137, 139
Steinbeck, John, **I:** 107, 288, 301, 378, 495, 519; **II:** 272; **III:** 382, 453, 454, 589; **IV:** **49–72;** **Retro. Supp. II:** 19, 196; **Supp. IV Part 1:** 102, 225; **Supp. IV Part 2:** 502; **Supp. IX:** 33, 171; **Supp. V:** 290, 291; **Supp. VIII:** 10; **Supp. XI:** 169; **Supp. XIII:** 1, 17; **Supp. XIV:** 21, 181; **Supp. XVII:** 228; **Supp. XVIII:** 90, 102, 254
Steinbeck, Olive Hamilton, **IV:** 51
Steinberg, Saul, **Supp. VIII:** 272
Steinberg, Sybil, **Supp. XVII:** 165, 166
Steinem, Gloria, **Supp. IV Part 1:** 203
Steiner, George, **Retro. Supp. I:** 327; **Supp. IV Part 1:** 286; **Supp. XVI:** 230
Steiner, Nancy, **Supp. I Part 2:** 529
Steiner, Stan, **Supp. IV Part 2:** 505
Steinfels, Margaret, **Supp. XVII:** 170
Steinhoff, Eirik, **Supp. XVI:** 290
Steinman, Michael, **Supp. VIII:** 172
Steinmetz, Charles Proteus, **I:** 483
Steinway Quintet Plus Four, The (Epstein), **Supp. XII:** 159, **162–166**
Stekel, Wilhelm, **III:** 554
Stella (Goethe), **Supp. IX:** 133, 138
Stella (Kushner), **Supp. IX:** 133
Stella, Joseph, **I:** 387
"Stellaria" (Francis), **Supp. IX:** 83
Stelligery and Other Essays (Wendell), **Supp. I Part 2:** 414
Stendhal, **I:** 316; **III:** 465, 467; **Supp. I Part 1:** 293; **Supp. I Part 2:** 445
Stepanchev, Stephen, **Supp. XI:** 312
Stephen, Leslie, **IV:** 440
Stephen, Saint, **II:** 539; **IV:** 228
Stephen, Sir Leslie, **IV:** 440; **Supp. I Part 1:** 306
Stephen Crane (Berryman), **I:** 169–170, 405
Stephen King, The Second Decade: "Danse Macabre" to "The Dark Half" (Magistrale), **Supp. V:** 138, 146, 151
Stephen King: The Art of Darkness (Winter), **Supp. V:** 144
Stephens, Jack, **Supp. X:** 11, 14, 15, 17
Stephenson, Gregory, **Supp. XII:** 120, 123
"Stepping Out" (Dunn), **Supp. XI:** 140, 141
Steps (Kosinski), **Supp. VII:** 215, 221–222, 225
"Steps" (Nye), **Supp. XIII:** 288
Steps to the Temple (Crashaw), **IV:** 145
"Steps Toward Poverty and Death" (R. Bly), **Supp. IV Part 1:** 60
Stepto, Robert B., **Retro. Supp. II:** 116, 120, 123
Sterile Cuckoo, The (Nichols), **Supp. XIII:** 258, **259–263,** 264
Sterling, Bruce, **Supp. XVI:** 118, 121, 123, 124, 128–129
Sterling, George, **I:** 199, 207, 208, 209; **II:** 440; **Supp. V:** 286
Stern, Bernhard J., **Supp. XIV:** 202, 213
Stern, Daniel, **Supp. VIII:** 238
Stern, Frederick C., **Supp. X:** 114, 115, 117
Stern, Gerald, **Supp. IX:** **285–303;** **Supp. XI:** 139, 267; **Supp. XV:** 211, 212
Stern, Madeleine B., **Supp. I Part 1:** 35
Stern, Maurice, **IV:** 285
Stern, Philip Van Doren, **Supp. XIII:** 164
Stern, Richard, **Retro. Supp. II:** 291
Stern, Richard G., **Retro. Supp. II:** 204
Stern, Steven, **Supp. XVII:** 42, 48, 49
"Sterne" (Schwartz), **Supp. II Part 2:** 663
Sterne, Laurence, **II:** 302, 304–305, 308; **III:** 454; **IV:** 68, 211, 465; **Supp. I Part 2:** 714; **Supp. IV Part 1:** 299; **Supp. V:** 127; **Supp. X:** 324; **Supp. XV:** 232
Sterritt, David, **Supp. IV Part 2:** 574
Stetson, Caleb, **IV:** 178
Stetson, Charles Walter, **Supp. XI:** 195, 196, 197, 202, 204, 209
Steve Nelson, American Radical (Nelson), **Supp. XVIII:** 226
Stevens, Mrs. Wallace (Elsie Kachel), **IV:** 75
Stevens, Wallace, **I:** 60, 61, 266, 273, 462, 521, 528, 540–541; **II:** 56, 57, 530, 552, 556; **III:** 19, 23, 194, 216, 270–271, 272, 278, 279, 281, 453, 463, 493, 509, 521, 523, 600, 605, 613, 614; **IV:** **73–96,** 140, 141, 332, 402, 415; **Retro. Supp. I:** 67, 89, 193, 284, 288, **295–315,** 335, 403, 411, 416, 417, 422; **Retro. Supp. II:** 40, 44, 326; **Supp. I Part 1:** 80, 82, 257; **Supp. II Part 1:** 9, 18; **Supp. III Part 1:** 2, 3, 12, 20, 48, 239, 318, 319, 344; **Supp. III Part 2:** 611; **Supp. IV Part 1:** 72, 393; **Supp. IV Part 2:** 619, 620, 621, 634; **Supp. IX:** 41; **Supp. V:** 337; **Supp. VIII:** 21, 102, 195, 271, 292; **Supp. X:** 58; **Supp. XI:** 123, 191, 312; **Supp. XIII:** 44, 45; **Supp. XV:** 39, 41, 92, 115, 250, 261, 298, 302, 306, 307; **Supp. XVI:** 64, 158, 202, 210, 288; **Supp. XVII:** 36, 42, 110, 129, 130, 240, 241
"Stevens and the Idea of the Hero" (Bromwich), **Retro. Supp. I:** 305
Stevenson, Adlai, **II:** 49; **III:** 581
Stevenson, Anne, **Supp. XV:** 121; **Supp. XVII:** 74
Stevenson, Burton E., **Supp. XIV:** 120
Stevenson, David, **Supp. XI:** 230
Stevenson, Robert Louis, **I:** 2, 53; **II:** 283, 290, 311, 338; **III:** 328; **IV:** 183–184, 186, 187; **Retro. Supp. I:** 224, 228; **Supp. I Part 1:** 49; **Supp. II Part 1:** 404–405; **Supp. IV Part 1:** 298, 314; **Supp. VIII:** 125; **Supp. XIII:** 75; **Supp. XIV:** 40; **Supp. XVII:** 69
Stevick, Robert D., **III:** 509
Stewart, Dugald, **II:** 8, 9; **Supp. I Part 1:** 151, 159; **Supp. I Part 2:** 422
Stewart, George, **Supp. XVIII:** 138
Stewart, Jeffrey C., **Supp. XIV:** 196, 209, 210
Stewart, Randall, **II:** 244
Stewart, Robert E., **Supp. XI:** 216
Stickeen (Muir), **Supp. IX:** 182
"Sticks and Stones" (L. Michaels), **Supp. XVI:** 205
Sticks and Stones (Mumford), **Supp. II Part 2:** 475, 483, 487–488
Sticks & Stones (Matthews), **Supp. IX:** 154, 155, 157, 158
Stieglitz, Alfred, **Retro. Supp. I:** 416; **Retro. Supp. II:** 103; **Supp. VIII:** 98; **Supp. XVII:** 96
"Stigmata" (Oates), **Supp. II Part 2:** 520
Stiles, Ezra, **II:** 108, 122; **IV:** 144, 146, 148
Still, William Grant, **Retro. Supp. I:** 203
"Stillborn" (Plath), **Supp. I Part 2:** 544
"Still Here" (Hughes), **Retro. Supp. I:** 211
"Still Just Writing" (Tyler), **Supp. IV Part 2:** 658
"Still Life" (Hecht), **Supp. X:** 68
"Still Life" (Malamud), **Supp. I Part 2:** 450
"Still Life" (Sandburg), **III:** 584
"Still Life: Moonlight Striking up on a Chess-Board" (Lowell), **II:** 528
"Still Life Or" (Creeley), **Supp. IV Part 1:** 141, 150, 158
Still Life with Oysters and Lemon (Doty), **Supp. XI:** 119, 121, **133–134**
Still Life with Woodpecker (Robbins), **Supp. X:** 260, **271–274,** 282
"Still Moment, A" (Welty), **IV:** 265; **Retro. Supp. I:** 347
Stillness (Gardner), **Supp. VI:** 74
"Stillness in the Air" (Dickinson), **Supp. XV:** 261
Stillness of Dancing, The (Bierds), **Supp. XVII:** **27–28**
"Still Small Voices, The" (Fante), **Supp. XI:** 164
Still Such (Salter), **Supp. IX:** 246
"Still the Place Where Creation Does Some Work on Itself" (Davis), **Supp. IV Part 1:** 68
Stimpson, Catharine R., **Supp. IV Part 2:** 686
Stimson, Eleanor Kenyon. *See* Brooks, Mrs. Van Wyck
"Stimulants, Poultices, Goads" (Wright), **Supp. XV:** 349
"Stings" (Plath), **Retro. Supp. II:** 255; **Supp. I Part 2:** 541
"Stirling Street September" (Baraka), **Supp. II Part 1:** 51
Stirner, Max, **II:** 27
"Stirrup-Cup, The" (Lanier), **Supp. I Part 1:** 364
Stitt, Peter, **Supp. IV Part 1:** 68; **Supp. IV Part 2:** 628; **Supp. IX:** 152, 163, 291, 299; **Supp. XI:** 311, 317; **Supp. XIII:** 87; **Supp. XV:** 98, 99
Stivers, Valerie, **Supp. X:** 311
St. John, David, **Supp. XV:** 73, 253
Stock, Noel, **III:** 479
Stockton, Frank R., **I:** 201
Stoddard, Charles Warren, **I:** 193, 195, 196; **Supp. II Part 1:** 192, 341, 351

Stoddard, Elizabeth, **II:** 275; **Supp. XV: 269–291**
Stoddard, Richard, **Supp. I Part 1:** 372
Stoddard, Richard Henry, **Supp. XV:** 269, 271, 272, 273, 274, 278, 279, 286
Stoddard, Solomon, **I:** 545, 548; **IV:** 145, 148
Stoffman, Judy, **Supp. XVIII:** 97
Stoic, The (Dreiser), **I:** 497, 502, 508, 516; **Retro. Supp. II:** 95, 96, 101, 108
Stokes, Geoffrey, **Supp. XV:** 256
Stokes, Olivia Egleston Phelps, **Supp. XVIII:** 261
"Stolen Calf, The" (Dunbar), **Supp. II Part 1:** 196
Stolen Jew, The (Neugeboren), **Supp. XVI: 222–224,** 225
Stolen Past, A (Knowles), **Supp. XII:** 249
Stollman, Aryeh Lev, **Supp. XVII:** 49
Stolmar, Thomas, **Supp. XVIII:** 138
"Stone" (Ozick), **Supp. XVII:** 50
Stone, Edward, **III:** 479
Stone, I. F., **Supp. XIV:** 3
Stone, Irving, **II:** 463, 466, 467
Stone, Oliver, **Supp. XIV:** 48, 316
Stone, Phil, **II:** 55
Stone, Richard, **Supp. XIV:** 54
Stone, Robert, **Supp. V: 295–312; Supp. X:** 1
Stone, Rosetta (pseudonym). *See* Geisel, Theodor Seuss (Dr. Seuss)
Stone, Wilmer, **Supp. I Part 1:** 49
Stone and the Shell, The (Hay), **Supp. XIV:** 122, 123, 127, 130
"Stone Bear, The" (Haines), **Supp. XII:** 206–207, 212
"Stone City" (Proulx), **Supp. VII:** 251–253
Stone Country (Sanders), **Supp. XVI:** 271–272
Stone Diaries, The (Shields), **Supp. VII:** 307, 315, 324–326, 327
"Stone Dreams" (Kingsolver), **Supp. VII:** 203
Stone Harp, The (Haines), **Supp. XII: 204,** 205, 206, 207
Stonemason, The (McCarthy), **Supp. VIII:** 175, 187
"Stones" (Hoffman), **Supp. XVIII:** 86
"Stones" (Kumin), **Supp. IV Part 2:** 447
"Stones, The" (Plath), **Supp. I Part 2:** 535, 539
"Stones in My Passway, Hellhounds on My Trail" (Boyle), **Supp. VIII:** 15
Stones of Florence, The (McCarthy), **II:** 562
"Stone Walls" (Sarton), **Supp. VIII:** 259
"Stop" (Wilbur), **Supp. III Part 2:** 556
"Stop Me If You've Heard This One" (Lardner), **II:** 433
Stopover: Tokyo (Marquand), **III:** 53, 57, 61, 70
Stoppard, Tom, **Retro. Supp. I:** 189
"Stopping by Woods" (Frost), **II:** 154
"Stopping by Woods on a Snowy Evening" (Frost), **Retro. Supp. I:** 129, 133, 134, 135, 139
Stopping Westward (Richards), **II:** 396
"Stop Player. Joke No. 4" (Gaddis), **Supp. IV Part 1:** 280
Stop-Time (Conroy), **Supp. XVI: 63–71,** 72, 75, 76–77
Store, The (Stribling), **Supp. VIII:** 126
"*Store* and *Mockingbird:* Two Pulitzer Novels about Alabama" (Going), **Supp. VIII:** 126
Storer, Edward, **Supp. I Part 1:** 261, 262
Stories, Fables and Other Diversions (Nemerov), **III:** 268–269, 285
Stories: Elizabeth Stoddard, **Supp. XV:** 270
"Stories for Sale" (Kolba), **Supp. XVIII:** 257
Stories for the Sixties (Yates, ed.), **Supp. XI:** 343
Stories from Our Living Past (Prose), **Supp. XVI:** 251
Stories from the Italian Poets (Hunt), **Supp. XV:** 175
Stories from the Old Testament Retold (L. P. Smith), **Supp. XIV:** 342
Stories from World Literature, **Supp. IX:** 4
"Stories in the Snow" (Leopold), **Supp. XIV:** 183
Stories of an Imaginary Childhood (Bukiet), **Supp. XVII: 41–44,** 45
Stories of F. Scott Fitzgerald, The (Cowley, ed.), **Retro. Supp. I:** 115
Stories of F. Scott Fitzgerald, The (Fitzgerald), **II:** 94
Stories of Modern America, **Supp. IX:** 4
Stories of Stephen Dixon, The (Dixon), **Supp. XII:** 152
Stories of the Spanish Civil War (Hemingway), **II:** 258
Stories Revived (James), **II:** 322
Stories that Could Be True (Stafford), **Supp. XI: 325–327**
Storm, The (Buechner), **Supp. XII: 54–57**
"Storm, The" (Chopin), **Retro. Supp. II:** 60, 68; **Supp. I Part 1:** 218, 224
"Storm Fear" (Frost), **II:** 153; **Retro. Supp. I:** 127
"Storm Ship, The" (Irving), **II:** 309
"Storm Warnings" (Kingsolver), **Supp. VII:** 207–208
"Stormy Weather" (Ellison), **Supp. II Part 1:** 233
"Story" (Everwine), **Supp. XV:** 89
"Story, A" (Jarrell), **II:** 371
Story, Richard David, **Supp. IV Part 2:** 575, 588
"Story about Chicken Soup, A" (Simpson), **Supp. IX: 272–273**
"Story about the Anteater, The" (Benét), **Supp. XI:** 53
"Story About the Body, A" (Hass), **Supp. VI: 107–108**
"Story Hearer, The" (Paley), **Supp. VI:** 230, 231
"Story Hour" (Hay), **Supp. XIV:** 124
"Story Hour" (Jarman), **Supp. XVII:** 116
Story Hour: A Second Look at Cinderella, Bluebeard, and Company (Hay), **Supp. XIV:** 119, 124, 125, 132, 133
Story of a Country Town, The (Howe), **I:** 106
Story of a Lover, The (Hapgood), **Supp. XVII:** 99, 100, 104
Story of an American Family, The (N. Boyce), **Supp. XVII:** 97
"Story of an Hour, The" (Chopin), **Retro. Supp. II:** 72; **Supp. I Part 1:** 212–213, 216
Story of a Novel, The (Wolfe), **IV:** 456, 458
"Story of a Proverb, The" (Lanier), **Supp. I Part 1:** 365
"Story of a Proverb, The: A Fairy Tale for Grown People" (Lanier), **Supp. I Part 1:** 365
Story of a Story and Other Stories, The: A Novel (Dixon), **Supp. XII:** 155
Story of a Wonder Man, The (Lardner), **II:** 433–434
"Story of a Year, The" (James), **Retro. Supp. I:** 218
Story of G.I. Joe, The (film, Wellman), **Supp. XVII:** 61, 62
"Story of Gus, The" (A. Miller), **III:** 147–148
"Story of How a Wall Stands, A" (Ortiz), **Supp. IV Part 2:** 499, 507
Story of Mount Desert Island, Maine, The (Morison), **Supp. I Part 2:** 494
Story of My Boyhood and Youth, The (Muir), **Supp. IX: 172–174,** 176
Story of My Father, The: A Memoir (Miller), **Supp. XII:** 301
Story of O, The (Réage), **Supp. XII:** 9, 10
Story of Our Lives, The (Strand), **Supp. IV Part 2:** 620, 628–629, 629
"Story of Poppy Van Buster, The" (Briggs), **Supp. XVIII:** 8
Story of the Normans, The, Told Chiefly in Relation to Their Conquest of England (Jewett), **II:** 406
Story of the Telegraph, The (Briggs, and Maverick), **Supp. XVIII:** 4
"Story of Toby, The" (Melville), **III:** 76
"Story of To-day, A" (Davis), **Supp. XVI:** 88, 89. *See also Margret Howth*
Story of Utopias, The (Mumford), **Supp. II Part 2:** 475, 483–486, 495
Story of Wine in California, The (M. F. K. Fisher), **Supp. XVII:** 88
Story on Page One, The (Odets), **Supp. II Part 2:** 546
"Storyteller" (Silko), **Supp. IV Part 2:** 569
Storyteller (Silko), **Supp. IV Part 2:** 558, 559, 560, 561, **566–570**
"*Storyteller:* Grandmother Spider's Web" (Danielson), **Supp. IV Part 2:** 569
"Storyteller's Notebook, A" (Carver), **Supp. III Part 1:** 142–143
Story Teller's Story, A: The Tale of an American Writer's Journey through His Own Imaginative World and through the World of Facts ... (Anderson), **I:** 98, 101, 114, 117
"Story That Could Be True, A" (Stafford), **Supp. XI:** 326
"Stout Gentleman, The" (Irving), **II:** 309
Stover at Yale (Johnson), **III:** 321
Stowe, Calvin, **IV:** 445; **Supp. I Part 2:** 587, 588, 590, 596, 597
Stowe, Charles, **Supp. I Part 2:** 581, 582

Stowe, Eliza, **Supp. I Part 2:** 587
Stowe, Harriet Beecher, **II:** 274, 399, 403, 541; **Retro. Supp. I:** 34, 246; **Retro. Supp. II:** 4, 138, 156; **Supp. I Part 1:** 30, 206, 301; **Supp. I Part 2: 579–601; Supp. III Part 1:** 154, 168, 171; **Supp. IX:** 33; **Supp. X:** 223, 246, 249, 250; **Supp. XI:** 193; **Supp. XIII:** 141, 295; **Supp. XV:** 278; **Supp. XVI:** 82, 85
Stowe, Samuel Charles, **Supp. I Part 2:** 587
Stowe, William, **Supp. IV Part 1:** 129
Strachey, Lytton, **I:** 5; **IV:** 436; **Retro. Supp. I:** 59; **Supp. I Part 2:** 485, 494; **Supp. XIV:** 342; **Supp. XVI:** 191
"Stradivari" (Bierds), **Supp. XVII:** 28
Straight Cut (Bell), **Supp. X:** 5, **6–7,** 10
Straight Man (Russo), **Supp. XII: 335–339,** 340
Straits: Poems (Koch), **Supp. XV:** 184
Strand, Mark, **Supp. IV Part 2: 619–636; Supp. IX:** 155; **Supp. V:** 92, 332, 337, 338, 343; **Supp. XI:** 139, 145; **Supp. XII:** 254; **Supp. XIII:** 76; **Supp. XV:** 74
Strand, Paul, **Supp. VIII:** 272
Strandberg, Victor, **Supp. V:** 273
"Strange Beautiful Woman, A" (Nelson), **Supp. XVIII:** 173
Strange Case of Dr. Jekyll and Mr. Hyde, The (Stevenson), **II:** 290
Strange Children, The (Gordon), **II:** 196, 197, 199, 211–213
Strange Fire (Bukiet), **Supp. XVII: 46**
"Strange Fruit" (Harjo), **Supp. XII:** 224, 225
"Strange Fruit" (song), **Supp. I Part 1:** 80; **Supp. XVIII:** 228
Strange Interlude (O'Neill), **III:** 391, 397–398; **IV:** 61
Stranger, The (Camus), **I:** 53, 292; **Supp. VIII:** 11; **Supp. XV:** 352
"Stranger, The" (Rich), **Supp. I Part 2:** 555, 560
"Stranger, The" (Salinger), **III:** 552–553
"Stranger in My Own Life, A: Alienation in American Indian Poetry and Prose" (Gunn Allen), **Supp. IV Part 1:** 322
"Stranger in the Village" (Baldwin), **Retro. Supp. II:** 3; **Supp. I Part 1:** 54; **Supp. IV Part 1:** 10
"Stranger in Town" (Hughes), **Supp. I Part 1:** 334
"Strangers" (Howe), **Supp. VI:** 120
Strangers and Wayfarers (Jewett), **Retro. Supp. II:** 138
"Strangers from the Horizon" (Merwin), **Supp. III Part 1:** 356
Strangers on a Train (Highsmith), **Supp. IV Part 1:** 132
"Strange Story, A" (Taylor), **Supp. V:** 323
"Strange Story, A" (Wylie), **Supp. I Part 2:** 723
Strange Things (Atwood), **Supp. XIII:** 35
"Strato in Plaster" (Merrill), **Supp. III Part 1:** 328
Straus, Ralph, **Supp. XIII:** 168
Straus, Roger, **Supp. VIII:** 82; **Supp. XV:** 59
Strauss, Harold, **Supp. XV:** 137
Strauss, Johann, **I:** 66
Strauss, Richard, **IV:** 316
Strauss, Robert, **Supp. XI:** 141, 142
Stravinsky (De Schloezer), **III:** 474
Stravinsky, Igor, **Retro. Supp. I:** 378; **Supp. IV Part 1:** 81; **Supp. XI:** 133; **Supp. XV:** 265
"Stravinsky's Three Pieces 'Grotesques,' for String Quartet" (Lowell), **II:** 523
Straw, The (O'Neill), **III:** 390
"Stray Document, A" (Pound), **II:** 517
Streaks of the Tulip, The: Selected Criticism (W. J. Smith), **Supp. XIII:** 333, 334, 344, **347–348**
Streamline Your Mind (Mursell), **Supp. I Part 2:** 608
"Street, Cloud" (Ríos), **Supp. IV Part 2:** 549
Street, The (Petry), **Supp. XVIII:** 286
Streetcar Named Desire, A (T. Williams), **IV:** 382, 383, 385, 386, 387, 389–390, 395, 398; **Supp. IV Part 1:** 359
Street in Bronzeville, A (Brooks), **Retro. Supp. I:** 208; **Supp. III Part 1:** 74–78
"Street Moths" (X. J. Kennedy), **Supp. XV:** 170
"Street Musicians" (Ashbery), **Supp. III Part 1:** 18
"Street off Sunset, A" (Jarrell), **II:** 387
"Streets" (Dixon), **Supp. XII: 145–146**
Streets in the Moon (MacLeish), **III:** 5, 8–11, 15, 19
Streets of Laredo (McMurtry), **Supp. V:** 230
"Streets of Laredo" (screenplay) (McMurtry and Ossana), **Supp. V:** 226, 230
Streets of Night (Dos Passos), **I:** 478, 479–480, 481, 488
Streitfield, David, **Supp. XIII:** 234; **Supp. XVI:** 63
"Strength of Fields, The" (Dickey), **Supp. IV Part 1:** 176, 184–185
Strength of Fields, The (Dickey), **Supp. IV Part 1:** 178
"Strength of Gideon, The" (Dunbar), **Supp. II Part 1:** 212
Strength of Gideon and Other Stories, The (Dunbar), **Supp. II Part 1:** 211, 212
"Strenuous Artistry" (Zagarell), **Supp. XV:** 281
Strether, Lambert, **II:** 313
Stribling, T. S., **Supp. VIII:** 126
Strickland, Joe (pseudonym). *See* Arnold, George W.
"Strictly Bucolic" (Simic), **Supp. VIII:** 278
Strictly Business (O. Henry), **Supp. II Part 1:** 410
"Strike, The" (Olsen), **Supp. XIII:** 292, 297
"Strikers" (Untermeyer), **Supp. XV:** 296
Strindberg, August, **I:** 78; **III:** 145, 165, 387, 390, 391, 392, 393; **IV:** 17; **Supp. XVII:** 100
"String, The" (Dickey), **Supp. IV Part 1:** 179
String Light (Wright), **Supp. XV: 345–346**
"Strivings of the Negro People" (Du Bois), **Supp. II Part 1:** 167
Stroby, W. C., **Supp. XIV:** 26
Strohbach, Hermann, **Supp. XI:** 242
"Stroke of Good Fortune, A" (O'Connor), **III:** 344; **Retro. Supp. II:** 229, 232
Strom, Stephen, **Supp. XII:** 223
Strong, Anna Louise, **Supp. XVIII:** 238
Strong, George Templeton, **IV:** 321
Strong, Josiah, **Supp. XIV:** 64
"Strong Draughts of Their Refreshing Minds" (Dickinson), **Retro. Supp. I:** 46
Strong Opinions (Nabokov), **Retro. Supp. I:** 263, 266, 270, 276
"Strong Women" (Dorman), **Supp. XI:** 240
Strout, Elizabeth, **Supp. X:** 86
Structure of Nations and Empires, The (Niebuhr), **III:** 292, 308
"Structure of Rime, The" (Duncan), **Supp. XVI:** 287
Struggle, The (film; Griffith), **Supp. XVI:** 191
"Strumpet Song" (Plath), **Retro. Supp. II:** 246; **Supp. I Part 2:** 536
Strunk, William, **Supp. I Part 2:** 652, 662, 670, 671, 672
Strunsky, Anna, **II:** 465
"Strut for Roethke, A" (Berryman), **I:** 188
Strychacz, Thomas F., **Supp. XVI:** 69–70
Stuart, Dabney, **Supp. XVIII:** 79
Stuart, Gilbert, **I:** 16
Stuart, J. E. B., **III:** 56
Stuart, Michael, **Supp. XV:** 140
Stuart Little (White), **Supp. I Part 2:** 655–658
"Student, The" (Moore), **III:** 212, 215
"Student of Salmanaca, The" (Irving), **II:** 309
"Student's Wife, The" (Carver), **Supp. III Part 1:** 141
Studies in American Indian Literature: Critical Essays and Course Designs (Gunn Allen), **Supp. IV Part 1:** 324, 333
Studies in Classic American Literature (Lawrence), **II:** 102; **III:** 33; **IV:** 333; **Retro. Supp. I:** 421
Studies in Short Fiction (Malin), **Supp. XVI:** 71
"Studs" (Farrell), **II:** 25, 28, 31
Studs Lonigan: A Trilogy (Farrell), **II:** 25, 26, 27, 31–34, 37, 38, 41–42
"Study of Images" (Stevens), **IV:** 79
"Study of Lanier's Poems, A" (Kent), **Supp. I Part 1:** 373
Study of Milton's Prosody (Bridges), **II:** 537
"Study of the Negro Problems, The" (Du Bois), **Supp. II Part 1:** 165
Stuewe, Paul, **Supp. IV Part 1:** 68
Stuhlmann, Gunther, **Supp. X:** 182, 184, 185, 187
Stultifera Navis (Brant), **III:** 447
Sturak, John Thomas, **Supp. XIII:** 162, 163, 165, 168
Sturgeon, Theodore, **Supp. XVIII:** 145

Sturgis, George, **III:** 600
Sturgis, Howard, **IV:** 319; **Retro. Supp. I:** 367, 373
Sturgis, Susan, **III:** 600
Sturm, Margaret. *See* Millar, Margaret
Stuttaford, Genevieve, **Supp. IX:** 279
Stuyvesant, Peter, **II:** 301
"Style" (Nemerov), **III:** 275
Styles of Radical Will (Sontag), **Supp. III Part 2:** 451, 459, 460–463
Styne, Jule, **Supp. XVI:** 193
Styron, William, **III:** 40; **IV:** 4, **97–119,** 216; **Supp. IX:** 208; **Supp. V:** 201; **Supp. X:** 15–16, 250; **Supp. XI:** 229, 231, 343; **Supp. XIV:** 82; **Supp. XVI:** 235–236
Suares, J. C., **Supp. IV Part 1:** 234
Suarez, Ernest, **Supp. IV Part 1:** 175; **Supp. V:** 180
"Sub, The" (Dixon), **Supp. XII:** 146
Subjection of Women, The (Mill), **Supp. XI:** 196, 203
"Subjective Necessity for Social Settlements" (Addams), **Supp. I Part 1:** 4
"Subject of Childhood, A" (Paley), **Supp. VI:** 221
"Submarginalia" (Howe), **Supp. IV Part 2:** 422
Substance and Shadow (James), **II:** 344
"Subterranean Homesick Blues" (song, Dylan), **Supp. XVIII:** 25
Subterraneans, The (Kerouac), **Supp. III Part 1:** 225, 227–231
"Subtitle" (Kees), **Supp. XV:** 139
Subtreasury of American Humor, A (White and White), **Supp. I Part 2:** 668
"Suburban Culture, Imaginative Wonder: The Fiction of Frederick Barthelme" (Brinkmeyer), **Supp. XI:** 38
Suburban Sketches (Howells), **II:** 274, 277
"Subversive Element, The" (Ryan as Quin), **Supp. XVIII:** 230
"Subverted Flower, The" (Frost), **Retro. Supp. I:** 139
"Subway, The" (Tate), **IV:** 128
"Subway Singer, The" (Clampitt), **Supp. IX:** 45
"Success" (Mora), **Supp. XIII:** 217
Successful Love and Other Stories (Schwartz), **Supp. II Part 2:** 661, 665
Succession, The: A Novel of Elizabeth and James (Garrett), **Supp. VII:** 104–107, 108
"Success is counted sweetest" (Dickinson), **Retro. Supp. I:** 30, 31–32, 38; **Supp. XV:** 126
Success Stories (Banks), **Supp. V:** 14–15
"Success Story" (Banks), **Supp. V:** 15
"Such Counsels You Gave to Me" (Jeffers), **Supp. II Part 2:** 433
Such Silence (Milburn), **Supp. XI:** 242
"Such Things Happen Only in Books" (Wilder), **IV:** 365
Suddenly, Last Summer (film) (Vidal), **Supp. IV Part 2:** 683
Suddenly Last Summer (T. Williams), **I:** 73; **IV:** 382, 383, 385, 386, 387, 389, 390, 391, 392, 395–396, 397, 398
Suder (Everett), **Supp. XVIII: 54–55**
Sudermann, Hermann, **I:** 66
Sugg, Richard P., **Supp. IV Part 1:** 68
"Suggestion from a Friend" (Kenyon), **Supp. VII:** 171
"Suicide" (Barnes), **Supp. III Part 1:** 33
"Suicide off Egg Rock" (Plath), **Supp. I Part 2:** 529, 538
Suicides and Jazzers (Carruth), **Supp. XVI:** 46
"Suicide's Note" (Hughes), **Retro. Supp. I:** 199
"Suitable Surroundings, The" (Bierce), **I:** 203
"Suitcase, The" (Ozick), **Supp. V:** 262, 264
"Suite for Augustus, A" (Dove), **Supp. IV Part 1:** 245
"Suite for Lord Timothy Dexter" (Rukeyser), **Supp. VI:** 283, 285
"Suite from the Firebird" (Stravinsky), **Supp. XI:** 133
"Suitor, The" (Kenyon), **Supp. VII:** 164–165
Sukarno, **IV:** 490
Sukenick, Ronald, **Supp. V:** 39, 44, 46; **Supp. XII:** 139
Sula (Morrison), **Supp. III Part 1:** 362, 364, 367, 368, 379; **Supp. VIII:** 219
Sullivan, Andrew, **Supp. IX:** 135
Sullivan, Frank, **Supp. IX:** 201
Sullivan, Harry Stack, **I:** 59
Sullivan, Jack, **Supp. X:** 86; **Supp. XII:** 331
Sullivan, Noel, **Retro. Supp. I:** 202; **Supp. I Part 1:** 329, 333
Sullivan, Richard, **Supp. VIII:** 124
Sullivan, Walter, **Supp. VIII:** 168
"Sullivan County Sketches" (Crane), **I:** 407, 421
"Sumach and Goldenrod: An American Idyll" (Mumford), **Supp. II Part 2:** 475
Suma Genji (Play), **III:** 466
Sumerian Vistas (Ammons), **Supp. VII:** 34, 35
"Summer" (Emerson), **II:** 10
Summer (Gioia), **Supp. XV:** 117
"Summer" (Lowell), **II:** 554
Summer (Wharton), **IV:** 317; **Retro. Supp. I:** 360, 367, 374, **378–379,** 382
Summer, Bob, **Supp. X:** 1, 5, 6, 42
Summer and Smoke (T. Williams), **IV:** 382, 384, 385, 386, 387, 395, 397, 398; **Supp. IV Part 1:** 84
Summer Anniversaries, The (Justice), **Supp. VII:** 115, 117
"Summer Commentary, A" (Winters), **Supp. II Part 2:** 808
"Summer Day" (O'Hara), **III:** 369
"Summer Days, The" (Oliver), **Supp. VII:** 239
"Summer Night" (Hughes), **Supp. I Part 1:** 325
"Summer Night, A" (Auden), **Supp. II Part 1:** 8
"Summer Night——Broadway" (Untermeyer), **Supp. XV:** 296
"Summer Noon: 1941" (Winters), **Supp. II Part 2:** 811
"Summer of '82" (Merwin), **Supp. III Part 1:** 355–356
Summer on the Lakes in 1843 (Fuller), **Supp. II Part 1:** 279, 295–296
"Summer People" (Hemingway), **II:** 258–259
"Summer People, The" (Jackson), **Supp. IX:** 120
"Summer People, The" (Merrill), **Supp. III Part 1:** 325–326
"Summer Ramble, A" (Bryant), **Supp. I Part 1:** 162, 164
Summers, Claude J., **Supp. IV Part 2:** 680–681; **Supp. XIV:** 161, 169
Summers, Robert, **Supp. IX:** 289
"Summer Solstice, New York City" (Olds), **Supp. X:** 207
"Summer's Reading, A" (Malamud), **Supp. I Part 2:** 430–431, 442
"Summer Storm" (Gioia), **Supp. XV:** 127
"Summer Storm" (Simpson), **Supp. IX:** 268
"'Summertime and the Living ...'" (Hayden), **Supp. II Part 1:** 363, 366
Summertime Island (Caldwell), **I:** 307–308
"Summer: West Side" (Updike), **Retro. Supp. I:** 320
"Summer with Tu Fu, A" (Carruth), **Supp. XVI:** 55, 58
"Summit Beach, 1921" (Dove), **Supp. IV Part 1:** 249
Summoning of Stones, A (Hecht), **Supp. X:** 57, 58, **58–59**
"Summons" (Untermeyer), **Supp. XV:** 296
Summons to Memphis, A (Taylor), **Supp. V:** 313, 314, 327
Summons to the Free, A (Benét), **Supp. XI:** 47
Sumner, Charles, **I:** 3, 15; **Supp. I Part 2:** 685, 687
Sumner, John, **Retro. Supp. II:** 95
Sumner, John B., **I:** 511
Sumner, William Graham, **III:** 102, 108; **Supp. I Part 2:** 640
"Sumptuous Destination" (Wilbur), **Supp. III Part 2:** 553
"Sun" (Moore), **III:** 215
"Sun" (Swenson), **Supp. IV Part 2:** 640
"Sun, Sea, and Sand" (Marquand), **III:** 60
Sun Also Rises, The (Hemingway), **I:** 107; **II:** 68, 90, 249, 251–252, 260, 600; **III:** 36; **IV:** 35, 297; **Retro. Supp. I:** 171, **177–180,** 181, 189; **Supp. I Part 2:** 614; **Supp. XIII:** 263; **Supp. XVIII:** 74
"Sun and Moon" (Kenyon), **Supp. VII:** 168
"Sun and the Still-born Stars, The" (Southern), **Supp. XI:** 295
Sun at Midnight (Soseki; Merwin and Shigematsu, trans.), **Supp. III Part 1:** 353
"Sun Crosses Heaven from West to East Bringing Samson Back to the Womb, The" (R. Bly), **Supp. IV Part 1:** 73
"Sun Dance Shield" (Momaday), **Supp. IV Part 2:** 491

Sunday, Billy, **II:** 449
"Sunday Afternoons" (Komunyakaa), **Supp. XIII:** 127
Sunday after the War (H. Miller), **III:** 184
"Sunday at Home" (Hawthorne), **II:** 231–232
"Sunday Morning" (Stevens), **II:** 552; **III:** 278, 463, 509; **IV:** 92–93; **Retro. Supp. I:** 296, 300, 301, 304, 307, 313; **Supp. XV:** 120; **Supp. XVI:** 210; **Supp. XVII:** 42
"Sunday Morning Apples" (Crane), **I:** 387
"Sunday Morning Prophecy" (Hughes), **Supp. I Part 1:** 334
"Sundays" (B. Kelly), **Supp. XVII:** 124–125
"Sundays" (Salter), **Supp. IX:** 257
"Sundays, They Sleep Late" (Rukeyser), **Supp. VI:** 278
"Sundays of Satin-Legs Smith, The" (Brooks), **Supp. III Part 1:** 74, 75
"Sundays Visiting" (Ríos), **Supp. IV Part 2:** 541
Sundial, The (Jackson), **Supp. IX: 126–127**
Sundog (Harrison), **Supp. VIII: 46–48**
Sun Dogs (R. O. Butler), **Supp. XII: 64–65**
Sun Do Move, The (Hughes), **Supp. I Part 1:** 339
Sundquist, Eric, **Supp. XIV:** 66, 71
"Sunfish" (C. Frost), **Supp. XV:** 100–101, 102
"Sunflower Sutra" (Ginsberg), **Supp. II Part 1:** 317, 321; **Supp. XV:** 215
Sunlight Dialogues, The (Gardner), **Supp. VI:** 63, **68,** 69, 70
"Sunlight Is Imagination" (Wilbur), **Supp. III Part 2:** 549
Sun Out: Selected Poems, 1952–1954 (Koch), **Supp. XV:** 179
"Sunrise" (Lanier), **Supp. I Part 1:** 370
"Sunrise runs for Both, The" (Dickinson), **Retro. Supp. I:** 45
Sunrise with Seamonsters: Travels and Discoveries, 1964–1984 (Theroux), **Supp. VIII:** 311, 313, 323, 325
"Sun Rising" (Donne), **Supp. VIII:** 164
"Sunset" (Ransom), **III:** 484
"Sunset from Omaha Hotel Window" (Sandburg), **III:** 584
Sunset Gun (Parker), **Supp. IX:** 192
Sunset Limited (Burke), **Supp. XIV:** 32, 33
Sunset Limited (Harrison), **Supp. VIII:** 51
"Sunset Maker, The" (Justice), **Supp. VII:** 123
Sunset Maker, The: Poems, Stories, a Memoir (Justice), **Supp. VII:** 116, 118, 119, 123–124
Sunshine Boys, The (film), **Supp. IV Part 2:** 589
Sunshine Boys, The (Simon), **Supp. IV Part 2:** 575, 584–585
"Sunthin' in the Pastoral Line" (Lowell), **Supp. I Part 2:** 415–416
Sun to Sun (Hurston), **Supp. VI:** 154
Sun Tracks (Ortiz), **Supp. IV Part 2:** 499, 500
Sun Under Wood (Hass), **Supp. VI:** 103, 108–109
"Superb Lily, The" (Pinsky), **Supp. VI:** 250
"Super Goat Man" (Lethem), **Supp. XVIII:** 148
"Superman Comes to the Supermarket" (Mailer), **Retro. Supp. II:** 204
"Supermarket in California, A" (Ginsberg), **Supp. XI:** 135
"Supernatural Love" (Schnackenberg), **Supp. XV:** 257, 259–260
Supernatural Love: Poems 1976–1992 (Schnackenberg), **Supp. XV:** 253, 256, 260, 263
Suplee, Curt, **Supp. XVI:** 202
"Supper After the Last, The" (Kinnell), **Supp. III Part 1:** 239
"Supposedly Fun Thing I'll Never Do Again, A" (Wallace), **Supp. X:** 315
Supposedly Fun Thing I'll Never Do Again, A: Essays and Arguments (Wallace), **Supp. X: 314–316**
Suppressed Desires (Glaspell), **Supp. III Part 1:** 178
Suppression of the African Slave Trade to the United States of America, 1638–1870 (Du Bois), **Supp. II Part 1:** 157, 162
Supreme Fiction, The (Stevens), **Supp. XVI:** 158
"Supremes, The" (Jarman), **Supp. XVII:** 115
Sure Hand of God, The (Caldwell), **I:** 297, 302
"Surety and Fidelity Claims" (Stevens), **Retro. Supp. I:** 296, 309
Surface of Earth, The (Price), **Supp. VI:** 261–262
"Surfaces" (Ammons), **Supp. VII:** 36
Surfacing (Atwood), **Supp. XIII:** 20, 21, **22–23,** 24, 33, 35
"Surgeon at 2 A.M." (Plath), **Supp. I Part 2:** 545
Surmmer Knowledge (Schwartz), **Supp. II Part 2:** 662, 665
"Surprise" (Kenyon), **Supp. VII:** 173
Surprised by Sin: The Reader in Paradise Lost (Fish), **Supp. XIV:** 15
"Surround, The Imagining Herself as the Environment,/She Speaks to James Wright at Sundow" (Dickey), **Supp. IV Part 1:** 185
"Survey of Literature" (Ransom), **III:** 480
"Surveyor, The" (H. Roth), **Supp. IX:** 233, 234
Survival (Atwood), **Supp. XIII:** 20, 22, 35
"Survival as Tao, Beginning at 5:00 A.M." (Carruth), **Supp. XVI:** 56
Survival of the Bark Canoe, The (McPhee), **Supp. III Part 1:** 301, 302, 308, 313
Survival This Way: Interviews with American Indian Poets (Bruchac), **Supp. IV Part 2:** 506
"Surviving Love" (Berryman), **I:** 173
Survivor (O. Butler), **Supp. XIII:** 62, 63
Susan and Anna Warner (Foster), **Supp. XVIII:** 265
Susan and God (film; Cukor), **Supp. XVI:** 192
Susanna Moodie: Voice and Vision (Shields), **Supp. VII:** 313
Susan Warner ("Elizabeth Wetherell") (A. Warner), **Supp. XVIII:** 259, 260
Suspect in Poetry, The (Dickey), **Supp. IV Part 1:** 177
"Sustained by Fiction" (Hoffman), **Supp. X:** 90, 92
"Susto" (Ríos), **Supp. IV Part 2:** 553
Sutherland, Donald, **IV:** 38, 44; **Supp. IX:** 254
Sutherland, Efua, **Supp. IV Part 1:** 9, 16
Sutherland-Smith, James, **Supp. X:** 211, 212
Sut Lovingood's Yarns (Harris), **II:** 70
Sutton, Roger, **Supp. X:** 266
Sutton, Walter, **III:** 479
Suttree (McCarthy), **Supp. VIII: 178–180,** 189
Suvero, Mark di, **Supp. IX:** 251
Svevo, Italo, **Supp. XIV:** 112
Swados, Harvey, **Supp. XI:** 222
Swallow, Alan, **Supp. X:** 112, 115, 116, 120, 123
Swallow Barn (J. P. Kennedy), **II:** 313
"Swamp Boy" (Bass), **Supp. XVI:** 20
Swan, Barbara, **Supp. IV Part 2:** 447
Swan, Jon, **Supp. IV Part 1:** 176
Swan Lake (Tchaikovsky), **Supp. IX:** 51
"Swan Legs" (Stern), **Supp. IX:** 299
Swann (Shields), **Supp. VII:** 315, 318–323, 326
Swann, Brian, **Supp. IV Part 2:** 500
Swanson, Gloria, **II:** 429
Swanson, Stevenson, **Supp. XIV:** 111
Swanton, John Reed, **Supp. VIII:** 295
Swan Watch (Schulberg), **Supp. XVIII:** 254
Swanwick, John, **Supp. XV:** 237
Swanwick, Michael, **Supp. XVI:** 128
"Swarm, The" (Plath), **Retro. Supp. II:** 255
"Sway" (Simpson), **Supp. IX:** 276
Sweat (Hurston), **Supp. VI:** 152
Swedenborg, Emanuel, **II:** 5, 10, 321, 342, 343–344, 396
Sweeney Agonistes (Eliot), **I:** 580; **Retro. Supp. I:** 64, 65; **Retro. Supp. II:** 247
"Sweeney Among the Nightingales" (Eliot), **III:** 4
Sweet, Blanche, **Supp. I Part 2:** 391
Sweet, Timothy, **Supp. IV Part 1:** 330
Sweet and Lowdown (film; Allen), **Supp. XV:** 11
Sweet and Sour (O'Hara), **III:** 361
"Sweet Armageddon" (Hoffman), **Supp. XVIII:** 85, 86
Sweet Bird of Youth (T. Williams), **IV:** 382, 383, 385, 386, 387, 388, 389, 390, 391, 392, 395, 396, 398; **Supp. IV Part 1:** 84, 89
Sweet Charity (musical), **Supp. IV Part 2:** 575
Sweet Flypaper of Life, The (Hughes), **Supp. I Part 1:** 335–336

"Sweetheart of the Song Tra Bong, The" (O'Brien), **Supp. V:** 243, 249
"Sweethearts" (Ford), **Supp. V:** 69
Sweet Hereafter, The (Banks), **Supp. V:** 15–16
Sweet Machine (Doty), **Supp. XI:** 121, **131–132,** 135
Sweet Sue (Gurney), **Supp. V:** 105, 107–108
Sweet Sweetback's Baadasss Song (Peebles; film), **Supp. XI:** 17
Sweet Thursday (Steinbeck), **IV:** 50, 52, 64–65
"Sweet Will" (Levine), **Supp. V:** 190
Sweet Will (Levine), **Supp. V:** 178, 187, 189, 190
"Sweet Words on Race" (Hughes), **Retro. Supp. I:** 211
Sweezy, Paul, **Supp. I Part 2:** 645
"Swell-Looking Girl, A" (Caldwell), **I:** 310
Swenson, May, **Retro. Supp. II:** 44; **Supp. IV Part 2: 637–655**
"Swift" (Schwartz), **Supp. II Part 2:** 663
Swift, Jonathan, **I:** 125, 194, 209, 441; **II:** 110, 302, 304–305, 577; **III:** 113; **IV:** 68; **Retro. Supp. I:** 66; **Supp. I Part 2:** 406, 523, 603, 656, 665, 708, 714; **Supp. IV Part 1:** 51; **Supp. IV Part 2:** 692; **Supp. XI:** 105, 209; **Supp. XII:** 276; **Supp. XV:** 258; **Supp. XVI:** 110; **Supp. XVIII:** 2, 12
"Swimmer" (Francis), **Supp. IX:** 82
"Swimmer, The" (Cheever), **Supp. I Part 1:** 185, 187
"Swimmer, The" (Glück), **Supp. V:** 82
"Swimmers" (Untermeyer), **Supp. XV:** 300
"Swimmers, The" (Fitzgerald), **Retro. Supp. I:** 110, 111
"Swimmers, The" (Tate), **IV:** 136
"Swimming" (Harjo), **Supp. XII:** 218
Swinburne, Algernon C., **I:** 50, 384, 568; **II:** 3, 4, 129, 400, 524; **IV:** 135; **Retro. Supp. I:** 100; **Supp. I Part 1:** 79; **Supp. I Part 2:** 422, 552; **Supp. XIV:** 120, 344
"Swinburne as Poet" (Eliot), **I:** 576
Swinger of Birches, A: A Portrait of Robert Frost (Cox), **Retro. Supp. I:** 132
"Swinging on a Birch-Tree" (Larcom), **Supp. XIII:** 147
Switch, The (Dixon), **Supp. XII:** 141
Swope, D. B., **Supp. IX:** 95
Sword Blades and Poppy Seed (Lowell), **II:** 518, 520, 522, 532
Sword of God, The: Jeanne D'Arc (Endore), **Supp. XVII:** 55
Sybil (Auchincloss), **Supp. IV Part 1:** 25
Sybil and Chryssa (S. and A. Warner), **Supp. XVIII:** 264
"Sycamore" (Stern), **Supp. IX:** 294
"Sycamore, The" (Moore), **III:** 216
"Sycamores, The" (Whittier), **Supp. I Part 2:** 699
Sylvester, Johnny, **Supp. I Part 2:** 438
Sylvester, Joshua, **I:** 178, 179; **II:** 18; **III:** 157; **Supp. I Part 1:** 98, 104, 114, 116
Sylvia (Gurney), **Supp. V:** 105
"Sylvia" (Larcom), **Supp. XIII:** 144
"Sylvia" (L. Michaels), **Supp. XVI:** 202, 213
"Sylvia" (Stern), **Supp. IX:** 297
Sylvia: A Fictional Memoir (L. Michaels), **Supp. XVI:** 202, 213
Sylvia Plath: Method and Madness (Butscher), **Supp. I Part 2:** 526
Sylvia Plath: Poetry and Existence (Holbrook), **Supp. I Part 2:** 526–527
"Sylvia's Death" (Sexton), **Supp. II Part 2:** 671, 684, 685
"Symbol and Image in the Shorter Poems of Herman Melville" (Dickey), **Supp. IV Part 1:** 176
Symbolist Movement in Literature, The (Symons), **I:** 50, 569; **Retro. Supp. I:** 55
Symonds, John Addington, **I:** 241, 242, 251, 259; **IV:** 334; **Supp. XIV:** 329, 335
Symons, Arthur, **I:** 50, 569; **Retro. Supp. I:** 55
Symons, Julian, **Supp. IV Part 1:** 343, 351
"Sympathy" (Dunbar), **Supp. IV Part 1:** 15
Sympathy of Souls, A (Goldbarth), **Supp. XII:** 175, 176, **186–187**
"Symphony, The" (Lanier), **Supp. I Part 1:** 352, 360–361, 364; **Supp. I Part 2:** 416
Symposium (Plato), **Retro. Supp. II:** 31; **Supp. IV Part 1:** 391
Symposium: To Kill a Mockingbird (Alabama Law Review), **Supp. VIII:** 127, 128
Symptoms of Being 35 (Lardner), **II:** 434
Synanon (Endore), **Supp. XVII:** 65
Synanon (film, Quine), **Supp. XVII:** 65
Synanon City (Endore), **Supp. XVII:** 65
Synge, John Millington, **I:** 434; **III:** 591–592; **Supp. III Part 1:** 34; **Supp. VIII:** 155
Synthetic Philosophy (Spencer), **II:** 462–463
"Syringa" (Ashbery), **Supp. III Part 1:** 19–21, 25
"Syrinx" (Clampitt), **Supp. IX:** 53
"Syrinx" (Merrill), **Supp. III Part 1:** 328
Syrkin, Marie, **Supp. XIV:** 279, 288, 291
"System, The" (Ashbery), **Supp. III Part 1:** 14, 15, 18, 21–22
System of Dante's Hell, The (Baraka), **Supp. II Part 1:** 39–41, 55
"System of Dante's Inferno, The" (Baraka), **Supp. II Part 1:** 40
"System of Doctor Tarr and Professor Fether, The" (Poe), **III:** 419, 425
System of General Geography, A (Brown), **Supp. I Part 1:** 146
Sze, Mai-mai, **Supp. X:** 291
Szentgyorgyi, Tom, **Supp. IX:** 135, 136, 140, 141–142
Szulc, Tad, **Supp. XVI:** 154
Szymborka, Wislawa, **Supp. XI:** 267
Szymborska, Wislawa, **Supp. XVIII:** 29

T

"T-2 Tanker Blues" (Snyder), **Supp. VIII:** 294
Tabios, Eileen, **Supp. XV:** 214, 225, 226
"Table of Delectable Contents, The" (Simic), **Supp. VIII:** 276
Tabloid Dreams (R. O. Butler), **Supp. XII: 70–72,** 74
Tacey Cromwell (Richter), **Supp. XVIII: 211,** 215, 217
Tacitus, Cornelius, **I:** 485; **II:** 113
Tadic, Novica, **Supp. VIII:** 272
Taft (Patchett), **Supp. XII:** 307, 312, **314–317**
"Tag" (Hughes), **Supp. I Part 1:** 341
Taggard, Genevieve, **IV:** 436
Taggart, John, **Supp. IV Part 2:** 421
Tagore, Rabindranath, **I:** 383
"Taibele and Her Demon" (Singer), **Retro. Supp. II:** 307
Taibl, Erika, **Supp. XV:** 255
"Tailor Shop, The" (H. Miller), **III:** 175
"Tails" (Dixon), **Supp. XII:** 154
Taine, Hippolyte, **I:** 503; **II:** 271; **III:** 323; **IV:** 440, 444
"Tain't So" (Hughes), **Supp. I Part 1:** 330
Takasago (play), **III:** 466
Take Away the Darkness (Bynner), **Supp. XV:** 51
Take Me Back: A Novel (Bausch), **Supp. VII:** 41, 43–45, 46, 49
"Take My Saddle from the Wall: A Valediction" (McMurtry), **Supp. V:** 219
"'Take No for an Answer'" (Didion), **Supp. IV Part 1:** 203
"Take Pity" (Malamud), **Supp. I Part 2:** 427, 428, 435, 436, 437
"Takers, The" (Olds), **Supp. X:** 205
"Take the I Out" (Olds), **Supp. X:** 213
Take the Money and Run (film; Allen), **Supp. XV: 3–4,** 6
"Taking Away the Name of a Nephew" (Ríos), **Supp. IV Part 2:** 545–546
Taking Care of Mrs. Carroll (Monette), **Supp. X:** 153
"Taking of Captain Ball, The" (Jewett), **Retro. Supp. II:** 134
"Taking Out the Lawn Chairs" (Karr), **Supp. XI:** 241
"Taking the Bypass" (J. Epstein), **Supp. XIV:** 110; **Supp. XVI:** 230
"Taking the Forest" (Howe), **Supp. IV Part 2:** 433
"Taking the Lambs to Market" (Kumin), **Supp. IV Part 2:** 455
"Tale, A" (Bogan), **Supp. III Part 1:** 50, 51
Taleb-Khyar, Mohamed, **Supp. IV Part 1:** 242, 243, 244, 247, 257
"Tale of Jerusalem, A" (Poe), **III:** 411
Tale of Possessors Self-Dispossessed, A (O'Neill), **III:** 404
Tale of the Body Thief, The (Rice), **Supp. VII:** 290, 293–294, 297
Tale of Two Cities, A (film), **Supp. I Part 1:** 67
"Tale of Two Liars, A" (Singer), **IV:** 12
Tales (Baraka), **Supp. II Part 1:** 39, 55
Tales (Poe), **III:** 413

Tales and Stories for Black Folks (Bambara, ed.), **Supp. XI:** 1
Tales before Midnight (Benét), **Supp. XI:** 46, 53, 57
Talese, Gay, **Supp. XVI:** 273; **Supp. XVII: 199–211**
Tales of a Traveller (Irving), **II:** 309–310
Tales of a Wayside Inn (Longfellow), **II:** 489, 490, 501, 502, 504–505; **Retro. Supp. II:** 154, **162–165**
Tales of Glauber-Spa (Bryant, ed.), **Supp. I Part 1:** 157
Tales of Manhattan (Auchincloss), **Supp. IV Part 1:** 23
Tales of Men and Ghosts (Wharton), **IV:** 315; **Retro. Supp. I:** 372
Tales of Rhoda, The (Rice), **Supp. VII:** 288
Tales of Soldiers and Civilians (Bierce), **I:** 200–203, 204, 206, 208, 212
Tales of the Argonauts (Harte), **Supp. II Part 1:** 337, 348, 351
Tales of the Fish Patrol (London), **II:** 465
Tales of the Grotesque and Arabesque (Poe), **II:** 273; **III:** 412, 415; **Retro. Supp. II:** 270
Tales of the Jazz Age (Fitzgerald), **II:** 88; **Retro. Supp. I:** 105; **Supp. IX:** 57
"Talisman, A" (Moore), **III:** 195–196
Talisman, The (King), **Supp. V:** 140, 144, 152
"Talkin Bout Sonny" (Bambara), **Supp. XI:** 6–7
"Talking" (Merwin), **Supp. III Part 1:** 354
Talking All Morning (R. Bly), **Supp. IV Part 1:** 59, 60, 61, 62, 64, 65
Talking Dirty to the Gods (Komunyakaa), **Supp. XIII: 130–131**
"Talking Horse" (Malamud), **Supp. I Part 2:** 435
Talking Soft Dutch (McCarriston), **Supp. XIV: 260–263,** 266, 270, 271
"Talking to Barr Creek" (Wagoner), **Supp. IX:** 328
"Talking to Sheep" (Sexton), **Supp. II Part 2:** 695
Talking to the Sun: An Illustrated Anthology of Poems for Young People (Koch and Farrell, eds.), **Supp. XV:** 188
"Talk of Heroes" (C. Bly), **Supp. XVI:** 34
"Talk of the Town" (*The New Yorker* column), **IV:** 215; **Supp. IV Part 1:** 53, 54
"Talk with the Yellow Kid, A" (Bellow), **I:** 151
Tallent, Elizabeth, **Supp. IV Part 2:** 570
Tallman, Warren, **Supp. IV Part 1:** 154
TallMountain, Mary, **Supp. IV Part 1:** 324–325
Talma, Louise, **IV:** 357
Talmadge, Constance, **Supp. XVI:** 186, 187, 196
Talmadge, Norma, **Supp. XVI:** 186, 187, 196
Talmadge Girls, The (Loos), **Supp. XVI:** 186, 196
Talmey, Allene, **Supp. IV Part 1:** 197; **Supp. XIII:** 172
Talmud, **IV:** 8, 17
Taltos: Lives of the Mayfair Witches (Rice), **Supp. VII:** 299–300
"Tamar" (Jeffers), **Supp. II Part 2:** 427–428, 436
Tamar and Other Poems (Jeffers), **Supp. II Part 2:** 416, 419
Tambourines to Glory (Hughes), **Supp. I Part 1:** 338–339
"Tame Indians" (Jewett), **Retro. Supp. II:** 141
"Tamerlane" (Poe), **III:** 426
Tamerlane and Other Poems (Poe), **III:** 410
"Tammany Man, The" (Hapgood), **Supp. XVII:** 103
"Tam O'Shanter" (Burns), **II:** 306
Tan, Amy, **Supp. X: 289–300**
Tangential Views (Bierce), **I:** 209
"Tangier 1975" (Bowles), **Supp. IV Part 1:** 94
"Tankas" (McClatchy), **Supp. XII:** 266
Tanner, Laura E., **Supp. X:** 209
Tanner, Tony, **I:** 260, 261; **Retro. Supp. II:** 205; **Supp. IV Part 1:** 285; **Supp. XVI:** 65, 69
Tannhäuser (Wagner), **I:** 315
"Tan Ta Ra, Cries Mars...," (Wagoner), **Supp. IX:** 325
Tao of Physics, The (Capra), **Supp. X:** 261
Tao Teh Ching (Bynner, trans.), **Supp. XV:** 46, 47
Tapahonso, Luci, **Supp. IV Part 1:** 404; **Supp. IV Part 2:** 499, 508
Tape for the Turn of the Year (Ammons), **Supp. VII:** 31–33, 35
"Tapestry" (Ashbery), **Supp. III Part 1:** 22–23
"Tapiama" (Bowles), **Supp. IV Part 1:** 89–90
"Tapiola" (W. C. Williams), **Retro. Supp. I:** 429
Tappan, Arthur, **Supp. I Part 2:** 588
Tapping the White Cane of Solitude (F. Wright), **Supp. XVII:** 243
Taps at Reveille (Fitzgerald), **II:** 94, 96; **Retro. Supp. I:** 113
Tar: A Midwest Childhood (Anderson), **I:** 98, 115; **II:** 27
Tarantino, Quentin, **Supp. IV Part 1:** 356
Tarantula (Dylan), **Supp. XVIII:** 21, 29, **31–32**
Tar Baby (Morrison), **Supp. III Part 1:** 364, 369–372, 379; **Supp. IV Part 1:** 13
Tarbell, Ida, **III:** 322, 580; **Retro. Supp. II:** 101
"Target Study" (Baraka), **Supp. II Part 1:** 49–50, 54
Tarkington, Booth, **II:** 444; **III:** 70; **Retro. Supp. I:** 100; **Supp. XV:** 41
Tarpon (film), **Supp. VIII:** 42
Tarr, Rodger L., **Supp. X:** 222, 224, 226
Tartt, Donna, **Supp. XVIII:** 135
Tartuffe (Molière; Wilbur, trans.), **Supp. III Part 2:** 560
Tarumba, Selected Poems of Jaime Sabines (Levine and Trejo, trans.), **Supp. V:** 178
"Tarzan Is an Expatriate" (Theroux), **Supp. VIII:** 313
Task, The (Cowper), **II:** 304
Tasso, Torquato, **I:** 276
Taste of Palestine, A: Menus and Memories (Shihab), **Supp. XIII:** 273
Tate, Alan, **Supp. XV:** 141
Tate, Allen, **I:** 48, 49, 50, 67, 69, 381, 382, 386, 390, 396, 397, 399, 402, 441, 468; **II:** 197–198, 367, 536, 537, 542, 551, 554; **III:** 424, 428, 454, 482, 483, 485, 493, 495, 496, 497, 499, 500, 517; **IV: 120–143,** 236, 237, 433; **Retro. Supp. I:** 37, 41, 90; **Retro. Supp. II:** 77, 79, 82, 83, 89, 176, 178, 179; **Supp. I Part 1:** 364, 371; **Supp. I Part 2:** 423; **Supp. II Part 1:** 90–91, 96, 98, 103–104, 136, 139, 144, 150, 151, 318; **Supp. II Part 2:** 643; **Supp. III Part 2:** 542; **Supp. V:** 315, 331; **Supp. X:** 1, 52; **Supp. XIV:** 2
Tate, Benjamin Lewis Bogan, **IV:** 127
Tate, Greg, **Supp. XIII:** 233, 237
Tate, James, **Supp. V:** 92, 338; **Supp. VIII:** 39, 279; **Supp. XV:** 250; **Supp. XVII:** 242
Tate, John Allen, **IV:** 127
Tate, Michael Paul, **IV:** 127
Tate, Mrs. Allen (Caroline Gordon). *See* Gordon, Caroline
Tate, Mrs. Allen (Helen Heinz), **IV:** 127
Tate, Mrs. Allen (Isabella Gardner), **IV:** 127
Tate, Nancy, **II:** 197
Tattooed Countess, The (Van Vechten), **I:** 295; **Supp. II Part 2:** 726–728, 738, 742
Tattooed Feet (Nye), **Supp. XIII:** 274
"Tattoos" (McClatchy), **Supp. XII:** 266–267, 268
"Tattoos" (Wright), **Supp. V:** 335, 340
Tatum, Anna, **I:** 516
Tatum, James, **Supp. IV Part 2:** 684
Taupin, René, **II:** 528, 529; **Supp. III Part 2:** 614, 615, 617, 621
Tawney, Richard Henry, **Supp. I Part 2:** 481
Taylor, Bayard, **II:** 275; **Supp. I Part 1:** 350, 361, 362, 365, 366, 372; **Supp. XV:** 269
Taylor, Cora. *See* Howarth, Cora
Taylor, Deems, **III:** 138
Taylor, Edward, **III:** 493; **IV: 144–166; Supp. I Part 1:** 98; **Supp. I Part 2:** 375, 386, 546
Taylor, Eleanor Ross, **Supp. V:** 317, 318
Taylor, Elizabeth, **II:** 588
Taylor, Frank, **III:** 81
Taylor, Frederick Winslow, **Supp. I Part 2:** 644
Taylor, Graham, **Supp. I Part 1:** 5
Taylor, Henry, **Retro. Supp. I:** 212; **Supp. XI:** 317; **Supp. XIII:** 333
Taylor, Henry W., **IV:** 144
Taylor, Jeremy, **II:** 11; **III:** 487; **Supp. I Part 1:** 349; **Supp. XII:** 45; **Supp. XIV:** 344, 345
Taylor, John, **IV:** 149
Taylor, Katherine, **Supp. VIII:** 251
Taylor, Kezia, **IV:** 148

Taylor, Mrs. Edward (Elizabeth Fitch), **IV:** 147, 165
Taylor, Mrs. Edward (Ruth Wyllys), **IV:** 148
Taylor, Nathaniel W., **Supp. I Part 2:** 580
Taylor, Paul, **I:** 293
Taylor, Peter, **Retro. Supp. II:** 179; **Supp. V: 313–329; Supp. XIV:** 3
Taylor, Raynor, **Supp. XV:** 238
Taylor, Richard, **IV:** 146
Taylor, Robert, **Supp. I Part 1:** 294; **Supp. XV:** 135, 138; **Supp. XVI:** 277
Taylor, Stephan, **Supp. XVI:** 203
Taylor, Thomas, **II:** 10
Taylor, William, **IV:** 145–146
Taylor, Zachary, **I:** 3; **II:** 433–434
Tchelitchew, Peter, **II:** 586
Tea and Sympathy (Anderson), **Supp. I Part 1:** 277; **Supp. V:** 108
"Tea at the Palaz of Hoon" (Stevens), **Retro. Supp. I:** 300, 302, 306
"Teacher's Pet" (Thurber), **Supp. I Part 2:** 605–606
"Teaching and Story Telling" (Maclean), **Supp. XIV:** 234
Teaching a Stone to Talk: Expeditions and Encounters (Dillard), **Supp. VI:** 23, 26, 28, 32, 33, 34–35
Teachings of Don B., The (Barthelme), **Supp. IV Part 1:** 53
Teale, Edwin Way, **Supp. XIII:** 7
Teall, Dorothy, **I:** 221
Team Team Team (film), **Supp. IX:** 251
"Tea on the Mountain" (Bowles), **Supp. IV Part 1:** 90
"Tea Party, The" (MacLeish), **III:** 11
"Tears, Idle Tears" (Lord Tennyson), **Supp. XIV:** 8
"Tears of the Pilgrims, The" (McClatchy), **Supp. XII:** 256
Teasdale, Sara, **Retro. Supp. I:** 133; **Supp. I Part 2:** 393, 707; **Supp. XIV:** 127; **Supp. XV:** 295, 297, 301, 305, 307, 308; **Supp. XVII:** 69, 75
Tebeaux, Elizabeth, **Supp. IX:** 109
Technics and Civilization (Mumford), **Supp. I Part 2:** 638; **Supp. II Part 2:** 479, 493, 497
Technics and Human Development (Mumford), **Supp. I Part 2:** 638; **Supp. II Part 2:** 497
"Teddy" (Salinger), **III:** 561–563, 571
"Te Deum" (Reznikoff), **Supp. XIV:** 281
Tedlock, Dennis, **Supp. IV Part 2:** 509
"Teeth Mother Naked at Last, The" (R. Bly), **Supp. IV Part 1:** 63, 68, 73
Teggart, Richard, **Supp. I Part 2:** 650
Tegnér, Esaias, **Retro. Supp. II:** 155
Teilhard de Chardin, Pierre, **Supp. I Part 1:** 314
Telephone, The (film), **Supp. XI:** 309
"Telephone Call, A" (Parker), **Supp. IX: 202–203**
"Telephone Number of the Muse, The" (Justice), **Supp. VII:** 124–125
Telephone Poles and Other Poems (Updike), **IV:** 214, 215
"Television" (Beattie), **Supp. V:** 33
Teller, Edward, **I:** 137
"Telling" (Ortiz), **Supp. IV Part 2:** 509
"Telling It in Black and White: The Importance of the Africanist Presence in *To Kill a Mockingbird*" (Baecker), **Supp. VIII:** 128
Telling Secrets (Buechner), **Supp. XII:** 53–54
"Telling Stories" (Didion), **Supp. IV Part 1:** 197
Telling Stories (Didion), **Supp. IV Part 1:** 197
"Telling the Bees" (Whittier), **Supp. I Part 2:** 694–695
Telling the Little Secrets (J. Burstein), **Supp. XVII:** 44
Telling the Truth: The Gospel as Tragedy, Comedy, and Fairy Tale (Buechner), **Supp. XII:** 53
"Tell Me" (Hughes), **Supp. VIII:** 213
Tell Me, Tell Me (Moore), **III:** 215
Tell Me Again How the White Heron Rises and Flies across the Nacreous River at Twilight toward the Distant Islands (Carruth), **Supp. XVI:**56
Tell Me a Riddle (film), **Supp. XIII:** 295
"Tell Me a Riddle" (Olsen), **Supp. XIII:** 294, 297, 298, **300–302,** 305
Tell Me a Riddle (Olsen), **Supp. XIII:** 294, 296, **298–302,** 303, 305
"Tell Me a Story" (McDermott), **Supp. XVIII:** 177
Tell Me How Long the Train's Been Gone (Baldwin), **Retro. Supp. II:** 9, **11–12,** 14; **Supp. I Part 1:** 48, 52, 63–65, 67
"Tell Me My Fortune" (Epstein), **Supp. XII:** 163
Tell Me Your Answer True (Sexton), **Supp. II Part 2:** 683
Tell My Horse (Hurston), **Supp. VI:** 149, 156, 158
"Tell-Tale Heart, The" (Poe), **III:** 413, 414–415, 416; **Retro. Supp. II:** 267, 269, 270
"Tell the Women We're Going" (Carver), **Supp. III Part 1:** 138, 144
"Telluride Blues——A Hatchet Job" (Abbey), **Supp. XIII:** 10
Telushkin, Dvorah, **Retro. Supp. II:** 317
Temblor (Howe), **Supp. IV Part 2:** 431
Tempering of Eugene O'Neill, The (D. Alexander), **Supp. XVII:** 99
"Temper of Steel, The" (Jones), **Supp. XI:** 218
Tempers, The (W. C. Williams), **Retro. Supp. I: 413–414,** 415, 416, 424
Tempest, The (Shakespeare), **I:** 394; **II:** 12; **III:** 40, 61, 263; **Retro. Supp. I:** 61; **Supp. IV Part 2:** 463; **Supp. V:** 302–303; **Supp. XII:** 54–57; **Supp. XV:** 255, 256
Temple, Minnie, **II:** 323
Temple, The (Herbert), **IV:** 145, 153
Temple, William, **III:** 303
Temple House (E. Stoddard), **Supp. XV:** 273, **284–286**
Temple of My Familiar, The (Walker), **Supp. III Part 2:** 521, 527, 529, 535, 537; **Supp. IV Part 1:** 14
"Temple of the Holy Ghost, A" (O'Connor), **III:** 344, 352; **Retro. Supp. II:** 232
Templin, Charlotte, **Supp. V:** 116
"Temporary Shelter" (Gordon), **Supp. IV Part 1:** 306
Temporary Shelter (Gordon), **Supp. IV Part 1:** 299, 305–307
Temptation Game, The (Gardner), **Supp. VI:** 72
"Temptation of St. Anthony, The" (Barthelme), **Supp. IV Part 1:** 47
Temptations, The, **Supp. X:** 242
"Tenancy, A" (Merrill), **Supp. III Part 1:** 322, 323
"Tenant" (Hoffman), **Supp. XVIII:** 86
Tenants, The (Malamud), **Supp. I Part 2:** 448–450
Ten Commandments (McClatchy), **Supp. XII: 262–265**
Ten Days That Shook the World (Reed), **II:** 577; **Supp. X:** 136; **Supp. XVIII:** 225
Tendencies in Modern American Poetry (Lowell), **II:** 529
"Tender, Hilarious Reminiscences of Life in Mythical Lake Wobegon" (MacDougall), **Supp. XVI:** 174
Tender Buttons (G. Stein), **I:** 103, 105; **IV:** 27, 42–43; **Retro. Supp. II:** 331; **Supp. XV:** 347
"Tenderfoot" (Haines), **Supp. XII:** 209
Tender Is the Night (Fitzgerald), **I:** 375; **II:** 79, 84, 91, 95–96, 97, 98, 420; **Retro. Supp. I:** 105, 108, 109, **110–112,** 114; **Supp. IX:** 59, 60, 61; **Supp. XV:** 197
"Tenderloin" (Crane), **I:** 408
"Tenderly" (Dobyns), **Supp. XIII:** 86–87
'Tender Man, A" (Bambara), **Supp. XI:** 9–10
"Tenderness" (Dunn), **Supp. XI:** 149, 150
"Tender Offer, The" (Auchincloss), **Supp. IV Part 1:** 34
"Tender Organizations, The" (C. Bly), **Supp. XVI:** 40, 42
"Tenebrae" (Komunyakaa), **Supp. XIII:** 132
"Ten Forty-Four" (Kingsolver), **Supp. VII:** 208
Ten Indians (Bell), **Supp. X:** 7, **12**
"Ten Neglected American Writers Who Deserve to Be Better Known" (Cantor), **Supp. IV Part 1:** 285
Tennent, Gilbert, **I:** 546
Tennessee Day in St. Louis (Taylor), **Supp. V:** 324
"Tennessee's Partner" (Harte), **Supp. II Part 1:** 345, 348–350
"Tennis" (Pinsky), **Supp. VI:** 241, 242
Tennis Court Oath, The (Ashbery), **Supp. III Part 1:** 7, 9, 12, 14, 26
Ten North Frederick (O'Hara), **III:** 361
Tennyson, Alfred, Lord, **I:** 587–588; **II:** 18, 82, 273, 338, 404, 439, 604; **III:** 5, 409, 469, 485, 511, 521, 523; **Retro. Supp. I:** 100, 325; **Retro. Supp. II:** 135; **Supp. I Part 1:** 349, 356; **Supp. I Part 2:** 410, 416, 552; **Supp. IX:**

19; **Supp. X:** 157; **Supp. XIII:** 111; **Supp. XIV:** 40, 120; **Supp. XV:** 275; **Supp. XVIII:** 78
"Ten O'Clock News" (Ortiz), **Supp. IV Part 2:** 503–504
Ten Poems (Dove), **Supp. IV Part 1:** 244
Ten Poems of Francis Ponge Translated by Robert Bly and Ten Poems of Robert Bly Inspired by the Poems by Francis Ponge (R. Bly), **Supp. IV Part 1:** 71
"Tension in Poetry" (Tate), **IV:** 128, 129, 135
Tenth Muse, The (Bradstreet), **Supp. I Part 1:** 102, 103, 114
"Tent on the Beach, The" (Whittier), **Supp. I Part 2:** 703
"Teodoro Luna Confesses after Years to His Brother, Anselmo the Priest, Who Is Required to Understand, But Who Understands Anyway, More Than People Think" (Ríos), **Supp. IV Part 2:** 552
Teodoro Luna's Two Kisses (Ríos), **Supp. IV Part 2:** 550–552, 553
"Tepeyac" (Cisneros), **Supp. VII:** 69
"Terce" (Auden), **Supp. II Part 1:** 22
Terence, **IV:** 155, 363; **Supp. I Part 2:** 405
Terkel, Studs, **Supp. IV Part 1:** 364
"Term" (Merwin), **Supp. III Part 1:** 356–357
"Terminal Days at Beverly Farms" (Lowell), **Retro. Supp. II:** 189
Terminating, or Sonnet LXXV, or "Lass Meine Schmerzen nicht verloren sein, or Ambivalence" (Kushner), **Supp. IX:** 132
Terminations (James), **Retro. Supp. I:** 229
"Terminus" (Emerson), **II:** 13, 19
"Terminus" (Wharton), **Retro. Supp. I:** 371
"Terms in Which I Think of Reality, The" (Ginsberg), **Supp. II Part 1:** 311
Terms of Endearment (film), **Supp. V:** 226
Terms of Endearment (McMurtry), **Supp. V:** 224–225
"Terrace, The" (Wilbur), **Supp. III Part 2:** 550
Terrarium (Sanders), **Supp. XVI:** 270
"Terrence McNally" (Bryer), **Supp. XIII:** 200
"Terrence McNally" (Di Gaetani), **Supp. XIII:** 200
Terrence McNally: A Casebook (Zinman), **Supp. XIII:** 209
"Terrible Peacock, The" (Barnes), **Supp. III Part 1:** 33
Terrible Threes, The (Reed), **Supp. X:** 241, 253
Terrible Twos, The (Reed), **Supp. X:** 241, **252–253**
"Terrific Mother" (Moore), **Supp. X:** 178
Territory Ahead, The (Morris), **III:** 228–229, 236
"Terrorism" (Wright), **Supp. XV:** 341
Terrorism (Wright), **Supp. XV:** 341, 342
Terry, Edward A., **II:** 128, 129
Terry, Rose, **Supp. I Part 2:** 420
Tertium Organum (Ouspensky), **I:** 383
Tess of the d'Ubervilles (Hardy), **II:** 181; **Retro. Supp. II:** 100
"Testament" (Berry), **Supp. X:** 36
"Testament" (Carruth), **Supp. XVI:** 59
"Testament (Or, Homage to Walt Whitman)" (Jong), **Supp. V:** 130
"Testament of Flood" (Warren), **IV:** 253
Testament of François Villon, The (Pound, opera), **Retro. Supp. I:** 287
"Testament: Vermeer in December" (Bierds), **Supp. XVII:** 33
"Testimonia on the Question of Stesichoros' Blinding by Helen" (Carson), **Supp. XII:** 107
"Testimonies of a Roasted Chicken" (Jarman), **Supp. XVII:** 120
"Testimony" (Komunyakaa), **Supp. XIII:** 129
"Testimony of James Apthorp, The" (Kees), **Supp. XV:** 146
Testimony: The United States (1885–1890): Recitative (Reznikoff), **Supp. XIV:** 279, 280, 281, 285, **289–291**
Testimony: The United States (1891–1900): Recitative (Reznikoff), **Supp. XIV:** 291
"Testing-Tree, The" (Kunitz), **Supp. III Part 1:** 269
Testing-Tree, The (Kunitz), **Supp. III Part 1:** 260, 263, 264, 267, 268
Test of Poetry, A (Zukofsky), **Supp. III Part 2:** 618, 622
"Teutonic Scholar" (X. J. Kennedy), **Supp. XV:** 161
"Texas Moon, and Elsewhere, The" (McMurtry), **Supp. V:** 225
Texas Poets in Concert: A Quartet (Gwynn, ed.), **Supp. XIII:** 277
Texas Summer (Southern), **Supp. XI:** 309
Texasville (McMurtry), **Supp. V:** 228, 233
Thacher, Molly Day, **IV:** 381
Thackeray, William Makepeace, **I:** 194, 354; **II:** 182, 271, 282, 288, 316, 321, 322; **III:** 64, 70; **IV:** 326; **Retro. Supp. I:** 218; **Supp. I Part 1:** 307; **Supp. I Part 2:** 421, 495, 579; **Supp. IV Part 1:** 297; **Supp. IX:** 200; **Supp. XI:** 277; **Supp. XIV:** 306
Thaddeus, Janice Farrar, **Supp. IV Part 1:** 299
"Thailand" (Barthelme), **Supp. IV Part 1:** 41
Thalberg, Irving, **Retro. Supp. I:** 109, 110, 114; **Supp. XVI:** 191, 192
Thales, **I:** 480–481
Thalia Trilogy (McMurtry), **Supp. V:** 220–223, 234
Tham, Claire, **Supp. VIII:** 79
"Thanatopsis" (Bryant), **Supp. I Part 1:** 150, 154, 155, 170
Thanatos Syndrome, The (Percy), **Supp. III Part 1:** 385, 397–399
"Thanksgiving" (Glück), **Supp. V:** 83
"Thanksgiving, A" (Auden), **Supp. II Part 1:** 26
"Thanksgiving for a Habitat" (Auden), **Supp. II Part 1:** 24
Thanksgivings (Traherne), **Supp. XVI:** 288
"Thanksgiving Spirit" (Farrell), **II:** 45
Thanksgiving Visitor, The (Capote), **Supp. III Part 1:** 116, 118, 119
Thank You, Fog (Auden), **Supp. II Part 1:** 24
"Thank You, Lord" (Angelou), **Supp. IV Part 1:** 15
Thank You, Mr. Moto (Marquand), **III:** 57, 58
Thank You and Other Poems (Koch), **Supp. XV:** 180–181
"Thank You in Arabic" (Nye), **Supp. XIII:** 273, 281
"Thar's More in the Man Than Thar Is in the Land" (Lanier), **Supp. I Part 1:** 352–353, 359–360
"That Evening Sun" (Faulkner), **II:** 72; **Retro. Supp. I:** 75, 83
That Horse (Hogan), **Supp. IV Part 1:** 397, 404, 405
"That I Had the Wings" (Ellison), **Supp. II Part 1:** 238
That Night (McDermott), **Supp. XVIII:** 155, **158–160,** 162, 163, 166
"That's the Place Indians Talk About" (Ortiz), **Supp. IV Part 2:** 511
"That the Soul May Wax Plump" (Swenson), **Supp. IV Part 2:** 650
"That the Universe Is Chrysalid" (Sobin), **Supp. XVI:** 284
"That Tree" (Porter), **III:** 434–435, 446, 451
That Was the Week That Was (television program), **Supp. XIV:** 125
"That Year" (Olds), **Supp. X:** 203
"Thaw" (C. Frost), **Supp. XV:** 93, 104, 105
Thaxter, Celia, **Retro. Supp. II:** 136, 147; **Supp. XIII:** 143, 153
Thayer, Abbott, **I:** 231
Thayer, Scofield, **I:** 231; **Retro. Supp. I:** 58
Thayer and Eldridge, **Retro. Supp. I:** 403
"Theater" (Toomer), **Supp. IX:** 309, 317–318
"Theater Chronicle" (McCarthy), **II:** 562
"Theater Problems? Call Dr. Chekhov" (Wasserstein), **Supp. XV:** 320
Theatricals (James), **Retro. Supp. I:** 228
"Theft" (Porter), **III:** 434, 435
Theft, A (Bellow), **Retro. Supp. II:** 31–32, 34
The Harder They Fall (Schulberg), **Supp. XVIII: 247,** 253
The Harder They Fall: Celebrities Tell Their Real-Life Stories of Addiction and Recovery (F. Wright), **Supp. XVII:** 240
Their Eyes Were Watching God (Hurston), **Supp. VI:** 149, 152, 156–157
Their Heads Are Green and Their Hands Are Blue: Scenes from the Non-Christian World (Bowles), **Supp. IV Part 1:** 89
"Their Losses" (Taylor), **Supp. V:** 320
Their Wedding Journey (Howells), **II:** 277–278; **Retro. Supp. I:** 334

them (Oates), **Supp. II Part 2:** 503, 511–514
Theme Is Freedom, The (Dos Passos), **I:** 488–489, 492, 494
Theme Time Radio Hour (radio show, Dylan), **Supp. XVIII:** 28
"Theme with Variations" (Agee), **I:** 27
"Then" (Barthelme), **Supp. IV Part 1:** 48
"Then It All Came Down" (Capote), **Supp. III Part 1:** 125, 131
Theocritus, **II:** 169; **Retro. Supp. I:** 286
"Theodore the Poet" (Masters), **Supp. I Part 2:** 461
Theological Position, A (Coover), **Supp. V:** 44
Theophrastus, **I:** 58
"Theoretical and Scientific Conceptions of Race, The" (Locke), **Supp. XIV:** 209
Theory and Practice of Rivers and Other Poems, The (Harrison), **Supp. VIII:** 47, 49
Theory of Business Enterprise, The (Veblen), **Supp. I Part 2:** 638, 641, 644
"Theory of Flight" (Rukeyser), **Supp. VI:** 277–278
Theory of Flight (Rukeyser), **Supp. VI:** 272, 275, **277–278,** 284
Theory of Moral Sentiments, The (A. Smith), **Supp. I Part 2:** 634
Theory of the Leisure Class, The (Veblen), **I:** 475–476; **Supp. I Part 2:** 629, 633, 641, 645; **Supp. IV Part 1:** 22
"There" (Taylor), **Supp. V:** 323
"There Are No Such Trees in Alpine California" (Haines), **Supp. XII:** 207
"There Goes (Varoom! Varoom!) That Kandy-Kolored Tangerine-Flake Streamline Baby" (Wolfe), **Supp. III Part 2:** 569–571
"There Is a Lesson" (Olsen), **Supp. XIII:** 292, 297
"There Is Only One of Everything" (Atwood), **Supp. XIII:** 34
There Is Something Out There (McNally). *See And Things That Go Bump in the Night* (McNally)
"There's a certain Slant of light" (Dickinson), **Retro. Supp. I:** 38
There's a Wocket in My Pocket! (Geisel), **Supp. XVI:** 111
Thérèse de Lisieux, Saint, **Supp. VIII:** 195
"There She Is She Is Taking Her Bath" (Anderson), **I:** 113, 114
"There Was a Child Went Forth" (Whitman), **IV:** 348
"There Was a Man, There Was a Woman" (Cisneros), **Supp. VII:** 70
"There Was an Old Woman She Had So Many Children She Didn't Know What to Do" (Cisneros), **Supp. VII:** 60
"There Was a Youth Whose Name Was Thomas Granger" (Olson), **Supp. II Part 2:** 558, 560, 563
There Were Giants in the Land (Benét), **Supp. XI:** 50
"There You Are" (Simpson), **Supp. IX:** 279
There You Are (Simpson), **Supp. IX: 279–280**
"Thermopylae" (Clampitt), **Supp. IX:** 43
Theroux, Alexander, **Supp. VIII:** 312
Theroux, Marcel, **Supp. VIII:** 325
Theroux, Paul, **Supp. V:** 122; **Supp. VIII: 309–327**
"These Are My People" (Hayden), **Supp. II Part 1:** 365
"These are the days when Birds come back" (Dickinson), **Retro. Supp. I:** 30
"These Days" (Olds), **Supp. X:** 215
"These Flames and Generosities of the Heart: Emily Dickinson and the Illogic of Sumptuary Values" (Howe), **Supp. IV Part 2:** 431
These Low Grounds (Turpin), **Supp. XVIII:** 283
"These saw Visions" (Dickinson), **Retro. Supp. I:** 46
These Thirteen (Faulkner), **II:** 72
These Three (film), **Supp. I Part 1:** 281
"These Times" (Untermeyer), **Supp. XV:** 300
These Times (Untermeyer), **Supp. XV: 299–300,** 303
"Thessalonica: A Roman Story" (Brown), **Supp. I Part 1:** 133
Thévenaz, Paul, **Supp. XV:** 42
Thew, Harvey, **Supp. XIII:** 166
"They Ain't the Men They Used To Be" (Farrell), **II:** 45
"They Burned the Books" (Benét), **Supp. XI:** 46
They Came Like Swallows (Maxwell), **Supp. VIII: 155–159,** 168, 169
"They Can't Turn Back" (Baldwin), **Supp. I Part 1:** 52
They Do Not: The Letters of a Non-Professional Lady Arranged for Public Consumption (Clements), **Supp. XVI:** 190
"They Feed They Lion" (Levine), **Supp. V:** 188
They Feed They Lion (Levine), **Supp. V:** 178, 179, 181, 184–185, 186
"They Lion Grow" (Levine), **Supp. V:** 184–185
"They're Not Your Husband" (Carver), **Supp. III Part 1:** 141, 143
They're Playing Our Song (musical), **Supp. IV Part 2:** 589
They Shall Inherit the Laughter (Jones), **Supp. XI:** 217, 218, 232
"They Shall Not Die" (Ryan as Quin), **Supp. XVIII:** 228–229
They Shoot Horses (film), **Supp. XIII:** 159
They Shoot Horses, Don't They? (McCoy), **Supp. XIII:** 159, **164–166,** 168, 171, 172, 174
"They Sing, They Sing" (Roethke), **III:** 544
They Stooped to Folly (Glasgow), **II:** 175, 186–187
They Were Expendable (film), **Supp. XVIII:** 247
They Whisper (R. O. Butler), **Supp. XII: 72–73**
Thidwick the Big-Hearted Moose (Geisel), **Supp. XVI:** 104
"Thief's Philosophy of Life, The" (Hapgood), **Supp. XVII:** 103
"Thief's Wife, The" (B. Kelly), **Supp. XVII:** 125–126
"Thieves" (Yates), **Supp. XI:** 349
Thieves of Paradise (Komunyakaa), **Supp. XIII:** 113, **128–130,** 132
"Thimble, The" (Kenyon), **Supp. VII:** 164
"Thing and Its Relations, The" (James), **II:** 357
"Things" (Haines), **Supp. XII:** 207
"Things" (Kenyon), **Supp. VII:** 169
"Things, The" (Kinnell), **Supp. III Part 1:** 246
Things As They Are (Stein), **IV:** 34, 37, 40
"Things Don't Stop" (Nye), **Supp. XIII:** 287
Things Gone and Things Still Here (Bowles), **Supp. IV Part 1:** 91
"Things of August" (Stevens), **Retro. Supp. I:** 309
Things of This World (Wilbur), **Supp. III Part 2:** 552–555
Things Themselves: Essays and Scenes (Price), **Supp. VI:** 261
Things They Carried, The (O'Brien), **Supp. V:** 238, 239, 240, 243, 248–250
Things They Carried, The (T. O'Brien), **Supp. XVII:** 14
"Thing That Killed My Father Off, The" (Carver), **Supp. III Part 1:** 143
"Think about It" (Conroy), **Supp. XVI:** 75
Think Back on Us ... (Cowley), **Supp. II Part 1:** 139, 140, 142
Think Fast, Mr. Moto (Marquand), **III:** 57, 58
"Thinking about Barbara Deming" (Paley), **Supp. VI:** 227
"Thinking about Being Called Simple by a Critic" (Stafford), **Supp. XI:** 328
Thinking about the Longstanding Problems of Virtue and Happiness: Essays, a Play, Two Poems, and a Prayer (Kushner), **Supp. IX:** 131, 134, 135
"Thinking about the Past" (Justice), **Supp. VII:** 123–124
"Thinking about Western Thinking" (Didion), **Supp. IV Part 1:** 204, 206
"'Thinking against Oneself': Reflections on Cioran" (Sontag), **Supp. III Part 2:** 459–460
"Thinking Back Through Our Mothers: Traditions in Canadian Women's Writing" (Shields), **Supp. VII:** 307–308
"Thinking for Berky" (Stafford), **Supp. XI:** 320
"Thinking like a Mountain" (Leopold), **Supp. XIV:** 188, 189
"Thinking of the Lost World" (Jarrell), **II:** 338–389
Thinking Out Loud (Quindlen), **Supp. XVII:** 167, **169–170**

Thin Man, The (film), **Supp. IV Part 1:** 342, 355
Thin Man, The (Hammett), **Supp. IV Part 1:** 354–355
"Thinnest Shadow, The" (Ashbery), **Supp. III Part 1:** 5
"Thin People, The" (Plath), **Supp. I Part 2:** 538, 547
Thin Red Line, The (film; Malick), **Supp. V:** 249; **Supp. XV:** 351
Thin Red Line, The (Jones), **Supp. XI:** 219, **224–225,** 229, 231, 232, 233, 234
"Thin Strips" (Sandburg), **III:** 587
"Third Avenue in Sunlight" (Hecht), **Supp. X:** 61
"Third Body, A" (R. Bly), **Supp. IV Part 1:** 71
Third Circle, The (Norris), **III:** 327
"Third Expedition, The" (Bradbury), **Supp. IV Part 1:** 103, 106
Third Generation, The (C. Himes), **Supp. XVI:** 135, **140–141**
Third Life of Grange Copeland, The (Walker), **Supp. III Part 2:** 520, 527–536
Third Mind, The (Burroughs), **Supp. XII:** 3
Third Rose, The (Brinnin), **IV:** 26
"Third Sermon on the Warpland, The" (Brooks), **Supp. III Part 1:** 85
"Third Thing That Killed My Father Off, The" (Carver), **Supp. III Part 1:** 144
Third Violet, The (Crane), **I:** 408, 417–418
Thirlwall, John C., **Retro. Supp. I:** 430
"Thirst: Introduction to Kinds of Water" (Carson), **Supp. XII: 103**
"13, 1977, 21" (Lethem), **Supp. XVIII:** 148
13 by Shanley (Shanley), **Supp. XIV:** 316
Thirteen Hands: A Play in Two Acts (Shields), **Supp. VII:** 322–323
Thirteen O'Clock (Benét), **Supp. XI:** 46
Thirteen Other Stories (Purdy), **Supp. VII:** 278
Thirteen Stories and Thirteen Epitaphs (Vollmann), **Supp. XVII:** 226
"Thirteenth and Pennsylvania" (Stafford), **Supp. XI:** 324
Thirteenth Month, The (Pedersen; Nelson, trans.), **Supp. XVIII:** 179–180
"Thirteen Ways of Looking at a Blackbird" (Stevens), **IV:** 94; **Supp. IX:** 47; **Supp. XVII:** 130
30/6 (poetry chapbook), **Supp. V:** 5, 6
"30. Meditation. 2. Cor. 5.17. He Is a New Creature" (Taylor), **IV:** 144
30: Pieces of a Novel (Dixon), **Supp. XII:** 152, **153–154**
"Thirty Bob a Week" (Davidson), **Retro. Supp. I:** 55
"Thirty Delft Tiles" (Doty), **Supp. XI:** 131
"35/10" (Olds), **Supp. X:** 206
"35,000 Feet——The Lanterns" (Goldbarth), **Supp. XII:** 182
31 Letters and 13 Dreams (Hugo), **Supp. VI:** 141–144
Thirty Poems (Bryant), **Supp. I Part 1:** 157, 158
Thirty-Six Poems (Warren), **IV:** 236, 239, 240
"33" (Alvarez), **Supp. VII:** 4
"3275" (Monette), **Supp. X:** 148, 159
Thirty Years (Marquand), **III:** 56, 60–61
Thirty Years of Treason (Bentley), **Supp. I Part 1:** 297
This, My Letter (Hay), **Supp. XIV:** 121, 122, 129, 131
"This, That & the Other" (Nemerov), **III:** 269
This Body Is Made of Camphor and Gopherwood (R. Bly), **Supp. IV Part 1:** 63–65, 66, 71
This Boy's Life: A Memoir (T. Wolff), **Supp. VII:** 334–339, 340, 343; **Supp. XI:** 246, 247
"This Bright Dream" (Benét), **Supp. XI:** 55
This Coffin Has No Handles (McGrath), **Supp. X:** 117
"This Configuration" (Ashbery), **Supp. III Part 1:** 22
"This Corruptible" (Wylie), **Supp. I Part 2:** 727, 729
"This Crutch That I Love" (Nye), **Supp. XIII:** 288
"This Gentile World" (H. Miller), **III:** 177
"This Hand" (Wylie), **Supp. I Part 2:** 713
"This Hour" (Olds), **Supp. X:** 212
"This House I Cannot Leave" (Kingsolver), **Supp. VII:** 208
This Hunger (Nin), **Supp. X:** 185
"This Is a Photograph of Me" (Atwood), **Supp. XIII:** 33
"This Is a Poem, Good Afternoon" (Keillor), **Supp. XVI:** 167
"This Is It" (Stern), **Supp. IX:** 290
"This Is Just to Say" (W. C. Williams), **Supp. XI:** 328
"This Is My Heart" (Harjo), **Supp. XII:** 230
This Is Not a Novel (Markson), **Supp. XVII:** 145–146
"This Is Not Who We Are" (Nye), **Supp. XIII:** 285, 286
"This Is What I Said" (Salinas), **Supp. XIII:** 322
This Journey (Wright), **Supp. III Part 2:** 605–606
This Man and This Woman (Farrell), **II:** 42
"This Morning" (Kenyon), **Supp. VII:** 164
"This Morning, This Evening, So Soon" (Baldwin), **Supp. I Part 1:** 63
"This Morning Again It Was in the Dusty Pines" (Oliver), **Supp. VII:** 240
This Music Crept by Me upon the Waters (MacLeish), **III:** 21
This People Israel: The Meaning of Jewish Existence (Baeck), **Supp. V:** 260
"This Personal Maze Is Not the Prize" (Selinger), **Supp. XI:** 248
"This Place in the Ways" (Rukeyser), **Supp. VI:** 273–274
This Property Is Condemned (T. Williams), **IV:** 378
This Proud Heart (Buck), **Supp. II Part 1:** 119–120
This Same Sky: A Collection of Poems from around the World (Nye, ed.), **Supp. XIII:** 280
"This Sandwich Has No Mayonnaise" (Salinger), **III:** 552–553
"This Shape We're In" (Lethem), **Supp. XVIII:** 148
This Shape We're In (Lethem), **Supp. XVIII:** 145
This Side of Paradise (Fitzgerald), **I:** 358; **II:** 77, 80, 81, 82–83, 84, 85–87, 88; **Retro. Supp. I:** 99–100, **101–102,** 103, 105, 106, 110, 111; **Supp. XVIII:** 248
This Singing World: An Anthology of Modern Poetry for Young People (Untermeyer, ed.), **Supp. XV:** 306
This Stubborn Self: Texas Autobiographies (Almon), **Supp. XIII:** 288
This Thing Don't Lead to Heaven (Crews), **Supp. XI: 112**
This Time: New and Selected Poems (Stern), **Supp. IX:** 290–291, **299**
"Thistle Seed in the Wind" (Francis), **Supp. IX:** 81
"Thistles in Sweden, The" (Maxwell), **Supp. VIII:** 169
"This Tokyo" (Snyder), **Supp. VIII:** 298
This Tree Will Be Here for a Thousand Years (R. Bly), **Supp. IV Part 1:** 65–66, 71, 72
This Tree Will Be Here for a Thousand Years (revised edition) (R. Bly), **Supp. IV Part 1:** 66
This Very Earth (Caldwell), **I:** 297, 302
This Wheel's on Fire: Levon Helm and the Story of the Band (Helm), **Supp. XVIII:** 26
Thoens, Karen, **Supp. V:** 147
Thomas, Brandon, **II:** 138
Thomas, Debra, **Supp. XIII:** 114
Thomas, D. M., **Supp. VIII:** 5
Thomas, Dylan, **I:** 49, 64, 382, 432, 526, 533; **III:** 21, 521, 528, 532, 534; **IV:** 89, 93, 136; **Supp. I Part 1:** 263; **Supp. III Part 1:** 42, 47; **Supp. IX:** 114; **Supp. V:** 344; **Supp. VIII:** 21; **Supp. X:** 115; **Supp. XV:** 74; **Supp. XVII:** 135
Thomas, Edna Lewis, **Supp. XVIII:** 281
Thomas, Edward, **II:** 154; **Retro. Supp. I:** 127, 131, 132; **Supp. I Part 1:** 263; **Supp. II Part 1:** 4
Thomas, James, **Supp. XVI:** 268
Thomas, Joseph, **Supp. XVIII:** 183
Thomas, J. Parnell, **Supp. I Part 1:** 286; **Supp. XV:** 198
Thomas, Lewis, **Retro. Supp. I:** 323
Thomas, Rob, **Supp. XVIII:** 100, 101
Thomas, William I., **Supp. I Part 2:** 641
Thomas-a-Kempis, **Retro. Supp. I:** 247
Thomas and Beulah (Dove), **Supp. IV Part 1:** 242, 247–248, 249; **Supp. XVIII:** 174
Thomas Aquinas (Saint), **I:** 13, 14, 265, 267; **III:** 270; **Retro. Supp. II:** 222; **Supp. IV Part 2:** 526

"Thomas at the Wheel" (Dove), **Supp. IV Part 1:** 248
"Thomas McGrath: Words for a Vanished Age" (Vinz), **Supp. X:** 117
Thomas Merton on Peace, **Supp. VIII:** 208
Thomas Merton Studies Center, The, **Supp. VIII:** 208
Thompson, Barbara, **Supp. V:** 322
Thompson, Cy, **I:** 538
Thompson, Dorothy, **II:** 449–450, 451, 453; **Supp. XV:** 307
Thompson, E. P., **Supp. X:** 112, 117
Thompson, Francis, **Retro. Supp. I:** 55
Thompson, Frank, **II:** 20
Thompson, George, **Supp. I Part 2:** 686
Thompson, Hunter S., **Supp. VIII:** 42; **Supp. XI:** 105; **Supp. XIII:** 1, 17; **Supp. XVII:** 95, 102, 228
Thompson, James R., **Supp. IV Part 1:** 217
Thompson, John, **Supp. V:** 323
Thompson, Lawrance, **II:** 508
Thompson, Lawrance Roger, **Retro. Supp. I:** 138, 141
Thompson, Morton, **Supp. XIII:** 170
Thompson, Theresa, **Supp. V:** 141
Thompson, William T., **Supp. I Part 2:** 411
Thomson, James, **II:** 304; **Supp. I Part 1:** 150, 151
Thomson, Virgil, **IV:** 45; **Supp. IV Part 1:** 81, 83, 84, 173; **Supp. XVI:** 195
"Thoreau" (Lowell), **Supp. I Part 2:** 420, 422
Thoreau, Henry David, **I:** 98, 104, 228, 236, 257, 258, 261, 305, 433; **II:** 7, 8, 13, 17, 101, 159, 224, 273–274, 295, 312–313, 321, 457–458, 540, 546–547; **III:** 171, 174, 186–187, 189, 208, 214–215, 453, 454, 507, 577; **IV: 167–189,** 191, 341; **Retro. Supp. I:** 51, 62, 122; **Retro. Supp. II:** 13, 96, 142, 158; **Supp. I Part 1:** 29, 34, 116, 188, 299, 358; **Supp. I Part 2:** 383, 400, 420, 421, 507, 540, 579, 580, 655, 659, 660, 664, 678; **Supp. III Part 1:** 340, 353; **Supp. IV Part 1:** 236, 392, 416; **Supp. IV Part 2:** 420, 430, 433, 439, 447; **Supp. IX:** 25, 90, 171; **Supp. V:** 200, 208; **Supp. VIII:** 40, 42, 103, 105, 198, 201, 204, 205, 292, 303; **Supp. X:** 21, 27, 28–29, 101, 102; **Supp. XI:** 155; **Supp. XIII:** 1, 17; **Supp. XIV:** 40, 54, 106, 177, 181; **Supp. XVIII:** 4
Thoreau, John, **IV:** 171, 182
Thoreau, Mrs. John, **IV:** 172
"Thorn, The" (Gordon), **Supp. IV Part 1:** 314
Thorne, Francis, **Supp. XII:** 253
"Thorn Merchant, The" (Komunyakaa), **Supp. XIII:** 119–120
Thornton, Billy Bob, **Supp. VIII:** 175
Thornton, Lionel, **III:** 291
"Thorofare" (Minot), **Supp. VI: 209–210**
"Thorow" (Howe), **Supp. IV Part 2:** 419, 420, 421, 431, 433–434
Thorp, Willard, **Supp. XIII:** 101
Thorslev, Peter L., Jr., **I:** 524
Thorstein Veblen (Dowd), **Supp. I Part 2:** 650
Thorstein Veblen (Qualey, ed.), **Supp. I Part 2:** 650
Thorstein Veblen: A Chapter in American Economic Thought (Teggart), **Supp. I Part 2:** 650
Thorstein Veblen: A Critical Interpretation (Riesman), **Supp. I Part 2:** 649, 650
Thorstein Veblen: A Critical Reappraisal (Dowd, ed.), **Supp. I Part 2:** 650
Thorstein Veblen and His America (Dorfman), **Supp. I Part 2:** 631, 650
Thorstein Veblen and the Institutionalists: A Study in the Social Philosophy of Economics (Seckler), **Supp. I Part 2:** 650
"Those before Us" (Lowell), **II:** 550
"Those Being Eaten by America" (R. Bly), **Supp. IV Part 1:** 62
Those Bones Are Not My Child (Bambara), **Supp. XI:** 1, 14, **20–22**
Those Extraordinary Twins (Twain), **IV:** 205–206
"Those Graves in Rome" (Levis), **Supp. XI:** 266
"Those of Us Who Think We Know" (Dunn), **Supp. XI:** 146
"Those Times ..." (Sexton), **Supp. II Part 2:** 670, 684
"Those Various Scalpels" (Moore), **III:** 202
"Those Were the Days" (Levine), **Supp. V:** 190
"Those Who Don't" (Cisneros), **Supp. VII:** 60
"Those Who Thunder" (Hogan), **Supp. IV Part 1:** 406
"Thought, A" (Sarton), **Supp. VIII:** 262
Thought and Character of William James (Perry), **II:** 362
Thoughtbook of Francis Scott Key Fitzgerald (Fitzgerald), **Retro. Supp. I:** 99
"Thoughtful Roisterer Declines the Gambit, The" (Hecht), **Supp. X:** 63
"Thought of Heaven, The" (Stern), **Supp. IX:** 297
"Thoughts after Lambeth" (Eliot), **I:** 587; **Retro. Supp. I:** 324
Thoughts and Reflections (Lord Halifax), **II:** 111
Thoughts in Solitude (Merton), **Supp. VIII:** 207
"Thoughts on Being Bibliographed" (Wilson), **IV:** 435
"Thoughts on the Establishment of a Mint in the United States" (Paine), **Supp. I Part 2:** 512
"Thoughts on the Gifts of Art" (Kenyon), **Supp. VII:** 167
Thousand Acres, A (Smiley), **Supp. VI:** 292, **301–303**
"Thousand and Second Night, The" (Merrill), **Supp. III Part 1:** 324
"Thousand Dollar Vagrant, The" (Olsen), **Supp. XIII:** 292, 297
"Thousand Faces of Danny Torrance, The" (Figliola), **Supp. V:** 143
"Thousand Genuflections, A" (McCarriston), **Supp. XIV:** 266
Thousand-Mile Walk to the Gulf, A (Muir), **Supp. IX: 177–178**
"Thou Shalt Not Steal" (McClatchy), **Supp. XII:** 264
"Thread, The" (Merwin), **Supp. III Part 1:** 351
Three (film), **Supp. IX:** 253
3-3-8 (Marquand), **III:** 58
"Three Academic Pieces" (Stevens), **IV:** 90
"Three Agee Wards, The" (Morris), **III:** 220–221
"Three American Singers" (Cather), **Retro. Supp. I:** 10
"Three Around the Old Gentleman" (Berryman), **I:** 188
"Three Avilas, The" (Jeffers), **Supp. II Part 2:** 418
Three Books of Song (Longfellow), **II:** 490
"Three Bushes" (Yeats), **Supp. I Part 1:** 80
Three Cantos (Pound), **Retro. Supp. I:** 290
Three Centuries of Harvard (Morison), **Supp. I Part 2:** 485
Three Comrades (Remarque), **Retro. Supp. I:** 113
"Three Corollaries of Cultural Relativism" (Locke), **Supp. XIV:** 202
"Three-Day Blow, The" (Hemingway), **II:** 248
Three Essays on America (Brooks), **I:** 246
Three Farmers on Their Way to a Dance (Powers), **Supp. IX:** 211–212, **213–214,** 222
"Three Fates, The" (Benét), **Supp. XI:** 48–49, 50
"Three Generations of Secrets" (A. Finch), **Supp. XVII:** 73
Three Gospels (Price), **Supp. VI:** 267
"Three Kings, The: Hemingway, Faulkner, and Fitzgerald" (Ford), **Supp. V:** 59
Three Lives (Auchincloss), **Supp. IV Part 1:** 25
Three Lives (Stein), **I:** 103; **IV:** 26, 27, 31, 35, 37–41, 42, 45, 46; **Supp. IX:** 306
"THREE MOVEMENTS AND A CODA" (Baraka), **Supp. II Part 1:** 50
Three One Act Plays (Riverside Drive, Old Saybrook, and *Central Park West)* (Allen), **Supp. XV:** 3
Three on the Tower: The Lives and Works of Ezra Pound, T. S. Eliot, and William Carlos Williams (Simpson), **Supp. IX:** 276
Three Papers on Fiction (Welty), **IV:** 261
Three-Penny Opera (Brecht), **I:** 301; **Supp. XIV:** 162
"Three Percent Own All the Wealth" (Ryan as Quin), **Supp. XVIII:** 231–232
Three Philosophical Poets (Santayana), **III:** 610–612

"Three Pigs in Five Days" (Prose), **Supp. XVI:** 257, 258
"Three Players of a Summer Game" (T. Williams), **IV:** 383
Three Poems (Ashbery), **Supp. III Part 1:** 2, 3, 14, 15, 18, 24–26
"Three Pokes of a Thistle" (Nye), **Supp. XIII:** 281
Three Roads, The (Macdonald, under Millar), **Supp. IV Part 2:** 466, 467
"Three Silences of Molinos, The" (Longfellow), **Retro. Supp. II:** 169
Three Sisters, The (Chekhov), **Supp. XV:** 323
"Three Sisters, The" (Cisneros), **Supp. VII:** 64
Three Soldiers (Dos Passos), **I:** 477–478, 480, 482, 488, 493–494
"Three Songs at the End of Summer" (Kenyon), **Supp. VII:** 169–170
"Three Steps to the Graveyard" (Wright), **Supp. III Part 2:** 593, 596
Three Stories and Ten Poems (Hemingway), **II:** 68, 263; **Supp. XVII:** 105
"Three Taverns, The" (Robinson), **III:** 521, 522
Three Taverns, The (Robinson), **III:** 510
Three Tenant Families (Agee), **I:** 37–38
Three Tenors, One Vehicle: A Book of Songs (X. J. Kennedy, Camp, and Waldrop), **Supp. XV:** 165
"Three Types of Poetry" (Tate), **IV:** 131
"Three Vagabonds of Trinidad" (Harte), **Supp. II Part 1:** 338
"Three Waterfalls, The" (Lanier), **Supp. I Part 1:** 350
"Three-Way Mirror" (Brooks), **Supp. III Part 1:** 69–70
"Three Women" (Plath), **Supp. I Part 2:** 539, 541, 544, 545, 546
Three Young Poets (Swallow, ed.), **Supp. X:** 116
"Threnody" (Emerson), **II:** 7
Threnody (Emerson), **Supp. I Part 2:** 416
"Threnody for a Brown Girl" (Cullen), **Supp. IV Part 1:** 166
"Threshing-Floor, The" (Baldwin), **Supp. I Part 1:** 50
Threshold (film), **Supp. IX:** 254
"Threshold" (Goldbarth), **Supp. XII:** 175
Threshold (Jackson), **Supp. IX:** 117
"Throat" (Goldbarth), **Supp. XII:** 177–178
Throne of Labdacus, The (Schnackenberg), **Supp. XV:** 260, **263–266**
Thrones (Pound), **Retro. Supp. I:** 293
Through Dooms of Love (Kumin), **Supp. IV Part 2:** 444
"Through the Black Curtain" (Kingston), **Supp. V:** 169
Through the Forest: New and Selected Poems, 1977–1987 (Wagoner), **Supp. IX: 330–331**
"Through the Hills of Spain" (Salinas), **Supp. XIII:** 315
"Through the Hole in the Mundane Millstone" (West), **Retro. Supp. II:** 321, 322
Through the Ivory Gate (Dove), **Supp. IV Part 1:** 242, 243, 251, 252, 253–254, 254
"Through the Kitchen Window, Chiapas" (Nye), **Supp. XIII:** 277
Through the Safety Net (C. Baxter), **Supp. XVII:** 17, 22
"Through the Smoke Hole" (Snyder), **Supp. VIII:** 299
Thucydides, **II:** 418; **IV:** 50; **Supp. I Part 2:** 488, 489, 492; **Supp. IV Part 1:** 391; **Supp. XIII:** 233
Thunderbolt and Lightfoot (film), **Supp. X:** 126
"Thunderhead" (MacLeish), **III:** 19
Thurber, James, **I:** 487; **II:** 432; **IV:** 396; **Supp. I Part 2: 602–627**, 653, 654, 668, 672, 673, 679; **Supp. II Part 1:** 143; **Supp. IV Part 1:** 349; **Supp. IX:** 118; **Supp. XIV:** 104; **Supp. XVI:** 167; **Supp. XVII:** 4
Thurber, Mrs. James (Althea Adams), **Supp. I Part 2:** 613, 615, 617
Thurber, Mrs. James (Helen Muriel Wismer), **Supp. I Part 2:** 613, 617, 618
Thurber, Robert, **Supp. I Part 2:** 613, 617
Thurber, Rosemary, **Supp. I Part 2:** 616
Thurber, William, **Supp. I Part 2:** 602
Thurber Album, The (Thurber), **Supp. I Part 2:** 611, 619
Thurber Carnival, The (Thurber), **Supp. I Part 2:** 620; **Supp. XIV:** 104
Thurman, Judith, **Supp. IV Part 1:** 309
Thurman, Wallace, **Retro. Supp. I:** 200; **Supp. I Part 1:** 325, 326, 328, 332; **Supp. IV Part 1:** 164; **Supp. X:** 136, 139; **Supp. XVI:** 135; **Supp. XVIII:** 279, 281
"Thursday" (Millay), **III:** 129
"Thurso's Landing" (Jeffers), **Supp. II Part 2:** 433
"Thus Do I Refute Gioia" (Junker), **Supp. XV:** 116
"Thus Far by Faith" (Nelson), **Supp. XVIII:** 177
Thus Spake Zarathustra (Nietzsche), **II:** 463; **Supp. IV Part 1:** 110; **Supp. IV Part 2:** 519
Thwaite, Lady Alicia. *See* Rawlings, Marjorie Kinnan
Thy Neighbor's Wife (Talese), **Supp. XVII:** 204, 205–206, 207, 208, 210
"Tiara" (Doty), **Supp. XI:** 122
"Tibetan Time" (Prose), **Supp. XVI:** 255
Ticket for a Seamstitch, A (Harris), **II:** 424–425
Tickets for a Prayer Wheel (Dillard), **Supp. VI:** 22, 34
Ticket That Exploded, The (Burroughs), **Supp. III Part 1:** 93, 103, 104
Tickless Time (Glaspell), **Supp. III Part 1:** 179
Ticknor, George, **II:** 488; **Supp. I Part 1:** 313
Ticknor, William, **Supp. XVIII:** 258
"Ti Démon" (Chopin), **Supp. I Part 1:** 225
Tide of Time, The (Masters), **Supp. I Part 2:** 471
"Tide Rises, the Tide Falls, The" (Longfellow), **I:** 498
"Tides" (Hoffman), **Supp. XVIII:** 86
Tidewater Blood (Hoffman), **Supp. XVIII: 82–83**
Tidyman, Ernest, **Supp. V:** 226
Tietjens, Eunice, **Supp. XV:** 47, 297
"Tiger" (Blake), **Supp. I Part 1:** 80; **Supp. VIII:** 26
Tiger (Bynner), **Supp. XV:** 42, 50
"Tiger, The" (Buechner), **Supp. XII:** 48
Tiger in the House, The (Van Vechten), **Supp. II Part 2:** 736
Tiger Joy (Benét), **Supp. XI:** 45
Tiger-Lilies (Lanier), **Supp. I Part 1:** 350–351, 357, 360, 371
Tiger Who Wore White Gloves, The: or, What You Are, You Are (Brooks), **Supp. III Part 1:** 86
Till, Emmett, **Supp. I Part 1:** 61
Tillich, Paul, **II:** 244; **III:** 291, 292, 303, 309; **IV:** 226; **Retro. Supp. I:** 325, 326, 327; **Supp. V:** 267; **Supp. XIII:** 74, 91
Tillie Olsen: A Study of the Short Fiction (Frye), **Supp. XIII:** 292, 296, 298, 299, 302
Tillman, Lynne, **Supp. XII:** 4
Tillotson, John, **II:** 114
Tillotson, Kristen, **Supp. XVII:** 23
Tillstrom, Burr, **Supp. XIV:** 125
Till the Day I Die (Odets), **Supp. II Part 2:** 530, 533–536, 552
Tilton, Eleanor, **Supp. I Part 1:** 317
Tilton, Theodore, **Supp. XVIII:** 4
Timaeus (Plato), **II:** 10; **III:** 609
Timber (Jonson), **II:** 16
Timberg, Scott, **Supp. XV:** 116
Timbuktu (Auster), **Supp. XII:** 34, **35–36**
"Time" (Matthews), **Supp. IX: 165–166**
"Time" (Merrill), **Supp. III Part 1:** 325
"Time and Again" (Sanders), **Supp. XVI:** 269
Time and a Place, A (Humphrey), **Supp. IX:** 95, 98, **100–102**
"Time and the Garden" (Winters), **Supp. II Part 2:** 801, 809
"Time and the Liturgy" (Merton), **Supp. VIII:** 199
Time and Tide: A Walk through Nantucket (Conroy), **Supp. XVI:** 63, 71, **76–77**
"Time Exposure" (C. Baxter), **Supp. XVII:** 20–21
Time in the Rock (Aiken), **I:** 65
Time Is Noon, The (Buck), **Supp. II Part 1:** 129, 130–131
Time & Money (Matthews), **Supp. IX:** 155, **165–167**
"Time of Friendship, The" (Bowles), **Supp. IV Part 1:** 90–91
"Time of Her Time, The" (Mailer), **III:** 37, 45; **Retro. Supp. II:** 200
Time of Our Time, The (Mailer), **Retro. Supp. II:** 213–214
Time of the Assassins, The: A Study of Rimbaud (H. Miller), **III:** 189
Time Out of Mind (album, Dylan), **Supp. XVIII:** 28

"Time Past" (Morris), **III:** 232
"Time Present" (Morris), **III:** 232
"Times" (Beattie), **Supp. V:** 31
"Times, The" (Emerson), **II:** 11–12
Times Are Never So Bad, The (Dubus), **Supp. VII:** 87–88
Time's Arrow (Amis), **Retro. Supp. I:** 278
"Time Shall Not Die" (Chandler), **Supp. IV Part 1:** 120
Times of Melville and Whitman, The (Brooks), **I:** 257
Times They Are A-Changin', The (album, Dylan), **Supp. XVIII:** 20, 25
"Times They Are A-Changin,' The" (song, Dylan), **Supp. XVIII:** 30
"Timesweep" (Sandburg), **III:** 595–596
Time to Act, A (MacLeish), **III:** 3
Time to Go (Dixon), **Supp. XII:** 147
Time to Kill (film), **Supp. IV Part 1:** 130
Time to Speak, A (MacLeish), **III:** 3
Time Will Darken It (Maxwell), **Supp. VIII:** 159, **162–164,** 169
"Timing of Sin, The" (Dubus), **Supp. VII:** 91
Tim O'Brien (Herzog), **Supp. V:** 239
Timoleon (Melville), **III:** 93; **Retro. Supp. I:** 257
Timothy Dexter Revisited (Marquand), **III:** 55, 62, 63
Timrod, Henry, **Supp. XVIII:** 31, 33
"Tin Can, The" (W. J. Smith), **Supp. XIII: 337–339**
Tin Can, The (W. J. Smith), **Supp. XIII:** 334, **Supp. XIII:** 336, 337
Tin Can Tree, The (Tyler), **Supp. IV Part 2:** 659–660
Tinguely, Jean, **Supp. XV:** 187
Tinker, Chauncey Brewster, **Supp. XIV:** 12
Tintern Abbey (Wordsworth), **Supp. I Part 2:** 673, 675
Tiny Alice (Albee), **I:** 81–86, 87, 88, 94
"Tiny Mummies! The True Story of the Ruler of 43rd Street's Land of the Walking Dead" (Wolfe), **Supp. III Part 2:** 573, 574
"Tip-Top Club, The" (Keillor), **Supp. XVI:** 172
"Tired" (Hughes), **Supp. I Part 1:** 331
"Tired and Unhappy, You Think of Houses" (Schwartz), **Supp. II Part 2:** 649
"Tiresias" (Garrett), **Supp. VII:** 96–97
'Tis (McCourt), **Supp. XII:** 271, **279–286**
Tisch (Dixon), **Supp. XII:** 141, **155–156**
Titan, The (Dreiser), **I:** 497, 501, 507–508, 509, 510; **Retro. Supp. II:** 94, 101, 102
Titian, **Supp. I Part 2:** 397, 714
"Tito's Goodbye" (García), **Supp. XI:** 190
"To a Blossoming Pear Tree" (Wright), **Supp. III Part 2:** 604
To a Blossoming Pear Tree (Wright), **Supp. III Part 2:** 602–605
"To Abolish Children" (Shapiro), **Supp. II Part 2:** 717
To Abolish Children and Other Essays (Shapiro), **Supp. II Part 2:** 703
"To a Caty-Did, the Precursor of Winter" (Freneau), **Supp. II Part 1:** 274–275
"To a Chameleon" (Moore), **III:** 195, 196, 215
"To a Conscript of 1940" (Read), **II:** 372–373, 377–378
"To a Contemporary Bunk Shooter" (Sandburg), **III:** 582
"To a Cough in the Street at Midnight" (Wylie), **Supp. I Part 2:** 727, 729–730
"To a Defeated Savior" (Wright), **Supp. III Part 2:** 593–594, 596
"To a Face in the Crowd" (Warren), **IV:** 239
"To a Fish Head Found on the Beach near Malaga" (Levine), **Supp. V:** 185
"To a Friend" (Nemerov), **III:** 272
"To a Friend Whose Work Has Come to Triumph" (Sexton), **Supp. II Part 2:** 683
To a God Unknown (Steinbeck), **I:** 107; **IV:** 51, 59–60, 67
"To a Greek Marble" (Aldington), **Supp. I Part 1:** 257
"To a Locomotive in Winter" (Whitman), **IV:** 348
"To a Military Rifle" (Winters), **Supp. II Part 2:** 810, 811, 815
"To a Mouse" (Burns), **Supp. IX:** 173
"To an Athlete Dying Young" (Houseman), **Supp. XVII:** 121
"To a Negro Jazz Band in a Parisian Cabaret" (Hughes), **Supp. I Part 1:** 325
"To an Old Philosopher in Rome" (Stevens), **III:** 605; **Retro. Supp. I:** 312
"To an Old Poet in Peru" (Ginsberg), **Supp. II Part 1:** 322
"To a Now-Type Poet" (X. J. Kennedy), **Supp. XV:** 161
"To Answer Your Question" (Jarman), **Supp. XVII:** 114–115
"To Any Would-Be Terrorists" (Nye), **Supp. XIII:** 285, 286
"To a Poet" (Rich), **Supp. I Part 2:** 571
"To a Prize Bird" (Moore), **III:** 215
"To a Republican, with Mr. Paine's Rights of Man" (Freneau), **Supp. II Part 1:** 267
"To a Shade" (Yeats), **III:** 18
"To a Skylark" (Shelley), **Supp. I Part 2:** 720; **Supp. X:** 31
"Toast to Harlem, A" (Hughes), **Supp. I Part 1:** 338
"To Aunt Rose" (Ginsberg), **Supp. II Part 1:** 320
"To Autumn" (Keats), **Supp. IX:** 50
"To a Waterfowl" (Bryant), **Supp. I Part 1:** 154, 155, 162, 171
"To a Young Poet" (X. J. Kennedy), **Supp. XV:** 161
"To a Young Writer" (Stegner), **Supp. X:** 24
Tobacco Road (Caldwell), **I:** 288, 289, 290, 295–296, 297, 298, 302, 307, 309, 310; **IV:** 198
"To Be a Monstrous Clever Fellow" (Fante), **Supp. XI:** 167
To Bedlam and Part Way Back (Sexton), **Retro. Supp. II:** 245; **Supp. II Part 2:** 672–678; **Supp. IV Part 2:** 441; **Supp. XI:** 317
"To Beethoven" (Lanier), **Supp. I Part 1:** 364
To Begin Again: Stories and Memoirs, 1908–1929 (M. F. K. Fisher), **Supp. XVII:** 92
Tobey, Mark, **Supp. X:** 264
To Be Young, Gifted, and Black: Lorraine Hansberry in Her Own Words (Nemiroff), **Supp. IV Part 1:** 372, 374
"To Big Mary from an Ex-Catholic" (Mora), **Supp. XIII:** 217, 224, 228
"Tobin's Palm" (O. Henry), **Supp. II Part 1:** 408; **Supp. XV:** 40
Tobit (apocryphal book), **I:** 89
"To Build a Fire" (London), **II:** 468
Toby Tyler: or, Ten Weeks with a Circus (Otis), **III:** 577
"To Change in a Good Way" (Ortiz), **Supp. IV Part 2:** 511
"To Charlotte Cushman" (Lanier), **Supp. I Part 1:** 364
"To Cole, the Painter, Departing for Europe" (Bryant), **Supp. I Part 1:** 157, 161
Tocqueville, Alexis de, **III:** 261; **IV:** 349; **Retro. Supp. I:** 235; **Supp. I Part 1:** 137; **Supp. I Part 2:** 659, 660; **Supp. II Part 1:** 281, 282, 284; **Supp. XIV:** 306, 312
"To Crispin O'Conner" (Freneau), **Supp. II Part 1:** 268
"To Da-Duh, In Memoriam" (Marshall), **Supp. XI:** 276
"TODAY" (Baraka), **Supp. II Part 1:** 55
"Today" (Ginsberg), **Supp. II Part 1:** 328
"Today Is a Good Day To Die" (Bell), **Supp. X:** 7
Todd, Mabel Loomis, **I:** 454, 470; **Retro. Supp. I:** 33, 34, 35, 39, 47
"To Death" (Levertov), **Supp. III Part 1:** 274
"To Delmore Schwartz" (Lowell), **II:** 547; **Retro. Supp. II:** 188
"to disembark" (Brooks), **Supp. III Part 1:** 86
"To Dorothy on Her Exclusion from The Guinness Book of Records" (X. J. Kennedy), **Supp. XV:** 166
"To Dr. Thomas Shearer" (Lanier), **Supp. I Part 1:** 370
"To Earthward" (Frost), **II:** 154
"To Edwin V. McKenzie" (Winters), **Supp. II Part 2:** 801
"To Eleonora Duse" (Lowell), **II:** 528
"To Elizabeth Ward Perkins" (Lowell), **II:** 516
"To Elsie" (W. C. Williams), **Retro. Supp. I:** 419
"To Emily Dickinson" (H. Crane), **Retro. Supp. II:** 76
"To E. T." (Frost), **Retro. Supp. I:** 132
"To Feel These Things" (L. Michaels), **Supp. XVI:** 214

To Feel These Things (L. Michaels), **Supp. XVI:** 205, **213–214**
Toffler, Alvin, **Supp. IV Part 2:** 517
"To Fill" (Moore), **Supp. X:** 168, 169
"To Gabriela, a Young Writer" (Mora), **Supp. XIII:** 220
To Have and Have Not (film), **Supp. XV:** 347
To Have and Have Not (Hemingway), **I:** 31; **II:** 253–254, 264; **Retro. Supp. I:** 182, **183,** 187
"To Helen" (Poe), **III:** 410, 411, 427; **Retro. Supp. II:** 102
"To Hell With Dying" (Walker), **Supp. III Part 2:** 523
"To His Father" (Jeffers), **Supp. II Part 2:** 415
Toilet, The (Baraka), **Supp. II Part 1:** 37, 40–42
"To James Russell Lowell" (Holmes), **Supp. I Part 1:** 311
To Jerusalem and Back (Bellow), **Retro. Supp. II:** 29
"To Jesus on His Birthday" (Millay), **III:** 136–137
"To John Keats" (Lowell), **II:** 516
"To Judge Faolain, Dead Long Enough: A Summons" (McCarriston), **Supp. XIV:** 264–265
"To Justify My Singing" (Wright), **Supp. III Part 2:** 590
"To Kill a Deer" (C. Frost), **Supp. XV:** 102
To Kill a Mockingbird (film), **Supp. VIII:** 128–129
To Kill a Mockingbird (Lee), **Supp. VIII: 113–129; Supp. XVI:** 259
"*To Kill a Mockingbird:* Harper Lee's Tragic Vision" (Dave), **Supp. VIII:** 126
To Kill a Mockingbird: Threatening Boundaries (Johnson), **Supp. VIII:** 126
Toklas, Alice B., **IV:** 27; **Supp. IV Part 1:** 81, 91; **Supp. XVI:** 187
"Tokyo Story" (Wasserstein), **Supp. XV:** 328
"To Light" (Hogan), **Supp. IV Part 1:** 402
"To Live and Diet" (Wasserstein), **Supp. XV:** 328
Tolkien, J. R. R., **Supp. V:** 140
Tolkin, Michael, **Supp. XI:** 160
Toller, Ernst, **I:** 479
"To Lose the Earth" (Sexton), **Supp. II Part 2:** 684, 685
Tolson, Melvin, **Retro. Supp. I:** 208, 209, 210
Tolstoy, Leo, **I:** 6, 7, 58, 103, 312, 376; **II:** 191–192, 205, 271, 272, 275, 276, 281, 285, 286, 320, 407, 542, 559, 570, 579, 606; **III:** 37, 45, 61, 323, 467, 572; **IV:** 17, 21, 170, 285; **Retro. Supp. I:** 91, 225; **Retro. Supp. II:** 299; **Supp. I Part 1:** 2, 3, 6, 20; **Supp. IV Part 1:** 392; **Supp. IX:** 246; **Supp. V:** 277, 323; **Supp. XI:** 68; **Supp. XII:** 310, 322; **Supp. XIV:** 87, 97, 98
"To Lu Chi" (Nemerov), **III:** 275
Tom (Cummings), **I:** 430
"Tom" (Oliver), **Supp. VII:** 232
"Tom, Tom, the Piper's Son" (Ransom), **Supp. X:** 58
"To M, with a Rose" (Lanier), **Supp. I Part 1:** 364
To Make a Prairie (Kumin), **Supp. IV Part 2:** 440, 441
"To Make Words Disappear" (Simpson), **Supp. IX:** 265–266
Tomás and the Library Lady (Mora), **Supp. XIII:** 216, 221
"Tomatoes" (Francis), **Supp. IX:** 82
"Tom Brown at Fisk" (Du Bois), **Supp. II Part 1:** 160
Tom Brown's School Days (Hughes), **Supp. I Part 2:** 406
"Tomb Stone" (Dickey), **Supp. IV Part 1:** 185
"Tombstone Blues" (song, Dylan), **Supp. XVIII:** 30
Tomcat in Love (O'Brien), **Supp. V:** 238, 240, 243, 252–254
"Tomcat's Wife, The" (C. Bly), **Supp. XVI:** 40
Tomcat's Wife and Other Stories, The (C. Bly), **Supp. XVI:** 40–41
"Tom Fool at Jamaica" (Moore), **III:** 215
To Mix with Time (Swenson), **Supp. IV Part 2:** 637, 643–645, 645
Tom Jones (Fielding), **I:** 131; **Supp. V:** 127
Tomlinson, Charles, **Supp. XVI:** 284
Tommy Gallagher's Crusade (Farrell), **II:** 44
Tommyknockers, The (King), **Supp. V:** 139, 144
"Tommy's Burglar" (Henry), **Supp. II Part 1:** 399, 401
Tomo Cheeki (pseudonym). *See* Freneau, Philip
Tomorrow is Another Day (film, Feist), **Supp. XVII:** 62
"Tomorrow the Moon" (Dos Passos), **I:** 493
"Tom Outland's Story" (Cather), **I:** 325–326
Tompkins, Jane, **Supp. XVI:** 89; **Supp. XVIII:** 258, 259, 263
Tompson, Benjamin, **Supp. I Part 1:** 110, 111
Tom Sawyer (musical) (Gurney), **Supp. V:** 96
Tom Sawyer (Twain). *See Adventures of Tom Sawyer, The* (Twain)
Tom Sawyer Abroad (Twain), **II:** 482; **IV:** 19, 204
Tom Sawyer Detective (Twain), **IV:** 204
"Tom's Husband" (Jewett), **Retro. Supp. II:** 132, 141
Tom Swift (Stratemeyer), **III:** 146
"Tom Wolfe's Guide to Etiquette" (Wolfe), **Supp. III Part 2:** 578
"To My Brother Killed: Haumont Wood: October, 1918" (Bogan), **Supp. III Part 1:** 58
"To My Class, on Certain Fruits and Flowers Sent Me in Sickness" (Lanier), **Supp. I Part 1:** 370
"To My Father's Ghost" (Everwine), **Supp. XV:** 76
"To My Ghost Reflected in the Auxvasse River" (Levis), **Supp. XI:** 265
"To My Greek" (Merrill), **Supp. III Part 1:** 326
"To My Mother" (Berry), **Supp. X:** 23
"To My Small Son, at the Photographer's" (Hay), **Supp. XIV:** 121
"To My Small Son, on Certain Occasions" (Hay), **Supp. XIV:** 121
"To Name is to Possess" (Kincaid), **Supp. VII:** 194
Tone, Aileen, **I:** 21–22
"Tongue Is, The" (Komunyakaa), **Supp. XIII:** 113
"Tongue of the Jews" (Bukiet), **Supp. XVII:** 47
Tongues (Shepard and Chaikin), **Supp. III Part 2:** 433
Tongues of Angels, The (Price), **Supp. VI:** 265
Tongues Untied (Riggs; film), **Supp. XI:** 19, 20
"Tonight" (Lowell), **II:** 538
"Tonight Is the Night of the Prom" (Jarman), **Supp. XVII:** 113
Tonight Is the Night of the Prom (Jarman), **Supp. XVII:** 110, **112–113**
Tony Kushner in Conversation (Vorlicky, ed.), **Supp. IX:** 132
"Too Anxious for Rivers" (Frost), **II:** 162
"Too Blue" (Hughes), **Retro. Supp. I:** 207
"Too Damn Close: Thresholds and Their Maintenance in Rick Bass's Work" (Kerridge), **Supp. XVI:** 26
"Too Early" (Leopold), **Supp. XIV:** 186
"Too Early Spring" (Benét), **Supp. XI:** 53
"Too Far from Home" (Bowles), **Supp. IV Part 1:** 94–95
Too Far from Home: Selected Writings of Paul Bowles (Halpern, ed.), **Supp. IV Part 1:** 94, 95
Too Far to Go: The Maples Stories (Updike), **Retro. Supp. I:** 321
"Too Good To Be True": The Life and Art of Leslie Fiedler (Winchell), **Supp. XIII:** 94, 98, 99, 101
Toohey, John Peter, **Supp. IX:** 190
Toolan, David, **Supp. IV Part 1:** 308
Too Late (Dixon), **Supp. XII: 143–144**
"Too-Late Born, The" (Hemingway), **III:** 9
Toole, John Kennedy, **Supp. XIV:** 21
Toomer, Jean, **Retro. Supp. II:** 79; **Supp. I Part 1:** 325, 332; **Supp. III Part 2: 475–491; Supp. IV Part 1:** 16, 164, 168; **Supp. IX: 305–322; Supp. XIII:** 305; **Supp. XVIII:** 122
Toomer, Nathan Eugene Pinchback. *See* Toomer, Jean
Too Much Johnson (film), **Supp. IV Part 1:** 83
"To One Who Said Me Nay" (Cullen), **Supp. IV Part 1:** 166
"Tooth, The" (Jackson), **Supp. IX:** 122
Tooth of Crime, The (Shepard), **Supp. III Part 2:** 432, 441–445, 447
"Too Young" (O'Hara), **III:** 369

"Top Israeli Official Hints at 'Shared' Jerusalem" (Nye), **Supp. XIII:** 287
"To P. L., 1916–1937" (Levine), **Supp. V:** 185
"To Please a Shadow" (Brodsky), **Supp. VIII:** 30
"Top of the Hill" (Jewett), **II:** 406
"Topography" (Olds), **Supp. X:** 208
Topper (T. Smith), **Supp. IX:** 194
Torah, **IV:** 19
"Torch Songs" (Wrigley), **Supp. XVIII:** 296
"Torquemada" (Bukiet), **Supp. XVII:** 44
"Torquemada" (Longfellow), **II:** 505; **Retro. Supp. II:** 164
Torrence, Ridgely, **III:** 507
Torrent and the Night Before, The (Robinson), **III:** 504
Torrents of Spring, The (Hemingway), **I:** 117; **II:** 250–251
Torres, Héctor A., **Supp. XIII:** 225
Torres, Louis, **Supp. IV Part 2:** 529, 530
Torsney, Cheryl, **Retro. Supp. I:** 224
Tortilla Curtain, The (Boyle), **Supp. VIII: 9–10**
Tortilla Flat (Steinbeck), **IV:** 50, 51, 61, 64
Tory Lover, The (Jewett), **II:** 406; **Retro. Supp. II:** 144–145
"Toscana" (Dixon), **Supp. XII:** 154
"To Sir Toby" (Freneau), **Supp. II Part 1:** 269
"To Sophy, Expectant" (Mumford), **Supp. II Part 2:** 475
"To Speak of Woe That Is in Marriage" (Lowell), **II:** 550
"To Statecraft Embalmed" (Moore), **III:** 197
To Stay Alive (Levertov), **Supp. III Part 1:** 280–282
"Total Eclipse" (Dillard), **Supp. VI:** 28
Toth, Emily, **Retro. Supp. II:** 71
Toth, Susan Allan, **Retro. Supp. II:** 138
"To the Americans of the United States" (Freneau), **Supp. II Part 1:** 271
"To the Apennines" (Bryant), **Supp. I Part 1:** 157, 164
"To the Bleeding Hearts Association of American Novelists" (Nemerov), **III:** 281
"To the Botequim & Back" (Bishop), **Retro. Supp. II:** 51
To the Bright and Shining Sun (Burke), **Supp. XIV:** 22, 25
"To the Citizens of the United States" (Paine), **Supp. I Part 2:** 519–520
"To the Dandelion" (Lowell), **Supp. I Part 2:** 424
"To the End" (Haines), **Supp. XII:** 212–213
To the Ends of the Earth: The Selected Travels of Paul Theroux, **Supp. VIII:** 324
To the Finland Station: A Study in the Writing and Acting of History (Wilson), **IV:** 429, 436, 443–444, 446
"To the Governor & Legislature of Massachusetts" (Nemerov), **III:** 287
To the Green Man (Jarman), **Supp. XVII:** 110, 120–121
To the Holy Spirit (Winters), **Supp. II Part 2:** 810
"To the Keeper of the King's Water Works" (Freneau), **Supp. II Part 1:** 269
"To the Lacedemonians" (Tate), **IV:** 134
"To the Laodiceans" (Jarrell), **Retro. Supp. I:** 121, 140
To the Lighthouse (Woolf), **I:** 309; **II:** 600; **Retro. Supp. II:** 337; **Supp. VIII:** 155
"To the Man on Trail" (London), **II:** 466
"To the Memory of the Brave Americans Under General Greene" (Freneau), **Supp. II Part 1:** 262, 274
"To the Muse" (Wright), **Supp. III Part 2:** 601
"To the Nazi Leaders" (Hay), **Supp. XIV:** 121
"To the New World" (Jarrell), **II:** 371
"To the One of Fictive Music" (Stevens), **IV:** 89; **Retro. Supp. I:** 297, 300
"To the One Upstairs" (Simic), **Supp. VIII:** 283
"To the Peoples of the World" (Du Bois), **Supp. II Part 1:** 172
To the Place of Trumpets (B. Kelly), 132; **Supp. XVII: 123–127**
"To the Pliocene Skull" (Harte), **Supp. II Part 1:** 343–344
"To the Reader" (Baudelaire), **II:** 544–545
"To The Reader" (Jarman), **Supp. XVII:** 115
"To the Reader" (Levertov), **Supp. III Part 1:** 277
"To the River Arve" (Bryant), **Supp. I Part 1:** 163
"To the Snake" (Levertov), **Supp. III Part 1:** 277
"To the Stone-Cutters" (Jeffers), **Supp. II Part 2:** 420
"To the Unseeable Animal" (Berry), **Supp. X:** 31
"To the Western World" (Simpson), **Supp. IX:** 269, 270
To the White Sea (Dickey), **Supp. IV Part 1:** 186, 190–191
"To the Young Who Want to Die" (Brooks), **Supp. III Part 1:** 85–86
"To Tlaoc of the Rain" (Everwine), **Supp. XV:** 77
"To Train a Writer" (Bierce), **I:** 199
"Touch, The" (Sexton), **Supp. II Part 2:** 687
Touch and Go (M. F. K. Fisher and D. Parrish), **Supp. XVII:** 84
"Touching the Tree" (Merwin), **Supp. III Part 1:** 355
Touching the World (Eakin), **Supp. VIII:** 167
Touch of Danger, A (Jones), **Supp. XI:** 226, **228–229**
Touch of the Poet, A (O'Neill), **III:** 385, 401, 404
Touchstone, The (Wharton), **Retro. Supp. I:** 365
"Touch-up Man" (Komunyakaa), **Supp. XIII:** 119
Tough Guys Don't Dance (Mailer), **Retro. Supp. II:** 211
Toulet, Paul Jean, **IV:** 79
Tour (McNally), **Supp. XIII:** 197
"Tour 5" (Hayden), **Supp. II Part 1:** 381
To Urania (Brodsky), **Supp. VIII:** 22, 28–29
Tourgée, Albion W., **Supp. XIV:** 63
"Tour Guide" (Komunyakaa), **Supp. XIII:** 114
"Tourist Death" (MacLeish), **III:** 12
Tourmaline (J. Scott), **Supp. XVII: 192–194,** 195
Tour of Duty (Dos Passos), **I:** 489
Touron the Prairies, A (Irving), **II:** 312–313
Tovey, Donald Francis, **Supp. XIV:** 336
To Walk a Crooked Mile (McGrath), **Supp. X:** 117
Toward a New Synthesis (Begiebing), **Retro. Supp. II:** 210
"Toward Nightfall" (Simic), **Supp. VIII:** 277
Towards a Better Life (Burke), **I:** 270
"Towards a Chicano Poetics: The Making of the Chicano Subject, 1969–1982" (Saldívar), **Supp. IV Part 2:** 544
Towards an Enduring Peace (Bourne), **I:** 232
"Towards Morning" (Pedersen; Nelson, trans.), **Supp. XVIII:** 180
Toward the Blanched Alphabets (Sobin), **Supp. XVI:** 290
Toward the Gulf (Masters), **Supp. I Part 2:** 465–466
"Toward the Solstice" (Rich), **Supp. I Part 2:** 575–576
Toward Wholeness in Paule Marshall's Fiction (Pettis), **Supp. XI:** 276
"Tower" (Merwin), **Supp. III Part 1:** 343
"Tower Beyond Tragedy, The" (Jeffers), **Supp. II Part 2:** 429–430
Tower of Ivory (MacLeish), **III:** 3–4
Towers, Robert, **Supp. IX:** 259; **Supp. XVI:** 211
"To What Red Hell" (C. Himes), **Supp. XVI:** 137
"To Whistler, American" (Pound), **III:** 465–466
"To Wine" (Bogan), **Supp. III Part 1:** 57, 58
Town, Caren J., **Supp. XVIII:** 195, 199
Town, The (Faulkner), **II:** 57, 73; **Retro. Supp. I:** 74, 82
Town, The (Richter), **Supp. XVIII:** 207, **214–215,** 217
Town and the City, The (Kerouac), **Supp. III Part 1:** 222–224; **Supp. XIV:** 143
"Town Crier" (Bierce), **I:** 193, 194, 195, 196
"*Town Crier* Exclusive, Confessions of a Princess Manqué: 'How Royals Found Me"Unsuitable"to Marry Their Larry'" (Elkin), **Supp. VI:** 56
Town Down the River, The (Robinson), **III:** 508
"Town Dump, The" (Nemerov), **III:** 272, 275, 281
Towne, Robert, **Supp. XI:** 159, 172, 174

"Townhouse Interior with Cat" (Clampitt), **Supp. IX:** 40
"Townies" (Dubus), **Supp. VII:** 86
"Town of the Sound of a Twig Breaking" (Carson), **Supp. XII: 102**
"Town Poor, The" (Jewett), **Retro. Supp. II:** 138, 139, 143
Townsend, Alison, **Supp. XIII:** 222
Townsend, Ann, **Supp. V:** 77
"Towns in Colour" (Lowell), **II:** 523–524
Townsman, The (Sedges), **Supp. II Part 1:** 124–125
"To World War Two" (Koch), **Supp. XV:** 184
"Toys in a Field" (Komunyakaa), **Supp. XIII:** 122
Toys in a Field (Komunyakaa), **Supp. XIII: 121–122**
Toys in the Attic (Hellman), **Supp. I Part 1:** 289–290
Tracer (F. Barthelme), **Supp. XI:** 31–32, 33
Traces of Thomas Hariot, The (Rukeyser), **Supp. VI:** 273, 274, 283
"Tracing Life with a Finger" (Caldwell), **I:** 291
Tracker (Wagoner), **Supp. IX:** 329, **336–337**
"Tracking" (Wagoner), **Supp. IX:** 329
"Track Meet, The" (Schwartz), **Supp. II Part 2:** 665
Tracks (Erdrich), **Supp. IV Part 1:** 259, 262–263, 269, 272, 273–274, 274, 275
"Tract" (W. C. Williams), **Retro. Supp. I:** 414
"Tract against Communism, A" (Twelve Southerners), **IV:** 125, 237
Tractatus (Wittgenstein), **Supp. XVII:** 143
Tracy, Benjamin, **Supp. XVIII:** 4
Tracy, D. H., **Supp. XVIII:** 178
Tracy, Lee, **IV:** 287, 288
Tracy, Steven, **Retro. Supp. I:** 195
"Trade, The" (Levine), **Supp. V:** 193
Trading Twelves (Callahan and Murray, eds.), **Retro. Supp. II:** 119
"Tradition and Industrialization" (Wright), **IV:** 489–490
"Tradition and Mythology: Signatures of Landscape in Chicana Poetry" (Rebolledo), **Supp. XIII:** 214
"Tradition and the Individual Talent" (Eliot), **I:** 441, 574, 585; **Retro. Supp. I:** 59, 286
Tragedies, Life and Letters of James Gates Percival (Swinburne), **Supp. I Part 2:** 422
Tragedy of Don Ippolito, The (Howells), **II:** 279
"Tragedy of Error, A" (James), **II:** 322; **Retro. Supp. I:** 218
Tragedy of Pudd'nhead Wilson, The (Twain), **IV:** 206–207
Tragic America (Dreiser), **Retro. Supp. II:** 95
"Tragic Dialogue" (Wylie), **Supp. I Part 2:** 724
Tragic Ground (Caldwell), **I:** 297, 306
Tragic Muse, The (James), **Retro. Supp. I:** 227
Traherne, Thomas, **IV:** 151; **Supp. III Part 1:** 14; **Supp. V:** 208; **Supp. XV:** 212; **Supp. XVI:** 282, 288, 295
"Trail, The" (W. J. Smith), **Supp. XIII:** 342
Trailerpark (Banks), **Supp. V:** 12
"Trailing Arbutus, The" (Whittier), **Supp. I Part 2:** 691
Trail of the Lonesome Pine, The (Fox), **Supp. XIII:** 166
"Train, The" (O'Connor), **Retro. Supp. II:** 225
"Train Rising Out of the Sea" (Ashbery), **Supp. III Part 1:** 22
"Trains" (Banks), **Supp. V:** 8
"Train Tune" (Bogan), **Supp. III Part 1:** 64
"Traits of Indian Character" (Irving), **II:** 303
Trakl, Georg, **Supp. XVII:** 241
Tramp Abroad, A (Twain), **IV:** 200
Tramping With a Poet in the Rockies (S. Graham), **Supp. I Part 2:** 397
Tramp's Excuse, The (Lindsay), **Supp. I Part 2:** 379, 380, 382
"Transatlantic" (Toomer), **Supp. III Part 2:** 486
Transatlantic Sketches (James), **II:** 324; **Retro. Supp. I:** 219
"Transcendental Etude" (Rich), **Supp. I Part 2:** 576
"Transcontinental Highway" (Cowley), **Supp. II Part 1:** 141
"Transducer" (Ammons), **Supp. VII:** 28
"Transfiguration" (Jarman), **Supp. XVII:** 118, 119
"Transfigured Bird" (Merrill), **Supp. III Part 1:** 320–321
"Transformations" (Harjo), **Supp. XII:** 226
Transformations (Sexton), **Supp. II Part 2:** 689–691; **Supp. IV Part 2:** 447; **Supp. XIV:** 125
Transforming Madness: New Lives for People Living with Mental Illness (Neugeboren), **Supp. XVI:** 229
"Transit" (Conroy), **Supp. XVI:** 72
Transit to Narcissus, A (Mailer), **Retro. Supp. II:** 196
"Translation and Transposition" (Carne-Ross), **Supp. I Part 1:** 268–269
"Translation of a Fragment of Simonides" (Bryant), **Supp. I Part 1:** 153, 155
"Translations" (Rich), **Supp. I Part 2:** 563
Translations of Ezra Pound, The (Kenner, ed.), **III:** 463
Translations of the Gospel Back into Tongues (Wright), **Supp. XV: 342–343,** 346
"Trans-National America" (Bourne), **I:** 229, 230
"Transparency" (X. J. Kennedy), **Supp. XV:** 159–160
"Transparent Itineraries: 1983" (Sobin), **Supp. XVI:** 287
"Transparent Itineraries: 1984" (Sobin), **Supp. XVI:** 287
"Transparent Itineraries: 1992" (Sobin), **Supp. XVI:** 289
"Transparent Itineraries" poems (Sobin), **Supp. XVI:** 290
"Transparent Man, The" (Hecht), **Supp. X: 69–70**
Transparent Man, The (Hecht), **Supp. X:** 57, **69–71**
Transparent Things (Nabokov), **Retro. Supp. I:** 266, 270, 277
"Transport" (Simic), **Supp. VIII:** 282
Transport to Summer (Stevens), **IV:** 76, 93; **Retro. Supp. I:** 309–312
Tranströmer, Thomas, **Supp. IV Part 2:** 648
"Traps for the Unwary" (Bourne), **I:** 235
Trash Trilogy (McMurtry), **Supp. V:** 225–226, 231
Traubel, Horace, **IV:** 350
"Travel: After a Death" (Kenyon), **Supp. VII:** 169
Travel Alarm (Nye), **Supp. XIII:** 277
"Traveler, The" (Haines), **Supp. XII:** 203–204, 210
"Traveler, The" (Stegner), **Supp. IV Part 2:** 605
Traveler at Forty, A (Dreiser), **I:** 515
Traveler from Altruria, a Romance A, (Howells), **II:** 285, 287
Traveler's Tree, The: New and Selected Poems (W. J. Smith), **Supp. XIII:** 332, 347
"Traveling" (Paley), **Supp. VI:** 230
"Traveling Light" (Wagoner), **Supp. IX:** 329
"Traveling Onion, The" (Nye), **Supp. XIII:** 276
"Traveling through the Dark" (Stafford), **Supp. XI:** 318–320, 321, 323, 329
Traveling through the Dark (Stafford), **Supp. XI:** 311, 316, **318–321**
Travelling in Amherst: A Poet's Journal, 1931–1954, **Supp. IX: 88–89**
Travels in Alaska (Muir), **Supp. IX:** 182, 185–186
"Travels in Georgia" (McPhee), **Supp. III Part 1:** 293–294
"Travels in North America" (Kees), **Supp. XV:** 133–134
Travels in the Congo (Gide), **III:** 210
"Travels in the South" (Ortiz), **Supp. IV Part 2:** 506
Travels with Charley (Steinbeck), **IV:** 52
"Travel Writing: Why I Bother" (Theroux), **Supp. VIII:** 310
Travis, Merle, **Supp. V:** 335
Travisano, Thomas, **Retro. Supp. II:** 40
Treasure Hunt (Buechner), **Supp. XII:** 52
Treasure Island (Stevenson), **Supp. X:** 230
"Treasure of the Redwoods, A" (Harte), **Supp. II Part 1:** 337
Treasury of Art Masterpieces, A: From the Renaissance to the Present Day (Craven), **Supp. XII:** 44
Treasury of English Aphorisms, A (L. P. Smith), **Supp. XIV:** 344
Treasury of English Prose, A (L. P. Smith, ed.), **Supp. XIV:** 341
Treasury of the Theatre, A (Gassner), **Supp. I Part 1:** 292

Treasury of Yiddish Stories, A (Howe and Greenberg, eds.), **Supp. I Part 2:** 432
Treat 'Em Rough (Lardner), **II:** 422–423
Treatise Concerning Religious Affections (Edwards), **I:** 547, 552, 554, 555, 557, 558, 560, 562
Treatise Concerning the Lord's Supper (Doolittle), **IV:** 150
"Treatise on Poetry" (Milosz), **Supp. VIII:** 20
Treatise on Right and Wrong, A (Mencken), **III:** 110, 119
"Treatise on Tales of Horror, A" (Wilson), **IV:** 438
Treatise on the Gods, A (Mencken), **III:** 108–109, 119
"Treatment" (Wright), **Supp. XV:** 343
Trece poetas del mundo azteca (León-Portilla), **Supp. XV:** 77
Tre Croce (Tozzi), **Supp. III Part 2:** 616
"Tree, a Rock, a Cloud, A" (McCullers), **II:** 587
"Tree, The" (Pound), **Retro. Supp. I:** 286; **Supp. I Part 1:** 255
"Tree, the Bird, The" (Roethke), **III:** 548
"Tree at My Window" (Frost), **II:** 155
Tree Grows in Brooklyn, A (B. Smith), **Supp. XVII:** 9
Tree Grows in Brooklyn, A (film; Kazan), **Supp. XVI:** 193
"Tree House at Night, The" (Dickey), **Supp. IV Part 1:** 179
Tree Is Older Than You Are, The (Nye, ed.), **Supp. XIII:** 280
"Tree of Laughing Bells, The" (Lindsay), **Supp. I Part 2:** 376
"Tree of Night, A" (Capote), **Supp. III Part 1:** 114, 120
Tree of Night and Other Stories, A (Capote), **Supp. III Part 1:** 114
"Trees, The" (Rich), **Supp. I Part 2:** 555
Trees, The (Richter), **Supp. XVIII: 212–213,** 220
"Trees Listening to Bach" (Merrill), **Supp. III Part 1:** 336
Tree That Came to Stay, The (Quindlen), **Supp. XVII:** 167
Tree Where Man Was Born, The (Matthiessen), **Supp. V:** 199, 203, 204
Trejo, Ernesto, **Supp. V:** 178, 180; **Supp. XIII:** 313, 316; **Supp. XV:** 73
Trelawny, Edward John, **Supp. I Part 2:** 721
"Trellis for R., A" (Swenson), **Supp. IV Part 2:** 647
Tremblay, Bill, **Supp. XIII:** 112
Tremble (Wright), **Supp. XV: 348–349**
"Trespass" (Frost), **Retro. Supp. I:** 139
"Tretitoli, Where the Bomb Group Was" (Hugo), **Supp. VI:** 138
Trevelyan, Robert C., **Supp. XIV:** 334
Trevor-Roper, Hugh, **Supp. XIV:** 348
Trial, The (Kafka), **IV:** 113; **Retro. Supp. II:** 20
"Trial, The" (Rukeyser), **Supp. VI:** 278
"Trial by Existence, The" (Frost), **II:** 166
Trial of a Poet, The (Shapiro), **Supp. II Part 2:** 710
Trial of the Hawk, The: A Comedy of the Seriousness of Life (Lewis), **II:** 441
Trials of the Human Heart (Rowson), **Supp. XV:** 237, 239
Tribal Secrets: Recovering American Indian Intellectual Traditions (Warrior), **Supp. IV Part 1:** 329
"Tribute" (A. Finch), **Supp. XVII:** 72, 73–74
"Tribute (To My Mother)" (Cullen), **Supp. IV Part 1:** 166
"Tribute, A" (Easton), **Supp. IV Part 2:** 461
"Tribute, The" (Doolittle), **Supp. I Part 1:** 267
Tribute to Freud (Doolittle), **Supp. I Part 1:** 253, 254, 258, 259, 260, 268
Tribute to the Angels (Doolittle), **Supp. I Part 1:** 272
"Trick on the World, A" (Ríos), **Supp. IV Part 2:** 553
"Tricks" (Olds), **Supp. X:** 203–204
"Trick Scenery" (F. Barthelme), **Supp. XI:** 26
Trifler, The (Masters), **Supp. I Part 2:** 459–460
Trifles (Glaspell), **Supp. III Part 1:** 175, 178, 179, 182, 186, 187; **Supp. X:** 46
Trifonov, Iurii V., **Retro. Supp. I:** 278
Triggering Town, The: Lectures and Essays on Poetry and Writing (Hugo), **Supp. VI:** 133, 140
Trilling, Diana, **II:** 587, 600; **Supp. I Part 1:** 297; **Supp. XII:** 126
Trilling, Lionel, **I:** 48; **II:** 579; **III:** 308, 310, 319, 327; **IV:** 201, 211; **Retro. Supp. I:** 19, 97, 121, 216, 227; **Supp. III Part 2: 493–515; Supp. IX:** 266, 287; **Supp. V:** 259; **Supp. VIII:** 93, 98, 190, 231, 236, 243; **Supp. XIII:** 100–101; **Supp. XIV:** 280, 288–289; **Supp. XV:** 20, 140, 152
Trilogy (Doolittle), **Supp. I Part 1:** 271, 272
Trilogy of Desire (Dreiser), **I:** 497, 508; **Retro. Supp. II:** 94, 96, **101–102**
Trimberger, Ellen Kay, **Supp. XVII:** 96, 106
Trimmed Lamp, The (O. Henry), **Supp. II Part 1:** 410
"Trinc" (McGrath), **Supp. X:** 127
Trio (Baker), **Supp. I Part 1:** 277
"Triolets for Triolet" (Nelson), **Supp. XVIII:** 179
"*Trip*" (F. Barthelme), **Supp. XI:** 26
Triple Thinkers, The: Ten Essays on Literature (Wilson), **IV:** 428, 431; **Supp. II Part 1:** 146
"Triplex" (Doolittle), **Supp. I Part 1:** 271
Tripmaster Monkey: His Fake Book (Kingston), **Supp. V:** 157, 158, 169, 170–173
Trippings in Authorland (Forrester), **Supp. XVIII:** 13
Trippings of Tom Pepper, The (Briggs), **Supp. XVIII:** 3, **13–14**
"Trip to Hanoi" (Sontag), **Supp. III Part 2:** 460–462
Trip to Parnassus, A; or, The Judgement of Apollo on Dramatic Authors and Performers (Rowson), **Supp. XV: 232–233**
"Triptych" (Eberhart), **I:** 522, 539
Tristan and Iseult, **Retro. Supp. I:** 328, 329, 330, 331
Tristessa (Kerouac), **Supp. III Part 1:** 225, 227, 229
Tristram (Robinson), **III:** 521, 522, 523
Tristram Shandy (Sterne), **I:** 299; **IV:** 465–466; **Supp. V:** 127; **Supp. XVIII:** 60
"Triumphal March" (Eliot), **I:** 580; **III:** 17; **Retro. Supp. I:** 64
Triumph of Achilles, The (Glück), **Supp. V:** 79, 84–86, 92
"Triumph of a Modern, The, or, Send for the Lawyer" (Anderson), **I:** 113, 114
"Triumph of the Egg, The" (Anderson), **I:** 113
Triumph of the Egg, The: A Book of Impressions from American Life in Tales and Poems (Anderson), **I:** 112, 114
Triumph of the Spider Monkey, The (Oates), **Supp. II Part 2:** 522
Triumphs of the Reformed Religion in America (Mather), **Supp. II Part 2:** 453
Trivial Breath (Wylie), **Supp. I Part 2:** 709, 722–724
Trivia; or, the Art of Walking the Streets of London (Gay), **Supp. XIV:** 337
Trivia: Printed from the Papers of Anthony Woodhouse, Esq. (L. P. Smith), **Supp. XIV:** 336, **337–340**
Trocchi, Alexander, **Supp. XI:** 294, 295, 301
Troilus and Criseyde (Chaucer), **Retro. Supp. I:** 426
Trois contes (Flaubert), **IV:** 31, 37
Trojan Horse, The: A Play (MacLeish), **III:** 21
"Trojan Women, The" (Maxwell), **Supp. VIII:** 169
Troll Garden, The (Cather), **I:** 313, 314–316, 322; **Retro. Supp. I:** 5, 6, 8, 14
"Trolling for Blues" (Wilbur), **Supp. III Part 2:** 563–564
Trollope, Anthony, **I:** 10, 375; **II:** 192, 237; **III:** 51, 70, 281, 382; **Retro. Supp. I:** 361
Trombly, Albert Edmund, **Supp. I Part 2:** 403
Trombold, John, **Supp. XVIII:** 111
"Troop Train" (Shapiro), **Supp. II Part 2:** 707
"Tropes of the Text" (Gass), **Supp. VI:** 88
Tropic of Cancer (H. Miller), **III:** 170, 171, 174, 177, 178–180, 181, 182, 183, 187, 190; **Supp. V:** 119; **Supp. X:** 187
Tropic of Capricorn (H. Miller), **III:** 170, 176–177, 178, 182, 183, 184, 187, 188–189, 190
Trotsky, Leon, **I:** 366; **II:** 562, 564; **IV:** 429
Trotter, W., **I:** 249
Troubled Island (opera; Hughes and Still), **Retro. Supp. I:** 203
Troubled Lovers in History (Goldbarth), **Supp. XII:** 176, **192–193**

Trouble Follows Me (Macdonald, under Millar), **Supp. IV Part 2:** 466
Trouble in July (Caldwell), **I:** 297, 304–305, 306, 309
Trouble Island (Hughes), **Supp. I Part 1:** 328
"Trouble of Marcie Flint, The" (Cheever), **Supp. I Part 1:** 186
Trouble with Francis, The: An Autobiography (Francis), **Supp. IX:** 76, 77, 82, **84–85**
Trouble with God, The (Francis), **Supp. IX:** 88
"Trouble with the Stars and Stripes" (Nye), **Supp. XIII:** 277
Trouillot, Michel-Rolphe, **Supp. X:** 14–15
Troupe, Quincy, **Retro. Supp. II:** 15, 111; **Supp. X:** 242
"Trout" (Hugo), **Supp. VI:** 135
Trout Fishing in America (Brautigan), **Supp. VIII:** 43
"Trouvée" (Bishop), **Retro. Supp. II:** 49
"Truce of the Bishop, The" (Frederic), **II:** 139–140
"Truck Stop: Minnesota" (Dunn), **Supp. XI:** 145–146
True and False: Heresy and Common Sense for the Actor (Mamet), **Supp. XIV:** 241, 243
Trueblood, Valerie, **Supp. XIII:** 306
True Confessions (Dunne), **Supp. IV Part 1:** 198
True Confessions (film), **Supp. IV Part 1:** 198
True History of the Conquest of New Spain, The (Castillo), **III:** 13
True Intellectual System of the Universe, The (Cuddleworth), **II:** 10
"True Love" (Olds), **Supp. X:** 212
Trueman, Matthew (pseudonym). *See* Lowell, James Russell
"True Morality" (Bell), **Supp. X:** 13
"True Romance" (Everett), **Supp. XVIII:** 65
"True Stories" (Atwood), **Supp. XIII:** 34
True Stories (Atwood), **Supp. XIII:** 34–35
"True Stories of Bitches" (Mamet), **Supp. XIV:** 246, 252
"Truest Sport, The: Jousting with Sam and Charlie" (Wolfe), **Supp. III Part 2:** 581–582
"True Vine" (Wylie), **Supp. I Part 2:** 723
True West (Shepard), **Supp. III Part 2:** 433, 441, 445, 447, 448
Truman, Harry, **III:** 3
Truman Capote: In Which Various Friends, Enemies, Acquaintances, and Detractors Recall His Turbulent Career (Plimpton), **Supp. XVI:**245
Truman Show, The (film), **Supp. XVI:** 271
Trumbo, Dalton, **Supp. I Part 1:** 295; **Supp. XIII:** 6; **Supp. XVII:** 63
Trumbull, John, **Supp. II Part 1:** 65, 69, 70, 268
Trump, Donald, **Supp. IV Part 1:** 393
Trumpener, Katie, **Retro. Supp. I:** 380
"Trumpet Player" (Hughes), **Supp. I Part 1:** 333
Trumpet Shall Sound, The (Wilder), **IV:** 356
Trumpet Unblown, The (Hoffman), **Supp. XVIII:** 71, **74–75**
"Truro Bear, The" (Oliver), **Supp. VII:** 234
Truscott, Lucian K., **Supp. IV Part 2:** 683
Trust (Ozick), **Supp. V:** 257–258, 259, 260–263, 270, 272
Trust Me (Updike), **Retro. Supp. I:** 322
"Trust Yourself" (Emerson), **II:** 10
"Truth" (Emerson), **II:** 6
"Truth, The" (Jarrell), **II:** 381–382
"Truth about God, The" (Carson), **Supp. XII: 105–106**
"Truthful James" (Harte), **IV:** 196
"Truth Is, The" (Hogan), **Supp. IV Part 1:** 401–402
"Truth Is Forced, The" (Swenson), **Supp. IV Part 2:** 652
"Truth of the Matter, The" (Nemerov), **III:** 270
Truth Serum (Cooper), **Supp. XI:** 129
"Truth the Dead Know, The" (Sexton), **Supp. II Part 2:** 681
Trying to Save Piggy Sneed (Irving), **Supp. VI: 19–165**
"Trying to Talk with a Man" (Rich), **Supp. I Part 2:** 559
"Tryptich I" (Bell), **Supp. X:** 7
"Tryst, The" (Wharton), **Retro. Supp. I:** 378
"Try the Girl" (Chandler), **Supp. IV Part 1:** 125
"Ts'ai Chih" (Pound), **III:** 466
T. S. Eliot and American Philosophy (Jain), **Retro. Supp. I:** 58
T. S. Eliot's Silent Voices (Mayer), **Retro. Supp. I:** 58
Tsuji, Shizuo, **Supp. XVII:** 90
Tsvetayeva, Marina, **Supp. VIII:** 30
"Tuberoses" (E. Stoddard), **Supp. XV:** 282
Tuckerman, Frederick Goddard, **IV:** 144
"Tuesday, November 5th, 1940" (Benét), **Supp. XI:** 46, 52
"Tuesday April 25th 1966" (Olson), **Supp. II Part 2:** 585
"Tuesday Night at the Savoy Ballroom" (Komunyakaa), **Supp. XIII:** 132
Tuffield, Aviva, **Supp. XVI:** 147, 148
"Tuft of Flowers, The" (Frost), **II:** 153; **Retro. Supp. I:** 126, 127
Tufts, James Hayden, **Supp. I Part 2:** 632
Tu Fu, **II:** 526; **Supp. XV:** 47
Tu Fu (Ayscough), **II:** 527
Tugwell, Rexford Guy, **Supp. I Part 2:** 645
"Tulip" (Hammett), **Supp. IV Part 1:** 356
"Tulip Man, The" (McCarriston), **Supp. XIV:** 261
"Tulips" (Nye), **Supp. XIII:** 281
"Tulips" (Plath), **Retro. Supp. II:** 252–253; **Supp. I Part 2:** 540, 542, 544
"Tulips" (Snodgrass), **Supp. VI:** 325
Tulips and Chimneys (Cummings), **I:** 436, 437, 440, 445, 447
Tully, Jim, **III:** 103, 109
Tumble Tower (Modarressi and Tyler), **Supp. IV Part 2:** 657
"Tuned in Late One Night" (Stafford), **Supp. XI:** 327–328
Tunnel, The (Gass), **Supp. V:** 44; **Supp. VI: 89–91,** 94
"Tunnel, The" (Strand), **Supp. IV Part 2:** 622
"Tunnels" (Komunyakaa), **Supp. XIII:** 123
Tuqan, Fadwa, **Supp. XIII:** 278
Tura, Cosimo, **III:** 474–475
Turandot and Other Poems (Ashbery), **Supp. III Part 1:** 3
Turco, Lewis, **Supp. XV:** 118
Turgenev, Ivan Sergeevich, **I:** 106; **II:** 263, 271, 275, 280, 281, 288, 319, 320, 324–325, 338, 407; **III:** 461; **IV:** 17, 277; **Retro. Supp. I:** 215, 222; **Supp. VIII:** 167
Turgot, Anne Robert Jacques, **II:** 103; **Supp. I Part 1:** 250
"Turkey and Bones and Eating and We Liked It" (Stein), **IV:** 44
Turman, Glynn, **Supp. IV Part 1:** 362
Turnbull, Dr. George, **II:** 113
Turnbull, Lawrence, **Supp. I Part 1:** 352
"Turned" (Gilman), **Supp. XI:** 207
Turner, Addie, **IV:** 123
Turner, Darwin, **Supp. I Part 1:** 339; **Supp. IV Part 1:** 165
Turner, Frederick Jackson, **Supp. I Part 2:** 480, 481, 632, 640; **Supp. IV Part 2:** 596
Turner, Nat, **IV:** 113–114, 115, 116, 117
Turner, Patricia, **Supp. XIII:** 237
Turner, Russell. *See* Lacy, Ed
Turner, Victor, **Supp. IV Part 1:** 304
"Turning Away Variations on Estrangement" (Dickey), **Supp. IV Part 1:** 183
Turning Point, The (McCoy), **Supp. XIII:** 175
"Turning Thirty, I Contemplate Students Bicycling Home" (Dove), **Supp. IV Part 1:** 250
Turning Wind, A (Rukeyser), **Supp. VI:** 272–273, 279–280
"Turn of the Screw, The" (H. James), **II:** 331–332; **Retro. Supp. I:** 228, 229, 231, 232; **Supp. XVII:** 143
Turn of the Screw, The (H. James), **Retro. Supp. I:** 219, 231; **Supp. IV Part 2:** 682
Turns and Movies and Other Tales in Verse (Aiken), **I:** 65
"Turn with the Sun, A" (Knowles), **Supp. XII:** 237–238
Turow, Scott, **Supp. V:** 220; **Supp. XVII: 213–224**
Turpin, E. Walters, **Supp. XVIII:** 283
Turrinus, Lucius Mamilius, **IV:** 373
"Turtle" (Hogan), **Supp. IV Part 1:** 401
"Turtle, Swan" (Doty), **Supp. XI:** 121–122
Turtle, Swan (Doty), **Supp. XI: 121–122**
Turtle Island (Snyder), **Supp. VIII: 300–303**

Turtle Moon (Hoffman), **Supp. X:** 77, **87–88,** 89
"Turtle Shrine near Chittagong, The" (Nye), **Supp. XIII:** 277
Turturro, John, **Supp. XI:** 174
Tuscan Cities (Howells), **II:** 280
Tuskegee movement, **Supp. II Part 1:** 169, 172
Tuten, Frederic, **Supp. VIII:** 75, 76; **Supp. XIII:** 237, 249
Tuten, James, **Supp. XVIII:** 195
Tuthill, Louisa Cavolne, **Supp. I Part 2:** 684
"Tutored Child, The" (Kunitz), **Supp. III Part 1:** 264
Tuttleton, James W., **Supp. IV Part 1:** 166, 168
"T.V.A." (Agee), **I:** 35
Tvedten, Brother Benet, **Supp. IV Part 2:** 505
"TV Men" (Carson), **Supp. XII: 105, 112**
Twain, Mark, **I:** 57, 103, 107, 109, 190, 192, 193, 195, 197, 203, 209, 245, 246, 247–250, 255, 256, 257, 260, 261, 292, 342, 418, 469, 485; **II:** 70, 140, 259, 262, 266–268, 271, 272, 274–275, 276, 277, 280, 285–286, 287, 288, 289, 301, 304, 306, 307, 312, 415, 432, 434, 436, 446, 457, 467, 475, 476, 482; **III:** 65, 101, 102, 112–113, 114, 220, 347, 357, 409, 453, 454, 504, 507, 554, 558, 572, 575, 576; **IV: 190–213,** 333, 349, 451; **Retro. Supp. I:** 169, 194, 195; **Retro. Supp. II:** 123; **Supp. I Part 1:** 37, 39, 44, 247, 251, 313, 317; **Supp. I Part 2:** 377, 385, 393, 410, 455, 456, 457, 473, 475, 579, 602, 604, 618, 629, 651, 660; **Supp. II Part 1:** 193, 344, 354, 385; **Supp. IV Part 1:** 386, 388; **Supp. IV Part 2:** 463, 468, 603, 607, 693; **Supp. IX:** 14, 171; **Supp. V:** 44, 113, 131; **Supp. VIII:** 40, 189; **Supp. X:** 51, 227; **Supp. XII:** 343; **Supp. XIII:** 1, 17; **Supp. XV:** 41; **Supp. XVI:** 66, 208; **Supp. XVIII:** 1, 9, 13
"Twa Sisters, The" (ballad), **Supp. I Part 2:** 696
Twelfth Night (Shakespeare), **Supp. IV Part 1:** 83; **Supp. IX:** 14
"12 O'Clock News" (Bishop), **Retro. Supp. II:** 48
Twelve Men (Dreiser), **Retro. Supp. II:** 94, 104
Twelve Moons (Oliver), **Supp. VII:** 231, 233–236, 238, 240
Twelve Southerners, **IV:** 125; **Supp. X:** 25
Twelve Years a Slave (Northup), **Supp. XIV:** 32
Twentieth Century Authors, **I:** 376, 527
"Twentieth Century Fiction and the Black Mask of Humanity" (Ellison), **Retro. Supp. II:** 118
Twentieth Century Pleasures (Hass), **Supp. VI:** 103, 106, 109
"28" (Levine), **Supp. V:** 187, 191
"Twenty-Four Poems" (Schwartz), **Supp. II Part 2:** 646, 649
"2433 Agnes, First Home, Last House in Missoula" (Hugo), **Supp. VI:** 139–140
"Twenty Hill Hollow" (Muir), **Supp. IX:** 178
"Twenty Minutes" (Salter), **Supp. IX:** 260
"Twenty-One Love Poems" (Rich), **Supp. I Part 2:** 572–573
"Twenty-One Poems" (MacLeish), **III:** 19
Twenty Poems (Haines), **Supp. XII:** 204, **205–206**
Twenty Poems of Anna Akhmatova (Kenyon), **Supp. VII:** 165–166
Twenty Questions: (Posed by Poems) (McClatchy), **Supp. XII:** 254, **259–262**
27 Wagons Full of Cotton and Other One-Act Plays (T. Williams), **IV:** 381, 383
Twenty Thousand Leagues under the Sea (Verne), **I:** 480; **Supp. XI:** 63
"Twenty Years Ago" (Lindsay), **Supp. I Part 2:** 384, 399
Twenty Years at Hull-House (Addams), **Supp. I Part 1:** 3, 4, 11, 16
Twice over Lightly: New York Ten and Now (Hayes and Loos), **Supp. XVI:** 195
Twice-Told Tales (Hawthorne), **I:** 354; **II:** 224; **III:** 412, 421; **Retro. Supp. I:** 154–155, 160
Twichell, Chase, **Supp. V:** 16; **Supp. XVII:** 110, 112
Twilight (Frost), **II:** 151
"Twilight's Last Gleaming" (Burroughs and Elvins), **Supp. III Part 1:** 93, 94, 101
Twilight Sleep (Wharton), **IV:** 320–322, 324–325, 327, 328; **Retro. Supp. I:** 381
"Twin, The" (Olds), **Supp. X:** 207
"Twin Beds in Rome" (Updike), **Retro. Supp. I:** 332
"Twins of Table Mountain, The" (Harte), **Supp. II Part 1:** 355
"Twist, The" (Olson), **Supp. II Part 2:** 570
Twitch and Shout (film), **Supp. XVIII:** 143
Twitchel-Waas, Jeffrey, **Supp. XVIII:** 99
Two Admirals, The (Cooper), **I:** 350
Two against One (F. Barthelme), **Supp. XI:** 32, 33, 36
"Two Boys" (Moore), **Supp. X:** 173
"Two Brothers, The" (Jewett), **Retro. Supp. II:** 132
Two-Character Play, The (T. Williams), **IV:** 382, 386, 393, 398
Two Citizens (Wright), **Supp. III Part 2:** 602–604
"Two Deer" (Bass), **Supp. XVI:** 24
"Two Domains, The" (Goldbarth), **Supp. XII:** 192
"Two Environments, The" (Trilling), **Supp. III Part 2:** 510
"Two-Fisted Self Pity" (Broyard), **Supp. XI:** 348
Two for Texas (Burke), **Supp. XIV:** 25, 34
"Two Friends" (Cather), **I:** 332
"Two Gardens in Linndale" (Robinson), **III:** 508
Two Gentlemen in Bonds (Ransom), **III:** 491–492
Two: Gertrude Stein and Her Brother (Stein), **IV:** 43
"Two Ghosts" (Francis), **Supp. IX:** 87
"Two Hangovers" (Wright), **Supp. III Part 2:** 596
Two-Headed Poems (Atwood), **Supp. XIII:** 34
Two Hot to Handle (Lacy), **Supp. XV:** 206
Two Hours to Doom (Bryant), **Supp. XI:** 302
"Two Kitchens in Provence" (M. F. K. Fisher), **Supp. XVII:** 88, 91
"Two Ladies in Retirement" (Taylor), **Supp. V:** 320
Two Letters to the Citizens of the United States, and One to General Washington (Barlow), **Supp. II Part 1:** 80
"Two Lives, The" (Hogan), **Supp. IV Part 1:** 400, 402, 403, 406, 411
Two Long Poems (Stern), **Supp. IX:** 296
"Two Lovers and a Beachcomber by the Real Sea" (Plath), **Supp. I Part 2:** 536
Two Men (E. Stoddard), **Supp. XV:** 272, 273, **283–284**
"Two Men" (McClatchy)", **Supp. XII:** 269
Two Men of Sandy Bar (Harte), **Supp. II Part 1:** 354
Twomey, Jay, **Supp. XVII:** 111
"Two Moods of Love"(Cullen), **Supp. IV Part 1:** 166
"Two Morning Monologues"(Bellow), **I:** 150; **Retro. Supp. II:** 20
Two-Ocean War, The (Morison), **Supp. I Part 2:** 491
"Two of Hearts"(Hogan), **Supp. IV Part 1:** 410
"Two on a Party"(T. Williams), **IV:** 388
"Two or Three Things I Dunno About John Cassavetes"(Lethem), **Supp. XVIII:** 148
"Two Pendants: For the Ears"(W. C. Williams), **Retro. Supp. I:** 423
"Two Poems of Going Home"(Dickey), **Supp. IV Part 1:** 182–183
"Two Portraits"(Chopin), **Supp. I Part 1:** 218
"Two Presences, The"(R. Bly), **Supp. IV Part 1:** 65
"Two Rivers"(Stegner), **Supp. IV Part 2:** 605
Tworkov, Jack, **Supp. XII:** 198
"Two Scenes"(Ashbery), **Supp. III Part 1:** 4
Two Serious Ladies (Jane Bowles), **Supp. IV Part 1:** 82
"Two Silences"(Carruth), **Supp. XVI:** 55
"Two Sisters"(Farrell), **II:** 45
Two Sisters: A Memoir in the Form of a Novel (Vidal), **Supp. IV Part 2:** 679
"Two Sisters of Persephone"(Plath), **Retro. Supp. II:** 246
"Two Songs on the Economy of Abundance"(Agee), **I:** 28

"Two Tales of Clumsy"(Schnackenberg), **Supp. XV:** 258
"Two Temples, The"(Melville), **III:** 89–90
Two Thousand Seasons (Armah), **Supp. IV Part 1:** 373
Two Towns in Provence (M. F. K. Fisher), **Supp. XVII:** 91
Two Trains Running (Wilson), **Supp. VIII: 345–348**
"Two Tramps in Mudtime"(Frost), **II:** 164; **Retro. Supp. I:** 137; **Supp. IX:** 261
"Two Views of a Cadaver Room"(Plath), **Supp. I Part 2:** 538
"Two Villages"(Paley), **Supp. VI:** 227
"Two Voices in a Meadow"(Wilbur), **Supp. III Part 2:** 555
"Two Witches"(Frost), **Retro. Supp. I:** 135
"Two Words"(Francis), **Supp. IX:** 81
Two Years before the Mast (Dana), **I:** 351
"Tyger, The"(Blake), **Supp. XVII:** 128
Tyler, Anne, **Supp. IV Part 2: 657–675; Supp. V:** 227, 326; **Supp. VIII:** 141; **Supp. X:** 1, 77, 83, 85; **Supp. XII:** 307; **Supp. XVI:** 37; **Supp. XVIII:** 157, 195
Tyler, Royall, **I:** 344; **Retro. Supp. I:** 377
Tymms, Ralph, **Supp. IX:** 105
Tyndale, William, **II:** 15
Tyndall, John, **Retro. Supp. II:** 93
Typee: A Peep at Polynesian Life (Melville), **III:** 75–77, 79, 84; **Retro. Supp. I:** 245–246, 249, 252, 256
Types From City Streets (Hapgood), **Supp. XVII:** 103
"Typewriter, The"(D. West), **Supp. XVIII:** 279
Typewriter Town (W. J. Smith), **Supp. XIII:** 332
"Typhus"(Simpson), **Supp. IX:** 277
"Tyranny of the Normal"(Fiedler), **Supp. XIII:** 107–108
Tyranny of the Normal (Fiedler), **Supp. XIII: 107–108**
"Tyrant of Syracuse"(MacLeish), **III:** 20
"Tyrian Businesses"(Olson), **Supp. II Part 2:** 567, 568, 569
Tytell, John, **Supp. XIV:** 140
Tzara, Tristan, **Supp. III Part 1:** 104, 105

U

U and I (Baker), **Supp. XIII: 45–47,** 48, 52, 55
Überdie Seelenfrage (Fechner), **II:** 358
Ubik (Dick), **Supp. XVIII:** 136
Ubu Roi (Jarry), **Supp. XV:** 178, 186
Ueland, Brenda, **Supp. XVII:** 13
"Ulalume"(Poe), **III:** 427; **Retro. Supp. II:** 264, 266
Ulin, David, **Supp. XIII:** 244; **Supp. XVI:** 74
Ullman, Leslie, **Supp. IV Part 2:** 550; **Supp. XVIII:** 175
Ultimate Good Luck, The (Ford), **Supp. V:** 57, 61–62
Ultimate Punishment: A Lawyer's Reflections on Dealing with the Death Penalty (Turow), **Supp. XVII:** 220–221
Ultima Thule (Longfellow), **II:** 490; **Retro. Supp. II:** 169
"Ultima Thule"(Nabokov), **Retro. Supp. I:** 274
Ultramarine (Carver), **Supp. III Part 1:** 137, 138, 147, 148
Ulysses (Joyce), **I:** 395, 475–476, 478, 479, 481; **II:** 42, 264, 542; **III:** 170, 398; **IV:** 103, 418, 428, 455; **Retro. Supp. I:** 59, 63, 290, 291; **Retro. Supp. II:** 121; **Supp. I Part 1:** 57; **Supp. III Part 2:** 618, 619; **Supp. IV Part 1:** 285; **Supp. IV Part 2:** 424; **Supp. IX:** 102; **Supp. V:** 261; **Supp. X:** 114; **Supp. XIII:** 43, 191; **Supp. XV:** 305; **Supp. XVII:** 140, 227
"*Ulysses,* Order and Myth"(Eliot), **Retro. Supp. I:** 63
Unaccountable Worth of the World, The (Price), **Supp. VI:** 267
Unamuno y Jugo, Miguel de, **III:** 310; **Supp. XV:** 79
"Unattached Smile, The"(Crews), **Supp. XI:** 101
"Unbelievable Thing Usually Goes to the Heart of the Story, The: Magic Realism in the Fiction of Rick Bass"(Dwyer), **Supp. XVI:** 16
"Unbeliever, The"(Bishop), **Retro. Supp. II:** 43
"Unborn Song"(Rukeyser), **Supp. VI:** 274
Unbought Spirit: A John Jay Chapman Reader (Stone, ed.), **Supp. XIV:** 54
Uncalled, The (Dunbar), **Supp. II Part 1:** 200, 211, 212
Uncentering the Earth: Copernicus and The Revolutions of the Heavenly Spheres (Vollmann), **Supp. XVII:** 226
Uncertain Certainty, The: Interviews, Essays, and Notes on Poetry (Simic), **Supp. VIII:** 270, 273, 274
Uncertainty and Plenitude: Five Contemporary Poets (Stitt), **Supp. IX:** 299
"Uncle"(Levine), **Supp. V:** 186
"Uncle Christmas"(Ríos), **Supp. IV Part 2:** 552
"Uncle Jim's Baptist Revival Hymn"(Lanier and Lanier), **Supp. I Part 1:** 353
"Uncle Lot"(Stowe), **Supp. I Part 2:** 585–586
Uncle Remus Tales (Harris), **Supp. II Part 1:** 201
"Uncle Tomitudes"(Briggs), **Supp. XVIII:** 14
Uncle Tom's Cabin (Stowe), **II:** 291; **Supp. I Part 1:** 49; **Supp. I Part 2:** 410, 579, 582, 589–592; **Supp. II Part 1:** 170; **Supp. III Part 1:** 154, 171; **Supp. IX:** 19; **Supp. X:** 246, 249, 250; **Supp. XIII:** 95; **Supp. XVI:** 82, 85, 88; **Supp. XVIII:** 14
Uncle Tom's Children (Wright), **IV:** 476, 478, 488; **Supp. II Part 1:** 228, 235; **Supp. XVIII:** 283
"Uncle Wiggily in Connecticut"(Salinger), **III:** 559–560, 563
"Unclouded Day, The"(Proulx), **Supp. VII:** 254–255
"Uncommon Visage"(Brodsky), **Supp. VIII:** 31
"Uncommon Woman: An Interview with Wendy Wasserstein"(Cohen), **Supp. XV:** 323
Uncommon Women and Others (Wasserstein), **Supp. XV:** 320–321, **322–323**
Uncompromising Fictions of Cynthia Ozick (Pinsker), **Supp. V:** 272
"Unconscious Came a Beauty"(Swenson), **Supp. IV Part 2:** 646
"Uncreation, The"(Pinsky), **Supp. VI:** 245
"Undead, The"(Wilbur), **Supp. III Part 2:** 556
"Undefeated, The"(Hemingway), **II:** 250; **Retro. Supp. I:** 180
Under a Glass Bell (Nin), **Supp. X:** 186
"Under Ben Bulben"(Yeats), **Supp. V:** 220
Undercliff: Poems 1946–1953 (Eberhart), **I:** 528, 536–537
Under Cover (Goldbarth), **Supp. XII:** 177, 180, 193
Undercover Doctor (film), **Supp. XIII:** 170
"Under Cygnus"(Wilbur), **Supp. III Part 2:** 558
"Under Forty"(Trilling), **Supp. III Part 2:** 494
Underground Man, The (film), **Supp. IV Part 2:** 474
Underground Man, The (Macdonald), **Supp. IV Part 2:** 474, 475
"Under Libra: Weights and Measures"(Merrill), **Supp. III Part 1:** 328
Under Milk Wood (D. Thomas), **III:** 21
"Undersea"(Carson), **Supp. IX:** 21
Understanding Cynthia Ozick (Friedman), **Supp. V:** 273
Understanding Drama (Brooks and Heilman), **Supp. XIV:** 12
Understanding E. L. Doctorow (Fowler), **Supp. IV Part 1:** 226
Understanding Fiction (Brooks and Warren), **IV:** 279; **Supp. XIV:** 11
Understanding Flannery O'Connor (Whitt), **Retro. Supp. II:** 226
Understanding Nicholson Baker (Saltzman), **Supp. XIII:** 48
Understanding Poetry: An Anthology for College Students (Brooks and Warren), **IV:** 236; **Retro. Supp. I:** 40, 41; **Supp. XIV:** 4–5
Understanding Tim O'Brien (Kaplan), **Supp. V:** 241
Understanding To Kill a Mockingbird: A Student Casebook to Issues, Sources, and Documents (Johnson), **Supp. VIII:** 127
Undertaker's Garland, The (Wilson and Bishop), **IV:** 427

Under the Banner of Heaven: A Story of Violent Faith (Krakauer), **Supp. XVIII:** 105, **114–116,** 117
"Under the Cedarcroft Chestnut"(Lanier), **Supp. I Part 1:** 364
"Under the Harbour Bridge"(Komunyakaa), **Supp. XIII:** 125
"Under the Influence"(Sanders), **Supp. XVI:** 274, 277
Under the Lilacs (Alcott), **Supp. I Part 1:** 42–43, 44
"Under the Maud Moon"(Kinnell), **Supp. III Part 1:** 246–247
Under the Mountain Wall: A Chronicle of Two Seasons in the Stone Age (Matthiessen), **Supp. V:** 202
Under the Red Flag (Jin), **Supp. XVIII:** 89, **94–95**
"Under the Rose"(Pynchon), **Supp. II Part 2:** 620
Under the Sea-Wind: A Naturalist's Picture of Ocean Life (Carson), **Supp. IX:** 19, **22–23**
"Under the Sign of Saturn"(Sontag), **Supp. III Part 2:** 470
Under the Sign of Saturn (Sontag), **Supp. III Part 2:** 451, 452, 458, 470–471
"Under the Sky"(Bowles), **Supp. IV Part 1:** 87
Under the Volcano (M. Lowry), **Supp. XVII:** 135, 139, 140
"Under the Willows"(Lowell), **Supp. I Part 2:** 416
Under the Willows and Other Poems (Lowell), **Supp. I Part 2:** 424
Underwood, Wilbur, **Retro. Supp. II:** 79
Underworld (DeLillo), **Supp. VI:** 2, 4–5, 6–7, 8, 9, 10, 11, **13–15; Supp. XI:** 68
Undine (La Motte-Fouqué), **II:** 212; **III:** 78
Undiscovered Country, The (Howells), **II:** 282
"Undressing, The"(C. Frost), **Supp. XV:** 98
Uneasy Chair, The (Stegner), **Supp. IV Part 2:** 599
"Unemployed, Disabled, and Insane, The"(Haines), **Supp. XII:** 211–212
Unending Blues (Simic), **Supp. VIII: 278–279**
"Unexpressed"(Dunbar), **Supp. II Part 1:** 199
"Unfinished Bronx, The"(Paley), **Supp. VI:** 228
"Unfinished Poems"(Eliot), **I:** 579
"Unfinished Song"(C. Frost), **Supp. XV:** 97
Unfinished Woman, An (Hellman), **Supp. I Part 1:** 292, 293, 294; **Supp. IV Part 1:** 12, 353–354; **Supp. IX:** 196, 200–201
Unforeseen Wilderness, The: An Essay on Kentucky's Red River Gorge (Berry), **Supp. X:** 28, 29, 30, 36
Unforgotten Years (L. P. Smith), **Supp. XIV:** 333, 334, 335, 336, 347
"Unfortunate Coincidence"(Parker), **Supp. IX:** 190
Unframed Originals (Merwin), **Supp. III Part 1:** 341
Ungar, Sanford, **Supp. XI:** 228
Ungaretti, Giuseppe, **Supp. V:** 337
Unguided Tour (Sontag), **Supp. III Part 2:** 452
"Unheimliche, Das"(The Uncanny) (Freud), **Supp. XVI:** 157–158
"Unholy Sonnets"(Jarman), **Supp. XVII:** 118, 119–120
Unholy Sonnets (Jarman), **Supp. XVII:** 109, 110, **119–120; Supp. XVIII:** 178
"Unidentified Flying Object"(Hayden), **Supp. II Part 1:** 368
"Unifying Principle, The"(Ammons), **Supp. VII:** 28
"Unimportant Man, An"(D. West), **Supp. XVIII:** 280
"Union"(Hughes), **Supp. I Part 1:** 331
"Union Street: San Francisco, Summer 1975" (Carver), **Supp. III Part 1:** 138
United States Army in World War II (Morison), **Supp. I Part 2:** 490
United States Constitution, **I:** 6, 283
United States Essays, 1951–1991 (Vidal), **Supp. IV Part 2:** 678, 687
United States of Poetry, The (television series), **Supp. XIII:** 274
"Unity through Diversity" (Locke), **Supp. XIV:** 212, 213
Universal Baseball Association, Inc., J. Henry Waugh, Prop., The (Coover), **Supp. V:** 39, 41–42, 44, 46
Universal Passion (Young), **III:** 111
"Universe of Death, The" (H. Miller), **III:** 184
Universe of Time, A (Anderson), **II:** 27, 28, 45, 46, 48, 49
"Universities" (Emerson), **II:** 6
"Universities: A Mirage?" (Mora), **Supp. XIII:** 219
"University" (Shapiro), **Supp. II Part 2:** 704–705, 717
"University Avenue" (Mora), **Supp. XIII:** 216
"University Days" (Thurber), **Supp. I Part 2:** 605
"University Hospital, Boston" (Oliver), **Supp. VII:** 235
"Unknowable, The" (Levine), **Supp. V:** 195
"Unknown Girl in the Maternity Ward" (Sexton), **Supp. II Part 2:** 676
"Unknown Love, The" (Chandler), **Supp. IV Part 1:** 120
Unknown Rilke, The (Rilke; F. Wright, trans.), **Supp. XVII:** 244
"Unknown War, The" (Sandburg), **III:** 594
Unleashed (anthology), **Supp. XI:** 132
"Unlighted Lamps" (Anderson), **I:** 112
Unloved Wife, The (Alcott), **Supp. I Part 1:** 33
Unmarried Woman, An (film), **Supp. IV Part 1:** 303
"Unnatural Mother, The" (Gilman), **Supp. XI:** 207
"Unnatural State of the Unicorn" (Komunyakaa), **Supp. XIII:** 119
"Unparalleled Adventure of One Hans Pfaall, The" (Poe), **III:** 424
"Unpleasant Profession of Jonathan Hoag, The" (Heinlein), **Supp. XVIII:** 149
Unprecedented Era, The (Goebbels), **III:** 560
"Unprofitable Servant, The" (O. Henry), **Supp. II Part 1:** 403
Unpublished Poems of Emily Dickinson (Bianchi and Hampson, ed.), **Retro. Supp. I:** 35
Unpunished (Gilman), **Supp. XI:** 208
"Unreal City" (Eliot), **Supp. XV:** 218
"Unreasoning Heart" (Untermeyer), **Supp. XV:** 309
"Unsaid (Gioia), **Supp. XV:** 129
"Unseen, The"(Pinsky), **Supp. VI:** 243–244
"Unseen, The"(Singer), **Retro. Supp. II:** 307
Unseen Hand, The (Shepard), **Supp. III Part 2:** 439, 445–446
Unselected Poems (Levine), **Supp. V:** 179
Unsettling of America, The: Culture and Agriculture (Berry), **Supp. X:** 22, 26, 29, 32, 33, 35; **Supp. XIV:** 177, 179
Unspeakable Gentleman, The (Marquand), **III:** 53–54, 60, 63
Unspeakable Practices, Unnatural Acts (Barthelme), **Supp. IV Part 1:** 39
"Unspeakable Things Unspoken: The Afro-American Presence in American Literature"(Morrison), **Supp. III Part 1:** 375, 377–379
"Untelling, The"(Strand), **Supp. IV Part 2:** 629
Unterecker, John, **I:** 386
Untermeyer, Jean Starr, **II:** 530; **Supp. XV:** 294, 295, 303, 307, 308, 310
Untermeyer, Louis, **II:** 516–517, 530, 532; **III:** 268; **Retro. Supp. I:** 124, 133, 136; **Supp. III Part 1:** 2; **Supp. IX:** 76; **Supp. XIV:** 119, 123; **Supp. XV: 293–318**
Untimely Papers (Bourne), **I:** 218, 233
"Untitled"(C. Frost), **Supp. XV:** 103
"Untitled Blues"(Komunyakaa), **Supp. XIII:** 117
Unto the Sons (Talese), **Supp. XVII:** 199–200, **206–207,** 208, 209, 210
"Untrustworthy Speaker, The"(Glück), **Supp. V:** 86
"Unused"(Anderson), **I:** 112, 113
Unvanquished, The (Faulkner), **II:** 55, 67–68, 71; **Retro. Supp. I:** 84; **Supp. I Part 2:** 450
"Unvexed Isles, The"(Warren), **IV:** 253
"Unwedded"(Larcom), **Supp. XIII:** 144
"Unweepables, The"(Karr), **Supp. XI:** 243
"Unwelcome Guest, An"(Papernick), **Supp. XVII:** 50
"Unwelcome Words"(Bowles), **Supp. IV Part 1:** 94, 95
Unwelcome Words (Bowles), **Supp. IV Part 1:** 93, 94
Unwin, T. Fisher, **Supp. XI:** 202

"Unwithered Garland, The"(Kunitz), **Supp. III Part 1:** 265
Unwobbling Pivot, The (Pound, trans.), **III:** 472
"Unwritten, The"(Merwin), **Supp. III Part 1:** 352
"Unwritten Law"(Glück), **Supp. V:** 91
Up (Sukenick), **Supp. V:** 39
Up Above the World (Bowles), **Supp. IV Part 1:** 82, 91, 92
"Up and Down"(Merrill), **Supp. III Part 1:** 328
Upanishads, **IV:** 183
Up Country: Poems of New England (Kumin), **Supp. IV Part 2:** 446, 447–448, 453
"Update"(Dunn), **Supp. XI:** 150–151
Updike, John, **I:** 54; **III:** 572; **IV: 214–235; Retro. Supp. I:** 116, **317–338; Retro. Supp. II:** 213, 279, 280; **Supp. I Part 1:** 186, 196; **Supp. IV Part 2:** 657; **Supp. IX:** 208; **Supp. V:** 23, 43, 95, 119; **Supp. VIII:** 151, 167, 236; **Supp. XI:** 65, 66, 99, 140; **Supp. XII:** 140, 296, 298, 310; **Supp. XIII:** 45–46, 47, 52; **Supp. XIV:** 79, 93, 111; **Supp. XVI:** 205, 207, 220
Updike, Mrs. Wesley, **IV:** 218, 220
Up from Slavery (Washington), **Supp. II Part 1:** 169; **Supp. IX:** 19
Upham, Thomas Goggswell, **II:** 487
"Upholsterers, The"(Lardner), **II:** 435
"Up in Michigan"(Hemingway), **II:** 263
Upjohn, Richard, **IV:** 312
"Upon a Spider Catching a Fly"(Taylor), **IV:** 161
"Upon a Wasp Child with Cold"(Taylor), **IV:** 161
"Upon Meeting Don L. Lee, in a Dream"(Dove), **Supp. IV Part 1:** 244
"Upon My Dear and Loving Husband His Going into England, Jan. 16, 1661" (Bradstreet), **Supp. I Part 1:** 110
"Upon Returning to the Country Road" (Lindsay), **Supp. I Part 2:** 382
"Upon the Burning of Our House, July 10th, 1666" (Bradstreet), **Supp. I Part 1:** 107–108, 122
"Upon the Sweeping Flood" (Taylor), **IV:** 161
"Upon Wedlock, and Death of Children" (Taylor), **IV:** 144, 147, 161
"Upset, An" (Merrill), **Supp. III Part 1:** 336
Upstairs and Downstairs (Vonnegut), **Supp. II Part 2:** 757
Upstate (Wilson), **IV:** 447
Upton, Lee, **Supp. X:** 209
"Upturned Face" (Crane), **I:** 423
Upward, Allen, **Supp. I Part 1:** 262
Upward, Edward, **Supp. XIV:** 159, 160
"Upward Moon and the Downward Moon, The" (R. Bly), **Supp. IV Part 1:** 71
Urania: A Rhymed Lesson (Holmes), **Supp. I Part 1:** 300
"Urban Convalescence, An" (Merrill), **Supp. III Part 1:** 322–324
"Urban Renewal" (Komunyakaa), **Supp. XIII:** 113
Urdang, Constance, **Supp. XV:** 74
"Urganda and Fatima" (Rowson), **Supp. XV:** 234
Urial Accosta: A Play (Reznikoff), **Supp. XIV:** 282, 288
Urich, Robert, **Supp. V:** 228
"Uriel" (Emerson), **II:** 19
Uris, Leon, **Supp. IV Part 1:** 285, 379
Uroff, Margaret D., **Supp. I Part 2:** 542
"Us" (Sexton), **Supp. II Part 2:** 687
U.S. 1 (Rukeyser), **Supp. VI:** 272, 278, 283, 285
U.S.A. (Dos Passos), **I:** 379, 475, 478, 482–488, 489, 490, 491, 492, 493, 494, 495; **Retro. Supp. II:** 197; **Supp. I Part 2:** 646; **Supp. III Part 1:** 104, 105; **Supp. XIV:** 24
"U.S.A. School of Writing, The" (Bishop), **Retro. Supp. II:** 43
"U.S. Commercial Orchid, The" (Agee), **I:** 35
"Used-Boy Raisers, The" (Paley), **Supp. VI:** 218, 228
"Used Cars on Oahu" (Nye), **Supp. XIII:** 282
"Used Side of the Sofa, The" (Ríos), **Supp. IV Part 2:** 551
Use of Fire, The (Price), **Supp. VI:** 265
"Use of Force, The" (W. C. Williams), **Retro. Supp. I:** 424
Use of Poetry and the Use of Criticism, The (Eliot), **Retro. Supp. I:** 65
Uses of Enchantment, The: The Meaning and Importance of Fairy Tales (Bettelheim), **Supp. XIV:** 126
Uses of Enchantment, The: The Meaning and Importance of Fairy Tales (Bettleheim), **Supp. X:** 77
"Uses of Hell, The" (E. Hoffman), **Supp. XVI:** 154
"Uses of Hell, The: An Exchange"(Novick, Katz, and Szulc), **Supp. XVI:** 154
Uses of Literacy, The (Hoggart), **Supp. XIV:** 299
"Uses of Poetry, The" (W. C. Williams), **Retro. Supp. I:** 412
"Uses of the Blues, The" (Baldwin), **Retro. Supp. II:** 8
"USFS 1919: The Ranger, the Cook, and a Hole in the Sky" (Maclean), **Supp. XIV:** 230, 234
Ushant: An Essay (Aiken), **I:** 49, 54, 55, 56, 57
"Usher 11" (Bradbury), **Supp. I Part 2:** 622
"Using Parrots to Kill Mockingbirds: Yet Another Racial Prosecution and Wrongful Conviction in Maycomb" (Fair), **Supp. VIII:** 128
Usual Star, The (Doolittle), **Supp. I Part 1:** 270
"Usurpation (Other People's Stories)" (Ozick), **Supp. V:** 268, 271
Utopia 14 (Vonnegut), **Supp. II Part 2:** 757

V

V. (Pynchon), **Supp. II Part 2:** 618, 620–622, 627–630; **Supp. IV Part 1:** 279
"Vacation" (Stafford), **Supp. XI:** 321, 322
"Vacation Trip" (Stafford), **Supp. XI:** 322
Vachel Lindsay: A Poet in America (Masters), **Supp. I Part 2:** 473, 474
"Vachel Lindsay: The Midwest as Utopia" (Whitney), **Supp. I Part 2:** 403
"Vachel Lindsay Writes to Floyd Dell" (Tanselle), **Supp. I Part 2:** 403
"Vacillation" (Yeats), **Supp. XV:** 253
Vadim, Roger, **Supp. XI:** 293, 307
"Vag" (Dos Passos), **I:** 487–488
Valentine, Jean, **Supp. V:** 92
Valentine, Saint, **IV:** 396
Valentino, Rudolph, **I:** 483
Valéry, Paul, **II:** 543, 544; **III:** 279, 409, 428, 609; **IV:** 79, 91, 92, 428, 443; **Retro. Supp. II:** 187
"Valhalla" (Francis), **Supp. IX:** 77
Valhalla and Other Poems (Francis), **Supp. IX:** 76
Validity in Interpretation (Hirsch), **Supp. XIV:** 15
Valitsky, Ken, **Supp. XII:** 7
Vallejo, César, **Supp. IX:** 271; **Supp. V:** 332; **Supp. XIII:** 114, 315, 323
"Valley, The" (Bass), **Supp. XVI:** 20, 22
"Valley Between, The" (Marshall), **Supp. XI:** 278
Valley of Decision, The (Wharton), **IV:** 311, 315; **Retro. Supp. I:** 365–367
Valley of the Moon, The (London), **II:** 467, 481
"Valley of Unrest, The" (Poe), **III:** 411
Valli, Alida, **Supp. IV Part 2:** 520
"Valor" (Bausch), **Supp. VII:** 54
Valparaiso (DeLillo), **Supp. VI:** 4, 12
"Value of a Place, The" (Bass), **Supp. XVI:** 18
"Values and Fictions" (Toomer), **Supp. III Part 2:** 485–486
"Values and Imperatives" (Locke), **Supp. XIV:** 199, 202, 212
Values of Veblen, The: A Critical Appraisal (Rosenberg), **Supp. I Part 2:** 650
"Vampire" (Karr), **Supp. XI:** 241
Vampire Armand, The (Rice), **Supp. VII:** 290, 294–295
Vampire Chronicles, The (Rice), **Supp. VII:** 290
Vampire Lestat, The (Rice), **Supp. VII:** 290–292, 298, 299
Van Buren, Martin, **II:** 134, 312; **III:** 473
Vande Kieft, Ruth M., **IV:** 260
Vanderbilt, Cornelius, **III:** 14
Van Dine, S. S., **Supp. IV Part 1:** 341
Van Doren, Carl, **I:** 252–253, 423; **II:** 103, 111, 112; **Supp. I Part 2:** 474, 486, 707, 709, 717, 718, 727; **Supp. II Part 1:** 395; **Supp. VIII:** 96–97
Van Doren, Mark, **I:** 168; **III:** 4, 23, 589; **Supp. I Part 2:** 604; **Supp. III Part 2:** 626; **Supp. IX:** 266, 268; **Supp. VIII:** 231; **Supp. XV:** 152, 305, 307
Vandover and the Brute (Norris), **III:** 314, 315, 316, 320–322, 328, 333, 334
Van Duyn, Mona, **Supp. IX:** 269
Van Dyke, Annette, **Supp. IV Part 1:** 327
Van Dyke, Henry, **I:** 223; **II:** 456

Van Gogh, Vincent, **I:** 27; **IV:** 290; **Supp. I Part 2:** 451; **Supp. IV Part 1:** 284

Van Gogh's Room at Arles (Elkin), **Supp. VI: 56**

"Vanilla Dunk" (Lethem), **Supp. XVIII:** 139

"Vanisher, The" (Whittier), **Supp. I Part 2:** 691

Vanishing Point (Markson), **Supp. XVII:** 135, 137, 138, 145–146

"Vanishing Red, The" (Frost), **Retro. Supp. II:** 47

"Vanity" (B. Diop), **Supp. IV Part 1:** 16

Vanity Fair (Thackeray), **I:** 354; **II:** 91; **III:** 70; **Supp. IX:** 200

"Vanity of All Wordly Things, The" (Bradstreet), **Supp. I Part 1:** 102, 119

Vanity of Duluoz (Kerouac), **Supp. III Part 1:** 221, 222

"Vanity of Existence, The" (Freneau), **Supp. II Part 1:** 262

Van Matre, Lynn, **Supp. V:** 126

Vann, Barbara, **Supp. XV:** 187

Vanquished, The (Faulkner), **I:** 205

Van Rensselaer, Stephen, **I:** 351

Van Vechten, Carl, **I:** 295; **IV:** 76; **Supp. I Part 1:** 324, 327, 332; **Supp. I Part 2:** 715; **Supp. II Part 2: 725–751; Supp. X:** 247; **Supp. XVI:** 135; **Supp. XVII:** 96, 97, 101, 104; **Supp. XVIII:** 123, 131, 132, 279, 280

Vanzetti, Bartolomeo, **I:** 482, 486, 490, 494; **II:** 38–39, 426; **III:** 139–140; **Supp. I Part 2:** 446, 610, 611; **Supp. IX:** 199; **Supp. V:** 288–289

"Vapor Trail Reflected in the Frog Pond" (Kinnell), **Supp. III Part 1:** 242–243

"Vapor Trails" (Snyder), **Supp. VIII:** 298

"Variation: Ode to Fear" (Warren), **IV:** 241

"Variation on a Sentence" (Bogan), **Supp. III Part 1:** 60

"Variation on Gaining a Son" (Dove), **Supp. IV Part 1:** 248

"Variation on Pain" (Dove), **Supp. IV Part 1:** 248

"Variations: The air is sweetest that a thistle guards" (Merrill), **Supp. III Part 1:** 321

"Variations: White Stag, Black Bear" (Merrill), **Supp. III Part 1:** 321

"Varick Street" (Bishop), **Supp. I Part 1:** 90, 92

Varieties of Metaphysical Poetry, The (Eliot), **Retro. Supp. I:** 65

Varieties of Religious Experience, The (William James), **II:** 344, 353, 354, 359–360, 362; **IV:** 28, 291; **Supp. IX:** 19

Variety (film), **Supp. XII:** 7

Variorum (Whitman), **Retro. Supp. I:** 406

Various Antidotes (J. Scott), **Supp. XVII: 188–189**

"Various Miracles" (Shields), **Supp. VII:** 318–319, 324

Various Miracles (Shields), **Supp. VII:** 318–320, 323, 324

Various Poems (Zach), **Supp. XV:** 86

"Various Tourists" (Connell), **Supp. XIV:** 79

"Varmint Question, The" (Leopold), **Supp. XIV:** 180–181

Vasari, Giorgio, **Supp. I Part 2:** 450; **Supp. III Part 1:** 5

Vasquez, Robert, **Supp. V:** 180

Vassall Morton (Parkman), **Supp. II Part 2:** 595, 597–598

Vasse, W. W., **III:** 478

Vaudeville for a Princess (Schwartz), **Supp. II Part 2:** 661–662

Vaughan, Henry, **IV:** 151; **Supp. XV:** 251

Vaughn, Robert, **Supp. XI:** 343

"Vaunting Oak" (Ransom), **III:** 490

Vazirani, Reetika, **Supp. XIII:** 133

Veblen (Hobson), **Supp. I Part 2:** 650

Veblen, Andrew, **Supp. I Part 2:** 640

Veblen, Mrs. Thorstein (Ellen Rolfe), **Supp. I Part 2:** 641

Veblen, Oswald, **Supp. I Part 2:** 640

Veblen, Thorstein, **I:** 104, 283, 475–476, 483, 498, 511; **II:** 27, 272, 276, 287; **Supp. I Part 2: 628–650; Supp. IV Part 1:** 22

Veblenism: A New Critique (Dobriansky), **Supp. I Part 2:** 648, 650

"Veblen's Attack on Culture" (Adorno), **Supp. I Part 2:** 650

Vechten, Carl Van, **Retro. Supp. I:** 199

Vedanta for Modern Man (Isherwood, ed.), **Supp. XIV:** 164

Vedanta for the Western World (Isherwood, ed.), **Supp. XIV:** 164

Vedas, **IV:** 183

Vega, Janine Pommy, **Supp. XIV:** 148

Vega, Lope de, **Retro. Supp. I:** 285; **Supp. III Part 1:** 341, 347

Vegetable, The (Fitzgerald), **Retro. Supp. I:** 105; **Supp. IX:** 57

Vegetable, The, or From President to Postman (Fitzgerald), **II:** 91

"Vegetable Love" (Apple), **Supp. XVII:** 4

Veinberg, Jon, **Supp. V:** 180; **Supp. XIII:** 313; **Supp. XV:** 76–77, 86

Vein of Iron (Glasgow), **II:** 175, 186, 188–189, 191, 192, 194

Vein of Riches, A (Knowles), **Supp. XII:** 249

Velie, Alan R., **Supp. IV Part 2:** 486

Velocities: New and Selected Poems, 1966–1992 (Dobyns), **Supp. XIII:** 86–87, 87, 88

"Velorio" (Cisneros), **Supp. VII:** 66

"Velvet Shoes" (Wylie), **Supp. I Part 2:** 711, 714

Venant, Elizabeth, **Supp. XI:** 343

Vencloca, Thomas, **Supp. VIII:** 29

Vendler, Helen H., **Retro. Supp. I:** 297; **Retro. Supp. II:** 184, 191; **Supp. I Part 1:** 77, 78, 92, 95; **Supp. I Part 2:** 565; **Supp. IV Part 1:** 245, 247, 249, 254, 257; **Supp. IV Part 2:** 448; **Supp. V:** 78, 82, 189, 343; **Supp. XII:** 187, 189; **Supp. XV:** 20, 184

"Venetian Blind, The" (Jarrell), **II:** 382–383

Venetian Glass Nephew, The (Wylie), **Supp. I Part 2:** 707, 709, 714, 717–719, 721, 724

Venetian Life (Howells), **II:** 274, 277, 279

"Venetian Vespers, The" (Hecht), **Supp. X:** 65, **66–67**

Venetian Vespers, The (Hecht), **Supp. X:** 57, **65–69**

Venice Observed (McCarthy), **II:** 562

Ventadorn, Bernard de, **Supp. IV Part 1:** 146

"Ventriloquists' Conversations" (Gentry), **Supp. IV Part 1:** 236

"Venus, Cupid, Folly and Time" (Taylor), **Supp. V:** 322–323

Venus and Adonis (film), **Supp. IV Part 1:** 82

"Venus and Don Juan" (C. Frost), **Supp. XV:** 103

Venus and Don Juan (C. Frost), **Supp. XV:** 93, **102–103,** 104, 107

Venus Blue (Sobin), **Supp. XVI: 293–294,** 294

Venus in Sparta (Auchincloss), **Supp. IV Part 1:** 25

"Venus's-flytraps" (Komunyakaa), **Supp. XIII:** 126, 127

"Veracruz" (Hayden), **Supp. II Part 1:** 371, 373

Verga, Giovanni, **II:** 271, 275

Verghese, Abraham, **Supp. X:** 160

Verhaeren, Emile, **I:** 476; **II:** 528, 529

Verlaine, Paul, **II:** 529, 543; **III:** 466; **IV:** 79, 80, 86, 286; **Retro. Supp. I:** 56, 62; **Retro. Supp. II:** 326

"Vermeer" (Nemerov), **III:** 275, 278, 280

Vermeer, Jan, **Retro. Supp. I:** 335

"Vermont" (Carruth), **Supp. XVI:** 54

Vermont Notebook, The (Ashbery), **Supp. III Part 1:** 1

"Vernal Ague, The" (Freneau), **Supp. II Part 1:** 258

Verne, Jules, **I:** 480; **Retro. Supp. I:** 270; **Supp. XI:** 63

Vernon, John, **Supp. X:** 15

Verplanck, Gulian C., **Supp. I Part 1:** 155, 156, 157, 158

Verrazano, Giovanni da, **Supp. I Part 2:** 496, 497

Verse (Zawacki), **Supp. VIII:** 272

"Verse for Urania" (Merrill), **Supp. III Part 1:** 329, 330

Verses (Wharton), **Retro. Supp. I:** 362

Verses, Printed for Her Friends (Jewett), **II:** 406

"Verses for Children" (Lowell), **II:** 516

"Verses Made at Sea in a Heavy Gale" (Freneau), **Supp. II Part 1:** 262

"Verses on the Death of T. S. Eliot" (Brodsky), **Supp. VIII:** 19

"Version of a Fragment of Simonides" (Bryant), **Supp. I Part 1:** 153, 155

Verulam, Baron. *See* Bacon, Francis

Very, Jones, **III:** 507

"Very Hot Sun in Bermuda, The" (Jackson), **Supp. IX:** 126

Very Old Bones (W. Kennedy), **Supp. VII:** 133, 148, 150–153

"Very Proper Gander, The" (Thurber), **Supp. I Part 2:** 610

"Very Short Story, A" (Hemingway), **II:** 252; **Retro. Supp. I:** 173
"Vesalius in Zante" (Wharton), **Retro. Supp. I:** 372
Vesey, Denmark, **Supp. I Part 2:** 592
Vesey, Desmond, **Supp. XIV:** 162
"Vespers" (Auden), **Supp. II Part 1:** 23
"Vespers" (Glück), **Supp. V:** 88
Vestal Lady on Brattle, The (Corso), **Supp. XII:** 119, **120–121,** 134
Vested Interests and the Common Man, The (Veblen), **Supp. I Part 2:** 642
"Vesuvius at Home" (Rich), **Retro. Supp. I:** 42
"Veteran, The" (Crane), **I:** 413
"Veterans' Cemetery" (Gioia), **Supp. XV:** 117
"Veteran Sirens" (Robinson), **III:** 512, 524
"Veterinarian" (X. J. Kennedy), **Supp. XV:** 168
"Vetiver" (Ashbery), **Supp. III Part 1:** 26
"Via Dieppe-Newhaven" (H. Miller), **III:** 183
"Via Negativa" (Salter), **Supp. IX:** 257
Vicar of Wakefeld, The (Goldsmith), **I:** 216
Vicious Circle, The (film, Wilder), **Supp. XVII:** 62
"Vicissitudes of the Avant-Garde, The" (Gass), **Supp. VI:** 91
Victim, The (Bellow), **I:** 144, 145, 147, 149, 150, 151, 152, 153, 155, 156, 158, 159, 164; **IV:** 19; **Retro. Supp. II:** 21, 22, 34
"Victor" (Mumford), **Supp. II Part 2:** 476
Victoria (Rowson), **Supp. XV:** 231
Victorian in the Modern World, A (Hapgood), **Supp. XVII:** 95, 97, 100, 101, 103, 105, 106
"Victories" (Untermeyer), **Supp. XV:** 300
"Victory at Sea" (television series), **Supp. I Part 2:** 490
"Victory comes late" (Dickinson), **Retro. Supp. I:** 45
"Victory of the Moon, The" (Crane), **I:** 420
Vidal, Gore, **II:** 587; **IV:** 383; **Supp. IV Part 1:** 22, 35, 92, 95, 198; **Supp. IV Part 2: 677–696; Supp. IX:** 96; **Supp. X:** 186, 195; **Supp. XIV:** 156, 170, 338
Viebahn, Fred, **Supp. IV Part 1:** 248
Viera, Joseph M., **Supp. XI:** 178, 186
Viereck, Peter, **Supp. I Part 2:** 403
Viertel, Berthold, **Supp. XIV:** 165
Viertel, Salka, **Supp. XVI:** 192
Viet Journal (Jones), **Supp. XI: 230–231**
Vietnam (McCarthy), **II:** 578–579
"Vietnam in Me, The" (O'Brien), **Supp. V:** 241, 252
Vie unanime, La (Romains), **I:** 227
"View, The" (Roussel), **Supp. III Part 1:** 15, 16, 21
View from 80, The (Cowley), **Supp. II Part 1:** 141, 144, 153
"View from an Institution" (F. Wright), **Supp. XVII:** 244
View from the Bridge, A (A. Miller), **III:** 147, 148, 156, 158, 159–160
View of My Own, A: Essays in Literature and Society (Hardwick), **Supp. III Part 1:** 194, 200
"View of the Capital from the Library of Congress" (Bishop), **Retro. Supp. II:** 45
View of the Soil and Climate of the United States, A (Brown, trans.), **Supp. I Part 1:** 146
"View of the Woods, A" (O'Connor), **III:** 349, 351, 358; **Retro. Supp. II:** 237
"Views of the Mysterious Hill: The Appearance of Parnassus in American Poetry" (Strand), **Supp. IV Part 2:** 631
"Vigil" (Karr), **Supp. XI:** 241
"Vigil, The" (Dante), **III:** 542
Vigny, Alfred Victor de, **II:** 543
Vildrac, Charles, **Supp. XV:** 50
Vile Bodies (Waugh), **Supp. I Part 2:** 607
Villa, Pancho, **I:** 210; **III:** 584
"Village Blacksmith, The" (Longfellow), **Retro. Supp. II:** 167, 168; **Supp. I Part 2:** 409
Village Hymns, a Supplement to Dr. Watts's Psalms and Hymns (Nettleton), **I:** 458
"Village Improvement Parade, The" (Lindsay), **Supp. I Part 2:** 388, 389
Village Magazine, The (Lindsay), **Supp. I Part 2:** 379–380, 382
Village Virus, The (Lewis), **II:** 440
"Villanelle at Sundown" (Justice), **Supp. VII:** 119, 122–123
"Villanelle of Change" (Robinson), **III:** 524
Villard, Oswald, **Supp. I Part 1:** 332
"Villa Selene" (Simpson), **Supp. IX:** 279
Villon, François, **II:** 544; **III:** 9, 174, 592; **Retro. Supp. I:** 286; **Supp. I Part 1:** 261; **Supp. III Part 1:** 235, 243, 249, 253; **Supp. III Part 2:** 560; **Supp. IX:** 116
"Villonaud for This Yule" (Pound), **Retro. Supp. I:** 286
Vindication of the Rights of Woman (Wollstonecraft), **Supp. I Part 1:** 126; **Supp. XI:** 203
Vines, Lois Davis, **Retro. Supp. II:** 261
Vintage Book of Amnesia, The (Lethem, ed.), **Supp. XVIII:** 138
"Vintage Thunderbird, A" (Beattie), **Supp. V:** 27
Vinz, Mark, **Supp. X:** 117
Violence (Bausch), **Supp. VII:** 48–49, 54
Violent Bear It Away, The (O'Connor), **III:** 339, 345–348, 350, 351, 354, 355, 356, 357; **Retro. Supp. II:** 233, **234–236**
"Violent Vet, The" (O'Brien), **Supp. V:** 238
Violin (Rice), **Supp. VII:** 302
Viorst, Judith, **Supp. X:** 153
Viper Run (Karr), **Supp. XI: 248–251**
Virgil, **I:** 312, 322, 587; **II:** 133, 542; **IV:** 137, 359; **Retro. Supp. I:** 135; **Supp. I Part 1:** 153; **Supp. I Part 2:** 494; **Supp. IV Part 2:** 631
"Virgin and the Dynamo" (Adams), **III:** 396
"Virgin Carrying a Lantern, The" (Stevens), **IV:** 80
Virginia (Glasgow), **II:** 175, 178, 181–182, 193, 194
"Virginia" (Lindsay), **Supp. I Part 2:** 398
"Virginia Britannia" (Moore), **III:** 198, 208–209
"Virginians Are Coming Again, The" (Lindsay), **Supp. I Part 2:** 399
Virginia Reels (Hoffman), **Supp. XVIII:** 79, 86
"Virgin Violeta" (Porter), **III:** 454
"Virility" (Ozick), **Supp. V:** 262, 265
Virtual Light (W. Gibson), **Supp. XVI:** 124, **129,** 130
Virtue of Selfishness, The: A New Concept of Egoism (Rand), **Supp. IV Part 2:** 527, 530–532
"Virtuoso" (Francis), **Supp. IX:** 82
Virtuous Woman, A (Gibbons), **Supp. X: 44–45,** 46, 50
Visconti, Luchino, **Supp. V:** 51
Visible Saints: The History of a Puritan Idea (Morgan), **IV:** 149
"Vision, A" (Olds), **Supp. X:** 214
"Vision, A" (Winters), **Supp. II Part 2:** 785, 795
"Vision and Prayer" (D. Thomas), **I:** 432
"Visionary, The" (Poe), **III:** 411
Visionary Farms, The (Eberhart), **I:** 537–539
Visioning, The (Glaspell), **Supp. III Part 1:** 175–177, 180, 187, 188
Vision in Spring (Faulkner), **Retro. Supp. I:** 79
Vision of Columbus (Barlow), **Supp. I Part 1:** 124; **Supp. II Part 1:** 67, 68, 70–75, 77, 79
Vision of Sir Launfal, The (Lowell), **Supp. I Part 1:** 311; **Supp. I Part 2:** 406, 409, 410
"Vision of the World, A" (Cheever), **Supp. I Part 1:** 182, 192
Visions of Cody (Kerouac), **Supp. III Part 1:** 225–227
Visions of Gerard (Kerouac), **Supp. III Part 1:** 219–222, 225, 227, 229
"Visions of the Daughters of Albion" (Blake), **III:** 540
"Visit" (Ammons), **Supp. VII:** 28–29
"Visit, The" (Kenyon), **Supp. VII:** 169
"Visitant, The" (Dunn), **Supp. XI:** 147
"*Visitation, The*/La Visitación" (Mora), **Supp. XIII:** 217, 224, 228
"Visit Home, A" (Stafford), **Supp. XI:** 318
Visit in 2001, The (musical, McNally), **Supp. XIII:** 207
"Visiting My Own House in Iowa City" (Stern), **Supp. IX:** 300
"Visit of Charity, A" (Welty), **IV:** 262
"Visitors" (Salinas), **Supp. XIII:** 318
"Visitors, The/Los Visitantes" (Kingsolver), **Supp. VII:** 208
"Visits to St. Elizabeths" (Bishop), **Retro. Supp. II:** 47
"Visit to a Small Planet" (teleplay) (Vidal), **Supp. IV Part 2:** 682

Visit to a Small Planet: A Comedy Akin to Vaudeville (Vidal), **Supp. IV Part 2:** 682–683
"Visit to Avoyelles, A" (Chopin), **Supp. I Part 1:** 213
"Vissi d'Arte" (Moore), **Supp. X: 173–174**
Vistas of History (Morison), **Supp. I Part 2:** 492
"Vita" (Stafford), **Supp. XI:** 330
Vital, David, **Supp. XVI:** 160
Vital Provisions (Price), **Supp. VI:** 262–263
"Vitamins" (Carver), **Supp. III Part 1:** 138
Vita Nova (Glück), **Supp. V:** 90–92
Vitruvius, **Supp. XVI:** 292
Vittorio, the Vampire (Rice), **Supp. VII:** 295–296
Viudas (Dorfman), **Supp. IX:** 138
"Viva Vargas!" (Allen), **Supp. XV:** 15
Viviparous Quadrupeds of North America, The (Audubon and Bachman), **Supp. XVI:** 10
Vizenor, Gerald, **Supp. IV Part 1:** 260, 262, 329, 404; **Supp. IV Part 2:** 502
Vladimir Nabokov: The American Years (Nabokov), **Retro. Supp. I:** 275
Vlag, Piet, **Supp. XV:** 295
"Vlemk, the Box Painter" (Gardner), **Supp. VI:** 73
"V-Letter" (Shapiro), **Supp. II Part 2:** 707
V-Letter and Other Poems (Shapiro), **Supp. II Part 2:** 702, 706
"Vocabulary of Dearness" (Nye), **Supp. XIII:** 284
"Vocation" (Stafford), **Supp. XI:** 312, 321
"Vocation and a Voice, A" (Chopin), **Retro. Supp. II:** 72; **Supp. I Part 1:** 200, 220, 224, 225
Vocation and a Voice, A (Chopin), **Retro. Supp. II:** 67, 72
Vogel, David, **Supp. XV:** 88
Vogel, Speed, **Supp. IV Part 1:** 390
"Voice" (F. Wright), **Supp. XVII:** 245
"Voice, The" (Dunn), **Supp. XI:** 152
Voiced Connections of James Dickey, The (Dickey), **Supp. IV Part 1:** 177
"Voice from the Wilderness" (Ray), **Supp. XVIII:** 202
"Voice from the Woods, A" (Humphrey), **Supp. IX:** 101
"Voice from Under the Table, A" (Wilbur), **Supp. III Part 2:** 553, 554
Voice of Reason, The: Essays in Objectivist Thought (Rand), **Supp. IV Part 2:** 527, 528, 532
"Voice of Rock, The" (Ginsberg), **Supp. II Part 1:** 313
Voice of the Butterfly, The (Nichols), **Supp. XIII:** 270
Voice of the City, The (O. Henry), **Supp. II Part 1:** 410
"Voice of the Mountain, The" (Crane), **I:** 420
Voice of the Negro (Barber), **Supp. II Part 1:** 168
Voice of the People, The (Glasgow), **II:** 175, 176
Voice of the Turtle: American Indian Literature 1900–1970 (Gunn Allen, ed.), **Supp. IV Part 1:** 332, 334
Voices from the Moon (Dubus), **Supp. VII:** 88–89
"Voices from the Other World" (Merrill), **Supp. III Part 1:** 331
Voices in the House (Sedges), **Supp. II Part 1:** 125
Voices of the Night (Longfellow), **II:** 489, 493; **Retro. Supp. II:** 154, 157, 168
"Voices of Village Square, The" (Wolfe), **Supp. III Part 2:** 571–572
Voice That Is Great within Us, The (Caruth, ed.), **Supp. XIII:** 112
Voigt, Ellen Bryan, **Supp. XIII:** 76
Volkening, Henry, **Retro. Supp. II:** 117; **Supp. XV:** 142
Vollmann, William T., **Supp. XIV:** 96; **Supp. XVII: 225–237**
Volney, Constantin François de Chasseboeuf, **Supp. I Part 1:** 146
Voltaire, **I:** 194; **II:** 86, 103, 449; **III:** 420; **IV:** 18; **Retro. Supp. II:** 94; **Supp. I Part 1:** 288–289; **Supp. I Part 2:** 669, 717; **Supp. XV:** 258
Voltaire! Voltaire! (Endore), **Supp. XVII:** 65
Volunteers, The (Rowson and Reinagle), **Supp. XV:** 238
Vonnegut, Kurt, **Retro. Supp. I:** 170; **Supp. II Part 2:** 557, 689, **753–784; Supp. IV Part 1:** 227, 392; **Supp. V:** 40, 42, 237, 244, 296; **Supp. X:** 260; **Supp. XI:** 104; **Supp. XII:** 139, 141; **Supp. XVIII:** 242, 252
Vonnegut, Kurt, Jr., **Supp. XVII:** 41, 135
"Voracities and Verities" (Moore), **III:** 214
Vore, Nellie, **I:** 199
Vorlicky, Robert, **Supp. IX:** 132, 135, 136, 141, 144, 147
Vorse, Mary Heaton, **Supp. XVII:** 99
"Vorticism" (Pound), **Retro. Supp. I:** 288
Voss, Richard, **I:** 199–200
"Vow, The" (Hecht), **Supp. X:** 64
"Vowels 2" (Baraka), **Supp. II Part 1:** 51
Vow of Conversation, A: Journal, 1964–1965 (Merton), **Supp. VIII:** 206
Vox (Baker), **Supp. XIII: 47–49,** 50, 52, 53
"Voyage" (MacLeish), **III:** 15
"Voyage, The" (Irving), **II:** 304
Voyage, The, and Other Versions of Poems by Baudelaire (Lowell), **Retro. Supp. II:** 187
Voyage dans la Haute Pennsylvanie et dans l'état de New-York (Crèvecoeur), **Supp. I Part 1:** 250–251
Voyage of the Beagle (Darwin), **Supp. IX:** 211
Voyage Out, The (Woolf), **Supp. XV:** 65
"Voyager, The" (Everwine), **Supp. XV:** 75
"Voyages" (H. Crane), **I:** 393–395; **Retro. Supp. II:** 78, 80, 81
"Voyages" (Levine), **Supp. V:** 190
Voyages and Discoveries of the Companions of Columbus (Irving), **II:** 310
Voyage to Pagany, A (W. C. Williams), **IV:** 404; **Retro. Supp. I:** 418–419, **420–421,** 423
Voyaging Portraits (Sobin), **Supp. XVI:** 282, 287
"Voyeur, The" (Gioia), **Supp. XV:** 125
Voznesensky, Andrei, **II:** 553; **Supp. III Part 1:** 268; **Supp. III Part 2:** 560
Vrbovska, Anca, **Supp. IV Part 2:** 639
V. S. Naipaul: An Introduction to His Work (Theroux), **Supp. VIII:** 314, 318
"V. S. Pritchett's Apprenticeship" (Maxwell), **Supp. VIII:** 172
"Vulgarity in Literature" (Huxley), **III:** 429–430
"Vultures" (Oliver), **Supp. VII:** 235
"V. V." (Alcott), **Supp. I Part 1:** 37

W

W (Viva) (Cummings), **I:** 429, 433, 434, 436, 443, 444, 447
Wabash (R. O. Butler), **Supp. XII:** 61, **68–69**
Wade, Grace, **I:** 216
"Wading at Wellfleet" (Bishop), **Retro. Supp. II:** 42, 43; **Supp. I Part 1:** 80, 85, 86
Wadsworth, Charles, **I:** 454, 470; **Retro. Supp. I:** 32, 33
Wagenknecht, Edward, **II:** 508; **Supp. I Part 2:** 408, 584; **Supp. IV Part 2:** 681
"Wages of Poetry, The" (Wright), **Supp. XV:** 337
Wagner, Jean, **Supp. I Part 1:** 341, 346; **Supp. IV Part 1:** 165, 167, 171
Wagner, Richard, **I:** 284, 395; **II:** 425; **III:** 396, 507; **Supp. IV Part 1:** 392
Wagner, Robert, **Supp. IX:** 250
"Wagnerians, The" (Auchincloss), **Supp. IV Part 1:** 23
"Wagner Matinee, A" (Cather), **I:** 315–316; **Retro. Supp. I:** 5, 8
Wagoner, David, **Supp. IX: 323–340; Supp. XII:** 178
Waid, Candace, **Retro. Supp. I:** 360, 372, 373
Waif, The (Longfellow, ed.), **Retro. Supp. II:** 155
"Waif of the Plains, A" (Harte), **Supp. II Part 1:** 354
Wain, John, **Supp. XIV:** 166
"Wait" (Kinnell), **Supp. III Part 1:** 250
"Waiting" (Dubus), **Supp. VII:** 87
Waiting (Jin), **Supp. XVIII:** 89, **96–97,** 99
"Waiting" (W. C. Williams), **Retro. Supp. I:** 418
"Waiting, The" (L.-Y. Lee), **Supp. XV:** 218
"Waiting, The" (Olds), **Supp. X:** 209
"Waiting between the Trees" (Tan), **Supp. X:** 290
"Waiting by the Gate" (Bryant), **Supp. I Part 1:** 171
Waiting for God (Weil), **I:** 298
Waiting for Godot (Beckett), **I:** 78, 91, 298; **Supp. IV Part 1:** 368–369

Waiting for Lefty (Odets), **Supp. I Part 1:** 277; **Supp. II Part 2:** 529, 530–533, 540; **Supp. V:** 109
Waiting for the End of the World (Bell), **Supp. X: 4–5,** 11
Waiting for the Verdict (Davis), **Supp. XVI:** 85, 89, 90
"Waiting in a Rain Forest" (Wagoner), **Supp. IX:** 329
Waiting Room, The (Kees), **Supp. XV:** 133, 148
Waiting to Exhale (McMillan), **Supp. XIII:** 184, 185, **189–190,** 191
"Waiting to Freeze" (Banks), **Supp. V:** 5, 6
Waiting to Freeze: Poems (Banks), **Supp. V:** 6, 8
Waits, Tom, **Supp. VIII:** 12
Wait until Spring, Bandini (Fante), **Supp. XI:** 160, 161, 164, 165, **166–167**
Wait until Spring, Bandini (film), **Supp. XI:** 173
"Wake, The" (Dove), **Supp. IV Part 1:** 250
"Wakefield" (Hawthorne), **Retro. Supp. I:** 154, 159
Wakefield, Dan, **Supp. VIII:** 43; **Supp. XVI:** 220
Wakefield, Richard, **Supp. IX:** 323
"Wake Island" (Rukeyser), **Supp. VI:** 273
Wakeman, Frederic, **Supp. IX:** 247
Wake Up and Live! (Brande), **Supp. I Part 2:** 608
"Waking" (C. Frost), **Supp. XV:** 93
Waking, The (Roethke), **III:** 541
"Waking Early Sunday Morning" (Lowell), **II:** 552; **Retro. Supp. II:** 190
"Waking in the Blue" (Lowell), **II:** 547; **Retro. Supp. II:** 180
"Waking in the Dark" (Rich), **Supp. I Part 2:** 559
"Waking Up the Rake" (Hogan), **Supp. IV Part 1:** 415–416, 416
Wakoski, Diane, **Supp. V:** 79; **Supp. XII:** 184; **Supp. XV:** 252; **Supp. XVII:** 112
Walcott, Charles C., **II:** 49
Walcott, Derek, **Supp. VIII:** 28; **Supp. X:** 122, 131; **Supp. XV:** 256
Walcott, Jersey Joe, **Supp. V:** 182
Wald, Alan, **Supp. XV:** 202; **Supp. XVIII:** 223
Wald, Lillian, **Supp. I Part 1:** 12
Walden (Thoreau), **Supp. XIV:** 177, 227; **Supp. XV:** 275; **Supp. XVIII:** 14, 80, 189
Walden, Daniel, **Supp. IV Part 2:** 584, 591; **Supp. V:** 272
Walden; or, Life in the Woods (Thoreau), **I:** 219, 305; **II:** 8, 142, 159, 312–313, 458; **IV:** 168, 169, 170, 176, 177–178, 179–182, 183, 187; **Retro. Supp. I:** 62; **Supp. I Part 2:** 579, 655, 664, 672; **Supp. VIII:** 296; **Supp. X:** 27, 101; **Supp. XIII:** 152
Waldman, Anne, **Supp. XIV:** 150
Waldmeir, Joseph, **III:** 45
Waldmeir, Joseph J., **Supp. I Part 2:** 476
Waldo (Theroux), **Supp. VIII:** 313, 314, **314–315**
Waldron, Jeremy, **Supp. XVII:** 235
Waldrop, Keith, **Supp. XV:** 153, 165
Waley, Arthur, **II:** 526; **III:** 466; **Supp. V:** 340
"Walk, A" (Snyder), **Supp. VIII:** 297
"Walk at Sunset, A" (Bryant), **Supp. I Part 1:** 155
"Walk before Mass, A" (Agee), **I:** 28–29
Walker, Alice, **Retro. Supp. I:** 215; **Supp. I Part 2:** 550; **Supp. III Part 2:** 488, **517–540; Supp. IV Part 1:** 14; **Supp. IX:** 306, 311; **Supp. VIII:** 141, 214; **Supp. X:** 85, 228, 252, 325, 330; **Supp. XIII:** 179, 185, 291, 295; **Supp. XVI:** 39; **Supp. XVIII:** 200, 283
Walker, Cheryl, **Supp. XI:** 145
Walker, David, **Supp. V:** 189; **Supp. XVII:** 246
Walker, Franklin D., **III:** 321
Walker, Gue, **Supp. XII:** 207
Walker, Margaret, **Supp. XVIII:** 282
Walker, Marianne, **Supp. VIII:** 139
Walker, Obadiah, **II:** 113
Walker, Scott, **Supp. XV:** 92
Walker in the City, A (Kazin), **Supp. VIII: 93–95,** 99
Walk Hard (Blum and Hill), **Supp. XV:** 194
Walk Hard-Talk Loud (Zinberg), **Supp. XV:** 194, 202
"Walking" (Hogan), **Supp. IV Part 1:** 416
"Walking" (Thoreau), **Supp. IV Part 1:** 416; **Supp. IX:** 178
"Walking Along in Winter" (Kenyon), **Supp. VII:** 167
"Walking around the Block with a Three-Year-Old" (Wagoner), **Supp. IX:** 331–332
"Walking Backwards into the Future" (R. Williams), **Supp. IX:** 146
Walking Down the Stairs: Selections from Interviews (Kinnell), **Supp. III Part 1:** 235, 249
"Walking Home" (Schnackenberg). *See* "Laughing with One Eye" (Schnackenberg)
"Walking Home at Night" (Ginsberg), **Supp. II Part 1:** 313
Walking Light (Dunn), **Supp. XI:** 140, 141, 153
"Walking Man of Rodin, The" (Sandburg), **III:** 583
"Walking Sticks and Paperweights and Water Marks" (Moore), **III:** 215
Walking Tall (Dunn), **Supp. XI:** 140
Walking the Black Cat (Simic), **Supp. VIII:** 280, **282–284**
Walking to Martha's Vineyard (F. Wright), **Supp. XVII:** 240, 241, 245, 246
"Walking to Sleep" (Wilbur), **Supp. III Part 2:** 544, 557, 559, 561, 562
Walking to Sleep (Wilbur), **Supp. III Part 2:** 557–560
Walkin' the Dog (Mosley), **Supp. XIII:** 242
"Walk in the Moonlight, A" (Anderson), **I:** 114
Walk Me to the Distance (Everett), **Supp. XVIII: 55–56,** 57
Walk on the Wild Side, A (Algren), **Supp. IX:** 3, **12–13,** 14; **Supp. V:** 4
"Walks in Rome" (Merrill), **Supp. III Part 1:** 337
Walk to the River, A (Hoffman), **Supp. XVIII: 77–78**
Walk with Tom Jefferson, A (Levine), **Supp. V:** 179, 187, 190–191
"Wall, The" (Brooks), **Supp. III Part 1:** 70, 71, 84
Wall, The (Hersey), **IV:** 4
"Wall, The" (Roethke), **III:** 544
"Wall, The" (Sexton), **Supp. II Part 2:** 696
Wallace, David Foster, **Retro. Supp. II:** 279; **Supp. X: 301–318; Supp. XVII:** 226
Wallace, Henry, **I:** 489; **III:** 111, 475; **Supp. I Part 1:** 286; **Supp. I Part 2:** 645
Wallace, Mike, **Supp. IV Part 1:** 364; **Supp. IV Part 2:** 526
Wallace, Richard, **Supp. XVIII:** 101–102
Wallace Stevens (Kermode), **Retro. Supp. I:** 301
Wallace Stevens: The Poems of our Climate (Bloom), **Retro. Supp. I:** 299
Wallace Stevens: Words Chosen out of Desire (Stevens), **Retro. Supp. I:** 297
Wallach, Eli, **III:** 161
Wallant, Edward Lewis, **Supp. XVI:** 220
Wallas, Graham, **Supp. I Part 2:** 643
"Walled City" (Oates), **Supp. II Part 2:** 524
Wallenstein, Anna. *See* Weinstein, Mrs. Max (Anna Wallenstein)
Waller, Edmund, **III:** 463
Waller, Fats, **IV:** 263
Walling, William English, **Supp. I Part 2:** 645; **Supp. XV:** 295
Wall of the Sky, the Wall of the Eye, The (Lethem), **Supp. XVIII:** 139
Walls Do Not Fall, The (Doolittle), **Supp. I Part 1:** 271, 272
"Wall Songs" (Hogan), **Supp. IV Part 1:** 413
Wall Writing (Auster), **Supp. XII:** 23–24
Walpole, Horace, **I:** 203; **Supp. I Part 2:** 410, 714
Walpole, Hugh, **Retro. Supp. I:** 231
Walpole, Robert, **IV:** 145
Walsh, David M., **Supp. XV:** 5
Walsh, Ed, **II:** 424
Walsh, George, **Supp. IV Part 2:** 528
Walsh, Raoul, **Supp. XIII:** 174
Walsh, Richard J., **Supp. II Part 1:** 119, 130
Walsh, William, **Supp. IV Part 1:** 242, 243, 246, 248, 252, 254, 257
"Walt and Will" (Apple), **Supp. XVII:** 6
Walter, Eugene, **Supp. XVI:** 230
Walter, Joyce, **Supp. XV:** 121
Walter Benjamin at the Dairy Queen: Reflections at Sixty and Beyond (McMurtry), **Supp. V:** 232
Walters, Barbara, **Supp. XIV:** 125

Walters, Marguerite. *See* Smith, Mrs. Lamar (Marguerite Walters)
"Walter T. Carriman" (O'Hara), **III:** 368
Walton, Izaak, **Supp. I Part 2:** 422
"Walt Whitman" (Masters), **Supp. I Part 2:** 458
"Walt Whitman at Bear Mountain" (Simpson), **Supp. IX:** 265
Walt Whitman Bathing (Wagoner), **Supp. IX: 331–332**
Walt Whitman Handbook (Allen), **IV:** 352
Walt Whitman Reconsidered (Chase), **IV:** 352
"Waltz, The" (Parker), **Supp. IX:** 204
"Waltzer in the House, The" (Kunitz), **Supp. III Part 1:** 258
Walzer, Kevin, **Supp. XII:** 202; **Supp. XV:** 118; **Supp. XVIII:** 174
Wambaugh, Joseph, **Supp. X:** 5
Wampeters, Foma, & Granfalloons (Vonnegut), **Supp. II Part 2:** 758, 759–760, 776, 779
Wand, David Hsin-fu, **Supp. X:** 292
"Wanderer, The" (W. C. Williams), **Retro. Supp. I:** 414, 421
"Wanderers, The" (Welty), **IV:** 273–274
"Wandering Jew, The" (Robinson), **III:** 505, 516–517
Wanderings of Oisin (Yeats), **Supp. I Part 1:** 79
Wang, Dorothy, **Supp. X:** 289
Wang Wei, **Supp. XV:** 47
Waniek, Marilyn Nelson, **Supp. IV Part 1:** 244. *See also* Nelson, Marilyn
"Wan Lee, the Pagan" (Harte), **Supp. II Part 1:** 351
"Want, The" (Olds), **Supp. X:** 210
Want Bone, The (Pinsky), **Supp. VI:** 236–237, 244–245, 247
"Wanted: An Ontological Critic" (Ransom), **III:** 498
"Wanting to Die" (Sexton), **Supp. II Part 2:** 684, 686; **Supp. XIV:** 132
"Wants" (Paley), **Supp. VI:** 219
Waples, Dorothy, **I:** 348
Wapshot Chronicle, The (Cheever), **Supp. I Part 1:** 174, 177–180, 181, 196
Wapshot Scandal, The (Cheever), **Supp. I Part 1:** 180–184, 187, 191, 196
"War" (Jin), **Supp. XVIII:** 93
"War" (Kingston), **Supp. V:** 169
"War" (Simic), **Supp. VIII:** 282
"War, Response, and Contradiction" (Burke), **I:** 283
"War and Peace" (Sanders), **Supp. XVI:** 277
War and Peace (Tolstoy), **I:** 6, 7; **II:** 191, 205, 291; **IV:** 446; **Supp. V:** 277; **Supp. XI:** 68; **Supp. XIV:** 97
War and War (F. Barthelme), **Supp. XI:** 25
"War Between Men and Women, The" (Thurber), **Supp. I Part 2:** 615
War Bulletins (Lindsay), **Supp. I Part 2:** 378–379
Ward, Aileen, **II:** 531
Ward, Artemus (pseudonym). *See* Browne, Charles Farrar
Ward, Douglas Turner, **Supp. IV Part 1:** 362
Ward, Henry, **Supp. I Part 2:** 588
Ward, Leo R., **Supp. VIII:** 124
Ward, Lester F., **Supp. I Part 2:** 640; **Supp. XI:** 202, 203
Ward, Lynn, **I:** 31
Ward, Mrs. Humphry, **II:** 338
Ward, Nathaniel, **Supp. I Part 1:** 99, 102, 111, 116
Ward, Theodora, **I:** 470; **Retro. Supp. I:** 28
Ward, William Hayes, **Supp. I Part 1:** 371
"War Debt, A" (Jewett), **Retro. Supp. II:** 138, 141
"War Diary" (N. Boyce), **Supp. XVII:** 104
"War Diary, A" (Bourne), **I:** 229
War Dispatches of Stephen Crane, The (Crane), **I:** 422
"Ward Line, The" (Morris), **III:** 220
Warfel, Harry R., **Supp. I Part 1:** 366
War Games (Morris), **III:** 238
War in Heaven, The (Shepard and Chaikin), **Supp. III Part 2:** 433
"War Is Kind" (Crane), **I:** 419
War Is Kind (Crane), **I:** 409; **III:** 585
Warlock (Harrison), **Supp. VIII:** 45, **46**
Warm as Wool (Sanders), **Supp. XVI:** 269
Warner, Anna, **Supp. XVIII:** 258–275
Warner, Charles Dudley, **II:** 405; **IV:** 198
Warner, Jack, **Supp. XII:** 160–161; **Supp. XVIII:** 249
Warner, John R., **III:** 193
Warner, Oliver, **I:** 548
Warner, Susan, **Retro. Supp. I:** 246; **Supp. XV:** 275; **Supp. XVIII: 257–275**
Warner, Sylvia Townsend, **Supp. VIII:** 151, 155, 164, 171
Warner, W. Lloyd, **III:** 60
Warner Family and the Warner Books, The (Baker), **Supp. XVIII:** 259, 267
"Warning" (Hughes), **Supp. I Part 1:** 343
"Warning" (Pound), **III:** 474
"Warning, The" (Creeley), **Supp. IV Part 1:** 150
"Warning, The" (Longfellow), **II:** 498
Warning Hill (Marquand), **III:** 55–56, 60, 68
"War of Eyes, A" (Coleman), **Supp. XI:** 93–94
War of Eyes and Other Stories, A (Coleman), **Supp. XI: 91–92**
War of the Classes (London), **II:** 466
"War of the Wall, The" (Bambara), **Supp. XI:** 15–16
"War of Vaslav Nijinsky, The" (Bidart), **Supp. XV:** 21–22, **27–29**
"War Poems" (Sandburg), **III:** 581
Warren, Austin, **I:** 265, 268, 271; **Supp. I Part 2:** 423
Warren, Earl, **III:** 581
Warren, Gabriel, **IV:** 244
Warren, Mercy Otis, **Supp. XV:** 230
Warren, Mrs. Robert Penn (Eleanor Clark), **IV:** 244
Warren, Robert Penn, **I:** 190, 211, 517; **II:** 57, 217, 228, 253; **III:** 134, 310, 382–383, 454, 482, 485, 490, 496, 497; **IV:** 121, 122, 123, 125, 126, **236–259,** 261, 262, 279, 340–341, 458; **Retro. Supp. I:** 40, 41, 73, 90; **Retro. Supp. II:** 220, 235; **Supp. I Part 1:** 359, 371; **Supp. I Part 2:** 386, 423; **Supp. II Part 1:** 139; **Supp. III Part 2:** 542; **Supp. IX:** 257; **Supp. V:** 261, 316, 318, 319, 333; **Supp. VIII:** 126, 176; **Supp. X:** 1, 25, 26; **Supp. XI:** 315; **Supp. XII:** 254, 255; **Supp. XIV:** 1, 2, 3, 4, 11, 14, 15; **Supp. XVIII:** 77, 78–79
Warren, Rosanna, **IV:** 244; **Supp. XV:** 251, 261, 262, 263
Warrington Poems, The (Ríos), **Supp. IV Part 2:** 540
Warrior, Robert Allen, **Supp. IV Part 1:** 329
"Warrior, The" (Gunn Allen), **Supp. IV Part 1:** 326
"Warrior: 5th Grade" (Olds), **Supp. X:** 214
"Warrior Road" (Harjo), **Supp. XII:** 217
Warshavsky, Isaac (pseudonym). *See* Singer, Isaac Bashevis
Warshow, Robert, **Supp. I Part 1:** 51
Wars I Have Seen (Stein), **IV:** 27, 36, 477
Wartime (Fussell), **Supp. V:** 241
War Trash (Jin), **Supp. XVIII:** 89, **100–101**
"War Widow, The" (Frederic), **II:** 135–136
"Was" (Creeley), **Supp. IV Part 1:** 155
"Was" (Faulkner), **II:** 71
"Wash" (Faulkner), **II:** 72
Wash, Richard, **Supp. XII:** 14
"Washboard Wizard" (Nelson), **Supp. XVIII:** 182
"Washed in the Rain" (Fante), **Supp. XI:** 165
Washington, Booker T., **Supp. I Part 2:** 393; **Supp. II Part 1:** 157, 160, 167, 168, 171, 225; **Supp. XIV:** 198, 199, 201; **Supp. XVIII:** 121–122
Washington, D.C. (Vidal), **Supp. IV Part 2:** 677, 684, 686–687, 690
Washington, George, **I:** 453; **II:** 313–314; **Supp. I Part 2:** 399, 485, 508, 509, 511, 513, 517, 518, 520, 599
Washington, Mary Helen, **Supp. XVIII:** 119, 284
Washington Crossing the Delaware (Rivers), **Supp. XV:** 186
Washington Post Book World (Lesser), **Supp. IV Part 2:** 453; **Supp. VIII:** 80, 84, 241; **Supp. X:** 282
Washington Square (James), **II:** 327, 328; **Retro. Supp. I:** 215, 220, **222–223**
"Washington Square, 1946" (Ozick), **Supp. V:** 272
Washington Square Ensemble, The (Bell), **Supp. X:** 1, **3–4**
"Was Lowell an Historical Critic?" (Altick), **Supp. I Part 2:** 423
Wasserman, Earl R., **Supp. I Part 2:** 439, 440
Wasserman, Jakob, **Supp. I Part 2:** 669
Wasserstein, Wendy, **Supp. IV Part 1:** 309; **Supp. XV: 319–336**
Wasson, Ben, **Retro. Supp. I:** 79, 83

"Waste Carpet, The" (Matthews), **Supp. IX: 158–159**
Waste Land, The (Eliot), **I:** 107, 266, 298, 395, 396, 482, 570–571, 572, 574–575, 577–578, 580, 581, 584, 585, 586, 587; **III:** 6–8, 12, 196, 277–278, 453, 471, 492, 586; **IV:** 122, 123, 124, 140, 418, 419, 420; **Retro. Supp. I:** 51, 60, **60–62,** 63, 64, 66, 210, 290, 291, 299, 311, 420, 427; **Retro. Supp. II:** 85, 121, 190; **Supp. I Part 1:** 272; **Supp. I Part 2:** 439, 455, 614; **Supp. II Part 1:** 4, 5, 11, 96; **Supp. III Part 1:** 9, 10, 41, 63, 105; **Supp. IV Part 1:** 47, 284; **Supp. IX:** 158, 305; **Supp. V:** 338; **Supp. X:** 125; **Supp. XIII:** 341–342, 344, 346; **Supp. XIV:** 6, 284; **Supp. XV:** 21, 181, 261, 306; **Supp. XVI:** 204; **Supp. XVII:** 140–141, 144, 227; **Supp. XVIII:** 78, 79–80
"Waste Land, The": A Facsimile and Transcript of the Original Drafts Including the Annotations of Ezra Pound (Eliot, ed.), **Retro. Supp. I:** 58
Waste Land and Other Poems, The (Eliot), **Supp. XV:** 305
Wat, Alexander, **Supp. XVI:** 155, 161
Watch, The (Bass), **Supp. XVI: 16–17**
"Watch, The,——" (Bass), **Supp. XVI:** 17
Watch and Ward (James), **II:** 323; **Retro. Supp. I:** 218, **219,** 220
"Watcher, The" (R. Bly), **Supp. IV Part 1:** 71
"Watcher by the Dead, A" (Bierce), **I:** 203
Watchfires (Auchincloss), **Supp. IV Part 1:** 23
"Watching Crow, Looking toward the Manzano Mountains" (Harjo), **Supp. XII:** 219
"Watching the Oregon Whale" (A. Finch), **Supp. XVII:** 77
"Watching the Sunset" (Coleman), **Supp. XI:** 92
Watch on the Rhine (Hellman), **Supp. I Part 1:** 276, 278, 279–281, 283–284; **Supp. IV Part 1:** 83
"Water" (Emerson), **II:** 19
"Water" (Komunyakaa), **Supp. XIII:** 132
"Water" (Lowell), **II:** 550
"Waterbird" (Swenson), **Supp. IV Part 2:** 651
"Water Borders" (Dillard), **Supp. VI:** 27
"Water Buffalo" (Komunyakaa), **Supp. XIII:** 122
"Watercolor of Grantchester Meadows" (Plath), **Supp. I Part 2:** 537
Water Cure, The (Everett), **Supp. XVIII: 64–66**
"Waterfall, The" (Clampitt), **Supp. IX:** 44
Waterfront (Schulberg), **Supp. XVIII: 251–252**
"Water Hose Is on Fire, The" (Simic), **Supp. XV:** 185
Waterhouse, Keith, **Supp. VIII:** 124
"Waterlily Fire" (Rukeyser), **Supp. VI:** 285, 286
Waterlily Fire: Poems 1935–1962 (Rukeyser), **Supp. VI:** 274, 283, 285
Watermark (Brodsky), **Supp. VIII:** 29
Water-Method Man, The (Irving), **Supp. VI:** 163, **167–179,** 180
Water Music (Boyle), **Supp. VIII:** 1, 3–5, 8, 14
"Water Music for the Progress of Love in a Life-Raft Down the Sammamish Slough" (Wagoner), **Supp. IX:** 326
"Water People" (Burke), **Supp. XIV:** 21
"Water Picture" (Swenson), **Supp. IV Part 2:** 641
"Water Rising" (Hogan), **Supp. IV Part 1:** 400
Waters, Ethel, **II:** 587
Waters, Frank, **Supp. X:** 124
Waters, Muddy, **Supp. VIII:** 345
Watershed (Everett), **Supp. XVIII: 58–59,** 64
"Watershed" (Kingsolver), **Supp. VII:** 208
"Watershed" (Warren), **IV:** 239
"Watershed, The" (Auden), **Supp. II Part 1:** 5
Waters of Kronos, The (Richter), **Supp. XVIII:** 207, 208, **218–219,** 220
Waters of Siloe, The (Merton), **Supp. VIII:** 196, 208
Waterston, Sam, **Supp. IX:** 253
Water Street (Merrill), **Supp. III Part 1:** 321–323
"Water Walker" (Wilbur), **Supp. III Part 2:** 548, 560
Water-Witch, The (Cooper), **I:** 342–343
"Water Works, The" (Doctorow), **Supp. IV Part 1:** 234
Waterworks, The (Doctorow), **Supp. IV Part 1:** 218, 222, 223, 231–233, 234
Watkin, E. I., **Retro. Supp. II:** 187
Watkins, Floyd C., **IV:** 452
Watkins, James T., **I:** 193, 194
Watkins, Maureen, **Supp. XVI:** 188
Watkins, Mel, **Supp. X:** 330; **Supp. XIII:** 246
Watrous, Peter, **Supp. VIII:** 79
Watson, Burton, **Supp. XV:** 47
Watson, James Sibley, Jr., **I:** 261
Watson, Jay, **Supp. XVIII:** 195
Watson, J. B., **II:** 361
Watson, Richard, **Supp. I Part 2:** 516, 517
Watson, William, **II:** 114
Watt, Ian, **Supp. VIII:** 4
Watteau, Jean Antoine, **III:** 275; **IV:** 79
Watts, Emily Stipes, **Supp. I Part 1:** 115
Waugh, Evelyn, **I:** 480; **III:** 281; **Supp. I Part 2:** 607; **Supp. IV Part 2:** 688; **Supp. XI:** 305, 306
"Wave" (Snyder), **Supp. VIII:** 299
"Wave, A" (Ashbery), **Supp. III Part 1:** 9, 19, 24–25
Wave, A (Ashbery), **Supp. III Part 1:** 1, 4, 24–26
"Wave, The" (MacLeish), **III:** 19
"Wave, The" (Untermeyer), **Supp. XV:** 300
"Waxwings" (Francis), **Supp. IX:** 82
Way, The (Steiner and Witt, eds.), **Supp. IV Part 2:** 505
"Way Down, The" (Kunitz), **Supp. III Part 1:** 263
"Way It Is, The" (Ellison), **Supp. II Part 1:** 245
"Way It Is, The" (Jones), **Supp. XI:** 229
Way It Is, The (Stafford), **Supp. XIII:** 274
"Way It Is, The" (Strand), **Supp. IV Part 2:** 627
"Wayland" (Sanders), **Supp. XVI:** 275
Wayne, John, **Supp. IV Part 1:** 200
Way of Chuang-Tzu, The (Merton), **Supp. VIII:** 208
"Way of Exchange in James Dickey's Poetry, The" (Weatherby), **Supp. IV Part 1:** 175
Way of Life According to Laotzu, The (Bynner), **Supp. XV:** 46, 48
Way Out, A (Frost), **Retro. Supp. I:** 133
Wayside Motor Inn, The (Gurney), **Supp. V:** 96, 105, 109
"Ways of Talking" (Jin), **Supp. XVIII:** 93
Ways of the Hour, The (Cooper), **I:** 354
Ways of White Folks, The (Hughes), **Retro. Supp. I:** 203, 204; **Supp. I Part 1:** 329, 330, 332
Way Some People Die, The (Macdonald), **Supp. IV Part 2:** 470, 471, 472, 474
Way Some People Live, The (Cheever), **Supp. I Part 1:** 175
"Way the Cards Fall, The" (Komunyakaa), **Supp. XIII:** 117
"Way Things Are, The" (Turow, unpub.), **Supp. XVII:** 215, 218
Way to Rainy Mountain, The (Momaday), **Supp. IV Part 2:** 485–486, 487–489, 491, 493
Way to Wealth, The (Franklin), **II:** 101–102, 110
Wayward and the Seeking, The: A Collection of Writings by Jean Toomer (Toomer), **Supp. III Part 2:** 478–481, 484, 487
Wayward Bus, The (Steinbeck), **IV:** 51, 64–65
"Way We Live Now, The" (Sontag), **Supp. III Part 2:** 467–468
"Way You'll Never Be, A" (Hemingway), **II:** 249
"W. D. Sees Himself Animated" (Snodgrass), **Supp. VI:** 327
"W. D. Sits in Kafka's Chair and Is Interrogated Concerning the Assumed Death of Cock Robin" (Snodgrass), **Supp. VI:** 319
"W. D. Tries to Warn Cock Robin" (Snodgrass), **Supp. VI:** 319
"We" (Alexander), **Supp. XVIII:** 185
Weaks, Mary Louise, **Supp. X:** 5
Weales, Gerald, **II:** 602
"Wealth," from *Conduct of Life, The* (Emerson), **II:** 2, 3–4
"Wealth," from *English Traits* (Emerson), **II:** 6
Wealth of Nations, The (A. Smith), **II:** 109
"We Are Looking at You, Agnes" (Caldwell), **I:** 309

We Are Still Married: Stories and Letters (Keillor), **Supp. XVI:** 176, 177
"We Are the Crazy Lady and Other Feisty Feminist Fables" (Ozick), **Supp. V:** 259
"Weary Blues, The" (Hughes), **Retro. Supp. I:** 198, 199; **Supp. I Part 1:** 324, 325
Weary Blues, The (Hughes), **Retro. Supp. I:** 195, 197, 198, 199, 200, 203, 205; **Supp. I Part 1:** 325
"Weary Kingdom" (Irving), **Supp. VI:** 163
Weasels and Wisemen: Ethics and Ethnicity in the Work of David Mamet (Kane), **Supp. XIV:** 250
Weather and the Women Treat Me Fair, The (Everett), **Supp. XVIII:** 66
Weatherby, H. L., **Supp. IV Part 1:** 175
"Weathering Out" (Dove), **Supp. IV Part 1:** 248
"Weather Within, The" (M. F. K. Fisher), **Supp. XVII:** 88, 91
Weaver, Harriet, **III:** 471
Weaver, James, **Supp. XVIII:** 72
Weaver, Michael, **Supp. XVIII:** 176, 177
Weaver, Mike, **Retro. Supp. I:** 430
Weaver, Will, **Supp. XVI:** 39
"Weaving" (Larcom), **Supp. XIII:** 142, **Supp. XIII:** 144–145, 150, 151
"Web" (Oliver), **Supp. VII:** 236
Web and the Rock, The (Wolfe), **IV:** 451, 455, 457, 459–460, 462, 464, 467, 468
Webb, Beatrice, **Supp. I Part 1:** 5
Webb, Mary, **I:** 226
Webb, Sidney, **Supp. I Part 1:** 5
Webb, W. P., **Supp. V:** 225
Weber, Brom, **I:** 383, 386
Weber, Carl, **Supp. IX:** 133, 138, 141
Weber, Max, **I:** 498; **Supp. I Part 2:** 637, 648
Weber, Sarah, **Supp. I Part 1:** 2
Weberman, A. J., **Supp. XVIII:** 27
Web of Earth, The (Wolfe), **IV:** 451–452, 456, 458, 464, 465
"Web of Life, The" (Nemerov), **III:** 282
Webster, Brenda, **Supp. XVI:** 157, 161
Webster, Daniel, **II:** 5, 9; **Supp. I Part 2:** 659, 687, 689, 690
Webster, John, **I:** 384; **Supp. I Part 2:** 422
Webster, Noah, **Supp. I Part 2:** 660; **Supp. II Part 1:** 77
Wector, Dixon, **II:** 103
Wedding, The (D. West), **Supp. XVIII:** 277**, 287–289**
"Wedding, The" (Everwine), **Supp. XV:** 83
Wedding, The (television miniseries), **Supp. XVIII:** 277, 289
"Wedding Cake" (Nye), **Supp. XIII:** 283
"Wedding in Brownsville, A" (Singer), **IV:** 15
Wedding in Hell, A (Simic), **Supp. VIII:** 280, **282**
"Wedding of the Rose and Lotus, The" (Lindsay), **Supp. I Part 2:** 387
"Wedding Supper, The" (Rowson), **Supp. XV:** 243
"Wedding Toast, A" (Wilbur), **Supp. III Part 2:** 561
Wedekind, Frank, **III:** 398
Wedge, The (W. C. Williams), **Retro. Supp. I:** 424
"Wednesday at the Waldorf" (Swenson), **Supp. IV Part 2:** 647
"We Don't Live Here Anymore" (Dubus), **Supp. VII:** 78–79, 85
"Weed" (McCarriston), **Supp. XIV:** 259, 273
"Weed, The" (Bishop), **Supp. I Part 1:** 80, 88–89
"Weeds, The" (McCarthy), **II:** 566
"Weekend" (Beattie), **Supp. V:** 27
Weekend, The (Cameron), **Supp. XII:** 80, 81, **86–88**
"Weekend at Ellerslie, A" (Wilson), **IV:** 431
Weekend Edition (National Public Radio), **Supp. IX:** 299; **Supp. XVII:** 240, 242
Week on the Concord and Merrimack Rivers, A (Thoreau), **IV:** 168, 169, 177, 182–183; **Supp. I Part 2:** 420; **Supp. XIV:** 227
Weeks, Edward, **III:** 64
Weeks, Jerome, **Supp. VIII:** 76
"Weeping Burgher" (Stevens), **IV:** 77
"Weeping Women" (Levertov), **Supp. III Part 1:** 282
We Fished All Night (W. Motley), **Supp. XVII: 155–158,** 159**,** 160
We Fly Away (Francis), **Supp. IX: 79–80,** 84
We Have Always Lived in the Castle (Jackson), **Supp. IX:** 121, 126, **127–128**
"We Have Our Arts So We Won't Die of Truth" (Bradbury), **Supp. IV Part 1:** 105
Weich, Dave, **Supp. XII:** 321; **Supp. XVIII:** 91
"Weight" (Wideman), **Supp. X:** 321
"Weights" (C. Baxter), **Supp. XVII:** 16
Weigl, Bruce, **Supp. VIII:** 269, 274; **Supp. XV:** 342
Weil, Dorothy, **Supp. XV:** 231
Weil, Robert, **Supp. IX:** 236
Weil, Simone, **I:** 298; **Supp. XV:** 259
Weiland (C. B. Brown), **Supp. XIII:** 100
Weinauer, Ellen, **Supp. XV:** 270, 284
Weinberger, Eliot, **Supp. IV Part 1:** 66; **Supp. VIII:** 290, 292; **Supp. XVI:** 284
Weininger, Otto, **Retro. Supp. I:** 416
Weinreb, Mindy, **Supp. X:** 24
Weinreich, Regina, **Supp. XIV:** 22
Weinstein, Cindy, **Supp. XVIII:** 261
Weinstein, Hinda, **IV:** 285
Weinstein, Max, **IV:** 285
Weinstein, Mrs. Max (Anna Wallenstein), **IV:** 285, 287
Weinstein, Nathan. *See* West, Nathanael
Weisheit, Rabbi, **IV:** 76
Weismuller, Johnny, **Supp. X:** 264
Weiss, David, **Supp. XVI:** 55
Weiss, Jane, **Supp. XVIII:** 267, 269
Weiss, Peter, **IV:** 117
Weiss, Theodore, **Supp. IV Part 2:** 440; **Supp. IX:** 96
Weist, Dianne, **Supp. X:** 80
Weithas, Art, **Supp. XI:** 231
Welch, James, **Supp. IV Part 1:** 404; **Supp. IV Part 2:** 503, 513, 557, 562
Welch, Lew, **Supp. V:** 170; **Supp. VIII:** 303
"Welcome from War" (Rukeyser), **Supp. VI:** 286
"Welcome Morning" (Sexton), **Supp. II Part 2:** 696
"Welcome the Wrath" (Kunitz), **Supp. III Part 1:** 261
Welcome to Hard Times (Doctorow), **Supp. IV Part 1:** 218, 219–220, 222, 224, 230, 238
Welcome to Hard Times (film), **Supp. IV Part 1:** 236
"Welcome to New Dork" (Leonard), **Supp. XVIII:** 148
Welcome to Our City (Wolfe), **IV:** 461
Welcome to the Monkey House (Vonnegut), **Supp. II Part 2:** 758
Welcome to the Moon (Shanley), **Supp. XIV:** 318
Welcome to the Moon and Other Plays (Shanley), **Supp. XIV:** 315, **316–319**
Weld, Theodore, **Supp. I Part 2:** 587, 588
Weld, Tuesday, **Supp. XI:** 306
Welded (O'Neill), **III:** 390
"Well, The" (Momaday), **Supp. IV Part 2:** 483
"Well Dressed Man with a Beard, The" (Stevens), **Retro. Supp. I:** 297
Wellek, René, **I:** 253, 261, 282; **II:** 320; **Supp. XIV:** 12, 14
Weller, George, **III:** 322
Welles, Gideon, **Supp. I Part 2:** 484
Welles, Orson, **IV:** 476; **Supp. I Part 1:** 67; **Supp. IV Part 1:** 82, 83; **Supp. V:** 251; **Supp. VIII:** 46; **Supp. XI:** 169, 307
"Wellfleet Whale, The" (Kunitz), **Supp. III Part 1:** 263, 269
Wellfleet Whale and Companion Poems, The (Kunitz), **Supp. III Part 1:** 263
Wellink, Yvonne, **Supp. XVIII:** 257
Wellman, Flora, **II:** 463–464, 465
"Well Rising, The" (Stafford), **Supp. XI:** 318
Wells, H. G., **I:** 103, 226, 241, 243, 253, 405, 409, 415; **II:** 82, 144, 276, 337, 338, 458; **III:** 456; **IV:** 340, 455; **Retro. Supp. I:** 100, 228, 231; **Supp. XVI:** 190
Wellspring, The (Olds), **Supp. X: 211–212**
Well Wrought Urn, The: Studies in the Structure of Poetry (Brooks), **Supp. XIV:** 1, **8–9,** 14, 15, 16
Welsh, Mary. *See* Hemingway, Mrs. Ernest (Mary Welsh)
Welty, Eudora, **II:** 194, 217, 606; **IV: 260–284; Retro. Supp. I:** 339–358; **Retro. Supp. II:** 235; **Supp. IV Part 2:** 474; **Supp. V:** 59, 315, 336; **Supp. VIII:** 94, 151, 171; **Supp. X:** 42, 290; **Supp. XII:** 310, 322; **Supp. XIV:** 3; **Supp. XV:** 338

Weltzien, O. Alan, **Supp. XVI:** 20–21, 28
"We miss Her, not because We see——" (Dickinson), **Retro. Supp. I:** 46
We Must Dance My Darlings (Trilling), **Supp. I Part 1:** 297
Wendell, Barrett, **III:** 507; **Supp. I Part 2:** 414; **Supp. XIV:** 197
Wendell, Sarah. *See* Holmes, Mrs. Abiel (Sarah Wendell)
Wendy Wasserstein: A Casebook (Barnett), **Supp. XV:** 323, 330
"Wendy Wasserstein's Three Sisters: Squandered Privilege" (Brewer), **Supp. XV:** 330
Wept of Wish-ton-Wish, The (Cooper), **I:** 339, 342, 350
Werbe, Peter, **Supp. XIII:** 236
"We Real Cool" (Brooks), **Supp. III Part 1:** 80
We're Back! A Dinosaur's Story (screenplay, Shanley), **Supp. XIV:** 316
"We're Friends Again" (O'Hara), **III:** 372–373
"Were the Whole Realm of Nature Mine" (Watts), **I:** 458
Werewolf (M. Sommers), **Supp. XVII:** 55
Were-Wolf, The (C. Housman), **Supp. XVII:** 55
Werewolf of Paris, The (Endore), **Supp. XVII:** 55–56
Werewolves in Their Youth (Chabon), **Supp. XI:** 66, **76–77**
Werlock, Abby, **Supp. XIII:** 293
Werthman, Michael, **Supp. V:** 115
"Wer-Trout, The" (Proulx), **Supp. VII:** 255–256
Wescott, Glenway, **I:** 288; **II:** 85; **III:** 448, 454; **Supp. VIII:** 156; **Supp. XIV:** 342; **Supp. XVI:** 195
"We Shall All Be Born Again But We Shall Not All Be Saved" (Matthews), **Supp. IX:** 162
West, Anthony, **Supp. IV Part 1:** 284
West, Benjamin, **Supp. I Part 2:** 511
West, Dorothy, **Supp. XIII:** 295; **Supp. XVIII: 277–291**
West, James, **II:** 562
West, Nathanael, **I:** 97, 107, 190, 211, 298; **II:** 436; **III:** 357, 425; **IV: 285–307; Retro. Supp. II: 321–341; Supp. IV Part 1:** 203; **Supp. VIII:** 97; **Supp. XI:** 85, 105, 159, 296; **Supp. XII:** 173, 310; **Supp. XIII:** 106, 170; **Supp. XVIII:** 251, 253, 254
West, Ray, **Supp. XV:** 142
West, Rebecca, **II:** 412, 445; **Supp. XVI:** 152, 153
Westall, Julia Elizabeth. *See* Wolfe, Mrs. William Oliver (Julia Elizabeth Westall)
"We Stand United" (Benét), **Supp. XI:** 46
"West Authentic, The: Willa Cather" (Stegner), **Supp. IV Part 2:** 608
"West Coast, The: Region with a View" (Stegner), **Supp. IV Part 2:** 608–609
Westcott, Edward N., **II:** 102
"Western Association of Writers" (Chopin), **Supp. I Part 1:** 217
"Western Ballad, A" (Ginsberg), **Supp. II Part 1:** 311
Western Borders, The (Howe), **Supp. IV Part 2:** 424–425
Western Canon: The Books and Schools of the Ages (Bloom), **Supp. IX:** 146
Western Lands, The (Burroughs), **Supp. III Part 1:** 106
Western Star (Benét), **Supp. XI:** 46, 47, 57
"Westland" (C. Baxter), **Supp. XVII:** 18, 19
"West Marginal Way" (Hugo), **Supp. VI:** 131, 135
West of Eden: Writers in Hollywood, 1928–1940 (Fine), **Supp. XVIII:** 248
West of Yesterday, East of Summer: New and Selected Poems, 1973–1993 (Monette), **Supp. X:** 159
West of Your City (Stafford), **Supp. XI:** 316, **317–318,** 321, 322
Weston, Jessie L., **II:** 540; **III:** 12; **Supp. I Part 2:** 438
"West Real" (Ríos), **Supp. IV Part 2:** 539, 540
"West-running Brook" (Frost), **II:** 150, 162–164
West-running Brook (Frost), **II:** 155; **Retro. Supp. I:** 136, 137
"West Wall" (Merwin), **Supp. III Part 1:** 355
"Westward Beach, A" (Jeffers), **Supp. II Part 2:** 418
Westward Ho (Harrison), **Supp. VIII:** 51, **52**
Westward the Course of Empire (Leutze), **Supp. X:** 307
"Westward the Course of Empire Takes Its Way" (Wallace), **Supp. X: 307–308**
"West Wind" (Oliver), **Supp. VII:** 246
"West Wind, The" (Bryant), **Supp. I Part 1:** 155
West Wind: Poems and Prose Poems (Oliver), **Supp. VII:** 243, 246–248
"Wet Casements" (Ashbery), **Supp. III Part 1:** 18–20
We the Living (film), **Supp. IV Part 2:** 520
We the Living (Rand), **Supp. IV Part 2:** 520–521
Wetherell, Elizabeth (pseudonym). *See* Warner, Susan
Wet Parade (Sinclair), **Supp. V:** 289
"We've Adjusted Too Well" (O'Brien), **Supp. V:** 247
Wevill, David, **Retro. Supp. II:** 247, 249
"We Wear the Mask" (Dunbar), **Supp. II Part 1:** 199, 207, 209–210
Weybright, Victor, **Supp. XIII:** 172
Weyden, Rogier van der, **Supp. IV Part 1:** 284
Whalen, Marcella, **Supp. I Part 1:** 49
Whalen, Philip, **Supp. VIII:** 289
Whalen-Bridge, John, **Retro. Supp. II:** 211–212
"Whales off Wales, The" (X. J. Kennedy), **Supp. XV:** 163
"Whales Weep Not!" (D. H. Lawrence), **Supp. XVII:** 77
Wharton, Edith, **I:** 12, 375; **II:** 96, 180, 183, 186, 189–190, 193, 283, 338, 444, 451; **III:** 69, 175, 576; **IV:** 8, 53, 58, **308–330; Retro. Supp. I:** 108, 232, **359–385; Supp. IV Part 1:** 23, 31, 35, 36, 80, 81, 310; **Supp. IX:** 57; **Supp. XII:** 308; **Supp. XIV:** 337, 347; **Supp. XVI:** 189; **Supp. XVIII:** 278
Wharton, Edward Robbins, **IV:** 310, 313–314, 319
"What" (Dunn), **Supp. XI:** 144
What a Kingdom It Was (Kinnell), **Supp. III Part 1:** 235, 238, 239
"What America Would Be Like without Blacks" (Ellison), **Retro. Supp. II:** 123
What Are Masterpieces (Stein), **IV:** 30–31
"What Are Years?" (Moore), **III:** 211, 213
What Are Years (Moore), **III:** 208–209, 210, 215
What a Way to Go (Morris), **III:** 230–232
"What a Wonder among the Instruments Is the Walloping Trombone!" (Carruth), **Supp. XVI:** 51
"What Became of the Flappers?" (Zelda Fitzgerald), **Supp. IX:** 71
"What Can I Tell My Bones?" (Roethke), **III:** 546, 549
"What Child Is This?" (Jarman), **Supp. XVII:** 113–114, 115
"What Do We Have Here" (Carson), **Supp. XII: 101**
"What Do We See" (Rukeyser), **Supp. VI:** 282
What Do Women Want? Bread Roses Sex Power (Jong), **Supp. V:** 115, 117, 129, 130
"What Do You Do in San Francisco?" (Carver), **Supp. III Part 1:** 143
What D'Ya Know for Sure (Zinberg), **Supp. XV:** 196
Whatever Happened to Gloomy Gus of the Chicago Bears? (Coover), **Supp. V:** 51, 52
Whatever Happened to Jacy Farrow? (Cleveland), **Supp. V:** 222
"What Every Boy Should Know" (Maxwell), **Supp. VIII:** 169
"What Feels Like the World" (Bausch), **Supp. VII:** 46
"What Fort Sumter Did for Me" (E. Stoddard), **Supp. XV:** 282
"What Girls Read" (Salmon), **Supp. XVIII:** 258
"What God Is Like to Him I Serve" (Bradstreet), **Supp. I Part 1:** 106–107
"What Happened Here Before" (Snyder), **Supp. VIII:** 302
"What Happened to Georgia" (Ray), **Supp. XVIII:** 194
What Have I Ever Lost by Dying? (R. Bly), **Supp. IV Part 1:** 71–72
What Have You Lost? (Nye, ed.), **Supp. XIII:** 280

"What I Believe" (Mumford), **Supp. II Part 2:** 479
"What I Call What They Call Onanism" (Goldbarth), **Supp. XII:** 175
What I Did Last Summer (Gurney), **Supp. V:** 96, 100, 107, 108
"What if God" (Olds), **Supp. X:** 208
"What I Have to Defend, What I Can't Bear Losing" (Stern), **Supp. IX:** 286, 287, 288, 298
"What I Knew" (Nelson), **Supp. XVIII:** 178
"What I Know about Being a Playwright" (McNally), **Supp. XIII:** 195, 207
"What I Mean" (Ortiz), **Supp. IV Part 2:** 497
"What Is an Emotion" (James), **II:** 350
What Is Art? (Tolstoy), **I:** 58
"What Is Civilization? Africa's Answer" (Du Bois), **Supp. II Part 1:** 176
"What Is College For?" (Bourne), **I:** 216
"What Is Exploitation?" (Bourne), **I:** 216
What Is Found There: Notebooks on Poetry and Politics (A. Rich), **Supp. XVII:** 74
"What Is It?" (Carver), **Supp. III Part 1:** 139
What Is Man? (Twain), **II:** 434; **IV:** 209
"What Is Poetry" (Ashbery), **Supp. III Part 1:** 19
"What Is Seized" (Moore), **Supp. X:** 164, 168, 169, 172, 175
"What Is the Earth?" (Olds), **Supp. X:** 213
"What Is This Poet" (Stern), **Supp. IX:** 295
"What I Think" (Hogan), **Supp. IV Part 1:** 406
What Maisie Knew (H. James), **II:** 332; **Retro. Supp. I:** 229, **230; Supp. XVIII:** 160
What Makes Sammy Run? (NBC broadcast, Schulberg and Schulberg), **Supp. XVIII:** 254
"What Makes Sammy Run?" (Schulberg), **Supp. XVIII:** 241
What Makes Sammy Run? (Schulberg), **Supp. XIII:** 170; **Supp. XVIII:** 241, **244–247**, 248, 249, 253
What Moon Drove Me to This? (Harjo), **Supp. XII: 218–220**
"What Must" (MacLeish), **III:** 18
"What My Father Believed" (Wrigley), **Supp. XVIII: 298–299**
What My Father Believed (Wrigley), **Supp. XVIII:** 298–300
What Price Hollywood? (film), **Supp. XVIII:** 243
"What Sally Said" (Cisneros), **Supp. VII:** 63
"What's Happening in America" (Sontag), **Supp. III Part 2:** 460–461
"What's in Alaska?" (Carver), **Supp. III Part 1:** 141, 143
What's New, Pussycat? (film; Allen), **Supp. XI:** 307; **Supp. XV:** 1, 2, 14
"What's New in American and Canadian Poetry" (R. Bly), **Supp. IV Part 1:** 67
What's O'Clock (Lowell), **II:** 511, 527, 528
What's Up, Tiger Lily? (film; Allen), **Supp. XV:** 2, **3**
"What the Arts Need Now" (Baraka), **Supp. II Part 1:** 47
"What the Brand New Freeway Won't Go By" (Hugo), **Supp. VI:** 132–133
"What the Gypsies Told My Grandmother While She Was Still a Young Girl" (Simic), **Supp. VIII:** 283
"What the Prose Poem Carries with It" (R. Bly), **Supp. IV Part 1:** 64
"What They Wanted" (Dunn), **Supp. XI:** 151
What Thou Lovest Well (Hugo), **Supp. VI:** 140, 141
"What Thou Lovest Well Remains American" (Hugo), **Supp. VI:** 140, 141
What Time Collects (Farrell), **II:** 46, 47–48
What to Do? (Chernyshevsky), **Retro. Supp. I:** 269
What Use Are Flowers? (Hansberry), **Supp. IV Part 1:** 359, 368–369, 374
What Was Literature? (Fiedler), **Supp. XIII:** 96–97, **105–106**
What Was Mine (Beattie), **Supp. V:** 33, 35
What Was the Relationship of the Lone Ranger to the Means of Production? (Baraka), **Supp. II Part 1:** 58
"What We Came Through" (Goldbarth), **Supp. XII:** 179–180
What We Talk About When We Talk About Love (Carver), **Supp. III Part 1:** 142–146
What We Talk about When We Talk about Love (Carver), **Supp. XII:** 139
"What Why When How Who" (Pinsky), **Supp. VI:** 244
What Will Suffice: Contemporary American Poets on the Art of Poetry (Buckley and Young, eds.), **Supp. XIII:** 313
What Work Is (Levine), **Supp. V:** 181, 187, 192–193
"What You Hear from Em" (Taylor), **Supp. V:** 314, 320, 324
"What You Want" (O. Henry), **Supp. II Part 1:** 402
Wheatley, Phyllis, **Supp. XVII:** 74–75
Wheatly, Phyllis, **Supp. XIII:** 111
Wheeler, David, **Supp. XVI:** 277
Wheeler, John, **II:** 433
Wheeler, Monroe, **Supp. XV:** 295
Wheelock, John Hall, **IV:** 461; **Supp. IX:** 268; **Supp. XIV:** 120; **Supp. XV:** 301
Wheel of Life, The (Glasgow), **II:** 176, 178, 179, 183
Wheelwright, Philip, **Supp. XV:** 20
"When" (Olds), **Supp. X:** 207
When Boyhood Dreams Come True (Farrell), **II:** 45
"When Death Came April Twelve 1945" (Sandburg), **III:** 591, 593
"When Death Comes" (Oliver), **Supp. VII:** 241
"When De Co'n Pone's Hot" (Dunbar), **Supp. II Part 1:** 202–203
"When God First Said" (Zach; Everwine trans.), **Supp. XV:** 87
"When Grandma Died——1942" (Shields), **Supp. VII:** 311
"When Howitzers Began" (Carruth), **Supp. XVI:** 55
"When I Buy Pictures" (Moore), **III:** 205
"When I Came from Colchis" (Merwin), **Supp. III Part 1:** 343
"When I Left Business for Literature" (Anderson), **I:** 101
"When in Rome——Apologia" (Komunyakaa), **Supp. XIII:** 120
"When It Comes" (Olds), **Supp. X:** 213
"When I Was Seventeen" (Kincaid), **Supp. VII:** 181
"When I Was Twenty-five" (Talese), **Supp. XVII:** 202
When Knighthood Was in Flower (Major), **III:** 320
"[When] Let by rain" (Taylor), **IV:** 160–161
"When Lilacs Last in the Dooryard Bloom'd" (Whitman), **IV:** 347–348, 351; **Retro. Supp. I:** 406; **Supp. IV Part 1:** 16; **Supp. XV:** 215
"When Malindy Sings" (Dunbar), **Supp. II Part 1:** 200, 204–205
When Peoples Meet: A Study of Race and Culture (Locke and Stern), **Supp. XIV:** 202, 213
When She Was Good (P. Roth), **Retro. Supp. II:** 282, 283, 284; **Supp. III Part 2:** 403, 405, 410–413
"When Sue Wears Red" (Hughes), **Retro. Supp. I:** 195, 204
"When the Dead Ask My Father about Me" (Olds), **Supp. X:** 210
"When the Frost Is on the Punkin" (Riley), **Supp. II Part 1:** 202
When the Jack Hollers (Hughes), **Retro. Supp. I:** 203; **Supp. I Part 1:** 328
"When the Last Riders" (Zach; Everwine, trans.), **Supp. XV:** 75, 86
"When the Light Gets Green" (Warren), **IV:** 252
"When the Peace Corps Was Young" (Theroux), **Supp. VIII:** 314
"When the Sun Tries to Go On" (Koch), **Supp. XV:** 179, 180
When the Sun Tries to Go On (Koch), **Supp. XV:** 185
"When the World Ended as We Knew It" (Harjo), **Supp. XII:** 231
When Time Was Born (Farrell), **II:** 46, 47
"When We Dead Awaken: Writing as Re-Vision" (Rich), **Supp. I Part 2:** 552–553, 560
"When We Gonna Rise" (Baraka), **Supp. II Part 1:** 48
"When We Have To" (Salinas), **Supp. XIII:** 322–323
"WHEN WE'LL WORSHIP JESUS" (Baraka), **Supp. II Part 1:** 54
"When we speak of God, is it God we speak of?" (J. Logan), **Supp. XVII:** 113
"When Women Throw Down Bundles: Strong Women Make Strong Nations" (Gunn Allen), **Supp. IV Part 1:** 328

"'When You Finally See Them': The Unconquered Eye in *To Kill a Mockingbird*" (Champion), **Supp. VIII:** 128
"When You Lie Down, the Sea Stands Up" (Swenson), **Supp. IV Part 2:** 643
Where Does One Go When There's No Place Left to Go? (Crews), **Supp. XI:** 103
"Where Go the Boats" (R. Stevenson), **Supp. XVII:** 69
"Where I Come from Is Like This" (Gunn Allen), **Supp. IV Part 1:** 319
"Where I'm Calling From" (Carver), **Supp. III Part 1:** 145
Where I'm Calling From: New and Selected Stories (Carver), **Supp. III Part 1:** 138, 148
"Where I Ought to Be" (Erdrich), **Supp. IV Part 1:** 265
Where Is My Wandering Boy Tonight? (Wagoner), **Supp. IX: 335–336**
"Where Is the Island?" (Francis), **Supp. IX:** 78
"Where Is the Voice Coming From?" (Welty), **IV:** 280; **Retro. Supp. I:** 355
Where Joy Resides (Isherwood), **Supp. XIV:** 156
"Where Knock Is Open Wide" (Roethke), **III:** 533–535
"Where My Sympathy Lies" (H. Roth), **Supp. IX:** 234
Where's My Money? (Shanley), **Supp. XIV:** 316, 328, **330–331**
Where the Bluebird Sings to the Lemonade Springs (Stegner), **Supp. IV Part 2:** 596, 597, 598, 600, 604, 606, 613
Where the Cross Is Made (O'Neill), **III:** 388, 391
"Where the Sea Used to Be" (Bass), **Supp. XVI:** 20, 21
Where the Sea Used to Be (Bass), **Supp. XVI:** 21
"*Where the Sea Used to Be:* Rick Bass and the Novel of Ecological Education" (Dixon), **Supp. XVI:** 21
"Where the Soft Air Lives" (Nye), **Supp. XIII:** 275
Where the Twilight Never Ends (Haines), **Supp. XII:** 211
Where the Wild Grape Grows: Selected Writings, 1930–1950 (D. West; Mitchell and Davis, eds.), **Supp. XVIII:** 283, 286
Where the Wild Things Are (Sendak), **Supp. IX:** 207
"Wherever Home Is" (Wright), **Supp. III Part 2:** 605, 606
Where Water Comes Together With Other Water (Carver), **Supp. III Part 1:** 147, 148
"Where We Crashed" (Hugo), **Supp. VI:** 138
"Where You Are" (Doty), **Supp. XI:** 131
Where You'll Find Me, and Other Stories (Beattie), **Supp. V:** 30–31
Whicher, Stephen, **II:** 20
"Which Is More Than I Can Say for Some People" (Moore), **Supp. X:** 177, 178
Which Ones Are the Enemy? (Garrett), **Supp. VII:** 98
"Which Theatre Is the Absurd One?" (Albee), **I:** 71
"Which Way to the Future?" (Rehder), **Supp. IV Part 1:** 69
While I Was Gone (Miller), **Supp. XII:** 290, **301–303**
"While Seated in a Plane" (Swenson), **Supp. IV Part 2:** 645
While the Messiah Tarries (Bukiet), **Supp. XVII:** 43, **46–47**
Whilomville Stories (Crane), **I:** 414
"Whip, The" (Robinson), **III:** 513
Whipple, Thomas K., **II:** 456, 458; **IV:** 427
"Whippoorwill, The" (Francis), **Supp. IX:** 90
"Whip-poor-will, The" (Thurber), **Supp. I Part 2:** 616
Whirlpool (film, Preminger), **Supp. XVII:** 62
"Whispering Gallery, The" (Komunyakaa), **Supp. XIII:** 132
"Whispering Leaves" (Glasgow), **II:** 190
Whispering to Fool the Wind (Ríos), **Supp. IV Part 2:** 540–541, 544, 545
"Whispers in the Next Room" (Simic), **Supp. VIII:** 278
"Whispers of Heavenly Death" (Whitman), **IV:** 348
"Whispers of Immortality" (Eliot), **Supp. XI:** 242
Whistle (Jones), **Supp. XI:** 219, 224, **231–234**
"Whistle, The" (Franklin), **II:** 121
"Whistle, The" (Komunyakaa), **Supp. XIII:** 111, 126
"Whistle, The" (Welty), **IV:** 262
Whistler, James, **I:** 484; **III:** 461, 465, 466; **IV:** 77, 369
Whistler, James Abbott McNeill, **Supp. XIV:** 335–336
"Whistling Dick's Christmas Stocking" (O. Henry), **Supp. II Part 1:** 390, 392
Whistling in the Dark (Garrett), **Supp. VII:** 111
Whistling in the Dark: True Stories and Other Fables (Garrett), **Supp. VII:** 95
Whitcher, Frances Miriam Berry, **Supp. XIII:** 152
"White" (Simic), **Supp. VIII: 275–276**
White, Barbara, **Retro. Supp. I:** 379
White, E. B., **Retro. Supp. I:** 335; **Supp. I Part 2:** 602, 607, 608, 612, 619, 620, **651–681; Supp. II Part 1:** 143; **Supp. IX:** 20, 32; **Supp. VIII:** 171; **Supp. XVI:** 167
White, Elizabeth Wade, **Supp. I Part 1:** 100, 103, 111
White, Henry Kirke, **Supp. I Part 1:** 150
White, James L., **Supp. XI:** 123
White, Joel, **Supp. I Part 2:** 654, 678
White, Katharine. (Katharine Sergeant Angell), **Supp. I Part 2:** 610, 653, 655, 656, 669; **Supp. VIII:** 151, 171
White, Lillian, **Supp. I Part 2:** 651
White, Lucia, **I:** 258
White, Maria. *See* Lowell, Mrs. James Russell (Maria White)
White, Morton, **I:** 258; **Supp. I Part 2:** 647, 648, 650
White, Roberta, **Supp. XII:** 293
White, Stanford, **Supp. IV Part 1:** 223
White, Stanley, **Supp. I Part 2:** 651, 655
White, T. H., **III:** 522
White, T. W., **III:** 411, 415
White, Walter, **Supp. I Part 1:** 345; **Supp. XVIII:** 123, 127
White, William, **Retro. Supp. II:** 326
White, William A., **I:** 252
"White Album, The" (Didion), **Supp. IV Part 1:** 205, 206
White Album, The (Didion), **Supp. IV Part 1:** 198, 202, 205–207, 210
"White Angel" (Cunningham), **Supp. XV:** 59
"White Apache" (Markson), **Supp. XVII:** 136
White Buildings (H. Crane), **I:** 385, 386, 390–395, 400; **Retro. Supp. II:** 77–78, **80–81,** 82, 83, 85
White Butterfly (Mosley), **Supp. XIII:** 237, 238, 240
"White Center" (Hugo), **Supp. VI:** 144, 146
White Center (Hugo), **Supp. VI:** 144–145
Whited, Stephen, **Supp. XI:** 135
White Deer, The (Thurber), **Supp. I Part 2:** 606
White Doves at Morning (Burke), **Supp. XIV:** 22–23, 32, 35–36
"White Eagle, The" (Chopin), **Retro. Supp. II:** 72
White Fang (London), **II:** 471–472, 481
Whitefield, George, **I:** 546
White-Footed Deer and Other Poems (Bryant), **Supp. I Part 1:** 157
White Goddess, The (Graves), **Supp. IV Part 1:** 280
White-Haired Lover (Shapiro), **Supp. II Part 2:** 703, 717
Whitehead, Alfred North, **III:** 605, 619, 620; **IV:** 88; **Supp. I Part 2:** 554, 647
Whitehead, Colson, **Supp. XIII:** 233, 241
Whitehead, James, **Supp. XV:** 339
Whitehead, Margaret, **IV:** 114, 115, 116
Whitehead, Mrs. Catherine, **IV:** 116
White Heat (Walsh), **Supp. XIII:** 174
"White Heron, A" (Jewett), **II:** 409; **Retro. Supp. II:** 17
White Heron and Other Stories, A (Jewett), **II:** 396
White Horses (Hoffman), **Supp. X: 83–85,** 90, 92
White House Diary, A (Lady Bird Johnson), **Supp. IV Part 1:** 22
White-Jacket; or, The World in a Man-of-War (Melville), **III:** 80, 81, 84, 94; **Retro Supp. I:** 248, 249, 254; **Supp. XVIII:** 7, 9
White Lantern, The (Connell), **Supp. XIV:** 97
"White Lights, The" (Robinson), **III:** 524
"White Lilies, The" (Glück), **Supp. V:** 88
White Man, Listen! (Wright), **IV:** 478, 488, 489, 494
"White Mulberry Tree, The" (Cather), **I:** 319; **Retro. Supp. I:** 7, 9, 17

White Mule (W. C. Williams), **Retro. Supp. I:** 423
"White Negro, The" (Mailer), **III:** 36–37; **Retro. Supp. II:** 202
"Whiteness of the Whale, The" (Melville), **III:** 84, 86
"White Night" (Oliver), **Supp. VII:** 236
"White Nights" (Auster), **Supp. XII:** 23–24
White Noise (DeLillo), **Supp. VI:** 1, 3–4, 5–7, 10, 11–12, 16; **Supp. XVIII:** 140
White Oxen and Other Stories, The (Burke), **I:** 269, 271
White Paper on Contemporary American Poetry (McClatchy), **Supp. XII:** 253, **259–260**
"White Pine" (Oliver), **Supp. VII:** 244
White Pine: Poems and Prose Poems (Oliver), **Supp. VII:** 243–246
"White Silence, The" (London), **II:** 468
"White Silk" (Nye), **Supp. XIII:** 275
"White Snake, The" (Sexton), **Supp. II Part 2:** 691
"White Spot" (Anderson), **I:** 116
"White-Tailed Hornet, The" (Frost), **Retro. Supp. I:** 138
Whitfield, Raoul, **Supp. IV Part 1:** 345
Whitlock, Brand, **II:** 276
Whitman (Masters), **Supp. I Part 2:** 473, 475, 476
Whitman, George, **IV:** 346, 350
Whitman, Sarah Wyman, **Retro. Supp. II:** 136
Whitman, Walt, **I:** 61, 68, 98, 103, 104, 109, 219, 220, 227, 228, 242, 246, 250, 251, 260, 261, 285, 381, 384, 386, 396, 397, 398, 402, 419, 430, 459, 460, 483, 485, 486, 577; **II:** 7, 8, 18, 127, 140, 273–274, 275, 289, 295, 301, 320, 321, 373, 445, 446, 451, 457, 494, 529, 530, 552; **III:** 171, 175, 177, 181–182, 189, 203, 234, 260, 426, 430, 453, 454, 461, 505, 507–508, 511, 528, 548, 552, 555, 559, 567, 572, 576, 577, 579, 584, 585, 595, 606, 609; **IV:** 74, 169, 191, 192, 202, **331–354,** 405, 409, 416, 444, 450–451, 457, 463, 464, 469, 470, 471; **Retro. Supp. I:** 8, 52, 194, 254, 283, 284, 333, **387–410,** 412, 417, 427; **Retro. Supp. II:** 40, 76, 93, 99, 155, 156, 158, 170, 262; **Supp. I Part 1:** 6, 79, 167, 311, 314, 325, 365, 368, 372; **Supp. I Part 2:** 374, 384, 385, 387, 389, 391, 393, 399, 416, 436, 455, 456, 458, 473, 474, 475, 525, 540, 579, 580, 582, 682, 691; **Supp. III Part 1:** 6, 20, 156, 239–241, 253, 340; **Supp. III Part 2:** 596; **Supp. IV Part 1:** 16, 169, 325; **Supp. IV Part 2:** 597, 625; **Supp. IX:** 8, 9, 15, 38, 41, 44, 48, 53, 131, 292, 298, 299, 308, 320; **Supp. V:** 113, 118, 122, 130, 170, 178, 183, 277, 279, 332; **Supp. VIII:** 42, 95, 105, 126, 198, 202, 269; **Supp. X:** 36, 112, 203, 204; **Supp. XI:** 83, 123, 132, 135, 203, 321; **Supp. XII:** 132, 185, 190, 256; **Supp. XIII:** 1, 77, 115, 153, 221, 304, 335; **Supp. XIV:** 89, 312, 334, 335, 338; **Supp. XV:** 41, 93, 181, 183, 212, 213, 218, 250, 275, 301, 302, 303, 309, 352; **Supp. XVI:** 209; **Supp. XVII:** 42, 71, 112, 133; **Supp. XVIII:** 4, 194, 196, 304
"Whitman: The Poet and the Mask" (Cowley), **Supp. II Part 1:** 143
Whitmarsh, Jason, **Supp. VIII:** 283
Whitmer, Peter, **Supp. X:** 264, 265
Whitney, Blair, **Supp. I Part 2:** 403
Whitney, Josiah, **Supp. IX:** 180, 181
Whitt, Margaret Earley, **Retro. Supp. II:** 226
Whittemore, Reed, **III:** 268; **Supp. XI:** 315
Whittier, Elizabeth, **Supp. I Part 2:** 700, 701, 703; **Supp. XIII:** 141, 142
Whittier, John Greenleaf, **I:** 216; **II:** 275; **III:** 52; **Retro. Supp. I:** 54; **Retro. Supp. II:** 155, 163, 169; **Supp. I Part 1:** 168, 299, 313, 317, 372; **Supp. I Part 2:** 420, 602, **682–707; Supp. VIII:** 202, 204; **Supp. XI:** 50; **Supp. XIII:** 140, 145; **Supp. XV:** 246
Whittier, Mary, **Supp. I Part 2:** 683
"Whittier Birthday Speech" (Twain), **Supp. I Part 1:** 313
"Who" (Kenyon), **Supp. VII:** 174
"Who" (Sobin), **Supp. XVI:** 284–285
"Who Am I——Who I Am" (Corso), **Supp. XII:** 134
"Who Be Kind To" (Ginsberg), **Supp. II Part 1:** 323
"Whoever Was Using This Bed" (Carver), **Supp. III Part 1:** 148
"Whoever You Are Holding Me Now in Hand" (Whitman), **IV:** 342; **Retro. Supp. I:** 52
Who Gathered and Whispered behind Me (Goldbarth), **Supp. XII:** 181, 182
"Who in One Lifetime" (Rukeyser), **Supp. VI:** 276, 279
Who Is Witter Bynner? (Kraft), **Supp. XV:** 40, 52
"Who Is Your Mother? Red Roots of White Feminism" (Gunn Allen), **Supp. IV Part 1:** 329
Whole Hog (Wagoner), **Supp. IX: 337–338**
"Whole Mess...Almost, The" (Corso), **Supp. XII:** 135
"Whole Moisty Night, The" (R. Bly), **Supp. IV Part 1:** 69
Whole New Life, A (Price), **Supp. VI:** 265, **266,** 267
"Whole Self, The" (Nye), **Supp. XIII:** 275
"Whole Soul, The" (Levine), **Supp. V:** 192
"Whole Story, The" (Strand), **Supp. IV Part 2:** 622
Whole Town's Talking, The (Loos), **Supp. XVI:** 187
"Whole World Knows, The" (Welty), **IV:** 272; **Retro. Supp. I:** 343
Who'll Stop the Rain (film), **Supp. V:** 301
Who Lost an American? (Algren), **Supp. IX: 15–16**
Who Owns America? (symposium), **Supp. XIV:** 4
"Who Puts Together" (Hogan), **Supp. IV Part 1:** 403, 405, 412–413
"Whore of Mensa, The" (Allen), **Supp. XV:** 15
Whores for Gloria (Vollmann), **Supp. XVII:** 226, 230
Whorf, Benjamin Lee, **Supp. XVI:** 283
Who's Afraid of Virginia Woolf? (Albee), **I:** 71, 77–81, 83, 85, 86, 87, 94; **IV:** 230
Who Shall Be the Sun? Poems Based on the Lore, Legends, and Myths of the Northwest Coast and Plateau Indians (Wagoner), **Supp. IX:** 328, **329–330,** 337
"Whosis Kid, The" (Hammett), **Supp. IV Part 1:** 344
"Who Sit Watch in Daylight" (Wright), **Supp. XV:** 342
"Who's Passing for Who?" (Hughes), **Supp. I Part 1:** 330
"Who Speak on the Page?" (Sanders), **Supp. XVI:** 278
Who Will Run the Frog Hospital?: A Novel (Moore), **Supp. X:** 163, 165, 169, **175–177**
Why Are We in Vietnam? (Mailer), **III:** 27, 29, 30, 33, 34–35, 39, 42, 44; **Retro. Supp. II:** 205–206
"Why Did the Balinese Chicken Cross the Road?" (Walker), **Supp. III Part 2:** 527
"Why Do the Heathens Rage?" (O'Connor), **III:** 351
"Why Do You Write About Russia?" (Simpson), **Supp. IX:** 277
"Why I Am a Danger to the Public" (Kingsolver), **Supp. VII:** 204
Why I Am Not a Christian (Russell), **Supp. I Part 2:** 522
"Why I Entered the Gurdjieff Work" (Toomer), **Supp. III Part 2:** 481
"Why I Like Laurel" (Patchett), **Supp. XII:** 309
"Why I Live at the P.O." (Welty), **IV:** 262; **Retro. Supp. I:** 345
"Why Is Economics Not an Evolutionary Science?" (Veblen), **Supp. I Part 2:** 634
"Why I Write" (Didion), **Supp. IV Part 1:** 201, 203
Why Johnny Can't Read: And What You Can Do About It (Flesch), **Supp. XVI:** 105
"Why Negro Women Leave Home" (Brooks), **Supp. III Part 1:** 75
"Why the Little Frenchman Wears His Hand in a Sling" (Poe), **III:** 425
Why We Behave Like Microbe Hunters (Thurber), **Supp. I Part 2:** 606
Why We Were in Vietnam (Podhoretz), **Supp. VIII:** 241
"Why Write?" (Updike), **Retro. Supp. I:** 317
"Wichita Vortex Sutra" (Ginsberg), **Supp. II Part 1:** 319, 321, 323–325, 327
Wickes, George, **Supp. XIV:** 165
Wickford Point (Marquand), **III:** 50, 58, 64–65, 69
Wicks, Robert Russell, **Supp. XII:** 49

Wide, Wide World, The (S. Warner as Wetherell), **Supp. XV:** 275; **Supp. XVIII:** 257, 260, **262–264,** 265
"Wide Empty Landscape with a Death in the Foreground" (Momaday), **Supp. IV Part 2:** 492
Wideman, John Edgar, **Retro. Supp. II:** 123; **Supp. X:** 239, 250, **319–336; Supp. XI:** 245; **Supp. XIII:** 247; **Supp. XVIII:** 89
Widener, Jeff, **Supp. XVIII:** 91
"Wide Net, The" (Welty), **IV:** 266
Wide Net and Other Stories, The (Welty), **IV:** 261, 264–266, 271; **Retro. Supp. I: 347–349,** 352, 355
Widening Spell of the Leaves, The (Levis), **Supp. XI:** 258, 259, 261, **268–269,** 271
"Wide Prospect, The" (Jarrell), **II:** 376–377
Wide Sargasso Sea (Rhys), **Supp. XVIII:** 131
Widow for One Year, A (Irving), **Supp. VI:** 165, **179–181**
Widows of Thornton, The (Taylor), **Supp. V:** 320, 321
"Widow's Wish, The" (Briggs), **Supp. XVIII:** 15
Wieland; or, The Transformation. An American Tale (Brown), **Supp. I Part 1:** 128–132, 133, 137, 140
Wiene, Robert, **Retro. Supp. I:** 268
Wiener, John, **Supp. IV Part 1:** 153
Wieners, John, **Supp. II Part 1:** 32
Wiesel, Elie, **Supp. XVII:** 47, 48, 49
Wiest, Dianne, **Supp. XV:** 12
"Wife, Forty-five, Remembers Love, A" (Shields), **Supp. VII:** 310
"Wifebeater, The" (Sexton), **Supp. II Part 2:** 693
"Wife for Dino Rossi, A" (Fante), **Supp. XI:** 165
"Wife of His Youth, The" (Chesnutt), **Supp. XIV: 63–66**
Wife of His Youth and Other Stories of the Color Line, The (Chesnutt), **Supp. XIV:** 62, 63
"Wife of Jesus Speaks, The" (Karr), **Supp. XI:** 250–251
"Wife of Nashville, A" (Taylor), **Supp. V:** 320
"Wife's Story, The" (Davis), **Supp. XVI:** 85, 91, 92–93
Wife's Story, The (Shields), **Supp. VII:** 316. *See also* Happenstance
"Wife-Wooing" (Updike), **IV:** 226
Wigan, Gareth, **Supp. XI:** 306
Wiget, Andrew, **Supp. IV Part 2:** 509
Wigglesworth, Michael, **IV:** 147, 156; **Supp. I Part 1:** 110, 111
Wilbur, Richard, **III:** 527; **Retro. Supp. II:** 50; **Supp. III Part 1:** 64; **Supp. III Part 2: 541–565; Supp. IV Part 2:** 626, 634, 642; **Supp. V:** 337; **Supp. VIII:** 28; **Supp. X:** 58, 120; **Supp. XII:** 258; **Supp. XIII:** 76, 336; **Supp. XV:** 51, 251, 256; **Supp. XVII:** 26; **Supp. XVIII:** 178
Wilcocks, Alexander, **Supp. I Part 1:** 125
Wilcox, Ella Wheeler, **Supp. II Part 1:** 197
Wild, John, **II:** 362, 363–364
Wild, Peter, **Supp. V:** 5
Wild, Robert, **IV:** 155
"Wild, The" (Berry), **Supp. X:** 30
Wild 90 (film) (Mailer), **Retro. Supp. II:** 205
Wild and Woolly (film), **Supp. XVI:** 185
Wild Boy of Aveyron, The (Itard). *See* De l'éducation d'un homme sauvage
Wild Boys, The: A Book of the Dead (Burroughs), **Supp. III Part 1:** 106–107
Wild Card Quilt: Taking A chance on Home (Ray), **Supp. XVIII:** 189, 192, 193, 196, 198, **200–202,** 204
Wilde, Oscar, **I:** 50, 66, 381, 384; **II:** 515; **IV:** 77, 350; **Retro. Supp. I:** 56, 102, 227; **Retro. Supp. II:** 76, 326; **Supp. IV Part 2:** 578, 679, 683; **Supp. IX:** 65, 66, 68, 189, 192; **Supp. V:** 106, 283; **Supp. X:** 148, 151, 188–189; **Supp. XIV:** 324, 334; **Supp. XV:** 350
Wilder, Amos Parker, **IV:** 356
Wilder, Billy, **Supp. IV Part 1:** 130; **Supp. XI:** 307
Wilder, Isabel, **IV:** 357, 366, 375
Wilder, Mrs. Amos Parker (Isabella Thornton Niven), **IV:** 356
Wilder, Thornton, **I:** 360, 482; **IV: 355–377,** 431; **Retro. Supp. I:** 109, 359; **Supp. I Part 2:** 609; **Supp. IV Part 2:** 586; **Supp. IX:** 140; **Supp. V:** 105; **Supp. XII:** 236–237
"Wilderness" (Leopold), **Supp. XIV:** 190
"Wilderness" (Sandburg), **III:** 584, 595
Wilderness (Warren), **IV:** 256
"Wilderness, The" (Merwin), **Supp. III Part 1:** 340, 345
"Wilderness, The" (Robinson), **III:** 524
Wilderness of Vision, The: On the Poetry of John Haines (Bezner and Walzer, eds.), **Supp. XII:** 202
Wilderness Plots: Tales about the Settlement of the American Land (Sanders), **Supp. XVI:** 267–268, 269
Wilderness World of Anne LaBastille, The (LaBastille), **Supp. X: 105,** 106
Wild Flag, The (White), **Supp. I Part 2:** 654
"Wildflower, The" (W. C. Williams), **Retro. Supp. I:** 420
"Wild Flowers" (Caldwell), **I:** 310
"Wildflowers" (Minot), **Supp. VI:** 208
"Wild Geese" (Oliver), **Supp. VII:** 237
"Wild Honey Suckle, The" (Freneau), **Supp. II Part 1:** 253, 264, 266
Wild in the Country (Odets), **Supp. II Part 2:** 546
Wild Iris, The (Glück), **Supp. V:** 79, 87–89, 91
Wildlife (Ford), **Supp. V:** 57, 69–71
Wildlife in America (Matthiessen), **Supp. V:** 199, 201, 204
"Wildlife in American Culture" (Leopold), **Supp. XIV:** 190, 191
"Wildness" (Sanders), **Supp. XVI:** 276
Wild Old Wicked Man, The (MacLeish), **III:** 3, 20
"Wild Palms, The" (Faulkner), **II:** 68
Wild Palms, The (Faulkner), **II:** 68–69; **Retro. Supp. I:** 85
"Wild Peaches" (Wylie), **Supp. I Part 2:** 707, 712
Wild Roses of Cape Ann and Other Poems (Larcom), **Supp. XIII:** 142, 147
Wild Seed (O. Butler), **Supp. XIII:** 62, 63
"Wild Swans at Coole, The" (W. B. Yeats), **Supp. XVI:** 48
"Wild Swans at Norfolk, The" (Carruth), **Supp. XVI:** 48
Wild Thorn (Hoffman), **Supp. XVIII: 84–85**
Wild to the Heart (Bass), **Supp. XVI:** 16
"Wild Turkeys: Dignity of the Damned" (B. Kelly), **Supp. XVII:** 129
"Wildwest" (MacLeish), **III:** 14
Wiley, Craig, **Supp. VIII:** 313
Wilhelm Meister (Goethe), **II:** 291
Wilkes, John, **Supp. I Part 2:** 503, 519, 522
Wilkie, Curtis, **Supp. V:** 11
Wilkins, Roy, **Supp. I Part 1:** 345
Wilkinson, Alec, **Supp. VIII:** 164, 168, 171
Wilkinson, Max, **Supp. IX:** 251
Willard, Samuel, **IV:** 150
Willard Gibbs (Rukeyser), **Supp. VI:** 273, 283, 284
Willcutts, Tim, **Supp. XVII:** 239, 241, 246
Willett, Ralph, **Supp. XIV:** 27
Willey, Basil, **Retro. Supp. II:** 243
William Carlos Williams (Koch), **Retro. Supp. I:** 428
William Carlos Williams: An American Artist (Breslin), **Retro. Supp. I:** 430
William Carlos Williams and Alterity (Ahearn), **Retro. Supp. I:** 415
William Carlos Williams and the Meanings of Measure (Cushman), **Retro. Supp. I:** 430
William Carlos Williams: The American Background (Weaver), **Retro. Supp. I:** 430
William Faulkner: A Critical Study (Howe), **Supp. VI:** 119–120, 125
William Faulkner: Early Prose and Poetry (Faulkner), **Retro. Supp. I:** 80
William Faulkner: First Encounters (Brooks), **Supp. XIV:** 13
"William Faulkner's Legend of the South" (Cowley), **Supp. II Part 1:** 143
"William Faulkner: The Stillness of *Light in August*" (Kazin), **Supp. VIII:** 104
William Faulkner: The Yoknapatawpha Country (Brooks), **Supp. XIV: 12–13,** 16
William Faulkner: Toward Yoknapatawpha and Beyond (Brooks), **Supp. XIV:** 13
"William Humphrey, 73, Writer of Novels about Rural Texas" (Gussow), **Supp. IX:** 93
William Humphrey, Destroyer of Myths (Almon), **Supp. IX:** 93

William Humphrey. Boise State University Western Writers Series (Winchell), **Supp. IX:** 109
"William Humphrey Remembered" (Masters), **Supp. IX:** 96
William Humphrey. Southwestern Series (Lee), **Supp. IX:** 109
"William Ireland's Confession" (A. Miller), **III:** 147–148
William James and Phenomenology: A Study of the "Principles of Psychology" (Wilshire), **II:** 362
William Lloyd Garrison (Chapman), **Supp. XIV:** 46–51, 52, 53, 55
William Maxwell Portrait, A: Memories and Appreciations (C. Baxter, Collier, and Hirsch, eds.), **Supp. XVII:** 23
Williams, Annie Laurie, **Supp. IX:** 93
Williams, Blanch Colton, **Supp. XVIII:** 279
Williams, Cecil, **II:** 508
Williams, Charles, **Supp. II Part 1:** 15, 16
Williams, C. K., **Supp. XIII:** 114; **Supp. XVII:** 112
Williams, Dakin, **IV:** 379
Williams, David Reichard, **Supp. XIII:** 162
Williams, Edward, **IV:** 404
Williams, Edwina Dakin, **IV:** 379
Williams, Esther, **Supp. XII:** 165
Williams, Fannie Barrier, **Supp. XIV:** 201
Williams, George, **Supp. V:** 220
Williams, Horace, **IV:** 453
Williams, Joan, **Supp. IX:** 95
Williams, John A., **Supp. XVI:** 143
Williams, John Sharp, **IV:** 378
Williams, Lyle, **Supp. XIV:** 22
Williams, Michael, **Supp. V:** 286
Williams, Miller, **Supp. XIV:** 126; **Supp. XV:** 339; **Supp. XVIII:** 177
Williams, Mrs. William Carlos (Florence Herman), **IV:** 404
Williams, Paul, **IV:** 404
Williams, Raymond, **Supp. IX:** 146
Williams, Roger, **Supp. I Part 2:** 699
Williams, Rose, **IV:** 379
Williams, Sherley Anne, **Supp. V:** 180
Williams, Solomon, **I:** 549
Williams, Stanley T., **II:** 301, 316; **Supp. I Part 1:** 251
Williams, Stephen, **IV:** 148
Williams, Ted, **IV:** 216; **Supp. IX:** 162
Williams, Tennessee, **I:** 73, 81, 113, 211; **II:** 190, 194; **III:** 145, 147; **IV:** 4, **378–401; Supp. I Part 1:** 290, 291; **Supp. IV Part 1:** 79, 83, 84, 359; **Supp. IV Part 2:** 574, 682; **Supp. IX:** 133; **Supp. XI:** 103; **Supp. XIII:** 331; **Supp. XIV:** 250, 315; **Supp. XVI:** 194
Williams, Terry Tempest, **Supp. XIII:** 16; **Supp. XVIII:** 189
Williams, Walter L., **Supp. IV Part 1:** 330, 331
Williams, William, **IV:** 404, 405
Williams, William Carlos, **I:** 61, 62, 229, 255, 256, 261, 285, 428, 438, 446, 539; **II:** 133, 536, 542, 543, 544, 545; **III:** 194, 196, 198, 214, 269, 409, 453, 457, 458, 464, 465, 591; **IV:** 30, 74, 75, 76, 94, 95, 286, 287, **402–425; Retro. Supp. I:** 51, 52, 62, 209, 284, 285, 288, 296, 298, **411–433; Retro. Supp. II:** 178, 181, 189, 250, 321, 322, 326, 327, 328, 334, 335; **Supp. I Part 1:** 254, 255, 259, 266; **Supp. II Part 1:** 9, 30, 308, 318; **Supp. II Part 2:** 421, 443; **Supp. III Part 1:** 9, 147, 239, 271, 275, 276, 278, 350; **Supp. III Part 2:** 542, 610, 613, 614, 615, 616, 617, 621, 622, 626, 628; **Supp. IV Part 1:** 151, 153, 246, 325; **Supp. IX:** 38, 268, 291; **Supp. V:** 180, 337; **Supp. VIII:** 195, 269, 272, 277, 292; **Supp. X:** 112, 120, 204; **Supp. XI:** 311, 328; **Supp. XII:** 198; **Supp. XIII:** 77, 90, 335; **Supp. XIV:** 280, 284, 285, 293; **Supp. XV:** 42, 51, 182, 250, 306, 307; **Supp. XVI:** 48, 282; **Supp. XVII:** 36, 113, 227, 243
Williams, Wirt, **Supp. XIV:** 24
Williamson, Alan, **Retro. Supp. II:** 185
William Styron's Nat Turner: Ten Black Writers Respond (Clarke, ed.), **IV:** 115
Williams-Walsh, Mary Ellen, **Supp. IV Part 2:** 611
William the Conqueror, **Supp. I Part 2:** 507
William Wetmore Story and His Friends (James), **Retro. Supp. I:** 235
William Wilson (Gardner), **Supp. VI:** 72
"William Wilson" (Poe), **II:** 475; **III:** 410, 412; **Retro. Supp. II:** 269; **Supp. IX:** 105
"Willie" (Angelou), **Supp. IV Part 1:** 15
Willie Masters' Lonesome Wife (Gass), **Supp. VI:** 77, **84–85, 86–87**
"Willing" (Moore), **Supp. X:** 178
Willis, Bruce, **Supp. IV Part 1:** 236
Willis, Gordon, **Supp. XV:** 7
Willis, Mary Hard, **Supp. V:** 290–291
Willis, Nathaniel Parker, **II:** 313; **Supp. I Part 2:** 405; **Supp. XVIII:** 12
Williwaw (Vidal), **Supp. IV Part 2:** 677, 680, 681
"Willow Woman" (Francis), **Supp. IX:** 78
Wills, Garry, **Supp. I Part 1:** 294; **Supp. IV Part 1:** 355
Wills, Ridley, **IV:** 122
Wills, Ross B., **Supp. XI:** 169
"Will to Believe, The" (James), **II:** 352; **Supp. XIV:** 50
Will to Believe, The, and Other Essays in Popular Philosophy (James), **II:** 356; **IV:** 28
Will to Change, The: Poems, 1968–1970 (Rich), **Supp. I Part 2:** 551, 557–559
"Will We Plug Chips into Our Brains?" (W. Gibson), **Supp. XVI:** 117–118
"Will You Please Be Quiet, Please?" (Carver), **Supp. III Part 1:** 137, 141
Will You Please Be Quiet, Please? (Carver), **Supp. III Part 1:** 138, 140, 144
"Will You Tell Me?" (Barthelme), **Supp. IV Part 1:** 42, 47
Wilsdorf, Anne, **Supp. XVI:** 177
Wilshire, Bruce, **II:** 362, 364
Wilshire, Gaylord, **Supp. V:** 280
Wilson, Adrian, **Supp. XV:** 147
Wilson, Alexander, **Supp. XVI:** 4, 6
Wilson, Angus, **IV:** 430, 435
Wilson, August, **Supp. VIII: 329–353**
Wilson, Augusta Jane Evans, **Retro. Supp. I:** 351
Wilson, Earl, **Supp. X:** 264
Wilson, Edmund, **I:** 67, 185, 236, 247, 260, 434, 482; **II:** 79, 80, 81, 86, 87, 91, 97, 98, 146, 276, 430, 530, 562, 587; **III:** 588; **IV:** 308, 310, **426–449; Retro. Supp. I:** 1, 97, 100, 101, 103, 104, 105, 115, 274; **Retro. Supp. II:** 321, 327, 329; **Supp. I Part 1:** 372; **Supp. I Part 2:** 407, 646, 678, 709; **Supp. II Part 1:** 19, 90, 106, 136, 137, 143; **Supp. III Part 2:** 612; **Supp. IV Part 2:** 693; **Supp. IX:** 55, 65, 190; **Supp. VIII:** 93, 95, 96, 97, 98–99, 100, 101, 103, 105, 162; **Supp. X:** 186; **Supp. XI:** 160; **Supp. XIII:** 170; **Supp. XIV:** 338; **Supp. XV:** 142, 308; **Supp. XVI:** 194
Wilson, Edmund (father), **IV:** 441
Wilson, E. O., **Supp. X:** 35
Wilson, Henry, **Supp. XIV:** 48
Wilson, Reuel, **II:** 562
Wilson, Robert, **Supp. XI:** 144
Wilson, Sloan, **Supp. IV Part 1:** 387
Wilson, Thomas, **IV:** 153
Wilson, Tracy, **Supp. XVIII:** 101
Wilson, Victoria, **Supp. X:** 166
Wilson, Woodrow, **I:** 245, 246, 490; **II:** 183, 253; **III:** 105, 581; **Supp. I Part 1:** 21; **Supp. I Part 2:** 474, 643; **Supp. V:** 288
Wilton, David, **IV:** 147
Wiman, Christian, **Supp. XV:** 251, 253, 264; **Supp. XVII:** 74; **Supp. XVIII:** 173, 174
Wimberly, Lowry, **Supp. XV:** 136, 137
Wimsatt, William K., **Supp. XIV:** 12
Winchell, Mark, **Supp. VIII:** 176, 189
Winchell, Mark Royden, **Supp. IX:** 97, 98, 109; **Supp. VIII:** 241; **Supp. XIII:** 94, 98, 99, 101; **Supp. XIV:** 103, 106, 111
Winckelmann, Johann Joachim, **Supp. XII:** 178
Wind, Sand, and Stars (Saint-Exupéry), **Supp. IX:** 247
Wind Across the Everglades (film, Ray), **Supp. XVIII:** 253
Wind Chrysalid's Rattle (Sobin), **Supp. XVI:** 283
"Windfall" (B. Kelly), **Supp. XVII:** 132
Windham, Donald, **IV:** 382
"Windhover" (Hopkins), **I:** 397; **II:** 539; **Supp. IX:** 43
Winding Stair and Other Poems, The (Yeats), **Supp. XV:** 253
"Winding Street, The" (Petry), **Supp. XI:** 6
"Window" (Pinsky), **Supp. VI:** 237, 247
Windows (Creeley), **Supp. IV Part 1:** 157, 158
"Windows" (Jarrell), **II:** 388, 389

"Window Seat, A" (Goldbarth), **Supp. XII:** 185
Wind Remains, The (opera) (Bowles), **Supp. IV Part 1:** 83
"Winds, The" (Welty), **IV:** 265; **Retro. Supp. I:** 348, 350
"Winds and Clouds over a Funeral" (Jin), **Supp. XVIII:** 94
"Wind up Sushi" (Goldbarth), **Supp. XII:** 186–187
"Windy Day at the Reservoir, A" (Beattie), **Supp. V:** 33
Windy McPherson's Son (Anderson), **I:** 101, 102–103, 105, 111
"Wine" (Carver), **Supp. III Part 1:** 138
"Wine Menagerie, The" (H. Crane), **I:** 389, 391; **Retro. Supp. II:** 82
Wine of the Puritans, The: A Study of Present-Day America (Brooks), **I:** 240
"Wine of Wizardry, A" (Sterling), **I:** 208
Winer, Linda, **Supp. IV Part 2:** 580; **Supp. XV:** 332
Winesburg, Ohio: A Group of Tales of Ohio Small Town Life (Anderson), **I:** 97, 102, 103, 104, 105–108; **III:** 112, 113, 114, 116, 224, 579; **Supp. IX:** 306, 308; **Supp. V:** 12; **Supp. XI:** 164; **Supp. XVI:** 17
Wing-and-Wing, The (Cooper), **I:** 350, 355
Winged Seed, The: A Remembrance (L.-Y. Lee), **Supp. XV:** 211, **220–223**
Winged Words: American Indian Writers Speak (Coltelli), **Supp. IV Part 2:** 493, 497
"Wingfield" (Wolff), **Supp. VII:** 341–342
"Wings, The" (Doty), **Supp. XI:** 124
Wings of the Dove, The (James), **I:** 436; **II:** 320, 323, 333, 334–335; **Retro. Supp. I:** 215, 216, 217, 232, **233–234; Supp. II Part 1:** 94–95; **Supp. IV Part 1:** 349
Winner Take Nothing (Hemingway), **II:** 249; **Retro. Supp. I:** 170, 175, 176, 181
"Winnie" (Brooks), **Supp. III Part 1:** 86
Winokur, Maxine. *See* Kumin, Maxine
Winslow, Art, **Supp. XVIII:** 102
Winslow, Devereux, **II:** 547
Winslow, Harriet, **II:** 552–553
Winslow, Ola Elizabeth, **I:** 547
Winslow, Warren, **II:** 540
Winston, Andrew, **Supp. XII:** 189
Winston, Michael R., **Supp. XIV:** 197
Winter, Douglas, **Supp. V:** 144
Winter, Johnny and Edgar, **Supp. V:** 334
Winter, Kate, **Supp. X:** 104
"Winter Branch, A" (Irving), **Supp. VI:** 163
"Winter Burial, A" (Clampitt), **Supp. IX:** 48
Winter Carnival (film), **Retro. Supp. I:** 113
"Winter Daybreak at Vence, A" (Wright), **Supp. III Part 1:** 249–250
Winter Diary, A (Van Doren), **I:** 168
"Winter Dreams" (Fitzgerald), **II:** 80, 94; **Retro. Supp. I:** 108
"Winter Drive, A" (Jewett), **Retro. Supp. II:** 147
"Winter Eden, A" (Frost), **Retro. Supp. I:** 137
"Winter Father, The" (Dubus), **Supp. VII:** 83, 87
Winter Hours: Prose, Prose Poems, and Poems (Oliver), **Supp. VII:** 230, 247
"Winter in Dunbarton" (Lowell), **II:** 547; **Retro. Supp. II:** 187
"Wintering" (Plath), **Retro. Supp. II:** 255
Winter Insomnia (Carver), **Supp. III Part 1:** 138
Winter in the Blood (Welch), **Supp. IV Part 2:** 562
"Winter Landscape" (Berryman), **I:** 174; **Retro. Supp. I:** 430
Winter Lightning (Nemerov), **III:** 269
Winter News (Haines), **Supp. XII:** 199, **201–204,** 207–208, 208
Winternitz, Mary. *See* Cheever, Mrs. John (Mary Winternitz)
Winter: Notes from Montana (Bass), **Supp. XVI:** 17–18
Winter of Our Discontent, The (Steinbeck), **IV:** 52, 65–66, 68
"Winter on Earth" (Toomer), **Supp. III Part 2:** 486
"Winter Piece, A" (Bryant), **Supp. I Part 1:** 150, 155
"Winter Rains, Cataluña" (Levine), **Supp. V:** 182
"Winter Remembered" (Ransom), **III:** 492–493
Winterrowd, Prudence, **I:** 217, 224
Winters, Jonathan, **Supp. XI:** 305
Winters, Yvor, **I:** 59, 63, 386, 393, 397, 398, 402, 471; **III:** 194, 498; **IV:** 153; **Retro. Supp. II:** 76, 77, 78, 82, 83, 85, 89; **Supp. I Part 1:** 268; **Supp. II Part 2:** 416, 666, **785–816; Supp. IV Part 2:** 480; **Supp. V:** 180, 191–192; **Supp. XIV:** 287; **Supp. XV:** 74, 341
"Winter Scenes" (Bryant). *See* "Winter Piece, A"
Winterset (Anderson), **III:** 159
"Winter Skyline Late" (F. Wright), **Supp. XVII:** 245
"Winter Sleep" (Wylie), **Supp. I Part 2:** 711, 729
Winter's Tale, The (Shakespeare), **Supp. XIII:** 219
"Winter Stars" (Levis), **Supp. XI:** 267–268
Winter Stars (Levis), **Supp. XI:** 259, **266–268**
"Winter Stop-Over" (Everwine), **Supp. XV:** 76
Winter Stop-Over (Everwine), **Supp. XV:** 74, 76
"Winter Swan" (Bogan), **Supp. III Part 1:** 52
"Winter Thunder" (X. J. Kennedy), **Supp. XV:** 169
Winter Thunder (X. J. Kennedy), **Supp. XV:** 167
"Winter Trees" (Pedersen; Nelson, trans.), **Supp. XVIII:** 180
Winter Trees (Plath), **Retro. Supp. II:** 257; **Supp. I Part 2:** 526, 539, 541
"Winter Weather Advisory" (Ashbery), **Supp. III Part 1:** 26
"Winter Wheat" (Hoffman), **Supp. XVIII:** 86, 87
"Winter without Snow, The" (C. Frost), **Supp. XV:** 96, 105–106
"Winter Words" (Levine), **Supp. V:** 192
Winthrop, John, **Supp. I Part 1:** 99, 100, 101, 102, 105; **Supp. I Part 2:** 484, 485
Winthrop Covenant, The (Auchincloss), **Supp. IV Part 1:** 23
Wirt, William, **I:** 232
Wirth, Louis, **IV:** 475
"Wisdom Cometh with the Years" (Cullen), **Supp. IV Part 1:** 166
Wisdom of the Desert, The: Sayings from the Desert Fathers of the Fourth Century (Merton), **Supp. VIII:** 201
Wisdom of the Heart, The (H. Miller), **III:** 178, 184
Wise Blood (O'Connor), **III:** 337, 338, 339–343, 344, 345, 346, 350, 354, 356, 357; **Retro. Supp. II:** 219, 221, 222, 223, **225–228**
Wise Men, The (Price), **Supp. VI:** 254
"Wiser Than a God" (Chopin), **Retro. Supp. II:** 61; **Supp. I Part 1:** 208
Wishes, Lies, and Dreams: Teaching Children to Write Poetry (Koch), **Supp. XV:** 176, 189
"Wish for a Young Wife" (Roethke), **III:** 548
Wishful Thinking: A Theological ABC (Buechner), **Supp. XII:** 53
Wishing Tree, The: Christopher Isherwood on Mystical Religion (Adjemian, ed.), **Supp. XIV:** 164, 173
Wismer, Helen Muriel. *See* Thurber, Mrs. James (Helen Muriel Wismer)
Wisse, Ruth, **Supp. XII:** 167, 168
Wister, Owen, **I:** 62; **Retro. Supp. II:** 72; **Supp. XIV:** 39
Wit (Edson), **Supp. XVIII:** 35–36, 37, **38–51**
"Witchbird" (Bambara), **Supp. XI:** 11
"Witch Burning" (Plath), **Supp. I Part 2:** 539
Witchcraft of Salem Village, The (Jackson), **Supp. IX:** 121
"Witch Doctor" (Hayden), **Supp. II Part 1:** 368, 380
Witches of Eastwick, The (Updike), **Retro. Supp. I:** 330, 331
Witching Hour, The (Rice), **Supp. VII:** 299–300
"Witch of Coös, The" (Frost), **II:** 154–155; **Retro. Supp. I:** 135; **Retro. Supp. II:** 42
"Witch of Owl Mountain Springs, The: An Account of Her Remarkable Powers" (Taylor), **Supp. V:** 328
"Witch of Wenham, The" (Whittier), **Supp. I Part 2:** 694, 696
Witek, Terri, **Supp. XVII:** 117
"With a Little Help from My Friends" (Kushner), **Supp. IX:** 131
With Bold Knife and Fork (M. F. K. Fisher), **Supp. XVII:** 89, 91
"With Che at Kitty Hawk" (Banks), **Supp. V:** 6

"With Che at the Plaza" (Banks), **Supp. V:** 7
"With Che in New Hampshire" (Banks), **Supp. V:** 6
"Withdrawal Symptoms" (Mora), **Supp. XIII:** 216
"Withered Skins of Berries" (Toomer), **Supp. III Part 2:** 485; **Supp. IX:** 320
Withers, Harry Clay, **Supp. XIII:** 161
Witherspoon, John, **Supp. I Part 2:** 504
With Eyes at the Back of Our Heads (Levertov), **Supp. III Part 1:** 276–277
With Her in Ourland (Gilman), **Supp. XI:** 208–209
With His Pistol in His Hand (Paredes), **Supp. XIII:** 225
"Within the Words: An Apprenticeship" (Haines), **Supp. XII:** 197
"With Kit, Age 7, at the Beach" (Stafford), **Supp. XI:** 323
"With Mercy for the Greedy" (Sexton), **Supp. II Part 2:** 680
With My Trousers Rolled (Epstein), **Supp. XIV:** 101, 105
Without a Hero (Boyle), **Supp. VIII:** 16
Without Feathers (Allen), **Supp. XV:** 3, 14, 15
Without Stopping (Bowles), **Supp. IV Part 1:** 79, 81, 85, 90, 91, 92
"Without Tradition and within Reason: Judge Horton and Atticus Finch in Court" (Johnson), **Supp. VIII:** 127
With Shuddering Fall (Oates), **Supp. II Part 2:** 504–506
"With the Dog at Sunrise" (Kenyon), **Supp. VII:** 170
With the Empress Dowager of China (Carl), **III:** 475
"With the Horse in the Winter Pasture" (McCarriston), **Supp. XIV:** 262
With the Old Breed: At Peleliu and Okinawa (Sledge), **Supp. V:** 249–250
"With the Violin" (Chopin), **Retro. Supp. II:** 61
"Witness" (Clampitt), **Supp. IX:** 42–43, 45, 46
"Witness" (Dubus), **Supp. VII:** 89
"Witness" (Harjo), **Supp. XII:** 227–228
Witness (McNally), **Supp. XIII:** 197
"Witness" (Nelson), **Supp. XVIII:** 186
"Witness, The" (Porter), **III:** 443–444
"Witness for Poetry, A" (Stafford), **Supp. XI:** 324
"Witness for the Defense" (Hay), **Supp. XIV:** 124
"Witnessing My Father's Will" (Karr), **Supp. XI:** 241
"Witnessing to a Shared World" (Sanders), **Supp. XVI:** 278
Witness to the Times! (McGrath), **Supp. X:** 118
Witness Tree, A (Frost), **II:** 155; **Retro. Supp. I:** 122, 137, 139
Wit's End: Days and Nights of the Algonquin Round Table (Gaines), **Supp. IX:** 190
Wits Recreations (Mennes and Smith), **II:** 111
Witt, Shirley Hill, **Supp. IV Part 2:** 505
Wittels, Anne F., **Supp. XV:** 59
Wittenberg, Judith Bryant, **Retro. Supp. II:** 146
Wittgenstein, Ludwig, **Retro. Supp. I:** 53; **Supp. III Part 2:** 626–627; **Supp. X:** 304; **Supp. XII:** 21; **Supp. XV:** 344, 346
Wittgensteins' Mistress (Markson), **Supp. XVII:** 135, 142, 143, 145
Wittliff, William, **Supp. V:** 227
"Witty War, A" (Simpson), **Supp. IX:** 268
"Wives and Mistresses" (Hardwick), **Supp. III Part 1:** 211–212
Wizard of Loneliness, The (Nichols), **Supp. XIII:** 259, 263, 264
Wizard of Oz, The (Baum), **Supp. IV Part 1:** 113
Wizard of Oz, The (film), **Supp. X:** 172, 214
Wizard's Tide, The: A Story (Buechner), **Supp. XII:** 54
"WLT (The Edgar Era)" (Keillor), **Supp. XVI:** 172
WLT: A Radio Romance (Keillor), **Supp. XVI:** 176
Wobegon Boy (Keillor), **Supp. XVI:** 177
Wodehouse, P. G., **Supp. IX:** 195
Woiwode, Larry, **Supp. VIII:** 151; **Supp. XVI:** 206
Wojahn, David, **Supp. IX:** 161, 292, 293
Wolcott, James, **Supp. IX:** 259
Wolf, Christa, **Supp. IV Part 1:** 310, 314
Wolf, Daniel, **Retro. Supp. II:** 202
Wolf: A False Memoir (Harrison), **Supp. VIII:** 40, **41–42,** 45
Wolfe, Ben, **IV:** 454
Wolfe, Gregory, **Supp. XIV:** 307
Wolfe, James, **Supp. I Part 2:** 498
Wolfe, Linnie, **Supp. IX:** 176
Wolfe, Mabel, **IV:** 454
Wolfe, Mrs. William Oliver (Julia Elizabeth Westall), **IV:** 454
Wolfe, Thomas, **I:** 288, 289, 374, 478, 495; **II:** 457; **III:** 40, 108, 278, 334, 482; **IV:** 52, 97, 357, **450–473; Retro. Supp. I:** 382; **Supp. I Part 1:** 29; **Supp. IV Part 1:** 101; **Supp. IX:** 229; **Supp. X:** 225; **Supp. XI:** 213, 216, 217, 218; **Supp. XIII:** 17; **Supp. XIV:** 122; **Supp. XVIII:** 78
Wolfe, Tom, **Supp. III Part 2: 567–588; Supp. IV Part 1:** 35, 198; **Supp. V:** 296; **Supp. X:** 264; **Supp. XI:** 239; **Supp. XV:** 143; **Supp. XVII:** 202; **Supp. XVIII:** 72, 117
Wolfe, William Oliver, **IV:** 454
"Wolfe Homo Scribens" (Cowley), **Supp. II Part 1:** 144
Wolfert's Roost (Irving), **II:** 314
Wolff, Cynthia Griffin, **Retro. Supp. I:** 379; **Supp. IV Part 1:** 203
Wolff, Donald, **Supp. XIII:** 316, 317, 326
Wolff, Geoffrey, **Supp. II Part 1:** 97; **Supp. XI:** 239, 245, 246
Wolff, Tobias, **Retro. Supp. I:** 190; **Supp. V:** 22; **Supp. VII: 331–346; Supp. X:** 1; **Supp. XI:** 26, 239, 245, 246, 247; **Supp. XV:** 223; **Supp. XVI:** 39, 41, 63, 70, 77
Wolfreys, Julian, **Supp. XVIII:** 61
Wolfson, P. J., **Supp. XIII:** 172
"Wolf Town" (Carson), **Supp. XII: 102**
Wolf Willow: A History, a Story, and a Memory of the Last Plains Frontier (Stegner), **Supp. IV Part 2:** 595, 596, 597, 598, 599, 600, 601, 604, 606, 611, 613, 614
Wolitzer, Hilma, **Supp. XV:** 55
Wolitzer, Meg, **Supp. XV:** 65
Wollaston, William, **II:** 108
Wollstonecraft, Mary, **Supp. I Part 1:** 126; **Supp. I Part 2:** 512, 554
"Woman" (Bogan), **Supp. X:** 102
"Woman, I Got the Blues" (Komunyakaa), **Supp. XIII:** 117
"Woman, Why Are You Weeping?" (Kenyon), **Supp. VII:** 174–175
"Woman, Young and Old, A" (Paley), **Supp. VI:** 222, 225
Woman Aroused, The (Lacy), **Supp. XV:** 199–200
Woman at the Washington Zoo, The (Jarrell), **II:** 367, 386, 387, 389
"Womand and the Woman's Movement" (Briggs), **Supp. XVIII:** 14
"Woman Dead in Her Forties, A" (Rich), **Supp. I Part 2:** 574–575
"Woman Hanging from the Thirteenth Floor Window, The" (Harjo), **Supp. XII:** 216, 221
"Woman Hollering Creek" (Cisneros), **Supp. VII:** 70
Woman Hollering Creek and Other Stories (Cisneros), **Supp. VII:** 58, 68–70
"Womanhood" (Brooks), **Supp. III Part 1:** 77
"Woman in Rain" (X. J. Kennedy), **Supp. XV:** 168
Woman in the Dark (Hammett), **Supp. IV Part 1:** 343
"Woman in the House, A" (Caldwell), **I:** 310
Woman in the Nineteenth Century (Fuller), **Retro. Supp. I:** 156; **Supp. II Part 1:** 279, 292, 294–296; **Supp. XI:** 197, 203; **Supp. XVIII:** 3, 11
"Woman in the Shoe, The" (Ryan as Quin), **Supp. XVIII:** 231
Woman in White, The (Collins), **Supp. I Part 1:** 35, 36
"Womanizer, The" (Ford), **Supp. V:** 71, 72
"Woman Like Yourself, A" (C. Frost), **Supp. XV:** 107
Woman Lit by Fireflies, The (Harrison), **Supp. VIII: 50–51**
"Woman Loses Cookie Bake-Off, Sets Self on Fire" (R. O. Butler), **Supp. XII:** 72
Woman of Andros, The (Wilder), **IV:** 356, 363–364, 367, 368, 374
Woman of Means, A (Taylor), **Supp. V:** 319–320
Woman on the Edge of Time (Piercy), **Supp. XIII:** 29
Woman on the Porch, The (Gordon), **II:** 199, 209–211
"Woman on the Stair, The" (MacLeish), **III:** 15–16

"Woman's Dream, A" (E. Stoddard), **Supp. XV:** 278
Woman's Fiction: A Guide to Novels By and About Women in America, 1820–1870 (Baym), **Supp. XVIII:** 258
"Woman's Heartlessness" (Thaxter), **Retro. Supp. II:** 147
Woman's Honor (Glaspell), **Supp. III Part 1:** 179
"Woman Singing" (Ortiz), **Supp. IV Part 2:** 513
Woman's Share in Primitive Culture (Mason), **Supp. I Part 1:** 18
"Woman Struck by Car Turns into Nymphomaniac" (R. O. Butler), **Supp. XII:** 72
"Woman's Work" (Alvarez), **Supp. VII:** 4
"Woman Uses Glass Eye to Spy on Philandering Husband" (R. O. Butler), **Supp. XII:** 70, 72
Woman Warrior (Kingston), **Supp. IV Part 1:** 12; **Supp. V:** 157, 158, 159, 160–164, 166, 169; **Supp. X:** 291–292; **Supp. XIV:** 162
Woman Warrior, The (Kingston), **Supp. XV:** 220
Woman Who Fell from the Sky, The (Harjo), **Supp. XII: 226–228**
"Woman Who Fell From the Sky, The" (Iroquois creation story), **Supp. IV Part 1:** 327
Woman Who Owned the Shadows, The (Gunn Allen), **Supp. IV Part 1:** 320, 322, 326, 327–328
Woman Within, The (Glasgow), **II:** 183, 190–191
"Womanwork" (Gunn Allen), **Supp. IV Part 1:** 326
Women (Bukowski), **Supp. XI:** 172
"Women" (Didion), **Supp. IV Part 1:** 205
"Women" (Swenson), **Supp. IV Part 2:** 647
Women, The (film), **Retro. Supp. I:** 113
Women, The (film; Cukor), **Supp. XVI:** 181, 192
"Women and Children First" (Prose), **Supp. XVI:** 254
Women and Children First: Stories (Prose), **Supp. XVI:** 254
Women and Economics (Gilman), **Supp. I Part 2:** 637; **Supp. V:** 284; **Supp. XI:** 200, **203–204,** 206
Women and Thomas Harrow (Marquand), **III:** 50, 61, 62, 66, 68, 69–70, 71
Women and Vodka (Markson as Merrill, ed.), **Supp. XVII:** 136
Women and Wilderness (LaBastille), **Supp. X:** 97, **102–104**
"Women as They Are" (Rowson), **Supp. XV:** 243
Women at Point Sur, The (Jeffers), **Supp. II Part 2:** 430–431
Women in Love (Lawrence), **III:** 27, 34
Women of Brewster Place, The: A Novel in Seven Stories (Naylor), **Supp. VIII:** 213, **214–218**
Women of Manhattan: An Upper West Side Story (Shanley), **Supp. XIV:** 315, **326–327**
"Women of My Color" (Coleman), **Supp. XI:** 88–89
Women of Trachis (Pound, trans.), **III:** 476
Women on the Wall, The (Stegner), **Supp. IV Part 2:** 599, 605, 606
Women Poets in English (Stanford, ed.), **Retro. Supp. I:** 41
"Women Reformers and American Culture, 1870–1930" (Conway), **Supp. I Part 1:** 19
"Women's Movement, The" (Didion), **Supp. IV Part 1:** 206
"Women Waiting" (Shields), **Supp. VII:** 320
"Women We Love Whom We Never See Again" (R. Bly), **Supp. IV Part 1:** 66
"Women We Never See Again" (R. Bly), **Supp. IV Part 1:** 66
Women with Men (Ford), **Supp. V:** 57, 71–72
"Wonder" (Olds), **Supp. X:** 210
Wonder Boys (Chabon), **Supp. XI:** 67, **73–75,Supp. XI:** 78; **Supp. XVI:** 259
Wonder Boys (film), **Supp. XI:** 67
Wonderful O, The (Thurber), **Supp. I Part 2:** 612
"Wonderful Old Gentleman, The" (Parker), **Supp. IX:** 197
"Wonderful Pen, The" (Swenson), **Supp. IV Part 2:** 650
Wonderful Words, Silent Truth: Essays on Poetry and a Memoir (Simic), **Supp. VIII:** 270
Wonderland (Oates), **Supp. II Part 2:** 511, 512, 514–515
Wonders Hidden (Sanders), **Supp. XVI:** 269
Wonders of the Invisible World, The (Mather), **Supp. II Part 2:** 456–459, 460, 467
Wonder-Working Providence (Johnson), **IV:** 157
Wong, Hertha, **Supp. IV Part 1:** 275
Wong, Jade Snow, **Supp. X:** 291
Wong, Nellie, **Supp. XVII:** 72
Wong, Shawn, **Supp. XV:** 221
Wong, Timothy, **Supp. XVIII:** 94
"Wood" (Nye), **Supp. XIII:** 276
Wood, Audrey, **IV:** 381
Wood, Charles Erskine Scott, **Supp. XV:** 301
Wood, Clement, **Supp. XV:** 298
Wood, Clement Biddle, **Supp. XI:** 307
Wood, James, **Supp. XIV:** 95–96
Wood, Mabel, **I:** 199
Wood, Michael, **Supp. IV Part 2:** 691
Wood, Mrs. Henry, **Supp. I Part 1:** 35
Wood, Norman Barton, **Supp. XIV:** 201
Wood, Susan, **Supp. XVI:** 123
Woodard, Calvin, **Supp. VIII:** 128
Woodard, Charles L., **Supp. IV Part 2:** 484, 493
Woodard, Deborah, **Supp. XIII:** 114
Woodberry, George Edward, **III:** 508
Woodbridge, Frederick, **I:** 217, 224
Woodbridge, John, **Supp. I Part 1:** 101, 102, 114
"Wood-Choppers, The" (Chopin), **Retro. Supp. II:** 72
Woodcock, George, **Supp. XIII:** 33
Woodcome, Beth, **Supp. XVII:** 240
"Wood Dove at Sandy Spring, The" (MacLeish), **III:** 19
"Wooden Spring" (Rukeyser), **Supp. VI:** 285
"Wooden Umbrella, The" (Porter), **IV:** 26
Woodhull, Victoria, **Supp. XVIII:** 4
"Woodnotes" (Emerson), **II:** 7, 19
"Wood-Pile, The" (Frost), **Retro. Supp. I:** 128; **Supp. IV Part 2:** 445
Woodrow, James, **Supp. I Part 1:** 349, 366
"Woods, Books, and Truant Officers, The" (Maclean), **Supp. XIV:** 221, 225
Woods, Robert A., **Supp. I Part 1:** 19
Woods, The (Mamet), **Supp. XIV:** 241, 254–255
Woodswoman (LaBastille), **Supp. X:** 95, **96–99,** 108
Woodswoman III: Book Three of the Woodswoman's Adventures (LaBastille), **Supp. X:** 95, **106–107**
"Wood Thrush" (Kenyon), **Supp. VII:** 172
Woodward, C. Vann, **IV:** 114, 470–471; **Retro. Supp. I:** 75, 76
"Wooing the Inanimate" (Brodsky), **Supp. VIII:** 32
Woolcott, Alexander, **Supp. IX:** 197
Wooley, Bryan, **Supp. V:** 225
Woolf, Leonard, **Supp. IX:** 95
Woolf, Virginia, **I:** 53, 79, 112, 309; **II:** 320, 415; **IV:** 59; **Retro. Supp. I:** 59, 75, 170, 215, 291, 359; **Supp. I Part 2:** 553, 714, 718; **Supp. IV Part 1:** 299; **Supp. IX:** 66, 109; **Supp. V:** 127; **Supp. VIII:** 5, 155, 251, 252, 263, 265; **Supp. XI:** 134, 193; **Supp. XII:** 81, 98, 289; **Supp. XIII:** 305; **Supp. XIV:** 341–342, 342, 343, 346, 348; **Supp. XV:** 55, 65
Woollcott, Alexander, **IV:** 432; **Retro. Supp. II:** 327; **Supp. I Part 2:** 664; **Supp. IX:** 190, 194
Woollstonecraft, Mary, **Supp. XVI:** 184
"Woolly Mammoth" (X. J. Kennedy), **Supp. XV:** 163–164
Woolman, John, **Supp. VIII:** 202, 204, 205
Woolson, Constance Fenimore, **Retro. Supp. I:** 224, 228
Worcester, Samuel, **I:** 458
Word and Idioms: Studies in the English Language (L. P. Smith), **Supp. XIV:** 343
Word of God and the Word of Man, The (Barth), **Retro. Supp. I:** 327
"Word out of the Sea, A" (Whitman), **IV:** 344
"Words" (Creeley), **Supp. IV Part 1:** 152
Words (Creeley), **Supp. IV Part 1:** 139, 150–153, 154, 155, 158
"Words" (Gioia), **Supp. XV:** 125
"Words" (Merwin), **Supp. III Part 1:** 352

"Words" (Plath), **Supp. I Part 2:** 547
"Words" (Shields), **Supp. VII:** 323
"Words, The" (Wagoner), **Supp. IX:** 326
"Words above a Narrow Entrance" (Wagoner), **Supp. IX:** 325
"Words for a Bike-Racing, Osprey-Chasing Wine-Drunk Squaw Man" (Gunn Allen), **Supp. IV Part 1:** 325
Words for Dr. Y (Sexton), **Supp. II Part 2:** 698
"Words for Hart Crane" (Lowell), **I:** 381; **II:** 547; **Retro. Supp. II:** 188
"Words for Maria" (Merrill), **Supp. III Part 1:** 327
"Words for the Unknown Makers" (Kunitz), **Supp. III Part 1:** 264
"Words for the Wind" (Roethke), **III:** 542–543
Words for the Wind (Roethke), **III:** 529, 533, 541, 543, 545
"Words in the Mourning Time" (Hayden), **Supp. II Part 1:** 370–371
Words in the Mourning Time (Hayden), **Supp. II Part 1:** 361, 366, 367
"Words into Fiction" (Welty), **IV:** 279
"Words Like Freedom" (Hughes), **Retro. Supp. I:** 207
"Words of a Young Girl" (Lowell), **II:** 554
Words under the Words: Selected Poems (Nye), **Supp. XIII:** 277
Wordsworth, Dorothy, **Supp. IX:** 38
Wordsworth, William, **I:** 283, 522, 524, 525, 588; **II:** 7, 11, 17, 18, 97, 169, 273, 303, 304, 532, 549, 552; **III:** 219, 263, 277, 278, 511, 521, 523, 528, 583; **IV:** 120, 331, 343, 453, 465; **Retro. Supp. I:** 121, 196; **Supp. I Part 1:** 150, 151, 154, 161, 163, 312, 313, 349, 365; **Supp. I Part 2:** 375, 409, 416, 422, 607, 621, 622, 673, 674, 675, 676, 677, 710–711, 729; **Supp. II Part 1:** 4; **Supp. III Part 1:** 12, 15, 73, 279; **Supp. IV Part 2:** 597, 601; **Supp. IX:** 38, 41, 265, 274; **Supp. V:** 258; **Supp. VIII:** 273; **Supp. X:** 22, 23, 65, 120; **Supp. XI:** 248, 251, 312; **Supp. XIII:** 214; **Supp. XIV:** 184; **Supp. XV:** 93, 250
Work (Alcott), **Supp. I Part 1:** 32–33, 42
Work (Dixon), **Supp. XII:** 141, **143**
"Work" (Oliver), **Supp. VII:** 243
Work and Love (Dunn), **Supp. XI: 147–148**
"Worker" (Coleman), **Supp. XI:** 89
Working a Passage; or, Life on a Liner (Briggs), **Supp. XVIII:** 2, **9–10**
Working Class Movement in America, The (E. Marx and E. Aveling), **Supp. XVI:** 85
Working Papers: Selected Essays and Reviews (Carruth), **Supp. XVI:** 46
"Working the Landscape" (Dunn), **Supp. XI:** 151
Workin' on the Chain Gang: Shaking Off the Dead Hand of History (Mosley), **Supp. XIII:** 247, 248
"Work Notes '66" (Baraka), **Supp. II Part 1:** 47
Work of Art (Lewis), **II:** 453–454
"Work of Shading, The" (Simic), **Supp. VIII:** 277–278
Work of Stephen Crane, The (Follett, ed.), **I:** 405
"Work on Red Mountain, The" (Harte), **Supp. II Part 1:** 339
Works of Love, The (Morris), **III:** 223–224, 225, 233
Works of Witter Bynner, The (Kraft, ed.), **Supp. XV:** 52
"World, The" (Simic), **Supp. VIII:** 282
World According to Garp, The (Irving), **Supp. VI:** 163, 164, **170–173,** 181
World and Africa, The: An Inquiry into the Part Which Africa Has Played in World History (Du Bois), **Supp. II Part 1:** 184–185
"World and All Its Teeth, The" (Nye), **Supp. XIII:** 282
"World and the Door, The" (O. Henry), **Supp. II Part 1:** 402
"World and the Jug, The" (Ellison), **Retro. Supp. II:** 112, 119, 123
"World as We Know It, The" (Barresi), **Supp. XV:** 100
World Authors 1950–1970, **Supp. XIII:** 102
World Below, The (Miller), **Supp. XII: 303–304**
World Below the Window, The: Poems 1937–1997 (W. J. Smith), **Supp. XIII:** 332, 340, 345
World Doesn't End, The (Simic), **Supp. VIII:** 272, **279–280**
World Elsewhere, A: The Place of Style in American Literature (Poirier), **I:** 239
"World Ends Here, The" (Harjo), **Supp. XII:** 227–228
World Enough and Time (Warren), **IV:** 243, 253–254
World Gone Wrong (album, Dylan), **Supp. XVIII:** 28
"World I Live In, The" (T. Williams), **IV:** 388
World I Never Made, A (Farrell), **II:** 34, 35, 424
World in the Attic, The (Morris), **III:** 222–223, 224
World in the Evening, The (Isherwood), **Supp. XIV:** 157, 164, 165, **166–167,** 170
"World Is a Wedding, The" (Schwartz), **Supp. II Part 2:** 655–656, 657
World Is a Wedding, The (Schwartz), **Supp. II Part 2:** 643, 654–660
"World Is Too Much with Us, The" (Wordsworth), **Supp. I Part 1:** 312
Worldly Hopes (Ammons), **Supp. VII:** 34
Worldly Philosophers, The (Heilbroner), **Supp. I Part 2:** 644, 650
World of Apples, The (Cheever), **Supp. I Part 1:** 191, 193
World of David Wagoner, The (McFarland), **Supp. IX:** 323
"World of Easy Rawlins, The" (Mosley), **Supp. XIII:** 234, 236
World of Gwendolyn Brooks, The (Brooks), **Supp. III Part 1:** 83, 84
World of H. G. Wells, The (Brooks), **I:** 240, 241, 242
World of Light, A: Portraits and Celebrations (Sarton), **Supp. III Part 1:** 62; **Supp. VIII:** 249, 253, 262
World of Our Fathers: The Journey of the Eastern European Jews to America and the Life They Found and Made (Howe), **Sup p. XIV:**104; **Supp. VI:** 113, 114, 116, 118, 119, **120–125**
"World of Pure Experience, A" (James), **II:** 356–357
World of Raymond Chandler, The (Spender), **Supp. IV Part 1:** 119
World of Sex, The (H. Miller), **III:** 170, 178, 187
"World of the Perfect Tear, The" (McGrath), **Supp. X:** 116, 118
World of the Ten Thousand Things, The: Selected Poems (Wright), **Supp. V:** 333
"World of Tomorrow, The" (White), **Supp. I Part 2:** 663
World of Washington Irving, The (Brooks), **I:** 256–257
World Over, The (Wharton), **Retro. Supp. I:** 382
"Worlds" (Goldbarth), **Supp. XII:** 183, 189
World's Body, The (Ransom), **III:** 497, 499; **Supp. II Part 1:** 146
World's End (Boyle), **Supp. VIII: 11–12**
World's End and Other Stories (Theroux), **Supp. VIII:** 322
"World's Fair" (Berryman), **I:** 173
World's Fair (Doctorow), **Supp. IV Part 1:** 217, 224, 227–229, 234, 236–237
World's Fair, The (Fitzgerald), **II:** 93
"Worlds of Color" (Du Bois), **Supp. II Part 1:** 175
Worlds of Color (Du Bois), **Supp. II Part 1:** 185–186
World So Wide (Lewis), **II:** 456
"World's Worst Boyfriends, The" (Wasserstein), **Supp. XV:** 328
"World-Telegram" (Berryman), **I:** 173
World to Come, The (D. Horn), **Supp. XVII:** 50
World View on Race and Democracy: A Study Guide in Human Group Relations (Locke), **Supp. XIV:** 205, 206
World within the Word, The (Gass), **Supp. VI:** 77
"World Without Objects Is a Sensible Place, A" (Wilbur), **Supp. III Part 2:** 550
"World Without Rodrigo, The" (Cisneros), **Supp. VII:** 68
"Worm Moon" (Oliver), **Supp. VII:** 234
"Worn Path, A" (Welty), **IV:** 262; **Retro. Supp. I:** 345–346
"Worsening Situation" (Ashbery), **Supp. III Part 1:** 17–18
"Worship" (Emerson), **II:** 2, 4–5
"Worship and Church Bells" (Paine), **Supp. I Part 2:** 521
Worster, Donald, **Supp. IX:** 19
Worthington, Marjorie, **Supp. XII:** 13

Wouldn't Take Nothing for My Journey Now (Angelou), **Supp. IV Part 1:** 10, 12, 14, 15, 16
"Wound" (Pedersen; Nelson, trans.), **Supp. XVIII:** 180
Wound and the Bow, The: Seven Studies in Literature (Wilson), **IV:** 429
Wounded (Everett), **Supp. XVIII:** 54, **64,** 65
Wounds in the Rain (Crane), **I:** 409, 414, 423
Woven Stone (Ortiz), **Supp. IV Part 2:** 501, 514
Woven Stories (Ortiz), **Supp. IV Part 2:** 503
"Wraith, The" (Roethke), **III:** 542
"Wrath of God, The" (Fante), **Supp. XI:** 160, 164
"Wreath for a Bridal" (Plath), **Supp. I Part 2:** 537
"Wreath for Emmet Till, A" (Nelson), **Supp. XVIII:** 177
Wreath for Emmett Till, A (Nelson), **Supp. XVIII:** 171, 173, 175, 181, **183–185**
Wreath for Garibaldi and Other Stories, A (Garrett), **Supp. VII:** 99–101
"Wreath of Women" (Rukeyser), **Supp. VI:** 280
Wreckage (Jin), **Supp. XVIII: 98–99**
Wreckage of Agathon, The (Gardner), **Supp. VI:** 63, **65–66**
Wrecking Crew (Levis), **Supp. XI: 259–260**
"Wreck of Rivermouth, The" (Whittier), **Supp. I Part 2:** 694, 696–697
"Wreck of the Deutschland" (Hopkins), **Supp. X:** 61
"Wreck of the Hesperus, The" (Longfellow), **Retro. Supp. II:** 168, 169
Wrestler's Cruel Study, The (Dobyns), **Supp. XIII: 82–83**
"Wrestler with Sharks, A" (Yates), **Supp. XI:** 341
Wright, Bernie, **I:** 191, 193
Wright, C. D. (Carolyn Doris), **Supp. XV: 337–355**
Wright, Charles, **Supp. V:** 92, **331–346; Supp. VIII:** 272; **Supp. XIII:** 114; **Supp. XVII:** 71
Wright, Chauncey, **II:** 344
Wright, Frank Lloyd, **I:** 104, 483
Wright, Franz, **Supp. XVII: 239–249**
Wright, George, **III:** 479
Wright, Harold Bell, **II:** 467–468
Wright, Holly, **Supp. VIII:** 272
Wright, James, **I:** 291; **Supp. III Part 1:** 249; **Supp. III Part 2:** 541, **589–607; Supp. IV Part 1:** 60, 72; **Supp. IV Part 2:** 557, 558, 561, 566, 571, 623; **Supp. IX:** 152, 155, 159, 265, 271, 290, 293, 296; **Supp. V:** 332; **Supp. X:** 69, 127; **Supp. XI:** 150; **Supp. XII:** 217; **Supp. XIII:** 76; **Supp. XV:** 79, 93, 212; **Supp. XVII:** 239, 241, 243, 244
Wright, Mrs. Richard (Ellen Poplar), **IV:** 476
Wright, Nathalia, **IV:** 155
Wright, Philip Green, **III:** 578, 579, 580
Wright, Richard, **II:** 586; **IV:** 40, **474–497; Retro. Supp. II:** 4, 111, 116, 120; **Supp. I Part 1:** 51, 52, 64, 332, 337; **Supp. II Part 1:** 17, 40, 221, 228, 235, 250; **Supp. IV Part 1:** 1, 11, 84, 374; **Supp. IX:** 316; **Supp. VIII:** 88; **Supp. X:** 131, 245, 254; **Supp. XI:** 85; **Supp. XII:** 316; **Supp. XIII:** 46, 233; **Supp. XIV:** 73; **Supp. XVI:** 135, 139, 141, 143; **Supp. XVIII:** 277, 282, 286
Wright, Sarah, **Supp. IV Part 1:** 8; **Supp. XIII:** 295
Wright, William, **Retro. Supp. II:** 76, 77
Wrigley, Robert, **Supp. XVIII: 293–308**
"Writer" (Sanders), **Supp. XVI:** 277
"Writer, The" (Wilbur), **Supp. III Part 2:** 561, 562
"Writer as Alaskan, The" (Haines), **Supp. XII:** 199
Writer in America, The (Brooks), **I:** 253, 254, 257
Writer in America, The (Stegner), **Supp. IV Part 2:** 597, 599, 607
"Writers" (Lowell), **II:** 554
Writer's Almanac, The (Keillor, radio program), **Supp. XIII:** 274; **Supp. XVI:** 178
Writer's America, A: Landscape in Literature (Kazin), **Supp. VIII:** 106
Writer's Capital, A (Auchincloss), **Supp. IV Part 1:** 21, 23, 24, 31
"Writer's Credo, A" (Abbey), **Supp. XIII:** 1, 17
Writer's Eye, A: Collected Book Reviews (Welty), **Retro. Supp. I:** 339, 354, 356
Writers in America (Schulberg), **Supp. XVIII:** 242, 243, 250, 254
Writers in Revolt (Southern, Seaver, and Trocchi, eds.), **Supp. XI:** 301
Writer's Life, A (Talese), **Supp. XVII:** 208–209, 210
Writer's Notebook, A (Maugham), **Supp. X:** 58
Writers on America (U.S. Department of State, ed.), **Supp. XIII:** 288
Writers on the Left (Aaron), **IV:** 429; **Supp. II Part 1:** 137
Writers on Writing (Prose), **Supp. XVI:** 259
"Writer's Prologue to a Play in Verse" (W. C. Williams), **Retro. Supp. I:** 424
"Writer's Quest for a Parnassus, A" (T. Williams), **IV:** 392
Writers' Workshop (University of Iowa), **Supp. V:** 42
"Writers Workshop, The" (Conroy), **Supp. XVI:** 76
"Writing" (Nemerov), **III:** 275
"Writing About the Universe" (Mosley), **Supp. XIII:** 247
"Writing American Fiction" (P. Roth), **Retro. Supp. II:** 279; **Supp. I Part 1:** 192; **Supp. I Part 2:** 431; **Supp. III Part 2:** 414, 420, 421; **Supp. V:** 45
"Writing and a Life Lived Well" (Patchett), **Supp. XII:** 308
Writing a Woman's Life (Heilbrun), **Supp. IX:** 66
Writing Chicago: Modernism, Ethnography, and the Novel (Cappetti), **Supp. IX:** 4, 8
Writing Creative Nonfiction: The Literature of Reality (Talese and Lounsberry, eds.), **Supp. XVII:** 208
Writing Dylan: The Songs of a Lonesome Traveler (Smith), **Supp. XVIII:** 22
Writing from the Center (Sanders), **Supp. XVI:** 266, 275–276
"Writing from the Inside Out: Style Is Not the Frosting; It's the Cake" (Robbins), **Supp. X:** 266
"Writing here last autumn of my hopes of seeing a hoopoe" (Updike), **Retro. Supp. I:** 335
Writing in Restaurants (Mamet), **Supp. XIV:** 246
"Writing Lesson, The" (Gordon), **Supp. IV Part 1:** 306
Writing Life, The (Dillard), **Supp. VI:** 23, 31
"Writing of Apollinaire, The" (Zukofsky), **Supp. III Part 2:** 616, 617
"Writing of *Fearless Jones,* The" (Mosley), **Supp. XIII:** 242
Writing on the Wall, The, and Literary Essays (McCarthy), **II:** 579
Writings to an Unfinished Accompaniment (Merwin), **Supp. III Part 1:** 352
"Writing the Universe-Mind" (Tabios), **Supp. XV:** 225
Writing the World (Stafford), **Supp. XI:** 314
"Writing to Save Our Lives" (Milligan), **Supp. XIII:** 274
Writin' Is Fightin' (Reed), **Supp. X:** 241
"Writ on the Eve of My 32nd Birthday" (Corso), **Supp. XII:** 129–130
"Written History as an Act of Faith" (Beard), **Supp. I Part 2:** 492
"Wrong Man, The" (Larsen), **Supp. XVIII:** 124
"Wrong Notes" (S. Kauffmann), **Supp. XVI:** 74
"Wrought Figure" (McCarriston), **Supp. XIV:** 272
"Wunderkind" (McCullers), **II:** 585
Wunderlich, Mark, **Supp. XI:** 119, 132
Wundt, Wilhelm, **II:** 345
Wurster, William Wilson, **Supp. IV Part 1:** 197
WUSA (film), **Supp. V:** 301
Wuthering Heights (E. Brontë), **Supp. V:** 305; **Supp. X:** 89
WWII (Jones), **Supp. XI:** 219, 231
Wyandotté (Cooper), **I:** 350, 355
Wyatt, Robert B., **Supp. V:** 14
Wyatt, Thomas, **Supp. I Part 1:** 369
Wycherly Woman, The (Macdonald), **Supp. IV Part 2:** 473
Wych Hazel (S. and A. Warner), **Supp. XVIII:** 267, **268–269**
Wydra, Ewa. *See* Hoffman, Eva
Wyler, William, **Supp. XV:** 195
Wylie, Elinor, **IV:** 436; **Supp. I Part 2: 707–730; Supp. III Part 1:** 2, 63, 318–319; **Supp. XI:** 44; **Supp. XIV:** 127; **Supp. XV:** 307
Wylie, Horace, **Supp. I Part 2:** 708, 709

Wylie, Philip, **III:** 223
Wyllys, Ruth. *See* Taylor, Mrs. Edward (Ruth Wyllys)
"Wyoming Valley Tales" (Crane), **I:** 409
Wyzewa, Théodore de, **Supp. XIV:** 336

X
Xaipe (Cummings), **I:** 430, 432–433, 447
Xenogenesis trilogy (O. Butler), **Supp. XIII: 63–66,** 69
Xenophon, **II:** 105
X Factor, The: A Quest for Excellence" (Plimpton), **Supp. XVI:** 241
X Files (television series), **Supp. XVI:** 125
Xiaojing, Zhou, **Supp. XV:** 214
Xingu and Other Stories (Wharton), **IV:** 314, 320; **Retro. Supp. I:** 378
Xionia (Wright), **Supp. V:** 333
XLI Poems (Cummings), **I:** 429, 432, 440, 443

Y
Yacoubi, Ahmed, **Supp. IV Part 1:** 88, 92, 93
Yage Letters, The (Burroughs), **Supp. III Part 1:** 94, 98, 100
Yagoda, Ben, **Supp. VIII:** 151
Yamamoto, Isoroku, **Supp. I Part 2:** 491
Yancey's War (Hoffman), **Supp. XVIII:** 71, **75–76**
Yankee City (Warner), **III:** 60
Yankee Clipper (ballet) (Kirstein), **Supp. IV Part 1:** 82
Yankee in Canada, A (Thoreau), **IV:** 188
Yankey in London (Tyler), **I:** 344
"Yánnina"(Merrill), **Supp. III Part 1:** 329
"Yanosz Korczak's Last Walk"(Markowick-Olczakova), **Supp. X:** 70
Yarboro, Chelsea Quinn, **Supp. V:** 147
Yardley, Jonathan, **Supp. V:** 326; **Supp. XI:** 67
"Yard Sale"(Kenyon), **Supp. VII:** 169
Yates, Richard, **Supp. XI: 333–350**
"Year, The"(Sandburg), **III:** 584
"Year Between, The"(Neugeboren), **Supp. XVI:** 226
Year in Provence, A (Mayle), **Supp. XVI:** 295
Yearling, The (Rawlings), **Supp. X:** 219, **230–231,** 233, 234
Year of Happy, A (Goldbarth), **Supp. XII:** 180
"Year of Mourning, The"(Jeffers), **Supp. II Part 2:** 415
Year of Silence, The (Bell), **Supp. X:** 1, **5–6,** 7
"Year of the Double Spring, The"(Swenson), **Supp. IV Part 2:** 647
Year's Best Science Fiction, The (Merril, ed.), **Supp. XVI:** 123
Year's Life, A (Lowell), **Supp. I Part 2:** 405
"Years of Birth"(Cowley), **Supp. II Part 1:** 149
Years of My Youth (Howells), **II:** 276
"Years of Wonder"(White), **Supp. I Part 2:** 652, 653
Years With Ross, The (Thurber), **Supp. I Part 2:** 619
Yeats, Jack, **Supp. XVI:** 190
Yeats, John Butler, **III:** 458
Yeats, William Butler, **I:** 69, 172, 384, 389, 403, 434, 478, 494, 532; **II:** 168–169, 566, 598; **III:** 4, 5, 8, 18, 19, 20, 23, 29, 40, 205, 249, 269, 270–271, 272, 278, 279, 294, 347, 409, 457, 458–460, 472, 473, 476–477, 521, 523, 524, 527, 528, 533, 540, 541, 542, 543–544, 591–592; **IV:** 89, 93, 121, 126, 136, 140, 271, 394, 404; **Retro. Supp. I:** 59, 66, 127, 141, 270, 283, 285, 286, 288, 290, 311, 342, 350, 378, 413; **Retro. Supp. II:** 185, 331; **Supp. I Part 1:** 79, 80, 254, 257, 262; **Supp. I Part 2:** 388, 389; **Supp. II Part 1:** 1, 4, 9, 20, 26, 361; **Supp. III Part 1:** 59, 63, 236, 238, 253; **Supp. IV Part 1:** 81; **Supp. IV Part 2:** 634; **Supp. IX:** 43, 119; **Supp. V:** 220; **Supp. VIII:** 19, 21, 30, 155, 156, 190, 239, 262, 292; **Supp. X:** 35, 58, 119, 120; **Supp. XI:** 140; **Supp. XII:** 132, 198, 217, 266; **Supp. XIII:** 77, **Supp. XIII:** 87; **Supp. XIV:** 7; **Supp. XV:** 36, 41, 181, 186; **Supp. XVI:** 47–48, 159; **Supp. XVII:** 36
Yee, Amy, **Supp. XVIII:** 93, 94
Yellin, Jean Fagan, **Supp. XVI:** 88, 89
Yellow Back Radio Broke-Down (Reed), **Supp. X:** 240, 242, **243–245**
"Yellow Dog Café"(Komunyakaa), **Supp. XIII:** 126
"Yellow Girl"(Caldwell), **I:** 310
"Yellow Glove"(Nye), **Supp. XIII:** 276
Yellow Glove (Nye), **Supp. XIII:** 275, **276–277**
"Yellow Gown, The"(Anderson), **I:** 114
Yellow House on the Corner, The (Dove), **Supp. IV Part 1:** 244, 245, 246, 254
"Yellow Raft, The"(Connell), **Supp. XIV: 85–86**
"Yellow River"(Tate), **IV:** 141
"Yellow Violet, The"(Bryant), **Supp. I Part 1:** 154, 155
"Yellow Wallpaper, The"(Gilman), **Supp. XI: 198–199,** 207; **Supp. XVI:** 84
"Yellow Woman"(Keres stories), **Supp. IV Part 1:** 327
"Yellow Woman"(Silko), **Supp. IV Part 2:** 567–568
Yelverton, Theresa, **Supp. IX:** 181
Yenser, Stephen, **Supp. X:** 207, 208; **Supp. XV:** 113–114
"Yentl the Yeshiva Boy"(Singer), **IV:** 15, 20
Yerkes, Charles E., **I:** 507, 512
Yerma (opera) (Bowles), **Supp. IV Part 1:** 89
Yertle the Turtle and Other Stories (Geisel), **Supp. XVI:** 109
"Yes"(Stafford), **Supp. XI:** 329
Yes, Mrs. Williams (W. C. Williams), **Retro. Supp. I:** 423
Yes, Yes, No, No (Kushner), **Supp. IX:** 133
"Yes and It's Hopeless"(Ginsberg), **Supp. II Part 1:** 326
Yesenin, Sergey, **Supp. VIII:** 40
"Yes! No!"(Oliver), **Supp. VII:** 243–244
Yesterday and Today: A Comparative Anthology of Poetry (Untermeyer, ed.), **Supp. XV:** 309
Yesterday's Self: Nostalgia and the Immigrant Identity (Ritivoi), **Supp. XVI:** 148
Yesterday Will Make You Cry (C. Himes), **Supp. XVI:** 137
"Yet Another Example of the Porousness of Certain Borders"(Wallace), **Supp. X:** 309
"Yet Do I Marvel"(Cullen), **Supp. IV Part 1:** 165, 169
Yet Other Waters (Farrell), **II:** 29, 38, 39, 40
Yevtushenko, Yevgeny, **Supp. III Part 1:** 268
Yezzi, David, **Supp. XII:** 193
Yizkor Book, **Supp. XVI:** 154
Y no se lo trago la tierra (And the Earth Did Not Cover Him) (Rivera), **Supp. XIII:** 216
¡Yo! (Alvarez), **Supp. VII:** 1, 15–17
"Yogurt of Vasirin Kefirovsky, The"(Apple), **Supp. XVII:** 3, 4
Yohannan, J. D., **II:** 20
"Yoke, The"(Bidart), **Supp. XV:** 33
Yonge, Charlotte, **II:** 174
"Yonnondio"(Whitman), **Supp. XIII:** 304
Yonnondio: From the Thirties (Olsen), **Supp. XIII:** 295, 295, **Supp. XIII:** 292, 296, **303–304,** 305
"Yore"(Nemerov), **III:** 283
"York Beach"(Toomer), **Supp. III Part 2:** 486
Yorke, Dorothy, **Supp. I Part 1:** 258
Yorke, Henry Vincent. *See* Green, Henry
"York Garrison, 1640" (Jewett), **Retro. Supp. II:** 141
Yosemite, The (Muir), **Supp. IX:** 185
"Yosemite Glaciers: Ice Streams of the Great Valley" (Muir), **Supp. IX:** 181
Yoshe Kalb (Singer), **IV:** 2
"You, Andrew Marvell" (MacLeish), **III:** 12–13
"You, Dr. Martin" (Sexton), **Supp. II Part 2:** 673
You, Emperors, and Others: Poems 1957–1960 (Warren), **IV:** 245
"You, Genoese Mariner" (Merwin), **Supp. III Part 1:** 343
"You All Know the Story of the Other Woman" (Sexton), **Supp. II Part 2:** 688
"You Are Happy" (Atwood), **Supp. XIII:** 34
You Are Happy (Atwood), **Supp. XIII:** 34
"You Are in Bear Country" (Kumin), **Supp. IV Part 2:** 453, 455
"You Are Not I" (Bowles), **Supp. IV Part 1:** 87
"You Begin" (Atwood), **Supp. XIII:** 34
You Bright and Risen Angels (Vollmann), **Supp. XVII:** 225, 226
"You Bring Out the Mexican in Me" (Cisneros), **Supp. VII:** 71

You Came Along (film), **Supp. IV Part 2:** 524
"You *Can* Go Home Again" (TallMountain), **Supp. IV Part 1:** 324–325
"You Can Have It" (Levine), **Supp. V:** 188–189
You Can't Go Home Again (Wolfe), **IV:** 450, 451, 454, 456, 460, 462, 468, 469, 470
You Can't Keep a Good Woman Down (Walker), **Supp. III Part 2:** 520, 525, 531
You Can't Take It with You (Kaufman and Hart), **Supp. XIV:** 327
"You Can't Tell a Man by the Song He Sings" (P. Roth), **Supp. III Part 2:** 406
"You Don't Know What Love Is" (Carver), **Supp. III Part 1:** 147
You Don't Love Me Yet (Lethem), **Supp. XVIII: 149–150**
"You Have Left Your Lotus Pods on the Bus" (Bowles), **Supp. IV Part 1:** 91
You Have Seen Their Faces (Caldwell), **I:** 290, 293–294, 295, 304, 309
You Know Me, Al: A Busher's Letters (Lardner), **Supp. XVI:** 189
You Know Me Al (comic strip), **II:** 423
You Know Me Al (Lardner), **II:** 26, 415, 419, 422, 431
"You Know What" (Beattie), **Supp. V:** 33
"You Know Who You Are" (Nye), **Supp. XIII:** 275
You Might As Well Live: The Life and Times of Dorothy Parker (Keats), **Supp. IX:** 190
"You Must Relax!" (J. Scott), **Supp. XVII:** 189
You Must Revise Your Life (Stafford), **Supp. XI:** 312–313, 313–314, 315
"Young" (Sexton), **Supp. II Part 2:** 680
Young, Al, **Supp. X:** 240
Young, Art, **IV:** 436
Young, Brigham, **Supp. IV Part 2:** 603
Young, Edward, **II:** 111; **III:** 415, 503
Young, Gary, **Supp. XV:** 88
Young, Mary, **Supp. XIII:** 236, 238, 239, 240
Young, Philip, **II:** 306; **Retro. Supp. I:** 172
Young Adventure (Benét), **Supp. XI:** 44
"Young America" (Brooks), **Supp. XV:** 298
"Young Child and His Pregnant Mother, A" (Schwartz), **Supp. II Part 2:** 650
Young Christian, The (Abbott), **Supp. I Part 1:** 38
"Young Dr. Gosse" (Chopin), **Supp. I Part 1:** 211, 216
Younger Choir, The (anthology), **Supp. XV:** 294
Younger Quire, The (Untermeyer), **Supp. XV:** 294, 297
"Young Folks, The" (Salinger), **III:** 551
Young Folk's Cyclopaedia of Persons and Places (Champlin), **III:** 577
"Young Girl's Lament, A" (Jin), **Supp. XVIII:** 99
"Young Goodman Brown" (Hawthorne), **II:** 229; **Retro. Supp. I:** 151–152, 153, 154; **Supp. XI:** 51; **Supp. XIV:** 48, 50
Young Harvard: First Poems of Witter Bynner (Bynner), **Supp. XV:** 41
Young Hearts Crying (Yates), **Supp. XI:** 348
"Young Housewife, The" (W. C. Williams), **Retro. Supp. I:** 415
Young Immigrants, The (Lardner), **II:** 426
"Young Lady's Friend, The: Verses, Addressed to a Young Lady, on Her Leaving School" (Rowson), **Supp. XV:** 234
Young Lonigan: A Boyhood in Chicago Streets (Farrell), **II:** 31, 41
Young Manhood of Studs Lonigan, The (Farrell), **II:** 31, 34
Young Men and Fire (Maclean), **Supp. XIV:** 221, **231–233**
Young People's Pride (Benét), **Supp. XI:** 44
Young Poet's Primer (Brooks), **Supp. III Part 1:** 86
Youngren, J. Alan, **Supp. XVI:** 174
"Young Sammy's First Wild Oats" (Santayana), **III:** 607, 615
"Young Sor Juana, The" (Mora), **Supp. XIII:** 218
"Your Arkansas Traveler" (Schulberg), **Supp. XVIII:** 252
"Your Death" (Dove), **Supp. IV Part 1:** 250
You're Only Old Once! (Geisel), **Supp. XVI:** 111
"You're Ugly, Too" (Moore), **Supp. X:** 171
"Your Face on the Dog's Neck" (Sexton), **Supp. II Part 2:** 686
"Your Hand, Your Hand" (Hoffman), **Supp. XVIII:** 79
Your Job in Germany (film, Capra), **Supp. XVI:** 102
Your Job in Japan (film, Capra), **Supp. XVI:** 102
"Your Life" (Stafford), **Supp. XI:** 329
"Your Mother's Eyes" (Kingsolver), **Supp. VII:** 209
"You Take a Train through a Foreign Country" (Dobyns), **Supp. XIII:** 90
"Youth" (Hughes), **Supp. I Part 1:** 321
"Youth" (Huncke), **Supp. XIV:** 145
Youth and Life (Bourne), **I:** 217–222, 232
Youth and the Bright Medusa (Cather), **I:** 322; **Retro. Supp. I:** 14
"Youthful Religious Experiences" (Corso), **Supp. XII:** 117
Youth of Parnassus, and Other Stories, The (L. P. Smith), **Supp. XIV:** 336
Youth's First Steps in Geography (Rowson), **Supp. XV:** 243
You Touched Me! (Williams and Windham), **IV:** 382, 385, 387, 390, 392–393
"You Touch Me" (X. J. Kennedy), **Supp. XV:** 166
Yurchenco, Henrietta, **Supp. XVIII:** 20
Yurka, Blanche, **Supp. I Part 1:** 67
Yutang, Adet, **Supp. X:** 291
Yutang, Anor, **Supp. X:** 291
Yutang, Lin, **Supp. X:** 291; **Supp. XVI:** 190
Yutang, Mei-mei, **Supp. X:** 291
Yvernelle: A Legend of Feudal France (Norris), **III:** 314
Y & X (Olson), **Supp. II Part 2:** 556

Z

Zabel, Morton Dauwen, **II:** 431; **III:** 194, 215; **Supp. I Part 2:** 721
Zach, Natan, **Supp. XV:** 75, 82, 85
Zagajewski, Adam, **Supp. XVII:** 241
Zagarell, Sandra, **Supp. XV:** 269, 270, 278, 281, 282
Zagarell, Sandra A., **Retro. Supp. II:** 140, 143
"Zagrowsky Tells" (Paley), **Supp. VI:** 229
Zakrzewska, Marie, **Retro. Supp. II:** 146
Zaleski, Jeff, **Supp. XI:** 143
Zall, Paul, **Supp. XIV:** 156
Zaltzberg, Charlotte, **Supp. IV Part 1:** 374
"Zambesi and Ranee" (Swenson), **Supp. IV Part 2:** 647
Zamir, Israel, **Retro. Supp. II:** 303, 317
Zamora, Bernice, **Supp. IV Part 2:** 545
Zamoyski, Adam, **Supp. XV:** 257
Zangwill, Israel, **I:** 229
Zanita: A Tale of the Yosemite (Yelverton), **Supp. IX:** 181
Zanuck, Darryl F., **Supp. XI:** 170; **Supp. XII:** 165
Zapata, Emiliano, **Supp. XIII:** 324
"Zapatos" (Boyle), **Supp. VIII:** 15
Zapruder, Matthew, **Supp. XVI:** 55
Zarathustra, **III:** 602
Zawacki, Andrew, **Supp. VIII:** 272
"Zaydee" (Levine), **Supp. V:** 186
Zebra-Striped Hearse, The (Macdonald), **Supp. IV Part 2:** 473
Zechariah (biblical book), **IV:** 152
Zeidner, Lisa, **Supp. IV Part 2:** 453
"Zeitl and Rickel" (Singer), **IV:** 20
Zeke and Ned (McMurtry and Ossana), **Supp. V:** 232
Zeke Proctor, Cherokee Outlaw (Conley), **Supp. V:** 232
Zelda: A Biography (Milford), **Supp. IX:** 60
"Zelda and Scott: The Beautiful and Damned" (National Portrait Gallery exhibit), **Supp. IX:** 65
Zelig (film; Allen), **Supp. XV:** 4, 6, **8–9**
Zen and the Birds of Appetite (Merton), **Supp. VIII:** 205–206, 208
Zend-Avesta (Fechner), **II:** 358
Zeno, **Retro. Supp. I:** 247
Zero db and Other Stories (Bell), **Supp. X:** 1, 5, 6
"Zeus over Redeye" (Hayden), **Supp. II Part 1:** 380
Zevi, Sabbatai, **IV:** 6
Ziegfeld, Florenz, **II:** 427–428
Zigrosser, Carl, **I:** 226, 228, 231
Zimmerman, Paul D., **Supp. IV Part 2:** 583, 589, 590
Zimmerman, Robert Allen. *See* Dylan, Bob

Zinberg, Leonard S. *See* Lacy, Ed
Zinman, Toby Silverman, **Supp. XIII:** 207–208, 209
Zinn, Howard, **Supp. V:** 289
Zinsser, Hans, **I:** 251, 385
Zip: A Novel of the Left and Right (Apple), **Supp. XVII: 4–5**
Zipes, Jack, **Supp. XIV:** 126
"Zipper, The" (L. Michaels), **Supp. XVI:** 214
"Zizi's Lament" (Corso), **Supp. XII:** 123
Zodiac, The (Dickey), **Supp. IV Part 1:** 178, 183–184, 185
Zola, Émile, **I:** 211, 411, 474, 500, 502, 518; **II:** 174, 175–176, 182, 194, 275, 276, 281, 282, 319, 325, 337, 338; **III:** 315, 316, 317–318, 319–320, 321, 322, 323, 393, 511, 583; **IV:** 326; **Retro. Supp. I:** 226, 235; **Retro. Supp. II:** 93; **Supp. I Part 1:** 207; **Supp. II Part 1:** 117
Zolotow, Maurice, **III:** 161
"Zone" (Bogan), **Supp. III Part 1:** 60–61
Zone Journals (Wright), **Supp. V:** 332–333, 342–343
"Zooey" (Salinger), **III:** 564–565, 566, 567, 569, 572
"Zoo Revisited" (White), **Supp. I Part 2:** 654
Zoo Story, The (Albee), **I:** 71, 72–74, 75, 77, 84, 93, 94; **III:** 281
Zorach, William, **I:** 260
Zuccotti, Susan, **Supp. XVI:** 154
Zuckerman Bound: A Trilogy and Epilogue (P. Roth), **Supp. III Part 2:** 423
Zuckerman Unbound (P. Roth), **Retro. Supp. II:** 283; **Supp. III Part 2:** 421–422
Zueblin, Charles, **Supp. I Part 1:** 5
Zuger, Abigail, **Supp. X:** 160
Zukofsky, Celia (Mrs. Louis), **Supp. III Part 2:** 619–621, 623, 625, 626–629, 631
Zukofsky, Louis, **IV:** 415; **Retro. Supp. I:** 422; **Supp. III Part 2: 619–636; Supp. IV Part 1:** 154; **Supp. XIV:** 279, 282, 285, 286–287
Zukofsky, Paul, **Supp. III Part 2:** 622, 623–626, 627, 628
Zuleika Dobson (Beerbohm), **Supp. I Part 2:** 714
Zulus (Everett), **Supp. XVIII:** 54, **56–57**
"Zuni Potter: Drawing the Heartline" (Bierds), **Supp. XVII:** 26
Zverev, Aleksei, **Retro. Supp. I:** 278
Zwinger, Ann, **Supp. X:** 29
Zyda, Joan, **Retro. Supp. II:** 52

A Complete Listing of Authors in *American Writers*

Abbey, Edward Supp. XIII
Acker, Kathy Supp. XII
Adams, Henry Vol. I
Addams, Jane Supp. I
Agee, James Vol. I
Aiken, Conrad Vol. I
Albee, Edward Vol. I
Alcott, Louisa May Supp. I
Algren, Nelson Supp. IX
Allen, Woody Supp. XV
Alvarez, Julia Supp. VII
Ammons, A. R. Supp. VII
Anderson, Sherwood Vol. I
Angelou, Maya Supp. IV
Apple, Max Supp. XVII
Ashbery, John Supp. III
Atwood, Margaret Supp. XIII
Auchincloss, Louis Supp. IV
Auden, W. H. Supp. II
Audubon, John James Supp. XVI
Auster, Paul Supp. XII
Baker, Nicholson Supp. XIII
Baldwin, James Supp. I
Baldwin, James Retro. Supp. II
Bambara, Toni Cade Supp. XI
Banks, Russell Supp. V
Baraka, Amiri Supp. II
Barlow, Joel Supp. II
Barnes, Djuna Supp. III
Barth, John Vol. I
Barthelme, Donald Supp. IV
Barthelme, Frederick Supp. XI
Bass, Rick Supp. XVI
Bausch, Richard Supp. VII
Baxter, Charles Supp. XVII
Beattie, Ann Supp. V
Bell, Madison Smartt Supp. X
Bellow, Saul Vol. I
Bellow, Saul Retro. Supp. II
Benét, Stephen Vincent Supp. XI
Berry, Wendell Supp. X
Berryman, John Vol. I
Bidart, Frank Supp. XV
Bierce, Ambrose Vol. I
Bierds, Linda Supp. XVII
Bishop, Elizabeth Supp. I
Bishop, Elizabeth Retro. Supp. II
Blackmur, R. P. Supp. II
Bly, Carol Supp. XVI
Bly, Robert Supp. IV
Bogan, Louise Supp. III
Bourne, Randolph Vol. I
Bowles, Paul Supp. IV
Boyle, T. C. Supp. VIII
Bradbury, Ray Supp. IV
Bradstreet, Anne Supp. I
Briggs, Charles Frederick Supp. XVIII
Brodsky, Joseph Supp. VIII
Brooks, Cleanth Supp. XIV
Brooks, Gwendolyn Supp. III
Brooks, Van Wyck Vol. I
Brown, Charles Brockden Supp. I
Bryant, William Cullen Supp. I
Buck, Pearl S. Supp. II
Buechner, Frederick Supp. XII
Bukiet, Melvin Jules Supp. XVII
Burke, James Lee Supp. XIV
Burke, Kenneth Vol. I
Burroughs, William S. Supp. III
Butler, Octavia Supp. XIII
Butler, Robert Olen Supp. XII
Bynner, Witter Supp. XV
Caldwell, Erskine Vol. I
Cameron, Peter Supp. XII

Capote, Truman Supp. III
Carruth, Hayden Supp. XVI
Carson, Anne Supp. XII
Carson, Rachel Supp. IX
Carver, Raymond Supp. III
Cather, Willa Vol. I
Cather, Willa Retro. Supp. I
Chabon, Michael Supp. XI
Chandler, Raymond Supp. IV
Chapman, John Jay Supp. XIV
Cheever, John Supp. I
Chesnutt, Charles W. Supp. XIV
Chopin, Kate Supp. I
Chopin, Kate Retro. Supp. II
Cisneros, Sandra Supp. VII
Clampitt, Amy Supp. IX
Coleman, Wanda Supp. XI
Connell, Evan S. Supp. XIV
Conroy, Frank Supp. XVI
Cooper, James Fenimore Vol. I
Coover, Robert Supp. V
Corso, Gregory Supp. XII
Cowley, Malcolm Supp. II
Cozzens, James Gould Vol. I
Crane, Hart Vol. I
Crane, Hart Retro. Supp. II
Crane, Stephen Vol. I
Creeley, Robert Supp. IV
Crèvecoeur, Michel-Guillaume Jean de Supp. I
Crews, Harry Supp. XI
Cullen, Countee Supp. IV
Cummings, E. E. Vol. I
Cunningham, Michael Supp. XV
Davis, Rebecca Harding Supp. XVI
DeLillo, Don Supp. VI
Dickey, James Supp. IV
Dickinson, Emily Vol. I
Dickinson, Emily Retro. Supp. I
Didion, Joan Supp. IV
Dillard, Annie Supp. VI
Dixon, Stephen Supp. XII
Dobyns, Stephen Supp. XIII
Doctorow, E. L. Supp. IV
Doolittle, Hilda (H.D.) Supp. I
Dos Passos, John Vol. I
Doty, Mark Supp. XI
Douglass, Frederick Supp. III
Dove, Rita Supp. IV
Dreiser, Theodore Vol. I
Dreiser, Theodore Retro. Supp. II
Du Bois, W. E. B. Supp. II
Dubus, Andre Supp. VII
Dunbar, Paul Laurence Supp. II
Dunn, Stephen Supp. XI
Dylan, Bob Supp. XVIII
Eberhart, Richard Vol. I
Edson, Margaret Supp. XVIII
Edwards, Jonathan Vol. I
Eliot, T. S. Vol. I
Eliot, T. S. Retro. Supp. I
Elkin, Stanley Supp. VI
Ellison, Ralph Supp. II
Ellison, Ralph Retro. Supp. II
Emerson, Ralph Waldo Vol. II
Endore, Guy Supp. XVII
Epstein, Joseph Supp. XIV
Epstein, Leslie Supp. XII
Erdrich, Louise Supp. IV
Everett, Percival Supp. XVIII
Everwine, Peter Supp. XV
Fante, John Supp. XI
Farrell, James T. Vol. II
Faulkner, William Vol. II
Faulkner, William Retro. Supp. I
Fiedler, Leslie Supp. XIII
Finch, Annie Supp. XVII
Fisher, M.F.K. Supp. XVII
Fitzgerald, F. Scott Vol. II
Fitzgerald, F. Scott Retro. Supp. I
Fitzgerald, Zelda Supp. IX
Ford, Richard Supp. V
Francis, Robert Supp. IX
Franklin, Benjamin Vol. II
Frederic, Harold Vol. II
Freneau, Philip Supp. II
Frost, Carol Supp. XV
Frost, Robert Vol. II
Frost, Robert Retro. Supp. I

Fuller, Margaret Supp. II
Gaddis, William Supp. IV
García, Cristina Supp. XI
Gardner, John Supp. VI
Garrett, George Supp. VII
Gass, William Supp. VI
Geisel, Theodor Seuss Supp. XVI
Gibbons, Kaye Supp. X
Gibson, William Supp. XVI
Gilman, Charlotte Perkins Supp. XI
Ginsberg, Allen Supp. II
Gioia, Dana Supp. XV
Glasgow, Ellen Vol. II
Glaspell, Susan Supp. III
Goldbarth, Albert Supp. XII
Glück, Louise Supp. V
Gordon, Caroline Vol. II
Gordon, Mary Supp. IV
Gunn Allen, Paula Supp. IV
Gurney, A. R. Supp. V
Haines, John Supp. XII
Hammett, Dashiell Supp. IV
Hansberry, Lorraine Supp. IV
Hapgood, Hutchins Supp. XVII
Hardwick, Elizabeth Supp. III
Harjo, Joy Supp. XII
Harrison, Jim Supp. VIII
Harte, Bret Supp. II
Hass, Robert Supp. VI
Hawthorne, Nathaniel Vol. II
Hawthorne, Nathaniel Retro. Supp. I
Hay, Sara Henderson Supp. XIV
Hayden, Robert Supp. II
Hearon, Shelby Supp. VIII
Hecht, Anthony Supp. X
Heller, Joseph Supp. IV
Hellman, Lillian Supp. I
Hemingway, Ernest Vol. II
Hemingway, Ernest Retro. Supp. I
Henry, O. Supp. II
Hijuelos, Oscar Supp. VIII
Himes, Chester Bomar Supp. XVI
Hoffman, Alice Supp. X
Hoffman, Eva Supp. XVI
Hoffman, William Supp. XVIII
Hogan, Linda Supp. IV
Holmes, Oliver Wendell Supp. I
Howe, Irving Supp. VI
Howe, Susan Supp. IV
Howells, William Dean Vol. II
Hughes, Langston Supp. I
Hughes, Langston Retro. Supp. I
Hugo, Richard Supp. VI
Humphrey, William Supp. IX
Huncke, Herbert Supp. XIV
Hurston, Zora Neale Supp. VI
Irving, John Supp. VI
Irving, Washington Vol. II
Isherwood, Christopher Supp. XIV
Jackson, Shirley Supp. IX
James, Henry Vol. II
James, Henry Retro. Supp. I
James, William Vol. II
Jarman, Mark Supp. XVII
Jarrell, Randall Vol. II
Jeffers, Robinson Supp. II
Jewett, Sarah Orne Vol. II
Jewett, Sarah Orne Retro. Supp. II
Jin, Ha Supp. XVIII
Johnson, Charles Supp. VI
Jones, James Supp. XI
Jong, Erica Supp. V
Justice, Donald Supp. VII
Karr, Mary Supp. XI
Kazin, Alfred Supp. VIII
Kees, Weldon Supp. XV
Keillor, Garrison Supp. XVI
Kelly, Brigit Pegeen Supp. XVII
Kennedy, William Supp. VII
Kennedy, X. J. Supp. XV
Kenyon, Jane Supp. VII
Kerouac, Jack Supp. III
Kincaid, Jamaica Supp. VII
King, Stephen Supp. V
Kingsolver, Barbara Supp. VII
Kingston, Maxine Hong Supp. V
Kinnell, Galway Supp. III
Knowles, John Supp. XII

Koch, Kenneth Supp. XV
Komunyakaa, Yusef Supp. XIII
Kosinski, Jerzy Supp. VII
Krakauer, Jon Supp. XVIII
Kumin, Maxine Supp. IV
Kunitz, Stanley Supp. III
Kushner, Tony Supp. IX
LaBastille, Anne Supp. X
Lacy, Ed Supp. XV
Lanier, Sidney Supp. I
Larcom, Lucy Supp. XIII
Lardner, Ring Vol. II
Larsen, Nella Supp. XVIII
Lee, Harper Supp. VIII
Lee, Li-Young Supp. XV
Leopold, Aldo Supp. XIV
Lethem, Jonathan Supp. XVIII
Levertov, Denise Supp. III
Levine, Philip Supp. V
Levis, Larry Supp. XI
Lewis, Sinclair Vol. II
Lindsay, Vachel Supp. I
Locke, Alain Supp. XIV
London, Jack Vol. II
Longfellow, Henry Wadsworth Vol. II
Longfellow, Henry Wadsworth Retro. Supp. II
Loos, Anita Supp. XVI
Lowell, Amy Vol. II
Lowell, James Russell Supp. I
Lowell, Robert Vol. II
Lowell, Robert Retro. Supp. II
Markson, David Supp. XVII
McCarriston, Linda Supp. XIV
McCarthy, Cormac Supp. VIII
McCarthy, Mary Vol. II
McClatchy, J. D. Supp. XII
McCourt, Frank Supp. XII
McCoy, Horace Supp. XIII
McCullers, Carson Vol. II
McDermott, Alice Supp. XVIII
Macdonald, Ross Supp. IV
McGrath, Thomas Supp. X
McKay, Claude Supp. X
Maclean, Norman Supp. XIV
MacLeish, Archibald Vol. III
McMillan, Terry Supp. XIII
McMurty, Larry Supp. V
McNally, Terrence Supp. XIII
McPhee, John Supp. III
Mailer, Norman Vol. III
Mailer, Norman Retro. Supp. II
Malamud, Bernard Supp. I
Mamet, David Supp. XIV
Marquand, John P. Vol. III
Marshall, Paule Supp. XI
Mason, Bobbie Ann Supp. VIII
Masters, Edgar Lee Supp. I
Mather, Cotton Supp. II
Matthews, William Supp. IX
Matthiessen, Peter Supp. V
Maxwell, William Supp. VIII
Melville, Herman Vol. III
Melville, Herman Retro. Supp. I
Mencken, H. L. Vol. III
Merrill, James Supp. III
Merton, Thomas Supp. VIII
Merwin, W. S. Supp. III
Michaels, Leonard Supp. XVI
Millay, Edna St. Vincent Vol. III
Miller, Arthur Vol. III
Miller, Henry Vol. III
Miller, Sue Supp. XII
Minot, Susan Supp. VI
Momaday, N. Scott Supp. IV
Monette, Paul Supp. X
Moore, Lorrie Supp. X
Moore, Marianne Vol. III
Mora, Pat Supp. XIII
Morison, Samuel Eliot Supp. I
Morris, Wright Vol. III
Morrison, Toni Supp. III
Mosley, Walter Supp. XIII
Motley, Willard Supp. XVII
Muir, John Supp. IX
Mumford, Lewis Supp. III
Nabokov, Vladimir Vol. III
Nabokov, Vladimir Retro. Supp. I
Naylor, Gloria Supp. VIII

Nelson, Marilyn Supp. XVIII
Nemerov, Howard Vol. III
Neugeboren, Jay Supp. XVI
Nichols, John Supp. XIII
Niebuhr, Reinhold Vol. III
Nin, Anaïs Supp. X
Norris, Frank Vol. III
Nye, Naomi Shihab Supp. XIII
Oates, Joyce Carol Supp. II
O'Brien, Tim Supp. V
O'Connor, Flannery Vol. III
O'Connor, Flannery Retro. Supp. II
Odets, Clifford Supp. II
O'Hara, John Vol. III
Olds, Sharon Supp. X
Oliver, Mary Supp. VII
Olsen, Tillie Supp. XIII
Olson, Charles Supp. II
O'Neill, Eugene Vol. III
Ortiz, Simon J. Supp. IV
Ozick, Cynthia Supp. V
Paine, Thomas Supp. I
Paley, Grace Supp. VI
Parker, Dorothy Supp. IX
Parkman, Francis Supp. II
Patchett, Ann Supp. XII
Percy, Walker Supp. III
Pinsky, Robert Supp. VI
Plath, Sylvia Supp. I
Plath, Sylvia Retro. Supp. II
Plimpton, George Supp. XVI
Podhoretz, Norman Supp. VIII
Poe, Edgar Allan Vol. III
Poe, Edgar Allan Retro. Supp. II
Porter, Katherine Anne Vol. III
Pound, Ezra Vol. III
Pound, Ezra Retro. Supp. I
Powers, Richard Supp. IX
Price, Reynolds Supp. VI
Prose, Francine Supp. XVI
Proulx, Annie Supp. VII
Purdy, James Supp. VII
Pynchon, Thomas Supp. II
Quindlen, Anna Supp. XVII
Rand, Ayn Supp. IV
Ransom, John Crowe Vol. III
Rawlings, Marjorie Kinnan Supp. X
Ray, Janisse Supp. XVIII
Reed, Ishmael Supp. X
Reznikoff, Charles Supp. XIV
Rice, Anne Supp. VII
Rich, Adrienne Supp. I
Rich, Adrienne Retro. Supp. II
Richter, Conrad Supp. XVIII
Ríos, Alberto Álvaro Supp. IV
Robbins, Tom Supp. X
Robinson, Edwin Arlington Vol. III
Rodriguez, Richard Supp. XIV
Roethke, Theodore Vol. III
Roth, Henry Supp. IX
Roth, Philip Supp. III
Roth, Philip Retro. Supp. II
Rowson, Susanna Supp. XV
Rukeyser, Muriel Supp. VI
Russo, Richard Supp. XII
Ryan, Paul William Supp. XVIII
Salinas, Luis Omar Supp. XIII
Salinger, J. D. Vol. III
Salter, James Supp. IX
Sandburg, Carl Vol. III
Sanders, Scott Russell Supp. XVI
Santayana, George Vol. III
Sarton, May Supp. VIII
Schnackenberg, Gjertrud Supp. XV
Schulberg, Budd Supp. XVIII
Schwartz, Delmore Supp. II
Scott, Joanna Supp. XVII
Sexton, Anne Supp. II
Shanley, John Patrick Supp. XIV
Shapiro, Karl Supp. II
Shepard, Sam Supp. III
Shields, Carol Supp. VII
Silko, Leslie Marmon Supp. IV
Simic, Charles Supp. VIII
Simon, Neil Supp. IV
Simpson, Louis Supp. IX
Sinclair, Upton Supp. V
Singer, Isaac Bashevis Vol. IV

Singer, Isaac Bashevis Retro. Supp. II
Smiley, Jane Supp. VI
Smith, Logan Pearsall Supp. XIV
Smith, William Jay Supp. XIII
Snodgrass, W. D. Supp. VI
Snyder, Gary Supp. VIII
Sobin, Gustaf Supp. XVI
Sontag, Susan Supp. III
Southern, Terry Supp. XI
Stafford, William Supp. XI
Stegner, Wallace Supp. IV
Stein, Gertrude Vol. IV
Steinbeck, John Vol. IV
Stern, Gerald Supp. IX
Stevens, Wallace Vol. IV
Stevens, Wallace Retro. Supp. I
Stoddard, Elizabeth Supp. XV
Stone, Robert Supp. V
Stowe, Harriet Beecher Supp. I
Strand, Mark Supp. IV
Styron, William Vol. IV
Swenson, May Supp. IV
Talese, Gay Supp. XVII
Tan, Amy Supp. X
Tate, Allen Vol. IV
Taylor, Edward Vol. IV
Taylor, Peter Supp. V
Theroux, Paul Supp. VIII
Thoreau, Henry David Vol. IV
Thurber, James Supp. I
Toomer, Jean Supp. IX
Trilling, Lionel Supp. III
Turow, Scott Supp. XVII
Twain, Mark Vol. IV
Tyler, Anne Supp. IV
Untermeyer, Louis Supp. XV
Updike, John Vol. IV
Updike, John Retro. Supp. I
Van Vechten, Carl Supp. II
Veblen, Thorstein Supp. I
Vidal, Gore Supp. IV
Vollmann, William T. Supp. XVII
Vonnegut, Kurt Supp. II
Wagoner, David Supp. IX
Walker, Alice Supp. III
Wallace, David Foster Supp. X
Warner, Susan Supp. XVIII
Warren, Robert Penn Vol. IV
Wasserstein, Wendy Supp. XV
Welty, Eudora Vol. IV
Welty, Eudora Retro. Supp. I
West, Dorothy Supp. XVIII
West, Nathanael Vol. IV
West, Nathanael Retro. Supp. II
Wharton, Edith Vol. IV
Wharton, Edith Retro. Supp. I
White, E. B. Supp. I
Whitman, Walt Vol. IV
Whitman, Walt Retro. Supp. I
Whittier, John Greenleaf Supp. I
Wilbur, Richard Supp. III
Wideman, John Edgar Supp. X
Wilder, Thornton Vol. IV
Williams, Tennessee Vol. IV
Williams, William Carlos Vol. IV
Williams, William Carlos Retro. Supp. I
Wilson, August Supp. VIII
Wilson, Edmund Vol. IV
Winters, Yvor Supp. II
Wolfe, Thomas Vol. IV
Wolfe, Tom Supp. III
Wolff, Tobias Supp. VII
Wright, C. D. Supp. XV
Wright, Charles Supp. V
Wright, Franz Supp. XVII
Wright, James Supp. III
Wright, Richard Vol. IV
Wrigley, Robert Supp. XVIII
Wylie, Elinor Supp. I
Yates, Richard Supp. XI
Zukofsky, Louis Supp. III

ISBN-13: 978-0-684-31552-2
ISBN-10: 0-684-31552-1